French Technical Dictionary

Dictionnaire technique anglais

Routledge
French Technical Dictionary
Dictionnaire technique anglais

VOLUME 1

FRENCH–ENGLISH
FRANÇAIS–ANGLAIS

London and New York

First published 1994
by Routledge
11 New Fetter Lane, London EC4P 4EE

Simultaneously published in the USA and Canada
by Routledge
29 West 35th Street, New York, NY 10001

Conversion tables adapted from *Dictionary of Scientific Units*, H. G. Jerrard and
D. B. McNeill, London: Chapman & Hall, 1992.

Typeset in Monotype Times, Helvetica Neue and Bauer Bodoni
by Routledge

Printed in Great Britain by TJ Press (Padstow), Cornwall

Printed on acid-free paper

British Library Cataloguing-in-Publication Data
A catalogue record for this book is available from the British Library

Library of Congress Cataloging-in-Publication Data
Applied for

ISBNs:
Vol 1 French–English 0–415–11224–9
Vol 2 English–French 0–415–11225–7
2-volume set 0–415–05670–5

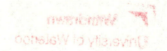

Contents/Table des matières

Editorial staff/Direction éditoriale

General Editor/Direction rédactionnelle
Yves Arden

Managing Editor/Chef de projet
Neil Clements

Programme Management/Direction de collection
Flavia Hodges   **Sinda López**
Wendy Morris   **Elizabeth Handford**

Market Research/Etude de marché
Judith Watts   **Rachel Miller**
Jane Gardner   **Nadia Lovell**
Susanne Jordans   **Perdita Geier**
Rebecca Moy

Systems/Informatique
George Allard   **Julian Zinovieff**
Simon Thompson   **Phoebe Bright**
Michael Al-Nassir

Administration/Secrétariat
Gemma Marren   **Kristoffer Blegvad**
Hazel Egerton   **Jessica Ramage**

Subeditorial/Rédaction
Martin Barr

Production/Production
Nigel Marsh

Contributors and lexicographers/
Collaborateurs et lexicographes

Contributors/Collaborateurs

Réjane Amery

Yves Arden

Josephine Bacon

John P. Bryon

Michael Carpenter

Anna Cordon

Maguy Couette

Elisabeth Coyne

P. J. Doyle

J. V. Drazil

Bill Duffin

James Dunster

Christopher Freeland

Crispin Geoghegan

Susan Green

Freda Klipstein

C. A. Lagall

David Larcher

Virginia Lester

Pamela Mayorcas

James Millard

Charles Polley

Michael Rawson

Louis Rioual

Tom Williams

Stephen Wilson

Stewart Wittering

Lexicographers/Lexicographes

Tom Bartlett

Hazel Curties

Charles Denroche

Anna Howes

Duncan Marshall

Valerie Smith

John Williams

Specialist consultants/
Spécialistes consultés

Chris Buchanan
Abbey Road Studios

Gérard Mercier
Air France

Maryline Grellier
Apple France

Hélène Mateescu
Association Française de Normalisation

Jean-Jacques Bisson
AT&T/NCR

Alain de Kermoysan
Automobiles Citroën

Patrick Leggatt
formerly/anciennement BBC Engineering
Information Department

John Camm
British Ceramic Research Limited

A.J. Wardle
British Coal Corporation

Annick Piant
Centre Audiovisuel Simone de Beauvoir

Dr Gilles Pinay
Centre d'Ecologie des Systèmes Fluviaux

Dr Bertrand Fritz
Dr Christine Mosser
Centre de Géochimie de la Surface

Jean-Louis Astor
Centre National d'Etudes Spatiales

Dr Nicole Kurtz-Newell
Centre National de la Recherche Scientifique

Prof. Roland Triay
Centre de Physique Théorique/Université de
Provence

Dr Christian Voltolini
Centre de Recherches Nucléaires

Dr Francis Saupé
Centre de Recherches Pétrographiques et
Géochimiques

Dr Frank Roux
Centre de Recherches en Physique de
l'Environnement Terrestre et Planétaire

Juliette Kohiyama
Charbonnages de France

Ronald Ridout
Chartered Institute of Building

Hans Bamert
Chemins de Fer Fédéraux Suisses

Gerald Cameron
Ciba-Geigy Limited

Christine Nunes
Compagnie Générale Maritime

Philippe Chambin
CREAR

Kevin Colcomb-Heiliger
Department of Transport
Marine Pollution
Control Unit

Héloïse Neefs
Dictionnaires Hachette

Ripple Linant
Elf Aquitaine Production

Nicolette Walshe
Energy Technology Support Unit

Bertrand Humbert
France 2

Josette Mell
France Télécom

Colin Andrews
Gambica

Marie-Dominique Agay
Sandra Buder
GRETA Alpes Dauphiné

Dr Gilles Zumbach
Harvard University

Prof. Michael Worthington
Imperial College London

Ray Griffiths
Institut Français pour l'Exploitation de la Mer

Dr Gilbert Binder
Institut National Polytechnique de
Grenoble/Université Joseph Fourrier

Jean-Pierre Michel
Institut National Polytechnique de Lorraine

Philip Maylor
Brian Patterson
Institute of Data Processing Management

J. E. H. Leach
Institute of Energy

Celia Kirby
D. B. Smith
Institute of Hydrology

J. H. Durran
Institute of Mathematics and its Applications

Dr Peter Collar
Institute of Oceanographic Sciences

Christopher Wolfe
Institute of Physics

Malcolm Horlick
Institute of Refrigeration

Chris Murphy
Institute of Wastes Management

Derek Chapman
Malcolm J. Raven
Institution of Gas Engineers

Don Goodsell
Institution of Mechanical Engineers

Michael White
formerly/anciennement International Maritime
Organization

Jean-Pierre Portier
Isabelle Prat
IRFIP

Dr Norman Borrett
Dr Michael Clode
Janine Lajudie
King's College London

Peter Sutherst
Kodak Limited

Dr Michel Vauclin
Laboratoire d'Etude des Transferts en
Hydrologie et Environnement

R. N. Avis
Lafarge Réfractaires Monolithiques

François Ducellier
Lesieur Alimentaire/Céréol

J. E. Lunn
Locomotive & Carriage Institution

Bernard Agnard
Georges Dive
Matra Défense

Jacques Siméon
Météo France

Dave Farlow
Michelin Tyre plc

Kevin Murphy
Mineralogical Society

Jean-Marie Massin
Ministère de l'Environnement

Thierry Berthaux
Ministère de l'Industrie
et du Commerce Extérieur

Claude Lannoy
Moulinex

Gill Wilkinson
National Radiological Protection Board

Gillian Strachan-Gray
Optical Information Council

Dr Graham Moore
Diana Deavin
Pira International

Dr Jim Smith
Prince Edward Island Food Technology Centre

Patrick Pigault
Régie Autonome des Transports Parisiens

Jean-Marc Pelletier
Renault Automation

R. G. Lee
formerly/anciennement Royal Military College
of Science

D. J. Elliott
Rubber Consultants

Jean-Louis Richard
Saunier Duval Electricité

Philippe de La Cotardière
Société Astronomique de France

Prof. Antoine Chaigne
Société Française d'Acoustique

Paul Dinsdale
Society of Dyers and Colourists

Phil Thompson
Andrew Melvin
Gwyneth Hughes
Texaco Limited

Michel Baeckelandt
Thomson-CSF

Dr Alan Williams
Université de Genève

Dr Minh-Tâm Tran
Université de Lausanne

Dr Bernard Junod
Université de Neuchâtel

Simon Achenbaum
Université de Paris V

Prof. Georges Calas
Université de Paris VII

Dr Alain Mauffret
Université Pierre et Marie Curie/Groupe
d'Etude de la Marge Continentale

Dr Roger Marchand
Dr Odile Merdrignac
Université de Rennes I

Michel Deblock
Université des Sciences et Technologies de Lille

Prof. Yves Gourinard
Université de Toulouse III

Mark Hempsell
University of Bristol

Dr Philippe Sarda
University of Cambridge

Elizabeth Fraser
University of Edinburgh

Dr John A Elliott
University of Manchester Institute of Science
and Technology

Line Fiquet
Witco

We are also particularly indebted to the following people for their assistance during the compilation of this dictionary:

Nous tenons aussi particulièrement à exprimer nos remerciements à ceux et celles qui nous ont apporté leur concours lors de la rédaction de ce dictionnaire:

Serge Bouchval

John Chillingworth

Catherine Maryan Green

Jason Miles

Dr Jacqueline Mitton

Thomas Stengel

John W. Thristan

Suzy Vergez

Preface/Préface

The two factors that have enabled us to create a completely new bilingual technical dictionary that sets new standards in its field are the database system and the method of compilation.

It would not have been possible to compile this dictionary within a realistic timescale, and to the standard that we have achieved, without the use of a highly sophisticated, custom-designed database. During the initial planning stages we looked closely at all the dictionary development systems then available, but concluded that none was sufficiently flexible for our purposes. As a result, we have had a completely unique system developed to our own specifications.

Its most significant feature is that it is designed as a relational database: term records for each language are held in separate files, with further files consisting only of link records. Links between terms in different language files represent translations and enable us to handle, in a sophisticated way, various types of one-to-many and many-to-one translation equivalences. Links between terms within a single language file represent cross-references, themselves of a wide variety of types: synonyms, antonyms, spelling variants, geographical variants and abbreviations.

The content of the database for this dictionary was created in three principal phases: the terms and their translations were originally solicited from a panel of professional translators with current practical experience of a narrowly defined specialist subject area and an interest in the collection and dissemination of terminology; the terms in each language were then vetted by native-speaker subject specialists working at the leading edge of the respective technology in order to ensure their currency, the accuracy of explanations, and the adequacy of coverage. Finally, each language file was reviewed by regional editors to ensure worldwide coverage of usage. British and North American forms and spellings are clearly labelled and distinguished, and careful attention is also paid to Canadian, Swiss and Belgian French.

The creation and editing of the database of terms was, however, only the first stage in the making of the dictionary. Within the database

Les deux facteurs qui nous ont permis de créer un dictionnaire technique bilingue totalement nouveau, posant des normes nouvelles, sont un système de base de données et une méthode de compilation parfaitement adaptés aux résultats souhaités.

La sortie de ce dictionnaire dans les délais et conformément aux critères prévus imposait la compilation d'une base de données spécifique extrêmement sophistiquée. Au début du projet, nous avons soigneusement étudié tous les systèmes de développement de dictionnaire existants. Aucun n'étant suffisamment flexible, nous avons opté pour le développement intégral d'un nouveau système, totalement adapté à nos exigences.

Ce système a pour caractéristique essentielle d'être conçu comme une base de données relationnelle: dans chaque langue, les termes sont stockés dans des fichiers séparés, tandis que d'autres fichiers ne se composent que de liens. Les liens entre les termes de fichiers de langues séparés représentent des traductions et nous permettent de gérer de manière très sophistiquée différents types d'équivalences de traduction 'un à plusieurs' et 'plusieurs à un'. Les liens entre les différents termes d'un même fichier de langue représentent des renvois, eux-mêmes de différents types: synonymes, antonymes, variantes orthographiques, variantes géographiques et abréviations.

La base de données a été créée en trois phases principales: tout d'abord, les termes et leurs traductions ont été sélectionnés par une équipe de traducteurs professionnels, ayant une connaissance pratique approfondie du domaine concerné et intéressés par la compilation et la diffusion de la terminologie. Ces termes regroupés ont ensuite été approuvés dans les différents pays par des spécialistes techniques de haut niveau, ayant pour mission de garantir l'actualité et la précision des termes, ainsi que l'étendue des sujets traités. Enfin, chaque fichier de langue a été contrôlé par des lexicographes des pays concernés, chargés de veiller au respect des variantes géographiques. Dans chaque langue, les formes et l'orthographe (anglaises ou américaines, canadiennes, suisses ou belges) sont clairement identifiées.

the distinction between source and target languages is not meaningful, but for this printed dictionary it has been necessary to format the data to produce separate French–English and English–French volumes. The data were processed by a further software module to produce two alphabetic sequences, of French headwords with English translations and vice versa, each displaying the nesting of compounds, ordering of translations, style for cross-references of different types, and other features according to a complex algorithm.

At this stage the formatted text was edited by a team of experienced lexicographers whose task it was to eliminate duplication or inconsistency; edit the contextual information and explanations; and remove terms that were on the one hand too general, or on the other, too specialized for inclusion in a 'general technical' dictionary.

This phased method of working has enabled us to set extremely high standards of quality control, and eliminate the idiosyncrasy often characteristic of 'general technical' dictionaries compiled by individuals or small teams, with the result that we can claim this to be an entirely new type of specialist bilingual dictionary.

The Publisher

La création et la vérification de la base de données terminologique n'ont cependant représenté que la première étape de la constitution du dictionnaire. La distinction entre les langues cible et source n'étant pas significative au niveau de la base de données, nous avons dû, pour la version imprimée, mettre les données en forme pour obtenir des volumes français–anglais et anglais–français séparés. Les données ont alors été traitées par un logiciel permettant de produire deux séquences alphabétiques, des mots-clés français avec leurs traductions anglaises – et vice versa – avec, dans chaque cas, indication de l'imbrication des composants, de l'ordre des traductions, du style des renvois de différents types, et d'autres fonctions, selon un algorithme complexe.

A ce stade, le texte mis en forme a été vérifié par une équipe de lexicographes expérimentés, qui avaient pour mission d'éliminer les doublons et les incohérences, de vérifier les informations et les explications contextuelles, et de supprimer les termes soit trop généraux, soit trop spécialisés pour être inclus dans un dictionnaire de 'technique générale'.

Cette méthodologie nous a permis d'établir des normes de contrôle de qualité extrêmement élevées et d'éliminer le manque d'homogénéité dont souffrent généralement les dictionnaires 'techniques généraux' compilés par des individus isolés ou de petites équipes, et d'offrir à nos clients un dictionnaire bilingue spécialisé d'un type entièrement nouveau.

Les éditeurs

Features of the dictionary/
Caractéristiques du dictionnaire

The main features of the dictionary are highlighted in the text extracts on the opposite page. For a more detailed explanation of each of these features and information on how to get the most out of the dictionary, see pages xxi–xxiii.

Les principales caractéristiques de ce dictionnaire sont mentionnées ci-contre dans les éclatés. Pour une explication détaillée de chacune de ces caractéristiques et pour tirer le meilleur parti de votre dictionnaire, reportez-vous aux pages xxv–xxvii

The abbreviation is expanded in both French and English	**DCO** *abrév (demande chimique d'oxygène)* CHIMIE, HYDROLOGIE, POLLUTION COD *(chemical oxygen demand)*	*Signification de l'abréviation indiquée pour le terme anglais ainsi que pour la traduction française*
	DCV *abrév (dépôt chimique en phase vapeur)* ELECTRON, OPTIQUE, TELECOM CVD *(chemical vapor deposition, chemical vapour deposition)*	
	ddp *abrév (différence de potentiel)* PHYSIQUE pd *(potential difference)*	*Renvois applicables*
Cross-references specific to a particular subject area follow the subject area label	**dé** *m* CONS MECA pillow, MINES die, PHYSIQUE *(D)* dee; ~ **d'entraînement** *m* CONS MECA drive bit	*uniquement à un domaine technique particulier fournis immédiatement après le domaine*
	déaminase *f* CHIMIE deaminase	
	débâcle *f* HYDROLOGIE breaking-up, OCEANO debacle, glacial outburst, ice breakup	
	déballastage *m* PETR dewatering	
	débandage *m* CERAM VER deburring	
	débarcadère *m* NAUT wharf	
British English and American English translations are given in full and labelled accordingly	**débarder** *vt* NAUT unload	*Variantes anglaises et françaises fournies intégralement et signalées par des codes géographiques*
	débardeur *m* NAUT docker (BrE), longshoreman (AmE), stevedore	
	débarquement *m* NAUT disembarkation, paying off, TRANSPORT landing	
	débarquer[1] *vt* NAUT disembark, *des passagers* land, *des marins* pay off, *une cargaison, l'équipage* discharge, land, unship	
A colon introduces a compound where the headword has no technical value	**débarquer**[2] *vi* NAUT land	*Deux-points indiquant un mot dépourvu de valeur technique et introduisant un mot composé*
	débarrassé *adj* MATERIAUX clear, free	
	débarrasser: se ~ de *v réfl* PRODUCTION scrap	
Compound terms are nested alphabetically at the first element	**débattement** *m* AERONAUT deflection, CONS MECA displacement; ~ **de gouverne de direction** *m* AERONAUT rudder travel; ~ **horizontal** *m* PRODUCTION horizontal travel	*Termes composés imbriqués en ordre alphabétique sous le premier élément*
	débavurer *vt* PLAST CAOU *plastiques* deflash	*Domaines en ordre alphabétique indiquant la traduction appropriée à chaque domaine*
	débillarder *vt* CONSTR wreath	
Subject area labels given in alphabetical order show appropriate translation	**débit** *m* AGRO ALIM delivery, CHARBON feed rate, yield, CINEMAT pace, CONS MECA delivery, CONSTR *des bois en grume* breaking down, DISTRI EAU discharge, flow rate, outflow, rate of flow, *d'une pompe* capacity,	
Contexts give supplementary information to help locate the right translation	*d'un cours d'eau, d'un déversoir* discharge, EN RENOUV yield, GAZ flow rate, sendout, HYDROLOGIE flow rate, INFORMAT rate, throughput, INST HYDR feed, flow, MECANIQUE *hydraulique* flow rate, NUCLEAIRE *d'une pompe, d'un compresseur, d'un ventilateur* delivery, discharge, ORDINAT rate, throughput, PAPIER flow, *d'une pompe* delivery, discharge, output, PETROLE yield, PHYS FLUID flow rate, PHYSIQUE flow rate, rate of flow, PRODUCTION output, throughput, yield, RECYCLAGE discharge rate, REFRIG rate of flow, TRANSPORT traffic volume; ~ **d'accumulateurs** *m*	*Contextes fournissant des informations supplémentaires pour faciliter la sélection de la traduction exacte*
Common articles are ignored for the purposes of ordering terms	ESPACE *énergie* battery drain; ~ **d'air** *m* AERONAUT airflow, MAT CHAUFF airflow rate; ~ **de l'année moyenne** *m pl* HYDROLOGIE average yearly flow; ~ **annuel** *m* DISTRI EAU annual flow; ~ **après convergence** *m* TRANSPORT diverging volume, merge volume; ~ **de base** *m* HYDROLOGIE base flow, TELECOM	*Articles non pris en compte lors du classement des termes*
British English and American English spelling variants are given in full and followed by regional labels	basic bit rate, TRANSPORT base volume; ~ **binaire** *m* INFORMAT, ORDINAT bit rate, TELECOM bit rate, data signaling rate (AmE), data signalling rate (BrE); ~ **binaire constant** *m* TELECOM constant bit rate; ~	*Informations complètes sur les variantes orthographiques américaines et anglaises suivies de codes géographiques*
Cross-references to abbreviations are shown for both the French term and the English translation	**binaire variable** *m (DBV)* TELECOM variable bit rate *(VBR)*; ~ **brut** *m* NUCLEAIRE gross flow; ~ **calorifique** *m* THERMODYN heat emission, heat output, rate of heat release; ~ **de canal** *m* INFORMAT channel address word, channel capacity; ~ **caractéristique** *m* HYDROLOGIE characteristic flow; ~ **caractéristique de 3 mois** *m* HYDROLOGIE three-month characteristic flow rate; ~ **caractéristique de crue** *m (DCC)* HYDROLOGIE	*Renvois aux abréviations fournis pour le terme français et pour la traduction anglaise*

Using the dictionary

Range of coverage

This is one volume (the French–English volume) of a general technical dictionary that covers the whole range of modern technology and the scientific knowledge that underlies it. It contains a broad base of terminology drawn from traditional areas of technology such as mechanical engineering, construction, electrical and electronic engineering, but also includes the vocabulary of newly prominent subject areas such as fuelless energy sources, safety engineering and quality assurance.

Selection of terms

We have aimed to include the essential vocabulary of each subject area, and the material has been checked by leading subject experts to ensure that both the English and the French terms are accurate and current, that the translations are valid equivalents, and that there are no gaps in coverage.

We have been careful about including only genuine technical terms and not allowing general vocabulary with no technical value. At the same time, we have entered the core vocabulary of technical discourse in its totality, although some of these items may also be found in general dictionaries. Although other variant translations would often be permissible in a particular subject area, we have given the term most widely preferred by specialists in the area.

Placement of terms

All terms are ordered alphabetically, beginning with their first element. Compound terms are never entered under their second or third element, regardless of the semantic structure of the unit.

Stoplists

Terms in French are not entered under the following elements:

à, au, aux, avec, c', ça, ce, cet, cette, chose, d', dans, de, des, dont, du, d'un, d'une, d'y, en, est, et, être, ici, l', la, là, laquelle, le, lequel, les,

lesquelles, lesquels, ne, ni, nul, nulle, on, ou, où, par, pendant, personne, peu, pour, que, qu', quelqu', quelque, qui, rien, s', se, si, sont, sous, sur, tous, tout, toute, toutes, très, trop, un, une, y

Open compounds consisting of more than one element are listed at their first element. In these nested listings, the simple form is replaced by a swung dash (~). For example:

alimenté: ~ **en blanc** *adj* IMPRIM blank-fed; ~ **en parallèle** *adj* AERONAUT parallel-fed; ~ **à la main** *adj* IMPRIM hand-fed; ~ **par batterie** *adj* CINEMAT, ELECTROTEC battery-powered; ~ **par courroie** *adj* GENIE CHIM belt-fed; ~ **par énergie solaire** *adj* EN RENOUV solar-powered

When this first element is itself a headword with one or more technical senses, compounds follow the simple form in alphabetical order. For example:

document *m* INFORMAT, ORDINAT document; ~ **administratif en plusieurs parties** *m* IMPRIM *continu* formset; ~ **dactylographié** *m* IMPRIM typescript proof; ~ **duplicata** *m* PHOTO duplicate; ~ **écrit réglementant la sûreté** *m* SECURITE written policy statement on health and safety

If the first element is not itself translated, a colon (:) precedes the compounds. For example:

guidé: ~ **par infrarouge** *adj* ESPACE *véhicules*, THERMODYN heat-seeking; ~ **par laser** *adj* ELECTRON laser-guided; ~ **par menu** *adj* INFORMAT, ORDINAT menu-driven

Ordering of terms

Hyphenated and solid compounds are entered in alphabetical sequence, and will thus follow a nest of open compounds with the same first element. For example:

brise *f* METEO breeze; ~ **établie** *f* NAUT steady breeze; ~ **folle** *f* METEO baffling wind; ~ **du large** *f* METEO sea breeze; ~ **légère** *f* METEO gentle breeze, light breeze; ~ **de mer** *f* METEO sea breeze; ~ **de montagne** *f* METEO mountain breeze; ~ **de terre** *f* METEO, NAUT land breeze; ~ **de vallée** *f* METEO valley breeze
brise-copeaux *m* CONS MECA chip breaker
brise-glace *m* MILITAIRE, NAUT icebreaker

Articles (*l', la, le, les, un, une*), the prepositions *à* and *de/d'*, and their contractions (*au, aux, du, des*) are ignored in determining the sequence of nested open compounds. For example:

bride: ~ **de fixation du radiateur** *f* AUTO radiator flange; ~ **de liaison** *f* ESPACE *véhicules* connecting flange; ~ **à moyeu** *f* CONS MECA hub-type flange; ~ **à moyeu lisse** *f* CONS MECA plain hub flange; ~ **d'obturation** *f* CONS MECA blind flange; ~ **à piège** *f* ELECTROTEC choke flange

The reflexive pronoun *se/s'* is also ignored for the purposes of ordering. For example:

amarrer:[2] **s'~** *v réfl* ESPACE *véhicules* dock; **s'~ à nouveau** *v réfl* ESPACE *véhicules* redock

In the case of very long nests of compounds, marginal markers have been used to make it easy to find a term more quickly. For example:

filtre:

~ f ~ **à faible temps de réponse** *m* PRODUCTION short-time constant filter; ~ **FI** *m* ELECTRON, TELECOM IF filter; ~ **à flancs raides** *m* ELECTRON sharp cutoff filter; ~ **à fréquence intermédiaire** *m* ELECTRON, TELECOM intermediate frequency filter;

~ g ~ **à gain fixe** *m* ELECTRON fixed gain filter; ~ **gris neutre** *m* CINEMAT neutral density filter; ~ **gros** *m* DISTRI EAU coarse filter;

~ h ~ **d'harmonique** *m* ELECTRON, ESPACE *communications* harmonic filter, PHYS RAYON harmonic suppressor; ~ **à huile** *m* AUTO, CONS MECA, MECANIQUE, VEHICULES *lubrification* oil filter; ~ **à huile à cartouche jetable**

Abbreviations and acronyms written in upper case appear after vocabulary words of the same form written in lower case. For example:

cap[3] *m* AERONAUT heading, ESPACE course, *véhicules* heading, NAUT boat's heading, cape, course, heading, headland, OCEANO cape, headland; ~ **de collision** *m* NAUT collision course; ~ **au compas** *m* NAUT compass heading; ~ **compas** *m* AERONAUT compass heading; ~ **d'éloignement** *m* AERONAUT outbound heading; ~ **magnétique** *m* AERONAUT magnetic heading, NAUT magnetic course; ~ **d'une piste** *m* AERONAUT localizer beam heading; ~ **radar** *m* AERONAUT radar heading; ~**retour** *m* AERONAUT inbound heading; ~ **vrai** *m* NAUT true course
CAP *abrév (capacité d'absorption des protons)* PHYS RAYON proton absorptive capacity

Terms containing figures and symbols are alphabetized according to the usual expansion when written out in full. For example:

lampe: ~ **à halogène** *f* ELECTR *éclairage* halogen lamp; ~ **HMI** *f* CINEMAT HMI lamp; ~ **800 watts sur batterie** *f* CINEMAT hand basher;

Homographs

Every term is accompanied by a label indicating its part of speech. For a complete list of these labels and their expansions, please see page xxix.

A term that has more than one part of speech is listed in a separate entry for each. Such entries are distinguished by a raised number immediately following the headword. The sequence is abbreviation, adjective, adverb, noun, verb, followed by less frequent parts of speech. For example:

électronique[1] *adj* ELECTR, ELECTRON electronic
électronique[2] *f* ELECTROTEC, INFORMAT, ORDINAT, PRODUCTION electronics

Ordering of translations

Every term is accompanied by one or more labels indicating the technological area in which it is used. For a complete list of these labels and their expansions, please see pages xxxi–xxxii.

Where the same term is used in more than one technological area, multiple labels are given as appropriate. These labels appear in alphabetical order.

Where a term has the same translation in more than one technological area, this translation is given after the sequence of labels. For example:

bruit *m* ACOUSTIQUE, ELECTRON, ENREGISTR, INFORMAT, ORDINAT, PHYS ONDES, PHYSIQUE, SECURITE, TELECOM noise

Where a term has different translations according to the technological area in which it is used, the appropriate translation is given after each label or set of labels. For example:

enfoncement *m* CONSTR driving, recess, recessing, *d'un clou* driving in, ESSAIS hollow, NAUT *augmentation du tirant d'eau* sinkage

Supplementary information

The gender is given for every French noun term. In the case of compound terms this is the gender of the term as a whole (that is, its noun head) rather than the final element. For example:

égout: ~ **d'évacuation des eaux pluviales** *m* RECYCLAGE storm drain

In very many cases additional data is given about a term in order to show how it is used. Such contextual information can be:

(a) the typical subject or object of a verb, for example:

flèche *f* CINEMAT boom arm, CONS MECA *d'un ressort* compression, *résistance des ressorts* set, CONSTR deflection, rise, *d'une grue* boom, *d'une ligne aérienne* dip, *d'une voûte* height above impost level, *d'une grue* jib, DISTRI EAU *d'une porte d'écluse* balance bar, EMBALLAGE *pour dispositif de fermeture* arrowhead, ESPACE *véhicules* boom, sweep, MECANIQUE deflection, *matériel de levage* boom, NUCLEAIRE boom, jib, deflection, sag, OCEANO harpoon, TRANSPORT derrick boom

(b) typical nouns used with an adjective, for example:

irisé *adj* CERAM VER *verre* iridescent

(c) words indicating the reference of a noun, for example:

cale *f* CONS MECA block, key, scotch, packing piece, shim, wedge, CONSTR needle, wedge, MECANIQUE *véhicules* chock, MINES holing prop, *placée dans la sous-cave* punch prop, NAUT chock, hold, *de construction* slip, *de carénage* slipway, OCEANO hold, PRODUCTION block, chock, TRANSPORT cargo hold

(d) a narrower subject area than indicated by the label, for example:

enduiseuse *f* PLAST CAOU *matériel* coating machine, REVETEMENT spreading machine; **~ avec barre d'application** *f* PLAST CAOU *revêtement* bar coater

(e) a paraphrase or broad equivalent

étançon *m* CONSTR prop, shore, shoring, stanchion, EMBALLAGE *partie d'un conteneur* strut

When various different translations apply in the same subject area, contextual information is also used to show which translation is appropriate in different circumstances. For example:

anneau *m* CHIMIE ring, CONS MECA *d'une chaîne* link, *pour cylindres de broyeur à cylindres* shell, CONSTR *d'une clef* bow

Cross-references

Coverage includes Belgian, Canadian and Swiss terms. All terms not universally applicable are accompanied by a label. For a complete list of these labels and their expansions, please see page xxxiii.

In the case of lexical variants, full information – including translations and cross-references to other regional forms – is given at each entry.

baie: **~ d'emballeur** *f* (Bel) *(cf loge d'emballeur)* CERAM VER packer's bay
loge: **~ d'emballeur** *f* (Fra) *(cf baie d'emballeur)* CERAM VER packer's bay

In the case of spelling variants not differentiated by region, the less common form is cross-referred to the dominant form. Full information is given at that entry only. For example:

clef *f voir* clé

Geographical variants, both spelling and lexical, are given in full when they are translations. For example:

frisure *f* CERAM VER chill mark (BrE), chill wrinkle (AmE), ENREGISTR *de la bande* curl, TEXTILE crimp

Both abbreviations and their full forms are entered in the main body of the dictionary in alphabetical sequence. Full information – including translations and cross-references to the full form or abbreviation as appropriate – is given at each entry. For example:

CNS *abrév (concentrateur numérique satellite)* TELECOM digital satellite concentrator
concentrateur: **~ numérique satellite** *m (CNS)* TELECOM digital satellite concentrator

Abbreviations are also listed in a separate alphabetical sequence at the back of this volume, to allow browsing in cases where the exact form of the abbreviation is not known.

Where appropriate, mention is made of antonyms or opposing terms. Full information is given at each entry. For example:

objectif: **~ à immersion** *m (cf objectif sec)* EQUIP LAB *microscope* immersion lens, **~ sec** *m (cf objectif à immersion)* EQUIP LAB *microscope* dry lens.

Comment utiliser ce dictionnaire

Domaines traités

Ce dictionnaire est un ouvrage technique 'général' qui couvre l'ensemble des nouvelles technologies et des connaissances scientifiques sur lesquelles elles reposent. Il comporte une importante base terminologique extraite des disciplines traditionnelles comme la mécanique, le bâtiment, l'électro-technique, l'électronique appliquée, ainsi que les nouvelles technologies comme les sources d'énergie renouvelable, la sécurité appliquée et l'assurance de la qualité.

Sélection des termes

Les termes qu'il contient se rapportent au vocabulaire de base de chaque discipline, et ont été minutieusement vérifiés par des spécialistes de haut niveau, chargés de veiller à l'exactitude et à l'actualité des termes anglais et français; à la parfaite correspondance des termes, et à la cohérence de l'ensemble.

Nous avons également veillé à n'inclure que des termes véritablement techniques, à l'exclusion de tout vocabulaire général dépourvu de valeur technique. Nous avons cependant inclus le vocabulaire technique de base dans son intégralité, bien que certains termes puissent également figurer dans des dictionnaires généraux. Nous avons eu pour principe de donner les traductions préférées par les spécialistes bien qu'il y ait souvent d'autres variantes possibles.

Classement des termes

Tous les termes sont classés par ordre alphabétique. Les termes composés apparaissent sous leur premier élément, quelle que soit la structure sémantique de l'ensemble.

Termes ignorés

Les termes français qui ne sont pas pris en compte lors du classement sont les suivants:

à, au, aux, avec, c', ça, ce, cet, cette, chose, d', dans, de, des, dont, du, d'un, d'une, d'y, en, est, et, être, ici, l', la, là, laquelle, le, lequel, les, lesquelles, lesquels, ne, ni, nul, nulle, on, ou, où, par, pendant, personne, peu, pour, que, qu', quel-

qu', quelque, qui, rien, s', se, si, sont, sous, sur, tous, tout, toute, toutes, très, trop, un, une, y

Les locutions ou les syntagmes figurent sous le premier élément. Dans les listes imbriquées, la forme simple est remplacée par un 'tilde' (~). Exemple:

alimenté: ~ **en blanc** *adj* IMPRIM blank-fed; ~ **en parallèle** *adj* AERONAUT parallel-fed; ~ **à la main** *adj* IMPRIM hand-fed; ~ **par batterie** *adj* CINEMAT, ELECTROTEC battery-powered; ~ **par courroie** *adj* GENIE CHIM belt-fed; ~ **par énergie solaire** *adj* EN RENOUV solar-powered

Lorsque ce premier élément est un mot-vedette ayant un ou plusieurs sens techniques, les mots composés suivent la forme simple et sont classés par ordre alphabétique. Exemple:

document *m* INFORMAT, ORDINAT document; ~ **administratif en plusieurs parties** *m* IMPRIM *continu* formset; ~ **dactylographié** *m* IMPRIM typescript proof; ~ **duplicata** *m* PHOTO duplicate; ~ **écrit réglementant la sûreté** *m* SECURITE written policy statement on health and safety

Si le premier élément n'est pas traduit, ses composants sont précédés de deux-points. Exemple:

guidé: ~ **par infrarouge** *adj* ESPACE *véhicules*, THERMODYN heat-seeking; ~ **par laser** *adj* ELECTRON laser-guided; ~ **par menu** *adj* INFORMAT, ORDINAT menu-driven

Ordre des termes

Les locutions ou termes comportant des traits-d'union sont entrés en ordre alphabétique, et suivent donc les locutions ou termes ayant le même premier élément. Exemple:

brise *f* METEO breeze; ~ **établie** *f* NAUT steady breeze; ~ **folle** *f* METEO baffling wind; ~ **du large** *f* METEO sea breeze; ~ **légère** *f* METEO gentle breeze, light breeze; ~ **de mer** *f* METEO sea breeze; ~ **de montagne** *f* METEO mountain breeze; ~ **de terre** *f* METEO, NAUT land breeze; ~ **de vallée** *f* METEO valley breeze
brise-copeaux *m* CONS MECA chip breaker
brise-glace *m* MILITAIRE, NAUT icebreaker

Les articles (*l'*, *la*, *le*, *les*, *un*, *une*), les prépositions *à* et *de*/*d'* et leurs contractions (*au*, *aux*, *du*, *des*) ne sont pas pris en compte lors du tri. Exemple:

bride: *~ de fixation du radiateur f* AUTO radiator flange; **~ de liaison** *f* ESPACE *véhicules* connecting flange; **~ à moyeu** *f* CONS MECA hub-type flange; **~ à moyeu lisse** *f* CONS MECA plain hub flange; **~ d'obturation** *f* CONS MECA blind flange; **~ à piège** *f* ELECTROTEC choke flange

Le pronom réfléchi *se/s'* n'est pas non plus pris en compte. Exemple:

amarrer:[2] **s'~** *v réfl* ESPACE *véhicules* dock; **s'~ à nouveau** *v réfl* ESPACE *véhicules* redock

Lorsque des composants ont de nombreuses imbrications, des repères en marge facilitent la recherche. Exemple:

filtre:

~ f **~ à faible temps de réponse** *m* PRODUCTION short-time constant filter; **~ FI** *m* ELECTRON, TELECOM IF filter; **~ à flancs raides** *m* ELECTRON sharp cutoff filter; **~ à fréquence intermédiaire** *m* ELECTRON, TELECOM intermediate frequency filter;

~ g **~ à gain fixe** *m* ELECTRON fixed gain filter; **~ gris neutre** *m* CINEMAT neutral density filter; **~ gros** *m* DISTRI EAU coarse filter;

~ h **~ d'harmonique** *m* ELECTRON, ESPACE *communications* harmonic filter, PHYS RAYON harmonic suppressor; **~ à huile** *m* AUTO, CONS MECA, MECANIQUE, VEHICULES *lubrification* oil filter; **~ à huile à cartouche jetable**

Les abréviations et acronymes en majuscules figurent après les termes de même forme en minuscules. Exemple:

cap[3] *m* AERONAUT heading, ESPACE *course, véhicules* heading, NAUT boat's heading, cape, course, heading, headland, OCEANO cape, headland; **~ de collision** *m* NAUT collision course; **~ au compas** *m* NAUT compass heading; **~ compas** *m* AERONAUT compass heading; **~ d'éloignement** *m* AERONAUT outbound heading; **~ magnétique** *m* AERONAUT magnetic heading, NAUT magnetic course; **~ d'une piste** *m* AERONAUT localizer beam heading; **~ radar** *m* AERONAUT radar heading; **~retour** *m* AERONAUT inbound heading; **~ vrai** *m* NAUT true course
CAP *abrév (capacité d'absorption des protons)* PHYS RAYON proton absorptive capacity

Les termes contenant des chiffres ou des symboles sont classés comme s'ils étaient écrits en lettres. Exemple:

lampe: **~ à halogène** *f* ELECTR éclairage halogen lamp; **~ HMI** *f* CINEMAT HMI lamp; **~ 800 watts sur batterie** *f* CINEMAT hand basher;

Homographes

Chaque terme est accompagné d'une abréviation indiquant sa fonction grammaticale. La liste complète de ces abréviations figure page xxix.

Un terme ayant plusieurs fonctions grammaticales figure sous une entrée séparée. Ces entrées se distinguent par un chiffre en exposant qui suit immédiatement le mot-vedette. La séquence est la suivante: abréviation, adjectif, adverbe, nom, verbe, suivie des fonctions moins fréquentes. Exemple:

électronique[1] *adj* ELECTR, ELECTRON electronic
électronique[2] *f* ELECTROTEC, INFORMAT, ORDINAT, PRODUCTION electronics

Ordre des traductions

Chaque terme est accompagné d'une ou plusieurs abréviations indiquant le domaine auquel il se rapporte. La liste complète de ces abréviations figure page xxxi–xxxii.

Lorsqu'un terme est utilisé dans plusieurs disciplines, il est suivi des abréviations appropriées, en ordre alphabétique.

Lorsqu'un terme est traduit de la même manière dans différentes disciplines, la traduction figure après la liste des abréviations. Exemple:

bruit *m* ACOUSTIQUE, ELECTRON, ENREGISTR, INFORMAT, ORDINAT, PHYS ONDES, PHYSIQUE, SECURITE, TELECOM noise

Lorsqu'un terme peut se traduire de différentes façons, selon les disciplines, sa traduction figure après chaque abréviation ou série d'abréviations. Exemple:

enfoncement *m* CONSTR driving, recess, recessing, *d'un clou* driving in, ESSAIS hollow, NAUT *augmentation du tirant d'eau* sinkage

Informations complémentaires

Le genre de chaque nom est indiqué. Pour les expressions ou termes composés, le genre est celui du terme dans son ensemble (c'est-à-dire de son mot-vedette), et non celui de l'élément final. Exemple:

égout *m* **~ d'évacuation des eaux pluviales** *m* RECYCLAGE storm drain

Dans de très nombreux cas, des informations complémentaires expliquent l'utilisation du terme concerné. Exemple:

(a) le sujet ou l'objet typique d'un verbe, par exemple:

flèche *f* CINEMAT boom arm, CONS MECA *d'un ressort*
compression, *résistance des ressorts* set, CONSTR deflection, rise, *d'une grue* boom, *d'une ligne aérienne*
dip, *d'une voûte* height above impost level, *d'une grue*
jib, DISTRI EAU *d'une porte d'écluse* balance bar, EM-
BALLAGE *pour dispositif de fermeture* arrowhead,
ESPACE *véhicules* boom, sweep, MECANIQUE deflection, *matériel de levage* boom, NUCLEAIRE boom, jib,
deflection, sag, OCEANO harpoon, TRANSPORT derrick
boom

(b) les noms typiques utilisés avec un adjectif, par
exemple:

irisé *adj* CERAM VER *verre* iridescent

(c) les mots indiquant la référence d'un nom, par
exemple:

cale *f* CONS MECA block, key, scotch, packing piece,
shim, wedge, CONSTR needle, wedge, MECANIQUE
véhicules chock, MINES holing prop, *placée dans la
sous-cave* punch prop, NAUT chock, hold, *de construction* slip, *de carénage* slipway, OCEANO hold,
PRODUCTION block, chock, TRANSPORT cargo hold

(d) un domaine plus limité que celui indiqué par
l'abréviation, par exemple:

enduiseuse *f* PLAST CAOU *matériel* coating machine,
REVETEMENT spreading machine; ~ **avec barre d'application** *f* PLAST CAOU *revêtement* bar coater

(e) une paraphrase ou un équivalent d'ordre
général, par exemple:

étançon *m* CONSTR prop, shore, shoring, stanchion,
EMBALLAGE *partie d'un conteneur* strut;

Lorsqu'un terme peut donner lieu à différentes
traductions, des informations contextuelles indi-
quent également la traduction appropriée.
Exemple:

anneau *m* CHIMIE ring, CONS MECA *d'une chaîne* link,
pour cylindres de broyeur à cylindres shell, CONSTR
d'une clef bow

Renvois

Les variantes linguistiques (entre l'anglais et
l'américain ou entre le français de France, du
Canada, de Suisse et de Belgique) sont toujours
indiquées. Tous les termes non universels sont
accompagnés de la mention typique. La liste

complète de ces mentions figure à la page xxxiii.

En cas de variantes lexicales, les informations
les concernant – et notamment les traductions et
renvois à d'autres formes régionales – sont four-
nies systématiquement à chaque entrée.
Exemple:

baie: ~ **d'emballeur** *f* (Bel) *(cf loge d'emballeur)* CERAM
VER packer's bay
loge: ~ **d'emballeur** *f* (Fra) *(cf baie d'emballeur)* CERAM
VER packer's bay

Lorsque les variantes orthographiques ne sont
pas différenciées par région ou par pays, la forme
la moins courante renvoie à la forme dominante.
Les informations complètes figurent uniquement
sous cette entrée. Exemple:

clef *f voir* clé

Les variantes géographiques, tant orthographiques que lexicales, sont indiquées
intégralement lorsqu'il s'agit de traductions.
Exemple:

frisure *f* CERAM VER chill mark (BrE), chill wrinkle
(AmE), ENREGISTR *de la bande* curl, TEXTILE crimp

Les abréviations et leurs formes intégrales figurent dans le corps principal du dictionnaire,
classées par ordre alphabétique. Les informations complètes – et notamment leurs traductions
et les renvois à leur abréviation ou à leur forme
intégrale, le cas échéant – sont indiquées pour
chaque entrée. Exemple:

CNS *abrév (concentrateur numérique satellite)* TELECOM
digital satellite concentrator
concentrateur *m* ~ **numérique satellite** *m (CNS)* TELE-
COM digital satellite concentrator

La liste alphabétique des abréviations contenues
dans ce dictionnaire figure à la fin de ce volume.
Dans certains cas, les antonymes ou termes contraires sont également spécifiés. Les
informations complètes figurent sous chaque entrée. Exemple:

objectif *m* ~ **à immersion** *m (cf objectif sec)* EQUIP LAB
microscope immersion lens, ~ **sec** *m (cf objectif à
immersion)* EQUIP LAB *microscope* dry lens.

Parts of speech/
Catégories grammaticales

abrév	abréviation	abbreviation
adj	adjectif	adjective
adv	adverbe	adverb
f	féminin	feminine
f pl	féminin pluriel	feminine plural
loc	locution	phrase
m	masculin	masculine
m pl	masculin pluriel	masculine plural
préf	préfixe	prefix
prép	préposition	preposition
vi	verbe intransitif	intransitive verb
v réfl	verbe réfléchi	reflexive verb
vt	verbe transitif	transitive verb
vti	verbe transitif et intransitif	transitive and intransitive verb

---

Registered trademarks

Every effort has been made to label terms which we believe constitute trademarks. The legal status of these, however, remains unchanged by the presence or absence of any such label.

(MD)   marque déposée

Marques déposées

Nous avons fait le maximum pour faire suivre de la mention appropriée les termes que nous estimons protégés par un dépôt de marque. Néanmoins, l'absence ou la présence de cette mention est sans effet sur leur statut légal.

registered trademark (TM)

Subject Labels/Domaines

ACOUSTIQUE	Acoustique	Acoustics
AERONAUT	Aéronautique	Aeronautics
AGRO ALIM	Alimentation	Food Technology
ASTRONOMIE	Astronomie	Astronomy
AUTO	Génie automobile	Automotive Engineering
BREVETS	Brevets et marques de fabrique	Patents and Trademarks
CERAM VER	Céramique et verre	Ceramics and Glass
CHARBON	Technologie du charbon	Coal Technology
CHAUFFAGE	Appareils de chauffage	Heat Engineering Components
CH DE FER	Chemins de fer	Railway Engineering
CHIMIE	Chimie	Chemistry
CINEMAT	Cinématographie	Cinematography
COMMANDE	Contrôle et automatisation	Control Technology
CONS MECA	Construction mécanique	Mechanical Engineering
CONSTR	Construction	Construction
COULEURS	Couleurs	Colours Technology
CRISTALL	Cristallographie	Crystallography
DISTRI EAU	Distribution de l'eau	Water Supply Engineering
ELECTR	Electricité	Electricity
ELECTRON	Electronique industrielle	Electronic Engineering
ELECTROTEC	Electrotechnique	Electrical Engineering
EMBALLAGE	Emballage	Packaging
ENREGISTR	Enregistrement	Recording Engineering
EN RENOUV	Sources d'énergie renouvelable	Fuelless Energy Sources
EQUIP LAB	Equipement de laboratoire	Laboratory Equipment
ESPACE	Technologie spatiale	Space Technology
ESSAIS	Essais	Testing
GAZ	Technologie du gaz	Gas Technology
GENIE CHIM	Génie chimique	Chemical Technology Process
GEOLOGIE	Géologie	Geology
GEOMETRIE	Géométrie	Geometry
GEOPHYS	Géophysique	Geophysics
HYDROLOGIE	Hydrologie	Hydrology
IMPRIM	Imprimerie	Printing
INFORMAT	Informatique	Data Processing
INST HYDR	Matériel hydraulique	Hydraulic Equipment
INSTRUMENT	Instrumentation	Instrumentation
LESSIVES	Détergents	Detergents
MAT CHAUFF	Installations de chauffage	Heating Equipment
MATERIAUX	Propriétés des matériaux	Properties of Materials
MATH	Mathématiques	Mathematics
MECANIQUE	Mécanique	Mechanics
METALL	Métallurgie	Metallurgy
METEO	Météorologie	Meteorology
METROLOGIE	Métrologie	Metrology
MILITAIRE	Armement et défense	Military Technology
MINERAUX	Minéralogie	Mineralogy

MINES	Exploitation minière	Mining
NAUT	Transport par voie d'eau	Water Transport Engineering
NUCLEAIRE	Energie nucléaire	Nuclear Technology
OCEANO	Océanographie	Oceanography
OPTIQUE	Optique	Optics
ORDINAT	Ordinateurs	Computer Technology
PAPIER	Papeterie	Paper Technology
PETR	Pétrologie	Petrology
PETROLE	Technologie du pétrole	Petroleum Technology
PHOTO	Photographie	Photography
PHYSIQUE	Physique	Physics
PHYS FLUID	Physique des fluides	Fluid Physics
PHYS PART	Physique des particules	Particle Physics
PHYS RAYON	Physique des rayonnements	Radiation Physics
PHYS ONDES	Physique ondulatoire	Wave Physics
PLAST CAOU	Plastiques et caoutchouc	Plastics and Rubber
POLLU MER	Pollution de la mer	Marine Pollution
POLLUTION	Pollution	Pollution
PRODUCTION	Gestion de la production	Production Engineering
QUALITE	Assurance de la qualité	Quality Assurance
RECYCLAGE	Recyclage	Recycling
REFRIG	Réfrigération	Refrigeration
RESSORTS	Ressorts	Springs
REVETEMENT	Revêtements	Coatings Technology
SECURITE	Sécurité	Safety Engineering
TELECOM	Télécommunications	Telecommunications
TEXTILE	Textile	Textiles
THERMODYN	Thermodynamique	Thermodynamics
TRANSPORT	Transport	Transport
TV	Télévision	Television
VEHICULES	Pièces détachées pour véhicules	Vehicle Components

Geographic codes/
Codes géographiques

	Varieties of English	**Variantes d'anglais**
(AmE)	American English	anglais américain
(BrE)	British English	anglais britannique
(Can)	Canadian English	anglais canadien

	Varieties of French	**Variantes de français**
(Belg)	Belgium	Belgique
(Can)	Canada	Canada
(Fra)	France	France
(Sui)	Switzerland	Suisse

A

A *abrév (ampère)* ELECTR, ELECTROTEC, METROLOGIE, PHYSIQUE A *(ampere)*

aalénien *adj* GEOLOGIE Aalenian

abaissé *adj* GEOLOGIE downfaulted

abaisse-bobines *m* PAPIER lowering cradle, lowering table

abaissement *m* PHYSIQUE *de la température* lowering, THERMODYN temperature drop, *de la température* heat drop; **~ du pH** *m* POLLUTION pH depression

abaisser *vt* CONSTR *nappe phréatique* lower, IMPRIM *héliogravure* drop, SECURITE *charge* lower

abandon *m* ORDINAT abort; **~ du navire** *m* NAUT abandonment of ship

abandonner[1] *vt* BREVETS abandon, ESPACE, ORDINAT abort

abandonner:[2] **~ le navire** *vi* NAUT abandon ship

abaque *m* MINES abacus major, ORDINAT abacus, PHYSIQUE chart, nomograph, PRODUCTION *pour le calcul des ressorts à boudin* diagram

abats *m pl* AGRO ALIM offal

abattage *m* CHARBON blasting, breaking down, coal winning, broken working, coal getting, mining, MINES breaking ground, stoping, *du minerai* breaking, ore extraction; **~ combiné** *m* MINES combined stoping; **~ conduit parallèlement à la descenderie** *m* MINES side stoping; **~ à l'eau** *m* MINES spatter work; **~ en carrière** *m* MINES quarrying; **~ en filon** *m* MINES lode mining; **~ en gradins** *m* MINES stoping; **~ en gradins renversés** *m* MINES overhand stoping; **~ à l'explosif** *m* MINES blasting; **~ hydraulique** *m* MINES spatter work; **~ latéral** *m* MINES side stoping; **~ mécanique du charbon** *m* CHARBON machine coal mining, mechanized coal-winning; **~ montant** *m* MINES overhand stoping; **~ par explosifs** *m* MINES blasting, shot-firing; **~ par gradins latéraux** *m* MINES side stoping; **~ par longs trous** *m* MINES long hole blasting; **~ par mines longues** *m* MINES long hole blasting; **~ par pans** *m* MINES bench blasting; **~ par trous profonds** *m* MINES long hole blasting; **~ de la roche** *m* CHARBON stoneworking

abattant *m* CONSTR flap

abattée *f* NAUT lee lurch; **~ d'urgence** *f* NAUT emergency turn

abattement *m* IMPRIM *gestion* abatement

abatteuse: **~ en veine** *f* MINES in-seam miner; **~ à tambour** *f* MINES shearer

abatteuse-chargeuse: **~ universelle** *f* MINES universal ripper-loader

abattoir *m* REFRIG abattoir

abattre[1] *vt* CONSTR break down, cut up, tip, tip up, MINES cut, mine, stope, *minerai* break down, NAUT cast, turn, *voile* pay off; **~ les arêtes** *vt* MECANIQUE break edges; **~ en carène** *vt* NAUT *un navire* careen; **~ à l'explosif** *vt* CHARBON, CONSTR blast; **~ la poussière** *vt* MINES lay the dust

abattre[2] *vi* NAUT bear away; **~ sous le vent** *vi* NAUT fall off

abattre:[3] **s'~** *v réfl* NAUT abate, drop

abée *f* PRODUCTION flume, leat

abélien *adj* MATH abelian

aber *m* HYDROLOGIE drowned river valley, river mouth

aberration *f* ASTRONOMIE, METALL, OPTIQUE, PHYS ONDES aberration; **~ chromatique** *f* ASTRONOMIE *d'un téléobjectif*, PHOTO, PHYSIQUE chromatic aberration, TV chromaticity aberration; **~ chromatique longitudinale** *f* PHYSIQUE longitudinal chromatic aberration; **~ chromatique transversale** *f* PHYSIQUE transverse chromatic aberration; **~ de coma** *f* ASTRONOMIE *d'un télescope* coma aberration; **~ optique** *f* TELECOM optical aberration; **~ de réfraction** *f* PHYSIQUE Newtonian aberration; **~ de sphéricité** *f* ASTRONOMIE *d'un télescope à réflection*, PHYSIQUE *d'un télescope à réflection* spherical aberration; **~ sphérique** *f* CINEMAT, PHOTO, TELECOM spherical aberration

abiétate *m* CHIMIE abietate

abîmé *adj* MECANIQUE worn

abîmer *vt* SECURITE *organes, système respiratoire* damage

ablatif *adj* ESPACE *véhicules* ablative

ablation *f* HYDROLOGIE, ORDINAT *enregistrement optique*, PHYSIQUE ablation; **~ de terre ferme** *f* HYDROLOGIE coastal erosion

abluant *m* GENIE CHIM detergent

abondance *f* PHYSIQUE abundance; **~ annuelle** *f* DISTRI EAU annual flow; **~ isotopique** *f* PHYSIQUE isotopic abundance; **~ nucléaire** *f* PHYSIQUE nuclear abundance; **~ relative** *f* PHYSIQUE relative abundance

abonné *m* CH DE FER season ticket holder, ELECTR, INFORMAT, ORDINAT, TELECOM subscriber; **~ absent** *m* TELECOM absent subscriber; **~ à bord** *m* TELECOM *maritime mobile* on-board subscriber; **~ itinérant** *m* TELECOM roaming subscriber; **~ résiliateur** *m* TELECOM ceased subscriber

abonnement *m* TELECOM line rental

abord *m* CONSTR, NAUT approach

abordage *m* ESPACE *véhicules* docking, NAUT collision, *dans un assaut* boarding; **~ aérien** *m* AERONAUT aerial collision; **~ à quai** *m* NAUT berthing

aborder[1] *vt* NAUT board, go alongside, ram, run down

aborder[2] *vi* NAUT collide; **~ à quai** *vi* NAUT berth

abords *m pl* OCEANO approaches

aboucher *vt* CONSTR *des tuyaux* join up

about *m* CONSTR butt, butt end, NAUT butt

aboutement *m* CONSTR abutment, butting, MECANIQUE butt

abouter[1] *vt* CONSTR abut, butt-joint

abouter:[2] **s'~** *v réfl* CONSTR abut

aboutir *vi* TELECOM terminate

abrasif[1] *adj* CHARBON, IMPRIM, MATERIAUX, MECANIQUE, PAPIER, PRODUCTION, SECURITE abrasive

abrasif[2] *m* CHARBON abradant, MATERIAUX abradant, abrasive, grinding medium, MECANIQUE *matériaux* abrasive, PAPIER abrasive material, PRODUCTION, SECURITE abrasive; **~ appliqué** *m* CONS MECA coated abrasive; **~ de décapage** *m* MECANIQUE grit; **~ de doucissage** *m* CERAM VER grinding agent; **~ sur support papier imperméable** *m* CONS MECA waterproof abrasive paper

abrasimètre *m* MECANIQUE *matériaux* abrasion tester, PAPIER abraser, abrasion tester, PLAST CAOU *instrument d'essai* abrasion tester

abrasion *f* CHARBON, GEOLOGIE, HYDROLOGIE abrasion, IMPRIM abrasion, abrasiveness, MATERIAUX, MECANIQUE, PAPIER, PLAST CAOU *terme physique* abrasion; ~ **Taber** *f* PLAST CAOU Taber abrasion

abrasivité *f* CHARBON abrasiveness

abrégé *m* BREVETS abstract

abreuver *vt* DISTRI EAU *une pompe* prime

abri *m* CH DE FER *véhicules* driver's cab (BrE), engineer's cab (AmE), CHARBON blast shelter, CONSTR manhole, refuge hole, shelter, ESPACE *véhicules*, MILITAIRE shelter, NAUT lee, shelter, TRANSPORT shelter; ~ **antigaz** *m* MILITAIRE antigas shelter; ~ **antiretombées** *m* NUCLEAIRE fallout shelter; ~ **collectif souple** *m* MILITAIRE *guerre chimique* collective protection shelter; ~ **contre le vent** *m* NAUT lee; ~ **de défense** *m* MILITAIRE dug-out; ~ **du mécanicien** *m* CH DE FER *véhicules* driver's cab (BrE), engineer's cab (AmE); ~ **de protection** *m* MILITAIRE dug-in; ~ **de rampe** *m* ESPACE *véhicules* launch ramp shelter; ~ **de sondeur** *m* PETROLE doghouse; ~ **de téléphone** *m* MILITAIRE telephone dugout

abrité *adj* CONS MECA drip-proof

abrité-grillagé *adj* CONS MECA drip-proof screen-protected

abriter *vt* NAUT shelter

abscisique *adj* CHIMIE abscissic

abscisse *f* INFORMAT abscissa, PHYSIQUE x-coordinate; ~ **curviligne** *f* PHYSIQUE curvilinear coordinate

absence *f* ACOUSTIQUE *d'harmoniques*, ESPACE *thermique* absence; ~ **systématique** *f* CRISTALL systematic absence; ~ **totale de réflexion** *f* IMPRIM *papier, encres* black

absinthe *f* CHIMIE absinth

absolu *adj* CHIMIE, INFORMAT, ORDINAT absolute

absorbable *adj* MATERIAUX, PAPIER absorbable

absorbance *f* PHYS RAYON, PHYSIQUE absorbance

absorbant[1] *adj* MATERIAUX PAPIER absorbent, absorptive

absorbant[2] *m* CHARBON, CHIMIE, MATERIAUX, MECANIQUE *matériaux*, PAPIER absorbent, POLLU MER sorbent, POLLUTION absorbent; ~ **de neutrons** *m* NUCLEAIRE neutron absorber; ~ **poreux** *m* ACOUSTIQUE porous absorber

absorbe: qui ~ la chaleur *adj* TEXTILE, THERMODYN heat-absorbing

absorber *vt* CHARBON absorb, CHIMIE *un métal* occlude, CONS MECA, PAPIER absorb

absorbeur *m* PAPIER, REFRIG absorber; ~ **articulé** *m* NUCLEAIRE articulated absorber; ~ **de chute libre** *m* NUCLEAIRE gravity drop absorber rod; ~ **composite** *m* NUCLEAIRE composite absorber; ~ **d'humidité** *m* CONSTR moisture absorber, EMBALLAGE humidity absorber; ~ **de résonance** *m* AUTO resonance damper; ~ **solaire** *m* ESPACE *thermique* solar absorber

absorbeur-neutralisateur *m* ESPACE scrubber, NUCLEAIRE gas scrubber, gas washer

absorptance *f* PHYSIQUE absorptance

absorptif *adj* CHIMIE absorbent

absorptiomètre *m* PAPIER absorptiometer, absorption tester

absorptiométrie *f* NUCLEAIRE absorptiometry

absorption *f* AGRO ALIM, CHARBON, ELECTROTEC, GENIE CHIM, OPTIQUE, PAPIER, PETR, PHYS RAYON *fréquences hertziennes et optiques*, PLAST CAOU absorption; ~ **acoustique** *f* ACOUSTIQUE sound absorption, ENREGISTR acoustic absorption; ~ **atmosphérique** *f* METEO, PHYS RAYON atmospheric absorption; ~ **de chaleur** *f* THERMODYN heat absorption; ~ **diélectrique** *f* ELECTROTEC dielectric absorption; ~ **d'eau** *f* ESSAIS water absorption, TEXTILE water inhibition; ~ **d'énergie** *f* TELECOM energy absorption; ~ **de gaz** *f* GAZ, PETROLE *raffinage* gas absorption; ~ **hyperfréquence** *f* TELECOM microwave absorption; ~ **de lumière** *f* PHYS RAYON absorption of light, extinction of light; ~ **optique** *f* PHYS RAYON optical absorption; ~ **par ozone** *f* PHYS RAYON ozone absorption; ~ **par le sol** *f* DISTRI EAU absorption in the soil; ~ **photon-photon** *f* PHYS PART photon-photon absorption; ~ **photosphérique** *f* PHYS RAYON *photosphère solaire* photospheric absorption; ~ **propre** *f* CHIMIE self-absorption; ~ **de rayonnement** *f* PHYS ONDES absorption of radiation; ~ **de rayonnement ionisant** *f* PHYS RAYON absorption of ionizing radiation; ~ **de rayons X** *f* PHYS RAYON X-ray absorption; ~ **résonante** *f* TELECOM resonant absorption; ~ **du son** *f* ENREGISTR sound absorption; ~ **spécifique** *f* METEO specific absorption; ~ **sur charbon actif** *f* POLLUTION active carbon absorption

absorptivité *f* CHAUFFAGE parameterization, DISTRI EAU water absorption capacity, PAPIER absorption factor, absorptiveness, absorptivity, TV absorptivity; ~ **solaire** *f* EN RENOUV solar absorptivity

abstraction *f* INFORMAT abstraction; ~ **de données** *f* INFORMAT, ORDINAT data abstraction

abstrait *adj* INFORMAT, ORDINAT abstract

abus *m* BREVETS abuse

Ac *(actinium)* CHIMIE Ac *(actinium)*

acanthikon *m* MINERAUX acanthicone, akanticone

acanthite *f* MINERAUX acanthite

accalmie *f* NAUT lull

accastillage *m* NAUT fittings; ~ **de pont** *m* NAUT deck fittings

accastiller *vt* NAUT fit out

accéder: ~ à *vti* ORDINAT access

accélérateur[1] *adj* PAPIER accelerating, accelerative

accélérateur[2] *m* AGRO ALIM accelerator, CHAUFFAGE circulating pump, ELECTROTEC, ESPACE *propulsion*, GENIE CHIM, MECANIQUE *véhicules*, NAUT accelerator, PAPIER accelerating agent, PHYS PART, PLAST CAOU *ingrédient de mélange*, TELECOM, VEHICULES *carburateur* accelerator; ~ **d'électrons** *m* PHYS PART electron accelerator; ~ **à impulsion** *m* PHYS RAYON pulse accelerator; ~ **à induction** *m* PHYS RAYON betatron, induction accelerator; ~ **d'ions** *m* PHYS PART ion accelerator; ~ **linéaire** *m* ELECTROTEC, PHYS PART, PHYSIQUE linear accelerator; ~ **linéaire d'électrons** *m* PHYS PART electron linear accelerator; ~ **de particules** *m* PHYS PART, PHYSIQUE particle accelerator; ~ **de prise** *m* CONSTR accelerator; ~ **à propagation d'ondes** *m* PHYS RAYON wave-propagating accelerator; ~ **surrégénérateur** *m* NUCLEAIRE accelerator breeder; ~ **surrégénérateur au sel fondu** *m* NUCLEAIRE accelerator molten salt breeder; ~ **tandem** *m* PHYSIQUE tandem generator

accélération *f* ESPACE *propulsion*, MECANIQUE, PAPIER, PHYSIQUE acceleration, PRODUCTION expediting, VEHICULES acceleration; ~ **acoustique** *f* ACOUSTIQUE sound acceleration; ~ **acoustique de référence** *f* ACOUSTIQUE reference sound acceleration; ~ **centrifuge** *f* AERONAUT centrifugal acceleration; ~ **centripète** *f* AERONAUT centripetal acceleration; ~ **de**

Coriolis *f* ESPACE *propulsion*, MECANIQUE Coriolis acceleration; ~ **due à la gravité** *f* PHYSIQUE gravity acceleration; ~ **du faisceau d'électrons** *f* ELECTRON electron beam acceleration; ~ **lente** *f* PRODUCTION *automatisme industriel* long acceleration; ~ **linéaire temporisée** *f* PRODUCTION *automatisme industriel* linear timed acceleration; ~ **négative** *f* CONS MECA minus acceleration, retardation, retarded acceleration; ~ **par la pesanteur** *f* GEOLOGIE gravitational acceleration; ~ **d'une particule** *f* ACOUSTIQUE particle acceleration; ~ **de la pesanteur** *f* ESPACE, PHYSIQUE gravity acceleration; ~ **séculaire** *f* ASTRONOMIE secular acceleration; ~ **tangentielle** *f* MECANIQUE, PHYSIQUE tangential acceleration; ~ **uniforme** *f* PAPIER uniform acceleration

accéléré *adj* PHYSIQUE accelerated

accélérer *vt* ESPACE *propulsion*, MECANIQUE boost, PAPIER accelerate, speed up, PHYSIQUE, PRODUCTION accelerate

accéléromètre *m* AERONAUT, ELECTROTEC, MECANIQUE, PAPIER, PETR, PHYSIQUE accelerometer; ~ **inertiel** *m* ESPACE inertial accelerometer; ~ **transversal** *m* AERONAUT lateral accelerometer

accent *m* IMPRIM accent; ~ **flottant** *m* IMPRIM floating accent; ~ **séparé** *m* IMPRIM floating accent, loose accent (BrE), piece accent (AmE); ~ **superposé** *m* IMPRIM floating accent, loose accent (BrE), piece accent (AmE)

accentuation: ~ **des contours** *f* TV edge enhancement; ~ **des images** *f* ASTRONOMIE, ESPACE *communications* image enhancement

accentuer *vt* IMPRIM *composition* accentuate, enhance

acceptation *f* QUALITE acceptance; ~ **d'adresses étendues** *f* TELECOM long address acceptance; ~ **de débordement** *f* TELECOM OA, overflow accept; ~ **pour remise** *f* TELECOM ITD, input transaction accepted for delivery

accepteur *m* CHIMIE, ELECTR *induction, circuit*, ELECTRON, ORDINAT *semi-conducteurs* acceptor; ~ **d'acide** *m* PLAST CAOU *ingrédient de mélange* acid acceptor

accès *m* CHARBON access, CONSTR approach, ESPACE *communications*, ORDINAT, TELECOM access; ~ **aléatoire** *m* ESPACE *communications*, IMPRIM, INFORMAT, ORDINAT random access; ~ **aléatoire à la mémoire** *m* INFORMAT, ORDINAT memory random access; ~ **d'arrivée** *m* TELECOM inlet; ~ **de base** *m* TELECOM *ISDN* basic access; ~ **au débit de base** *m* TELECOM *ISDN* BRA, basic rate access; ~ **au débit primaire** *m* TELECOM PRA, primary rate access; ~ **au débit primaire au RNIS** *m* TELECOM ISDN primary rate access; ~ **de départ** *m* TELECOM outlet; ~ **direct** *m* INFORMAT, ORDINAT direct access, immediate access, random access; ~ **direct à l'arrivée** *m* TELECOM DID (AmE), direct inward dialing (AmE); ~ **direct à la mémoire** *m* INFORMAT, ORDINAT DMA, direct memory access; ~ **direct à un poste** *m* TELECOM direct inward dialing (AmE), direct inward dialling (BrE); ~ **direct au réseau** *m* TELECOM DOD, direct outward dialling; ~ **à distance** *m* INFORMAT, ORDINAT remote access; ~ **de données numériques** *m* TELECOM data port; ~ **en mode asynchrone** *m* TELECOM asynchronous port; ~ **en mode paquet** *m* TELECOM packet port; ~ **fichier** *m* INFORMAT, ORDINAT file access; ~ **instantané** *m* INFORMAT random access; ~ **intégré** *m* TELECOM integrated access; ~ **au lexique** *m* TELECOM lexical access; ~ **mémoire** *m* INFORMAT, ORDINAT memory access; ~ **à la mémoire** *m*

ELECTROTEC memory access; ~ **monoutilisateur** *m* INFORMAT, ORDINAT single user access; ~ **multiple** *m* ESPACE *communications*, TELECOM multiple access; ~ **multiple aléatoire** *m* TELECOM random multiple access; ~ **multiple par détection de collision** *m* (*CSMA-CD*) INFORMAT carrier sense multiple access with collision detection (*CSMA-CD*); ~ **multiple par détection de porteuse** *m* (*CSMA*) TELECOM carrier sense multiple access (*CSMA*); ~ **multiple par détection de porteuse avec détection de collision** *m* (*CSMA-CD*) ELECTRON, ORDINAT carrier sense multiple access with collision detection (*CSMA-CD*); ~ **multiple par étalement du spectre** *m* (*AMES*) ESPACE *communications* spread spectrum multiple access (*SSMA*); ~ **multiple par répartition en code** *m* (*AMRC*) ESPACE *communications* code-division multiple access (*CDMA*); ~ **multiple à répartition en fréquence** *m* (*AMRF*) ESPACE, TELECOM frequency-division multiple access (*FDMA*); ~ **multiple temporel** *m* ELECTRON, TELECOM time-division multiple access; ~ **multiple par répartition dans le temps** *m* (*AMRT*) ELECTRON, ESPACE *communications*, INFORMAT, TELECOM time-division multiple access (*TDMA*); ~ **octet** *m* PRODUCTION *automatisme industriel* get byte; ~ **aux octets de surdébit** *m* TELECOM OHA, overhead access; ~ **parallèle** *m* INFORMAT, ORDINAT parallel access; ~ **par file d'attente** *m* INFORMAT, ORDINAT queued access; ~ **par liaison spécialisée** *m* TELECOM dedicated port; ~ **par réseau commuté** *m* TELECOM dial-up port; ~ **primaire** *m* TELECOM primary access; ~ **privé par réseau commuté** *m* TELECOM private dial-up port; ~ **aux quais** *m* CH DE FER access to platforms; ~ **au RNIS** *m* TELECOM ISDN access; ~ **sélectif** *m* INFORMAT random access; ~ **sélectif à la mémoire** *m* ORDINAT memory random access; ~ **séquentiel** *m* INFORMAT, ORDINAT sequential access, serial access; ~ **séquentiel indexé** *m* INFORMAT, ORDINAT indexed sequential access; ~ **séquentiel sélectif** *m* INFORMAT, ORDINAT selective sequential access; ~ **au surdébit** *m* TELECOM OHA, overhead access; ~ **d'usager** *m* TELECOM user access

accessibilité *f* MECANIQUE, QUALITE accessibility

accessoire *m* CHARBON attachment, CONS MECA attachment, fitting, MECANIQUE fitting, PRODUCTION option, *d'une machine* attachment; ~ **brisable** *m* CINEMAT breakaway prop; ~ **de projection** *m* INSTRUMENT projector attachment

accessoires *m pl* CONS MECA fittings; ~ **d'auto** *m pl* VEHICULES car accessories; ~ **de chaudière** *m pl* INST HYDR boiler fittings; ~ **de chaudières** *m pl* PRODUCTION boiler fittings; ~ **de circuit hydraulique** *m pl* INST HYDR hydraulic fittings; ~ **de générateur** *m pl* INST HYDR boiler fittings; ~ **d'installation** *m pl* PRODUCTION installation accessories; ~ **pour automobile** *m pl* VEHICULES car accessories; ~ **de voiture** *m pl* VEHICULES car accessories

accessoiriste *m* PRODUCTION component manufacturer

accident *m* MINES leap; ~ **causé par réfrigération** *m* REFRIG chilling injury; ~ **causé par refroidissement brusque** *m* REFRIG chilling injury; ~ **à déclarer obligatoirement** *m* SECURITE notifiable accident, reportable accident; ~ **de dépressurisation** *m* NUCLEAIRE blowdown accident, depressurization accident; ~ **dû au froid** *m* REFRIG cold injury; ~ **électrique** *m* SECURITE electrical accident; ~ **mortel** *m* SECURITE fatal accident; ~ **potentiel** *m* SECURITE potential accident; ~ **du travail** *m* CONSTR accident at work, SECURITE industrial accident, industrial injury

accidentellement *adv* SECURITE accidentally

accidents: ~ **de fonctionnement** *m pl* SECURITE running accidents; ~ **de levage** *m pl* SECURITE lifting accidents; ~ **au personnel ouvrier** *m pl* SECURITE accidents to workers; ~ **du travail** *m pl* SECURITE accidents to workers

acclimatation *f* CHAUFFAGE, METEO acclimatization

acclimaté *adj* MATERIAUX acclimatized

acclimater[1] *vt* METEO acclimatize

acclimater:[2] **s'~** *v réfl* METEO acclimatize

accolades *f pl* IMPRIM brackets

accompagnateur: ~ **de wagons-lit** *m pl* CH DE FER sleeping car attendant

accord *m* ACOUSTIQUE chord, concord, ELECTRON, NAUT, TELECOM tuning; ~ **adaptatif** *m* ELECTRON adaptive tuning; ~ **capacitif** *m* ELECTROTEC capacitive tuning; ~ **continu** *m* ELECTRON continuous tuning; ~ **d'échange** *m* TELECOM communications agreement; ~ **électrique** *m* ELECTRON electric tuning; ~ **électromagnétique** *m* ELECTRON electromagnetic tuning; ~ **électronique** *m* ELECTRON, TELECOM electronic tuning; ~ **en fréquence** *m* TELECOM frequency tuning; ~ **en phase** *m* TELECOM phase tuning; ~ **fin** *m* ELECTRON fine tuning; ~ **fixe** *m* ELECTRON fixed tuning; ~ **fondamental** *m* ACOUSTIQUE fundamental chord; ~ **gros** *m* ELECTR *d'instrument* coarse adjustment; ~ **multioctave** *m* ELECTRON multioctave tuning; ~ **numérique** *m* ELECTRON digital tuning; ~ **optique** *m* TELECOM optical tuning; ~ **par commande unique** *m* ELECTROTEC ganged tuning; ~ **par cristal YIG** *m* ELECTRON YIG tuning; ~ **par diode varicap** *m* ELECTRON varactor tuning; ~ **parfait majeur** *m* ACOUSTIQUE major common chord; ~ **par noyau plongeur** *m* ELECTROTEC slug tuning; ~ **par noyau réglable** *m* ELECTROTEC slug tuning; ~ **par paliers** *m* ELECTRON incremental tuning; ~ **par variation de capacité** *m* ELECTROTEC capacitive tuning; ~ **par YIG** *m* ELECTRON YIG tuning; ~ **sinusoïdal** *m* ELECTRON sine wave tuning; ~ **sur plusieurs octaves** *m* ELECTRON multioctave tuning; ~ **thermique** *m* ELECTRON thermal tuning

accordage *m* ACOUSTIQUE tuning

accordé *adj* PHYS RAYON tuned

accorder *vt* ELECTRON, TELECOM tune

accore *f* NAUT *construction navale* shore, OCEANO bluff, bold shore, steep coast, escarpment, sea scarp; ~ **de bouchain** *f* NAUT bilge shore

accorer *vt* NAUT shore up

accostage *m* ESPACE berthing, docking, NAUT berthing, drawing alongside, landing

accoster[1] *vt* ESPACE *véhicules* dock, NAUT dock, *le long du quai* berth, *le quai* haul alongside, *à quai* go alongside; ~ **à nouveau** *vt* ESPACE *véhicules* redock

accoster[2] *vi* NAUT board

accotement *m* CONSTR shoulder; ~ **stabilisé** *m* CONSTR hard shoulder

accoudoir *m* VEHICULES *de siège* armrest

accouplé: **être ~** *vi* ELECTROTEC be coupled

accouplement *m* AERONAUT coupling, CINEMAT clutch, CONS MECA coupling box, *de deux arbres* coupling, ELECTR *raccordement, induction* coupling, *résistances* ganging, ELECTROTEC coupling, *d'axes* shaft coupling, MECANIQUE, NAUT coupling; ~ **d'arbres** *m* CONS MECA shaft coupling; ~ **articulé** *m* CONS MECA flexible shaft coupling; ~ **d'axes** *m* ELECTROTEC shaft coupling; ~ **à bande** *m* CONS MECA band coupling; ~ **à cardan** *m*

AERONAUT cardan; ~ **à cliquet** *m* CONS MECA pawl coupling; ~ **à débrayage** *m* CONS MECA clutch coupling; ~ **à déclic** *m* CONS MECA impulse coupling; ~ **à déconnexion par traction** *m* ELECTR *raccordement* pull-off coupling; ~ **à dents crémaillère** *m* NUCLEAIRE toothed rack; ~ **direct** *m* EN RENOUV direct coupling; ~ **élastique** *m* CONS MECA compensating coupling, flexible coupling; ~ **élastique pour arbre de transmission** *m* CONS MECA resilient shaft coupling; ~ **flexible** *m* CONS MECA flexible coupling; ~ **à griffe** *m* CONS MECA dog coupling; ~ **à manchon** *m* CONS MECA box coupling, butt coupling, muff coupling, sleeve coupling; ~ **Oldham** *m* MECANIQUE Oldham coupling; ~ **à plateaux** *m* CONS MECA faceplate coupling, flange coupling, plate coupling; ~ **pneumatique** *m* CONS MECA *transmission d'énergie* pneumatic coupling; ~ **rigide** *m* CONS MECA rigid coupling; ~ **à rotule** *m* CONS MECA ball and socket joint; ~ **synchrone** *m* ELECTR *de bobine* synchronous coupling

accoupler[1] *vt* CH DE FER *véhicules* couple, CONS MECA attach, ELECTROTEC couple, PAPIER *des machines* connect, couple

accoupler:[2] **s'~** *v réfl* ELECTROTEC be coupled

accrétion *f* ASTRONOMIE, DISTRI EAU, METEO accretion; ~ **continentale** *f* GEOLOGIE continental accretion; ~ **littorale** *f* OCEANO progradation; ~ **de matière** *f* ASTRONOMIE accretion of matter; ~ **des terrains** *f* DISTRI EAU land accretion

accroc *m* ENREGISTR scratch, TEXTILE snag

accrochage *m* AERONAUT *sur un faisceau* lock-on, ELECTRON singing, ELECTROTEC crawling, IMPRIM *impression* bond, MINES landing stage, landing station, lodge, onsetting, pit landing, plane table, platt, PRODUCTION hang, TELECOM squealing; ~ **à barre** *m* CONS MECA bar hanger; ~ **de la charge** *m* AERONAUT load hook-up; ~ **de l'impression** *m* IMPRIM trapping; ~ **du jour** *m* MINES bank; ~ **de la nappe** *m* TEXTILE batt anchorage; ~ **normal de l'encre sur papier** *m* IMPRIM *impression* hold-out; ~ **de phase** *m* TV phase locking; ~ **de la porteuse** *m* ELECTRON carrier acquisition; ~ **sec sur sec** *m* IMPRIM *impression* dry tapping; ~ **train bas** *m* AERONAUT landing gear downlock; ~ **train rentré** *m* AERONAUT landing gear uplock; ~ **des trappes de train** *m* AERONAUT landing gear door latch

accroche *f* IMPRIM catchline, *presse, publicité* tag

accrochement *m* SECURITE trapping

accrocher[1] *vt* PETROLE *tige sur les élévateurs* latch

accrocher:[2] **s'~** *v réfl* PRODUCTION hang

accroche-tube *m* CONSTR casing grab, pipe grab

accrocheur *m* MINES dog, grab, hoisting dog, onsetter (BrE), platman (AmE), PETR derrick man, PETROLE derrick man, derrick monkey

accroissement *m* GEOLOGIE *de la croûte continentale* continental accretion

accroupissement *m* TRANSPORT squat

accumulateur *m* ELECTR accumulator, ELECTROTEC accumulator, battery, secondary cell, storage cell, ESPACE battery, secondary battery, storage cell, INST HYDR accumulator, battery, NAUT battery, *d'électricité* accumulator, ORDINAT accumulator, battery, PAPIER accumulator, accumulator tank, battery, PHOTO battery pack, powerpack unit, PHYSIQUE accumulator, battery, storage battery, TRANSPORT storage battery, VEHICULES accumulator, battery, lead-acid battery; ~ **aérohydraulique** *m* CHAUFFAGE *chaufferie à eau chaude* air bottle; ~ **alcalin** *m* ELECTR alkaline storage battery, ELECTROTEC alkaline storage cell; ~ à l'argent *m* ELECTROTEC silver cell; ~ **argent-cadmium** *m* ELECTROTEC silver cadmium cell; ~ **argent-zinc** *m* ELECTROTEC silver zinc cell, silver zinc storage cell, TRANSPORT silver zinc storage battery; ~ **argent-zinc amorçable** *m* ELECTROTEC silver zinc primary cell; ~ **d'aspiration antibélier** *m* REFRIG suction line accumulator; ~ **autonome** *m* INST HYDR self-contained accumulator; ~ **au cadmium nickel** *m* CINEMAT nickel cadmium battery; ~ **cadmium-nickel** *m* ELECTROTEC cadmium nickel cell; ~ **de chaleur** *m* THERMODYN heat accumulator, TRANSPORT thermal energy storage system; ~ **de démarrage** *m* TRANSPORT starter battery; ~ **Edison** *m* ELECTROTEC ferronickel cell; ~ **à électrolyte alcalin** *m* ELECTROTEC alkaline storage cell; ~ **à électrolyte gélifié** *m* ELECTROTEC gel cell; ~ **à électrolyte non-aqueux** *m* TRANSPORT nonaqueous electrolyte battery; ~ **fer-nickel** *m* ELECTR *pile* Edison cell; ~ **à grillage** *m* PAPIER grid-type accumulator, grid-type battery; ~ **hydraulique** *m* AERONAUT hydraulic accumulator, hydraulic battery, CONS MECA hydraulic accumulator, hydropneumatic accumulator, PLAST CAOU *presse* hydraulic accumulator; ~ **hydropneumatique** *m* CONS MECA gas-loaded accumulator; ~ **inversible** *m* VEHICULES *système électrique* nonspill battery (BrE), sealed battery (AmE); ~ **lithium-chlore** *m* TRANSPORT lithium-chlorine storage battery; ~ **métal-air** *m* TRANSPORT metal-air battery; ~ **négatif** *m* TELECOM negative battery; ~ **nickel-cadmium** *m* TRANSPORT nickel cadmium battery; ~ **nickel-fer** *m* ELECTROTEC ferronickel cell, TRANSPORT nickel iron storage battery; ~ **nickel-zinc** *m* TRANSPORT nickel zinc storage battery; ~ **à oxyde d'argent** *m* TRANSPORT silver oxide storage battery; ~ **performant** *m* TRANSPORT high-performance battery; ~ **à plaques de nickel et de cadmium** *m* PHOTO Nicad battery; ~ **au plomb** *m* ELECTR lead-acid accumulator, ELECTROTEC lead-acid cell, PHYSIQUE lead accumulator, TRANSPORT lead-acid battery; ~ **positif** *m* TELECOM positive battery; ~ **de pression** *m* PAPIER pressure accumulator; ~ **de pression hydraulique inversé** *m* INST HYDR inverted pattern accumulator; ~ **rechargeable** *m* CINEMAT, ELECTROTEC, TV rechargeable battery; ~ **sec** *m* ELECTR dry-storage battery, ELECTROTEC gel cell; ~ **aux sels fondus à haute température** *m* TRANSPORT high-temperature molten salts fuel battery (AmE); ~ **sodium soufre** *m* TRANSPORT sodium sulfur storage battery (AmE), sodium sulphur storage battery (BrE); ~ **tampon** *m* REFRIG accumulator, battery; ~ **de vapeur** *m* INST HYDR, PAPIER steam accumulator; ~ **zinc-air** *m* TRANSPORT zinc-air storage battery

accumulation *f* METEO accumulation; ~ **de chaleur** *f* THERMODYN heat accumulation; ~ **de charges** *f* ELECTROTEC charge build-up; ~ **d'énergie** *f* ELECTROTEC, THERMODYN energy storage

accumulé *adj* CONSTR heaped

accusé: ~ **de réception** *m (AR)* INFORMAT, ORDINAT, TELECOM acknowledgement *(ACK);* ~ **de réception de message d'entrée** *m* TELECOM IMA, input message acknowledgment; ~ **de réception négatif** *m* INFORMAT, ORDINAT NAK, negative acknowledgment; ~ **de réception positif** *m* INFORMAT, ORDINAT positive acknowledgment; ~ **de réception des produits** *m* QUALITE receipt for goods; ~ **de réception technique** *m* TELECOM technical acknowledgement

accuser: ~ **réception de** *vt* ORDINAT acknowledge re-

ceipt of

acerdèse *f* MINERAUX manganite

acétal[1] *adj* AGRO ALIM acetal

acétal[2] *m* PLAST CAOU acetal

acétaldéhyde *m* AGRO ALIM acetaldehyde

acétanilide *m* CHIMIE acetanilide

acétate *m* AGRO ALIM, CHIMIE, IMPRIM, TEXTILE acetate; ~ **d'amyle** *m* PAPIER, PLAST CAOU *solvant* amyl acetate; ~ **de bornyle** *m* CHIMIE bornyl acetate; ~ **de butyle** *m* PLAST CAOU *solvant* butyl acetate; ~ **de cellulose** *m* PLAST CAOU *plastiques, peintures* cellulose acetate; ~ **d'éthyle** *m* AGRO ALIM, PLAST CAOU *solvant* ethyl acetate; ~ **de méthyle** *m* CHIMIE, LESSIVES methyl acetate; ~ **de vinyle** *m* MATERIAUX vinyl acetate

acétification *f* CHIMIE acetification

acétifier *vt* CHIMIE acetify

acétine *f* AGRO ALIM acetoin, glyceryl monacoleate, CHIMIE acetin

acétique *adj* CHIMIE acetic

acétobacter *m* AGRO ALIM acetobacter

acétobutyrate: ~ **de cellulose** *m* PLAST CAOU cellulose acetobutyrate

acétoglycéride *f* AGRO ALIM fatty acid glyceride

acétolyse *f* AGRO ALIM, CHIMIE acetolysis

acétone *f* AGRO ALIM acetone, ketone, CHIMIE, IMPRIM, PLAST CAOU *solvant* acetone

acétonitrile *m* CHIMIE acetonitrile

acétonurie *f* CHIMIE acetonuria

acétophénone *f* CHIMIE acetophenone

acétoxy- *préf* CHIMIE acetoxy-

acétylation *f* PAPIER acetylation

acétyle *m* PAPIER acetyl

acétylène *m* CHIMIE *gaz*, CONSTR, GAZ, PAPIER, PRODUCTION *matériaux*, SECURITE acetylene

acétylénique *adj* CHIMIE acetylenic

acétyler *vt* PAPIER acetylate

acétylsalicylique *adj* CHIMIE acetylsalicylic

acétylure *m* CHIMIE acetylide

acheminement *m* INFORMAT, ORDINAT route, routing, TELECOM routing; ~ **adaptatif** *m* INFORMAT adaptive routing; ~ **détourné** *m* TELECOM alternative routing; ~ **intérieur** *m* TRANSPORT inland haulage; ~ **des messages** *m* INFORMAT, ORDINAT message routing; ~ **par le chargeur** *m* TRANSPORT merchant haulage; ~ **retour** *m* TELECOM reverse routing; ~ **section par section** *m* TELECOM link-by-link traffic routing

acheteur *m* PRODUCTION vendor scheduler, QUALITE purchaser

achèvement: ~ **de l'affinage** *m* CERAM VER seed-free time

achever *vt* PRODUCTION finish

achondrites *f pl* ASTRONOMIE achondrites

achrématite *f* MINERAUX achrematite

achroïte *f* MINERAUX achroite

achromat *m* PHYSIQUE achromat

achromatique *adj* IMPRIM, PHYSIQUE achromatic

aciculaire *adj* METALL acicular, needle-shaped

aciculiforme *adj* CHIMIE aciform

aciculite *f* MINERAUX aciculite

acide[1] *adj* CHIMIE, PETROLE acidic

acide[2] *m* AGRO ALIM, CHIMIE, PAPIER, TEXTILE acid; ~ **abiétique** *m* PAPIER abietic acid; ~ **acétique** *m* AGRO ALIM acetic acid, ethanoic acid, white vinegar, PLAST CAOU acetic acid; ~ **acétique crystallisable** *m* AGRO ALIM glacial acetic acid; ~ **acétique glacial** *m* CHIMIE glacial acetic acid; ~ **acrylique** *m* MATERIAUX acrylic acid; ~ **alcanesulfonique** *m* LESSIVES alkyl sulfonic acid

(AmE), alkyl sulphonic acid (BrE); ~ **alginique** *m* AGRO ALIM alginic acid; ~ **aminé** *m* AGRO ALIM, CHIMIE amino acid; ~ **arachidonique** *m* AGRO ALIM arachidonic acid; ~ **aspartique** *m* AGRO ALIM aspartic acid; ~ **azotique** *m* CHIMIE nitric acid; ~ **barbiturique** *m* CHIMIE barbituric acid; ~ **benzoïque** *m* AGRO ALIM benzoic acid; ~ **biliaire** *m* CHIMIE bile acid; ~ **borique** *m* CERAM VER, CHIMIE boric acid; ~ **butyrique** *m* AGRO ALIM butyric acid; ~ **caféique** *m* AGRO ALIM caffeic acid; ~ **carbonique** *m* CHIMIE carbon dioxide, MINES stythe; ~ **de chambre** *m* GENIE CHIM chamber acid; ~ **chlorhydrique** *m* AGRO ALIM acid chloride, chloric acid, CHIMIE, LESSIVES hydrochloric acid; ~ **chlorocarbonique** *m* CHIMIE carbonyl chloride; ~ **citrique** *m* AGRO ALIM, LESSIVES citric acid; ~ **comestible** *m* AGRO ALIM edible acid; ~ **désoxyribonucléique** *m* *(ADN)* CHIMIE deoxyribonucleic acid *(DNA)*; ~ **dialurique** *m* CHIMIE tartronylurea; ~ **ellagitannique** *m* CHIMIE ellagitannin; ~ **éthanoïque** *m* CHIMIE ethanoic acid; ~ **éthylène-diamino-tétracétique** *m* LESSIVES EDTA, ethylenediamino tetra-acetic acid; ~ **folique** *m* AGRO ALIM folic acid; ~ **gluconique** *m* LESSIVES gluconic acid; ~ **gras** *m* CHIMIE, LESSIVES, PAPIER fatty acid; ~ **gras essentiel** *m* AGRO ALIM EFA, essential fatty acid; ~ **hydantoïque** *m* CHIMIE hydantoic acid; ~ **hydrosulfureux** *m* CHIMIE hydrosulfurous acid (AmE), hydrosulphurous acid (BrE); ~ **hypochloreux** *m* CHIMIE hypochlorous acid; ~ **hyposulfureux** *m* CHIMIE hyposulfurous acid (AmE), hyposulphurous acid (BrE); ~ **linoléique** *m* AGRO ALIM, PLAST CAOU *matière première* linoleic acid; ~ **maléique** *m* CHIMIE maleic acid; ~ **malique** *m* AGRO ALIM malic acid; ~ **de la même famille** *m* CHIMIE parent acid; ~ **nicotinique** *m* CHIMIE niacinamide; ~ **nitrique** *m* CHIMIE, POLLUTION nitric acid; ~ **oléique** *m* AGRO ALIM fatty acid, oleic acid; ~ **organique** *m* CHIMIE organic acid; ~ **orthophosphorique** *m* LESSIVES orthophosphoric acid; ~ **oxalique** *m* PHOTO oxalic acid; ~ **parabanique** *m* CHIMIE oxalylurea, parabanic acid; ~ **périodique** *m* CHIMIE periodic acid; ~ **phosphorique** *m* CHIMIE phosphoric acid; ~ **phtalique** *m* PLAST CAOU *matière première* phthalic anhydride; ~ **phytique** *m* AGRO ALIM phytic acid; ~ **polyphosphorique** *m* LESSIVES polyphosphoric acid; ~ **prussique** *m* CHIMIE prussic acid; ~ **pyrophosphorique** *m* LESSIVES pyrophosphoric acid; ~ **de récupération** *m* TEXTILE spent acid; ~ **silicique** *m* CHIMIE silicic acid; ~ **sorbique** *m* CHIMIE sorbic acid; ~ **styphnique** *m* CHIMIE styphnic acid; ~ **sulfamique** *m* LESSIVES sulfamic acid (AmE), sulphamic acid (BrE); ~ **sulfonique** *m* MATERIAUX sulfonic acid (AmE), sulphonic acid (BrE); ~ **sulfureux** *m* POLLUTION sulfurous acid (AmE), sulphurous acid (BrE); ~ **sulfurique** *m* CHIMIE oil of vitriol, sulfuric acid (AmE), sulphuric acid (BrE), vitriol, vitriolic acid, LESSIVES, POLLUTION sulfuric acid (AmE), sulphuric acid (BrE); ~ **sulfurique fumant** *m* CHIMIE fuming sulfuric acid (AmE), fuming sulphuric acid (BrE), oleum sulfuric acid (AmE), oleum sulphuric acid (BrE), LESSIVES oleum; ~ **sulphydrique** *m* POLLUTION hydrogen sulfide (AmE), hydrogen sulphide (BrE); ~ **tartrique** *m* LESSIVES tartaric acid; ~ **titanique** *m* CHIMIE titanic acid; ~ **urique** *m* CHIMIE trioxypurine; ~ **usagé** *m* LESSIVES spent acid; ~ **vitriolique** *m* CHIMIE oil of vitriol, sulfuric acid (AmE), sulphuric acid (BrE), vitriol, vitriolic acid
acide-aldéhyde *m* AGRO ALIM, CHIMIE aldehyde acid
acidifère *adj* CHIMIE, MATERIAUX, PAPIER acidiferous

acidifiable *adj* CHIMIE, PAPIER acidifiable
acidifiant[1] *adj* PAPIER, POLLUTION acidifying
acidifiant[2] *m* PAPIER acidifier, PETROLE acidizer
acidificateur *m* CHIMIE acidifier, TEXTILE acidifier, acidifying agent
acidification *f* CHIMIE, GENIE CHIM, HYDROLOGIE, PAPIER *de la pâte* acidification, PETROLE AWT, acid well treatment, acidization, POLLUTION acidification; ~ **anthropique** *f* POLLUTION anthropogenic acidification; ~ **anthropogène** *f* POLLUTION anthropogenic acidification; ~ **artificielle** *f* POLLUTION artificial acidification; ~ **des eaux** *f* POLLUTION aquatic acidification; ~ **expérimentale** *f* POLLUTION artificial acidification; ~ **hydrique** *f* POLLUTION aquatic acidification; ~ **naturelle** *f* POLLUTION natural acidification
acidifier[1] *vt* AGRO ALIM, CHIMIE acidify, PAPIER acidify, acidize, POLLUTION, TEXTILE acidify
acidifier:[2] **s'~** *v réfl* CHIMIE acidify
acidimètre *m* CHIMIE acidimeter, acidometer, GENIE CHIM, PAPIER acidimeter
acidimétrie *f* CHIMIE, GENIE CHIM, PAPIER acidimetry
acidimétrique *adj* CHIMIE, PAPIER acidimetric
acidité *f* CHIMIE, HYDROLOGIE, MATERIAUX, PAPIER, POLLUTION acidity; ~ **de l'air** *f* POLLUTION atmospheric acidity; ~ **libre** *f* CHIMIE free acidity
acidogène *adj* POLLUTION acidifying
acidolyse *f* AGRO ALIM acidolysis
acidomètre *m* PAPIER acid tester
acidophile *adj* CHIMIE oxyphilic, oxyphilous
acidulé *adj* CHIMIE acidulated
aciduler *vt* AGRO ALIM, CHIMIE acidulate
acier *m* CONS MECA steel; ~ **affiné** *m* MATERIAUX high-grade steel; ~ **allié** *m* CHARBON alloyed steel, MATERIAUX alloy steel; ~ **austénitique** *m* MECANIQUE *matériaux* austenitic steel; ~ **bas carbone** *m* CONS MECA low-carbon steel; ~ **Bessemer** *m* PRODUCTION Bessemer steel; ~ **bleui en bain de salpêtre** *m* CONS MECA niter-blued steel (AmE), nitre-blued steel (BrE); ~ **calmé à l'aluminium** *m* MECANIQUE *matériaux* aluminium-killed steel (BrE), aluminum-killed steel (AmE); ~ **au carbone** *m* CHARBON, CONS MECA, MECANIQUE *matériaux*, NUCLEAIRE carbon steel; ~ **cémenté** *m* MECANIQUE *matériaux* case-hardened steel; ~ **à conductivité élevée** *m* MATERIAUX high-conductivity steel; ~ **de construction** *m* CONSTR structural steel; ~ **contenant du manganèse** *m* MATERIAUX manganese steel; ~ **coulé par le fond** *m* MATERIAUX bottom-poured steel; ~ **doux** *m* CONS MECA low-carbon steel, mild steel; ~ **en attente** *m* CONSTR starter bar; ~ **en bande** *m* MATERIAUX strip steel; ~ **faiblement allié** *m* METALL low-alloy steel; ~ **à faible teneur de manganèse** *m* MATERIAUX low-manganese steel; ~ **à haute résistance** *m* MECANIQUE *matériaux* high-tensile steel; ~ **hypereutectoïde** *m* METALL hypereutectoid steel; ~ **inoxydable** *m* MATERIAUX, PAPIER, VEHICULES stainless steel; ~ **inoxydable austénitique** *m* CONS MECA austenitic stainless steel; ~ **inoxydable ferritique** *m* CONS MECA ferritic stainless steel; ~ **inoxydable trempé** *m* PRODUCTION hardened stainless steel; ~ **laminé** *m* MATERIAUX rolled steel; ~ **liquide** *m* MATERIAUX liquid steel; ~ **au manganèse** *m* MECANIQUE *matériaux* manganese steel; ~ **manufacturé en procédé duplex** *m* MATERIAUX duplex steel; ~ **maraging** *m* METALL maraging steel; ~ **moulé** *m* PAPIER, PRODUCTION cast steel; ~ **nitruré** *m* PRODUCTION nitrided steel; ~ **noir** *m* NUCLEAIRE carbon steel; ~ **non allié** *m* RESSORTS

unalloyed steel; ~ **de piquage** *m* CONSTR tamping rod; ~ **plaqué** *m* MATERIAUX clad steel; ~ **pour fleurets** *m* MINES drill steel; ~ **pour forets** *m* CONS MECA drill steel; ~ **pour mèches** *m* CONS MECA drill steel; ~ **pour ressorts de soupape** *m* RESSORTS valve spring steel; ~ **rapide** *m* MECANIQUE *matériaux* high-speed steel; ~ **recuit** *m* PAPIER annealed steel; ~ **au silicium** *m* ELECTROTEC silicon steel; ~ **trempé à l'air** *m* RESSORTS air-hardened steel; ~ **trempé en bain de sels** *m* RESSORTS salt-bath-hardened steel; ~ **usiné avec précision** *m* MATERIAUX precision-machined steel

aciérie *f* PRODUCTION steelwork

aciforme *adj* CHIMIE aciform

acmite *f* MINERAUX acmite

aconitase *f* CHIMIE aconitase

aconitate *m* CHIMIE aconitate

aconitine *f* AGRO ALIM aconitine

aconitique *adj* CHIMIE aconitic

à-côté: ~ **de coupe** *m* PAPIER offcut; ~ **de fabrication** *m* PAPIER side run

à-coup *m* AERONAUT impact load, CONS MECA jerk; ~ **de réactivité** *m* NUCLEAIRE reactivity surge

acouphène *m* ACOUSTIQUE acouphene

à-coups *m pl* ESPACE *véhicules* nudging

acoustique[1] *adj* ENREGISTR acoustic

acoustique[2] *f* ENREGISTR acoustic, acoustics, audio, PHYSIQUE, SECURITE acoustics; ~ **sous-marine** *f* OCEANO marine acoustics, underwater acoustics

acquisition *f* ESPACE *communications* acquisition; ~ **d'attitude** *f* ESPACE *véhicules* acquisition of attitude, attitude acquisition; ~ **de données** *f* ELECTRON, INFORMAT, ORDINAT data acquisition; ~ **du mode normal** *f* ESPACE *véhicules* acquisition of normal mode, normal mode acquisition

acquitter *vt* BREVETS *une taxe* pay

acre *f* METROLOGIE acre

acrobaties: ~ **aériennes** *f pl* AERONAUT aerobatics

acroléine *f* AERONAUT, MATERIAUX *chimie* acrolein

acronyme *m* INFORMAT, ORDINAT acronym

acrylate *m* PLAST CAOU *groupe, chimie* acrylate

acrylique[1] *adj* CONSTR, MECANIQUE *matériaux*, TEXTILE acrylic

acrylique[2] *m* CONSTR, TEXTILE acrylic

acrylonitrile *m* CHIMIE acrylonitrile

actangulaire *adj* GEOMETRIE acute-angular

acte: ~ **dangereux pour la sécurité** *m* SECURITE unsafe act; ~ **de francisation** *m* NAUT certificate of registry; ~ **d'immatriculation** *m* NAUT certificate of registration; ~ **d'invention** *m* BREVETS notice of opposition; ~ **de recours** *m* BREVETS notice of appeal

actif *adj* ELECTROTEC, INFORMAT, ORDINAT active

actine *f* AGRO ALIM actin

actinide *m* PHYSIQUE actinide

actinides *m pl* CHIMIE actinides, PHYS RAYON actinide series, actinides

actinique *adj* IMPRIM *photogravure*, PHOTO, PHYSIQUE actinic

actinisme *m* PHYSIQUE actinism

actinium *m (Ac)* CHIMIE actinium *(Ac)*

actinomètre *m* ASTRONOMIE, PHYS RAYON, PHYSIQUE actinometer

actinométrie *f* METEO, PHYS RAYON, PHYSIQUE actinometry

actinon *m* CHIMIE actinon

actinote *f* MINERAUX actinolite, actinote

action *f* MECANIQUE action, effect, PHYSIQUE action; ~

corrective *f* QUALITE corrective action; ~ **de couvrir** *f* PRODUCTION coating; ~ **d'entité fonctionnelle** *f* TELECOM FEA, functional entity action; ~ **d'épaissir** *f* IMPRIM *encres, impression* bodying; ~ **frigorifique utile** *f* REFRIG useful refrigerating effect; ~ **momentanée** *f* ELECTROTEC momentary action; ~ **de préparer la forme imprimante** *f* IMPRIM *copie* imaging; ~ **préventive** *f* QUALITE preventive action; ~ **de la racle sur un rouleau** *f* IMPRIM wiping; ~ **refroidissante totale** *f* REFRIG sensible cooling effect, total cooling effect; ~ **de retour** *f* ELECTRON feedback

actionné: ~ **à la main** *adj* SECURITE *d'une machine* handheld; ~ **par chaîne** *adj* CONS MECA chain-driven; ~ **par moteur** *adj* PRODUCTION engine-driven

actionnement: ~ **à distance** *m* COMMANDE remote actuation; ~ **intempestif** *m* PRODUCTION unintended actuation; ~ **par bouton-poussoir à deux positions** *m* PRODUCTION push-on push-off operation

actionner[1] *vt* CONS MECA actuate, run, MECANIQUE actuate, PRODUCTION operate, TEXTILE drive

actionner[2] *vi* PHYSIQUE act; ~ **une perforatrice par air comprimé** *vi* CONS MECA run a drill by compressed air

actionneur *m* ELECTR *transducteur*, ELECTROTEC, INFORMAT, MECANIQUE, ORDINAT *servomécanisme* actuator, PRODUCTION *automatisme industriel* output device; ~ **analogique** *m* ELECTROTEC analog actuator (AmE), analogue actuator (BrE); ~ **axial** *m* ESPACE *véhicules* axial actuator; ~ **électrique** *m* ESPACE *véhicules* electric actuator; ~ **numérique** *m* ELECTROTEC digital actuator; ~ **oscillant** *m* PRODUCTION *système hydraulique* semirotary actuator; ~ **à tige** *m* PRODUCTION rod actuator

activant: ~ **le frittage** *adj* GENIE CHIM sinter-activating

activateur *m* CHARBON activator, CHIMIE activator, promoter, ELECTROTEC, PLAST CAOU *ingrédient de mélange* activator

activation *f* CHARBON activation, ELECTRON dither, HYDROLOGIE, METALL, PAPIER, TELECOM activation; ~ **par radiation** *f* PHYS RAYON radiation-induced activation; ~ **photonucléaire** *f* PHYS RAYON gamma photon activation; ~ **thermique** *f* METALL thermal activation

activer *vt* CHARBON activate, CONS MECA, IMPRIM actuate, PAPIER activate, PRODUCTION energize, *automatisme industriel* enable, *la combustion par une machine soufflante* accelerate, *un bit* set

activeur *m* PAPIER activator

activité *f* INFORMAT, ORDINAT, PHYSIQUE activity; ~ **absolue** *f* PHYSIQUE absolute activity; ~ **du catalyseur** *f* MATERIAUX catalyst activity; ~ **déclassée** *f* PRODUCTION out-of-sequence activity, out-of-sequence operation; ~ **globale** *f* TELECOM ensemble activity; ~ **hors séquence** *f* PRODUCTION out-of-sequence activity; ~ **inventive** *f* BREVETS inventive step; ~ **linéique** *f* NUCLEAIRE linear activity; ~ **massique de l'élément** *f* NUCLEAIRE element specific activity; ~ **nucléaire** *f* PHYS RAYON nuclear activity; ~ **optique** *f* CHIMIE, PHYSIQUE optical activity; ~ **sismique lunaire** *f* ASTRONOMIE lunar seismic activity; ~ **solaire** *f* ASTRONOMIE, PHYSIQUE solar activity; ~ **spécifique** *f* PHYSIQUE specific activity

actomyosine *f* AGRO ALIM actomyosin

actualisation *f* INFORMAT, ORDINAT update

actualiser *vt* INFORMAT, ORDINAT update

acuité *f* CONS MECA *du tranchant d'un outil* sharpness, CONSTR *du tranchant d'un outil* keenness, GEOMETRIE acuteness, *d'un angle* sharpness; ~ **de résonance** *f*

PHYSIQUE sharpness

acutangle *adj* GEOMETRIE acute-angled

acyclique *adj* CHIMIE acyclic

acylation *f* CHIMIE acylation

acyle *m* CHIMIE acyl

acyler *vt* CHIMIE acylate

ADAC *abrév* AERONAUT, TRANSPORT *(avion à décollage et attérissage court)* STOL aircraft *(short takeoff and landing aircraft)*

adamine *f* MINERAUX adamine, adamite

adamsite *f* MINERAUX adamsite

ADAO *abrév (avion à décollage et atterrissage ordinaires)* AERONAUT CTOL aircraft *(conventional takeoff and landing aircraft)*

adaptateur *m* CONS MECA, ELECTR *raccordement* adaptor, ELECTROTEC adaptor, plug adaptor, EQUIP LAB *verrerie* adaptor, INFORMAT adaptor, MECANIQUE, ORDINAT adaptor; ~ **d'accostage** *m* ESPACE *véhicules* docking adaptor; ~ **de canal asynchrone** *m* ORDINAT asynchronous channel adaptor; ~ **de culot** *m* ELECTROTEC socket adaptor; ~ **de douille** *m* ELECTROTEC socket adaptor; ~ **d'écran** *m* INFORMAT, ORDINAT display adaptor; ~ **d'écran graphique** *m* INFORMAT graphic display adaptor; ~ **des E/S** *m* PRODUCTION *automatisme industriel* I/O adaptor; ~ **de fiche** *m* ELECTROTEC plug adaptor; ~ **graphique couleur** *m (EGA)* ORDINAT *carte* enhanced graphic adaptor *(EGA)*; ~ **d'impédance** *m* ELECTR impedance corrector; ~ **d'interface périphérique** *m* INFORMAT, ORDINAT peripheral interface adaptor; ~ **à lame quart d'onde** *m* ELECTROTEC waveguide transformer; ~ **à ligne** *m* ELECTROTEC stub; ~ **de lignes** *m* ORDINAT line adaptor, modem; ~ **de phase** *m* ELECTR *courant alternatif* phase adaptor; ~ **de phonographe** *m* ENREGISTR phono adaptor; ~ **pour photomicrographie** *m* PHOTO microscope adaptor; ~ **de prise de courant** *m* ELECTROTEC plug adaptor; ~ **pour reproduction de diapositives** *m* PHOTO slide-copying attachment; ~ **secteur** *m* ELECTROTEC current adaptor (AmE), mains adaptor (BrE); ~ **de support** *m* TELECOM MA, medium adaptor; ~ **de terminal** *m* TELECOM TA, terminal adaptor; ~ **de terminal pour le RNIS-LB** *m* TELECOM B-ISDN terminal adaptor, TA-LB; ~ **de tuyère** *m* CONS MECA nozzle adaptor

adaptatif *adj* COMMANDE, INFORMAT, MECANIQUE, ORDINAT *régulation* adaptive

adaptation *f* CONS MECA fitting, IMPRIM adaptation; ~ **client** *f* PRODUCTION customerization; ~ **de conduit d'ordre inférieur** *f* TELECOM LPA, lower-order path adaptation; ~ **de conduit d'ordre supérieur** *f* TELECOM HPA, higher-order path adaptation; ~ **d'impédance** *f* ELECTROTEC, ENREGISTR, PHYSIQUE impedance matching, TELECOM aerial matching; ~ **du logiciel** *f* INFORMAT, ORDINAT software adaptation; ~ **par sonde réglable** *f* ELECTROTEC slug tuning; ~ **plastique** *f* PLAST CAOU plastic flow properties; ~ **de section** *f* TELECOM SA, section adaptation; ~ **à l'usager** *f* PRODUCTION customization

adapté *adj* PHYSIQUE matched, PRODUCTION *procédé* suitable

adapter[1] *vt* CONS MECA fit, MECANIQUE fit

adapter:[2] **s'~** *v réfl* CONS MECA fit

ADAR *abrév (avion à décollage et atterrissage réduits)* AERONAUT RTOL aircraft *(reduced takeoff and landing aircraft)*

ADAS *abrév (avion à décollage et atterrissage silen-* *cieux)* AERONAUT QTOL aircraft *(quiet takeoff and landing aircraft)*

ADAV *abrév (avion à décollage et atterrissage verticaux)* AERONAUT VTOL aircraft *(vertical takeoff and landing aircraft)*

addendum *m* IMPRIM addendum

additif[1] *adj* MATH additive

additif[2] *m* AGRO ALIM additive, CHARBON adjuvant, CHIMIE, LESSIVES, MATERIAUX, MECANIQUE *matériaux* additive, PETR dope, PETROLE additive, defoaming agent, PLAST CAOU additive; ~ **d'adhésivité** *m* CHIMIE tackiness agent; ~ **alimentaire** *m* AGRO ALIM food additive; ~ **anticorrosif** *m* AUTO corrosion inhibitor; ~ **anticorrosion** *m* PETROLE anticorrosion additive, anticorrosion agent; ~ **antidétonant** *m* POLLUTION antiknock additive, VEHICULES *carburant* antiknock agent; ~ **antimoussant** *m* CHIMIE defoaming agent; ~ **antimousse** *m* GENIE CHIM foam inhibitor, PETROLE defoaming agent; ~ **au détergent** *m* LESSIVES detergent additive; ~ **extrême pression** *m* PETROLE *forage, raffinage* extreme pressure additive; ~ **au plomb** *m* POLLUTION lead additive

addition *f* CONS MECA, MATH, ORDINAT addition; ~ **binaire** *f* ELECTRON binary addition; ~ **logique** *f* ELECTRON logic addition

additionnel *adj* IMPRIM additional

additionner *vt* MATH add

additionneur *m* ELECTRON, ORDINAT adder; ~ **avec report** *m* INFORMAT, ORDINAT ripple carry adder; ~ **binaire** *m* ELECTRON, ORDINAT binary adder; ~ **complet** *m* INFORMAT front-end processor, full adder, ORDINAT full adder; ~ **en cascade** *m* INFORMAT, ORDINAT ripple carry adder; ~ **numérique** *m* ELECTRON digital adder; ~ **parallèle** *m* ELECTRON, INFORMAT, ORDINAT parallel adder; ~ **série** *m* ELECTRON, INFORMAT, ORDINAT serial adder; ~ **simultané** *m* INFORMAT ripple carry adder

additionneuse *f* ORDINAT calculator

addressage: ~ **calculé** *m* ORDINAT hashing

adduction *f* CHIMIE adduction, HYDROLOGIE adduction, conduction; ~ **d'air** *f* AERONAUT air supply, CONS MECA air ducting; ~ **de chaleur** *f* THERMODYN heat supply; ~ **d'eau** *f* DISTRI EAU water delivery

adelpholite *f* MINERAUX adelpholite

adelpholithe *f* MINERAUX adelpholite

adénine *f* AGRO ALIM, CHIMIE adenine

adénosine *f* CHIMIE adenosine

adent *m* CONSTR indent

adhérence *f* CH DE FER *des roues à la surface des rails*, CHARBON adhesion, CONSTR adhesion, bond, EMBALLAGE adherence, PAPIER adherence, adhesion, PLAST CAOU bonding, *d'un adhésif* adhesion, PRODUCTION sticking; ~ **de contact** *f* PLAST CAOU blocking; ~ **des couches** *f* PLAST CAOU *contreplaqué, stratifié, caoutchouté* plybond strength; ~ **à la paroi** *f* PHYS FLUID wall attachment, *écoulement* Coanda effect; ~ **spécifique** *f* PLAST CAOU *d'un adhésif* specific adhesion

adhérent *adj* PAPIER adherent

adhérer[1] *vt* CONSTR *menuiserie* stick

adhérer[2] *vi* EMBALLAGE, PAPIER, PLAST CAOU adhere

adhérisation *f* TEXTILE dip

adhériser *vt* TEXTILE dip

adhésif[1] *adj* MATERIAUX self-adhering, PAPIER adhesive, sticky, PLAST CAOU adhesive

adhésif[2] *m* CERAM VER sealant, IMPRIM, MECANIQUE *matériaux* adhesive, PLAST CAOU adhesive, bonding

agent, cement, glue, PRODUCTION adhesive; ~ anaérobie *m* PLAST CAOU anaerobic adhesive; ~ avec
acétate *m* EMBALLAGE acetate adhesive; ~ chimique *m*
IMPRIM glue; ~ de contact *m* PLAST CAOU contact
adhesive; ~ durcissant à chaud *m* PLAST CAOU hot-setting adhesive; ~ durcissant à froid *m* PLAST CAOU
cold-setting adhesive; ~ fort autocollant *m* EMBALLAGE
high-tack pressure-sensitive adhesive; ~ pour contre-
plaqué *m* EMBALLAGE plywood adhesive; ~ pour
palettisation *m* EMBALLAGE palletizing adhesive; ~
synthétique *m* IMPRIM *colle* synthetic adhesive; ~ thermoplastique *m* IMPRIM *brochure, reliure* hot-melt
adhesive; ~ thermosoudable *m* EMBALLAGE heat-sealing adhesive

adhésiomètre *m* PLAST CAOU *instrument* adherometer

adhésion *f* CHARBON attachment, PLAST CAOU adhesion,
bonding, PRODUCTION sticking; ~ des contacts *f*
ELECTR *de relais* sticking contacts; ~ entre les couches
f PLAST CAOU *contreplaqué, stratifiés, caoutchouc* plybond strength

adhésivité *f* MATERIAUX, PAPIER adhesiveness, REVETE-
MENT tackiness

adiabatique *adj* MECANIQUE, PHYS FLUID, PHYSIQUE,
THERMODYN adiabatic

adiabatiquement *adv* PHYS FLUID, PHYSIQUE, THERMO-
DYN adiabatically

adiabatisme *m* THERMODYN adiabatism

adinole *f* GEOLOGIE *cornéenne à albite* adinole

adipique *adj* CHIMIE adipic

adipocérite *f* PHYSIQUE adipocerite

adjacence *f* GEOMETRIE adjacence, adjacency

adjacent *adj* GEOMETRIE adjacent

adjonction *f* CONS MECA addition

adjuvant *m* CHARBON adjuvant, CHIMIE additive, CONSTR
du béton admixture, PLAST CAOU additive; ~ de filtrage
m GENIE CHIM filter aid; ~ au froid *m* REFRIG supplement to refrigeration

administrateur: ~ de base de données *m* INFORMAT,
ORDINAT DBA, database administrator; ~ de réseau
m INFORMAT, ORDINAT network manager

administration: ~ chargée de l'examen préliminaire *f*
BREVETS preliminary examining authority; ~ chargée
de la recherche internationale *f* BREVETS international
searching authority

admissibilité: ~ à l'affrètement *f* AERONAUT *transport
aérien* charterworthiness

admission *f* AERONAUT *moteur* intake, CONS MECA inlet,
intake, CONSTR *d'eau* ingress, INST HYDR input, steam
port, MECANIQUE, MINES inlet, VEHICULES *moteur, carburation* induction; ~ d'air *f* CONS MECA air inlet, air
intake; ~ anticipée *f* INST HYDR preadmission, PRO-
DUCTION early admission; ~ avant *f* CONS MECA
crank-end dead center (AmE), crank-end dead centre
(BrE); ~ différée *f* INST HYDR retarded admission; ~ de
vapeur *f* INST HYDR steam admission

admittance *f* ELECTR *circuit à courant alternatif*, ELEC-
TROTEC, PHYSIQUE admittance; ~ acoustique *f*
ACOUSTIQUE, ELECTROTEC acoustic admittance; ~ caractéristique *f* ELECTR *circuit à courant alternatif*
characteristic admittance; ~ complexe *f* ELECTR *circuit à courant alternatif*, PHYSIQUE complex
admittance; ~ électrique *f* TELECOM electrical admittance; ~ d'électrode *f* ELECTR electrode admittance; ~
d'entrée *f* ELECTROTEC input admittance; ~ inverse de
transfert *f* COMMANDE feedback admittance; ~ mécanique *f* ACOUSTIQUE mechanical admittance; ~ de

sortie *f* ELECTROTEC output admittance; ~ supplémentaire due à la réaction d'anode *f* COMMANDE
électronique feedback admittance

ADN *abrév (acide désoxyribonucléique)* CHIMIE DNA
(deoxyribonucleic acid)

adobe *m* THERMODYN unburnt brick

adonner *vi* NAUT free, veer aft, *le vent* free off

adossé *adj* CONSTR back-to-back

adossement *m* CERAM VER batter

adoucir *vt* CONSTR soften, PRODUCTION *une surface avec
de la toile d'émeri* rub down

adoucissement *m* MATERIAUX softening, PETROLE
sweetening; ~ d'acier *m* MATERIAUX steel softening; ~
d'eau *m* GENIE CHIM water softening; ~ de l'eau d'a-
limentation *m* CHAUFFAGE feedwater softening; ~ par
déformation *m* METALL work softening; ~ par fatigue
m METALL fatigue softening

adoucisseur *m* TEXTILE *eau* softener; ~ d'eau *m* CONSTR,
GENIE CHIM, IMPRIM, PAPIER, TEXTILE water softener

adressable *adj* ORDINAT addressable

adressage *m* ORDINAT, TELECOM addressing; ~ associatif *m* ORDINAT associative addressing; ~ autorelatif *m*
INFORMAT self-relative addressing; ~ calculé *m* INFOR-
MAT hashing; ~ différé *m* INFORMAT, ORDINAT deferred
addressing; ~ différentiel *m* ORDINAT self-relative addressing; ~ direct *m* INFORMAT, ORDINAT direct
addressing; ~ d'E/S complémentaire *m* PRODUCTION
complementary I/O addressing; ~ étendu *m* INFOR-
MAT, ORDINAT extended addressing; ~ extensible *m*
INFORMAT, ORDINAT extensible addressing; ~ immédiat *m* INFORMAT, ORDINAT immediate addressing; ~
implicite *m* INFORMAT, ORDINAT implied addressing; ~
indexé *m* INFORMAT, ORDINAT indexed addressing; ~
indirect *m* INFORMAT, ORDINAT indirect addressing; ~
intrinsèque *m* INFORMAT, ORDINAT inherent addressing; ~ logique *m* INFORMAT, ORDINAT logical
addressing; ~ par complémentaire des E/S *m* PRODUC-
TION *automatisme industriel* duplicate I/O addressing;
~ relatif *m* INFORMAT, ORDINAT relative addressing; ~
symbolique *m* INFORMAT, ORDINAT symbolic addressing; ~ unique de l'emplacement des E/S *m*
PRODUCTION *automatisme industriel* unique I/O location addressing

adresse *f* IMPRIM *courrier, informatique*, ORDINAT address; ~ absolue *f* ORDINAT absolute address; ~
d'acheminement *f* TELECOM routing address; ~ d'a-
cheminement retour *f* TELECOM reverse routing
address; ~ de base *f* ORDINAT base address; ~ de bit de
verrouillage *f* PRODUCTION *automatisme industriel*
latch address; ~ calculée *f* INFORMAT, ORDINAT generated address; ~ du correspondant *f* TELECOM party
address; ~ de début de zone *f* PRODUCTION *automatisme industriel* start address field; ~ directe *f*
INFORMAT, ORDINAT direct address; ~ dont les change-
ments d'état sont temporisés de 1 à 0 *f* PRODUCTION
automatisme industriel address which pulses on and
off; ~ effective *f* INFORMAT effective address; ~ émettrice *f* INFORMAT, ORDINAT source address; ~
d'emplacement *f* PRODUCTION *automatisme industriel*
location address; ~ d'emplacement de borne d'E/S *f*
PRODUCTION *automatisme industriel* I/O terminal location address; ~ explicite *f* INFORMAT, ORDINAT
explicit address; ~ de fin *f* PRODUCTION *automatisme
industriel* end statement address; ~ de fin de zone *f*
PRODUCTION *automatisme industriel* end address field;
~ immédiate *f* INFORMAT, ORDINAT immediate ad-

dress; ~ **de livraison** *f* PRODUCTION receiving address; ~ **de mémoire** *f* ORDINAT storage location; ~ **mémoire** *f* ORDINAT memory location; ~ **de mots de la table de données** *f* PRODUCTION *automatisme industriel* data table word address; ~ **d'origine** *f* INFORMAT source address; ~ **réelle** *f* INFORMAT, ORDINAT real address; ~ **de retour** *f* INFORMAT, ORDINAT return address; ~ **au sol** *f* TELECOM ground address; ~ **source** *f* INFORMAT source address; ~ **du temporisateur** *f* PRODUCTION *automatisme industriel* timer address; ~ **unique** *f* INFORMAT, ORDINAT single address

adresser *vt* ORDINAT address

adsorbant *m* CHIMIE adsorbent

adsorber *vt* CHARBON adsorb

adsorbeur *m* GAZ adsorber

adsorption *f* AGRO ALIM, CHARBON, CHIMIE, DISTRI EAU, HYDROLOGIE, MATERIAUX, PLAST CAOU adsorption

adulaire *f* MINERAUX adularia

adultérant *m* AGRO ALIM adulterant

adultéré *adj* AGRO ALIM adulterated

adultérer *vt* AGRO ALIM adulterate

advection *f* METEO, PHYSIQUE advection

aegirine *f* MINERAUX aegirine, aegirite, aegyrite

aegyrine *f* MINERAUX aegirine, aegirite, aegyrite

aenigmatite *f* MINERAUX aenigmatite

aérage *m* CHARBON aeration, CONSTR draft (AmE), draught (BrE), ventilating, ventilation, MINES, SECURITE ventilation; ~ **artificiel** *m* SECURITE artificial ventilation; ~ **distinct** *m* MINES separate ventilation; ~ **mécanique par aspiration** *m* CONS MECA exhaust draft (AmE), exhaust draught (BrE), induced draft (AmE), induced draught (BrE); ~ **négatif** *m* CONS MECA exhaust draft (AmE), exhaust draught (BrE), induced draft (AmE), induced draught (BrE); ~ **positif** *m* CONS MECA forced draft (AmE), forced draught (BrE), pressure draft (AmE), pressure draught (BrE)

aérateur *m* AERONAUT aerator, PAPIER air exchanger, ventilator, RECYCLAGE aerator, REFRIG ventilator; ~ **de cale** *m* NAUT bilge blower; ~ **à cascades** *m* HYDROLOGIE cascade aerator; ~ **par contact** *m* HYDROLOGIE contact aerator; ~ **pour la conduite forcée** *m* EN RENOUV *hydroélectricité* antivacuum valve

aération *f* CHARBON aeration, ventilation, CONSTR, HYDROLOGIE aeration, IMPRIM air vent, MINES, NAUT ventilation, RECYCLAGE aeration, SECURITE, THERMODYN ventilation

aéraulique *f* GAZ aeraulics

aéré *adj* THERMODYN ventilated

aérémie *f* PETROLE *sécurité du personnel* bends

aérer *vt* AGRO ALIM aerate, CHARBON aerate, ventilate, CONSTR, IMPRIM *papier* aerate, NAUT air, RECYCLAGE aerate, SECURITE air, ventilate, THERMODYN ventilate

aérien *adj* AERONAUT aerial

aérification *f* CHIMIE aerification

aérobe *adj* AGRO ALIM aerobic

aérobie[1] *adj* AGRO ALIM, HYDROLOGIE, RECYCLAGE aerobic

aérobie[2] *m* AGRO ALIM aerobic; ~ **facultatif** *m* AGRO ALIM facultative aerobe; ~ **strict** *m* AGRO ALIM obligate aerobe

aérobiologie *f* METEO aerobiology

aérobiose *f* RECYCLAGE aerobiosis

aérobus *m* TRANSPORT aerobus

aérodrome *m* AERONAUT aerodrome (BrE), airdrome (AmE)

aérodynamique[1] *adj* AERONAUT, PHYS FLUID streamlined, PHYSIQUE, TRANSPORT aerodynamic

aérodynamique[2] *f* METEO, NAUT, PHYSIQUE, TRANSPORT aerodynamics

aérodyne: ~ **à voilure tournante** *m* AERONAUT helicopter

aéroélasticité *f* EN RENOUV *éolienne*, NUCLEAIRE aeroelasticity

aéroélectronique *f* AERONAUT avionics

aéroembolisme *m* OCEANO aeroembolism, gas embolism, air embolism

aérofrein *m* AERONAUT air brake, TRANSPORT drag brake, speed brake

aérogare *f* TRANSPORT air terminal; ~ **de fret** *f* AERONAUT cargo terminal, TRANSPORT cargo warehouse

aéroglisseur *m* AERONAUT hovercraft, NAUT air cushion vehicle, hovercraft, TRANSPORT hovercraft; ~ **guidé** *m* TRANSPORT, guided air-cushion vehicle, tracked air cushion vehicle TACV, tracked hovercraft; ~ **à jupes rigides** *m* TRANSPORT rigid sidewall hovercraft, rigid skirt hovercraft; ~ **marin** *m* TRANSPORT marine air-cushion vehicle, marine hovercraft, seagoing hovercraft; ~ **non-amphibie** *m* TRANSPORT nonamphibious hovercraft; ~ **à parois latérales** *m* TRANSPORT sidewall hovercraft, sidewall-type hovercraft; ~ **à propulsion marine** *m* TRANSPORT air-propelled hovercraft, water-propelled hovercraft; ~ **semi-amphibie** *m* TRANSPORT semiamphibious air cushion vehicle, semiamphibious hovercraft; ~ **à sustentation aérodynamique** *m* TRANSPORT aerodynamic-type air cushion vehicle; ~ **à sustentation aérostatique** *m* TRANSPORT aerostatic-type air cushion vehicle; ~ **terrestre** *m* TRANSPORT land air-cushion vehicle

aérographe *m* IMPRIM aerograph, airbrush, PHOTO airbrush

aérographie *f* CERAM VER aerography

aérolithe *m* ASTRONOMIE aerolite

aérologie *f* METEO aerology

aéromagnétique *adj* PETR aeromagnetic

aéromagnétométrique *adj* GEOLOGIE aeromagnetic

aéromètre *m* GEOPHYS gravimeter, PAPIER aerometer, airspeed indicator, PHYSIQUE aerometer

aérométrie *f* PAPIER, PHYSIQUE aerometry

aéronaval *adj* NAUT air-and-sea

Aéronavale *f* NAUT Fleet Air Arm (BrE), Naval Air Service (AmE)

aéronef *m* AERONAUT aircraft, aircraft category; ~ **tout-cargo** *m* AERONAUT all-cargo aircraft; ~ **à voilure tournante** *m* AERONAUT rotary wing aircraft, TRANSPORT rotary wing aircraft, rotating wing aircraft

aéronef-kilomètre: ~ **réalisé** *m* AERONAUT aircraft-kilometer performed (AmE), aircraft-kilometre performed (BrE)

aéronomie *f* ESPACE aeronomy

aéroport *m* AERONAUT airport; ~ **international** *m* AERONAUT international airport; ~ **régional** *m* AERONAUT regional airport

aéroporté *adj* TRANSPORT airborne

aéroréfrigérant *m* NUCLEAIRE air coolant, air cooler, REFRIG fluid cooler

aérorefroidisseur *m* REFRIG fluid cooler

aérosilicagel: ~ **opacifié** *m* REFRIG opacified silica aerogel

aérosite *f* MINERAUX aerosite

aérosol *m* EMBALLAGE, MATERIAUX, METEO, PHYSIQUE, POLLUTION aerosol; ~ **acide** *m* POLLUTION acid aerosol

aérospatial *adj* ESPACE aerospace, aerospatial

aérostatique *f* METEO aerostatics

aérotherme _m_ CONS MECA air heater, THERMODYN unit heater

aérotrain _m_ TRANSPORT aerotrain, hovercraft train, hovertrain

aeschynite _f_ MINERAUX aeschynite, eschinite

aesculine _f_ CHIMIE aesculin

affaiblir _vt_ PHOTO _éclairage_ dim, reduce

affaiblissant: ~ **le signal local** _adj_ TELECOM antisidetone

affaiblissement _m_ CINEMAT fading, ELECTR _d'un signal_ attenuation, ELECTRON attenuation, fading, ENREGISTR attenuation, decay, roll off, ESPACE _communications_ attenuation, IMPRIM _photogravure, impression_ fading, _photogravures, encres_ reducing, OPTIQUE attenuation, loss, PHYSIQUE attenuation, TELECOM attenuation, loss, TV attenuation; ~ **acoustique** _m_ ACOUSTIQUE transmission loss; ~ **d'adaptation** _m_ ELECTRON matching attenuation; ~ **d'adaptation optique** _m_ TELECOM ORL, optical return loss; ~ **copolaire** _m_ ESPACE _communications_ copolar attenuation; ~ **de couplage** _m_ TELECOM coupling loss; ~ **de coupleur** _m_ OPTIQUE, TELECOM coupler loss; ~ **dû à la pénétration dans les bâtiments** _m_ TELECOM building penetration loss; ~ **dû au pointage de l'antenne** _m_ TELECOM _satellite maritime_ antenna pointing loss; ~ **élevé** _m_ TELECOM high loss; ~ **en espace libre** _m_ TELECOM free space basic loss; ~ **d'épissure** _m_ TELECOM splice loss; ~ **d'espace libre** _m_ ESPACE _communications_ free space loss; ~ **d'image** _m_ CINEMAT film fading, picture fading; ~ **d'insertion** _m_ OPTIQUE, TELECOM insertion loss; ~ **linéique** _m_ ACOUSTIQUE, OPTIQUE attenuation coefficient, PHYSIQUE attenuation coefficient, linear coefficient, TELECOM attenuation coefficient; ~ **modal différentiel** _m_ OPTIQUE, TELECOM differential mode attenuation; ~ **par couplage de polarisation** _m_ TELECOM polarization coupling loss; ~ **par macrocourbures** _m_ OPTIQUE, TELECOM macrobend loss; ~ **par microcourbures** _m_ OPTIQUE, TELECOM microbend loss; ~ **de propagation** _m_ PHYSIQUE propagation loss, TV path attenuation; ~ **réduit** _m_ TELECOM low loss; ~ **spécifique** _m_ ESPACE _communications_ specific attenuation; ~ **sur images** _m_ ELECTRON image attenuation coefficient; ~ **de transmission** _m_ ESPACE _communications_ transmission attenuation, OPTIQUE _d'un trajet optique_, TELECOM transmission loss

affaiblisseur _m_ ELECTRON attenuator, PHOTO reducer, TELECOM attenuator; ~ **à absorption** _m_ TELECOM absorptive attenuator; ~ **de champ** _m_ ELECTR field suppressor; ~ **de Farmer** _m_ PHOTO Farmer's reducer; ~ **non-réciproque** _m_ PHYSIQUE isolator; ~ **à piston** _m_ PHYSIQUE piston attenuator; ~ **proportionnel** _m_ PHOTO proportional reducer; ~ **résistif** _m_ TELECOM resistive attenuator; ~ **sélectif** _m_ PHOTO selective reducer

affaires: ~ **maritimes** _f pl_ NAUT shipping trade

affaissement _m_ CH DE FER subsidence, CONS MECA _résistance des ressorts_ set, CONSTR _d'un édifice, d'une montagne_ subsidence, _de la surface_ subsidence, GEOLOGIE collapse, MINES _du toit_ subsidence, POLLUTION subsidence; ~ **latéral** _m_ NUCLEAIRE lateral yielding; ~ **du sommet** _m_ ELECTRON droop; ~ **tectonique** _m_ GEOLOGIE downbuckle

affaisser[1] _vt_ CONSTR cause to subside, EMBALLAGE press down

affaisser:[2] **s'~** _v réfl_ CONSTR subside, GEOLOGIE collapse, MINES sink

affaler _vt_ NAUT _les voiles_ lower, _un pavillon, une voile_ haul down

affectation _f_ ESPACE assignment, INFORMAT, ORDINAT allocation, PRODUCTION allocation, allotment; ~ **adaptable de voies** _f_ ORDINAT adaptive channel allocation; ~ **aléatoire de la mémoire** _f_ INFORMAT scatter load; ~ **des broches** _f_ PRODUCTION _automatisme industriel_ pin assignment; ~ **à la demande** _f_ ESPACE _communications_ demand assignment; ~ **diffuse de la mémoire** _f_ ORDINAT scatter load; ~ **dynamique** _f_ INFORMAT, ORDINAT dynamic allocation; ~ **ferme** _f_ PRODUCTION _production_ firm allocation; ~ **mémoire** _f_ INFORMAT storage allocation; ~ **des ressources** _f_ INFORMAT, ORDINAT resource allocation; ~ **statique** _f_ ORDINAT static allocation; ~ **du trafic** _f_ TRANSPORT traffic assignment; ~ **de la voie** _f_ CH DE FER track allocation

affecté: **être ~ à un navire** _vi_ NAUT be posted to a ship

affecter _vt_ GEOMETRIE modify, INFORMAT allocate, assign, ORDINAT assign

affichage _m_ ELECTR display, read-out, ESPACE, IMPRIM display, INFORMAT, ORDINAT, TELECOM display, read-out; ~ **alphagéométrique** _m_ TELECOM alphageometric display; ~ **alphanumérique** _m_ TELECOM alphanumeric display; ~ **à cristaux liquides** _m_ ELECTR, ELECTRON, INFORMAT, ORDINAT, PHYSIQUE, TV LCD, liquid crystal display; ~ **digital** _m_ ELECTR _d'un instrument_, INFORMAT, ORDINAT digital readout; ~ **à l'écran du texte illisible** _m_ IMPRIM _montage_ text greeking; ~ **électrolytique** _m_ ELECTRON electrolytic display; ~ **en couleur** _m_ AERONAUT, ESPACE, INFORMAT color display (AmE), colour display (BrE); ~ **matriciel** _m_ TELECOM matrix display; ~ **menu** _m_ INFORMAT, ORDINAT menu screen; ~ **numérique** _m_ ELECTRON digital display, INFORMAT digital readout, INSTRUMENT digital display, digital readout, ORDINAT digital readout; ~ **du numéro appelé** _m_ TELECOM called number display; ~ **par électroluminescence** _m_ ELECTRON electroluminescent display; ~ **par électroluminescence en couches épaisses** _m_ ELECTRON thick-film electroluminescent display; ~ **par panneau** _m_ ELECTRON flat panel display; ~ **à plusieurs lignes** _m_ PRODUCTION _automatisme industriel_ multiple-rung display; ~ **radar** _m_ TRANSPORT radar display; ~ **récurrent** _m_ INFORMAT raster display; ~ **du schéma à relais** _m_ PRODUCTION _automatisme industriel_ ladder-diagram display; ~ **sur écran** _m_ ORDINAT screen display; ~ **tramé** _m_ INFORMAT raster display

affiche: **qui s'~ à l'écran** _adj_ IMPRIM screen-displayed

afficher _vt_ ESPACE, INFORMAT, ORDINAT display, SECURITE _sur une plaque_ show, TELECOM display

afficheur: ~ **à cristaux liquides** _m_ ELECTRON liquid crystal display; ~ **à cristaux liquides dichroïques** _m_ ELECTRON dichroic LCD; ~ **à cristaux liquides à joint plastique** _m_ ELECTRON plastic-sealing LCD; ~ **à cristaux liquides à réflexion** _m_ ELECTRON reflective LCD; ~ **à cristaux liquides à transflexion** _m_ ELECTRON transflective LCD; ~ **à cristaux liquides à transmission** _m_ ELECTROTEC transmissive LCD; ~ **dichroïque** _m_ ELECTRON dichroic LCD; ~ **électroluminescent** _m_ ELECTRON electroluminescent display; ~ **électroluminescent à couches épaisses** _m_ ELECTRON thick-film electroluminescent display; ~ **LCD dichroïque** _m_ ELECTRON dichroic LCD; ~ **à transmission** _m_ ELECTROTEC transmissive LCD

affilage _m_ CONS MECA setting

affilé _adj_ IMPRIM _photogravure, impression_ keen

affilement _m_ CONS MECA setting

affiler *vt* CONS MECA set, PRODUCTION draw

affiloir *m* CONS MECA sharpener

affiloire *f* PRODUCTION hone, honestone, oilstone, whetstone

affinage *m* CERAM VER planing (AmE), refining (BrE), CHIMIE *métaux* refinement, MATERIAUX refining; ~ **sans laitier** *m* MATERIAUX slag-free refining; ~ **d'uranium** *m* NUCLEAIRE uranium refining; ~ **au vent** *m* MATERIAUX, METALL air blast refining

affinement *m* CHIMIE, CRISTALL refinement; ~ **des grains** *m* METALL grain refinement

affiner *vt* AGRO ALIM cure

affinerie *f* PRODUCTION finery, finery furnace

affinité *f* CHIMIE affinity; ~ **tinctoriale** *f* TEXTILE dyeing affinity

affirmation: ~ **de connexion** *f* ORDINAT handshaking

affleurement *m* GEOLOGIE, MINES outcrop

affleurer[1] *vt* CONS MECA make flush, PRODUCTION flush, flush up

affleurer:[2] **s'~ avec** *v réfl* PRODUCTION be flush with

affleureuse *f* PAPIER attrition mill

affluence *f* HYDROLOGIE concourse

affluent *m* HYDROLOGIE *de premier ordre ou secondaire*, NAUT *d'une rivière* tributary, TELECOM TR, tributary

affluer *vi* HYDROLOGIE *dans la mer* run; ~ **dans la mer** *vi* HYDROLOGIE discharge into the sea, outfall to sea

affouillement *m* CONSTR undermining, EN RENOUV *barrages* scour, HYDROLOGIE eroding, scour, OCEANO scouring, underwashing, PETR scouring

affouiller *vt* EN RENOUV scour, HYDROLOGIE erode, scour

affrètement *m* NAUT charter, charter party, charterage, chartering; ~ **coque nue** *m* NAUT bare boat charter; ~ **en coque nue** *m* PETROLE *navigation* bare boat charter; ~ **en travers** *m* PETROLE lump sum freight; ~ **à forfait** *m* PETROLE *commerce, transport maritime* lump sum freight; ~ **à temps** *m* NAUT, PETROLE time charter; ~ **au voyage** *m* NAUT, PETROLE *commerce, transport maritime* voyage charter

affréter *vt* NAUT charter

affréteur *m* NAUT charterer, freighter, shipper

affusion *f* CHIMIE affusion

affût *m* CONS MECA standard, MINES bar; ~ **à berceau** *m* MILITAIRE cradle mounting; ~ **de canon** *m* MILITAIRE gun carriage; ~ **pour creusement de tunnels** *m* CONSTR tunnel bar; ~ **pour fonçage de puits** *m* MINES shaft-sinking bar; ~ **à roues** *m* MILITAIRE *d'un canon* wheeled carriage

affûtage *m* CONS MECA sharpening, PRODUCTION grinding; ~ **d'outils** *m* CONS MECA tool grinding, tool sharpening

affût-colonne *m* CONS MECA post, MINES column

affûté *adj* CONS MECA sharp, sharpened

affûter *vt* CONS MECA sharpen, PRODUCTION grind

affûteur *m* CONS MECA sharpener, PRODUCTION grinder

affûteuse *f* CONS MECA grinding machine, sharpener, sharpening machine, PAPIER defiberer (AmE), defibrer (BrE), grinder, grinding machine, sharpening machine

affût-trépied *m* MINES tripod

aflatoxine *f* AGRO ALIM aflatoxin

afwillite *f* MINERAUX afwillite

Ag *(argent)* CHIMIE Ag *(silver)*

agalite *f* MINERAUX, PAPIER agalite

agalmatolite *f* MINERAUX agalmatolite

agalmatolithe *f* MINERAUX agalmatolite

agar *m* AGRO ALIM agar-agar

agar-agar *m* AGRO ALIM agar-agar

agaric: ~ **fossile** *m* MINERAUX agaphite, agaric mineral; ~ **minéral** *m* MINERAUX agaphite, agaric mineral

agarice *f* MINERAUX agaphite, agaric mineral

agate *f* CERAM VER, MINERAUX agate; ~ **mousse** *f* MINERAUX moss agate

agaté *adj* MINERAUX agaty

âge *m* GEOLOGIE age, date, PETR age; ~ **absolu** *m* GEOLOGIE date; ~ **de mise en place** *m* GEOLOGIE emplacement age; ~ **de refroidissement** *m* GEOLOGIE cooling age; ~ **de l'univers** *m* ASTRONOMIE age of the universe

agence *f* MATERIAUX *action*, TEXTILE agency; ~ **maritime** *f* NAUT shipping agency; ~ **pour la protection de l'environnement** *f* POLLUTION environmental protection agency; ~ **spatiale** *f* ESPACE space agency

Agence: ~ **nationale de l'aéronautique et de l'espace** *f* *(NASA)* ESPACE National Aeronautics and Space Administration *(NASA)*; ~ **spatiale européenne** *f* *(ASE)* ASTRONOMIE, ESPACE European Space Agency *(ESA)*

agencement *m* CONS MECA fitting, layout; ~ **de goulottes pour fils** *m* PRODUCTION duct layout

agencements *m pl* CONSTR fittings, fixtures and fittings

agencer[1] *vt* CONS MECA fit

agencer:[2] **s'~** *v réfl* CONS MECA fit

agène *m* AGRO ALIM agene

agent *m* CHARBON, CHIMIE, TEXTILE agent; ~ **absorbant** *m* CHIMIE sorbent; ~ **d'accompagnement de train** *m* CH DE FER *véhicules* conductor (AmE); ~ **actif de surface** *m* LESSIVES surface-active agent; ~ **activant** *m* CHARBON activating agent; ~ **additif** *m* IMPRIM additive; ~ **adsorbant** *m* AGRO ALIM adsorbent; ~ **améliorant** *m* PETROLE improver; ~ **antiblocant** *m* PLAST CAOU *adhésifs* antiblocking agent; ~ **anticorrosif** *m* EMBALLAGE corrosion preventive; ~ **anticorrosion** *m* MATERIAUX corrosion inhibitor; ~ **antiéclaboussant** *m* AGRO ALIM antispattering agent; ~ **antiflottation** *m* PLAST CAOU *additif pour peintures* antiflooding agent; ~ **antigrilleur** *m* PLAST CAOU antiscorching agent; ~ **antimicrobien** *m* MATERIAUX *auxiliaire plastique* biological agent; ~ **antimottant** *m* AGRO ALIM anticaking agent; ~ **antimoussant** *m* GENIE CHIM foam breaker; ~ **antimousse** *m* CHARBON, IMPRIM *impression* antifoaming agent, PETROLE defoaming agent, PLAST CAOU *revêtements, adhésifs* antifoaming agent; ~ **antipeau** *m* IMPRIM *encres* antiskinning agent, PLAST CAOU *peintures* antiskinning agent; ~ **antiredéposition** *m* LESSIVES antiredeposition agent; ~ **antistatique** *m* LESSIVES, PLAST CAOU *additif ou traitement*, TEXTILE antistatic agent; ~ **atmosphérique** *m* PETROLE atmospheric agent; ~ **augmentant la synergie** *m* LESSIVES synergist; ~ **d'azurage** *m* PLAST CAOU *peinture* optical brightener; ~ **biologique** *m* POLLUTION biological agent; ~ **de blanchiment** *m* AGRO ALIM, LESSIVES bleaching agent; ~ **de brevets** *m* CONS MECA patent agent; ~ **de brevets d'invention** *m* CONS MECA patent agent; ~ **caloporteur** *m* THERMODYN heat-exchanging medium; ~ **chelatant** *m* HYDROLOGIE chelating agent; ~ **chélateur** *m* LESSIVES chelating agent; ~ **chimique** *m* PLAST CAOU *chimie* reagent, POLLUTION, TEXTILE chemical agent; ~ **clarifiant** *m* AGRO ALIM clarifier; ~ **coagulant** *m* PLAST CAOU *caoutchouc* coagulating agent; ~ **collant** *m* PLAST CAOU *caoutchouc, adhésifs* tackifying agent; ~ **collecteur** *m* CHARBON collecting agent; ~ **de combustion** *m* POLLU MER burning agent; ~ **complexant** *m* NUCLEAIRE complexing agent; ~ **de coulage** *m* POLLU MER sinking agent; ~ **coulant** *m* POLLU MER sinking agent; ~ **de crémage** *m* PLAST CAOU *caoutchouc* creaming agent; ~ **décolorant** *m* LESSIVES bleaching agent; ~ **défloculant** *m* PLAST CAOU *peintures* deflocculating agent; ~ **de démoulage** *m* PLAST CAOU release agent; ~ **désémulsifiant** *m* MATERIAUX desemulsifying agent; ~ **déshydratant** *m* GENIE CHIM dehydrating agent, dehydrator; ~ **dessiccateur** *m* AGRO ALIM desiccant; ~ **dispersant** *m* AGRO ALIM, HYDROLOGIE dispersing agent, LESSIVES peptizer, PLAST CAOU *pigments, polymère,* POLLUTION dispersing agent; ~ **de dopage** *m* ELECTRON doping agent, impurity; ~ **durcissant** *m* IMPRIM *chimie graphique* alum; ~ **de durcissement** *m* PLAST CAOU *plastiques, adhésifs, revêtements* curing agent; ~ **émulseur** *m* PRODUCTION emulsifying agent; ~ **émulsifiant** *m* GENIE CHIM emulsifier, emulsifying agent; ~ **d'encollage** *m* TEXTILE sizing agent; ~ **entraîneur d'air** *m* CONSTR *béton* air-entraining admixture; ~ **épaississant** *m* IMPRIM *chimie* bodying agent; ~ **d'étalement** *m* PLAST CAOU *mélange* extender; ~ **d'étanchéité** *m* CHIMIE sealant; ~ **extincteur d'incendie** *m* SECURITE fire-extinguishing agent; ~ **de gélification** *m* PLAST CAOU *additif* gelling agent; ~ **de gonflement** *m* PLAST CAOU *mélange* blowing agent; ~ **hydrofuge** *m* REVETEMENT water-repellent impregnation means; ~ **d'imprégnation** *m* CHIMIE impregnant; ~ **inhibiteur de voile coloré** *m* CINEMAT antistain agent; ~ **de lavage** *m* LESSIVES detergent, washing agent; ~ **lixiviant** *m* NUCLEAIRE leachant, leaching agent; ~ **de manoeuvre** *m* CH DE FER shunter; ~ **de manutention** *m* CH DE FER freight porter (AmE), goods porter (BrE); ~ **maritime** *m* NAUT shipping agent; ~ **mouillant** *m* AGRO ALIM, CERAM VER, CHIMIE, CINEMAT, IMPRIM, PHYSIQUE, POLLU MER, TEXTILE wetting agent; ~ **moussant** *m* AGRO ALIM foaming agent, GENIE CHIM foamer, foaming agent, LESSIVES foamer; ~ **neutralisant** *m* SECURITE neutralizing agent; ~ **opacifiant** *m* LESSIVES opacifying agent; ~ **d'oxydation** *m* THERMODYN oxidant; ~ **photorésistant** *m* ELECTRON photoresist; ~ **physique** *m* POLLUTION physical agent; ~ **de planning** *m* PRODUCTION planner; ~ **de polissage** *m* CERAM VER polishing agent; ~ **de précipitation** *m* HYDROLOGIE coagulant; ~ **préservatif** *m* EMBALLAGE preservative; ~ **de préservation** *m* PRODUCTION preservative; ~ **producteur de mousse** *m* AERONAUT foam compound; ~ **protecteur** *m* EMBALLAGE protective agent; ~ **de réception** *m* PRODUCTION receiver; ~ **réducteur** *m* CHARBON, CHIMIE reducing agent, CINEMAT reducer; ~ **réfrigérant** *m* THERMODYN refrigerant; ~ **de refroidissement** *m* REFRIG cooling medium; ~ **renforçant** *m* PLAST CAOU *plastiques, caoutchouc* reinforcing agent; ~ **repousseur** *m* POLLU MER herding agent, POLLUTION oil-concentrating agent; ~ **résistant au gel** *m* EMBALLAGE frost-preventive agent; ~ **retardant le rassissement** *m* AGRO ALIM antistaling agent; ~ **de retard de la prise** *m* CONSTR retarding agent; ~ **de réticulation** *m* PLAST CAOU *polymérisation* cross-linking agent; ~ **salin** *m* NUCLEAIRE salting agent; ~ **séchant** *m* IMPRIM *encres* dryer; ~ **de la sécurité** *m* SECURITE safety representative; ~ **de séparation** *m* GENIE CHIM separating agent; ~ **de surface** *m* LESSIVES surfactant, PLAST CAOU surfactant, *additif* wetting agent, POLLU MER surface-active agent, POLLUTION surfactant; ~ **de surface anionique** *m* LESSIVES anionic surface active agent; ~ **surfactant** *m* POLLU MER sinking agent, surface-active agent; ~ **surfactif** *m* POLLU MER sinking agent, surface-active agent; ~ **tampon** *m* CINEMAT buffering agent; ~ **technique de saturation** *m* (*ATS*) OCEANO caisson master, life support technician; ~ **télématique** *m* TELECOM TLMA, telematic agent; ~ **tensio-actif** *m* AGRO ALIM, CHARBON, LESSIVES, PLAST CAOU surfactant, POLLU MER sinking agent, surface-active agent, surfactant; ~ **de traitement d'appel** *m* TELECOM CCA, call control agent; ~ **de transfert de messages** *m* TELECOM MTA, message transfer agent; ~ **d'usager** *m* TELECOM UA, user agent; ~ **d'usager d'annuaire** *m* TELECOM directory user agent; ~ **d'usager EDI** *m* TELECOM EDI user agent, EDI-UA; ~ **utilisateur** *m* TELECOM UA, user agent; ~ **d'utilisateur EDI** *m* TELECOM EDI user agent, EDI-UA; ~ **de la voie** *m* CH DE FER track layer

agents: ~ **d'intempérisme** *m pl* MATERIAUX weathering agencies

agglo *m* (*aggloméré*) CONSTR permanent concrete shuttering

agglomérant *m* AGRO ALIM binding agent, CONSTR binder, cement, matrix, POLLU MER binding agent; ~ **par frittage** *m* CHARBON cherry coal

agglomérat *m* PETR agglomerate

agglomératif *adj* PAPIER agglomerative

agglomération *f* AGRO ALIM caking, GENIE CHIM agglomeration, sintering, METALL clustering, PAPIER agglomeration, PLAST CAOU *pigments, charges* agglomeration, *plastiques* pelletizing; ~ **de grain** *f* PHOTO grain clumping

aggloméré[1] *adj* GENIE CHIM sintered, PAPIER agglomerated

aggloméré[2] *m* CHARBON briquette, CONSTR conglomerate, CONSTR permanent concrete shuttering; ~ **de béton** *m* CONSTR concrete masonry; ~ **de goudron** *m* POLLU MER tar ball

agglomérer:[1] ~ **par frittage** *vt* GENIE CHIM sinter

agglomérer:[2] *vti* CHARBON, GENIE CHIM, PAPIER agglomerate

agglomérer:[3] **s'~** *v réfl* GEOLOGIE cohere, *particules* aggregate, cluster together

agglomérés: ~ **banchés** *m pl* CONSTR permanent concrete shuttering

agglutinant[1] *adj* GENIE CHIM, MATERIAUX agglutinative

agglutinant[2] *m* AGRO ALIM, GENIE CHIM binding agent, PRODUCTION *d'une meule en émeri* bond

agglutination *f* AGRO ALIM agglutination, caking, CHIMIE, GENIE CHIM agglutination, PLAST CAOU *pigment, charge* caking

agglutiner[1] *vt* GENIE CHIM agglutinate

agglutiner:[2] **s'~** *v réfl* CHIMIE agglutinate

agglutinine *f* AGRO ALIM agglutinin

aggradation *f* DISTRI EAU aggradation

agilité: ~ **en fréquence** *f* ELECTRON frequency agility

agir: ~ **sur** *vt* PHYSIQUE act upon, PRODUCTION adjust

agitateur *m* AGRO ALIM agitator, CHARBON agitator, impeller, mixer, CINEMAT paddle, stirring rod, CONS MECA agitator, EQUIP LAB stirrer, GENIE CHIM agitating machine, agitator, PAPIER agitator, stirrer, PETROLE agitator, PLAST CAOU stirrer; ~ **antidéflagrant** *m* EQUIP LAB *mélange* fireproof stirrer, flameproof stirrer; ~ **à hélice** *m* GENIE CHIM mixing propeller; ~ **magnétique** *m* EQUIP LAB *mélange* magnetic stirrer; ~ **mélangeur** *m* GENIE CHIM agitating mixer; ~ **secoueur** *m* EQUIP LAB *récipients, tamis* shaker; ~ **vibrant** *m* EQUIP LAB vibrating stirrer

agitation *f* CHIMIE stirring, CONS MECA shaking, METEO swell; ~ **effectuée par intervalles** *f* PHOTO intermittent agitation; ~ **localisée** *f* PHYS FLUID localized disturbance; ~ **thermique** *f* ELECTROTEC *des électrons*, METALL, PHYSIQUE thermal agitation

agité *adj* PHYS FLUID turbulent

agiter *vt* AGRO ALIM churn, CHIMIE stir, GENIE CHIM, IMPRIM agitate, PAPIER agitate, stir, PHOTO *un bain* agitate

agrafage *m* IMPRIM stapling; ~ **latéral** *m* EMBALLAGE lateral stapling; ~ **simple** *m* CONS MECA single overlap; ~ **supérieur et inférieur** *m* EMBALLAGE top and bottom stapling; ~ **sur coin** *m* EMBALLAGE corner stapling

agrafe *f* CERAM VER *pour bouteilles* closure, CONS MECA clasp, clip, hook, CONSTR casement fastener, cramp, cramp iron, EMBALLAGE staple, PAPIER clamp, staple, PRODUCTION fastener, *pour oreilles de châssis, etc* dog, TEXTILE hook; ~ **à clavette** *f* CONSTR cottered joint; ~ **de collets** *f* MINES collar grab; ~ **et porte** *f* CONS MECA hook and eye; ~ **d'isolateur** *f* ELECTROTEC insulator clamp; ~ **de manoeuvre** *f* MINES clamp; ~ **pour sac** *f* EMBALLAGE bag staple; ~ **à scellement** *f* CONSTR cramp iron with stone hook; ~ **à T** *f* CONSTR T-cramp; ~ **à talon** *f* CONSTR cramp with turned-down ends

agrafer[1] *vt* CONS MECA clasp, hook; ~ **avec une fermeture éclair** *vt* TEXTILE *doublure* zip in

agrafer[2] **s'~** *v réfl* CONS MECA clasp

agrafes: ~ **à griffes pour courroies** *f pl* CONS MECA steel belt lacing, PRODUCTION belt lacing

agrafeuse *f* EMBALLAGE stapling machine; ~ **électrique** *f* PRODUCTION electric stapling machine; ~ **sur coins** *f* EMBALLAGE corner stapling machine

agrandir *vt* PHOTO blow up, *une plaque* enlarge

agrandissement *m* CINEMAT optical enlargement, IMPRIM, PHOTO enlargement; ~ **photographique** *m* IMPRIM *photographie* blowup

agrandisseur *m* IMPRIM enlarging camera, *photo* enlarger, PHOTO enlarger; ~ **à mise au point automatique** *m* PHOTO automatic enlarger

agravité *f* PHYSIQUE weightlessness

agréer *vt* SECURITE approve

agrégat *m* CERAM VER, CHARBON, CONSTR, IMPRIM *pigments, encres*, MATERIAUX, METALL aggregate; ~ **de données** *m* INFORMAT, ORDINAT data aggregate; ~ **gros** *m* CONSTR coarse aggregate; ~ **de laitier mousseux** *m* CHAUFFAGE foamed slag aggregate

agréger: s'~ *v réfl* GEOLOGIE *particules* aggregate, cluster together

agrément *m* QUALITE acceptance

agrès *m pl* PRODUCTION gin tackle, hoisting tackle, tackle; ~ **de chèvre** *m pl* PRODUCTION gin tackle

agressé: ~ **par la pollution acide** *adj* POLLUTION acid-stressed

agression: ~ **acide** *f* POLLUTION acid stress

agressivité *f* HYDROLOGIE aggression

agréyeur *m* PRODUCTION wiredrawer

agricolite *f* MINERAUX agricolite

agricolithe *f* MINERAUX agricolite

agrippe-col *m* EMBALLAGE clip-on carrier

agripper *vt* PRODUCTION grip

agrippeur *m* TRANSPORT spreader

agroindustrie *f* AGRO ALIM agrobusiness

agrumier *m* NAUT fruit carrier

aidant *m* CERAM VER foot carrier

aide:[1] ~ **foreur** *m* PETR assistant driller

aide[2] *f* CONS MECA assistance, INFORMAT, ORDINAT support, SECURITE assistance; ~ **autonome à la navigation** *f* AERONAUT self-contained navigational aid; ~ **à la conception** *f* INFORMAT, ORDINAT design aid; ~ **directionnelle** *f* TRANSPORT directional aid; ~ **de pointage radar automatique** *f* NAUT ARPA, automatic radar plotting aid

aide-mémoire *m* CONS MECA handbook, PRODUCTION manual

aider *vt* INFORMAT, ORDINAT support

aides: ~ **antiabordage** *f pl* NAUT collision avoidance aids; ~ **d'approche par radio** *f pl* AERONAUT radio approach aids; ~ **de dépassement** *f pl* TRANSPORT passing aids; ~ **électroniques à la circulation routière** *f pl* TRANSPORT electronic traffic aids; ~ **et engins nécessaires à la manoeuvre des pièces** *f pl* CONS MECA necessary assistance and appliances for handling machinery; ~ **à la navigation** *f pl* NAUT aids to navigation, navigational instruments; ~ **d'urgence** *f pl* TRANSPORT emergency aids

Aigle *m* ASTRONOMIE Aquila

aigrette *f* GEOPHYS aigrette, terminal aigrette; ~ **lumineuse** *f* ELECTR *d'une chine électrique* brush discharge

aigu *adj* CONS MECA sharp, ENREGISTR treble, IMPRIM *photogravure, impression* keen

aiguemarine *f* MINERAUX aquamarine

aiguillage *m* CH DE FER points switching, set of points, CONSTR set of points, switch, ELECTRON *programme* directing, ELECTROTEC switch, INFORMAT jump, switch, ORDINAT switch; ~ **automatique** *m* TRANSPORT automatic switching; ~ **à deux voies symétriques** *m* CH DE FER dual control switch; ~ **semi-automatique** *m* CH DE FER semiautomatic points switching; ~ **simple** *m* CH DE FER ordinary points (BrE), ordinary switch (AmE); ~ **tangentiel** *m* CH DE FER *tramway, caténaire* overhead line knuckle; ~ **d'un train** *m* CH DE FER switching a train (AmE)

aiguille *f* CERAM VER bird cage, tapered pad, CH DE FER point switch, turnout, *installations fixes* points, switch, CONS MECA index, *d'un compteur* pointer, *d'un injecteur* spindle, *d'une balance* tongue, CONSTR breaker point, king rod, breaker steel, ELECTR, ELECTROTEC pointer, ENREGISTR needle, stylus, EQUIP LAB *d'un instrument* pointer, *index d'un instrument* hand, needle, MINES aiguille, nail, needle, picker, pricker, shooting needle, PAPIER, TEXTILE, VEHICULES *carburateur* needle; ~ **à acier huilé** *f* PAPIER oil-tempered needle; ~ **aimantée** *f* GEOPHYS magnetic needle, mariner's needle, NAUT compass needle; ~ **de bifurcation** *f* CH DE FER junction points; ~ **de boussole** *f* PHYSIQUE compass needle; ~ **de carburateur** *f* VEHICULES carburetor needle (AmE), carburettor needle (BrE); ~ **à clapet** *f* TEXTILE latch needle; ~ **de déraillement** *f* CH DE FER catch points, derailing points (BrE), derailing switch (AmE); ~ **à dissection** *f* EQUIP LAB *biologie* dissection needle; ~ **d'essai** *f* CONS MECA test needle, touch needle; ~ **à filet** *f* OCEANO fisherman's needle, netting needle; ~ **d'inclinaison** *f* GEOPHYS dip circle needle, dip needle, magnetic inclinometer; ~ **de mesure** *f* PHOTO indicator needle; ~ **de posemètre** *f* PHOTO exposure meter needle; ~ **de réglage** *f* CONS MECA spindle; ~ **de relieur** *f* IMPRIM bookbinder's needle; ~ **à repriser** *f* TEXTILE darning needle; ~ **à retirer les pièces battues** *f* PRODUCTION draw hook, draw spike, draw stick; ~ **semi-automatique** *f* CH DE FER ground frame; ~ **à tracer** *f* CONS MECA scriber, CONSTR scratch awl; ~ **trotteuse** *f* CONS MECA second hand; ~ **à trous d'air** *f* PRODUCTION piercer, pricker; ~ **vibrante** *f* CONSTR poker vibrator

aiguillé *adj* MATERIAUX acicular, aciculate, aciculated, aciculiform

aiguiller *vt* INFORMAT *programme*, ORDINAT *programme* branch, TELECOM direct

aiguilletage *m* TEXTILE needling

aiguillette *f* NAUT lanyard, sennet

aiguilleur: ~ **du ciel** *m* AERONAUT air traffic controller

aiguillot *m* NAUT *de gouvernail* pintle

aiguisage *m* CONS MECA sharpening, PRODUCTION grinding

aiguisé *adj* CONS MECA sharp

aiguisement *m* PRODUCTION grinding

aiguiser *vt* CONS MECA sharpen, PRODUCTION grind

aiguiseur *m* CONS MECA sharpener, PRODUCTION grinder

aiguisoir *m* CONS MECA sharpener

aikinite *f* MINERAUX aikinite

aile *f* CONS MECA blade, *d'un ventilateur* vane, *d'une vis ailée* wing, CONSTR *d'un bâtiment* wing, NAUT *d'hélice, de turbine* blade, OCEANO trawl wing, wing, PHYSIQUE wing, VEHICULES *carrosserie* fender (AmE), mudguard (BrE), wing (BrE); ~ **arrière** *f* AUTO rear fender (AmE), rear wing (BrE); ~ **avant** *f* AUTO front fender (AmE), front wing (BrE); ~ **de cornière** *f* CONS MECA extrusion flange; ~ **critique** *f* AERONAUT *navigabilité* critical wing; ~ **de dérive** *f* NAUT drop keel, leeboard; ~ **effilée** *f* AERONAUT tapered wing; ~ **en delta** *f* AERONAUT delta wing; ~ **en flèche** *f* AERONAUT swept wing; ~ **en flèche négative** *f* AERONAUT forward-swept wing; ~ **en flèche positive** *f* AERONAUT swept-back wing; ~ **à fente** *f* AERONAUT slotted wing; ~ **d'hydroptère** *f* TRANSPORT hydrofoil; ~ **inférieure** *f* CONSTR bottom flange; ~ **médiane** *f* AERONAUT mid-wing; ~ **mi-haute** *f* AERONAUT shoulder wing; ~ **profilée** *f* AERONAUT swept wing; ~ **rotor à cycle chaud** *f* AERONAUT hot-cycle rotor wing; ~ **de seine** *f* OCEANO wing end; ~ **semi-haute** *f* AERONAUT shoulder wing; ~ **de senne** *f* OCEANO wing end; ~ **supérieure** *f* CONSTR top flange

aileron *m* AERONAUT aileron, CONS MECA *d'un ventilateur, d'une roue hydraulique* paddle, paddle board, DISTRI EAU float, floatboard, NAUT fin keel, fin, skeg, TRANSPORT spoiler; ~ **compensé** *m* AERONAUT balanced aileron; ~ **intérieur** *m* TRANSPORT all-speed aileron

ailettage: ~ **de turbine** *m* MECANIQUE blading

ailette *f* AERONAUT cooling fin, CERAM VER fin, CONS MECA blade, vane, *de ventilateur, de turbine* blade, ESPACE *véhicules* blade, MECANIQUE fin, NAUT *de ventilateur, de turbine* blade, NUCLEAIRE fin, rib, *en chevrons* herringbone fin, REFRIG fin; ~ **gaufrée** *f* REFRIG staggered fin; ~ **protégée par vinyle** *f* REFRIG vinyl-coated fin; ~ **de radiateur** *f* AUTO, VEHICULES *refroidissement* radiator fin; ~ **de refroidissement** *f* AERONAUT cooling fin, CINEMAT cooling rib, CONS MECA, NUCLEAIRE cooling fin; ~ **de turbine** *f* EN RENOUV, NAUT turbine blade

aimant *m* ELECTR, ELECTROTEC, ENREGISTR, EQUIP LAB, PHYS PART, PHYSIQUE, TELECOM magnet; ~ **d'actionnement** *m* PRODUCTION operating magnet; ~ **de Bitter** *m* PHYSIQUE Bitter magnet; ~ **de blindage** *m* TV field neutralizing magnet; ~ **CC à faible consommation** *m* PRODUCTION economized DC magnet; ~ **de champ** *m* ELECTROTEC, ENREGISTR field magnet; ~ **de compensation** *m* NAUT corrector magnet; ~ **de concentration** *m* ELECTROTEC, ESPACE *communications* focusing mag-

net; ~ **de convergence** *m* TV beam-positioning magnet; ~ **de déviation** *m* TV deflection magnet; ~ **droit** *m* PHYSIQUE bar magnet; ~ **en fer à cheval** *m* CONS MECA U-magnet, horseshoe magnet, ELECTR, PHYSIQUE horseshoe magnet; ~ **du faisceau bleu** *m* TV blue beam magnet; ~ **du faisceau rouge** *m* TV red-beam magnet; ~ **feuilleté** *m* ELECTR laminated magnet; ~ **de focalisation** *m* TV focusing magnet; ~ **de guidage** *m* TRANSPORT guidance magnet; ~ **à lames** *m* ELECTR laminated magnet; ~ **de levage** *m* ELECTR lifting magnet, TRANSPORT lift magnet; ~ **permanent** *m* CONS MECA, ELECTR, ELECTROTEC, PHYSIQUE, TELECOM, TRANSPORT permanent magnet; ~ **de signalisation** *m* CONS MECA magnetic needle; ~ **supraconducteur** *m* PHYS PART, TRANSPORT superconducting magnet; ~ **torique** *m* PHYSIQUE annular magnet, toroidal magnet; ~ **de traction** *m* TRANSPORT propulsion magnet; ~ **d'uniformisation de la trame de couleurs** *m* TV color field corrector (AmE), colour field corrector (BrE)

aimantation *f* ELECTR, ELECTROTEC, ENREGISTR, GEOLOGIE, PETR, PHYSIQUE, TELECOM, TV magnetization; ~ **par induction** *f* ELECTR cross-magnetizing effect; ~ **rémanente** *f* PHYS RAYON residual magnetization, PHYSIQUE remanent magnetization; ~ **à saturation** *f* ELECTROTEC saturation magnetization; ~ **spontanée** *f* PHYS RAYON, PHYSIQUE spontaneous magnetization

aimanté *adj* ELECTR magnetized

aimanter *vt* ELECTROTEC, PHYSIQUE magnetize

ainalite *f* MINERAUX ainalite

air: ~ **ambiant** *m* POLLUTION, REFRIG ambient air; ~ **calme** *m* EN RENOUV still air; ~ **chaud forcé** *m* MAT CHAUFF forced warm air; ~ **de combustion** *m* THERMODYN combustion air; ~ **comprimé** *m* CONS MECA, CONSTR, MINES compressed air; ~ **continental** *m* METEO continental air; ~ **de dégivrage** *m* AERONAUT de-icing air; ~ **de dilution** *m* AERONAUT engine bypass air; ~ **de dilution moteur** *m* AERONAUT engine bypass air; ~ **dynamique** *m* REFRIG ram air; ~ **équatorial maritime** *m* METEO maritime equatorial air; ~ **forcé** *m* CONS MECA induced air, ram air; ~ **humide** *m* METEO humid air; ~ **impropre à la respiration** *m* SECURITE air unfit for respiration; ~ **inclus** *m* EMBALLAGE entrapped air; ~ **instable** *m* METEO unstable air; ~ **libre** *m* CONSTR open air; ~ **liquide** *m* THERMODYN liquid air; ~ **maritime** *m* METEO maritime air; ~ **occlus** *m* PLAST CAOU entrapped air; ~ **polaire** *m* METEO polar air; ~ **de réchauffage** *m* AERONAUT heating air; ~ **de refroidissement** *m* CONS MECA cooling air, NUCLEAIRE air coolant; ~ **respirable** *m* SECURITE air fit to breathe, breathable air; ~ **salin** *m* REFRIG salted atmosphere; ~ **saturé** *m* METEO, REFRIG saturated air; ~ **sec** *m* METEO dry air; ~ **de séchage** *m* CHARBON drying air; ~ **secondaire** *m* AUTO, CHAUFFAGE secondary air; ~ **soufflé** *m* CONS MECA forced draft (AmE), forced draught (BrE); ~ **stable** *m* METEO stable air; ~ **sursaturé** *m* METEO supersaturated air; ~ **tropical** *m* METEO tropical air; ~ **vicié** *m* MINES bad air

airage *m* MINES airhead, airheading, airway, ventilation drive

airbus *m* TRANSPORT airbus

aire *f* CONSTR *d'un bâtiment* area, *d'un bassin, d'un réservoir* floor, *d'un pont* floor, ESPACE pad, GEOMETRIE *d'un cercle*, MATH area, PHYSIQUE surface, PRODUCTION floor, *d'une enclume* crown, *d'un marteau* face, *d'une enclume* face; ~ **d'absorption équivalente** *f* ACOUSTIQUE equivalent absorption area;

~ d'activation ƒ METALL activation area; ~ d'alimenta-tion ƒ DISTRI EAU, HYDROLOGIE watershed; ~ d'atterrissage ƒ AERONAUT, ESPACE *véhicules* landing area, POLLU MER helicopter pad, TRANSPORT landing area; ~ d'atterrissage pour hélicoptère ƒ AERONAUT helipad; ~ d'audition ƒ ACOUSTIQUE auditory sensation area; ~ brute ƒ EN RENOUV *d'un récepteur* gross area; ~ de chargement ƒ AERONAUT *d'aéroport* loading area, NUCLEAIRE charge area, charge face, reactor charging face; ~ de cohérence ƒ OPTIQUE coherence area, coherent area, TELECOM coherent area; ~ du collecteur ƒ ELECTROTEC collector region; ~ de compensation de compas ƒ AERONAUT compass compensation base; ~ de coulée ƒ PRODUCTION pig bed; ~ damée ƒ NU-CLEAIRE rammed area; ~ de décollage ƒ AERONAUT takeoff area; ~ d'empilage ƒ CONSTR storage area; ~ d'évolution ƒ TRANSPORT apron; ~ de génération de la houle ƒ OCEANO wave-generating area; ~ de lancement ƒ ESPACE *véhicules* launch area, launch pad, MILITAIRE rocket launching site; ~ latérale ƒ GEOMETRIE lateral area; ~ de lavoir ƒ CHARBON strake; ~ de manutention de conteneurs ƒ TRANSPORT marshalling area (BrE); ~ nette ƒ EN RENOUV *d'un récepteur* net area; ~ normale d'audition ƒ ACOUSTIQUE normal auditory sensation area; ~ de nutrition ƒ OCEANO fattening ground, feed-ing ground; ~ de pluie ƒ DISTRI EAU rainfall area; ~ de point fixe ƒ AERONAUT *d'un aéroport* run-up area; ~ de ralentissement ƒ NUCLEAIRE, PHYSIQUE slowing-down area; ~ de séchage ƒ PRODUCTION drying floor; ~ de sécurité d'extrémité de piste ƒ AERONAUT runway end safety area; ~ de stationnement ƒ AERONAUT parking area; ~ de stockage ƒ CONSTR storage area, PETR pipe deck; ~ de stockage amont ƒ PRODUCTION inbound stock point

aires: ~ d'alluvions ƒ pl CONSTR alluvial areas; ~ de vent ƒ pl NAUT points of the compass

ais *m* CONSTR board, deal

aisselier *m* CONSTR angle brace, angle tie, strut

ajointer *vt* CONSTR *des tuyaux* join up

ajout *m* CONS MECA addition, IMPRIM *composition* ad-dendum; ~ de tige *m* PETROLE making a connection

ajouté: ~ à l'emballage *m* EMBALLAGE add-on to the packaging

ajouter *vt* ENREGISTR *musique, son* overdub, ORDINAT add; ~ des améliorations *vt* EN RENOUV *sur équipement ancien* retrofit; ~ une espace fine *vt* IMPRIM add thin space; ~ et effacer *vt* IMPRIM add and delete

ajustable *adj* COMMANDE adjustable, adjusting, CONS MECA, MECANIQUE adjustable

ajustage *m* COMMANDE adjustment, CONS MECA fitting, METROLOGIE adjustment; ~ dynamique *m* ELECTROTEC dynamic trimming; ~ de format *m* TV aspect ratio adjustment; ~ de gain *m* ELECTRON gain trimming; ~ glissant *m* MECANIQUE sliding fit; ~ au laser *m* ELEC-TRON laser trimming; ~ laser *m* ELECTRON laser trimming; ~ d'une machine *m* CONS MECA setting up; ~ du palier du noir *m* TV pedestal adjustment; ~ de piste *m* TV track adjustment; ~ de résistance *m* ELECTROTEC resistor trimming

ajustement *m* CRISTALL, METROLOGIE *d'une balance* ad-justment; ~ avec serrage *m* CONS MECA interference fit; ~ à chaud *m* CONS MECA hot shrink fit; ~ à force *m* CONS MECA drive fit; ~ à froid *m* CONS MECA cold shrink fit; ~ à frottement dur *m* CONS MECA force fit; ~ glissant juste *m* CONS MECA close sliding fit; ~ libre *m* CONS MECA loose fit; ~ lisse *m* CONS MECA plain fitting; ~

d'une machine *m* CONS MECA setting up; ~ à la presse *m* PRODUCTION press fit; ~ de résistance *m* ELECTRO-TEC resistor trimming; ~ de stock *m* PRODUCTION stock transaction; ~ de zéro mécanique *m* ELECTR *d'un instrument* mechanical zero adjustment

ajuster[1] *vt* CONS MECA fit, *couvercle à une boîte* fit, IMPRIM set, MECANIQUE fit, *physique* adjust, SECURITE adjust

ajuster:[2] s'~ *v réfl* CONS MECA fit

ajusteur *m* CONS MECA, MECANIQUE fitter

ajusteur-monteur *m* CONS MECA fitter, MECANIQUE mill-wright, PRODUCTION erector

ajutage *m* CONS MECA air nozzle, nozzle, DISTRI EAU jet, PRODUCTION nose, nosepiece, *système hydraulique* drilling; ~ d'automaticité *m* AUTO air correction jet; ~ convergent *m* CONS MECA *d'un injecteur* combining nozzle; ~ cylindrique *m* INST HYDR cylindrical mouth-piece, opening in thick wall, short pipe; ~ divergent *m* PRODUCTION *d'un injecteur* delivery cone, delivery nozzle, delivery tube; ~ de remplissage *m* EMBALLAGE filling nozzle; ~ rentrant de Borda *m* INST HYDR Borda mouthpiece; ~ de robinet *m* CONSTR bib nozzle; ~ à vapeur *m* INST HYDR steam nozzle

akanthicone *m* MINERAUX acanthicone, akanticone

akérite ƒ PETR akerite

akermanite ƒ MINERAUX åkermanite

Al *(aluminium)* CHIMIE Al *(aluminium)*

alaise ƒ TEXTILE waterproof sheet

alalite ƒ MINERAUX alalite

alambic *m* AGRO ALIM, EQUIP LAB *distillation* still, GENIE CHIM distillation flask, distilling flask, still, THERMO-DYN distillation flask, distillation retort

alandier: ~ d'attrempage *m* CERAM VER startup burner

alanine ƒ CHIMIE alanine

alarme ƒ CONS MECA *signal acoustique ou optique*, SE-CURITE alarm; ~ antieffraction ƒ SECURITE burglar alarm; ~ automatique d'incendie ƒ SECURITE automat-ic fire alarm; ~ de basse pression ƒ PRODUCTION *de système hydraulique* low-pressure alarm; ~ de chau-dière ƒ INST HYDR boiler alarm; ~ de débit ƒ PRODUCTION *de système hydraulique* flow alarm; ~ à la fumée ƒ SECURITE smoke alarm; ~ de groupe de voies ƒ TELECOM CGA, carrier group alarm; ~ lumineuse ƒ ELECTROTEC warning light; ~ majeure ƒ TELECOM major alarm; ~ mineure ƒ TELECOM minor alarm; ~ pour fuite d'eau ƒ MINES water leakage alarm; ~ de pression ƒ PRODUCTION *de système hydraulique* press-ure alarm; ~ sonore ƒ TELECOM audible alarm; ~ de surchauffe ƒ PRODUCTION *de système hydraulique* tem-perature alarm; ~ visuelle ƒ TELECOM visual alarm

alaskaïte ƒ MINERAUX alaskaite

alaskite ƒ PETR alaskite

albâtre *m* MINERAUX alabaster; ~ onychite *m* MINERAUX oriental alabaster

albédo *m* ASTRONOMIE, ESPACE *astronomie*, GEOPHYS, METEO albedo; ~ géométrique *m* ESPACE *astronomie* geometric albedo

albertite ƒ MINERAUX albertite

albien *m* GEOLOGIE Albian

albite ƒ CERAM VER, MINERAUX albite

albraque ƒ MINES lodge

albumen *m* AGRO ALIM albumen

albuminate *m* AGRO ALIM, CHIMIE albuminate

albumine ƒ AGRO ALIM, CHIMIE albumin; ~ de sang ƒ AGRO ALIM blood albumin

albuminoïde *adj* CHIMIE albuminoid

albumose *f* AGRO ALIM, CHIMIE albumose

alcali *m* CHIMIE, PAPIER, PETROLE, TEXTILE alkali; ~ caustique *m* LESSIVES caustic alkali; ~ cellulose *m* PAPIER alkali cellulose

alcalimètre *m* AGRO ALIM, PAPIER alkalimeter

alcalimétrie *f* CHIMIE, LESSIVES alkalimetry

alcalin[1] *adj* CHIMIE alkaline, GEOLOGIE *minéral, série magmatique* alkalic, alkaline, HYDROLOGIE alkaline

alcalin[2] *m* CHARBON alkali

alcalinisation *f* CHIMIE alkalization

alcaliniser *vt* CHIMIE alkalinize

alcalinité *f* CHIMIE, HYDROLOGIE, LESSIVES, MATERIAUX, PAPIER, POLLUTION alkalinity; ~ antérieure *f* POLLUTION preacidification alkalinity; ~ de carbonate *f* HYDROLOGIE carbonate alkalinity; ~ initiale *f* POLLUTION preacidification alkalinity; ~ originelle *f* POLLUTION preacidification alkalinity

alcalisation *f* CHIMIE alkalization

alcaliser *vti* HYDROLOGIE alkalize

alcaloïde *m* CHIMIE alkaloid; ~ de lobélie *m* CHIMIE lobelia alkaloid; ~ de poivre *m* CHIMIE pepper alkaloid

alcaloïdes: ~ de l'ergot *m pl* CHIMIE ergot alkaloids

alcane *m* CHIMIE, LESSIVES alkane; ~ sulfonate *m* LESSIVES alkane sulfonate (AmE), alkane sulphonate (BrE)

alcanes *m pl* PETROLE alkanes

alcaptone *f* CHIMIE alkaptone

alcène *m* CHIMIE alkene, LESSIVES alkene, alkylene, PETROLE alkene

alcényle *adj* CHIMIE alkenyl

alcool *m* CHIMIE alcohol, spirit, IMPRIM, PLAST CAOU, TEXTILE alcohol; ~ absolu *m* CHIMIE absolute alcohol; ~ allylique *m* CHIMIE allyl alcohol; ~ amylique *m* CHIMIE pentanol, PAPIER amyl alcohol; ~ benzylique *m* CHIMIE benzyl alcohol; ~ de bois *m* THERMODYN wood alcohol; ~ à brûler *m* CHIMIE methylated spirit; ~ butylique *m* LESSIVES butyl alcohol; ~ décylique *m* CHIMIE decyl alcohol; ~ dénaturé *m* AGRO ALIM denatured alcohol, industrial alcohol, CHIMIE denatured alcohol, methylated spirit, COULEURS methylated spirits; ~ eicosylique *m* CHIMIE eicosyl alcohol; ~ enhydre *m* CHIMIE absolute alcohol; ~ éthylique *m* AGRO ALIM ethanol, ethyl alcohol, grain alcohol, CHIMIE, PETROLE, PHOTO ethyl alcohol; ~ gras *m* CHIMIE, LESSIVES fatty alcohol; ~ hexylique *m* CHIMIE hexyl alcohol; ~ isobutylique *m* CHIMIE isopropylcarbinol; ~ isopropylique *m* AGRO ALIM isopropyl alcohol, IMPRIM IPA, isopropylic alcohol, LESSIVES IPA, isopropanol, isopropyl acid; ~ laurique *m* LESSIVES lauryl alcohol; ~ méthylique *m* CHIMIE methanol, methyl alcohol, PLAST CAOU methyl alcohol; ~ myristique *m* LESSIVES myristic alcohol; ~ nonylique *m* LESSIVES nonyl alcohol; ~ ordinaire *m* COULEURS methylated spirits; ~ ordinaire dénaturé par méthylation *m* COULEURS methylated spirits; ~ oxo *m* LESSIVES oxo alcohol; ~ polyvinylique *m* IMPRIM, PLAST CAOU polyvinyl alcohol; ~ propylique *m* CHIMIE propanol; ~ thuylique *m* CHIMIE thujyl alcohol; ~ de Ziegler *m* LESSIVES Ziegler alcohol

alcoolat *m* CHIMIE alcoholate

alcoolisé *adj* AGRO ALIM alcoholic

alcoolomètre *m* AGRO ALIM spirit poise

alcoolyse *f* CHIMIE alcoholysis

alcôve *f* CONSTR bay

alcoxy- *préf* CHIMIE alkoxy-

alcoxyde *m* CHIMIE alkoxide

alcoylamine *f* LESSIVES alkylamine

alcoylation *f* MATERIAUX alkylation

alcoyle *m* CHIMIE, LESSIVES, MATERIAUX, PETROLE alkyl

alcoylène *m* CHIMIE alkylene, LESSIVES alkene, alkylene

alcyne *m* CHIMIE alkyne

alcynes *m pl* PETROLE alkynes

aldéhyde *m* AGRO ALIM, CHIMIE, PLAST CAOU *composé chimique,groupe* aldehyde; ~ anisique *m* CHIMIE anisaldehyde; ~ crotonique *m* CHIMIE crotonaldehyde; ~ cuminique *m* CHIMIE cumaldehyde; ~ salicylique *m* CHIMIE salicylaldehyde

aldéhydique *adj* CHIMIE aldehydic

aldohexose *m* AGRO ALIM, CHIMIE aldohexose

aldol *m* CHIMIE aldol

aldose *m* AGRO ALIM, CHIMIE aldose

aldostérone *f* AGRO ALIM aldosterone

aléatoire[1] *adj* CHIMIE random, PRODUCTION unplanned

aléatoire:[2] ~ complexe *f* GEOPHYS random noise

alêne *f* CONSTR awl

alerte *f* SECURITE alarm, emergency, TELECOM *maritime mobile* alerting, THERMODYN *alarme d'incendie* fire alarm; ~ en cas de détresse *f* TELECOM distress alerting; ~ à la fumée *f* SECURITE smoke alarm; ~ aux gaz *f* MILITAIRE gas alert; ~ météorologique *f* METEO, NAUT weather warning; ~ navire-navire *f* TELECOM ship-to-ship alerting; ~ navire-terre *f* TELECOM ship-to-shore alerting; ~ passive *f* TELECOM *maritime mobile* passive alerting; ~ terre-navire *f* TELECOM shore-to-ship alerting

alésage *m* AUTO bore, CONS MECA boring, reaming, reaming out, *diamètre d'un trou cylindrique* bore, PRODUCTION boring, boring out, VEHICULES *de moteur,de cylindre* bore; ~ de diffuseur *m* GENIE CHIM atomizer nozzle; ~ en coordonnées *m* CONS MECA jig boring; ~ des trous profonds *m* CONS MECA deep-hole boring; ~ de vérin *m* CONS MECA cylinder bore

aléser *vt* CONS MECA bore, broach, MECANIQUE bore, *outillage* ream, PETR ream, PRODUCTION bore, bore out

aléseur: ~ en coordonnées à commande numérique *m* CONS MECA NC jig borer

aléseuse *f* CONS MECA, MECANIQUE boring machine

aléseuse-fraiseuse *f* MECANIQUE boring mill

alésoir *m* CONS MECA broach, opening bit, reamer, CONSTR *plomberie* turnpin, MECANIQUE *outillage* reamer, MINES broaching bit, reamer, PRODUCTION, VEHICULES *outil* reamer; ~ à bout fileté pour l'amorçage *m* CONS MECA self-feeding reamer; ~ à cannelures torses *m* CONS MECA reamer with spiral flutes; ~ de chaudronnerie *m* CONS MECA bridge reamer; ~ à cinq pans *m* CONS MECA five-sided broach; ~ creux avec alésage conique *m* CONS MECA shell reamer with taper bore; ~ en bout *m* CONS MECA chucking reamer; ~ expansible *m* CONS MECA adjustable reamer; ~ extensible *m* PRODUCTION expansion reamer; ~ de finition *m* CONS MECA finishing reamer; ~ de finition pour cônes Morse *m* CONS MECA finishing reamer for Morse tapers; ~ à lames mobiles *m* CONS MECA adjustable blade reamer, adjustable reamer, PRODUCTION expansion reamer; ~ à lames rapportées *m* CONS MECA adjustable blade reamer, adjustable reamer, PRODUCTION expansion reamer; ~ à main en hélice *m* CONS MECA twist hand reamer; ~ à main à quatre tranchants en hélice *m* CONS MECA four-flute twist hand reamer; ~ pour machine à goujures longues *m* CONS MECA long-fluted machine reamer; ~ à queue *m* CONS MECA chucking reamer; ~ à rainures torses *m* CONS MECA reamer with spiral flutes; ~ **réglable** *m* CONS MECA adjustable blade reamer, adjustable reamer

alésoir-fraise *m* CONS MECA *creux* shell reamer

aleurite *f* GEOLOGIE silt

aleuronite *f* GEOLOGIE siltstone

alevinage *m* OCEANO stocking

alevinier *m* OCEANO fish farmer

alexandrite *f* MINERAUX alexandrite

alèze *f* OCEANO lint, netting, webbing

alfa *m* IMPRIM alfa

algèbre *f* MATH, ORDINAT algebra; ~ **de Boole** *f* INFORMAT, ORDINAT Boolean algebra; ~ **booléenne** *f* MATH Boolean algebra; ~ **linéaire** *f* INFORMAT line termination equipment, linear algebra, ORDINAT linear algebra; ~ **logique** *f* ELECTRON logic algebra

algébrique *adj* MATH algebraic

algicide[1] *adj* HYDROLOGIE algicide

algicide[2] *m* HYDROLOGIE algicide

alginate *m* PLAST CAOU alginate; ~ **de sodium** *m* AGRO ALIM sodium alginate

algoculture *f* OCEANO algoculture

algodonite *f* MINERAUX algodonite

Algol *f* ASTRONOMIE Algol

algologie *m* OCEANO algology

algorithme *m* ESPACE *communications*, MATH, ORDINAT algorithm; ~ **d'ordonnancement** *m* INFORMAT, ORDINAT scheduling algorithm; ~ **parallèle** *m* ORDINAT parallel algorithm

algorithmique *adj* INFORMAT, ORDINAT algorithmic

algue *f* POLLU MER seaweed

algues *f pl* HYDROLOGIE, PETR algae; ~ **calcaires** *f pl* GEOLOGIE *Corallinaceae* lime-secreting algae

alias *m* INFORMAT alias

alichen *m* CONS MECA *d'un ventilateur, d'une roue hydraulique* paddle, paddle board, DISTRI EAU float, floatboard

alichon *m* CONS MECA *d'un ventilateur, d'une roue hydraulique* paddle, paddle board, DISTRI EAU float, floatboard

alidade *f* CONSTR alidade, sight rule, INSTRUMENT alidade, NAUT alidade, bearing marker, index bar, sight bar; ~ **à éclimètre** *f* INSTRUMENT clinometer alidade; ~ **électronique** *f* NAUT electronic bearing cursor, electronic bearing line, electronic bearing marker; ~ **à lunette** *f* INSTRUMENT telescopic alidade; ~ **nivelatrice** *f* CONSTR leveling alidade (AmE), levelling alidade (BrE); ~ **à pinnules** *f* CONSTR sighted alidade, INSTRUMENT open-sight alidade

aligné *adj* CONS MECA aligned, in-line

alignement *m* CINEMAT registration, CONSTR *projection horizontale*, IMPRIM *mise en page* alignment, INFORMAT registration, MECANIQUE alignment, NAUT alignment, leading line, transit, PETR line-up, TELECOM tracking, TV registration; ~ **des cellulos** *m* CINEMAT registration of artwork; ~ **de descente** *m* AERONAUT glide path; ~ **de descente minimal** *m* AERONAUT minimum glide path; ~ **de la direction** *m* MINES line of strike; ~ **en approche** *m* AERONAUT approach path; ~ **du faisceau** *m* TV beam alignment; ~ **de hausse** *m* COMMANDE sights adjustment; ~ **des impulsions de synchronisation** *m* TV sync line-up; ~ **local** *m* ELECTRON local alignment; ~ **magnétique** *m* ENREGISTR magnetic alignment; ~ **du masque** *m* ELECTRON mask alignment; ~ **du motif** *m* ELECTRON pattern registration; ~ **oblique** *m* AERONAUT *système d'atterrissage aux instruments* slant course line; ~ **des pales** *m* AERO-

NAUT blade tracking, TRANSPORT tracking; ~ **par griffe** *m* CINEMAT pin registration; ~ **par laser** *m* CONS MECA laser alignment; ~ **de piste** *m* AERONAUT runway alignment, *système d'atterrissage aux instruments* course line; ~ **des roues** *m* TRANSPORT wheel alignment; ~ **des signaux chromatiques** *m* TV scan registration; ~ **structural** *m* GEOLOGIE lineament; ~ **de tête** *m* ENREGISTR head alignment; ~ **des têtes** *m* TV head alignment; ~ **des têtes sur la synchronisation de trame** *m* TV field sync alignment; ~ **vertical** *m* CONSTR vertical alignment

aligner[1] *vt* CINEMAT align, line up, CONS MECA, CONSTR align, IMPRIM *typographie* align, line up

aligner:[2] ~ **un instrument en plan horizontale** *vi* CONSTR *arpentage* orient an instrument horizontally; ~ **un instrument en plan verticalement** *vi* CONSTR *arpentage* orient an instrument vertically

aliment *m* AGRO ALIM nutrient; ~ **de base** *m* AGRO ALIM staple food, staple; ~ **congelé** *m* THERMODYN frozen food; ~ **diététique** *m* AGRO ALIM health food; ~ **à teneur réduit en sel** *m* AGRO ALIM reduced salt food

alimentateur *m* PRODUCTION feeder; ~ **à courroie** *m* GENIE CHIM belt feeder; ~ **de minerai** *m* MINES ore feeder; ~ **rotatif et table de collection** *m* EMBALLAGE rotary feeder and collecting table; ~ **vibrant** *m* PRODUCTION vibrating feeder

alimentation *f* AGRO ALIM nutrition, AUTO feed, CH DE FER power supply, CHARBON feed, DISTRI EAU supply, ELECTR *réseau* feed, *énergie électrique* supply, ELECTROTEC feed, *en courant* power supply, ENREGISTR power supply, GAZ supply, INFORMAT feed, INST HYDR *par opposition à collecteur ou évacuation* source, METEO accretion, ORDINAT feed, PAPIER feed, feeding, PHYSIQUE power supply, PLAST CAOU *moulage* feed, PRODUCTION feed, feeding, power supply unit, TELECOM power feed, power feeding, power supply, TEXTILE feeding, TV feed; ~ **artificielle** *f* HYDROLOGIE *de nappe aquifère* artificial recharge; ~ **automatique** *f* CERAM VER automatic feeding, CONS MECA *outil de coupe* automatic feed; ~ **avec plaque tournante** *f* EMBALLAGE turntable feed; ~ **axiale** *f* TELECOM vertex feed; ~ **bilatérale** *f* ELECTR two-way feed; ~ **bipolaire** *f* ELECTROTEC bipolar power supply; ~ **de chaudière** *f* INST HYDR boiler feeding; ~ **de colle sous pression** *f* EMBALLAGE pressurized glue feed; ~ **continue** *f* ELECTR direct current supply, *réseau* DC supply; ~ **à courant alternatif** *f* ELECTR alternating current supply; ~ **à courant continu** *f* ELECTROTEC DC supply; ~ **à découpage** *f* ELECTROTEC switching power supply; ~ **à découpage monotension** *f* ELECTROTEC single output switching power supply; ~ **à découpage nue** *f* ELECTROTEC open-frame switching power supply; ~ **double** *f* ELECTROTEC dual power supply; ~ **d'eau** *f* PRODUCTION *pour foreuse* water feed; ~ **électrique** *f* CINEMAT power supply, CONSTR electricity supply; ~ **en boîte** *f* EMBALLAGE canned food (AmE), tinned food (BrE); ~ **en combustible moteur** *f* NAUT engine fuel supply; ~ **en courant** *f* CINEMAT, TV power supply; ~ **en courant alternatif** *f* ESPACE *véhicules* AC power system; ~ **en double paraison** *f* CERAM VER double gobbing; ~ **en eau** *f* HYDROLOGIE, PRODUCTION, TEXTILE water supply; ~ **en eau à distance** *f* DISTRI EAU distant water supply; ~ **en eau individuelle** *f* DISTRI EAU individual water supply; ~ **en eau potable** *f* DISTRI EAU, HYDROLOGIE drinking water supply; ~ **en électricité** *f* ELECTR *réseau* electricity supply; ~ **en énergie** *f* ELECTR *réseau* power supply; ~ **en énergie électrique** *f* ELECTROTEC electrical power supply; ~ **énergétique commutée** *f* PRODUCTION switch-mode power supply; ~ **d'énergie** *f* THERMODYN energy supply; ~ **en fibres primaires** *f* CERAM VER fiber feeder (AmE), fibre feeder (BrE); ~ **en huile** *f* VEHICULES *lubrification* oil feed; ~ **en oxygène** *f* ESPACE *propulsion* oxygen supply; ~ **en papier** *f* IMPRIM, ORDINAT FF, form feed; ~ **en parallèle** *f* ELECTR, ELECTROTEC shunt feed; ~ **en secteur** *f* ELECTROTEC power supply; ~ **en simple paraison** *f* CERAM VER single gob feeding (BrE), single gob process (AmE); ~ **en tension négative** *f* ELECTROTEC negative voltage supply; ~ **et soutirage** *f* NUCLEAIRE feed and bleed; ~ **feuille à feuille** *f* INFORMAT, ORDINAT sheet feeding; ~ **forcée** *f* PETROLE *d'un matériau* automatic feed; ~ **haute tension** *f* ELECTR HT supply; ~ **intégrée** *f* PRODUCTION integral power supply; ~ **manuelle** *f* EMBALLAGE hand feed; ~ **massique** *f* PRODUCTION weight feeding; ~ **de microphone** *f* ENREGISTR microphone power supply; ~ **mixte** *f* TRANSPORT mixed power supply; ~ **monophasée** *f* ELECTR, ELECTROTEC single-phase supply; ~ **monotension** *f* ELECTROTEC single output power supply; ~ **de la nappe souterraine** *f* HYDROLOGIE aquifer recharge; ~ **négative** *f* ELECTROTEC negative power supply; ~ **non stabilisée** *f* PRODUCTION unregulated input; ~ **nue** *f* ELECTROTEC open-frame power supply; ~ **par bobine** *f* ELECTR choke feed; ~ **par distributeur** *f* CERAM VER gob feeding; ~ **par pile** *f* ELECTROTEC battery operation; ~ **par le secteur** *f* ELECTROTEC line operation; ~ **par une seule tension** *f* ELECTROTEC single supply; ~ **par succion** *f* CERAM VER suction feeding; ~ **positive** *f* ELECTROTEC positive power supply; ~ **à régulation série** *f* ELECTROTEC series-regulated power supply; ~ **régulée** *f* ELECTROTEC electronic power supply, regulated power supply; ~ **régulée en tension** *f* ELECTROTEC voltage-regulated power supply; ~ **régulée série** *f* ELECTROTEC series-regulated power supply; ~ **des sacs sur bobine** *f* EMBALLAGE reel feed bags; ~ **sans coffret** *f* ELECTROTEC open-frame power supply; ~ **sans coupure** *f* ESPACE *énergie* no-break power supply; ~ **sans transformateur** *f* ELECTR *réseau* transformerless power supply; ~ **de secours** *f* ELECTR emergency power supply, PRODUCTION *automatisme industriel* backup power, TELECOM backup power supply; ~ **de secours par batterie** *f* ELECTROTEC battery backup; ~ **secteur** *f* CINEMAT power adaptor, ELECTR *réseau* electrical supply (BrE), mains (BrE), mains supply (BrE), supply network (AmE), ELECTROTEC mains (BrE), supply network (AmE), power supply, PHYSIQUE electrical supply (AmE), mains supply (BrE), PRODUCTION AC power, line input power, TV mains (BrE), supply network (AmE); ~ **séparée** *f* ELECTR *réseau* floating supply; ~ **série** *f* ELECTROTEC linear power supply, series feed; ~ **série à incorporer** *f* ELECTROTEC linear power supply; ~ **série nue** *f* ELECTROTEC open-frame linear power supply; ~ **sous pression** *f* IMPRIM slot feeding; ~ **stabilisée** *f* ELECTR *réseau* voltage-stabilized power supply; ~ **THT** *f* TV EHT supply; ~ **à thyristors** *f* ELECTROTEC SCR-regulated power supply; ~ **à très haute tension** *f* ELECTROTEC high-voltage power supply, kickback power supply; ~ **triphasée** *f* ELECTROTEC three-phase supply; ~ **vibratoire** *f* EMBALLAGE vibratory feeder

alimentation-dosage *f* EMBALLAGE dosing feeder

alimenté: ~ **en blanc** *adj* IMPRIM blank-fed; ~ **en parallèle** *adj* AERONAUT parallel-fed; ~ **à la main** *adj* IMPRIM hand-fed; ~ **par batterie** *adj* CINEMAT, ELECTROTEC battery-powered; ~ **par courroie** *adj* GENIE CHIM belt-fed; ~ **par énergie solaire** *adj* EN RENOUV solar-powered; ~ **par le secteur** *adj* ELECTROTEC electrically-operated (AmE), mains-operated (BrE), line-operated; ~ **du réseau** *adj* ELECTR *appareil* electrically-operated (AmE), mains-operated (BrE)

alimenter *vt* ELECTR *énergie électrique* supply, ELECTROTEC energize, feed, INFORMAT, MECANIQUE, ORDINAT feed, PHYSIQUE supply, TV feed; ~ **en charbon** *vt* CHARBON coal; ~ **en combustible** *vt* THERMODYN fuel; ~ **en eau** *vt* DISTRI EAU water

aliphatique *adj* PETROLE aliphatic

alizé *m* METEO trade wind

alkoxy- *préf* CHIMIE alkoxy-

alkoxyde *m* CHIMIE alkoxide

alkyd *m* CHIMIE alkyd, PLAST CAOU *liant de peinture* glyptal resin; ~ **court en huile** *m* PLAST CAOU *résine pour peintures* short-oil alkyd; ~ **long en huile** *m* PLAST CAOU *résine pour peintures* long-oil alkyd

alkylamine *f* LESSIVES alkylamine

alkylaromatiques *m pl* PETROLE alkylaromatics

alkylation *f* CHIMIE, LESSIVES alkylation

alkylbenzène *m* LESSIVES alkyl benzene

alkyle *m* CHIMIE, LESSIVES, PETROLE alkyl

alkylène *m* CHIMIE alkylene, LESSIVES alkene, alkylene

allactite *f* MINERAUX allactite

allagite *f* MINERAUX allagite

allanite *f* MINERAUX allanite

allantoïne *f* CHIMIE allantoin

allée: ~ **de desserte** *f* CHARBON gate road, MINES stall road

allège *f* CERAM VER spandrel glass, NAUT barge, lighter, TRANSPORT barge, dumb barge

allégement *m* POLLU MER lightening, lightering; ~ **à gaz** *m* PETROLE *récupération du pétrole* gas lift

alléger *vt* CONSTR *une planche* reduce, PRODUCTION thin, thin out, *une planche* thin down

allélotropique *adj* CHIMIE allelotropic

allemontite *f* MINERAUX allemontite

allène *m* CHIMIE allene, diene

aller:[1] ~ **de** *vt* TELECOM range from

aller[2] *vi* CONS MECA fit; ~ **à bord de** *vi* NAUT *passagers* board; ~ **en amont** *vi* HYDROLOGIE go upstream

aller-retour *m* PETR round trip, PETROLE round trip, trip

alliage *m* CHIMIE, PAPIER, PRODUCTION alloy; ~ **d'acier** *m* CHARBON steel alloy; ~ **d'aluminium** *m* CONS MECA *pour paliers massifs*, MATERIAUX aluminium alloy (BrE), aluminum alloy (AmE); ~ **antifriction** *m* CONS MECA antifriction lining; ~ **à base de zirconium** *m* NUCLEAIRE zirconium base alloy; ~ **binaire** *m* MATERIAUX binary alloy; ~ **de brasage tendre** *m* CONS MECA soft-solder alloy; ~ **de cuivre corroyé pour paliers lisses** *m* CONS MECA wrought-copper alloy for plain bearings; ~ **léger** *m* MECANIQUE *matériaux* light alloy; ~ **de magnésium** *m* MATERIAUX magnesium alloy; ~ **métallique** *m* MATERIAUX metal alloy; ~ **métallique superplastique** *m* MATERIAUX superplastic ceramic material; ~ **moulé de plomb et d'étain** *m* CONS MECA lead-tin alloy; ~ **ordonné** *m* METALL ordered alloy; ~ **pour hautes températures** *m* MECANIQUE *matériaux* high-temperature alloy; ~ **à satellites** *m* METALL sideband alloy; ~ **spinodal** *m* MATERIAUX spinodal alloy; ~ **ternaire** *m* METALL three-component alloy; ~ **de titane** *m* ESPACE titanium alloy; **~ ultra-léger** *m* ESPACE ultralight alloy

alliage-mère *m* MATERIAUX master alloy

allier *vt* CHIMIE alloy

allocation *f* PRODUCTION allocation, allotment; **~ des canaux** *f* TV channel allocation; **~ dynamique** *f* INFORMAT dynamic allocation; **~ de fréquence** *f* ENREGISTR, TELECOM frequency allocation; **~ mémoire** *f* INFORMAT storage allocation; **~ statique** *f* INFORMAT static allocation; **~ de temps** *f* INFORMAT, ORDINAT time slicing

allochem *m* GEOLOGIE *élément clastique carbonaté* allochem

allochroïte *f* MINERAUX allochroite

allochtone[1] *adj* PETR allochthonous, POLLUTION external

allochtone[2] *m* GEOLOGIE allochthon

allomorphite *f* MINERAUX allomorphite

allonge *f* CONS MECA extension piece, lengthening piece, lengthening rod, lengthening tube; **~ réglable pour pied de cadre** *f* MINES adjustable stilt

allongé *adj* GEOMETRIE *dans le sens d'un diamètre polaire* prolate, IMPRIM, MECANIQUE elongated

allongement *m* AERONAUT *d'une aile* aspect ratio, *d'un corps fuselé* fineness ratio, CONS MECA stretch, METALL *d'un échantillon* elongation, PAPIER elongation, stretch, PHYSIQUE aspect ratio, elongation, extension, PLAST CAOU stretch; **~ du bord** *m* METALL edgewise growth; **~ élastique** *m* EMBALLAGE elastic elongation, elastic stretch; **~ du fil à l'encollage** *m* TEXTILE stretch of yarn in sizing; **~ au noeud** *m* TEXTILE knot extensibility; **~ de la pale** *m* AERONAUT blade aspect ratio; **~ de pale** *m* AERONAUT *hélicoptère* blade width ratio; **~ à la rupture** *m* PLAST CAOU elongation at break, ultimate elongation; **~ de rupture par fluage** *m* METALL creep rupture elongation; **~ à la rupture par traction** *m* PAPIER stretch at break, stretch at breaking point, stretch length

allonger *vt* IMPRIM, ORDINAT extend

allopalladium *m* MINERAUX allopalladium

allophane *f* MINERAUX allophane

allotissement: ~ spectral *m* NAUT spectrum allocation

allotriomorphe *adj* GEOLOGIE *structure ou agencement des minéraux*, PETR allotriomorphic

allotropie *f* CHIMIE, CRISTALL allotropy

allotropique *adj* CHIMIE, CRISTALL allotropic

allotropisme *m* CHIMIE allotropy

allouer *vt* INFORMAT allocate, assign, ORDINAT allocate, assign

alluaudite *f* MINERAUX alluaudite

alluchon *m* CONS MECA cog

allumage *m* AERONAUT, AUTO, CHIMIE, CINEMAT *d'un arc*, ELECTR *moteur à combustion interne* ignition, ELECTROTEC turn-on, ESPACE *véhicules,propulsion* ignition, MATERIAUX arcing, MECANIQUE *véhicules* ignition, MINES firing, PLAST CAOU, VEHICULES ignition; **~ anticipé** *m* VEHICULES preignition; **~ automatique** *m* GAZ automatic ignition; **~ classique** *m* AUTO capacitor ignition; **~ commandé** *m* AUTO, ELECTR *d'automobile* spark ignition; **~ à double circuit** *m* AUTO two-circuit ignition system; **~ électrique** *m* MINES electric firing, electrical blasting, electrical shot-firing; **~ électromagnétique** *m* AUTO electromagnetic ignition; **~ électronique** *m* AUTO, TRANSPORT, VEHICULES electronic ignition; **~ électrostatique** *m* AUTO capacitor ignition; **~ par batterie** *m* AUTO battery ignition; **~ par capacité** *m* AUTO capacitor ignition; **~ par magnéto** *m* AUTO magneto ignition; **~ par mèche de sûreté** *m*

MINES safety fuse initiation; **~ par rupteur** *m* AUTO make-and-break ignition; **~ prématuré** *m* AUTO premature ignition; **~ séquentiel** *m* ESPACE *véhicules, propulsion* phased ignition; **~ spontané** *m* ESPACE *véhicules* hypergolic ignition, VEHICULES *moteur* auto-ignition; **~ transistorisé** *m* AUTO transistorized ignition system; **~ transistorisé sans rupteur** *m* AUTO contactless transistorized ignition (BrE), electronic ignition, pointless ignition (AmE), solid-state ignition

allumé *adj* ELECTROTEC on

allume-feu *m* CHAUFFAGE firelighter

allume-gaz *m* CHAUFFAGE gas lighter

allumer *vt* CHIMIE ignite, DISTRI EAU *une pompe* start in operation, ELECTROTEC turn on, ESPACE *véhicules, propulsion* ignite, THERMODYN set ablaze, *chaudière, brûleur* fire up, *feu* kindle, TV switch on

allumeur *m* CHIMIE primer, CONS MECA, ESPACE *véhicules, propulsion* igniter; **~ électrique** *m* ELECTR *appareil à gaz* electric lighter; **~ de fusée** *m* MILITAIRE rocket igniter

allure *f* NAUT rate of sailing, PRODUCTION throughput, working; **~ froide** *f* PRODUCTION cold working; **~ lente** *f* CONS MECA low-speed; **~ de ralenti** *f* MECANIQUE idling speed; **~ rapide** *f* CONS MECA high-speed

allures: aux ~ portantes *adj* NAUT off the wind

alluvion *f* OCEANO, PETR alluvium; **~ aurifère** *f* MINES pay dirt, placer dirt

alluvionner *vt* GEOLOGIE aggrade

alluvions: ~ fluviales *f pl* DISTRI EAU fluvial alluvium; **~ sédimentées dans les chenaux** *f pl* GEOLOGIE channel fill

allyle *m* CHIMIE allyl

almandin *m* MINERAUX almandine, almandite

alnoeite *f* MINERAUX alnoeite, alnoite

aloïne *f* CHIMIE aloin

alphabet *m* INFORMAT alphabet; **~ télégraphique international** *m* AERONAUT international telegraph alphabet

alphabétique *adj* INFORMAT alphabetic

alpha-cellulose *f* PAPIER alpha cellulose

alphamosaïque *adj* INFORMAT alphamosaic

alphanumérique *adj* INFORMAT alphameric, alphanumeric

alquifoux *m* CERAM VER potter's ore, MINERAUX alquifou, alquifoux

alstonite *f* MINERAUX alstonite

altaïte *f* MINERAUX altaite

altération *f* ACOUSTIQUE alteration, CERAM VER corrosion, INFORMAT, ORDINAT corruption, POLLU MER *par les agents atmosphériques* weathering; **~ accidentelle** *f* ACOUSTIQUE accidental alteration; **~ de bord** *f* CERAM VER edge creep; **~ chimique** *f* GEOLOGIE *des roches*, PETR chemical weathering; **~ constitutive** *f* ACOUSTIQUE constitutive alteration; **~ de la couleur** *f* CERAM VER discoloration (AmE), discolouration (BrE); **~ deutérique** *f* GEOLOGIE deuteric alteration; **~ due au froid** *f* AGRO ALIM cold storage injury; **~ due aux intempéries** *f* GEOLOGIE *par les agents atmosphériques*, TEXTILE weathering; **~ en profondeur** *f* REFRIG bone taint; **~ mécanique** *f* PETR mechanical weathering; **~ météorique** *f* GEOLOGIE *des roches* chemical weathering; **~ postmagmatique** *f* GEOLOGIE *des roches ignées* deuteric alteration; **~ sous-marine** *f* GEOLOGIE halmyrolysis

altérer[1] *vt* GEOLOGIE weather, ORDINAT corrupt

altérer:[2] **s'~ par l'atmosphère** *v réfl* CONSTR weather
alternance *f* CONS MECA alternation, ELECTROTEC half
cycle, GEOMETRIE reciprocation
alternateur *m* ELECTR *générateur* alternating current
generator, alternator, ELECTROTEC, EN RENOUV *hydro-
électricité-éolien* alternator, PHYSIQUE alternative
current generator, alternator, VEHICULES *système
électrique* generator; **~ asynchrone** *m* ELECTR induction generator, *générateur* asynchronous generator,
ELECTROTEC asynchronous alternator, induction generator; **~ bulbe** *m* ELECTR bulb alternator, bulb
generator; **~ à courant triphasé** *m* ELECTR *générateur*
three-phase alternator; **~ diphasé** *m* ELECTR *générateur* two-phase alternator; **~ à double enroulement** *m*
ELECTR *générateur* double-wound generator; **~ en
cloche** *m* ELECTR *générateur* umbrella-type alternator; **~ à fer tournant** *m* ELECTR *générateur* induction
generator, inductor alternator, ELECTROTEC inductor
alternator; **~ de fréquences radio** *m* ELECTROTEC RF
alternator; **~ pilote à aimants permanent** *m* ELECTR
générateur dynamometric dynamo; **~ pilote à aimants
permanents** *m* ELECTR *générateur* cradle dynamo; **~ à
pôles intérieurs** *m* ELECTR internal pole dynamo,
générateur internal pole generator; **~ à pôles saillants**
m ELECTR *machine* salient pole generator; **~ polyphasé**
m ELECTROTEC polyphase generator; **~ synchrone** *m*
ELECTR synchronous generator, synchronous machine, *générateur* synchronous alternator
alternatif *adj* CONS MECA alternating, reciprocating,
ELECTR *courant, tension* alternating, MECANIQUE reciprocating, PETROLE reciprocal
alternating: ~ current *adj* ELECTR periodic
alternation *f* CONS MECA alternation; **~ d'un mouvement**
f CONS MECA alternation of a movement
altimètre *m* AERONAUT, ESPACE *véhicules, propulsion* altimeter, GEOPHYS altimeter, height gage (AmE),
height gauge (BrE), PHYSIQUE, TRANSPORT altimeter;
~ anéroïde *m* AERONAUT aneroid altimeter; **~ asservi** *m*
AERONAUT servoaltimeter; **~ barométrique** *m* AERO-
NAUT pressure altimeter; **~ de cabine** *m* AERONAUT
cabin altimeter; **~ codeur** *m* AERONAUT encoding altimeter; **~ de précision** *m* AERONAUT sensitive
altimeter; **~ à tambour** *m* AERONAUT drum altimeter
altimétrie *f* PHYSIQUE altimetry; **~ radar** *f* ASTRONOMIE
utilisée pour tracer la surface des planètes intérieures
radar altimetry
altitude *f* CONSTR elevation, ESPACE altitude, PHYSIQUE
altitude, height; **~ au-dessus du niveau de la mer** *f*
METEO elevation above sea level; **~ cabine** *f* AERONAUT
cabin altitude; **~ de croisière** *f* AERONAUT cruising
altitude; **~ d'exploitation** *f* AERONAUT operating altitude;
~ fictive *f* AERONAUT cabin altitude; **~ géopotentielle** *f*
GEOPHYS geopotential height; **~ maximum en exploitation** *f* AERONAUT maximum operating altitude; **~
minimale de descente** *f* AERONAUT minimum descent
altitude; **~ minimale de sécurité** *f* AERONAUT minimum
safe altitude; **~ nominale** *f* AERONAUT rated altitude; **~
de l'optimum pluvial** *f* METEO altitude of optimum
rainfall; **~ de pression** *f* AERONAUT pressure height; **~
relative** *f* AERONAUT relative altitude; **~ de rentrée** *f*
ESPACE *des satellites terrestres* Earth reentry altitude;
~ de rétablissement *f* AERONAUT critical altitude
altitude-pression *f* AERONAUT pressure altitude
altocumulus *m* AERONAUT, METEO altocumulus
altostratus *m* AERONAUT, METEO altostratus
alumiane *f* MINERAUX alumian

aluminage *m* PAPIER alumination
aluminate *m* CHIMIE aluminate
alumine *f* CHIMIE alumina, aluminium oxide (BrE), aluminum oxide (AmE), MINERAUX, PAPIER alumina
aluminé *adj* REVETEMENT aluminium-coated (BrE), alu-
minum-coated (AmE)
aluminer *vt* CHIMIE, PAPIER aluminate
alumineux *adj* CHIMIE aluminous
aluminiate *m* CHIMIE aluminate
aluminifère *adj* CHIMIE aluminiferous
aluminite *f* MINERAUX aluminite
aluminium *m* (Al) CHIMIE aluminium (BrE), aluminum
(AmE) (Al); **~ mince pour emboutissage profond** *m*
EMBALLAGE deep drawing foil
aluminosilicate *m* CHIMIE, MINERAUX aluminosilicate
alun *m* CHIMIE, IMPRIM *chimie graphique*, MINERAUX,
PAPIER alum; **~ ammoniacal** *m* CHIMIE, PAPIER ammonia alum; **~ de chrome** *m* CHIMIE chrome alum; **~
de fer** *m* CHIMIE iron alum; **~ des papetiers** *m* PAPIER
alum; **~ de potasse** *m* CHIMIE potash-alum; **~ de sodium** *m* CHIMIE soda-alum; **~ de soude** *m* CHIMIE
soda-alum
alunage *m* CHIMIE alumination
aluner *vt* CHIMIE aluminate
alunifère *adj* CHIMIE aluminiferous
alunite *f* MINERAUX alunite, alunogen
alurgite *f* MINERAUX alurgite
alvéolage: ~ du pain *m* AGRO ALIM bread texture
alvéolaire *adj* AERONAUT cellular
alvéole *f* IMPRIM *héliogravure* cell; **~ entre lames de
cylindre de pile** *f* PAPIER roll pocket; **~ ronde** *f* IMPRIM
héliogravure round cell
alvite *f* MINERAUX alvite
Am (américium) CHIMIE Am (americium)
amagnétique *adj* CHIMIE, ELECTR, MATERIAUX nonmagnetic
amaigrir[1] *vt* CONSTR *planche* reduce, PRODUCTION thin,
thin out
amaigrir:[2] **s'~** *v réfl* CERAM VER shrink
amaigrissement *m* CONSTR reducing, PRODUCTION thinning, thinning down, thinning out
amalgamateur *m* CHARBON amalgam barrel, amalgamator, CONS MECA amalgamator; **~ à cuve** *m*
PRODUCTION pan amalgamator
amalgamation *f* CHARBON amalgamation; **~ à plaques** *f*
CHARBON plate amalgamation; **~ au tonneau** *f* PRO-
DUCTION barrel amalgamation
amalgame *m* CHARBON, CHIMIE, MINERAUX amalgam
amalgamer *vt* CHARBON amalgamate
amarine *f* CHIMIE amarine
amarrage *m* ESPACE *véhicules* docking, NAUT lashing, *de
couteau* lanyard, *d'action* mooring, POLLU MER mooring; **~ doux** *m* ESPACE soft landing; **~ dur** *m* ESPACE hard
landing; **~ à fouet** *m* NAUT rolling hitch; **~ du point
d'écoute** *m* NAUT outhaul; **~ à point unique** *m* PETROLE
SBM, single buoy mooring, *distribution, transport
maritime* ELSBM, exposed location single buoy
mooring
amarre *f* NAUT line, mooring line, painter, *équipement*
mooring, POLLU MER mooring; **~ debout de l'arrière** *f*
NAUT stern line; **~ debout de l'avant** *f* NAUT bowline,
headline; **~ en belle** *f* NAUT bow spring, cross spring; **~
de poste** *f* NAUT shoreline; **~ traversière** *f* NAUT breast
line
amarrer[1] *vt* NAUT belay, lash, make fast, secure, seize,
tie up, *navire, bouée* moor, POLLU MER moor; **~ la barre**

vt NAUT lash the helm

amarrer:[2] **s'~** *v réfl* ESPACE *véhicules* dock; **s'~ à nouveau** *v réfl* ESPACE *véhicules* redock

amas *m* ASTRONOMIE *de galaxies, d'étoiles* cluster, CONSTR heap, pile, ESPACE *de galaxies,* MATERIAUX *catalyse* cluster; **~ d'étoiles** *m* ASTRONOMIE star cluster; **~ de galaxies Persée** *m* ASTRONOMIE Perseus cluster of galaxies; **~ globulaire** *m* ASTRONOMIE globule, *étoiles* globular cluster; **~ d'ions** *m* PHYS RAYON ion cluster; **~ ouvert** *m* ASTRONOMIE open cluster; **~ ouvert d'étoiles** *m* ASTRONOMIE open cluster of stars

amasser[1] *vt* CONSTR bank

amasser:[2] **s'~** *v réfl* CONSTR bank, bank up

amausite *f* MINERAUX amausite

amazonite *f* MINERAUX Amazon stone, amazonite

ambérite *f* MINERAUX ambrite

ambiance *f* PHYSIQUE surroundings, PRODUCTION environ-ment; **~ hyperbare** *f* OCEANO atmospheric hyperbare, hyperbaric environment

ambiant *adj* REFRIG ambient

amblygonite *f* MINERAUX amblygonite

ambre *m* MINERAUX amber

ambréine *f* CHIMIE ambrain

ambrite *f* MINERAUX ambrite

ambroïne *f* MINERAUX amberoid, ambroid

ambulance *f* TRANSPORT ambulance

âme *f* AERONAUT *d'un longeron* web, CONS MECA *diamètre intérieur d'un canon* bore, CONSTR *d'un fer à T, d'un rail de chemin de fer* web, ELECTR *conducteur d'un câble* conductor, *d'un câble* core (BrE), insulated conductor (AmE), ELECTROTEC, EMBALLAGE *d'une bobine* core, MECANIQUE *d'une poutre* web, NAUT *d'une corde,* PHYSIQUE, TEXTILE core; **~ armée de métal** *f* ELECTR *conducteur d'un câble* metal-clad conductor; **~ de câble** *f* ELECTROTEC, PLAST CAOU *caoutchouc, plastiques* cable core; **~ câblée** *f* ELECTR *conducteur d'un câble* stranded conductor; **~ circulaire câblée à couches concentriques** *f* ELECTR *conducteur d'un câble* concentrically-stranded circular conductor; **~ compacte** *f* ELECTR *conducteur d'un câble* compacted conductor; **~ concentrique** *f* ELECTR *conducteur d'un câble* concentric conductor; **~ creuse** *f* ELECTR *conducteur d'un câble* hollow conductor; **~ en cuivre** *f* ELECTR *d'un câble* copper conductor; **~ en tôle** *f* NAUT plate web; **~ en torons** *f* ELECTR *conducteur d'un câble* multiple-stranded conductor; **~ étamée** *f* ELECTR *conducteur d'un câble* tinned conductor; **~ massive** *f* ELECTR *conducteur d'un câble à fil unique* solid conductor; **~ nue** *f* ELECTR *conducteur d'un câble* plain conductor; **~ plaquée** *f* ELECTR *conducteur d'un câble* metal-clad conductor; **~ de poutre de fuselage** *f* AERONAUT fuselage box beam wall; **~ profilée** *f* ELECTR *conducteur d'un câble* shaped conductor; **~ de rail** *f* CH DE FER rail web; **~ rétreinte** *f* ELECTR *conducteur d'un câble* compacted conductor; **~ revêtue d'une couche métallique** *f* ELECTR *conducteur d'un câble* metal-coated conductor; **~ sectorale** *f* ELECTR *conducteur d'un câble* sector shaped conductor; **~ segmentée** *f* ELECTR *conducteur d'un câble* Millikan conductor; **~ souple** *f* ELECTR *conducteur d'un câble* flexible conductor; **~ tordonnée** *f* ELECTR *conducteur d'un câble* bunched conductor (BrE), bundled conductor (AmE)

améliorant *m* AGRO ALIM improver; **~ de boulangerie** *m* AGRO ALIM bread improver; **~ d'indice de viscosité** *m* PETROLE viscosity index improver

amélioration *f* CHIMIE upgrading, TELECOM enhance-ment; **~ de la carte** *f* NAUT chart correction; **~ des images** *f* ASTRONOMIE, ELECTRON, ESPACE *communica-tions,* TV image enhancement; **~ matérielle** *f* ORDINAT hardware upgrade; **~ de la qualité** *f* QUALITE quality improvement

amenage *m* PRODUCTION feed, feeding; **~ automatique** *m* CONS MECA *outil de coupe* automatic feed; **~ par crémaillère** *m* CONS MECA rack feed; **~ rapide automat-ique** *m* CONS MECA power rapid traverse

aménagement *m* CONS MECA accommodation, *d'un ate-lier* arrangement, CONSTR furnishings, DISTRI EAU *d'une chute d'eau* harnessing, INFORMAT housekeep-ing, NAUT accommodation, ORDINAT housekeeping; **~ cabine** *m* AERONAUT cabin layout; **~ du courant d'air** *m* MINES coursing, coursing the air; **~ des cours d'eau** *m* DISTRI EAU river works; **~ de l'environnement** *m* POL-LUTION environmental planning; **~ fixe de soute** *m* AERONAUT cargo compartment equipment; **~ fixe des soutes** *m* AERONAUT cargo compartment equipment; **~ général** *m* CONSTR general arrangement; **~ hôtelier de bord** *m* AERONAUT galley; **~ hydro-électrique** *m* ELECTROTEC hydroelectric generating station; **~ multiple** *m* EN RENOUV multiple development; **~ office** *m* AERONAUT galley furnishings; **~ de pente** *m* CONSTR grading; **~ du terrain** *m* CONSTR development

aménagements: ~ commerciaux *m pl* CONSTR furnish-ings; **~ de gestion de crue** *m pl* EN RENOUV flood control measures; **~ de lutte des inondations** *m pl* EN RENOUV flood control measures; **~ de maîtrise de crue** *m pl* HYDROLOGIE flood control measures, flood miti-gation measures, flood relief measures; **~ de sécurité** *m pl* SECURITE safety fittings

aménager:[1] **~ la pente de** *vt* CONSTR grade

aménager:[2] **~ une mine** *vi* MINES lay out a mine, lay out a shaft; **~ un puits** *vi* MINES lay out a mine, lay out a shaft

amendement *m* CONS MECA amendment

amenée *f* HYDROLOGIE conduction; **~ d'air de soufflage** *f* CERAM VER air inlet; **~ de courant** *f* ELECTROTEC cur-rent lead

amener[1] *vt* NAUT *les voiles, les embarcations* lower; **~ à ébullition** *vt* THERMODYN boil; **~ à quai** *vt* NAUT berth

amener:[2] **~ la bulle d'air entre ses repères** *vi* CONSTR bring the air bubble to the center of its run (AmE), bring the air bubble to the centre of its run (BrE); **~ les couleurs** *vi* NAUT strike colors (AmE), strike colours (BrE); **~ son pavillon** *vi* NAUT strike colors (AmE), strike colours (BrE)

amenuisement *m* CONSTR reducing, PRODUCTION thin-ning, thinning down, thinning out

amenuiser *vt* CONSTR *planche* reduce, PRODUCTION thin, thin out, *planche* thin down

amer *m* ESPACE seamark, NAUT landmark, mark, sea-mark, OCEANO landmark, seamark

américium *m (Am)* CHIMIE americium *(Am)*

amerrissage *m* AERONAUT landing on water, splash-down, ESPACE splashdown; **~ forcé** *m* AERONAUT ditch, ditching

AMES *abrév (accès multiple par étalement du spectre)* ESPACE SSMA *(spread spectrum multiple access)*

amésite *f* MINERAUX amesite

améthyste *f* MINERAUX amethyst

amiante *m* CERAM VER, CHIMIE, IMPRIM, MECANIQUE as-bestos, MINERAUX amiant, amianthus, PAPIER, PLAST CAOU *charge,* SECURITE, TEXTILE asbestos

amiante-ciment *m* CONSTR, PAPIER asbestos cement

amianthinite *f* MINERAUX amianthinite

amide *m* CHIMIE, LESSIVES, PLAST CAOU amide; ~ **d'acide** *m* CHIMIE amic acid; ~ **de sodium** *m* CHIMIE sodamide
amidine *f* CHIMIE amidine
amidogène *m* CHIMIE amidogen
amidon *m* AGRO ALIM, CHIMIE, IMPRIM *colles et papiers*, PAPIER starch, TEXTILE starch, stiffener; ~ **modifié** *m* AGRO ALIM modified starch
amidure: ~ **de sodium** *m* CHIMIE sodamide
amination *f* CHIMIE amination
amincir *vt* CONSTR *une planche* reduce, PRODUCTION thin out, *une plaque en la passant au laminoir* reduce, *une planche* thin down, *une plaque* thin down, RESSORTS taper
amincissement *m* CONSTR reducing, GEOLOGIE thinning, PRODUCTION thinning, thinning down, thinning out, RESSORTS tapering
amine *f* LESSIVES, PLAST CAOU amine; ~ **cycloaliphatique** *f* PLAST CAOU *durcissement* cycloaliphatic amine; ~ **grasse** *f* LESSIVES fatty amine
amino:[1] ~ **acide** *m* CHIMIE amino acid
amino:[2] ~ **résine** *f* PLAST CAOU *plastiques, peintures, adhésifs* amino resin
amino- *préf* CHIMIE amino-
aminoplaste *m* PLAST CAOU *plastiques, peintures, adhésifs* amino resin
amiral *m* NAUT admiral; ~ **d'escadre** *m* NAUT fleet admiral
Amis: ~ **de la Terre** *m pl* POLLUTION FoE, Friends of the Earth
ammine *f* CHIMIE ammine
ammiolite *f* MINERAUX ammiolite
ammonal *m* CHIMIE ammonal
ammoniac *m* CHIMIE, HYDROLOGIE, POLLUTION ammonia; ~ **anhydre** *m* PETROLE anhydrous ammonia
ammoniacal *adj* CHIMIE ammoniacal
ammoniaque *f* CHIMIE, ELECTRON, ESPACE *véhicules*, LESSIVES, PAPIER ammonia, PETROLE ammonium hydroxide; ~ **liquide** *f* THERMODYN liquid ammonia
ammonite *f* GEOLOGIE *paléontologie* ammonite
ammonium *m* CHIMIE ammonium
ammonolyse *f* MATERIAUX *chimie* ammonolysis
amodiation *f* PETROLE *commerce, permis* farming out
amollir *vt* PAPIER soften
amollisse *f* CERAM VER step
amonceler[1] *vt* CONSTR bank
amonceler:[2] **s'**~ *v réfl* CONSTR bank, bank up, METEO *nuages* bank up
amoncellement *m* CONSTR drifting
amont:[1] **d'**~ *adj* CONSTR, EN RENOUV, HYDROLOGIE, NAUT *rivière*, PHYS FLUID, PHYSIQUE, TRANSPORT, TV upstream
amont:[2] **en** ~ *adv* EN RENOUV, ESPACE, GAZ, NAUT *rivière*, PHYS FLUID upstream, PRODUCTION backward
amont:[3] **d'**~ *m* HYDROLOGIE upstream HYDROLOGIE *d'une rivière* upper part, PRODUCTION backward
amont-pendage:[1] **en** ~ *adv* GEOLOGIE updip
amont-pendage[2] *m* GEOLOGIE updip, MINES back, PETROLE *géologie* updip
amorçage:[1] **d'**~ *adj* PHYSIQUE breakdown
amorçage[2] *m* AERONAUT choking, *d'une pompe* priming, CHIMIE *d'une réaction* promoting, CONS MECA starting, ELECTRON breakdown, ELECTROTEC firing, flashover, ignition, striking, ENREGISTR lacing, INFORMAT start, INST HYDR, MILITAIRE priming, MINES initiation, priming, NUCLEAIRE *d'une rupture, germination* initiation of fracture, nucleation, ORDINAT bootstrapping, start, PHYSIQUE breakdown, PRODUCTION scarfing; ~ **antérieur** *m* MINES direct initiation; ~ **d'arc** *m* CINEMAT arc ignition, ELECTR arc discharge, arc ignition, arc striking, ELECTROTEC arc ignition, arcing; ~ **basse fréquence** *m* ELECTRON motorboating; ~ **du débit** *m* CONSTR inducing flow; ~ **du déchirement** *m* PLAST CAOU *essai, défaut* tear initiation; ~ **de l'écoulement** *m* CONSTR inducing flow; ~ **inverse** *m* MINES inverse initiation; ~ **postérieur** *m* MINES indirect initiation, indirect priming; ~ **à retardement** *m* MINES delay firing
amorce *f* ACOUSTIQUE leader, CERAM VER edge crack, CINEMAT leader, spacing, CONSTR cap, DISTRI EAU priming, IMPRIM *bande magnétique* bootstrap, INFORMAT *de bande* leader, MILITAIRE fuse, MINES blasting cap, detonator, exploder, squib, *d'une galerie* mouth, OPTIQUE launching fiber (AmE), launching fibre (BrE), optical fiber pigtail (AmE), optical fibre pigtail (BrE), ORDINAT bootstrap, PETR cap, PRODUCTION *soudure* scarf, TELECOM optical fiber pigtail (AmE), optical fibre pigtail (BrE), TV leader; ~ **à allumage retardé** *f* MINES delay-action detonator; ~ **de bande** *f* INFORMAT, TV tape leader; ~ **blanche** *f* CINEMAT white leader; ~ **cadrée** *f* CINEMAT frame line leader; ~ **de chargement** *f* CINEMAT machine leader; ~ **de coulée** *f* PRODUCTION gate, ingate; ~ **de crique** *f* AERONAUT incipient crack; ~ **départ** *f* CINEMAT head leader; ~ **électrique** *f* MINES electric blasting cap, electric detonator; ~ **à étincelle** *f* MINES spark fuse; ~ **d'étirage** *f* CERAM VER bait; ~ **étoilée** *f* CERAM VER star crack; ~ **à fil** *f* MINES battery fuse, quantity fuse; ~ **de fin** *f* CINEMAT end leader, tail leader; ~ **finale** *f* CINEMAT end leader; ~ **de fin de bobine** *f* CINEMAT run out leader; ~ **de fissure** *f* NUCLEAIRE incipient crack; ~ **de fissure de fatigue** *f* NUCLEAIRE fatigue precrack; ~ **fonctionnant avec retardement ou par choc** *f* MILITAIRE retard and impact fuse; ~ **à friction** *f* MINES friction fuse; ~ **à microretard** *f* MINES millisecond delay cap, millisecond delay detonator, short-delay detonator; ~ **noire** *f* CINEMAT black leader, black spacing; ~ **normalisée** *f* CINEMAT standard leader; ~ **opaque** *f* CINEMAT opaque leader; ~ **opérateur** *f* CINEMAT head leader; ~ **passe-partout** *f* CINEMAT universal leader; ~ **de pellicule** *f* PHOTO film leader; ~ **à percussion** *f* MILITAIRE percussion fuse; ~ **de quantité** *f* MINES battery fuse, quantity fuse; ~ **à retard** *f* MINES delay cap, delay detonator, delay-action detonator; ~ **télévision** *f* TV TV academy leader; ~ **de tension** *f* MINES spark fuse; ~ **transparente** *f* CINEMAT clear leader
amorcer[1] *vt* CERAM VER start, CINEMAT *arc* arc, CONS MECA *injecteur* start, DISTRI EAU *pompe* prime, start in operation, ENREGISTR lace up, INFORMAT start, INST HYDR *pompe*, MINES *cartouche* prime, ORDINAT bootstrap, boot, start, PHYSIQUE supply, PRODUCTION *trou* start
amorcer:[2] ~ **un siphon** *vi* DISTRI EAU start the flow of water in a siphon
amorceur *m* DISTRI EAU priming cock, ESPACE squib
amorçoir *m* CONSTR boring bit; ~ **à mortaises** *m* CONSTR mortise boring bit
amorphe *adj* CHARBON, CHIMIE, CRISTALL, GEOLOGIE amorphous
amorphie *f* CHIMIE amorphism
amorphisme *m* CHIMIE amorphism
amorti *adj* PHYSIQUE damped
amortir *vt* CONS MECA deaden, ELECTR *oscillation*, ELECTROTEC damp, INST HYDR cushion

amortissement *m* AERONAUT choking, CONSTR deadening, ELECTR *d'une oscillation*, ELECTROTEC damping, ENREGISTR decay, MATERIAUX damping, METALL dampening, ORDINAT, PETR, PHYSIQUE damping, PRODUCTION *système hydraulique* cushioning, TV damping; ~ **avec bulles d'air** *m* EMBALLAGE air bubble cushioning; ~ **critique** *m* ELECTROTEC, PETR, PHYSIQUE critical damping; ~ **électromagnétique** *m* ELECTR *d'oscillation* electromagnetic damping; ~ **de haut-parleur** *m* ENREGISTR loudspeaker damping; ~ **de la houle** *m* OCEANO swell abatement, wave damping, wave decay; ~ **interne** *m* AERONAUT internal damping; ~ **magnétique** *m* GEOPHYS magnetic damping; ~ **des matériaux** *m* MATERIAUX material damping; ~ **optimal** *m* ELECTROTEC optimum damping; ~ **par courants de Foucault** *m* ELECTROTEC magnetic damping; ~ **périodique** *m* ELECTROTEC periodic damping; ~ **périphérique** *m* ENREGISTR edge damping; ~ **sur le bord** *m* EMBALLAGE edge cushion; ~ **de surface** *m* ENREGISTR surface damping; ~ **visqueux** *m* MECANIQUE viscous damping

amortisseur *m* AUTO, CONSTR shock absorber, ESPACE *véhicules* attenuator, damper, shock absorber, snubber, MECANIQUE snubber, *véhicules* shock absorber, NUCLEAIRE dashing vessel, dashpot, OCEANO wave damper, VEHICULES *suspension* damper, shock absorber; ~ **à air** *m* MECANIQUE dashpot; ~ **avant** *m* AUTO front shock absorber; ~ **de bruit** *m* ACOUSTIQUE silencer, VEHICULES *échappement* muffler (AmE), silencer (BrE); ~ **de bruit à absorption** *m* SECURITE absorption silencer; ~ **de bruits à résonance** *m* SECURITE resonance silencer; ~ **de chocs** *m* CONSTR shock absorber; ~ **de commande** *m* AERONAUT control damper; ~ **contre le bruit** *m* SECURITE *pour conduites* silencer; ~ **électrodynamique passif** *m* ESPACE *véhicules* passive electrodynamic damper; ~ **électromagnétique** *m* GEOPHYS electromagnetic damper; ~ **à fluide** *m* TRANSPORT, VEHICULES dashpot; ~ **de friction** *m* AERONAUT friction damper; ~ **à friction** *m* CONS MECA friction draft gear (AmE), friction draught gear (BrE), MECANIQUE frictional damper; ~ **hydraulique télescopique** *m* AUTO, VEHICULES *suspension* telescopic shock absorber; ~ **de nutation** *m* ESPACE *véhicules* nutation damper; ~ **d'oscillations** *m* ELECTR shock absorber, *courant alternatif, galvanomètre* oscillating damper; ~ **de palonnier** *m* AERONAUT pedal damper assembly; ~ **du papillon** *m* VEHICULES *carburateur* dashpot, throttle dashpot; ~ **pneumatique** *m* AERONAUT air dashpot; ~ **principal** *m* AERONAUT landing gear main shock strut; ~ **de shimmy** *m* AERONAUT *d'un aéronef* shimmy damper; ~ **de tangage** *m* AERONAUT pitch damper; ~ **de traînée** *m* AERONAUT drag damper; ~ **de vibrations** *m* AERONAUT *d'un aéronef* vibration damper, AUTO *d'un moteur* damper, shock absorber, CONS MECA, REFRIG, VEHICULES *d'un moteur* vibration damper; ~ **de vibrations et de chocs** *m* SECURITE vibration damper and shock absorber

amovible *adj* CONS MECA detachable, interchangeable, removable, OPTIQUE removable, PHOTO detachable

amovibles *m pl* AERONAUT removables

ampélite *f* GEOLOGIE black shale

ampérage *m* ELECTROTEC amperage, PHOTO ampere-hour capacity

ampère *m* ELECTR, ELECTROTEC, METROLOGIE, PHYSIQUE ampere; ~ **tour** *m* METROLOGIE ampere turn

ampère-conducteur *m* ELECTR ampere conductor

ampère-heure *m* ELECTR *quantité*, PHYSIQUE ampere-hour

ampèremètre *m* ELECTR, ELECTROTEC, EQUIP LAB *courant électrique*, PHYSIQUE, TV, VEHICULES *système électrique* ammeter; ~ **alternatif** *m* ELECTR AC meter, ELECTROTEC AC ammeter; ~ **analogique** *m* ELECTROTEC analog ammeter (AmE), analogue ammeter (BrE); ~ **astatique** *m* ELECTR astatic ammeter; ~ **continu** *m* ELECTROTEC DC ammeter; ~ **différentiel** *m* ELECTR differential ammeter; ~ **digital** *m* ELECTR digital ammeter; ~ **ferrodynamique** *m* ELECTR iron-core ammeter; ~ **à fil chaud** *m* ELECTR hot wire ammeter; ~ **magnéto-électrique** *m* ELECTR moving coil ammeter; ~ **numérique** *m* ELECTR digital ammeter; ~ **à pinces** *m* PRODUCTION *électricité* clamp-on-type amp probe; ~ **pour courant alternatif** *m* ELECTROTEC AC ammeter; ~ **pour courant continu** *m* ELECTROTEC DC ammeter; ~ **thermique** *m* ELECTR thermal ammeter, thermoammeter; ~ **thermique à fil** *m* ELECTR hot wire ammeter

ampère-seconde *m* ELECTR ampere-second

ampère-tour *m* ELECTR *d'un enroulement*, PHYSIQUE ampere-turn

amphibie *adj* NAUT amphibian

amphibole *f* CHIMIE, MINERAUX amphibole

amphibolifère *adj* MINERAUX amphiboliferous

amphibolique *adj* MINERAUX amphibolic

amphibolite *f* PETR amphibolite

amphiboloïde *adj* MINERAUX amphiboloid

amphiphile *adj* LESSIVES amphiphilic

amphitalite *f* MINERAUX amphitalite

amphodélite *f* MINERAUX amphodelite

ampholyte *m* CHIMIE ampholyte

amphotère *adj* CHIMIE, LESSIVES amphoteric

ampli *m* NAUT amplifier; ~ **FI** *m* NAUT intermediate frequency amplifier; ~ **de synchronisation** *m* TV sync amplifier

amplidyne *f* ELECTROTEC amplidyne

amplificateur[1] *adj* ELECTR *intensité* amplifying

amplificateur[2] *m* ELECTR *appareil* amplifier, ELECTRON amplifier, booster, ENREGISTR, INFORMAT, NAUT, ORDINAT, PHYS ONDES, TELECOM amplifier; **– a** ~ **accordé** *m* ELECTRON band-pass amplifier, tuned amplifier; ~ **acoustique** *m* ENREGISTR acoustic amplifier; ~ **acoustique à ondes progressives** *m* ENREGISTR traveling-wave acoustic amplifier (AmE), travelling-wave acoustic amplifier (BrE); ~ **d'adaptation** *m* ELECTRON matching amplifier; ~ **d'asservissement** *m* ELECTRON servoamplifier; ~ **d'attaque de ligne** *m* ORDINAT analog line driver; ~ **audiofréquence** *m* ELECTRON audio amplifier, audio frequency amplifier; ~ **automatique** *m* COMMANDE servoamplifier; **– b** ~ **à bande élargie** *m* ELECTRON double-tuned amplifier; ~ **à bande étroite** *m* ELECTRON narrow band amplifier; ~ **à base commune** *m* ELECTRON common base amplifier; ~ **basse fréquence** *m* ELECTRON low-frequency amplifier, ENREGISTR audio amplifier; ~ **bilatéral** *m* ELECTRON bilateral amplifier; ~ **bipolaire** *m* ELECTRON bipolar amplifier; ~ **de brillance** *m* INSTRUMENT image intensifier; **– c** ~ **à champs croisés** *m* ELECTRON, TELECOM crossed field amplifier; ~ **de charge** *m* ELECTRON charge amplifier; ~ **de chrominance** *m* ELECTRON chrominance amplifier; ~ **à circuits décalés** *m* ELECTRON stagger-tuned amplifier; ~ **civil** *m* ELECTRON commercial amplifier; ~ **classe A** m ELECTRON, PHYSIQUE class A amplifier; ~ **à collecteur commun** m ELECTRON common collector amplifier; ~ **à contre-réaction** m ELECTRON feedback amplifier; ~ **à contreréaction sélective** m ELECTRON selective feedback amplifier; ~ **de contrôle** m ENREGISTR monitoring amplifier; ~ **correcteur** m TV equalizing amplifier; ~ **de courant** m ELECTR, ELECTRON current amplifier; ~ **de courant alternatif** m ELECTRON AC amplifier; ~ **à courant continu** m ELECTRON DC amplifier, PRODUCTION *électricité* DC boost; ~ **à courant porteur** m ELECTRON carrier amplifier; ~ **à courbe de réponse plate** m ELECTRON flat amplifier;

~ d ~ **à découpage** m ELECTRON chopper amplifier; ~ **déphaseur** m ELECTRON phase splitter amplifier, TV paraphase amplifier; ~ **de déviation** m ELECTRON deflection amplifier; ~ **de différence** m ELECTRON difference amplifier; ~ **différentiel** m ELECTRON, PHYSIQUE, TELECOM differential amplifier; ~ **à diode Gunn** m ELECTRON Gunn amplifier; ~ **à diode tunnel** m ESPACE *communications* tunnel-diode amplifier; ~ **discret** m ELECTRON discrete amplifier; ~ **de distribution** m TV distribution amplifier; ~ **de distribution vidéo** m TV VDA, video distribution amplifier; ~ **à drain commun** m ELECTRON common drain amplifier;

~ e ~ **à échantillonnage** m ELECTRON sampling amplifier; ~ **à effet de champ** m ELECTRON field-effect amplifier; ~ **d'électromètre** m ELECTRON electrometer amplifier; ~ **à émetteur commun** m ELECTRON common emitter amplifier; ~ **en cascade** m ELECTRON cascade amplifier; ~ **en contrephase** m TV paraphase amplifier; ~ **en ondes millimétriques** m ELECTRON millimeter wave amplifier (AmE), millimetre wave amplifier (BrE); ~ **d'enregistrement** m ENREGISTR record amplifier, TV record driver; ~ **d'entrée** m ELECTRON input amplifier; ~ **équilibré** m ENREGISTR balanced amplifier; ~ **à un étage** m ELECTR *électronique*, ELECTRON single stage amplifier; ~ **exponentiel** m ELECTRON exponential amplifier;

~ f ~ **à faible bruit** m ELECTRON, ESPACE *communications* LNA, low-noise amplifier, PHYS RAYON low-noise preamplifier, TELECOM LNA, low-noise amplifier; ~ **à faible gain** m ELECTRON low-gain amplifier, small-gain amplifier; ~ **à faisceau droit** m ELECTRON linear beam amplifier; ~ **ferromagnétique** m ELECTRON ferromagnetic amplifier; ~ **FI** m ELECTRON, TELECOM IF amplifier; ~ **de filtre actif** m ELECTRON filter amplifier; ~ **à fréquence intermédiaire** m ELECTRON, TELECOM intermediate frequency amplifier; ~ **de fréquences audibles** m ENREGISTR audio frequency amplifier; ~ **de fréquences radioélectriques** m ELECTRON RF amplifier;

~ g ~ **à gain unité** m ELECTRON unity gain amplifier; ~ **à gain variable** m ELECTRON variable gain amplifier; ~ **à grand gain** m ELECTRON high-gain amplifier; ~ **à grille commune** m ELECTRON common gate amplifier; ~ **de gyro** m AERONAUT gyro amplifier;

~ h ~ **haute fréquence** m ELECTRON preselector; ~ **horizontal** m ELECTRON horizontal amplifier; ~ **hyperfréquence** m ELECTRON, PHYSIQUE microwave amplifier; ~ **à hyperfréquences** m TELECOM microwave amplifier;

~ i ~ **d'impulsion** m ELECTRON pulse amplifier; ~ **d'impulsions** m ESPACE power amplifier, PRODUCTION gate amplifier; ~ **d'impulsions linéaire** m ELECTRON linear pulse amplifier; ~ **incorporé** m ELECTRON on-chip amplifier; ~ **d'intégration** m AERONAUT integrator amplifier; ~ **inverseur** m ELECTRON inverting amplifier; ~ **d'isolement** m ELECTRON isolation amplifier;

~ l ~ **à large bande** m ELECTRON broadband amplifier, wide band amplifier; ~ **de lecture** m ELECTRON read amplifier, sense amplifier, ENREGISTR playback amplifier; ~ **à liaison directe** m ELECTRON DC-coupled amplifier, direct-coupled amplifier; ~ **de ligne** m ELECTRON, ENREGISTR line amplifier, ORDINAT line driver; ~ **limiteur** m ELECTRON clipper amplifier, limiting amplifier, ENREGISTR limiter amplifier, TV clipper amplifier; ~ **linéaire** m ELECTRON, TELECOM linear amplifier; ~ **logarithmique** m ELECTRON logarithmic amplifier; ~ **de lumière** m ELECTRON light amplifier; ~ **de luminance** m ELECTRON luminance amplifier;

~ m ~ **magnétique** m ELECTROTEC magamp, magnetic amplifier, ESPACE *véhicules* magnetic amplifier, PHYSIQUE magnetic amplifier, saturable reactor, transductor; ~ **de mélange** m TV mixer amplifier; ~ **mélangeur** m ELECTRON mixing amplifier; ~ **de mesure** m ELECTRON data amplifier, instrumentation amplifier, measuring amplifier; ~ **de microphone** m ENREGISTR microphone amplifier; ~ **de mise en forme** m ELECTRON shaping amplifier; ~ **de modulation** m ELECTRON modulation amplifier; ~ **à modulation de vitesse** m ELECTRON velocity-modulated amplifier; ~ **monocanal** m ENREGISTR mono amplifier; ~ **monolithique** m ELECTRON monolithic amplifier; ~ **monovoie** m ELECTRON single channel amplifier; ~ **de moyenne puissance** m ELECTRON medium-power amplifier; ~ **multivoie** m ELECTRON multichannel amplifier;

~ n ~ **neutrodyné** m ELECTRON neutralized amplifier; ~ **non-linéaire** m ELECTRON nonlinear amplifier; ~ **non-symétrique** m ELECTRON single-ended amplifier;

~ o ~ **à ondes progressives** m TELECOM traveling-wave amplifier (AmE), travelling-wave amplifier (BrE); ~ **opérationnel** m ELECTRON op amp, operational amplifier, INFORMAT, ORDINAT, PHYSIQUE, TELECOM op amp, operational amplifier; ~ **opérationnel quadruple** m ELECTRON quad operational amplifier; ~ **optique** m ELECTRON, TELECOM optical amplifier; ~ **optoélectronique** m ELECTRON optoelectronic amplifier;

~ p ~ **paramagnétique** m ELECTRON paramagnetic amplifier; ~ **paramétrique** m ELECTRON parametric amplifier, paramp, ESPACE *communications*, PHYSIQUE, TELECOM parametric amplifier; ~ **paramétrique à diode** m ELECTRON diode amplifier; ~ **paramétrique à faisceau d'électrons** m ELECTRON electron beam parametric amplifier; ~ **par tout ou rien** m ELECTRON discontinuous amplifier; ~ **passe-bande** m ENREGISTR band-pass amplifier; ~ **de petits signaux** m ELECTRON small-signal amplifier; ~ **photoélectrique** m ELECTRON photoelectric amplifier; ~ **à plusieurs étages** m ELECTRON cascade amplifier, multistage amplifier; ~ **de pont** m ELECTRON bridge amplifier; ~ **ponté** m ENREGISTR bridging amplifier; ~ **à première fréquence intermédiaire** m ELECTRON first IF amplifier; ~ **propre** m ELECTRON basic amplifier; ~ **de puissance** m ELECTRON final amplifier, power amplifier, ELECTROTEC, ENREGISTR power amplifier, ESPACE power amplifier, *communications* high-power amplifier, PHYSIQUE power amplifier, TELECOM PA, power amplifier; ~ **de puissance basse fréquence** m ELECTRON audio power amplifier; ~ **de puissance à grand gain** m ELECTRON high-gain power amplifier; ~ **de**

puissance hyperfréquence *m* ELECTRON microwave power amplifier; ~ **de puissance à large bande** *m* ELECTRON wide band power amplifier; ~ **de puissance linéaire** *m* ELECTRON, TELECOM linear power amplifier; ~ **de puissance à transistor** *m* ELECTRON transistor power amplifier; ~ **push-pull** *m* ELECTRON push-pull amplifier;

~ q ~ **à quatre voies** *m* ELECTRON four-channel amplifier;

~ r ~ **à radiofréquence** *m* TELECOM RF amplifier; ~ **à réaction** *m* ELECTRON regenerative amplifier; ~ **de réglage** *m* COMMANDE regulating amplifier, servoamplifier; ~ **régulateur de niveau** *m* ELECTRON leveling amplifier (AmE), levelling amplifier (BrE); ~ **de reportage** *m* ELECTRON remote amplifier; ~ **à résistance négative** *m* ELECTRON negative resistance amplifier;

~ s ~ **de salve** *m* ELECTRON, TV burst amplifier; ~ **sans contreréaction** *m* ELECTRON forward amplifier; ~ **à seconde fréquence intermédiaire** *m* ELECTRON second IF amplifier; ~ **sélecteur de fréquence** *m* ELECTRON frequency selective amplifier; ~ **de sélection** *m* ENREGISTR gating amplifier; ~ **à semi-conducteurs** *m* TELECOM semiconductor amplifier, solid-state amplifier; ~ **séparateur** *m* ELECTRON, ENREGISTR buffer amplifier; ~ **séparateur d'entrée** *m* ELECTRON input buffer amplifier; ~ **du signal d'arrêt** *m* COMMANDE shutdown amplifier, trip amplifier; ~ **de signaux à bas niveau** *m* ELECTRON low-level amplifier; ~ **de sonorisation** *m* ENREGISTR PA amplifier, public address amplifier; ~ **de sortie** *m* ELECTRON, TV output amplifier; ~ **à source commune** *m* ELECTRON common source amplifier; ~ **stabilisé par découpage** *m* ELECTRON chopper-stabilized amplifier; ~ **symétrique** *m* ELECTRON balanced amplifier, push-pull amplifier; ~ **de synchro d'erreur de cap** *m* AERONAUT heading error synchronizer amplifier; ~ **synchrone** *m* ELECTRON lock-in amplifier;

~ t ~ **à TEC** *m* ELECTRON, ESPACE FET amplifier; ~ **téléphonique** *m* TELECOM voice amplifier; ~ **de tension** *m* ELECTRON voltage amplifier; ~ **à thyristor** *m* ELECTRON SCR amplifier; ~ **à TOP** *m* ELECTRON TWT amplifier; ~ **tournant** *m* ELECTROTEC *magnétique* rotary amplifier; ~ **à transistor** *m* ELECTRON transistor amplifier; ~ **à transistor à effet de champ** *m* ESPACE *communications* field-effect transistor amplifier; ~ **à transistor hyperfréquence** *m* ELECTRON microwave transistor amplifier; ~ **à très large bande** *m* ELECTRON compensated amplifier; ~ **à trois étages** *m* ELECTRON three-stage amplifier; ~ **à tube** *m* ELECTRON vacuum tube amplifier; ~ **à tube électronique** *m* ELECTRON vacuum tube amplifier; ~ **à tube à ondes progressives** *m (ATOP)* ELECTRON, ESPACE *communications* traveling-wave tube amplifier (AmE), travelling-wave tube amplifier (BrE) *(TWTA)*; ~ **à tubes à ondes progressives** *m* TELECOM traveling waveguide amplifier (AmE), travelling waveguide amplifier (BrE);

~ v ~ **vertical** *m* ELECTRON vertical amplifier; ~ **vertical à échantillonnage** *m* ELECTRON sampling vertical amplifier; ~ **vidéo** *m* ELECTRON, PHYSIQUE, TV video amplifier; ~ **vidéo logarithmique** *m* ELECTRON logarithmic video amplifier; ~ **de voie** *m* TV channel amplifier

amplification *f* ELECTR *d'un signal* amplification, gain, ELECTRON amplification, ENREGISTR amplification, gain; ~ **avec réaction** *f* ELECTRON regenerative amplification; ~ **à bas niveau** *f* ELECTRON low-level amplification; ~ **basse fréquence** *f* ELECTRON low-frequency amplification; ~ **BF** *f* ELECTRON low-frequency amplification; ~ **de courant** *f* ELECTRON, ENREGISTR current amplification; ~ **d'un courant continu** *f* ELECTRON DC amplification; ~ **différentielle** *f* TV differential gain; ~ **à faible bruit** *f* ELECTRON low-noise amplification; ~ **FI** *f* ELECTRON, TELECOM IF amplification; ~ **du flux de photons** *f* PHYS PART photon amplification; ~ **à fréquence intermédiaire** *f* ELECTRON, TELECOM intermediate frequency amplification; ~ **de fréquences radioélectriques** *f* ELECTRON RF amplification; ~ **à haute fréquence** *f* ELECTRON high-frequency amplification; ~ **hyperfréquence** *f* ELECTRON microwave amplification; ~ **d'impulsion** *f* ELECTRON pulse amplification; ~ **incorporée** *f* ELECTRON on-chip amplification; ~ **à large bande** *f* ELECTRON wide band amplification; ~ **linéaire** *f* ELECTRON linear amplification; ~ **de la lumière par rayonnement stimulé** *f* PHYS RAYON LASER, light amplification by stimulated emission of radiation; ~ **non-linéaire** *f* TELECOM nonlinear amplification; ~ **d'onde** *f* TELECOM wave amplification; ~ **des ondes millimétriques** *f* ELECTRON millimeter wave amplification (AmE), millimetre wave amplification (BrE); ~ **paramétrique** *f* ELECTRON parametric amplification; ~ **par transistor** *f* ELECTRON transistor amplification; ~ **par tube** *f* ELECTRON vacuum tube amplification; ~ **de petits signaux** *f* ELECTRON small-signal amplification; ~ **des photons** *f* PHYS RAYON photon amplification; ~ **de puissance** *f* ELECTRON final amplification, power amplification, INFORMAT line driver, TV gain; ~ **de puissance hyperfréquence** *f* ELECTRON microwave power amplification; ~ **sur la puce** *f* ELECTRON on-chip amplification; ~ **de tension** *f* ELECTRON voltage amplification; ~ **vidéo** *f* ELECTRON video amplification

amplifier *vt* ELECTRON amplify, boost, INFORMAT, ORDINAT, PHYS ONDES amplify

amplitron *m* ELECTRON, PHYSIQUE amplitron

amplitude *f* ACOUSTIQUE, ASTRONOMIE *d'une étoile*, ELECTR *d'une onde*, ELECTRON, EN RENOUV *énergie marémotrice*, ENREGISTR *d'une onde* amplitude, GEOMETRIE *d'un arc* length, NAUT, ORDINAT amplitude, PHYS ONDES amplitude, height, PHYSIQUE amplitude; ~ **constante** *f* ELECTRON fixed amplitude; ~ **de crête** *f* ELECTRON peak amplitude; ~ **crête-à-crête** *f* ACOUSTIQUE peak-to-peak value; ~ **crête-à-crête du signal** *f* TV peak-to-peak signal amplitude; ~ **de crête à crête** *f* ELECTRON peak-to-peak amplitude; ~ **crête d'une impulsion** *f* ELECTRON peak pulse amplitude; ~ **dynamique** *f* PETR dynamic range; ~ **de la houle** *f* NAUT height of swell, OCEANO wave amplitude; ~ **d'impulsion** *f* ELECTRON pulse amplitude, pulse height, ENREGISTR pulse amplitude, INFORMAT, ORDINAT pulse height; ~ **de la marée** *f* NAUT tidal range; ~ **maximale** *f* ELECTRON peak amplitude; ~ **maximale du signal** *f* ELECTRON maximum signal amplitude, peak signal amplitude; ~ **maximale de tension** *f* ELECTR potential loop; ~ **maximum de l'intensité de rafale** *f* AERONAUT derived gust velocity; ~ **moyenne annuelle** *f* NAUT mean annual variation; ~ **de pointe** *f* ENREGISTR peak amplitude; ~ **de pointe à pointe** *f* ENREGISTR peak-to-peak amplitude; ~ **de référence** *f* ENREGISTR reference volume; ~ **de refroidissement** *f* REFRIG cooling range; ~ **relative du signal** *f* ELECTRON relative signal amplitude; ~ **du signal** *f* ELECTRON signal amplitude; ~ **totale d'oscillation** *f* ACOUSTIQUE total oscillation amplitude; ~ **d'une vague** f OCEANO wave amplitude; ~ **verticale** f TV vertical amplitude

ampoule f CERAM VER ampoule (BrE), ampule (AmE), CHIMIE flask, CINEMAT bulb, lamp, ELECTR *lampe électrique* bulb, ELECTRON envelope, ELECTROTEC bulb, EMBALLAGE, EQUIP LAB *verrerie* ampoule, TV envelope; ~ **à décanter** f CHIMIE separation funnel, separator funnel, EQUIP LAB *verrerie* separating funnel; ~ **de flash** f PHOTO flash bulb; ~ **de laboratoire** f CHIMIE flask; ~ **pour lampe à incandescence** f CERAM VER lamp bulb; ~ **de télévision** f CERAM VER TV bulb

AMRC *abrév (accès multiple par répartition en code)* ESPACE *communications* CDMA *(code-division multiple access)*

AMRF *abrév (accès multiple à répartition en fréquence)* ESPACE, TELECOM FDMA *(frequency-division multiple access)*

AMRT *abrév (accès multiple par répartition dans le temps)* ELECTRON, ESPACE, INFORMAT, TELECOM TDMA *(time-division multiple access)*

amure f NAUT tack

amylacé *adj* AGRO ALIM, CHIMIE starchy, PAPIER amylaceous

amyle m CHIMIE, PAPIER amyl

amylique *adj* PAPIER amylic

amyloïde *adj* CHIMIE starchy

amylopectine f TEXTILE amylopectin

anaérobie[1] *adj* HYDROLOGIE, RECYCLAGE anaerobic

anaérobie[2] f AGRO ALIM anaerobe, HYDROLOGIE anaerobe, anaerobium (AmE), OCEANO, RECYCLAGE anaerobe

anaérobiose f RECYCLAGE anaerobiosis

anaérobique *adj* AGRO ALIM, HYDROLOGIE anaerobic

analogique *adj* ELECTRON analog (AmE), analogue (BrE), ORDINAT analog, PETR, TELECOM analog (AmE), analogue (BrE)

analogique-numérique *adj* TV A-to-D, analog-to-digital (AmE), analogue-to-digital (BrE)

analyse f CHARBON analysis, CHIMIE analysis, assay, *des minéraux* assaying, CONS MECA, DISTRI EAU, QUALITE, TEXTILE analysis, TV scan, scanning, sweep; ~ **d'absorption par spectrophotométrie** f PHYS RAYON absorption spectroanalysis; ~ **approximative** f TV coarse scanning; ~ **de bruit** f PETR noise analysis; ~ **de carbone 14** f PHYS RAYON carbon 14 analysis, carbon dating; ~ **des carottes** f PETROLE core analysis; ~ **du champ lointain** f TELECOM far-field analysis; ~ **du champ proche** f TELECOM near field analysis; ~ **chimique** f CHARBON chemical analysis; ~ **chromatique** f TV color separation (AmE), colour separation (BrE); ~ **de chronologie** f ELECTRON logic timing analysis; ~ **des circuits** f ELECTROTEC circuit analysis; ~ **de la circulation** f TRANSPORT traffic survey; ~ **combinatoire** f MATH combinatorial analysis; ~ **contradictoire** f CHIMIE check analysis, check assay; ~ **de contraintes** f ESPACE *véhicules* stress analysis; ~ **de contraintes et tensions** f CONS MECA stress and strain analysis; ~ **de contrôle** f CHARBON control assay; ~ **de corrélation par le temps** f NUCLEAIRE time correlation analysis; ~ **des correspondances** f MATH correspondence analysis; ~ **de couleur** f TV color analysis (AmE), colour analysis (BrE); ~ **cryptographique** f INFORMAT, TELECOM cryptanalysis; ~ **de défaut** f PHYS RAYON defect analysis; ~ **densimétrique par liqueurs denses** f CHARBON float-and-sink analysis; ~ **densimétrique par liquides denses** f CHARBON heavy liquid test; ~

densimétrique par liquides lourds f CHARBON heavy liquid test; ~ **différée** f TV delayed scanning; ~ **de la distribution des espacements** f TRANSPORT headway distribution analysis; ~ **des données de temps de vol** f PHYS RAYON *expériences de radioactivité* time-of-flight data analysis; ~ **des eaux usées** f DISTRI EAU sewage analysis; ~ **élastoplastique** f MATERIAUX elastoplastic analysis; ~ **électrographique** f PHYS RAYON electrographic analysis; ~ **électrolytique** f CHIMIE electroanalysis; ~ **en temps réel** f ELECTRON real-time analysis; ~ **en trace** f DISTRI EAU *des éléments* trace analysis; ~ **entrelacée** f TV interlaced scanning, line-interlaced scanning; ~ **entrelacée double** f TV twin interlaced scanning; ~ **entrelacée point par point** f TV dot interlace scanning; ~ **entrelacée progressive** f TV progressive interlace; ~ **entrelacée séquentielle** f TV sequential interlace; ~ **d'erreurs** f INFORMAT, ORDINAT error analysis; ~ **d'états logiques** f ELECTRON logic state analysis; ~ **factorielle** f MATH factor analysis; ~ **de fluorescence de rayonnement X** f PHYS RAYON X-ray fluorescence analysis; ~ **des flux critiques** f TEXTILE critical path analysis; ~ **fonctionnelle** f MATH functional analysis; ~ **de Fourier** f ELECTRON, PHYSIQUE Fourier analysis; ~ **fractionnée** f GENIE CHIM distillation test; ~ **de gaz** f PETROLE gas analysis; ~ **granulométrique** f CERAM VER granule size distribution, granulometric analysis (BrE), screen analysis (AmE), CHARBON screen analysis, sieve analysis, CONSTR grading analysis, GENIE CHIM particle size analysis; ~ **gravimétrique** f PETROLE *prospection* gravimetric analysis; ~ **harmonique** f ELECTRON harmonic analysis, MATH Fourier analysis, MECANIQUE, PHYSIQUE, TELECOM harmonic analysis; ~ **de l'huile brute** f PETROLE crude oil analysis; ~ **hypothétique** f PRODUCTION assumption analysis; ~ **de l'image** f TELECOM image analysis; ~ **d'image négative** f TV negative scanning; ~ **d'images de dislocations** f MATERIAUX *cristallographie* dislocation image analysis; ~ **immédiate** f CHIMIE proximate analysis; ~ **d'impédance** f ESSAIS impedance analysis; ~ **isotopique** f PHYS RAYON isotopic analysis; ~ **lexicale** f INFORMAT, ORDINAT lexical analysis; ~ **ligne par ligne non entrelacée** f TV sequential scanning; ~ **logique** f ELECTRON, INFORMAT, ORDINAT logic analysis; ~ **des marées** f NAUT tidal signature; ~ **des minerais** f NUCLEAIRE ore assaying, ore testing; ~ **minérale** f CHIMIE mineral analysis; ~ **de modulation** f ESSAIS modulation analysis; ~ **du niveau de risque** f QUALITE criticality analysis; ~ **numérique** f INFORMAT, ORDINAT numerical analysis; ~ **numérique des signaux** f ELECTRON digital signal analysis; ~ **optique spectrale** f ELECTRON optical spectral analysis; ~ **orthogonale** f TV orthogonal scanning; ~ **oscillante** f TV oscillatory scanning; ~ **par absorption** f NUCLEAIRE radiation absorption analysis; ~ **par absorption atomique** f PHYS RAYON *spectrophotométrie* atomic absorption analysis; ~ **par absorption des rayons bêta** f PHYS RAYON beta particle absorption analysis; ~ **par absorption des rayons gamma** f PHYS RAYON gamma ray absorption analysis; ~ **par absorption de rayons X** f PHYS RAYON X-ray absorption analysis; ~ **par activation** f PHYSIQUE activation analysis; ~ **par activation dans les photons gamma** f PHYS RAYON gamma ray activation analysis, photoactivation analysis; ~ **par activation aux particules chargées** f PHYS RAYON charged particle activation analysis; ~ **paramétrique** f ELECTRON, MATERIAUX parametric analysis; ~ **par dif-**

fraction à rayons X *f* PHYS RAYON X-ray diffraction analysis; ~ **par électrons de haute vitesse** *f* TV high-velocity scanning; ~ **par entraîneur** *f* NUCLEAIRE carrier analysis; ~ **par fluorescence** *f* PHYS RAYON fluorescence analysis; ~ **par fluorescence atomique** *f* PHYS RAYON *spectrométrie* atomic fluorescence analysis; ~ **par incinération** *f* THERMODYN combustion analysis; ~ **par lignes** *f* TV rectilinear scanning; ~ **de la parole** *f* TELECOM speech analysis; ~ **par précipitation** *f* GENIE CHIM precipitation analysis; ~ **par radioactivité** *f* PHYS RAYON radioactivation analysis; ~ **par rayons positifs** *f* NUCLEAIRE *de canaux* canal ray analysis; ~ **par rétrodiffusion des rayons bêta** *f* PHYS RAYON beta particle backscattering analysis; ~ **par sédimentation** *f* CHARBON sedimentation analysis; ~ **par spectroscopie d'émission** *f* PHYS RAYON emission spectral analysis; ~ **par spectroscopie de masse** *f* PHYS RAYON mass spectrum analysis; ~ **par tamisage** *f* GENIE CHIM sieve analysis; ~ **par télécinéma** *f* TV telecine scan; ~ **par voie humide** *f* CHARBON wet assay; ~ **du pétrole brut** *f* PETROLE crude oil analysis; ~ **des phénomènes dangereux** *f* QUALITE hazard analysis; ~ **préalable** *f* INFORMAT, ORDINAT feasibility study; ~ **PVT** *f* PETR PVT analysis; ~ **qualitative** *f* DISTRI EAU qualitative analysis; ~ **quantitative** *f* DISTRI EAU, MATERIAUX quantitative analysis; ~ **radiométrique** *f* PHYS RAYON radiometric analysis; ~ **à rayons X** *f* INSTRUMENT, PHYS RAYON X-ray analysis; ~ **des réseaux** *f* ELECTR *réseau d'alimentation*, ELECTROTEC network analysis; ~ **des réseaux à haute fréquence** *f* ELECTROTEC high-frequency network analysis; ~ **du risque** *f* QUALITE hazard analysis; ~ **de roche totale** *f* PETR whole rock analysis; ~ **de routine** *f* QUALITE *des données quantitatives* routine analysis; ~ **routinière** *f* QUALITE *des données quantitatives* automatic verification; ~ **scalaire des réseaux** *f* ELECTROTEC scalar network analysis; ~ **sémantique** *f* INFORMAT, ORDINAT semantic analysis; ~ **de sensibilité** *f* PRODUCTION sensitivity analysis; ~ **de séries temporelles** *f* ELECTRON time-series analysis; ~ **de signaux** *f* ELECTRON, TELECOM signal analysis; ~ **spectrale** *f* INFORMAT, MATERIAUX, ORDINAT spectral analysis, PHYS RAYON spectrum analysis, PHYSIQUE, TELECOM spectral analysis; ~ **spectrale en temps réel** *f* ELECTRON real-time spectral analysis; ~ **spectrale à lecture directe** *f* PHYS RAYON spectrometric analysis; ~ **du spectre sismique** *f* GEOPHYS seismic spectral analysis; ~ **spectrographique** *f* MATERIAUX, PHYS RAYON spectrographic analysis; ~ **spectrométrique** *f* PHYS RAYON spectrometric analysis; ~ **statistique** *f* INFORMAT, ORDINAT statistical analysis; ~ **syntaxique** *f* INFORMAT, ORDINAT parsing, syntax analysis, TELECOM syntactic analysis; ~ **système** *f* INFORMAT, ORDINAT systems analysis; ~ **au tamis** *f* GENIE CHIM sieve analysis; ~ **temporelle** *f* INFORMAT, ORDINAT timing analysis; ~ **thermique** *f* CHIMIE thermal analysis, thermoanalysis, MATERIAUX, THERMODYN thermal analysis; ~ **thermique différentielle** *f (ATD)* CONSTR, PLAST CAOU, POLLUTION, THERMODYN differential thermal analysis *(DTA)*; ~ **du trafic** *f* TELECOM traffic analysis; ~ **des transitoires** *f* ELECTRON transient analysis; ~ **de la valeur** *f* PRODUCTION value analysis; ~ **de la variance** *f* ORDINAT ANOVA, analysis of variance; ~ **vectorielle des réseaux** *f* ELECTROTEC vector network analysis; ~ **de verre** *f* CERAM VER glass analysis; ~ **vibratoire** *f* MECANIQUE vibration analysis; ~ **volumétrique** *f* ESSAIS volumetric analysis, LESSIVES titration

analyser[1] *vt* CHIMIE analyze, INFORMAT monitor, parse, ORDINAT parse, TV scan

analyser:[2] ~ **les couleurs** *vi* IMPRIM *photogravure* break for colors (AmE), break for colours (BrE)

analyseur *m* ELECTRON, METALL, PHYSIQUE analyzer, TELECOM analyzer, scanner, TV scanner; ~ **de bruit de choc** *m* ENREGISTR impact noise analyzer; ~ **couleur** *m* CINEMAT color film analyzer (AmE), colour film analyzer (BrE), PHOTO color analyzer (AmE), colour analyzer (BrE); ~ **de diapositives** *m* TV slide pickup, slide scanner; ~ **de dimensions des particules** *m* GENIE CHIM particle size analyzer; ~ **en temps réel** *m* ACOUSTIQUE real-time analyzer; ~ **de film** *m* TV telecine machine; ~ **de gaz** *m* GAZ, PETROLE gas analyzer; ~ **de gaz d'échappement à rayons infrarouges** *m* AUTO infrared exhaust gas analyzer; ~ **de gaz à ionisation alpha** *m* NUCLEAIRE alpha ionization gas analyzer; ~ **harmonique** *m* ELECTRON harmonic analyzer; ~ **d'harmoniques** *m* PHYSIQUE harmonic analyzer; ~ **d'image** *m* TELECOM image analyzer, TV image scanner; ~ **d'indices** *m* PETROLE *prospection* oil show analyzer; ~ **logique** *m* ELECTRON, ORDINAT logic analyzer; ~ **logique mixte** *m* ELECTRON logic state and timing analyzer; ~ **multicanaux** *m* PHYSIQUE multichannel analyzer; ~ **numérique de signaux** *m* ELECTRON digital signal analyzer; ~ **d'ondes** *m* ELECTRON wave analyzer; ~ **optique** *m* TV OSD, optical scanning device; ~ **optique spectral** *m* ELECTRON optical spectral analyzer; ~ **de réseaux** *m* ELECTR *réseau d'alimentation*, ELECTROTEC, INFORMAT, ORDINAT, TELECOM network analyzer; ~ **de réseaux scalaire** *m* ELECTROTEC scalar network analyzer; ~ **scalaire** *m* ELECTROTEC scalar network analyzer; ~ **de signaux** *m* ELECTRON, PHYS RAYON *spectres atomiques*, TELECOM signal analyzer; ~ **de son** *m* ACOUSTIQUE sound analyzer; ~ **de son hétérodyne** *m* ENREGISTR heterodyne sound analyzer; ~ **spectral en temps réel** *m* ELECTRON real-time spectral analyzer; ~ **de spectre** *m* TELECOM spectrum analyzer; ~ **de spectres à échantillonnage** *m* ELECTRON sampling spectrum analyzer; ~ **à spot mobile** *m* TV flying-spot scanner; ~ **syntactique** *m* TELECOM syntactic analyzer; ~ **syntaxique** *m* INFORMAT, ORDINAT analyzer, syntax analyzer, parser; ~ **thermogravimétrique** *m* EQUIP LAB TGA, thermogravimetric analyzer; ~ **de titres** *m* TV caption scanner; ~ **de trafic** *m* TRANSPORT traffic analyzer; ~ **de transitoires** *m* ELECTRON transient analyzer; ~ **vectoriel de réseaux** *m* ELECTROTEC vector network analyzer

analyste *m* CHIMIE analyst

analytique *adj* CHIMIE analytic, analytical

anamésite *f* PETR anamesite

anamorphose *f* CINEMAT squeeze, TELECOM anamorphosis

anamorphosé *adj* CINEMAT anamorphic

anamorphoseur[1] *adj* CINEMAT anamorphic

anamorphoseur[2] *m* PHOTO anamorphic lens

anastigmat *m* PHOTO, PHYSIQUE anastigmat; ~ **symétrique** *m* PHOTO symmetrical anastigmat

anatexie *f* GEOLOGIE anatexis

anatto *m* AGRO ALIM anatto

ancêtre *m* INFORMAT ancestor

anche *f* CONSTR *d'une chèvre* mast

anches *f pl* CONSTR shear legs

anchoitage *m* OCEANO brine fermentation, brine pickling

ancrage m CERAM VER bracing, CONS MECA fixing, CONSTR anchoring, CRISTALL pinning, ESPACE anchoring, MECANIQUE anchor, METALL pinning, MINES *de la cheminée* chute hang-up, clogging; ~ **du brin mort** m PETROLE dead line anchor; ~ **de la ceinture de sécurité** m VEHICULES *accessoire de sécurité* safety belt anchorage, seat belt attachment; ~ **de la colonne de protection** m PETROLE tubing anchor; ~ **de haubanage** m PETROLE *du derrick* guy anchor; ~ **tubulaire** m CONS MECA pipe anchor

ancre[1] f CONSTR *building*, NAUT anchor; ~ **à bascule** f NAUT Danforth anchor; ~ **de bossoir** f NAUT bow anchor; ~ **de cape** f NAUT drogue; ~ **champignon** f NAUT mushroom anchor; ~ **charrue** f NAUT CQR anchor, plough anchor (BrE), plow anchor (AmE); ~ **CQR** f NAUT CQR anchor, ploughshare (BrE), plowshare (AmE); ~ **engagée** f NAUT foul anchor, fouled anchor; ~ **flottante** f NAUT drogue, sea anchor; ~ **à jas** f NAUT stock anchor; ~ **à jet** f NAUT kedge anchor; ~ **à pattes articulées** f NAUT stockless anchor; ~ **principale** f NAUT bow anchor; ~ **à soc de charrue** f NAUT plough anchor (BrE), plow anchor (AmE); ~ **surjalée** f NAUT foul anchor, fouled anchor; ~ **surpattée** f NAUT foul anchor, fouled anchor

ancre:[2] **être à l'**~ vi NAUT lie at anchor, ride at anchor

ancrer[1] vt CONSTR fix, secure, *solive de plancher* anchor, *une solive de planches à un mur* fix, ESPACE *véhicules*, NAUT anchor

ancrer:[2] ~ **en rade** vi NAUT anchor in the roads

andaillot m NAUT hank

andésite f PETR andesite

andésitique adj PETR andesitic

Andromède f ASTRONOMIE Andromeda

anélasticité f METALL, PHYSIQUE anelasticity

anémoclinomètre m METEO wind inclination meter

anémographe m METEO anemograph

anémomètre m AERONAUT airspeed indicator, EN RENOUV *éolien* anemometer, wind gage (AmE), wind gauge (BrE), EQUIP LAB *vélocité d'air*, HYDROLOGIE *vélocité d'air* anemometer, METEO, NAUT anemometer, wind sensor, PAPIER, PHYSIQUE anemometer, TRANSPORT airspeed indicator; ~ **bidirectionnel** m METEO bidirectional wind vane; ~ **enregistreur** m METEO wind recorder; ~ **à fil chaud** m PHYSIQUE hot wire anemometer; ~ **à plaque** m METEO plate anemometer; ~ **de pression** m METEO pressure anemometer; ~ **à résistance électrique** m PHYSIQUE hot wire anemometer

anémométrie f METEO, PHYSIQUE anemometry

anémométrique adj PAPIER anemometric

anéthole m CHIMIE anethole

aneurine f CHIMIE aneurin

anfractuosités f pl MATERIAUX roughness

angiographie f INSTRUMENT angiography

angle m CINEMAT *d'un objectif*, GEOMETRIE angle, PHYSIQUE *de déviation* angle, *de raccordement* angle; **~ a** ~ **d'admission** m ELECTRON, ELECTROTEC, OPTIQUE, TELECOM acceptance angle; ~ **aigu** m GEOMETRIE acute angle; ~ **d'arrivée** m TELECOM angle of arrival; ~ **d'attaque** m EN RENOUV *d'hélice, d'orbite* pitch angle, MINES *de l'outil* attack angle; ~ **d'attaque de pale** m AERONAUT blade pitch angle, feathering angle; ~ **d'atterrissage** m AERONAUT ground angle; ~ **d'auge** m EN RENOUV *hydroélectricité, turbines* bucket angle; ~ **d'avance** m ELECTR *phase* advance angle, VEHICULES *allumage* timing angle; ~ **d'avance à l'admission** m CONS MECA *avance angulaire* angle of lead; ~ **d'avance**

à l'échappement m CONS MECA angle of prerelease; ~ **azimutal** m EN RENOUV azimuth angle; **~ b** ~ **de basculement** m AERONAUT flapping angle; ~ **battant** m AERONAUT flapping angle; ~ **de battement** m AERONAUT flapping angle; ~ **de battement cyclique** m AERONAUT cyclic flapping angle; ~ **de battement de pale** m AERONAUT *d'hélicoptère* blade flapping angle; ~ **de biellette de pas** m AERONAUT pitch control rod angle; ~ **de Bragg** m CRISTALL Bragg angle; ~ **de braquage** m NAUT angle, steering angle, VEHICULES *direction* steer angle; ~ **de braquage des gouvernes** m AERONAUT control surface angle; ~ **de Brewster** m OPTIQUE Brewster's angle; ~ **de bridage** m RESSORTS seat angle;

~ c ~ **de calage** m AUTO *allumage* angle of advance, CONS MECA angle of keying, VEHICULES *allumage* timing angle; ~ **de calage de pale** m AERONAUT blade setting angle, blade tilt; ~ **de calage de la voilure** m AERONAUT angle of wing setting; ~ **de came** m AUTO cam angle; ~ **de cap** m AERONAUT course angle; ~ **de charge** m ELECTR *d'une machine* load angle; ~ **de cintrage** m PRODUCTION bend angle; ~ **de commettage** m MECANIQUE *cordages métalliques* angle of twist; ~ **complémentaire** m GEOMETRIE complementary angle; ~ **de conduction** m ELECTROTEC conduction angle; ~ **de conicité** m AERONAUT coning angle, MECANIQUE *outillage* angle of taper; ~ **de contact** m CHARBON contact angle, PRODUCTION angle of contact, VEHICULES *allumage* dwell angle; ~ **de contingence** m PRODUCTION angle of contact; ~ **de convergence** m AERONAUT *des feux de piste* toe-in angle, CINEMAT angle of coverage; ~ **de coupe** m AGRO ALIM, CONS MECA cutting angle; ~ **de crabe** m AERONAUT crab angle;

~ d ~ **de décalage** m ELECTR *balais d'un moteur* angle of lead, *des balais d'un moteur* angle of brush lag; ~ **de déclinaison** m AERONAUT declination angle; ~ **de décrochage** m AERONAUT angle of stall; ~ **de dégagement** m CONS MECA top rake, *d'un outil de coupe* angle of rake; ~ **de départ** m TELECOM angle of departure; ~ **de déphasage** m ELECTROTEC angle of phase difference; ~ **de dérive** m AERONAUT, TRANSPORT drift angle; ~ **de déviation** m TV deflection angle; ~ **dièdre** m CRISTALL interfacial angle, GEOMETRIE, METALL dihedral angle; ~ **de diffusion** m PHYSIQUE scattering angle; ~ **droit** m GEOMETRIE right angle; ~ **dwell** m VEHICULES *allumage* dwell angle;

~ e ~ **d'éclairement** m IMPRIM *photogravure* illumination angle; ~ **d'élévation** m GEOMETRIE angle of elevation; ~ **d'empiètement** m ELECTR *d'un redresseur* angle of overlap; ~ **en radians** m GEOMETRIE angle in radians; ~ **d'enroulement** m CONS MECA *de la courroie* arc of contact; ~ **de l'entaille** m METALL notch angle; ~ **d'entrée** m NUCLEAIRE *d'ions* angle of acceptance; ~ **entre faces** m CRISTALL interfacial angle; ~ **entre flancs** m GEOLOGIE *d'un pli* interlimb angle; ~ **entre vitesse d'un point de pale et vitesse relative** m AERONAUT inflow angle; ~ **d'équilibre instable** m NAUT angle of loll; ~ **extérieur** m GEOMETRIE exterior angle; ~ **externe** m GEOMETRIE outward angle;

~ f ~ **de fermeture** m AUTO dwell angle; ~ **de flèche** m AERONAUT *d'une cellule* sweep angle; ~ **de frottement** m CHARBON, CONSTR angle of friction, EMBALLAGE angle of repose, PHYSIQUE, PRODUCTION angle of friction;

~ g ~ **de gîte** m NAUT angle of heel; ~ **de gîte per-**

manente *m* NAUT angle of loll; ~ **de gravure** *m* ENREGISTR groove angle;

~ h ~ **horaire** *m* ASTRONOMIE hour angle; ~ **horizontal de projection** *m* CINEMAT angle of rake;

~ i ~ **d'incidence** *m* AERONAUT incidence angle, CINEMAT angle of incidence, CONS MECA clearance angle, relief, *d'un outil de coupe* angle of relief, relief angle, EN RENOUV angle of incidence, IMPRIM pick-up angle, OPTIQUE, PHYS ONDES angle of incidence, PHYSIQUE angle of attack, angle of incidence, PRODUCTION angle of clearance, angle of incidence, TELECOM angle of incidence; ~ **d'incidence arrière** *m* CONS MECA bank clearance angle; ~ **d'incidence de pale** *m* AERONAUT blade pitch angle, feathering angle; ~ **d'inclinaison** *m* CINEMAT angle of tilt, GEOLOGIE angle of hade, PRODUCTION angle of inclination; ~ **d'inclinaison des balais** *m* ELECTR *d'une machine* brush angle; ~ **d'inclinaison longitudinale** *m* AERONAUT pitch angle; ~ **d'inclinaison de récepteur** *m* EN RENOUV collector tilt angle; ~ **d'induit** *m* AERONAUT inflow angle; ~ **induit** *m* AERONAUT induced angle of attack; ~ **interne** *m* GEOMETRIE internal angle, IMPRIM *d'un cahier* gusset; ~ **d'intersection** *m* CONSTR intersection angle;

~ l ~ **de lacet** *m* ESPACE *véhicules*, TRANSPORT yaw angle; ~ **de levée de pale** *m* AERONAUT flapping angle; ~ **de liaison** *m* CRISTALL bond angle; ~ **limite** *m* CHIMIE, OPTIQUE, PETR, PHYSIQUE, TELECOM critical angle;

~ m ~ **de mesure** *m* IMPRIM *optique, photogravure* acceptance angle; ~ **de modulation** *m* ACOUSTIQUE modulation angle; ~ **mort** *m* AERONAUT blind angle;

~ n ~ **négatif** *m* GEOMETRIE negative angle; ~ **négatif de dépouille** *m* CONS MECA negative rake;

~ o ~ **oblique** *m* GEOMETRIE oblique angle; ~ **d'observation** *m* CINEMAT angle of view; ~ **de l'obturateur** *m* CINEMAT shutter angle; ~ **d'obturation** *m* CINEMAT angle of cutoff; ~ **obtus** *m* GEOMETRIE obtuse angle; ~ **optimal de montée** *m* AERONAUT best climb angle; ~ **ouvert** *m* GEOMETRIE open angle; ~ **d'ouverture** *m* AUTO *d'un moteur* cylinder bank angling, CINEMAT acceptance angle, aperture angle; ~ **d'ouverture du faisceau** *m* ELECTRON beam angle;

~ p ~ **parallactique** *m* ASTRONOMIE parallactic angle; ~ **de pas** *m* AERONAUT pitch angle; ~ **du pas** *m* AERONAUT blade angle; ~ **de pas de filet** *m* CONS MECA thread lead angle; ~ **de pas de pale** *m* AERONAUT blade pitch angle; ~ **de pertes** *m* ELECTR *d'un condensateur*, PHYSIQUE loss angle; ~ **de pertes diélectriques** *m* ELECTR dielectric loss angle; ~ **de phase** *m* AERONAUT, ELECTR *courant alternatif*, ELECTRON, EN RENOUV, ESSAIS, PHYS ONDES *d'une oscillation*, PHYSIQUE phase angle; ~ **de phase du signal de chrominance** *m* TV color phase (AmE), colour phase (BrE); ~ **de pincement dynamique** *m* VEHICULES *de la direction* dynamic toe angle; ~ **plan** *m* GEOMETRIE plane angle; ~ **de plané** *m* AERONAUT gliding angle; ~ **du plan de pendage avec la verticale** *m* GEOLOGIE hade; ~ **plat** *m* GEOMETRIE flat angle; ~ **de polarisation** *m* OPTIQUE polarization angle, polarizing angle; ~ **polyèdre** *m* GEOMETRIE polyhedral angle, solid angle; ~ **positif** *m* GEOMETRIE positive angle; ~ **de position** *m* ASTRONOMIE position angle; ~ **de précession** *m* EN RENOUV angle of precession; ~ **de pression** *m* CONS MECA angle of obliquity, pressure angle, MECANIQUE *des engrenages* angle of pressure; ~ **de prise** *m* CHARBON angle of nip; ~ **de prise de vue** *m* CINEMAT camera angle;

~ r ~ **de radiation** *m* ELECTRON beam angle; ~ **de**

rayonnement *m* OPTIQUE, TELECOM radiation angle; ~ **de recouvrement** *m* CONS MECA *avance angulaire à l'admission d'un tiroir* angle of lap; ~ **rectiligne** *m* GEOMETRIE plane angle; ~ **de réflexion** *m* PHYS ONDES, PHYSIQUE angle of reflection; ~ **de réfraction** *m* PHYSIQUE angle of refraction; ~ **de réfraction limite** *m* PHYSIQUE critical angle; ~ **rentrant** *m* GEOMETRIE reflex angle; ~ **de retard** *m* AERONAUT lag angle, ELECTR *des balais d'un moteur* angle of lag; ~ **de route** *m* AERONAUT course angle;

~ s ~ **saillant** *m* CERAM VER arris; ~ **de site** *m* CONSTR elevation angle, TELECOM angle of elevation, angle of sight, elevation angle; ~ **solide** *m* GEOMETRIE, PHYSIQUE solid angle; ~ **au sommet de l'alvéole** *m* IMPRIM, TELECOM vertex angle; ~ **de sortie** *m* INST HYDR *d'une turbine* exit angle, OPTIQUE, TELECOM output angle; ~ **supplémentaire** *m* GEOMETRIE supplementary angle;

~ t ~ **de tangage** *m* AERONAUT pitch angle, CERAM VER, NAUT angle of pitch; ~ **tg** *m* ELECTR *d'un condensateur* loss angle; ~ **de tir** *m* MILITAIRE *artillerie* angle of sight; ~ **de tire** *m* NAUT angle of pull; ~ **de traction** *m* MECANIQUE angle of pull, angle of traction; ~ **de traînée** *m* AERONAUT drag angle, lag angle; ~ **de trame** *m* IMPRIM *photogravure* screen angle; ~ **du tranchant** *m* AGRO ALIM cutting angle;

~ v ~ **de visualisation** *m* IMPRIM *optique* pick-up angle; ~ **de vue** *m* CINEMAT angle of view;

~ z ~ **zénithal** *m* EN RENOUV zenith angle

angledozer *m* CONSTR angledozer

angler *vt* PAPIER angle

angles: ~ **adjacents** *m pl* GEOMETRIE adjacent angles, contiguous angles; ~ **alternes-externes** *m pl* GEOMETRIE alternate exterior angles; ~ **alternes-internes** *m pl* GEOMETRIE alternate interior angles; ~ **correspondants** *m pl* GEOMETRIE corresponding angles; ~ **d'Euler** *m pl* PHYSIQUE Euler angles; ~ **eulériens** *m pl* PHYSIQUE Euler angles; ~ **intérieurs** *m pl* GEOMETRIE interior angles; ~ **opposés** *m pl* GEOMETRIE vertical angles

angloir *m* METROLOGIE bevel square

anglomètre *m* METROLOGIE angle meter, angulometer

angstroem *m* METROLOGIE angstrom

angström *m* IMPRIM *lecture optique* angstrom

anguiller *m* NAUT limber hole

anguillule *f* AGRO ALIM eelworm

angulaire *adj* GEOMETRIE, MECANIQUE angular

anhydre *adj* AGRO ALIM anhydrous, CHIMIE anhydrous, unslaked, water-free, LESSIVES waterless, PAPIER, PETROLE anhydrous, TEXTILE water-free

anhydride *m* CHIMIE, LESSIVES, PAPIER anhydride; ~ **acétique** *m* AGRO ALIM acetic anhydride; ~ **arsénieux** *m* CERAM VER flaky arsenic, white arsenic; ~ **borique** *m* CERAM VER boric oxide; ~ **carbonique** *m* CONS MECA carbon dioxide; ~ **hypo-azoteux** *m* POLLUTION nitrous oxide; ~ **nitrique** *m* POLLUTION nitrogen pentoxide; ~ **sulfocarbonique** *m* CHIMIE carbon bisulfide (AmE), carbon bisulphide (BrE), carbon disulfide (AmE), carbon disulphide (BrE); ~ **sulfureux** *m* CHIMIE sulfur dioxide, sulfur dioxyde (AmE), sulphur dioxide (BrE), POLLUTION sulfur dioxide (AmE), sulphur dioxide (BrE); ~ **sulfurique** *m* CHIMIE sulfur trioxyde (AmE), sulphur trioxide (BrE), POLLUTION sulfur dioxide (AmE), sulphur dioxide (BrE), sulfuric anhydride (AmE), sulphuric anhydride (BrE)

anhydrisation *f* CHIMIE anhydration, dehydration, PAPIER anhydration

anhydrite f GAZ, PETR, PETROLE anhydrite; ~ **d'azote** f POLLUTION nitrogen pentoxide

anicolite f MINERAUX niccolite

anilide f CHIMIE anilide

aniline f CHIMIE phenylamine, PAPIER aniline

animation: ~ **assistée par ordinateur** f TV computer animation; ~ **avec image virtuelle** f CINEMAT aerial image animation; ~ **par cellulose** f CINEMAT peg animation; ~ **par ordinateur** f CINEMAT, ORDINAT computer animation; ~ **sur écran d'épingles** f CINEMAT pin screen animation; ~ **sur plusieurs plans** f CINEMAT multiplane animation

animer vt CINEMAT animate

anion m AGRO ALIM, CHARBON, CHIMIE, ELECTR particule chargée, ELECTROTEC, PHYS RAYON anion, PHYSIQUE anion, negative ion; ~ **dominant** m POLLUTION dominant anion; ~ **majeur** m POLLUTION dominant anion; ~ **principal** m POLLUTION dominant anion

anionique adj CHARBON, CHIMIE anionic

anionotropie f CHIMIE anionotropy

anisentropique adj THERMODYN anisentropic

anisidine f CHIMIE anisidine

anisien m GEOLOGIE stratigraphie Anisian

anisochrone adj INFORMAT, ORDINAT anisochronous

anisoélasticité f ESPACE mécanique anisoelasticity

anisoélastique adj ESPACE mécanique anisoelastic

anisol m AGRO ALIM anisole, CHIMIE anisole, methoxybenzene

anisotrope adj ASTRONOMIE, CRISTALL, MATERIAUX, OPTIQUE, PLAST CAOU, TELECOM anisotropic

anisotropie f CRISTALL, GEOLOGIE, MATERIAUX anisotropy; ~ **diamagnétique** f PHYS RAYON diamagnetic anisotropy; ~ **de la turbulence** f PHYS FLUID anisotropy of turbulence

ankérite f GEOLOGIE minéral ferroan dolomite, MINERAUX ankerite

annabergite f MINERAUX nickel bloom, nickel ocher (AmE), nickel ochre (BrE)

annaline f PAPIER annaline

annatto m AGRO ALIM annatto

anneau m CHIMIE ring, CONS MECA d'une chaîne link, pour cylindres de broyeur à cylindres shell, CONSTR d'une clef bow, GEOMETRIE annulus, INFORMAT, MECANIQUE ring, NAUT eyeplate, ORDINAT, RESSORTS, TEXTILE ring; ~ **agrandi** m RESSORTS enlarged loop; ~ **allemand** m RESSORTS full-twisted loop; ~ **d'amarrage au sol** m AERONAUT mooring ring; ~ **aminci** m RESSORTS tapered loop; ~ **anglais** m RESSORTS full-centered loop (AmE), full-centred loop (BrE); ~ **d'antiprotons de basse énergie** m (LEAR) PHYS PART low-energy antiproton ring (LEAR); ~ **d'arrêt de la cage à bille** m CONS MECA lock ring for ball bearings; ~ **d'autorisation d'écriture** m INFORMAT, ORDINAT write permit ring; ~ **d'azimut** m AERONAUT outer axis gimbal; ~ **de béton** m CONSTR concrete ring; ~ **de boue** m PETROLE mud ring; ~ **de broyeur** m GENIE CHIM grinding ring; ~ **de butée** m AUTO thrust washer; ~ **de calibrage** m RESSORTS gaging ring (AmE), gauging ring (BrE); ~ **de Cambridge** m ORDINAT Cambridge ring; ~ **de centrage magnétique** m ESPACE véhicules magnetic centering ring (AmE), magnetic centring ring (BrE); ~ **collecteur** m CONS MECA, ELECTROTEC collector ring; ~ **de cueillage** m CERAM VER ring; ~ **de cylindre** m PRODUCTION de broyeur à cylindres roll shell; ~ **dépoli** m PHOTO ground glass circle; ~ **à détacher** m CERAM VER cracking ring; ~ **de dilatation** m

PETROLE forage expansion ring; ~ **double** m RESSORTS double loop; ~ **d'écriture** m INFORMAT, ORDINAT write ring; ~ **élargi** m RESSORTS enlarged loop; ~ **élastique** m VEHICULES d'un moteur circlip; ~ **d'étanchéité** m AERONAUT d'une turbomachine shroud ring, AUTO, CONS MECA, PAPIER sealing ring; ~ **fermé** m RESSORTS closed loop; ~ **de garde** m ELECTR d'un champ électrique guard ring, ELECTROTEC channel stopper, guard ring, PHYSIQUE guard ring; ~ **de graissage** m PRODUCTION oil ring; ~ **de haubanage** m PETROLE du derrick guy ring; ~ **de hissage** m AERONAUT hoisting ring; ~ **intermédiaire** m CINEMAT adaptor ring; ~ **à jeton** m ORDINAT token ring; ~ **joint** m NUCLEAIRE joint ring; ~ **laminé sans soudure** m CONS MECA seamless rolled ring; ~ **de levage** m AERONAUT hoisting ring, CONS MECA lifting eyebolt, MECANIQUE eyebolt; ~ **de manoeuvre** m MINES spider and slips; ~ **ouvert** m RESSORTS opened loop; ~ **d'ouverture de boîte** m EMBALLAGE lever ring; ~ **passe-jarretières** m TELECOM jumper ring; ~ **postaccélérateur** m TV intensifier ring; ~ **de préhension** m EMBALLAGE pull ring; ~ **de puits** m EN RENOUV géothermie well casing; ~ **ramené au centre** m RESSORTS full-centered loop (AmE), full-centred loop (BrE); ~ **rapporté** m RESSORTS added loop; ~ **réciproque** m CONS MECA droop restraining ring; ~ **de relance** m CERAM VER flag build; ~ **relevé** m RESSORTS raised loop; ~ **de retenue** m PETROLE baffle ring, d'un forage, d'un puits casing clamp, VEHICULES d'un moteur circlip; ~ **de roue libre** m CONS MECA freewheel-driven head; ~ **de stockage des électrons** m PHYS PART electron storage ring; ~ **supérieur** m INSTRUMENT front ring; ~ **sur platine** m NAUT flush lifting ring; ~ **de synchronisation** m CONS MECA synchronizing cone; ~ **à tige** m CONS MECA pour levage eyebolt; ~ **torique** m VEHICULES lubrification O-ring; ~ **tournant** m PHYS FLUID rotating annulus; ~ **de vitesse** m REFRIG speed track

anneaux: ~ **de Newton** m pl CINEMAT, PHOTO, PHYSIQUE Newton's rings; ~ **de Saturne** m pl ASTRONOMIE Saturn's rings

année: ~ **anomalistique** f ASTRONOMIE anomalistic year; ~ **cosmique** f ASTRONOMIE cosmic year; ~ **dracontique** f ASTRONOMIE eclipse year; ~ **hydrologique** f HYDROLOGIE hydrologic year; ~ **martienne** f ASTRONOMIE Martian year; ~ **prévisionnelle** f PRODUCTION planned year; ~ **sidérale** f ASTRONOMIE, PHYSIQUE sidereal year; ~ **solaire** f ASTRONOMIE solar year; ~ **tropique** f ASTRONOMIE tropical year

année-lumière f ASTRONOMIE, PHYSIQUE light year

annexe f IMPRIM mise en page appendix, NAUT dinghy, tender

annihilation f PHYS PART, PHYSIQUE annihilation; ~ **électron-positron** f PHYS PART electron positron annihilation; ~ **de paires** f NUCLEAIRE pair annihilation

annonce f IMPRIM advertisement; ~ **pleine page** f IMPRIM full-page advertisement

annonciateur m ELECTROTEC annunciator

annotation f INFORMAT annotation; ~ **vocale** f TELECOM voice annotation

annuaire m TELECOM telephone directory; ~ **électronique** m TELECOM electronic directory; ~ **hydrologique** m HYDROLOGIE hydrologic yearbook; ~ **des marées** m NAUT, OCEANO tide table; ~ **téléphonique** m TELECOM telephone directory

annulaire[1] adj ASTRONOMIE annular, CONS MECA shaped,

ESPACE *véhicules* annular, GEOMETRIE annular, ring-shaped, MECANIQUE annular

annulaire² *m* PETROLE annulus, *d'un puits* annular space

annulation: **~ de la conduction** *f* ELECTROTEC turn-off

annuler¹ *vt* INFORMAT delete; **~ la conduction** *vt* ELECTROTEC turn off

annuler² *vi* PHYSIQUE vanish

anode *f* CHIMIE, ELECTR *pile*, ELECTROTEC, NAUT, PHYSIQUE, TV anode; **~ d'accélération** *f* ELECTROTEC accelerating anode; **~ accélératrice** *f* ELECTROTEC, PHYS RAYON accelerating anode, TV second anode; **~ cloisonnée** *f* ELECTROTEC vane-type anode; **~ de concentration** *f* ELECTROTEC focusing anode; **~ creuse** *f* ELECTR *électrode* hollow anode; **~ à disque perforé** *f* TV perforated disc anode (BrE), perforated disk anode (AmE); **~ en aluminium** *f* ELECTROTEC aluminium anode (BrE), aluminum anode (AmE); **~ en tantale** *f* ELECTROTEC tantalum anode; **~ en tantale frittée** *f* ELECTROTEC tantalum slug; **~ d'entretien** *f* ELECTROTEC excitation anode, holding anode; **~ finale** *f* TV final anode; **~ de focalisation** *f* ELECTROTEC focusing anode; **~ frittée** *f* ELECTROTEC sintered anode, slug; **~ massive** *f* ELECTROTEC heavy anode; **~ principale** *f* ELECTROTEC main anode; **~ rugueuse** *f* ELECTROTEC rough anode; **~ sacrificielle** *f* PETR, PETROLE sacrificial anode; **~ de shuntage** *f* ELECTROTEC bypass anode; **~ zéro** *f* ELECTROTEC zero anode

anodique *adj* ELECTR *pile* anodic

anodiser *vt* CHIMIE, NAUT anodize

anomalie *f* AGRO ALIM blemish, ASTRONOMIE *distance angulaire* anomaly, CONS MECA discrepancy, GEOLOGIE anomaly, INFORMAT, ORDINAT exception, PETR anomaly; **~ à l'air libre** *f* GEOLOGIE, GEOPHYS free air anomaly; **~ de Bouguer** *f* GEOLOGIE, GEOPHYS Bouguer anomaly; **~ climatique** *f* METEO climatic anomaly; **~ excentrique** *f* ASTRONOMIE, ESPACE eccentric anomaly; **~ gravimétrique** *f* GEOPHYS gravity anomaly; **~ de la gravité** *f* GEOPHYS gravity anomaly; **~ isotopique** *f* PHYSIQUE isotopic anomaly; **~ magnétique** *f* GEOLOGIE, GEOPHYS magnetic anomaly; **~ moyenne** *f* ASTRONOMIE, ESPACE mean anomaly; **~ de la pesanteur** *f* GEOPHYS gravity anomaly; **~ thermostérique** *f* OCEANO thermosteric anomaly; **~ vraie** *f* ASTRONOMIE, ESPACE *mécanique céleste* true anomaly

anomère *m* CHIMIE anomer

anorogénique *adj* GEOLOGIE *site géotectonique en dehors de l'orogène* anorogenic

anorthite *f* CERAM VER anorthite

anorthosite *f* PETR anorthosite

anse *f* CONSTR *d'un cadenas* bow, shackle, *d'une benne* lifting bow, HYDROLOGIE inlet, NAUT bight, cove, creek, inlet, loop, OCEANO cove, PRODUCTION bail, bull, bull handle, *d'une poche de fonderie* bottom die, bow, bow handle, *d'un panier, d'un seau* handle

ANSI *abrév* (*Institut américain de normalisation*) TELECOM ANSI (*American National Standards Institute*)

aspect *m* CONS MECA handspike

antécédent *m* MATH inverse image

antenne:¹ **à l'~** *adj* TV on air; **sur l'~** *adj* TV on air

antenne² *f* CH DE FER feeder line, ESPACE *communications* antenna, NAUT aerial, antenna, PHYSIQUE aerial, antenna, TELECOM, TV aerial, VEHICULES *accessoire* aerial, antenna, radio aerial, radio antenna; **~ acoustique** *f* TELECOM acoustic antenna; **~ adaptative** *f* TELECOM adaptive antenna; **~ à balayage** *f* TELECOM sweep antenna; **~ biconique** *f* TELECOM biconical antenna; **~ blindée** *f* TV screened aerial; **~ cadre** *f* TELECOM loop aerial, loop antenna; **~ Cassegrain** *f* ESPACE *communications* Cassegrain antenna, PHYSIQUE Cassegrain aerial; **~ à champ magnétique** *f* GEOPHYS magnetic field antenna; **~ cierge** *f* ESPACE *communications* dielectric antenna; **~ cigare** *f* ESPACE *communications* cigar antenna; **~ coaxiale** *f* TELECOM coaxial antenna; **~ collective** *f* TELECOM collective aerial, collective antenna, common aerial, TV community aerial, community antenna; **~ conformée** *f* ESPACE *communications* conformal antenna; **~ cornet** *f* ESPACE *communications* horn antenna; **~ déployable** *f* ESPACE *communications* deployable antenna; **~ dièdre** *f* TELECOM dihedral antenna; **~ diélectrique** *f* TELECOM dielectric antenna; **~ dipôle** *f* NAUT, TV dipole aerial; **~ de dipôle à demi-onde** *f* PHYS RAYON half-wave dipole aerial; **~ directionnelle** *f* TV directional aerial, directional antenna; **~ directive** *f* ESPACE *communications*, TELECOM directional antenna; **~ à disque** *f* TELECOM disk antenna (AmE); **~ à double réflecteur** *f* TELECOM double reflector antenna; **~ émettrice** *f* PHYSIQUE transmitting aerial antenna, TELECOM transmit antenna; **~ d'émission** *f* TV transmitting aerial, transmitting antenna; **~ à empreinte modelée** *f* ESPACE *communications* contoured beam antenna; **~ encastrée** *f* AERONAUT flush aerial, ESPACE flush mounted antenna, TELECOM flush antenna; **~ en hélice** *f* NAUT helical scanner, TELECOM helical antenna; **~ en réseau de doublet** *f* TELECOM dipole antenna; **~ en V** *f* TELECOM V-shaped antenna; **~ équidirective** *f* ESPACE *communications*, TELECOM omnidirectional antenna; **~ escamotable** *f* TV retractable aerial, retractable antenna; **~ à faisceau conformé** *f* ESPACE *communications* shaped beam antenna; **~ à faisceau étroit** *f* ESPACE *communications* spot beam antenna; **~ à faisceau modelé** *f* ESPACE *communications* shaped beam antenna; **~ à fente** *f* ESPACE *communications*, TELECOM slot antenna; **~ à fil** *f* TELECOM wire aerial; **~ fouet** *f* ESPACE whip antenna, NAUT whip aerial, whip antenna; **~ fouet quart d'onde** *f* TELECOM quarter wave whip antenna; **~ de guidage** *f* ESPACE *véhicules* guidance antenna; **~ à guide d'ondes** *f* TELECOM waveguide antenna; **~ hélice** *f* ESPACE *communications* helix antenna; **~ hélicoïdale** *f* TELECOM corkscrew antenna, helical antenna; **~ à hyperfréquences** *f* TELECOM microwave aerial, microwave antenna; **~ d'incidence** *f* AERONAUT incidence probe; **~ intérieure** *f* ELECTROTEC indoor antenna; **~ isotrope** *f* ESPACE *communications* isotropic antenna, omnidirectional antenna; **~ à large bande** *f* ESPACE wide band antenna, TV broadband aerial; **~ à lentille** *f* ESPACE *communications*, TELECOM lens antenna; **~ mortaise** *f* AERONAUT flush aerial; **~ multibande** *f* TELECOM multifrequency antenna, PHYSIQUE multiband antenna; **~ multifaisceau** *f* ESPACE *communications* multibeam antenna, PHYSIQUE, TELECOM multiple beam antenna; **~ noyée** *f* AERONAUT flush aerial; **~ à ondes gravitationnelles** *f* PHYS RAYON gravitational wave aerial; **~ à ondes progressives** *f* TELECOM, TV traveling-wave antenna, travelling-wave aerial; **~ orientable** *f* TELECOM rotatable antenna, steerable beam antenna; **~ à ouverture** *f* TELECOM aperture antenna; **~ parabolique** *f* ASTRONOMIE dish antenna, ESPACE *communications* dish antenna, parabolic antenna, paraboloidal antenna, TELECOM dish aerial, parabolic reflector antenna, TV dishpan, satellite dish; **~ parabolique à mailles** *f* ES-

PACE *communications* parabolic mesh antenna; ~ **parabolique réceptrice** *f* TV receiving dish aerial, receiving dish antenna; ~ **de pente** *f* AERONAUT glide aerial, glide antenna, glide slope antenna; ~ **périscopique** *f* PHYSIQUE periscope aerial antenna; ~ **à pinceau étroit** *f* ESPACE *communications* spot beam antenna; ~ **plane** *f* TELECOM flat antenna; ~ **plaquée** *f* TELECOM flush antenna; ~ **pliante** *f* ESPACE *communications* collapsible antenna; ~ **pour la réception communautaire** *f* TELECOM community aerial, community antenna; ~ **de poursuite** *f* ESPACE tracking antenna; ~ **radar** *f* NAUT radar scanner, TELECOM radar aerial, radar antenna, TRANSPORT radar antenna, radar scanner; ~ **radio** *f* TRANSPORT radio antenna; ~ **radioastronomique** *f* TELECOM radioastronomical antenna; ~ **radiogoniométrique** *f* TRANSPORT RDF antenna, aural null loop, direction finder antenna, radio direction finder antenna; ~ **à rayon longitudinal** *f* TELECOM endfire array antenna; ~ **à rayonnement longitudinal** *f* ESPACE *communications* endfire antenna, TELECOM endfire array antenna; ~ **à rayonnement transversal** *f* ESPACE *communications* broadside antenna, TELECOM broadside array antenna; ~ **réceptrice** *f* PHYSIQUE receiving aerial , TELECOM receive antenna, TV receiving aerial, receiving antenna; ~ **rectiligne** *f* TELECOM rectilinear antenna; ~ **à réflecteur** *f* ESPACE *communications* reflector antenna, TELECOM reflecting antenna; ~ **à réflecteur cylindrique** *f* TELECOM cylindrical reflecting antenna; ~ **à réflecteur en parapluie** *f* ESPACE *communications* umbrella reflector antenna; ~ **à réflecteur grégorien** *f* TELECOM Gregorian reflector antenna; ~ **à réflecteurs multiples** *f* TELECOM multiple-reflector antenna; ~ **réseau** *f* ESPACE, TELECOM array antenna; ~ **réseau à commande de phase** *f* ESPACE *communications* phased array antenna; ~ **rétrodirective** *f* ESPACE backfire antenna; ~ **à source décalée** *f* ESPACE *communications* offset antenna; ~ **sphérique** *f* TELECOM spherical antenna; ~ **spirale** *f* TELECOM spiral antenna; ~ **toroïdale** *f* TELECOM toroidal antenna; ~ **type ouverture rayonnante** *f* TELECOM aperture antenna; ~ **unipolaire** *f* TELECOM monopole antenna, unipole antenna; ~ **Yagi** *f* ESPACE, TELECOM Yagi antenna

anthracène *m* CHIMIE anthracene

anthracine *f* CHIMIE anthracene

anthracite *m* CHARBON anthracite, anthracite coal, hard coal, MINES stone coal

anthragallol *m* CHIMIE anthragallol

antiacide[1] *adj* MATERIAUX acid-proof

antiacide[2] *m* CHIMIE antacid

antiadhérent *adj* PAPIER nonstick

antialiassage *m* TV anti-aliasing

antiarc *adj* ELECTROTEC nonarcing

antibaryon *m* PHYS PART antibaryon

antibruit *adj* ACOUSTIQUE antinoise

antibuée *m* AERONAUT demister

anticapacitif *adj* ELECTR *charge* noncapacitive

anticatalyseur *m* AGRO ALIM anticatalyst

anticathode *f* ELECTR *tube à rayons X*, PHYSIQUE anticathode

antichlore *m* CHIMIE, PAPIER antichlor

antichoc *adj* CINEMAT shockproof

anticlinal[1] *adj* GAZ anticlinal

anticlinal[2] *m* GEOLOGIE, PETROLE *géologie* anticline; ~ **à coeur érodé** *m* GEOLOGIE breached anticline; ~ **de compensation** *m* GEOLOGIE *retournement des couches*

contre faille roll-over anticline; ~ **de croissance** *m* GEOLOGIE growth anticline

anticlinorium *m* GEOLOGIE anticlinorium

anticoïncidence *f* ELECTRON anticoincidence

anticorrosif *adj* MECANIQUE *matériaux* anticorrosive

anticorrosion[1] *adj* MATERIAUX corrosion-resistant

anticorrosion[2] *f* IMPRIM anticorrosive, PAPIER anticorrosion agent, anticorrosive, corrosion inhibitor

anticrénelage *m* ORDINAT anti-aliasing

anticyclogenèse *f* METEO anticyclogenesis

anticyclone *m* METEO anticyclone, high, high-pressure area, high-pressure zone; ~ **de blocage** *m* METEO blocking anticyclone; ~ **continental** *m* METEO continental anticyclone; ~ **permanent** *m* METEO permanent anticyclone; ~ **semi-permanent** *m* METEO semipermanent anticyclone; ~ **subtropical** *m* METEO subtropical anticyclone

anticyclonique *adj* METEO anticyclonic

antidéflagrant *adj* AERONAUT explosion-proof, fireproof, flameproof, ELECTR *sécurité* fireproof, flameproof, EMBALLAGE, MECANIQUE, MINES explosion-proof, SECURITE, THERMODYN fireproof, flameproof

antidépôt *adj* PLAST CAOU *additif* antisettling

antidérapant *adj* CHIMIE skidproof, NAUT nonslip

antidérapeur *m* VEHICULES *freinage* antiskid device

antidétonant *m* AUTO antiknock additive

antidote *m* CHIMIE, SECURITE antidote

antiéblouissement *adj* SECURITE antidazzle, glare-free

antiemballement *m* PRODUCTION *automatisme industriel* antireset wind-up

antienrayeur *m* VEHICULES *freinage* antiskid device

antienzyme *f* AGRO ALIM anti-enzyme

antifading *m* ELECTRON automatic gain control, ELECTROTEC automatic volume control

antiferromagnétique *adj* PHYSIQUE antiferromagnetic

antiferromagnétisme *m* ELECTR, PHYSIQUE antiferromagnetism

antifeu *adj* PLAST CAOU *peinture, plastiques* fire-retardant, THERMODYN protecting against fire

antifriction[1] *adj* CONS MECA, MECANIQUE antifriction

antifriction[2] *m* PAPIER antifriction

antigel *m* AERONAUT, AUTO antifreeze, REFRIG antifreeze agent, VEHICULES *refroidissement* antifreeze

antigène *m* CHIMIE antigen

antigivrage *m* ESPACE *véhicules* anti-icing

antigravité *adj* ESPACE anti-G, *mécanique céleste* antigravity

antigrippant *adj* MECANIQUE antiseize

antigrisouteux *adj* ELECTR *sécurité* fireproof, flameproof, MINES explosion-proof

antihalo *m* IMPRIM *photogravure, plaques* nonhalation

anti-inductif *adj* ELECTR *charge* noninductive

antilogarithme *m* MATH antilogarithm

antimaculateur: ~ **liquide** *m* IMPRIM liquid spray

antimaculeur *m* IMPRIM *impression* anti-offset spray; ~ **à poudre** *m* IMPRIM *impression* dusting unit

antimagnétique *adj* ELECTR nonmagnetic

antimatière *f* PHYS PART, PHYSIQUE antimatter

antimoine *m* (*Sb*) CHIMIE antimony, stibium

antimonial *adj* CHIMIE antimonial

antimoniate *m* CHIMIE antimoniate

antimonique *adj* CHIMIE antimonic

antimonite *m* CHIMIE antimonite

antimoniure *m* CHIMIE antimonide

antimoussant *m* PETROLE antifoam agent

antimousse¹ *adj* EMBALLAGE antifoam
antimousse² *m* AGRO ALIM defoaming agent, CHIMIE antifroth, GENIE CHIM foam breaker, PAPIER antifoam, antifroth, defoamer, foam inhibitor
antineutrino *m* PHYS PART antineutrino
antineutron *m* PHYSIQUE antineutron
antinoeud *m* ELECTR antinode
antioxydant *m* AGRO ALIM, IMPRIM antioxidant, PAPIER rust inhibitor, PLAST CAOU *ingrédient de mélange* antioxidant
antioxygène *m* PLAST CAOU *ingrédient de mélange* antioxidant
antiozone *adj* EMBALLAGE antioxidant
antiparallèle *adj* GEOMETRIE antiparallel
antiparasitage *m* ELECTROTEC spark suppression, suppression, ENREGISTR RF shielding, PRODUCTION *électricité* contact noise suppression, TELECOM interference suppression, TV RF shielding; ~ **à diode** *m* ELECTRON diode suppression; ~ **d'interface** *m* PRODUCTION *automatisme industriel* interface suppression
antiparasite¹ *adj* ELECTR *protection* anti-interference; ~ **de façon transitoire** *adj* PRODUCTION transient-suppressed
antiparasite² *m* ELECTRON suppressor, ELECTROTEC spark suppressor, suppressor, PRODUCTION suppressor, surge suppressor
antiparticule *f* PHYS PART, PHYSIQUE antiparticle
antiperthite *f* MINERAUX antiperthite
antiphase: en ~ *adj* TV antiphase
antipodes *m pl* GEOMETRIE antipodes
antiproton *m* PHYS PART, PHYSIQUE antiproton
antiquark *m* PHYS PART, PHYSIQUE antiquark
antirassissant *m* AGRO ALIM antistaling agent
antiréactivité *f* NUCLEAIRE deficit reactivity, negative reactivity
antiredéposition *f* LESSIVES antiredepositing
antireflet *m* CINEMAT antiglare, IMPRIM antiflare
antirepliement *m* TV anti-aliasing; ~ **du spectre** *m* ELECTRON anti-aliasing
antirésonance *f* ACOUSTIQUE antiresonance, ELECTRON antiresonance, parallel resonance
antiretour: ~ **de flamme** *m* AERONAUT, SECURITE flame trap
antiripage *m* ENREGISTR antiskating
antirouille¹ *adj* MECANIQUE *matériel* antirust
antirouille² *m* EMBALLAGE rust preventive, NAUT rust inhibitor
antistatique *adj* CINEMAT, ELECTR *matériel*, PHOTO antistatic
antitartrage *m* REFRIG scale inhibitor
antiusure *adj* REVETEMENT abrasion-proof
anti-UV *adj* CERAM VER *verre* UV-absorbing
antivol¹ *adj* EMBALLAGE, QUALITE antitheft, SECURITE antitheft, burglar-proof, thief-proof
antivol² *m* QUALITE loss prevention; ~ **coupe-contact** *m* AUTO antitheft ignition lock
Antlia *f* ASTRONOMIE Antlia
antozonite *f* MINERAUX antozonite
apatélite *f* MINERAUX apatelite
apatite *f* MINERAUX apatite
apériodique *adj* ELECTR *galvanomètre*, ELECTRON *circuit*, PHYSIQUE aperiodic
apesanteur *f* ESPACE weightlessness, zero gravity, zero-g, PHYSIQUE weightlessness
apex *m* ASTRONOMIE solar apex, CHARBON, ESPACE apex

aphanèse *f* MINERAUX aphanesite
aphanésite *f* MINERAUX aphanesite
aphanite *f* PETR aphanite
aphanitique *adj* GEOLOGIE *texture* aphanitic, aphyric
aphélie *m* ASTRONOMIE, ESPACE, PHYSIQUE aphelion
aphrite *f* MINERAUX aphrite
aphrizite *f* MINERAUX aphrizite
aphrodite *f* MINERAUX aphrodite
aphrosidérite *f* MINERAUX aphrosiderite
aphtalose *f* MINERAUX aphthalose, aphthitalite
aphthalose *f* MINERAUX aphthalose, aphthitalite
aphthitalite *f* MINERAUX aphthalose, aphthitalite
aphthonite *f* MINERAUX aphthonite
aphyrique *adj* GEOLOGIE aphyric
apiine *f* CHIMIE apiin
apionol *m* CHIMIE apionol
apjohnite *f* MINERAUX apjohnite
aplaneur *m* CONS MECA planisher
aplani *adj* CONSTR struck
aplanir *vt* PRODUCTION level
aplanissement *m* CONSTR leveling (AmE), levelling (BrE), GEOLOGIE flattening; ~ **des interfluves** *m* GEOLOGIE lateral planation
aplat *m* IMPRIM solid
à-plat *m* IMPRIM *photogravure* flat tint
aplati *adj* GEOMETRIE oblate
aplatissage *m* CERAM VER flattening
aplatissement *m* ASTRONOMIE oblateness, CONS MECA collapsing, VEHICULES *d'un pneu* flattening; ~ **de pavement** *m* CONSTR pavement surface evenness; ~ **de surface de pavé** *m* CONSTR pavement surface evenness
aplatisserie *f* PRODUCTION flatting mill, flatting works
aplatissoir *m* PRODUCTION flatter, flatting mill
aplite *f* PETR aplite, haplite
aplomb:¹ **d'** ~ *adj* CONSTR plumb
aplomb² *m* CONSTR plumb
aplome *m* MINERAUX aplome
apnée *f* OCEANO apnea (AmE), apnoea (BrE), breath-holding
apoastre *m* ASTRONOMIE, ESPACE apastron
apochromatique *adj* IMPRIM *optique* apochromatic
apogée *m* ASTRONOMIE, ESPACE *mécanique céleste*, PHYSIQUE apogee
apophyllite *f* MINERAUX apophyllite
apostilb *m* METROLOGIE apostilb
apostrophe *f* IMPRIM apostrophe
apothème *m* GEOMETRIE apothem
apotome *f* ACOUSTIQUE apotome
appairage *m* TV pairing
appairement: ~ **des formes** *m* PRODUCTION pattern matching
apparaux: ~ **d'amarrage** *m pl* NAUT mooring gear; ~ **auxiliaires** *m pl* NAUT auxiliary machinery; ~ **de charge** *m pl* NAUT cargo gear; ~ **de levage** *m pl* NAUT cargo gear; ~ **de mouillage** *m pl* NAUT ground tackle
appareil *m* CONS MECA apparatus, appliance, device, gear, instrument, tackle, CONSTR turnout, *de brique, de pierre* bond, ELECTROTEC instrument, EQUIP LAB apparatus, PHOTO, PHYSIQUE *photographique* camera, PRODUCTION appliance, device;
~ a ~ **d'ajustage** *m* CONS MECA fitting device; ~ **d'alimentation** *m* EMBALLAGE feeding device, MAT CHAUFF *d'un fourneau* mechanical stoker, PRODUCTION feed gear; ~ **analogique** *m* TELECOM analog device (AmE), analogue device (BrE); ~ **à annonce enregistrée** *m* TELECOM recorded announcement machine;

~ d'annonce de trains *m* CH DE FER train supervision; ~ antistatique *m* TEXTILE static eliminator; ~ d'arrêt et de mise en marche *m* CONS MECA stopping-and-starting gear; ~ d'arrosage *m* DISTRI EAU sprinkler, SECURITE fire sprinkler, sprinkler; ~ d'asservissement *m* PHYSIQUE servomechanism; ~ automatique *m* TELECOM automatic device;

~ b ~ de battage *m* MINES percussion rig; ~ à braser les scies à ruban *m* CONS MECA band-saw brazing apparatus;

~ c ~ à cadre mobile *m* ELECTROTEC moving coil meter; ~ à cellule couplée *m* PHOTO camera with coupled exposure meter; ~ de changement de marche *m* CONS MECA reversing gear; ~ de chargement distributeur *m* PRODUCTION stock distributor; ~ de chauffage *m* CHAUFFAGE heating appliance, THERMODYN heater; ~ de chauffage d'air *m* CONS MECA air heater, air preheater; ~ de chauffage non raccordé *m* CHAUFFAGE flueless heater; ~ chercheur de câble *m* ELECTR cable detector, cable locator; ~ de choc *m* CH DE FER buffing gear, MATERIAUX drop test machine; ~ de choc compensateur *m* CH DE FER compensating buffer; ~ à cintrer les rails *m* CH DE FER rail-bending device, rail-bending machine; ~ de commande *m* COMMANDE control device, regulator, ELECTR *réglage*, ELECTROTEC control gear; ~ à commutation vocale *m* TELECOM voice-switching equipment; ~ de concentration *m* MINES concentrator; ~ de connexion à semi-conducteur *m* ELECTR *commutateur* semiconductor switching device; ~ de contrôle *m* ELECTROTEC control gear, ENREGISTR monitor; ~ de contrôle de continuité *m* ELECTR continuity tester; ~ de contrôle d'état de surface *m* METROLOGIE surface geometry meter; ~ de contrôle de rupture de fil *m* ELECTR *sécurité* electric wire break alarm; ~ de correction auditive *m* ACOUSTIQUE hearing aid; ~ coupe-circuit *m* SECURITE *sécurité électrique* cutout device; ~ de court-circuit *m* ELECTR short-circuiting device; ~ Cowper *m* CERAM VER Cowper stove; ~ à cuire à faisceau tubulaire *m* GENIE CHIM calandria; ~ de cuisson *m* THERMODYN cooker;

~ d ~ Dean Stark *m* EQUIP LAB *teneur en eau* Dean and Stark apparatus; ~ à déboucher et à nettoyer les tuyaux *m* CONSTR drain testing and cleaning equipment; ~ à décanter *m* GENIE CHIM decanter; ~ à démagnétiser *m* PRODUCTION demagnetizing equipment; ~ de démarrage *m* CONS MECA starting gear; ~ détecteur de défaut de masse *m* PRODUCTION *électricité* earth sensing apparatus (BrE), ground sensing apparatus (AmE); ~ de détente *m* CONSTR pressure-reducing valve; ~ à deux cercles *m* NUCLEAIRE two-circle instrument; ~ à deux objectifs *m* PHOTO twin-lens reflex camera; ~ à diaphragme *m* GAZ diaphragm meter; ~ de diffusion *m* GENIE CHIM diffusion apparatus; ~ digestif *m* RECYCLAGE digestive system; ~ de distillation *m* EQUIP LAB *verrerie* distillation apparatus, GENIE CHIM distilling apparatus, still; ~ distillatoire *m* GENIE CHIM still; ~ à distiller *m* AGRO ALIM, GENIE CHIM still; ~ de distribution de vapeur *m* INST HYDR valve motion; ~ diviseur *m* CONS MECA dividing attachment, index centers (AmE), index centres (BrE), *pour fraiser entre pointes* dividing heads, PRODUCTION *pour écrous à 6 et 8 pans* dividing apparatus; ~ domestique *m* ELECTR domestic appliance (BrE), home appliance (BrE);

~ e ~ d'éclairage *m* ELECTROTEC light fitting, EQUIP LAB illuminating apparatus; ~ électrique *m* TEXTILE electrical appliance; ~ électrodynamique *m* ELECTR electrodynamic instrument; ~ électroménager *m* ELECTR electrical household appliance; ~ électronique *m* ELECTRON electronic instrument; ~ émetteur-récepteur *m* INFORMAT ASR, automatic send-receive; ~ en boutisses *m* CONSTR heading bond; ~ enregistreur *m* CONS MECA self-registering apparatus; ~ enregistreur de température *m* TEXTILE temperature recorder; ~ enregistreur de vitesse *m* TEXTILE speed recorder; ~ d'essai d'induit *m* ELECTR armature tester, growler; ~ étanche *m* PHOTO waterproof sealed camera; ~ à évaporer *m* GENIE CHIM evaporating apparatus, evaporator; ~ d'extraction sans câble *m* MINES ropeless hoisting apparatus;

~ f ~ de façonnage *m* INSTRUMENT *des verres de lunettes* edging machine; ~ de fond de puits *m* PETROLE bottom hole assembly; ~ de forage *m* PETROLE drilling rig, rig; ~ de forage géothermique *m* EN RENOUV geothermal drilling equipment; ~ de fractionnement *m* GENIE CHIM fractionating apparatus; ~ de fragmentation *m* GENIE CHIM crushing machine; ~ à fraiser les angles et les axes *m* CONS MECA cherrying attachment; ~ à fraiser circulairement *m* CONS MECA circular milling attachment; ~ à fraiser verticalement *m* CONS MECA vertical milling attachment; ~ frigorifique *m* CONS MECA refrigerating system, PRODUCTION freezing machine; ~ frigorifique à plaques *m* CONS MECA slab-freezing apparatus;

~ g ~ de gazage *m* TEXTILE singeing machine; ~ gazifère *m* PRODUCTION gas-making apparatus; ~ à gouverner *m* NAUT steering system;

~ h ~ d'hydrogénation *m* AGRO ALIM hydrogenator;

~ i ~ d'impression *m* IMPRIM print maker; ~ à imprimer *m* IMPRIM printing apparatus; ~ indicateur analogique *m* ELECTROTEC analog meter (AmE), analogue meter (BrE); ~ à induction *m* ELECTROTEC induction instrument;

~ k ~ de Kipp *m* CHIMIE, EQUIP LAB Kipp's apparatus;

~ l ~ de lavage *m* GENIE CHIM washer; ~ à lecture directe *m* ELECTR direct read-out instrument, direct reading instrument; ~ de levage *m* CONS MECA lifting apparatus, lifting gear, lifting tackle, NAUT lifting tackle, PRODUCTION hoist, hoisting tackle, tackle, SECURITE hoist, lifting appliance, lifting gear, lifting tackle; ~ de levage pneumatique *m* CONS MECA air hoist; ~ de limite de liquidité *m* CHARBON liquid limit device;

~ m ~ à mandriner les tubes *m* CONSTR tube expander; ~ de manutention de charbon *m* CHARBON coal-handling plant; ~ mécanique *m* CONS MECA instrument; ~ à mélanger *m* GENIE CHIM mixer; ~ ménager *m* ELECTR domestic appliance (BrE), home appliance (BrE); ~ ménager à gaz *m* MAT CHAUFF domestic gas appliance; ~ de mesure *m* CONSTR measuring apparatus, ELECTR instrument, measuring equipment, measuring instrument, METROLOGIE measuring instrument; ~ de mesure à affichage numérique *m* METROLOGIE digital readout measuring instrument; ~ de mesure analogique *m* METROLOGIE analog measuring instrument (AmE), analogue measuring instrument (BrE); ~ de mesure à calibres multiples *m* ELECTR multirange meter; ~ de mesure électrique *m* SECURITE electrical measuring apparatus; ~ de mesure de l'épair *m* PAPIER formation tester; ~ de mesure de fuite *m* ELECTR leakage meter; ~

de mesure du lissé *m* PAPIER smoothness tester; ~ **de mesure du niveau des audiofréquences** *m* ENREGISTR audio level meter; ~ **de mesure numérique** *m* ELECTR digital instrument, METROLOGIE digital readout measuring instrument; ~ **de mesure à pince** *m* ELECTR clip-on instrument, tong-test instrument; ~ **de mesure à plusieurs gammes** *m* ELECTR multirange meter; ~ **de mesure du point d'éclair** *m* EQUIP LAB *liquides inflammables* flash point apparatus; ~ **de mesure pour CA** *m* ELECTR AC meter; ~ **de mesure pour courant continu** *m* ELECTR DC meter; ~ **de mesure de puissance active** *m* ELECTR active power meter; ~ **de microscope automatique** *m* INSTRUMENT automatic microscope camera; ~ **de mise en marche** *m* CONS MECA starting gear; ~ **de mise au point** *m* COMMANDE regulating device; ~ **à mise au point fixe** *m* PHOTO fixed focus camera; ~ **de montage** *m* CONS MECA fitting device; ~ **à monture rentrante** *m* PHOTO camera with collapsible mount; ~ **muni de décentrement** *m* PHOTO camera with rising and swinging front;

~ n ~ **de navigation par satellites** *m (satnav)* NAUT satellite navigator *(satnav)*; ~ **de nettoyage aux ultrasons** *m* CINEMAT sonic cleaner;

~ o ~ **à ombroscopie** *m* CERAM VER shadowgraph; ~ **à optique interchangeable** *m* PHOTO camera with interchangeable lens;

~ p ~ **panoramique** *m* PHOTO panoramic camera ~ **à paraffiner** *m* CINEMAT *pour protection des copies* waxing machine; ~ **de photogrammétrie** *m* INSTRUMENT photogrammetric camera; ~ **photo grand format** *m* INSTRUMENT large format camera; ~ **photographique** *m* PHOTO camera, still camera; ~ **photographique de microformat** *m* PHOTO subminiature camera; ~ **photographique petit format** *m* PHOTO miniature camera; ~ **photographique à soufflet** *m* PHOTO bellows-type folding camera; ~ **à photomètre incorporé** *m* PHOTO camera with built-in exposure meter; ~ **photo de microscope** *m* INSTRUMENT microscope camera; ~ **photo petit format** *m* INSTRUMENT miniature camera; ~ **photo à rayons X** *m* PHYS RAYON X-ray camera; ~ **de pointage** *m* PRODUCTION time recorder; ~ **à point de goutte** *m* EQUIP LAB *graisses de lubrification* drop point apparatus; ~ **de polissage continu** *m* CERAM VER continuous polisher; ~ **portatif** *m* ELECTR portable appliance; ~ **pour chromatographie sur papier** *m* EQUIP LAB *analyse* paper chromatography apparatus; ~ **pour injection de produits de contraste** *m* INSTRUMENT contrast medium injector; ~ **pour mesurer l'épaisseur de films** *m* METROLOGIE coating thickness measurement apparatus; ~ **pour mesures de dureté** *m* METROLOGIE hardness tester; ~ **de préhension** *m* NUCLEAIRE gripper tool; ~ **à pression** *m* MECANIQUE pressure vessel; ~ **de prise d'échantillons en bout** *m* CHARBON tip sampler; ~ **de prises de vue cinématographique** *m* CINEMAT motion picture camera; ~ **de prise de vue** *m* PHOTO camera; ~ **de production d'eau pure à échange d'ions** *m* EQUIP LAB *analyse* ion exchange water purifier; ~ **programmable** *m* TELECOM programmable device; ~ **de projection** *m* CINEMAT projector; ~ **de projection d'analyse** *m* CINEMAT analytic projector; ~ **de projection à boucle sans fin** *m* CINEMAT continuous loop projector; ~ **de projection double bande** *m* CINEMAT double-band projector (AmE), double-headed projector (BrE); ~ **de projection à lampe au xénon** *m* CINEMAT xenon arc projector; ~ **de projection multiformat** *m* CINEMAT multigage

projector (AmE), multigauge projector (BrE); ~ **de projection pour étude de mouvement** *m* CINEMAT analyzing projector; ~ **de propulsion** *m* CONS MECA propelling gear; ~ **à pulvérisation d'eau** *m* DISTRI EAU pulverizer; ~ **de purification** *m* GENIE CHIM purifying apparatus;

~ r ~ **radiographique** *m* INSTRUMENT X-ray apparatus; ~ **ralentisseur de vitesse** *m* CONS MECA speed-checking appliance; ~ **de ramassage** *m* POLLU MER collection device; ~ **à rayons X** *m* INSTRUMENT X-ray apparatus; ~ **de récupération** *m* POLLU MER recovery device; ~ **de redistillation** *m* AGRO ALIM secondary still; ~ **de réenregistrement** *m* ENREGISTR rerecording machine; ~ **reflex à deux objectifs** *m* PHOTO twin-lens reflex; ~ **reflex mono-objectif** *m* PHOTO SLR, single-lens reflex camera; ~ **de réfrigération** *m* CONS MECA cooling equipment; ~ **de réglage** *m* COMMANDE regulating device; ~ **de réglage automatique** *m* PETROLE automatic control equipment; ~ **de réglage de débit de fluide** *m* REFRIG refrigerant metering device; ~ **de repérage acoustique** *m* ACOUSTIQUE sound locator; ~ **de reportage grand format** *m* PHOTO press camera; ~ **à reproduire** *m* CONS MECA copying unit; ~ **de respiration à oxygène** *m* SECURITE oxygen breathing apparatus; ~ **respiratoire** *m* CHARBON breathing apparatus, OCEANO breathing apparatus, respirator, PETROLE *sécurité du personnel*, SECURITE breathing apparatus; ~ **respiratoire avec alimentation d'air** *m* SECURITE supplied-air breathing apparatus; ~ **respiratoire à oxygène** *m* SECURITE oxygen breathing apparatus;

~ s ~ **de sauvetage** *m* CONSTR fire escape, NAUT life-saving apparatus, rescue apparatus, SECURITE life-saving apparatus; ~ **à sécher la vapeur** *m* INST HYDR steam dryer; ~ **de secours** *m* PRODUCTION stand-by; ~ **de serrage et de desserrage de robot** *m* CONS MECA robot gripping device; ~ **de sondage** *m* MINES drill rig, drilling rig; ~ **sous-marin** *m* PHOTO underwater camera; ~ **de stéréométrie** *m* INSTRUMENT stereometric camera; ~ **stéréoscopique** *m* PHOTO stereoscopic camera; ~ **de sûreté** *m* CONS MECA safety apparatus, MINES safety apparatus, safety appliance, SECURITE safety apparatus; ~ **de surveillance** *m* ELECTR monitor; ~ **de suspension à arc** *m* PRODUCTION bow hanger; ~ **de suspension à étrier** *m* CONS MECA stirrup hanger;

~ t ~ **de tamponnement** *m* CH DE FER buffing gear; ~ **à teindre sur ensouple** *m* TEXTILE beam dyeing machine; ~ **de télémesure** *m* ELECTR *mesure* telemeter; ~ **à télémètre couplé** *m* PHOTO camera with coupled rangefinder; ~ **téléphonique** *m* TELECOM telephone instrument; ~ **terminal** *m* INFORMAT, ORDINAT terminal device; ~ **de traction** *m* PLAST CAOU *essai* tensile tester; ~ **transistorisé** *m* ELECTR *composant* solid-state device; ~ **à trousser** *m* PRODUCTION rig, spindle and sweep;

~ v ~ **de vérification** *m* EMBALLAGE checking apparatus; ~ **à visée reflex** *m* PHOTO camera with mirror-reflex focusing; ~ **à visée reflex amovible** *m* PHOTO camera with detachable reflex viewfinder; ~ **de voie** *m* CH DE FER points and crossing, switch and crossing

appareillage *m* CONS MECA fittings, CONSTR *de briques, de pierres* bonding, PHOTO *d'un photographe* outfit; ~ **de commutation** *m* ELECTR *commutateur, interrupteur,* ELECTROTEC switchgear; ~ **de coupure** *m* ELECTR *com-*

mutateur, interrupteur switchgear; ~ **débrochable** *m* ELECTR *interrupteur* draw-out switchgear; ~ **électrique** *m* ELECTR *commutateur, interrupteur* switchgear; ~ **à haute tension** *m* ELECTR *interrupteur* high-voltage switch gear; ~ **de mesure** *m* CONSTR measuring apparatus; ~ **de moteurs** *m* CONS MECA engine fittings; ~ **de prélèvement** *m* ESSAIS sampling equipment; ~ **de protection contre l'électricité** *m* SECURITE electrical protection equipment; ~ **de radiodétection** *m* NAUT radar imager; ~ **de secours** *m* SECURITE emergency equipment

appareiller[1] *vt* CONSTR bond, *la pierre de taille* bed out, NAUT weigh

appareiller[2] *vi* NAUT get under way, set sail

appareilleur: ~ **à gaz** *m* PRODUCTION gas fitter

appareils *m pl* CONS MECA fittings, gear, PRODUCTION plant; ~ **d'autosauvetage à oxygène** *m pl* SECURITE oxygen self-rescue apparatus, oxygen self-rescuers; ~ **de dépoussiérage individuels** *m pl* SECURITE individual dust removal apparatus; ~ **de distribution du gaz** *m pl* PRODUCTION gas fittings; ~ **d'équilibrage sur site** *m pl* CONS MECA *essai de vibration* field balancing equipment; ~ **d'extraction** *m pl* PRODUCTION hoisting appliances, hoisting gear; ~ **de lavage** *m pl* PRODUCTION washing plant; ~ **de levage** *m pl* CONS MECA lifting machinery, PRODUCTION hoisting appliances, hoisting gear; ~ **de mesure du bruit et des vibrations** *m pl* SECURITE noise and vibration measuring equipment; ~ **de mesure et d'analyse pour aérosols et poussières** *m pl* SECURITE aerosol and dust measuring and analysis apparatus; ~ **pour la lutte contre le crime** *m pl* SECURITE crime prevention devices; ~ **pour la prévention des infractions** *m pl* SECURITE crime prevention devices; ~ **de protection respiratoire** *m pl* SECURITE respiratory protective equipment; ~ **de ventilation de garage** *m pl* SECURITE garage ventilating apparatus; ~ **de voie** *m pl* CH DE FER switch gears

apparence *f* MATERIAUX look; ~ **soignée** *f* TEXTILE finished appearance

apparente *f* IMPRIM bulk density

apparié *adj* CHIMIE paired

apparier *vt* PRODUCTION match

appartenance *f* INFORMAT, ORDINAT membership

appauvri *adj* NUCLEAIRE depleted

appauvrir *vt* NUCLEAIRE strip, *combustible* deplete

appauvrissement *m* CHIMIE, ELECTRON, GEOLOGIE depletion, METALL denudation

appel *m* CONS MECA intake, INFORMAT selection, ORDINAT call, polling, TELECOM call; ~ **d'air** *m* CONS MECA draft (AmE), draught (BrE), indraught (BrE), indraught of air (BrE), inlet; ~ **avec préavis** *m* TELECOM personal call; ~ **ayant abouti** *m* TELECOM successful call; ~ **carte de crédit** *m* TELECOM credit card call; ~ **commandant de bord** *m* AERONAUT captain call; ~ **de courant** *m* ELECTROTEC inrush current; ~ **de détresse** *m* AERONAUT distress call; ~ **à émettre** *m* ORDINAT *téléphone* polling; ~ **en attente** *m* TELECOM waiting call; ~ **en instance** *m* TELECOM CW, call waiting; ~ **en PCV** *m* TELECOM collect call (AmE), reverse charge call (BrE), transfer charge call; ~ **erroné** *m* TELECOM false call; ~ **à frais virés** *m* (Can) *(cf appel en PCV)* TELECOM collect call (AmE), reverse charge call (BrE), transfer charge call; ~ **global** *m* TELECOM global call; ~ **gratuit** *m* TELECOM freephone call (BrE), toll-free call (AmE); ~ **inefficace** *m* TELECOM ineffective call; ~ **intérieur** *m* TELECOM inland call; ~ **de klaxon** *m* COMMANDE blast

on the horn; ~ **local** *m* TELECOM local call; ~ **malveillant** *m* TELECOM malicious call; ~ **de note** *m* IMPRIM *composition* callout, footnote call-out; ~ **obscène** *m* TELECOM obscene call; ~ **par magnéto** *m* ELECTROTEC generator signaling (AmE), generator signalling (BrE); ~ **par nom** *m* ORDINAT call by name; ~ **par référence** *m* ORDINAT call by reference; ~ **par sonnerie** *m* ELECTROTEC ringing; ~ **par valeur** *m* ORDINAT call by value; ~ **de personnes** *m* TELECOM paging; ~ **à prix partagé** *m* TELECOM local charge rate call, local charge rate trunk call; ~ **de rendez-vous** *m* TELECOM reminder call; ~ **réservé** *m* TELECOM booked call; ~ **resté sans réponse** *m* TELECOM unanswered call; ~ **sans frais** *m* (Can) TELECOM freephone call (BrE), toll-free call (AmE); ~ **sans réponse** *m* TELECOM unanswered call; ~ **sélectif** *m* INFORMAT, ORDINAT polling; ~ **sélectif numérique** *m* TELECOM DSC, selective calling, digital selective calling; ~ **d'un sous-programme** *m* INFORMAT, ORDINAT subroutine call; ~ **du superviseur** *m* INFORMAT, ORDINAT SVC, supervisor call; ~ **à trois** *m* TELECOM three-way call; ~ **de trompe** *m* COMMANDE blast on the horn; ~ **d'urgence** *m* TELECOM emergency call

appeler *vt* INFORMAT, ORDINAT poll, TELECOM make a call to; ~ **la bulle d'air entre ses repères** *vt* CONSTR bring the air bubble to the centre of its run (BrE); ~ **en PCV** *vt* TELECOM make a collect call (AmE), make a reverse charge call to (BrE)

appels: ~ **de départ** *m pl* TELECOM outgoing calls; ~ **par seconde** *m pl* TELECOM CS, calls per second

appendice *m* IMPRIM *mise en page* appendix

appentis *m* CONSTR lean-to, shed

appertisation *f* AGRO ALIM canning

applicateur: ~ **de colle** *m* EMBALLAGE adhesive applicator

application *f* ELECTRON injection, inputting, MECANIQUE, ORDINAT application; ~ **d'antireflet** *f* REVETEMENT antireflective coating; ~ **asservie** *f* INFORMAT machine learning; ~ **automatique des freins** *f* COMMANDE automatic application of the brakes; ~ **d'une charge** *f* ELECTROTEC loading; ~ **des charges** *f* AERONAUT load application; ~ **à chaud** *f* CERAM VER prunt; ~ **de couche antireflet** *f* CERAM VER antireflecting treatment, blooming; ~ **en mode asservi** *f* INFORMAT, ORDINAT slave application; ~ **industrielle** *f* BREVETS exploitation in industry, industrial application

applications: ~ **particulières** *f pl* CONS MECA special requirements; ~ **possibles** *f pl* PRODUCTION application considerations; ~ **de surveillance** *f pl* INFORMAT watchdog applications

applique *f* CONSTR, ELECTROTEC bracket

appliquer *vt* CONSTR *du mortier* bed out, ELECTRON input, ELECTROTEC *une tension*, MECANIQUE apply, PHYSIQUE exert; ~ **une couche réfléchissante à** *vt* REVETEMENT metal-coat

appointage *m* CONSTR pointing

appointer *vt* CONSTR point

appointir *vt* CONSTR point

appointissage *m* CONSTR pointing

appontage *m* NAUT landing

appontement *m* NAUT wharf, TRANSPORT ferry landing stage

apponter *vi* NAUT land

apport *m* GEOLOGIE input, supply; ~ **allogène** *m* POLLUTION external input; ~ **atmosphérique** *m* POLLUTION atmospheric fallout; ~ **de chaleur** *m* REFRIG heat pickup; ~ **thermique** *m* THERMODYN heat input

apporter *vt* HYDROLOGIE drift

appréciation: ~ **réservée** *f* PRODUCTION conservative estimate

appréhender *vt* CONSTR *un projet* address

apprentissage *m* PRODUCTION apprenticeship; ~ **automatique** *m* INFORMAT, ORDINAT machine learning; ~ **d'une machine** *m* ORDINAT machine learning

apprêt *m* CHIMIE sizing agent, CONSTR primer, COULEURS size, sizing agent, sizing preparation, undercoat, PAPIER finish, PLAST CAOU *fibre de verre* size, PRODUCTION primer, REVETEMENT primer, size, TEXTILE finish; ~ **à l'air chaud** *m* REVETEMENT hot air finish; ~ **antifroisse** *m* REVETEMENT crease-resistant finish, wrinkle-resistant finish; ~ **antiglissant** *m* REVETEMENT slip-proof finish; ~ **antiglisse** *m* REVETEMENT slip-proof finish; ~ **antigonflant** *m* REVETEMENT swell-resistant finish; ~ **antimoissisure** *m* REVETEMENT mildewproofing; ~ **antiretrait** *m* REVETEMENT shrinkproof finish; ~ **antisalissant** *m* REVETEMENT soil-release finish; ~ **de brillant permanent** *m* REVETEMENT permanent sheen finish; ~ **complet** *m* REVETEMENT full finish; ~ **craquant** *m* REVETEMENT scroop finish; ~ **à l'eau** *m* PAPIER water finish, water finishing, water finishing, PRODUCTION water finish, REVETEMENT luster finish (AmE), lustre finish (BrE); ~ **éliminant le repassage** *m* REVETEMENT noniron finish; ~ **envers** *m* REVETEMENT back finish; ~ **hydrofuge** *m* TEXTILE water-repellent finish; ~ **d'infroissabilité** *m* TEXTILE crease-resist finish; ~ **par enduction** *m* REVETEMENT coating finish

apprêté *adj* AGRO ALIM cooked, dressed, prepared, TEXTILE *lin* crisp

approbation *f* QUALITE approval

approche *f* CINEMAT *d'un sujet* angle, ESPACE *véhicules* approach; ~ **courbe** *f* AERONAUT curved approach; ~ **directe** *f* AERONAUT straight-in approach; ~ **en ligne droite** *f* AERONAUT straight-in approach; ~ **en régime stabilisé** *f* AERONAUT steady approach; ~ **espace acceptable entre deux caractères** *f* IMPRIM *composition* escapement; ~ **finale** *f* AERONAUT final approach; ~ **de fin de papier** *f* INFORMAT, ORDINAT paper low; ~ **indirecte** *f* AERONAUT circling approach; ~ **initiale** *f* AERONAUT initial approach; ~ **aux instruments** *f* AERONAUT instrument approach; ~ **intermédiaire** *f* AERONAUT intermediate approach; ~ **interrompue** *f* AERONAUT discontinued approach; ~ **au radar** *f* AERONAUT, TRANSPORT radar approach; ~ **radioguidée** *f* TRANSPORT radio homing; ~ **rectiligne** *f* AERONAUT straight-in approach; ~ **stabilisée** *f* AERONAUT steady approach; ~ **sur radar de précision** *f* AERONAUT precision approach; ~ **visuelle** *f* AERONAUT visual approach

approcher: ~ **de** *vt* MINES approach

approches *f pl* IMPRIM *composition informatique* kern, *composition* letter spacing

approfondissement *m* MINES deepening; ~ **d'un puits** *m* MINES shaft deepening

approuver *vt* QUALITE, SECURITE approve

approvisionnement *m* DISTRI EAU individual water supply, supply, PRODUCTION procurement, supplying; ~ **des composants** *m* ESPACE *gestion* component procurement; ~ **en eau domestique** *m* DISTRI EAU domestic water supply; ~ **en eau public** *m* DISTRI EAU public water supply; ~ **en eaux rurales** *m* DISTRI EAU rural water supply; ~ **énergétique** *m* EN RENOUV energy supply

approvisionner *vt* NAUT provision; ~ **en charbon** *vt* CHARBON coal; ~ **en combustible** *vt* PRODUCTION stoke

approvisionneur: ~ **de la marine** *m* NAUT ship chandler

approximatif *adj* MATH approximate

approximation *f* MATH approximation; ~ **asymptomatique** *f* TELECOM asymptomatic approximation, asymptomatical approximation; ~ **linéaire** *f* TELECOM linear approximation; ~ **au millimètre près** *f* MATH approximation to the nearest millimeter (AmE), approximation to the nearest millimetre (BrE); ~ **quasi-chimique** *f* METALL quasi-chemical approximation; ~ **semi-classique** *f* NUCLEAIRE semiclassical approximation

approximations: ~ **successives** *f pl* INFORMAT, ORDINAT stepwise refinement

appui *m* CONSTR pole, sill, *d'une voûte* support; ~ **de fenêtre** *m* CONSTR windowsill; ~ **gravitationnel** *m* ESPACE *mécanique spatiale* swing-by; ~ **à pivot** *m* NUCLEAIRE king journal, pivot, trunnion; ~ **de porte** *m* CONSTR door sill; ~ **vertical** *m* CONS MECA prop

appui-tête *m* VEHICULES *de siège* headrest

appulse *m* ASTRONOMIE appulse

appuyer:[1] ~ **pour parler** *adj* TELECOM push-to-talk

appuyer[2] *vt* CONS MECA carry, hold up, support

après: ~ **rétrécissement** *adj* EMBALLAGE after-shrinkage; ~ **vieillissement** *adj* PLAST CAOU after ageing (BrE), after aging (AmE)

apside *f* ASTRONOMIE apse, apsis, *le plus éloigné* apoapsis

apte: ~ **à la mise en circulation** *adj* TRANSPORT roadworthy; ~ **à la trempe et au revenu** *adj* THERMODYN heat-treatable

aptien *m* GEOLOGIE *stratigraphie* Aptian

aptitude *f* MATERIAUX ability, QUALITE capability; ~ **au brasage** *f* CONS MECA brazeability; ~ **au broyage** *f* GENIE CHIM grindability; ~ **au bullage** *f* CERAM VER seeding potential; ~ **à la conservation** *f* REFRIG keeping quality; ~ **au décollage** *f* AERONAUT takeoff ability; ~ **à l'égouttage** *f* PAPIER drainability; ~ **à l'enlèvement** *f* CHARBON excavatability; ~ **à l'impression** *f* PAPIER printability; ~ **au raffinage** *f* PAPIER beatability, refining characteristics; ~ **au rebullage** *f* CERAM VER tendency to reboil; ~ **au vol** *f* AERONAUT airworthiness

apyre *adj* CHIMIE apyrous

aquaculteur *m* OCEANO aquaculturist

aquaculture *f* OCEANO aquaculture

aquanaute *m* OCEANO aquanaut

aquaplanage *m* AERONAUT, AUTO aquaplaning

aquatique *adj* HYDROLOGIE aquatic, MATERIAUX *qui contient beaucoup d'eau* watery

aqueduc *m* CONSTR, DISTRI EAU, EN RENOUV, HYDROLOGIE aqueduct

aqueux *adj* CHIMIE *solution, mélange* hydrous, DISTRI EAU aqueous, MATERIAUX aqueous, watery, PAPIER, PETROLE, PHYS FLUID aqueous

aquiclude *f* DISTRI EAU aquiclude

aquiculture *f* DISTRI EAU aquiculture, OCEANO aquaculture

aquifère[1] *adj* DISTRI EAU aquiferous, HYDROLOGIE aquiferous, water-bearing, MATERIAUX water-bearing

aquifère[2] *m* HYDROLOGIE aquafer, aquifer; ~ **captif** *m* DISTRI EAU confined aquifer; ~ **karstique** *m* HYDROLOGIE karstic aquifer; ~ **multicouche** *m* HYDROLOGIE multilayer aquifer

aquifuge *m* DISTRI EAU aquifuge

aquitard *m* DISTRI EAU aquitard

Ar *(argon)* CHIMIE Ar *(argon)*

AR *abrév* CONS MECA *(arrière)* head-end, INFORMAT *(accusé de réception)*, ORDINAT *(accusé de réception)*, TELECOM *(accusé de réception)* ACK *(acknowledgement)*

arabinose *m* CHIMIE arabinose, pectinose

arabitol *m* CHIMIE arabitol

arachique *adj* CHIMIE *acide* arachic

aragonite *f* MINERAUX, PETR aragonite

araignée *f* CINEMAT crawfoot, crowfoot, spider, spreader, PETR spider; **~ de changement de pas** *f* AERONAUT pitch change spider

aramide *m* PLAST CAOU *type de polymère* aramid

arasement *m* CONSTR grading, *des têtes de pieux* cutting-off

araser *vt* CONS MECA machine-flush, CONSTR grade, PRODUCTION strike

arbalétrier *m* CONSTR principal, principal rafter

arbitre: ~ de bus *m* TELECOM bus arbitrator

arborer *vt* NAUT *le mât* step; **~ le pavillon** *vt* NAUT hoist the colors (AmE), hoist the colours (BrE)

arborescence *f* IMPRIM *dessinée par le carbone* treeing, INFORMAT, ORDINAT tree, tree structure

arbre *m* CONS MECA arbor, mandrel, mandril, shaft, spindle, *de la poupée mobile* dead spindle, CONSTR post, *d'une grue* jib post, IMPRIM *mécanique* spindle, INFORMAT tree, MECANIQUE shaft, MINES *d'une molette* gudgeon, NAUT shaft, ORDINAT tree, VEHICULES *moteur, transmission* shaft; **~ d'allumeur** *m* AUTO, VEHICULES *allumage* distributor shaft; **~ d'articulation** *m* CONS MECA hinge shaft; **~ d'attaque** *m* CONS MECA driving shaft, VEHICULES *arbre de transmission* drive pinion shaft; **~ binaire** *m* ORDINAT binary tree; **~ de boîte de vitesses** *m* VEHICULES drive shaft (AmE); propeller shaft (BrE); **~ bridé** *m* CONS MECA flanged shaft; **~ à cames** *m* AUTO camshaft, CONS MECA camshaft, tumbling shaft, wiper shaft, MECANIQUE, NAUT, VEHICULES *moteur* camshaft; **~ à cames en tête** *m* AUTO, MECANIQUE, VEHICULES *moteur* OHC, overhead camshaft; **~ à cames en tête à attaque directe** *m* AUTO direct acting overhead camshaft; **~ à cames en tête à attaque indirecte** *m* AUTO indirect overhead camshaft; **~ à cames préfabriqué** *m* CONS MECA camshaft; **~ cardan** *m* MECANIQUE cardan shaft; **~ à cardan longitudinal** *m* AUTO cardan shaft; **~ de changement de marche** *m* CONS MECA lifting shaft, reversing shaft, tumbling shaft; **~ à collerette** *m* CONS MECA flanged shaft; **~ de commande** *m* AUTO drive shaft (AmE), propeller shaft (BrE), CONS MECA driving shaft; **~ de commande de la pompe à huile** *m* AUTO oil pump spindle; **~ de couche** *m* CONS MECA driving shaft; **~ coudé** *m* CONS MECA crankshaft; **~ creux** *m* CONS MECA hollow shaft; **~ creux cylindrique** *m* CONS MECA *torsion* hollow circular shaft; **~ de décision** *m* INFORMAT decision tree; **~ de décomposition** *m* PRODUCTION product tree; **~ de défaillance** *m* COMMANDE fault tree; **~ de défaut** *m* COMMANDE fault tree; **~ à deux manivelles** *m* CONS MECA two-throw crank shaft; **~ de Diane** *m* CHIMIE arbor; **~ de différentiel** *m* AUTO rear axle shaft; **~ de direction** *m* AUTO steering shaft; **~ d'échauffement** *m* THERMODYN overheating; **~ d'embrayage** *m* AUTO clutch shaft; **~ d'entraînement** *m* CONS MECA drive shaft (AmE); **~ d'entrée** *m* CONS MECA input shaft; **~ d'entrée de boîte d'engrenages** *m* CONS MECA gearbox input shaft; **~ d'essieu** *m* VEHICULES *trans-mission* halfshaft; **~ de l'essieu arrière** *m* VEHICULES *transmission* rear axle drive shaft; **~ à excentrique** *m* CONS MECA eccentric shaft; **~ flexible** *m* CONS MECA flexible shaft; **~ flottant** *m* AUTO full-floating axle, CONS MECA floating shaft, free shaft, floating spindle; **~ de frein** *m* VEHICULES *système de freinage* brake shaft; **~ d'hélice** *m* NAUT propeller shaft; **~ d'induit** *m* ELECTR *d'un générateur* rotor shaft; **~ d'information d'annuaire** *m* TELECOM DIT, directory information tree; **~ intermédiaire** *m* AUTO countershaft, CONS MECA countershaft, lay shaft; **~ de ligne** *m* CONS MECA line, line shaft; **~ mandrin** *m* CONS MECA live spindle; **~ à manivelle** *m* CONS MECA crankshaft; **~ de marche arrière** *m* AUTO, VEHICULES *de la boîte de vitesses* reverse idler shaft; **~ menant** *m* CONS MECA driving shaft; **~ de montage pour fraises** *m* CONS MECA cutter adaptor; **~ de montage pour mandrin** *m* CONS MECA chuck adaptor; **~ moteur** *m* CONS MECA driving shaft, *machine-outil* motor shaft, NAUT driving shaft; **~ à mouvement planétaire** *m* CONS MECA planet spindle, planet-action spindle; **~ de Noël** *m* PETR Christmas tree; **~ de nomenclature** *m* PRODUCTION *production* product tree; **~ non-ordonné** *m* ORDINAT unordered tree; **~ non-porteur** *m* AUTO full-floating axle; **~ ordonné** *m* INFORMAT, ORDINAT ordered tree; **~ de pignon conique d'attaque** *m* AERONAUT input bevel pinion shaft; **~ de poignon** *m* CONS MECA gear shaft; **~ de pont** *m* VEHICULES *transmission* halfshaft; **~ du pont arrière** *m* VEHICULES *transmission* rear axle drive shaft; **~ porte-enduit** *m* ELECTR *d'une machine* armature shaft; **~ porte-foret** *m* CONS MECA drilling spindle; **~ porte-foret équilibré** *m* CONS MECA counterbalanced drilling spindle; **~ porte-fraise** *m* CONS MECA milling machine arbor, PRODUCTION milling machine arbor, milling machine cutter arbor; **~ porte-galet** *m* AERONAUT main shaft, AUTO roller shaft; **~ porte-hélice** *m* AERONAUT propeller shaft; **~ porte-meule** *m* CONS MECA grinding spindle, wheel spindle, PRODUCTION emery wheel spindle; **~ porte-scie** *m* CONS MECA saw arbor (AmE), saw arbour (BrE); **~ port-hélice** *m* NAUT propeller shaft; **~ de la poupée fixe** *m* CONS MECA *d'un tour* live spindle; **~ de la poupée mobile** *m* CONS MECA *d'un tour* dead spindle, tailspindle; **~ primaire** *m* AERONAUT *mécanique* main shaft, AUTO primary shaft, VEHICULES *de l'embrayage* clutch shaft, input shaft, *de la boîte de vitesses* drive shaft (AmE); **~ principal** *m* AERONAUT, AUTO, CONS MECA, MECANIQUE, VEHICULES *boîte de vitesses* main shaft; **~ de recherche** *m* INFORMAT, ORDINAT search tree; **~ de relais** *m* AERONAUT connecting rod, connecting shaft; **~ de relevage** *m* CONS MECA lifting shaft, reversing shaft, tumbling shaft, PRODUCTION *d'un bocard* jackshaft; **~ de renvoi** *m* CONS MECA countershaft, jackshaft; **~ de repérage** *m* CONS MECA locating arbor; **~ de rotor** *m* AERONAUT main rotor shaft; **~ de roue** *m* AUTO rear axle shaft, VEHICULES *transmission* axle shaft; **~ de Saturne** *m* CHIMIE lead tree; **~ secondaire** *m* AUTO third-motion shaft, CONS MECA countershaft, lay shaft, intermediate shaft, jackshaft, second motion shaft, VEHICULES *de la boîte de vitesses* output shaft; **~ semi-flottant** *m* VEHICULES *essieu arrière* semi-floating axle; **~ semi-porteur** *m* AUTO semi-floating axle; **~ de sortie** *m* AUTO output shaft; **~ du tambour** *m* CONS MECA drum shaft; **~ de tiroir** *m* INST HYDR stem; **~ de transmission** *m* CONS MECA shaft, transmission shaft, VEHICULES drive shaft (AmE), propeller shaft (BrE); **~ de transmission hori-**

zontal *m* CONS MECA lying shaft; ~ **de transmission principale** *m* AERONAUT main drive shaft; ~ **de transmission à relais** *m* AUTO two-piece drive shaft, two-piece propeller shaft; ~ **de transmission verticale** *m* CONS MECA upright shaft; ~ **à trois manivelles** *m* CONS MECA three-throw crank shaft; ~ **à trousser** *m* PRODUCTION spindle; ~ **vertical de douci** *m* CERAM VER grinder spindle; ~ **à vilebrequin** *m* CONS MECA crankshaft

arbre-manivelle *m* CONS MECA, MECANIQUE crankshaft

arbres *m pl* CONS MECA shafting; ~ **à came** *m pl* METROLOGIE *instruments de mesure* cam measuring equipment; ~ **cylindriques** *m pl* CONS MECA *torsion* circular shafts; ~ **de transmission en acier comprimé** *m pl* CONS MECA compressed steel shafting; ~ **de transmissions** *m pl* CONS MECA shafting

arc: [1] **en ~** *adj* CONSTR arched

arc [2] *m* CINEMAT arc, CONSTR arch, ELECTR *décharge*, ELECTROTEC, GEOMETRIE *de cercle* arc, PRODUCTION *électricité* arcing; ~ **aplati** *m* CONSTR four-centered arch (AmE), four-centred arch (BrE); ~ **bombé** *m* CONSTR segmental arch; ~ **de cercle** *m* GEOMETRIE circular arc; ~ **à charbon** *m* ELECTR, ELECTROTEC carbon arc; ~ **dans le vide** *m* ELECTROTEC vacuum arc; ~ **de décharge** *m* CONSTR arch of discharge, discharging arch, safety arch; ~ **de développante** *m* GEOMETRIE involute arc; ~ **électrique** *m* ELECTR *éclairage*, ELECTROTEC, GAZ, PHYSIQUE electric arc; ~ **elliptique** *m* CONSTR elliptical arch; ~ **en air libre** *m* ELECTROTEC open arc; ~ **en anse de panier** *m* CONSTR basket handle arch; ~ **en briques** *m* CONSTR *d'un fourneau, d'une boîte à feu* brick arch; ~ **en chaînette** *m* GEOMETRIE catenary; ~ **en courant alternatif** *m* ELECTR alternating current arc; ~ **en décharge** *m* CONSTR arch of discharge, discharging arch, safety arch; ~ **en fer à cheval** *m* CONSTR horseshoe arch; ~ **d'engrènement** *m* CONS MECA pitch arc; ~ **en segment de cercle** *m* CONSTR segmental arch; ~ **exhaussé** *m* CONSTR stilted arch; ~ **de flammes** *m* ELECTROTEC flame arc; ~ **à haute intensité** *m* ELECTR high-intensity electric arc; ~ **insulaire** *m* GEOLOGIE, OCEANO island arc; ~ **majeur** *m* GEOMETRIE *d'un cercle* major arc; ~ **au mercure** *m* ELECTROTEC mercury arc; ~ **mineur** *m* GEOMETRIE *d'un cercle* minor arc; ~ **outrepassé** *m* CONSTR horseshoe arch; ~ **plein cintre** *m* CONSTR Roman arch, round arch, semicircular arch, semicircular arch; ~ **de prise** *m* CONS MECA pitch arc; ~ **à quatre centres** *m* CONSTR four-centered arch (AmE), four-centred arch (BrE); ~ **rampant** *m* CONSTR rising arch; ~ **renversé** *m* CONSTR inflected arch, inverted arch; ~ **romain** *m* CONSTR Roman arch, round arch, semicircular arch; ~ **de rupture** *m* ELECTROTEC breaking arc; ~ **surbaissé** *m* CONSTR diminished arch, scheme arch, segmental arch, skene arch; ~ **surhaussé** *m* CONSTR stilted arch; ~ **de suspension** *m* PRODUCTION bow hanger; ~ **triangulaire** *m* CONSTR triangular arch; ~ **à trois centres** *m* CONSTR three-centered arch (AmE), three-centred arch (BrE); ~ **tubulaire au carbone** *m* NUCLEAIRE tubular carbon arc

arcade *f* CERAM VER arch, pillar arch, CONSTR arcade

arcanite *f* MINERAUX arcanite

arc-boutant *m* CONSTR brace, flying buttress, raker, raking shore, spur, strut

arc-boutement *m* CONS MECA interference; ~ **en voûte** *m* MINES arching

arc-bouter *vt* CONSTR buttress

arceau *m* CONSTR arch; ~ **de sécurité** *m* TRANSPORT

camions crushproof safety bonnet (BrE), crushproof safety hood (AmE), safety bonnet (BrE), safety hood (AmE), VEHICULES *carrosserie* roll bar, roll-over bar; ~ **support de réacteur** *m* AERONAUT engine support arch

arche *f* CERAM VER tunnel lehr, CONSTR arch; ~ **biaise** *f* CONSTR oblique arch; ~ **bombée** *f* CONSTR segmental arch; ~ **à convection forcée** *f* CERAM VER forced convection lehr; ~ **de décharge pour les hautes eaux** *f* DISTRI EAU flood arch; ~ **à décorer** *f* CERAM VER decorating lehr; ~ **elliptique** *f* CONSTR elliptical arch; ~ **en anse de panier** *f* CONSTR basket handle arch; ~ **en segment de cercle** *f* CONSTR segmental arch; ~ **exhaussée** *f* CONSTR stilted arch; ~ **mouflée** *f* CERAM VER muffle lehr; ~ **plein cintre** *f* CONSTR round arch, semicircular arch; ~ **de pont ferroviaire** *f* CONSTR railroad arch (AmE), railway arch (BrE); ~ **à pots** *f* CERAM VER pot arch; ~ **à recyclage** *f* CERAM VER continuous recirculation lehr; ~ **surbaissée** *f* CONSTR diminished arch, segmental arch; ~ **surélevée** *f* CONSTR stilted arch; ~ **surhaussée** *f* CONSTR stilted arch; ~ **à tapis** *f* CERAM VER conveyor belt lehr; ~ **à tirer** *f* CERAM VER pan lehr

archéen *m* GEOLOGIE Archaean, Archean

archet *m* CH DE FER *véhicules*, CONS MECA bow

archipel *m* NAUT, OCEANO archipelago

architecte: ~ **naval** *m* NAUT marine architect, naval architect, ship designer

architecture *f* ORDINAT architecture; ~ **à coeur réparti spécialisé** *f* TELECOM function division system architecture; ~ **distribuée** *f* ORDINAT distributed architecture; ~ **en tranches** *f* INFORMAT, ORDINAT slice architecture; ~ **navale** *f* NAUT naval architecture; ~ **orientée objet** *f* INFORMAT, ORDINAT object-oriented architecture; ~ **de pile** *f* INFORMAT, ORDINAT stack architecture; ~ **répartie** *f* INFORMAT, ORDINAT distributed architecture; ~ **de réseau** *f* ELECTR system configuration, INFORMAT, ORDINAT network architecture; ~ **de réseau informatique** *f* ORDINAT computer network architecture; ~ **de réseau informatisé** *f* INFORMAT computer network architecture; ~ **de systèmes ouverts** *f* TELECOM OSA, open systems architecture; ~ **systolique** *f* TELECOM systolic architecture; ~ **unifiée de réseau** *f* INFORMAT, ORDINAT SNA, systems network architecture

archivage *m* IMPRIM storage, INFORMAT archiving, filing, ORDINAT filing; ~ **électronique** *m* INFORMAT electronic filing, ORDINAT electronic filing; ~ **des messages** *m* TELECOM message storing; ~ **optique** *m* OPTIQUE optic storage, optical storage

archive *f* INFORMAT archive

archivé *adj* TELECOM put on file

archiver *vt* INFORMAT archive

archives *f pl* ORDINAT repository; ~ **cinématographiques** *f pl* CINEMAT stock shot library; ~ **photographiques** *f pl* PHOTO picture library

arcs: ~ **intersectés** *m pl* GEOMETRIE intersecting arcs

ardennite *f* MINERAUX ardennite

ardent *adj* NAUT hard on the helm, THERMODYN blazing, burning

ardoise *f* CINEMAT, CONSTR, GEOLOGIE slate

ardoiserie *f* MINES slate industry

ardoisière *f* MINES slate quarry

ardu *adj* CONSTR uphill

are *m* METROLOGIE are

arécaïne *f* CHIMIE arecaine

aréique *adj* DISTRI EAU arheic

arénacé *adj* EN RENOUV *roches* arenaceous, GEOLOGIE sandy

arendalite *f* MINERAUX arendalite

arène *f* PETR sand

aréner *vi* MINES sink

arénite: ~ **quartzique** *f* GEOLOGIE quartzarenite

aréomètre *m* AGRO ALIM *d'un accumulateur*, ELECTR *d'accumulateur* hydrometer, HYDROLOGIE hydromètre, PETROLE *hydromètre*, PHYSIQUE *hydromètre* araeometer, areometer, VEHICULES *d'accumulateur* hydrometer

aréométrie *f* HYDROLOGIE, PHYSIQUE araeometry, areometry

arête *f* CERAM VER sharp edge, CONS MECA *d'un tiroir, d'une lumière de cylindre* edge, CONSTR groin, ridge, hip, CRISTALL, GEOMETRIE *d'un cube*, MECANIQUE, PHYSIQUE edge; ~ **centrale** *f* EN RENOUV *turbines* central splitter edge, METALL midrib; ~ **de coupe** *f* MECANIQUE *outillage* cutting edge; ~ **de dérive** *f* AERONAUT fin leading edge; ~ **dorsale fuselage** *f* AERONAUT fuselage dorsal fin; ~ **rapportée** *f* CONS MECA *outils* built-up edge; ~ **de sortie** *f* NUCLEAIRE outlet edge; ~ **tranchante** *f* CONS MECA, CONSTR *d'un outil*, TEXTILE cutting edge

arêtier *m* CONS MECA ledge, CONSTR angle rafter, hip, hip rafter

arêtière *f* CONSTR hip tile

arfvedsonite *f* MINERAUX arfvedsonite

argent *m* (*Ag*) CHIMIE silver (*Ag*); ~ **brillant** *m* CERAM VER bright silver; ~ **à polir** *m* CERAM VER burnishing silver; ~ **sterling** *m* MATERIAUX sterling silver; ~ **telluré** *m* MINERAUX hessite

argentage *m* PRODUCTION silver plating, silvering

argenter: ~ **par galvanoplastie** *vt* ELECTROTEC electrosilver

argentifère *adj* MINERAUX argentiferous

argentique *adj* CHIMIE argentic

argentite *f* CHIMIE argentite, silver glance, MINERAUX argentite, argyrite

argentopyrite *f* MINERAUX argentopyrite

argenture *f* ACOUSTIQUE, CERAM VER silvering, MATERIAUX silver coating, PRODUCTION silver plating, silvering; ~ **en bandes** *f* CERAM VER striped silvering; ~ **galvanique** *f* ELECTROTEC electrosilvering

argile *f* CERAM VER clay, potter's earth, CHARBON, CHIMIE, CONSTR, GAZ, GEOLOGIE, PETROLE clay; ~ **alluviale glaciaire** *f* CHARBON glacial clay; ~ **alluviale postglaciaire** *f* CHARBON postglacial clay; ~ **bleue** *f* CERAM VER blue clay; ~ **à blocaux** *f* CHARBON, GEOLOGIE *sédiment glaciaire* boulder clay; ~ **à briques** *f* CONSTR brick clay; ~ **collante** *f* PETROLE sticky clay; ~ **cuite** *f* CERAM VER burnt clay, fired clay; ~ **en poudre** *f* CERAM VER clay dust, clay powder; ~ **à faible rendement** *f* PETR low-yield clay; ~ **fluante** *f* PETROLE *forage* gumbo; ~ **fluide** *f* CHARBON quick clay; ~ **fusible** *f* CERAM VER fusible clay; ~ **du gault** *f* CONSTR Gault clay; ~ **gonflante** *f* PETR, PETROLE swelling clay; ~ **grasse** *f* CERAM VER fatty clay, highly-plastic clay, rich clay, PETROLE *géologie* fat clay; ~ **gypsifère** *f* GEOLOGIE gypsiferous shale; ~ **maigre** *f* CERAM VER lean-plasticity clay, low-plasticity clay, meager clay (AmE), meagre clay (BrE); ~ **malaxée** *f* MINES pug; ~ **marneuse** *f* DISTRI EAU marly clay; ~ **à modeler** *f* PRODUCTION modeling clay (AmE), modelling clay (BrE); ~ **morainique** *f* CHARBON till; ~ **mouvante** *f* PETR sloughing shale; ~ **ocreuse** *f* CERAM VER ochery clay (AmE),

ochry clay (BrE); ~ **de pipe** *f* CONSTR pipe clay; ~ **plastique** *f* CERAM VER pipe clay, GEOLOGIE ball clay, plastic clay, PETROLE ball clay; ~ **à pot** *f* CERAM VER pot clay; ~ **à poterie** *f* CONSTR argil, pottery clay; ~ **de potier** *f* CONSTR argil, pottery clay; ~ **réfractaire** *f* CERAM VER, GEOLOGIE, THERMODYN fireclay; ~ **rouge** *f* PETR red clay; ~ **sableuse** *f* CONSTR, GEOLOGIE sandy clay; ~ **salifère** *f* CERAM VER saliferous clay; ~ **schisteuse** *f* CERAM VER schistous clay, shale; ~ **à sidérose** *f* GEOLOGIE sideritic mudstone; ~ **à silex** *f* GEOLOGIE clay-with-flints; ~ **smectique** *f* CHIMIE smectite; ~ **smectique décolorante** *f* LESSIVES bleaching earth; ~ **à tuiles** *f* GEOLOGIE tile clay

argiles: ~ **de delta** *f pl* GEOLOGIE prodelta clays

argileux *adj* EN RENOUV *roches* argillaceous, GEOLOGIE shaly

argilite *f* GEOLOGIE claystone, mudstone, PETR argillite, shale

argilocinèse *f* GEOLOGIE clay flowage, PETROLE shale diapirism

arginase *f* CHIMIE arginase

arginine *f* CHIMIE *acide aminé* arginine

argon *m* (*Ar*) CHIMIE argon (*Ar*)

argue *f* PRODUCTION draw bench, drawing bench, wiredrawing bench

arguer *vt* PRODUCTION draw

argument *m* MATH *d'un nombre complexe*, ORDINAT argument

argyrique *adj* CHIMIE argyric

argyrite *f* CHIMIE silver glance

argyrodite *f* MINERAUX argyrodite

argyropyrite *f* MINERAUX argyropyrite

argyrose *f* CHIMIE silver glance

arithmétique *f* INFORMAT, MATH, ORDINAT arithmetic; ~ **binaire** *f* ELECTRON, ORDINAT binary arithmetic; ~ **des congruences** *f* MATH congruence arithmetic; ~ **en double précision** *f* INFORMAT, ORDINAT double precision arithmetic; ~ **en virgule fixe** *f* INFORMAT, ORDINAT fixed point arithmetic; ~ **en virgule flottante** *f* INFORMAT, ORDINAT floating point arithmetic; ~ **modulaire** *f* INFORMAT modular arithmetic, residue arithmetic, MATH modular arithmetic, ORDINAT modular arithmetic, residue arithmetic; ~ **parallèle** *f* INFORMAT, ORDINAT parallel arithmetic

arizonite *f* MINERAUX arizonite

arkansite *f* MINERAUX arkansite

arkose *f* GEOLOGIE *grès feldspathique*, PETR arkose

arksutite *f* MINERAUX arksutite

armateur *m* NAUT shipowner

armature *f* CONS MECA gear, stirrup, stirrup bolt, stirrup piece, stirrup strap, strap, CONSTR bracing, fastening, reinforcement, reinforcing, strap, strap bolt, trussing, ELECTR *d'une machine* armature, ELECTROTEC armature, armor (AmE), armour (BrE), PHYSIQUE armature, keeper, PRODUCTION grate, grating, grid, tie rod, *de châssis, de noyau* spider, VEHICULES *de génératrice* winding; ~ **de charpente** *f* CONSTR fastening, strap, strap bolt; ~ **dans le sens longitudinal** *f* CONSTR longitudinal reinforcement; ~ **du dessous** *f* PRODUCTION loam plate, *d'un moule en terre* bottom plate; ~ **du dessus** *f* PRODUCTION cope ring; ~ **feuilletée** *f* ELECTR *de moteur* laminated armature; ~ **interne** *f* ELECTRON internal shield; ~ **longitudinale** *f* CONSTR longitudinal reinforcement; ~ **montée sur pivots** *f* ELECTROTEC pivoted armature; ~ **de noyau** *f* PRODUCTION core grid, core iron; ~ **de pompe** *f* DISTRI EAU,

PRODUCTION pump gear; ~ **de porte-balais** f ELECTR *de moteur, de générateur* brush yoke; ~ **principale** f CONSTR main reinforcement; ~ **de relais** f ELECTROTEC relay armature; ~ **de stratifié verre-résine** f CERAM VER glass fiber reinforcement (AmE), glass fibre reinforcement (BrE); ~ **transversale** f CONSTR distribution steel; ~ **de treillis métallique** f CONSTR wire mesh reinforcement

armatures f pl PHYSIQUE capacitor plates

arme: ~ **atomique** f MILITAIRE atomic weapon; ~ **à implosion** f MILITAIRE, NUCLEAIRE implosion weapon; ~ **intelligente** f MILITAIRE smart weapon; ~ **laser** f ELECTRON laser weapon

armé adj ELECTR *câble* armored (AmE), armoured (BrE); ~ **de fibre de verre** adj PRODUCTION glass reinforced

armée: ~ **de mer** f NAUT naval forces

armement m NAUT armament, fitting-out, manning, OCEANO *d'un filet* hanging, setting; ~ **en personnel** m NAUT manning; ~ **léger** m MILITAIRE light armament; ~ **Lorrain** m ELECTROTEC rectangular wiring; ~ **manuel** m PHOTO *d'un obturateur* manual cocking

armer vt CINEMAT *un obturateur* cock, set, CONSTR *une poutre* brace, ELECTROTEC *un câble* sheathe, MINES equip, NAUT equip, fit out, man, *un navire* put into commission, OCEANO *un filet* hang, ORDINAT arm, PHOTO cock; ~ **d'un équipage** vt NAUT crew; ~ **un navire** vt NAUT put a ship into commission

armes: ~ **portatives** f pl MILITAIRE small arms

armoire f MECANIQUE cabinet, PRODUCTION enclosure, TELECOM cabinet; ~ **à baie unique** f PRODUCTION single bay enclosure; ~ **de conversion** f TELECOM converter cabinet; ~ **à déshydrater sous vide** f AGRO ALIM vacuum shelf dryer; ~ **de distribution** f ELECTROTEC distribution cabinet; ~ **en acier** f EQUIP LAB *meuble* steel locker; ~ **frigorifique à chariots** f REFRIG roll-in refrigerator; ~ **d'incubation** f EQUIP LAB *microbiologie* incubator; ~ **à poisons** f EQUIP LAB *meuble, sécurité* poisons cupboard; ~ **de premier secours** f SECURITE first-aid cabinet; ~ **réfrigérée** f REFRIG cold chamber; ~ **réfrigérée négative** f REFRIG negative cold chamber; ~ **réfrigérée positive** f REFRIG positive cold chamber; ~ **sanitaire** f SECURITE first-aid cabinet; ~ **de séchage** f CINEMAT, PLAST CAOU *matériel, peintures, plastiques* drying cabinet; ~ **de séchage sous vide** f CONS MECA vacuum drying cabinet; ~ **à sécher** f CONS MECA drying cabinet, *les électrodes de soudure* drying cabinet; ~ **à sécher sous vide** f AGRO ALIM vacuum shelf dryer; ~ **séchoir** f AGRO ALIM drying cupboard; ~ **de sous-répartiteur** f TELECOM cabinet, cross-connect cabinet (AmE); ~ **de stockage** f EQUIP LAB *meuble* storage cupboard

armurage m TEXTILE patterning

armure f ELECTR *de conducteur de câble*, ELECTROTEC armor (AmE), armour (BrE), TEXTILE pattern, style, *d'un tissu* weave; ~ **chevronnée** f TEXTILE herringbone weave; ~ **de clef** f ACOUSTIQUE key signature; ~ **unie** f TEXTILE plain weave

armures: ~ **en relief** f pl TEXTILE relief weaves

aromaticité f CHIMIE aromaticity

aromatique adj PETROLE aromatic

aromatisation f CHIMIE, MATERIAUX aromatization

aromatiser vt AGRO ALIM flavor (AmE), flavour (BrE), CHIMIE aromatize

arôme m AGRO ALIM flavor (AmE), flavoring (AmE), flavour (BrE), flavouring (BrE)

arpège m ACOUSTIQUE arpeggio

arpentage m CONSTR land measuring, land survey, land surveying, survey, surveying, METROLOGIE *de terrain* measurement, measuring; ~ **sismique** m CONSTR seismic survey

arpenter vt METROLOGIE measure

arpenteur m CONSTR surveyor; ~ **du cadastre** m CONSTR ordnance surveyor

arqué adj NAUT *navire* broken-backed

arquer[1] vt CONSTR arch, *une pièce de bois* bend, MINES arch, PRODUCTION bend

arquer[2] vi CONSTR bend

arquer:[3] **s'** ~ v réfl NAUT hog

arquérite f MINERAUX arquerite

arrachage m CONS MECA *d'un clou* pulling out, CONSTR *d'un clou* drawing, extraction, IMPRIM *du papier par les encres* picking, *impression* flaking, PAPIER flaking, picking, picking resistance, surface bonding strength; ~ **de fibre** m TEXTILE peeling, picking, plucking; ~ **du tubage d'isolement** m CONSTR drawing casting, DISTRI EAU pulling casing

arraché m CERAM VER bottom tear, tear

arrache-aiguille m CONS MECA pointer jack

arrache-clou m CONSTR nail extractor

arrachement m CONSTR *maçonnerie* toothing, NUCLEAIRE *de revêtements durs* galling; ~ **au col** m CERAM VER danny neck; ~ **de métal** m PRODUCTION metal pick-up

arrache-moyeu m CONS MECA hub extractor, MECANIQUE hub puller

arrache-pieux m CONSTR pile drawer, pile extractor

arrache-pignon m VEHICULES *outil* gear puller

arracher vt CONS MECA *un clou* pull out, CONSTR extract, *un clou* pull out, PAPIER pick; ~ **le filet de** vt PRODUCTION strip

arrache-sonde m MINES drill rod grab

arrache-tire-fond m CH DE FER sleeper screw extractor (BrE), spike puller (AmE)

arrache-tuyau m CONSTR casing spear, MINES dog

arraisonner vt NAUT inspect

arrangement m CONS MECA arrangement, INFORMAT *configuration*, ORDINAT layout; ~ **général** m CONSTR general arrangement; ~ **au hasard** m METALL random arrangement

arrêt m CONS MECA off, stop, standstill, CONSTR *de chanfrein* stop, ELECTROTEC turn-off, ESPACE *véhicules, propulsion* shutdown, INFORMAT halt, stop, *d'un programme* close down, INST HYDR *de l'admission de vapeur* cutoff, *de la vapeur* shutting-off, NUCLEAIRE *d'un réacteur* shutdown, *de la réaction en chaîne* disruption, ORDINAT halt, stop, PRODUCTION *situation* stand-by, TEXTILE stop; ~ **de l'aérage** m CHARBON ventilation breakdown; ~ **automatique** m ENREGISTR automatic stop; ~ **de chanfrein** m CONSTR chamfer stop; ~ **de débit** m CONSTR cutoff valve; ~ **au décollage** m AERONAUT aborted takeoff; ~ **en cours de route** m AERONAUT stopover; ~ **en roue libre** m PRODUCTION *automatisme libre* coast-to-stop; ~ **d'étincelage** m MINES spark-out stop; ~ **et rebobinage automatique** m PHOTO auto stop and rewind; ~ **d'excentricité** m MECANIQUE *d'une came* dwell; ~ **de fabrication** m CERAM VER call-down; ~ **de fin de papier** m ORDINAT form stop; ~ **de flamme** m CONSTR flame arrester; ~ **du four** m CERAM VER shutdown; ~ **immédiat** m ORDINAT dead halt; ~ **imprévu** m INFORMAT, ORDINAT hang-up; ~ **de machine** m CERAM VER machine stop, PRODUCTION machine shutdown; ~ **machine** *m* PRODUCTION hang-up; ~ **d'une manoeuvre retardatrice** *m* MILITAIRE recoil break; ~ **manuel** *m* NUCLEAIRE manual shutdown; ~ **d'un moteur en vol** *m* AERONAUT engine shutdown in flight; ~ **par épuisement** *m* ESPACE burnout; ~ **par extinction** *m* ESPACE *véhicules, propulsion* flameout; ~ **par rampe** *m* PRODUCTION *automatisme industriel* rated stop; ~ **périodique** *m* NUCLEAIRE periodic shutdown; ~ **de porte** *m* VEHICULES door catch; ~ **pour fin de papier** *m* INFORMAT form stop; ~ **pour procéder à des réparations** *m* PRODUCTION stoppage for repairs; ~ **pour réparations** *m* PRODUCTION stoppage for repairs; ~ **de poussée** *m* ESPACE thrust cutoff; ~ **sûr en cas de séisme** *m* NUCLEAIRE safe shutdown earthquake; ~ **sur image** *m* CINEMAT still frame, TV freeze-frame, pause; ~ **système** *m* PRODUCTION hang-up; ~ **du système de la machine** *m* PRODUCTION *automatisme industriel* machine system shutdown; ~ **de tramway** *m* TRANSPORT streetcar stop (AmE), tram stop; ~ **d'urgence** *m* INFORMAT, NUCLEAIRE *d'un réacteur*, ORDINAT emergency shutdown, SECURITE emergency stop; ~ **d'urgence partiel** *m* NUCLEAIRE partial trip; ~ **d'urgence du réacteur** *m* NUCLEAIRE emergency shutdown of the reactor, reactor trip

arrêt-barrage *m* DISTRI EAU dam, MINES barrier, stopping; ~ **d'eau** *m* MINES damp sheet, water barrier, water curtain; ~ **des tailings** *m* CONSTR tailings dam

arrêté *adj* CONSTR off

arrêter[1] *vt* AUTO *moteur* turn off, CERAM VER *une casse* stop, CONSTR fix, ELECTROTEC turn off, ESPACE *véhicules, propulsion moteur* shut down, INFORMAT, ORDINAT halt, stop, TEXTILE stop

arrêter:[2] ~ **les travaux** *vi* MINES cease work

arrêter:[3] s'~ *v réfl* CONS MECA come to a standstill; **s'~ doucement** *v réfl* ORDINAT quiesce; **s'~ progressivement** *v réfl* INFORMAT quiesce

arrêtoir-butoir: ~ **magnétique** *m* CONSTR magnetic doorstop

arrhénite *f* MINERAUX arrhenite

arrière[1] *adj* (*AR*) CONS MECA head-end

arrière:[2] **à l'~** *adv* ESPACE aft, NAUT abaft, aft, astern; **en ~** *adv* NAUT astern; **en ~ demie** *adv* NAUT half astern; **en ~ lente** *adv* NAUT slow astern; **en ~ toute** *adv* NAUT full astern; **en ~ très lente** *adv* NAUT dead slow astern; **sur l'~** *adv* NAUT abaft

arrière[3] *m* IMPRIM *impression, reliure* backside, NAUT aft, stern, PAPIER *d'une machine* rear, PHOTO back; ~ **à canoë** *m* NAUT canoe stern; ~ **carré** *m* NAUT square transom stern; ~ **de croiseur** *m* NAUT cruiser stern; ~ **de cylindre** *m* INST HYDR *de locomotive, de machine à vapeur fixe* back cylinder cover; ~ **en tableau** *m* NAUT counterstern; ~ **de fabrication** *m* PRODUCTION backlog; ~ **plat** *m* NAUT flat stern; ~ **rond** *m* NAUT elliptical stern; ~ **à tableau** *m* NAUT counterstern, transom stern; ~ **à voûte** *m* NAUT counterstern

arrière:[4] **à l'~ de** *prép* NAUT abaft; **sur l'~ de** *prép* NAUT abaft

arrière-bec *m* DISTRI EAU *d'une pile de pont* downstream cutwater

arrière-bief *m* DISTRI EAU aft bay

arrière-corps *m* ESPACE afterbody

arrière-cylindre *m* CONS MECA head-end of cylinder

arrière-pays *m* GEOLOGIE hinterland

arrière-plage *f* OCEANO backshore

arrière-plan *m* IMPRIM, PHOTO background

arrière-pont *m* NAUT afterdeck

arrière-port *m* NAUT inner harbor (AmE), inner harbour (BrE), inner port

arrière-taille *f* MINES goaf, gob

arrimage *m* AERONAUT *de la cargaison, de l'avion* trim, ESPACE, NAUT *de la cargaison, du navire* stowage, trim; ~ **en breton** *m* NAUT aburton stowage; ~ **en travers** *m* NAUT aburton stowage

arrimer *vt* AERONAUT *cargaison, avion* stow, trim, ESPACE *véhicule* stow, trim, NAUT *cargaison, navire* stow, trim

arrimeur *m* NAUT docker (BrE), stevedore

arrisement *m* CONSTR roads which cross

arrivage *m* PRODUCTION consignment

arrivages *m pl* CH DE FER freight inwards (AmE), goods inwards (BrE)

arrivée *f* MECANIQUE, PRODUCTION inlet, TV incoming feed; ~ **d'air** *f* CONS MECA air inlet; ~ **d'eau froide** *f* INSTRUMENT cool water inlet; ~ **de météorites** *f* ESPACE *astronomie* meteorite influx; ~ **de la pâte sur machine** *f* PAPIER stock inlet; ~ **de vapeur** *f* INST HYDR steam inlet; ~ **du vent** *f* CONS MECA air inlet

arriver:[1] ~ **à** *vt* MINES approach

arriver:[2] ~ **à** *vi* NAUT *à un port* make; ~ **au bassin** *vi* NAUT dock; ~ **aux docks** *vi* NAUT dock; ~ **à quai** *vi* NAUT dock

arrondi[1] *adj* PHYSIQUE streamlined

arrondi[2] *m* AERONAUT flare-out, INFORMAT, ORDINAT rounding

arrondir *vt* INFORMAT round, NAUT *un cap* double, round, ORDINAT round, round off, PRODUCTION *à l'entier le plus proche* round; ~ **au chiffre supérieur** *vt* MATH, PRODUCTION round up; ~ **par défaut** *vt* INFORMAT, MATH *au chiffre inférieur*, ORDINAT, PRODUCTION *à l'entier inférieur* round down; ~ **par excès** *vt* INFORMAT, ORDINAT round up; ~ **au plus près** *vt* INFORMAT round off

arrondissage *m* CERAM VER rounding of rim, MATH rounding

arrondissure *f* IMPRIM *reliure* rounding; ~ **et endossure** *f* IMPRIM back rounding

arrosage *m* CONS MECA cooling, DISTRI EAU sprinkling, ELECTRON flooding

arrosement *m* DISTRI EAU sprinkling

arroser *vt* CONSTR water, DISTRI EAU sprinkle

arroseur *m* DISTRI EAU sprinkler; ~ **rotatif** *m* DISTRI EAU rotating sprayer

arrosoir: ~ **rotatif** *m* CONSTR sprinkler

arrow-root *m* AGRO ALIM arrowroot

arsenal: ~ **maritime** *m* NAUT naval dockyard, *de la marine nationale* dockyard

arséniate *m* CHIMIE arsenate, arseniate

arsenic *m* (*As*) CHIMIE arsenic (*As*); ~ **blanc** *m* CHIMIE arsenic trioxide; ~ **sulfuré rouge** *m* CHIMIE red arsenic

arsénié *adj* CHIMIE arseniuretted

arsénifère *adj* MINERAUX arseniferous

arséniopléite *f* MINERAUX arseniopleite

arséniosidérite *f* MINERAUX arseniosiderite

arsénite *m* CHIMIE arsenite, MINERAUX arsenite, arsenolite

arséniure *m* CHIMIE arsenide; ~ **de gallium** *m* ELECTRON, OPTIQUE, PHYSIQUE gallium arsenide; ~ **de nickel** *m* CHIMIE nickel arsenide

arsennickel *m* MINERAUX copper nickel

arsénolite *f* MINERAUX arsenite, arsenolite

arsénopyrite *f* MINERAUX arsenopyrite

arsine *f* CHIMIE arsine

art: ~ **céramique** *m* CERAM VER ceramic art; ~ **de l'ingé-**

nieur *m* CONS MECA engineering; ~ **de la manoeuvre** *m* NAUT seamanship; ~ **des mines** *m* MINES mining engineering; ~ **typographique** *m* IMPRIM art of printing

artère *f* ELECTR *réseau* feeder, feeder cable, ELECTROTEC lead, INFORMAT, ORDINAT bus (BrE), trunk (AmE); ~ **d'alimentation** *f* ELECTR balanced line; ~ **finale** *f* ELECTR *alimentation* radial feeder; ~ **d'interconnexion** *f* ELECTR interconnecting line, *alimentation* interconnecting feeder; ~ **parallèle** *f* ELECTR *alimentation* parallel feeder; ~ **principale** *f* ELECTR trunk main, *alimentation* trunk feeder; ~ **de retour** *f* ELECTR *alimentation* negative feeder; ~ **de transmission** *f* TELECOM transmission highway

artésien *adj* DISTRI EAU, PETROLE artesian

article *m* CONS MECA item, part, INFORMAT item, record, ORDINAT data item, item, record, TEXTILE item; ~ **de boulonnerie** *m* MECANIQUE threaded fastener; ~ **fantôme** *m* PRODUCTION pseudo item; ~ **fictif** *m* PRODUCTION pseudo item; ~ **sous-traité** *m* PRODUCTION subcontracting item; ~ **standard** *m* PRODUCTION standard item; ~ **de tamponnage** *m* EMBALLAGE cushioning product

article-label *m* INFORMAT label record

articles: ~ **en agate** *m pl* CERAM VER agate ware; ~ **en faïence** *m pl* CERAM VER earthenware; ~ **en porcelaine** *m pl* CERAM VER porcelain goods; ~ **de majolique** *m pl* CERAM VER majolica ware

articulation *f* CONS MECA connection, coupling, hinge, hinging, CONSTR joint, MECANIQUE knuckle, link; ~ **de battement** *f* AERONAUT flapping hinge; ~ **de battement excentrée** *f* AERONAUT offset flapping hinge; ~ **à genouillère** *f* CONS MECA knuckle, knuckle joint; ~ **de pas** *f* AERONAUT blade pitch change hinge; ~ **de repliage des pales** *f* AERONAUT blade folding hinge; ~ **à rotule** *f* CONS MECA ball, ball and socket joint, ball joint; ~ **sphérique** *f* MECANIQUE ball and socket joint, VEHICULES *direction* ball joint, spherical joint

articulé *adj* MECANIQUE, TRANSPORT articulated

artifice *m* COMMANDE light signal

artificiel *adj* PAPIER artificial, imitation

artificier *m* MILITAIRE artificer, technician

artillerie *f* MILITAIRE artillery; ~ **de campagne** *f* MILITAIRE field artillery; ~ **côtière** *f* MILITAIRE coastal artillery; ~ **légère** *f* MILITAIRE light artillery; ~ **lourde** *f* MILITAIRE heavy armament, heavy artillery; ~ **portée** *f* MILITAIRE mounted artillery; ~ **de siège** *f* MILITAIRE siege artillery

artinskien *adj* GEOLOGIE *stratigraphie* Artinskian

arts: ~ **traînants** *m pl* OCEANO trawling and dredging gear, troll

arylamine *f* CHIMIE arylamine

aryle *f* CHIMIE aryl

As *(arsenic)* CHIMIE As *(arsenic)*

asbeste *m* CHIMIE, MECANIQUE, MINERAUX, SECURITE, TEXTILE asbestos

asbestose *f* CONSTR asbestosis

asbolane *f* MINERAUX asbolane, asbolite

asbolite *f* MINERAUX asbolane, asbolite

ascaricide *m* CHIMIE ascaricide

ascendance *f* METEO, PHYS FLUID, THERMODYN uplift

ascendantes *f pl* IMPRIM ascenders

ascenseur *m* CONSTR elevator, lifter, MECANIQUE, PRODUCTION elevator; ~ **d'avions** *m* TRANSPORT aircraft lift; ~ **à bateaux** *m* TRANSPORT boat elevator, boat lift; ~ **horizontal** *m* TRANSPORT horizontal elevator; ~ **personnes** *m* TRANSPORT passenger elevator (AmE),

passenger lift (BrE); ~ **à piston plongeur** *m* CONSTR plunger elevator

ascension: ~ **capillaire** *f* PAPIER capillary rise; ~ **droite** *f* ASTRONOMIE right ascension, vertical ascent, ESPACE *astronomie* right ascension, vertical ascent; ~ **de panaches** *f* POLLUTION plume rise

aschiste *adj* PETR aschistic

ASCII *abrév* IMPRIM, INFORMAT, ORDINAT ASCII, American Standard Code for Information Interchange

ascorbique *adj* CHIMIE ascorbic

ASE *abrév (Agence spatiale européenne)* ASTRONOMIE, ESPACE ESA *(European Space Agency)*

aseptique *adj* AGRO ALIM, EMBALLAGE aseptic

askarel *m* ELECTROTEC askarel

asmanite *f* MINERAUX asmanite

aspartame *m* AGRO ALIM aspartame

aspartique *adj* CHIMIE aspartic

aspect *m* ESSAIS appearance, PAPIER *du papier* appearance, *du papier sous éclairage oblique* look-down, TEXTILE look; ~ **technique** *m* TELECOM technical viewpoint

aspérolite *f* MINERAUX asperolite

aspersion: ~ **de saumure** *f* REFRIG brine sparge

asphaltage *m* CONSTR asphalting

asphalte *m* CONSTR asphalt, mineral pitch, MINERAUX, PETROLE asphalt

asphaltène *m* MINERAUX asphaltene

asphalter *vt* CONSTR asphalter, bituminize

asphaltisation *f* CHIMIE inspissation

asphaltite *f* MINERAUX asphaltite

asphyxie *f* SECURITE suffocation; ~ **due aux émissions de fumées** *f* SECURITE suffocation by fumes; ~ **par les fumées** *f* SECURITE suffocation by fumes

aspidolite *f* MINERAUX aspidolite

aspirail *m* CONSTR vent, vent hole, PRODUCTION air flue, air hole

aspirant *m* DISTRI EAU rose, strainer, tailpiece, wind bore, NAUT midshipman

aspirateur *m* CONS MECA exhauster, sucker, PRODUCTION aspirator; ~ **centrifuge** *m* GENIE CHIM centrifugal exhauster; ~ **mobile** *m* ELECTROTEC roller dust collector; ~ **pour usages industriels** *m* SECURITE *nettoyage* vacuum cleaner for industrial purposes; ~ **de poussière** *m* CHARBON dust exhaust fan, EMBALLAGE dust aspirator, SECURITE dust exhaust fan; ~ **de poussières dangereuses pour la santé** *m* SECURITE vacuum cleaner for dusts hazardous to health

aspirateur-diffuseur *m* EN RENOUV draft tube (AmE), draught tube (BrE)

aspiration *f* CONS MECA intake, suction, MECANIQUE suction, MINES *de l'air* exhausting, PAPIER aspiration, suction, REFRIG, TEXTILE suction

aspirer *vt* TEXTILE suck

assainir *vt* DISTRI EAU cleanse, MINES degas, RECYCLAGE clean up, drain; ~ **un chantier contaminé** *vt* MINES degas workings, ventilate gas-filled workings

assainissement *m* DISTRI EAU cleansing, drainage, sanitation, INFORMAT, ORDINAT sanitization, RECYCLAGE cleanup, drainage, sewerage; ~ **agricole** *m* DISTRI EAU arterial drainage; ~ **écologique** *m* POLLU MER, POLLUTION ecological recovery

asseau *m* CONSTR roofer's hammer

assèchement *m* CONSTR dewatering, DISTRI EAU drainage, draining, pumping, pumping out, GENIE CHIM desiccation, MINES dewatering, draining, NUCLEAIRE dry-out, THERMODYN drying

assécher[1] *vt* CONSTR drain, DISTRI EAU pump, pump out, *un étang* drain, MINES *une mine* dewater, drain, NAUT bail out, pump out, RECYCLAGE drain, REFRIG dehumidify, THERMODYN *terrain* dry, dry out

assécher:[2] **s'~** *v réfl* HYDROLOGIE run dry

assemblage *m* CONS MECA assembling, assembly, CONSTR joining, joint, ELECTR assembly, *constituant d'un câble* lay, GAZ, IMPRIM, MECANIQUE assembly, NUCLEAIRE joining, joint, ORDINAT *d'un programme* assembly, PRODUCTION jointing, TEXTILE cluster; ~ **d'angle** *m* CONSTR angle joint; ~ **d'arrêt d'urgence** *m* NUCLEAIRE emergency shutdown of the reactor, shim assembly; ~ **automatique** *m* EMBALLAGE automatic assembly work, automatic collation; ~ **boulonné** *m* ESPACE *véhicules* bolted connection; ~ **bout à bout** *m* CONSTR heading joint; ~ **à bride** *m* CONS MECA flange joint; ~ **à bride boulonnée** *m* CONS MECA flange joint; **à charnière** *m* CONSTR folding joint, hinge joint; **à clé** *m* CONS MECA key joint; ~ **à clin** *m* CONSTR lap joint; **à collier** *m* CONS MECA collar joint; ~ **combustible** *m* NUCLEAIRE, PHYSIQUE fuel assembly; ~ **combustible détérioré** *m* NUCLEAIRE *endommagé* damaged fuel assembly; ~ **combustible à grille d'espacement** *m* NUCLEAIRE grid-spaced fuel assembly; ~ **combustible inétanche** *m* NUCLEAIRE leaking fuel assembly; ~ **combustible limiteur** *m* NUCLEAIRE limiting fuel assembly; ~ **combustible non-instrumenté** *m* NUCLEAIRE uninstrumented fuel assembly; ~ **combustible périphérique** *m* NUCLEAIRE edge control assembly, peripheral fuel assembly; ~ **combustible sans boîtier** *m* NUCLEAIRE canless fuel assembly; ~ **combustible ventilé** *m* NUCLEAIRE vented fuel assembly; ~ **à la commande** *m* PRODUCTION assemble to order; ~ **à cornières** *m* CONSTR angle iron joint; ~ **à couvre-joints** *m* PRODUCTION butt strap joint, welted joint; ~ **croisé** *m* ORDINAT cross assembly; ~ **à double-entaille** *m* CONSTR notch joint; ~ **à double tenon** *m* CONSTR double tenon joint; ~ **à douille** *m* CONS MECA socket bushed with gun metal, socket joint; ~ **à emboîtement** *m* CONSTR faucet joint, spigot joint, spigot-and-faucet joint, spigot-and-faucet joint pipes; ~ **à embrèvement** *m* CONSTR joggle joint; ~ **à embrèvements anglais** *m* CONSTR bridle joint; ~ **à embrèvements séparés par un plat joint** *m* CONSTR bridle joint; ~ **en about** *m* CONSTR, PETROLE *canalisation* abutting joint; ~ **à encastrement** *m* CONSTR housed joint; ~ **en coupe d'onglets** *m* CONS MECA bevel joint; ~ **à enfourchement** *m* CONSTR slit mortise joint, slot mortise joint; ~ **d'engrenages** *m* CONS MECA gear assembly; ~ **en onglet** *m* CONSTR chamfered joint, miter joint (AmE), mitre joint (BrE); ~ **en queue d'hironde** *m* CONSTR fantail joint; ~ **en sifflet** *m* CONSTR splayed joint; ~ **à entaille** *m* CONSTR notch joint, single notch joint; ~ **à enture** *m* CONSTR scarf, scarf joint, scarf jointing; ~ **à enture à vis** *m* CONS MECA screw-and-socket joint; ~ **à étrier** *m* CONS MECA stirrup joint; ~ **à fausse languette** *m* CONSTR grooved and feathered joint, loose-tongue joint, ploughed and feathered joint (BrE), plowed and feathered joint (AmE), ploughed and tongued joint (BrE), plowed and tongued joint (AmE), slip-tongue joint; ~ **à feuillure** *m* CONSTR fillistered joint, rabbeted joint, rebated joint; ~ **de la fonte** *m* CONSTR cast-iron joint; ~ **à franc-bord** *m* PRODUCTION butt joint; ~ **à grain-d'orge** *m* CONSTR angular grooved-and-tongued joint; ~ **hybride rapide de puissance nulle** *m* NUCLEAIRE fast fusion-fission assembly at zero thermal power; ~ **à languette rapportée** *m* CONSTR filleted joint, grooved and feathered joint, loose-tongue joint, ploughed and tongued joint (BrE), plowed and tongued joint (AmE), slip-tongue joint, plowed and feathered joint (AmE); ~ **à manchon** *m* CONS MECA sleeve joint; ~ **à mi-bois** *m* CONSTR halved joint, halving, lap joint, overleap joint, step joint; ~ **à mi-fer** *m* PRODUCTION halved joint, halving; ~ **à mi-fonte** *m* PRODUCTION halved joint, halving; ~ **oblique à tenon et mortaise avec embrèvement** *m* CONSTR mortise-and-tenon heel joint; ~ **à onglet** *m* CONSTR chamfered joint, miter joint (AmE), mitre joint (BrE); ~ **à onglet en sifflet** *m* CONSTR splayed miter joint (AmE), splayed mitre joint (BrE); ~ **par boulons** *m* CONS MECA bolted joint; ~ **par brides** *m* PRODUCTION flange mounting; ~ **par clavette en coin** *m* CONSTR cottered joint; ~ **par contraction frigorifique** *m* REFRIG cold shrink fitting; ~ **par rivets** *m* CONSTR rivet joint; ~ **à plat** *m* CONS MECA straight joint, CONSTR butt joint, square joint; ~ **à plat joint** *m* CONS MECA straight joint, CONSTR butt joint, square joint; ~ **de prismes diffractant la lumière** *m* IMPRIM *optique* beam splitter; ~ **à queue** *m* CONSTR dovetail joint, swallow-tail joint, fantail joint; ~ **à queue d'aronde** *m* CONSTR dovetail joint, fantail joint, swallow-tail joint, MECANIQUE dovetail joint; ~ **à queue d'aronde à mi-bois** *m* CONSTR dovetail halved joint; ~ **à queue d'aronde à recouvrement** *m* CONSTR dovetail lap joint; ~ **à queue d'hirondelle** *m* CONSTR dovetail joint, swallow-tail joint; ~ **à rainure et languette** *m* CONSTR angular grooved-and-tongued joint, feather joint, ploughed and tongued joint (BrE), plowed and tongued joint (AmE), tongue-and-groove joint, tongued-and-grooved joint; ~ **de rallonges** *m* MINES drill joint, drill pole joint, drill rod joint, pipe joint; ~ **à recouvrement** *m* CONS MECA step joint, CONSTR lap joint, overlap joint, MECANIQUE *soudage* lap joint; ~ **soudé** *m* MECANIQUE *soudage* weldment; ~ **supérieur** *m* EN RENOUV top assembly; ~ **suspendu** *m* CONSTR suspended joint; ~ **à tenon** *m* CONSTR tenon joint, tenoned and housed joint; ~ **à tenon avec chaperon et renfort** *m* CONSTR tusk tenon joint; ~ **à tenon avec cheville** *m* CONSTR pinned tenon joint; ~ **à tenon avec renfort** *m* CONSTR tusk tenon joint; ~ **à tenon avec renfort carré** *m* CONSTR haunched mortise-and-tenon joint; ~ **à tenon et à mortaise** *m* CONSTR mortise joint, mortise-and-tenon joint, tenon joint, tenoned and housed joint; ~ **à tenon et mortaise doubles** *m* CONSTR double mortise-and-tenon joint, double tenon joint; ~ **à tenon mortaise et cale** *m* CONSTR wedged mortise-and-tenon joint; ~ **à tenon passant avec clef** *m* CONSTR pegged tenon joint, pinned tenon joint; ~ **à tenon renforcé** *m* CONSTR tusk tenon joint; ~ **à tenon de repos** *m* CONSTR tusk tenon joint; ~ **de tuyauterie** *m* CONSTR pipe joint; ~ **à vis** *m* CONS MECA screw joint

assemblages: ~ **de charpente** *m pl* CONSTR carpenters' joint; ~ **de charpente en fer** *m pl* CONSTR smithery; ~ **de plomberie** *m pl* CONSTR plumber's joints

assemblé: ~ **en usine** *adj* PRODUCTION factory assembled; ~ **et équipé** *adj* CONS MECA complete-assembly

assembler *vt* CONSTR assemble, join, EMBALLAGE *les boîtes pliantes* erect, IMPRIM, ORDINAT assemble; ~ **à queue d'aronde** *vt* CONSTR dovetail

assembleur *m* ORDINAT assembler; ~ **croisé** *m* ORDINAT cross assembler

assembleur-désassembleur: ~ **de paquets** *m* INFORMAT,

ORDINAT PAD, packet assembler-disassembler, TELE-COM PAD, packet assembler-disassembler, packetizer-depacketizer

assembleuse *f* IMPRIM collating press, gatherer, gathering machine, *façonnage* collator; ~ **de cartons** *f* EMBALLAGE folding box erecting machine, folding box setting machine; ~ **de grandes caisses** *f* EMBALLAGE large-case erector; ~ **jumelée** *f* IMPRIM twin-stream collator

asseoir[1] *vt* CONSTR *les fondements* bed

asseoir:[2] ~ **une pièce** *vi* MILITAIRE *artillerie* bed in a gun

asservi *adj* COMMANDE servo-driven; ~ **à rester en quadrature** *adj* ELECTRON locked in phase quadrature

asservissement *m* AERONAUT coupling, COMMANDE automatic control, interlock, ELECTRON closed-loop control, loop lock, ELECTROTEC automatic guidance system, feedback control, ORDINAT servomechanism, TV interlock, slaving; ~ **automatique** *m* TV picture lock; ~ **du cabestan** *m* CINEMAT capstan servolock, TV servo capstan; ~ **de commutation** *m* TV switch lock; ~ **au compteur de défilement** *m* TV tachometer lock; ~ **de disque de têtes** *m* TV servo wheel; ~ **électrique** *m* ELECTR *sécurité* electric interlocking system; ~ **électronique auto-adaptable** *m* COMMANDE adaptive control electronics; ~ **horizontal** *m* TV horizontal lock; ~ **de moteur** *m* TV motor control; ~ **numérique** *m* TELECOM digital feedback; ~ **de phase** *m* ELECTRON phase locking; ~ **programmé** *m* ESPACE *communications* programed servosystem (AmE), programmed servosystem (BrE); ~ **radial** *m* OPTIQUE radial control; ~ **des sorties** *m* PRODUCTION *automatisme industriel* output override; ~ **sous-porteuse** *m* TV subcarrier lock; ~ **du tambour des têtes** *m* TV head servo lock; ~ **tangentiel** *m* OPTIQUE tangential control; ~ **de tension** *m* TV tension servo; ~ **vertical** *m* OPTIQUE vertical control, TV vertical lock

asservisseur *m* CINEMAT synchrolock

assette *f* CONSTR roofer's hammer

assiette *f* AERONAUT trim, CERAM VER Hager disc (BrE), spinner, whirler, CONS MECA set, CONSTR foundation, location, seat, seating, NAUT *d'un navire* trim; ~ **autour de l'axe longitudinal** *f* AERONAUT pitch attitude; ~ **longitudinale** *f* AERONAUT pitch attitude; ~ **pour le pied** *f* CONSTR foothold, footing; ~ **de rails** *f* CH DE FER railbed; ~ **des traverses** *f* CH DE FER sleeper bed (BrE), tie bed (AmE); ~ **de la voie** *f* CH DE FER track bed; ~ **de vol** *f* AERONAUT flight attitude

assignation *f* ESPACE *de fréquence* assignment

assimilable: ~ **par l'organisme** *adj* RECYCLAGE digestible

assimilation: ~ **des roches encaissantes** *f* GEOLOGIE magmatic stoping

assise *f* CERAM VER course, CONSTR bed, course, foundation, MILITAIRE *d'une pièce d'artillerie* bedding, PRODUCTION bedplate; ~ **de boutisses** *f* CONSTR heading, heading course; ~ **de carreaux** *f* CONSTR stretching course; ~ **houillère** *f* CHARBON coal bed; ~ **de panneresses** *f* CONSTR *maçonnerie* stretching course; ~ **de retombée** *f* CONSTR springing course

assistance *f* INFORMAT support, SECURITE assistance

assistance-annuaire *f* (Can) TELECOM directory assistance, directory enquiries (BrE), directory information (AmE)

assistant: ~ **radiographe** *m* INSTRUMENT radiographer

assisté *adj* COMMANDE servo-assisted; ~ **par ordinateur** *adj* ORDINAT computer-aided, computer-assisted

assister *vt* INFORMAT, ORDINAT support

association *f* CHIMIE association, CONSTR connection, TELECOM association; ~ **d'application** *f* TELECOM application association; ~ **stellaire** *f* ASTRONOMIE stellar association

Association: ~ **européenne pour le recyclage et la récupération** *f* EMBALLAGE ERRA, European Recycling and Recovery Association

associer *vt* ORDINAT *adresse* bind

assombrir *vt* CINEMAT dim

assombrissement: ~ **atmosphérique** *m* METEO overcast; ~ **du bord** *m* ASTRONOMIE limb darkening

assortiment *m* CERAM VER mixed ware, IMPRIM *fournitures* batch, PRODUCTION assortment; ~ **d'outils** *m* CONS MECA set of tools

assortir *vt* PRODUCTION match; ~ **à la couleur** *vt* TEXTILE sort by color (AmE), sort by colour (BrE), sort by shade

assujetti *adj* PRODUCTION secured

assujettir *vt* CONSTR fix, *une poutre* fix

assurance: ~ **contre les accidents du travail** *f* SECURITE industrial insurance; ~ **maritime** *f* NAUT marine insurance, underwriting; ~ **de la qualité** *f* CONS MECA, CONSTR, ESPACE, MECANIQUE, NUCLEAIRE, PRODUCTION, QUALITE QA, quality assurance; ~ **de la qualité en contrôle et essais finals** *f* QUALITE quality assurance in final inspection and test; ~ **sur corps** *f* NAUT hull insurance

assurer *vt* CONS MECA *opération* perform

assureur: ~ **maritime** *m* NAUT underwriter

astaki *m* PETR astatki

astate *m (At)* CHIMIE astatine *(At)*

astatique *adj* PHYSIQUE astatic

astéonécrose: ~ **dysbarique** *f* OCEANO ascepticone necrosis

astérisme *m* ASTRONOMIE asterism

astérisque *f* IMPRIM *composition* footnote call-out

astéroïde *m* ASTRONOMIE *petite planète* asteroid, minor planet, ESPACE *astronomie* asteroid

astéroïdes *m pl* ASTRONOMIE planetesimals

asthénosphère *f* GEOLOGIE, PETR asthenosphere

astigmatique *m* PHYSIQUE astigmatic

astigmatisme *m* PHYSIQUE, TV astigmatism

astragale *m* CONSTR astragal

astrakanite *f* MINERAUX astrakanite

astre *m* ASTRONOMIE celestial body, ESPACE celestial body, star

astrobiologie *f* ASTRONOMIE astrobiology

astrochimie *f* ASTRONOMIE astrochemistry

astrocompas *m* ESPACE astrocompass

astrodrome *m* ESPACE astrodrome

astrodynamique *f* ESPACE astrodynamics

astrographe *m* ASTRONOMIE astrograph

astrolabe *m* ASTRONOMIE astrolabe

astrométrie *f* ASTRONOMIE, ESPACE astrometry

astromobile *m* ESPACE *véhicules* rover

astronaute *m* ESPACE astronaut, cosmonaut

astronef *m* ESPACE spacecraft, spaceship

astronome *m* ASTRONOMIE, ESPACE astronomer

astronomie: ~ **dans l'ultraviolet** *f* ASTRONOMIE ultraviolet astronomy; ~ **gamma** *f* ASTRONOMIE, ESPACE gamma ray astronomy; ~ **des hautes énergies** *f* ASTRONOMIE high-energy-astronomy; ~ **infrarouge** *f* ASTRONOMIE infrared astronomy; ~ **millimétrique** *f* ASTRONOMIE millimeter astronomy (AmE), millimetre astronomy (BrE); ~ **onde-millimétrique** *f* ASTRONOMIE millimeter wave astronomy (AmE), mil-

limetre wave astronomy (BrE); ~ **optique** *f* ASTRON-
OMIE optical astronomy; ~ **par satellite** *f* ASTRONOMIE
satellite astronomy; ~ **radar** *f* ASTRONOMIE radar astronomy; ~ **à rayons X** *f* ASTRONOMIE X-ray
astronomy; ~ **spatiale** *f* ESPACE space astronomy; ~
sub-millimétrique *f* ASTRONOMIE submillimeter astronomy (AmE), submillimetre astronomy (BrE)

astronomique *adj* NAUT celestial

astronophysique: ~ **à énergie haute** *f* ASTRONOMIE high-
energy-astrophysics

astrophotographie *f* ASTRONOMIE astrophotography

astrophyllite *f* MINERAUX astrophyllite

astrophysique *f* ASTRONOMIE, ESPACE astrophysics

asymétrie *f* CHIMIE asymmetry, dissymmetry, MATH
asymmetry

asymétrique *adj* GEOMETRIE asymmetric, asymmetrical,
INFORMAT, MATH, ORDINAT asymmetric

asymptote *f* GEOMETRIE, MATH asymptote

asymptotique *adj* GEOMETRIE asymptotic

asynchrone *adj* CINEMAT nonsync, ELECTR *moteur*, IN-
FORMAT, ORDINAT, PHYSIQUE asynchronous, TV
asynchronous, nonsync

asynchronisme *m* PHYSIQUE asynchronism

At *(astate)* CHIMIE At *(astatine)*

atacamite *f* MINERAUX atacamite

atactique *adj* CHIMIE, MATERIAUX atactic

ATD *abrév (analyse thermique différentielle)* CONSTR,
PLAST CAOU, POLLUTION, THERMODYN DTA *(differential thermal analysis)*

atélestite *f* MINERAUX atelestite

atelier *m* MECANIQUE shop, workshop, PRODUCTION
mill, shop floor, shop, workshop, works, SECURITE
workshop; ~ **d'ajustage** *m* CONS MECA fitting shop; ~
d'assemblage *m* MECANIQUE assembly shop; ~ **des
bocards** *m* MINES battery house, stamp house; ~ **de
broyage** *m* GENIE CHIM grinding plant; ~ **de chaudronnerie** *m* INST HYDR boiler works; ~ **de composition** *m*
CERAM VER batch house, mixing room; ~ **de concentration des grenailles et sables** *m* MINES jig mill; ~ **de
congélation** *m* REFRIG freezing section; ~ **de découpe**
m (Fra) *(cf magasin de découpe)* CERAM VER cutting
shop; ~ **de dessablage** *m* PRODUCTION cleaning shop,
dressing shop; ~ **d'enrichissement** *m* MINES concentrator, dressing works; ~ **d'entretien** *m* CONSTR
maintenance shop; ~ **d'essai** *m* CONS MECA test shop,
testing shop; ~ **de filtration** *m* CHARBON filtration
plant, NUCLEAIRE filter house; ~ **de flottation** *m* GENIE
CHIM flotation plant; ~ **de forge** *m* CONSTR smithy,
PRODUCTION forge; ~ **de forgeron** *m* CONS MECA blacksmith's forge, blacksmith's shop, CONSTR smithy,
PRODUCTION forge; ~ **de galvanisation** *m* REVETEMENT
hot-coating shop; ~ **d'imprimerie** *m* IMPRIM print
shop; ~ **de lavage** *m* PRODUCTION wash house; ~ **de
maréchal ferrant** *m* CONSTR smithy, PRODUCTION
forge; ~ **de modelage** *m* PRODUCTION pattern shop; ~
de montage *m* MECANIQUE, NAUT, PRODUCTION erecting shop; ~ **de montage final** *m* PRODUCTION *système
hydraulique* final assembly; ~ **de moulage** *m* PRODUC-
TION molding shop (AmE), moulding shop (BrE); ~
orbital *m* ESPACE orbital workshop; ~ **d'outillage** *m*
MECANIQUE toolroom; ~ **de polissage** *m* CERAM VER
polishing shop; ~ **pour la protection de la respiration** *m*
SECURITE respiratory protection workshop; ~ **de préparation** *m* MINES processing plant; ~ **de préparation de
la lessive** *m* PAPIER acid plant; ~ **de préparation mécanique** *m* MINES dressing works, PRODUCTION mill; ~

de réparation des joints *m* CERAM VER jointing yard; ~
de réparations *m* PRODUCTION repair shop; ~ **de réparation de wagons** *m* CH DE FER car repair shop (AmE),
workshop (BrE); ~ **spatial** *m* ESPACE manned workshop, space workshop; ~ **de tôlerie** *m* MECANIQUE
fabricating shop; ~ **des tôles** *m* NAUT plater's shop; ~
de travail des fines *m* PRODUCTION fine concentration
mill; ~ **de travail des grenailles et sables** *m* MINES
coarse concentration mill; ~ **de zingage** *m* REVETE-
MENT hot-coating shop

Atelier: ~ **du Sculpteur** *m* ASTRONOMIE Sculptor

atélite *f* MINERAUX atelite

athermal *adj* CHIMIE athermal

athermane *adj* PHYSIQUE heat-insulating

athermanéité *f* PHYSIQUE athermancy

atlantique *m* NAUT ocean liner

atlas: ~ **céleste** *m* ASTRONOMIE celestial atlas; ~ **des
courants** *m* NAUT tidal stream atlas; ~ **des étoiles** *m*
ASTRONOMIE star atlas; ~ **stellaire** *m* ASTRONOMIE star
atlas

atlasite *f* MINERAUX atlasite

atmolyse *f* CHIMIE atmolysis

atmosphère *f* ASTRONOMIE, METEO, PHYSIQUE atmosphere; ~ **contrôlée** *f* MAT CHAUFF controlled
atmosphere; ~ **corrosive** *f* PRODUCTION corrosive atmosphere; ~ **explosive** *f* SECURITE explosive
atmosphere; ~ **inflammable** *f* SECURITE flammable atmosphere; ~ **ionique** *f* PHYS RAYON ionic atmosphere;
~ **jovienne** *f* ASTRONOMIE Jovian atmosphere; ~ **libre** *f*
METEO free atmosphere; ~ **normale de référence** *f* CONS
MECA *transmission pneumatique* standard reference
atmosphere; ~ **de référence** *f* ESPACE reference atmosphere; ~ **solaire** *f* ASTRONOMIE sun's atmosphere; ~ **du
soleil** *f* ASTRONOMIE solar atmosphere; ~ **standard** *f*
METEO standard atmosphere; ~ **terrestre** *f* ESPACE
météorologie Earth's atmosphere

atmosphérique *adj* METEO, PHYSIQUE atmospheric

atoll *m* NAUT, OCEANO atoll

atome *m* CHIMIE hexad, INFORMAT, ORDINAT, PHYS PART,
PHYSIQUE atom; ~ **accepteur** *m* ELECTRON, PHYSIQUE
acceptor atom; ~ **donneur** *m* ELECTRON, PHYSIQUE
donor atom; ~ **excité** *m* PHYS PART excited atom; ~
interstitiel *m* CRISTALL interstitial atom; ~ **ionisé** *m*
PHYS PART ionized atom; ~ **métastable** *m* PHYS RAYON
metastable atom; ~ **neutre** *m* PHYS PART neutral atom;
~ **percuté** *m* NUCLEAIRE knocked-on atom; ~ **stimulé**
m PHYS PART excited atom; ~ **terminal** *m* CHIMIE terminal atom

atomicité *f* CHIMIE, INFORMAT, ORDINAT, PHYSIQUE ato-
micity

atomique *adj* CHIMIE, PHYS PART, PHYSIQUE atomic

atomisation *f* CHIMIE atomization, GENIE CHIM atomizing process, NUCLEAIRE, PETROLE atomization

atomiser *vt* CHIMIE atomize

atomiseur *m* GENIE CHIM atomizer; ~ **de combustible à
ultrasons** *m* TRANSPORT ultrasonic fuel atomizer

ATOP *abrév (amplificateur à tube à ondes progressives)*
ELECTRON, ESPACE *communications* TWTA *(traveling-wave tube amplifier, travelling-wave tube
amplifier)*

atopite *f* MINERAUX atopite

âtre *m* CONSTR hearth

atropique *adj* CHIMIE atropic

ATS *abrév (agent technique de saturation)* OCEANO caisson master, life support technician

attache *f* CONS MECA clamp, clip, tie, CONSTR binder,

bond, ESPACE fastener, MECANIQUE clip, fastener, PRODUCTION fastening, VEHICULES *de voiture décapotable* top catch; ~ **de bielle** *f* CONS MECA rod linkage; ~ **capot** *f* VEHICULES *carrosserie* bonnet catch (BrE), hood catch (AmE); ~ **de courroie** *f* PAPIER belt fastener; ~ **DZUS** *f* ESPACE *véhicules* DZUS fastener; ~ **à élément fileté** *f* RESSORTS threaded plug end; ~ **à élément inséré** *f* RESSORTS swivel loop; ~ **par courroies** *f* PRODUCTION belt fastener; ~ **pilote** *f* AERONAUT *d'avion militaire* seat belt; ~ **de rail direct** *f* CH DE FER direct rail fastening

attachement: ~ **d'un électron** *m* NUCLEAIRE electron attachment

attacher *vt* CONSTR bind, INFORMAT attach, MECANIQUE fasten, ORDINAT attach, TEXTILE fasten; ~ **avec une pince** *vt* EMBALLAGE clip

attache-rail *m* CH DE FER rail clip

attaches *f pl* TEXTILE fastenings

attacolite *f* MINERAUX attacolite

attapulgite *f* MINERAUX, PETR attapulgite, PETROLE attapulgite, polygorskite, *forage* attapulgite

attaque *f* ACOUSTIQUE, CHARBON attack, CONS MECA driving, PRODUCTION input voltage; ~ **acide** *f* CHIMIE etching; ~ **angulaire** *f* MECANIQUE *engrenages* angular meshing; ~ **de la base** *f* ELECTRON base drive; ~ **cathodique** *f* METALL cathodic etching; ~ **chimique** *f* ELECTRON, MATERIAUX *métallurgie* etching; ~ **directe** *f* EN RENOUV direct coupling; ~ **d'un faisceau** *f* AERONAUT beam intercept; ~ **de grille** *f* TV drive voltage; ~ **au plasma** *f* ELECTRON plasma etching, reactive plasma etching; ~ **de sulfate** *f* CONSTR sulfate attack (AmE), sulphate attack (BrE); ~ **thermique** *f* METALL thermal etching

attaqué: ~ **par les acides** *adj* POLLUTION attacked by acids

attaquer *vt* CONS MECA engage, MECANIQUE drive, METALL etch

attaqueur: ~ **de ligne** *m* INFORMAT line driver; ~ **MOS** *m* ELECTRON MOS driver, metal-oxide semiconductor driver

atteindre *vt* MINES strike, NAUT *un port* fetch; ~ **le bedrock** *vt* MINES bottom; ~ **la criticité** *vt* NUCLEAIRE *réacteur* go critical

atteint: ~ **du mal de l'espace** *adj* ESPACE space sick

attelage *m* CH DE FER attachment, *véhicules* coupling, ESPACE docking, NAUT running gear, VEHICULES connector, *d'une remorque* coupling; ~ **à l'américaine** *m* CH DE FER *véhicules* buckeye drophead coupling; ~ **articulé** *m* TRANSPORT articulated coupling; ~ **automatique** *m* CH DE FER *véhicules*, TRANSPORT automatic coupling; ~ **automatique rigide** *m* TRANSPORT rigid automatic coupling; ~ **automatique semi-rigide** *m* TRANSPORT semirigid automatic coupling; ~ **à boulon** *m* VEHICULES *dispositif d'attelage* shackle; ~ **à chaîne** *m* CONS MECA chain coupling; ~ **à tampon central** *m* TRANSPORT central buffer coupling; ~ **à vis et tampons latéraux** *m* TRANSPORT side buffer screw coupling; ~ **Willison** *m* TRANSPORT Willison coupling

atteler *vt* CH DE FER *véhicules* couple, CONS MECA *une remorque à un tracteur* attach, MECANIQUE *véhicules* hitch

attendrisseur *m* AGRO ALIM tenderizer

attente:[1] **en** ~ *adj* INFORMAT, ORDINAT stand-by

attente:[2] **en** ~ *adv* POLLU MER on stand-by

attente[3] *f* AERONAUT holding, CONSTR toothing stone, MECANIQUE *soudage* hub, MILITAIRE stand-by; ~ **après**

numérotation *f* TELECOM postdialing delay (AmE), postdialling delay (BrE); ~ **mauvaise** *f* PETROLE WOW, waiting on weather; ~ **opérationnelle** *f* ESPACE *véhicules* hot stand-by

atténuateur *m* ELECTR *réglage de la lumière* dimmer, ELECTRON attenuator, fader, ENREGISTR attenuator, volume equalizer, TELECOM attenuator, pad; ~ **à absorption** *m* ELECTRON, TELECOM absorptive attenuator; ~ **basse fréquence** *m* ELECTRON audio attenuator; ~ **coaxial** *m* ELECTRON coaxial attenuator; ~ **coaxial variable** *m* ELECTRON variable coaxial attenuator; ~ **à diode PIN** *m* ELECTRON PIN diode attenuator; ~ **à dix positions** *m* ELECTRON decade attenuator; ~ **en échelle** *m* ELECTRON ladder attenuator; ~ **d'entrée** *m* ELECTRON input attenuator; ~ **fixe** *m* ELECTRON fixed attenuator; ~ **hyperfréquence** *m* ELECTRON variable microwave attenuator, TELECOM microwave attenuator; ~ **hyperfréquence variable** *m* ELECTRON microwave attenuator; ~ **à lame** *m* ELECTRON flap attenuator; ~ **à lame parallèle** *m* ELECTRON parallel vane attenuator; ~ **numérique** *m* ELECTRON digital attenuator; ~ **optique** *m* TELECOM optical attenuator; ~ **à piston** *m* ELECTRON, PHYSIQUE piston attenuator; ~ **réactif** *m* ELECTRON reactance attenuator; ~ **résistif** *m* (Can) TELECOM resistive attenuator; ~ **de sortie** *m* ELECTRON output attenuator; ~ **unidirectionnel** *m* PHYSIQUE isolator; ~ **variable** *m* ELECTRON variable attenuator; ~ **à variation continue** *m* ELECTRON continuously-variable attenuator

atténuation *f* ELECTR attenuation, ELECTRON attenuation, rejection, ENREGISTR attenuation, OPTIQUE attenuation, loss, ORDINAT attenuation, PETR attenuation, muting, PHYS ONDES, PHYSIQUE attenuation, POLLU MER mitigation, TELECOM loss; ~ **acoustique** *f* ELECTRON acoustic attenuation; ~ **d'une bande latérale** *f* ELECTRON sideband attenuation; ~ **du bruit** *f* IMPRIM *ergonomie* noise abatement; ~ **de contraste** *f* PHOTO contrast reduction; ~ **dans la bande passante** *f* ELECTRON pass band attenuation; ~ **en fréquence** *f* TV frequency losses; ~ **en hyperfréquence** *f* ELECTRON microwave attenuation; ~ **faible** *f* TELECOM low loss; ~ **du faisceau** *f* ELECTRON beam attenuation; ~ **de filtre** *f* ELECTRON filter attenuation; ~ **forte** *f* TELECOM high loss; ~ **à la fréquence intermédiaire** *f* ELECTRON, TELECOM IF rejection, intermediate frequency rejection; ~ **d'une harmonique** *f* ELECTRON harmonic attenuation; ~ **des harmoniques** *f* ELECTRON harmonic rejection; ~ **infinie** *f* ELECTRON infinite attenuation; ~ **de l'ondulation résiduelle** *f* CONSTR ripple attenuation; ~ **des parasites** *f* ELECTRON interference rejection; ~ **par la pluie** *f* ESPACE *communications* rain attenuation; ~ **de sortie** *f* ELECTRON output attenuation; ~ **variable** *f* ELECTRON variable attenuation

atténuer *vt* ELECTRON, ENREGISTR attenuate, IMPRIM keep down, *la couleur* tone down, PHOTO reduce

atterrir *vi* AERONAUT *véhicules* land, touch down, ESPACE touch down, *véhicules* land, MINES bank, land, NAUT ground, run ashore

atterrissage *m* AERONAUT landing, ESPACE landing, touchdown, MINES landing, *de la cage* banking, NAUT landfall, landing, TRANSPORT landing; ~ **brutal** *m* AERONAUT hard landing, rough landing; ~ **doux** *m* ESPACE soft landing; ~ **dur** *m* AERONAUT hard landing, rough landing, ESPACE hard landing; ~ **en arrondi** *m* AERONAUT flared landing; ~ **en catastrophe** *m* AERONAUT, ESPACE *véhicules* crash landing; ~ **forcé** *m*

AERONAUT forced landing, ESPACE *véhicules* emergency landing; ~ **aux instruments** *m* AERONAUT instrument landing; ~ **par mauvaise visibilité** *m* AERONAUT low visibility landing; ~ **par parachute** *m* MILITAIRE parachute landing; ~ **par vent de travers** *m* AERONAUT crosswind landing; ~ **ripé** *m* AERONAUT lateral drift landing; ~ **sans moteur** *m* AERONAUT dead stick landing; ~ **sans visibilité** *m* AERONAUT blind landing; ~ **sur le ventre** *m* AERONAUT belly landing, wheels-up landing; ~ **train rentré** *m* AERONAUT belly landing, wheels-up landing; ~ **à trois points** *m* AERONAUT three-point landing; ~ **trop court** *m* AERONAUT undershoot; ~ **trop long** *m* AERONAUT overshoot; ~ **d'urgence** *m* AERONAUT *véhicules*, ESPACE *véhicules* emergency landing

atterrissement *m* DISTRI EAU aggradation, OCEANO alluviation

atterrisseur *m* AERONAUT landing gear; ~ **à flotteurs** *m* AERONAUT floating gear; ~ **principal** *m* AERONAUT main landing gear; ~ **Viking** *m* ASTRONOMIE Viking lander

attirail *m* PHOTO apparatus, *d'un photographe* apparatus

attirer: s'~ *v réfl* PHYSIQUE attract

attisage *m* PRODUCTION poking

attisement *m* PRODUCTION poking

attisoir *m* PRODUCTION poker, prick bar, pricker

attisonnoir *m* PRODUCTION prick bar, pricker

attitude *f* ESPACE *véhicules* attitude, trim; ~ **latérale** *f* ESPACE *véhicules* roll attitude; ~ **longitudinale** *f* ESPACE *véhicules* pitch attitude

atto- *préf* METROLOGIE atto-

attractif *adj* PHYSIQUE attractive

attraction *f* ESPACE, PHYSIQUE attraction, gravitation; ~ **électrostatique** *f* ELECTR, ELECTROTEC electrostatic attraction; ~ **magnétique** *f* ELECTR magnetic attraction

attrape *f* NAUT heaving line

attrempage *m* CERAM VER heating-up; ~ **des pots** *m* CERAM VER pot arching

attremper *vt* CERAM VER heat up, THERMODYN *verre* fire up, heat up

attribuer *vt* INFORMAT, ORDINAT allocate, assign

attribut *m* INFORMAT, ORDINAT, TELECOM attribute; ~ **à un ensemble de valeurs** *m* TELECOM set-valued attribute; ~ **gras** *m* PRODUCTION bold type

attribution *f* INFORMAT, ORDINAT allocation; ~ **dynamique** *f* INFORMAT, ORDINAT dynamic allocation; ~ **de fréquence** *f* TV frequency allocation; ~ **de fréquences** *f* INFORMAT frequency distribution; ~ **de mémoire** *f* INFORMAT, ORDINAT storage allocation; ~ **des priorités** *f* INFORMAT, ORDINAT priority sequencing

attributs: ~ des feuilles de style *m pl* IMPRIM *composition* style attributes

attrition *f* CERAM VER, CHARBON, CONSTR, IMPRIM *broyage extra-fin des pigments des encres* attrition

atypique *adj* CHIMIE *caractère* paratypical

Au *(or)* CHIMIE Au *(gold)*

aubage *m* MECANIQUE *de turbine* blading

aube *f* AERONAUT *turbomachines* vane, CONS MECA *d'un ventilateur, d'une roue hydraulique* paddle, paddle board, *d'une turbine* vane, *de ventilateur, de turbine* blade, DISTRI EAU float, floatboard, EN RENOUV *turbines* runner blade, ESPACE blade, INST HYDR curved vane, runner blade, runner vane, *de turbine* blade, MECANIQUE vane, NAUT *hydraulique* blade, PRODUCTION vane; ~ **à cols multiples** *f* AERONAUT multithroat vane; ~ **du compresseur** *f* AERONAUT compressor blade; ~ **directrice** *f* AERONAUT intake guide vane, EN RENOUV *turbines* guide vane, INST HYDR guide vane, stationary vane, *aube fixe de turbine* guide blade, MECANIQUE, REFRIG guide vane; ~ **directrice d'entrée** *f* AERONAUT intake guide vane; ~ **fixe** *f* INST HYDR guide vane, stationary vane, MECANIQUE guide vane; ~ **fixe de stator** *f* AERONAUT fixed stator vane, stator vane; ~ **de guidance** *f* AERONAUT intake guide vane; ~ **mobile de rotor** *f* AERONAUT movable rotor blade; ~ **de prérotation** *f* AERONAUT intake guide vane; ~ **de stator** *f* AERONAUT *d'un compresseur* stator vane; ~ **de turbine** *f* NAUT turbine blade

aubes *f pl* CERAM VER spiral runner bars; ~ **d'admission variables** *f pl* NUCLEAIRE *à pas variables* variable pitch inlet vanes

aubette *f* TRANSPORT bus shelter, shelter

audibilité *f* TELECOM clarity

audimètre *m* ENREGISTR audibility meter

audio[1] *adj* ELECTRON, ENREGISTR audio

audio[2] *m* INFORMAT, ORDINAT audio

audiofréquence *f* ACOUSTIQUE, ELECTRON, ENREGISTR, PHYS ONDES, TELECOM AF, audio frequency

audiogramme *m* ACOUSTIQUE audiogram; ~ **d'un effet de masque** *m* ACOUSTIQUE masking level audiogram; ~ **tonal** *m* ACOUSTIQUE pure tone audiogram; ~ **vocal** *m* ACOUSTIQUE speech audiogram

audiomessagerie *f* TELECOM voice mail

audiomètre *m* ACOUSTIQUE, PHYS ONDES audiometer; ~ **vocal** *m* ACOUSTIQUE speech audiometer

audiométrie *f* ACOUSTIQUE, ENREGISTR audiometry; ~ **liminaire** *f* SECURITE threshold audiometry; ~ **vocale** *f* ACOUSTIQUE speech audiometry

audiovidéographie *f* TELECOM audio-videotex

audit *m* QUALITE, TELECOM audit; ~ **qualité** *m* QUALITE quality audit; ~ **de sécurité** *m* TELECOM security audit; ~ **de sécurité du cycle de travail** *m* CONSTR job cycle safety audit

audité *m* QUALITE auditee

auditeur: ~ normal *m* ACOUSTIQUE normal listener; ~ **qualité** *m* QUALITE quality auditor

audition: ~ stéréophonique *f* ENREGISTR stereo sound

auditorium *m* ENREGISTR auditorium

auge *f* CONSTR trough, DISTRI EAU sluice box, *d'une roue hydraulique* bucket, EN RENOUV *turbine* bucket, PRODUCTION flume, leat, trough

augélite *f* MINERAUX augelite

auget *m* CONSTR *d'un élévateur, d'une drague*, DISTRI EAU *d'une roue hydraulique* bucket; ~ **d'élévateur** *m* PRODUCTION elevator bucket, elevator cup; ~ **de turbine** *m* MECANIQUE *turbine hydraulique* bucket

augite *f* MINERAUX augite

augmentateur: ~ de poussée *m* AERONAUT *d'aéronef* thrust augmenter

augmentation *f* ELECTRON *de dynamique* expansion, NUCLEAIRE growth, TEXTILE increment; ~ **brusque de section** *f* INST HYDR sudden enlargement of cross section; ~ **du contraste** *f* PHOTO increase in contrast; ~ **différentielle** *f* TEXTILE step increment; ~ **de pas** *f* AERONAUT pitch increase

augmenter *vt* TEXTILE increment; ~ **la productivité** *vt* TEXTILE boost productivity; ~ **progressivement** *vt* ENREGISTR fade up

aulacogène *m* GEOLOGIE aulacogen

aulne *m* PAPIER alder

aune *m* PAPIER alder

auralite *f* MINERAUX auralite

auréole *f* MINES gas cap, show, testing flame; **~ de contact** *f* GEOLOGIE contact aureole; **~ de dispersion** *f* NUCLEAIRE dispersion train, halo of dispersion; **~ métamorphique** *f* GEOLOGIE contact aureole

aureux *adj* CHIMIE aurous

aurichalcite *f* MINERAUX aurichalcite

aurifère *adj* MINERAUX auriferous, MINES auriferous, gold-bearing

aurocyanure *m* CHIMIE aurocyanide

aurore *f* ASTRONOMIE, ESPACE, GEOPHYS aurora; **~ australe** *f* ASTRONOMIE, METEO, NAUT aurora australis; **~ australis** *f* GEOPHYS aurora australis; **~ boréale** *f* ASTRONOMIE, GEOPHYS, METEO aurora borealis, NAUT aurora borealis, northern lights; **~ polaire** *f* METEO polar aurora, NAUT aurora polaris

auscultation: **~ par courant de Foucault** *f* CH DE FER eddy current inspection; **~ de qualité de l'eau** *f* DISTRI EAU water quality monitoring; **~ des rails** *f* CH DE FER rail inspection

aussière *f* CONS MECA, NAUT hawser; **~ de halage** *f* NAUT warp

austénite: **~ résiduelle** *f* METALL residual austenite; **~ restante** *f* METALL residual austenite

austénitique *adj* MATERIAUX austenitic

autel *m* PRODUCTION bridge, fire bridge, flame bridge, furnace bridge

Autel *m* ASTRONOMIE Ara

authentification *f* INFORMAT, ORDINAT authentication, QUALITE authentication, certification, TELECOM authentication, authentication procedure; **~ de l'entité homologue** *f* TELECOM peer entity authentication; **~ inverse** *f* INFORMAT, ORDINAT reverse authentication; **~ de l'origine de données** *f* TELECOM data origin authentication

authentifier *vt* QUALITE authenticate

authigène *adj* PETR authigenic

authigenèse *f* GEOLOGIE *de roche sédimentaire* authigenesis

auto: **~ blindée** *f* MILITAIRE armored car (AmE), armoured car (BrE); **~ blindée amphibie** *f* MILITAIRE amphibious armored car (AmE), amphibious armoured car (BrE); **~ blindée de reconnaissance** *f* MILITAIRE armored reconnaissance car (AmE), armoured reconnaissance car (BrE); **~ des sables** *f* TRANSPORT dune buggy

auto-absorption *f* PHYS RAYON *de la radiation* self-absorption

auto-adaptatif *adj* INFORMAT, ORDINAT self-adapting

auto-ajustable *adj* COMMANDE self-adjusting

auto-allumage *m* AERONAUT auto-ignition, AUTO self-firing, self-ignition, VEHICULES auto-ignition

autobloquant *adj* EMBALLAGE, VEHICULES self-locking

autobroyage *m* CHARBON autogenous milling, crushing

autobroyeur *m* CHARBON autogenous mill, coal crusher

autobus: **~ à accumulateur** *m* TRANSPORT battery bus; **~ articulé** *m* TRANSPORT articulated bus; **~ bimodal** *m* TRANSPORT bimodal bus, dual-mode bus, road rail bus; **~ au cadran** *m* TRANSPORT demand-scheduled bus service; **~ à la demande** *m* TRANSPORT demand-responsive system, dial-a-bus, on-call bus system; **~ électrique** *m* TRANSPORT electric bus; **~ à gaz** *m* TRANSPORT gas-fueled bus (AmE), gas-fuelled bus (BrE); **~ à gaz liquéfié** *m* TRANSPORT liquid petroleum gas bus; **~ à gaz naturel comprimé** *m* TRANSPORT pressurized natural gas bus; **~ à gaz naturel liquéfié** *m* TRANSPORT LNG bus, liquid natural gas bus; **~ guidé** *m* TRANSPORT railbus; **~ souterrain** *m* TRANSPORT underground bus; **~ sur voie de chemin de fer** *m* TRANSPORT bus on railroad tracks (AmE), bus on railway tracks (BrE); **~ sur wagon de chemin de fer** *m* TRANSPORT bus on railroad car (AmE), bus on railway wagon (BrE); **~ à traction électrique avec montage hybride** *m* TRANSPORT hybrid bus; **~ à turbine à gaz** *m* TRANSPORT gas turbine bus; **~ à vapeur** *m* TRANSPORT steambus

autocabrage *m* AERONAUT pitch-up

autocar *m* TRANSPORT coach, long-distance bus, motorcoach; **~ à turbine** *m* TRANSPORT turbocruiser

autocaravane *f* TRANSPORT motor home

autocatalyse *f* CHIMIE autocatalysis, METALL autocatalytic effect

autocentrage *m* ELECTRON self-tracking; **~ de la bande passante** *m* ELECTRON self-tracking

autochtonal *adj* POLLUTION autochtonous

autochtone[1] *adj* PETR autochtonal, autochtonous, POLLUTION autochtonous

autochtone[2] *m* GEOLOGIE autochthon

autocicatrisation *f* ELECTROTEC self-healing

autoclave *m* AGRO ALIM, CERAM VER, CHARBON, CHIMIE, EQUIP LAB *chaleur, pression* autoclave, THERMODYN digester; **~ à blanchiment** *m* TEXTILE kier; **~ continu** *m* AGRO ALIM continuous cooker

autocollant *adj* EMBALLAGE self-sealing

autocollimateur *m* METROLOGIE autocollimator

autocommutateur *m* ELECTROTEC *téléphonique* telephone switch, ORDINAT switching equipment; **~ crossbar** *m* TELECOM crossbar exchange; **~ électromécanique** *m* TELECOM electromechanical exchange, electromechanical switching unit; **~ électronique à commande centralisée** *m* TELECOM centralized control system; **~ à intégration voix-données** *m* TELECOM integrated voice-data switch; **~ multiservice** *m* TELECOM multiservice-switching system; **~ numérique** *m* TELECOM digital exchange, digital switch; **~ numérique à intégration de services** *m* TELECOM integrated services exchange; **~ privé** *m* TELECOM PABX, private automatic branch exchange, PBX, private branch exchange; **~ privé pour le RNIS-LB** *m* TELECOM B-ISDN PBX, PBXIS-LB; **~ privé à programme enregistré** *m* TELECOM stored program control PABX (AmE), stored programme control PABX (BrE); **~ privé réparti** *m* TELECOM distributed PBX; **~ privé voix-données** *m* TELECOM integrated voice-data PABX; **~ à quatre fils** *m* TELECOM four-wire switch, four-wire switching system; **~ à relais à tige** *m* TELECOM reed relay electronic exchange; **~ à relais à tiges** *m* ELECTROTEC reed relay switch; **~ RNIS** *m* TELECOM ISDN switch; **~ temporel** *m* TELECOM time switch; **~ visiophonique** *m* TELECOM videophone switching system

autoconstruction *f* CONSTR self-help housing

autocontrôle *m* QUALITE self-inspection

autocorrélation *f* ELECTRON, TELECOM autocorrelation

autocuiseur *m* AGRO ALIM, CONS MECA pressure cooker

autodécharge *f* AUTO, ELECTROTEC, ESPACE *véhicules* self-discharge

autodestructeur *m* MILITAIRE self-destruct

autodiffusion *f* PHYSIQUE self-scattering

autodirecteur *m* MILITAIRE homing device

autodocumentant *adj* INFORMAT, ORDINAT self-documenting

autodurcissement *m* METALL self-hardening

auto-échauffement *m* ELECTROTEC self-heating

auto-épuration *f* DISTRI EAU self-purification

auto-excitation *f* ELECTROTEC self-excitation, NUCLEAIRE self-excitation, spontaneous excitation, squitter

autogène *adj* CHARBON, CONS MECA autogenous

autogire *m* AERONAUT autogiro, autogyro

autogonflant *adj* POLLU MER self-inflating

autoguidage *m* COMMANDE automatic control, ESPACE *véhicules* autopilot, homing; **~ actif** *m* AERONAUT homing active guidance; **~ passif** *m* AERONAUT homing passive guidance; **~ semi-actif** *m* AERONAUT homing semi-active guidance

autogyre *m* AERONAUT, TRANSPORT autogiro, autogyro, gyroplane

auto-identification *f* TELECOM self-identification

auto-induction *f* AUTO, ELECTROTEC, PHYSIQUE self-induction

auto-ionisation *adj* PHYSIQUE auto-ionization

autolyse *f* AGRO ALIM autolysis

automanette *f* AERONAUT autothrottle

automate *m* INFORMAT, ORDINAT automaton, PRODUCTION *automatisme industriel* controller; **~ industriel** *m* PRODUCTION industrial controller; **~ programmable** *m* ELECTROTEC process controller, PRODUCTION programmable logic controller, *automatisme industriel* programmable controller; **~ programmable à E/S locales** *m* PRODUCTION *automatisme industriel* local I/O PC; **~ programmable indépendant** *m* PRODUCTION *automatisme industriel* stand-alone controller

automation *f* CONSTR automation

automatique *adj* CONS MECA fully-automatic, ESPACE *véhicules* unmanned, INFORMAT automatic, INSTRUMENT fully-automatic, MECANIQUE, ORDINAT automatic

Automatique: **~ International** *m* TELECOM IDD, IDDD, ISD, International Direct Dialing (AmE), International Direct Distance Dialing (AmE), International Subscriber Dialling (BrE)

automatisation *f* CONS MECA, CONSTR, ESPACE, INFORMAT, NAUT, ORDINAT, PRODUCTION automation; **~ de bibliothèque** *f* INFORMAT, ORDINAT library automation; **~ de la conception** *f* INFORMAT design automation; **~ industrielle** *f* CONS MECA industrial automation, INFORMAT process automation; **~ de navire** *f* NAUT ship automation

automatisé *adj* PRODUCTION automated, computer-based, computerized

automatiser *vt* COMMANDE automate, CONSTR automate, automatize, INFORMAT, ORDINAT automate

automatisme *m* ELECTR automatic control, ESPACE *véhicules* automatic system; **~ industriel** *m* INFORMAT, ORDINAT process automation

automatismes: **~ programmables** *m pl* PRODUCTION programmable controls; **~ traditionnels** *m pl* PRODUCTION traditional controls

autométamorphisme *m* EN RENOUV autometamorphism

automobile[1] *adj* TRANSPORT automobile, automotive

automobile[2] *f* AUTO automobile, car, TRANSPORT automobile, motorcar, VEHICULES automobile, car; **~ isoélectrique** *f* TRANSPORT isoelectric vehicle

automodulation *f* TELECOM automodulation

automorphe *adj* GEOLOGIE *dans roches métamorphiques* idioblastic, *texture* automorphic, euhedral, PETR automorphic, automorphous

automoteur *adj* NAUT, POLLU MER self-propelled

automotrice[1] *adj* TRANSPORT turboelectric

automotrice[2] *f* TRANSPORT driving motor car, motorcoach, power car; **~ à accumulateurs** *f* TRANSPORT accumulator railcar; **~ à adhérence** *f* TRANSPORT adhesion railcar; **~ articulée** *f* TRANSPORT articulated railcar, articulated tramcar; **~ diesel** *f* CH DE FER *véhicule* railcar; **~ électrique** *f* ELECTR *véhicule* electric railcar; **~ intermédiaire** *f* TRANSPORT driving trailer car; **~ à turbine à gaz** *f* TRANSPORT gas turbine motorcoach (BrE), gas turbine railcar (AmE)

autonome *adj* ELECTROTEC self-powered, ESPACE *véhicules* autonomous, self-contained, INFORMAT, ORDINAT off-line, stand-alone, PHYSIQUE self-contained, TELECOM off-line

autonomie *f* AERONAUT endurance, ESPACE *véhicules* autonomy, cruising range, endurance; **~ de données** *f* INFORMAT, ORDINAT data independence; **~ pétrolière** *f* PETROLE oil self-sufficiency; **~ théorique** *f* AERONAUT endurance

auto-obturant *adj* ESPACE *véhicules* self-sealing

auto-oxydation *f* CHIMIE auto-oxidation

autopropulsé *adj* NAUT, POLLU MER self-propelled

autopropulsion *f* ESPACE self-propulsion

autoprotecteur *adj* PRODUCTION self-shielding

autoradiographie *f* PHYS RAYON, PHYSIQUE autoradiography; **~ qualitative** *f* NUCLEAIRE qualitative autoradiography

autoradiolyse *f* PHYS RAYON autoradiolysis

autorail *m* TRANSPORT rail coach; **~ diesel-électrique** *m* CH DE FER *véhicules* diesel-electric railcar (AmE)

autoréglable *adj* COMMANDE self-adjusting

autoréglage *m* COMMANDE, TV self-adjustment

autorégression *f* ORDINAT autoregression

autorégulateur[1] *adj* COMMANDE automatically-controlled

autorégulateur[2] *m* CONS MECA automatic regulator, self-acting regulator

autorégulé *adj* COMMANDE automatically-controlled, autoregulating, self-adjusting

autorisation *f* BREVETS authorization, *nationale* authority, INFORMAT, ORDINAT, TELECOM authorization; **~ d'approche** *f* AERONAUT approach clearance; **~ du contrôle de la circulation aérienne** *f* AERONAUT air traffic control clearance; **~ d'exploitation** *f* AERONAUT *transport aérien* operating permit; **~ d'exploitation de route** *f* AERONAUT route licence (BrE), route licencing (BrE), route license (AmE), route licensing (AmE); **~ de transfert** *f* TELECOM TFA, transfer allowed; **~ de vol** *f* AERONAUT flight clearance

autorisé *adj* AERONAUT *à décoller* cleared

Autorité: **~ internationale des fonds marins** *f* OCEANO International Sea Bed Authority

autorité: **~ accordant des permis de construire** *f* CONSTR chief building authority

autorités: **~ du bassin fluvial** *f pl* DISTRI EAU river authority; **~ de gestion des eaux** *f pl* DISTRI EAU water authority; **~ portuaires** *f pl* NAUT port authorities

autorotation: **~ du réacteur** *f* AERONAUT engine windmilling

autoroute *f* CONSTR freeway (AmE), motorway (BrE), TRANSPORT highway (BrE), motorway (BrE), roadway; **~ automatique** *f* TRANSPORT automatic highway (AmE), automatic motorway (BrE); **~ d'informations** *f* ORDINAT, TELECOM information highway; **~ urbaine** *f* TRANSPORT freeway (AmE)

autoroutier *adj* CONSTR freeway (AmE), motorway

(BrE)

autoserrant *adj* COMMANDE automatically-closing, self-closing, EMBALLAGE self-closing

autosilencieux *adj* CINEMAT self-blimped

autosynchronisation *f* TELECOM autosynchronization

autotransformateur *m* ELECTR one-coil transformer, ELECTROTEC, PHYSIQUE autotransformer; **~ abaisseur de tension** *m* ELECTROTEC step-down autotransformer; **~ de démarrage** *m* ELECTR autotransformer starter; **~ élévateur de tension** *m* ELECTROTEC step-up autotransformer

autotrophe *m* AGRO ALIM autotroph

autovideur *adj* NAUT self-draining

autovulcanisation *f* PLAST CAOU *caoutchouc* self-vulcanization

autoxydation *f* AGRO ALIM autoxidation

autunite *f* MINERAUX autunite

auvent *m* AERONAUT cowl, CONSTR hood, porch roof; **~ d'éclairage** *m* AERONAUT glare shield

auxiliaire[1] *adj* CONS MECA auxiliary, ESPACE *véhicules* ancillary, strap-on, PRODUCTION ancillary

auxiliaire[2] *m* PRODUCTION utility; **~ pousser pour relâcher** *m* PRODUCTION twist-to-release push unit; **~ tirer pour relâcher** *m* PRODUCTION twist-to-release pull unit; **~ tourner pour relâcher** *m* PRODUCTION *automatisme industriel* twist to release unit

auxochrome *m* CHIMIE auxochrome

AV *m (avant)* CONS MECA crank-end

aval[1] *adj* CONSTR, HYDROLOGIE, PHYS FLUID downstream; **d'~** *adj* HYDROLOGIE downstream; **en ~** *adj* NAUT, PHYSIQUE downstream

aval:[2] **en ~** *adv* CONSTR, ESPACE, GAZ, HYDROLOGIE, MECANIQUE, NAUT, PHYS FLUID, TRANSPORT downstream; **en ~ pendage** *adv* GEOLOGIE downdip

aval[3] *m* TEXTILE downstream; **~ pendage** *m* MINES *d'un chantier d'abattage d'une galerie* bottom, footwall, PETROLE down dip; **~ pendage d'une galerie** *m* MINES footwall

avalaison *f* HYDROLOGIE freshet, spate

avalanche *f* ELECTROTEC, METEO avalanche

avalasse *f* HYDROLOGIE freshet, spate

avalent *adj* CHIMIE avalent

avaleresse *f* DISTRI EAU shaft in water-bearing ground

avalite *f* MINERAUX avalite

avance *f* ASTRONOMIE *du périphélie*, CHARBON advance, CONS MECA *travail au tour* traverse feed, *à l'allumage* advance, lead, ELECTR *phase* advance, ELECTRON *de phase* lead, MECANIQUE feed, OCEANO *de la marée* priming, PHYSIQUE *du périhélie* advance, PRODUCTION *travail au tour* feed, VEHICULES *à l'allumage* advance; **~ à l'admission** *f* AUTO cam angle, INST HYDR outside lead, preadmission, PRODUCTION early admission; **~ à l'allumage** *f* AERONAUT ignition advance, spark advance, AUTO angle of advance; **~ angulaire** *f* CONS MECA angle of advance; **~ angulaire à l'admission** *f* CONS MECA angular lead; **~ angulaire à l'échappement** *f* CONS MECA angle of prerelease, angular prerelease; **~ automatique** *f* COMMANDE automatic advance, CONS MECA power feed, *outil de coupe* automatic feed, PETROLE *du trépan* automatic feed, PHOTO auto winding; **~ automatique à dépression** *f* AUTO, VEHICULES *à l'allumage* vacuum advance mechanism; **~ automatique en plongée** *f* CONS MECA *machines-outils* automatic down feed; **~ descendante** *f* CONS MECA downfeed; **~ à l'échappement** *f* INST HYDR exhaust lead, inside lead slide valve; **~ à l'émission** *f* INST HYDR inside lead slide valve, PRODUCTION early release; **~ en plongée** *f* CONS MECA, PRODUCTION infeed; **~ initiale à l'allumage** *f* AUTO initial advance; **~ linéaire à l'admission** *f* INST HYDR outside lead; **~ linéaire à l'échappement** *f* INST HYDR exhaust lead, inside lead slide valve; **~ manuelle** *f* CONS MECA hand feed; **~ par tour** *f* AERONAUT *de l'hélice* effective pitch; **~ de phase** *f* ELECTR *courant alternatif*, ELECTRON, PHYSIQUE phase lead; **~ rapide** *f* CONS MECA coarse feed, fast feed, ENREGISTR, TV fast forward; **~ de la tête** *f* CONS MECA head feed; **~ tiroir** *f* INST HYDR lead; **~ transversale** *f* CONS MECA crossfeed, PRODUCTION cross-traverse

avancée *f* CONS MECA heading, MINES head

avancement *m* CONS MECA heading, MINES head, heading, PRODUCTION feed, feeding; **~ automatique** *m* PETROLE *du trépan* automatic feed; **~ des charbons** *m* CINEMAT arc feed, carbon advancing; **~ horizontal au bouclier** *m* CH DE FER shield tunneling (AmE), shield tunnelling (BrE); **~ de pellicule** *m* CINEMAT film transport; **~ rapide** *m* PETR drilling break

avance-papier *m* IMPRIM, ORDINAT FF, form feed

avancer:[1] **~ rapidement** *vt* TV fast forward

avancer:[2] **s'~ vers le large** *v réfl* GEOLOGIE prograde

avant[1] *adj* AERONAUT forward, NAUT fore, forward; **de l'~** *adj* NAUT fore, forward; **~ du navire en haut** *adj* NAUT head-up; **sur l'~** *adj* NAUT forward

avant[2] *adv* NAUT fore, forward; **de l'~** *adv* NAUT ahead, forward; **en ~** *adv* ESPACE, NAUT ahead; **de l'~ à l'arrière** *adv* NAUT fore and aft; **en ~ demie** *adv* NAUT half-ahead; **en ~ lente** *adv* NAUT slow ahead; **en ~ toute** *adv* NAUT full ahead; **en ~ très lente** *adv* NAUT dead slow ahead; **sur l'~** *adv* NAUT ahead, forward; **sur l'~ du travers** *adv* NAUT forward of the beam

avant[3] *m* CONS MECA crank-end, CONSTR front, NAUT bow; **~ en cuiller** *m* NAUT spoon bow

avantage *m* BREVETS advantage

avant-bassin *m* CERAM VER working end

avant-clou *m* CONSTR gimlet

avant-corps *m* CONSTR projection

avant-creuset *m* PRODUCTION forehearth, *de cubilot* receiver

avant-cylindre *m* CONS MECA crank-end of cylinder

avant-étude *f* CONSTR preliminary design

avant-fosse *f* GEOLOGIE fore deep

avant-lancement *m* ESPACE *véhicules* prefiring

avant-métré *m* CONSTR preliminary cost estimate

avant-pays *m* GEOLOGIE foreland; **~ marin** *m* OCEANO foreland

avant-pieu *m* CONSTR punch, set

avant-plan:[1] **d'~** *adj* INFORMAT, ORDINAT foreground

avant-plan[2] *m* CINEMAT foreground

avant-port *m* NAUT outer harbor (AmE), outer harbour (BrE), OCEANO forebay, outer harbor (AmE), outer harbour (BrE), outer port, outport

avant-projet *m* CONSTR preliminary design, PRODUCTION draft (AmE)

avant-puits *m* PETROLE derrick cellar

avant-trou *m* CONS MECA, PETR pilot hole

avarie *f* NAUT damage; **~ de barre** *f* NAUT helm damage

avarié: ~ pendant le transport par mer *adj* NAUT sea-damaged

avaser *vt* CONSTR *lime ou sable sur une surface* bite

AV-cylindre *m* CONS MECA crank-end of cylinder

avenant *m* CONSTR variation order

avénéine *f* CHIMIE avenin, avenine

avénine *f* CHIMIE avenin, avenine

aventurine *f* MINERAUX aventurine quartz

avérer *v réfl* TELECOM perform

avernérite *f* MINERAUX wernerite

averse *f* METEO shower; ~ **cosmique** *f* ESPACE *astronomie* cosmic shower; ~ **nominale** *f* HYDROLOGIE design storm

avertissement *m* CH DE FER caution signal, PRODUCTION warning; ~ **de brume** *m* NAUT fog warning

avertisseur *m* AUTO horn, CONS MECA *signal acoustique ou optique* alarm, PAPIER alarm bell, SECURITE alarm; ~ **automatique** *m* COMMANDE automatic alarm; ~ **avant la mise en route** *m* CONS MECA prestart warning; ~ **de collision** *m* ESPACE *véhicules* collision warning system; ~ **de décrochage** *m* AERONAUT stall warning device; ~ **détecteur** *m* AERONAUT ice detector; ~ **de fuite** *m* SECURITE leakage warning; ~ **de fumée et de gaz** *m* SECURITE smoke and gas alarm installation; ~ **de givrage** *m* AERONAUT ice detector; ~ **d'incendie** *m* COMMANDE, ELECTR *appareil*, NAUT, SECURITE fire alarm; ~ **infrarouge des mouvements** *m* SECURITE infrared motion alarm, infrared movement-sensing alarm; ~ **lumineux** *m* CH DE FER telltale lamp, *véhicules* indicator lamp, VEHICULES *éclairage* headlamp flasher; ~ **optique** *m* CH DE FER, COMMANDE warning sign, VEHICULES *éclairage* headlamp flasher; ~ **de panne** *m* CINEMAT failure indicator; ~ **de proximité** *m* AERONAUT proximity warning indicator; ~ **de proximité de bord** *m* AERONAUT airborne proximity warning indicator; ~ **sonore** *m* SECURITE warning bell, VEHICULES *accessoire de sécurité* horn; ~ **de surcharge** *m* ELECTR *réseau, appareil* overload indicator

aveugle *adj* ESPACE blind

aveugler *vt* DISTRI EAU *voie d'eau* stop, stop a leak in, PRODUCTION stop, stop up

avide: ~ **d'eau** *adj* MATERIAUX absorbent of water, hygroscopic, *absorbant* thirsty, *argile* greedy of water

avion *m* AERONAUT aeroplane (BrE), aircraft (AmE), airplane (AmE), airplane (AmE), plane, TRANSPORT airplane (AmE), plane; ~ **d'affaires** *m* AERONAUT business aircraft, executive aircraft; ~ **à aile basse** *m* AERONAUT low-wing plane; ~ **à aile demi-surélevée** *m* AERONAUT mid-wing plane; ~ **à aile haute** *m* AERONAUT high-wing plane; ~ **à aile propulsive** *m* AERONAUT aircraft with powered lift; ~ **à ailes inclinables** *m* AERONAUT tilt-wing plane; ~ **à ailes repliables** *m* AERONAUT folding wing aircraft; ~ **allongé** *m* AERONAUT stretched aircraft; ~ **d'appui sol** *m* MILITAIRE strike aircraft; ~ **cargo** *m* AERONAUT cargo plane; ~ **de chasse** *m* MILITAIRE pursuit plane; ~ **de combat** *m* MILITAIRE combat aircraft; ~ **combiné** *m* AERONAUT composite aircraft; ~ **à conversion rapide** *m* AERONAUT quick change aircraft; ~ **convertible** *m* AERONAUT convertiplane; ~ **à couloir unique** *m* AERONAUT single aisle aircraft; ~ **à décollage et attérissage court** *m* (*ADAC*) TRANSPORT short takeoff and landing aircraft (*STOL aircraft*); ~ **à décollage et atterrissage courts** *m* (*ADAC*) AERONAUT short takeoff and landing aircraft (*STOL aircraft*); ~ **à décollage et atterrissage courts et silencieux** *m* AERONAUT QSTOL aircraft, quiet short takeoff and landing aircraft; ~ **à décollage et atterrissage ordinaires** *m* (*ADAO*) AERONAUT conventional takeoff and landing aircraft (*CTOL aircraft*); ~ **à décollage et atterrissage réduits** *m* (*ADAR*) AERONAUT reduced takeoff and landing aircraft (*RTOL aircraft*); ~ **à décollage et atterrissage silencieux** *m* (*ADAS*) AERO-

NAUT quiet takeoff and landing aircraft (*QTOL aircraft*); ~ **à décollage et atterrissage verticaux** *m* (*ADAV*) AERONAUT vertical takeoff and landing aircraft (*VTOL aircraft*); ~ **embarqué** *m* MILITAIRE carrier-borne aircraft; ~ **à flèche variable** *m* AERONAUT variable geometry aircraft; ~ **fusée** *m* AERONAUT rocket plane; ~ **à fuselage portant** *m* AERONAUT lifting-body aircraft; ~ **à géométrie variable** *m* AERONAUT variable geometry aircraft; ~ **gros porteur** *m* AERONAUT jumbo jet, wide-bodied aircraft, wide-body aircraft, TRANSPORT wide-bodied aircraft, wide-body aircraft; ~ **hypersonique** *m* AERONAUT hypersonic aircraft; ~ **de ligne** *m* AERONAUT airliner, passenger plane; ~ **lisse** *m* AERONAUT clean configuration; ~ **long-courrier** *m* AERONAUT long-haul airliner; ~ **à nez basculant** *m* AERONAUT droop-nose aircraft; ~ **d'observation** *m* MILITAIRE artillery spotter, POLLU MER spotter plane; ~ **de pénétration** *m* MILITAIRE strike aircraft; ~ **porteur** *m* ESPACE launching aircraft; ~ **de présérie** *m* AERONAUT preproduction aircraft; ~ **rapidement convertible** *m* AERONAUT quick change aircraft; ~ **ravitailleur** *m* MILITAIRE supply aircraft, *en carburant* refueling aircraft (AmE), refuelling aircraft (BrE); ~ **à réaction** *m* TRANSPORT jet, jet aeroplane (BrE), jet airplane (AmE), jet plane; ~ **à réaction propulseur** *m* AERONAUT jet; ~ **de recherche tout-temps** *m* MILITAIRE all-weather search aircraft; ~ **de réglage de tir** *m* POLLU MER spotter plane; ~ **de repérage** *m* POLLU MER spotter plane; ~ **de série** *m* AERONAUT production aircraft; ~ **à une seule travée** *m* AERONAUT single aisle aircraft; ~ **spatial** *m* ESPACE *véhicules* space plane; ~ **subsonique** *m* AERONAUT subsonic aircraft; ~ **supersonique** *m* AERONAUT supersonic aircraft; ~ **tout-cargo** *m* AERONAUT all-cargo aircraft; ~ **à transformation rapide** *m* AERONAUT *pour utilisation passager, fret* quick change aircraft; ~ **de transport et de liaison** *m* AERONAUT transport and communications aircraft; ~ **de transport exclusif de fret** *m* AERONAUT all-cargo aircraft; ~ **à trois plans** *m* AERONAUT triplane; ~ **à voilure canard** *m* AERONAUT canard-wing aircraft, tail-first configuration aircraft; ~ **à voilure fixe** *m* AERONAUT fixed wing aircraft

avion-cible *m* MILITAIRE *sans pilote* pilotless target aircraft, pilotless target plane

avion-citerne *m* AERONAUT refueling craft (AmE), refuelling craft (BrE)

avionique *f* AERONAUT avionics

aviron *m* NAUT oar, scull

avis: ~ **d'amélioration** *m* SECURITE improvement notice; ~ **de chaîne de service** *m* TELECOM service string advice; ~ **de coup de vent** *m* METEO, NAUT gale warning; ~ **de forte brise** *m* NAUT gale warning; ~ **d'interdiction** *m* SECURITE HASAWA (BrE), prohibition notice; ~ **de modification** *m* PRODUCTION modification proposal; ~ **de tempête** *m* METEO gale warning, storm warning, NAUT storm warning

aviso *m* NAUT *marine* sloop; ~ **de croisière** *m* NAUT cruising cutter

aviso-torpilleur *m* NAUT torpedo gunboat

avisse *f* CONS MECA screw piece

avitaillement *m* AERONAUT fueling (AmE), fuelling (BrE), NAUT ship chandling

avitailleur *m* AERONAUT bowser, ESPACE bowser, fueling vehicle (AmE), fuelling vehicle (BrE), POLLU MER tender; ~ **de navire** *m* NAUT ship chandler

aviver *vt* CERAM VER *la feuille d'étain* burnish

avoir: ~ **de la bande** *vi* NAUT heel, *navire* list; ~ **du contre-arc** *vi* NAUT sag; ~ **de la gîte** *vi* NAUT heel; ~ **de la main** *vi* PAPIER bulk

avorter *vi* ESPACE abort

avoyage *m* CONS MECA *des dents d'une scie* setting

avoyé *adj* CONS MECA set

avoyer *vi* CONS MECA set, PRODUCTION *une scie* jump

awaruite *f* MINERAUX awaruite

axe:[1] **d'~ en axe** *adv* CONS MECA from center-to-center (AmE), from centre-to-centre (BrE)

axe[2] *m* CINEMAT spindle, CONS MECA center line (AmE), centre line (BrE), shaft, spindle, *d'un cylindre* spindle, CRISTALL axis, GEOLOGIE *du pli anticlinal* crest, GEOMETRIE axial line, axis, IMPRIM *mécanique* spindle, MECANIQUE center line (AmE), centre line (BrE), shaft, *d'un couple* axis, *d'une roue, d'une poulie* axis, METEO *d'une dépression* axis, PAPIER axle, spindle, PHYSIQUE axis, PRODUCTION spindle, TV I-axis, wide band axis, VEHICULES *moteur, transmission* shaft; ~ **des l'abscisses** *m* PHYSIQUE x-axis; ~ **des abscisses** *m* MATH abscissa, x-axis, horizontal axis; ~ **d'aéronef** *m* AERONAUT aircraft axis; ~ **d'anticyclone** *m* METEO axis of an anticyclone; ~ **d'articulation** *m* CONS MECA hinge pin, *sans tête* clevis pin; ~ **d'articulation de train principal** *m* AERONAUT landing gear shaft; ~ **d'attelage** *m* VEHICULES *d'une semi-remorque* fifth wheel kingpin; ~ **de battement** *m* AERONAUT flapping hinge pin; ~ **binaire** *m* CRISTALL twofold rotation axis; ~ **binaire hélicoïdal** *m* CRISTALL twofold screw axis; ~ **de bobine** *m* CINEMAT, ENREGISTR reel spindle; ~ **B-Y** *m* TV B-Y axis; ~ **cannelé** *m* PRODUCTION knurled operating shaft; ~ **céleste** *m* ASTRONOMIE celestial axis; ~ **de changement de pas** *m* AERONAUT pitch change rod; ~ **de chape** *m* CONS MECA clevis pin; ~ **de charnière** *m* REFRIG hinge spindle; ~ **du codeur** *m* PRODUCTION encoder shaft; ~ **de commutation** *m* ELECTR *machine* axis of commutation; ~ **du coulisseau** *m* CONS MECA link block pin; ~ **creux** *m* CONS MECA hollow pin; ~ **de culbuteur** *m* AUTO rocker arm shaft, rocker shaft; ~ **de déclinaison** *m* ASTRONOMIE axis of declination, declination axis, INSTRUMENT declination axis; ~ **en approche** *m* AERONAUT approach path; ~ **d'ensouple** *m* TEXTILE beam shaft; ~ **d'entraînement** *m* CONS MECA drive pin; ~ **d'étai** *m* NAUT forestay pin; ~ **de la fibre** *m* OPTIQUE fiber axis (AmE), fibre axis (BrE), TELECOM fiber axis (AmE), fibre axis (BrE), optical axis; ~ **de la fibre optique** *m* OPTIQUE optical axis; ~ **de fixation** *m* CONS MECA fitting bolt; ~ **de fusée** *m* VEHICULES *d'une remorque* pivot pin; ~ **de guidage** *m* CONS MECA guide pin; ~ **de haute pression** *m* METEO axis of an anticyclone; ~ **hélicoïdal** *m* CRISTALL screw axis; ~ **horaire** *m* INSTRUMENT polar axis; ~ **horizontal** *m* CONSTR, MATH horizontal axis; ~ **d'incidence** *m* AERONAUT pitch change axis; ~ **d'inertie** *m* MECANIQUE axis of inertia; ~ **d'inversion** *m* CRISTALL inversion axis; ~ **de lacet** *m* AERONAUT, ESPACE *véhicules* yaw axis; ~ **latéral** *m* AERONAUT lateral axis, ESPACE *véhicules* pitch axis; ~ **de levée de pale** *m* AERONAUT flapping hinge pin; ~ **du levier de débrayage** *m* AUTO release lever pin; ~ **longitudinal** *m* AERONAUT *d'un avion*, CONS MECA longitudinal axis, ESPACE center line (AmE), centre line (BrE), *véhicules* longitudinal axis, NAUT *d'un navire* fore-and-aft line, *étude d'un navire* center line (AmE), centre line (BrE); ~ **magnétique** *m* ASTRONOMIE, ESPACE, GEOPHYS magnetic axis; ~ **de la mèche du gouvernail** *m* NAUT center line of rudderstock

(AmE), centre line of rudderstock (BrE); ~ **du monde** *m* INSTRUMENT polar axis; ~ **neutre** *m* CONSTR, RESSORTS neutral axis; ~ **normal** *m* AERONAUT normal axis; ~ **de noyau** *m* PRODUCTION core arbor; ~ **optique** *m* CRISTALL, OPTIQUE *d'un milieu* optic axis, PHOTO optical axis, PHYSIQUE, TELECOM optic axis; ~ **de l'ordonnée** *m* PHYSIQUE y-axis; ~ **des ordonnées** *m* MATH ordinate, vertical axis, y-axis; ~ **d'ordre deux** *m* CRISTALL twofold rotation axis; ~ **d'ordre quatre** *m* CRISTALL fourfold rotation axis; ~ **d'ordre six** *m* CRISTALL six-fold rotation axis; ~ **d'ordre trois** *m* CRISTALL three-fold rotation axis; ~ **d'oscillation** *m* PHYSIQUE axis of oscillation; ~ **de la pale** *m* AERONAUT blade span axis; ~ **de piste** *m* AERONAUT runway center line (AmE), runway centre line (BrE); ~ **de piston** *m* MECANIQUE gudgeon pin, VEHICULES gudgeon pin (BrE), piston pin (AmE), wrist pin (AmE); ~ **de pivotement** *m* CONS MECA fulcrum pin; ~ **d'un pli** *m* GEOLOGIE fold axis; ~ **polaire** *m* ASTRONOMIE polar axis; ~ **porte-meule** *m* CONS MECA grinding spindle; ~ **de poussée** *m* CONS MECA aerodynamic axis; ~ **principal** *m* CONS MECA center line (AmE), centre line (BrE), main shaft, CRISTALL principal axis; ~ **principal d'inertie** *m* PHYSIQUE principal axis; ~ **de profondeur** *m* AERONAUT pitch axis; ~ **de projection** *m* CINEMAT axis of projection, projection axis; ~ **quadratique** *m* CRISTALL fourfold rotation axis; ~ **de quadrature** *m* ELECTR *d'une machine* quadrature axis; ~ **de radioalignement** *m* AERONAUT course line; ~ **de référence** *m* ACOUSTIQUE reference axis, CONS MECA datum line; ~ **de repliage** *m* AERONAUT folding axis; ~ **du ressort** *m* RESSORTS spring axis; ~ **de révolution** *m* MECANIQUE axis of revolution; ~ **de rotation** *m* ASTRONOMIE axis of rotation, CRISTALL rotation axis, ESPACE *véhicules* spin axis, MECANIQUE axis of rotation; ~ **de roulis** *m* ESPACE longitudinal axis, NAUT *d'un navire* center line (AmE), centre line (BrE); ~ **R-Y** *m* TV R-Y axis; ~ **secondaire** *m* CONS MECA countershaft, intermediate shaft, jackshaft, second motion shaft; ~ **du secteur denté** *m* AUTO sector shaft; ~ **de la sellette** *m* VEHICULES *d'une semi-remorque* fifth wheel kingpin axis; ~ **solidaire de la bielle** *m* AUTO piston locked to connecting rod; ~ **solidaire de piston** *m* AUTO piston pin locked to piston; ~ **de symétrie** *m* CONS MECA, CRISTALL, GEOMETRIE axis of symmetry; ~ **synclinal** *m* CONS MECA synclinal axis; ~ **de tangage** *m* AERONAUT, ESPACE *véhicules* pitch axis; ~ **ternaire** *m* CRISTALL three-fold rotation axis; ~ **de la Terre** *m* ESPACE *géographique* Earth's axis; ~ **de tête de mèche** *m* NAUT tiller axle; ~ **de traction** *m* METALL tensile axis; ~ **de traînée** *m* AERONAUT drag axis, drag hinge; ~ **transversal** *m* AERONAUT lateral axis; ~ **vertical** *m* MATH vertical axis, y-axis; ~ **de volant** *m* AUTO steering column; ~ **V-Y** *m* TV G-Y axis; ~ **X** *m* CONSTR x-axis; ~ **des x** *m* MATH abscissa, x-axis, PHYSIQUE, TV x-axis; ~ **des y** *m* CONSTR y-axis, MATH ordinate, y-axis, vertical axis, PHYSIQUE, TV y-axis; ~ **des z** *m* PHYSIQUE z-axis; ~ **de zone** *m* CRISTALL zone axis

axes: ~ **des coordonnées** *m pl* GEOMETRIE coordinate axes; ~ **cristallins** *m pl* CRISTALL crystal axes; ~ **obliques** *m* MATH oblique axes

axial *adj* GEOMETRIE, PAPIER axial

axinite *f* MINERAUX axinite

axiomatique *adj* GEOMETRIE axiomatic

axiome *m* GEOMETRIE axiom, MATH axiom, postulate

axisymétrique *adj* CRISTALL axially symmetric

ayant:[1] **~ cause** *m* BREVETS successor in title

ayant:[2] **~ pour action de renverser** *loc* SECURITE overturning

azélaïque *adj* CHIMIE azelaic

azéotrope *m* AGRO ALIM azeotropic mixture, REFRIG azeotrope

azéotropie *f* REFRIG azeotropy

azéotropique *adj* CHIMIE azeotropic

azimide *m* CHIMIE azimino compound

azimidé *adj* CHIMIE azimino

azimut *m* ASTRONOMIE, CONSTR, ESPACE *astronomie* azimuth, GEOLOGIE compass bearing, *orientation cardinale* bearing, line of bearing, NAUT azimuth, PETR azimuth, drift azimuth, PHYSIQUE, TV azimuth; **~ d'entrefer** *m* ENREGISTR gap azimuth; **~ de lancement** *m* ESPACE *véhicules* launch azimuth; **~ magnétique** *m* GEOPHYS magnetic azimuth; **~ solaire** *m* EN RENOUV solar azimuth

azoamidé *adj* CHIMIE aminoazo

azoaminé *adj* CHIMIE aminoazo

azobenzène *m* CHIMIE azobenzene

azobenzoïque *adj* CHIMIE azobenzoic

azohydrique *adj* CHIMIE hydrazoic

azorite *f* MINERAUX azorite

azotate *m* CHIMIE nitrate; **~ d'argent** *m* CHIMIE silver nitrate; **~ de potassium** *m* CHIMIE potassium nitrate; **~ de sodium** *m* CHIMIE sodium nitrate; **~ de soude** *m* CHIMIE sodium nitrate

azote *m* CHIMIE nitrogen; **~ liquide** *m* ESPACE liquid nitrogen

azoté *adj* CHIMIE nitrogenous

azoteux *adj* CHIMIE nitrous

azothydrique *adj* CHIMIE triazoic

azotique *adj* CHIMIE nitric

azoture *m* CHIMIE azide, hydrazoate

azulène *m* CHIMIE azulene

azuline *f* CHIMIE azulin

azulmine *f* CHIMIE azulmin

azurant: **~ optique** *m* LESSIVES optical brightener

azurer *vt* IMPRIM *papier* blue

azurite *f* CHIMIE chessylite, MINERAUX azurite

B

b *abrév (barn)* PHYS PART b *(barn)*
B *(bore)* CHIMIE B *(boron)*
Ba *(baryum)* CHIMIE Ba *(barium)*
babingtonite *f* MINERAUX babingtonite
bâbord *m* ESPACE *véhicules*, NAUT port
babordais *m* NAUT port watch
bac *m* CHARBON pit, shaft, CHIMIE precipitator, CONS
MECA pan, tray, EMBALLAGE tub, MINES keeve, kieve,
NAUT ferry, ferryboat, PRODUCTION bowl, trough,
tub, vat, TRANSPORT ferryboat, harbor ferry (AmE),
harbour ferry (BrE); **~ d'accumulateur** *m* CERAM VER
battery jar; **~ à accumulation de glace** *m* REFRIG ice
bank tank; **~ à acidifier** *m* TEXTILE acidifier, acidifying
beck; **~ aérien** *m* AERONAUT air ferry; **~ à agitation** *m*
GENIE CHIM agitating vessel; **~ à air comprimé** *m* CHAR-
BON Baum jig, Baum washbox, air jig; **~ antisuccion** *m*
CHARBON pulsator jig; **~ à bec** *m* PRODUCTION open
front bin; **~ à boue** *m* PETR slam tank, slurry trough,
PETROLE mud tank; **~ à boues** *m* DISTRI EAU silt trap; **~
à câble** *m* TRANSPORT cable ferry, chain ferry; **~ à
calcin** *m* CERAM VER catch pan; **~ à chaîne** *m* TRANS-
PORT cable ferry; **~ à chutes** *m* CINEMAT *film* bin, trim
bin; **~ de classe A** *m* HYDROLOGIE class A evaporating
pan; **~ collecteur** *m* MINES collecting vat; **~ de décantation** *m* DISTRI EAU sedimentation tank, PETROLE
settling tank; **~ de dégivrage** *m* REFRIG drip tray; **~ à
diaphragme** *m* CHARBON diaphragm jig, diaphragm-
type washbox; **~ de dissolution** *m* PAPIER dissolving
tank; **~ d'évaporation** *m* DISTRI EAU evaporation pan,
HYDROLOGIE evaporation tank; **~ évaporatoire** *m* HY-
DROLOGIE evaporation tank; **~ de filtration** *m* DISTRI
EAU filtration vat; **~ à glace** *m* REFRIG ice bunker; **~ de
jaugeage** *m* PETROLE gaging tank (AmE), gauging
tank (BrE); **~ jaugeur** *m* PETROLE gaging tank (AmE),
gauging tank (BrE); **~ de lavage** *m* GENIE CHIM sieve
jigger; **~ laveur** *m* GENIE CHIM sieve jigger; **~ de
manutention** *m* EMBALLAGE tote box; **~ à moteur** *m*
TRANSPORT motor ferry; **~ à mousse** *m* PAPIER foam
tank; **~ à passagers** *m* TRANSPORT passenger ferry; **~ à
piston** *m* CHARBON jig, piston jig, PRODUCTION fixed
sieve jig; **~ à piston mécanique** *m* CHARBON plunger-
type jig; **~ à pistonnage** *m* MINES jig; **~ à pistonnage de
type Baum** *m* CHARBON Baum jig; **~ de recette** *m*
PETROLE receiver, receiving drum; **~ de récupération**
m CONS MECA drain pen; **~ de refroidissement à la
ferme** *m* REFRIG refrigerated farm tank; **~ à saumure**
m REFRIG brine tank; **~ de sédimentation** *m* AUTO
batterie sediment space, CHARBON settling tank; **~
tampon** *m* PETR flow tank; **~ transbordeur** *m* CH DE
FER, NAUT train ferry; **~ de type Baum** *m* CHARBON
Baum box; **~ à voitures** *m* NAUT car ferry, TRANSPORT
vehicle ferry
bac-baratte *m* CERAM VER slough
bâche *f* CONSTR tarpaulin, *pour bois* cleaver, INST HYDR
enclosed casing, PRODUCTION feed tank; **~ d'alimentation** *f*
PRODUCTION feed tank; **~ d'aspiration** *f* INST HYDR
suction tank; **~ à eau** *f* DISTRI EAU water tank; **~ fermée**
f INST HYDR, PRODUCTION closed turbine chamber; **~**

de protection *f* CONS MECA cover
bacholle *f* PAPIER collection tray, save-all tray, tray,
wire-tray
bacille *m* AGRO ALIM bacillus
bacnure *f* MINES gallery in dead ground, stone drift
bactéricide[1] *adj* AGRO ALIM, HYDROLOGIE bactericidal
bactéricide[2] *m* AGRO ALIM, CHIMIE, HYDROLOGIE bacte-
ricide
bactérie *f* HYDROLOGIE, RECYCLAGE bacterium; **~ acétique** *f* AGRO ALIM acetic acid bacterium; **~ coliforme** *f*
AGRO ALIM coliform bacterium; **~ mangeuse de pétrole** *f* RECYCLAGE oil-eating bacterium; **~ de méthane**
f CHIMIE methane bacterium; **~ méthanophile** *f* CHIMIE
methane bacterium; **~ revivifiable** *f* DISTRI EAU viable
bacterium
bactériolyse *f* AGRO ALIM bacteriolysis
bactériophage *m* AGRO ALIM bacteriophage
bactériostatique *m* AGRO ALIM bacteriostat
bactériotoxine *f* CHIMIE bacteriotoxin
badge *m* INFORMAT badge
badigeon *m* CHIMIE whitewash
badigeonner *vt* COULEURS distemper, REVETEMENT coat;
~ à la chaux *vt* COULEURS whitewash
badin *m* AERONAUT airspeed indicator
badine *f* PRODUCTION elbow tongs
baffle *m* ENREGISTR baffle, GENIE CHIM vapor trap
(AmE), vapour trap (BrE); **~ à absorption parallèle** *m*
ENREGISTR parallel absorbent baffle; **~ à chapeau** *m*
GENIE CHIM vapor-catching cone cap (AmE), vapour-
catching cone cap (BrE); **~ de plafond** *m* ENREGISTR
ceiling baffle; **~ sphérique** *m* ENREGISTR spherical
baffle
bagages: ~ de cabine *m pl* AERONAUT cabin baggage; **~ à
main** *m pl* AERONAUT hand baggage
bag-in-box *m* IMPRIM bag in box
bague *f* CERAM VER finish, CONS MECA bushing, bush,
collar, external cylindrical gauge (BrE), *d'un excentrique* strap, *de broyeur à cylindres* shell, MECANIQUE
ring, NUCLEAIRE yoke, OPTIQUE ferrule, PRODUCTION
cylindrical gage (AmE), cylindrical gauge (BrE),
thimble, TELECOM ferrule; **~ d'adaptation** *f* PHOTO
adaptor ring; **~ d'appui** *f* AUTO thrust collar; **~ d'arbre
à cames** *f* AUTO camshaft bushing; **~ d'armement** *f*
PHOTO cocking ring; **~ d'arrêt** *f* CONS MECA set collar,
stop collar, MECANIQUE retaining ring; **~ d'arrêt en
deux pièces** *f* CONS MECA split-set collar; **~ d'articulation** *f* AUTO pivot ring; **~ de baïonnette** *f* CERAM VER
bayonet cap finish; **~ de blocage** *f* CINEMAT locking
ring; **~ de bossage de piston** *f* AUTO piston boss
bushing; **~ de butée** *f* CONS MECA set collar, stop collar;
~ calibre *f* RESSORTS gaging ring (AmE), gauging ring
(BrE); **~ de centrage** *f* CONS MECA centering bush
(AmE), centring bush (BrE), TV *du module de balayage* centering ring (AmE), centring ring(BrE); **~
champenoise** *f* CERAM VER champagne finish; **~ du
chapeau** *f* PRODUCTION follower bush; **~ de collecteur**
f ELECTR *commutateur* commutator ring; **~ collectrice**
f ELECTR *moteur*, ELECTROTEC, PHYSIQUE, VEHICULES

génératrice slip ring; ~ **collectrice de démarreur** *f* VEHICULES *moteur* starter slip ring; ~ **à collerette** *f* CONS MECA guide bush; ~ **à collerette centrale** *f* CONS MECA *plaque d'éjection* support pillar bush; ~ **de commande du diaphragme** *f* PHOTO aperture-setting ring; ~ **de correction dioptrique** *f* INSTRUMENT focusing ring; ~ **couronne** *f* CERAM VER crown finish; ~ **de cylindre** *f* PRODUCTION *de broyeur à cylindres* roll shell; ~ **cylindrique** *f* CONS MECA guide bush; ~ **décalée** *f* CERAM VER shifted finish; ~ **déformée** *f* CERAM VER saddled finish; ~ **dévêtisseuse** *f* CONS MECA *moule d'injection* stripper bush; ~ **dévêtisseuse de carotte d'injection** *f* CONS MECA *moule d'injection* sprue ejector pin guide; ~ **de diaphragme** *f* CINEMAT, PHOTO aperture ring; ~ **en alliage de cuivre** *f* CONS MECA copper alloy bush; ~ **d'entraînement** *f* CONS MECA coupling ring; ~ **d'étanchéité** *f* CONS MECA, MATERIAUX sealing ring; ~ **d'étanchéité à lèvres** *f* CONS MECA lip-type seal, *pour arbres tournants* lip seal, rotary shaft lip-type seal; ~ **d'étoupe** *f* NAUT *machine* grommet; ~ **d'excentrique** *f* CONS MECA eccentric collar, eccentric hoop, eccentric strap; ~ **excentrique** *f* CONS MECA eccentric bush; ~ **extérieure de roulement** *f* CONS MECA outer race; ~ **fendue** *f* CONS MECA split ring; ~ **filetée de guidage** *f* CONS MECA threaded bush; ~ **de fixation** *f* PHOTO retaining ring; ~ **de freinage** *f* CONS MECA brake ring; ~ **gonflée** *f* CERAM VER bulged finish; ~ **de graissage** *f* PRODUCTION oil ring; ~ **de guidage** *f* CONS MECA guide bush, *plaque d'éjection* ejection guide bush; ~ **de guidage en bronze** *f* CONS MECA bronze guide bush; ~ **incisée** *f* CERAM VER checked finish; ~ **des indices de lumination** *f* PHOTO light value setting ring; ~ **intérieure de roulement** *f* CONS MECA ball inner race; ~ **intermédiaire** *f* CINEMAT step down ring, PHOTO extension ring; ~ **d'inversion** *f* PHOTO reversing ring; ~ **isolante** *f* CONS MECA *pour matériaux de soudage par résistance* insulation bush; ~ **de manchon** *f* CERAM VER collar; ~ **de mise au point** *f* CINEMAT focusing ring, INSTRUMENT focusing sleeve, PHOTO focusing ring; ~ **ovalisée** *f* CERAM VER out-of-round finish; ~ **à pas de vis intérieur** *f* CERAM VER internal screw; ~ **penchée** *f* CERAM VER bent finish; ~ **percée** *f* CERAM VER swing stopper finish (BrE), wired stopper finish (AmE); ~ **de pied de bielle** *f* AUTO, VEHICULES small end bush; ~ **de piston** *f* CONS MECA piston ring; ~ **porte-oculaire** *f* INSTRUMENT fine focus sleeve; ~ **pour bouchage à levier** *f* CERAM VER pry-off finish; ~ **pour bouchage liège** *f* CERAM VER cork finish; ~ **de préinjection** *f* CONS MECA *moule d'injection* feed bush; ~ **de presse-étoupe** *f* CONS MECA gland; ~ **de protection** *f* CONS MECA oil slinger; ~ **rapportée en laiton** *f* PRODUCTION brass insert ring; ~ **de réglage** *f* COMMANDE adjusting ring; ~ **de réglage du zoom** *f* CINEMAT zoom ring; ~ **de repérage** *f* PRODUCTION identification strip; ~ **de retenue** *f* MECANIQUE retaining ring; ~ **retombée** *f* CERAM VER warped finish; ~ **de roulement** *f* CONS MECA ball race, bearing race; ~ **de roulement à billes** *f* VEHICULES ball bearing race; ~ **sale** *f* CERAM VER crizzled finish; ~ **de sécurité pour enfants** *f* CERAM VER childproof finish; ~ **de serrage** *f* CONS MECA collet, EMBALLAGE clamping ring; ~ **de sertissage** *f* CONS MECA crimping bush; ~ **de sortie d'étambot** *f* NAUT main shaft bearing; ~ **à tolérance** *f* CONS MECA limit external gage (BrE), limit external gauge (BrE); ~ **d'usure** *f* PETR wear bushing; ~ **à vis** *f* CERAM VER external screw thread finish
bague-aimant: ~ **circulaire** *f* TV annular magnet, ring

magnet
bague-batoir *f* CONS MECA knock-off link
bague-guide *f* AUTO pilot bushing
baguer *vt* CONS MECA collar
baguette *f* CERAM VER rack mark, CONSTR bead, reed, rod, welding wire, IMPRIM, INFORMAT, ORDINAT wand, TELECOM preformed fiber (AmE), preformed fibre (BrE); ~ **chromée** *f* VEHICULES *carrosserie* chrome strip; ~ **en verre** *f* EQUIP LAB glass stirring rod, *verrerie* glass rod; ~ **étirée** *f* CERAM VER draw rod; ~ **de métal d'apport** *f* PRODUCTION filler rod; ~ **de moulure** *f* PRODUCTION molding (AmE), moulding (BrE); ~ **de séparation** *f* TEXTILE separating rod; ~ **de soudure** *f* PRODUCTION filler rod
baie *f* CONSTR aperture, opening, EN RENOUV, HYDROLOGIE, NAUT, TELECOM bay; ~ **d'emballeur** *f* (Bel) *(cf loge d'emballeur)* CERAM VER packer's bay; ~ **de fenêtre** *f* CONSTR window opening; ~ **magnétique** *f* GEOPHYS magnetic bay; ~ **de porte** *f* CONSTR door opening, doorway; ~ **de la régie** *f* TV control room window
baignoire *f* NAUT *sous-marin* bridge
baïkalite *f* MINERAUX baikalite
bailer *m* PETR bailer
bâillement *m* CONS MECA, RESSORTS gap
bain *m* CERAM VER, CINEMAT, IMPRIM *chimie du développement*, TEXTILE bath; ~ **accélérateur** *m* CINEMAT accelerator; ~ **acide** *m* PAPIER, PHOTO acid bath; ~ **d'arrêt** *m* CINEMAT short stop, stop bath, PHOTO stop bath; ~ **d'arrêt acide** *m* CINEMAT, PHOTO acid stop bath; ~ **d'arrêt durcissant** *m* PHOTO acid hardening bath; ~ **de blanchiment** *m* CINEMAT, PHOTO bleaching bath; ~ **de clarification** *m* CINEMAT clearing bath; ~ **de coagulation** *m* GENIE CHIM coagulating bath; ~ **de couche** *m* PAPIER coating mixture; ~ **désensibilisateur** *m* PHOTO desensitizing bath; ~ **détergent** *m* LESSIVES washing bath; ~ **de développement** *m* CINEMAT, PHOTO developing bath; ~ **de durcissement** *m* IMPRIM *chimie* hardening bath; ~ **électrolytique** *m* ELECTR *électrolyse*, ELECTROTEC electrolytic bath, REVETEMENT electroplating bath; ~ **d'encollage** *m* TEXTILE size bath; ~ **de fixage** *m* CINEMAT fixer, fixing bath; ~ **fixateur acide** *m* PHOTO acid fixing bath; ~ **fluidisé** *m* GENIE CHIM fluid bed, fluidized bed; ~ **de fusion** *m* PRODUCTION *soudage* molten pool, THERMODYN melting bath; ~ **galvanoplastique** *m* REVETEMENT electroplating bath; ~ **de givrage** *m* CERAM VER frosting bath; ~ **de gravure lisse** *m* CERAM VER clear etching bath; ~ **d'huile** *m* EQUIP LAB *chauffage* oil bath; ~ **inverseur** *m* PHOTO reversing bath; ~ **pour gravure profonde** *m* CERAM VER deep-etching bath; ~ **pour histologie** *m* EQUIP LAB *montage* histology bath, mounting bath; ~ **préliminaire** *m* PHOTO preliminary bath; ~ **de recuit** *m* THERMODYN annealing bath; ~ **de refroidissement** *m* REFRIG cooling bath; ~ **retardateur** *m* PHOTO restrainer; ~ **révélateur** *m* PHOTO developing bath; ~ **de sable** *m* EQUIP LAB *chauffage* sand bath; ~ **sensibilisateur** *m* PHOTO sensitizing bath; ~ **stabilisateur** *m* CINEMAT stabilizing bath; ~ **tannant** *m* CINEMAT hardener; ~ **thermostaté** *m* EQUIP LAB thermostatically-controlled bath; ~ **de trempe** *m* METALL quenching bath; ~ **à ultrasons** *m* EQUIP LAB *nettoyage* ultrasonic bath; ~ **unique** *m* CINEMAT monobath; ~ **de vapeur** *m* GENIE CHIM vapor bath (AmE), vapour bath (BrE); ~ **de virage** *m* CINEMAT, PHOTO toning bath
bainite *f* METALL, RESSORTS bainite; ~ **inférieure** *f* METALL

lower bainite; ~ **supérieure** ƒ METALL upper bainite

bain-marie m CHIMIE, EQUIP LAB *chauffage* water bath

baïonnette ƒ CONSTR bayonet fitting, ELECTROTEC bayonet

baisse ƒ HYDROLOGIE decline, *d'un fleuve* fall, OCEANO, PHYSIQUE *de température* fall; ~ **de l'eau** ƒ NAUT fall of the tide; ~ **de la marée** ƒ NAUT ebb, tidal fall, OCEANO tidal fall; ~ **de la nappe phréatique** ƒ HYDROLOGIE falling water table, receding water table; ~ **de niveau** ƒ CONS MECA level drop; ~ **du niveau aquifère** ƒ EN RENOUV draw-down of water in aquifer; ~ **du pH** ƒ POLLUTION pH depression; ~ **de pression** ƒ INST HYDR pressure drop; ~ **de réactivité** ƒ NUCLEAIRE decrement in reactivity; ~ **d'une rivière** ƒ HYDROLOGIE subsidence; ~ **de tension** ƒ ELECTROTEC, PRODUCTION *de l'alimentation* brownout

baisser *vi* HYDROLOGIE recede, subside

bajocien *adj* GEOLOGIE *stratigraphie* Bajocian

bajoyer m CONSTR dock wall, DISTRI EAU river wall, *d'une écluse, du coursier d'une roue hydraulique* sidewall, NAUT dock wall

bakélite ƒ ELECTR *isolation*, PLAST CAOU *plastiques* bakelite

baladeur m CONS MECA, VEHICULES *boîte de vitesses* sliding gear

baladeuse ƒ CINEMAT extension lead, ELECTR *éclairage* portable lamp, ELECTROTEC inspection lamp, portable lamp

balai m ELECTR commutator brush, *machine* brush, ELECTROTEC brush, carbon brush, current-collecting brush, MECANIQUE *électrique*, PRODUCTION *charbon* brush; ~ **d'alternateur** m VEHICULES *système électrique* generator brush; ~ **au carbone** m CONS MECA carbon brush; ~ **de démarreur** m AUTO starter brush; ~ **en charbon** m ELECTR *moteur, générateur*, ELECTROTEC carbon brush; ~ **en graphite** m ELECTR *machine* graphite brush; ~ **d'essuie-glace** m VEHICULES *accessoire* wiper blade; ~ **à lames** m ELECTR *machine* laminated brush; ~ **de moteur** m IMPRIM *moteurs* motor brush; ~ **multilame** m ELECTROTEC laminated brush

balais m pl AUTO brush

balance ƒ CONS MECA scales, ENREGISTR, EQUIP LAB *analyse* balance, IMPRIM weighing machine, METROLOGIE balance, scale, weighing scale, OCEANO hand lift net, scoop net, PHYSIQUE balance; ~ **aérodynamique** ƒ AERONAUT aerodynamic balance, wind tunnel balance; ~ **d'analyse** ƒ PHYSIQUE analytical balance; ~ **automatique du blanc** ƒ TV automatic white balance; ~ **des blancs** ƒ TV white balance; ~ **chimique** ƒ PHYSIQUE chemical balance; ~ **à colonne** ƒ CONSTR pillar balance, EQUIP LAB pillar scales; ~ **de Cotton** ƒ PHYSIQUE Cotton balance; ~ **de courant** ƒ ELECTR, PHYSIQUE current balance; ~ **électrodynamique** ƒ ELECTR ampere balance, current balance; ~ **électronique** ƒ EMBALLAGE electronic weighing scales, EQUIP LAB electronic balance; ~ **d'ensachage** ƒ EMBALLAGE sack scales; ~ **d'Eötvös** ƒ PHYSIQUE Eötvös balance; ~ **d'essai** ƒ CHIMIE assay balance; ~ **à fléau** ƒ METROLOGIE beam and scales, beam balance, beam scales; ~ **à gaz** ƒ GAZ gas balance; ~ **hydrostatique** ƒ PHYS FLUID hydrostatic balance; ~ **de Kelvin** ƒ ELECTR *mesure* Kelvin balance; ~ **de laboratoire** ƒ EQUIP LAB *analyse* chemical balance; ~ **magnétique** ƒ GEOPHYS magnetic balance; ~ **à ressort** ƒ CONS MECA, PHYSIQUE spring balance; ~ **romaine** ƒ CONS MECA lever scales, PHYSIQUE steelyard; ~ **sèche à**

simple effet ƒ PRODUCTION single gravity hoist; ~ **sensible** ƒ EQUIP LAB analytical balance; ~ **de soufflerie** ƒ AERONAUT wind tunnel balance; ~ **de torsion** ƒ CONS MECA, GEOPHYS, PHYSIQUE torsion balance; ~ **de torsion de Coulomb** ƒ PHYSIQUE Coulomb's torsion balance; ~ **de vérification** ƒ EMBALLAGE checkweigher

Balance ƒ ASTRONOMIE Libra, Scales

balance-cuvette ƒ PHOTO dish rocker

balancement m CERAM VER *de la canne* swinging, CONS MECA swaying, swinging

balancer *vt* CONSTR *une marche* dance

balancier m AERONAUT *commande de volet* balance arm, CONS MECA beam, compensating beam, logging head, walking beam, working beam, DISTRI EAU *d'une porte d'écluse* balance bar, PRODUCTION fly press, lifting beam, sling beam, *d'une machine à balancier* bob; ~ **de battage** m MINES walking beam; ~ **à boules** m PRODUCTION fly bar with two balls; ~ **à contrepoids** m MINES balance bob; ~ **d'équerre** m CONS MECA V-bob, MINES *d'une pompe* quadrant; ~ **de répartition** m CONS MECA compensating beam, CONSTR rock lever; ~ **de suspension** m CONS MECA compensating beam, CONSTR rock lever

balancine ƒ AERONAUT outrigger, NAUT topping lift

balant m NAUT bight

balata m PLAST CAOU balata

balayage m AERONAUT *radar* scan, scanning, DISTRI EAU scavenging, ELECTRON scanning, sweep, ESPACE scanning, sweep, INFORMAT scan, scanning, MECANIQUE scavenging, NAUT scanning, scavenging, NUCLEAIRE scavenging, ORDINAT scanning, scan, PETROLE scanning, scavenging, sweep, PHYS RAYON, PHYSIQUE, TELECOM, TV scanning; ~ **adaptatif** m ELECTRON adaptive sweep; ~ **antérieur** m TV front scanning; ~ **asymétrique** m TV asymmetrical deflection; ~ **avec loupe** m ELECTRON expanded sweep; ~ **cavalier** m ELECTRON vector scanning, ORDINAT random scan; ~ **circulaire** m ELECTRON circular scan; ~ **défectueux** m TV scanning error; ~ **dilaté** m ELECTRON delayed sweep, expanded sweep; ~ **électronique** m NUCLEAIRE electron scanning; ~ **électronique du faisceau** m ELECTRON electronic beam steering; ~ **en fréquence** m ELECTRON frequency sweep; ~ **en ligne** m TELECOM line scanning; ~ **entrelacé** m ELECTRON, TV interlaced scanning; ~ **fragmenté** m TV segmented scanning; ~ **de fréquence** m ENREGISTR frequency scanning, TELECOM frequency scanning, frequency sweep; ~ **hélicoïdal** m ELECTRON helical scanning, INFORMAT, ORDINAT helical scan; ~ **horizontal** m TV horizontal scanning, horizontal sweep; ~ **inversé** m TV reverse scan; ~ **de ligne** m ORDINAT line scanning, TV line sweep; ~ **ligne à ligne** m ELECTRON line scanning, raster scanning, INFORMAT, ORDINAT, TV raster scanning; ~ **ligne par ligne** m IMPRIM *photogravure* line scanning; ~ **logarithmique** m ELECTRON logarithmic sweep; ~ **omnidirectionnel** m ORDINAT random scan; ~ **par contact** m ORDINAT contact scanning; ~ **par faisceau** m ELECTRON beam scanning; ~ **par faisceau d'électrons** m ELECTRON electron beam scanning; ~ **par fente** m TV slit scanning; ~ **radar** m TRANSPORT radar scan; ~ **rapide** m ELECTRON fast sweep; ~ **rectiligne** m ELECTRON linear scan; ~ **récurrent** m ELECTRON repetitive sweep, INFORMAT, ORDINAT raster scanning; ~ **retardant** m ELECTRON delaying sweep; ~ **d'un secteur** m MILITAIRE *radar* sector scan; ~ **séquentiel** m TV sequential scanning; ~ **télévision** m ELECTRON, INFORMAT, ORDINAT, TV raster scanning; ~ **tramé** *m* ELECTRON raster scanning; ~ **des trames** *m* ELECTRON vertical sweep; ~ **vertical** *m* ELECTRON vertical sweep, TV vertical scanning; ~ **à vitesse rapide** *m* TV variable speed scanning

balayer *vt* IMPRIM, INFORMAT, ORDINAT, PHYS ONDES, TRANSPORT *radar*, TV scan

balayeur: ~ **de fréquence** *m* TELECOM frequency scanner; ~ **radar** *m* TRANSPORT radar scanner

balayeuse *f* TRANSPORT street cleaning lorry (BrE), street cleaning truck (AmE); ~ **mécanique** *f* CONSTR mechanical broom

balayures *f pl* PRODUCTION sweepings

balcon *m* CERAM VER balcony, PRODUCTION burr, fin; ~ **arrière** *m* NAUT pushpit, stern pulpit; ~ **avant** *m* NAUT pulpit

balconnet *m* REFRIG door rack; ~ **de pied de mât** *m* NAUT mast foot safety rail

Baleine *f* ASTRONOMIE Cetus

baleinier *m* OCEANO factory ship, whaler, whaling ship

baleinière *f* OCEANO whale boat

balène *f* PRODUCTION burr, fin

balètre *f* PRODUCTION burr, fin

balèvre *f* PRODUCTION burr, scab, scale

balisage *m* AERONAUT ground lighting, CONSTR beaconing; ~ **d'un chenal** *m* TRANSPORT channel markings; ~ **lumineux d'approche** *m* AERONAUT approach lighting system; ~ **maritime** *m* NAUT seamarking

balise *f* CH DE FER beacon, track magnet, CONSTR, ESPACE *communications* beacon, IMPRIM *composition* flag, NAUT beacon, TRANSPORT marker; ~ **de bord de voie de circulation** *f* AERONAUT taxiway edge marker; ~ **de circulation** *f* TRANSPORT road marker cone; ~ **de codification** *f* IMPRIM *codes et marques* sentinel; ~ **de détresse** *f* ESPACE emergency beacon, *communications* distress beacon, NAUT distress beacon; ~ **émettrice radar** *f* NAUT radar marker beacon, TRANSPORT ramark; ~ **d'entrée de piste** *f* AERONAUT landing strip marker; ~ **extérieure** *f* AERONAUT outer marker; ~ **d'extrémité** *f* AERONAUT boundary light; ~ **fixe** *f* NAUT fixed beacon; ~ **flottante** *f* IMPRIM *d'appel de composants* floating pick-up, NAUT floating beacon; ~ **d'identification** *f* IMPRIM *codes et marques* sentinel; ~ **intérieure** *f* AERONAUT inner marker; ~ **de localisation portable** *f* NAUT personal locator beacon; ~ **de marquage** *f* IMPRIM *codes et marques* sentinel; ~ **radar** *f* AERONAUT, NAUT, PHYS RAYON, TELECOM radar beacon; ~ **radio** *f* NAUT radio beacon; ~ **de radio ralliement** *f* TRANSPORT radio homing beacon; ~ **remark** *f* TRANSPORT ramark; ~ **répondeuse** *f* ESPACE transponder beacon; ~ **répondeuse radar** *f* AERONAUT, NAUT radar transponder beacon; ~ **rétroréfléchissante** *f* AERONAUT *aéroport* retroreflective marker

balisement *m* CONSTR beaconing

baliser *vt* CONSTR beacon, NAUT *chenal* buoy, POLLU MER mark

baliseur *m* NAUT buoy tender

balistique[1] *adj* ESPACE *mécanique céleste* ballistic

balistique[2] *m* ESPACE *mécanique céleste* ballistics

baliveau *m* CONSTR scaffold pole, standard

ballast *m* CH DE FER ballast, CONSTR ballast, ballasting, ELECTROTEC ballast, NAUT ballast tank, TRANSPORT ballast

ballastage *m* CONSTR *matériel* ballasting; ~ **en vrac** *m* CH DE FER loose ballasting

ballastière *f* CONSTR quarry

balle *f* AGRO ALIM chaff, CERAM VER convex optical tool, EMBALLAGE, TEXTILE bale; ~ **de fusil** *f* MILITAIRE rifle bullet; ~ **de pâte** *f* PAPIER bale; ~ **perdue** *f* MILITAIRE lost bullet; ~ **perforante** *f* MILITAIRE armor-piercing bullet (AmE), armour-piercing bullet (BrE); ~ **de puddlage** *f* PRODUCTION puddle ball; ~ **traçante** *f* MILITAIRE tracer bullet; ~ **vive** *f* MILITAIRE live round

ballon *m* AGRO ALIM flask, CHIMIE balloon, flask, EQUIP LAB *verrerie* flask, GENIE CHIM boiling flask, MILITAIRE *formation des parachutistes* balloon system; ~ **d'air comprimé** *m* CONS MECA air receiver; ~ **antipulsatoire** *m* GAZ antipulse flask; ~ **à col court** *m* EQUIP LAB *verrerie* bolthead flask (BrE), matrass (AmE); ~ **à col large** *m* EQUIP LAB *verrerie* wide-necked flask; ~ **à col long** *m* EQUIP LAB *verrerie* long-necked flask; ~ **de décantage** *m* CHIMIE funnel; ~ **de détente** *m* MECANIQUE *procédé* flash drum; ~ **à distillation** *m* EQUIP LAB *verrerie* distillation flask; ~ **à fond plat** *m* EQUIP LAB *verrerie* flat-bottomed flask; ~ **de levage** *m* AERONAUT lifting bag; ~ **marqueur aéroporté** *m* MILITAIRE airborne marker balloon; ~ **pilote** *m* AERONAUT pilot balloon; ~ **stratosphérique** *m* ASTRONOMIE stratospheric balloon; ~ **de surveillance** *m* MILITAIRE surveillance balloon; ~ **de transmission de données** *m* MILITAIRE, TELECOM data transmission balloon; ~ **tricol** *m* EQUIP LAB *verrerie* three-necked flask

ballonnement *m* NUCLEAIRE *de gaine* ballooning

ballon-sonde *m* AERONAUT pilot balloon, ESPACE sounding balloon, METEO sounding balloon, weather balloon

ballot: ~ **de laine** *m* TEXTILE woolpack

ballotte *f* CERAM VER flashing knob

ballottement *m* PRODUCTION rapping, rattling; ~ **de liquide** *m* ESPACE sloshing, *véhicules* liquid sloshing

ballotter *vt* PRODUCTION rap

balourd *m* CONS MECA, MECANIQUE unbalance; ~ **résiduel admissible** *m* CONS MECA *des rotors rigides* permissible residual unbalance

balthazar *m* CERAM VER belshazzar

baltimorite *f* MINERAUX baltimorite

balustrade *f* CONSTR balustrade

balustre *m* CONSTR baluster

bambou *m* CERAM VER bamboo

banc *m* CONS MECA bed, CONSTR bank, bench, NAUT bank, shelf, OCEANO bank, flat shelf, school, shoal; ~ **d'animation** *m* CINEMAT animation bench; ~ **d'assemblage** *m* CONS MECA assembly jig; ~ **à broches** *m* TEXTILE roving frame; ~ **à broches en gros** *m* TEXTILE slubbing frame; ~ **à broches intermédiaires** *m* TEXTILE intermediate frame; ~ **de brouillard** *m* METEO fog bank; ~ **de cellules** *m* CHARBON bank of cells; ~ **de charpentier** *m* CONSTR carpenters' bench; ~ **demi-rompu** *m* CONS MECA half gap bed; ~ **d'essai** *m* CONS MECA test bench, test rig, ELECTR test bed, ESPACE test bed, test stand, *mesures* test rig, INFORMAT, MECANIQUE test bed, NUCLEAIRE test bay, test stand, testing bed, ORDINAT test bed, RESSORTS test jig, TELECOM test bench; ~ **d'essai moteur** *m* ESPACE *véhicules, propulsion* engine test stand; ~ **d'essai réacteur** *m* AERONAUT engine test stand; ~ **d'essai volant** *m* AERONAUT flying test bench; ~ **d'étalonnage de compteur** *m* GAZ meter calibration bench; ~ **d'étirage** *m* PRODUCTION draw bench, drawing bench, TEXTILE drawframe; ~ **à étirer** *m* PRODUCTION draw bench, drawing bench; ~ **de filtres** *m* ELECTRON filter bank; ~ **long** *m* RESSORTS long bed; ~ **médian** *m* NAUT middle ground; ~ **de menuisier** *m* CONSTR joiner's bench; ~ **de milieu** *m* NAUT middle ground; ~ **de moulage** *m* PRODUCTION molding bench (AmE), moulding bench (BrE); ~ **optique** *m* CINEMAT, IMPRIM, METROLOGIE, PHOTO, PHYSIQUE optical bench; ~ **à rectifier** *m* CONS MECA straightener, straightening machine; ~ **de redressage** *m* CONS MECA straightener, straightening machine; ~ **de reproduction** *m* CINEMAT copy stand, IMPRIM reproduction camera, PHOTO copying stand; ~ **rompu** *m* CONS MECA gap bed; ~ **stérile** *m* CHARBON dirt band, stone band; ~ **de tirage à chenilles** *m* PRODUCTION take-up unit; ~ **à tirer** *m* PRODUCTION draw bench; ~ **titre** *m* CINEMAT title printer, TV caption stand; ~ **de tour** *m* MECANIQUE lathe bed; ~ **de tour renforcé par des nervures d'entretoisage** *m* CONS MECA lathe bed braced by cross-girths; ~ **à tréfiler les gros fils** *m* CONS MECA bull block; ~ **de tréfilerie** *m* PRODUCTION wiredrawing bench; ~ **de trucages** *m* TV effects bank; ~ **de verrier** *m* CERAM VER chair

bandage *m* CH DE FER tire (AmE), *véhicules* tyre (BrE), CONS MECA band, shell, IMPRIM *flexographie* band; ~ **de cylindre** *m* PRODUCTION *de broyeur à cylindres* roll shell; ~ **pneumatique** *m* VEHICULES pneumatic tire (AmE), pneumatic tyre (BrE)

bande:[1] ~ **large** *adj* TELECOM wideband

bande[2] *f* CONS MECA *d'un ressort* tension, CONSTR band, ELECTR *enregistrement* tape, IMPRIM *rotatives* web, *édition* band, INFORMAT band, tape, MINES *de minerai* streak, NAUT heel, list, ORDINAT band, tape, PAPIER web, PHYSIQUE band, RESSORTS nip;

~ **a** ~ **abrasive** *f* CERAM VER, CONS MECA abrasive belt; ~ **d'absorption** *f* PHYS RAYON, PHYSIQUE absorption band; ~ **adhésif** *f* PLAST CAOU self-adhesive tape; ~ **d'aimantation** *f* GEOLOGIE *du plancher océanique, à polarité définie* magnetic stripe; ~ **d'alignement** *f* TV line-up tape; ~ **amorce** *f* ENREGISTR leader tape; ~ **d'arrachage** *f* EMBALLAGE tear strip; ~ **d'arrêt d'urgence** *f* TRANSPORT escape lane; ~ **d'atténuation de filtre** *f* ENREGISTR filter attenuation band; ~ **atténuée** *f* ELECTRON attenuation band; ~ **d'atterrissage** *f* AERONAUT landing strip, strip, strip; ~ **audio** *f* INFORMAT voice-band; ~ **audio-numérique** *f* ORDINAT DAT, digital audio tape;

~ **b** ~ **de base** *f* ELECTRON, ORDINAT, TELECOM, TV baseband; ~ **basse** *f* TELECOM low-pass band;

~ **c** ~ **cache** *f* CINEMAT masking tape; ~ **de Carson** *f* ESPACE *communications* Carson's rule bandwidth; ~ **de chargement** *f* TRANSPORT loading conveyor; ~ **au chrome** *f* TV chrome dioxide tape; ~ **cisaillée** *f* RESSORTS sheared strip; ~ **colorée** *f* EMBALLAGE colored strapping (AmE), coloured strapping (BrE); ~ **de commande** *f* INFORMAT control tape; ~ **commentaire** *f* CINEMAT commentary track, narration track, ENREGISTR narration track; ~ **commune** *f* TV frequency overlap; ~ **de conduction** *f* PHYSIQUE conduction band; ~ **de conductivité** *f* PHYS RAYON conduction band; ~ **de convoyeur de sortie** *f* PRODUCTION outgoing conveyor belt; ~ **correctrice** *f* CINEMAT control film band; ~ **couchée** *f* IMPRIM *rotative* coated web; ~ **couchée PVC** *f* IMPRIM *papiers* PVC-coated web; ~ **coupée** *f* ELECTRON rejection band; ~ **crantée** *f* CONS MECA notched band; ~ **critique** *f* ACOUSTIQUE, ENREGISTR critical band;

~ **d** ~ **de décalage vitesse** *f* TV velocity banding; ~ **de défilement** *f* INFORMAT scroll bar; ~ **de départ** *f* INFORMAT master tape; ~ **de dorsale polyester** *f* ENREGISTR polyester tape; ~ **à dorsale pvc** *f* ENREGISTR PVC tape;

~ **double durée** *f* ENREGISTR double play tape; ~ **de durée standard** *f* ENREGISTR standard-play tape;

~ **e** ~ **échantillon** *f* TEXTILE sample strip; ~ **à écrous prisonniers** *f* CONS MECA gang channel; ~ **effets sonores** *f* ENREGISTR Foley track, atmos track; ~ **d'émission** *f* PHYSIQUE emission band; ~ **en cartouche** *f* ENREGISTR cartridge tape; ~ **enduite** *f* ENREGISTR coated tape; ~ **à enduit en bioxyde de chrome** *f* TV chrome dioxide tape; ~ **d'énergie permise** *f* PHYS RAYON allowed energy band; ~ **en papier** *f* ELECTR *isolation* paper tape; ~ **enregistrée** *f* TV recording; ~ **enregistreuse** *f* ELECTR chart strip; ~ **entrant dans la machine** *f* IMPRIM *rotatives* incoming web; ~ **d'essai** *f* ACOUSTIQUE test tape; ~ **essai** *f* PHOTO test strip; ~ **étalon** *f* CINEMAT reference strip, ENREGISTR test tape, TV reference tape, standard tape, test tape; ~ **d'étalonnage** *f* CINEMAT grading band, TV alignment tape; ~ **d'étalonnage en temps** *f* ENREGISTR timing tape; ~ **étroite** *f* IMPRIM *de papier* strip, *rotatives* narrow web;

~ **f** ~ **finisseuse** *f* CERAM VER finishing belt; ~ **de fixation de film** *f* IMPRIM *pour mise en repérage* goldenrod; ~ **Flaman** *f* CH DE FER speed recording tape; ~ **de flottaison** *f* NAUT boot topping; ~ **de frein** *f* CONS MECA brake band, brake strap, MECANIQUE, VEHICULES *embrayage* brake band; ~ **de fréquence** *f* ELECTR *signal*, ELECTRON, INFORMAT, NAUT, ORDINAT, TELECOM frequency band; ~ **de fréquence banalisée** *f* TELECOM CB, citizen's band; ~ **de fréquence publique** *f* TELECOM CB, citizen's band; ~ **de fréquences** *f* ELECTR *courant alternatif* frequency range, PHYS ONDES waveband; ~ **de fréquences audibles** *f* ENREGISTR audio frequency band; ~ **de fréquence VHF** *f* TV VHF frequency band; ~ **de frottement** *f* AERONAUT chafing strip, CH DE FER pantograph-wearing strip;

~ **g** ~ **de glissement** *f* CRISTALL slip band, METALL glide band;

~ **h** ~ **de haute énergie** *f* TV high-energy tape; ~ **hectométrique** *f* NAUT MW band, medium wave band;

~ **i** ~ **d'incertitude des fréquences** *f* TELECOM frequency uncertainty band; ~ **interdite** *f* PHYS RAYON forbidden band, PHYSIQUE forbidden band, gap; ~ **intermédiaire satellite** *f* TELECOM intermediate satellite band;

~ **l** ~ **L** *f* ELECTRON, ESPACE *communications* L-band; ~ **large** *f* ORDINAT, TELECOM wide band; ~ **latérale** *f* ELECTRON, ENREGISTR, INFORMAT, ORDINAT, PHYSIQUE, TELECOM, TV sideband; ~ **latérale atténuée** *f* ELECTRON vestigial sideband; ~ **latérale inférieure** *f* ELECTRON, TELECOM LSB, lower sideband; ~ **latérale résiduelle** *f* TELECOM residual sideband; ~ **latérale restante** *f* TELECOM, TV vestigial sideband; ~ **latérale supérieure** *f* ELECTRON, TELECOM USB, upper sideband; ~ **latérale unique** *f* ELECTRON, TELECOM, TV single sideband; ~ **longue durée** *f* ENREGISTR long-play tape; ~ **lubrifié** *f* ENREGISTR lubricated tape;

~ **m** ~ **magnétique** *f* ACOUSTIQUE magnetic tape, CINEMAT magnetic film, ELECTR, ENREGISTR, GEOPHYS, IMPRIM *enregistrement de données*, INFORMAT, ORDINAT, TELECOM, TV magnetic tape; ~ **magnétique à haute coercivité** *f* TV chrome dioxide tape; ~ **magnétique de niveau** *f* ACOUSTIQUE level magnetic tape; ~ **magnétique à niveau de sortie élevée** *f* ENREGISTR high output tape; ~ **magnétique pré-enregistré** *f* ENREGISTR prerecorded magnetic tape; ~ **magnétique vierge** *f* TV blank magnetic tape, raw magnetic tape; ~ **magnétos-**

copique f PHYSIQUE videotape; ~ **maîtresse** f ENREGISTR, INFORMAT master tape; ~ **de manoeuvre** f INFORMAT, ORDINAT scratch tape; ~ **mère** f TV master tape; ~ **de métallisation** f PRODUCTION bonding strip; ~ **de modulation** f ELECTRON modulation band; ~ **des mouvements** f ORDINAT change tape;

~ o ~ **d'un octave** f ELECTRON octave band; ~ **optique laser** f OPTIQUE laser-optic tape; ~ **originale** f INFORMAT, TV master tape;

~ p ~ **de papier** f INFORMAT paper tape; ~ **de passage** f TRANSPORT through band; ~ **passante** f CONS MECA, ELECTRON, INFORMAT pass band, OPTIQUE bandwidth, ORDINAT, PHYSIQUE, TELECOM pass band, TV bandwidth; ~ **passante de l'amplificateur vertical** f ELECTRON vertical amplifier bandwidth; ~ **passante de canal** f TV channel bandwidth; ~ **passante de la chrominance** f TV chrominance bandwidth; ~ **passante Doppler** f ELECTRON Doppler bandwidth; ~ **passante en grands signaux** f ELECTRON large-signal bandwidth; ~ **passante en puissance** f ELECTRON power bandwidth; ~ **passante de filtre** f ELECTRON filter pass band; ~ **passante résultante** f ELECTRON composite pass band; ~ **perforée** f ENREGISTR perforated tape, INFORMAT perforated tape, punched tape, ORDINAT punched tape; ~ **à perforer** f INFORMAT, ORDINAT punch tape; ~ **photographique** f PHOTO strip; ~ **pilote** f INFORMAT control tape; ~ **pleine** f PHYSIQUE full band; ~ **de pliage** f METALL kink, kink band; ~ **pour l'enregistrement** f ELECTR chart strip; ~ **pré-enregistrée** f ENREGISTR prerecorded magnetic tape; ~ **de première génération** f TV master, original; ~ **de protection** f INFORMAT group separator, guard band, ORDINAT, TV guard band; ~ **de protection de collier de serrage** f CONS MECA clamping band, cushion;

~ r ~ **radar maritime** f NAUT marine radar band, marine radar frequency; ~ **de recouvrement** f CONSTR cover, PRODUCTION butt strap, butt strip, covering plate, strap, welt; ~ **de référence** f ACOUSTIQUE reference tape, INFORMAT master tape; ~ **de réglage** f CINEMAT *dans une tireuse* control band, exposure control tape, TV line-up tape; ~ **de ris** f OCEANO reef band; ~ **de roulement** f CH DE FER *véhicules* tread, PLAST CAOU *caoutchouc* tire tread (AmE), tyre tread (BrE), VEHICULES *pneu* tread; ~ **rythmo** f ENREGISTR timing track; ~ **rythmo-son** f ENREGISTR click track;

~ s ~ **S** f ELECTRON S-band; ~ **sans fin** f TV tape loop; ~ **de sauvegarde** f INFORMAT backing tape; ~ **de serrage par pince** f EMBALLAGE clip band; ~ **sismique** f GEOPHYS seismic zone; ~ **son internationale** f CINEMAT M and E track, Music and Effects track, international soundtrack; ~ **son synchrone** f CINEMAT dialogue track; ~ **sortant de la machine** f IMPRIM *rotatives* outgoing web; ~ **souple de transport** f PRODUCTION apron, conveyor belt, traveling apron (AmE), travelling apron (BrE); ~ **stéréophonique à enregistrement aligné** f ENREGISTR in-line stereophonic tape; ~ **stratifiée** f PLAST CAOU *plastiques* laminated strip; ~ **stroboscopique** f ENREGISTR stroboscopic tape;

~ t ~ **tachygraphique** f CH DE FER speed recording tape; ~ **téléphonique** f ORDINAT, TELECOM voice-band; ~ **témoin** f CINEMAT control strip, control wedge; ~ **de transfert de charge** f PHYS RAYON charge transfer band; ~ **transporteuse** f CONS MECA belt conveyor, CONSTR, MECANIQUE conveyor belt, TRANSPORT pedestrian conveyor; ~ **transporteuse pour piétons** f TRANSPORT passenger conveyor; ~ **transporteuse pour**

sacs f TRANSPORT bag conveyor; ~ **transporteuse à vitesse variable** f TRANSPORT variable speed conveyor belt; ~ **de type parallèle** f PHYS RAYON *spectres de vibration* parallel band;

~ u ~ **d'usure** f CH DE FER pantograph contact strip, pantograph-wearing strip; ~ **d'usure pantographe** f CH DE FER pantograph contact strip, pantograph-wearing strip;

~ v ~ **de valence** f PHYSIQUE valence band; ~ **vide** f PHYSIQUE empty band; ~ **vidéo** f TELECOM, TV videotape; ~ **vocale** f TELECOM voice-band;

~ x ~ **X** f ELECTRON X-band;

~ z ~ **zéro** f NUCLEAIRE zero band; ~ **zodiacale** f ASTRONOMIE zodiacal band

bandeau m IMPRIM *édition* band

bande-L: ~ **de fréquences** f NAUT L-band frequency

bander vt RESSORTS stretch

banderole f EMBALLAGE banderole

bandes: ~ **de l'atmosphère jovienne** f pl ASTRONOMIE Jovian bands; ~ **de saturation** f pl TV saturation banding; ~ **spectrales** f pl PHYS ONDES bands of the spectrum

bandeuse f EMBALLAGE banding machine

bandothèque f INFORMAT, ORDINAT tape library

banette f NAUT bunk

bang: ~ **supersonique** m AERONAUT, PHYSIQUE, SECURITE sonic boom

banket m MINES banket

banque: ~ **de données** f ELECTRON, INFORMAT, ORDINAT databank; ~ **d'os** f REFRIG bone bank; ~ **de sang** f REFRIG blood bank; ~ **de tissus** f REFRIG tissue bank

banquette f AERONAUT console, CERAM VER seat, CONSTR banquette, bench, berm, *de terre* bank, VEHICULES *sièges* bench seat; ~ **de brûleur** f CERAM VER port sill; ~ **de halage** f CONSTR tow path; ~ **de poste de pilotage** f AERONAUT pilot's console

banquise f NAUT, OCEANO ice field, ice pack; ~ **flottante** f NAUT ice floe

baquet m AERONAUT bottom structure, CERAM VER bosh, CONSTR bucket, PRODUCTION trough, VEHICULES *siège* bucket seat

bar m METROLOGIE *unité de pression*, PETROLE *unité de pression*, PHYSIQUE *unité de pression* bar

baraque f CONSTR barracks, shed; ~ **d'outils** f CONSTR tool shed

baraquement m CONSTR, MILITAIRE barracks

baratte f AGRO ALIM churn

baratter vt AGRO ALIM churn

barbacane f CONSTR weephole

barbe f CONS MECA burr, CONSTR notch, MECANIQUE, PRODUCTION burr

barbiturate m CHIMIE barbiturate

barbiturique[1] adj CHIMIE barbituric

barbiturique[2] m CHIMIE barbiturate

barboche f CONS MECA frame saw file

barbotage m CHIMIE sparging, IMPRIM dipping, PHYSIQUE bubbling

barboter vi PHYSIQUE bubble through

barboteur m CONS MECA patouillet, IMPRIM *machines à imprimer* dipping roller, PHYSIQUE bubbler

barbotin m NAUT chain grab

barbotine f CERAM VER slip; ~ **de coulage** f CERAM VER casting slip

barbule f METEO wind speed barb

barbure f PRODUCTION burr, scale

bardage m CONSTR siding

bardeau *m* CONSTR, shingle
bardelle *f* CERAM VER chair arm
barégine *f* CHIMIE glairin
barème *m* CONSTR scale of charges, table
barette: ~ **de masse** *f* PRODUCTION *électricité* earth bus (BrE), ground bus (AmE)
barge *f* NAUT, PETR barge; ~ **d'ensouillage** *f* PETROLE *canalisations sous-marines* bury barge; ~ **de forage** *f* PETROLE drill barge; ~ **LASH** *f* TRANSPORT LASH lighter; ~ **de levage** *f* PETROLE crane barge; ~ **de navire** *f* TRANSPORT ship-borne lighter; ~ **de plongée** *f* OCEANO diving support barge; ~ **porte-conteneurs** *f* TRANSPORT container lighter; ~ **de pose** *f* PETR *canalisations sous-marines* PETROLE *canalisations sous-marines* lay barge, laying barge, pipe laying barge; ~ **de reconditionnement** *f* PETROLE *forage* workover barge; ~ **transocéanique** *f* TRANSPORT seagoing barge; ~ **de travail** *f* PETROLE work barge; ~ **type EBCS** *f* TRANSPORT EBCS lighter
baril *m* AGRO ALIM barrel, CONS MECA *d'un vilebrequin* socket, PETR barrel, PRODUCTION *système hydraulique* drum, TRANSPORT barrel; ~ **équivalent pétrole** *m* PETROLE BOE, barrel oil equivalent
barillet *m* CINEMAT lens barrel, CONS MECA *de pompe* barrel, DISTRI EAU pump barrel, pump cylinder, INST HYDR *d'indicateur de pression* drum, INSTRUMENT cell, PRODUCTION cluster, *d'une pompe* cylinder, TRANSPORT cluster; ~ **de la lentille frontale** *m* PHOTO mount of front element; ~ **d'objectif** *m* PHOTO lens barrel; ~ **de stockage** *m* NUCLEAIRE *des assemblages combustibles neufs* new element storage drum
bariolé *adj* GEOLOGIE mottled
barkévicite *f* MINERAUX barkevikite
barn *m (b)* METROLOGIE, PHYSIQUE barn *(b)*
barnhardite *f* MINERAUX barnhardite, barnhardtite
barographe *m* EQUIP LAB, METEO, NAUT barograph, PHYSIQUE barograph, recording barometer
baromètre *m* EQUIP LAB, METEO, NAUT, PHYSIQUE barometer; ~ **anéroïde** *m* AERONAUT, EQUIP LAB, METEO, PHYSIQUE aneroid barometer; ~ **anéroïde de nivellement** *m* CONSTR surveying aneroid barometer; ~ **enregistreur** *m* METEO, NAUT barograph, PHYSIQUE barograph, recording barometer; ~ **Fortin** *m* EQUIP LAB, PHYSIQUE Fortin barometer; ~ **à mercure** *m* EQUIP LAB, METEO, METROLOGIE, PHYSIQUE mercury barometer
barométrique *adj* PHYSIQUE barometric
baroscope *m* PHYSIQUE baroscope
barostat *m* AERONAUT barostat
barothermographe *m* PHYSIQUE barothermograph
barotraumatisme *m* ACOUSTIQUE barotrauma
barque *f* AERONAUT bottom structure, NAUT boat, TEXTILE winch; ~ **de pêche** *f* NAUT fishing smack; ~ **de pêcheur** *f* NAUT fishing boat
barquette *f* EMBALLAGE food tray, punnet tray (BrE); ~ **en carton** *f* EMBALLAGE cardboard tray; ~ **wraparound** *f* EMBALLAGE wraparound tray
barrage *m* CONSTR barrage, dam, DISTRI EAU dam, damming, weir, EN RENOUV dam, HYDROLOGIE barrage, dam, dike (AmE), dyke (BrE), MINES stopping, NAUT dam, OCEANO barrage, PETROLE boom; ~ **à aiguilles** *m* DISTRI EAU needle dam, pin weir; ~ **antipollution** *m* PETROLE containment boom; ~ **d'arrêt** *m* MINES stopping; ~ **à barreaux** *m* DISTRI EAU bar weir; ~ **barrière** *m* POLLU MER fence boom; ~ **à bulles d'air** *m* POLLU MER bubble barriers; ~ **à contreforts** *m* CONSTR buttress dam; ~ **cyclopéen** *m* DISTRI EAU cyclopic barrage; ~ **de dérivation** *m* HYDROLOGIE diversion dam; ~ **déversoir** *m* DISTRI EAU, HYDROLOGIE overflow dam; ~ **à déversoir** *m* POLLU MER weir boom; ~ **d'écrémage** *m* POLLU MER skimming barrier; ~ **écrémeur** *m* POLLU MER skimming barrier; ~ **en conteneur** *m* POLLU MER boom pack; ~ **en maçonnerie** *m* HYDROLOGIE masonry dam; ~ **en maçonnerie et terre** *m* HYDROLOGIE masonry earth dam; ~ **en terre** *m* DISTRI EAU, HYDROLOGIE earth dam; ~ **à fermettes** *m* DISTRI EAU needle dam; ~ **fixe** *m* CERAM VER bridge; ~ **flottant** *m* CERAM VER floater, NAUT *l'entrée du port* boom, POLLU MER, POLLUTION floating boom; ~ **flottant autoréglable** *m* POLLU MER self-adjusting floating weir; ~ **mobile** *m* DISTRI EAU, EN RENOUV weir; ~ **poids** *m* HYDROLOGIE gravity dam; ~ **poids déversoir** *m* CONSTR gravity spillway dam; ~ **poids en béton cyclopéen** *m* HYDROLOGIE cyclopean concrete gravity dam; ~ **poids évidé** *m* HYDROLOGIE hollow gravity dam; ~ **pour retenir les tailings** *m* CONSTR tailings dam; ~ **provisoire** *m* DISTRI EAU temporary dam; ~ **récupérateur** *m* POLLU MER skimming barrier; ~ **de retenue** *m* DISTRI EAU retaining dam; ~ **de retenue des tailings** *m* CONSTR tailings dam; ~ **rideau** *m* POLLU MER curtain boom; ~ **à segment** *m* DISTRI EAU sector weir; ~ **thermique** *m* CERAM VER thermal barrier; ~ **voûte** *m* CONSTR, DISTRI EAU arch dam
barrandite *f* MINERAUX barrandite
barratage *m* AGRO ALIM churning
barre *f* CHARBON band, bar, CONSTR rail, HYDROLOGIE *d'un port* bar, *d'un fleuve* bar, MECANIQUE rod, MINES bar, NAUT bar, helm, OCEANO bore, sand bar, tidal bore, TEXTILE bar, barriness; ~ **d'accouplement** *f* AUTO relay rod, VEHICULES *direction* drag link, *remorque* drawbar; ~ **d'aiguilles** *f* TEXTILE needle bar; ~ **à air** *f* IMPRIM *mécanique* air bar; ~ **à air décalé en quinconce** *f* IMPRIM *sécheur* staggered air bar; ~ **d'alésage** *f* CONS MECA boring bar; ~ **d'alimentation** *f* ELECTR feeder bar, ESPACE *véhicules* power bus, MATERIAUX runner, TELECOM busbar; ~ **d'ancrage** *f* AERONAUT *hélicoptère* dog bone, tie bar; ~ **antiroulis** *f* AUTO antiroll bar; ~ **d'appui** *f* CONSTR window bar; ~ **d'arrêt d'urgence** *f* NUCLEAIRE emergency shutdown rod; ~ **d'arrêt d'urgence injectée** *f* NUCLEAIRE inserted scram rod, scrammed rod; ~ **bus** *f* ELECTROTEC busbar; ~ **de carrière** *f* MINES jumper, quarry bar; ~ **de chariotage** *f* CONS MECA feed shaft; ~ **collectrice** *f* CONS MECA collector ring; ~ **colorée** *f* TV color bar (AmE), colour bar (BrE); ~ **de combustible** *f* PHYSIQUE fuel rod; ~ **de commande de chariotage** *f* CONS MECA feed shaft; ~ **de commande** *f* PHYSIQUE control rod; ~ **de commutation** *f* TV switching bar; ~ **de compensation et d'arrêt d'urgence** *f* NUCLEAIRE scram rod, shim, shim safety rod; ~ **de compensation-sécurité** *f* NUCLEAIRE scram rod, shim, shim safety rod; ~ **de connexion** *f* VEHICULES *direction* tie rod, track rod; ~ **de contrôle** *f* couleur wedge, photogravure color key (AmE), colour key (BrE), PHYSIQUE control rod; ~ **de contrôle avec diverses plages** *f* IMPRIM step wedge; ~ **de couleur** *f* TV color bar (AmE), colour bar (BrE); ~ **de débrayage** *f* CONS MECA fork bar, strap bar; ~ **de défilement** *f* ORDINAT scroll bar; ~ **déplisseuse** *f* PAPIER camber bar, spreader bar; ~ **diagonale** *f* NUCLEAIRE diagonal, diagonal member rod; ~ **de dopage** *f* NUCLEAIRE booster rod; ~ **d'eau** *f* HYDROLOGIE bore; ~ **d'ébranlage** *f* PRODUCTION loosening bar; ~ **d'écartement** *f* CONSTR

gage bar (AmE), gauge bar (BrE); ~ d'écoute de grande voile *f* NAUT main sheet track; ~ d'écrémage *f* CERAM VER skim bar; ~ espacée *f* PAPIER *provoquée par des vibrations* baring; ~ d'état *f* INFORMAT status bar, tool status, tool status, ORDINAT status bar; ~ d'excentrique *f* CONS MECA eccentric rod; ~ de fermeture *f* CONSTR window bar; ~ de flèche *f* NAUT crosstree; ~ flottante *f* NAUT *du port* boom; ~ de force *f* VEHICULES *suspension* radius arm; ~ franche *f* NAUT tiller; ~ de guidage en l'air *f* CONS MECA overhead pilot bar; ~ à haute tension *f* ELECTR *distribution* high-voltage bus; ~ horizontale *f* TV horizontal bar; ~ d'induit *f* ELECTR *machine*, ELECTROTEC armature bar; ~ intérieure de renforcement *f* EMBALLAGE interior strengthening bar; ~ littorale *f* OCEANO bay-mouth bar, spit; ~ longue *f* CH DE FER continuous welded rail; ~ de masse *f* AERONAUT grounding bar; ~ Meyer *f* IMPRIM *sécheurs* Meyer bar; ~ à mine *f* MINES jumper, jumper drill, jumping drill, miners' bar, scaling bar; ~ de mineur *f* MINES jumper, jumper drill, jumping drill, miners' bar, scaling bar; ~ omnibus *f* CONS MECA, ELECTR *raccordement* busbar; ~ omnibus principale *f* TELECOM main busbar; ~ omnibus de terre *f* ELECTR *raccordement* earth bus (BrE), ground bus (AmE); ~ d'outils *f* INFORMAT, ORDINAT tool bar; ~ de passettes *f* TEXTILE guide bar; ~ de pilotage *f* CONS MECA fine control rod; ~ de platines *f* TEXTILE sinker bar; ~ de plongée *f* OCEANO depth rudder, diving plate, hydrofoil rudder; ~ de porte *f* CONSTR door bar, door brand; ~ porte-couteau *f* CHARBON cutter arm; ~ porteuse *f* PAPIER carrying bar; ~ pour cadre d'extrémité *f* EMBALLAGE *dans un conteneur* end frame member; ~ de poussée *f* VEHICULES *suspension* torque arm; ~ principale *f* ELECTROTEC main bar; ~ de rallonge *f* CONS MECA extension piece, lengthening piece, lengthening rod; ~ de rappel *f* AERONAUT drag link; ~ de relevage *f* CONS MECA reversing lever rod, reversing rod; ~ de remorquage *f* MECANIQUE *véhicules*, VEHICULES tow bar; ~ de remorque *f* VEHICULES drawbar; ~ de renvoi *f* CONS MECA flat rod, string rod, transmission rod; ~ de réparation *f* CONSTR *armature* distribution steel; ~ de retournement *f* IMPRIM turner bar, *lignes de production, mécanique* air turn, angle bar, turner bar; ~ de rivière *f* HYDROLOGIE river bar; ~ ronde *f* MATERIAUX round bar; ~ de ronflement *f* TV hum bar; ~ à roue *f* NAUT wheel; ~ à roulis *f* NAUT fiddle; ~ sectionnée *f* ELECTR *alimentation* sectionalized busbar; ~ de serrage *f* IMPRIM *machines* tensioning bar; ~ de shuntage *f* CH DE FER *véhicules* shunt bar; ~ de sinus *f* METROLOGIE sine bar; ~ de sonde *f* MINES drill rod; ~ soufflante *f* IMPRIM air bar; ~ de soutien extensible *f* CINEMAT polecat; ~ de stabilisateur *f* AERONAUT antiroll bar; ~ de stabilisation *f* AUTO torque stabilizer; ~ stabilisatrice *f* MECANIQUE antiroll bar, stabilizer bar, VEHICULES *suspension* antiroll bar, stabilizer bar; ~ de surcharge *f* MINES sinker bar; ~ de surréactivité *f* NUCLEAIRE booster rod; ~ de tendance *f* AERONAUT horizontal and vertical bar of flight direction; ~ de tension *f* TEXTILE tension bar; ~ de terre *f* ELECTR *raccordement* earthing bus (BrE), grounding bus (AmE); ~ de torsion *f* AUTO torsion bar; ~ de traction *f* CH DE FER draft bar (AmE), draught bar (BrE), *véhicules* drawbar; ~ de trame *f* TEXTILE barriness in the weft; ~ transversale de feux *f* AERONAUT *balisage lumineux d'approche* crossbar; ~ de treillis *f* CONSTR window bar; ~ au vent *f* NAUT weather helm; ~ de verrouillage de l'alimentation *f* PRODUCTION *automatisme industriel* power interlock bar

barreau *m* CONSTR rail, step, *d'une échelle* round, rung; ~ aimanté *m* PHYSIQUE bar magnet; ~ de battement *m* CONSTR shutting post; ~ à chevrons *m* PRODUCTION herringbone bar; ~ de côtière *m* CONSTR hinge post, hinging post, swinging post; ~ dormant *m* PRODUCTION *d'un foyer* bearer; ~ en uranium naturel *m* NUCLEAIRE natural uranium slug; ~ d'essai *m* CONS MECA, MATERIAUX test bar; ~ de fenêtre *m* CONSTR window bar; ~ de ferrasse *m* CERAM VER runner bar; ~ de grille *m* CONSTR railing, PRODUCTION furnace bar, grid bar; ~ à pique *m* CONSTR spear-headed railing; ~ rectifié en acier *m* CONS MECA steel tool bit; ~ traité *m* CONS MECA tool bit

barre-levier *f* CONS MECA jimmy bar

barrémien *adj* GEOLOGIE *stratigraphie* Barremian

barrer *vt* CONSTR *route* close, DISTRI EAU dam, NAUT helm, *navire* steer

barrette *f* AUTO plate strap, CONS MECA *d'un châssis de fonderie* bar, crossbar, ELECTRON linear array, PRODUCTION stay, *d'un châssis de fonderie* crossbar, *du tiroir* face flange, TV frame line; ~ à bornes *f* ELECTROTEC terminal strip; ~ de connexion *f* TELECOM connection strip; ~ de fixation *f* PHOTO mounting bracket; ~ flash *f* PHOTO flash bar; ~ de guidage *f* CINEMAT aperture guide

barretter *m* ELECTR *stabilisateur de tension*, ELECTROTEC, PHYSIQUE barretter

barricade *f* CONSTR, SECURITE barricade

barricader *vt* CONSTR, SECURITE barricade

barrière *f* CONSTR barrier, gate, window bar, SECURITE barricade, guard, TRANSPORT railroad gate (AmE), railway gate (BrE); ~ antibruit *f* CONSTR noise barrier; ~ antisouffle *f* AERONAUT blast fence; ~ d'arrêt *f* TRANSPORT crash barrier, emergency crash barrier; ~ à bascule *f* CONSTR lift gate; ~ de confinement *f* NUCLEAIRE engineered barrier; ~ de contrôle *f* CONSTR control barrier; ~ corallienne *f* OCEANO coral reef; ~ à déclic *f* SECURITE trip guard; ~ à enclenchement *f* SECURITE interlocking guard; ~ flottante *f* POLLU MER boom; ~ de glace *f* OCEANO ice barrier; ~ à guillotine *f* MINES guillotine gate; ~ du micron *f* ELECTRON micron barrier; ~ oscillante *f* CONSTR lift gate; ~ pare-neige *f* CONSTR snow barrier; ~ photo-électrique *f* SECURITE photoelectric guard; ~ à pivot *f* CONSTR swing gate; ~ de potentiel *f* ELECTROTEC, PHYSIQUE potential barrier; ~ pour la buée *f* EMBALLAGE water vapor barrier (AmE), water vapour barrier (BrE); ~ protectrice pour machine *f* SECURITE machine fence; ~ roulante *f* CONSTR sliding gate; ~ de Schottky *f* ELECTRON, PHYSIQUE Schottky barrier; ~ de sécurité *f* SECURITE crush barrier, guardrail; ~ de sûreté *f* SECURITE safety barrier; ~ technique *f* NUCLEAIRE engineered barrier; ~ thermique *f* CHAUFFAGE, ESPACE thermal barrier, NUCLEAIRE heat barrier; ~ à tournante *f* CONSTR swing gate

barrique *f* AGRO ALIM barrel

barrot *m* NAUT beam; ~ de pont *m* NAUT deck beam; ~ transversal *m* NAUT deck transverse

barrotin *m* NAUT crossbeam, half beam

barycentre *m* ASTRONOMIE, ESPACE *véhicules*, MATH barycenter (AmE), barycentre (BrE), MECANIQUE center of mass (AmE), centre of mass (BrE), PHYSIQUE centroid

barylite *f* MINERAUX barylite

baryon *m* PHYS PART, PHYSIQUE baryon
barysphère *f* GEOPHYS barysphere, centrosphere, core, earth core
baryte *f* CERAM VER, CHIMIE, MINERAUX , PETR, PETROLE *forage*, PLAST CAOU *pigment* barite, barytes
barytique *adj* CHIMIE baric
barytocalcite *f* MINERAUX barytocalcite
barytocélestine *f* MINERAUX barytocelestine, barytocelestite
baryum *m (Ba)* CHIMIE barium *(Ba)*
bas:[1] **en ~** *adj* NAUT below, below decks
bas:[2] **en ~** *adv* NAUT below
bas[3] *m* CONSTR *d'une colline* bottom, HYDROLOGIE *aquifère* bed, IMPRIM bottom; **~ fourneau** *m* CHARBON low kiln; **~ de garniture** *m* PETROLE BHA, bottom hole assembly; **~ hauban** *m* NAUT lower shroud; **~ logique** *m* ELECTRON logic low; **~ niveau de signal** *m* ELECTRON low signal level; **~ titre** *m* MATERIAUX low grade
basal *adj* GEOLOGIE basal
basalte *m* GEOLOGIE, MATERIAUX *géologie*, MINERAUX, PETR basalt; **~ de plateau** *m* GEOLOGIE flood basalt; **~ vitreux** *m* PETR basalt glass
basaltine *f* MINERAUX basaltine
basane *f* IMPRIM basan
basanite *f* PETR basanite
basculage *m* CONS MECA seesawing, PRODUCTION tilting
bascule *f* CONS MECA bascule, scales, CONSTR trap, ELECTRON flip-flop, INFORMAT flip-flop, latch, switch, toggle, METROLOGIE scale, ORDINAT flip-flop, latch, toggle, trigger, PHYSIQUE trigger circuit, PRODUCTION weighing machine; **~ asynchrone** *f* ELECTRON unclocked flip-flop; **~ de battage** *f* MINES walking beam; **~ binaire** *f* ELECTRON binary pair; **~ bistable** *f* PHYSIQUE flip-flop; **~ commandée par porte** *f* ELECTRON gated flip-flop; **~ D** *f* ELECTRON D-type flip-flop; **~ déclenchée par front** *f* ELECTRON edge-triggered flip-flop; **~ électronique** *f* ORDINAT trigger; **~ maître-esclave** *f* ELECTRON master-slave flip-flop; **~ RS** *f* ELECTR RS flip-flop, reset-set flip-flop; **~ RST** *f* ELECTR RST flip-flop, reset-set-toggle flip-flop; **~ sur rotule** *f* PHOTO tilt head; **~ synchrone** *f* ELECTRON clocked flip-flop; **~ synchronisée** *f* ELECTRON clocked flip-flop; **~ T** *f* ELECTRON T-flip-flop; **~ de type D** *f* ELECTRON D-type flip-flop
basculement *m* CONSTR dumping (AmE), tipping (BrE), ELECTROTEC firing
basculer[1] *vt* CINEMAT tilt, INFORMAT, ORDINAT toggle
basculer[2] *vi* CONS MECA swing, CONSTR tip up
basculer[3] *vti* CONS MECA overturn
basculeur *m* CONSTR dump (AmE), tip (BrE), dump truck (AmE), tipper (BrE), PRODUCTION tilter; **~ en bout** *m* CONSTR end dump; **~ à mouleaux de glace** *m* REFRIG ice tip; **~ de train principal** *m* AERONAUT main gear axle beam
bas-de-casse *m* IMPRIM lower case
base *f* CHIMIE base, CONSTR base, foundation, baseline, datum, datum line, *d'une colline* bottom, ELECTROTEC, GEOMETRIE base, INFORMAT base, radix, INSTRUMENT baseplate, MATH base, NUCLEAIRE base, base frame, ORDINAT base, radix, PHYSIQUE base, RESSORTS seat, TELECOM base; **~ active** *f* MATERIAUX active dope; **~ aérienne** *f* TRANSPORT air base; **~ d'alliage** *f* METALL bare metal; **~ du col** *f* CERAM VER base; **~ de connaissances** *f* INFORMAT, ORDINAT knowledge base; **~ de contrôle** *f* CONSTR base of verification; **~ côtière** *f* PETROLE *installations à terre* onshore base; **~ de coul-**

isse *f* EMBALLAGE skid base; **~ de données** *f* ELECTRON, INFORMAT, ORDINAT, TELECOM database; **~ de données en ligne** *f* INFORMAT, ORDINAT on-line database; **~ de données en réseau** *f* INFORMAT, ORDINAT network database; **~ de données de gestion** *f* TELECOM MIB, management information base; **~ de données relationnelles** *f (BDR)* INFORMAT, ORDINAT, TELECOM relational database *(RDB)*; INFORMAT ; **~ de données répartie** *f* ORDINAT distributed database; **~ de données sur disque optique** *f* OPTIQUE optical database; **~ dopée P** *f* ELECTRON p-type base; **~ d'une figure** *f* GEOMETRIE *géométrique* base of figure; **~ d'informations de gestion** *f* TELECOM MIB, management information base; **~ d'informations de gestion de sécurité** *f* TELECOM SMIB, security management information base; **~ de lancement** *f* ESPACE *infrastructure* cosmodrome, launching base, range; **~ monobloc** *f* PRODUCTION one-piece base; **~ navale** *f* NAUT naval base; **~ nuageuse** *f* METEO cloudbase; **~ d'opérations** *f* CONSTR baseline, datum, datum line, PRODUCTION base of operations; **~ organique** *f* CHIMIE organic base; **~ oxygénée** *f* CHIMIE basyl, basyle; **~ P** *f* ELECTRON p-type base; **~ de payer-par-utilisation** *f* TELECOM pay-by-use basis; **~ plate temporaire** *f* PETR template drilling; **~ de règles** *f* INFORMAT, ORDINAT rule base; **~ des ressources accessibles** *f* EN RENOUV accessible resource base; **~ de temps** *f* ELECTRON, NUCLEAIRE, PHYSIQUE, PRODUCTION time base, TELECOM time base, timing, TV time base; **~ de temps de ligne** *f* TV line output; **~ de temps linéaire** *f* ELECTRON linear time base; **~ de temps pilotée par quartz** *f* ELECTRON crystal time base; **~ de temps pour les éléments de signal** *f* TELECOM signal element timing; **~ de temps retardante** *f* ELECTRON delaying time base; **~ de transistor** *f* ELECTRON, TELECOM transistor base; **~ de type P** *f* ELECTRON p-type base
bas-fond *m* HYDROLOGIE *cours d'eau* bed, PRODUCTION shoal
BASIC *abrév* INFORMAT, ORDINAT BASIC, beginner's all-purpose symbolic instruction code
basicité *f* CHIMIE, MATERIAUX basicity
basique *adj* CHIMIE basic
bas-joyer *m* DISTRI EAU *d'une écluse, d'une roue hydraulique* sidewall
bas-parc *m* OCEANO stake net
basse *f* ACOUSTIQUE bass, GEOLOGIE, NAUT shoal, OCEANO bank, sandbank, shoal; **~ fréquence** *f (BF)* ELECTR *onde*, ELECTRON, ELECTROTEC, PHYS RAYON, TELECOM low-frequency *(LF)*; **~ mer** *f* HYDROLOGIE low water, NAUT low tide, low water, OCEANO low tide, low water; **~ pression** *f* PHYSIQUE low pressure; **~ résistance nuque/terre** *f* TELECOM low B to earth, low ring to ground; **~ résistance pointe/nuque** *f* TELECOM low A to B, low tip to ring; **~ résistance pointe/nuque/terre** *f* TELECOM low A to B to earth; **~ résistance pointe/terre** *f* TELECOM low A to earth, low tip to ground; **~ température** *f* REFRIG low temperature; **~ teneur** *f* MINES baseness, low grade, poor grade; **~ teneur de minerai** *f* MINES low tenor of ore; **~ tension** *f* ELECTR LV, low voltage, low tension, ELECTROTEC LV, low tension, low voltage, TELECOM LV, low voltage
basses: **~ eaux** *f pl* EN RENOUV low-water, HYDROLOGIE, NAUT low water
bassier *m* OCEANO shore fisherman, shrimper
bassin *m* CERAM VER basin, dish, tank, CHARBON basin,

pan, pond, CONS MECA scale, scale pan, DISTRI EAU, EQUIP LAB, GEOLOGIE basin, HYDROLOGIE basin, reservoir, METROLOGIE *d'une balance* bowl, NAUT dock, PETROLE pit, *géologie* basin, PRODUCTION casting pit; ~ **d'activation** *m* HYDROLOGIE activated sludge tank; ~ **d'aération** *m* DISTRI EAU aeration basin, RECYCLAGE aeration tank; ~ **d'air** *m* POLLUTION air shed; ~ **d'amortissement** *m* HYDROLOGIE stilling basin; ~ **arrière-arc** *m* GEOLOGIE, OCEANO back-arc basin; ~ **atmosphérique** *m* POLLUTION air shed; ~ **à boue** *m* CHARBON slurry pond, PETROLE mud tank; ~ **calibré** *m* POLLUTION calibrated watershed; ~ **charbonnier** *m* CHARBON coal basin; ~ **de chasse** *m* DISTRI EAU flush pond, OCEANO flushing basin, scouring basin; ~ **de chloration** *m* HYDROLOGIE chlorination tank, chlorination vessel, chlorine contact chamber; ~ **à circulation radiale** *m* HYDROLOGIE radial flow tank; ~ **de clarification** *m* PETROLE clarifying basin; ~ **à clarifier** *m* GENIE CHIM settling basin, settling cistern, settling reservoir; ~ **collecteur** *m* POLLU MER *d'huile* collection basin; ~ **de compensation** *m* DISTRI EAU compensating reservoir, equalizing tank, HYDROLOGIE compensation basin; ~ **de concentration** *m* OCEANO concentration basin; ~ **de coulée** *m* PRODUCTION casting pit, runner basin; ~ **de cristallisation** *m* GENIE CHIM crystallizing pond; ~ **de curage** *m* GENIE CHIM settling basin, settling cistern, settling pool; ~ **de décantation** *m* CHARBON clear pond, sedimentation pond, settling basin, settling pond, GENIE CHIM precipitating tank, precipitation tank, HYDROLOGIE clarifier, settling basin, settling tank, MINES settling basin, RECYCLAGE sedimentation basin, sedimentation tank; ~ **de décantation des boues** *m* CHARBON settling pond, slurry pond; ~ **de décharge** *m* NUCLEAIRE discharge pond; ~ **de dégrossissage** *m* HYDROLOGIE intake chamber; ~ **de désiltage** *m* HYDROLOGIE desilting basin; ~ **de dessablement** *m* HYDROLOGIE desilting basin, settling basin; ~ **de drainage** *m* HYDROLOGIE catchment basin; ~ **d'eau souterraine** *m* DISTRI EAU ground water basin; ~ **d'effondrement** *m* GEOLOGIE, PETROLE fault basin; ~ **en eaux profondes** *m* CONSTR deep-water dock; ~ **en pull-apart** *m* GEOLOGIE pull-apart basin; ~ **en subsidence** *m* PETROLE subsident basin; ~ **d'entremont** *m* GEOLOGIE intramontane basin; ~ **d'essai** *m* DISTRI EAU test basin, NAUT *de carènes, de modèles, de moteurs* testing tank; ~ **d'essai des carènes** *m* NAUT ship model test tank; ~ **d'essai générateur de vagues** *m* NAUT wave-generating test tank; ~ **d'évaporation** *m* HYDROLOGIE evaporation tank; ~ **d'évitage** *m* NAUT turning basin; ~ **fermé** *m* DISTRI EAU blind drainage area; ~ **de filtrage** *m* RECYCLAGE filter basin; ~ **de filtration** *m* DISTRI EAU filter bed, filter tank; ~ **à flot** *m* EN RENOUV tidal basin; ~ **fluvial** *m* DISTRI EAU, EN RENOUV, HYDROLOGIE river basin; ~ **d'homogénéisation** *m* DISTRI EAU mixing basin; ~ **houiller** *m* CHARBON, GEOLOGIE coal basin; ~ **hydrographique** *m* DISTRI EAU catchment basin, GEOLOGIE hydrographic basin, HYDROLOGIE catchment area, drainage area, drainage basin; ~ **hydrologique** *m* DISTRI EAU drainage area, drainage basin; ~ **d'infiltration** *m* HYDROLOGIE infiltration basin; ~ **jaugé** *m* POLLUTION calibrated watershed; ~ **de marée** *m* OCEANO tidal basin; ~ **à marée** *m* NAUT tidal dock; ~ **de maturation** *m* DISTRI EAU maturation pond; ~ **mélangeur** *m* HYDROLOGIE mixing basin; ~ **de neutralisation** *m* NUCLEAIRE neutralization pond; ~ **océanique** *m* HYDROLOGIE oceanic basin, OCEANO

ocean basin, oceanic basin; ~ **pétrolifère** *m* PETROLE petroleum basin, *géologie* oil basin; ~ **de radoub** *m* NAUT dry dock, repair dock; ~ **de réfrigération** *m* DISTRI EAU cooling pond; ~ **de retenue** *m* DISTRI EAU detention basin, HYDROLOGIE compensation basin; ~ **à schlamms** *m* CHARBON slurry pond; ~ **secondaire** *m* PETROLE sedimentary basin; ~ **sédimentaire** *m* GAZ sedimentary basin, GENIE CHIM sedimentation basin, sedimentation pit, sedimentation tank, GEOLOGIE sedimentary basin; ~ **de sédimentation** *m* GENIE CHIM sedimentation basin, sedimentation pit, sedimentation tank; ~ **solaire** *m* EN RENOUV solar pond; ~ **de stabilisation** *m* DISTRI EAU equalizing tank; ~ **à stériles** *m* CHARBON settling pond, tailing pond; ~ **structural** *m* GEOLOGIE intermount basin; ~ **de tranquillisation** *m* HYDROLOGIE settling basin; ~ **de transtension** *m* GEOLOGIE pull-apart basin; ~ **urbain** *m* DISTRI EAU urban catchment; ~ **versant** *m* CONSTR catchment area, DISTRI EAU drainage area, drainage basin, EN RENOUV catchment area, HYDROLOGIE catchment basin, drainage basin; ~ **versant calibré** *m* POLLUTION calibrated watershed; ~ **versant expérimental** *m* DISTRI EAU experimental basin

bassine *f* GENIE CHIM evaporating boiler, evaporating vessel, IMPRIM *machine* fountain, *machines* pan; ~ **de couchage** *f* IMPRIM coating pan

bastague *f* NAUT runner

bastite *f* MINERAUX bastite, schiller spar

bastnaésite *f* MINERAUX bastnaesite

bâtardeau *m* CONSTR batardeau, cofferdam, DISTRI EAU, HYDROLOGIE cofferdam; ~ **cellulaire** *m* HYDROLOGIE cellular cofferdam; ~ **cellulaire à cellules gabionnées** *m* HYDROLOGIE diaphragm cellular cofferdam

batch *m* AGRO ALIM batch

bateau *m* CERAM VER concave bow, NAUT boat, ship, TRANSPORT boat; ~ **à aubes** *m* NAUT paddle boat; ~ **caboteur** *m* NAUT coaster; ~ **charbonnier** *m* CHARBON coal ship; ~ **de croisière** *m* NAUT cruise ship; ~ **diurne** *m* NAUT day boat; ~ **dragueur** *m* MINES dredge boat, floating dredge; ~ **feu** *m* TRANSPORT lightship; ~ **fluvial** *m* NAUT river boat; ~ **de forage** *m* PETROLE drill ship; ~ **d'intervention** *m* PETROLE stand-by boat; ~ **mixte** *m* NAUT motor sailer; ~ **à moteur** *m* NAUT motorboat; ~ **de pêche** *m* NAUT fishing boat, fishing smack; ~ **de pêche à filets traînants** *m* NAUT drifter; ~ **de plaisance** *m* NAUT *avec cabines* cabin cruiser; ~ **pliant** *m* NAUT collapsible boat; ~ **pneumatique** *m* NAUT inflatable boat, rubber boat; ~ **de ravitaillement** *m* PETR supply boat; ~ **de sauvetage** *m* NAUT rescue boat; ~ **de soutien** *m* NAUT support boat; ~ **usine** *m* OCEANO factory ship; ~ **à vapeur** *m* NAUT steamboat; ~ **à voiles** *m* NAUT sailboat (AmE), sailing boat (BrE)

bateau-drague *m* MINES dredge boat, floating dredge

bateau-feu *m* NAUT light vessel, lightship, THERMODYN fireship, TRANSPORT light vessel

bateau-phare *m* NAUT light vessel, lightship

bateau-pilote *m* NAUT pilot boat, pilot cutter

bateau-pompe *m* NAUT fireboat

bateau-porte *m* NAUT *de bassin de radoub* caisson

bateau-rabot *m* MINES dredge boat, floating dredge

batée *f* MINES pan, PAPIER batch

batelage *m* NAUT lighterage, waterage

batelée *f* NAUT *de marchandises* boatload

batelier *m* NAUT bargee (BrE), bargeman (AmE), boatman, waterman; ~ **de chaland** *m* NAUT lighterman

batellerie *f* NAUT canal transport, inland navigation,

inland water transport, lighterage, river fleet, river traffic

batholite *m* GEOPHYS batholic, PETR batholith

bathomètre *m* OCEANO, PHYSIQUE bathometer, bathymeter

bathonien *adj* GEOLOGIE *stratigraphie* Bathonian

bathycélérimétrie *f* OCEANO bathytachymetry

bathymètre *m* OCEANO, PHYSIQUE bathometer, bathymeter

bathymétrie *f* EN RENOUV, NAUT, OCEANO bathymetry

bathyscaphe *m* OCEANO bathyscaph

bathysphère *f* OCEANO bathysphere

bathythermie *f* OCEANO bathythermy

bathythermographe *m* OCEANO bathythermograph

bathythermographie *f* OCEANO bathythermography

bâti *m* CINEMAT rack, CONS MECA mount, *de machine* base, *de machine-outil* bed, *de machine ou analogue* frame, CONSTR casing, frame, ELECTROTEC, MECANIQUE rack, PAPIER frame, TELECOM rack, TEXTILE frame; ~ **d'agrandisseur** *m* PHOTO enlarger support; ~ **des aiguilles à bec** *m* TEXTILE bearded needle frame; ~ **d'assise du moteur** *m* NAUT engine bed-plate; ~ **de croisée** *m* CONSTR window frame; ~ **dormant** *m* CONSTR casing, door case, door casing, doorframe, frame, window frame; ~ **en bois** *m* PRODUCTION *système hydraulique* wooden cradle; ~ **en C** *m* INSTRUMENT C-shaped frame; ~ **en caisson** *m* CONS MECA *machines-outils* box frame; ~ **en col** *m* INSTRUMENT C-shaped frame; ~ **latéral** *m* CONS MECA *pour tables de déplacement rectiligne* wing base; ~ **de machine** *m* CONS MECA engine frame; ~ **mécanique** *m* AERONAUT main gearbox support; ~ **moteur** *m* AERONAUT engine cradle, NAUT engine frame; ~ **nervuré** *m* CONSTR ribbed frame; ~ **de la partie de mesure** *m* NUCLEAIRE indicator bay; ~ **de porte** *m* CONSTR door case, door casing, doorframe; ~ **de réception moteur** *m* AERONAUT engine stand; ~ **de reprise** *m* CONS MECA out-of-jig cradle; ~ **de soupape** *m* CONS MECA valve yoke; ~ **de toile** *m* PAPIER wire frame

bâti-baïonnette *m* PRODUCTION *d'une machine à vapeur* girder-type frame

bâtiment *m* CONSTR building, NAUT ship, vessel; ~ **administratif** *m* MINES administration building; ~ **d'escorte** *m* NAUT escort ship; ~ **de fosse** *m* MINES pithead building; ~ **de fret et de poste** *m* TRANSPORT mail and cargo terminal; ~ **des machines** *m* MINES engine winding house, hoist room, PRODUCTION engine house; ~ **des moteurs** *m* CONS MECA power station, PRODUCTION engine house; ~ **de pompe** *m* DISTRI EAU pump house; ~ **de puits** *m* MINES pithead building

bâtir *vt* CONSTR construct, *maison* build

bâtisse *f* CONSTR structure

bâtisseur *m* CONSTR builder

batiste *f* TEXTILE chambray; ~ **de Cambrai** *f* TEXTILE chambray

batitures *f pl* PRODUCTION cinder, scale

bâton: ~ **d'affûtage à la main** *m* CONS MECA hand finishing stick; ~ **rodoir** *m* CONS MECA honing stone, slip stone

bâtonnet: ~ **de ferrite** *m* ELECTROTEC, PHYSIQUE ferrite rod

bâton-pilote *m* CH DE FER single line token

battage *m* PRODUCTION beating, hammering, ramming; ~ **d'essai de pieux** *m* CHARBON test piling; ~ **au large** *m* MINES broaching; ~ **de pieux** *m* CHARBON, CONSTR pile driving; ~ **de pieux par compaction** *m* CHARBON compaction piling; ~ **de pieux pour remblai** *m* CHARBON embankment piling; ~ **de pilots** *m* CONSTR pile driving

battant *m* CONSTR *d'une porte* leaf, *d'un loquet de porte* lift

batte *f* CERAM VER potter's beetle, CONSTR bossing mallet, *de plombier* beater, PRODUCTION mallet, rammer; ~ **à bourre** *f* PRODUCTION tamper; ~ **des chemins de fer** *f* CONSTR beater, beating pick; ~ **de mouleur** *f* PRODUCTION rammer; ~ **de plombier** *f* PRODUCTION lead dresser

battellement *m* CERAM VER eaves course

battement *m* ACOUSTIQUE beat, AERONAUT flapping, CONS MECA *de piston ou analogue* stroke, ELECTRON beat, beating, ENREGISTR flutter, PHYSIQUE beat, PRODUCTION jar, jarring; ~ **d'un clapet** *m* REFRIG valve flutter; ~ **nul** *m* TV zero beat; ~ **de piston** *m* CONS MECA piston stroke; ~ **régulier** *m* AERONAUT *d'un moteur* beat; ~ **au terminus** *m* CH DE FER *véhicules* turnaround time at terminus; ~ **vertical** *m* AERONAUT flapping; ~ **de vibration** *m* AERONAUT, ESPACE buffeting

batte-plate *f* CONSTR beater, bossing mallet, PRODUCTION flat rammer, lead dresser

batterie *f* AUTO, CHIMIE battery, CONS MECA *de cylindres* battery, *ensemble de dispositifs* battery, ELECTR *de piles* battery, ELECTRON *de filtres* bank, ELECTROTEC bank, battery, ESPACE *véhicules*, MINES *de pilons*, NAUT *artillerie, électricité* battery, PHOTO battery, *de lampes* bank, VEHICULES accumulator, battery, lead-acid battery; ~ **d'accumulateurs** *f* AUTO, ELECTR storage battery, ELECTROTEC battery, storage battery, TELECOM accumulator battery, battery; ~ **d'accumulateurs alcalins** *f* ELECTROTEC alkaline storage battery; ~ **d'accumulateurs argent-zinc amorçables** *f* ELECTROTEC silver zinc primary battery; ~ **d'accumulateurs au nickel-cadmium** *f* ESPACE *véhicules* nickel cadmium battery; ~ **d'accumulateurs au nickel-fer** *f* ESPACE *véhicules* nickel iron battery; ~ **d'accumulateurs au plomb** *f* ELECTROTEC lead-acid battery; ~ **alcaline** *f* ELECTROTEC alkaline storage battery; ~ **à l'argent** *f* ELECTROTEC silver battery; ~ **argent-cadmium** *f* ELECTROTEC silver cadmium battery; ~ **argent-zinc** *f* ELECTROTEC silver zinc battery, silver zinc storage battery; ~ **blindée** *f* TRANSPORT armored battery (AmE), armoured battery (BrE); ~ **de bocards** *f* PRODUCTION stamp battery; ~ **de bord** *f* AERONAUT main battery; ~ **cadmium-nickel** *f* ELECTROTEC nickel cadmium battery; ~ **de campagne** *f* MILITAIRE *artillerie* field battery; ~ **cartouche** *f* ELECTROTEC power pack; ~ **de ceinture** *f* CINEMAT Pag belt, battery belt, power belt; ~ **de condensateurs** *f* ELECTROTEC bank of capacitors, capacitor bank; ~ **côtière** *f* MILITAIRE coast battery; ~ **de cylindres** *f* CONS MECA train of rolls, PRODUCTION set of rolls; ~ **de démarrage** *f* ELECTR *automobile*, ELECTROTEC starter battery; ~ **électrique** *f* PHYSIQUE battery; ~ **en boîtier DIP** *f* ELECTROTEC DIP battery; ~ **d'étais** *f* CONSTR frame, set of shores, system of shoring; ~ **fer-nickel** *f* ELECTROTEC nickel iron battery; ~ **frigorifique** *f* REFRIG cooling battery; ~ **de fusibles** *f* ELECTROTEC fuse array; ~ **locale** *f* ELECTROTEC local battery; ~ **de longue durée** *f* ELECTROTEC long-life battery; ~ **nucléaire** *f* CONSTR nuclear battery; ~ **d'ordinateurs** *f* ORDINAT, TELECOM computer bank; ~ **d'oscillateurs** *f* ELECTRON oscillator bank; ~ **de pilons** *f* PRODUCTION stamp battery; ~ **au plomb** *f* ELECTROTEC, PHYSIQUE, VEHICULES lead-acid battery;

~ de projecteurs *f* CINEMAT bank of lights; **~ de projecteurs au plafond** *f* CINEMAT overhead bank; **~ de puits** *f* DISTRI EAU set of wells; **~ de RAMs** *f* ELECTROTEC bank of RAMs; **~ de refroidissement** *f* NUCLEAIRE cooling coil; **~ de renfort** *f* TRANSPORT booster battery; **~ sèche** *f* ELECTROTEC dry battery, gel cell; **~ secondaire** *f* ELECTROTEC, TRANSPORT secondary battery; **~ de secours** *f* ELECTR *accumulateur*, ELECTROTEC emergency battery; **~ solaire** *f* EN RENOUV, TV solar battery; **~ tampon** *f* ELECTROTEC, TRANSPORT buffer battery; **~ thermoélectrique** *f* ELECTROTEC thermal battery; **~ de traction** *f* TRANSPORT booster battery, drive battery; **~ de trois pilons** *f* MINES three-head battery, three-stamp mill; **~ ventilée** *f* REFRIG fan coil unit

batterie-tampon *f* ELECTROTEC floating battery

batteur: **~ de chiffons** *m* PAPIER rag duster, rag thrasher; **~ électrique** *m* AGRO ALIM electric mixer; **~ de feutre** *m* PAPIER felt whipper, thrasher, whipper; **~ finisseur** *m* TEXTILE finisher scutcher

battitures *f pl* MATERIAUX rolling mill scale, PRODUCTION forge scale, hammer slag, hammer scale, iron scale, nill; **~ de fer** *f pl* PRODUCTION iron scale

battre *vt* CONS MECA drive, drive in, ELECTRON beat, NAUT *pavillon* fly, PRODUCTION ram, TEXTILE beat; **~ en neige** *vt* AGRO ALIM *blanc d'oeuf* aerate; **~ à la masse** *vt* CONSTR sledge

battu: **~ par la tempête** *adj* NAUT weather-beaten; **~ par les vents** *adj* NAUT weather-beaten

bau *m* NAUT *navire* beam

baud *m* IMPRIM, INFORMAT, ORDINAT baud

baulite *f* PETR baulite

bauquière *f* OCEANO shelf

bauxite *f* CERAM VER, CHIMIE, MINERAUX, PETR bauxite

bavette *f* TEXTILE flap, TRANSPORT spoiler; **~ garde-boue** *f* VEHICULES *accessoire* mudflap

bavure *f* CONS MECA burr, wire edge, MECANIQUE burr, PLAST CAOU *moulage* flash, PRODUCTION burr, fin; **~ de bague** *f* CERAM VER flanged press finish; **~ au fond** *f* CERAM VER flanged bottom

BDR *abrév (base de données relationnelles)* INFORMAT, ORDINAT, TELECOM RDB *(relational database)*

Be *(béryllium)* CHIMIE Be *(beryllium)*

beaumontite *f* PETR beaumontite

beaupré *m* NAUT bowsprit

bec *m* CERAM VER spout, CONS MECA jaw, nozzle, *d'un outil* nose, CONSTR *d'une pile de pont* cutwater, EQUIP LAB *chauffage* burner, *d'un vase, d'une éprouvette* lip, *verrerie* spout, MECANIQUE *outillage* jaw, NAUT *d'ancre* peak, PRODUCTION nose, nosepiece, *d'une burette* spout; **~ d'ancre** *m* NAUT anchor bill; **~ d'âne** *m* CONS MECA crosscut, CONSTR framing chisel, heading chisel, mortise chisel, PRODUCTION chipping chisel, crosscut chisel; **~ d'attaque** *m* AERONAUT leading edge; **~ de bord d'attaque** *m* AERONAUT *aéronef* leading edge slat; **~ Bunsen** *m* EQUIP LAB *chauffage* Bunsen burner; **~ de cane** *m* CONS MECA eccentric hook, CONSTR lever handle, INST HYDR hook gear valve motion, *pour manoeuvrer une vanne* gab, gab hook, PRODUCTION flat-nose pliers, flat-nosed pliers; **~ de compensation** *m* AERONAUT balance horn; **~ de descente** *m* CONSTR downspout; **~ de diffuseur anti-incendie** *m* SECURITE fire hose nozzle; **~ de gaz** *m* PRODUCTION, THERMODYN gas burner; **~ à gaz** *m* PRODUCTION gas burner; **~ Meker** *m* EQUIP LAB *chauffage* Meker burner; **~ de nervure** *m* AERONAUT leading edge rib; **~ papillon** *m* EQUIP LAB *chauffage* flat flame burner; **~ pour verser** *m*

EMBALLAGE pour spout; **~ renversé** *m* PRODUCTION inverted burner; **~ de segment** *m* AUTO ring end; **~ de tuyaux d'incendie** *m* SECURITE fire hose nozzle; **~ d'une tuyère** *m* CONSTR nosepiece; **~ de tuyère** *m* PRODUCTION nozzle tip, tuyère nozzle

bécarre *m* ACOUSTIQUE natural

bécasse *f* PRODUCTION gage (AmE), gauge (BrE), stock indicator, test rod

bêche *f* CONSTR spade

bécher *m* AGRO ALIM, CERAM VER, CHIMIE, EQUIP LAB *verrerie*, PAPIER beaker; **~ à bec** *m* EQUIP LAB *verrerie* beaker with spout; **~ en acier inoxydable** *m* EQUIP LAB *récipient* stainless steel beaker

becquerel *m (Bq)* METROLOGIE, PHYS RAYON, PHYSIQUE becquerel *(Bq)*

becquet *m* TRANSPORT, VEHICULES *carrosserie* spoiler

bédane *m* CONS MECA crosscut, CONSTR framing chisel, *de menuisier* heading chisel, mortise chisel, MECANIQUE *outillage* groove-cutting chisel, PRODUCTION crosscut chisel, *de mécanicien* chipping chisel; **~ à froid** *m* CONS MECA cold chisel, crosscut, PRODUCTION chipping chisel; **~ à joues** *m* CONSTR self-coring chisel; **~ de menuisier** *m* CONSTR framing chisel

bed-rock *m* DISTRI EAU bedrock

bée *f* PRODUCTION flume, leat

beffroi *m* DISTRI EAU *d'une drague* gantry

béguettes *f pl* CONS MECA short-nose pliers, short-nosed pliers

béhénique *adj* CHIMIE *acide* behenic

beidellite *f* MINERAUX beidellite

beignet *m* GEOMETRIE doughnut

bel *m* ACOUSTIQUE, ELECTROTEC, PHYS RAYON, PHYSIQUE bel

Bélier *m* ASTRONOMIE Aries

bélier *m* CONSTR ram **~ aspirateur** *m* PRODUCTION suction ram; **~ hydraulique** *m* INST HYDR ram pump, NAUT ram

belle: **~ page** *f* IMPRIM *imposition* right-hand page

belle-fleur *f* MINES gallows frame, head frame, headstock, pithead frame

bélonite *f* MINERAUX belonite

bémol *m* ACOUSTIQUE flat

bénarde *f* CONSTR pinned key lock

benday *m* IMPRIM *photogravure* Ben Day, flat tint

benne *f* CONSTR *de grue ou analogue* bucket, MINES bucket, hudge, kibble, tub, NAUT grab, POLLU MER, TRANSPORT skip; **~ automatique** *f* CONSTR clamshell bucket, grab, grab bucket; **~ basculante** *f* CONSTR dump bucket (AmE), tipping bucket (BrE), dumping bucket, TRANSPORT dump bucket (AmE), tipping bucket (BrE), dumping bucket, skip, tilting body, tilting skip; **~ à bascule** *f* CONSTR dump bucket (AmE), tipping bucket (BrE), dumping bucket; **~ à culbutage automatique** *f* CONSTR self-dumping bucket; **~ à demi-coquelle** *f* CONSTR clamshell bucket; **~ d'extraction** *f* MINES mining bucket, PRODUCTION hoisting bucket; **~ à fond mobile** *f* CONSTR bucket with drop bottom; **~ à ordures** *f* RECYCLAGE dustbin lorry (BrE), garbage track (AmE), refuse collection vehicle; **~ piocheuse** *f* CONSTR clamshell bucket, grab, grab bucket; **~ preneuse** *f* CONSTR clamshell bucket, mechanical grab, grab, grab bucket; **~ racleuse** *f* TRANSPORT aggregate scraper, concrete scraper; **~ de ramassage** *f* POLLUTION scoop; **~ suspendue** *f* PRODUCTION hanging bucket

benthonique *adj* GEOLOGIE benthonic

bentonite *f* CHARBON, CONSTR, MATERIAUX *géologie*, MINERAUX, PETR, PETROLE *forage, smectite* bentonite

benzaldéhyde *m* CHIMIE benzaldehyde

benzaldoxime *f* CHIMIE benzaldoxime

benzamide *m* CHIMIE benzamide

benzanilide *m* CHIMIE benzanilide

benzène *m* CHIMIE, PETROLE benzene

benzénoïde *adj* CHIMIE benzenoid

benzidine *f* CHIMIE benzidine

benzile *m* CHIMIE benzil

benzoate *m* CHIMIE benzoate

benzohydrol *m* CHIMIE benzohydrol

benzoïne *f* CHIMIE benzoin

benzoïque *adj* CHIMIE benzoic

benzol *m* CHIMIE benzol, benzole

benzonaphtol *m* CHIMIE benzonaphthol

benzonitrile *m* CHIMIE benzonitrile

benzophénone *f* CHIMIE benzophenone

benzopyrène *m* CHIMIE benzopyrene

benzoquinone *f* CHIMIE benzoquinone

benzyne *m* CHIMIE benzyne

béquette *f* CONSTR devil's claw

béquille *f* AERONAUT drag link, NAUT beaching leg, *support* leg, PRODUCTION crutch handle, *d'un robinet* crutch key, TRANSPORT skid, *de semi-remorque* landing gear VEHICULES *motocyclette* stand; ~ **arrière** *f* AERONAUT tailskid; ~ **de combinateur** *f* AERONAUT mixer rod; ~ **de queue** *f* AERONAUT tailskid

béquilles: ~ **à roues** *f pl* TRANSPORT undercarriage

ber *m* NAUT cradle; ~ **de transport** *m* NAUT cradle

berceau *m* CINEMAT, CONS MECA cradle, CONSTR barrel vault, MECANIQUE cradle, MINES cradle, cradle rocker, mining cradle, rocker, NAUT cradle; ~ **commutateur** *m* ELECTROTEC gravity switch; ~ **moteur** *m* AERONAUT engine cradle, AUTO engine support; ~ **pour missile** *m* MILITAIRE missile cradle

berge *f* CONSTR *d'un canal, d'une route, d'un chemin de fer, d'un fossé,* HYDROLOGIE *d'une rivière, d'un fleuve,* NAUT bank; ~ **de fleuve** *f* CONSTR, HYDROLOGIE river bank

bergmannite *f* MINERAUX bergmannite

berkélium *m (Bk)* CHIMIE berkelium *(Bk)*

berlaine *f* MINES mine car, tram, tub

berline *f* MINES mine car, tram, tub, TRANSPORT mine car, saloon (BrE), sedan (AmE); ~ **accumulatrice** *f* MINES bunker car; ~ **de transport** *f* MINES transit car

berme *f* CHARBON berm, CONSTR bank, bench, banquette, berm, OCEANO berm

berne: en ~ *adj* NAUT half-mast, mourning

berthiérite *f* MINERAUX berthierite

bertrandite *f* MINERAUX bertrandite

béryl *m* CHIMIE, MINERAUX beryl; ~ **doré** *m* MINERAUX golden beryl

béryllium *m (Be)* CHIMIE beryllium *(Be)*

béryllonite *f* MINERAUX beryllonite

berzélianite *f* MINERAUX berzelianite

berzéliite *f* MINERAUX berzeliite

besoin: ~ **saisonnier** *m* GAZ seasonal demand

besoins: ~ **bruts** *m pl* PRODUCTION gross requirements; ~ **en chaleur** *m pl* CHAUFFAGE heat demand, THERMODYN heat consumption, heat demand; ~ **en dents de scie** *m pl* PRODUCTION lumpy demand; ~ **en mémoire** *m pl* ORDINAT storage requirement; ~ **en substances nutritives** *m* AGRO ALIM nutrient requirements; ~ **nutritifs alimentaires** *m pl* AGRO ALIM food nutritive requirements

bêta-amylase *f* AGRO ALIM beta-amylase

bêtatron *m* NUCLEAIRE, PHYS RAYON, PHYSIQUE betatron

béton *m* CERAM VER, CONSTR concrete; ~ **armé** *m* CONSTR ferroconcrete, reinforced concrete, MILITAIRE reinforced concrete; ~ **armé translucide** *m* CERAM VER glass reinforced concrete; ~ **asphaltique** *m* CONSTR asphalt concrete; ~ **avec occlusion d'air** *m* CONSTR air-entrained concrete; ~ **bitumineux** *m* CONSTR asphalt concrete; ~ **de chantier** *m* CONSTR site concrete; ~ **de ciment** *m* CONSTR cement concrete; ~ **coulé en place** *m* CONSTR in situ concrete; ~ **coulé sur place** *m* CONSTR in situ concrete; ~ **cyclopéen** *m* CONSTR cyclopean concrete; ~ **filé** *m* CONSTR spun concrete; ~ **frais** *m* CONSTR green concrete; ~ **fretté** *m* CONSTR hooped concrete, stirruped concrete; ~ **gras** *m* CONSTR fat concrete, fat mortar; ~ **immergé** *m* CONSTR submerged concrete; ~ **industriel** *m* CONSTR ready-mixed concrete; ~ **léger** *m* CONSTR lightweight concrete; ~ **de magnésium** *m* CONSTR magnesian concrete, magnesium concrete; ~ **maigre** *m* CONSTR blinding concrete, lean concrete; ~ **malaxé à la main** *m* CONSTR hand-mixed concrete; ~ **de masse** *m* CONSTR mass concrete; ~ **occlu** *m* CONSTR air-entrained concrete; ~ **poreux** *m* CONSTR no-fines concrete; ~ **précontraint** *m* CONSTR prestressed concrete; ~ **préfabriqué** *m* CONSTR precast concrete; ~ **préparé sur place** *m* CONSTR site concrete; ~ **prêt à l'emploi** *m* CONSTR ready-mixed concrete; ~ **de propreté** *m* CONSTR blinding concrete, lean concrete; ~ **de qualité à paver** *m* CONSTR PQC, pavement quality concrete; ~ **réfractaire** *m* CERAM VER castable; ~ **riche en ciment** *m* CONSTR fat concrete, fat mortar; ~ **sous-marin** *m* CONSTR submerged concrete; ~ **à la toupie** *m* CONSTR ready-mixed concrete; ~ **vibré** *m* CONSTR vibrated concrete

bétonnage *m* CONSTR concrete work, concreting, underpinning, NUCLEAIRE embedding in concrete

bétonner *vt* CONSTR concrete

bétonneuse *f* CONSTR concrete mixer

bétonnière *f* CONSTR concrete mixer

beudantine *f* MINERAUX beudantine

beudantite *f* MINERAUX beudantite

beurre: ~ **clarifié** *m* AGRO ALIM clarified butter; ~ **de tourbière** *m* CHARBON bog butter

beurtia *m* MINES internal shaft, staple, staple pit, staple shaft

bezier *m* IMPRIM bezier

BF *abrév (basse fréquence)* ELECTR, ELECTRON, ELECTROTEC, PHYS RAYON, TELECOM LF *(low-frequency)*

BHA *m (hydroxyanisol butylé)* AGRO ALIM BHA *(butylated hydroxyanisole)*

BHT *abrév (hydroxytoluène butylé)* AGRO ALIM BHT *(butylated hydroxytoluene)*

Bi *(bismuth)* CHIMIE Bi *(bismuth)*

biacide *m* CHIMIE biacid

biais:[1] **en** ~ *adj* IMPRIM askew

biais[2] *m* CONSTR skew, GEOMETRIE skewness, INFORMAT, MATH bias

biaisement *m* CONSTR skewing

biaiser *vt* CONSTR weather

biaxe *adj* CRISTALL, MATH biaxial

bibasique *adj* CHIMIE dibasic

bibliothèque *f* INFORMAT, ORDINAT library; ~ **de bandes** *f* INFORMAT, ORDINAT tape library; ~ **de procédures** *f* ORDINAT procedure library; ~ **de programmes** *f* INFORMAT, ORDINAT program library; ~ **de sous-programmes** *f* INFORMAT, ORDINAT subroutine library; **~ système** *f* IMPRIM , INFORMAT, ORDINAT systems library

bicarbonate *m* CHIMIE bicarbonate; **~ de sodium** *m* AGRO ALIM baking soda, bicarbonate of soda, sodium bicarbonate, CHIMIE, LESSIVES bicarbonate of soda, sodium bicarbonate

bicarbure: **~ d'uranium** *m* NUCLEAIRE uranium dicarbide

bichlorure *m* CHIMIE dichloride

bichromate *m* CHIMIE dichromate

bickford *m* MINES Bickford fuse

bicolore *adj* COULEURS bicolored (AmE), bicoloured (BrE)

bicône *m* CONS MECA cone union body, TEXTILE cheese

bicristal *m* METALL bicrystal

bicyclette: **~ électrique** *f* TRANSPORT battery-powered moped; **~ pliante** *f* TRANSPORT folding bicycle

bicyclique *adj* CHIMIE bicyclic

bicylindre: **~ à plat** *m* TRANSPORT flat twin

bidet *m* CONS MECA plain lathe, plain ungeared lathe

bidimensionnel *adj* INFORMAT, ORDINAT, PHYSIQUE two-dimensional

bidirectionnel *adj* INFORMAT, ORDINAT, TELECOM bidirectional

bidon *m* EMBALLAGE drum; **~ à eau** *m* TEXTILE water container; **~ en acier** *m* PRODUCTION steel pail; **~ en fer-blanc** *m* PRODUCTION tin plate pail; **~ à essence** *m* MILITAIRE jerry can; **~ de gaz** *m* THERMODYN gas bottle

biebérite *f* MINERAUX bieberite

bief *m* DISTRI EAU level, pond, raceway, race, reach, HYDROLOGIE reach; **~ d'amont** *m* DISTRI EAU forebay, head crown, headbay, headrace; **~ d'aval** *m* DISTRI EAU aft bay, mill tail, tail bay, tailrace; **~ de fuite** *m* DISTRI EAU tailrace; **~ de moulin** *m* DISTRI EAU mill course, mill race; **~ supérieur** *m* DISTRI EAU headwater reach

bielle *f* AUTO, CH DE FER connecting rod, CONS MECA connecting rod, connection, link, pitman, CONSTR strut, MECANIQUE connecting rod, rod, NAUT, VEHICULES *moteur* connecting rod; **~ d'accouplement** *f* CH DE FER coupling rod; **~ articulée** *f* CONS MECA knuckle-jointed connecting rod; **~ d'attaque** *f* AERONAUT actuating rod; **~ avec tête à cage fermée** *f* CONS MECA box-end connecting rod; **~ avec tête à chape** *f* CONS MECA strap-end connecting rod; **~ avec tête à fourche** *f* CONS MECA fork-end connecting rod; **~ de changement de marche** *f* CH DE FER *véhicules* axle guide, reversing rod; **~ à chape** *f* CONS MECA strap-end connecting rod; **~ de combinateur** *f* AERONAUT mixer rod; **~ de commande** *f* AERONAUT actuating rod, control rod; **~ de commande de direction** *f* VEHICULES drop arm, pitman arm; **~ de compensation** *f* AERONAUT landing gear compensation rod; **~ de connexion** *f* CH DE FER *véhicules* coupling rod, VEHICULES *direction* drag link, track rod; **~ de connexion pour levier de frein** *f* CONS MECA connecting brake lever rods; **~ à contact** *f* AERONAUT force link; **~ coulée** *f* AUTO run bearing; **~ déportée** *f* AUTO offset connecting rod; **~ diagonale** *f* AERONAUT landing gear diagonal truss; **~ de direction** *f* AUTO steering rod; **~ double** *f* AERONAUT dual rod; **~ élastique** *f* AERONAUT connecting rod; **~ en I** *f* AUTO I-connecting rod; **~ d'excentrique** *f* CONS MECA, MECANIQUE eccentric rod; **~ de force** *f* VEHICULES *suspension* radius arm; **~ à fourche** *f* CONS MECA fork-end connecting rod; **~ de liaison** *f* CONS MECA connecting rod, link rod; **~ de longueur infinie** *f* CONS MECA connecting rod of infinite length; **~ motrice** *f* CONS MECA main rod; **~ pendante** *f* AUTO drop

arm, pitman arm; **~ de poussée** *f* AUTO, VEHICULES *suspension* torque arm; **~ de recul** *f* AERONAUT drag brace; **~ de relevage** *f* CH DE FER *véhicules* reversing rod, CONS MECA *distribution* shifting rod; **~ de suspension de la coulisse** *f* CONS MECA link hanger, link support; **~ de tiroir** *f* INST HYDR rod, slide rod, valve rod; **~ vérin** *f* AERONAUT actuating rod

biellette *f* CONS MECA link, PRODUCTION crank link; **~ de commande de pas** *f* AERONAUT blade pitch change rod; **~ coupe-feu** *f* AERONAUT fuel shut-off cock control link; **~ de direction** *f* AUTO, VEHICULES tie rod; **~ double** *f* AERONAUT landing gear fork rod; **~ de liaison** *f* CONS MECA link; **~ de vitesse** *f* AERONAUT governor control link

bien: **~ en main** *adj* MECANIQUE *outillage* handy; **~ équilibré** *adj* PAPIER adjusted

biergol *m* ESPACE bipropellant, dual fuel

biez *m* DISTRI EAU level, pond, raceway, race; **~ d'amont** *m* DISTRI EAU forebay, head crown, headbay, headrace; **~ d'aval** *m* DISTRI EAU tail bay, tailrace; **~ de fuite** *m* DISTRI EAU mill tail; **~ de moulin** *m* DISTRI EAU mill course, mill race

bifil *m* TEXTILE twin cards

bifilaire *adj* ELECTR *enroulement*, PHYSIQUE bifilar

bifurcation *f* CONSTR fork, junction, TRANSPORT road junction; **~ de rails** *f* CH DE FER rail junction

Big: **~ Bang** *m* ASTRONOMIE Big Bang

bigarré *adj* GEOLOGIE mottled

bigorne *f* CONS MECA beak iron; **~ à gouttière** *f* PRODUCTION groove punch

biguanide *m* CHIMIE biguanide

bigue *f* CONSTR derrick, shear legs, MECANIQUE *levage* derrick, NAUT heavy-lift derrick, mast crane; **~ flottante** *f* CONSTR floating derrick

bilame: **~ métallique** *f* ELECTR *thermostat, thermomètre*, PHYSIQUE bimetallic strip, REFRIG bimetallic element

bilan *m* INFORMAT record; **~ calorifique** *m* PAPIER heat balance, THERMODYN calorific balance, thermal balance; **~ d'eau** *m* HYDROLOGIE, NAUT water balance; **~ énergétique** *m* GAZ energy balance, POLLUTION energy budget, THERMODYN energy balance; **~ énergétique du sol** *m* HYDROLOGIE energy balance of the soil; **~ d'énergie** *m* DISTRI EAU energy balance; **~ d'énergie en turbulence** *m* PHYS FLUID energy balance in turbulence; **~ gazeux** *m* GAZ gas balance; **~ global du soufre** *m* POLLUTION global sulfur budget (AmE), global sulphur budget (BrE); **~ hydraulique** *m* DISTRI EAU water budget; **~ hydrologique** *m* DISTRI EAU, HYDROLOGIE hydrologic balance; **~ ionique** *m* OCEANO salt balance, POLLUTION ion budget; **~ de liaison** *m* ESPACE *communications* link budget; **~ de masse** *m* ESPACE *communications* mass budget; **~ massique** *m* NUCLEAIRE mass balance; **~ de puissance d'une liaison** *m* TELECOM link power budget; **~ radiatif** *m* HYDROLOGIE energy balance of the soil; **~ radiatif du sol** *m* HYDROLOGIE energy balance of the soil; **~ salin** *m* OCEANO salt balance; **~ du soufre** *m* POLLUTION sulfur budget (AmE), sulphur budget (BrE); **~ thermique** *m* CHAUFFAGE heat balance, MATERIAUX thermal balance, REFRIG heat balance, THERMODYN heat balance, thermal balance, thermal balance

bilatéral *adj* TELECOM bidirectional

bilboquets *m pl* IMPRIM *impression* jobbing

bildstein *m* MINERAUX bildstein

bilentille: **~ de Billet** *f* PHYSIQUE Billet split lens

bilirubine *f* CHIMIE bilirubin

billage *m* CONS MECA brinelling

billblade *f* IMPRIM *papier* billblade

bille *f* CONSTR saw log; **~ de roulement** *f* CONS MECA ball; **~ routière** *f* CERAM VER road bead; **~ de verre** *f* CERAM VER glass bead, glass marble

billes: ~ doubles *f pl* CERAM VER twins

billot *m* CONS MECA *d'enclume* block; **~ d'enclume** *m* CONS MECA anvil block

bimbeloterie *f* CERAM VER Gablonz glassware, IMPRIM *impression* jobbing

bimoléculaire *adj* CHIMIE bimolecular

bimoteur *adj* AERONAUT, CONS MECA twin-engined

binaire[1] *adj* CHIMIE, ELECTRON, INFORMAT, MATH, METALL binary

binaire:[2] **~ astrométrique** *m* ASTRONOMIE astrometric binary

binaural *adj* ACOUSTIQUE binaural

binocle: ~ stéréoscopique *m* PHOTO stereo viewer

binoculaire *adj* PHYSIQUE binocular

binôme *m* MATH binomial

biocatalyseur *m* MATERIAUX biocatalyst

biocénose *f* POLLUTION biocenosis

bioclastique *adj* GEOLOGIE bioclastic

biodégradabilité *f* RECYCLAGE biodegradability

biodégradable *adj* MATERIAUX, POLLUTION, RECYCLAGE biodegradable

biodégradation *f* HYDROLOGIE, LESSIVES, MATERIAUX, POLLU MER, POLLUTION, RECYCLAGE biodegradation

biofiltre *m* POLLUTION biofilter

biogaz *m* GAZ biogas, RECYCLAGE digester gas, sludge gas

biogénique *adj* PETROLE biogenic

bioherme *m* OCEANO reef knoll

bio-indicateur *m* POLLUTION bioindicator

biologique *adj* AGRO ALIM organic

biomasse *f* EN RENOUV, GAZ, HYDROLOGIE biomass

biomicrite *f* PETR biomicrite

biophysique *f* PHYSIQUE biophysics

biose *m* CHIMIE biose

biosparite *f* PETR biosparite

biosphère *f* METEO, POLLUTION biosphere

biostratigraphie *f* GEOLOGIE biostratigraphy

biostrome *m* GEOLOGIE biostrome

biosynthèse *f* CHIMIE biosynthesis

biotechnologie *f* AGRO ALIM biotechnology

biotine *f* AGRO ALIM biotin

biotite[1] *adj* PETR biotite

biotite[2] *f* MINERAUX biotite

bioturbation *f* GEOLOGIE bioturbation

bioverre *m* CERAM VER bioglass

bioxyde *m* CHIMIE dioxide; **~ d'azote** *m* CHIMIE nitrogen dioxide; **~ de soufre** *m* POLLUTION sulfur dioxide (AmE), sulphur dioxide (BrE)

biozone *f* GEOLOGIE *stratigraphie* biozone

bip *m* CINEMAT beep tone, bleep, TELECOM tone pager; **~ sonore** *m* TELECOM pip

bipack *m* CINEMAT bipack

bipasse *m* PETROLE *forage* bypass

biphase *adj* ELECTROTEC two-phase

biplace *m* AERONAUT two-seat aircraft

bipolaire[1] *adj* ELECTR *moteur*, ORDINAT, PHYSIQUE bipolar

bipolaire:[2] **~ à deux directions** *f* ELECTR, ELECTROTEC DPDT, double-pole double-throw; **~ double course** *f* ELECTR, ELECTROTEC DPDT, double-pole double-throw

bipoulie *f* PRODUCTION two-step cone, two-step cone pulley

biprisme: ~ de Fresnel *m* PHYSIQUE Fresnel biprism

biquinaire *adj* INFORMAT biquinary

biréacteur *m* AERONAUT twin-engine jet aircraft

biréfringence *f* CRISTALL double refraction, OPTIQUE, PHYS RAYON birefringence

biréfringent *adj* CRISTALL birefringent, doubly refracting, OPTIQUE birefringent

biscuit *m* CERAM VER biscuit ware

biseau *m* CERAM VER bevel, miter (AmE), mitre (BrE), CONS MECA bevel, bevel edge, CONSTR side chisel, IMPRIM *façonnage, reliure, carton* miter (AmE), mitre (BrE), INSTRUMENT, MECANIQUE, METROLOGIE, PRODUCTION bevel; **~ antique** *m* CERAM VER Vauxhall bevel; **~ arrêté droit** *m* CERAM VER tapered stop bevel; **~ arrêté en arrondi** *m* CERAM VER diminishing stop bevel; **~ assez tranché** *m* CERAM VER steep bevel; **~ avec olives** *m* CERAM VER beaded bevel; **~ contourné** *m* CERAM VER shaped bevel; **~ croisé** *m* CERAM VER cross bevel; **~ diamant** *m* CERAM VER taper bevel; **~ double** *m* CERAM VER double bevel; **~ écailles** *m* CERAM VER scalloped bevel; **~ marbre** *m* CERAM VER flat edge and bevel

biseautage *m* CERAM VER, INSTRUMENT beveling (AmE), bevelling (BrE), PETROLE pinch-out trap

biseauter *vt* INSTRUMENT bevel

biseautoir *m* INSTRUMENT beveling tool (AmE), bevelling tool (BrE)

bismite *f* MINERAUX bismite

bismuth *m* (*Bi*) CHIMIE bismuth (*Bi*)

bismuthate *m* CHIMIE bismuthate

bismuthine *f* MINERAUX bismuthine, bismuthinite

bismuthite *f* MINERAUX bismuthite, bismutite

bisphénol: ~ A *m* PLAST CAOU *matière première* bisphenol A

bissecteur *adj* GEOMETRIE bisecting

bissection *f* GEOMETRIE *d'un angle* bisection

bissectrice *f* GEOMETRIE bisector

bistabilité *f* TELECOM bistability; **~ optique** *f* TELECOM optical bistability

bistable *adj* ELECTRON, ORDINAT, PHYSIQUE bistable

bistouri *m* EQUIP LAB scalpel

bisulfate *m* CHIMIE bisulfate (AmE), bisulphate (BrE)

bisulfite *m* CHIMIE bisulfite (AmE), bisulphite (BrE)

bisulfure *m* CHIMIE bisulfide (AmE), bisulphide (BrE), disulfide (AmE), disulphide (BrE)

bit *m* ELECTRON, IMPRIM, INFORMAT, ORDINAT, PETR, TELECOM bit; **~ d'alarme pour chaque outil** *m* PRODUCTION *automatisme industriel* individual tool range alarm bit; **~ d'arrêt** *m* INFORMAT, ORDINAT stop bit; **~ de continuation** *m* TELECOM M-bit, more bit; **~ de contrôle** *m* ELECTRON check bit, INFORMAT, ORDINAT control bit; **~ de début** *m* PRODUCTION start fence; **~ de défaut majeur** *m* PRODUCTION *automatisme industriel* major fault bit; **~ de densité** *m* PETR bit density; **~ de départ** *m* INFORMAT, ORDINAT start bit; **~ de droite** *m* ORDINAT low-order bit; **~ d'état du temporisateur** *m* PRODUCTION *automatisme industriel* timer status bit; **~ de fin** *m* PRODUCTION end fence, *automatisme industriel* done bit; **~ de fin de comptage** *m* PRODUCTION *automatisme industriel* count-up done bit; **~ de fin d'exécution** *m* PRODUCTION *automatisme industriel* step completion bit; **~ de fin de temporisation au déclenchement** *m* PRODUCTION *automatisme industriel* timer-off done bit; **~ de gauche** *m* INFORMAT,

ORDINAT high-order bit; **~ d'horloge de temporisateur** *m* PRODUCTION *automatisme industriel* timer clock bit; **~ indicateur** *m* INFORMAT, ORDINAT flag bit; **~ d'information** *m* INFORMAT, ORDINAT information bit; **~ interne** *m* PRODUCTION *automatisme industriel* flag bit; **~ d'interrogation** *m* TELECOM poll bit; **~ M** *m* TELECOM M-bit; **~ de mémoire** *m* PRODUCTION *automatisme industriel* store bit; **~ de parité** *m* INFORMAT, ORDINAT parity bit; **~ de plus faible poids** *m* ORDINAT LSB, least significant bit; **~ le plus significatif** *m* INFORMAT most significant bit; **~ de poids faible** *m* ORDINAT LSB; **~ de poids fort** *m* INFORMAT high-order bit, most significant bit, ORDINAT MSB, high-order bit, most significant bit, PRODUCTION *automatisme industriel*, TELECOM MSB, most significant bit; **~ de poids le plus faible** *m* PRODUCTION *automatisme industriel* LSB, least significant bit; **~ de service** *m* INFORMAT, ORDINAT service bit; **~ de signe** *m* INFORMAT, ORDINAT sign bit, sign digit; **~ de stop** *m* INFORMAT stop bit; **~ de temporisation** *m* PRODUCTION timer bit; **~ de temporisation en cours** *m* PRODUCTION *automatisme industriel* timer timing bit; **~ de validation de début de zone** *m* PRODUCTION start fence; **~ de validation de décompteur** *m* PRODUCTION *automatisme industriel* down-enable bit; **~ de verrouillage** *m* PRODUCTION *automatisme industriel* latch bit; **~ verrouillé** *m* PRODUCTION *automatisme industriel* latched bit

bitartrate: ~ de potasse *m* CHIMIE cream of tartar

bitord *m* TEXTILE spun yarn

bits: ~ d'en-tête *m pl* TELECOM overhead bits; **~ par pouce** *m pl* ORDINAT bits per inch; **~ par seconde** *m pl (BPS)* ORDINAT bits per second *(BPS)*

bitte *f* NAUT bitt; **~ d'amarrage** *f* NAUT mooring bitt, samson post, POLLU MER mooring bracket

bitture *f* NAUT range

bitumage *m* CONSTR asphalting, bituminization, tarring

bitumation *f* CONSTR bituminization

bitume *m* CHIMIE tar, CONS MECA bitumen, CONSTR bitumen, pitch, tar, ELECTR *isolation*, PETR, PETROLE, PLAST CAOU *matière première* bitumen; **~ fluxé** *m* CONSTR cutback; **~ glutineux** *m* MINERAUX mineral tar; **~ minéral** *m* CONSTR mineral pitch

bitumé *adj* CONSTR bituminized

bitumer *vt* CONSTR asphalt, bituminize

bituminé *adj* CONSTR bituminized

bituminer *vt* CONSTR asphalt, bituminize

bitumineux *adj* CONSTR bituminous

bituminisation *f* CONSTR bituminization

bituminiser *vt* CONSTR bituminize

biturbopropulseur *m* TRANSPORT propeller turbine plane

bivalence *f* CHIMIE bivalence

bivalent *adj* CHIMIE bivalent

bixine *f* AGRO ALIM bixin

Bk *(berkélium)* CHIMIE Bk *(berkelium)*

black: ~ shale *m* GEOLOGIE black shale

blaireau *m* PRODUCTION swab, swab brush; **~ pour dépoussiérage** *m* PHOTO duster, dusting brush; **~ pour épousseter** *m* PHOTO blower brush, duster, dusting brush

blanc[1] *adj* INFORMAT, ORDINAT blank

blanc[2] *m* IMPRIM *impression* blank; **~ de chaux** *m* CONSTR limewash, whitewash; **~ de couture** *m* IMPRIM back gutter, back margin; **~ dehors** *m* METEO white-out; **~ de gorge** *m* IMPRIM *imposition* back edge margin; **~ maximal** *m* TV peak white; **~ de papier** *m* IMPRIM

typographie head; **~ permanent** *m* IMPRIM barium monosulfite (AmE), barium monosulphite (BrE); **~ de prise** *m* IMPRIM gripper pad; **~ de référence** *m* TV reference white, white reference; **~ soudant** *m* THERMODYN white heat; **~ transversal** *m* IMPRIM *imposition* gutter; **~ travaux** *m* CH DE FER possession

blanchet *m* IMPRIM impression blanket, *de la régleuse* blanket; **~ de caoutchouc** *m* IMPRIM rubber blanket; **~ glacé** *m* IMPRIM glazed blanket; **~ gravé** *m* IMPRIM engraved blanket; **~ supérieur** *m* IMPRIM top blanket

blanchet-blanchet *adj* IMPRIM *impression* blanket-to-blanket

blancheur *f* PAPIER brightness, whiteness

blanchiment *m* AGRO ALIM, CHIMIE bleaching, CONSTR whitewashing, IMPRIM *papier*, LESSIVES, PAPIER bleaching; **~ à la chaux** *m* CONSTR limewashing, whitewashing; **~ au chlorure de chaux** *m* LESSIVES chloride of lime bleaching

blanchir[1] *vt* AGRO ALIM *légumes* blanch, CHIMIE, CINEMAT bleach, CONSTR *bois* clean up, IMPRIM keep out, *papier* bleach, PAPIER bleach, PHOTO bleach out, PRODUCTION *pièce de fonderie* clean up, TEXTILE launder

blanchir[2] *vti* IMPRIM *composition* lead

blanchissage *m* LESSIVES bleaching, TEXTILE laundering; **~ optique** *m* LESSIVES optical bleaching

blanchissement: ~ par agents fluorescents *m* PAPIER fluorescent whitening

blancs-de-pied *m pl* IMPRIM *mise en page* tail

blanc-soudant *m* PRODUCTION sparkling heat

blastomylonite *f* GEOLOGIE blastomylonite

blazar *m* ASTRONOMIE blazar

blé: ~ dur *m* AGRO ALIM durum wheat

blende *f* CHIMIE zinc blende, MINERAUX blende; **~ de zinc** *f* CHIMIE, MINERAUX zinc blende

blendeux *adj* PRODUCTION blendous, blendy

blessure *f* SECURITE injury; **~ causée par une fraise** *f* SECURITE cutter wound; **~ courante sur les lieux de travail** *f* SECURITE common injury in the workplace; **~ industrielle** *f* SECURITE industrial injury; **~ à l'oeil** *f* SECURITE eye injury; **~ aux yeux** *f* SECURITE eye injury

bleu *m* CERAM VER green patch distortion, CONSTR, PRODUCTION blueprint; **~ d'épreuves** *m* IMPRIM ozalid; **~ de faïence** *m* CERAM VER Chinese blue, English blue; **~ de méthylène** *m* PHYS FLUID gentian violet; **~ primaire** *m* TV blue primary; **~ de Prusse** *m* CHIMIE Prussian blue; **~ tirage** *m* TEXTILE blueprint; **~ de travail** *m* SECURITE overalls

bleutage *m* PHOTO blooming, lens coating

bleuté *adj* CERAM VER bloomed, REVETEMENT coated

blindage *m* CHARBON liner, sheet piling, CONSTR sheeting, ELECTR *d'un câble* shield, ELECTROTEC armor (AmE), armour (BrE), shield, ENREGISTR, ESPACE shield, shielding, INFORMAT screen, shield, MILITAIRE armor (AmE), armour (BrE), ORDINAT screen, PHYS RAYON screening, shielding, PHYSIQUE screening, shielding, PRODUCTION shield, SECURITE shielding, TV screen, *de câble* screening; **~ acoustique** *m* ENREGISTR acoustic shielding; **~ antimagnétique** *m* ELECTR magnetic screening; **~ électromagnétique** *m* PHYSIQUE electromagnetic screen; **~ électrostatique** *m* PHYSIQUE electrostatic screen; **~ entre pieux** *m* CHARBON interpile sheeting; **~ d'induit** *m* ELECTROTEC armature casing; **~ interne** *m* ELECTRON internal shield; **~ magnétique** *m* ELECTROTEC magnetic shielding; **~ de microphone** *m* ENREGISTR microphone shield; **~ de protection** *m* MILITAIRE protective armour; **~ de radia-**

tion *m* PHYS RAYON radiation shielding; ~ **de virole** *m* CHARBON shell liner

blindé *adj* ELECTROTEC armor-clad (AmE), armour-clad (BrE), MECANIQUE metal-clad, TELECOM armored (AmE), armoured (BrE)

blinder *vt* CONSTR sheet, ESPACE shield, MINES *un puits* line with metal

blindés *m pl* MILITAIRE *chars d'assaut, autres véhicules* armor (AmE), armour (BrE)

blister *m* IMPRIM *emballage* blister, blister pack; ~ **double coque** *m* EMBALLAGE clamshell blister

blizzard *m* METEO blizzard

BL-Lacs *m pl* ASTRONOMIE BL Lacertae

bloc *m* CERAM VER chunk glass, lump glass, CHARBON block, boulder, CONSTR lump, ESPACE block, *véhicules* power module, power package, IMPRIM *reliure* block, NUCLEAIRE unit, PETR boulder, PETROLE licence block (BrE), license block (AmE), *prospection, exploitation* block; ~ **d'accrochage mécanique** *m* PRODUCTION mechanical latch; ~ **additif** *m* PRODUCTION *électricité* auxiliary contact deck; ~ **d'alimentation** *m* CINEMAT power pack, ELECTROTEC power pack, power supply unit; ~ **d'angle** *m* CERAM VER corner block; ~ **basculé** *m* GEOLOGIE tilted block; ~ **de battage** *m* CONSTR driving block, MINES drive block; ~ **de batteries** *m* CINEMAT battery pack; ~ **de béton** *m* CERAM VER, CONSTR concrete block; ~ **de brûleur** *m* CERAM VER burner block; ~ **de butée** *m* NAUT thrust block; ~ **à colonnes** *m* CONS MECA *outils de découpage* die set; ~ **à colonnes arrière** *m* CONS MECA rear pillar; ~ **à colonnes rectangulaires** *m* CONS MECA rectangle die set; ~ **à colonnes rondes** *m* CONS MECA circular die set; ~ **de combustible** *m* NUCLEAIRE block-shaped fuel element; ~ **de commande** *m* CINEMAT control unit; ~ **de connexion** *m* ELECTROTEC, VEHICULES *système électrique* terminal block; ~ **de contacts** *m* ELECTROTEC pile-up; ~ **de contacts moulé** *m* PRODUCTION *automatisme industriel* molded contact block (AmE), moulded contact block (BrE); ~ **de convergence** *m* TV convergence assembly; ~ **de croix** *m* CINEMAT Maltese cross assembly; ~ **de culasse** *m* MILITAIRE breechblock; ~ **de cuve** *m* CERAM VER tank block; ~ **de déviation** *m* ELECTRON deflection yoke, TV deflection system; ~ **écrémeur** *m* CERAM VER skimmer block; ~ **électronique** *m* AUTO transistor control unit, INSTRUMENT remote electronics; ~ **encastré** *m* CONSTR base; ~ **en palissade** *m* CERAM VER soldier-block; ~ **erratique** *m* GEOLOGIE *glaciaire* erratic block; ~ **erroné** *m* TELECOM EB, erroneous block; ~ **erroné consécutif** *m* TELECOM CEB, consecutive error block; ~ **expérimental** *m* ESPACE experiment package; ~ **de flottaison** *m* CERAM VER flux line block; ~ **de fondation du mortier** *m* PRODUCTION mortar block; ~ **de graphite** *m* NUCLEAIRE graphite block; ~ **d'interverrouillage électrique** *m* PRODUCTION *automatisme industriel* electric interlock; ~ **d'interverrouillage mécanique** *m* PRODUCTION *automatisme industriel* mechanical interlock; ~ **isolant** *m* REFRIG block-type insulant; ~ **L** *m* CERAM VER L-block; ~ **à lames souples** *m* PRODUCTION logic reed block; ~ **de liaison montante** *m* TELECOM uplink block; ~ **logique** *m* INFORMAT, ORDINAT logical block; ~ **de longueur fixe** *m* INFORMAT, ORDINAT fixed length block; ~ **de mémoire** *m* ORDINAT memory bank; ~ **de messages pour le contrôle du CRC** *m* TELECOM CMB, CRC message bloc; ~ **de mesure gyrométrique tri-axiale** *m* ESPACE *véhicules* three-axis gyro unit; ~ **numérique** *m* INFORMAT, ORDI-

NAT numeric keypad; ~ **obturateur** *m* PETROLE blowout preventer; ~ **obturateur automatique** *m* PETROLE automatic blowout preventer; ~ **obturateur de puits** *m (BOP)* COMMANDE, OCEANO, PETROLE blowout preventer *(BOP)*; ~ **d'obturation de puits** *m (BOP)* GAZ blowout preventer *(BOP)*, well-plugging block, PETR blowout preventer *(BOP)*; ~ **optique** *m* AUTO sealed beam unit, CINEMAT picture head, projection head; ~ **d'organigramme** *m* INFORMAT flowchart block; ~ **de pavage** *m* CERAM VER paving block; ~ **de pilotage** *m* AERONAUT autopilot; ~ **de placage** *m* (Fra) *(cf placard)* CERAM VER patch block; ~ **porte-piles** *m* PRODUCTION *électricité* battery pack; ~ **de poudre** *m* ESPACE *véhicules* propellant grain; ~ **primaire** *m* ELECTRON mother crystal; ~ **de propulsion** *m* ESPACE propulsion unit; ~ **de puissance** *m* ELECTROTEC power module, ESPACE power module, power package; ~ **quadriprise** *m* ELECTROTEC four-way extension socket; ~ **récepteur** *m* NUCLEAIRE receiving assembly; ~ **de sole** *m* CERAM VER bottom block; ~ **de sorties** *m* ELECTR *raccordement* terminal block; ~ **standard** *m* RESSORTS loading block; ~ **technique** *m* AERONAUT *aéroport* service area; ~ **de têtes** *m* ENREGISTR, TV head assembly; ~ **de têtes vidéo** *m* TV video head assembly; ~ **de tête de tubage** *m* MINES drive head; ~ **de touches** *m* INFORMAT, ORDINAT keypad; ~ **de touches tactiles** *m* INFORMAT touchpad; ~ **de transmission** *m* INFORMAT, ORDINAT transmission block; ~ **tubulaire** *m* NUCLEAIRE tubular slug; ~ **d'uranium** *m* NUCLEAIRE uranium slug; ~ **de verre** *m* NUCLEAIRE glass block

blocage *m* CHARBON blocking, CONS MECA clamping mechanism, locking, locking mechanism, CONSTR filling, hardcore, rubble, rubble stone, CRISTALL pinning, ELECTRON jamming, ELECTROTEC blocking, cutoff, turn-off, ENREGISTR clamping, INFORMAT deadlock, interlock, interlock, MECANIQUE clamping, *outillage* chucking, METALL locking, ORDINAT lockout, *canal* interlock, PLAST CAOU blocking, PRODUCTION clamping, TELECOM, TV blocking; ~ **à l'aubinage** *m* CH DE FER block signal locked; ~ **à la clé** *m* PETROLE *forage* backup; ~ **complet** *m* ORDINAT deadlock, deadly embrace; ~ **externe** *m* TELECOM external blocking; ~ **du faisceau** *m* TV beam gate; ~ **de gouverne** *m* AERONAUT control surface locking; ~ **des gouvernes** *m* AERONAUT gust lock; ~ **des gyros** *m* AERONAUT gyro caging; ~ **interne** *m* TELECOM internal blocking; ~ **partiel de l'accès à l'interurbain** *m* TELECOM CTD, conditionally toll denied; ~ **de phase** *m* TV phase lock; ~ **thermique** *m* ELECTRON thermal shutdown, THERMODYN heat barrier; ~ **de la zone de Fresnel** *m* TELECOM Fresnel zone blockage

blocageux *adj* CONSTR rubbly

blocaille *f* CONSTR ballast, rubble, rubble stone

blocailleux *adj* CONSTR rubbly

bloc-bouteilles *m* OCEANO diving cylinder, diving tank, scuba tank

bloc-cylindres *m* AUTO cylinder block, VEHICULES engine block

block *m* CH DE FER block system; ~ **d'assentiment** *m* CH DE FER permissive block; ~ **à circulation intéressée** *m* CH DE FER lock and block, lock and block system

blockhaus *m* MILITAIRE blockhouse

bloc-moteur *m* CONS MECA, MECANIQUE engine block

bloc-notes *m* INFORMAT, ORDINAT scratch pad

blocs: ~ **éventuellement supprimables** *m pl* TELECOM optionally droppable blocks; ~ **non supprimables** *m pl*

TELECOM nondroppable blocks; ~ **de référence de dureté** *m pl* CONS MECA hardness reference standards

blocus *m* NAUT blockade

bloedite *f* MINERAUX blodite

bloqué *adj* CONSTR off, PRODUCTION clamped, *automatisme industriel* gated off; ~ **en état de désactivation** *adj* PRODUCTION *automatisme industriel* clamped in off-state; ~ **par les glaces** *adj* NAUT *navire* icebound

bloquer[1] *vt* CINEMAT lock off, CONS MECA block, lock, ELECTROTEC turn off, MECANIQUE clamp, jam, wedge, NAUT block, blockade, jam, PRODUCTION *tourelle d'une tour* clamp

bloquer[2] *vi* NUCLEAIRE seize

bloquer:[3] **se ~** *v réfl* CONS MECA lock, MECANIQUE jam, PRODUCTION be clamped

blouse: ~ **antipoussière** *f* SECURITE dust blouse; ~ **de protection** *f* EQUIP LAB *sécurité* laboratory coat

BLU *abrév (bande latérale unique)* TELECOM SSB *(single sideband)*

blutage *m* CONSTR bolting

bluter *vt* AGRO ALIM *farine* sieve, sift, CONSTR bolt

bobierrite *f* MINERAUX bobierrite

bobinage *m* CONS MECA winding, ELECTR coil winding, *moteur, générateur* winding, ELECTROTEC reeling, PAPIER reeling, winding, PRODUCTION coiling, winding process, TEXTILE winding process, TV spooling; ~ **à air** *m* ESPACE *véhicule spatial* air core winding; ~ **bifilaire** *m* ELECTR *bobine* bifilar winding; ~ **de champ** *m* ELECTR *machine* field coil; ~ **en fond de panier** *m* ELECTROTEC basket coil; ~ **en nid d'abeilles** *m* ELECTROTEC honeycomb winding, lattice-wound coil; ~ **en plusieurs galettes** *m* ELECTROTEC pie winding; ~ **d'excitation** *m* ELECTR *machine* field coil; ~ **extra-plat** *m* ELECTROTEC banked winding, pancake coil; ~ **haute fréquence** *m* ELECTROTEC RF coil; ~ **d'induit** *m* ELECTROTEC armature winding; ~ **monophasé** *m* ELECTROTEC single-phase winding; ~ **de moteur** *m* PRODUCTION *automatisme industriel* motor winding; ~ **primaire** *m* AUTO primary winding; ~ **du rotor** *m* ELECTROTEC rotor winding; ~ **rotorique** *m* ELECTROTEC rotor winding; ~ **rotorique diphasé** *m* ELECTROTEC two-phase rotor winding; ~ **rotorique triphasé** *m* ELECTROTEC three-phase rotor winding; ~ **sans fer** *m* ESPACE *véhicule spatiale* air core winding; ~ **secondaire** *m* AUTO secondary winding; ~ **à spires serrées** *m* PHOTO tight spooling; ~ **du stator** *m* ELECTROTEC stator winding; ~ **statorique** *m* ELECTROTEC stator winding; ~ **statorique diphasé** *m* ELECTROTEC two-phase stator winding; ~ **statorique triphasé** *m* ELECTROTEC three-phase stator winding; ~ **sur mandrin** *m* PAPIER center winding; ~ **d'une tête** *m* TV head winding

bobine:[1] **de ~ à bobine** *adj* CINEMAT, ENREGISTR reel-to-reel

bobine[2] *f* ACOUSTIQUE, CERAM VER spool, CINEMAT reel, roll, spool, CONS MECA bobbin, CONSTR reel, ELECTR coil, ELECTROTEC coil, reel, ENREGISTR reel, spool, IMPRIM reel, INFORMAT reel, spool, MECANIQUE coil, ORDINAT reel, spool, PETR *câble* reel, PHOTO *de pellicules* spool, PHYSIQUE, RESSORTS coil, TEXTILE bobbin, TV reel, spool, VEHICULES *allumage* coil; ~ **d'accord** *f* MILITAIRE tuning coil; ~ **d'ajustage de la largeur de l'image** *f* TV width choke; ~ **d'allumage** *f* AERONAUT ignition coil, AUTO ignition coil, induction coil, ELECTROTEC ignition coil, spark coil; ~ **d'amortissement** *f* ELECTR, ELECTROTEC damping coil; ~ **annulaire** *f* ESSAIS encircling coil; ~ **antironflement** *f*

ELECTROTEC, ENREGISTR, TV hum-bucking coil; ~ **d'arrêt** *f* ELECTR choke, choke coil, retardation coil, ELECTROTEC choke, choke coil, impedance coil, PRODUCTION lockout coil; ~ **avec espace d'air** *f* ELECTR air gap coil; ~ **de balayage** *f* TV scanning coil; ~ **de bande** *f* ENREGISTR tape reel; ~ **à boucles** *f* ELECTR loop coil; ~ **de câble** *f* EMBALLAGE cable reel; ~ **de cadrage** *f* TV image control coil; ~ **de carton** *f* IMPRIM Rinco process; ~ **de champ** *f* ELECTR *machine*, ELECTROTEC, ENREGISTR field coil; ~ **de charge** *f* ELECTROTEC loading coil; ~ **de choc** *f* ELECTR choke, choke coil; ~ **de concentration** *f* ELECTROTEC focusing coil, INSTRUMENT projector lens pole piece; ~ **de couplage** *f* ELECTR coupling coil, mutual inductor; ~ **à culasse** *f* ESSAIS yoked coil; ~ **débitrice** *f* CINEMAT feed reel, feed spool, supply reel, supply spool, takeoff reel, INFORMAT, TV supply reel; ~ **de déclenchement** *f* ELECTR trip coil; ~ **de déflexion** *f* NUCLEAIRE PHYSIQUE, deflecting coil; ~ **de démagnétisation** *f* TV degaussing coil; ~ **de démarrage** *f* TRANSPORT booster coil; ~ **démontable** *f* CINEMAT split reel, split spool; ~ **détectrice** *f* PHYSIQUE search coil; ~ **détériorée aux extrémités** *f* PAPIER starred roll; ~ **de déviation** *f* ELECTROTEC deflection coil, yoke coil; ~ **de déviation horizontale** *f* ELECTROTEC horizontal deflection coil; ~ **de déviation verticale** *f* ELECTROTEC vertical deflection coil; ~ **déviatrice** *f* INSTRUMENT double condenser pole piece; ~ **différentielle** *f* ELECTR differential coil; ~ **égalisatrice** *f* ELECTROTEC static balancer; ~ **électrique** *f* ELECTROTEC electric coil; ~ **d'électro-aimant** *f* ELECTROTEC magnet coil, VEHICULES solenoid coil; ~ **élémentaire** *f* RESSORTS wap; ~ **en bout de machine** *f* PAPIER batch roll; ~ **encerclée de matériau à essayer** *f* ESSAIS internal coil; ~ **en dérivation** *f* ELECTROTEC shunt coil; ~ **d'équilibrage** *f* ELECTR balance coil; ~ **d'essai** *f* CINEMAT test reel; ~ **d'excitation** *f* ELECTROTEC drive coil, field coil; ~ **exploratrice** *f* ELECTR search coil, *magnétique* exploring coil, ELECTROTEC flip coil, search coil, ESSAIS search coil; ~ **d'extinction** *f* ELECTR *relais* arc suppression coil, ELECTROTEC arc breaker; ~ **d'extraction** *f* MINES *pour câble plat* hoisting reel; ~ **fantôme** *f* ELECTROTEC phantom coil; ~ **fixe** *f* ELECTR fixed coil; ~ **de focalisation** *f* ELECTROTEC, TV focusing coil; ~ **formée sur gabarit** *f* ELECTR *enroulement* form-wound coil; ~ **de Helmholtz** *f* PHYSIQUE Helmholtz coil; ~ **image** *f* CINEMAT picture reel; ~ **d'impédance** *f* ELECTROTEC impedance coil; ~ **imprégnée** *f* ELECTROTEC impregnated coil; ~ **d'inductance** *f* ELECTR *électromagnétisme* inductance coil, ELECTROTEC inductance coil, inductor, reactance coil, THERMODYN *chauffage* heating coil; ~ **d'inductance hermétique** *f* ELECTR sealed reactor; ~ **d'inductance de puissance** *f* ELECTROTEC power inductor; ~ **d'inductance triphasée de mise à la terre** *f* ELECTR three-phase neutral reactor; ~ **d'inductance de type sec à enroulement non encapsulé** *f* ELECTR nonencapsulated winding dry-type reactor; ~ **d'induction** *f* AUTO, ELECTR induction coil, ELECTROTEC induction coil, *téléphonique* telephone induction coil, PHYSIQUE, VEHICULES *allumage* induction coil; ~ **d'induit** *f* ELECTR *machine* armature coil; ~ **interchangeable** *f* ELECTROTEC plug-in coil; ~ **isolateur** *f* ELECTROTEC bobbin; ~ **à joues** *f* CINEMAT loading spool; ~ **de lissage** *f* ELECTROTEC filter choke, smoothing choke; ~ **magnétisante** *f* ELECTR *électromagnétisme* magnetizing coil; ~ **de magnétisation** *f* ELECTROTEC magnetizing coil; ~ **mère** *f* CINEMAT parent roll; ~ **mobile** *f* ELECTR *galvanomètre*, ELECTROTEC moving coil; ~ **non rebobinée** *f* PAPIER jumbo roll; ~ **d'objectif** *f* INSTRUMENT objective pole piece; ~ **oscillatrice** *f* CINEMAT oscillator coil; ~ **de papier** *f* PAPIER reel of paper; ~ **parcourue par un courant** *f* PHYSIQUE current-carrying coil; ~ **de pellicule** *f* PHOTO film spool; ~ **plate** *f* ELECTR pancake coil, slab coil; ~ **plate** *f* ELECTR pancake coil; ~ **à plusieurs couches** *f* ELECTR multilayer coil; ~ **de présentation** *f* CINEMAT demo reel; ~ **primaire** *f* ESSAIS primary coil; ~ **à prise** *f* ELECTROTEC tapped coil; ~ **protégée** *f* ESSAIS shielded coil; ~ **de pupinisation** *f* ELECTR, PHYSIQUE loading coil; ~ **de réactance** *f* ELECTR reactor, ELECTROTEC reactance coil, reactor; ~ **de réactance réactive** *f* ELECTR adjustable inductance coil; ~ **de réaction** *f* ELECTROTEC feedback coil, oscillator coil; ~ **réceptrice** *f* CINEMAT lower spool, take-up reel, ENREGISTR take-up spool, INFORMAT take-up reel, PHOTO take-up drum, TV take-up spool; ~ **de relais** *f* ELECTROTEC, PRODUCTION *électricité* relay coil; ~ **à résistance** *f* ELECTROTEC resistance coil; ~ **sans noyau de fer** *f* ELECTR air core inductance; ~ **saturable** *f* ELECTROTEC swinging choke; ~ **secondaire** *f* ELECTROTEC, ESSAIS secondary coil; ~ **sectionnelle** *f* TEXTILE *tricot chaîne* sectional beam; ~ **série** *f* ELECTR series coil; ~ **solénoïde** *f* ELECTR solenoid coil; ~ **de soufflage** *f* ELECTROTEC arc suppression coil, blowout coil; ~ **du stator** *f* ELECTROTEC stator coil; ~ **statorique** *f* ELECTROTEC stator coil; ~ **supraconductrice** *f* TRANSPORT superconducting coil; ~ **de Tesla** *f* ELECTROTEC Tesla coil; ~ **thermique** *f* THERMODYN heating coil; ~ **de tirerie** *f* PRODUCTION drawing block; ~ **toroïdale** *f* ELECTR toroidal coil, ELECTROTEC toroid, NUCLEAIRE toroid, toroidal coil; ~ **à trembleur** *f* ELECTR make-and-break coil; ~ **de verrou** *f* CONSTR lock bush; ~ **voisine** *f* ELECTR adjacent coil

bobineau *m* IMPRIM dinky reel

bobiner *vt* CONS MECA, PAPIER wind, PRODUCTION coil, TEXTILE wind

bobineuse *f* CINEMAT winding machine, PAPIER winder, PHOTO bulk film loader

bobineuse-refendeuse *f* PAPIER slitter rewinder

bobinoir *m* CERAM VER winder, PRODUCTION coiler; ~ **roving** *m* CERAM VER roving winder

bocage *m* PRODUCTION foundry scrap; ~ **de fonte** *m* PRODUCTION cast scrap, foundry scrap; ~ **de poterie** *m* PRODUCTION pot scrap

bocal: [1] **en ~** *adj* AGRO ALIM bottled

bocal [2] *m* AGRO ALIM, EMBALLAGE jar; ~ **à conserves** *m* CERAM VER canning jar (AmE), preserving jar (BrE); ~ **en matière plastique** *m* PHOTO plastic bottle

bocard *m* CHARBON, PRODUCTION mill, stamp, stamp mill, stamping mill; ~ **à 3 pilons** *m* MINES three-head battery, three-stamp mill; ~ **à minerai** *m* MINES ore stamp; ~ **à simple pilon** *m* PRODUCTION single stamp mill

bocardage *m* MINES milling, PRODUCTION stamp milling, stamping

bocarder *vt* PRODUCTION mill, stamp

bocfil *m* PRODUCTION fret saw, fret saw frame

boehmite *f* MINERAUX boehmite

boette *f* OCEANO gurry bait, live bait

boghead *m* CHARBON boghead

bogie *m* CH DE FER *véhicules* bogie, bogie truck (AmE), CONS MECA bogie (BrE), trailer (AmE), truck (AmE), CONSTR bogie, cart (AmE), truck (AmE), VEHICULES

remorque bogie (BrE), trailer (AmE), truck (AmE); ~ **monomoteur** *m* TRANSPORT monomotor bogie (BrE), monomotor truck (AmE); ~ **moteur** *m* CH DE FER motor bogie (BrE), motor truck (AmE); ~ **porteur** *m* CH DE FER *véhicules* carrying bogie, trailer bogie (BrE), trailer car (AmE)

bogue *f* ORDINAT bug

bois *m* CONS MECA *d'un rabot* stock, CONSTR timber; ~ **carré** *m* CONSTR square timber; ~ **de charpente** *m* CONSTR timber; ~ **composite** *m* CONSTR plywood; ~ **de construction** *m* CONSTR builders' timber; ~ **de contreplacage** *m* CONSTR plywood; ~ **contreplaqué** *m* CONSTR plywood; ~ **débité** *m* CONSTR broken-down timber; ~ **déjeté** *m* CONSTR warped timber; ~ **desséché** *m* NAUT seasoned timber, seasoned wood; ~ **déversé** *m* CONSTR warped timber; ~ **doux** *m* NAUT softwood; ~ **dur** *m* CONSTR hardwood; ~ **en état** *m* CONSTR standing timber; ~ **en feuillu** *m* PAPIER deciduous wood; ~ **équarri** *m* CONSTR balk (AmE), baulk (BrE), squared timber; ~ **d'étais** *m* CONSTR propwood; ~ **de feuillu** *m* PAPIER hardwood; ~ **flottant** *m* NAUT driftwood; ~ **de gaïac** *m* MECANIQUE *matériaux* lignum vitae; ~ **gauchi** *m* CONSTR warped timber; ~ **gravé** *m* IMPRIM xylograph; ~ **à limer** *m* CONS MECA vice cap (BrE), vice clamp (BrE), vice jaw (BrE), vise cap (AmE), vise clamp (AmE), vise jaw (AmE); ~ **de mine** *m* MINES mine timber, mining timber, pit wood; ~ **de montagne** *m* MINERAUX mountain wood; ~ **moulé** *m* NAUT cold molded wood (AmE), cold moulded wood (BrE); ~ **non-résineux** *m* NAUT wood reinforcements; ~ **d'oeuvre** *m* CONSTR timber suitable for conversion into market forms; ~ **à pâte** *m* PAPIER pulpwood; ~ **pelard** *m* CONSTR barked timber; ~ **d'une pioche** *m* CONSTR pick handle; ~ **plaqué triplé** *m* CONSTR three-ply wood; ~ **propre à la construction** *m* CONSTR wood suitable for building; ~ **raboteux** *m* CONSTR rough wood; ~ **de refend** *m* CONSTR lath wood; ~ **de résineux** *m* PAPIER softwood; ~ **de sciage** *m* CONSTR saw timber; ~ **séché à l'air** *m* NAUT seasoned timber, seasoned wood; ~ **de soutènement** *m* CONSTR propwood; ~ **de stère** *m* CONSTR cordwood; ~ **tendre** *m* CONSTR softwood; ~ **voilé** *m* CONSTR warped timber

boisage *m* CONSTR timbering; ~ **armé** *m* MINES double timbering, herringbone timbering, reinforced timbering; ~ **jointif** *m* MINES close timbering; ~ **serré** *m* MINES close timbering; ~ **de voie maîtresse** *m* MINES entry timbering

boiser *vt* CONSTR timber

boiserie *f* CONSTR woodwork

boisseau *m* AGRO ALIM bushel, CONSTR *d'un robinet* dome, EQUIP LAB *verrerie* cock, METROLOGIE bushel

boitage *m* CERAM VER warp

boîte: [1] **en ~** *adj* AGRO ALIM tinned

boîte [2] *f* CONS MECA, CONSTR *d'une serrure* case, IMPRIM book case, *reliure, emballage, façonnage* casing, TRANSPORT box; ~ **aérosol** *f* CONS MECA aerosol container, EMBALLAGE aerosol can; ~ **à air** *f* CONS MECA, PETROLE air box; ~ **d'alimentation** *f* PRODUCTION feed box; ~ **d'aluminium** *f* EMBALLAGE aluminium can (BrE), aluminum can (AmE); ~ **automatique** *f* AUTO, VEHICULES automatic transmission; ~ **des avances** *f* CONS MECA feed box; ~ **avec bord métallique** *f* EMBALLAGE metal edging case; ~ **avec fond plié** *f* EMBALLAGE folded bottom box; ~ **avec ouverture par clé** *f* EMBALLAGE key-opening can; ~ **des barres** *f* TEXTILE bar frame; ~ **à borne du compresseur** *f* REFRIG compressor terminal box; ~ **à boue** *f* PETR, PETROLE mud box; ~ **à bourrage** *f* PRODUCTION gland, stuffing box; ~ **brochée** *f* EMBALLAGE stitched box; ~ **à câble** *f* ELECTR *connection* cable box; ~ **de capacités** *f* ELECTROTEC capacitance box, decade capacitance box; ~ **de carton ondulé** *f* EMBALLAGE corrugated board box; ~ **à cendre** *f* MAT CHAUFF ash box; ~ **de changement d'avance** *f* CONS MECA change feed box; ~ **de changement de vitesse** *f* CONS MECA gearbox; ~ **chaude** *f* CH DE FER *jargon ferroviaire* hot box; ~ **à clapet** *f* CONS MECA clack box, INST HYDR valve chest; ~ **de claquage** *f* CONS MECA flash tester; ~ **de collecteur d'air** *f* AUTO plenum chamber; ~ **collée** *f* EMBALLAGE glued box; ~ **de commande d'accessoires** *f* AERONAUT accessory gearbox; ~ **de commande** *f* CONS MECA control box, control unit; ~ **à commande manuelle** *f* VEHICULES manual gearbox; ~ **de commande de pilote automatique** *f* AERONAUT autopilot control unit; ~ **de commande train** *f* AERONAUT landing gear control unit; ~ **de commutation gyro** *f* AERONAUT gyro data switching control; ~ **à concentrés** *f* MINES concentrates box; ~ **de connexions** *f* ELECTROTEC conduit box; ~ **des coussinets** *f* CONS MECA journal box, pedestal box; ~ **à débourbage** *f* PRODUCTION mud box; ~ **à décades** *f* AERONAUT, ELECTROTEC decade box; ~ **de démarrage réacteur** *f* AERONAUT engine starting control box; ~ **de dérivation** *f* ELECTR *raccordement* branch box; ~ **de dérivation en porcelaine** *f* CERAM VER porcelain conduit box, porcelain junction box; ~ **de détente** *f* INST HYDR expansion box; ~ **de dilatation** *f* INST HYDR expansion box, MINES slip box; ~ **de direction** *f* VEHICULES steering gearbox; ~ **de distribution** *f* CINEMAT switch box, ELECTR distribution box, *raccordement* outlet box, ELECTROTEC distribution box, INST HYDR valve chest; ~ **de distribution de vapeur** *f* INST HYDR steam box, steam case, steam chamber, steam chest; ~ **à eau** *f* CERAM VER water box; ~ **en carton pour conteneur** *f* EMBALLAGE container board box; ~ **en fer blanc** *f* IMPRIM tin; ~ **d'engrenage** *f* CONS MECA, NAUT gearbox; ~ **d'entrée** *f* TELECOM block terminal; ~ **en verre** *f* INFORMAT, ORDINAT glass box; ~ **d'essieu** *f* CH DE FER journal box (AmE), *véhicules* axle box (BrE), PRODUCTION grease box, oil box; ~ **d'essieu à coussinets** *f* CH DE FER *véhicules* bearing axle box (BrE), bearing journal box (AmE); ~ **à étoupe** *f* PRODUCTION stuffing box; ~ **et vis** *f* MINES *de sonde* box and pin; ~ **d'expansion carburant** *f* AERONAUT fuel expansion box, fuel ullage box; ~ **d'extinction d'arc** *f* ELECTROTEC arc quench chamber; ~ **factice** *f* EMBALLAGE display box; ~ **à feu** *f* MAT CHAUFF, THERMODYN firebox; ~ **de film** *f* CINEMAT film can; ~ **à forets** *f* CONS MECA drill socket, piercer; ~ **à fumée** *f* CH DE FER *véhicules* smoke box, CHAUFFAGE smoke arch, smoke box, CONSTR smoke box; ~ **à fusible** *f* ELECTR *sécurité*, ELECTROTEC fuse box; ~ **à gants** *f* NUCLEAIRE, VEHICULES *habitacle* glove box; ~ **à garniture** *f* PRODUCTION stuffing box; ~ **de graissage** *f* PRODUCTION grease box, oil box; ~ **à graisse** *f* CONS MECA grease packing gland; ~ **de gyromètre pour pilote automatique** *f* AERONAUT angular three-axis rate sensor; ~ **à huile** *f* PRODUCTION grease box; ~ **d'inductances** *f* ELECTROTEC decade inductance box, inductance box; ~ **inférieure de décharge** *f* DISTRI EAU drop box; ~ **à jacks** *f* CONS MECA jack box; ~ **de joint** *f* CONSTR joint box; ~ **de jonction** *f* ELECTR junction box,

raccordement joint box, ELECTROTEC junction box, terminal box, ESPACE *véhicules* junction box; ~ **de jonction de câble** *f* ELECTR splice box, *raccordement* cable junction box; ~ **aux lettres** *f* CERAM VER fore-hearth entrance; ~ **à lettres** *f* TELECOM text mailbox; ~ **aux lettres électronique** *f* INFORMAT, ORDINAT, TELECOM electronic mailbox; ~ **à lettres électronique** *f* ELECTRON, TELECOM electronic mailbox; ~ **à lettres vocale** *f* TELECOM voice mail box; ~ **à lumière** *f* CINEMAT light box, INSTRUMENT lamphouse, PHOTO lamphousing, light box; ~ **mécanique** *f* AUTO manual transmission; ~ **de mesure** *f* CONS MECA meter; ~ **métallique** *f* EMBALLAGE canister, metal box (BrE), metal can (AmE); ~ **noire** *f* AERONAUT, INSTRUMENT, ORDINAT black box; ~ **à noyaux** *f* PRODUCTION core box, core stock; ~ **à noyaux en deux parties** *f* PRODUCTION split core box; ~ **d'onglet** *f* CONSTR miter board (AmE), miter box (AmE), mitre board (BrE), mitre box (BrE); ~ **à onglets** *f* CONSTR miter board (AmE), miter box (AmE), mitre board (BrE), mitre box (BrE); ~ **à outils** *f* CONS MECA tool box, INFORMAT, ORDINAT tool-kit; ~ **de pansement** *f* SECURITE first-aid box; ~ **de Pétri** *f* EQUIP LAB *verrerie, microbiologie* Petri dish; ~ **à platine** *f* PAPIER bedplate box; ~ **pliante** *f* EMBALLAGE fold carton, folding carton, folding box, PAPIER folding box; ~ **à plongeur** *f* MINES slip box; ~ **pour ampoules** *f* EMBALLAGE ampoule box; ~ **pour emboîtement** *f* EMBALLAGE nesting box; ~ **pour emplettes** *f* EMBALLAGE carrier box; ~ **de pression** *f* PRODUCTION pressure box; ~ **de protection** *f* NUCLEAIRE glove box; ~ **de pulvérisateur par pression** *f* CONS MECA aerosol spray container; ~ **de queue** *f* DISTRI EAU end box, tail box; ~ **de raccordement** *f* ELECTROTEC cable box, connection box, TELECOM block terminal; ~ **récupérable** *f* EMBALLAGE reusable box; ~ **réfrigérante** *f* PRODUCTION cooler, jumbo; ~ **de regard** *f* PRODUCTION inspection fitting; ~ **de relais d'alimentation et d'interdiction de pilote** *f* AERONAUT power and interlock relay box; ~ **de renvoi d'angle** *f* IMPRIM *mécanique* angle box; ~ **à réparations** *f* PRODUCTION repair outfit; ~ **de répartition** *f* CONS MECA distribution chamber; ~ **de répartition d'air** *f* AUTO plenum chamber; ~ **de résistance** *f* ELECTROTEC decade resistance box, resistance box; ~ **rigide** *f* EMBALLAGE rigid box; ~ **de séparation** *f* ELECTR splitter box, *câble* dividing box; ~ **de sonde** *f* MINES pole box; ~ **à soupape** *f* INST HYDR valve chest, PETROLE valve cage, valve chest; ~ **sous vapeur** *f* AGRO ALIM exhaustion box; ~ **synchro** *f* AUTO synchronized transmission; ~ **de tête** *f* DISTRI EAU head box; ~ **tirage** *f* ELECTR *installation* pull box; ~ **à tiroir** *f* INST HYDR steam box, steam case, steam chamber, steam chest; ~ **de transmission** *f* NAUT gearbox; ~ **de transmission principale** *f* AERONAUT main gearbox; ~ **à vapeur** *f* INST HYDR slide box, steam box, steam case, steam chamber, steam chest, *d'un tiroir de distribution* valve chest; ~ **à vent** *f* CONS MECA air box; ~ **de vitesse** *f* AUTO gearbox, transmission, CONS MECA, MECANIQUE *véhicules*, VEHICULES *transmission* gearbox; ~ **de vitesses à commande manuelle** *f* VEHICULES manual gearbox; ~ **de vitesses semi-automatique** *f* VEHICULES semiautomatic transmission; ~ **de vitesses synchronisées** *f* AUTO synchromesh transmission, synchronized transmission; ~ **de vitesses à trains baladeurs** *f* AUTO sliding gear transmission; ~ **vocale** *f* TELECOM voice mailbox

boîte-guide *f* NUCLEAIRE guide bushing

boîte-magasin: ~ débitrice *f* CINEMAT feed magazine

boîtes: ~ pliantes *f pl* PAPIER folding boxboard

boîtier:[1] en ~ hermétique *adj* ELECTROTEC hermetically-sealed

boîtier[2] *m* CINEMAT *d'une caméra* casing, ELECTROTEC package, MECANIQUE case, casing, PHOTO *de caméra* body, housing, PRODUCTION enclosure; ~ d'accrochage train rentré *m* AERONAUT landing gear uplock box; ~ d'accrochage trappes de train *m* AERONAUT landing gear door uplock; ~ d'acquisition de données de vol *m* AERONAUT FDAU, flight data acquisition unit; ~ de circuit intégré *m* ELECTRON integrated circuit package; ~ de cloche *m* AERONAUT coupling cover; ~ de commande électronique *m* AUTO digital control box; ~ de convertisseur de couple *m* AUTO torque converter housing; ~ de démarrage *m* AERONAUT automatic starting unit; ~ à deux rangées de broches *m* ELECTROTEC, INFORMAT, ORDINAT DIP, dual-in-line package; ~ de différentiel *m* AUTO differential case; ~ DIP *m* ELECTROTEC, INFORMAT, ORDINAT DIP, dual-in-line package; ~ de direction *m* AUTO steering gearbox; ~ électronique *m* AUTO transistor ignition unit; ~ enfichable *m* ELECTROTEC drop-in package; ~ en polyester armé de fibre de verre *m* PRODUCTION glass polyester enclosure; ~ en tôle d'acier *m* PRODUCTION sheet steel case; ~ étanche *m* PHOTO underwater housing; ~ de filtre *m* VEHICULES *carburateur* filter bowl; ~ à fusible *m* VEHICULES *système électrique* fuse box; ~ de mini-rupteurs *m* AERONAUT microswitch box; ~ de montre *m* CONS MECA watch casing; ~ plat *m* ELECTRON flat pack; ~ de plate-forme météorologique *m* NAUT weather station cabinet; ~ de préaffichage *m* AERONAUT presetting controls; ~ de préaffichage de carburant *m* AERONAUT fuel level presetting controls; ~ programmable *m* CONSTR programmable box; ~ à quatre rangées de broches *m* ELECTRON QUIP, quad-in-line package; ~ de raccordement *m* ESPACE *véhicules* junction box; ~ à une rangée de broches *m* ELECTRON, INFORMAT, ORDINAT SILP, SIP, single-in-line package; ~ relais d'hélice *m* AERONAUT propeller relay unit; ~ SIP *m* ELECTRON SILP, SIP; ~ standard *m* PRODUCTION gang; ~ tour *m* INFORMAT, ORDINAT deskside system; ~ de verrou *m* CONSTR lock casing

bol *m* CHARBON bowl; ~ vibrant *m* MECANIQUE vibratory feeder

boléite *f* MINERAUX boleite

bolide *m* ASTRONOMIE bolide

bolinche *f* OCEANO purse seine

bollard *m* NAUT bitt, bollard

bolomètre *m* ASTRONOMIE, ELECTROTEC, ESPACE, PHYSIQUE, REFRIG bolometer; ~ à semi-conducteur *m* ASTRONOMIE, PHYSIQUE semiconductor bolometer

bombage *m* AGRO ALIM *boîte* swell, CERAM VER bending

bombardement *m* GAZ bombardment, MILITAIRE bombardment, bombing; ~ à basse altitude *m* AERONAUT low-altitude bombing; ~ électronique *m* PHYS PART electron bombardment; ~ ionique *m* ELECTRON ionic bombardment, PHYSIQUE ion bombardment; ~ par électrons *m* ELECTRON electron bombardment

bombe *f* CONS MECA aerosol container; ~ atomique *f* NUCLEAIRE atomic bomb; ~ d'attaque *f* EQUIP LAB reaction bomb; ~ calorimétrique *f* EQUIP LAB calorimetric bomb, PHYSIQUE bomb calorimeter; ~ catalytique *f* GENIE CHIM catalytic bomb; ~ fumigène *f* MILITAIRE smoke bomb; ~ guidée *f* MILITAIRE smart

bomb; ~ à hydrogène *f* NUCLEAIRE H-bomb; ~ à mater *f* CINEMAT dulling spray; ~ napalm *f* MILITAIRE *guerre chimique* napalm bomb; ~ non-explosée *f* MILITAIRE unexploded bomb; ~ à retardement *f* MILITAIRE time bomb

bombé *m* PAPIER camber; ~ à petit rayon de carré *m* NUCLEAIRE hemiellipsoidal bottom, hemiellipsoidal head; ~ de presse *m* PAPIER crown

bombement *m* AERONAUT *piste* camber, AGRO ALIM *boîtes* blowing, CONSTR belly, bulge, bulging, cambering, *d'un mur* bulge, *d'une route* camber, ENREGISTR cupping, GEOLOGIE upwarp, PRODUCTION crowning, crown; ~ d'une chaussée *m* VEHICULES road camber

bomber[1] *vt* CONSTR camber, PRODUCTION dish

bomber[2] *vi* CONSTR belly, belly out, bulge, camber

bomber:[3] se ~ *v réfl* CONS MECA bulge, CONSTR bulge, camber

bombonne: ~ à gaz *f* PRODUCTION gas bottle

bombure *f* CONS MECA bulge

bôme *f* NAUT boom; ~ à rouleau *f* NAUT roller boom

bon:[1] en ~ état de navigation *adj* TRANSPORT seaworthy

bon:[2] ~ aller-retour *m* PRODUCTION turnaround document; ~ d'embarquement *m* NAUT shipping order; ~ frais *m* METEO strong breeze; ~ de livraison *m* PRODUCTION delivery ticket; ~ de livraison fournisseur *m* PRODUCTION packing slip; ~ de mélange *m* PRODUCTION bland formula; ~ d'outillage *m* PRODUCTION tool requisition; ~ de production *m* PRODUCTION job ticket, operation ticket; ~ de réalisation *m* PRODUCTION job ticket, operation ticket; ~ de rejet *m* PRODUCTION rejection note; ~ de sortie *m* PRODUCTION tool requisition; ~ de sortie matière *m* PRODUCTION material issue note; ~ de travail *m* PRODUCTION job ticket, operation ticket

bonace *f* OCEANO calm sea

bonbonne *f* AGRO ALIM, EQUIP LAB *verrerie* carboy; ~ d'ammoniaque *f* LESSIVES ammonia carboy

bonde *f* CONSTR plug, DISTRI EAU shut, shut-off, EQUIP LAB bung, MECANIQUE plug, PRODUCTION plug, *d'un baril* bung; ~ de bouchon *f* AGRO ALIM bunghole

bonhomme *m* NAUT deadman; ~ de verrouillage *m* CONS MECA locking plunger

bonification *f* DISTRI EAU land reclamation

bonne: ~ assiette *f* NAUT even keel, level keel; ~ épreuve *f* IMPRIM clean proof; ~ feuille *f* IMPRIM *tirage* pull

bonnet: ~ de protection *m* SECURITE protective hood; ~ de protection pour travaux au pistolet *m* SECURITE dust and spray protective hood

bonneterie *f* TEXTILE hosiery

bonnette *f* CINEMAT auxiliary close-up lens, plus diopter (AmE), plus dioptre (BrE), supplementary lens; ~ d'approche *f* CINEMAT close-up attachment, portrait attachment, proxar, PHOTO close-up attachment; ~ diffusante *f* PHOTO soft-focus lens; ~ dioptrique *f* CINEMAT diopter lens (AmE), dioptre lens (BrE); ~ de flou *f* CINEMAT diffusion effect filter; ~ paravent *f* ENREGISTR windscreen (BrE), windshield (AmE); ~ à portrait *f* PHOTO portrait attachment; ~ positive convergente *f* PHOTO wide-angle converter; ~ à trèfle *f* AERONAUT dimmer cap

booléen *adj* INFORMAT Boolean

boomerang *m* PHYS FLUID boomerang

booster *m* MINES booster

BOP *abrév* COMMANDE *(bloc obturateur de puits)*, GAZ *(bloc d'obturation de puits)*, OCEANO *(bloc obturateur de puits)*, PETR *(bloc d'obturation de puits)*, PETROLE *(bloc obturateur de puits)* BOP *(blowout preventer)*

boracite *f* MINERAUX boracite

borane *m* CHIMIE borane

borate *m* CHIMIE borate; ~ **de sodium** *m* CHIMIE sodium borate; ~ **de soude** *m* CHIMIE sodium borate

borax *m* CERAM VER, CHIMIE, LESSIVES, MINERAUX borax

Borazon *m* (MD) CHIMIE Borazon (TM)

bord:[1] ~ **à bord** *adj* CONS MECA edge-to-edge

bord:[2] ~ **à bord** *adv* NAUT alongside

bord[3] *m* CONS MECA *d'un tiroir, d'une lumière de cylindre,* EMBALLAGE edge, GEOLOGIE boundary, HYDROLOGIE margin, *d'une rivière, d'un fleuve* bank, INFORMAT *d'une carte* edge, NAUT bank, board, tack, *de la mer, d'un fleuve* shore, OCEANO seaboard, shore, PHYSIQUE edge; ~ **à angle vif** *m* CONSTR feather edge; ~ **d'attaque** *m* AERONAUT leading edge, INST HYDR exhaust edge, steam edge, MILITAIRE *d'un parachute* peripheral hem, PHYSIQUE leading edge; ~ **d'attaque de pale** *m* AERONAUT blade leading edge; ~ **biseauté** *m* CONS MECA bevel edge; ~ **bridé** *m* EMBALLAGE flanged edge; ~ **brut de coupe** *m* CERAM VER edge as cut, rough edge; ~ **de carafe** *m* CERAM VER reinforced rim (BrE), turned rim (AmE); ~ **côte** *m* TEXTILE ribbing; ~ **croqué** *m* CONS MECA pinked edge; ~ **à la cuve** *m* PAPIER deckle edge; ~ **en biseau** *m* CONSTR feather edge; ~ **évasé** *m* CERAM VER flared end; ~ **de feuille** *m* CERAM VER border, edge of the sheet; ~ **de fuite** *m* AERONAUT *aile,* PHYSIQUE trailing edge; ~ **de fuite de pale** *m* AERONAUT blade trailing edge; ~ **gommé** *m* EMBALLAGE gummed edge; ~ **de goulotte** *m* CERAM VER trough lip; ~ **de guidage** *m* CINEMAT leading edge; ~ **intérieur** *m* INST HYDR *d'un distributeur à tiroir* exhaust edge; ~ **marge** *m* IMPRIM lay edge; ~ **de piste vidéo en amont** *m* TV trailing-edge video track; ~ **rebrûlé** *m* CERAM VER fire-polished edge; ~ **de référence** *m* TV *de la bande* reference edge; ~ **renforcé** *m* CERAM VER conical reinforced rim; ~ **ridé** *m* CERAM VER wrinkled rim; ~ **de rivière** *m* HYDROLOGIE river bank, riverside; ~ **de roue** *m* VEHICULES wheel flange; ~ **rouge** *m* CERAM VER red edge; ~ **à sceller** *m* CERAM VER sealing edge; ~ **soudé** *m* EMBALLAGE welded body seam; ~ **tombé** *m* CONS MECA flanged edge; ~ **du vent** *m* NAUT weather side; ~ **vif** *m* RESSORTS sharp edge

bord:[4] ~ **à bord avec** *prép* NAUT alongside

bordage *m* INST HYDR cleading, MATERIAUX flanging, NAUT plank, PRODUCTION flanging

bordages *m pl* NAUT king

bordé:[1] ~ **à clin** *adj* NAUT clinker-built

bordé[2] *m* NAUT plating, skin; ~ **de bouchain** *m* NAUT bilge plating; ~ **de coque** *m* NAUT shell plating; ~ **en fer** *m* NAUT iron plating; ~ **extérieur** *m* NAUT outer hull, outer skin, shell; ~ **de fond** *m* NAUT bottom plating; ~ **à franc-bord** *m* NAUT flush plating; ~ **intérieur** *m* NAUT inner skin; ~ **de muraille** *m* NAUT side plating; ~ **de pont** *m* NAUT deck plating

bordée *f* NAUT tack, *navigation* leg

border *vt* CONSTR *deux extrémités* bind, NAUT *avirons* ship, *cordage* haul in, *navire* plate, *voile* trim, PRODUCTION flange

bordereau *m* PRODUCTION docket; ~ **d'approvisionnement** *m* PRODUCTION pick list, picking list; ~ **de livraison** *m* PRODUCTION delivery ticket, internal delivery slip; ~ **de réception** *m* PRODUCTION receipt ticket, stock receipt

bordeuse *f* PAPIER edge cutter

bordigue *f* OCEANO fish corral

bord-queue *m* IMPRIM *plaques et blanchets* tail edge

bordure *f* CERAM VER banding, CONSTR curb (AmE), curbstone (AmE), kerb (BrE), kerbstone (BrE), GEOLOGIE boundary, IMPRIM border, ornamental border, NAUT foot; ~ **continentale** *f* OCEANO continental borderland, continental fringe, continental margin; ~ **d'encadrement** *f* CONS MECA frame edging; ~ **de trottoir** *f* CONSTR curb (AmE), curb stone (AmE), kerb (BrE), kerb stone (BrE)

bore *m* (B) CHIMIE boron *(B)*

borgne *m* MATERIAUX blind hole

borique *adj* CHIMIE boric

bornage *m* CONSTR setting; ~ **superficielle** *m* CONSTR surface demarcation

borne *f* AUTO post, terminal, CERAM VER batch pile, CONSTR boundary, boundary mark, boundary stone, landmark, ELECTR *raccordement*, ELECTROTEC, PHYSIQUE, TELECOM terminal, TRANSPORT bollard, VEHICULES *système électrique* terminal; ~ **d'alimentation** *f* PRODUCTION line terminal; ~ **d'amarrage** *f* NAUT mooring pile, mooring post; ~ **d'amarrage à terre** *f* TRANSPORT mooring bollard; ~ **d'antenne** *f* TV aerial terminal; ~ **d'appel taxi** *f* TRANSPORT taxi telephone; ~ **d'arrivée** *f* ELECTROTEC input terminal; ~ **d'attache** *f* NAUT bollard; ~ **avec serre-fils** *f* PRODUCTION saddle clamp terminal; ~ **de batterie** *f* AUTO, ELECTROTEC, PHOTO battery terminal; ~ **de bougie** *f* AUTO spark plug terminal; ~ **de branchement électrique** *f* PRODUCTION wiring terminal; ~ **de branchement secteur** *f* PRODUCTION incoming power terminal; ~ **centrale** *f* AUTO main terminal; ~ **du circuit d'entrée** *f* PRODUCTION *électricité* input circuit terminal; ~ **côté charge** *f* PRODUCTION load terminal; ~ **côté secteur** *f* PRODUCTION line terminal; ~ **de départ** *f* ELECTROTEC output terminal; ~ **de dérivation** *f* ELECTR *raccordement* branch terminal; ~ **du drain** *f* ELECTROTEC drain terminal; ~ **à écrou** *f* ELECTROTEC binding post; ~ **d'entrée** *f* ELECTR *raccordement*, ELECTROTEC input terminal, PRODUCTION line terminal; ~ **d'entrée PTC** *f* PRODUCTION RTD input terminal; ~ **haute tension** *f* AUTO high-tension terminal; ~ **d'incendie** *f* SECURITE pillar fire hydrant; ~ **interactive** *f* TELECOM interactive terminal; ~ **de jonction** *f* ELECTR *câble, raccordement* connecting terminal; ~ **kilométrique** *f* TRANSPORT milestone; ~ **latérale** *f* AUTO side-mounted terminal; ~ **de ligne** *f* ELECTR *raccordement* line terminal; ~ **de masse** *f* ELECTROTEC earth terminal (BrE), ground terminal (AmE); ~ **de mesure** *f* ELECTROTEC test terminal; ~ **de métallisation** *f* PRODUCTION bonding strut; ~ **négative** *f* AUTO, ELECTR *pile*, ELECTROTEC, VEHICULES *système électrique* negative terminal; ~ **négative à la masse** *f* AUTO negative grounded terminal; ~ **neutre** *f* ELECTR *raccordement* neutral terminal; ~ **de phase** *f* ELECTR *raccordement* phase terminal; ~ **positive** *f* AUTO, ELECTR *raccordement*, VEHICULES *accumulateur* positive terminal; ~ **positive à la masse** *f* AUTO positive earthed terminal (BrE), positive grounded terminal (AmE); ~ **à prisonnier** *f* ELECTR *raccordement* captive head terminal; ~ **routière** *f* TRANSPORT road identification sign; ~ **de secondaire** *f* ELECTROTEC secondary terminal; ~ **de sortie** *f* ELECTR, ELECTROTEC output terminal, PRODUCTION load terminal; ~ **de sortie PTC** *f* PRODUCTION RTD output terminal; ~ **de terre** *f* ELECTR earth terminal (BrE), ground terminal (AmE), earthing clip (BrE), grounding clip (AmE), *raccordement* earth clamp (BrE), ground clamp

(AmE), ELECTROTEC, PRODUCTION *électricité* earth terminal (BrE), ground terminal (AmE); ~ **tubulaire** *f* PRODUCTION box lug; ~ **à vis** *f* CINEMAT, PRODUCTION screw terminal; ~ **à vis cruciforme** *f* PRODUCTION captive crosshead terminal screw, crosshead terminal screw

bornéol *m* CHIMIE borneol, bornyl alcohol, camphol

borne-signal *f* CONSTR monument, trig point

bornier *m* PRODUCTION strip, terminal block, terminal strip, termination, *automatisme industriel* power terminal bloc; ~ **de barrage** *m* PRODUCTION *automatisme industriel* terminal barrier strip; ~ **des entrées** *m* PRODUCTION *automatisme industriel* input terminal strip; ~ **de simulation des entrées** *m* PRODUCTION *automatisme industriel* input simulator strip

bornite *f* MINERAUX bornite

bornyle *m* CHIMIE bornyl

borofluorure *m* CHIMIE borofluoride

borosilicate *m* CHIMIE borosilicate, silicoborate

bort *m* PRODUCTION bort

borure *m* CHIMIE boride

bosco *m* NAUT boatswain

boson *m* PHYS PART, PHYSIQUE boson; ~ **de Higgs** *m* PHYS PART Higgs boson; ~ **Z** *m* PHYSIQUE Z-boson, Z-particle

bossage *m* CONS MECA boss, cam, sheave, *d'excentrique* disc (BrE), disk (AmE), MECANIQUE *de came* lobe, VEHICULES *roues* boss; ~ **de came** *m* AERONAUT, AUTO, VEHICULES cam lobe; ~ **de l'excentrique** *m* CONS MECA eccentric disc (BrE), eccentric sheave; ~ **de montage** *m* CONS MECA mounting pad; ~ **de piston** *m* AUTO piston boss

bosse *f* CERAM VER, CONS MECA boss, NAUT painter; ~ **due au gel** *f* CHARBON frost boil; ~ **à échappement** *f* NAUT senhouse slip

bosseler *vt* CONS MECA, MECANIQUE dent

bosselure *f* CONS MECA, MECANIQUE dent

bosser *vt* NAUT *une aussière* stop off

bossette: ~ **d'entrée d'air** *f* AERONAUT air scoop

bosseyeuse *f* MINES *de pilon de bucard* boss

bossoir *m* MECANIQUE *levage* davit, NAUT bow, davit; ~ **d'ancre** *m* NAUT anchor boss; ~ **d'embarcation** *m* TRANSPORT boat launching crane

botryogène *m* MINERAUX botryogen

botryoïde *adj* MINERAUX botryoidal

botte *f* CERAM VER fiber bundle (AmE), fibre bundle (BrE), EMBALLAGE bundle, PRODUCTION *de fil*, RESSORTS coil

botulisme *m* AGRO ALIM botulism

bouc *m* CONS MECA rag wheel

boucanage *m* AGRO ALIM smoking

boucassin *m* CERAM VER warming-in hole

bouchage *m* CERAM VER grinding in of a stopper, stopping, CONS MECA plugging, stopping, CONSTR obstruction, scaling, sealing up, stopping, PRODUCTION stoppage; ~ **par congélation** *m* REFRIG freeze-up; ~ **par gain du point** *m* IMPRIM *impression* plugging; ~ **pour arrêt momentané** *m* PRODUCTION damping down

bouchain *m* NAUT bilge

bouche *f* ACOUSTIQUE mouth, DISTRI EAU plug, HYDROLOGIE *d'un fleuve* mouth, MILITAIRE *d'une arme à feu* muzzle, MINES, NAUT *d'un fleuve*, PRODUCTION *d'un four, d'un convertisseur* mouth; ~ **d'air** *f* REFRIG air terminal device; ~ **artificielle** *f* ACOUSTIQUE artificial mouth; ~ **d'eau** *f* DISTRI EAU hydrant, plug, water hydrant, water plug; ~ **de fleuve** *f* HYDROLOGIE river

mouth; ~ **hydrante** *f* DISTRI EAU hydrant; ~ **d'incendie** *f* CONS MECA fire valve, CONSTR, NAUT, SECURITE, THERMODYN fire hydrant; ~ **porte-mèche** *f* CONS MECA drilling spindle; ~ **de puits** *f* MINES pit mouth, pithead; ~ **de sortie d'oxygène** *f* PRODUCTION oxygen outlet; ~ **de soufflage** *f* AERONAUT aerator; ~ **de ventilation individuelle** *f* AERONAUT aerator

bouché *adj* CONS MECA clogged

bouche-bouteilles *m* EMBALLAGE bottle-corking machine, corking machine

bouchée: ~ **à la reine** *f* AGRO ALIM single portion

bouche-pores *m* COULEURS filler, filler coat

boucher[1] *vt* DISTRI EAU clog, *une voie d'eau* stop, NAUT stop up, *trou* plug, POLLU MER foul, PRODUCTION choke, seal, seal up, stop up, stop

boucher:[2] **se** ~ *v réfl* PRODUCTION choke

bouche-trou *m* PRODUCTION stop gap

bouchon *m* AGRO ALIM bung, CONS MECA internal cylindrical gage (AmE), internal cylindrical gauge (BrE), CONSTR plug, plug gage (AmE), plug gauge (BrE), EMBALLAGE corking plug, EQUIP LAB cork, GEOLOGIE cap, INST HYDR plug, MECANIQUE plug, *véhicules* filler cap, NAUT *de trou* plug, PHOTO *pour objectif* cap, PRODUCTION cylindrical gage (AmE), cylindrical gauge (BrE), plug, *fonderie* boat, bott, TRANSPORT tailback, VEHICULES *de vidange* plug; ~ **d'air** *m* PHYS FLUID airlock; ~ **d'ajout de tige** *m* PETROLE CG, connection gas, trip gas; ~ **anti-éclaboussure** *m* AUTO splash-proof vent cap; ~ **antipoussière** *m* CONS MECA dust cap; ~ **de bouteille** *m* EQUIP LAB cork; ~ **canadien** *m* MINES burn cut, parallel cut, shatter cut; ~ **casquette** *m* CERAM VER mushroom stopper; ~ **de ciment** *m* PETROLE cement plug; ~ **de cimentation** *m* PETROLE cementing plug; ~ **de cimentation inférieur** *m* PETROLE bottom cementing plug; ~ **de cimentation supérieur** *m* PETROLE top cementing plug; ~ **conique** *m* MINES cone cut; ~ **convergent** *m* MINES wedge cut; ~ **coromant** *m* MINES coromant cut; ~ **de coulée** *m* CERAM VER tapout block; ~ **du couvercle de coeur** *m* NUCLEAIRE core head plug unit; ~ **en caoutchouc** *m* EQUIP LAB rubber stopper; ~ **en éventail** *m* MINES fan cut; ~ **en liège** *m* EQUIP LAB cork; ~ **en pyramide** *m* MINES pyramid cut; ~ **en V** *m* MINES V-cut; ~ **en verre** *m* EQUIP LAB glass stopper; ~ **en verre dépoli** *m* EMBALLAGE ground stopper; ~ **de forage sismique** *m* PETROLE shot hole plug; ~ **à gros trous** *m* MINES large hole-cut; ~ **de lavage** *m* PRODUCTION washout plug; ~ **de liège** *m* EQUIP LAB cork; ~ **magnétique** *m* CONS MECA magnetic drain plug; ~ **à mines parallèles** *m* MINES parallel cut, shatter cut; ~ **d'objectif** *m* CINEMAT, PHOTO lens cap; ~ **obturateur** *m* AERONAUT blanking cover, PETROLE plug; ~ **d'obturation de trou de coulée** *m* PRODUCTION boat, bott, plug; ~ **d'oreille** *m* SECURITE ear plug; ~ **parallèle** *m* MINES parallel cut, shatter cut; ~ **plastique** *m* EMBALLAGE plastic plug; ~ **poreux** *m* MATERIAUX *métallurgie* porous plug; ~ **pour la protection de l'ouïe** *m* SECURITE noise protective plug, soundproof plug; ~ **de purge** *m* CONS MECA bleed plug; ~ **pyramidal** *m* MINES pyramid cut; ~ **de radiateur** *m* AUTO pressure cap, radiator cap, radiator pressure cap, VEHICULES *refroidissement* radiator cap; ~ **de remplissage** *m* PRODUCTION filling plug, VEHICULES filler cap; ~ **de remplissage d'huile** *m* AUTO oil filter cap; ~ **de remplissage par gravité** *m* AERONAUT gravity filler plug; ~ **de réservoir** *m* AUTO, MECANIQUE *véhicules*, VEHICULES *carburant, huile* tank cap; ~ **à rodage** *m* EQUIP LAB *verrerie* ground stopper;

~ **supérieur** *m* NUCLEAIRE upper end plug; ~ **de tête de tubage** *m* PETROLE *forage* bradenhead cap for the casing; ~ **à tir de cratère** *m* MINES crater cut; ~ **à tolérance** *m* CONS MECA limit internal gage (AmE), limit internal gauge (BrE), plug gage (AmE), plug gauge (BrE); ~ **à trous parallèles** *m* MINES parallel cut, shatter cut; ~ **de tube** *m* CONS MECA pipe plug; ~ **de turbulence** *m* PHYS FLUID turbulent plug; ~ **utile** *m* IMPRIM *robinets, vidanges* plug; ~ **de valve** *m* VEHICULES *pneu* valve cap; ~ **de vapeur** *m* AUTO vapor lock (AmE), vapour lock (BrE), REFRIG gas lock, TRANSPORT airlock, vapor lock (AmE), vapour lock (BrE); ~ **vaseux** *m* OCEANO silt plug; ~ **de vidange** *m* AUTO, PRODUCTION, VEHICULES *moteur-transmission* drain plug; ~ **de vidange d'huile** *m* AUTO, MECANIQUE, VEHICULES *lubrification* oil drain plug; ~ **à vis** *m* PHOTO screw-on lens cap

bouchon-charrue *m* MINES V-cut

bouclage *m* COMMANDE, ELECTRON feedback, ELECTROTEC terminating, INFORMAT, ORDINAT wraparound; ~ **inertiel Doppler** *m* ESPACE *véhicules* Doppler inertial loop

boucle *f* ACOUSTIQUE, CERAM VER, CINEMAT loop, CONS MECA buckle, buckling, shackle, *d'une courroie* buckle, CONSTR handle, ELECTR antinode, *circuit* loop, *réseau* ring feeder, ELECTRON, ELECTROTEC loop, ENREGISTR tape loop, HYDROLOGIE loop, *d'une rivière* sweep, INFORMAT, NAUT *d'un cordage*, ORDINAT, PETR, PRODUCTION *automatisme industriel* loop, RESSORTS hook, TELECOM loop, loopback, TEXTILE curl, loop, TV tape; ~ **d'accrocheuse** *f* PAPIER festoon, loop; ~ **active** *f* NUCLEAIRE active test loop; ~ **d'amarrage** *f* NAUT ring bolt; ~ **d'ambiance** *f* ENREGISTR presence loop; ~ **d'asservissement** *f* CINEMAT, COMMANDE, TV servoloop; ~ **d'asservissement fermée** *f* COMMANDE closed servoloop; ~ **d'attente** *f* INFORMAT, ORDINAT wait loop; ~ **audio** *f* TELECOM audio loop; ~ **autorestaurée** *f* INFORMAT, ORDINAT self-resetting loop; ~ **de bande** *f* ENREGISTR tape loop; ~ **de bande de papier** *f* INFORMAT paper tape loop; ~ **à blocage de phase** *f* ELECTRON PLL, phase-locked loop; ~ **de contre-réaction** *f* MECANIQUE *régulation* feedback loop; ~ **de Costas** *f* TELECOM Costas loop; ~ **de couplage** *f* ELECTROTEC coupling loop; ~ **de courant** *f* PHYSIQUE current loop; ~ **de détection** *f* TRANSPORT detection loop; ~ **de détection incendie** *f* ESPACE *véhicules* fire detection loop; ~ **de dilatation** *f* REFRIG expansion loop; ~ **de dislocation** *f* CRISTALL dislocation loop; ~ **emboîtée** *f* INFORMAT nested loop; ~ **en pile** *f* NUCLEAIRE in-pile loop; ~ **d'essai active** *f* NUCLEAIRE active test loop; ~ **fermée** *f* AERONAUT, ELECTR *circuit*, ELECTRON closed loop; ~ **d'hystérésis** *f* ELECTR, PHYSIQUE hysteresis loop; ~ **d'hystérésis magnétique** *f* ELECTR magnetic hysteresis loop, *magnétisme* B/H loop; ~ **d'induction magnétique** *f* TELECOM magnetic induction current loop; ~ **inférieure** *f* CINEMAT lower loop; ~ **infinie** *f* ORDINAT infinite loop; ~ **d'irradiation** *f* PHYS RAYON irradiation loop; ~ **à longue distance** *f* TRANSPORT long loop; ~ **de masse** *f* PRODUCTION *électricité* earth loop (BrE), ground loop (AmE); ~ **noyée dans la chaussée** *f* TRANSPORT buried loop, embedded loop; ~ **numérique** *f* TELECOM digital loop; ~ **oméga** *f* TV omega loop; ~ **ouverte** *f* AERONAUT, ELECTR *circuit* open loop; ~ **à phase asservie** *f* ELECTRON PLL, phase-locked loop; ~ **de présence** *f* TRANSPORT presence loop; ~ **de propagation** *f* PETR propagating buckle; ~ **de la qualité** *f* QUALITE quality loop; ~ **de réacteur** *f* NUCLEAIRE in-pile loop, reactor loop; ~ **de régulation** *f* COMMANDE, PRODUCTION regulation loop; ~ **à retard de phase** *f* TELECOM delay lock loop; ~ **de rétroaction** *f* COMMANDE feedback control loop, feedback loop, PRODUCTION feedback loop; ~ **sans fin** *f* CINEMAT continuous loop; ~ **son** *f* ENREGISTR sound loop; ~ **de vapeur** *f* INST HYDR steam loop; ~ **à verrouillage** *f* TELECOM locked loop; ~ **à verrouillage de phase** *f* ESPACE *véhicules*, TELECOM, TV PLL, phase-locked loop; ~ **vidéo** *f* TELECOM video loop; ~ **vissée dans les spires** *f* RESSORTS screwed hook

bouclé *adj* ELECTR *circuit*, TELECOM *circuit* looped

boucle-oeil *f* RESSORTS eyeloop

boucler *vi* CONSTR bulge

boucles: ~ **entrecroisées** *f pl* TEXTILE intermeshed loops; ~ **liées par tricotage** *f pl* TEXTILE meshed loops

boucleur *m* CINEMAT loop former

bouclier *m* CERAM VER end door (BrE), pit door (AmE), CONSTR, ESPACE *thermique*, NUCLEAIRE shield; ~ **ablatif** *m* ESPACE *véhicules spatiaux, thermique* ablation shield; ~ **biologique** *m* NUCLEAIRE biological shield; ~ **continental** *m* GEOLOGIE continental shield; ~ **fixe de canon** *m* MILITAIRE gun shield; ~ **de freinage** *m* ESPACE braking shield; ~ **à graphite** *m* NUCLEAIRE graphite shielding; ~ **de lave** *m* GEOLOGIE Hawaiian-type volcano, lava shield; ~ **de soudeur** *m* SECURITE welder's shield; ~ **thermique** *m* ELECTROTEC thermal shield, ESPACE thermal shield, thermal shroud, *véhicules* thermal shield, THERMODYN thermal shield

boudin *m* CONS MECA flange, CONSTR ovolo, ovolo plane, quarter round; ~ **de dégivrage** *m* AERONAUT de-icer boot; ~ **de roue** *m* CH DE FER wheel flange

boudinage *m* GEOLOGIE boudinage, pinch and swell, PLAST CAOU *plastiques* extrusion

boudine *f* CERAM VER bullion

boudiner *vi* PLAST CAOU extrude

boudineuse *f* EMBALLAGE *pour tubes* extrusion machine, PLAST CAOU extruder, extruding machine, extrusion machine

boue *f* AGRO ALIM sludge, CERAM VER slime, CHARBON slime, slurry, CHIMIE sludge, CONS MECA slurry, CONSTR sludge, DISTRI EAU, HYDROLOGIE slime, sludge, MINES mud, OCEANO mud, ooze, PRODUCTION RECYCLAGE, REFRIG sludge; ~ **activée** *f* HYDROLOGIE, POLLUTION, RECYCLAGE activated sludge; ~ **aérée** *f* PETROLE *forage* aerated mud; ~ **allégée** *f* PETR, PETROLE *forage* aerated mud; ~ **à l'argile** *f* PETROLE clay base mud; ~ **argileuse** *f* PETROLE clay base mud; ~ **à base de chaux** *f* PETROLE *forage* lime-treated mud; ~ **à base d'eau** *f* PETROLE *forage* water base mud; ~ **à base d'huile** *f* PETR, PETROLE *forage* oil-base mud; ~ **brute** *f* RECYCLAGE raw sludge; ~ **calcaire** *f* GEOLOGIE calcareous ooze; ~ **carbonatée** *f* PETROLE *forage* lime mud; ~ **de chaux** *f* CERAM VER lime slurry; ~ **à la chaux** *f* PETROLE lime-treated mud; ~ **colloïdale** *f* PETROLE colloidal mud; ~ **concentrée** *f* CHARBON concentrated sludge; ~ **contaminée** *f* PETROLE contaminated mud; ~ **de démarrage** *f* PETROLE spud mud; ~ **digérée** *f* HYDROLOGIE digested sludge; ~ **à l'eau douce** *f* PETROLE *forage* freshwater mud; ~ **à l'eau salée** *f* PETROLE saltwater mud; ~ **émulsionnée** *f* PETR emulsion mud; ~ **à faible teneur en solides** *f* PETROLE *forage* low-solid mud; ~ **de forage** *f* PETR, PETROLE drilling mud; ~ **de forage à l'eau douce** *f* PETR freshwater drilling mud; ~ **de forage à l'eau salée** *f* PETR saltwater drilling mud; ~

à forte teneur en solides *f* PETROLE *forage* high-solid mud; ~ **fraîche** *f* DISTRI EAU raw sludge, HYDROLOGIE raw sewage, untreated sewage; ~ **glaciaire** *f* HYDROLOGIE glacier mud, glacier silt; ~ **à globigérines** *f* GEOLOGIE *des grands fonds* Globigerina ooze; ~ **d'injection** *f* PETROLE mud fluid; ~ **liquide** *f* CERAM VER slurry; ~ **de meule** *f* PRODUCTION grit, swarf, wheel swarf; ~ **pélagique** *f* GEOLOGIE pelagic ooze; ~ **recyclée et active** *f* HYDROLOGIE activated recycled sludge, activated return sludge; ~ **sèche** *f* PETROLE dry mud; ~ **aux surfactants** *f* PETROLE surfactant mud; ~ **du venturi** *f* CHARBON venturi sludge

bouée *f* NAUT, PETR buoy; ~ **d'amarrage** *f* NAUT mooring buoy; ~ **d'amarrage à point unique** *f* PETROLE ELSBM, exposed location single-buoy mooring; ~ **d'ancre** *f* NAUT anchor buoy; ~ **ancrée** *f* NAUT moored buoy; ~ **de balisage** *f* NAUT marker buoy; ~ **conique** *f* NAUT conical buoy; ~ **de corps mort** *f* NAUT mooring buoy; ~ **couronne** *f* NAUT lifebuoy; ~ **culotte** *f* NAUT breeches buoy; ~ **cylindrique** *f* NAUT can buoy; ~ **dérivante** *f* NAUT drifting buoy; ~ **en fer à cheval** *f* NAUT horseshoe lifebuoy; ~ **à espar** *f* NAUT spar buoy; ~ **extérieure** *f* NAUT sea buoy; ~ **à fuseau** *f* NAUT pillar buoy; ~ **lumineuse** *f* NAUT light buoy; ~ **monoposte** *f* PETROLE ELSBM, exposed location single-buoy mooring, single buoy mooring; ~ **de mouillage** *f* PETR mooring buoy; ~ **océanographique** *f* OCEANO oceanographic buoy; ~ **plate** *f* NAUT can buoy; ~ **radar** *f* TRANSPORT radar marker float; ~ **radiosonore** *f* NAUT radio sonobuoy; ~ **à réflexion de radar** *f* TRANSPORT radar reflector buoy; ~ **sonore à cloche** *f* NAUT bell buoy; ~ **sonore à sifflet** *f* NAUT whistle buoy; ~ **tonne** *f* NAUT barrel buoy, can buoy

bouée-fenzi *f* OCEANO buoyancy compensator

boues *f pl* POLLUTION turbid water; ~ **biologiques** *f pl* HYDROLOGIE biological sludge; ~ **de dragage** *f pl* HYDROLOGIE dredgings; ~ **d'égout** *f pl* RECYCLAGE sewage sludge; ~ **d'égout septique** *f pl* RECYCLAGE septic sludge; ~ **d'épuration** *f pl* DISTRI EAU sewage sludge; ~ **septiques** *f pl* RECYCLAGE septic sludge

bouette *f* OCEANO gurry bait, live bait

bouffant[1] *adj* PAPIER bulky

bouffant[2] *m* IMPRIM, PAPIER bulk (BrE), bulk index (BrE), bulking index (BrE), specific index (AmE), specific volume (AmE)

bouffée *f* NUCLEAIRE burst; ~ **de neutrons** *f* NUCLEAIRE neutron burst; ~ **turbulente** *f* PHYS FLUID turbulent spot

bouge *f* NAUT *de barrot* camber, round, PRODUCTION *de châssis* belly

bougie *f* AUTO, ELECTR *automobile* spark plug, VEHICULES plug, spark plug; ~ **d'allumage** *f* AUTO, MECANIQUE *véhicules*, VEHICULES ignition plug; ~ **antiparasite** *f* AUTO resistor-type spark plug; ~ **chaude** *f* AUTO hot spark plug; ~ **décimale** *f* METROLOGIE decimal candle; ~ **filtrante** *f* NUCLEAIRE filtering candle; ~ **de préchauffage** *f* AUTO glow plug, heat plug, THERMODYN glow plug, heat plug

bougie-mètre *f* PHOTO lux

bougie-pied *f* CINEMAT foot candle, METROLOGIE footcandle

bougniou *m* MINES sink, sump

bougran *m* IMPRIM buckram

bouillant *adj* PHYSIQUE boiling, THERMODYN boiling, scalding

bouilleur *m* AGRO ALIM boiler

bouillie *f* AGRO ALIM slurry, MINES slurry, watergel explosive; ~ **explosive** *f* MINES SBA, slurry-blasting agent, SE, slurry explosive, slurry, watergel explosive; ~ **neigeuse** *f* HYDROLOGIE slush; ~ **pompable** *f* MINES pourable slurry

bouillir[1] *vt* PHYSIQUE, THERMODYN boil

bouillir:[2] ~ **fort** *vi* THERMODYN boil fast; ~ **à gros bouillons** *vi* THERMODYN boil fast; ~ **à petits bouillons** *vi* THERMODYN boil slowly

bouillon *m* CERAM VER blister, PHYSIQUE bubble, PRODUCTION blow; ~ **crevé** *m* CERAM VER broken seed; ~ **de cueillage** *m* CERAM VER gathering bubble; ~ **de débiteuse** *m* CERAM VER debiteuse bubble; ~ **élongé** *m* CERAM VER blibe; ~ **de retassure** *m* CERAM VER vacuum bubble; ~ **de sel** *m* CERAM VER salt bubble; ~ **de sel allongé** *m* CERAM VER gray blibs (AmE), grey blibs (BrE); ~ **de surface** *m* CERAM VER skin blister

bouillonnage *m* CERAM VER bubbling, CHIMIE slugging

bouillonnant *adj* PHYSIQUE bubbling

bouillonnement *m* CHIMIE boiling, PHYSIQUE bubbling

bouillonneur *m* CERAM VER bubbler

bouillotte *f* MAT CHAUFF hot water bottle

boulance *f* CHARBON boil

boulangérite *f* MINERAUX boulangerite

boule *f* CONS MECA bead, IMPRIM pull-in wheel; ~ **de feu primordiale** *f* ASTRONOMIE primeval fireball; ~ **d'hystérésis** *f* METALL hysteresis loop; ~ **à mur** *f* CONSTR wall box; ~ **du passage-papier** *f* IMPRIM *rotative* trolley; ~ **de puddlage** *f* PRODUCTION puddle ball; ~ **de régulateur** *f* CONS MECA ball; ~ **roulante** *f* INFORMAT, ORDINAT trackball

boulet *m* CHARBON ovoid

bouletage *m* CHARBON balling

bouleter *vt* CHARBON ball

boulette *f* CHARBON boulet, pellet

boulin *m* CONSTR putlock, putlog

bouline *f* NAUT *noeud* bowline

boullochage *m* TEXTILE pilling

boullocher *vt* TEXTILE pill

boulon *m* CONS MECA bolt, pin, PRODUCTION, VEHICULES bolt; ~ **d'ancrage** *m* CONS MECA anchor bolt, CONSTR anchor bolt, anchoring bolt, rock dowel, rockbolt, MECANIQUE anchor bolt; ~ **d'assemblage** *m* CONS MECA assembling bolt; ~ **d'attelage** *m* CONS MECA coupling pin, VEHICULES *remorque* drawbar bolt; ~ **avec indication de charge** *m* CONS MECA load-indicating bolt; ~ **carrossier** *m* CONS MECA coach bolt; ~ **de chaîne** *m* CONS MECA chain bolt; ~ **de chape** *m* CONS MECA clevis bolt; ~ **à clavette** *m* CONS MECA cotter bolt, forelock bolt, key bolt; ~ **de courroie** *m* PRODUCTION belt bolt; ~ **creux de raccord** *m* CONS MECA banjo bolt; ~ **à croc** *m* CONS MECA hook block; ~ **à crochet** *m* CONS MECA hook block; ~ **de culasse** *m* AUTO cylinder head bolt; ~ **décolleté** *m* CONS MECA bright bolt; ~ **de dilatation** *m* CONS MECA expansion bolt; ~ **à écrou** *m* CONS MECA screw bolt; ~ **à ergot** *m* PRODUCTION feather-necked bolt, lip bolt; ~ **étrier** *m* NAUT U-bolt; ~ **explosif** *m* ESPACE *pyrotechnie*, MECANIQUE explosive bolt; ~ **à filetage** *m* CONS MECA unified bolt; ~ **fileté** *m* VEHICULES threaded bolt; ~ **de fixation** *m* PRODUCTION holding-down bolt; ~ **de fondation** *m* CONSTR foundation bolt; ~ **libre** *m* CONS MECA in-and-out bolt, through bolt; ~ **mécanicien** *m* CONS MECA machine bolt; ~ **mécanique** *m* CONS MECA machine bolt; ~ **de montage** *m* CONS MECA mounting bolt; ~ **à oeil** *m* CONS MECA banjo bolt, eye-bolt, MECANIQUE, PRODUCTION,

VEHICULES *embrayage* eyebolt; ~ **à oreilles** *m* CONS MECA thumb bolt, wing bolt; ~ **pour courroies** *m* PRODUCTION belt bolt; ~ **prisonnier** *m* CONS MECA standing bolt, stud, stud bolt; ~ **rectifié** *m* CONS MECA machine bolt; ~ **de scellement** *m* CONS MECA stone bolt, PAPIER anchor bolt; ~ **de scellement à crans** *m* CONSTR bar bolt, barbed bolt, bat bolt, bay bolt, jag bolt, jagged bolt, rag bolt, sprig bolt; ~ **de scellement ordinaire** *m* CONSTR fang bolt; ~ **à six pans** *m* CONS MECA hexagonal head bolt; ~ **de soc** *m* CONS MECA plough belt (BrE), plow belt (AmE); ~ **de suspension** *m* CONSTR spring hanger pin; ~ **à T** *m* CONS MECA T-bolt, T-headed bolt, tee bolt; ~ **taraudé** *m* CONS MECA tap bolt; ~ **à tête en biseau** *m* CONSTR bevel-headed bolt; ~ **à tête en goutte-de-suif** *m* CONS MECA button head bolt, mushroom head bolt; ~ **à tête en goutte de suif** *m* CONSTR button head bolt; ~ **à tête en T** *m* CONS MECA hammer drive screw; ~ **tête et écrou 6 pans** *m* CONS MECA hexagon head bolt and hexagon nut; ~ **à tête fraisée** *m* CONSTR countersunk head bolt, countersunk-headed bolt; ~ **à tête hémisphérique** *m* CONS MECA round-head bolt, round-headed bolt; ~ **à tête hexagonale** *m* PRODUCTION hex head bolt; ~ **à tête de marteau** *m* CONS MECA T-bolt, T-headed bolt, tee bolt; ~ **à tête noyée** *m* PRODUCTION flush bolt; ~ **à tête perdue** *m* PRODUCTION flush bolt; ~ **à tête plate** *m* CONS MECA flat-head bolt, flat-headed bolt; ~ **à tête ronde** *m* CONS MECA round-head bolt, round-headed bolt; ~ **à tête ronde fendue** *m* CONS MECA slotted round-head bolt; ~ **de timon** *m* VEHICULES *remorque* drawbar bolt

boulonnage *m* CONS MECA, SECURITE bolting
boulonner *vt* CONSTR, MECANIQUE bolt
boulonnerie *f* CONSTR nut and bolt works; ~ **à tête fendue** *f* CONS MECA slotted head fastener
boulonnière *f* PRODUCTION bolt header
bouniou *m* MINES sinkhole, standage, sump
bourbe *f* AGRO ALIM sludge, MINES mud
bourbier *m* PETROLE mud pit
bourdon *m* IMPRIM out, OCEANO seine staff
bourdonneau *m* CONSTR hook
bourdonnement *m* ACOUSTIQUE hum, TRANSPORT buzz
bourdonnière *f* CONSTR strap
bourlinguer *vt* NAUT make heavy weather
bournonite *f* MINERAUX bournonite, cogwheel ore, wheel ore
bourrage *m* CINEMAT buckle, jam, CONS MECA packing, CONSTR ramming, tamping, ELECTR *câble* filler, ELECTRON jamming, IMPRIM *machine* jam, MINES ramming, stemming, stemming material, tamping material, tamping, *de la cheminée* chute hang-up, clogging, PRODUCTION stuffing, tamping, TELECOM stuffing, traffic padding, TV blocking; ~ **de cartes** *m* INFORMAT card jam; ~ **de piston** *m* CONS MECA piston packing
bourrasque *f* METEO squall; ~ **de neige** *f* METEO snow flurry
bourre *f* CONSTR *d'argile* ram, MINES stemming, stemming material, tamping material, PAPIER fluff, PRODUCTION tamping, TEXTILE staple fiber (AmE), staple fibre (BrE); ~ **d'argile** *f* CONSTR clay tamping; ~ **de coton** *f* PLAST CAOU *charge* cotton linter, PRODUCTION cotton waste
bourrelet *m* CERAM VER bulb edge, CONS MECA bead; ~ **de défense** *m* NAUT rubbing strake; ~ **en caoutchouc** *m* VEHICULES *moteur* rubber weather seal; ~ **glacial** *m* OCEANO ice-pushed ridge; ~ **de rive** *m* OCEANO coastal ridge

bourrelotte *f* CERAM VER stop belt
bourrer *vt* MECANIQUE *de graisse* pack, MINES ram, stem, tamp, PRODUCTION ram, tamp; ~ **une charge de mine** *vt* MINES ram home a charge
bourreur *m* PRODUCTION tamper
bourreuse *f* CH DE FER tamping machine, MINES tamper
bourriche *f* OCEANO bass, fish basket, pad, shellfish basket
bourroir *m* CERAM VER packing stick, CONSTR beater, beating pick, rammer, MINES loading stick, ramming bar, stemmer, stemming rod, stemming stick, tamper, tamping rod, tamping stick, PRODUCTION tamper
boursage *m* OCEANO pursing
boursault *m* PRODUCTION lead dresser
bourseau *m* PRODUCTION lead dresser
boursouflement *m* MINES creep
boursoufler: se ~ *v réfl* MINES creep
boursouflure *f* PAPIER bloating
bousillé *m* (Bel) CERAM VER frigger
boussole *f* AERONAUT, CONSTR, ESPACE, GEOPHYS, MILITAIRE, NAUT, PHYSIQUE compass; ~ **d'arpenteur** *f* CONSTR surveyor's compass, surveyor's dial; ~ **de déclinaison** *f* GEOPHYS variation compass; ~ **d'inclinaison** *f* GEOPHYS dip circle, dip compass; ~ **magnétique** *f* INSTRUMENT magnetic compass; ~ **nivelante** *f* CONSTR leveling compass (AmE), levelling compass (BrE); ~ **de poche** *f* MILITAIRE pocket compass; ~ **du sinus** *f* PHYSIQUE sine galvanometer; ~ **des tangentes** *f* ELECTROTEC, PHYSIQUE tangent galvanometer
Boussole *f* ASTRONOMIE Pyxis
bout:[1] **de ~ en bout** *adj* INFORMAT, ORDINAT end-to-end
bout[2] *m* NUCLEAIRE end fitting, end section, TEXTILE ply; ~ **affranchi** *m* PRODUCTION crop end; ~ **d'arbre conique** *m* CONS MECA conical shaft end; ~ **chanfreiné** *m* RESSORTS chamfered end; ~ **de course** *m* CONS MECA *d'un outil, d'un piston* end of stroke, end of travel; ~ **décollé** *m* RESSORTS detached end; ~ **découpé** *m* RESSORTS trimmed end; ~ **droit** *m* RESSORTS square end; ~ **d'essai** *m* CINEMAT screen test, *développé à la main* slop test; ~ **de fil** *m* ELECTROTEC wire end; ~ **mort** *m* CONS MECA dead end; ~ **de pale** *m* AERONAUT blade tip; ~ **rejeté** *m* CONSTR *de bois* cut end; ~ **renforcé** *m* SECURITE *chaussure de protection* steel toecap; ~ **renforcé en acier** *m* SECURITE *chaussure de protection* steel toecap; ~ **trapézoïdal** *m* RESSORTS diamond point; ~ **de vergue** *m* NAUT yardarm
bout-dehors *m* NAUT bumpkin, *de foc* boom
boutée *f* CONSTR strut
boutefeu *m* CONSTR blasting foreman, MINES blasting foreman, shot firer
bouteille *f* EQUIP LAB reagent bottle, MECANIQUE *air comprimé* cylinder; ~ **d'acétylène** *f* PRODUCTION *outillage* acetylene cylinder, SECURITE acetylene bottle; ~ **d'air** *f* MECANIQUE *air comprimé* air cylinder; ~ **anti-coup de liquide** *f* REFRIG suction line accumulator; ~ **avec capsule à vis** *f* EMBALLAGE screw cap bottle; ~ **à cobalt** *f* CERAM VER cobalt bottle; ~ **consignée** *f* EMBALLAGE deposit bottle, returnable bottle; ~ **de Delf** *f* HYDROLOGIE Delf flask; ~ **en aluminium** *f* EMBALLAGE aluminium bottle (BrE), aluminum bottle (AmE); ~ **en polyéthylène** *f* EMBALLAGE PET bottle; ~ **en polyvinyle chloride** *f* EMBALLAGE PVC bottle; ~ **extincteur** *f* SECURITE fire extinguisher; ~ **extincteur portative** *f* SECURITE portable fire extinguisher; ~ **à filtre** *f* GENIE CHIM filter flask; ~ **à gaz** *f* CONS MECA gas cylinder,

NUCLEAIRE gas bottle, gas cylinder, PRODUCTION gas bottle, gas cylinder; ~ **à gaz transportable** *f* SECURITE transportable gas container; ~ **isolante** *f* CERAM VER vacuum flask; ~ **à jeter** *f* EMBALLAGE one-way bottle; ~ **de Klein** *f* GEOMETRIE *topologie* Klein bottle; ~ **de Leyde** *f* ELECTROTEC Leyden jar; ~ **magnétique** *f* PHYSIQUE magnetic bottle; ~ **non consignée** *f* EMBALLAGE no-return bottle; ~ **non récupérable** *f* CERAM VER single trip bottle; ~ **d'oxygène** *f* ESPACE *véhicules*, PRODUCTION oxygen cylinder; ~ **penchée** *f* CERAM VER leaner; ~ **qui ne répand pas** *f* EMBALLAGE antispill bottle; ~ **recyclée** *f* EMBALLAGE recycled bottle; ~ **soufflée** *f* EMBALLAGE blown bottle; ~ **tampon** *f* REFRIG accumulator, battery, suction accumulator; ~ **tampon échangeur** *f* REFRIG heat exchanger suction accumulator

bouter *vt* CONSTR shoot, MINES dump

bouterolle *f* CONS MECA die bar, CONSTR rivet set, rivet snap, riveting set, set; ~ **à oeil** *f* PRODUCTION eyed rivet snap

bouteur *m* CONSTR, MINES, TRANSPORT bulldozer; ~ **biais** *m* CONSTR angledozer; ~ **inclinable** *m* TRANSPORT tiltdozer (BrE), tilting dozer

boutique *f* CONS MECA set of tools

boutisse *f* CONSTR header

bouton *m* CERAM VER knob, COMMANDE button, CONS MECA knob, CONSTR button, knob, ELECTROTEC button, knob, MECANIQUE knob, PETR button; ~ **affleurant** *m* COMMANDE flush-type push button; ~ **d'arrêt** *m* COMMANDE stop button; ~ **d'avance à main** *m* CINEMAT inching knob; ~ **de blocage** *m* INSTRUMENT locking knob; ~ **de cadrage** *m* CINEMAT framing knob; ~ **de commande du chariot** *m* INSTRUMENT mechanical stage control; ~ **de commande** *m* CINEMAT control knob, COMMANDE control button, control knob, ELECTR *réglage* control knob; ~ **de commande du diaphragme** *m* TV iris control button; ~ **de commande de synchronisme vertical** *m* COMMANDE vertical hold button; ~ **commutateur tournant** *m* COMMANDE rotary switch; ~ **de contact** *m* COMMANDE, ELECTROTEC contact button; ~ **cranté** *m* CONS MECA dented knob; ~ **de déclenchement** *m* CINEMAT release button, COMMANDE activate button, release button, TV release button; ~ **de déclenchement d'obturateur** *m* PHOTO shutter release, shutter release button; ~ **de démarrage** *m* COMMANDE start button, starter button; ~ **de déplacement lent** *m* INSTRUMENT fine adjustment; ~ **de déplacement rapide** *m* INSTRUMENT coarse adjustment; ~ **à deux positions** *m* COMMANDE dual-position button; ~ **à effacer** *m* COMMANDE erase button; ~ **encastré** *m* COMMANDE flush-type push button; ~ **d'enregistrement** *m* ENREGISTR, TV record button; ~ **d'enroulement** *m* PHOTO film winder; ~ **floche** *m* TEXTILE slub; ~ **à friction** *m* CONS MECA *d'un plamer* ratchet stop; ~ **à index** *m* CONS MECA pointer knob; ~ **d'intercommunication** *m* COMMANDE transfer button; ~ **intérieur de condamnation** *m* COMMANDE inner locking button; ~ **d'interrupteur** *m* COMMANDE switch button; ~ **à levier à ailette** *m* PRODUCTION wing lever knob; ~ **de manivelle** *m* CONS MECA crankpin; ~ **de mire** *m* MILITAIRE *d'un fusil* front sight; ~ **de mise en marche** *m* CINEMAT start button; ~ **de mise à l'heure** *m* COMMANDE time setting knob; ~ **de mise au point** *m* CINEMAT focusing knob, GEOPHYS adjusting knob, pinion knob, INSTRUMENT coarse adjustment, PHOTO adjustment knob; ~ **de mise au point de l'oculaire** *m*

INSTRUMENT eyepiece focusing knob; ~ **de mise au point précise** *m* INSTRUMENT fine adjustment; ~ **moleté** *m* CONS MECA milled head, milled knob, INSTRUMENT focus knob, focusing knob; ~ **à olive** *m* CONSTR oval knob; ~ **ovale** *m* CONSTR *serrurerie* oval knob; ~ **de percussion** *m* CONS MECA discharge button; ~ **de porcelaine** *m* CERAM VER porcelain button; ~ **de porte** *m* COMMANDE panel button, panel knob, CONSTR door knob; ~ **pour courroies** *m* PRODUCTION button fastener; ~ **pousser-tourner** *m* COMMANDE push and turn-switch; ~ **pression** *m* COMMANDE press button, push button, TEXTILE press stud; ~ **à pression** *m* COMMANDE press button, push button; ~ **de rallumage réacteur** *m* AERONAUT engine relight push button; ~ **de réglage** *m* CINEMAT control knob, COMMANDE adjusting button, adjusting knob, adjustment button, GEOPHYS, MECANIQUE adjusting knob; ~ **de réglage du diaphragme** *m* PHOTO aperture-setting lever; ~ **de réglage du micromètre** *m* INSTRUMENT micrometer screw; ~ **de réglage du mouvement lent** *m* INSTRUMENT slow-motion control knob; ~ **de réglage de l'ouverture** *m* PHOTO aperture-setting lever; ~ **de réglage de temps de pose** *m* PHOTO speed setting knob; ~ **de réglage de la tonalité** *m* COMMANDE tone control button; ~ **de réglage de vitesse** *m* PHOTO speed setting knob; ~ **de réglage du volume** *m* COMMANDE volume control; ~ **de remise à zéro** *m* CINEMAT reset knob, INFORMAT reset button, TV reset knob; ~ **de restauration** *m* INFORMAT, ORDINAT reset button; ~ **rotatif** *m* ELECTROTEC rotary knob; ~ **de sélection de mode** *m* PRODUCTION *automatisme industriel* mode-setting knob; ~ **de sélection de programme** *m* COMMANDE program selection button (AmE), programme selection button (BrE); ~ **de sonnerie** *m* COMMANDE bell push; ~ **sphérique** *m* CONS MECA ball knob; ~ **tournant** *m* COMMANDE knob, turning knob; ~ **tournant pour sélection** *m* COMMANDE selector switch; ~ **d'urgence** *m* COMMANDE, ELECTR *sécurité* emergency button; ~ **à vernier** *m* COMMANDE vernier knob; ~ **de virage** *m* AERONAUT autopilot turn knob

bouton-flèche *m* CONS MECA pointer knob

boutonnière *f* GEOLOGIE exhumed anticlinal fold

bouton-poussoir *m* CHIMIE push button, COMMANDE press button, push button, ELECTR *commande*, ELECTROTEC, ENREGISTR push button, TELECOM press-button, push button; ~ **à accrochage** *m* PRODUCTION *automatisme industriel* maintained contact push button; ~ **d'avertisseur** *m* COMMANDE horn, horn button, warning button; ~ **concentrique** *m* COMMANDE concentric control button; ~ **à contact momentané** *m* PRODUCTION *automatisme industriel* momentary contact switch; ~ **à fermeture momentanée** *m* PRODUCTION *automatisme industriel* momentary close push button; ~ **à impulsions** *m* PRODUCTION *automatisme industriel* momentary contact push button; ~ **lumineux** *m* PRODUCTION backlit push button, illuminated push button; ~ **piétons** *m* TRANSPORT pedestrian push button; ~ **de réarmement** *m* PRODUCTION *automatisme industriel* reset push button; ~ **de réenclenchement** *m* COMMANDE reset button; ~ **à verrouillage** *m* COMMANDE locking push button

bouveau *m* MINES crosscut, rock drift, stone drift, gallery in dead ground

bouveleur *m* CHARBON stoneman

bouvet: ~ à approfondir *m* CONSTR plough (BrE), plough plane (BrE), plow (AmE), plow plane (AmE); ~ **de**

deux pièces *m* CONSTR plough (BrE), plough plane (BrE), plow (AmE), plow plane (AmE); ~ **en deux morceaux** *m* CONSTR matching planes, tonguing-and-grooving planes; ~ **femelle** *m* CONSTR grooving plane; ~ **à joindre** *m* CONSTR matching plane; ~ **à languette** *m* CONSTR tonguing plane; ~ **mâle** *m* CONSTR tonguing plane; ~ **à rainure** *m* CONSTR grooving plane

bouveter *vt* CONSTR match

Bouvier *m* ASTRONOMIE Boötes

bovette *f* MINES crosscut, rock drift, stone drift

bowénite *f* MINERAUX bowenite

bowette *f* MINES crosscut, rock drift, waste drive, gallery in dead ground, stone drift

bowetteur *m* CHARBON stoneman

bowlingite *f* MINERAUX bowlingite

bow-string *m* CONSTR bowstring bridge

box-tilts *m pl* IMPRIM *rotatives* box tilts

boyau *m* AGRO ALIM casing, PRODUCTION hose; ~ **d'accouplement** *m* CH DE FER *véhicules* coupling hose; ~ **de mine** *m* MINES breakthrough

BPS *abrév (bits par seconde)* ORDINAT BPS *(bits per second)*

Bq *abrév (becquerel)* METROLOGIE, PHYS RAYON, PHYSIQUE Bq *(becquerel)*

Br *(brome)* CHIMIE Br *(bromine)*

brachystocrone *f* GEOMETRIE brachistochrone

bracon *m* DISTRI EAU diagonal brace

brai *m* CHIMIE tar, CONSTR pitch; ~ **de pétrole** *m* CONSTR pitch; ~ **de pétrole fluxé** *m* CONSTR cutback

braise *f* CERAM VER cooling-down period, CHARBON breeze

bran: ~ **de scie** *m* CONSTR sawdust

branche *f* CONS MECA prong, *d'une tenaille* handle, CONSTR leaf, shackle, stem, strap, *d'un cadenas* bow, *d'une clef* shank, *d'une fourche* tine, ELECTROTEC, INFORMAT *circuit* branch, INSTRUMENT side, NUCLEAIRE leg, ORDINAT *circuit*, PHYSIQUE branch; ~ **acoustique** *f* PHYSIQUE acoustic branch; ~ **articulée** *f* PHOTO foldover leg; ~ **de compas mâle** *f* AERONAUT lower link of rotor shaft; ~ **conjuguée** *f* ELECTROTEC conjugate branch; ~ **coulissante** *f* PHOTO sliding leg, telescopic leg; ~ **à coulisse** *f* PHOTO sliding leg; ~ **droite** *f* PHOTO rigid leg; ~ **mutuelle** *f* ELECTR *réseau*, ELECTROTEC common branch; ~ **optique** *f* PHYSIQUE optical branch; ~ **de pied** *f* PHOTO tripod leg; ~ **du pont** *f* INSTRUMENT bridge arm; ~ **principale** *f* NUCLEAIRE main leg; ~ **de trépied** *f* CINEMAT tripod leg; ~ **vent arrière** *f* AERONAUT downwind leg; ~ **vent rabattant** *f* AERONAUT downwind leg

branché *adj* CONS MECA, ELECTR *circuit* connected, PHYSIQUE connected, live; ~ **sur le secteur** *adj* ELECTR *installation* connected to the electrical network (AmE), connected to the mains (BrE)

branchement *m* CH DE FER turnout, CONSTR branch, branch pipe, DISTRI EAU branching, ELECTR *alimentation pour le consommateur* line connection, *enroulement* tap, *raccordement* tapping, *réseau pour le consommateur* supply service, ELECTRON branch, ELECTROTEC connection, switch, tap, INFORMAT, ORDINAT jump, *de programme* branch, PHYSIQUE branching, connection; ~ **d'abonné** *m* ELECTROTEC service line; ~ **conditionnel** *m* ORDINAT conditional branch; ~ **en courbe** *m* CH DE FER turnout on the curve; ~ **en parallèle** *m* ELECTROTEC parallel arrangement; ~ **en série** *m* ELECTROTEC series arrangement, MINES series connection; ~ **inconditionnel** *m* INFORMAT, ORDI-NAT unconditional branch; ~ **par cosses à fiches** *m* PRODUCTION stab termination; ~ **spécial** *m* CH DE FER special turnout

brancher *vt* CINEMAT connect, patch, plug in, turn-on, CONSTR *tuyau* branch, branch off, ELECTROTEC connect, INFORMAT, ORDINAT branch, connect, PHYSIQUE connect, TV patch, plug in, switch on

brandisite *f* MINERAUX brandisite

braquage *m* VEHICULES *direction* steering circle, steering lock; ~ **d'ailerons** *m* AERONAUT aileron deflection; ~ **de profondeur** *m* AERONAUT elevator deflection; ~ **du train avant** *m* AERONAUT nose gear steering

bras *m* CONS MECA *d'une manivelle* web, MATH *d'un instrument* limb, MINES *d'une bobine* horn, NAUT guy, *d'ancre* arm, PAPIER, PETR arm; ~ **d'accès** *m* INFORMAT seek arm, ORDINAT access arm, seek arm; ~ **d'ancre** *m* NAUT anchor arm; ~ **articulé** *m* CINEMAT flexi arm; ~ **à bornes pivotant** *m* PRODUCTION terminal swing arm; ~ **de câblage** *m* PRODUCTION *automatisme industriel* wiring arm; ~ **de câblage extérieur** *m* PRODUCTION field wiring arm; ~ **de commande de pas** *m* AERONAUT pitch control arm; ~ **cryotechnique** *m* ESPACE cryotechnic arm; ~ **érecteur télescopique** *m* CONSTR telescopic erector arm; ~ **d'essuie-glace** *m* VEHICULES *accessoire* wiper arm; ~ **d'excentrage** *m* PETR excentering arm; ~ **extérieur** *m* PRODUCTION swing arm; ~ **d'extracteur** *m* CERAM VER takeout arm; ~ **à gradient de pesanteur** *m* ESPACE *véhicules* gravity gradient boom; ~ **d'une grue** *m* CINEMAT jib; ~ **de lecture** *m* ACOUSTIQUE pick-up arm; ~ **de levier** *m* CONS MECA lever arm, leverage of a force, moment arm, CONSTR lever arm; ~ **de levier de redressement** *m* NAUT righting lever, righting lever arm; ~ **de manivelle** *m* AUTO crank arm, CONS MECA crank arm, crank cheek, crankweb; ~ **de mer** *m* NAUT firth, sea loch; ~ **de mise à l'arche** *m* CERAM VER stacker arm; ~ **mort** *m* DISTRI EAU cutoff, HYDROLOGIE backwater, oxbow; ~ **oblique** *m* VEHICULES *essieu arrière* semitrailing arm; ~ **oscillant longitudinal** *m* VEHICULES *suspension* trailing arm; ~ **oscillant transversal** *m* VEHICULES *suspension* transverse control arm; ~ **de pickup** *m* ENREGISTR pick-up arm; ~ **pivotant** *m* INSTRUMENT swivel arm, PRODUCTION wiring arm; ~ **pivotant pour les échantillons** *m* NUCLEAIRE sample swivel arm; ~ **porte fusée** *m* AUTO wheel suspension lever; ~ **porte-outils oscillant** *m* CONS MECA floating bush; ~ **porte-profil** *m* PRODUCTION spindle arm; ~ **de réactance** *m* PHYSIQUE stub; ~ **de renvoi** *m* AUTO idler arm; ~ **robotisé** *m* PRODUCTION *automatisme industriel* robotic arm; ~ **rotatif** *m* POLLU MER rotatable arm; ~ **de signal** *m* COMMANDE signal arm; ~ **spiral** *m* ASTRONOMIE *d'une galaxie* spiral arm; ~ **spiral dans le Sagittaire** *m* ASTRONOMIE *de la Galaxie* Sagittarius arm; ~ **support** *m* CONS MECA overarm machine; ~ **de support horizontal** *m* INSTRUMENT horizontal arm, horizontal base; ~ **de suspension** *m* AUTO suspension arm, VEHICULES control arm; ~ **tangentiel** *m* ENREGISTR tangential arm; ~ **télémanipulateur** *m* ESPACE remote manipulator arm; ~ **télescopique** *m* CINEMAT telescopic arm; ~ **de tension** *m* INFORMAT, ORDINAT tension arm; ~ **d'un treuil** *m* AERONAUT jib

brasage *m* CONSTR brazing, soldering, MAT CHAUFF, PRODUCTION, SECURITE, THERMODYN brazing; ~ **au bain salin** *m* CONSTR salt bath brazing; ~ **au bain de sel** *m* CONSTR salt bath brazing; ~ **fort** *m* ESPACE, PRODUCTION hard soldering; ~ **fort par trempage** *m* CONSTR dip brazing; ~ **aux gaz** *m* CONSTR torch brazing; ~ **par**

fusion *m* ESPACE *véhicules* brazing; ~ **par induction à haute fréquence** *m* CONSTR high-frequency induction brazing; ~ **par trempage** *m* CONSTR dip brazing; ~ **sous vide** *m* CONSTR vacuum brazing; ~ **tendre** *m* ELECTR *raccordement*, PRODUCTION *raccordement* soft soldering

brasé *adj* THERMODYN brazed

brasement *m* CONSTR soldering, PRODUCTION, SECURITE brazing

braser *vt* CONS MECA braze, CONSTR solder, MECANIQUE, PRODUCTION *scie à ruban*, THERMODYN braze

bras-poussoir *m* CERAM VER ware pusher

brassage *m* AERONAUT cranking, AGRO ALIM mashing, PRODUCTION rabbling; ~ **à l'arc** *m* PRODUCTION arc brazing

brasse *f* NAUT, OCEANO fathom

brasser *vt* GENIE CHIM agitate, NAUT brace, TV patch

brasserie *f* AGRO ALIM brewing

brasseur *m* GENIE CHIM agitating machine, agitator, TELECOM cross-connect unit; ~ **de modes** *m* OPTIQUE, TELECOM mode mixer; ~ **de réseau à haut débit ATM** *m* TELECOM high bit-rate ATM network mixer

brasseur-répartiteur: ~ **numérique** *m* TELECOM DXC, digital cross-connect

brassiage *m* OCEANO sounding, water clearance

brassière: ~ **de sauvetage** *f* NAUT life jacket

brasure *f* CONSTR brass solder, PRODUCTION brazing solder, hard soldering, SECURITE brazing solder; ~ **douce** *f* PRODUCTION soft brass solder, soft-brazing solder; ~ **tendre** *f* PRODUCTION soft brass solder, soft-brazing solder

braunite *f* MINERAUX braunite

break *m* TRANSPORT shooting brake

brèche *f* ASTRONOMIE breccia, CONS MECA, CONSTR gap, DISTRI EAU breach, PETR breccia; ~ **diamantifère** *f* GEOLOGIE blueground; ~ **d'explosion volcanique** *f* GEOLOGIE explosion breccia; ~ **de friction** *f* GEOLOGIE crush breccia; ~ **volcanique à gros fragments** *f* GEOLOGIE agglomerate

bréchique *adj* GEOLOGIE autoclastic

bredindin *m* NAUT Spanish burton

bréguet *m* CONS MECA dog hook sling

breithauptite *f* MINERAUX breithauptite

brêler *vt* NAUT make fast

bremsstrahlung *f* PHYS RAYON, PHYSIQUE bremsstrahlung

brésiline *f* CHIMIE brasilin

bretelle *f* AERONAUT feeder line, CH DE FER scissor crossing, CONS MECA brace; ~ **de raccordement** *f* PRODUCTION drop line wiring, *automatisme industriel* drop line

bretzel *m* GEOMETRIE *topologie* pretzel

breunérite *f* MINERAUX breunnerite

brevet *m* BREVETS, CONS MECA patent; ~ **antérieur** *m* BREVETS prior patent; ~ **de capitaine** *m* NAUT master's certificate; ~ **dépendant** *m* BREVETS dependent patent; ~ **européen** *m* BREVETS European patent; ~ **d'invention** *m* BREVETS, CONS MECA patent; ~ **national** *m* BREVETS national patent; ~ **de perfectionnement** *m* BREVETS improvement patent, CONS MECA patent of improvement; ~ **régional** *m* BREVETS regional patent

brevetabilité *f* BREVETS patentability

breveté *adj* CONS MECA patented

brewstérite *f* MINERAUX brewsterite

bribe *f* ESPACE chip

bricole *f* CERAM VER sling

bridage *m* PRODUCTION clamping; ~ **à chaud** *m* RESSORTS hot clamping; ~ **à froid** *m* RESSORTS cold clamping; ~ **magnétique** *m* CONS MECA magnetic holding

bride *f* CONS MECA collar, cramp, flange, *de ressort à lames* buckle, buckling, *ressort* clamp, ELECTR clamp, *raccordement* flange, ELECTROTEC, MECANIQUE flange, NUCLEAIRE gland, stuffing box lid, PETR bridle, PETROLE *canalisation* flange, PRODUCTION clamp, strap, *d'un cylindre* flange, *d'un tube* flange, TEXTILE bar, VEHICULES *roue* flange; ~ **d'accouplement** *f* MECANIQUE coupling flange; ~ **d'assemblage** *f* ESPACE *véhicules*, POLLU MER flange; ~ **aveugle** *f* MECANIQUE blank; ~ **de câble armé** *f* ELECTR armor clamp (AmE), armour clamp (BrE); ~ **à capote** *f* CONS MECA G-clamp, G-cramp, cramp; ~ **centrale** *f* VEHICULES *suspension, ressort à lames* U-bolt; ~ **à collet** *f* CONS MECA neck flange; ~ **dressée sur face** *f* PRODUCTION faced flange; ~ **de fixation** *f* INSTRUMENT cradle; ~ **de fixation du radiateur** *f* AUTO radiator flange; ~ **de liaison** *f* ESPACE *véhicules* connecting flange; ~ **à moyeu** *f* CONS MECA hub-type flange; ~ **à moyeu lisse** *f* CONS MECA plain hub flange; ~ **d'obturation** *f* CONS MECA blind flange; ~ **à piège** *f* ELECTROTEC choke flange; ~ **pleine** *f* CONS MECA blank flange, blind flange; ~ **pour tuyaux flexibles** *f* CONS MECA hose clip; ~ **du ressort** *f* CONS MECA *pour ressort à lames superposées* spring band, spring buckle; ~ **de retenue de bague de guidage** *f* CONS MECA guide clamp; ~ **de serrage** *f* CONS MECA clamp, cramp; ~ **de serrage à vis sans fin** *f* CONS MECA worm-drive clamp; ~ **soudée** *f* RESSORTS welded buckle; ~ **de terre** *f* ELECTROTEC earthing strip (BrE), grounding strip (AmE)

bridé *adj* PRODUCTION clamped

brider[1] *vt* PRODUCTION *tuyaux* clamp together

brider:[2] **se** ~ *v réfl* PRODUCTION clamp together

brigade *f* ESPACE *communications* shift

brigadier: ~ **de manoeuvre** *m* CH DE FER foreman shunter

brillance *f* ELECTRON brightness, brilliance, IMPRIM *impression* brightness, OPTIQUE brightness, radiance, TEXTILE luster (AmE), lustre (BrE); ~ **de l'écran** *f* NAUT display brilliance

brillancemètre *m* PLAST CAOU *peintures* gloss meter

brillant[1] *adj* CINEMAT, IMPRIM, PLAST CAOU glossy, TEXTILE bright

brillant[2] *m* IMPRIM gloss, *impression* brightness, MATERIAUX, PAPIER gloss, PLAST CAOU gloss, *peinture* high gloss, PRODUCTION glossiness, TEXTILE sheen; ~ **de l'encre** *m* IMPRIM ink gloss; ~ **supérieur** *m* IMPRIM *impression* full gloss

brillantage *m* PRODUCTION brightening

brin *m* PHYSIQUE, PRODUCTION strand, TEXTILE hair; ~ **conducteur** *m* PRODUCTION driving side; ~ **conduit** *m* PRODUCTION idle side, slack length, slack portion, *de transmission* slack side; ~ **lâche** *m* PRODUCTION idle side, slack length, slack portion, *de transmission* slack side; ~ **libre** *m* PRODUCTION *de palan* free end; ~ **menant** *m* PRODUCTION driving side; ~ **mené** *m* PRODUCTION idle side, slack length, slack portion, *de transmission* slack side; ~ **moteur** *m* PRODUCTION driving side; ~ **mou** *m* PRODUCTION idle side, slack length, slack portion, *de transmission* slack side; ~ **tendu** *m* PRODUCTION driving side

brins: ~ **cassés** *m pl* TEXTILE projecting hairs

brion *m* NAUT forefoot

brique *f* CERAM VER, CONSTR brick; ~ **d'aération en verre** *f* CERAM VER glass ventilating brick; ~ **d'aluminosili-**

cate *f* MAT CHAUFF *four* aluminosilicate brick; ~ **de bois** *f* CONSTR wood brick; ~ **boutisse** *f* CONSTR header; ~ **de brûleur** *f* MAT CHAUFF burner brick; ~ **de carbone** *f* MAT CHAUFF carbon brick; ~ **de chamotte** *f* THERMODYN firebrick; ~ **à couteau** *f* CONSTR arch brick, feather-edged brick, gage brick (AmE), gauge brick (BrE); ~ **couvre-goulotte** *f* CERAM VER cover tile (BrE), spout cover (AmE); ~ **couvre-goulotte avec bec** *f* CERAM VER lipped cover tile (BrE), seal block (AmE); ~ **creuse** *f* CONSTR perforated brick; ~ **creuse en verre** *f* CERAM VER hollow glass block; ~ **crue** *f* CERAM VER adobe, sun-dried brick, clay brick, cob brick, CONSTR dried brick, sun-dried brick; ~ **cuite** *f* CONSTR burned brick; ~ **de diatomite** *f* CHAUFFAGE *isolation* diatomaceous brick; ~ **dinas** *f* CERAM VER dinas brick; ~ **de dolomie** *f* CONSTR dolomite brick; ~ **émaillée** *f* CONSTR glazed brick; ~ **d'empilage** *f* CERAM VER checker brick; ~ **en argile à feu** *f* EQUIP LAB *four* fireclay brick; ~ **fonctionnelle** *f* CERAM VER light-directing block; ~ **hollandaise** *f* CERAM VER clinker brick; ~ **intérieure de goulotte** *f* CERAM VER goal post (AmE), inside jamb block (BrE); ~ **isolante** *f* CHAUFFAGE insulating brick; ~ **de magnésite** *f* CONSTR magnesite brick; ~ **de main** *f* CERAM VER edger block (AmE), jamb block (BrE); ~ **de parement** *f* CONSTR facing brick; ~ **placée en parement** *f* CONSTR stretcher; ~ **pleine** *f* CONSTR solid brick; ~ **réfractaire** *f* CERAM VER, CONSTR firebrick, EQUIP LAB *four* refractory brick, MAT CHAUFF burner brick, firebrick, refractory brick, MATERIAUX *construction*, THERMODYN firebrick; ~ **séchée au soleil** *f* THERMODYN unburnt brick; ~ **de seuil** *f* CERAM VER sill block; ~ **simple** *f* CERAM VER glass brick; ~ **vernissée** *f* CONSTR glazed brick; ~ **vitrifiée** *f* GENIE CHIM clinker

briquet *m* CHAUFFAGE lighter, CONSTR flap hinge
briquetage *m* CONSTR brickwork
briqueter *vt* CONSTR brick, brick up
briqueterie *f* CERAM VER brick works, CONSTR brick field
briqueteur *m* CONSTR bricklayer
briqueton *m* CONSTR bat
briquette *f* CHARBON briquette; ~ **de composition** *f* CERAM VER briquette; ~ **de ferro-alliage** *f* MATERIAUX ferroalloy briquette
brisance *f* MINES brisance
brisant[1] *adj* MINES disruptive
brisant[2] *m* GEOLOGIE shoal, NAUT breaker, reef, shoal, OCEANO *vague* breaker, breaking wave
brise *f* METEO breeze; ~ **établie** *f* NAUT steady breeze; ~ **folle** *f* METEO baffling wind; ~ **du large** *f* METEO sea breeze; ~ **légère** *f* METEO gentle breeze, light breeze; ~ **de mer** *f* METEO sea breeze; ~ **de montagne** *f* METEO mountain breeze; ~ **de terre** *f* METEO, NAUT land breeze; ~ **de vallée** *f* METEO valley breeze
brise-béton *m* CONSTR concrete breaker
brise-copeau: ~ **meulé** *m* CONS MECA ground-in cutting rake
brise-copeaux *m* CONS MECA chip breaker
brise-glace *m* MILITAIRE, NAUT icebreaker
brise-lames *m* CONSTR, DISTRI EAU breakwater, NAUT breakwater, mole, OCEANO breakwater
briser[1] *vt* SECURITE break
briser:[2] **se** ~ *v réfl* CONSTR break
brise-roche *m* CONSTR rock breaker
briseur: ~ **d'émulsion** *m* POLLUTION emulsion breaker
brise-vent *m* METEO wind break
brisis *m* CONSTR *d'un comble* break

brisou *m* MINES marsh gas
bristol *m* PAPIER ivory board
brisure *f* CONS MECA offset, CONSTR *d'une charnière* break; ~ **de bord d'attaque** *f* AERONAUT leading edge glove; ~ **de riz** *f* AGRO ALIM broken rice
broc: ~ **en verre** *m* CERAM VER glass jug
brocart *m* TEXTILE brocade
brocatelle *f* MINERAUX brocatel, brocatello
brochage *m* CONS MECA broaching, drifting, MECANIQUE broaching
brochantite *f* MINERAUX brochantite
broche *f* CONS MECA arbor, drift, drift pin, driver, spindle, CONSTR drill pin, pin, pintle, spike, spike nail, stem, *d'une serrure* broach, *d'une charnière* pin, ELECTROTEC pin, MECANIQUE broaching tool, pin, spindle, PRODUCTION pricker, prod, *d'une plaque de fond, d'un moule en terre* dabber, pin, TELECOM bank contact; ~ **d'alésage** *f* CONS MECA *d'une aléseuse*, MECANIQUE boring spindle; ~ **d'assemblage** *f* CONS MECA drift, drift pin, driver; ~ **à billes circulantes** *f* CONS MECA circulating ball spindle; ~ **de câble de déclenchement** *f* MILITAIRE *parachute* rip pin; ~ **de charnière** *f* CONS MECA, CONSTR hinge pin; ~ **conique** *f* CONS MECA carrot wedge; ~ **de contact** *f* ELECTROTEC contact pin; ~ **de coulée** *f* PRODUCTION gate pin, gate stick, runner stick, runner pin, sprue; ~ **de déchassage** *f* CONS MECA center key (AmE), centre key (BrE), drift; ~ **à denture rapportée** *f* CONS MECA inserted tooth broach; ~ **à ergot de train** *f* AERONAUT landing gear lock pin; ~ **d'évent** *f* PRODUCTION riser pin, riser stick; ~ **de fermeture de câble automatique** *f* MILITAIRE static pin; ~ **de guidage** *f* MECANIQUE guide pin; ~ **de machine** *f* CERAM VER spindle; ~ **de machine-outil** *f* CONS MECA machine tool spindle; ~ **à mâchoires** *f* PRODUCTION clamping pin; ~ **de navette** *f* TEXTILE shuttle spindle; ~ **porte-fraise** *f* CONS MECA cutter arbor, milling machine arbor, PRODUCTION milling machine arbor, milling machine cutter arbor; ~ **porte-meule** *f* CONS MECA grinding spindle; ~ **de réglage** *f* COMMANDE adjusting spindle; ~ **type à moyeu** *f* CONS MECA hub-type spindle; ~ **de verrouillage** *f* CONS MECA locking pin
broché *adj* IMPRIM soft-bound, stitched
brocher *vt* IMPRIM bind
brocheuse *f* CONS MECA broaching machine; ~ **automatique sans couture** *f* IMPRIM perfect binder
bromal *m* CHIMIE bromal
bromargyrite *f* MINERAUX bromargyrite, bromite, bromyrite
bromate *m* CHIMIE bromate
bromatologie *f* AGRO ALIM food science
brome *m* (*Br*) CHIMIE bromine *(Br)*
broméline *f* AGRO ALIM bromelain
bromhydrate *m* CHIMIE hydrobromide
bromhydrique *adj* CHIMIE hydrobromic
bromique *adj* CHIMIE bromic
bromlite *f* MINERAUX bromlite
bromoacétique *adj* CHIMIE bromoacetic
bromoacétone *m* CHIMIE bromoacetone
bromobenzène *m* CHIMIE bromobenzene
bromoforme *m* CHIMIE bromoform
bromophénol *m* CHIMIE bromophenol
bromure *m* CHIMIE bromide, IMPRIM *composition* bromide print, glossy print, *surfaces sensibles* resin-coated paper, LESSIVES, PHOTO bromide; ~ **d'argent** *m* CHIMIE silver bromide; ~ **de décylique** *m* CHIMIE decyl bromide; ~ **de méthyle** *m* CHIMIE methyl bro-

mide

bronzage *m* IMPRIM *finition* bronzing

bronze *m* CHIMIE bronze; ~ **d'aluminium** *m* MECANIQUE *matériaux* aluminium bronze (BrE), aluminum bronze (AmE); ~ **à canon** *m* MATERIAUX, MILITAIRE gunmetal; ~ **coulé** *m* MECANIQUE *matériaux* cast bronze; ~ **en poudre** *m* COULEURS bronze pigment; ~ **au manganèse** *m* CHIMIE manganese bronze; ~ **phosphoreux** *m* CHIMIE, ELECTR, ELECTROTEC phosphor bronze; ~ **pour robinetterie** *m* CONSTR cock brass, cock metal; ~ **au zinc** *m* MECANIQUE *matériaux* gunmetal

bronzite *f* MINERAUX bronzite

brookite *f* MINERAUX brookite

broquette *f* CONS MECA tack

brosse *f* CONSTR broom, brush, MECANIQUE *outillage*, PAPIER brush; ~ **d'acier rotative** *f* PAPIER rotary wire brush; ~ **à badigeon** *f* COULEURS flat brush, whitewash brush; ~ **dite moignon** *f* PRODUCTION mop-end brush; ~ **en fil de fer** *f* PRODUCTION wire brush; ~ **à nettoyer** *f* IMPRIM cleaning brush; ~ **rotative** *f* PAPIER jacket brush, rotary brush; ~ **à son** *f* AGRO ALIM bran finisher; ~ **à tubes** *f* EQUIP LAB *nettoyage* tube brush

brosseuse: ~ **pour couché** *f* PAPIER brush polishing machine

brouettage *m* CONSTR barrowing

brouette *f* CONSTR barrow, hand barrow, wheelbarrow

brouettée *f* CONSTR barrowful, barrowload

brouillage *m* ELECTRON atmospherics, jamming, ESPACE *communications* interference, MILITAIRE jamming, scrambling, TELECOM breakthrough, interference, jamming, TV interference, noise; ~ **entre symboles** *m* TELECOM intersymbol interference; ~ **intentionnel** *m* TELECOM jamming; ~ **intersymbole** *m* TELECOM intersymbol interference; ~ **numérique** *m* TELECOM digital interference; ~ **radar** *m* NAUT clutter, radar interference; ~ **RF** *m* TV RF interference; ~ **solaire** *m* ESPACE *communications* sun interference

brouillard *m* IMPRIM *impression* fog, PETROLE, POLLUTION mist, REFRIG fog; ~ **acide** *m* POLLUTION acid fog; ~ **artificiel** *m* MILITAIRE smoke screen; ~ **d'encre** *m* IMPRIM misting; ~ **d'huile** *m* IMPRIM *lubrification* oil mist; ~ **mouillant** *m* METEO damp fog, wet fog; ~ **photochimique oxydant** *m* POLLUTION photochemical smog; ~ **salin** *m* COULEURS *épreuve pour peinture* salt spray, ESSAIS *essai de corrosion* salt mist

brouiller *vt* MILITAIRE, TELECOM jam

brouilleur *m* ELECTRON jammer, MILITAIRE jammer, scrambler telephone; ~ **de modes** *m* OPTIQUE mode mixer; ~ **numérique linéaire de la voix** *m* TELECOM linear digital voice scrambler; ~ **de parole** *m* TELECOM speech scrambler

brouillon *m* IMPRIM *prémaquette* scratch

broussailles *f pl* CONSTR brush

broutage *m* PRODUCTION chattering

broutement *m* ACOUSTIQUE grazing, PRODUCTION chattering; ~ **de l'embrayage** *m* AUTO grabbing clutch

brouter *vi* PRODUCTION chatter

broyabilité *f* GENIE CHIM grindability

broyage *m* CHARBON grinding, milling, CHIMIE grinding, GENIE CHIM breaking, comminution, milling, size reduction, METALL grinding, MINES crushing, grinding, milling, NUCLEAIRE comminution, PAPIER breaking, milling, PLAST CAOU *procédé* crushing, PRODUCTION grinding; ~ **au bocard** *m* PRODUCTION stamp milling; ~ **à boulets** *m* CHARBON ball milling; ~ **en circuit fermé** *m* CHARBON closed-circuit grinding; ~ **fin** *m* CHARBON fine grinding, PRODUCTION fine crushing; ~ **grossier** *m* CHARBON primary grinding, MINES coarse crushing, primary crushing; ~ **humide** *m* CHARBON wet grinding; ~ **des minéraux d'uranium** *m* NUCLEAIRE uranium milling; ~ **moyen** *m* PRODUCTION medium grinding; ~ **primaire** *m* CHARBON coarse grinding; ~ **à sec** *m* CHARBON dry crushing; ~ **secondaire** *m* CHARBON secondary grinding

broyage-dissolution *m* NUCLEAIRE grind and leach process

broyer *vt* AGRO ALIM crush, mill, pound, CHARBON crush, grind, CHIMIE grind, CONSTR crush, GENIE CHIM grind, PRODUCTION grind, mill

broyeur *m* AGRO ALIM disintegrator, grinder, CHARBON chat roller, crusher, crusher, CONS MECA breaker, grinding machine, CONSTR crusher, GENIE CHIM breaker, crushing mill, grinding mill, HYDROLOGIE comminutor, PAPIER beater-breaker, breaker, crushing mill, kneader pulper, PRODUCTION crusher, mill; ~ **à anneau cylindrique** *m* CHARBON ring roll crusher; ~ **à anneau de mouture** *m* CHARBON roller crusher; ~ **à barre** *m* CHARBON rod mill; ~ **à billes** *m* CHARBON, GENIE CHIM, PLAST CAOU *matériel* ball mill; ~ **à boules** *m* GENIE CHIM, PLAST CAOU *matériel* ball mill; ~ **à boules Fuller-Bonot** *m* CHARBON Fuller-Bonot mill; ~ **à boulets** *m* AGRO ALIM, CERAM VER, CHARBON, EQUIP LAB *préparation*, GENIE CHIM, MINES ball mill; ~ **bowl-mill** *m* CHARBON bowl mill crusher; ~ **à cascade** *m* CHARBON cascade mill; ~ **centrifuge** *m* GENIE CHIM centrifugal crusher, centrifuge mill; ~ **à ciment** *m* CONSTR cement mill; ~ **à coke** *m* CHARBON coke mill; ~ **à compartiments** *m* CHARBON compartment mill; ~ **conique** *m* CHARBON conical mill; ~ **à cylindres** *m* GENIE CHIM crushing roll, fine crushing mill, PRODUCTION crushing roll; ~ **cylindrique** *m* CHARBON tube mill; ~ **à disque** *m* AGRO ALIM, CHARBON disc mill (BrE), disk mill (AmE); ~ **d'émail** *m* CERAM VER glaze grinder; ~ **des fins** *m* PRODUCTION fine crusher; ~ **à galets** *m* CHARBON, PRODUCTION pebble mill; ~ **giratoire** *m* AGRO ALIM gyratory crusher, GENIE CHIM centrifugal crusher; ~ **à glace** *m* REFRIG ice crusher; ~ **des gros** *m* MINES coarse crusher, primary crusher; ~ **à mâchoires** *m* CONS MECA, PRODUCTION jaw crusher, jaw crusher; ~ **à marteaux** *m* AGRO ALIM hammer mill, CHARBON hammer crusher; ~ **à meules** *m* PLAST CAOU *peinture, matériel* edge mill; ~ **à meules horizontales** *m* PRODUCTION roller mill; ~ **à meules verticales** *m* CERAM VER edge runner mill, PRODUCTION edge mill; ~ **mixeur** *m* CHARBON ball mill; ~ **à mortier** *m* PRODUCTION mortar mill; ~ **de noeuds** *m* PAPIER knot breaker; ~ **par percussion** *m* CHARBON impact crusher; ~ **à peinture** *m* CERAM VER paint mill; ~ **à pendule** *m* CONS MECA swinging crusher; ~ **à percussion** *m* EQUIP LAB percussion mortar; ~ **planétaire** *m* EQUIP LAB planetary mill; ~ **pour colloïdes** *m* AGRO ALIM colloid mill; ~ **pour glace** *m* CONS MECA crushing machine for ice; ~ **pour minerai** *m* MINES ore crusher; ~ **de rocher** *m* CONSTR rock breaker; ~ **à sable** *m* PLAST CAOU *matériel, peinture* sand mill; ~ **à son** *m* AGRO ALIM ball mill; ~ **vibrant à barre** *m* CHARBON vibrating rod mill; ~ **vibrant à billes** *m* EQUIP LAB *broyage* vibrating ball mill

broyeur-concasseur *m* CHARBON crusher

broyeur-granulateur *m* GENIE CHIM granulating crusher

broyeur-malaxeur *m* PRODUCTION mixing mill

broyeur-mélangeur *m* PRODUCTION mixing mill; ~ **à meules** *m* GENIE CHIM mixing pan mill broyeur-sécheur *m* CHARBON dryer mill

broyeur-tamiseur *m* PRODUCTION combined grinder and sieve

brucelles *f pl* CERAM VER, EQUIP LAB tweezers

brucine *f* AGRO ALIM, CHIMIE brucine

brucite *f* MINERAUX brucite

bruine *f* METEO drizzle

bruit *m* ACOUSTIQUE, ELECTRON, ENREGISTR, INFORMAT, ORDINAT, PHYS ONDES, PHYSIQUE, SECURITE, TELECOM noise; ~ **acoustique** *m* TELECOM acoustic noise; ~ **acoustique aérien** *m* SECURITE airborne acoustical noise; ~ **additif** *m* TELECOM additive noise; ~ **aérien** *m* CONS MECA *engins de terrassement, scies* airborne noise; ~ **d'agitation thermique** *m* PHYSIQUE Johnson noise, thermal noise; ~ **d'aiguille** *m* ENREGISTR needle noise; ~ **aléatoire** *m* ELECTRON, ESPACE, PHYSIQUE, TELECOM random noise; ~ **d'ambiance** *m* ENREGISTR atmospheric noise; ~ **ambiant** *m* SECURITE environmental noise, TELECOM ambient noise; ~ **de l'amplificateur** *m* ELECTRON amplifier noise; ~ **artificiel** *m* ESPACE artificial noise, man-made noise, TELECOM artificial noise; ~ **atmosphérique** *m* ELECTRON atmospheric noise, atmospherics, ESPACE *communications* atmospheric noise, atmospherics; ~ **à bande étroite** *m* ELECTRON, TELECOM narrow band noise; ~ **de bande magnétique** *m* ENREGISTR magnetic tape noise; ~ **blanc** *m* ACOUSTIQUE, ELECTRON, ENREGISTR, ESPACE *communications*, INFORMAT, ORDINAT, PHYSIQUE, TELECOM white noise; ~ **de cellule** *m* AERONAUT aerodynamic noise; ~ **de choc normalisé** *m* ACOUSTIQUE standardized impact sound; ~ **de chrominance** *m* TV color noise (AmE), colour noise (BrE); ~ **cohérent** *m* ENREGISTR, GEOPHYS coherent noise; ~ **de collure dans le son** *m* CINEMAT bloop; ~ **cosmique** *m* ESPACE cosmic noise; ~ **de courant** *m* ENREGISTR current noise (AmE), mains noise (BrE); ~ **de courant alternatif** *m* ELECTR *alimentation* electrical hum (AmE), mains hum (BrE), *amplificateur* alternating current hum; ~ **diffus** *m* ENREGISTR random noise; ~ **dû aux brouillages** *m* ESSAIS interference noise; ~ **dû aux parasites** *m* ELECTRON interference noise; ~ **électrique** *m* ELECTRON electric noise, electrical noise (AmE), mains noise (BrE); ~ **d'émission secondaire** *m* ELECTRON secondary emission noise; ~ **d'enregistrement** *m* ENREGISTR recording noise; ~ **de l'environnement** *m* SECURITE environmental noise; ~ **externe** *m* ELECTRON external noise; ~ **fluctuant** *m* ACOUSTIQUE fluctuating noise; ~ **de fond** *m* ACOUSTIQUE background noise, ELECTRON background noise, ground noise, ENREGISTR, ESPACE *communications*, ESSAIS, GEOPHYS background noise, PHYS RAYON background radiation, PHYSIQUE, TELECOM background noise; ~ **de fond de rayonnement X** *m* PHYS RAYON X-ray background radiation; ~ **de fréquence** *m* ELECTRON frequency noise; ~ **galactique** *m* ELECTRON galactic noise; ~ **gaussien** *m* ELECTRON, INFORMAT, ORDINAT, PHYSIQUE, TELECOM Gaussian noise; ~ **de granulation** *m* TELECOM speckle noise; ~ **de grenaille** *m* ELECTRON, ESPACE *communications*, OPTIQUE shot noise, PHYSIQUE Schottky noise, shot noise, TELECOM granular noise, shot noise; ~ **impulsif** *m* ESPACE *communications*, TELECOM impulse noise; ~ **impulsionnel** *m* ACOUSTIQUE impulse noise, impulsive noise, INFORMAT, ORDINAT impulse noise; ~ **inhérent** *m* ENREGISTR inherent noise; ~ **inorganisé** *m* GEOPHYS random noise; ~ **intermittent** *m* ACOUSTIQUE intermittent noise; ~ **d'intermodulation** *m* ESPACE *communications* intermodulation noise; ~ **interne** *m* ELECTRON internal noise; ~ **d'ionisation** *m* ELECTRON gas noise; ~ **Johnson** *m* ELECTRON Johnson noise; ~ **à large bande** *m* ELECTRON wide band noise, ENREGISTR broadband noise, TELECOM wide band noise; ~ **de la ligne** *m* ELECTRON, ELECTROTEC line noise; ~ **de ligne** *m* ELECTRON circuit noise; ~ **de la mer** *m* OCEANO sea noise; ~ **modal** *m* OPTIQUE, TELECOM modal noise; ~ **de modulation** *m* ACOUSTIQUE, ELECTRON, ENREGISTR, TELECOM, TV modulation noise; ~ **de modulation d'amplitude** *m* ENREGISTR amplitude modulation noise; ~ **à modulation de fréquence** *m* TELECOM frequency modulation noise; ~ **modulé en amplitude** *m* ELECTRON AM noise; ~ **de moteur de bateau** *m* ELECTRON motorboating; ~ **non gaussien** *m* TELECOM non-Gaussian noise; ~ **organisé** *m* GEOPHYS coherent noise; ~ **d'origine galactique** *m* ELECTRON galactic noise; ~ **parasite** *m* ENREGISTR, TELECOM background noise, extraneous noise; ~ **de partage** *m* ELECTRON partition noise; ~ **des perforations** *m* CINEMAT sprocket noise; ~ **photonique** *m* OPTIQUE, TELECOM photon noise; ~ **physiologique** *m* ACOUSTIQUE physiological noise; ~ **de polarisation continue** *m* ENREGISTR DC noise; ~ **de la porteuse** *m* ELECTRON carrier noise; ~ **propre** *m* ELECTRON internal noise, intrinsic noise, OCEANO self-noise; ~ **pseudoaléatoire** *m* TELECOM pseudonoise, pseudorandom noise; ~ **de quantification** *m* ESPACE *communications*, INFORMAT, ORDINAT, TELECOM quantization noise; ~ **quantique** *m* ELECTRON, OPTIQUE, TELECOM quantum noise; ~ **de raccord de la piste sonore** *m* ENREGISTR bloop; ~ **radioélectrique** *m* ELECTRON radio noise; ~ **de référence** *m* ELECTRON reference noise; ~ **de répartition** *m* ELECTRON partition noise; ~ **résiduel** *m* INFORMAT, ORDINAT residual noise; ~ **rose** *m* ACOUSTIQUE, ENREGISTR, PHYSIQUE pink noise; ~ **rythmique** *m* ACOUSTIQUE cyclic noise; ~ **de scintillation** *m* ELECTRON flicker noise, ESPACE *communications* scintillation noise; ~ **de scintillement** *m* ELECTRON flicker noise; ~ **de secteur** *m* ENREGISTR electrical noise (AmE), mains noise (BrE); ~ **stable** *m* ACOUSTIQUE stable noise, steady noise; ~ **de surface** *m* ACOUSTIQUE, ELECTRON, ENREGISTR surface noise; ~ **de tacheture** *m* OPTIQUE speckle noise; ~ **thermique** *m* ELECTRON, ESPACE *communications* thermal noise; ~ **transmis par l'air** *m* SECURITE *machines-outils* airborne noise; ~ **de la voie** *m* ELECTRON channel noise

bruitages *m pl* CINEMAT effects, sound effects, ENREGISTR sound effects, TV effects, sound effects

brûlage *m* THERMODYN burning; ~ **à la torchère** *m* PETROLE flaring

brûlant *adj* THERMODYN burning, scalding

brûlé *adj* THERMODYN burnt, incinerated

brûler¹ *vt* AGRO ALIM fire, CH DE FER *gare, signal fermé* overrun, overshoot, THERMODYN burn; ~ **à la torche** *vt* THERMODYN burn off

brûler² *vi* THERMODYN burn; ~ **lentement** *vi* THERMODYN smolder (AmE), smoulder (BrE)

brûleur *m* CERAM VER port, CHAUFFAGE, GAZ, IMPRIM *sécheurs*, THERMODYN burner; ~ **à air soufflé** *m* GAZ forced air furnace (AmE), forced draft burner (AmE), forced draught burner (BrE); ~ **d'allumage** *m* CHAUFFAGE ignition burner, CONS MECA pilot flame; ~ **atmosphérique** *m* THERMODYN atmospheric burner; ~ **atomiseur** *m* THERMODYN atomizing burner; ~ **automatique à mazout à jet sous pression** *m* CHAUFFAGE automatic oil burner; ~ **à combustion interne** *m* CERAM VER internal burner; ~ **côté feu** *m* CERAM VER inlet port (BrE), intake port (AmE); ~ **côté fumées** *m* CERAM VER burner outlet port; ~ **à courant d'air** *m* CONS MECA air blast burner; ~ **à courant d'air forcé** *m* CONS MECA forced draft burner (AmE), forced draught burner (BrE); ~ **à couronne** *m* CONSTR ring burner, rose burner; ~ **à courte flamme** *m* CHAUFFAGE short flame burner; ~ **de déchets** *m* CONSTR incinerator; ~ **à double débit** *m* TRANSPORT duplex burner; ~ **à évaporation** *m* THERMODYN atomizing burner; ~ **à gaz** *m* CHAUFFAGE, PRODUCTION gas burner; ~ **de gaz à basse pression** *m* CHAUFFAGE low-pressure gas burner; ~ **infrarouge** *m* GAZ infrared burner; ~ **à jet de gaz** *m* PRODUCTION gas jet; ~ **à mazout** *m* CONS MECA, THERMODYN oil burner; ~ **de pied de feuille** *m* CERAM VER piccolo burner; ~ **de postcombustion** *m* THERMODYN *réacteur* afterburner; ~ **principal** *m* CHAUFFAGE main burner; ~ **de pulvérisation** *m* CONS MECA pulverization burner; ~ **à tirage induit** *m* CONS MECA induced draft burner (AmE), induced draught burner (BrE); ~ **à vaporisation** *m* THERMODYN vaporizing burner; ~ **à vaporisation de fuel** *m* CHAUFFAGE atomizing oil burner; ~ **à ventilateur** *m* CONS MECA fan-powered burner

brûlure *f* IMPRIM *préimpression*, SECURITE *d'une personne* burn; ~ **de balayage** *f* TV scan burn; ~ **chimique** *f* SECURITE chemical burn; ~ **de congélation** *f* REFRIG freezer burn; ~ **au premier degré** *f* SECURITE first degree burn; ~ **de radiation** *f* PHYS RAYON radiation burn

brume *f* IMPRIM *encres, impression* misting, METEO, POLLUTION haze, mist; ~ **sèche** *f* METEO, THERMODYN heat haze

brumeux *adj* METEO hazy

brun: ~ **de Bismark** *m* CHIMIE vesuvin

brunissage *m* CERAM VER burnishing, watermark, IMPRIM *finition*, MATERIAUX, MECANIQUE, PRODUCTION burnishing; ~ **galvanique** *m* PRODUCTION black finishing

brunissoir *m* CERAM VER burnisher

brunissure *f* AGRO ALIM scald mark

brushite *f* MINERAUX brushite

brut[1] *adj* CHARBON crude, raw, unwashed, CHIMIE crude, CONS MECA coarse, HYDROLOGIE *eau* raw, untreated; ~ **de coulée** *adj* PRODUCTION as cast; ~ **d'estampage** *adj* PRODUCTION as stamped, rough stamped; ~ **de fonderie** *adj* PRODUCTION as cast; ~ **de fonte** *adj* PRODUCTION as cast; ~ **de forge** *adj* PRODUCTION as forged, rough forged; ~ **de laminage** *adj* PRODUCTION as rolled, rough rolled

brut[2] *m* PETROLE crude, crude oil; ~ **acide** *m* PETROLE sour crude; ~ **étêté** *m* PETROLE tipped crude; ~ **léger** *m* PETROLE light crude; ~ **lourd** *m* PETROLE heavy crude; ~ **non-sulfuré** *m* PETROLE sweet crude; ~ **de synthèse** *m* PETROLE synthetic crude; ~ **synthétique** *m* PETROLE synthetic crude

bûche *f* CERAM VER stick

bûchette *f* PAPIER shive

bucholzite *f* MINERAUX bucholzite

buddle *m* MINES buddle

buée *f* METEO, REFRIG mist

buffêtement: ~ **à grande vitesse** *m* AERONAUT high-speed buffeting

buffeting: ~ **à grande vitesse** *m* AERONAUT high-speed buffeting

bufotoxine *f* CHIMIE bufotoxin

bulbe *m* CONS MECA bulb; ~ **de détendeur** *m* AUTO thermal bulb; ~ **d'étrave** *m* TRANSPORT ram bow

bulk *vi* IMPRIM avoir de la main

bulldozer *m* CONSTR, TRANSPORT bulldozer

bulle *f* CERAM VER, CHARBON bubble, CHIMIE void, GENIE CHIM bubble, IMPRIM *bande dessinée* balloon, PAPIER blister, bubble, PHYSIQUE bubble, PLAST CAOU void, *imperfection* bubble; ~ **d'air** *f* CERAM VER, CINEMAT air bell, IMPRIM *emballage, impression* air bubble, NAUT blister, PHYSIQUE air bubble; ~ **ascendante** *f* CHARBON coursing bubble; ~ **capillaire** *f* CERAM VER airline; ~ **facettée** *f* NUCLEAIRE faceted bubble (AmE), facetted bubble (BrE); ~ **de rebullage** *f* CERAM VER reboil bubble; ~ **de vapeur** *f* GENIE CHIM vapor bubble (AmE), vapour bubble (BrE)

bulletin: ~ **d'expédition** *m* TRANSPORT parcel registration card; ~ **météo** *m* METEO, NAUT weather report; ~ **météorologique** *m* ESPACE, METEO, NAUT weather report; ~ **des routes** *m* TRANSPORT road news

bunsénine *f* MINERAUX bunsenine

bunsénite *f* MINERAUX bunsenite

Bunter *m* PETR Bunter

buntsandstein *m* PETROLE *géologie* bunter

buratite *f* MINERAUX buratite

bure *m* MINES internal shaft, staple, staple pit

bureau: ~ **des cartes et plans** *m* NAUT hydrographic office; ~ **de contrôle d'approche** *m* AERONAUT approach control office; ~ **des départs** *m* TRANSPORT forwarding office (BrE), freight office (AmE); ~ **de dessin** *m* PRODUCTION design department; ~ **des douanes** *m* TRANSPORT port custom house; ~ **électronique** *m* INFORMAT, ORDINAT electronic office; ~ **d'essais** *m* CHIMIE assay office; ~ **d'études** *m* CONS MECA engineering and design department, CONSTR design office, MECANIQUE engineering office, NAUT design department, design office, PRODUCTION engineering department; ~ **maritime** *m* NAUT shipping office; ~ **météorologique** *m* METEO weather bureau

bureautique *f* ORDINAT, PRODUCTION OA, office automation; ~ **intégrée** *f* ORDINAT IOS, integrated office system

bureaux: ~ **du port** *m pl* TRANSPORT port administration offices

burette *f* CHIMIE, EQUIP LAB *analyse* burette, PRODUCTION can, oilcan, oiler; ~ **automatique** *f* EQUIP LAB *analyse* automatic burette; ~ **à gaz** *f* EQUIP LAB *analyse* gas burette; ~ **de graissage** *f* PRODUCTION oilcan, oiler; ~ **à huile** *f* PRODUCTION oilcan, oiler; ~ **de séparation** *f* GENIE CHIM separating burette

burin *m* CONS MECA flat chisel, MECANIQUE *outillage* chisel, MINES borer, drill, jackhammer, rock drill, chisel, NAUT caulking iron, PRODUCTION chipping chisel, chisel; ~ **bédane** *m* CONS MECA crosscut, PRODUCTION chipping chisel; ~ **en pointe de diamant** *m* CONS MECA diamond cold chisel, diamond, diamond nose chisel, diamond point chisel; ~ **à froid** *m* CONS MECA flat cold chisel, PRODUCTION flat chipping chiesel, flat cold chisel; ~ **grain-d'orge** *m* CONS MECA round-nosed chisel, round-nosed cold chisel, PRODUCTION chipping chisel; ~ **de gravure** *m* ACOUSTIQUE cutting stylus, engraving, ENREGISTR recording stylus

Burin *m* ASTRONOMIE Caelum

burinage *m* PRODUCTION chipping, chiseling (AmE), chiselling (BrE)

buriner *vt* CONSTR chip

burineur *m* CONSTR chipper, PRODUCTION chiseler

(AmE), chiseller (BrE)

bus *m* ELECTROTEC, ESPACE *véhicules* bus, INFORMAT bus, busbar, highway, ORDINAT busbar, highway, TELECOM bus, highway, busbar; **~ d'adresses** *m* INFORMAT, ORDINAT address bus; **~ d'alimentation** *m* ELECTROTEC busbar; **~ de chaînage en guirlande** *m* ORDINAT daisy chain bus; **~ de commande** *m* ORDINAT control bus; **~ de contrôle** *m* INFORMAT control bus; **~ de données** *m* ESPACE *communications*, INFORMAT, ORDINAT data bus; **~ d'eau** *m* TRANSPORT river bus; **~ en chaîne** *m* INFORMAT daisy chain bus; **~ d'entrée/sortie** *m* INFORMAT, ORDINAT input/output bus; **~ à jeton** *m* INFORMAT, ORDINAT token bus; **~ optique** *m* OPTIQUE, TELECOM optical data bus; **~ principal** *m* INFORMAT backbone bus; **~ de transfert d'énergie** *m* ESPACE *véhicules* battery transfer bus

busc *m* DISTRI EAU clap sill, lock sill, miter sill (AmE), mitre sill (BrE); **~ d'amont** *m* DISTRI EAU head miter sill (AmE), head mitre sill (BrE); **~ d'aval** *m* DISTRI EAU tail miter sill (AmE), tail mitre sill (BrE)

buse *f* CONSTR nozzle, *en béton* pipe, EN RENOUV, EQUIP LAB *verrerie* nozzle, IMPRIM *projections, mécaniques* slot, MINES air pipe, PAPIER nozzle, PLAST CAOU sprue bush, *extrudeuse* nozzle, PRODUCTION blast nozzle, leat, nosepiece, *d'une soufflerie* nozzle, *du porte-vent d'une tuyère* nose, *soufflerie* flume, nose; **~ d'air** *f* VEHICULES *carburateur* venturi; **~ d'alimentation sous pression** *f* IMPRIM slot die; **~ d'atomisation** *f* AGRO ALIM atomizing nozzle; **~ de carburant** *f* CONS MECA fuel nozzle; **~ chambre chaude** *f* CONS MECA sprue bush; **~ chauffante** *f* CONS MECA hot sprue brushing; **~ à débit variable** *f* CONS MECA adjustable nozzle; **~ en béton** *f* CONSTR concrete pipe; **~ d'entrée** *f* CONS MECA, ESPACE *véhicules* bell mouth; **~ à film d'air** *f* IMPRIM *séchage* airfoil nozzle; **~ d'insufflation d'air** *f* CONS MECA air inlet nozzle; **~ de moule chambre chaude** *f* CONS MECA sprue bush; **~ pour envoi sous pression de la solution de couchage** *f* IMPRIM *papier* die; **~ réglable** *f* CONS MECA adjustable nozzle; **~ de sablage** *f* CERAM VER sandblasting nozzle; **~ de tuyau flexible** *f* CONS MECA hose nozzle; **~ à vapeur** *f* INST HYDR *d'un injecteur* steam nozzle

buselure: **~ en bronze** *f* CONS MECA gunmetal bush, gunmetal bushing

busillon *m* PRODUCTION blast nozzle, nozzle, *du porte-vent d'une tuyère* nose

bustamite *f* MINERAUX bustamite

buste *m* TEXTILE bustline

butadiène *m* CHIMIE, PETROLE butadiene

butane *m* CHIMIE, PETROLE butane

butanier *m* PETROLE, TRANSPORT butane carrier, butane tanker

butanol *m* CHIMIE butanol

butanone *f* PLAST CAOU butanone

butée *f* CONS MECA stop, thrust, thrust bearing, thrust block, *de micromètre* anvil, CONSTR abutment, shore, thrust, MECANIQUE stop, POLLU MER thrust, VEHICULES stop; **~ d'accrochage** *f* CONS MECA lock stop; **~ d'affaissement** *f* CONS MECA droop restrainer; **~ arrière** *f* IMPRIM *mécanique* backstop; **~ à l'arrière** *f* CONS MECA end thrust bearing, thrust bearing, tailpin thrust; **~ à billes** *f* CONS MECA axial thrust bearing, ball bearing reactor, ball stop, thrust ball bearing, thrust ball bearing, MECANIQUE thrust ball bearing, PAPIER thrust ball bearing; **~ de came d'éjecteur rapide** *f* CONS MECA *fonderie* kicker actuator; **~ de débrayage** *f* AUTO release bearing, release bearing sleeve, throw-out bearing, throw-out bearing sleeve, VEHICULES clutch release bearing; **~ de direction** *f* VEHICULES steering circle, steering lock; **~ d'éjection** *f* CONS MECA *fonderie* bumper rod; **~ élastique du train** *f* AERONAUT landing gear bumper; **~ de fin de course** *f* CONS MECA limit strip; **~ fixe** *f* CONS MECA fixed stop; **~ de front** *f* IMPRIM *machines* front stop; **~ d'inclinaison de moyeu** *f* AERONAUT hub tilt stop; **~ mécanique** *f* CONS MECA mechanical stop unit; **~ mobile** *f* CONS MECA movable stop; **~ de moyeu** *f* AERONAUT hub spacer; **~ de pale** *f* AERONAUT blade stop; **~ de pas** *f* AERONAUT pitch stop; **~ plein gaz** *f* AERONAUT full-open throttle; **~ ralentie** *f* AERONAUT idle throttle stop; **~ réacteur éteint** *f* AERONAUT engine shut-off stop; **~ réglable** *f* CINEMAT, CONS MECA, MECANIQUE adjustable stop; **~ régulateur** *f* AERONAUT governor control stop; **~ à ressort** *f* CONS MECA spring stop; **~ de signalisation** *f* CONS MECA indicating stop; **~ statique** *f* CONS MECA droop restrainer; **~ des terres** *f* CHARBON passive earth pressure; **~ de traînée** *f* AERONAUT drag stop

butenal *m* CHIMIE butenal, crotonaldehyde

butène *m* CHIMIE, LESSIVES butene, butylene

butoir *m* CH DE FER buffer, buffer stop, CONS MECA, MECANIQUE buffer, PHOTO stop pin; **~ de pare-chocs** *m* VEHICULES *carrosserie* overrider

butte *f* CONSTR knoll, MINES post, prop, shore, tree

butteroil *m* AGRO ALIM butter oil

buttes *f pl* CONSTR shoring

buttoir *m* CONS MECA pawl head

butyl *m* PLAST CAOU butyl rubber

butyl-caoutchouc *m* PLAST CAOU butyl rubber

butylène *m* CHIMIE, LESSIVES butene, butylene

butyral: **~ de polyvinyle** *m* PLAST CAOU polyvinyl butyral

butyraldéhyde *m* CHIMIE butyraldehyde

butyrate *m* CHIMIE butyrate

butyrellite *f* CHARBON butyrite

butyrine *f* CHIMIE butyrin

butyrique *adj* CHIMIE butyric

buvable *adj* DISTRI EAU drinkable, potable

buvant *m* CERAM VER lip

bypass *m* CONS MECA, ELECTR *circuit*, GAZ, PETROLE *forage* bypass

byssolite *f* MINERAUX byssolite

bytownite *f* MINERAUX bytownite

C

c *abrév (centi-)* METROLOGIE c *(centi-)*

C¹ *(carbone)* CHIMIE C *(carbon)*

C² *abrév (coulomb)*, ELECTR (coulomb), ELECTROTEC *(coulomb)*, C *(coulomb)*, METROLOGIE *(centigrade)* C *(centigrade)*, METROLOGIE *(Celsius)* C *(Celsius)*, METROLOGIE *(coulomb)*, PHYSIQUE *(coulomb)* C *(coulomb)*

Ca *(calcium)* CHIMIE Ca *(calcium)*

CA *abrév (courant alternatif)* ELECTR, ELECTRON, ELECTROTEC, ENREGISTR, PHYSIQUE, TELECOM, TV AC *(alternating current)*

cabestan *m* ACOUSTIQUE, CINEMAT, CONS MECA, ELECTROTEC, ENREGISTR, INFORMAT, MECANIQUE, NAUT, TV capstan; **~ à dépression** *m* ENREGISTR, TV vacuum capstan

cabillot *m* NAUT belaying pin, *de tournage* belaying pin; **~ d'amarrage** *m* NAUT toggle

cabine *f* AERONAUT cabin, CH DE FER cabin, driver's cab (BrE), driver's cabin, engineer's cab (AmE), CINEMAT booth, CONSTR cabin, house, *d'une grue* cab, ESPACE *véhicules* cabin, IMPRIM *téléphone, visualisation* booth, NAUT cabin, saloon, TRANSPORT cab, gondola, VEHICULES *carrosserie* cab; **~ audiométrique** *f* ACOUSTIQUE audiometric room, ENREGISTR audiometric booth; **~ avancée** *f* VEHICULES *carrosserie* cab-over-engine; **~ à cartes** *f* TELECOM card-operated payphone, cardphone; **~ des cartes** *f* NAUT chartroom; **~ circulante** *f* TRANSPORT cab; **~ de conduite** *f* CH DE FER *véhicules* cabine, driver's cab (BrE), driver's cabin, engineer's cab (AmE); **~ de contrôle** *f* ENREGISTR control cubicle, control room; **~ d'enregistrement** *f* ENREGISTR recording booth; **~ insonorisante** *f* SECURITE noise protection booth, soundproof booth; **~ insonorisée** *f* ENREGISTR soundproofed booth; **~ de luxe** *f* NAUT stateroom; **~ de mixage** *f* ENREGISTR mixing booth, mixing room; **~ des passagers** *f* TRANSPORT passenger cabin; **~ à pièces** *f* TELECOM coin-operated payphone; **~ de prise de son** *f* ENREGISTR sound booth; **~ de projection** *f* CINEMAT projection box, screening booth; **~ de réduction** *f* ENREGISTR reduction room; **~ de réenregistrement** *f* ENREGISTR dubbing room; **~ de son** *f* CINEMAT sound booth; **~ technique** *f* CINEMAT sound booth; **~ téléphonique** *f* TELECOM telephone kiosk

cabine-conteneur *f* TRANSPORT container capsule

câblage *m* ELECTR *alimentation* cabling, *raccordement* wiring, ELECTROTEC cabling, wiring, ESPACE *véhicules* wiring, TELECOM cabling, wiring; **~ du bâti** *m* ELECTROTEC rack wiring; **~ des circuits de commande** *m* PRODUCTION line wiring; **~ direct** *m* ELECTROTEC point-to-point wiring; **~ électrique** *m* ELECTROTEC, VEHICULES electrical wiring; **~ encastré** *m* ELECTR *réseau* flush wiring; **~ en paires** *m* ELECTR pairing; **~ en série** *m* PRODUCTION serial wiring; **~ extérieur** *m* PRODUCTION field wiring; **~ intérieur** *m* TELECOM internal wiring; **~ à liaison directe** *m* TEXTILE direct link wiring; **~ ligne principale** *m* PRODUCTION trunkline wiring; **~ des lignes de puissance** *m* PRODUCTION power wiring; **~ point par point** *m* ELECTR *alimentation* point-to-point wiring; **~ de puissance** *m* PRODUCTION power wiring

câble *m* ELECTR *conducteur*, ELECTROTEC, ENREGISTR cable, MECANIQUE, NAUT cable, rope, ORDINAT cable, PAPIER rope, PETR, PLAST CAOU, TELECOM cable, TEXTILE cord, tow, VEHICULES *système électrique, commande* cable;

~ a **~ d'accélérateur** *m* AUTO carburetor control cable (AmE), carburettor control cable (BrE); **~ d'acier** *m* NAUT steel wire; **~ aérien** *m* CONSTR overhead line, ELECTR *réseau* overhead cable, ELECTROTEC aerial cable, overhead cable, TELECOM aerial cable, TRANSPORT airline; **~ aérien isolé** *m* ELECTR aerial insulated cable; **~ d'alimentation** *m* ELECTROTEC feed cable, INFORMAT, ORDINAT feeder cable, PRODUCTION supply cable, TV feeder cable; **~ à âme divisée** *m* ELECTROTEC stranded cable; **~ armé** *m* CONS MECA armored cable (AmE), armoured cable (BrE), shielded cable, ELECTROTEC armored cable (AmE), armoured cable (BrE), shielded cable; **~ armé multiple** *m* ELECTR separate lead cable; **~ d'arrivée** *m* TV drop cable; **~ assemblé** *m* OPTIQUE cable assembly, spun cable, TELECOM cable assembly, optical cable assembly; **~ d'atterrissage** *m* ELECTROTEC shore end; **~ ayant une armature métallique** *m* CONS MECA armored cable (AmE), armoured cable (BrE);

~ b **~ à basse tension** *m* ELECTR *alimentation* low-voltage cable; **~ de batterie** *m* CINEMAT battery cable; **~ biaxial** *m* ELECTR, PRODUCTION biaxial cable; **~ bifilaire** *m* ORDINAT cable pair; **~ bifilaire torsadé** *m* ELECTR, ORDINAT twisted-pair cable; **~ blindé** *m* ELECTR, ELECTROTEC screened cable, shielded cable, ENREGISTR shielded cable, ORDINAT screened cable, PHYSIQUE screened cable, shielded cable, PRODUCTION shielded cable, TELECOM armored cable (AmE), armoured cable (BrE), TV shielded cable; **~ de bougie** *m* AUTO spark plug cable; **~ Bowden** *m* MECANIQUE Bowden cable, VEHICULES *embrayage, freins* Bowden cable, brake cable, clutch cable; **~ de branchement** *m* TV outside plant cable;

~ c **~ chargé** *m* ELECTROTEC, TELECOM loaded cable; **~ à charge continue** *m* ELECTROTEC continuously-loaded cable; **~ à charge discontinue** *m* ELECTROTEC coil-loaded cable; **~ de chauffage par le plancher** *m* CONS MECA floor-warming cable; **~ chauffant** *m* ELECTR heating cable; **~ classique** *m* OPTIQUE concentric optical cable, conventional cable; **~ classique à fibres enrobées** *m* OPTIQUE direct strand cable; **~ classique à fibres libres** *m* OPTIQUE, TELECOM loose tube cable; **~ de clé** *m* PETROLE backup line, tong line; **~ coaxial** *m* ELECTR, ELECTROTEC, ENREGISTR, ORDINAT, PHYSIQUE, TELECOM, TV coax, coaxial cable; **~ de commande** *m* CONS MECA control cable; **~ de commande d'embrayage** *m* AUTO clutch cable; **~ composite** *m* ELECTROTEC composite cable; **~ conducteur** *m* TV feeder cable; **~ à un conducteur** *m* ELECTR single conductor cable, single core cable, ELECTROTEC single conductor cable; **~ à conducteur de cuivre** *m*

TELECOM copper cable; ~ à conducteurs métalliques *m* TELECOM metallic conductor cable; ~ de connexion *m* CINEMAT connecting cable; ~ de connexion d'accumulateurs *m* VEHICULES *système électrique* jump lead, jumper; ~ de contrepoids *m* MINES load rope; ~ à courte distance *m* ELECTROTEC short-haul cable; ~ de curage *m* PETR sand line; ~ cylindrique rainuré *m* TELECOM grooved cable;

~ d ~ de déclenchement *m* MILITAIRE *parachute* rip cord; ~ déconnecté *m* PRODUCTION open wire; ~ de démarreur *m* AUTO starter cable; ~ à deux âmes torsadées *m* ELECTR duplex cable; ~ à deux conducteurs *m* ELECTR double core cable; ~ de distribution *m* ELECTR, ELECTROTEC distribution cable;

~ e ~ élastique *m* TRANSPORT sandow; ~ électrique *m* CONS MECA electrical cable; ~ d'embarquement *m* PAPIER rope carrier; ~ d'énergie *m* ELECTR *réseau*, ELECTROTEC power cable; ~ en faisceaux *m* OPTIQUE unit-type cable; ~ en fer *m* PRODUCTION iron wire rope; ~ en fibres optiques *m* OPTIQUE fiberoptic cable (AmE), fibreoptic cable (BrE); ~ en fil de fer *m* PRODUCTION iron wire rope; ~ en nappe *m* ELECTROTEC flat cable; ~ d'entrée *m* ELECTR lead-in cable; ~ en tuyau *m* ELECTR pipe-type cable; ~ épissé *m* NAUT spliced rope; ~ d'équilibre *m* MINES load rope; ~ d'équipartition *m* AERONAUT blade spacing system; ~ d'extension *m* PRODUCTION expansion cable; ~ d'extraction *m* MINES hoisting rope;

~ f ~ à faibles pertes *m* ELECTR *alimentation* low-loss cable; ~ à fibre en plastique *m* ELECTROTEC *optique* plastic fiber cable (AmE), plastic fibre cable (BrE); ~ à fibre optique *m* ELECTROTEC fiberoptic cable (AmE), fibreoptic cable (BrE), light cable, INFORMAT fiberoptic cable (AmE), fibreoptic cable (BrE), OPTIQUE fiberoptic cable (AmE), fibreoptic cable (BrE), optical fiber cable (AmE), optical fibre cable (BrE), ORDINAT fiberoptic cable (AmE), fibreoptic cable (BrE); ~ à fibre optique en verre *m* ELECTROTEC glass fibre cable; ~ à fibres enrobées *m* OPTIQUE tight construction cable, tight-jacketed cable, TELECOM tight-jacketed cable; ~ à fibres libres *m* OPTIQUE, TELECOM loose structure cable; ~ à fibres optiques *m* TELECOM optical fiber cable, optical fibre cable (BrE); ~ à fils armés *m* ELECTROTEC metal-sheathed cable; ~ flexible *m* ELECTROTEC flexible cable; ~ de forage *m* MINES drill rope, drilling cable, PETR, PETROLE drilling line; ~ de frein *m* VEHICULES brake cable; ~ de frein à main *m* AUTO handbrake cable; ~ de fréquence pilote *m* CINEMAT pilot tone cable;

~ g ~ à grande distance *m* ELECTROTEC long-distance cable; ~ des grandes profondeurs *m* NAUT deep-sea cable; ~ groupé *m* ELECTR bunched cable (BrE), bundled cable (AmE); ~ de guidage *m* PRODUCTION guide rope; ~ guide *m* PRODUCTION guide rope;

~ h ~ de haubanage *m* CONSTR guy rope; ~ à haute fréquence *m* ELECTR *alimentation en courant alternatif* high-frequency cable; ~ à haute tension *m* ELECTR *alimentation*, INSTRUMENT high-voltage cable; ~ à huile *m* ELECTR oil-filled cable; ~ à huile en tuyau *m* ELECTR oil-filled pipe-type cable;

~ i ~ imprégné *m* ELECTR impregnated cable; ~ d'interconnexion *m* ELECTROTEC interconnection cable; ~ interurbain *m* ELECTROTEC long-distance cable, trunk cable, TELECOM trunk cable; ~ à isolation minérale *m* ELECTR, ELECTROTEC mineral-insulated cable; ~ isolé *m* ELECTR, ELECTROTEC insulated cable; ~ isolé au

plastique *m* ELECTROTEC, TELECOM plastic-insulated cable;

~ j ~ à jonc rainuré *m* OPTIQUE grooved cable; ~ de jonction *m* ELECTROTEC junction cable;

~ k ~ krarupisé *m* ELECTROTEC continuously-loaded cable, krarup cable;

~ l ~ de levage *m* PRODUCTION *d'un transporteur aérien à voie unique* hoisting rope; ~ de liaison *m* ELECTROTEC connecting cable;

~ m ~ mal serti *m* PRODUCTION loose cable; ~ métallique *m* NAUT steel wire, PRODUCTION stranded wire, wire rope, TELECOM metal conductor cable; ~ de microphone *m* ENREGISTR microphone cable; ~ mini-bundle *m* OPTIQUE mini-bundle cable; ~ de mise à la masse *m* AUTO earth connection (BrE), ground connection (AmE), ELECTROTEC, VEHICULES *système électrique* earth cable (BrE), ground cable (AmE); ~ monoconducteur *m* ELECTROTEC single conductor cable; ~ monofibre *m* ELECTROTEC *optique* single fiber cable (AmE), single fibre cable (BrE); ~ monomode *m* ELECTROTEC single mode cable; ~ monotoron *m* PRODUCTION stranded wire; ~ multiconducteur *m* ELECTR multiconductor cable, ELECTROTEC multiconductor cable, multicore cable; ~ multifibre *m* ELECTROTEC, OPTIQUE, TELECOM multifiber cable (AmE), multifibre cable (BrE); ~ multifibres *m* TV multicore cable; ~ multipaires *m* TV multicore cable; ~ multiple *m* ELECTR, ELECTROTEC multicore cable; ~ multipolaire *m* ELECTR multiconductor cable;

~ n ~ à n conducteur *m* ELECTROTEC n-core cable; ~ non chargé *m* TELECOM unloaded cable; ~ non pupinisé *m* TELECOM unloaded cable;

~ o ~ OF *m* ELECTR oil-filled cable; ~ oléostatique *m* ELECTR oil-filled pipe-type cable; ~ ombilical *m* ESPACE umbilical cable; ~ optique *m* OPTIQUE optical cable, optical fiber cable (AmE), optical fibre cable (BrE), TELECOM, TV optical cable;

~ p ~ à une paire *m* ELECTROTEC single pair cable; ~ à paires *m* ELECTR, ELECTROTEC, TV paired cable; ~ à paires coaxiales *m* ELECTROTEC coaxial pair cable; ~ à paires symétriques *m* ELECTROTEC twin cable, TELECOM symmetrical pair cable, twisted-pair cable; ~ à paires torsadées *m* ELECTR twisted-pair cable; ~ de pédale de débrayage *m* VEHICULES *embrayage* clutch cable; ~ à peigne *m* ELECTROTEC fanned cable; ~ à pertes de couplage *m* TELECOM grading coupling loss cable; ~ plat *m* ELECTR flat cable, ribbon cable, ELECTROTEC flat cable, mass-terminated cable, PRODUCTION ribbon cable; ~ plat à paires torsadées *m* ELECTROTEC twisted-pair flat cable; ~ à plusieurs conducteurs *m* ELECTROTEC bunched cable (BrE), bundled cable (AmE); ~ porteur *m* CONSTR supporting rope, TRANSPORT track cable; ~ pour l'éclairage *m* ELECTRON lighting cable; ~ pour l'extérieur *m* ELECTR outdoor cable; ~ pour installation intérieure *m* ELECTR indoor cable; ~ à pression *m* ELECTR pressure cable; ~ à pression externe de gaz *m* ELECTR external gas pressure cable; ~ à pression interne de gaz *m* ELECTR internal gas pressure cable; ~ à pression sous gaine métallique *m* ELECTR self-contained pressure cable; ~ prolongateur *m* AERONAUT extension cord, CINEMAT extension cable; ~ protégé *m* PHYSIQUE screened cable, shielded cable; ~ protégé par une gaine en fils métalliques *m* CONS MECA armored cable (AmE), armoured cable (BrE); ~ de puissance *m* ELECTR power cable; ~ pupinisé *m* ELECTROTEC coil-loaded cable,

TELECOM loaded cable;
~ q ~ à quartes *m* ELECTROTEC quadded cable; ~ à quartes en étoile *m* ELECTROTEC star quadded cable; ~ à quatre paires *m* ELECTROTEC quadruple pair cable;
~ r ~ de raccordement *m* CONSTR interconnecting cable, PHOTO connecting cord, TELECOM local distribution cable; ~ de rallonge *m* CINEMAT extension cable; ~ de rechange pour interconnexion de terminal de programmation *m* PRODUCTION *automatisme industriel* replacement programmer interconnect cable; ~ de remorque *m* NAUT tow rope, towline, POLLU MER towline; ~ à remplissage d'huile *m* ELECTROTEC oil-filled cable; ~ de renvoi *m* CONS MECA return rope; ~ de réseau *m* TELECOM network cable, TV outside plant cable; ~ à retard *m* TV delay cable; ~ de retenue *m* TRANSPORT safety stop cable; ~ à ruban *m* ELECTR, OPTIQUE, TELECOM ribbon cable; **~ ruban à fibres libres** *m* OPTIQUE loose ribbon cable; ~ à rubans à fibres libres *m* OPTIQUE loose ribbon cable; ~ à rubans jumelés *m* TRANSPORT twin-ribbon cable;
~ s ~ sans fin *m* TRANSPORT endless cable; ~ de secours *m* TRANSPORT emergency cable; ~ secteur *m* ELECTROTEC mains cable (BrE), supply cable (AmE); ~ de sondage *m* MINES drill rope, drilling cable; ~ soufflé *m* TELECOM blown fiber (AmE), blown fibre (BrE); ~ souple *m* ELECTR flexible cable; ~ sous caoutchouc *m* ELECTROTEC rubber cable, rubber-insulated cable; ~ sous huile *m* ELECTROTEC oil-filled cable; ~ sous-marin *m* ELECTROTEC, NAUT, OCEANO, TELECOM submarine cable; ~ sous papier *m* ELECTROTEC paper-insulated cable; ~ sous plomb *m* ELECTR, ELECTROTEC lead-covered cable, lead-sheathed cable; ~ sous pression de gaz *m* ELECTR gas-filled cable; ~ souterrain *m* ELECTR *réseau*, ELECTROTEC underground cable; ~ à structure classique *m* OPTIQUE concentric optical cable, conventional cable; ~ à structure lâche *m* OPTIQUE, TELECOM loose structure cable; ~ à structure libre *m* OPTIQUE loose construction cable; ~ à structure ruban *m* OPTIQUE, TELECOM ribbon cable; ~ à structure serrée *m* OPTIQUE tight construction cable, TELECOM tight-jacketed cable; ~ supraconducteur *m* TELECOM superconductor cable; ~ de synchronisation *m* CINEMAT sync cable, sync pulse cable, synchronisation cable;
~ t ~ de télécommunications *m* ELECTROTEC communications cable, TELECOM, TV telecommunications cable; ~ de télévision *m* ELECTROTEC television cable; ~ de terre *m* ELECTROTEC earth cable (BrE), ground cable (AmE); ~ terrestre *m* TELECOM land cable; ~ de tirage *m* CONS MECA pulling rope, traction rope; ~ toronné *m* ELECTR *conducteur d'un câble* stranded cable; ~ tracteur *m* CONS MECA pulling rope, traction rope, TRANSPORT haulage cable, traction cable, traction rope; ~ de traction *m* CONS MECA pulling rope; ~ à très haute tension *m* ELECTR *réseau* extra high-voltage cable; ~ triplomb *m* ELECTR SL cable, separately lead-sheathed cable; ~ à trois brins *m* ELECTR triple-core cable; ~ à trois conducteurs *m* ELECTR triple-core cable, ELECTROTEC three-conductor cable; ~ à tubes assemblés *m* OPTIQUE, TELECOM loose tube cable;
~ u ~ unipolaire *m* ELECTR single conductor cable, single core cable;
~ v ~ vidéo *m* ELECTROTEC video cable; ~ de vissage *m* PETROLE spinning line
câblé *adj* ELECTROTEC, INFORMAT, ORDINAT hardwired; ~ en étoile *adj* TELECOM star-wired

câble-chaîne *m* CONS MECA chain cable, MINES, NAUT cable chain; ~ à étais *m* CONSTR stud-link chain cable, studded link chain cable; ~ à mailles étançonnées *m* CONSTR stud-link chain cable, studded link chain chain
câbler *vt* PRODUCTION hardwire, TV wire; ~ en fibres *vt* OPTIQUE make a cable with fibers (AmE), make a cable with fibres (BrE)
câbles: ~ à signaux *m pl* CH DE FER signaling wires (AmE), signalling wires (BrE)
câblier *m* NAUT cable ship, cable-laying ship
cabochon *m* AERONAUT dimmer cap, PRODUCTION lens, *d'interrupteur* lens; ~ de couleur *m* PRODUCTION color cap (AmE), colour cap (BrE)
cabotage *m* HYDROLOGIE coastal navigation, coastal trade, NAUT coastal navigation, coastal trade, coasting trade, coastwise trade, home trade
caboter *vi* NAUT coast
caboteur *m* NAUT coaster, TRANSPORT coastal vessel, coaster, coasting vessel
cabotier *m* NAUT coaster
cabré: en ~ *adj* AERONAUT in a nose-up attitude
cabrérite *f* MINERAUX cabrerite
cabriolet *m* NAUT spray hood, VEHICULES *type de véhicule* cabriolet, convertible
CAC *abrév (contrôle automatique de chrominance)* TV ACC *(automatic chrominance control)*
cache *m* CINEMAT mask, matte, matt, vignette, IMPRIM frisket, MECANIQUE cover, PHOTO mask, printing mask; ~ à bords francs *m* CINEMAT hard-edged matte; ~ dans fenêtre de prise de vue *m* CINEMAT cutoff; ~ écran *m* CINEMAT screen mask; ~ électronique *m* TV electronic matting; ~ en forme de trou de serrure *m* CINEMAT keyhole mask; ~ et contrecache *m* CINEMAT matte and counter-matte; ~ normalisé *m* CINEMAT academy mask; ~ peint *m* CINEMAT painted matte; ~ projetable *m* CINEMAT ulcer; ~ de protection *m* CONS MECA cover; ~ réducteur *m* PHOTO reduction mask; ~ ruban *m* EMBALLAGE masking tape; ~ de sécurité *m* CONS MECA guard; ~ sommet *m* TELECOM vertex plate
cache-borne *m* PRODUCTION terminal cover
cache-clavier *m* ORDINAT keytop overlay
cache-courroie *m* SECURITE belt guard
cache-culbuteurs *m* AUTO rocker cover
cache-entrée *m* CONSTR drop, key drop, keyhole guard
cache-moyeu *m* VEHICULES *roue* hub cap
cache-poussière[1] *adj* PRODUCTION dustproof
cache-poussière[2] *m* CONS MECA dust cover, EMBALLAGE dust guard, SECURITE dust cover
cacher *vt* PHOTO *un tirage photographique* dodge
cacheter *vt* PAPIER seal
cacholong *m* MINERAUX cacholong
cachon *m* CERAM VER chest
cacorcénite *f* MINERAUX cacoxenite
cadavérine *f* CHIMIE cadaverine
cadenas *m* CONSTR padlock
cadence *f* AERONAUT rate of turn, PRODUCTION throughput; ~ de balayage *f* AERONAUT *radar* scanning rate; ~ de comptage *f* ELECTRON counting rate; ~ de distribution *f* CERAM VER machine speed; ~ d'échantillonnage *f* ELECTRON, INFORMAT, ORDINAT sampling rate; ~ de forage *f* CONSTR drilling rate; ~ de la main-d'oeuvre *f* PRODUCTION labor rate (AmE), labour rate (BrE); ~ de numérisation *f* ELECTRON digitizing rate; ~ de prise de vue *f* CINEMAT filming speed; ~ de tir *f* MILITAIRE rate of fire; ~ utile de transfert de données *f*

ORDINAT effective data transfer rate

cadencement *m* ELECTRON clocking, timing, PRODUCTION time phasing

cadencer *vt* ELECTRON clock, time

cadenceur *m* ELECTRON clock

cadène *f* NAUT chain plate

cadmié *adj* MECANIQUE *traitement de surface* cadmium-plated

cadmium *m (Cd)* CHIMIE cadmium *(Cd)*

cadrage *m* CINEMAT camera viewpoint, IMPRIM *illustration* cropping, INFORMAT registration, TV framing; ~ **de la page sur écran** *m* IMPRIM justification; ~ **serré** *m* CINEMAT tight framing; ~ **télévision** *m* TV safe action area; ~ **TV** *m* TV TV cutoff; ~ **vertical** *m* ELECTRON vertical centring; ~ **visible à l'écran** *m* CINEMAT picture safety area

cadran *m* CONS MECA dial, dial plate, ELECTR dial, scale, INSTRUMENT, TELECOM, VEHICULES dial; ~ **à aiguille** *m* EQUIP LAB *instrument* needle dial; ~ **d'ajustage des fréquences** *m* ENREGISTR tuning dial; ~ **à clavier** *m* TELECOM keypad; ~ **du compas** *m* NAUT compass dial; ~ **divisé** *m* CONS MECA divided dial; ~ **gradué** *m* CINEMAT scale dial, CONS MECA divided dial, graduated dial, INSTRUMENT graduated dial, PRODUCTION *système hydraulique* calibrated dial; ~ **lumineux** *m* PHOTO illuminated dial; ~ **solaire** *m* ASTRONOMIE sundial; ~ **de transmission d'ordres** *m* NAUT engine room telegraph

cadrat *m* IMPRIM quad

cadre *m* CINEMAT image, CONS MECA frame, CONSTR stirrup, EMBALLAGE frame, EN RENOUV housing, IMPRIM box, frame, INFORMAT, MECANIQUE frame, MINES durn, timber frame, timber set, NAUT frame, pipe cot, *équipage* berth, ORDINAT, PHOTO frame, TELECOM loop aerial, TV, VEHICULES *carrosserie* frame; ~ **avant** *m* VEHICULES *carrosserie* subframe; ~ **avec tendard** *m* CONSTR set with stretcher piece; ~ **de boisage** *m* CONSTR set of timber; ~ **à dépoli** *m* PHOTO focusing screen frame; ~ **en matière plastique** *m* PHOTO plastic mount; ~ **en pointillé** *m* IMPRIM *composition* dotted frame; ~ **d'étambot** *m* NAUT stern frame; ~ **de fantaisie** *m* IMPRIM *composition* fancy frame; ~ **de fenêtre** *m* CONSTR window sash, VEHICULES *carrosserie* window frame; ~ **filtreur** *m* GENIE CHIM filter frame; ~ **latéral** *m* EMBALLAGE *d'un conteneur* side frame; ~ **margeur** *m* PHOTO printing mask; ~ **mobile** *m* ELECTROTEC moving coil; ~ **de montage** *m* PRODUCTION *automatisme industriel* mounting bezel; ~ **ordinaire** *m* MINES ordinary timber set, three-piece timber set; ~ **à oreilles** *m* MINES crib, curb; ~ **de page** *m* INFORMAT, ORDINAT page frame; ~ **périmétrique** *m* AUTO perimeter frame; ~ **porteur** *m* MINES bearer set, crib, curb; ~ **de positionnement** *m* CINEMAT register mount; ~ **pour développement de film** *m* PHOTO film rack; ~ **pour tissu** *m* TEXTILE stretcher; ~ **presseur** *m* CINEMAT, PHOTO pressure gate; ~ **à pression** *m* CINEMAT pressure gate; ~ **de puits** *m* CONSTR trestle; ~ **de radiateur** *m* AUTO radiator frame; ~ **à renversement** *m* OCEANO reversing frame; ~ **de séchage** *m* PHOTO drying frame; ~ **à un seul montant** *m* MINES half set; ~ **de soufflet** *m* PHOTO bellows frame; ~ **de superficie** *m* MINES head frame, *d'un puits de mine* shaft collar; ~ **surbaissé** *m* VEHICULES *châssis* drop bed frame; ~ **tectonique** *m* GEOLOGIE tectonic setting; ~ **de vitre** *m* VEHICULES *carrosserie* window frame

cadrer *vt* IMPRIM crop, INFORMAT, ORDINAT register, PHOTO frame

cadres: ~ **jointifs** *m pl* MINES close sets, skin-to-skin timbering

cadreur *m* CINEMAT cameraman, TV cameraman, phaser

CAF *abrév* COMMANDE *(contrôle automatique de fréquence)*, ELECTR *(commande automatique de fréquence)*, ELECTRON *(commande automatique de fréquence)*, ENREGISTR *(contrôle automatique de fréquence)*, PHYSIQUE *(commande automatique de fréquence)*, PRODUCTION *(commande automatique de fréquence)*, TELECOM *(commande automatique de fréquence)*, TV *(contrôle automatique de fréquence)* AFC *(automatic frequency control)*

caféine *f* CHIMIE caffeine

caféique *adj* CHIMIE caffeic

cafétannique *adj* CHIMIE caffetannic

CAG[1] *abrév* COMMANDE *(contrôle automatique de gain)*, ELECTRON *(commande automatique de gain)*, GEOPHYS *(contrôle automatique de gain)*, TELECOM *(commande automatique de gain)* AGC *(automatic gain control)*

CAG:[2] ~ **à contre-réaction** *f* TELECOM feedback AGC; ~ **avec réaction vers l'avant** *f* TELECOM feedforward AGC

cage *f* CONS MECA standard, *d'un laminoir* housing, METROLOGIE case, PRODUCTION holster; ~ **d'ascenseur** *f* AERONAUT lift shaft; ~ **à billes** *f* CONS MECA ball bearing cage, ball cage, IMPRIM *mécanique* ball race; ~ **de condensateur variable** *f* ELECTROTEC variable capacitor section; ~ **d'écrou** *f* CONS MECA nut cage; ~ **d'écureuil** *f* ELECTROTEC squirrel cage; ~ **en fil de fer** *f* PRODUCTION wire guard; ~ **d'escalier** *f* CONSTR staircase, stairway, stairwell; ~ **d'extraction** *f* CONSTR *mining* hoisting compartment; ~ **de Faraday** *f* ELECTR écran, ELECTROTEC, NUCLEAIRE, PHYSIQUE Faraday cage; ~ **de filière radiale** *f* CONS MECA radial diehead; ~ **de filière tangentielle** *f* CONS MECA tangential diehead; ~ **de laminoir** *f* CONS MECA bearer; ~ **de renversement** *f* NUCLEAIRE tilting basket; ~ **de rotule** *f* CONS MECA ball joint cage; ~ **de roulement** *f* CONS MECA bearing cage; ~ **de tourelle** *f* OCEANO protection cage; ~ **de la vanne** *f* HYDROLOGIE gate chamber

cagoule *f* OCEANO diving hood; ~ **antipoussière** *f* SECURITE dust hood; ~ **de protection** *f* SECURITE protective hood

cahier *m* IMPRIM gathering, section, signature; ~ **de charges** *m* RESSORTS specification; ~ **des charges** *m* CONSTR specifications, PRODUCTION, VEHICULES specification, specification sheet; ~ **des charges unifié** *m* PRODUCTION standard specification; ~ **de nivellement** *m* CONSTR level book; ~ **sortant d'une rotative** *m* IMPRIM *impression* form; ~ **de suivis** *m* PRODUCTION record book

cahiers: ~ **sortant 2 à 2** *m pl* IMPRIM *rotatives* two-on signatures

caillage *m* AGRO ALIM clotting, coagulating

caillasse *f* GEOLOGIE brackish marl and limestone, INST HYDR *pour infrastructures hydrauliques* rock rubble

caillé[1] *adj* GENIE CHIM coagulated

caillé[2] *m* AGRO ALIM curd

caillebotis *m* CONSTR duckboard, NAUT gratings

caillebotte *f* AGRO ALIM curd

caille-lait *m* AGRO ALIM lady's bedstraw

caillou *m* CONSTR boulder, GEOLOGIE cobble

cailloutage *m* CONSTR pebble paving

cailloutis *m* CONSTR crushed stone, roadstones, DISTRI EAU break stone, GEOPHYS scree

cailloux: ~ **concassés** *m pl* CONSTR stone chippings

caisse *f* CH DE FER, DISTRI EAU *d'une voiture, d'un wagon* body, PRODUCTION packet, VEHICULES body; ~ **d'alimentation** *f* PAPIER feed box; ~ **antichoc** *f* CH DE FER *véhicules* shock-absorbing body; ~ **d'arrivée multijet** *f* PAPIER multilayer headbox, multistock headbox; ~ **d'arrivée ouverte** *f* PAPIER open headbox; ~ **d'arrivée de pâte** *f* PAPIER breast box, flow box, head box; ~ **d'arrivée primaire** *f* PAPIER primary headbox; ~ **d'arrivée à rouleaux** *f* PAPIER roll headbox; ~ **d'arrivée secondaire** *f* PAPIER secondary headbox; ~ **aspirante** *f* PAPIER flat box, pump box, suction box, vacuum box; ~ **aspirante bombée** *f* PAPIER cambered suction box; ~ **aspirante à courroies mobiles** *f* PAPIER moving belt flat box; ~ **autoporteuse** *f* VEHICULES *carrosserie* unit construction body, unitized body; ~ **de ballast** *f* NAUT ballast tank; ~ **de cémentation** *f* PRODUCTION converting pot; ~ **à châssis intégré** *f* VEHICULES *carrosserie* unit construction body; ~ **à claire-voies** *f* EMBALLAGE crate; ~ **de criblage** *f* PRODUCTION screening box; ~ **à débourber** *f* MINES trunk; ~ **à eau de rouleau de calandre** *f* PAPIER calender water box; ~ **d'égouttage** *f* PAPIER drainage chest, straining chest, drainer; ~ **d'emballage** *f* TEXTILE packing case; ~ **d'empilage** *f* EMBALLAGE stacking box; ~ **en contreplaqué** *f* EMBALLAGE plywood case; ~ **isolée** *f* REFRIG insulated body; ~ **isotherme** *f* REFRIG insulated body; ~ **à latte double** *f* EMBALLAGE double-battened case; ~ **de mélange** *f* PAPIER mixing box, mixing chest; ~ **pour raffermir la barbotine** *f* CERAM VER slip kiln; ~ **profonde** *f* TRANSPORT deep tank; ~ **de service** *f* NUCLEAIRE day tank, day-fuel tank

caisses: ~ **mobiles** *f pl* CH DE FER *véhicules* swap bodies

caisson *m* AERONAUT box-type structure, CERAM VER tower section, CHARBON sunk well, CONS MECA case, CONSTR, DISTRI EAU caisson, GAZ tank, MINES bunker, ore bin, NAUT caisson, locker; ~ **d'aérage** *m* MINES air box, air reservoir, PETROLE air box; ~ **d'air** *m* PETROLE air tank; ~ **à air** *m* NAUT air tank, buoyancy tank, caisson, camel; ~ **de bordure** *m* AERONAUT edge box member; ~ **de chaudière** *m* INST HYDR boiler jacket; ~ **congélateur** *m* REFRIG freezer compartment; ~ **de décompression** *m* PETROLE decompression chamber; ~ **de dérive** *m* AERONAUT fin spar box; ~ **étanche** *m* CINEMAT *pour prise de vues sous-marines* underwater housing; ~ **de flottabilité** *m* NAUT air tank, buoyancy tank, flotation tank; ~ **de fuselage** *m* AERONAUT fuselage box; ~ **humide** *m* OCEANO wet chamber; ~ **hyperbare** *m* OCEANO, PETROLE hyperbaric chamber; ~ **insonore** *m* CINEMAT blimp; ~ **à minerai** *m* MINES ore bin; ~ **d'observation** *m* PETROLE *plongée* observation chamber; ~ **de pale** *m* AERONAUT blade pocket; ~ **de pistonnage** *m* CHARBON compression chamber; ~ **raidisseur** *m* AERONAUT box-type stiffener; ~ **de réacteur** *m* NUCLEAIRE reactor tank, reactor vessel, PHYSIQUE reactor vessel

cake *m* PETR mud cake

calage: [1] **avec** ~ **automatique** *adj* COMMANDE self-adjusting

calage [2] *m* AERONAUT *instrument* setting, CONS MECA adjustment, fixing, keying, scotching, shimming, ELECTR *courant alternatif* phasing, ELECTRON adjustment, ELECTROTEC lead, IMPRIM make-ready, PRODUCTION clamping, TV registration, VEHICULES *allumage, soupape* timing; ~ **d'allumage** *m* AUTO ignition setting, ignition timing, VEHICULES ignition timing; ~ **altimétrique** *m* AERONAUT altimeter setting; ~ **altimé-**

trique standard *m* AERONAUT standard altimeter setting; ~ **automatique** *m* COMMANDE self-adjustment, self-setting; ~ **du compresseur** *m* AERONAUT *turbomachines* compressor stall; ~ **de la distribution** *m* AUTO timing adjustment; ~ **d'essieu** *m* CONS MECA axle fit; ~ **de pas** *m* AERONAUT *hélice* pitch setting

calamine *f* AUTO oil-carbon deposit, MECANIQUE *matériaux* scale, MINERAUX calamine, electric calamine

calamite *f* MINERAUX calamite

calandrage *m* CERAM VER rolling process, PAPIER, PLAST CAOU *opération* calendering; ~ **à chaud** *m* PAPIER hot calendering; ~ **humide** *m* PAPIER water finish, TEXTILE water finishing

calandre *f* GENIE CHIM calandria, IMPRIM *papier*, PAPIER, PLAST CAOU, TEXTILE calender; ~ **à bâti fermé** *f* PAPIER closed-face calender; ~ **à bâti ouvert** *f* PAPIER open-frame super calender; ~ **à feuilles** *f* PAPIER sheet calender; ~ **à friction** *f* PAPIER friction calender; ~ **gaufrée** *f* EMBALLAGE embossed calender; ~ **de radiateur** *f* VEHICULES *refroidissement* radiator grille; ~ **de satinage** *f* PAPIER gloss calender; ~ **à satiner** *f* EMBALLAGE glazing calender; ~ **à vapeur** *f* TEXTILE steam calender

calandré: ~ **à l'eau** *adj* PAPIER *industrie du papier* water-finished; ~ **humide** *adj* PAPIER water-finished

calandrer *vt* PLAST CAOU calender, TEXTILE surface

calanque *f* OCEANO creek, inlet

calavérite *f* MINERAUX calaverite

calcaire [1] *adj* CHIMIE calcareous, GEOLOGIE calcareous, limy

calcaire [2] *m* CERAM VER limestone, CHIMIE lime rock, CONSTR, GEOLOGIE, PETR limestone; ~ **à algues** *m* PETR algal limestone; ~ **avec grains jointifs liés par la micrite** *m* GEOLOGIE packstone; ~ **à ciment** *m* CONSTR cement stone; ~ **construit** *m* GEOLOGIE boundstone, constructed limestone, PETR boundstone; ~ **coquillier** *m* GEOLOGIE shelly limestone; ~ **à crinoïdes** *m* GEOLOGIE crinoidal limestone, encrinitic limestone; ~ **cristallin** *m* GEOLOGIE crystalline limestone; ~ **dolomitique** *m* GEOLOGIE dolomitic limestone; ~ **à éléments jointifs liés par la sparite** *m* GEOLOGIE grainstone; ~ **à encrines** *m* GEOLOGIE encrinitic limestone; ~ **graveleux** *m* GEOLOGIE lump limestone, pellet limestone; ~ **gréseux** *m* GEOLOGIE sandy limestone; ~ **magnésien** *m* GEOLOGIE magnesian limestone; ~ **microcristallin** *m* GEOLOGIE microcrystalline limestone; ~ **noduleux** *m* GEOLOGIE knobbly limestone, nodular limestone; ~ **à nummulites** *m* GEOLOGIE nummulitic limestone; ~ **oolithique** *m* GEOLOGIE oolitic limestone; ~ **oolithique** *m* GEOLOGIE pisolite limestone, pisolitic limestone, PETR grapestone; ~ **pisolitique** *m* GEOLOGIE pisolite limestone, pisolitic limestone; ~ **de précipitation chimique** *m* GEOLOGIE orthochemical limestone; ~ **récifal** *m* GEOLOGIE constructed limestone; ~ **sableux** *m* GEOLOGIE sandy limestone; ~ **siliceux** *m* GEOLOGIE cherty limestone

calcarénite *f* GEOLOGIE calcarenite, lime sandrock

calcarifère *adj* CHIMIE calciferous

calcédoine *f* MINERAUX chalcedony

calcédonix *m* MINERAUX chalcedonyx

calcifère *adj* GEOLOGIE calciferous

calciférol *m* CHIMIE calciferol

calcifier *vt* CHIMIE calcify

calcilutite *f* GEOLOGIE lime mudrock

calcin *m* CERAM VER cullet, PRODUCTION fur, scale; ~ **étranger** *m* CERAM VER foreign cullet; ~ **recyclé** *m*

CERAM VER, RECYCLAGE ecology cullet; ~ **tiré à l'eau** *m* (Fra) *(cf calcinures)* CERAM VER quenched cullet (BrE), shredded cullet (AmE); ~ **d'usine** *m* CERAM VER factory cullet

calcination *f* CHARBON calcination, MAT CHAUFF calcining, PRODUCTION roasting, THERMODYN burning

calciné *adj* PRODUCTION, THERMODYN burnt

calciner *vt* CHARBON, CHIMIE calcine, THERMODYN burn

calcinures *f pl* (Bel) *(cf calcin tiré à l'eau)* CERAM VER quenched cullet (BrE), shredded cullet (AmE)

calciocélestite *f* MINERAUX calciocelestine

calcioferrite *f* MINERAUX calcioferrite

calciothorite *f* MINERAUX calciothorite

calcique *adj* CHIMIE, GEOLOGIE calcic

calcite *f* MINERAUX, PETR calcite

calcium *m* (Ca) CHIMIE calcium (Ca)

calco-alcalin *adj* GEOLOGIE *roche ou série magmatique* calc-alkaline

calcschiste *m* GEOLOGIE *marne métamorphisée* calcschist

calcul *m* INFORMAT computation, computing, MATH calculation, calculus, ORDINAT computation, computing; ~ **d'adresse** *m* ORDINAT address generation; ~ **analogique** *m* ORDINAT analog calculation; ~ **des charges** *m* PRODUCTION capacity requirement planning; ~ **des charges globales** *m* PRODUCTION rough-cut capacity planning; ~ **différentiel** *m* MATH differential calculus; ~ **d'extrapolation linéaire** *m* TELECOM linear scaling calculation; ~ **d'orbite** *m* ESPACE orbit determination; ~ **des ouvrages** *m* CONSTR structural analysis; ~ **par tâtonnement** *m* GEOMETRIE trial and error calculation; ~ **tensoriel** *m* MATH tensor calculus; ~ **des variations** *m* MATH calculus of variations, variational calculus

calculateur *m* INFORMAT computer, MATH calculator, ORDINAT computer, TELECOM call processor; ~ **analogique** *m* TELECOM analog call processor (AmE), analogue call processor (BrE); ~ **de bord** *m* ESPACE *véhicules* on-board computer; ~ **central** *m* TELECOM central processor; ~ **de commutation** *m* TELECOM switching system processor; ~ **électronique** *m* INFORMAT, ORDINAT electronic calculator; ~ **d'exécution** *m* ORDINAT target computer; ~ **d'exploitation et de maintenance** *m* TELECOM maintenance processor; ~ **de gestion** *m* TELECOM administrative processor; ~ **hybride** *m* TELECOM hybrid call processor; ~ **métrage-temps** *m* CINEMAT time-footage calculator; ~ **numérique** *m* INFORMAT, ORDINAT digital computer; ~ **périphérique** *m* TELECOM PP, peripheral processor; ~ **de posemètre** *m* PHOTO light meter scale; ~ **à programme enregistré** *m* TELECOM stored program computer (AmE), stored programme computer; ~ **de route** *m* NAUT tracker register; ~ **sériel** *m* INFORMAT serial computer; ~ **spécialisé** *m* ORDINAT special-purpose computer; ~ **synchrone** *m* ORDINAT synchronous computer; ~ **de temps de pose** *m* CINEMAT exposure calculator; ~ **universel** *m* INFORMAT, ORDINAT GP computer, general-purpose computer; ~ **de vol** *m* AERONAUT flight computer

calculatrice *f* ELECTRON, MATH, ORDINAT calculator; ~ **de poche** *f* INFORMAT, ORDINAT pocket calculator

calculer *vt* MATH calculate

calculette *f* TELECOM pocket calculator

caldeira *f* GEOLOGIE *cratère volcanique* caldera

cale *f* CONS MECA block, key, scotch, packing piece, shim, wedge, CONSTR needle, wedge, MECANIQUE *vé*-

hicules chock, MINES holing prop, *placée dans la souscave* punch prop, NAUT chock, hold, *de construction* slip, *de carénage* slipway, OCEANO hold, PRODUCTION block, chock, TRANSPORT cargo hold; ~ **d'appui** *f* CONS MECA packing piece, shim; ~ **d'arbre** *f* CONS MECA shaft key; ~ **de centrage** *f* CONS MECA positioning block; ~ **de construction** *f* NAUT building berth, building slip; ~ **à eau** *f* NAUT water tank; ~ **en béton** *f* CONSTR spacer block; ~ **d'entrefer** *f* ENREGISTR gap spacer; ~ **en V** *f* CONS MECA *traçage*, METROLOGIE *traçage* V-block; ~ **d'épaisseur** *f* MECANIQUE *outillage* shim; ~ **étalon** *f* MECANIQUE, METROLOGIE gage block (AmE), gauge block (BrE); ~ **étalon en céramique** *f* CONS MECA ceramic slip gage (AmE), ceramic slip gauge (BrE); ~ **de forme** *f* CONS MECA form shim; ~ **froide** *f* TRANSPORT refrigerating hold; ~ **Johansson** *f* MECANIQUE *outillage* Johansson gage (AmE), Johansson gauge (BrE); ~ **lamellée** *f* CONS MECA peel shim; ~ **pelable** *f* CONS MECA strip shim, strip washer; ~ **de précision** *f* CONS MECA precision shim; ~ **sec** *f* CONSTR dry dock; ~ **sèche** *f* NAUT dry dock, graving dock; ~ **de sécurité** *f* CONS MECA heel block; ~ **d'usure** *f* CONS MECA wear strip

calédonite *f* MINERAUX caledonite

caléfaction *f* NUCLEAIRE film boiling, sheet boiling

calendrier *m* ESPACE, PRODUCTION schedule; ~ **d'exécution** *m* CONSTR construction program (AmE), construction programme (BrE), construction schedule; ~ **des insertions** *m* IMPRIM *presse* insertion schedule; ~ **julien** *m* ASTRONOMIE Julian calendar; ~ **de livraison** *m* PRODUCTION delivery schedule; ~ **lunaire musulman** *m* ASTRONOMIE Islamic lunar calendar; ~ **de production** *m* CINEMAT production schedule

caler[1] *vt* CINEMAT lock, CONS MECA block, cog, key, CONSTR fix, *instrument de nivellement* clamp, IMPRIM adjust, set, *presse* make ready, INST HYDR *une soupape* jam, MECANIQUE jam, wedge, NAUT draw, OCEANO bottom, *filet* set, shoot, *un filet* lay, PRODUCTION chock, VEHICULES *moteur* stall

caler[2] ~ **un appareil altimétriquement** *vi* CONSTR *arpentage* orient an instrument vertically; ~ **un appareil planimétriquement** *vi* CONSTR *arpentage* orient an instrument horizontally

caler[3] **se** ~ *v réfl* CONSTR bind

caleur *m* CH DE FER shunter

calfait *m* CONS MECA, NAUT caulking iron

calfat *m* CONS MECA, NAUT caulker

calfatage *m* CONS MECA, MECANIQUE, NAUT, PRODUCTION caulking

calfater *vt* CONS MECA, NAUT caulk

calibrage *m* CHARBON, ELECTRON calibration, IMPRIM calibration, wordage, character count, METROLOGIE *d'un appareil de mesure* gaging (AmE), gauging (BrE), NUCLEAIRE, PRODUCTION calibration; ~ **de l'amplitude** *m* ELECTRON amplitude calibration; ~ **de la copie** *m* IMPRIM *composition, mise en page* copy fitting; ~ **en ligne** *m* RESSORTS on-line gaging (AmE), on-line gauging (BrE); ~ **de modèle** *m* POLLUTION model calibration; ~ **par radar** *m* PHYS ONDES radar calibration

calibrateur *m* ELECTRON calibrator; ~ **d'amplitude** *m* ELECTRON amplitude calibrator

calibre *m* CONS MECA caliper (AmE), calliper (BrE), gage (AmE), gauge (BrE), jig, template, templet, GENIE CHIM particle size, INSTRUMENT former, MECANIQUE *indicateur*, METROLOGIE gage (AmE), gauge (BrE), PAPIER caliper (AmE), calliper (BrE), template, former, PETR caliber (AmE), calibre (BrE), PHYSIQUE rating, PRODUCTION former, patron, pattern, *d'un fusible* size, QUALITE gage (AmE), gauge (BrE); ~ **d'affûtage** m CONS MECA drill gage (AmE), drill gauge (BrE); ~ **d'alésage** m METROLOGIE bore gage (AmE), bore gauge (BrE); ~ **de bague** m CERAM VER, METROLOGIE ring gage (AmE), ring gauge (BrE); ~ **à bague** m CONS MECA external cylindrical gage (AmE), external cylindrical gauge (BrE), PRODUCTION cylindrical gage (AmE), cylindrical gauge (BrE); ~ **à bouchon** m CONS MECA internal cylindrical gage (AmE), internal cylindrical gauge (BrE), CONSTR plug, plug gage (AmE), plug gauge (BrE), PRODUCTION cylindrical gage (AmE), cylindrical gauge (BrE); ~ **à cadran indicateur** m METROLOGIE dial indicating gage (AmE), dial indicating gauge (BrE); ~ **de contrôle** m CONS MECA inspection gage (AmE), inspection gauge (BrE); ~ **à coulisse** m CONS MECA sliding caliper gage (AmE), sliding calipers (AmE), sliding caliper gauge (BrE), sliding callipers (BrE), METROLOGIE beam caliper (AmE), beam caliper gage (AmE), beam calliper (BrE),beam caliper gauge (BrE); ~ **de détail** m CONS MECA detail gage (AmE), detail gauge (BrE); ~ **électronique** m METROLOGIE *fréquence unique* electronic gage (AmE), electronic gauge (BrE); ~ **d'ensemble** m CONS MECA master gage (AmE), master gauge (BrE); ~ **d'épaisseur** m CONS MECA sheet gage (AmE), sheet gauge (BrE), sheet iron gage (AmE), sheet iron gauge (BrE), METROLOGIE plate gage (AmE), plate gauge (BrE), VEHICULES feeler gage (AmE), feeler gauge (BrE); ~ **étalon** m CONS MECA reference gage (AmE), reference gauge (BrE), standard gage (AmE), standard gauge (BrE), METROLOGIE gage block (AmE), gauge block (BrE), slip gage (AmE), slip gauge (BrE); ~ **fileté** m METROLOGIE screw gage (AmE), screw gauge (BrE); ~ **de forage** m CONS MECA drilling jig, drilling template; ~ **de forme** m CONS MECA jig, PRODUCTION former; ~ **de fraisage** m CONS MECA milling jig; ~ **de hauteur** m METROLOGIE *micrométrique* height gage (AmE), height gauge (BrE); ~ **à lames** m CONS MECA thickness gage (AmE), thickness gauge (BrE), METROLOGIE feeler gage (AmE), feeler gauge (BrE); ~ **à languette** m METROLOGIE spline gage (AmE), spline gauge (BrE); ~ **à limites** m CONS MECA limit gage (AmE), limit gauge (BrE); ~ **de longueur** m METROLOGIE length gage (AmE), length gauge (BrE); ~ **à mâchoires** m METROLOGIE gap gage (AmE), gap gauge (BrE), *fixe, simple* gap gage (AmE), gap gauge (BrE), snap gage (AmE), snap gauge (BrE); ~ **mâle** m CONS MECA internal caliper gage (AmE), internal caliper gauge (BrE); ~ **mère** m CONS MECA master gage (AmE), master gauge (BrE); ~ **passe pas** m CONS MECA no-go gage (AmE), no-go gauge (BrE); ~ **pneumatique** m METROLOGIE air-operated gage (AmE), air-operated gauge (BrE); ~ **pour lamelles couvre-objet** m CERAM VER cover glass gage (AmE), cover glass gauge (BrE); ~ **de préréglage** m METROLOGIE air-operated gage (AmE), air-operated gauge (BrE), pneumatic gage (AmE), pneumatic gauge, presetting gage (AmE), presetting gauge (BrE); ~ **prismatique** m CONS MECA measuring block; ~ **de profondeur** m METROLOGIE depth gage (AmE), depth gauge (BrE); ~ **de référence** m CONS MECA reference gage (AmE), reference gauge (BrE), standard gage (AmE), standard gauge (BrE); ~ **reproducteur** m PRODUCTION former; ~ **simple** m CONS

MECA internal caliper gage (AmE), internal calliper gauge (BrE); ~ **simple femelle** m CONS MECA external caliper gage (AmE), external caliper gauge (BrE); ~ **simple mâle** m CONS MECA male caliper gage (AmE), male caliper gauge (BrE); ~ **tampon** m METROLOGIE plug gage (AmE), plug gauge (BrE); ~ **à tige coulissante et vis micrométrique** m CONS MECA internal micrometer; ~ **de tolérance** m CONS MECA, METROLOGIE limit gage (AmE), limit gauge (BrE); ~ **de vérification des vis** m CONS MECA screw gage (AmE), screw gauge (BrE), screw thread gage (AmE), screw thread gauge (BrE), thread gage (AmE), thread gauge (BrE); ~ **à vis micrométrique** m CONS MECA micrometer, micrometer calipers (AmE), micrometer callipers (BrE)

calibre-mâchoires: ~ **à 3 points** m CONS MECA three-point snap gage (AmE), three-point snap gauge (BrE)

calibrer vt AGRO ALIM *fruits* grade, CHARBON size, CONS MECA gage (AmE), gauge (BrE), EQUIP LAB calibrate, IMPRIM calibrate, cast off, PAPIER, PHYSIQUE calibrate, PRODUCTION gage (AmE), gauge (BrE)

calibres m pl METROLOGIE *trusquin à lecture numérique, vernier* calipers (AmE), callipers (BrE); ~ **à cadran indicateur** m pl METROLOGIE dial indicating calipers (AmE), dial indicating callipers (BrE)

calibreur m CONS MECA tube gage (AmE), tube gauge (BrE), MINES coal sizer

calicot m IMPRIM *reliure* calico

californium m *(Cf)* CHIMIE californium *(Cf)*

caliorne m NAUT winding tackle

callaïnite f MINERAUX callainite

callovien adj GEOLOGIE *stratigraphie* Callovian

calmant m METALL killing agent

calme[1] adj HYDROLOGIE, METEO calm

calme[2] m HYDROLOGIE calm; ~ **plat** m HYDROLOGIE, NAUT *météorologie* dead calm

calmes: ~ **équatoriaux** m pl METEO doldrums, equatorial calms, OCEANO doldrums, equatorial calms; ~ **subtropicaux** m pl METEO, OCEANO subtropical calms; ~ **tropicaux** m pl METEO, OCEANO tropical calms

caloduc m ELECTRON thermal diode, ESPACE *thermique, véhicules,* TRANSPORT heat pipe

calomel m CHIMIE, MINERAUX calomel

caloporteur m THERMODYN heat-exchanging medium; ~ **de secours** m NUCLEAIRE emergency core coolant

calorie f AGRO ALIM, PHYSIQUE, THERMODYN calorie; ~ **Britannique** f METROLOGIE BTU, BThU, British thermal unit

calorifère m CHAUFFAGE hot air heater

calorifiant adj PRODUCTION calorific

calorifieur m CONS MECA calorifier

calorifique adj PHYSIQUE, PRODUCTION calorific, THERMODYN calorific, thermic

calorifuge[1] adj MATERIAUX insulated against heat, SECURITE heat-proof, THERMODYN heat-insulating

calorifuge[2] m MATERIAUX *chaleur* nonconductor, MECANIQUE heat insulation, lagging

calorifugé adj CHAUFFAGE heat-insulated, MECANIQUE heat-insulated, lagged, PHYSIQUE heat-insulating, SECURITE heat-resistant, THERMODYN heat-insulated

calorifugeage m EMBALLAGE heat insulation, MATERIAUX heat insulation, lagging, PETROLE heat insulation, *raffinerie* lagging, THERMODYN heat insulation, insulation against heat loss, lagging, thermal lagging; ~ **frigorifique** m THERMODYN insulation against heat gain, low-temperature insulation

calorimètre *m* CHIMIE, CONS MECA, EQUIP LAB *mesure de chaleur*, PHYS PART, PHYSIQUE, REFRIG, THERMODYN calorimeter; ~ **à condensation** *m* GENIE CHIM condensation calorimeter; ~ **électromagnétique** *m* PHYS PART, PHYS RAYON electromagnetic calorimeter; ~ **hadronique** *m* PHYS PART, PHYS RAYON hadronic calorimeter; ~ **quasiadiabatique** *m* NUCLEAIRE quasiadiabatic calorimeter

calorimétrie *f* CHIMIE, PHYSIQUE, REFRIG, THERMODYN calorimetry; ~ **différentielle à balayage** *f* PHYS RAYON, THERMODYN differential scanning calorimetry; ~ **différentielle programmée** *f* THERMODYN differential scanning calorimetry; ~ **par analyse différentielle** *f* PLAST CAOU, THERMODYN differential scanning calorimetry

calorimétrique *adj* CHIMIE calorimetric

calorique *adj* THERMODYN caloric

calotte *f* CERAM VER cap, dome, moil, CONSTR *d'une chèvre* cap; ~ **de barbotage** *f* PETROLE *raffinerie* bubble cap; ~ **à barbotage** *f* NUCLEAIRE bubble cap, bubble hood; ~ **diffusante** *f* PHOTO *pour mesure en lumière incidente* diffuser; ~ **glaciaire** *f* OCEANO ice cap, ice sheet; ~ **polaire** *f* ASTRONOMIE polar cap, polar tip

calquage *m* CONS MECA tracing

calque *m* IMPRIM traced design, tracing; ~ **de préparation** *m* IMPRIM overlay; ~ **de travail** *m* IMPRIM mechanical overlay

calquer *vt* CONS MECA trace

CAM *abrév (corde aérodynamique moyenne)* AERONAUT MAC *(mean aerodynamic chord)*

cambrage *m* CONSTR cambering

cambre *f* CONSTR camber

cambrer[1] *vt* CONSTR camber

cambrer:[2] **se ~** *v réfl* CONSTR camber

cambrien *adj* GEOLOGIE *stratification* Cambrian

cambriolage *m* SECURITE burglary

cambrure *f* CONSTR camber, *de bois* camber, OCEANO *d'une vague* camber, steepness

cambuse *f* NAUT storeroom

came *f* AUTO, CINEMAT cam, CONS MECA cam, wipe, lifter, wiper, INST HYDR valve eccentric, MECANIQUE, VEHICULES cam; ~ **des axes** *f* PRODUCTION spindle cam; ~ **de blocage** *f* CONS MECA locking cam; ~ **de butée** *f* CONS MECA knock-off cam; ~ **à cylindre** *f* PRODUCTION cylinder cam, drum cam; ~ **à cylindre à rainure** *f* CONS MECA grooved cylinder cam; ~ **cylindrique** *f* CONS MECA barrel cam; ~ **désaxée** *f* CONS MECA eccentric cam; ~ **à développement** *f* CONS MECA involute cam; ~ **d'éjecteur rapide** *f* CONS MECA kicker box; ~ **de frein** *f* AUTO, MECANIQUE brake cam; ~ **d'impression** *f* IMPRIM printing cam; ~ **de rupture** *f* VEHICULES *allumage* distributor cam; ~ **à tambour** *f* PRODUCTION cylinder cam, drum cam; ~ **à tambour à languettes** *f* PRODUCTION strake drum cam

camée: ~ **en verre** *m* CERAM VER glass cameo

Caméléon *m* ASTRONOMIE Chamaeleon

camembert *m* INFORMAT pie chart

caméra *f* CINEMAT, IMPRIM *optique*, INSTRUMENT, PHYSIQUE *ciné*, TV camera; ~ **d'animation** *f* CINEMAT animation camera, rostrum camera; ~ **à l'antenne** *f* TV hot camera, live camera; ~ **autonome** *f* TV mobile camera; ~ **autosilencieuse** *f* CINEMAT blimped camera; ~ **avec intervallomètre** *f* CINEMAT low-speed camera; ~ **avec moteur à ressort** *f* CINEMAT clockwork camera; ~ **banc titre** *f* CINEMAT rostrum camera; ~ **biformat** *f* PHOTO dual-format camera; ~ **à chargeur** *f* CINEMAT magazine camera; ~ **à chargeurs parallèles** *f* CINEMAT parallel magazine camera; ~ **à compteur de photons** *f* PHYS PART photon-counting camera; ~ **électronographique** *f* PHYS PART electronographic camera; ~ **à l'épaule** *f* CINEMAT hand-held camera; ~ **à fente** *f* CINEMAT streak camera; ~ **à fente avec convertisseur d'image** *f* CINEMAT streak image converter camera; ~ **à fente et miroir tournant** *f* CINEMAT rotating mirror streak camera; ~ **à fente à tambour tournant** *f* CINEMAT rotating drum streak camera; ~ **grande vitesse** *f* CINEMAT high-speed camera; ~ **image-son** *f* CINEMAT double-headed camera; ~ **insonorisée** *f* CINEMAT sound camera; ~ **lucida** *f* PHOTO camera lucida; ~ **mal équilibrée** *f* TV mismatched camera; ~ **à manivelle** *f* CINEMAT hand cranked camera; ~ **miniature** *f* TV minicam; ~ **non synchrone** *f* CINEMAT wild camera; ~ **numérique** *f* TV digital camera; ~ **pour analyse de mouvement** *f* CINEMAT motion analysis camera; ~ **pour effets spéciaux** *f* CINEMAT process camera; ~ **pour mémoire ccd** *f* EMBALLAGE charge-coupled device camera; ~ **pour prise de vue aérienne** *f* CINEMAT aerial camera; ~ **de poursuite** *f* ESPACE tracking camera; ~ **pour trucages** *f* CINEMAT process camera; ~ **prenant la place de la personne** *f* CINEMAT subjective camera; ~ **à prisme diviseur** *f* CINEMAT split beam camera; ~ **reflex** *f* CINEMAT reflex camera; ~ **de reportage** *f* CINEMAT hand-held camera; ~ **à ressort** *f* CINEMAT spring-drive camera; ~ **sans tube** *f* ELECTRON solid-state camera; ~ **son** *f* CINEMAT sound camera; ~ **son optique** *f* CINEMAT optical sound camera; ~ **sonore** *f* CINEMAT newsreel camera; ~ **de studio** *f* PHOTO studio camera; ~ **télécommandée** *f* TV remote-controlled camera; ~ **de télévision** *f* ELECTRON, PHYSIQUE television camera; ~ **thermique** *f* MILITAIRE thermal imager; ~ **titre** *f* TV caption scanner; ~ **titres** *f* TV insert camera; ~ **tourelle** *f* CINEMAT turret camera; ~ **tritube** *f* TV three-tube camera; ~ **à trois bandes** *f* CINEMAT three-strip camera; ~ **à tube vidicon** *f* TV vidicon camera; ~ **TV** *f* PHYSIQUE television camera; ~ **à visée reflex** *f* CINEMAT reflex camera; ~ **à vitesse variable** *f* CINEMAT multiple speed camera, variable speed camera

cameraman *m* CINEMAT cameraman

camion *m* MECANIQUE truck, TRANSPORT, VEHICULES lorry (BrE), truck (AmE); ~ **à accumulateur** *m* TRANSPORT battery truck; ~ **articulé** *m* VEHICULES articulated lorry (BrE), articulated truck (AmE), tractor-trailer truck (AmE); ~ **d'assainissement** *m* POLLU MER gulley sucker, vacuum truck; ~ **avec malaxeur** *m* CONSTR mixer truck; ~ **benne** *m* POLLU MER skip lorry, TRANSPORT dumper, skip lorry, skip truck; ~ **à bestiaux** *m* TRANSPORT cattle truck; ~ **bétonnière** *m* CONSTR mixer truck; ~ **chute de poids** *m* PETR thumper; ~ **citerne** *m* CONSTR tanker truck, water tanker, water truck, PETROLE tanker, POLLU MER road tanker, TRANSPORT RTC, road tank car, tank truck, tanker, vehicle tanker, VEHICULES tanker; ~ **citerne de ravitaillement** *m* TRANSPORT refueling tanker (AmE), refuelling tanker (BrE); ~ **de collecte** *m* TRANSPORT refuse collection lorry (BrE), refuse collection truck (AmE); ~ **de déménagement** *m* TRANSPORT removal van; ~ **dépanneur** *m* TRANSPORT salvage car (AmE), salvage lorry (BrE), salvage truck (AmE); ~ **élévateur** *m* EMBALLAGE lifting vehicle; ~ **important autres camions semi-portés** *m* TRANSPORT saddle mount combination; ~ **et remorque** *m* TRANSPORT trailer train; ~ **de fret** *m* TRANSPORT freight truck (AmE), goods lorry

(BrE); ~ **frigorifique** m REFRIG refrigerated lorry (BrE), refrigerated truck (AmE), THERMODYN insulated lorry (BrE), insulated truck (AmE), refrigerated lorry (BrE), refrigerated truck (AmE); ~ **à hayon élévateur** m TRANSPORT tail-lift truck; ~ **isolé** m REFRIG insulated lorry (BrE), insulated truck (AmE); ~ **isotherme** m REFRIG insulated lorry (BrE), insulated truck (AmE), TRANSPORT refrigerated truck (AmE) ~ **isothésure** m THERMODYN heat-insulated truck; ~ **laitier** m TRANSPORT milk tanker; ~ **plateau** m TRANSPORT rack body truck; ~ **plate-forme** m TRANSPORT pick-up truck (AmE), pick-up van (BrE); ~ **porte-conteneur** m TRANSPORT container carrier lorry (BrE), container carrier truck (AmE); ~ **à propulsion électrique** m TRANSPORT electric propulsion lorry (BrE), electric propulsion truck (AmE); ~ **ravitailleur** m PETROLE *aéroport* fueler (AmE), fueller (BrE); ~ **régie** m CINEMAT control van; ~ **semi-remorque** m VEHICULES articulated lorry (BrE), articulated truck (AmE), tractor-trailer truck (AmE); ~ **tout-terrain** m TRANSPORT cross-country lorry (BrE), cross-country truck (AmE); ~ **à turbine** m TRANSPORT turbine-engined lorry (BrE), turbine-engined truck (AmE); ~ **de vidange des fosses septiques** m RECYCLAGE sludge gulper; ~ **'mille pattes'** m TRANSPORT multiaxle heavy freight vehicle (AmE), multiaxle heavy goods vehicle (BrE)

camionnage m CH DE FER collection and delivery, door-to-door delivery

camionnette f TRANSPORT light lorry (BrE), light truck (AmE); ~ **électrique** f TRANSPORT electric delivery lorry (BrE), electric delivery truck (AmE), electric transport vehicle, electrovan; ~ **plateau** f TRANSPORT platform truck

camion-tracteur m TRANSPORT tractor unit

campagne f CERAM VER campaign, working life, PRODUCTION campaign, mill run, *d'un haut-fourneau* run; ~ **de combustion de réacteur** f NUCLEAIRE operating fuel cycle; ~ **contre les accidents** f SECURITE safety first campaign; ~ **de haut-fourneau** f PRODUCTION blast furnace campaign; ~ **de pêche** f OCEANO fishing trip; ~ **sismique** f PETROLE seismic survey

campanien adj GEOLOGIE Campanian

camphane m CHIMIE camphane

camphène m CHIMIE camphene

camphol m CHIMIE camphol

camphorate m CHIMIE camphorate

camphorique adj CHIMIE camphoric

camphre m CHIMIE camphor

camphré adj CHIMIE camphorated

campylite f MINERAUX campylite

CAN abrév (*convertisseur analogique-numérique*) ELECTRON ADC (*analog-to-digital converter, analogue-to-digital converter*) ORDINAT ADC (*analog-to-digital converter*), PHYSIQUE, TELECOM ADC (*analog-to-digital converter, analogue-to-digital converter*)

canal m CERAM VER canal, CONSTR channel, ditch, pipe, DISTRI EAU sluiceway, sluice, ELECTROTEC, EN RENOUV, ENREGISTR, ESPACE *communications*, INFORMAT channel, INST HYDR raceway, race, MINES *aérage des mines* air pipe, NAUT canal, channel, OCEANO, ORDINAT, TELECOM, TV channel; ~ **adjacent** m TV adjacent channel; ~ **d'alimentation** m PLAST CAOU feed runner; ~ **alluvial** m DISTRI EAU alluvial bed; ~ **d'amenée** m DISTRI EAU flume, head race, inflow canal, intake

canal, leat, penstock, pentrough, INST HYDR head race, PRODUCTION leat; ~ **d'amont** m EN RENOUV headrace canal; ~ **annulaire** m NUCLEAIRE annular channel; ~ **d'assèchement** m DISTRI EAU drainage channel; ~ **audio** m ENREGISTR audio channel; ~ **B** m TELECOM *information* B-channel; ~ **de bande** m TV canoe, ~ **à bande réduite** m INFORMAT band-limited channel; ~ **à bief de partage** m DISTRI EAU summit canal; ~ **de chauffe** m EMBALLAGE heating channel; ~ **collecteur** m DISTRI EAU *d'une pompe centrifuge* volute chamber; ~ **de commande** m TELECOM CC, control channel; ~ **de commande intégré** m TELECOM ECC, embedded control channel; ~ **de communication de données** m TELECOM DCC, data communication channel; ~ **court** m ELECTRON short channel; ~ **D** m TELECOM D-channel; ~ **décentralisé** m PRODUCTION remote channel; ~ **de décharge** m DISTRI EAU emergency spillway, tailrace, HYDROLOGIE discharge channel; ~ **découvert** m INST HYDR *conduite* open channel; ~ **de dérivation** m DISTRI EAU diversion canal, flume, HYDROLOGIE diversion canal, diversion channel, diversion cut, INST HYDR head race, PRODUCTION leat; ~ **de dessèchement** m DISTRI EAU drainage channel; ~ **de déversement** m RECYCLAGE discharge pipe; ~ **de différence** m ENREGISTR difference channel; ~ **direct** m TV channel using upper sideband; ~ **discret** m TELECOM discrete channel; ~ **distributeur** m DISTRI EAU delivery channel, delivery race, distributing canal; ~ **de distribution** m CERAM VER forehearth; ~ **éclusé** m DISTRI EAU locked canal; ~ **à écluses et à lac intérieur** m DISTRI EAU lock and inland lake canal; ~ **d'émission** m TELECOM transmit channel; ~ **en bois** m DISTRI EAU *supporté par chevalets* flume; ~ **en planches** m DISTRI EAU flume; ~ **d'enregistrement** m CINEMAT track, ENREGISTR recording channel; ~ **en surface** m ELECTRON surface channel; ~ **enterré** m ELECTRON bulk channel; ~ **d'entrée/sortie** m INFORMAT input/output channel; ~ **d'épuisement** m DISTRI EAU drainage ditch; ~ **d'éruption** m GEOLOGIE volcanic vent; ~ **d'essai** m DISTRI EAU test flume; ~ **d'étalonnage** m DISTRI EAU calibration flume; ~ **d'évacuation** m DISTRI EAU discharge canal, tailrace, RECYCLAGE discharge pipe; ~ **d'exploitation intégré** m TELECOM EOC, embedded operations channel; ~ **à forte pente** m EN RENOUV chute spillway; ~ **de fréquence** m TELECOM frequency channel; ~ **à fréquence vocale** m INFORMAT speech channel; ~ **de fuite** m DISTRI EAU tailrace; ~ **de graissage** m CONS MECA oil groove; ~ **de groupement de signalisation** m TELECOM SGC, signaling grouping channel (AmE), signalling grouping channel (BrE); ~ **incliné** m NUCLEAIRE inclined channel; ~ **interocéanique** m OCEANO interocean channel, sea canal; ~ **d'interrogation** m ESPACE *communications* request channel; ~ **interurbain** m TELECOM trunk channel; ~ **interurbain intermédiaire** m TELECOM IT, intermediate trunk; ~ **inversé** m TV channel using lower sideband; ~ **d'irrigation** m DISTRI EAU catch feeder, irrigation canal; ~ **de jaugeage** m DISTRI EAU discharge flume; ~ **de lecture-écriture** m INFORMAT, ORDINAT read-write channel; ~ **linéaire** m TELECOM linear channel; ~ **de maintenance des exploitants de réseau** m TELECOM NOMC, network operators maintenance channel; ~ **maritime** m NAUT ship canal, OCEANO interocean channel, sea canal, ship canal; ~ **multiplexeur** m INFORMAT, ORDINAT multiplexer channel; ~ **N** m ELECTRON n-channel; ~ **de navigation** m DISTRI EAU navigation channel; ~ **à ni-**

veau *m* DISTRI EAU ditch canal; ~ **P** *m* ELECTRON p-channel; ~ **à point de partage** *m* DISTRI EAU summit canal; ~ **de prise** *m* DISTRI EAU flume, penstock, pentrough, PRODUCTION leat; ~ **de prise d'eau** *m* DISTRI EAU intake, INST HYDR head race; ~ **de prise de vue** *m* ESPACE channel; ~ **radio** *m* AERONAUT radio channel; ~ **de réaction nucléaire** *m* PHYS RAYON nuclear reaction channel; ~ **de réception** *m* TELECOM receive channel; ~ **de retour** *m* ENREGISTR feedback channel, return channel; ~ **satellite** *m* TV satellite channel; ~ **sélecteur** *m* INFORMAT, ORDINAT selector channel; ~ **sémaphore** *m* TELECOM signaling channel (AmE), signalling channel (BrE); ~ **son** *m* ENREGISTR, TV audio channel, sound channel; ~ **spécialisé pour la signalisation** *m* TELECOM dedicated signaling channel (AmE), dedicated signalling channel (BrE); ~ **stéréo de droite** *m* ENREGISTR right stereo channel; ~ **stéréophonique de gauche** *m* ENREGISTR left stereo channel; ~ **supplémentaire stéréo** *m* ENREGISTR stereo subchannel; ~ **sur appuis** *m* CONSTR flume; ~ **de surcharge** *m* TELECOM overload channel; ~ **de télécommande** *m* ESPACE *communications* command channel; ~ **téléphonique** *m* INFORMAT voice-band; ~ **de transmission de données** *m* TELECOM DCC, data communication channel; ~ **de transmission des E/S** *m* PRODUCTION *automatisme industriel* I/O channel communication; ~ **de ventilation** *m* CONS MECA cooling duct; ~ **Venturi-Parshall** *m* HYDROLOGIE Venturi-Parshall flume; ~ **de vidange** *m* CONSTR channel; ~ **vidéo** *m* TV video channel; ~ **virtuel** *m* TELECOM VC, virtual channel; ~ **virtuel de signalisation** *m* TELECOM SVC, signaling virtual channel (AmE), signalling virtual channel (BrE); ~ **vocal** *m* ORDINAT speech channel

canal: ~ **d'entrée-sortie** *m* ORDINAT input-output channel

canalisation *f* AUTO passage, CONSTR pipage, piping, pipeline, piping, system of pipes, DISTRI EAU conduit, ditch line, pipeline, sewerage, ELECTR *alimentation* conduit, EN RENOUV pipeline, *barrages, géothermie* channeling (AmE), channelling (BrE), GAZ pipeline, MECANIQUE duct, PETROLE pipeline, transmission main, *en tête de puits* flow line, PRODUCTION *production* raceway, *système hydraulique* line, TELECOM duct, THERMODYN line, TRANSPORT channelization; ~ **d'aérage** *f* MINES ventilation ducting; ~ **d'air** *f* CONS MECA air pipeline, airline; ~ **d'air comprimé** *f* CONS MECA compressed air line; ~ **d'amenée** *f* DISTRI EAU flume; ~ **d'aspiration** *f* PRODUCTION *système hydraulique* suction line; ~ **de carburant** *f* AUTO, VEHICULES fuel line, fuel pipe; ~ **d'eau** *f* CONSTR water line; ~ **enterrée** *f* GAZ buried pipeline; ~ **d'essence** *f* VEHICULES carburant fuel line; ~ **d'évacuation** *f* RECYCLAGE sewer; ~ **de frein** *f* VEHICULES *système de freinage* brake line; ~ **de gaz** *f* CONSTR gas pipeline; ~ **de graissage** *f* AUTO oil channel, oil gallery, oil line; ~ **d'intercommunication** *f* AERONAUT crossfeed line; ~ **de pompage** *f* INSTRUMENT vacuum manifold; ~ **principale** *f* CONSTR main; ~ **principale d'adduction d'air** *f* CONS MECA air main; ~ **de retour des vapeurs** *f* AUTO vapor return line (AmE), vapour return line (BrE); ~ **sans pression** *f* CONS MECA nonpressure pipeline; ~ **de tuyaux** *f* CONSTR system of pipes; ~ **de vapeur** *f* INST HYDR steam pipeline, steam pipe

canalisations: ~ **sous pression** *f pl* CONS MECA pressure main lines

canaliser *vt* CONSTR pipe, DISTRI EAU canalize, EN RE-

NOUV channel

canal-séchoir *m* AGRO ALIM drying cupboard

canard *m* MINES *aérage des mines* air pipe

Cancer *m* ASTRONOMIE Cancer

cancérigène[1] *adj* CHIMIE carcinogenic

cancérigène[2] *m* CHIMIE carcinogen

cancérogène *adj* CHIMIE carcinogenic

cancrinite *f* MINERAUX cancrinite

candela *m (cd)* ELECTROTEC, METROLOGIE, OPTIQUE, PHYSIQUE candela *(cd)*

candélabre *m* AERONAUT landing gear hinge beam fitting

candite *f* MINERAUX candite

canette *f* CERAM VER pirn, TEXTILE pirn, spindle

canevas *m* IMPRIM *reliure* canvas, TEXTILE layer, scrim screen; ~ **huilé** *m* EMBALLAGE oiled canvas; ~ **inférieur** *m* TEXTILE under layer; ~ **intermédiaire** *m* TEXTILE middle layer; ~ **supérieur** *m* TEXTILE top layer

canicule *f* METEO heatwave

Canis: ~ **major** *m* ASTRONOMIE Canis Major; ~ **minor** *m* ASTRONOMIE Canis Minor

caniveau *m* CONS MECA gutter, CONSTR channel, gutter, *de drainage* channel, DISTRI EAU, EN RENOUV flume, EQUIP LAB sump, NUCLEAIRE raceway, PRODUCTION duct; ~ **pour câbles** *m* ELECTROTEC cable conduit, cable duct, cable trough

cannage *m* TEXTILE cannage

canne *f* CERAM VER blowpipe, glass tube; ~ **de niveau** *f* ESPACE level sensor; ~ **pyrométrique** *f* ELECTR pyrometer probe

cannelé *adj* MECANIQUE fluted, splined, PAPIER fluted, PRODUCTION fluted, grooved

canneler *vt* CONSTR channel

canneleuse *f* PAPIER fluter

cannelle *f* CONSTR butt cock

cannelure *f* CERAM VER flute, CONS MECA spline, *dans un cylindre de laminoir* groove, CONSTR flute, fluting, ESPACE *véhicules* flute, groove, spline, GEOLOGIE furrow, IMPRIM *de carton ondulée* flute, MECANIQUE flute, spline, PAPIER *ondulée* flute, PRODUCTION channeling (AmE), channelling (BrE), groove, pass; ~ **carrée** *f* PRODUCTION box pass; ~ **ébaucheuse** *f* PRODUCTION roughing pass; ~ **emboîtée** *f* PRODUCTION closed pass; ~ **en développante** *f* CONS MECA involute spline; ~ **et dentelure** *f* CONS MECA spline and serration; ~ **fermée** *f* PRODUCTION closed pass; ~ **ouverte** *f* PRODUCTION open pass; ~ **roulante** *f* PRODUCTION open pass

cannetière *f* TEXTILE pirn-winding machine

cannibalisme: ~ **galactique** *m* ASTRONOMIE galactic cannibalism; ~ **stellaire** *m* ASTRONOMIE stellar cannibalism

canon *m* CERAM VER cylinder, rod, CONS MECA guide, CONSTR pipe, tube, *d'une clef* barrel, *d'une serrure* barrel, *d'une vis d'Archimède* barrel, EQUIP LAB *seringue*, MECANIQUE barrel, MILITAIRE gun; ~ **à air** *m* PETR air-gun; ~ **à air comprimé** *m* GEOPHYS air-gun; ~ **antichar** *m* MILITAIRE antitank gun; ~ **antichar léger** *m* MILITAIRE light antitank gun; ~ **antichar lourd** *m* MILITAIRE heavy antitank gun; ~ **d'arrosage** *m* ELECTRON flooding gun; ~ **automatique** *m* MILITAIRE automatic gun; ~ **automoteur** *m* MILITAIRE automatic gun; ~ **du bleu** *m* TV blue gun; ~ **de centrage** *m* CONS MECA centering bush (AmE), centring bush (BrE); ~ **contre-avion** *m* MILITAIRE air defence gun; ~ **d'écriture** *m* ELECTRON writing gun; ~ **électronique à faisceau toroïdal** *m* TV toroidal electron gun; ~ **à électrons** *m*

ELECTRON, INSTRUMENT, PHYS RAYON, PHYSIQUE, TV electron gun; ~ **à électrons à pulsation** *m* PHYS RAYON pulsed electron gun; ~ **d'entrée de clé** *m* CONSTR *d'une serrure* barrel; ~ **d'essai** *m* NUCLEAIRE test jack; ~ **du faisceau vert** *m* ELECTRON, TV green gun; ~ **de fusil rayé** *m* MILITAIRE rifle barrel; ~ **à gaz** *m* PETR gas exploder; ~ **de guidage** *m* CONS MECA guide bush, headed guide bush, *d'un pointeau* barrel; ~ **de guidage cylindrique** *m* CONS MECA headless guide bush; ~ **d'inscription** *m* ELECTRON writing gun; ~ **à ions** *m* PRODUCTION ion gun; ~ **lance-harpon** *m* OCEANO harpon gun; ~ **de lecture** *m* ELECTRON flooding gun, reading gun; ~ **léger contre-avion** *m* MILITAIRE light air defence gun; ~ **à longue portée** *m* MILITAIRE long-range weapon; ~ **lourd contre-avion** *m* MILITAIRE heavy anti-aircraft gun; ~ **à neige** *m* CINEMAT snow machine, REFRIG snow gun; ~ **nylon** *m* PLAST CAOU nylon bush; ~ **de perçage** *m* MECANIQUE drill bushing; ~ **sans recul** *m* MILITAIRE recoilless gun; ~ **à tir rapide** *m* MILITAIRE rapid fire gun; ~ **à tourelle** *m* MILITAIRE turret gun

canot *m* NAUT boat; ~ **hors-bord** *m* TRANSPORT outboard motorboat, outboard speedboat; ~ **à moteur** *m* TRANSPORT motorboat; ~ **pneumatique** *m* AERONAUT inflatable dinghy, NAUT dinghy, inflatable dinghy, rubber dinghy; ~ **de sauvetage** *m* NAUT lifeboat; ~ **à voiles** *m* NAUT sailboat (AmE), sailing boat (BrE)

cantharadine *f* CHIMIE cantharadine

cantilever *adj* CH DE FER, CONSTR, PHYSIQUE cantilever

canton *m* CH DE FER section; ~ **de block** *m* CH DE FER block section

cantonite *f* MINERAUX cantonite

cantonnement *m* CH DE FER block system; ~ **de pêche** *m* OCEANO fishery conservation zone, fishery reserve

cantre *m* TEXTILE creel, warping creel; ~ **magasin** *m* TEXTILE magazine creel

canyon *m* NUCLEAIRE canyon

CAO *abrév (conception assistée par ordinateur)* ELECTR, IMPRIM, MECANIQUE, ORDINAT, PRODUCTION, TELECOM CAD *(computer-aided design)*

caoutchouc *m* CHIMIE caoutchouc, rubber, ELECTROTEC, IMPRIM, PAPIER, PLAST CAOU rubber; ~ **acrylique** *m* EMBALLAGE acrylic rubber; ~ **antistatique** *m* PLAST CAOU antistatic rubber; ~ **brut** *m* PLAST CAOU crude rubber, raw rubber; ~ **butadiène** *m* PLAST CAOU butadiene rubber; ~ **butadiène acrylonitrile** *m* PLAST CAOU butadiene acrylonitrile rubber; ~ **cellulaire** *m* CHAUFFAGE, REFRIG cellular rubber; ~ **chloré** *m* PLAST CAOU chlorinated rubber; ~ **chloroprène** *m* PLAST CAOU chloroprene rubber; ~ **durci** *m* PLAST CAOU ebonite; ~ **éthylène propylène** *m* PLAST CAOU ethylene propylene rubber; ~ **expansé** *m* PLAST CAOU expanded rubber, foamed rubber; ~ **à graver** *m* IMPRIM *flexographie* engraving rubber; ~ **microcellulaire** *m* PLAST CAOU microcellular rubber; ~ **minéral** *m* MINERAUX mineral caoutchouc; ~ **mousse** *m* PLAST CAOU expanded rubber, foamed rubber; ~ **naturel** *m* PLAST CAOU natural rubber; ~ **nerveux** *m* PLAST CAOU snappy rubber; ~ **nitrile** *m* PLAST CAOU nitrile rubber; ~ **de nitrile acrylique** *m* PLAST CAOU *type d'élastomère*, PRODUCTION *matériaux* acrylonitrile rubber; ~ **plastifié à l'huile** *m* PLAST CAOU oil-softened rubber; ~ **régénéré** *m* PLAST CAOU reclaimed rubber, regenerated rubber; ~ **silicone** *m* ELECTROTEC *isolant* silicone rubber; ~ **au styrène butadiène** *m* PLAST CAOU styrene butadiene rubber; ~ **synthétique** *m* PETROLE, PLAST CAOU *élastomère* synthetic rubber; ~ **thermoplastique** *m* PLAST

CAOU thermoplastic rubber; ~ **vulcanisé** *m* ELECTR *isolation* vulcanite

caoutchouc-crêpe *m* PLAST CAOU crepe rubber

caoutchoucs: ~ **expansés à cellules ouvertes** *m pl* PLAST CAOU open-cell cellular plastic; ~ **mousses à cellules ouvertes** *m pl* PLAST CAOU open-cell cellular plastic

caoutchoutage *m* REVETEMENT rubber coating

caoutchouté *adj* ELECTR *isolation*, PLAST CAOU rubberized, REVETEMENT rubber-coated, rubber-covered

caoutchouter *vt* REVETEMENT rubberize

cap:[1] ~ **en haut** *adj* NAUT course-up

cap:[2] ~ **en haut** *adv* NAUT course-up

cap[3] *m* AERONAUT heading, ESPACE course, *véhicules* heading, NAUT boat's heading, cape, course, heading, headland, OCEANO cape, headland; ~ **de collision** *m* NAUT collision course; ~ **au compas** *m* NAUT compass heading; ~ **compas** *m* AERONAUT compass heading; ~ **d'éloignement** *m* AERONAUT outbound heading; ~ **magnétique** *m* AERONAUT magnetic heading, NAUT magnetic course; ~ **d'une piste** *m* AERONAUT localizer beam heading; ~ **radar** *m* AERONAUT radar heading; ~ **retour** *m* AERONAUT inbound heading; ~ **vrai** *m* NAUT true course

CAP *abrév (capacité d'absorption des protons)* PHYS RAYON proton absorptive capacity

capabilité *f* QUALITE capability

capacimètre *m* ELECTROTEC capacitance meter

capacitance *f* ELECTROTEC capacitive reactance; ~ **acoustique** *f* ENREGISTR acoustic compliance; ~ **entre spires** *f* ELECTR *bobine* interturn capacitance; ~ **à l'état bloqué** *f* ENREGISTR clamped capacitance; ~ **thermique** *f* EN RENOUV thermal capacitance

capacité *f* CONS MECA, CONSTR capacity, ELECTR capacitance, ELECTROTEC capacitance, capacity, EMBALLAGE holding capacity, EN RENOUV *tube* carrying capacity, INFORMAT, NUCLEAIRE, ORDINAT capacity, PETROLE throughput, PHYSIQUE capacitance, PRODUCTION, REFRIG capacity, TELECOM capability, capacitance; ~ **d'absorption** *f* EMBALLAGE *industrie du papier*, HYDROLOGIE *puits* absorptive capacity; ~ **d'absorption d'eau** *f* DISTRI EAU water absorption capacity; ~ **d'absorption des protons** *f* (*CAP*) PHYS RAYON proton absorptive capacity; ~ **d'accrochage de la colle** *f* IMPRIM *finition* grab; ~ **de base** *f* TRANSPORT basic capacity; ~ **d'une bobine** *f* CINEMAT reel capacity; ~ **de bobine** *f* ELECTR winding capacitance; ~ **calorifique** *f* THERMODYN caloric content, heat capacity; ~ **de canal** *f* TELECOM channel capacity; ~ **de capture** *f* OCEANO catch index, catchability coefficient; ~ **de charge** *f* CONS MECA carrying capacity, ELECTR current-carrying capacity; ~ **de la charge** *f* ELECTROTEC load capacitance; ~ **chauffante** *f* THERMODYN heating capacity; ~ **de chauffe** *f* CHAUFFAGE, THERMODYN heating capacity; ~ **concentrée** *f* ELECTR *condensateur* lumped capacitance; ~ **de conduite** *f* EN RENOUV conduit capacity; ~ **de congélation** *f* REFRIG freezing capacity; ~ **de correction des paquets d'erreur** *f* TELECOM burst error correcting capability; ~ **cyclique** *f* TRANSPORT tidal capacity; ~ **de débit solide** *f* HYDROLOGIE transport capacity for solids; ~ **différentielle** *f* ELECTR incremental capacitance; ~ **d'échange cationique** *f* (*CEC*) GEOLOGIE, PETROLE, POLLUTION cation exchange capacity (*CEC*); ~ **d'écoulement** *f* TRANSPORT capacity of a road; ~ **effective** *f* PRODUCTION demonstrated capacity; ~ **électrique** *f* CONS MECA capacity, TELECOM electrical capacitance; ~ **en becs**

parallèles *f* CONS MECA parallel jaw capacity; ~ en parallèle *f* ELECTROTEC shunt capacitance; ~ de l'enroulement *f* ELECTROTEC winding capacitance; ~ en série *f* ELECTROTEC series capacitance; ~ entre broches *f* ELECTROTEC pin-to-pin capacitance; ~ d'entrée *f* ELECTROTEC input capacitance; ~ entre électrodes *f* ELECTROTEC interelectrode capacitance; ~ de fixation *f* CHARBON loaded capacity; ~ de fixation des protons *f* POLLUTION proton absorptive capacity; ~ fonctionnelle locale *f* TELECOM LFC, local function capabilities; ~ de fusion *f* CERAM VER maximum melting rate; ~ grille-cathode *f* ELECTROTEC grid cathode capacitance; ~ grille-drain *f* ELECTROTEC gate-to-drain capacitance; ~ grille-source *f* ELECTROTEC gate-to-source capacitance; ~ grille-substrat *f* ELECTROTEC gate-to-substrate capacitance; ~ hebdomadaire *f* PRODUCTION man-year; ~ hebdomadaire par semaine *f* PRODUCTION man-week; ~ horaire par employé *f* PRODUCTION man-hour; ~ de jonction *f* ELECTROTEC junction capacitance; ~ journalière par employé *f* PRODUCTION man-day; ~ de levage *f* NUCLEAIRE *crochet* lifting capacity with hook; ~ limite *f* AERONAUT load capacity; ~ locale *f* TRANSPORT local capacity; ~ localisée *f* ELECTROTEC lumped capacitance; ~ de manoeuvre *f* NAUT maneuverability (AmE), manoeuvrability (BrE); ~ de mémoire *f* ELECTROTEC memory capacity, INFORMAT capacity, memory capacity, ORDINAT memory capacity, storage capacity; ~ momentanée *f* TRANSPORT capacity under prevailing conditions, momentaneous capacity; ~ de neutralisation des acides *f (CNA)* POLLUTION acid neutralizing capacity *(ANC)*; ~ nominale *f* CERAM VER nominal capacity, CHARBON, DISTRI EAU rated capacity; ~ d'oxygénation *f* HYDROLOGIE oxygenation capacity; ~ parasite *f* ELECTROTEC parasitic capacitance, PHYSIQUE stray capacitance; ~ de pêche *f* OCEANO fishing power; ~ de pointe *f* CONSTR peak capacity; ~ de pointe maximum *f* PAPIER maximum capacity, top capacity; ~ portante *f* CONSTR bearing capacity; ~ possible *f* TRANSPORT absolute capacity, possible capacity; ~ pratique *f* TRANSPORT practical capacity; ~ pratique rurale *f* TRANSPORT practical capacity under rural conditions; ~ pratique urbaine *f* TRANSPORT practical capacity under urban conditions; ~ de production *f* ELECTR *fourniture* generating capacity, PETR potential; ~ de production de glace *f* REFRIG ice-making capacity; ~ de production d'un puits *f* PETR well potential; ~ propre *f* ELECTR *bobine*, PHYSIQUE self-capacitance; ~ de puissance musicale soutenue *f* ENREGISTR music-power-handling capacity; ~ de puissance soutenue *f* ENREGISTR power handling capacity; ~ à ras-bord *f* CERAM VER brim capacity; ~ réelle *f* PRODUCTION demonstrated capacity; ~ répartie *f* ELECTROTEC distributed capacitance; ~ de réponse à une pollution par les hydrocarbures *f* POLLU MER oilspill response; ~ résiduelle *f* ELECTROTEC residual capacitance, zero capacitance; ~ de rétention *f* HYDROLOGIE *milieu* retentive capacity, PRODUCTION *système hydraulique* holding capacity; ~ de sortie *f* ELECTROTEC output capacitance; ~ spécifique *f* ELECTR *condensateur* specific capacitance, EN RENOUV *d'un puits* specific capacity; ~ de stockage *f* DISTRI EAU storage capacity, POLLU MER storage facility; ~ du support *f* TELECOM bearer capacity; ~ de tamisage *f* GENIE CHIM sieving rate; ~ tampon *f* GAZ buffer tank; ~ thermique *f* CHAUFFAGE thermal capacity, PHYSIQUE heat capacity, THERMODYN thermal capacity; ~ thermique électronique *f* PHYSIQUE electronic heat capacity; ~ thermique massique *f* PHYSIQUE specific heat capacity; ~ thermique massique à pression constante *f* PHYSIQUE specific heat capacity at constant pressure; ~ thermique massique à volume constant *f* PHYSIQUE specific heat capacity at constant volume; ~ thermique molaire *f* PHYSIQUE molar heat capacity; ~ de transport *f* EMBALLAGE carrying capacity, HYDROLOGIE transport capacity for solids; ~ de transport d'eau *f* TEXTILE water-carrying capacity; ~ utile *f* TELECOM payload; ~ d'une voie *f* INFORMAT channel capacity, ORDINAT channel capacity; ~ volumétrique *f* NAUT cubic capacity

capaciteur *m* ELECTR *composant*, EQUIP LAB capacitor; ~ série *m* ELECTR series capacitor

cape:[1] à la ~ sèche *adj* NAUT *navire* ahull

cape:[2] à la ~ sèche *adv* NAUT *navire* ahull

capelage *m* NAUT hounds

capeler *vt* NAUT make fast

capillaire *adj* CONS MECA capillary

capillarimètre *m* CHARBON capillarimeter, PAPIER bibliometer, capillary rise tester

capillarité *f* CHARBON, CHIMIE, CONSTR, PETROLE, PHYSIQUE capillarity

capitaine *m* NAUT shipmaster; ~ de frégate *m* NAUT commander; ~ marchand *m* NAUT master mariner; ~ de port *m* NAUT harbor master (AmE), harbour master (BrE); ~ de vaisseau *m* NAUT captain

capitainerie *f* NAUT harbor master's office (AmE), harbour master's office (BrE)

capital: ~ équipement *m* PRODUCTION equipment; ~ travail *m* PRODUCTION manpower

capitale *f* IMPRIM *composition* capital, capital letter

capitales: ~ dressées *f pl* IMPRIM stand-up capitals

capitonnage: ~ de siège *m* VEHICULES seat upholstery

capnite *f* MINERAUX kapnite

caponnière *f* CONSTR manhole, refuge hole, shelter

capot *m* AUTO bonnet (BrE), hood (AmE), CONS MECA cover, guard, ELECTROTEC *d'une lampe* hood, MECANIQUE cover, cowl, NAUT casing, hatch, tarpaulin; ~ d'aspiration *m* GENIE CHIM fume cupboard, fume hood; ~ de buse réacteur *m* AERONAUT nozzle cowl; ~ de carénage *m* AERONAUT fairing; ~ couvre-courroie *m* SECURITE belt guard; ~ couvre-mandrin *m* CONS MECA chuck guard; ~ couvre-meule *m* SECURITE wheel guard; ~ insonorisant *m* SECURITE noise protective hood, soundproof hood; ~ d'instrument *m* CONS MECA hood; ~ isolant *m* PRODUCTION insulating cover; ~ d'isolateur *m* ELECTR insulator cap; ~ moteur *m* AERONAUT cowl; ~ de plombage *m* PRODUCTION antitamper cover; ~ pour palette *m* EMBALLAGE pallet hood; ~ de protection *m* CONS MECA, MECANIQUE guard; ~ de sécurité *m* PRODUCTION safety cover; ~ transparent de plombage *m* PRODUCTION transparent antitamper cover; ~ de verrouillage *m* PRODUCTION locking cover

capotage *m* AERONAUT cowling, *aéronef* fairing, NAUT capsizing, TRANSPORT overturning, roll-over

capote *f* AUTO top of convertible, CONSTR cowl

capoter *vi* NAUT capsize, turn turtle

capot-moteur *m* VEHICULES *carrosserie* bonnet (BrE), hood (AmE)

Capricorne *m* ASTRONOMIE Capricornus

caprique *adj* CHIMIE capric

caproïne *f* CHIMIE caproin

caproïque *adj* CHIMIE caproic

caprolactame *m* CHIMIE, MATERIAUX *polymères* caprolactam

caproyle *m* CHIMIE caproyl

capryle *m* CHIMIE capryl

caprylique *adj* CHIMIE caprylic

capsaïcine *f* CHIMIE capsaicin

capsicine *f* CHIMIE capsicin

capsulation *f* EMBALLAGE capping

capsulatrice: ~ **automatique** *f* EMBALLAGE automatic capper

capsule *f* CHIMIE dish, CONSTR cap, EQUIP LAB *évaporation* basin, dish, IMPRIM *emballage, métal* cap, MINES capsule, detonator, exploder, squib, PETR cap; ~ **d'aérosol** *f* EMBALLAGE aerosol cap; ~ **d'aluminium** *f* EMBALLAGE aluminium capsule (BrE), aluminum capsule (AmE), ~ **d'atterrissage** *f* ESPACE *véhicules* landing capsule; ~ **autopénétrante à charnière** *f* EMBALLAGE hinged plug orifice closure; ~ **de bouteille** *f* EMBALLAGE bottle cap, bottle capsule; ~ **bridée** *f* EMBALLAGE flanged cap; ~ **éjectable** *f* ESPACE *véhicules* ejectable capsule; ~ **à encliqueter** *f* EMBALLAGE friction snap-on cap, snap cap; ~ **d'évacuation** *f* ESPACE *véhicules* emergency capsule; ~ **d'évaporation** *f* GENIE CHIM evaporating basin, evaporating dish, evaporating pan; ~ **fulminante** *f* MILITAIRE percussion cap; ~ **de garantie** *f* EMBALLAGE guarantee cap; ~ **gélatineuse** *f* EMBALLAGE gelatin capsule, gelatine capsule; ~ **à levier** *f* EMBALLAGE flip spout closure; ~ **pour la protection de l'ouïe** *f* SECURITE noise protective capsule, soundproof capsule; ~ **de pression** *f* CHARBON pressure cell; ~ **réceptrice** *f* TELECOM receiver inset; ~ **rétractable** *f* EMBALLAGE shrink capsule; ~ **de sauvetage** *f* PETROLE *exploitation en mer* escape capsule; ~ **spatiale** *f* ESPACE space capsule, *véhicules* capsule; ~ **téléphonique** *f* ACOUSTIQUE telephone transmitter; ~ **verrou** *f* EMBALLAGE sealing cap; ~ **à vis** *f* EMBALLAGE screw cap; ~ **à vis préfiletée** *f* EMBALLAGE continuous thread cap, continuous thread closure

capsule-couronne *f* EMBALLAGE crown closure, crown cork, crown cup

capsuleuse: ~ **de bouteilles** *f* CERAM VER bottle-casing machine

captage *m* DISTRI EAU catching, catchment, collection, *de l'eau souterraine* capture, NUCLEAIRE sensing; ~ **de l'eau** *m* DISTRI EAU tapping, water catchment; ~ **de l'eau souterraine** *m* DISTRI EAU ground water catchment; ~ **de poussière** *m* GENIE CHIM dust control; ~ **de rivière** *m* HYDROLOGIE river capture; ~ **de ronflement** *m* ENREGISTR hum pickup

captation *f* DISTRI EAU catching, catchment, ELECTROTEC collection; ~ **de courant** *f* TRANSPORT pick-up, power collection system

capter *vt* DISTRI EAU *les eaux* collect, TELECOM pick up

capteur *m* AUTO sensor, CONS MECA transducer, ELECTR *mesure* pick-up, ELECTRON, ESPACE sensor, ESSAIS sensor, transducer, INFORMAT, METEO, METROLOGIE, NAUT *météorologie* sensor, NUCLEAIRE pick-up, sensing element, sensor, ORDINAT sensor, PHYSIQUE probe, sensor, POLLU MER sensing element, TELECOM, VEHICULES *instrumentation* sensor; ~ **acoustique** *m* ELECTRON acoustic sensor, ENREGISTR acoustic pickup; ~ **actif** *m* ESPACE active sensor; ~ **d'attitude** *m* ESPACE attitude sensor; ~ **de courant** *m* CH DE FER *véhicules* current collector; ~ **à courant continu** *m* ELECTROTEC DC transducer; ~ **de courant par arc** *m* TRANSPORT plasma arc power collector; ~ **de débit** *m*

PAPIER flow transmitter; ~ **différentiel** *m* ELECTROTEC differential transducer; ~ **à distance** *m* CONSTR remote sensor; ~ **d'échantillonnage** *m* QUALITE *eau* sample captor; ~ **en forme de tige** *m* NUCLEAIRE bar-type pickup base; ~ **d'entrée** *m* PRODUCTION *automatisme industriel* input sensor; ~ **à fibre optique** *m* ELECTROTEC fiberoptic transducer (AmE), fibreoptic transducer (BrE); ~ **inductif** *m* CONS MECA induction pickup; ~ **laser** *m* ELECTRON laser sensor; ~ **linéaire** *m* ELECTROTEC linear transducer; ~ **de lumière** *m* ELECTRON light sensor; ~ **météorologique** *m* NAUT meteorological sensor; ~ **optique** *m* ELECTRON optical sensor; ~ **optoélectronique** *m* CONS MECA optoelectronic pickup; ~ **passif** *m* ESPACE passive sensor; ~ **pelliculaire** *m* ESPACE *mesure* film transducer; ~ **piézoélectrique** *m* CONS MECA piezoelectric pick-up; ~ **piézosensible** *m* OPTIQUE piezoelectric sensor; ~ **pneumatique** *m* IMPRIM *contrôle* pneumatic sensor; ~ **de poussière** *m* CHARBON, GENIE CHIM dust catcher, dust collector; ~ **de pression** *m* GAZ pressure detector; ~ **des profilomètres d'état de surface de contact** *m* CONS MECA pick-up for contact meter; ~ **de repère** *m* AUTO reference sensor; ~ **sans contact** *m* ELECTR contactless pickup; ~ **solaire** *m* CONS MECA, CONSTR, EN RENOUV solar collector, GEOPHYS sun sensor; ~ **de tassement** *m* CHARBON settlement gage (AmE), settlement gauge (BrE); ~ **de température** *m* PRODUCTION *système hydraulique* temperature sensor; ~ **à tubes évacués** *m* EN RENOUV evacuated tube collector; ~ **de vibrations et de chocs** *m* CONS MECA vibration and shock pick-up; ~ **de vitesse axiale** *m* ESPACE *véhicules* axial velocity sensor; ~ **Winston** *m* EN RENOUV Winston collector

capture *f* ESPACE *d'un satellite* capture, OCEANO catch, landings, PHYSIQUE capture; ~ **coupe transversale** *f* PETR capture cross-section; ~ **électronique** *f* PHYS RAYON, PHYSIQUE electron capture; ~ **des électrons** *f* PHYSIQUE electron capture; ~ **K** *f* PHYSIQUE K-capture; ~ **des neutrons** *f* PHYSIQUE neutron capture; ~ **parasite** *f* NUCLEAIRE *de neutrons* parasitic capture; ~ **par unité d'effort** *f* OCEANO catch per unit effort; ~ **radiative** *f* PHYSIQUE radiative capture; ~ **radiative du neutron** *f* PHYS RAYON neutron radiative capture; ~ **unitaire** *f* PETR capture unit

capuchon *m* CHAUFFAGE *cheminée* cowl, ELECTROTEC cap, *d'une lampe* hood; ~ **conique** *m* CINEMAT conical snoot; ~ **en verre** *m* CERAM VER socket cap; ~ **isolant** *m* CONS MECA insulation cap; ~ **pour meules d'émeri** *m* PRODUCTION hood for emery wheels; ~ **protecteur** *m* MILITAIRE *guerre chimique* protective hood, PHOTO cap; ~ **de protection** *m* INSTRUMENT protective hood, turret cap; ~ **de visée** *m* PHOTO finder hood; ~ **de visée interchangeable** *m* PHOTO interchangeable waist-level finder; ~ **vissé** *m* CERAM VER screw cap

caque *f* AGRO ALIM barrel

caquer *vt* AGRO ALIM cure

car: ~ **long courrier** *m* TRANSPORT coach; ~ **régie** *m* TV OB van, OB vehicle; ~ **de reportage** *m* CINEMAT mobile unit; ~ **vidéo** *m* TV OB van

carabine *f* MILITAIRE rifle

caracole *f* MINES pole hook

caractère *m* IMPRIM body type, typeface, *abrégé d'oeil de caractère* face, INFORMAT character, QUALITE characteristic; ~ **accusé de réception** *m* ORDINAT acknowledge character; ~ **alphanumérique** *m* INFORMAT alphanumeric character; ~ **d'annonce** *m* IMPRIM ad face; ~ **d'arrêt** *m* ORDINAT terminator; ~ **d'attente** *m*

INFORMAT, ORDINAT idle character; ~ **blanc** *m* INFORMAT, ORDINAT blank; ~ **de bourrage** *m* TELECOM stuffing character; ~ **de changement de code** *m* INFORMAT code extension character, shift character; ~ **de changement de page** *m* INFORMAT, ORDINAT form feed character; ~ **de commande** *m* ORDINAT control character; ~ **de code normal** *m* INFORMAT SI character, shift-in character, ORDINAT SI character, shift in character; ~ **de contrôle** *m* INFORMAT, ORDINAT check character, control character; ~ **de contrôle d'erreurs** *m* TELECOM error check character, error check signal; ~ **de code spécial** *m* INFORMAT, ORDINAT SO character, shift-out character; ~ **distinctif** *m* BREVETS distinctiveness; ~ **d'échappement** *m* ORDINAT escape character; ~ **en-code** *m* ORDINAT shift in character; ~ **en cuivre** *m* IMPRIM brass type; ~ **espace** *m* INFORMAT, ORDINAT blank, space character; ~ **espace arrière** *m* ORDINAT BS, backspace; ~ **d'état** *m* INFORMAT, ORDINAT status character; ~ **étroit** *m* IMPRIM condensed face; ~ **de face Didot** *m* IMPRIM *typographie* modern face; ~ **de fin** *m* INFORMAT, ORDINAT terminator; ~ **fonctionnel** *m* IMPRIM functional character; ~ **générique** *m* INFORMAT, ORDINAT wildcard character; ~ **graphique** *m* INFORMAT, ORDINAT graphic character; ~ **hors-code** *m* ORDINAT SO character, shift-out character; ~ **d'identification** *m* INFORMAT, ORDINAT identification character; ~ **interdit** *m* INFORMAT, ORDINAT illegal character; ~ **d'interrogation** *m* ORDINAT ENQ, enquiry character; ~ **d'interruption** *m* PRODUCTION *automatisme industriel* break character; ~ **italique** *m* INFORMAT italic character; ~ **laineux** *m* TEXTILE woolliness; ~ **non valide** *m* INFORMAT, ORDINAT illegal character; ~ **nul** *m* INFORMAT, ORDINAT NUL, null character; ~ **d'omission** *m* INFORMAT, ORDINAT ignore character; ~ **de passage en code normal** *m* INFORMAT SI character, shift-in character; ~ **de passage en code spécial** *m* INFORMAT shift-out character; ~ **permanent du mouvement irrotationnel** *m* PHYS FLUID permanence of irrotational motion; ~ **de plomb** *m* IMPRIM *typographie* casting; ~ **le plus significatif** *m* INFORMAT, ORDINAT most significant character; ~ **de présentation** *m* INFORMAT layout character; ~ **principal** *m* IMPRIM *composition* body type; ~ **de remplissage** *m* INFORMAT, ORDINAT filler character; ~ **de retour arrière** *m* INFORMAT backspace character; ~ **de retour chariot** *m* ORDINAT CR, carriage return; ~ **de sonnerie** *m* INFORMAT bell character; ~ **spécial** *m* INFORMAT, ORDINAT special character; ~ **spécial du vol** *m* AERONAUT flight status; ~ **de substitution** *m* INFORMAT, ORDINAT SUB character, substitute character; ~ **de suppression** *m* INFORMAT, ORDINAT DEL, delete character; ~ **de synchronisation** *m (SYN)* INFORMAT, ORDINAT synchronous idle character *(SYN)*; ~ **de titrage** *m* IMPRIM supertype; ~ **travaux de ville** *m* IMPRIM jobbing face; ~ **visqueux** *m* AGRO ALIM ropiness

caractère: ~ **d'échappement** *m* INFORMAT escape character; ~ **de mise en page** *m* TELECOM FE, format effector

caractères: ~ **antiques** *m pl* IMPRIM sanserif face; ~ **casseaux** *m pl* IMPRIM pi characters; ~ **digitaux** *m pl* IMPRIM numerics; ~ **écran dans les systèmes WYSIWYG** *m pl* IMPRIM display type; ~ **d'édition** *m pl* IMPRIM *composition* book faces; ~ **en indice** *m pl* IMPRIM inferior characters, inferior figures, inferior letters, subscript; ~ **de fantaisie** *m pl* IMPRIM display faces, *composition* fancy type; ~ **gothiques** *m pl* IMPRIM antique face, gothic face; ~ **gras** *m pl* IMPRIM bold face, bold type; ~ **d'imprimerie** *m pl* IMPRIM printing types; ~ **inhabituels** *m pl* IMPRIM pi characters, *composition, typographie* pi types; ~ **italiques** *m pl* IMPRIM italic type; ~ **de labeur** *m pl* IMPRIM commercial type, jobbing type; ~ **large** *m* IMPRIM extended type; ~ **à machine à écrire** *m pl* IMPRIM typewriter face; ~ **maigres** *m pl* IMPRIM, INFORMAT light face; ~ **par pouce** *m pl* IMPRIM CPI, characters per inch; ~ **par seconde** *m pl (CPS)* IMPRIM, ORDINAT characters per second *(CPS)*; ~ **personnalisés** *m pl* IMPRIM *composition, typographie* pi types; ~ **pleins** *m pl* IMPRIM full-face type; ~ **prétentieux** *m pl* IMPRIM *typographie* swatch type; ~ **qualitatifs** *m pl* QUALITE qualitative characteristics; ~ **quantitatifs** *m pl* QUALITE quantitative characteristics; ~ **sur bois** *m pl* IMPRIM woodtypes; ~ **de titrage** *m pl* IMPRIM display faces, *affichage* display type; ~ **de transfert sec** *m pl* IMPRIM *maquette* dry transfer

caractérisation *f* SECURITE *du bruit ambiant* description

caractéristique *f* BREVETS feature, CHIMIE property, CONS MECA characteristic, ELECTRON characteristic curve, characteristic, response curve, ELECTROTEC *nominale* rating, INFORMAT characteristic, feature, *notation en virgule flottante* biased exponent, MATH characteristic, NAUT specification, ORDINAT, PHYS FLUID, PRODUCTION feature, QUALITE, TELECOM characteristic; ~ **additionnelle** *f* BREVETS additional feature; ~ **d'anode** *f* ELECTROTEC anode characteristic; ~ **de la charge** *f* ELECTROTEC load characteristic; ~ **de commande** *f* ELECTROTEC control characteristic; ~ **de construction** *f* NAUT constructional features; ~ **conversion** *f* ELECTRON gamma characteristic; ~ **courant-tension** *f* ELECTROTEC, ESPACE *véhicules* current-voltage characteristic; ~ **de diode** *f* ELECTRON diode characteristic; ~ **directe** *f* ELECTRON forward characteristic; ~ **directionnelle** *f* ENREGISTR directional characteristic; ~ **électrique** *f* ELECTRON, ELECTROTEC electrical characteristic; ~ **d'électrode** *f* ELECTROTEC electrode characteristic; ~ **en charge** *f* AERONAUT load characteristic; ~ **d'enregistrement** *f* ACOUSTIQUE, ENREGISTR, TV recording characteristic; ~ **d'enregistrement-lecture** *f* ACOUSTIQUE reproducing-recording characteristic; ~ **essentielle** *f* BREVETS essential feature; ~ **de fiabilité** *f* MATERIAUX reliability parameter; ~ **fréquentielle** *f* TELECOM frequency characteristic; ~ **gain-fréquence** *f* ELECTRON gain frequency characteristic; ~ **de grille** *f* ELECTRON grid characteristic; ~ **d'impédance** *f* ELECTROTEC impedance characteristic; ~ **de lecture** *f* ACOUSTIQUE reproducing characteristic, ENREGISTR playback characteristic; ~ **logarithmique** *f* ELECTRON logarithmic characteristic; ~ **optique** *f* TELECOM optical characteristic; ~ **de persistance** *f* ELECTRON persistence characteristic, ELECTROTEC decay characteristic; ~ **phase-amplitude** *f* TELECOM phase-amplitude characteristic; ~ **de pression** *f* METEO pressure characteristic; ~ **d'un produit** *f* PRODUCTION product feature; ~ **rectiligne** *f* ELECTRON linear characteristic; ~ **de réponse harmonique** *f* PHYS ONDES harmonic response characteristic; ~ **de reproduction** *f* ENREGISTR playback characteristic, TV playback characteristic, replay characteristic, reproduction characteristic; ~ **à rotor bloqué** *f* ELECTR *machine asynchrone* locked rotor impedance characteristic; ~ **de saut** *f* TV surge characteristic, transient response; ~ **spectrale** *f* ELECTRON spectral characteristic; ~ **statique** *f* ELECTROTEC static characteristic; ~ **temporelle** *f* TELECOM time characteristic; ~ **tension-courant** *f* ELECTROTEC voltage-current characteristic; ~ **thermique** *f* TELECOM thermal characteristic, THERMODYN thermal property; ~ **de transfert** *f* ELECTRON, PHYSIQUE transfer characteristic; ~ **de transmission** *f* TELECOM transmission characteristic; ~ **à vide** *f* AERONAUT no-load characteristic

caractéristiques: ~ **à circuit ouvert** *f pl* ELECTR *matériel* open circuit characteristics; ~ **électriques** *f pl* PRODUCTION electrical ratings; ~ **de fatigue** *f pl* MECANIQUE *matériaux* fatigue properties; ~ **de fluage** *f pl* MECANIQUE *matériaux* creep properties; ~ **des impulsions** *f pl* ELECTRON pulse characteristics; ~ **mécaniques** *f pl* CONS MECA mechanical properties; ~ **optiques** *f pl* MATERIAUX optical properties; ~ **des performances** *f pl* CONS MECA performance properties; ~ **de pilotage** *f pl* ESPACE *véhicules* handling characteristics; ~ **qualitatives** *f pl* QUALITE qualitative characteristics; ~ **quantitatives** *f pl* QUALITE quantitative characteristics; ~ **de réglage** *f pl* PHYS RAYON *d'un laser monofréquence* tuning characteristics; ~ **de saturation** *f pl* PHYS RAYON *cavité laser* saturation characteristics; ~ **d'un transistor** *f pl* ELECTRON transistor characteristics

carambolage *m* TRANSPORT multiple pile-up

caranguer *vi* NAUT *pendant un coup de vent* heave to

carapace: ~ **d'air annulaire** *f* NUCLEAIRE *interstice* annular air gap

carat *m* METROLOGIE carat; ~ **de fin** *m* METROLOGIE carat fine; ~ **métrique** *m* METROLOGIE metric carat

caravane *f* TRANSPORT caravan (BrE), trailer (AmE); ~ **de camping** *f* VEHICULES camper, caravan (BrE), house trailer (AmE), trailer (AmE)

carbamate *m* CHIMIE carbamate

carbamide *m* CHIMIE urea

carbamique *adj* CHIMIE carbamic

carbamyle *m* CHIMIE carbamyl, carbamyle

carbanile *m* CHIMIE carbanil

carbanion *m* CHIMIE carbanion

carbazide *m* CHIMIE carbazide

carbazol *m* CHIMIE carbazole

carbazole *m* CHIMIE carbazole

carbène *m* CHIMIE carbene

carbinol *m* CHIMIE carbinol

carbocyclique *adj* CHIMIE carbocyclic

carboglace *f* AGRO ALIM dry ice

carbohydrase *f* AGRO ALIM, CHIMIE carbohydrase

carbolique *adj* CHIMIE carbolic

carbonado *m* MINERAUX carbonado, MINES bort, industrial diamond

carbonatation *f* CHIMIE carbonatation, carbonation, GEOLOGIE *néoformation* carbonatation, carbonation, HYDROLOGIE carbonation

carbonate *m* CHIMIE, LESSIVES carbonate; ~ **de calcium** *m* AGRO ALIM calcium carbonate; ~ **de chaux** *m* CHIMIE whiting; ~ **de fer** *m* CHIMIE iron carbonate; ~ **de magnésie** *m* CHAUFFAGE magnesium carbonate; ~ **de potassium** *m* LESSIVES pearl ash, potassium carbonate; ~ **de sodium** *m* LESSIVES sodium carbonate; ~ **de soude** *m* CHIMIE, LESSIVES sodium carbonate, PAPIER soda ash, sodium carbonate

carbonaté *adj* GEOLOGIE carbonated, limy

carbonater *vt* CHIMIE carbonate

carbone *m (C)* CHIMIE carbon *(C)*; ~ **activé** *m* PAPIER activated carbon; ~ **fixe** *m* CHIMIE fixed carbon; ~

inorganique dissous *m* POLLUTION dissolved inorganic carbon; ~ **organique dissous** *m (COD)* POLLUTION dissolved organic carbon; ~ **sulfuré** *m* POLLUTION carbonyl sulfide (AmE), carbonyl sulphide (BrE)

carboné *adj* GEOLOGIE, MATERIAUX carbonaceous

carbonifère[1] *adj* CHARBON coal-bearing, MINERAUX carboniferous

carbonifère[2] *m* PETROLE carboniferous

carbonification *f* CHARBON carbonization

carbonique *adj* CHIMIE carbonic

carbonisage *m* CONSTR charring

carbonisation *f* CHARBON carbonization, CHIMIE charring

carbonisé *adj* CHIMIE charred, THERMODYN blackened, burnt, incinerated

carboniser[1] *vt* CHARBON carbonize, THERMODYN blacken, carbonize

carboniser:[2] **se** ~ *v réfl* CHARBON carbonize

carbonyle[1] *adj* MATERIAUX carbonyl

carbonyle[2] *m* CHIMIE carbonyl

Carborundum *m (MD)* CHIMIE, CONS MECA Carborundum (TM)

carbostyryle *m* CHIMIE carbostyril

carboxylate *m* CHIMIE carboxylate

carboxyle *m* CHIMIE carboxyl

carboxylé *adj* PLAST CAOU *terme chimique* carboxylated

carboxylique *adj* CHIMIE carboxylic

carboxyméthylcellulose *f* AGRO ALIM, LESSIVES, PLAST CAOU CMC, carboxymethyl cellulose

carboy *f* EQUIP LAB bonbonne

carburant *m* ESPACE, NAUT, PETROLE, THERMODYN, VEHICULES *combustible* fuel; ~ **auto** *m* PETROLE motor spirit; ~ **diesel** *m* TRANSPORT diesel oil; ~ **embarqué** *m* AERONAUT fuel load; ~ **émulsifié** *m* AERONAUT emulsified fuel; ~ **émulsionné** *m* AERONAUT emulsified fuel; ~ **non utilisable récupérable** *m* AERONAUT drainable unusable fuel; ~ **tertiaire** *m* AUTO tertiary fuel

carburateur *m* AUTO, CERAM VER, CONS MECA, MECANIQUE *véhicules*, NAUT, PRODUCTION, VEHICULES carburetor (AmE), carburretor (BrE); ~ **compensé** *m* AUTO zenith carburetor (AmE), zenith carburretor (BrE); ~ **à dépression** *m* AUTO suction carburetor (AmE), suction carburretor (BrE); ~ **à diffuseur variable** *m* AUTO variable venturi carburetor (AmE), variable venturi carburretor (BrE); ~ **double corps** *m* AUTO twin carburetor (AmE), twin carburretor (BrE), twin-barreled carburetor (AmE), twin-barrelled carburretor (BrE), twin-choke carburetor (AmE), twin-choke carburretor (BrE); ~ **à double corps** *m* AUTO dual carburetor (AmE), dual carburretor (BrE), MECANIQUE *véhicules* dual carburetor (AmE), dual carburretor (BrE); ~ **électronique** *m* TRANSPORT electronic carburetor (AmE), electronic carburretor (BrE); ~ **à deux étages** *m* AUTO two-phase carburetor (AmE), two-phase carburretor (BrE); ~ **horizontal** *m* AUTO, VEHICULES sidedraft carburetor (AmE), sidedraft carburretor (BrE); ~ **inversé** *m* VEHICULES downdraft carburetor (AmE), downdraught carburretor (BrE); ~ **quadruple** *m* AUTO four-barrel carburetor (AmE), four-barrel carburretor (BrE), quad carburretor (BrE); ~ **à tirage par bas** *m* AUTO downdraft carburetor (AmE), downdraught carburretor (BrE); ~ **zénith** *m* AUTO zenith carburetor (AmE), zenith carburettor (BrE)

carbure *m* CHIMIE carbide, MATERIAUX carbide; ~ **allié** *m*

METALL alloy carbide; ~ **de calcium** *m* CHIMIE calcium carbide; ~ **d'hydrogène** *m* CHIMIE hydrocarbon; ~ **métallique** *m* MECANIQUE *matériaux* carbide; ~ **primaire** *m* METALL primary carbide; ~ **de silicium** *m* CONS MECA Carborundum (TM), ELECTROTEC, PHYSIQUE silicon carbide; ~ **de tungstène** *m* CONS MECA, PETROLE tungsten carbide

carburéacteur *m* AERONAUT jet engine fuel, jet fuel, PETROLE ATK, aviation turbine kerosene, TRANSPORT aviation fuel

carburer *vt* CHIMIE carburet

carbures: ~ **saturés** *m pl* GAZ methane series

carbylamine *f* CHIMIE carbylamine, isocyanide

carcas *m* PRODUCTION bear, horse, sow

carcasse *f* CONS MECA skeleton, CONSTR carcass, frame, skeleton, ELECTROTEC carcass, frame, NAUT *d'un navire* frame, TEXTILE carcass; ~ **de bobine** *f* ELECTROTEC coil form; ~ **de navire** *f* NAUT hulk; ~ **de recuisson** *f* CERAM VER annealing kiln; ~ **de stator** *f* ELECTROTEC stator frame

carcinogène[1] *adj* CHIMIE carcinogenic

carcinogène[2] *m* AGRO ALIM carcinogen

carcinotron *m* (MD)ELECTRON carcinotron, TELECOM carcinotron (TM); ~ **O** *m* PHYSIQUE backward wave oscillator; ~ **de type M** *m* PHYSIQUE type-M carcinotron; ~ **de type O** *m* ELECTRON O-type carcinotron

cardage *m* TEXTILE carding

cardan *m* CONS MECA cardan coupling, gimbal joint; ~ **de roue** *m* AUTO universal joint; ~ **de transmission** *m* VEHICULES drive shaft (AmE), propeller shaft (BrE)

carde *f* TEXTILE card

carder *vt* TEXTILE card

carderie *f* TEXTILE cardroom

cardioïde *f* CONS MECA cardioid

carénage *m* AERONAUT, ESPACE fairing, NAUT careening, REFRIG fairing; ~ **amont** *m* REFRIG upstream fairing; ~ **aval** *m* REFRIG downstream fairing; ~ **de bout de pale** *m* AERONAUT blade tip fairing; ~ **de raccordement** *m* AERONAUT *cellule* fillet

Carène *f* ASTRONOMIE Carina

caréné *adj* AERONAUT faired

carène[1] *m* CHIMIE carene

carène[2] *f* AERONAUT hull, NAUT body; ~ **liquide** *f* NAUT free surface; ~ **sale** *f* NAUT *d'un bateau* foul bottom

caréner[1] *vt* AUTO streamline

caréner[2] *vti* NAUT careen, repair

cargaison *f* ESPACE *véhicules* cargo, NAUT cargo, shipload, shipment; ~ **d'avion** *f* EMBALLAGE air cargo; ~ **diverse** *f* EMBALLAGE general cargo; ~ **réfrigérée** *f* TRANSPORT refrigerated cargo

cargneule *f* GEOLOGIE *unité sédimentaire* alveolar dolomite, cellular dolomite

cargo *m* NAUT, TRANSPORT cargo ship, freighter; ~ **brise-glace** *m* TRANSPORT icebreaking cargo ship; ~ **frigorifique** *m* NAUT reefer ship, refrigerated cargo ship, TRANSPORT refrigerated cargo ship; ~ **à manutention horizontale** *m* NAUT roll-on/roll-off vessel; ~ **mixte** *m* TRANSPORT combined cargo and passenger liner, passenger-cargo ship; ~ **mixte passagers-marchandises** *m* TRANSPORT combined cargo and passenger ship; ~ **polytherme** *m* TRANSPORT polythermal cargo ship; ~ **polyvalent** *m* NAUT multipurpose ship, TRANSPORT multipurpose carrier; ~ **pour marchandises diverses** *m* TRANSPORT general cargo ship; ~ **à roulage direct** *m* TRANSPORT roll-on/roll-off ship; ~ **satellite** *m* ESPACE *véhicules* cargo satellite; ~ **spatial** *m* ESPACE *véhicules* heavy-lift vehicle

carie *f* CONSTR *du bois* rotting; ~ **humide** *f* CONSTR wet rot

carier *vt* CONSTR rot

carlingage: ~ **des machines** *m* NAUT engine seating; ~ **de turbine** *m* NAUT turbine seating

carlingue *f* NAUT keelson

carmin *m* AGRO ALIM carmine

carminique *adj* CHIMIE *acide* carminic

carnallite *f* MINERAUX carnallite

carneau *m* CHAUFFAGE, PRODUCTION flue; ~ **à air** *m* PRODUCTION air flue; ~ **de cheminée** *m* CERAM VER flue; ~ **à gaz** *m* NUCLEAIRE gas vent, issue, PRODUCTION gas flue; ~ **intérieur** *m* PRODUCTION *d'une chaudière* flue; ~ **de sole** *m* CHAUFFAGE bottom flue

carnet: ~ **de bord** *m* AERONAUT journey logbook; ~ **de commandes** *m* PRODUCTION backlog of orders; ~ **de douane** *m* CINEMAT carnet; ~ **de route** *m* AERONAUT journey logbook; ~ **à souches** *m* IMPRIM *façonnage* stubook; ~ **de vol** *m* AERONAUT flight log

carnien *adj* GEOLOGIE Carnian

carnieule *f* GEOLOGIE *unité sédimentaire* alveolar dolomite, cellular dolomite

carnitine *f* CHIMIE carnitine

carnotite *f* MINERAUX carnotite

carone *f* CHIMIE carone

carotène *m* AGRO ALIM, CHIMIE carotene

carottage *m* CONSTR core sampling, PETR core drilling, core drilling, coring, PETROLE coring; ~ **latéral** *m* PETR sidewall coring

carotte *f* CERAM VER stack, CHARBON core sample, CONSTR core, GAZ core sample, MINES core, core sample, drill core, PETROLE core, PLAST CAOU *moulage* sprue; ~ **latérale** *f* PETR sidewall core, PETROLE sidewell core; ~ **orientée** *f* PETR oriented core

carotte-échantillon *f* MINES core sample

carotter *vt* GEOLOGIE *forage* core

carotte-témoin *f* MINES core sample, core, drill core

carottier *m* PETROLE core barrel, core drill, corer, coring tool; ~ **au diamant** *m* PETROLE diamond core drill; ~ **latéral** *m* PETR sidewall core; ~ **à piston** *m* CHARBON piston sampler; ~ **à rubans** *m* CHARBON foil sampler

carottière: ~ **latérale** *f* PETR core slicer

caroube *f* AGRO ALIM carob

carpholite *f* MINERAUX carpholite

carré *m* (Fra) CH DE FER absolute stop signal, CONS MECA square, CONSTR landing, quirk, square head, NAUT saloon, wardroom; ~ **de Berne** *m* CH DE FER carriage key; ~ **conducteur** *m* CONS MECA square drive; ~ **d'entraînement** *m* CONS MECA *outillage* square bit drive; ~ **d'entraînement de cable de compteur de vitesse** *m* AUTO speedometer drive gear; ~ **d'entraînement de la tige carrée** *m* PETROLE kelly bushing; ~ **parfait** *m* MATH perfect square; ~ **violet** *m* CH DE FER violet square signal

carreau *m* CONS MECA square file, CONSTR square, stretcher, tile, *de verre* pane, MINES *d'une carrière* head, *mine* mouth; ~ **de carrelage** *m* CONSTR flooring tile; ~ **de carrelage céramique** *m* CERAM VER ceramic pavement slab; ~ **de carrière** *m* MINES quarry head; ~ **céramique** *m* CERAM VER Dutch tile; ~ **de faïence** *m* CERAM VER earthenware slab; ~ **de majolique** *m* CERAM VER majolica tile; ~ **de mine** *m* MINES bankhead, plat, pit, pit bank; ~ **de la mine** *m* MINES pithead; ~ **de revêtement céramique** *m* CERAM VER ceramic wall tile

carreaux *m pl* TEXTILE checks; ~ **d'absorption acoustique** *m pl* SECURITE soundproof tiles; ~ **quadrillés** *m pl* TEXTILE lumberback checks

carrefour *m* CONSTR crossroads, roads which cross; ~ **giratoire** *m* CONSTR rotary (AmE), roundabout (BrE), traffic circle (AmE)

carrelage *m* CONSTR brick pavement, brick paving, decking, floor, tile floor, tile flooring; ~ **en briques** *m* CONSTR brick pavement, brick paving

carreler *vt* CONSTR floor

carrelet *m* CONS MECA square file, square ruler, CONSTR batten, OCEANO dip net, lift net; ~ **pour mosaïque** *m* CERAM VER tessera

carrer[1] *vt* PRODUCTION square

carrer:[2] **se ~** *v réfl* PRODUCTION be square, be squared

carrhagénine *m* AGRO ALIM carrageen

carrier *m* MINES quarryman

carrière *f* CONSTR quarry, MINES pit, quarry, stone pit, stone quarry; ~ **abandonnée** *f* MINES disused quarry; ~ **d'ardoise** *f* MINES slate quarry; ~ **d'argile** *f* MINES clay pit; ~ **à ciel ouvert** *f* MINES open quarry; ~ **en entonnoir** *f* MINES open pit mine; ~ **exploitée en chassant** *f* MINES strip mine; ~ **de gravier** *f* CONSTR gravel pit; ~ **de marbre** *f* MINES marble quarry; ~ **de pierre calcaire** *f* MINES lime pit, limestone quarry; ~ **de pierre à chaux** *f* MINES lime pit, limestone quarry; ~ **de pierre à plâtre** *f* MINES gypsum quarry; ~ **de pierre de taille** *f* CONSTR cut-stone quarry; ~ **de terre à porcelaine** *f* CERAM VER china clay quarry

carrossage *m* VEHICULES *roues* camber

carrosserie *f* REFRIG casing, VEHICULES body; ~ **autoporteuse** *f* VEHICULES unit construction body

carrousel *m* AERONAUT turntable, PHOTO rotary magazine

carte *f* ELECTRON card, IMPRIM *électronique, papier* board, INFORMAT card, ORDINAT board; ~ **80 colonnes** *f* INFORMAT eighty-column card; ~ **accélératrice** *f* ORDINAT accelerator card; ~ **aéronautique** *f* AERONAUT aeronautical chart (BrE), sectional chart (AmE); ~ **d'alarme** *f* TELECOM alarm card; ~ **aller-retour** *f* PRODUCTION turnaround card; ~ **analogique** *f* ELECTRON analog board (AmE), analogue board (BrE); ~ **d'approche** *f* AERONAUT approach chart; ~ **d'approche aux instruments** *f* AERONAUT instrument approach chart; ~ **d'assignation** *f* TELECOM assignment map; ~ **d'atterrissage** *f* AERONAUT, NAUT landing chart; ~ **bathymétrique** *f* NAUT bathymetric chart; ~ **cadastrale** *f* CONSTR cadastral survey; ~ **de circuit imprimé** *f* INFORMAT, ORDINAT, TELECOM PCB, printed circuit board; ~ **à circuit imprimé** *f* ELECTRON PC board; ~ **de circuit imprimé** *f* ELECTRON PCB, printed circuit board; ~ **à circuit imprimé** *f* ELECTRON printed wiring board; ~ **de circuit imprimé** *f* ELECTR PCB, printed circuit board; ~ **à circuit imprimé double face** *f* ELECTRON double-sided printed circuit board; ~ **à circuit imprimé en verre-époxy** *f* ELECTRON glass epoxy-printed circuit board; ~ **à circuit imprimé haute fréquence** *f* ELECTRON high-frequency printed circuit board; ~ **climatique** *f* METEO climatic graph; ~ **de commande** *f* PRODUCTION driver card; ~ **commande gachette** *f* PRODUCTION gate drive board, gate driving board; ~ **de contrôle** *f* QUALITE control chart, inspection card; ~ **couchée** *f* IMPRIM artboard; ~ **couleur** *f* ORDINAT color adaptor (AmE), colour adaptor (BrE); ~ **des couleurs** *f* INFORMAT, ORDINAT color map (AmE), colour map (BrE); ~ **des courants** *f* NAUT current chart; ~ **de décharge du bus** *f* PRODUCTION bus discharge board; ~ **demi-longueur** *f* ELECTRON half-sized board; ~ **de détail** *f* NAUT plan; ~ **d'émission radio** *f* ASTRONOMIE contour map of a radio source; ~ **en courbes de niveau** *f* CONSTR contour map; ~ **enfichable** *f* ELECTRON daughter board; ~ **d'entretien** *f* PRODUCTION maintenance data card; ~ **d'état-major** *f* MILITAIRE ordnance survey map; ~ **des étoiles** *f* NAUT star chart; ~ **d'extension** *f* ELECTRON add-in board, expansion card, INFORMAT expansion board, expansion card, ORDINAT expanded memory specification, expansion board, expansion card; ~ **à fenêtre** *f* INFORMAT aperture card; ~ **fille** *f* ELECTRON daughter board; ~ **de grande cercle** *f* NAUT great circle chart; ~ **graphique** *f* ORDINAT graphic display adaptor; ~ **graphique couleur** *f* ORDINAT CGA, color graphics adaptor (AmE), colour graphics adaptor (BrE); ~ **Hollerith** *f* INFORMAT, ORDINAT Hollerith card; ~ **hydrogéologique** *f* HYDROLOGIE hydrogeological map; ~ **hydrographique** *f* HYDROLOGIE hydrographic chart, NAUT Admiralty chart (BrE), hydrographic chart; ~ **hypsométrique** *f* HYDROLOGIE hypsometric map; ~ **imprimée** *f* ELECTRON board, circuit board; ~ **d'incident** *f* AERONAUT failure data card; ~ **infrarouge** *f* ASTRONOMIE infrared map; ~ **d'interface** *f* ELECTRON interface card; ~ **d'interface réseau** *f* INFORMAT, ORDINAT network interface card; ~ **d'interface S** *f* TELECOM S-universal interface card; ~ **isobarique** *f* METEO isobaric map; ~ **isopache** *f* GEOLOGIE isopach map; ~ **d'isopaques** *f* GEOLOGIE isopach map; ~ **des isoplèthes de la nappe phréatique** *f* HYDROLOGIE ground water contour map; ~ **ivoire contrecollée** *f* PAPIER pasted ivory board; ~ **de Karnaugh** *f* INFORMAT Karnaugh map; ~ **logique** *f* ELECTRON, INFORMAT, ORDINAT logic card; ~ **à logique mixte** *f* ELECTRON mixed-logic board; ~ **logique de modulation** *f* PRODUCTION *automatisme industriel* modulator logic board; ~ **magnétique** *f* GEOPHYS magnetic map, IMPRIM *cartes de commande, de paiement* mag card, INFORMAT, ORDINAT magnetic card; ~ **maîtresse** *f* INFORMAT, ORDINAT master card; ~ **marine** *f* NAUT chart, TRANSPORT sea chart; ~ **marine électronique** *f* NAUT electronic chart; ~ **de mémoire** *f* INFORMAT, ORDINAT memory card, memory map, storage map; ~ **à mémoire** *f* INFORMAT, ORDINAT smart card, TELECOM swipe card; ~ **à mémoire optique** *f* OPTIQUE optical memory card; ~ **Mercator** *f* NAUT Mercator chart; ~ **mère** *f* ELECTRON, INFORMAT, ORDINAT motherboard; ~ **météo** *f* METEO weather chart; ~ **météorologique** *f* METEO weather chart, NAUT weather map; ~ **mixte** *f* ELECTRON mixed-logic board; ~ **modem** *f* ELECTRON modem board; ~ **de navigation** *f* AERONAUT aeronautical route chart; ~ **de navigation côtière** *f* NAUT coastal chart; ~ **particulière** *f* NAUT plan; ~ **pastel** *f* TELECOM chargecard; ~ **perforée** *f* IMPRIM *façonnage, finition* tab card, INFORMAT, ORDINAT punched card; ~ **perforée douze lignes** *f* INFORMAT twelve-row punched card; ~ **à perforer** *f* INFORMAT, ORDINAT punch card; ~ **piézométrique** *f* PETROLE piezometric map; ~ **de pointage** *f* NAUT plotting sheet, PRODUCTION time card; ~ **potentiométrique** *f* PETROLE potentiometric map; ~ **à puce** *f* ORDINAT chip card; ~ **du radio** *f* ASTRONOMIE radio map; ~ **récepteur** *f* ELECTRON receiver board; ~ **de réception** *f* ELECTRON receiver board; ~ **réceptrice** *f* ELECTRON receiver board; ~ **réseau** *f* ORDINAT network card; ~ **de route** *f* NAUT pilot chart; ~ **routière** *f*

AUTO road map, NAUT routing chart; ~ **sismique** *f* GEOPHYS seismological map; ~ **à somme cumulée** *f* QUALITE *statistique* cusum chart; ~ **spectraloïde** *f* ESPACE spectral map; ~ **structurale** *f* GEOLOGIE structural map, tectonic map; ~ **structurale de subsurface** *f* GEOLOGIE *en isohypses,en isobathes* structure contour map, structure subsurface contour map; ~ **de surface isobare** *f* METEO surface pressure chart; ~ **thermoformée** *f* EMBALLAGE blister card; ~ **de tracé de navigation** *f* NAUT plotting chart; ~ **de traitement** *f* TELECOM processing card; ~ **universelle** *f* ELECTRON general-purpose board; ~ **des vents** *f* METEO, NAUT wind chart

carte-lettre *f* PAPIER lettercard; ~ **illustrée** *f* PAPIER illustrated lettercard

carter *m* AUTO oil pan, CINEMAT *d'une caméra* casing, CONS MECA case, casing, cover, guard, housing, wheel guard, ELECTR *moteur*, VEHICULES *moteur, transmission* casing; ~ **d'allumeur** *m* AUTO distributor housing; ~ **de la boîte de vitesses** *m* VEHICULES gearbox housing; ~ **de chaîne** *m* VEHICULES *transmission, motocyclette* chaincase; ~ **de la chaîne primaire** *m* VEHICULES *transmission d'une motocyclette* primary chaincase; ~ **de courroie** *m* CONS MECA belt guard; ~ **de différentiel** *m* AUTO differential carrier; ~ **de distribution** *m* AUTO timing cover, timing-gear housing; ~ **d'embrayage** *m* AUTO clutch housing, VEHICULES clutch casing; ~ **en cloche** *m* PRODUCTION *système hydraulique* bellhousing; ~ **d'engrenage** *m* CONS MECA case, casing, cover, guard, wheel guard; ~ **en spirale** *m* AUTO volute casing; ~ **d'entrée** *m* CONS MECA inlet case; ~ **en volute** *m* AUTO volute casing; ~ **d'essieu** *m* VEHICULES *transmission* axle casing, axle housing; ~ **d'essieu arrière** *m* VEHICULES *transmission* rear axle housing; ~ **de filtre d'huile** *m* AUTO oil filter; ~ **du frein** *m* AUTO brake housing; ~ **d'huile** *m* MECANIQUE oil pan, VEHICULES *lubrification du moteur* sump; ~ **intermédiaire** *m* AERONAUT intermediate case; ~ **interne** *m* AERONAUT internal wheel case; ~ **moteur** *m* MECANIQUE crankcase; ~ **de pompe** *m* AUTO pump housing; ~ **du pont arrière** *m* VEHICULES *transmission* rear axle housing; ~ **de protection** *m* SECURITE guard; ~ **de protection des glissières** *m* CONS MECA apron of a lathe; ~ **réacteur** *m* AERONAUT case; ~ **récepteur** *m* CINEMAT bottom spool box; ~ **sec** *m* VEHICULES dry sump; ~ **de sécurité** *m* CONS MECA guard; ~ **de sortie** *m* AERONAUT exhaust case; ~ **de ventilateur** *m* INST HYDR fan casing; ~ **de vilebrequin** *m* VEHICULES crankcase; ~ **de volant** *m* VEHICULES flywheel housing

cartographe *m* CONSTR mapper

cartographie *f* CONSTR mapping

carton *m* AGRO ALIM tetrapak (TM), EMBALLAGE paperboard, IMPRIM cardboard, *papier* board, PAPIER board; ~ **affiché** *m* PAPIER pasted ivory board, pasted lined board; ~ **d'amiante** *m* PAPIER asbestos board; ~ **d'asbeste** *m* CONSTR asbestos millboard; ~ **avec compartiments** *m* EMBALLAGE compartment case; ~ **bitumé** *m* CONSTR roofing felt, tarred felt; ~ **blanc avec revêtement** *m* EMBALLAGE white lined board; ~ **blanchi** *m* PAPIER *pour boîte pliante* bleached lined board; ~ **bois** *m* IMPRIM pulp board, PAPIER mechanical pulp board; ~ **bois brun** *m* PAPIER brown mechanical pulp board; ~ **calandré humide** *m* IMPRIM water-finished carton, PAPIER water-finished board; ~ **chiné** *m* PAPIER veined board; ~ **coloré deux faces** *m* PAPIER two-side colored board (AmE), two-side coloured board (BrE); ~ **coloré une face** *m* PAPIER one-side

colored board (AmE), one-side coloured board (BrE); ~ **compact** *m* PAPIER carton compact; ~ **comprimé** *m* ELECTR pressboard, *insolation* insulating board; ~ **contrecollé** *m* IMPRIM pasteboard, PAPIER pasted board; ~ **couché** *m* REVETEMENT coated board; ~ **couché pour boîtes pliantes** *m* PAPIER coated folding board; ~ **à couches multiples** *m* EMBALLAGE duplex board; ~ **deux couches** *m* PAPIER two-layer board; ~ **diélectrique** *m* PAPIER electrical insulating board; ~ **doublé à la cuve** *m* PRODUCTION vat lined board; ~ **double toile** *m* PAPIER twin-wire board; ~ **duplex imperméable** *m* EMBALLAGE duplex waterproof board; ~ **dur** *m* PAPIER glazed millboard; ~ **d'emboutissage** *m* EMBALLAGE molded board (AmE), moulded board (BrE); ~ **à l'enrouleuse** *m* IMPRIM, PAPIER millboard; ~ **entre-deux fils** *m* PAPIER cloth-centered board (AmE), cloth-centred board (BrE); ~ **entre-deux toiles** *m* PAPIER cloth-centered board (AmE), cloth-centred board (BrE); ~ **extérieur** *m* EMBALLAGE outer case; ~ **feutre** *m* PAPIER felt board; ~ **feutré** *m* PAPIER felt board; ~ **fossile** *m* MINERAUX mountain paper; ~ **frictionné** *m* PAPIER MG board, machine-glazed board; ~ **de générique** *m* CINEMAT title card; ~ **glacé** *m* EMBALLAGE enamel board, glazed board; ~ **gris** *m* EMBALLAGE board mill, chipboard, millboard, IMPRIM, PAPIER chipboard; ~ **gris mixte** *m* PAPIER lined chipboard; ~ **homogène** *m* PAPIER solid board; ~ **imitation chromo** *m* EMBALLAGE imitation chromoboard; ~ **imperméable à la graisse** *m* EMBALLAGE, PAPIER grease-resistant board; ~ **imprimé pliant** *m* EMBALLAGE printed folding carton; ~ **isolant** *m* CHAUFFAGE insulating board; ~ **jacquard** *m* EMBALLAGE, PAPIER jacquard board; ~ **un jet** *m* PAPIER single ply board; ~ **kraft** *m* EMBALLAGE kraft board; ~ **mécanique** *m* EMBALLAGE machine-made board; ~ **minéral** *m* MINERAUX mountain paper; ~ **de montagne** *m* MINERAUX mountain paper; ~ **moulé** *m* PAPIER molded board (AmE), moulded board (BrE); ~ **multicouche** *m* PAPIER multilayer board; ~ **multiple** *m* EMBALLAGE multiply board; ~ **multiple** *m* EMBALLAGE multiple board; ~ **ondulé** *m* EMBALLAGE corrugated board, corrugated cardboard, corrugated fiberboard (AmE), corrugated fibreboard (BrE), PAPIER corrugated board, corrugated cardboard; ~ **ondulé avec cannelures espacées** *m* EMBALLAGE corrugated board with broadly spaced flutes; ~ **ondulé avec cannelures serrées** *m* EMBALLAGE corrugated board with narrowly spaced flutes; ~ **ondulé à double cannelure** *m* EMBALLAGE double-wall corrugated fibreboard (BrE), double-wall corrugated fiberboard (AmE); ~ **ondulé à double face** *m* EMBALLAGE double-face corrugated board; ~ **ondulé à paroi simple** *m* EMBALLAGE single-wall corrugated fibreboard; ~ **ondulé à plusieurs épaisseurs de cannelures** *m* IMPRIM *transformation* multiwall corrugated board; ~ **paille** *m* EMBALLAGE, IMPRIM strawboard; ~ **de paille mixte** *m* PAPIER mixed strawboard; ~ **palettisé** *m* EMBALLAGE palletized board; ~ **paraffiné** *m* PAPIER waxed board; ~ **de pâte brune mixte** *m* PAPIER brown mixed pulp board; ~ **de pâte mécanique** *m* EMBALLAGE mechanical pulp board, PAPIER mechanical pulp board, mechanical woodpulp board; ~ **de pâte mécanique brune** *m* PAPIER brown mechanical pulp board, unbleached mechanical pulp board; ~ **plaqué bois** *m* PRODUCTION veneer board; ~ **pour chaussures** *m* PAPIER shoe board; ~ **pour emboutissage** *m* PAPIER board for pressing; ~ **pour étiquettes** *m* TEXTILE tagboard; ~ **pour flan de clicherie** *m* PAPIER flong; ~ **pour reliure** *m* PAPIER bookbinding board; ~ **pour valise** *m* PAPIER suitcase board; ~ **recouvert par entrecollage** *m* PAPIER pasted ivory board, pasted lined board; ~ **récupéré lavé et comprimé** *m* EMBALLAGE washed and squashed consumer waste carton; ~ **renforcé** *m* PAPIER reinforced board; ~ **résistant aux liquides** *m* EMBALLAGE liquid-proof carton; ~ **rigide pliant** *m* EMBALLAGE rigid and folding cartons; ~ **triplex** *m* EMBALLAGE triple-wall corrugated board; ~ **trois couches** *m* PAPIER three-layer board, triplex board; ~ **vernis d'un côté** *m* EMBALLAGE one-side coated board

cartonnage: ~ **combiné pour bouteilles** *m* EMBALLAGE coupled lid-base bottle tray

cartonneuse *f* EMBALLAGE cardboard machine

cartouche *f* IMPRIM, INFORMAT, MINES, PHOTO, TV *renfermant une bobine* cartridge, VEHICULES *lubrification* filter; ~ **à aimant mobile** *f* ENREGISTR moving magnet cartridge; ~ **annexe** *f* CONS MECA annex block (AmE), annexe block (BrE); ~ **de bande** *f* INFORMAT tape cartridge; ~ **de bande magnétique** *f* INFORMAT, ORDINAT magnetic tape cartridge; ~ **à blanc** *f* MILITAIRE blank cartridge; ~ **chauffante** *f* CONS MECA *moules d'injection* cartridge heater; ~ **d'un dessin** *f* CONS MECA engineering drawing block; ~ **de disque** *f* INFORMAT, ORDINAT disk cartridge; ~ **de données** *f* INFORMAT data cartridge; ~ **de dynamite** *f* MINES dynamite cartridge; ~ **à extraction** *f* EQUIP LAB *appareil de Soxhlet* extraction thimble; ~ **filtrante** *f* GENIE CHIM filter cartridge; ~ **de filtre** *f* MECANIQUE, VEHICULES *huile* filter cartridge; ~ **à grenaille** *f* MILITAIRE fragmenting shell; ~ **à plaquette amovible** *f* CONS MECA *pour outils de coupe* cartridge for indexable inserts; ~ **pour bande magnétique sans fin** *f* ACOUSTIQUE endless magnetic loop cartridge

cartouche-amorce *f* MINES primer cartridge, primer

cartoucherie *f* MILITAIRE cartridge depot, cartridge factory

cas:[1] ~ **dimensionnant** *m* ESPACE *véhicules* design basis case; ~ **d'urgence** *m* SECURITE emergency; ~ **urgent** *m* SECURITE emergency

cas:[2] **en ~ d'incendie** *loc* SECURITE in case of fire; **en ~ de panne** *loc* SECURITE in the event of breakdown

cascade *f* CHARBON, ELECTROTEC cascade, HYDROLOGIE cascade, waterfall; ~ **d'électrons** *f* NUCLEAIRE electron cascade, electron shower; ~ **d'énergie** *f* PHYS FLUID energy cascade; ~ **générique** *f* NUCLEAIRE generic cascade; ~ **incorporée** *f* REFRIG mixed refrigerant cascade; ~ **radiative** *f* PHYS RAYON radiative cascade; ~ **sans mélange** *f* NUCLEAIRE no-mixing cascade

case *f* CONS MECA compartment, MINES bunker, ore bin; ~ **à cocher** *f* IMPRIM *composition, continu* X-box; ~ **à minerai** *f* MINES ore bin; ~ **de train** *f* AERONAUT wheel well

caséinate: ~ **de sodium** *m* AGRO ALIM sodium caseinate

caséine *f* AGRO ALIM, CHIMIE, PLAST CAOU *protéine naturelle* casein; ~ **acide** *f* AGRO ALIM casein acid; ~ **de présure** *f* AGRO ALIM rennet casein

caséique *adj* CHIMIE lactic

caserne *f* CONSTR barracks

casette *f* CERAM VER fireclay mold (AmE), fireclay mould (BrE)

caseyage *m* OCEANO creel fishing

caseyeur *m* OCEANO basket trap, creel, pot

casier *m* EMBALLAGE bin, *à bouteille* crate, PRODUCTION

bin; ~ **destinataire** *m* PRODUCTION destination bin

casque *m* ENREGISTR headphones, OCEANO diving helmet, SECURITE helmet; ~ **antibruit** *m* CONSTR earmuffs, EQUIP LAB *sécurité* ear protectors, earmuffs, SECURITE earmuffs; ~ **antifumée** *m* SECURITE smoke helmet; ~ **d'écoute** *m* ENREGISTR headphones; ~ **à infrarouges** *m* ENREGISTR wireless infrared headphones; ~ **de protection** *m* PETR, SECURITE safety helmet, protective helmet, TRANSPORT safety helmet; ~ **de protection pour l'industrie** *m* SECURITE industrial safety helmet; ~ **respiratoire** *m* SECURITE smoke helmet; ~ **de sécurité** *m* SECURITE safety helmet; ~ **de sécurité pour soudeurs** *m* SECURITE welder's safety helmet; ~ **de soudeur** *m* CONSTR welding helmet, SECURITE welder's hood, welding helmet, welding helmet; ~ **stéréo** *m* ENREGISTR stereo headphones; ~ **téléphonique** *m* TELECOM headset; ~ **ventilé pour équipage de char** *m* MILITAIRE ventilated tank crew helmet

cassage *m* CONSTR breaking

cassant *adj* GEOLOGIE *déformation*, MATERIAUX, MECANIQUE *matériaux*, PAPIER, PLAST CAOU brittle

casse *f* CERAM VER *de pot* breaking down, IMPRIM case, PAPIER wet break, TEXTILE broken end; ~ **annulaire** *f* CERAM VER annular crack; ~ **de bande** *f* IMPRIM *impression* web break; ~ **en long** *f* CERAM VER snake; ~ **en spirale** *f* CERAM VER spiral fracture; ~ **en travers** *f* CERAM VER crossbreak, tranverse fracture; ~ **étoilée** *f* CERAM VER star fracture; ~ **du fil de trame** *f* TEXTILE weft stop motion; ~ **mécanique** *f* CERAM VER pad break; ~ **de teinture** *f* TEXTILE rope marking

cassé[1] *adj* NAUT *bôme* broken

cassé:[2] ~ **en trame** *f* TEXTILE weft break; ~ **de fil** *f* TEXTILE break

casse-coke *m* CHARBON coke breaker

casse-écrous *m* CONS MECA nut splitter

casse-fil *m* CERAM VER strand break detector; ~ **de chaîne** *m* TEXTILE warp stop motion; ~ **sur cantre** *m* TEXTILE stop motion on creel

casse-gueuse *m* PRODUCTION pig iron breaker

casse-pierre *m* CONSTR rock breaker, stone breaker, stone crusher

casser[1] *vt* CONSTR break

casser[2] *vi* MECANIQUE fail

casser:[3] **se ~** *v réfl* CONSTR break

casserole: ~ **d'hélice** *f* AERONAUT spinner

cassés: ~ **de fabrication** *m pl* PAPIER broke; ~ **humides** *m pl* PAPIER wet broke; ~ **secs** *m pl* PAPIER dry broke

cassette *f* CERAM VER saggar, CINEMAT, ENREGISTR cassette, IMPRIM cartridge, INFORMAT, PHOTO, TV *avec deux bobines* cassette; ~ **compacte** *f* ENREGISTR compact cassette; ~ **coplanaire** *f* ACOUSTIQUE coplanar cartridge; ~ **numérique** *f* ENREGISTR DAT, digital audio tape, ORDINAT digital cassette; ~ **pour magnétoscope** *f* ENREGISTR tape cassette; ~ **pour urographie** *f* INSTRUMENT pyelogram cassette; ~ **radiographique** *f* INSTRUMENT X-ray cartridge; ~ **réceptrice** *f* PHOTO take-up cassette

casseur *m* CONSTR breaker steel; ~ **d'émulsion** *m* POLLU MER emulsion breaker

Cassiopée *f* ASTRONOMIE Cassiopeia

cassitérite *f* MINERAUX cassiterite

cassure *f* CHARBON break, fracture, CONSTR *d'un pont* failure, CRISTALL, EN RENOUV fracture, GENIE CHIM breaking, MECANIQUE *matériaux* fracture; ~ **conchoïdale** *f* CRISTALL conchoidal fracture; ~ **à éclats** *f* CHARBON splintery fracture; ~ **de fatigue** *f* CRISTALL fatigue fracture; ~ **d'image** *f* TV picture breakup

castorine *f* CHIMIE castorin

cataclase *f* GEOLOGIE cataclasis

cataclysme *m* GEOLOGIE cataclasm, cataclysm

catadioptre *m* AUTO reflector, CONSTR *sur la route* cat's eye (BrE), TRANSPORT rear reflector, VEHICULES reflex reflector

catadioptrique *adj* ASTRONOMIE, PHYSIQUE catadioptric

catalase *f* AGRO ALIM, CHIMIE catalase

catalogue *m* INFORMAT catalog (AmE), catalogue (BrE), ORDINAT catalog (AmE), catalogue (BrE), directory; ~ **d'étoiles** *m* ASTRONOMIE star catalog (AmE), star catalogue (BrE); ~ **de Messier** *m* ASTRONOMIE Messier catalogue

catalyse *f* AGRO ALIM, CHIMIE, MATERIAUX catalysis; ~ **sous irradiation** *f* PHYS RAYON radiation catalysis

catalyser *vt* CHIMIE, PLAST CAOU catalyze

catalyseur *m* CHIMIE catalyst, catalyzer, GAZ, MATERIAUX, NAUT, PETROLE, PLAST CAOU, TEXTILE, VEHICULES *échappement* catalyst; ~ **de Ziegler** *m* CHIMIE Ziegler catalyst

catalytique *adj* CHIMIE catalytic

catamaran *m* NAUT catamaran, TRANSPORT catamaran, twin-hull ship

catamétamorphisme *m* GEOLOGIE high-grade metamorphism

cataphote *m* CERAM VER cat's eye, VEHICULES reflex reflector

catapléite *f* MINERAUX catapleiite, catapleite

cataracte *f* CERAM VER *du verrier*, CHARBON, DISTRI EAU cataract

catastrophe: ~ **ultraviolet** *f* PHYSIQUE ultraviolet catastrophe

catéchinamine *f* CHIMIE catecholamine

catéchine *f* CHIMIE catechol

catéchutannique *adj* CHIMIE catechutannic

catégorie *f* BREVETS category, CONS MECA class; ~ **d'aéronef** *f* AERONAUT aircraft category; ~ **produit** *f* PRODUCTION product group

caténaire[1] *adj* GEOMETRIE catenary

caténaire[2] *f* CH DE FER catenary, crossover, overhead crossover, CHIMIE *de réactions* serie, PHYSIQUE catenary

caténoïde *f* GEOMETRIE catenoid

catergol *m* ESPACE *véhicules* catergol

cathartique *adj* CHIMIE *acide* cathartic

cathathermomètre *m* CHAUFFAGE *courants d'air* katathermometer

cathepsine *f* CHIMIE cathepsin

cathétomètre *m* EQUIP LAB *mesure de longueur, d'écartement* cathetometer, traveling microscope (AmE), travelling microscope (BrE), PHYSIQUE cathetometer

cathode *f* ELECTR, ELECTROTEC, PHYSIQUE, TV cathode; ~ **à bain de mercure** *f* ELECTROTEC mercury pool cathode; ~ **au césium** *f* ELECTROTEC caesium cathode (BrE), cesium cathode (AmE); ~ **chaude** *f* ELECTROTEC hot cathode; ~ **à chauffage direct** *f* ELECTROTEC directly-heated cathode, TV rapid heat-up cathode; ~ **à chauffage indirect** *f* ELECTROTEC indirect heater-type cathode, indirectly-heated cathode; ~ **chauffée** *f* ELECTROTEC hot cathode; ~ **commune** *f* ELECTROTEC common cathode; ~ **à décharge luminescente** *f* ELECTROTEC glow discharge cathode; ~ **à émission thermoélectrique** *f* ELECTROTEC thermionic cathode; ~ **à émission thermoélectronique** *f* ELECTROTEC hot cathode; ~ **en tungstène thorié** *f* ELECTROTEC thoriated

tungsten filament; ~ **équipotentielle** *f* ELECTROTEC indirectly-heated cathode; ~ **froide** *f* ELECTROTEC cold cathode; ~ **imprégnée** *f* ELECTROTEC impregnated cathode; ~ **liquide** *f* ELECTROTEC pool cathode; ~ **à mercure** *f* ELECTROTEC mercury pool cathode; ~ **à oxydes** *f* ELECTROTEC oxide-coated cathode; ~ **photoémissive** *f* ELECTROTEC photocathode; ~ **de réserve** *f* ELECTROTEC dispenser cathode

cathodoluminescence *f* ELECTROTEC, PHYSIQUE cathodoluminescence

cation *m* CHIMIE, ELECTR, HYDROLOGIE, PHYS RAYON, PHYSIQUE cation; ~ **basique** *m* POLLUTION base cation; ~ **dominant** *m* POLLUTION dominant cation; ~ **échangeable** *m* POLLUTION exchangeable cation; ~ **majeur** *m* POLLUTION dominant cation; ~ **principal** *m* POLLUTION dominant cation

cationique *adj* CHARBON, CHIMIE, HYDROLOGIE cationic

cause: ~ **attribuable** *f* QUALITE assignable cause; ~ **courante d'accidents** *f* SECURITE common cause of accidents; ~ **de défaillance humaine** *f* QUALITE human failure cause; ~ **de suspension** *f* PRODUCTION reason for hold

causticité *f* CHIMIE causticity

caustifier *vt* CHIMIE causticize

caustique[1] *adj* CHIMIE caustic

caustique[2] *m* CHIMIE, PHYSIQUE caustic

CAV *abrév (commande automatique de volume)* COMMANDE, ELECTROTEC, OPTIQUE, PHYSIQUE AVC *(automatic volume control)*

cavalier *m* CHARBON waling, CONS MECA tangent plate, *d'un tour à fileter* swing frame, CONSTR staple, wire staple, ELECTROTEC jack plug, *ordinateur* jumper, EMBALLAGE header label, EQUIP LAB *balance* rider, PRODUCTION *électricité* jumper, TEXTILE drop wire; ~ **de déblais** *m* CONSTR spoil heap

cave *f* CONSTR vault, PETR *avant-puits* cellar

caver *vt* CONSTR, MINES hollow, hollow out

caverne: ~ **cavité** *f* NUCLEAIRE cavity, flaw

caverneux *adj* GEOLOGIE cavernous

cavernosité *f* CONSTR hollowness

cavitant *adj* MECANIQUE *hydraulique* cavitating

cavitation *f* CONSTR, EN RENOUV, MECANIQUE *hydraulique*, METALL, PETROLE, PHYS FLUID, PHYSIQUE cavitation

cavité *f* CHARBON cavity, CONSTR cavity, hollow, ELECTRON, GAZ cavity, MATERIAUX cavity, void, METALL cavity, void, MINES, PETR, PHYSIQUE cavity; ~ **aimant sphérique** *f* ESPACE *géophysique* magnet spheric cavity; ~ **coaxiale** *f* ELECTRON coaxial cavity; ~ **à deux fréquences d'accord** *f* ELECTRON double-tuned cavity; ~ **d'entrée** *f* ELECTRON buncher resonator, input cavity; ~ **hyperfréquence** *f* ELECTRON microwave cavity; ~ **laser** *f* ELECTRON laser cavity; ~ **optique** *f* OPTIQUE optical cavity, PHYS RAYON *création laser* optical cavity, *des lasers à gaz* optical cavity, *formée par miroirs plans à réflexion forte* optical cavity, TELECOM optical cavity; ~ **optique résonnante** *f* OPTIQUE resonant optical cavity, TELECOM cavity resonator; ~ **résonnante** *f* ELECTRON cavity resonator, resonant cavity, OPTIQUE cavity resonator, resonant cavity, PHYSIQUE cavity resonator, resonant cavity, TELECOM cavity resonator, resonant cavity, cavity resonator, TV cavity resonator; ~ **résonnante à accord fixe** *f* ELECTRON fixed tuned cavity resonator; ~ **résonnante annulaire** *f* ELECTRON annular resonator; ~ **résonnante d'entrée** *f* ELECTRON buncher resonator; ~ **résonnante de laser** *f*

ELECTRON laser cavity; ~ **résonnante ouverte** *f* ELEC-
TRON open resonator; ~ **résonnante de sortie** *f*
ELECTRON catcher cavity; ~ **saline** *f* GAZ salt cavity; ~
de sortie *f* ELECTRON output cavity

caviter *vi* PRODUCTION cavitate

cavités: ~ **accélératrices** *f pl* PHYS PART *installation*
accelerator cavities

cayat *m* CHARBON running jig

caye *f* OCEANO cay, key, sandbank

Cc *abrév (cirro-cumulus)* METEO Cc *(cirrocumulus)*

CC *abrév (courant continu)* CH DE FER, ELECTRON, ELEC-
TROTEC, ENREGISTR, PRODUCTION, TELECOM, TV DC
(direct current)

CCD:[1] *abrév (dispositif à couplage de charge, circuit
CCD)*, ASTRONOMIE, ELECTRON, ELECTROTEC, ORDI-
NAT, PHYSIQUE, TELECOM, TV CCD *(charge-coupled
device)*

CCD[2] ~ **à canaux enterrés** *m* ELECTRON buried channel
CCD

CCIR *abrév (Comité consultatif international des radio-
communications)* TELECOM CCIR *(International
Radio Consultative Committee)*

CCITT *abrév (Comité consultatif international télégraphique*et *téléphonique)* TELECOM CCITT *(International Telegraph and Telephone Consultative
Committee)*

CCL *abrév (contrôle de charge de ligne)* TELECOM LLC
(line load control)

CCV *abrév (commutateur de circuits virtuels)* TELECOM
VCS *(virtual-circuit switch)*

cd *abrév (candela)* ELECTROTEC, METROLOGIE, OPTIQUE,
PHYSIQUE cd *(candela)*

Cd *(cadmium)* CHIMIE Cd *(cadmium)*

CDA *abrév (couche de demi-atténuation)* NUCLEAIRE,
PHYSIQUE HVL *(half value layer)*

CD-ROM *abrév (disque compact ROM)* INFORMAT, OP-
TIQUE, ORDINAT CD-ROM *(compact disk-read only
memory)*

Ce *(cérium)* CHIMIE Ce *(cerium)*

CEC *abrév (capacité d'échange cationique)* GEOLOGIE,
PETROLE, POLLUTION CEC *(cation exchange capacity)*

cédant *m* BREVETS assignor

cédation: ~ **locale** *f* METALL local yielding

céder *vi* CONSTR give way

cédrène *m* CHIMIE cedrene

cédrol *m* CHIMIE cedrol

ceintreuse *f* CH DE FER rail-bending device

ceinture *f* IMPRIM *flexographie* band, MECANIQUE, VE-
HICULES *sécurité* belt; ~ **d'astéroïdes** *f* ASTRONOMIE
asteroid belt; ~ **cartouchière** *f* MILITAIRE cartridge
belt; ~ **chauffante** *f* CHAUFFAGE heating belt; ~ **et étuis
pour outils** *f* CONS MECA tool belt and pouches; ~
facettée *f* NUCLEAIRE faceted ring (AmE), facetted
ring (BrE); ~ **de lest** *f* OCEANO weight belt; ~ **d' Orion** *f*
ASTRONOMIE Orion's belt; ~ **orogénique** *f* GEOLOGIE
orogenic belt; ~ **de rayonnements** *f* ESPACE *géophysique* radiation belt; ~ **de rayonnements de Van Allen** *f*
ASTRONOMIE, GEOPHYS, PHYS RAYON, PHYSIQUE Van
Allen radiation belt; ~ **de roches vertes** *f* GEOLOGIE
greenstone belt; ~ **de sauvetage** *f* NAUT lifebelt; ~ **de
sécurité** *f* AERONAUT seat belt, SECURITE safety belt,
seat belt, TRANSPORT safety belt, seat belt, VEHICULES
safety belt, seat belt; ~ **de sécurité à trois points** *f*
TRANSPORT three-point seat belt; ~ **de siège** *f* AERO-
NAUT *d'avion militaire* seat belt

céladonite *f* MINERAUX celadonite

célérité *f* PHYSIQUE speed; ~ **de la lumière** *f* PHYSIQUE
speed of light; ~ **du son** *f* PHYSIQUE speed of sound; ~
des vagues *f* OCEANO wave velocity

céleste *adj* ASTRONOMIE celestial

célestin *m* MINERAUX celestine, celestite

célestine *f* MINERAUX celestine, celestite

célibataire *adj* PHYSIQUE *électron* unpaired

cello *m* IMPRIM acetate proof

cellulaire *adj* MATERIAUX cellular; ~ **toéton** *adj* MATERI-
AUX cellular

cellule *f* CINEMAT cell

cellule *f* CHARBON cell, compartment, ELECTROTEC cell,
ESPACE *énergie* cell, secondary battery, storage cell,
IMPRIM *héliogravure*, INFORMAT, ORDINAT, TELECOM
cell; ~ **d'animation** *f* CINEMAT animation cell; ~ **de
batterie** *f* ELECTROTEC battery cell; ~ **de Bragg** *f* ELEC-
TROTEC Bragg cell; ~ **de conductance** *f* EQUIP LAB
analyse conductance cell; ~ **à couche d'arrêt** *f* ELEC-
TROTEC barrier layer cell; ~ **couplée au diaphragme** *f*
PHOTO coupled exposure meter; ~ **débrochable** *f*
ELECTR draw-out unit; ~ **de diffusion** *f* GENIE CHIM
diffusion cell; ~ **électrochimique** *f* THERMODYN fuel
cell; ~ **d'électrolyse** *f* ELECTROTEC, PHYSIQUE electrolytic cell; ~ **électrolytique** *f* ELECTROTEC, PHYSIQUE
electrolytic cell; ~ **élémentaire** *f* CRISTALL, NUCLEAIRE
unit cell; ~ **en H** *f* ELECTROTEC H-cell; ~ **en L** *f* ELEC-
TRON L-section; ~ **en T** *f* ELECTRON T-section; ~
d'épuisement *f* CHARBON scavenger cell; ~ **d'essai en
cuivre** *f* PHYS RAYON copper test cell; ~ **de fabrication** *f*
PRODUCTION manufacturing location; ~ **fermée** *f*
PLAST CAOU closed cell; ~ **de filtre** *f* ELECTRON filter
section; ~ **galvanique** *f* CHIMIE galvanic cell; ~ **de Golay**
f PHYSIQUE Golay cell; ~ **incorporée** *f* CINEMAT built-in
light meter, PHOTO built-in exposure meter; ~ **de Kerr** *f*
PHYSIQUE Kerr cell; ~ **magnétique** *f* INFORMAT, ORDI-
NAT magnetic cell; ~ **à multiplication des électrons** *f*
INSTRUMENT multiplier phototube, photomultiplier;
~ **OAM de la couche physique** *f* TELECOM PL-OAM,
physical layer operations and maintenance; ~ **OAM de
la physique** *f* TELECOM PL-OAM, physical layer operations and maintenance; ~ **ouverte** *f* PLAST CAOU open
cell; ~ **passe-bas** *f* ELECTRON low-pass section; ~
photoconductrice *f* ELECTRON photoconductive cell; ~
photoélectrique *f* CINEMAT photocell, ELECTR, ELEC-
TRON *pile* PEC, photocell, photoelectric cell,
ELECTROTEC electric eye, ESPACE *énergie* PEC, photoelectric cell, IMPRIM photocell, PHOTO meter cell, PHYS
RAYON PEC, photoelectric cell, PHYSIQUE PEC,
photoelectric cell, photocell, PRODUCTION *automatisme industriel* light sensor, TV PEC, photoelectric
cell; ~ **photoélectrique antérieure** *f* ELECTROTEC front-
wall photovoltaic cell; ~ **photoélectrique à métal alcalin** *f* PHOTO alkaline photocell; ~ **photogalvanique** *f*
EN RENOUV photogalvanic cell; ~ **photorésistante** *f*
PHYSIQUE photoconductive cell; ~ **photovoltaïque** *f*
ESPACE *véhicules*, PHYSIQUE photovoltaic cell; ~ **photovoltaïque à couche antérieure** *f* ELECTROTEC
front-wall photovoltaic cell; ~ **photovoltaïque à
couche postérieure** *f* ELECTROTEC back wall photovoltaic cell; ~ **pneumatique** *f* CHARBON pneumatic cell;
~ **de posemètre** *f* PHOTO light meter cell; ~ **de production** *f* PRODUCTION manufacturing location; ~ **de
redresseur** *f* ELECTROTEC rectifier cell; ~ **relaveuse** *f*
CHARBON cleaner cell; ~ **au sélénium** *f* ELECTROTEC,
PHYSIQUE selenium cell; ~ **au silicium** *f* ELECTROTEC, EN
RENOUV silicon cell; ~ **solaire** *f* ELECTROTEC, EN RE-

NOUV solar cell, ESPACE solar cell, *véhicules* photovoltaic cell, PHYSIQUE, TELECOM, THERMODYN solar cell; ~ **solaire à l'arséniure de gallium** *f* ELECTRON gallium arsenide solar cell; ~ **solaire sans concentrateur** *f* ELECTROTEC nonconcentrator solar cell; ~ **solaire au silicium** *f* ELECTROTEC silicon solar cell; ~ **TR** *f* NAUT TR cell; ~ **TTL** *f* CINEMAT through-the-lens meter

celluloïd *m* CHIMIE, CINEMAT, EMBALLAGE celluloid

cellulose *f* CHIMIE, EMBALLAGE, MATERIAUX, PLAST CAOU cellulose; ~ **blanchie** *f* EMBALLAGE bleached pulp; ~ **régénérée** *f* MATERIAUX regenerated cellulose; ~ **technique** *f* EMBALLAGE wood pulp

cellulosique *adj* CHIMIE, TEXTILE cellulosic

célomètre *m* AERONAUT ceilometer

Celsius *adj (C)* METROLOGIE *thermodynamique* Celsius *(C)*

cémentation *f* CERAM VER staining, CONS MECA, MECANIQUE *procédé* case hardening; ~ **à l'argent** *f* CERAM VER silver staining; ~ **au carbone** *f* CONS MECA, MAT CHAUFF carburizing; ~ **au cuivre** *f* CERAM VER copper staining; ~ **en noir** *f* CERAM VER black staining; ~ **gazeuse** *f* THERMODYN gas carburizing

cémentite *f* MATERIAUX *métallurgie* cementite

cendre *f* PAPIER, PLAST CAOU, POLLUTION, THERMODYN ash; ~ **de houille** *f* CHARBON coal ash; ~ **d'os** *f* CERAM VER, CHIMIE bone ash; ~ **de soude** *f* CHIMIE soda ash; ~ **volante** *f* CHARBON flue dust, fly ash, POLLUTION fly ash; ~ **volatile** *f* PAPIER fly ash

cendres *f pl* PAPIER, PLAST CAOU, THERMODYN ash; ~ **exclues** *f pl* POLLUTION ash-free; ~ **volantes** *f pl* CHARBON flue dust, fly ash, POLLUTION fly ash; ~ **volatiles** *f pl* PAPIER fly ash; ~ **volcaniques** *f pl* GEOLOGIE volcanic cinders

cendrier *m* NUCLEAIRE core catcher, melting core catcher, PRODUCTION ash bin, ash pit

cendrure *f* PRODUCTION cinder pit

cénomanien *adj* GEOLOGIE *stratigraphie* cenomanian

cénozoïque[1] *adj* GEOLOGIE *stratigraphie* Cainozoic

cénozoïque[2] *m* PETR Tertiary era

Centaure *f* ASTRONOMIE Centaurus

centi- *préf (c)* METROLOGIE centi-*(c)*

centiare *m* METROLOGIE centiare

centigrade *adj (C)* METROLOGIE centigrade *(C)*

centigramme *m* METROLOGIE centigram (AmE), centigramme (BrE)

centilitre *m* METROLOGIE centiliter (AmE), centilitre (BrE)

centimètre *m* METROLOGIE centimeter (AmE), centimetre (BrE); ~ **carré** *m* METROLOGIE square centimeter (AmE), square centimetre (BrE); ~ **cube** *m* METROLOGIE cubic centimeter (AmE), cubic centimetre (BrE)

centimètre-gramme-seconde *m (CGS)* METROLOGIE centimeter-gram-second (AmE), centimetre-gramme-second (BrE) *(CGS)*

centinormal *adj* CHIMIE centinormal

centipoise *m* PLAST CAOU *unité physique* centipoise

centrage:[1] ~ **sur flancs** *adj* CONS MECA side fit

centrage[2] *m* AERONAUT aircraft balance, CONS MECA centering (AmE), centring (BrE), ENREGISTR tracking, MECANIQUE centering (AmE), centring (BrE); ~ **automatique des têtes** *m* TV autotracking; ~ **et biais** *m* TEXTILE bow and bias; ~ **de faisceau** *m* TV X-Y alignment, beam alignment; ~ **de l'image par aimants permanents** *m* TV permanent magnet centering (BrE), permanent magnet centring (AmE); ~ **de piste** *m* TV

tracking; ~ **des têtes** *m* TV head tracking

central: ~ **d'arrivée** *m* TELECOM terminating exchange; ~ **automatique local** *m* TELECOM CDO, community dial office; ~ **automatique de localité** *m* TELECOM UAX, unit automatic exchange; ~ **automatique privé** *m* TELECOM PAX, private automatic exchange; ~ **automatique rural** *m* TELECOM rural automatic exchange; ~ **autonome** *m* TELECOM stand-alone exchange; ~ **de départ** *m* TELECOM originating exchange; ~ **électromécanique** *m* TELECOM electromechanical exchange; ~ **électronique** *m* TELECOM electronic exchange; ~ **interurbain** *m* TELECOM trunk exchange; ~ **manuel** *m* TELECOM manual exchange; ~ **manuel privé** *m* TELECOM private manual exchange; ~ **d'origine** *m* TELECOM home exchange; ~ **à sélecteurs rotatifs** *m* TELECOM rotary exchange; ~ **serveur** *m* TELECOM serving exchange; ~ **de télécommande** *m* COMMANDE remote control center (AmE), remote control centre (BrE), remote control office; ~ **téléphonique** *m* TELECOM telephone exchange; ~ **téléphonique automatique** *m* TELECOM automatic telephone exchange; ~ **temporel** *m* TELECOM time-division exchange

centrale *f* PHYSIQUE power station; ~ **aérodynamique** *f* AERONAUT air data computer; ~ **alimentée au gaz** *f* ELECTR gas turbine power station; ~ **atomique** *f* CONSTR nuclear power plant, nuclear power station; ~ **baro-altimétrique** *f* AERONAUT barometric altitude controller; ~ **à béton** *f* CONSTR concrete batching and mixing plant; ~ **bigyroscopique** *f* AERONAUT dual platform; ~ **de cap** *f* AERONAUT heading data generator; ~ **de chauffage urbain** *f* THERMODYN district heating station; ~ **combinée** *f* THERMODYN combined heat and power station; ~ **de commande d'attitude** *f* ESPACE *véhicules* attitude control unit; ~ **construite après 1975** *f* POLLUTION new plant; ~ **diesel** *f* ELECTROTEC diesel-electric power station; ~ **d'eau lourde** *f* NUCLEAIRE heavy water plant; ~ **d'électricité thermique** *f* THERMODYN thermal power station; ~ **électrique** *f* CONSTR electricity generating station, ELECTR *alimentation* power plant, *réseau* electric power station, ELECTROTEC electric power station, power plant, EN RENOUV powerhouse, MINES, TELECOM electric power station; ~ **électrique au mazout** *f* ELECTR *alimentation* oil-fired power station; ~ **électrique à mazout** *f* THERMODYN oil-fired power station; ~ **électrosolaire** *f* ELECTROTEC solar electric power plant, solar electric power station; ~ **d'énergie** *f* TELECOM power plant; ~ **d'enrobage** *f* CONSTR asphalt plant; ~ **éolienne** *f* ELECTROTEC wind-electric power station; ~ **de force motrice** *f* ELECTROTEC central power plant; ~ **froide** *f* REFRIG cold store; ~ **au fuel** *f* NUCLEAIRE oil-fired power plant; ~ **à gâchage** *f* CONSTR batch plant; ~ **génératrice** *f* ELECTROTEC central power plant, power plant; ~ **géothermique** *f* ELECTR *alimentation* geothermal plant, ELECTROTEC geothermal power station; ~ **gyroscopique** *f* AERONAUT gyroscopic platform; ~ **à haute tension** *f* ELECTROTEC high-tension power supply; ~ **héliogénératrice** *f* ELECTROTEC solar electric power plant, solar electric power station; ~ **hydraulique** *f* ESPACE hydraulic generator, *véhicules* hydraulic power pack, HYDROLOGIE hydroelectric power station, INST HYDR hydraulic generator, MINES hydraulic power pack; ~ **hydro-électrique** *f* ELECTR *alimentation* hydroelectric power station, ELECTROTEC hydroelectric power plant, hydroelectric power station; ~ **hydroélectrique** f ELECTROTEC water power station, HYDROLOGIE hydroelectric power station; ~ **inertielle** f ESPACE *véhicules* inertial unit; ~ **non surveillée** f TELECOM unattended exchange, unmanned exchange; ~ **nucléaire** f CONSTR nuclear power plant, nuclear power station, ELECTR *générateur* nuclear power station, PHYSIQUE nuclear power plant, nuclear power station; ~ **nucléaire à deux circuits** f NUCLEAIRE two-circuit nuclear power plant; ~ **nucléaire à deux réacteurs** f NUCLEAIRE twin-reactor station; ~ **nucléaire de pointe** f NUCLEAIRE *production d'électricité* peak load nuclear power plant; ~ **nucléaire à trois circuits** f NUCLEAIRE three-circuit nuclear power plant; ~ **de pointe** f ELECTR *réseau* peak load power plant; ~ **de référence d'attitude** f ESPACE *véhicules* attitude reference unit; ~ **de référence de direction et d'attitude** f ESPACE *véhicules* TADG, heading and vertical reference unit system, three-axis data generator; ~ **de référence de verticale** f ESPACE *véhicules* vertical reference unit; ~ **solaire** f EN RENOUV solar farm; ~ **solaire photovoltaïque** f ELECTROTEC photovoltaic solar power plant; ~ **thermique** f ELECTROTEC thermal electric power plant, thermal electric power station, NUCLEAIRE *usine* thermal power plant, THERMODYN heat flow diagram; ~ **thermique à combustibles fossiles** f ELECTR, THERMODYN fossil-fuel power station; ~ **thermique à vapeur** f ELECTROTEC steam-electric power plant, steam-electric power station; ~ **à turbine à gaz** f ELECTR *alimentation* gas turbine power station

centralisé *adj* ORDINAT centralized

centre:[1] ~ **à centre** *adj* CONS MECA center-to-center (AmE), centre-to-centre (BrE); **au ~ du navire** *adj* NAUT midship

centre:[2] **au ~ du navire** *adv* NAUT amidships

centre[3] *m* CONS MECA center (AmE), centre (BrE), center hole (AmE), centre hole (BrE), GEOMETRIE, TELECOM center (AmE), centre (BrE); ~ **d'acidité** *m* POLLUTION acidic area; ~ **acoustique effectif** *m* ENREGISTR effective acoustic center (AmE), effective acoustic centre (BrE); ~ **acoustique d'une source** *m* ACOUSTIQUE effective center of acoustic source (AmE), effective centre of acoustic source (BrE); ~ **automatique de commutation de messages** *m* TELECOM automatic message switching center (AmE), automatic message switching centre (BrE); ~ **avec chanfrein de protection** *m* CONS MECA center hole with protecting chamfer (AmE), centre hole with protecting chamfer (BrE); ~ **de basse pression** *m* METEO center of low pressure (AmE), centre of low pressure (BrE); ~ **de carène** f NAUT center of buoyancy (AmE), centre of buoyancy (BrE); ~ **du cercle circonscrit** *m* GEOMETRIE circumcenter (AmE), circumcentre (BrE); ~ **de charge** *m* PRODUCTION work center (AmE), work centre (BrE); ~ **du coeur** *m* OPTIQUE, TELECOM core center (AmE), core centre (BrE); ~ **de collecte de données** *m* TELECOM DCC, data collection center (AmE), data collection centre (BrE); ~ **de commutation** *m* TELECOM switching center (AmE), switching centre (BrE); ~ **de commutation de circuits** *m* TELECOM circuit switching center (AmE), circuit switching centre (BrE); ~ **de commutation de données** *m* ORDINAT, TELECOM DSE, data switching exchange; ~ **de commutation en mode virtuel** *m* TELECOM virtual-circuit switching node; ~ **de commutation international** *m* TELECOM ISC, international switching

center (AmE), international switching centre (BrE); ~ **de commutation maritime** *m* TELECOM MSC, maritime switching center (AmE), maritime switching centre (BrE); ~ **de commutation de messages** *m* INFORMAT store-and-forward switching center (AmE), store-and-forward switching centre (BrE), TELECOM message switching center (AmE), message switching centre (BrE); ~ **de commutation mobile** *m* TELECOM MSC, mobile switching center (AmE), mobile switching centre (BrE); ~ **de commutation numérique** *m* TELECOM digital switching center (AmE), digital switching centre (BrE); ~ **de commutation numérique du réseau principal** *m* TELECOM DMNSC, digital main network switching center (AmE), digital main network switching centre (BrE); ~ **de commutation de paquets** *m* TELECOM PSE, packet switching exchange; ~ **de contrôle** *m* ESPACE *véhicules* control center (AmE), control centre (BrE); ~ **de contrôle de la circulation aérienne** *m* AERONAUT air traffic control center (AmE), air traffic control centre (BrE); ~ **de contrôle et de commandement** *m* NAUT command and control center (AmE), command and control centre (BrE); ~ **de contrôle radar d'approche** *m* TRANSPORT radar approach control center (AmE), radar approach control centre (BrE); ~ **de coordination de sauvetage** *m* AERONAUT, NAUT rescue coordination center (AmE), rescue coordination centre (BrE); ~ **de courbure** *m* GEOMETRIE, PHYS RAYON *de lentille ou miroir*, PHYSIQUE center of curvature (AmE), centre of curvature (BrE); ~ **de coûts** *m* PRODUCTION cost center (AmE), cost centre (BrE); ~ **de décision** *m* PRODUCTION control center (AmE), control centre (BrE); ~ **dépressionnaire** *m* METEO center of low pressure (AmE), centre of low pressure (BrE); ~ **de dérive** *m* NAUT center of lateral resistance (AmE), centre of lateral resistance (BrE); ~ **de direction** *m* ESPACE control center (AmE), control centre (BrE); ~ **de distribution** *m* TELECOM distribution center (AmE), distribution centre (BrE); ~ **éruptif** *m* GEOLOGIE *volcanisme* eruption point; ~ **d'essais en vol** *m* AERONAUT flight test center (AmE), flight test centre (BrE); ~ **d'exploitation** *m* TELECOM operations center (AmE), operations centre (BrE); ~ **de facturation** *m* TELECOM billing center (AmE), billing centre (BrE); ~ **fixe** *m* MECANIQUE center of motion (AmE), centre of motion (BrE); ~ **de frais** *m* PRODUCTION cost center (AmE), cost centre (BrE); ~ **de la gaine** *m* OPTIQUE, TELECOM cladding center (AmE), cladding centre (BrE); ~ **galactique** *m* ASTRONOMIE galactic center (AmE), galactic centre (BrE); ~ **de gestion** *m* TELECOM NCC, management center (AmE), management centre (BrE), network control center (AmE), network control centre (BrE); ~ **de gestion d'exploitation et de maintenance** *m* TELECOM OAMC, operation administration and maintance center (AmE), operation administration and maintenance centre (BrE); ~ **de gestion de réseau** *m* TELECOM NCC, NMC, network control center (AmE), network control centre (BrE), network management center (AmE), network management centre (BrE); ~ **de gravité** *m* CONSTR, ESPACE *véhicules*, MECANIQUE, NAUT, PHYSIQUE center of gravity (AmE), centre of gravity (BrE); ~ **de gravité de la flottaison** *m* NAUT center of flotation (AmE), centre of flotation (BrE), center of waterplane area (AmE), centre of waterplane area (BrE); ~ **hyperbare** *m* OCEANO hyperbaric center (AmE), hyperbaric centre

(BrE); ~ **d'inertie** *m* MECANIQUE, PHYSIQUE center of inertia (AmE), centre of inertia (BrE); ~ **d'information de vol** *m* AERONAUT flight information center (AmE), flight information centre (BrE); ~ **informatique** *m* INFORMAT DPC, data processing center (AmE), data processing centre (BrE); ~ **international automatique** *m* TELECOM international switching center (AmE), international switching centre (BrE); ~ **international de commutation de données** *m* TELECOM IDSE, international data switching exchange; ~ **international de transit principal** *m* TELECOM main international switching center (AmE), main international switching centre (BrE), main international trunk switching center (AmE), main international trunk switching centre (BrE); ~ **interurbain** *m* TELECOM trunk exchange; ~ **d'inversion** *m* CRISTALL inversion center (AmE), inversion centre (BrE); ~ **de maintenance des accès client** *m* TELECOM CAMC, customer access maintenance center (AmE), customer access maintenance centre (BrE); ~ **de masse** *m* ESPACE barycentre (BrE), barycenter (AmE), center of mass (AmE), centre of mass (BrE), MECANIQUE center of gravity (AmE), centre of gravity (BrE), center of mass (AmE), centre of mass (BrE), PHYSIQUE center of mass (AmE), centre of mass (BrE); ~ **nodal** *m* TV switching center (AmE), switching centre (BrE); ~ **d'opérateurs** *m* TELECOM operator center (AmE), operator centre (BrE); ~ **d'opérations** *m* ESPACE *véhicules* operation center (AmE), operation centre (BrE); ~ **optique** *m* PHYSIQUE optical center (AmE), optical centre (BrE); ~ **d'oscillation** *m* PHYSIQUE center of oscillation (AmE), centre of oscillation (BrE); ~ **de percussion** *m* MECANIQUE center of impact (AmE), centre of impact (BrE), PHYSIQUE center of percussion (AmE), centre of percussion (BrE); ~ **de poussée** *m* AERONAUT *aérodynamique* center of pressure (AmE), centre of pressure (BrE), ESPACE *véhicules* center of thrust (AmE), centre of thrust (BrE), HYDROLOGIE center of buoyancy (AmE), center of displacement (AmE), centre of buoyancy (BrE), centre of displacement (BrE), NAUT aerodynamic center (AmE), aerodynamic centre (BrE), center of buoyancy (AmE), centre of buoyancy (BrE), PHYSIQUE center of pressure (AmE), centre of pressure (BrE); ~ **de poussée de la pale** *m* AERONAUT blade center of pressure (AmE), blade centre of pressure (BrE); ~ **de pression** *m* AERONAUT center of pressure (AmE), centre of pressure (BrE); ~ **de radar** *m* MILITAIRE radar station; ~ **de rattachement** *m* TELECOM local exchange, serving exchange; ~ **de recherche sur les communications** *m* TELECOM CRC, communications research center (AmE), communications research centre (BrE); ~ **de rectification** *m* CONS MECA grinding center (AmE), grinding centre (BrE); ~ **de rectification à 7 axes** *m* CONS MECA grinding center with 7 axis (AmE), grinding centre with 7 axis (BrE); ~ **de relaxation** *m* METALL relaxation center (AmE), relaxation centre (BrE); ~ **RNIS** *m* TELECOM ISDN exchange, integrated digital services exchange; ~ **satellite** *m* TELECOM RSU, remote switching unit, dependent exchange; ~ **secondaire de perturbation** *m* PHYS ONDES secondary center of disturbance (AmE), secondary centre of disturbance (BrE); ~ **spatial** *m* ESPACE space center (AmE), space centre (BrE); ~ **de sustentation** *m* AERONAUT lift center (AmE), lift centre (BrE); ~ **de symétrie** *m* CRISTALL center of symmetry (AmE), centre of symmetry

(BrE); ~ **thermique** *m* REFRIG thermal center (AmE), thermal centre (BrE); ~ **de traitement de données** *m* INFORMAT, TELECOM DPC, data processing center (AmE), data processing centre (BrE); ~ **de traitement d'informations** *m* INFORMAT DPC, data processing center (AmE), data processing centre (BrE); ~ **de transit** *m* TELECOM GSC, group switching center (AmE), group switching centre (BrE), transit switching center (AmE), transit switching centre (BrE), trunk switching center (AmE), trunk switching centre (BrE), TELECOM *(CT)* trunk transit exchange; ~ **de transit principal** *m* TELECOM main trunk switching center (AmE), main trunk switching centre (BrE); ~ **de transit privé** *m* TELECOM hub; ~ **d'usinage** *m* CONS MECA machine center (AmE), machine centre (BrE), MECANIQUE machining center (AmE), machining centre (BrE); ~ **vélique** *m* NAUT center of wind pressure (AmE), centre of wind pressure (BrE)

Centre: ~ **de contrôle technique et opérationnel** *m* ESPACE *communications* TOCC, Technical and Operational Control Centre; ~ **européen pour la recherche nucléaire** *m* PHYS PART European Centre for Nuclear Research; ~ **d'exploitation Intelsat** *m* ESPACE *communications* IOS, Intelsat Operations Centre; ~ **de transit international** *m* ESPACE *communications* International Transit Centre

centrer *vt* PHOTO align

centreur *m* CONS MECA centering pin (AmE), centring pin (BrE), PETROLE centralizer; ~ **de foret** *m* CONS MECA drill locater

centrifugation *f* CHARBON centrifuging, CHIMIE, DISTRI EAU, HYDROLOGIE centrifugation

centrifuge *adj* GENIE CHIM, MECANIQUE, PHYSIQUE centrifugal

centrifuger[1] *vt* CHARBON, GENIE CHIM, PLAST CAOU *opération* centrifuge

centrifugeur *m* CHIMIE, EQUIP LAB *séparation* centrifuge, GENIE CHIM centrifugal machine; ~ **à main** *m* EQUIP LAB *séparation* hand centrifuge; ~ **à supra vitesse** *m* EQUIP LAB *séparation* ultracentrifuge

centrifugeuse *f* GENIE CHIM centrifugal machine, centrifuge, MECANIQUE, PHYSIQUE, PLAST CAOU centrifuge; ~ **à bol perforé** *f* CHARBON basket centrifuge; ~ **à bol plein** *f* CHARBON bowl centrifuge

centripète *adj* PHYSIQUE centripetal

centroïde *adj* GEOMETRIE centroid

centro-symétrique *adj* METALL space-centered (AmE), space-centred (BrE)

centrosymétrique *adj* CRISTALL centrosymmetric

céphalopode *m* GEOLOGIE *paléontologie* cephalopod

céphalosporine *f* CHIMIE cephalosporin

Céphée *f* ASTRONOMIE Cepheus

Céphéide *f* ASTRONOMIE Cepheid

cepstre *m* ELECTRON cepstrum

céramique *f* CERAM VER, CHIMIE ceramic; ~ **dentaire** *f* CERAM VER dental ceramic

céramiques: ~ **superplastiques** *f pl* MATERIAUX superplastic ceramics

céramiste *m* CERAM VER ceramist, clay worker

céramo-plastiques *m pl* MATERIAUX ceramoplastics

cérargyrite *f* MINERAUX cerargyrite, kerargyrite

cérasine *f* CHIMIE cerasin

cerceau *m* MECANIQUE, PRODUCTION *d'un tonneau* hoop

cerclage *m* EMBALLAGE banding, hooping, steel band strapping, PRODUCTION hooping; ~ **en polypropylène** *m* EMBALLAGE polypropylene strap

cercle *m* CERAM VER plunger ring, CONS MECA *de galets, de billes*, EMBALLAGE, MECANIQUE, PRODUCTION *d'un tonneau* hoop; **~ de base** *m* CONS MECA *d'un engrenage à denture en développante* base circle; **~ de boulonnage** *m* PRODUCTION bolt circle; **~ de calage horaire** *m* INSTRUMENT polar axis circle; **~ circonscrit** *m* GEOMETRIE circumcircle, circumscribed circle; **~ concentrique** *m* GEOMETRIE concentric circle; **~ de confusion** *m* CINEMAT, PHOTO circle of confusion; **~ de contact** *m* CONS MECA dividing circle, pitch circle, pitch line; **~ de couronne** *m* CONS MECA addendum circle, outside circle, point circle; **~ de déclinaison** *m* INSTRUMENT, PHYSIQUE declination circle; **~ de distance fixe** *m* NAUT calibration ring; **~ de distance variable** *m* NAUT variable range marker; **~ de division** *m* CONS MECA dividing circle, pitch circle, pitch line; **~ d'échanfreinement** *m* CONS MECA outside circle, point circle; **~ en feuillard** *m* EMBALLAGE band iron; **~ d'évidement** *m* CONS MECA dedendum circle; **~ extérieur** *m* CONS MECA addendum circle, blank circle, outside circle, point circle; **~ de glissement** *m* CONSTR, GEOLOGIE slip circle; **~ gradué** *m* GEOMETRIE, INSTRUMENT divided circle, graduated circle; **~ horaire** *m* METROLOGIE hour circle; **~ inscrit** *m* GEOMETRIE inscribed circle; **~ limite** *m* CONS MECA clearance circle; **~ méridien** *m* INSTRUMENT meridian circle; **~ de moindre aberration** *m* PHOTO circle of least confusion; **~ osculateur** *m* GEOMETRIE kissing circle; **~ de perçage** *m* PRODUCTION bolt circle; **~ primitif** *m* CONS MECA dividing circle, pitch circle, pitch line; **~ de Rowland** *m* PHYSIQUE Rowland circle; **~ tangent** *m* GEOMETRIE tangent circle; **~ de tête** *m* CONS MECA addendum circle, blank circle, outside circle, point circle

cerclé *m*: **~ de fer** *adj* PRODUCTION ironbound

cercler *vt* MECANIQUE hoop

cercleuse *f* EMBALLAGE strapping machine

cerco *m* OCEANO purse seine

céréales: **~ panifiables** *f pl* AGRO ALIM bread grain

céréaline *f* CHIMIE cerealin, diastase

céréalose *m* CHIMIE cerealose

cérérite *f* MINERAUX cererite, cerite

cérésine *f* CHIMIE ceresin, ceresine

céreux *adj* CHIMIE cerous

cerf-volant *m* AERONAUT kite

cérine *f* CHIMIE, MINERAUX cerin

cérique *adj* CHIMIE ceric

ceri-rouge *m* CERAM VER ceri-rouge

cérite *f* MINERAUX cererite, cerite

cérium *m* (Ce) CHIMIE cerium (Ce)

CERN *abrév* (*Conseil européen pour la recherche nucléaire*) PHYS PART CERN (*European Organization for Nuclear Research*)

cérotique *adj* CHIMIE cerotic

certificat *m* BREVETS certificate; **~ d'acceptation** *m* QUALITE acceptance certificate; **~ agréé de premiers secours** *m* SECURITE approved first aid certificate; **~ d'assurance de la qualité** *m* CONS MECA quality assurance certificate; **~ de brevet** *m* BREVETS patent certificate; **~ de conformité** *m* CONS MECA certificate of conformity, QUALITE certificate of compliance, certificate of conformity; **~ de construction** *m* NAUT builder's certificate; **~ d'homologation** *m* AERONAUT approval certificate; **~ d'immatriculation** *m* AERONAUT certificate of registration, NAUT ship's register; **~ de navigabilité** *m* AERONAUT certificate of airworthiness, NAUT certificate of seaworthiness; **~ de réception** *m*

QUALITE acceptance certificate; **~ d'utilité** *m* BREVETS utility certificate

certification *f* INFORMAT, ORDINAT, QUALITE certification

certifier *vt* AERONAUT *en état de navigabilité* certify, QUALITE authenticate, certify

céruléum *m* CHIMIE ceruleum

céruse *f* CHIMIE ceruse, white lead

cérusite *f* MINERAUX cerusite, cerussite

cervantite *f* MINERAUX cervantite

cérylique *adj* CHIMIE cerylic

césium *m* CHIMIE cesium (AmE), caesium (BrE)

cession *f* BREVETS assignment; **~ de licence** *f* QUALITE transfer of license

cessionnaire *m* BREVETS assignee

cétane *m* CHIMIE cetane

cétazine *f* CHIMIE ketazine

cétène *m* CHIMIE keten, ketene

cétimine *f* CHIMIE ketimine

céto-acides *m pl* CHIMIE keto-acids

cétone *f* CHIMIE, PLAST CAOU ketone

cétonique *adj* CHIMIE ketonic

cétose *m* CHIMIE ketose

cétyle *m* CHIMIE cetyl

ceylanite *f* MINERAUX ceylanite, ceylonite

ceylonite *f* MINERAUX ceylanite, ceylonite

Cf (*californium*) CHIMIE Cf (*californium*)

CFAO *abrév* (*conception et fabrication assistées par ordinateur*) ORDINAT, PRODUCTION CADCAM (*computer-aided design and manufacture*)

CFC *abrév* CHIMIE (*cubique à faces centrées*), CRISTALL (*cubique à faces centrées*) FCC (*face-centered cubic, face-centred cubic*), EMBALLAGE (*chlorofluorocarbone*) POLLUTION (*chlorofluorocarbone*), CFC (*chlorofluorocarbon*)

CG *abrév* (*convertisseur de gestion*) TELECOM charge-metering converter

CGL *abrév* (*chromatographie gaz-liquide*) POLLUTION, THERMODYN gas liquid chromatography

CGS *abrév* METROLOGIE (*centimètre-gramme-seconde*) CGS (*centimetre-gramme-second*), POLLUTION (*chromatographie gaz-solide*) gas solid chromatography

chabasite *f* MINERAUX chabasite, chabazite

chabotte *f* CONS MECA *de marteau-pilon* anvil block

chaille *f* GEOLOGIE *concentration locale de silice* chert nodule

chaînage *m* CONSTR chainage, chaining, ORDINAT chaining; **~ de données** *m* INFORMAT, ORDINAT data chaining; **~ de données de commandes répétitives** *m* IMPRIM concatenation; **~ de programmes** *m* ORDINAT program linking

chaîne *f* CHIMIE, CONS MECA, GEOLOGIE chain, IMPRIM string, *de caractères au-dessus de la ligne normale de texte* superscript, INFORMAT chain, string, MECANIQUE, METROLOGIE chain, NAUT chain cable, chain, ORDINAT chain, string, PAPIER warp, TEXTILE chain, warp, TV *de diffusion TV* channel, network, VEHICULES *distribution, transmission* chain; **~ d'action** *f* ELECTROTEC forward path; **~ d'allongement** *f* MINES drill chain; **~ d'amarrage** *f* POLLU MER mooring chain; **~ d'ancre** *f* NAUT anchor chain; **~ d'approvisionnement** *f* GAZ distribution system; **~ d'arpentage** *f* CONSTR engineer's chain, land measuring chain, measuring chain, surveyor's chain; **~ d'arpenteur** *f* CONSTR measuring chain, surveyor's chain; **~ à articu-**

lations *f* CONS MECA pintle chain; ~ **d'asservissement** *f* COMMANDE servoloop; ~ **à augets** *f* CONSTR bucket chain; ~ **avec axes sans douilles** *f* CONS MECA pintle chain; ~ **binaire** *f* INFORMAT, ORDINAT bit string; ~ **de bits** *f* INFORMAT, ORDINAT bit string; ~ **calibrée** *f* CONS MECA pitch chain, pitched chain; ~ **de caractères** *f* IMPRIM *composition électronique*, INFORMAT character string; ~ **de charge** *f* CONS MECA *d'un palan, d'un monte-charge* load chain, CONSTR *d'un palan, d'un monte-charge* lifting chain, PRODUCTION, SECURITE load chain; ~ **charnière** *f* CONS MECA *pour convoyeur* flat-top chain; ~ **cinématique** *f* AUTO power train, MECANIQUE kinematic chain; ~ **de codes** *f* IMPRIM *composition, informatique* code string; ~ **de commande** *f* ESPACE command link; ~ **compacte** *f* ENREGISTR three-in-one stereo component system; ~ **de connexion** *f* TELECOM connection; ~ **de contrepoids** *f* CONS MECA balance chain; ~ **de contrôle d'un rayonnement** *f* NUCLEAIRE radiation channel; ~ **convoyeuse** *f* CONS MECA conveyor chain; ~ **dédiée** *f* TV dedicated channel; ~ **de désintégration** *f* PHYSIQUE decay chain; ~ **désordonnée** *f* CHIMIE *polymère* disordered chain; ~ **de diodes** *f* ELECTRON diode string; ~ **directe** *f* ELECTROTEC forward path; ~ **de distribution** *f* AUTO timing chain, EMBALLAGE distribution chain, VEHICULES *moteur* camshaft drive chain; ~ **de distribution à rouleaux** *f* AUTO roller timing chain; ~ **de distribution silencieuse** *f* AUTO noiseless-timing chain; ~ **dragueuse** *f* MINES, NAUT dredge chain; ~ **droite** *f* CHIMIE straight chain; ~ **duplex** *f* AUTO, VEHICULES *transmission* duplex chain; ~ **dynamique** *f* AERONAUT power train; ~ **électroacoustique** *f* ACOUSTIQUE electroacoustic chain; ~ **d'éléments** *f* ELECTRON daisy chain; ~ **d'emballage** *f* EMBALLAGE packaging line; ~ **d'emballage pour liquides** *f* EMBALLAGE liquid-packaging line; ~ **d'emballage thermoformé** *f* EMBALLAGE blister packing line; ~ **d'émetteurs** *f* ELECTROTEC network; ~ **encollée** *f* TEXTILE sized warp; ~ **en gerbe** *f* CONS MECA indented chain; ~ **en mailles d'acier moulé à goujons** *f* CONS MECA pintle chain; ~ **d'enregistrement** *f* TV recording chain; ~ **en S** *f* PRODUCTION curbed chain; ~ **d'entraînement** *f* VEHICULES *transmission* drive chain; ~ **d'entraînement d'arbre à cames** *f* VEHICULES *moteur* camshaft drive chain; ~ **éprouvée** *f* CONS MECA tested chain; ~ **d'équilibrage** *f* CONS MECA balance chain; ~ **fermée** *f* CONS MECA closed chain, ring; ~ **frigorifique** *f* REFRIG cold chain; ~ **froide** *f* REFRIG cold chain; ~ **à fuseau** *f* CONS MECA stud chain, CONSTR pin chain; ~ **Galle** *f* CONS MECA, MECANIQUE sprocket chain; ~ **à godets** *f* CONSTR bucket chain; ~ **de Gunter** *f* CONSTR Gunter's chain; ~ **d'informations** *f* TV news network; ~ **d'isolateurs suspendus** *f* ELECTROTEC cap and pin insulator; ~ **latérale** *f* CHIMIE *d'atomes* side chain; ~ **de lecture** *f* ENREGISTR playback system; ~ **de levage** *f* CONS MECA *d'un palan, d'un monte-charge* lifting chain, load chain, CONSTR *d'un palan, d'un monte-charge*, PRODUCTION, SECURITE lifting chain; ~ **de levage à mailles jointives** *f* CONS MECA leaf chain; ~ **Loran** *f* AERONAUT *navigation* Loran chain; ~ **à maillons** *f* CONS MECA, PAPIER, PRODUCTION link chain; ~ **à maillons courts** *f* CONS MECA short-link chain; ~ **à maillons non-rivés forgés par estampage** *f* CONS MECA drop-forged rivetless chain; ~ **à maillons ouverts** *f* PRODUCTION link chain; ~ **à maillons plats** *f* CONS MECA block chain; ~ **à main** *f* CONSTR hand chain; ~ **de manoeuvre** *f* PRODUCTION *d'un palan, d'un monte-*

charge hand chain; ~ **de mesure de la constante de temps** *f* NUCLEAIRE period measuring channel; ~ **de mise en bouteilles** *f* EMBALLAGE bottling line; ~ **de montage** *f* CONS MECA, EMBALLAGE, MECANIQUE, NAUT, PRODUCTION assembly line; ~ **de montagne** *f* GEOLOGIE mountain chain; ~ **de mouillage** *f* NAUT anchor chain, POLLU MER mooring chain; ~ **non-ramifiée** *f* CHIMIE straight chain; ~ **ordonnée** *f* CHIMIE ordered chain; ~ **ouverte** *f* CHIMIE open chain, PRODUCTION link chain; ~ **de pilotage** *f* ESPACE *véhicule spatial* attitude control unit; ~ **de pointeurs** *f* INFORMAT, ORDINAT pointer chain; ~ **porte-couteau** *f* CHARBON cutter chain; ~ **de précision à rouleaux et roue dentée** *f* CONS MECA precision roller chain and chain wheel; ~ **de production** *f* EMBALLAGE, NAUT production line; ~ **de production à marche continue** *f* EMBALLAGE continuous production line; ~ **de production pour fermetures** *f* EMBALLAGE closure production line; ~ **radioactive** *f* PHYSIQUE radioactive series; ~ **ramifiée** *f* CHIMIE branched chain; ~ **de Ramsden** *f* CONSTR Ramsden's chain; ~ **de réaction** *f* COMMANDE feedback chain; ~ **de recherche** *f* IMPRIM search string; ~ **de refroidissement** *f* REFRIG cold chain; ~ **de remplissage** *f* EMBALLAGE filling line; ~ **de remplissage de boîtes** *f* EMBALLAGE can filling line (AmE), tin filling line (BrE); ~ **de remplissage de sacs** *f* EMBALLAGE sack filling line; ~ **de reproduction** *f* TV reproducing chain; ~ **de résistances** *f* ELECTROTEC resistor string; ~ **de retour** *f* ELECTRON feedback loop; ~ **de rétroaction** *f* ELECTRON feedback loop; ~ **à rouleaux** *f* CONS MECA roller chain; ~ **de roulis** *f* AERONAUT *pilote automatique* roll channel; ~ **à ruban d'acier** *f* CONSTR band chain, band tape, steel band chain; ~ **sans fin** *f* PAPIER, VEHICULES endless chain; ~ **sans fin à picots** *f* TEXTILE endless pin chain; ~ **de sécurité** *f* SECURITE safety chain; ~ **serrée** *f* CONS MECA short-link chain; ~ **spécialisée** *f* TV dedicated channel; ~ **de sûreté** *f* CONS MECA safety chain, MINES bridle chain; ~ **de suspension** *f* PRODUCTION chain sling, sling, SECURITE chain sling; ~ **de symboles** *f* INFORMAT symbol string; ~ **de tangage** *f* AERONAUT pitch channel; ~ **de télécinéma** *f* CINEMAT telecine chain; ~ **d'un tissu** *f* PAPIER, TEXTILE warp; ~ **torse** *f* PRODUCTION curbed chain; ~ **traînante** *f* MINES creeper chain; ~ **de transmission à douilles** *f* CONS MECA transmission bush chain; ~ **de transmission à maillons coudés** *f* CONS MECA cranked link transmission chain; ~ **de TV à péage** *f* TELECOM pay television network; ~ **unitaire** *f* INFORMAT, ORDINAT unit string; ~ **de Vaucanson** *f* PRODUCTION ladder chain; ~ **de vernissage** *f* REVETEMENT enameling line (AmE), enamelling line (BrE); ~ **vide** *f* INFORMAT, ORDINAT empty string, null string

chaîne-câble *f* MINES cable chain; ~ **à mailles serrées** *f* CONS MECA short-link chain cable

chaînée *f* METROLOGIE chain

chaîne-Galle: ~ **à fuseau** *f* CONS MECA stud chain

chaîner *vt* CONSTR chain, INFORMAT, ORDINAT concatenate

chaînetier *m* PRODUCTION chainsmith

chaînette *f* CONS MECA chain, GEOMETRIE, MECANIQUE, NAUT catenary; ~ **à boules** *f* CONS MECA beaded chain

chaîneur *m* CONSTR chainman

chaînier *m* PRODUCTION chain maker, chainsmith

chaîniste *m* PRODUCTION chain maker, chainsmith

chaînon *m* CONS MECA *d'une chaîne* link, *d'un câble-chaîne* link

chair *f* CERAM VER orange peel; ~ **fossile** *f* MINERAUX mountain flesh; ~ **minérale** *f* MINERAUX mountain flesh

chaise *f* CONS MECA hanger, seat, seating, MECANIQUE bracket, PRODUCTION *de laminoir* chock; ~ **console** *f* MINES bracket hanger, wall bracket; ~ **à deux jambages** *f* PRODUCTION sling hanger; ~ **en bout** *f* CONSTR angle bracket, MINES *pour transmissions* end bracket, end wall bracket; ~ **en U** *f* PRODUCTION sling hanger; ~ **de gabier** *f* NAUT boatswain's chair; ~ **grillage** *f* REFRIG unit housing; ~ **d'hélice** *f* NAUT propeller bracket; ~ **palier** *f* CONS MECA hanger with bearings, PRODUCTION plummer block; ~ **pendante** *f* MINES pendant bracket; ~ **pendante à deux jambes** *f* PRODUCTION sling hanger; ~ **de sol** *f* MINES floor hanger, standard

chaise-applique *f* MINES bracket hanger, wall bracket

chaland *m* NAUT barge, lighter, PETR barge, TRANSPORT barge, freight barge; ~ **automoteur** *m* NAUT self-propelled barge; ~ **à clapets** *m* NAUT hopper, hopper barge; ~ **de débarquement** *m* MILITAIRE landing barge; ~ **d'écrémage** *m* POLLU MER skimming barge; ~ **écrémeur** *m* POLLU MER skimming barge; ~ **récupérateur** *m* POLLU MER skimming barge; ~ **sans moteur** *m* NAUT dumb barge

chaland-citerne *m* TRANSPORT tank barge

chalcanthite *f* MINERAUX chalcanthite, cyanose, cyanosite

chalcocite *f* MINERAUX chalcocite, chalcosine, chalcosine

chalcolite *f* MINERAUX chalcolite, NUCLEAIRE copper uranite, torbernite

chalcoménite *f* MINERAUX chalcomenite

chalcomorphite *f* MINERAUX chalkomorphite

chalcone *f* CHIMIE chalcone

chalcophanite *f* MINERAUX chalcophanite

chalcophile *adj* MATERIAUX chalcophilous

chalcophyllite *f* MINERAUX chalcophyllite

chalcopyrite *f* MATERIAUX copper pyrites, MINERAUX chalcopyrite

chalcopyrrhotite *f* MINERAUX chalcopyrrhotine, chalcopyrrhotite

chalcosidérite *f* MINERAUX chalcosiderite

chalcostibite *f* MINERAUX chalcostibite

chalcotrichite *f* MINERAUX chalcotrichite

chaleur[1] *f* CHIMIE, ESPACE, MAT CHAUFF, PAPIER, PHYSIQUE, REFRIG, TEXTILE, THERMODYN heat; ~ **d'absorption** *f* THERMODYN heat of absorption; ~ **d'activation** *f* THERMODYN heat of activation; ~ **d'adsorption** *f* NUCLEAIRE adsorption heat; ~ **ardente** *f* THERMODYN burning heat; ~ **blanche** *f* THERMODYN white heat; ~ **de combinaison** *f* THERMODYN heat of combination; ~ **de combustion** *f* CHIMIE heat of combustion, THERMODYN combustion heat; ~ **de compression** *f* THERMODYN heat of compression; ~ **de condensation** *f* METEO, THERMODYN heat of condensation; ~ **de convection** *f* THERMODYN convection heat; ~ **de décomposition** *f* CHIMIE heat of decomposition; ~ **de dilatation** *f* THERMODYN heat of dilatation; ~ **de dissociation** *f* THERMODYN heat of dissociation; ~ **de dissolution** *f* THERMODYN heat of solution; ~ **douce** *f* THERMODYN warmth; ~ **efficace** *f* THERMODYN available heat; ~ **enlevée** *f* REFRIG heat removed; ~ **évacuée au condenseur** *f* REFRIG condenser heat; ~ **d'évaporation** *f* THERMODYN heat of vaporization; ~ **d'expansion** *f* THERMODYN heat of expansion; ~ **de fond** *f* CERAM VER bottom heat; ~ **de formation** *f* CHIMIE, THERMODYN heat of formation; ~ **de friction** *f* THERMODYN heat caused by friction; ~ **de fusion** *f* THERMODYN heat of fusion, melting heat; ~ **des gaz brûlés** *f* THERMODYN waste gas heat; ~ **de haute qualité** *f* NUCLEAIRE high-grade heat; ~ **d'hydratation** *f* CONSTR, THERMODYN heat of hydration; ~ **d'incandescence** *f* THERMODYN glowing heat; ~ **latente** *f* CHAUFFAGE, CONSTR, MECANIQUE, METEO, PETROLE *raffinage*, PHYSIQUE, REFRIG, THERMODYN latent heat; ~ **latente de compression** *f* THERMODYN latent heat of compression; ~ **latente de cristallisation** *f* THERMODYN latent heat of solidification; ~ **latente d'évaporation** *f* THERMODYN latent heat of evaporation; ~ **latente d'expansion** *f* THERMODYN latent heat of expansion; ~ **latente de fusion** *f* PHYSIQUE, THERMODYN latent heat of fusion; ~ **latente de la glace** *f* REFRIG ice melting equivalent; ~ **latente massique** *f* PHYSIQUE specific latent heat; ~ **latente de transformation** *f* THERMODYN latent heat of transformation; ~ **latente de vaporisation** *f* PHYSIQUE, THERMODYN latent heat of vaporization; ~ **massique** *f* CHAUFFAGE, PHYSIQUE, REFRIG specific heat; ~ **de mélange** *f* THERMODYN heat of mixing; ~ **modérée** *f* THERMODYN gentle heat; ~ **moléculaire** *f* THERMODYN molecular heat; ~ **de neutralisation** *f* THERMODYN heat of neutralization; ~ **perdue** *f* CHAUFFAGE, NUCLEAIRE, POLLUTION, THERMODYN waste heat; ~ **de prise** *f* CONSTR *ciment* heat of hydration; ~ **rayonnante** *f* PHYS RAYON *rayons infrarouges*, THERMODYN radiant heat; ~ **de réaction** *f* CHIMIE, THERMODYN heat of reaction; ~ **reflétée** *f* THERMODYN reflected heat; ~ **rémanente** *f* AERONAUT afterheat; ~ **résiduelle** *f* AERONAUT afterheat; ~ **rouge** *f* THERMODYN glowing heat; ~ **sèche** *f* TEXTILE dry heat; ~ **sensible** *f* CHAUFFAGE, GEOPHYS, PHYSIQUE sensible heat, THERMODYN free heat; ~ **solaire** *f* EN RENOUV solar heat; ~ **de solution** *f* THERMODYN heat of solution; ~ **spécifique** *f* ESPACE, PLAST CAOU, THERMODYN specific heat; ~ **spécifique atomique** *f* PHYS RAYON atomic heat capacity; ~ **transportée par convection** *f* THERMODYN convected heat; ~ **utile** *f* CHAUFFAGE useful heat, THERMODYN available heat

chaleur:[2] **être à ~ rouge** *vi* THERMODYN glow

chaloupe *f* NAUT longboat, ship's boat

chalumeau *m* CHAUFFAGE blowlamp, CONS MECA blowlamp, blowpipe, blowtorch, CONSTR blowpipe, blowtorch, GAZ burner, MECANIQUE torch, TELECOM burner, THERMODYN flame cutting torch, welding torch; ~ **à acétylène** *m* CONSTR acetylene blowpipe; ~ **acétylénique** *m* CONSTR acetylene blowpipe; ~ **à basse pression** *m* CONSTR low-pressure blowpipe; ~ **braseur** *m* CONSTR brazing blowpipe, soldering blowpipe; ~ **chauffeur** *m* CONSTR heating blowpipe; ~ **de coupe** *m* MECANIQUE flame cutter; ~ **coupeur** *m* CONSTR cutting blowpipe; ~ **coupeur sous l'eau** *m* CONSTR underwater cutting blowpipe; ~ **à découper** *m* CONS MECA cutting torch; ~ **à gaz** *m* PRODUCTION gas blowpipe; ~ **goujeur** *m* CONSTR gouging blowpipe; ~ **à haute pression** *m* CONSTR high-pressure blowpipe; ~ **manuel** *m* CONS MECA *pour soudage, coupage* manual blowpipe; ~ **oxhydrique** *m* PRODUCTION compound blowpipe; ~ **oxyacétylénique** *m* CONSTR, MECANIQUE, PRODUCTION oxyacetylene blowpipe; ~ **oxycoupeur** *m* CONSTR cutting blowpipe; ~ **soudage** *m* CONSTR soldering blowpipe; ~ **soudeur** *m* CONSTR welding blowpipe

chalut *m* NAUT trawl, trawl net, OCEANO dragnet, trawl, trawl net, POLLU MER trawl net, TEXTILE trawl

chalutage *m* OCEANO trawl fishing, trawling; **~ de barrage flottant** *m* POLLU MER boom towing

chaluter *vt* NAUT, OCEANO trawl

chalutier *m* NAUT, OCEANO trawler

chalybite *f* MINERAUX chalybite

chambrage *m* CONS MECA counterbore, MECANIQUE counterboring; **~ arrière** *m* CONS MECA back spotfacing

chambranle *m* CONSTR jamb lining

chambre *f* CHIMIE, CONS MECA *d'un injecteur* chamber, CONSTR room, DISTRI EAU chamber, coffer, MECANIQUE chamber, MINES room, NAUT cabin, PHOTO plate camera; **~ d'accélération** *f* GENIE CHIM accelerating chamber; **~ d'accrochage** *f* MINES landing stage, landing station, lodge, onsetting, pit landing, plane table, plat, winding inset; **~ d'accumulation des gaz de fission** *f* NUCLEAIRE fission gas plenum; **~ d'agrandissement** *f* PHOTO enlarger camera, enlarging camera; **~ d'air** *f* MINES *dans un trou* airspace; **~ à air** *f* MINES *dans un trou* airspace, VEHICULES *pneu* inner tube; **~ anéchoïque** *f* TELECOM echoless chamber; **~ annulaire** *f* AERONAUT, ESPACE *véhicules* annulus; **~ annulaire en forme de beignet** *f* NUCLEAIRE pancakeshaped annular chamber; **~ d'aspiration** *f* CONS MECA suction box, INST HYDR *d'une turbine* draft box (AmE), draft tube (AmE), draught box (BrE), draught tube (BrE); **~ d'asservissement** *f* AERONAUT pilot pressure chamber; **~ d'astrophotographie** *f* PHOTO astronomical camera; **~ d'atelier** *f* PHOTO studio camera; **~ avec conditionnement de l'air** *f* EMBALLAGE climatic chamber; **~ box** *f* PHOTO box camera; **~ à brouillard** *f* PHYS PART *détection des particules chargées*, PHYSIQUE Wilson cloud chamber; **~ à bulles** *f* PHYS PART, PHYSIQUE bubble chamber; **~ à câbles** *f* ELECTR *alimentation* cable manhole; **~ de carburation** *f* AUTO, VEHICULES mixing chamber; **~ des cartes** *f* NAUT chartroom; **~ de chauffe** *f* THERMODYN heating chamber; **~ claire** *f* PHOTO camera lucida; **~ climatique** *f* REFRIG climatic chamber; **~ de combustion** *f* AUTO, CONS MECA combustion chamber, ESPACE burner can, combustor, thrust chamber, *propulsion* combustion chamber, INST HYDR combustion chamber, fire chamber, MAT CHAUFF, NAUT combustion chamber, THERMODYN combustion chamber, *locomotive* firebox, *moteur, soupape* combustion chamber; **~ de combustion en coin** *f* AUTO wedge-type combustion chamber; **~ de combustion hémisphérique** *f* AUTO hemispherical combustion chamber; **~ de combustion du moteur** *f* CONS MECA engine combustion chamber; **~ de compensation** *f* EN RENOUV surge tank; **~ de compression** *f* ACOUSTIQUE closed diaphragm, AUTO, INST HYDR, PETROLE *plongée* compression chamber; **~ de congélation** *f* REFRIG freezing room, walk-in freezer; **~ à court tirage** *f* PHOTO camera with short bellows extension; **~ à dards** *f* PHYS PART streamer chamber; **~ de Debye-Scherrer** *f* NUCLEAIRE X-ray powder camera; **~ de décantation** *f* NUCLEAIRE settler chamber, POLLUTION decanter; **~ de décintrage** *f* CONSTR dismantling chamber; **~ de décompression** *f* NAUT, PETR, PETROLE decompression chamber; **~ de décompression d'un distributeur à tiroir** *f* INST HYDR exhaust cavity; **~ de démontage** *f* CONSTR dismantling chamber; **~ de dépoussiérage** *f* CHARBON dust chamber; **~ à dépression** *f* TV vacuum chamber; **~ de dessablage au jet de sable** *f* PRODUCTION sandblast cleaning room; **~ de dessiccation à étagères** *f* REFRIG tray drying chamber; **~ de détente** *f* CONS MECA expansion chamber; **~ de diffraction X** *f* NUCLEAIRE *caméra* X-ray camera, X-ray diffraction camera; **~ de digestion des boues** *f* THERMODYN digestion tank; **~ de distillation** *f* GENIE CHIM distillation chamber; **~ de distribution** *f* INST HYDR steam box, steam case, steam chamber, steam chest, valve chest; **~ d'eau** *f* DISTRI EAU flume; **~ à eau** *f* INST HYDR *réservoir, alimentation d'une turbine* forebay; **~ d'eau ouverte** *f* PRODUCTION open flume; **~ d'eau de turbine** *f* DISTRI EAU open turbine chamber, INST HYDR open turbine chamber, open turbine pit; **~ d'écho** *f* ENREGISTR echo chamber, reverb, reverberation unit; **~ d'écluse** *f* DISTRI EAU chamber, lock chamber; **~ d'élutriation** *f* GENIE CHIM elutriation chamber; **~ d'émission** *f* INSTRUMENT emission chamber; **~ d'envoyage** *f* MINES landing stage, landing station, lodge, onsetting, pit landing, plane table, plat; **~ d'épuration** *f* PRODUCTION skim gate, skimming chamber; **~ d'équilibre** *f* EN RENOUV surge tank, INST HYDR forebay; **~ d'essai acoustique** *f* CONS MECA acoustic testing room; **~ à étincelles** *f* ASTRONOMIE, PHYSIQUE spark chamber; **~ d'expansion** *f* CERAM VER expansion space; **~ d'explosion du moteur** *f* CONS MECA engine combustion chamber; **~ à feu** *f* INST HYDR fire chamber; **~ de filtration** *f* CHARBON baghouse; **~ de flottaison** *f* POLLU MER flotation chamber; **~ de flotteur** *f* VEHICULES *carburateur* float chamber; **~ de flotteur de carburateur** *f* VEHICULES carburetor float chamber (AmE), carburettor float chamber (BrE); **~ de format moyen** *f* PHOTO half plate camera; **~ française à soufflet carré** *f* PHOTO square bellows camera; **~ frigorifique** *f* CONS MECA, REFRIG, THERMODYN coldroom; **~ froide** *f* CONS MECA coldroom, REFRIG cold chamber, coldroom, THERMODYN coldroom; **~ froide démontable** *f* REFRIG portable coldroom; **~ froide à double paroi** *f* REFRIG jacket coldroom; **~ froide gonflable** *f* REFRIG inflatable coldroom; **~ froide à plantes** *f* REFRIG nursery cold store; **~ froide préfabriquée** *f* REFRIG sectional coldroom; **~ grand format à soufflet** *f* PHOTO large format folding camera; **~ de grillage du minerai** *f* MINES stall; **~ hydropneumatique** *f* OCEANO hydropneumatic chamber; **~ insonorisée** *f* ENREGISTR soundproof room; **~ d'ionisation** *f* PHYS PART, PHYSIQUE ionization chamber; **~ d'ionisation à fission** *f* NUCLEAIRE fission ionization chamber; **~ d'ionisation interne du coeur** *f* NUCLEAIRE in-core ionization chamber; **~ d'irradiation** *f* PHYS RAYON irradiation chamber; **~ isolée** *f* CHARBON panel, room; **~ jumelée pour stéréophotographie** *f* PHOTO stereoscopic camera; **~ de Kanne** *f* NUCLEAIRE Kanne chamber; **~ à long tirage** *f* PHOTO camera with long bellows extension; **~ des machines** *f* NAUT engine room; **~ de maturation** *f* REFRIG ageing room (BrE), aging room (AmE); **~ de mélange** *f* GAZ mixing chamber; **~ de mesure** *f* INSTRUMENT measurement chamber; **~ métrique universelle de photogrammétrie** *f* INSTRUMENT phototheodolite; **~ de mine** *f* MINES blast hole, borehole, mine opening, mining hole, chamber, mine chamber, shot hole; **~ du moteur** *f* NAUT engine compartment, PRODUCTION engine room; **~ de navigation** *f* NAUT chartroom; **~ noire** *f* CHIMIE camera, CINEMAT darkroom, loading room, PHOTO darkroom; **~ à nuages** *f* PHYS ONDES *détection de radiation* cloud chamber; **~ d'observation** *f* INSTRUMENT viewing chamber; **~ à obturateur central** *f* PHOTO camera with diaphragm shutter; **~ à oscillation** *f* CRIS-

TALL oscillation camera; ~ **de photogrammétrie aérienne** *f* PHOTO aerial mapping camera; ~ **photographique** *f* INSTRUMENT camera, photo chamber; ~ **pliante** *f* PHOTO folding camera; ~ **de pompe** *f* DISTRI EAU pump room; ~ **portative** *f* PHOTO field camera; ~ **des portes** *f* DISTRI EAU chamber, lock chamber; ~ **de postcombustion** *f* CHARBON postcombustion chamber, MATERIAUX *catalyse*, THERMODYN *réacteur* afterburner; ~ **de poudre** *f* CRISTALL powder camera; ~ **pour fermeture hermétique** *f* EMBALLAGE chamber-type vacuum sealing; ~ **à poussières** *f* CERAM VER side pocket; ~ **de précombustion** *f* AUTO *moteur diesel*, THERMODYN *moteur diesel*, VEHICULES *moteur diesel* precombustion chamber; ~ **de pression** *f* PAPIER pocket, pressure pocket; ~ **propre** *f* ESPACE clean room; ~ **de pulvérisation** *f* GENIE CHIM pulverizing chamber, REFRIG spray chamber; ~ **de réfrigération** *f* REFRIG chill room; ~ **réfrigérée** *f* REFRIG chill room; ~ **de régénération** *f* CERAM VER checker chamber; ~ **de réverbération** *f* ENREGISTR echo chamber, reverb, reverberant room, reverberation unit, reverb, reverberation chamber, ESPACE *véhicules* reverberation chamber; ~ **de réverbération à ressort** *f* ENREGISTR spring reverberation unit; ~ **de salaison** *f* REFRIG curing cellar; ~ **de séchage** *f* PRODUCTION drying chamber, drying house, drying room; ~ **de séchage par congélation** *f* GENIE CHIM freeze-dryer; ~ **de sédimentation** *f* AUTO sediment chamber; ~ **à sillages lumineux** *f* PHYS PART streamer chamber; ~ **de simulation spatiale** *f* ESPACE *essais* space simulation chamber; ~ **sonore** *f* ACOUSTIQUE echo chamber; ~ **sourde** *f* ENREGISTR dead room, PHYSIQUE anechoic room, dead room; ~ **souterraine** *f* TELECOM underground chamber; ~ **à sténopé** *f* PHOTO pinhole camera; ~ **de stockage frigorifique** *f* REFRIG cold storage room; ~ **de stockage de produits congelés** *f* REFRIG frozen food storage room; ~ **de sustentation** *f* TRANSPORT suction chamber; ~ **de tranquillisation** *f* AERONAUT plenum chamber, HYDROLOGIE settling basin; ~ **de turbulence** *f* AUTO turbulence chamber, turbulence combustion chamber; ~ **de vapeur d'une chaudière** *f* INST HYDR steam space; ~ **de Weissenberg** *f* CRISTALL Weissenberg camera; ~ **de Wilson** *f* PHYS PART, PHYSIQUE Wilson cloud chamber

chambre-laboratoire *f* PHOTO copy camera
chambrer *vt* CERAM VER soak, CONS MECA counterbore
chambrière *f* MINES drag, safety drag bar
chameau *m* NAUT *caisson à air* camel
chamois *m* CONSTR, PRODUCTION chamois
chamoisite *f* MINERAUX chamosite
chamotte *f* CERAM VER chamotte, THERMODYN fireclay
champ *m* ACOUSTIQUE field, CINEMAT angle, field, ELECTR *électromagnétisme* field, ELECTROTEC field, *dans un conducteur* field, INFORMAT, ORDINAT, PETR, PETROLE field; ~ **acoustique** *m* ACOUSTIQUE acoustical field; ~ **d'action** *m* CINEMAT field of action, NUCLEAIRE operation area; ~ **de l'adresse du mot** *m* PRODUCTION *automatisme industriel* word address field; ~ **d'aimantation** *m* ELECTR *magnétisme* magnetizing force; ~ **aléatoire** *m* TELECOM random field; ~ **alternatif** *m* ELECTROTEC alternating field; ~ **d'analyse** *m* TV scanning field; ~ **aurifère** *m* MINES gold field; ~ **banalisé** *m* INFORMAT free field; ~ **de bruit** *m* TELECOM noise field; ~ **de clé** *m* INFORMAT key field; ~ **coercible** *m* ELECTROTEC coercive force; ~ **coercitif** *m* PHYSIQUE, TV coercivity; ~ **de commande UIH** *m* TELECOM UIH

control field; ~ **continu** *m* ELECTR constant field; ~ **de courant alternatif** *m* ELECTR *électromagnétisme* alternating current field; ~ **cristallin** *m* PHYS RAYON crystal field; ~ **critique** *m* ELECTROTEC critical field; ~ **croisé** *m* TELECOM crossed field; ~ **démagnétisant** *m* ELECTR, PHYSIQUE demagnetizing field; ~ **dépolarisant** *m* ENREGISTR, PHYSIQUE depolarizing field; ~ **diamantifère** *m* MINES diamond field; ~ **diffus** *m* ACOUSTIQUE diffuse field; ~ **de dispersion** *m* ELECTR *machine, transformateur* stray field; ~ **de données** *m* INFORMAT data field; ~ **de dragage** *m* MINES dredging field; ~ **électrique** *m* ELECTR, ELECTROTEC, ENREGISTR, PHYSIQUE, TELECOM, TV electric field; ~ **électrique alternatif** *m* ELECTROTEC alternating electric field; ~ **électrique atmosphérique** *m* GEOPHYS atmospheric electric field; ~ **électrique radial** *m* PHYS RAYON radial electrical field; ~ **électrique statique** *m* ELECTROTEC static electric field; ~ **électromagnétique** *m* ELECTR, ELECTROTEC, PHYS ONDES, PHYSIQUE electromagnetic field, TELECOM eletromagnetic field; ~ **électromagnétique du courant d'excitation** *m* ESSAIS exciting field; ~ **électrostatique** *m* ELECTR, PHYSIQUE electrostatic field; ~ **d'épandage** *m* DISTRI EAU, RECYCLAGE sewage farm, spreading field; ~ **évanescent** *m* OPTIQUE, TELECOM evanescent field; ~ **d'excitation** *m* ELECTROTEC excitation field; ~ **fixe** *m* INFORMAT, ORDINAT fixed field; ~ **de forces** *m* ELECTROTEC field of force; ~ **de forces nucléaires** *m* NUCLEAIRE field of nuclear forces; ~ **de fuite** *m* TELECOM leakage field; ~ **de gaz naturel** *m* PETROLE gas field; ~ **géomagnétique** *m* ELECTR *magnétisme*, GEOPHYS, PHYSIQUE Earth's magnetic field; ~ **géomagnétique extérieur** *m* GEOPHYS external geomagnetic field; ~ **géothermique** *m* EN RENOUV geothermal field; ~ **de gravitation** *m* ASTRONOMIE, PHYSIQUE gravitational field; ~ **gravitationnel** *m* ASTRONOMIE, PHYSIQUE gravitational field; ~ **de Hall** *m* PHYSIQUE Hall field; ~ **hyperthermique** *m* EN RENOUV hyperthermal field; ~ **d'image** *m* CINEMAT field of image, image field; ~ **d'induction** *m* ELECTROTEC, TV induction field; ~ **d'induit** *m* ELECTR *générateur* rotor field, *machine* armature field; ~ **induit** *m* ELECTR *électromagnétisme* induced field; ~ **irrotationnel** *m* PHYSIQUE irrotational field; ~ **de lave** *m* GEOLOGIE, PETR lava plateau; ~ **lointain** *m* TELECOM distant field; ~ **magnétique** *m* ELECTR, ELECTROTEC, ENREGISTR, ESSAIS, GEOLOGIE, PHYSIQUE, TELECOM, TV magnetic field; ~ **magnétique alternatif** *m* ELECTROTEC alternating magnetic field; ~ **magnétique extérieur** *m* ELECTR external magnetic field; ~ **magnétique galactique** *m* ASTRONOMIE galactic magnetic field; ~ **magnétique interstellaire** *m* ASTRONOMIE interstellar magnetic field; ~ **magnétique parasite** *m* GEOPHYS magnetic interference field; ~ **magnétique solaire** *m* ASTRONOMIE solar magnetic field; ~ **magnétique du soleil** *m* ASTRONOMIE solar magnetic field; ~ **magnétique terrestre** *m* ESPACE *géophysique*, GEOPHYS Earth's magnetic field; ~ **magnétisant** *m* ELECTROTEC magnetizing field; ~ **de mines** *m* MILITAIRE minefield; ~ **moléculaire** *m* PHYSIQUE molecular field; ~ **de netteté** *m* CINEMAT field of sharpness; ~ **opposé** *m* ELECTR *électromagnétisme* opposing field; ~ **optique** *m* ASTRONOMIE field of view; ~ **d'or** *m* MINES gold field; ~ **à périodicité temporelle** *m* ELECTROTEC time-periodic field; ~ **perturbateur** *m* TV noise field; ~ **perturbé** *m* METEO disturbed field; ~ **de pesanteur** *m* PHYSIQUE gravitational field; ~ **de pétrole** *m* PETR, PETROLE oilfield; ~ **pétrolifère** *m*

PETR petroleum field, PETROLE oilfield; ~ **proche** *m* TELECOM near field; ~ **protégé** *m* INFORMAT, ORDINAT protected field; ~ **quadripolaire** *m* NUCLEAIRE quadrupole field; ~ **de rayonnement** *m* PHYS RAYON radiation field; ~ **réservé** *m* TELECOM RES, reserved field; ~ **réverbéré** *m* ACOUSTIQUE reverberant field; ~ **sinusoïdal** *m* ELECTROTEC sinusoidal field; ~ **solénoïdal** *m* PHYSIQUE solenoidal field; ~ **stable** *m* METEO stable field; ~ **stationnaire** *m* ELECTROTEC stationary field; ~ **statique** *m* ELECTROTEC, TELECOM static field; ~ **de tir** *m* MILITAIRE shooting range; ~ **de tir au fusil** *m* MILITAIRE rifle range; ~ **tourbillonnaire** *m* ELECTROTEC curl field; ~ **tournant** *m* ELECTR *électromagnétisme* rotating field, ELECTROTEC rotary field, TELECOM rotating field; ~ **de tri** *m* INFORMAT, ORDINAT sort field; ~ **uniforme** *m* PHYSIQUE uniform field; ~ **utile** *m* PHOTO effective image field; ~ **variable** *m* ELECTROTEC, INFORMAT, ORDINAT variable field; ~ **vectoriel** *m* ELECTR *électromagnétisme*, ELECTROTEC vector field; ~ **visible** *m* PHYSIQUE visible region; ~ **visuel** *m* CINEMAT field of view, lens coverage

champignon *m* CONS MECA *d'un essieu* collar; ~ **d'aération** *m* NAUT mushroom ventilator; ~ **du rail** *m* CH DE FER *véhicules* railhead

chance *f* MATH odds

chandelier *m* NAUT stanchion, PRODUCTION pedestal

chandelle *f* CONS MECA positioning screw jack, CONSTR prop, vertical shore, MINES post, prop, shore, tree; ~ **de pression** *m* CONS MECA *bloc à colonnes* pressure pin

chandelles *f pl* CONSTR shoring

chanfrein *m* CONS MECA cant, CONSTR chamfer, MECANIQUE *soudage* edge; ~ **d'ajustage** *m* CERAM VER miter return (AmE), mitre return (BrE); ~ **arrêté** *m* CONSTR stopped chamfer; ~ **d'entrée** *m* CONS MECA leading chamfer; ~ **extérieur** *m* RESSORTS external chamfer; ~ **interne** *m* RESSORTS internal chamfer; ~ **plat** *m* CERAM VER miter bevel (AmE), mitre bevel (BrE); ~ **de protection** *m* CONS MECA protecting chamfer

chanfreinage *m* CONSTR, PETR beveling (AmE), bevelling (BrE), chamfering

chanfreiné *adj* RESSORTS chamfered

chanfreiner *vt* CONS MECA, CONSTR, IMPRIM chamfer

chanfreineuse *f* CONS MECA plate edge planing machine

changement *m* CONS MECA variation, *de marche* reversing, ELECTROTEC switch, MATH substitution, PHYSIQUE change; ~ **adiabatique** *m* THERMODYN adiabatic change; ~ **d'aspect** *m* IMPRIM *de l'encre en cours de séchage* dry back; ~ **automatique de canette** *m* TEXTILE automatic pirn change; ~ **de cap** *m* ESPACE *pilotage*, NAUT *navigation* alteration of course; ~ **de code** *m* INFORMAT code extension; ~ **de contexte** *m* INFORMAT, ORDINAT context switching; ~ **de direction** *m* ESPACE *pilotage* alteration of course; ~ **d'état** *m* PHYSIQUE, THERMODYN change of state; ~ **de fréquence** *m* ELECTRON frequency conversion; ~ **de fréquence hétérodyne** *m* ELECTROTEC heterodyne conversion; ~ **de gain** *m* ELECTRON gain change; ~ **de ligne** *m* IMPRIM *imprimantes, photocomposeuses*, INFORMAT, ORDINAT, TELECOM LF, line feed; ~ **de la ligne de base** *m* PETR baseline shift; ~ **de marche** *m* CONS MECA *d'un tour* reversing gear, reversing motion; ~ **de marche du mouvement de pression** *m* CONS MECA feed-reversing gear; ~ **de marche pour fileter à droite et à gauche** *m* CONS MECA screw cutting reverse; ~ **de marche à vis** *m* CONS MECA screw reversing gear; ~ **de mode** *m* ELECTRON mode jump, INFORMAT, ORDINAT mode change;

~ **d'outil** *m* PETROLE bit change, *forage* BC; ~ **de phase** *m* ELECTRON phase shift; ~ **de plaque** *m* IMPRIM *tirage* plate changeover; ~ **de prises en charge** *m* ELECTR *transformateur* on-load tap changing; ~ **radioactif** *m* PHYS RAYON radioactive transformation; ~ **de route** *m* NAUT alteration of course; ~ **simple** *m* CH DE FER right-hand turnoff; ~ **de teinte** *m* CERAM VER color change (AmE), colour change (BrE), loss of color (AmE), loss of colour (BrE); ~ **de vitesse** *m* CONS MECA change speed gear, gear change (BrE), gearshift (AmE), VEHICULES gear change (BrE), gearshift (AmE); ~ **de voie** *m* CH DE FER points, switch, turnout; ~ **de voie automatique** *m* COMMANDE automatic alternative routing; ~ **de volume** *m* METALL volume change

changer[1] *vt* NAUT *de bateau* transship, *le cap* change

changer[2] *vi* NAUT *vent* shift

changer:[3] ~ **un charbon** *vti* CINEMAT *sur une lampe à arc* trim; ~ **d'échelle** *vti* INFORMAT scale; ~ **la phase** *vti* ELECTRON phase shift; ~ **de position** *vti* TEXTILE shift; ~ **le sens de la marche** *vti* CONS MECA reverse

changeur *m* TELECOM *de fréquence* frequency converter; ~ **abaisseur de fréquence** *m* TELECOM down converter; ~ **automatique de disques** *m* OPTIQUE optical disc exchanger (BrE), optical disk exchanger (AmE); ~ **de disques** *m* ACOUSTIQUE, ENREGISTR record changer; ~ **élévateur de fréquence** *m* TELECOM upconverter; ~ **de fréquence** *m* ELECTRON first detector, frequency changer, mixer, ELECTROTEC converter, frequency transducer; ~ **de fréquence hétérodyne** *m* ELECTROTEC heterodyne conversion transducer; ~ **de grossissement** *m* INSTRUMENT magnification changer; ~ **pentagrille** *m* ELECTROTEC pentagrid converter; ~ **de phase** *m* ELECTR *courant alternatif*, ELECTRON phase changer; ~ **de prises** *m* ELECTR tap changer; ~ **de prises en charge** *m* ELECTR load tap changer, on-load tap changer

chanlate *f* CONSTR eaves board, fascia, fascia board

chant: ~ **vif** *m* RESSORTS sharp edge

chantier:[1] **sur le** ~ *adv* CONSTR on site

chantier[2] *m* CONSTR construction site, yard, MINES labor (AmE), labour (BrE), stope, PRODUCTION *d'une fonderie* floor; ~ **abandonné** *m* MINES abandoned workings, mined-out area; ~ **d'abatage** *m* MINES stope; ~ **accidenté** *m* CHARBON broken working; ~ **de bois** *m* CONSTR timberyard; ~ **chassant** *m* MINES drift stope; ~ **à ciel ouvert** *m* MINES openwork; ~ **de construction** *m* NAUT construction yard, slipway; ~ **de construction navale** *m* NAUT dockyard, shipyard; ~ **contaminé** *m* MINES gas-filled workings; ~ **de dépôt** *m* CONSTR dump (AmE), tip (BrE), MINES dump, dump site (AmE), dumping ground, tailings area, tip area (BrE); ~ **d'embarcation** *m* NAUT boat chock; ~ **en gradins** *m* MINES stope; ~ **en mort-terrain** *m* MINES dead-working; ~ **en remonte** *m* MINES raise stope; ~ **épuisé** *m* MINES stoped-out workings; ~ **d'exploitation borgne** *m* CONSTR blind workings; ~ **du fond** *m* MINES bottom workings; ~ **de houille** *m* CHARBON coal yard; ~ **inférieur** *m* MINES lower workings; ~ **de manoeuvres** *m* CH DE FER shunting yard; ~ **maritime** *m* NAUT shipyard; ~ **de moulage** *m* PRODUCTION molding floor (AmE), moulding floor (BrE); ~ **de moulage en sable** *m* PRODUCTION sand floor; ~ **naval** *m* NAUT shipyard, *constructions* dockyard; ~ **de préfabrication** *m* CONSTR precasting works; ~ **de triage** *m* CH DE FER classification yard, marshalling yard (BrE), sorting siding, switching yard (AmE), TRANSPORT classification yard; ~ **de versage** *m* CONSTR dump (AmE), tip (BrE), MINES dump (AmE), dump site, dumping ground, tailings area, tip area (BrE)

chantournage: ~ **à la fraise** *m* CONS MECA form milling

chantournement *m* CONSTR jigsawing

chantourner *vt* CONSTR jigsaw

chanvre *m* NAUT hemp

chaos: ~ **de glace** *m* OCEANO hummocked ice

chape *f* CONS MECA clevis, jaw, strap, *d'une articulation à genouillère* fork, *d'une poulie* shell, CONSTR coating, feather edge, INSTRUMENT cover, MECANIQUE clevis, METROLOGIE *d'une balance* bearings, PRODUCTION cheek, middle, middle part, *d'un moule en terre* cope, RESSORTS shackle; ~ **de bielle** *f* CONS MECA strap; ~ **de châssis** *f* PRODUCTION cheek, middle; ~ **de poulie** *f* CONS MECA pulley shell; ~ **sur moyeu** *f* CONS MECA hub grip

chapeau *m* CONS MECA *d'un palier* pedestal cover, CONSTR collar, flange, flange plate, hood, *d'une poutre composée* boom, boom plate, *d'un pieu* cap, DISTRI EAU *d'une vanne* cap still, ELECTROTEC cap, *d'une lampe* hood, GEOLOGIE *d'un gisement, d'un réservoir* cap rock, INST HYDR *de valve, de clapet, de soupape*, MECANIQUE cap, MINES cap, cap piece, crown, crown piece, head piece, NAUT bonnet, PRODUCTION gland, *d'un presse-étoupe* follower; ~ **d'allumeur** *m* VEHICULES distributor cap; ~ **altéré** *m* GEOLOGIE gossan; ~ **de bielle** *m* AUTO connecting rod cap; ~ **de châssis** *m* PRODUCTION top part of flask; ~ **de couple** *m* CONS MECA frame cap; ~ **ferrugineux** *m* GEOLOGIE gossan; ~ **de filon** *m* MINES capping, rock capping; ~ **de gaz** *m* PETR, PETROLE *géologie* gas cap; ~ **de gaz secondaire** *m* PETR secondary gas cap; ~ **de moyeu** *m* AERONAUT hub cover plate, AUTO axle cap; ~ **de palier** *m* AUTO bearing cap, crankshaft bearing cap, CONS MECA bearing cap; ~ **de pieu** *m* CHARBON, CONSTR pile cap; ~ **de roue** *m* VEHICULES wheel cover

chapelet *m* CONSTR *d'un élévateur, d'une drague* bucket; ~ **de godets** *m* CONSTR line of buckets; ~ **hydraulique** *m* DISTRI EAU chapelet, paternoster pump

chapelle *f* CONS MECA clack box; ~ **à clapet** *f* HYDROLOGIE valve chamber; ~ **d'échappement** *f* AUTO exhaust passage; ~ **de refoulement** *f* PRODUCTION delivery box; ~ **de sortie** *f* AUTO exhaust passage; ~ **à soupape** *f* HYDROLOGIE valve chamber; ~ **de structure** *f* AERONAUT fin stub frame; ~ **de tiroir** *f* INST HYDR slide box, steam box, steam chamber, steam chest

chaperon *m* CONSTR coping

chaperonner *vt* CONSTR cope

chapiteau *m* AERONAUT landing gear hinge beam, EQUIP LAB head

chaptalisation *f* AGRO ALIM sugaring

char: ~ **d'assaut** *m* MILITAIRE tank; ~ **d'assaut amphibie** *m* MILITAIRE amphibious tank; ~ **d'assaut lourd** *m* MILITAIRE heavy tank; ~ **poseur de ponts** *m* MILITAIRE bridge-layer tank

charbon *m* CHARBON coal, mineral, CHIMIE coke, GEOLOGIE coal, IMPRIM motor brush; ~ **actif** *m* AGRO ALIM activated charcoal, CHIMIE, DISTRI EAU, GAZ, HYDROLOGIE activated carbon, MATERIAUX activated charcoal; ~ **activé** *m* CHIMIE activated carbon, activated charcoal, PLAST CAOU *charge* activated carbon, activated charcoal; ~ **d'agglomération** *m* CHARBON sintering coal; ~ **agglutinant** *m* CHARBON caking coal; ~ **agglutiné** *m* CHARBON rich coal; ~ **anthraciteux** *m* CHARBON hard coal, lean coal, THERMODYN lean coal;

~ **ardent** *m* CHARBON burning coal, live coal; ~ **barré** *m* CHARBON bone coal; ~ **bitumineux** *m* CHARBON bituminous coal, flaming coal; ~ **de bois** *m* CHARBON charcoal, wood charcoal, wood coal, CHIMIE charcoal, wood charcoal; ~ **brut** *m* CHARBON raw coal; ~ **calibré** *m* CHARBON graded coal; ~ **à coke** *m* CHARBON coking coal; ~ **à coke boursouflé** *m* CHARBON rich coal, swelled coking coal; ~ **de contact** *m* AUTO brush; ~ **de cornue** *m* CHARBON gas carbon, retort coal; ~ **criblé** *m* CHARBON screened coal, sifted coal; ~ **demi-gras** *m* CHARBON semibituminous coal; ~ **à détacher** *m* CERAM VER cracking coal; ~ **domestique** *m* CHARBON domestic coal, household coal; ~ **d'électrode** *m* ELECTROTEC electrode carbon; ~ **en gros morceaux** *m* CHARBON lump coal; ~ **en morceaux** *m* CHARBON best coal; ~ **en parc** *m* CHARBON stock coal, stockyard coal; ~ **en stock** *m* CHARBON stock coal, stockpile coal; ~ **épuré** *m* CHARBON cleaned coal; ~ **d'exploitation souterraine** *m* CHARBON deep-mined coal; ~ **extra pur** *m* CHARBON super clean coal; ~ **filtrant** *m* GENIE CHIM filtering charcoal; ~ **à filtrer** *m* CHARBON filtering charcoal; ~ **à gaz** *m* CHARBON gas coal; ~ **gras** *m* CHARBON fat coal, flaming coal, medium-volatile coal, soft coal; ~ **lamelleux** *m* CHARBON foliated coal, slate-foliated lignite, paper coal, papyraceous lignite; ~ **limoneux** *m* CHARBON coal sludge, slimes, mud coal; ~ **maigre** *m* CHARBON lean coal, low-volatile coal, uninflammable coal, nonbituminous coal; ~ **maigre sableux** *m* CHARBON sintering sand coal; ~ **marchand** *m* CHARBON commercial coal, saleable coal; ~ **mat** *m* CHARBON candel coal, cannel coal, dull coal, kennel coal; ~ **menu** *m* CHARBON coal slack, pea coal, small coal, MINES small, small coal; ~ **de mine** *m* CHARBON pit coal; ~ **minéral** *m* CHARBON mineral coal; ~ **non-collant** *m* CHARBON noncaking coal; ~ **nu** *m* AGRO ALIM loose smut; ~ **piciforme** *m* CHARBON pitch coal; ~ **pour arc** *m* CINEMAT arc carbon; ~ **pour gazogène** *m* CHARBON generator coal, producer coal; ~ **pour lampes à arc** *m* CONS MECA arc lamp carbon; ~ **pulvérisé** *m* CHARBON coal dust, coal powder, pulverized coal, pulverized charcoal, MATERIAUX coal dust; ~ **pulvérulent** *m* CHARBON duff, dust coal, fine coal; ~ **pur** *m* CHARBON pure coal; ~ **pur sans cendre et sec** *m* CHARBON clean coal, cleans; ~ **reconnu** *m* CHARBON known coal deposit; ~ **de sang** *m* AGRO ALIM blood black; ~ **schisteux** *m* CHARBON schistous coal; ~ **de soute** *m* CHARBON bunker coal; ~ **tendre** *m* CHARBON soft coal; ~ **de terre** *m* CHARBON bright coal, glance coal, coal; ~ **de tourbe** *m* CHARBON peat coal; ~ **toutvenant** *m* CHARBON pit coal, rough coal, run-of-mine coal, unscreened coal, MINES run-of-mine, run-of-mine coal; ~ **à vapeur** *m* CHARBON boiler coal, steam raising coal

charboniser *vt* CHARBON char

charbonnage *m* CHARBON coal mine, coal mining, mining of coal, MINES coal mine, colliery, pit

charbonnaille *f* CHARBON coal slack, fines, MINES small coal

charbonné *adj* CHARBON carbonized

charbonner[1] *vt* CHARBON carbonize, char, NAUT bunker

charbonner:[2] **se** ~ *v réfl* CHARBON carbonize

charbonneux *adj* CHIMIE carbonaceous

charbonnier *m* CHARBON coal ship, NAUT collier

char-bulldozer *m* MILITAIRE tank bulldozer

chardage *m* TEXTILE hairiness, raising, scratching

charder *vt* TEXTILE raise, scratch

chardonnet *m* CONSTR hanging post

charge:[1] **en ~** *adj* NAUT loaded, VEHICULES under load

charge[2] *f* AGRO ALIM batch, CERAM VER filler, CHARBON, CONSTR load, ELECTR charge, *alimentation* load, ELECTROTEC charge, charging, load, HYDROLOGIE load, INST HYDR head of water pressure, pressure, MECANIQUE, METALL load, MINES charge, NAUT bulk, load, ORDINAT load, PAPIER filler, load, PETROLE feed, feedstock, PHYSIQUE load, PLAST CAOU batch, filler, *mélange* extender, POLLU MER payload, PRODUCTION load, stock, REFRIG capacity, load, SECURITE care, TELECOM charge, load;

~ a ~ **d'accumulateur** *f* ELECTR accumulator charge, battery charge; ~ **des accumulateurs** *f* ESPACE *véhicules* battery charging; ~ **accumulée** *f* ELECTROTEC integrated charge; ~ **acide** *f* POLLUTION acid loading; ~ **active** *f* ELECTR *machine* resistive load, *ohmique, résistive* active load, ELECTROTEC active load, PLAST CAOU active filler, *matière première* reinforcing filler; ~ **adaptée** *f* ELECTROTEC, PHYSIQUE matched load; ~ **additionnelle** *f* CHARBON surcharge load; ~ **admissible** *f* CHARBON permissible load, safe load, ELECTR allowable load; ~ **admissible de fonctionnement** *f* SECURITE safe working load; ~ **aérodynamique** *f* AERONAUT aerodynamic load; ~ **alaire** *f* AERONAUT wing loading; ~ **d'alimentation** *f* PETROLE *hydrocarbures de base* feedstock; ~ **d'amorçage** *f* ESPACE *pyrotechnie*, MINES priming charge; ~ **amorce** *f* MILITAIRE primer; ~ **annuelle** *f* DISTRI EAU annual load; ~ **d'appoint** *f* CINEMAT trickle charge, ELECTROTEC topping charge; ~ **atmosphérique** *f* POLLUTION atmospheric load, atmospheric loading; ~ **automatique** *f* PRODUCTION automatic feeder;

~ b ~ **de batterie** *f* ELECTROTEC battery charge; ~ **d'un broyeur** *f* CHARBON crop load;

~ c ~ **de calcul par roue** *f* AERONAUT *navigabilité* design wheel load; ~ **calorifique** *f* REFRIG cooling load, THERMODYN fire load; ~ **calorifique d'exploitation** *f* REFRIG service load; ~ **calorifique du produit** *f* REFRIG product load; ~ **des canaux** *f* TELECOM channel loading; ~ **capacitive** *f* ELECTR *circuit à courant alternatif*, ELECTROTEC, TELECOM capacitive load; ~ **au cheval** *f* METROLOGIE power loading; ~ **circulante** *f* CHARBON circulating load; ~ **coaxiale** *f* ELECTROTEC coaxial load; ~ **coaxiale fixe** *f* ELECTROTEC coaxial fixed load; ~ **de colonne** *f* MINES column charge, columnar charge; ~ **complète** *f* TRANSPORT carload (AmE), wagonload (BrE); ~ **de conduction** *f* PHYSIQUE conduction charge; ~ **d'un congélateur** *f* REFRIG freezer capacity; ~ **constante** *f* ELECTR constant load; ~ **continue** *f* ELECTR *machine* constant load, *moteur* continuous load, ELECTROTEC continuous loading; ~ **à courant alternatif** *f* ELECTROTEC AC load; ~ **au crochet** *f* PETROLE *forage* hook load;

~ d ~ **diélectrique** *f* TELECOM dielectric charge; ~ **du disque balayé** *f* AERONAUT disc loading (BrE), disk loading (AmE);

~ e ~ **d'eau** *f* DISTRI EAU water pressure, INST HYDR pressure; ~ **efficace** *f* EMBALLAGE effective load; ~ **électrique** *f* ELECTR, ELECTROTEC electrical charge, PHYS PART charge, electrical charge, PHYSIQUE, TELECOM electrical charge; ~ **électrostatique** *f* ELECTR, MATERIAUX electrostatic charge; ~ **élémentaire** *f* PHYSIQUE elementary charge; ~ **en guide d'ondes** *f* ELECTROTEC waveguide load; ~ **en suspension** *f* HYDROLOGIE load in suspension, suspended load; ~

d'entretien *f* ELECTROTEC floating charge; ~ **d'épreuve** *f* AERONAUT *navigabilité* proof load, CONS MECA test load, *des éléments de fixation* proof load; ~ **équilibrée** *f* ELECTROTEC balanced load; ~ **d'espace** *f* PHYSIQUE space charge; ~ **d'essai** *f* CHARBON test loading, CONS MECA test load; ~ **d'étalonnage** *f* CONS MECA preload; ~ **excessive** *f* CONSTR overload; ~ **d'exploitation** *f* CONSTR live load; ~ **explosive** *f* MINES blasting charge;

~ f ~ **du faisceau** *f* TV beam loading; ~ **fixe** *f* ELECTROTEC fixed load; ~ **fixe en guide d'ondes** *f* ELECTROTEC waveguide fixed load; ~ **de flambement** *f* MECANIQUE *matériaux* buckling load; ~ **de fond** *f* GEOLOGIE bed load; ~ **du four** *f* CERAM VER furnace charge, furnace fill; ~ **de frigorigène** *f* REFRIG refrigerant charge;

~ g ~ **générale d'écoulement** *f* METALL general yield load; ~ **géostatique** *f* PETROLE *géologie* overburden; ~ **de grande puissance** *f* ELECTROTEC high-power load;

~ h ~ **hydraulique** *f* INST HYDR hydraulic head; ~ **hydrodynamique** *f* HYDROLOGIE hydrodynamic load; ~ **hydrostatique** *f* HYDROLOGIE hydrostatic load, PETROLE *géologie de forage* hydrostatic head;

~ i ~ **d'incendie** *f* THERMODYN fire load; ~ **incomplète** *f* NUCLEAIRE underload; ~ **inductive** *f* ELECTR *courant alternatif*, ELECTROTEC, TELECOM inductive load; ~ **induite** *f* CHIMIE, ELECTR, ELECTROTEC induced charge; ~ **intermittente** *f* ELECTR *générateur* intermittent load;

~ l ~ **lente** *f* CINEMAT, ELECTROTEC trickle charge; ~ **libre** *f* PHYSIQUE free charge; ~ **limite** *f* AERONAUT maximum load, *de pale* limit load, ELECTR *appareil* limit load, NAUT maximum load, TRANSPORT loading capacity; ~ **liquide** *f* MATERIAUX, REFRIG liquid charge; ~ **à la longueur** *f* RESSORTS load at length;

~ m ~ **de manoeuvre** *f* AERONAUT *navigabilité* maneuvering load (AmE), manoeuvring load (BrE); ~ **marchande** *f* AERONAUT payload; ~ **marchande maximum** *f* AERONAUT maximum payload; ~ **marchande normale estimée** *f* AERONAUT estimated normal payload; ~ **massique** *f* PHYSIQUE charge mass ratio, specific charge; ~ **maximale** *f* CHARBON bearing capacity, ELECTROTEC, PAPIER peak load; ~ **maximum de réaction élastique** *f* AERONAUT maximum spring back load; ~ **de même signe** *f* ELECTR like charge; ~ **militaire** *f* MILITAIRE missile warhead; ~ **de mine** *f* MINES charge; ~ **de missile** *f* ESPACE *véhicules* missile warhead; ~ **mobile** *f* ELECTROTEC moving charge; ~ **moyenne** *f* ELECTR average load;

~ n ~ **négative** *f* ELECTR, ELECTROTEC, PHYSIQUE negative charge; ~ **nominale** *f* ELECTROTEC rated load; ~ **non-inductive** *f* ELECTR noninductive load, nonreactive load; ~ **normale** *f* ELECTROTEC off-peak load; ~ **nucléaire** *f* PHYS PART nuclear charge;

~ o ~ **offerte** *f* AERONAUT allowable load; ~ **opposée** *f* CHIMIE opposite charge;

~ p ~ **de pale** *f* AERONAUT blade loading; ~ **par essieu** *f* CONSTR axle load; ~ **par roue** *f* CONSTR wheel load; ~ **partagée** *f* ELECTROTEC partitioned charge; ~ **partielle** *f* AUTO, TRANSPORT part load; ~ **à passage unique** *f* NUCLEAIRE once-through charge; ~ **passive** *f* ELECTROTEC passive load; ~ **payante** *f* AERONAUT payload; ~ **permanente** *f* CHARBON permanent load, ELECTR *moteur* continuous load; ~ **de pied** *f* MINES bottom charge; ~ **de polarisation** *f* PHYSIQUE polarization charges; ~ **de polluants atmosphériques** *f* POLLUTION atmospheric load, atmospheric loading; ~ **ponctuelle** *f* ELECTR, PHYSIQUE point charge; ~ **positive** *f* ELECTR,

ELECTROTEC, PHYSIQUE positive charge; ~ **pratique** f CONS MECA working load; **de la ~ primaire** f MILITAIRE percussion priming; **~ primaire** f ESPACE priming charge, *véhicules* primer charge; **~ principale** f CONSTR main load; **~ propulsive** f MILITAIRE propelling charge; **~ provoquant un calage moteur** f PRODUCTION stall load;

~ r ~ **radiale** f MATERIAUX radial load; **~ de rafales limite** f AERONAUT gust load limit; **~ rapide** f TRANS-PORT boost charge, quick charge; **~ réactive** f ELECTROTEC, PHYSIQUE, TELECOM reactive load; **~ re-couvrée** f ELECTROTEC recovered charge; **~ réglable** f ELECTROTEC sliding load; **~ réglable en guide d'ondes** f ELECTROTEC waveguide sliding load; **~ rémanente** f ELECTROTEC remanent charge; **~ remorquée** f TRANS-PORT trailing load; **~ renforçante** f PLAST CAOU *matière première* reinforcing filler; **~ répartie** f ELECTROTEC continuous loading; **~ résiduelle** f ELECTR, ELECTRO-TEC, TV residual charge; **~ résistive** f ELECTROTEC, TELECOM resistive load; **~ du ressort** f RESSORTS spring load; **~ résultante** f ELECTROTEC net charge; **~ de ruissellement** f HYDROLOGIE surface water load; **~ de rupture** f CHARBON breaking load, failure load, ulti-mate load, CONS MECA, EMBALLAGE, MECANIQUE, NAUT, PAPIER breaking load; **~ à la rupture** f PLAST CAOU load at break; **~ de rupture en fatigue** f METALL fatigue strength; **~ de rupture rationnelle** f MATERIAUX fracture stress;

~ s ~ **de sécurité** f CONS MECA safe load; **~ de sécurité par flexion** f CONS MECA safe stress under bending; **~ de signes contraires** f ELECTR opposite charge; **~ de signes opposés** f ELECTR opposite charge; **~ solide** f HYDROLOGIE solids loading; **~ à la sortie** f ELECTROTEC output charge; **~ soulevée** f AERONAUT lifted load; **~ sous-marine** f MILITAIRE depth charge; **~ spatiale** f PHYSIQUE space charge; **~ spécifique** f PHYS PART *d'un électron*, PHYSIQUE specific charge; **~ spécifique d'é-lectrons** f NUCLEAIRE electron specific charge; **~ stabilisatrice** f ELECTROTEC bleeder; **~ statique** f ELEC-TROTEC static charge; **~ statique d'eau** f INST HYDR static head; **~ superficielle** f ELECTR, PHYSIQUE surface charge; **~ surfacique** f PHYSIQUE surface charge den-sity; **~ sur le foret** f PETR bit load; **~ sur la mèche** f PETR bit load; **~ sur l'outil** f PETR bit load; **~ sur le trépan** f PETR bit load; **~ du système** f TELECOM system load;

~ t ~ **temporaire** f CHARBON temporary load; **~ thé-orique** f AERONAUT design load; **~ théorique à spires jointives** f RESSORTS theoretical solid load; **~ thermique** f THERMODYN heat load; **~ totale de combustible** f NUCLEAIRE fuel charge, total charge; **~ totale maxi-male** f CONSTR maximum total load; **~ de trafic** f TELECOM, TRANSPORT traffic load; **~ de traitement** f INFORMAT, ORDINAT processing load; **~ transversale** f RESSORTS transverse load; **~ de travail** f CONS MECA working load, PRODUCTION load, TEXTILE work load; **~ de travail moyenne** f TEXTILE average workload;

~ u ~ **utile** f AERONAUT payload, DISTRI EAU service load, ESPACE *véhicules* payload, MECANIQUE *véhicules* carrying capacity, POLLU MER, TELECOM, VEHICULES payload; **~ utile d'un satellite** f ESPACE useful satellite load; **~ d'utilisation** f TRANSPORT degree of utilization

~ v ~ **verticale maximum sur roues** f AERONAUT maximum wheel vertical load

chargé *adj* EMBALLAGE reinforced, REVETEMENT *d'une couche* coated; **~ en poids et en cubage** *adj* NAUT full and down; **~ de poussière** *adj* CHARBON, SECURITE

atmosphère dust-laden

charge-image f ELECTROTEC image charge

chargement m CINEMAT *du film* film threading, ESPACE *propulsion*, INFORMAT *fichier ou programme* loading, MINES charging, loading, NAUT cargo, load, loading, shipload, shipment, shipping, ORDINAT *fichier ou pro-gramme* loading, PAPIER *d'un appareil* feeding, loading, PHYSIQUE, PRODUCTION, TRANSPORT loading; **~ amont** m PRODUCTION backward scheduling; **~ ar-rimé** m NAUT bulk; **~ automatique** m CINEMAT self-threading, ORDINAT autoload; **~ automatique de pellicule** m CINEMAT automatic film-threading; **~ aval** m PRODUCTION forward scheduling; **~ avec arrêt** m NUCLEAIRE *du réacteur* off-load charging; **~ axial** m METALL axial loading; **~ de la bande** m ENREGISTR tape threading; **~ biaxial** m METALL biaxial loading; **~ de cartouche** m INFORMAT cartridge loading; **~ concen-trique** m CONSTR concentric loading; **~ dynamique** m CONSTR dynamic loading; **~ en discontinu** m NU-CLEAIRE *combustible* batch fuel loading; **~ en métal dur** m MECANIQUE *matériaux* hardfacing; **~ excen-trique** m CONSTR eccentric loading; **~ à froid** m NUCLEAIRE off-load charging; **~ à la lumière du jour** m CINEMAT daylight loading; **~ manuel** m CINEMAT ma-nual threading; **~ de palette** m EMBALLAGE pallet load; **~ par cassette** m CINEMAT cassette loading; **~ par-dessus** m MINES load on top; **~ par zones** m NUCLEAIRE zoned fuel loading; **~ au plus tard** m PRODUCTION backward scheduling; **~ au plus tôt** m PRODUCTION forward scheduling; **~ quasi-statique** m ESPACE *vé-hicules* quasi-statical loading; **~ sans arrêt** m NUCLEAIRE *du réacteur* on-load charging, on-load fueling (AmE), on-load fuelling (BrE); **~ séquenceur** m PRODUCTION sequencer load; **~ de silo de puits** m MINES shaft bunker loading; **~ sur résidus** m POLLU-TION load on top process

charger[1] *vt* CINEMAT lace up, load, thread, CONS MECA strain, CONSTR, ELECTROTEC load, ENREGISTR lace up, load, thread, IMPRIM load, INFORMAT load, set, ME-CANIQUE load, NAUT load, *une cargaison* ship, ORDINAT load, set

charger[2] *vi* MINES squeeze

chargeur m CINEMAT, CONS MECA magazine, ELECTRO-TEC charger, EMBALLAGE feeder, NAUT shipper, ORDINAT disk pack, loader, PRODUCTION charger, TRANSPORT *sur réseau* loader; **~ absolu** m ORDINAT absolute loader; **~ d'arche** m CERAM VER stacker; **~ de balles** m TRANSPORT bale loader; **~ à bande sans fin** m TV tape loop cassette; **~ de batterie** m ELECTROTEC, PHOTO, TRANSPORT battery charger; **~ co-axial** m CINE-MAT concentric magazine; **~ de disques** m INFORMAT disk pack; **~ embarqué** m TRANSPORT built-in charger; **~ d'entretien** m ELECTROTEC trickle charger; **~ frontal** m POLLU MER front-end loader; **~ mécanique** m PRO-DUCTION stoker; **~ mécanique à alimentation par le dessus** m CONS MECA overfeed stoker; **~ de palettes** m EMBALLAGE pallet loader; **~ à poste fixe** m TRANSPORT stationary charger; **~ à régime lent** m ELECTR *accumu-lateur* trickle charger

chargeur-éditeur: **~ de liens** m ORDINAT link loader

chargeurs: **~ jumelés** m pl PHOTO twin magazine

chargeuse f PRODUCTION charging machine, loader, TRANSPORT loader; **~ mécanique** f CONSTR power loader

chargeuse-pelle f CONSTR backhoe loader

chargeuse-pelleteuse f CONSTR, TRANSPORT backhoe

loader

chariot *m* CONS MECA carriage, EQUIP LAB *meuble* trolley, IMPRIM *de machine à écrire*, INFORMAT carriage, INSTRUMENT mechanical stage, MECANIQUE carriage, truck, NUCLEAIRE crab, trolley, TRANSPORT car, carriage, wagon, *à bagages* barrow; ~ **d'alésage** *m* CONS MECA boring head; ~ **automoteur** *m* SECURITE *code de sécurité* industrial truck; ~ **à benne basculante** *m* TRANSPORT dump lorry (BrE), dump truck (AmE); ~ **de chargement** *m* MINES larry, larry car; ~ **à civières** *m* SECURITE *premier secours* stretcher cart; ~ **de contrepoids** *m* MINES counterbalance carriage; ~ **de découpe** *m* CERAM VER automatic cutter; ~ **dépalettisateur** *m* EMBALLAGE depalletizer; ~ **des dunes** *m* TRANSPORT beach buggy, buggy; ~ **électrique** *m* TRANSPORT electric trolley; ~ **Elemack** *m* CINEMAT cricket dolly, elemack, spider dolly; ~ **élévateur** *m* EMBALLAGE, MECANIQUE lift truck; ~ **élévateur à fourche** *m* CONSTR, EMBALLAGE forklift truck, TRANSPORT fork truck, forklift truck, forklift truck; ~ **d'étuve à noyaux** *m* PRODUCTION core carriage; ~ **de guidage volets** *m* AERONAUT flap roller carriage; ~ **de hissage** *m* AERONAUT hoisting carriage; ~ **de levage à commande manuelle** *m* EMBALLAGE manual lift truck; ~ **monorail à grappin** *m* TRANSPORT monorail grab trolley; ~ **omnidirectionnel** *m* CINEMAT crab dolly; ~ **de palan** *m* CONS MECA *d'un pont roulant* block carriage; ~ **de pont roulant** *m* MECANIQUE *matériel de levage* crab; ~ **porte-griffe** *m* CINEMAT claw carriage; ~ **porte-meule** *m* CONS MECA wheel carriage; ~ **porte-outil** *m* CONS MECA *d'un étau-limeur* ram, *d'une machine-outil* tool carriage; ~ **porte-tourelle** *m* CONS MECA turret slide; ~ **de précision** *m* CONS MECA *pour machine-outil* precision slide; ~ **récepteur** *m* TRANSPORT receiving trunk; ~ **roulant** *m* CONS MECA runner, PRODUCTION traveling runner (AmE), traveling trolley (AmE), travelling runner (BrE), travelling trolley (BrE), trolley; ~ **de roulement** *m* CONS MECA runner, PRODUCTION monkey carriage, traveling runner (AmE), traveling trolley (AmE), travelling runner (BrE), travelling trolley (BrE), trolley, *d'un pont roulant* jenny; ~ **de service à bord** *m* AERONAUT service trolley; ~ **de tour** *m* MECANIQUE lathe saddle, lathe slide; ~ **de transport** *m* MECANIQUE dolly; ~ **de transport réacteur** *m* AERONAUT engine trolley; ~ **transversal** *m* CONS MECA cross-slide; ~ **de travelling** *m* CINEMAT dolly; ~ **de travelling à écartement variable** *m* CINEMAT scorpion dolly; ~ **de travelling sur pneumatiques** *m* CINEMAT billyboy dolly; ~ **à tronçonner** *m* CONS MECA cutting-off slide

chariotage *m* CONS MECA traverse; ~ **longitudinal** *m* CONS MECA sliding; ~ **transversal** *m* CONS MECA surfacing, PRODUCTION cross-traverse

chariot-crabe *m* CINEMAT crab dolly

chariot-grue *m* CINEMAT crab

charme *m* PAPIER hornbeam, PHYSIQUE charm

charmeuse *f* TEXTILE lock-knit

charmonium *m* PHYSIQUE charmonium

charnière: ~ **et gond** *f* CONSTR hinge and pin

charnière *f* CONS MECA hinge, CONSTR butt, butt hinge, GEOLOGIE hinge, INSTRUMENT hinge, side joint, MECANIQUE, VEHICULES hinge; ~ **et pivot** *f* CONSTR hinge and pin; ~ **porte-moule** *f* CERAM VER mold holder (AmE), mould holder (BrE); ~ **universelle** *f* CONS MECA universal joint

charnières: sur ~ *adj* MECANIQUE hinged

charnon *m* CONSTR *d'une charnière* knuckle

charpente *f* CONS MECA frame, CONSTR framing, *d'un comble, d'un pont* frame, *d'une grue* framework, MECANIQUE frame; ~ **de cintre** *f* CONSTR center (AmE), centering (AmE), centre (BrE), centring (BrE); ~ **de comble** *f* CONSTR roof frame; ~ **à croisillons** *f* CONSTR lattice bracing; ~ **en bois** *f* CONSTR carpentry; ~ **en fer** *f* CONSTR ironwork; ~ **en forme de portique** *f* CONSTR gantry

charpenterie *f* CONSTR carpentry; ~ **en fer** *f* CONSTR ironworking

charpentier *m* CONSTR carpenter; ~ **du bord** *m* NAUT shipwright; ~ **de marine** *m* NAUT shipwright

charrette *f* CONSTR design office

charriage *m* GEOLOGIE overthrust; ~ **de fond** *m* HYDROLOGIE bed load transport, bottom transport

charrié: ~ **par l'eau** *adj* HYDROLOGIE waterborne

charrier *vt* HYDROLOGIE drift, transport, wash away

charrue *f* IMPRIM plough (BrE), plow (AmE); ~ **défonceuse** *f* CONSTR ripper

charte: ~ **d'affrètement à temps** *f* PETROLE time charter; ~ **chromatique** *f* TV color chart (AmE), colour chart (BrE); ~ **des couleurs** *f* IMPRIM *photogravure* color key (AmE), colour key (BrE); ~ **de couleurs et gamme de gris** *f* CINEMAT color chart and grey scale (AmE), colour chart and grey scale (BrE); ~ **de gris normalisé** *f* CINEMAT standard gray card (AmE), standard grey card (BrE); ~ **des marées** *f* NAUT tide chart

charte-partie *f* NAUT, PETROLE charter party

chas *m* PRODUCTION *d'une aiguille* eye

chassage *m* MINES development, drift, level, strike drive, drifting level, driving level, drifting, driving, tunneling (AmE), tunnelling (BrE), drivage, drive, level running along the strike; ~ **des clavettes** *m* CONS MECA driving out of keys, driving out of wedges

chassante *f* MINES drift, level, strike drive, drivage, drive, driving level, level running along the strike

chasse *f* CONS MECA clearance, set, DISTRI EAU flush, scouring, *d'eau* scour, IMPRIM width, OCEANO scouring, *sédimentation* fishery, fishing; ~ **d'air** *f* MINES air blast, rush of air; ~ **du caractère** *f* IMPRIM character pitch, character width; ~ **à coins** *f* PRODUCTION keying hammer; ~ **d'eau** *f* DISTRI EAU scour, scouring; ~ **par reflux** *f* DISTRI EAU backblowing; ~ **sous-marine** *f* OCEANO underwater fishing

chasse-bestiaux *m* CH DE FER cowcatcher, pilot

chasse-boulon *m* CONS MECA teeming pouch, PRODUCTION drift bolt, drive bolt

chasse-clavette *m* CONS MECA drift, driver, key drift

chasse-clé *m* CONS MECA drift, driver, key drift

chasse-clou *m* CONSTR bradawl, nail punch, nail set, set

chasse-goupille *m* CONS MECA pin drift, CONSTR pin punch, MECANIQUE pin driver, *outillage* drift

chasse-goupilles *m* CONS MECA drift punch

chasse-marée *m* NAUT coasting lugger

chasse-neige *m* METEO blower, drifting snow; ~ **rotatif** *m* TRANSPORT snow blower

chasse-pâte *f* PAPIER banger, pulp charge

chasse-pierres *m* CH DE FER cow-catcher, *véhicules* guard iron

chasse-pointe *m* CONSTR bradawl, nail punch, nail set, set

chasser[1] *vt* CONS MECA drive, drive in, drive into, ESPACE drive, *véhicules* blow, PRODUCTION *un rivet* knock out; ~ **par distillation** *vt* THERMODYN distil off (BrE), distill off (AmE)

chasser:[2] ~ **sur l'ancre** *vi* NAUT drag anchor

chasse-rivet *m* CONSTR rivet set, rivet snap, riveting set, set

chasses: ~ **proportionnelles** *f pl* IMPRIM proportional widths

chasse-tampon *m* CONS MECA plugging bar

châssis *m* CH DE FER underframe, *véhicules* frame, CINEMAT rack, CONS MECA frame, underframe, CONSTR sash, ELECTROTEC frame, IMPRIM chase, frame, printing frame, MECANIQUE frame, MINES durn, timber frame, timber set, NAUT frame, NUCLEAIRE base frame, underframe, PHOTO slide holder, slide, PRODUCTION box, molding flask (AmE), moulding flask (BrE), casting box, flask, molding box (AmE), moulding box (BrE), VEHICULES *carrosserie* chassis; ~ **de bogie** *m* CH DE FER *véhicules* bogie frame, bogie truck frame (AmE); ~ **de charpente** *m* CONSTR frame, skeleton; ~ **à colonnes** *m* PRODUCTION column box; ~ **dormant** *m* CONSTR window frame; ~ **d'E/S** *m* PRODUCTION *automatisme industriel* I/O chassis; ~ **en métal** *m* PHOTO metal dark slide; ~ **de fenêtre** *m* CONSTR sash, window frame, window sash; ~ **de fonderie** *m* PRODUCTION box, molding flask (AmE), moulding flask (BrE), casting box, flask, foundry flask, molding box (AmE), moulding box (BrE); ~ **de guidage** *m* PETROLE template; ~ **à guillotine** *m* CONSTR sliding sash; ~ **inverseur** *m* PHOTO *pour tirage de couple stéréoscopique* transposing frame; ~ **de mine** *m* MINES durn, timber frame, timber set; ~ **mobile** *m* CONSTR sash, window sash; ~ **à molettes** *m* MINES gallows frame, head frame, headstock, pithead frame; ~ **de montage** *m* IMPRIM chase, frame; ~ **de moulage** *m* PRODUCTION box, molding flask (AmE), moulding flask (BrE), casting box, flask, foundry flask, molding box (AmE), moulding box (BrE); ~ **négatif** *m* PHOTO slide holder, slide; ~ **à négatif** *m* IMPRIM chase; ~ **à pivot** *m* CONSTR pivot-hung sash; ~ **pneumatique** *m* IMPRIM airframe, vacuum frame; ~ **de porte** *m* CONSTR doorframe, jamb lining; ~ **porte-plaque** *m* PHOTO plate holder, slide holder, slide; ~ **processeur** *m* PRODUCTION *automatisme industriel* processor chassis; ~ **processeur primaire** *m* PRODUCTION *automatisme industriel* primary processor chassis; ~ **à rideau** *m* PHOTO roller blind dark slide; ~ **séparé** *m* PHOTO dark slide; ~ **surbaissé** *m* VEHICULES *châssis* drop bed frame; ~ **à trois parties** *m* PRODUCTION *dessous, chape, dessus* three-part flask, three-parted box; ~ **tubulaire** *m* VEHICULES *motocyclette* tubular frame; ~ **à tuyaux** *m* PRODUCTION pipe box; ~ **à verre** *m* CERAM VER casement; ~ **vitré** *m* CONSTR glazed frame, glazed sash

châssis-cabine *m* VEHICULES chassis cab

châssis-presse *m* PHOTO contact printing frame; ~ **à margeur mobile** *m* PHOTO masking frame

châssis-support *m* CONS MECA mounting

chat *m* PRODUCTION break-out

château *m* NAUT bridge castle; ~ **d'eau** *m* CONSTR, HYDROLOGIE, MINES water tower; ~ **de réfrigération** *m* MINES cooling tower; ~ **de transport pour un seul assemblage combustible** *m* NUCLEAIRE shielded coffin, single element shipping cask

chatoiement *m* ESPACE speckle

chatoyant *adj* MINERAUX chatoyant, TEXTILE lustrous

chatterton *m* CINEMAT camera tape; ~ **grande largeur** *m* CINEMAT gaffer tape

chaude: ~ **blanche** *f* THERMODYN white heat; ~ **blanc-soudant** *f* PRODUCTION sparkling heat

chaudière *f* AGRO ALIM, CH DE FER *véhicules*, CHIMIE, CONS MECA, INST HYDR, MECANIQUE, NAUT, PHYSIQUE, REFRIG, THERMODYN boiler; ~ **aquatubulaire** *f* CHAUFFAGE water tube boiler; ~ **auxiliaire** *f* MAT CHAUFF auxiliary boiler; ~ **de base** *f* NUCLEAIRE base load boiler; ~ **à basse pression** *f* MAT CHAUFF low-pressure hot water boiler; ~ **de bitumier** *f* CONSTR asphalt boiler, tar boiler; ~ **à bouilleur** *f* MAT CHAUFF shell-type boiler; ~ **à bouilleurs** *f* INST HYDR elephant boiler; ~ **à bouilleurs croisés** *f* MAT CHAUFF cross tube boiler; ~ **à carneau intérieur** *f* PRODUCTION flue boiler; ~ **à charbon** *f* MAT CHAUFF coal-fired boiler; ~ **de chauffage central** *f* MAT CHAUFF central heating boiler; ~ **à chauffage extérieur** *f* PRODUCTION outside-fired boiler; ~ **à chauffage intérieur** *f* PRODUCTION inside-fired boiler; ~ **chauffée chaleur perdue** *f* AERONAUT waste heat boiler; ~ **chauffée par chaleur perdue** *f* THERMODYN waste heat boiler; ~ **à circulation** *f* INST HYDR circulating boiler; ~ **à circulation d'eau forcée** *f* MAT CHAUFF forced circulation boiler; ~ **cylindrique** *f* INST HYDR cylinder boiler; ~ **cylindrique simple** *f* INST HYDR plain cylindrical boiler; ~ **à deux ballons** *f* MAT CHAUFF bi-drum boiler; ~ **à deux passes** *f* MAT CHAUFF double-pass boiler; ~ **à eau chaude** *f* CONS MECA hot water boiler; ~ **à écorces** *f* PAPIER bark boiler, bark burner, bark power boiler; ~ **électrique** *f* CONS MECA electric heater; ~ **à évaporation rapide** *f* THERMODYN flash boiler; ~ **fixe** *f* PRODUCTION stationary boiler; ~ **à flamme directe** *f* PRODUCTION direct draft boiler (AmE), direct draught boiler (BrE); ~ **à fonds bombés** *f* INST HYDR dish-ended boiler; ~ **à foyer cylindrique** *f* INST HYDR cylindrical flue boiler; ~ **à foyer extérieur** *f* PRODUCTION outside-fired boiler; ~ **à foyer intérieur** *f* PRODUCTION inside-fired boiler; ~ **à foyer intérieur cylindrique** *f* PRODUCTION flue boiler; ~ **à foyer tubulaire** *f* INST HYDR tubular furnace boiler; ~ **inexplosible** *f* PRODUCTION safety boiler; ~ **de locomotive** *f* MAT CHAUFF locomotive boiler; ~ **marine** *f* MAT CHAUFF marine boiler; ~ **marine à rayonnement** *f* MAT CHAUFF marine radiant boiler; ~ **marine à réchauffer à rayonnement** *f* MAT CHAUFF marine radiant reheat boiler; ~ **à mazout** *f* CHAUFFAGE, MAT CHAUFF oil-fired boiler; ~ **monobloc** *f* CHAUFFAGE packaged boiler; ~ **multitubulaire** *f* PRODUCTION safety boiler; ~ **à passage unique** *f* MAT CHAUFF once-through boiler; ~ **à petits éléments** *f* PRODUCTION sectional boiler; ~ **placée à demeure** *f* PRODUCTION stationary boiler; ~ **à rayonnement** *f* MAT CHAUFF radiant boiler; ~ **de réserve** *f* CHAUFFAGE stand-by boiler; ~ **à retour de flamme** *f* PRODUCTION return flue boiler, return tube boiler, return tubular boiler; ~ **sectionnelle** *f* MAT CHAUFF, PRODUCTION sectional boiler; ~ **sectionnelle aquatubulaire** *f* MAT CHAUFF water tube boiler; ~ **à trois passes** *f* MAT CHAUFF treble-pass boiler; ~ **à tube-foyer** *f* PRODUCTION flue boiler, single flue boiler; ~ **à tubes d'eau** *f* CHAUFFAGE water tube boiler; ~ **à tubes de fumée** *f* MAT CHAUFF fire-tube boiler; ~ **tubulaire** *f* AGRO ALIM, PRODUCTION tubular boiler; ~ **tubulaire à retour de flamme** *f* PRODUCTION return flue boiler, return tube boiler, return tubular boiler; ~ **à vapeur** *f* INST HYDR, THERMODYN steam boiler; ~ **à vapeur électrique** *f* CONS MECA electric steam boiler; ~ **à vaporisation instantanée** *f* INST HYDR flash boiler, flasher

chaudron *m* PRODUCTION cauldron

chaudronnerie *f* INST HYDR boiler works, boilermaking

chaudronnier *m* INST HYDR boilermaker, boilersmith, MECANIQUE boilermaker

chauffage *m* AUTO heater system, CHAUFFAGE, GAZ, MECANIQUE heating, PRODUCTION heating, stoking, TEXTILE, THERMODYN heating, VEHICULES *accessoires* heating system; ~ **à basse fréquence** *m (chauffage BF)* ELECTROTEC low-frequency induction heating; ~ **à basse pression** *m* CHAUFFAGE low-pressure heating; ~ **BF** *m (chauffage à basse fréquence)* ELECTROTEC low-frequency induction heating; ~ **central** *m* CONSTR, MAT CHAUFF, THERMODYN central heating; ~ **central au mazout** *m* CHAUFFAGE oil-fired central heating system; ~ **au charbon pulvérisé** *m* MAT CHAUFF pulverized coal firing; ~ **combustible** *m* THERMODYN fuel; ~ **à conduit de cheminée** *m* CONS MECA flued heater; ~ **diélectrique** *m* ELECTR, ELECTROTEC, MAT CHAUFF dielectric heating; ~ **dynamique** *m* THERMODYN dynamic heating; ~ **à eau chaude** *m* MAT CHAUFF hot water heating system; ~ **électrique** *m* CHAUFFAGE, ELECTR electric heating, THERMODYN heating; ~ **électrique de surface** *m* CONS MECA electric surface heater; ~ **électronique** *m* ELECTROTEC electronic heating; ~ **au gaz** *m* PRODUCTION gas heating, THERMODYN gas heating, heating; ~ **d'un groupe d'îlots** *m* MAT CHAUFF district heating; ~ **à haute fréquence** *m* ELECTROTEC *(chauffage HF)* high-frequency heating, MAT CHAUFF power frequency heating; ~ **à haute pression** *m* MAT CHAUFF high-pressure heating system; ~ **HF** *m (chauffage à haute fréquence)* ELECTROTEC high-frequency heating; ~ **inductif** *m* THERMODYN inductive heating; ~ **infrarouge** *m* PHYS RAYON infrared heating; ~ **des locaux** *m* GAZ space heating; ~ **au mazout** *m* CONSTR oil firing, MAT CHAUFF oil heating; ~ **mécanique** *m* CONS MECA mechanical firing; ~ **MF** *m (chauffage à moyenne fréquence)* ELECTROTEC medium-frequency heating; ~ **à moyenne fréquence** *m (chauffage MF)* ELECTROTEC medium-frequency heating; ~ **mural** *m* THERMODYN panel heating; ~ **ohmique** *m* ELECTR resistance heating, NUCLEAIRE *par effet Joule* Joule heating, THERMODYN resistance heating; ~ **par arc électrique** *m* ELECTROTEC arc heating; ~ **par effet joule** *m* THERMODYN resistance heating; ~ **par haute fréquence** *m* ELECTR high-frequency heating; ~ **par induction** *m* ELECTROTEC, MATERIAUX, MECANIQUE, PLAST CAOU induction heating; ~ **par jaquette électrique** *m* CHAUFFAGE electric blanket heating; ~ **par plancher chauffant** *m* THERMODYN underfloor heating; ~ **par radiation** *m* PHYS RAYON radiation heating, THERMODYN radiant heating; ~ **par le sol** *m* CHAUFFAGE floor heating, underfloor heating; ~ **préalable** *m* CH DE FER *véhicules* preheating; ~ **à radiation d'air chaud** *m* SECURITE hot air radiation heating system; ~ **rapide** *m* AGRO ALIM flash heating; ~ **à rayonnement** *m* MAT CHAUFF radiant heating; ~ **à rayons gamma** *m* PHYS RAYON gamma ray heating; ~ **aux rayons infrarouges** *m* CHAUFFAGE infrared heating; ~ **à récupération de chaleur** *m* REFRIG regenerative heating; ~ **sans conduit de cheminée** *m* CONS MECA flueless heater; ~ **solaire** *m* ASTRONOMIE solar heating, EN RENOUV solar heating system; ~ **urbain** *m* THERMODYN district heating; ~ **à vapeur** *m* CONSTR steam heating; ~ **de voiture** *m* MAT CHAUFF car heater

chauffagiste *m* THERMODYN heating engineer

chauffe *f* PRODUCTION fire chamber, stoking

chauffé: ~ **à blanc** *adj* THERMODYN white-hot; ~ **au charbon** *adj* CHARBON coal-fired; ~ **au coke** *adj* PRODUCTION coke-fired; ~ **à gaz** *adj* CHAUFFAGE, PRODUCTION gas-fired; ~ **au rouge** *adj* THERMODYN red-hot

chauffe-bain *m* PHOTO dish heater; ~ **à gaz** *m* MAT CHAUFF *salle de bain* gas geyser

chauffe-ballon *m* EQUIP LAB heating mantle

chauffe-eau *m* EQUIP LAB, THERMODYN *chauffage* water heater; ~ **à électrode** *m* CHAUFFAGE electrode boiler; ~ **à gaz** *m* THERMODYN gas boiler, gas water heater; ~ **instantané** *m* MAT CHAUFF instantaneous water heater; ~ **ménager** *m* CONS MECA domestic boiler; ~ **solaire** *m* CONS MECA solar water heater

chauffe-entonnoir *m* EQUIP LAB funnel heater

chauffe-liant *m* CONSTR binder heater

chauffer[1] *vt* CHIMIE, PHYSIQUE heat, PRODUCTION stoke, *une chaudière* serve, TEXTILE, THERMODYN heat

chauffer[2] *vi* CONS MECA run hot; ~ **à vide** *vi* CERAM VER fire over

chauffe-règle *m* CONSTR screed heater

chaufferie *f* INST HYDR boiler house, boiler room; ~ **d'appoint** *f* EN RENOUV *géothermie* booster heating system; ~ **à gaz** *f* CHAUFFAGE gas heating system

chauffeur *m* PRODUCTION stoker

chaufour *m* PRODUCTION lime kiln, lime pit

chaufournerie *f* PRODUCTION lime burning

chaufrein *m* MECANIQUE *soudage* gap

chaulage *m* CONSTR liming; ~ **de lac** *m* POLLUTION lake liming

chauler *vt* COULEURS whitewash

chaulmoogra *m* CHIMIE *huile* chaulmoogra

chaumard *m* NAUT fairlead; ~ **à rouleau** *m* NAUT roller fairlead

chaussée *f* CONSTR roadway, *d'un pont* deck, floor, *en béton* pavement (BrE), NAUT causeway, TRANSPORT roadway, VEHICULES road; ~ **empierrée** *f* CONSTR metalled road (BrE), paved road (AmE)

chaussette *f* IMPRIM *rouleaux* sleeve, NUCLEAIRE thimble

chaussures: ~ **agréées** *f pl* SECURITE approved footwear; ~ **antistatiques** *f pl* SECURITE antistatic footwear; ~ **en plastique moulé** *f pl* SECURITE plastic-molded footwear (AmE), plastic-moulded footwear (BrE); ~ **de protection** *f pl* SECURITE protective footwear; ~ **de travail** *f pl* SECURITE work boots

chaux *f* AGRO ALIM lime, CERAM VER chalk, CHARBON, CHIMIE, CONSTR lime; ~ **anhydre** *f* CHIMIE quicklime; ~ **chlorée** *f* AGRO ALIM chlorinated lime, LESSIVES bleaching lime, bleaching powder, chlorinated lime; ~ **éteinte** *f* AGRO ALIM, CHIMIE, CONSTR slaked lime; ~ **grasse** *f* PAPIER fat lime; ~ **hydratée** *f* CONSTR hydrated lime; ~ **sodée** *f* CHIMIE soda lime; ~ **sulfatée** *f* CHIMIE sulfate of lime (AmE), sulphate of lime (BrE); ~ **vive** *f* CERAM VER, CHIMIE, CONSTR, POLLU MER quicklime

chavibétol *m* CHIMIE chavibetol

chavicol *m* CHIMIE chavicol

chavirement *m* CONSTR dumping (AmE), tipping (BrE)

chavirer[1] *vt* CONSTR shoot, tip, tip up, NAUT capsize

chavirer[2] *vi* NAUT capsize

cheddite *f* MINES chlorate explosive

chef *m* PRODUCTION foreman; ~ **animateur** *m* CINEMAT animation director; ~ **de base** *m* CONSTR *d'une ardoise* tail; ~ **de bureau d'études** *m* CONSTR chief designer; ~ **de caisson** *m* OCEANO caisson master; ~ **de chantier** *m* PETROLE tool pusher; ~ **d'équipe** *m* PRODUCTION charge hand, foreman; ~ **d'escadre** *m* NAUT commodore; ~ **de forage** *m* PETR drilling superintendent; ~ **du gisement** *m* MINES rock capping; ~ **machiniste** *m* CINEMAT boss grip; ~ **mécanicien** *m* NAUT chief engineer; ~

opérateur *m* CINEMAT chief cameraman; ~ **de palan-quée** *m* OCEANO diving supervisor; ~ **de place** *m* CERAM VER foreman, gaffer; ~ **de plongée** *m* OCEANO diving supervisor; ~ **de pose** *m* CH DE FER track-laying foreman; ~ **de poste** *m* PRODUCTION foreman; ~ **son-deur** *m* PETR driller; ~ **de tête** *m* CONSTR *d'une ardoise* head; ~ **de traction** *m* CH DE FER head driver; ~ **de train** *m* CH DE FER *véhicules* conductor (AmE), guard (BrE); ~ **de triage** *m* CH DE FER freight yard foreman (AmE), goods yard foreman (BrE)

chélate *m* CHIMIE, LESSIVES chelate

chélater *vt* CHIMIE chelate

chélateur *m* CHIMIE chelating agent

chélation *f* CHIMIE chelation; ~ **séquestration** *f* NU-CLEAIRE chelate formation, chelation

chemin *m* CONSTR road, way, GEOMETRIE, INFORMAT, ORDINAT, PHYSIQUE path, VEHICULES road; ~ **d'accès** *m* ORDINAT access path; ~ **anfractueux** *m* CONSTR rough road; ~ **de câble** *m* ELECTR *alimentation* cable run; ~ **de cartes** *m* INFORMAT card bed; ~ **creux** *m* CONSTR sunken road; ~ **critique** *m* CONSTR, INFORMAT, ORDINAT critical path; ~ **détourné** *m* CONSTR byway; ~ **de données** *m* ELECTRON, INFORMAT data path; ~ **en déblai** *m* CH DE FER railroad cutting (AmE), railway cutting (BrE); ~ **de fer** *m* TRANSPORT railroad (AmE), railway (BrE); ~ **de fer à crémaillère** *m* TRANSPORT cog railroad (AmE), cog railway (BrE), rack railroad (AmE), rack railway (BrE), rack-and-pinion railroad (AmE), rack-and-pinion railway (BrE); ~ **de fer mini-ature** *m* CH DE FER model railroad (AmE), model railway (BrE); ~ **de fer minier** *m* TRANSPORT mine railroad (AmE), mine railway (BrE); ~ **de fer modèle réduit** *m* CH DE FER model railroad (AmE), model railway (BrE); ~ **de fer de montagne** *m* CH DE FER, TRANSPORT mountain railroad (AmE), mountain rail-way (BrE); ~ **de fer de montagne à crémaillère** *m* TRANSPORT rack mountain railroad (AmE), rack mountain railway (AmE); ~ **de fer suspendu** *m* CONS MECA runway, PRODUCTION overhead runway, over-head track, TRANSPORT overhead runway; ~ **de fer à voie étroite** *m* CH DE FER narrow gage railroad (AmE), narrow gauge railway (BrE), TRANSPORT light rail-road (AmE), narrow gage track system (AmE), narrow gauge track system (BrE); ~ **de fer à voie large** *m* CH DE FER broad-gage railroad (AmE), broad-gauge railway (BrE); ~ **de fer à voie normale** *m* CH DE FER standard gage railroad (AmE), standard gauge railway (BrE); ~ **à forte pente** *m* CONSTR steep road; ~ **de halage** *m* CONSTR tow path; ~ **de mise à la terre** *m* PRODUCTION *électricité* earthing path (BrE), ground-ing path (AmE); ~ **de nivellement** *m* OCEANO survey traverse; ~ **optimal** *m* TELECOM optimal path; ~ **op-tique** *m* OPTIQUE optical path, *dans un milieu homogène et isotrope* optical path length, TELECOM optical path, optical path length; ~ **du papier** *m* IM-PRIM *dans la machine* lead; ~ **de retenue** *m* PRODUCTION *voie logique d'accrochage* hold-in path; ~ **de roulement** *m* CONS MECA runway, *pour billes* race, MECANIQUE race; ~ **de roulement pour billes** *m* CONS MECA ball race; ~ **rude** *m* CONSTR rough road; ~ **suivi par le bouton de manivelle** *m* CONS MECA crankpath

cheminée *f* CHAUFFAGE chimney, CONS MECA chamber, CONSTR chimney stack, chimney, funnel, shaft, stack, GEOLOGIE *volcanique* vent, MECANIQUE funnel, MINES chimney, chute, mill, mill hole, pass, NAUT funnel, PETR stack, PRODUCTION chimney; ~ **d'aérage** *f* MINES air stack, surface ventilation chimney, surface venti-lation duct; ~ **à charbon** *f* CHARBON chute, drop hole, coal chute; ~ **de chaudière** *f* INST HYDR *carneau* boiler flue; ~ **en acier** *f* CONSTR steel chimney; ~ **en tôle** *f* CONSTR steel chimney; ~ **d'équilibre** *f* EN RENOUV surge shaft, HYDROLOGIE surge shaft, surge tank; ~ **à minerai** *f* MINES mill, mill hole, ore pass; ~ **d'usine** *f* CONSTR chimney stack; ~ **de ventilation** *f* CONSTR vent pipe; ~ **volcanique** *f* GEOLOGIE volcanic vent; ~ **volcanique diatrème** *f* GEOLOGIE diatreme

cheminement *m* CONSTR meandering, PETROLE creep; ~ **aléatoire** *m* INFORMAT, ORDINAT random walk; ~ **d'arc** *m* ELECTR *défaut d'isolateur* tracking; ~ **horizontal au bouclier** *m* CH DE FER shield tunneling (AmE), shield tunnelling (BrE); ~ **littoral** *m* HYDROLOGIE littoral drift

chemisage *m* INST HYDR clothing, lagging, NUCLEAIRE jacketing; ~ **extérieur de chaudière** *m* INST HYDR boiler jacket, chauffage

chemise *f* AUTO cylinder liner, CERAM VER casing, skirt, CONS MECA *élément* liner, DISTRI EAU *d'une pompe* lining, ESPACE *véhicules* jacket, MECANIQUE cylinder liner, jacket, liner, NUCLEAIRE jacket, PRODUCTION jacket, lining, sheathing, *d'un fourneau* shirt; ~ **de chauffage** *f* THERMODYN heating jacket; ~ **à circulation d'eau** *f* PRODUCTION water jacket; ~ **de cylindre** *f* AUTO cylinder sleeve, VEHICULES *moteur* cylinder liner; ~ **d'eau** *f* AUTO, PRODUCTION, THERMODYN, VEHICULES *système de refroidissement* water jacket; ~ **extérieure** *f* PRODUCTION building, *d'un haut fourneau* mantle; ~ **humide** *f* AUTO wet cylinder liner; ~ **à vapeur** *f* CHAUFF-AGE, INST HYDR steam jacket

chemisé *adj* MECANIQUE jacketed

chenal *m* CONSTR, DISTRI EAU channel, EN RENOUV chan-nel, fairway, GEOLOGIE, HYDROLOGIE channel, NAUT channel, fairway, OCEANO channel; ~ **d'accès** *m* NAUT approach channel; ~ **acoustique** *m* OCEANO acoustic channel, acoustic waveband, sound channel; ~ **d'ap-proche** *m* AERONAUT approach path, NAUT approach channel; ~ **de coulée** *m* PRODUCTION main gate, main runner, runner; ~ **de coulée en chute directe** *m* PRO-DUCTION direct pouring gate, drop runner, plump gate, pop gate; ~ **de coulée en source** *m* PRODUCTION fountain runner, horn gate; ~ **de coulée à talon** *m* PRODUCTION side gate; ~ **de cours d'eau** *m* DISTRI EAU channelway, HYDROLOGIE streamway; ~ **de déverse-ment** *m* DISTRI EAU drainage channel; ~ **filonien** *m* MINES lode channel; ~ **à huile** *m* CONS MECA oil channel; ~ **de marée** *m* OCEANO tidal channel; ~ **de navigation** *m* HYDROLOGIE navigation channel, OCEANO fairway, shipping channel, TRANSPORT navigation channel; ~ **de rivière** *m* HYDROLOGIE river channel; ~ **sonore** *m* OCEANO acoustic channel, sound channel

chenalage *m* NAUT fairway navigation

chéneau *m* CONSTR gutter; ~ **à l'anglaise** *m* CONSTR parapet gutter; ~ **encaissé** *m* CONSTR box gutter, parallel gutter, secret gutter, trough gutter

chenet *m* MAT CHAUFF firedog

chenillards *f pl* ENREGISTR sound bars

chenille *f* MILITAIRE *d'un char d'assaut* caterpillar

chenilles *f pl* CONS MECA *pour véhicules* crawler tracks

cherche-pôles *m* ELECTR *connexions* polarity tester

chercher *vt* INFORMAT, ORDINAT seek

chercheur *m* ASTRONOMIE auxiliary telescope, finder, CONSTR *des travaux publics* surveyor, INSTRUMENT finder, MINES digger; ~ **de ligne** *m* TELECOM LF, line finder; ~ **d'opérateur** *m* TELECOM access matrix; ~ **de**

pôle m ELECTR polarity tester

chert m GEOLOGIE chert; **~ ferrugineux rubané** m GEOLOGIE jaspilite

chessylite f CHIMIE, MINERAUX chessylite

cheval m CONS MECA horsepower, METROLOGIE metric horsepower, MINES horsepower; **~ dynamique** m CONS MECA horsepower; **~ effectif** m CONS MECA BHP, brake horsepower, actual horsepower, PRODUCTION BHP, brake horsepower, effective horsepower; **~ de force** m CONS MECA horsepower; **~ heure** m CONS MECA horsepower hour; **~ heure effectif** m CONS MECA brake horsepower hour, effective horsepower hour, MECANIQUE actual horsepower hour, PRODUCTION brake horsepower hour; **~ indiqué** m CONS MECA gross horsepower; **~ de Troie** m INFORMAT, ORDINAT Trojan horse; **~ vapeur** m AUTO horsepower, hp, CONS MECA, METROLOGIE horsepower

chevalement m MINES gallows frame, head frame, headstock, pithead gear, pithead frame

chevalement-abri m MINES head house

chevalet m CERAM VER buck (AmE), horse (BrE), storage rack, CONSTR trestle, PRODUCTION horse; **~ d'extraction** m MINES gallows frame, head frame, headstock, pithead frame; **~ de scieur** m CONSTR buck, jack, sawbuck, sawhorse

Chevalet: ~ du Peintre m ASTRONOMIE Pictor

chevauchement m ACOUSTIQUE overcutting, CONS MECA straddling, CONSTR overlap, overlapping, ELECTRON pipelining, ELECTROTEC overlapping, GEOLOGIE overlap, overthrust, thrusting, INFORMAT, ORDINAT overlap, PETROLE overthrust, PRODUCTION overriding; **~ aveugle** m GEOLOGIE *structure sans affleurement* blind thrust; **~ des soupapes** m AUTO valve lap

chevelure: ~ cométaire f ASTRONOMIE coma fail; **~ hydrographique** f PETR braided stream

Chevelure: ~ de Bérénice f ASTRONOMIE Coma Berenices

chevet m MINES foot, footwall

chevêtre m CONSTR trimmer, trimmer beam; **~ sous la marche palière** m CONSTR landing trimmer

cheville f CONS MECA pin, CONSTR brad, draw bore pin, hinge pin, peg, pin, MECANIQUE peg; **~ antiexpansion** f CONSTR through bolt; **~ d'assemblage** f CONS MECA drift pin; **~ d'attache** f PRODUCTION hitch pin; **~ d'attelage** f CONS MECA *pour une remorque* coupling pin; **~ autoforeuse** f CONSTR self-drill anchor; **~ barbelée** f CONSTR sprig bolt; **~ de bois** f CONSTR treenail (AmE), trenail (BrE), trunnel (AmE); **~ cadre** f CONSTR frame fixing; **~ clou** f CONSTR hammer plug; **~ douille** f CONSTR sleeve anchor; **~ métallique corps creux** f CONSTR metal cavity fixing umbrella; **~ ouvrière** f CONS MECA kingbolt, kingpin, main pin, pintle; **~ de sécurité** f CONS MECA safety bolt

cheviller vt CONSTR bolt, peg, PRODUCTION dowel

chèvre f CONSTR derrick, derrick crane, gin, jack, sawbuck, sawhorse, shear legs, PRODUCTION horse; **~ à véhicule** f CONS MECA *pour le remplacement de bogies* lifting jack; **~ verticale** f CONSTR derrick, derrick crane

chevron m CONS MECA chevron, herringbone, CONSTR rafter; **~ arêtier** m CONSTR hip, hip rafter; **~ intermédiaire** m CONSTR common rafter; **~ de long pan** m CONSTR hip rafter; **~ principal** m CONSTR principal, principal rafter

chevronnage: ~ à tenon m CONSTR bridle joint

chevrons m pl CERAM VER chevron runner bars

chez: ~ le destinataire adv TELECOM at the far end; **~ l'émetteur** adv TELECOM at the near end

chiastolite f MINERAUX chiastolite

chicane f CINEMAT light trap, CONS MECA baffle, CONSTR baffle, baffle plate, GENIE CHIM baffle, vapor trap (AmE), vapour trap (BrE), NUCLEAIRE, PAPIER, VEHICULES *silencieux* baffle; **~ pour retenue de l'huile** f NUCLEAIRE oil baffle

chicanes f pl REFRIG baffle plates

chien m CONS MECA click, detent, dog, pawl, ratchet, trigger, CONSTR devil's claw, lion's claw; **~ de garde** m ORDINAT watchdog timer

Chiens: ~ de Chasse m pl ASTRONOMIE Canes Venatici

chiffon m PAPIER rag; **~ non-pelucheux** m MECANIQUE lint-free cloth

chiffrage m CERAM VER figuring, ELECTRON encipherment, ORDINAT encryption

chiffraison: ~ d'une échelle f METROLOGIE scale numbering

chiffre m IMPRIM numeral, INFORMAT, ORDINAT digit; **~ binaire** m CONS MECA binary number, INFORMAT, ORDINAT binary digit, bit; **~ de bourrage** m TELECOM *maritime mobile* stuffing digit; **~ de contrôle** m INFORMAT, ORDINAT check digit; **~ en index** m IMPRIM inferior character, inferior figure, inferior letter, subscript; **~ d'identification de nationalité** m TELECOM NID, national identification digit; **~ le plus significatif** m INFORMAT, ORDINAT MSD, most significant digit; **~ de poids faible** m PRODUCTION *automatisme industriel* LSD, least significant digit; **~ de poids fort** m INFORMAT, PRODUCTION *automatisme industriel* MSD, most significant digit; **~ de poids le plus faible** m INFORMAT, ORDINAT LSD, least significant digit; **~ romain** m IMPRIM, MATH Roman numeral; **~ significatif** m MATH significant figure; **~ supplémentaire** m TELECOM extra digit

chiffrement m TELECOM encipherment, encryption; **~ de bout en bout** m TELECOM end-to-end encipherment; **~ de données** m ORDINAT data encryption; **~ de liaison** m TELECOM link-by-link encipherment; **~ de liaison par liaison** m TELECOM link-by-link encipherment

chiffrer vt ELECTR digitize, ELECTRON encipher, TELECOM encode, TV code

chiffres: ~ après la virgule m pl MATH significant figures; **~ arabes** m pl IMPRIM modern figures; **~ et signes digitaux** m pl IMPRIM numerics

chignole f CONS MECA hand brace

childrénite f MINERAUX childrenite

chiléite f MINERAUX chileite

chimico-analytique adj CHIMIE chemico-analytical

chimico-électrique adj CHIMIE chemico-electrical

chimico-métallurgique adj CHIMIE chemicometallurgical

chimico-minéralogique adj CHIMIE chemicomineralogical

chimico-physique adj CHIMIE chemicophysical

chimie: ~ alimentaire f AGRO ALIM food chemistry; **~ appliquée** f CHIMIE applied chemistry; **~ de l'atmosphère** f POLLUTION atmospheric chemistry; **~ atmosphérique** f POLLUTION atmospheric chemistry; **~ inorganique** f CHIMIE mineral chemistry; **~ minérale** f CHIMIE inorganic chemistry, mineral chemistry; **~ organique** f CHIMIE organic chemistry; **~ physiologique** f CHIMIE physiochemistry; **~ pure** f CHIMIE theoretical chemistry; **~ radioactive** f CHIMIE, PHYS RAYON radiochemistry; **~ sous rayonnement** f NUCLEAIRE radiation chemistry; **~ de la teinture** f COULEURS teintochemistry

chimioluminescence f PHYS RAYON, PHYSIQUE chemiluminescence

chimiothérapie *f* CHIMIE chemotherapy

chimique *adj* CHIMIE, TEXTILE chemical

chimiquier *m* NAUT chemical tanker

chinois *m* AGRO ALIM conical sieve

chiolite *f* MINERAUX chiolite

chiral *adj* CHIMIE chiral

chiralité *f* CRISTALL, MATERIAUX *catalyse* chirality

chitine *f* CHIMIE chitin

chitosamine *f* CHIMIE chitosamine

chiviatite *f* MINERAUX chiviatite

chloanthite *f* MINERAUX chloanthite

chloracétate *m* CHIMIE chloracetate

chloracétique *adj* CHIMIE chloracetic

chlorage *m* LESSIVES chlorination

chloral *m* CHIMIE chloral

chloralamide *m* CHIMIE chloralamide

chloralbenzène *m* CHIMIE chloralbenzene

chloralbutol *m* CHIMIE chloralbutol

chloralformiate *m* CHIMIE chloralformate

chloralose *m* CHIMIE chloralose

chloranile *m* CHIMIE chloranil

chlorastrolite *f* MINERAUX chlorastrolite

chlorate *m* CHIMIE chlorate; ~ **de potasse** *m* CHIMIE potassium chlorate; ~ **de potassium** *m* CHIMIE potassium chlorate

chloration *f* CHIMIE, HYDROLOGIE chlorination; ~ **au point optimal** *f* HYDROLOGIE breakpoint chlorination

chlore *m (Cl)* CHIMIE chlorine *(Cl)*; ~ **actif** *m* LESSIVES, PAPIER active chlorine; ~ **liquide** *m* THERMODYN liquid chlorine

chloré *adj* HYDROLOGIE, LESSIVES chlorinated

chlorer *vt* HYDROLOGIE chlorinate

chloreux *adj* CHIMIE chlorous

chlorhydraté *adj* CHIMIE muriated

chlorhydrique *adj* CHIMIE *acide* hydrochloric

chlorique *adj* CHIMIE chloric

chlorite *f* CHARBON, CHIMIE, MINERAUX, PETROLE *minéral* chlorite

chloritoïde *f* MINERAUX chlorite spar, chloritoid

chlorobutadiène *m* CHIMIE chloroprene

chlorocalcite *f* MINERAUX chlorocalcite

chlorofibres *f pl* TEXTILE chlorofibers (AmE), chlorofibres (BrE)

chlorofluorocarbone *m (CFC)* EMBALLAGE chlorofluorocarbon *(CFC)*

chlorohydrine *f* CHIMIE chlorohydrin

chloromélanite *f* MINERAUX chloromelanite

chloropale *f* MINERAUX chloropal

chlorophane *f* MINERAUX chlorophane

chlorophénol *m* CHIMIE chlorophenol

chlorophylle *f* CHIMIE chlorophyll

chloropicrine *f* CHIMIE chloropicrin, nitrochloroform

chloroplatinate *m* CHIMIE chloroplatinate

chloroprène *m* CHIMIE chloroprene

chlorospinelle *m* MINERAUX chlorospinel

chlorosulfonation *f* LESSIVES chlorosulfonation (AmE), chlorosulphonation (BrE)

chlorosulfoné *adj* LESSIVES chlorosulfonated (AmE), chlorosulphonated (BrE)

chloruration *f* CHIMIE chlorination

chlorure *m* CHARBON, CHIMIE, MATERIAUX *chimie* chloride; ~ **acide** *m* CHIMIE acidic chloride; ~ **d'acide** *m* CHIMIE acid chloride; ~ **d'acyle** *m* MATERIAUX acyl chloride; ~ **d'ammonium** *m* CHIMIE ammonium chloride; ~ **d'argent** *m* CHIMIE, ELECTROTEC silver chloride; ~ **de benzoyle** *m* CHIMIE benzoyl chloride; ~ **de calcium** *m* AGRO ALIM, CHIMIE calcium chloride; ~ **de carbonyle** *m* CHIMIE carbonyl chloride; ~ **de chaux** *m* AGRO ALIM chlorinated lime, LESSIVES bleaching lime, bleaching powder, chlorinated lime, PAPIER bleaching powder; ~ **de cobalt** *m* CERAM VER cobalt chloride; ~ **décolorant** *m* LESSIVES bleaching agent, chlorine bleaching agent; ~ **de méthyle** *m* CHIMIE methyl chloride; ~ **de méthylrosalinium** *m* CHIMIE viocid; ~ **d'or** *m* CHIMIE gold chloride; ~ **de polyvinyle** *m* CONSTR, ELECTROTEC, MATERIAUX, PLAST CAOU polyvinyl chloride; ~ **de polyvinyle chloré** *m* PLAST CAOU chlorinated polyvinyl chloride; ~ **de polyvinyle non plastifié** *m* PLAST CAOU unplasticized polyvinyl chloride; ~ **de polyvinylidène** *m* PLAST CAOU polyvinylidene chloride; ~ **de potassium** *m* CHIMIE potassium chloride; ~ **de sodium** *m* CHIMIE, LESSIVES sodium chloride; ~ **de xénon** *m* ELECTRON xenon chloride; ~ **de zinc** *m* ELECTROTEC zinc chloride

chlorurer *vt* CHIMIE chlorinate

choc *m* CHARBON impact, CONS MECA shock, CONSTR, MECANIQUE impact, PHYSIQUE impact, shock, PRODUCTION jar, jarring; ~ **acide** *m* POLLUTION acid shock; ~ **acide printanier** *m* POLLUTION spring acid shock; ~ **acide du printemps** *m* POLLUTION spring acid shock; ~ **avant** *m* ESPACE bow shock; ~ **élastique** *m* PHYSIQUE elastic collision; ~ **électrique** *m* ELECTROTEC, SECURITE electric shock; ~ **en retour** *m* MECANIQUE recoil, PHYSIQUE return stroke; ~ **inélastique** *m* PHYSIQUE inelastic collision; ~ **lointain** *m* NUCLEAIRE distant collision, range collision; ~ **pyrotechnique** *m* ESPACE *véhicules* pyrotechnic shock; ~ **thermique** *m* ESPACE thermal shock, NUCLEAIRE heat flush, THERMODYN thermal shock

chocage *m* NUCLEAIRE chugging

choisir *vt* INFORMAT, ORDINAT select

choisisseuse *f* CERAM VER slitter

choix *m* CERAM VER inspection, selection, sorting, IMPRIM select; ~ **des composants** *m* ESPACE *véhicules* component selection; ~ **du fabricant** *m* CONS MECA manufacturer's discretion

cholate *m* CHIMIE cholate

cholécystographie *f* INSTRUMENT cholecystography

cholestérique *adj* CHIMIE cholesteric

cholestérol *m* AGRO ALIM, CHIMIE cholesterol

choline *f* AGRO ALIM choline

cholinergique *adj* CHIMIE cholinergic

cholinestérase *f* CHIMIE cholinesterase

cholique *adj* CHIMIE *acide* cholic

chômage:[1] **en ~** *adj* PRODUCTION idle

chômage[2] *m* PRODUCTION *d'une usine* closing

chondrine *f* CHIMIE chondrin

chondrite *f* ASTRONOMIE chondrite; ~ **charbonneuse** *f* ASTRONOMIE carbonaceous chondrite

chondritique *adj* GEOLOGIE chondritic

chondroarsénite *f* MINERAUX chondrarsenite

chondrodite *f* MINERAUX chondrodite

choquage *m* ESPACE chugging

choquer *vt* NAUT *marine* check, *un cordage* slip

christianite *f* MINERAUX christianite

chromage *m* MATERIAUX chromium plating, chromizing, VEHICULES chromium plating

chromate *m* CHIMIE chromate; ~ **de fer** *m* CHIMIE iron chromate

chromaté: ~ **au bronze** *adj* PRODUCTION bronze chromate finished

chromaticité *f* TV chromaticity

chromatique *adj* PHOTO, PHYSIQUE, TV chromatic

chromatisation *f* MATERIAUX chromizing

chromatographe *m* EQUIP LAB *pour phase gazeuse* gas chromatograph, *pour l'analyse des ions* ion chromatograph

chromatographie *f* CHIMIE chromatography; ~ **d'adsorption gaz-solide** *f* POLLUTION gas solid chromatography; ~ **à couches minces** *f* EQUIP LAB *analyse* thin-layer chromatography; ~ **en phase gazeuse** *f (CPG)* AGRO ALIM, CHIMIE, MATERIAUX gas chromatography; ~ **en phase liquide** *f* POLLUTION liquid chromatography; ~ **gazeuse** *f* THERMODYN gas chromatography; ~ **gaz-liquide** *f (CGL)* POLLUTION, THERMODYN gas liquid chromatography; ~ **gaz-solide** *f (CGS)* POLLUTION gas solid chromatography; ~ **liquéfiée** *f* POLLUTION liquid chromatography; ~ **liquide à grande vitesse** *f* POLLUTION high-performance liquid chromatography; ~ **liquide à haute performance** *f* POLLUTION high-performance liquid chromatography; ~ **liquide à haute pression** *f (CLHP)* AGRO ALIM, CHIMIE, EQUIP LAB, POLLUTION high-pressure liquid chromatography *(HPLC)*; ~ **par partition** *f* CHIMIE partition chromatography; ~ **par perméation du gel** *f* EQUIP LAB *analyse* gel permeation chromatography; ~ **sur couches minces** *f* CHIMIE TLC, thin-layer chromatography; ~ **sur gel perméable** *f* CHIMIE gel permeation chromatography; ~ **sur papier** *f* CHIMIE paper chromatography

chrome *m* CHIMIE *(Cr)* chromium *(Cr)*

chromer *vt* GENIE CHIM chrome

chromeux *adj* CHIMIE chromous

chrominance *f* ELECTRON chrominance, TV chroma; ~ **retardée** *f* TV lagging chrominance

chromique *adj* CHIMIE chromic

chromite *f* CERAM VER, MINERAUX chromite

chromodynamique: ~ **quantique** *f* PHYS PART, PHYSIQUE quantum chromodynamics

chromogène *m* CHIMIE chromogen

chromophorique *adj* CHIMIE chromophoric

chromosphère *f* ASTRONOMIE, ESPACE chromosphere

chromotropique *adj* CHIMIE chromotropic

chromotypie *f* PHOTO color printing process (AmE), colour printing process (BrE)

chronogramme *m* INFORMAT, ORDINAT timing diagram

chronologie *f* ELECTRON *de circuits logiques* logic timing, ESPACE *de lancement* chronology

chronométrage *m* CINEMAT timing

chronomètre *m* EQUIP LAB chronometer, *durée* timer, NAUT chronometer, PHYSIQUE chronometer, timer; ~ **à déclic** *m* PHYSIQUE stopclock, stopwatch

chronométrer *vt* PRODUCTION time

chronophotographie *f* CINEMAT motion analysis

chrysène *m* CHIMIE chrysene

chrysobéryl *m* MINERAUX chrysoberyl, cymophane

chrysocolle *f* MINERAUX chrysocolla

chrysoïdine *f* CHIMIE chrysoidine

chrysolite *f* MINERAUX chrysolite

chrysolithe *f* MINERAUX chrysolite

chrysophanique *adj* CHIMIE chrysophanic

chrysoprase *f* MINERAUX chrysoprase

chrysotile *m* MINERAUX chrysotile

chuck *f* CONS MECA *d'un tour* chuck

chute *f* CINEMAT cut, offcut, reject, throw-away, trim, *de pellicule vierge* short end, DISTRI EAU fall, lift, HYDROLOGIE *écluse* lift, waterfall, INST HYDR head, *différence négative de niveau* fall, MECANIQUE discard, NAUT leech, PHYSIQUE *de température* fall, TEXTILE feeder; ~ **anodique** *f* GAZ anode drop; ~ **de barre** *f* PRODUCTION crop end; ~ **cathodique** *f* GAZ cathode drop; ~ **de comble** *f* CONSTR pitch of roof, roof pitch; ~ **d'eau** *f* HYDROLOGIE waterfall head, INST HYDR water fall height; ~ **d'eau utile** *f* EN RENOUV effective head; ~ **en ligne** *f* ELECTR *de tension*, ELECTROTEC *de tension* line drop; ~ **d'un filet** *f* OCEANO net depth; ~ **de fréquence** *f* ELECTR frequency fall-off; ~ **d'impédance** *f* ELECTR *tension* impedance drop; ~ **inductive** *f* ELECTR inductive drop; ~ **inductive de tension** *f* ELECTR reactance drop; ~ **libre** *f* AERONAUT, EMBALLAGE free fall; ~ **de neige** *f* METEO snowfall; ~ **de papier** *f* IMPRIM *façonnage* offcut; ~ **du pH** *f* POLLUTION pH drop; ~ **de potentiel** *f* ELECTROTEC, PHYSIQUE potential drop; ~ **de potentiel thermique** *f* THERMODYN heat drop, thermal head; ~ **de pression** *f* EN RENOUV pressure drop, INST HYDR pressure drop, pressure loss, PAPIER, PRODUCTION *système hydraulique* pressure drop; ~ **de pression hydraulique** *f* HYDROLOGIE fall in hydraulic head; ~ **réactive** *f* ELECTROTEC reactance drop; ~ **de résistance** *f* ELECTR IR-drop, ohmic drop, resistance drop; ~ **du sommet** *f* ELECTRON droop; ~ **de température** *f* THERMODYN heat drop, temperature drop; ~ **de tension** *f* CINEMAT power drop, ELECTR potential drop, voltage drop, voltage loss, ELECTROTEC, PHYSIQUE, PRODUCTION voltage drop

chutes: ~ **non imprimées** *f pl* IMPRIM *façonnage, récupération du papier* blank trimmings

chutier *m* CINEMAT *pour film* bin, editing rack, film bin, film tree, trim bin

chymosine *f* AGRO ALIM rennin

Ci *abrév (cirrus)* METEO Ci *(cirrus)*

CI *abrév* ELECTR *(circuit intégré)*, ELECTRON *(circuit intégré)* IC *(integrated circuit)*, ELECTRON *(circuit imprimé)*, INFORMAT *(circuit intégré)* IC *(integrated circuit)*, INFORMAT *(circuit imprimé)* PC *(printed circuit)*, ORDINAT *(circuit intégré)* IC *(integrated circuit)*, ORDINAT *(circuit imprimé)* PC *(printed circuit)*, PHYSIQUE *(circuit intégré)* IC *(integrated circuit)*, PHYSIQUE *(circuit imprimé)* PC *(printed circuit)*, TELECOM *(circuit intégré)* IC *(integrated circuit)*, TELECOM *(circuit imprimé)* PC *(printed circuit)*, TV *(circuit intégré)* IC *(integrated circuit)*, TV *(circuit imprimé)* PC *(printed circuit)*

cible *f* ESPACE, PHYS PART, TV target; ~ **d'absorption totale** *f* PHYS RAYON total absorption target; ~ **creuse** *f* NUCLEAIRE hollow target; ~ **à émission secondaire** *f* ELECTRON secondary emission target; ~ **en glace** *f* NUCLEAIRE ice target; ~ **à fils** *f* PHYS RAYON wire mesh target; ~ **multiplicatrice au silicium** *f* ELECTRON silicon-intensifier target

cible-mannequin *f* MILITAIRE dummy target

cicatrice: ~ **de coulée** *f* CERAM VER casting scar

CIE *f (Commission internationale de l'éclairage)* PHYSIQUE International Commission on Illumination

ciel:[1] **à ~ ouvert** *adj* MINES open cast

ciel[2] *m* MINES *d'une mine*, PRODUCTION *d'un foyer* roof; ~ **de gorge** *m* CERAM VER throat cover

cigale: ~ **d'ancre** *f* NAUT anchor ring

ciment *m* CERAM VER cement, CHIMIE cement, glue, CONSTR cement, GEOLOGIE binder, *d'une roche sédimentaire* cement, MATERIAUX, PLAST CAOU *construction* cement; ~ **armé** *m* CONSTR reinforced concrete; ~ **à durcissement rapide** *m* CONSTR quick-setting cement, rapid-hardening cement; ~ **en vrac** *m* CONSTR bulk cement; ~ **fondu** *m* CHIMIE lumnite; ~ **de haut-fourneau** *m* CONSTR blast furnace cement; ~ **isolant** *m* REFRIG insulating cement; ~ **Portland artificiel à haute résistance aux sulfates** *m* CONSTR Portland sulfate-resisting cement (AmE), Portland sulphate-resisting cement (BrE); ~ **Portland ordinaire** *m* CONSTR ordinary Portland cement; ~ **à la pouzzolane** *m* CONSTR pozzolanic cement; ~ **à prise lente** *m* CONSTR slow-setting cement; ~ **à prise rapide** *m* CONSTR quick-setting cement, rapid-hardening cement

cimentage *m* CONSTR cementing

cimentaire *adj* CONSTR cementing

cimentation *f* CONSTR, PETR, PETROLE cementation, cementing; ~ **sous pression** *f* PETROLE squeeze

cimenter *vt* CERAM VER cement, CONSTR bed out, cement

cimenterie *f* CONSTR cement works

cimentier *m* CONSTR cement maker, cement manufacturer

cimolite *f* MINERAUX cimolite

cinabre *m* CHIMIE, MINERAUX cinnabar, MINES mercury ore

cinchonidine *f* CHIMIE cinchonidine

cinchonine *f* CHIMIE cinchonia, cinchonin

cinchonique *adj* CHIMIE *acide* quinic

cinéaste *m* CINEMAT cinematographer, film-maker; ~ **indépendant** *m* CINEMAT independent film-maker; ~ **pigiste** *m* CINEMAT independent film-maker

Cinémascope *m* (MD) CINEMAT Cinemascope (TM)

cinématique *f* MECANIQUE, PHYSIQUE kinematics

cinématographier *vt* CINEMAT film

cinémodérivomètre *m* AERONAUT drift indicator

cinémomètre *m* PHYSIQUE tachometer; ~ **radar** *m* TRANSPORT road traffic radar

cinéol *m* CHIMIE cineol

cinéolique *adj* CHIMIE cineolic

cinéradiographie *f* CINEMAT X-ray cinematography, cineradiography

Cinérama *m* (MD) CINEMAT Cinerama (TM)

cinérite *f* GEOLOGIE flinty ash, vitric tuff

cinétique[1] *adj* ESPACE kinetic

cinétique[2] *f* CHIMIE, GAZ, MATERIAUX, MECANIQUE, METALL, NUCLEAIRE, PHYSIQUE kinetics; ~ **des gaz** *f* THERMODYN gas kinetics; ~ **de réaction** *f* MATERIAUX reaction kinetics

cinnamate *m* CHIMIE cinnamate; ~ **de benzyle** *m* AGRO ALIM benzyl cinnamate; ~ **d'éthyle** *m* AGRO ALIM ethyl cinnamate; ~ **éthylique** *m* AGRO ALIM ethyl cinnamate

cinnamique *adj* CHIMIE cinnamic

cinnamyle *m* CHIMIE cinnamyle

cinnoline *f* CHIMIE cinnoline

cinquième: ~ **génération** *f* INFORMAT, ORDINAT fifth generation

cintrage *m* CONSTR *du toit* arching, IMPRIM *papier* curl, PHOTO *des pellicules photographiques* buckling; ~ **à froid** *m* MECANIQUE cold bending

cintre:[1] **en** ~ *adj* CONSTR arched

cintre[2] *m* CONS MECA former, CONSTR arch, center (AmE), centering (AmE), centre (BrE), centring (BrE), *d'une voûte* curve; ~ **de lancement** *m* CONSTR launching gantry

cintré *adj* CONSTR arched

cintrer *vt* CONSTR arch, *un tuyau* bend, *une pièce de bois* bend, MINES arch, PRODUCTION bend

cintreur: ~ **à tubes** *m* CONSTR pipe bender

cintreuse *f* CH DE FER rail-bending machine, CONS MECA bending press

cipolin *m* GEOLOGIE patterned marble

circlip *m* MECANIQUE circlip

circonférence *f* GEOMETRIE circumference; ~ **primitive** *f* CONS MECA pitch circumference

circonscription *f* CONSTR area, TELECOM local exchange area; ~ **administrative** *f* CONSTR administrative area

circonscrire *vt* GEOMETRIE circumscribe

circuit:[1] **en** ~ *adj* ELECTR connected; **en** ~ **ouvert** *adj* PHYSIQUE open circuit

circuit[2] *m* ELECTR, ELECTRON, ORDINAT circuit, PHYSIQUE circuit, network;
en ~ *m* ELECTR in circuit *(cct)* TELECOM circuit;

▪ a ~ **d'absorption** *m* ELECTR absorption circuit, suction circuit, *relais* spark absorber; ~ **d'accès** *m* TELECOM access circuit; ~ **d'accord** *m* ELECTRON, ELECTROTEC, TELECOM tuning circuit; ~ **à accord décalé** *m* ELECTRON double-tuned circuit; ~ **accordé** *m* ELECTRON, PHYSIQUE tuned circuit; ~ **actif** *m* PHYSIQUE active circuit; ~ **additionneur** *m* ELECTR adding network; ~ **d'air comprimé** *m* AERONAUT pressure air system; ~ **d'alarme** *m* TELECOM alarm circuit; ~ **d'alimentation** *m* ELECTR feed circuit, ELECTROTEC power supply circuit, ESPACE feed system; ~ **d'allumage** *m* ESPACE *pyrotechnie* ignition circuit, PHOTO triggering circuit; ~ **d'amortissement** *m* ELECTROTEC snubber circuit; ~ **amplifié** *m* TELECOM amplified circuit; ~ **analogique** *m* ELECTRON analog circuit (AmE), analogue circuit (BrE), linear circuit, ELECTROTEC, TELECOM analog circuit (AmE), analogue circuit (BrE); ~ **d'annulation de la suppression** *m* TV unblanking circuit; ~ **de l'anode** *m* ELECTROTEC anode circuit; ~ **anodique** *m* ELECTROTEC anode circuit, plate circuit; ~ **à anticoïncidence** *m* PHYSIQUE anticoincidence circuit; ~ **antirésonnant** *m* ELECTRON, PHYSIQUE antiresonant circuit; ~ **arithmétique** *m* ELECTRON arithmetic circuit; ~ **d'arrêt à distance** *m* PRODUCTION *automatisme industriel* remote shutdown circuit; ~ **d'arrêt de la machine** *m* PRODUCTION machine shutdown circuit; ~ **d'asservissement** *m* CINEMAT servoloop; ~ **astable** *m* ELECTRON astable circuit; ~ **asymétrique** *m* ELECTR asymmetric circuit, asymmetrical circuit; ~ **asynchrone** *m* ORDINAT, TELECOM asynchronous circuit; ~ **d'attaque de ligne** *m* INFORMAT line driver; ~ **d'attente** *m* AERONAUT holding pattern, holding stack; ~ **d'attente en hippodrome** *m* AERONAUT racetrack holding pattern; ~ **d'attente en vol** *m* AERONAUT flight holding pattern; ~ **d'augmentation de la pente** *m* TV peaking circuit; ~ **autoélévateur** *m* TV bootstrap;

▪ b ~ **de balayage linéaire** *m* TV sweep circuit; ~ **à bande étroite** *m* ELECTRON narrow band circuit; ~ **basculant** *m* TV dumping circuit; ~ **binaire** *m* ELECTRON binary circuit; ~ **bipolaire** *m* ELECTRON bipolar integrated circuit; ~ **bistable** *m* ELECTRON bistable circuit; ~ **bouchon** *m* AERONAUT, PHYSIQUE antiresonant circuit; ~ **bouclé** *m* ELECTR, ELECTROTEC ring circuit (AmE), ring main (BrE); ~ **des boues** *m* PETROLE mud system; ~ **de Burgers** *m* METALL Burgers circuit;

▪ c ~ **cadencé** *m* ELECTRON clocked circuit; ~ **carburant** *m* AERONAUT fuel system; ~ **cathodique** *m* ELECTROTEC cathode circuit; ~ **CCD** *m* (*CCD*) ASTRONOMIE, ELECTRON, ELECTROTEC, ORDINAT, PHYSIQUE, TELECOM, TV charge-coupled device (*CCD*); ~ **de champ** *m* ELECTR *machine* field circuit; ~

de charge *m* ELECTR *accumulateur* charging circuit, TELECOM load circuit; ~ de chauffage *m* MAT CHAUFF heating circuit; ~ de circulation du gaz *m* NUCLEAIRE gas circulation loop; ~ de clamp *m* TV clamping circuit; ~ cloche *m* TV Gaussian circuit; ~ codeur *m* PRODUCTION encoder; ~ à coïncidence *m* ELECTRON, PHYSIQUE coincidence circuit; ~ combinateur *m* TELECOM, TV combining circuit; ~ combinatoire *m* ELECTRON, ORDINAT combinational circuit (AmE), combinatorial circuit (BrE), TELECOM combining circuit; ~ de commande *m* CINEMAT control circuit, COMMANDE control circuit, signal circuit, ELECTR, ORDINAT, TELECOM control circuit; ~ à commande unique *m* ELECTROTEC ganged circuit, single drive circuit, TV ganged circuit; ~ de commutation *m* ELECTROTEC switching circuit; ~ commuté *m* TELECOM switched circuit; ~ comparateur *m* ELECTRON comparator circuit; ~ compensateur *m* TV corrector circuit; ~ de compensation *m* ELECTR compensating circuit, ELECTROTEC adjusting circuit, TELECOM compensation circuit; ~ de compensation de câble *m* TV cable compensation circuit; ~ de comptage *m* ELECTRON counter circuit; ~ conformateur *m* TV squaring circuit; ~ de connexion *m* TELECOM junctor, trunk; ~ de connexion local *m* TELECOM intraoffice junctor circuit (AmE), own-exchange supervisory circuit; ~ à constantes localisées *m* ELECTROTEC lumped element circuit; ~ à constantes réparties *m* ELECTROTEC distributed element circuit; ~ de contrôle *m* ELECTR, REFRIG control circuit; ~ de convergence *m* TV convergence circuit; ~ correcteur *m* TV corrector circuit; ~ correcteur de distorsion *m* TV equalizer; ~ de correction *m* ELECTRON peaking circuit; ~ couplé *m* ELECTR, ELECTROTEC coupled circuit; ~ de courant alternatif *m* ELECTR alternating current circuit; ~ à courant alternatif *m* ELECTROTEC AC circuit; ~ à courant continu *m* ELECTROTEC DC circuit; ~ à courant de Foucault *m* ELECTR eddy current circuit;

~ d ~ de décharge *m* ELECTROTEC discharge circuit; ~ de déclenchement *m* ELECTR trigger circuit, trip circuit, ELECTRON, ESSAIS, PHYSIQUE trigger circuit; ~ déclencheur de trame *m* TV field gating circuit; ~ défectueux *m* NUCLEAIRE failed circuit, failed loop; ~ de démarrage *m* TELECOM startup circuit; ~ de départ *m* ELECTR leading-out wire, outgoing circuit; ~ de dérivation *m* PRODUCTION *automatisme industriel* branch circuit; ~ de dérivation de moteur *m* PRODUCTION *automatisme industriel* motor branch circuit; ~ dérivé *m* ELECTR, ELECTROTEC derived circuit; ~ de détection *m* ELECTRON detector circuit; ~ de détection d'incendie *m* NAUT fire detection system; ~ à deux fils *m* ELECTR, INFORMAT, ORDINAT two-wire circuit; ~ différentiateur *m* ELECTRON differentiating circuit; ~ de différentiation *m* TV peaking network; ~ diviseur *m* ELECTRON dividing circuit, scaler, scaling circuit; ~ à double sens *m* TELECOM both-way circuit;

~ e ~ d'eau *m* NAUT water system; ~ échantillonneur *m* ELECTROTEC sample-and-hold circuit; ~ d'échappement moteur *m* NAUT engine exhaust system; ~ d'éclairage *m* ELECTR lighting circuit; ~ d'écrêtage *m* ELECTRON clipper circuit, TV amplitude limiter circuit; ~ électrique *m* ELECTR electric circuit, ELECTRON, TELECOM electrical circuit; ~ électronique *m* ELECTRON, TELECOM electronic circuit; ~ enchaîné *m* ELECTR linked circuit; ~ d'enclenchement *m* ELECTROTEC interlock circuit; ~ en dérivation *m* ELECTR derived

circuit, ELECTROTEC derived circuit, shunt circuit; ~ en parallèle *m* MINES, TELECOM parallel circuit; ~ en pont *m* ELECTROTEC bridge circuit; ~ de l'enroulement secondaire *m* ELECTROTEC secondary circuit; ~ en séries parallèles *m* MINES series-parallel circuit; ~ entièrement personnalisé *m* ELECTRON full custom circuit; ~ entrant *m* TELECOM incoming circuit; ~ d'entrée *m* ELECTR, ELECTROTEC input circuit; ~ d'entrée à TEC *m* ELECTRON FET front end; ~ équivalent *m* ELECTR, PHYSIQUE equivalent circuit; ~ ET *m* ELECTRON AND circuit; ~ ET inclusif *m* ELECTRON inclusive AND circuit; ~ d'évacuation de la chaleur *m* NUCLEAIRE heat removal loop; ~ d'excitation *m* ELECTROTEC energizing circuit, excitation circuit; ~ extérieur *m* ELECTR external circuit;

~ f ~ fantôme *m* ELECTROTEC, TELECOM phantom circuit; ~ fermé *m* CHARBON, CONS MECA closed circuit, ELECTR closed circuit, closed loop, ELECTROTEC, PHYSIQUE closed circuit; ~ fermé d'usagers *m* INFORMAT, ORDINAT closed user group; ~ ferrorésonnant *m* ELECTROTEC ferroresonance circuit; ~ de filtrage RC *m* ELECTRON RC filter-circuit; ~ de fixation de niveau *m* ELECTRON clamping circuit; ~ fixe aéronautique *m* AERONAUT aeronautical fixed circuit; ~ de freinage *m* CONS MECA brake system; ~ de freinage double circuit *m* AUTO L-split system;

~ g ~ de garde *m* ELECTROTEC guard circuit; ~ gaussien *m* TV Gaussian circuit; ~ gaz *m* MAT CHAUFF gas circuit; ~ géothermique *m* EN RENOUV geothermal circuit; ~ de graissage *m* CONS MECA lubricating system;

~ h ~ à haut débit *m* TELECOM megastream circuit; ~ à haut débit par satellite *m* TELECOM Satstream circuit (TM); ~ d'horloge *m* ELECTRON clock circuit; ~ hybride *m* ELECTRON, PHYSIQUE hybrid circuit; ~ hybride à couches épaisses *m* ELECTRON thick-film hybrid circuit; ~ hybride à couches minces *m* ELECTRON thin-film hybrid circuit; ~ hybride hyperfréquence *m* ELECTRON MIC, microwave integrated circuit; ~ hybride optique *m* ELECTRON optical hybrid circuit; ~ hybride à puces nues connectées par fils *m* ELECTRON chip-and-wire hybrid circuit; ~ hybride simple *m* ELECTRON simple hybrid circuit; ~ hydraulique *m* AUTO, INST HYDR hydraulic system; ~ hyperfréquence *m* ELECTRON microwave circuit;

~ i ~ imprimé *m* ELECTRON printed wiring, ELECTRON *(CI)*, INFORMAT *(CI)*, ORDINAT *(CI)*, PHYSIQUE *(CI)*, TELECOM *(CI)*, TV *(CI)* printed circuit *(PC)*; ~ imprimé double face *m* ELECTRON double-sided printed circuit; ~ imprimé haute fréquence *m* ELECTRON high-frequency printed circuit; ~ imprimé hyperfréquence *m* ELECTRON microwave printed circuit; ~ imprimé multicouche *m* ELECTRON, TELECOM multilayer printed circuit; ~ imprimé au polyimide *m* ELECTRON polyimide printed circuit; ~ imprimé à rubans étroits *m* ELECTRON fine line printed circuit; ~ imprimé simple face *m* ELECTRON single-sided printed circuit; ~ imprimé souple *m* ELECTRON flexible printed circuit; ~ imprimé à substrat souple *m* ELECTRON flexible printed circuit; ~ à impulsion *m* ELECTRON, ELECTROTEC pulse circuit; ~ incorporé *m* ELECTRON on-chip circuit; ~ inducteur *m* ELECTR inductive circuit, primary circuit; ~ d'induit *m* ELECTR *machine* armature circuit; ~ intégrateur *m* ELECTROTEC integrating circuit; ~ à intégration à échelle moyenne *m* TELECOM MSI circuit; ~ intégré *m* ELECTR, ELECTRON, ORDINAT,

PHYSIQUE integrated circuit, TELECOM chip, TELECOM, TV integrated circuit; ~ **intégré analogique** m ELECTRON analog integrated circuit (AmE), analogue integrated circuit (BrE), linear integrated circuit; ~ **intégré bipolaire** m ELECTRON, ORDINAT bipolar integrated circuit; ~ **intégré bipolaire analogique** m ELECTRON analog bipolar integrated circuit (AmE), analogue bipolar integrated circuit (BrE); ~ **intégré bipolaire Schottky** m ELECTRON Schottky bipolar integrated circuit; ~ **intégré bipolaire au silicium** m ELECTRON silicon bipolar integrated circuit; ~ **intégré CMOS à grilles métalliques** m ELECTRON metal gate CMOS integrated circuit; ~ **intégré à couche épaisse** m TELECOM thick-layer integrated circuit; ~ **intégré électronique** m ELECTRON electronic integrated circuit; ~ **intégré à grande échelle** m PHYSIQUE large-scale integrated circuit, TELECOM large-scale integration circuit; ~ **intégré Hall** m AUTO Hall integrated circuit; ~ **intégré à haute densité** m ELECTRON high-density integrated circuit; ~ **intégré hybride** m ELECTRON, TELECOM hybrid integrated circuit; ~ **intégré hyperfréquence actif** m ELECTRON active microwave integrated circuit; ~ **intégré logique** m ELECTRON logic integrated circuit, TELECOM integrated office system; ~ **intégré micro-onde** m PHYSIQUE MIC, microwave integrated circuit; ~ **intégré monolithique** m ELECTRON monolithic integrated circuit; ~ **intégré monolithique micro-ondes** m PHYSIQUE MMIC, monolithic microwave integrated circuit; ~ **intégré monolithique à semi-conducteurs** m TELECOM monolithic integrated circuit; ~ **intégré NMOS** m ELECTRON NMOS integrated circuit; ~ **intégré numérique** m ELECTRON digital integrated circuit; ~ **intégré optique** m ELECTRON optical integrated circuit, OPTIQUE, TELECOM IOC, integrated optical circuit; ~ **intégré optique monomode** m ELECTRON single-mode optical integrated circuit; ~ **intégré planar** m ELECTRON planar integrated circuit; ~ **intégré à semi-conducteur** m ELECTRON semiconductor integrated circuit; ~ **intégré au silicium** m ELECTRON silicon-integrated circuit; ~ **intégré à très grande échelle** m PHYSIQUE very large-scale integrated circuit; ~ **intégré tridimensionnel** m ELECTRON three-dimensional integrated circuit; ~ **intégré de type planar** m ELECTRON planar integrated circuit; ~ **intégré unipolaire** m ELECTRON unipolar integrated circuit; ~ **d'interface** m ELECTRON, TELECOM interface circuit; ~ **intermédiaire** m TV buffer; ~ **inverseur de phase** m ELECTR à courant alternatif-continu phase inverter; ~ **inverseur à semi-conducteurs** m ELECTR semiverter;

~ j ~ **de jonction** m TELECOM trunk;

~ l ~ **à large bande** m TELECOM wide band circuit; ~ **de ligne** m TELECOM line circuit; ~ **linéaire** m ELECTR, ELECTRON, TELECOM linear circuit; ~ **de lissage** m ELECTR smoothing circuit; ~ **logique** m ELECTRON, INFORMAT, ORDINAT, TELECOM logic circuit; ~ **logique combinatoire** m ELECTRON combinatorial circuit; ~ **logique intégré** m ELECTRON integrated logic circuit; ~ **logique MOS** m ELECTRON MOS logic circuit, metal-oxide semiconductor logic circuit; ~ **logique optique** m ELECTRON optical logic circuit; ~ **logique programmable** m INFORMAT, ORDINAT PAL, programmable array logic, TELECOM programmable logic circuit; ~ **LSI** m PHYSIQUE, TELECOM LSI circuit, large-scale integration circuit;

~ m ~ **magnétique** m ELECTR magnetic circuit, ma-chine électrique, transformateur core, ELECTROTEC, ESPACE véhicules, PHYSIQUE magnetic circuit; ~ **matriciel** m TELECOM matrix circuit; ~ **mélangeur** m ELECTRON combiner circuit, TV adder; ~ **mélangeur pour le bleu** m TV blue adder; ~ **mélangeur pour le rouge** m TV red adder; ~ **mélangeur pour le vert** m TV green adder; ~ **de mémoire** m TELECOM memory circuit; ~ **métallique** m ELECTROTEC metallic circuit; ~ **micronique** m ELECTRON micron circuit; ~ **de mise au point** m COMMANDE adjustment circuit, regulator circuit; ~ **mixte** m TELECOM both-way circuit; ~ **monolithique** m ELECTRON monolithic integrated circuit; ~ **monostable** m ELECTRON one-shot circuit; ~ **MOS à grille métallique et oxyde secondaire** m ELECTRON thick oxide metal gate MOS circuit; ~ **moyen débit** m TELECOM kilostream circuit; ~ **MSI** m TELECOM MSI circuit; ~ **multiétage** m TELECOM multistage circuit; ~ **de multiplexage** m PRODUCTION automatisme industriel multiplex circuit;

~ n ~ **NI** m ELECTRON NOR circuit; ~ **NI exclusif** m ELECTRON exclusive NOR circuit; ~ **NON** m ELECTRON NOT circuit; ~ **NON-ET** m ELECTRON NAND circuit; ~ **non-inductif** m ELECTR noninductive circuit; ~ **non-linéaire** m TELECOM nonlinear circuit; ~ **non réciproque** m TELECOM nonreciprocal circuit; ~ **numérique** m ELECTRON, INFORMAT, ORDINAT, TELECOM digital circuit; ~ **numérique de synchronisation** m TV digital framer;

~ o ~ **optique** m ELECTRON optical integrated circuit; ~ **d'optique intégré** m OPTIQUE, TELECOM IOC, integrated optical circuit; ~ **optoélectronique** m ELECTRON optical integrated circuit; ~ **optoélectronique intégré** m TELECOM integrated optoelectronic circuit; ~ **d'ordres** m TV talkback circuit; ~ **oscillant** m ELECTR oscillating circuit, ELECTRON resonant circuit, TV oscillating circuit; ~ **oscillant parallèle** m ELECTRON parallel resonant circuit; ~ **OU** m ELECTRON OR circuit; ~ **OU exclusif** m ELECTRON exclusive OR circuit; ~ **OU inclusif** m ELECTRON inclusive OR circuit; ~ **ouvert** m CHARBON open circuit, ELECTR open circuit, open loop, ELECTROTEC broken circuit, open circuit, PHYSIQUE, PRODUCTION open circuit;

~ p ~ **parallèle** m ELECTR, TELECOM parallel circuit; ~ **de parole** m TELECOM speech circuit; ~ **passif** m PHYSIQUE, TELECOM passive circuit; ~ **physique** m ELECTROTEC physical circuit; ~ **de polarisation** m ELECTROTEC bias circuit; ~ **polyphasé** m ELECTR à courant alternatif polyphase circuit; ~ **prédiffusé** m INFORMAT, ORDINAT, TELECOM gate array; ~ **primaire** m ELECTR primary circuit; ~ **principal** m ELECTR réseau main circuit; ~ **protecteur** m ELECTR protective circuit; ~ **de protection** m ELECTROTEC ballasting circuit, protection circuit, shutdown circuit, TELECOM protection circuit; ~ **de puissance** m ELECTR power circuit; ~ **push-pull** m ENREGISTR push-pull circuit;

~ q ~ **de quantification** m ELECTRON quantizer; ~ **quatre fils** m INFORMAT, ORDINAT four-wire circuit;

~ r ~ **de rayonnement** m TV radiating circuit; ~ **de réactance** m ELECTR choke circuit, reactance circuit; ~ **à réactance** m ELECTROTEC reactive circuit; ~ **réactif** m ELECTROTEC reactive circuit; ~ **de réaction** m COMMANDE, TV feedback circuit; ~ **réalisé sur la carte** m ELECTRON on-board circuitry; ~ **réalisé sur la puce** m ELECTRON on-chip circuit; ~ **réciproque** m TELECOM reciprocal circuit; ~ **de recoupement** m ENREGISTR crossover network; ~ **de redressement** m ELECTROTEC rectifying circuit; ~ **réel** m ELECTROTEC side circuit; ~

du **réfrigérant** *m* REFRIG refrigerant circuit; **~ de réfrigération** *m* REFRIG refrigerating circuit; **~ de refroidissement** *m* AUTO cooling system; **~ de refroidissement moteur** *m* NAUT engine cooling system; **~ de refroidissement à réservoir d'expansion** *m* AUTO closed and sealed cooling system; **~ de refroidissement de saumure** *m* NUCLEAIRE *système* brine cooling system; **~ de réglage** *m* COMMANDE regulator circuit; **~ de régularisation** *m* CINEMAT servoloop; **~ de régulation** *m* TRANSPORT closed-loop traffic control system, TV servoloop; **~ résistif** *m* ELECTROTEC, TELECOM resistive circuit; **~ de résonance** *m* ELECTR *induction* acceptor circuit; **~ résonnant** *m* ELECTRON, PHYSIQUE, TELECOM resonant circuit; **~ résonnant parallèle** *m* ELECTRON parallel resonant circuit; **~ résonnant série** *m* ELECTROTEC series resonant circuit; **~ à retard** *m* ELECTR delay circuit, ELECTRON delay circuit, time-delay circuit, TV delay circuit; **~ de retour** *m* ELECTR return conductor, return wire, ELECTROTEC return circuit; **~ de retour vidéo** *m* TV video feedback circuit;

~ s **~ sans perte** *m* TELECOM zero loss circuit; **~ secondaire** *m* ELECTROTEC secondary circuit; **~ de secours** *m* AERONAUT emergency system, PRODUCTION backup circuit; **~ semi-personnalisé** *m* ELECTRON semicustom circuit; **~ série** *m* ELECTROTEC, MINES, TELECOM series circuit; **~ série-parallèle** *m* ELECTROTEC series-parallel circuit; **~ sortant** *m* TELECOM outgoing circuit; **~ de sortie** *m* ELECTROTEC, TELECOM output circuit; **~ de sortie en court-circuit** *m* PRODUCTION shorted output circuit; **~ de soudage** *m* CONSTR welding circuit; **~ souple** *m* ELECTRON flexible printed circuit; **~ sous forme intégrée** *m* ELECTRON integrated circuitry; **~ sous tension** *m* ELECTROTEC live circuit; **~ spécifique à une application** *m* ORDINAT ASIC, application-specific integrated circuit; **~ de suppression** *m* TV blanking circuit; **~ symétrique** *m* ENREGISTR balanced circuit; **~ synchrone** *m* TELECOM synchronous circuit;

~ t **~ tampon** *m* ELECTRON buffer circuit; **~ de tarage** *m* ELECTR bucking circuit; **~ de télécommunications** *m* ELECTROTEC communications circuit; **~ de temporisation** *m* ELECTRON time-delay circuit; **~ à thermistance** *m* PRODUCTION *automatisme industriel* thermistor circuit; **~ de tir** *m* MINES firing circuit, shot-firing circuit; **~ total** *m* ELECTR full circuit; **~ de trafic** *m* TELECOM traffic circuit; **~ de traitement de matières fertiles** *m* NUCLEAIRE blanket reprocessing circuit; **~ à très bas niveau** *m* ELECTROTEC dry circuit; **~ à très grande intégration** *m* TELECOM VLSI circuit, very large-scale integration circuit; **~ triphasé** *m* TELECOM three-phase circuit; **~ de tri de signaux** *m* TV separation circuit;

~ u **~ ULSI** *m* TELECOM ultra large scale integration circuit; **~ utilisateur** *m* ELECTR load circuit; **~ d'utilisation** *m* ELECTR load circuit;

~ v **~ de ventilation moteur** *m* NAUT engine ventilation system; **~ de verrouillage** *m* PRODUCTION *automatisme industriel* latch circuit, TV clamping circuit; **~ de vidange** *m* ESPACE *véhicules* fuel dumping system; **~ de vide-vite** *m* ESPACE *véhicules* fuel dumping system; **~ virtuel** *m* INFORMAT, ORDINAT, TELECOM virtual circuit; **~ virtuel commuté** *m* TELECOM SVC, switched virtual circuit; **~ virtuel permanent** *m* INFORMAT, ORDINAT, TELECOM PVC, permanent virtual circuit; **~ virtuel sur canal D** *m* TELECOM D-channel virtual circuit; **~ VLSI** *m* TELECOM VLSI circuit, very large-scale circuit; **~ de voie** *m* CH DE FER track circuit

circuitage: **~ électrique** *m* ELECTROTEC electric wiring

circuit-pilote *m* COMMANDE control circuit, signal circuit

circuits: **à ~ intégrés** *adj* ORDINAT solid-state

circulaire: **~ d'information aéronautique** *f* AERONAUT aeronautical information circular; **~ de pointage** *f* MILITAIRE *artillerie* training rack

circularisation *f* ESPACE *d'une orbite* circularization

circulariser *vt* ESPACE *une orbite* circularize

circulateur *m* ESPACE *communications*, TELECOM circulator; **~ à effet Faraday** *m* ELECTROTEC Faraday circulator; **~ à hyperfréquences** *m* TELECOM microwave circulator; **~ optique** *m* TELECOM optical circulator

circulation *f* CONSTR traffic flow, DISTRI EAU circulation, INFORMAT flow, PETROLE *boues de forage* circulation, PHYSIQUE circulation, flow, TRANSPORT traffic flow, traffic, VEHICULES traffic; **~ anticyclonique** *f* METEO anticyclonic circulation; **~ arrêtée** *f* TRANSPORT stationary traffic; **~ atmosphérique** *f* METEO general atmospheric circulation; **~ de boue** *f* PETR mud circulation; **~ à contre-voie** *f* CH DE FER running on wrong line, wrong direction running; **~ cyclonique** *f* METEO cyclonic circulation; **~ en mouvement** *f* TRANSPORT moving traffic; **~ en navette** *f* TRANSPORT shuttle traffic; **~ forcée** *f* MAT CHAUFF fanned circulation; **~ de l'information** *f* INFORMAT, ORDINAT information flow; **~ locale** *f* CONSTR local traffic; **~ de matériel** *f* EMBALLAGE material flow; **~ perdue** *f* PETR lost circulation, PETROLE *forage* loss of returns, lost circulation; **~ des poids lourds** *f* TRANSPORT heavy freight vehicle traffic (AmE), heavy goods vehicle traffic (BrE); **~ routière** *f* TRANSPORT road traffic; **~ à la surface** *f* AERONAUT taxiing; **~ tourbillonaire** *f* METEO vorticity; **~ à voie unique** *f* CH DE FER single line working

circuler *vi* INFORMAT, ORDINAT, PHYSIQUE flow; **~ en sens opposés** *vi* PHYS PART *faisceaux* circulate in opposite directions

circumnavigation *f* TRANSPORT circumnavigation

circumpolaire *adj* TRANSPORT circumpolar

CIRD *abrév* (*code d'identification de réseau de données*) TELECOM DNIC (*data network identification code*)

cire *f* IMPRIM wax; **~ de carnauba** *f* AGRO ALIM carnauba wax; **~ d'enduction** *f* REVETEMENT coating wax; **~ à enduire** *f* REVETEMENT coating wax; **~ d'enrobage** *f* REVETEMENT coating wax; **~ à imprégner** *f* EMBALLAGE impregnating wax; **~ isolante** *f* ELECTROTEC insulating wax; **~ microcristalline** *f* PETROLE microcrystalline wax; **~ de paraffine** *f* CHIMIE, ELECTR *isolateur* paraffin wax; **~ perdue** *f* CERAM VER lost wax; **~ de pétrole** *f* PETROLE *raffinage* petroleum wax

ciré *m* NAUT foul weather gear, oilskin

cirer *vt* REVETEMENT coat

cirro-cumulus *m* (*Cc*) METEO cirrocumulus (*Cc*)

cirrolite *f* MINERAUX cirrolite

cirro-stratus *m* (*Cs*) METEO cirrostratus (*Cs*)

cirrus *m* (*Ci*) METEO cirrus (*Ci*); **~ infrarouge** *m* ASTRONOMIE infrared cirrus

CIRT *abrév* (*code d'identification de réseau télex*) TELECOM telex network identification code

cis *adj* CHIMIE *forme d'un composé* cis

cisaille *f* CONS MECA shear, MECANIQUE *outillage* shears, PHOTO trimmer; **~ à barres** *f* CONS MECA bar shear; **~ à billettes** *f* CONS MECA billet shears; **~ à blooms** *f* CONS MECA bloom shears; **~ de câble de treuil** *f* AERONAUT hoist cable cutter; **~ à guillotine** *f* MECANIQUE *outillage* guillotine shears, PRODUCTION guillotine, guillotine shears, SECURITE guillotine; ~ **de mise à longuer des barres** f CONS MECA bar shears; ~ **pour feuilles** f EMBALLAGE sheet cutting machine

cisaille-déchiqueteuse f PHOTO jagged edge trimmer

cisaillement m CONS MECA shearing, slide, *résistance des matériaux* shear, GEOLOGIE shear, shearing, wrench fault, MATERIAUX shearing, MECANIQUE shear, PAPIER shearing effect, PHYSIQUE, PLAST CAOU *rhéologie* shear; ~ **critique** m METALL critical shear strain; ~ **horizontal du vent** m AERONAUT horizontal wind shear; ~ **de maclage** m METALL twinning shear; ~ **simple** m CONS MECA *résistance des matériaux* single shear; ~ **de vent** m METEO wind shear

cisailler vt CONS MECA shear, PRODUCTION clip; ~ **à froid** vt CONS MECA cold-shear

cisailles f pl CONS MECA shear, shearing machine, shears; ~ **à anneaux** f pl CONS MECA ring shears; ~ **à brames** f pl PRODUCTION slab shears; ~ **chantourneuses** f pl CONS MECA scroll shears; ~ **d'établi** f pl CONSTR bench shears; ~ **de ferblantier** f pl PRODUCTION tinman's shears, tinman's snips; ~ **à goupilles** f pl CONSTR pin shears; ~ **grignotantes** f pl CONS MECA nibbler; ~ **à levier à contrepoids** f pl PRODUCTION lever shearing machine with counterweight; ~ **à main** f pl PRODUCTION hand shears; ~ **à métaux** f pl PRODUCTION metal shears; ~ **passe-franc** f pl CONS MECA panel shears; ~ **à tôles** f pl CONS MECA plate shears; ~ **universelles** f CONS MECA universal shears

ciseau m CONSTR, MINES, PRODUCTION chisel; ~ **automatique** m ENREGISTR tape splicer; ~ **bédane** m CONSTR mortise chisel; ~ **biseauté** m CONS MECA beveled chisel (AmE), bevelled chisel (BrE); ~ **à la charrue** m CONSTR bolster; ~ **de deux chanfreins** m CONSTR double-beveled chisel (AmE), double-bevelled chisel (BrE); ~ **à froid** m CONS MECA flat chisel, flat cold chisel, PRODUCTION flat cold chisel; ~ **à gouge** m CONSTR gouge; ~ **long** m CONSTR paring chisel; ~ **qui se grippe** m CONSTR *dans une rainure* chisel which binds

ciseaux m pl CERAM VER shears, CONS MECA scissors; ~ **de couturière** m pl TEXTILE shears; ~ **à cranter** m CONS MECA pinking shears; ~ **à dissection** m pl EQUIP LAB *biologie* dissecting scissors

ciseleur m PRODUCTION chiseler (AmE), chiseller (BrE)

ciselure f PRODUCTION chiseling (AmE), chiselling (BrE)

cislunaire adj ASTRONOMIE cislunar

cission f PHYSIQUE shear; ~ **réduite** f METALL resolved shear stress; ~ **résolue** f METALL resolved shear stress

cis-trans adj CHIMIE cis-trans

citation f BREVETS citation, IMPRIM quotation

citer vt BREVETS cite

citerne f CONSTR tank, DISTRI EAU cistern, water tank, ESPACE, MECANIQUE, PRODUCTION tank; ~ **de cargaison** f POLLUTION cargo tank; ~ **de dégraissage** f AGRO ALIM degreasing tank; ~ **de livraison** f PRODUCTION delivery tanker; ~ **souple flottante** f POLLU MER dracone, floating flexible tank; ~ **de stockage** f POLLUTION, PRODUCTION *système hydraulique* storage tank

citral m CHIMIE citral

citrate m CHIMIE citrate

citrine f MINERAUX citrine, citrine quartz, false topaz

citrique adj CHIMIE citric

citronellal m CHIMIE citronellal

citronyle f CHIMIE citronyl

citrulline f CHIMIE citrulline

civettone f CHIMIE civetone

civière f SECURITE stretcher

Cl *(chlore)* CHIMIE Cl *(chlorine)*

CL50 abrév *(concentration létale à 50%)* POLLUTION median lethal concentration

claie f HYDROLOGIE *électricité* grid, PRODUCTION screen

claim m MINES claim; ~ **minier** m MINES mining claim, mining concession

clair[1] adj GEOLOGIE light-colored (AmE), light-coloured (BrE); **en** ~ adj TELECOM uncoded

clair:[2] ~ **de lune** m ASTRONOMIE moonlight; ~ **de Terre** m ASTRONOMIE, ESPACE *astronomie* earthshine

claire f OCEANO claire, oyster bed, oyster fattening pond; ~ **de coupelle** f CHIMIE bone ash; ~ **soudure** f ELECTR *raccordement* soft solder

claire-voie f CONSTR paling, NAUT skylight

clairières f pl CERAM VER thin ware

clair-obscur m CINEMAT chiaroscuro

clameau m PRODUCTION dog iron

clameaux m pl CONS MECA clamp, CONSTR cramp, cramp iron, joint cramp, PRODUCTION clamp

clamp m TV clamping

clampe f CONS MECA clamp, CONSTR cramp, cramp iron, joint cramp, timber dogs, PRODUCTION clamp

clamping: ~ **sur le palier arrière** m TV back porch clamping

clap m CINEMAT clapper board, slate, ENREGISTR clapper; ~ **à l'envers** m CINEMAT upside down slate; ~ **micro** m CINEMAT mike tap

clapet m CONS MECA clack, clack valve, flap valve, INST HYDR clack valve, clapper valve, deflecting valve, delivery valve, drop valve gear, flap valve, valve, MINES, PETROLE *raffinerie*, PHYSIQUE valve, PRODUCTION *système hydraulique* poppet; ~ **d'admission** m INST HYDR inlet valve, relief valve; ~ **d'aérosol** m EMBALLAGE aerosol valve; ~ **d'air** m CONS MECA air valve; ~ **anti-retour** m CONS MECA, ESPACE *véhicules* check valve, INST HYDR nonreturn valve, MECANIQUE check valve; ~ **anti-retour piloté** m PRODUCTION *système hydraulique* pilot-operated check valve; ~ **d'appel d'air** m INST HYDR relief valve; ~ **d'aspiration** m AUTO, INST HYDR suction valve; ~ **d'aspiration d'air** m CONS MECA air sniffing valve; ~ **à bille** m CONS MECA ball valve, INST HYDR ball valve, globe valve; ~ **à charnière** m INST HYDR leaf valve; ~ **commandé** m AERONAUT lockout valve; ~ **coupe-feu** m CHAUFFAGE *protection contre les incendies* fire damper; ~ **de décharge** m AUTO relief valve, CONS MECA discharge valve, INST HYDR blow valve, discharge valve, escape valve, exhaust valve, outlet valve, relief valve, PRODUCTION *système hydraulique*, VEHICULES *lubrification* relief valve; ~ **de dépression** m CONS MECA depressurization valve; ~ **de détente** m CONS MECA auxiliary valve, INST HYDR expansion valve; ~ **d'échappement** m INST HYDR eduction valve, exhaust valve; ~ **équilibré** m INST HYDR balanced valve; ~ **d'expansion** m INST HYDR expansion valve; ~ **d'expiration** m AERONAUT exhalation valve; ~ **à flotteur** m CONS MECA float valve; ~ **de freinage** m INST HYDR retaining valve; ~ **de gonflage** m AERONAUT air charging valve; ~ **d'intercommunication d'air** m AERONAUT air cross bleed valve; ~ **d'intercommunication de carburant** m AERONAUT fuel cross feed valve; ~ **de levage** m INST HYDR lifting valve; ~ **à levier** m INST HYDR lever valve; ~ **de mise à l'air libre** m AERONAUT air vent valve; ~ **de mise**

à l'air libre étanche au carburant *m* AERONAUT air-no-fuel vent valve; **~ de non-retour** *m* CONS MECA check valve, return valve, EN RENOUV check valve, nonreturn valve, PRODUCTION nonreturn valve, VEHICULES *lubrification* check valve; **~ à opercule soulevé** *m* INST HYDR *distributeur à soupape* poppet valve; **~ de pied** *m* CONS MECA foot valve; **~ de pied d'aspiration** *m* INST HYDR suction valve; **pilote** *m* CONS MECA pilot valve; **~ plat** *m* CONS MECA clapper; **~ de pompe** *m* PETROLE pump valve; **~ de pompe à boue** *m* PETROLE mud pump valve; **~ préférentiel** *m* INST HYDR priority valve; **~ de pressurisation** *m* AERONAUT pressurizing valve; **~ prioritaire** *m* INST HYDR priority valve; **~ de purge** *m* CONS MECA bleed valve; **~ réducteur de pression** *m* INST HYDR pressure-reducing valve; **~ de refoulement** *m* AUTO outlet valve; **~ à ressort** *m* INST HYDR spring valve; **~ de retenue** *m* AUTO vacuum check valve, CONSTR nonreturn valve, DISTRI EAU check valve, INST HYDR back pressure valve, nonreturn valve, retaining valve; **~ de soupape** *m* NUCLEAIRE flap, valve flap; **~ de sûreté** *m* INST HYDR escape valve; **~ de surpression** *m* INST HYDR blow valve, pressure relief valve, relief valve; **~ taré** *m* CONS MECA calibrated valve; **~ de trop plein** *m* INST HYDR overflow valve; **~ de verrouillage** *m* PRODUCTION locking lab; **~ de vidange** *m* CONS MECA drain valve

clapiste *m* CINEMAT clapper person

clapot *m* NAUT, OCEANO choppy sea

clapotis *m* NAUT swash, OCEANO choppiness, ripple

claquage *m* ELECTR *diélectrique* breakdown, ELECTRON breakdown, punch-through, puncture, ELECTROTEC breakdown, electrical breakdown, PHYSIQUE, PLAST CAOU *électrique* breakdown, THERMODYN *appareillage* flashover; **~ destructif** *m* ELECTRON, ELECTROTEC destructive breakdown; **~ électrique** *m* ELECTROTEC electrical breakdown; **~ entre broches** *m* ELECTROTEC pin-to-pin breakdown; **~ de l'isolant** *m* ELECTROTEC insulation breakdown; **~ de la jonction émetteur-base** *m* ELECTRON emitter base breakdown; **~ d'un magnétron** *m* ELECTROTEC magnetron arcing; **~ par avalanche** *m* ELECTR *diode semi-conductrice*, ELECTRON avalanche breakdown; **~ par effet Zener** *m* ELECTRON Zener breakdown; **~ par emballement thermique** *m* ELECTRON thermal breakdown; **~ par surtension** *m* ELECTROTEC overvoltage breakdown

claque: ~ de collage *f* CINEMAT bloop

claquement *m* ACOUSTIQUE click, CONSTR backfire, PRODUCTION rattling; **~ de pales** *m* AERONAUT *hélicoptère* blade slap; **~ du piston** *m* AUTO, VEHICULES *moteur* piston slap

claquer[1] *vt* THERMODYN *appareillage* flash over

claquer[2] *vi* CRISTALL crack

claquette *f* CINEMAT clapper board, slate; **~ du début** *f* CINEMAT head slate; **~ de fin** *f* CINEMAT end slate, endboard, tail slate, upside down slate; **~ image** *f* CINEMAT camera slate, picture clap, vision clap

clarifiant *m* AGRO ALIM clarifier

clarificateur[1] *adj* CHIMIE clarifying

clarificateur[2] *m* HYDROLOGIE clarifier, settling tank

clarification *f* CHARBON, CHIMIE clarification, GENIE CHIM defecation, purification, QUALITE clarification; **~ de l'eau** *f* GENIE CHIM water purification

clarifier *vt* AGRO ALIM *beurre, liquide*, CHARBON, CHIMIE clarify, GENIE CHIM clarify, settle on, *par filtre* filter

clarite *f* MINERAUX clarite

clarkéite *f* MINERAUX clarkeite

clarté *f* DISTRI EAU *de l'eau* clearness, IMPRIM *photogravure* lightness

classe *f* BREVETS, CONS MECA, CRISTALL, INFORMAT, ORDINAT class, PRODUCTION, QUALITE *excellence technique* grade; **~ d'un amplificateur** *f* ELECTRON amplifier class; **~ de durabilité** *f* CERAM VER staining class; **~ erreur de protocole** *f* TELECOM protocol error class; **~ d'exploitation asymétrique en mode réponse normal** *f* TELECOM UNC, unbalanced operation normal response mode class; **~ holoédrique** *f* CRISTALL holohedral class; **~ d'isolation** *f* ELECTR insulation class; **~ d'objet géré** *f* TELECOM MOC, managed object class; **~ de précision** *f* METROLOGIE class of accuracy; **~ de protocole** *f* TELECOM protocol class; **~ ressource indisponible** *f* TELECOM resource unavailable class; **~ service-ou-option indisponible** *f* TELECOM service-or-option not available class; **~ service-ou-option non mis en oeuvre** *f* TELECOM service-or-option not implemented class; **~ situation normale** *f* TELECOM normal situation class; **~ spectrale** *f* ASTRONOMIE spectral type

classement *m* CH DE FER *véhicules* marshaling (AmE), marshalling (BrE), CHARBON size grading, sizing, GEOLOGIE sorting, PHYSIQUE rating, PRODUCTION, QUALITE, TELECOM grading; **~ granulométrique** *m* GENIE CHIM particle classification, particle sizing, MATERIAUX *métallurgie* grain size classification

classer *vt* AGRO ALIM grade, CHARBON, GENIE CHIM classify, GEOLOGIE, PRODUCTION grade, QUALITE classify, QUALITY grade

classeur *m* CERAM VER classifier, CONS MECA sizer, PAPIER screen; **~ conique** *m* PRODUCTION cone classifier; **~ à courant ascendant** *m* CHARBON countercurrent classifier, upward current classifier; **~ mécanique** *m* CHARBON mechanical classifier

classeur-trieur *m* CONS MECA sizer

classificateur *m* CHARBON classifier, CONS MECA sizer, GENIE CHIM classifier; **~ à contre-courant** *m* CHARBON counterflow classifier; **~ à coupe** *m* CHARBON bowl classifier

classification *f* ASTRONOMIE classification, CHARBON sizing, QUALITE classification; **~ des caractères** *f* IMPRIM classification of type design; **~ en énergie des photons** *f* ASTRONOMIE photon energy classification; **~ de Hubble** *f* ASTRONOMIE *des galaxies* Hubble classification; **~ hydraulique** *f* CHARBON hydraulic classification; **~ des masses d'air** *f* METEO air mass classification

classique *adj* CONS MECA standard

claste *m* GEOLOGIE clast

clastique *adj* GEOLOGIE clastic

claudétite *f* MINERAUX claudetite

clause: ~ de capacité *f* AERONAUT capacity clause; **~ de rétrocession** *f* PETROLE relinquishment requirement

clausthalite *f* MINERAUX clausthalite

clavage *m* CONSTR *d'une voûte* keying, keying in, keying up

claveau *m* CONSTR arch stone, voussoir, PRODUCTION quoin

clavetage *m* CONS MECA cottering, forelocking, keying, keyway; **~ par clavettes disques** *m* CONS MECA woodruff keys and keyways; **~ par clavettes inclinées** *m* CONS MECA taper keys and keyways; **~ par clavettes tangentielles** *m* CONS MECA tangential keys and keyways

claveté *adj* MECANIQUE keyed

claveter *vt* CONS MECA cotter, key

clavette *f* AUTO insert, CINEMAT key, CONS MECA cotter, forelock, key, pin, CONSTR wedge, MECANIQUE key, PAPIER key bolt, pin, pinhole, TV key, VEHICULES *moteur, carburateur* collet; ~ **d'arbre** *f* CONS MECA shaft key; ~ **d'assemblage** *f* MECANIQUE locating key; ~ **de calage** *f* CONS MECA shaft key, steady pin; ~ **creuse** *f* CONS MECA saddle key; ~ **disque** *f* VEHICULES Woodruff key; ~ **à disque** *f* CONS MECA disc key (BrE), disk key (AmE); ~ **et contre-clavette** *f* CONS MECA gib and cotter, gib and key; ~ **évidée** *f* CONS MECA saddle key; ~ **fendue** *f* CONS MECA spring cotter, spring forelock, spring key; ~ **à friction** *f* CONS MECA saddle key; ~ **inclinée** *f* CONS MECA taper key; ~ **inclinée avec talon** *f* CONS MECA taper key with gib head; ~ **inclinée mince** *f* CONS MECA thin taper key; ~ **inclinée sans talon** *f* CONS MECA taper key without gib head; ~ **linguiforme** *f* CONS MECA feather, spline; ~ **à mantonnet** *f* CONS MECA gib head key; ~ **à méplat** *f* CONS MECA key on flat; ~ **noyée** *f* CONS MECA sunk key; ~ **parallèle** *f* NUCLEAIRE *fixée par vis* feather key, spline key; ~ **posée à plat** *f* CONS MECA key on flat; ~ **d'une soupape** *f* NUCLEAIRE valve off, valving out; ~ **à talon** *f* CONS MECA gib head key; ~ **tangentielle** *f* CONS MECA tangent key; ~ **à tête** *f* CONS MECA gib head key

clavetter *vt* CONS MECA key

clavettes: ~ **parallèles carrées** *f pl* CONS MECA square parallel keys; ~ **parallèles rectangulaires** *f pl* CONS MECA rectangular parallel keys

claviature *f* PETROLE manifold, pipe manifold

clavier *m* CINEMAT, ELECTR *commande*, IMPRIM, INFORMAT, ORDINAT keyboard, PHYSIQUE keyboard, keypad, TELECOM keyboard, keypad, push-button dial, TV keyboard; ~ **amovible** *m* INFORMAT detachable keyboard; ~ **auxiliaire** *m* IMPRIM additional keyboard; ~ **aveugle** *m* IMPRIM blind keyboard; ~ **AZERTY** *m* INFORMAT, ORDINAT AZERTY keyboard; ~ **détachable** *m* PRODUCTION detachable keyboard; ~ **indépendant** *m* PRODUCTION detachable keyboard; ~ **à membrane** *m* ELECTROTEC, PRODUCTION *automatisme industriel* membrane keyboard; ~ **numérique** *m* ENREGISTR, INFORMAT, ORDINAT, TV keypad; ~ **programmable** *m* INFORMAT, ORDINAT soft keyboard; ~ **QWERTY** *m* INFORMAT, ORDINAT QWERTY keyboard

clé *f* ACOUSTIQUE, CINEMAT key, CONS MECA key, spanner (BrE) wrench (AmE), CONSTR, ELECTROTEC, INFORMAT key, MECANIQUE *outil* spanner (BrE), wrench (AmE), NAUT chock, *cordage* hitch, ORDINAT, TELECOM, TV key, VEHICULES *outil* spanner (BrE), wrench (AmE); ~ **Allen mâle** *f* IMPRIM Allen key (BrE), Allen wrench (AmE); ~ **anglaise** *f* CONS MECA coach wrench; ~ **anglaise simple à marteau** *f* CONS MECA single bar coach wrench; ~ **à béquille** *f* CONS MECA sliding tee socket wrench, socket wrench, tee socket wrench; ~ **de Berne** *f* CH DE FER Berne key; ~ **de bocage** *f* PETROLE tongs; ~ **à bougies** *f* CONS MECA spark plug wrench; ~ **de calibre** *f* CONS MECA spanner (BrE), wrench (AmE); ~ **à chaîne pour tubes** *f* CONS MECA chain pipe wrench; ~ **à chocs pneumatique** *f* CONS MECA pneumatic impact wrench; ~ **cintrée en S** *f* CONS MECA S-shaped spanner (BrE), S-wrench (AmE), curved spanner; ~ **à cliquet** *f* CONS MECA ratchet spanner (BrE), ratchet wrench (AmE); ~ **à col de cygne** *f* CONS MECA gooseneck wrench; ~ **coudée** *f* CONS MECA bent spanner (BrE), cranked spanner (BrE), offset wrench; ~ **cro-**

codile *f* CONS MECA alligator wrench; ~ **à douille** *f* CONS MECA socket wrench, CONSTR crutch key, MECANIQUE socket spanner (BrE), socket wrench (AmE); ~ **dynamométrique** *f* CONS MECA torque wrench, NUCLEAIRE metric key, torque spanner (BrE), torque wrench (AmE), VEHICULES *outil* torque spanner (BrE), torque wrench (AmE); ~ **emmanchée** *f* CONS MECA nut spinner; ~ **en croix** *f* CONS MECA wheel nut cross brace; ~ **en deux pièces pour tubes** *f* CONS MECA grip pipe wrench; ~ **en main** *f* CONSTR turnkey; ~ **en S** *f* CONS MECA S-shaped spanner (BrE), S-wrench (AmE), curved spanner (BrE); ~ **en tube** *f* CONS MECA angle box wrench; ~ **d'épaisseur** *f* CERAM VER V-gage (AmE), V-gauge, thickness gage (AmE), thickness gauge; ~ **à ergot** *f* CONS MECA pin spanner (BrE), pin wrench (AmE); ~ **à ergots** *f* CONS MECA C-wrench (BrE), open end wrench, hook and pin wrench; ~ **à fer creux** *f* CONS MECA tube wrench; ~ **fermée** *f* CONS MECA spanner (BrE), wrench (AmE); ~ **à fourche** *f* CONS MECA fork wrench, gap spanner (BrE), open end wrench, MECANIQUE *outillage* open end wrench; ~ **à fourche extra-plate** *f* CONS MECA low-profile open-end wrench; ~ **à griffe** *f* CONS MECA hook spanner (BrE), hook wrench (AmE); ~ **hexagonale coudée** *f* VEHICULES *outil* Allen key (BrE), Allen wrench (AmE); ~ **à mâchoires mobiles** *f* CONS MECA screw wrench, shifting spanner (BrE); ~ **mâle** *f* CONS MECA Allen key (BrE), Allen wrench (AmE), hexagonal key; ~ **mâle coudée** *f* CONS MECA angled key; ~ **à marteau** *f* CONS MECA screw hammer; ~ **à molette** *f* CONS MECA adjustable spanner (BrE), screw wrench, adjustable wrench (AmE), shifting spanner (BrE), MECANIQUE *outillage*, VEHICULES *outil* adjustable spanner (BrE), adjustable wrench (AmE); ~ **à molette façon Clyburn** *f* CONS MECA Clyburn wrench; ~ **à molette à une seule mâchoire mobile** *f* CONS MECA Clyburn wrench; ~ **à pipes** *f* CONS MECA angled socket spanner (BrE), angled socket wrench; ~ **à pipes débouchées** *f* CONS MECA angled open socket spanner (BrE), angled open socket wrench; ~ **polygonale** *f* CONS MECA ring wrench, VEHICULES *outil* ring spanner (BrE), ring wrench (AmE); ~ **polygonale contre-coudée** *f* CONS MECA offset ring spanner (BrE), offset ring wrench; ~ **polygonale demie-lune** *f* CONS MECA half-moon ring spanner (BrE); ~ **polygonale à frapper** *f* CONS MECA slogging ring spanner (BrE), slogging ring wrench; ~ **polygonale à tuyauterie** *f* CONS MECA split ring flare nut spanner (BrE), split ring flare nut wrench; ~ **pour vis à six-pans creux** *f* CONS MECA Allen key (BrE), Allen wrench (AmE); ~ **qui va à une serrure** *f* CONSTR key which fits a lock; ~ **de rallonge** *f* CONS MECA *pour clé à douille* lengthening bar; ~ **de recherche** *f* INFORMAT, ORDINAT search key; ~ **de réglage** *f* COMMANDE adjustment spanner (BrE), adjustment wrench (AmE); ~ **de réglage des culbuteurs** *f* CONS MECA tappet adjuster; ~ **à rochet** *f* CONS MECA ratchet spanner (BrE), ratchet wrench (AmE); ~ **à sangle** *f* CONS MECA strap spanner (BrE), strap wrench; ~ **serre-tubes** *f* CONS MECA pipe spanner (BrE), pipe wrench; ~ **serre-tubes à chaîne** *f* CONS MECA chain pipe spanner (BrE), chain pipe wrench; ~ **de serrure** *f* CONSTR lock key; ~ **simple** *f* CONS MECA single-ended spanner (BrE), single-ended wrench; ~ **simple à fourche** *f* CONS MECA single-ended spanner (BrE), single-ended wrench; ~ **six-pans** *f* MECANIQUE *outillage* hex head wrench; ~ **à six pans** *f* CONS MECA spanner for hexagon nuts; ~ **à tiges** *f*

PETROLE pipe tongs, tongs; ~ **à tubes** *f* CONS MECA tube wrench, CONSTR pipe spanner (BrE), pipe wrench; ~ **à tuyauter** *f* CONS MECA pipe spanner (BrE), pipe wrench; ~ **à tuyauterie à cliquet** *f* CONS MECA ratchet flare nut wrench; ~ **à vis** *f* CONS MECA screw key; ~ **de voiture** *f* CONS MECA coach wrench

clé-étau *f* CONS MECA lock grip wrench

clef *f voir clé*

clenche *f* CONSTR *de loquet de porte* bar, catch

clenchette *f* CONSTR *de loquet de porte* bar

clés: ~ **d'encrier** *f pl* IMPRIM *machines* fountain keys

clévéite *f* MINERAUX cleveite

CLF *abrév (combustion sur lit fluidisé)* POLLUTION fluidized bed combustion

CLHP *abrév (chromatographie liquide à haute pression)* AGRO ALIM, CHIMIE, EQUIP LAB, POLLUTION HPLC *(high-pressure liquid chromatography)*

clic *m* TELECOM transient

clichage *m* MINES catch, dog, prop, kep, rest, *de plan incliné* tub controller

clichages *m pl* MINES cage sheets, cage shuts, fangs

cliché *m* ASTRONOMIE negative, *d'un corps céleste* photographic negative, IMPRIM block, stereoplate, stereotype plate, PHOTO image, photograph, picture, negative, PHYSIQUE negative, REVETEMENT electroplate; ~ **d'archives** *m* PHOTO file picture; ~ **développé** *m* PHOTO developed image; ~ **à dorer** *m* IMPRIM block; ~ **électrotypique** *m* IMPRIM electrotype; ~ **latéral** *m* INSTRUMENT lateral view; ~ **manqué** *m* PHOTO spoiled negative; ~ **de poudre** *m* CRISTALL powder photograph; ~ **de projection** *m* CINEMAT lantern slide, slide; ~ **simili** *m* PHOTO halftone block; ~ **sous-exposé** *m* PHOTO underexposed picture; ~ **stéréo** *m* IMPRIM *presse* electrotype; ~ **surexposé** *m* PHOTO overexposed picture; ~ **au trait** *m* IMPRIM line block, line cut, line plate; ~ **typographique** *m* IMPRIM block print, *impression* block

clicherie: ~ **typographique** *f* IMPRIM *typographie* block-making

clichés: ~ **pour dorure** *m pl* IMPRIM *reliure* gold blocking

clicheur *m* MINES onsetter (BrE), platman (AmE)

client *m* INFORMAT, ORDINAT client; ~ **grand compte** *m* TELECOM major account holder; ~ **pilote** *m* TELECOM test customer

client/serveur *m* ORDINAT client/server

clignotant *m* IMPRIM *électronique* blinker, VEHICULES blinker, *accessoire* flasher

clignotement *m* ORDINAT blinking

clignoter *vi* ELECTRON flicker, ORDINAT *visualisation graphique* blink

clignoteur *m* AERONAUT indicator, VEHICULES blinker, *accessoire* direction indicator, flasher; ~ **avant** *m* AUTO front flasher

climagramme *m* METEO climagram, climatic graph, climatogram

climat *m* METEO climate; ~ **continental** *m* METEO continental climate; ~ **équatorial** *m* METEO equatorial climate; ~ **maritime** *m* METEO maritime climate; ~ **méditerranéen** *m* METEO mediterranean climate; ~ **de montagne** *m* METEO mountain climate; ~ **de moussons** *m* METEO monsoon climate; ~ **polaire** *m* METEO polar climate; ~ **tropical** *m* METEO tropical climate; ~ **de type méditerranéen** *m* METEO mediterranean climate

climatisation *f* CONS MECA, MAT CHAUFF, METEO, PAPIER, REFRIG air conditioning; ~ **toutes saisons** *f* REFRIG all year air conditioning

climatiser *vt* MAT CHAUFF, REFRIG air-condition

climatiseur *m* AUTO air conditioner, REFRIG air conditioning unit, VEHICULES *habitacle* air conditioner; ~ **à air et ventilation libre** *m* REFRIG free flow air conditioning unit; ~ **à condenseur à air** *m* REFRIG air-cooled air conditioning unit; ~ **à condenseur à eau** *m* REFRIG water-cooled air conditioning unit; ~ **à encastrer** *m* REFRIG through-the-wall air conditioning unit; ~ **de fenêtre** *m* REFRIG window air conditioning unit; ~ **mobile** *m* REFRIG room air conditioning unit; ~ **monobloc** *m* REFRIG self-contained air conditioning unit; ~ **mural** *m* REFRIG console air conditioning unit; ~ **de toiture** *m* REFRIG rooftop air conditioning unit; ~ **à ventilation libre** *m* REFRIG free flow air conditioning unit; ~ **de zone** *m* REFRIG zone air conditioning unit

climatologie *f* METEO climatology

clinker *m* CONSTR clinker

clinochlore *m* MINERAUX clinochlore

clinoclase *f* MINERAUX clinoclase, clinoclasite

clinoclasite *f* MINERAUX clinoclase, clinoclasite

clinoédrite *f* MINERAUX clinohedrite

clinohumite *f* MINERAUX clinohumite

clinomètre *m* CHARBON clinometer, inclinometer, CONSTR, GEOLOGIE clinometer, GEOPHYS clinometer, tiltmeter, METROLOGIE clinometer, PHYSIQUE inclinometer

clinométrie *f* CONSTR clinometry

clinozoïsite *f* MINERAUX clinozoisite

clinquant *m* PRODUCTION foil

clintonite *f* MINERAUX clintonite

clip *m* CINEMAT *vidéo* clip

clique *f* TELECOM clique

cliquet *m* CONS MECA click, detent, dog, keeper, ratchet spanner (BrE), ratchet wrench (AmE), ratchet, ratchet brace, trigger, *d'un treuil* pawl, CONSTR brace, latch, MECANIQUE pawl, ratchet, NUCLEAIRE latch; ~ **d'arrêt** *m* CONS MECA *d'un treuil* pawl; ~ **à canon** *m* CONS MECA ratchet, ratchet brace; ~ **à douilles débouchées** *m* CONS MECA open socket ratchet; ~ **simple** *m* CONS MECA ratchet spanner (BrE), ratchet wrench (AmE); ~ **de stationnement** *m* AUTO *frein* parking pawl; ~ **universel** *m* CONS MECA reversible ratchet; ~ **de verrouillage** *m* CONS MECA catch

cliquetage *m* VEHICULES *moteur* pinging (AmE), pinking (BrE)

cliqueter *vi* CONS MECA chatter

cliquetis *m* AUTO pinging (AmE), pinking (BrE), piston knock, PETROLE knock, piston, VEHICULES *moteur* pinging (AmE), pinking (BrE)

clivage *m* CONSTR cleaving, CRISTALL, GEOLOGIE, METALL cleavage; ~ **ardoisier** *m* GEOLOGIE slaty cleavage; ~ **ardoisier axial** *m* GEOLOGIE axial plane cleavage; ~ **de crénulation** *m* GEOLOGIE slip cleavage; ~ **de diamant** *m* PRODUCTION diamond cleaving; ~ **de flux** *m* GEOLOGIE flow cleavage; ~ **de fracture** *m* GEOLOGIE fracture cleavage; ~ **par pli-fracture** *m* GEOLOGIE strain slip cleavage

cliver *vt* CONSTR cope

cloche *f* CHIMIE bell jar, CONS MECA *de cabestan* barrel, CONSTR pothole, *de la surface* subsidence, EQUIP LAB *verrerie* bell jar, MINES cauldron, sludge pump, sludger, *d'une carrière* opening, PRODUCTION bell, *d'un cabestan* drum; ~ **d'avertissement** *f* COMMANDE signal bell; ~ **de barbotage** *f* AGRO ALIM bubble cap, NUCLEAIRE bubble cap, bubble hood; ~ **de curage** *f* MINES sludge pump, sludger; ~ **à échantillon** *f* MINES core breaker, core catcher, core extractor, core lifter, core plunger, core pusher; **~ en porcelaine** *f* CERAM VER porcelain cup; **~ de gueulard** *f* PRODUCTION cone; **~ de liaison** *f* AUTO input shell; **~ de mesure** *f* AERONAUT drag cup; **~ de plongée** *f* OCEANO, PETR, PETROLE diving bell; **~ à plongeur** *f* NAUT, OCEANO diving bell; **~ de refroidissement** *f* CERAM VER soaking pit; **~ de repêchage** *f* MINES horn socket; **~ de tachymètre** *f* AERONAUT drag cup

cloison *f* CONS MECA bulkhead, CONSTR division, partition, ESPACE *véhicules*, MECANIQUE bulkhead, MINES brattice, NAUT bulkhead; **~ d'aérage** *f* MINES air brattice; **~ antiballast** *f* AERONAUT antisurge baffle; **~ axiale** *f* NAUT center line bulkhead (AmE), centre line bulkhead (BrE); **~ coupe-feu** *f* NAUT fire bulkhead, THERMODYN fire-resistant bulkhead, fire-resisting bulkhead; **~ de décrochage** *f* AERONAUT stall fence; **~ en décharge** *f* CONSTR self-supporting partition; **~ en madriers** *f* CONSTR plank partition; **~ en porte-à-faux** *f* CONSTR self-supporting partition; **~ en toile grossière** *f* CONSTR canvas brattice; **~ à entretoise** *f* CONSTR stud partition; **~ étanche** *f* AERONAUT *aéronef* pressure bulkhead, MECANIQUE bulkhead; **~ d'incendie** *f* THERMODYN fire-resistant bulkhead, fire-resisting bulkhead; **~ médiane** *f* MINES midwall; **~ médiane de brûleur** *f* CERAM VER midfeather; **~ pare-feu** *f* AERONAUT fire wall, fireproof bulkhead, ESPACE fire bulkhead, fire wall, fireproof bulkhead, NAUT fire bulkhead; **~ de planches** *f* CONSTR boarding; **~ pressurisée** *f* AERONAUT *aéronef* pressure bulkhead; **~ de séparation** *f* CONSTR partition; **~ transversale** *f* NAUT transverse bulkhead

cloisonnage *m* CONSTR partitioning, REFRIG baffle plates

cloisonné *adj* INFORMAT, ORDINAT partitioned

cloisonnement *m* CONSTR partitioning, INFORMAT, ORDINAT compartmentalization

clonage *m* PHYSIQUE cloning

clone *m* INFORMAT, ORDINAT, PHYSIQUE clone

cloquage *m* IMPRIM blistering, PAPIER blistering, bubbling

cloque *f* ESSAIS, IMPRIM, NAUT, PAPIER, PLAST CAOU, PRODUCTION blister

clos[1] *adj* GEOMETRIE, MATH closed

clos[2] *m* CHIMIE retort

closet *m* CERAM VER closet

clotte *f* CERAM VER flooding

clôture *f* CONSTR enclosure, ELECTR *relais* closing operation; **~ de bornage** *f* CONSTR boundary fence; **~ en fil de fer** *f* CONSTR wire fence; **~ de machine** *f* SECURITE machine fence; **~ murée** *f* CONSTR walled enclosure

clôturer *vt* CONSTR fence in

clou *m* CONSTR nail, rivet, MECANIQUE nail; **~ ardoise** *m* CONS MECA clout nail, slate nail; **~ barbelé** *m* CONSTR barbed wire nail; **~ de couvreur** *m* CONS MECA slate nail; **~ à crochet** *m* CONSTR tenterhook, wall holdfast; **~ à deux pointes** *m* CONSTR staple, wire staple; **~ fondu** *m* CONSTR cast nail; **~ à latter** *m* CONSTR lath nail; **~ maçonnerie** *m* CONSTR masonry nail; **~ de mouleur** *m* PRODUCTION gagger, lifter; **~ à parquet** *m* CONSTR flooring nail; **~ à patte** *m* CONSTR wall holdfast, PRODUCTION holdfast; **~ pour noyaux** *m* CONSTR core nail; **~ réflectorisé** *m* CONSTR reflecting stud; **~ à river** *m* CONSTR rivet; **~ à roc** *m* CHARBON rock dowel, rock tip

clouage *m* CONSTR nailing

clouement *m* CONSTR nailing

clouer *vt* CONSTR drive in, nail

clouterie *f* PRODUCTION nailmaking

clouure *f* CONSTR nailing

clupéine *f* CHIMIE clupeine

Cm *(curium)* CHIMIE Cm *(curium)*

CMI *abrév (concentration maximale d'immixtion)* POLLUTION maximum emission concentration

CMS *abrév (composant monté en surface)* ELECTRON, TELECOM SMC *(surface-mounted component)*

CN *abrév (commande numérique)* COMMANDE, CONS MECA, PRODUCTION NC *(numerical control)*

CNA *abrév* ELECTRON *(convertisseur numérique-analogique)* DAC *(digital-to-analog converter, digital-to-analogue converter)*, ORDINAT *(convertisseur numérique-analogique)* DAC *(digital-to-analog converter)*, POLLUTION *(capacité de neutralisation des acides)* ANC *(acid neutralizing capacity)*, TV *(convertisseur numérique-analogique)* DAC *(digital-to-analog converter, digital-to-analogue converter)*

CNC *abrév (concentration numérique des conversations)* TELECOM DSI *(digital speech interpolation)*

CNP *abrév (concentration numérique de la parole)* TELECOM digital speech compression

CNS *abrév (concentrateur numérique satellite)* TELECOM digital satellite concentrator

Co *(cobalt)* CHIMIE Co *(cobalt)*

coacervat *m* CHIMIE coacervate

coacervation *f* CHIMIE coacervation

coagulant *m* GENIE CHIM, HYDROLOGIE coagulant

coagulation *f* AGRO ALIM coagulating, CHIMIE clotting, coagulation, GENIE CHIM, HYDROLOGIE, PLAST CAOU coagulation

coaguler[1] *vt* GENIE CHIM thicken

coaguler:[2] **se ~** *v réfl* CHIMIE gel, GENIE CHIM coagulate

coagulum *m* PLAST CAOU *caoutchouc* coagulum

coalescence *f* METEO coalescence; **~ des cavités** *f* METALL void coalescence

coaltar *m* CHARBON coal tar

coarmateur *m* NAUT part owner

coaxial *adj* ELECTROTEC, GEOMETRIE coaxial

cobalamine *f* CHIMIE cobalamin

cobalt *m* *(Co)* CHIMIE cobalt *(Co)*; **~ arséniaté** *m* MINERAUX red cobalt; **~ oxydé noir** *m* MINERAUX black cobalt ocher (AmE), black cobalt ochre (BrE)

cobaltammine *f* CHIMIE cobaltammine

cobaltiammine *f* CHIMIE cobaltammine

cobaltique *adj* CHIMIE cobaltic

cobaltite *f* MINERAUX cobalt glance, cobaltine, cobaltite

cobaltoammine *f* CHIMIE cobaltammine

cocaïne *f* CHIMIE cocaine

cocanalisation *f* TV interleaving

coccolite *f* MINERAUX coccolite

coccolithe *f* GEOLOGIE coccolith

coche: ~ de plaisance *m* TRANSPORT houseboat

cochenille *f* AGRO ALIM cochineal

Cocher *m* ASTRONOMIE Auriga

cochon *m* PRODUCTION bear, horse, sow

cochonnet *m* PETROLE pig, *canalisation* go devil

cockpit *m* ESPACE, NAUT cockpit

coco *m* NAUT coir

cocotte: ~ minute *f* AGRO ALIM pressure cooker

COD *abrév (carbone organique dissous)* POLLUTION dissolved organic carbon

codage *m* ELECTRON coding, encoding, ESPACE *communications*, INFORMAT encoding, ORDINAT encoding, encryption, TELECOM coding, encoding; ~ **adaptif** *m* TELECOM adaptive coding; ~ **de base** *m* INFORMAT, ORDINAT basic coding; ~ **binaire** *m* TELECOM binary coding; ~ **bit à bit** *m* TELECOM bit-by-bit encoding; ~ **convolutif** *m* TELECOM convolutional coding; ~ **à débit réduit** *m* TELECOM LRE, low rate encoding; ~ **de détection d'erreurs** *m* TELECOM error detection coding; ~ **à faible débit** *m* TELECOM LRE, low rate encoding; ~ **à fréquence** *m* TELECOM frequency encoding; ~ **intertrame** *m* TELECOM interframe coding; ~ **intratrame** *m* TELECOM in-frame coding; ~ **numérique** *m* ELECTRON digital coding; ~ **par blocs** *m* TELECOM block coding; ~ **par convolution auto-orthogonal** *m* TELECOM self-orthogonal convolutional coding; ~ **par convolution à débit moitié** *m* TELECOM rate one half convolutional coding; ~ **par modulation de largeur** *m* ELECTRON width coding; ~ **de la parole** *m* ESPACE *communications*, TELECOM speech coding, speech encoding; ~ **pour correction d'erreurs** *m* TELECOM error correcting code; ~ **prédictif** *m* TELECOM predictive coding; ~ **prédictif linéaire** *m* ELECTRON linear predictive coding, TELECOM LPC, linear predicting coding; ~ **de signal composite** *m* TELECOM composite signal coding; ~ **sous forme numérique** *m* TELECOM digital coding; ~ **à tonalités séquentielles** *m* TELECOM sequential tone coding; ~ **de la voix** *m* TELECOM vocoding

code *m* ELECTRON, IMPRIM, INFORMAT, ORDINAT, TELECOM code; ~ **absolu** *m* ORDINAT absolute code; ~ **alphabétique** *m* INFORMAT alphabetic code; ~ **alphanumérique** *m* INFORMAT alphanumeric code; ~ **d'arrêt** *m* INFORMAT, ORDINAT stop code; ~ **arrondi** *m* PRODUCTION rounding code; ~ **ASCII** *m* IMPRIM, INFORMAT, ORDINAT ASCII code; ~ **ASME** *m* MECANIQUE ASME code; ~ **d'authentification** *m* INFORMAT authentication code; ~ **à barres** *m* EMBALLAGE, IMPRIM, INFORMAT, TELECOM bar code; ~ **binaire** *m* INFORMAT binary code; ~ **bipolaire** *m* TELECOM bipolar code; ~ **bipolaire avec substitution de trois zéros** *m* TELECOM B3ZS, bipolar code with three-zero substitution; ~ **bipolaire à haute densité d'ordre 2** *m* TELECOM HDB2, high-density bipolar of order 2 code; ~ **biquinaire** *m* INFORMAT biquinary code; ~ **de bruit pseudoaléatoire** *m* TELECOM pseudorandom noise code; ~ **de caractère** *m* INFORMAT character code; ~ **CMI** *m* TELECOM CMI, coded mark inversion; ~ **complémentaire** *m* TELECOM complementary code; ~ **considéré** *m* TELECOM given code; ~ **de contact pour chaîne de production** *m* EMBALLAGE in-line contact coding; ~ **convolutif** *m* TELECOM convolutive code; ~ **de convolution** *m* TELECOM convolution code, convolutional code; ~ **correcteur d'erreurs** *m* ELECTRON, ESPACE *communications*, INFORMAT, ORDINAT, TELECOM ECC, error correcting code; ~ **cyclique** *m* TELECOM cyclic code; ~ **dateur** *m* EMBALLAGE date code; ~ **décimal codé binaire étendu** *m (code EBCDIC)* ELECTRON, INFORMAT, ORDINAT extended binary coded decimal interchange code *(EBCDIC)*; ~ **détecteur d'erreurs** *m* ELECTRON, INFORMAT, ORDINAT error detecting code, self-checking code; ~ **EBCDIC** *m (code décimal codé binaire étendu)* ELECTRON, INFORMAT, ORDINAT EBCDIC, EBCDIC code; ~ **d'emplacement** *m* EMBALLAGE site code; ~ **à enchaînement** *m* ORDINAT chain code; ~ **en ligne** *m* TELECOM line code; ~ **d'erreur** *m* INFORMAT, ORDINAT error code; ~ **de fonction** *m* INFORMAT function code; ~ **de Gray** *m* ESPACE *communications* Gray code; ~ **de Hamming** *m* ESPACE *communications* Hamming code;

~ **Hollerith** *m* INFORMAT, ORDINAT Hollerith code; ~ **horaire SMPTE** *m* CINEMAT SMPTE time code; ~ **à huit moments** *m* ELECTRON eight-level code; ~ **d'identification** *m* INFORMAT, ORDINAT, TELECOM identification code; ~ **d'identification du destinataire** *m* TELECOM recipient identification code; ~ **d'identification de réseau de données** *m (CIRD)* TELECOM data network identification code *(DNIC)*; ~ **d'identification de réseau télex** *m (CIRT)* TELECOM telex network identification code; ~ **d'impulsion** *m* ELECTRON pulse code; ~ **d'instructions** *m* INFORMAT, ORDINAT instruction code; ~ **d'instructions machine** *m* INFORMAT, ORDINAT machine instruction code; ~ **laser** *m* ELECTRON laser code; ~ **linéaire** *m* EMBALLAGE line code, TELECOM linear code; ~ **à longueur variable** *m* TELECOM variable length code; ~ **de lot** *m* EMBALLAGE batch code; ~ **machine** *m* INFORMAT, ORDINAT machine code; ~ **national de destination** *m* TELECOM NDC, national destination code; ~ **non binaire** *m* TELECOM nonbinary code; ~ **numérique** *m* ELECTRON digital code, INFORMAT, ORDINAT numerical code; ~ **objet** *m* INFORMAT, ORDINAT object code; ~ **op** *m (code d'opération)* INFORMAT, ORDINAT, PRODUCTION op code *(operation code)*; ~ **d'opération** *m* INFORMAT, ORDINAT operation code, PRODUCTION *automatisme industriel* operation number, PRODUCTION *automatisme industriel* operation code; ~ **d'option** *m* ORDINAT option code; ~ **optionnel** *m* INFORMAT option code; ~ **de point** *m* TELECOM point code; ~ **du point d'origine** *m* TELECOM OPC, originating point code; ~ **de priorité de traitement** *m* TELECOM processing priority code; ~ **de priorité de la transmission** *m* TELECOM transmission priority code; ~ **de production** *m* CINEMAT production code; ~ **de protection contre les erreurs** *m* TELECOM error protection code; ~ **de redondance cyclique** *m* TELECOM cyclic redundancy code; ~ **redondant** *m* INFORMAT, ORDINAT redundant code; ~ **à réponse partielle** *m* TELECOM partial response code; ~ **retour** *m* INFORMAT, ORDINAT return code; ~ **de sécurité** *m* CONS MECA, SECURITE safety code; ~ **séparateur** *m* PRODUCTION *automatisme industriel* fence code; ~ **de service** *m* INFORMAT function code; ~ **source** *m* INFORMAT, ORDINAT source code; ~ **temporel** *m* CINEMAT address code, time code, ENREGISTR, TV time code; ~ **temporel incrusté** *m* TV burnt-in time code; ~ **temporel à piste centrale** *m* ENREGISTR center track time code (AmE), centre track time code (BrE); ~ **temporel SMPTE** *m* TV SMPTE time code; ~ **unité de temps** *m* PRODUCTION time key

code-barre *m* IMPRIM *emballage* wedge

codec *m* ELECTRON, TELECOM codec

codéine *f* CHIMIE codeine

codemandeur *m* BREVETS joint applicant

coder *vt* ELECTRON, INFORMAT, ORDINAT, TELECOM encode, TV code, encode, scramble

codes: ~ de blocs cycliques *m pl* TELECOM cyclic block codes

codeur *m* ELECTRON, INFORMAT coder, encoder, TELECOM coder, TV coder, encoder; ~ **de clavier** *m* INFORMAT, ORDINAT keyboard encoder; ~ **à fréquences vocales** *m* ENREGISTR vocoder, TELECOM linear predicting coding vocoder, vocoder; ~ **à fréquences vocales activé par la hauteur du son** *m* TELECOM pitch-excited vocoder; ~ **à fréquences vocales de formants** *m* TELECOM formant vocoder; ~ **à fréquences vocales de voies** *m* TELECOM channel vocoder; ~ **d'impulsions** *m* ELECTRON pulse coder; ~ **MICDA** *m* TELECOM ADPCM encoder; ~ **multitours** *m* PRODUCTION *automatisme industriel* multiturn encoder; ~ **optique** *m* ESPACE *communications* optical encoder; ~ **à réinjection** *m* COMMANDE feedback encoder; ~ **simple tour** *m* PRODUCTION *automatisme industriel* single turn encoder

codeur/décodeur *m* ELECTRON, ORDINAT, TELECOM codec, coder/decoder

coefficient:[1] **à ~ d'uniformité moyen** *adj* CHARBON *sol* medium-graded

coefficient[2] *m* ELECTR, INST HYDR coefficient, MATH coefficient, modulus, PHYSIQUE coefficient, PRODUCTION factor;

~ a ~ **d'abondance** *m* DISTRI EAU coefficient of abundance; ~ **d'abrasion de gravier** *m* CONSTR AA, aggregate abrasion value; ~ **d'absorption** *m* PAPIER absorbency value, absorption rate, PHYS RAYON, PHYSIQUE absorption coefficient; ~ **d'absorption linéique** *m* PHYSIQUE linear absorption coefficient; ~ **d'absorption massique** *m* PHYSIQUE mass absorption coefficient; ~ **d'absorption solaire** *m* EN RENOUV solar absorption coefficient; ~ **d'activité** *m* PHYSIQUE activity coefficient; ~ **d'adhérence** *m* AUTO adhesion coefficient; ~ **aérodynamique** *m* AERONAUT aerodynamic factor, ESPACE aerodynamic coefficient; ~ **d'affaiblissement** *m* ENREGISTR attenuation factor, PHYSIQUE attenuation coefficient, linear coefficient; ~ **d'affaiblissement linéique** *m* PHYSIQUE linear attenuation coefficient; ~ **d'amortissement** *m* PHYSIQUE damping coefficient; ~ **d'amplification** *m* ELECTRON amplification factor, gain, gas ratio; ~ **d'anamorphose** *m* CINEMAT anamorphic squeeze; ~ **d'armement** *m* OCEANO hang ratio, hanging ratio; ~ **d'atténuation** *m* ELECTRON attenuation coefficient, PHYSIQUE attenuation coefficient, linear coefficient; ~ **d'atténuation linéique** *m* PHYSIQUE linear attenuation coefficient; ~ **d'atténuation de rafale** *m* AERONAUT gust alleviation factor; ~ **d'attrition** *m* PRODUCTION scrapping factor; ~ **d'augmentation de pression** *m* EN RENOUV pressure coefficient; ~ **d'auto-échauffement** *m* ELECTROTEC self-heating coefficient; ~ **d'auto-induction** *m* ELECTROTEC self-induction;

~ b ~ **binomial** *m* MATH binomial coefficient; ~ **de Brewster** *m* CERAM VER stress-optical coefficient;

~ c ~ **de capacité** *m* PHYSIQUE coefficient of capacitance; ~ **de capturabilité** *m* OCEANO catchability coefficient, coefficient of capture; ~ **de chaleur** *m* REFRIG heat ratio; ~ **de charge** *m* AERONAUT load factor; ~ **de cisaillement** *m* PHYSIQUE modulus of rigidity, rigidity modulus, shear modulus; ~ **de compressibilité** *m* CHARBON, PHYSIQUE compressibility coefficient; ~ **de conductibilité thermique** *m* MECANIQUE *mécanique, physique* coefficient of thermal conductivity, PHYSIQUE coefficient of thermal conduction, PLAST CAOU coefficient of thermal conductivity; ~ **de consolidation** *m* CHARBON coefficient of consolidation; ~ **de contraction** *m* CONS MECA, EN RENOUV, INST HYDR contraction coefficient; ~ **de convection** *m* CHAUFFAGE convection heat transfer coefficient; ~ **de conversion AM-PM** *m* ESPACE *communications* AM-PM conversion coefficient; ~ **de corrélation** *m* INFORMAT, ORDINAT, PHYS FLUID correlation coefficient; ~ **de couplage** *m* ELECTR *bobine*, PHYSIQUE coefficient of coupling; ~ **de couplage électromécanique** *m* ACOUSTIQUE electromechanical coupling factor; ~ **de couplage magnétique** *m* ELECTR *transformateur* magnetic coupling coefficient; ~ **de couple de rotation** *m* EN RENOUV coefficient of torque;

~ d ~ **de débit** *m* EN RENOUV discharge coefficient, flow coefficient, ESPACE discharge coefficient, PHYS FLUID flow coefficient; ~ **de décharge** *m* INST HYDR coefficient of efflux; ~ **de désadaptation** *m* ELECTROTEC mismatch factor; ~ **différentiel** *m* MATH differential coefficient; ~ **de diffusion** *m* ELECTRON, PHYSIQUE diffusion coefficient, TELECOM scattering coefficient; ~ **de diffusion apparente** *m* MATERIAUX apparent diffusion coefficient; ~ **de diffusion thermique** *m* PHYSIQUE thermal diffusion coefficient; ~ **de dilatation** *m* CONSTR, MECANIQUE *mécanique, physique*, PLAST CAOU coefficient of expansion, TV expansion coefficient; ~ **de dilatation linéique** *m* PHYSIQUE linear expansion coefficient; ~ **de dilatation thermique** *m* MATERIAUX, MECANIQUE, PHYSIQUE, THERMODYN thermal expansion coefficient; ~ **de dilatation volumique** *m* PHYSIQUE cubic expansion coefficient, cubic expansivity, volume expansion coefficient; ~ **de dispersion magnétique** *m* ELECTR coefficient of magnetic dispersion; ~ **de dispersion du matériau** *m* OPTIQUE material dispersion coefficient, TELECOM material dispersion parameter; ~ **de dissipation** *m* PHYSIQUE dissipation coefficient;

~ e ~ **d'écaillement** *m* CONSTR flakiness index; ~ **d'écoulement** *m* DISTRI EAU runoff coefficient, HYDROLOGIE coefficient of run-off; ~ **d'écrasement** *m* NAUT modulus of compression; ~ **d'écrasement de gravier** *m* CONSTR aggregate crushing value; ~ **d'écrouissage** *m* METALL work-hardening coefficient; ~ **d'effet utile** *m* MECANIQUE *mécanique, physique*, PHYSIQUE coefficient of efficiency, PRODUCTION commercial coefficiency; ~ **d'Einstein** *m* PHYS RAYON Einstein coefficient; ~ **d'élancement** *m* CONSTR slenderness ratio; ~ **d'élasticité** *m* MATERIAUX, METALL coefficient of elasticity, NAUT modulus of elasticity, PLAST CAOU coefficient of elasticity; ~ **d'emmagasinement** *m* HYDROLOGIE water storage coefficient; ~ **d'équilibrage** *m* ELECTROTEC return current coefficient; ~ **d'équivalence en UVP** *m* TRANSPORT passenger car equivalent;

~ f ~ **de filtre** *m* CINEMAT filter factor; ~ **de finesse** *m* NAUT coefficient of fineness; ~ **de force latérale** *m* AERONAUT lateral force coefficient; ~ **de forme** *m* CHAUFFAGE *isolation thermique* shape factor; ~ **de friction** *m* PLAST CAOU coefficient of friction; ~ **de frottement** *m* CONSTR, MECANIQUE, PHYSIQUE, PLAST CAOU coefficient of friction; ~ **de frottement par glissement** *m* PHYSIQUE sliding friction coefficient; ~ **de frottement de roulement** *m* PHYSIQUE rolling friction coefficient; ~ **de frottement statique** *m* PHYSIQUE static friction coefficient; ~ **de fuite** *m* GENIE CHIM dispersion coefficient;

~ g ~ **de glissement** *m* EN RENOUV, TRANSPORT lift-to-drag ratio; ~ **de gravier poli** *m* CONSTR polished stone value;

~ h ~ **d'hystérésis** *m* ELECTR *magnétisation* hysteresis coefficient;

~ i ~ **d'induction mutuelle** *m* ELECTR coefficient of mutual induction; ~ **d'induction propre** *m* ELECTROTEC self-induction; ~ **d'infiltration** *m* HYDROLOGIE coefficient of infiltration; ~ **d'influence** *m* PHYSIQUE coefficient of induction; ~ **d'isolation thermique** *m* PHYSIQUE coefficient of thermal insulance, thermal insulation coefficient;

~ l **~ de lixiviation** m NUCLEAIRE leaching coefficient; **~ m** **~ de majoration** m PRODUCTION scrapping factor; **~ de mobilité** m PETR mobility ratio; **~ de moment** m CONS MECA moment coefficient; **~ de montage** m PRODUCTION assembly coefficient;

~ n **~ numérique forfaitaire** m CONS MECA empirical operation factor;

~ o **~ d'occupation** m AERONAUT loading factor;

~ p **~ de partage** m CHIMIE partition coefficient; **~ de Peltier** m PHYSIQUE Peltier coefficient; **~ de pénétration** m VEHICULES *carrosserie* drag coefficient; **~ de perméabilité** m CHARBON, HYDROLOGIE coefficient of permeability; **~ de perte** m INST HYDR coefficient of efflux; **~ de plénitude** m AERONAUT *d'une hélice* solidity; **~ de Poisson** m CONSTR, MECANIQUE *matériaux*, PHYSIQUE Poisson's ratio; **~ de pondération de gain** m ELECTRON gain weighting factor; **~ de portance** m AERONAUT, EN RENOUV, PHYSIQUE lift coefficient; **~ de portance de pale** m AERONAUT *d'un hélicoptère* blade lift coefficient; **~ de pose** m PHOTO exposure factor; **~ de potentiel** m PHYSIQUE coefficient of potential; **~ de pression** m PHYSIQUE pressure coefficient; **~ de pression des terres** m CHARBON earth pressure coefficient; **~ de production** m PETROLE recovery factor; **~ de puissance** m EN RENOUV *énergie éolienne* power coefficient;

~ q **~ de qualité** m INSTRUMENT magnification factor; **~ r** **~ de rayonnement** m CHAUFFAGE radiation heat transfer coefficient; **~ de rayonnement de l'antenne** m TV aerial efficiency; **~ de rebut** m PRODUCTION scrapping factor, shrinkage factor; **~ de réciprocité électroacoustique** m ACOUSTIQUE electroacoustical reciprocity coefficient; **~ de recombinaison** m PHYSIQUE recombination coefficient; **~ de réduction** m NAUT *d'échantillonnage* coefficient of reduction; **~ de réflectivité** m ESPACE reflectivity coefficient, *communications* TWT transfer coefficient; **~ de réflexion** m ELECTRON, OPTIQUE, PHYSIQUE reflection coefficient; **~ de réflexion spéculaire** m TELECOM specular reflection coeficient; **~ relatif de pression** m PHYSIQUE relative pressure coefficient; **~ de remplissage** m NAUT coefficient of fineness, TELECOM filling coefficient; **~ de remplissage tout-cargo** m AERONAUT all-cargo load factor; **~ de rendement** m PRODUCTION commercial coefficiency; **~ de répartition** m METALL partition coefficient; **~ de réserve de capacité** m TRANSPORT reserve capacity; **~ de résistance à la conductibilité de chaleur** m THERMODYN heat insulation factor; **~ de restitution** m PHYSIQUE restitution coefficient; **~ de rugosité** m HYDROLOGIE coefficient of roughness; **~ de ruissellement** m CONSTR runoff coefficient; **~ de ruissellement utile** m HYDROLOGIE coefficient of usable groundwater;

~ s **~ de sécurité** m CHARBON, CONSTR, ELECTR, NAUT, SECURITE safety factor; **~ de Seebeck** m PHYSIQUE Seebeck coefficient; **~ de soudure** m CONSTR joint efficiency; **~ de Steinmetz** m PHYSIQUE Steinmetz coefficient; **~ de sustentation** m TRANSPORT lift coefficient;

~ t **~ de tarissement** m HYDROLOGIE coefficient of drainage; **~ de température** m ELECTROTEC, THERMODYN temperature coefficient; **~ de température de la capacité** m ELECTROTEC temperature coefficient of capacitance; **~ de température de résistance** m ELECTR, ELECTROTEC temperature coefficient of resist-

ance; **~ de Thomson** m PHYSIQUE Thomson coefficient; **~ de torsion** m TEXTILE twist factor; **~ de traction d'hélice** m TRANSPORT propeller thrust coefficient; **~ de traînée** m AERONAUT, AUTO, EN RENOUV, NAUT, PHYS FLUID *dans des fluides*, PHYSIQUE, TRANSPORT drag coefficient; **~ de transfert AM-PM** m ESPACE *communications* AM-PM transfer coefficient; **~ de transfert d'énergie** m PHYSIQUE energy transfer coefficient; **~ de transfert d'énergie massique** m PHYSIQUE mass energy transfer coefficient; **~ de transfert sur images** m ELECTRON image transfer coefficient; **~ de transmission** m PHYSIQUE transmission coefficient, POLLUTION coefficient of haze; **~ de transmission thermique** m PHYSIQUE, THERMODYN heat transfer coefficient; **~ de turbidité** m EN RENOUV turbidity coefficient;

~ u **~ d'uniformité** m CHARBON uniformity coefficient; **~ d'utilisation** m PRODUCTION duty cycle, material quantity per unit; **~ d'utilitière pratique** m *(CUP)* MINES weight strength *(WS)*;

~ v **~ de viscosité** m PHYS FLUID, THERMODYN viscosity coefficient; **~ viscosité-température** m THERMODYN viscosity-temperature coefficient; **~ de vitesse** m EN RENOUV velocity coefficient; **~ de vitesse au pointeau** m EN RENOUV nozzle velocity coefficient; **~ du volume d'émission et d'absorption** m PHYS RAYON volume emission and absorption coefficient

coelostat m ASTRONOMIE coelostat

coembranché m CH DE FER co-owner of private siding

co-entreprise f CONSTR joint venture

coenzyme f AGRO ALIM coenzyme

coéquipier m ESPACE *véhicules* crewmate

coercivité f ENREGISTR coercivity, MATERIAUX retentivity, PHYSIQUE, TV coercivity

coeur m CONSTR, ELECTROTEC, ESPACE *pilotage,* GEOLOGIE *d'un pli* core, NUCLEAIRE active lattice, core, OPTIQUE, PHYSIQUE, TELECOM core; **~ annulaire** m NUCLEAIRE annular core; **~ de l'atome** m NUCLEAIRE atomic core; **~ bien modéré** m NUCLEAIRE well moderated core; **~ de chaîne** m TELECOM BU, base unit; **~ de comète** m ESPACE *astronomie* comet core; **~ de croisement** m CH DE FER common crossing; **~ de croisement courbe** m CH DE FER curved common crossing; **~ de croisement droit** m CH DE FER straight common crossing; **~ de dislocation** m METALL dislocation core; **~ de fibre** m OPTIQUE fiber core (AmE), fibre core (BrE); **~ à gradient d'indice** m ELECTROTEC graded index core; **~ du matériau** m MATERIAUX *chimie analytique* bulk of material

coffrage m CONSTR formwork, shuttering, DISTRI EAU coffering, NAUT casing, PRODUCTION form; **~ en acier** m CONSTR steel forms; **~ glissant** m CONSTR moving formwork, sliding formwork, slip form; **~ mobile** m CONSTR moving formwork, sliding formwork, slip form; **~ perdu** m CONSTR permanent concrete shuttering; **~ permanent du béton** m CONSTR permanent concrete shuttering

coffre m AUTO boot (BrE), trunk (AmE), CONSTR *d'une serrure* case, DISTRI EAU chamber, coffer, MINES bunker, ore bin, NAUT locker, VEHICULES *carrosserie* boot (BrE), trunk (AmE); **~ d'amarrage** m NAUT, POLLU MER mooring buoy; **~ à bagages** m AUTO, TRANSPORT boot (BrE), trunk (AmE), VEHICULES *carrosserie* luggage compartment; **~ de batterie** m AUTO battery box; **~ congélateur** m REFRIG chest freezer; **~ d'écluse** m DISTRI EAU lock chamber; **~ de gouttière** m CONSTR rainwater head; ~ **à minerai** *m* MINES ore bin; ~ **à munitions** *m* MILITAIRE ammunition box; ~ **à signaux** *m* NAUT signal locker

coffre-fort *m* SECURITE safe

coffrer *vt* MINES coffer, seal

coffret *m* IMPRIM *reliure, emballage, façonnage* casing, MECANIQUE case; ~ **de chantier** *m* MINES gate end box; ~ **classeur pour diapos** *m* PHOTO slide box; ~ **de commande et de visualisation** *m* ESPACE *pilotage* control and display unit; ~ **d'extrémité** *m* ELECTR *accessoire de câble* terminal box; ~ **à montage mural** *m* PRODUCTION wall mount enclosure assembly; ~ **pour montage en surface** *m* PRODUCTION surface-mounted enclosure; ~ **de télévision** *m* TV television cabinet

cognement *m* AUTO dieseling, CHIMIE bumping, CONS MECA *des moteurs à explosion* knocking

cogner[1] *vt* CONS MECA drive, drive in, drive into

cogner[2] *vi* CHIMIE bump, CONS MECA knock

cognitique *f* ORDINAT knowledge engineering

cohérence *f* ELECTRON coherence, INFORMAT consistency, MATERIAUX, OPTIQUE *rayonnement* coherence, ORDINAT consistency, PHYS ONDES coherence; ~ **d'onde** *f* TELECOM wave coherence; ~ **optique** *f* TELECOM optical coherence; ~ **partielle** *f* OPTIQUE, TELECOM partial coherence; ~ **spatiale** *f* PHYSIQUE, TELECOM spatial coherence; ~ **temporelle** *f* OPTIQUE, PHYSIQUE, TELECOM temporal coherence

cohérent *adj* ELECTRON, OPTIQUE coherent

cohésif *adj* CONSTR cohesive

cohésion *f* CHARBON, CONSTR, PHYSIQUE cohesion

cohobation *f* CHIMIE cohobation, redistillation

cohober *vt* CHIMIE cohobate, redistil

coiffe *f* CONSTR *d'une chèvre* cap, ESPACE nose cone, shroud, *véhicules* fairing, IMPRIM *reliure* head cap, TEXTILE cap; ~ **du bord d'attaque** *f* AERONAUT leading edge glove; ~ **éjectable** *f* ESPACE *véhicules* nose cone; ~ **de fusée** *f* MILITAIRE fuse cap; ~ **mobile de train** *f* AERONAUT landing gear sliding valve

coiffée: ~ **par hydroxie** *adj* CHIMIE hydroxy-capped

coiffer *vt* CONSTR *puits* cap, GEOLOGIE drape

coin *m* CONS MECA quoin, wedge, CONSTR plug, quoin, wedge, IMPRIM, MECANIQUE wedge, MINES gad, spike, wedge, RESSORTS key; ~ **de calage** *m* CONS MECA keying wedge; ~ **de calfat** *m* CONSTR reaming iron; ~ **de centrage** *m* IMPRIM *typographie* centering wedge (AmE), centring wedge (BrE); ~ **demi-rond** *m* CONSTR plug; ~ **de desserrage** *m* CONS MECA loosening wedge; ~ **en quartz** *m* CRISTALL quartz wedge; ~ **étroit** *m* CONSTR tight corner; ~ **à fendre le bois** *m* CONSTR timber-splitting wedge; ~ **grippeur** *m* PETROLE slip; ~ **gris neutre** *m* CINEMAT neutral wedge; ~ **mouché** *m* CERAM VER dubbed corner; ~ **multiple** *m* MINES compound wedge, multiple wedge; ~ **photométrique** *m* PHOTO step wedge; ~ **à pierre** *m* CONSTR plug, stone wedge; ~ **prisonnier** *m* CONS MECA set key; ~ **de rattrapage de jeu** *m* CONS MECA slip for taking up wear; ~ **salé** *m* OCEANO saltwater wedge; ~ **sensitométrique** *m* CINEMAT gamma strip, sensitometric step wedge, step wedge; ~ **de serrage** *m* CONS MECA tightening wedge; ~ **de surface intérieure** *m* EMBALLAGE inside corner edge

coinçage *m* CONS MECA jamming, keying, wedging, CONSTR binder

coincé *adj* CONS MECA jammed

coincement *m* CONS MECA jam, jamming, wedging, CONSTR binder, PETROLE *problème de forage* key seating

coincer[1] *vt* CONS MECA jam, wedge, key, MECANIQUE jam, wedge

coincer:[2] **se** ~ *v réfl* MECANIQUE jam, NUCLEAIRE seize

coïncidence *f* INFORMAT, ORDINAT hit

coins: ~ **gommés** *m pl* PHOTO corner mounts; ~ **de retenue** *m pl* PETR slips

coistresse *f* MINES counter gangway, counter level, subdrift

coke *m* CHARBON, CHIMIE, THERMODYN coke; ~ **de gaz** *m* CHARBON gas coke; ~ **métallurgique** *m* CHARBON furnace coke, metallurgic coke, oven coke; ~ **d'usine à gaz** *m* CHARBON gas coke

cokéfaction *f* CHARBON coking; ~ **différée** *f* THERMODYN delayed coking

cokéfiant *adj* CHARBON coking

cokéfier *vt* CHARBON coke

cokerie *f* CHAUFFAGE, MINES coking plant

col *m* CERAM VER, ELECTRON neck, EQUIP LAB *d'une cornue* neck, *verrerie* neck, ESPACE *propulsion* throat, MECANIQUE neck; ~ **d'admission** *m* AERONAUT *d'un moteur* inlet throat; ~ **d'ampoule** *m* ELECTRON electron tube neck; ~ **de bouteille** *m* EMBALLAGE bottleneck; ~ **creux** *m* CERAM VER hollow neck; ~ **de cygne** *m* CINEMAT, CONSTR swan neck, MECANIQUE gooseneck; ~ **penché** *m* CERAM VER bent neck; ~ **protecteur** *m* SECURITE neck shield; ~ **trop étroit** *m* CERAM VER choke; ~ **de tube** *m* TV tube neck; ~ **de tuyère** *m* ESPACE *propulsion* nozzle throat

colain *m* CONSTR collar

colchicéine *f* CHIMIE colchiceine

colchicine *f* CHIMIE colchicine

colcotar *m* CHIMIE colcothar

colémanite *f* MINERAUX colemanite

colibacille *m* HYDROLOGIE colon bacillus

colinéaire *adj* GEOMETRIE collinear

colinéarité *f* GEOMETRIE collinearity

colique: ~ **des scaphandriers** *f* OCEANO colics, diver's cramps, stomach cramps

collaboration: ~ **européenne pour la physique du muon** *f* PHYS PART European collaboration for muon physics

collage *m* CERAM VER joining, laminating, pluck, sticking, sticking mark, ELECTROTEC sticking, EMBALLAGE glueing, MECANIQUE bonding, PAPIER pasting, sizing, PLAST CAOU bonding, PRODUCTION gluing, sticking; ~ **de la bande neuve sur la bande finissante** *m* IMPRIM *dérouleurs* splice; ~ **à chaud** *m* EMBALLAGE hot gluing, THERMODYN hot bonding; ~ **des contacts** *m* ELECTR *relais* sticking contacts; ~ **dans la pâte** *m* PAPIER stock sizing, stuff sizing; ~ **en marche au dérouleur** *m* IMPRIM flying paster; ~ **en surface** *m* PAPIER surface sizing; ~ **à froid** *m* THERMODYN cold bonding; ~ **mécanique** *m* MECANIQUE, TV splice; ~ **parallèle** *m* EMBALLAGE parallel glueing; ~ **physique** *m* TV mechanical splice; ~ **de poinçon** *m* CERAM VER plunger spike (AmE), plunger sticking (BrE)

collagène *m* AGRO ALIM, CHIMIE collagen

collagimètre *m* PAPIER size tester, sizing tester

collant *adj* EMBALLAGE adhesive, GENIE CHIM agglutinative, PLAST CAOU *adhésifs* tacky

collapse: ~ **gravitationnel** *m* ESPACE gravitation collapse

collargol *m* CHIMIE collargol

collationner *vt* IMPRIM collate

colle *f* CHIMIE glue, sizing agent, COULEURS size, sizing agent, sizing preparation, EMBALLAGE bonding agent, glue, IMPRIM glue, PAPIER glue, size, PLAST CAOU cement, glue, PRODUCTION adhesive, TEXTILE glue, size;

~ **acide** *f* IMPRIM acid size; ~ **acrylique** *f* TEXTILE acrylic size; ~ **à l'alcool polyvinyle** *f* TEXTILE polyvinyl alcohol size; ~ **d'amidon** *f* IMPRIM starch paste; ~ **animale** *f* COULEURS animal size, IMPRIM *façonnage*, PAPIER, PLAST CAOU animal glue; ~ **à base d'acétate** *f* EMBALLAGE acetate glue; ~ **à base de caséine** *f* AGRO ALIM casein glue, caseinate gum; ~ **à base de deux polymères** *f* MATERIAUX two-polymer adhesive; ~ **blanche** *f* COULEURS white size; ~ **à chaud** *f* IMPRIM *brochure, reliure* hot-melt adhesive; ~ **de contact** *f* EMBALLAGE, PLAST CAOU *adhésif* contact adhesive; ~ **durcissante à chaud** *f* EMBALLAGE, PLAST CAOU hot-setting glue; ~ **durcissante à froid** *f* PLAST CAOU cold-setting glue; ~ **d'emballage à base d'eau** *f* EMBALLAGE water-based backing adhesive; ~ **en émulsion** *f* EMBALLAGE emulsion adhesive; ~ **époxy à l'or** *f* ELECTRON gold epoxy; ~ **faite sur demande** *f* EMBALLAGE purpose-formulated adhesive; ~ **à film** *f* CINEMAT splicing cement; ~ **flexible qui ne craquèle pas en séchant** *f* IMPRIM nonwarp glue; ~ **forte** *f* IMPRIM glue; ~ **à froid** *f* IMPRIM starch paste; ~ **fusible** *f* PLAST CAOU *adhésif* hot-melt adhesive; ~ **hot-melt** *f* IMPRIM hot-melt glue; ~ **à l'hydrate de carbone** *f* TEXTILE carbohydrate size; ~ **de mélange** *f* EMBALLAGE mixed adhesive; ~ **naturelle** *f* SECURITE natural adhesive; ~ **neutre** *f* PHOTO acid-free glue; ~ **de peau** *f* COULEURS glue size, PLAST CAOU animal glue; ~ **permanente résistante à la réfrigération** *f* EMBALLAGE chill permanent adhesive; ~ **de poisson** *f* AGRO ALIM finings, isinglass; ~ **pour film** *f* CINEMAT cement; ~ **protéique** *f* TEXTILE protein size; ~ **servant à la fabrication de blocs papetiers** *f* IMPRIM padding emulsion; ~ **synthétique** *f* TEXTILE synthetic size; ~ **thermofusible** *f* EMBALLAGE hot-melt adhesive; ~ **thermofusible autoadhésive** *f* EMBALLAGE pressure-sensitive hot-melt adhesive; ~ **à usages multiples** *f* EMBALLAGE all-purpose adhesive; ~ **végétale** *f* COULEURS vegetable size, PRODUCTION vegetable glue

collé: **très** ~ *adj* IMPRIM hard sized

collecte *f* PETR flow line, RECYCLAGE refuse collection, waste collection; ~ **de données** *f* INFORMAT, ORDINAT data collection, data gathering, TELECOM data collection; ~ **des positions inutiles** *f* ORDINAT garbage collection; ~ **sélective** *f* RECYCLAGE selective collection, separate collection

collecteur *m* CHARBON collector, CONS MECA *d'un surchauffeur* manifold, CONSTR head, main, ELECTROTEC collector, commutator, EQUIP LAB *verrerie* manifold, MECANIQUE header pipe, manifold, NUCLEAIRE header, manifold, PETROLE pipe manifold, PHYSIQUE collector, POLLU MER manifold system, PRODUCTION *de surchauffeur* header, *système hydraulique* manifold, TELECOM collector, TRANSPORT collector, commutator; ~ **d'admission** *m* AERONAUT *moteur*, MECANIQUE intake manifold, VEHICULES *moteur* inlet manifold (BrE), intake manifold (AmE); ~ **d'alimentation** *m* NUCLEAIRE feeder header; ~ **annulaire** *m* AERONAUT annulus; ~ **de la batterie** *m* REFRIG coil header; ~ **de boue** *m* CONS MECA *pour conduites et robinetterie* dirt trap; ~ **de démarreur** *m* AUTO starter collector ring, starter commutator, starter slip ring, VEHICULES *moteur* starter slip ring; ~ **à deux augets** *m* POLLUTION double bucket collector; ~ **de données** *m* TELECOM data sink; ~ **d'eau** *m* MINES sinkhole, standage, sump; ~ **d'échappement** *m* AERONAUT, AUTO, MECANIQUE, VEHICULES exhaust manifold; ~ **d'entrée**

m CONS MECA inlet manifold (BrE), intake manifold (AmE); ~ **des gaz brûlés** *m* THERMODYN exhaust manifold; ~ **d'huile** *m* CONS MECA oil cup; ~ **mécanique** *m* ELECTROTEC commutator; ~ **de messages** *m* INFORMAT, ORDINAT message sink; ~ **de poussière** *m* CHARBON dust collector; ~ **de précipitation** *m* POLLUTION precipitation collector; ~ **de pressurisation** *m* AERONAUT pressurizing manifold; ~ **principal** *m* HYDROLOGIE, RECYCLAGE main sewer; ~ **du radiateur** *m* AUTO radiator header; ~ **de saumure** *m* REFRIG brine header; ~ **secondaire** *m* DISTRI EAU branch sewer; ~ **solaire** *m* CONS MECA solar collector; ~ **de surchauffeur** *m* PRODUCTION superheater header, superheater manifold; ~ **de tête** *m* AUTO radiator header; ~ **de transistor** *m* TELECOM transistor collector; ~ **de type P** *m* ELECTRON p-type collector; ~ **de vapeur** *m* PAPIER steam header

collecteur-fossé *m* DISTRI EAU drainage ditch

colle-émail *f* IMPRIM fish glue

coller *vt* AGRO ALIM clarify, CINEMAT join, splice, CONSTR *menuiserie* stick, MECANIQUE bond, ORDINAT *raccord* splice, TEXTILE size; ~ **à chaud** *vt* THERMODYN hot-bond; ~ **à froid** *vt* THERMODYN cold-bond; ~ **à sec** *vt* PHOTO dry-mount

collerette:[1] **à** ~ *adj* MECANIQUE flanged

collerette[2] *f* ESPACE flange, IMPRIM *emballage* collar, MECANIQUE collar, flange, PRODUCTION *autour de l'écran d'un ordinateur* bezel, *d'un tube* flange, VEHICULES *phare* rim; ~ **bas profil** *f* PRODUCTION *automatisme industriel* low-profile bezel; ~ **de la cuvette d'avant-corps** *f* CERAM VER curb

collerettes *f pl* TEXTILE paper collars

colles: ~ **à chaud maintenues à une température de fusion** *f pl* IMPRIM hot-melts

collet *m* CONS MECA collet, *d'un essieu* collar, *d'un cylindre de laminoir* journal, CONSTR *d'un ciseau* neck, NUCLEAIRE gland, stuffing box lid, PRODUCTION flange, *d'un cylindre de laminoir* neck; ~ **du palier de butée** *m* CONS MECA thrust collar; ~ **rabattu** *m* PRODUCTION turned-up flange; ~ **à souder** *m* CONS MECA welded collar; ~ **tombé** *m* PRODUCTION turned-up flange

colleuse *f* CINEMAT joiner, splicer, PAPIER pasting machine, TELECOM splicer; ~ **bout à bout** *f* CINEMAT butt end splicer; ~ **en biais** *f* CINEMAT diagonal joiner; ~ **à pathéine** *f* CINEMAT cement splicer; ~ **à pédale** *f* CINEMAT machine splicer; ~ **à scotch** *f* CINEMAT guillotine splicer, tape splicer; ~ **sèche** *f* CINEMAT dry splicer

colleuse-plieuse: ~ **flexible** *f* EMBALLAGE flexo-folder-gluer

collidine *f* CHIMIE collidin, collidine

collier *m* CONS MECA collar, *d'un excentrique* strap, CONSTR *fixé sur un chevron* gutter bracket, MECANIQUE collar, VEHICULES clamp; ~ **d'arbre** *m* CONS MECA shaft collar; ~ **d'arrêt** *m* CONS MECA set collar, stop collar; ~ **d'attache** *m* PRODUCTION tie wrap; ~ **de brûleur** *m* CERAM VER port mouth; ~ **de butée** *m* CONS MECA thrust collar; ~ **de câble** *m* ELECTR *fixation* cable clip; ~ **de câbles** *m* ELECTROTEC cable clamp; ~ **chauffant** *m* CONS MECA *moule d'injection* band heater; ~ **à coins** *m* PETR spider; ~ **d'embrayage** *m* CONS MECA clutch collar; ~ **d'excentrique** *m* CONS MECA eccentric collar, eccentric hoop, eccentric strap; ~ **de flottaison** *m* ESPACE *véhicules* flotation collar; ~ **de frein** *m* TEXTILE ruffle; ~ **à garniture de protection** *m* CONS MECA lined clamp; ~ **de jonction** *m* CONS MECA coupling sleeve; ~

de mise à la terre *m* ELECTR *raccordement* earth clip (BrE), ground clip (AmE); ~ par tuyau *m* CONSTR hose coupler; ~ positionneur *m* PETR line-up clamp; ~ de retenue *m* CONSTR *pour la descente des tubages de puits* casing clamp, MINES *pour la descente des tubages de puits* pipe clamp; ~ à segments *m* AUTO piston ring compressor; ~ de serrage *m* CONS MECA, MECANIQUE cable clamp, hose clamp; ~ de serrage pour tubes *m* CONS MECA pipe clip; ~ de serrage pour tuyaux flexibles *m* CONS MECA hose clamp; ~ de tuyau *m* CONSTR pipe-collar

colligatif *adj* CHIMIE colligative

collimater *vt* ASTRONOMIE, ELECTRON, INSTRUMENT collimate

collimateur *m* ASTRONOMIE, CINEMAT, INSTRUMENT, PHOTO, PHYSIQUE, TELECOM collimator; ~ de pilotage *m* AERONAUT head-up display, INSTRUMENT HUD, head-up display; ~ de spectroscope *m* INSTRUMENT spectroscope collimator

collimation *f* ASTRONOMIE, ELECTRON, INSTRUMENT, OPTIQUE collimation

colline: ~ abyssale *f* OCEANO abyssal hill, sea high, sea knoll

collision *f* CHARBON collision, ESPACE *véhicules* docking, INFORMAT collision, METALL impingement, ORDINAT collision, PHYSIQUE shock, SECURITE collision, TELECOM clashing, TRANSPORT collision; ~ aérienne *f* AERONAUT aerial collision; ~ atome-atome *f* NUCLEAIRE atom-atom collision; ~ avec réarrangement *f* NUCLEAIRE rearrangement collision; ~ élastique *f* NUCLEAIRE billiard ball collision, elastic collision, elastic impact; ~ d'électrons *f* TELECOM electron collision; ~ en chaîne *f* TRANSPORT multiple pile-up; ~ en vol *f* AERONAUT aerial collision; ~ de flanc *f* TRANSPORT side collision; ~ galactique *f* ASTRONOMIE galactic collision; ~ inélastique *f* PHYS RAYON inelastic collision; ~ inélastique en profondeur *f* NUCLEAIRE deep inelastic collision; ~ ion-ion *f* PHYS PART ion-ion collision; ~ latérale *f* TRANSPORT side on collision; ~ lointaine *f* NUCLEAIRE distant collision, range collision; ~ par l'arrière *f* TRANSPORT rear end collision; ~ de particules *f* PHYS PART particle collision; ~ primaire *f* TRANSPORT primary collision; ~ proton-antiproton *f* PHYS PART proton-antiproton collision; ~ proton-proton *f* PHYS PART proton-proton collision; ~ radiative *f* PHYS RAYON radiative collision; ~ rasante *f* NUCLEAIRE glancing collision; ~ secondaire *f* TRANSPORT secondary collision

collisionneur: ~ linéaire électron-positron *m* PHYS PART electron-positron collider; ~ proton-antiproton *m* PHYS PART proton-antiproton collider

collodion *m* CHIMIE collodion

colloïdal *adj* CHIMIE colloidal

colloïde *m* AGRO ALIM, CERAM VER, CHARBON colloid, CHIMIE *coagulé* colloid, gel, HYDROLOGIE, PLAST CAOU *état physique* colloid; ~ protecteur *m* CHIMIE protective colloid

colloïdes: ~ irréversibles *m pl* CHIMIE irreversible colloids

colloir *m* CERAM VER squeegee

colloxyline *f* CHIMIE colloxylin

collure *f* CINEMAT join, patch splice, splice, tape splice, ENREGISTR tape splice, PAPIER paster, splice, PLAST CAOU *adhésif* glue line; ~ en biais *f* CINEMAT diagonal splice; ~ à la pathéine *f* CINEMAT cement splice

collyre *m* SECURITE eyewash

collyrite *f* MINERAUX collyrite

colmatage *m* CHARBON, CONS MECA binding, clogging, DISTRI EAU binding, blocking, clogging, PRODUCTION filling up, silting, *système hydraulique* blocking, TEXTILE plugging; ~ des parois *m* PETR skin effect; ~ d'une tête *m* TV head clogging

colmater[1] *vt* DISTRI EAU clog

colmater:[2] se ~ *v réfl* PRODUCTION clog up

Colombe *f* ASTRONOMIE Columba

colonne *f* CONS MECA standard, *d'un laminoir* housing, CONSTR pillar, ELECTRON column, EN RENOUV *forage géothermique* tubing, IMPRIM, INFORMAT, ORDINAT column, PRODUCTION holster, TEXTILE wale; ~ d'absorption *f* AGRO ALIM absorption tower, CHARBON, GENIE CHIM absorption column, absorption tower, PETROLE absorption tower, *raffinerie* absorber, absorption column; ~ acoustique *f* ACOUSTIQUE sound column; ~ d'agrandisseur *f* PHOTO enlarger column; ~ barométrique *f* PAPIER barometric column, barometric leg, drop leg; ~ binaire *f* INFORMAT, ORDINAT binary column; ~ de boue *f* PETROLE mud column; ~ de carte *f* INFORMAT card column; ~ centrale *f* PHOTO *de trépied* central column; ~ à chromatographie *f* EQUIP LAB *analyse* chromatography column; ~ de cimentation *f* PETROLE cementing string; ~ de coke *f* CHARBON coke column; ~ de combustible *f* NUCLEAIRE pellet stack; ~ de concentration *f* GENIE CHIM concentration column; ~ de condensation *f* GENIE CHIM condensation column; ~ à corps de remplissage *f* GENIE CHIM packed column, packed tower; ~ couchée *f* MINES *de minerai* course of ore; ~ à dessécher *f* EQUIP LAB *verrerie* drying column; ~ de direction *f* AUTO, VEHICULES steering column; ~ de direction cédant sous l'impact *f* AUTO collapsible steering column; ~ de direction télescopique *f* TRANSPORT axially collapsing steering column; ~ de distillation *f* GENIE CHIM distillation column, distillation tower, PETROLE, THERMODYN distillation tower; ~ d'eau *f* EN RENOUV, HYDROLOGIE head of water; ~ d'eau différentielle *f* EN RENOUV differential head; ~ d'eau élevée *f* EN RENOUV high head; ~ d'eau en amont *f* EN RENOUV upstream head; ~ d'eau moyenne *f* EN RENOUV medium head; ~ d'eau peu élevée *f* EN RENOUV low head; ~ en charge *f* CONSTR wet standpipe; ~ entretoise *f* CONS MECA support pillar; ~ épaulée *f* CONS MECA guide pillar; ~ d'épuisement *f* REFRIG stripping column; ~ d'exploitation *f* PETR perforated casing, production string; ~ d'extraction *f* GENIE CHIM extractor; ~ de fermeture d'eau *f* PETROLE water string; ~ de fractionnement *f* EQUIP LAB *distillation*, GENIE CHIM, PETROLE *raffinerie* fractionating column; ~ à fractionner *f* GENIE CHIM separating column; ~ garnie *f* GENIE CHIM packed column, packed tower; ~ à garnissage *f* CHIMIE packed column, GENIE CHIM packed column, packed tower, PETROLE packed column; ~ géologique *f* GEOLOGIE geological column; ~ de guidage *f* CONS MECA *bloc à colonnes* guide pillar, *de plaque d'éjection* ejection guide pillar, *moule d'injection* guide pillar; ~ guide *f* PETR guidepost; ~ d'incendie *f* CONS MECA pillar hydrant; ~ inclinée *f* PHOTO angled column; ~ de laminoir *f* CONS MECA bearer; ~ lisse *f* CONSTR plain column; ~ de mise en contact *f* HYDROLOGIE contact column; ~ de mise au point des faisceaux d'ions *f* PHYS RAYON ion beam focusing column; ~ montante *f* CONSTR riser, riser pipe, rising main, ELECTR riser, *alimentation* rising main, PETR riser pipe, riser, standpipe, PETROLE riser, standpipe; ~ **moyenne d'eau** *f* EN RENOUV medium head; ~ **perdue** *f* PETR, PETROLE liner; ~ **perdue non crépinée** *f* PETROLE *forage* blank liner; ~ **des petites annonces classées** *f* IMPRIM *presse* ad-stack; ~ **à plateaux** *f* PETROLE plate column; ~ **à plateaux de barbotage** *f* GENIE CHIM bubble tray column; ~ **positive** *f* ELECTRON, PHYSIQUE positive column; ~ **de production** *f* PETR, PETROLE production string, production tubing; ~ **réservée aux dernières nouvelles** *f* IMPRIM newshole; ~ **sèche** *f* CONSTR dry standpipe; ~ **de sel** *f* PETROLE salt column; ~ **sonore** *f* ENREGISTR sound column; ~ **stratigraphique** *f* GEOLOGIE geological column, log, *d'un forage* composite log; ~ **de surforage** *f* PETROLE washover string; ~ **télescopique** *f* CINEMAT polecat; ~ **thermique** *f* NUCLEAIRE thermal column; ~ **de tubage** *f* CONSTR casing line, string of casing, tube column; ~ **de tubes** *f* CONSTR casing line, string of casing, tube column

colonnes: ~ **en serpent comportant des lézardes** *f pl* IMPRIM *composition* snaking columns

colophane *f* CHIMIE colophony, PLAST CAOU *matière première pour peinture* rosin, *matière première* wood rosin

colophène *m* CHIMIE colophene

colophon *m* IMPRIM imprint

colophonite *f* MINERAUX colophonite

coloradoïte *f* MINERAUX coloradoite

colorant *m* AGRO ALIM color (AmE), coloring (AmE), colour (BrE), colouring (BrE), CERAM VER coloring agent (AmE), colouring agent (BrE), CHIMIE dye, COULEURS coloring agent (AmE), coloring matter (AmE), colouring agent (BrE), colouring matter (BrE), TEXTILE dye, dyestuff; ~ **acide** *m* CHIMIE, TEXTILE acid dye; ~ **d'acridine** *m* COULEURS acridine dye; ~ **d'aniline** *m* COULEURS aniline dye; ~ **azoïque** *m* CHIMIE azo dye, TEXTILE azoic dye; ~ **basique** *m* CHIMIE basic dye, PAPIER basic color (AmE), basic colour (BrE), basic dye, TEXTILE basic dye; ~ **benzoïque** *m* COULEURS benzo dyestuff; ~ **de cuve** *m* TEXTILE vat dye; ~ **diazoïque** *m* CHIMIE bis-azo dye; ~ **direct** *m* TEXTILE direct dye; ~ **dispersé** *m* TEXTILE disperse dye; ~ **en poudre** *m* COULEURS powdered dye; ~ **pour beurre** *m* COULEURS butter coloring (AmE), butter colouring (BrE); ~ **pour encre d'imprimerie** *m* COULEURS printer's color (AmE), printer's colour (BrE), printing color (AmE), printing colour (BrE); ~ **prémétallisé** *m* TEXTILE pre-metallized dye; ~ **réactif** *m* TEXTILE reactive dye

colorants: ~ **anthracéniques** *m pl* CHIMIE anthracene dyes

coloration *f* CHIMIE staining, CINEMAT tinting, COULEURS dyeing; ~ **acoustique** *f* ENREGISTR acoustic coloring (AmE), acoustic colouring (BrE); ~ **due aux rayons X** *f* NUCLEAIRE X-ray coloration (AmE), X-ray colouration (BrE); ~ **en surface** *f* PAPIER surface coloring (AmE), surface colouring (BrE); ~ **par immersion** *f* PAPIER padding

coloré *adj* TELECOM colored (AmE), coloured (BrE)

colorer *vt* CHIMIE stain, PAPIER color (AmE), colour (BrE), dye, stain, TEXTILE dye

coloriage *m* INFORMAT, ORDINAT painting

colorimètre *m* CHIMIE, EQUIP LAB *analyse*, HYDROLOGIE, PAPIER, PHYS RAYON, PHYSIQUE, PLAST CAOU *instrument* colorimeter

colorimétrie *f* CHIMIE, DISTRI EAU, PHYS RAYON, PHYSIQUE colorimetry

coloris *m* TEXTILE shade; ~ **clair** *m* TEXTILE light shade; ~

foncé *m* TEXTILE dark shade, deep shade, overall shade; ~ **naturel** *m* TEXTILE natural color (AmE), natural colour (BrE), natural shade; ~ **neutre** *m* TEXTILE neutral shade

coltinage: ~ **du charbon** *m* CHARBON coal backing

colures *m pl* ASTRONOMIE colures

coma *m* ELECTRON, PHOTO, PHYSIQUE coma

comagmatique *adj* GEOLOGIE comagmatic

combinaison *f* CHIMIE combination, CONS MECA contrivance, INFORMAT, MATH, ORDINAT combination; ~ **anti-g** *f* ESPACE *véhicules* anti-G suit; ~ **d'images** *f* IMPRIM combo; ~ **logique** *f* ELECTRON logic pattern; ~ **de plongée** *f* OCEANO diving suit, wetsuit; ~ **de protection** *f* SECURITE protective suit; ~ **spatiale pressurisée** *f* ESPACE extra-vehicular pressure garment; ~ **de travail** *f* TEXTILE overall

combinateur: ~ **d'inversion et de freinage** *m* TRANSPORT reversing braking switchgroup; ~ **optique** *m* OPTIQUE, TELECOM optical combiner; ~ **de pas** *m* AERONAUT mixing unit; ~ **de pas général et cyclique** *m* AERONAUT collective pitch synchronizer; ~ **de shuntage** *m* CH DE FER shunt controller

combination: ~ **de plongée** *f* NAUT wetsuit

combinatoire *f* MATH combinatorics

combinatorique *f* MATH combinatorics

combiné[1] *adj* AERONAUT gyrodyne

combiné[2] *m* CHIMIE combination, compound, PRODUCTION handset, TELECOM handset, receiver; ~ **téléphonique à écoute amplifiée** *m* TELECOM amplified handset

combiner[1] *vt* CINEMAT marry up, INFORMAT, ORDINAT combine, PLAST CAOU blend

combiner:[2] **se ~** *v réfl* CHIMIE coalesce, unite

combineur *m* TELECOM combiner

comble *m* CONSTR roof; ~ **avec avant-toit** *m* CONSTR umbrella roof; ~ **brisé** *m* CONSTR curb roof, gambrel roof (AmE), mansard roof (BrE); ~ **à deux égouts** *m* CONSTR double pitch roof, pitch roof, ridge roof, ridged roof, span roof; ~ **à deux longs pans** *m* CONSTR pitch roof, ridge roof, ridged roof, span roof; ~ **à deux longs pans avec croupes** *m* CONSTR hip roof with ridge, hip-and-ridge roof, hipped ridge roof; ~ **à deux longs pans sans fermes** *m* CONSTR couple roof; ~ **à deux pans symétriques** *m* CONSTR double pitch roof; ~ **à deux pentes** *m* CONSTR double pitch roof, pitch roof, ridge roof, ridged roof, span roof; ~ **à deux rampants** *m* CONSTR double pitch roof; ~ **à deux rampes** *m* CONSTR ridge roof, ridged roof, span roof; ~ **à deux versants** *m* CONSTR double pitch roof, pitch roof, ridge roof, ridged roof, span roof; ~ **en appentis** *m* CONSTR lean-to roof, pent roof; ~ **en croupe** *m* CONSTR hip roof, hipped roof; ~ **en dent de scie** *m* CONSTR sawtooth roof, shed roof, square to roof; ~ **en dôme** *m* CONSTR dome roof; ~ **en mansarde** *m* CONSTR gambrel roof (AmE), mansard roof (BrE); ~ **à la française** *m* CONSTR curb roof; ~ **à la Mansard** *m* CONSTR curb roof, gambrel roof (AmE), mansard roof (BrE); ~ **à une pente** *m* CONSTR single pitch roof; ~ **à pignon** *m* CONSTR gable roof; ~ **retroussé** *m* CONSTR collar roof; ~ **sans ferme** *m* CONSTR untrussed roof; ~ **à une seule pente** *m* CONSTR single pitch roof; ~ **sur fermes** *m* CONSTR trussed roof; ~ **à un versant** *m* CONSTR single pitch roof

combler *vt* CONSTR *fossé* fill up

combles: ~ **s'intersectant** *m pl* CONSTR hip-and-valley roof

comble-shed *m* CONSTR sawtooth roof, shed roof, square to roof

comburable *adj* CHIMIE combustible

comburant[1] *adj* CHIMIE combustive

comburant[2] *m* AERONAUT, ESPACE *propulsion* oxidizer, THERMODYN oxidant

combustibilité *f* EMBALLAGE, SECURITE combustibility, THERMODYN combustibility, inflammability

combustible[1] *adj* CHIMIE combustive, THERMODYN combustible, inflammable

combustible[2] *m* ESPACE *propulsion* fuel, propellant fuel, THERMODYN combustible, fuel, VEHICULES fuel; **~ aluminure d'uranium** *m* NUCLEAIRE uranium aluminide fuel; **~ d'appoint** *m* NUCLEAIRE make-up fuel; **~ de bioxyde** d'uranium *m* NUCLEAIRE U02fuel, uranium dioxide fuel; **~ en dispersion** *m* NUCLEAIRE dispersion fuel; **~ enrichi** *m* NUCLEAIRE enriched fuel, enriched nuclear fuel; **~ fossile** *m* POLLUTION, THERMODYN fossil fuel; **~ de gueulard** *m* PRODUCTION furnace gas; **~ liquide** *m* THERMODYN *fusées* liquid fuel; **~ de matrice** *m* NUCLEAIRE matrix fuel; **~ de ménage** *m* CHARBON household fuel; **~ neuf** *m* NUCLEAIRE fresh fuel, new fuel; **~ non fumigène** *m* POLLUTION smokeless fuel; **~ non irradié** *m* NUCLEAIRE fresh fuel, new fuel; **~ nucléaire** *m* MILITAIRE nuclear fuel; **~ de référence** *m* PETROLE reference fuel; **~ solide** *m* NUCLEAIRE solid nuclear fuel; **~ d'U02** *m* NUCLEAIRE U02 fuel, uranium dioxide fuel; **~ d'uranium naturel** *m* NUCLEAIRE natural uranium fuel

combustibles *m pl* CHARBON combustibles, fuels; **~ gazeux** *m pl* PETROLE gaseous fuels; **~ pour soutes** *m pl* TRANSPORT bunker oils; **~ sulfureux** *m pl* POLLUTION sulfurous combustibles (AmE), sulphurous combustibles (BrE)

combustion[1] **~ à d'huile** *adj* THERMODYN oil-burning; **à ~ de mazout** *adj* THERMODYN oil-fired

combustion[2] *f* CHIMIE, PLAST CAOU, SECURITE combustion, THERMODYN burning, combustion; **~ du carbone** *f* NUCLEAIRE carbon burning; **~ à co-courant** *f* PETR forward combustion; **~ complète** *f* GAZ complete combustion; **~ à contre-courant** *f* PETR reverse combustion; **~ en avance** *f* PETR forward combustion; **~ érosive** *f* ESPACE *propulsion* erosive burning; **~ in situ** *f* PETR in situ combustion; **~ inversée** *f* PETR reverse combustion; **~ lente** *f* AUTO slow combustion; **~ massique cible** *f* NUCLEAIRE target burn-up, target irradiation; **~ massique finale** *f* NUCLEAIRE final fuel burn-up, ultimate burn-up; **~ massique moyenne du coeur** *f* NUCLEAIRE core average burn-up; **~ massique de préférence** *f* NUCLEAIRE design burn-up, design irradiation level; **~ massique réalisable** *f* NUCLEAIRE achievable burn-up; **~ optimale** *f* NUCLEAIRE optimum burn-up; **~ pulsatoire** *f* THERMODYN resonant burning; **~ spontanée** *f* SECURITE spontaneous combustion; **~ submergée** *f* GAZ submerged combustion; **~ sur lit fluidisé** *f* (CLF) POLLUTION fluidized bed combustion

coménique *adj* CHIMIE comenic

comète *f* ASTRONOMIE, ESPACE *astronomie*, IMPRIM comet; **~ de Halley** *f* ASTRONOMIE Halley's comet; **~ périodique** *f* ASTRONOMIE periodic comet

Comité: ~ consultatif international des radiocommunications *m* (CCIR) TELECOM International Radio Consultative Committee (CCIR); **~ consultatif international télégraphique et téléphonique** *m* (CCITT) TELECOM International Telegraph and Telephone Consultative Committee (CCITT); **~ international**

d'enregistrement des fréquences *m* ESPACE *communications* IFRB, International Frequency Registration Board

comité: ~ de sûreté d'aéroport *m* AERONAUT airport security committee

comma *m* ACOUSTIQUE comma; **~ d'Aristoxène** *m* ACOUSTIQUE Aristoxene comma; **~ de Didyme** *m* ACOUSTIQUE Didyme comma; **~ holdérien** *m* ACOUSTIQUE Holder comma; **~ de Pythagore** *m* ACOUSTIQUE Pythagorean comma; **~ syntonique** *m* ACOUSTIQUE syntonous comma

commandant: ~ de bord *m* AERONAUT captain, pilot, ESPACE*véhicules* commander; **~ d'un navire amiral** *m* NAUT flag captain; **~ des opérations sur le terrain** *m* POLLU MER OSC, on-scene commander

commande:[1] **à ~ automatique** *adj* CONS MECA push-button; **à ~ électronique** *adj* ELECTRON electronically-controlled; **à ~ manuelle** *adj* COMMANDE, ELECTROTEC manually-controlled, MECANIQUE hand-operated; **à ~ numérique** *adj* COMMANDE, CONS MECA numerically-controlled; **à ~ numérique par ordinateur** *adj* CONS MECA CNC-controlled, computerized numerical control; **à ~ par le bas** *adj* CONS MECA underdriven; **à ~ par chaîne** *adj* CONS MECA chain-driven; **à ~ pédestre** *adj* COMMANDE pedestrian-controlled; **à ~ au pied** *adj* COMMANDE pedestrian-controlled; **à ~ vocale** *adj* COMMANDE voice-operated

commande:[2] **à ~ manuelle** *adv* ESPACE hand-operated

commande:[3] **~ de liaison de données à haut niveau** *f* ORDINAT HDLC, high-level data link control

commande[4] *f* AERONAUT actuation, COMMANDE control, CONS MECA drive, driving gear, driving, ELECTR, ESPACE control, ORDINAT command, control, PAPIER, TEXTILE drive, VEHICULES control;

~ a **~ ACC** *f* (*contrainte de commande adaptative*) COMMANDE ACC (*adaptive control constraint*); **~ d'accès au support** *f* TELECOM MAC, medium access control; **~ adaptative** *f* COMMANDE, ELECTROTEC adaptive control, TRANSPORT vehicle-actuated control; **~ adaptative des signaux** *f* TRANSPORT vehicle-actuated signalization, vehicle-actuated traffic signals; **~ adaptative de la vitesse** *f* COMMANDE adaptive speed control; **~ d'allumeur** *f* VEHICULES distributor drive; **~ d'arrêt** *f* TV pause control; **~ asservie** *f* TV programed control (AmE), programmed control (BrE); **~ attendue** *f* PRODUCTION scheduled receipt; **~ automatique** *f* COMMANDE, CONS MECA, CONSTR, ELECTR, EMBALLAGE automatic control; **~ automatique de l'espacement entre les véhicules** *f* TRANSPORT automatic control of headway; **~ automatique de fréquence** *f* (CAF) ELECTRON, PHYSIQUE, PRODUCTION, TELECOM automatic frequency control (AFC); **~ automatique de gain** *f* (CAG) ELECTRON, TELECOM automatic gain control (AGC); **~ automatique de gain à seuil** *f* ELECTRON delayed automatic gain control; **~ automatique d'incendie** *f* CONSTR automatic fire alarm; **~ automatique de marche et de freinage** *f* TRANSPORT automatic running and braking control; **~ automatique de phase** *f* ELECTRON automatic phase control; **~ automatique des trains** *f* TRANSPORT ATO, automatic train operation, automatic train control; **~ automatique de volume** *f* (CAV) COMMANDE automatic amplitude control, automatic volume control (AVC), ELECTROTEC, OPTIQUE, PHYSIQUE automatic volume control (AVC); **~ de l'avance** *f* VEHICULES *allumage, soupapes* timing;

~ b ~ de boucle "demande de boucle audio" *f* TELECOM LCA, loopback command "audio loop request"; ~ de boucle "demande de boucle numérique" *f* TELECOM LCD, loopback command "digital loop request"; ~ de boucle "demande de boucle vidéo" *f* TELECOM LCV, loopback command "video loop request"; ~ à boucle fermée *f* COMMANDE closed-loop control; ~ de bout en bout *f* INFORMAT end-to-end control;

~ c ~ à cabestan *f* TV capstan drive; ~ de chauffage *f* AUTO heater control; ~ à clavier *f* NUCLEAIRE keyboard; ~ de compensation *f* AERONAUT trim control, TV peaking control; ~ à contacteurs *f* COMMANDE current contactor control; ~ continue *f* ELECTR stepless control; ~ de contrôle de poussée *f* ESPACE TVC, thrust vector control; ~ de correction *f* TV peaking control; ~ de courant *f* ELECTROTEC current control; ~ cyclique *f* AERONAUT azimuthal control; ~ cyclique de pas *f* AERONAUT cyclic pitch control;

~ d ~ de démarrage *f* AUTO starter control; ~ directe *f* CONS MECA, ELECTROTEC direct control; ~ de direction *f* AERONAUT rudder control; ~ à distance *f* COMMANDE, ELECTR, ESPACE *communications*, PHOTO, VEHICULES remote control; ~ à distance par caméra *f* TRANSPORT remote control by television camera; ~ à distance par radio *f* TRANSPORT radio steering; ~ à distance sans fil *f* CINEMAT wireless remote control; ~ de distributeur Joy *f* INST HYDR Joy's valve-gear; ~ de la distribution *f* AUTO camshaft drive; ~ à double position *f* ELECTR on/off control;

~ e ~ d'éclairage de réticule *f* INSTRUMENT reticle illumination knob; ~ électrique *f* ELECTROTEC electric control, NUCLEAIRE electrical drive; ~ électronique *f* NAUT, TRANSPORT electronic control; ~ électronique de fréquence *f* ELECTRON electronic frequency control; ~ électronique de zoom *f* CINEMAT servozoom; ~ de l'embrayage *f* VEHICULES clutch linkage; ~ d'émission numérique *f* TELECOM digital transit command; ~ en temps réel *f* TRANSPORT real-time control; ~ d'entrée/sortie *f* INFORMAT, ORDINAT input/output control;

~ f ~ flexible *f* CONS MECA flexible control; ~ de flux *f* INFORMAT, ORDINAT, TELECOM flow control; ~ de forçage à "1" *f* PRODUCTION *automatisme industriel* force-on command; ~ de forçage à "O" *f* PRODUCTION force-off command; ~ de formatage *f* INFORMAT template command; ~ de fréquence *f* TELECOM frequency control;

~ g ~ de gain *f* ELECTRON gain control; ~ de gauchissement *f* AERONAUT aileron control; ~ générale de gain *f* ELECTRON master gain control; ~ de groupe préréglé *f* TV subpreset master;

~ h ~ hydraulique *f* AUTO hydraulic linkage;

~ i ~ imprimante *f* IMPRIM printer command; ~ indirecte *f* ELECTROTEC indirect control; ~ individuelle *f* CONS MECA *pour machines outils* individual drive; ~ d'intensité *f* ELECTROTEC current control; ~ d'interdiction *f* AERONAUT interlock control; ~ d'invalidation de forçage *f* PRODUCTION force disable command;

~ l ~ de lecture *f* ENREGISTR playback control; ~ de liaison de données *f* AERONAUT, INFORMAT, TELECOM DLC, data link control; ~ de liaison de données à haut niveau *f* TELECOM HDLC, high-level data link control; ~ de liaison logique *f* TELECOM LLC, logical link control; ~ locale *f* MECANIQUE local control; ~ de

luminosité *f* TV brightness control;

~ m ~ de machine à papier *f* PAPIER paper machine drive; ~ à la main *f* COMMANDE, ELECTR hand control, manual control; ~ manuelle *f* AERONAUT, COMMANDE, CONSTR, ELECTR, MECANIQUE manual control; ~ manuelle à distance *f* AERONAUT manual remote control; ~ manuelle des gaz *f* AUTO hand throttle control; ~ mécanique *f* CONS MECA *d'une soupape* mechanical operation; ~ de mélange *f* AERONAUT mixture control; ~ à microprocesseur *f* ELECTRON microprocessor control; ~ de mise au point *f* TV focusing control; ~ multipoint d'assignation de jeton *f* TELECOM MCA, multipoint command assign token; ~ multipoint de conférence *f* TELECOM MCC, multipoint command conference; ~ multipoint de demande de jeton *f* TELECOM MCT, multipoint command token claim; ~ multipoint d'imposition de visualisation *f* TELECOM MCV, multipoint command visualization forcing; ~ multipoint de libération de jeton *f* TELECOM MCR, multipoint command release token; ~ multipoint de neutralisation de MCS *f* TELECOM MCN, multipoint command negating MCS; ~ multipoint de transmission symétrique des données *f* TELECOM MCS, multipoint command symmetrical data transmission;

~ n ~ de netteté *f* TV focusing control; ~ numérique *f* (CN) COMMANDE, CONS MECA, ELECTR *ordinateur*, INFORMAT, ORDINAT, PRODUCTION, TELECOM, TV digital control, numerical control; ~ numérique à cinq axes *f* CONS MECA five-axis numerical control; ~ numérique directe *f* INFORMAT, ORDINAT DDC, direct digital control;

~ o ~ opérateur *f* INFORMAT, ORDINAT, TELECOM operator command; ~ optimale *f* TELECOM optimal control; ~ d'orientation *f* TELECOM orientation control; ~ d'ouverture de boucle *f* TELECOM LCO, loopback command off;

~ p ~ par arbre *f* VEHICULES *transmission* shaft drive; ~ par autocalibrage *f* PRODUCTION dimensional control; ~ par balancier *f* CONS MECA beam drive; ~ par chaîne *f* CONS MECA chain drive; ~ par cône *f* CONS MECA cone pulley drive, step cone drive; ~ par cône-poulie *f* CONS MECA cone pulley drive; ~ par cônes de friction *f* CONS MECA cone drive, cone gear; ~ par cônes à friction *f* CONS MECA friction cone drive; ~ par courroie *f* PAPIER, PRODUCTION belt drive; ~ par électro-aimant à noyau-plongeur *f* ELECTROTEC solenoid actuation; ~ par engrenages *f* CONS MECA gear drive; ~ par microprocesseurs *f* TELECOM microprocessor control; ~ par monopoulie *f* CONS MECA single pulley drive; ~ par moteur *f* ELECTROTEC motor drive; ~ par programme *f* INFORMAT program control; ~ par relais ampèremétriques *f* COMMANDE current contactor control; ~ par tambour *f* CONS MECA drum drive; ~ par tension d'induit *f* ELECTR *machine* armature control; ~ par thermistances *f* ELECTROTEC thermistor control; ~ par touches *f* PHOTO push-button operation; ~ par la voix *f* TELECOM voice activation, voice control; ~ de pas *f* AERONAUT pitch control; ~ de pas général *f* AERONAUT collective pitch control; ~ de pause *f* ENREGISTR pause control; ~ de phase *f* ELECTRON, TELECOM phase control; ~ au pied *f* COMMANDE pedestrian control, CONS MECA foot-operated control, pedal-operated control; ~ au plancher *f* VEHICULES *boîte de vitesses* floor shift; ~ de point *f* TV focusing control; ~ pour ascenseurs *f* CONS MECA lift drive; ~ à présélection *f* VEHICULES *boîte de vitesses* preselection gear change; ~ **de processus** *f* ELECTROTEC process control; ~ **de profondeur** *f* AERONAUT elevator control, pitch control; ~ **programmable** *f* TELECOM programmable control; ~ **à programme enregistré** *f* TELECOM SPC, stored program control (AmE), stored programme control (BrE);

~ r ~ **de la rampe de sortie** *f* PRODUCTION *automatisme industriel* output ramp control; ~ **du réacteur** *f* AERONAUT, COMMANDE reactor control; ~ **de réapprovisionnement** *f* PRODUCTION replenishment order; ~ **de richesse** *f* AERONAUT *d'un moteur* mixture control; ~ **de richesse du carburant** *f* AERONAUT fuel control, mixture control; ~ **de richesse du mélange** *f* AERONAUT mixture control; ~ **de rotation du prisme inverseur** *f* INSTRUMENT inverter knob;

~ s ~ **de secours** *f* AERONAUT, SECURITE emergency control; ~ **sectionnelle** *f* PAPIER sectional drive; ~ **sensible à l'effleurement** *f* INFORMAT touch-sensitive control; ~ **séquentielle** *f* INFORMAT sequence control; ~ **du servomoteur de cabestan** *f* CINEMAT capstan motor control; ~ **des soupapes** *f* VEHICULES *moteur* valve gear, valve train; ~ **à soupapes** *f* AUTO valve control; ~ **de synchronisation verticale** *f* COMMANDE vertical hold;

~ t ~ **téléflex** *f* CONS MECA flexible control; ~ **à temps fixe** *f* TRANSPORT traffic forecasting; ~ **tout-ou-rien** *f* COMMANDE all-or-nothing control, ESPACE on/off control; ~ **du trafic** *f* TRANSPORT traffic control; ~ **de transmission** *f* INFORMAT transmission control; ~ **de transmission synchrone** *f* ORDINAT SDLC, synchronous data link control; ~ **transparente** *f* AERONAUT override control; ~ **de trim** *f* AERONAUT trim control;

~ v ~ **de validation de forçage** *f* PRODUCTION force enable command; ~ **vidéo de demande de gel de l'image** *f* TELECOM VCF, video command freeze-picture request; ~ **vidéo de demande de rafraîchissement rapide** *f* TELECOM VCU, video command fast-update request; ~ **de vitesse à présélection** *f* VEHICULES *boîte de vitesses* preselection gear change; ~ **des vitesses au pied** *f* VEHICULES *boîte de vitesses de motocyclette* foot change lever (BrE), foot gearshift (AmE); ~ **vocale** *f* COMMANDE voice operation; ~ **de voie** *f* TELECOM channel control;

~ z ~ **zonale du trafic** *f* TRANSPORT traffic network control; ~ **de zoom** *f* TV zoom lever

commandé: ~ **à distance** *adj* COMMANDE remote-controlled; ~ **à la main** *adj* COMMANDE manually-controlled; ~ **par courroie** *adj* PRODUCTION belt-driven; ~ **par électro-aimant** *adj* ELECTROTEC electromagnetically-operated; ~ **par fréquence vocale** *adj* TELECOM voice-activated; ~ **par moteur** *adj* PRODUCTION engine-driven; ~ **par piétons** *adj* COMMANDE pedestrian-controlled; ~ **par radar** *adj* TRANSPORT radar-controlled; ~ **par touche** *adj* ORDINAT key-driven; ~ **par la voix** *adj* COMMANDE voice-operated

commander *vt* MECANIQUE drive, *mécanique, physique* actuate, NAUT navigate, sail, ORDINAT, TELECOM control

commandes: ~ **de compensateur de gouvernes** *f pl* AERONAUT trim controls; ~ **conjuguées** *f pl* AERONAUT interconnected controls; ~ **électroniques** *f pl* PRODUCTION solid-state controls; ~ **en cours** *f pl* PRODUCTION backlog of orders; ~ **et contrôles** *f pl* AERONAUT controls and indicating; ~ **inversées** *f pl* AERONAUT reversed controls; ~ **de trim** *f pl* AERONAUT trim con-

trols; ~ **de vol** *f pl* AERONAUT, ESPACE flight controls; ~ **de vol doubles** *f pl* AERONAUT dual flight control system

commencement *m* CONS MECA starting; ~ **de l'échappement** *m* INST HYDR release point

commencer: ~ **à descendre** *vi* NAUT set out; ~ **à monter** *vi* NAUT set in; ~ **à se retirer** *vi* NAUT set out

commensurable *adj* MATH commensurable

commentaire *m* IMPRIM *en LDS* comment, INFORMAT, ORDINAT narrative, PAPIER *en LDS* comment

commerce: ~ **caboteur** *m* NAUT coastal trade; ~ **maritime** *m* NAUT sea trade, seaborne trade, shipping trade

commettre *vt* NAUT *cordage* lay

comminuer *vt* CHARBON mill

comminution *f* GENIE CHIM comminution, milling, size reduction; ~ **des particules** *f* GENIE CHIM particle size reduction

commis:[1] ~ **en aussière** *adj* NAUT *cordage* cable-laid; ~ **en grelin** *adj* NAUT *cordage* cable-laid

commis:[2] ~ **aux vivres** *m* NAUT purser

commissaire *m* NAUT purser; ~ **d'avarie** *m* NAUT surveyor

commission:[1] **en** ~ *adj* NAUT *d'un navire* in commission

commission:[2] ~ **chargée des questions de sécurité** *f* SECURITE safety committee

Commission: ~ **internationale de l'éclairage** *f (CIE)* PHYSIQUE International Commission on Illumination; ~ **internationale pour la protection radiologique** *f* PHYS RAYON ICRP, International Commission on Radiological Protection

commissionnaire: ~ **chargeur** *m* NAUT shipping agent; ~ **expéditeur** *m* NAUT shipping agent

communauté: ~ **maritime** *f* NAUT maritime community; ~ **vivante** *f* POLLUTION living community

communicant *adj* TELECOM networked

communicateur: ~ **de mouvement puissance** *m* CONS MECA transmitter of motive power

communication[1] *f* CH DE FER crossover, railroad junction (AmE), railway junction (BrE), TELECOM call; ~ **d'arrivée** *f* TELECOM incoming call; ~ **défectueuse** *f* TELECOM faulty call, faulty connection; ~ **de départ** *f* TELECOM outgoing call; ~ **en redondance** *f* PRODUCTION *automatisme industriel* backup communication; ~ **enroulée** *f* CH DE FER crossover between curved track; ~ **entre deux puits** *f* CONS MECA connection between two shafts; ~ **locale** *f* TELECOM local call; ~ **au moyen d'essaims de météores** *f* ESPACE *communications* meteor burst communication; ~ **par paquets** *f* ELECTROTEC, INFORMAT, ORDINAT packet switching; ~ **de redondance** *f* PRODUCTION *automatisme industriel* backup communication; ~ **téléphonique** *f* TELECOM telephone call; ~ **urbaine** *f* TELECOM local call; ~ **de voies** *f* CH DE FER crossover, rail crossover, railroad junction (AmE), railway junction (BrE)

communication:[2] **être en** ~ **avec** *vi* TELECOM to be talking to

communications *f pl* INFORMAT, ORDINAT communications; ~ **dans le sens sol-air** *f pl* AERONAUT ground-to-air communication; ~ **mobiles par satellite** *f pl* NAUT mobile satellite communications; ~ **numériques** *f pl* INFORMAT, ORDINAT digital communications; ~ **numérisées** *f pl* INFORMAT, ORDINAT digital communications; ~ **par satellite** *f pl* (*satcom*) NAUT satellite communications (*satcom*); ~ **sur place** *f pl* TELECOM *maritime mobile* OSC, on-scene communications

communiquant *adj* TELECOM networked

communiquer: ~ **l'énergie à** *vt* PHYSIQUE, THERMODYN impart energy to

commutable *adj* ELECTROTEC, PRODUCTION switch selectable, TV switchable

commutateur *m* CINEMAT switch, ELECTR changeover switch, *circuit* switch, *machine* commutator, ELECTROTEC multiposition switch, selector switch, ELECTR, ENREGISTR, INFORMAT, ORDINAT, PHYSIQUE switch, TELECOM switching unit, switch, TV switch;

~ a ~ **d'abonnés** *m* TELECOM local exchange; ~ **à accès flexible** *m* TELECOM FAS, flexible access switch; ~ **à action fugitive** *m* ELECTR touch contact switch; ~ **actionné par la pression** *m* ELECTR manometric switch; ~ **d'appareil** *m* ELECTROTEC instrument switch; ~ **automatique** *m* ELECTR automatic switch, ELECTROTEC self-acting switch; ~ **à autonomie d'acheminement** *m* TELECOM GSC, group switching center (AmE), group switching centre (BrE); ~ **auxiliaire** *m* TELECOM auxiliary switch, auxiliary switching unit;

~ b ~ **à bain d'huile** *m* PRODUCTION oil switch; ~ **à bande étroite** *m* TELECOM narrow band switch; ~ **barométrique** *m* AERONAUT barometric switch; ~ **à bascule** *m* CINEMAT rocker switch, COMMANDE toggle switch, tumbler switch, ELECTR *interrupteur* rocker switch, ELECTROTEC reversible switch; ~ **à batterie centrale** *m* TELECOM CB switchboard, central battery switchboard, common battery switchboard; ~ **bipolaire à bascule** *m* ELECTR DPSS, double-pole snap switch; ~ **bipolaire à couteaux** *m* ELECTR double-pole double-throw knife switch; ~ **de bits** *m* TELECOM bit switch; ~ **de bouclage** *m* ELECTR busbar coupler;

~ c ~ **à cames** *m* ELECTR camshaft controller, drum controller, drum starter; ~ **caractère par caractère** *m* TELECOM character coupling switch; ~ **de caractères** *m* TELECOM character switch; ~ **du champ de mesure** *m* ELECTR range switch, scale switch; ~ **de charge** *m* COMMANDE regulator breaker, regulator cutout, ELECTR *automobile* regulator cutout; ~ **à chevauchement** *m* ELECTROTEC shorting contact switch; ~ **de circuits** *m* ELECTRON circuit switch, TELECOM circuit switching unit, circuit-switched exchange; ~ **de circuits rapides** *m* TELECOM fast circuit switch; ~ **de circuits virtuels** *m (CCV)* TELECOM virtual-circuit switch *(VCS)*; ~ **à clef de protection de mémoire** *m* PRODUCTION *automatisme industriel* memory protect keyswitch; ~ **des clignotants** *m* AUTO direction indicator; ~ **de commande** *m* ELECTR, ELECTROTEC control switch; ~ **commandé par la voix** *m* TELECOM voice-operated switch; ~ **de commande et d'accusé de réception** *m* ELECTR control discrepancy switch; ~ **conjoncteur** *m* ELECTROTEC circuit closer, self-acting switch; ~ **à contactage progressif** *m* ELECTR continuity switch; ~ **à contacts à chevauchement** *m* ELECTROTEC shorting contact switch; ~ **à contacts sans court-circuit** *m* CONSTR nonshorting switch; ~ **à couteaux à deux directions** *m* ELECTR double-throw knife switch; ~ **cyclique mécanique** *m* ELECTROTEC scanning switch; ~ **cylindrique** *m* ELECTR drum switch;

~ d ~ **de démarrage** *m* ELECTR starting changeover switch; ~ **à déplacement de fibre** *m* TELECOM moving fiber switch (AmE), moving fibre switch (BrE); ~ **de dérivation** *m* ELECTR shunting switch; ~ **de desserrage** *m* ELECTR release switch; ~ **à deux directions** *m*

ELECTR, PHYSIQUE double-throw switch; ~ **à deux fils** *m* TELECOM two-wire switch, two-wire switching system, two-wire system; ~ **à dicorde** *m* TELECOM double-cord switchboard; ~ **à diode** *m* TV diode switch; ~ **de direction** *m* ELECTR direction commutator, *machine-outil* direction switch; ~ **à une direction** *m* PHYSIQUE single throw switch; ~ **disjoncteur** *m* ELECTR circuit breaker; ~ **de données** *m* TELECOM DSE, data switch;

~ e ~ **d'éclairage** *m* ELECTR light switch; ~ **électronique** *m* INFORMAT, ORDINAT electronic switch, TELECOM electronic exchange; ~ **électronique de messages** *m* TELECOM electronic message switch; ~ **électro-optique** *m* TELECOM electro-optic switch; ~ **en boîtier DIP** *m* ELECTROTEC DIP switch; ~ **encastré** *m* ELECTR flush switch, recessed switch; ~ **d'enclenchement** *m* ELECTROTEC interlock switch; ~ **en étoile** *m* TELECOM star switch; ~ **en fréquence** *m* TELECOM frequency-division switching system; ~ **en longueur d'onde** *m* TELECOM wavelength division switch; ~ **en parallèle** *m* ELECTR multiple switch; ~ **en série** *m* ELECTR series switch; ~ **d'enveloppes** *m* TELECOM envelope switch; ~ **d'escalier** *m* ELECTR three-point switch, three-position switch, three-way switch; ~ **d'étage** *m* ELECTR *ascenseur* floor switch, landing switch; ~ **étoile-triangle** *m* ELECTR star-delta starter, star-delta starting switch; ~ **étoile triangle** *m* ELECTR y-delta starter, y-delta starting switch;

~ f ~ **fermé** *m* ELECTROTEC sealed wafer rotary switch; ~ **à fiche** *m* ELECTROTEC plug switch; ~ **à fiches** *m* COMMANDE jack switch; ~ **à fiches et jacks** *m* TELECOM plug and cord switchboard; ~ **de fin de course** *m* ELECTR limit switch; ~ **de flash** *m* PHOTO flash switch; ~ **de flux** *m* ELECTR flow switch; ~ **de fonctions** *m* ELECTR function selector;

~ g ~ **à galette** *m* ELECTROTEC deck switch, gang switch, wafer switch; ~ **à galette fermé** *m* ELECTROTEC sealed wafer rotary switch; ~ **à galette non fermé** *m* ELECTROTEC open wafer rotary switch; ~ **glissant** *m* ELECTROTEC sliding switch; ~ **à glissière** *m* ELECTROTEC slide switch; ~ **à gradins** *m* ELECTR multiple contact switch, step switch; ~ **de groupe préréglé** *m* TV subpreset switch;

~ h ~ **holographique** *m* TELECOM holographic exchange; ~ **hybride** *m* TELECOM hybrid switch;

~ i ~ **interurbain** *m* TELECOM toll switch, trunk exchange; ~ **inverseur** *m* TV normal reverse switch; ~ **à inversion** *m* ELECTR reversing drum switch;

~ j ~ **à jacks** *m* ELECTR jack switchboard;

~ l ~ **à large bande** *m* TELECOM broadband switch; ~ **à levier** *m* ELECTROTEC lever switch; ~ **de ligne** *m* ELECTR line commutator; ~ **local** *m* TELECOM LE, local exchange, local switch;

~ m ~ **MA** *m* PHYSIQUE on/off switch; ~ **à manette** *m* CONS MECA handle switch, ELECTR double-throw knife switch, lever commutator switch; ~ **à manivelle** *m* CONS MECA handle switch; ~ **manuel** *m* TELECOM exchange switchboard, switchboard; ~ **manuel à fiches et jacks** *m* TELECOM plug and cord switchboard; ~ **manuel sans cordons** *m* TELECOM cordless switchboard; ~ **marche/arrêt** *m* PHYSIQUE on/off switch; ~ **de mémoire** *m* PRODUCTION memory store switch; ~ **de messages** *m* TELECOM message switch; ~ **de mesure** *m* ELECTROTEC test switch; ~ **minuterie** *m* ELECTR clock relay; ~ **de mise en phase** *m* ENREGISTR phasing switch; ~ **de mise en veilleuse** *m* ELECTR dimmer switch; ~ **de mise à la terre** *m* ELECTR, ELECTROTEC earthing switch (BrE), grounding switch (AmE); ~ **multiple** *m* ELECTR series switch; ~ **multiplex** *m* TELECOM multiple switchboard;

~ n ~ **à n directions** *m* ELECTR n-way switch; ~ **à n positions** *m* ELECTROTEC n-position switch; ~ **numérique** *m* TELECOM digital exchange, digital switch;

~ o ~ **d'octets** *m* TELECOM byte switch; ~ **optique** *m* TELECOM optical exchange, optical switch; ~ **optique à coupleur directif** *m* TELECOM directional coupler switch; ~ **optique intégré** *m* TELECOM integrated optical switch; ~ **optomécanique** *m* TELECOM mechanical optical switch; ~ **d'ordre** *m* ENREGISTR push-to-talk switch; ~ **ordre-écoute** *m* ENREGISTR talk-listen switch;

~ p ~ **de paquets** *m* ELECTR, TELECOM PS, packet switch; ~ **de paquets rapide** *m* TELECOM FPS, fast packet switch; ~ **de paquets téléphonie-données** *m* TELECOM voice-data packet switch; ~ **par bouton-poussoir** *m* PRODUCTION push-button switch; ~ **par enveloppes** *m* TELECOM envelope switch; ~ **pas à pas** *m* COMMANDE selector switch, ELECTROTEC stepping switch; ~ **de phares** *m* AUTO headlight switch; ~ **à plots** *m* ELECTR step switch; ~ **à plusieurs directions** *m* ELECTR series switch; ~ **du point de mesure** *m* ELECTR check switch, scanner; ~ **de position** *m* ELECTR position switch; ~ **à poussoir** *m* ELECTR rocker switch; ~ **de précision** *m* ELECTR power switch; ~ **préselecteur à disque "multiswitch"** *m* ELECTR thumbwheel switch; ~ **principal** *m* ELECTROTEC master switch, TELECOM main exchange (BrE); ~ **à prises** *m* ELECTR tap switch, ELECTROTEC tap changer; ~ **privé manuel** *m* TELECOM PMBX, private manual branch exchange; ~ **à programme enregistré** *m* TELECOM stored program control exchange (AmE), stored programme control exchange (BrE); ~ **public** *m* TELECOM central exchange switch (BrE), central office switch (AmE), public telephone exchange (BrE);

~ q ~ **à quatre fils** *m* TELECOM four-wire switch, four-wire switching system;

~ r ~ **rapide** *m* ELECTR quick throwover switch; ~ **à rappel automatique** *m* ELECTR *d'une automobile* self-canceling steering column switch (AmE), self-canceling turn signal switch (AmE), self-cancelling steering column switch (BrE), self-cancelling turn signal switch (BrE); ~ **de rattachement** *m* TELECOM host exchange, main exchange, serving exchange; ~ **à relais** *m* CINEMAT relay switch; ~ **de réseau privé** *m* TELECOM PNX, private network exchange; ~ **à ressort** *m* ELECTR spring commutator; ~ **rotatif** *m* COMMANDE, ELECTR rotary switch, ELECTROTEC rotary switch, stepping switch, uniselector, PRODUCTION thumbwheel switch; ~ **rotatif à plots** *m* ELECTROTEC rotary wafer switch; ~ **rural** *m* TELECOM rural exchange, rural switch;

~ s ~ **S** *m* TELECOM space switch; ~ **sans blocage** *m* ELECTROTEC nonblocking switch; ~ **satellite** *m* TELECOM satellite exchange; ~ **de secteur** *m* ELECTR current switch (AmE), mains switch (BrE); ~ **de sécurité** *m* ELECTR earthed switch (BrE), grounded switch (AmE); ~ **de sélection** *m* COMMANDE selector switch, ELECTR selective switch, ELECTRON, PRODUCTION selector switch; ~ **de sensibilité** *m* PHOTO light scale switch; ~ **de sens de marche** *m* ELECTR commutator switch; ~ **de séquence repos-travail** *m* TV break-before-make switch; ~ **à séquence travail-repos** *m* TV

gapping switch; ~ **des signaux des têtes** *m* TV switcher; ~ **spatial** *m* TELECOM space switch; ~ **spatial multiplex** *m* TELECOM multiplex space switch;

~ t ~ **T** *m* TELECOM TSI, time slot interchanger; ~ **à tambour** *m* ELECTR drum switch; ~ **téléphonique** *m* TELECOM telephone exchange; ~ **téléphonique privé** *m* TELECOM PBX, private branch exchange; ~ **télex** *m* TELECOM telex exchange; ~ **temporel** *m* TELECOM TSI, time slot interchanger, time switch; ~ **temporisé** *m* ELECTR clock relay; ~ **à temps** *m* ELECTR switch clock; ~ **à tige** *m* ELECTR joystick selector; ~ **à tourner-pousser** *m* ELECTR lock-down switch; ~ **tout à relais** *m* TELECOM relay system; ~ **de trame** *m* TV field shift switch; ~ **de transit** *m* TELECOM tandem exchange, transit exchange; ~ **de transit international** *m* TELECOM INTTR, international transit exchange, international gateway exchange; ~ **de transit urbain** *m* TELECOM junction tandem exchange; ~ **à trois positions** *m* ELECTR three-way switch;

~ u ~ **unipolaire** *m* ELECTR single-pole double-throw switch; ~ **universel** *m* TELECOM universal switch; ~ **urbain** *m* TELECOM central exchange, central switching unit, metropolitan switch;

~ v ~ **vidéo** *m* TELECOM video switch;

~ z ~ **des zones de mesure** *m* ELECTR range switch, scale switch

commutatif *adj* MATH commutative

commutation *f* ELECTROTEC commutation, switching, ESPACE *communications*, INFORMAT switching, MATH commutation, ORDINAT, TELECOM switching; ~ **accélérée** *f* ELECTR *machine* accelerated commutation; ~ **des appels en cours** *f* TELECOM switching call-in-progress; ~ **automatique** *f* ELECTR *commutateur* automatic changeover, ELECTROTEC automatic switching; ~ **automatique sur liaison de réserve** *f* TELECOM APS, automatic protection switching; ~ **de blocs mémoire** *f* ORDINAT bank switching; ~ **à bord** *f* ESPACE *communications* on-board switching; ~ **à bord du satellite** *f* ESPACE *communications* satellite switching; ~ **des caméras** *f* TV camera switching; ~ **de circuits** *f* ELECTRON, INFORMAT, ORDINAT CS, circuit switching; ~ **à commande vocale** *f* TELECOM voice-controlled operation, voice-operated relay, voice-operated switching; ~ **de courant alternatif** *f* ELECTROTEC AC switching; ~ **de courant continu** *f* ELECTROTEC DC switching; ~ **de données** *f* TELECOM data switching; ~ **électromécanique** *f* TELECOM electromechanical switching; ~ **électronique** *f* TELECOM electronic switching, TRANSPORT electronic commutation; ~ **d'entrées/sorties** *f* INFORMAT, ORDINAT input/output switching; ~ **de faisceaux** *f* ESPACE *communications* beam switching; ~ **de gammes d'ondes** *f* TV waveband switching; ~ **à haute fréquence** *f* ELECTROTEC high-frequency switching; ~ **de lignes** *f* INFORMAT, ORDINAT line switching; ~ **à longueur d'onde** *f* TELECOM wavelength switching; ~ **manuelle** *f* ELECTROTEC manual switching, TELECOM manual working; ~ **manuelle automatique** *f* NUCLEAIRE hand automatic switch; ~ **de messages** *f* INFORMAT, ORDINAT, TELECOM message switching; ~ **numérique** *f* TELECOM digital switching; ~ **optique** *f* ELECTROTEC, INFORMAT, ORDINAT, TELECOM optical switching; ~ **du palier avant** *f* TV front porch switch; ~ **de paquets** *f* ELECTROTEC, INFORMAT, ORDINAT, TELECOM packet switching; ~ **par relais à tiges** *f* ELECTROTEC reed relay switching; ~ **par répartition** *f* TELECOM time-division switching; ~ **au passage par**

zéro *f* ELECTROTEC zero-crossing switching; ~ **de primaire de transformateurs** *f* PRODUCTION *automatisme industriel* transformer primary switching; ~ **de protection automatique** *f* TELECOM APS, automatic protection switching; ~ **de Q** *f* ELECTRON Q-switching; ~ **spatiale** *f* INFORMAT, ORDINAT, TELECOM space division switching; ~ **téléphonique automatique** *f* ELECTROTEC automatic telephone switching; ~ **temporelle** *f* INFORMAT, ORDINAT time-division switching, TELECOM time switching, time-division switching; ~ **de transit** *f* TELECOM trunk switching; ~ **des voies entre cellules** *f* TELECOM intercell switching; ~ **au zéro de la tension** *f* ELECTROTEC zero voltage switching

commutator *f* ELECTROTEC collector

commutatrice *f* ELECTR *alimentation en courant alternatif* synchronous converter, *courant alternatif* rotary converter, ELECTROTEC dynamotor, rotary converter, synchronous converter; ~ **inversée** *f* ELECTROTEC synchronous inverter

commuté *adj* TELECOM switched; ~ **par la voix** *adj* TELECOM voice-switched

commuter *vt* CINEMAT change over, INFORMAT, ORDINAT, TELECOM switch

compacité *f* INFORMAT packing density

compact[1] *adj* INFORMAT high-density

compact:[2] ~ **vert** *m* NUCLEAIRE *avant frittage* green compact, green pellet

compactage *m* CHARBON, CONSTR, MATERIAUX compaction, TELECOM condensing; ~ **d'échantillons** *m* CHARBON laboratory compaction

compacter *vt* PRODUCTION compact

compacteur: ~ **à cylindre vibrant** *m* CONSTR vibrating roller; ~ **à pneus** *m* CONSTR rubber tired roller (AmE), rubber tyred roller (BrE); ~ **vibrant en tandem** *m* CONSTR tandem vibrating roller

compaction *f* GEOLOGIE compaction, INFORMAT, ORDINAT compaction, compression, PETROLE compaction; ~ **de mémoire** *f* INFORMAT, ORDINAT memory compaction, memory compression

compagnie: ~ **aérienne** *f* AERONAUT airline; ~ **d'affrètement** *f* AERONAUT, NAUT charter company; ~ **maritime** *f* NAUT shipping company; ~ **de navigation** *f* NAUT shipping company; ~ **opératrice Bell** *f* (MD) TELECOM BOC, Bell operating company (TM); ~ **subsidiaire** *f* AERONAUT feeder airline

companseur *m* ELECTRON compander

compansion *f* ELECTRON companding

comparaison: ~ **de signaux** *f* ELECTRON signal comparison; ~ **de tension** *f* ELECTROTEC voltage comparison

comparateur *m* ELECTRON comparator, signal comparator, INFORMAT, METROLOGIE, ORDINAT, PHYSIQUE comparator, TELECOM comparator, comparison circuit; ~ **à amplificateur opérationnel** *m* ELECTRON operational amplifier comparator; ~ **analogique** *m* ELECTRON analog comparator (AmE), analogue comparator (BrE); ~ **à cadran** *m* CONS MECA dial gage (AmE), dial gauge (BrE); ~ **différentiel** *m* ELECTRON differential comparator; ~ **électronique** *m* CONS MECA *mesurage dimensionnel* electronic comparator; ~ **mécanique** *m* METEO dial gage (AmE), dial gauge (BrE); ~ **optique** *m* METROLOGIE optical comparator; ~ **de phase** *m* ELECTRON phase comparator, phase detector, TV phase comparator; ~ **de signaux** *m* ELECTRON signal comparator; ~ **de tension** *m* ELECTROTEC voltage comparator

comparer *vt* INFORMAT, ORDINAT compare

compartiment *m* ORDINAT bucket, compartment, REFRIG compartment; ~ **abaissé d'une faille** *m* GEOLOGIE downfaulted side, dropped side; ~ **à bagages** *m* TRANSPORT baggage room (AmE), luggage compartment (BrE); ~ **à basse température** *m* REFRIG low-temperature compartment; ~ **congélateur** *m* REFRIG freezer compartment; ~ **des échelles** *m* MINES ladder road, ladder shaft, ladder way, manway; ~ **emboîtable** *m* EMBALLAGE compartmented insert; ~ **de l'exhaure** *m* DISTRI EAU *d'un puits* pump compartment; ~ **d'extraction** *m* CONSTR *d'un puits* hoisting compartment; ~ **à glace carbonique** *m* REFRIG dry ice bunker; ~ **à marchandises** *m* TRANSPORT cargo space; ~ **des pompes** *m* DISTRI EAU *d'un puits* pump compartment; ~ **de production de glace** *m* CONS MECA ice-making compartment; ~ **relevé** *m* GEOLOGIE upfaulted block; ~ **de travail** *m* CERAM VER gathering end; ~ **des voyageurs** *m* TRANSPORT passenger compartment

compartimentage *m* CONSTR partitioning, GEOLOGIE block faulting, MINES *d'un puits*, NAUT compartmentation

compartimentation *f* CONSTR partitioning

compartiment-moteur *m* VEHICULES engine compartment

compas *m* AERONAUT *atterrisseur* torque link, CONS MECA compasses, ESPACE compass, GEOMETRIE compasses, METROLOGIE compass, compasses, NAUT, PHYSIQUE compass; ~ **azimutal** *m* NAUT azimuth compass; ~ **à balustre** *m* CONS MECA, CONSTR bow compass, bow compasses; ~ **de calibre** *m* METROLOGIE caliper compasses (AmE), calliper compasses (BrE), calipers (AmE), callipers (BrE); ~ **à coulisse** *m* CONS MECA sliding caliper gage (AmE), sliding calipers (AmE), sliding calliper gauge (BrE), sliding callipers (BrE), METROLOGIE beam caliper (AmE), beam caliper gage (AmE), beam calliper (BrE), beam calliper gauge (BrE); ~ **dit 1/2 huit de chiffre** *m* CONS MECA egg calipers (AmE), egg callipers (BrE); ~ **dit huit** *m* CONS MECA hourglass calipers (AmE), hourglass callipers (BrE); ~ **dit huit de chiffre** *m* CONS MECA hourglass calipers (AmE), hourglass callipers (BrE); ~ **à diviser** *m* CONS MECA, PRODUCTION divider, dividers, pair of dividers; ~ **droit** *m* CONS MECA, PRODUCTION divider, dividers, pair of dividers; ~ **droit à pointes** *m* CONS MECA, PRODUCTION divider, dividers, pair of dividers; ~ **d'ellipse** *m* CONS MECA oval compass; ~ **elliptique** *m* CONS MECA oval compass; ~ **d'épaisseur** *m* CONS MECA outside calipers (AmE), outside callipers (BrE), CONSTR double calipers (AmE), double callipers (BrE), METROLOGIE spring adjusting caliper (AmE), spring adjusting calliper (BrE); ~ **étalon** *m* NAUT standard compass; ~ **d'extérieur** *m* CONS MECA outside calipers (AmE), outside callipers (BrE); ~ **gyroscopique** *m* AERONAUT, NAUT gyroscopic compass; ~ **gyrosyn** *m* AERONAUT, NAUT gyrosyn compass; ~ **d'habitacle** *m* NAUT binnacle compass; ~ **d'intérieur** *m* CONS MECA inside calipers (AmE), inside callipers (BrE); ~ **à lame tranchante** *m* CONS MECA washer cutter; ~ **liquide** *m* NAUT liquid compass; ~ **magnétique** *m* AERONAUT magnetic compass; ~ **maître-à-danser** *m* CONS MECA in-and-out calipers (AmE), in-and-out callipers (BrE), inside-and-outside calipers (AmE), inside-and-outside callipers (BrE); ~ **maître de danse** *m* CONS MECA in-and-out calipers (AmE), in-and-out callipers (BrE), inside-and-outside calipers (AmE), inside-and-outside callipers (BrE), CONSTR double calipers

(AmE), double callipers (BrE); ~ **de mer** *m* NAUT mariner's compass; ~ **à pointes sèches** *m* CONS MECA divider, pair of dividers, GEOMETRIE, METROLOGIE dividers, NAUT dividers, pair of dividers, PRODUCTION divider, dividers, pair of dividers; ~ **à pompe** *m* CONS MECA pump spring bow, rotational compass; ~ **à porte-crayon** *m* CONS MECA compasses with pencil point; ~ **quart de cercle** *m* CONS MECA wing compasses; ~ **qui s'affole** *m* NAUT disturbed compass; ~ **de réduction** *m* CONS MECA reduction compass; ~ **de relèvement** *m* NAUT azimuth compass, bearing compass; ~ **répétiteur** *m* ESPACE *véhicules*, NAUT repeater compass; ~ **à répétition optique** *m* NAUT projector compass; ~ **à ressort** *m* CONS MECA spring dividers; ~ **de route** *m* NAUT steering compass; ~ **sphérique** *m* CONSTR bow calipers (AmE), bow callipers (BrE); ~ **à tire-ligne** *m* CONS MECA compasses with pen point; ~ **de train** *m* AERONAUT torque link; ~ **de variation** *m* GEOPHYS variation compass; ~ **à verge** *m* CONS MECA beam dividers, trammel, METROLOGIE beam compasses

Compas *m* ASTRONOMIE Circinus

compas-balustre *m* CONSTR bow, bow compass, bow compasses; ~ **à pincettes** *m* CONSTR bow spring compasses; ~ **à pointes sèches** *m* CONSTR bow dividers; ~ **à pompe** *m* CONS MECA pump spring bow, rotational compass

compatibilité:[1] **à ~ ascendante** *adj* INFORMAT, ORDINAT upward compatible; **à ~ descendante** *adj* INFORMAT, ORDINAT downward compatible

compatibilité[2] *f* CONS MECA, INFORMAT, ORDINAT, PLAST CAOU, PRODUCTION, QUALITE, TV *de format* compatibility; ~ **ascendante** *f* INFORMAT upward compatibility; ~ **avec l'environnement** *f* POLLUTION environmental compatibility; ~ **descendante** *f* INFORMAT downward compatibility; ~ **dimensionnelle** *f* TELECOM dimensional compatibility; ~ **électromagnétique** *f* ELECTROTEC electromagnetic compatibility, ESPACE EMC, electromagnetic compatibility; ~ **des fluides avec les caoutchoucs** *f* CONS MECA compatibility between elastometric materials and fluids; ~ **totale** *f* ELECTROTEC plug compatibility; ~ **vers le bas** *f* ORDINAT downward compatibility; ~ **vers le haut** *f* ORDINAT upward compatibility

compatible *adj* INFORMAT, ORDINAT, QUALITE compatible

compensateur *m* ELECTR, ELECTRON compensator, ELECTROTEC balancer, compensator, PHYSIQUE compensator; ~ **Babinet** *m* PHYSIQUE Babinet compensator; ~ **de commande de pas** *m* AERONAUT blade pitch control compensator; ~ **de courant alternatif** *m* ELECTR alternating current balancer; ~ **de dilatation à soufflet** *m* CONS MECA bellow expansion joint; ~ **de direction** *m* AERONAUT rudder trim; ~ **d'erreur de vitesse de têtes** *m* TV velocity error compensator; ~ **d'évolution** *m* AERONAUT balance tab, horn balance; ~ **de freinage** *m* AUTO proportioning valve; ~ **hydraulique de pilonnement** *m* PETROLE *plateforme en mer* hydraulic compensator; ~ **d'impédance** *m* ENREGISTR impedance compensator; ~ **de perte de niveau** *m* TV drop-out compensator; ~ **de phase** *m* ELECTR *moteur* phase advancer; ~ **de pilonnement** *m* PETR, PETROLE *exploitation en mer* heave compensator; ~ **pneumatique** *m* AERONAUT pneumatic cylinder; ~ **de présence** *m* ENREGISTR presence equalizer; ~ **à ressort** *m* CONS MECA spring tab; ~ **à tube ondulé** *m* NUCLEAIRE *de dilatation* corrugated expansion joint, corrugated tube compensator

compensateurs *m pl* IMPRIM *périphériques de rotatives* box tilts

compensation *f* AERONAUT counterbalance, trimming, ELECTRON, ELECTROTEC compensation, MECANIQUE equalization, PHYSIQUE compensation; ~ **des aigus** *f* ENREGISTR treble compensation; ~ **des basses** *f* ENREGISTR bass compensation; ~ **de compas** *f* AERONAUT compass compensating; ~ **à corne débordante** *f* AERONAUT horn balance; ~ **de direction** *f* AERONAUT rudder trim; ~ **en fréquence** *f* ENREGISTR frequency compensation; ~ **de fréquence** *f* ELECTRON frequency compensation; ~ **de gauchissement** *f* AERONAUT lateral trim; ~ **des hautes fréquences** *f* ENREGISTR high-frequency compensation; ~ **isostatique** *f* GEOLOGIE isostatic adjustment; ~ **par dopage** *f* ELECTRON doping compensation; ~ **de pas** *f* AERONAUT pitch compensation; ~ **de phase** *f* ELECTR *courant alternatif*, TELECOM phase compensation; ~ **de profondeur** *f* AERONAUT pitch trim; ~ **de la réaction d'induit** *f* ELECTROTEC armature reaction compensation; ~ **de température** *f* ELECTRON, ELECTROTEC, THERMODYN temperature compensation; ~ **thermique** *f* ELECTRON, THERMODYN temperature compensation; ~ **de l'usure** *f* MECANIQUE compensation for wear

compenser[1] *vt* ESPACE *véhicules* trim, NAUT compensate, *compas* adjust, OCEANO equalize, PHYSIQUE compensate; ~ **le diaphragme** *vt* CINEMAT follow F-stop

compenser:[2] ~ **l'usure** *vi* MECANIQUE compensate for wear

compilateur *m* ORDINAT, TELECOM compiler; ~ **C** *m* ORDINAT C-compiler; ~ **de compilateur** *m* ORDINAT compiler-compiler; ~ **croisé** *m* ORDINAT cross compiler; ~ **incrémentiel** *m* ORDINAT incremental compiler

compilation *f* ORDINAT compilation; ~ **croisée** *f* ORDINAT cross compilation

compiler *vt* ORDINAT compile

complément *m* ELECTRON, INFORMAT, ORDINAT complement; ~ **à la base** *m* IMPRIM, INFORMAT, ORDINAT radix complement; ~ **à deux** *m* INFORMAT, ORDINAT two's complement; ~ **d'épuration** *m* POLLUTION supplementary purification; ~ **de ligne numérique** *m* TELECOM digital pad; ~ **à neuf** *m* INFORMAT, ORDINAT nine's complement; ~ **nutritionnel** *m* AGRO ALIM nutritional supplement; ~ **restreint** *m* INFORMAT, ORDINAT radix-minus-one complement; ~ **à un** *m* INFORMAT, ORDINAT one's complement

complémentaire *adj* BREVETS supplementary, CONS MECA additional

complémenteur *m* INFORMAT, ORDINAT negator

complétion *f* PETROLE *d'un puits foré* completion; ~ **en trou ouvert** *f* PETR barefoot completion, open hole completion; ~ **sous-marine** *f* PETROLE subsea completion

complexant *adj* CHIMIE sequestering agent

complexe[1] *adj* CONS MECA intricate

complexe[2] *m* GEOLOGIE *d'unités lithologiques, structurales* complex; ~ **activé** *m* METALL activated complex; ~ **Epoxy** *m* IMPRIM glass epoxy laminate; ~ **frigorifique** *m* REFRIG cold store complex; ~ **intrusif annulaire** *m* GEOLOGIE cone sheet; ~ **magmatique** *m* GEOLOGIE igneous complex; ~ **à orbitales externes** *m* PHYS RAYON *structure atomique* outer orbital complex; ~ **à orbitales internes** *m* PHYS RAYON *structure atomique* inner orbital complex; ~ **de studios** *m* CINEMAT lot

complexer *vt* CHIMIE sequester
complexes: **~ stratifiés** *m pl* IMPRIM laminate
complexité *f* INFORMAT, ORDINAT complexity; **~ de la puce** *f* ELECTRON chip complexity
comportant: **~ un balourd** *adj* CONS MECA, METROLOGIE out-of-balance
comportement *m* CONSTR behavior (AmE), behaviour (BrE), IMPRIM *du papier* runnability, *matières premières* behavior (AmE), behaviour (BrE), POLLU MER behavior (AmE), behaviour (BrE); **~ d'un avion** *m* AERONAUT aircraft behavior (AmE), aircraft behaviour (BrE); **~ dans le temps** *m* COMMANDE time response; **~ aux efforts de longue durée** *m* MATERIAUX long-term stress behavior (AmE), long-term stress behaviour (BrE); **~ en compression** *m* MATERIAUX compressive behavior (AmE), compressive behaviour (BrE); **~ en mer** *m* TRANSPORT seakeeping; **~ en traction** *m* MATERIAUX tensile behavior (AmE), tensile behaviour (BrE); **~ au feu** *m* SECURITE *études d'incendie* burning behavior (AmE), burning behaviour (BrE); **~ linéaire** *m* ELECTRON linear behavior (AmE), linear behaviour (BrE); **~ mécanique de matériaux** *m* ESSAIS mechanical behavior of materials (AmE), mechanical behaviour of materials (BrE); **~ du réacteur** *m* NUCLEAIRE reactor behavior (AmE), reactor behaviour (BrE); **~ à la rupture** *m* METALL fracture behavior (AmE), fracture behaviour (BrE)
composant[1] *adj* CONS MECA component
composant[2] *m* CHARBON, ELECTR *pièce*, ELECTRON, NUCLEAIRE, PRODUCTION, TELECOM component; **~ active** *m* TELECOM active component; **~ à l'arséniure de gallium** *m* ELECTRON gallium arsenide component; **~ chimique** *m* GEOLOGIE *d'un système chimique* chemical component; **~ à conducteurs poutres** *m* ELECTRON beam lead device; **~ à couches épaisses** *m* ELECTRON thick-film device; **~ à couches minces** *m* ELECTRON thin-film device; **~ discret** *m* ELECTROTEC, TELECOM discrete component; **~ électrique** *m* ELECTROTEC electrical component; **~ électronique** *m* ELECTRON, INFORMAT, ORDINAT, TELECOM electronic component; **~ électronique actif** *m* ELECTROTEC active component; **~ en bande** *m* ELECTROTEC bandoliered component, taped component; **~ en boîtier DIP** *m* ELECTRON DIP component; **~ enfichable** *m* ELECTROTEC plug-in component; **~ en guide d'ondes** *m* ELECTROTEC waveguide component; **~ fileté** *m* CONS MECA threaded component; **~ fourni** *m* PRODUCTION consigned component; **~ hybride intégré** *m* ELECTRON integrated hybrid component; **~ logique** *m* ELECTRON logic component; **~ monolithique** *m* MATERIAUX solid-state semiconductor component; **~ monté en surface** *m* (CMS) ELECTRON, TELECOM surface-mounted component (SMC); **~ NMOS** *m* ELECTRON NMOS component; **~ optoélectronique** *m* ELECTROTEC optoelectronic coupler; **~ parasite** *m* ELECTROTEC parasitic component; **~ passif** *m* ELECTRON, NUCLEAIRE, PHYSIQUE, TELECOM passive component; **~ à pattes** *m* ELECTRON beam lead device; **~ de puissance discret** *m* ELECTROTEC direct power component; **~ à quatre couches** *m* ELECTRON p-n-p-n component, p-n-p-n device; **~ d'un réacteur** *m* NUCLEAIRE reactor component; **~ de réglage** *m* COMMANDE servocomponent; **~ Schottky** *m* ELECTRON Schottky device; **~ à semi-conducteur** *m* ELECTRON, MATERIAUX semiconductor component; **~ à semi-conducteur discret** *m* ELECTRON discrete semiconductor device; **~ au silicium** *m* ELECTROTEC silicon device; **~ thermique** *m* METALL thermal component; **~ de type N** *m* ELECTRON n-type component

composante *f* ACOUSTIQUE fundamental, ELECTR *d'une force, d'un courant* component, ELECTRON component, frequency component, MECANIQUE, PHYSIQUE *d'un vecteur* component; **~ active** *f* ELECTR active component, ELECTROTEC active component, real component, PHYSIQUE active component; **~ alternative** *f* ELECTR *courant alternatif* alternating component; **~ alternative d'un courant** *f* ELECTR alternating current component; **~ capacitive** *f* ELECTR capacitive component; **~ chromatique** *f* TV chromatic component; **~ de la chromatologie** *f* IMPRIM *photogravure* chroma; **~ de chrominance** *f* TV chrominance component; **~ constante de pertes** *f* ELECTR *machine* fixed loss; **~ continue** *f* TELECOM DC component; **~ de courant continu** *f* ELECTR direct current component; **~ déwattée** *f* ELECTR wattless component, *courant alternatif* idle component, ELECTROTEC wattless component; **~ directe** *f* ELECTR *courant* direct component; **~ en phase** *f* ELECTRON in-phase component; **~ en quadrature** *f* ELECTRON quadrature component, ELECTROTEC reactive component; **~ fondamentale** *f* PHYSIQUE fundamental component; **~ à fréquence élevée** *f* ELECTRON high-frequency component; **~ fréquencielle** *f* ELECTRON frequency component; **~ horizontale** *f* GEOLOGIE *du rejet d'une faille* heave, PHYSIQUE horizontal component; **~ horizontale de déplacement** *f* GEOLOGIE offset; **~ horizontale du rejet** *f* GEOLOGIE normal horizontal separation; **~ longitudinale** *f* PHYSIQUE longitudinal component; **~ longitudinale du vent** *f* AERONAUT longitudinal wind component; **~ lunaire** *f* ESPACE *communications spatiales* moon segment; **~ de la marée** *f* OCEANO harmonic tidal constituent, tidal component; **~ martienne** *f* ESPACE *communications spatiales* Mars segment; **~ de portance** *f* AERONAUT lift component; **~ principale** *f* MATH principal component; **~ radiale** *f* PHYSIQUE radial component; **~ réactive** *f* ELECTR *courant alternatif* wattless component, ELECTROTEC idle component, wattless component, reactive component; **~ du signal** *f* ELECTRON signal component; **~ de la sous-porteuse** *f* TV subcarrier component; **~ spatiale** *f* ESPACE *communications spatiales* space segment; **~ tangentielle** *f* PHYSIQUE tangential component; **~ terrienne** *f* ESPACE *communications spatiales* ground segment; **~ transversale** *f* ELECTR *courant alternatif* quadrature axis component, quadrature component, PHYSIQUE transverse component; **~ verticale** *f* PHYSIQUE vertical component; **~ wattée** *f* ELECTROTEC real component; **~ Zeeman** *f* PHYSIQUE Zeeman component

composantes: **~ trichromatiques** *f pl* PHYSIQUE tristimulus values
composé:[1] **~ plein** *adj* IMPRIM set solid
composé[2] *m* CHIMIE compound; **~ d'addition** *m* CHIMIE adduct; **~ amphiphile** *m* LESSIVES amphiphilic compound; **~ amphotère** *m* LESSIVES amphoteric compound; **~ aromatique** *m* AGRO ALIM, MATERIAUX, PETROLE aromatic compound; **~ électronique** *m* METALL electronic compound; **~ ignifuge moussant** *m* SECURITE intumescence compound; **~ inorganique de chrome** *m* CHIMIE inorganic chromium compound; **~ d'insertion** *m* CHIMIE clathrate compound; **~ inter-halogène** *m* CHIMIE interhalogen compound; **~ intermétallique** *m* MATERIAUX, METALL intermetallic

compound; ~ **interstitiel** *m* CHIMIE interstitial compound; ~ **marqué** *m* NUCLEAIRE isotopically tagged compound, labeled compound (AmE), labelled compound (BrE); ~ **métallo-céramique** *m* MECANIQUE *outillage* cermet; ~ **métamère** *m* CHIMIE metamer; ~ **nitré** *m* CHIMIE nitro-compound; ~ **organique** *m* CHIMIE organic compound; ~ **orgomagnésien** *m* CHIMIE organomagnesium compound; ~ **soufré** *m* GAZ sulfur compound (AmE), sulphur compound (BrE); ~ **stoechiométrique** *m* CRISTALL stoichiometric compound; ~ **d'uranium** *m* NUCLEAIRE uranium compound

composer *vt* CONSTR *poutre* build up, IMPRIM compose, set, *colonnes de chiffres* digitize, TELECOM *numéro* dial; ~ **en capitales** *vt* IMPRIM keep up

composés: ~ **organochlorés** *m pl* RECYCLAGE organochlorines; ~ **soufrés** *m pl* PETROLE petrosulfur compounds (AmE), petrosulphur compounds (BrE)

composeur *m* CERAM VER mixer; ~ **vocal** *m* TELECOM voice dialler

composite[1] *adj* MATERIAUX composite

composite[2] *m* METALL composite; ~ **intermétallique** *m* MATERIAUX intermetallic composite; ~ **à matrice métallique** *m* MATERIAUX metal matrix composite; ~ **renforcé** *m* MATERIAUX *matières plastiques* reinforced composite; ~ **satellite-moteur d'apogée** *m* ESPACE *véhicules* satellite apogee motor combination; ~ **zircone-alumine** *m* MATERIAUX zirconia-alumina composite

compositeur *m* IMPRIM comp, compositor, typesetter, composing stick, setting stick; ~ **typographique** *m* IMPRIM typo

composition *f* CERAM VER batch, charge, mix, CHIMIE composition, IMPRIM body matter, composition, MECANIQUE *des forces*, PAPIER *papier ou carton* composition, TELECOM dialing (AmE), dialling (BrE); ~ **abrégée** *f* TELECOM abbreviated dialling (BrE), short code dialing (AmE), short code dialling (BrE); ~ **à l'américaine** *f* IMPRIM flush setting; ~ **assistée par ordinateur** *f* IMPRIM computer-assisted typesetting; ~ **à base d'argile** *f* CERAM VER clay composition; ~ **au clavier** *f* TELECOM keying; ~ **au début de vie** *f* NUCLEAIRE beginning of life; ~ **dégraissante** *f* EMBALLAGE degreasing compound; ~ **à distance** *f* IMPRIM teletypesetting; ~ **en drapeau** *f* IMPRIM ragged setting; ~ **de fabrication** *f* PAPIER furnish; ~ **de fermeture pour boîtes** *f* EMBALLAGE can sealing compound; ~ **fibreuse** *f* EMBALLAGE, IMPRIM, PAPIER fiber composition (AmE), fibre composition (BrE); ~ **de garnissage** *f* EMBALLAGE lining compound; ~ **granulométrique** *f* CONSTR grading; ~ **initiale** *f* NUCLEAIRE composition; ~ **à la main** *f* IMPRIM hand composition; ~ **mécanique** *f* IMPRIM mechanical setting; ~ **minéralogique** *f* GEOLOGIE *d'une roche* mode; ~ **pour enduire** *f* EMBALLAGE coating compound; ~ **pour fermeture avec capsule** *f* EMBALLAGE cap sealing compound; ~ **pour fermeture de couvercle** *f* EMBALLAGE lid-sealing compound; ~ **sans renfoncement ni à droite à gauche** *f* IMPRIM full out; ~ **stoechiométrique** *f* METALL stoichiometric composition; ~ **sur film** *f* IMPRIM film composition; ~ **du train** *f* CH DE FER train consist (AmE), train formation (BrE); ~ **typographique** *f* IMPRIM typesetting

compostage *m* POLLUTION composting

composteuse: ~ **pour repiquage d'étiquettes** *f* EMBALLAGE label overprinting machine

compoundage *m* ELECTROTEC compounding

compresseur *m* AUTO supercharger, CONS MECA, CONSTR, ELECTRON, ENREGISTR, EQUIP LAB, GAZ, MECANIQUE, PAPIER, PETROLE *plongée, pompe, moteurs*, REFRIG, VEHICULES *moteur* compressor; ~ **d'air** *m* CONS MECA air compressor, CONSTR compressor, EQUIP LAB, INST HYDR, MECANIQUE *air comprimé* air compressor; ~ **alternatif** *m* REFRIG reciprocating compressor; ~ **automatique** *m* ENREGISTR dialogue equalizer; ~ **axial** *m* AERONAUT axial compressor, CONS MECA low-pressure compressor, MECANIQUE axial compressor; ~ **centrifuge** *m* AUTO centrifugal supercharger, CONS MECA centrifugal compressor; ~ **compound** *m* PRODUCTION stage compressor; ~ **à contre-courant** *m* REFRIG return flow compressor; ~ **à cylindres jumelés** *m* INST HYDR duplex compressor; ~ **double** *m* CONS MECA dual compressor; ~ **entièrement hermétique** *m* CONS MECA hermetic compressor; ~ **entraîné par moteur diesel** *m* CONS MECA diesel-powered compressor; ~ **à équicourant** *m* REFRIG uniflow compressor; ~ **étagé** *m* CONS MECA, PRODUCTION stage compressor; ~ **à flux inversé** *m* REFRIG return flow compressor; ~ **de frein** *m* AUTO air compressor; ~ **frigorifique** *m* REFRIG refrigerating compressor; ~ **à gaz** *m* PRODUCTION gas compressor; ~ **à groupe unique de cylindres en tandem** *m* PRODUCTION straight-line compressor; ~ **haute pression** *m* CONS MECA high-pressure compressor; ~ **à injection** *m* PRODUCTION spray compressor; ~ **à injection d'air** *m* INST HYDR air injection compressor; ~ **à injection d'eau** *m* INST HYDR water injection compressor, PRODUCTION spray compressor; ~ **à injection pneumatique** *m* INST HYDR air injection compressor; ~ **lent** *m* INST HYDR slow-speed compressor; ~ **à marche sèche** *m* CONS MECA dry-running compressor; ~ **à membrane** *m* CONS MECA diaphragm compressor; ~ **monocylindrique** *m* INST HYDR single stage compressor; ~ **monocylindrique simple** *m* PRODUCTION straight-line compressor; ~ **à piston** *m* CONS MECA, GAZ piston compressor; ~ **à piston à basse pression** *m* CONS MECA low-pressure piston compressor; ~ **à piston à haute pression** *m* CONS MECA high-pressure piston compressor; ~ **à plusieurs étages** *m* CONS MECA multistage compressor, NUCLEAIRE compound compressor; ~ **pour fluides frigorigènes** *m* CONS MECA refrigerant compressor; ~ **de réfrigération** *m* CONS MECA refrigerant compressor; ~ **refroidi par air** *m* REFRIG air-cooled compressor; ~ **refroidi par gaz réfrigérant** *m* REFRIG refrigerant-cooled compressor; ~ **rotatif** *m* REFRIG rotary compressor; ~ **rotatif stationnaire à un arbre** *m* CONS MECA single shaft stationary rotary compressor; ~ **rotatif à vis** *m* PRODUCTION rotary screw compressor; ~ **sans huile** *m* REFRIG oil-free compressor; ~ **sec** *m* CONS MECA dry-running compressor; ~ **à simple effet** *m* INST HYDR single stage compressor, REFRIG single-acting compressor; ~ **de suralimentation** *m* MECANIQUE supercharger; ~ **à vis** *m* CONS MECA, GAZ screw compressor; ~ **de volume** *m* ENREGISTR volume compressor; ~ **volumétrique** *m* CONS MECA positive displacement compressor

compresseur-expanseur *m* ELECTRON, INFORMAT, ORDINAT compander

compresseur-extenseur *m* ESPACE *communications* compander, TELECOM compander, compressor-expander

compressibilité *f* CHAUFFAGE, METALL, PAPIER, PHYS FLUID, PHYSIQUE compressibility; ~ **des gaz** *f* THERMODYN compressibility of gases; ~ **isentropique** *f*

PHYSIQUE isentropic compressibility; ~ **isotherme** *f*
PHYSIQUE isothermal compressibility
compressiomètre *m* CHARBON compressometer; ~ **pour**
moteur diesel *m* AUTO diesel compression tester
compression *f* CINEMAT squeeze, CONSTR, ELECTRON,
ENREGISTR compression, INFORMAT compaction,
compression, INST HYDR, MATERIAUX, NUCLEAIRE
compression, ORDINAT compaction, compression,
PHYS ONDES *des ondes sonores*, PHYSIQUE, PLAST CAOU,
REFRIG compression; ~ **adiabatique** *f* PHYS FLUID,
THERMODYN adiabatic compression; ~ **automatique**
de volume *f* ENREGISTR automatic volume compression; ~ **de bande** *f* ELECTRON bandwidth
compression; ~ **de bande passante** *f* TV bandwidth
compression; ~ **du blanc** *f* TV white compression; ~ **de**
blocs *f* ORDINAT block compaction (BrE), block compression (AmE); ~ **compound** *f* PRODUCTION stage
compression; ~ **de données** *f* INFORMAT data compaction, data compression; ~ **de la dynamique** *f* ELECTRON
volume compression; ~ **en deux étages** *f* CONS MECA
two-space compression; ~ **à un étage** *f* REFRIG single
stage compression; ~ **étagée** *f* CONS MECA compound
compression, PRODUCTION stage compression; ~ **de**
gain *f* ELECTRON gain compression; ~ **d'image** *f* TV
picture compression; ~ **d'images** *f* ELECTRON image
compression; ~ **d'impulsion** *f* TELECOM pulse compression; ~ **d'information** *f* ELECTRON data
compression; ~ **de mémoire** *f* INFORMAT memory compaction, memory compression; ~ **des noirs** *f* TV black
compression, black crush; ~ **à plusieurs étages** *f* RE-
FRIG multistage compression; ~ **de signal** *f* TELECOM
signal compression; ~ **de télécopie** *f* TELECOM facsimile compression; ~ **temporelle** *f* TELECOM time
compression; ~ **des tonalités** *f* IMPRIM *photogravure*
tone compression; ~ **de la vapeur** *f* GENIE CHIM vapor
compression (AmE), vapour compression (BrE)
compression-extension *f* ESPACE *communications*, TELE-
COM companding; ~ **syllabique** *f* TELECOM
maritime-satellite syllabic companding
compressomètre *m* PAPIER compression tester, compressometer
comprimer *vt* CONSTR, INFORMAT, ORDINAT compress,
PRODUCTION press
comptabilisation: ~ **des travaux** *f* INFORMAT, ORDINAT
job accounting
comptabiliser: ~ **en stock** *vt* PRODUCTION post to stock
comptabilité: ~ **des produits** *f* PRODUCTION product
accounting
comptage *m* ELECTRON counting, GAZ metering, INFOR-
MAT tally, PRODUCTION *automatisme industriel* up
count, TELECOM metering; ~ **des accès** *m* TRANSPORT
access road census (AmE), slip road census (BrE),
access road count (AmE), slip road count (BrE),
ramp metering; ~ **des appels** *m* TELECOM call metering; ~ **de la circulation** *m* TRANSPORT traffic census,
traffic count; ~ **de défaut** *m* QUALITE defect counting;
~ **directionnel** *m* TRANSPORT directional census; ~
électronique *m* ELECTRON electronic counting; ~ **des**
mouvements *m* COMMANDE traffic count
compte: ~ **de la chaîne** *m* TEXTILE warp setting; ~ **de**
justification de pointeur *m* TELECOM PJC, pointer justification count; ~ **à rebours** *m* ESPACE *véhicules*
countdown, TV back timing; ~ **rendu** *m* ESPACE payoff;
~ **rendu de données d'accident** *m* AERONAUT accident
data reporting; ~ **rendu de données d'incident** *m*
AERONAUT incident data reporting; ~ **rendu d'essai** *m*

INFORMAT, ORDINAT test report; ~ **rendu pour l'atter-**
rissage *m* AERONAUT *météorologie* report for landing;
~ **rendu pour le décollage** *m* AERONAUT report for
takeoff; ~ **temps** *m* PHOTO timer
compte-fils *m* IMPRIM *contrôle de qualité* line tester,
magnifying glass, magnifying lens, PAPIER line tester,
thread counter
compte-gouttes *m* CONS MECA drip-feed lubricator, EM-
BALLAGE drop counter, EQUIP LAB *verrerie*, PAPIER
dropper; ~ **capillaire** *m* EQUIP LAB dropping tube
compte-pas *m* PHYSIQUE pedometer
compte-pose *m* PHOTO darkroom timer
comptes: ~ **lainiers** *m pl* TEXTILE wool counts
compte-tours *m* AUTO tachometer, CONS MECA revolution counter, speed counter. VEHICULES *moteur,*
accessoire rev counter (BrE), tachometer (AmE)
compteur *m* CONS MECA counter, ELECTR meter, ELEC-
TRON counter, ENREGISTR tape counter, INFORMAT
counter, METROLOGIE meter (AmE), ORDINAT
counter, PRODUCTION *automatisme industriel* up
counter, TELECOM counter, meter, TV tape counter,
VEHICULES *accessoire* speedometer; ~ **d'abonné** *m*
TELECOM subscriber's meter; ~ **additif** *m* ELECTRON up
counter; ~ **d'appels** *m* TELECOM CR, call register; ~
bidirectionnel *m* ELECTRON bidirectional counter, up-
down counter; ~ **binaire** *m* ELECTRON, ORDINAT binary
counter; ~ **Cerenkov** *m* ASTRONOMIE, PHYS RAYON
Cerenkov counter; ~ **à cliquet** *m* CINEMAT click footage counter; ~ **de consommation** *m* ELECTROTEC
demand meter; ~ **de contamination** *m* SECURITE contamination meter; ~ **de débit** *m* INST HYDR current
meter; ~ **de débit d'air** *m* CONS MECA air meter; ~ **à**
diaphragme *m* GAZ diaphragm meter; ~ **à domicile** *m*
TELECOM subscriber's private meter; ~ **d'eau** *m* TEX-
TILE water meter; ~ **à eau** *m* DISTRI EAU water meter; ~
d'éclairs *m* GEOPHYS lightning flash counter; ~ **élec-**
trique *m* ELECTR, ELECTROTEC electricity meter; ~
électronique *m* ELECTRON electronic counter; ~ **en**
anneau *m* TV ring counter; ~ **en cascade** *m* ORDINAT
cascadable counter; ~ **d'énergie** *m* ELECTROTEC energy
meter, integrating meter; ~ **d'énergie active** *m* ELECTR
active energy meter; ~ **d'énergie apparente** *m* ELECTR
apparent energy meter; ~ **en pieds** *m* CINEMAT film
footage counter, footage counter; ~ **d'étincelles** *m*
PHYS RAYON spark counter; ~ **à gaz** *m* EQUIP LAB,
PRODUCTION gas meter, THERMODYN flowmeter, gas
meter; ~ **Geiger** *m* NUCLEAIRE, PHYS PART, PHYSIQUE
Geiger counter; ~ **d'heures de marche** *m* NAUT engine
hours indicator, operating hours indicator; ~ **d'-**
heures de travail *m* SECURITE working hours counter;
~ **horaire** *m* PHYSIQUE timer; ~ **d'images** *m* CINEMAT
frame counter, PHOTO exposure counter, frame
counter; ~ **d'impulsion** *m* ELECTRON pulse counter; ~
d'impulsions *m* ELECTR impulse counter; ~ **d'instruc-**
tions *m* INFORMAT, ORDINAT sequence control register;
~ **journalier** *m* AUTO trip mileage indicator; ~ **kilomé-**
trique *m* AUTO mileage recorder (BrE), odometer
(AmE); ~ **de manoeuvres** *m* ELECTR *changeur de prise*
operation counter; ~ **métreur** *m* METROLOGIE length
meter; ~ **à neuf chiffres** *m* EMBALLAGE nine digit
counter; ~ **de noyaux de condensation** *m* POLLUTION
condensation nucleus counter; ~ **d'orbites** *m* ESPACE
mesures orbit counter; ~ **à paiement préalable** *m* CONS
MECA slot counter; ~ **pas à pas** *m* INFORMAT step
counter; ~ **à piston rotatif** *m* GAZ rotary piston meter;
~ **de poses** *m* PHOTO frame counter; ~ **de poussière**

micrométrique *m* INSTRUMENT dust counter; ~ de programme *m* INFORMAT, ORDINAT program counter; ~ progressif *m* ELECTRON accumulating counter, adding counter, count-up counter, up counter; ~ proportionnel *m* PHYSIQUE proportional counter; ~ de puissance apparente *m* ELECTR apparent power meter; ~ de radiation *m* PHYS ONDES radiation counter, PHYS RAYON radiation counter, radiation monitor; ~ de renvois *m* TELECOM redirecting counter; ~ à scintillation *m* ASTRONOMIE, PHYS RAYON, PHYSIQUE scintillation counter; ~ séquentiel *m* INFORMAT, ORDINAT step counter; ~ au silicium *m* PHYS RAYON silicon counter; ~ soustractif *m* ELECTRON down counter; ~ de surplus d'énergie *m* ELECTR excess energy meter; ~ de taxes *m* TELECOM message register, subscriber's meter; ~ de taxes d'abonné *m* TELECOM subscriber's meter; ~ de taxes à domicile *m* TELECOM subscriber's private meter; ~ de tours *m* CONS MECA revolution counter, speed counter, stroke counter; ~ de tours manuel *m* EMBALLAGE hand tachometer; ~ de trafic *m* TRANSPORT traffic counter; ~ à turbine *m* GAZ turbine meter; ~ à ultrason *m* GAZ ultrasound meter; ~ de vapeur *m* PAPIER steam flowmeter; ~ de vitesse *m* AUTO, VEHICULES speedometer; ~ de vitesse linéaire *m* CONS MECA surface speed indicator; ~ à vortex *m* GAZ vortex meter; ~ de vues *m* PHOTO frame counter

compteur-décompteur *m* ELECTRON increment-decrement counter, up-down counter, PRODUCTION *automatisme industriel* up-down counter, TV forward-backward counter

compteur-fréquencemètre *m* ELECTRON frequency counter

compteurs: ~ en cascade *m pl* PRODUCTION cascading counters

comptoir: ~ frigorifique *m* REFRIG refrigerated counter

concassage *m* CHARBON breaking down, crushing, CONSTR breaking; ~ en circuit ouvert *m* CHARBON open circuit crushing; ~ fin *m* CHARBON fine crushing; ~ grossier *m* CHARBON coarse crushing; ~ tertiaire *m* CHARBON tertiary crushing

concasser *vt* AGRO ALIM grind, CHARBON crush, CONSTR break, crush

concasseur *m* CHARBON crusher, CONS MECA breaker, CONSTR crusher, rock breaker, stone breaker, stone crusher, stone mill, PRODUCTION crusher; ~ à calcin *m* CERAM VER cullet crusher; ~ centrifuge *m* GENIE CHIM centrifugal crusher; ~ à charbon *m* CHARBON coal breaker, cracker, coal cracker; ~ de charbon et de pierre *m* MINES coal and stone breaker; ~ à cône *m* CHARBON cone crusher; ~ dégrossisseur *m* CHARBON primary crusher; ~ giratoire *m* AGRO ALIM gyratory crusher, GENIE CHIM centrifugal crusher; ~ à impact *m* CHARBON impact breaker; ~ à mâchoires *m* CHARBON jaw crusher, CONS MECA jaw breaker, jaw crusher, EQUIP LAB *préparation*, PRODUCTION jaw crusher; ~ à mâchoires à cadence rapide *m* CHARBON impact crusher; ~ à minerai *m* MINES ore crusher; ~ mobile *m* CHARBON mobile crusher; ~ à pointes *m* CHARBON pick breaker; ~ primaire *m* CHARBON coarse crusher, primary crusher; ~ secondaire *m* CHARBON secondary crusher

concaténation *f* ELECTROTEC, IMPRIM, INFORMAT, ORDINAT, TELECOM concatenation

concaténer *vt* ORDINAT concatenate

concave *m* CHARBON concave

concavité *f* ENREGISTR *de la bande* cupping, PETR sag

bend, under bend

concentrateur *m* ELECTRON, EN RENOUV, MAT CHAUFF, MINES, ORDINAT concentrator, TELECOM CON, concentrator; ~ d'abonnés *m* TELECOM line concentrator, local line concentrator; ~ d'abonnés distant *m* TELECOM remote line concentrator; ~ d'abonnés local *m* TELECOM collocated concentrator; ~ distant *m* TELECOM remote concentrator; ~ de données *m* INFORMAT, ORDINAT data concentrator; ~ de lignes *m* TELECOM line concentrator; ~ numérique satellite *m (CNS)* TELECOM digital satellite concentrator; ~ satellite numérique *m* TELECOM RCU, remote concentration unit; ~ solaire *m* EN RENOUV solar concentrator; ~ de voies asynchrones *m* TELECOM access concentrator

concentration *f* AERONAUT *contrôle de la circulation aérienne* bunching, CHARBON concentration, ELECTRON concentration, focusing, PLAST CAOU concentration; ~ acide *f* POLLUTION acid concentration; ~ ambiante *f* POLLUTION background concentration; ~ atmosphérique *f* POLLUTION atmospheric concentration; ~ des boues *f* HYDROLOGIE sludge bulking, sludge thickening; ~ des conversations *f* ESPACE *communications* speech interpolation; ~ des électrons liants *f* NUCLEAIRE electron-to-atom ratio, valence electron concentration; ~ électrostatique *f* ELECTROTEC electrostatic focusing; ~ en acides *f* POLLUTION acid concentration; ~ en masse *f* SECURITE mass concentration; ~ en masse de dioxyde de soufre *f* SECURITE *dans l'air ambiant* mass sulfur dioxide concentration (AmE), mass sulphur dioxide concentration (BrE); ~ en ozone *f* POLLUTION ozone concentration; ~ d'erreurs *f* TELECOM error density; ~ du faisceau d'électrons *f* ELECTRON electron beam focusing; ~ de fond *f* POLLUTION background concentration; ~ d'impuretés *f* ELECTRON impurity concentration; ~ instantanée *f* POLLUTION instantaneous concentration; ~ ionique *f* GEOPHYS ionic concentration; ~ des ions d'hydrogène *f* CHIMIE hydrogen ion concentration; ~ létale *f* POLLUTION lethal concentration; ~ létale à 50% *f (CL50)* POLLUTION median lethal concentration; ~ locale d'un polluant *f* POLLUTION ambient pollutant concentration; ~ magnétique *f* ELECTROTEC magnetic focusing; ~ magnétique du faisceau *f* PHYS PART magnetic beam compressing; ~ maximale admissible *f* POLLUTION MAC, maximum allowable concentration, TLV, TLV at place of work, threshold limit value, occupational MAC, occupational maximum allowable concentration, occupational TLV, occupational threshold limit value, *dans l'air ambiant* MAC, maximum allowable concentration; ~ maximale admissible dans l'air ambiant *f* POLLUTION TLV in the free environment, threshold limit value in the free environment; ~ maximale d'immixtion *f (CMI)* POLLUTION maximum emission concentration; ~ mécanique *f* PRODUCTION mechanical concentration; ~ au niveau du sol *f* POLLUTION ground level concentration; ~ nominale *f* MATERIAUX bulk concentration, nominal concentration; ~ numérique des conversations *f (CNC)* TELECOM digital speech interpolation *(DSI)*; ~ numérique de la parole *f (CNP)* TELECOM digital speech compression; ~ par congélation *f* GENIE CHIM, REFRIG freeze concentration; ~ par les gaz résiduels *f* ELECTRON gas focusing; ~ de pointe *f* POLLUTION peak concentration; ~ des poussières en suspension dans l'air *f* SECURITE airborne dust concentration; ~ **des signaux vocaux** *f* TELECOM interpolation of speech signals; ~ **sûre** *f* NUCLEAIRE safe concentration; ~ **volumique critique de pigment** *f* *(CVCP)* REVETEMENT *peinture* critical pigment volume concentration *(CPVC)*

concentré¹ *adj* AGRO ALIM concentrated, PHYSIQUE lumped

concentré² *m* AGRO ALIM, CHARBON concentrate; ~ **de levure** *m* AGRO ALIM yeast extract; ~ **de petit-lait** *m* AGRO ALIM whey concentrate; ~ **de produit de boulangerie** *m* AGRO ALIM bakery concentrate; ~ **de protéines de lactosérum** *m* AGRO ALIM whey concentrate; ~ **de protéines de poisson** *m* *(CPP)* OCEANO fish protein concentrate *(FPC)*; ~ **uranifère** *m* NUCLEAIRE uranium concentrate, yellow cake

concentrer *vt* AGRO ALIM, CHARBON concentrate, ELECTRON focus, GENIE CHIM concentrate, PRODUCTION consolidate; ~ **par ébullition** *vt* AGRO ALIM boil down

concentricité *f* MECANIQUE concentricity

concentrique *adj* MECANIQUE concentric

concept: ~ **de pale avançante** *m* AERONAUT advancing blade concept

conception *f* CONSTR, INFORMAT, ORDINAT, PRODUCTION, SECURITE design; ~ **assistée par ordinateur** *f* *(CAO)* ELECTR, IMPRIM, MECANIQUE, ORDINAT, PRODUCTION, TELECOM computer-aided design *(CAD)*; ~ **automatisée** *f* ORDINAT design automation; ~ **de base** *f* NUCLEAIRE base design; ~ **des circuits** *f* ELECTRON, ELECTROTEC circuit design; ~ **des circuits analogiques** *f* ELECTRON analog circuit design (AmE), analogue circuit design (BrE); ~ **des circuits intégrés** *f* ELECTRON integrated circuit design; ~ **des circuits numériques** *f* ELECTRON digital circuit design; ~ **et fabrication assistées par ordinateur** *f* *(CFAO)* ORDINAT, PRODUCTION computer-aided design and manufacture *(CADCAM)*; ~ **fonctionnelle** *f* INFORMAT, ORDINAT functional design; ~ **hiérarchique orientée objet** *f* ORDINAT HOOD, hierarchical object-oriented design; ~ **logicielle** *f* INFORMAT, ORDINAT software design; ~ **logique** *f* ELECTRON, INFORMAT, ORDINAT logic design; ~ **orientée objet** *f* *(COO)* INFORMAT, ORDINAT object-oriented design *(OOD)*; ~ **de programme** *f* INFORMAT, ORDINAT program design; ~ **des puces** *f* ELECTRON chip design; ~ **des réacteurs** *f* NUCLEAIRE reactor design; ~ **de satellite** *f* ESPACE satellite design; ~ **structurée** *f* INFORMAT, ORDINAT structured design; ~ **sûre en cas de défaillance** *f* NUCLEAIRE fail-safe design

conceptuel *adj* INFORMAT, ORDINAT conceptual

concession *f* MINES claim, PETROLE concession; ~ **de mines** *f* MINES mining claim, mining concession; ~ **minière** *f* MINES mining claim, mining concession

concevoir *vt* MECANIQUE design

conchage *m* AGRO ALIM conching

concher *vt* AGRO ALIM conche

conchyliculteur *m* OCEANO shellfish farmer

conchyliculture *f* OCEANO shellfish culture

concordance *f* GEOLOGIE conformity, OCEANO concordance, PETROLE conformity; ~ **des couleurs** *f* COULEURS color match (AmE), colour match (BrE); ~ **de marée** *f* OCEANO concordance

concréfier *vt* CONSTR concrete

concret *m* CONSTR concrete

concrétation *f* AGRO ALIM caking

concrétion *f* AGRO ALIM caking, GEOLOGIE concretion, nodule, PETR concretion

concurrent *adj* INFORMAT, ORDINAT concurrent

condamnation: ~ **centrale** *f* VEHICULES central locking; ~ **des portières** *f* CH DE FER *véhicules* door blocking

condamner *vt* NAUT *les panneaux* batten down

condensable *adj* CHIMIE *gaz*, PHYSIQUE condensable

condensat *m* CHAUFFAGE, GENIE CHIM, PETROLE, THERMODYN condensate

condensateur *m* AUTO capacitor, CINEMAT condenser, CONS MECA *électrique seulement* capacitor, ELECTR *composant* capacitor, *composante* condenser, ELECTROTEC capacitor, condenser, EQUIP LAB *électrique* condenser, ORDINAT, PAPIER, PHYSIQUE capacitor, PRODUCTION *électrique* condenser, TELECOM, TV capacitor, VEHICULES *allumage* capacitor, condenser; ~ **d'accord** *m* ELECTROTEC tuning capacitor; ~ **d'accord à cages** *m* ELECTROTEC gang tuning capacitor; ~ **accouplé** *m* ELECTROTEC gang capacitor; ~ **accumulateur d'énergie** *m* ELECTROTEC energy storage capacitor; ~ **à air** *m* ELECTR, PHYSIQUE air capacitor; ~ **ajustable** *m* ELECTROTEC adjustable capacitor, trimmer capacitor; ~ **ajustable à air** *m* ELECTROTEC air trimmer capacitor; ~ **d'allumage** *m* AUTO ignition capacitor; ~ **à l'aluminium** *m* ELECTROTEC aluminium electrolytic capacitor (BrE), aluminum electrolytic capacitor (AmE); ~ **à l'aluminium à électrolyte liquide** *m* ELECTROTEC wet-aluminium capacitor (BrE), wet-aluminum capacitor (AmE); ~ **à l'aluminium à électrolyte solide** *m* ELECTROTEC solid aluminium capacitor (BrE), solid aluminum capacitor (AmE); ~ **d'amortissement** *m* ELECTROTEC damping capacitor, snubber capacitor; ~ **à anneau de garde** *m* ELECTROTEC guard ring capacitor; ~ **d'arrêt** *m* ELECTR, PHYSIQUE blocking capacitor; ~ **autocicatrisant** *m* ELECTROTEC self-healing capacitor; ~ **à bande plastique** *m* ELECTROTEC film capacitor; ~ **de blocage** *m* PHYSIQUE blocking capacitor; ~ **bouton** *m* ELECTROTEC disc capacitor (BrE), disk capacitor (AmE); ~ **calculable** *m* PHYSIQUE calculable capacitor; ~ **céramique** *m* ELECTR, ELECTROTEC, PHYSIQUE, TELECOM ceramic capacitor; ~ **céramique ajustable** *m* ELECTROTEC adjustable ceramic capacitor; ~ **céramique à enrobage verre** *m* ELECTROTEC glass-coated ceramic capacitor; ~ **céramique monocouche** *m* ELECTROTEC single layer ceramic capacitor; ~ **céramique tubulaire** *m* ELECTROTEC tubular ceramic capacitor; ~ **de charge** *m* ELECTROTEC reservoir capacitor; ~ **commandé en tension** *m* ELECTROTEC voltage-controlled capacitor; ~ **de compensation thermique** *m* ELECTROTEC temperature-compensating capacitor; ~ **à couche épaisse** *m* ELECTRON thick-film capacitor; ~ **à couche mince** *m* ELECTR thin-film capacitor; ~ **à couches minces** *m* TELECOM thin-layer capacitor; ~ **de couplage** *m* ELECTR, PHYSIQUE coupling capacitor; ~ **cylindrique** *m* PHYSIQUE cylindrical capacitor; ~ **dans l'huile** *m* ELECTR oil-immersed capacitor; ~ **à décharge** *m* ELECTROTEC discharge capacitor; ~ **de découplage** *m* ELECTROTEC decoupling capacitor, PHYSIQUE bypass capacitor; ~ **de démarrage** *m* ELECTR starting capacitor; ~ **déphaseur** *m* ELECTR phase-shifting capacitor; ~ **de dérivation** *m* PHYSIQUE bypass capacitor; ~ **diélectrique** *m* ELECTR dielectric condenser; ~ **à diélectrique métallisé** *m* ELECTROTEC metalized film capacitor (AmE), metallized film capacitor (BrE); ~ **discret** *m* ELECTROTEC discrete capacitor; ~ **double** *m* ELECTR two-cell capacitor; ~ **électrique** *m* PAPIER electrical condenser; ~ **électrochimique** *m* ELECTROTEC wet-aluminium capacitor (BrE), wet-aluminum capacitor (AmE), PHYSIQUE electrolytic capacitor, TELECOM electrochemical capacitor; ~ **électrochimique à l'aluminium** *m* ELECTROTEC aluminium electrolytic capacitor (BrE), aluminum electrolytic capacitor (AmE); ~ **à électrolyte solide** *m* ELECTROTEC solid electrolyte capacitor; ~ **électrolytique** *m* ELECTR, ELECTROTEC, PHYSIQUE electrolytic capacitor; ~ **électrolytique à l'aluminium** *m* ELECTROTEC aluminium electrolytic capacitor (BrE), aluminum electrolytic capacitor (AmE); ~ **électrolytique non polarisé** *m* CONSTR non-polarized electrolytic capacitor; ~ **électrolytique polarisé** *m* ELECTROTEC polarized electrolytic capacitor; ~ **en bande** *m* ELECTROTEC reeled capacitor; ~ **en plastique** *m* ELECTROTEC plastic capacitor; ~ **d'entrée** *m* ELECTROTEC input capacitor; ~ **en verre** *m* ELECTROTEC glass capacitor; ~ **étalon** *m* ELECTR reference capacitor, ELECTROTEC standard capacitor; ~ **à film** *m* ELECTROTEC film capacitor; ~ **à film plastique** *m* ELECTROTEC plastic film capacitor; ~ **de filtrage** *m* ELECTR *capaciteur* smoothing capacitor, ELECTROTEC filter capacitor; ~ **fixe** *m* ELECTROTEC, PHYSIQUE fixed capacitor; ~ **à fortes fuites** *m* ELECTROTEC leaky capacitor; ~ **de forte valeur** *m* ELECTROTEC large-value capacitor; ~ **de fuite de grille** *m* ELECTROTEC grid capacitor; ~ **d'impulsion** *m* ELECTR pulse capacitor; ~ **inductif** *m* ELECTROTEC inductive capacitor; ~ **intégrateur** *m* ELECTROTEC integrating capacitor; ~ **d'intégration** *m* ELECTROTEC integrating capacitor; ~ **intégré** *m* ELECTROTEC integrated capacitor, on-chip capacitor; ~ **interdigital** *m* PHYSIQUE interdigital capacitor; ~ **à jonction** *m* ELECTROTEC junction capacitor; ~ **à lames** *m* ELECTR plate capacitor; ~ **à lames multiples** *m* ELECTR multiple plate capacitor; ~ **de Lampard et Thomson** *m* PHYSIQUE Lampard and Thomson capacitor; ~ **de liaison** *m* ELECTROTEC blocking capacitor; ~ **localisé** *m* ELECTROTEC lumped capacitor; ~ **de mémorisation** *m* ELECTROTEC storage capacitor; ~ **métallisé** *m* ELECTROTEC metalized film capacitor (AmE), metallized film capacitor (BrE); ~ **au mica** *m* ELECTR mica dielectric capacitor, ELECTROTEC mica capacitor; ~ **au mica argenté** *m* ELECTROTEC silvered mica capacitor; ~ **au mica métallisé** *m* ELECTROTEC metalized mica capacitor (AmE), metallized mica capacitor (BrE); ~ **mis en parallèle** *m* PHYSIQUE shunt capacitor; ~ **monté en série** *m* ELECTROTEC series capacitor; ~ **MOS** *m* ELECTROTEC MOS capacitor, metal-oxide semiconductor capacitor; ~ **optique** *m* CINEMAT optical condenser; ~ **oscillant** *m* ELECTR oscillating capacitor; ~ **à l'oxyde de tantale** *m* ELECTROTEC tantalum oxide capacitor; ~ **au papier** *m* ELECTR, ELECTROTEC paper capacitor; ~ **au papier imprégné d'huile** *m* ELECTROTEC oil paper capacitor; ~ **au papier métallisé** *m* ELECTR metalized paper capacitor (AmE), metallized paper capacitor (BrE); ~ **pare-étincelles** *m* ELECTROTEC spark capacitor; ~ **pastille céramique** *m* ELECTROTEC ceramic chip capacitor; ~ **plan** *m* ELECTROTEC parallel plate capacitor; ~ **à plaques parallèles** *m* PHYSIQUE parallel plate capacitor; ~ **pliant** *m* ELECTR book capacitor; ~ **polarisé** *m* ELECTROTEC polarized capacitor; ~ **pour accumulation d'énergie** *m* ELECTROTEC energy storage capacitor; ~ **pour courant alternatif** *m* ELECTROTEC AC capacitor; ~ **de protection** *m* ELECTROTEC protection capacitor; ~ **de puissance** *m* ELECTR, ELECTROTEC power capacitor; ~ **à rebord** *m* ELECTR rim capacitor; ~ **à refluement** *m* NUCLEAIRE refluxer; ~

réglable *m* PHYSIQUE variable capacitor; ~ **rotatif** *m* ELECTR rotary capacitor; ~ **sans blocage** *m* ELECTROTEC nonblocking concentrator; ~ **de sortie** *m* ELECTROTEC output capacitor; ~ **à sorties radiales** *m* ELECTROTEC radial lead capacitor; ~ **synchrone** *m* ELECTROTEC synchronous capacitor; ~ **au tantale** *m* ELECTROTEC tantalum capacitor; ~ **au tantale à anode frittée** *m* ELECTROTEC tantalum slug capacitor; ~ **au tantale à anode frittée et électrolyte gélifiée** *m* ELECTROTEC wet-slug tantalum capacitor; ~ **au tantale bobiné** *m* ELECTROTEC tantalum foil capacitor; ~ **au tantale au boîtier en argent** *m* ELECTROTEC silver case tantalum capacitor; ~ **au tantale à électrolyte gélifiée** *m* ELECTROTEC wet-slug tantalum capacitor; ~ **au tantale à électrolyte liquide** *m* ELECTROTEC tantalum wet capacitor; ~ **au tantale à électrolyte solide** *m* ELECTROTEC solid tantalum capacitor, tantalum solid capacitor; ~ **au tantale sec** *m* ELECTROTEC solid tantalum capacitor; ~ **tout tantale** *m* ELECTROTEC all-tantalum capacitor; ~ **de traversée** *m* ELECTROTEC feedthrough capacitor; ~ **de vapeur** *m* PAPIER steam condenser; ~ **variable** *m* ELECTR adjustable capacitor, *capaciteur* variable capacitor, ELECTROTEC, PHYSIQUE variable capacitor; ~ **variable à air** *m* ELECTROTEC air variable capacitor; ~ **variable différentiel** *m* ELECTROTEC differential capacitor; ~ **variable à rotor commun** *m* ELECTROTEC split stator variable capacitor; ~ **à vide** *m* ELECTROTEC vacuum capacitor

condensateurs: ~ **jumelés** *m pl* ELECTR gang capacitors, ELECTROTEC ganged capacitors; ~ **à rapport de capacité** *m pl* ELECTROTEC ratioed capacitors

condensation *f* CERAM VER, CHAUFFAGE, CHIMIE, CONSTR, EMBALLAGE, GENIE CHIM, HYDROLOGIE, PHYSIQUE, REFRIG, THERMODYN condensation; ~ **de Bose-Einstein** *f* PHYSIQUE Bose-Einstein condensation; ~ **de Claisen** *f* CHIMIE Claisen condensation; ~ **d'eau** *f* IMPRIM, REFRIG sweating; ~ **par injection** *f* GENIE CHIM condensation by injection; ~ **par refroidissement de la surface** *f* GENIE CHIM condensation by surface cooling; ~ **statistique de Bose-Einstein** *f* PHYSIQUE Bose-Einstein condensation; ~ **des vapeurs** *f* NUCLEAIRE vapor condensation (AmE), vapour condensation (BrE); ~ **du zinc** *f* CHARBON zinc condensation

condensé *adj* PHYSIQUE, THERMODYN condensed

condenser *vt* CHIMIE occlude, *gaz* condense, EMBALLAGE condensate, GAZ, GENIE CHIM condense, INFORMAT, ORDINAT pack, THERMODYN condense

condenseur *m* CHARBON, CHAUFFAGE, CHIMIE, EQUIP LAB, GENIE CHIM, PETROLE, REFRIG condenser; ~ **à air** *m* REFRIG air-cooled condenser; ~ **à air forcé** *m* REFRIG forced draft air-cooled condenser (AmE), forced draught air-cooled condenser (BrE); ~ **à air par convection** *m* REFRIG natural air-cooled condenser; ~ **à autorefroidissement** *m* REFRIG evaporative condenser; ~ **des buées** *m* NUCLEAIRE off-gas condenser; ~ **à calandre et serpentin** *m* REFRIG shell and coil condenser; ~ **éjecteur** *m* INST HYDR ejector condenser; ~ **à éjection** *m* INST HYDR ejector condenser; ~ **en sous-sol** *m* NUCLEAIRE underfloor condenser; ~ **à glace** *m* NUCLEAIRE ice condenser; ~ **à immersion** *m* REFRIG submerged condenser; ~ **à injection** *m* INST HYDR injection condenser, jet condenser; ~ **à jet** *m* GAZ spray condenser, INST HYDR injection condenser, jet condenser; ~ **à lanières** *m* TEXTILE tape condenser; ~ **à mélange** *m* PRODUCTION direct contact condenser; ~

par injection *m* INST HYDR injection condenser; ~ **par mélange** *m* PRODUCTION direct contact condenser; ~ **par surface** *m* PRODUCTION surface condenser; ~ **pour microscopes** *m* EQUIP LAB microscope condenser; ~ **à purgeur** *m* REFRIG bleeder-type condenser; ~ **refroidi par l'eau** *m* CHAUFFAGE water-cooled condenser; ~ **à refroidissement** *m* CHAUFFAGE air-cooled condenser; ~ **à refroidissement par chaleur latente d'évaporation** *m* REFRIG evaporative condenser; ~ **à surface** *m* PRODUCTION surface condenser; ~ **à trompe** *m* INST HYDR ejector condenser; ~ **universel** *m* INSTRUMENT universal condenser

condition *f* INFORMAT, ORDINAT condition; ~ **de ballastage maximal** *f* NAUT deepest ballast condition; ~ **de Bragg** *f* CRISTALL Bragg's law; ~ **de branche** *f* PRODUCTION *automatisme industriel* branching condition; ~ **en parallèle** *f* PRODUCTION *automatisme industriel* parallel condition; ~ **d'essai** *f* METROLOGIE, PRODUCTION test condition; ~ **fausse** *f* PRODUCTION *automatisme industriel* off condition; ~ **de freinage de référence** *f* AERONAUT *d'une piste* reference friction condition; ~ **initiale** *f* MATERIAUX initial condition; ~ **de liaison** *f* INFORMAT, ORDINAT interface requirement; ~ **de non-glissement** *f* PHYS FLUID no-slip condition; ~ **de régime permanent** *f* ELECTROTEC, TELECOM steady-state condition; ~ **requise** *f* SECURITE requirement; ~ **de sécurité requise** *f* SECURITE safety requirement; ~ **vraie** *f* PRODUCTION *automatisme industriel* on condition

conditionné *adj* TEXTILE conditioned; ~ **pour expédition postale** *adj* AGRO ALIM mail-order packed; ~ **sous atmosphère contrôlée** *adj* AGRO ALIM controlled atmosphere packed; ~ **sous gaz** *adj* AGRO ALIM gas-packed; ~ **sous-vide** *adj* AGRO ALIM vacuum-packed

conditionnel *adj* INFORMAT, ORDINAT conditional

conditionnement *m* AGRO ALIM packaging, CERAM VER, CHARBON conditioning, IMPRIM packaging, PAPIER *de l'humidité ou la température*, PLAST CAOU procédé conditioning, PRODUCTION, TEXTILE packaging; ~ **de l'air** *m* CONS MECA, MAT CHAUFF, SECURITE air conditioning; ~ **aseptique** *m* AGRO ALIM aseptic filling; ~ **des boues** *m* DISTRI EAU, HYDROLOGIE sludge conditioning; ~ **de l'eau** *m* DISTRI EAU water conditioning; ~ **et traitement** *m* POLLUTION *des déchets* conditioning; ~ **industriel** *m* NUCLEAIRE industrial packaging; ~ **du papier** *m* PAPIER paper conditioning; ~ **par unité** *m* EMBALLAGE unit pack; ~ **sous atmosphère contrôlée** *m* EMBALLAGE CA packaging, controlled atmosphere packaging CAP; ~ **sous carte** *m* EMBALLAGE carded packaging; ~ **sous matériaux barrière** *m* EMBALLAGE barrier packaging; ~ **sous vide** *m* EMBALLAGE vacuum pack

conditionner *vt* CHARBON, PRODUCTION condition

conditionneur *m* CHARBON conditioning tank; ~ **d'air** *m* CONS MECA air conditioner, REFRIG air conditioning unit; ~ **à air de pièce** *m* REFRIG room air conditioning unit; ~ **à air de type armoire** *m* REFRIG self-contained air conditioning unit; ~ **à air de type fenêtre** *m* REFRIG window air conditioning unit; ~ **à air de zone** *m* REFRIG zone air conditioning unit; ~ **de feutre** *m* PAPIER felt conditioner

conditions:[1] ~ **ambiantes dangereuses** *f pl* SECURITE unsafe environmental conditions; ~ **atmosphériques** *f pl* MATERIAUX, METEO, NAUT atmospheric conditions; ~ **climatiques** *f pl* EMBALLAGE climatic conditions; ~ **du**

contrat de transport *f pl* NAUT shipping terms; ~ **contrôlées** *f pl* MATERIAUX controlled conditions; ~ **dimensionnelles** *f pl* SECURITE dimensional requirements; ~ **d'écoulement** *f pl* MATERIAUX flow behavior (AmE), flow behaviour (BrE); ~ **en champ libre** *f pl* ENREGISTR free field conditions; ~ **d'environnement** *f pl* METROLOGIE, PRODUCTION environmental conditions; ~ **d'essai** *f pl* EMBALLAGE, ESSAIS, MATERIAUX test conditions; ~ **de fonctionnement** *f pl* ELECTR *d'un matériel*, ELECTROTEC operating conditions; ~ **de fond** *f pl* PETROLE *forage* bottom hole conditions, downhole conditions; ~ **idéales** *f pl* TRANSPORT ideal conditions; ~ **d'injections d'équilibre** *f pl* TELECOM steady-state launching conditions; ~ **de livraison** *f pl* PRODUCTION terms of delivery; ~ **maritimes** *f pl* NAUT sea conditions; ~ **météorologiques** *f pl* METEO meteorological conditions; ~ **nominales** *f pl* ELECTROTEC rated conditions; ~ **pour la similitude dynamique de deux écoulements** *f pl* PHYS FLUID conditions for dynamic similarity of two flows; ~ **de référence** *f pl* METROLOGIE reference conditions; ~ **requises pour la santé et la sûreté** *f pl* SECURITE *au travail* health and safety requirements; ~ **requises de sécurité et surveillance** *f pl* SECURITE safety requirements and supervision; ~ **requises de sécurité pour alimentation en électricité** *f pl* SECURITE electrical safety requirements; ~ **requises techniques de sécurité** *f pl* SECURITE technical safety requirements; ~ **de réservoir** *f pl* PETR reservoir conditions; ~ **de service** *f pl* ELECTR *d'un matériel* operating conditions; ~ **de sous-sol** *f pl* PETROLE subsurface conditions; ~ **de trafic** *f pl* TRANSPORT traffic conditions; ~ **de travail** *f pl* PRODUCTION, SECURITE working conditions; ~ **d'utilisation prévues** *f pl* AERONAUT anticipated operating conditions; ~ **de validité** *f pl* PRODUCTION effectivity terms

conditions:[2] **dans les ~ usuelles d'utilisation** *loc* PRODUCTION under normal conditions of use

conductance *f* ELECTR, ELECTROTEC, IMPRIM, PHYSIQUE, TELECOM conductance; ~ **directe** *f* ELECTR *semi-conducteur* forward conductance; ~ **électrique** *f* TELECOM electrical conductance; ~ **en l'état passant** *f* ELECTR *semi-conducteur* forward conductance; ~ **équivalente** *f* PHYSIQUE equivalent conductance; ~ **mutuelle** *f* ELECTROTEC transconductance; ~ **négative** *f* ELECTR *semi-conducteur* negative conductance; ~ **superficielle** *f* CHAUFFAGE surface conductance; ~ **thermique** *f* CHAUFFAGE, PHYSIQUE thermal conductance

conducteur[1] *adj* ELECTR conducting, MATERIAUX conducting, conductive, PETROLE conducting

conducteur[2] *m* CH DE FER *véhicules* driver (BrE), engineer (AmE), CONSTR foreman, operator, ELECTR conductor, *câble, raccordement* conductor, ELECTROTEC conductor, IMPRIM rotary printer, PETROLE *électrique, thermal*, PHYSIQUE conductor, TELECOM conductor, leg; ~ **d'arche** *m* CERAM VER lehr attendant; ~ **d'autobus** *m* TRANSPORT bus driver; ~ **central** *m* TELECOM inner conductor; ~ **de chaleur** *m* MATERIAUX thermal conductor, PRODUCTION heat conductor; ~ **de chantiers** *m* CONSTR chief superintendent engineer; ~ **de la charge** *m* ELECTROTEC load leads; ~ **chauffant** *m* CONS MECA conduction heater, contact heater; ~ **de connexion** *m* ELECTROTEC connecting lead; ~ **coupé** *m* ELECTROTEC open conductor; ~ **creux** *m* ELECTR hollow conductor; ~ **de distribution** *m* ELECTR distributor; ~ **divisé** *m* ELECTROTEC stranded conductor; ~ **écran** *m* ELECTR *d'un câble* shielding conductor;

~ **d'électricité** m PHYSIQUE electrical conductor; ~ **électrique** m ELECTROTEC, PHYSIQUE electrical conductor; ~ **d'émission** m TV continuity log; ~ **en aluminium** m ELECTR aluminium conductor (BrE), aluminum conductor (AmE); ~ **en couche épaisse** m ELECTRON thick-film conductor; ~ **en couches minces** m ELECTRON thin-film conductor; ~ **d'entrée** m ELECTROTEC input lead; ~ **extérieur** m TELECOM outer conductor; ~ **à fils armés** m ELECTROTEC metal-sheathed conductor; ~ **flexible** m ELECTROTEC flexible conductor; ~ **d'induit** m ELECTR *machine* armature conductor; ~ **isolé** m ELECTR *d'un câble* core, insulated conductor, insulated core, ELECTROTEC insulated conductor; ~ **linéaire** m PHYSIQUE ohmic conductor; ~ **de lingots** m CONS MECA traveling table (AmE), travelling table (BrE); ~ **de masse** m ELECTROTEC earth lead (BrE), ground lead; ~ **massif** m ELECTROTEC solid conductor; ~ **métallique** m ELECTROTEC metallic conductor; ~ **de métallisation** m ELECTROTEC bonding jumper; ~ **de mise à la masse** m ESPACE *véhicules* bonding strap; ~ **de mise à la terre** m PRODUCTION *électricité* earthing electrode conductor (BrE), grounding electrode conductor (AmE); ~ **négatif** m ELECTROTEC negative conductor; ~ **neutre** m ELECTROTEC neutral conductor, zero conductor; ~ **nu** m ELECTR bare conductor; ~ **de nuque** m TELECOM B-leg, ring; ~ **ohmique** m PHYSIQUE ohmic conductor; ~ **de poids lourds** m CONSTR HG driver; ~ **de pointe** m TELECOM A-leg; ~ **principal** m ELECTROTEC main conductor; ~ **de protection** m ELECTR *d'un câble* shielding conductor; ~ **de terre** m ELECTR earth conductor (BrE), ground conductor (AmE), ELECTROTEC earth lead (BrE), ground lead (AmE), PRODUCTION earth wire (BrE), *électricité* ground wire (AmE); ~ **thermique** m MATERIAUX thermal conductor; ~ **tubulaire** m MINES conductor pipe, drill casing, guide tube; ~ **volant** m PRODUCTION flying lead

conductibilité f ELECTR, ELECTROTEC, PHYSIQUE conductivity; ~ **calorifique** f THERMODYN heat conductivity, thermal conductivity, thermal conductivity; ~ **électrique** f ELECTROTEC electrical conductivity; ~ **électrolytique** f ELECTR electrolytic conductivity; ~ **à l'état passant** f ELECTROTEC on-state conductivity; ~ **extrinsèque** f ELECTROTEC extrinsic conductivity; ~ **intrinsèque** f ELECTR, ELECTROTEC intrinsic conductivity; ~ **thermique** f CONSTR thermal conductivity, THERMODYN caloric conductibility, thermal conductibility, thermal conductivity; ~ **thermique électronique** f NUCLEAIRE electronic heat conductivity

conductible adj ELECTR conducting

conductimètre m EQUIP LAB *analyse* conductivity meter

conduction f CONSTR, ELECTROTEC, MAT CHAUFF, PHYSIQUE conduction; ~ **aérienne** f ACOUSTIQUE air conduction; ~ **de chaleur** f THERMODYN heat conduction; ~ **électrique** f ELECTROTEC electric conduction, electrical conduction; ~ **lacunaire** f ELECTROTEC defect conduction, hole conduction; ~ **d'obscurité** f ELECTROTEC dark conduction; ~ **osseuse** f ACOUSTIQUE bone conduction; ~ **par trous** f ELECTROTEC p-type conductivity; ~ **thermique** f THERMODYN thermal conduction

conductivité f DISTRI EAU, ELECTROTEC, ENREGISTR, PETR, PHYSIQUE *quantité*, PLAST CAOU, TELECOM conductivity; ~ **calorifique** f THERMODYN thermal conductivity; ~ **capillaire** f HYDROLOGIE capillary conductivity; ~ **électrique** f ELECTR conductivity; ~

électronique f PHYS RAYON electron conductivity; ~ **hydraulique** f EN RENOUV, HYDROLOGIE hydraulic conductivity; ~ **ionique équivalente** f PHYS RAYON ionic conductance; ~ **moléculaire** f THERMODYN molecular conductivity; ~ **spécifique** f ELECTR specific conductance; ~ **thermique** f CHAUFFAGE, GAZ, PETROLE, PHYSIQUE, PLAST CAOU, THERMODYN thermal conductivity; ~ **thermique équivalente** f CHAUFFAGE equivalent thermal conductivity

conduire vt DISTRI EAU *un canal* carry, ESPACE drive, NUCLEAIRE operate, PAPIER drive, TRANSPORT drive, steer

conduit m CONSTR conduit, conduit pipe, pipe, ELECTR *alimentation* conduit, MINES air passage, air passageway, airway, PHYS FLUID pipe, PRODUCTION *de câble*, REFRIG, TELECOM duct, THERMODYN *d'une cheminée* flue; ~ **d'air** m CONS MECA air conduit, CONSTR vent; ~ **de câbles** m ELECTROTEC cable conduit, conduit; ~ **de dérivation** m AERONAUT *turbosoufflante* secondary duct; ~ **distributeur d'eau d'alimentation** m NUCLEAIRE distribution ring, feedwater manifold; ~ **en fonte** m CONSTR cast-iron pipe; ~ **de gaz** m CONSTR gas pipe; ~ **karstique** m HYDROLOGIE karstic conduit; ~ **de lumière** m ELECTROTEC light pipe; ~ **de pale** m AERONAUT blade duct; ~ **principal** m NUCLEAIRE distributing pipe, manifold, PETR trunk line; ~ **secondaire de dérivation** m AERONAUT secondary duct; ~ **à vent** m CONS MECA air conduit; ~ **de ventilation de poche d'air** m PAPIER pocket-ventilating duct; ~ **virtuel** m TELECOM VP, virtual path

conduite f CH DE FER *véhicules* driving, CONS MECA ducting, duct, CONSTR conduit, conduit pipe, main, pipe, pipeline, DISTRI EAU conduit, EN RENOUV conduit, pipeline, ESPACE *véhicules* handling; ~ **d'air** f CHARBON air duct, CONS MECA air duct, air pipe, MAT CHAUFF air duct, PAPIER airline, REFRIG air duct; ~ **d'alimentation** f AUTO delivery pipe, NUCLEAIRE feedline; ~ **d'amenée** f CONSTR supply pipe, INST HYDR head pipe; ~ **d'amenée d'eau** f DISTRI EAU water supply pipe; ~ **d'amenée de secteur** f ELECTROTEC mains lead (BrE), supply lead (AmE); ~ **d'arrivée** f PRODUCTION inlet pipe; ~ **ascendante pour les bouches d'incendie** f THERMODYN fire riser, fire rising main; ~ **d'aspiration** f CONS MECA eductor, HYDROLOGIE, TRANSPORT suction pipe; ~ **automatique des trains par mini-ordinateur** f CH DE FER ATOMIC, automatic train operation by mini computer; ~ **à bride** f CONSTR flange pipe; ~ **circulaire de vent** f PRODUCTION bustle pipe, circular blast aim, *haut fourneau* horseshoe main; ~ **de condensation** f REFRIG condensate line; ~ **dangereuse** f SECURITE unsafe act; ~ **de décharge du gaz de couverture** f NUCLEAIRE cover gas discharge line; ~ **de distribution d'eau** f DISTRI EAU water main; ~ **d'eau** f DISTRI EAU water pipe; ~ **d'eau de refroidissement** f CONS MECA cooling water pipe; ~ **d'échantillonnage** f QUALITE *d'eau* sampling line; ~ **d'écoulement** f PETR, PETROLE flow line; ~ **à emboîtement** f CONSTR socket pipe; ~ **d'émission** f TV cue sheet; ~ **en fonte** f CONSTR iron pipe; ~ **d'évacuation** f RECYCLAGE drain; ~ **d'évacuation d'air** f PETROLE air exhaust; ~ **de fer** f CONSTR iron pipe; ~ **forcée** f EN RENOUV *barrages*, HYDROLOGIE penstock, INST HYDR full pipe, NUCLEAIRE penstock; ~ **de frein** f AUTO brake line; ~ **de gaz** f CONSTR, TRANSPORT gas pipe; ~ **générale** f CH DE FER main brake hose (AmE), main brake pipe (BrE); ~ **hydraulique** f AUTO hydraulic linkage; ~ **à joints à emboîtements** f CONSTR socket pipe; ~ **maîtresse** *f* CONSTR main; ~ **maîtresse de gaz** *f* PRODUCTION gas main; ~ **maîtresse de vapeur** *f* INST HYDR main steam pipe; ~ **du moteur** *f* NAUT engine operation; ~ **de pression** *f* AUTO pressure tube; ~ **principale** *f* CH DE FER main air supply hose (AmE), main air supply pipe (BrE), CONSTR main; ~ **principale d'eau** *f* DISTRI EAU water main; ~ **principale de gaz** *f* PRODUCTION gas main; ~ **de refoulement** *f* DISTRI EAU delivery main, delivery pipe; ~ **sans pression** *f* NU-CLEAIRE *tuyauterie* unpressurized line; ~ **de saumure** *f* REFRIG brine line; ~ **souple** *f* CONS MECA flexible pipe, PRODUCTION hose; ~ **sous-marine** *f* TRANSPORT under-sea pipeline; ~ **de succion** *f* CONS MECA *appareils d'aspiration* eductor; ~ **de trop plein** *f* AUTO overflow pipe; ~ **de vapeur** *f* INST HYDR steam pipe; ~ **de vent** *f* PRODUCTION blast main; ~ **de ventilation** *f* CONSTR ventilation duct

conduites *f pl* CONSTR piping; ~ **de fer** *f pl* CONSTR iron piping

conduits *m pl* CONSTR piping; ~ **de fer** *m pl* CONSTR iron piping

condurrite *f* MINERAUX condurrite

cône *m* CERAM VER reamer, CHARBON slug, CONS MECA cone, cone pulley, speed cone, step cone, ELECTRON cone, funnel, ESPACE, GEOMETRIE cone, IMPRIM *plieuse* former, MATERIAUX bell, cone, MATH cone, MILITAIRE *d'une torpille* nose, PRODUCTION, TEXTILE, TV cone; ~ **d'ablation** *m* ESPACE *thermique* ablating cone; ~ **d'alluvion** *m* HYDROLOGIE alluvial cone; ~ **d'appel** *m* DISTRI EAU depression cone; ~ **d'avancement** *m* MINES sink; ~ **avertisseur** *m* CONSTR traffic cone; ~ **de cendres** *m* GEOLOGIE cinder cone; ~ **central** *m* ESPACE *propulsion* thrust cone; ~ **circulaire droit** *m* GEOMETRIE right circular cone; ~ **classeur** *m* CHARBON cone classifier; ~ **de confusion** *m* AERONAUT confusion cone; ~ **à corde** *m* CONS MECA cone sheave, grooved cone; ~ **creux** *m* CERAM VER bell cone; ~ **de décantation** *m* CHARBON settling cone, GENIE CHIM settling cone, settling tank; ~ **de déjections** *m* GEOLOGIE cone delta; ~ **de diffuseur** *m* GENIE CHIM atomizer injection nozzle; ~ **de dispersion** *m* GENIE CHIM dispersion cone; ~ **divergent** *m* PRODUCTION *d'un injecteur* delivery cone, delivery nozzle, delivery tube; ~ **de division** *m* CONS MECA pitch cone; ~ **d'éboulis** *m* DISTRI EAU alluvial cone; ~ **d'échappement** *m* AERONAUT exhaust cone; ~ **d'élution** *m* GENIE CHIM elutriating funnel; ~ **d'entrée d'air** *m* TRANSPORT spike; ~ **épaississeur** *m* CHARBON thickening cone; ~ **érodable** *m* ESPACE *thermique* ablating cone, nose cone; ~ **à faible conicité** *m* CONS MECA *pour emmanchements d'outils* self-holding taper; ~ **à filtrer** *m* GENIE CHIM filtering cone; ~ **de fracturation** *m* CERAM VER fracture cone; ~ **d'hélice** *m* AERONAUT spinner; ~ **de Hertz** *m* CERAM VER Hertzian fracture; ~ **mâle** *m* CONS MECA male cone; ~ **de mer profonde** *m* GEOLOGIE deep-sea fan; ~ **Morse** *m* CONS MECA Morse taper; ~ **de nez** *m* AERONAUT nose cone; ~ **de nez amovible** *m* AERONAUT detachable nose cone; ~ **de nez démontable** *m* AERONAUT detachable nose cone; ~ **oblique** *m* GEOMETRIE oblique cone; ~ **d'occultation du coronographe** *m* ASTRONOMIE occultation cone for coronograph; ~ **pour le slump-test** *m* CONSTR slump cone; ~ **primitif** *m* CONS MECA pitch cone; ~ **de projection** *m* GENIE CHIM atomizing cone; ~ **de pulvérisateur** *m* GENIE CHIM atomizer injection nozzle; ~ **pyroscopique** *m* CERAM VER Seger cone; ~ **de renvoi** *m* CONS MECA cone for overhead motion, countershaft cone,

overhead cone, overhead cone pulley; ~ **de révolution** *m* GEOMETRIE cone of revolution; ~ **scalène** *m* GEOMETRIE scalene cone; ~ **de scories** *m* GEOLOGIE cinder cone; ~ **à sédimentation d'Imhof** *m* EQUIP LAB *verrerie* Imhof sedimentation cone; ~ **séparateur** *m* CHARBON cone separator; ~ **des signaux** *m* COMMANDE signal cone; ~ **de silence** *m* CONS MECA cone of silence; ~ **sous-marin** *m* OCEANO abyssal cone, deep-sea fan; ~ **support** *m* TEXTILE cone tube; ~ **Taylor** *m* PHYS RAYON Taylor cone; ~ **de télévision** *m* CERAM VER cone (BrE), funnel (AmE); ~ **de transmission** *m* CONS MECA cone, cone pulley, speed cone, step cone; ~ **à trois gradins** *m* CONS MECA three-lift cone pulley, three-step cone pulley; ~ **d'usure** *m* CHARBON mantle; ~ **de vitesse** *m* CONS MECA cone, cone pulley, speed cone, step cone; ~ **volcanique** *m* GEOPHYS volcanic cone

cône-poulie *m* CONS MECA cone, cone pulley, speed cone, step cone; ~ **à trois étages** *m* CONS MECA three-lift cone pulley, three-step cone pulley

confection *f* CONSTR *d'une route*, *du béton armé* making, PRODUCTION *des joints*, TEXTILE making up; ~ **artisanale** *f* AGRO ALIM hand baking; ~ **des noyaux** *f* PRODUCTION core making; ~ **de routes** *f* CONSTR road making

confectionner *vt* PRODUCTION *outil* make

conférence *f* TELECOM conference call; ~ **rendez-vous** *f* TELECOM meet-me conference call; ~ **téléphonique** *f* TELECOM conference call, telephone conference

confetti *m* INFORMAT chad

confidentialité *f* INFORMAT, ORDINAT privacy, TELECOM confidentiality; ~ **de données** *f* INFORMAT, ORDINAT data privacy (BrE), data security (AmE); ~ **du flux de données** *f* TELECOM traffic flow confidentiality

configuration *f* CONS MECA outline, CONSTR lie, *du pays* lay, ELECTRON, ESPACE configuration, pattern, INFORMAT, ORDINAT configuration, PRODUCTION layout, TV setup; ~ **de base de données** *f* ORDINAT database mapping; ~ **binaire** *f* INFORMAT bit pattern; ~ **de câblage** *f* PRODUCTION wiring configuration; ~ **du champ magnétique** *f* NUCLEAIRE, PHYS RAYON magnetic field configuration; ~ **chargée** *f* ESPACE *véhicules* full-load configuration; ~ **déchargée** *f* ESPACE *véhicules* reduced load configuration; ~ **d'écoulement** *f* PHYS FLUID, REFRIG flow pattern; ~ **d'électrode** *f* TELECOM electrode configuration; ~ **électronique** *f* PHYSIQUE electronic configuration; ~ **en anneau** *f* TELECOM ring configuration; ~ **en étoile** *f* TELECOM star configuration; ~ **en grappes** *f* NUCLEAIRE banked configuration; ~ **d'erreurs** *f* TELECOM error pattern; ~ **de lancement** *f* ESPACE *véhicules* launching configuration; ~ **de la ligne** *f* ELECTROTEC line configuration; ~ **des lignes de courant** *f* PHYS FLUID streamline pattern; ~ **lisse** *f* AERONAUT clean configuration; ~ **logicielle** *f* INFORMAT, ORDINAT software configuration; ~ **matérielle** *f* INFORMAT, ORDINAT hardware configuration; ~ **mémoire** *f* PRODUCTION *informatique* memory map; ~ **des partitions** *f* ORDINAT, PRODUCTION *informatique* setting-up partitions; ~ **des pôles** *f* PRODUCTION *automatisme industriel* pole arrangement; ~ **de pose** *f* PETR pipe string; ~ **de pose de barrage** *f* POLLU MER boom-laying configuration; ~ **quadripolaire** *f* NUCLEAIRE quadrupolar configuration; ~ **de redondance** *f* PRODUCTION backup configuration; ~ **d'un réseau** *f* ELECTR system configuration; ~ **spatiale** *f* POLLUTION spatial pattern; ~ **de stockage** *f* ESPACE *véhicules* storage configuration; ~ **du système** *f* PRODUCTION system setup; ~ **du type canal** *f* NUCLEAIRE channel configuration; ~ **de l'utilisateur** *f* INFORMAT, ORDINAT user operating environment

configurer *vt* ORDINAT configure, PRODUCTION *informatique* install, TV set up

confinement *m* GEOLOGIE, MINES, PETROLE *géologie* confinement, PHYSIQUE confinement, containment; ~ **inertiel** *m* PHYSIQUE inertial confinement; ~ **magnétique** *m* PHYSIQUE magnetic confinement; ~ **des quarks** *m* PHYS PART quark confinement

confirmation *f* PRODUCTION authorization, TELECOM confirmation, confirm; ~ **de connexion** *f* TELECOM CC, connect confirm; ~ **primitive** *f* TELECOM confirm

confirmer *vt* TELECOM confirm

confisquer *vt* NAUT seize

conflit: ~ **d'accès** *m* ELECTRON, INFORMAT, ORDINAT, TELECOM contention; ~ **du travail** *m* PRODUCTION industrial dispute

confluent *m* DISTRI EAU, HYDROLOGIE confluence

confluer *vi* DISTRI EAU meet

conformateur: ~ **pneumatique** *m* TV vacuum guide system

conformation: ~ **d'impulsion** *f* ORDINAT pulse shaping

conformer *vt* CINEMAT, TV conform, match

conformité *f* CONS MECA accordance, INFORMAT, ORDINAT conformance, QUALITE compliance, conformity; ~ **des couleurs** *f* COULEURS color match (AmE), colour match (BrE)

congé *m* CONSTR fillet, neck mold (AmE), neck molding (AmE), neck mould (BrE), neck moulding (BrE), neck molding plane (AmE), neck moulding plane (BrE); ~ **de bandage** *m* CH DE FER *véhicules* tire groove (AmE), tyre groove (BrE); ~ **de raccord** *m* CH DE FER fillet radius; ~ **de raccordement** *m* AERONAUT *cellule*, CONSTR fillet; ~ **de raccord de la table de roulement** *m* CH DE FER rail shoulder

congélateur *m* AGRO ALIM deepfreeze, freezer, CONS MECA freezer, frozen food storage cabinet, OCEANO deep-freeze ship, freezer trawler, freezer vessel, REFRIG deepfreeze, freezer, THERMODYN deepfreeze, quick freezer, *domestique* freezer; ~ **à air forcé** *m* REFRIG air blast freezer; ~ **à aspersion** *m* REFRIG spray freezer; ~ **continu** *m* REFRIG continuous freezer; ~ **à crème glacée** *m* REFRIG batch-type freezer; ~ **discontinu** *m* AGRO ALIM batch freezer, REFRIG batch-type freezer; ~ **domestique** *m* REFRIG domestic freezer; ~ **à étagères** *m* REFRIG shelf freezer; ~ **horizontal** *m* AGRO ALIM deepfreeze; ~ **à liquide** *m* REFRIG liquid chiller; ~ **ménager** *m* REFRIG domestic freezer; ~ **navire** *m* OCEANO deep-freeze ship, freezer trawler, freezer vessel; ~ **par contact** *m* REFRIG contact freezer; ~ **à plaque** *m* REFRIG plate freezer; ~ **à racleur** *m* REFRIG scraped surface freezer; ~ **vertical** *m* REFRIG upright freezer

congélation:[1] **à ~ rapide** *adj* AGRO ALIM quick-freezing

congélation[2] *f* MATERIAUX congealment, congelation, PHYSIQUE freezing, solidification, REFRIG freezing; ~ **en masse divisée** *f* REFRIG loose freezing; ~ **en vrac** *f* REFRIG bulk freezing; ~ **lente** *f* AGRO ALIM, REFRIG slow freezing; ~ **par contact** *f* REFRIG contact freezing; ~ **par immersion** *f* EMBALLAGE, REFRIG immersion freezing; ~ **par jet d'air** *f* REFRIG jet freezing; ~ **par pulvérisation** *f* REFRIG spray freezing; ~ **par immersion** *f* REFRIG quick freezing; ~ **sans circulation d'air** *f* REFRIG still-air freezing; ~ **sous courant d'air** *f* AGRO ALIM blast freezing; ~ **superficielle** *f* REFRIG crust freezing; ~ **sur bande** *f* REFRIG belt freezing; ~ **sur plaque réfrigérante** *f* REFRIG fluidized bed freezing; ~ **ventilée** *f* REFRIG air blast freezing

congelé *adj* REFRIG frozen, THERMODYN frozen, frozen solid; ~ **à basse température** *adj* AGRO ALIM deepfrozen

congeler[1] *vt* AGRO ALIM, PHYSIQUE, REFRIG, THERMODYN freeze

congeler:[2] **se ~** *v réfl* THERMODYN freeze

congère *f* METEO snowdrift

conglomérat *m* CONSTR, EN RENOUV conglomerate, GEOLOGIE conglomerate, lithic tuff; ~ **aurifère** *m* MINES banket, gold conglomerate, gold reef; ~ **de faille** *m* MINES fault conglomerate; ~ **de friction** *m* GEOLOGIE crush conglomerate; ~ **polygénique** *m* GEOLOGIE polygenetic conglomerate, polymictic conglomerate, PETR interformational conglomerate

conglutiner *vt* GENIE CHIM coagulate

congru *adj* MATH congruent

congruent *adj* MATH congruent

coniacien *adj* GEOLOGIE *stratigraphie* Coniacian

conicité *f* AERONAUT coning angle, taper ratio, CONS MECA *d'un angle* gear cone angle, MECANIQUE taper; ~ **du rotor** *f* AERONAUT coning angle

coniférine *f* CHIMIE coniferin

coniine *f* CHIMIE coniine, conine

conine *f* CHIMIE coniine, conine

coniques *f pl* GEOMETRIE conics

conjoncteur *m* ELECTROTEC circuit closer

conjoncteur-disjoncteur *m* COMMANDE regulator breaker, regulator cutout

conjonction *f* ASTRONOMIE, ELECTRON, INFORMAT *opération ET*, ORDINAT *opération ET* conjunction; ~ **inférieure** *f* ASTRONOMIE inferior conjunction; ~ **supérieure** *f* ASTRONOMIE superior conjunction

conjugaison *f* AERONAUT combination, CH DE FER *véhicules* blending

conjugation *f* CHIMIE conjugation

conjugué[1] *adj* CHIMIE conjugated, GEOMETRIE conjugate, MATERIAUX twin, MATH conjugated

conjugué[2] *m* MATH conjugate

connaissances: ~ **en informatique** *f pl* INFORMAT computer literacy

connaissement *m* NAUT bill of lading, shipping bill, PETROLE *transport* bill of lading; ~ **aérien** *m* TRANSPORT airway bill; ~ **avec réserves** *m* NAUT claused bill of lading; ~ **net** *m* NAUT clean bill of lading; ~ **sans réserve** *m* NAUT clean bill of lading

connecté *adj* INFORMAT, ORDINAT on-line; ~ **par jack** *adj* ELECTROTEC jacked in

connecter[1] *vt* ELECTROTEC connect, patch, INFORMAT attach, connect, ORDINAT attach, connect, PHYSIQUE, PRODUCTION connect

connecter:[2] **se ~ au système** *v réfl* INFORMAT log on

connecteur *m* CINEMAT connector, coupler, jack plug, ELECTROTEC, ORDINAT, TELECOM connector; ~ **d'accouplement** *m* PRODUCTION *automatisme industriel* mating connector; ~ **d'amplificateur de ligne** *m* PRODUCTION line drive connector; ~ **banalisé** *m* ELECTROTEC hermaphroditic connector; ~ **de boucle** *m* PRODUCTION *automatisme industriel* loopback connector; ~ **à broches** *m* CINEMAT pin connector; ~ **de câbles** *m* ELECTROTEC cable connector; ~ **de carte enfichable** *m* ELECTROTEC edge connector; ~ **de circuit imprimé** *m* ELECTROTEC printed circuit connector; ~ **coaxial** *m* ELECTROTEC coaxial connector; ~ **de con-**

figuration m PRODUCTION *automatisme industriel* configuration plug; ~ **à contacts protégés** m ELECTROTEC dead-front connector; ~ **à effort nul** m ELECTRON zero insertion force connector; ~ **électrique** m ELECTROTEC electrical connector; ~ **encartable** m ELECTROTEC edge socket connector; ~ **en deux parties** m ELECTROTEC two-piece connector; ~ **enfichable** m TELECOM plug-type connector; ~ **en une partie** m ELECTROTEC one-piece connector; ~ **d'entrée** m TELECOM in-connector; ~ **en Y** m ENREGISTR, TV y-cable, y-lead; ~ **d'extension** m INFORMAT, ORDINAT expansion slot; ~ **à faible effort** m ELECTROTEC *d'emboîtement* low-insertion force connector; ~ **femelle** m ELECTROTEC female connector; ~ **de fibres optiques** m OPTIQUE optical fiber connector (AmE), optical fibre connector (BrE); ~ **mâle** m ELECTROTEC male connector; ~ **mâle-femelle** m PRODUCTION plug and socket; ~ **du module mémoire** m PRODUCTION *automatisme industriel* memory module socket; ~ **multicontact** m ELECTROTEC multicore cable; ~ **ombilical** m ESPACE umbilical connector; ~ **optique** m TELECOM optical connector, optical fiber connector (AmE), optical fibre connector (BrE); ~ **phonographique** m ENREGISTR phono plug; ~ **polarisé** m ELECTROTEC polarized connector; ~ **pour fibre optique** m ELECTROTEC fiberoptic connector (AmE), fibreoptic connector (BrE); ~ **rapide** m ESPACE *véhicules* quick coupler; ~ **sec** m ELECTROTEC dry connector; ~ **de sortie** m INFORMAT, ORDINAT out-connector, TELECOM out connector; ~ **de terminaison** m PRODUCTION terminator; ~ **verrouillable** m ELECTROTEC lockable connector

connectez: ~ **le poste de données sur la ligne** *loc* TELECOM connect data set to line

connectif m INFORMAT, ORDINAT connective

connection: ~ **inductive** f CH DE FER impedance bond; ~ **inductive accordée** f CH DE FER tuned impedance bond

connectique f TELECOM easy connection

connectivité f INFORMAT, ORDINAT connectivity

connexion f CONSTR connection, ELECTROTEC connection, joint, patch, INFORMAT, ORDINAT attachment, connection; ~ **antiparallèle** f ELECTR antiparallel connection; ~ **à câbles blindés** f PRODUCTION shielded cable connection; ~ **de canal virtuel** f TELECOM VCC, virtual channel connection; ~ **de circuit intégré** f ELECTROTEC integrated circuit connection; ~ **conductrice** f EN RENOUV ohmic contact; ~ **de conduit d'ordre inférieur** f TELECOM LPC, lower-order path connection; ~ **de conduit d'ordre supérieur** f TELECOM HPC, higher-order path connection; ~ **de conduit virtuel** f TELECOM VPC, virtual path connection; ~ **défectueuse** f SECURITE faulty connection; ~ **directe** f ELECTR *connexions d'écrans* solid bond; ~ **électrique** f ELECTROTEC electrical connection; ~ **en cascade** f ELECTROTEC cascade connection, NUCLEAIRE cascade connection, tandem connection; ~ **en étoile** f PHYSIQUE Y-connection, star connection; ~ **en guirlande** f PRODUCTION *électricité* daisy chain; ~ **en polygone** f ELECTR polygon connection; ~ **en réseau** f INFORMAT, ORDINAT networking; ~ **enroulée** f CONS MECA wire-wrap; ~ **en série** f ELECTROTEC series connection; ~ **en triangle** f ELECTR, PHYSIQUE delta connection, mesh connection; ~ **en triangle ouvert** f ELECTR open delta connection; ~ **en V** f ELECTR V-connection; ~ **en zigzag** f ELECTR *transformateur, bobine* zigzag connection; ~ **équipotentielle** f ELECTROTEC equipotential connection; ~ **étoile** f ELECTR wye connection, *transformateur, bobine* Y-connection; ~ **étoilée** f ELECTR, TELECOM star connection; ~ **étoile-étoile** f ELECTR star-star connection; ~ **à fibre optique** f ELECTROTEC fiberoptic connection (AmE), fibreoptic connection (BrE); ~ **frontale d'induit** f ELECTR *machine* armature end connections; ~ **globale** f OPTIQUE multi-fiber joint (AmE), multifibre joint (BrE); ~ **de grille** f ELECTRON top cap; ~ **inversée sur bande** f ELECTROTEC face-down TAB; ~ **longitudinale de rail** f CH DE FER *voie* railbond; ~ **N** f TELECOM N-connection; ~ **normale sur bande** f ELECTROTEC face-up TAB; ~ **numérique** f TELECOM digital connection; ~ **par dicorde** f ELECTROTEC patching; ~ **par enroulement** f ELECTROTEC wire wrapping; ~ **par pression** f ELECTROTEC pressurized connection; ~ **physique** f TELECOM PhC, physical connection; ~ **à plusieurs masses** f PRODUCTION *électricité* multiple earthing connection (BrE), multiple grounding connection (AmE); ~ **polygonale** f ELECTR mesh connection; ~ **pour liaison de données** f TELECOM DLC, data link connection; ~ **provisoire** f IMPRIM patch; ~ **de rail** f CH DE FER *voie* railbond; ~ **réactive** f CH DE FER reactance bond; ~ **de roue** f CH DE FER *véhicules* wheel bond; ~ **à sec** f ELECTROTEC dry connection; ~ **sertie** f ELECTROTEC crimped connection; ~ **superficielle** f TELECOM surface connection; ~ **sur bande** f ELECTROTEC TAB, tape automated bonding; ~ **temporaire** f ELECTROTEC jumper; ~ **de terre** f ELECTROTEC earth connection (BrE), ground connection (AmE); ~ **de trajet virtuel** f TELECOM VPC, virtual path connection; ~ **transversale de rail** f CH DE FER crossbond; ~ **triangle-étoile** f ELECTR delta star connection; ~ **virtuelle** f INFORMAT, ORDINAT virtual connection; ~ **de voie virtuelle** f TELECOM VCC, virtual channel connection; ~ **volante** f ELECTR jumper

connexions: ~ **d'écrans** f pl ELECTR *câble* shield bonding

connexité: ~ **numérique de bout en bout** f TELECOM end-to-end digital connectivity

conode f METALL tie line

conscience f PRODUCTION conscience; ~ **de perceuse** f CONS MECA breastplate

consécutif adj INFORMAT, ORDINAT consecutive

Conseil: ~ **européen pour la recherche nucléaire** m *(CERN)* PHYS PART European Organization for Nuclear Research *(CERN)*

conseiller: ~ **de sécurité** m CONSTR safety advisor

conseils: ~ **de montage** m pl EMBALLAGE handling and installing instructions

conservateur: ~ **de cap** m AERONAUT course indicator; ~ **d'huile** m ELECTROTEC oil conservator; ~ **ménager de denrées congelées** m REFRIG freezer, household frozen food storage cabinet

conservation f PETROLE, SECURITE conservation; ~ **de charge** f PHYSIQUE conservation of charge; ~ **de charges électriques** f ELECTROTEC charge storage; ~ **des eaux** f HYDROLOGIE water conservation; ~ **de l'énergie** f PHYSIQUE conservation of energy; ~ **de l'information** f ELECTROTEC data retention; ~ **de la luminance** f OPTIQUE conservation of brightness, conservation of radiance, TELECOM conservation of radiance; ~ **de la masse** f PHYSIQUE conservation of mass; ~ **des matériaux inflammables** f SECURITE care of flammable stores; ~ **du moment angulaire** f ASTRONOMIE conservation of angular momentum; ~ **de la parité** f PHYSIQUE conservation of parity; ~ **de quantité de mouvement** f PHYSIQUE conservation of momentum; ~ **sous gaz** f AGRO ALIM gas storage; ~ **de la trace** f

ELECTRON display retention

conserve:[1] **qui ~ la chaleur** *adj* THERMODYN heat-retaining

conserve[2] *f* AGRO ALIM preserve; **~ souple** *f* EMBALLAGE flexible package

conserver:[1] **à ~** *adj* IMPRIM alive

conserver[2] *vt* AGRO ALIM preserve

conserver:[3] **~ les conditions des locaux aseptisées** *vi* SECURITE maintain aseptic area conditions

conserverie *f* OCEANO fishery conservation zone, fishery reserve

consignateur: **~ d'état** *m* ELECTR *enregistreur* event recorder

consignation *f* EMBALLAGE bottle deposit, deposit; **~ emballage** *f* PRODUCTION return of empties; **~ des pannes** *f* INFORMAT, ORDINAT failure logging

consigne *f* PRODUCTION guide line; **~ emballage** *f* PRODUCTION return of empties; **~ de sécurité** *f* PRODUCTION safety warning; **~ d'utilisation** *f* PRODUCTION operating procedure

consigner *vt* INFORMAT, ORDINAT log

consignes: **~ en cas d'incendie** *f pl* SECURITE fire regulations

consistance *f* AGRO ALIM, CHARBON consistency, IMPRIM *d'une encre* body

console *f* CONS MECA, CONSTR bracket, INFORMAT console, MECANIQUE bracket, ORDINAT console; **~ d'exploitation** *f* TELECOM operating console, operator's console; **~ de mixage** *f* ENREGISTR mixing desk, sound console, TV mixing desk; **~ murale** *f* CONSTR wall bracket; **~ opérateur** *f* INFORMAT, ORDINAT operator console; **~ principale** *f* INFORMAT, ORDINAT master console; **~ de programmation** *f* PRODUCTION *automatisme industriel* programmer; **~ son** *f* ENREGISTR audio console, dubbing console; **~ de visualisation** *f* ESPACE *communications* display terminal, INFORMAT, ORDINAT, TELECOM VDU, display console, visual display unit, TV VDU, video display unit; **~ de visualisation de données** *f* TV data display terminal

console-équerre *f* CONSTR knee bracket

consolidation *f* CHARBON, PETR consolidation, PRODUCTION strengthening

consolider *vt* PRODUCTION strengthen

consommable *adj* ESPACE, MECANIQUE expendable

consommateur *m* GAZ consumer; **~ de courant domestique** *m* ELECTR domestic consumer

consommation *f* ELECTROTEC input power, *d'énergie* power consumption, MECANIQUE, VEHICULES *carburant* consumption; **~ de carburant** *f* THERMODYN *combustible* fuel consumption; **~ de chaleur** *f* THERMODYN heat consumption; **~ de circuit** *f* ELECTR, PRODUCTION circuit power requirement; **~ dynamique** *f* ELECTROTEC dynamic power consumption; **~ d'eau moyenne** *f* HYDROLOGIE average consumption of water; **~ en courant** *f* ELECTR, PRODUCTION current requirement; **~ d'énergie** *f* ELECTR *réseau* power consumption, PHYSIQUE, THERMODYN energy consumption; **~ en watts** *f* ELECTROTEC wattage; **~ d'essence** *f* VEHICULES *moteur* gasoline consumption (AmE), petrol consumption (BrE); **~ du four à vide** *f* CERAM VER no-load heat consumption; **~ journalière** *f* DISTRI EAU daily consumption; **~ journalière par habitant** *f* HYDROLOGIE daily specific consumption; **~ minimale** *f* HYDROLOGIE *d'eau* minimum consumption; **~ d'oxygène** *f* HYDROLOGIE oxygen

consumption; **~ par habitant** *f* DISTRI EAU per capita consumption; **~ de pointe** *f* DISTRI EAU peak demand, HYDROLOGIE *d'eau* maximum consumption

consommer: **à ~ avant** *loc* EMBALLAGE best before

consonance *f* ACOUSTIQUE consonance

constant *adj* PHYSIQUE constant

constantan *m* ELECTR *thermocouple* constantan

constante:[1] **à une ~ arbitraire près** *adv* PHYSIQUE to within an arbitrary constant

constante[2] *f* INFORMAT, MATH, ORDINAT, PHYSIQUE constant; **~ d'affaiblissement** *f* OPTIQUE, PHYSIQUE attenuation constant; **~ arbitraire** *f* PHYSIQUE arbitrary constant; **~ d'atténuation** *f* ELECTRON attenuation constant; **~ d'atténuation acoustique** *f* ELECTRON acoustic attenuation constant; **~ de Boltzmann** *f* ESPACE *communications*, PHYSIQUE Boltzmann constant; **~ calorifique** *f* THERMODYN heat constant; **~ de couplage** *f* NUCLEAIRE, PHYSIQUE coupling constant; **~ critique** *f* CHIMIE critical constant; **~ de Curie** *f* PHYS RAYON, PHYSIQUE Curie constant; **~ de désintégration** *f* GEOLOGIE, PHYS RAYON, PHYSIQUE decay constant; **~ diélectrique** *f* ELECTROTEC dielectric constant, relative permittivity, PLAST CAOU dielectric constant, TV specific inductive capacity; **~ de dissociation** *f* CHIMIE dissociation constant; **~ de dose** *f* PHYS RAYON dose constant; **~ d'effet d'écran** *f* NUCLEAIRE screening constant, screening number; **~ élastique** *f* METALL, PHYS FLUID elastic constant; **~ électrique** *f* ELECTROTEC, PHYSIQUE electric constant; **~ d'équilibre** *f* CHIMIE *d'une réaction* equilibrium constant; **~ de Faraday** *f* PHYSIQUE Faraday constant; **~ figurative** *f* INFORMAT, ORDINAT figurative constant; **~ de gaz parfait** *f* PHYSIQUE gas constant; **~ de gravitation** *f* ASTRONOMIE, GEOPHYS, PHYSIQUE gravitational constant; **~ gravitationnelle** *f* ESPACE gravitation constant; **~ de Hall** *f* PHYSIQUE Hall coefficient; **~ de Hubble** *f* ASTRONOMIE, ESPACE *communications* Hubble's constant; **~ de Josephson** *f* PHYSIQUE Josephson constant; **~ localisée** *f* ELECTROTEC lumped element; **~ de Lorenz** *f* PHYSIQUE Lorenz constant; **~ magnétique** *f* ELECTROTEC, PHYSIQUE magnetic constant; **~ molaire des gaz** *f* PHYSIQUE molar gas constant; **~ numérique** *f* INFORMAT numeric literal; **~ de phase** *f* ACOUSTIQUE, ELECTRON, OPTIQUE, PHYSIQUE, TV phase constant; **~ de Planck** *f* PHYS RAYON, PHYSIQUE Planck's constant; **~ de propagation** *f* OPTIQUE, PHYSIQUE propagation constant; **~ de propagation acoustique** *f* ACOUSTIQUE acoustic propagation constant; **~ de rayonnement** *f* CHAUFFAGE Stefan's constant, radiation constant; **~ réduite de Planck** *f* PHYSIQUE Dirac constant, h-bar; **~ du réseau** *f* ELECTROTEC network constant; **~ de Rydberg** *f* PHYSIQUE Rydberg constant; **~ solaire** *f* ASTRONOMIE, EN RENOUV, ESPACE *communications*, GEOPHYS solar constant; **~ de Stefan-Boltzmann** *f* PHYSIQUE Stefan-Boltzmann constant; **~ de structure fine** *f* PHYSIQUE fine structure constant; **~ de temps** *f* ELECTR *circuit à courant alternatif*, PHYSIQUE time constant; **~ de temps d'autodécharge** *f* ELECTROTEC self-discharge time constant; **~ de temps inverse** *f* NUCLEAIRE reciprocal period; **~ de torsion** *f* PHYSIQUE torsional constant; **~ viscosité-gravité** *f* THERMODYN viscosity-gravity constant; **~ de vitesse** *f* METALL rate constant

constantes: **~ de réseau** *f pl* PHYSIQUE network parameters

constat: **~ d'avaries** *m* NAUT damage assessment; **~**

d'impact *m* POLLUTION impact statement; ~ **d'impact sur l'environnement** *m* POLLUTION environmental impact statement

constellation *f* ASTRONOMIE asterism, constellation

constituant[1] *adj* CONS MECA component

constituant:[2] ~ **détritique** *m* GEOLOGIE clast

constituer: ~ **une contrefaçon** *vt* BREVETS constitute an infringement; ~ **un danger pour** *vt* SECURITE be a danger to

constitutif *adj* CONS MECA component

constriction *f* METALL constriction, NUCLEAIRE denting

constringence *f* PHYSIQUE constringence

constructeur *m* CONSTR builder, PRODUCTION maker; ~ **de bâtiments** *m* CONSTR builder; ~ **de machines** *m* CONS MECA engine builder; PRODUCTION engine maker; ~ **de maisons** *m* CONSTR house builder; ~ **de modèle réduit** *m* CINEMAT model builder; ~ **de navires** *m* NAUT shipbuilder, shipwright

construction *f* CONSTR building, construction, structure, *de bâtiments* erection, GEOMETRIE construction; ~ **alvéolée** *f* EMBALLAGE honeycomb structure; ~ **de cordes** *f* PHYS RAYON *physique théorique* string construction; ~ **en acier** *f* CONSTR steel construction; ~ **en nid d'abeilles** *f* AERONAUT honeycomb structure; ~ **en série** *f* NAUT mass production, series production; ~ **de haut en bas** *f* CONSTR top-down construction; ~ **mécanique** *f* PRODUCTION mechanical engineering; ~ **moderne** *f* CONSTR modern construction; ~ **des murailles** *f* NAUT side construction; ~ **navale** *f* NAUT shipbuilding; ~ **parasismique** *f* CONSTR earthquake-proof construction; ~ **de puits** *f* EN RENOUV well sinking; ~ **des réacteurs nucléaires** *f* NUCLEAIRE reactor art; ~ **rigide** *f* CONSTR rigid construction; ~ **de routes** *f* CONSTR road making; ~ **routière** *f* TRANSPORT road building, road making; ~ **transversale** *f* NAUT transverse framing

construire *vt* CONSTR construct, put up, *maison* build; ~ **la carcasse** *vt* NAUT *d'un navire* frame

consultation *f* INFORMAT inquiry, look-up, query, ORDINAT inquiry, query; ~ **de données** *f* INFORMAT data query, interrogation, inquiry, look-up, ORDINAT data query, interrogation, look-up; ~ **des fournisseurs** *f* PRODUCTION quotation request, request for quotation; ~ **des messages** *f* TELECOM message retrieval; ~ **de table** *f* INFORMAT, ORDINAT table lookup, table search

consulter *vt* INFORMAT, ORDINAT query

contact *m* AERONAUT contact point, ELECTR *relais, interrupteur, etc*, ELECTROTEC contact, INFORMAT switch, VEHICULES *allumage* point; ~ **"F"** *m* PRODUCTION NO contact; ~ **"F" à fermeture** *m* PRODUCTION NO contact; ~ **"F" à fermeture avancée** *m* PRODUCTION NO early make contact; ~ **"O"** *m* PRODUCTION NC contact, normally closed contact; ~ **"O" à ouverture** *m* PRODUCTION NC contact; ~ **"O" à ouverture retardée** *m* PRODUCTION NO late break contact; ~ **d'arc** *m* ELECTR *interrupteur* arcing contact; ~ **argenté** *m* ELECTROTEC silver-plated contact; ~ **auxiliaire** *m* ELECTROTEC auxiliary contact, PRODUCTION auxiliary switch; ~ **auxiliaire en accessoire** *m* ELECTR, PRODUCTION auxiliary contact accessory; ~ **banalisé** *m* ELECTROTEC hermaphroditic contact; ~ **basculant à mercure** *m* COMMANDE mercury switch, wet reed relay; ~ **de base** *m* ELECTROTEC base contact; ~ **bimétallique** *m* ELECTROTEC bimetallic contact; ~ **brûlé** *m* VEHICULES *allumage* burnt contact; ~ **central pour flash** *m* PHOTO

hot-shoe flash contact; ~ **chevauchant** *m* PRODUCTION *automatisme industriel* overlap contact; ~ **à chevauchement** *m* ELECTROTEC bridging contact, shorting contact; ~ **du collecteur** *m* ELECTROTEC collector contact; ~ **de connexion en bande** *m* ELECTROTEC reeled contact; ~ **à court-circuit** *m* ELECTROTEC bridging contact; ~ **de déclenchement** *m* AUTO, CONS MECA trigger contact, PRODUCTION trip contact; ~ **à déclic** *m* PRODUCTION snap-action contact; ~ **à deux directions** *m* ELECTROTEC DPST, double-pole single-throw switch; ~ **de drain** *m* ELECTROTEC drain contact; ~ **électrique** *m* ELECTR *relais*, ELECTROTEC electrical contact; ~ **d'émetteur** *m* ELECTROTEC emitter contact; ~ **en argent** *m* ELECTROTEC silver contact; ~ **en bande** *m* ELECTROTEC reeled contact; ~ **en charbon** *m* ELECTROTEC carbon contact; ~ **d'enclenchement** *m* ELECTROTEC interlock contact; ~ **femelle** *m* ELECTROTEC female contact, socket contact; ~ **à fermeture** *m* ELECTR *relais* make contact; ~ **à fiches** *m* ELECTROTEC plug connector; ~ **fixe** *m* ELECTR *relais*, ELECTROTEC fixed contact, PRODUCTION stationary contact; ~ **fixe de voie** *m* CH DE FER contact ramp, crocodile; ~ **glissant** *m* ELECTROTEC sliding contact; ~ **à grand pouvoir de coupure** *m* ELECTROTEC heavy-duty contact; ~ **de grille** *m* ELECTROTEC gate contact; ~ **à interrupteur scellé** *m* PRODUCTION *automatisme industriel* sealed switch contact; **à un** ~ **interrupteur** *m* ELECTR, ELECTROTEC, SPST, single-pole single-throw; ~ **inverseur** *m* ELECTROTEC double-throw contact, reverse contact; **à un** ~ **inverseur** *m* ELECTR, ELECTROTEC SPDT, single-pole double-throw; ~ **jumelé à pression** *m* ELECTR, PRODUCTION bifurcated mating contact; ~ **à lames souples** *m* PRODUCTION reed contact, *automatisme industriel* logic reed contact, TELECOM reed contact; ~ **de mise en court-circuit** *m* ELECTROTEC shorting contact; ~ **mobile** *m* ELECTR movable contact, ELECTROTEC moving contact, PRODUCTION movable contact; ~ **mobile à double portée** *m* PRODUCTION bifurcated movable contact; ~ **mouillé au mercure** *m* ELECTROTEC mercury-wetted contact; ~ **normalement ouvert** *m* ELECTR *relais* make contact; ~ **ohmique** *m* ELECTROTEC, PHYSIQUE ohmic contact; ~ **à ouverture** *m* ELECTR *relais* break contact, PRODUCTION normally closed contact; ~ **à ouverture retardée** *m* PRODUCTION *automatisme industriel* late break contact; ~ **par radio** *m* NAUT radiocommunication; ~ **de passage** *m* ELECTR *transformateur* transition contact; ~ **ponctuel** *m* ELECTROTEC point contact; ~ **à portée sur la tranche** *m* ELECTROTEC side-wipe contact; ~ **potentiel différence** *m* ELECTR *entre deux métaux* contact emf; ~ **à pression directe** *m* ELECTR *relais* butt contact; ~ **de relais** *m* ELECTR, ELECTROTEC, PRODUCTION relay contact; ~ **de repos** *m* ELECTR *relais* back contact, break contact, normally closed contact, open contact, resting contact, ELECTROTEC break contact; ~ **repos** *m* ELECTROTEC, PRODUCTION break contact; ~ **repos-travail** *m* ELECTROTEC make-and-break contact; ~ **de rupture** *m* ELECTR *relais* break contact, VEHICULES *allumage* breaker contact; ~ **à rupture brusque** *m* PRODUCTION snap-action contact; ~ **sans chevauchement** *m* ELECTROTEC nonbridging contact; ~ **sans court-circuit** *m* ELECTROTEC nonbridging contact; ~ **scellé** *m* ELECTROTEC sealed contact, TELECOM reed; ~ **sec** *m* ELECTR, PRODUCTION hard contact; ~ **à simple rupture** *m* ELECTROTEC single break contact; ~ **à soufflage mag-**

nétique *m* CONS MECA magnetic arc blowout contact; ~ **de source** *m* ELECTROTEC source contact; ~ **tête-bande** *m* TV head-to-tape contact; ~ **de travail** *m* CONSTR normally open contact; ~ **de travail** *m* ELECTR closing contact, normally open contact, ELECTROTEC make contact; ~ **à vis** *m* ELECTR screw contact

contacteur *m* ELECTR *relais*, ELECTROTEC contactor; ~ **avec blocs additifs temporisés** *m* ELECTR contactor with timer adder desk; ~ **avec blocs instantanés** *m* ELECTR contactor with auxiliary adder desk; ~ **avec relais de protection thermique à bilames** *m* ELECTR, PRODUCTION contactor with overload relay; ~ **barométrique** *m* INST HYDR pressure switch; ~ **CA** *m* PRODUCTION AC contactor; ~ **centrifuge** *m* CONS MECA centrifugal switch; ~ **de débit** *m* PRODUCTION flow switch; ~ **manométrique** *m* INST HYDR pressure switch; ~ **marche arrière** *m* PRODUCTION *automatisme industriel* reverse contactor; ~ **marche avant** *m* PRODUCTION forward contactor; ~ **mécanique** *m* ELECTR *relais* mechanical contactor; ~ **moyenne tension à coupure sous vide** *m* PRODUCTION *automatisme industriel* medium-voltage vacuum contactor; ~ **de niveau de liquide** *m* PRODUCTION fluid-level switch; ~ **de papillon d'air** *m* AUTO throttle valve switch; ~ **de porte** *m* COMMANDE emergency door switch; ~ **de préalimentation** *m* PRODUCTION precharge contactor; ~ **à semi-conducteur** *m* ELECTRON semiconductor contactor; ~ **de stop** *m* AUTO stop light switch; ~ **supplémentaire** *m* PHOTO auxiliary shoe; ~ **de switch** *m* PRODUCTION *système hydraulique* level switch; ~ **thermique** *m* PRODUCTION *système hydraulique* temperature switch; ~ **variométrique** *m* AERONAUT pressure rate-of-change switch

contacts: ~ **en contact** *m pl* ELECTROTEC mated contacts; ~ **mis en contact** *m pl* ELECTROTEC mated contacts; ~ **à placage sélectif** *m pl* ELECTROTEC selectively-plated contacts; ~ **principaux** *m pl* ELECTR *transformateur* main contacts; ~ **principaux de coupure** *m pl* ELECTR main switching contacts

contaminamètre *m* MILITAIRE *guerre nucléaire* contamination meter, radiation meter

contamination *f* CHARBON, CHIMIE contamination, ESPACE contamination, pollution, HYDROLOGIE, NUCLEAIRE *radioactive*, QUALITE *nourriture* contamination, SECURITE pollution; ~ **des eaux** *f* DISTRI EAU water pollution; ~ **radioactive** *f* PHYS RAYON, PHYSIQUE radioactive contamination, SECURITE radioactive pollution

contaminer *vt* CHARBON contaminate

contemporain *adj* GEOLOGIE coeval

contenance *f* CONS MECA capacity, CONSTR *d'un champ* content

conteneur *m* CHARBON, EMBALLAGE container, TELECOM CT, container, TRANSPORT container; ~ **assemblable** *m* TRANSPORT joinable container; ~ **avec porte latérale** *m* TRANSPORT open wall container; ~ **bâché** *m* TRANSPORT tarpaulin covered container; ~ **à bâches** *m* TRANSPORT tilt container, tiltainer; ~ **de boîtes de conserve à recycler** *m* RECYCLAGE can bank; ~ **de boîtes en aluminium** *m* RECYCLAGE aluminium can bank (BrE), aluminum can bank (AmE); ~ **buse** *m* CONS MECA pouring sleeve; ~ **calorifique** *m* TRANSPORT heated container; ~ **citerne** *m* TRANSPORT tank container; ~ **à claire-voie** *m* TRANSPORT lattice-sided container, skeleton container; ~ **de collecte** *m* RECYCLAGE bank; ~ **de collecte de verre usé** *m* RECYCLAGE

bottle bank; ~ **collico** *m* TRANSPORT collico; ~ **en acier pouvant être mis en pièces détachées** *m* EMBALLAGE steel reusable CKD container; ~ **fermé** *m* TRANSPORT closed container, covered container; ~ **ferroviaire** *m* TRANSPORT railroad container (AmE), railway container (BrE); ~ **flottant** *m* TRANSPORT barge container; ~ **frigorifique** *m* THERMODYN heat-insulated container, TRANSPORT refrigerated container; ~ **gerbable** *m* TRANSPORT stackable container; ~ **de grande capacité** *m* EMBALLAGE large size container; ~ **hors-cotes** *m* *(HC)* TRANSPORT high-cube container *(HC)*; ~ **intermédiaire à pulvérents** *m* EMBALLAGE intermediate bulk container; ~ **isotherme** *m* TRANSPORT insulated container; ~ **multimodal** *m* TRANSPORT intermodal container; ~ **non normalisé** *m* TRANSPORT dravos, odd container; ~ **non retour** *m* EMBALLAGE one-way container; ~ **normalisé** *m* TRANSPORT standard container; ~ **ouvert** *m* TRANSPORT open-top container; ~ **palette** *m* TRANSPORT pallet container; ~ **à paroi ouverte** *m* TRANSPORT open wall container; ~ **à porteur aménagé** *m* TRANSPORT PA container; ~ **pour trafic d'outre-mer** *m* TRANSPORT overseas container, transcontainer; ~ **à pulvérulents** *m* TRANSPORT dry bulk container; ~ **à pulvérulents à vidange par air pulsé** *m* TRANSPORT bulk container with pressure discharge; ~ **à pulvérulents à vidange par gravité** *m* TRANSPORT bulk container with gravity discharge; ~ **repliable** *m* TRANSPORT collapsible freight container; ~ **à roues fixes** *m* TRANSPORT container with fixed wheels; ~ **sans toit** *m* TRANSPORT tilt-top container; ~ **spécial hors-cotes** *m* *(SHC)* TRANSPORT superhigh cube *(SHC)*; ~ **terrestre** *m* TRANSPORT land container; ~ **à toit ouvert** *m* TRANSPORT tilt-top container; ~ **à toit ouvrant** *m* TRANSPORT container with opening top; ~ **de transport** *m* TRANSPORT freight container; ~ **virtuel** *m* *(CTV)* TELECOM virtual container; ~ **virtuel-n** *m* TELECOM VC-n, virtual container-n

conteneurisation *f* EMBALLAGE, TRANSPORT containerization

conteneuriser *vt* TRANSPORT containerize

conteneur-n *m* TELECOM C-n, container-n

contention *f* ORDINAT content-addressable storage (AmE), content-addressable store (BrE), contention

contenu *m* BREVETS *de l'abrégé*, INFORMAT, ORDINAT, TELECOM, TEXTILE content; ~ **décisionnel** *m* ORDINAT decision content; ~ **énergétique** *m* THERMODYN energy content; ~ **en harmoniques** *m* ELECTRON harmonic content; ~ **en vapeur d'eau** *m* METEO specific humidity, water content; ~ **informationnel** *m* ORDINAT information content; ~ **nominal** *m* EMBALLAGE, IMPRIM nominal content; ~ **salin** *m* OCEANO salt content

contexte *m* INFORMAT, ORDINAT context; ~ **d'application** *m* TELECOM application context

contextuel *adj* INFORMAT, ORDINAT context-sensitive

contexture: ~ **d'un tissu** *f* TEXTILE fabric construction

contigu *adj* GEOMETRIE, INFORMAT, ORDINAT contiguous

continu *adj* INFORMAT, ORDINAT continuous; **en** ~ *adj* IMPRIM *impression, traitements complémentaires* in-line

continuité: ~ **de contact** *f* ELECTR, PRODUCTION contact continuity; ~ **dialoguée** *f* CINEMAT scenario; ~ **électrique** *f* ELECTROTEC electrical continuity

continuité-discontinuité *f* ESSAIS continuity-discontinuity

continuum: ~ **espace-temps** *m* ESPACE space-time continuum

conti-snap *m* IMPRIM conti-snap

contour *m* CONS MECA outline, CONSTR *d'une colonne* contour, *d'un dôme* contour; ~ **d'un caractère** *m* INFORMAT, ORDINAT character outline; ~ **de flux constant** *m* GEOPHYS isodynamic flux lines

contourage *m* PRODUCTION contour grinding

contournement *m* ELECTR, ELECTROTEC, THERMODYN flashover; ~ **par un arc** *m* ELECTR, ELECTROTEC arc over

contractabilité *f* CHARBON contractancy, contractibility

contracter: se ~ *v réfl* PHYSIQUE, TEXTILE contract

contractile *adj* TEXTILE contractile

contraction *f* CINEMAT shrinkage, CONSTR shrinking, METALL shrinkage, PHYSIQUE contraction, shrinkage, PRODUCTION shrinkage, TEXTILE contraction, shrinkage; ~ **due au froid** *f* THERMODYN contraction due to cold; ~ **de Fitzgerald et Lorentz** *f* PHYSIQUE Lorentz-Fitzgerald contraction; ~ **gravitationnelle** *f* ASTRONOMIE gravitational contraction; ~ **d'image** *f* TV cramping; ~ **lanthanide** *f* CHIMIE lanthanide contraction; ~ **latérale** *f* HYDROLOGIE *écoulement de l'eau par déversoir* end contraction, METALL lateral contraction; ~ **des longueurs** *f* PHYSIQUE length contraction; ~ **thermique** *f* THERMODYN thermal contraction

contraindre *vt* CONS MECA stress

contrainte *f* CERAM VER, CONS MECA, CONSTR stress, GEOLOGIE strain, stress, INFORMAT constraint, MECANIQUE *matériaux*, METALL stress, ORDINAT constraint, PETROLE stress, PHYSIQUE strength, stress, PLAST CAOU, RESSORTS stress; ~ **appliquée** *f* METALL applied stress, working stress; ~ **au choc** *f* EMBALLAGE impact stress; ~ **circonférentielle** *f* METALL circumferential stress; ~ **circonférentielle de flexion** *f* NAUT bending circumferential stress; ~ **de cisaillement** *f* CONSTR, PHYSIQUE, PLAST CAOU, RESSORTS shear stress; ~ **de cisaillement réduite** *f* MATERIAUX resolved shear stress; ~ **de cisaillement simple** *f* METALL simple shear stress; ~ **de commande adaptative** *f* *(commande ACC)* COMMANDE adaptive control constraint *(ACC)*; ~ **de compression** *f* EMBALLAGE, MECANIQUE *matériaux*, METALL compression stress; ~ **corrigée** *f* RESSORTS corrected stress; ~ **de courroie de transmission** *f* CONS MECA belt stress; ~ **critique** *f* METALL critical stress; ~ **critique de rupture** *f* METALL critical fracture stress; ~ **dans le rail** *f* CH DE FER rail stress; ~ **directe** *f* CONS MECA direct stress; ~ **dynamique** *f* CONS MECA dynamic stress; ~ **d'écoulement** *f* PHYSIQUE flow stress, yield stress; ~ **effective** *f* PETROLE *géologie* effective stress; ~ **en retour** *f* METALL back stress; ~ **finale** *f* RESSORTS ultimate stress; ~ **de flexion** *f* MECANIQUE, RESSORTS bending stress; ~ **de frottement** *f* METALL friction stress; ~ **hydrostatique** *f* METALL hydrostatic stress; ~ **initiale** *f* RESSORTS initial stress; ~ **interne** *f* METALL internal stress; ~ **locale** *f* METALL local stress; ~ **longitudinale** *f* METALL longitudinal stress; ~ **maximale** *f* IMPRIM *mécanique, papiers* maximal stress; ~ **maximum admissible de la courroie** *f* CONS MECA maximum allowable belt stress; ~ **minimale** *f* METALL minimum stress; ~ **moyenne** *f* METALL mean stress; ~ **nominale** *f* METALL nominal stress; ~ **non corrigée** *f* RESSORTS uncorrected stress; ~ **oscillante** *f* RESSORTS oscillating stress; ~ **permanente** *f* CERAM VER permanent stress; ~ **réelle** *f* METALL true stress; ~ **réelle de rupture** *f* METALL true fracture stress; ~ **résiduelle** *f* CERAM VER, CONSTR, MATERIAUX, RESSORTS residual stress; ~ **de Reynolds** *f* PHYS FLUID Reynolds stress; ~ **de rupture** *f* CONS MECA breaking stress, ultimate stress, MECANIQUE *matéri-*

aux breaking stress; ~ **statique** *f* CONS MECA strain; ~ **technologique** *f* ESPACE technological restriction; ~ **temporaire** *f* CERAM VER temporary stress; ~ **de tension** *f* PHYSIQUE tensile stress; ~ **thermique** *f* MATERIAUX, THERMODYN thermal stress; ~ **de torsion** *f* RESSORTS torsional strain; ~ **totale** *f* RESSORTS total stress; ~ **de traction** *f* MECANIQUE *matériaux*, METALL, PHYSIQUE, RESSORTS tensile stress; ~ **variable** *f* METALL fluctuating stress; ~ **visqueuse** *f* PHYS FLUID viscous stress

contraintes: ~ dues à l'environnement *f pl* ESPACE *véhicules* environmental stress

contrarotatif *adj* ESPACE *antenne* despun

contraste *m* CINEMAT lighting ratio, IMPRIM *photogravure* gradation, OPTIQUE, PHYSIQUE contrast; ~ **d'indice** *m* OPTIQUE index contrast; ~ **d'indice de réfraction** *m* TELECOM refractive index contrast; ~ **lumineux** *m* CINEMAT lighting contrast

contrasté *adj* CINEMAT contrasty, hard

contrat: ~ d'affrètement *m* NAUT charter party

contre:[1] **à ~** *adj* NAUT aback

contre:[2] **~ le vent** *adv* NAUT upwind

contre:[3] **~ pression** *f* INST HYDR, PAPIER back pressure

contré *adj* NAUT *bois* laminated

contre-alizés *m pl* NAUT antitrades

contre-arc *m* NAUT sagging

contre-bague *f* CERAM VER bead

contrebalancer *vt* MECANIQUE counterbalance

contre-balancier *m* MINES balance bob

contre-bateau *m* CERAM VER convex bow

contre-bouterolle *f* AERONAUT backing bar, bucking bar

contre-bride *f* MECANIQUE, NUCLEAIRE counterflange, mating flange

contre-câble: ~ d'équilibre *m* MINES counterbalancing rope

contre-cache *m* CINEMAT complementary matte, reverse mask, countermatte

contre-came *f* MECANIQUE cam follower

contre-champ *m* CINEMAT countershot, reverse angle

contre-clavette *f* CONS MECA gib, nose key

contrecollage *m* IMPRIM alignment, lining-up, PAPIER glueing, pasting

contre-cône *m* CONS MECA cone for overhead motion, countershaft cone, overhead cone, overhead cone pulley

contrecoup *m* CONS MECA recoil, MINES *d'une explosion* backlash, SECURITE repercussion

contre-courant *m* CHARBON counterflow, CHIMIE, HYDROLOGIE countercurrent, INST HYDR counterstream line, OCEANO countercurrent; ~ **de fond** *m* NAUT undertow; ~ **sous-marin** *m* NAUT undercurrent

contre-coussinet *m* CONS MECA top brass

contre-dessin *m* CERAM VER image

contre-dupli *m* CINEMAT reversal master print, second generation dupe

contre-échelle *f* CONS MECA diagonal scale

contre-écrou *m* CONS MECA checknut, jam nut, keeper, locknut, locknut, pinch nut, safety nut, set nut, IMPRIM *mécanique* backnut, MECANIQUE locknut, PRODUCTION grip nut, locknut

contre-électrode *f* TV backplate

contre-entrefer *m* ENREGISTR back gap

contre-essai *m* CONS MECA countertest

contre-étrave *f* NAUT apron

contrefaçon *f* BREVETS infringement

contrefacteur *m* BREVETS infringer

contre-fer *m* CONSTR *d'un rabot* back iron

contrefiche *f* CONS MECA brace strut, CONSTR brace, raker, raking shore, spur, strut; ~ de couple *f* CONS MECA frame cross member; ~ diagonale de train *f* AERONAUT landing gear diagonal truss; ~ horizontale *f* AERONAUT horizontal strut; ~ longitudinale *f* AERONAUT drag link; ~ de train principal *f* AERONAUT main landing gear brace-strut; ~ de verrouillage du train *f* AERONAUT drag brace

contre-flèche *f* RESSORTS reverse deflection

contrefort *m* CONSTR buttress, close buttress

contre-fossé *m* DISTRI EAU berm ditch

contre-fruit *m* CONSTR inner batter

contre-griffe *f* CINEMAT pilot claw

contregyrer *vt* ESPACE *véhicules* despin

contre-hublot *m* NAUT deadlight

contre-jour:[1] à ~ *adj* CINEMAT, PHOTO backlit

contre-jour[2] *adv* CINEMAT, PHOTO against the light

contre-lame *f* PAPIER bed knife

contre-latte *f* CONSTR counter lath

contre-lèvre *f* PAPIER apron lip

contre-limon *m* CONSTR wall string

contremaître *m* CONSTR, PRODUCTION foreman; ~ de forage *m* PETR tool pusher; ~ de production *m* PETROLE roustabout

contre-manivelle *f* PRODUCTION fly crank

contremarche *f* CONSTR riser, rise, riser, rise; ~ palière *f* CONSTR landing riser

contre-mesures: ~ électroniques *f pl* MILITAIRE electronic countermeasures

contre-moule *m* NAUT inner lining

contrepartie: ~ optique *f* ASTRONOMIE *des radiosources intenses* optical counterpart

contre-plaque *f* CONS MECA backing plate, counterplate; ~ dévêtisseuse *f* CONS MECA *moule d'injection* core plate; ~ d'éjection *f* CONS MECA ejector retaining plate

contreplaqué *m* CONSTR plywood, wall plate, *article* plywood, EMBALLAGE plywood; ~ à la résine *m* PLAST CAOU *bois* resin-bonded plywood

contre-plateau: ~ pour le montage des mandrins *m* CONS MECA chuck back

contrepoids *m* CONS MECA balance weight, counterweight, CONSTR, INSTRUMENT counterweight, MECANIQUE balance weight, counterweight; ~ arrière *m* CONS MECA back balance; ~ d'équilibrage *m* ENREGISTR counterweight; ~ de maintien de la tension *m* CONS MECA balanced tension block

contre-poinçon *m* CONS MECA counterpunch

contre-poinçonner *vt* CONS MECA counterpunch

contre-pointe *f* CONS MECA back puppet, backhead, deadhead, footstock, headstock, loose head, loose headstock, sliding headstock, sliding poppet, tailstock; ~ à fourreau *f* PRODUCTION cylinder poppet head, cylinder tailstock; ~ d'un tour *f* CONS MECA back center (AmE), back centre (BrE)

contrepoison *m* CHIMIE antidote

contre-poupée *f* CONS MECA back puppet, backhead, deadhead, footstock, headstock, loose head, loose headstock, sliding headstock, sliding poppet, tailstock

contre-pression *f* IMPRIM *mécanique* back pressure; ~ à l'échappement *f* AERONAUT exhaust back pressure

contre-rail *m* CONSTR checkrail

contre-réaction *f* ELECTRON inverse feedback, negative feedback, ELECTROTEC inverse feedback, ENREGISTR, MECANIQUE *régulation* feedback, PHYS ONDES negative feedback, PHYSIQUE, TELECOM feedback; ~ de courant *f* ELECTROTEC current feedback; ~ parallèle *f* ELECTROTEC shunt feedback; ~ sélective *f* ELECTRON selective feedback; ~ série *f* ELECTROTEC series feedback; ~ de synchronisation *f* TV sync feedback; ~ de tension *f* ELECTROTEC voltage feedback

contre-rouleau *m* CERAM VER trang roll

contre-signal *m* COMMANDE, PRODUCTION feedback signal

contre-tension *f* PHYSIQUE stopping potential

contre-tige *f* CONS MECA tailrod; ~ de piston *f* CONS MECA extended piston rod, tail piston rod

contre-torpilleur *m* NAUT destroyer

contretypage *m* COULEURS color matching (AmE), colour matching (BrE), IMPRIM *reproduction* optical printing

contre-type *m* CINEMAT interdupe, *pour tirage des copies d'exploitation* release negative, IMPRIM *photogravure*, PHOTO duplicate; ~ couleur *m* CINEMAT color dupe neg (AmE); ~ négatif *m* CINEMAT dupe negative, intermediate negative

contretyper *vt* CINEMAT dupe, PHOTO duplicate

contre-vapeur *f* INST HYDR reversed steam

contrevenir: ~ aux règlements *vi* SECURITE contravene regulations

contrevent *m* CONSTR wind brace

contreventement *m* CONSTR bracing against wind pressure; ~ diagonal de chaudière *m* INST HYDR diagonal stay

contreventer *vt* CONSTR *comble, ferme* brace against wind pressure

contrôlable *adj* COMMANDE controllable

contrôle:[1] sous ~ *adj* COMMANDE, CONS MECA under control; à ~ centrifuge *adj* EN RENOUV centrifugally operated

contrôle[2] *m* ELECTR, ELECTRON control, ENREGISTR monitoring, ESPACE check, control, inspection, INFORMAT check, MECANIQUE examination, inspection, ORDINAT check, control, PAPIER *régulation* control, *vérification* checking, PRODUCTION, QUALITE inspection, REFRIG check, TELECOM, TEXTILE control, TV monitoring;

~ a ~ d'accélération *m* AERONAUT acceleration control unit; ~ d'accès *m* TELECOM access control; ~ d'accès au média *m* TELECOM MAC, medium access control; ~ d'accès au réseau *m* INFORMAT, ORDINAT network access control; ~ actif *m* ESPACE *véhicules* active control; ~ d'aérage *m* COMMANDE ventilation control; ~ des aigus *m* ENREGISTR treble control; ~ d'alignement *m* TV registration control; ~ alimentaire *m* QUALITE food control; ~ de l'alimentation du fil *m* TEXTILE yarn feed control; ~ de l'amiante à l'usine *m* SECURITE asbestos control in the workplace; ~ annexe *m* COMMANDE minor control; ~ d'approche *m* AERONAUT approach control; ~ d'assemblage *m* COMMANDE assembly line inspection; ~ d'assiette *m* TRANSPORT trim control; ~ attentif *m* SECURITE close supervision; ~ automatique *m* COMMANDE automatic control, automatic monitoring, INFORMAT machine check; ~ automatique d'approche *m* AERONAUT automatic approach control; ~ automatique de chrominance *m (CAC)* TV automatic chrominance control *(ACC)*; ~ automatique de fréquence *m (CAF)* COMMANDE, ENREGISTR, TV automatic frequency control *(AFC)*; ~ automatique de gain *m (CAG)* COMMANDE automatic gain control, automatic gain monitoring, GEOPHYS automatic gain control *(AGC)*; ~ **automatique de luminance** *m* COMMANDE, TV automatic brightness control; ~ **automatique de la marche** *m* CH DE FER automatic train monitoring; ~ **automatique du niveau d'enregistrement** *m* ENREGISTR automatic recording level control; ~ **automatique de phase** *m* ELECTRON, TV APC, automatic phase control; ~ **automatique de sélectivité** *m* COMMANDE automatic selectivity control; ~ **automatique de sensitivité** *m* COMMANDE automatic sensitivity control; ~ **automatique à séquence** *m* COMMANDE ASC, automatic sequence control; ~ **automatique des trains** *m* CH DE FER ATC, automatic train control; ~ **d'avancement** *m* COMMANDE feed check, progress check; ~ **des avancements** *m* COMMANDE progress control; ~ **d'avaries** *m* COMMANDE malfunction detection;

~ b ~ **des basses** *m* ENREGISTR bass control; ~ **de bout en bout** *m* ORDINAT end-to-end control; ~ **du bruit des avions** *m* COMMANDE aircraft noise monitoring;

~ c ~ **de capacité** *m* AERONAUT *transport aérien* capacity control; ~ **cent-pour-cent** *m* COMMANDE hundred per cent inspection; ~ **de charge de batterie** *m* CINEMAT battery check; ~ **de charge de ligne** *m* *(CCL)* TELECOM line load control *(LLC)*; ~ **de chauffe** *m* NAUT combustion control; ~ **de la circulation** *m* COMMANDE traffic control; ~ **de la circulation aérienne** *m* AERONAUT, COMMANDE air traffic control; ~ **à claviers** *m* COMMANDE keyboard tuning; ~ **de configuration** *m* INFORMAT, ORDINAT CM, configuration management; ~ **de conformité** *m* PRODUCTION configuration control; ~ **de continuité** *m* COMMANDE continuity check, ELECTR *circuit* continuity test; ~ **du contraste** *m* COMMANDE contrast control; ~ **de la couche limite** *m* TRANSPORT boundary layer control; ~ **à cycle fermé** *m* COMMANDE closed-loop control; ~ **cyclique de la superfluité** *m* MATH cyclic redundancy check;

~ d ~ **du débit** *m* COMMANDE rate control; ~ **de dérangements** *m* COMMANDE malfunction detection; ~ **de déroulement** *m* TV continuity control; ~ **de la déviation** *m* COMMANDE deviation control; ~ **dimensionnel** *m* COMMANDE dimensional check, dimensional inspection, CONS MECA gaging (AmE), gauging (BrE); ~ **à distance** *m* COMMANDE remote control, remote monitoring; ~ **de la durée de stockage** *m* EMBALLAGE shelf life test; ~ **dynamique de la charge** *m* TELECOM dynamic load control;

~ e ~ **d'échappement de moteur** *m* CONS MECA engine emission control; ~ **d'éclairage** *m* COMMANDE light control, lighting control; ~ **d'écoute** *m* COMMANDE audio check; ~ **d'émission** *m* COMMANDE emission control; ~ **en cours d'enregistrement** *m* OPTIQUE DRAW, direct read after write; ~ **en cours de fabrication** *m* COMMANDE production control, QUALITE in-process inspection in manufacturing; ~ **de l'énergie atomique** *m* COMMANDE atomic energy control, nuclear energy control; ~ **en orbite** *m* ESPACE *essais* orbit control; ~ **en première inspection** *m* COMMANDE first-time inspection, initial inspection; ~ **en première présentation** *m* QUALITE original inspection; ~ **d'entrée** *m* PRODUCTION good inwards test; ~ **en usine** *m* COMMANDE, MECANIQUE factory inspection; ~ **de l'environnement** *m* POLLUTION environmental control, pollution control; ~ **d'équilibrage de niveau** *m* ENREGISTR balance control; ~ **d'erreur d'en-tête** *m* TELECOM HEC, header error control; ~ **d'erreurs** *m* TELECOM

error check; ~ **d'erreur sur l'en-tête** *m* TELECOM HEC, header error control; ~ **à l'étage supérieur** *m* COMMANDE major control; ~ **d'étanchéité** *m* REFRIG leak test; ~ **d'état** *m* COMMANDE condition monitoring; ~ **de l'état d'avancement** *m* PRODUCTION progress control; ~ **d'exposition aux vapeurs de soudage et brasage** *m* SECURITE control of exposure to fumes from welding and brazing;

~ f ~ **de fabrication** *m* COMMANDE manufacturing control; ~ **de fatigue** *m* AERONAUT fatigue inspection; ~ **final** *m* COMMANDE, QUALITE final inspection; ~ **de flux** *m* INFORMAT, ORDINAT flow control; ~ **de flux générique** *m* TELECOM GFC, generic flow control; ~ **de fréquence** *m* TELECOM frequency control; ~ **des fumées** *m* SECURITE smoke control;

~ g ~ **de gain automatique retardé** *m* ENREGISTR delayed automatic gain control; ~ **de gaz brulé** *m* COMMANDE exhaust gas test; ~ **de gaz d'échappement** *m* COMMANDE exhaust gas test; ~ **de granulométrie par tamisage** *m* NUCLEAIRE sieve analysis;

~ h ~ **holographique de la qualité** *m* COMMANDE holographic quality control; ~ **d'homogénéité** *m* COMMANDE consistency check;

~ i ~ **d'image** *m* COMMANDE video check, video monitoring; ~ **d'imparité** *m* COMMANDE odd parity check; ~ **d'inflammabilité** *m* SECURITE fire test; ~ **intégral** *m* COMMANDE integral control;

~ l ~ **de lacet** *m* EN RENOUV yaw control; ~ **de la largeur de ligne** *m* TV line amplitude control; ~ **de levage par interrupteur pendant** *m* SECURITE *palan roulant* pendant switch control; ~ **de liaison** *m* ORDINAT data link control; ~ **logique** *m* ELECTRON logic test; ~ **de la longueur développée** *m* CONS MECA peripheral length checking; ~ **de lot** *m* COMMANDE batch control;

~ m ~ **magnétoscopique** *m* CONS MECA magnetic particle inspection; ~ **majeur** *m* COMMANDE major control; ~ **manuel** *m* COMMANDE, CONSTR manual control; ~ **marginal** *m* COMMANDE marginal testing; ~ **du matériel** *m* COMMANDE hardware acceptance test; ~ **des mesures** *m* COMMANDE dimensional check, measurement control; ~ **du milieu naturel** *m* COMMANDE environmental control; ~ **du milieu vital** *m* COMMANDE environmental control; ~ **mineur** *m* COMMANDE minor control; ~ **minimums-maximums** *m* COMMANDE minima-maxima check; ~ **minutieux** *m* COMMANDE tight inspection; ~ **du montage à la chaîne** *m* COMMANDE assembly line inspection; ~ **multiple** *m* COMMANDE multiple control; ~ **multivoies** *m* NAUT multichannel monitoring;

~ n ~ **de niveau** *m* COMMANDE level control; ~ **du niveau de bruit** *m* SECURITE noise control; ~ **du niveau d'un liquide** *m* EMBALLAGE liquid level control; ~ **du niveau de rayonnement** *m* COMMANDE radiation monitoring; ~ **au niveau inférieur** *m* COMMANDE minor control; ~ **noir-blanc** *m* TV black-white monitoring; ~ **non destructif des matériaux** *m* NUCLEAIRE *examen* nondestructive materials testing; ~ **normal** *m* QUALITE normal inspection; ~ **de nourriture** *m* QUALITE food inspection;

~ o ~ **d'opération** *m* COMMANDE process control, process monitoring; ~ **orthographique** *m* INFORMAT spellchecker;

~ p ~ **par attributs** *m* QUALITE inspection by attributes; ~ **par bloc** *m* COMMANDE block check; ~ **par bon ou mauvais** *m* COMMANDE quality inspection; ~

par courant de Foucault *m* ELECTROTEC eddy current inspection; ~ par détection de code interdit *m* COMMANDE forbidden combination check; ~ par différences *m* COMMANDE difference check control; ~ par duplication *m* COMMANDE duplication check; ~ par échantillonnage *m* QUALITE sampling inspection; ~ par écho *m* INFORMAT, ORDINAT echo check; ~ par induction électrique *m* COMMANDE electric induction check; ~ par interrupteur pendant *m* SECURITE *palan roulant* pendant switch control; ~ de parité *m* COMMANDE parity check, INFORMAT, ORDINAT odd-even check, parity check, TELECOM parity check; ~ par multiprocesseur *m* COMMANDE multiprocessor control; ~ par l'opérateur *m* COMMANDE operator control; ~ par paramètres *m* QUALITE inspection by variables; ~ par processeur *m* COMMANDE processor control; ~ par redondance *m* COMMANDE, INFORMAT, ORDINAT redundancy check; ~ par redondance longitudinale *m* ORDINAT LRC, longitudinal redundancy check; ~ par redondance verticale *m* INFORMAT, ORDINAT VRC, vertical redundancy check; ~ par sonnage *m* ELECTR ringing test; ~ particulier *m* COMMANDE special examination; ~ par vidage *m* ORDINAT dump check; ~ passif *m* ESPACE *véhicules* passive control; ~ des phases *m* COMMANDE phase monitoring; ~ de pistage *m* COMMANDE tracking control, ENREGISTR clamped capacitance; ~ de piste *m* COMMANDE track check, ENREGISTR channel separation; ~ de la pollution atmosphérique *m* POLLUTION air pollution control; ~ de positionnement *m* COMMANDE positioning control; ~ pour l'assurance de qualité *m* COMMANDE quality assurance control; ~ poussé *m* COMMANDE extended inspection; ~ de présence *m* PRODUCTION timekeeping; ~ de pression hydraulique *m* PRODUCTION hydraulic pressure test, COMMANDE hydraulic pressure test; ~ principal *m* COMMANDE major control; ~ de processus industriel *m* TELECOM process control; ~ programmé *m* COMMANDE programed check (AmE), programmed check (BrE);

~ q ~ de qualité *m* CONSTR, EMBALLAGE, IMPRIM, METROLOGIE *des produits fabriqués*, NUCLEAIRE, PRODUCTION quality control; ~ de la qualité de l'air ambiant *m* SECURITE quality monitoring of ambient air;

~ r ~ radar *m* AERONAUT, COMMANDE, TRANSPORT radar control; ~ radio *m* COMMANDE radio monitoring; ~ radiographique *m* COMMANDE radiation test, ESPACE *véhicules* X-ray inspection; ~ de réception *m* COMMANDE, CONS MECA acceptance inspection, PRODUCTION receiving inspection, QUALITE acceptance inspection, receiving inspection; ~ de redondance cyclique *m* COMMANDE, ELECTRON, ORDINAT cyclic redundancy check, ORDINAT cyclical redundancy check; ~ réduit *m* QUALITE reduced inspection; ~ relais maître *m* PRODUCTION *automatisme industriel* MCR, master control reset; ~ de rendement *m* COMMANDE efficiency survey; ~ renforcé *m* COMMANDE, QUALITE tightened inspection; ~ de résistance à la soudure *m* PRODUCTION weld strength check; ~ de routage *m* TELECOM routing control;

~ s ~ secondaire *m* COMMANDE minor control; ~ sélectif *m* COMMANDE, QUALITE screening inspection; ~ de sensation d'intensité *m* ENREGISTR loudness control; ~ de séquence *m* COMMANDE, INFORMAT, ORDINAT sequence check; ~ serré *m* COMMANDE severe control; ~ de siccité *m* REFRIG dryness test; ~ simple de

parité *m* COMMANDE single parity check; ~ de sortie *m* TV output control; ~ statistique *m* METROLOGIE statistical check; ~ statistique de la fabrication *m* COMMANDE statistical manufacturing quality control; ~ statistique par attributs *m* ESSAIS statistical control by attributes; ~ strict *m* COMMANDE tight inspection; ~ de survitesse *m* EN RENOUV overspeed control;

~ t ~ de température *m* TEXTILE temperature control; ~ des textes *m* TELECOM text editing; ~ des tolérances *m* INFORMAT marginal check, marginal test, ORDINAT marginal check, marginal test; ~ de tonalité *m* COMMANDE tone control, TV hue control, phase control; ~ de toxicité à l'usine *m* SECURITE control of toxicity at work; ~ du trafic aérien *m* AERONAUT, TRANSPORT ATC, air traffic control; ~ de trame *m* COMMANDE field monitoring, frame monitoring; ~ de transmission *m* COMMANDE transmission control; ~ des travaux *m* INFORMAT job control;

~ u ~ aux ultrasons *m* PHYS ONDES ultrasonic inspection; ~ d'uniformité *m* COMMANDE consistency check;

~ v ~ de validité *m* COMMANDE, INFORMAT, ORDINAT, TELECOM validity check; ~ de vibration *m* COMMANDE vibration test; ~ de vidage *m* INFORMAT dump check; ~ visuel *m* COMMANDE visual inspection; ~ visuel d'étanchéité *m* REFRIG visual leak test; ~ de vitesse *m* TEXTILE speed control; ~ de volume *m* ENREGISTR volume control

contrôlé: ~ par impulsions *adj* COMMANDE pulse-controlled; ~ par l'opérateur *adj* COMMANDE operator-controlled; ~ par ordinateur *adj* PRODUCTION computer-controlled; ~ à partir du sol *adj* ESPACE *véhicules* ground-controlled

contrôler *vt* CINEMAT monitor, COMMANDE check, control, inspect, monitor, verify, CONSTR check, ENREGISTR monitor, ESPACE control, inspect, INFORMAT monitor, test, NAUT check, ORDINAT control, monitor, POLLU MER, PRODUCTION, TEXTILE monitor; ~ au calibre *vt* CERAM VER put down in color work (AmE), put down in colour work (BrE); ~ de nouveau *vt* METROLOGIE recheck

contrôles: ~ électroniques *m pl* PRODUCTION solid-state controls

contrôleur *m* COMMANDE controller, *vérification* inspector, CONS MECA controller, *instrument* telltale, ESPACE, INFORMAT controller, MECANIQUE inspector, OPTIQUE, ORDINAT controller, PRODUCTION checker, timekeeper, QUALITE inspector; ~ acrylique *m* EMBALLAGE acrylic tester; ~ d'altitude *m* AERONAUT altitude controller; ~ de batteries "entre bornes" *m* ELECTROTEC load tester; ~ à cames *m* ELECTR *commutateur* cam switch; ~ de circuit *m* COMMANDE line tester; ~ de la circulation aérienne *m* AERONAUT, COMMANDE air traffic controller; ~ à cylindre *m* COMMANDE drum-type controller; ~ de débit *m* COMMANDE flow control device; ~ de démarrage *m* COMMANDE starter control; ~ de dérouleurs *m* COMMANDE tape control unit; ~ de disque *m* INFORMAT, ORDINAT disk controller; ~ à distance *m* COMMANDE remote-controlled switch; ~ d'écran *m* INFORMAT, ORDINAT display controller; ~ d'entrée/sortie *m* COMMANDE input/output controller; ~ de flammes *m* COMMANDE automatic flame guard; ~ de fréquence *m* COMMANDE frequency monitor; ~ de gonflage *m* COMMANDE pressure gage (AmE), pressure gauge (BrE); ~ de grappe *m* INFORMAT, ORDINAT *de terminaux* cluster controller; ~ d'incendie *m* CONSTR, SECURITE automatic fire alarm; ~ d'indicatif numérique *m* COMMANDE check digit verifier; ~ **inverseur universel** *m* COMMANDE universal inverter controller; ~ **d'isolement** *m* COMMANDE insulation tester; ~ **de levage** *m* COMMANDE hoist controller; ~ **logique** *m* ELECTRON logic tester; ~ **de modulation** *m* COMMANDE modulation monitor; ~ **moteur** *m* PRODUCTION *automatisme industriel* motor controller; ~ **multifonction** *m* ELECTROTEC multifunction tester; ~ **pas à pas** *m* PRODUCTION *automatisme industriel* stepper controller; ~ **de périphériques** *m* ORDINAT, TELECOM device controller; ~ **photoélectrique de flammes** *m* COMMANDE photoelectric flame-failure detector; ~ **de piste** *m* COMMANDE runway controller; ~ **de pression d'huile** *m* COMMANDE oil pressure controller, oil pressure gage (AmE), oil pressure gauge (BrE); ~ **de pression des pneus** *m* COMMANDE tire pressure gage (AmE), tyre pressure gauge (BrE); ~ **de projet** *m* ESPACE project controller; ~ **radar** *m* AERONAUT radar controller; ~ **de réseau** *m* INFORMAT, ORDINAT network controller; ~ **de ronde** *m* PRODUCTION time recorder, watchman's clock; ~ **de séquence** *m* INFORMAT sequencer; ~ **de station de base** *m* TELECOM base station controller; ~ **de surveillance** *m* PRODUCTION monitoring controller; ~ **à tambour** *m* COMMANDE drum-type controller; ~ **de température** *m* COMMANDE temperature controller; ~ **de tension** *m* COMMANDE tension control; ~ **du trafic aérien** *m* COMMANDE air traffic controller; ~ **universel** *m* COMMANDE multimeter; ~ **de vitesse** *m* CONS MECA speed controller, speed reducer; ~ **de vol** *m* AERONAUT flight controller, COMMANDE flight instrument system

contrôlographe *m* COMMANDE tachograph

convecteur *m* THERMODYN convector, convector heater; ~ **à ailettes** *m* THERMODYN finned heater; ~ **électrique** *m* THERMODYN electric convector

convectif *adj* MAT CHAUFF, THERMODYN convective

convection:[1] **par ~** *adj* MAT CHAUFF, THERMODYN convective

convection[2] *f* CONSTR, MAT CHAUFF, PETROLE *liquides et gaz*, PHYS FLUID, PHYSIQUE, THERMODYN convection; ~ **dans un anneau tournant** *f* PHYS FLUID rotating annulus convection; ~ **forcée** *f* CHAUFFAGE, GAZ, PHYS FLUID, PHYSIQUE forced convection; ~ **naturelle** *f* CHAUFFAGE, GAZ, PHYS FLUID, PHYSIQUE natural convection

convention: ~ **de données** *f* AERONAUT data convention; ~ **typographique** *f* IMPRIM, PRODUCTION notation convention

convergence *f* TRANSPORT merging; ~ **dynamique** *f* TV dynamic convergence; ~ **dynamique horizontale** *f* TV horizontal dynamic convergence; ~ **par courant sinusoïdal** *f* TV sine wave convergence; ~ **radiale** *f* ELECTRON vertical convergence; ~ **de trame** *f* TV field convergence; ~ **de transmission** *f* TELECOM transmission convergence

convergent[1] *adj* GEOMETRIE, OPTIQUE, PHYSIQUE convergent

convergent[2] *m* CONS MECA *d'un injecteur* combining cone, combining nozzle, combining tube

convergent-divergent *m* MECANIQUE venturi nozzle

conversation: ~ **en clair** *f* TELECOM clear speech; ~ **impossible** *f* TELECOM CI, conversation impossible; ~ **à trois** *f* TELECOM three-way conversation

conversationnel *adj* INFORMAT conversational, interactive, ORDINAT conversational

conversion *f* INFORMAT, ORDINAT conversion; ~ **additive**

f ELECTRON additive mixing; ~ **d'adresses** *f* ORDINAT address mapping; ~ **alternatif-continu** *f* ELECTROTEC AC-to-DC conversion; ~ **d'alternatif en continu** *f* ELECTROTEC AC-to-DC conversion; ~ **analogique-numérique** *f* ELECTR, ENREGISTR analog-to-digital conversion (AmE), analogue-to-digital conversion (BrE), ORDINAT analog-to-digital conversion; ~ **automatique de données** *f* INFORMAT, ORDINAT automatic data conversion; ~ **à bas coût** *f* PHYS RAYON low cost conversion; ~ **ca-cc** *f* ELECTROTEC AC-to-DC conversion; ~ **cc-ca** *f* ELECTROTEC DC-to-AC conversion; ~ **de code** *f* INFORMAT, ORDINAT code conversion; ~ **continu-alternatif** *f* ELECTROTEC DC-to-AC conversion; ~ **continu-continu** *f* ELECTROTEC DC-to-DC conversion; ~ **de continu en alternatif** *f* ELECTROTEC DC-to-AC conversion; ~ **décimale-binaire** *f* ELECTRON decimal-to-binary conversion; ~ **directe** *f* EN RENOUV direct conversion; ~ **directe d'énergie** *f* ELECTROTEC direct energy conversion; ~ **de données** *f* ELECTRON data conversion; ~ **d'énergie** *f* ELECTROTEC, THERMODYN energy conversion; ~ **d'énergie électrique** *f* ELECTR *réseau* conversion of electricity; ~ **de l'énergie solaire** *f* ELECTROTEC solar energy conversion; ~ **de fréquence** *f* ELECTRON, TELECOM frequency conversion; ~ **d'images** *f* ELECTRON, TELECOM image conversion; ~ **d'impédance** *f* ELECTROTEC impedance conversion; ~ **d'information** *f* ELECTRON data conversion; ~ **interne** *f* PHYSIQUE internal conversion; ~ **de la lumière artificielle en lumière du jour** *f* CINEMAT tungsten-to-daylight; ~ **magnétohydrodynamique** *f* (*conversion MHD*) ELECTROTEC, GEOPHYS magnetohydrodynamic conversion; ~ **MHD** *f* (*conversion magnétohydrodynamique*) ELECTROTEC, GEOPHYS MHD conversion; ~ **numérique-analogique** *f* ELECTRON, ENREGISTR digital-to-analog conversion (AmE), digital-to-analogue conversion (BrE), ORDINAT digital-to-analog conversion, TELECOM digital-analog conversion (AmE), digital-analogue conversion (BrE); ~ **parallèle** *f* ELECTRON flash conversion, parallel conversion; ~ **de parallèle en série** *f* ELECTROTEC parallel-to-serial conversion; ~ **parallèle-série** *f* ELECTROTEC parallel-to-serial conversion; ~ **de rayons gamma** *f* PHYS RAYON gamma ray conversion; ~ **série** *f*, ELECTRON serial analog-to-digital conversion (AmE), serial analogue-to-digital conversion (BrE); ~ **de série en parallèle** *f* ELECTROTEC serial-to-parallel conversion; ~ **série-parallèle** *f* ELECTROTEC serial-to-parallel conversion; ~ **de signaux** *f* ELECTRON data conversion, TELECOM signal conversion; ~ **des signaux optiques** *f* ELECTROTEC optical signal conversion; ~ **tension-fréquence** *f* ELECTROTEC voltage-to-frequency conversion; ~ **thermodynamique de l'énergie solaire** *f* EN RENOUV solar thermal conversion; ~ **thermodynamique de l'océan** *f* EN RENOUV ocean thermal conversion; ~ **thermodynamique du rayonnement solaire** *f* EN RENOUV solar thermal conversion; ~ **thermoélectrique** *f* ELECTROTEC thermoelectric conversion; ~ **thermoionique** *f* ELECTROTEC, NUCLEAIRE thermionic conversion

convertir *vt* ELECTROTEC, INFORMAT, ORDINAT convert; ~ **en circuit intégré monolithique** *vt* ELECTRON commit to silicon; ~ **en numérique** *vt* ELECTRON, TV digitize; ~ **de parallèle en série** *vt* ELECTROTEC serialize

convertisseur *m* AGRO ALIM converter, CINEMAT converter, inverter, ELECTR *courant alternatif-continu*, ELECTRON, ELECTROTEC, MAT CHAUFF, TELECOM converter; ~ **d'alimentation** *m* ESPACE *véhicules* power converter; ~ **alternatif-continu** *m* ELECTROTEC AC-to-DC converter; ~ **analogique-numérique** *m (CAN)* ELECTRON analog-to-digital converter (AmE), analogue-to-digital converter (BrE) *(analog-to-digital converter)*, ORDINAT analog-to-digital converter *(ADC)*, PHYSIQUE, TELECOM analog-to-digital converter (AmE), analogue-to-digital converter (BrE) *(analog-to-digital converter)*; ~ **à arc de mercure** *m* ELECTR *courant alternatif* mercury arc converter; ~ **de balayage** *m* ELECTRON scan converter; ~ **Bessemer** *m* CONS MECA, PRODUCTION Bessemer converter; ~ **câble-ruban** *m* TEXTILE tow-to-top converter; ~ **ca-cc** *m* ELECTROTEC AC-to-DC converter; ~ **à cascade** *m* ELECTROTEC motor converter; ~ **catalytique** *m* POLLUTION catalytic converter (BrE), TRANSPORT, VEHICULES catalytic converter (BrE), catalytic muffler (AmE); ~ **cc-ac** *m* ELECTROTEC DC-to-AC converter; ~ **à champ magnétique rotatif** *m* ELECTR rotary field converter; ~ **de code** *m* ELECTROTEC code converter; ~ **à commutation automatique** *m* ELECTR self-commutated converter; ~ **à commutation par la charge** *m* ELECTR load commutated converter; ~ **continu-alternatif** *m* ELECTROTEC DC-to-AC converter; ~ **continu-continu** *m* ELECTROTEC DC-to-DC converter, ESPACE *véhicules* DC/DC converter; ~ **de continu en alternatif** *m* ELECTROTEC DC-to-AC converter; ~ **de couple** *m* AUTO torque converter, VEHICULES torque converter; ~ **de courant** *m* ELECTROTEC power converter; ~ **de courant alternatif en courant continu** *m* ELECTROTEC AC-to-DC converter; ~ **courant continu** *m* TELECOM direct current converter; ~ **à courant continu** *m* TELECOM direct current converter; ~ **de courant continu en courant alternatif** *m* ELECTR inverted converter; ~ **décimal-binaire** *m* ELECTRON decimal-to-binary converter; ~ **direct de courant alternatif** *m* ELECTR direct AC converter; ~ **direct de courant continu** *m* ELECTR direct DC converter; ~ **de données** *m* ELECTRON data converter; ~ **en courant continu** *m* ELECTR DC converter; ~ **d'énergie** *m* ELECTROTEC, TELECOM, THERMODYN energy converter; ~ **d'étalonnage** *m* NUCLEAIRE calibrating transformer; ~ **de fréquence** *m* ELECTR frequency changer, frequency converter, ELECTRON frequency converter; ~ **de fréquence à collecteur** *m* ELECTR commutator-type frequency converter; ~ **fréquence-courant** *m* ELECTR frequency current converter; ~ **de fréquence à induction** *m* ELECTR induction frequency converter; ~ **de fréquence rotatif** *m* ELECTR rotary frequency converter; ~ **de fréquence UHF** *m* TV UHF converter; ~ **de gestion** *m (CG)* TELECOM charge-metering converter; ~ **hydraulique de couple** *m* CONS MECA torque converter; ~ **d'images** *m* CINEMAT, ELECTRON, INSTRUMENT image converter; ~ **d'impédance** *m* PHYSIQUE impedance transformer; ~ **d'impédance négative** *m* ELECTROTEC negative impedance converter; ~ **à inductance série** *m* ELECTROTEC series converter; ~ **d'information** *m* ELECTRON data converter; ~ **magnétohydrodynamique** *m (convertisseur MHD)* ELECTROTEC, ESPACE, NUCLEAIRE magnetohydrodynamic converter; ~ **MHD** *m (convertisseur magnétohydrodynamique)* ELECTROTEC, ESPACE, NUCLEAIRE MHD converter; ~ **de mode à réseau** *m* ELECTROTEC grating converter; ~ **de neutrons** *m* NUCLEAIRE neutron converter doughnut; ~ **numérique** *m* ELECTRON digital converter; ~ **numérique-analogique**

m ELECTRON *(CNA)*, ORDINAT *(CNA)* digital-to-analog converter, TELECOM, TV *(CNA)* digital-to-analog converter (AmE), digital-to-analogue converter (BrE) *(DAC)*; ~ **parallèle** *m* ELECTRON flash converter, parallel converter; ~ **parallèle-série** *m* ELECTROTEC parallel-to-serial converter; ~ **de phase** *m* ELECTR *courant alternatif*, ELECTRON phase converter; ~ **de protocole** *m* INFORMAT, ORDINAT, TELECOM protocol converter; ~ **à résistances pondérées** *m* ELECTRON ladder adder; ~ **rotatif** *m* ELECTR *courant alternatif* rotary converter; ~ **rotatif à induit unique** *m* ELECTROTEC rotary converter; ~ **série** *m* CONSTR serial converter, ELECTRON serial analog-to-digital converter (AmE), serial analogue-to-digital converter (BrE); ~ **série-parallèle** *m* ELECTROTEC serial-to-parallel converter; ~ **de signal** *m* TELECOM signal converter; ~ **de signaux** *m* ELECTRON data converter; ~ **soufflé à l'oxygène au sol** *m* MATERIAUX *métallurgie* bottom-blown oxygen converter; ~ **statique** *m* ELECTR, ELECTROTEC, ESPACE *véhicules* static converter; ~ **synchrone** *m* ELECTROTEC synchronous converter; ~ **tension-fréquence** *m* ELECTROTEC voltage-to-frequency converter; ~ **thermique** *m* ELECTROTEC thermal converter; ~ **à thermocouples** *m* ELECTROTEC thermocouple converter; ~ **thermoionique** *m* ELECTROTEC thermionic converter; ~ **à thyristor** *m* ELECTROTEC SCR converter

convexité *f* PETR overbend
convivial *adj* INFORMAT, ORDINAT user friendly
convoi *m* NAUT convoy; ~ **à marchandises** *m* CH DE FER *véhicules* freight train; ~ **poussé** *m* TRANSPORT multiple barge convoy set, tow train; ~ **remorqué** *m* TRANSPORT tow train; ~ **tracté** *m* TRANSPORT towed convoy; ~ **de wagons** *m* MINES rake of hutches
convoluteur *m* ELECTRON convolver
convolution *f* ELECTRON, PETR convolution
convolvuline *f* CHIMIE convolvulin
convoyage *m* AERONAUT ferry flight
convoyer *vt* NAUT convoy
convoyeur *m* CONS MECA transporter, CONSTR, MINES, PRODUCTION *automatisme industriel* conveyor; ~ **accumulateur** *m* MINES bunker conveyor; ~ **actionné par moteur** *m* PRODUCTION *automatisme industriel* motor-driven conveyor; ~ **d'argenture** *m* CERAM VER conveyor for silvering; ~ **blindé de taille** *m* MINES armored face conveyor (AmE), armoured face conveyor (BrE); ~ **à câble** *m* PAPIER cable conveyor; ~ **à courroie** *m* PAPIER belt conveyor; ~ **à godets** *m* CONSTR bucket conveyor; ~ **de grumes** *m* PRODUCTION log conveyor; ~ **monorail** *m* MINES monorail conveyor; ~ **à palettes** *m* PRODUCTION flight conveyor, push-plate conveyor, scraper conveyor, trough conveyor; ~ **pneumatique** *m* TRANSPORT pneumatic pipe conveyor; ~ **de quai** *m* TRANSPORT quayside conveyor, quayside railway, quayside roadway; ~ **à raclette** *m* MINES scraper chain conveyor; ~ **vibrant** *m* SECURITE oscillating conveyor; ~ **à vis sans fin** *m* PRODUCTION screw conveyor, spiral conveyor
COO *abrév (conception orientée objet)* INFORMAT, ORDINAT OOD *(object-oriented design)*
coopérant *adj* TELECOM networked
coordinat *m* CHIMIE ligand
coordination: ~ **inductive** *f* ELECTROTEC inductive coordination; ~ **du travail** *f* PRODUCTION work assembly
coordinence *f* CRISTALL coordination number
coordonnée *f* INFORMAT, MATH, ORDINAT, PHYSIQUE CO-

ordinate; ~ **cartésienne** *f* CONSTR, MATH, PHYSIQUE Cartesian coordinate

coordonnées *f pl* CONSTR coordinates; ~ **atomiques** *f pl* CRISTALL atomic coordinates; ~ **de chromaticité** *f pl* PHYSIQUE chromaticity coordinates; ~ **chromatiques** *f pl* PHYSIQUE chromatic coordinates; ~ **colorimétriques** *f pl* PHYS RAYON color coordinates (AmE), colour coordinates (BrE); ~ **cylindriques** *f pl* PHYSIQUE cylindrical coordinates; ~ **généralisées** *f pl* PHYSIQUE generalized coordinates; ~ **normales** *f pl* PHYSIQUE normal coordinates; ~ **paramétriques** *f pl* GEOMETRIE parametric coordinates; ~ **polaires** *f pl* ELECTRON, PHYSIQUE polar coordinates; ~ **réduites** *f pl* PHYSIQUE reduced coordinates; ~ **sphériques** *f pl* PHYSIQUE spherical coordinates

copal: ~ **fossile** *m* MINERAUX fossil copal

copaline *f* MINERAUX copaline, copalite

copeau *m* CONSTR chip, chipping, shaving, GEOLOGIE slice, GEOLOGIE flake, MECANIQUE, PAPIER chip, PRODUCTION chip, chipping, cutting, scrap

copeaux: ~ **de bois** *m pl* CONSTR wood shavings; ~ **de forage** *m pl* CHARBON borings, drillings; ~ **de fraisage** *m pl* CHARBON turnings; ~ **de métal** *m pl* PRODUCTION swarf

copiapite *f* MINERAUX copiapite

copie *f* CINEMAT print, IMPRIM copy, manuscript, matter, INFORMAT, ORDINAT copy, PHOTO print, TV copy, dub; ~ **"O"** *f* CINEMAT first answer print, grading copy; ~ **"O" standard** *f* CINEMAT composite check print, trial composite print; ~ **à l'aniline** *f* IMPRIM aniline print; ~ **anamorphique** *f* CINEMAT anamorphic print; ~ **d'antenne** *f* CINEMAT, TV transmission copy; ~ **d'avance** *f* IMPRIM advance copy; ~ **contact** *f* CINEMAT direct print; ~ **de contrôle** *f* PHOTO test print; ~ **de deuxième génération** *f* CINEMAT second generation copy; ~ **d'écran** *f* INFORMAT, ORDINAT screen dump; ~ **en couleurs** *f* PHOTO color print (AmE), colour print (BrE); ~ **en radiofréquence** *f* TV RF dub; ~ **en version originale** *f* CINEMAT original language print; ~ **d'étalonnage** *f* CINEMAT answer print, approval print; ~ **étalonnée** *f* CINEMAT timed print; ~ **étalonnée pour projection à 5.400 K** *f* CINEMAT xenon print; ~ **d'exploitation** *f* CINEMAT release positive; ~ **faite sur tireuse optique** *f* CINEMAT optical print; ~ **fraîche** *f* CINEMAT green print; ~ **gonflée** *f* CINEMAT enlargement print; ~ **à grande fixité** *f* CINEMAT register print; ~ **à grande vitesse** *f* TV high-speed duplication; ~ **image** *f* CINEMAT mute film; ~ **image et son** *f* CINEMAT combined print; ~ **imprimée** *f* INFORMAT hard copy; ~ **inversible** *f* CINEMAT reversal dupe, reversal print; ~ **inversible couleur** *f* CINEMAT color dupe print (AmE), colour dupe print (BrE); ~ **locale** *f* TELECOM local copy; ~ **à lumière unique** *f* CINEMAT one-light print; ~ **de montage** *f* CINEMAT cutting copy, edit master; ~ **montée** *f* CINEMAT edited print; ~ **négative** *f* PHOTO negative print; ~ **papier** *f* INFORMAT, ORDINAT hard copy; ~ **par réduction** *f* CINEMAT reduction print; ~ **de présentation** *f* CINEMAT final trial composite; ~ **prête à la reproduction** *f* IMPRIM CRC, camera-ready copy; ~ **de projection marquée pour doublage** *f* CINEMAT cue print; ~ **de référence** *f* CINEMAT reference print; ~ **de secours** *f* CINEMAT protection copy; ~ **de série** *f* CINEMAT release positive; ~ **son optique** *f* CINEMAT optical sound positive; ~ **sons magnétique et optique** *f* CINEMAT mag-optical print; ~ **standard** *f* CINEMAT combined print, composite print, married print, release positive; ~ **standard avec étalonnage définitif** *f* CINEMAT final trial print; ~ **standard son magnétique** *f* CINEMAT commag; ~ **standard son optique** *f* CINEMAT comopt; ~ **sur bande** *f* INFORMAT tape copy; ~ **sur écran** *f* ORDINAT screen image; ~ **tirée en vitesse** *f* CINEMAT slash print; ~ **tirée d'internégatif** *f* CINEMAT CRI print; ~ **tirée par contact** *f* CINEMAT contact print; ~ **de travail** *f* CINEMAT cutting copy, work print; ~ **trop claire** *f* CINEMAT thin print; ~ **trop contrastée** *f* CINEMAT soot-and-whitewash print; ~ **virée** *f* CINEMAT toned print; ~ **zéro** *f* CINEMAT check print, first answer print

copier *vt* CINEMAT, ENREGISTR dub, IMPRIM, INFORMAT, ORDINAT copy, TV dub, duplicate

copilote *m* AERONAUT copilot

coplanaire *adj* GEOMETRIE coplanar

copolymère *m* CHIMIE, MATERIAUX, PETROLE, PLAST CAOU, TEXTILE copolymer; ~ **block** *m* LESSIVES block polymer; ~ **butadiène-styrène** *m* PETROLE butadiene styrene copolymer; ~ **en masse** *m* PLAST CAOU block copolymer

copolymérisation *f* MATERIAUX, PLAST CAOU copolymerization; ~ **en bloc** *f* MATERIAUX block polymerization

copperasine *f* MINERAUX copperasine

coprécipitation *f* NUCLEAIRE coprecipitation

coprocesseur *m* ORDINAT coprocessor

coprolite *m* GEOLOGIE coprolite

coprostérine *f* CHIMIE coprostanol

cops *m* CERAM VER cop

copulant *m* CINEMAT coupler, PLAST CAOU coupling agent

coque *f* DISTRI EAU *de la drague* hull, ESPACE *véhicules* shell, NAUT hull, kink, VEHICULES *carrosserie* body in white, body shell; ~ **à ailes aériennes** *f* NAUT aerofoil hull (BrE), airfoil hull (AmE); ~ **en zircaloy** *f* NUCLEAIRE zircaloy hull; ~ **extérieure** *f* NAUT outer hull, outer skin, shell; ~ **nue** *f* AERONAUT bare hull

coqueron *m* NAUT *de la cale* peak; ~ **arrière** *m* NAUT lazarette

coquille *f* IMPRIM literal error, misprint, PRODUCTION chill mold (AmE), chill mould (BrE), *d'un moule* part; ~ **en bronze** *f* CONS MECA gunmetal bush, gunmetal bushing; ~ **de garniture** *f* NUCLEAIRE packing bush; ~ **lunetterie** *f* CERAM VER coquille; ~ **à montage forcé** *f* CONS MECA forced fit bush; ~ **de plastique** *f* IMPRIM *emballage* blister pack; ~ **sphérique avec parois minces** *f* CONS MECA thin-walled spherical shell

coquiller *vt* PRODUCTION chill, chill harden

coracite *f* MINERAUX, NUCLEAIRE coracite

corail *m* GEOLOGIE coral

corallien *adj* GEOLOGIE coralline

corbeau *m* CERAM VER, CONSTR corbel

Corbeau *m* ASTRONOMIE Corvus

corbeille *f* IMPRIM bin; ~ **arrivée** *f* PRODUCTION in tray; ~ **de coulée** *f* PRODUCTION *pour moulage en mottes* slip jacket

cordage *m* MECANIQUE cable, NAUT cordage, line, rope, PAPIER, SECURITE, TEXTILE rope; ~ **de chanvre** *m* EMBALLAGE hemp rope; ~ **en nylon** *m* NAUT nylon line; ~ **goudronné** *m* NAUT tarred rope; ~ **à quatre torons** *m* NAUT three-stranded line; ~ **qui ne fait pas de coque** *m* NAUT nonkinking rope

corde *f* CERAM VER cord, CONSTR line, EN RENOUV, GEOMETRIE *d'une courbe* chord, NAUT line, rope, TEXTILE twine; ~ **aérodynamique moyenne** *f* (CAM)

AERONAUT mean aerodynamic chord *(MAC)*; ~ **d'a-
miante** *f* CONSTR asbestos-plaited packing; ~
d'asbeste *f* CONSTR asbestos-plaited packing; ~ **en
foin** *f* PRODUCTION hay band, hay rope; ~ **en sisal** *f*
CONS MECA sisal rope; ~ **entre appuis** *f* RESSORTS length
inside supports; ~ **d'évacuation** *f* AERONAUT escape
rope; ~ **de fibre** *f* CONS MECA fiber rope (AmE), fibre
rope (BrE); ~ **géométrique moyenne** *f* GEOMETRIE
mean geometric chord; ~ **de levage** *f* PRODUCTION
hoisting rope; ~ **de manoeuvre** *f* PRODUCTION hand
rope; ~ **mobile** *f* CERAM VER seam line; ~ **moyenne de la
gouverne** *f* AERONAUT mean chord of the control
surface; ~ **nylon** *f* CONS MECA nylon rope; ~ **de la pale** *f*
AERONAUT blade chord; ~ **de piano** *f* CONS MECA piano
wire; ~ **de profil** *f* AERONAUT aerofoil chord (BrE),
airfoil chord (AmE); ~ **de tension** *f* CONS MECA tightening cord; ~ **vibrante** *f* PHYSIQUE vibrating string
cordeau *m* CONSTR line, MINES fuse; ~ **Bickford** *m* MINES
Bickford fuse, common fuse, safety fuse; ~ **détonant**
m MINES Primacord, detonating fuse, detonating
cord; ~ **détonant de mineur** *m* MINES detonating cord,
detonating fuse; ~ **fusant** *m* ESPACE *véhicules* fuse
cord, Primacord fuse; ~ **ordinaire** *m* MINES ordinary
fuse; ~ **de transmission** *m* ESPACE *véhicules* detonating
cord
cordeau-maître *m* MINES master fuse
cordée *f* MINES hoist, lift, SECURITE hoist; ~ **de bois** *f*
METROLOGIE cord of wood
cordeline *f* voir *piqûre*
cordiérite *f* CERAM VER, MINERAUX cordierite
cordon *m* CONS MECA, ELECTR *câble* cord, MINES stringer,
PAPIER piping, ribbing, TELECOM handset cord, TEX-
TILE cord, lease band ~ **de bavure** *m* PLAST CAOU
moulage flash; ~ **de connexion** *m* INFORMAT, ORDINAT
patch cord; ~ **de cylindre** *m* IMPRIM *mécanique, machines* bearer; ~ **détecteur d'incendie** *m* AERONAUT fire
wire; ~ **d'engagement de la bande** *m* IMPRIM *rotatives*
leading-in tape; ~ **d'essai** *m* ELECTROTEC test lead; ~
flexible *m* TELECOM instrument cord; ~ **de jonction
enfichable** *m* INFORMAT patch cord; ~ **littoral** *m* GEO-
LOGIE barrier beach, offshore bar, OCEANO beach
ridge, offshore bar; ~ **littoral sableux** *m* GEOLOGIE sand
bar, *dans la zone intertidale* longshore bar; ~ **oléophile**
m POLLU MER oil mop; ~ **prolongateur** *m* ELECTROTEC
extension cable; ~ **de silice** *m* CERAM VER batch melting line (AmE), batch meltout line, silica scum line
(BrE); ~ **de soudabilité** *m* NUCLEAIRE welding seam; ~
de soudure *m* MECANIQUE bead
cordon-sur-cordon *m* IMPRIM *rotatives* bearer-to-bearer
corindon *m* CERAM VER, MINERAUX corundum; ~ **adamantin** *m* MINERAUX adamantine spar
corne *f* ASTRONOMIE cusp, NAUT gaff; ~ **de charge** *f* NAUT
cargo boom; ~ **de chargement** *f* NAUT loading boom;
~ **de compensation** *f* AERONAUT horn balance; ~ **de
gouverne** *f* AERONAUT horn; ~ **de salabarde** *f* NAUT
brailer boom
cornéenne *f* GEOLOGIE hornfels; ~ **calco-silicatée** *f* GEO-
LOGIE calco-silicate hornfels
cornet *m* ESPACE *communications* horn
corniche *f* CONSTR cornice, ledge
cornière *f* CONS MECA *perçage* angle, CONSTR L-iron,
angle, angle iron, MECANIQUE angle section, NAUT
angle; ~ **d'acier** *f* MECANIQUE *matériaux* angle steel; ~
de gouttière *f* NAUT stringer angle; ~ **de membrure** *f*
NAUT frame angle; ~ **perforée** *f* MECANIQUE *matériaux*
perforated angle; ~ **de renforcement** *f* MECANIQUE

angle bracket; ~ **de reprise** *f* CONS MECA pick-up angle
cornières: ~ **à ailes égales** *f pl* CONSTR equal-sided
angles, PRODUCTION even-sided angles; ~ **à angles vifs**
f pl METROLOGIE square root and edge angles; ~ **à
branches égales** *f pl* CONSTR equal-sided angles, PRO-
DUCTION even-sided angles
cornue *f* CHIMIE, EQUIP LAB *verrerie*, MAT CHAUFF, PE-
TROLE retort; ~ **Bessemer** *f* MAT CHAUFF *sidérurgie*
Bessemer converter; ~ **à gaz** *f* PRODUCTION gas retort;
~ **à refroidissement à l'eau** *f* MAT CHAUFF water-cooled
retort
corollaire *m* MATH corollary
corolle: ~ **de flammes** *f* GAZ ring of flame
coronène *m* CHIMIE coronene
coronographe *m* ASTRONOMIE coronagraph
corps *m* CHIMIE substance, CONS MECA *d'un piston*
crown, head, *d'un palier* pillow, *d'une manivelle* web,
de pompe barrel, HYDROLOGIE *de minerai* body, IM-
PRIM type size, *d'un caractère* body, INST HYDR *de
cylindre, de cylindre à vapeur, de vérin hydraulique*
barrel, INSTRUMENT body, PRODUCTION drag, nowel,
d'une pompe cylinder, *d'un marteau* head, *de châssis*
bottom part, TELECOM body; ~ **d'appareil de prise de
vue** *m* CINEMAT camera body; ~ **d'arrière** *m* PHOTO
back; ~ **avant** *m* PHOTO camera front, front frame; ~ **de
bielle** *m* AUTO connecting rod shank; ~ **broyant** *m*
CHARBON grinding media; ~ **du broyeur** *m* GENIE CHIM
crushing bowl; ~ **de caractère** *m* IMPRIM type size,
composition body size; ~ **de carburateur** *m* AUTO carburetor barrel (AmE), carburettor barrel (BrE); ~
céleste *m* ASTRONOMIE celestial body, heavenly body,
ESPACE celestial body, heavenly body; ~ **de chaudière**
m INST HYDR boiler shell; ~ **de chauffe** *m* MAT CHAUFF
chauffe-eau heating body; ~ **colorant** *m* COULEURS
coloring body (AmE), colouring body (BrE); ~ **de
coronographe** *m* ASTRONOMIE coronagraph body; ~
de cylindre *m* PRODUCTION, VEHICULES *moteur* cylinder barrel; ~ **de cylindre à vapeur** *m* INST HYDR steam
cylinder casing; ~ **cylindrique** *m* CONS MECA *d'une
chaudière* barrel, PRODUCTION *d'une chaudière* shell; ~
diélectrique *m* ELECTROTEC dielectric material; ~ **en
métal moulé** *m* PRODUCTION die cast body; ~ **en
mouvement** *m* MECANIQUE body in motion; ~ **en rotation rapide** *m* PHYS FLUID spinning bodies; ~
ferromagnétique *m* ELECTROTEC ferromagnetic material; ~ **de filtre** *m* GENIE CHIM filter frame; ~ **gris** *m* TV
gray body (AmE), grey body (BrE); ~ **d'interrupteur**
m PRODUCTION switch body; ~ **intrusif igné** *m* GEO-
LOGIE pluton; ~ **isolant** *m* ELECTROTEC insulating
material; ~ **magnétique** *m* ELECTROTEC magnetic material; ~ **magnétostrictif** *m* ELECTROTEC
magnetostrictive material; ~ **de manivelle** *m* CONS
MECA crank arm, crank cheek, crankweb; ~ **mort** *m*
NAUT mooring buoy; ~ **de moteur** *m* NAUT engine
body; ~ **de moule** *m* CERAM VER body mold (AmE),
body mould (BrE); ~ **de moyeu** *m* AERONAUT hub; ~
noir *m* CINEMAT, ESPACE *communications*, IMPRIM *optique*, PHYS RAYON, PHYSIQUE, TV black body; ~ **octavalent** *m* CHIMIE octad; ~ **pentavalent** *m* CHIMIE
pentad; ~ **de piston** *m* AUTO piston body, CONS MECA
piston, piston head; ~ **de poignée** *m* CONS MECA handgrip; ~ **de pompe** *m* DISTRI EAU pump barrel, pump
cylinder; ~ **de pompe centrifuge** *m* INST HYDR centrifuge pump casing; ~ **de pompe à eau** *m* VEHICULES
refroidissement water pump housing; ~ **primaire** *m*
AUTO primary barrel; ~ **de programme** *m* ORDINAT

program body; ~ **de propulseur** *m* ESPACE engine body, jet body, motor case; ~ **radioactif** *m* PHYS RAYON radioactive body; ~ **au repos** *m* MECANIQUE body at rest; ~ **de roue à rayons** *m* VEHICULES spoke wheel center (AmE), spoke wheel centre (BrE); ~ **semi-conducteur** *m* ELECTRON semiconductor material; ~ **de siphon** *m* EN RENOUV *barrages* siphon barrel; ~ **solide** *m* PRODUCTION solid object; ~ **de sonde** *m* MINES rods; ~ **de soupapes** *m* AUTO valve body; ~ **tournant rapidement** *m* PHYS FLUID spinning bodies; ~ **de turbine** *m* INST HYDR casing; ~ **de vanne** *m* CONS MECA valve body; ~ **volatil** *m* CHARBON volatile body; ~ **X désintégrant en deux jets** *m* PHYS RAYON X-body decaying into two jets

correcteur *m* IMPRIM reader, TELECOM equalizer; ~ **adaptatif de phase** *m* COMMANDE adaptive delay equalizer; ~ **adaptatif de temps de propagation** *m* COMMANDE adaptive delay equalizer; ~ **altimétrique** *m* AUTO altitude corrector; ~ **d'amplitude** *m* TV amplitude corrector; ~ **d'assiette** *m* AUTO automatic level control; ~ **automatique de base de temps couleur** *m* TV color automatic time-base corrector (AmE), colour automatic time base corrector (BrE); ~ **de base de temps** *m* TV TBC, time-base corrector; ~ **de détails** *m* TV image enhancer; ~ **dioptrique** *m* CINEMAT dioptric adjuster; ~ **d'effort** *m* AERONAUT pitch-correcting unit; ~ **de gamma** *m* TV gamma corrector; ~ **de Mach** *m* AERONAUT Mach compensator; ~ **de pailles** *m* TV drop-out compensator; ~ **de phases** *m* ELECTR *courant alternatif* phase equalizer

correction *f* ACOUSTIQUE correction, equalization, BREVETS, ORDINAT correction; ~ **d'absorption** *f* CRISTALL absorption correction; ~ **à l'air libre** *f* GEOPHYS free air correction; ~ **d'altitude** *f* GEOPHYS height correction; ~ **apochromatique** *f* PHOTO apochromatic correction; ~ **auditive** *f* ACOUSTIQUE hearing correction; ~ **automatique des erreurs** *f* AERONAUT, TELECOM automatic error correction; ~ **des basses fréquences** *f* ELECTRON low-frequency compensation; ~ **de Bouguer** *f* GEOPHYS Bouguer correction; ~ **colorimétrique** *f* TV color correction (AmE), colour correction (BrE); ~ **de la configuration du spot** *f* TV spot-shape corrector; ~ **de contour** *f* TV edge correction; ~ **de copie** *f* IMPRIM *contrôle qualité* proofreading; ~ **de diamètre** *f* ACOUSTIQUE diameter equalization; ~ **de distorsion** *f* TELECOM error correction; ~ **dynamique** *f* GEOLOGIE move-out correction, PETR dynamic correction, PETROLE *forage, prospection* move-out correction; ~ **en première** *f* IMPRIM house correction; ~ **d'erreur de base de temps** *f* TV time-base error correction; ~ **d'erreur de chrominance** *f* TV color correction (AmE), colour correction (BrE); ~ **d'erreurs** *f* COMMANDE, ELECTRON, INFORMAT, ORDINAT, TELECOM error correction; ~ **d'erreurs sans voie de retour** *f* ORDINAT FEC, forward error correction, TELECOM *satellite maritime* forward error correction; ~ **du facteur de puissance** *f* ELECTROTEC power factor correction; ~ **des fréquences élevées** *f* ELECTRON peaking; ~ **du gamma** *f* CINEMAT gamma correction; ~ **minime** *f* IMPRIM *composition* minus correction; ~ **d'orbite** *f* ESPACE orbit trimming, *mécanique céleste* orbit correction; ~ **de parallaxe** *f* CINEMAT parallax correction; ~ **pour eau douce** *f* NAUT freshwater allowance; ~ **pour la rétrodiffusion saturée** *f* NUCLEAIRE saturation backscattering correction; ~ **statique** *f* PETR static correction; ~ **de trajet** *f* MILITAIRE *d'une fusée* path correction

corrections: ~ **d'auteur** *f pl* IMPRIM author's alterations; ~ **de franc-bord** *f pl* NAUT *étude du navire* freeboard allowances; ~ **de marée** *f pl* OCEANO tidal corrections

corrélateur *m* ELECTRON, TELECOM correlator; ~ **optique** *m* ELECTRON optical correlator

corrélation *f* ELECTRON, INFORMAT, MATH, PHYS FLUID, PHYSIQUE, TELECOM correlation; ~ **spatio-temporelle** *f* TELECOM space-time correlation; ~ **temporelle** *f* TELECOM time correlation

corrélé *adj* ELECTRON, PHYSIQUE correlated

correspondance *f* ACOUSTIQUE correspondence, CH DE FER interchange, train connection, INFORMAT complementarity, correlation, hit, register, ORDINAT complementarity, correlation, hit; ~ **des couleurs** *f* IMPRIM color matching (AmE), colour matching (BrE); ~ **des réseaux** *f* METALL lattice correspondence

correspondant *m* TELECOM called party

corriger *vt* ESPACE *véhicules* trim, ORDINAT *un programme* patch, PAPIER *teint* adjust

corrodable *adj* CHIMIE corrodible

corrodant *m* CHIMIE corrodent

corrompre *vt* INFORMAT corrupt

corrosif[1] *adj* SECURITE corrosive

corrosif[2] *m* CHIMIE corrodent

corrosion *f* CHARBON, CHIMIE, PETROLE, QUALITE, VEHICULES *carrosserie* corrosion; ~ **de bord** *f* ESSAIS edge corrosion; ~ **due à l'usure par frottement** *f* MECANIQUE abrasion fretting corrosion; ~ **noduleuse** *f* NUCLEAIRE nodular corrosion; ~ **par courants vagabonds** *f* ELECTROTEC stray current corrosion; ~ **par friction** *f* RESSORTS fretting corrosion; ~ **de surface** *f* ESSAIS surface corrosion; ~ **uniforme** *f* METALL uniform corrosion

corroyer *vt* CONSTR trim

corruption *f* INFORMAT corruption

corsage *m* TEXTILE shirting

corset *m* CONS MECA collar

corsite *f* PETR corsite

cortège: ~ **électronique** *m* CHIMIE, NUCLEAIRE electron cloud; ~ **ophiolitique** *m* GEOLOGIE ophiolite suite; ~ **de roches ignées** *m* GEOLOGIE igneous suite

corticoïde *m* CHIMIE corticoid

corticostéroïde *m* CHIMIE corticosteroid

corticostérone *f* CHIMIE corticosterone

corticotrope *adj* CHIMIE corticotrophic, corticotropic

corticotrophine *f* CHIMIE corticotrophin, corticotropin

corticotropine *f* CHIMIE corticotrophin, corticotropin

cortisol *m* CHIMIE hydrocortisone

cortisone *f* CHIMIE cortisone

corundellite *f* MINERAUX corundellite

corundophilite *f* MINERAUX corundophilite

corundophyllite *f* MINERAUX corundophilite

corynite *f* MINERAUX corynite

cos *m* (*cosinus*) GEOMETRIE cos (*cosine*), PHYSIQUE power factor; ~ **phi** *m* PHYSIQUE power factor

cosalite *f* MINERAUX cosalite

cosec *f* (*cosécante*) GEOMETRIE cosec (*cosecant*)

cosécante *f* (*cosec*) GEOMETRIE cosecant (*cosec*)

cosinus *m* (*cos*) CONSTR, GEOMETRIE, MATH, ORDINAT cosine (*cos*), PHYSIQUE power factor

cosmique *adj* ASTRONOMIE cosmic

cosmochimie *f* ASTRONOMIE cosmochemistry

cosmodrome *m* ESPACE cosmodrome

cosmogonie *f* ASTRONOMIE, ESPACE cosmogony

cosmographie *f* ASTRONOMIE, ESPACE cosmography

cosmologie *f* ASTRONOMIE, ESPACE cosmology
cosmonaute *m* ESPACE cosmonaut
Cosmos *m* ASTRONOMIE Cosmos
cosse *f* NAUT cringle, thimble, PRODUCTION lug, spade lug, thimble; ~ **de câble** *f* ELECTROTEC cable lug; ~ **à fiches** *f* PRODUCTION stab terminal; ~ **de mise à la terre** *f* ELECTR, PRODUCTION earth lug (BrE), ground lug (AmE); ~ **ovale** *f* PRODUCTION egg-shaped thimble; ~ **à sertir** *f* ELECTROTEC crimp terminal lug; ~ **à souder** *f* PRODUCTION solder tag; ~ **à vis** *f* PRODUCTION screw lug
cosse-câble: ~ **de serrage** *f* VEHICULES *système électrique, commande* cable clip
cossyrite *f* MINERAUX cossyrite
costière *f* MINES drift, level, strike drive, drifting level, driving level, level running along the strike
costresse *f* MINES counter, counter gangway, counter level, subdrift
cot *f (cotangente)* CONSTR, GEOMETRIE cot *(cotangent)*
cotangente *f (cot)* CONSTR, GEOMETRIE *d'un angle* cotangent *(cot)*
cotation *f* CONS MECA *dessins techniques*, PRODUCTION dimensioning
cote *f* CONSTR, ESSAIS reading, PHYSIQUE height; ~ **d'alerte** *f* SECURITE danger point; ~ **limite** *f* MECANIQUE limit size; ~ **lue sur la mire** *f* CONSTR staff reading; ~ **d'un navire** *f* NAUT classification of ship; ~ **nominale** *f* CONS MECA nominal size; ~ **de trusquinage** *f* CONS MECA edge distance; ~ **Z** *f* PHYSIQUE Z-coordinate
côte *f* CONSTR slope, GEOLOGIE coast, shore, HYDROLOGIE, NAUT coast, shore, POLLU MER shoreline, TEXTILE rib; ~ **abordable** *f* NAUT accessible coast; ~ **creuse** *f* CERAM VER flute; ~ **plate** *f* CERAM VER flat facet
côté *m* GEOMETRIE *d'un triangle, cube* side; ~ **adhésif** *m* EMBALLAGE adhesive side; ~ **d'admission** *m* NUCLEAIRE inlet end; ~ **chair** *m* PRODUCTION *d'une courroie* flesh side; ~ **commande** *m* IMPRIM *rotatives* DS, drive side; ~ **composant** *m* TELECOM component side; ~ **conducteur** *m* PAPIER front side, operating side, tending side; ~ **cuir** *m* PRODUCTION *d'une courroie* grain side; ~ **émulsion** *m* CINEMAT emulsion side; ~ **enregistrement** *m* CINEMAT, TV *d'une bande magnétique* oxide side; ~ **entraînement** *m* ELECTROTEC drive end; ~ **envers d'un papier** *m* PAPIER wire side; ~ **feutre** *m* PAPIER felt side; ~ **fonction** *m* IMPRIM *rotatives* operator's side; ~ **four** *m* CERAM VER *d'une feuille étiré* back surface; ~ **de la génératrice** *m* NUCLEAIRE generation end; ~ **grain du papier** *m* PAPIER top side; ~ **inférieur** *m* IMPRIM *impression* lower side; ~ **oxyde** *m* TV *d'une bande magnétique* oxide side; ~ **plat** *m* IMPRIM broadside; ~ **de première** *m* IMPRIM *imposition* outer side; ~ **du refoulement** *m* INST HYDR pressure side, NUCLEAIRE delivery side, outlet side; ~ **secondaire** *m* NUCLEAIRE secondary side; ~ **de soudure** *m* TELECOM soldered side; ~ **sous le vent** *m* METEO leeward side, NAUT lee; ~ **supérieur** *m* IMPRIM *impression* upper side; ~ **support** *m* CINEMAT cell side; ~ **toile** *m* IMPRIM wire side; ~ **transmission** *m* PAPIER drive side, *arrière d'une machine papier* backside; ~ **du vent** *m* CONSTR windward side
côté: **à ~ de** *prép* NAUT alongside
côtelé *adj* TEXTILE ribbed
coter *vt* PRODUCTION number, *un plan* dimension
cotes: ~ **d'encombrement** *f pl* CONS MECA overall dimensions; ~ **horizontales et verticales** *f pl* PRODUCTION horizontal and vertical dimensioning

côtes: ~ **épaisses** *f pl* CERAM VER heavy panels; ~ **minces** *f pl* CERAM VER light panels; ~ **sans trame** *f pl* TEXTILE crosswise ribs
côtés: ~ **adjacents** *m pl* GEOMETRIE adjacent sides; ~ **opposés** *m pl* GEOMETRIE *d'un carré* opposite sides; ~ **pliants** *m pl* EMBALLAGE folding sides
cotidal *adj* GEOPHYS cotidal
côtier *adj* GEOLOGIE coastal, nearshore, HYDROLOGIE coastal, NAUT coastal, *navigation, pêche* inshore, PETROLE onshore
coton *m* TEXTILE cotton; ~ **minéral** *m* CHAUFFAGE mineral wool, PRODUCTION cinder wool
coton-poudre *m* MINES guncotton
cotre *m* NAUT cutter
cotret *m* CERAM VER lens holder
cotunnite *f* MINERAUX cotunnite
couchage *m* CINEMAT *d'une émulsion*, PAPIER, PLAST CAOU, PRODUCTION coating; ~ **à l'argile** *m* IMPRIM *papier* clay coating; ~ **à la barre filetée** *m* PAPIER rod coating kiss applicator; ~ **à la brosse** *m* PAPIER brush coating; ~ **à froid** *m* IMPRIM *transformation, finition* coldseal coating; ~ **au glacis** *m* IMPRIM *papier*, PAPIER cast coating; ~ **hors machine** *m* PAPIER off-machine coating; ~ **au hot-melt** *m* IMPRIM *brochure, emballage* hot-melt coating; ~ **à la lame** *m* IMPRIM, PAPIER blade coating; ~ **à lame traînante** *m* PAPIER trailing-blade coating; ~ **par brosses** *m* PAPIER brush coating; ~ **par coulage à chaud** *m* PAPIER hot-melt coating; ~ **par effleurage** *m* IMPRIM *papiers, films, vernissage* kiss coating; ~ **par extrusion** *m* IMPRIM, PAPIER extrusion coating; ~ **par fusion** *m* PAPIER hot-melt coating; ~ **par gravure** *m* PAPIER gravure coating; ~ **par gravure offset** *m* IMPRIM offset gravure coating; ~ **par gravure transfert** *m* IMPRIM offset gravure coating; ~ **par immersion** *m* PAPIER dip coating; ~ **par lame d'air** *m* PAPIER air knife coating; ~ **par presse encolleuse** *m* PAPIER size-press coating; ~ **par rouleaux** *m* PAPIER roller coating; ~ **par rouleaux lisseurs** *m* PAPIER smoothing roll coating; ~ **par thermocollage** *m* REVETEMENT heat seal laminating; ~ **par thermosoudage** *m* REVETEMENT heat seal laminating; ~ **par vaporisation** *m* IMPRIM *finition* spray coating; ~ **de protection** *m* PAPIER protective coating; ~ **à la racle** *m* IMPRIM *papiers* blade coating; ~ **sur bande** *m* PLAST CAOU coil coating; ~ **de surface** *m* IMPRIM top sizing; ~ **sur machine** *m* PAPIER on-machine coating
couche:[1] **à ~ unique** *adj* REVETEMENT single-layer
couche[2] *f* CHARBON bed, layer, seam, CONSTR coat, course, layer, sole piece, DISTRI EAU, ELECTRON layer, ESPACE ply, *véhicules* coat, layer, GAZ layer, GEOLOGIE bed, layer, IMPRIM coat, INFORMAT, METALL, NAUT layer, PAPIER coat, PLAST CAOU *peinture, adhésif, plastique* coat, layer, PRODUCTION coat, coating, TEXTILE layer;
~ a ~ **absolument stable** *f* METEO completely stable layer; ~ **absolument stable non saturée** *f* METEO unsaturated completely stable layer; ~ **d'accrochage** *f* PRODUCTION priming coat; ~ **d'accrochage primaire** *f* PLAST CAOU wash primer; ~ **active** *f* ELECTRON active layer; ~ **d'adaptation AAL** *f* TELECOM AAL, ATM adaptation layer; ~ **adhésive** *f* IMPRIM adhesive coating, REVETEMENT adhesive coating, tie coat, bonding layer; ~ **alluvionnaire** *f* DISTRI EAU aggradational deposit; ~ **amorphe** *f* ELECTRON amorphous layer; ~ **anodique** *f* REVETEMENT anodic coat; ~ **anti-abrasive** *f* CINEMAT anti-abrasion coating, REVETEMENT anti-ab-

rasion layer; ~ **antiacide** *f* REVETEMENT anti-acid film; ~ **anticapillaire** *f* CHARBON capillarity breaking layer, CONSTR anticapillary course; ~ **anticorrosive** *f* REVETEMENT protective coat of paint, protective coating of paint; ~ **antidérapante** *f* REVETEMENT nonskid coating; ~ **antihalo** *f* CINEMAT antihalation layer, rem jet backing, IMPRIM *chimie plaques et films* antihalation backing, PHOTO antihalation backing, antihalo layer, REVETEMENT antihalation backing; ~ **antiréfléchissante** *f* CERAM VER, REVETEMENT antireflection coating; ~ **antireflet** *f* CINEMAT, OPTIQUE, PHOTO, REVETEMENT, TELECOM antireflection coating; ~ **antirouille** *f* REVETEMENT antirust coating; ~ **antiusure** *f* CONSTR *soudure* hardfacing, REVETEMENT wear-resistant coating; ~ **d'Appleton** *f* GEOPHYS, PHYSIQUE Appleton layer, F-layer; ~ **d'application** *f* INFORMAT, TELECOM *interconnexion de systèmes ouverts* application layer; ~ **d'apprêt** *f* PRODUCTION priming coat, REVETEMENT subcoating; ~ **aquifère** *f* DISTRI EAU aquifer, water-bearing stratum; ~ **arable** *f* CHARBON topsoil; ~ **d'argile** *f* CONSTR bed of clay; ~ **d'arrêt** *f* ELECTRON barrier layer, PHYSIQUE depletion layer, TELECOM barrier layer; ~ **autocopiante** *f* IMPRIM *papiers et enductions complémentaires* microencapsulated coating;

~ **b** ~ **barrière** *f* OPTIQUE barrier layer; ~ **de base** *f* CONSTR base course, REVETEMENT ground coat, undercoating;

~ **c** ~ **cachée** *f* PETR hidden layer; ~ **de carbone** *f* ELECTROTEC carbon film; ~ **de chaînage de données** *f* TELECOM data link layer; ~ **de charbon** *f* CHARBON coal bed; ~ **chaude** *f* METEO warm layer; ~ **de chrome** *f* REVETEMENT chromium deposit; ~ **de la cible** *f* TV target layer; ~ **de colle** *f* REVETEMENT glue layer; ~ **commutée** *f* TELECOM switched network layer; ~ **conditionnellement instable non saturée** *f* METEO conditionally unstable unsaturated layer; ~ **de conversion** *f* COULEURS conversion layer, REVETEMENT conversion coating; ~ **coupe-feu** *f* REVETEMENT fire-resistant coating; ~ **de craie** *f* CONSTR chalk strata;

~ **d** ~ **D** *f* GEOPHYS, PHYSIQUE D-layer; ~ **de demi-atténuation** *f* *(CDA)* NUCLEAIRE half value layer *(HVL)*, PHYSIQUE half thickness, half value layer, half value thickness *(HVL)*; ~ **déposée** *f* ELECTRON deposited layer; ~ **déposée sous vide** *f* ELECTRON vacuum-deposited film; ~ **à deux électrons** *f* NUCLEAIRE K-shell, two-electron innermost shell; ~ **diazoïque** *f* IMPRIM *chimie* diazo coating; ~ **diffusante profonde** *f* OCEANO DSL, deep scattering layer; ~ **diffusée** *f* ELECTRON diffused layer; ~ **de discontinuité** *f* OCEANO discontinuity layer; ~ **de doublage** *f* CERAM VER flash; ~ **double** *f* REVETEMENT double-layer; ~ **double électrique** *f* CHIMIE *surface* electrical double layer; ~ **durcie** *f* CHARBON dry crust;

~ **e** ~ **E** *f* GEOPHYS E-layer, PHYSIQUE E-layer, Kennelly-Heaviside layer; ~ **d'eau** *f* INST HYDR *d'une chaudière* film; ~ **d'eau superficielle** *f* CHARBON surface water layer; ~ **Ekman** *f* HYDROLOGIE, OCEANO Ekman layer; ~ **électronique** *f* CHIMIE, NUCLEAIRE, PHYS PART, PHYSIQUE electron shell; ~ **d'enduit** *f* REVETEMENT coating film; ~ **épaisse** *f* ELECTRON thick film; ~ **épaisse en multicouche** *f* ELECTRON multilayer thick film; ~ **épitaxiale** *f* CRISTALL, ELECTRON, MATERIAUX, TELECOM epitaxial layer; ~ **épitaxiale en phase vapeur** *f* ELECTRON vapor phase grown epitaxial layer (AmE), vapour phase grown epitaxial layer (BrE); ~

épitaxiale magnétique *f* ELECTRON magnetic epitaxial layer; ~ **épitaxiale de silicium** *f* ELECTRON silicon epitaxial layer; ~ **épitaxiale de type N** *f* ELECTRON n-type epitaxial layer; ~ **épitaxiale de type P** *f* ELECTRON p-type epitaxial layer; ~ **d'équipement** *f* TELECOM equipment layer; ~ **évaporée** *f* ELECTRON evaporated layer;

~ **f** ~ **F** *f* GEOPHYS Appleton layer, F-layer, PHYSIQUE Appleton layer, F-layer; ~ **fertile sous-modérée** *f* NUCLEAIRE undermoderated blanket; ~ **fibreuse** *f* PAPIER fibrous layer, furnish layer, REVETEMENT furnish layer; ~ **filtrante** *f* GENIE CHIM filter bed, filter layer; ~ **filtrante jaune** *f* IMPRIM *photogravure* yellow filter layer; ~ **filtre** *f* CINEMAT *d'une émulsion* filter layer; ~ **de finition** *f* COULEURS final coat, top coat; ~ **fluidifiée** *f* GENIE CHIM fluid bed, fluidized bed; ~ **de fond** *f* CONSTR prime coat, PLAST CAOU base coat; ~ **de fond au phosphate** *f* REVETEMENT reaction primer, self-etching primer, wash primer; ~ **de forme** *f* CONSTR selected fill; ~ **de fort pendage** *f* MINES highly-inclined seam; ~ **de frottement** *f* CONSTR friction course;

~ **g** ~ **galvanique** *f* REVETEMENT electrodeposit, electroplating; ~ **galvanoplastique** *f* REVETEMENT electrodeposit, electroplating; ~ **de gel** *f* PLAST CAOU *polyesters*, REVETEMENT gel coat; ~ **géologique** *f* GAZ geological layer; ~ **de gravier** *f* DISTRI EAU channel bed, GEOLOGIE *dans le lit d'un cours d'eau* channel lag;

~ **h** ~ **de houille** *f* CHARBON coal bed, coal seam; ~ **hydratée** *f* CERAM VER hydrated layer;

~ **i** ~ **ignifuge** *f* REVETEMENT fire-resistant layer; ~ **imperméable** *f* CONSTR clamp course, DISTRI EAU aquifuge; ~ **implantée de type P** *f* ELECTRON p-type implanted layer; ~ **d'impression** *f* PRODUCTION priming coat; ~ **d'impression à l'atelier** *f* REVETEMENT shop priming; ~ **d'impression pour bois** *f* REVETEMENT wood primer; ~ **inférieure** *f* PRODUCTION base coat, REVETEMENT lower ply; ~ **infiniment épaisse** *f* PHYS RAYON infinitely thick layer; ~ **d'interconnexions** *f* ELECTRON interconnection layer; ~ **intérieure** *f* EMBALLAGE interior coating; ~ **intermédiaire** *f* GEOPHYS sima, REVETEMENT intermediate coat, intermediate layer; ~ **d'inversion** *f* ELECTRON, POLLUTION, TELECOM inversion layer; ~ **ionisante** *f* ELECTR *charge* ionizing layer; ~ **ionosphérique** *f* GEOPHYS ionosphere layer; ~ **isolante** *f* ELECTROTEC, EMBALLAGE, REVETEMENT insulating layer; ~ **isolante imperméable** *f* CONSTR damp-proof course; ~ **d'isolement** *f* CONSTR damp-proof course; ~ **isotherme** *f* METEO isothermal layer;

~ **k** ~ **K** *f* NUCLEAIRE K-shell, two-electron innermost shell, PHYSIQUE K-shell; ~ **de Kennelly-Heaviside** *f* PHYSIQUE Kennelly-Heaviside layer;

~ **l** ~ **L** *f* PHYSIQUE L-shell; ~ **de laque** *f* REVETEMENT coat of varnish; ~ **de liage** *f* REVETEMENT bonding layer; ~ **de liaison** *f* CONSTR binder course; ~ **de liaison de données** *f* INFORMAT, TELECOM data link layer; ~ **de limite** *f* REVETEMENT boundary film, boundary layer; ~ **limite** *f* AERONAUT, EN RENOUV, IMPRIM *papiers, film*, MECANIQUE *hydraulique*, OCEANO, PHYS FLUID, PHYSIQUE, REFRIG boundary layer; ~ **limite atmosphérique** *f* METEO surface boundary level; ~ **limite planétaire** *f* METEO planetary boundary layer; ~ **limite de surface** *f* METEO ground layer, surface boundary layer; ~ **limite turbulente** *f* PHYS FLUID turbulent boundary layer;

~ **m** ~ **M** *f* PHYSIQUE M-shell; ~ **métallique** *f* ELECTRON metal film; ~ **de métallisation** *f* ELECTRON metalization layer (AmE), metallization layer (BrE); ~ de métal lustré *f* REVETEMENT metal glaze film; ~ à microcapsules *f* IMPRIM *papiers et productions complémentaires* microencapsulated coating; ~ mince *f* ELECTRON thin film, MECANIQUE, REVETEMENT film; ~ mince de colle *f* EMBALLAGE adhesive film, glue film, REVETEMENT adhesive film; ~ mince déposée sous vide *f* REVETEMENT vacuum-coated film; ~ mince en multicouche *f* ELECTRON multilayer thin film; ~ mince magnétique *f* ELECTRON magnetic thin film; ~ mince résistive *f* ELECTRON resistive thin film; ~ mince de rouille *f* REVETEMENT rust film; ~ mitoyenne *f* REVETEMENT boundary film, boundary layer; ~ monomoléculaire *f* CHIMIE monomolecular layer; ~ de mortier *f* CONSTR bedding mortar; ~ de mousse *f* TEXTILE foam layer;

■ n ~ N *f* TELECOM N-layer; ~ néphéloïde *f* OCEANO turbidity layer; ~ nuageuse *f* ESPACE cloud layer;

■ o ~ obtenue par condensation de vapeur *f* GENIE CHIM vapor deposited layer (AmE), vapour deposited layer (BrE); ~ d'oxyde de bande *f* TV tape oxide layer; ~ d'oxyde *f* ORDINAT oxide layer, REVETEMENT oxide film; ~ d'oxyde protectrice *f* REVETEMENT protective oxide coat; ~ d'oxyde de silicium *f* ELECTRON silicon dioxide layer; ~ d'ozone *f* ESPACE ozonosphere, POLLUTION ozone layer;

■ p ~ passivante à phosphate *f* REVETEMENT reaction primer, self-etching primer, wash primer; ~ de passivation *f* ELECTRON passivation layer; ~ de peinture *f* REVETEMENT coat of paint; ~ perméable *f* GAZ permeable layer, porous layer, HYDROLOGIE aquifer, water-bearing stratum; ~ de phosphate insoluble *f* REVETEMENT phosphate coating; ~ photoconductrice *f* OPTIQUE photoconducting layer; ~ photoélectrique *f* REVETEMENT photoelectric layer; ~ photoémissive *f* ELECTRON photoemissive layer; ~ photographique *f* REVETEMENT emulsion layer; ~ photopolymère *f* IMPRIM photopolymer coating; ~ de photorésist *f* ELECTRON photoresist coating; ~ de photosynthèse *f* OCEANO photosynthetic layer; ~ physique *f* INFORMAT, TELECOM physical layer; ~ de polysilicium *f* ELECTRON polysilicon layer; ~ poreuse *f* GAZ permeable layer, porous layer; ~ postérieure semi-transparente *f* ELECTRON transflective back coating; ~ de présentation *f* INFORMAT presentation layer; ~ primaire *f* IMPRIM *surfaces sensibles*, PLAST CAOU *caoutchouc, adhésifs* primer; ~ productrice *f* PETROLE production layer; ~ de protection *f* CINEMAT anti-abrasion coating, EMBALLAGE protective coating, protective layer, IMPRIM *reliure, emballage* protective lining, REVETEMENT protective coating, protective finish, protective layer; ~ protectrice *f* REVETEMENT protective coating, protective layer; ~ protectrice anti-feu *f* REVETEMENT flameproof protective coating; ~ protectrice galvanisée *f* REVETEMENT galvanized protective coating; ~ protectrice de peinture *f* REVETEMENT protective coat of paint, protective coating of paint;

■ q ~ Q *f* NUCLEAIRE Q-shell;

■ r ~ de radiation *f* PHYS RAYON radiation belt; ~ remplie *f* PHYSIQUE closed shell; ~ repère *f* GEOLOGIE key bed; ~ de réseau *f* INFORMAT, ORDINAT network layer; ~ réseau de transmission *f* TELECOM transmission layer; ~ résistante à l'abrasion *f* REVETEMENT abrasion-resistant coating; ~ résistante aux attaques chimiques *f* REVETEMENT chemical-resistant coating; ~ résistante à la chaleur *f* REVETEMENT heat-resistant coating; ~ résistante au feu *f* REVETEMENT fire-resis-

tant coating; ~ résistante à l'usure *f* REVETEMENT wear-resistant coating; ~ résistive vitrifiée *f* ELECTRON metal glaze; ~ de roche *f* CHARBON stone bed; ~ rocheuse *f* DISTRI EAU rock layer; ~ de roulement *f* CONSTR carpet, wearing course;

■ s ~ saturée *f* METEO saturated layer; ~ de saut *f* OCEANO discontinuity layer; ~ de scellage *f* EMBALLAGE heat seal coating; ~ de scellement *f* CONSTR seal coat; ~ de sédiment *f* GAZ sediment layer; ~ de semiconducteur *f* ELECTRON semiconductor layer; ~ semi-conductrice *f* ELECTRON semiconductor layer; ~ semi-imperméable *f* DISTRI EAU semi-impermeable layer; ~ de séparation *f* GENIE CHIM separation layer, REVETEMENT boundary film; ~ de services *f* TELECOM service layer; ~ de session *f* INFORMAT, ORDINAT session layer; ~ de silicium *f* ELECTRON silicon layer; ~ superficielle *f* POLLU MER surface layer; ~ superficielle d'eau chaude *f* OCEANO surface layer, warm-water sphere; ~ supérieure *f* IMPRIM *papiers, film* boundary layer;

■ t ~ de transport *f* INFORMAT transport layer; ~ de turbidité *f* OCEANO turbidity layer; ~ turbulente *f* GENIE CHIM fluid bed, fluidized bed, METEO turbulent layer;

■ u ~ d'usage *f* REVETEMENT use-surface;

■ v ~ de vernis *f* REVETEMENT coat of varnish; ~ visqueuse *f* REFRIG slime;

■ z ~ de zinc *f* REVETEMENT zinc coating

couché: ~ à l'émulsion *adj* EMBALLAGE emulsion-coated; ~ à haut brillant *adj* PAPIER *papier, carton* cast-coated; ~ léger *adj* IMPRIM *papiers* lightweight-coated; ~ machine *adj* EMBALLAGE machine-coated

couche-barrage *f* POLLUTION barrier layer

couche-image *f* PHOTO emulsion

couche-piège *f* ELECTROTEC wave duct

coucher:[1] ~ héliaque *m* ASTRONOMIE heliacal setting; ~ de lune *m* ASTRONOMIE moonset

coucher[2] *vt* PAPIER *feuille* couch, REVETEMENT coat

coucher:[3] ~ les sons sur des pistes *vi* ENREGISTR lay tracks

coucher:[4] se ~ *v réfl* NAUT *navire* careen

couches: ~ à chailles *f pl* GEOLOGIE cherty beds; ~ à chert *f pl* GEOLOGIE cherty beds; ~ cisaillées *f pl* PHYS FLUID *dans les fluides tournants* shear layers; ~ déformées *f pl* GEOLOGIE contorted beds; ~ deltaïques de fond *f pl* GEOLOGIE bottomset beds; ~ deltaïques peu profondes *f pl* GEOLOGIE topset beds; ~ de fond *f pl* GEOLOGIE bottomset beds; ~ ionisées de la zone aurorale *f pl* ASTRONOMIE auroral zone ionized layers; ~ OSI *f pl* TELECOM OSI layers, open systems interconnection layers; ~ plissées *f pl* GEOLOGIE contorted beds; ~ de transition *f pl* GEOLOGIE passage beds

couchette *f* NAUT bunk, *passagers* berth; ~ de quart *f* NAUT quarter berth

coucheuse *f* PAPIER, REVETEMENT coater, coating machine; ~ à brosses *f* PAPIER brush coater; ~ hors machine *f* PAPIER off machine coater; ~ à lame *f* PAPIER blade coater; ~ à lame d'air *f* PAPIER air jet coater, airbrush coater, air knife coater; ~ par pulvérisation *f* PAPIER spray coater; ~ par rideau liquide *f* PLAST CAOU *revêtement* curtain coater; ~ à racles *f* PAPIER knife coater; ~ à rouleau essoreur *f* PAPIER squeeze roll coater; ~ à rouleau gravé *f* PAPIER offset coater; ~ à rouleaux tournant en sens inverse *f* PAPIER reverse roll coater

couchis *m* CONSTR footing block, sole piece, wall piece

coude *m* CONS MECA bend, crank, CONSTR, ELECTROTEC

bend, EQUIP LAB *verrerie* elbow, MECANIQUE bend, elbow, NAUT *d'une rivière, d'un tuyau* bend, NU-CLEAIRE elbow; ~ **circulaire** *m* CONS MECA wheel crank, PRODUCTION disc crank (BrE), disk crank (AmE); ~ **conique** *m* CONS MECA taper bend; ~ **en coquille** *m* CONS MECA shell-type elbow; ~ **en E** *m* ELECTROTEC E-bend; ~ **en fonte** *m* CONSTR cast-iron elbow; ~ **en H** *m* ELECTROTEC H-plane bend, edgewise bend; ~ **d'é-querre** *m* CONS MECA right-angled bend; ~ **d'essieu** *m* CONS MECA axle crank; ~ **de piquage** *m* CONS MECA bleed elbow; ~ **plan E** *m* ELECTROTEC E-plane bend; ~ **du porte-vent** *m* PRODUCTION gooseneck; ~ **de raccord** *m* CONSTR union elbow; ~ **de tube** *m* CONS MECA tube bend; ~ **vertical supérieur** *m* PETR sag bend

coudé *adj* PRODUCTION angled

couder[1] *vt* PRODUCTION *barre de fer* bend

couder:[2] **se ~** *v réfl* CONSTR, PRODUCTION bend

coudeuse: ~ **de plaques** *f* IMPRIM *préimpression* bender

coudre[1] *vt* TEXTILE sew, stitch; ~ **à points de surjet** *vt* TEXTILE overlock

coudre[2] *vi* CERAM VER chatter

couffe: ~ **à charbon** *f* CHARBON coal basket

coufflée *f* MINES leap

coulage *m* CERAM VER casting, CONSTR leak, leakage, DISTRI EAU *d'eau* leakage, IMPRIM *du texte dans le blanc du papier* sinkage, PRODUCTION break-out, casting, pouring, runout, teeming; ~ **dans les moules** *m* PRO-DUCTION casting in molds (AmE), casting in moulds (BrE); ~ **en barbotine** *m* CERAM VER slip casting; ~ **de feuille** *m* PLAST CAOU *procédé* film casting; ~ **des nappes** *m* POLLUTION oil slick sinking; ~ **à noyaux** *m* PRODUCTION core casting; ~ **par fusion** *m* CERAM VER fusion casting; ~ **plein** *m* PRODUCTION solid casting

coulant[1] *adj* DISTRI EAU *eau*, HYDROLOGIE flowing, running

coulant[2] *m* CONS MECA slider, MINES guide

coulantage *m* MINES cage guides, cage slides, guides, pit guides

coulants *m pl* MINES cage guides, cage slides, pit guides

coulé[1] *adj* PRODUCTION cast; ~ **sous pression** *adj* ME-CANIQUE *matériaux* die-cast

coulé[2] *m* PRODUCTION casting

coulée *f* CERAM VER casting, *pot* cast, pouring, CHAR-BON, ESPACE *véhicules* heat, MATERIAUX *au four* tapping, PLAST CAOU *procédé de moulage* casting, PRODUCTION cast, cast gate, down runner, pouring hole, runner stick, sprue hole, drawhole, gate stick, flow, funnel, gate pin, gate, header, jet, mouth, pour-ing gate, pouring, runner pin, runner, running gate, sprue, tap, tap hole, teeming, *d'un lingot* casting, *d'un creuset* lip, SECURITE pouring, THERMODYN fusing, melting; ~ **de boue** *f* GEOLOGIE *dans débris volcaniques* lahar; ~ **boueuse** *f* GEOLOGIE debris flow, mud flow; ~ **à la cire perdue** *f* PRODUCTION lost wax casting; ~ **continue** *f* CERAM VER, MATERIAUX *métallurgie*, ME-CANIQUE *matériaux* continuous casting; ~ **à la descente** *f* PRODUCTION top pouring; ~ **en chute di-recte** *f* PRODUCTION top pouring; ~ **en matrice** *f* PRODUCTION die casting, die cast; ~ **en première fusion** *f* PRODUCTION direct casting; ~ **en source** *f* PRODUC-TION bottom pouring; ~ **en source directe** *f* PRODUCTION bottom pouring; ~ **de fonte** *f* PRODUC-TION tapping the metal; ~ **au four** *f* CERAM VER leak; ~ **du four** *f* CERAM VER tapping; ~ **de lave** *f* GEOLOGIE, PETR lava flow, lava stream; ~ **du métal en fusion** *f* SECURITE pouring of molten metal; ~ **des moules** *f*

PRODUCTION running molds (AmE), running moulds (BrE); ~ **par injection** *f* MATERIAUX die casting; ~ **ratée** *f* THERMODYN *fonderie* off heat; ~ **semi-continue** *f* CERAM VER semicontinuous casting; ~ **sous pression** *f* PRODUCTION die casting; ~ **sous vide** *f* NUCLEAIRE vacuum casting; ~ **sur métal** *f* PRODUCTION burning, casting on; ~ **sur table** *f* CERAM VER table casting; ~ **à talon** *f* PRODUCTION side casting; ~ **de terres** *f* MINES run of ground

coulée-arrière *f* OCEANO run

coulées: ~ **de blancs** *f pl* TV bleeding whites

couler[1] *vt* CERAM VER tap, teem, *glaces* cast, CINEMAT *émulsion* apply, CONS MECA cast, CONSTR grout, *béton* pour, DISTRI EAU *l'eau d'une bâche* run off, ELECTR *soudure* run, PRODUCTION run, tap, teem, *métal d'un four* run off, *un lingot* cast; ~ **à découvert** *vt* PRODUC-TION cast in open sand; ~ **à travers** *vt* HYDROLOGIE run through

couler[2] *vi* CHIMIE run, CONSTR leak, HYDROLOGIE *dans la mer* run, *rivière* flow, MINES run, NAUT founder, go down, sink, PHYS FLUID flow, PRODUCTION break out, run

couler:[3] **se ~** *v réfl* PRODUCTION be cast

couleur:[1] **de ~ acier** *adj* COULEURS steel-colored (AmE), steel-coloured (BrE); **de ~ cuivre** *adj* COULEURS cop-per-colored (AmE), copper-coloured (BrE); **de ~ éclatante** *adj* COULEURS colorful (AmE), colourful (BrE); **de ~ vive** *adj* COULEURS colorful (AmE), col-ourful (BrE)

couleur[2] *m* PRODUCTION caster, pourer

couleur[3] *f* CHIMIE color (AmE), colour (BrE), IMPRIM color (AmE), colour (BrE), *photogravure* chroma, MINES color (AmE), colour (BrE), PAPIER color (AmE), colour (BrE), dye, TELECOM, TEXTILE color (AmE), colour (BrE); ~ **d'accompagnement** *f* IMPRIM spot color (AmE), spot colour (BrE); ~ **achromatique** *f* IMPRIM achromatic color (AmE), achromatic colour (BrE); ~ **d'addition** *f* COULEURS additive color (AmE), additive colour (BrE); ~ **additive** *f* COULEURS additive color (AmE), additive colour (BrE); ~ **argentée** *f* COULEURS argentine, silver color (AmE), silver colour (BrE); ~ **de base** *f* COULEURS primary color (AmE), primary colour (BrE); ~ **à base d'aniline** *f* PHOTO aniline dye; ~ **broyée** *f* COULEURS ground color (AmE), ground colour (BrE); ~ **du caractère** *f* IMPRIM type color (AmE), type colour (BrE); ~ **chromatique** *f* COULEURS chromatic color (AmE), chromatic colour (BrE); ~ **de chrome** *f* COULEURS chrome color (AmE), chrome colour (BrE); ~ **citron** *f* COULEURS citrine color (AmE), citrine colour (BrE), lemon chrome, lemon color (AmE), lemon colour (BrE); ~ **au cobalt** *f* COULEURS cobalt color (AmE), cobalt colour (BrE); ~ **complémentaire** *f* PHOTO complementary color (AmE), complementary colour (BrE); ~ **désaturée** *f* TV desaturated color (AmE), desaturated colour (BrE); ~ **détectrice** *f* COULEURS sighting color (AmE), sighting colour (BrE); ~ **à détrempe** *f* COULEURS dis-temper; ~ **à détrempe à base d'huile** *f* COULEURS oil-bound distemper; ~ **éclatante** *f* MATERIAUX bright color (AmE), bright colour (BrE); ~ **élémentaire** *f* COULEURS principal color (AmE), principal colour (BrE); ~ **émail** *f* CERAM VER enamel color (AmE), enamel colour (BrE); ~ **en poudre** *f* COULEURS dry color (AmE), dry colour (BrE), powdered color (AmE), powdered colour (BrE); ~ **en tube** *f* COULEURS tube paint; ~ **de fond** *f* CERAM VER ground color

(AmE), ground colour (BrE); ~ **de gluon** *f* PHYS PART gluon color (AmE), gluon colour (BrE); ~ **de goudron** *f* COULEURS coal tar dye, tar dye; ~ **irisée** *f* COULEURS interference color (AmE), interference colour (BrE); ~ **jaune** *f* TEXTILE yellowness; ~ **lithographique** *f* COULEURS lithographic color (AmE), lithographic colour (BrE); ~ **marengo** *f* COULEURS Oxford grey (BrE), Oxford gray (AmE); ~ **de marquage** *f* COULEURS indicator color (AmE), indicator colour (BrE); ~ **minérale** *f* COULEURS mineral color (AmE), mineral colour (BrE); ~ **naturelle** *f* COULEURS inherent color (AmE), inherent colour (BrE), natural color (AmE), natural colour (BrE); ~ **non transparente** *f* COULEURS opaque color (AmE), opaque colour (BrE); ~ **opaque** *f* COULEURS opaque color (AmE), opaque colour (BrE); ~ **pour céramique** *f* COULEURS ceramic color (AmE), ceramic colour (BrE); ~ **pour ciment** *f* COULEURS cement paint; ~ **pour porcelaine** *f* CERAM VER porcelain color (AmE), porcelain colour (BrE); ~ **primaire** *f* COULEURS, CINEMAT, PHYS RAYON, PHYSIQUE primary color (AmE), primary colour (BrE); ~ **primaire rouge** *f* TV red primary; ~ **propre** *f* COULEURS perceived color (AmE), perceived colour (BrE), surface color (AmE), surface colour (BrE); ~ **des quarks** *f* PHYS PART quark color (AmE), quark colour (BrE); ~ **résistante** *f* COULEURS nonfading color (AmE), nonfading colour (BrE); ~ **résistant au feu** *f* COULEURS fireproof color (AmE), fireproof colour (BrE); ~ **résistant à la lumière** *f* IMPRIM fast color (AmE), fast colour (BrE); ~ **secondaire** *f* IMPRIM *photogravure* secondary color (AmE), secondary colour (BrE); ~ **semi-transparente** *f* CERAM VER semitransparent color (AmE), semitransparent colour (BrE); ~ **de signalisation** *f* COULEURS warning color (AmE), warning colour (BrE); ~ **solide** *f* COULEURS permanent color (AmE), permanent colour (BrE); ~ **solide à la lumière** *f* COULEURS nonfading color (AmE), nonfading colour (BrE); ~ **stable** *f* COULEURS permanent color (AmE), permanent colour (BrE); ~ **tranchante** *f* COULEURS warning color (AmE), warning colour (BrE); ~ **trop épaisse** *f* CERAM VER false body; ~ **au verre soluble** *f* REVETEMENT silicate paint, waterglass color (AmE), waterglass colour (BrE); ~ **vitrifiable** *f* CERAM VER glass color (AmE), glass colour (BrE); ~ **vitrifiable mate** *f* CERAM VER matt vitrifiable color (AmE), matt vitrifiable colour (BrE); ~ **vitrifiable simple** *f* CERAM VER flat color (AmE), flat colour (BrE)

couleurs:[1] **de** ~ **différentes** *adj* COULEURS varicolored (AmE), varicoloured (BrE); **de** ~ **diverses** *adj* COULEURS multicolored (AmE), multicoloured (BrE)

couleurs[2] *f pl* NAUT colors, colours (BrE); ~ **acides** *f pl* IMPRIM acid colors (AmE), acid colours (BrE); ~ **complémentaires** *f pl* PHYSIQUE complementary colors (AmE), complementary colours (BrE); ~ **illisibles** *f pl* IMPRIM *impression* drop-out; ~ **imprimées en complément sur les autres** *f pl* IMPRIM overprint colors (AmE), overprint colours (BrE); ~ **métamériques** *f pl* IMPRIM metameric colors (AmE), metameric colours (BrE); ~ **pour majolique** *f pl* CERAM VER majolica colors (AmE), majolica colours (BrE); ~ **primaires additives** *f pl* CINEMAT additive primaries; ~ **primaires dans la synthèse additive** *f pl* IMPRIM additive primaries; ~ **primaires de la quadrichromie** *f pl* IMPRIM process colors (AmE), process colours (BrE); ~ **primaires soustractives** *f pl* CINEMAT, TV subtractive primaries; ~ **de référence** *f pl* IMPRIM *photogravure*

memory colors (AmE), memory colours (BrE); ~ **des règlements de sécurité** *f pl* SECURITE safety colors (AmE), safety colours (BrE); ~ **spectrales** *f pl* PHYS RAYON spectral colors (AmE), spectral colours (BrE); ~ **vitrifiables** *f pl* CERAM VER vitrifiable colors (AmE), vitrifiable colours (BrE)

couleurs-mémoire *f pl* IMPRIM *photogravure, composition* memory colors (AmE), memory colours (BrE)

coulis:[1] ~ **basaltique** *m* GEOLOGIE flood basalt

coulis[2] *m* CONSTR grouting; ~ **de ciment** *m* CONSTR cement slurry; ~ **hydraulique d'injection** *m* CONSTR grout

coulissage: ~ **de plaques** *m* GEOLOGIE strike-slip movements

coulissant *adj* MECANIQUE telescopic

coulisse *f* CONS MECA link gear, link motion, link valve motion, slide, slider, *de distribution à coulisse* link, MINES drill jar, drilling jar, jar, OCEANO purse line; ~ **à barres croisées** *f* CONS MECA link motion with crossed rods; ~ **à barres droites** *f* CONS MECA link motion with open rods; ~ **à barres fermées** *f* CONS MECA link motion with crossed rods; ~ **à barres ouvertes** *f* CONS MECA link motion with open rods; ~ **de changement de marche** *f* CONS MECA reversing link; ~ **fixe** *f* CONS MECA stationary link; ~ **à flasques** *f* CONS MECA plate link; ~ **mobile** *f* CONS MECA shifting link

coulisseau *m* CONS MECA die, link block, slide block, slide, slider, slipper block; ~ **de crosse** *m* CONS MECA crosshead block, crosshead body; ~ **du diaphragme d'ouverture** *m* INSTRUMENT aperture top slide; ~ **incliné** *m* CONS MECA *moule d'injection* angled core slide; ~ **porte-outil** *m* CONS MECA tool ram, tool slide; ~ **porte-outils** *m* CONS MECA tool-holding slide

coulisser *vi* CONS MECA slide

coulisseur *m* CONSTR tonguing-and-grooving planes

couloir *m* CONSTR chute, TRANSPORT lane; ~ **aérien** *m* AERONAUT air corridor; ~ **central** *m* TRANSPORT central gangway; ~ **à charbon** *m* CHARBON coal chute; ~ **de chargement** *m* MINES loading chute; ~ **du film** *m* CINEMAT film gate; ~ **maritime** *m* NAUT sea lane; ~ **de montée** *m* AERONAUT climb corridor; ~ **de navigation** *m* OCEANO sea lane, shipping corridor, traffic lane; ~ **optimal de rentrée** *m* ESPACE optimum re-entry corridor; ~ **oscillant** *m* CONSTR swinging chute; ~ **presseur** *m* CINEMAT film channel; ~ **réservé aux bus** *m* TRANSPORT bus lane

coulomb *m (C)* ELECTR *unité*, ELECTROTEC, METROLOGIE, PHYSIQUE coulomb *(C)*

coulombmètre *m* ELECTR coulombmeter, ELECTROTEC coulometer

coulomètre *m* ELECTR coulombmeter, ELECTROTEC coulometer

coulure *f* PLAST CAOU *défaut de peinture* sagging, PRODUCTION break-out, runout; ~ **de peinture** *f* REVETEMENT varnish run, varnish tear, varnish tit; ~ **de vernis** *f* REVETEMENT varnish run, varnish tear, varnish tit

coumaline *f* CHIMIE coumalin, coumaline

coumalique *adj* CHIMIE coumalic

coumaranne *m* CHIMIE coumaran, coumarane

coumarine *f* CHIMIE coumarin, coumarine

coumarique *adj* CHIMIE coumaric

coup *m* CERAM VER bruise, CONS MECA *de piston, analogue* stroke, CONSTR observation, sight, MILITAIRE round, MINES shot; ~ **d'air** *m* MINES rush of air; ~ **arrière** *m* CONSTR back observation, backsight, MINES backsight; ~ **avant** m CONSTR fore observation, foresight, MINES foresight; ~ **de bélier** m INST HYDR pressure surge, PETROLE, PHYS FLUID water hammer, REFRIG hammering; ~ **bref** m NAUT short blast; ~ **de ciseaux** m CERAM VER shear cut; ~ **complet** m MILITAIRE round of ammunition; ~ **d'eau** m DISTRI EAU water inflow, HYDROLOGIE flood of water; ~ **de feu** m IMPRIM rush order, MILITAIRE shot; ~ **de foudre** m ELECTR lightning discharge, lightning stroke, METEO lightning strike, thunderbolt; ~ **de gouge** m GEOLOGIE chatter mark; ~ **de grisou** m CHARBON gas explosion; ~ **du lapin** m TRANSPORT whiplash effect; ~ **de liquide** m REFRIG slugging; ~ **long** m NAUT long blast; ~ **de lunette** m CONSTR observation, sight; ~ **de mer** m OCEANO breaker, breaking wave, waterwall; ~ **de mine** m MINES shot; ~ **de piston** m CONS MECA piston stroke; ~ **de pointeau** m CONS MECA punch mark, PRODUCTION center pop (AmE), center punch mark (AmE), centre pop (BrE), centre punch mark (BrE); ~ **de poussière** m CHARBON dust explosion; ~ **de relevage** m MINES bottom shot; ~ **de rouleau** m CERAM VER in-line variation; ~ **de roulis** m NAUT lurch; ~ **de sabre** m CERAM VER flux line attack; ~ **de sonde** m CONSTR borehole; ~ **de souffle** m CERAM VER puff; ~ **de tonnerre** m METEO thunderclap

coupage m PRODUCTION blending, *des jets de fonderie* cutting-off; ~ **à l'acétylène** m MECANIQUE *procédé* acetylene cutting; ~ **à l'arc** m CONSTR, PRODUCTION arc cutting; ~ **à l'arc avec oxygène** m CONSTR oxygen arc cutting; ~ **à l'arc électrique** m THERMODYN electric arc cutting; ~ **à gaz** m CONSTR flame cutting; ~ **laser** m CONSTR laser cutting; ~ **plasma** m CONSTR plasma arc cutting, plasma cutting

coupant m CONS MECA edge, CONSTR *d'un outil* cutting edge

coupe f CHARBON cut, CONS MECA cross section, cut, gap, sectional drawing, GEOLOGIE cross section, section, IMPRIM *rotatives* cutoff, MINES cutting, cut, PAPIER cutting, PETROLE *raffinage, distillation* fraction, PHYSIQUE cross section, PRODUCTION *des métaux par un jet d'oxygène* cutting; ~ **confection** f TEXTILE cutting; ~ **consistométrique** f EQUIP LAB *viscosité des liquides* flow cup; ~ **délibérée** f IMPRIM *dans une bande* split; ~ **de desserrage** f CERAM VER auxiliary cut; ~ **diagonale** f PAPIER angle cut; ~ **du diamant** f CERAM VER diamond cutting edge; ~ **en travers** f CONS MECA cross section, PRODUCTION cross cut; ~ **franche** f CERAM VER clean cut; ~ **géologique** f GEOLOGIE geological section; ~ **longitudinale** f NAUT profile; ~ **losange** f PAPIER angle cutting; ~ **au maître** f NAUT midship section; ~ **à mi-bois** f CONSTR halved joint, halving, lap joint, overleap joint, step joint; ~ **négative** f CONS MECA negative rake; ~ **à ras** f PRODUCTION flush cut; ~ **de segment** f AUTO ring gap; ~ **transversale** f CONS MECA, NAUT, PAPIER, PRODUCTION cross section; ~ **transversale d'absorption** f PHYS RAYON *d'un atome* absorption cross section; ~ **très douce** f PRODUCTION dead-smooth cut

Coupe f ASTRONOMIE Crater

coupé adj ELECTROTEC off; ~ **court** adj TEXTILE cropped; ~ **dans le biais** adj TEXTILE cut on the bias; ~ **à la longueur** adj PRODUCTION cut-to-length

coupe-béton m CONSTR concrete saw

coupe-bordure m CONS MECA edge trimmer, PAPIER edge cutter

coupe-boulons m CONS MECA bolt cropper, bolt cutter,

MECANIQUE bolt cutter, NAUT bolt cropper

coupe-câble m ESPACE *véhicules* cable cutter; ~ **acier** m CONS MECA steel cable cutter

coupe-cercle m CONS MECA washer cutter

coupe-circuit m COMMANDE, CONSTR circuit breaker, ELECTROTEC cutout, TV fuse; ~ **à expulsion dirigée** m ELECTROTEC expulsion fuse; ~ **à lame** m ELECTR *fusible* link fuse; ~ **protecteur de ligne** m GEOPHYS line protector cutout; ~ **sectionneur** m ELECTROTEC switch fuse; ~ **de surtension** m ELECTROTEC overvoltage protection

coupe-coulées m CONS MECA gate cutter, PRODUCTION gate cutter, sprue cutter

coupée f NAUT accommodation ladder

coupe-épreuves m PHOTO trimmer

coupe-feu adj MECANIQUE fireproof

coupe-feuilles: ~ **hydraulique** m PAPIER edge cutter, edge spray, edge squirt, hydraulic sheet cutter, spray cutter

coupe-flamme m PETROLE *sécurité* flame arrester

coupe-flux: ~ **cylindrique** m CINEMAT snoot

coupe-gazon m CONSTR edging iron

coupelle f CERAM VER edge bowl, CHIMIE cupel, EMBALLAGE base cup, EQUIP LAB dish, *analyse* boat, INST HYDR valve spring washer, THERMODYN melting crucible, melting pot; ~ **d'appui du ressort** f AUTO spring retainer; ~ **creuse** f NUCLEAIRE well-type planchet; ~ **d'étanchéité** f AUTO secondary cup; ~ **de pesée** f EQUIP LAB weighing dish; ~ **principale** f AUTO primary cup; ~ **de protection** f CONS MECA protective cap; ~ **de rotule** f CONS MECA ball cup; ~ **serre-gaine** f CONS MECA ferrule

coupe-odeur f CONSTR stench trap, stink trap, trap

couper vt CINEMAT kill, turn off, DISTRI EAU *l'eau* turn off, ELECTROTEC *circuit* break, turn off, ESPACE *moteur* shut down, IMPRIM *une photo sans réduire* crop, INST HYDR *l'arrivée de vapeur* cut off, MECANIQUE *outillage*, PLAST CAOU *viscosité* cut, PRODUCTION cut off; ~ **le contact** vt AERONAUT *réacteur* shut down; ~ **le courant d'excitation de** vt ELECTROTEC de-energize; ~ **en dés** vt AGRO ALIM dice; ~ **en deux parties égales** vt GEOMETRIE bisect; ~ **en travers** vt PRODUCTION cross-cut; ~ **à la longueur voulue** vt PRODUCTION tube cut to the required length; ~ **la route** vt NAUT *d'un navire* cross the bows

couper-coller vt IMPRIM *composition, montage électronique* cut and paste

coupé-rebrûlé m CERAM VER burning-off

coupe-rondelle m CONS MECA washer cutter

couperose f CHIMIE copperas; ~ **bleue** f CHIMIE blue vitriol, bluestone, copper sulfate (AmE), copper sulphate (BrE)

coupe-tubage m CONSTR casing cutter

coupe-tubes m CONS MECA tube cutter, CONSTR pipe cutter, EQUIP LAB tube cutter; ~ **à trois molettes** m CONS MECA three-wheel tube cutter

coupe-tuiles m CONSTR tile cutter

coupe-tuyaux m CONSTR pipe cutter

coupeur: ~ **de verre** m CERAM VER glass cutter

coupeuse f MINES heading machine; ~ **à bois** f PAPIER chipper, chopper; ~ **de copeaux** f PAPIER chipper; ~ **à deux couteaux** f PAPIER double blade cutter, dual-knife cutter; ~ **en feuilles** f IMPRIM sheeter; ~ **en long** f PAPIER slitter; ~ **de rails** f CH DE FER rail-cutting machine; ~ **rotative** f CHARBON rotary heading machine, IMPRIM *façonnage* rotary cutter

coupeuse-rebrûleuse f CERAM VER burning-off and edge-melting machine (BrE), remelting machine (AmE)

coupe-verre: ~ **à molette** *m* CERAM VER wheeled glass cutter

couplage:[1] **à ~ direct** *adj* INFORMAT, ORDINAT direct-coupled

couplage[2] *m* CHIMIE coupling, CINEMAT interlock, ELECTR *circuits à courant alternatif* direct coupling, *raccordement, induction* coupling, ELECTROTEC, ORDINAT, PHYSIQUE, TELECOM coupling; ~ **acoustique** *m* ELECTRON, TELECOM acoustic coupling; ~ **de câbles** *m* ELECTROTEC cable coupling; ~ **came-poinçon** *m* CERAM VER plunger assist mechanism; ~ **capacitif** *m* ELECTR capacitive coupling, ELECTROTEC capacitance coupling, TELECOM capacitive coupling; ~ **directif** *m* ELECTROTEC directional coupling; ~ **électromagnétique** *m* ELECTROTEC electromagnetic coupling; ~ **électronique** *m* ELECTRON, ELECTROTEC electron coupling; ~ **en cascade** *m* ELECTROTEC cascade connection; ~ **en parallèle** *m* ELECTROTEC, MINES parallel connection; ~ **en série** *m* ELECTROTEC series connection, tandem connection; ~ **en triangle** *m* ELECTR *raccordement* delta connection; ~ **en zigzag double** *m* ELECTR *raccordement* forked connection; ~ **faible** *m* NUCLEAIRE normal coupling, weak coupling; ~ **de flux magnétique** *m* EN RENOUV magnetic flux linkage; ~ **inductif** *m* ELECTR *bobine*, ELECTROTEC inductive coupling; ~ **j-j** *m* NUCLEAIRE, PHYSIQUE j-j coupling; ~ **lâche** *m* ELECTROTEC, INFORMAT, ORDINAT, PHYSIQUE loose coupling; ~ **de ligne** *m* ELECTROTEC line coupling; ~ **magnétique** *m* ELECTR *transformateur* magnetic coupling; ~ **des modes** *m* OPTIQUE, TELECOM mode coupling; ~ **mutuel** *m* TELECOM mutual coupling; ~ **normal** *m* NUCLEAIRE normal coupling, weak coupling; ~ **d'ondes** *m* TELECOM wave coupling; ~ **optique** *m* ELECTROTEC optical coupling; ~ **oxydant** *m* GAZ oxidative coupling; ~ **parallèle** *m* MINES parallel connection; ~ **parasite** *m* ELECTROTEC cross coupling, parasitic coupling, stray coupling, TELECOM parasitic coupling; ~ **par boucle** *m* ELECTROTEC loop coupling; ~ **par inductance mutuelle** *m* ELECTROTEC mutual inductance coupling; ~ **par induction** *m* ELECTROTEC inductive coupling; ~ **par résistance** *m* ELECTROTEC resistive coupling; ~ **par transformateur** *m* ELECTR transformer coupling; ~ **de Racah** *m* NUCLEAIRE Racah coupling; ~ **RC** *m* ELECTRON RC coupling; ~ **de référence** *m* ELECTROTEC reference coupling; ~ **R-S** *m* PHYSIQUE R-S coupling, Russell-Saunders coupling; ~ **Russell-Saunders** *m* PHYSIQUE R-S coupling, Russell-Saunders coupling; ~ **serré** *m* ELECTR *inductance* close coupling, ELECTROTEC tight coupling, ORDINAT close coupling, PHYSIQUE tight coupling; ~ **spin-orbite** *m* PHYSIQUE spin orbit coupling; ~ **transversal** *m* ELECTROTEC cross coupling; ~ **vectoriel** *m* PHYS RAYON *orbites d'électron* vector coupling; ~ **des voisins les plus proches** *m* NUCLEAIRE nearest neighbor coupling (AmE), nearest neighbour coupling (BrE)

couple:[1] **à ~ bas** *adj* PRODUCTION low-torque; **à ~ élevé** *adj* MECANIQUE high-torque

couple:[2] **à ~** *adv* NAUT *navire* alongside

couple[3] *m* AERONAUT *d'un aéronef* ring frame, CONS MECA couple, frame, torque, ELECTROTEC couple, torque, MATH ordered pair, MECANIQUE *mécanique, physique*, PETROLE torque, PHYSIQUE couple, torque, PRODUCTION *système hydraulique*, VEHICULES *moteur* torque; ~ **antagoniste** *m* AERONAUT antagonistic torque; ~ **conique** *m* AUTO bevel gearing, ring and pinion, VEHICULES *pont arrière* bevel gear set, crown and pinion, crown wheel and pinion; ~ **conique à denture hypoïde** *m* AUTO hypoid gearing, VEHICULES *différentiel* hypoid gearing; ~ **conique à denture spirale** *m* AUTO spiral bevel gearing; ~ **de construction** *m* NAUT bulkhead; ~ **de démarrage** *m* CONS MECA, PRODUCTION starting torque; ~ **à deux rapports** *m* AUTO two-speed final drive; ~ **en autorotation** *m* AERONAUT windmill torque; ~ **étanche** *m* CONS MECA pressure bulkhead; ~ **final** *m* AUTO final drive; ~ **fléchissant** *m* PHYSIQUE bending moment; ~ **de flexion** *m* PHYSIQUE, RESSORTS bending moment; ~ **de freinage** *m* AERONAUT brake torque; ~ **de frottement** *m* ESPACE *véhicules* frictional torque; ~ **fuselage** *m* AERONAUT ring fuselage; ~ **galvanique** *m* ELECTROTEC galvanic couple; ~ **gyroscopique** *m* AERONAUT gyroscopic torque; ~ **d'hélice** *m* AERONAUT propeller torque; ~ **moteur** *m* AERONAUT, AUTO engine torque, CONS MECA engine couple, engine torque; ~ **perturbateur dû à l'environnement** *m* ESPACE environmental torque; ~ **de rappel** *m* MECANIQUE restoring torque, NAUT righting moment; ~ **de réaction** *m* AUTO rear end torque; ~ **résistant** *m* AUTO resisting torque; ~ **rotor** *m* AERONAUT *hélicoptère* rotor torque; ~ **de serrage avec lubrifiant** *m* CONS MECA lubricated thread torque; ~ **de service** *m* PRODUCTION running torque; ~ **stéréoscopique** *m* PHOTO stereoscopic pair; ~ **thermoélectrique** *m* METALL, PHYSIQUE thermocouple; ~ **thermoélectrique différentiel** *m* THERMODYN differential thermocouple; ~ **de torsion** *m* RESSORTS torque; ~ **de tracé** *m* NAUT body section; ~ **à vis sans fin** *m* AUTO worm gear final drive

couple:[4] **à ~ de** *prép* NAUT alongside

couplé *adj* ELECTROTEC coupled, MECANIQUE linked; ~ **par le petit côté** *adj* ELECTROTEC sidewall-coupled

coupler *vt* CONS MECA gang, ELECTROTEC couple

couples: ~ **de tracé** *m pl* NAUT ordinates

couplet *m* CONSTR strap hinge

coupleur *m* ACOUSTIQUE, CINEMAT *en réaction chimique*, CONS MECA, ELECTROTEC, ORDINAT, TELECOM coupler; ~ **acoustique** *m* ELECTRON, ORDINAT acoustic coupler; ~ **alternatif** *m* TELECOM alternating current coupler; ~ **de batteries** *m* AUTO battery changeover relay; ~ **bidirectionnel** *m* ELECTROTEC bidirectional coupler; ~ **directif** *m* ELECTROTEC directional coupler, OPTIQUE directional coupler, TELECOM direct current coupler, directional coupler; ~ **directionnel** *m* PHYSIQUE directional coupler; ~ **en étoile** *m* OPTIQUE, TELECOM star coupler; ~ **en té** *m* OPTIQUE, TELECOM tee coupler; ~ **en Y** *m* OPTIQUE, TELECOM y-coupler; ~ **étoile-triangle** *m* ELECTROTEC star-delta switch; ~ **de faisceau latéral** *m* AERONAUT lateral beam coupler; ~ **de faisceau longitudinal** *m* AERONAUT longitudinal beam coupler; ~ **hydraulique** *m* PRODUCTION fluid coupling; ~ **Mach-Zehnder** *m* TELECOM balanced bridge interferometer switch; ~ **optique** *m* ELECTROTEC optical coupler, optocoupler, OPTIQUE, TELECOM optical coupler, optical fiber coupler (AmE), optical fibre coupler (BrE); ~ **optique directif** *m* OPTIQUE directional optical coupler; ~ **sélectif** *m* TV separation filter; ~ **série-parallèle** *m* ELECTROTEC series parallel switch; ~ **téléphonique** *m* ELECTRON dataphone (TM), modem; ~ **de vol stationnaire** *m* AERONAUT hover flight coupler

coupole *f* AERONAUT *structural* blister, GEOLOGIE *corps intrusif* cupola

coupon *m* CONS MECA section, test bar

coupure *f* CONSTR cutting, ELECTR disconnection, ELEC-

TROTEC cutoff, GEOLOGIE division, IMPRIM break, INST HYDR *de l'arrivée de vapeur* cutting-off, MINES cut, cutting, PHYSIQUE, TELECOM breakdown, TV cutoff; ~ **d'alimentation** *f* INFORMAT, ORDINAT power supply interrupt, PRODUCTION power down; ~ **d'antenne** *f* TV dead air; ~ **automatique** *f* IMPRIM *en fin de colonne ou de page* automatic jump; ~ **automatique du laser** *f* TELECOM ALS, automatic laser shutdown; ~ **des basses** *f* ENREGISTR bass cut; ~ **de circuit** *f* ELECTROTEC turn-off; ~ **de courant** *f* CINEMAT, ELECTROTEC power failure; ~ **du courant d'excitation** *f* ELECTROTEC de-energization; ~ **en basse fréquence** *f* ENREGISTR low-frequency cut-off; ~ **du faisceau** *f* TV beam cutoff; ~ **de ligne** *f* ELECTR *réseau d'alimentation* line break; ~ **de méandre** *f* DISTRI EAU cutoff; ~ **d'un moteur en vol** *f* AERONAUT engine shutdown in flight; ~ **non-sensible** *f* TV match cut

courant *m* CONSTR *dans une cheminée* draft (AmE), draught (BrE), ELECTR, ELECTROTEC current, HYDROLOGIE current, flow, NAUT current, PHYS FLUID stream, PHYSIQUE current; ~ **a** ~ **absorbé** *m* ELECTROTEC current input; ~ **d'absorption** *m* ELECTR absorption current; ~ **d'accrochage** *m* ELECTROTEC latching current; ~ **actif** *m* ELECTR *courant alternatif* active current, actual current, PHYSIQUE active current; ~ **admissible** *m* ELECTROTEC contact rating; ~ **admissible de coupure** *m* ELECTR *disjoncteur* admissible interrupting current; ~ **d'air** *m* CONS MECA, CONSTR airflow, draft (AmE), draught (BrE), PHYS FLUID airflow, PRODUCTION blast; ~ **d'air chaud** *m* METEO warm air stream; ~ **d'air descendant** *m* AERONAUT, CONS MECA downdraft (AmE), downdraught (BrE), MINES downcast; ~ **d'air entrant** *m* MINES ingoing air current; ~ **d'air forcé** *m* CONS MECA forced draft (AmE), forced draught (BrE); ~ **d'air rabattant** *m* AERONAUT downdraft (AmE), downdraught (BrE); ~ **d'air sortant** *m* MINES outgoing air current; ~ **d'alimentation** *m* ELECTROTEC supply current; ~ **alternant** *m* OCEANO reversing current; ~ **alternatif** *m (CA)* ELECTR, ELECTRON, ELECTROTEC, ENREGISTR, PHYSIQUE, TELECOM, TV alternating current *(AC)*; ~ **alternatif brut** *m* ELECTR unrectified AC; ~ **alternatif redressé** *m* ELECTROTEC rectified alternating current; ~ **ampérien** *m* PHYSIQUE Amperian current; ~ **anodique** *m* ELECTROTEC anode current; ~ **d'appel** *m* TELECOM ringing current; ~ **d'arc** *m* ELECTR arc current; ~ **d'arrachement** *m* OCEANO rip current; ~ **assigné** *m* ELECTR rated current; ~ **d'auto-induction** *m* ELECTROTEC self-induction current; ~ **b** ~ **de bruit induit** *m* PRODUCTION *électricité* induced noise current; ~ **c** ~ **de charge** *m* ELECTR *accumulateur* charging current; ~ **de chauffage** *m* ELECTR *tube*, ELECTROTEC filament current, THERMODYN heating current; ~ **de choc** *m* ELECTR impulse current, PRODUCTION surge current; ~ **de circulation** *m* TRANSPORT traffic stream; ~ **à clapotage** *m* OCEANO rip current; ~ **commuté** *m* ELECTR *commutateur* switched current; ~ **compensateur** *m* ELECTR compensating current; ~ **de compensation** *m* OCEANO compensation current; ~ **de conduction** *m* ELECTR, PHYSIQUE conduction current; ~ **constant** *m* ELECTROTEC constant current; ~ **continu** *m (CC)* CH DE FER, ELECTR, ELECTRON, ELECTROTEC, ENREGISTR, PHYSIQUE, PRODUCTION, TELECOM, TV direct current *(DC)*; ~ **continu pulsé** *m* ELECTROTEC pulsating current; ~ **de convection** *m* CERAM VER,

ELECTROTEC, PHYSIQUE, THERMODYN convection current; ~ **de coupure** *m* ELECTR *interrupteur* cutoff current; ~ **de courte durée assigné** *m* ELECTR rated short-time current; ~ **de courte durée nominal** *m* ELECTR rated short-time current; ~ **de crête** *m* ELECTR *réseau*, ELECTROTEC, PHYSIQUE peak current; ~ **d** ~ **dans le filament** *m* ELECTROTEC filament current; ~ **débité** *m* ELECTROTEC current output; ~ **de décharge** *m* ELECTR *condensateur*, ELECTROTEC discharge current; ~ **de déclenchement réglable** *m* PRODUCTION adjustable trip setting; ~ **de défaut de mise à la terre** *m* PRODUCTION *électricité* earth fault current (BrE), ground fault current (AmE); ~ **de densité** *m* HYDROLOGIE density current; ~ **de déplacement** *m* ELECTR *diélectrique*, ELECTROTEC, PHYSIQUE displacement current; ~ **de dérive** *m* OCEANO drift current; ~ **dérivé** *m* DISTRI EAU undercurrent, underflow, ELECTR *branchement* derived current, ELECTROTEC shunt current; ~ **descendant** *m* AERONAUT downdraft (AmE), downdraught (BrE); ~ **déwatté** *m* ELECTR *courant alternatif* idle current, reactive current, wattless current, ELECTROTEC wattless current; ~ **diélectrique** *m* ELECTROTEC dielectric current, displacement current; ~ **de diffusion** *m* ELECTR *électrolyse* diffusion current; ~ **diphasé** *m* ELECTR biphase current, ELECTROTEC two-phase current; ~ **direct** *m* ELECTR *semi-conducteur*, ELECTROTEC forward current, TRANSPORT straight-through traffic; ~ **de drain** *m* ELECTROTEC drain current; ~ **e** ~ **d'eau souterraine** *m* HYDROLOGIE underground flow; ~ **d'effacement** *m* ENREGISTR, TV erasing current; ~ **électrique** *m* ELECTR, ELECTROTEC, PHYSIQUE, TELECOM electric current; ~ **électronique** *m* ELECTROTEC electron current; ~ **d'électrons** *m* ELECTROTEC electron current; ~ **d'émission à champ nul** *m* NUCLEAIRE field free emission current; ~ **d'emploi** *m* PRODUCTION operational current; ~ **en charge** *m* ELECTROTEC on-load current; ~ **en dents de scie** *m* TV sawtooth current; ~ **en phase avec la tension** *m* ELECTR in-phase current; ~ **d'enregistrement** *m* TV record current; ~ **d'enregistrement audiofréquence** *m* ENREGISTR recording audio-frequency current; ~ **d'enregistrement vidéo** *m* TV video record current; ~ **d'entraînement** *m* OCEANO entrainment current, inshore current; ~ **d'entrée** *m* ELECTR input current; ~ **entre les phases** *m* ELECTROTEC mesh current; ~ **équilibré** *m* ELECTROTEC balanced current; ~ **établi** *m* OCEANO permanent current, stable current; ~ **à l'état passant** *m* ELECTROTEC on-state current; ~ **d'étoiles** *m* ASTRONOMIE stellar stream; ~ **d'excitation** *m* ELECTR *machine* field current, *électro-aimant* excitation current, ELECTROTEC energizing current, field current; ~ **f** ~ **à la fermeture** *m* ELECTROTEC make current; ~ **de flamme** *m* PRODUCTION *d'une chaudière* path of a flame; ~ **de flot** *m* NAUT, OCEANO flood stream; ~ **de fonctionnement** *m* ELECTR, ELECTROTEC operating current; ~ **de fond** *m* DISTRI EAU bottom current, bottom flow, OCEANO bottom current, underflow; ~ **de Foucault** *m* ELECTR, ELECTROTEC, ESSAIS, PHYSIQUE, TV eddy current; ~ **de foudre** *m* ELECTROTEC lightning current; ~ **de fuite** *m* ELECTR, ELECTROTEC, TELECOM leakage current; ~ **de fuite d'un condensateur** *m* ELECTROTEC capacitor leakage current; ~ **de fuite dans la jonction** *m* ELECTROTEC junction leakage current; ~ **de fuite de la grille** *m* ELECTROTEC gate leakage current; ~ **de fuite à la terre** *m* ELECTR earth leakage current

(BrE), ground leakage current (AmE);

~ g ~ **galvanique** *m* ELECTROTEC galvanic current; ~ **géostrophique** *m* OCEANO geostrophic current, geostrophic flow; ~ **giratoire** *m* OCEANO rotary current, rotary tidal current; ~ **global du faisceau** *m* TV electron gun current; ~ **de grille** *m* ELECTROTEC grid current;

~ h ~ **à haute fréquence** *m* ELECTR *courant alternatif* high-frequency current, ELECTROTEC RF current; ~ **hexaphasé** *m* ELECTROTEC six-phase current; ~ **HF** *m* ELECTROTEC RF current;

~ i ~ **d'impulsion** *m* ELECTR impulse current; ~ **d'induction** *m* ELECTROTEC induction current; ~ **d'induit** *m* ELECTR *machine*, ELECTROTEC armature current; ~ **induit** *m* ELECTR *électromagnétisme* induced current, ELECTROTEC induction current, TELECOM induced current; ~ **d'inertie** *m* OCEANO inertial current; ~ **initial** *m* ELECTR, ELECTROTEC initial current; ~ **initial de charge** *m* AUTO initial forming charge; ~ **initial de démarrage** *m* ELECTR breakaway starting current; ~ **instantané** *m* ELECTR instantaneous current; ~ **inverse** *m* ELECTROTEC reverse current; ~ **ionique** *m* PHYS RAYON ion current; ~ **d'ionisation** *m* ELECTRON ionization current;

~ j ~ **de jusant** *m* NAUT, OCEANO ebb stream;

~ l ~ **limite** *m* ELECTR limiting current, *transformateur* limiting overload current; ~ **limite de fonctionnement** *m* PRODUCTION run current limit; ~ **longitudinal** *m* CERAM VER longitudinal current;

~ m ~ **magellanique** *m* ASTRONOMIE Magellanic stream; ~ **magnétisant** *m* ELECTROTEC magnetizing current; ~ **de maintien** *m* ELECTR maintenance current, *relais, thyristor* hold current, ELECTROTEC holding current; ~ **de marée** *m* EN RENOUV tidal current, NAUT tidal current, tidal stream, OCEANO tidal current; ~ **de masse** *m* PRODUCTION *électricité* ground current; ~ **maximal** *m* ELECTR maximum current; ~ **à mesurer** *m* ELECTR measured current; ~ **monophasé** *m* CINEMAT single-phase current, CONSTR single-phase electric current, ELECTROTEC *alternatif* single-phase current; ~ **montant** *m* NUCLEAIRE *écoulement* upflow, upward flow;

~ n ~ **neutre** *m* PHYSIQUE neutral current; ~ **de noeud** *m* ELECTR *circuit* nodal current; ~ **nominal** *m* ELECTR rated current, PRODUCTION current rating; ~ **nominal d'emploi** *m* PRODUCTION rated operational current; ~ **non pulsé** *m* ELECTROTEC continuous current; ~ **nul** *m* ELECTROTEC zero current;

~ o ~ **d'obscurité** *m* ELECTROTEC, OPTIQUE, PHYSIQUE, TELECOM dark current; ~ **océanique** *m* METEO oceanic current, NAUT ocean current; ~ **opposé** *m* ELECTROTEC countercurrent, return current;

~ p ~ **de palan** *m* CONS MECA purchase fall, PRODUCTION tackle fall; ~ **parasite** *m* ELECTROTEC parasitic current, PHYSIQUE eddy current; ~ **partiel** *m* MINES split; ~ **de pâte** *m* PAPIER *en avant de la machine* approach flow; ~ **de pente** *m* OCEANO gradient current, slope current; ~ **de phase** *m* ELECTR *réseau*, ELECTROTEC phase current; ~ **de phase moteur** *m* PRODUCTION motor phase current; ~ **photoélectrique** *m* ELECTR, OPTIQUE photoelectric current, TELECOM light current, photoelectric current; ~ **photovoltaïque** *m* ELECTROTEC photovoltaic current; ~ **pleine charge** *m* PRODUCTION full-load current; ~ **de polarisation** *m* PHYSIQUE polarization current; ~ **polyphasé** *m* ELECTR *courant alternatif* polyphase current; ~ **porteur** *m*

ELECTRON carrier; ~ **de prémagnétisation** *m* TV biasing current; ~ **primaire** *m* ELECTR *transformateur*, ELECTROTEC primary current; ~ **de prise** *m* ELECTR *d'un enroulement* tapping current; ~ **profond** *m* OCEANO underflow; ~ **pulsatoire** *m* ELECTROTEC pulsatory current; ~ **pulsé** *m* ELECTR pulsating current, pulsed current, ELECTROTEC pulsating current;

~ r ~ **réactif** *m* ELECTR *courant alternatif* wattless current, ELECTROTEC reactive current, wattless current; ~ **de recombinaison dans la base** *m* ELECTRON recombination base current; ~ **redressé** *m* ELECTROTEC rectified current; ~ **réfléchi** *m* ELECTRON feedback current; ~ **de relâchement** *m* ELECTR, ELECTROTEC drop-out current; ~ **résiduel** *m* ELECTR, ELECTROTEC residual current; ~ **de retombée** *m* ELECTR, ELECTROTEC drop-out current; ~ **de retour** *m* ELECTRON feedback current, ELECTROTEC return current, HYDROLOGIE back eddy, return current, NAUT rip tide, OCEANO eddying current, rip current; ~ **rétrograde** *m* HYDROLOGIE back eddy, return current; ~ **à rotor bloqué** *m* ELECTR *machine asynchrone* locked rotor current; ~ **de rupture** *m* ELECTR *relais* breaking current;

~ s ~ **sagittal** *m* OCEANO rip current; ~ **de saturation** *m* ELECTRON, PHYSIQUE saturation current; ~ **secondaire** *m* ELECTR *transformateur*, ELECTROTEC secondary current; ~ **de secteur** *m* ELECTROTEC line current; ~ **secteur** *m* ELECTROTEC current (AmE), mains current (BrE), supply current; ~ **de service** *m* ELECTR operating current; ~ **de seuil** *m* ELECTROTEC, OPTIQUE *d'un laser semiconducteur*, PHYS RAYON, TELECOM threshold current; ~ **sinusoïdal** *m* ELECTROTEC *alternatif*, PHYSIQUE sinusoidal current; ~ **de sortie** *m* ELECTR output current; ~ **de sortie régulé** *m* ELECTROTEC regulated output current; ~ **de soudage maximal** *m* CONSTR maximum welding current; ~ **de soudage minimal** *m* CONSTR minimum welding current; ~ **de soudage nominal** *m* CONSTR rated welding current; ~ **sous-marin** *m* EN RENOUV undercurrent; ~ **stationnaire** *m* PHYSIQUE steady current; ~ **superficiel** *m* TELECOM surface current; ~ **de surcharge** *m* ELECTR *réseau, appareil*, ELECTROTEC overload current; ~ **de surface** *m* NAUT drift current, surface current;

~ t ~ **tellurique** *m* GEOPHYS earth current (BrE), ground current (AmE); ~ **temporaire admissible** *m* PRODUCTION withstand current; ~ **à la terre** *m* ELECTR earth current (BrE), ground current (AmE); ~ **thermique** *m* METEO thermal current; ~ **thermique nominal** *m* PRODUCTION rated thermal current; ~ **thermoélectrique** *m* NUCLEAIRE thermocurrent; ~ **de tirée** *m* CERAM VER pull current (BrE), withdrawal current (AmE); ~ **tournant** *m* TRANSPORT turning traffic; ~ **tourne-à-droite** *m* TRANSPORT right turning traffic; ~ **tourne-à-gauche** *m* TRANSPORT left turning traffic; ~ **transitoire** *m* TRANSPORT *circulation* transient current; ~ **transitoire en arc étincelant** *m* PRODUCTION showering arc transient; ~ **transversal** *m* CERAM VER transverse current; ~ **traversant assigné** *m* ELECTR *changeur de prises* rated through-current; ~ **traversant assigné maximal** *m* ELECTR *contacts* maximum rated through-current; ~ **traversant nominale** *m* ELECTR *changeur de prises* rated through-current; ~ **triphasé** *m* ELECTROTEC three-phase current; ~ **de turbidité** *m* GEOLOGIE, OCEANO turbidity current;

~ v ~ **vagabond** *m* ELECTROTEC stray current; ~ **à vide** *m* ELECTR no-load current, open circuit current, mo-

teur idle current;

~ w ~ **watté** *m* ELECTR *circuit à courant alternatif* actual current, *courant alternatif* active current, ELECTROTEC effort current

courant-jet *m* METEO jet stream

courantomètre *m* DISTRI EAU, EN RENOUV, NAUT current meter; ~ **acoustique** *m* OCEANO acoustic current meter; ~ **électromagnétique** *m* OCEANO electromagnetic current meter

courants: ~ **de circulation non conflictuels** *m pl* TRANSPORT nonconflicting traffic flows

courbe[1] *adj* GEOMETRIE curved

courbe[2] *f* CONS MECA pipe bend, CONSTR bend, GEOMETRIE curve, curved line, INFORMAT line graph, MATH curve, NAUT knee; ~ **adiabatique** *f* PHYSIQUE, THERMODYN adiabatic curve; ~ **d'aimantation** *f* ELECTROTEC magnetization curve; ~ **d'amplitude-fréquence** *f* ACOUSTIQUE magnitude-frequency curve; ~ **aplatie** *f* GEOMETRIE flat curve; ~ **caractéristique** *f* CINEMAT *d'une émulsion* characteristic curve, sensitometric curve, ELECTR characteristic curve, ELECTRON characteristic curve, sensitometric curve, ESPACE, PHYSIQUE characteristic curve; ~ **caustique** *f* PHYSIQUE caustic curve; ~ **de charge** *f* ELECTR *réseau*, ELECTROTEC load curve; ~ **de chauffage** *f* PLAST CAOU *moulage, durcissage* heating curve; ~ **de compaction normale** *f* GEOLOGIE, PETROLE *géologie du pétrole* normal trend; ~ **de compressibilité** *f* THERMODYN compressibility curve; ~ **de compression** *f* CHARBON compression curve; ~ **de contact** *f* CONS MECA *engrenages* curve of contact; ~ **de contrainte-déformation** *f* MATERIAUX, PLAST CAOU stress-strain curve; ~ **à coussin d'air** *f* IMPRIM air turn; ~ **dans l'espace** *f* GEOMETRIE *hélice* space curve; ~ **des débits cumulés** *f* HYDROLOGIE discharge mass curve; ~ **des déclenchements** *f* PRODUCTION trip curve; ~ **de décroissance** *f* ENREGISTR decay curve; ~ **de décrue** *f* DISTRI EAU recession curve; ~ **densimétrique** *f* CHARBON specific gravity curve; ~ **des densités** *f* IMPRIM *photogravure* density curve; ~ **de désintégration** *f* PHYS RAYON decay curve; ~ **de distribution** *f* MATH frequency curve; ~ **de distribution de fréquence** *f* MATH *statistiques* frequency distribution curve; ~ **durée de charge** *f* PRODUCTION *automatisme industriel* life-load curve; ~ **durée de vie** *f* PRODUCTION *automatisme industriel* life-load curve; ~ **d'échauffement** *f* THERMODYN heating curve; ~ **d'égalisation** *f* ELECTRON equalization curve; ~ **en chaînette** *f* GEOMETRIE catenary; ~ **de l'énergie de liaison** *f* NUCLEAIRE binding energy curve; ~ **en flocon de neige** *f* GEOMETRIE snowflake curve; ~ **en forme de cloche** *f* GEOMETRIE bell-shaped curve, MATH bell-shaped curve, normal curve; ~ **enveloppe** *f* MECANIQUE envelope curve; ~ **d'expérience** *f* TEXTILE experience curve; ~ **fermée** *f* GEOMETRIE closed curve; ~ **fermée non-simple** *f* GEOMETRIE nonsimple closed curve; ~ **filetée avec manchon** *f* CONS MECA screwed and socketed bend; ~ **de flottabilité** *f* NAUT buoyancy curve; ~ **de flux lumineux** *f* PHOTO time-light output curve; ~ **de fréquence** *f* CINEMAT frequency response; ~ **de fusion** *f* THERMODYN melting point curve; ~ **de gain** *f* ELECTRON gain curve; ~ **de gamma** *f* ELECTRON gamma characteristic; ~ **de Gauss** *f* MATH Gaussian curve, bell-shaped curve, normal curve; ~ **gaussienne** *f* MATH Gaussian curve, bell-shaped curve, normal curve; ~ **de giration** *f* NAUT, VEHICULES turning circle; ~ **à grand rayon** *f* GEOMETRIE flat curve, long radius

curve; ~ **granulométrique** *f* CERAM VER particle size curve, CHARBON grading curve; ~ **hypsographique** *f* GEOLOGIE hypsographic curve; ~ **d'hystérésis** *f* ELECTR hysteresis curve; ~ **isobare météorologique** *f* INST HYDR pressure curve; ~ **isodynamique** *f* GEOPHYS isodynamic line; ~ **d'isofaciès** *f* GEOLOGIE isofacies; ~ **isopoids** *f* AERONAUT isoweight curve; ~ **isosiste** *f* GEOLOGIE isoseismic line; ~ **isotherme** *f* PHYSIQUE isothermal curve; ~ **de luminosité** *f* TV brightness curve; ~ **manométrique** *f* INST HYDR pressure curve; ~ **de marée** *f* OCEANO tide curve; ~ **de mise à température** *f* THERMODYN heating-up curve; ~ **de niveau** *f* CONSTR contour line, GEOLOGIE contour, contour line, subsurface contour; ~ **normale de répartition** *f* MATH bell-shaped distribution curve, normal distribution curve; ~ **pantocarène** *f* NAUT crosscurve; ~ **à petit rayon** *f* GEOMETRIE sharp curve; ~ **piézométrique** *f* INST HYDR piezometric pressure curve; ~ **des points d'ébullition** *f* THERMODYN liquid vapor equilibrium diagram (AmE), liquid vapour equilibrium diagram (BrE); ~ **de la première aimantation** *f* PHYSIQUE initial magnetization curve; ~ **de la première magnétisation** *f* PHYSIQUE initial magnetization curve; ~ **de pression** *f* INST HYDR pressure curve; ~ **des probabilités** *f* MATH probability curve; ~ **de puissance de ventilateur** *f* CHAUFFAGE fan performance curve; ~ **de raccordement** *f* CONSTR transition curve; ~ **raide** *f* CONSTR tight corner; ~ **des rayons sonores** *f* OCEANO sound path, sound ray curve; ~ **de réponse** *f* ELECTRON, ENREGISTR response curve, TV response characteristic; ~ **de réponse amplitude-fréquence** *f* ELECTRON amplitude-frequency response curve; ~ **de réponse électroacoustique enregistrement lecture** *f* ENREGISTR recording-reproducing electroacoustical frequency response; ~ **de réponse en amplitude** *f* ELECTRON amplitude response curve; ~ **de réponse en fréquence** *f* ELECTRON, ENREGISTR frequency response curve; ~ **de réponse d'un filtre elliptique** *f* ELECTRON elliptic response curve; ~ **de réponse phase-fréquence** *f* ACOUSTIQUE phase-frequency response curve; ~ **de réponse spectrale** *f* ELECTRON spectral characteristic; ~ **de réponse totale** *f* ACOUSTIQUE overall response curve; ~ **de résonance** *f* TV resonance curve; ~ **de rotation** *f* ASTRONOMIE *d'une galaxie* rotation curve; ~ **de sensibilité** *f* PHOTO characteristic curve; ~ **sensitométrique** *f* ACOUSTIQUE, CINEMAT characteristic curve, sensitometric curve; ~ **de stabilité** *f* NAUT crosscurve, stability curve; ~ **de tarissement** *f* DISTRI EAU recession curve; ~ **de température** *f* THERMODYN temperature curve; ~ **de température de chauffage** *f* THERMODYN heating temperature curve; ~ **des températures critiques** *f* THERMODYN critical temperature curve; ~ **temps-température** *f* CINEMAT time-temperature curve; ~ **de tension** *f* INSTRUMENT pressure graph; ~ **des tonalités** *f* IMPRIM *photogravure* tone curve; ~ **d'une trajectoire** *f* MILITAIRE *d'un obus* trajectory; ~ **des trames** *f* IMPRIM *photogravure* screen curve; ~ **de travers** *f* GEOMETRIE skewed curve; ~ **d'utilisation** *f* EN RENOUV utilization curve; ~ **vitesse-débit** *f* TRANSPORT speed-volume curve; ~ **vitesses-profondeur** *f* PETROLE *levé sismique* velocity-depth curve

courbement *m* CONSTR *des bois* bending

courber[1] *vt* CONSTR *une pièce de bois*, PRODUCTION bend

courber:[2] ~ **sous une charge** *vi* CONSTR *poutre* bend under a load

courber:[3] **se** ~ *v réfl* CONSTR bend

courbes: ~ **de correction** *f pl* PETR departure curves; ~ **filetées avec manchon** *f pl* CONS MECA screwed and socketed, pipe bends; ~ **hydrostatiques** *f pl* NAUT hydrostatic curves; ~ **de Lissajous** *f pl* PHYSIQUE Lissajous figures; ~ **osculatrices** *f pl* GEOMETRIE osculating curves

courbure *f* CONSTR *des bois* bending, ELECTROTEC bend, GEOMETRIE *de la trajectoire*, MATH curvature, NAUT *d'un chenal* bend, OPTIQUE bending, PHYSIQUE curvature; ~ **de la bande** *f* ENREGISTR, TV tape curvature; ~ **de champ** *f* CINEMAT, PHYSIQUE curvature of field; ~ **de Gauss** *f* GEOMETRIE Gaussian curvature; ~ **de Gauss négative** *f* GEOMETRIE negative Gauss curvature; ~ **de Gauss positive** *f* GEOMETRIE positive Gauss curvature; ~ **intrinsèque** *f* GEOMETRIE intrinsic curvature; ~ **négative** *f* GEOMETRIE negative curvature; ~ **positive** *f* GEOMETRIE positive curvature; ~ **secondaire** *f* CERAM VER secondary curvature; ~ **sectionnelle** *f* GEOMETRIE sectional curvature; ~ **des surfaces** *f* GEOMETRIE curvature of surfaces; ~ **de la Terre** *f* ESPACE Earth's curvature; ~ **transversale de la bande** *f* ENREGISTR, TV tape cupping

courir[1] *vt* HYDROLOGIE flow along; ~ **sur** *vt* NAUT bear down on

courir[2] *vi* NAUT run; ~ **vent arrière** *vi* NAUT run before the wind

couronne *f* ASTRONOMIE corona, MECANIQUE ring, MINES drill bit, PRODUCTION dome, *d'un fourneau* crown, *d'un cabestan* drumhead, *de fil* coil, RESSORTS coil, VEHICULES *différentiel* ring gear; ~ **à barres** *f* PRODUCTION *d'un cabestan* drumhead; ~ **de butée basse** *f* CONS MECA droop restraining ring; ~ **de centrage** *f* CONS MECA location spigot; ~ **de concassage** *f* GENIE CHIM grinding ring; ~ **de démarrage** *f* VEHICULES *moteur* starter ring gear; ~ **dentée** *f* AUTO bevel gearing, ring gear, CONS MECA annular gear; ~ **diamantée** *f* GAZ diamond drill; ~ **de différentiel** *f* AUTO, VEHICULES *transmission* crown wheel; ~ **directrice** *f* INST HYDR *turbine* guide ring; ~ **fixe** *f* INST HYDR *de turbine* guide ring; ~ **fixe de réducteur** *f* AERONAUT fixed ring gear; ~ **de forage** *f* CHARBON drill bit; ~ **de lancement** *f* CONS MECA flywheel ring gear; ~ **des linguets** *f* CONS MECA pawl rim, pawl ring; ~ **mobile** *f* CONS MECA *d'une turbine, d'une pompe centrifuge* runner, PRODUCTION *d'une pompe centrifuge* impeller, *d'une turbine* wheel; ~ **mobile de réduction** *f* AERONAUT first-stage sun gear; ~ **pivotante** *f* CONS MECA *à rouleaux* slewing rim; ~ **de pivotement** *f* TRANSPORT turntable; ~ **planétaire** *f* ASTRONOMIE annulus; ~ **à pointes de diamant** *f* MINES diamond boring crown, diamond crown set, PRODUCTION diamond boring crown; ~ **de renfort** *f* CONSTR *moulage en terre* building ring; ~ **solaire** *f* GEOPHYS solar corona; ~ **de soufflage** *f* CERAM VER blowing crown, blowing ring; ~ **de turbine** *f* INST HYDR turbine ring; ~ **du volant** *f* VEHICULES *moteur* flywheel starter ring gear

Couronne: ~ **australe** *f* ASTRONOMIE Corona Australis; ~ **boréale** *f* ASTRONOMIE Corona Borealis

couronnement *m* CONSTR coping, crest, crowning, DISTRI EAU *des bajoyers d'une écluse* coping, EN RENOUV *barrages*, HYDROLOGIE crest; ~ **de siphon** *m* EN RENOUV *barrages* siphon crest

couronner *vt* CONSTR cap, *le faîte d'un comble* ridge

courrier ~ **électronique** *m* ELECTRON, INFORMAT, ORDINAT, TELECOM E-mail, EM, electronic mail

courroie *f* CERAM VER recirculation, IMPRIM *mécanique*, MECANIQUE belt, PAPIER belt, strap, PHOTO strap, PRODUCTION belt, strap, SECURITE belt-type sling, TEXTILE webbing, VEHICULES belt; ~ **balata** *f* CONS MECA balata belt; ~ **de commande** *f* CONS MECA driving belt; ~ **crantée** *f* CONS MECA toothed drive belt, MECANIQUE timing belt, VEHICULES *distribution* cog belt, notched belt; ~ **à créneaux** *f* CONS MECA cog belt; ~ **croisée** *f* PRODUCTION halved belt (BrE); ~ **de cuir** *f* PRODUCTION leather belt; ~ **demi-tordue** *f* PRODUCTION halved belt (BrE), half belt (AmE); ~ **dentée** *f* VEHICULES *distribution* cog belt; ~ **de distribution** *f* VEHICULES *commande de l'arbre à cames* timing belt; ~ **droite** *f* PAPIER open belt; ~ **en cuir** *f* PRODUCTION leather belt; ~ **d'ensimage** *f* CERAM VER apron applicator; ~ **hexagonale sans fin** *f* CONS MECA endless hexagonal belt; ~ **à hydrocarbures** *f* POLLU MER oleophilic belt; ~ **oléophile** *f* POLLU MER oleophilic belt; ~ **ouverte** *f* PRODUCTION open belt; ~ **plate de transmission** *f* CONS MECA flat transmission belt; ~ **sans fin** *f* PRODUCTION continuous belt, VEHICULES *système de refroidissement* endless belt; ~ **semi-croisée** *f* PRODUCTION quarter belt (AmE), quarter turn belt, quarter twist belt, quartered belt (BrE); ~ **synchrone** *f* CONS MECA synchronous belt; ~ **tordue d'un demi-tour** *f* PRODUCTION half belt (AmE), halved belt (BrE); ~ **tordue d'un quart** *f* PRODUCTION quarter belt (AmE), quarter turn belt, quarter twist belt, quartered belt (BrE); ~ **de transmission** *f* CONS MECA banding, band, belt, driving belt, PAPIER transmission belting, TEXTILE V-belting; ~ **transporteuse** *f* CONS MECA, MINES conveyor belt, PRODUCTION apron, conveyor belt, traveling apron (AmE), travelling apron (BrE), TEXTILE conveyor belt; ~ **transporteuse à cables d'acier** *f* CONS MECA steel cord conveyor belt; ~ **transporteuse à carcasse textile** *f* CONS MECA conveyor belt with a textile carcass; ~ **transporteuse résistant aux flammes** *f* CONS MECA flame-retardant conveyor belt; ~ **trapézoïdale** *f* AUTO, CONS MECA, MECANIQUE, PRODUCTION, VEHICULES *système de refroidissement* V-belt; ~ **trapézoïdale large sans fin** *f* CONS MECA endless wide V-belt; ~ **trapézoïdale sans fin** *f* CONS MECA *antiélectrostatique* endless V-belt; ~ **trapézoïdale striée** *f* CONS MECA ribbed V-belt; ~ **de ventilateur** *f* AUTO, MECANIQUE, VEHICULES *système de refroidissement* fan belt; ~ **de ventilation** *f* AUTO fan belt

courroie-guide *f* PAPIER deckle strap

courroies *f pl* CONS MECA, PRODUCTION belting; ~ **en cuir articulé** *f pl* PLAST CAOU *machine* link belting, PRODUCTION leather-link belting; ~ **en huit épaisseurs** *f pl* PRODUCTION eight-ply belting; ~ **en six épaisseurs** *f pl* PRODUCTION six-ply belting; ~ **à huit plis** *f pl* PRODUCTION eight-ply belting; ~ **à six plis** *f pl* PRODUCTION six-ply belting; ~ **de transmission** *f pl* PRODUCTION belting; ~ **de transmission en caoutchouc** *f pl* CONS MECA rubber belting; ~ **de transmission en cuir** *f pl* PRODUCTION leather belting

cours *m* HYDROLOGIE flow, *d'une rivière* course, MINES run, trend, PHYSIQUE flow; ~ **d'eau** *m* CONSTR watercourse, HYDROLOGIE stream, watercourse, POLLUTION watercourse; ~ **d'eau affluent** *m* HYDROLOGIE tributary channel; ~ **d'eau émissif** *m* HYDROLOGIE influent stream, losing stream; ~ **d'eau perché** *m* HYDROLOGIE perched watercourse; ~ **d'eau tributaire** *m pl* HYDROLOGIE tributary channel; ~ **d'eau au stade de maturité** *m* HYDROLOGIE mature river; ~ **de secourisme** *m pl* SECURITE first-aid course; ~ **des sluices** *m* DISTRI EAU run of sluices; ~ **supérieur** *m* HYDROLOGIE *d'une rivière* upper part

course *f* AERONAUT takeoff run, CONS MECA length of stroke, stroke, *du chariot, du tiroir* travel, CONSTR *d'un piston* stroke, *des pilons* lift, INST HYDR *d'un tiroir* stroke, NUCLEAIRE length of stroke, lift, stroke, travel, TEXTILE traverse; ~ **d'admission** *f* VEHICULES *moteur* induction stroke; ~ **aller** *f* INST HYDR outstroke; ~ **arrière** *f* CONS MECA return stroke; ~ **ascendante** *f* AUTO, CONS MECA, VEHICULES *moteur, piston* upstroke; ~ **à l'atterrissage** *f* AERONAUT landing run; ~ **avant** *f* INST HYDR outstroke; ~ **de la balade** *f* IMPRIM *d'une table d'encrage ou de mouillage* stroke; ~ **à blanc** *f* CONS MECA noncutting stroke, *outil* idle stroke; ~ **du clapet** *f* INST HYDR valve travel; ~ **de combustion** *f* AUTO power stroke; ~ **de compression** *f* AUTO, THERMODYN, VEHICULES *moteur* compression stroke; ~ **descendante** *f* AUTO downstroke, CONS MECA, MECANIQUE downstroke, downward stroke, VEHICULES *moteur* downstroke; ~ **de détente** *f* CONS MECA, THERMODYN expansion stroke; ~ **directe** *f* INST HYDR outstroke; ~ **d'échappement** *f* AUTO, VEHICULES *moteur* exhaust stroke; ~ **d'essai** *f* NUCLEAIRE precommissioning checks, proving run, trial run; ~ **de gouverne de direction** *f* AERONAUT rudder travel; ~ **morte** *f* AUTO free travel, ELECTROTEC pretravel; ~ **motrice** *f* THERMODYN expansion stroke; ~ **de l'outil** *f* CONS MECA length of stroke; ~ **d'ouverture** *f* PRODUCTION opening travel; ~ **du piston** *f* CONS MECA piston stroke, stroke of ram, CONSTR length of piston stroke; ~ **piston** *f* PHYSIQUE stroke; ~ **de recul** *f* CONS MECA backward stroke; ~ **de retour** *f* CONS MECA return stroke, INST HYDR *du piston* instroke; ~ **de retour du piston** *f* INST HYDR piston back stroke; ~ **rétrograde** *f* CONS MECA return stroke; ~ **du tiroir** *f* INST HYDR valve travel; ~ **utile** *f* CONS MECA cutting stroke; ~ **verticale** *f* CONS MECA *de l'arbre porte-foret* traverse, PRODUCTION *d'un porte-foret, d'un porte-outil* fall; ~ **à vide** *f* CONS MECA noncutting stroke, *outil* idle stroke

coursive *f* NAUT alleyway, gangway

court[1] *adj* CERAM VER steep; **à ~ de personnel** *adj* PRODUCTION, TRANSPORT undermanned

court:[2] ~ **courrier** *m* TRANSPORT short-haul airliner; ~ **métrage** *m* CINEMAT short; ~ **terme** *m* PRODUCTION short term

court-circuit[1] *adj* PHYSIQUE short-circuit, short-circuited, TELECOM short-circuit

court-circuit[2] *m* ELECTR short circuit, ELECTROTEC short, short circuit, INFORMAT, ORDINAT, PHYSIQUE, TELECOM short circuit; ~ **entre phases** *m* ELECTR interphase short circuit; ~ **entre phases en sortie** *m* ELECTR, PRODUCTION output phase-to-phase short circuit; ~ **franc** *m* ELECTROTEC dead short circuit; ~ **magnétique** *m* ELECTR *aimant* keeper; ~ **réglable** *m* ELECTROTEC adjustable short circuit

court-circuitage *m* ELECTROTEC shorting

court-circuiter *vt* ELECTROTEC short

court-circuiteur: ~ **de mise à la terre** *m* GEOPHYS earth arrester (BrE), ground arrester (AmE)

courtier: ~ **d'affrètement** *m* NAUT chartering broker; ~ **maritime** *m* NAUT ship broker

co-usager *m* TELECOM joint user

coussin *m* AUTO pad; ~ **d'air** *m* AERONAUT, CONS MECA *engin de manutention*, NAUT, TRANSPORT air cushion; ~ **d'air à cloche** *m* TRANSPORT plenum chamber air cushion system; ~ **d'air à gonflage instantané** *m* TRANSPORT air cushion restraint system; ~ **d'air à jet périphérique** *m* TRANSPORT peripheral jet air cushion; ~ **d'air à jupes rigides** *m* TRANSPORT rigid sidewall air cushion; ~ **d'air multiple à jupes souples** *m* TRANSPORT multiple-skirted plenum chamber; ~ **d'air négatif** *m* TRANSPORT negative air cushion; ~ **d'air statique** *m* TRANSPORT static air cushion; ~ **anticoulissant** *m* PRODUCTION antislide pad; ~ **antidérapant** *m* PRODUCTION antislide pad; ~ **à bulles d'air captives** *m* TRANSPORT sidewall air cushion; ~ **électrique** *m* THERMODYN electric heating pad; ~ **de guidage** *m* TRANSPORT guidance cushion; ~ **magnétique** *m* TRANSPORT magnetic cushion, magnetic cushion train; ~ **de siège** *m* VEHICULES seat cushion

coussinet *m* CH DE FER bearing, CONS MECA bearing bush, bearing, bottom brass, pillow, screwing die, CONSTR springer, springer stone, springing, IMPRIM bearing, MECANIQUE bearing, bushing, PRODUCTION die head, TEXTILE pad, VEHICULES bearing; ~ **à auto-alignement** *m* CONS MECA self-aligning bearing; ~ **autolubrifiant** *m* CONS MECA oilless bearing; ~ **d'axe** *m* VEHICULES *transmission* axle bush, axle bushing; ~ **d'axe de piston** *m* AUTO piston pin bushing; ~ **de balancier de renvoi** *m* CONS MECA rocker bearing; ~ **de bielle** *m* AUTO connecting rod bearing; ~ **en deux pièces** *m* CONS MECA die in two halves; ~ **en une pièce** *m* CONS MECA one-part die; ~ **fendu** *m* CONS MECA split die; ~ **de filière** *m* RESSORTS adjustable screw die; ~ **de filière radial** *m* CONS MECA radial threading die; ~ **de filière tangentiel** *m* CONS MECA tangential threading die; ~ **gazeux** *m* NUCLEAIRE gas lubricated bearing; ~ **à graissage automatique** *m* CONS MECA self-lubricating bearing; ~ **inférieur** *m* CONS MECA bottom brass; ~ **lisse** *m* VEHICULES plain bearing; ~ **non fendu** *m* CONS MECA unsplit bush; ~ **de palier** *m* AUTO crankshaft bearing, main bearing bushing; ~ **à rapprochement concentrique** *m* CONS MECA self-centering die (AmE), self-centring die (BrE); ~ **d'une seule pièce** *m* CONS MECA one-part die; ~ **supérieur** *m* CONS MECA top brass; ~ **de tête de bielle** *m* AUTO, VEHICULES big end bearing

coussinet-lunette *m* PRODUCTION die

coussinets: ~ **à coude** *m pl* SECURITE elbow pads; ~ **en bronze** *m pl* CONS MECA *d'un mandrin* gunmetal bearings; ~ **en fonte garnis d'un alliage antifriction** *m pl* CONS MECA babbitted cast-iron bearings; ~ **pour coudes** *m pl* SECURITE elbow pads; ~ **pour genoux** *m pl* SECURITE knee pads

coût: ~ **assurance fret** *m* PRODUCTION CIF, cost insurance freight; ~ **d'évaluation** *m* QUALITE appraisal cost; ~ **de fonctionnement** *m* QUALITE operating cost; ~ **d'homologation** *m* QUALITE approval cost; ~ **d'investissement** *m* QUALITE capital cost; ~ **main-d'oeuvre** *m* PRODUCTION labor cost (AmE), labour cost (BrE); ~ **de maintenance** *m* QUALITE maintenance cost; ~ **de prévention** *m* QUALITE prevention cost; ~ **de production** *m* PRODUCTION labor cost (AmE), labour cost (BrE); ~ **de la qualité** *m* QUALITE quality cost; ~ **de stockage** *m* PRODUCTION warehousing charge; ~ **supplémentaire** *m* IMPRIM additional charge; ~ **travail** *m* PRODUCTION labor cost (AmE), labour cost (BrE); ~ **de l'unité d'oeuvre** *m* CONSTR accounting ratio

couteau *m* CERAM VER cutter blade, CHARBON scraper, CONS MECA cutter, *d'une mèche à trois pointes* router, MECANIQUE *outillage* knife, PRODUCTION *d'une balance* knife edge, TEXTILE knife; ~ **d'air** *m* IMPRIM air knife; ~

central *m* CONS MECA middle knife-edge, METROLOGIE center knife edge (AmE), centre knife edge (BrE); ~ **de coupeuse** *m* PAPIER chipper knife; ~ **de coupure** *m* ELECTR *relais* contact blade; ~ **de déclenche** *m* CONS MECA trip catch; ~ **à délisser** *m* PAPIER rag cutter; ~ **à démastiquer** *m* CONSTR hacking knife, putty knife; ~ **d'encrier** *m* IMPRIM ink knife; ~ **à fendre** *m* SECURITE riving knife; ~ **du fléau** *m* CONS MECA middle knife-edge, METROLOGIE center knife edge (AmE), centre knife edge (BrE); ~ **générateur** *m* CONS MECA generating cutter; ~ **à lame rétractable** *m* CONS MECA retractable blade knife; ~ **à mastiquer** *m* CONSTR putty knife, stopping knife; ~ **nettoyeur** *m* EMBALLAGE doctor blade; ~ **à palette** *m* EQUIP LAB *peinture* palette knife (BrE), pallet knife (AmE); ~ **à parer** *m* CONSTR putty knife; ~ **de peintre à enduire** *m* CONS MECA palette knife (BrE), pallet knife (AmE); ~ **pour sacs** *m* EMBALLAGE sack knife; ~ **universel** *m* CONS MECA utility knife

couteaux: ~ **du fléau** *m pl* METROLOGIE *d'une balance* knife edges

coutellerie *f* AGRO ALIM silverware

coûteux: ~ **en combustible** *adj* ESPACE *véhicules* fuel-costly

coûts: ~ **d'exploitation** *m pl* TEXTILE running costs

couture *f* CERAM VER mold mark (AmE), mould mark (BrE), seam, CONS MECA seam, IMPRIM sewing, PAPIER *de la toile de machine*, TEXTILE seam; ~ **à cheval** *f* IMPRIM pamphlet stitching; ~ **ébaucheur** *f* CERAM VER blank mold seam (AmE), blank mould seam (BrE), blank seam; ~ **au fil textile** *f* IMPRIM pamphlet stitching; ~ **de fond ébaucheur** *f* CERAM VER baffle mark; ~ **longue** *f* IMPRIM seam; ~ **rivetée** *f* EMBALLAGE riveted seam; ~ **soudée** *f* PAPIER welded seam

coutures: ~ **inégales** *f pl* TEXTILE mismatched seams

couver *vi* PRODUCTION breed, THERMODYN smolder (AmE), smoulder (BrE)

couvercle *m* CERAM VER stopper, CONS MECA cover, EMBALLAGE lid, EN RENOUV *d'un récepteur* cover plate, EQUIP LAB *récipient* lid, IMPRIM *emballage, métal* cap, INST HYDR cover, *de boîte à vapeur* cap, MECANIQUE cap, coupling sleeve, cover, lid, NAUT bonnet, POLLUTION lid, SECURITE chaincase; ~ **articulé** *m* PRODUCTION hinge cover; ~ **d'aspiration** *m* REFRIG suction cover; ~ **avant de cylindre** *m* INST HYDR *locomotive ou machine à vapeur fixe* front cylinder cover, front cylinder head; ~ **avec ouverture par clé** *m* EMBALLAGE key-opening lid; ~ **avec patte d'arrachage** *m* EMBALLAGE tear tab lid; ~ **de bornes** *m* PRODUCTION terminal coverplate; ~ **à charnières** *m* EMBALLAGE hinged lid; ~ **à crochet** *m* EMBALLAGE hooked lid; ~ **de distribution** *m* AUTO timing cover; ~ **du dôme** *m* PRODUCTION dome cap, dome head; ~ **à enclenchement** *m* EMBALLAGE snap-on lid; ~ **du logement de la pile** *m* PHOTO battery chamber cover, battery compartment cover; ~ **mobile** *m* EMBALLAGE sliding lid; ~ **de palier** *m* CONS MECA bearing cap; ~ **du piston** *m* CONS MECA follower, PRODUCTION junk ring; ~ **plat** *m* PRODUCTION straight hood; ~ **porte-gicleur** *m* AERONAUT fuel jet support cover; ~ **rentrant** *m* EMBALLAGE lever lid; ~ **à vis** *m* EMBALLAGE screw lid, screw top

couvert *adj* METEO overcast

couverte *f* PAPIER deckle

couverture:[1] **à ~ souple** *adj* IMPRIM *reliure* limpbound

couverture[2] *f* CONSTR application rate, coating, roof, roofing, ESPACE *véhicules* blanket, GEOLOGIE cover, IMPRIM cover, *d'un livre* case, PETROLE cap rock, SECURITE cover, TELECOM coverage, TEXTILE blanket, cover; ~ **d'argon** *f* NUCLEAIRE argon gas blanket; ~ **avec gaz inerte** *f* NUCLEAIRE inert gas blanketing, inerting system; ~ **d'azote** *f* NUCLEAIRE nitrogen cover gas; ~ **de la boîte à étoupe** *f* NUCLEAIRE gland, stuffing box lid; ~ **du carton** *f* PAPIER liner; ~ **électrique** *f* CHAUFFAGE electric blanket; ~ **d'un émetteur** *f* TV station coverage; ~ **en caoutchouc** *f* REVETEMENT rubber coating; ~ **en encre** *f* IMPRIM *impression* ink lay-down, *processus* ink coverage; ~ **en zinc** *f* REVETEMENT hot covering; ~ **étanche** *f* GAZ impermeable layer; ~ **globale** *f* TELECOM, TRANSPORT global coverage; ~ **hémisphérique** *f* TELECOM hemispherical coverage; ~ **imperméable** *f* GAZ impermeable layer; ~ **d'incendie** *f* SECURITE fire blanket; ~ **insonorisante pour caméra** *f* CINEMAT barney; ~ **kraft** *f* PAPIER kraft liner; ~ **neigeuse** *f* METEO snow cover; ~ **nuageuse** *f* AERONAUT cloud cover, METEO cloud amount, cloud cover; ~ **de l'orifice d'échappement** *f* INST HYDR *d'un distributeur à tiroir* exhaust cover, exhaust lap; ~ **par faisceaux ponctuels** *f* TELECOM spot beam coverage; ~ **par radar** *f* TRANSPORT radar range; ~ **piquée** *f* TEXTILE quilt; ~ **réfrigérante** *f* REFRIG hypothermic blanket; ~ **d'un réseau** *f* TV network coverage; ~ **de sauvetage** *f* SECURITE rescue blanket; ~ **spéciale pour cartonnage** *f* EMBALLAGE test liner board; ~ **de survie** *f* SECURITE rescue blanket

couvinien *adj* GEOLOGIE Couvinian

couvre-culasse *m* MILITAIRE breech cover

couvre-engrenages *m* CONS MECA case, casing, cover, guard, wheel guard

couvre-joint *m* CONS MECA cover strip, CONSTR cover, MECANIQUE butt plate, butt strap, PRODUCTION butt strap, butt strip, covering plate

couvre-meule *m* PRODUCTION hood for emery wheel

couvre-objet *m* CERAM VER cover glass, cover slip

couvre-roue *m* CONS MECA guard, wheel guard, SECURITE guard, machine guard

couvreur *m* CONSTR roofer

couvrir[1] *vt* CINEMAT *objectif* cap up, PHYSIQUE cover; ~ **de fondant** *vt* MATERIAUX *soudure* flux

couvrir:[2] **se ~ de nuages** *v réfl* METEO cloud over

covalence *f* CHIMIE, NUCLEAIRE covalence, covalency

covalent *adj* CHIMIE covalent

covariance *f* ORDINAT covariance

covellite *f* MINERAUX covelline, covellite

covoiturage *m* TRANSPORT car pool, car pooling

coyau *m* CONSTR furring, furring piece

CPG *abrév* (*chromatographie en phase gazeuse*) AGRO ALIM, CHIMIE, MATERIAUX gas chromatography

CPP *abrév* (*concentré de protéines de poisson*) OCEANO FPC (*fish protein concentrate*)

CPS *abrév* (*caractères par seconde*) IMPRIM, ORDINAT CPS (*characters per second*)

CPUE *abrév* (*prise par unité d'effort*) OCEANO CUE (*catch per unit effort*)

Cr (*chrome*) CHIMIE Cr (*chromium*)

crabot *m* AUTO clutch sleeve, sliding sleeve, CONS MECA dog

crabotage *m* AUTO jaw clutching, CONS MECA dog clutch

crachat *m* CERAM VER dirt, feather

crachement *m* ~ **aux balais** *m* ELECTR commutator sparking, *machine* brush sparking

cracher *vi* ELECTROTEC arc, THERMODYN flash over

crachin m METEO drizzle

cradle m MINES cradle, cradle rocker, mining cradle, rocker

craie f GEOLOGIE chalk; ~ **bleue** f CONSTR chalk marl; ~ **fracturée et faillée** f CONSTR fractured and faulted chalk; ~ **marneuse** f CONSTR, GEOLOGIE chalk marl; ~ **sableuse** f GEOLOGIE sandy chalk

crain m MINES leap

craint: ~ **l'humidité** loc EMBALLAGE keep dry

crampon m CH DE FER voie dog spike, CONS MECA clamp, holdfast, CONSTR cramp, cramp iron, hook, spike, staple, timber dogs, PRODUCTION dog iron; ~ **à deux pointes** m CONSTR staple; ~ **de fermeture** m CONSTR sash fastener, window catch, window fastener; ~ **à scellement** m CONSTR cramp iron with stone hook

cramponner vt CONS MECA cramp

cran m CONS MECA notch, CRISTALL jog, leap, METALL jog, MINES leap, PRODUCTION fault, notch; ~ **absorbeur de lacunes** m METALL vacancy absorbing jog; ~ **d'arrêt** m CONS MECA catch; ~ **de détente d'un secteur denté** m INST HYDR expansion notch; ~ **émetteur de lacunes** m METALL vacancy emitting jog; ~ **d'immobilisation** m PHOTO click stop; ~ **de point mort** m CONS MECA secteur denté dead-center notch (AmE), dead-centre notch (BrE); ~ **de repos** m CONS MECA safety catch; ~ **de sûreté** m CONS MECA, MILITAIRE safety catch

cranté adj CONS MECA notched

cranter vt CONS MECA notch

crapaud m CH DE FER rail clip, voie rail clip; ~ **de patinage** m CH DE FER voie wheel slide mark, wheel slip mark on rails

crapaudine f CH DE FER center casting (AmE), centre casting (BrE), center plate (AmE), centre plate (BrE), pivot bearing, CONS MECA footstep, footstep bearing, shaft step, step, step bearing, step box, PRODUCTION main casting, plug

craquage m PETROLE cracking; ~ **avec fixation du coke** m CHARBON coking cracking; ~ **catalytique** m CHIMIE, PETROLE catalytic cracking; ~ **catalytique fluide** m GENIE CHIM fluid cracking; ~ **catalytique à lit fluide** m GENIE CHIM fluid-catalyst process; ~ **thermique** m PETROLE thermal cracking; ~ **à la vapeur d'eau** m PETROLE steam cracking

craquelage m MATERIAUX, PLAST CAOU défaut cracking

craquelé m CONSTR crazing

craquelure f CERAM VER crizzle, CONSTR, PLAST CAOU crazing

craquelures f pl CONS MECA fine cracks

craquer vi CRISTALL crack

crasse f PRODUCTION cinder; ~ **de fonte** f PRODUCTION clinker

crasses f pl PRODUCTION dans poches ou moules sullage; ~ **des chaudières** f pl PRODUCTION fur, scale

crassier m MINES dump, slack heap, spoil heap, tip heap, PRODUCTION cinder bank, slag dump, slag heap, slag tip

cratère m ASTRONOMIE, ESPACE géophysique, GEOLOGIE, MINES, PLAST CAOU défaut de peinture crater; ~ **adventif** m GEOLOGIE volcanique lateral crater, parasitic crater; ~ **d'effondrement** m GEOLOGIE sinkhole, swallow hole; ~ **d'impact** m ESPACE géophysique impact crater; ~ **météorique** m ASTRONOMIE meteor crater; ~ **d'un volcan éteint** m GEOLOGIE maar

cratères: ~ **de la lune** m pl ASTRONOMIE lunar craters

craton m GEOLOGIE craton

crayeuse f IMPRIM impression chalking

crayeux adj GEOLOGIE chalky

crayon m IMPRIM wand; ~ **absorbant** m NUCLEAIRE absorber rod; ~ **absorbant noir** m NUCLEAIRE black absorber rod; ~ **d'angle** m NUCLEAIRE bundle corner rod, corner rod, fuel assembly corner rod; ~ **de code à barres** m INFORMAT bar code pen; ~ **combustible défectueux** m NUCLEAIRE defective fuel rod; ~ **combustible en forme de javelot** m NUCLEAIRE javelin-shaped fuel rod; ~ **combustible ventilé** m NUCLEAIRE vented fuel rod; ~ **gras** m CINEMAT chinagraph, grease pencil; ~ **lumineux** m PHYSIQUE light pen; ~ **optique** m INFORMAT, ORDINAT light gun, TV light pen; ~ **segmenté** m NUCLEAIRE de combustible segmented fuel rod

crayon-lecteur m INFORMAT, ORDINAT wand scanner

CRC abrév (contrôle de redondance cyclique) COMMANDE, ELECTRON, ORDINAT CRC (cyclical redundancy check)

création: ~ **de données** f INFORMAT, ORDINAT data origination; ~ **d'enregistrement** f INFORMAT, ORDINAT record creation; ~ **de fichier** f INFORMAT, ORDINAT file creation; ~ **d'une tonalité parasite** f IMPRIM tinting

creep m PLAST CAOU creep

créer vt INFORMAT, ORDINAT create, TEXTILE style

crémage m PLAST CAOU opération creaming

crémaillère:[1] à ~ adj MECANIQUE rack-and-pinion

crémaillère[2] f CH DE FER rack rail, rail, CINEMAT rackover, CONS MECA cog rail, rack, rack, slip joint, CONSTR cut string, open string, INSTRUMENT rack-and-pinion, MECANIQUE rack, rack-and-pinion, PAPIER rack, PRODUCTION rack-and-pinion, système hydraulique rack, TRANSPORT rack, rack rail, rack track, VEHICULES direction rack; ~ **d'avance** f CONS MECA feed rack; ~ **et pignon** f CONS MECA rack-and-pinion; ~ **de fixation** f INSTRUMENT focus knob, focusing knob; ~ **qui engrène avec un pignon** f CONS MECA rack which engages with a pinion, ~ **de référence** f CONS MECA engrenages basic rack; ~ **à vis sans fin** f CONS MECA worm rack

crème f AGRO ALIM slurry; ~ **de noix de coco** f AGRO ALIM coconut cream; ~ **de protection pour le travail** f SECURITE occupational safety cream; ~ **protectrice** f SECURITE protective cream, skin cream; ~ **de tartre** f AGRO ALIM, CHIMIE cream of tartar

crémone f CONSTR lock bolt; ~ **de sûreté** f SECURITE panic bolt

crénage m IMPRIM typographie kern

créneau m CINEMAT position, ESPACE véhicules slot, TRANSPORT gap, TV slot; ~ **de dépassement** m TRANSPORT divided highway (AmE), dual carriageway (BrE); ~ **horaire** m TV airtime; ~ **de pointe** m TV prime time slot; ~ **publicitaire** m TV advertising slot; ~ **de sensibilisation** m ELECTRON indicator gate; ~ **temporel** m TELECOM, TV time slot; ~ **de temps** m ESPACE communications time slot; ~ **de voie** m CH DE FER distance between sleepers

crénelage m CONS MECA toothing, ORDINAT aliasing

créneler vt CONS MECA ratch

crénulation f GEOLOGIE crenulation, microfold

créosote f CHIMIE creosote

crêpage m PAPIER creping; ~ **hors machine** m PAPIER off-machine creping; ~ **humide** m PAPIER wet creping; ~ **à sec** m PAPIER dry creping; ~ **sur machine** m PAPIER on-machine creping

crêpe[1] m CHIMIE, TEXTILE crepe; ~ **lourd** m PAPIER heavy crepe

crêpe:[2] **~ de glace** *f* OCEANO pancake ice

crêpé *adj* PAPIER, TEXTILE creped

crépi *m* CONSTR roughcast

crépine *f* AUTO oil strainer, strainer, CH DE FER *véhicules* water strainer, DISTRI EAU rose, strainer, tailpiece, wind bore, GAZ strainer; **~ d'aspiration** *f* DISTRI EAU rose, strainer, tailpiece, wind bore, PRODUCTION suction strainer, *système hydraulique* inlet strainer

crépitement *m* ENREGISTR crackle

crésol *m* CHIMIE o-cresol

crétacé *m* GEOLOGIE, PETROLE Cretaceous Period

crête:[1] **~ à crête** *adv* TV peak-to-peak

crête[2] *f* CONSTR crest, ridge, DISTRI EAU *d'un barrage, d'un déversoir*, GEOLOGIE *d'un pli anticlinal*, HYDROLOGIE crest, NAUT ridge; **~ du blanc** *f* TV peak white, white peak; **~ de courant** *f* ELECTR current peak; **~ monoclinale symétrique** *f* GEOLOGIE hogback; **~ de niveau** *f* TV peak; **~ du noir** *f* TV black peak; **~ de plage** *f* OCEANO beach ridge; **~ de pression** *f* OCEANO pressure ridge; **~ d'une vague** *f* EN RENOUV, OCEANO wave crest

crêtemètre *m* TV peak meter

creusage *m* CONSTR digging, MINES sinking

creusé *adj* MILITAIRE dug-out

creusement *m* CHARBON digging, redriving, CONSTR digging, excavating, excavation, hollowing, hollowing out, MINES sinking; **~ contrôlé** *m* CHARBON control driving; **~ en tranchées** *m* CONSTR cut and cover; **~ de fossés** *m* CONSTR trenching; **~ de tranchées** *m* CONSTR trenching

creuser *vt* GEOLOGIE channel, PRODUCTION hollow, hollow out

creuset *m* CHIMIE crucible, melting pot, EQUIP LAB *récipient* crucible, GAZ hearth, IMPRIM *composition chaude* pot, MAT CHAUFF crucible, *four* hearth, PRODUCTION hearth, melter, melting pot, *d'un haut fourneau* crucible, THERMODYN crucible, melting crucible, melting pot; **~ en graphite** *m* PRODUCTION blue pot, plumbago crucible; **~ en mine de plomb** *m* PRODUCTION black lead crucible, blue pot, plumbago crucible; **~ en platine** *m* EQUIP LAB *récipient* platinum crucible; **~ en plombagine** *m* PRODUCTION blue pot, plumbago crucible; **~ en porcelaine** *m* CERAM VER, EQUIP LAB *récipient* porcelain crucible; **~ en terre réfractaire** *m* CERAM VER clay crucible, fireclay crucible; **~ filtrant à plaque de verre fritté** *m* EQUIP LAB *verrerie, filtration* sintered glass filter crucible; **~ à filtration Gooch** *m* EQUIP LAB Gooch crucible; **~ de plombagine** *m* PRODUCTION black lead crucible, blue pot; **~ réducteur** *m* PRODUCTION reduction crucible

creux *m* CERAM VER undercut, CHIMIE *d'un réservoir* ullage, CONS MECA dent, hole, space, CONSTR hollow, hollowness, MECANIQUE *engrenages* dedendum, MINES cavity, NAUT *architecture* depth, *houle* trough, *voile* belly, OCEANO *ondes* hollow, trough, PETROLE *d'un réservoir* ullage, PRODUCTION mold (AmE), mould (BrE), pass, *d'une vis* groove, tooth; **~ du bandage** *m* CH DE FER *véhicules* hollow tread; **~ barométrique** *m* METEO barometric trough, trough; **~ de cale** *m* NAUT registered depth; **~ central d'indice** *m* OPTIQUE, TELECOM index dip; **~ du cylindre** *m* IMPRIM *hauteur des cordons* bearer height, *rotatives* undercut; **~ dépressionnaire** *m* METEO trough; **~ de franc-bord** *m* NAUT depth for freeboard; **~ sur quille** *m* NAUT molded depth (AmE), moulded depth (BrE); **~ de tension** *m* ELECTROTEC brownout, drop-out

crevaison *f* CONSTR bursting

crevasse *f* CERAM VER tearing, GEOPHYS fissure, MATERIAUX split, OCEANO cleft, fissure

crevassé *adj* MATERIAUX cracked, fractured

crevasser[1] *vi* CH DE FER, CONS MECA split

crevasser:[2] **se ~** *v réfl* CH DE FER, CONS MECA split

crever *vt* CONSTR *les tuyaux* burst

crevettier *m* NAUT shrimp boat, OCEANO shrimp boat, shrimper

criblage *m* CERAM VER pitting, CONSTR filtering, screening, sieving, sifting, MINES jigging, POLLU MER screening, sieving, sifting, PRODUCTION griddling, riddling, screening, sifting; **~ du ballast** *m* CH DE FER ballast screening; **~ à l'eau** *m* CHARBON wet screening

crible *m* CHARBON screen, CONSTR screen, sieve, HYDROLOGIE screen, MINES jigger screen, PRODUCTION cribble, griddle, riddle, screen; **~ à barreaux** *m* CHARBON grizzly; **~ à bascule** *m* CHARBON swing sieve; **~ à chocs** *m* CHARBON impact screen; **~ classeur** *m* PRODUCTION sizing screen; **~ déschlammeur** *m* CHARBON desliming screen; **~ d'égouttage** *m* CHARBON draining screen; **~ en toile métallique** *m* PRODUCTION wire cloth screen, wire sieve, wire screen, wire-wove screen; **~ en tôle perforée** *m* CONSTR punched plate screen; **~ de fil de fer** *m* PRODUCTION wire screen, wire sieve; **~ à grille filtrante** *m* PRODUCTION filter screen; **~ à grille fixe** *m* MINES jig, PRODUCTION fixed sieve jig; **~ à grille mobile** *m* MINES jig; **~ à grosses mailles** *m* CHARBON coarse mesh screen, cribble, coarse screen, riddle; **~ hydraulique** *m* CHARBON, MINES jig; **~ hydraulique à piston** *m* MINES jig, PRODUCTION fixed sieve jig, plunger jig; **~ à manivelle** *m* CHARBON swing sieve; **~ oscillant** *m* NUCLEAIRE *vibration* jig table, PRODUCTION swinging screen; **~ à percussion** *m* PRODUCTION impact screen, percussion sieve; **~ à piston** *m* MINES jig, PRODUCTION fixed sieve jig, plunger jig; **~ de reclassement** *m* CHARBON nut sizing screen; **~ à résonance** *m* CHARBON resonance screen; **~ de rinçage** *m* CHARBON spraying screen; **~ rotatif** *m* PRODUCTION rotary screen; **~ à rouleaux** *m* CHARBON roll screen; **~ scalpeur** *m* CHARBON scalping screen; **~ à secousse** *m* PRODUCTION bumping screen, push screen, shaking screen; **~ à tambour** *m* GENIE CHIM sieve drum; **~ à tout-venant** *m* CHARBON raw coal screen; **~ vibrant** *m* CHARBON vibrating screen; **~ à vibrations circulaires** *m* CHARBON circular vibrating screen

cribler *vt* CHARBON screen, CONSTR honeycomb, screen, sift, GENIE CHIM separate, sieve, HYDROLOGIE sieve, POLLU MER screen, sift

criblés: **~ 80** *m* CHARBON lump coal

cribleuse *f* PRODUCTION riddler, sand riddler, sand sifter, sifter

cric *m* CONS MECA jack, lifting jack, MECANIQUE jack, PRODUCTION hoisting jack, VEHICULES *outil* jack; **~ de charpentier** *m* CONSTR timber jack; **~ à crémaillère** *m* CONS MECA rack-and-pinion jack; **~ hydraulique** *m* INST HYDR hydraulic jack; **~ à levier** *m* CONS MECA lifting jack, PRODUCTION lever jack

crichtonite *f* MINERAUX crichtonite

cric-tenseur *m* CONS MECA strainer, CONSTR tumbuckle, wire strainer, wire stretcher

crin *m* MINES stringer

crique *f* CONSTR crazing, CRISTALL crack, HYDROLOGIE inlet, MECANIQUE *matériaux* crack, NAUT creek; **~ initiale** *f* NUCLEAIRE fatigue precrack

crise: **~ d'ébullition** *f* NUCLEAIRE critical heat flow, departure from nuclear boiling; ~ **énergétique** *f* THER-MODYN energy crisis; ~ **d'énergie** *f* THERMODYN energy crisis

crispage *m* PAPIER cockle finish

cristal *m* CERAM VER, CHIMIE, CRISTALL, ELECTRON crystal, PAPIER glassine; ~ **aciculaire** *m* MATERIAUX acicular crystal; ~ **allongé et mince** *m* GEOLOGIE lath; ~ **blanc** *m* CHIMIE alban; ~ **de Bohème** *m* CERAM VER Bohemian crystal; ~ **de Bragg** *m* CRISTALL Bragg cell; ~ **colonnaire** *m* METALL columnar crystal; ~ **en forme de lattes** *m* GEOLOGIE lath; ~ **ferroélectrique** *m* ELEC-TROTEC ferroelectric crystal; ~ **germe** *m* CRISTALL seed crystal; ~ **idiomorphe** *m* METALL idiomorphic crystal; ~ **liquide** *m* CRISTALL, NUCLEAIRE, TELECOM liquid crystal; ~ **parfait** *m* METALL perfect crystal; ~ **piézoé-lectrique** *m* ELECTROTEC, MATERIAUX, TELECOM piezoelectric crystal; ~ **au plomb** *m* CERAM VER lead crystal glass; ~ **presque parfait** *m* METALL nearly perfect crystal; ~ **de quartz** *m* ELECTR *horloge électrique*, ELECTRON, INFORMAT, ORDINAT quartz crystal; ~ **semi-conducteur** *m* ELECTRON semiconductor crystal; ~ **de silicium** *m* ELECTRON silicon crystal; ~ **de sucre** *m* AGRO ALIM sugar nucleus; ~ **supérieur** *m* CERAM VER full-lead crystal glass

cristallin *adj* CERAM VER crystallin, CHIMIE, CRISTALL, MATERIAUX crystalline

cristallisation *f* CRISTALL, PLAST CAOU *procédé* crystallization; ~ **fractionnée** *f* GEOLOGIE *processus magmatique* fractional crystallization; ~ **isotherme** *f* MATERIAUX isothermal crystallization; ~ **partielle** *f* MATERIAUX partial crystallization

cristallisé: ~ **en phase vapeur** *adj* GENIE CHIM vapor-grown (AmE), vapour-grown (BrE)

cristalliser *vi* GENIE CHIM crystallize out

cristallisoir *m* CERAM VER glass dish, EQUIP LAB dish, crystallizing dish, GENIE CHIM crystallization basin, crystallizer, MATERIAUX *processus* crystallizer

cristallite *f* CRISTALL crystallite

cristallochimie *f* MATERIAUX crystal chemistry

cristallographie *f* METALL crystallography

cristallographique *adj* MATERIAUX crystallographic

cristaux: ~ **de chambre** *m pl* GENIE CHIM chamber crystals; ~ **liquides** *m pl* ELECTRON, PETROLE liquid crystals; ~ **liquides dichroïques** *m pl* ELECTRON dichroic liquid crystals; ~ **liquides nématiques** *m pl* ELECTRON nematic liquid crystals; ~ **liquides smectiques** *m pl* ELECTRON smectic liquid crystals; ~ **de soude** *m pl* LESSIVES soda ash

cristobalite *f* MINERAUX cristobalite

critère *m* INFORMAT, ORDINAT criterion; ~ **d'acceptation** *m* ESPACE *véhicules* acceptance criterion, PRODUCTION allowance; ~ **de conception** *m* NUCLEAIRE, PRODUC-TION design criterion; ~ **de Griffith** *m* NUCLEAIRE Griffith's fracture criterion; ~ **de Rayleigh** *m* PHYSIQUE Rayleigh criterion; ~ **de ruine** *m* MECANIQUE criterion of failure; ~ **de rupture** *m* METALL fracture criterion

critères: ~ **de conception et d'essais** *m pl* PRODUCTION design specification and requirements; ~ **d'implanta-tion** *m pl* POLLUTION site criteria; ~ **de qualité** *m pl* CONS MECA quality acceptance criteria; ~ **de risque** *m pl* QUALITE risk criteria

criticité: ~ **initiale** *f* NUCLEAIRE first criticality, initial criticality

critique *adj* CHIMIE, PHYSIQUE, QUALITE critical

croc *m* CONS MECA hook, hook with eye, PRODUCTION

eyehook; ~ **de boucherie** *m* AGRO ALIM meat hook; ~ **à ciseaux** *m* CONS MECA clip hook, CONSTR match hooks; ~ **à cosse** *m* PRODUCTION eyehook and thimble; ~ **à émerillon** *m* NAUT swivel hook

crocéine *f* CHIMIE crocein

crochet *m* CH DE FER turnaround time, CONS MECA cranked tool, hook, CONSTR hook, lifting hook, *d'une grue* jib, MECANIQUE *matériel de levage* hook, METALL yield point, *sur une dislocation* cusp, NAUT grappling hook, PETR hook, PRODUCTION hanging tool, staff, RESSORTS, TEXTILE *d'une aiguille* hook; ~ **à ancre** *m* CONS MECA change hook; ~ **d'assemblage** *m* CONSTR cramp, cramp iron, joint cramp, PRODUCTION dog iron; ~ **d'attelage** *m* CONS MECA coupling hook, ME-CANIQUE, VEHICULES hitch; ~ **de balancier** *m* PRODUCTION beam hook; ~ **délesteur de fret** *m* AERO-NAUT cargo release hook; ~ **double** *m* CONS MECA change hook; ~ **en queue de cochon** *m* PRODUCTION pigtail hook; ~ **en S** *m* CONS MECA S-hook, S-shaped hook; ~ **à feu** *m* PRODUCTION rake; ~ **de fonderie** *m* PRODUCTION gagger, lifter; ~ **de gouttière** *m* CONSTR gutter bracket; ~ **de gouttière à queue en pointe** *m* CONSTR gutter bracket; ~ **de grue** *m* CONSTR crane hook; ~ **de levage** *m* CONS MECA lifting hook, CONSTR crane hook, NAUT cargo hook; ~ **de levage en acier forgé** *m* CONS MECA forged steel lifting hook; ~ **mural** *m* CONSTR wall holdfast; ~ **de palan** *m* CONS MECA pulley block hook, PRODUCTION tackle hook; ~ **pour établis de menuisiers** *m* CONSTR bench stop; ~ **pour la pose des courroies** *m* PRODUCTION belt mounter, belt shif-ter, belt shipper; ~ **pour tenir la fenêtre ouvert** *m* CONSTR casement fastener; ~ **pour tiges** *m* PETROLE pipe hook; ~ **pour tuyaux** *m* CONSTR pipe hook; ~ **à ramasser** *m* PRODUCTION lifter; ~ **de remorquage** *m* VEHICULES tow hook; ~ **à ressort** *m* CONS MECA clevis, clip hook; ~ **de sécurité** *m* AUTO, VEHICULES *capot* safety catch; ~ **de sûreté** *m* CONS MECA clevis, clip hook, safety hook, spring hook, MINES detaching hook, humble hook; ~ **de suspension** *m* CONS MECA hook, suspension hook, PRODUCTION hanger; ~ **de suspension des boyaux** *m* PRODUCTION hose hanger; ~ **à talon** *m* PRODUCTION *pour lisser* cleaner; ~ **à tête de bélier** *m* CONS MECA change hook; ~ **tournant** *m* CONS MECA swivel hook; ~ **de traction** *m* CH DE FER *véhicules* coupling hook, draw hook, NUCLEAIRE grip hook; ~ **de traction aigu** *m* METALL sharp yield point; ~ **de traction répété** *m* METALL repeated yield point; ~ **à trempe** *m* CERAM VER straight pincers; ~ **à tuiles** *m* CERAM VER tile cramp; ~ **de verrouillage** *m* CONS MECA catch; ~ **à vis** *m* CONSTR screw hook; ~ **vissé dans les spires** *m* RESSORTS screwed hook

crocheter *vt* AERONAUT *faisceau* capture, CONSTR *ser-rure* pick

crochets *m pl* IMPRIM *composition* brackets

crochon: ~ **de faille** *m* GEOLOGIE drag fold

crocidolite *f* MINERAUX crocidolite

crocine *f* CHIMIE crocin

crocodile *m* CH DE FER contact ramp, crocodile, MINES crocodile

crocoïte *f* MINERAUX crocoisite, crocoite

croconique *adj* CHIMIE *acide* croconic

croisée *f* CONSTR window; ~ **de fils** *f* INSTRUMENT gra-ticule

croisement: ~ **à coeur mobile** *m* TRANSPORT swing nose crossing

croiser[1] *vt* CONSTR bridge, GEOLOGIE cross

croiser² *vi* NAUT cruise
croiser:³ **se ~** *v réfl* CONSTR cross
croisette *f* GEOLOGIE, MINES cross stone
croiseur *m* MINES contralode, crosslode, counterlode, counter, cross vein; **~ de bataille** *m* NAUT battle cruiser, *marine* cruiser
croisière¹ *f* AERONAUT, NAUT cruise; **~ ascendante** *f* AERONAUT climb cruise, cruise climb, cruise climb drift up; **~ descendante** *f* AERONAUT cruise descent; **~ en palier** *f* AERONAUT level cruise
croisière:² **être en ~** *vi* NAUT cruise
croisillon *m* AERONAUT brace, CERAM VER spider, CONS MECA starwheel, CONSTR brace, PETR, VEHICULES *joint de cardan* spider; **~ de cardan** *m* MECANIQUE journal cross; **~ de changement de pas** *m* AERONAUT pitch change spider; **~ de différentiel** *m* VEHICULES *transmission* differential spider; **~ d'induit** *m* ELECTR *machine* field spider, ELECTROTEC armature spider; **~ à poignées** *m* CONS MECA starwheel; **~ à treillis en fer** *m* CONSTR window bar
croissance *f* NUCLEAIRE, PHYS FLUID *d'une perturbation* growth; **~ des cavités** *f* METALL void growth; **~ concourante** *f* METALL competition growth; **~ d'une couche épitaxiale** *f* ELECTRON epitaxial growth; **~ cristalline** *f* CRISTALL, METALL crystal growth; **~ épitaxiale** *f* ELECTRON, MATERIAUX epitaxial growth; **~ à facettes** *f* METALL faceted growth (AmE), facetted growth (BrE); **~ initiale d'une fissure** *f* NUCLEAIRE initial crack growth, pop-in; **~ orientée** *f* METALL oriented growth
croissant:¹ **en ~** *adj* GEOMETRIE crescent-shaped
croissant² *m* NAUT crutch; **~ de lune** *m* ASTRONOMIE crescent moon; **~ de plage** *m* OCEANO beach cusp
croisure: ~ du fil sur le support *f* TEXTILE wind
croix *f* CONSTR *d'un tuyau* cross; **~ de centrage** *f* CINEMAT cross hair; **~ de Malte** *f* CONS MECA Geneva wheel, MECANIQUE Maltese cross; **~ du Nord** *f* ASTRONOMIE Northern Cross; **~ du Sud** *f* ASTRONOMIE Crux
cronstedtite *f* MINERAUX cronstedtite
croquage *m* CERAM VER crimp, snap; **~ par cisaillement** *m* CERAM VER snapping; **~ à pédale** *m* CERAM VER cracking, foot-operated score
croquer *vt* CERAM VER break off (BrE), cap (AmE), CONS MECA pink, CONSTR sketch
croqueur *m* CERAM VER capper (AmE), cutoff man (BrE)
croquis *m* CONSTR sketch; **~ coté** *m* PRODUCTION dimensioned sketch; **~ quadrangulaire** *m* EMBALLAGE four-sided sketch
crosse *f* CINEMAT rifle grip; **~ d'épaule** *f* CINEMAT gunpod, shoulder brace; **~ de piston** *f* CONS MECA slipper block, MECANIQUE, PRODUCTION piston crosshead
crossette: ~ de piston *f* CONS MECA slipper block, MECANIQUE, PRODUCTION piston crosshead
crossite *f* MINERAUX crossite
crotonique *adj* CHIMIE crotonique
crotylique *adj* CHIMIE crotylic
croupe *f* CONSTR hip
croûte *f* PRODUCTION coating; **~ de composition** *f* CERAM VER batch crust; **~ océanique** *f* GEOLOGIE, OCEANO ocean crust, oceanic crust; **~ terrestre** *f* EN RENOUV Earth's crust, ESPACE terrestrial crust, PETR Earth's crust
croûtes: ~ de coke *f pl* MINES coked coal dust
crowdion *m* METALL crowdion
crown: ~ dense *m* CERAM VER dense crown; **~ léger** *m* CERAM VER light crown

cru *adj* CHARBON *charbon* unwashed, MATERIAUX raw, THERMODYN unbaked
crue:¹ **en ~** *adj* HYDROLOGIE in flood
crue² *f* HYDROLOGIE flood, inundation, spate, increasing flow; **~ annuelle** *f* DISTRI EAU annual flood; **~ nominale** *f* HYDROLOGIE design flood; **~ de plage** *f* OCEANO beach growth; **~ subite** *f* HYDROLOGIE flash flood
crues *f pl* HYDROLOGIE floods
cryobiologie *f* REFRIG cryobiology
cryochirurgie *f* REFRIG cryosurgery
cryodécapage *m* REFRIG cryoetching
cryodessiccation *f* AGRO ALIM freeze-drying
cryogénie *f* ESPACE, PHYSIQUE, REFRIG, THERMODYN cryogenics
cryogénique *adj* ESPACE, PHYSIQUE, THERMODYN cryogenic
cryolite *f* CHIMIE cryolite
cryolithe *f* CERAM VER, CHIMIE, MINERAUX cryolite
cryologie *f* REFRIG cryology
cryomagnétisme *m* REFRIG cryomagnetism
cryomarquage *m* REFRIG cryobranding
cryomédicine *f* REFRIG cryomedicine
cryomètre *f* THERMODYN low-temperature thermometer
cryophysique *f* PHYSIQUE, REFRIG cryophysics
cryoréfrigérateur *m* REFRIG cryogenic refrigerator
cryorefroidissement *m* REFRIG cryocooling
cryoscopie *f* REFRIG cryoscopy
cryostat *m* COMMANDE cryostat, cryostatic temperature control, ESPACE, MATERIAUX, PHYSIQUE cryostat
cryotechnique *f* ESPACE, PHYSIQUE cryogenics
cryothermostat *m* EQUIP LAB *contrôle de refroidissement, température* cryostat
cryotron *m* ELECTROTEC cryotron
cryptage *m* ELECTRON, TV encryption; **~ de données** *m* INFORMAT data encryption
cryptanalyse *f* INFORMAT, ORDINAT cryptanalysis
crypter *vt* ELECTRON encrypt, TV scramble
cryptogramme *m* TELECOM ciphertext
cryptographie *f* ESPACE *communications*, INFORMAT, ORDINAT, TELECOM cryptography
cryptographique *adj* ESPACE *communications* cryptographic
Cs¹ *(césium)* CHIMIE Cs *(caesium)*
Cs² *abrév (cirro-stratus)* METEO Cs *(cirrostratus)*
CSMA *abrév (accès multiple par détection de porteuse)* TELECOM CSMA *(carrier sense multiple access)*
CSMA-CD *abrév (accès multiple par détection de porteuse avec détection de collision)*, ELECTRON, INFORMAT, ORDINAT CSMA-CD *(carrier sense multiple access with collision detection)*
CT *abrév (centre de transit)* TELECOM trunk transit exchange
CTV *abrév (conteneur virtuel)* TELECOM virtual container
Cu¹ *(cuivre)* CHIMIE Cu *(copper)*
Cu² *abrév (cumulus)* METEO Cu *(cumulus)*
cubage *m* METROLOGIE cubage, cubic measurement, gaging (AmE), gauging (BrE), measurement, measuring, yardage, NAUT volume, PETROLE gaging (AmE), gauging (BrE)
cubanite *f* MINERAUX cubanite
cubature *f* CONSTR earthworks cubature, earthworks cubing
cube *m* GEOMETRIE, MATH cube; **~ d'essai** *m* CONSTR test cube; **~ de la vitesse du vent** *m* EN RENOUV wind

velocity cubed

cubébine *f* CHIMIE cubebin

cube-flash *m* PHOTO flash cube

cuber *vt* MATH cube, METROLOGIE measure, PRODUCTION gage (AmE), gauge (BrE)

cubilot *m* CERAM VER cupola furnace, CHARBON cupola, PRODUCTION cupola, cupola furnace; ~ **à avant-creuset** *m* PRODUCTION cupola with receiver

cubique *adj* CRISTALL cubic, isometric; ~ **centré** *adj* CHIMIE body-centered cubic (AmE), body-centred cubic (BrE); ~ **à faces centrées** *adj (CFC)* CHIMIE, CRISTALL face-centered cubic (AmE), face-centred cubic (BrE) *(FCC)*

cubizite *f* MINERAUX cubicite

cuboctaèdre *m* GEOMETRIE cubic octahedron

cuboïde *m* GEOMETRIE cuboid

cueillage *m* CERAM VER, PRODUCTION gathering

cueilleur: ~ **de jambe** *m* CERAM VER stem carrier; ~ **de paraison** *m* CERAM VER parison gatherer

cueillir *vt* CERAM VER, PRODUCTION gather

cuffat *m* MINES bucket, kibble, tub, PRODUCTION hoisting bucket; ~ **d'épuisement** *m* DISTRI EAU bailing tank; ~ **à vidange automatique** *m* DISTRI EAU self-discharging water bucket

cuiller *f* CHARBON earth grab, earthdrill, overburden drill, CONSTR ladle, MINES earth auger, earth borer, mud bit, shell and auger, shell auger, surface auger; ~ **écumoire** *f* PRODUCTION skimmer, skimming ladle; ~ **rotative** *f* CERAM VER gob distributor

cuillère *f* CONSTR ladle, MINES earth auger, earth borer, shell and auger, shell auger

cuir: ~ **embouti** *m* PRODUCTION cup leather; ~ **de montagne** *m* MINERAUX mountain leather

cuirasse *f* CERAM VER packing piece, CONS MECA saddle, ELECTROTEC armor (AmE), armour (BrE), shield

cuirassé *adj* MECANIQUE metal-clad

cuire *vt* CERAM VER bake, fire, PRODUCTION burn, kiln, TEXTILE bake, THERMODYN bake, cook; ~ **à la vapeur** *vt* AGRO ALIM steam

cuisine *f* NAUT galley

cuisson *f* CERAM VER baking, firing, burning, firing on, kilning, ELECTRON, ELECTROTEC firing, IMPRIM burning in, PAPIER cooking, PLAST CAOU cure, curing, *peinture* baking, *peintures, plastiques, caoutchouc* hardening, PRODUCTION burning, *des briques* baking, TEXTILE baking, THERMODYN burning, cooking; ~ **de la chaux** *f* PRODUCTION lime burning; ~ **en couverte** *f* CERAM VER hardening on the glazing

cuit: ~ **à l'avance** *adj* AGRO ALIM precooked; ~ **à mort** *adj* THERMODYN dead-burned

cuite *f* CERAM VER batch, PRODUCTION burning, *des briques* baking

cuit-vite *adj* PLAST CAOU *plastiques, caoutchouc* fast-curing

cuivrage *m* CERAM VER coppering

cuivre *m* CHIMIE *(Cu)* copper *(Cu)*, PRODUCTION *d'un fer à souder* copper bit; ~ **gris** *m* MINERAUX gray copper ore (AmE), grey copper ore (BrE); ~ **jaune** *m* CONS MECA brass, IMPRIM bookbinder's brass; ~ **vitreux rouge** *m* CHIMIE red copper ore

cuivré *adj* ELECTR copper-clad

cuivrerie *f* CONSTR brass foundry, brassworks, PRODUCTION copper works

cuivreux *adj* CHIMIE cupreous, cuprous

cul:[1] **sur** ~ *adj* NAUT down by the stern, trimmed by the stern

cul:[2] ~ **de poche** *m* PRODUCTION scull, skull; ~ **de porc** *m* NAUT back splice

culasse *f* AUTO cylinder head, MILITAIRE breech, NAUT cylinder head, NUCLEAIRE *d'un aimant*, PHYSIQUE *d'un aimant* yoke, REFRIG, VEHICULES *moteur* cylinder head; ~ **de balayage** *f* TV scanning yoke

culbutage *m* CONSTR dumping (AmE), tipping (BrE), PRODUCTION tilting

culbutement *m* CONSTR dumping (AmE), tipping (BrE)

culbuter[1] *vt* CONSTR shoot, tip, tip up, MINES dump

culbuter[2] *vi* CONSTR tip, tip up

culbuter:[3] **se** ~ *v réfl* CONSTR tip

culbuteur *m* AUTO rocker arm, CONSTR dump, tip (BrE), dump truck (AmE), tipper (BrE), tipping device, MECANIQUE rocker, PRODUCTION tilter, TRANSPORT dump truck (AmE), tipper (BrE), VEHICULES *moteur, soupape* rocker arm; ~ **des wagons** *m* CONSTR dump site

cul-de-sac *m* CONSTR blind alley

culée *f* CONSTR abutment

culicide *m* CHIMIE mosquitocide

culmination: ~ **inférieure** *f* ASTRONOMIE lower culmination; ~ **d'un pli** *f* GEOLOGIE axial culmination, high; ~ **supérieure** *f* ASTRONOMIE upper culmination

culot:[1] ~ **en bas** *adj* CINEMAT base down

culot[2] *m* CONS MECA center bearing plate (AmE), centre bearing plate (BrE), CONSTR baffle brick, ELECTRON base, ELECTROTEC cap, *de lampe* lamp cap, MINES *d'un trou de mine* socket; ~ **à baïonnette** *m* ELECTR *ampoule électrique* bayonet cap, ELECTROTEC, PHOTO bayonet base; ~ **de bougie** *m* AUTO spark plug body, spark plug shell; ~ **de fusible** *m* ELECTROTEC fuse base; ~ **de lampe** *m* CINEMAT lamp base; ~ **loctal** *m* ELECTRON loctal base; ~ **octal** *m* CONS MECA octal base; ~ **de plomb** *m* CHIMIE lead button; ~ **de poche** *m* CERAM VER scull; ~ **de tube électronique** *m* ELECTRON electron tube base, electron tube holder; ~ **à vis** *m* CINEMAT screw base, ELECTROTEC screw cap

culotte *f* CONS MECA breeches pipe, CONSTR y-branch, MECANIQUE, PRODUCTION breeches pipe; ~ **de tuyère de réacteur** *f* AERONAUT exhaust nozzle breech

culottes: ~ **de la cheminée** *f pl* PRODUCTION breeching

cumarine *f* CHIMIE cumarin

cumène *m* CHIMIE cumene

cumengéite *f* MINERAUX cumengeite, cumengite

cuminique *adj* CHIMIE cumic

cummingtonite *f* MINERAUX cummingtonite

cumulande *m* ORDINAT augend

cumulateur *m* ORDINAT addend

cumulo-dôme *m* GEOLOGIE cumulo-dome, tholoid dome

cumulo-volcan *m* GEOLOGIE cumulo-volcano

cumulus *m (Cu)* METEO cumulus *(Cu)*; ~ **congestus** *m* METEO cumulus congestus; ~ **humilis** *m* METEO cumulus humilis

cumyle *m* CHIMIE cumyl

cunette *f* CONSTR gutter

cup *m* PRODUCTION hopper; ~ **et cône** *m* PRODUCTION cup-and-cone

CUP *abrév (coefficient d'utilisation pratique)* MINES WS *(weight strength)*

cuprammonium *m* CHIMIE, TEXTILE cuprammonium

cuprate *m* CHIMIE cuprate

cupride *m* CHIMIE cupride

cuprifère *adj* MINES copper-bearing

cuprique *adj* CHIMIE cupric

cuprite *f* MINERAUX cuprite, red copper ore
cuproapatite *f* MINERAUX cuproapatite
cuprodescloizite *f* MINERAUX cuprodescloizite
cupromagnésite *f* MINERAUX cupromagnesite
cupromanganèse *m* CHIMIE cupromanganese
cuproplumbite *f* MINERAUX cuproplumbite
cuproscheelite *f* MINERAUX cuproscheelite
cuprotungstite *f* MINERAUX cuprotungstite
cupule *f* METALL dimple
curage *m* DISTRI EAU cleaning out, cleansing, flushing, PETROLE sand-washing, *sous pression* snubbing, PRODUCTION scraping; **~ des égouts** *m* DISTRI EAU, HYDROLOGIE sewer cleaning
curbature *f* CONSTR *d'un toit* break
curcuma *m* AGRO ALIM, CHIMIE turmeric
curcumine *f* CHIMIE curcumine
cure: ~ par faisceau d'électrons *f* NUCLEAIRE *béton* electron beam curing
cure-feu *m* PRODUCTION poker, prick bar, pricker
curer[1] *vt* DISTRI EAU cleanse, *une rivière* cleanse, NAUT dredge, PRODUCTION clean out
curer[2] *vi* DISTRI EAU flush
curette *f* CONS MECA clearer, scraper, DISTRI EAU cleaner, MINES cleaner, scraper, drag, hole scraper, POLLU MER scraper
curie *m* PHYS RAYON, PHYSIQUE curie
curium *m (Cm)* CHIMIE curium *(Cm)*
curl *m* PHYSIQUE curl
curseur *m* AUTO rheostat sliding contact, CONS MECA slider, traveler (AmE), traveller (BrE), IMPRIM cursor, hairline, pointer, INFORMAT, ORDINAT cursor, PHYSIQUE sliding contact, PRODUCTION *d'une cuve d'amalgamation* spider; **~ du diaphragme d'ouverture** *m* INSTRUMENT aperture top slide; **~ en croix** *m* IMPRIM cross hair; **~ de potentiomètre** *m* ELECTR résistance potentiometer slider; **~ de rhéostat** *m* ELECTR *résistance* rheostat slider; **~ virtuel** *m* PRODUCTION *automatisme industriel* invisible cursor
curviligne *adj* GEOMETRIE curvilinear
custode *f* VEHICULES *carrosserie* rear end, tail
cuve *f* AGRO ALIM vat, CHARBON bowl, CHIMIE vat, CONSTR tank, EQUIP LAB *analyse* cell, *verrerie* trough, ESPACE, MECANIQUE tank, MINES kieve, PAPIER pond, tank, vat, POLLU MER bucket, PRODUCTION fire room, tank, tub, vat, *d'une plaque tournante* basin, *d'un haut fourneau* tunnel, TEXTILE vat; **~ d'accumulateur** *f* PAPIER accumulator box, battery box; **~ d'acide** *f* PAPIER acid vat; **~ d'agglomération** *f* GENIE CHIM sintering furnace; **~ d'amalgamation** *f* PRODUCTION grinding pan, pan mill, pan; **~ de broyage** *f* PRODUCTION grinding pan, pan mill, pan; **~ à chargement en plein jour** *f* PHOTO daylight loading tank; **~ collectrice** *f* MINES collecting vat; **~ de décantation** *f* MINES dewaterer; **~ à défécation** *f* GENIE CHIM settling vat; **~ de développement** *f* CINEMAT, PHOTO developing tank, development tank; **~ à développement multiple** *f* PHOTO multiunit developing tank; **~ d'effondrement** *f* GEOLOGIE sink; **~ d'électrophorèse** *f* EQUIP LAB *analyse* electrophoresis cell; **~ en grès** *f* CERAM VER earthenware tank; **~ en matière plastique** *f* PHOTO plastic developing tank; **~ en porcelaine** *f* CERAM VER porcelain cell; **~ en verre** *f* EQUIP LAB glass tank; **~ extérieure** *f* REFRIG cabinet shell; **~ de fermentation** *f* AGRO ALIM fermenter, mash tun; **~ filtrante** *f* DISTRI EAU filtration vat; **~ de filtration** *f* DISTRI EAU filtration vat; **~ de filtre** *f* CHARBON, GENIE CHIM filter feed trough; **~ à huile** *f*

ELECTROTEC oil tank; **~ intégrée** *f* TRANSPORT *de méthanier* integrated tank; **~ interne** *f* REFRIG liner; **~ de lavage** *f* PHOTO wash tank; **~ à niveau constant** *f* AUTO float chamber; **~ à niveau constant de carburateur** *f* VEHICULES carburetor float chamber (AmE), carburettor float chamber (BrE); **~ pour chromatographie** *f* EQUIP LAB *analyse* chromatography tank; **~ pour chromatographie sur papier** *f* EQUIP LAB *analyse* paper chromatography tank; **~ de précipitation** *f* CHIMIE precipitator; **~ de préparation des bains** *f* CINEMAT mixing tank; **~ de réacteur** *f* NUCLEAIRE reactor tank, reactor vessel, PHYSIQUE reactor vessel; **~ de refroidissement** *f* CINEMAT cooling tank, PRODUCTION cooling basin; **~ à rides** *f* PHYS ONDES *pour créer des ondes* ripple tank; **~ de sécurité** *f* NUCLEAIRE guard vessel, leakage interception vessel; **~ sphérique** *f* TRANSPORT *de méthanier* spherical container; **~ de stockage de câble** *f* TELECOM cable storage hold; **~ suspendue** *f* POLLU MER slung bucket; **~ universelle** *f* PHOTO universal developing tank; **~ à vide** *f* EQUIP LAB vacuum pan
cuve-cylindre *f* PRODUCTION *pour malaxage, lavage* drum
cuvelage *m* GAZ casing, MINES tubbing, PETROLE casing; **~ en maçonnerie** *m* CHARBON stone tubbing; **~ en pierre** *m* MINES stone tubbing
cuveler *vt* CONSTR *puits* case, line, MINES tub
cuvellement *m* MINES tubbing
cuve-mélangeur *f* GENIE CHIM mixing tank
cuvette *f* CONSTR head, hopper head, DISTRI EAU basin, EQUIP LAB cup, trough, *verrerie* basin, GEOLOGIE intermount basin, PHOTO dish, tray; **~ d'avant-corps** *f* CERAM VER feeder nose; **~ de boussole** *f* PHYSIQUE compass bowl; **~ de coucheuse** *f* REVETEMENT coater pan, coater trough, coating trough; **~ coupelle** *f* EQUIP LAB dish; **~ de développement à thermostat** *f* PHOTO thermostatically-controlled developing dish; **~ à dissection** *f* EQUIP LAB *biologie* dissecting tray; **~ d'écoulement de distributeur** *f* CERAM VER orifice ring; **~ d'égouttage** *f* CONSTR drip cup, PRODUCTION drain cup; **~ en matière plastique** *f* PHOTO plastic dish; **~ d'évaporation** *f* GENIE CHIM evaporating basin, evaporating pan, vaporization dish, evaporating dish; **~ d'évaporation en porcelaine** *f* CERAM VER porcelain evaporating basin; **~ de gouttière** *f* CONSTR rainwater head; **~ de poignée** *f* CONS MECA handle plate; **~ de refroidissement par l'eau** *f* CINEMAT water-cooled heat trap; **~ de retenue** *f* DISTRI EAU reservoir basin; **~ à température constante** *f* PHOTO thermostatically-controlled developing dish; **~ tournante** *f* CERAM VER rotating bowl; **~ de vaporisation** *f* GENIE CHIM evaporating basin, evaporating dish, evaporating pan, vaporization dish; **~ de verrou** *f* CONSTR lock cup
cuvier *m* PAPIER chest; **~ de blanchiment** *m* PAPIER bleaching chest; **~ de machine** *m* PAPIER machine chest; **~ de mélange** *m* PAPIER blending chest; **~ à pâte** *m* PAPIER stock chest; **~ de tête** *m* IMPRIM machine chest, PAPIER machine chest, stuff chest
CVCP *abrév (concentration volumique critique de pigment)* REVETEMENT *peinture* CPVC *(critical pigment volume concentration)*
cyamélide *m* CHIMIE cyamelid, cyamelide
cyanacétique *adj* CHIMIE cyanacetic
cyanamide *m* CHIMIE cyanamide
cyanate *m* CHIMIE cyanate
cyanhydrique *adj* CHIMIE hydrocyanic
cyanique *adj* CHIMIE cyanic

cyanite *f* MINERAUX cyanite, kyanite

cyanofer *m* CHIMIE ferrocyanogen

cyanoferrate *m* CHIMIE ferrocyanate, ferrocyanide

cyanogène *m* CHIMIE cyanogen

cyanotrichite *f* MINERAUX cyanotrichite

cyanuration *f* CHARBON cyanidation, CHIMIE *des matières organiques* cyanization

cyanure *m* CHIMIE cyanide; ~ **d'argent** *m* CHIMIE silver cyanide; ~ **d'or** *m* CHIMIE gold cyanide; ~ **de potassium** *m* CHIMIE potassium cyanide

cybernétique *f* ESPACE, ORDINAT cybernetics

cyclamate *m* CHIMIE cyclamate

cyclane *m* PETROLE cycloalkane

cycle *m* ACOUSTIQUE, ELECTR *tension*, ELECTROTEC, INFORMAT, ORDINAT, PLAST CAOU, REFRIG cycle; ~ **à 6 éléments** *m* CHIMIE six-membered ring; ~ **à air à turbo-détendeur** *m* REFRIG brake turbine air cycle; ~ **d'analyse** *m* TV scanning cycle; ~ **d'approvisionnement** *m* PRODUCTION procurement lead time, replenishment lead time; ~ **Beau de Rochas** *m* VEHICULES *moteur* Otto cycle, four-stroke cycle; ~ **biogéochimique** *m* GEOLOGIE biogeochemical cycling; ~ **de Brückner** *m* METEO Brückner cycle; ~ **du carbone** *m* AGRO ALIM, ASTRONOMIE carbon cycle; ~ **de Carnot** *m* MAT CHAUFF *thermodynamique*, PHYSIQUE, THERMODYN Carnot cycle; ~ **de Carnot inverse** *m* THERMODYN vapor compression cycle (AmE), vapour compression cycle (BrE); ~ **du champ magnétique solaire** *m* ASTRONOMIE sun's magnetic field cycle; ~ **de charge-décharge** *m* TRANSPORT charge discharge cycle; ~ **de Clausius-Rankine** *m* MAT CHAUFF *thermodynamique*, THERMODYN Rankine cycle; ~ **de combustible** *m* ESPACE fuel cycle; ~ **à combustible avancé** *m* NUCLEAIRE advanced fuel cycle; ~ **du combustible en pile** *m* NUCLEAIRE in-core fuel cycle; ~ **des composés soufrés** *m* POLLUTION sulfur cycle (AmE), sulphur cycle (BrE); ~ **de conduite urbaine** *m* VEHICULES urban cycle; ~ **de dégivrage** *m* REFRIG defrost cycle; ~ **de l'eau** *m* GEOLOGIE hydrologic cycle; ~ **de fabrication** *m* PRODUCTION manufacturing cycle, manufacturing lead time; ~ **fermé** *m* CHIMIE closed ring; ~ **fermé de combustibles** *m* NUCLEAIRE closed fuel cycle; ~ **de fonctionnement** *m* AUTO working cycle, TRANSPORT operating cycle; ~ **frigorifique à air** *m* REFRIG air refrigeration cycle; ~ **frigorifique à compression** *m* REFRIG compression refrigerating cycle; ~ **géochimique** *m* GEOLOGIE geochemical cycle; ~ **d'horloge** *m* ELECTRON, INFORMAT, ORDINAT clock cycle; ~ **hydrologique** *m* DISTRI EAU hydrologic cycle; ~ **d'hystérésis** *m* ELECTROTEC, METALL, PHYSIQUE, PLAST CAOU, TV hysteresis loop; ~ **d'hystérésis rectangulaire** *m* ELECTROTEC rectangular hysteresis loop; ~ **d'immersion-séchage** *m* CONSTR soaking-drying cycle; ~ **d'instruction** *m* INFORMAT, ORDINAT instruction cycle; ~ **d'intervalles** *m* ACOUSTIQUE cycle of intervals; ~ **machine** *m* INFORMAT, ORDINAT machine cycle; ~ **magnétique** *m* ASTRONOMIE *du soleil*, GEOPHYS *du soleil* magnetic cycle; ~ **des marées de forts et faibles coefficients** *m* EN RENOUV spring neap cycle; ~ **de mémoire** *m* INFORMAT, ORDINAT memory cycle; ~ **de Meton** *m* ASTRONOMIE Metonic cycle; ~ **de moulage** *m* PLAST CAOU molding cycle (AmE), moulding cycle (BrE); ~ **opératoire** *m* MECANIQUE duty cycle; ~ **orogénique** *m* GEOLOGIE orogenic cycle, orogenic phase; ~ **ouvert** *m* NUCLEAIRE once-through, open fuel cycle; ~ **placé en amont** *m* NUCLEAIRE topping cycle; ~ **de**

production *m* PRODUCTION manufacturing cycle, manufacturing lead time; ~ **à quatre temps** *m* AUTO Otto cycle, four-stroke cycle, VEHICULES *moteur* four-stroke cycle; ~ **de rafraîchissement** *m* INFORMAT, ORDINAT refresh cycle, refresh rate; ~ **rectangulaire** *m* ELECTROTEC square loop; ~ **de référence** *m* REFRIG standard rating cycle; ~ **de réfrigération** *m* REFRIG refrigeration cycle; ~ **de réfrigération à absorption** *m* REFRIG absorption refrigerating cycle; ~ **de réfrigération à éjection de vapeur** *m* REFRIG vapor jet refrigerating cycle (AmE), vapour jet refrigerating cycle (BrE); ~ **de service** *m* PRODUCTION *système hydraulique* duty; ~ **solaire** *m* ASTRONOMIE, GEOPHYS solar cycle; ~ **à sortir après passage unique** *m* NUCLEAIRE *charge* OTTO, once-through-then-out; ~ **de soudage** *m* CONSTR welding cycle; ~ **du soufre** *m* POLLUTION sulfur cycle (AmE), sulphur cycle (BrE); ~ **surrégénérateur** *m* NUCLEAIRE breeding cycle; ~ **des taches solaires** *m* ASTRONOMIE, GEOPHYS sunspot cycle; ~ **de température** *m* THERMODYN temperature cycle; ~ **thermique** *m* THERMODYN thermal cycle; ~ **thermodynamique** *m* MAT CHAUFF thermodynamic cycle; ~ **de traitement thermique** *m* THERMODYN heat cycle; ~ **triazinique** *m* CHIMIE triazine ring; ~ **d'uranium-plutonium** *m* NUCLEAIRE U-Pu cycle, uranium-plutonium cycle; ~ **de visites** *m* AERONAUT inspection cycle

cyclène *m* PETROLE cycloalkene

cyclique *adj* CHIMIE, PETROLE cyclic

cyclisation *f* CHIMIE cyclization

cycloalcane *m* PETROLE cycloalkane

cyclohéxane *m* PETROLE cyclohexane

cycloïde *f* GEOMETRIE cycloid

cyclomoteur *m* TRANSPORT moped, motor-assisted bicycle; ~ **électrique** *m* TRANSPORT electric moped

cyclone *m* AGRO ALIM, CHARBON, METEO, PETROLE *séparateur de poussière*, POLLUTION cyclone; ~ **chaud** *m* CHARBON hot cyclone; ~ **filtre** *m* GENIE CHIM filter cyclone; ~ **de séparation** *m* GENIE CHIM settling cyclone; ~ **tropical** *m* METEO hurricane, tropical cyclone, tropical revolving storm

cyclooléfine *f* PETROLE cycloolefin

cycloparaffine *f* PETROLE cycloparaffin

cyclorama *m* CINEMAT cyclorama

cyclothème *m* GEOLOGIE cyclothem

cyclotron *m* ELECTROTEC, PHYS PART, PHYSIQUE cyclotron; ~ **à électrons** *m* PHYS PART electron cyclotron

cylindrage *m* CONS MECA straight turning, CONSTR *des chaussées empierrées*, PRODUCTION rolling; ~ **des rouleaux en bois** *m* PRODUCTION rounding wooden rollers

cylindre *m* AUTO cylinder, CONS MECA *de laminoir* roll, *de pompe* barrel, GEOMETRIE cylinder, INFORMAT platen, *lecteur de disque* cylinder, MECANIQUE, MINES, NAUT cylinder, ORDINAT platen, *lecteur de disque* cylinder, PLAST CAOU *calandre, enduiseuse* cylinder, *matériel* roller, *presse* cylinder, PRODUCTION drum, roller, *d'une pompe* cylinder, VEHICULES *moteur* cylinder, engine capacity; ~ **accumulateur** *m* IMPRIM *rotatives* collect cylinder; ~ **à air comprimé** *m* CONS MECA compressed air cylinder; ~ **aspirant** *m* PAPIER suction couch roll; ~ **à bagasse** *m* AGRO ALIM bagasse roller; ~ **blanchet** *m* IMPRIM *impression* blanket cylinder; ~ **de broyage** *m* AGRO ALIM break roller, GENIE CHIM grinding cylinder; ~ **broyeur** *m* GENIE CHIM crusher roll, grinding cylinder, PRODUCTION crusher roll, crushing roll; ~ **cannelé** *m* CONS MECA grooved roll, GENIE CHIM granulating roller, PRODUCTION corrugated roll; ~ **à cannelures** m CONS MECA grooved roll, PRODUCTION corrugated roll; ~ **de la cathode** m TV shield; ~ **à cintrer** m CONS MECA bending roll; ~ **circulaire droit** m GEOMETRIE right circular cylinder; ~ **collecteur** m IMPRIM *rotatives* gathering cylinder; ~ **compresseur** m CONSTR roller; ~ **de contre-pression** m IMPRIM impression cylinder; ~ **cuivré** m IMPRIM copper-plated cylinder; ~ **de dégrossissement** m PRODUCTION roughing roll, roughing-down roll; ~ **dégrossisseur** m CONS MECA breaking-down roll, PRODUCTION puddle roll, roughing roll, roughing-down roll; ~ **désagré-geur** m AGRO ALIM break roller; ~ **du dessous** m PRODUCTION *laminoir* bottom roll; ~ **du dessus** m CONS MECA top roll, upper roll; ~ **ébaucheur** m CONS MECA breaking-down roll, PRODUCTION puddle roll, roughing roll, roughing-down roll; ~ **en fonte trem-pée** m PRODUCTION chilled iron roll; ~ **enregistreur** m GEOPHYS rotating drum; ~ **d'entraînement** m CONS MECA feed roll, feed roller; ~ **entraîneur** m CONS MECA feed roll, feed roller; ~ **d'épreuve** m CONSTR test cylinder; ~ **d'équerrage** m METROLOGIE squareness cylinder; ~ **espatard** m CONS MECA planishing roll; ~ **de Faraday** m ELECTR *électrostatique*, PHYSIQUE Faraday cylinder; ~ **femelle** m CONS MECA *laminoir* lower roll, PRODUCTION *laminoir* bottom roll; ~ **forgeur** m PRODUCTION forge roll; ~ **de format** m PAPIER size roll; ~ **de frein** m AUTO, CONS MECA, VEHICULES brake cylinder; ~ **de friction** m CONS MECA friction wheel; ~ **frictionneur** m PAPIER glazing cylinder, PRODUCTION *industrie du papier* yankee cylinder; ~ **à gaz comprimé** m THERMODYN gas bottle; ~ **géométrique** m CONS MECA *transmissions hydrauliques* geometric displacement; ~ **de glissement** m METALL slip cylinder; ~ **à gradins** m CONS MECA stepped roll; ~ **à granuler** m GENIE CHIM granulating roller; ~ **hélio** m IMPRIM gravure roller; ~ **hydraulique** m CONS MECA hydraulic cylinder, hydraulic jack; ~ **d'impression** m PLAST CAOU *matériel* impression cylinder; ~ **à imprimer** m IMPRIM, PAPIER printing cylinder; ~ **d'imprimerie** m PLAST CAOU *matériel* printing roll; ~ **intermédiaire de machine à vapeur** m INST HYDR intermediate pressure cylinder, intermediate steam engine cylinder; ~ **à lames enga-geantes** m IMPRIM tucking blades cylinder; ~ **lamineur** m PRODUCTION roller, rolling mill roll; ~ **de laminoir** m PRODUCTION rolling mill roll; ~ **de laminoir à blooms** m CONS MECA blooming roll; ~ **lisse** m CONSTR smooth roller, PRODUCTION plain roll; ~ **malaxeur** m PRODUCTION mixing cylinder; ~ **mâle** m CONS MECA *laminoir* top roll, upper roll; ~ **de mesure d'engrenages** m METROLOGIE gear measuring cylinder; ~ **de mesure de**

filetages m METROLOGIE screw thread measuring cylinder; ~ **à moyenne pression** m INST HYDR intermediate pressure cylinder, intermediate steam engine cylinder; ~ **à parois minces** m CONS MECA thin-walled cylinder; ~ **de pile raffineuse** m PAPIER beater roll; ~ **à piston effet** m CONS MECA double-ended piston rod cylinder; ~ **plieur** m IMPRIM *machine* folding cylinder; ~ **pneumatique** m CONS MECA pneumatic cylinder; ~ **polisseur** m CONS MECA planishing roll; ~ **de pompe** m DISTRI EAU pump barrel, pump cylinder; ~ **porte-couteaux** m PAPIER knife cylinder; ~ **de pression** m TEXTILE quetch roller, squeezing roller; ~ **de pulvérisation** m AGRO ALIM break roller; ~ **qui en effleure un autre pratiquement sans pression** m IMPRIM kissing cylinder; ~ **de ralentissement** m IMPRIM *rotatives* slow-down cylinder; ~ **récepteur** m AUTO clutch output cylinder, slave cylinder, wheel cylinder, VEHICULES *freins, embrayage* slave cylinder; ~ **refroid-isseur** m PAPIER cooling cylinder, sweat roll, PLAST CAOU *matériel* chill roll; ~ **de révolution** m GEOMETRIE cylindrical solid of revolution; ~ **de roue** m AUTO brake wheel cylinder; ~ **de séchage** m LESSIVES drying cylinder, drying drum; ~ **sécheur** m PAPIER drying cylinder; ~ **de taille-douce** m IMPRIM intaglio cylinder; ~ **télescopique** m CONS MECA telescopic cylinder; ~ **à tige de piston traversante** m CONS MECA through-rod cylinder; ~ **à tôles** m CONS MECA plate roll; ~ **de transmission hydraulique** m CONS MECA fluid-power cylinder; ~ **à vapeur** m INST HYDR steam cylinder; ~ **de verre d'humecteur** m CERAM VER glass roll dampener; ~ **yankee** m PRODUCTION *industrie du papier* yankee cylinder

cylindrée f AUTO cylinder capacity, displacement, MECANIQUE *véhicules* cubic capacity, VEHICULES *moteur* capacity; ~ **totale** f AUTO displacement

cylindre-plaque m IMPRIM plate cylinder

cylindrer vt CONS MECA turn, PRODUCTION round

cylindres: ~ **d'alimentation** m pl AGRO ALIM feed rollers, feed rolls; ~ **en ligne** m pl AUTO in-line cylinders; ~ **en V** m pl AUTO V-shaped cylinders; ~ **opposés** m pl AUTO opposed cylinders; ~ **placés côte à côte** m pl CONS MECA side-by-side cylinders

cylindreur m CONSTR roller

cylindrique adj GEOLOGIE cylindrical, PRODUCTION tubular

cylindroconique adj PRODUCTION cylindroconic

cymène m CHIMIE cymene

cymogène m PETR cymogene

cyprine f MINERAUX cyprine

cytisine f CHIMIE cytisine, ulexine

D

D *abrév (dé)* PHYSIQUE dee
da *abrév (déca)* METROLOGIE da *(deca-)*
dacite *f* PETR dacite
dactylographié *adj* BREVETS typewritten
daguerréotype *m* PHOTO daguerreotype
dallage *m* CONSTR flagging, flagstone pavement, pavement (BrE), paving (AmE); ~ en terre cuite *m* CERAM VER terracotta floor; ~ de sol *m* CERAM VER bottom paving
dalle *f* CERAM VER cover tile, floor tile, glass paving slab, CONSTR flag, slab, flagstone, ELECTRON faceplate, GEOLOGIE flag, flagstone; ~ brute *f* CERAM VER thick roughcast plate glass; ~ continue *f* CONSTR continuous slab; ~ de couverture *f* NUCLEAIRE cover plate, cover slab, roof shielding plate; ~ en béton translucide *f* CERAM VER glass concrete panel; ~ de plafond *f* CONSTR ceiling tile; ~ polie *f* CERAM VER thick polished plate glass; ~ PVC autocollante pour sol et mur *f* PLAST CAOU floor and wall self-adhesive PVC tile
dalleur *m* CONSTR pavior (AmE), paviour (BrE)
dalot *m* CONSTR box culvert, flat-top culvert, NAUT drain
dalots *m pl* NAUT scuppers
dalton *m* PHYS RAYON dalton
dame *f* CHARBON pile hammer, CONSTR earth rammer, rammer, PRODUCTION dam plate, dam; ~ de nage *f* NAUT oarlock (AmE), rowlock
dame-jeanne *f* AGRO ALIM carboy, CERAM VER carboy, demijohn
damer *vt* CH DE FER *du ballast* tamp, CONSTR batter, ram, PRODUCTION tamp
damiers: ~ de silicium *m pl* PHYS RAYON *détecteurs de particule* silicon checkers
damourite *f* MINERAUX damourite
danaïte *f* MINERAUX danaite
danalite *f* MINERAUX danalite
danburite *f* MINERAUX danburite
danger[1] *m* QUALITE hazard, SECURITE danger, hazard; ~ d'incendie *m* AERONAUT, SECURITE, THERMODYN fire hazard; ~ majeur *m* QUALITE major hazard; ~ pour l'environnement *m* QUALITE environmental hazard
danger:[2] être un ~ pour *vt* SECURITE be a danger to
dangers: ~ dûs aux dispositifs mécaniques *m pl* SECURITE mechanical hazards; ~ dûs aux machines *m pl* SECURITE machinery hazards; ~ des machines *m pl* SECURITE machinery hazards; ~ non-mécaniques *m pl* SECURITE *comprennent les poussières et les accidents électriques* nonmechanical hazards; ~ des ondes radio *m pl* SECURITE radio wave hazards; ~ du rayonnement *m pl* SECURITE radiation hazards; ~ des rayons laser *m pl* SECURITE laser radiation hazards; ~ des ultrasons *m pl* SECURITE ultrasonic hazards; ~ des vibrations *m pl* SECURITE vibration hazards
danien *adj* GEOLOGIE *stratigraphie* Danian
dannemorite *f* MINERAUX dannemorite
danse *f* CH DE FER instability
daphnétine *f* CHIMIE daphnetin
daphnine *f* CHIMIE daphnin

daphnite *f* MINERAUX daphnite
darcy *m* HYDROLOGIE darcy
dard: ~ de chalumeau *m* THERMODYN darting flame
dartre *f* PRODUCTION scab
dashpot *m* CONS MECA, MECANIQUE dashpot
datagramme *m* INFORMAT, ORDINAT, TELECOM datagram
datarom *m* (MD) OPTIQUE datarom (TM)
datation *f* GEOLOGIE age dating, dating, PHYSIQUE dating; ~ K-Ar *f* GEOLOGIE K-Ar dating; ~ par la méthode K-Ar *f* GEOLOGIE K-Ar dating; ~ par radioactivité *f* PHYSIQUE radioactive dating; ~ par traces de fission *f* GEOLOGIE, PHYSIQUE fission track dating; ~ au radiocarbone *f* PHYSIQUE radiocarbon dating; ~ radiométrique *f* GEOLOGIE radiometric age determination
date: ~ d'arrivée usine *f* PRODUCTION shop arrival date, *production* date freight inward; ~ de début de fabrication *f* PRODUCTION production start date; ~ de délivrance *f* BREVETS date of grant; ~ de dépôt *f* BREVETS date of filling; ~ de dernier retour *f* PRODUCTION last feedback rate; ~ d'échange *f* TELECOM interchange date; ~ en calendrier usine *f* PRODUCTION shop date; ~ d'enregistrement *f* BREVETS date of registration; ~ et heure de transmission *f* TELECOM date and time of transmission; ~ d'exigibilité *f* PRODUCTION due date; ~ d'expiration *f* CINEMAT expiry date; ~ de fabrication *f* EMBALLAGE date of manufacture; ~ limite *f* CINEMAT, TV deadline; ~ de livraison *f* EMBALLAGE delivery date; ~ ou heure de préparation *f* TELECOM date or time of preparation; ~ de passage à l'antenne *f* TV air date; ~ de production *f* PRODUCTION production date; ~ de retombée *f* ESPACE *véhicules* decay date; ~ usine *f* PRODUCTION shop date
datiscine *f* CHIMIE datiscin
datolite *f* MINERAUX datholite, datolite
dauphin *m* CONSTR boot, shoe
Dauphin *m* ASTRONOMIE Delphinus
DAV *abrév (dépôt axial en phase vapeur)* OPTIQUE, TELECOM VAD *(vapor phase axial deposition, vapour phase axial deposition)*
davyne *f* MINERAUX davyne
dB *abrév (décibel)* ACOUSTIQUE, ENREGISTR, PHYS RAYON, PHYSIQUE, POLLUTION dB *(decibel)*
DBE *abrév (densité de boue équivalente)* PETROLE *forage* EMW *(Equivalent Mud Weight)*
DBO *abrév (demande biochimique d'oxygène)* AGRO ALIM, HYDROLOGIE, PETROLE, POLLUTION BOD *(biochemical oxygen demand)*
DBV *abrév (débit binaire variable)* TELECOM VBR *(variable bit rate)*
DCA *abrév (défense contre avions)* MILITAIRE air defence
DCB *abrév (décimal codé binaire)* ORDINAT BCD *(binary-coded decimal)*
DCO *abrév (demande chimique d'oxygène)* CHIMIE, HYDROLOGIE, POLLUTION COD *(chemical oxygen demand)*
DCV *abrév (dépôt chimique en phase vapeur)* ELECTRON,

OPTIQUE, TELECOM CVD *(chemical vapor deposition, chemical vapour deposition)*

ddp *abrév (différence de potentiel)* PHYSIQUE pd *(potential difference)*

dé *m* CONS MECA pillow, MINES die, PHYSIQUE *(D)* dee; **~ d'entraînement** *m* CONS MECA drive bit

déaminase *f* CHIMIE deaminase

débâcle *f* HYDROLOGIE breaking-up, OCEANO debacle, glacial outburst, ice breakup

déballastage *m* PETR dewatering

débandage *m* CERAM VER deburring

débarcadère *m* NAUT wharf

débarder *vt* NAUT unload

débardeur *m* NAUT docker (BrE), longshoreman (AmE), stevedore

débarquement *m* NAUT disembarkation, paying off, TRANSPORT landing

débarquer[1] *vt* NAUT disembark, *des passagers* land, *des marins* pay off, *une cargaison, l'équipage* discharge, land, unship

débarquer[2] *vi* NAUT land

débarrassé *adj* MATERIAUX clear, free

débarrasser: se ~ de *v réfl* PRODUCTION scrap

débattement *m* AERONAUT deflection, CONS MECA displacement; **~ de gouverne de direction** *m* AERONAUT rudder travel; **~ horizontal** *m* PRODUCTION horizontal travel

débavurer *vt* PLAST CAOU *plastiques* deflash

débillarder *vt* CONSTR wreath

débit *m* AGRO ALIM delivery, CHARBON feed rate, yield, CINEMAT pace, CONS MECA delivery, CONSTR *des bois en grume* breaking down, DISTRI EAU discharge, flow rate, outflow, rate of flow, *d'une pompe* capacity, *d'un cours d'eau, d'un déversoir* discharge, EN RENOUV yield, GAZ flow rate, sendout, HYDROLOGIE flow rate, INFORMAT rate, throughput, INST HYDR feed, flow, MECANIQUE *hydraulique* flow rate, NUCLEAIRE *d'une pompe, d'un compresseur, d'un ventilateur* delivery,discharge, ORDINAT rate, throughput, PAPIER flow, *d'une pompe* delivery, discharge, output, PETROLE yield, PHYS FLUID flow rate, PHYSIQUE flow rate, rate of flow, PRODUCTION output, throughput, yield, RECYCLAGE discharge rate, REFRIG rate of flow, TRANSPORT traffic volume; **~ d'accumulateurs** *m* ESPACE *énergie* battery drain; **~ d'air** *m* AERONAUT airflow, MAT CHAUFF airflow rate; **~ de l'année moyenne** *m pl* HYDROLOGIE average yearly flow; **~ annuel** *m* DISTRI EAU annual flow; **~ après convergence** *m* TRANSPORT diverging volume, merge volume; **~ de base** *m* HYDROLOGIE base flow, TELECOM basic bit rate, TRANSPORT base volume; **~ binaire** *m* INFORMAT, ORDINAT bit rate, TELECOM bit rate, data signaling rate (AmE), data signalling rate (BrE); **~ binaire constant** *m* TELECOM constant bit rate; **~ binaire variable** *m (DBV)* TELECOM variable bit rate *(VBR)*; **~ brut** *m* NUCLEAIRE gross flow; **~ calorifique** *m* THERMODYN heat emission, heat output, rate of heat release; **~ de canal** *m* INFORMAT channel capacity; **~ caractéristique** *m* HYDROLOGIE characteristic flow; **~ caractéristique de 3 mois** *m* HYDROLOGIE three-month characteristic flow rate; **~ caractéristique de crue** *m (DCC)* HYDROLOGIE characteristic floodwater flow rate; **~ caractéristique d'étiage** *m* HYDROLOGIE characteristic low water flow rate; **~ caractéristique maximal** *m (DCM)* HYDROLOGIE characteristic floodwater flow rate; **~ de carburant** *m* AERONAUT mass fuel

rate of flow; **~ de chaleur** *m* THERMODYN heat throughput; **~ de chaleur de la radioactivité** *m* PHYS RAYON heat of radioactivity; **~ de la circulation** *m* TRANSPORT traffic flow; **~ constant** *m* TELECOM constant bit rate; **~ de copeaux** *m* CONS MECA stock removal; **~ du courant** *m* CERAM VER flow; **~ cumulatif** *m* EN RENOUV cumulative discharge; **~ directionnel** *m* TRANSPORT turning movements; **~ de dose** *m* PHYS RAYON, PHYSIQUE dose rate; **~ de dose absorbée** *m* PHYSIQUE absorbed dose rate; **~ d'eau** *m* CONSTR *d'une pompe* flow of water, MAT CHAUFF water flow rate; **~ d'écoulement** *m* PETROLE *forage, production, etc* flow rate; **~ des éléments** *m* TELECOM chip rate; **~ élevé** *m* PRODUCTION *système hydraulique* high flow rate; **~ en bits** *m* INFORMAT, ORDINAT bit rate; **~ de l'encre** *m* IMPRIM *impression* ink flow; **~ d'étiage** *m* DISTRI EAU low-water discharge; **~ de fluence énergétique** *m* PHYSIQUE energy fluence rate, radiant energy fluence rate, radiant flux density; **~ de fluence de particules** *m* PHYSIQUE particle fluence rate; **~ garanti** *m* EN RENOUV guaranteed draw off; **~ globale** *m* HYDROLOGIE *d'une nappe* total flow, total rate; **~ à l'heure de pointe** *m* TRANSPORT vehicular flow at rush hour; **~ horaire maximal** *m* TRANSPORT maximum hourly volume; **~ d'huile** *m* PRODUCTION *système hydraulique* oil flow; **~ d'infiltration** *m* MAT CHAUFF infiltration rate; **~ d'information garanti** *m* TELECOM CIR, committed information rate; **~ journalier** *m* DISTRI EAU daily water flow; **~ journalier moyen** *m* DISTRI EAU mean daily flow, HYDROLOGIE average daily flow, TRANSPORT average daily traffic ADT; **~ journalier moyen d'une année** *m* TRANSPORT average annual daily traffic; **~ de kerma** *m* PHYSIQUE kerma rate; **~ masse** *m* AERONAUT *d'air* mass airflow, REFRIG mass flow rate; **~ massique** *m* AERONAUT, NUCLEAIRE mass flow, PHYSIQUE mass rate; **~ de matière fondue** *m* PHYS FLUID melt flow rate; **~ minimal horaire** *m* HYDROLOGIE minimum hourly runoff; **~ minimal journalier** *m* HYDROLOGIE minimum daily runoff; **~ moyen annuel** *m* HYDROLOGIE average annual flow; **~ moyen caractéristique** *m* HYDROLOGIE average characteristic flow; **~ moyen horaire** *m* HYDROLOGIE mean hourly runoff; **~ moyen mensuel** *m* HYDROLOGIE average monthly flow; **~ nominal** *m* HYDROLOGIE design flow; **~ numérique** *m* ESPACE *communications* bit rate; **~ de pointe** *m* DISTRI EAU peak water flow, GAZ sendout rate, HYDROLOGIE peak flow, peak rate, TRANSPORT peak traffic volume; **~ de pointe horaire** *m* HYDROLOGIE maximum hourly runoff; **~ de pointe journalier** *m* HYDROLOGIE maximum daily runoff; **~ de purge** *m* PRODUCTION *système hydraulique* bleed flow; **~ de refroidissement du coeur par réfrigérant** *m* NUCLEAIRE core coolant flow rate; **~ de rouage** *m* CONS MECA speed; **~ de service** *m* TRANSPORT service volume; **~ solide** *m* DISTRI EAU sediment discharge, silt discharge; **~ de la source sur la plaque** *m* NUCLEAIRE name plate source strength; **~ sous pression** *m* INST HYDR pressure delivery; **~ spécifique de pointe** *m* HYDROLOGIE specific peak flow; **~ thermique** *m* THERMODYN heat throughput; **~ de transfert de données** *m* ORDINAT data transfer rate; **~ de transfert d'informations** *m* TELECOM information transfer rate; **~ volume** *m* REFRIG volume flow rate; **~ volumique** *m* PHYSIQUE volume rate

débitage *m* CHARBON breaking down, precrushing, CONSTR sawing, *des bois* breaking down

débiter *vt* CONSTR *bois, tronc d'arbre* break down, cut up; **~ en feuillets** *vt* CONSTR *de l'ardoise* split into thin sheets

débiteur *m* CHARBON primary crusher, IMPRIM *rotatives* infeed

débiteuse *f* CERAM VER debiteuse

débitmètre *m* CHARBON, CONSTR, DISTRI EAU, ELECTROTEC, EQUIP LAB *débit de fluides*, HYDROLOGIE, PAPIER, PETROLE *raffinerie, canalisation etc*, PHYSIQUE flowmeter; **~ à aimant permanent** *m* NUCLEAIRE permanent magnet flowmeter; **~ d'air** *m* AUTO airflow sensor; **~ à bulle de gaz** *m* GENIE CHIM bubble gage (AmE), bubble gauge (BrE); **~ à bulle de savon** *m* EQUIP LAB *débit de gaz* bubble flowmeter; **~ capillaire** *m* EQUIP LAB *débit de fluides* capillary flowmeter; **~ à courant de Foucault** *m* NUCLEAIRE eddy current flow meter; **~ électromagnétique** *m* ELECTROTEC electromagnetic flowmeter; **~ à flotteur** *m* EQUIP LAB *débit de fluides*, PETROLE rotameter; **~ instantané** *m* DISTRI EAU instant flowmeter; **~ totaliseur** *m* AERONAUT fuel consumption meter, integrating flowmeter

débituminisation *f* CHARBON debitumization

déblai *m* CH DE FER excavated material, railroad cutting (AmE), railway cutting (BrE), spoil, CONSTR cut, excavating, excavation, spoil, MINES excavation; **~ à flanc de coteau** *m* CONSTR sidehill cut; **~ de forage** *m* GAZ drill cutting

déblaiement *m* MINES *des éboulements* clearing, fall cleanup

déblais *m pl* GEOLOGIE debris, PETR, PETROLE cuttings, PRODUCTION waste; **~ de mine** *m pl* MINES barren ground, deads, waste ground, waste rock; **~ mis en dépôt** *m pl* CONSTR spoil to waste

déblayage *m* CONSTR digging

déblayer[1] *vt* CONSTR clear out, *un banc de sable* clear away, MINES *le front de taille* clear, *un éboulement* clear

déblayer:[2] **~ une chambre d'accrochage** *vi* MINES cut a landing, cut a plat, cut a station

déblayeur: **~ mécanique** *m* CONSTR mechanical broom

déblocage *m* ELECTROTEC turn-on, PETROLE *forage* break-out; **~ du faisceau** *m* ELECTRON unblanking; **~ instantané** *m* ESPACE *véhicules* quick release; **~ manuel** *m* PRODUCTION *automatisme industriel* manual bypass

débloqué *adj* ELECTROTEC on

débloquer *vt* MECANIQUE, PRODUCTION release

débloqueur *m* PETROLE *forage* bit breaker

débobinage *m* PAPIER reeling off, winding off

débobiner *vt* CINEMAT unwind

débobinoir *m* PRODUCTION decoiler

déboguer *vt* INFORMAT, ORDINAT debug

débogueur *m* ORDINAT debugger

déboisage *m* MINES prop drawing, removal of timbering

déboîtement *m* TRANSPORT lane switching, leaving a line of traffic

déboîter *vt* CONS MECA disengage

débordage *m* CERAM VER edging

débordement *m* CHIMIE, CONS MECA overflow, IMPRIM *d'encriers, de réservoirs* flood, ORDINAT overflow; **~ de données de connexion** *m* TELECOM CDO, connect data overflow; **~ toléré** *m* TV *pour satellite* agreed spillover

déborder[1] *vi* DISTRI EAU run over, HYDROLOGIE burst its bank, overflow its banks, overtop its banks, *fleuve* flood, NAUT *rivière* flood, THERMODYN boil over

déborder[2] *vti* HYDROLOGIE overflow

déborder:[3] **se ~** *v réfl* DISTRI EAU run over

débordure *f* TEXTILE edge trim, trimming

débouchage *m* CERAM VER bore (BrE), corkage (AmE); **~ et réamorçage** *m* CERAM VER picking down

débouché *m* PRODUCTION outlet

déboucher[1] *vt* CONSTR *un tuyau* unstop

déboucher[2] *vi* HYDROLOGIE *dans la mer* run; **~ dans la mer** *vi* HYDROLOGIE discharge into the sea, outfall to sea

débouchoir *m* CERAM VER pick

débouchonneuse *f* EMBALLAGE uncorking machine

débouchure *f* PRODUCTION punching

déboulonnage *m* CONS MECA unbolting

déboulonnement *m* CONS MECA unbolting

déboulonner *vt* NUCLEAIRE unbolt

débourbage *m* CHAUFFAGE *chaudières* blowdown, DISTRI EAU cleaning out, cleansing

débourber *vt* CHAUFFAGE *chaudières* blowdown, DISTRI EAU cleanse, GENIE CHIM clarify, PRODUCTION clean out

débourbeur *m* CHARBON scrubber

débourrage *m* GENIE CHIM elutriation, MINES unramming

déboutonner[1] *vt* PRODUCTION peel off

déboutonner:[2] **se ~** *v réfl* PRODUCTION fly, fly off

débranchement: **~ en palier** *m* TRANSPORT shunting on level tracks

débrancher *vt* CINEMAT turn off, CONS MECA disconnect, switch off, ELECTR *circuit* disconnect from the circuit, *raccordement* unplug, ELECTROTEC disconnect, TELECOM unplug, TV switch off, unplug

débrayage *m* AUTO clutch throwout, CONS MECA stop motion, strike gear, striker, striking gear, tripping, *par excentrique* release, PRODUCTION belt fork; **~ instantané** *m* CONS MECA instantaneous release; **~ de pilote automatique** *m* AERONAUT autopilot disengagement; **~ sur le devant** *m* CONS MECA disengaging gear in front

débrayer *vt* AUTO unclutch, CONS MECA declutch, throw out of feed, throw out of gear, unclutch, throw out of action, *une courroie* throw off, PRODUCTION *une courroie* lay off, VEHICULES declutch; **~ une courroie** *vt* CONS MECA fork a belt off

débrayeur *m* CONS MECA strike gear, striker, striking gear, PRODUCTION belt fork

débreffage *m* ESPACE debriefing, report

débrider *vt* CONS MECA unclamp, NAUT *la voile* free off

débris *m* GEOLOGIE, METALL debris, PRODUCTION scrap; **~ carbonaté remanié** *m* GEOLOGIE lithoclast; **~ de dislocations** *m* METALL dislocation debris; **~ de fer** *m* PRODUCTION scrap iron; **~ de fonte** *m* PRODUCTION cast scrap, foundry scrap, scrap; **~ de fonte de poterie** *m* PRODUCTION pot scrap; **~ de forage** *m pl* PETR cuttings, PETROLE drill cuttings; **~ métallique** *m* PRODUCTION scrap metal; **~ de rocher** *m* CHARBON blasted stone

débrouiller *vt* TV unscramble

débroussaillement *m* CONSTR clearing and grubbing

début:[1] **en ~ de forage** *adv* PETROLE spudding in

début[2] *m* CINEMAT *d'une bobine* head, INFORMAT *d'entête, de message, de texte*, ORDINAT *d'en-tête, de message, de texte* SOH, start of header, TELECOM *de transmission* start, THERMODYN *d'incendie* outbreak; **~ avancé** *m* TV early start; **~ de bande** *m* INFORMAT, ORDINAT BOT, beginning of tape; **~ de bobine** *m* CINEMAT head out; **~ de branche** *m* PRODUCTION *automatisme industriel* branch start; **~ brusque d'orage**

magnétique *m* ESPACE SSC, sudden storm commencement; ~ **de la demande d'appel** *m* TELECOM beginning of call demand; ~ **de descente** *m* AERONAUT top of descent; ~ **de forage** *m* PETROLE spudding in; ~ **image avancé** *m* TV early start video; ~ **de message** *m* INFORMAT SOM, start of message, ORDINAT BOM, beginning of message, SOM, start of message, TELECOM BOM, beginning of message; ~ **de rupture** *m* AERONAUT incipient fatigue failure; ~ **de session** *m* INFORMAT log-in, log-on; ~ **de soirée** *m* TV prime time slot; ~ **son avancé** *m* TV early start audio; ~ **de texte** *m* INFORMAT, ORDINAT STX, start of text; ~ **de vie** *m* NUCLEAIRE *d'un cœur* beginning of life

débuter *vt* PETR spud in

déca *préf (da)* METROLOGIE deca-*(da)*

décadré *adj* IMPRIM *mise en page* out-of-frame

décaèdre[1] *adj* GEOMETRIE decahedral

décaèdre[2] *m* GEOMETRIE decahedron

décaféiné *adj* AGRO ALIM decaffeinated

décagement *m* MINES clearing the cage, discharging of the cage, unloading the cage

décagone *m* GEOMETRIE decagon

décagramme *m* METROLOGIE decagram (AmE), decagramme (BrE)

décahydronaphtalène *m* CHIMIE decahydronaphthalene, decalin

décalage *m* CINEMAT offset, CONS MECA driving out of keys, driving out of wedges, unkeying, ELECTROTEC lag, GEOLOGIE displacement, lateral shift, offset, INFORMAT shift, MECANIQUE offset, ORDINAT shift, PETR drift, PRODUCTION offsetting, TELECOM out-of-sync error, out-of-synchronization error, TRANSPORT offset, TV staggering; ~ **à angle droit** *m* TV *entre les quatre têtes* quadrature displacement; ~ **arithmétique** *m* ORDINAT arithmetic shift; ~ **axial des têtes** *m* TV axial displacement; ~ **de chiffres** *m* INFORMAT figures shift; ~ **circulaire** *m* ELECTRON circular shift, INFORMAT circular shift, cyclic redundancy check, cyclic shift, ORDINAT circular shift, cyclic shift; ~ **à droite** *m* INFORMAT, ORDINAT right shift; ~ **en entrée** *m* PRODUCTION *automatisme industriel* feedforward; ~ **en sortie** *m* PRODUCTION *automatisme industriel* output biasing; ~ **des flancs arrières** *m* ELECTRON end distortion; ~ **des fréquences porteuses** *m* TELECOM carrier frequency offset; ~ **à gauche** *m* INFORMAT, ORDINAT left shift; ~ **image** *m* CINEMAT advance; ~ **de ligne** *m* TV pulling; ~ **logique** *m* INFORMAT, ORDINAT logical shift; ~ **de niveau** *m* ELECTRON level shifting; ~ **de l'ouverture de fissure** *m* NUCLEAIRE crack opening displacement, crack opening stretch; ~ **de pale** *m* AERONAUT out-of-pitch blade; ~ **de phase** *m* PHYSIQUE, TV phase shift; ~ **son** *m* CINEMAT advance; ~ **de la sous-porteuse de chrominance** *m* TV subcarrier offset; ~ **spectral vers le bleu** *m* ASTRONOMIE blue shift; ~ **spectral vers le rouge** *m* ASTRONOMIE *augmentation de la longueur d'onde d'une source de lumière s'éloignant de la Terre,* redshift; ~ **temporel** *m* ELECTRON time shift; ~ **transversal des spires** *m* TV pop stranding; ~ **vertical** *m* TV frame slip

décalaminage *m* CHIMIE decarbonizing, LESSIVES descaling, THERMODYN decarbonization

décalaminer *vt* LESSIVES, MECANIQUE descale, THERMODYN decarbonize

décalcification *f* HYDROLOGIE decalcification

décalcifier *vt* CHIMIE decalcify

décalcomanie *f* CERAM VER covercoat, decal (AmE),

transfer (BrE); ~ **à chaud** *f* CERAM VER heat release decal; ~ **pour porcelaine** *f* CERAM VER ceramic transfer

décalé[1] *adj* CONS MECA displaced, offset, IMPRIM, VEHICULES *moteur* offset

décalé[2] *m* CONSTR, IMPRIM offset

décaler *vt* CH DE FER hold back, ELECTROTEC displace, IMPRIM offset, INFORMAT, ORDINAT, PRODUCTION shift; ~ **l'axe** *vt* CONSTR move the center line (AmE), move the centre line (BrE)

décaline *f* CHIMIE decahydronaphthalene, decalin, naphthalene

décalitre *m* METROLOGIE decaliter (AmE), decalitre (BrE)

décalque *m* IMPRIM transfer

décalqué *adj* IMPRIM offset

décalquer *vt* IMPRIM offset, transfer

décamètre *m* METROLOGIE decameter (AmE), decametre (BrE); ~ **à ruban** *m* METROLOGIE measure, measuring tape, tape line

décane *m* CHIMIE decane

décanoïque *adj* CHIMIE decanoic

décanol *m* CHIMIE decanol

décantage *m* GENIE CHIM decantation

décantation *f* AGRO ALIM decantation, CHIMIE decanting, GENIE CHIM decantation, purification, MATERIAUX decantation, settling, PETROLE decantation; ~ **composée** *f* HYDROLOGIE compound clarification; ~ **primaire** *f* DISTRI EAU primary clarification, HYDROLOGIE preliminary sedimentation, settling; ~ **sédimentaire** *f* PHYSIQUE settling

décanter *vt* CHIMIE decant, *un dépôt* separate, GENIE CHIM decant, elutriate

décanteur *m* CHARBON settling tank, DISTRI EAU settling basin, GENIE CHIM decantation glass, decantation vessel, decanting glass, precipitation vessel, NUCLEAIRE settler chamber; ~ **secondaire** *m* DISTRI EAU final settling tank, humus tank

décapage *m* CHIMIE etching, pickling, CONSTR grading, removing an overburden, NAUT pickling, sandblasting, PRODUCTION scouring; ~ **à l'acide** *m* CHIMIE pickling; ~ **au bain acidulé** *m* GENIE CHIM acid dipping; ~ **chimique** *m* CONSTR pickling; ~ **aux gaz** *m* CONSTR flame cleaning; ~ **au jet à haute pression** *m* POLLU MER high-pressure washing; ~ **par corrosion** *m* NUCLEAIRE corrosion pickling; ~ **par flamme** *m* CONSTR flame cleaning; ~ **par projection** *m* MECANIQUE grit blasting; ~ **à la sableuse** *m* POLLU MER sandblasting; ~ **de terre végétale** *m* CONSTR topsoil stripping

décapant *m* CONSTR paint stripper; ~ **pour peintures** *m* COULEURS paint remover; ~ **solvant** *m* COULEURS paint remover; ~ **de soudure** *m* PRODUCTION flux

décapelage *m* MINES baring

décapeler: ~ **le gîte** *vi* MINES remove an overburden

décaper *vt* CONSTR scarify, scrape, *à la sableuse* sandblast, POLLU MER scrape, PRODUCTION scour

décapeuse *f* CONSTR grader, scraper, POLLU MER scraper, TRANSPORT caterpillar hauling scraper; ~ **sur chenilles** *f* TRANSPORT caterpillar hauling scraper

décapitation *f* HYDROLOGIE headwater capture

décarbonatation *f* GEOLOGIE *décomposition des minéraux carbonatés* decarbonation

décarbonater *vt* CHARBON, GENIE CHIM decarbonate

décarbonisation *f* CHARBON, THERMODYN decarbonization

décarboniser *vt* CHARBON decarb (AmE), decarbonize, GENIE CHIM, THERMODYN decarbonize

décarboxylase *f* CHIMIE decarboxylase
décarboxylation *f* CHIMIE decarboxylation
décarburation *f* CHIMIE decarbonization, MATERIAUX decarburization
décarburer *vt* CHIMIE decarbonize
décatir *vt* TEXTILE decatize
décatiseur *m* TEXTILE decatizing machine
décatissage *m* TEXTILE decatizing; ~ **au bouillon** *m* TEXTILE roll boiling
décélération *f* ESPACE, MECANIQUE, PHYSIQUE deceleration; ~ **de freinage** *f* TRANSPORT braking deceleration
décéléré *adj* PHYSIQUE decelerated
décélérer *vti* MECANIQUE, PHYSIQUE decelerate
décéléromètre *m* ESPACE decelerometer
décentralisé *adj* INFORMAT, ORDINAT decentralized, PRODUCTION distributed
décentré *adj* CONS MECA, ESPACE off-center (AmE), off-centre (BrE), IMPRIM *mise en page* out-of-frame
décentrement *m* PHOTO *d'un objectif* lens movement
décentrer *vt* CONS MECA throw off center (AmE), throw off centre (BrE)
décharge *f* CHARBON discharge, dump, landfill, CONSTR brace, dump (AmE), tip (BrE), DISTRI EAU discharge, outflow, ELECTR *condensateur, arc, etc*, ELECTROTEC discharge, IMPRIM *impression* marring, MECANIQUE relief, METALL unloading, MILITAIRE *d'une arme à feu ou d'un canon* volley, PHYSIQUE discharge, POLLU MER landfill site, POLLUTION dumping, tipping, RECYCLAGE discharge, dump, refuse dump, waste dump, dumping, tipping; ~ **d'accumulateur** *f* ELECTR accumulator discharge, battery discharge; ~ **des accumulateurs** *f* ESPACE *véhicules* battery discharge; ~ **d'arc** *f* ELECTR, ELECTROTEC, GAZ arc discharge; ~ **d'arc avec transfert** *f* GAZ arc discharge with transfer; ~ **d'arc sans transfert** *f* GAZ arc discharge without transfer; ~ **autonome** *f* ELECTROTEC self-sustained discharge; ~ **brusque** *f* ELECTROTEC disruptive discharge; ~ **brute** *f* RECYCLAGE open dump; ~ **d'un condensateur** *f* ELECTROTEC capacitor discharge; ~ **contrôlée** *f* POLLUTION controlled dumping, RECYCLAGE controlled dumping, controlled tipping, landfilling; ~ **corona** *f* PHYSIQUE, PLAST CAOU *physique* corona discharge; ~ **couronne** *f* GAZ corona discharge; ~ **dans un gaz** *f* ELECTRON gas discharge; ~ **dans le vide** *f* ELECTROTEC vacuum discharge; ~ **de déchets** *f* RECYCLAGE waste dump; ~ **disruptive** *f* ELECTROTEC disruptive discharge, TV sparking; ~ **d'effluent** *f* RECYCLAGE effluent discharge; ~ **électrique** *f* ELECTR *sécurité* electric shock, ELECTROTEC electric discharge; ~ **en aigrette** *f* ELECTROTEC brush discharge; ~ **en courant alternatif** *f* ELECTROTEC AC discharge; ~ **en couronne** *f* ELECTROTEC corona discharge; ~ **en rayons canaux** *f* NUCLEAIRE canal ray discharge; ~ **en surface** *f* ELECTROTEC flashover; ~ **excessive** *f* ELECTROTEC overdischarging; ~ **fulgurante** *f* ELECTROTEC lightning discharge; ~ **haute fréquence** *f* GAZ high-frequency discharge; ~ **illégale** *f* RECYCLAGE fly tipping; ~ **à l'impression** *f* IMPRIM set-off; ~ **de lueur** *f* PHYS RAYON glow discharge; ~ **à lueur** *f* ELECTROTEC glow discharge; ~ **luminescente** *f* ELECTR *ionisation de gaz*, ELECTRON, ELECTROTEC glow discharge, GAZ luminescent discharge, PHYSIQUE glow discharge; ~ **micro-onde** *f* GAZ microwave discharge; ~ **municipale** *f* RECYCLAGE municipal dump; ~ **non autonome** *f* CONSTR non-self-sustained discharge; ~ **non condensée** *f* ELECTROTEC noncondensed discharge; ~ **non**

contrôlée *f* RECYCLAGE indiscriminate dumping; ~ **par effet corona** *f* ELECTROTEC, PHYSIQUE corona discharge; ~ **par étincelles** *f* PHYSIQUE spark discharge; ~ **partielle** *f* ELECTR *condensateur* partial discharge; ~ **publique** *f* DISTRI EAU refuse dumping (AmE), refuse tipping (BrE); ~ **sauvage** *f* RECYCLAGE uncontrolled dump site; ~ **secondaire** *f* ELECTROTEC residual discharge; ~ **spontanée** *f* ESPACE *véhicules* self-discharge; ~ **thermique** *f* PRODUCTION *système hydraulique* thermal relief; ~ **de Townsend** *f* ELECTRON Townsend discharge
déchargé *adj* ELECTR discharged
déchargement *m* CONSTR dumping (AmE), PHYSIQUE unloading, PRODUCTION off-load; ~ **de la cage** *m* MINES clearing the cage, discharging of the cage, unloading the cage
décharger *vt* CINEMAT unthread, INFORMAT unload, INST HYDR *une soupape* relieve, MILITAIRE *une arme à feu* discharge, unload, NAUT *une cargaison* discharge, land, unload, ORDINAT, POLLU MER unload, TELECOM discharge
déchargeur: ~ **de piston** *m* CONSTR piston relief duct
déchausser *vt* CONSTR dislodge
déchénite *f* MINERAUX dechenite
déchet *m* PRODUCTION scrap, waste product, RECYCLAGE waste product; ~ **de coton** *m* PRODUCTION cotton waste; ~ **de la marée** *m* OCEANO ebb; ~ **métallurgique** *m* CHARBON metallurgical waste; ~ **oxydé** *m* CHARBON oxidic waste; ~ **sous forme gazeuse** *m* POLLUTION gaseous waste
déchets *m pl* AGRO ALIM kitchen waste, waste, CERAM VER scrap, waste, CHARBON dross, refuse, DISTRI EAU recirculating water economy, refuse, MINES barren ground, waste, deads, waste ground, waste rock, PAPIER refuse, waste, POLLUTION waste, PRODUCTION garbage (AmE), rubbish, refuse, scrap, waste, RECYCLAGE garbage (AmE), refuse, rubbish (BrE), trash, waste, TEXTILE waste; ~ **alcalins d'activité intermédiaire** *m pl* NUCLEAIRE alkaline medium-level radioactive waste; ~ **de broyage** *m pl* AGRO ALIM break tailings; ~ **combustibles** *m pl* POLLUTION combustible waste; ~ **combustibles semi-solides** *m pl* POLLUTION semisolid combustible waste; ~ **contaminés** *m pl* RECYCLAGE *des hôpitaux* pathological waste; ~ **de criblages** *m pl* CHIMIE screenings; ~ **déshydratés** *m pl* NUCLEAIRE dewatered waste; ~ **domestiques** *m pl* DISTRI EAU domestic waste; ~ **encombrants** *m pl* RECYCLAGE bulky waste; ~ **d'épuration** *m pl* PAPIER screenings, tailings; ~ **de faible activité** *m pl* RECYCLAGE low-level waste; ~ **de faible et moyenne activité** *m pl* RECYCLAGE indeterminate waste; ~ **fibreux** *m pl* TEXTILE fibrous waste; ~ **de film** *m pl* CINEMAT reject; ~ **de fonderie** *m pl* PRODUCTION cast scrap, foundry scrap, scrap; ~ **de forte activité** *m pl* RECYCLAGE high-level waste; ~ **huileux** *m pl* POLLUTION oil waste; ~ **industriels** *m pl* DISTRI EAU, RECYCLAGE industrial waste; ~ **métalliques** *m pl* MATERIAUX metal scrap, PRODUCTION scrap metal; ~ **monstres** *m pl* RECYCLAGE bulky waste; ~ **nucléaires** *m pl* POLLUTION, RECYCLAGE nuclear waste; ~ **d'orge** *m pl* AGRO ALIM tailings; ~ **pathogènes** *m pl* RECYCLAGE pathological waste; ~ **radioactifs** *m pl* NUCLEAIRE, PHYS RAYON radioactive waste; ~ **radioactifs contenant des transuraniens** *m pl* NUCLEAIRE transuranic waste; ~ **résiduels** *m pl* AGRO ALIM tailings; ~ **solides** *m pl* POLLUTION solid waste; ~ **urbains** *m pl* DISTRI EAU municipal waste

déchiffrage *m* ELECTRON deciphering, TELECOM decryption

déchiffrement *m* TELECOM decipherment, decoding

déchiffrer *vt* ELECTRON decipher, TELECOM decode

déchiffreur: ~ de radar *m* PHYS RAYON radar scanner

déchiqueté *adj* SECURITE jagged

déchiqueteur *m* PAPIER kneader

déchiqueteuse *f* EMBALLAGE shredding machine, PAPIER shredder

déchirement *m* PAPIER, PLAST CAOU *essai, défaut* tear; ~ horizontal *m* TV line tear

déchirer *vt* PAPIER, PLAST CAOU tear

déchiromètre *m* PAPIER tearing tester

déchirure *f* PAPIER tear, tearing, PLAST CAOU *essai, défaut* tear, TV *de l'image* tearing; ~ des fibres *f* IMPRIM *papier* fiber tear (AmE), fibre tear (BrE); ~ des plages claires *f* TV highlight tearing

déchirures: ~ de bords *f pl* CERAM VER rip in

déchloration *f* HYDROLOGIE dechlorination

déci *préf* METROLOGIE d, deci

décibel *m (dB)* ACOUSTIQUE, ENREGISTR, PHYS RAYON, PHYSIQUE, POLLUTION decibel *(dB)*

décibelomètre *m* IMPRIM *ergonomie* noisemeter

décigramme *m* METROLOGIE decigram (AmE), decigramme (BrE)

décilitre *m* METROLOGIE deciliter (AmE), decilitre (BrE)

décimal[1] *adj* INFORMAT, MATH decimal

décimal:[2] ~ codé binaire *m* IMPRIM, ORDINAT binary-coded decimal; ~ condensé *m* INFORMAT packed decimal

décimètre *m* METROLOGIE decimeter (AmE), decimetre (BrE); ~ carré *m* METROLOGIE square decimeter (AmE), square decimetre (BrE); ~ cube *m* METROLOGIE cubic decimeter (AmE), cubic decimetre (BrE)

décinéper *m* ACOUSTIQUE decineper

décinormal *adj* CHIMIE decinormal

décintrage *m* CONSTR *d'une voûte* falsework, striking the centering (AmE), striking the centring (BrE)

décintrement *m* CONSTR *d'une voûte* falsework, striking the centering (AmE), striking the centring (BrE)

décintroir: ~ de talus *m* CONSTR mattock; ~ à talus *m* CONSTR mattock, PRODUCTION pick mattock

décision *f* INFORMAT, ORDINAT decision

déclaration *f* INFORMAT, ORDINAT declaration, declarative; ~ d'avaries *f* NAUT ship's protest; ~ de conformité *f* PRODUCTION conformance statement; ~ de conformité de mise en oeuvre du protocole *f* TELECOM PICS, protocol implementation conformance statement; ~ du contenu *f* EMBALLAGE contents declaration; ~ de données *f* ORDINAT data declaration

déclarations: ~ dénigrantes *f pl* BREVETS disparaging statements

déclarative *f* INFORMAT, ORDINAT declarative

déclarer[1] *vt* INFORMAT, ORDINAT declare; ~ nul *vt* BREVETS revoke

déclarer:[2] se ~ aux autorités du port *v réfl* NAUT report to the port authorities

déclassé[1] *adj* TEXTILE off-quality

déclassé[2] *m* CHARBON misplaced size, outsize; ~ inférieur *m* CHARBON undersize; ~ supérieur *m* CHARBON oversize

déclassement *m* NUCLEAIRE decommissioning, proper shutdown, PRODUCTION downgrading

déclassés: ~ des gros *m pl* CHARBON nutty slack

déclenche *f* CONS MECA release, trip, trip gear, tripper, tripping device, tripping

déclenché: ~ par événement *adj* PRODUCTION *automatisme industriel* event-driven; ~ par le temps *adj* PRODUCTION *automatisme industriel* time-driven

déclenchement[1] *m* CONS MECA release, trip, trip gear, tripping, INFORMAT, ORDINAT gating, triggering, PHYS RAYON activation, TV gating; ~ automatique *m* COMMANDE automatic disconnection, automatic tripping; ~ du champ magnétique *m* PHYS RAYON *expériences de la désintégration de particules* onset of magnetic field; ~ comprenant trois niveaux de décision successifs *m* PHYS RAYON activation comprising three successive levels of decision; ~ au doigt *m* PHOTO finger release; ~ à doigt *m* PHOTO trigger release; ~ induit par électrons *m* PHYS RAYON electron induced activation; ~ intempestif *m* ELECTR *relais* false tripping; ~ du mouvement de pression *m* CONS MECA release of the feed motion; ~ par impulsion *m* TV pulse triggering; ~ par rupteur *m* AUTO breaker triggering; ~ périodique *m* TV gating; ~ du réacteur *m* NUCLEAIRE reactor trip; ~ retardé *m* ELECTROTEC delayed-action circuit-breaking; ~ sans rupteur *m* AUTO breakerless triggering; ~ shunt *m* PRODUCTION shunt trip; ~ à tension nulle *m* ELECTROTEC no-volt release

déclenchement:[2] à ~ libre *loc* PRODUCTION trip-free

déclencher[1] *vt* CONS MECA disconnect, INFORMAT trigger, MECANIQUE *physique* actuate, ORDINAT trigger; ~ à vide *vt* PHOTO operate the camera

déclencher:[2] ~ une alarme *vi* TELECOM set off an alarm, trigger an alarm

déclencher:[3] se ~ *v réfl* CONS MECA trigger, trip

déclencheur *m* CINEMAT release button, shutter release, trigger, ELECTR trigger, trip gear, ELECTROTEC release, INFORMAT actuator, trigger, PHOTO shutter release button, trigger, TV release button; ~ à action instantanée *m* CONS MECA fast-acting trip; ~ automatique *m* COMMANDE automatic-tripping equipment, PHOTO automatic timer; ~ direct à maximum de courant *m* ELECTR direct overcurrent release; ~ à distance *m* CINEMAT remote control; ~ à effet Hall *m* AUTO Hall generator; ~ électromagnétique *m* PHOTO electromagnetic shutter release; ~ de fin de course *m* CONS MECA limit strip; ~ indirect à maximum de courant *m* ELECTR indirect overcurrent release; ~ instantané *m* ELECTR *interrupteur* instantaneous release; ~ à maxima *m* ELECTR overcurrent circuit breaker; ~ mécanique *m* ELECTR *disjoncteur* mechanical tripping device; ~ métallique *m* PHOTO cable release; ~ d'obturateur *m* PHOTO shutter release; ~ par tension de défaut *m* ELECTR fault voltage circuit breaker; ~ pneumatique *m* PHOTO pneumatic release; ~ à retardement *m* PHOTO delayed-action release, self-timer; ~ souple *m* CINEMAT shutter release cable; ~ souple double *m* PHOTO double cable release; ~ à surintensité *m* ELECTROTEC overcurrent circuit breaker, overcurrent trip; ~ de tension *m* ELECTR overvoltage release; ~ thermique *m* ELECTR thermal circuit breaker

déclic *m* CONS MECA click, release, trip dog, trip, trip gear, tripper, tripping device, CONSTR *d'une sonnette* releasing hook, SECURITE trip device; ~ d'attelage *m* MINES detaching hook, humble hook

déclinaison *f* ASTRONOMIE, EN RENOUV declination, MILITAIRE slant angle, NAUT declination, variation, PETR, PHYSIQUE declination; ~ magnétique *f* GEOPHYS magnetic declination, magnetic variation, variation, NAUT magnetic declination, magnetic variation, PHYSIQUE angle of magnetic declination, magnetic declination; ~ **magnétique locale** ƒ NAUT compass variation

déclinateur m CONSTR long compass, PRODUCTION trough compass

déclinatoire m CONSTR long compass, PRODUCTION trough compass

déclinomètre m PHYSIQUE declinometer

déclivité ƒ CH DE FER gradient, CONSTR slope; ~ **vers le bas** ƒ CONSTR downhill slope

décochage m PRODUCTION stripping

décocher vt PRODUCTION strip

décoction ƒ AGRO ALIM decoction

décodage m ELECTRON, ESPACE *communications*, INFORMAT, ORDINAT, TELECOM, TV decoding; ~ **à décision douce** m TELECOM soft decision decoding; ~ **à décision dure** m TELECOM hard decision decoding; ~ **à décision programmable** m TELECOM *satellite maritime* soft decision decoding; ~ **séquentiel** m TELECOM sequential decoding; ~ **de Viterbi** m TELECOM Viterbi decoding

décoder vt ELECTRON, ESPACE *communications*, INFORMAT, ORDINAT, TELECOM, TV decode, unscramble

décoder-coder vt TV decode-encode

décodeur m ELECTRON, INFORMAT, ORDINAT, TELECOM decoder, TV decoder, unscrambler; ~ **couleur** m TV color decoder (AmE), colour decoder (BrE); ~ **d'instructions** m INFORMAT, ORDINAT instruction decoder; ~ **MICDA** m TELECOM ADPCM decoder; ~ **stéréo** m ENREGISTR stereo decoder; ~ **stéréophonique** m ENREGISTR stereophonic decoder

décoffrer vt CONSTR strip formwork

décohésion ƒ MATERIAUX *perte de cohésion* debonding, METALL decohesion

décoincement m CONS MECA driving out of keys, driving out of wedges, unkeying

décollage m AERONAUT takeoff, CONS MECA parting, ESPACE *véhicules* liftoff, IMPRIM stripping, MATERIAUX debonding, PLAST CAOU *adhésifs, caoutchouc* bond separation; ~ **arrière** m AERONAUT *hélicoptère* backward takeoff, rearward takeoff; ~ **assisté** m TRANSPORT JATO, jet-assisted takeoff; ~ **avant** m AERONAUT *hélicoptères* forward takeoff; ~ **avec vitesse initiale** m AERONAUT rolling takeoff; ~ **et atterrissage verticaux** m TRANSPORT vertical takeoff and landing; ~ **interrompu** m AERONAUT aborted takeoff; ~ **sauté** m AERONAUT jump takeoff; ~ **vertical** m MILITAIRE *d'un avion* vertical takeoff

décollement m AERONAUT *compresseur, turbomachine* stall, CERAM VER delamination, CONS MECA parting, *d'une soupape* cracking open, GEOLOGIE detachment, PHYSIQUE separation, PLAST CAOU *adhésifs, caoutchouc* bond separation; ~ **de la couche limite** m PHYS FLUID boundary layer separation; ~ **des filets d'air** m AERONAUT airstream separation; ~ **laminaire** m PHYS FLUID laminar separation; ~ **du noir** m TV black lift; ~ **du pantographe** m CH DE FER pantograph slippage; ~ **turbulent** m PHYS FLUID turbulent separation

décoller[1] vt CONSTR dislodge

décoller[2] vi AERONAUT take off

décoller:[3] **se** ~ v réfl CONS MECA part

décolletage m PRODUCTION cutting-off

décolleté: ~ **dans la barre** adj PRODUCTION cut from bar

décolleter vt PRODUCTION cutoff

décolleur m IMPRIM stripper

décolleuse: ~ **de papier peint électrique** ƒ ELECTROTEC steam stripper for wall paper

décolmatage m DISTRI EAU backblowing

décolorant m AGRO ALIM bleaching agent, CERAM VER decolorizer (AmE), decolourizer (BrE), TEXTILE bleaching agent

décoloration ƒ CHIMIE, IMPRIM *papier*, LESSIVES bleaching, PAPIER, PLAST CAOU *défaut* discoloration (AmE), discolouration (BrE)

décolorer vt AGRO ALIM, CHIMIE, EMBALLAGE, TEXTILE bleach

décommettage m CH DE FER *câble* unwinding

décommutateur m ELECTRON decommutator

décommutation ƒ ELECTRON decommutation

décompilateur m ORDINAT decompiler

décomposant m CHIMIE decomposing agent

décomposer vt CHIMIE decompose

décomposition ƒ AGRO ALIM decomposition, CHIMIE breakdown, decomposition, CRISTALL dissociation, splitting, GENIE CHIM separation, GEOLOGIE *d'une roche ou d'un minéral* breakdown, INFORMAT, MATERIAUX, ORDINAT, PETROLE decomposition, PHYSIQUE breakdown, splitting, PRODUCTION breakdown; ~ **anaérobie** ƒ HYDROLOGIE, RECYCLAGE anaerobic decomposition; ~ **de couleurs** ƒ TV color break-up (AmE), colour break-up (BrE); ~ **de l'eau sous rayonnement** ƒ NUCLEAIRE water decomposition under irradiation, water radiolysis; ~ **fonctionnelle** ƒ INFORMAT, ORDINAT functional decomposition; ~ **photochimique** ƒ MATERIAUX photodecomposition; ~ **spinodale** ƒ METALL spinodal decomposition; ~ **thermique** ƒ MATERIAUX, PLAST CAOU thermal decomposition, THERMODYN decomposition by heat, thermal decomposition

décompresseur m AERONAUT pressure reducer

décompressimètre m OCEANO decompression meter

décompression ƒ OCEANO, PETR decompression; ~ **explosive** ƒ OCEANO blowup ascent, explosive decompression, THERMODYN explosive decompression

décomprimer vt INFORMAT, ORDINAT unpack, PETR bleed off

décompte: ~ **des lignes de trame** ƒ IMPRIM *photogravure* screen count

décompteur m ELECTRON countdown counter, PRODUCTION *automatisme industriel* down counter

décondenser vt INFORMAT, ORDINAT unpack

décongélation ƒ AGRO ALIM defrosting, REFRIG thawing; ~ **diélectrique** ƒ REFRIG dielectric thawing; ~ **par hyperfréquence** ƒ REFRIG ultrahigh frequency thawing

décongeler vt AGRO ALIM defrost, thaw, REFRIG thaw

déconnecter[1] vt ELECTROTEC, INFORMAT disconnect, MECANIQUE disengage, ORDINAT disconnect

déconnecter:[2] **se** ~ **du système** v réfl INFORMAT log off

déconnexion ƒ ELECTR disconnection; ~ **rapide** ƒ AERONAUT *hydraulique* quick disconnect

déconsolidation: ~ **de la voie** ƒ CH DE FER loss of track compactness

déconstruction ƒ CONS MECA taking to pieces

décontamination ƒ CHIMIE, GENIE CHIM, MATERIAUX, PHYS RAYON decontamination

déconvolué adj ELECTRON *traité par déconvolution* deconvolved

déconvolution ƒ ELECTR, ELECTRON *traitement du signal* deconvolution, NUCLEAIRE *d'un spectre* deconvolution, unfolding, TELECOM deconvolution

décor m CINEMAT set; ~ **sur verre** m CINEMAT glass shot

décoration: ~ **au four** ƒ CERAM VER decoration firing, enamel firing; ~ **de la porcelaine** ƒ CERAM VER porcelain decoration; ~ **de porcelaine** *f* CERAM VER china decoration

décorrélation *f* TELECOM decorrelation

décortiqué *adj* AGRO ALIM husked, shelled

décortiquer *vt* AGRO ALIM *noix* husk

décortiqueuse *f* AGRO ALIM decorticator

découler *vi* DISTRI EAU run out

découpage *m* ORDINAT scissoring, PRODUCTION cutting-off, fret cutting, punching out, fret sawing, punching, *des métaux au moyen d'un jet d'oxygène* cutting; ~ **à l'arc avec oxygène** *m* CONSTR *soudure* oxygen arc cutting; ~ **de la bande selon un code de brassage** *m* TELECOM rolling code band splitting; ~ **au chalumeau** *m* THERMODYN gas cutting; ~ **chronostratigraphique** *m* GEOLOGIE chronostratigraphic division; ~ **du cuir** *m* PRODUCTION leather cutting; ~ **définitif** *m* CINEMAT editing shot list; ~ **à l'emporte-pièce** *m* PRODUCTION punch out, punching, punching out; ~ **en partitions** *m* ORDINAT partitioning; ~ **en voies** *m* TELECOM channeling (AmE), channelling (BrE); ~ **à la flamme** *m* THERMODYN flame cutting; ~ **au laser** *m* ELECTRON laser cutting; ~ **laser** *m* ELECTRON laser cutting; ~ **mécanique** *m* CONS MECA machine cutting; ~ **par faisceau d'électrons** *m* ELECTRON electron beam cutting; ~ **à la presse** *m* PRODUCTION blanking, press cutting; ~ **technique** *m* CINEMAT action outline, scenario, screenplay, script, shooting script; ~ **technique définitif** *m* CINEMAT final shooting script; ~ **du temps** *m* ELECTRON, INFORMAT, ORDINAT time slicing

découpe *f* CERAM VER cutting, ELECTRON scribing, IMPRIM *transformation, façonnage, emballage* box die, MECANIQUE cutout, PRODUCTION breakdown; ~ **des bords** *f* CERAM VER cutting off the edges; ~ **au couteau** *f* IMPRIM *façonnage, emballage* knifecut; ~ **à l'emporte-pièce** *f* IMPRIM *transformation* die cutting; ~ **en coin** *f* IMPRIM *façonnage et continu* corner cut; ~ **et mise au poids** *f* CERAM VER chipping to the weight; ~ **de film** *f* PRODUCTION *production* film cutting; ~ **au fil de verre chaud** *f* CERAM VER hot glass wire cutting; ~ **à la lame de scie** *f* IMPRIM *façonnage, emballage* knifecut; ~ **au laser** *f* ELECTRON laser scribing; ~ **des marges** *f* IMPRIM *façonnages* trim; ~ **de la plage de montage** *f* PRODUCTION flange cutout; ~ **pointillée** *f* CERAM VER perforation

découpe-joints *m* CONS MECA wad punch

découper *vt* CERAM VER cutoff, ELECTRON chop, MECANIQUE punch out, PRODUCTION cutoff, punch out, cutout, punch; ~ **à l'emporte-pièce** *vt* IMPRIM *transformation* die-cut, PRODUCTION punch; ~ **en partitions** *vt* ORDINAT partition

découpeur *m* AERONAUT, ELECTRON chopper; ~ **de carottes** *m* MINES core bit, core cutter, core lifter; ~ **optique** *m* ELECTRON light chopper; ~ **de témoins** *m* MINES core bit, core cutter, core lifter; ~ **à transistor** *m* ELECTRON electronic chopper

découpeuse *f* CONS MECA punching machine

découplage *m* CHIMIE, ELECTR *circuit en courant alternatif*, ELECTROTEC decoupling, ESPACE disconnecting, isolation, uncoupling, *communications* decoupling, NUCLEAIRE uncoupling, unlatching, TELECOM decoupling; ~ **dynamique** *m* ESPACE quasi-stellar decoupling; ~ **en fréquence** *m* ESPACE *véhicules* frequency decoupling; ~ **de polarisation** *m* ESPACE *communications* polarization isolation

découplé *adj* INFORMAT, ORDINAT decoupled

découpler *vt* CH DE FER *remorques, wagons* uncouple

découpoir *m* CONS MECA punch, PRODUCTION socket punch; ~ **à col de cygne** *m* CONS MECA swan neck fly press, swan neck screw press; ~ **à la main** *m* PRODUCTION fly press

découpure *f* PRODUCTION fretwork

déc006ronnement *m* CONS MECA uncapping

découvert *m* PRODUCTION clearance; ~ **intérieur d'un tiroir** *m* INST HYDR inside clearance slide valve

découverte *f* PETR discovery; ~ **de pétrole** *f* PETROLE oil discovery

découverture *f* CONSTR removing an overburden, MINES baring

décraber *vt* AERONAUT decrab

décrassage *m* MATERIAUX *métallurgie* slagging, PRODUCTION pricking, slicing

décrasse-meule *m* CONS MECA wheel dresser, PRODUCTION dresser, emery wheel dresser

décrasser *vt* LESSIVES scour

décrasseur *m* GAZ poker

décrément *m* ELECTRON decrement, PHYSIQUE damping factor, decrement; ~ **logarithmique** *m* ELECTRON, PHYSIQUE logarithmic decrement

décrémenter *vt* INFORMAT, ORDINAT decrement

décrémenteur *m* INFORMAT, ORDINAT *microprocesseur* decrementer

décreuser *vt* TEXTILE *la soie* degum

décrochage *m* AERONAUT *d'un aéronef* stall, CONS MECA unhooking, ELECTR *de synchronisme* loss, EN RENOUV stall; ~ **de bout de pale** *m* AERONAUT blade tip stall; ~ **d'image** *m* CINEMAT picture slip; ~ **manuel du train** *m* AERONAUT landing gear manual release; ~ **à pale reculante** *m* AERONAUT *hélicoptère* retreating blade stall; ~ **des pales** *m* AERONAUT blade stall; ~ **du train** *m* AERONAUT landing gear unlocking; ~ **des trappes de train** *m* AERONAUT landing gear door unlatching; ~ **vertical de l'image** *m* TV loss of picture lock

décroché *adj* TELECOM off-the-hook

décrochement *m* CONS MECA detachment, unhooking, CRISTALL kink, GEOLOGIE lateral shift, offset, strike slip, transcurrent fault, wrench fault, METALL kink; ~ **sur une dislocation** *m* METALL dislocation kink

décrocher[1] *vt* CH DE FER *remorques, wagons* uncouple, CINEMAT black out

décrocher[2] *vi* EN RENOUV stall, TELECOM lift, pick up, unhook

décro-chevauchement *m* GEOLOGIE strike-slip thrust, transcurrent thrust, transpressive thrust

décroissance *f* ELECTRON droop, ENREGISTR, NUCLEAIRE *radioactivité* decay; ~ **exponentielle** *f* ELECTRON exponential decay; ~ **de luminescence** *f* TV decay; ~ **radioactive** *f* PHYSIQUE radioactive decay

décroûtage *m* PRODUCTION skinning

décrue *f* HYDROLOGIE receding flood, *d'un fleuve* fall, *d'une rivière* subsidence

décryptage *m* INFORMAT, ORDINAT decryption, TV decoding

décrypter *vt* ELECTRON, INFORMAT, ORDINAT decrypt, TV unscramble

déculasser *vt* MILITAIRE *artillerie* unlock

décutage *m* CERAM VER breaking-off of base

décyle *m* CHIMIE decyl

dédié *adj* INFORMAT, ORDINAT dedicated

dédommagement *m* BREVETS, SECURITE compensation

dédommager *vt* BREVETS, SECURITE compensate for damage

dédouanement *m* NAUT clearance, customs clearance

dédoublement: ~ **de structure fine** m NUCLEAIRE fine structure splitting, multiple splitting

dédoubler[1] vt CINEMAT du négatif break down

dédoubler[2] vi NAUT single up

dédoubleur m CINEMAT du négatif breakdown operator

défaillance f CONSTR, ELECTR matériel, ELECTROTEC, ESPACE qualité, GAZ failure, INFORMAT failure, fault, malfunction, MECANIQUE failure, METROLOGIE malfunction, ORDINAT failure, fault, malfunction, PHYSIQUE breakdown, QUALITE, TELECOM failure; ~ **accidentelle** f ELECTROTEC random failure; ~ **catastrophique** f ELECTROTEC catastrophic failure; ~ **due à la température** f ELECTROTEC temperature-related failure; ~ **due à l'usure** f ELECTROTEC wear-out failure; ~ **humaine** f QUALITE human failure; ~ **d'une installation** f AERONAUT facility failure; ~ **intrinsèque de base** f AERONAUT basic failure; ~ **du matériel** f PRODUCTION automatisme industriel component failure; ~ **non révélée** f QUALITE unrevealed failure; ~ **par vieillissement** f ELECTROTEC time-related failure; ~ **prématurée** f ELECTROTEC early failure; ~ **révélée** f QUALITE revealed failure; ~ **de signal** f TELECOM SF, signal fail; ~ **technique** f TELECOM technical breakdown

défaillir vi CONSTR fail

défaire vt CHIMIE émulsion break, CONS MECA un joint unmake, CONSTR fail

défausser vt CONS MECA true, true up, PRODUCTION straighten, une tige straighten

défaut:[1] **par ~** adj INFORMAT, ORDINAT default

défaut[2] m AGRO ALIM blemish, CHIMIE, CRISTALL defect, ELECTR fault, ELECTROTEC defect, fault, INFORMAT fault, MECANIQUE failure, fault, matériaux flaw, METALL defect, NUCLEAIRE d'un matériau defect, flaw, ORDINAT fault, PAPIER defect, PHYSIQUE breakdown, PRODUCTION fault, QUALITE defect, failure, flaw, TELECOM, TEXTILE fault; ~ **d'adaptation** m ELECTROTEC mismatch; ~ **affectant le système processeur** m PRODUCTION automatisme industriel processor hardware fault; ~ **d'alignement** m CONS MECA misalignment, MECANIQUE offset, TELECOM alignment fault; ~ **d'amorçage** m ELECTROTEC misfire; ~ **de bas niveau** m PRODUCTION automatisme industriel low-level fault; ~ **de boucle** m PRODUCTION automatisme industriel loop fault; ~ **de câble** m ELECTROTEC cable defect; ~ **de calage** m TV misregistration; ~ **de collimation** m PHOTO collimating fault; ~ **de conception** m NUCLEAIRE design-related defect; ~ **de contact** m ELECTROTEC contact fault; ~ **de continuité** m TELECOM continuity fault; ~ **cristallin** m QUALITE crystal defect; ~ **critique** m QUALITE critical defect; ~ **de cuisson** m AGRO ALIM baking fault; ~ **de diffusion** m ELECTRON diffusion defect; ~ **dû à un défaut de masse** m PRODUCTION électricité ground fault trip; ~ **dû à l'usure** m NUCLEAIRE wear-out defect; ~ **électrique** m QUALITE electrical fault; ~ **d'empilement** m CRISTALL stacking fault; ~ **en exploitation** m NUCLEAIRE operations-related defect; ~ **en ligne** m ELECTROTEC line fault; ~ **en réception à l'extrémité distante** m TELECOM FERF, far-end receive failure; ~ **d'épiderme** m AGRO ALIM skin blemish; ~ **d'équilibrage** m MECANIQUE unbalance; ~ **de fabrication** m NUCLEAIRE fabrication-related fuel defect; ~ **de flamme** m THERMODYN flame failure; ~ **de fonctionnement du moteur** m NAUT engine malfunction; ~ **fragile** m NUCLEAIRE brittle failure; ~ **de Frenkel** m CRISTALL Frenkel defect; ~ **d'impression formant une trace allongée** m

IMPRIM flexographie comet; ~ **inhérent au bois** m QUALITE wood defect; ~ **intercristallin** m MATERIAUX defect fracture, intergranular fracture; ~ **intermittent** m ELECTR intermittent fault; ~ **d'isolement** m ELECTROTEC insulation defect; ~ **linéaire** m METALL linear defect; ~ **de masse** m PHYSIQUE mass defect; ~ **de masse relatif** m PHYSIQUE packing fraction; ~ **de mise à la terre sur deux phases** m ELECTR double earth fault (BrE), double ground fault (AmE); ~ **monophasé à la terre** m ELECTR courant alternatif phase-to-earth fault (BrE), phase-to-ground fault (AmE); ~ **du papier** m IMPRIM corrugation, PAPIER flaw; ~ **du papier provenant du rouleau coucheur** m IMPRIM couch mark; ~ **de poids** m EMBALLAGE short weight; ~ **ponctuel** m CRISTALL, METALL point defect; ~ **des produits cuits au four** m AGRO ALIM baking fault; ~ **provenant de la fabrication du papier** m IMPRIM imprimerie cockle; ~ **de répartition** m CERAM VER defect in distribution; ~ **du réseau** m ELECTRON lattice defect; ~ **réticulaire** m METALL lattice defect; ~ **de Schottky** m CRISTALL Schottky defect; ~ **de surface** m QUALITE surface defect; ~ **de la table de données** m PRODUCTION automatisme industriel data table failure; ~ **de temps d'exécution** m PRODUCTION run-time error; ~ **de terre** m PRODUCTION earth fault (BrE), ground fault (AmE); ~ **à la terre** m ELECTR earth fault (BrE), ground fault (AmE); ~ **de verrouillage trame** m (DVT) TELECOM out-of-frame

défauts: ~ **de matière** m pl CONS MECA material defects; ~ **de surface** m pl CONS MECA surface discontinuities

défécation f GENIE CHIM defecation; ~ **au lait de chaux** f AGRO ALIM lime defecation

défectueux[1] adj ELECTR, MECANIQUE faulty, QUALITE defective, TEXTILE faulty

défectueux[2] m IMPRIM contrôle de qualité misregistration

défectuosité f AGRO ALIM blemish, NUCLEAIRE defect, flaw

défense[1] f INFORMAT security, NAUT, POLLU MER fender; ~ **aérienne active** f MILITAIRE active air defence (BrE), active air defense (AmE); ~ **aérienne passive** f MILITAIRE passive air defence; ~ **anti-sous-marine** f NAUT antisubmarine defence (BrE), antisubmarine defense (AmE); ~ **contre avions** f (DCA) MILITAIRE air defence; ~ **côtière** f MILITAIRE, NAUT coastal defence (BrE), coastal defense (AmE); ~ **d'étrave** f NAUT bow fender, noseband; ~ **passive** f MILITAIRE civil defence (BrE), civil defense (AmE)

défense:[2] ~ **d'utiliser des crochets** loc EMBALLAGE inscription ou étiquette de manutention use no hooks

déferlement m OCEANO ondes breaking

déferler[1] vt NAUT drapeau break

déferler[2] vi NAUT vague break

déferrisation: ~ **magnétique** f CERAM VER de-ironing, magnetting, removal of iron

défibrage m PAPIER defibering (AmE), defibring (BrE), grinding; ~ **longitudinal** m PAPIER longitudinal grinding; ~ **transversal** m PAPIER cross grinding, defibration

défibreur m PAPIER grinder; ~ **à chaîne** m PAPIER caterpillar grinder; ~ **à chaînes** m PAPIER chain grinder; ~ **en continu** m PAPIER continuous grinder, defibrer (AmE), defibrer (BrE); ~ **multipresse** m PAPIER pocket grinder

déficit: ~ **hydrique** m DISTRI EAU water deficiency; ~ **d'oxygène** m HYDROLOGIE oxygen deficit; ~ **à satura-**

tion *m* METEO saturation deficit

défilé *m* CONSTR defile

défilement *m* INFORMAT, ORDINAT scrolling, TV shuttle; **~ de la bande** *m* ENREGISTR, TV tape run; **~ à l'écran** *m* IMPRIM scrolling

défiler *vi* INFORMAT, ORDINAT scroll

défileur: **~ cinéma** *m* TV film pick-up; **~ son optique** *m* CINEMAT optical sound reproducer

défileuse: **~ à chiffons** *f* PAPIER rag breaker

défini: **~ par l'utilisateur** *adj* INFORMAT, ORDINAT user-defined

définition *f* CINEMAT definition, resolution, sharpness, ELECTRON definition, resolution, INFORMAT *graphique* definition, ORDINAT definition, PHOTO definition, TV resolution; **~ de données** *f* INFORMAT, ORDINAT data definition; **~ de l'écran** *f* IMPRIM screen resolution, screen ruling; **~ en fréquence** *f* ELECTRON frequency resolution; **~ horizontale** *f* TV horizontal resolution; **~ d'image** *f* TELECOM picture definition; **~ du problème** *f* INFORMAT, ORDINAT problem definition; **~ de la structure de données** *f* INFORMAT, ORDINAT data set definition; **~ des travaux** *f* INFORMAT, ORDINAT job definition; **~ des zones** *f* IMPRIM *sur un document* zoning

déflagration *f* MINES deflagration, explosive combustion; **~ aérienne** *f* CHARBON air blast

déflagrer *vi* CHIMIE deflagrate, MINES combust, deflagrate, SECURITE *flamber avec des flammes soudaines* deflagrate

défléchir *vt* CONS MECA deflect

déflecter *vt* PHYS RAYON deflect

déflecteur *m* AERONAUT deflector, CERAM VER deflector chute, delivery, CONS MECA, CONSTR *plaque ou mur pour défléchir les gaz, les liquides* baffle, EN RENOUV deflector, ESPACE deflection plate, GENIE CHIM baffle, deflector, NUCLEAIRE deflecting coil, TELECOM deflector, TRANSPORT spoiler; **~ à chicanes** *m* GENIE CHIM baffle plate; **~ de la gaine d'étirage** *m* CERAM VER baffle; **~ de gaz** *m* NUCLEAIRE gas baffle; **~ d'huile** *m* CONS MECA oil slinger; **~ de jet** *m* ESPACE *véhicules* jet deflector; **~ de porte avant** *m* AERONAUT quarter light (BrE), quarter window (AmE), vent window

déflecteurs *m pl* REFRIG baffle plates

déflection *f* PHYS RAYON, PHYSIQUE deflection

déflegmateur *m* NUCLEAIRE dephlegmator, reflux condenser, refluxer

déflegmer *vt* CHIMIE dephlegmate

déflexion *f* CONS MECA, ELECTRON, METALL deflection; **~ magnétique** *f* PHYS PART magnetic deflection; **~ vers le bas** *f* AERONAUT *navigabilité* downwash; **~ vers le haut** *f* AERONAUT *navigabilité* upwash

défloculant *m* CHIMIE deflocculant

défloculation *f* CHIMIE, HYDROLOGIE deflocculation

défocalisation *f* ELECTRON, MATERIAUX defocusing

défocalisé *adj* PHOTO out-of-focus

défocaliser *vt* CINEMAT, MATERIAUX defocus

défoliant *m* CHIMIE defoliant

défoncement *m* CONSTR recess, recessing

défoncer *vt* CONSTR recess

défonceuse *f* CONSTR recessing machine; **~ portée** *f* CONSTR ripper; **~ portée à l'arrière** *f* TRANSPORT rear-mounted ripper

déformant *adj* CERAM VER, INSTRUMENT distorting

déformation *f* CERAM VER strain, CHARBON, CHIMIE deformation, CINEMAT distortion, CONS MECA distortion, set, strain, GEOLOGIE deformation, strati-graphie strain, IMPRIM expansion, *papier* curl, *reliure de livres* warping, MATERIAUX deformation, MECANIQUE deformation, *matériaux* strain, METALL deformation, shape change, strain, NUCLEAIRE *d'un noyau atomique*, PHYS RAYON *d'un noyau atomique* deformation, PHYSIQUE strain, PLAST CAOU deformation, set, strain, PRODUCTION buckling, *des pièces coulées* warping; **~ causée par la compression** *f* GEOLOGIE compressive strain; **~ de champ** *f* TV fringing; **~ creuse** *f* CONS MECA dent; **~ due à la chaleur** *f* THERMO-DYN heat distortion; **~ due au cisaillement** *f* CONS MECA, PHYSIQUE shear strain; **~ due à la torsion** *f* CONS MECA torsional strain; **~ due à la traction** *f* CONS MECA tensile strain; **~ élastique** *f* CONS MECA lag, temporary set, EMBALLAGE, MATERIAUX elastic deformation; **~ homogène** *f* GEOLOGIE homogeneous deformation; **~ momentanée** *f* CONS MECA lag, temporary set; **~ non élastique** *f* PLAST CAOU plastic yield; **~ nucléaire** *f* NUCLEAIRE nuclear deformation; **~ de la pale** *f* AERONAUT blade distortion; **~ par fluage** *f* METALL creep strain; **~ permanente** *f* CONS MECA permanent set, METALL permanent deformation, RESSORTS permanent set; **~ permanente par sollicitation de compression** *f* PLAST CAOU compression set; **~ des plaquettes** *f* ELECTRON wafer distortion; **~ plastique** *f* CONSTR, CRISTALL, METALL, PHYSIQUE, PLAST CAOU plastic deformation; **~ réelle** *f* METALL true strain; **~ résiduelle** *f* PLAST CAOU residual set; **~ réticulaire** *f* METALL lattice deformation; **~ sous compression** *f* MECANIQUE *matériaux* compressive strain; **~ de la structure de ligne** *f* TV line crawl; **~ tangentielle** *f* CONS MECA tangential strain; **~ thermoélastique** *f* ESPACE *véhicules* thermoelastic distorsion; **~ de traction** *f* METALL tensile strain; **~ volumétrique** *f* CONS MECA volumetric strain

déformé[1] *adj* CERAM VER out-of-shape, ELECTRON distorted, IMPRIM out-of-true

déformé[2] *m* CERAM VER freak

déformer *vt* CONS MECA buckle, MATERIAUX injure, MECANIQUE deform, POLLU MER wring

défournement *m* PRODUCTION drawing the charge

défourner *vt* PRODUCTION draw the charge, *des briques* draw out of a kiln

défourneuse *f* CERAM VER goose-necked pot carriage

défraîchi *adj* AGRO ALIM withered

défrichage *m* CONSTR *bitume* aggregate stripping

défricher *vt* CONSTR rip

défroissabilité *f* TEXTILE crease recovery

dégagé *adj* PHYSIQUE released

dégagement *m* CHIMIE *de chaleur* liberation, *de gaz* evolution, release, separation, CONS MECA backing-off, clearance, relief, *d'une tête porte-outil* disengagement, INST HYDR clearance, clearance space, MECANIQUE clearance, PHYSIQUE evolution, THERMODYN *de chaleur* development; **~ de chaleur résiduelle** *m* NUCLEAIRE afterheat release; **~ extérieur** *m* INST HYDR outside clearance; **~ gazeux** *m* GAZ gas leak, GENIE CHIM degasifying; **~ du rouleau-support** *m* IMPRIM *machines* backing roller gap

dégagements *m pl* PHYS RAYON *monitorage de radiation* emissions

dégager[1] *vt* CHIMIE isolate, *de la chaleur* evolve, *un gaz* release, CONS MECA back off, relieve, MECANIQUE disengage, NAUT *ancre* clear, PHYSIQUE give off, liberate, PRODUCTION *une forêt* clear, THERMODYN emit, *de la chaleur, de la vapeur, de la fumée* give off; **~ du**

gaz *vt* GENIE CHIM degas

dégager:[2] **se ~** *v réfl* NAUT float off, PRODUCTION clear

dégainage: ~ mécanique *m* NUCLEAIRE mechanical decanning, mechanical decladding; **~ retraitement** *m* NUCLEAIRE *des combustibles* decanning, decladding

dégât: ~ par rayonnement *m* PHYS RAYON radiation damage

dégâts: ~ d'incendie *m pl* SECURITE fire damage; **~ occasionnés par un incendie** *m pl* SECURITE loss caused by fire

dégauchir *vt* CONS MECA surface, true, true up, PRODUCTION *une tige* straighten

dégauchissage *m* CONS MECA surface planing, surfacing, CONSTR taking out of wind, PRODUCTION straightening

dégauchissement *m* CONS MECA surface planing, surfacing, CONSTR taking out of wind, PRODUCTION straightening

dégauchisseuse *f* CONS MECA surface planer, surface-planing machine

dégazage *m* ELECTRON degassing, GENIE CHIM degasifying, degassing, HYDROLOGIE degasification, OCEANO degassing, desaturation, gas expulsion, gas extraction, REFRIG gas purging

dégazé *adj* THERMODYN gas-free

dégazement: ~ atmosphérique *m* HYDROLOGIE atmospheric degassing

dégazer *vt* CHIMIE outgas, ELECTRON, GENIE CHIM degas, THERMODYN free from gas

dégazeur *m* CHAUFFAGE, GENIE CHIM degasser, GEOLOGIE degasser, getter (AmE), NUCLEAIRE gas stripper, REFRIG gas purger, TELECOM getter; **~ d'eau lourde** *m* NUCLEAIRE heavy water degasifier

dégel *m* METEO thaw; **~ par micro-ondes** *m* REFRIG microwave thawing; **~ par radio fréquence** *m* REFRIG high-frequency thawing

dégeler *vti* METEO, REFRIG thaw

dégénération *f* ELECTRON degeneration

dégénéré *adj* ELECTRON, METALL, PHYSIQUE degenerate

dégénérescence *f* ELECTRON degeneracy, PHYS RAYON degeneration, PHYSIQUE degeneracy

dégivrage *m* AERONAUT de-icing, AGRO ALIM, CONS MECA defrosting, ESPACE, MAT CHAUFF de-icing, REFRIG defrosting; **~ automatique** *m* REFRIG autodefrost; **~ chronocommandé** *m* REFRIG timed defrosting; **~ électrique** *m* REFRIG electric defrosting; **~ manuel** *m* REFRIG manual defrost; **~ naturel cyclique** *m* REFRIG off-cycle defrosting; **~ par aspersion d'eau** *m* REFRIG water defrosting; **~ par cycle inversé** *m* REFRIG reverse cycle defrosting; **~ par l'extérieur** *m* REFRIG external defrosting; **~ par gaz chauds** *m* REFRIG hot gas defrosting; **~ par l'intérieur** *m* REFRIG internal defrosting; **~ par micro-ondes** *m* REFRIG microwave thawing; **~ par thermoaccumulateur** *m* REFRIG thermobank defrosting; **~ planeur** *m* AERONAUT aerofoil de-icing (BrE), airfoil de-icing (AmE); **~ réacteur** *m* AERONAUT engine de-icing

dégivrer:[1] *vt* AERONAUT, ESPACE *véhicules*, MAT CHAUFF de-ice, REFRIG defrost

dégivrer:[2] **se ~** *v réfl* AGRO ALIM, REFRIG defrost

dégivreur *m* AERONAUT, ESPACE *véhicules*, MAT CHAUFF de-icer, VEHICULES *accessoire* defroster; **~ pneumatique** *m* ESPACE *véhicules* de-icer boot

dégommage *m* AERONAUT cranking, *d'un moteur* priming, AGRO ALIM degumming

dégonflement *m* VEHICULES *pneu* deflation

dégonfler *vt* CONS MECA deflate

dégorgement *m* IMPRIM *des pigments dans le papier* bleeding, flooding, PLAST CAOU *défaut de peinture* running

dégorgeoir *m* CONS MECA round-nosed chisel, round-nosed cold chisel, CONSTR boring bit, DISTRI EAU outlet, PRODUCTION chipping chisel, spout; **~ des eaux résiduaires** *m* DISTRI EAU wastewater outfall; **~ à mortaises** *m* CONSTR mortise boring bit

dégorger[1] *vt* TEXTILE bleed off

dégorger[2] *vi* PLAST CAOU *imperfection de peinture* bleed

dégoujonneuse *f* CONS MECA stud driver

dégoulottage *m* PETROLE debottlenecking

dégourdi *m* CERAM VER biscuit-baked porcelain, biscuit-fired porcelain

dégradation:[1] **à ~ contrôlée** *adj* INFORMAT, ORDINAT fail-soft

dégradation:[2] **à ~ restreinte** *adv* ESPACE fail-soft

dégradation[3] *f* CONS MECA, ESPACE *qualité* degradation, HYDROLOGIE eroding, INFORMAT degradation, NUCLEAIRE *par choc* degradation, energy degradation, thindown, PHYSIQUE degradation, PLAST CAOU *défaut* degradation, *physique, chimie* breakdown, POLLU MER *sous l'effet des intempéries* weathering, QUALITE, TV degradation; **~ anaérobie** *f* HYDROLOGIE anaerobic decomposition; **~ biologique** *f* EMBALLAGE, HYDROLOGIE, LESSIVES, POLLU MER, POLLUTION biodegradation; **~ écologique** *f* POLLU MER, POLLUTION ecological damage; **~ harmonieuse** *f* INFORMAT graceful degradation; **~ interne** *f* REFRIG internal breakdown; **~ de l'orbite** *f* ESPACE *mécanique* orbital decay; **~ par radiation** *f* PHYS RAYON radiation degradation; **~ photochimique** *f* MATERIAUX photochemical decomposition; **~ progressive** *f* INFORMAT graceful degradation; **~ du signal** *f* TELECOM SD, signal degradation, signal weakening; **~ des sols** *f* POLLUTION land degradation

dégradé *adj* CERAM VER shaded

dégrader *vt* HYDROLOGIE erode

dégraissage *m* CERAM VER, CONS MECA, CONSTR, MECANIQUE degreasing, PRODUCTION scouring; **~ alcalin** *m* LESSIVES alkaline cleaning; **~ d'un feutre** *m* PAPIER scouring

dégraissant *m* CHIMIE scouring agent, ELECTR degreasing agent, *nettoyage* degreaser, LESSIVES detergent, MECANIQUE degreaser, degreasing agent; **~ pour tapis** *m* LESSIVES carpet cleaner, carpet shampoo

dégraissé *adj* AGRO ALIM nonfat

dégraisser *vt* AGRO ALIM, ELECTR *nettoyage*, MECANIQUE degrease, PRODUCTION scour, *une lime* clean

dégraisseur *m* CONS MECA separator

degré *m* ACOUSTIQUE *échelle musicale* pitch, CONSTR step, GEOMETRIE degree, PHYSIQUE degree, *de liberté* degree, TRANSPORT *de congestion* level; **~ absolu** *m* IMPRIM *photogravure* Kelvin degree; **~ d'acidité** *m* IMPRIM acidity; **~ d'adhésivité** *m* EMBALLAGE tack level; **~ d'arrondi** *m* GEOLOGIE roundness; **~ Celsius** *m* METROLOGIE, PHYSIQUE degree Celsius; **~ de chaleur** *m* THERMODYN degree of heat; **~ de cohérence** *m* OPTIQUE, TELECOM degree of coherence; **~ de compactage** *m* CHARBON, CONSTR degree of compaction; **~ de congestion** *m* TRANSPORT overloading; **~ de consolidation** *m* CHARBON degree of consolidation; **~ de dureté** *m* PRODUCTION *d'une meule en émeri* grade; **~ de dureté Brinell** *m* CONS MECA Brinell hardness number; **~ de dureté dur** *m* PRODUCTION hard grade;

~ **de deureté moyen** *m* PRODUCTION medium grade; ~ **de dureté tendre** *m* PRODUCTION soft grade; ~ **de dureté tendre moyen** *m* PRODUCTION medium-soft grade; ~ **d'émoussage** *m* GEOLOGIE roundness; ~ **d'épuration** *m* DISTRI EAU degree of purification; ~ **d'évaporation** *m* REVETEMENT rate of evaporation; ~ **de fissures** *m* GEOLOGIE fracturing; ~ **de flèche** *m* RESSORTS deflection ratio; ~ **de frisure** *m* TEXTILE degree of crimp; ~ **d'humidité** *m* GAZ water content; ~ **hydrométrique** *m* HYDROLOGIE, METEO hydrometric state; ~ **hygrométrique** *m* PAPIER, REFRIG relative humidity; ~ **hygrométrique de l'air** *m* THERMODYN air humidity; ~ **d'incombustibilité** *m* PAPIER degree of incombustibility; ~ **d'ininflammabilité** *m* PAPIER degree of non-flammability; ~ **Kelvin** *m* IMPRIM *photogravure* Kelvin degree, METROLOGIE degree Kelvin; ~ **de marche** *m* COMMANDE regulating step; ~ **de métamorphisme** *m* GEOLOGIE metamorphic grade; ~ **d'occupation des voies** *m* TELECOM channel occupancy; ~ **de pollution** *m* POLLUTION degree of pollution; ~ **de polymérisation** *m* PLAST CAOU degree of polymerization; ~ **de saturation** *m* CHARBON, TRANSPORT degree of saturation; ~ **de séchage** *m* CONSTR degree of drying; ~ **de siccité** *m* CONSTR degree of drying; ~ **de subtilité** *m* RESSORTS slenderness ratio; ~ **de température** *m* THERMODYN degree of temperature; ~ **de trempe** *m* CERAM VER temper; ~ **d'utilisation** *m* TRANSPORT degree of utilization

dégréement *m* NAUT unrigging

dégréer *vt* NAUT unrig

degrés: ~ **conjoints** *m pl* ACOUSTIQUE conjoined pitches

dégrillage *m* POLLU MER screening

dégriller *vt* POLLU MER screen

dégrossi *adj* CONSTR rough-hewn

dégrossir *vt* CHARBON rough, CONSTR *du bois* rough down

dégrossissage *m* CERAM VER rough grinding, CHARBON roughing, CONS MECA facing tool for roughing, PRODUCTION roughing, roughing-down

dégrossissement *m* PRODUCTION roughing, roughing-down

dégrossisseur *m* DISTRI EAU roughing tank, PRODUCTION puddle roll, roughing roll, roughing-down roll

dégroupage *m* CONS MECA disassembly, INFORMAT, ORDINAT deblocking

dégroupement *m* ELECTRON debunching

dégrouper *vt* INFORMAT, ORDINAT deblock

dégustation *f* AGRO ALIM tasting

dégyrer *vt* ESPACE despin, *véhicules* retard

déhouillement: ~ **des piliers** *m* CHARBON broken working, pillar working

déhouilleuse *f* CHARBON coal cutter, MINES coal cutter, coal-cutting machine, mining machine

déhourdage *m* MINES *d'une cheminée* starting

déhydrase *f* LESSIVES dehydrogenase

déhydrogénase *f* LESSIVES dehydrogenase

déjettement *m* CONSTR *du bois* warping, MATERIAUX springing, PRODUCTION *d'une tôle de chaudière* buckling

DEL[1] *abrév (diode électroluminescente)* ELECTR *affichage*, ELECTRON, INFORMAT, OPTIQUE, ORDINAT, PHYS RAYON, PHYSIQUE, TELECOM, TV LED *(light-emitting diode)*

DEL:[2] ~ **à émission frontale** *f* OPTIQUE surface-emitting electroluminescent diode; ~ **seuil bas de pile** *f* PRODUCTION *électricité* battery low LED

délai *m* BREVETS time limit, CONS MECA lead time, CONSTR construction time, ELECTRON, ESPACE *communications*, INFORMAT, ORDINAT delay; ~ **d'acheminement** *m* PRODUCTION move time; ~ **d'approvisionnement** *m* PRODUCTION procurement lead time, replenishment lead time; ~ **d'attente** *m* INFORMAT, ORDINAT rotational delay; ~ **constant** *m* ELECTR *relais, commutateur* fixed delay; ~ **de cure** *m* CONSTR cure period; ~ **d'exécution** *m* CONSTR completion time, construction program (AmE), construction programme (BrE), INFORMAT, PRODUCTION turnaround time; ~ **de fabrication** *m* PRODUCTION manufacturing cycle, manufacturing lead time, production time; ~ **de garantie** *m* CONSTR maintenance period; ~ **de groupe** *m* ELECTROTEC group delay; ~ **de livraison** *m* PRODUCTION delivery cycle, delivery lead time, delivery time; ~ **de manoeuvre** *m* NAUT time to manoeuvre; ~ **médian** *m* PHOTO *d'un éclair* flash duration; ~ **d'obtention** *m* PRODUCTION lead time; ~ **d'option** *m* CONSTR validity period; ~ **de passage en autorotation** *m* AERONAUT autorotation transition time; ~ **de production** *m* PRODUCTION manufacturing cycle, manufacturing lead time, run-time; ~ **de propagation** *m* INFORMAT, ORDINAT propagation delay; ~ **de réalisation** *m* PRODUCTION lead time; ~ **de réapprovisionnement** *m* PRODUCTION lead time; ~ **de réponse d'un bassin versant** *m* HYDROLOGIE catchment area response lag; ~ **de réseau** *m* INFORMAT, ORDINAT network delay; ~ **rotationnel** *m* OPTIQUE rotational delay; ~ **de sécurité** *m* PRODUCTION safety time; ~ **supplémentaire** *m* BREVETS period of grace; ~ **de transmission de paquets** *m* INFORMAT, ORDINAT, TELECOM packet delay

délaissé *m* DISTRI EAU cutoff

délaissement: ~ **du navire** *m* NAUT abandonment of ship

délaissés: ~ **de crue** *m pl* HYDROLOGIE flood deposits

délaminage *m* MATERIAUX, PLAST CAOU *plastiques, adhésifs* delamination

délaminer *vt* PLAST CAOU *plastiques, adhésifs* delaminate

délangeur: ~ **vidéo** *m* TV switcher

délavé *adj* CINEMAT washed out, IMPRIM *photogravure, impression, documents* washed, TEXTILE faded

délayage: ~ **des écumes** *m* GENIE CHIM foam dilution

délayant *m* GENIE CHIM diluting agent

délayer *vt* GENIE CHIM dilute

deleatur *m* IMPRIM *préparation de copie* deleatur

délégué: ~ **mineur** *m* MINES deputy

délessite *f* MINERAUX delessite

délestage *m* CONSTR liftoff, ELECTROTEC load shedding; ~ **de consommation** *m* ELECTR *alimentation* load shedding

délester *vt* AERONAUT jettison, NAUT discharge, *cargaison* jettison

délesteur: ~ **de charges** *m* AERONAUT cargo sling

délétère *adj* PETROLE toxic

déliasser *vt* INFORMAT, ORDINAT decollate

déliasseuse *f* IMPRIM *façonnage*, INFORMAT, ORDINAT decollator

délié *m* IMPRIM *caractère* hairline

délimitation *f* CONSTR boundary, OCEANO *des espaces maritimes* demarcation

délimiter *vt* PRODUCTION locate

délimiteur *m* IMPRIM, INFORMAT, ORDINAT delimiter; ~ **de champ** *m* INFORMAT, ORDINAT field delimiter; ~ **de mot** *m* INFORMAT word delimiter

déliquescence *f* AGRO ALIM, CHIMIE deliquescence
déliquescent *adj* CHIMIE deliquescent
délisseuse *f* PAPIER rag shredder
déliter: se ~ en poudre *v réfl* MATERIAUX crumble to powder; **se ~ par exposition à l'air** *v réfl* MATERIAUX crumble on exposure to the air
délivrance *f* BREVETS grant; **~ des bagages** *f* TRANSPORT baggage retrieval
délivrer: ~ un brevet *vt* BREVETS grant a licence
delorenzite *f* NUCLEAIRE delorenzite
delphinine *f* CHIMIE delphinin, delphinine
delphinite *f* MINERAUX delphinite
delta *m* ELECTROTEC, HYDROLOGIE, PETROLE delta; **~ abyssal** *m* OCEANO deep-sea fan; **~ de marée** *m* OCEANO flow delta, tidal delta; **~ de tempête** *m* PETR wave delta
deltaïque *adj* GEOLOGIE, PETROLE deltaic
déluge *m* METEO deluge
délustrer *vt* TEXTILE deluster (AmE), delustre (BrE)
démagnétisateur *m* CONS MECA demagnetizer
démagnétisation *f* ELECTR, MATERIAUX demagnetization, ORDINAT degaussing, PHYSIQUE demagnetization, TV degaussing, demagnetization; **~ adiabatique** *f* PHYSIQUE adiabatic demagnetization
démagnétiser *vt* CHARBON demagnetize, CONS MECA, ENREGISTR degauss, MATERIAUX demagnetize, ORDINAT degauss, PHYSIQUE demagnetize, PRODUCTION degauss, TV degauss, demagnetize
démagnétiseur *m* ENREGISTR degausser, TV bulk eraser, eraser
démaigrissement *m* OCEANO littoral retreat; **~ littoral** *m* OCEANO littoral retreat
démailler *vt* OCEANO unmesh, unravel
demande:[1] **à la ~** *adj* PRODUCTION as required
demande[2] *f* BREVETS application, INFORMAT request, MECANIQUE de permis application, ORDINAT request, TELECOM req, request; **~ d'accusé de réception** *f* TELECOM acknowledgement request; **~ d'achat** *f* PRODUCTION procurement request, procurement requisition; **~ antérieure** *f* BREVETS earlier application; **~ biochimique d'oxygène** *f (DBO)* AGRO ALIM, HYDROLOGIE, POLLUTION biochemical oxygen demand *(BOD)*; **~ biologique d'oxygène** *f (DBO)* PETROLE biochemical oxygen demand *(BOD)*; **~ de brevet** *f* BREVETS patent application; **~ de brevet déposée** *f* TEXTILE patents applied for; **~ de brevet européen** *f* BREVETS European patent application; **~ calorifique** *f* THERMODYN heat consumption, heat demand; **~ de chaleur** *f* THERMODYN heat demand; **~ chimique d'oxygène** *f (DCO)* CHIMIE, HYDROLOGIE, POLLUTION chemical oxygen demand *(COD)*; **~ de connexion** *f* TELECOM CR, connection request; **~ discontinue** *f* PRODUCTION lumpy demand; **~ de droit de passage** *f* TRANSPORT demand right of way; **~ en chlore** *f* HYDROLOGIE chlorine demand; **~ en dents de scie** *f* PRODUCTION lumpy demand; **~ énergétique** *f* THERMODYN energy demand; **~ d'énergie** *f* THERMODYN energy demand; **~ fermée** *f* PRODUCTION closed demand; **~ de gel de l'image** *f* TELECOM freeze-picture request; **~ intermittente** *f* PRODUCTION lumpy demand; **~ internationale** *f* BREVETS international application; **~ interne** *f* PRODUCTION internal demand; **~ de libération** *f* INFORMAT, ORDINAT clear request; **~ de ligne** *f* INFORMAT bid; **~ maximale** *f* ELECTR *alimentation* maximum demand; **~ maximum** *f* ELECTROTEC maximum demand; **~ de modification d'appel** *f (MAD)* TELECOM call modification request message *(CMR)*; **~ pour émettre** *f*

TELECOM request to send; **~ de prestation** *f* TELECOM request for service; **~ de rafraîchissement rapide** *f* TELECOM fast update request; **~ de recherche** *f* INFORMAT, ORDINAT search query; **~ soldée** *f* PRODUCTION closed demand; **~ de trafic** *f* TRANSPORT traffic demand; **~ de travail** *f* INFORMAT, ORDINAT job request
demande:[3] **~ est en instance** *loc* BREVETS application is pending
demandé *m* TELECOM called party
demander *vt* BREVETS *permis* apply for, INFORMAT, ORDINAT request, PRODUCTION *permis* apply for
demandes: ~ concurrentes *f pl* PRODUCTION competing demands
demandeur *m* BREVETS applicant, TELECOM caller; **~ de l'association** *m* TELECOM association initiator
démantèlement *m* CONS MECA dismantling, MILITAIRE *d'une fortification* dismantlement, NUCLEAIRE *d'une installation nucléaire* dismantling
démantoïde *f* MINERAUX demantoid
démarcation *f* CONSTR boundary line; **~ superficielle** *f* CONSTR surface demarcation
démargariner *vt* CHIMIE *huile* winterize
démarrage *m* CONS MECA starting, INFORMAT start, NAUT unmooring, ORDINAT start; **~ autonome** *m* NUCLEAIRE black start-up; **~ avec surchauffe** *m* AERONAUT hot start; **~ à chaud** *m* INFORMAT, ORDINAT warm start; **~ énergétique** *m* NUCLEAIRE energetic start-up; **~ à froid** *m* THERMODYN cold start; **~ sous pleine tension** *m* ELECTR *moteur* direct starting; **~ sous tension réduite** *m* ELECTR *moteur* partial voltage starting; **~ sur fraction d'enroulement** *m* ELECTR *moteur* part winding starting; **~ à vide** *m* ELECTR *moteur* no-load start
démarrer[1] *vt* INFORMAT, ORDINAT start
démarrer[2] *vi* NAUT *navire* cast off, unmoor
démarreur *m* AUTO starter, starter motor, ELECTROTEC starter motor, starter, VEHICULES starter, *moteur* starter button, starter, starter motor; **~ à base d'électro-aimant** *m* PRODUCTION magnetic starter; **~ Bendix** *m* (MD) AUTO Bendix-type starter, VEHICULES *moteur* Bendix starter (TM); **~ à bouton-poussoir** *m* ELECTR *moteur* push-button starter; **~ à combustion** *m* AERONAUT combustion starter; **~ à contacteur** *m* ELECTR *machine* contactor starter; **~ à déplacement d'induit** *m* ELECTR sliding gear starting motor; **~ direct** *m* ELECTR across-the-line starter; **~ électrique** *m* ELECTR *automobile* electric starter; **~ étoile-triangle** *m* ELECTROTEC star-delta starter; **~ à l'huile** *m* ELECTR oil hydraulic starter; **~ magnétique** *m* ELECTR *moteur* magnetic starter; **~ de moteur** *m* ELECTROTEC motor starter; **~ à n étages** *m* ELECTR n-step starter; **~ par changement du nombre de pôles** *m* ELECTR *moteur* pole-changing starter; **~ à plots** *m* ELECTR *moteur* faceplate starter; **~ pneumatique** *m* CONS MECA air starter; **~ régulateur** *m* ELECTR regulating starter; **~ au rhéostat** *m* ELECTROTEC rheostat starter; **~ de rotor** *m* ELECTR rotor starter; **~ rotorique** *m* ELECTR rotor starter; **~ à solénoïde** *m* AUTO screw push starter; **~ statique** *m* PRODUCTION *automatisme industriel* solid-state motor controller; **~ stator-rotor** *m* ELECTR *moteur* stator rotor starter motor; **~ très lent** *m* ELECTR time-delay starter
démasquer *vt* MILITAIRE *artillerie* unmask
démâtage *m* NAUT dismasting
démâter *vt* NAUT dismast, unstep
dématérialisation *f* PHYSIQUE annihilation
démêlage: ~ horizontal *m* PLAST CAOU *imperfection de*

peinture flooding; ~ **vertical** *m* PLAST CAOU *imperfection de peinture* floating

déméthylation *f* CHIMIE demethylation

déméthyliser *vt* CHIMIE demethylate

demi-additionneur *m* ELECTRON half adder, one-digit adder, INFORMAT, ORDINAT half adder

demi-amplitude: ~ **d'impulsion** *f* ELECTRON half pulse

demi-arbre *m* AUTO *pont moteur* rear axle shaft; ~ **inférieur** *m* AUTO lower shaft

demi-bague *f* CONS MECA half bushing

demi-bande *f* IMPRIM narrow web, *rotatives* ribbon

demi-boisage *m* CONSTR half timbering

demi-cadratin *m* IMPRIM en space

demi-carter: ~ **inférieur** *m* AUTO crankcase bottom half, oil pan; ~ **supérieur** *m* AUTO crankcase top half

demi-cercle *m* CONSTR, GEOMETRIE semicircle

demi-collerette *f* CONS MECA half flange

demi-collier *m* CONS MECA half clamp

demi-coupe *f* PRODUCTION half section

demi-coussinet: ~ **inférieur** *m* CONS MECA bottom brass; ~ **mince** *m* CONS MECA thin-walled half-bearing; ~ **supérieur** *m* CONS MECA top brass

demi-cuvette *f* CONS MECA half cup

demi-droite *f* GEOMETRIE half line

demi-écrémé *adj* AGRO ALIM semiskimmed

demi-ensouple: ~ **sectionnelle** *f* TEXTILE *tricot chaîne* half sectional beam

demi-ferme *f* CONSTR half truss

demi-fixe *adj* CONS MECA semiportable

demi-flasque: ~ **de butée** *f* CONS MECA half thrust washer

demi-flasques: ~ **de butée bimétalliques découpées à la presse** *f pl* CONS MECA pressed bimetallic half-thrust washers

demi-grand: ~ **axe** *m* ESPACE *astronomie* semimajor axis

demi-gras *adj* CHARBON semibituminous

demi-intérieur *m* PAPIER underliner

demi-largeur *f* PHYS RAYON *spectrométrie*, PHYSIQUE half-width

demi-masque *m* SECURITE half mask

demi-métal *m* CHIMIE semimetal

demi-métallique *adj* CHIMIE semimetallic

demi-mot *m* INFORMAT, ORDINAT half word

déminéralisateur *m* EQUIP LAB *de l'eau* deionizer

déminéralisation *f* CHAUFFAGE demineralization, GENIE CHIM demineralizing, desalting, HYDROLOGIE demineralization, desalination

déminéralisé *adj* HYDROLOGIE demineralized

déminéraliser[1] *vt* GENIE CHIM demineralize, desalt

déminéraliser[2] *vti* HYDROLOGIE demineralize

déminéraliseur *m* NUCLEAIRE demineralizing plant

demi-noeud *m* NAUT overhand knot

demi-onde *f* ELECTR *courant alternatif* half-wave

demi-peigne *m* CONS MECA half cleat

demi-période *f* GEOLOGIE half life; ~ **de radioactivité** *f* NUCLEAIRE half life

demi-petit: ~ **fût** *m* AGRO ALIM firkin

demi-pincette *f* CONS MECA half elliptic spring

demi-plage: ~ **de synchronisation** *f* ELECTRON lock-in range

demi-pont *m* CONS MECA *tour* half bridge piece, ELECTROTEC half bridge

demi-raccord *m* CONS MECA half union

demi-rame *f* IMPRIM *papier* token

demi-reliure:[1] **en** ~ *adj* IMPRIM half-bound

demi-reliure[2] *f* IMPRIM quarter-binding

demi-ressort *m* RESSORTS quarter elliptic spring

demi-soustracteur *m* ELECTRON half subtractor, one-digit subtractor, INFORMAT, ORDINAT half subtractor

demi-teinte *f* IMPRIM *photogravure* halftone; ~ **à trame fine** *f* IMPRIM *photogravure* fine screen halftone

demi-teintes *f pl* IMPRIM *photogravure* middletones

demi-toile: ~ **avec coins** *f* IMPRIM *reliure* half-binding

demi-ton[1] *adj* IMPRIM *reliure* half-bound

demi-ton[2] *m* IMPRIM *photogravure* halftone, PHYSIQUE semitone; ~ **chromatique** *m* ACOUSTIQUE chromatic semitone; ~ **diatonique** *m* ACOUSTIQUE diatonic semitone; ~ **mineur** *m* ACOUSTIQUE minor semitone; ~ **tempéré** *m* ACOUSTIQUE halftone, semitone

demi-tons *m pl* IMPRIM middletones

demi-tordu *m* PRODUCTION half twist

demi-tour *m* AERONAUT *d'aéronef* turnaround, CONSTR latch bolt, spring bolt

demi-varlope *f* CONSTR jack plane

demi-vie *f* CHIMIE half life, NUCLEAIRE half cycle, PHYS PART *d'un isotope radioactif* half life

demi-vue: ~ **du plan des formes** *f* NAUT half-breadth plan

démodulateur *m* ELECTRON, ESPACE *communications*, ORDINAT, PHYSIQUE, TELECOM, TV demodulator; ~ **de la composante en quadrature** *m* ELECTRON quadrature demodulator; ~ **à compression de fréquence** *m* ESPACE *communications* frequency compressive feedback demodulator; ~ **couleur** *m* TV chrominance demodulator; ~ **à diode** *m* ELECTRON diode modulator; ~ **à estimation de la fréquence instantanée** *m* ESPACE *communications* instantaneous frequency estimation demodulator; ~ **à filtre asservi** *m* ESPACE *communications* tracking filter demodulator; ~ **de fréquence** *m* ELECTRON, TELECOM frequency demodulator; ~ **I** *m* TV I-demodulator; ~ **à oscillateur synchronisé par injection** *m* ESPACE *communications* injection-locked oscillator demodulator; ~ **de phase** *m* ELECTRON phase demodulator; ~ **Q** *m* ELECTRON Q-demodulator; ~ **à seuil amélioré** *m* ESPACE *communications*, TELECOM threshold extension demodulator; ~ **de la sous-porteuse de chrominance** *m* ELECTRON chrominance subcarrier demodulator; ~ **à talon** *m* TV Nyquist demodulator; ~ **à verrouillage de phase** *m* ESPACE *communications* phase-locked demodulator; ~ **de la voie Q** *m* ELECTRON Q-demodulator

démodulation *f* ELECTRON, ESPACE *communications*, ORDINAT, PHYSIQUE, TELECOM, TV demodulation; ~ **d'amplitude** *f* ELECTRON amplitude demodulation; ~ **à bande étroite** *f* ELECTRON narrow band demodulation; ~ **cohérente** *f* ELECTRON synchronous detection; ~ **de fréquence** *f* ELECTRON, TELECOM frequency demodulation; ~ **par diode** *f* ELECTRON diode modulation; ~ **de phase** *f* ELECTRON, TELECOM phase demodulation; ~ **de la sous-porteuse de chrominance** *f* ELECTRON chrominance subcarrier demodulation

démodulé *adj* ELECTRON *signal* demodulated

démoduler *vt* ELECTRON, TV demodulate

demoiselle *f* CONSTR earth rammer, rammer

démolition: ~ **du navire** *f* NAUT shipbreaking

démontable *adj* CONS MECA removable, sectional, PRODUCTION made in sections

démontage *m* CONS MECA disassembly, dismantling, taking to pieces, MINES *de la sonde* unmaking, PRODUCTION teardown

démonter[1] *vt* CONS MECA *un joint* unmake, *une machine* dismantle, dismount

démonter:[2] ~ **un décor** *vi* CINEMAT kill a set, strike

démoulage *m* CERAM VER demold (AmE), demould (BrE), takeout, MATERIAUX stripping, NAUT removal, PLAST CAOU demolding (AmE), demoulding (BrE), PRODUCTION drawing, stripping; ~ **par poussoir** *m* (Bel) *(cf démoulage par soupape)* CERAM VER takeout with push-up; ~ **par soupape** *m* (Fra) *(cf démoulage par poussoir)* CERAM VER takeout with push-up

démouler *vt* NAUT remove, PRODUCTION strip

démultiplexage *m* ELECTRON, INFORMAT, ORDINAT, TELECOM demultiplexing; ~ **temporel** *m* ELECTRON time-division demultiplexing

démultiplexer *vt* ELECTRON demultiplex

démultiplexeur *m* ELECTRON, INFORMAT, ORDINAT, TELECOM demultiplexer, demultiplexor

démultiplicateur *m* VEHICULES *boîte de vitesses* reduction gear; ~ **de fréquence** *m* ELECTR frequency divider

démultiplication *f* AUTO transmission reduction

dendrite *f* CRISTALL, METALL, MINERAUX dendrite

dendritique *adj* CHIMIE, CRISTALL, METALL dendritic

dénébulation *f* AERONAUT fog dispersal

déni *m* TELECOM *de service* denial

denier *m* TEXTILE denier; ~ **du brin** *m* TEXTILE filament denier; ~ **total** *m* TEXTILE total denier

dénitrification *f* HYDROLOGIE, POLLUTION denitrification

dénivellation *f* CONSTR dislevelment, oscillations of level

dénivellement *m* CONSTR dislevelment, oscillations of level

dénominateur *m* MATH denominator

dénomination: ~ **des pièces** *f* PRODUCTION names of parts

dénoyage *m* CONSTR dewatering

dénoyauter *vt* AGRO ALIM stone

denrée: ~ **alimentaire** *f* AGRO ALIM foodstuff; ~ **principale** *f* AGRO ALIM staple food

densimètre *m* AGRO ALIM densimeter, CHARBON, ELECTR *accumulateur*, EQUIP LAB *densité, liquides* hydrometer, PETROLE densimeter, PHYSIQUE hydrometer; ~ **bêta** *m* NUCLEAIRE beta density gage (AmE), beta density gauge (BrE)

densimétrie *f* AGRO ALIM densimetry

densité *f* CHIMIE, CONSTR, GAZ density, IMPRIM *papier* bulk density, INFORMAT, MATERIAUX density, MATH *probabilité* frequency distribution, MECANIQUE density, NAUT *de l'eau de mer* specific gravity, ORDINAT, PETROLE density, PHYSIQUE relative density, specific gravity, PLAST CAOU density, TEXTILE density, specific gravity; ~ **API** *f* PETR, PETROLE API gravity; ~ **apparente** *f* CERAM VER bulk density, CHARBON apparent density, MATERIAUX bulk density, PAPIER apparent specific gravity, PETROLE bulk density, PLAST CAOU apparent density, bulk density; ~ **après damage** *f* PLAST CAOU tamped density; ~ **argile** *f* PETROLE shale density; ~ **atomique** *f* PHYS RAYON atomic density; ~ **binaire** *f* INFORMAT bit density; ~ **de bits** *f* INFORMAT bit density; ~ **de boue** *f* PETR mud density, mud weight, PETROLE mud weight; ~ **de boue équivalente** *f* PETROLE equivalent density, PETROLE *(DBE) forage* Equivalent Mud Weight *(EMW)*; ~ **calorifique** *f* THERMODYN heat density; ~ **de chaleur** *f* THERMODYN heat density; ~ **de charge** *f* ELECTR *condensateur*, PHYS RAYON *d'une particule*, PHYSIQUE charge density; ~ **de chargement** *f* MINES loading density; ~ **de charge superficielle** *f* ELECTR *électrostatique* surface charge density; ~ **des collisions** *f* PHYS RAYON collision density; ~ **de composants** *f* ELECTRON component density; ~ **de courant** *f*

ELECTR ampere density, current density, ELECTROTEC, GEOPHYS, METALL, PHYSIQUE current density; ~ **critique** *f* ASTRONOMIE, TRANSPORT critical density; ~ **critique de la matière dans l'Univers** *f* ASTRONOMIE critical density of matter in the universe; ~ **de dislocations** *f* METALL dislocation density; ~ **de drainage** *f* HYDROLOGIE drainage density; ~ **électronique** *f* PHYSIQUE electron density; ~ **d'électrons** *f* CHIMIE, PHYSIQUE electron density; ~ **d'électrons libres** *f* PHYS RAYON free electron density; ~ **d'émission** *f* ELECTROTEC specific emission; ~ **d'empilement** *f* CRISTALL packing density; ~ **d'énergie cinétique** *f* ACOUSTIQUE kinetic energy density; ~ **d'énergie totale** *f* ACOUSTIQUE total energy density; ~ **en lumière diffuse** *f* OPTIQUE diffuse light density; ~ **en lumière dirigée** *f* ACOUSTIQUE specular density; ~ **d'enregistrement** *f* INFORMAT packing density, recording density, ORDINAT packing density, recording density, storage density, TV packing density; ~ **d'équilibre** *f* PETROLE *forage* equilibrium density; ~ **équivalente** *f* PETROLE *forage* equivalent density; ~ **équivalente de la boue** *f* PETROLE equivalent density; ~ **équivalente de circulation** *f* PETROLE *forage* ECD, equivalent circulating density; ~ **d'états** *f* PHYSIQUE density; ~ **de flux** *f* PHYSIQUE flux density; ~ **de flux électrostatique** *f* ELECTR electrostatic flux density; ~ **de flux énergétique** *f* NUCLEAIRE radiation flux density, PHYSIQUE radiant energy fluence rate, radiant flux density; ~ **de flux lumineux émis** *f* ELECTROTEC luminance; ~ **de flux magnétique** *f* ELECTR magnetic induction density, ELECTROTEC magnetic induction, PHYSIQUE magnetic flux density, magnetic induction; ~ **du flux magnétique** *f* ESSAIS magnetic flux density; ~ **de flux de radiation** *f* OPTIQUE, PHYS RAYON radiant flux density; ~ **de flux thermique critique** *f* PRODUCTION critical heat flux; ~ **d'implantation** *f* TEXTILE packing density; ~ **d'intégration** *f* ELECTRON integration density, packing density; ~ **linéique de charge** *f* PHYSIQUE linear charge density; ~ **massique** *f* PLAST CAOU density; ~ **de mémorisation** *f* INFORMAT storage density; ~ **moyenne** *f* TRANSPORT average density; ~ **moyenne de la matière** *f* ASTRONOMIE mean density of matter; ~ **neutre** *f* IMPRIM *photogravure, impression* neutral density; ~ **neutre équivalente** *f* IMPRIM *photogravure* equivalent neutral density; ~ **d'occupation** *f* TRANSPORT occupancy rate; ~ **optique** *f* OPTIQUE optical density; ~ **optique d'un aplat à 100%** *f* IMPRIM *contrôle de qualité* solid ink density; ~ **optique par réflexion** *f* OPTIQUE transmittance density; ~ **optique par transmission** *f* OPTIQUE reflectance density; ~ **de partage** *f* CHARBON partition density; ~ **de la pâte** *f* PAPIER consistency; ~ **de pistes** *f* OPTIQUE track density; ~ **du poil** *f* TEXTILE density of pile; ~ **de population des atomes excités** *f* PHYS RAYON population density of excited atoms; ~ **de portes** *f* ELECTRON gate density; ~ **de probabilité** *f* PHYSIQUE probability density; ~ **de puissance** *f* TELECOM power density; ~ **de puissance du faisceau** *f* ELECTRON beam power density; ~ **de ralentissement** *f* NUCLEAIRE, PHYSIQUE slowing-down density; ~ **de référence d'un document opaque** *f* IMPRIM RDR, reflection density reference; ~ **relative frittée** *f* GENIE CHIM sintered density ratio; ~ **sèche** *f* CONSTR dry density; ~ **de séparation** *f* CHARBON separation density; ~ **spectrale** *f* ACOUSTIQUE, ELECTRON, PHYSIQUE spectral density; ~ **spectrale d'éclairement** *f* OPTIQUE, TELECOM spectral irradiance; ~ **spectrale d'éclairement énergétique** *f*

OPTIQUE, TELECOM spectral irradiance; ~ **spectrale de luminance** f TELECOM spectral radiance; ~ **spectrale de luminance énergétique** f TELECOM spectral radiance; ~ **spectrale de puissance** f ESPACE *communications* power spectral density; ~ **superficielle** f ELECTROTEC surface density; ~ **superficielle de charge** f PHYSIQUE surface charge density; ~ **de support** f CINEMAT base density; ~ **surfacique de puissance** f ESPACE *véhicules*, OPTIQUE power flux density; ~ **de tassement** f PLAST CAOU packing density; ~ **théorique** f NUCLEAIRE TD, theoretical density, true density; ~ **du trafic** f TRANSPORT traffic concentration, traffic density; ~ **de vapeur** f CHIMIE, PHYSIQUE, THERMODYN vapor density (AmE), vapour density (BrE); ~ **volumique de charge** f PHYSIQUE volume charge density

densités: ~ **énergiques de rayonnement** f pl PHYS RAYON energy densities of radiation

densitomètre m ACOUSTIQUE, CINEMAT densiometer, PAPIER color densitometer (AmE), colour densitometer (BrE), densitometer, PHYSIQUE densitometer; ~ **à coin gris** m PHOTO wedge densitometer; ~ **comparateur** m CINEMAT comparator densitometer

densitométrie f PHOTO, PHYSIQUE densitometry; ~ **gamma de discontinuité d'absorption K** f NUCLEAIRE K-edge gamma densitometry

dent f CONS MECA cog, prong, tooth, CONSTR *d'une fourche* tine, MECANIQUE cog; ~ **à crochet** f CONS MECA hook tooth, hooked tooth; ~ **crochue** f CONS MECA hook tooth, hooked tooth; ~ **droite** f CONS MECA fleam tooth, fleam-tooth saw, peg tooth; ~ **d'engrenage** f CONS MECA gear tooth, wheel tooth; ~ **en porcelaine** f CERAM VER porcelain tooth; ~ **d'entraînement** f CINEMAT sprocket tooth; ~ **d'induit** f ELECTR *machine* armature tooth; ~ **mère** f CONS MECA master spline; ~ **pour couper en travers** f PRODUCTION crosscut tooth; ~ **de repère** f CONS MECA guide tooth; ~ **triangulaire** f PRODUCTION crosscut tooth

denté adj MECANIQUE cogged

dentelle f TEXTILE lace

dentelure f CONS MECA serration, PRODUCTION indentation

denter vt CONS MECA cog, ratch

dents f pl CONS MECA *d'une roue d'engrenages, d'une scie, d'une crémaillère, d'une lime, d'une fourche* teeth; ~ **chevronnées** f pl CONS MECA herringbone teeth; ~ **de coupe** f pl CONSTR cutting teeth; ~ **dégagées** f pl CONS MECA relieved teeth, *d'engrenage ou de crémaillère* backed-off teeth; ~ **de fouille de la pelle** f pl TRANSPORT digging bucket teeth; ~ **de requin** f pl CERAM VER serration hackle; ~ **de trépan** f pl PETROLE drill bit studs

denture f CONS MECA *d'une roue d'engrenage* teeth; ~ **de blocage du planétaire** f AUTO sun gear lock-out teeth; ~ **dégagée** f CONS MECA *d'engrenage ou de crémaillère* backed-off teeth; ~ **à dépouille** f CONS MECA relieved teeth; ~ **intérieure** f AUTO internal gear

dénudation f GEOLOGIE denudation

dénudé adj PRODUCTION *électricité* bare

dénumériseur m ELECTRON reconverter

dépaler vi NAUT drift

dépalettisation f EMBALLAGE depalletization

dépannage m ELECTROTEC fault-finding, ORDINAT corrective maintenance

dépanneur m CONS MECA artificer; ~ **frigoriste** m REFRIG refrigeration service engineer

dépanneuse: ~ **lourde** f MILITAIRE wrecker

dépaqueteur m TELECOM depacketizer

départ m CHIMIE parting, *d'une réaction* onset, INFORMAT, ORDINAT start; ~ **en batterie** m CH DE FER flighted departure; ~ **à froid** m THERMODYN cold start

dépassant[1] m IMPRIM *finition, façonnage* foldover edge, *impression, emballage* overlap

dépassant:[2] ~ **la surcharge normale de fonctionnement** loc PRODUCTION excess of operating overload

dépassement m AERONAUT overshooting, ELECTROTEC, METALL overshoot, ORDINAT overflow; ~ **de capacité inférieur** m ORDINAT underflow; ~ **de course** m AERONAUT overrun; ~ **inférieur** m PRODUCTION *automatisme industriel* underrange; ~ **négatif** m ELECTRON undershoot, INFORMAT underflow; ~ **négatif de capacité** m INFORMAT underflow; ~ **supérieur** m PRODUCTION *automatisme industriel* overrange; ~ **du temps imparti** m INFORMAT time-out; ~ **des têtes** m TV tip height, tip projection

dépasser[1] vt MECANIQUE overshoot, NAUT *navigation* overhaul

dépasser[2] vi PRODUCTION time-out

dépastilleur m PAPIER centrifiner, fiberizer (BrE), fibrizer (AmE), deflaker

dépècement m MINES *du massif* excavation, stoping of the seam

dépendances f pl CONSTR outbuildings

dépendant: ~ **de la machine** adj INFORMAT, ORDINAT machine-dependent

dépendre: ~ **d'un port** vi NAUT hail from a port

dépense f DISTRI EAU efflux; ~ **de chaleur** f THERMODYN heat consumption; ~ **d'énergie** f THERMODYN energy consumption

déperdition f PRODUCTION wastage, waste; ~ **de chaleur** f PHYSIQUE heat loss

déperditions: ~ **calorifiques de paroi** f pl REFRIG wall losses

déphasage m ELECTR angular displacement, phase shift, *courant alternatif* angle of phase difference, displacement of phase, phase displacement, *transformateur* phase difference, ELECTRON, ESPACE *communications*, NUCLEAIRE phase shift, PHYSIQUE phase difference, phase shift, TELECOM phase difference, TRANSPORT phase shift, TV lag, phase difference, shift; ~ **en arrière** m ELECTRON lag, phase lag, PHYSIQUE phase lag; ~ **en avant** m ELECTRON lead, phase lead, PHYSIQUE phase lead; ~ **inductif** m ELECTR *courant alternatif* induction displacement; ~ **linéique** m OPTIQUE phase constant, TELECOM phase coefficient, phase constant; ~ **linéique de propagation acoustique** m ACOUSTIQUE dephasing coefficient; ~ **numérique** m ELECTRON digital phase shifting; ~ **par bague** m ELECTR *générateur, moteur* pole shading; ~ **sur images** m ELECTRON image phase-change coefficient

déphasé adj ELECTR out-of-phase, *courant alternatif* dephased, ELECTRON out-of-phase, phase shifted, TV out-of-phase; ~ **en arrière** adj ELECTROTEC lagging

déphaser vt ELECTRON phase shift

déphaseur m AERONAUT phasing unit, ELECTR *courant alternatif* phase shifter, ELECTRON phase changer, phase shifter, ENREGISTR phase splitter, TELECOM phase changer, phase shifter, TV phase converter; ~ **coaxial** m ELECTROTEC coaxial phase shifter; ~ **à diode** m ELECTRON diode phase shifter; ~ **à diode PIN** m ELECTRON PIN-diode phase shifter; ~ **en guide d'ondes** m ELECTROTEC, NUCLEAIRE waveguide phase shifter; ~ **à ferrite** *m* ELECTROTEC ferrite phase shifter; ~ **hyperfréquence** *m* TELECOM microwave phase changer; ~ **de régulation rotor par le pas général** *m* AERONAUT *hélicoptère* collective pitch anticipator

déphosphoration *f* GENIE CHIM, MATERIAUX dephosphorization

dépilage: ~ **des piliers** *m* CHARBON broken working, pillar extraction

dépiler *vt* ORDINAT pop

déplacé *adj* NUCLEAIRE *atome* displaced

déplacement *m* CONS MECA movement, *de machines* removal, CONSTR *de bornes* removing, DISTRI EAU, ELECTROTEC, GAZ, GEOLOGIE displacement, GEOPHYS dislocation, displacement, INFORMAT *adresses*, NAUT displacement, NUCLEAIRE shift, ORDINAT shift, *adresses* displacement, PETR drift, PHYSIQUE displacement; ~ **atomique** *m* METALL atomic displacement; ~ **à la base** *m* ORDINAT base displacement; ~ **du centre de gravité** *m* NAUT shift of G; ~ **de chaleur** *m* THERMODYN heat displacement; ~ **de cisaillement** *m* MATERIAUX shearing displacement, shift; ~ **Doppler** *m* ASTRONOMIE Doppler shift; ~ **Doppler-Fizeau** *m* ACOUSTIQUE Doppler-Fizeau displacement shift; ~ **électrique** *m* ELECTROTEC, PHYSIQUE electric displacement; ~ **en charge** *m* NAUT load displacement, loaded displacement; ~ **en cours de communication** *m* TELECOM call portability; ~ **en phases miscibles** *m* PETR miscible slug flooding; ~ **de fréquence** *m* INFORMAT, ORDINAT frequency shift, TELECOM frequency displacement, frequency shift; ~ **hors membres** *m* NAUT molded displacement (AmE), moulded displacement (BrE); ~ **de l'image** *m* TV picture shift; ~ **de Knight** *m* NUCLEAIRE Knight shift; ~ **de Lamb** *m* PHYSIQUE Lamb shift; ~ **latéral** *m* NAUT crabbing; ~ **léger** *m* NAUT light displacement; ~ **lourd** *m* NAUT *architecture* heavy displacement; ~ **de niveau** *m* NUCLEAIRE level displacement, level shift; ~ **de l'ouverture de fissure** *m* NUCLEAIRE crack opening displacement, crack opening stretch; ~ **permanent de seuil** *m* ACOUSTIQUE permanent threshold shift; ~ **relativiste vers le rouge** *m* ASTRONOMIE *des raies* Einstein displacement; ~ **sur un plan** *m* PRODUCTION translation on a drawing; ~ **de tangage d'une bouée** *m* EN RENOUV heaving displacement of buoy; ~ **temporaire de seuil** *m* ACOUSTIQUE temporary threshold shift; ~ **à vide** *m* NAUT light displacement; ~ **du zéro** *m* CERAM VER zero displacement

déplacer[1] *vt* CONS MECA *machines* remove, INFORMAT drag, NUCLEAIRE displace

déplacer:[2] **se** ~ *v réfl* PHYS ONDES travel, PRODUCTION shift; **se** ~ **latéralement** *v réfl* CINEMAT crab

déplétion *f* ELECTRON depletion; ~ **profonde** *f* ELECTROTEC deep depletion

dépliant: ~ **français** *m* IMPRIM French folder

déployable *adj* TELECOM *antenne* unfurlable

dépolarisant *m* ELECTR *pile* depolarizing agent

dépolarisateur *m* CHIMIE depolarizer

dépolarisation *f* CHIMIE, ELECTROTEC, ESPACE *communications* depolarization; ~ **magnétique de la radiation de résonance** *f* PHYS RAYON magnetic depolarization of resonance radiation

dépolariser *vt* ELECTROTEC depolarize

dépoli *m* CINEMAT ground glass

dépollué *adj* POLLUTION *eau* depolluted

dépolymérisation *f* CHIMIE, EMBALLAGE, PLAST CAOU depolymerization

dépontillage *m* CERAM VER puntying

déport *m* CONS MECA mismatch; ~ **dans l'avancement** *m* AERONAUT blade tilt; ~ **dans le plan de rotation** *m* AERONAUT blade sweep; ~ **horizontal** *m* GEOPHYS offset

déporté *adj* CONS MECA offset

déporteur *m* AERONAUT *aéronef*, TRANSPORT spoiler

déposable *adj* PRODUCTION removable

déposant *m* BREVETS applicant

déposé: ~ **par sédimentation** *adj* GENIE CHIM sedimented

déposer[1] *vt* BREVETS apply for, GENIE CHIM settle, GEOLOGIE lay down

déposer:[2] ~ **un brevet** *vi* TEXTILE file a patent application; ~ **une demande** *vi* BREVETS file an application; ~ **son rassis** *vi* GENIE CHIM settle

déposer:[3] **se** ~ *v réfl* GENIE CHIM precipitate, settle

déposition *f* ELECTRON deposition; ~ **axiale** *f* TELECOM ALDP, axial plasma deposition; ~ **latérale** *f* TELECOM lateral plasma deposition

dépôt *m* BREVETS deposit, filing, CHARBON deposit, CHIMIE deposit, sediment, settling, CONSTR shed, stockpile, yard, DISTRI EAU deposit, ELECTRON deposition, GENIE CHIM sediment, GEOLOGIE deposit, INST HYDR boiler scale, MECANIQUE *brevets* application, MINES dumping, magazine, POLLUTION deposition, repository, PRODUCTION storeroom, *système hydraulique* drag, RECYCLAGE dump, refuse dump, waste dump; ~ **acide** *m* POLLUTION acid fallout; ~ **acide humide** *m* POLLUTION wet acidic fallout; ~ **d'acides** *m* POLLUTION acid deposit, acid fallout; ~ **acide sec** *m* POLLUTION dry acidic fallout; ~ **d'acide sec** *m* POLLUTION dry acid deposit; ~ **alluvial** *m* OCEANO alluvial deposit; ~ **alluvionnaire** *m* DISTRI EAU alluvial deposit; ~ **atmosphérique** *m* POLLUTION atmospheric fallout; ~ **axial** *m* CERAM VER axial deposition; ~ **axial en phase vapeur** *m* *(DAV)* OPTIQUE, TELECOM vapor phase axial deposition (AmE), vapour phase axial deposition (BrE) *(VAD)*; ~ **de bois** *m* CONSTR timberyard; ~ **brut** *m* POLLUTION bulk deposition; ~ **de carburant** *m* MILITAIRE fuel dump; ~ **des cendres** *m* PRODUCTION ash dump; ~ **chimique en phase vapeur** *m* ELECTRON, OPTIQUE chemical vapor deposition (AmE), chemical vapour deposition (BrE), TELECOM vapor phase chemical deposition (AmE), vapour phase chemical deposition (BrE), TELECOM chemical vapor deposition (AmE), chemical vapour deposition (BrE); ~ **clastique résiduel** *m* GEOLOGIE lag deposit; ~ **contrôlé de déchets** *m* POLLUTION controlled dumping; ~ **côtier** *m* DISTRI EAU coastal deposit; ~ **d'une couche** *m* ELECTRON layer deposition; ~ **de couches réfléchissantes** *m* REVETEMENT metal coating of reflectors; ~ **dans les conduites** *m* PAPIER slime; ~ **des déblais** *m* CONSTR dump (AmE), tip (BrE), MINES dump, dump site (AmE), dumping ground, tailings area, tip area (BrE); ~ **de déchets** *m* POLLUTION dumping, tipping, RECYCLAGE waste dump; ~ **électrolytique** *m* REVETEMENT electroplated coating; ~ **en phase gazeuse par procédé physique** *m* MATERIAUX physical vapor deposition (AmE), physical vapour deposition (BrE); ~ **en phase vapeur** *m* ELECTRON vapor phase deposition (AmE), vapour deposition (BrE); ~ **en phase vapeur interne** *m* TELECOM IVPO, inside vapor phase oxidation (AmE), inside vapour phase oxidation (BrE); ~ **épitaxial** *m* ELECTRON epitaxial deposition; ~ **d'essence** *m* MILITAIRE gasoline dump (AmE), petrol dump (BrE); ~ **d'explosifs** *m* MINES explosives magazine, powder store; ~ **de givre** *m* REFRIG frost deposit;

~ global *m* POLLUTION bulk deposition; **~ houiller** *m* CHARBON coal deposit; **~ humide** *m* POLLUTION wet deposition; **~ hydrothermal** *m* GEOLOGIE hydrothermal deposit; **~ de locomotives** *m* CH DE FER engine shed, locomotive shed; **~ magnétique** *m* TV magnetic coating; **~ de marchandises** *m* CH DE FER freight yard (AmE), goods yard (BrE); **~ d'une mince couche** *m* ELECTRON striking; **~ de munitions** *m* MILITAIRE ammunition depot, ammunition dump; **~ d'oxyde** *m* ENREGISTR, TV oxide build-up; **~ par évaporation** *m* CERAM VER vapor deposition (AmE), vapour deposition (BrE); **~ par pyrolyse** *m* CERAM VER pyrolytic coating; **~ de pellicule** *m* CINEMAT emulsion pile-up; **~ de plage induré** *m* GEOLOGIE beach rock; **~ pyroclastique soudé** *m* GEOLOGIE ignimbrite, welded tuff; **~ réglementé** *m* POLLUTION regulated deposition; **~ de résidus** *m* RECYCLAGE refuse dump; **~ de revêtement par soudage** *m* MECANIQUE overlay cladding; **~ sapropélitique** *m* GEOLOGIE sapropel deposit, sapropelic deposit; **~ des schistes** *m* CHARBON spoil tip, tip; **~ sec** *m* POLLUTION dry deposition; **~ sous vide** *m* ELECTRON vacuum deposition; **~ total** *m* POLLUTION total deposition; **~ de wagons** *m* CH DE FER car shed (AmE), wagon shed (BrE)

dépotage *m* TRANSPORT container destuffing, container stripping, container unpacking, unstuffing

dépoter *vt* TRANSPORT unstuff

dépotoir *m* DISTRI EAU refuse dump

dépôts *m pl* CHIMIE settlings, PRODUCTION fur, scale; **~ acides** *m pl* POLLUTION acid pollution; **~ deltaïques frontaux** *m pl* GEOLOGIE foreset beds; **~ intercotidaux** *m pl* GEOLOGIE intertidal deposits; **~ intertidaux** *m pl* GEOLOGIE intertidal deposits; **~ de lagon** *m pl* GEOLOGIE lagoonal deposits; **~ phosphatés** *m pl* GEOLOGIE phosphatic deposits; **~ phosphorites** *m pl* GEOLOGIE phosphatic deposits; **~ supratidaux** *m pl* GEOLOGIE supratidal deposits

dépouille:[1] **à ~ rapide** *adj* IMPRIM *encres* quick-release

dépouille[2] *f* CONS MECA backing-off, clearance, relief, PRODUCTION delivery, draft (AmE), draught (BrE), draw taper, strip, taper

dépouillé *adj* IMPRIM *photogravure, impression* keen

dépouillement *m* CINEMAT shot breakdown, MINES baring, PRODUCTION stripping; **~ du gîte** *m* MINES stripping

dépouiller *vt* CONS MECA relieve, *un foret* back, *un taraud* back, *une fraise* back off, PRODUCTION *un foret* clear

dépoussiérage *m* PRODUCTION dust removal, removing dust; **~ à fonctionnement sec** *m* SECURITE dry dust removal

dépoussiérer *vt* CHARBON dedust, SECURITE remove

dépoussiéreur *m* CHARBON deduster, dust filter, PLAST CAOU *matériel* dust collector, SECURITE *séparateurs aérauliques* dust separator; **~ à chicane** *m* POLLUTION baffle collector; **~ électrique** *m* POLLUTION ESP, electrostatic precipitator; **~ humide** *m* POLLUTION wet scrubber; **~ mécanique** *m* POLLUTION mechanical collector; **~ à tissu** *m* SECURITE fabric dust collector; **~ à tissu filtrant** *m* POLLUTION baghouse

dépoussiéreurs: ~ individuels *m pl* SECURITE individual dust removal apparatus

dépréciation *f* PETROLE depreciation; **~ des capitaux** *f* PRODUCTION depreciation; **~ de stock** *f* PRODUCTION inventory wipe-off

dépresseur *m* CERAM VER depression bar, OCEANO depressor

dépression *f* AUTO vacuum, CONS MECA depression, negative pressure, MECANIQUE vacuum, METEO cyclone, depression, NAUT dip, OCEANO *d'une vague* hollow, PETROLE vacuum; **~ axiale** *f* GEOLOGIE axial depression; **~ de l'horizon** *f* GEOPHYS dip angle; **~ moléculaire du point de congélation** *f* THERMODYN molecular depression of freezing point; **~ motrice** *f* CONS MECA depression; **~ orographique** *f* METEO lee depression; **~ du pH** *f* POLLUTION pH depression; **~ de régime** *f* CH DE FER *véhicules* normal brake application, working vacuum; **~ sous le vent** *f* METEO lee depression

dépressurisation *f* ESPACE *véhicules*, PRODUCTION depressurization

dépressuriser *vt* AERONAUT, ESPACE, PRODUCTION depressurize

déprimer *vt* CHARBON depress

dépurer *vt* GENIE CHIM purify

dépuration *f* CHIMIE depuration

déradage *m* NAUT *bouée* dragging

déraillement *m* CH DE FER derailment

déramer *vt* IMPRIM *papier* aerate

dérangé *adj* CONS MECA out-of-order

dérangement:[1] **en ~** *adv* TELECOM out-of-order

dérangement[2] *m* TELECOM disruption to service; **~ d'une ligne** *m* TELECOM line fault; **~ de réception à l'extrémité** *m* TELECOM FERF, far-end receive failure

déranger: se ~ *v réfl* PRODUCTION fall out of order

dérapage *m* AERONAUT skidding, NAUT *ancre* dragging, PHYSIQUE sideslip

déraper *vi* AERONAUT skid, NAUT trip anchor, *ancre* drag, VEHICULES *circulation* skid

dérapeur *m* TRANSPORT skid car

dératage *m* ELECTROTEC derating

déréglage:[1] **en pas** *adj* AERONAUT out-of-pitch

déréglage:[2] **~ de la compensation** *m* AERONAUT *avion* out-of-trim; **~ des pales en rotation** *m* AERONAUT out-of-track

déréglé *adj* CONS MECA out-of-order

dérivateur *m* ELECTR *alimentation* shunting device

dérivation:[1] **en ~** *adj* ELECTROTEC shunt, PHYSIQUE bypass

dérivation:[2] **en ~** *adv* ELECTROTEC shunt, PHYSIQUE bypass

dérivation[3] *f* CH DE FER *véhicules* shunt, CHARBON, CONS MECA bypass, DISTRI EAU diversion, penstock, pentrough, diverting, flume, ELECTR spur, *circuit* bypass, *raccordement* tapping, *réseau* branch, branch line, ELECTRON branch, ELECTROTEC shunt, GAZ, INST HYDR bypass, MATH differentiation, MINES split, PETR bypassing, PETROLE *forage* bypass, PHYSIQUE shunt, PRODUCTION leat, *système hydraulique* bypass, TELECOM bridge; **~ en té** *f* ELECTR *liaison de câble* T-joint, tee joint; **~ en Y** *f* ELECTR *liaison de câble* breeches joint, y-joint; **~ de filtre** *f* PRODUCTION *système hydraulique* filter bypass; **~ tangente** *f* ELECTR *liaison de câble* breeches joint, y-joint

dérive:[1] **en ~** *adj* NAUT adrift; **à la ~** *adj* CH DE FER *véhicules* runaway, NAUT adrift

dérive:[2] **en ~** *adv* NAUT adrift; **à la ~** *adv* CH DE FER *véhicules* runaway, NAUT adrift

dérive[3] *f* ACOUSTIQUE drift, AERONAUT *aéronef* tail fin, *motion* drift, ELECTR, ESPACE *mesures* drift, HYDROLOGIE velocity, INFORMAT shift, METROLOGIE *d'un appareil de mesure* drift, NAUT center plate (AmE), centre plate (BrE), centerboard (AmE), centreboard

(BrE), daggerboard, drift, leeway, PETR, POLLU MER, PRODUCTION drift, TELECOM deviation, drift; ~ **d'alignement** *f* TV registration drift; ~ **anisoélastique** *f* ESPACE *gyroscopes, mesures* anisoelastic drift; ~ **de l'asservissement** *f* ESPACE *communications* servosystem drift; ~ **des continents** *f* GEOLOGIE continental drift; ~ **de courant** *f* TELECOM current drift; ~ **à court terme** *f* ELECTRON short-term drift; ~ **Doppler** *f* ESPACE *mesures* Doppler shift; ~ **des électrons** *f* NUCLEAIRE electron drift; ~ **en vol** *f* AERONAUT drift in flight; ~ **de fréquence** *f* ELECTR, ELECTRON, TELECOM frequency drift; ~ **de fréquence à long terme** *f* ELECTRON fractional frequency deviation; ~ **de la fréquence du quartz** *f* ELECTRON crystal frequency drift; ~ **de gain** *f* ELECTRON gain drift; ~ **littorale** *f* OCEANO littoral current, longshore current; ~ **nord-atlantique** *f* OCEANO North Atlantic Current, North Atlantic Drift; ~ **nord-pacifique** *f* OCEANO North Pacific Current, North Pacific Drift; ~ **de l'oscillateur** *f* ELECTRON oscillator drift; ~ **temporelle** *f* ELECTRON time drift

dérivé *m* CHIMIE derivative, derived product, ELECTRON derivative, POLLUTION by-product

dérivée *f* MATH derivative; ~ **de la courbe d'analyse thermique à l'échauffement** *f* THERMODYN heat rate curve; ~ **temporelle** *f* PHYSIQUE time derivative

dériver[1] *vt* CHIMIE derive, HYDROLOGIE drift

dériver[2] *vi* NAUT drift; ~ **sur son ancre** *vi* NAUT club

dériveur *m* NAUT dinghy, OCEANO drifter

dérivomètre *m* AERONAUT drift indicator, driftmeter

dernbachite *f* MINERAUX dernbachite

dernier: ~ **entré premier sorti** *m* INFORMAT, ORDINAT, PRODUCTION LIFO, last-in first-out; ~ **état** *m* PRODUCTION *d'une sortie, automatisme industriel* last state; ~ **quartier** *m* ASTRONOMIE last quarter, ASTRONOMIE third quarter; ~ **renseignement** *m* PRODUCTION last feedback

dernière: ~ **couche** *f* CONSTR finishing coat; ~ **épreuve** *f* IMPRIM *photogravure* final proof; ~ **passe** *f* PETR cap

dernières: ~ **lueurs** *f pl* PHYS RAYON *désintégration radiative* afterglow

dérouillage *m* CONS MECA derusting

dérouillant *m* CONS MECA rust remover

dérouillement *m* PRODUCTION rubbing off rust

dérouiller *vt* PRODUCTION *couteau* rub rust off

déroulable *adj* ESPACE *antenne* unfurlable

déroulant *m* CINEMAT roller caption; ~ **titre** *m* CINEMAT caption roller

déroulement *m* CONS MECA unwinding, INFORMAT *d'un programme*, ORDINAT *d'un programme* running; ~ **en sens inverse** *m* INFORMAT, ORDINAT reverse direction flow; ~ **des pas de séquenceur** *m* PRODUCTION *automatisme industriel* sequencer step instruction

dérouler *vt* CINEMAT unwind, PHOTO unspool, unwind, POLLU MER reel out

dérouleur *m* PETROLE *géophysique* jug hustler, PLAST CAOU *revêtement* reeling machine, POLLU MER reel, TEXTILE unwinder; ~ **automatique** *m* IMPRIM *rotatives* stripper; ~ **de bande** *m* INFORMAT, ORDINAT streamer, streaming tape drive, tape transport, tape unit; ~ **de bande magnétique** *m* INFORMAT deck, tape deck, ORDINAT tape deck; ~ **à collage automatique** *m* IMPRIM *rotatives* autopaster; ~ **à collage en marche** *m* IMPRIM flying paster; ~ **pour générique** *m* CINEMAT crawl title machine

dérouleuse *f* EMBALLAGE unwinding machine

déroutement *m* INFORMAT trap, NAUT rerouting, ORDI-

NAT trap

dérouter *vt* NAUT reroute

derrick *m* CONSTR derrick, derrick crane, PETR, PETROLE derrick

dés: ~ **en bronze** *m pl* CONS MECA gunmetal bearings

désaccentuation *f* ACOUSTIQUE, ELECTRON, ENREGISTR, ESPACE *communications*, TV de-emphasis

désaccord *m* ELECTRON detuning; ~ **gyro** *m* AERONAUT gyro unbalance; ~ **de réseau** *m* METALL misfit

désaccorder *vt* ELECTRON detune

désacidification *f* CHIMIE basification

désactivation *f* CHIMIE deactivation; ~ **d'état excité** *f* PHYS RAYON excited state deactivation; ~ **nucléaire** *f* REFRIG nuclear cooling

désactiver[1] *vt* CHARBON deactivate, INFORMAT, ORDINAT disable

désactiver[2] *vi* PRODUCTION reset

désadaptation *f* ELECTROTEC mismatch

désadapté *adj* ELECTR, PHYSIQUE mismatched

désaérateur *m* AERONAUT, PETROLE deaerator

désagrégation *f* MATERIAUX decomposition; ~ **par les intempéries** *f* CHARBON, CONSTR, MATERIAUX weathering; ~ **physique** *f* GEOLOGIE *des roches* mechanical weathering

désagréger[1] *vt* GEOLOGIE weather

désagréger:[2] se ~ **par les intempéries** *v réfl* CONSTR weather

désaimantation *f* ELECTR, MATERIAUX, PHYSIQUE, TV demagnetization; ~ **adiabatique** *f* PHYSIQUE adiabatic demagnetization

désaimanter *vt* MATERIAUX, PHYSIQUE, TV demagnetize

désaisonnaliser *vt* PRODUCTION deseasonalize

désalcalinisation *f* CERAM VER dealkalization

désalignement *m* IMPRIM misalignment; ~ **de la poussée** *m* ESPACE *propulsion* thrust misalignment

désamorçage *m* CONS MECA *d'un injecteur* stopping, PRODUCTION *d'un injecteur* failure

désamorcer[1] *vt* DISTRI EAU *une pompe* drain, INST HYDR *une pompe* dewater, PHYSIQUE de-energize

désamorcer:[2] se ~ *v réfl* PRODUCTION fail

désanamorphoser *vt* CINEMAT unsqueeze

désanamorphoseur *m* CINEMAT deanamorphoser

désancrage *m* METALL unpinning, MINES *d'une cheminée* starting

désarmé *adj* NAUT decommissioned, inactive, *navire* laid-up

désarmement: ~ **manuel** *m* ESPACE *véhicules* manual disarming

désarmer[1] *vt* MILITAIRE disarm, NAUT lay up

désarmer[2] *vti* INFORMAT, ORDINAT disarm

désarrimer *vt* NAUT *cargaison* shift

désassemblage *m* CONS MECA disjointing, NUCLEAIRE *d'un assemblage combustible* breakdown, dismantling; ~ **des rallonges** *m* MINES uncoupling rods

désassembler *vt* CONS MECA disassemble, disjoint, dismantle

désassembleur *m* ORDINAT disassembler; ~ **de paquets** *m* TELECOM depacketizer

désattelage *m* CONS MECA detachment

désaturation *f* OCEANO desaturation

désaturer *vt* TV desaturate

désaxage *m* CONS MECA setting-over

désaxé *adj* CONS MECA off-center (AmE), off-centre (BrE), VEHICULES *moteur* offset

désaxer *vt* CONS MECA set over, throw off center (AmE), throw off centre (BrE)

descellage *m* CERAM VER stripping

descendant *m* INFORMAT *arbre*, ORDINAT *arbre* descendant; **~ radioactif** *m* PHYS RAYON, PHYSIQUE daughter product

descendante *f* IMPRIM descender, OCEANO ebb tide, falling tide

descenderie *f* CONSTR mine access, MINES winze; **~ de remblai** *f* MINES fill raise, filling raise

descendre[1] *vt* SECURITE *une charge* lower

descendre[2] *vi* NAUT *la marée* ebb

descenseur: **~ hélicoïdal** *m* MINES spiral chute

descente *f* AERONAUT let-down, CONSTR leader, stack pipe, ESPACE descent, IMPRIM *d'un caractère ou d'un texte au dessous de la ligne* sinkage, NAUT hatch, hatchway, *du navire* ladder, PRODUCTION *d'un arbre porte-foret, d'un porte-outil* fall; **~ d'antenne** *f* TV aerial lead; **~ d'eau** *f* CONSTR leader, rainwater downpipe (BrE), rainwater downspout (AmE), stack pipe; **~ en parachute** *f* MILITAIRE parachute drop; **~ en spirale** *f* AERONAUT spiral glide; **~ fluviale** *f* CONSTR rainwater pipe; **~ manuelle** *f* CONS MECA hand downfeed; **~ à pente faible** *f* AERONAUT shallow descent; **~ progressive** *f* AERONAUT cruise descent; **~ rapide** *f* AERONAUT emergency descent; **~ sous pression** *f* PETROLE snubbing; **~ de tiges** *f* PETROLE *foret* going in hole; **~ du train** *f* AERONAUT landing gear extension

déschlammage *m* CHARBON desliming, deslurrying

déschlammer *vt* CHARBON deslime, deslurry

descloizite *f* MINERAUX descloizite

descripteur *m* INFORMAT, ORDINAT descriptor

descriptif *adj* BREVETS descriptive

description *f* BREVETS description; **~ de cellule de maintenance** *f* TELECOM MCD, maintenance cell description; **~ de données** *f* INFORMAT, ORDINAT data description; **~ de fichier** *f* INFORMAT, ORDINAT file description; **~ du problème** *f* INFORMAT, ORDINAT problem description; **~ de route** *f* AERONAUT *circulation aérienne* route description

déséchafauder: **~ un bâtiment** *vi* CONSTR take down scaffolding from a building

déséchouer[1] *vt* NAUT refloat

déséchouer[2] **se ~** *v réfl* NAUT float off

désembiellage *m* CH DE FER *véhicules* removal of locomotive rods

désembrayage: **~ automatique** *m* COMMANDE automatic disconnection, automatic tripping

désembrayer *vt* CONS MECA throw out of action, MECANIQUE disengage

désembrouillage *m* ESPACE *communications*, TELECOM descrambling

désembrouiller *vt* ESPACE *communications*, TELECOM descramble

désembrouilleur *m* ESPACE *communications*, TELECOM descrambler, TV unscrambler

désembueur-dégivreur *m* AUTO demister

désempilement *m* EMBALLAGE *des palettes* destacking

désempiler *vt* INFORMAT pop

désémulsifiant *m* POLLU MER de-emulsifier, emulsion breaker

désémulsification *f* MATERIAUX demulsification

désémulsionnant *m* AGRO ALIM de-emulsifier, de-emulsifying agent

désencollage *m* TEXTILE desizing

désencoller *vt* TEXTILE desize

désencrage *m* PAPIER deinking

désenfumage *m* SECURITE smoke control

désengrené *adj* CONS MECA out-of-gear

désengrener *vt* CONS MECA throw out of action

désenrobage *m* CONSTR *bitume* aggregate stripping

désensableur *m* MINES sludge pump

désensibilisateur *m* PHOTO desensitizer

désensibilisation *f* MINES, PHOTO, TELECOM desensitization

désensibiliser *vt* MINES desensitize, phlegmatize

désensimage *m* CERAM VER desizing

désentrelacement *m* ELECTRON deinterleaving

désentrelacer *vt* ELECTRON deinterleave

déséquilibre *m* CONS MECA unbalance, IMPRIM *impression, encres, eau* imbalance, MECANIQUE unbalance; **~ de phase** *m* PRODUCTION *automatisme industriel* phase unbalance; **~ thermique** *m* THERMODYN thermal imbalance; **~ du trafic** *m* TELECOM traffic distribution imbalance, traffic load imbalance

déséquilibré *adj* ELECTR unbalanced

désétiquetage: **~ de boîte** *m* EMBALLAGE can delabeling (AmE), can delabelling (BrE)

désexcitation *f* ELECTROTEC de-energization, GEOPHYS de-excitation, PRODUCTION *automatisme industriel* drop-out time

désexciter *vt* CONS MECA deactivate, ELECTROTEC de-energize

déshabillage *m* CONS MECA disassembly

désherbeuse: **~ électrique** *f* CONSTR strimmer

désheurement *m* CH DE FER out-of-course running

déshuileur *m* CONS MECA separator, DISTRI EAU oil trap, HYDROLOGIE oil separator, oil trap, PAPIER oil separator

déshumidificateur *m* REFRIG dehumidifier; **~ à action de surface** *m* REFRIG surface dehumidifier

déshumidificateurs: **~ d'air** *m pl* SECURITE air dehumidifiers

déshuntage *m* CH DE FER de-shunting

déshydratage *f* THERMODYN drying

déshydratant[1] *adj* GENIE CHIM desiccative

déshydratant[2] *m* CHIMIE desiccant, GENIE CHIM dehydrating agent, dehydrator, REFRIG desiccant

déshydratation *f* CHIMIE dehydration, dewatering, GENIE CHIM, GEOLOGIE dehydration, PETROLE dehydration, desiccation, dewatering, TEXTILE dewatering, hydroextraction; **~ des boues** *f* HYDROLOGIE sludge dewatering; **~ par aspiration** *f* TEXTILE suction dewatering, suction hydroextraction

déshydratation-congélation *f* AGRO ALIM, REFRIG dehydrofreezing

déshydraté *adj* AGRO ALIM desiccated, dried, THERMODYN desiccated, dried, dry

déshydrater *vt* CHIMIE dehydrate, desiccate, GEOLOGIE, REFRIG dehydrate, TEXTILE dewater, hydroextract, THERMODYN dry out, dry

déshydrateur *m* NUCLEAIRE dehumidifier, REFRIG dehydrator, THERMODYN dryer; **~ filtre** *m* REFRIG filter dryer; **~ d'hélium** *m* NUCLEAIRE helium dehydrator unit

déshydrogénase *f* AGRO ALIM dehydrogenase

déshydrogénation *f* CHIMIE, MATERIAUX dehydrogenation

déshydrogéné *adj* CHIMIE dehydrogenated

déshydrogéner *vt* CHIMIE dehydrogenate

déshydroluminostérol *m* CHIMIE dehydroluminosterol

désignation *f* ACOUSTIQUE, BREVETS designation, INFORMAT, ORDINAT selection; **~ de borne** *f* PRODUCTION terminal designation; **~ conjointe** *f* BREVETS joint designation; **~ double** *f* PRODUCTION double legend; **~ de la variante produit** *f* PRODUCTION product variant option descriptions

désiliciage *m* MATERIAUX desilication, desiliconizing

désiliciation *f* MATERIAUX desiliconization

désilteur *m* PETROLE desilter

désincrustant *m* CH DE FER *véhicules* boiler-scaling appliance, scale solvent, MAT CHAUFF *traitement des eaux de chaudière* boiler-cleaning compound, scale solvent, PRODUCTION disincrustant

désincrustation *f* PRODUCTION removing, scaling

désincruster *vt* PRODUCTION fur, *une chaudière* descale

désincrusteur: ~ de chaudière *m* CH DE FER *véhicules* boiler-scaling appliance

désinfecter *vt* HYDROLOGIE, SECURITE disinfect

désinfection *f* DISTRI EAU, SECURITE disinfection

désinfester *vt* SECURITE disinfest

désintégrateur *m* AGRO ALIM disintegrator, PAPIER disintegrator, hog, pulper, PRODUCTION disintegrator

désintégration *f* NUCLEAIRE, PHYS RAYON *radioactive*, TV decay; **~ alpha** *f* PHYS PART, PHYSIQUE alpha decay; **~ bêta** *f* PHYSIQUE beta decay; **~ bêta moins** *f* PHYS PART beta decay; **~ radioactive** *f* PHYS PART radioactive decay, PHYSIQUE radioactive disintegration; **~ spontanée** *f* PHYS RAYON *élément radioactif* spontaneous decay

désintégrer[1] *vt* EMBALLAGE disintegrate

désintégrer:[2] **se ~** *v réfl* PHYS RAYON decay, disintegrate, PHYSIQUE decay

desktop *adj* INFORMAT, ORDINAT desktop

desmine *f* MINERAUX desmine

desmotropie *f* CHIMIE desmotropy

désodorisation *f* HYDROLOGIE deodorizing

désorber *vt* CHIMIE desorb

désordre *m* METALL disorder

désorientation *f* METALL disorientation

désorption *f* CHARBON, CHIMIE, MATERIAUX desorption

désoufrage *m* CHIMIE desulfuration (AmE), desulfurization (AmE), desulphuration (BrE), desulphurization (BrE)

désoufrer *vt* CHIMIE desulfurize (AmE), desulphurize (BrE)

désoxydant *m* CHIMIE deoxidizer

désoxydation *f* CHIMIE deoxidization, *d'un oxyde* reduction, MATERIAUX deoxidation; **~ de l'air** *f* MINES deoxidation, oxygen depletion of air

desquamation *f* GEOLOGIE *en écailles* exfoliation

dessablage *m* PRODUCTION dressing, *des pièces coulées* cleaning; **~ au tonneau** *m* PRODUCTION rattling, tumbling

dessabler *vt* PRODUCTION *une pièce coulée* clean; **~ au tonneau** *vt* PRODUCTION rattle

dessableur *m* DISTRI EAU sand trap, HYDROLOGIE grit trap, sand trap, PETR, PETROLE desander, PRODUCTION cleaner, dresser

dessableur-dégraveur *m* HYDROLOGIE sand and gravel trap

dessalage *m* PETROLE desalting

dessalé *adj* GENIE CHIM, HYDROLOGIE desalinated

dessalement *m* DISTRI EAU saline water conversion, GENIE CHIM desalination, desalinization, HYDROLOGIE *de l'eau de mer* demineralization, desalination, NAUT *de l'eau de mer*, OCEANO desalination

dessaler *vti* GENIE CHIM desalinate, desalinize, desalt, HYDROLOGIE desalinate

desséchant *m* CHIMIE, EMBALLAGE *gel de silice* desic-

cant, GENIE CHIM dehydrating agent, dehydrator, THERMODYN desiccant

desséché *adj* THERMODYN desiccated, dried, scorched

dessèchement *m* DISTRI EAU drainage, draining, EMBALLAGE, GENIE CHIM, PETROLE desiccation, THERMODYN drying out

dessécher *vt* AGRO ALIM desiccate, DISTRI EAU *un étang* drain, MAT CHAUFF dehumidify, desiccate, MATERIAUX dry, THERMODYN desiccate, dry out, scorch

dessécheur *m* CONS MECA dryer

desserrage *m* CH DE FER *d'un attelage* loosening, *véhicules* brakes off, releasing, CONS MECA *d'un écrou* slacking, PAPIER release, release-coated paper, PRODUCTION *d'un écrou* looseness; **~ automatique** *m* CONS MECA automatic release; **~ du frein** *m* CH DE FER *véhicules* brake release; **~ spontané** *m* NUCLEAIRE self-loosening

desserré *adj* ELECTR *borne*, PRODUCTION *écrou* loose

desserrer *vt* MECANIQUE loosen, release, PRODUCTION *un écrou* loosen, VEHICULES *frein* release

desserte *f* CH DE FER service, TELECOM serving; **~ des abonnés** *f* TELECOM subscriber service

dessiccant *m* THERMODYN siccative

dessiccateur *m* AGRO ALIM, CHIMIE desiccator, CONS MECA dryer, EQUIP LAB *séchage*, GENIE CHIM, MAT CHAUFF desiccator, THERMODYN dryer; **~ centrifuge** *m* GENIE CHIM centrifugal dryer, centrifugal hydroextractor; **~ de vapeur** *m* INST HYDR steam dryer; **~ à vide** *m* EQUIP LAB, MAT CHAUFF vacuum desiccator

dessiccatif *adj* GENIE CHIM desiccative, MAT CHAUFF desiccant

dessiccation *f* AGRO ALIM, CHIMIE desiccation, CONSTR *des bois* seasoning, GENIE CHIM dehydration, desiccation, PETROLE drying, REFRIG desiccation, THERMODYN desiccation, drying; **~ dans les paquets** *f* REFRIG in-package desiccation; **~ par congélation** *f* GENIE CHIM freeze-drying, lyophilization

dessin:[1] **~ flou** *adj* CERAM VER not molded (AmE), not moulded (BrE)

dessin[2] *m* BREVETS design, drawing, CONSTR drawing print, GEOMETRIE, NAUT drawing; **~ animé** *m* CINEMAT animated cartoon, cartoon; **~ de caractère** *m* INFORMAT typeface; **~ des circuits intégrés** *m* ELECTRON integrated circuit layout; **~ de coupe** *m* CONS MECA section drawing; **~ demi-nature** *m* PRODUCTION half-size drawing; **~ de diffraction** *m* METALL diffraction pattern; **~ à l'échelle** *m* GEOMETRIE scale drawing; **~ en demi-grandeur naturelle** *m* PRODUCTION half-size drawing; **~ d'étude** *m* CONS MECA engineering drawing; **~ de fabrication** *m* PRODUCTION production drawing; **~ flou** *m* CERAM VER dim letters (BrE); **~ de fragmentation** *m* CERAM VER fracture pattern; **~ géométrique** *m* PRODUCTION mechanical drawing; **~ industriel** *m* NAUT engineering drawing; **~ des lignes de courant** *m* PHYS FLUID flow pattern; **~ schématique** *m* CONS MECA scheme, PRODUCTION diagram; **~ au trait** *m* CONS MECA outline, GEOMETRIE, IMPRIM line drawing; **~ de trempe** *m* CERAM VER checker pattern

dessinateur *m* IMPRIM, NAUT draftsman (AmE), draughtsman (BrE), PRODUCTION designer, draftsman (AmE), draughtsman (BrE); **~ concepteur** *m* CONS MECA design draftsman (AmE), design draughtsman (BrE); **~ industriel** *m* MECANIQUE draftsman (AmE), draughtsman (BrE)

dessinateur-projeteur *m* CONS MECA project design manager

dessiner *vt* CONSTR design

dessoudure *f* CONS MECA unsoldering

dessous *m* PRODUCTION drag, nowel, *de châssis* bottom part; **~ de carrosserie** *m* VEHICULES underbody; **~ de châssis** *m* PRODUCTION drag, nowel; **~ d'étampe** *m* PRODUCTION bottom swage; **~ froid statique** *m* REFRIG cold static base

dessus *m* PRODUCTION *d'un moule en terre* cope; **~ de caisse aspirante** *m* PAPIER suction box cover; **~ de châssis** *m* PRODUCTION cope, top part of flask; **~ d'étampe** *m* CONS MECA top rounding-tool, top swage

destinataire *m* ORDINAT addressee, TELECOM recipient, transmission recipient; **~ de l'échange** *m* TELECOM interchange recipient

destination: **à ~ de** *adj* NAUT bound for; **à ~ de son port d'attache** *adj* NAUT *bateau* homeward-bound

destocker *vt* DISTRI EAU draw-down

destroyer *m* NAUT destroyer

destruction: **~ de la cathode** *f* ELECTROTEC cathode disintegration

désulfonation *f* CHIMIE desulfonation (AmE), desulphonation (BrE)

désulfuration *f* CHARBON desulfurization (AmE), desulphurization (BrE), CHIMIE desulfuration (AmE), desulphuration (BrE), MATERIAUX, PETROLE, POLLUTION desulfurization (AmE), desulphurization (BrE); **~ des effluents gazeux** *f* POLLUTION flue gas desulfurization (AmE), flue gas desulphurisation (BrE); **~ de gaz** *f* POLLUTION gas desulfurization (AmE), gas desulphurisation (BrE); **~ des gaz de combustion** *f* POLLUTION flue gas desulfurization (AmE), flue gas desulphurisation (BrE)

désulfurer *vt* CHIMIE desulfurize (AmE), desulphurize (BrE)

désurchauffer *vt* CHAUFFAGE desuperheat

désurchauffeur *m* CHAUFFAGE desuperheater

désynchronisation *f* CINEMAT picture slip

désynchronisé *adj* TV out-of-sync

détachable *adj* CONS MECA detachable

détachage: **~ au fer** *m* CERAM VER cracking-off; **~ par soufflage au mince** *m* CERAM VER bursting-off

détachement: **~ d'abordage** *m* NAUT *dans un assaut* boarding party; **~ de bord** *m* CERAM VER edge flaking, edge peeling, edge shelling; **~ de visite** *m* NAUT *visite autorisée* boarding party

détacher *vt* CONSTR dislodge

détail: **~ estimatif préliminaire** *m* CONSTR preliminary cost estimate; **~ de la maille** *m* TEXTILE stitch detail

détaillant *m* PRODUCTION retailer

détalonnage *m* CONS MECA backing-off

détartrage *m* LESSIVES , PRODUCTION descaling

détartrer *vt* LESSIVES descale, PRODUCTION fur, *une chaudière* descale

détecté *adj* ELECTRON *signal* detected

détecter *vt* ELECTRON, PHYS PART detect

détecteur *m* CONS MECA, ELECTR *démodulation* detector, ELECTRON detector, sensor, ELECTROTEC detector, ESPACE *communications, véhicules spatiaux* sensor, OCEANO *poissons* fish detector, OPTIQUE detector, photodetector, PHYSIQUE demodulator, detector, sensor, POLLU MER sensing element, TELECOM detector, sensor, TV discriminator; **~ d'accélération** *m* AERONAUT acceleration detector; **~ d'accidents** *m* TRANSPORT accident detector; **~ d'analyse de la circulation** *m* TRANSPORT traffic analysis detector; **~ angulaire trois axes** *m* AERONAUT angular three-axis

rate sensor; **~ d'arrêt moteur** *m* ESPACE *véhicules* shutdown sensor; **~ à barrette** *m* ESPACE *véhicules* strip-type detector; **~ de battement** *m* ELECTRON beat note detector; **~ de boîte chaude** *m* CH DE FER, TRANSPORT hot box detector; **~ à boucle d'induction** *m* TRANSPORT induction loop detector; **~ à boucle à induction à circuit résonnant** *m* TRANSPORT resonant circuit induction loop detector; **~ à boucle à induction à déphasage** *m* TRANSPORT phase displacement induction loop detector; **~ à boucle magnétique** *m* TRANSPORT magnetic loop detector; **~ de bulles** *m* OCEANO bubble detector; **~ de câbles** *m* ELECTR cable locator; **~ à capacité** *m* TRANSPORT objective detector; **~ à capture électronique** *m* POLLUTION electron capture detector; **~ à capture d'électrons** *m* POLLUTION electron capture detector; **~ des caractéristiques des véhicules** *m* TRANSPORT vehicle characteristic detector; **~ carré** *m* PRODUCTION block sensor; **~ Cerenkov** *m* PHYS RAYON Cerenkov detector; **~ de chaleur** *m* THERMODYN heat detector; **~ de classification** *m* TRANSPORT *des véhicules* classification detector; **~ de classification des véhicules** *m* TRANSPORT selective vehicle detector; **~ climatique** *m* TRANSPORT climatic detector; **~ de compteur de jeu** *m* PRODUCTION *automatisme industriel* set counter sensor; **~ à contact** *m* TRANSPORT contact detector; **~ de contamination chimique miniature** *m* MILITAIRE *guerre chimique* miniature chemical agent detector; **~ de créneaux** *m* TRANSPORT gap detector; **~ cylindrique** *m* PRODUCTION tubular sensor; **~ de débit** *m* TRANSPORT traffic volume meter; **~ de défaut** *m* ELECTR fault detector; **~ DELPHI** *m* PHYS PART DELPHI detector; **~ de déplacement** *m* AERONAUT travel follow-up; **~ directionnel** *m* TRANSPORT directional detector; **~ de données à fréquence vocale** *m* TELECOM voice-band data detector; **~ de double feuille** *m* IMPRIM *impression* double sheet detector; **~ d'écart** *m* AERONAUT deviation detector; **~ d'écartométrie** *m* ESPACE *communications* RF sensor; **~ d'écart radioélectrique** *m* ESPACE *communications* RF sensor; **~ électrique de métaux** *m* CONSTR metal detector; **~ électronique de hauteur de pile** *m* IMPRIM *machines* pile scanner; **~ embrayable** *m* AERONAUT *hélicoptère* collective pitch follow up; **~ d'embrayage** *m* AERONAUT clutch pick-off; **~ d'erreurs** *m* TELECOM error detector; **~ à état solide** *m* PHYS RAYON solid-state detector; **~ à fil continu** *m* AERONAUT fire wire; **~ de file d'attente** *m* TRANSPORT queue detector; **~ à filtre et échantillonnage** *m* TELECOM filter-and-sample detector; **~ de fissures** *m* CONS MECA, NUCLEAIRE crack detector; **~ de flambement** *m* PETR buckle detector; **~ de flamme** *m* COMMANDE, MAT CHAUFF flame detector; **~ de flux** *m* AERONAUT flux gate (AmE), flux valve (BrE); **~ de fréquence différentielle** *m* ELECTRON frequency detector; **~ de fuite** *m* ELECTR earth leakage detector (BrE), ground leakage detector (AmE); **~ de fuite de gaz** *m* EQUIP LAB, THERMODYN gas leak detector; **~ de fuites** *m* MAT CHAUFF leak detector; **~ de fuites à spectromètre de masse** *m* CONS MECA *technique du vide* mass spectrometer-type leak detector; **~ de fumée** *m* SECURITE smoke detector; **~ de gaz** *m* COMMANDE, EQUIP LAB *analyse, sécurité*, MILITAIRE gas detector; **~ de givrage** *m* AERONAUT ice detector; **~ gravimétrique** *m* AERONAUT leveling unit (AmE), levelling unit (BrE); **~ de grisou** *m* MINES gas detector, methanometer, methane detector, methane indicator, pit gas indicator; ~ **d'horizon** *m* ESPACE *véhicules* horizon sensor; ~ **hydraulique** *m* TRANSPORT hydraulic detector; ~ **d'image** *m* TELECOM image sensor; ~ **d'incendie** *m* COMMANDE, SECURITE fire detector; ~ **d'incidence** *m* AERONAUT incidence probe; ~ **inertiel** *m* ESPACE *véhicules* inertial sensor; ~ **d'infrarouge** *m* ESPACE infrared sensor; ~ **à infrarouge** *m* TRANSPORT infrared detector, passive infrared detector; ~ **à infrarouge actif** *m* TRANSPORT active infrared detector; ~ **d'interruption de la porteuse de données** *m* TELECOM data carrier failure detector; ~ **Jodel** *m* NUCLEAIRE Jodel detector; ~ **de lasers** *m* ELECTRON laser warning receiver; ~ **de LEP** *m* PHYS PART LEP detector; ~ **linéaire** *m* ELECTRON linear detector; ~ **logique** *m* INFORMAT logical sensor; ~ **de lumière** *m* PHYS RAYON light detector; ~ **magnétique** *m* TRANSPORT magnetic detector; ~ **de métaux** *m* EMBALLAGE metal detector; ~ **de minces** *m* CERAM VER thin-spot detector; ~ **de mines** *m* MILITAIRE mine detector; ~ **de neige** *m* TRANSPORT snow detector; ~ **de neutrons à résonance** *m* PHYS RAYON resonance neutron detector; ~ **de niveau** *m* CHARBON level detector; ~ **d'occupation** *m* TRANSPORT continuous presence detector, occupancy detector; ~ **OPAL** *m* PHYS PART OPAL detector; ~ **optique** *m* ELECTRON optical detector, ESPACE *véhicules* optical sensor, OPTIQUE, TELECOM optical detector; ~ **optique de vitesse** *m* TRANSPORT optical speed trap detector; ~ **d'orientation terrestre** *m* GEOPHYS earth sensor; ~ **par ionisation** *m* PHYS RAYON ionization detector; ~ **de parole** *m* ESPACE *communications* voice detector, TELECOM speech detector; ~ **de particules neutres** *m* NUCLEAIRE neutral particle detector; ~ **de passage** *m* TRANSPORT dynamic movement detector, motion detector, passage detector; ~ **de passage d'étoile** *m* ESPACE *véhicules* star transit detector; ~ **de phase** *m* ELECTRON, TELECOM phase detector; ~ **photoélectrique** *m* TRANSPORT photoelectric detector, reflected beam photo-electric detector; ~ **à photométrie de flamme** *m* POLLUTION flame photometric detector; ~ **photométrique à flamme** *m* POLLUTION flame photometric detector; ~ **de photons** *m* PHYS PART photon detector; ~ **photosensible** *m* ELECTRON photodetector; ~ **piézoélectrique** *m* TRANSPORT piezoelectric detector; ~ **pneumatique** *m* IMPRIM *contrôles* pneumatic sensor, TRANSPORT pneumatic detector; ~ **de position** *m* PRODUCTION limit switch; ~ **de position angulaire** *m* MECANIQUE angle sensor; ~ **de présence dynamique** *m* TRANSPORT dynamic presence detector; ~ **d'une présence intruse** *m* TELECOM intruder presence detector; ~ **de présence limitée** *m* TRANSPORT limited presence detector; ~ **à pression** *m* TRANSPORT pressure-sensitive detector; ~ **de proximité inductif** *m* ELECTROTEC inductive proximity switch; ~ **pyrométrique** *m* THERMODYN temperature sensor; ~ **quadratique** *m* ELECTROTEC square-law detector; ~ **radar** *m* PHYS RAYON radar sensor; ~ **de radiation** *m* EQUIP LAB, PHYS RAYON radiation detector; ~ **à rayonnement de transition** *m* PHYS RAYON transition radiation detector; ~ **des rayons cosmiques** *m* ASTRONOMIE cosmic ray detector; ~ **RF** *m* ESPACE *communications* RF sensor; ~ **de signal** *m* TELECOM signal detector; ~ **de signalisation** *m* TELECOM signaling detector (AmE), signalling detector (BrE); ~ **du signal de ligne reçu sur la voie de données** *m* TELECOM data channel received line signal detector; ~ **au silicium** *m* ELECTRON, PHYS RAYON *diffusion des particules*

silicon detector; ~ **solaire** *m* ESPACE *véhicules* solar sensor, GEOPHYS sun sensor; ~ **de son** *m* MILITAIRE sound detector; ~ **sonique** *m* TRANSPORT sonic detector; ~ **stellaire** *m* ESPACE *véhicules* star sensor; ~ **de température** *m* THERMODYN heat sensor, *thermique* temperature sensor; ~ **de température et d'humidité** *m* TRANSPORT moisture and temperature detector; ~ **de terre** *m* ELECTROTEC earth detector (BrE), ground detector (AmE); ~ **à la terre** *m* ELECTR earth leakage detector (BrE), ground leakage detector (AmE); ~ **thermovélocimétrique** *m* THERMODYN rate of rise detector; ~ **de trafic** *m* TRANSPORT traffic detector; ~ **à trois axes** *m* AERONAUT angular three-axis rate sensor; ~ **à ultrason à pulsation** *m* TRANSPORT pulsed ultrasonic detector; ~ **à ultrasons** *m* TRANSPORT ultrasonic detector; ~ **à ultrasons à ondes continues** *m* TRANSPORT continuous wave ultrasonic detector; ~ **de vitesse** *m* TRANSPORT speed detector, speed trap; ~ **de vitesse angulaire** *m* AERONAUT angular velocity rate sensor

détecteurs: ~ **de casse** *m pl* IMPRIM web break detectors; ~ **de mouvements à infrarouges** *m pl* SECURITE infrared motion alarm

détection *f* ACOUSTIQUE, ELECTRON, ESPACE *communications* detection, INFORMAT sensing, OCEANO echo detection, echo ranging, echo sounding, echolocation, ORDINAT sense, sensing, PHYS RAYON *d'un rayonnement radioactif* detection; ~ **d'anomalie** *f* GAZ, INFORMAT, ORDINAT fault detection; ~ **de la cible** *f* PHYS PART target detection; ~ **cohérente** *f* ELECTRON coherent detection; ~ **de collisions** *f* INFORMAT, ORDINAT, TELECOM CD, collision detection; ~ **de courant** *f* ELECTROTEC current sensing; ~ **de défauts** *f* TELECOM fault detection; ~ **à distance** *f* POLLU MER remote sensing; ~ **d'électrons** *f* PHYS PART electron detection; ~ **d'erreurs** *f* COMMANDE, ELECTRON, INFORMAT, ORDINAT, TELECOM, TV error detection; ~ **de fuite** *f* GAZ leak detection; ~ **de fuites** *f* EMBALLAGE leakage detection; ~ **de fuites à l'hélium** *f* NUCLEAIRE helium leak detection; ~ **de hadrons** *f* PHYS PART hadron detection; ~ **hétérodyne** *f* TELECOM heterodyne detection; ~ **des indices dans la boue** *f* PETR mud logging; ~ **linéaire** *f* ELECTRON linear detection; ~ **de modification** *f* TELECOM manipulation detection; ~ **de mot unique** *f* ESPACE *communications* unique word detection; ~ **optique** *f* ELECTRON optical detection, optical sensing; ~ **de panne de sensation musculaire** *f* AERONAUT artificial feel failure detector; ~ **par la méthode ultrasonique** *f* CONS MECA nondestructive ultrasonic testing; ~ **de parole** *f* ESPACE *communications* speech detection, voice sensor; ~ **par photostyle** *f* INFORMAT, ORDINAT light pen detection; ~ **par radar** *f* TRANSPORT radar contact; ~ **de phase cohérente** *f* ELECTRON coherent detection; ~ **de porteuse** *f* ELECTRON, TELECOM CD, carrier detect; ~ **de porteuse de données** *f* TELECOM DCD, data carrier detect; ~ **de position angulaire** *f* INFORMAT, ORDINAT rotation position sensing; ~ **au radar** *f* NAUT radar detection; ~ **de rupture de gaine à collection électrostatique** *f* NUCLEAIRE electrostatic collector, failed fuel element monitor; ~ **de rupture de gaine par neutrons différés** *f* NUCLEAIRE delayed neutron failed fuel element monitor; ~ **de signal** *f* TELECOM signal detection; ~ **de surcourse** *f* PRODUCTION *automatisme industriel* overtravel detection; ~ **synchrone** *f* ELECTRON synchronous detection

détectivité *f* OPTIQUE detectability, TELECOM detectivity;

~ normée *f* OPTIQUE D-star, normalized detectivity, TELECOM D-star; **~ spécifique** *f* OPTIQUE D-star, normalized detectivity, specific detectivity, TELECOM specific detectivity

dételage *m* CH DE FER *véhicules* uncoupling, CONS MECA detachment; **~ automatique des wagons** *m* TRANSPORT automatic uncoupling of rolling stock

dételer *vt* CH DE FER *remorques, motrices, wagons* uncouple

détendeur *m* AERONAUT pressure reducer, CONSTR pressure regulator, ESPACE *véhicules* pressure reducer, INST HYDR escape valve, pressure-reducing valve, relief valve, MAT CHAUFF gas pressure regulator, REFRIG expansion valve; **~ à braser** *m* REFRIG sweat-type expansion valve; **~ à égalisation extérieure de pression** *m* REFRIG external equalizer valve; **~ manuel** *m* REFRIG hand expansion valve; **~ pour gaz sous pression** *m* THERMODYN gas pressure reducing valve; **~ de sensation musculaire** *m* AERONAUT feel simulator valve; **~ thermostatique** *m* REFRIG thermostatic expansion valve; **~ de vapeur** *m* INST HYDR steam relief valve

détendre[1] *vt* MECANIQUE, TEXTILE relax

détendre:[2] **se ~** *v réfl* INST HYDR expand

détendu *adj* ESPACE *véhicules* expanded, RESSORTS, TEXTILE relaxed

détente *f* CONS MECA click, detent, dog, expansion gear, keeper, link gear, link motion, link valve motion, pawl, trigger, ESPACE *véhicules*, INST HYDR, MECANIQUE *physique* expansion, MILITAIRE *d'une arme à feu* trigger, PHYSIQUE pressure reduction, REFRIG, RESSORTS, THERMODYN expansion; **~ adiabatique** *f* AERONAUT, PHYS FLUID adiabatic pressure drop, THERMODYN adiabatic expansion; **~ automatique** *f* CONS MECA automatic expansion gear; **~ directe** *f* REFRIG direct expansion; **~ de Gay-Lussac** *f* PHYSIQUE Gay-Lussac expansion; **~ de Joule** *f* PHYSIQUE Joule expansion; **~ de Joule-Kelvin** *f* PHYSIQUE Joule-Kelvin expansion, Joule-Thomson expansion; **~ de Joule-Thomson** *f* PHYSIQUE Joule-Kelvin expansion, Joule-Thomson expansion

détergence *f* CHIMIE detergency

détergent *m* CHIMIE, GENIE CHIM, MATERIAUX, PETROLE detergent; **~ anionique** *m* LESSIVES anionic detergent; **~ liquide** *m* LESSIVES liquid detergent; **~ synthétique** *m* LESSIVES non-soapy detergent, synthetic detergent

détérioration *f* CONS MECA degradation, EMBALLAGE, PLAST CAOU deterioration, TV degradation; **~ due aux intempéries** *f* MATERIAUX weathering; **~ de la qualité** *f* TV quality degradation

détériorer *vt* EMBALLAGE deteriorate

déterminant *m* INFORMAT, MATH, ORDINAT determinant

détermination *f* SECURITE *de la concentration du dioxyde d'azote*, THERMODYN *de la puissance calorifique* determination; **~ de l'âge radioactif** *f* PHYS RAYON radioactive dating; **~ du centrage** *f* AERONAUT computation of center of gravity (AmE), computation of centre of gravity (BrE); **~ de la contamination** *f* QUALITE *nourriture* contaminant determination; **~ de l'élément contaminant** *f* QUALITE *nourriture* contaminant determination; **~ de l'humidité** *f* EMBALLAGE moisture determination; **~ du nombre de masse** *f* NUCLEAIRE mass assignment; **~ de l'orbite** *f* ESPACE *orbitographie* orbit determination, orbit prediction; **~ quantitative** *f* MATERIAUX quantitative determination

déterminer: ~ un point *vi* NAUT plot the position

déterministe *adj* INFORMAT, ORDINAT deterministic

détersif *m* CHIMIE cleaner, detergent, GENIE CHIM, TEXTILE detergent

détonant *adj* MINES capable of detonation, detonatable

détonateur *m* CONSTR cap, ESPACE *pyrotechnie* detonator, MINES detonator, detonator cap, *de mine* cap, exploder, PETR cap, THERMODYN detonator; **~ à basse intensité** *m* MINES low-tension detonator; **~ BI** *m* MINES low-tension detonator; **~ à BI** *m* MINES low-tension detonator; **~ électrique** *m* MINES electric detonator; **~ électrique à court retard** *m* MINES short-delay electric detonator; **~ électrique instantané** *m* MINES instantaneous detonator, instantaneous electric blasting cap; **~ électrique à retardement** *m* MINES electric delay detonator cap; **~ à haute intensité** *m* MINES high-tension detonator; **~ à HI** *m* MINES high-tension detonator; **~ instantané** *m* MINES instantaneous detonator, instantaneous electric blasting cap; **~ à mèche** *m* MINES ordinary detonator; **~ à microretard** *m* MINES millisecond delay cap, millisecond delay detonator, short-delay detonator; **~ de mine** *m* MINES blasting cap, detonator; **~ ordinaire** *m* MINES ordinary detonator; **~ à retardement** *m* MINES delay cap, delay detonator, delay-action detonator

détonation *f* MINES detonation, report, PETROLE knock, SECURITE, THERMODYN detonation, VEHICULES *allumage anticipé* detonation, knocking; **~ par influence** *f* MINES sympathetic detonation; **~ par sympathie** *f* MINES sympathetic detonation; **~ supersonique** *f* PHYSIQUE, SECURITE *causée par des avions supersoniques* sonic boom

détoner *vt* MINES, THERMODYN detonate

détorsion *f* CONS MECA untwisting

détourage *m* CINEMAT silhouetting, IMPRIM *photogravure* cutout, *typographie, mise en page* blockout, INFORMAT clipping, scissoring, ORDINAT clipping; **~ de fenêtre** *m* INFORMAT, ORDINAT window clipping; **~ à gabarit** *m* SECURITE cut with a jig

détourer *vt* CONS MECA cutout, IMPRIM outline

détournement *m* DISTRI EAU *d'une rivière* diversion, diverting

détourner *vt* CONS MECA deflect, CONSTR divert, DISTRI EAU *un cours d'eau* deflect; **~ une corde roulée sur un tambour** *vt* CONS MECA wind off a cord rolled round a drum

détrempage: ~ de l'argile *m* CERAM VER clay wetting

détrempe *f* PRODUCTION distemper

détresse:[1] **de ~** *adj* ESPACE *véhicules* emergency; **en ~** *adj* NAUT in distress

détresse[2] *f* AERONAUT last emergency action

détret *m* CONS MECA hand vice (BrE), hand vise (AmE)

détritiation *f* NUCLEAIRE tritium extraction

détritique *adj* PETR detrital

détritus *m* CHARBON debris, overburden, CONSTR *pour la construction* rubble, EMBALLAGE garbage (AmE), rubbish (BrE), PRODUCTION garbage (AmE), rubbish, RECYCLAGE garbage (AmE), rubbish (BrE); **~ de criblage** *m pl* HYDROLOGIE screenings

détroit *m* NAUT *géographie* sound, OCEANO sound, strait

détrompage *m* ELECTROTEC mounting polarization

détrompeur *m* CONS MECA locating pin, PRODUCTION keying band

détroquage *m* OCEANO mollusc detaching, mollusc harvesting

détroqueuse *f* OCEANO mollusc detacher

détruire: ~ au feu *vt* THERMODYN destroy by fire

deutéride *m* CHIMIE deuteride

deutérium *m* CHIMIE, NUCLEAIRE, PHYSIQUE deuterium

deutéron *m* CHIMIE deuton, PHYS PART, PHYSIQUE deuteron, deuton

deutéroprotéose *f* CHIMIE deuteroproteose

deuton *m* CHIMIE, PHYS PART, PHYSIQUE deuton

deux:[1] **à ~ contacts interrupteurs** *adj* ELECTR, ELECTROTEC DPST, double-pole single-throw; **à ~ contacts inverseurs** *adj* ELECTR, ELECTROTEC DPDT, double-pole double-throw; **à ~ couches** *adj* REVETEMENT double-layer; **de ~ couleurs** *adj* COULEURS bicolored (AmE), bicoloured (BrE); **à ~ faces** *adj* MATERIAUX two-sided; **à ~ filets** *adj* CONSTR *vis* double-threaded; **à ~ phases** *adj* ELECTR *alimentation*, ELECTROTEC two-phase

deux:[2] **~ bouts d'un fil retors** *m pl* TEXTILE two plies of a two-ply yarn; **~ dents qui sont complètement en prise** *m pl* CONS MECA two teeth which engage completely; **~ étoiles entourées de halos** *m pl* ASTRONOMIE two stars surrounded by halos; **~ fils parallèles** *m pl* TEXTILE twin ends

deuxième:[1] **~ canot** *m* NAUT *de navire de guerre* barge; **~ faux pont** *m* NAUT third deck; **~ harmonique** *m* ELECTRON second harmonic; **~ moment d'aire** *m* CONS MECA *moment d'inertie* second moment of area; **~ petit quart** *m* MILITAIRE *de marine* second dog watch; **~ principe de la thermodynamique** *m* PHYSIQUE second law of thermodynamics; **~ quartier** *m* ASTRONOMIE second quarter

deuxième:[2] **~ classe** *f* TRANSPORT cabin class, coach class; **~ cuisson** *f* CERAM VER second reducing firing; **~ équipe** *f* CINEMAT location unit, second unit; **~ feuille d'une série dans une liasse** *f* IMPRIM duplicata; **~ loi de Kepler** *f* ESPACE *orbitographie* Kepler's law of areas; **~ passe** *f* PETR hot pass; **~ vitesse cosmique** *f* ESPACE *astronomie* Earth escape velocity

devant[1] *adv* NAUT ahead

devant[2] *m* CONSTR front; **~ de la marche** *m* CONSTR riser

devanture *f* CERAM VER wicket wall; CONSTR, PRODUCTION *d'une chaudière, d'un foyer, etc* front; **~ frigorifique** *f* REFRIG refrigerated window

dévaser *vt* NAUT *un canal* dredge

dévastation: **~ du sol** *f* POLLUTION land degradation, land disturbance

développante:[1] **de ~** *adj* GEOMETRIE involute; **à ~** *adj* GEOMETRIE involute; **de ~ de cercle** *adj* GEOMETRIE involute; **à ~ de cercle** *adj* GEOMETRIE involute

développante[2] *f* GEOMETRIE involute; **~ de cercle** *f* GEOMETRIE involute of a circle

développée *f* GEOMETRIE evolute

développement *m* CERAM VER *du cylindre* opening, CONS MECA development, MATH expansion, PHOTO processing; **~ d'un anticyclone** *m* METEO anticyclonic generation; **~ avec révélateur utilisable une seule fois** *m* IMPRIM *plaques, films* total loss processing; **~ au cadre** *m* CINEMAT rack-and-pin processing; **~ de chaleur** *m* THERMODYN heat build-up; **~ chimique** *m* PHOTO chemical development; **~ chromogène** *m* CINEMAT coupler development, PHOTO color development (AmE), colour development (BrE); **~ du cliché** *m* IMPRIM *flexographie* plate processing; **~ de couleur** *m* CERAM VER color striking (AmE), colour striking (BrE); **~ en cours** *m* PRODUCTION active development; **~ en cuve** *m* CINEMAT tank developing; **~ en cuves profondes** *m* PHOTO tank development; **~ en deux bains** *m* IMPRIM *surfaces sensibles* two-bath processing; **~ en un seul bain** *m* IMPRIM *films et plaques*

one-bath development; **~ d'une expression** *m* MATH expansion of an expression; **~ à grande vitesse** *m* CINEMAT high-speed film processing; **~ de logiciel** *m* INFORMAT, ORDINAT software development; **~ par inversion** *m* CINEMAT reversal development, IMPRIM reversal process, PHOTO reversal processing; **~ de la plaque** *m* IMPRIM *copie* plate processing; **~ poussé** *m* CINEMAT forced development; **~ de programme** *m* INFORMAT, ORDINAT program development; **~ superficiel** *m* PHOTO surface development; **~ sur tambour** *m* CINEMAT drum development; **~ thermique** *m* THERMODYN heat build-up

développer *vt* CINEMAT, CONSTR, GEOMETRIE *une figure solide, une fonction algébrique, etc* develop

développeur *m* PHOTO developer

développeuse: **~ automatique à rouleau** *f* PHOTO machine processor

déverminage *m* PRODUCTION burn-in

déverrouillage *m* INFORMAT, ORDINAT unlocking

déverrouiller *vt* CINEMAT unlock

dévers[1] *adj* CONS MECA out-of-plumb, out-of-true

dévers[2] *m* CH DE FER cant, superelevation of track, CONSTR cant, *de lame d'une machine* inclination, NAUT *de l'étrave* flare, TRANSPORT banking, superelevation of the outer rail

déversement *m* CONSTR dumping (AmE), tipping (BrE), *du bois* warping, DISTRI EAU, PETROLE spillage, POLLU MER discharge, spill, PRODUCTION tilting; **~ en mer** *m* POLLU MER oilspill; **~ d'hydrocarbures** *m* POLLU MER oilspill; **~ illégal** *m* DISTRI EAU illegal dumping; **~ naturel** *m* DISTRI EAU natural drainage; **~ de pétrole** *m* POLLUTION oilspill

déverser *vt* CONSTR shoot, HYDROLOGIE discharge, overflow, overtop, PAPIER pour

déversoir *m* CERAM VER pot spout, weir, CONSTR spillway, DISTRI EAU weir, EN RENOUV spillway channel, *barrages* spillway, HYDROLOGIE outlet, overflow, spillway, weir, INST HYDR spillway canal, weir, PETROLE downcomer, PRODUCTION cutoff; **~ à arête vive** *m* INST HYDR sharp-crested weir, thin-edged weir; **~ de barrage** *m* DISTRI EAU shaft spillway; **~ circulaire** *m* DISTRI EAU roller weir; **~ à contraction** *m* DISTRI EAU contracted weir; **~ à crête épaisse** *m* DISTRI EAU broad-crested weir, INST HYDR flat-crested weir; **~ à crête mince** *m* INST HYDR sharp-crested weir, thin-edged weir; **~ dénoyé** *m* HYDROLOGIE free overall weir; **~ à échancrure** *m* HYDROLOGIE notched weir; **~ d'égout** *m* RECYCLAGE outfall, outfall pipe, outfall sewer; **~ en biais** *m* HYDROLOGIE diagonal weir; **~ en mince paroi** *m* DISTRI EAU notch, sharp-crested weir; **~ à équation linéaire** *m* HYDROLOGIE proportional weir; **~ flottant autoréglable** *m* POLLU MER self-adjusting floating weir; **~ gonflable** *m* DISTRI EAU inflatable weir; **~ à hausses** *m* DISTRI EAU lever weir; **~ à immersion réglable** *m* POLLUTION adjustable submersion weir; **~ de jaugeage** *m* INST HYDR weir; **~ libre** *m* HYDROLOGIE ungated spillway; **~ de mesure** *m* DISTRI EAU measuring weir, HYDROLOGIE measuring weir, notched weir; **~ à nappe noyée** *m* DISTRI EAU drowned weir, INST HYDR submerged weir; **~ noyé** *m* DISTRI EAU, HYDROLOGIE drowned weir; **~ d'orage** *m* RECYCLAGE storm sewer; **~ à paroi** *m* INST HYDR sharp-crested weir; **~ à paroi mince** *m* INST HYDR thin-edged weir; **~ à poutrelles** *m* DISTRI EAU stop log weir; **~ principal** *m* HYDROLOGIE main spillway; **~ de réglage** *m* DISTRI EAU control weir; **~ submergé** *m* INST HYDR submerged weir; ~ **de superficie** *m* NUCLEAIRE effluent weir, leaping weir; ~ **sur seuil** *m* DISTRI EAU broad-crested weir, INST HYDR flat-crested weir

déviant: ~ **de la ligne centrale** *adj* IMPRIM *machines, plaques* askew

déviateur *m* ELECTRON deflection yoke, PETROLE diverter

déviation *f* CONSTR *d'un trou de sonde* drift, *route* bypass, CRISTALL cross-slip, ESPACE *véhicules*, GEOPHYS deflection, NAUT *compas* deviation, PETR deviation well, PHYSIQUE deflection, *d'un rayon lumineux* deviation, TRANSPORT *de la circulation* diversion; ~ **électromagnétique** *f* ELECTROTEC electromagnetic deflection; ~ **en azimut** *f* ENREGISTR azimuth deviation; ~ **de forage** *f* PETROLE sidetracking; ~ **de la forme d'onde** *f* PHYS ONDES waveform error; ~ **horizontale** *f* ELECTRON horizontal deflection; ~ **magnétique** *f* GEOPHYS *du compteur* magnetic deflection, magnetic deviation, NUCLEAIRE magnetic deflection; ~ **par champs électriques** *f* PHYS RAYON deflection by electric fields; ~ **par champs magnétiques** *f* PHYS RAYON deflection by magnetic fields; ~ **recommandée** *f* TRANSPORT advisory diversion; ~ **sélective** *f* TRANSPORT *de la circulation* selective diversion; ~ **totale de circulation** *f* TRANSPORT complete diversion; ~ **de la trame** *f* TV vertical deflection; ~ **verticale** *f* ELECTRON, TV vertical deflection; ~ **x** *f* TV x-deflection; ~ **y** *f* TV y-deflection

dévider[1] *vt* CONS MECA wind, POLLU MER reel out

dévider:[2] **se** ~ *v réfl* CONS MECA wind

dévideur *m* INFORMAT streaming tape drive, ORDINAT streamer, streaming tape drive

dévidoir *m* CINEMAT spool, PLAST CAOU *revêtement* reeling machine, POLLU MER reel, TEXTILE swift; ~ **à bobine** *m* PRODUCTION hose reel; ~ **de câble** *m* PETR reel; ~ **mobile** *m* SECURITE *matériel de lutte contre l'incendie* mobile hose reel; ~ **à tuyaux** *m* PRODUCTION hose reel; ~ **de tuyaux d'incendie** *m* SECURITE fire hose reel

dévié *adj* CONS MECA out-of-true, ESPACE off-course; ~ **de sa route** *adj* ESPACE off-course

dévier[1] *vt* CONS MECA deflect, run out of true, CONSTR divert, TV deflect

dévier:[2] ~ **de la ligne verticale** *vi* CONS MECA run out of the vertical; ~ **de la route** *vi* NAUT veer off course

devis *m* PRODUCTION estimate; ~ **descriptif** *m* CONSTR specifications; ~ **estimatif** *m* PRODUCTION estimate; ~ **de poids et de centrage** *m* AERONAUT *aéronef* load and trim sheet; ~ **préliminaire** *m* CONSTR preliminary cost estimate; ~ **de tracé** *m* NAUT offset

dévissage *m* CONS MECA unscrewing, PETROLE breakout, screwing-out, *forage* unscrewing pipe

dévisser *vt* NUCLEAIRE unscrew

dévitrification *f* CERAM VER devitrification

dévitrifier *vi* CERAM VER devitrify

dévolter *vi* ELECTROTEC drop the voltage, lower

dévolteur *m* ELECTROTEC booster, negative booster

dévonien *adj* GEOLOGIE Devonian

dévrillement: ~ **automatique** *m* EMBALLAGE automatic decurling

déwatté *adj* ELECTR *courant alternatif* wattless

deweylite *f* MINERAUX deweylite

dextrane *f* CHIMIE dextran

dextrine *f* AGRO ALIM, CHIMIE, IMPRIM *colles*, PLAST CAOU *adhésifs* dextrin

dextrogyre *adj* AGRO ALIM clockwise-rotating, dextrorotary, CHIMIE, PHYSIQUE dextrorotatory

dextrose *m* CHIMIE dextrose

diabase *f* PETR diabase (AmE), dolerite (BrE)

diable *m* EMBALLAGE sack barrow, PRODUCTION hand truck; ~ **brouette** *m* PRODUCTION hand truck; ~ **à pots** *m* CERAM VER pot carriage

diabolo *m* AERONAUT *train d'atterrissage* dual wheels, PRODUCTION dolly

diacétate *m* TEXTILE secondary acetate

diacétique *adj* CHIMIE *acide* diacetic

diacétylacétone *f* CHIMIE diacetylacetone

diacétyle *m* CHIMIE diacetyl

diacétylène *m* CHIMIE diacetylene

diachromie *f* TV cross color noise (AmE), cross colour noise (BrE)

diachrone *adj* GEOLOGIE diachronous

diaclasage *m* GEOLOGIE jointing

diaclase *f* GEOLOGIE joint

diaclasite *f* MINERAUX diaclasite

diacritique *adj* INFORMAT, ORDINAT diacritical

diadochite *f* MINERAUX diadochite

diagénèse *f* EN RENOUV, GEOLOGIE, PETR, PETROLE diagenesis

diagénétique *adj* PETROLE diagenetic

diagnostic:[1] **de** ~ *adj* INFORMAT, ORDINAT diagnostic

diagnostic[2] *m* INFORMAT, ORDINAT diagnosis, diagnostic report, diagnostics, TELECOM diagnostics; ~ **du compilateur** *m* ORDINAT compiler diagnostic; ~ **d'erreurs** *m* INFORMAT, ORDINAT error diagnostic, TELECOM error diagnosis; ~ **de panne** *m* INFORMAT, ORDINAT fault diagnosis; ~ **aux rayons X** *m* INSTRUMENT X-ray diagnostics

diagnostique *adj* INFORMAT, ORDINAT diagnostic

diagomètre *m* THERMODYN heat conductivity meter

diagonal *adj* GEOMETRIE diagonal

diagonale:[1] **en** ~ *adv* GEOMETRIE diagonally

diagonale[2] *f* CH DE FER crossover, overhead crossover, GEOMETRIE diagonal, NUCLEAIRE diagonal, diagonal member rod

diagonalement *adv* GEOMETRIE diagonally

diagramme *m* ESPACE pattern, INFORMAT, ORDINAT diagram, PETR log, PHYSIQUE chart, PRODUCTION, TELECOM diagram; ~ **acoustique** *m* GEOPHYS acoustical log; ~ **d'Applegate** *m* ELECTRON Applegate diagram; ~ **d'autopolarisation** *m* GEOPHYS self-potential log; ~ **de Basov** *m* NUCLEAIRE Basov diagram; ~ **des boues** *m* GEOPHYS mud log; ~ **cardioïde** *m* ENREGISTR cardioid diagram; ~ **de charge** *m* MECANIQUE load diagram; ~ **de charges classées** *m* ELECTR *réseau* load duration curve; ~ **de constitution** *m* CHIMIE phase diagram; ~ **des contraintes-déformations** *m* NAUT stress-strain diagram; ~ **contrapolaire** *m* ESPACE *communications* cross-polar pattern; ~ **copolaire** *m* ESPACE *communications* copolar pattern; ~ **de densité** *m* GEOPHYS density log; ~ **détaillé** *m* PETR detail log; ~ **de diffraction** *m* CRISTALL, METALL diffraction pattern; ~ **de diffraction électronique** *m* CRISTALL electron diffraction pattern; ~ **de diffraction en champ lointain** *m* OPTIQUE far-field diffraction pattern; ~ **de diffraction en champ proche** *m* OPTIQUE, TELECOM near field diffraction pattern; ~ **de diffraction de Fraunhofer** *m* OPTIQUE Fraunhofer diffraction pattern, far-field diffraction pattern, TELECOM Fraunhofer diffraction pattern; ~ **de diffraction de Fresnel** *m* OPTIQUE, TELECOM Fresnel diffraction pattern; ~ **de diffraction des rayons X** *m* CRISTALL X-ray diffraction pattern, INSTRUMENT X-ray diagram, X-ray diffraction pattern; ~ **directionnel**

m ACOUSTIQUE directional pattern; ~ **de distribution** *m* AUTO valve-timing diagram, CONS MECA, HYDROLOGIE distribution diagram; ~ **de la distribution Corliss** *m* PRODUCTION diagram of Corliss valve gear; ~ **de distribution cumulé** *m* HYDROLOGIE cumulative distribution diagram; ~ **double induction** *m* PETR dual induction log; ~ **d'écoulement** *m* DISTRI EAU flow pattern; ~ **d'écoulement de la circulation** *m* TRANSPORT traffic flow diagram; ~ **électrique** *m* PETR electrical log; ~ **en bâtons** *m* MATH *pour statistiques* bar chart; ~ **d'engorgement** *m* GEOPHYS flooding pattern; ~ **en oeil** *m* TELECOM eye diagram, eyeshape pattern; ~ **d'équilibre** *m* MATERIAUX equilibrium diagram, METALL phase diagram; ~ **d'état** *m* INFORMAT, ORDINAT state diagram; ~ **d'Euler-Venn** *m* MATH Venn diagram; ~ **de Feynman** *m* PHYSIQUE Feynman diagram; ~ **du flux énergétique** *m* THERMODYN energy flow chart; ~ **du flux thermique** *m* THERMODYN heat balance chart, heat balance diagram, heat flow diagram; ~ **focalisé** *m* PETR focused log; ~ **de fracture** *m* PETR fracture log; ~ **de Fresnel** *m* ELECTROTEC phasor representation; ~ **de Gantt** *m* PRODUCTION Gantt chart; ~ **gardé** *m* PETR guard log; ~ **de Hertzsprung-Russell** *m* *(cf diagramme HR)* ASTRONOMIE Hertzsprung-Russell diagram; ~ **HR** *m* *(cf diagramme de Hertzsprung-Russell)* ASTRONOMIE Hertzsprung-Russell diagram; ~ **de Hubble** *m* ASTRONOMIE Hubble diagram; ~ **d'impédance de charge** *m* ELECTRON Rieke diagram; ~ **de l'indicateur** *m* PHYSIQUE indicator diagram; ~ **d'induction** *m* PETR induction log; ~ **isochrone** *m* GEOLOGIE isochrone diagram; ~ **de Laue** *m* CRISTALL Laue pattern, PHYS RAYON Laue diagram; ~ **de la luminosité stellaire en fonction de la température** *m* ASTRONOMIE graph of stellar luminosity plotted against temperature; ~ **de manoeuvre et de rafales** *m* AERONAUT flight envelope; ~ **de microrésistivité** *m* GEOPHYS microresistivity log; ~ **moyen de distribution** *m* HYDROLOGIE average distribution diagram; ~ **neutron** *m* PETR neutron log; ~ **neutron de paroi latérale** *m* PETR sidewall neutron log; ~ **de Nicolaysen** *m* GEOLOGIE isochrone, isochrone diagram; ~ **nucléaire de cimentation** *m* PETR nuclear cement log; ~ **nucléaire magnétique** *m* PETR nuclear magnetic log; ~ **de l'oeil** *m* TELECOM eye diagram; ~ **oxygène-salinité** *m* OCEANO oxygen-salinity diagram; ~ **par induction** *m* PETR induction log; ~ **de phase** *m* CHIMIE phase diagram; ~ **de phase de couleur** *m* TV color phase diagram (AmE), colour phase diagram (BrE); ~ **de phases** *m* NUCLEAIRE, TRANSPORT phase diagram; ~ **polaire** *m* PHYSIQUE polar diagram; ~ **de polarisation spontanée** *m* GEOPHYS self-potential log, spontaneous potential log; ~ **de poudre** *m* CRISTALL powder pattern; ~ **pression-température d'équilibre de phases minérales** *m* GEOLOGIE *métamorphisme* petrogenetic grid; ~ **de production** *m* PRODUCTION output diagram; ~ **de proximité** *m* PETR, PETROLE proximity log; ~ **de puits** *m* GEOPHYS well log; ~ **radiométrique** *m* PETR radiometric log; ~ **de rafales en V-n** *m* AERONAUT gust V-n diagram; ~ **rankinisé** *m* CONS MECA combined diagram; ~ **de rayonnement** *m* ESPACE *communications*, OPTIQUE, PHYSIQUE, TELECOM radiation pattern; ~ **de rayonnement en champ lointain** *m* OPTIQUE far-field diffraction pattern, far-field radiation pattern, TELECOM far-field pattern; ~ **de rayonnement en champ proche** *m* OPTIQUE near field diffraction pattern, TELECOM near field pattern, near field radiation pattern; ~

de rayonnement à l'équilibre *m* OPTIQUE, TELECOM equilibrium radiation pattern; ~ **de rayons gamma** *m* GEOPHYS gamma ray log; ~ **de résistivité** *m* GEOPHYS resistivity log; ~ **de Rieke** *m* ELECTRON Rieke diagram; ~ **à secteurs** *m* INFORMAT pie chart; ~ **de Segrè** *m* PHYS PART Segrè chart; ~ **de sensation d'intensité** *m* ENREGISTR loudness pattern; ~ **séquentiel de comptage-décomptage** *m* PRODUCTION *automatisme industriel* timing diagram; ~ **des signaux lumineux** *m* TRANSPORT phasing diagram; ~ **de Smith** *m* PHYSIQUE Smith chart; ~ **sonique** *m* PETR sonic log; ~ **T/S** *m* OCEANO T/S diagram; ~ **température potentielle-salinité** *m* OCEANO potential temperature-salinity diagram; ~ **température-salinité** *m* OCEANO T/S diagram, temperature-salinity diagram; ~ **de temps** *m* INFORMAT timing diagram; ~ **temps-distance** *m* TRANSPORT time-space diagram; ~ **de traitement thermique** *m* THERMODYN heat treatment diagram; ~ **de transition d'état** *m* TELECOM state transition diagram; ~ **de Veitch** *m* INFORMAT, ORDINAT Veitch diagram; ~ **de Venn** *m* INFORMAT, ORDINAT Venn diagram; ~ **vitesse débit** *m* TRANSPORT speed flow diagram; ~ **des vitesses** *m* EN RENOUV velocity diagram

diagraphie *f* PETROLE *prospection* log, logging; ~ **acoustique** *f* PETROLE *exploration* acoustic log, acoustic well logging; ~ **activation** *f* PETR activation logging; ~ **à activation neutronique** *f* NUCLEAIRE neutron activation logging; ~ **d'adhésivité** *f* PETROLE CBL, cement bond log; ~ **d'adhésivité du ciment** *f* PETROLE CBL, cement bond log; ~ **d'analyse des boues** *f* PETROLE mud analysis log, mud log; ~ **de boue de forage** *f* PETROLE mud log; ~ **de contact** *f* PETROLE contact log; ~ **de densité** *f* PETROLE density log; ~ **de densité variable** *f* PETR three-D log; ~ **de diamétrage** *f* PETROLE *puits, forage* caliper log (AmE), calliper log (BrE); ~ **différée** *f* PETROLE *forage, prospection* wireline log; ~ **électrique** *f* PETROLE *forage, prospection* electric log; ~ **électrique à espacements** *f* PETROLE multiple special electrical logging; ~ **de forage** *f* GEOLOGIE, PETROLE *forage, prospection* well logging; ~ **gamma-gamma** *f* PETROLE *forage, prospection* gamma-gamma log; ~ **des gaz** *f* PETR gas log; ~ **géophysique** *f* GEOLOGIE, PETROLE *forage, prospection* geophysical log; ~ **géothermique** *f* PETROLE *forage, prospection* geothermal log; ~ **de neutron** *f* PETROLE neutron logging; ~ **neutron** *f* GAZ neutron logging, PETROLE neutron log; ~ **neutron-gamma** *f* PETROLE *prospection* neutron-gamma log; ~ **neutron-neutron** *f* PETROLE neutron-neutron log; ~ **nucléaire** *f* PETROLE radioactive log, *prospection* nuclear log; ~ **par activation** *f* PETROLE *exploration* activation log; ~ **par impulsion de neutron** *f* PETROLE pulsed neutron log; ~ **par neutron pulsé** *f* PETROLE pulsed neutron log; ~ **par rayons gamma** *f* PETROLE gamma ray well logging; ~ **par résonance magnétique nucléaire** *f* PETROLE *prospection* nuclear magnetic resonance; ~ **de perméabilité** *f* PETROLE permeability logging; ~ **de polarisation spontanée** *f* PETROLE self-potential log, spontaneous potential log; ~ **de porosité** *f* PETROLE porosity log; ~ **pseudosonique** *f* PETROLE pseudosonic log; ~ **de rayons gamma** *f* PETROLE gamma ray log; ~ **de résistivité** *f* PETR resistivity logging, PETROLE contact log, resistivity log; ~ **de résonance magnétique nucléaire** *f* PETR NML, nuclear magnetic logging; ~ **RMN** *f* PETROLE NMR log; ~ **sonique** *f* PETROLE sonic log; ~ **de température** *f* PETROLE temperature logging, temperature well logging; ~ **du trou de sondage** f GEOPHYS borehole logging, well logging

diallage m MINERAUX diallage

diallogite f MINERAUX diallogite

dialogite f MINERAUX dialogite

dialogue m INFORMAT, ORDINAT dialog (AmE), dialogue (BrE); ~ **homme-machine** m INFORMAT, ORDINAT man-machine interaction

dialysate m CHIMIE dialysate

dialyse f CHIMIE dialysis

dialyser vt CHIMIE dialyse

dialytique adj CHIMIE dialytic

diamagnétique adj MATERIAUX, PETR, PHYSIQUE diamagnetic

diamagnétiques f pl PHYS RAYON diamagnetics

diamagnétisme m CHIMIE, ELECTR, ELECTROTEC, PHYS RAYON, PHYSIQUE diamagnetism

diamant m CERAM VER cutting diamond, diamond, MINERAUX diamond, NAUT d'ancre crown; ~ **noir** m MINERAUX black diamond, MINES bort, industrial diamond; ~ **pour couper le verre** m CERAM VER diamond pencil; ~ **tenu droit** m CERAM VER diamond held upright; ~ **tenu piquant** m CERAM VER diamond held with firm grip; ~ **tenu traînant** m CERAM VER diamond-held trailing; ~ **de vitrier** m CONSTR diamond pencil, diamond point, diamond tool, glass cutter, glass cutter's diamond, glazier's diamond, point

diamantaire m PRODUCTION diamond cutter

diamantifère adj MINES diamond-bearing, diamondiferous

diamants: ~ **de tournage** m pl CONS MECA turning diamonds

diamétral adj ELECTR diametrical, GEOMETRIE diametric, diametrical

diamétralement: ~ **opposé** adv GEOMETRIE diametrically opposed

diamètre m GEOMETRIE d'un cercle diameter; ~ **admis au-dessus des chariots** m CONS MECA swing of the rest, swing over saddle; ~ **admissible au-dessus du banc** m CONS MECA swing of the bed, swing over bed; ~ **angulaire** m ESPACE mesures angular diameter; ~ **de bobine effectif** m ESSAIS effective coil diameter; ~ **de cercle primitif** m AERONAUT pitch circle diameter; ~ **du champ de mode** m OPTIQUE, TELECOM mode field diameter; ~ **du coeur** m OPTIQUE core diameter; ~ **critique** m MINES critical diameter; ~ **du cylindre** m TEXTILE roll diameter; ~ **dans oeuvre** m CONS MECA inside diameter; ~ **d'enroulement** m RESSORTS coil diameter; ~ **extérieur** m CONS MECA, MECANIQUE OD, outside diameter; ~ **extérieur d'enroulement** m RESSORTS outside coil diameter; ~ **d'un faisceau** m OPTIQUE beam diameter; ~ **du faisceau guidé** m OPTIQUE guided beam diameter, TELECOM mode field diameter; ~ **du fil** m RESSORTS wire diameter; ~ **de fond de filet** m CONS MECA minor diameter; ~ **de la gaine** m OPTIQUE cladding diameter; ~ **intérieur** m MECANIQUE ID, inner diameter, inside diameter, PRODUCTION d'un tuyau internal diameter; ~ **intérieur d'enroulement** m RESSORTS inside coil diameter; ~ **de jet** m EN RENOUV jet diameter; ~ **maximum admis** m CONS MECA swing; ~ **maximum admis dans le rompu** m CONS MECA swing in gap; ~ **moyen du coeur** m OPTIQUE, TELECOM average core diameter; ~ **moyen de la gaine** m OPTIQUE, TELECOM average cladding diameter; ~ **nominal** m CONS MECA nominal diameter, NUCLEAIRE NB, nominal bore; ~ **de perçage** m AERONAUT pitch center

diameter (AmE), pitch centre diameter (BrE); ~ **primitif** m AERONAUT, CONS MECA pitch diameter; ~ **de rotor** m EN RENOUV rotor diameter; ~ **sans dimension** m EN RENOUV nondimensional diameter; ~ **de serrage** m CONS MECA d'un mandrin holding capacity; ~ **de la spire** m RESSORTS coil diameter; ~ **de stockage** m TELECOM stock diameter; ~ **de la surface de référence** m OPTIQUE reference surface diameter; ~ **sur flancs de filets** m AERONAUT pitch diameter; ~ **sur plats** m CONS MECA diameter across flats; ~ **de tige de rivet** m CONS MECA rivet shank diameter; ~ **utile du diaphragme** m PHOTO effective aperture

diamétreur m PETR caliper log (AmE), calliper log (BrE); ~ **électronique** m PETR photon log

diamide m CHIMIE diamide

diamine f CHIMIE diamine

diaminodiphénylméthane m PLAST CAOU agent de durcissement diaminodiphenylmethane

diapason m ACOUSTIQUE, ENREGISTR, PHYS ONDES, PHYSIQUE tuning fork

diaphane adj MATERIAUX diaphanous

diaphasique adj TRANSPORT jet diaphasic

diaphone m NAUT diaphone

diaphonie f ACOUSTIQUE, ENREGISTR, INFORMAT, ORDINAT, PHYSIQUE, TELECOM, TV crosstalk; ~ **magnétique** f ENREGISTR magnetic printing echo

diaphonomètre m ENREGISTR crosstalk meter

diaphorite f MINERAUX diaphorite

diaphragmation: ~ **en oeil de chat** f PHOTO vignetting

diaphragme m CINEMAT diaphragm, lens stop, ELECTROTEC septum, INSTRUMENT field lens, MECANIQUE diaphragm, PHOTO aperture, diaphragm, PHYSIQUE aperture, stop; ~ **antérieur** m PHOTO front diaphragm; ~ **automatique** m CINEMAT auto-iris; ~ **de champ** m METALL field diaphragm, PHYSIQUE field stop; ~ **couplé à l'obturateur** m PHOTO coupled speed and F-stop setting; ~ **d'éclatement** m MECANIQUE bursting disc (BrE), bursting disk (AmE); ~ **en fente** m PHOTO slit diaphragm; ~ **iris** m INSTRUMENT iris diaphragm; ~ **de mesure** m REFRIG orifice plate; ~ **de microphone** m ENREGISTR microphone diaphragm; ~ **d'ouverture** m METALL aperture diaphragm; ~ **présélectif à fermeture automatique** m PHOTO fully-automatic diaphragm; ~ **réglable** m PHYSIQUE adjustable aperture

diaphragmer vt CINEMAT fermer le diaphragme close down, stop down, PHOTO stop down

diaphtorèse f GEOLOGIE retrograde metamorphism

diapir m GEOLOGIE diapir, PETROLE diapir, salt dome

diapo f PHOTO slide

diapositive f CINEMAT transparency, IMPRIM transparency, photographie slide, PHOTO diapositive, slide, transparency; ~ **de réglage** f CINEMAT line-up slide; ~ **de transition** f TV cut slide

diaschiste adj PETR diaschistic

diaspore m MINERAUX diaspore

diastase f AGRO ALIM, CHIMIE diastase

diastème f PETR diastem

diastéreo-isomère m CHIMIE diastereoisomer

diathermane adj PHYSIQUE paroi diathermal, THERMODYN diathermanous, diathermic

diatherme adj PHYSIQUE paroi diathermal

diatomée f PETR diatom

diatomique adj CHIMIE diatomic

diatomite f CHAUFFAGE isolation diatomite, GEOLOGIE diatomaceous earth, kieselguhr, diatomite, MINERAUX diatomite

diatonique *adj* ACOUSTIQUE *gamme* diatonic
diazo *m* CHIMIE *composé* diazo
diazoacétique *adj* CHIMIE diazoacetic
diazobenzène *m* CHIMIE diazobenzene
diazoïmide *m* CHIMIE diazoimide
diazoïque *m* CHIMIE diazo compound, IMPRIM diazo
diazole *m* CHIMIE diazole
diazominé *m* CHIMIE diazomine
diazonium *m* CHIMIE diazonium
diazoter *vt* CHIMIE diazotize
dibasique *adj* CHIMIE dibasic
dibenzanthracène *m* CHIMIE dibenzanthracene
dibenzopyrrole *m* CHIMIE dibenzopyrrole
dibenzoyle *m* CHIMIE dibenzoyl
dibenzylamine *f* CHIMIE dibenzylamine
dibromobenzène *m* CHIMIE dibromobenzene
dibromohydrine *f* CHIMIE dibromohydrin
dibromosuccinique *adj* CHIMIE dibromosuccinic
dibutyrine *f* CHIMIE dibutyrin
dichloracétique *adj* CHIMIE dichloracetic
dichloroacétone *f* CHIMIE dichloroacetone
dichlorobenzène *m* CHIMIE dichlorobenzene
dichloroéthane *f* CHIMIE dichloroethane
dichlorohydrine *f* CHIMIE dichlorohydrin
dichotomie *f* ASTRONOMIE dichotomy
dichroïque *adj* PHYSIQUE dichroic
dichroïsme *m* CHIMIE, CRISTALL, PHYSIQUE dichroism
dichroïte *f* MINERAUX dichroïte
dichromate *m* CHIMIE dichromate
dickinsonite *f* MINERAUX dickinsonite
dicorde *m* ELECTROTEC patch cord, TELECOM cord, cord circuit
Dictaphone *m* (MD) ENREGISTR Dictaphone (TM), dictation machine
dictionnaire *m* INFORMAT, ORDINAT dictionary; ~ **de données** *m* INFORMAT, ORDINAT data dictionary
didacticiel *m* ORDINAT courseware
didyme *m* CHIMIE didymium
didymium *m* CHIMIE didymium
dièdre[1] *adj* GEOMETRIE dihedral
dièdre[2] *m* AERONAUT dihedral
dieldrine *f* AGRO ALIM, CHIMIE dieldrin
diélectrique[1] *adj* CHIMIE, ELECTR *condensateur*, IMPRIM *reproduction* dielectric
diélectrique[2] *m* ELECTROTEC, PHYSIQUE, TELECOM dielectric; ~ **à absorption** *m* ELECTR absorptive dielectric; ~ **à air** *m* ELECTR air dielectric; ~ **à faible pertes** *m* ELECTR low-loss dielectric; ~ **de la grille** *m* ELECTROTEC gate dielectric; ~ **imparfait** *m* ELECTR imperfect dielectric; ~ **non polaire** *m* PHYSIQUE nonpolar dielectric; ~ **parfait** *m* ELECTR *condensateur* perfect dielectric; ~ **à pertes** *m* ELECTR lossy dielectric; ~ **polaire** *m* PHYSIQUE polar dielectric; ~ **solide** *m* ELECTROTEC solid dielectric
diène *m* CHIMIE diene, PETROLE dialkene
diergol *m* ESPACE *propulsion* bipropellant
dièse *f* ACOUSTIQUE sharp
diesel: ~ **lent** *m* NAUT low-speed engine; ~ **oil** *m* PETROLE diesel fuel; ~ **rapide** *m* NAUT high-speed engine; ~ **de secours** *m* NUCLEAIRE emergency diesel generator; ~ **semi-rapide** *m* NAUT medium-speed engine
diéséliser *vt* TRANSPORT convert to diesel
diéthanolamine *f* CHIMIE, LESSIVES diethanolamine
diéthylène *m* LESSIVES diethylene
diéthylénique *adj* CHIMIE diethylenic
différé: en ~ *adv* INFORMAT, ORDINAT, TELECOM off-line
différence:[1] **en ~ négative** *adj* NAUT trimmed by the head; **en ~ positive** *adj* NAUT trimmed by the stern
différence[2] *f* INFORMAT, ORDINAT difference; ~ **commune** *f* MATH common difference; ~ **couleur** *f* TV color difference (AmE), colour difference (BrE); ~ **focale** *f* TV depth of focus; ~ **d'intervalles** *f* ACOUSTIQUE interval difference; ~ **de marche** *f* PHYSIQUE path difference; ~ **à la masse critique** *f* NUCLEAIRE off critical amount; ~ **moyenne de température** *f* MAT CHAUFF mean temperature difference; ~ **de phase** *f* ELECTRON, ENREGISTR, ESSAIS phase difference, NUCLEAIRE phase shift, PETR, PHYS ONDES, PHYSIQUE phase difference; ~ **de potentiel** *f* ELECTR potential difference, voltage difference, ELECTROTEC, PHYSIQUE potential difference; ~ **de pression** *f* CHARBON pressure head, INST HYDR pressure difference; ~ **de température** *f* PHYSIQUE temperature difference; ~ **de temps entre canaux** *f* ENREGISTR interchannel time difference
différenciation: ~ **magmatique** *f* GEOLOGIE magmatic differentiation; ~ **métamorphique** *f* GEOLOGIE metamorphic differentiation
différencié *adj* GEOLOGIE differentiated
différentiateur *m* ELECTRON differentiating circuit
différentiation *f* MATH differentiation; ~ **implicite** *f* MATH *d'une fonction* implicit differentiation
différentié *adj* ELECTRON *signal*, MATH differentiated
différentiel[1] *adj* MATH differential
différentiel[2] *m* AUTO, CERAM VER differential, CONS MECA balance gear, compensating gear, differential, equalizing gear, MECANIQUE *véhicules*, VEHICULES *transmission* differential; ~ **autobloquant** *m* AUTO traction differential, VEHICULES *transmission* limited slip differential; ~ **à blocage automatique** *m* AUTO nonslip differential; ~ **à glissement contrôlé** *m* MECANIQUE *véhicules*, VEHICULES controlled slip differential; ~ **à glissement limité** *m* AUTO limited slip differential; ~ **train planétaire** *m* AUTO planetary gear differential
différentielle *f* MATH differential, increment
diffraction *f* ACOUSTIQUE scattering, CRISTALL, ELECTROTEC, OPTIQUE diffraction, PETR diffraction, scattering, PHOTO, PHYS ONDES *d'ondes*, PHYSIQUE, TELECOM diffraction; ~ **acoustique** *f* ACOUSTIQUE acoustic diffraction; ~ **électronique** *f* CRISTALL, PHYS RAYON electron diffraction; ~ **d'électrons de grande énergie** *f* PHYS PART high-energy electron diffraction; ~ **des faisceaux atomiques** *f* NUCLEAIRE atomic beam diffraction; ~ **de Fraunhofer** *f* PHYSIQUE Fraunhofer diffraction; ~ **de Fresnel** *f* PHYSIQUE Fresnel diffraction; ~ **multiple** *f* TELECOM multiple diffraction; ~ **de neutrons** *f* CRISTALL neutron diffraction; ~ **d'onde** *f* TELECOM wave diffraction; ~ **des rayons X** *f* CRISTALL, ELECTRON, ESPACE, METALL, PHYS ONDES X-ray diffraction; ~ **spectroscopique des électrons** *f* PHYS RAYON electron spectroscopic diffraction
diffractomètre *m* CRISTALL, MATERIAUX diffractometer; ~ **de poudre** *m* CRISTALL powder diffractometer; ~ **à quatre cercles** *m* CRISTALL four-circle diffractometer; ~ **des rayons X** *m* CRISTALL, PHYS RAYON X-ray diffractometer; ~ **à rayons X pour les substances pulvérulentes** *m* NUCLEAIRE X-ray powder diffractometer
diffractométrie *f* PETROLE diffractometry
diffus *adj* MATERIAUX diffuse
diffusant[1] *adj* CERAM VER *verre* diffusing
diffusant[2] *m* MATERIAUX diffusing substance
diffusat *m* MATERIAUX *chimie* diffusate

diffuser *vt* PHOTO diffuse, PHYS ONDES, TELECOM broadcast, TV air, broadcast; ~ **par la télévision** *vt* TV telecast

diffuseur *m* AUTO venturi, CINEMAT frost, light softener, scrim, EN RENOUV, GENIE CHIM diffuser, POLLU MER spray gun, REFRIG, TELECOM diffuser, VEHICULES *carburateur* venturi; ~ **d'air** *m* REFRIG air diffuser; ~ **anti-incendie** *m* SECURITE fire sprinkler; ~ **chambre chaude** *m* CONS MECA *moule pour fonderie sous pression* sprue pin; ~ **champignon** *m* GENIE CHIM atomizer; ~ **linéaire** *m* REFRIG slot diffuser; ~ **parfait par réflexion** *m* PAPIER perfect reflecting diffuser; ~ **plafonnier** *m* REFRIG ceiling diffuser; ~ **de son** *m* ENREGISTR sound diffuser

diffusiomètre *m* OCEANO diffusiometer, scattering meter, scatterometer

diffusion *f* CHARBON, CHIMIE *d'un fluide* diffusion, CINEMAT scattering, CONS MECA distribution, CONSTR diffusion, CRISTALL scattering, ELECTRON diffusion, scattering, ESPACE broadcasting, *communications* scatter, scattering, GEOPHYS scattering, INFORMAT broadcast, MATERIAUX diffusion, NUCLEAIRE, OPTIQUE, PETR, PHYS RAYON *des faisceaux* scattering, PHYSIQUE, POLLUTION diffusion, TELECOM broadcasting, scattering, TV broadcasting, broadcast; ~ **acoustique** *f* ENREGISTR acoustic scattering; ~ **aléatoire** *f* NUCLEAIRE random scattering; ~ **anomale** *f* CRISTALL anomalous scattering; ~ **atomique** *f* NUCLEAIRE *par collision* atomic scattering; ~ **de la base** *f* ELECTRON base diffusion; ~ **capillaire** *f* HYDROLOGIE capillary diffusion; ~ **Compton** *f* PHYS RAYON Compton effect, PHYSIQUE Compton scattering; ~ **au dedans** *f* NUCLEAIRE inscattering, scattering in; ~ **différée** *f* TELECOM store-and-forward facility; ~ **directe par satellite** *f* TV direct satellite broadcasting; ~ **élastique** *f* PHYS PART, PHYS RAYON, PHYSIQUE elastic scattering; ~ **de fibrage** *f* OPTIQUE, TELECOM fiber scattering (AmE), fibre scattering (BrE); ~ **géographique** *f* IMPRIM *presse* geographical circulation; ~ **aux grands angles** *f* NUCLEAIRE large angle scattering, wide angle scattering; ~ **d'impuretés** *f* ELECTRON impurity diffusion; ~ **inélastique** *f* PHYSIQUE inelastic scattering; ~ **inélastique des neutrons** *f* PHYSIQUE inelastic neutron scattering; ~ **intergranulaire** *f* METALL grain boundary diffusion; ~ **des lacunes** *f* METALL vacancy diffusion; ~ **latérale** *f* ELECTRON lateral diffusion; ~ **le long des lignes de dislocations** *f* METALL pipe diffusion; ~ **de matériaux** *f* OPTIQUE, TELECOM material scattering; ~ **moyenne** *f* IMPRIM *presse* average circulation; ~ **des neutrons** *f* PHYS PART neutron scattering; ~ **non-linéaire** *f* OPTIQUE, TELECOM nonlinear scattering; ~ **à ondes décimétriques** *f* TV UHF broadcasting; ~ **par câble** *f* TV cablecast; ~ **par défaut** *f* NUCLEAIRE defect scattering; ~ **par les deux faces** *f* ELECTRON top-bottom diffusion; ~ **par les impuretés** *f* ELECTRON impurity scattering; ~ **par un mécanisme lacunaire** *f* METALL vacancy diffusion; ~ **par la pluie** *f* ESPACE *communications* rain scatter; ~ **aux petits angles** *f* CRISTALL small angle scattering; ~ **planar** *f* ELECTRON planar diffusion; ~ **pour public ciblé** *f* TV narrowcasting; ~ **radiative** *f* ASTRONOMIE radiative diffusion; ~ **Raman** *f* PHYS RAYON, PHYSIQUE Raman scattering; ~ **Raman anti-Stokes cohérente** *f (DRASC)* PHYSIQUE coherent anti-Stokes Raman scattering *(CARS)*; ~ **de Rayleigh** *f* OPTIQUE, PHYS RAYON, PHYSIQUE Rayleigh scattering; ~ **des rayons X** *f* CRISTALL X-ray scattering; ~ **rétrograde** *f* PHYS RAYON backscattering;

~ **de Rutherford** *f* PHYSIQUE Rutherford scattering; ~ **sélective** *f* ELECTRON selective diffusion; ~ **simultanée** *f* TV simulcast broadcasting; ~ **sous pression** *f* NUCLEAIRE barodiffusion; ~ **de télévision** *f* TELECOM television broadcasting; ~ **thermique** *f* THERMODYN thermal diffusion, thermodiffusion; ~ **de Thomson** *f* PHYSIQUE Thomson scattering; ~ **à travers le champ magnétique** *f* NUCLEAIRE diffusion across the magnetic field; ~ **troposphérique** *f* TELECOM tropospheric scatter; ~ **turbulente** *f* NUCLEAIRE eddy diffusion, turbulent diffusion; ~ **de type P** *f* ELECTRON p-type diffusion; ~ **de volume** *f* METALL volume diffusion; ~ **volumique** *f* METALL bulk diffusion, volume diffusion

diffusivité *f* MATERIAUX, PHYS FLUID diffusivity; ~ **hydraulique** *f* HYDROLOGIE hydraulic diffusivity; ~ **thermique** *f* CHAUFFAGE, PHYSIQUE, THERMODYN thermal diffusivity

digérer *vt* RECYCLAGE digest

digesteur *m* HYDROLOGIE digester, digestion tank, RECYCLAGE digester; ~ **aérobie** *m* RECYCLAGE aerobic digester; ~ **Kjeldahl minéralisateur** *m* EQUIP LAB *d'analyse d'azote* Kjeldahl digestion apparatus

digestible *adj* RECYCLAGE digestible

digestif *adj* RECYCLAGE digestive

digestion *f* RECYCLAGE digestion; ~ **aérobie** *f* RECYCLAGE aerobic digestion; ~ **aérobie des boues** *f* DISTRI EAU aerobic sludge digestion; ~ **anaérobie** *f* RECYCLAGE anaerobic digestion; ~ **des boues** *f* HYDROLOGIE, RECYCLAGE sludge digestion

digital *adj* ENREGISTR digital

digitaline *f* AGRO ALIM digitalis, CHIMIE digitalin

digitaliser *vt* INFORMAT, ORDINAT digitize

digitation *f* GEOLOGIE *d'un gisement, des couches*, PETR fingering

diguanide *m* CHIMIE diguanide

digue *f* CONSTR breakwater, dike (AmE), dyke (BrE), sea wall, DISTRI EAU, EN RENOUV dam, dike (AmE), dyke (BrE), HYDROLOGIE dike (AmE), dyke (BrE), NAUT sea wall, *de canal* dam; ~ **anti-bruit** *f* CONSTR noise bund; ~ **déversoir** *f* DISTRI EAU, HYDROLOGIE overflow dam; ~ **fluviale** *f* DISTRI EAU river dam; ~ **maritime** *f* DISTRI EAU sea dike (AmE), sea dyke (BrE); ~ **sans centrale** *f* EN RENOUV dead dike (AmE), dead dyke (BrE)

dihydroacridine *f* CHIMIE dihydroacridine

dihydrobenzène *m* CHIMIE dihydrobenzene

dihydrocarvéol *m* CHIMIE dihydrocarveol

dihydrocarvone *f* CHIMIE dihydrocarvone

dihydroergotamine *f* CHIMIE dihydroergotamine

dihydronaphtalène *m* CHIMIE dihydronaphthalene

dihydrostreptomycine *f* CHIMIE dihydrostreptomycin

dihydrotachystérol *m* CHIMIE dihydrotachysterol

dihydroxyacétone *f* CHIMIE dihydroxyacetone

diisocyanate: ~ **de diphénylméthane** *m* PLAST CAOU *agent de durcissement* diphenylmethane diisocyanate; ~ **de toluène** *m* PLAST CAOU *agent de durcissement* TDI, toluene diisocyanate

dilatabilité *f* CHARBON dilatancy

dilatable *adj* CHARBON dilatable, *sol* dilatant

dilatance *f* PLAST CAOU *viscosité* dilatancy

dilatation *f* GAZ dilation, GEOMETRIE dilation, dilator, MATERIAUX dilatation, MECANIQUE *physique*, PHYSIQUE, PLAST CAOU, THERMODYN expansion; ~ **adiabatique** *f* PHYSIQUE adiabatic expansion; ~ **de contrainte** *f* CH DE FER stress expansion; ~ **cubique** *f* METALL cubical expansion; ~ **des durées** *f* PHYSIQUE time dilation; ~ **isotherme** *f* PHYSIQUE isothermal expansion; ~ **du masque** *f* ELECTRON mask run-out; ~ **thermique** *f* MATERIAUX, PLAST CAOU, TELECOM, THERMODYN thermal expansion

dilateur *m* CONSTR tube expander

dilation *f* CHIMIE *d'un gaz* expansion

dilatomètre *m* PHYSIQUE dilatometer

diluant *m* CHIMIE diluent, thinner, COULEURS paint thinner, thinner, GENIE CHIM diluting agent, LESSIVES solvent, MATERIAUX blending agent, diluting agent, PAPIER, PLAST CAOU *revêtements, adhésifs* diluent

dilué *adj* MATERIAUX *alliage*, METALL *alliage* dilute

diluer *vt* CHARBON dilute, CHIMIE water, GENIE CHIM, PAPIER, PLAST CAOU *revêtements, adhésifs* dilute

dilution *f* CHIMIE dilution, thinning, GENIE CHIM, PETROLE dilution

dimension *f* IMPRIM format, size, INFORMAT dimension, METROLOGIE measurement, ORDINAT, PHYSIQUE dimension; ~ **des grains** *f* CHARBON grain size; ~ **nominale** *f* EMBALLAGE nominal size; ~ **de séparation** *f* CHARBON partition size; ~ **type** *f* PRODUCTION standard size

dimensionnement *m* INFORMAT, ORDINAT dimensioning, sizing; ~ **de chaussées** *m* CONSTR pavement design; ~ **au flambage** *m* ESPACE *véhicules* design to buckling strength; ~ **à la limite élastique** *m* ESPACE *véhicules* design to yield point; ~ **au point du système** *m* ESPACE *véhicules spatiaux* design to yield point; ~ **à la rupture** *m* ESPACE *véhicules* design to ultimate strength

dimensionner *vt* PRODUCTION *table de données* adjust

dimensions: ~ **d'encombrement** *f pl* CONS MECA boundary dimensions, connecting dimensions; ~ **d'encombrement des mandrins** *f pl* CONS MECA connecting dimensions of chucks; ~ **extérieures** *f pl* EMBALLAGE outside dimensions; ~ **hors-tout** *f pl* CONS MECA overall dimensions; ~ **d'interchangeabilité** *f pl* CONS MECA fitting dimensions; ~ **des lits** *f pl* TEXTILE bed sizes; ~ **supérieures** *f pl* GEOMETRIE higher dimensions; ~ **totales** *f pl* EMBALLAGE overall dimensions

dimère[1] *adj* CHIMIE dimeric

dimère[2] *m* CHIMIE, MATERIAUX dimer

diméthylacétique *adj* CHIMIE dimethylacetic

diméthylamine *f* CHIMIE dimethylamine

diméthylaniline *f* CHIMIE dimethylaniline

diméthylarsine *f* CHIMIE dimethylarsine

diméthylbenzène *m* CHIMIE dimethylbenzene, xylene

diméthyle *m* CHIMIE dimethyl

diméthylformamide *m* CHIMIE dimethylformamide

diméthylglyoxime *f* CHIMIE dimethylglyoxime

diminuer[1] *vt* PRODUCTION thin, thin out; ~ **par fractions régulières** *vt* IMPRIM decrement

diminuer[2] *vi* NAUT abate; ~ **progressivement le niveau** *vi* ENREGISTR fade down

diminuteur *m* INFORMAT, ORDINAT subtrahend

diminution *f* POLLU MER mitigation; ~ **brusque de section** *f* INST HYDR sudden contraction of cross section; ~ **de crue** *f* DISTRI EAU flood abatement; ~ **de la netteté** *f* PHOTO decrease in definition; ~ **de température** *f* GAZ temperature drop

dimorphie *f* CHIMIE dimorphism

dimorphisme *m* CHIMIE dimorphism

DIN *abrév (Deutsche Industrienorm)* CONS MECA DIN *(Deutsche Industrienorm)*

dinaphtyle *m* CHIMIE dinaphthyl

dinghy *m* NAUT dinghy; ~ **à moteur hors-bord** *m* TRANS-

PORT outboard inflatable; ~ **à voile** *m* NAUT sailing dinghy

dinitrobenzène *m* CHIMIE dinitrobenzene

dinitrocrésol *m* CHIMIE dinitrocresol

dinitronaphtalène *m* CHIMIE dinitronaphthalene

dinitrophénol *m* CHIMIE dinitrophenol

dinitrotoluène *m* CHIMIE dinitrotoluene

dinucléotide *m* CHIMIE dinucleotide

diode *f* ELECTR *redresseur*, ELECTRON, INFORMAT diode, NUCLEAIRE diode, diode tube, ORDINAT, PHYSIQUE, TELECOM, VEHICULES *système électrique d'allumage* diode; ~ **antiparasite** *f* ELECTRON diode suppressor; ~ **à l'arséniure de gallium** *f* ELECTRON gallium arsenide diode; ~ **d'atténuation** *f* ELECTRON attenuator diode; ~ **atténuatrice PIN** *f* ELECTRON PIN attenuator diode; ~ **à avalanche** *f* ELECTRON, PHYSIQUE avalanche diode; ~ **à avalanche au silicium** *f* ELECTRON silicon avalanche diode; ~ **à avalanche à temps de propagation** *f (diode Impatt)* ELECTRON, PHYSIQUE impact avalanche transit-time diode *(IMPATT diode)*; ~ **à avalanche à temps de transit** *f* PHYSIQUE avalanche transit-time diode; ~ **BARITT** *f* PHYSIQUE BARITT diode; ~ **à barrière de Schottky** *f* ELECTRON Schottky barrier diode; ~ **à bruit** *f* ELECTRON noise diode; ~ **de Burrus** *f* OPTIQUE, TELECOM Burrus diode; ~ **à capacité variable** *f* TV varactor diode, variable capacitance diode; ~ **de clamp** *f* TV DC clamp diode; ~ **coaxiale** *f* ELECTRON coaxial diode; ~ **de commutation** *f* ELECTRON, TELECOM switching diode; ~ **de commutation rapide** *f* ELECTRON high-speed switching diode; ~ **à couche intrinsèque** *f* ELECTRON intrinsic barrier diode; ~ **à coupure brusque** *f* ELECTRON charge storage diode, snap-off diode, step recovery diode; ~ **à court temps de transition** *f* ELECTRON fast-recovery diode; ~ **à cristal** *f* ELECTRON crystal diode; ~ **débloquée par intervalles** *f* ELECTRON gated diode; ~ **de déclenchement** *f* ELECTRON trigger diode; ~ **à déclenchement périodique** *f* ELECTRON gated diode; ~ **de détection** *f* ELECTRON detector diode; ~ **de détection à barrière de Schottky** *f* ELECTRON Schottky barrier detector diode; ~ **de détection à pointe** *f* ELECTRON point contact detector diode; ~ **de détection au silicium** *f* ELECTRON silicon detector diode; ~ **détectrice** *f* ELECTRON detector diode; ~ **dopée à l'or** *f* ELECTRON gold-doped diode; ~ **double base** *f* ELECTRON double-base diode; ~ **écrêteuse** *f* ELECTRON clipper diode, limiter diode; ~ **à effet Gunn** *f* ELECTRON Gunn diode, Gunn effect diode, PHYSIQUE Gunn diode effect; ~ **à effet tunnel** *f* ELECTRON tunnel diode; ~ **d'efficacité** *f* ELECTRON efficiency diode; ~ **électroluminescente** *f (DEL)* ELECTR *affichage*, ELECTRON, INFORMAT, OPTIQUE, ORDINAT, PHYS RAYON, PHYSIQUE, TELECOM, TV light-emitting diode *(LED)*; ~ **électroluminescente à émission frontale** *f* OPTIQUE surface-emitting electroluminescent diode; ~ **électroluminescente à émission longitudinale** *f* OPTIQUE ELED, edge-emitting light-emitting diode; ~ **électroluminescente à émission par la surface** *f* TELECOM surface-emitting light-emitting diode; ~ **électroluminescente à émission par la tranche** *f* TELECOM ELED, edge-emitting light-emitting diode; ~ **émettrice** *f* ELECTRON light-emitting diode; ~ **émissive** *f* ELECTRON emissive diode, light-emitting diode; ~ **en bande S** *f* ELECTRON S-band diode; ~ **Esaki** *f* ELECTRON, PHYSIQUE Esaki diode; ~ **à faibles fuites** *f* ELECTRON low-leakage diode; ~ **de fixation de niveau** *f* ELECTRON clamping diode; ~ **à fort courant** *f* ELECTRON high-current diode; ~ **à gaz** *f* ELECTRON gas diode; ~ **au germanium** *f* ELECTR, ELECTRON germanium diode; ~ **Gunn** *f* ELECTRON Gunn diode, Gunn effect diode, PHYSIQUE Gunn diode, Gunn diode effect; ~ **à haute conductance** *f* ELECTRON high-conductance diode; ~ **à homojonction PN** *f* ELECTRON p-n homojunction diode; ~ **hyperfréquence** *f* ELECTRON microwave diode; ~ **Impatt** *f* (*diode à avalanche à temps de propagation*) ELECTRON, PHYSIQUE IMPATT diode *(impact avalanche transit-time diode)*; ~ **inverse** *f* ELECTRON backward diode; ~ **ionique à gaz** *f* ELECTR gas-filled rectifier diode; ~ **d'isolement** *f* ELECTRON isolation diode; ~ **à jonction** *f* ELECTR *semi-conducteur*, ELECTRON junction diode; ~ **à jonction classique** *f* ELECTRON bipolar diode; ~ **à jonction par alliage** *f* ELECTRON alloy diode; ~ **à jonction PN** *f* ELECTRON p-n junction diode; ~ **à jonction PN** *f* ELECTR *semi-conducteur* p-n junction diode; ~ **à jonction au silicium** *f* ELECTRON silicon junction diode; ~ **laser** *f* ELECTRON laser diode, OPTIQUE ILD, diode laser, injection laser diode, laser diode, TELECOM laser diode; ~ **laser à émission continue** *f* ELECTRON CW laser diode; ~ **laser à faible puissance** *f* TELECOM low-power laser diode; ~ **laser à simple hétérojonction** *f* ELECTRON single heterojunction laser diode; ~ **de limitation d'amplitude** *f* ELECTRON limiter diode; ~ **de limitation Schottky** *f* ELECTRON Schottky clamping diode; ~ **limitatrice** *f* TV limiter diode; ~ **limiteuse** *f* ELECTRON limiter diode; ~ **luminescente** *f* ELECTRON light-emitting diode, luminescent diode; ~ **lumineuse** *f* ELECTRON light-emitting diode; ~ **lumineuse infrarouge** *f* ELECTRON infrared LED; ~ **mélangeuse** *f* ELECTRON mixer diode; ~ **mélangeuse à pointe** *f* ELECTRON point contact mixer diode; ~ **mélangeuse Schottky** *f* ELECTRON Schottky barrier mixer diode; ~ **mélangeuse au silicium** *f* ELECTRON silicon mixer diode; ~ **mésa** *f* ELECTRON mesa diode; ~ **modulatrice** *f* ELECTRON modulator diode; ~ **de niveau** *f* ELECTRON clamping diode, TV DC clamp diode; ~ **paramétrique à l'arséniure de gallium** *f* ELECTRON gallium arsenide parametric amplifier diode; ~ **parasite** *f* ELECTRON parasitic diode; ~ **PIN** *f* ELECTRON PIN diode, PHYSIQUE p-i-n diode; ~ **planar** *f* ELECTRON planar diode; ~ **planar épitaxiale** *f* ELECTRON planar epitaxial diode; ~ **à pointe** *f* ELECTRON point contact diode; ~ **à pointe au silicium** *f* ELECTRON point contact silicon diode; ~ **à porteurs chauds** *f* ELECTRON hot carrier diode; ~ **à porteurs majoritaires** *f* ELECTRON majority carrier diode; ~ **pour amplificateur paramétrique** *f* ELECTRON parametric amplifier diode; ~ **pour signaux à bas niveau** *f* ELECTRON low-power diode; ~ **de protection** *f* ELECTRON protection diode, PRODUCTION freewheeling diode; ~ **de puissance** *f* ELECTRON power diode; ~ **à quatre couches** *f* ELECTRON four-layer diode; ~ **à rayonnement lumineux** *f* PHYS RAYON light-emitting diode; ~ **réceptrice** *f* ELECTRON receiver diode; ~ **de redressement** *f* ELECTRON rectifier diode; ~ **de redressement Schottky** *f* ELECTRON Schottky barrier rectifier diode; ~ **de référence de tension** *f* ELECTRON voltage reference diode; ~ **de référence de tension compensée en température** *f* ELECTRON temperature-compensated Zener diode; ~ **régulatrice de tension** *f* ELECTRON voltage regulator diode; ~ **à résistance négative** *f* ELECTRON negative resistance diode; ~ **de roue libre** *f* ELECTRON freewheeling diode; ~ **Schottky** *f* ELECTRON, PHYSIQUE Schottky diode; ~ **à semi-conducteur** *f* ELECTRON, ORDINAT semiconduc-

tor diode; ~ **Shockley** *f* ELECTRON Shockley diode; ~ **au silicium** *f* ELECTR *semi-conducteur*, ELECTRON silicon diode; ~ **superluminescente** *f* OPTIQUE SRD, super-radiant diode, OPTIQUE superluminescent diode, TELECOM SRD, superradiant diode, TELECOM superluminescent LED, superluminescent diode; ~ **à temps de transit** *f* ELECTRON transit-time diode; ~ **à transfert d'électrons** *f* ELECTRON transferred electron diode, PHYSIQUE electron transfer diode; ~ **Trapatt** *f* ELECTRON, PHYSIQUE trapatt diode; ~ **tunnel** *f* ELECTRON, PHYSIQUE tunnel diode; ~ **de type planar** *f* ELECTRON planar diode; ~ **unitunnel** *f* ELECTRON backward diode; ~ **varactor** *f* PHYSIQUE varactor diode; ~ **varactor hyperabrupt** *f* PHYSIQUE hyperabrupt varactor diode; ~ **varicap** *f* ELECTRON varicap; ~ **varicap pour génération d'harmoniques** *f* ELECTRON harmonic generator varactor; ~ **de verrouillage** *f* PHYSIQUE clamping diode; ~ **à vide** *f* ELECTRON vacuum diode; ~ **de Zener** *f* ELECTRON, PHYSIQUE, TELECOM Zener diode; ~ **Zener compensée en température** *f* ELECTRON temperature-compensated Zener diode

diodes: ~ appariées *f pl* ELECTRON matched diodes

diol *m* CHIMIE diol

dioléfine *f* PETROLE diolefin

diopside *m* MINERAUX diopside

dioptase *m* MINERAUX dioptase, emerald copper

dioptre *m* ESPACE *mesures* diopter (AmE), dioptre (BrE), PHYSIQUE surface

dioptrie *f* PHYSIQUE diopter (AmE), dioptre (BrE)

diorite *f* PETR diorite

dioxine *f* CHIMIE dioxin

dioxyde *m* CHIMIE dioxide; ~ **d'azote** *m* POLLUTION, SECURITE *air sur les lieux de travail* nitrogen dioxide; ~ **de carbone** *m* CHARBON carbon dioxide; ~ **de manganèse** *m* ELECTROTEC manganese dioxide; ~ **de silice** *m* MATERIAUX silicon dioxide; ~ **de silicium** *m* ELECTRON, MATERIAUX silicon dioxide; ~ **de silicium colloïdal** *m* LESSIVES colloidal silica; ~ **de soufre** *m* AGRO ALIM, POLLUTION sulfur dioxide (AmE), sulphur dioxide (BrE); ~ **de titane** *m* PLAST CAOU *pigment* titanium dioxide

dioxytartarique *adj* CHIMIE dioxytartaric

dipalmitine *f* CHIMIE dipalmitin

diparachlorobenzyle *m* CHIMIE diparachlorobenzyl

diphasé *adj* ELECTR *courant* biphase, ELECTROTEC diphase, two-phase

diphénol: ~ A *m* PLAST CAOU bisphenol A

diphénylamine *f* CHIMIE diphenylamine

diphényle *m* CHIMIE biphenyl; ~ **chloriné** *m* ELECTROTEC askarel

diphénylurée *f* CHIMIE carbanilide

diphtongue *f* IMPRIM diphthong

diplacousie *f* ACOUSTIQUE diplacusis

diplexeur *m* TELECOM diplexer

dipolaire *adj* CHIMIE dipolar

dipôle *m* ELECTR *charge, antenne*, ELECTROTEC, METALL dipole; ~ **actif** *m* ELECTR *pièce* active impeder, ELECTROTEC active dipole; ~ **demi-onde** *m* PHYSIQUE half-wave dipole; ~ **électrique** *m* ELECTROTEC, PHYSIQUE electric dipole; ~ **électrocinétique** *m* PHYSIQUE two-terminal network; ~ **magnétique** *m* PHYSIQUE magnetic dipole; ~ **omnidirectionnel** *m* NAUT omnidirectional dipole; ~ **passif** *m* ELECTROTEC passive dipole

dipyre *m* MINERAUX dipyre

direct[1] *adj* DISTRI EAU, INFORMAT, ORDINAT direct; **en ~**

adj IMPRIM, TELECOM on-line, TV live; **~ modulateur-démodulateur** *adj* TV *transfert E-E*, E-to-E, electronic-to-electronic

direct[2] *adv* INFORMAT, ORDINAT, TELECOM direct; **en ~** *adv* INFORMAT, ORDINAT, TELECOM on-line

directeur *m* ESPACE director; **~ de l'aéroport** *m* AERONAUT airport manager; **~ de photographie** *m* CINEMAT lighting cameraman; **~ du plan** *m* PRODUCTION master scheduler; **~ de projet** *m* PRODUCTION project manager; **~ de vol** *m* AERONAUT flight director

direction:[1] **dans la ~ du vent** *adv* POLLUTION downwind

direction[2] *f* AUTO steering gear, steering system, HYDROLOGIE *d'un courant* drift, MINES run, trend, *d'un filon, d'une galerie de mine* bearing, *d'un filon* course, *d'un filon souterrain* strike, NAUT *d'un courant* drift, VEHICULES steering; **~ assistée** *f* AUTO, TRANSPORT, VEHICULES power-assisted steering; **~ automatique** *f* COMMANDE automatic control, automatic direction; **~ de champ** *f* ELECTROTEC field direction; **~ à circulation de billes** *f* AUTO recirculating ball steering gear; **~ du courant** *f* NAUT current set; **~ de courant ancien** *f* GEOLOGIE palaeocurrent direction (BrE), paleocurrent direction (AmE); **~ à crémaillère et pignon** *f* VEHICULES rack-and-pinion steering; **~ de paléocourant** *f* GEOLOGIE palaeocurrent direction (BrE), paleocurrent direction (AmE); **~ de pendage** *f* GEOLOGIE line of dip; **~ des traces d'usinage** *f* CONS MECA lay; **~ du vent** *f* AERONAUT, METEO, NAUT wind direction; **~ de vergence** *f* GEOLOGIE facing direction

direction:[3] **en ~** *prép* MINES along the line of strike, along the strike

directive *f* INFORMAT direct memory access, directive, ORDINAT direct memory access, directive; **~ d'aller-retour** *f* PRODUCTION turnaround directive; **~ d'assemblage** *f* ORDINAT assembler directive; **~ de compilateur** *f* ORDINAT compiler directive

directives: **~ de sécurité** *f pl* SECURITE safety instructions

directivité *f* ESPACE *communications* directivity, TV directional selectivity; **~ d'antenne** *f* TV aerial directivity

directrice *f* CONS MECA directing line, INST HYDR *de turbine* guide

dirigé: **~ vers** *adj* GEOLOGIE facing

diriger *vt* CINEMAT direct, HYDROLOGIE flow along

disaccharide *m* CHIMIE disaccharide

disclinaison *f* METALL disclination; **~ coincée** *f* METALL wedge disclination; **~ torse** *f* METALL twist disclination

discontinuité *f* GEOLOGIE discontinuity; **~ d'absorption** *f* NUCLEAIRE K-absorption edge, absorption edge; **~ Gutenberg** *f* EN RENOUV Gutenberg discontinuity; **~ hydraulique** *f* HYDROLOGIE hydraulic discontinuity, leach; **~ magnétique** *f* GEOPHYS magnetic discontinuity; **~ de Mohorovicic** *f* GEOLOGIE Moho discontinuity, Mohovicic discontinuity; **~ sédimentaire** *f* OCEANO sediment break, sedimentation break

discordance *f* ACOUSTIQUE discordance, GEOLOGIE disconformity, discordance, nonconformity, PETROLE *géologie* unconformity; **~ angulaire** *f* GEOLOGIE angular disconformity, angular unconformity; **~ d'érosion** *f* GEOLOGIE erosional unconformity; **~ de ravinement** *f* GEOLOGIE disconformity, erosional unconformity

discothèque *f* ENREGISTR record library

discret *adj* INFORMAT, ORDINAT discrete

discriminant *m* CONS MECA discriminant

discriminateur *m* CONS MECA, ELECTRON, OPTIQUE discriminator, TELECOM call-barring equipment, discriminator, restrictor (AmE); **~ de fréquence** *m* TV discriminator; **~ de phase** *m* ELECTRON phase discriminator, TV phase detector; **~ de protocole** *m (DP)* TELECOM protocol discriminator *(PD)*

discrimination *f* ELECTRON discrimination, ESPACE *communications* isolation, ESSAIS discrimination

disharmonique *adj* GEOLOGIE *pli* disharmonic

disilane *m* CHIMIE disilane

disjoint *adj* MATH disjoint

disjoncteur *m* CINEMAT circuit breaker, ELECTR cutout switch, *commutateur, interrupteur* circuit breaker, ELECTROTEC circuit breaker, disconnecting switch; **~ à air** *m* ELECTR air breaker, air circuit breaker; **~ à air comprimé** *m* ELECTR air blast breaker, air blast switch, ELECTROTEC air blast circuit breaker; **~ anodique** *m* ELECTR anode circuit breaker; **~ à bain d'huile** *m* ELECTR bulk oil circuit breaker; **~ de batterie** *m* COMMANDE battery load switch, battery switch; **~ à boîtier isolant** *m* ELECTR all-insulated switch; **~ du circuit** *m* ELECTROTEC circuit breaker; **~ à coupure dans l'air** *m* ELECTR air breaker, air circuit breaker; **~ à coupure multiple** *m* ELECTR multibreak circuit breaker; **~ différentiel** *m* ELECTR earth leakage circuit breaker (BrE), ground leakage circuit breaker (AmE); **~ à l'huile** *m* ELECTR *interrupteur* oil circuit breaker, ELECTROTEC oil switch; **~ limiteur de courant** *m* ELECTR current-limiting circuit breaker; **~ à maxima** *m* COMMANDE overload cutout; **~ à maximum** *m* ELECTROTEC maximum cutout; **~ miniature** *m* ELECTR microswitch, miniature circuit breaker, ELECTROTEC miniature circuit breaker; **~ par surintensité de courant** *m* COMMANDE overload cutout; **~ pneumatique** *m* ELECTR air blast breaker, ELECTROTEC air blast circuit breaker, air break switch; **~ de shuntage** *m* ELECTR bypass switch; **~ de sortie** *m* ELECTROTEC overcurrent circuit breaker; **~ à soufflage d'air** *m* ELECTR air blast breaker, air blast switch; **~ à soufflage magnétique** *m* ELECTR magnetic blowout circuit breaker; **~ de surintensité** *m* ELECTROTEC overcurrent trip; **~ thermique** *m* THERMODYN thermal circuit breaker

disjonction *f* ELECTRON disjunction, INFORMAT exjunction, nonequivalence operation, *opération* disjunction, ORDINAT exjunction, *opération* disjunction; **~ électrique indépendante** *f* ELECTR *déclencheur* trip-free release; **~ exclusive** *f* ORDINAT exjunction

dislocation *f* CRISTALL dislocation, GEOPHYS dislocation, displacement, MATERIAUX *cristallographie* dislocation, MECANIQUE breaking-up, METALL dislocation; **~ du bord** *f* METALL edge dislocation; **~ coin** *f* CRISTALL edge dislocation; **~ en hélice** *f* CRISTALL helical dislocation; **~ en zigzag** *f* METALL zigzag dislocation; **~ épitaxiale** *f* METALL epitaxial dislocation; **~ glissile** *f* METALL glissile dislocation; **~ hélicale** *f* METALL helical dislocation; **~ image** *f* METALL image dislocation; **~ immobile** *f* METALL immobile dislocation; **~ mixte** *f* CRISTALL, METALL mixed dislocation; **~ non décorée** *f* METALL undecorated dislocation; **~ originelle** *f* METALL grown-in dislocation; **~ parfaite** *f* CRISTALL perfect dislocation; **~ partielle** *f* CRISTALL, METALL partial dislocation; **~ polygonale** *f* METALL polygonal dislocation; **~ sessile** *f* CRISTALL sessile dislocation; **~ Shockley** *f* METALL Shockley dislocation; **~ tringle** *f* METALL stair rod dislocation; **~ vis** *f* CRISTALL, MATERIAUX, METALL screw dislocation; **~ vis crantée** *f* METALL jogged screw dislocation; **~ de Volterra** *f* METALL Volterra dislocation

disloquer *vt* CONSTR dislodge

dismutation *f* CHIMIE dismutation

disomose *m* MINERAUX disomose

disparaître: ~ **en fondu** *vi* CINEMAT fade out

dispersant *m* CHARBON dispersing agent, PETROLE dispersant, PLAST CAOU *pigments, polymères* dispersing agent, POLLU MER, POLLUTION dispersant

dispersé *adj* TELECOM *système* dispersed

disperser: **se** ~ *vi* POLLU MER, POLLUTION disperse

dispersion *f* CHARBON dispersion, CHIMIE mull, CINEMAT scattering, CRISTALL dispersion, ELECTR *courant, charge* leak, leakage, EN RENOUV scattering, ESPACE spread, GENIE CHIM dispersion, GEOPHYS scattering, INFORMAT spread, *variation* dispersion, MATERIAUX dispersion, MATH deviation, METALL dispersion, scattering, OPTIQUE dispersion, ORDINAT spread, *variation* dispersion, PETR scattering, PHYS RAYON, PHYSIQUE, PLAST CAOU, TELECOM dispersion; ~ **acoustique** *f* ACOUSTIQUE acoustic dispersion; ~ **anomale** *f* PHYSIQUE anomalous dispersion; ~ **de chaleur** *f* THERMODYN heat dissipation; ~ **chromatique** *f* OPTIQUE chromatic dispersion; ~ **colloïdale** *f* AGRO ALIM macromolecular dispersion, POLLUTION colloid disperse system; ~ **des couleurs** *f* PHYS ONDES *à cause de la réfraction* dispersion; ~ **d'énergie** *f* ESPACE *communications* energy dispersal; ~ **de guidage d'ondes** *f* OPTIQUE, TELECOM waveguide dispersion; ~ **de guide d'ondes** *f* OPTIQUE, TELECOM waveguide dispersion; ~ **d'une impulsion** *f* OPTIQUE impulse dispersion; ~ **linéaire** *f* PHYS RAYON *de la spectrographie* linear dispersion; ~ **macromoléculaire** *f* AGRO ALIM macromolecular dispersion; ~ **de matériaux** *f* OPTIQUE, TELECOM material dispersion; ~ **modale** *f* OPTIQUE modal dispersion; ~ **multimode** *f* OPTIQUE multimode distortion; ~ **d'onde** *f* TELECOM wave dispersion; ~ **par le vent** *f* GAZ, POLLUTION wind dispersion; ~ **d'un peloton** *f* TRANSPORT platoon dispersion; ~ **de profil** *f* OPTIQUE, TELECOM profile dispersion; ~ **de vapeur** *f* GAZ vapor dispersion (AmE), vapour dispersion (BrE); ~ **verticale** *f* POLLUTION vertical dispersion

dispersivité *f* GENIE CHIM dispersivity

dispnée *f* OCEANO choke, dyspnea, dyspnoea

disponibilité *f* INFORMAT availability, NUCLEAIRE *d'un élément combustible* serviceability, ORDINAT, TELECOM availability; ~ **d'un circuit** *f* TELECOM circuit availability; ~ **de l'installation** *f* AERONAUT facility availability; ~ **intrinsèque** *f* AERONAUT inherent availability; ~ **opérationnelle** *f* PRODUCTION operational availability; ~ **réalisable** *f* PRODUCTION achievable availability

disponible *adj* QUALITE available

disposé: ~ **en gradins** *adj* CONS MECA stepped

disposer *vt* CONSTR *une rangée de pierres* set out

dispositif *m* CONS MECA apparatus, appliance, arrangement, device, layout, INFORMAT, ORDINAT device, PAPIER apparatus, device, POLLU MER device, PRODUCTION appliance, device, TELECOM device;

~**a** ~ **d'absorption du bruit** *m* CONS MECA noise absorption device; ~ **à accès direct** *m* INFORMAT random access device; ~ **à accès sélectif** *m* ORDINAT random access device; ~ **à accès série** *m* ORDINAT serial access device; ~ **d'accord** *m* TV tuner; ~ **d'accouplement à bille** *m* NUCLEAIRE ball coupling; ~ **d'accrochage sur picots** *m* TEXTILE pinning-up device; ~ **actif d'excursion haute** *m* ELECTRON active pullup device; ~ **actionné hydrauliquement** *m* CONS MECA hydrauli-

cally-operated device; ~ **d'ajustage** *m* COMMANDE adjusting device, adjustment device; ~ **d'alésage** *m* CONS MECA boring head; ~ **d'alimentation** *m* CONS MECA feeder; ~ **d'allumage** *m* CHAUFFAGE ignition device; ~ **alpha** *m* NUCLEAIRE alpha device; ~ **d'amortissement** *m* ELECTROTEC damper; ~ **amortisseur** *m* CONS MECA damper, damping device; ~ **d'analyse** *m* TV scanner; ~ **antiblocage** *m* AUTO antiblocking system; ~ **antibuée** *m* AERONAUT demister; ~ **anticouple** *m* AERONAUT antitorque device; ~ **antidérapant** *m* ACOUSTIQUE antiskating, AERONAUT antiskid unit; ~ **antiécho parasite** *m* NAUT anticlutter control; ~ **antieffraction** *m* SECURITE burglar alarm; ~ **antiencastrement** *m* VEHICULES *carrosserie* underrun bar, underrun bumper, underrun guard; ~ **antienrayeur intégral** *m* AUTO antiskid braking system; ~ **antigivrage** *m* ESPACE *véhicules* anti-icing system; ~ **d'antiparasitage pour allumeur** *m* VEHICULES distributor suppressor; ~ **antiparasite** *m* ELECTRON, ELECTROTEC suppressor, PRODUCTION suppression device; ~ **antipatinage** *m* AUTO antiskid braking system; ~ **antiretour de flamme** *m* THERMODYN flame trap; ~ **antiroulis** *m* NAUT antirolling device; ~ **antivol** *m* SECURITE theft prevention device; ~ **d'arrêt d'urgence** *m* SECURITE *sécurité des machines* emergency-stopping device; ~ **d'asservissement** *m* COMMANDE automatic controller, TV slave unit; ~ **automatique de désemboîtement** *m* EMBALLAGE denesting magazine; ~ **d'avance** *m* VEHICULES *allumage* advance mechanism; ~ **d'avance automatique** *m* COMMANDE automatic advance device, automatic advance; ~ **d'avance centrifuge** *m* VEHICULES *allumage* centrifugal advance mechanism; ~ **avertisseur d'espacement** *m* TRANSPORT headway warning device; ~ **avertisseur de proximité** *m* AERONAUT proximity warning indicator;

~**b** ~ **de balayage** *m* ELECTRON scanner, TV scanner, scanning device; ~ **à balayage cavalier** *m* INFORMAT random scan device; ~ **à balayage omnidirectionnel** *m* ORDINAT random scan device; ~ **à balayage récurrent** *m* INFORMAT, ORDINAT raster scan device; ~ **à bas niveau** *m* ELECTRON low-level device; ~ **de blocage** *m* CONS MECA locking device, ELECTROTEC blocking device; ~ **de blocage à déclic** *m* PRODUCTION snap lock; ~ **de bloc par surintensité** *m* ELECTR *commande par moteur* overcurrent blocking device; ~ **de bourrage** *m* TELECOM stuffing device;

~**c** ~ **de cadrage** *m* CINEMAT frame adjuster; ~ **de calibrage** *m* ELECTRON calibrator; ~ **de calibrage en cours de service** *m* METROLOGIE in-process gaging (AmE), in-process gauging (BrE); ~ **à canal N** *m* ELECTRON n-channel device; ~ **à canal P** *m* ELECTRON p-channel device; ~ **de changement de vitesse** *m* CONS MECA speed-changing device, speed-changing mechanism; ~ **de chauffage** *m* CONS MECA heating device, VEHICULES *accessoires* heater; ~ **de circonstance** *m* PRODUCTION makeshift; ~ **de codage** *m* TRANSPORT coding device, TV coder; ~ **codeur de fond** *m* EMBALLAGE bottom coder; ~ **de commande automatique** *m* COMMANDE automatic control device; ~ **de commande** *m* INST HYDR *de tiroir ou de distributeur de vapeur, à action positive* valve gear, valve motion; ~ **commandé en courant** *m* ELECTROTEC current-controlled device; ~ **de commande de marche en parallèle** *m* ELECTR *changeur de prises* parallel control device; ~ **de commande de pale** *m* AERONAUT blade control system; ~ **de commande des soupapes en tête** *m* AUTO I-head valve train; ~ **de commande des soupapes latérales** *m* AUTO T-head valve train; ~ **de commande de tiroir** *m* INST HYDR valve gear; ~ **de commutation** *m* ELECTRO-TEC, TELECOM switching device; ~ **de comptage** *m* ELECTRON counter; ~ **de contrarotation** *m* ESPACE *véhicules* despin system; ~ **de contrôle de débit** *m* MAT CHAUFF flow control; ~ **de contrôle des décollages** *m* AERONAUT takeoff monitoring system; ~ **de contrôle de flamme** *m* MAT CHAUFF flame control; ~ **de contrôle optique du train** *m* AERONAUT landing gear downlock visual check installation; ~ **de contrôle de pression** *m* MAT CHAUFF pressure control; ~ **de contrôle de la tension d'entrée** *m* PRODUCTION *électricité* incoming voltage monitor; ~ **à couplage de charge** *m (CCD)* ASTRONOMIE, ELECTRON, ELECTROTEC, ORDINAT, PHYSIQUE, TELECOM, TV charge-coupled device *(CCD)*;

~ **d** ~ **de décalage des balais** *m* ELECTROTEC brush rocker; ~ **de décentrement** *m* TV horizontal centering control (AmE), horizontal centring control (BrE); ~ **de déclenchement** *m* CONS MECA tripper, tripping device, PRODUCTION tripping advice; ~ **de décodage** *m* TRANSPORT decoding device; ~ **de décollage** *m* IMPRIM *des morceaux de papier* stripper; ~ **de délestage** *m* REFRIG unloader; ~ **de démarrage** *m* ELECTR *moteur* starter, starting device; ~ **de démarrage à froid** *m* VEHICULES *carburateur* cold start device; ~ **de démonstration** *m* CONS MECA test facility, tryout facility; ~ **déprimogène** *m* PETROLE *canalisations* orifice; ~ **de désattelage** *m* CONS MECA detachment device; ~ **détecteur aux rayons X** *m* INSTRUMENT industrial X-ray apparatus; ~ **de dételage** *m* CONS MECA detachment device; ~ **de déversement** *m* NUCLEAIRE *des assemblages combustibles* fuel transfer table, tiltingd e v i c e, upender; ~ **de disjonction** *m* SECURITE cutout device; ~ **de dosage** *m* EMBALLAGE dosing apparatus;

~ **e** ~ **à eau diffusée sur pont** *m* NAUT deck sprinkler system; ~ **électromécanique** *m* ELECTROTEC electro-mechanical device; ~ **électronique** *m* ELECTRON electronic device; ~ **à électrons** *m* ELECTROTEC electron device; ~ **à enclenchement** *m* SECURITE trip device; ~ **d'encollage** *m* EMBALLAGE gluing device; ~ **enfichable** *m* ELECTROTEC plug-in unit; ~ **enregistreur Campbell-Stokes** *m* EN RENOUV Campbell-Stokes recorder; ~ **d'entrée** *m* ELECTROTEC, INFORMAT, ORDINAT input device; ~ **d'entrée/sortie** *m* INFORMAT, ORDINAT input/output device; ~ **d'entrée de la bande dans le feston** *m* IMPRIM *dérouleurs* web into festoon; ~ **d'essai** *m* ESSAIS test equipment; ~ **des essais** *m* CONS MECA tryout facility; ~ **d'étanchéité** *m* NAUT seal; ~ **d'exploration** *m* TV scanner; ~ **externe** *m* INFORMAT, ORDINAT external device; ~ **d'extinction à mousse** *m* SECURITE foam extinguisher; ~ **d'extrémité de fibre optique** *m* TELECOM fiberoptic terminal device (AmE), fibreoptic terminal device (BrE); ~ **d'extrémité de liaison optique** *m* OPTIQUE fiberoptic terminal device (AmE), fibreoptic terminal device (BrE);

~ **f** ~ **de fermeture du capot** *m* AUTO bonnet lock (BrE), hood latch (AmE), hood lock (AmE); ~ **de fluidification** *m* PAPIER fluidification device; ~ **fluidique** *m* CONS MECA fluidic device; ~ **de fortune** *m* PRODUCTION makeshift; ~ **de fraisage** *m* CONS MECA milling attachment;

~ **g** ~ **GEK** *m* OCEANO GEK, geomagnetic electro-kinetograph; ~ **de géophones** *m* GEOLOGIE seismic array;

~ **h** ~ **de hissage des volets de profondeur** *m* AERONAUT elevator hoist; ~ **de l'homme mort** *m* TRANSPORT dead man's control; ~ **humectant** *m* EMBALLAGE moistening device; ~ **d'humidification pour ruban** *m* EMBALLAGE tape moistening device;

~ **i** ~ **à injection de charge** *m* TELECOM CID, charge injection device; ~ **d'insertion de dépliants** *m* EMBALLAGE leaflet insertor; ~ **d'ionisation** *m* IMPRIM *séchage* ionization unit;

~ **l** ~ **de lavage des blanchets** *m* IMPRIM *impression* blanket washer; ~ **de lavage des tamis** *m* IMPRIM *sérigraphie* screen washer; ~ **de levage** *m* CONS MECA *d'une capacité de 10 tonnes* lifting equipment; ~ **de levage des bobines** *m* EMBALLAGE reel lifter; ~ **à levée verticale** *m* EN RENOUV lift-type device; ~ **de libération du lanceur** *m* ESPACE *véhicules* launcher release gear; ~ **logique** *m* ELECTRON, INFORMAT, ORDINAT logic device; ~ **lumineux à voie étroite** *m* AERONAUT *piste* narrow gage lighting system (AmE), narrow gauge lighting system (BrE);

~ **m** ~ **de maintien** *m* COMMANDE governor; ~ **de manoeuvre** *m* CONS MECA manipulating device; ~ **de manutention de câbles** *m* ELECTROTEC cable-handling system; ~ **de marche cran par cran** *m* ELECTR *commande par moteur* step-by-step control; ~ **de médiation** *m* TELECOM MD, mediation device; ~ **mélangeur** *m* CONSTR mixer; ~ **de mesure** *m* INSTRUMENT, METROLOGIE measuring device; ~ **de mesure de la distance de l'avion à la station** *m* AERONAUT distance-measuring equipment; ~ **de microphotographie** *m* PHOTO microscope adaptor; ~ **de mise en attente** *m* TELECOM queueing device; ~ **de mise en phase** *m* ENREGISTR phasing plug; ~ **de mise en phase de l'obturateur** *m* CINEMAT shutter-phasing device; ~ **de mise au point** *m* COMMANDE focusing device, PHOTO focusing aid; ~ **de mise sous tension constante d'une colonne montante** *m* PETR riser tensioner; ~ **de mise sous tension constante de lignes guides** *m* PETR guide line tensioner; ~ **mortaiseuse** *m* CONSTR mortising machine;

~ **n** ~ **numérique** *m* ELECTRON digital device;

~ **o** ~ **à ondes acoustiques de surface** *m* ELECTRON SAW device, surface acoustic wave device, TELECOM SAW device, surface acoustic wave device; ~ **d'optimisation de courant d'enregistrement** *m* TV record current optimizer; ~ **optoélectronique** *m* ELECTROTEC, OPTIQUE optoelectronic device; ~ **d'ouverture de sachets** *m* EMBALLAGE bag opener;

~ **p** ~ **de perçage** *m* CONS MECA drilling attachment; ~ **de perforation pour la mise en repérage des films** *m* IMPRIM *copie* film register punch; ~ **à photoconduction** *m* ELECTRON photoconductive cell; ~ **photoélectrique** *m* ELECTRON photoelectric device; ~ **de pointage** *m* INFORMAT pointer; ~ **de pompage** *m* POLLU MER pumping unit; ~ **de positionnement des billes** *m* CONS MECA ball register; ~ **de postcombustion** *m* VEHICULES *moteur* afterburner; ~ **pour colonne de tubage perdue** *m* PETR liner hanger; ~ **pour compter** *m* EMBALLAGE counting device; ~ **pour déceler les capsules manquantes** *m* EMBALLAGE missing cap detector; ~ **pour la mise en oeuvre de** *m* BREVETS apparatus for carrying out; ~ **programmable** *m* INFORMAT, ORDINAT programmable device; ~ **programmable par l'utilisateur** *m* INFORMAT, ORDINAT field-programmable device; ~ **de protection du circuit de dérivation** *m* PRODUCTION *automatisme industriel* branch circuit protective device; ~ **de protection contre les claquages** *m* ELECTROTEC blowout fuse; ~ **de protection contre les erreurs** *m* TELECOM ECD, error control device; ~ **de protection contre les surcharges** *m* ELECTROTEC overload protection device; ~ **de protection contre les surtensions** *m* ELECTROTEC overvoltage protection device, surge arrester; ~ **de purification de l'air** *m* SECURITE *propreté de l'environnement* clean air device;

~ q ~ **Q** *m* NUCLEAIRE Q-device; ~ **QP** *m* NUCLEAIRE QP device; ~ **à quatre couches** *m* ELECTRON p-n-p-n device;

~ r ~ **racleur d'huile** *m* NUCLEAIRE oil scraper, oil wiper; ~ **du ralenti** *m* AUTO idle and low speed circuit; ~ **de ralenti variable** *m* TV variable slow motion; ~ **de réchauffe** *m* TRANSPORT afterburner; ~ **de récupération** *m* NUCLEAIRE recovery system, POLLU MER recovery device; ~ **de réfrigération** *m* POLLUTION cooling system; ~ **de réglage** *m* COMMANDE adjusting device, adjustment device; ~ **de réglage de caméra** *m* TV CCU, camera control unit; ~ **de réglage à distance** *m* COMMANDE remote-adjusting device; ~ **de réglage de vitesse** *m* TV variable speed control; ~ **régulateur** *m* COMMANDE regulating device; ~ **de régulation et de sécurité** *m* MAT CHAUFF control and safety device; ~ **de remise à zéro électrique** *m* ELECTR, INSTRUMENT electrical zero adjuster; ~ **de remplissage** *m* EMBALLAGE feeding device, filling device; ~ **de renvoi** *m* TELECOM *d'appels* call diverter; ~ **de repérage** *m* CONS MECA locating device; ~ **de repliage automatique de pales** *m* AERONAUT automatic blade-folding system; ~ **de reproduction** *m* CONS MECA copying attachment; ~ **de reproduction des diapositives** *m* PHOTO slide-copying device; ~ **de retournement aéroporté** *m* IMPRIM air turn; ~ **de retournement de la bande** *m* IMPRIM web-turning device; ~ **de roue libre** *m* CONS MECA freewheel mechanism; ~ **de rupture** *m* REFRIG rupture member;

~ s ~ **de sauvetage pour aviateurs naufragés** *m* MILITAIRE air-sea rescue equipment; ~ **de secours** *m* ELECTROTEC backup; ~ **de section de la bande** *m* IMPRIM *rotatives* web severer; ~ **de sécurité** *m* CONS MECA, SECURITE safety device; ~ **de sécurité et d'armement à distance** *m* ESPACE *véhicules* remote arming and safety unit; ~ **de sécurité et de téléarmement** *m* ESPACE *véhicules* remote arming and safety unit; ~ **sécurité routière** *m* SECURITE road safety device; ~ **à semi-conducteurs** *m* ORDINAT semiconductor device, PHYSIQUE, TELECOM solid-state device; ~ **séparant la vapeur de l'eau** *m* INST HYDR steam separator; ~ **de séparation du trafic** *m* NAUT traffic separation scheme; ~ **de serrage** *m* CONS MECA holding device, EMBALLAGE clam pack; ~ **de serrage électromagnétique** *m* CONS MECA electromagnetic fixing device; ~ **silencieux** *m* TELECOM *maritime mobile* muting device; ~ **silencieux à commande par tonalité** *m* TELECOM CTCSS, continuous tone-controlled squelch system; ~ **de sortie** *m* IMPRIM, INFORMAT, ORDINAT, PRODUCTION *automatisme industriel* output device; ~ **de sortie de secours** *m* SECURITE escape device; ~ **de stabilisation** *m* TRANSPORT stabilization device; ~ **de stockage** *m* ORDINAT storage device; ~ **de stockage d'énergie** *m* ESPACE *véhicules* energy storage device; ~ **à supraconduction** *m* ELECTRON superconducting device; ~ **de sûreté** *m* CONS MECA safety device, ELECTR *sécurité*, SECURITE guard; ~ **de sûreté télescopique** *m* SECURITE *utilisé avec les raboteuses* telescopic guard; ~ **de surfaçage** *m* CONS MECA facing attachment; ~ **de surveillance** *m* ESSAIS monitor; ~ **de suspension** *m* MINES suspension gear; ~ **de suspension de liner** *m* PETR casing hanger, liner hanger; ~ **de suspension pour tubage perdu** *m* PETR liner hanger; ~ **de suspension de tubage** *m* PETR casing hanger;

~ t ~ **de télécommande** *m* ENREGISTR remote control device; ~ **de téléréunion** *m* TELECOM meet-me bridge; ~ **à temps de transit** *m* ELECTROTEC transit-time device; ~ **de tension** *m* TEXTILE tension device, tensioner; ~ **terminal de déclenchement** *m* NUCLEAIRE final trip assembly, trip logic signalconverter; ~ **test d'accrochage** *m* TEXTILE batt anchorage testing device; ~ **de thermosoudage** *m* EMBALLAGE heat-sealing device; ~ **de traitement de signal** *m* TV SP, signal processor; ~ **de traitement des signaux** *m* TELECOM signal processor; ~ **de transfert à la chaîne** *m* ELECTROTEC, TELECOM BBD, bucket brigade device; ~ **à transfert de charges** *m* *(DTC)* ELECTROTEC, ESPACE *véhicules*, PHYSIQUE, TELECOM charge transfer device *(CTD)*; ~ **transistorisé** *m* ELECTRON solid-state device;

~ v ~ **de verrouillage** *m* CONS MECA, ELECTR *sécurité* locking device, PRODUCTION locking attachment; ~ **de verrouillage de diabolo train avant** *m* AERONAUT nose gear steer lock; ~ **de verrouillage du dos** *m* PHOTO back cover release; ~ **de verrouillage de pas** *m* AERONAUT pitch-locking system; ~ **de verrouillage pour portes coupe-feu** *m* SECURITE locking device for fire-resisting doors; ~ **de vigilance** *m* CH DE FER vigilance device; ~ **de vissage** *m* NUCLEAIRE screwing device

dispositif-extracteur: ~ **de poussière** *m* EMBALLAGE dust exhausting device

dispositifs: ~ **de copiage pour tours** *m pl* CONS MECA copying attachments for lathes; ~ **de mines** *m pl* MINES dead-work, development work; ~ **de protection des oreilles** *m pl* SECURITE ear protectors; ~ **à reproduire pour fraiseuses** *m pl* CONS MECA copying attachments for milling machines

disposition *f* CONS MECA arrangement, ELECTR *circuit*, INFORMAT *schéma*, ORDINAT *scheme* layout; ~ **des composants** *f* ELECTRON component layout; ~ **des contacts** *f* ELECTROTEC contact arrangement; ~ **en nappe** *f* ELECTR *configuration de câble* flat formation; ~ **en trèfle** *f* ELECTR *configuration de câble* trefoil formation; ~ **parallèle** *f* ELECTROTEC parallel lay

disproportionnement *m* CHIMIE disproportionation

disque *m* ACOUSTIQUE record, CH DE FER disc signal (BrE), disk signal (AmE), CONS MECA *d'excentrique* disc (BrE), disk (AmE), sheave, ENREGISTR disc (BrE), disk (AmE), record, INFORMAT, ORDINAT disk, TEXTILE flange, TV disc (BrE), disk (AmE); ~ **abrasif** *m* CONS MECA abrasive disc (BrE), abrasive disk (AmE); ~ **abrasif en fibre vulcanisée** *m* CONS MECA vulcanized fiber disk (AmE), vulcanized fibre disc (BrE); ~ **d'accouplement** *m* VEHICULES *embrayage automatique* clutch plate; ~ **d'accrétion** *m* ASTRONOMIE accretion disc (BrE), accretion disk (AmE); ~ **adhésif** *m* EMBALLAGE adhesive disc (BrE), adhesive disk (AmE); ~ **d'Airy** *m* PHYSIQUE Airy disc (BrE), Airy disk (AmE); ~ **amorçable** *m* PRODUCTION *automatisme industriel* bootable disc (BrE), bootable disk (AmE); ~ **amovible** *m* INFORMAT, ORDINAT exchangeable disk, removable disk; ~ **d'analyse à hélices multiples** *m* TV multispiral scanning disc (BrE), multispiral scanning disk (AmE); ~ **aplati des étoiles** *m* ASTRONOMIE flattened disc of stars (BrE), flattened disk of stars (AmE); ~ **d'appui** *m* CONS MECA bearing plate;

~ **d'arrêt** *m* (Fra) CH DE FER stop signal disc shunting (BrE), stop signal disk shunting (AmE); ~ **arrière** *m* REFRIG impeller backplate; ~ **audionumérique** *m* OPTIQUE audio compact disc (BrE), audio compact disk (AmE), compact audio disc (BrE), compact audio disk (AmE), compact music disc (BrE), compact music disk (AmE), ORDINAT CD, compact disk; ~ **capacitif** *m* OPTIQUE capacitance disc (BrE), capacitance disk (AmE); ~ **compact** *m* ENREGISTR CD, compact disc (BrE), compact disk (AmE), INFORMAT CD, compact disk, OPTIQUE CD, compact disc (BrE), compact disk (AmE), ORDINAT CD, compact disk; ~ **compact audio** *m* OPTIQUE CD audio disc (BrE), CD audio disk (AmE), audio compact disc (BrE), audio compact disk (AmE), compact audio disc (BrE), compact audio disk (AmE), compact music disc (BrE), compact music disk (AmE); ~ **compact audio-numérique** *m* OPTIQUE CD audio disc (BrE), CD audio disk (AmE), audio compact disc (BrE), audio compact disk (AmE), compact audio disc (BrE), compact audio disk (AmE), compact music disc (BrE), compact music disk (AmE); ~ **compact interactif** *m* OPTIQUE CD-I, compact disc-interactive (BrE), compact disk-interactive (AmE), interactive compact disc (BrE), interactive compact disk (AmE); ~ **compact ROM** *m* *(CD-ROM)* INFORMAT compact disk-read only memory *(CD-ROM)*, OPTIQUE compact disc-read only memory (BrE), compact disk-read only memory (AmE) *(CD-ROM)*, ORDINAT compact disk-read only memory *(CD-ROM)*; ~ **double face** *m* INFORMAT double-sided disk, OPTIQUE two-sided disc (BrE), two-sided disk (AmE); ~ **dur** *m* INFORMAT, ORDINAT hard disk, TELECOM hard disc (BrE), hard disk (AmE); ~ **électrostatique** *m* *(disque VHD)* OPTIQUE video high-density disc (BrE), video high-density disk (AmE); ~ **d'embrayage** *m* AUTO clutch disc (BrE), clutch disk (AmE), VEHICULES clutch disc (BrE), clutch disk (AmE), clutch plate, driven plate; ~ **en buffle** *m* PRODUCTION buff wheel; ~ **en drap** *m* PRODUCTION calico mop, rag wheel; ~ **d'enregistrement** *m* ENREGISTR recording disc (BrE), recording disk (AmE); ~ **en sisal** *m* CONS MECA *polissage* sisal wheel; ~ **d'entraînement** *m* CONS MECA driving disc (BrE), driving disk (AmE); ~ **étalon** *m* ENREGISTR test record; ~ **étalon de recuisson** *m* CERAM VER strain disc (BrE), strain disk (AmE); ~ **d'excentrique** *m* CONS MECA eccentric disc (BrE), eccentric disk (AmE), eccentric sheave; ~ **explorateur** *m* TV *pour enregistrement héli-coïdal* drum scanner; ~ **de Faraday** *m* PHYSIQUE Faraday's disc (BrE), Faraday's disk (AmE); ~ **fil-treur** *m* GENIE CHIM filter frame; ~ **fixe** *m* INFORMAT, ORDINAT fixed disk; ~ **de frein** *m* MECANIQUE, VEHICULES *système de freinage* brake disc (BrE), brake disk (AmE); ~ **de fréquence** *m* ENREGISTR frequency record; ~ **de fréquences à bande de tonalité** *m* ENREGISTR tone-band frequency record; ~ **à gravure directe** *m* OPTIQUE direct disc (BrE), direct disk (AmE); ~ **imprimant** *m* IMPRIM printing disc (BrE), printing disk (AmE); ~ **d'initiation** *m* PRODUCTION tutorial disc (BrE), tutorial disk (AmE); ~ **inscriptible une seule fois** *m* OPTIQUE, ORDINAT WORM, write-once read many times; ~ **interactif** *m* OPTIQUE interactive disc (BrE), interactive disk (AmE); ~ **isolant** *m* ELECTR, ELECTROTEC insulating washer; ~ **de lacunes** *m* METALL vacancy disc (BrE), vacancy disk (AmE); ~ **laser** *m* OPTIQUE laser disc (BrE), laser disk (AmE); ~ **laser-**

vision *m* OPTIQUE LV disc (BrE), LV disk (AmE), laservision disc (BrE), laservision disk (AmE), laser-vision videodisc (BrE), laservision videodisk (AmE); ~ **à lecture laser** *m* OPTIQUE laser disc (BrE), laser disk (AmE); ~ **linéaire** *m* OPTIQUE linear disc (BrE), linear disk (AmE); ~ **longue durée** *m* ENREGISTR long-playing record; ~ **magnétique** *m* ELECTR, ELECTROTEC, ENREGISTR magnetic disc (BrE), magnetic disk (AmE), INFORMAT magnetic disk; ~ **magnéto-optique** *m* ENREGISTR magneto-optical disc (BrE), magneto-optical disk (AmE), INFORMAT magneto-optical disk, OPTIQUE m-o disc (BrE), m-o disk (AmE), magneto-optical disc (BrE), magneto-optical disk (AmE); ~ **magnétoscopique** *m* ENREGISTR, OPTIQUE m-o disc (BrE), m-o disk (AmE), magneto-optical disc (BrE), magneto-optical disk (AmE); ~ **matrice** *m* OPTIQUE master disc (BrE), master disk (AmE); ~ **menant d'embrayage** *m* VEHICULES clutch drive plate; ~ **mené** *m* CONS MECA driven disc (BrE), driven disk (AmE); ~ **mère métallique** *m* ENREGISTR metal master; ~ **de mesure** *m* ACOUSTIQUE test record; ~ **microsillon** *m* ENREGISTR long-playing record, microgroove record; ~ **monoface** *m* OPTIQUE single-sided disc (BrE), single-sided disk (AmE); ~ **monoral** *m* ENREGISTR monaural record; ~ **moteur d'embrayage** *m* VEHICULES clutch drive plate; ~ **moulé** *m* ACOUSTIQUE processed disc (BrE), processed disk (AmE); ~ **non inscriptible** *m* OPTIQUE, ORDINAT read-only disc (BrE), read-only disk (AmE); ~ **optique** *m* ENREGISTR, INFORMAT, OPTIQUE, ORDINAT optical disc (BrE), optical disk (AmE); ~ **optique effaçable** *m* OPTIQUE erasable optical disc (BrE), erasable optical disk (AmE); ~ **optique inscriptible** *m* OPTIQUE recordable optical disc (BrE), recordable optical disk (AmE), writable optical disc (BrE), writable optical disk (AmE); ~ **optique magnétique** *m* INFORMAT magneto-optical disk; ~ **optique non effaçable** *m* *(DON)* INFORMAT write-once optical disk *(WOOD)*; ~ **optique non-réinscriptible** *m* INFORMAT write-once optical disk (WOOD); ~ **optique numérique** *m* INFORMAT *(DON)* digital optical disk, OPTIQUE optical data disc (BrE), optical data disk (AmE), optical digital data disc (BrE), optical digital data disk (AmE), OPTIQUE *(DON)* digital optical disc (BrE), digital optical disk (AmE), ORDINAT *(DON)* digital optical disk; ~ **optique numérique inscriptible** *m* ORDINAT write-once disk; ~ **optique numérique inscriptible une seule fois** *m* OPTIQUE write-once data disc (BrE), write-once data disk (AmE); ~ **optique numérique non effaçable** *m* OPTIQUE nonerasable data disc (BrE), nonerasable data disk (AmE), write-once data disc (BrE), write-once data disk (AmE), write-once disc (BrE), write-once disk (AmE), ORDINAT write-once disk; ~ **optique réinscriptible** *m* OPTIQUE erasable optical disc (BrE); ~ **optique réutilisable** *m* OPTIQUE erasable optical disc (BrE), erasable optical disk (AmE), reusable optical disc (BrE), reusable optical disk (AmE); ~ **optique vidéo** *m* OPTIQUE laser optic disc (BrE), laser optic disk (AmE), optical vide-odisc (BrE), optical videodisk (AmE), TV laser disc (BrE), laser disk (AmE); ~ **original** *m* ACOUSTIQUE original disc (BrE), original disk (AmE), INFORMAT master disk; ~ **à polir** *m* CONS MECA, METALL polishing wheel, PRODUCTION buffing wheel; ~ **de polissage** *m* METALL polishing wheel; ~ **porte-filtres** *m* IMPRIM *photogravure* filter turret; ~ **porte-têtes** *m* TV drum, head wheel; ~ **45 tours** *m* ENREGISTR forty-five rpm record; ~ **de ralenti** *m* TV slow-motion disc (BrE), slow-motion disk (AmE); ~ **de Rayleigh** *m* ACOUSTIQUE Rayleigh disc (BrE), Rayleigh disk (AmE); ~ **réflecteur** *m* OPTIQUE reflective disc (BrE), reflective disk (AmE); ~ **rotor** *m* AERONAUT *hélicoptère* rotor disc (BrE), rotor disk (AmE); ~ **rouge** *m* (Fra) CH DE FER semipermissive stop signal; ~ **de rupture** *m* MECANIQUE bursting disk; ~ **simple face** *m* INFORMAT single-sided disk; ~ **souple** *m* INFORMAT, ORDINAT flexible disk, floppy disk; ~ **stéréophonique** *m* ENREGISTR stereophonic record; ~ **sustentateur** *m* AERONAUT actuator disc (BrE), actuator disk (AmE); ~ **synchrone** *m* OPTIQUE synchronous videodisc (BrE), synchronous videodisk (AmE); ~ **système** *m* INFORMAT, ORDINAT system disk; ~ **de test** *m* ENREGISTR test record; ~ **à trancher** *m* CERAM VER slitting disc (BrE), slitting disk (AmE); ~ **transparent** *m* OPTIQUE transmissive disc (BrE), transmissive disk (AmE), transparent disc (BrE), transparent disk (AmE); ~ **verni** *m* ACOUSTIQUE lacquer disc (BrE), lacquer disk (AmE); ~ **VHD** *m (disque électrostatique)* OPTIQUE VHD *(video high-density disc)*; ~ **vidéo longue durée** *m* OPTIQUE VLP, video long play; ~ **à vitesse angulaire constante** *m* OPTIQUE CAV disc (BrE), CAV disk (AmE), constant angular velocity disc (BrE), constant angular velocity disk (AmE); ~ **à vitesse linéaire constante** *m* OPTIQUE constant linear velocity disc (BrE), constant linear velocity disk (AmE); ~ **Winchester** *m* INFORMAT, ORDINAT Winchester disk

disques: ~ **circumstellaires** *m pl* ASTRONOMIE *de protoétoiles* circumstellar discs (BrE), circumstellar disks (AmE)

disque-scie *m* CONS MECA circular saw

disquette *f* INFORMAT, ORDINAT, TELECOM diskette, floppy disk; ~ **double face** *f* ORDINAT double-sided disk; ~ **à secteurs définis par programme** *f* ORDINAT soft-sectored disk; ~ **à sectorisation logicielle** *f* INFORMAT soft-sectored disk; ~ **simple face** *f* ORDINAT single-sided disk

disqueuse *f* CONS MECA disc sander (BrE), disk sander (AmE)

disruptif *adj* ELECTROTEC disruptive, PHYSIQUE breakdown

dissection *f* GEOMETRIE dissection

dissimulation: ~ **d'information** *f* ORDINAT information-hiding

dissipateur: ~ **de chaleur** *m* ELECTR *diode Zener*, THERMODYN heat sink; ~ **d'énergie** *m* HYDROLOGIE energy dissipator

dissipation *f* ELECTROTEC dissipation; ~ **de chaleur** *f* THERMODYN heat dissipation; ~ **d'énergie** *f* PHYS RAYON *thermodynamique* dissipation; ~ **de puissance** *f* PRODUCTION *automatisme industriel* power dissipation

dissociable *adj* CHIMIE dissociable

dissociation *f* CHARBON, CHIMIE dissociation, MECANIQUE *procédé* breaking-up; ~ **de gaz** *f* GAZ gas dissociation; ~ **thermique** *f* THERMODYN thermolysis

dissocié *adj* GAZ dissociated

dissocier: se ~ *v réfl* CHIMIE dissociate

dissolubilité *f* CHIMIE dissolubility, dissolubleness

dissolution *f* CHIMIE dissolution, dissolving, solution, GENIE CHIM dissolution, dissolving, MATERIAUX dissolution; ~ **sursaturée** *f* CHIMIE supersaturated solution

dissolvant *m* AGRO ALIM, CHIMIE, CINEMAT solvent, GENIE CHIM dissolvent, dissolver, LESSIVES solvent, PAPIER dissolvent

dissonance *f* ACOUSTIQUE, PHYS ONDES dissonance

dissoudre[1] *vt* CHIMIE, CINEMAT, GAZ dissolve, THERMODYN melt

dissoudre[2] *vi* GENIE CHIM dissolve away, dissolve out

dissous *adj* CHIMIE dissolved, GENIE CHIM dissolute; ~ **en solution** *adj* CHIMIE solute

dissymétrie *f* GEOMETRIE dissymmetry, MATH asymmetry

dissymétrique *adj* ESPACE *communications* unbalanced, GEOMETRIE dissymmetric, dissymmetrical, RESSORTS asymmetrical

distance[1] **à** ~ *adj* ORDINAT remote

distance[2] *f* CH DE FER block headway, train spacing, ELECTRON, MILITAIRE, NAUT *navigation* range, PHYSIQUE distance; ~ **d'accélération-arrêt** *f* AERONAUT accelerate-stop distance; ~ **d'arrêt** *f* AUTO braking distance; ~ **d'arrêt du véhicule** *f* TRANSPORT braking distance; ~ **d'atterrissage** *f* AERONAUT landing distance; ~ **d'avertissement** *f* CH DE FER presignaling distance (AmE), presignalling distance (BrE), warning distance; ~ **des centres** *f* CONS MECA center distance (AmE), centre distance (BrE), distance between centers (AmE), distance between centres (BrE); ~ **des centres d'une roue d'engrenage et d'un pignon** *f* CONS MECA distance between centers of gear wheel and pinion (AmE), distance between centres of gear wheel and pinion (BrE); ~ **critique** *f* PETR critical distance; ~ **de décollage** *f* AERONAUT takeoff run; ~ **disruptive** *f* ELECTROTEC sparking distance; ~ **entre contacts** *f* ELECTROTEC gap; ~ **entre deux cahiers sortant de la rotative** *f* IMPRIM shingle distance; ~ **entre pointes** *f* CONS MECA distance between centers (AmE), distance between centres (BrE); ~ **entre les signaux** *f* TRANSPORT signaling distance (AmE), signalling distance (BrE); ~ **des faces d'une faille** *f* GEOLOGIE lateral separation; ~ **focale** *f* PHOTO, PHYSIQUE focal length; ~ **focale de lentille électronique** *f* TV focal time; ~ **de formation d'une rafale** *f* AERONAUT gust gradient distance; ~ **franchissable** *f* AERONAUT *performance d'avion* range; ~ **de freinage** *f* TRANSPORT braking distance less brake lag distance; ~ **de Hamming** *f* TELECOM Hamming distance; ~ **d'horizon** *f* ASTRONOMIE horizon distance; ~ **intercanal** *f* INFORMAT, ORDINAT channel spacing; ~ **interparticulaire** *f* METALL interparticle spacing; ~ **d'isolement** *f* ELECTROTEC insulation distance; ~ **métacentrique** *f* NAUT metacentric height; ~ **minimale de croisement** *f* NAUT closest approach distance; ~ **de mise au point minimum** *f* CINEMAT minimum-focusing distance; ~ **nécessaire au décollage** *f* AERONAUT takeoff distance required; ~ **nécessaire pour l'accélération-arrêt** *f* AERONAUT accelerate-stop distance required; ~ **nominale de détection** *f* PRODUCTION *automatisme industriel* rated sensing distance; ~ **d'ouverture** *f* ELECTROTEC break distance; ~ **parcourue** *f* NAUT distance logged, distance run; ~ **de plané** *f* AERONAUT gliding distance; ~ **de prise de vues** *f* PHOTO shooting distance; ~ **de projection** *f* CINEMAT throw; ~ **de réutilisation des fréquences dans une même voie** *f* TELECOM co-channel reuse distance; ~ **de saut** *f* PHYS ONDES *onde hertzienne réfléchie* skip distance; ~ **de sécurité** *f* TRANSPORT safe headway, safety headway; ~ **à travailler** *f* METALL working distance; ~ **utilisable à l'atterrissage** *f* AERONAUT landing distance available;

~ **utilisable au décollage** *f* AERONAUT takeoff distance available; ~ **utilisable pour l'accélération-arrêt** *f* AERO-NAUT accelerate-stop distance available; ~ **verticale** *f* PRODUCTION vertical separation; ~ **de visibilité** *f* TRANSPORT sight distance, visibility distance; ~ **de visibilité d'arrêt** *f* TRANSPORT stopping sight distance; ~ **de visibilité de dépassement** *f* CONSTR sight distance; ~ **zénithale** *f* ASTRONOMIE zenith distance, ESPACE co-altitude, *astronomie* zenith distance

distant *adj* ORDINAT remote

disthène *m* MINERAUX cyanite, disthene, kyanite

distillat *m* CHIMIE, MATERIAUX distillation, PETROLE, THERMODYN distillate, distillation; ~ **moyen** *m* PE-TROLE middle distillate; ~ **de tête** *m* PETROLE LDF, light distillate feedstock

distillateur *m* GENIE CHIM distiller, NAUT freshwater con-denser; ~ **d'alcool** *m* AGRO ALIM still

distillation *f* CHIMIE distillate, distillation, MATERIAUX, PETROLE, THERMODYN distillation; ~ **azéotrope** *f* AGRO ALIM azeotropic distillation; ~ **dans le vide** *f* CHIMIE, PHYSIQUE vacuum distillation; ~ **à détentes multiples** *f* THERMODYN flash distillation; ~ **discontinue** *f* NU-CLEAIRE batch distillation; ~ **droite** *f* GENIE CHIM, THERMODYN distillation by ascent; ~ **éclair** *f* CHIMIE flash distillation; ~ **extractive** *f* AGRO ALIM extractive distillation; ~ **flash** *f* AGRO ALIM, THERMODYN flash distillation; ~ **fractionnée** *f* GENIE CHIM, PETROLE *raffinage* fractional distillation; ~ **instantanée** *f* DISTRI EAU flash distillation; ~ **par entraînement à la vapeur** *f* GENIE CHIM distillation by steam entraining; ~ **par extraction** *f* AGRO ALIM extractive distillation; ~ **sèche** *f* CHIMIE dry distillation; ~ **solaire** *f* EN RENOUV solar distillation; ~ **sous vide** *f* AGRO ALIM, GENIE CHIM vacuum distillation; ~ **à la vapeur** *f* CHIMIE steam distillation; ~ **vers le bas** *f* GENIE CHIM, THERMODYN distillation by descent

distillats: ~ **légers** *m pl* PETROLE light distillates, light fractions; ~ **moyens** *m pl* PETROLE medium distillates

distillé *adj* CHIMIE, HYDROLOGIE, VEHICULES distilled

distiller[1] *vt* CHIMIE distil (BrE), distill (AmE), GENIE CHIM distil off (BrE), distill off (AmE)

distiller[2] *vi* THERMODYN distil (BrE), distill (AmE); ~ **à la vapeur** *vi* CHIMIE steam distil (BrE), steam distill (AmE)

distiller:[3] **se** ~ *v réfl* CHIMIE distil (BrE), distill (AmE)

distillerie *f* AGRO ALIM, GENIE CHIM distillery

distorsion *f* ACOUSTIQUE distortion, CONS MECA buckle, buckling, ELECTR, ELECTRON, ENREGISTR, MATERIAUX distortion, MECANIQUE deformation, PHYSIQUE, PLAST CAOU *physique*, TELECOM, TV distortion; ~ **d'affaiblissement** *f* ELECTRON attenuation distortion, PHYSIQUE attenuation distortion, frequency distortion; ~ **d'amplitude** *f* ELECTRON amplitude distortion, amplitude-amplitude distortion, ENREGISTR, PHYS ONDES, PHYSIQUE, TELECOM amplitude distortion; ~ **amplitude-fréquence** *f* ELECTRON amplitude-frequency distortion; ~ **d'amplitude non linéaire** *f* ENREGISTR amplitude frequency distortion; ~ **angulaire** *f* CINEMAT angular distortion; ~ **d'atténuation** *f* ENREGISTR attenuation distortion; ~ **d'azimut** *f* TV azimuth distortion; ~ **de centrage** *f* ENREGISTR track-ing distortion; ~ **de contact** *f* ACOUSTIQUE tracing distortion; ~ **de crête** *f* TV peak distortion; ~ **cubique** *f* METALL cubical distortion; ~ **de demi-teintes** *f* TV gamma error; ~ **due à l'écho** *f* ELECTRON echo distor-tion; ~ **dynamique** *f* ACOUSTIQUE dynamic distortion;

~ **en arête de hareng** *f* CERAM VER herringbone distor-tion; ~ **en barillet** *f* CINEMAT barrel distortion, positive distortion, PHOTO, PHYSIQUE barrel distortion; ~ **en courant continu** *f* NUCLEAIRE direct current distortion; ~ **en coussin** *f* PHYSIQUE pincushion distortion; ~ **en coussinet** *f* CINEMAT cushion distortion, pillow distor-tion, pincushion distortion, PHOTO, TV pincushion distortion; ~ **en S** *f* TV S-distortion; ~ **en trapèze** *f* ELECTRON keystone distortion; ~ **de fréquence** *f* EN-REGISTR frequency distortion; ~ **harmonique** *f* ELECTRON, MATERIAUX, TELECOM harmonic distor-tion; ~ **harmonique en enregistrement-lecture** *f* ENREGISTR recording-reproducing harmonic distor-tion; ~ **de l'image** *f* TV flagging; ~ **d'intermodulation** *f* ELECTRON, ENREGISTR intermodulation distortion; ~ **intramodale** *f* OPTIQUE chromatic distortion, intramo-dal distortion, TELECOM intramodal distortion; ~ **linéaire** *f* CINEMAT, ENREGISTR, TELECOM linear distor-tion; ~ **linéaire de phase** *f* ESPACE *communications* group delay linear distortion; ~ **de linéarité** *f* TV li-nearity error; ~ **modale** *f* OPTIQUE modal dispersion, TELECOM intermodal distortion, modal distortion, mode distortion, multimode distortion; ~ **non-li-néaire** *f* ELECTRON delay distortion, nonlinear distortion, nonlinear distortion, ENREGISTR, TELECOM nonlinear distortion; ~ **non-linéaire de phase** *f* ESPACE *communications* phase non-linear distortion; ~ **op-tique** *f* CERAM VER optical distortion; ~ **d'ouverture** *f* ELECTRON aperture distortion; ~ **par dispersion** *f* OP-TIQUE intramodal distortion, TELECOM chromatic distortion; ~ **par harmonique deux** *f* ELECTRON second harmonic distortion; ~ **par harmonique trois** *f* ELEC-TRON third harmonic distortion; ~ **de phase** *f* ELECTRON delay distortion, phase distortion, ENREG-ISTR delay distortion, PHYSIQUE, TELECOM, TV phase distortion; ~ **de quantification** *f* ELECTRON quantiza-tion distortion; ~ **de recoupement** *f* ENREGISTR crossover distortion; ~ **du signal** *f* ELECTRON, TELECOM signal distortion; ~ **du son** *f* ENREGISTR sound distor-tion; ~ **sphérique** *f* CINEMAT spherical distortion; ~ **de suroscillation** *f* TV overshoot distortion; ~ **tangentielle** *f* MATERIAUX tangential distortion; ~ **de temps de groupe** *f* ESPACE *communications* envelope delay dis-tortion; ~ **du temps de propagation** *f* ELECTRON, TV delay distortion; ~ **du temps de retard** *f* ELECTRON time-delay distortion; ~ **du temps de transit** *f* TV delay distortion; ~ **du temps de transit de groupe** *f* ELEC-TRON delay distortion; ~ **de transitoire** *f* ENREGISTR transient distortion; ~ **trapézoïdale** *f* CINEMAT key-stone distortion, ELECTRON keystone distortion, trapezoidal distortion

distorsions: ~ **géométriques** *f pl* TV geometric error

distribué *adj* INFORMAT, ORDINAT, TELECOM distributed

distribuer *vt* CINEMAT release

distributeur *m* AGRO ALIM dispenser, CERAM VER feeder, CONS MECA distributor, ignition distributor, EMBAL-LAGE dispenser, distributor, EQUIP LAB *analyse* dispenser, INST HYDR slide valve, valve, MECANIQUE distributor, PAPIER distributor, flow distributor, spreader, PRODUCTION *système hydraulique* direc-tional control valve, VEHICULES *allumage* distributor; ~ **d'allumage** *m* AUTO ignition distributor; ~ **analyseur** *m* TELECOM scanner distributor; ~ **d'appel** *m* TELECOM call distributor; ~ **automatique** *m* CONS MECA slot machine; ~ **automatique d'appels** *m* TELECOM ACD, automatic call distributor; ~ **automatique de billets** *m*

TRANSPORT ticket machine, ticket slot machine; ~ **à boisseau** *m* INST HYDR rotary valve; ~ **de boissons** *m* REFRIG beverage dispenser; ~ **de buse chaude** *m* CONS MECA hot runner manifold; ~ **de câble** *m* ELECTROTEC cable distributor; ~ **de commande** *m* INST HYDR control valve; ~ **d'eau** *m* POLLUTION water supplier; ~ **équilibré** *m* CONS MECA balanced slide valve; ~ **d'essence** *m* VEHICULES *carburant* gas pump (AmE), gasoline pump (AmE), petrol pump (BrE); ~ **d'étiquettes** *m* EMBALLAGE label dispenser; ~ **de frigorigène** *m* REFRIG refrigerant distributor; ~ **glissant à robinets** *m* PRODUCTION swinging valve; ~ **lent** *m* TELECOM signal distributor; ~ **oscillant** *m* PRODUCTION swinging valve; ~ **quadruple de freins** *m* AERONAUT landing gear master brake cylinder, master cylinder; ~ **à quatre orifices** *m* CONS MECA four-port directional control valve; ~ **rapide** *m* TELECOM central pulse distributor; ~ **rotatif** *m* CONS MECA rotary feeder, VEHICULES *moteur à deux-temps* rotary disc valve (BrE), rotary disk valve (AmE); ~ **de servodyne** *m* AERONAUT actuator control valve; ~ **à tambour alvéolé** *m* PAPIER airlock feeder; ~ **à tambour cylindrique** *m* CONS MECA rotary drum feeder; ~ **à tiroir** *m* INST HYDR slide, slide valve; ~ **à tiroir coulissant** *m* INST HYDR circular slide valve, slide valve; ~ **à tiroir rotatif** *m* INST HYDR circular slide valve, slide valve; ~ **tournant** *m* PRODUCTION swinging valve; ~ **à trois voies** *m* INST HYDR switch valve, three-way valve; ~ **de turbine** *m* INST HYDR guide ring; ~ **de vapeur** *m* INST HYDR steam valve, *commandé par expansion d'un fluide* valve gear

distributeurs: ~ **et transporteurs vibrants** *m pl* CONS MECA vibrating feeders and conveyors

distribution *f* AUTO timing, CONS MECA link gear, link motion, link valve motion, ELECTR *alimentation*, GAZ distribution, INST HYDR valve gear, valve motion, *série d'opérations* distribution, MATH frequency distribution, VEHICULES *allumage* distribution, *allumage, soupapes* timing; ~ **de l'alimentation** *f* PRODUCTION *automatisme industriel* power distribution; ~ **d'amplitude de bruit** *f* TELECOM NAD, noise amplitude distribution; ~ **arborescente** *f* TELECOM tree distribution; ~ **binomiale** *f* PHYSIQUE binomial distribution; ~ **de Bose-Einstein** *f* PHYSIQUE Bose-Einstein distribution; ~ **canonique** *f* PHYSIQUE canonical distribution; ~ **Compton** *f* PHYS RAYON Compton continuum; ~ **à coulisse** *f* CONS MECA link gear, link motion, link valve motion; ~ **de courant** *f* ELECTR current distribution; ~ **à déclic** *f* CONS MECA trip valve gear; ~ **de densité électronique** *f* CRISTALL electron density distribution; ~ **d'eau** *f* CONSTR water distribution, DISTRI EAU water distribution, water supply; ~ **d'eau potable** *f* HYDROLOGIE drinking water supply; ~ **d'électricité** *f* ELECTR *réseau* power supply; ~ **de l'encre par la racle** *f* IMPRIM *hélioflexo* metering; ~ **de l'encre par des rouleaux distributeurs** *f* IMPRIM metering; ~ **de l'encre sur la forme imprimante** *f* IMPRIM *impression* ink lay-down; ~ **en énergie transversale** *f* PHYS RAYON transverse energy distribution; ~ **d'énergie électrique** *f* ELECTR *réseau* electricity distribution; ~ **en étoile** *f* TELECOM star distribution; ~ **exponentielle** *f* ORDINAT exponential distribution; ~ **de Fermi-Dirac** *f* PHYSIQUE Fermi-Dirac distribution; ~ **de fréquences** *f* INFORMAT, ORDINAT frequency distribution; ~ **de Gauss** *f* ENREGISTR Gaussian distribution, PHYSIQUE Gaussian distribution, normal distribution; ~ **gaussienne** *f* ORDINAT Gaussian distribution; ~ **géographique** *f*

POLLUTION spatial distribution; ~ **granulométrique** *f* CONSTR particle size distribution; ~ **au hasard** *f* METALL random distribution; ~ **d'intensité** *f* CRISTALL intensity distribution; ~ **Joy** *f* INST HYDR Joy's valvegear; ~ **de Maxwell** *f* PHYSIQUE Maxwell distribution; ~ **normale** *f* ORDINAT normal distribution, PHYSIQUE Gaussian distribution, normal distribution; ~ **par chaîne et roues dentées** *f* AUTO sprocket and chain timing; ~ **par courroie crantée** *f* AUTO cogged belt timing, notched belt timing; ~ **par soupapes** *f* INST HYDR poppet valve gear; ~ **par système d'Allan** *f* CONS MECA Allan's link motion; ~ **des phases** *f* METALL phase distribution; ~ **de Poisson** *f* INFORMAT, ORDINAT, PHYSIQUE Poisson distribution; ~ **de probabilité des amplitudes** *f* TELECOM APD, amplitude probability distribution; ~ **à programme variable** *f* TRANSPORT variable valve timing; ~ **quasi-état-fermé** *f* METALL quasi-steady state distribution; ~ **radiale de puissance** *f* NUCLEAIRE radial power distribution; ~ **à soupape** *f* INST HYDR poppet valve gear; ~ **spatiale** *f* POLLUTION spatial distribution; ~ **spectrale d'énergie** *f* EN RENOUV spectral energy distribution; ~ **à tiroir** *f* INST HYDR slide valve gear

distributrice *f* EMBALLAGE dispensing machine

district: ~ **aurifère** *m* MINES gold field; ~ **houiller** *m* CHARBON coal field

disulfure *m* CHIMIE disulfide (AmE), disulphide (BrE)

dithiobenzoïque *adj* CHIMIE dithiobenzoic

dithionate *m* CHIMIE dithionate

dithionique *adj* CHIMIE dithionic

diurne *adj* ASTRONOMIE, GEOPHYS, METEO *amplitude* diurnal

divalence *f* CHIMIE divalence

divalent *adj* CHIMIE divalent

divergence *f* NUCLEAIRE divergence, OPTIQUE *d'un faisceau* beam divergence, PHYSIQUE divergence, TELECOM *d'un faisceau* beam divergence, TRANSPORT diverging; ~ **de sortie** *f* TELECOM output divergence; ~ **thermique** *f* ELECTRON thermal blooming

divergent[1] *adj* MATH, OPTIQUE divergent

divergent[2] *m* ESPACE *véhicules spatiaux, propulsion* deviation, divergence, flared section, PHYSIQUE divergent nozzle, PRODUCTION *d'un injecteur* delivery cone, delivery nozzle, delivery tube; ~ **conique** *m* PHYSIQUE exit cone; ~ **à la réception** *m pl* (Fra) *(cf bec)* CERAM VER spout

diverger *vt* NUCLEAIRE *réacteur* go critical

divers *adj* GEOMETRIE *topologie* manifold

diversion: ~ **par imitation de signaux** *f* ELECTRON imitative deception

diversité *f* TELECOM diversity; ~ **de fréquence** *f* TELECOM frequency diversity; ~ **de site** *f* ESPACE *communications* site diversity

divertisseur: ~ **de surtension** *m* ELECTR *ligne* surge diverter

dividende *m* INFORMAT, MATH, ORDINAT dividend

divinyle *m* CHIMIE divinyl

diviser[1] *vt* INFORMAT, ORDINAT divide; ~ **en deux parties égales** *vt* GEOMETRIE bisect

diviser[2] *vti* MATH divide

diviser:[3] **se ~ en lamelles** *v réfl* PAPIER flake

diviseur *m* CHARBON, CINEMAT splitter, ELECTRON divider, INFORMAT divider, divisor, MATH divisor, ORDINAT divider, divisor, TELECOM divider; ~ **audiofréquence** *m* TELECOM audio splitter; ~ **binaire** *m* ELECTRON binary divider; ~ **capacitif** *m* ELECTROTEC capacitive voltage divider; ~ **de courant** *m* ELECTR *circuit* current divider; ~ **de débit** *m* PRODUCTION *système hydraulique* flow divisor; ~ **du faisceau** *m* CINEMAT, OPTIQUE, TV beam splitter; ~ **de fréquence** *m* TELECOM frequency divider; ~ **de fréquence de lignes** *m* TV line divider; ~ **de fréquence de trame** *m* TV field divider; ~ **par deux** *m* ELECTRON binary scaler; ~ **par dix** *m* ELECTRON decade scaler; ~ **de phase** *m* ELECTR *courant alternatif* phase splitter; ~ **de puissance** *m* ELECTR *alimentation*, ELECTROTEC, TELECOM power divider; ~ **de tension** *m* ELECTR, ELECTROTEC voltage divider, PHYSIQUE potential divider, voltage divider, TELECOM, TV voltage divider; ~ **de tension d'ajustement** *m* ELECTR adjustable voltage divider; ~ **de tension capacitif** *m* ELECTROTEC capacitive voltage divider; ~ **de tension par résistance** *m* ELECTR resistive voltage divider; ~ **de tension à résistances** *m* ELECTROTEC resistor voltage divider

divisibilité *f* CH DE FER couplability

divisible *adj* MATH divisible

division *f* CONSTR, INFORMAT, MATH, ORDINAT division, PHYSIQUE *d'amplitude* division, *du front d'onde* division; ~ **d'algorithmes** *f* ORDINAT procedure division; ~ **binaire** *f* ELECTRON binary division; ~ **Cassini** *f* ASTRONOMIE *des anneaux de Saturne* Cassini division; ~ **chromatique** *f* TV chromatic splitting; ~ **du cycle** *f* TRANSPORT cycle split adjustment; ~ **de données** *f* ORDINAT *COBOL* data division; ~ **d'environnement** *f* ORDINAT *COBOL* environment division; ~ **de faisceau** *f* ELECTRON beam splitting; ~ **d'identification** *f* ORDINAT *COBOL* identification division; ~ **de phase** *f* ELECTR *courant alternatif*, ELECTRON phase splitting; ~ **procédure** *f* INFORMAT procedure division; ~ **de traitement** *f* ORDINAT procedure division

DL *abrév (dose létale)* PHYSIQUE, POLLUTION LD *(lethal dose)*

DL50 *abrév (dose létale médiane, dose létale 50%)* NUCLEAIRE, PHYS RAYON, POLLUTION, SECURITE LD50 *(median lethal dose)*

DLM *abrév (dose létale moyenne)* NUCLEAIRE, PHYS RAYON, POLLUTION, SECURITE MLD *(mean lethal dose)*

dock *m* NAUT dock, dock warehouse; ~ **de carénage** *m* NAUT dry dock; ~ **en mer** *m* TRANSPORT offshore dock; ~ **flottant** *m* CONSTR floating dock, NAUT floating dock, wet dock, TRANSPORT pontoon dock; ~ **à immersion** *m* CONSTR floating dock; ~ **sec** *m* CONSTR dry dock

docker *m* NAUT docker (BrE), longshoreman (AmE), stevedore

docteur *m* PLAST CAOU *revêtement* doctor; ~ **à eau** *m* PRODUCTION *industrie du papier* water doctor; ~ **à lame d'air** *m* PAPIER air doctor; ~ **oscillant** *m* PAPIER oscillating doctor

document *m* INFORMAT, ORDINAT document; ~ **administratif en plusieurs parties** *m* IMPRIM *continu* formset; ~ **dactylographié** *m* IMPRIM typescript proof; ~ **duplicata** *m* PHOTO duplicate; ~ **écrit réglementant la sûreté** *m* SECURITE written policy statement on health and safety; ~ **prêt** *m* IMPRIM CRC, camera-ready copy; ~ **source** *m* INFORMAT, ORDINAT source document; ~ **sous-développé** *m* IMPRIM *photogravure* high key document; ~ **surexposé** *m* IMPRIM *photogravure* high key document; ~ **au trait** *m* IMPRIM *photogravure* line copy; ~ **transparent** *m* IMPRIM slide

documentaire *m* CINEMAT documentary

documentariste *m* CINEMAT documentary film-maker

documentation *f* INFORMAT, ORDINAT documentation; ~ **technique des produits** *f* SECURITE technical product documentation; ~ **de vol** *f* AERONAUT flight documentation

documents: ~ **de bord** *m pl* NAUT ship's papers; ~ **d'expédition** *m pl* NAUT shipping documents

dodécaèdre[1] *adj* GEOMETRIE dodecahedral

dodécaèdre[2] *m* GEOMETRIE dodecahedron

dodécagone *m* GEOMETRIE dodecagon

dodécane *m* CHIMIE, LESSIVES dodecane

dodécylbenzène *m* LESSIVES dodecyl benzene

doéglique *adj* CHIMIE *acide* doeglic

doguin *m* CONS MECA dog, driver, lathe carrier, lathe dog, turning carrier

doigt *m* CONS MECA finger, finger bar, trigger, MECANIQUE cog; ~ **absorbant** *m* NUCLEAIRE absorber finger; ~ **d'accrochage** *m* CONS MECA catch; ~ **d'allumeur** *m* VEHICULES distributor arm, rotor arm; ~ **butée** *m* CONS MECA ejector stop piece; ~ **de butée d'affaissement** *m* CONS MECA droop restraining shaft; ~ **de démoulage** *m* CONS MECA *moule pour fonderie sous pression* angle pin; ~ **de distributeur** *m* VEHICULES *allumage* rotor arm; ~ **de distribution** *m* AUTO distributor finger, distributor rotor; ~ **d'encliquetage** *m* CONS MECA click, dog, pawl, ratchet; ~ **d'entraînement** *m* CONS MECA catch pin, drive pin, MECANIQUE dog; ~ **de gant** *m* PETROLE salt column; ~ **de gaut** *m* NUCLEAIRE thimble; ~ **de retenue** *m* CONS MECA finger, finger bar; ~ **de verrouillage** *m* CONS MECA locking pin

doigtier *m* SECURITE finger stall

dolérite *f* GEOLOGIE, PETR diabase (BrE), dolerite (AmE)

dolérophanite *f* MINERAUX dolerophane, dolerophanite

doline *f* DISTRI EAU doline

dolly *m* CINEMAT dolly

doloire *f* CONSTR adze

dolomie *f* GEOLOGIE dolostone, *roche* dolomite, MATERIAUX, MINERAUX dolomite; ~ **calcaire** *f* GEOLOGIE calcareous dolomite, calcitic dolomite; ~ **ferrifère** *f* GEOLOGIE *roche* ferroan dolomite

dolomite *f* CERAM VER, CHIMIE, GEOLOGIE *minéral*, MINERAUX, PETR, PETROLE dolomite

domaine *m* CONSTR area, ELECTRON, PHYSIQUE domain; ~ **d'application** *m* CONS MECA *d'une norme* scope; ~ **côtier** *m* GEOLOGIE *milieu de sédimentation* coastal zone, littoral zone; ~ **de définition d'une fonction** *m* MATH function domain; ~ **de divergence** *m* NUCLEAIRE period range; ~ **élastique** *m* MECANIQUE *matériaux* elastic range; ~ **des fréquences audibles** *m* ACOUSTIQUE audible frequency range; ~ **fréquenciel** *m* ELECTRON frequency domain; ~ **de fusion** *m* THERMODYN melting range; ~ **de gestion** *m* TELECOM MD, management domain; ~ **de gestion privé** *m* TELECOM PRMD, private management domain; ~ **logique** *m* ELECTRON data domain; ~ **magnétique** *m* ELECTROTEC magnetic domain; ~ **minier** *m* MINES mining area; ~ **de mouvement** *m* NUCLEAIRE range of movement; ~ **nominal** *m* NUCLEAIRE rated range; ~ **numérique** *m* ELECTRON digital domain; ~ **paléogéographique** *m* GEOLOGIE palaeogeographic province (BrE), paleogeographic province (AmE); ~ **de réglage** *m* COMMANDE regulating range; ~ **de saturation** *m* ELECTRON saturation region; ~ **spatial** *m* ELECTRON spatial domain; ~ **technique** *m* BREVETS technical field; ~ **de température effective** *m* THERMODYN effective temperature range; ~ **de températures** *m* THERMODYN

temperature range; ~ **des températures critiques** *m*
THERMODYN critical temperature range; ~ **temporel** *m*
ELECTRON time domain; ~ **de tolérance du coeur** *m*
OPTIQUE, TELECOM core tolerance field; ~ **de tolérance
de la gaine** *m* OPTIQUE, TELECOM cladding tolerance
field; ~ **de tolérance de la surface de référence** *m*
OPTIQUE reference surface tolerance field; ~ **de transformation** *m* CERAM VER transformation range; ~ **de
travail** *m* CERAM VER working range; ~ **de vol** *m* AERO-
NAUT flight envelope; ~ **de Weiss** *m* ELECTROTEC
magnetic domain, PHYSIQUE Weiss domain

dôme *m* ASTRONOMIE dome, CERAM VER roof light,
CONSTR, GAZ dome, GEOLOGIE dome, *corps intrusif*
cupola, INST HYDR dome, steam dome, MAT CHAUFF
four cupola, PRODUCTION *d'un fourneau* dome; ~ **d'argile** *m* PETROLE shale dome; ~ **de cuve** *m* NAUT tank
hatch; ~ **de prise de vapeur** *m* INST HYDR dome, steam
dome; ~ **de radar** *m* NAUT radar dome; ~ **de sel** *m*
GEOLOGIE salt dome, PETROLE salt dome, salt pillow; ~
à vapeur *m* INST HYDR dome, steam dome

domeykite *f* MINERAUX domeykite

dominant *adj* ACOUSTIQUE dominant

dominante: ~ **colorée** *f* CINEMAT color cast (AmE),
colour cast (BrE); ~ **de couleur** *f* PHOTO color cast
(AmE), colour cast (BrE)

dommage *m* BREVETS, QUALITE damage; ~ **auditif induit
par le bruit** *m* SECURITE noise-induced hearing impairment; ~ **causé par le feu** *m* QUALITE fire damage; ~
causé par réfrigération *m* REFRIG chilling injury; ~
causé par refroidissement brusque *m* REFRIG chilling
injury

dommages-intérêts *m pl* SECURITE *pour un accident*
compensation

domotique *f* GAZ home automation, ORDINAT IHS, integrated home system

DON: ~ **effaçable** *m* OPTIQUE erasable data disc (BrE),
erasable data disk (AmE); ~ **à enregistrement effaçable** *m* OPTIQUE erasable data disc (BrE), erasable
data disk (AmE); ~ **inscriptible une seule fois** *m* OP-
TIQUE write-once data disc (BrE), write-once data
disk (AmE); ~ **non-effaçable** *m* OPTIQUE write-once
data disc (BrE), write-once data disk (AmE)

DON *abrév* INFORMAT *(disque optique non effaçable)*
WOOD *(write-once optical disk)*, OPTIQUE *(disque
optique numérique)* digital optical disc (BrE), digital
optical disk (AmE)

donnée *f* CHIMIE record, ESSAIS, INFORMAT, ORDINAT
datum; ~ **en puissance** *f* ENREGISTR power rating

données *f pl* ASTRONOMIE, ELECTRON, ESPACE, ESSAIS,
GEOLOGIE, INFORMAT, ORDINAT, QUALITE data; ~ **analogiques** *f pl* ELECTRON analog data (AmE), analogue
data (BrE); ~ **antérieures** *f pl* POLLUTION historical
data; ~ **brutes** *f pl* ELECTRON, INFORMAT, ORDINAT raw
data; ~ **corrigée** *f pl* ORDINAT corrected data; ~ **de
contrôle** *f pl* INFORMAT, ORDINAT control data; ~ **différentielles GPS** *f pl* NAUT differential GPS data; ~
directes *f pl* INFORMAT, ORDINAT immediate data; ~
élaborée *f pl* ORDINAT processed data; ~ **élémentaire** *f
pl* INFORMAT, ORDINAT data item; ~ **d'émission** *f pl*
POLLUTION emission data; ~ **en puissance musicale** *f
pl* ENREGISTR music power rating; ~ **en temps réel** *f pl*
ORDINAT real-time data; ~ **d'entrée** *f pl* INFORMAT,
ORDINAT input data; ~ **d'essai** *f pl* ESSAIS, INFORMAT,
ORDINAT test data; ~ **géométriques** *f pl* CONSTR geometric data; ~ **historiques** *f pl* POLLUTION historical
data; ~ **introduites du compas** *f pl* NAUT compass

input; ~ **lisibles par ordinateur** *f pl* INFORMAT, ORDINAT
machine-readable data; ~ **de masque** *f pl* PRODUCTION
mask data; ~ **météorologiques** *f pl* POLLUTION meteorological data; ~ **numériques** *f pl* ELECTRON digital
data; ~ **numérisées** *f pl* ELECTRON, TELECOM digitized
data; ~ **de plan de vol** *f pl* AERONAUT flight plan data; ~
relatives aux pas *f pl* PRODUCTION *automatisme industriel* step data; ~ **de sortie** *f pl* INFORMAT, ORDINAT
output data; ~ **statistiques** *f pl* INFORMAT, ORDINAT
statistical data; ~ **techniques** *f pl* PRODUCTION engineering data; ~ **de test** *f pl* INFORMAT test data; ~
utilisateur-N *f pl* TELECOM N-user data; ~ **de vol** *f pl*
AERONAUT flight data

donner[1] *vt* PRODUCTION return

donner[2] *vi* MINES squeeze; ~ **l'alarme** *vi* SECURITE give the
alarm; ~ **de l'arc à** *vi* NAUT hog; ~ **de la bande** *vi* NAUT
heel; ~ **le bon à tirer** *vi* IMPRIM pass; ~ **une chasse à** *vi*
DISTRI EAU flush; ~ **la couche d'impression** *vi* COU-
LEURS prime; ~ **le départ** *vi* CINEMAT cue; ~ **à fret** *vi*
NAUT freight; ~ **du fruit à** *vi* CONSTR batter; ~ **du jeu** *vi*
NAUT *à une corde* loosen; ~ **du mou** *vi* NAUT *à une corde*
loosen; ~ **les tendances** *vi* TEXTILE give directions; ~ **de
la voie à** *vi* CONS MECA set, PRODUCTION *une scie* jump

donneur *m* CHIMIE *atome*, ELECTRON, ORDINAT *fabrication de puces* donor; ~ **d'une licence** *m* BREVETS
licenser

dopage *m* ELECTRON, MATERIAUX, PHYSIQUE, TELECOM
doping; ~ **de la base** *m* ELECTRON base doping; ~ **du
canal** *m* ELECTRON channel doping; ~ **du collecteur** *m*
ELECTRON collector doping; ~ **à l'or** *m* ELECTRON gold
doping; ~ **par diffusion** *m* ELECTRON diffusion doping;
~ **au phosphore** *m* ELECTRON phosphorus doping; ~
des semi-conducteurs *m* ELECTRON semiconductor
doping; ~ **du silicium** *m* ELECTRON silicon doping

dopamine *f* CHIMIE dopamine

dopant *m* ELECTRON impurity, OPTIQUE, PHYSIQUE, TELE-
COM dopant

dopé *adj* ELECTRON, ORDINAT *fabrication des puces*,
PHYSIQUE doped

doper *vt* CHIMIE *cristal*, OPTIQUE, PHYSIQUE, TELECOM
dope

dopeur *m* ORDINAT *fabrication des puces* dopant

dopplérite *f* MINERAUX dopplerite

dorade *f* NAUT *accastillage de pont* ventilator

Dorade *f* ASTRONOMIE Dorado

doré: ~ **sur tranche** *adj* IMPRIM gilt-edged

doreur: ~ **sur porcelaine** *m* CERAM VER porcelain gilder

dormant *m* CONS MECA *d'un palan* standing end, CONSTR
frame, window frame; ~ **de fenêtre** *m* CONSTR window
frame; ~ **de porte** *m* CONSTR door case, door casing,
doorframe

dorsale *f* ENREGISTR, TV tape backing; ~ **médio-
océanique** *f* GEOLOGIE midocean ridge; ~ **océanique** *f*
OCEANO oceanic ridge, ridge, rise

dorure *f* CERAM VER, IMPRIM *reliure, façonnage* gilding,
MATERIAUX gold plating, PRODUCTION gilding; ~ **électrolytique** *f* ESPACE *véhicules* gold plating; ~ **par
projection** *f* ESPACE *véhicules* gold flashing

dos *m* CONS MECA back, IMPRIM spine, *impression, reliure* backside, OCEANO baiting, PHOTO *de l'appareil*
back cover; ~ **amovible** *m* PHOTO removable back; ~
arrondi *m* IMPRIM *reliure* rounded back; ~ **avec enregistrement de données de prise de vue** *m* PHOTO data
recording back; ~ **carré** *m* IMPRIM flat back, square
back; ~ **couché** *m* IMPRIM *papier autocopiant* coated
back; ~ **cousu** *m* IMPRIM sawn-in back; ~ **du livre** *m*

IMPRIM shelfback; ~ **magasin** *m* PHOTO magazine back; ~ **pivotant** *m* PHOTO *d'un appareil photographique* revolving back, swinging back; ~ **à ressort** *m* IMPRIM false back

DOS *abrév* (MD) *(système d'exploitation à disque)* INFORMAT, ORDINAT DOS (TM) *(disk operating system)*

dos-à-dos[1] *adj* CONSTR, PRODUCTION back-to-back

dos-à-dos[2] *m* TEXTILE back-to-back

dosage *m* CHARBON dosage, CHIMIE assay, measurement, measuring, *des ingrédients* dosing, proportioning, SECURITE *de composés* determination, TEXTILE dispensing; ~ **de l'acidité** *m* PAPIER acid determination; ~ **manuel** *m* EMBALLAGE hand dosing; ~ **du mélange** *m* AUTO mixture ratio, CONSTR mix proportions; ~ **parfait** *m* AUTO ideal mixture ratio, perfect mixture ratio; ~ **potentiométrique** *m* CHIMIE electrometric titration; ~ **de puissance maximum** *m* AUTO maximum output mixture ratio; ~ **volumétrique** *m* CONSTR batch mix, EMBALLAGE volume dosing

dose *f* CHIMIE dose, measure, proportion; ~ **absorbée** *f* PHYS RAYON *de radiation ionisante*, PHYSIQUE absorbed dose; ~ **accumulée par les travailleurs** *f* PHYS RAYON *radioactivité* dose accumulated by workers; ~ **effet** *f* POLLUTION dose response; ~ **en profondeur** *f* PHYS RAYON depth dose; ~ **enregistrée** *f* PHYS RAYON recorded dose; ~ **d'exposition** *f* PHYS RAYON *radiation ionisante* exposure dose; ~ **génétiquement significative** *f* POLLUTION genetically significant dose; ~ **d'impuretés implantées** *f* ELECTRON implant dose; ~ **d'irradiation** *f* ESPACE radiation dose; ~ **létale** *f (DL)* PHYSIQUE, POLLUTION lethal dose *(LD)*; ~ **létale 50%** *f (DL50)* NUCLEAIRE, PHYS RAYON, POLLUTION, SECURITE median lethal dose *(LD50)*; ~ **létale médiane** *f (DL50)* NUCLEAIRE, PHYS RAYON *radiation ionisante*, POLLUTION, SECURITE median lethal dose *(LD50)*; ~ **létale minimale** *f* POLLUTION minimum lethal dose; ~ **létale moyenne** *f (DLM)* NUCLEAIRE, PHYS RAYON, POLLUTION, SECURITE mean lethal dose *(MLD)*; ~ **maximale d'activité professionnelle** *f* PHYS RAYON maximum permissible occupational whole-body dose; ~ **maximale admissible** *f* PHYS RAYON *radiation ionisante* maximum permissible dose; ~ **de rayonnement** *f* PHYS RAYON, POLLUTION radiation dose; ~ **sonore** *f* SECURITE noise dose; ~ **totale pour une population** *f* POLLUTION population dose

doser *vt* CHIMIE measure

doseur *m* PAPIER proportioner

doseuse: ~ **par poids** *f* EMBALLAGE weight filling machine

dosimètre *m* PHYS RAYON, PHYSIQUE dosimeter; ~ **de film** *m* PHYS RAYON *radiation ionisante* film dosimeter; ~ **photographique** *m* PHYS RAYON *radiation ionisante* film dosimeter; ~ **de poche gradué** *m* PHYS RAYON graduated pocket dosimeter; ~ **à rayons X** *m* INSTRUMENT X-ray dosimeter; ~ **sonore de radiation** *m* PHYS RAYON sound alarm radiation dosimeter; ~ **thermoluminescent** *m* PHYS RAYON thermoluminescent dosimeter

dosimétrie *f* PHYS RAYON, PHYSIQUE dosimetry; ~ **chimique** *f* PHYS RAYON *radioactivité* chemical dosimetry; ~ **de haut niveau** *f* PHYS RAYON high-level dosimetry; ~ **individuelle** *f* PHYS RAYON *mesure de radiation* personal dosimetry; ~ **de radiation** *f* PHYS RAYON radiation dosimetry

dosse *f* CONSTR *de bois* slab

dosseret *m* AERONAUT backing

dossier *m* AUTO backrest, PRODUCTION brief, VEHICULES *sièges* backrest, seat back; ~ **atelier** *m* PRODUCTION manufacturing papers, shop papers; ~ **de calcul** *m* CONS MECA engineering calculations record; ~ **de fabrication** *m* PRODUCTION manufacturing documents, shop packet; ~ **latex** *m* TEXTILE latex backing

dotation: ~ **de personnel** *f* NAUT manning

doté: ~ **de** *adj* TELECOM fitted with

doter *vt* MINES equip

doublage *m* CERAM VER flashing (BrE), overlaying (AmE), PETR double joint, PRODUCTION lining, TV dubbing; ~ **en boucle** *m* CINEMAT dialogue replacement; ~ **par gain excessif du point** *m* IMPRIM *impression* slur

double[1] *adj* GEOMETRIE dual; **en** ~ *adj* INFORMAT standby; **à** ~ **alimentation** *adj* ELECTR *moteur* double-fed; **à** ~ **bombage** *adj* CERAM VER *verre* double-bended; **à** ~ **capsule** *adj* ENREGISTR *micro* double-button; ~ **couche** *adj* REVETEMENT double-layer; **à** ~ **densité** *adj* INFORMAT, ORDINAT double-density; **à** ~ **effet** *adj* AUTO *amortisseur*, CONS MECA *cylindre*, EN RENOUV *servomoteur*, MECANIQUE, PRODUCTION *vérin*, REFRIG *compresseur* double-acting; **à** ~ **parois** *adj* CONS MECA *réservoir à pression* double-skinned; ~ **piste** *adj* ENREGISTR twin-track; **à** ~ **taille** *adj* PRODUCTION *lime* double-cut; **à** ~ **torsade** *adj* GEOMETRIE double-twist; **à** ~ **usage** *adj* COMMANDE dual-purpose

double[2]: ~ **arbre à cames en tête** *m* VEHICULES *moteur* double overhead camshaft; ~ **bémol** *m* ACOUSTIQUE double flat; ~ **chanfrein** *m* CERAM VER miter bevel both sides (AmE), mitre bevel both sides (BrE); ~ **changement de fréquence** *m* ELECTRON double conversion; ~ **circuit de freinage** *m* TRANSPORT double circuit brake, dual-circuit brake, separated-braking circuits; ~ **décalque** *m* IMPRIM retransfer; ~ **décamètre à ruban** *m* METROLOGIE tape line; ~ **dièse** *m* ACOUSTIQUE double sharp; ~ **duo** *m* PRODUCTION four-high; ~ **état** *m* ELECTRON double rail; ~ **filet** *m* IMPRIM double rule; ~ **filet très fin pour délimiter une zone** *m* IMPRIM *composition, montage* double hairline; ~ **fond** *m* NAUT double bottom, inner bottom, PRODUCTION false bottom; ~ **griffe** *m* CINEMAT double claw; ~ **hélical** *m* CONS MECA herringbone gear; ~ **mamelon** *m* CONS MECA *raccord pour tubes* barrel nipple; ~ **quartier tournant** *m* CONSTR half space; ~ **spectromètre à rayons-X** *m* NUCLEAIRE WDX, wavelength dispersive double X-ray spectrometer; ~ **talon** *m* IMPRIM *impression de chèques et continu* double stub; ~ **tamponnage** *m* ORDINAT double buffering; ~ **tirage de la chambre** *m* PHOTO double camera extension; ~ **vanne de pression** *m* PRODUCTION *système hydraulique* dual pressure valve; ~ **vitrage** *m* CHAUFFAGE, CONSTR double glazing, REFRIG sandwich-paned insulating panel

double[3]: ~ **action hétérodyne** *f* TV double super effect; ~ **chape** *f* CONS MECA dual clevis; ~ **commande** *f* AERONAUT dual control; ~ **coque** *f* NAUT double hull, double skin; ~ **décomposition** *f* LESSIVES ester interchange; ~ **diffusion** *f* ELECTRON double diffusion; ~ **enveloppe** *f* CONS MECA double casing; ~ **étoile** *f* ASTRONOMIE Aries, The Ram; ~ **exposition** *f* CINEMAT, PHOTO double exposure; ~ **face** *f* PAPIER two-sidedness; ~ **fraction** *f* MATH complex fraction; ~ **image** *f* CINEMAT ghost image; ~ **mise en mémoire tampon** *f* ORDINAT double buffering; ~ **modulation** *f* ELECTRON double modulation; ~ **page** *f* IMPRIM *maquette* double spread; **~ perforation** *f* CINEMAT double perforation; **~ pompe** *f* PRODUCTION *système hydraulique* double pump; **~ précision** *f* INFORMAT, ORDINAT double precision; **~ rupture** *f* PRODUCTION *électricité* double break; **~ sauvegarde** *f* IMPRIM *des données* backing up; **~ sensibilité** *f* AERONAUT autopilot pitch sensitivity system; **~ teinture** *f* TEXTILE double dyeing; **~ tension d'alimentation** *f* ELECTROTEC dual supply voltage; **~ triode** *f* ELECTRON double triode

doublé *adj* IMPRIM pasted; **~ de matière plastique** *adj* REVETEMENT plastic-coated

doubler *vt* CINEMAT dub, postsynchronize, ENREGISTR dub, NAUT *les amarres* double, *un cap* round, REVETEMENT line; **~ de fer-blanc** *vt* PRODUCTION *une boîte* line with tin

doublés *m pl* PHOTO double exposure

doublet *m* CHIMIE *spectroscopie*, EN RENOUV *géothermie*, PHYSIQUE doublet; **~ achromatique** *m* PHYSIQUE achromatic doublet; **~ électrique** *m* ELECTROTEC electric dipole; **~ de Hertz** *m* ESPACE *communications* Hertzian dipole; **~ libre** *m* CHIMIE lone pair

doubleur *m* TELECOM doubler; **~ de fréquence** *m* ELECTR, ELECTRON, PHYSIQUE, TELECOM frequency doubler; **~ de tension** *m* ELECTR *circuit redresseur* voltage doubler

doublon *m* IMPRIM doublet

doublure *f* EMBALLAGE liner, lining paper, IMPRIM *reliure, emballage* lining, MECANIQUE liner, PAPIER lining; **~ de boîtes de carton** *f* IMPRIM *reliure, emballage* liner; **~ de couverture** *f* IMPRIM *reliure, emballage* liner; **~ du dos d'un livre** *f* IMPRIM *reliure* back lining; **~ intermédiaire** *f* TEXTILE interlining; **~ plastique** *f* EMBALLAGE plastic liner

douci *m* CERAM VER grinder

doucine *f* CONSTR ogee, ogee plane; **~ renversée** *f* CONSTR reversed ogee

douci-poli *m* CERAM VER grinding and polishing; **~ continu** *m* CERAM VER continuous grinder and polisher

doucir *vt* CONS MECA set

douci-rond *m* CERAM VER disc grinding (BrE), disk grinding (AmE)

doucissage *m* CERAM VER grinding, smooth grinding, CONS MECA setting; **~ d'un joint** *m* CERAM VER edge fine grinding

douelle *f* CONSTR soffit, *d'une voûte* intrados

douille *f* AUTO adjusting sleeve, CINEMAT jack socket, socket, lamp holder, CONS MECA bush, bushing, socket, CONSTR *d'une pelle* socket, ELECTROTEC holder, socket, *de lampe* lamp holder, MECANIQUE bushing, sleeve, socket, PRODUCTION pin, TV socket; **~ à air comprimé** *f* CONS MECA compressed air socket; **~ allonge** *f* CONS MECA extension socket; **~ d'axe** *f* VEHICULES *transmission* axle bush; **~ à baïonnette** *f* CINEMAT bayonet socket, ELECTR *lampe* bayonet lamp holder, bayonet socket, PHOTO bayonet socket; **~ banane** *f* ELECTROTEC banana jack; **~ à billes** *f* CONS MECA ball bushing; **~ de cartouche** *f* MILITAIRE cartridge case; **~ de centrage** *f* CONS MECA centering sleeve (AmE), centring sleeve (BrE); **~ de chandelier** *f* NAUT stanchion deck fitting; **~ à encliqueter** *f* ELECTROTEC snap-in socket; **~ filetée** *f* CONS MECA screw socket, thread insert; **~ de jack** *f* ELECTROTEC jack bush; **~ de lampe** *f* PHOTO lamp socket; **~ lisse** *f* CONS MECA bushing; **~ de mesure** *f* ELECTROTEC test jack; **~ à percer** *f* CONS MECA drill bushing; **~ de pied de bielle** *f* VEHICULES small end bush; **~ porte-outil** *f* CONS MECA

chuck bushing; **~ pour forets** *f* CONS MECA drill socket; **~ de pression** *f* CONS MECA pressure sleeve; **~ de protection pour sonde** *f* PRODUCTION *automatisme industriel* thermostat well; **~ de protection type immersion** *f* PRODUCTION immersion well; **~ de réduction** *f* CONS MECA reduction sleeve, taper sleeve; **~ de réglage** *f* CONS MECA *pour têtes multibroches* adjustable adaptor; **~ de secours** *f* MINES horn socket; **~ de verrou** *f* CONSTR lock bush; **~ à vis** *f* CONS MECA screw socket, ELECTROTEC screw base

douve *f* PRODUCTION stave

doux *adj* CHIMIE sweet, MATERIAUX *de l'eau* fresh

DP *abrév (discriminateur de protocole)* TELECOM PD *(protocol discriminator)*

drachme *f* METROLOGIE dram

dragage *m* MINES dredging, NAUT dredging, *rivière* dragging, OCEANO dredging; **~ hydrographique** *m* OCEANO hydrographic dredging, wire dragging, wiredrag survey; **~ de mines** *m* NAUT *marine* minesweeping; **~ à la traîne** *m* NAUT trail dredging

dragline: **~ à chenilles** *f* CONSTR crawler dragline excavator; **~ sur patins** *f* CONSTR crawler dragline excavator, walking dragline excavator

Dragon *m* ASTRONOMIE Draco

drague *f* CONSTR dredge, MINES drag, dredge, dredger, NAUT dredge, POLLU MER, TRANSPORT dredger; **~ aspirante** *f* DISTRI EAU suction dredge, NAUT pump dredger, suction dredger, TRANSPORT suction dredger; **~ à aspiration** *f* DISTRI EAU suction dredge; **~ à benne piocheuse** *f* NAUT grab dredger; **~ à benne preneuse** *f* NAUT grab dredger; **~ à chapelets** *f* CONSTR bucket dredger; **~ coupeuse** *f* NAUT cutter dredger; **~ à cuiller** *f* DISTRI EAU spoon dredge, spoon dredger; **~ dérocheuse** *f* NAUT rock-cutting dredger; **~ à élinde** *f* NAUT ladder dredge; **~ en catamaran** *f* DISTRI EAU catamaran dredge; **~ flottante** *f* OCEANO floating hydrographic dredge, floating wire drag; **~ fluviale** *f* DISTRI EAU river dredge; **~ à godets** *f* CONSTR, NAUT bucket dredger; **~ hydrographique** *f* OCEANO floating hydrographic dredge, floating wire drag; **~ à mâchoires** *f* CONSTR clam shell bucket dredger, grab dredge, grab dredger; **~ mixte** *f* NAUT dual-purpose dredger; **~ océanographique** *f* OCEANO oceanographic dredge; **~ à pelle** *f* NAUT dipper dredge; **~ pompe** *f* CONSTR pump dredge, pump dredger; **~ porteuse** *f* NAUT hopper dredger; **~ de prospection** *f* MINES prospecting dredge; **~ à succion** *f* DISTRI EAU suction dredge, NAUT pump dredger, suction dredger; **~ suceuse** *f* DISTRI EAU suction dredge, NAUT pump dredger, suction dredger, TRANSPORT suction dredger; **~ suceuse porteuse** *f* NAUT suction hopper dredger

draguer[1] *vt* NAUT dredge

draguer[2] *vi* NAUT *le fond* drag

dragueur *m* NAUT dredger; **~ d'huîtres** *m* NAUT oyster dredger; **~ de mines** *m* MILITAIRE, NAUT minesweeper

drain *m* CHARBON drain, CONSTR drain, watercourse, ELECTROTEC, HYDROLOGIE drain, PETR carrier bed, PETROLE, PHYSIQUE drain; **~ collecteur** *m* CONSTR main drain

drainage *m* DISTRI EAU drainage, draining, HYDROLOGIE, PETROLE drainage; **~ annulaire** *m* DISTRI EAU annular drainage; **~ à la charrue taupe** *m* CONSTR mole drainage; **~ par expansion de gaz dissous** *m* PETROLE solution gas drive; **~ par expansion du gaz libre** *m* PETROLE *récupération du pétrole* gas cap drive; **~ par**

fossés *m* HYDROLOGIE ditch drainage; ~ **profond** *m* DISTRI EAU underground drainage; ~ **sous l'action de la pesanteur** *m* PETR gravity draining; ~ **vertical** *m* CHARBON vertical drainage

drainer[1] *vt* CONSTR *des terres*, DISTRI EAU drain, MINES dewater, drain, RECYCLAGE drain

drainer[2] *vti* HYDROLOGIE drain

drains: ~ **chimiques** *m pl* NUCLEAIRE *résiduaires chimiques* chemical drains

draisine *f* CONSTR manrider, railroad inspection trolley (AmE), railway inspection trolley (BrE)

drame: ~ **vécu** *m* CINEMAT docudrama

drap *m* TEXTILE sheet; ~ **de sauvetage** *m* SECURITE rescue blanket

drapage *m* CERAM VER corrugation

drapé *m* TEXTILE drape

drapeau:[1] **en ~** *adj* AERONAUT *hélice* feathered; **en ~ à droite** *adj* IMPRIM rag-right (AmE), ragged right (BrE); **en ~ à gauche** *adj* IMPRIM *composition* rag-left (AmE), ragged left (BrE)

drapeau[2] *m* CERAM VER cullet catcher, scum, CINEMAT flag, nigger, INFORMAT, NAUT, ORDINAT flag; ~ **code** *m* IMPRIM *composition* flag

draper *vt* TEXTILE drape

DRASC *abrév (diffusion Raman anti-Stokes cohérente)* PHYSIQUE CARS *(coherent anti-Stokes Raman scattering)*

dravite *f* MINERAUX dravite

drèche *f* AGRO ALIM pomace; ~ **de brasserie** *f* AGRO ALIM brewer's grain

dressage *m* CONS MECA surfacing, CONSTR dressing, *d'un échafaud* erection, *des pavés* squaring, PRODUCTION straightening; ~ **en profil de la voie** *m* CH DE FER surfacing of the track (BrE)

dressant *m* CHARBON edge seam, MINES highly-inclined seam, rearer, steep vein

dressants: ~ **de houille** *m pl* CHARBON edge coals

dresse-meule *f* PRODUCTION emery wheel dresser

dresser *vt* CONS MECA true, true up, CONSTR trim, *le champ d'une planche* shoot, MECANIQUE plane, PRODUCTION face, square, *une tige* straighten; ~ **sur face** *vt* PRODUCTION face

dresseuse: ~ **de tôles** *f* CH DE FER plate-straightening machine

drille *f* CONS MECA lightning brace, *porte-foret à main* drill

drisse *f* AERONAUT, NAUT halyard

drogue: ~ **à godet** *f* NAUT bucket drogue

droit[1] *adj* CONSTR plumb

droit:[2] ~ **derrière** *adv* NAUT dead astern; ~ **devant** *adv* NAUT dead ahead

droit[3] *m* BREVETS, NAUT right; ~ **d'antenne** *m* TV broadcasting right; ~ **au brevet** *m* BREVETS right to a patent; ~ **de diffusion** *m* TV broadcasting right; ~ **de l'environnement** *m* POLLUTION environmental law; ~ **exclusif** *m* BREVETS exclusive right; ~ **de hauteur** *m* NAUT *navigation* baseline; ~ **d'interdire** *m* BREVETS prohibition right; ~ **maritime** *m* NAUT maritime law; ~ **de la mer** *m* NAUT maritime law; ~ **de passage** *m* CONSTR, NAUT, TRANSPORT right of way; ~ **de priorité** *m* BREVETS priority right; ~ **de sauvetage** *m* NAUT salvage award

droite:[1] **de ~** *adj* INFORMAT low-order; **à ~** *adj* MECANIQUE right-hand

droite[2] *f* GEOMETRIE, PHYSIQUE straight line; ~ **de charge** *f* ELECTROTEC load line; ~ **de compaction** *f* PETROLE *argiles* compaction trend; ~ **de compaction normale** *f* PETROLE normal trend; ~ **de conjugaison** *f* METALL tie line; ~ **des cornes** *f* ASTRONOMIE line of cusps; ~ **d'évidement** *f* CONS MECA dedendum line; ~ **primitive** *f* CONS MECA pitch line

droits:[1] ~ **de bassin** *m pl* NAUT dockage; ~ **de batelage** *m pl* NAUT waterage; ~ **de diffusion** *m pl* TV television rights; ~ **de dock** *m pl* NAUT dockage; ~ **d'écluse** *m pl* NAUT lock dues; ~ **miniers** *m pl* PETROLE mineral rights; ~ **de pêche** *m pl* NAUT fishing rights; ~ **de phare** *m pl* NAUT light dues; ~ **de port** *m pl* NAUT harbor dues (AmE), harbour dues (BrE), port charges; ~ **de propriété intellectuelle** *m pl* PRODUCTION proprietary information; ~ **de sas** *m pl* NAUT lock dues; ~ **d'utilisation hors antenne** *m pl* TV nonbroadcast rights

droits:[2] ~ **conférés par** *loc* BREVETS rights afforded by

drone *m* ESPACE drone

drop *m* ENREGISTR *de signal* drop-out; ~ **audio** *m* ENREGISTR audio drop-out

drosse *f* NAUT rudder cable, steering chain, steering wire, tiller rope, transmission wire

drupe *f* AGRO ALIM stone fruit

drusique: ~ **à géodes** *adj* GEOLOGIE drusy

DSL *abrév (diode superluminescente)* OPTIQUE, TELECOM SLD *(superluminescent diode)*

DTC *abrév (dispositif à transfert de charges)* ELECTROTEC, ESPACE *véhicules*, PHYSIQUE, TELECOM CTD *(charge transfer device)*

dualité: ~ **onde-corpuscule** *f* PHYSIQUE wave particle duality; ~ **onde-particule** *f* PHYS ONDES wave particle duality

duc: ~ **d'Albe** *m* NAUT dolphin

ductile *adj* CRISTALL, MATERIAUX, METALL ductile

ductilité *f* CRISTALL, METALL ductility; ~ **en traction** *f* MATERIAUX tensile ductility

dudgeon *m* CONSTR tube expander

dufrénite *f* MINERAUX dufrenite

dufrénoysite *f* MINERAUX dufrenoysite

duite *f* TEXTILE pick; ~ **lâche** *f* TEXTILE loose pick

duites: ~ **par pouce** *f pl* TEXTILE picks per inch

dulçaquicole *adj* GEOLOGIE *milieu sédimentaire ou faune* freshwater

dulcine *f* CHIMIE dulcin, dulcine

dulcitol *m* CHIMIE melampyrite

dumortiérite *f* MINERAUX dumortierite

dumper *m* CONSTR dumper

dunette *f* NAUT afterdeck

dunite *f* PETR dunite

duo *m* PRODUCTION two-high rolls, two-high train

duperie *f* ORDINAT spoofing

duplex[1] *adj* ELECTROTEC, INFORMAT, ORDINAT, TELECOM duplex; ~ **intégral** *adj* INFORMAT full-duplex, ORDINAT FDX, full-duplex

duplex[2] *m* CONSTR maisonette

duplexeur *m* TELECOM duplexer; ~ **de polarisation** *m* ESPACE *communications* polarization diplexer

duplicata *m* CINEMAT reversal print, PHOTO duplicate

duplication *f* ACOUSTIQUE duplication; ~ **à grande vitesse** *f* TV high-speed duplication

dupliquer *vt* INFORMAT duplicate

dur *adj* CINEMAT, MATERIAUX hard

durabilité *f* PLAST CAOU, QUALITE durability; ~ **du béton** *f* CONSTR concrete durability; ~ **chimique** *f* CERAM VER chemical durability, chemical resistance

durable *adj* QUALITE durable

duralumin *m* MECANIQUE *matériaux* duralumin

durangite *f* MINERAUX durangite

durci *adj* PRODUCTION embrittled; ~ **à froid** *adj* THERMO-DYN cold-cured

durcibilité *f* METALL hardenability

durcir *vt* PLAST CAOU cure, PRODUCTION harden; ~ **à froid** *vt* THERMODYN cold cure, cold harden; ~ **par précipitation** *vt* THERMODYN artificially age, precipitation harden

durcissable: ~ **par précipitation** *adj* THERMODYN *aluminium* heat-treatable

durcissage: ~ **à froid** *m* PLAST CAOU *adhésifs* cold-setting

durcissant: ~ **amidique** *m* PLAST CAOU amide hardener; ~ **aminique** *m* PLAST CAOU amine-curing agent; ~ **anhydrique** *m* PLAST CAOU *résines, adhésifs, revêtements* anhydride hardener

durcissement *m* CHARBON, CONSTR, ESPACE hardening, GEOLOGIE, MATERIAUX induration, METALL hardening, NUCLEAIRE *spectre de neutrons* leakage hardening, PLAST CAOU cure, curing, *peintures, plastiques, caoutchouc* hardening, REFRIG hardening; ~ **chimique** *m* METALL chemical hardening; ~ **dépassé** *m* METALL overageing (BrE), overaging (AmE); ~ **en tunnel** *m* REFRIG tunnel hardening; ~ **à froid** *m* CRISTALL work hardening, THERMODYN cold curing; ~ **par contact** *m* REFRIG contact hardening; ~ **par déformation** *m* METALL strain hardening; ~ **par diffusion** *m* NUCLEAIRE *du spectre de neutrons* diffusion hardening; ~ **par dispersion** *m* METALL dispersion hardening; ~ **par fatigue** *m* METALL fatigue hardening; ~ **par irradiation** *m* METALL irradiation hardening; ~ **par obstacles** *m* METALL obstacle hardening; ~ **par ordination** *m* METALL order hardening; ~ **par particules** *m* METALL particle reinforcement; ~ **par phase dispersée** *m* GENIE CHIM dispersion strengthening; ~ **par précipitation** *m* CRISTALL, METALL, PRODUCTION precipitation hardening, THERMODYN artificial ageing (BrE), artificial aging (AmE); ~ **par produits chimiques et congélation** *m* MINES chemical grouting and freezing; ~ **par rayonnement** *m* NUCLEAIRE radiation hardening; ~ **par saturation** *m* METALL saturation hardening; ~ **par trempe** *m* METALL quench hardening; ~ **par trichites** *m* MATERIAUX whisker toughening; ~ **par vieillissement** *m* CRISTALL, METALL, PLAST CAOU *plastiques* age hardening; ~ **structural** *m* MATERIAUX *métallurgie*, RESSORTS age hardening; ~ **superficiel** *m* METALL surface hardening; ~ **de travail linéaire** *m* METALL linear work hardening

durcisseur *m* PLAST CAOU *ingrédient de mélange* hardener, POLLU MER solidifier; ~ **amidique** *m* PLAST CAOU amide hardener; ~ **aminique** *m* PLAST CAOU *adhésifs, revêtements* amine-curing agent; ~ **anhydrique** *m* PLAST CAOU anhydride hardener

durée *f* ELECTRON time, ESPACE durability, endurance, INST HYDR *de compression de la vapeur* duration, MINES *d'une mine* life, lifetime, PHYSIQUE time, TEXTILE endurance; ~ **d'arc** *f* ELECTR *pôle, fusible, interrupteur* arcing time; ~ **d'attaque** *f* CHARBON leaching time; ~ **d'attente de tonalité** *f* TELECOM dial tone delay; ~ **d'attribution des canaux** *f* TELECOM channel allocation time; ~ **d'autorotation** *f* AERONAUT *d'un réacteur* engine coasting down time; ~ **du brevet** *f* BREVETS term of patent; ~ **de cohérence** *f* OPTIQUE, PHYSIQUE, TELECOM coherence time; ~ **de la communication** *f* TELECOM call duration; ~ **de compilation** *f* ORDINAT compilation time; ~ **de conservation** *f* CINEMAT shelf life, PHOTO storage period, PLAST CAOU *stockage* shelf life, REFRIG keeping time; ~ **de coupure** *f* ELECTR *relais* break time;

~ **d'un cycle** *f* INFORMAT cycle time; ~ **de désactivation** *f* NUCLEAIRE cooling-down period; ~ **de développement** *f* CINEMAT development time; ~ **des émissions sans effet** *f* TELECOM ineffective airtime; ~ **d'emmagasinage** *f* EMBALLAGE storage durability; ~ **estimée** *f* AERONAUT estimated elapsed time; ~ **d'établissement** *f* ELECTR *relais* make time; ~ **d'établissement d'une communication** *f* TELECOM call setup delay; ~ **d'exécution** *f* INFORMAT run-time, ORDINAT execution time, run-time; ~ **de fermeture** *f* ELECTR *relais* closing time; ~ **de fonctionnement prévue** *f* TELECOM scheduled operating time; ~ **de formation d'une rafale** *f* AERONAUT gust formation time; ~ **de frittage** *f* GENIE CHIM sintering time; ~ **de fusion** *f* THERMODYN melting time; ~ **de gâchage** *f* CONSTR mixing time; ~ **de garantie** *f* ESPACE *gestion* guarantee period; ~ **d'impulsion** *f* ELECTRON pulse duration, pulse length, PHYSIQUE pulse width, TELECOM pulse length, TV pulse width; ~ **d'interruption** *f* PRODUCTION interrupt period, TELECOM downtime; ~ **de la ligne** *f* TV trace interval; ~ **limite de stockage** *f* PLAST CAOU shelf life; ~ **de marche** *f* TRANSPORT running time; ~ **de la marée** *f* OCEANO tide duration; ~ **à mi-crête** *f* OPTIQUE *d'une impulsion* full-duration half-maximum, *impulsion* FDHM, TELECOM FDHM, full-duration half-maximum; ~ **de mise en température** *f* THERMODYN heating time, heating-up curve, heating-up time; ~ **moyenne avant défaillance** *f* QUALITE MTTF, mean time to failure; ~ **moyenne de réparation** *f* ESPACE *qualité*, MECANIQUE MTTR, mean time to repair; ~ **de numérotation** *f* TELECOM dialing period (AmE), dialling period (BrE); ~ **d'occupation** *f* TELECOM holding time; ~ **d'ouverture** *f* ELECTR *relais* opening time; ~ **de pénétration de la chaleur** *f* THERMODYN heat penetration time; ~ **d'une période** *f* ELECTRON periodic time; ~ **de pose** *f* PHOTO exposure time, printing time, exposure; ~ **de préchauffage** *f* THERMODYN warm-up time; ~ **de projection** *f* CINEMAT playing time, running time, screen time, screening time; ~ **de prolongation** *f* TRANSPORT vehicle extension period; ~ **de propulsion** *f* MILITAIRE burn time; ~ **de recharge** *f* PHOTO recharge time, recycle time; ~ **de réparation** *f* INFORMAT, ORDINAT repair time; ~ **de réponse** *f* ESSAIS response time; ~ **de reproduction** *f* ENREGISTR playing time; ~ **de rétablissement d'une coupure** *f* ELECTR *relais* make-break time; ~ **de retard** *f* ELECTR *interrupteur* delay time; ~ **de retour du spot** *f* TV return interval; ~ **de réverbération** *f* ACOUSTIQUE reverberation time; ~ **de sélection d'un commutateur** *f* TELECOM switching delay; ~ **de service** *f* ELECTROTEC service life, NUCLEAIRE *entre deux nettoyages* filter run; ~ **de la sonnerie** *f* TELECOM ringing duration; ~ **de stockage** *f* EMBALLAGE shelf life; ~ **de la totalité** *f* ASTRONOMIE *éclipse solaire* duration of totality; ~ **du trajet** *f* TRANSPORT journey time (BrE), trip time (AmE); ~ **de la traversée** *f* NAUT crossing time; ~ **d'utilisation** *f* PRODUCTION operating time, service time; ~ **de vert** *f* TRANSPORT green time; ~ **de vie** *f* CHARBON, CONSTR service life, ELECTROTEC, ESPACE *véhicules* lifetime, MATERIAUX durability, lifetime, METALL time to rupture, NUCLEAIRE operating lifetime, service life, PHYSIQUE lifetime, mean life, PRODUCTION mechanical endurance, QUALITE life, TELECOM life expectancy, lifetime, lifetime expectancy; ~ **de vie dans l'atmosphère** *f* POLLUTION atmospheric lifetime; ~ **de vie en fonctionnement** *f* ELECTROTEC operating life; ~ **de vie en profondeur** *f* ELECTRON bulk lifetime; ~ **de vie**

en service *f* ELECTROTEC service life; ~ **de vie en tampon** *f* ELECTROTEC float life; ~ **de vie lumineuse** *f* PHYS RAYON luminosity lifetime; ~ **de vie mécanique** *f* ELECTROTEC, PRODUCTION mechanical life; ~ **de vie moyenne** *f* PHYSIQUE average life, mean lifetime, QUALITE mean life; ~ **de vie d'un outil** *f* CONS MECA tool life; ~ **de vie de la pale** *f* AERONAUT blade life; ~ **de vie radiative** *f* PHYS RAYON radiative lifetime; ~ **de vie sur l'étagère** *f* IMPRIM shelf life; ~ **de vulcanisation** *f* PLAST CAOU curing time

durène *m* CHIMIE durene

dureté *f* CHIMIE, CRISTALL, MECANIQUE *matériaux*, METALL, PAPIER, PLAST CAOU hardness; ~ **Brinell** *f* MECANIQUE *matériaux* Brinell hardness; ~ **carbonatée** *f* HYDROLOGIE carbonate hardness; ~ **à coeur** *f* RESSORTS full hardness, through hardness; ~ **de l'eau** *f* CONSTR hardness, DISTRI EAU water hardness; ~ **non carbonatée** *f* HYDROLOGIE noncarbonate hardness; ~ **par pénétration** *f* PLAST CAOU indentation hardness; ~ **pendulaire** *f* PLAST CAOU *essai, revêtements* pendulum hardness; ~ **à la pénétration de la bille** *f* PLAST CAOU indentation hardness; ~ **Shore** *f* PLAST CAOU Shore hardness; ~ **superficielle** *f* CONS MECA surface hardness; ~ **Sward rocker** *f* PLAST CAOU *essai, revêtements* Sward rocker hardness

durit: ~ **de radiateur** *f* (MD) AUTO, VEHICULES *refroidissement* radiator hose

duromètre *m* CONS MECA hardness tester, EQUIP LAB *instrument* hardness tester, *mesure de la dureté* durometer, IMPRIM plastometer, *photogravure* durometer, PAPIER durometer, hardness tester, PLAST CAOU *instrument* durometer, hardness tester; ~ **Shore** *m* EQUIP LAB *instrument*, INSTRUMENT Shore hardness tester

duse *f* PETR bean, choke, PETROLE *canalisation* choke

DVT *abrév (défaut de verrouillage trame)* TELECOM out-of-frame

dy *m* CHARBON dy

Dy *(dysprosium)* CHIMIE Dy *(dysprosium)*

dyadique *adj* INFORMAT dyadic

dynamique[1] *adj* INFORMAT dynamic, METALL *recouvrement* dynamical, ORDINAT dynamic, PHYS FLUID *processus* dynamical

dynamique[2] *f* ACOUSTIQUE dynamic range, MECANIQUE, PHYSIQUE dynamics, TV dynamic range; ~ **de l'amplificateur vertical** *f* ELECTRON vertical amplifier dynamic range; ~ **des fluides** *f* PHYS FLUID fluid dynamics; ~ **du mouvement des particules** *f* NUCLEAIRE particle dynamics; ~ **des océans** *f* NAUT ocean dynamics; ~ **structurale** *f* CONS MECA structural dynamics

dynamiser: ~ **le signal** *vi* ELECTRON serrodyne

dynamite *f* MINES dynamite; ~ **antigel** *f* MINES low-freezing dynamite; ~ **gélatinée** *f* MINES gelatin, gelatin dynamite, gelatine, gelatine dynamite; ~ **gélatinisée** *f* MINES gelatin, gelatin dynamite, gelatine, gelatine dynamite; ~ **gomme** *f* MINES blasting gelatine; ~ **plastique** *f* MINES plastic explosive; ~ **pulvérulente** *f* MINES powder explosive

dynamitière *f* MINES dynamite store, explosives magazine

dynamo *f* ELECTR *générateur*, ELECTROTEC dynamo, NAUT dynamo, generator, VEHICULES *système électrique* alternator (AmE), dynamo (BrE), generator; ~ **amplificatrice** *f* ELECTROTEC rotary amplifier; ~ **à anneau plat** *f* ELECTR *générateur* flat ring dynamo; ~ **auxiliaire** *f* ELECTR *générateur* booster dynamo, booster generator; ~ **compensatrice** *f* ELECTR *générateur* DC balancer; ~ **compound à excitation différentielle** *f* ELECTR *générateur* differentially-excited compound generator; ~ **à courant constant** *f* ELECTR constant current dynamo; ~ **à courant continu** *f* PHYSIQUE DC generator; ~ **dynamométrique** *f* ELECTR *générateur* brake dynamo; ~ **en série** *f* ELECTR *générateur* series-wound dynamo; ~ **à excitation séparée** *f* ELECTROTEC separate excited dynamo; ~ **excitatrice** *f* ELECTR exciting dynamo, *générateur* exciter; ~ **pilote** *f* ELECTR variable voltage generator, *générateur* control dynamo; ~ **à pôles extérieurs** *f* ELECTR *générateur* exterior pole generator, external pole generator; ~ **quadripolaire** *f* ELECTR *générateur* four-pole generator; ~ **série** *f* ELECTROTEC series dynamo, series-wound dynamo; ~ **shunt** *f* ELECTROTEC shunt dynamo, shunt-wound dynamo; ~ **tampon** *f* ELECTR regulating dynamo, *générateur* buffer dynamo; ~ **à tension constante** *f* ELECTR *générateur* constant voltage dynamo; ~ **tétrapolaire** *f* ELECTR four-pole generator; ~ **unipolaire** *f* ELECTR *générateur* acyclic dynamo, acyclic generator

dynamo-électrique *adj* ELECTROTEC dynamo-electric

dynamo-frein *f* ELECTR *générateur* brake dynamo

dynamographe *m* MECANIQUE dynamograph

dynamo-magnéto *f* ELECTR *automobile* mag-dyno

dynamométamorphisme *m* GEOLOGIE dynamic metamorphism

dynamomètre *m* ELECTR, EQUIP LAB *énergie*, MECANIQUE dynamometer, PAPIER tensile strength tester; ~ **de machine à vapeur** *m* INST HYDR indicator; ~ **de traction** *m* PAPIER breaking strength tester

dynamoteur *m* ELECTR dynamotor

dyne *f* METROLOGIE dyne

dynode *f* PHYSIQUE dynode

dysanalyte *f* MINERAUX dysanalyte

dysbarique *adj* OCEANO *arthropathie* dysbaric, hyperbaric arthralgia, *emphysème* dysbaric

dysbarisme *m* OCEANO dysbarism

dysclasite *f* MINERAUX dysclasite

dyscrase *f* MINERAUX dyscrase

dyscrasite *f* MINERAUX dyscrasite

dysluite *f* MINERAUX dysluite

dysodile *f* MINERAUX dysodile

dysprosium *m (Dy)* CHIMIE dysprosium *(Dy)*

E

E *abrév (exa-)* METROLOGIE E *(exa-)*

E/S[1] *abrév (entrée/sortie)* ORDINAT, PRODUCTION I/O *(input/output)*

E/S:[2] ~ **immédiate** *f* PRODUCTION immediate I/O

EAA *abrév (équipement d'appel automatique)* INFORMAT, ORDINAT ACU *(automatic calling unit)*

EAO *abrév (enseignement assisté par ordinateur)* ORDINAT CAL *(computer-assisted learning)*

eau:[1] d'~ douce *adj* GEOLOGIE freshwater

eau:[2]

~ a ~ **acide** *f* POLLUTION acid water; ~ **d'adduction** *f* INST HYDR headwater; ~ **aggressive** *f* DISTRI EAU, HYDROLOGIE aggressive water; ~ **d'alimentation** *f* CHAUFFAGE, DISTRI EAU, HYDROLOGIE, MECANIQUE *procédé*, NAUT, PAPIER feedwater; ~ **d'alimentation de chaudière** *f* HYDROLOGIE feedwater, PETROLE boiler feed water; ~ **ammoniacale** *f* PAPIER ammonical water; ~ **d'amont** *f* HYDROLOGIE, INST HYDR headwater; ~ **d'appoint** *f* AGRO ALIM make-up water, DISTRI EAU make-up, REFRIG make-up water; ~ **artésienne** *f* CHARBON artesian water, ground water; ~ **d'aval** *f* DISTRI EAU, EN RENOUV, INST HYDR tailwater;

~ b ~ **de bordure** *f* PETR edge water; ~ **de brassage** *f* AGRO ALIM brewing liquor; ~ **brute** *f* DISTRI EAU raw water;

~ c ~ **de cale** *f* NAUT bilge water; ~ **calme** *f* DISTRI EAU quiet water, HYDROLOGIE still water; ~ **capillaire** *f* CHARBON, HYDROLOGIE capillary water; ~ **capillaire du sol** *f* HYDROLOGIE capillary soil water; ~ **chargée de flottation** *f* GENIE CHIM flotation liquid; ~ **de chaux** *f* CHIMIE lime water; ~ **chlorée** *f* HYDROLOGIE, PRODUCTION chlorinated water; ~ **claire** *f* DISTRI EAU clear water; ~ **commerciale** *f* HYDROLOGIE commercial water; ~ **de compensation** *f* HYDROLOGIE make-up water; ~ **de conduite ordinaire** *f* HYDROLOGIE ordinary tap water; ~ **connée** *f* GEOLOGIE, HYDROLOGIE connate water; ~ **de consommation** *f* DISTRI EAU consumption water; ~ **de constitution** *f* DISTRI EAU combined water, GEOLOGIE connate water, PETR bound water; ~ **corrosive** *f* DISTRI EAU active water, corrosive water; ~ **courante** *f* DISTRI EAU, HYDROLOGIE running water; ~ **crue** *f* DISTRI EAU raw water;

~ d ~ **de déballastage** *f* POLLUTION deballasting water; ~ **de dégivrage** *f* REFRIG condensate; ~ **déionisée** *f* ELECTR *électrolyte* deionized water; ~ **déminéralisée** *f* CONSTR, HYDROLOGIE demineralized water; ~ **de distribution** *f* DISTRI EAU domestic water; ~ **domestique** *f* HYDROLOGIE domestic water; ~ **dormante** *f* HYDROLOGIE standing water, still water; ~ **douce** *f* DISTRI EAU freshwater, soft water, GAZ, HYDROLOGIE, NAUT, PETR freshwater; ~ **dure** *f* DISTRI EAU hard water;

~ e ~ **d'écoulement** *f* POLLUTION stem flow; ~ **d'égout** *f* DISTRI EAU sewage, HYDROLOGIE wastewater, RECYCLAGE sewage waste, sewage; ~ **d'égout brute** *f* RECYCLAGE raw sewage; ~ **d'égout non traitée** *f* RECYCLAGE raw sewage; ~ **d'empâtage** *f* AGRO ALIM mash liquor; ~ **en excès** *f* DISTRI EAU surplus water; ~

épurée *f* HYDROLOGIE purified water; ~ **d'étanchéité** *f* NUCLEAIRE seal water; ~ **exclue** *f* POLLUTION water-free;

~ f ~ **de fissure** *f* CHARBON cleft water, fissure water, joint water; ~ **fluviale** *f* HYDROLOGIE river water; ~ **de fond** *f* OCEANO bottom water; ~ **de fonte** *f* DISTRI EAU snow melt (AmE), snow water (BrE); ~ **de formation** *f* PETR, PETROLE *géologie* formation water; ~ **fossile** *f* GEOLOGIE connate water, HYDROLOGIE fossil water, PETR connate water; ~ **de fuite** *f* DISTRI EAU leak water, HYDROLOGIE tailwater; ~ **de fusion** *f* DISTRI EAU snow melt (AmE), snow water (BrE); ~ **de fusion de la glace** *f* REFRIG ice water;

~ g ~ **glycolée** *f* REFRIG glycol solution; ~ **gravitaire** *f* HYDROLOGIE gravity water;

~ h ~ **hydrothermale marine** *f* OCEANO hot spring water; ~ **hygroscopique** *f* DISTRI EAU, HYDROLOGIE hygroscopic water; ~ **hyperhaline** *f* OCEANO hypersaline water; ~ **hypogée** *f* GEOLOGIE juvenile water;

~ i ~ **industrielle** *f* DISTRI EAU industrial water, process water, HYDROLOGIE industrial process water, process water; ~ **d'infiltration** *f* CHIMIE seepage water, DISTRI EAU infiltrating water, percolating water, HYDROLOGIE infiltrating water, infiltration water; ~ **interstitielle** *f* CHARBON interstitial water, pore water, DISTRI EAU, HYDROLOGIE interstitial water, OCEANO interstitial water, pore water, PETR, PETROLE *géologie* interstitial water;

~ j ~ **juvénile** *f* DISTRI EAU, GEOLOGIE juvenile water;

~ l ~ **lacustre** *f* POLLUTION lake water; ~ **de lavage** *f* GENIE CHIM washings, HYDROLOGIE backwash water; ~ **à laver** *f* GENIE CHIM washings; ~ **libre** *f* DISTRI EAU unconfined water; ~ **liée** *f* AGRO ALIM bound water; ~ **limpide** *f* DISTRI EAU clear water; ~ **lourde** *f* CHIMIE, NUCLEAIRE, PHYSIQUE heavy water;

~ m ~ **de mer** *f* DISTRI EAU saltwater, NAUT, OCEANO sea water; ~ **météorique** *f* HYDROLOGIE meteoric water; ~ **minérale** *f* HYDROLOGIE mineral water; ~ **minérale naturelle** *f* HYDROLOGIE mineral water; ~ **morte** *f* HYDROLOGIE slack water, OCEANO dead water; ~ **municipale** *f* HYDROLOGIE municipal water;

~ n ~ **néritique** *f* OCEANO neritic water; ~ **noire** *f* HYDROLOGIE black liquor; ~ **normale** *f* OCEANO normal sea water, standard sea water;

~ o ~ **ordinaire** *f* NUCLEAIRE *naturelle légère* normal water, ordinary water; ~ **oxygénée** *f* CHIMIE hydrogen peroxide, HYDROLOGIE oxygenated water;

~ p ~ **pelliculaire** *f* CHARBON pellicular water; ~ **de pénétration** *f* CHARBON gravitational water, seepage, HYDROLOGIE *par de grands interstices* influent water; ~ **de pénétration par les frondaisons** *f* POLLUTION throughfall; ~ **perchée** *f* DISTRI EAU perched water; ~ **de percolation** *f* DISTRI EAU infiltrating water, percolating water, HYDROLOGIE percolating water; ~ **peu profonde** *f* OCEANO shallow water, shallows; ~ **phréatique** *f* HYDROLOGIE ground water, phreatic water; ~ **plate** *f* AGRO ALIM still water; ~ **pluviale** *f* HYDROLOGIE storm water; ~ **polluée** *f* DISTRI EAU polluted water; ~ **potable** *f* AGRO ALIM, CONSTR, DISTRI EAU, HYDROLOGIE drinking water; ~ **pour usage commerciaux** *f* HYDROLOGIE commercial water; ~ **précipitable** *f* METEO precipitable water; ~ **de précipitation** *f* METEO rainwater; ~ **précipitée** *f* METEO rainwater; ~ **primitive** *f* HYDROLOGIE fossil water; ~ **de procédé** *f* HYDROLOGIE process water; ~ **propre** *f* DISTRI EAU clean water; ~ **de puits** *f* DISTRI EAU pump water; ~ **pulvérisée** *f* HYDROLOGIE spray; ~ **pure** *f* DISTRI EAU clean water, pure water, HYDROLOGIE pure water;

~ r ~ **réceptrice** *f* DISTRI EAU receiving water; ~ **régale** *f* CHIMIE aqua regia; ~ **résiduaire** *f* DISTRI EAU, POLLUTION wastewater, RECYCLAGE industrial wastewater; ~ **résiduelle** *f* HYDROLOGIE wastewater; ~ **résiduelle industrielle** *f* DISTRI EAU industrial discharge, industrial effluent, HYDROLOGIE industrial effluent, industrial wastewater; ~ **de retour** *f* PAPIER backwater; ~ **de rinçage** *f* DISTRI EAU backwash water; ~ **de rivière** *f* HYDROLOGIE river water; ~ **de robinet ordinaire** *f* HYDROLOGIE ordinary tap water; ~ **de ruissellement** *f* HYDROLOGIE surface water, POLLU MER, POLLUTION runoff;

~ s ~ **saine** *f* DISTRI EAU wholesome water, NAUT safe water; ~ **sale** *f* RECYCLAGE foul water; ~ **salée** *f* DISTRI EAU saline water, HYDROLOGIE brine, saltwater; ~ **saline** *f* HYDROLOGIE saline water, saltwater; ~ **savonneuse** *f* SECURITE soap and water solution; ~ **du sol** *f* DISTRI EAU soil water; ~ **souillée** *f* RECYCLAGE foul water; ~ **de source** *f* DISTRI EAU, HYDROLOGIE spring water; ~ **sous pression** *f* DISTRI EAU water under pressure; ~ **souterraine** *f* DISTRI EAU ground water, HYDROLOGIE ground water, underground water, POLLUTION underground water; ~ **souterraine libre** *f* DISTRI EAU free ground water; ~ **souterraine profonde** *f* DISTRI EAU deep ground water; ~ **stagnante** *f* DISTRI EAU stagnant water, HYDROLOGIE stagnant water, still water, standing water; ~ **de subsurface** *f* DISTRI EAU subterranean water; ~ **superficielle** *f* CONSTR, HYDROLOGIE surface water; ~ **de surface** *f* CHARBON, DISTRI EAU, HYDROLOGIE, OCEANO, POLLUTION surface water; ~ **surfondue** *f* HYDROLOGIE supercooled water;

~ t ~ **tellurique** *f* GEOLOGIE *magmatogène* juvenile water; ~ **thermale** *f* HYDROLOGIE thermal water; ~ **tranquille** *f* DISTRI EAU, HYDROLOGIE still water;

~ u ~ **usée** *f* CHIMIE, DISTRI EAU wastewater, HYDROLOGIE effluent, sewage, wastewater, POLLUTION black water, wastewater, RECYCLAGE wastewater; ~ **usée brute** *f* DISTRI EAU raw sewage; ~ **usée déposée** *f* DISTRI EAU settled sewage; ~ **usée domestique** *f* DISTRI EAU domestic waste water, sewage waste water, HYDROLOGIE domestic sewage, domestic waste water, RECYCLAGE domestic sewage; ~ **usée pluviale** *f* DISTRI EAU storm sewage; ~ **usée sanitaire** *f* DISTRI EAU sanitary waste water;

~ v ~ **vadose** *f* DISTRI EAU vadose water, HYDROLOGIE unsaturated zone water; ~ **de ville** *f* DISTRI EAU town water, HYDROLOGIE city water (AmE), mains water (BrE), municipal water; ~ **vive** *f* HYDROLOGIE running water

eau-mère *f* AGRO ALIM mother liquor

eaux: ~ **adjacentes** *f pl* OCEANO adjacent waters, contiguous waters; ~ **adjacentes aux côtes** *f pl* HYDROLOGIE coastal waters; ~ **continentales** *f pl* OCEANO continental shelf waters, inshore waters; ~ **côtières** *f pl* OCEANO coastal waters; ~ **intérieures** *f pl* DISTRI EAU inland waters, OCEANO internal waters; ~ **intermédiaires** *f pl* OCEANO intermediate waters; ~ **internationales** *f pl* NAUT international waters; ~ **mères** *f pl* CHIMIE bittern; ~ **pélagiques** *f pl* OCEANO pelagic waters; ~ **de pluie** *f pl* CHARBON storm water; ~ **de pluies polluées** *f pl* POLLUTION polluted rainwater; ~ **rouges** *f pl* OCEANO red tide, red waters; ~ **territoriales** *f pl* NAUT coastal waters, OCEANO territorial waters; ~ **usées** *f pl* DISTRI EAU, RECYCLAGE sewage

eaux-mères *f pl* OCEANO brine

eaux-vannes *f pl* RECYCLAGE domestic sewage

ébarbé *adj* PRODUCTION trimmed-off

ébarber *vt* CONS MECA *une pièce de métal* take the burr off, CONSTR *un joint* chip, wipe, IMPRIM trim, *mécanique* pare, PLAST CAOU *plastiques* deflash, PRODUCTION trim, trim off rough edges, trim off the burr from, *une pièce moulée* remove

ébarbeur *m* CONSTR chipper

ébarbeuse *f* CONS MECA grinding machine, trimming machine, RESSORTS deburring machine

ébarbure *f* PRODUCTION burr, fin

ébardoir *m* CONSTR shave hook

ébauchage *m* CERAM VER rough cutting, truing, CONS MECA blanking operations, PRODUCTION roughing, roughing-down

ébauche *f* PLAST CAOU preform, PRODUCTION blank; ~ **coulée** *f* CONSTR rough casting; ~ **d'engrenage** *f* CONS MECA gear blank; ~ **matricée** *f* PRODUCTION drop forging; ~ **des molettes de soudage** *f* CONS MECA seam welding wheel blank

ébauché[1] *adj* CONSTR rough-hewn, MECANIQUE rough-machined

ébauché:[2] ~ **de puddlage** *m* PRODUCTION puddle bar

ébauchement *m* RESSORTS slugging

ébaucher *vt* CONSTR *le bois* rough down

ébaucheur *m* PRODUCTION puddle roll, roughing roll, roughing-down roll

ébaucheuse *f* CHARBON rougher

ébauchoir *m* CONSTR boring bit; ~ **à mortaises** *m* CONSTR boring bit, mortise boring bit

ébavurage *m* CONS MECA, MECANIQUE deburring

ébavurer *vt* MECANIQUE debur, PLAST CAOU deflash

ébéniste *m* CONSTR cabinetmaker

ébénisterie *f* CONSTR cabinetmaking, cabinetwork

éblouissement *m* IMPRIM *photogravure* glare

ébonite *f* ELECTR *isolateur* ebonite, PLAST CAOU vulcanite, *caoutchouc* ebonite

éboueuse *f* TRANSPORT street cleaner

ébouillanter[1] *vt* THERMODYN scald

ébouillanter:[2] **s'** ~ *v réfl* SECURITE scald

ébouillir *vi* THERMODYN boil away

éboulé *adj* GEOLOGIE caved

éboulement *m* CH DE FER landslide, landslip, CHARBON slide, CONSTR fall of earth, fall of ground, GEOLOGIE landslide, landslip, rock slip, rockslide, MINES caving, caving in, collapse, PETR caving; ~ **de rocher** *m* CONSTR fall of rock; ~ **de terrain** *m* CH DE FER landslide, landslip, MINES run of ground; ~ **de terre** *m* CONSTR fall of earth, fall of ground; ~ **de terres** *m* CONSTR earth fall, landslide

éboulements *m pl* MINES caved area

ébouler[1] *vt* CONSTR cause to subside

ébouler:[2] **s'** ~ *v réfl* CONSTR fall in, GEOLOGIE collapse

éboulis *m* CONSTR fall of earth, fall of ground, GEOLOGIE debris, rubble, scree, GEOPHYS talus, MINES caved area, PETR rubble; ~ **de gravité** *m* GEOLOGIE gravity slide; ~ **de roches** *m* CONSTR fall of rock

ébranlage *m* PRODUCTION rapping

ébranlement *m* ESPACE *véhicules* judder

ébranler *vt* PRODUCTION rap

ébraser: s'~ *v réfl* CONSTR splay

ébréché *adj* MECANIQUE *outillage* jagged

ébullition *f* AGRO ALIM, CHIMIE, GENIE CHIM, PHYSIQUE, REFRIG boiling; ~ **libre** *f* REFRIG pool boiling; ~ **locale** *f* PRODUCTION subcooled boiling; ~ **nucléée** *f* REFRIG nucleate boiling; ~ **nucléée saturée** *f* NUCLEAIRE saturated boiling; ~ **par film** *f* NUCLEAIRE film boiling, sheet boiling; ~ **par film annulaire** *f* NUCLEAIRE annular film boiling; ~ **pelliculaire** *f* REFRIG film boiling; ~ **au reflux** *f* GENIE CHIM reflux boiling; ~ **saturée** *f* NUCLEAIRE saturated boiling; ~ **violente** *f* NUCLEAIRE violent boiling

écaillage *m* CERAM VER spalling, CHIMIE peeling off, CONSTR scaling, GEOLOGIE exfoliation, MATERIAUX chipping, peeling, scaling, NUCLEAIRE *de revêtements durs* galling, PRODUCTION scaling

écaille *f* CERAM VER chip, shell, CONSTR chip, chipping, GEOLOGIE slice, IMPRIM flaking, *impression* flake, PRODUCTION scale; ~ **tectonique** *f* GEOLOGIE upthrusted wedge

écaillement *m* CHIMIE peeling off, CONSTR spalling, MATERIAUX flaking, PRODUCTION scaling

écailler[1] *vt* OCEANO shuck, skin

écailler:[2] **s'~** *v réfl* CHIMIE peel off in flakes

écailles *f pl* PRODUCTION cinder, forge scale, hammer slag, hammer scale, nill; ~ **de fer** *f pl* PRODUCTION iron scale; ~ **de laminage** *f pl* PRODUCTION roll scale; ~ **de pots** *f pl* CERAM VER pot sherds

écart *m* CONS MECA deviation, variation, INFORMAT bias, exception, PRODUCTION deviation, THERMODYN *de température* difference; ~ **absolu moyen** *m* PRODUCTION mean absolute deviation; ~ **acceptable** *m* TRANSPORT *entre véhicules* tolerable gap; ~ **angulaire** *m* ELECTROTEC angular deviation; ~ **atonal** *m* ACOUSTIQUE atonal space, hearing threshold difference; ~ **de base de temps** *m* TV time-base error; ~ **de consommation** *m* PRODUCTION consumption deviation; ~ **de contraste** *m* IMPRIM key; ~ **de couleur** *m* PAPIER offshade; ~ **de coût** *m* PRODUCTION cost variance; ~ **de la criticité** *m* NUCLEAIRE deviation from criticality; ~ **des densités** *m* IMPRIM *photogravure* density range; ~ **énergétique** *m* NUCLEAIRE energy band gap, forbidden energy band, PHYSIQUE energy gap; ~ **à l'équilibre** *m* MATERIAUX equilibrium deviation; ~ **de fréquence** *m* ELECTRON frequency offset; ~ **intervoie** *m* INFORMAT, ORDINAT channel spacing; ~ **maximal admis de planéité** *m* CONS MECA maximum permissible flatness error; ~ **maximal toléré** *m* CONS MECA maximum permissible deviation; ~ **moyen** *m* ELECTR, MATH average deviation, mean deviation; ~ **moyen quadratique** *m* ELECTR root mean square deviation; ~ **moyen de température** *m* REFRIG mean temperature difference; ~ **d'ordre** *m* INFORMAT, ORDINAT ordering bias; ~ **de phase** *m* ELECTRON phase difference; ~ **du point de rosée** *m* REFRIG dew point depression; ~ **quadratique moyen** *m* ELECTRON standard deviation; ~ **de route transversal** *m* NAUT cross-track error; ~ **sur délai** *m* PRODUCTION lead time deviation; ~ **de température** *m* THERMODYN temperature difference; ~ **type** *m* ELECTRON, INFORMAT standard deviation, MATH average deviation, standard deviation, ORDINAT, PHYSIQUE, PRODUCTION standard deviation

écartement *m* CONS MECA clearance, distance apart, *des rivets d'axe en axe* pitch, CONSTR gap, *de rail, de wagon* gage (AmE), gauge (BrE), MECANIQUE gap; ~ **des charbons** *m* CINEMAT arc width; ~ **des contacts** *m* ELECTR *relais* contact gap; ~ **des électrodes** *m* AUTO spark plug gap; ~ **du foret à la colonne** *m* CONS MECA distance of drill from column; ~ **des garnitures** *m* AUTO brake clearance; ~ **des membrures** *m* NAUT frame spacing; ~ **minime d'exercice** *m* RESSORTS residual range; ~ **normal** *m* CH DE FER standard gage (AmE), standard gauge (BrE), standard rail gage (AmE), standard rail gauge (BrE), CONSTR standard gage (AmE), standard gauge (BrE); ~ **des perforations** *m* CINEMAT, PHOTO pitch; ~ **des rails** *m pl* CH DE FER distance between rails, rail gage (AmE), rail gauge (BrE), track gage (AmE), trackgauge (BrE), TRANSPORT rail gage (AmE), rail gauge (BrE); ~ **standard** *m* CH DE FER standard gauge (BrE), standard rail gage (AmE), standard rail gauge (BrE), CONSTR standard gage (AmE), standard gauge (BrE); ~ **des vis platinées** *m* AUTO contact gap; ~ **de la voie** *m* CH DE FER rail gage (AmE), rail gauge (BrE)

écarter: s'~ de la verticale *v réfl* CONS MECA run out of the vertical

écarteur *m* MECANIQUE *matériel de levage* spreader; ~ **de bande** *m* TV tape lifter

écartométrie *f* TELECOM deviation measurement

écarts *m pl* GEOMETRIE range of points; ~ **de réciprocité** *m pl* PHOTO reciprocity failure

ecdysone *f* CHIMIE ecdysone

ecgonine *f* CHIMIE ecgonine

échafaud *m* CONSTR scaffold, stage, staging; ~ **à bascule** *m* CONSTR flying scaffold; ~ **en encorbellement** *m* CONSTR flying scaffold; ~ **itinérant** *m* CONSTR boat; ~ **de maçon** *m* CONSTR common scaffold; ~ **ordinaire** *m* CONSTR common scaffold; ~ **simple** *m* CONSTR common scaffold; ~ **volant** *m* CONSTR boat, hanging stage, cradle, hanging scaffold, traveling cradle (AmE), travelling cradle (BrE)

échafaudage *m* CONSTR scaffold, scaffolding, stage, staging, SECURITE scaffolding; ~ **en bascule** *m* CONSTR flying scaffold; ~ **de fonçage** *m* CHARBON sinking trestle; ~ **itinérant** *m* CONSTR traveling cradle (AmE), travelling cradle (BrE); ~ **de montage** *m* CONSTR erection; ~ **suspendu** *m* CONSTR suspended scaffold; ~ **tubulaire** *m* CONSTR tubular scaffolding; ~ **volant** *m* CONSTR boat, cradle, hanging scaffold, hanging stage, traveling cradle (AmE), travelling cradle (BrE), MINES cradle, walling scaffold, walling stage

échalonnage: ~ vertical *m* AERONAUT *contrôle du trafic aérien* stacking

échancrer *vt* CONS MECA cutout

échancrure *f* CONS MECA cutout, DISTRI EAU notch, PRODUCTION indentation, notch

échange *m* INFORMAT, ORDINAT exchange, swapping, PRODUCTION trade-in; ~ **d'amplification d'impulsions** *m* PRODUCTION *automatisme industriel* hardware handshaking; ~ **d'authentification** *m* TELECOM authentication exchange; ~ **de cations** *m* HYDROLOGIE cation exchange; ~ **de chaleur** *m* THERMODYN heat exchange, heat transformation; ~ **convectif** *m* GAZ convective exchange; ~ **de documents informatisés** *m (EDI)* TELECOM electronic document interchange *(EDI)*; ~ **de données avec protocole** *m* INFORMAT, ORDINAT handshaking; ~ **de données commerciales** *m* TELECOM TDI, trade data interchange; ~ **de données informati-**

sées *m (EDI)* TELECOM electronic data interchange *(EDI)*; ~ **électronique de données** *m* TELECOM electronic data interchange; ~ **d'ions** *m* CHIMIE ion exchange; ~ **par modem** *m* INFORMAT, ORDINAT modem interchange; ~ **radiatif** *m* ESPACE *véhicules spatiaux, thermique* radiative heat transfer; ~ **thermique** *m* GAZ thermal exchange, thermic exchange

échanger *vt* INFORMAT, ORDINAT swap, TELECOM hold

échanges: ~ **intercompagnies** *m pl* AERONAUT *transport aérien* interlining

échangeur *m* CONSTR interchange; ~ **d'anion** *m* CHARBON anion exchanger; ~ **d'anions** *m* LESSIVES anionic exchanger; ~ **cationique** *m* CHARBON cation exchanger; ~ **de chaleur** *m* AGRO ALIM, EN RENOUV, MECANIQUE, NAUT, PAPIER, PETROLE *raffinerie*, REFRIG, THERMODYN heat exchanger; ~ **de chaleur d'air** *m* CONS MECA air-to-air heat exchanger; ~ **de chaleur à courant parallèle** *m* NUCLEAIRE parallel flow heat exchanger; ~ **de chaleur de grande superficie** *m* CONS MECA extended surface heat exchanger; ~ **de chaleur à tubes hélicoïdaux** *m* NUCLEAIRE helical coil-type heat exchanger; ~ **de chaleur tubulaire** *m* NUCLEAIRE shell and tube heat exchanger; ~ **à contre-courant** *m* AGRO ALIM counterflow heat exchanger; ~ **à courant parallèle** *m* CHAUFFAGE parallel flow heat exchanger; ~ **huile-kérosène** *m* AERONAUT fuel coolant heat exchanger; ~ **d'ions anioniques** *m* LESSIVES anionic exchanger; ~ **multitubulaire** *m* CHAUFFAGE multitube heat exchanger; ~ **de pression air-huile** *m* PRODUCTION air-oil actuator; ~ **de pression atmosphérique** *m* TRANSPORT cryptosteady pressure exchanger; ~ **primaire** *m* AERONAUT primary heat exchanger; ~ **solide** *m* CHARBON solid exchanger; ~ **thermique** *m* CHAUFFAGE, CONS MECA, PRODUCTION, THERMODYN heat exchanger; ~ **thermique à calandre** *m* REFRIG shell and tube heat exchanger; ~ **thermique à contre-courant** *m* REFRIG counterflow heat exchanger; ~ **thermique à courants croisés** *m* REFRIG crossflow heat exchanger; ~ **thermique à équicourant** *m* REFRIG parallel flow heat exchanger; ~ **thermique à liquide-vapeur** *m* REFRIG liquid suction heat exchanger; ~ **thermique à métal liquide** *m* THERMODYN liquid metal heat exchanger; ~ **thermique tubulaire** *m* CONS MECA tube-type heat exchanger

échantillon *m* CHARBON sample, specimen, CHIMIE sample, CONS MECA section, CONSTR bare, CRISTALL specimen, DISTRI EAU sample, ELECTRON sampled value, sample, ESPACE *communications* sample, INFORMAT read-out, sample, MATH *statistique* sample, METALL sample, test piece, ORDINAT read-out, sample, PAPIER, PHYSIQUE sample, PLAST CAOU sample, *essai* specimen, QUALITE, TELECOM sample, TEXTILE fabric sample, pattern; ~ **d'air** *m* SECURITE air sample; ~ **carotte** *m* CONSTR core sampling; ~ **de carotte** *m* PETR core sample; ~ **composite** *m* CHARBON, QUALITE composite sample; ~ **de contrôle** *m* CHIMIE check sample; ~ **à doser** *m* CHIMIE assay sample; ~ **d'entaille** *m* CHARBON channel sample; ~ **d'essai** *m* CHARBON analysis sample; ~ **au hasard** *m* AGRO ALIM, CHARBON random sample; ~ **intact** *m* CHARBON undisturbed sample; ~ **moyen** *m* HYDROLOGIE mixed average sample; ~ **primaire** *m* CHARBON primary sample; ~ **pris sur bobine à la machine** *m* PAPIER reel sample, reel specimen; ~ **remanié** *m* CHARBON remolded sample (AmE), remoulded sample (BrE); ~ **statistique des données de désintégrations** *m* PHYS RAYON statistical sample of

decay data; ~ **sur toute laize** *m* TEXTILE full-width sample; ~ **témoin** *m* CHARBON, CHIMIE check sample, ESSAIS reference piece; ~ **tiré au hasard** *m* MATH random sample

échantillonnage *m* AGRO ALIM, DISTRI EAU, ELECTRON, ENREGISTR, ESPACE *communications*, INFORMAT sampling, NAUT scantlings, ORDINAT, PETR, PETROLE, PHYSIQUE, PRODUCTION, TELECOM sampling; ~ **aléatoire** *m* TELECOM random sampling; ~ **automatique** *m* PRODUCTION, QUALITE automatic sampling; ~ **continu** *m* QUALITE continuous sampling; ~ **au hasard** *m* CHARBON, ESSAIS random sampling; ~ **intégral** *m* TELECOM integral sampling; ~ **isocinétique** *m* QUALITE isokinetic sampling; ~ **manuel** *m* CHARBON hand sampling; ~ **du minerai** *m* MINES ore sampling; ~ **multiple** *m* TELECOM multiple sampling; ~ **optimal** *m* TELECOM optimal sampling; ~ **proportionnel** *m* QUALITE proportional sampling; ~ **simple** *m* QUALITE discrete sampling; ~ **stratifié** *m* CHARBON, SECURITE stratified sampling; ~ **systématique** *m* INFORMAT, ORDINAT systematic sampling; ~ **à volume constant** *m* POLLUTION CVS, constant volume sampling

échantillonner *vt* ELECTRON, ESPACE *communications*, INFORMAT, ORDINAT, PHYSIQUE, QUALITE, TELECOM sample

échantillonneur *m* CHARBON sampler, ELECTROTEC sample-and-hold circuit, EQUIP LAB sampling device, PRODUCTION, TELECOM sampler; ~ **automatique** *m* CHARBON automatic sampler, EQUIP LAB *analyse* autosampler; ~ **conique** *m* CHARBON cone sampler; ~ **à curettes** *m* CHARBON spoon sampler; ~ **d'eau** *m* EQUIP LAB water sampler; ~ **latéral** *m* PETR sidewall sampler; ~ **mécanique** *m* CHARBON mechanical sampler; ~ **à riffles** *m* CHARBON riffle sampler

échantillonneuse *f* PRODUCTION *machine* sampler

échappée *f* CONSTR headroom

échappement *m* AERONAUT *moteur*, CHAUFFAGE exhaust, CONS MECA escapement mechanism, CONSTR leak, DISTRI EAU leakage, INFORMAT *(ESC)* escape *(ESC)*, INST HYDR release, ORDINAT *(ESC)* escape *(ESC)*, PAPIER, VEHICULES exhaust; ~ **accidentel** *m* POLLUTION accidental discharge; ~ **d'air** *m* MECANIQUE *système* air discharge; ~ **anticipé** *m* PRODUCTION early release; ~ **AV** *m* CONS MECA crank-end release; ~ **différé** *m* INST HYDR retarded release; ~ **en transmission** *m* INFORMAT, ORDINAT *caractère* DLE, data link escape; ~ **à manette** *m* CONS MECA *mécanisme à rochet* lever escapement; ~ **de moteur** *m* CONS MECA engine exhaust system; ~ **à la transmission** *m* INFORMAT, ORDINAT DLE, data link escape; ~ **de vapeur** *m* INST HYDR steam outlet

écharde *f* CONSTR splinter

écharpe *f* CINEMAT wall brace, CONSTR brace

échasse: ~ **d'échafaud** *f* CONSTR scaffold pole, standard

échaudage *m* CONSTR limewashing

échaudé *adj* THERMODYN scalded

échauder *vt* AGRO ALIM, THERMODYN scald

échaudure *f* AGRO ALIM, THERMODYN scald

échauffant *adj* PRODUCTION calorific

échauffement *m* CONS MECA overheating, POLLUTION temperature rise, thermal load, PRODUCTION heating; ~ **cinétique** *m* ESPACE *véhicules* aerodynamic heating, kinetic heating, air friction heating, PHYSIQUE kinetic heating; ~ **critique** *m* NUCLEAIRE critical heat flow, departure from nuclear boiling; ~ **par pertes diélectriques** *m* PLAST CAOU RF heating; ~ **propre** *m*

ELECTROTEC self-heating

échauffer[1] *vt* CHIMIE heat up, PHYSIQUE heat, THERMO-DYN heat, preheat, warm up

échauffer:[2] **s'~** *v réfl* CHIMIE heat up, THERMODYN heat up, overheat, *chaudière* fire up

échéancer *vt* PRODUCTION schedule

échéancier *m* PRODUCTION schedule

échec *m* ELECTROTEC failure

échelle *f* CONSTR ladder, scale, ELECTR dial, scale, GE-OMETRIE, IMPRIM scale, INFORMAT scale, scale factor, METROLOGIE scale, NAUT *du navire* ladder, ORDINAT scale; **~ absolue** *f* CHIMIE absolute scale of temperature; **~ accès au poste de pilotage** *f* AERONAUT flight compartment access stairway; **~ Baumé** *f* AGRO ALIM, PHYSIQUE Baumé scale; **~ Beaufort** *f* METEO, NAUT Beaufort scale; **~ binaire** *f* ELECTRON binary scaler; **~ de Brix** *f* AGRO ALIM Brix scale; **~ de charge** *f* NAUT deadweight scale; **~ chronostratigraphique** *f* GEOLOGIE geological timescale; **~ de commandement** *f* NAUT accommodation ladder; **~ de comptage** *f* ELECTRON scaler; **~ de comptage binaire** *f* ELECTRON binary scaler; **~ de comptage décimale** *f* ELECTRON decade scaler; **~ à coulisse** *f* CONSTR extension ladder; **~ à coulisse deux plans** *f* CONSTR double ladder; **~ à coulisses trois plans** *f* CONSTR triple ladder; **~ de coupée** *f* NAUT accommodation ladder; **~ décimale** *f* ELECTRON decade scaler; **~ de descente** *f* NAUT companionway, companionway ladder; **~ de deux** *f* ELECTRON binary scaler; **~ des diaphragmes** *f* PHOTO aperture scale; **~ dilatée** *f* METROLOGIE expanded scale; **~ de distances** *f* MILITAIRE *artillerie* range dial; **~ des distances** *f* CINEMAT distance scale; **~ divisée linéaire pour machines-outils** *f* CONS MECA linear-divided machine tool scale; **~ divisée ronde pour machines-outils** *f* CONS MECA machine tool scales; **~ de dix** *f* ELECTRON decade scaler; **~ double** *f* CONSTR stepladder, steps; **~ de dureté** *f* MECANIQUE *matériaux* hardness scale; **~ de dynamique** *f* ENREGISTR dynamic range; **~ d'écluses** *f* HYDROLOGIE flight of locks; **~ en chaîne** *f* CONSTR chain ladder; **~ en décibels** *f* ENREGISTR decibel scale; **~ en métal léger garantie contre les chutes** *f* SECURITE fall-safe light metal ladder; **~ d'étiage** *f* DISTRI EAU water gage (AmE), water gauge (BrE); **~ Fahrenheit** *f* PHYSIQUE Fahrenheit scale; **~ des fonctions d'ondes radiales** *f* PHYS RAYON scale of radial wavefunctions; **~ de fréquence** *f* ELECTRON frequency scale; **~ des gaz parfaits** *f* PHYSIQUE perfect gas scale; **~ de gradations** *f* TV gray scale (AmE), grey scale (BrE); **~ graduée** *f* INSTRUMENT instrument dial; **~ grandeur** *f* CONS MECA full scale; **~ de gris** *f* CINEMAT, IMPRIM, INFORMAT, TV gray scale (AmE), grey scale (BrE); **~ hédonique** *f* AGRO ALIM hedonic scale; **~ hybride** *f* PETR hybrid scale; **~ de l'image** *f* CINEMAT image scale, PHOTO scale of image; **~ à incendie** *f* SECURITE fire ladder; **~ K** *f* CHIMIE *acide* absolute scale of temperature; **~ Kelvin** *f* CINEMAT, CONSTR, ESPACE Kelvin scale; **~ linéaire** *f* ELECTR, ELECTRON, METROLOGIE linear scale; **~ linéaire des gris** *f* CINEMAT linear gray scale (AmE), linear grey scale (BrE); **~ logarithmique** *f* ELECTR *mesure*, ELECTRON logarithmic scale; **~ de magnitude de Pogson** *f* ASTRONOMIE Pogson scale of magnitude; **~ marchepied** *f* SECURITE stepladder; **~ de marée** *f* GEOPHYS tide level indicator, tide pole, OCEANO tidal scale, tide gage (AmE), tide gauge (BrE), tide scale; **~ mécanique** *f* CONSTR traveling ladderway (AmE), travelling ladderway (BrE); **~ de mise au point** *f* PHOTO distance scale; **~ mobile** *f* CONSTR traveling ladderway (AmE), travelling ladderway (BrE), PRODUCTION sliding scale; **~ musicale** *f* ACOUSTIQUE musical scale; **~ non linéaire** *f* CONSTR, METROLOGIE nonlinear scale; **~ portative** *f* SECURITE portable ladder; **~ pour machine-outil divisée par machine** *f* CONS MECA machine-divided machine tool scale; **~ de profondeur de champ** *f* PHOTO depth of field scale; **~ de profondeur de foyer** *f* PHOTO depth of focus scale; **~ de puits** *f* DISTRI EAU shaft ladder; **~ de réglage** *f* PRODUCTION trip scale; **~ de résistance** *f* ELECTROTEC resistor ladder; **~ de Richter** *f* CONSTR Richter scale; **~ de sauvetage** *f* CONSTR, SECURITE fire escape, fire ladder; **~ de sécurité** *f* SECURITE safety ladder; **~ suspendue** *f* CONSTR boat; **~ de température** *f* THERMODYN temperature scale; **~ des temps géologiques** *f* GEOLOGIE geological timescale; **~ des temps de pose** *f* PHOTO exposure scale; **~ thermodynamique** *f* ESPACE Kelvin scale; **~ de tirant d'eau** *f* NAUT draft marks (AmE), draught marks (BrE); **~ de tirets** *f* IMPRIM *composition* hyphen ladders; **~ des tonalités** *f* IMPRIM tone scale; **~ transversale** *f* CONS MECA diagonal scale; **~ à vernier** *f* CONS MECA vernier scale

échelles *f pl* SECURITE *méthodes de travail sûres* ladders

échelon *m* CONSTR rung, step, *d'une échelle* round, *d'une poutre* tread; **~ de commande cyclique** *m* AERONAUT cyclic control step; **~ de quantification** *m* ELECTRON quantization level; **~ de réglage** *m* ELECTR tapping step; **~ de tension** *m* PHYSIQUE voltage step

échelonné *adj* CONS MECA stepped

échelonnement *m* PRODUCTION time phase, time phasing

échelons: en ~ *adj* CONS MECA stepped

écheveau *m* TEXTILE hank

échine: ~ corallienne *f* OCEANO coral ridge

échinochromes *m pl* CHIMIE echinochromes

échinodermes *m* GEOLOGIE echinoderms

écho *m* CINEMAT ghost image, ELECTRON, ENREGISTR, ESPACE *communications*, INFORMAT, ORDINAT, PHYS ONDES *son réfléchi*, PHYSIQUE echo; **~ aléatoire** *m* NAUT random signal; **~ de deuxième balayage** *m* NAUT second trace echo; **~ fixe** *m* ESPACE *communications* permanent echo; **~ flottant** *m* ACOUSTIQUE flutter echo; **~ magnétique** *m* ENREGISTR magnetic echo, magnetic printing echo, TV magnetic print-through, printing echo; **~ de météores** *m* ESPACE meteor echo; **~ de météorites** *m* ESPACE meteor echo; **~ multiple** *m* ACOUSTIQUE, ENREGISTR, OCEANO multiple echo, TV flutter echo; **~ parasite** *m* NAUT, TELECOM clutter; **~ radar** *m* AERONAUT radar echo, NAUT radar blip; **~ secondaire** *m* NAUT second trace echo; **~ simple** *m* ACOUSTIQUE echo; **~ de vagues** *m* TELECOM sea clutter

échofantôme *m* ESPACE ghost echo

échogramme *m* PHYSIQUE echograph

échographe *m* PHYSIQUE echograph

échographie *f* PHYS ONDES scan, PHYS RAYON ultrasound scan

échointégration *f* OCEANO echo integration

écholocalisation *f* ACOUSTIQUE echolocation

échométrie *f* GAZ echometry

échoplex *m* INFORMAT, ORDINAT echoplex

échosondage *m* PHYS ONDES echo sounder

échosondeur *m* NAUT, OCEANO echo sounder

échouage *m* NAUT stranding, POLLU MER grounding

échoué *adj* NAUT stranded, *bateau* aground

échouement *m* POLLU MER grounding

échouer[1] *vt* ESPACE abort; ~ **volontairement** *vt* NAUT beach

échouer[2] *vi* NAUT go aground, run aground

échouerie *f* OCEANO stranding ground

éclaboussage *m* CHIMIE sputtering

éclabousser *vi* CHIMIE sputter

éclair *m* CINEMAT flash, ELECTR lightning discharge, ELECTROTEC lightning, IMPRIM *photogravure* flash, METEO lightning; ~ **d'appoint** *m* PHOTO fill-in flash; ~ **diffus** *m* METEO sheet lightning; ~ **en nappes** *m* METEO sheet lightning; ~ **de rayons X** *m* INSTRUMENT X-ray flash; ~ **vert** *m* ASTRONOMIE green flash

éclairage *m* CINEMAT illumination, lighting, METALL illumination; ~ **d'ambiance** *m* CINEMAT mood lighting; ~ **d'appoint** *m* CINEMAT accent light; ~ **de base** *m* CINEMAT keylight; ~ **à contre-jour** *m* CINEMAT backlight; ~ **de décrochement** *m* CINEMAT outline lighting; ~ **dirigé** *m* CINEMAT directional lighting; ~ **dominant** *m* CINEMAT key lighting; ~ **de l'échelle** *m* NAUT scale illumination; ~ **à effet** *m* CINEMAT effect lighting; ~ **électrique** *m* ELECTR *installation* electric lighting; ~ **faible** *m* CINEMAT low key; ~ **fluorescent** *m* ELECTR, ELECTROTEC, GAZ fluorescent lighting; ~ **de fond** *m* CINEMAT background light; ~ **à fond clair** *m* PHYSIQUE bright field illumination; ~ **inactinique** *m* CINEMAT darkroom lighting; ~ **incident** *m* INSTRUMENT incident illumination, incident top lighting, vertical illumination; ~ **indirect** *m* CINEMAT bounce lighting, indirect lighting, ELECTROTEC indirect illumination; ~ **des instruments** *m* INSTRUMENT instrument lighting; ~ **intense** *m* CINEMAT high key; ~ **intérieur** *m* ELECTROTEC indoor lighting; ~ **lumière artificielle** *m* CINEMAT tungsten lighting; ~ **mixte** *m* PHOTO mixed light; ~ **oblique** *m* IMPRIM oblique lighting, METALL oblique illumination; ~ **optimal d'un objet** *m* PHYS RAYON optimum object illumination; ~ **par l'arrière** *m* ELECTROTEC backlighting; ~ **par projection** *m* ELECTR, ELECTROTEC floodlighting; ~ **par réflection** *m* CINEMAT bounce lighting; ~ **par la tranche** *m* ELECTROTEC edge lighting; ~ **par transparence** *m* CINEMAT animation backlight, bottom lighting; ~ **de la plaque d'immatriculation** *m* AUTO rear license plate lamp (AmE), rear marker plate lamp (AmE), rear number plate lamp (BrE); ~ **plat** *m* CINEMAT, PHOTO flat lighting; ~ **du poste de pilotage** *m* AERONAUT flight compartment lights; ~ **principal** *m* PHOTO keylight; ~ **de relief** *m* CINEMAT modeling light (AmE), modelling light (BrE); ~ **sans relief** *m* CINEMAT flat lighting; ~ **de sécurité** *m* ELECTR emergency lighting; ~ **sur fond obscur** *m* PHYSIQUE dark ground illumination, dark-field illumination; ~ **uniforme** *m* CINEMAT flat lighting

éclaircir *vt* CERAM VER polish, PRODUCTION *la grille du foyer* clean

éclairement *m* ELECTROTEC, IMPRIM *photogravure, contrôle de qualité* illumination, OPTIQUE irradiance, *énergétique* intensity; ~ **énergétique** *m* OPTIQUE energy irradiance, TELECOM irradiance; ~ **énergétique spectrique** *m* OPTIQUE spectral energy irradiance, TELECOM spectral irradiance; ~ **lumineux** *m* PHYSIQUE illuminance, irradiance; ~ **spectrique** *m* OPTIQUE, TELECOM spectral irradiance

éclairer: ~ **à contre-jour** *vt* PHOTO backlight; ~ **de côté** *vt* PHOTO sidelight; ~ **de face** *vt* PHOTO front-light

éclat *m* ASTRONOMIE flare, *d'une étoile, d'une planète* brightness, CONSTR chip, chipping, splinter, split, *dans le bois* shake, GEOLOGIE *de verre volcanique* shard, MINERAUX luster (AmE), lustre (BrE), PHYS RAYON radiance, PRODUCTION chip, chipping, TEXTILE luster (AmE), lustre (BrE); ~ **adamantin** *m* MINERAUX adamantine luster (AmE), adamantine lustre (BrE); ~ **excessif** *m* IMPRIM *photogravure* glare; ~ **de limbe** *m* ASTRONOMIE limb brightening; ~ **métallique** *m* CHIMIE metallic luster (AmE), metallic lustre (BrE); ~ **d'obus** *m* MILITAIRE shell burst, shrapnel, shell splinter; ~ **photométrique** *m* PHYS RAYON photometric brightness; ~ **terne** *m* MATERIAUX dull luster (AmE), dull lustre (BrE)

éclaté: ~ **mécanique** *m* MECANIQUE exploded view

éclatement *m* CONSTR, IMPRIM *papiers* bursting, PAPIER, TEXTILE burst; ~ **des besoins** *m* PRODUCTION requirement explosion; ~ **en éventail** *m* PRODUCTION fanning out

éclater *vi* CONS MECA burst, CONSTR split, MECANIQUE, ORDINAT, PAPIER burst, SECURITE *incendie* break out, THERMODYN explode

éclateur *m* ELECTR *électrodes*, ELECTROTEC spark gap, GEOPHYS lightning arrester, PHYSIQUE spark gap; ~ **à intervalle micrométrique** *m* ELECTR *étincelle* micrometric spark discharger; ~ **de mesure** *m* ELECTROTEC measuring spark gap; ~ **de mise à la terre** *m* ELECTR *raccordement* earth terminal arrester (BrE), ground terminal arrester (AmE); ~ **parallèle** *m* ELECTR *étincelle* parallel spark gap; ~ **pare-étincelles** *m* ELECTR arc breaker, spark blowout, spark extinguisher, spark quencher, *relais* spark arrester; ~ **de protection** *m* ELECTR *étincelles* protective spark gap, *étincelle* reliefgap; ~ **rotatif** *m* ELECTR *étincelle* rotary discharger; ~ **à sphères** *m* ELECTROTEC sphere gap; ~ **de sûreté** *m* ELECTR *étincelle* coordinating gap, protective spark gap

éclatomètre *m* PAPIER Müllen tester, burst tester

éclipse *f* ASTRONOMIE, ESPACE *astronomie* eclipse; ~ **de la Lune** *f* ASTRONOMIE lunar eclipse; ~ **partielle** *f* ASTRONOMIE partial eclipse; ~ **pénombre** *f* ASTRONOMIE penumbral eclipse; ~ **solaire annulaire** *f* ASTRONOMIE annular solar eclipse; ~ **du soleil** *f* ASTRONOMIE solar eclipse; ~ **totale** *f* ASTRONOMIE total eclipse

écliptique *m* ASTRONOMIE, ESPACE ecliptic

éclissage *m* CH DE FER applying of joint bars (AmE), fishplating (BrE); ~ **angulaire** *m* CH DE FER angle fishplating (BrE), applying of angle joint bars (AmE); ~ **de fortune** *m* CH DE FER applying of emergency joint bars (AmE), emergency fishplating

éclisse *f* CH DE FER fishplate (BrE), joint bar (AmE), rail splice, splice bar (AmE), splice joint (AmE), CONS MECA batten; ~ **d'assemblage** *f* CONSTR *bois* cleat; ~ **cornière** *f* CH DE FER angle fishplate (BrE), applying of angle joint bar (AmE); ~ **électrique** *f* CH DE FER *voie* railbond; ~ **isolante** *f* CH DE FER insulating fishplate (BrE), insulating joint bar (AmE); ~ **magnétique réglable** *f* CONS MECA magnetic adjustable link; ~ **à patin** *f* CH DE FER angle fishplate (BrE), applying of angle joint bar (AmE)

éclogite *f* PETR eclogite

éclusage *m* DISTRI EAU locking, *d'un bateau* lockage

écluse *f* CONSTR lock, DISTRI EAU canal lock-gate, canal lock, lock, lock gate, sluice, *d'un caisson* airlock, HYDROLOGIE lock, navigation lock, NAUT lock, sluice, sluicegate, PAPIER reject gate, PRODUCTION gate shutter, shut, RECYCLAGE sluice; ~ **d'alimentation** *f* NUCLEAIRE feeder lock; ~ **de canal** *f* DISTRI EAU canal lock; ~ **double** *f* DISTRI EAU lift-lock; ~ **d'évacuation** *f*

DISTRI EAU discharge sluice; ~ **à grande chute** *f* HYDROLOGIE high lift-lock; ~ **à marée** *f* HYDROLOGIE tidal lock; ~ **de prise** *f* DISTRI EAU intake sluice; ~ **rotative** *f* CONS MECA *engins de rotation* rotary vane feeder; ~ **à sas** *f* DISTRI EAU lift-lock; ~ **à sas simple** *f* HYDROLOGIE single lift-lock

éclusée *f* DISTRI EAU feed

écluser[1] *vt* DISTRI EAU *un bateau* lock, NAUT *canal* install, PRODUCTION *le métal en fusion* shut off

écluser[2] *vi* NAUT pass through a lock

écluses: ~ **étagées** *f pl* HYDROLOGIE flight of locks; ~ **jumelées décalées** *f pl* HYDROLOGIE staggered locks

éclusier *m* NAUT lock keeper

écoin *m* MINES blocking board, headboard, bonnet, lid

école: ~ **industrielle** *f* PRODUCTION technical school

écologie *f* POLLU MER, POLLUTION ecology

économie: ~ **de carburant** *f* THERMODYN fuel economy; ~ **d'énergie** *f* PRODUCTION energy saving, THERMODYN energy conservation, energy saving; ~ **de la qualité** *f* QUALITE quality economics

économique: ~ **en combustible** *adj* ESPACE *véhicules*, THERMODYN *carburant* fuel-efficient

économiseur *m* INST HYDR, MAT CHAUFF economizer

écope *f* NAUT bailer, POLLU MER scoop

écoper *vt* NAUT bail out

écoperche *f* CONSTR scaffold pole, standard

écorage *m* OCEANO tally

écorçage *m* NUCLEAIRE chafing, PAPIER barking, peeling

écorce *f* GEOLOGIE crust, PAPIER bark; ~ **terrestre** *f* EN RENOUV lithosphere, ESPACE terrestrial crust, terrestrial surface, GEOLOGIE, GEOPHYS Earth's crust

écorceuse *f* PAPIER barker, peeler

écorné *m* CERAM VER chipped corner

écorner *vt* CONS MECA chamfer

écosphère *f* ASTRONOMIE ecosphere, POLLUTION biosphere

écossé *adj* AGRO ALIM husked, shelled

écosystème *m* POLLUTION ecosystem

écoulement *m* CHARBON flow, DISTRI EAU discharge, drainage, draining, flow, outflow, runoff, EN RENOUV flow, HYDROLOGIE flow, runoff, runoff, MECANIQUE *hydraulique*, METALL, PETROLE fluid flow, PHYS FLUID, PHYSIQUE, PLAST CAOU *plastiques, peintures* flow, POLLU MER discharge, leakage, POLLUTION runoff, stem flow, PRODUCTION *système hydraulique* outflow, REFRIG, TEXTILE, THERMODYN *débit de gaz* flow; ~ **aérodynamique** *m* ESPACE *véhicules* airflow; ~ **d'air** *m* AERONAUT airflow, slipstream, PHYS FLUID airflow; ~ **d'air transversal** *m* TRANSPORT crossflow; ~ **annuel** *m* DISTRI EAU annual runoff; ~ **avant relance** *m* CERAM VER starting down; ~ **axial** *m* AERONAUT axial flow; ~ **de base** *m* HYDROLOGIE base flow; ~ **biphasique** *m* GAZ biphasic flow; ~ **bipolaire** *m* ASTRONOMIE bipolar outflow; ~ **de chaleur** *m* THERMODYN heat flow; ~ **cisaillé** *m* PHYS FLUID shear flow; ~ **compressible** *m* PHYS FLUID compressible flow; ~ **continu** *m* TRANSPORT uninterrupted flow; ~ **convectif** *m* PHYS FLUID convective flow; ~ **convectif libre** *m* PHYS FLUID free convection flow; ~ **de Couette** *m* PHYS FLUID Couette flow; ~ **dans des canaux découverts** *m* PHYS FLUID flow in open channels; ~ **dans des conduites** *m* PHYS FLUID pipe flow; ~ **diaphasique** *m* REFRIG two-phase flow; ~ **direct** *m* HYDROLOGIE direct runoff; ~ **discontinu** *m* METALL jerky flow, TRANSPORT interrupted flow; ~ **de l'eau** *m* HYDROLOGIE current; ~

d'Ekman *m* HYDROLOGIE, OCEANO Ekman flow; ~ **en masse** *m* GEOLOGIE mass flow; ~ **extérieur** *m* PHYS FLUID free stream; ~ **fluage** *m* GEOLOGIE flowage; ~ **fluide** *m* PHYS FLUID fluid flow; ~ **de gaz** *m* PHYS FLUID gas flow; ~ **gazeux** *m* GAZ gas flow; ~ **gravitaire** *m* NUCLEAIRE gravity flow; ~ **d'huile** *m* PETROLE flow; ~ **hypersonique** *m* PHYS FLUID hypersonic flow; ~ **hypodermique** *m* HYDROLOGIE subsurface flow; ~ **incompressible** *m* PHYS FLUID, PHYSIQUE incompressible flow; ~ **instable** *m* PHYS FLUID, TRANSPORT unstable flow; ~ **instationnaire** *m* PHYS FLUID unstable flow; ~ **irrégulier** *m* METALL jerky flow, NUCLEAIRE unsteady flow; ~ **irrotationnel** *m* PHYS FLUID, PHYSIQUE irrotational flow; ~ **laminaire** *m* AERONAUT, MECANIQUE *hydraulique* laminar flow, PHYS FLUID laminar flow, laminar pipe flow, PHYSIQUE, REFRIG laminar flow; ~ **laminaire dans une conduite** *m* PHYS FLUID laminar pipe flow; ~ **libre** *m* MATERIAUX free flow; ~ **libre de convection** *m* PHYS FLUID free convection flow; ~ **libre du matériau** *m* MATERIAUX free flow conditions; ~ **liquide** *m* NUCLEAIRE, PHYS FLUID liquid flow; ~ **de marée** *m* DISTRI EAU tidal flow; ~ **non permanent** *m* HYDROLOGIE intermittent flow; ~ **normal** *m* TRANSPORT normal flow, stable flow; ~ **permanent** *m* AERONAUT steady flow, HYDROLOGIE permanent flow, PHYS FLUID steady flow; ~ **plastique** *m* GEOLOGIE flowage, METALL, PLAST CAOU plastic flow; ~ **de Poiseuille** *m* PHYS FLUID Poiseuille flow; ~ **pulsant** *m* PHYS FLUID pulsating flow; ~ **pulsatoire** *m* REFRIG pulsating flow; ~ **rampant** *m* PHYS FLUID creeping motion; ~ **retardé** *m* HYDROLOGIE retarded flow; ~ **rotationnel** *m* GAZ swirling flow; ~ **souterrain** *m* HYDROLOGIE underground flow; ~ **stabilisé** *m* AERONAUT *aérodynamique* steady flow; ~ **stationnaire** *m* PHYSIQUE steady flow; ~ **stratifié** *m* PHYS FLUID stratified flow; ~ **submergé** *m* PHYS FLUID drowned flow; ~ **de subsurface** *m* HYDROLOGIE subsurface flow; ~ **supercortical** *m* POLLUTION stem flow; ~ **superplastique** *m* MATERIAUX *céramiques* superplastic flow; ~ **à surface libre dans les canaux** *m* PHYS FLUID flow in open channels; ~ **thermique** *m* PHYS FLUID thermal flow; ~ **thermonucléaire** *m* NUCLEAIRE Knudsen effect; ~ **tourbillonnaire** *m* GAZ swirling stream; ~ **tournant de Couette** *m* PHYS FLUID rotating Couette flow; ~ **du trafic** *m* COMMANDE, TELECOM traffic flow; ~ **turbulent** *m* CHARBON eddy flow, PHYS FLUID, PHYSIQUE turbulent flow, REFRIG eddy flow; ~ **uniforme** *m* HYDROLOGIE uniform flow; ~ **varié** *m* HYDROLOGIE variable flow; ~ **vertical de l'eau** *m* TEXTILE vertical water flow; ~ **visqueux** *m* AGRO ALIM, METALL viscous flow, NUCLEAIRE *des fluides* frictional flow, viscous flow, PHYSIQUE viscous flow; ~ **visqueux incompressible** *m* PHYS FLUID viscous incompressible flow

écouler[1] *vt* EN RENOUV flow, TELECOM carry

écouler[2] **s'~** *v réfl* DISTRI EAU run out, HYDROLOGIE *rivière*, TEXTILE flow

écoute *f* ENREGISTR monitoring, NAUT *cordage* sheet; ~ **de grand-voile** *f* NAUT mainsheet; ~ **silencieuse** *f* TELECOM listening-in

écouteur *m* ACOUSTIQUE earphone, TELECOM headphones, receiver; ~ **circumaural** *m* ACOUSTIQUE circumaural earphone; ~ **à embout** *m* ACOUSTIQUE insert earphone

écoutille *f* ESPACE *véhicules* hatch, NAUT hatch, hatchway; ~ **d'accès** *f* ESPACE *véhicules* access panel; ~ **d'évacuation** *f* ESPACE escape hatch; ~ **de soute** *f*

ESPACE *véhicules* cargo hatch

écouvillon *m* MILITAIRE gun swab brush

écran:[1] **à ~** *adj* INFORMAT, ORDINAT screen-based

écran[2] *m* CERAM VER shade, CINEMAT screen, ELECTR *champ électronique* screening, *câble* shielding, ELECTRON screen, ESPACE screen, shield, INFORMAT, MECANIQUE screen, ORDINAT screen, video screen, PHYSIQUE screen, PRODUCTION fire screen, TV screen; **~ acoustique** *m* ACOUSTIQUE baffle, ENREGISTR acoustic screen; **~ d'aide** *m* INFORMAT, ORDINAT help screen; **~ aluminisé** *m* ELECTRON aluminized screen; **~ antiéblouissant** *m* VEHICULES *accessoire* antidazzle visor, antiglare visor, day-night mirror, sun visor; **~ antisouffle** *m* AERONAUT *barrière* blast fence; **~ argenté** *m* CINEMAT silver screen; **~ arrière** *m* CERAM VER rear lip tile; **~ avant** *m* CERAM VER front lip tile; **~ axial** *m* NUCLEAIRE axial shield; **~ biologique** *m* NUCLEAIRE biological shield; **~ d'un câble** *m* ELECTR *conducteur* cable screen; **~ cathodique** *m* TELECOM cathode ray screen, TV cathode screen; **~ de chaleur** *m* THERMODYN *aérospatial, Bouclier thermique* heat shield; **~ coffret automatique** *m* PHOTO self-erecting screen; **~ contre le rayonnement** *m* SECURITE radiation shield; **~ de contrôle** *m* TV preview monitor; **~ de contrôle couleur** *m* TV RGB monitor; **~ de contrôle studio** *m* TV studio monitor; **~ couleur** *m* INFORMAT, ORDINAT color display (AmE), colour display (BrE); **~ à cristaux liquides** *m* ELECTR, ELECTRON, INFORMAT, ORDINAT, PHYSIQUE LCD, liquid crystal display, TELECOM crystal liquid display, TV LCD, liquid crystal display; **~ diamagnétique du noyau** *m* PHYS RAYON diamagnetic shielding of the nucleus; **~ diffuseur** *m* CINEMAT diffuser, diffuser scrim, scrim, PHOTO incident light attachment; **~ électroluminescent** *m* INFORMAT, ORDINAT electroluminescent display; **~ électromagnétique** *m* ELECTR electromagnetic shielding, PHYSIQUE electromagnetic shielding; **~ électrostatique** *m* ELECTR static screen, ELECTRON, PHYSIQUE electrostatic screen; **~ en couleurs** *m* IMPRIM color screen (AmE), colour screen (BrE); **~ en tresse de cuivre** *m* ELECTR *câble* copper braid shielding; **~ en verre dépoli** *m* PHOTO ground glass screen; **~ d'extrémité** *m* ELECTRON end screen; **~ de Faraday** *m* ELECTROTEC Faraday screen; **~ filtre** *m* PRODUCTION filter screen; **~ fluorescent** *m* ELECTR *oscilloscope*, ELECTRON, INSTRUMENT, PHYSIQUE fluorescent screen; **~ gris neutre** *m* CINEMAT, PHOTO neutral density filter; **~ à haute luminosité** *m* ELECTRON high-brightness screen; **~ ignifuge** *m* PRODUCTION, SECURITE fire screen; **~ interne** *m* ELECTRON internal shield; **~ à longue persistance** *m* TV long-persistence screen; **~ luminescent** *m* TV phosphor screen; **~ luminescent à points** *m* TV phosphor dot faceplate; **~ à mémoire** *m* ELECTRON storage screen; **~ de menu** *m* INFORMAT, ORDINAT menu screen; **~ métallique** *m* PRODUCTION shield; **~ métallisé** *m* CINEMAT silver screen, ELECTRON metalized screen (AmE), metallized screen (BrE); **~ de microphone** *m* ENREGISTR microphone blanket; **~ de mise au point** *m* INSTRUMENT focusing screen; **~ opaque** *m* CINEMAT nigger; **~ orthochromatique** *m* PHOTO color screen (AmE), colour screen (BrE); **~ pare-douche** *m* CERAM VER shower screen; **~ pare-souffle** *m* AERONAUT *barrière* blast fence; **~ partagé** *m* INFORMAT, ORDINAT split screen; **~ partagé en régions** *m* INFORMAT, ORDINAT split screen; **~ à pénétration** *m* ELECTRON penetration screen; **~ perlé** *m* CINEMAT beaded screen, glass-

beaded screen, pearl screen, PHOTO beaded screen; **~ à plasma** *m* INFORMAT, ORDINAT plasma display; **~ plat** *m* INFORMAT, ORDINAT, TELECOM, TV flat screen; **~ plein jour** *m* CINEMAT daylight screen; **~ plongeant** *m* CERAM VER control tweel; **~ pour projection par transparence** *m* CINEMAT back projection screen; **~ de protection** *m* ELECTR *conducteur d'un câble* shield, EQUIP LAB safety screen, SECURITE *pour tubes à rayons cathodiques* protective screen; **~ de protection des mains** *m* SECURITE hand shield; **~ de protection du visage** *m* SECURITE face shield; **~ de radar** *m* AERONAUT radar screen, MILITAIRE radar display, NAUT radar screen, TRANSPORT radar scope, radar screen; **~ réflecteur** *m* CINEMAT reflecting screen, reflector, PHOTO reflecting screen; **~ rémanent** *m* TV long-persistence screen; **~ de repérage** *m* TV cue screen; **~ sensitif** *m* INFORMAT touch-sensitive screen; **~ de soie** *m* CERAM VER silk-screen; **~ sonore** *m* ENREGISTR sound screen; **~ de soudeur** *m* SECURITE welder's hand shield; **~ sur âme** *m* ELECTR *conducteur d'un câble* conductor screen; **~ sur enveloppe isolante** *m* ELECTR insulation screen, *conducteur d'un câble* core screen; **~ de sûreté** *m* PHOTO safelight filter, *chambre noire* safelight; **~ suspendu** *m* CERAM VER suspended curtain wall; **~ tactile** *m* INFORMAT touch-sensitive screen, ORDINAT touch screen, touch-sensitive screen; **~ témoin** *m* TV camera monitor, picture monitor; **~ thermique** *m* ESPACE heat screen, thermal screen; **~ à trace foncé** *m* ELECTRON dark-trace screen; **~ translucide** *m* CINEMAT rear projection screen; **~ de visualisation** *m* ELECTRON display screen, ESPACE display, INFORMAT VDU, visual display unit, PHYSIQUE visual display unit, TELECOM VDU, visual display unit, display screen, TV VDU, visual display unit; **~ vitré** *m* CINEMAT frost

écrans: ~ multiples *m pl* TV multiscreen; **~ publicitaires successifs** *m pl* TV back-to-back commercials

écrantage *m* TV *de câble* screening

écrasé *m* PAPIER crushing

écrasée *f* CONSTR collapse, MINES caving, caving in, collapse, *du toit* subsidence

écrasement *m* CONS MECA collapsing, CONSTR crushing, INFORMAT, ORDINAT crash, *données* overwriting, PRODUCTION flattening, *d'une chaudière* implosion, SECURITE *dangers mécaniques*, TEXTILE crushing; **~ éjection** *m* SECURITE crushing ejection; **~ d'un joint** *m* CONS MECA seal compression; **~ d'un pétard** *m* CH DE FER exploding of detonator; **~ système** *m* INFORMAT, ORDINAT system crash; **~ de tête** *m* INFORMAT, ORDINAT head crash

écraser[1] *vt* AGRO ALIM, PAPIER, TEXTILE crush

écraser:[2] **s'~** *v réfl* ESPACE crash

écrasure *f* CERAM VER rub (AmE), scrub mark (BrE)

écrémage *m* CERAM VER, PRODUCTION skimming

écrémer *vt* POLLUTION skim off, PRODUCTION skim, skim off

écrémeur *m* CERAM VER, PETROLE, POLLU MER skimmer; **~ à action centrifuge** *m* POLLU MER centrifugal skimmer; **~ autopropulsé** *m* POLLU MER self-propelled skimmer; **~ à bande** *m* POLLU MER belt skimmer; **~ centrifuge** *m* POLLU MER centrifugal skimmer; **~ à corde flottante** *m* POLLU MER rope skimmer; **~ à courroie oléophile** *m* POLLU MER oleophilic belt skimmer; **~ à déversoir** *m* POLLU MER weir skimmer; **~ à disque** *m* POLLU MER disc skimmer (BrE), disk skimmer (AmE); **~ dynamique** *m* POLLU MER hydrodynamic skimmer; **~ à effet de vortex** *m* POLLU MER weir with vortex skimmer; ~ **à seuil** *m* POLLU MER weir skimmer; ~ **à succion directe** *m* POLLU MER direct suction skimmer; ~ **à tambour** *m* POLLU MER drum skimmer; ~ **à vortex** *m* POLLU MER vortex skimmer

écrémeuse *f* AGRO ALIM cream separator, separator

écrémoir *m* PRODUCTION skimmer, skimming ladle

écrêtage *m* ELECTRON limiting, peak clipping, ENREGISTR clipping; ~ **numérique** *m* PETR flat topping; ~ **du signal** *m* ELECTRON signal clipping

écrêter *vt* ELECTRON limit, ELECTROTEC clip, HYDROLOGIE overtop

écrêteur *m* AERONAUT chopper, clipper, ELECTRON limiter, ENREGISTR clipper, TV clipper, peak limiter; ~ **du blanc** *m* TV white clip, white limiter; ~ **d'impulsion** *m* TV pulse clipper; ~ **à niveau constant** *m* ELECTRON hard limiter; ~ **de noir** *m* TV black clipper; ~ **du signal de parole** *m* ENREGISTR speech clipper

écrevisse *f* PRODUCTION lever grip tongs

écrire *vt* INFORMAT, ORDINAT write

écriteau *m* CONSTR board

écriture *f* INFORMAT, ORDINAT write; ~ **avec regroupement** *f* INFORMAT, ORDINAT gather write

écrou *m* CONS MECA, MECANIQUE, VEHICULES nut; ~ **à ailettes** *m* CONSTR butterfly nut; ~ **autofreiné** *m* CONS MECA elastic stop nut; ~ **à billes** *m* CONS MECA ball circulating nut; ~ **borgne** *m* AERONAUT acorn nut, CONS MECA cap nut; ~ **de calage** *m* COMMANDE adjusting nut, adjustment nut; ~ **de centrage** *m* CONS MECA centering nut (AmE), centring nut (BrE); ~ **à chapeau** *m* CONS MECA box nut, MECANIQUE cap nut; ~ **à collet** *m* CONS MECA flanged nut; ~ **conique** *m* NUCLEAIRE *fraisé* countersunk nut; ~ **à créneaux** *m* CONS MECA castle nut, CONSTR castellated nut, castle nut; ~ **crénelé** *m* CONS MECA castellated nut, CONSTR castellated nut, castle nut; ~ **cylindrique** *m* CONS MECA round nut; ~ **décolleté** *m* CONS MECA machine-made nut; ~ **à dents** *m* CONS MECA notched nut, slotted nut; ~ **de dôme** *m* CONS MECA dome nut; ~ **élastique** *m* CONS MECA elastic stop nut; ~ **à entailles** *m* CONS MECA notched nut, slotted nut; ~ **fendu** *m* PRODUCTION elastic nut; ~ **fileté** *m* CONS MECA threaded nut; ~ **flottant** *m* CONS MECA floating anchor nut; ~ **godronné** *m* CONS MECA knurled nut, milled nut, nurled nut; ~ **haut** *m* CONS MECA heavy nut, CONSTR deep nut; ~ **hexagonal** *m* CONS MECA hexagon nut; ~ **hexagonal à freinage interne avec couple préalable** *m* CONS MECA prevailing torque-type hexagon nut; ~ **indesserrable** *m* CONS MECA elastic stop nut, locknut; ~ **moleté** *m* CONS MECA knurled nut, milled nut, nurled nut; ~ **à molette** *m* CONS MECA knurled nut, milled nut, nurled nut; ~ **non taraudé** *m* PRODUCTION blank nut; ~ **normal** *m* CONS MECA ordinary hexagonal nut; ~ **nylstop** *m* CONS MECA nylstop self-locking nut; ~ **ordinaire** *m* CONS MECA standard nut; ~ **à oreilles** *m* CONS MECA thumbnut, wing nut (BrE), PRODUCTION fly nut, hand nut, VEHICULES wing nut (BrE); ~ **papillon** *m* CONS MECA thumbnut, CONSTR butterfly nut, PRODUCTION fly nut, hand nut; ~ **à patte de scellement** *m* CONS MECA anchor nut, press nut; ~ **de pied** *m* PHOTO tripod bush; ~ **à portée sphérique** *m* AERONAUT acorn nut; ~ **pression** *m* CONS MECA anchor nut, press nut; ~ **prisonnier** *m* MECANIQUE insert nut; ~ **de raccord** *m* CONS MECA coupling nut; ~ **à rainures** *m* CONS MECA notched nut, slotted nut; ~ **de réglage** *m* COMMANDE adjusting nut, adjustment nut, CONS MECA regulating nut, unscrewing bush; ~ **à river** *m* CONS MECA anchor nut,

press nut; ~ **de roue** *m* AUTO lug nut (AmE), wheel nut (BrE); ~ **de serrage** *m* CONS MECA maiden nut, PRODUCTION torque nut; ~ **à six pans** *m* CONS MECA hexagonal nut; ~ **sphérique** *m* NUCLEAIRE ball nut; ~ **de sûreté** *m* CONS MECA safety nut; ~ **taraudé** *m* CONS MECA tapped nut; ~ **taraudeur** *m* PRODUCTION die nut; ~ **tendeur** *m* COMMANDE adjusting nut, adjustment nut; ~ **à trous** *m* PRODUCTION holed nut; ~ **de vis-mère** *m* CONS MECA clasp nut; ~ **à 8 pans** *m* CONS MECA octagonal nut

écrou-frein *m* CONS MECA locknut

écrou-guide *m* CONS MECA guide nut

écroui *adj* RESSORTS cold-hardened, hammer-hardened, work-hardened

écrouissage *m* CRISTALL work hardening, MATERIAUX strain hardening, MECANIQUE *matériaux* work hardening, RESSORTS cold working, relaxing, work hardening

écroulement *m* CONSTR collapse; ~ **de gravitation** *m* ASTRONOMIE gravitational collapse

écrouler: **s'~** *v réfl* CONSTR give way, *pont* give way

écrous: ~ **et boulons** *m pl* CONSTR nuts and bolts

écru *adj* TEXTILE in the gray (AmE), in the grey (BrE), undyed

Ecu *m* ASTRONOMIE Scutum

écubier *m* NAUT hawse, hawse pipe

écueil *m* OCEANO reef

écuelle *f* MINES pan, PRODUCTION *d'une vis* groove

écumage *m* GENIE CHIM foaming, PRODUCTION skimming

écume *f* AGRO ALIM foam, scum, CHARBON froth, scum, CHIMIE, HYDROLOGIE scum, NAUT foam, OCEANO foam, white caps, white horses, PLAST CAOU frothing, PRODUCTION skim; ~ **de flottation** *f* GENIE CHIM flotation froth; ~ **de mer** *f* MINERAUX meerschaum, OCEANO sea foam; ~ **de silice** *f* CERAM VER silica scum

écumer[1] *vt* PRODUCTION skim, skim off

écumer[2] *vi* GENIE CHIM foam

écumeux *adj* GENIE CHIM foamy

écumoire *f* DISTRI EAU rose, strainer, PRODUCTION skimmer, skimming ladle

écurer *vt* PRODUCTION clean out

écusson *m* CERAM VER badge, CONSTR escutcheon (AmE), scutcheon (BrE), key plate

édénite *f* MINERAUX edenite

édestine *f* CHIMIE edestin

EDI *abrév* TELECOM *(échange de données informatisées, échange de documents informatisés)* EDI *(electronic document interchange)*

édifier *vt* CONSTR build

édingtonite *f* MINERAUX edingtonite

éditer *vt* INFORMAT, ORDINAT edit

éditeur *m* INFORMAT, ORDINAT editor; ~ **de liens** *m* INFORMAT link editor, linkage editor, ORDINAT link editor, linkage editor; ~ **pleine page** *m* INFORMAT, ORDINAT full screen editor; ~ **de texte** *m* INFORMAT, ORDINAT, TELECOM text editor

édition *f* INFORMAT, ORDINAT editing, edit; ~ **abrégée** *f* IMPRIM abridged edition; ~ **des alarmes** *f* TELECOM alarm printout facility; ~ **électronique** *f* ELECTRON electronic publishing; ~ **graphique** *f* INFORMAT, ORDINAT graphical editing; ~ **de l'inventaire** *f* PRODUCTION inventory reporting; ~ **de liens** *f* ORDINAT link editing; ~ **de luxe** *f* IMPRIM de luxe edition; ~ **optique** *f* OPTIQUE optical publishing; ~ **révisée** *f* IMPRIM revised edition

édredon *m* TEXTILE comforter, eiderdown

éduction *f* MAT CHAUFF *de vapeur* eduction
édulcorant *m* AGRO ALIM sweetener
édulcoré *adj* AGRO ALIM sweetened
effaçage: ~ **du raccord de la piste sonore** *m* ENREGISTR blooping
effacement *m* ACOUSTIQUE, ENREGISTR erasure, GAZ interruption, INFORMAT, ORDINAT clearing, TV blanking, erasure; ~ **à aimant permanent** *m* ENREGISTR permanent magnet erasing; ~ **par tête volante** *m* TV flying erase head; ~ **par ultraviolet** *m* INFORMAT, ORDINAT ultraviolet erasing; ~ **de la sécurité de train** *m* AERONAUT landing gear safety override; ~ **sélectif** *m* INFORMAT, ORDINAT selective erasure
effacer *vt* AERONAUT *la piste* overshoot, ENREGISTR erase, INFORMAT, ORDINAT clear, delete, erase
effaceur *m* TV bulk eraser, eraser; ~ **magnétique** *m* ENREGISTR, TV degausser; ~ **total** *m* ENREGISTR bulk eraser
effectif[1] *adj* ACOUSTIQUE, MECANIQUE effective
effectif:[2] ~ **cumulé** *m* METROLOGIE total size; ~ **de l'échantillon** *m* METROLOGIE sample size
effectuer:[1] ~ **un appel à** *vt* TELECOM make a call to
effectuer:[2] ~ **une nouvelle compilation** *vi* ORDINAT recompile; ~ **un relèvement** *vi* NAUT take a bearing; ~ **la tombée de front de taille** *vi* MINES bring down the face
effervescence *f* CHIMIE effervescence
effervescent *adj* AGRO ALIM effervescent
effet[1] *m* MECANIQUE effect, *mécanique, physique* action, PHYS FLUID, TELECOM effect;
◼ **a** ~ **d'accélération** *m* ESPACE fly-by effect; ~ **acousto-optique** *m* OPTIQUE acousto-optic effect; ~ **d'agrandissement** *m* IMPRIM *photogravure, composition, optique* zoom; ~ **aigu** *m* POLLUTION acute effect; ~ **d'anneau de diamants** *m* ASTRONOMIE diamond ring effect; ~ **d'apprêt glacé** *m* COULEURS gloss effect; ~ **d'arête** *m* PHYSIQUE edge effect; ~ **Auger** *m* PHYS RAYON, PHYSIQUE Auger effect;
◼ **b** ~ **bambou** *m* NUCLEAIRE bamboo effect; ~ **de bande de bord de piste** *m* TV edge of track banding; ~ **de bande** *m* TV banding, head banding; ~ **de bande sur le bruit** *m* TV banding on noise; ~ **de bande sur la saturation** *m* TV banding on saturation; ~ **de bande sur la teinte** *m* TV banding on hue; ~ **Barkhausen** *m* PHYSIQUE Barkhausen effect; ~ **Barnett** *m* PHYSIQUE Barnett effect; ~ **Becquerel** *m* ELECTR *pile électrolytique* Becquerel effect; ~ **biologique** *m* PHYS RAYON biological effect; ~ **de blindage négatif** *m* NUCLEAIRE deshielding effect; ~ **de bord** *m* ELECTROTEC edge effect, fringe effect, TV fringe effect; ~ **de bruit Schottky** *m* PHYSIQUE Schottky noise;
◼ **c** ~ **de cache** *m* CINEMAT vignetting; ~ **calorifique** *m* THERMODYN heat effect; ~ **capillaire** *m* PHYS FLUID capillary action; ~ **de capture** *m* TELECOM capture effect; ~ **des carènes liquides** *m* NAUT free surface effect; ~ **de cavité résonante** *m* ENREGISTR cavity resonance effect; ~ **de champ** *m* ELECTRON, TELECOM field effect; ~ **de la charge accumulée** *m* ELECTROTEC storage effect; ~ **de cheminée** *m* CHAUFFAGE *mouvement d'air ou de gaz* chimney effect; ~ **de chevrotement** *m* TV flutter effect; ~ **chronique** *m* POLLUTION chronic effect; ~ **Coanda** *m* PHYS FLUID *écoulement* Coanda effect; ~ **de coïncidence** *m* ENREGISTR coincidence effect; ~ **Compton** *m* PHYS RAYON, PHYSIQUE Compton effect; ~ **Compton inverse** *m* PHYSIQUE inverse Compton effect; ~ **de contournement** *m* ACOUSTIQUE

contour effect; ~ **de contraste** *m* TV contrast effect; ~ **de copie magnétique** *m* ENREGISTR magnetic print-through; ~ **corona** *m* ELECTR *décharge*, ELECTROTEC, ESPACE corona effect; ~ **Cotton-Mouton** *m* PHYSIQUE Cotton-Mouton effect; ~ **couronne** *m* ELECTR *décharge*, ELECTROTEC corona effect; ~ **de culot** *m* ESPACE base flow effect;
◼ **d** ~ **du débit de dose** *m* PHYS RAYON dose rate effect; ~ **détergent** *m* LESSIVES detergent effect; ~ **différentiel** *m* AERONAUT differential effect; ~ **Doppler** *m* ELECTRON Doppler effect, PETR Doppler effect, Doppler shift, PHYSIQUE Doppler effect; ~ **Doppler-Fizeau** *m* ACOUSTIQUE, PHYS ONDES Doppler-Fizeau effect; ~ **drapeau** *m* AERONAUT feathering effect; ~ **dynamo** *m* ESPACE dynamo effect;
◼ **e** ~ **Early** *m* ELECTRON Early effect; ~ **d'eau arrêtée** *m* EN RENOUV backwater effect; ~ **d'écho** *m* TV magnetic print-through; ~ **d'écho magnétique** *m* ENREGISTR magnetic printing echo; ~ **d'écran** *m* ELECTR screening effect, *champ électromagnétique* shielding effect, TELECOM screen effect; ~ **d'écran des vagues** *m* TELECOM wave shadowing effect; ~ **Einstein-de-Haas** *m* PHYSIQUE Einstein-de-Haas effect; ~ **d'élargissement et d'aplatissement** *m* IMPRIM *papier* winding and fanning; ~ **électroacoustique** *m* TELECOM acoustoelectric effect; ~ **électrodermal** *m* ACOUSTIQUE electrodermal effect; ~ **électromérique** *m* CHIMIE electromeric effect; ~ **électro-optique** *m* OPTIQUE electro-optic effect; ~ **électro-optique de Kerr** *m* PHYSIQUE Kerr electro-optical effect; ~ **d'empreinte magnétique** *m* ACOUSTIQUE magnetic printing effect, TV magnetic print-through; ~ **d'entaille** *m* CONS MECA notch effect; ~ **d'entrefer** *m* TV gap effect; ~ **d'épontes** *m* PETR adjacent bed effect, shoulder bed effect; ~ **d'étouffement** *m* ELECTRON capture effect;
◼ **f** ~ **Faraday** *m* ELECTROTEC Faraday effect, ESPACE Faraday rotation, PHYSIQUE Faraday effect; ~ **de flottement** *m* ACOUSTIQUE frequency flutter; ~ **de la force de Coriolis** *m* PHYS FLUID *fluides en rotation* Coriolis effect; ~ **des forces attractives** *m* TRANSPORT attractive effect;
◼ **g** ~ **géostatique** *m* PETR overburden effect; ~ **Gunn** *m* ELECTRON Gunn effect;
◼ **h** ~ **Hall** *m* ELECTR *électromagnétisme*, ESPACE, PHYS RAYON, PHYSIQUE Hall effect; ~ **Hall quantique** *m* PHYSIQUE quantum Hall effect; ~ **Hanle** *m* PHYS RAYON Hanle effect; ~ **Holden** *m* NUCLEAIRE Holden effect; ~ **d'hydroglisseur** *m* AERONAUT aquaplaning;
◼ **i** ~ **d'inclinaison magnétique** *m* GEOPHYS magnetic latitude effect; ~ **isotopique** *m* NUCLEAIRE kinetic isotope effect;
◼ **j** ~ **Josephson** *m* ELECTRON, NUCLEAIRE, PHYSIQUE Josephson effect; ~ **Josephson alternatif** *m* ELECTRON AC Josephson effect; ~ **Josephson continu** *m* ELECTROTEC, PHYSIQUE DC Josephson effect; ~ **Joule** *m* ELECTR, ELECTROTEC, PHYSIQUE Joule effect;
◼ **k** ~ **de Kelvin** *m* ELECTR Kelvin effect; ~ **Knudsen** *m* NUCLEAIRE Knudsen effect;
◼ **l** ~ **Langmuir** *m* METEO Langmuir effect; ~ **Larsen** *m* CINEMAT larsen effect, ENREGISTR audio feedback, howling, TV feedback; ~ **laser** *m* ELECTRON laser action; ~ **laser continu** *m* ELECTRON continuous laser action; ~ **létal** *m* POLLUTION lethal effect; ~ **local** *m* TELECOM sidetone; ~ **de longue ligne** *m* ELECTRON long-line effect; ~ **lumineux** *m* CINEMAT lighting effect;
◼ **m** ~ **magnéto-optique** *m* OPTIQUE magneto-optical

effect; ~ **magnéto-optique de Kerr** *m* PHYSIQUE Kerr magneto-optical effect; ~ **Magnus** *m* PHYSIQUE Magnus effect; ~ **de manche** *m* AERONAUT ram recovery; ~ **martelé** *m* PLAST CAOU *peinture, caractéristique* hammer finish; ~ **maser** *m* ESPACE *communications* microwave amplification by stimulated emission of radiation; ~ **de masque** *m* ACOUSTIQUE masking effect, CINEMAT vignetting; ~ **de masse** *m* NUCLEAIRE mass effect, packing effect; ~ **mécanothermique** *m* THERMODYN mechanothermal effect; ~ **Meissner** *m* ELECTRON, PHYSIQUE Meissner effect; ~ **de mer** *m* ESPACE sea clutter; ~ **microphonique cochléaire** *m* ACOUSTIQUE cochlear microphonic effect; ~ **Mössbauer** *m* PHYSIQUE Mössbauer effect; ~ **Mullin** *m* PLAST CAOU *caoutchouc* Mullin's effect;

~ n ~ **nocif** *m* POLLUTION harmful effect; ~ **nuisible** *m* POLLUTION harmful effect; ~ **de nuit** *m* CINEMAT day for night, night effect;

~ o ~ **d'obliquité** *m* INFORMAT skew; ~ **d'ombrage** *m* TV shading;

~ p ~ **pariétal** *m* PETR skin effect; ~ **de paroi** *m* CHARBON wall effect; ~ **de Paschen-Back** *m* PHYSIQUE Paschen-Back effect; ~ **de peau** *m* ELECTROTEC, ESSAIS, PHYSIQUE skin effect; ~ **pelliculaire** *m* AERONAUT fringe effect, skin effect, ELECTROTEC skin effect; ~ **Peltier** *m* ELECTR, PHYSIQUE Peltier effect; ~ **de persiennes** *m* TV venetian blind effect; ~ **photochimique** *m* EN RENOUV photochemical effect; ~ **photoélectrique** *m* ELECTRON, OPTIQUE, PHYS RAYON, PHYSIQUE, TELECOM photoelectric effect; ~ **photoélectrique externe** *m* OPTIQUE, TELECOM external photoelectric effect; ~ **photoélectrique interne** *m* ELECTRON, OPTIQUE, TELECOM internal photoelectric effect; ~ **photoélectrique inverse** *m* ELECTRON inverse photoelectric effect; ~ **photoélectronique** *m* PHYSIQUE photoelectric effect; ~ **photovoltaïque** *m* ELECTROTEC, EN RENOUV, ESPACE *véhicules*, OPTIQUE, PHYSIQUE, TELECOM photovoltaic effect; ~ **phugoïde** *m* AERONAUT phugoid effect; ~ **piézoélectrique** *m* ELECTROTEC, MATERIAUX, PHYSIQUE piezoelectric effect; ~ **piézoélectrique direct** *m* ELECTROTEC direct piezoelectric effect; ~ **piézoélectrique inverse** *m* ELECTROTEC, PHYSIQUE inverse piezoelectric effect; ~ **de pince** *m* ACOUSTIQUE pinch effect; ~ **de pincement** *m* ELECTRON pinch-off effect, PHYSIQUE pinch effect; ~ **POGO** *m* ESPACE POGO effect; ~ **de portance** *m* NAUT lift effect; ~ **de pression dynamique** *m* AERONAUT ram effect; ~ **de proximité** *m* ELECTROTEC proximity effect;

~ r ~ **Raman** *m* PHYS RAYON, PHYSIQUE Raman effect; ~ **de rayonnage** *m* NAUT backlash; ~ **de rayonnement de photons** *m* PHYS RAYON photoemissive effect; ~ **de récif** *m* PETROLE reef effect; ~ **de réciprocité** *m* CINEMAT reciprocity effect; ~ **repousseur** *m* POLLU MER herder effect; ~ **rétroactif sur la radioactivité** *m* NUCLEAIRE reactivity feed back; ~ **de rétrodiffusion** *m* NUCLEAIRE backscatter effect;

~ s ~ **Sabattier** *m* CINEMAT Sabattier effect; ~ **samarium** *m* NUCLEAIRE samarium effect; ~ **Schottky** *m* ELECTRON Schottky effect; ~ **Schwarzschild** *m* CINEMAT reciprocity law failure; ~ **secondaire** *m* INFORMAT, ORDINAT side effect; ~ **de Seebeck** *m* ELECTROTEC, PHYSIQUE Seebeck effect; ~ **du séisme** *m* GEOPHYS effects of earthquakes; ~ **de serre** *m* EN RENOUV, GEOPHYS, METEO, PHYSIQUE, POLLUTION, REFRIG greenhouse effect; ~ **de serre dû au dioxyde de carbone** *m* POLLUTION carbon dioxide greenhouse

effect; ~ **de serre dû au gaz carbonique** *m* POLLUTION carbon dioxide greenhouse effect; ~ **simple de séparation** *m* NUCLEAIRE elementary separation effect; ~ **au sol** *m* AERONAUT ground effect; ~ **solide** *m* NUCLEAIRE solid-state effect; ~ **Stark** *m* PHYSIQUE Stark effect; ~ **Stark linéaire** *m* PHYSIQUE linear Stark effect; ~ **Stark non-linéaire** *m* PHYSIQUE nonlinear Stark effect; ~ **de stéréophonie** *m* ENREGISTR stereo effect; ~ **de store vénitien** *m* TV skew error, venetian blind effect; ~ **de striction** *m* PHYSIQUE pinch effect; ~ **de striction néoclassique** *m* NUCLEAIRE neoclassical pinch effect; ~ **structural** *m* CONSTR structural effect; ~ **sublétal** *m* POLLUTION sublethal effect; ~ **synergique** *m* POLLUTION synergetic effect;

~ t ~ **thermique** *m* CHAUFFAGE thermal effect, GAZ thermal effect, thermic effect, PHYSIQUE thermal effect, THERMODYN heat effect, thermal effect; ~ **thermoélectrique** *m* ELECTR *circuit, température* thermoelectric effect; ~ **thermomécanique** *m* THERMODYN thermomechanical effect; ~ **Thomson** *m* PHYSIQUE Thomson effect; ~ **toxique** *m* POLLUTION toxic effect; ~ **toxique cumulatif** *m* POLLUTION cumulative toxic effect; ~ **triode** *m* ELECTRON triode action; ~ **de trou** *m* PETR borehole effect; ~ **de tunnel** *m* PHYSIQUE, TRANSPORT tunnel effect; ~ **tunnel** *m* ELECTRON tunnel effect; ~ **Tyndall** *m* PHYSIQUE Tyndall effect;

~ v ~ **venturi** *m* METEO venturi effect; ~ **de la viscosité** *m* PHYS FLUID viscous action; ~ **de viscosité entre la paroi et le fluide** *m* PHYS FLUID action of viscosity between wall and fluid; ~ **vortex** *m* GAZ vortex effect;

~ w ~ **Wigner** *m* PHYSIQUE Wigner effect;

~ x ~ **xénon d'empoisonnement** *m* NUCLEAIRE xenon poisoning effect;

~ z ~ **Zeeman** *m* NUCLEAIRE, PHYSIQUE Zeeman effect; ~ **Zeeman anomal** *m* PHYSIQUE anomalous Zeeman effect; ~ **Zeeman normal** *m* PHYSIQUE normal Zeeman effect; ~ **Zener** *m* ELECTRON Zener effect; ~ **de zoom** *m* INFORMAT, ORDINAT zooming

effet:[2] **sous l'~ de la gravitation** *loc* ASTRONOMIE under gravitational force

effets: ~ **biologiques** *m pl* SECURITE biological effects; ~ **de blocage** *m pl* TELECOM blockage effects; ~ **de compressibilité** *m pl* AERONAUT compressibility effects; ~ **gyromagnétiques** *m pl* PHYSIQUE gyromagnetic effects; ~ **d'ombre** *m pl* TV clouding; ~ **physiologiques** *m pl* SECURITE *dangers inhérents au travail* physiological effects; ~ **sonores** *m pl* CINEMAT, ENREGISTR sound effects; ~ **spéciaux** *m pl* CINEMAT effects, special effects, TV DVE, digital video effects; ~ **spéciaux numériques** *m pl* TV DVE, digital video effects; ~ **systématiques** *m pl* QUALITE systematic effects

efficace *adj* MECANIQUE effective, efficient, PHYSIQUE efficient

efficacité *f* ESPACE, MECANIQUE, PHYSIQUE efficiency, POLLU MER effectiveness; ~ **axiale** *f* ACOUSTIQUE axial efficiency; ~ **des canaux** *f* TELECOM channel efficiency; ~ **caractéristique** *f* ACOUSTIQUE characteristic efficiency; ~ **de combustion** *f* THERMODYN combustion efficiency; ~ **de concassage** *f* CHARBON crushing efficiency; ~ **de criblage** *f* CHARBON screening efficiency; ~ **différentielle** *f* NUCLEAIRE *d'une barre de commande* differential control rod worth; ~ **énergétique relative** *f* PHYSIQUE radiant efficiency; ~ **en tension** *f* ACOUSTIQUE tension efficiency; ~ **en tension en champ libre** *f* ACOUSTIQUE free field tension efficiency; ~ **hydrau-**

lique *f* HYDROLOGIE hydraulic efficiency; ~ **intrinsèque** *f* ACOUSTIQUE specific efficiency; ~ **lumineuse** *f* PHYSIQUE luminous efficacy; ~ **lumineuse relative** *f* PHYSIQUE relative luminous efficiency; ~ **lumineuse spectrale** *f* PHYSIQUE spectral luminous efficiency; ~ **paraphonique** *f* ACOUSTIQUE close talking efficiency; ~ **de pêche** *f* OCEANO fishing efficiency; ~ **relative** *f* ACOUSTIQUE *d'un transducteur* relative efficiency; **thermique** *f* GAZ thermal efficiency, thermic efficiency; ~ **d'un transducteur** *f* ACOUSTIQUE transducer efficiency; ~ **d'utilisation de l'eau** *f* HYDROLOGIE water-use efficiency; ~ **volumique** *f* ELECTROTEC volumetric efficiency

effilement: ~ **progressif** *m* CONS MECA tapering

effilocher *vt* CINEMAT bleed

effleurir *vi* CHIMIE effloresce

efflorescence *f* AGRO ALIM *fruits* bloom, CHIMIE efflorescence, PLAST CAOU *plastiques, peinture* bloom

efflorescent *adj* CHIMIE efflorescent

effluence *f* DISTRI EAU efflux, outflow

effluent *m* CHARBON wastewater, HYDROLOGIE, NUCLEAIRE, PETROLE *raffinerie* effluent, RECYCLAGE waste product; ~ **aqueux** *m* POLLUTION aqueous effluent; ~ **brut** *m* HYDROLOGIE raw sewage, untreated sewage; ~ **de l'eau d'égout** *m* RECYCLAGE sewage effluent; ~ **des eaux usées** *m* DISTRI EAU sewage effluent; ~ **gazeux** *m* GAZ gaseous effluent, POLLUTION exhaust gas, waste gas; ~ **industriel** *m* RECYCLAGE industrial waste; ~ **liquide** *m* GAZ liquid effluent, RECYCLAGE liquid waste; ~ **toxique** *m* RECYCLAGE toxic effluent

effluve *m* CHIMIE effluvium, ELECTROTEC brush discharge, PHYSIQUE brush discharge, glow discharge; ~ **électrique** *m* ELECTR *haute tension* corona discharge; ~ **en couronne** *m* ELECTR *haute tension* corona discharge, PHYSIQUE corona

effluves *f pl* CINEMAT static mark

effondré *adj* GEOLOGIE caved

effondrement *m* CONSTR, GEOLOGIE collapse, HYDROLOGIE subsidence, MINES caving, caving in, collapse, *du toit* subsidence, POLLUTION subsidence; ~ **gravitationnel** *m* ASTRONOMIE *de nuages compacts de gaz et poussières* gravitational collapse, ESPACE gravitation collapse

effondrer[1] *vt* CONSTR *un plancher, en le surchargeant* weigh down

effondrer:[2] **s'~** *v réfl* ASTRONOMIE *étoile* collapse, CONSTR give way, subside, GEOLOGIE collapse

effort *m* CONS MECA load, CONSTR, GEOLOGIE, NAUT stress, PHYSIQUE load; ~ **de cisaillement** *m* CONS MECA shear stress, shearing stress, CONSTR shearing stress; ~ **de commande de pas** *m* AERONAUT pitch control load; ~ **de compression** *m* CONS MECA compressive force, positive stress; ~ **direct** *m* CONS MECA direct force; ~ **de flexion** *m* PLAST CAOU bending stress; ~ **de freinage** *m* CONS MECA brake force; ~ **gyroscopique** *m* EN RENOUV gyroscopic force; ~ **longitudinal au manche cyclique** *m* AERONAUT longitudinal cyclic stick load; ~ **maximal** *m* IMPRIM *mécanique, papiers* maximal stress; ~ **de pêche** *m* OCEANO fishing effort; ~ **tangentiel** *m* CONS MECA, MATERIAUX tangential stress; ~ **de tension** *m* MATERIAUX yield stress; ~ **de torsion** *m* CONS MECA torsional stress; ~ **de traction** *m* CONS MECA pull, tensile stress; ~ **tranchant** *m* CONS MECA shearing stress, CONSTR shear force

effritement *m* MATERIAUX crumbling; ~ **de l'arête de coupe** *m* MATERIAUX cutting edge chipping; ~ **par les**

agents atmosphériques *m* CONSTR weathering; ~ **par les intempéries** *m* CONSTR weathering

effriter: **s'~** *v réfl* CONSTR *murs* crumble, MATERIAUX crack

effusion *f* NUCLEAIRE, PHYSIQUE effusion; ~ **de boue** *f* GEOPHYS solifluction lobe, solifluction tongue

EGA *abrév* *(adaptateur graphique couleur)* ORDINAT *carte EGA (enhanced graphics adaptor)*

égal *adj* GEOLOGIE even; **à égal** *adj* INFORMAT, ORDINAT peer-to-peer

égalisateur *m* INFORMAT, TELECOM equalizer; ~ **de pression** *m* REFRIG equalizer; ~ **du système de freinage** *m* VEHICULES brake compensator

égalisation *f* ELECTRON, ENREGISTR, INFORMAT, MECANIQUE, ORDINAT, TELECOM equalization; ~ **adaptative** *f* ELECTROTEC adaptive equalization; ~ **autoadaptative** *f* ELECTROTEC adaptive equalization; ~ **automatique** *f* ELECTROTEC, TV auto-equalization

égaliser *vt* PRODUCTION level

égaliseur *m* ELECTRON, ENREGISTR, ORDINAT, TELECOM, TV equalizer; ~ **actif** *m* ENREGISTR active equalizer; ~ **d'amplitude** *m* TELECOM amplitude equalizer; ~ **de courant alternatif** *m* ELECTR alternating current balancer; ~ **en cosinus** *m* TV cosine equalizer

égalité *f* INFORMAT, ORDINAT equality

égoïne *f* CONSTR *scie* handsaw

égout *m* CONSTR drain, eaves, sewer, *d'un comble* slope, DISTRI EAU, HYDROLOGIE, RECYCLAGE sewer; ~ **captant** *m* HYDROLOGIE interceptor sewer; ~ **collecteur** *m* CONSTR main sewer; ~ **conjoint** *m* HYDROLOGIE combined sewer; ~ **d'évacuation des eaux pluviales** *m* RECYCLAGE storm drain; ~ **pluvial** *m* CONSTR, HYDROLOGIE storm drain; ~ **principal** *m* HYDROLOGIE main sewer

égouts *m pl* HYDROLOGIE sewage

égouttage *m* PAPIER drainage

égouttamètre *m* PAPIER freeness tester

égoutter *vt* CONSTR *des terres*, DISTRI EAU, PAPIER drain

égouttoir *m* AGRO ALIM, EQUIP LAB *nettoyage* draining rack, REFRIG drain pan

égratignure *f* IMPRIM *surfaces* scratch

égrisé *m* MINES diamond dust, diamond powder, PRODUCTION bort

égrugeoir *m* AGRO ALIM kibbler

égruger *vt* AGRO ALIM crush, pound

égrugeures: ~ **de minerai** *f pl* MINES crushed ore

eicosane *m* CHIMIE eicosane

einsteinium *m (Es)* CHIMIE einsteinium *(Es)*

éjecta *m pl* GEOLOGIE ejecta, NUCLEAIRE *retombés dans le cratère* fallback, washback

éjecter *vt* AERONAUT, ESPACE jettison

éjecteur *m* CONS MECA, MECANIQUE, PLAST CAOU *presse* ejector; ~ **de carotte d'injection par retenue** *m* CONS MECA *moule d'injection* sprue puller pin; ~ **cylindrique** *m* CONS MECA ejection pin; ~ **lame** *m* CONS MECA flat ejector pin; ~ **tubulaire** *m* CONS MECA ejector sleeve, *moules pour fonderie sous pression* sleeve ejector; ~ **à vapeur** *m* INST HYDR steam ejector; ~ **de ventilation** *m* CHARBON air nozzle

éjection *f* AERONAUT *réacteur* exhaust, MECANIQUE ejection; ~ **des déchets** *f* IMPRIM stripping

ékebergite *f* MINERAUX ekebergite

ekta *m* IMPRIM transparency

élaboré: ~ **sur la puce** *adj* ELECTRON generated on chip

élaeolite *f* MINERAUX elaeolite

élaeostéarique *adj* CHIMIE *acide* elaeostearic

élaïdine *f* CHIMIE elaidin

élaïdique *adj* CHIMIE elaidic

élancement: ~ **arrière** *m* NAUT aft rake; ~ **de l'étrave** *m* NAUT stem rake

élargir:[1] ~ **un puits** *vt* MINES cut down a shaft

élargir:[2] **s'~ entre la première couche** *vi* IMPRIM *d'une page* feather

élargissement *m* ELECTRON *de faisceau* expansion, MINES underreaming; ~ **brusque de section** *m* INST HYDR sudden enlargement of cross section; ~ **Doppler** *m* PHYS RAYON *des raies spectrales*, PHYSIQUE Doppler broadening; ~ **d'impulsion** *m* OPTIQUE pulse broadening, pulse dispersion, TELECOM pulse broadening, pulse dispersion, pulse spreading, pulse widening; ~ **par pression** *m* PHYS RAYON *des raies spectrales*, PHYSIQUE pressure broadening; ~ **des raies** *m* CRISTALL line broadening; ~ **de résonance** *m* PHYS RAYON *raies spectrales* resonance broadening; ~ **du ruban** *m* CERAM VER spread

élargisseur *m* CONSTR casing expander

élasmose *f* MINERAUX elasmose, elasmosine

élasticité *f* MATERIAUX elasticity, springiness, MECANIQUE, METALL elasticity, NAUT elasticity, flexibility, PHYSIQUE, PLAST CAOU elasticity; ~ **acoustique** *f* ACOUSTIQUE acoustic capacitance; ~ **de gluten** *f* AGRO ALIM gluten extensibility; ~ **de la mie** *f* AGRO ALIM crumb elasticity; ~ **de torsion** *f* CONS MECA rotational elasticity, torsional elasticity

élastique *adj* CHIMIE rubbery, MECANIQUE *matériaux*, PLAST CAOU elastic

élastomère *m* CHIMIE, PETROLE, PLAST CAOU *caoutchouc*, REFRIG elastomer; ~ **synthétique** *m* PETROLE synthetic elastomer

élastoplastique *adj* MATERIAUX elastoplastic

élatérite *f* MINERAUX elastic bitumen, elaterite

électrète *m* PHYSIQUE electret

électricien *m* CINEMAT electrician, sparks

électricité *f* ELECTROTEC, PHYSIQUE electricity; ~ **atmosphérique** *f* GEOPHYS, METEO atmospheric electricity; ~ **solaire** *f* ELECTROTEC solar electricity; ~ **statique** *f* CONSTR, MATERIAUX, TEXTILE static electricity

électrification *f* ELECTR electrification

électrifier *vt* ELECTROTEC electrify

électrique *adj* ELECTR, ELECTRON electric, electrical

électrique-optique *adj* TELECOM E-O, electrical-optical

électrisation *f* PHOTO static on film, PHYSIQUE electrification

électriser *vt* ELECTROTEC electrify; ~ **par frottement** *vt* PHYSIQUE charge by friction

électroacoustique[1] *adj* ENREGISTR electroacoustic

électroacoustique[2] *f* ELECTROTEC electroacoustics

électro-aimant *m* CHIMIE, ELECTR, ELECTROTEC, PHYSIQUE electromagnet, TELECOM electric magnet, TV electromagnet, solenoid; ~ **de levage** *m* CONS MECA lifting magnet; ~ **à noyau-plongeur** *m* ELECTROTEC solenoid; ~ **porteur** *m* CONS MECA lifting magnet; ~ **de relais** *m* ELECTROTEC relay magnet; ~ **de soufflage** *m* ELECTROTEC arc breaker; ~ **de verrouillage** *m* ELECTR latching electromagnet

électro-analyse *f* CHIMIE electroanalysis

électrobus *m* TRANSPORT electrobus

électrocapillaire *adj* CHIMIE electrocapillary

électrocapillarité *f* CHIMIE electrocapillarity

électrochimie *f* CHIMIE, ELECTR electrochemistry

électrochimique *adj* CHIMIE electrochemical

électrocinétique[1] *adj* CHIMIE electrokinetic

électrocinétique[2] *f* ELECTROTEC, PHYSIQUE electrokinetics

électrocochléographie *f* ACOUSTIQUE electrocochleography

électrode *f* CHIMIE, CONSTR, ELECTR, ELECTROTEC, EQUIP LAB, MECANIQUE *soudure*, METALL, PHYSIQUE, TV electrode; ~ **accélératrice** *f* NUCLEAIRE accelerating electrode; ~ **d'amorçage** *f* ELECTROTEC initiating electrode, starter electrode; ~ **d'appoint** *f* CERAM VER auxiliary electrode; ~ **d'argent** *f* EQUIP LAB silver electrode; ~ **auxiliaire** *f* ELECTROTEC starter electrode; ~ **de base** *f* ELECTROTEC base electrode; ~ **bipolaire** *f* ELECTR bipolar electrode; ~ **de bougie** *f* AUTO spark plug electrode, spark plug point; ~ **de captage** *f* ELECTROTEC target electrode; ~ **de charbon** *f* ELECTR *pile* carbon electrode; ~ **collectrice** *f* ELECTROTEC collector electrode, POLLUTION collecting electrode; ~ **de commande** *f* ELECTROTEC control electrode, TV modulation electrode; ~ **à consommer** *f* MATERIAUX *soudure* consumable electrode; ~ **de déviation** *f* ELECTROTEC deflection electrode, NUCLEAIRE deflecting electrode; ~ **de déviation horizontale** *f* TV X-plate, horizontal deflection plate; ~ **à déviation radiale** *f* TV radial deflecting electrode; ~ **diviseuse de faisceau** *f* TV splitting electrode; ~ **émettrice** *f* ELECTROTEC emitter electrode; ~ **en forme de peigne** *f* ESPACE *véhicules* comb-shaped electrode; ~ **enrobée** *f* CONSTR covered electrode, MECANIQUE *soudure* coated electrode; ~ **d'entrée** *f* ELECTROTEC input electrode; ~ **d'entretien** *f* ELECTROTEC keep-alive electrode; ~ **en verre** *f* EQUIP LAB *analyse* glass electrode; ~ **de focalisation** *f* ELECTROTEC, TV focusing electrode; ~ **fusible** *f* CONSTR consumable electrode; ~ **de grille** *f* ELECTROTEC gate; ~ **de masse** *f* AUTO earth electrode (BrE), ground electrode (AmE); ~ **de mesure** *f* ELECTROTEC sensing electrode; ~ **de mise à la terre** *f* ELECTROTEC earth electrode (BrE), ground electrode (AmE); ~ **négative** *f* ELECTR *pile*, ELECTROTEC negative electrode; ~ **postaccélératrice** *f* TV intensifier electrode; ~ **de référence** *f* EQUIP LAB *électrochimie, analyse* reference electrode; ~ **réflectrice** *f* ELECTROTEC reflecting electrode, reflector electrode, repeller; ~ **de réflexion** *f* TV reflector electrode; ~ **réfractaire** *f* CONSTR nonconsumable electrode; ~ **sélective** *f* EQUIP LAB *électrochimie* ISE, ion selective electrode; ~ **de signal** *f* ELECTRON signal electrode; ~ **de sortie** *f* ELECTROTEC output electrode; ~ **de soudage** *f* MATERIAUX welding electrode; ~ **de soudage à arc** *f* ELECTR arc welding electrode; ~ **de terre** *f* ELECTR earth electrode (BrE), ground electrode (AmE); ~ **de Wehnelt** *f* INSTRUMENT, PHYSIQUE Wehnelt cylinder

électrodéposition *f* CONSTR electrodeposition, ELECTROTEC electrodeposition, electroplating, MATERIAUX electroplating, REVETEMENT electroplating, galvanoplastics

électrodialyse *f* CHIMIE electrodialysis

électrodistributeur *m* INST HYDR solenoid valve

électrodynamique *f* ELECTR, PHYSIQUE electrodynamics; ~ **quantique** *f* PHYS PART, PHYSIQUE quantum electrodynamics

électrodynamomètre *m* ELECTR, PHYSIQUE electrodynamometer

électro-érosion *f* PRODUCTION EDM, electrodischarge machining

électrofiltre *m* ELECTRON electrostatic filter, POLLUTION ESP, electrostatic precipitator

électroformage *m* ELECTROTEC electroforming
électrogalvanisation *f* MATERIAUX electrogalvanizing
électro-incandescence *f* ESPACE electroglow
électroluminescence *f* ELECTRON electroluminescence, NUCLEAIRE electrofluorescence, electroluminescence, OPTIQUE, PHYSIQUE, TELECOM electroluminescence; ~ **à couches minces** *f* ELECTRON TFEL, thin-film electroluminescence
électrolyse *f* CHIMIE, ELECTR *électrochimie*, ELECTROTEC, IMPRIM, MATERIAUX, PHYSIQUE electrolysis; ~ **de l'eau** *f* NUCLEAIRE water electrolysis
électrolyser *vt* CHIMIE, PHYSIQUE electrolyze
électrolyseur *m* CHIMIE electrolyzer, PHYSIQUE electrolytic unit
électrolyte *m* CHIMIE, ELECTR *électrochimie*, ELECTROTEC, PHYSIQUE, PLAST CAOU *chimie*, TELECOM electrolyte; ~ **sec** *m* ELECTROTEC dry electrolyte
électrolytique *adj* CHIMIE, ELECTR *électrochimie*, PHYSIQUE electrolytic
électromagnétique *adj* CHIMIE, ELECTR, MECANIQUE electromagnetic; ~ **transverse** *adj (TEM)* ELECTROTEC transverse electromagnetic *(TEM)*
électromagnétisme *m* CHIMIE, ELECTR, PHYSIQUE electromagnetism
électromécanique *f* ELECTR electromechanics
électromètre *m* ELECTR, ELECTROTEC, EQUIP LAB, GEOPHYS, PHYSIQUE electrometer; ~ **bifilaire** *m* ELECTR bifilar electrometer; ~ **de Hoffman** *m* ELECTR Hoffman electrometer; ~ **à quadrants** *m* ELECTR, ELECTROTEC quadrant electrometer; ~ **de torsion** *m* GEOPHYS torsion electrometer
électrométrie *f* ELECTROTEC electrometry
électromobile *m* TRANSPORT electromobile
électromoteur *m* ELECTROTEC electric motor
électron *m* CHIMIE, ELECTR, ELECTROTEC, GAZ, PHYS PART, PHYSIQUE electron; ~ **antiliant** *m* PHYS RAYON antibonding electron; ~ **Auger** *m* PHYS RAYON, PHYSIQUE Auger electron; ~ **de conduction** *m* PHYSIQUE free electron; ~ **de conversion** *m* PHYS RAYON conversion electron; ~ **de la couche-Q** *m* NUCLEAIRE Q-electron, Q-shell electron; ~ **délocalisé** *m* PETROLE delocalized electron; ~ **à haute énergie** *m* ELECTRON high-energy electron; ~ **interne** *m* PHYS RAYON inner electron; ~ **libre** *m* ELECTR, PHYS PART, PHYSIQUE free electron; ~ **lié** *m* PHYS PART bound electron; ~ **non-liant** *m* NUCLEAIRE nonbonding electron; ~ **optique** *m* PHYS RAYON optical electron; ~ **orbital** *m* PHYS RAYON orbital electron; ~ **oscillant** *m* NUCLEAIRE oscillating electron; ~ **de recul** *m* PHYSIQUE recoil electron; ~ **secondaire** *m* ELECTRON, PHYS RAYON secondary electron; ~ **de valence** *m* METALL, PHYSIQUE valence electron
électronégatif *adj* CHIMIE electronegative
électronique[1] *adj* ELECTR, ELECTRON electronic
électronique[2] *f* ELECTROTEC, INFORMAT, ORDINAT, PRODUCTION electronics; ~ **aérospatiale** *f* ESPACE, TRANSPORT avionics; ~ **appliquée aux avions** *f* TRANSPORT avionics; ~ **de conditionnement d'énergie** *f* ESPACE *véhicules* power conditioning unit; ~ **à découpage** *f* ESPACE *véhicules* chopper circuitry; ~ **de l'état solide** *f* ELECTRON solid-state electronics; ~ **grand public** *f* ELECTROTEC consumer electronics; ~ **industrielle** *f* ELECTROTEC industrial electronics; ~ **moléculaire** *f* ELECTRON molecular electronics; ~ **à semi-conducteurs** *f* ELECTRON solid-state electronics; ~ **spatiale** *f* ESPACE astrionics

électronographie *f* NUCLEAIRE electron radiography
électron-Q *m* NUCLEAIRE Q-electron, Q-shell electron
électrons: ~ **appariés** *m pl* PHYS RAYON paired electrons; ~ **couplés** *m pl* PHYS RAYON paired electrons
électron-volt *m (eV)* ELECTROTEC, METROLOGIE, PHYS PART, PHYSIQUE electronvolt *(eV)*
électro-optique *adj* ELECTRON electro-optical, OPTIQUE optoelectronic, TELECOM electro-optic
électro-osmose *f* CHIMIE electro-osmosis
électro-osmotique *adj* CHIMIE electro-osmotic
électrophile *adj* CHIMIE electrophilic
électrophilique *adj* CHIMIE electrophilic
électrophone *m* ENREGISTR record player
électrophore *m* ELECTROTEC electrophorus
électrophorèse *f* CHIMIE, ELECTR *électrolyse*, EQUIP LAB *analyse* electrophoresis
électrophotographie *f* IMPRIM electrophotography
électroplaquer *vt* REVETEMENT electroplate
électropositif *adj* CHIMIE, MATERIAUX electropositive
électroproduction: ~ **près du seuil** *f* NUCLEAIRE electroproduction at threshold
électroscope *m* ELECTR, PHYSIQUE electroscope; ~ **à feuilles d'or** *m* ELECTROTEC, PHYSIQUE gold leaf electroscope
électrostatique[1] *adj* ELECTR, TELECOM electrostatic
électrostatique[2] *f* ELECTR, ELECTROTEC, PHYSIQUE electrostatics
électrostriction *f* PHYSIQUE electrostriction
électrosynthèse *f* CHIMIE electrosynthesis
électrotechnique *f* ELECTR electrical engineering, electrotechnics, electrotechnology, ELECTRON electrical engineering
électrothermique *adj* ELECTR electrothermal
électrotrieuse *f* MINES magnetic separator
électrovanne *f* CONSTR electronically-controlled valve, PRODUCTION *système hydraulique* electrical solenoid, electrically-operated valve, solenoid valve; ~ **de coupure** *f* PRODUCTION solenoid-operated shut-off valve
éléis: ~ **de Guinée** *f* AGRO ALIM oil palm
élément *m* CHIMIE element, CONS MECA element, part, ELECTR *circuit*, ELECTRON element, ELECTROTEC cell, INFORMAT element, item, unit, MATH member, *théorie des ensembles* element, ORDINAT element, item, unit, PHYSIQUE element, PRODUCTION section, TELECOM chip; ~ **absorbant** *m* NUCLEAIRE absorber member; ~ **d'accumulateur** *m* ELECTR accumulator cell, battery cell, ELECTROTEC accumulator cell, battery cell, secondary cell, storage cell, ESPACE *énergie* battery cell; ~ **actif** *m* ELECTROTEC active element; ~ **actinide** *m* PHYS RAYON actinide element; ~ **alcalino-terreux** *m* MATERIAUX alkaline-earth element; ~ **d'alliage** *m* MATERIAUX alloying element; ~ **d'arrêt** *m* INFORMAT, ORDINAT stop element; ~ **atténuateur** *m* ELECTRON attenuating element; ~ **automoteur** *m* TRANSPORT rail motor unit; ~ **de batterie** *m* AUTO accumulator cell, battery cell; ~ **de batterie alcaline** *m* ELECTROTEC alkaline storage cell; ~ **binaire** *m* TELECOM bit; ~ **de calmage** *m* METALL killing agent; ~ **de chaudière modulaire** *m* INST HYDR element; ~ **de chauffage** *m* CHAUFFAGE heating element; ~ **de chauffage à ailettes** *m* MAT CHAUFF ribbed radiator; ~ **chauffant** *m* AERONAUT, ELECTR heating element; ~ **de circuit** *m* ELECTRON, ELECTROTEC, PHYSIQUE circuit element; ~ **de circuit intégré** *m* ELECTRON integrated circuit element; ~ **de circuit linéaire** *m* ELECTRON linear circuit element; ~ **combustible annulaire** *m* NUCLEAIRE annular fuel element; ~ **combustible à eau bouillant-**

surchauffé *m* NUCLEAIRE boiling assembly, superheat assembly; ~ **combustible en uranium** *m* NUCLEAIRE uranium fuel element; ~ **combustible à gaine en graphite** *m* NUCLEAIRE graphite clad fuel element; ~ **combustible neuf** *m* NUCLEAIRE new fuel element; ~ **combustible nu** *m* NUCLEAIRE uncanned fuel element; ~ **combustible semi-homogène** *m* NUCLEAIRE semihomogeneous fuel element; ~ **de commande périphérique** *m* NUCLEAIRE edge control element, peripheral control element; ~ **de compensation** *m* NUCLEAIRE shim element, shim member; ~ **concasseur** *m* GENIE CHIM crusher ball; ~ **de connexion** *m* TELECOM CE, connection element; ~ **de connexion d'accès** *m* TELECOM ACE, access connection element; ~ **de connexion de transit** *m* TELECOM TCE, transit connection element; ~ **consommable** *m* CONS MECA expendable item; ~ **à contact sous vide** *m* PRODUCTION vacuum contact element; ~ **de contrôle fin** *m* NUCLEAIRE fine control member; ~ **de courant** *m* PHYSIQUE current element; ~ **démontable** *m* ELECTR *circuit* removable part; ~ **de départ** *m* INFORMAT start element; ~ **déphaseur** *m* ELECTRON phase-shifting element; ~ **destructeur** *m* SECURITE destructive element; ~ **détritique** *m* GEOLOGIE clast; ~ **dissipatif** *m* ELECTROTEC terminating element; ~ **de donnée** *m* INFORMAT data element, data item; ~ **de dopage** *m* NUCLEAIRE booster element; ~ **de douci** *m* CERAM VER grinding unit; ~ **dynamique** *m* AERONAUT dynamic component; ~ **électrochimique** *m* ESPACE *énergie* battery cell; ~ **électropositif** *m* PHYS RAYON electropositive element; ~ **en forme de bloc** *m* NUCLEAIRE block-shaped fuel element; ~ **d'étanchéité** *m* EQUIP LAB seal; ~ **filtrant** *m* POLLUTION bag, filtering unit, PRODUCTION *système hydraulique* filter element; ~ **fini** *m* MATERIAUX finite element; ~ **de fixation** *m* CONS MECA attaching part, fastener, ESPACE, MECANIQUE fastener; ~ **de fixation fileté** *m* CONS MECA threaded fastener; ~ **de fixation fileté femelle** *m* CONS MECA internal thread fastener; ~ **de fixation fileté mâle** *m* CONS MECA external thread fastener; ~ **de fixation rapide** *m* CONS MECA quick-release fastener; ~ **de fixation à tête à créneaux** *m* CONS MECA castellated head fastener; ~ **de fixation à tête cylindrique** *m* CONS MECA cheese head fastener; ~ **de fixation à tête fraisée** *m* CONS MECA countersunk fastener; ~ **de fixation à tête fraisée bombée** *m* CONS MECA oval head fastener; ~ **de fixation à tête moletée** *m* CONS MECA knurled head fastener; ~ **à fixation à tête noyée** *m* CONS MECA recessed head fastener; ~ **à fixation à tête rectangulaire** *m* CONS MECA rectangle head fastener; ~ **fixe** *m* CONS MECA *d'un palan, d'une moufle* arse; ~ **à forte affinité pour l'oxygène** *m* GEOLOGIE lithophile element; ~ **de fusible** *m* ELECTROTEC fuse element; ~ **hygromagmatophile** *m* GEOLOGIE incompatible element; ~ **d'image** *m* INFORMAT, ORDINAT pixel; ~ **à impédance** *m* ELECTROTEC impedor; ~ **incompatible** *m* GEOLOGIE incompatible element; ~ **d'information** *m* ELECTRON data element, INFORMAT data item, ORDINAT data element; ~ **infrarouge** *m* CHAUFFAGE infrared element; ~ **de liaison** *m* CONS MECA attachment; ~ **limité** *m* CONS MECA finite element; ~ **logique** *m* ELECTRON, INFORMAT, ORDINAT logic element; ~ **longitudinal** *m* AERONAUT longitudinal member; ~ **mécanique d'asservissement** *m* COMMANDE mechanical servo-link device; ~ **de mémoire** *m* INFORMAT, ORDINAT storage element; ~ **de mémorisation** *m* ELECTROTEC storage element; ~ me-

nant *m* CONS MECA driving element; ~ **mené** *m* CONS MECA driven element; ~ **microcircuit** *m* MATERIAUX microcomponent; ~ **mobile** *m* POLLUTION mobile component; ~ **mural** *m* REFRIG wall coil; ~ **naturel** *m* NUCLEAIRE naturally-occurring element; ~ **neutre** *m* MATH identity element; ~ **non alimenté** *m* PHYSIQUE parasitic element; ~ **non linéaire** *m* CONSTR nonlinear element; ~ **non suspendu** *m* VEHICULES *roues, pneus, freins* unsprung weight; ~ **normalisé** *m* CONS MECA standard part; ~ **numérique de bourrage** *m* TELECOM stuffing digit; ~ **oligodynamique** *m* HYDROLOGIE micronutrient; ~ **pare-feu** *m* AERONAUT heat shield; ~ **passerelle de réseau** *m* TELECOM gateway network element; ~ **passif** *m* ELECTRON passive element, PHYSIQUE parasitic aerial, passive aerial; ~ **de pieu** *m* CHARBON pile segment; ~ **piézoélectrique** *m* ELECTROTEC piezoelectric element; ~ **de pile électrique** *m* ELECTROTEC primary cell; ~ **plafonnier** *m* REFRIG ceiling coil; ~ **de poli** *m* CERAM VER polishing unit; ~ **préfabriqué** *m* CONSTR precast unit; ~ **principal** *m* CONS MECA main unit; ~ **de radiateur** *m* AUTO radiator element; ~ **rapporté** *m* ESPACE *véhicules* added-on component; ~ **à réactance** *m* ELECTROTEC reactive element; ~ **réactif** *m* ELECTROTEC reactive element; ~ **de réduction** *m* COMMANDE reductor cell, regulator cell; ~ **de régulation** *m* COMMANDE regulator cell; ~ **de remplissage** *m* INFORMAT, ORDINAT filler; ~ **de repiquage** *m* IMPRIM *impression* imprinting unit; ~ **de réseau** *m* TELECOM NE, network element; ~ **de réseau non SDH** *m* TELECOM NNE, non-SDH network element; ~ **résistif** *m* ELECTROTEC resistive element; ~ **retard** *m* NUCLEAIRE delay component, delay unit; ~ **secondaire** *m* CHIMIE secondary element, PHYSIQUE parasitic aerial, passive aerial; ~ **à semi-conducteurs** *m* PRODUCTION solid-state component; ~ **sensible** *m* ELECTRON sensing element; ~ **de serrage pour tube** *m* CONS MECA pipe-clamping element; ~ **de service de l'accès aux transfert et manipulation** *m* TELECOM FTAMSE, file transfer access and manipulation service element; ~ **de service d'application** *m* TELECOM ASE, application service element; ~ **de service d'application pour la gestion de réseau** *m* TELECOM NM-ASE, network management application service element; ~ **de service de commande d'association** *m* TELECOM ACSE, association control service element; ~ **de service commun d'information de gestion** *m* TELECOM CMISE, common management information service element; ~ **de service commun de transfert d'informations de gestion** *m* TELECOM CMISE, common management information service element; ~ **de service de contrôle d'association** *m* TELECOM ACSE, association control service element; ~ **de service d'opération distante** *m* TELECOM ROSE, remote operation service element; ~ **simple** *m* CONS MECA part; ~ **standard** *m* CONS MECA modular unit; ~ **structural** *m* GEOLOGIE fabric element; ~ **surchauffeur** *m* PRODUCTION superheater element, superheater unit; ~ **sur chenilles** *m* MINES crawler base; ~ **de surréactivité** *m* NUCLEAIRE booster element; ~ **suspendu** *m* VEHICULES *carrosserie* sprung weight; ~ **de suspension élastique** *m* TRANSPORT sandow; ~ **de tension** *m* POLLU MER tension member; ~ **thermique** *m* PRODUCTION heater element; ~ **thermostatique** *m* REFRIG thermostatic element; ~ **trace** *m* GEOLOGIE trace element; ~ **de transition** *m* CHIMIE, MATERIAUX transition element; ~ **transplutonien** *m* NUCLEAIRE transplutonium element; **~ de tube** *m* PETR joint; **~ d'usure** *m* NUCLEAIRE wearing detail, wearing element, working part; **~ utilisable** *m* NUCLEAIRE valuable element; **~ à vide** *m* POLLU MER vacuum unit

éléments: **~ figurés** *m pl* GEOLOGIE visible grains, PETR allochem; **~ finis pour le dessin mécanique** *m pl* CONS MECA finite elements for mechanical engineering; **~ de fixation en acier inoxydable résistant à la corrosion** *m pl* CONS MECA corrosion-resistant stainless steel fasteners; **~ d'une machine** *m pl* CONS MECA parts of a machine; **~ de machines** *m pl* CONS MECA mechanical components; **~ à mouvement alternatif** *m pl* CONS MECA reciprocating parts; **~ orbitaux** *m pl* ASTRONOMIE *du mouvement d'un corps céleste* orbital elements; **~ de protection en matière plastique** *m pl* SECURITE plastic protective elements; **~ standard de contrôles multiples** *m pl* METROLOGIE standard multigaging elements (AmE), standard multigauging elements (BrE); **~ standard pour la construction des machines-outils** *m pl* CONS MECA modular units for machine-tool construction; **~ de symétrie** *m pl* CRISTALL symmetry elements; **~ tournants** *m pl* CONS MECA rotating parts; **~ de tuyauterie** *m pl* CONS MECA pipe components; **~ visibles à l'oeil nu** *m pl* GEOLOGIE visible grains

éléolite *f* MINERAUX elaeolite

élevage: **~ de coquillages** *m* OCEANO shellfish farm

élévateur *m* CONSTR elevator, lift, lifter, PETROLE *forage*, PRODUCTION elevator; **~ à chaîne** *m* CONS MECA chain elevator (AmE), chain lift (BrE), chain pump; **~ à chapelets** *m* CONSTR bucket elevator; **~ de drague** *m* MINES dredge elevator; **~ en queue** *m* DISTRI EAU tail elevator; **~ à godets** *m* CONS MECA bucket pump, CONSTR bucket elevator; **~ à godets oscillants** *m* TRANSPORT tilt bucket elevator; **~ de marchandises** *m* PRODUCTION goods lift; **~ de tailings** *m* CONSTR tailings elevator; **~ de tubage** *m* CONSTR casing elevator, casing lift; **~ à vis sans fin** *m* CONSTR screw elevator

élévateur-basculeur *m* PAPIER arm elevator

élévation *f* CONS MECA front elevation, lifting, CONSTR elevation, *d'un mur* raising, MINES raising, NAUT profile, *bureau d'études, navigation* elevation, NUCLEAIRE *du sol* upward heave, PHYSIQUE altitude, height; **~ moléculaire du point d'ébullition** *f* THERMODYN molecular elevation of boiling point; **~ du plan des formes** *f* NAUT sheer plan; **~ de la température** *f* PHYSIQUE temperature raising, temperature rise

élevée *f* CHIMIE vicidity

élèvement *m* CONSTR *d'un mur* raising

élever *vt* CONSTR put up; **~ au carré** *vt* MATH square; **~ au cube** *vt* MATH cube; **~ à une puissance** *vt* MATH raise to a power

élevon *m* TRANSPORT elevon

éligma *m* NUCLEAIRE electron-impregnated migma, eligma

élimé *adj* TEXTILE threadbare

élimination *f* ELECTRON rejection, POLLU MER disposal; **~ d'une bande latérale** *f* ELECTRON sideband suppression; **~ de CO2** *f* HYDROLOGIE deacidification; **~ des déchets** *f* RECYCLAGE waste disposal; **~ de défaut par recuit** *f* ELECTRON defect annealing; **~ des dislocations** *f* METALL dislocation annihilation; **~ de la dorsale** *f* CINEMAT backing removal; **~ des eaux d'égout** *f* RECYCLAGE sewage disposal; **~ d'erreur** *f* PRODUCTION fault recovery; **~ de fréquence** *f* ELECTRON frequency rejection; **~ des goûts** *f* DISTRI EAU taste control; **~ des interférences** *f* NAUT interference

rejection; **~ par transmutation nucléaire** *f* NUCLEAIRE *des déchets* disposal by nuclear transmutation; **~ des poisons** *f* NUCLEAIRE de-poisoning; **~ du réacteur des poisons nucléaires** *f* NUCLEAIRE nuclear reactor poison removal; **~ des rognures de bordure** *f* PAPIER trim removal; **~ de sels nutritifs** *f* HYDROLOGIE nutrient removal; **~ de silence** *f* TELECOM silence elimination; **~ des transitoires** *f* ELECTROTEC transient suppression

éliminer *vt* INFORMAT, ORDINAT delete; **~ par cache** *vt* CINEMAT matte out; **~ par lavage** *vt* CHIMIE wash

élinde *f* CONSTR *de la drague* bucket ladder, MINES digging ladder, NAUT suction pipe, *d'une drague* ladder; **~ de drague** *f* MINES dredge bucket ladder, dredge ladder; **~ flottante** *f* PETROLE stinger

élingue *f* NAUT, POLLU MER sling, SECURITE fiber-type sling (AmE), fibre-type sling (BrE), rope-type sling; **~ balançoire** *f* AERONAUT cargo swing; **~ à câble métallique** *f* SECURITE wire-rope sling; **~ de chargement** *f* AERONAUT cargo sling; **~ de fret** *f* AERONAUT cargo sling; **~ de hissage** *f* AERONAUT hoisting sling; **~ de levage** *f* AERONAUT hoisting sling; **~ à pattes** *f* CONS MECA dog hook sling; **~ du type câble** *f* SECURITE rope-type sling; **~ du type câble métallique** *f* SECURITE rope-type sling; **~ du type corde en fibre** *f* SECURITE fiber-type sling (AmE), fibre-type sling (BrE)

ellagique *adj* CHIMIE ellagic

ellipse *f* GEOMETRIE ellipse, IMPRIM ellipsis; **~ d'inertie** *f* MECANIQUE ellipse of inertia; **~ parallactique** *f* ASTRONOMIE parallactic ellipse

ellipsoïdal *adj* MATERIAUX ellipsoidal

ellipsoïde[1] *adj* GEOMETRIE ellipsoid

ellipsoïde[2] *m* GEOMETRIE, PHYSIQUE ellipsoid; **~ aplati** *m* GEOMETRIE, PHYSIQUE oblate ellipsoid; **~ de déformation** *m* CONS MECA strain ellipsoid, GEOLOGIE deformation ellipsoid, strain ellipsoid; **~ prolongé** *m* PHYSIQUE prolate ellipsoid

ellipsomètre *m* PHYSIQUE ellipsometer

ellipticité *f* ESPACE ellipticity

elliptique *adj* GEOMETRIE elliptic, elliptical

elliptone *f* CHIMIE elliptone

ellsworthite *f* NUCLEAIRE ellsworthite

éloigné *adj* INFORMAT, ORDINAT remote

éloignement: **~ des galaxies** *m* ASTRONOMIE recession of the galaxies

élongation *f* ACOUSTIQUE displacement, ASTRONOMIE elongation, PLAST CAOU elongation, stretch, stretch; **~ en traction** *f* MATERIAUX tensile elongation; **~ de l'est** *f* ASTRONOMIE elongation east; **~ de l'ouest** *f* ASTRONOMIE elongation west

éluant *m* CHIMIE eluent, NUCLEAIRE eluent, eluting agent

éluat *m* CHIMIE eluate

éluer *vt* CHIMIE elute

élution *f* CHIMIE, GENIE CHIM elution

élutriation *f* AGRO ALIM elution, CHIMIE elutriation

elvan *m* PETR elvan, elvanite

em *m* *(quadratin)* IMPRIM em *(emquad)*

émail *m* CERAM VER, PLAST CAOU *peinture*, PRODUCTION, REVETEMENT enamel; **~ au four** *m* COULEURS baked enamel, baking enamel, stove enamel, PLAST CAOU stoving enamel varnish, PRODUCTION baking enamel; **~ transparent** *m* CERAM VER transparent enamel; **~ vitrifié** *m* CERAM VER, REVETEMENT vitreous enamel

émaillage *m* MAT CHAUFF, PRODUCTION, REVETEMENT enameling (AmE), enamelling (BrE); **~ rideau** *m* CERAM VER curtain coating

émaillé *adj* REVETEMENT enameled (AmE), enamelled

(BrE)

émailler[1] *vt* REVETEMENT enamel

émailler:[2] ~ **au four** *vi* COULEURS stove enamel

émaillerie *f* REVETEMENT metal enameling works (AmE), metal enamelling works (BrE); ~ **industrielle** *f* REVETEMENT metal enameling works (AmE), metal enamelling works (BrE)

émaillure *f* REVETEMENT enameling (AmE), enamelling (BrE)

émanation *f* CHIMIE emanation, NUCLEAIRE active emanation, emanation; ~ **radioactive** *f* PHYS RAYON radioactive emanation; ~ **du radium** *f* PHYS RAYON radium emanation

émaner *vt* PRODUCTION give out

embâclement *m* HYDROLOGIE ice jam

emballage *m* AGRO ALIM packaging, EMBALLAGE package, packet, PAPIER packaging, wrapping, PRODUCTION packaging, wrapping, TEXTILE packing, wrapping; ~ **aérosol** *m* EMBALLAGE aerosol container, aerosol packing; ~ **alimentaire** *m* EMBALLAGE food packaging; ~ **antirouille** *m* EMBALLAGE rust preventive packaging; ~ **arrachable** *m* EMBALLAGE tear-off pack; ~ **attrayant** *m* EMBALLAGE shelf appeal, shelf impact; ~ **avec bulles d'air** *m* EMBALLAGE air bubble wrap; ~ **avec siccatif inclus** *m* EMBALLAGE packing with siccative; ~ **biodégradable** *m* RECYCLAGE biodegradable packaging; ~ **de bobine** *m* IMPRIM wrapping; ~ **composé** *m* EMBALLAGE combined packaging; ~ **consigné** *m* EMBALLAGE returnable packaging, PRODUCTION return of empties; ~ **contractuel** *m* EMBALLAGE contract packaging; ~ **convenant aux fours à hyperfréquence** *m* EMBALLAGE microwavable packaging; ~ **coque** *m* EMBALLAGE bubble pack; ~ **de détail** *m* EMBALLAGE retail package; ~ **dosé** *m* EMBALLAGE dosing packing; ~ **économique** *m* EMBALLAGE economy size pack; ~ **efficace** *m* EMBALLAGE efficient packaging; ~ **en atmosphère modifiée** *m* IMPRIM MAP, modified atmosphere packaging; ~ **en barquettes** *m* EMBALLAGE tray packaging; ~ **en carton** *m* EMBALLAGE cardboard packaging; ~ **en fin de chaîne de production** *m* EMBALLAGE end of line packaging; ~ **en papier** *m* EMBALLAGE paper wrapping; ~ **en plastique mousse** *m* EMBALLAGE plastic foam packaging; ~ **en polythène mousse** *m* EMBALLAGE expanded polythene packaging; ~ **en portions** *m* EMBALLAGE portion pack; ~ **en sacs** *m* EMBALLAGE bag packaging; ~ **d'étalage** *m* EMBALLAGE display packaging; ~ **et doublure en polythène pour palettes** *m* EMBALLAGE polyethylene pallet covers and liners; ~ **étirable** *m* EMBALLAGE stretch wrapping; ~ **extérieur** *m* EMBALLAGE overwrap; ~ **extérieur sur bobine** *m* EMBALLAGE reel overwrapper; ~ **familial** *m* EMBALLAGE family package; ~ **à fenêtre** *m* EMBALLAGE window packaging; ~ **fin et souple comme une peau** *m* IMPRIM skinpack; ~ **formé sous vide** *m* EMBALLAGE vacuum-formed package; ~ **horizontal** *m* EMBALLAGE horizontal wrapping; ~ **industriel** *m* EMBALLAGE industrial packing; ~ **intérieur** *m* EMBALLAGE interior packaging; ~ **à jeter** *m* EMBALLAGE one-way pack; ~ **jumelé** *m* EMBALLAGE twin pack; ~ **laminé** *m* EMBALLAGE laminated pack; ~ **manuel** *m* EMBALLAGE hand packing; ~ **mousse avec tampon amortisseur** *m* EMBALLAGE foam packaging and cushioning; ~ **multi-casse-croûte** *m* EMBALLAGE multisnack bagging; ~ **non alimentaire** *m* EMBALLAGE nonfood packaging; ~ **pelable** *m* EMBALLAGE peel-off wrapping; ~ **plié** *m* EMBALLAGE flat pack; ~ **pour**

l'exportation *m* EMBALLAGE export packaging; ~ **pour normalisation** *m* EMBALLAGE package for standardization; ~ **pour pousser les pastilles à travers** *m* EMBALLAGE push through pill pack; ~ **pour transport maritime** *m* EMBALLAGE overseas packaging, seaworthy packaging; ~ **pouvant être refermé** *m* EMBALLAGE reclosable pack; ~ **préfabriqué** *m* EMBALLAGE prefabricated package; ~ **profondément embouti** *m* EMBALLAGE deep-drawn packaging; ~ **de protection** *m* EMBALLAGE protective wrapper; ~ **de protection pour enfants** *m* EMBALLAGE child-resistant packaging; ~ **récupérable** *m* EMBALLAGE reusable packaging; ~ **d'un sachet dans une boîte** *m* EMBALLAGE bag in a box packaging; ~ **souple** *m* IMPRIM flexible packaging; ~ **sous atmosphère contrôlée** *m* EMBALLAGE controlled atmosphere packaging; ~ **sous film thermorétractable sans support** *m* EMBALLAGE unsupported shrink wrapping; ~ **sous manchon rétractable** *m* IMPRIM sleeve wrapping, stretch wrapping; ~ **stérilisé** *m* EMBALLAGE aseptic packaging; ~ **surgelé** *m* EMBALLAGE deep-freeze packaging, deep-frozen packaging; ~ **thermoformé** *m* EMBALLAGE blister pack; ~ **thermorétractable** *m* EMBALLAGE shrink pack, shrink wrapping; ~ **thermorétractable pour travail en chaîne** *m* EMBALLAGE shrink flow line wrappers; ~ **thermoscellé** *m* THERMODYN heat-sealed wrappings; ~ **transparent sur carton** *m* EMBALLAGE visual pack; ~ **triple** *m* EMBALLAGE triple pack; ~ **trompeur** *m* EMBALLAGE deceptive packaging; ~ **tropical** *m* EMBALLAGE tropical packaging; ~ **à usages multiples** *m* EMBALLAGE multipack; ~ **visuel** *m* EMBALLAGE see-through packaging

emballé: ~ **sous vide** *adj* AGRO ALIM, EMBALLAGE vacuum-packed

emballement *m* CONS MECA overspeed, racing, INFORMAT, ORDINAT thrashing; ~ **du rotor** *m* AERONAUT *hélicoptère* rotor overspeed; ~ **thermique** *m* ELECTRON thermal runaway

emballer[1] *vt* PAPIER pack, wrap, TEXTILE wrap

emballer:[2] ~ **le moteur** *vi* VEHICULES rev up

emballeur *m* EMBALLAGE packer, wrapper, TEXTILE packer, wrapper

emballeuse: ~ **sous vide** *f* EMBALLAGE vacuum packaging machine

embarcadère *m* NAUT landing pier, landing stage, wharf

embarcation *f* NAUT boat, craft, launch; ~ **de bord** *f* NAUT ship's boat; ~ **de débarquement** *f* MILITAIRE landing craft; ~ **pneumatique** *f* MILITAIRE rubber dinghy; ~ **de sauvetage** *f* NAUT lifeboat

embardée *f* AERONAUT gust, ESPACE *véhicules* yaw, NAUT lurch, PHYSIQUE yaw

embarqué *adj* MILITAIRE on-board; ~ **à bord** *adj* ESPACE *véhicules* on-board

embarquement *m* AERONAUT shipment, *des passagers* boarding, *des marchandises* shipping, NAUT shipment, *des passagers* boarding, *des marchandises* shipping

embarquer *vt* NAUT *de l'eau* ship, *une cargaison* ship; ~ **son eau** *vt* NAUT take on water

embarqueteuse *f* EMBALLAGE tray erector and loader, tray packing machine

embarqueur *m* PAPIER baby dryer, first dryer

embarreurs *m pl* IMPRIM *périphériques de rotatives* box tilts

embase *f* CINEMAT turtle, *support d'appareil* baseplate,

CONS MECA *d'un couteau, d'un ciseau* shoulder, CONSTR base, EMBALLAGE *fond d'une bouteille* base cup, INSTRUMENT base, baseplate, RESSORTS crop end, shoulder; ~ **de mât** *f* NAUT mast tabernacle; ~ **de palier** *f* CONS MECA base of plummer block; ~ **pour manche à air** *f* NAUT ventilator socket; ~ **de raccord** *f* CONS MECA pipe union

embaucher *vt* NAUT *de la main d'oeuvre* take on

embavurage *m* CERAM VER scarfing

embeline *m* CHIMIE embelin

embiellage *m* CONS MECA link mechanism, linkage; ~ **à embout sphérique** *m* CONS MECA ball-ended linkage

embobinage *m* PHOTO *d'une cassette* spooling

emboîtage *m* EMBALLAGE slip case, IMPRIM book case, *reliure, emballage, façonnage* casing, *reliure* casing-in, housing

emboîté *adj* INFORMAT, MATH, ORDINAT nested

emboîtement *m* CONS MECA *d'une pièce dans une autre* fitting, CONSTR housing, *des mortaises et des tenons d'une charpente* boxing, INFORMAT, ORDINAT nesting, PRODUCTION jointing; ~ **à baïonnette** *m* NUCLEAIRE bayonet closure; ~ **à bride** *m* CONS MECA socket flange; ~ **lisse** *m* CONS MECA plain socket

emboîter[1] *vt* CONS MECA engage, fit in, fit into, *une pièce dans une autre* fit, CONSTR house, *des tuyaux* socket, *un tenon dans une mortaise* box, INFORMAT, ORDINAT nest

emboîter:[2] **s'~** *v réfl* CONS MECA fit in, GEOMETRIE fit together

embolite *f* MINERAUX embolite

embotteler *vt* PAPIER bundle

embouage *m* MINES flushing

embouchure *f* CONS MECA opening, orifice, CONSTR *d'un concasseur*, DISTRI EAU *d'un fleuve*, HYDROLOGIE *d'un fleuve*, NAUT *d'un fleuve* mouth, TELECOM mouthpiece; ~ **de fleuve** *f* HYDROLOGIE river mouth

embourbement *m* PETROLE *forage* flounder point

embout *m* CONS MECA fitting, CONSTR tailpiece, ELECTROTEC cap, end cap, ESPACE end piece, nozzle, MECANIQUE nozzle, PRODUCTION end, RESSORTS end piece, tip; ~ **arrêtoir** *m* CONS MECA end stop; ~ **d'articulation** *m* CONS MECA hinge fitting; ~ **de bougie** *m* VEHICULES *allumage* plug socket; ~ **de câble** *m* ELECTROTEC cable end; ~ **de drain** *m* CONS MECA drain nipple; ~ **d'échappement** *m* AUTO tailpipe extension; ~ **en caoutchouc** *m* PHOTO *d'un trépied* rubber tip; ~ **fileté vissé** *m* RESSORTS screwed tip, threaded tip; ~ **de flexible** *m* CONS MECA flexible shaft adaptor; ~ **de levage mâle** *m* CONS MECA dome pad; ~ **à oeil** *m* CONS MECA eye end; ~ **à rotule** *m* CONS MECA swivel pipe connector; ~ **sphérique** *m* CONS MECA ball end; ~ **tournevis** *m* CONS MECA screwdriver bit; ~ **de tuyauterie** *m* CONS MECA nipple; ~ **de vissage** *m* CONS MECA bit

embouteillage *m* TRANSPORT road jam, traffic jam

embouteillé *adj* AGRO ALIM bottled

embouteilleuse *f* AGRO ALIM bottle filler, bottling machine

embouti *adj* MECANIQUE dished

emboutir *vt* IMPRIM *cylindre* indent, PRODUCTION shape, stamp, tip

emboutissage *m* PRODUCTION beating, shaping, stamping, swaging; ~ **profond** *m* MECANIQUE, RESSORTS deep drawing

emboutisseur *m* PRODUCTION shaper, stamper

emboutisseuse *f* CONS MECA shaping machine, EMBAL-LAGE flanging machine, PRODUCTION stamp, stamping machine, stamping press, swage

emboutissoir *m* CONS MECA shaping machine, PRODUCTION drift, stamp, swage

embranchement *m* CH DE FER *voie* rail junction, CONSTR branch, branch pipe, junction, DISTRI EAU branching; ~ **de conduite sous-marine** *m* PETROLE spur line; ~ **en T** *m* CONSTR T-junction

embrancher[1] *vt* CONSTR branch, branch off, *un tuyau sur un autre* branch

embrancher:[2] **s'~** *v réfl* CONSTR branch, branch off

embraquer *vt* NAUT haul in, haul taut

embrasement *m* CONSTR *d'un mur* reveal; ~ **du mur** *m* CONSTR reveal

embraser: **s'~** *v réfl* THERMODYN blaze up, flare up

embrasse *f* TEXTILE curtain loop, tieback

embrasure *f* CONSTR recess

embrayage *m* AUTO, CINEMAT clutch, CONS MECA clutch, coming into gear, engagement, engaging, *transmission* clutch, CONSTR connection, MECANIQUE, NAUT, VEHICULES clutch; ~ **automatique** *m* VEHICULES automatic clutch; ~ **à bande** *m* CONS MECA band clutch; ~ **bidisque** *m* AUTO two-disc clutch (BrE), two-disk clutch (AmE), two-plate clutch; ~ **bidisque à sec** *m* AUTO double plate dry clutch; ~ **centrifuge** *m* AUTO, VEHICULES centrifugal clutch; ~ **à coins** *m* CONS MECA V-groove clutch; ~ **à cône** *m* AUTO, CONS MECA, VEHICULES cone clutch; ~ **à diaphragme** *m* AUTO diaphragm clutch; ~ **à disque** *m* CONS MECA plate clutch, MECANIQUE, VEHICULES disc clutch (BrE), disk clutch (AmE); ~ **à disques** *m* CONS MECA multiplate clutch, multiple disc clutch (BrE), multiple disk clutch (AmE); ~ **électrique** *m* ELECTROTEC magnetic clutch; ~ **électromagnétique** *m* MECANIQUE electromagnetic clutch, TRANSPORT electromagnetic clutch, electromagnetic coupling; ~ **à enroulement** *m* CONS MECA coil clutch, scroll clutch, spiral clutch; ~ **à friction** *m* CONS MECA friction clutch; ~ **à griffe** *m* AUTO, VEHICULES *boîte de vitesses* dog clutch; ~ **à griffes** *m* CONS MECA claw clutch; ~ **hydraulique** *m* INST HYDR hydraulic clutch, VEHICULES *transmission* fluid coupling; ~ **hydromécanique** *m* CONS MECA hydromechanical clutch; ~ **à mâchoires** *m* CONS MECA jaw clutch, PAPIER clutch; ~ **magnétique** *m* CONS MECA, ELECTR *véhicule* magnetic clutch; ~ **métallique** *m* CONS MECA metal-to-metal clutch; ~ **monodisque à sec** *m* AUTO single dry plate clutch; ~ **multidisque** *m* AUTO multiple disc clutch; ~ **de pilote automatique** *m* AERONAUT autopilot engagement; ~ **à plateau** *m* CONS MECA plate clutch; ~ **à plateaux multiples** *m* CONS MECA multiple plate clutch; ~ **pneumatique** *m* CONS MECA air clutch, pneumatic clutch; ~ **à rattrapage de jeu automatique** *m* AUTO self-adjusting clutch; ~ **à ressort** *m* AUTO coil spring clutch; ~ **à roue libre** *m* AERONAUT overrunning clutch, AUTO roller clutch; ~ **à ruban** *m* CONS MECA strap clutch; ~ **à sec** *m* VEHICULES dry clutch; ~ **simultané de mouvements automatiques** *m* SECURITE automatic movements being put into operation at the same time; ~ **à spirale** *m* CONS MECA coil clutch, scroll clutch, spiral clutch

embrayé *adj* CONS MECA *moteur*, PRODUCTION *moteur* engaged

embrayer[1] *vt* CONS MECA engage, engage gear, throw into action, throw into gear, trip in, MECANIQUE engage, PRODUCTION connect; ~ **une courroie** *vt* CONS MECA fork a belt on, throw on, PRODUCTION lay on

embrayer:[2] **s'~** *v réfl* CONS MECA come into gear, engage

embrayeur *m* CONS MECA clutch fork, strike gear, striker, striking gear, *d'un manchon d'embrayage* fork, PRODUCTION belt fork

embrèvement *m* CONS MECA dimpling, CONSTR joggle, recess; **~ à froid** *m* CONS MECA cold dimpling process

embrever *vt* CONSTR joggle

embrochable *adj* PRODUCTION plug-in

embrocher *vt* ELECTR *raccordement* plug in

embrouillage *m* TELECOM, TV scrambling

embrouiller *vt* TELECOM, TV scramble

embrouilleur *m* ESPACE *communications*, TELECOM, TV scrambler; **~ de mode** *m* OPTIQUE mode mixer, mode scrambler, TELECOM mode scrambler

embrun: **~ courant** *m* HYDROLOGIE spindrift

embruns *m pl* NAUT spray

embuvage *m* TEXTILE contraction

EMCN *abrév (équipement de multiplication de circuit numérique)* TELECOM DCME *(digital circuit multiplication equipment)*

émeraude *f* CERAM VER beryl, MINERAUX emerald

émergé *adj* GEOLOGIE emerged

émergent *adj* GEOLOGIE emergent

émeri *m* CERAM VER, MECANIQUE *outillage*, PRODUCTION emery

émerillon *m* MECANIQUE, NAUT swivel

émerisage *m* TEXTILE emerizing

émersion *f* ASTRONOMIE emersion, GEOLOGIE *d'un fond de mer* emergence, OCEANO emergence, exposure at the surface

émerylite *f* MINERAUX emerylite, emeryllite

émétine *f* CHIMIE emetine

émettance *f* PHYS RAYON excitance

émetteur *m* ELECTROTEC emitter, ESPACE *communications* transmitter, INFORMAT emitter, NAUT transmitter, ORDINAT emitter, PHYS ONDES transmitter, PHYS RAYON emitter, PHYSIQUE emitter, transmitter, POLLUTION emission source, TELECOM emitter, sender, transmitter, TV transmitter; **~ alpha** *m* PHYS RAYON, PHYSIQUE alpha emitter; **~ Argos** *m* OCEANO Argos transmitter; **~ bêta** *m* PHYSIQUE beta emitter; **~ à clavier** *m* TELECOM keyboard sender; **~ à couverture locale** *m* TRANSPORT road-based transmitter; **~ de détresse de faible puissance** *m* TELECOM LPDT, low-power distress transmitter; **~ d'électrons** *m* ELECTRON electron emitter; **~ à fibre optique** *m* ELECTROTEC fiberoptic transmitter (AmE), fibreoptic transmitter (BrE); **~ de freinage** *m* AERONAUT *atterrissage* master cylinder; **~ d'informations** *m* ELECTROTEC data source; **~ K** *m* NUCLEAIRE K-emitter; **~ lié à la caméra** *m* TV pick-up transmitter; **~ de localisation d'urgence** *m* NAUT emergency locator transmitter, TELECOM ELT, emergency locator transmitter; **~ de messages routiers** *m* TRANSPORT traffic radio transmitter; **~ à numérotation automatique** *m* TELECOM automatic numbering equipment; **~ optique** *m* OPTIQUE optical emitter, TELECOM transmit fiber optic terminal device (AmE), transmit fibre optic terminal device (BrE); **~ orienté** *m* TV directional beam transmitter; **~ portatif** *m* TV portable transmitter; **~ de radiodiffusion** *m* TELECOM broadcast transmitter; **~ de radiodiffusion sonore** *m* TELECOM sound broadcast transmitter; **~ radioélectrique** *m* PHYSIQUE radio transmitter; **~ de la radionavigation** *m* AERONAUT radio beacon; **~ radio à source ponctuelle** *m* TRANSPORT point source radio transmitter; **~ relais** *m* TV network broadcast repeater station, relay transmitter, translator station; **~ au sol** *m* TRANSPORT roadside radio transmitter; **~ à suppression de porteuse** *m* ELECTRON suppressed carrier transmitter; **~ de télécinéma** *m* TV film transmitter; **~ de télévision** *m* TELECOM television transmitter; **~ X** *m* NUCLEAIRE X-emitter; **~ zonal** *m* TRANSPORT area broadcasting station

émetteur-récepteur[1] *adj* ELECTRON TR, transmit-receive

émetteur-récepteur[2] *m* INFORMAT sender-receiver, transceiver, NAUT transceiver, transmitter-receiver, ORDINAT sender-receiver, TELECOM transceiver, transmitter-receiver, TV transmitter-receiver; **~ automatique** *m* INFORMAT ASR, automatic send-receive; **~ à clavier** *m* ORDINAT KSR, keyboard send-receive

émettivité *f* PHYS RAYON emissivity

émettre[1] *vt* ELECTRON beam, INFORMAT emit, send, ORDINAT emit, send, transmit, PHYSIQUE give off, PRODUCTION give out, THERMODYN *dégager de la vapeur* emit, TV air, broadcast; **~ des étincelles** *vt* ELECTROTEC spark; **~ un signal** *vt* ELECTRON signal

émettre:[2] **~ un rayonnement** *vi* GAZ radiate

émeulage *m* PRODUCTION grinding

émeuler *vt* PRODUCTION grind

émissaire *m* DISTRI EAU outlet, HYDROLOGIE effluent, outfall, OCEANO drainage channel, outlet; **~ d'effluent** *m* DISTRI EAU effluent channel; **~ de rejet** *m* NUCLEAIRE waste outlet

émission *f* AERONAUT *moteur* emission, CHIMIE *de gaz* release, INFORMAT emission, sending, INST HYDR release, ORDINAT emission, sending, PHYS PART emission, PHYSIQUE transmission, POLLUTION emission, TELECOM BC, broadcast, TV broadcast, program (AmE), programme (BrE), transmission, VEHICULES *échappement* emission; **~ acoustique** *f* NUCLEAIRE acoustic emission; **~ à bande latérale unique** *f* PHYSIQUE, TV single sideband transmission; **~ brouilleuse** *f* TELECOM unwanted emission; **~ de chaleur** *f* THERMODYN heat emission; **~ de champ** *f* ELECTRON, PHYSIQUE field emission; **~ coopérative** *f* METALL cooperative emission; **~ de données** *f* INFORMAT data origination; **~ des données** *f* TELECOM transmitted data; **~ d'électrons** *f* ELECTRON, PHYS PART electron emission; **~ d'électrons par l'anode** *f* ELECTRON reverse emission; **~ d'électrons secondaires** *f* ELECTRON secondary emission; **~ en direct** *f* TV live broadcast; **~ en extérieur** *f* TV remote broadcast; **~ en stéréophonie et modulation de fréquence** *f* ENREGISTR FM stereo; **~ en studio** *f* TV studio broadcast; **~ d'un faisceau laser** *f* ELECTRON laser beam emission, lasing; **~ à froid** *f* ELECTRON field emission, ELECTROTEC cold emission; **~ de gaz d'échappement** *f* TRANSPORT exhaust gas emission; **~ induite** *f* ELECTRON stimulated emission; **~ ionique secondaire** *f* TELECOM secondary ionic emission; **~ laser** *f* ELECTRON laser emission, lasing; **~ locale** *f* POLLUTION local emission; **~ d'un ordre de fabrication** *f* PRODUCTION production order issue; **~ par effet de champ** *f* ELECTRON field emission; **~ photoélectrique** *f* ELECTRON photoelectric emission, TV photoemission; **~ de polluants atmosphériques** *f* POLLUTION air pollution emission; **~ primaire** *f* ELECTRON primary emission; **~ secondaire** *f* ELECTRON, PHYSIQUE secondary emission; **~ secondaire par la grille** *f* ELECTRON secondary grid emission; **~ de signal** *f* TELECOM signal transmission; ~ **spectrale** *f* MATERIAUX spectral emission; ~ **spontanée** *f* ELECTRON, PHYS RAYON, PHYSIQUE, TELECOM spontaneous emission; ~ **stimulée** *f* ELECTRON, OPTIQUE, PHYS RAYON *de radiation*, PHYSIQUE, TELECOM stimulated emission; ~ **thermoé-lectronique** *f* ELECTROTEC, PHYSIQUE thermionic emission; ~ **thermo-ionique** *f* ELECTROTEC, PHYS RAYON, PHYSIQUE thermionic emission; ~ **transmise de l'extérieur** *f* TV OB, outside broadcast; ~ **transmise par satellite** *f* TV satellite telecast; ~ **utile** *f* TELECOM wanted emission

émissions: ~ **étrangères** *f pl* POLLUTION foreign emissions; ~ **globales** *f pl* POLLUTION global emissions; ~ **intérieures** *f pl* POLLUTION domestic emission; ~ **de moteurs d'aviation** *f pl* AERONAUT aircraft engine emissions

émissivité *f* CHAUFFAGE, OPTIQUE, PHYSIQUE, TELECOM emissivity; ~ **spectrale** *f* PHYSIQUE spectral emissivity; ~ **thermique** *f* THERMODYN thermal emissivity

émittance *f* EN RENOUV emittance

émetteur *m* TELECOM transistor emitter

emmagasinage *m* PRODUCTION storage, warehousing, SECURITE storage; ~ **d'énergie** *m* THERMODYN energy storage; ~ **en réservoirs** *m* PRODUCTION tank storage

emmagasinement *m* PRODUCTION storage, warehousing; ~ **nival** *m* HYDROLOGIE snow storage; ~ **vidangeable** *m* DISTRI EAU live storage

emmagasiner *vt* GAZ store; ~ **l'air** *vt* PRODUCTION trap air

emmanché: ~ **à chaud** *adj* MECANIQUE heat-shrunk; ~ **sur roulements sans friction** *adj* CONS MECA mounted on frictionless bearings

emmanchement *m* CONS MECA coupling, fixing, CONSTR joining, PRODUCTION handling; ~ **à chaud** *m* CONS MECA shrinking on, MECANIQUE shrink fit, PRODUCTION shrinking, shrinking on, THERMODYN heat shrink fitting; ~ **direct** *m* CONS MECA direct fitting shank; ~ **à force** *m* MECANIQUE force fit; ~ **de tiges** *m* MINES rod coupling; ~ **de tige de sonde** *m* MINES drill pipe coupling, drill rod coupling

emmancher[1] *vt* CONS MECA *un piston solidement sur la tige*, CONSTR fix, MINES *des tiges de sonde* couple, PRODUCTION handle, mount; ~ **à chaud** *vt* PRODUCTION shrink on; ~ **par effort** *vt* CONS MECA force on

emmancher:[2] ~ **dans** *vi* CONS MECA slip in, slip into

emmarchement *m* CONSTR length of step

emmêler *vt* TEXTILE entangle, mat, snarl

émodine *f* CHIMIE emodin

émodique *adj* CHIMIE emodic

émondoir *m* CONS MECA pruner

émorfiler *vt* CONS MECA *un ciseau* take the wire edge off

émoudre *vt* PRODUCTION grind

émouleur *m* PRODUCTION grinder

émoussé *adj* CONS MECA, IMPRIM blunt, MECANIQUE *outillage* dull

émoussement: ~ **plastique** *m* METALL plastic blunting

émousser *vt* CONS MECA blunt, *un ciseau* take the edge off, IMPRIM blunt

empannon *m* CONSTR jack rafter

empattement *m* AERONAUT wheelbase, CONSTR footing, IMPRIM serif, VEHICULES *roue* wheelbase; ~ **en forme de barre** *m* IMPRIM slab serifs; ~ **oblique** *m* IMPRIM oblique serif

empêchement *m* SECURITE hindrance

empêcher *vt* CHIMIE *une réaction* inhibit

empennage *m* AERONAUT *queue d'avion* empennage, tail

unit, NAUT stabilizing fin; ~ **double** *m* AERONAUT twin-tail unit; ~ **en T** *m* AERONAUT T-tail; ~ **horizontal** *m* AERONAUT horizontal stabilizer, tailplane; ~ **papillon** *m* AERONAUT V-tail; ~ **de queue** *m* AERONAUT tail unit; ~ **vertical** *m* AERONAUT tail fin

empenneler *vt* NAUT *l'ancre* back

empenoir *m* CONSTR lock-mortise chisel

empeser *vt* TEXTILE stiffen

empierrement *m* CONSTR metaling (AmE), metalling (BrE), paving (AmE), surfacing (AmE)

empierrer *vt* CONSTR metal

empiètement *m* PHYSIQUE *des spectres* overlapping

empilable *adj* EMBALLAGE, PRODUCTION stackable

empilage *m* CERAM VER stacking, CONSTR piling, piling up, INFORMAT, ORDINAT stacking, PAPIER piling up, stacking, PRODUCTION piling, stacking; ~ **en cheminées** *m* CERAM VER smooth plain packing; ~ **en dominos droits** *m* CERAM VER straight packing; ~ **en dominos en simple chicane** *m* CERAM VER staggered packing; ~ **en tressage de panier** *m* CERAM VER basketweave packing

empilé *adj* CONSTR heaped

empilement *m* CONSTR piling, piling up, CRISTALL piling up, stacking, EMBALLAGE stacking up, stacking, GEOMETRIE stacking, PRODUCTION piling, stacking; ~ **compact** *m* CRISTALL close packing; ~ **de graphite** *m* NUCLEAIRE graphite structure; ~ **par compaction** *m* CHARBON compaction piling

empiler *vt* CONSTR stack, stockpile, INFORMAT, ORDINAT stack, PAPIER pile up, stack up, PRODUCTION stack

emplacement *m* CONSTR locating, location, INFORMAT, ORDINAT, PETR location, PRODUCTION *pour détrompeur* slot; ~ **de bit** *m* PRODUCTION *automatisme industriel* bit location; ~ **de bit de mémoire** *m* PRODUCTION *automatisme industriel* memory bit location; ~ **de canon** *m* MILITAIRE gun pit; ~ **de châssis d'E/S** *m* PRODUCTION *automatisme industriel* I/O chassis module slot; ~ **de forage** *m* CONSTR boring site, MINES drill site, drilling site; ~ **libre** *m* INFORMAT, ORDINAT expansion slot; ~ **de mémoire** *m* INFORMAT, ORDINAT storage location; ~ **pour carte d'extension** *m* ELECTRON expansion slot; ~ **pour les jambes** *m* VEHICULES *sièges, habitacle* legroom; ~ **protégé** *m* INFORMAT, ORDINAT protected location; ~ **de sondage** *m* CONSTR boring site, MINES drill site, drilling site, PETR drilling site; ~ **de stockage** *m* PRODUCTION stock location; ~ **de la table-image des sorties** *m* PRODUCTION *automatisme industriel* output image table location; ~ **de la zone primitive** *m* CONS MECA *courroies trapézoïdales* pitch zone location

emplanture *f* AERONAUT wing root; ~ **de mât** *f* NAUT mast step

emplectite *f* MINERAUX emplectite

emplir *vt* PRODUCTION *une citerne, une lampe, un tonneau vide* fill

emploi: ~ **final** *m* TEXTILE end use

employé *m* BREVETS employee

employée *f* BREVETS employee

employeur *m* BREVETS employer

employeuse *f* BREVETS employer

empochement *m* CONSTR bay

empointer *vt* CONSTR point

empois *m* AGRO ALIM starch; ~ **d'amidon** *m* AGRO ALIM boiled starch, starch slurry

empoise *f* PRODUCTION *de laminoir* chock

empoisonnement *m* CHIMIE poisoning; ~ **xénon** *m* NU-

CLEAIRE xenon buildup

empoissonnement *m* OCEANO stocking

empontiller *vi* CERAM VER put on the punty

emporte-pièce *m* CONS MECA punch, sheet metal punch, IMPRIM *transformation, façonnage, emballage* box die, *transformation* die, MINES core breaker, core extractor, core plunger, core pusher, PAPIER cutting die, punch, PRODUCTION socket punch

emporter *vt* HYDROLOGIE drift, remove, wash away

empotage *m* TRANSPORT stuffing

empoter *vt* MINES hitch, TRANSPORT stuff

empreinte *f* CONS MECA dent, indentation, ESPACE *d'un faisceau* footprint, METALL indentation, PAPIER imprint, mold printing (AmE), mould printing (BrE), PRODUCTION impression, print, TV *d'un satellite* footprint; ~ **cruciforme pour vis** *f* CONS MECA cross recess for screw; ~ **fossile** *f* GEOLOGIE fossil imprint; ~ **à la plaque** *f* IMPRIM stamping; ~ **rapportée** *f* CONS MECA *moules d'injection* cavity insert

emprise *f* CONSTR right of way, PRODUCTION grip

emprises: ~ **de la gare** *f pl* CH DE FER station area

emprunt *m* CONSTR borrow

emsien *adj* GEOLOGIE Emsian

émulateur *m* ELECTRON, INFORMAT, ORDINAT, TELECOM emulator; ~ **de protocol** *m* TELECOM PE, protocol emulator

émulation *f* ELECTRON, INFORMAT, ORDINAT emulation

émuler *vt* ELECTRON, INFORMAT, ORDINAT emulate

émulgateur *m* PAPIER emulsifier

émulseur *m* AERONAUT foam compound, CHIMIE emulsifier, PLAST CAOU emulsifier, emulsifying agent

émulsifiant[1] *adj* GENIE CHIM emulsifying

émulsifiant[2] *m* AGRO ALIM emulsifier, CHIMIE emulsifying agent, GENIE CHIM emulsifier, emulsifying agent, PLAST CAOU emulsifier, emulsifying agent

émulsificateur *m* CHIMIE emulsifier

émulsification *f* CHIMIE emulsification

émulsifier *vt* PAPIER emulsify

émulsine *f* GENIE CHIM emulsin

émulsion *f* CHIMIE, CINEMAT emulsion, IMPRIM foaming, PETROLE *boues de forage*, PHOTO, PHYSIQUE, PLAST CAOU *état physique* emulsion; ~ **de bitume** *f* CONS MECA, CONSTR bitumen emulsion; ~ **au chlorure d'argent** *f* PHOTO silver chloride emulsion; ~ **directe** *f* IMPRIM *sérigraphie* direct emulsion; ~ **d'eau de mer dans du pétrole brut** *f* POLLUTION sea water in crude oil emulsion; ~ **d'halogénures d'argent** *f* PHOTO silver halide emulsion; ~ **multicouche** *f* CINEMAT integral tripack; ~ **noircissement direct** *f* PHOTO printing-out emulsion; ~ **orthochromatique** *f* CINEMAT, PHOTO orthochromatic emulsion; ~ **panchromatique** *f* PHOTO panchromatic emulsion; ~ **sale** *f* IMPRIM *équilibre encre-eau* scum, scumming; ~ **sensible à l'infrarouge** *f* PHOTO, PHYS RAYON infrared emulsion, infrared-sensitive emulsion; ~ **servant à la fabrication de blocs papetiers** *f* IMPRIM *papeterie* padding emulsion; ~ **stable** *f* MATERIAUX stable emulsion

émulsionnabilité *f* GENIE CHIM emulsifiability

émulsionnable *adj* GENIE CHIM emulsifiable

émulsionnant[1] *adj* GENIE CHIM emulsifying

émulsionnant[2] *m* EMBALLAGE emulsifying agent, GENIE CHIM emulsifier, emulsifying agent

émulsionné *adj* GENIE CHIM emulsified

émulsionnement *m* CHIMIE, GENIE CHIM emulsification

émulsionner[1] *vt* CHIMIE, GENIE CHIM, PHOTO, PLAST CAOU, POLLUTION emulsify

émulsionner:[2] **s'~** *v réfl* IMPRIM *impression* emulsify

émulsionneuse *f* GENIE CHIM emulsifying machine, NUCLEAIRE emulsifier, emulsifying machine, PLAST CAOU *ingrédient de mélange* emulsifier

énantiomère *m* CHIMIE enantiomer

énantiomorphe *adj* CHIMIE enantiomorphic, enantiomorphous, CRISTALL enantiomorph

énantiomorphie *f* CHIMIE enantiomorphism

énantiomorphique *adj* CRISTALL enantiomorphic

énantiomorphisme *m* CHIMIE, CRISTALL enantiomorphism

énantiotrope *adj* CHIMIE, CRISTALL enantiotropic

énargite *f* MINERAUX enargite

encablure *f* NAUT cable, cable's length

encadrement: ~ **de porte** *m* CONSTR doorframe

encager *vt* MINES cage

encaissement *m* CONSTR *maçonnerie* toothing

encaisseuse: ~ **latérale** *f* EMBALLAGE horizontal case loader

encapsulé: ~ **sous vide** *adj* ELECTROTEC vacuum encapsulated

encart *m* CONS MECA insert, IMPRIM insert, inset-insert; ~ **double-face** *m* IMPRIM *impression* double-sided insert; ~ **en quadrichromie** *m* IMPRIM *impression* art insert; ~ **libre** *m* IMPRIM freestanding insert; ~ **de luxe** *m* IMPRIM *impression* art insert; ~ **volant** *m* IMPRIM flying insert; ~ **volant de petite taille** *m* IMPRIM inset

encartage *m* PAPIER *de feuilles* inserting, insetting

encartonnage: ~ **final** *m* EMBALLAGE film cartoning

encartonneuse *f* EMBALLAGE cartoner, cartoning machine; ~ **à chargement horizontal et par-dessus** *f* EMBALLAGE horizontal and top loader cartoner; ~ **horizontale** *f* EMBALLAGE horizontal cartoning machine; ~ **horizontale et verticale** *f* EMBALLAGE horizontal and vertical wrapping machine; ~ **verticale** *f* EMBALLAGE vertical cartoner

encastré *adj* CONS MECA built-in, embedded, inserted, CONSTR encased, INFORMAT embedded, MECANIQUE built-in, cantilevered; ~ **dans le mur** *adj* CONSTR embedded in the wall, sunk into the wall

encastrement *m* CONSTR housing; ~ **d'aile** *m* AERONAUT *aéronef* wing root

encastrer *vt* CONSTR house, tail, *un châssis dans un mur* embed, PRODUCTION mount flush

encaustique *m* LESSIVES floor polish; ~ **à parquets** *m* LESSIVES floor polish

enceinte *f* ACOUSTIQUE, CONSTR enclosure, ENREGISTR loudspeaker, NUCLEAIRE canyon, enclosure, PHYSIQUE enclosure; ~ **acoustique** *f* ACOUSTIQUE acoustic enclosure, baffle, ENREGISTR speaker system; ~ **à basse réflexe** *f* ENREGISTR bass reflex enclosure; ~ **blindée** *f* ELECTROTEC shielded enclosure; ~ **de haut-parleur** *f* ENREGISTR cabinet loudspeaker, loudspeaker enclosure, loudspeaker housing; ~ **de palissades** *f* CONSTR enclosure of palisades; ~ **pare-feu** *f* SECURITE fireproof enclosure, flameproof enclosure; ~ **de protection de machine** *f* SECURITE machine cage; ~ **réflexe** *f* ACOUSTIQUE reflex baffle; ~ **réfrigérée** *f* REFRIG cold chamber; ~ **vide** *f* NUCLEAIRE *d'un calorimètre* vacuum jacket

en-centre *adj* GEOMETRIE in-center (AmE), in-centre (BrE)

encercler *vt* POLLU MER corral

enchaîné: ~ **au flou** *m* CINEMAT defocus transition

enchaînement *m* CHIMIE catenation, chain formation, linking, ELECTRON, ELECTROTEC concatenation, TV changeover, wipe; ~ **des opérations** *m* PRODUCTION process chart; ~ **opératoire** *m* PRODUCTION process chart; ~ **de programme** *m* INFORMAT program linking

enchaîner *vt* INFORMAT, ORDINAT concatenate

enchâsser *vt* PRODUCTION mount

enchères: ~ **sous plis fermés** *f pl* PETROLE blind auction

enchevêtrement *m* CH DE FER *de tampons* overriding, GEOLOGIE *structure minérale* intergrowth, SECURITE entanglement

enchevêtrer *vt* CONSTR *solive* trim

encirage: ~ **à la cire** *m* IMPRIM *flexographie* wax laminating

enclave *f* DISTRI EAU offset, *d'une écluse* gate chamber, GEOLOGIE xenolith; ~ **de roche éruptive** *f* PETR enclave

enclaver[1] *vt* CONS MECA encompass, fit in, fit into, CONSTR *deux poutres l'une dans l'autre* fit

enclaver:[2] **s'~** *v réfl* CONS MECA fit in

enclenchement *m* AERONAUT interlocking, CONS MECA cutting-in, engagement, interlocking, ELECTROTEC interlock; ~ **automatique de réserve** *m* ELECTR *alimentation* automatic load transfer; ~ **intempestif** *m* ELECTR *commutateur* false switching; ~ **de transit** *m* CH DE FER route locking

enclencher *vt* CONS MECA actuate, engage, interlock, MECANIQUE latch, PRODUCTION snap

encliquetable *adj* PRODUCTION snap-on

encliquetage *m* CONS MECA ratchet, ratchet motion; ~ **à arc-boutement** *m* CONS MECA strut-action pawl motion; ~ **à frottement** *m* CONS MECA strut-action pawl motion; ~ **à levier** *m* CONS MECA lever ratchet motion; ~ **à rochet** *m* CONS MECA pawl-and-ratchet motion, ratchet-and-pawl motion

encliqueter *vt* CONS MECA ratch

enclos *m* CONSTR enclosure; ~ **marin** *m* OCEANO sea ranch; ~ **muré** *m* CONSTR walled enclosure

enclume *f* CONS MECA, IMPRIM *mécanique*, MECANIQUE *outillage*, MINES anvil

encoche *f* CERAM VER chipped edge, notch, CINEMAT edge notch, notch, CONS MECA, ELECTROTEC, IMPRIM *plaques, repérage* slot, PRODUCTION nick, notch, *automatisme industriel* keyslot, *sur conducteur de batterie* slot; ~ **d'extrémité** *f* RESSORTS slotted end notch; ~ **latérale** *f* CINEMAT edge notch; ~ **de protection écriture** *f* INFORMAT, ORDINAT write-protect notch; ~ **sonore** *f* CINEMAT blooping notch; ~ **de verrou** *f* CH DE FER *véhicules* locking notch

encochement *m* CONS MECA slotting, PRODUCTION nicking, notching

encocher *vt* CINEMAT notch, PRODUCTION nick

encocheuse *f* CINEMAT notcher, punch

encodage *m* EMBALLAGE, INFORMAT, ORDINAT encoding

encoder *vt* INFORMAT, ORDINAT encode

encodeur *m* INFORMAT, ORDINAT encoder; ~ **pour cartons recouverts d'aluminium mince** *m* EMBALLAGE hot foil carton coder

encoffrement: ~ **en charpente** *m* PRODUCTION crib, crib-work

encollage *m* EMBALLAGE sizing, IMPRIM *papiers* bond, PRODUCTION shutting together, shutting-up, TEXTILE sizing; ~ **de chaînes sectionnelles** *m* TEXTILE beam-to-beam sizing, sectional warp sizing, sectional warp slashing; ~ **du fil simple** *m* TEXTILE single end sizing; ~ **multi-ensouple** *m* TEXTILE multiple beam slashing; ~ **réunissage de bobines primaires** *m* TEXTILE slasher sizing; ~ **sur filé de fibre** *m* TEXTILE spun yarn sizing; ~ **total** *m* EMBALLAGE full glueing

encollé *adj* CERAM VER bonded

encoller *vt* PAPIER glue, paste, PRODUCTION shut up

encolleuse *f* EMBALLAGE glueing machine, IMPRIM *machines* glueing machine, *papier* billblade, PAPIER size press, TEXTILE sizing machine; ~ **à air-chaud** *f* TEXTILE hot air sizing machine; ~ **sur marge** *f* EMBALLAGE margin gluer; ~ **à tambour** *f* TEXTILE cylinder sizing machine

encombrement *m* CONS MECA space occupied, space taken up, space taken up, CONSTR floorspace, floorspace occupied, obstruction, EMBALLAGE floorspace, MECANIQUE, PHYSIQUE bulk, TELECOM congestion; ~ **intérieur en hauteur** *m* CONS MECA overall internal height; ~ **sur le plancher** *m* CONSTR floorspace, floorspace occupied

encorbellement *m* CONS MECA cantilever, CONSTR cantilever, cantilevering

encourbage: ~ **par coulée** *m* PRODUCTION potting

en-cours: ~ **de fabrication** *m* PRODUCTION in-process inventory; ~ **par employé** *m* PRODUCTION work-in-progress by employee; ~ **de production** *m* PRODUCTION in-process inventory

encrage *m* IMPRIM *machines* ink deck, PAPIER inking

encrassage: ~ **des chaudières** *m* INST HYDR calcin

encrassé *adj* PRODUCTION fouled

encrassement *m* PRODUCTION clogging, gumming, gumming up

encrasser[1] *vt* POLLU MER foul, PRODUCTION clog, gum, gum up

encrasser:[2] **s'~** *v réfl* PRODUCTION clog

encre *f* COULEURS, IMPRIM, PAPIER ink; ~ **à absorption** *f* COULEURS pressure set ink; ~ **à l'alcool** *f* IMPRIM alcohol ink; ~ **à autocopier** *f* COULEURS autographic ink; ~ **à base d'huile** *f* IMPRIM *impression* oil-based ink; ~ **à base de solvants** *f* IMPRIM solvent-based ink; ~ **brillante** *f* COULEURS gloss ink; ~ **de Chine** *f* COULEURS Chinese ink, Indian ink, drawing ink, IMPRIM India ink, drawing ink, REVETEMENT China water; ~ **coldset** *f* COULEURS cold-set ink; ~ **conductrice** *f* COULEURS electrographic ink; ~ **à copier** *f* COULEURS copying ink; ~ **demi-teinte** *f* IMPRIM halftone ink; ~ **déposée sur le papier** *f* IMPRIM *impression* downcolor (AmE), downcolour (BrE); ~ **à dessin** *f* IMPRIM India ink, drawing ink; ~ **double-ton** *f* COULEURS bitone ink, double tone ink, duotone ink, duplex ink, IMPRIM duple ink; ~ **à l'eau** *f* IMPRIM aqueous ink; ~ **à écrire** *f* COULEURS ferrogallic ink; ~ **en pâte** *f* COULEURS paste ink; ~ **en poudre** *f* COULEURS powdering ink; ~ **fixée à chaud** *f* IMPRIM thermosetting ink; ~ **flexographique** *f* IMPRIM flexographic ink; ~ **à forte viscosité** *f* IMPRIM heavy-bodied ink; ~ **grasse** *f* COULEURS printer's black, printing black; ~ **hectographique** *f* COULEURS autographic ink; ~ **hélio** *f* COULEURS gravure ink, gravure printing ink; ~ **hélioliquide** *f* COULEURS gravure ink, gravure printing ink; ~ **hypsométrique** *f* COULEURS hypsometric tint; ~ **illisible** *f* IMPRIM *impression* dropout; ~ **d'impression** *f* IMPRIM ink, printer's ink, printing ink; ~ **d'imprimerie** *f* COULEURS printer's black, printing black, PAPIER, PLAST CAOU printing ink; ~ **indélébile** *f* COULEURS indelible ink, permanent ink, record ink; ~ **labeur** *f* COULEURS book ink; ~ **magnétique** *f* IMPRIM, INFORMAT, ORDINAT magnetic ink; ~ **manquant de corps** *f* IMPRIM light-bodied ink; ~ **à marquer** *f* COULEURS marking ink; ~ **à marquer le linge** *f* COULEURS marking ink; ~ **de masquage** *f* COULEURS masking paste; ~ **mate** *f* COULEURS mat ink; ~

métallisée *f* COULEURS metallic ink; ~ **normalisée** *f* IMPRIM standard ink; ~ **oléique** *f* COULEURS oleic ink; ~ **pour gravure sur cuivre** *f* COULEURS copperplate engraving ink, photogravure ink; ~ **pour gravure sur verre** *f* COULEURS diamond ink; ~ **pour héliogravure** *f* COULEURS gravure ink, gravure printing ink; ~ **pour offset sèche** *f* IMPRIM dry offset ink; ~ **pour photocomposition** *f* COULEURS cold-set ink; ~ **pour retouche** *f* COULEURS retouching ink; ~ **pour les travaux de ville** *f* IMPRIM *typographie* jobbing ink; ~ **pour verre** *f* COULEURS etching ink; ~ **du premier groupe** *f* IMPRIM *impression* first down ink; ~ **pressure-set** *f* COULEURS pressure set ink; ~ **primaire d'imprimerie** *f* IMPRIM process ink; ~ **quadrichromique** *f* IMPRIM four-color process ink (AmE), four-colour process ink (BrE); ~ **qui s'imprime** *f* IMPRIM *impression* first down ink; ~ **à résistance électrique** *f* COULEURS resistor ink; ~ **à saupoudrer** *f* COULEURS powdering ink; ~ **séchant en milieu humide** *f* COULEURS moisture-set ink; ~ **séchant à froid** *f* COULEURS cold-set ink; ~ **séchant aux infrarouges** *f* IMPRIM infrared process ink; ~ **séchant par la chaleur** *f* COULEURS heat-set ink; ~ **sensible à la température** *f* COULEURS heat-set ink; ~ **sympathique** *f* COULEURS invisible ink, sympathetic ink; ~ **taille-douce** *f* COULEURS copperplate engraving ink, photogravure ink; ~ **à tampons** *f* COULEURS endorsing ink; ~ **à timbres** *f* COULEURS endorsing ink; ~ **tirante** *f* IMPRIM heavy ink

encrer *vt* COULEURS ink; ~ **par rouleaux** *vt* COULEURS roll ink on; ~ **la plaque** *vt* IMPRIM *impression* ink the image; ~ **le report** *vt* IMPRIM *copie* ink the plate; ~ **la surface imprimante** *vt* IMPRIM ink the image

encrier *m* COULEURS ink duct, ink fountain, IMPRIM ink fountain, *machine* fountain; ~ **à lame** *m* COULEURS ductor-type ink fountain

encroix *m* TEXTILE shed

encroûtement *m* GEOLOGIE encrustation; ~ **calcaire** *m* GEOLOGIE calcrete

encryptage *m* INFORMAT, ORDINAT encryption

endent *m* CONSTR indent

endentement *m* CONS MECA toothing

endenter *vt* CONS MECA cog, ratch

endigage *m* DISTRI EAU damming

endiguement *m* DISTRI EAU damming

endiguer *vt* CONSTR bank, DISTRI EAU dam, MINES bank up, dam, fill, pack, stow

endoatmosphérique *adj* ESPACE *véhicules* endoatmospheric

endogène *adj* PETR endogenic

endogénétique *adj* PETR endogenetic

endommagé *adj* TELECOM damaged; ~ **pendant le transport par mer** *adj* NAUT sea-damaged

endommagement: ~ **causé par la compression** *m* EMBALLAGE compression damage

endomorphe *m* MINERAUX endomorph

endoscope *m* ESPACE *mesures*, NUCLEAIRE, PHYSIQUE endoscope

endoscopie *f* ESPACE endoscopy, NUCLEAIRE endoscopy, introscopy, PHYSIQUE endoscopy

endosperme *m* AGRO ALIM endosperm

endosser *vt* IMPRIM back

endossure *f* IMPRIM *d'une reliure* casing-in, TEXTILE *d'un livre* backing

endothermique *adj* CERAM VER, CHIMIE, ESPACE endothermic

enducteur *m* TEXTILE coating

enduction *f* PAPIER surface application, PLAST CAOU, PRODUCTION coating; ~ **adhésive** *f* IMPRIM *papier* adhesive coating; ~ **à la cire** *f* IMPRIM *flexographie* wax laminating; ~ **au couteau** *f* PLAST CAOU knife spreading; ~ **électrostatique** *f* MATERIAUX electrostatic coating; ~ **envers** *f* TEXTILE backcoating; ~ **par matière plastique** *f* REVETEMENT plastic coating; ~ **par résine acrylique** *f* REVETEMENT acrylic resin coating; ~ **par vaporisation** *f* IMPRIM *finition* spray coating; ~ **de poudre** *f* PLAST CAOU *revêtements* powder coating

enduire *vt* CINEMAT *émulsion*, PLAST CAOU *procédé* coat, REVETEMENT coat, *de gomme* apply; ~ **de cire** *vt* REVETEMENT coat, wax; ~ **de gomme-laque** *vt* REVETEMENT shellac; ~ **de shellac** *vt* REVETEMENT shellac; ~ **de vernis** *vt* REVETEMENT varnish

enduisage *m* PRODUCTION coating

enduiseuse *f* PLAST CAOU *matériel* coating machine, REVETEMENT spreading machine; ~ **avec barre d'application** *f* PLAST CAOU *revêtement* bar coater

enduit[1] *adj* REVETEMENT coated; ~ **de vernis** *adj* REVETEMENT varnished

enduit[2] *m* CONSTR *route* coat, EMBALLAGE, PLAST CAOU *peintures, adhésifs* coating, PRODUCTION coating, compound, REVETEMENT film; ~ **d'accrochage** *m* CONSTR tack coat; ~ **acoustique** *m* REVETEMENT acoustic plaster; ~ **antiflamme moussant** *m* SECURITE foam layer-forming flame-proofing agent; ~ **antistatique** *m* ORDINAT antistatic spray; ~ **de caoutchouc** *m* REVETEMENT rubber coating; ~ **céramique de surface** *m* REVETEMENT ceramic coating; ~ **à la chaux** *m* REVETEMENT lime paint, lime work, whitewash; ~ **coupe-feu** *m* REVETEMENT fire-resistant coating; ~ **de débauche** *m* REVETEMENT ground coat, primer; ~ **dorsal** *m* CINEMAT backside coating; ~ **d'effaçage de raccord de la piste sonore** *m* ENREGISTR blooping patch; ~ **électrostatique** *m* PLAST CAOU *peinture* electrostatic powder coating; ~ **étanche à l'eau** *m* REVETEMENT waterproof coating; ~ **fouetté** *m* CONSTR roughcast; ~ **hydrofuge** *m* REVETEMENT water repellant coat; ~ **imperméable à l'eau** *m* REVETEMENT waterproof coating; ~ **de laque** *m* REVETEMENT coat of varnish; ~ **magnétique** *m* CINEMAT magnetic coating, ENREGISTR tape coating material, REVETEMENT magnetic film, TV magnetic coating, tape coating material; ~ **de noir** *m* REVETEMENT blackwash, founder's black; ~ **pare-feu** *m* THERMODYN fire-resistant coating, fire-resisting coating; ~ **pour isolation** *m* REFRIG insulation finish; ~ **protecteur** *m* CERAM VER resist, wax resist, REVETEMENT protective coating, protective finish; ~ **réfractaire** *m* REVETEMENT refractory coating, refractory wash; ~ **résistant aux attaques chimiques** *m* REVETEMENT chemical-resistant coating; ~ **résistant à la chaleur** *m* REVETEMENT heat-resistant coating; ~ **résistant à chaud** *m* REVETEMENT heat-resistant coating; ~ **résistant au feu** *m* REVETEMENT fire-resistant coating; ~ **de scellement** *m* CONSTR seal coat; ~ **superficiel** *m* CONSTR surface dressing; ~ **des tanneurs** *m* REVETEMENT dubbing, stuff; ~ **transparent** *m* REVETEMENT transparent coating

endurance *f* AERONAUT endurance, fatigue strength, CONS MECA life, ESPACE *véhicules*, MATERIAUX endurance

endurci *adj* MATERIAUX indurated

endurcir[1] *vt* MATERIAUX indurate, PRODUCTION harden

endurcir:[2] **s'**~ *v réfl* MATERIAUX harden

endurcissement *m* MATERIAUX hardening

énergétique *adj* PHYSIQUE, THERMODYN energy
énergie:[1] **à ~ solaire** *adj* ELECTROTEC, EN RENOUV solar-powered
énergie[2] *f* CHIMIE energy, CONS MECA power, CRISTALL, ELECTR energy, ELECTROTEC energy, power, MECANIQUE, PHYSIQUE, THERMODYN energy; **~ absorbée** *f* METALL, PHYS RAYON absorbed energy; **~ accumulée** *f* PHYS RAYON stored energy; **~ acoustique** *f* ELECTROTEC acoustic energy, sound energy, PETR air pulse; **~ d'activation** *f* CRISTALL, MATERIAUX, METALL, NUCLEAIRE *chaleur* activation energy; **~ active** *f* ELECTR *d'un système* active energy; **~ apparente** *f* ELECTR apparent energy; **~ calorifique** *f* THERMODYN heat energy; **~ de choc** *f* METALL impact energy; **~ cinétique** *f* CONS MECA, ESPACE, GEOPHYS, MECANIQUE, PHYSIQUE kinetic energy; **~ cinétique angulaire** *f* CONS MECA angular kinetic energy; **~ cinétique linéaire** *f* CONS MECA linear kinetic energy; **~ cinétique de vague par mètre de crête** *f* EN RENOUV wave momentum per metre of crest; **~ de cohésion** *f* METALL cohesive energy; **~ de collision** *f* PHYS PART collision energy; **~ de combustion** *f* THERMODYN combustion energy; **~ coulombienne** *f* PHYS RAYON *interaction électronique* coulomb energy; **~ de coupure géomagnétique** *f* ESPACE *géophysique* geomagnetic cutoff energy; **~ de déclenchement** *f* PHYS RAYON activation energy; **~ de désintégration alpha** *f* PHYSIQUE alpha disintegration energy; **~ de désintégration bêta** *f* PHYSIQUE beta disintegration energy; **~ de désintégration radioactive** *f* PHYS RAYON disintegration energy; **~ de dissociation** *f* GAZ dissociation energy; **~ d'échange** *f* METALL exchange energy; **~ électrique** *f* ELECTR electric energy, electric power, ELECTROTEC electrical energy, PHYSIQUE electric energy; **~ électrochimique** *f* ELECTROTEC electrochemical energy; **~ électrocinétique** *f* ELECTR electrokinetic energy; **~ électromagnétique** *f* ELECTROTEC, PHYSIQUE electromagnetic energy; **~ électrostatique** *f* MATERIAUX electrostatic energy; **~ emmagasinée** *f* METALL, PHYSIQUE stored energy, PRODUCTION stored up energy; **~ en courant alternatif** *f* ELECTROTEC AC power; **~ d'entrée** *f* PHYS RAYON input; **~ éolienne** *f* EN RENOUV wind energy, wind power, METEO wind power, PHYSIQUE wind energy, wind power; **~ d'excitation** *f* PHYS RAYON excitation energy; **~ d'extraction** *f* ELECTROTEC work function; **~ d'un faisceau laser** *f* ELECTRON laser-beam energy; **~ de Fermi** *f* PHYSIQUE Fermi energy; **~ fictive de liaison** *f* NUCLEAIRE fictitious binding energy; **~ de formation** *f* METALL formation energy; **~ gaspillée** *f* THERMODYN waste energy; **~ géothermique** *f* PHYSIQUE, POLLUTION geothermal energy; **~ de grande unification** *f* PHYS PART, PHYSIQUE grand unification energy; **~ de la houle** *f* OCEANO wave energy; **~ hydraulique** *f* ELECTR *alimentation* hydroelectric energy, INST HYDR hydraulic power, TEXTILE, THERMODYN water power; **~ hydroélectrique** *f* ELECTR *alimentation* hydroelectric power, EN RENOUV hydroelectric power, water power; **~ d'interaction** *f* METALL interaction energy; **~ interfaciale** *f* METALL interface energy; **~ interne** *f* PHYS RAYON *thermodynamique*, PHYSIQUE internal energy; **~ interne massique** *f* PHYSIQUE specific internal energy; **~ interne molaire** *f* PHYSIQUE molar internal energy; **~ d'ionisation** *f* GAZ, PHYS RAYON, PHYSIQUE ionization energy; **~ de liaison** *f* CHIMIE binding energy, CRISTALL binding energy, bond strength, METALL bond energy, PHYS PART *d'un noyau*, PHYS RAYON binding energy; **~**

libre *f* CHIMIE, METALL, PHYSIQUE, THERMODYN free energy; **~ libre de Gibbs** *f* PHYSIQUE Gibbs free energy; **~ libre de Helmholtz** *f* PHYSIQUE Helmholtz free energy; **~ libre massique** *f* PHYSIQUE specific Helmholtz function; **~ lumineuse** *f* PHYS ONDES *du soleil* luminous energy, PHYS RAYON light energy; **~ magnétique** *f* ELECTR, ELECTROTEC, PHYSIQUE magnetic energy; **~ des marées** *f* OCEANO tidal energy; **~ marémotrice** *f* OCEANO tidal energy, wave energy, PHYSIQUE tidal energy, tidal power; **~ massique** *f* PHYSIQUE specific energy; **~ mécanique** *f* CONS MECA mechanical energy; **~ moyenne de liaison** *f* NUCLEAIRE mean bond energy; **~ nucléaire** *f* ELECTR, PHYSIQUE nuclear energy; **~ nucléaire industrielle** *f* NUCLEAIRE industrial nuclear power; **~ ondulatoire** *f* PHYS ONDES wave energy; **~ du photon** *f* PHYS PART photon energy; **~ de pincement** *f* METALL constriction energy; **~ de point zéro** *f* PHYSIQUE zero point energy; **~ à point zéro** *f* PHYS RAYON *en électrodynamique quantique* zero point energy; **~ potentielle** *f* PHYSIQUE potential energy; **~ potentielle électrostatique** *f* GEOPHYS electrostatic potential energy; **~ radiante** *f* PHYS RAYON radiant energy; **~ rayonnante** *f* PHYSIQUE, TELECOM radiant energy; **~ rayonnante volumique** *f* PHYSIQUE radiant energy density; **~ rayonnée** *f* PHYS RAYON radiated energy, radiated output; **~ réactive** *f* ELECTR *réseau alternatif* reactive energy; **~ de référence** *f* ACOUSTIQUE reference energy; **~ réfléchie** *f* ELECTROTEC reflected power; **~ résiduelle** *f* MAT CHAUFF residual energy; **~ rotative** *f* PRODUCTION *système hydraulique* rotational energy; **~ de Rydberg** *f* PHYSIQUE Rydberg energy; **~ secondaire** *f* PETROLE derived energy, derived fuel; **~ sensible** *f* GAZ sensitive energy; **~ de séparation du champ cristallin** *f* PHYS RAYON crystal field splitting energy; **~ de seuil** *f* METALL threshold energy; **~ solaire** *f* ASTRONOMIE, ELECTROTEC, EN RENOUV solar energy, PHYSIQUE solar energy, solar power; **~ spécifique** *f* GAZ, PHYSIQUE specific energy; **~ superficielle** *f* PHYSIQUE surface energy; **~ de symétrie nucléaire** *f* PHYS RAYON nuclear symmetry energy; **~ thermique** *f* CHAUFFAGE thermal energy, THERMODYN heat energy, thermal energy; **~ thermique des océans** *f* OCEANO ocean thermal energy; **~ transformée** *f* PETROLE derived energy, derived fuel; **~ d'unification électrofaible** *f* PHYS PART electroweak unification energy; **~ de la vapeur** *f* INST HYDR steam power; **~ de vibration** *f* NUCLEAIRE vibrational energy; **~ volumique acoustique** *f* PHYSIQUE sound energy density; **~ volumique acoustique instantanée** *f* ACOUSTIQUE instantaneous acoustic energy per unit volume; **~ volumique cinétique acoustique instantanée** *f* ACOUSTIQUE instantaneous acoustic kinetic energy per unit volume; **~ volumique potentielle acoustique instantanée** *f* ACOUSTIQUE instantaneous acoustic potential energy per unit volume; **~ au zéro absolu** *f* PHYSIQUE zero point energy

énergies: ~ fossiles combustibles *f pl* POLLUTION combustible fossils
enfer *m* PRODUCTION stoke hole
enfermé *adj* CONS MECA enclosed
enferrure *f* MINES plugging
enfichable *adj* ELECTROTEC pluggable
enfichage *m* ELECTROTEC plugging
enficher[1] *vt* ELECTR, ELECTROTEC plug in, plug
enficher:[2] **s'~** *v réfl* TELECOM plug in
enfilage *m* MINES forepoling, lagging, poling

enflammé *adj* THERMODYN flaming

enflammer[1] *vt* NUCLEAIRE, POLLUTION ignite

enflammer:[2] **s'~** *v réfl* THERMODYN blaze up, flare up

enfoncement *m* CONSTR driving, recess, recessing, *d'un clou* driving in, ESSAIS hollow, NAUT *augmentation du tirant d'eau* sinkage; **~ de la barre d'étirage** *m* CERAM VER depth of the draw bar; **~ de calcin** *m* CERAM VER pushing down the cullet; **~ de pilots** *m* CONSTR pile driving; **~ du train** *m* AERONAUT landing gear shock strut compression

enfoncer[1] *vt* CONS MECA drive, drive in, drive into, CONSTR bite, recess, *porte* bite, break open, SECURITE break open

enfoncer:[2] **s'~** *v réfl* MINES sink

enfouissement *m* PETROLE burial

enfournage *m* PRODUCTION charging

enfournée *f* PRODUCTION charging

enfournement *m* CERAM VER charging, charging end, fill, setting-in, PRODUCTION charging; **~ de calcin** *m* (Fra) *(cf enfournement tout groisil)* CERAM VER charging cullet only; **~ en nappe** *m* CERAM VER blanket feed; **~ en tapis sectionné** *m* CERAM VER strip filling; **~ sans calcin** *m* (Fra) *(cf enfournement toute composition)* CERAM VER charge of batch without cullet; **~ toute composition** *m* (Bel) *(cf enfournement sans calcin)* CERAM VER charge of batch without cullet; **~ tout groisil** *m* (Bel) *(cf enfournement de calcin)* CERAM VER charging cullet only

enfourner *vt* CERAM VER fill, PRODUCTION, THERMODYN charge

enfourneur *m* PRODUCTION charger

enfourneuse *f* CERAM VER batch charger, PRODUCTION charging machine; **~ en tapis** *f* CERAM VER blanket charger; **~ à va-et-vient** *f* CERAM VER reciprocating charger

enfumage *m* POLLUTION fumigation

engagement *m* IMPRIM *de la bande dans la machine* threading-in, PRODUCTION commitment; **~ de la bande** *m* IMPRIM *impression, rotatives* webbing-in; **~ en roulis** *m* AERONAUT lateral divergence; **~ longitudinal** *m* AERONAUT longitudinal divergence, pitching; **~ du papier** *m* PAPIER *dans la machine* threading of paper; **~ positif des pointures** *m* IMPRIM *pliage* positive impalement

engager[1] *vt* NAUT *un cordage* foul

engager:[2] **~ la bande** *vi* IMPRIM thread

engendré: être ~ *vi* PRODUCTION be generated

engendrement *m* PRODUCTION generating, generation

engendrer[1] *vt* GEOMETRIE *une courbe* generate

engendrer:[2] **s'~** *v réfl* PRODUCTION be generated

engin *m* CONS MECA appliance, tackle, CONSTR plant, ESPACE craft; **~ autoguidé** *m* MILITAIRE guided weapon; **~ balistique** *m* ESPACE *véhicules* ballistic missile; **~ à câble** *m* OCEANO towed instrument, towed submersible; **~ de dégommage** *m* AERONAUT cranking; **~ extérieur** *m* MINES headwork; **~ de forage** *m* CHARBON drill; **~ lancé d'une rampe** *m* MILITAIRE launched missile; **~ de levage** *m* CH DE FER, CONS MECA, CONSTR lifting gear, PRODUCTION tackle; **~ de pêche** *m* OCEANO fishing gear; **~ de récupération** *m* POLLU MER recovery device; **~ de sauvetage** *m* CONSTR fire escape, SECURITE fire rescue appliance; **~ sol-air** *m* MILITAIRE SAM, surface-to-air missile; **~ sous-marin** *m* OCEANO submersible; **~ spatial** *m* ESPACE spacecraft; **~ subsonique téléguidé** *m* MILITAIRE guided subsonic missile; **~ de sûreté** *m* CONS MECA safety appliance, MINES safety

apparatus, safety appliance, SECURITE safety appliance

engins *m pl* CONS MECA gear; **~ de construction routière** *m pl* TRANSPORT road building machinery; **~ de levage** *m pl* CONS MECA hoisting gear, lifting tackle, PRODUCTION hoisting appliances, hoisting gear, hoisting tackle; **~ de manutention** *m pl* CONS MECA mechanical handling equipment; **~ de manutention continue** *m pl* CONS MECA continuous mechanical handling equipment; **~ de mines** *m pl* MINES mining appliances; **~ de sauvetage** *m pl* NAUT rescue apparatus; **~ de terrassement** *m pl* CONS MECA, CONSTR earthmoving machinery

engobe *m* CERAM VER colored clay (AmE), coloured clay (BrE), engobe

engober *vt* REVETEMENT coat, enamel

engommer *vt* REVETEMENT coat

engorgement *m* CHARBON congestion, CONSTR *dans un tuyau* obstruction, DISTRI EAU clogging, MINES *de la cheminée* chute hang-up, clogging, PRODUCTION blinding, choking, stoppage, *d'un haut fourneau, d'un cubilot* bunging up

engorger[1] *vt* POLLU MER foul, PRODUCTION choke

engorger:[2] **s'~** *v réfl* PRODUCTION choke

engouement *m* TEXTILE craze

engoujonnage *m* CONS MECA register

engoujonner *vt* CONS MECA register

engraissement *m* DISTRI EAU accretion

engrenage:[1] **à ~** *adj* CONS MECA, MECANIQUE geared

engrenage[2] *m* CONS MECA coming into gear, engagement, engaging, gear, gear wheel, gearing, mesh, meshing, pinion, pitching, MECANIQUE, NAUT, PAPIER gear; **~ d'angle** *m* CONS MECA bevel gearing, conical gear; **~ d'attaque** *m* CONS MECA driving gear; **~ à bride** *m* CONS MECA flanged gear; **~ à chaîne** *m* CONS MECA chain gear; **~ à chevrons** *m* CONS MECA V-gear, double helical gear, herringbone gear; **~ de commande** *m* CONS MECA driving gear; **~ conique** *m* CONS MECA bevel gear, bevel ring, conical gear, MECANIQUE bevel gear; **~ conique plat** *m* CONS MECA face gear; **~ à crémaillère** *m* CONS MECA rack-and-pinion gear, TRANSPORT rack gearing; **~ cycloïdal** *m* MECANIQUE cycloidal gear; **~ cylindrique** *m* AUTO cylindrical gear pair, CONS MECA circular gear, circular gearing; **~ de démarrage** *m* CONS MECA starter gear; **~ démultiplicateur** *m* CONS MECA reducing gear; **~ à denture croisée** *m* CONS MECA step tooth gear, stepped gear; **~ à denture droite** *m* VEHICULES *boîte de vitesses* sprung gear; **~ à denture en chevrons** *m* MECANIQUE herringbone gear; **~ à denture hélicoïdale** *m* AUTO, VEHICULES *transmission, différentiel* helical gear; **~ à développante** *m* CONS MECA involute gear, involute gearing; **~ à développante de cercle** *m* CONS MECA involute gear, involute gearing; **~ différentiel** *m* CONS MECA balance gear, compensating gear, equalizing gear, VEHICULES *transmission* differential; **~ échelonné** *m* CONS MECA step tooth gear, stepped gear; **~ elliptique** *m* CONS MECA elliptical gear; **~ épicycloïdal** *m* CONS MECA epicycloidal gear; **~ excentrique** *m* CONS MECA eccentric gear; **~ extérieur** *m* CONS MECA outside gear; **~ de fatigue** *m* CONS MECA heavy-duty gear; **~ à flanc** *m* CONS MECA flank gear; **~ à flancs rectilignes** *m* CONS MECA straight flank gear; **~ à fuseaux** *m* CONS MECA cog and round, lantern gear, lantern gearing; **~ gardé** *m* CONS MECA flanged gear, shrouded gear, shrouding gear; **~ globoïde** *m* CONS MECA curved-worm gear, globoid gear, PRODUCTION

hourglass screw gear; ~ **hélicoïdal** *m* CONS MECA screw gear, screw gearing, spiral gear, spiral gearing, MECANIQUE helical gear; ~ **hélicoïdal double** *m* CONS MECA V-gear, double helical gear, herringbone gear; ~ **hypoïde** *m* CONS MECA hypoid gear; ~ **intérieur** *m* CONS MECA inside gear, internal gear; ~ **inverseur de mouvement** *m* CONS MECA back gear, back speed; ~ **à joues** *m* CONS MECA flanged gear, shrouded gear, shrouding gear; ~ **à lanterne** *m* CONS MECA cog and round, lantern gear, lantern gearing; ~ **menant** *m* CONS MECA driving gear; ~ **mené** *m* CONS MECA following gear; ~ **multiplicateur** *m* CONS MECA multiplying gear, multiplying gearing, multiplying wheel; ~ **à onglet** *m* CONSTR miter gear (AmE), mitre gear (BrE); ~ **parallèle à développante** *m* CONS MECA parallel involute gear; ~ **partiellement denté** *m* CONS MECA mutilated gear; ~ **planétaire** *m* CONS MECA planet gear, planet gearing; ~ **à plateau** *m* CONS MECA flanged gear; ~ **de prise directe** *m* CONS MECA direct drive; ~ **à quarante cinq degrés** *m* CONSTR miter gear (AmE), mitre gear (BrE); ~ **de rechange** *m* CONS MECA change gear; ~ **réciproque** *m* CONS MECA reciprocal gear, reversible gear; ~ **réducteur** *m* CONS MECA reducing gear; ~ **de réduction de vitesse** *m* CONS MECA reducing gear; ~ **de renvoi** *m* CONS MECA counter gear; ~ **retardateur** *m* CONS MECA reducing gear; ~ **à retour** *m* CONS MECA reversible gear; ~ **à tour** *m* CONS MECA reciprocal gear; ~ **de transmission** *m* CONS MECA intermediate gear, transmission gear; ~ **à vis à filets convergents** *m* CONS MECA curved-worm gear; ~ **à vis globique** *m* CONS MECA curved-worm gear, globoid gear, PRODUCTION hourglass screw gear; ~ **à vis sans fin** *m* CONS MECA worm gear, worm gearing, MECANIQUE, NAUT worm gear; ~ **à vis sans fin globique** *m* CONS MECA curved-worm gear, PRODUCTION hourglass screw gear
engrenages *m pl* CONS MECA gear, gearing, PRODUCTION gears; ~ **baladeurs** *m pl* CONS MECA sliding gear; ~ **bruts de fonte** *m pl* PRODUCTION roughcast gears; ~ **coniques à denture droite et hélicoïdale** *m pl* CONS MECA bevel gears with straight and spiral tooth system; ~ **cylindriques** *m pl* CONS MECA cylindrical gears; ~ **cylindriques de grosse mécanique** *m pl* CONS MECA cylindrical gears for heavy engineering; ~ **enfermés dans des carters** *m pl* CONS MECA enclosed gears, guarded gears, SECURITE guarded gears; ~ **pour portes** *m pl* CONS MECA gate accentuator; ~ **protégés sous capot** *m pl* SECURITE guarded gears; ~ **protégés sous carter** *m pl* SECURITE guarded gears; ~ **recouverts de gaines protectrices** *m pl* CONS MECA enclosed gears, guarded gears; ~ **taillés** *m pl* CONS MECA cut gears; ~ **taillés à la machine** *m pl* CONS MECA cut gears
engrenant *adj* CONS MECA gearing
engrènement *m* CONS MECA engagement, engaging, meshing, mesh, pitching, MECANIQUE meshing
engrener[1] *vt* CONS MECA engage gear, throw into action, throw into gear, gear, mesh
engrener[2] *vi* CONS MECA come into gear, gear, interlock, mesh, pitch
engrener:[3] **s'~** *v réfl* CONS MECA come into gear, engage, gear, mesh, pitch
enhydre *m* MINERAUX enhydrite
enjoliveur *m* VEHICULES *roue* hub cap; ~ **de roue** *m* AUTO hub cap, VEHICULES wheel cover
enlevage *m* MINES lifting point
enlevé: ~ **par une vague** *adj* NAUT washed overboard
enlèvement *m* POLLU MER removal, PRODUCTION *des*

débris clearing away; ~ **du boisage** *m* MINES removal of timbering; ~ **de copeaux** *m* CONS MECA *usinage* chip removal; ~ **des cosses** *m* MINES quarry stripping; ~ **d'un gîte métallifère** *m* MINES removal; ~ **de matière sur la pièce** *m* CONS MECA metal removal; ~ **par lavage** *m* GENIE CHIM washing out; ~ **des piliers** *m* CHARBON broken working, pillar working, pillar drawing; ~ **des poussières** *m* PRODUCTION removing dust; ~ **des terrains de couverture** *m* CONSTR removing an overburden; ~ **des terrains stériles superposés** *m* CONSTR removing an overburden
enlever[1] *vt* HYDROLOGIE remove, PRODUCTION hoist; ~ **les dépôts** *vt* LESSIVES descale
enlever:[2] ~ **du malaxeur** *vi* GENIE CHIM batch off; ~ **les terrains de couverture** *vi* MINES remove an overburden
enneigé *adj* METEO snowed up
enneigement *m* METEO snow cover
ennoyage *m* OCEANO flooding, submergence
ennoyer: s'~ *v réfl* GEOLOGIE pitch, plunge
énol *m* CHIMIE enol
énolase *f* CHIMIE enolase
énolique *adj* CHIMIE enolic
énolisation *f* CHIMIE enolization
énoncé: ~ **de Clausius** *m* PHYSIQUE *du second principe* Clausius statement; ~ **de Kelvin du second principe** *m* PHYSIQUE Kelvin statement
enquête *f* CONS MECA investigation, QUALITE audit; ~ **cordon** *f* TRANSPORT cordon line survey; ~ **papillons** *f* TRANSPORT vehicle intercept survey; ~ **par papillons** *f* TRANSPORT precoded tag survey; ~ **par procédé aéro-cinématographique** *f* TRANSPORT time lapse survey
enrayage *m* CH DE FER *véhicules* braking, locking of wheels
enrayé *adj* ESPACE *véhicules* jammed
enrayer: s'~ *v réfl* MECANIQUE jam
enrayeur *m* (Fra) *(cf sabotier)* CH DE FER *personnel* shunter
enregistrement *m* ACOUSTIQUE recording, BREVETS registration, ESSAIS, GEOLOGIE, GEOPHYS recording, INFORMAT recording, record, ORDINAT record, recording, registration, PHYSIQUE record, TELECOM recording; ~ **à amplitude variable** *m* ACOUSTIQUE variable amplitude recording; ~ **analogique** *m* TELECOM analog recording (AmE), analogue recording (BrE); ~ **d'annulation** *m* INFORMAT, ORDINAT deletion record; ~ **d'audit** *m* TELECOM audit trail; ~ **avec marche avant-arrière** *m* ENREGISTR rock and roll recording; ~ **chronologique de données** *m* ORDINAT data logging; ~ **à demi-piste** *m* ENREGISTR half track recording; ~ **à densité variable** *m* ACOUSTIQUE variable density recording, TV variable area recording; ~ **direct** *m* ACOUSTIQUE instantaneous recording, ENREGISTR direct recording; ~ **de données** *m* INFORMAT data logging, data record, data recording, NUCLEAIRE data logging, ORDINAT data record, data recording, TELECOM data recording; ~ **des données d'appels** *m* TELECOM CDR, call data recording, call detail recording; ~ **électromécanique** *m* ENREGISTR electromechanical recording; ~ **en direct** *m* TV off-air recording; ~ **en double densité** *m* INFORMAT, ORDINAT double-density recording; ~ **en modulation de phase** *m* INFORMAT, ORDINAT PE, phase encoding; ~ **d'entrée** *m* INFORMAT, ORDINAT input record; ~ **de fin** *m* INFORMAT, ORDINAT trailer record; ~ **fractionnel** *m* ACOUSTIQUE multiplay; ~ **fragmenté** *m* TV segmented recording; ~ **hélicoïdal** *m* TV helical recording; ~ **ident-**

ificateur *m* INFORMAT label record; ~ **international** *m* BREVETS international registration; ~ **au laser** *m* TV laser beam recording; ~ **latéral** *m* ACOUSTIQUE, ENREGISTR lateral recording; ~ **logique** *m* INFORMAT, ORDINAT logical record; ~ **longitudinal** *m* ENREGISTR, TV longitudinal recording; ~ **longue durée** *m* ENREGISTR extended play record; ~ **de longueur fixe** *m* INFORMAT, ORDINAT fixed length record; ~ **de longueur variable** *m* INFORMAT, ORDINAT variable length record; ~ **low-band** *m* TV low-band recording; ~ **magnétique** *m* ACOUSTIQUE magnetic recording, ENREGISTR magnetic recording, tape recording, INFORMAT, ORDINAT, TELECOM magnetic recording, TV magnetic recording, recording; ~ **magnétique longitudinal** *m* ACOUSTIQUE longitudinal magnetic recording; ~ **magnétique perpendiculaire** *m* ACOUSTIQUE perpendicular magnetic recording, TV perpendicular magnetization; ~ **magnétique stéréo** *m* ENREGISTR stereo tape recording; ~ **magnétique transversal** *m* ACOUSTIQUE transverse magnetic recording; ~ **mécanique** *m* ACOUSTIQUE, ENREGISTR mechanical recording; ~ **mécanique à amplitude constante** *m* ACOUSTIQUE constant amplitude mechanical reading; ~ **mécanique à vélocité constante** *m* ACOUSTIQUE constant velocity mechanical reading; ~ **à microsillon** *m* ENREGISTR microgroove recording; ~ **à minisillon** *m* ENREGISTR minigroove recording; ~ **à modulation de fréquence** *m* ENREGISTR FM recording; ~ **monophonique** *m* ACOUSTIQUE, ENREGISTR monophonic recording; ~ **monotrace** *m* ACOUSTIQUE one-track recording; ~ **mouvement** *m* INFORMAT transaction record, ORDINAT change record, transaction record; ~ **multiple** *m* ACOUSTIQUE multitrack recording; ~ **non synchrone** *m* ENREGISTR wild recording; ~ **numérique** *m* ENREGISTR, TELECOM, TV digital recording; ~ **optique** *m* ACOUSTIQUE, ENREGISTR, TELECOM optical recording; ~ **optique au laser** *m* OPTIQUE laser-optic recording; ~ **original** *m* TV master, original; ~ **par ablation** *m* OPTIQUE ablative method recording; ~ **par codage de groupe** *m* ORDINAT GCR, group code recording; ~ **par faisceau laser** *m* INFORMAT, ORDINAT laser beam recording; ~ **par groupe** *m* ORDINAT GCR, group code recording; ~ **perpendiculaire** *m* ENREGISTR perpendicular recording; ~ **physique** *m* INFORMAT, ORDINAT physical record; ~ **pirate** *m* TV pirate recording; ~ **à piste unique** *m* ENREGISTR single track recording; ~ **pleine piste** *m* ENREGISTR full track recording; ~ **de la position de la station mobile** *m* TELECOM mobile location registration; ~ **principal** *m* ORDINAT master record; ~ **qualité** *m* QUALITE quality record; ~ **à quart de piste** *m* ENREGISTR four-track recording, quarter track recording; ~ **sans retour à zéro** *m* INFORMAT, ORDINAT NRZ recording, nonreturn to zero recording; ~ **à sillon repoussé** *m* ENREGISTR embossed groove recording; ~ **simultané** *m* ENREGISTR instantaneous recording; ~ **de son** *m* TV audio record; ~ **du son** *m* TELECOM sound recording; ~ **son optique** *m* CINEMAT optical sound recording; ~ **sonore** *m* CINEMAT, ENREGISTR sound recording; ~ **de sortie** *m* INFORMAT, ORDINAT output record; ~ **stéréo** *m* ENREGISTR stereo recording; ~ **stéréophonique** *m* ACOUSTIQUE, ENREGISTR stereophonic recording; ~ **sur laque** *m* ENREGISTR lacquer recording; ~ **sur vidéodisque** *m* TV videodisc recording (BrE), videodisk recording (AmE); ~ **synchrone** *m* ENREGISTR direct recording; ~ **témoin** *m* TV aircheck; ~ **témoin d'une émission simultané antenne** *m* TV aircheck tape; ~ **de température** *m* PETR temperature log; ~ **tétraphonique** *m* ACOUSTIQUE tetraphonic recording; ~ **transversal** *m* ENREGISTR, TV transverse recording; ~ **vertical** *m* ACOUSTIQUE vertical recording; ~ **vidéo** *m* TELECOM video recording, TV videotaping; ~ **à vitesse constante** *m* ENREGISTR constant velocity recording

enregistrement-label *m* ORDINAT label record

enregistrer[1] *vt* ENREGISTR, IMPRIM record, INFORMAT enter, record, NAUT log, ORDINAT, PHYSIQUE, TV record

enregistrer[2] *vi* ORDINAT enter; ~ **sur bande** *vi* ENREGISTR, TV tape

enregistreur *m* ACOUSTIQUE recorder, CONS MECA recorder, self-registering apparatus, ELECTR logger, recorder, ENREGISTR recorder, EQUIP LAB chart recorder, INFORMAT data logger, recorder, INSTRUMENT recorder, recording device, ORDINAT, TELECOM recorder; ~ **analyseur** *m* INSTRUMENT scanner printer; ~ **d'arrivée** *m* TELECOM incoming register; ~ **automatique** *m* INSTRUMENT logger; ~ **automatique d'infraction** *m* TRANSPORT automatic infringement recorder; ~ **à bande** *m* ELECTR strip chart recorder; ~ **à bande magnétique** *m* ENREGISTR magnetic tape recorder; ~ **de bord** *m* AERONAUT flight recorder; ~ **de caractéristiques** *m* INSTRUMENT character tracer; ~ **à cartouche** *m* INSTRUMENT cartridge recorder; ~ **de cassette** *m* INSTRUMENT cassette recorder; ~ **à cassette** *m* ENREGISTR cassette tape recorder; ~ **chronologique automatique** *m* INSTRUMENT logger; ~ **de conversation** *m* AERONAUT cockpit voice recorder; ~ **de conversation de poste de pilotage** *m* AERONAUT cockpit voice recorder; ~ **de conversations** *m* ESPACE *véhicules* voice recorder; ~ **de déformation** *m* CONSTR strain gauge; ~ **de degré de raffinage** *m* PAPIER freeness recorder; ~ **de départ** *m* TELECOM originating register; ~ **à diagramme polaire** *m* INSTRUMENT radial chart recorder; ~ **de diagrammes** *m* INSTRUMENT chart recorder; ~ **à disque** *m* ELECTR disk recorder, ENREGISTR disc recorder (BrE), disk recorder (AmE); ~ **de données** *m* ELECTR, INFORMAT data recorder, INSTRUMENT data logger, ORDINAT data logger, data recorder; ~ **de données de vol** *m* AERONAUT flight data recorder; ~ **à douze stylos** *m* INSTRUMENT twelve-point recorder; ~ **à douze traces** *m* INSTRUMENT twelve-point recorder; ~ **à encre** *m* INSTRUMENT ink recorder, ink writer, pen plotter, pen recorder; ~ **à étincelles** *m* INSTRUMENT spark recorder; ~ **de flèche de pont** *m* CONSTR bridge deflective recorder; ~ **à huit canaux** *m* INSTRUMENT eight-channel recorder; ~ **à huit courbes** *m* INSTRUMENT eight-point recorder; ~ **d'images** *m* INSTRUMENT telerecording equipment; ~ **d'impédance** *m* INSTRUMENT impedance recorder; ~ **d'information** *m* INSTRUMENT event recorder; ~ **de lumière dispersée** *m* INSTRUMENT diffuse light recorder; ~ **magnétique** *m* ACOUSTIQUE magnetic recorder; ~ **de maintenance** *m* AERONAUT maintenance recorder; ~ **mécanique** *m* ACOUSTIQUE mechanical recorder; ~ **multicourbe** *m* INSTRUMENT multipoint recorder; ~ **de niveau** *m* ENREGISTR level recorder; ~ **numérique** *m* NUCLEAIRE digital recorder; ~ **numérique de données de vol** *m* AERONAUT digital flight data recorder; ~ **numérique incrémentiel** *m* INSTRUMENT incremental digital recorder; ~ **optique à laser** *m* ELECTRON laser optical recorder; ~ **à papier déroulant** *m* INSTRUMENT continuous chart recorder, strip chart recorder; ~ **par**

points *m* INSTRUMENT point recorder; ~ phonographique *m* INSTRUMENT sound recorder; ~ à pistes multiples *m* INSTRUMENT multitrack recorder; ~ à plume *m* ELECTR, EQUIP LAB, INFORMAT pen plotter (AmE), pen recorder (BrE), INSTRUMENT ink recorder, ink writer, pen plotter (AmE), pen recorder; ~ à plusieurs voies *m* INSTRUMENT multivariable recorder; ~ à pointe sèche *m* INSTRUMENT stylus recording instrument; ~ potentiométrique *m* INSTRUMENT potentiometric recorder; ~ pour essais en vol *m* AERONAUT flight test recorder; ~ de pression de fond *m* PETR pressure bomb; ~ de productivité *m* INSTRUMENT production recorder; ~ du profil sismique *m* PHYS ONDES seismic profile recorder; ~ de puissance *m* INSTRUMENT output recorder; ~ de quantités *m* INSTRUMENT quantity recorder; ~ sonore optique *m* ENREGISTR optical sound recorder; ~ sur bande *m* INSTRUMENT continuous chart recorder, strip chart recorder; ~ sur bande magnétique *m* ENREGISTR magnetic tape recorder; ~ sur bande à pas de progressions *m* INSTRUMENT incremental tape recorder; ~ sur fil d'acier *m* ENREGISTR wire recorder; ~ sur microfilm *m* INFORMAT, ORDINAT microfilm recorder; ~ de temps *m* INSTRUMENT chronograph, time recorder; ~ à trace continue *m* INSTRUMENT line recorder; ~ de trajectoire de vol *m* INSTRUMENT black box, flight path recorder; ~ des valeurs moyennes *m* INSTRUMENT mean value recorder; ~ des vibrations *m* INSTRUMENT vibration recorder; ~ de vitesse *m* CONS MECA, INSTRUMENT speed recorder; ~ de vol *m* AERONAUT flight recorder, INSTRUMENT black box, flight path recorder; ~ X-Y *m* ELECTR, ESPACE X-Y recorder

enregistreur-duplicateur *m* INSTRUMENT duplicating recorder

enregistreur-lecteur *m* ENREGISTR recorder-player, OPTIQUE, ORDINAT read-write drive

enregistreur-traducteur *m* TELECOM register translator

enrichi *adj* AGRO ALIM fortified

enrichir *vt* AGRO ALIM, CHARBON enrich

enrichissement *m* AGRO ALIM enrichment, fortification, CERAM VER beneficiation, CHARBON, CHIMIE, MATERIAUX, PHYSIQUE *de l'uranium* enrichment; ~ en gaz *m* THERMODYN gas enrichment; ~ initial *m* NUCLEAIRE feed enrichment; ~ isotopique *m* PHYS PART isotopic enrichment

enrichisseur *m* AUTO, MECANIQUE *véhicules* choke

enrobage *m* CONSTR coating, ESPACE potting, NUCLEAIRE jacketing, *déchets nucléaires* encapsulation, OPTIQUE fiber jacket (AmE), fibre jacket (BrE), PLAST CAOU encapsulation, potting, *procédé* embedding, PRODUCTION coating, TELECOM fiber jacket (AmE), fibre jacket (BrE); ~ aux abrasifs *m* REVETEMENT abrasive coating; ~ à chaud *m* CONSTR hot mix; ~ au chocolat *m* AGRO ALIM chocolate coating; ~ à froid *m* CONSTR asphaltage cold mix

enrober *vt* CONSTR encase, MATERIAUX *isolation* lag, REVETEMENT coat, *de caoutchouc* coat

enrochement *m* CONSTR riprap, rock fill, DISTRI EAU rock fill

enrôler *vt* NAUT *un équipage* ship

enroulage *m* CONS MECA winding, PAPIER reeling, PRODUCTION coiling; ~ des poches *m* PRODUCTION bag rolling; ~ du tissu *m* TEXTILE wind-up

enroulé *adj* RESSORTS coiled, wound; ~ à chaud *adj* RESSORTS hot-coiled; ~ à froid *adj* RESSORTS cold-coiled; ~ sur ensouple *adj* TEXTILE wound onto the beam

enroulement *m* CINEMAT take-up, CONS MECA convolution, winding, wrapping, ELECTR *moteur, générateur* winding, ELECTROTEC reeling, winding, PHYSIQUE winding, PRODUCTION coiling, TV *trajet de la bande* alpha wrap; ~ B *m* CINEMAT B-wind; ~ à barres *m* ELECTR *induit* bar winding; ~ à basse tension *m* ELECTR low-voltage winding; ~ bipolaire *m* ELECTR *machine* bipolar winding; ~ à bobines *m* ELECTR wirewound coil; ~ à bobines concentriques *m* ELECTR cylindrical winding; ~ à bobines en U *m* ELECTR push-through winding; ~ à cage double *m* ELECTROTEC double squirrel cage winding; ~ de champ *m* ELECTROTEC field winding; ~ de circuit *m* ELECTR *transformateur* primary winding; ~ de commutation *m* ELECTR *machine* commutating winding; ~ de compensation *m* ELECTROTEC bucking coil, compensation winding; ~ compound *m* ELECTR *machine à courant direct*, ELECTROTEC compound winding; ~ concentrique *m* ELECTR *machine* concentric winding; ~ de contre-réaction *m* ELECTROTEC feedback winding; ~ dérivé *m* ELECTR *moteur* shunt winding, *réglage* bleeder winding; ~ à deux couches *m* ELECTR double-layer winding; ~ à deux rangées de billes *m* CONS MECA double row ball bearing; ~ diamétral *m* ELECTR *bobine* full-pitch coil, full-pitch winding, *machine* diametrical winding; ~ différentiel *m* ELECTROTEC differential winding; ~ en anneau *m* ELECTR ring winding, *bobine* Gramme ring, Gramme winding; ~ en barres posées sur chant *m* ELECTR *machine* edge winding; ~ en biais de la bande *m* TV skew; ~ en cage d'écureuil *m* ELECTROTEC squirrel cage winding; ~ en chaîne *m* ELECTROTEC chain winding; ~ en couronne *m* PRODUCTION coiling; ~ en cuivre plat *m* ELECTR *machine* strip-wound armature; ~ en dérivation *m* ELECTR *moteur* shunt winding, *réglage* bleeder winding, ELECTROTEC shunt winding; ~ en disque *m* ELECTR *bobine* pile-wound coil, *transformateur* disc winding (BrE), disk winding (AmE), ELECTROTEC disk winding (AmE); ~ en disques doubles *m* ELECTR *transformateur* double disc winding (BrE), double disk winding (AmE); ~ en épingle à cheveux *m* ELECTROTEC pi winding; ~ en losange *m* ELECTR *machine*, ELECTROTEC diamond winding; ~ en pattes de grenouilles *m* ELECTROTEC frogleg winding; ~ en tambour *m* ELECTROTEC drum winding; ~ en U *m* TV U-wrap; ~ en vrac *m* ELECTR random winding, *petites machines à courant alternatif* mush winding; ~ d'excitation *m* ELECTROTEC field coil; ~ excitation *m* ELECTR *électro-aimant* excitation winding; ~ extérieur *m* CINEMAT emulsion out; ~ fil à fil *m* ELECTR turn-to-turn winding, uniform layer winding; ~ à fils jetés *m* ELECTR random winding, *petites machines à courant alternatif* mush winding; ~ à fils semés par l'entaille *m* ELECTR fed-in winding; ~ à fils tirés *m* ELECTR pull-through winding; ~ à haute tension *m* ELECTR *transformateur* high-voltage winding; ~ imbriqué *m* ELECTR *machine*, ELECTROTEC lap winding; ~ imbriqué parallèle *m* ELECTR *machine* simplex lap winding; ~ imbriqué parallèle double *m* ELECTR *machine* duplex lap winding; ~ imbriqué parallèle multiple *m* ELECTR *machine* multiplex lap winding; ~ inducteur *m* ELECTR *machine* field coil, field winding, ELECTROTEC field winding; ~ d'induit *m* ELECTR *machine*, ELECTROTEC armature winding; ~ intérieur *m* CINEMAT emulsion in; ~ M *m* TV M-wrap; ~ de maintien *m* ELECTROTEC holding coil; ~

monophasé *m* ELECTROTEC single-phase winding; ~ **multiple** *m* ELECTR *transformateur*, ELECTROTEC multiple winding; ~ **à nombre fractionnaire par pôle et par phase** *m* ELECTROTEC fractional slot winding; ~ **oméga** *m* TV omega wrap; ~ **ouvert** *m* ELECTR *transformateur, machine* open circuit winding; ~ **du papier autour des cylindres lors d'une casse** *m* IMPRIM *rotatives* wraparound; ~ **à pas allongé** *m* ELECTR *bobine*, ELECTROTEC long pitch winding; ~ **à pas diamétral** *m* ELECTR *bobine* full-pitch coil, full-pitch winding, ELECTROTEC full-pitch winding; ~ **à pas partiel** *m* ELECTR *armature*, ELECTROTEC fractional pitch winding; ~ **de phase** *m* ELECTR phase winding; ~ **de polarisation** *m* ELECTROTEC bias winding; ~ **préformé** *m* ELECTR form-wound coil; ~ **primaire** *m* ELECTR *transformateur*, ELECTROTEC, PHYSIQUE primary winding; ~ **primaire à prises** *m* ELECTROTEC tapped primary winding; ~ **à prises** *m* ELECTROTEC tapped winding; ~ **progressif** *m* ELECTR *moteur* lazy coil; ~ **rangé** *m* ELECTR *bobine* bank winding, banked winding; ~ **de relais** *m* ELECTR relay winding; ~ **rotorique** *m* ELECTROTEC rotor winding; ~ **secondaire** *m* ELECTR *transformateur*, ELECTROTEC, PHYSIQUE secondary winding; ~ **secondaire à prises** *m* ELECTROTEC tapped secondary winding; ~ **série** *m* ELECTR, ELECTROTEC series winding; ~ **de sortie** *m* ELECTR *transformateur* output winding; ~ **spire** *m* CONS MECA convolution; ~ **à spires jointives** *m* ELECTROTEC layer winding; ~ **à spires non jointives** *m* ELECTROTEC random winding; ~ **de stabilisation** *m* ELECTR *bobine* stabilizing winding; ~ **sur gabarit** *m* CERAM VER former winding; ~ **à tension intermédiaire** *m* ELECTR intermediate voltage winding; ~ **tertiaire** *m* ELECTR *transformateur* tertiary winding; ~ **du texte** *m* IMPRIM *traitement de texte, saisie* word wrap; ~ **toroïdal** *m* ELECTR torus, *bobine* toroid; ~ **à trois rainures** *m* ELECTR three-slot winding

enroulements: ~ **alternés** *m pl* ELECTR sandwich windings; ~ **en disque** *m pl* ELECTR sandwich windings; ~ **de phase indépendants** *m pl* ELECTR *transformateur, bobine* open windings; ~ **secondaires montés en opposition** *m pl* ELECTROTEC phase-reversed secondaries

enrouler[1] *vt* CINEMAT spool, wind, CONS MECA wind, wrap, ELECTROTEC reel, NAUT coil, PAPIER reel, PHYSIQUE wind, POLLU MER reel in, TV spool

enrouler:[2] **s'**~ *v réfl* CONS MECA wind

enrouleur *m* CONSTR cable drum; ~ **de câble électrique** *m* ELECTROTEC extension reel; ~ **prolongateur téléphonique** *m* TELECOM telephone extension reel

enrouleuse *f* CINEMAT winding machine, EMBALLAGE winding machine, winding-on machine, PAPIER reel, winder; ~ **avec patin de serrage** *f* CINEMAT tight winder; ~ **électrique** *f* CINEMAT power rewinder; ~ **à entraînement axial** *f* PAPIER center wind reel (AmE), centre wind reel (BrE); ~ **à entraînement périphérique** *f* PAPIER friction reel, surface drive reel, frictionroller; ~ **à grande vitesse** *f* CINEMAT positive rewinder; ~ **pope** *f* PAPIER pope reel; ~ **pour carton** *f* PAPIER intermittent board machine

ensachement *m* EMBALLAGE bagging

ensacher *vt* AGRO ALIM bag

ensacheuse *f* EMBALLAGE bagging machine; ~ **tubulaire** *f* EMBALLAGE flow wrapping machine

enseigne: ~ **de vaisseau** *m* NAUT sublieutenant

enseignement: ~ **assisté par ordinateur** *m* (EAO) ORDINAT computer-assisted learning *(CAL)*, TELECOM computer-based training

ensellement *m* GEOLOGIE *d'un axe anticlinal* axial depression, low

ensemble *m* AERONAUT *d'avions en attente* stack, CONS MECA outfit, GEOLOGIE sequence, set, *d'unités lithologiques ou structurales* complex, IMPRIM batch, INFORMAT, MATH set, MECANIQUE assembly, ORDINAT, TEXTILE set, VEHICULES assembly; ~ **accéléromètre latéral** *m* AERONAUT lateral accelerometer; ~ **accéléromètre transversal** *m* AERONAUT lateral accelerometer; ~ **d'antenne** *m* ASTRONOMIE array; ~ **du bain et des rouleaux d'encollage** *m* TEXTILE quetsh unit; ~ **de branches** *m* PRODUCTION *automatisme industriel* branch group; ~ **de calandrage** *m* EMBALLAGE calender unit; ~ **du calorimètre** *m* PHYS RAYON *détecteurs de radiation des particules* calorimeter assembly; ~ **de camouflage contre les attaques aériennes** *m* MILITAIRE anti-air camouflage equipment; ~ **canonique** *m* PHYSIQUE canonical ensemble; ~ **de chaînes à raclette** *m* MINES scraper chain assembly; ~ **clés en main** *m* CONS MECA turnkey project; ~ **complémentaire** *m* MATH complementary set; ~ **des contextes définis** *m* TELECOM DCS, defined context set; ~ **de données** *m* INFORMAT data set, ORDINAT data array, data set; ~ **de données générées** *m* INFORMAT, ORDINAT generation data set; ~ **flou** *m* ORDINAT fuzzy set; ~ **de formations** *m* GEOLOGIE *dans un domaine géographique ou tectonique* terrain; ~ **d'instructions** *m* PRODUCTION *automatisme industriel* set of instructions; ~ **d'interrupteurs** *m* PRODUCTION switch assembly; ~ **de joints parallèles** *m* GEOLOGIE joint set; ~ **de lancement** *m* ESPACE launch site, launching complex, *véhicules* launching site; ~ **logique** *m* ELECTR *commande* logic unit; ~ **de modules** *m* PRODUCTION *automatisme industriel* module group; ~ **d'outils** *m* CONS MECA set of tools; ~ **pile** *m* PRODUCTION *électricité* battery assembly; ~ **pile de secours** *m* PRODUCTION replacement battery assembly; ~ **porte-piles** *m* PRODUCTION *électricité* battery pack; ~ **pour conditionnement d'air comprimé** *m* CONSTR compressed air conditioning unit; ~ **de propulsion** *m* CONS MECA drive system, ESPACE propulsion unit; ~ **de prospection de béryllium** *m* NUCLEAIRE beryllium prospecting meter; ~ **récepteur** *m* NUCLEAIRE receiving assembly; ~ **récupérateur** *m* MILITAIRE recoil brake; ~ **de récupération** *m* ESPACE *véhicules* recovery package; ~ **de réglage automatique** *m* NUCLEAIRE automatic control assembly; ~ **de relais** *m* PRODUCTION *automatisme industriel* bank of relays; ~ **de rouleaux** *m* PAPIER set of rolls; ~ **des rouleaux d'encrage** *m* IMPRIM *machines* ink deck; ~ **des signaux** *m* TV signal complex; ~ **de sismographes** *m* GEOLOGIE seismic array; ~ **symétrique** *m* CONS MECA handed assembly; ~ **terminal** *m* NUCLEAIRE final assembly, logic signal converter

ensemencement *m* CHIMIE seeding, NUCLEAIRE inoculation, seeding

ensimage *m* CERAM VER size, sizing, REFRIG bonding, TEXTILE oiling

ensimer *vi* REFRIG bond

ensoleillement *m* EN RENOUV insolation

ensouple *f* TEXTILE beam; ~ **dérouleuse** *f* TEXTILE yarn roll; ~ **d'ourdissage** *f* TEXTILE warp beam; ~ **primaire** *f* TEXTILE back beam; ~ **au tissage** *f* TEXTILE weaver's beam

enstatite *f* MINERAUX enstatite

entablement *m* PRODUCTION *d'un marteau-pilon, d'une*

presse à forger entablature

entaillage *m* CONS MECA slotting, PRODUCTION grooving, nicking, notching; ~ **des épontes** *m* MINES broaching

entaille *f* CONS MECA slot, MECANIQUE *matériaux*, METALL notch, PRODUCTION groove, nick, notch, *d'une lime, d'une râpe* cut; ~ **à affûter les scies** *f* CONS MECA saw clamp; ~ **en V** *f* NUCLEAIRE V-shaped notch, chevron notch; ~ **à mi-bois** *f* CONSTR halved joint, halving, lap joint, overleap joint, step joint; ~ **de profil** *f* GEOLOGIE knickpoint (BrE), nickpoint (AmE)

entaillé *adj* PRODUCTION grooved

entailler *vt* PRODUCTION nick

entartrage *m* DISTRI EAU scale formation, INST HYDR boiler scale, MATERIAUX furring

entartrer *vt* PRODUCTION fur, scale

entassement *m* PRODUCTION piling, stacking

entasser[1] *vt* CONSTR bank, PRODUCTION stack

entasser:[2] **s'~** *v réfl* CONSTR bank, bank up

entéromine *f* CHIMIE serotonin

enterré *adj* ELECTRON *canal* buried

en-tête *m* INFORMAT, ORDINAT header, heading, PRODUCTION, TELECOM header; ~ **de bande** *m* INFORMAT, ORDINAT tape header; ~ **d'échange** *m* TELECOM interchange header; ~ **d'ensemble transactionnel** *m* TELECOM transactional set-header; ~ **de groupe fonctionnel** *m* TELECOM functional group header; ~ **de message** *m* INFORMAT, ORDINAT, TELECOM message header

enthalpie *f* CHARBON, CHAUFFAGE *chaleur latente*, CHIMIE, EN RENOUV, ESPACE, GAZ, MECANIQUE *thermodynamique*, PHYS RAYON *fonction thermodynamique*, PHYSIQUE enthalpy, THERMODYN enthalpy, heat content; ~ **de formation** *f* THERMODYN enthalpy of formation; ~ **libre** *f* PHYSIQUE Gibbs free energy; ~ **libre massique** *f* PHYSIQUE specific Gibbs function; ~ **massique** *f* PHYSIQUE specific enthalpy; ~ **de transition** *f* NUCLEAIRE transition enthalpy; ~ **de vaporisation** *f* GENIE CHIM evaporation enthalpy, THERMODYN enthalpy of vaporization

entibois *m* CONS MECA vice cap (BrE), vice clamp (BrE), vice jaw (BrE), vise cap (AmE) vise clamp (AmE), vise jaw (AmE)

entier[1] *adj* AGRO ALIM shell-on

entier[2] *m* INFORMAT, MATH integer; ~ **naturel** *m* INFORMAT natural number; ~ **négatif** *m* MATH negative integer

entièrement: ~ **numérique** *adj* ELECTRON all digital; ~ **transistorisé** *adj* ELECTRON all-solid state

entité *f* INFORMAT, ORDINAT, QUALITE entity; ~ **d'application** *f* TELECOM AE, application entry; ~ **d'application de gestion** *f* TELECOM system management application entry; ~ **d'application de gestion de systèmes** *f* TELECOM SMAE, system management application entity; ~ **d'application ISCP** *f* TELECOM ISCP application entity, ISCPAE; ~ **fonctionnelle** *f* TELECOM FE, functional entity; ~ **de gestion de couche** *f* TELECOM LME, layer management entity; ~ **de maintenance d'installation de client** *f* TELECOM CIME, customer installation maintenance entities; ~ **N** *f* TELECOM N-entity

entités: ~ **homologues** *f pl* TELECOM peer entities

entonnoir *m* AGRO ALIM funnel, CHIMIE filter funnel, CONSTR chute, funnel, hollow, EQUIP LAB funnel, IMPRIM *plieuse* former, MECANIQUE funnel; ~ **de Buchner** *m* EQUIP LAB *filtration* Buchner funnel; ~ **de décanta-**tion *m* GENIE CHIM separating funnel; ~ **filtrant à plaque de verre fritté** *m* EQUIP LAB sintered glass filter funnel; ~ **à filtration** *m* EQUIP LAB *verrerie* filter funnel; ~ **à filtre** *m* EQUIP LAB filter funnel; ~ **de guidage** *m* PETR guide funnel; ~ **à robinet** *m* EQUIP LAB *verrerie* tap funnel; ~ **de séparation** *m* GENIE CHIM separating funnel; ~ **à séparation** *m* CHIMIE separation funnel, separator funnel; ~ **à tige** *m* EQUIP LAB *verrerie* thistle funnel

entonnoir-filtre *m* CERAM VER porcelain funnel, GENIE CHIM suction strainer

entourer *vt* CONSTR fence in, TEXTILE ring

entraîné: ~ **par un moteur** *adj* ELECTROTEC motor-driven

entraînement:[1] **à ~ direct** *adj* MECANIQUE gearless; **à ~ électrique** *adj* MECANIQUE, PHOTO electrically-driven

entraînement[2] *m* CHIMIE entrainment, CONS MECA drive, IMPRIM traction, MECANIQUE drive, MILITAIRE *d'antenne directionnelle* steering, NUCLEAIRE scavenging, *des produits de corrosion* carry-off, PAPIER draw, PHYS FLUID entrainment, POLLUTION below-cloud scavenging, PRODUCTION feed, feeding, VEHICULES *transmission* drive; ~ **de la bande** *m* ENREGISTR tape drive, TV tape advance, tape drive; ~ **de bande magnétique** *m* INFORMAT, ORDINAT tape drive; ~ **de cabestan** *m* ENREGISTR capstan drive; ~ **à chaîne** *m* VEHICULES *transmission, motocyclette* chain drive; ~ **à distance** *m* COMMANDE remote control operation; ~ **électrique** *m* PHOTO electric drive; ~ **en boucle fermée** *m* ENREGISTR closed-loop drive; ~ **de film** *m* CINEMAT film drive; ~ **de film à boucle roulant** *m* CINEMAT rolling loop film transport; ~ **de fréquence** *m* ELECTRON frequency pulling; ~ **intermittent** *m* CINEMAT *d'une tireuse, d'une caméra ou d'un projecteur* pull down; ~ **à main** *m* CINEMAT hand drive; ~ **de manche** *m* AERONAUT control column whip; ~ **mécanique** *m* CONS MECA mechanical drive; ~ **par arbre** *m* VEHICULES *transmission* shaft drive; ~ **par batterie** *m* CINEMAT battery drive; ~ **par chaîne** *m* AUTO chain and sprocket drive, MECANIQUE chain drive; ~ **par clavette** *m* CONS MECA *fraises à métaux* keydrive; ~ **par courroie** *m* MECANIQUE belt drive; ~ **par croix de Malte** *m* CINEMAT Maltese cross movement, CONS MECA Geneva mechanism, Maltese cross mechanism; ~ **par flexible** *m* MECANIQUE flexible drive; ~ **par friction** *m* CINEMAT friction drive, roller transport, tendency drive; ~ **par moteur** *m* ELECTROTEC, PHOTO motor drive; ~ **par tambour denté** *m* CINEMAT sprocket drive; ~ **par tenon** *m* CONS MECA tenon drive; ~ **positif du cône Morse** *m* CONS MECA positive drive of Morse tapers; ~ **pour tournevis automatique** *m* CONS MECA spiral ratchet screwdriver end; ~ **de poussières** *m* CERAM VER carry-over; ~ **à renvoi d'angle** *m* MECANIQUE angle drive; ~ **synchrone** *m* CINEMAT, TV synchronous drive; ~ **à tournevis** *m* AERONAUT blade and slot drive; ~ **à la vapeur** *m* GENIE CHIM steam distillation, steam entraining; ~ **de vis** *m* PLAST CAOU *boudineuse* screw drive; ~ **à vitesse constante** *m* CONS MECA constant speed drive

entraîner *vt* ESPACE *véhicules* drive, HYDROLOGIE drift, remove, transport, wash away, MECANIQUE drive, PAPIER draw; ~ **dans** *vt* HYDROLOGIE incorporate into; ~ **au large** *vt* HYDROLOGIE carry out to sea; ~ **au lavage** *vt* GENIE CHIM wash away

entraîneur: ~ **d'air** *m* CONSTR air-entraining admixture; ~ **primaire de vol aux instruments** *m* AERONAUT basic instrument flight trainer; ~ **synthétique de vol** *m* AERONAUT synthetic flight trainer entrait *m* CONSTR stretcher, *d'une ferme de comble* stringer, *d'une ferme de comble métallique* tie bar, tie rod, *d'une ferme de comble en bois* tie beam; ~ **retroussé** *m* CONS MECA collar, collar beam, collar tie, CONSTR span piece, straining beam, straining piece

entrance *f* ELECTROTEC, INFORMAT, ORDINAT fan in

entrant *adj* NAUT inward bound, TELECOM incoming

entrave *f* SECURITE hindrance

entre:[1] ~ **centraux** *adj* TELECOM interexchange (BrE), interoffice (AmE); ~ **deux eaux** *adj* NAUT *d'un navire* waterlogged

entre:[2] ~ **plats** *adv* CONS MECA across flats

entre:[3] ~ **le confort et la gêne** *loc* SECURITE between comfort and discomfort

entre-axe[1] *adj* CONS MECA center-to-center (AmE), centre-to-centre (BrE)

entre-axe[2] *adv* CONS MECA from center-to-center (AmE), from centre-to-centre (BrE)

entre-axe[3] *m* CONS MECA distance between centers (AmE), distance between centres (BrE); ~ **des fusées** *m* CONS MECA distance between centers of journals (AmE), distance between centres of journals (BrE); ~ **des pistes** *m* ENREGISTR, INFORMAT, TV track pitch

entrebarre *f* PRODUCTION interlock

entrebarré *adj* PRODUCTION interlocked

entre-basculer *vt* PRODUCTION toggle

entrecouper *vt* GEOLOGIE intersect

entrecroisement *m* TRANSPORT weaving

entrecroiser *vt* TEXTILE interlace

entrecroisure *f* TEXTILE interlacing; ~ **et frisure** *f* TEXTILE interlacing and crimping

entre-deux *m* CONS MECA parting

entrée:[1] **d'~** *adj* NAUT inward bound

entrée[2] *f* CONS MECA inlet, intake, CONSTR ingress, *d'un tunnel* portal, ELECTR *courant, tension, etc*, ELECTRON input, INFORMAT entry, input, MINES *d'une galerie* mouth, ORDINAT entry, input, PHYSIQUE input, PLAST CAOU *moulage* gate, PRODUCTION, TELECOM inlet, TV input; ~ **d'air** *f* AERONAUT air scoop, CONS MECA air inlet, draft (AmE), draught (BrE), indraft (AmE), indraft of air (AmE), indraught (BrE), indraught of air (BrE), inlet; ~ **d'air fuseau réacteur** *f* AERONAUT nacelle intake ring; ~ **d'air réacteur** *f* AERONAUT engine air intake; ~ **d'air variable** *f* TRANSPORT variable geometry inlet, variable geometry intake; ~ **d'alimentation** *f* PRODUCTION line voltage in; ~ **alternative** *f* ELECTROTEC AC input; ~ **de l'amplificateur vertical** *f* ELECTRON vertical amplifier input; ~ **asymétrique** *f* ELECTROTEC unbalanced input; ~ **de bouclage** *f* PRODUCTION *automatisme industriel* tieback input; ~ **de câble** *f* PRODUCTION conduit entry; ~ **calorifique** *f* THERMODYN heat input; ~ **du canal** *f* TRANSPORT canal entrance; ~ **du canal de distribution** *f* CERAM VER feeder opening; ~ **des cannelures** *f* PRODUCTION draft (AmE), draught (BrE); ~ **au clavier** *f* INFORMAT keyboard entry; ~ **de clé** *f* CONSTR pipe; ~ **commandée en tension** *f* ELECTROTEC voltage-controlled input; ~ **continue** *f* ELECTROTEC DC input; ~ **à couple thermoélectrique** *f* PRODUCTION *automatisme industriel* thermocouple input; ~ **différentielle** *f* ELECTRON differential input; ~ **directe** *f* ELECTRON direct input; ~ **directe de données** *f* INFORMAT, ORDINAT DDE, direct data entry; ~ **de données** *f* ORDINAT data entry; ~ **double** *f* PRODUCTION *automatisme industriel*, TV dual input; ~ **double à diode** *f* PRODUCTION *automatisme industriel* diode-type dual input; ~ **double à transfor-**

mateur *f* PRODUCTION *automatisme industriel* transformer-type dual input; ~ **d'eau** *f* NUCLEAIRE water ingress, REFRIG water inlet; ~ **électrique** *f* ELECTRON, ELECTROTEC electrical input; ~ **en courant alternatif** *f* ELECTROTEC AC input; ~ **en courant continu** *f* ELECTROTEC DC input; ~ **en ligne** *f* TELECOM interruption; ~ **en mémoire** *f* INFORMAT, ORDINAT storage entry; ~ **en stock** *f* PRODUCTION entry in stock; ~ **en temps réel** *f* INFORMAT, ORDINAT real-time input; ~ **en vigueur** *f* BREVETS entry into force; ~ **extérieure** *f* ELECTRON external input; ~ **flottante** *f* ELECTROTEC floating input; ~ **de fluides** *f* CONS MECA fluid inlet; ~ **de galerie** *f* MINES mine entrance; ~ **gardée** *f* ELECTROTEC guarded input; ~ **inverseuse** *f* ELECTRON inverting input; ~ **ligne** *f* ENREGISTR, TV line in; ~ **manuelle** *f* INFORMAT, ORDINAT manual input; ~ **non inverseuse** *f* CONSTR noninverting input; ~ **numérique** *f* ELECTRON digital input; ~ **optique** *f* ELECTROTEC optical input; ~ **par clavier** *f* INFORMAT keyboard entry; ~ **par traversée isolante** *f* ELECTROTEC isolated feed through input; ~ **de piste** *f* AERONAUT approach end of runway, runway threshold; ~ **prioritaire** *f* PRODUCTION *automatisme industriel* immediate input; ~ **des procédures autorisées** *f* ORDINAT action entry; ~ **RVB** *f* TV RGB input; ~ **séquenceur** *f* PRODUCTION *automatisme industriel* sequencer input; ~ **de serrure** *f* CONSTR escutcheon (AmE), scutcheon (BrE), key plate, keyhole; ~ **du signal d'interdiction** *f* ELECTRON inhibiting input; ~ **du signal de référence** *f* ELECTRON reference signal input; ~ **son** *f* ENREGISTR audio input; ~ **symétrique** *f* ELECTROTEC balanced input; ~ **de la synchronisation** *f* TV sync input; ~ **d'un TEC** *f* ELECTRON FET input; ~ **vidéo** *f* TV video input; ~ **vocale de données** *f* INFORMAT, ORDINAT voice-data entry

entrée/sortie *f (E/S)* ELECTR *tension, courant, etc*, ORDINAT, PRODUCTION input/output *(I/O)*; ~ **parallèle** *f* INFORMAT parallel input/output; ~ **séquentielle** *f* ORDINAT SIO, sequential input/output; ~ **série** *f* ORDINAT SIO, series input/output; ~ **tamponnée** *f* ORDINAT buffered input/output; ~ **tout ou rien** *f* PRODUCTION *automatisme industriel* discrete input/output

entrefer *m* CONS MECA gap, ELECTR air gap, ELECTROTEC air gap, gap, PHYSIQUE air gap, TV gap, head gap; ~ **arrière** *m* ACOUSTIQUE, TV back gap; ~ **avant** *m* ACOUSTIQUE front gap; ~ **effectif** *m* ENREGISTR effective gap length; ~ **frontal** *m* ENREGISTR front gap; ~ **résiduel** *m* ELECTROTEC residual gap; ~ **secondaire** *m* ENREGISTR back gap; ~ **de tête** *m* INFORMAT, ORDINAT head gap; ~ **d'une tête magnétique** *m* TV magnetic head gap

entrelacement: ~ **quadruple** *m* TV quadruple scanning; ~ **spectral** *m* TV frequency interlace

entrelacer *vt* CONSTR *menuiserie* wreath, ELECTRON, INFORMAT, ORDINAT interlace

entre-pointes *m* CONS MECA distance between centers (AmE), distance between centres (BrE)

entrepont:[1] **dans l'~** *adj* NAUT below, below decks

entrepont:[2] **dans l'~** *adv* NAUT below, between decks

entrepont[3] *m* NAUT between decks, tween deck

entreposage *m* PRODUCTION warehousing; ~ **des déchets sur le site** *m* NUCLEAIRE onsite waste disposal; ~ **définitif** *m* NUCLEAIRE ultimate waste disposal; ~ **frigorifique** *m* AGRO ALIM cold storage; ~ **à froid** *m* AGRO ALIM cold storage; ~ **sûr des liquides inflammables** *m* SECURITE safe storage of flammable liquids

entrepôt *m* NAUT, PRODUCTION warehouse; ~ **décentralisé** *m* PRODUCTION branch warehouse; ~ **en** douane *m* NAUT bonded warehouse; ~ **frigorifique** *m* CONS MECA cold store, REFRIG refrigerated warehouse, SECURITE cold storage; ~ **frigorifique de distribution** *m* REFRIG dispatching cold store; ~ **frigorifique polyvalent** *m* REFRIG multipurpose cold store; ~ **frigorifique portuaire** *m* REFRIG port cold store; ~ **frigorifique spécialisé** *m* REFRIG specialized cold store; ~ **de surgélation** *m* AGRO ALIM cold storage

entrepreneur *m* CONSTR builder, contractor; ~ **de bâtiments** *m* CONSTR builder; ~ **de constructions** *m* CONSTR builder; ~ **de forage** *m* PETR drilling contractor; ~ **de sondages** *m* CONSTR boring contractor; ~ **à la tâche** *m* CONSTR jobbing contractor

entreprise: ~ **certifiée** *f* QUALITE certified company; ~ **de transformation des produits alimentaires** *f* AGRO ALIM food-processing plant; ~ **de transport** *f* TRANSPORT haulage contractor, *routier* haulier; ~ **de transport aérien** *f* AERONAUT airline

entrer[1] *vi* ELECTRON input, INFORMAT enter; ~ **en collision avec** *vt* NAUT ram, *navire* foul

entrer[2] *vi* ORDINAT enter; ~ **dans le système** *vi* INFORMAT log in, log on, ORDINAT log in, log on, sign on; ~ **en cale sèche** *vi* NAUT dry-dock; ~ **en communication** *vi* INFORMAT log in; ~ **en ligne** *vi* TELECOM go into circuit; ~ **en session** *vi* PRODUCTION log in; ~ **en vigueur** *vi* CONS MECA become effective

entre-rails *m* CH DE FER space between rails

entreteneur *m* CONSTR maintainer

entretenir *vt* MECANIQUE, PHYSIQUE maintain; ~ **le feu de** *vt* PRODUCTION stoke

entretien *m* ELECTROTEC holding, ESPACE, MECANIQUE, PAPIER maintenance, PRODUCTION maintenance, upkeep, SECURITE maintenance, TEXTILE care, TV maintenance; ~ **à base de conditions** *m* QUALITE condition-based maintenance; ~ **d'une bonne efficacité économique** *m* PRODUCTION cost-effective maintenance; ~ **direct** *m* NUCLEAIRE direct maintenance; ~ **général** *m* NUCLEAIRE general maintenance, major overhaul; ~ **du moteur** *m* NAUT engine maintenance; ~ **périodique** *m* CONSTR *machines* scheduled service; ~ **préventif** *m* CONSTR preventive maintenance; ~ **de rampe** *m* AERONAUT ramp services; ~ **de tissu** *m* TEXTILE fabric care

entretoisage *m* PRODUCTION staying

entretoise *f* CH DE FER *véhicules* cross-member, crossbar, tie bar, CONSTR brace, bridging piece, crosspiece, girt, noggin (BrE), nogging (AmE), spur, stay, stay bolt, stay rod, strut, strut, *entre les barreaux d'une grille* distance piece, DISTRI EAU *d'une porte d'écluse* crosspiece, ESPACE *véhicules* brace, spacer, INST HYDR, MECANIQUE brace, PRODUCTION spacer, REFRIG stay block, VEHICULES *carrosserie, moteur* strut; ~ **calibrée** *f* CONS MECA close tolerance spacer; ~ **de chaudière** *f* CONS MECA boiler stay; ~ **conique** *f* CONS MECA conical spacer, dishpan spacer; ~ **de derrick** *f* CONSTR derrick girt; ~ **isolante** *f* REFRIG breaker strip; ~ **de pantographe** *f* CH DE FER pantograph tie bar; ~ **de parois latérales** *f* CH DE FER *véhicules* side stay bolt; ~ **de plaque de garde** *f* CH DE FER *véhicules* axle guide stay

entretoise-éclisse *f* CH DE FER *voie* fishplate block

entretoisement *m* CONSTR bracing, strutting, PRODUCTION staying

entretoiser *vt* CONS MECA, CONSTR *une charpente* brace

entretoises *f pl* CONSTR bridging, stiffening, strutting

entropie *f* ASTRONOMIE, CHIMIE, EN RENOUV, INFORMAT, MECANIQUE *thermodynamique*, ORDINAT, PHYSIQUE, TELECOM, THERMODYN entropy; ~ **d'activation** *f* METALL activation entropy; ~ **de configuration** *f* METALL configurational entropy; ~ **de fusion** *f* THERMODYN entropy of fusion; ~ **massique** *f* PHYSIQUE specific entropy; ~ **de vaporisation** *f* THERMODYN entropy of vaporization; ~ **de vibration** *f* METALL vibrational entropy

enture *f* CONSTR scarf, scarf joint, scarf jointing, splice joint; ~ **en paume** *f* CONSTR lapped scarf; ~ **à goujon** *f* CONSTR plug-tenon joint, spur tenon joint; ~ **à mi-bois avec abouts carrés** *f* CONSTR lapped scarf; ~ **à mi-bois avec tenons d'about et clef** *f* CONSTR lipped table scarf with key; ~ **à simple tenon** *f* CONSTR plug-tenon joint, spur tenon joint

énumération *f* INFORMAT, MATH, ORDINAT enumeration

envahi: ~ **par l'eau** *adj* HYDROLOGIE, NAUT flooded; ~ **par les eaux** *adj* HYDROLOGIE flooded

envasé *adj* HYDROLOGIE silted up

envasement *m* GENIE CHIM silting, HYDROLOGIE silting up, PRODUCTION *système hydraulique* silting

envaser[1] *vt* HYDROLOGIE silt up

envaser:[2] **s'~** *v réfl* HYDROLOGIE silt up, PRODUCTION *système hydraulique* clog up

enveloppe *f* CONS MECA *isolation* jacket, CONSTR coating, ELECTROTEC envelope, jacket, sheath, EMBALLAGE envelope, wraparound, EQUIP LAB *verrerie* jacket, ESPACE *véhicules* case, jacket, shell, GEOPHYS mantle, IMPRIM *reliure, emballage, façonnage* casing, INST HYDR closed turbine chamber, clothing, lagging, *de turbine* enclosed casing, MECANIQUE jacket, OPTIQUE sheath, PRODUCTION closed turbine chamber, deading, jacket, sheathing, sheath, TELECOM envelope, VEHICULES *pneu* cover; ~ **annulaire de la chambre de combustion** *f* AERONAUT combustion chamber annular case; ~ **de câble** *f* ELECTROTEC cable covering, cable sheath, PLAST CAOU *caoutchouc, plastiques* cable covering; ~ **calorifuge** *f* PRODUCTION insulating jacketing, insulating lagging; ~ **cinématique** *f* CH DE FER *véhicules* kinematic envelope; ~ **de cylindre** *f* PRODUCTION cylinder jacket; ~ **du dôme** *f* PRODUCTION dome casing, dome cover; ~ **d'eau** *f* PRODUCTION water jacket; ~ **en jute** *f* ELECTROTEC jute covering; ~ **en plomb** *f* ELECTROTEC lead sheath; ~ **en spirale** *f* PRODUCTION spiral casing; ~ **étanche en verre** *f* CERAM VER encapsulating glass; ~ **extérieure** *f* PRODUCTION building, *d'un haut fourneau* mantle; ~ **externe de cylindre à vapeur** *f* INST HYDR steam cylinder casing; ~ **d'extracteur** *f* AGRO ALIM extraction thimble; ~ **granulométrique** *f* CONSTR grading envelope; ~ **intérieure** *f* EMBALLAGE interior wrapping; ~ **isolante** *f* ELECTROTEC insulating covering, INST HYDR boiler lagging; ~ **isolante de chaudière** *f* INST HYDR lagging; ~ **métallique** *f* ELECTROTEC metal sheath; ~ **de modulation** *f* ENREGISTR modulation envelope; ~ **portefeuille** *f* EMBALLAGE wallet-type envelope; ~ **postale** *f* PAPIER correspondence envelope, correspondence pocket; ~ **pour palette** *f* EMBALLAGE pallet wrapper; ~ **de protection** *f* OPTIQUE cassette, optical disc cassette (BrE), optical disk cassette (AmE); ~ **protectrice** *f* EMBALLAGE protective cover; ~ **de rafale** *f* AERONAUT gust envelope; ~ **de signal** *f* TELECOM signal envelope; ~ **de silencieux** *f* AUTO muffler jacket, muffler shell; ~ **structurale** *f* ESPACE *propulsion* casing; ~ **thermorétractable pour palette** *f* EMBALLAGE pallet shrink-wrapping, shrink-wrapped pallet cover; ~ **de tôle** *f* PRODUCTION jacket; ~ **de tube électronique** *f*

ELECTRON electron tube envelope; ~ **de turbine** *f* NAUT turbine casing; ~ **à vapeur** *f* INST HYDR steam jacket
enveloppement: ~ **avec film** *m* EMBALLAGE film wrap
envelopper *vt* PRODUCTION jacket; ~ **d'un film protecteur** *vt* IMPRIM *la forme imprimante* bandage
enveloppeuse: ~ **pour manchons** *f* EMBALLAGE wraparound sleeving machine
enverguer *vt* NAUT *voile* bend
envergure *f* AERONAUT *ailes* span, NAUT luff, PHYSIQUE span, TRANSPORT wing span
enverjure *f* TEXTILE end-and-end lease; ~ **simple** *f* TEXTILE one-and-one lease
enverrer *vt* CERAM VER glaze
envers:[1] **à l'**~ *adv* CINEMAT tailout
envers[2] *m* PAPIER two-sidedness
environnement:[1] **pour l'**~ *adj* POLLUTION environmental
environnement[2] *m* ESPACE, INFORMAT, ORDINAT environment, PHYSIQUE surroundings, POLLUTION, QUALITE environment; ~ **électromagnétique** *m* ESPACE electromagnetic environment; ~ **de lancement** *m* ESPACE *véhicules* launch environment; ~ **de messagerie EDI** *m* TELECOM EDI messaging environment, EDIME; ~ **physiochimique** *m* POLLUTION physicochemical environment
envoi *m* TELECOM transmission sending, transmission; ~ **de détail** *m* TRANSPORT part-load consignment; ~ **de marchandises de détail** *m pl* CH DE FER *véhicules* less-than-carload freight shipment (AmE); ~ **aux molettes** *m* MINES overwind, overwinding, pulleying
envoyage *m* MINES landing stage, landing station, lodge, onsetting, pit landing, plane table, platt, plat
envoyer[1] *vt* INFORMAT, ORDINAT send; ~ **par canalisation** *vt* CONSTR pipe; ~ **par télécopieur** *vt* TELECOM fax; ~ **par voie de mer** *vt* NAUT ship
envoyer:[2] ~ **le grand pavois** *vi* NAUT dress ship overall
enzyme *f* AGRO ALIM, CHIMIE, LESSIVES enzyme; ~ **attendrissante** *f* AGRO ALIM tenderizer; ~ **digestive** *f* RECYCLAGE digestive enzyme; ~ **intracellulaire** *f* CHIMIE endoenzyme
eocène *adj* GEOLOGIE Eocene
éolien *adj* GEOLOGIE, PETR aeolian
éosine *f* CHIMIE eosin
épair *m* IMPRIM *papier*, PAPIER look-through; ~ **irrégulier** *m* PAPIER cloudy formation, wild formation, wild lookthrough
épais *adj* CERAM VER, MECANIQUE heavy, NAUT hazy, PAPIER thick
épaisseur *f* CERAM VER substance, thickness, CONS MECA ply, IMPRIM *papier* look-through, MECANIQUE thickness, NAUT *membres* depth, PAPIER look-through, thickness, PLAST CAOU thickness; ~ **de la base** *f* ELECTRON base width; ~ **compactée** *f* CONSTR compacted thickness; ~ **de la couche** *f* PLAST CAOU *peintures, adhésifs* coating thickness; ~ **de couche** *f* PLAST CAOU film thickness; ~ **curviligne** *f* CONS MECA circular thickness; ~ **de déplacement** *f* CONS MECA displacement thickness; ~ **de l'enduit** *f* EMBALLAGE coating thickness; ~ **de l'extrémité** *f* RESSORTS end thickness; ~ **de feuillard** *f* MATERIAUX strip thickness; ~ **d'une feuille seule** *f* PAPIER single sheet thickness; ~ **de garniture** *f* CONS MECA thickness of lining; ~ **moyenne d'une feuille en liasse** *f* PAPIER bulking thickness; ~ **nominale** *f* ESSAIS, QUALITE nominal thickness; ~ **optique** *f* ESPACE optical depth, optical thickness, TELECOM optical thickness; ~ **du papier** *f* PAPIER caliper (AmE), calliper (BrE); ~ **par gravité** *f* PAPIER gravity concen-

trator; ~ **de peau** *f* PHYSIQUE skin depth; ~ **de pénétration** *f* PHYSIQUE skin depth; ~ **précise du papier** *f* IMPRIM caliper (AmE), calliper (BrE); ~ **rectiligne** *f* AERONAUT chordal thickness; ~ **relative** *f* AERONAUT *profil aérodynamique* thickness-chord ratio; ~ **de revêtement** *f* REVETEMENT coating thickness; ~ **de serrage** *f* CONS MECA grip; ~ **théorique minimale** *f* NAUT minimum theoretical thickness; ~ **des traits** *f* METROLOGIE *d'une échelle* thickness of lines
épaissir[1] *vt* GENIE CHIM thicken
épaissir:[2] **s'**~ *v réfl* GENIE CHIM thicken
épaississage *m* CHARBON thickening
épaississant *m* AGRO ALIM thickener, thickening agent, thickening, CHIMIE stayput agent, LESSIVES thickening agent, PLAST CAOU *additif* thickener
épaississement *m* AGRO ALIM clotting, thickening, CHIMIE inspissation; ~ **de la base** *m* ELECTRON base widening; ~ **des boues** *m* DISTRI EAU sludge thickening, HYDROLOGIE sludge bulking, sludge thickening
épaississeur *m* AGRO ALIM, CHARBON thickener, CHIMIE thickener, thickening agent, GENIE CHIM thickener tank, thickener, PAPIER concentrator, decker, thickener
épanchement *m* CONSTR outpouring; ~ **de boue** *m* GEOPHYS solifluction lobe, solifluction tongue
épandage *m* CHIMIE spreading, GAZ spillage, POLLU MER spreading; ~ **de dispersants** *m* POLLU MER dispersant spraying
épandeur-régleur-dameur *m* TRANSPORT asphalt-spreading machine (AmE), pavement-spreading machine (AmE), road metal-spreading machine (BrE), macadam spreader, stone spreader
épandre *vt* POLLU MER spray
épanouir *vt* PRODUCTION flare
épar *m* NAUT spar
épargne: ~ **de l'eau** *adj* HYDROLOGIE water-saving
épaule *f* CERAM VER shoulder; ~ **sale** *f* CERAM VER dirty shoulder
épaulement *m* CONS MECA shoulder; ~ **de mesure** *m* PRODUCTION *système hydraulique* metering land
épaulette *f* TEXTILE shoulder pad
épave *f* NAUT wreck
épaves: ~ **flottantes** *f pl* NAUT flotsam; ~ **rejetées** *f pl* NAUT jetsam
épée *f* DISTRI EAU *d'une vanne* stem; ~ **coupe-argiles** *f* CERAM VER clay cutter; ~ **d'Orion** *f* ASTRONOMIE Orion's sword; ~ **de vanne** *f* INST HYDR gate stem
éperon *m* CONSTR buttress, spur, close buttress; ~ **corallien** *m* OCEANO reef spur, spit
éphédrine *f* CHIMIE ephedrine
éphéméride *f* ASTRONOMIE ephemeris
éphémérides *f pl* ESPACE *orbitographie* ephemerides; ~ **nautiques** *f pl* NAUT nautical almanac
épi *m* CONSTR finial, DISTRI EAU, NAUT groin (AmE), groyne (BrE), OCEANO groin (AmE), groyne (BrE), jetty, spur dike (AmE), spur dyke (BrE); ~ **en pieux** *m* DISTRI EAU pile groin (AmE), pile groyne (BrE)
épicéa *m* PAPIER spuce
épicentre *m* GEOLOGIE, GEOPHYS, PHYSIQUE epicenter (AmE), epicentre (BrE)
épichlorhydrine *f* CHIMIE epichlorhydrin
épicinchonine *f* CHIMIE epicinchonine
épiclastique *adj* PETR epiclastic
épicontinental *adj* PETR epicontinental
épicoprostérine *f* CHIMIE epicoprostanol
épicycle *m* ASTRONOMIE epicycle

épicyclique *adj* MECANIQUE epicyclic

épicycloïdal *adj* CONS MECA epicycloidal, MECANIQUE epicycloidal, *engrenages* epicyclic

épicycloïde *f* GEOMETRIE epicycloid

épidéhydroandrostérone *f* CHIMIE epidehydroandrosterone

épidiascope *m* PHOTO epidiascope

épidote *f* MINERAUX epidote

épierrage *m* CHARBON culling, stone picking

épigénique *adj* GEOLOGIE epigenic

épimère *m* CHIMIE epimer

épimérisation *f* CHIMIE epimerization

épimétamorphisme *m* GEOLOGIE *température et pression faibles* low-grade metamorphism

épinglage *m* CONS MECA fastening, PRODUCTION piercing; ~ **avant rivetage** *m* CONS MECA fastening

épingle: ~ **chauffante** *f* NUCLEAIRE heating pin; ~ **à l'eau** *f* CERAM VER hairpin cooler; ~ **de freinage** *f* CONS MECA lockpin

épingler *vt* PRODUCTION *un moule* pierce

épinglette *f* MINES aiguille, nail, picker, pricker, shooting needle

épirogénèse *f* GEOLOGIE epeirogenesis

épisode *m* POLLUTION episode; ~ **interglaciaire** *m* GEOLOGIE interglacial phase, interglacial stage; ~ **de pollution atmosphérique** *m* POLLUTION air pollution episode; ~ **de pollution météorologique** *m* POLLUTION air pollution episode

épissage: ~ **d'un fil cassé** *m* TEXTILE splicing

épisser *vt* TEXTILE splice

épisseur *m* TELECOM cable jointer, jointer, splicer cable (AmE)

épissoir *m* NAUT marlinspike

épissure *f* CERAM VER, NAUT, OPTIQUE, PRODUCTION splice, TELECOM cable joint, joint, optical splice, splice; ~ **de câble** *f* ELECTR cable splicing; ~ **longue** *f* NAUT long splice; ~ **mécanique** *f* OPTIQUE, TELECOM mechanical splice; ~ **à oeil** *f* NAUT eyesplice; ~ **à oeillet** *f* NAUT eyesplice; ~ **optique** *f* OPTIQUE, TELECOM optical fiber splice (AmE), optical fibre splice (BrE), optical splice; ~ **par fusion** *f* OPTIQUE, TELECOM fusion splice; ~ **par soudage** *f* OPTIQUE, TELECOM fusion splice

épissurer *vt* TELECOM splice, *un câble* splice

épistilbite *f* MINERAUX epistilbite

épitaxial *adj* ELECTRON, MATERIAUX *cristallographie* epitaxial

épitaxie *f* CRISTALL, ELECTRON, MATERIAUX *cristallographie*, METALL, PHYS RAYON epitaxy; ~ **en phase liquide** *f* ELECTRON liquid phase epitaxy; ~ **en phase vapeur** *f* ELECTRON, GENIE CHIM vapor phase epitaxy (AmE), vapour phase epitaxy (BrE); ~ **par faisceaux moléculaires** *f* ELECTRON molecular beam epitaxy

épithermal *adj* GEOLOGIE *minéralisation* epithermal

épizone *f* GEOLOGIE *métamorphisme* epizone

éplucher *vt* AGRO ALIM *légumes* peel

éponge: ~ **de zirconium** *f* NUCLEAIRE zirconium sponge

éponte *f* GEOLOGIE vein wall, MINES wall

épontille *f* NAUT deck pillar, pillar, samson post

épontiller *vt* NAUT shore up

époque *f* GEOLOGIE, PETR epoch; ~ **glaciaire** *f* GEOLOGIE glacial stage; ~ **de rayonnement** *f* ASTRONOMIE radiation era; ~ **de recombinaison** *f* ASTRONOMIE recombination era

épouser *vt* PRODUCTION conform in shape to; ~ **la forme de** *vt* PRODUCTION conform in shape to

époxyde[1] *adj* CHIMIE epoxide, epoxy

époxyde[2] *m* CHIMIE epoxide; ~ **à durcissement aminique** *m* PLAST CAOU *adhésifs, revêtements* amine-cured epoxy

EPR *abrév (exploitation privée reconnue)* TELECOM recognized private operating agency

épreuve:[1] **à l'~ des balles** *adj* MILITAIRE bulletproof; **à l'~ du feu** *adj* MECANIQUE, PRODUCTION, SECURITE fireproof, THERMODYN fireproof, flameproof; **à l'~ de l'humidité** *adj* EMBALLAGE moisture-proof; **à l'~ de la radiation** *adj* PHYS RAYON radiation-proof

épreuve[2] *f* CHIMIE testing, test, ESPACE hard copy, IMPRIM blueprint, brown print, proof, *photogravure* hard copy, *préimpression* blue key, *tirage* pull, INFORMAT hard copy, MECANIQUE test, PHOTO print, proof, PHYSIQUE test, PRODUCTION proof, TEXTILE test; ~ **d'abrasion** *f* CONSTR Los Angeles abrasion test; ~ **d'artiste** *f* IMPRIM artist's proof; ~ **auditive** *f* ACOUSTIQUE hearing test; ~ **d'autoredressement** *f* NAUT self-righting test; ~ **à la brosse** *f* IMPRIM *typographie* brush proof; ~ **de charge** *f* CONSTR loading test; ~ **conventionnelle sur machine** *f* IMPRIM press proof; ~ **couleur progressive** *f* IMPRIM *prépresse* scatter proof; ~ **écran** *f* IMPRIM *photogravure* soft proof; ~ **en page** *f* IMPRIM page proof; ~ **en placard** *f* IMPRIM galley proof, slip proof, string proof; ~ **en première** *f* IMPRIM galley proof, slip proof, string proof; ~ **en traits blancs sur fond bleu** *f* PRODUCTION blueprint; ~ **glacée** *f* PHOTO glossy print; ~ **hélio** *f* IMPRIM opal; ~ **d'homologation** *f* AERONAUT certification test; ~ **hydraulique** *f* MECANIQUE hydro-test; ~ **négative** *f* PHOTO negative; ~ **par agrandissement** *f* PHOTO enlargement print; ~ **par contact** *f* IMPRIM, PHOTO contact print; ~ **par rabattement** *f* PRODUCTION plating-out test; ~ **photographique** *f* IMPRIM photographic proof; ~ **de photograveur** *f* IMPRIM *prépresse* repro proof; ~ **pour bon-à-tirer** *f* IMPRIM *prépresse* repro proof; ~ **prélevée par déchirement de la bande** *f* IMPRIM *rotatives* tear-off; ~ **progressive** *f* IMPRIM progressive proof; ~ **de qualité** *f* IMPRIM *prépresse* repro proof; ~ **statique à la déformation** *f* CONS MECA static strain test; ~ **de style Cromalin** *f* IMPRIM *prépresse* prepress proof; ~ **sur machine** *f* IMPRIM press proof; ~ **sur papier couché** *f* IMPRIM *préparation* artpull; ~ **tierce** *f* IMPRIM *photogravure* final proof; ~ **trichrome par le procédé carbro** *f* PHOTO carbro color print (AmE), carbro colour print (BrE)

éprouvé: ~ **en clientèle** *adj* MECANIQUE field-tested

éprouver *vt* CHIMIE, CONS MECA test

éprouvette *f* CERAM VER, CHIMIE test tube, CONS MECA test bar, CONSTR test cube, EQUIP LAB *échantillonnage* sampling tube, MATERIAUX test piece, MECANIQUE *matériaux* specimen, METALL sample, PAPIER, PHYSIQUE test piece, PRODUCTION test tube; ~ **Almen** *f* RESSORTS Almen test strip; ~ **bouchée** *f* EQUIP LAB stoppered measuring cylinder; ~ **Charpy V** *f* NUCLEAIRE Charpy V-notch impact specimen; ~ **cylindrique** *f* CONSTR test cylinder; ~ **à entaille en V** *f* NUCLEAIRE Charpy V-notch impact specimen; ~ **à entailles latérales** *f* METALL sidegrooved specimen; ~ **d'essai** *f* ESSAIS test specimen; ~ **à fléchir à trois points** *f* NUCLEAIRE three-point bending specimen; ~ **graduée** *f* CHIMIE burette, EQUIP LAB measuring cylinder, MATERIAUX calibrated measure, calibrated measure tube, PHOTO measuring cylinder; ~ **de traction** *f* CONS MECA tensile test piece, RESSORTS tension test bar; ~ **type** *f* PRODUCTION standard test piece

epsomite *f* MINERAUX epsomite
épuisé *adj* CHIMIE spent
épuisement *m* CONSTR dewatering, DISTRI EAU depletion, drainage, draining, pumping, pumping out,
MINES dewatering, draining, drainage, mine pumping,
NUCLEAIRE depletion, exhaustion, impoverishment; ~
en répétitions *m* MINES multistage pumping, stage
pumping; ~ en un seul jet *m* MINES single stage pumping; ~ des neutres *m* NUCLEAIRE neutral burnout; ~
spécifique *m* NUCLEAIRE burnup
épuiser[1] *vt* CONSTR drain, DISTRI EAU drain, pump,
pump out, MINES dewater, drain
épuiser:[2] ~ les chantiers d'abattage *vi* MINES spend
ground
épuisette *f* OCEANO brailer, dip net, scoop net
épurateur *m* CHIMIE purifier, GENIE CHIM scrubber, PA-
PIER cleaner, screener; ~ d'air *m* CHARBON, CONS MECA,
VEHICULES *carburateur* air cleaner; ~ d'arrivée d'air *m*
PRODUCTION air inlet purifier; ~ centrifuge *m* GENIE
CHIM centrifuge screen; ~ d'eau *m* TEXTILE water purifier; ~ à force centrifuge *m* GENIE CHIM centrifugal
cleaner; ~ de gaz *m* PRODUCTION gas purifier, THERMO-
DYN gas scrubbing plant; ~ des gaz de fumée *m*
THERMODYN flue gas scrubber
épuration *f* CHIMIE scavenging, *des huiles* regeneration,
GENIE CHIM purification, scrubbing, HYDROLOGIE sewage sludge, PAPIER cleaning, screening, PETROLE
purification, POLLUTION *des matières huileuses dans
des séparateurs* removal, *des particules solides (par
sédimentation)* removal, *des matières organiques*
removal, THERMODYN *des gaz* scrubbing; ~ de l'air *f*
CHARBON air cleaning; ~ biologique *f* HYDROLOGIE
biological purification; ~ chimique *f* HYDROLOGIE
chemical purification; ~ chimique du charbon *f* POL-
LUTION chemical coal cleaning; ~ de l'eau *f* GENIE CHIM
water purification; ~ des eaux *f* DISTRI EAU water
purification, GENIE CHIM, HYDROLOGIE water treatment; ~ des eaux résiduaires *f* DISTRI EAU wastewater
purification; ~ en mélange des eaux usées *f* DISTRI
EAU mixed sewage and waste water treatment; ~ fine *f*
NUCLEAIRE *poussée* complete purification; ~ de gaz *f*
GAZ gas cleaning, purification; ~ de gaz d'échappement *f* THERMODYN *lavage* exhaust gas cleaning; ~ des
gaz de fumée *f* THERMODYN flue gas scrubbing; ~ de
l'huile *f* PETROLE *procédé de raffinage* oil scrubbing; ~
primaire *f* DISTRI EAU preliminary treatment, HYDRO-
LOGIE primary treatment
épure *f* PRODUCTION diagram; ~ de la distribution Corliss *f* PRODUCTION diagram of Corliss valve gear; ~ de
régulation *f* CONS MECA distribution diagram
épurer *vt* CHIMIE purify, DISTRI EAU purify plant, GENIE
CHIM, HYDROLOGIE, PAPIER, PETROLE, THERMODYN
purify
équarrir *vt* CONS MECA broach, PRODUCTION square
équarrissage *m* CONS MECA reaming, reaming out,
CONSTR scantling, squareness, squaring
équarrissement *m* CONS MECA reaming, reaming out,
CONSTR squareness, squaring
équarrisseur *m* AGRO ALIM knacker
équarrissoir *m* CONS MECA broach, opening bit, reamer,
MINES reamer; ~ à cinq pans *m* CONS MECA five-sided
broach; ~ à huit pans *m* CONS MECA eight-sided reamer, octagonal reamer
équateur *m* ASTRONOMIE, NAUT equator; ~ céleste *m*
ASTRONOMIE celestial equator; ~ géomagnétique *m*
GEOPHYS geomagnetic equator; ~ magnétique *m*

GEOPHYS dip equator, magnetic equator, PHYSIQUE
magnetic equator
équation *f* CHIMIE, MATH equation; ~ d'Arrhénius *f*
CHIMIE Arrhenius equation; ~ de Bernoulli *f* PHYS
FLUID Bernoulli's equation; ~ de Bethe-Goldstone *f*
NUCLEAIRE Bethe-Goldstone equation; ~ de
Boltzmann *f* PHYS RAYON *conservation particule*
Boltzmann equation; ~ de Bragg *f* CRISTALL Bragg's
law; ~ caractéristique *f* ESPACE characteristic equation; ~ de continuité *f* PHYSIQUE continuity equation; ~
différentielle *f* MATH differential equation; ~ de dimensions *f* PHYSIQUE dimensional equation; ~ de
dispersion *f* PHYSIQUE dispersion equation; ~ des
écoulements visqueux *f* PHYS FLUID viscous flow equation; ~ du énième degré *f* MATH nth degree equation;
~ d'équilibre *f* PHYSIQUE equilibrium equation; ~ équivalente *f* MATH simultaneous equation; ~ d'état *f*
PHYSIQUE state equation; ~ d'état thermique *f* THER-
MODYN thermal state equation; ~ des gaz *f* PHYSIQUE
gas equation; ~ générale du cercle *f* GEOMETRIE
general equation of the circle; ~ de Hamilton-Jacobi *f*
PHYSIQUE Hamilton-Jacobi equation; ~ de Kepler *f*
ASTRONOMIE Kepler's equation; ~ de Klein-Gordon *f*
PHYSIQUE Klein-Gordon equation; ~ de Laplace *f*
PHYSIQUE Laplace's equation; ~ de mouvement de
Schlueter *f* NUCLEAIRE Schlueter motion equation; ~
des mouvements rampants *f* PHYS FLUID *écoulement
visqueux* creeping motion equation; ~ de Navier-
Stokes *f* PHYSIQUE Navier-Stokes equation; ~
nucléaire d'état *f* PHYS RAYON nuclear equation of
state; ~ d'onde *f* PHYS RAYON, PHYSIQUE wave equa-
tion; ~ photo-électrique d'Einstein *f* ELECTROTEC
Einstein photoelectric equation; ~ de Poisson *f*
PHYSIQUE Poisson's equation; ~ de propagation *f*
PHYSIQUE propagation equation; ~ de Schrödinger *f*
PHYSIQUE Schrödinger equation; ~ de la tangente *f*
GEOMETRIE tangent equation; ~ du temps *f* ASTRON-
OMIE time equation; ~ thermodynamique d'état *f*
THERMODYN thermodynamic equation of state; ~ de
transfert radiatif *f* PHYS RAYON *stimulation électro-
magnétique* radiative transfer equation; ~ de Van der
Waals *f* PHYSIQUE Van der Waals equation; ~ de
vorticité *f* PHYS FLUID vorticity equation
équations: ~ canoniques *f pl* PHYSIQUE canonical equations; ~ des faisceaux hertziens *f pl* PHYS RAYON
electromagnetic wave equations; ~ de Hamilton *f pl*
PHYSIQUE Hamilton's equations; ~ de Lagrange *f pl*
PHYSIQUE Lagrange's equations; ~ de Maxwell *f pl*
PHYSIQUE Maxwell's equations
équerrage *m* PAPIER squaring
équerre *f* CONS MECA angle bracket, set square, CONSTR
L-iron, angle iron, angle, cross-staff, cross-staff head,
cross, METROLOGIE square; ~ d'angle *f* CONSTR corner
band, METROLOGIE *boîte* angle plate; ~ d'arpenteur *f*
CONSTR cross, cross-staff, cross-staff head; ~ assem-
blée à jour *f* CONS MECA framed set square; ~ à centrer
à téton *f* METEO center finder (AmE), centre finder
(BrE); ~ à coulisse *f* CONS MECA caliper square (AmE),
calliper square (BrE), sliding caliper gage (AmE),
sliding calipers (AmE), sliding calliper gauge (BrE),
sliding callipers (BrE), METROLOGIE beam caliper
(AmE), beam caliper gage (AmE), beam calliper
(BrE), beam calliper gauge (BrE); ~ à dessin *f* GEOME-
TRIE set square; ~ en T *f* CONS MECA T-square; ~ de
fixation *f* INST HYDR bracket, MECANIQUE angle
bracket; ~ à huit pans *f* CONS MECA octagonal nut

angle gage (AmE), octagonal nut angle gauge (BrE); **~ à lame d'acier** *f* CONS MECA try square; **~ de métallisation** *f* PRODUCTION bonding angle; **~ à onglet** *f* CONSTR miter square (AmE), mitre square (BrE)

équerre-applique *f* CONSTR angle bracket, MINES *pour transmissions* end bracket, end wall bracket

équiangle *adj* GEOMETRIE equiangular

équidimensionnel *adj* GEOLOGIE equant

équidistance *f* GEOLOGIE contour interval

équidistant *adj* CONS MECA equally spaced, equidistant, CONSTR, GEOMETRIE equidistant

équigranulaire *adj* GEOLOGIE *minéraux* equigranular

équilatéral *adj* GEOMETRIE equilateral

équilenine *f* CHIMIE equilenin

équilibrage *m* AERONAUT balancing, equalizing, trim, AUTO balancing, NAUT *par noyage d'un compartiment* counterflooding, NUCLEAIRE balancing, OCEANO pressure equalization, PAPIER, PHYSIQUE, TELECOM balancing; **~ des caméras** *m* TV camera matching, picture match; **~ colorimétrique** *m* CINEMAT color matching (AmE), colour matching (BrE); **~ dynamique** *m* AERONAUT dynamic balancing; **~ électronique des gris** *m* IMPRIM *photogravure, informatique* gray component replacement (AmE), grey component replacement(BrE); **~ d'entrefer** *m* TV gap setting; **~ de l'entrefer** *m* TV head adjustment; **~ des pales** *m* AERONAUT blade balance; **~ du pont** *m* ELECTROTEC bridge balancing; **~ des rotors flexibles** *m* CONS MECA flexible rotor balance; **~ de la sous-porteuse couleur** *m* TV carrier balance; **~ statique** *m* CONS MECA *des meules* static balance; **~ des températures** *m* THERMODYN temperature equalizing; **~ des voies** *m* ENREGISTR channel balancing

équilibre *m* GEOLOGIE equilibrium, graded profile, IMPRIM *mécanique, couleur* balance, MECANIQUE equilibrium, PAPIER balance, PETROLE *condition de puits en cours de forage* equilibrium, PHYSIQUE balance, equilibrium; **~ calco-carbonate** *m* HYDROLOGIE carbonic acid equilibrium; **~ chromatique** *m* TV chromatic balance; **~ des couleurs** *m* CINEMAT color balance (AmE), colour balance (BrE); **~ dynamique** *m* CONS MECA dynamic balance; **~ écologique** *m* POLLUTION biological equilibrium; **~ des gris** *m* IMPRIM *photogravure, impression* gray balance (AmE), grey balance(BrE); **~ hydrophile** *m* LESSIVES hydrophile balance; **~ hydrostatique** *m* THERMODYN hydrostatic equilibrium; **~ instable** *m* PHYSIQUE unstable equilibrium; **~ métastable** *m* PHYSIQUE metastable equilibrium; **~ des modes** *m* OPTIQUE equilibrium mode distribution, steady-state condition, TELECOM equilibrium mode distribution; **~ optique** *m* IMPRIM *contrôle à l'écran* optical balance; **~ de phase** *m* THERMODYN phase equilibrium; **~ de pression** *m* MECANIQUE equalization; **~ radioactif** *m* PHYS RAYON, PHYSIQUE radioactive equilibrium; **~ séculaire** *m* PHYSIQUE secular equilibrium; **~ stable** *m* PHYSIQUE stable equilibrium; **~ des températures** *m* THERMODYN temperature balance, temperature equalization; **~ de la tension** *m* ELECTR voltage balance; **~ thermique** *m* ESPACE thermodynamic equilibrium, THERMODYN thermal equilibrium; **~ thermodynamique** *m* ESPACE *véhicules* thermodynamic equilibrium, THERMODYN thermal equilibrium; **~ transitoire** *m* PHYSIQUE transient equilibrium; **~ visuel** *m* IMPRIM *contrôle à l'écran* optical balance

équilibré: ~ par rapport à la terre *adj* ELECTROTEC earth-balanced

équilibrer *vt* MECANIQUE counterbalance, OCEANO equalize, PAPIER balance

équilibreur *m* ENREGISTR fader

équimoléculaire *adj* CHIMIE equimolecular

équinoxe *m* ASTRONOMIE equinox; **~ de printemps** *m* ASTRONOMIE spring equinox; **~ vernal** *m* ASTRONOMIE spring equinox, vernal equinox, ESPACE vernal equinox

équipage *m* AERONAUT crew, CONS MECA outfit, *d'engrenages* cluster, nest, CONSTR equipment, plant, ELECTROTEC meter movement, ESPACE *véhicules* crew, NAUT crew, ship's hands, PRODUCTION mill, rig, rolls; **~ commercial** *m* AERONAUT cabin crew; **~ de conduite** *m* AERONAUT flight crew; **~ de cylindres** *m* CONS MECA train of rolls, PRODUCTION set of rolls; **~ dégrossisseur** *m* PRODUCTION puddle bar train, puddle train, roughing rolls, puddle rolls; **~ d'engrenage** *m* CONS MECA multiple of gearing; **~ d'engrenages** *m* CONS MECA gear train, train of gearing, gear work; **~ de laminoir** *m* PRODUCTION roll train, rolling mill roll, rolling mill train; **~ mobile** *m* ACOUSTIQUE moving armature; **~ d'outils** *m* CONS MECA set of tools; **~ de relève** *m* AERONAUT relief crew; **~ technique** *m* AERONAUT flight crew; **~ de vol** *m* AERONAUT flight crew

équipartition *f* PHYSIQUE equipartition

équipe *f* CINEMAT crew, unit, PETROLE crew, PRODUCTION crew, team, *travail posté* shift; **~ caméra** *f* CINEMAT camera crew; **~ de désamorçage de bombes** *f* MILITAIRE bomb disposal team; **~ de forage** *f* PETROLE drilling crew; **~ image** *f* CINEMAT camera crew; **~ pour combattre l'incendie** *f* SECURITE firefighting team; **~ principale** *f* CINEMAT first unit; **~ de prise de vues** *f* CINEMAT camera crew; **~ de sauvetage** *f* SECURITE rescue party; **~ de secours** *f* CONSTR breakdown gang; **~ volante** *f* CONSTR flying squad

équipement *m* CONS MECA apparatus, appliance, equipment, outfit, CONSTR, NAUT *d'un navire* fitting-out; **~ d'accès externe** *m* TELECOM EA, external access equipment; **~ d'agrafage** *m* EMBALLAGE stapling equipment; **~ d'alimentation de chaîne de fabrication** *m* EMBALLAGE line feeding equipment; **~ d'appel automatique** *m* INFORMAT, ORDINAT automatic calling unit *(ACU)*; **~ de bord** *m* AERONAUT aircraft equipment, ESPACE *véhicules* on-board system; **~ de calcul** *m* INFORMAT, ORDINAT computing device; **~ de canaux** *m* TELECOM CE, channel equipment; **~ de carottage** *m* GEOPHYS borehole logging equipment, NUCLEAIRE well logging equipment; **~ de cerclage** *m* EMBALLAGE strapping equipment; **~ de cerclage avec fil** *m* EMBALLAGE wire strapping equipment; **~ de collecte** *m* TELECOM data collection equipment; **~ de commande** *m* PRODUCTION, TELECOM control equipment; **~ commercial** *m* CONSTR furnishings; **~ de commutation** *m* INFORMAT switching equipment; **~ de contrôle** *m* ESPACE check out system; **~ de désintégration** *m* EMBALLAGE repulping equipment; **~ DME** *m* *(équipement de mesure de distance)* AERONAUT DME *(distance-measuring equipment)*; **~ embarqué** *m* ESPACE *véhicules* on-board system; **~ d'enroulement et de déroulement** *m* EMBALLAGE wind-unwind equipment; **~ de facturation** *m* TELECOM call charging equipment, charging equipment; **~ facultatif** *m* CONS MECA optional equipment; **~ fibre optique** *m* EQUIP LAB fiber optics equipment (AmE), *éclairage* fibre optics equipment (BrE); **~ de finissage sur chaîne de produc-**

tion *m* EMBALLAGE in-line finishing equipment; ~ **fixe** *m* CONSTR fixed equipment; ~ **fonctionnant sous pression** *m* CONS MECA pressure equipment; ~ **de forage** *m* PETROLE drilling rig; ~ **frontal de saisie** *m* IMPRIM *composition, photogravure* front-end equipment; ~ **à haute tension** *m* ELECTR *matériel* high-voltage equipment; ~ **d'inspection** *m* EMBALLAGE inspection equipment; ~ **d'instruments** *m* INSTRUMENT instrumentation; ~ **d'interception** *m* TELECOM interception equipment; ~ **d'une ligne** *m* CH DE FER permanent way installation; ~ **de ligne interautomatique** *m (cf équipement de ligne de jonction)* TELECOM tie circuit interface; ~ **de ligne de jonction** *m* (Can) *(cf équipement de ligne interautomatique)* TELECOM tie circuit interface; ~ **local d'abonnés** *m* TELECOM customer premises equipment; ~ **de lutte contre l'incendie** *m* SECURITE firefighting equipment; ~ **de manutention** *m* EMBALLAGE handling equipment; ~ **de manutention des emballages** *m* EMBALLAGE pack handling equipment; ~ **de manutention des emballages sur bobine** *m* EMBALLAGE reel wrapping and handling equipment; ~ **de manutention et de remplissage** *m* EMBALLAGE handling and filling equipment; ~ **de médiation** *m* TELECOM MD, mediation device; ~ **de mélange et de dosage** *m* EMBALLAGE mixing and blending equipment; ~ **de mesure de distance** *m (équipement DME)* AERONAUT distance-measuring equipment *(DME)*; ~ **de mesure de la distance de visibilité** *m* TRANSPORT visibility distance measuring equipment; ~ **mesureur** *m* EMBALLAGE metering equipment; ~ **multiplexeur-aiguilleur numérique** *m* TELECOM DXC, digital cross-connect equipment; ~ **de multiplication de circuit numérique** *m (EMCN)* TELECOM digital circuit multiplication equipment *(DCME)*; ~ **neutralisé** *m* TELECOM *maritime mobile* equipment disabled; ~ **ophtalmologique** *m* INSTRUMENT ophtalmic test stand; ~ **optoélectronique de réception** *m* TELECOM fiberoptic receiver (AmE), fibreoptic receiver (BrE); ~ **de pesage** *m* PETR weighting material; ~ **de plongée** *m* OCEANO, PETR diving equipment, diving gear; ~ **pour déceler les pilules manquantes** *m* EMBALLAGE missing pill equipment; ~ **pour l'extrusion de films** *m* EMBALLAGE film extrusion equipment; ~ **pour fermeture avec capsule** *m* EMBALLAGE cap sealing equipment; ~ **pour la fermeture des sacs** *m* EMBALLAGE bag sealing equipment; ~ **pour mettre en place les divisions** *m* EMBALLAGE *d'une emballage* division inserting equipment; ~ **pour rincer les conteneurs** *m* EMBALLAGE container rinsing equipment; ~ **pour la sécurité** *m* SECURITE safety appliance; ~ **de protection individuelle** *m* MILITAIRE *guerre chimique* IPE, individual protection equipment; ~ **de purification et de désodorisation de l'air** *m* SECURITE air purification and deodorization equipment; ~ **radar** *m* MILITAIRE radar equipment; ~ **à rayons X** *m* INSTRUMENT X-ray apparatus; ~ **de réanimation** *m* SECURITE resuscitation equipment; ~ **de refroidissement** *m* TEXTILE cooling equipment; ~ **de sauvetage** *m* AERONAUT rescue equipment; ~ **de sauvetage anti-incendie** *m* SECURITE fire rescue appliance; ~ **de secours** *m* AERONAUT emergency equipment; ~ **de sécurité** *m* SECURITE safety equipment, *pour bâtiments* safety facility; ~ **de signalisation de ligne** *m* TELECOM line signalling equipment; ~ **sonore** *m* ENREGISTR sound equipment, sound system; ~ **sonore monophonique** *m* ENREGISTR monophonic sound system; ~ **de soudure à**

haute fréquence *m* EMBALLAGE high-frequency welding equipment; ~ **standard de commande** *m* PRODUCTION *automatisme industriel* standard control equipment; ~ **de survie** *m* ESPACE survival kit; ~ **de taxation** *m* TELECOM call charging equipment, charging equipment; ~ **de taxation centralisée** *m* TELECOM central charging equipment; ~ **de terminaison de circuit de données** *m* TELECOM data circuit terminating equipment; ~ **de terminaison de ligne** *m* ORDINAT LTE, line termination equipment, TELECOM line-terminating equipment; ~ **terminal** *m* TELECOM terminal equipment, terminating equipment; ~ **terminal de circuit de données** *m (ETCD)* TELECOM data circuit terminal equipment *(DCE)*; ~ **terminal de données** *m (ETD)* AERONAUT, ORDINAT, TELECOM data terminal equipment *(DTE)*; ~ **terminal mobile terrestre de traitement de données** *m (ETTD-MT)* TELECOM mobile data processing terminal equipment; ~ **terminal pour le RNIS-LB** *m* TELECOM B-ISDN terminal equipment, TE-LB; ~ **terminal de réseau** *m* TELECOM NTE, network terminal equipment; ~ **terminal de traitement de données** *m (ETTD)* AERONAUT, ORDINAT data terminal equipment *(DTE)*, TELECOM data processing terminal equipment, data terminal equipment; ~ **terminal de traitement de données fixe** *m (ETTD-F)* TELECOM fixed data processing terminal equipment; ~ **de tête** *m* AERONAUT headgear; ~ **de tête de puits** *m* PETR wellhead equipment; ~ **de thermosoudage** *m* EMBALLAGE heat-sealing equipment; ~ **de traitement de messages** *m* NAUT message processing equipment; ~ **de transmission plésiochrone** *m* TELECOM plesiosynchronous transmission equipment; ~ **d'usager** *m* TELECOM CEQ, customer equipment; ~ **de vie** *m* ESPACE life support system

équipements: ~ **auxiliaires** *m pl* IMPRIM ancillaries

équiper *vt* CONS MECA fit out, NAUT *un canot* man, PRODUCTION fit out, rig, rig out, rig up, TELECOM equip; ~ **d'instruments** *vt* NAUT instrument

équipet *m* NAUT locker; ~ **cloisonné** *m* NAUT closed locker

équipotentiel[1] *adj* ELECTR equipotential, ELECTROTEC equipotential, *cathode* unipotential

équipotentiel[2] *m* PHYSIQUE equipotential

équipression *f* OCEANO equal pressure, equipressure

équivalence *f* INFORMAT, ORDINAT equivalence; ~ **masse-énergie** *f* PHYSIQUE mass energy equivalence

équivalent *m* PHYSIQUE equivalent; ~ **calorifique** *m* THERMODYN mechanical equivalent of heat; ~ **de dose** *m* PHYSIQUE dose equivalent; ~ **de dose pour un groupe** *m* POLLUTION group collective dose; ~ **de dose pour un sous-groupe** *m* POLLUTION subpopulation collective dose; ~ **en eau** *m* PHYSIQUE water equivalent; ~ **en roentgen pour l'homme** *m* PHYS RAYON rem, roentgen equivalent man; ~ **mécanique de calorie** *m* MECANIQUE Joule's equivalent, mechanical equivalent of heat, PHYSIQUE, THERMODYN Joule's equivalent; ~ **mécanique de la chaleur** *m* ELECTR *thermodynamique* Joule's equivalent, THERMODYN Joule's equivalent, heat equivalent, mechanical equivalent of heat, thermal equivalent; ~ **par million** *m* POLLUTION equivalent per million; ~ **de sable** *m* CONSTR sand equivalent; ~ **thermique** *m* THERMODYN thermal value; ~ **de vitesse** *m* AERONAUT equivalent airspeed; ~ **de vitesse de rafale verticale** *m* AERONAUT *navigabilité* equivalent vertical gust speed

équivalent-habitant *m* DISTRI EAU population equivalent

Er *(erbium)* CHIMIE Er *(erbium)*

éraflure *f* CERAM VER scuff mark, scuffing, TEXTILE scuff mark, scuffing

érathème *m* GEOLOGIE *systèmes lithostratigraphiques* erathem

erbium *m (Er)* CHIMIE erbium *(Er)*

ère *f* GEOLOGIE era; ~ **primaire** *f* GEOLOGIE Palaeozoic (BrE), Paleozoic (AmE); ~ **quaternaire** *f* GEOLOGIE Quaternary, Quaternary era; ~ **secondaire** *f* PETROLE mesozoic; ~ **spatiale** *f* ASTRONOMIE, ESPACE space age; ~ **tertiaire** *f* PETR Tertiary era

érecteur *m* CH DE FER erector

érection *f* CONSTR *de bâtiments* erection

erg *m* METROLOGIE erg

ergol *m* CHIMIE propellant, ESPACE *propulsion* ergol, fuel, THERMODYN ergol; ~ **cryotechnique** *m* ESPACE *propulsion* cryogenic fuel, cryogenic propellant; ~ **en bouillie** *m* ESPACE *propulsion* slush propellant; ~ **stockable** *m* ESPACE *propulsion* storable propellant

ergolier *m* ESPACE *véhicules* fuel man

ergomètre *m* METROLOGIE ergmeter

ergonome *m* CONS MECA ergonomist

ergonomie *f* CONS MECA, EMBALLAGE, ESPACE, INFORMAT, ORDINAT, PRODUCTION, SECURITE ergonomics

ergonomique *adj* EMBALLAGE, PRODUCTION ergonomic

ergot *m* AGRO ALIM ergot, CONS MECA lug, CONSTR stump, *du pêne d'une serrure à gorge* stub, ELECTROTEC pin, INFORMAT, ORDINAT sprocket; ~ **de détrompage** *m* PRODUCTION *automatisme industriel* keying band; ~ **de fixation** *m* CINEMAT register bar; ~ **de positionnement** *m* CINEMAT register peg, CONS MECA *bloc à colonnes* locating pin

ergothionéine *f* CHIMIE thiozene

ergotinine *f* CHIMIE ergotinine

Eridan *m* ASTRONOMIE Eridanus

ériger *vt* CONSTR put up

érinite *f* MINERAUX erinite

érodé: ~ **par l'eau** *adj* HYDROLOGIE wate-eroded; ~ **par la pluie** *adj* METEO rain-eroded; ~ **par le vent** *adj* METEO wind-eroded

éroder *vt* CONSTR, HYDROLOGIE, METEO erode

érosion *f* CHARBON, CHIMIE, CONSTR, EN RENOUV erosion, GAZ wear, GEOLOGIE abrasion, erosion, HYDROLOGIE erosion, MECANIQUE fretting; ~ **due à l'eau** *f* HYDROLOGIE water erosion; ~ **en surface** *f* HYDROLOGIE surface erosion; ~ **éolienne** *f* GEOLOGIE wind erosion; ~ **fluviale** *f* HYDROLOGIE river erosion; ~ **fluviatile** *f* HYDROLOGIE river erosion; ~ **interne** *f* CHARBON internal erosion, internal scour; ~ **mécanique** *f* GEOLOGIE mechanical weathering; ~ **par l'eau de surface** *f* CHARBON surface water erosion; ~ **par fil** *f* CONS MECA *usinage* wire erosion; ~ **par la pluie** *f* HYDROLOGIE water erosion, METEO rain erosion; ~ **par suintement** *f* DISTRI EAU piping seepage; ~ **pluviale** *f* METEO rain erosion; ~ **remontante** *f* CERAM VER pitting, upward drilling; ~ **souterraine** *f* DISTRI EAU subsurface erosion

erre *f* NAUT *d'un navire*, OCEANO way; ~ **en avant** *f* NAUT headway

erreur *f* ELECTRON error, IMPRIM bug, INFORMAT error, ORDINAT bug, error, PHYSIQUE error; ~ **absolue** *f* ORDINAT absolute error; ~ **aléatoire** *f* CHARBON, METROLOGIE, PHYSIQUE, TELECOM random error; ~ **d'analyse** *f* CHARBON analysis error; ~ **d'angle** *f* METROLOGIE angle error; ~ **d'approximation** *f* MATH rounding error, TELECOM approximation error; ~

d'arrondi *f* INFORMAT, ORDINAT rounding error; ~ **de base de temps** *f* TV time-base error; ~ **de base de temps due au guide** *f* TV guide error; ~ **de bloc à l'extrémité distante** *f* TELECOM FEBE, far-end block error; ~ **de câblage** *f* PRODUCTION wiring error; ~ **centrée** *f* INFORMAT balanced error; ~ **chromatique** *f* TV color error (AmE), colour error (BrE); ~ **de codage** *f* ELECTRON coding error; ~ **de collimation** *f* NAUT index error; ~ **de concentricité coeur-gaine** *f* OPTIQUE, TELECOM core-cladding concentricity error; ~ **de concentricité coeur-surface de référence** *f* OPTIQUE, TELECOM core-reference surface concentricity error; ~ **de convergence** *f* TV convergence error; ~ **de dérive** *f* AERONAUT *altimètre* drift error; ~ **de développement** *f* IMPRIM *chimie des films et plaques* processing error; ~ **de diamètre de fond de filet** *f* METROLOGIE *contrôle de filetages* minor diameter error; ~ **de diamètre sur flancs de filets** *f* METROLOGIE *contrôle de filetages* pitch diameter error; ~ **due à l'installation** *f* PRODUCTION installation error; ~ **due à l'instrument** *f* CONS MECA instrument error; ~ **due au mécanisme** *f* TV mechanical error; ~ **d'écart** *f* AERONAUT *système d'atterrissage aux instruments* displacement error; ~ **d'écriture** *f* INFORMAT, ORDINAT write error; ~ **fatale** *f* INFORMAT fatal error; ~ **de fluctuation de base de temps** *f* TV fluctuating error; ~ **de forme** *f* METROLOGIE *d'une pièce de travail* form error; ~ **de gamma** *f* TV gamma error; ~ **de géométrie** *f* TV geometric error; ~ **humaine** *f* QUALITE, SECURITE human error; ~ **d'hystérésis** *f* AERONAUT *altimètre* hysteresis error; ~ **d'implantation des trames** *f* IMPRIM *photogravure* angling error; ~ **instrumentale** *f* INSTRUMENT instrument error, NAUT index error; ~ **intrinsèque** *f* METROLOGIE *d'un instrument de mesure* intrinsic error; ~ **irrécupérable** *f* INFORMAT irrecoverable error, ORDINAT fatal error, irrecoverable error; ~ **de jeu** *f* AERONAUT *altimètre* backlash error; ~ **de lecture** *f* INFORMAT, ORDINAT read error; ~ **logicielle** *f* INFORMAT, ORDINAT soft error; ~ **longitudinale** *f* ESPACE *pilotage* along-track error; ~ **machine** *f* INFORMAT, ORDINAT machine check, machine error; ~ **matérielle** *f* INFORMAT, ORDINAT hard error; ~ **maximale tolérée** *f* METROLOGIE maximum permissible error, measurable quantity, *d'un instrument de mesure* limit of error; ~ **maximum d'intervalle de temps** *f* TELECOM MTIE, maximum time interval error; ~ **de mesurage** *f* METROLOGIE measuring error; ~ **moyenne** *f* ELECTR mean error; ~ **moyenne d'alignement de descente** *f* AERONAUT mean glide path error; ~ **non définie** *f* INFORMAT, ORDINAT undefined error; ~ **numérique** *f* TELECOM digital error; ~ **de numérotation** *f* TELECOM dialing error (AmE), dialling error (BrE), keying error; ~ **opératoire** *f* CHARBON operating error; ~ **d'orientation** *f* MATERIAUX *cristallographie* misorientation; ~ **par diffusion sur le support** *f* NUCLEAIRE backscatter error; ~ **de parité** *f* INFORMAT, ORDINAT parity error; ~ **de parité en mémoire** *f* PRODUCTION *automatisme industriel* memory parity error; ~ **par omission** *f* QUALITE error of omission; ~ **par troncature** *f* INFORMAT, ORDINAT truncation error; ~ **persistante** *f* INFORMAT, ORDINAT permanent error; ~ **de phase** *f* ELECTRON, TV phase error; ~ **de phase aléatoire** *f* TV random phase error; ~ **de phase de sous-porteuse couleur** *f* TV color error (AmE), colour error (BrE); ~ **de pistage** *f* ENREGISTR tracking error; ~ **de piste latérale** *f* ACOUSTIQUE lateral tracking angle error; ~ **de piste verticale** *f* ACOUSTIQUE vertical tracking angle error; ~ **de pointage** *f* ESPACE *communications* pointing error; ~ **de poursuite** *f* METROLOGIE *d'un instrument de mesure*, TELECOM tracking error; ~ **de poursuite instantanée** *f* ESPACE *communications* instantaneous tracking error; ~ **de programmation** *f* ORDINAT coding error; ~ **quadrantale** *f* AERONAUT quadrantal error; ~ **quadratique moyenne** *f* INFORMAT, MATH, ORDINAT MSE, mean square error; ~ **de quadrature** *f* TV quadrature error; ~ **de quantification** *f* ELECTRON, TELECOM quantization error; ~ **récupérable** *f* INFORMAT, ORDINAT recoverable error; ~ **relative** *f* INFORMAT, ORDINAT relative error; ~ **relative maximum d'intervalle de temps** *f* TELECOM MRTIE, maximum relative time interval error; ~ **statique de base de temps** *f* TV static error; ~ **de syntaxe** *f* INFORMAT, ORDINAT syntax error; ~ **systématique** *f* CHARBON bias, METROLOGIE, PHYSIQUE systematic error; ~ **technique de vol** *f* AERONAUT flight technical error; ~ **de teinte** *f* TV chromaticity aberration; ~ **de temps d'exécution** *f* PRODUCTION *automatisme industriel* run-time error; ~ **de tenue d'altitude** *f* AERONAUT height-keeping error; ~ **transitoire** *f* INFORMAT, ORDINAT transient error; ~ **de transmission** *f* TELECOM transmission error; ~ **transversale** *f* ESPACE *pilotage* across-track error; ~ **de tri** *f* CONS MECA missorting; ~ **typographique** *f* IMPRIM misprint; ~ **de vitesse de têtes** *f* TV velocity error

erse *f* CONS MECA, NAUT *cordage* grommet

erseau *m* NAUT *cordage* grommet

érubescite *f* MINERAUX erubescite, variegated copper ore

érucique *adj* CHIMIE erucic

éruption *f* GAZ eruption, PETR, PETROLE blowout, PHYS FLUID eruption, POLLUTION blowout; ~ **chromosphérique** *f* ASTRONOMIE chromatospherical eruption; ~ **solaire** *f* ESPACE *astronomie*, GEOPHYS solar flare

érythrine *f* CHIMIE erythrin

érythrite *f* MINERAUX cobalt bloom, erythrite

érythritol *m* CHIMIE erythritol

érythrose *m* CHIMIE erythrose

érythrosine *f* CHIMIE erythrosine

érythrulose *m* CHIMIE erythrulose

Es *(einsteinium)* CHIMIE Es *(einsteinium)*

ESC *abrév (échappement)* INFORMAT, ORDINAT ESC *(escape)*

escadre *f* NAUT fleet

escadrille *f* NAUT flotilla

escalator *m* CONSTR escalator, traveling staircase (AmE), travelling staircase (BrE)

escale *f* AERONAUT stopover, NAUT port of call; ~ **technique** *f* AERONAUT technical stop

escalier *m* CONSTR stair, staircase, stairway, TV *la forme d'un signal* staircase; ~ **à deux volées** *m* CONSTR dogleg stairs; ~ **à double quartier tournant** *m* CONSTR half turn stairs; ~ **droit** *m* CONSTR fliers, flyers; ~ **droit à une volée** *m* CONSTR straight flight of stairs; ~ **en encorbellement** *m* CONSTR hanging stairs, hanging steps; ~ **en escargot** *m* CONSTR corkscrew stairs, spiral stairs; ~ **en huit** *m* CONSTR figure-of-eight stairs; ~ **en limaçon** *m* CONSTR corkscrew stairs, spiral stairs; ~ **en spirale** *m* CONSTR corkscrew stairs, spiral stairs; ~ **en vis** *m* CONSTR corkscrew stairs, spiral stairs; ~ **hélicoïdal** *m* CONSTR corkscrew stairs, spiral stairs; ~ **intégré** *m* AERONAUT air stairs; ~ **à marches mobiles** *m* CONSTR escalator, moving staircase (BrE), moving stairway (BrE), traveling staircase (AmE), travelling staircase

(BrE); ~ **mécanique** *m* CONSTR escalator, TRANSPORT escalator (AmE); ~ **à noyau creux** *m* CONSTR open newel stair; ~ **à noyau plein** *m* CONSTR solid-newel stair; ~ **à rampe droite** *m* CONSTR fliers, flyers, straight flight of stairs; ~ **rampe-sur-rampe** *m* CONSTR dogleg stairs; ~ **rompu en paliers** *m* CONSTR stairs interrupted by landings; ~ **roulant** *m* CONSTR escalator (AmE), moving stairway (BrE), moving staircase (BrE), TRANSPORT escalator (AmE); ~ **de secours** *m* THERMODYN fire escape; ~ **suspendu** *m* CONSTR hanging stairs, hanging steps; ~ **tournant** *m* CONSTR corkscrew stairs, spiral stairs

escamotable *adj* CONS MECA foldaway, MECANIQUE retractable

escamotage: ~ **de phase** *m* TRANSPORT phase skipping; ~ **rapide** *m* TV fast pull-down

escarpement *m* CONSTR bluff, steepness, OCEANO escarpment, sea scarp

escaver: ~ **une recette** *vi* MINES cut a landing, cut a plat, cut a station

eschynite *f* MINERAUX aeschynite, eschinite

esclave *m* INFORMAT, ORDINAT slave; ~ **d'égal à égal** *m* PRODUCTION *automatisme industriel* peer-to-peer slave

escorter *vt* NAUT convoy

escorteur *m* NAUT escort ship, frigate

escramaisons *f pl* CERAM VER skimmings

esculine *f* CHIMIE esculin

ésérine *f* CHIMIE eserine

esker: ~ **en chapelet** *m* GEOLOGIE beaded esker

espace *m* ASTRONOMIE space, CONS MECA gap, ESPACE, GEOMETRIE space, INFORMAT, ORDINAT space character, PHYSIQUE space; ~ **d'adressage** *m* ORDINAT address space; ~ **aérien** *m* AERONAUT airspace; ~ **aérien contrôlé** *m* AERONAUT *aux instruments et à vue* controlled airspace; ~ **annulaire** *m* GAZ annular space, PETR annulus, PETROLE *d'un puits* annular space, annulus; ~ **arrière** *m* ORDINAT BS, backspace; ~ **cavité-réflecteur** *m* ELECTRON reflector space; ~ **de configuration** *m* GEOMETRIE, PHYSIQUE configuration space; ~ **confiné** *m* SECURITE confined space; ~ **coupe-feu** *m* NUCLEAIRE fire area, fire cell; ~ **creux** *m* MINES cavity; ~ **de Crookes** *m* PHYSIQUE Crookes dark space; ~ **disque** *m* INFORMAT, ORDINAT disk space; ~ **elliptique** *m* GEOMETRIE elliptical space; ~ **à empoussièrage contrôlé** *m* REFRIG clean space; ~ **entre les atomes** *m* NUCLEAIRE atomic interspace; ~ **entre blocs** *m* ORDINAT IBG, interblock gap; ~ **entre électrodes** *m* ELECTROTEC electrode gap; ~ **euclidien** *m* GEOMETRIE, PHYSIQUE euclidean space; ~ **d'excitation** *m* ELECTRON catcher space; ~ **extra-atmosphérique** *m* ESPACE cosmic space, outer space; ~ **fin** *m* IMPRIM matrix hairline, thin space; ~ **fort** *m* IMPRIM thick space, three-to-em space; ~ **de glissement** *m* ELECTRON drift space; ~ **de groupement** *m* ELECTRON bunching space; ~ **hyperbolique** *m* GEOMETRIE hyperbolic space; ~ **d'interaction** *m* ELECTRON interaction gap, interaction space; ~ **interbloc** *m* ORDINAT interblock gap; ~ **inter image** *m* CINEMAT rack line; ~ **intermédiaire** *m* CONS MECA receiver space; ~ **interpiste** *m* ENREGISTR track spacing; ~ **intersidéral** *m* ESPACE *astronomie* interstellar space; ~ **intersillon** *m* ENREGISTR land; ~ **interstellaire** *m* ASTRONOMIE, ESPACE *astronomie* interstellar space; ~ **justifiante** *m* IMPRIM variable space; ~ **libre** *m* CONS MECA piston clearance, NUCLEAIRE clearance, gap; ~ **lointain** *m* ESPACE far space, *communications* deep space; ~ **de Minkowski** *m* PHYSIQUE Minkowski space; ~ **de modulation** *m* ELECTRON buncher space, input gap; ~ **mort** *m* CONS MECA piston clearance, INST HYDR *dans un cylindre à vapeur, espace libre* waste space, *entre le piston et le fond du cylindre* space; ~ **neutre** *m* CONS MECA piston clearance; ~ **nuisible** *m* CONS MECA piston clearance; ~ **des phases** *m* PHYSIQUE phase space; ~ **de la planche** *m* CONSTR floorspace; ~ **d'un point** *m* IMPRIM hairline space; ~ **réciproque** *m* CRISTALL reciprocal space; ~ **de regroupement** *m* ELECTRON drift space; ~ **restreint** *m* SECURITE confined space; ~ **sombre cathodique** *m* PHYSIQUE Crookes dark space; ~ **sombre de Faraday** *m* PHYSIQUE Faraday dark space; ~ **sur rayons** *m* EMBALLAGE shelf space; ~ **de tête** *m* AGRO ALIM head space

espacé:[1] ~ **d'un point** *adj* IMPRIM *interlettrage* one point letter spaced

espacé[2] *adv* TELECOM spaced-out

espacement *m* AERONAUT *des aéronefs* spacing, MECANIQUE, OPTIQUE, TRANSPORT *des véhicules* spacing; ~ **arrière** *m* IMPRIM *clavier* backspace; ~ **des canaux** *m* INFORMAT channel spacing; ~ **des caractères** *m* INFORMAT, ORDINAT row pitch; ~ **entre canaux** *m* TV channel spacing; ~ **entre les éléments constitutifs** *m* PRODUCTION *automatisme industriel* component spacing; ~ **entre les lettres** *m* IMPRIM *composition* letter spacing; ~ **entre véhicules** *m* TRANSPORT headway; ~ **de garde** *m* TELECOM guard space; ~ **horizontal** *m* PRODUCTION horizontal spacing; ~ **idéal** *m* IMPRIM *entre deux chiffres d'un même corps* figure space; ~ **latéral** *m* TRANSPORT lateral clearance; ~ **des lignes** *m* TV raster pitch; ~ **réticulaire** *m* METALL lattice spacing; ~ **vertical** *m* PRODUCTION vertical spacing

espace-temps *m* ASTRONOMIE, PHYSIQUE space-time; ~ **courbe** *m*

espatard *m* CONS MECA planishing roll

espèce *f* PLAST CAOU *groupe d'atomes* radical ~ **excitée** *f* GAZ excited component; ~ **indicatrice** *f* POLLUTION indicator species

espérance *f* ORDINAT expectation; ~ **de vie** *f* CONSTR life expectancy

esperluète *f* IMPRIM ampersand

esprit *m* CHIMIE spirit; ~ **de compétition** *m* PRODUCTION competitive edge

esquichage *m* PETROLE squeeze

esquisse *f* IMPRIM outline

essai *m* CHARBON test, testing, CHIMIE analysis, assaying, assay, testing, test, CONS MECA testing, ESSAIS test, INFORMAT testing, test, MECANIQUE, METALL test, NUCLEAIRE proving trial, trial, ORDINAT test, testing, PHYSIQUE test, PRODUCTION proof, QUALITE testing, REFRIG test, TEXTILE trial;

~ **a** ~ **abrasif** *m* CONS MECA abrasion test; ~ **d'abrasion** *m* CONS MECA attrition test, PRODUCTION endurance test; ~ **accéléré d'emmagasinage** *m* EMBALLAGE accelerated storage test; ~ **acoustique** *m* SECURITE acoustical test; ~ **d'adhérence** *m* CONS MECA adhesion strength test, PLAST CAOU adhesion test, PRODUCTION bonding test; ~ **d'adhérence des câbles dans l'enrobage** *m* CONS MECA cord-to-coating bond test; ~ **d'ambiance** *m* ESPACE environmental test; ~ **d'aplatissement** *m* PHYSIQUE flattening test; ~ **d'arrachement** *m* MATERIAUX pullout test, PRODUCTION peeling test;

~ **b** ~ **bêta** *m* INFORMAT, ORDINAT beta test; ~ **de boucle** *m* ELECTR loop test; ~ **de boucle Allen** *m* ELECTR Allen's loop test; ~ **Brinell** *m* CONS MECA Brinell test;

~ **c** ~ **caméra** *m* CINEMAT camera test; ~ **censuré** *m* ESPACE censured test; ~ **de certification** *m* GAZ certification test; ~ **de charge** *m* ELECTR load test; ~ **Charpy** *m* PHYSIQUE Charpy test; ~ **Charpy sur éprouvette à entaille en V** *m* MECANIQUE *matériaux* Charpy V-notch test; ~ **au choc** *m* EMBALLAGE, METROLOGIE impact test, NUCLEAIRE impact check, notch impact test; ~ **de choc** *m* PHYSIQUE impact test, TRANSPORT collision test, impact test; ~ **de choc Charpy** *m* PLAST CAOU *instrument* Charpy impact tester; ~ **de choc mécanique** *m* METROLOGIE mechanical shock test; ~ **de choc au sac de lest** *m* CERAM VER shot bag test; ~ **de choc sur éprouvette à entaille de V** *m* PHYSIQUE Charpy test; ~ **de choc thermique** *m* CHAUFFAGE *circuits imprimés*, THERMODYN heat shock test; ~ **de choc à torpille** *m* CERAM VER dart impact test; ~ **de chute** *m* EMBALLAGE drop test; ~ **de chute limite de train** *m* AERONAUT landing gear drop test; ~ **de circuit magnétique** *m* ELECTR *machine* core test; ~ **à circuit ouvert** *m* ELECTR open circuit test; ~ **de cisaillement par compression** *m* CONS MECA block shear test; ~ **de cisaillement pour rivets** *m* CONS MECA shear test; ~ **de claquage** *m* ELECTROTEC flash test; ~ **climatique** *m* EMBALLAGE, ESPACE climatic test, MECANIQUE environmental testing; ~ **de cloquage** *m* ESSAIS blistering test, PAPIER bubble test; ~ **de collage** *m* EMBALLAGE bonding test; ~ **de combustion verticale** *m* ESSAIS vertical burning test; ~ **de compactage de Proctor** *m* CHARBON Proctor compaction test; ~ **comparatif** *m* PHYSIQUE comparative test; ~ **de comportement mécanique** *m* GAZ mechanical behavior test (AmE), mechanical behaviour test (BrE); ~ **de compression** *m* CHARBON, EMBALLAGE, MECANIQUE, METALL *matériaux* compression test; ~ **peu concluant** *m* PHYSIQUE inconclusive test; ~ **de condensation de vapeur d'eau** *m* CONS MECA *armoires frigorifiques* water vapor condensation test (AmE), water vapour condensation test (BrE); ~ **de conduit** *m* REFRIG in-duct method; ~ **de conformité** *m* QUALITE compliance test, conformity test; ~ **de consolidation** *m* CHARBON compression test, consolidation test; ~ **de continuité** *m* ELECTR *circuit* continuity test; ~ **contradictoire** *m* CHIMIE control assay; ~ **de courbure et vrillage** *m* ESSAIS curvature and twisting test; ~ **de court-circuit brusque** *m* ELECTR sudden short circuit test; ~ **de courte durée** *m* ELECTR short-time test;

~ **d** ~ **de déchirement** *m* PLAST CAOU tearing test; ~ **de décrépitation** *m* CERAM VER creep test, decrepitation test; ~ **de dégivrage** *m* CONS MECA *meubles frigorifiques* defrosting test; ~ **de densité** *m* CONSTR density test; ~ **de désenrobage** *m* CONSTR aggregate stripping test; ~ **destructif** *m* CONS MECA destructive test; ~ **de dispersion** *m* GAZ dispersion test; ~ **à distance** *m* INFORMAT, ORDINAT remote test; ~ **de durabilité** *m* EMBALLAGE durability test; ~ **de durée** *m* ESPACE *véhicules* endurance test; ~ **de durée de vie des outils** *m* CONS MECA tool-life testing; ~ **de dureté** *m* MATERIAUX *métallurgie* hardness testing, MECANIQUE *matériaux*, PHYSIQUE hardness test; ~ **de dureté à bille d'acier** *m* CONS MECA steel ball hardness test; ~ **de dureté Rockwell** *m* CONS MECA Rockwell hardness test; ~ **dynamique** *m* METALL dynamic test;

~ **e** ~ **d'échauffement et d'irradiation UV** *m* CERAM VER bake and UV-irradiation test; ~ **d'écrasement** *m* ESSAIS crushing test; ~ **électrique** *m* ELECTROTEC, ESSAIS electrical test; ~ **d'emballage** m EMBALLAGE package test; ~ **d'emballement** m ELECTR *machine* overspeed test; ~ **d'emboutissage** m PRODUCTION stamping test; ~ **d'émulsion** m GENIE CHIM emulsion test; ~ **en blanc** m IMPRIM *impression, façonnage* blank test; ~ **d'endurance** m CONS MECA endurance test, ELECTROTEC life test, ESPACE, METROLOGIE, QUALITE endurance test, RESSORTS durability test, endurance test; ~ **d'endurance haute température** m ESSAIS high-temperature strength test; ~ **en environnement** m ESPACE environmental test, QUALITE environmental testing; ~ **en pratique** m POLLU MER field trial; ~ **en soufflerie** m ESPACE *véhicules*, ESSAIS wind tunnel test; ~ **d'entraînement** m CONSTR elutriation test; ~ **d'environnement** m MECANIQUE environmental testing; ~ **en vol** m AERONAUT, ESPACE flight test; ~ **en vol libre** m ESPACE free flight test; ~ **en vraie grandeur** m ESPACE field trial; ~ **d'épaisseur totale** m ESSAIS total thickness test; ~ **d'étalonnage** m AERONAUT calibration test; ~ **d'étanchéité** m CONSTR leak testing, EMBALLAGE leakage test, GAZ tightness test, NUCLEAIRE leak test; ~ **d'étanchéité à l'hélium** m NUCLEAIRE helium leak test; ~ **d'exposition** m CINEMAT exposure test;

■**f** ~ **à facteur de puissance nul** m ELECTR zero power factor test; ~ **à faisceau d'électrons** m PHYS RAYON electron beam test; ~ **de fatigue** m AERONAUT, METALL fatigue test; ~ **de fatigue sous charge axiale** m CONS MECA axial load fatigue testing; ~ **de fiabilité** m ELECTROTEC reliability test, reliability testing; ~ **filmé** m CINEMAT screen test; ~ **de fissibilité** m CONS MECA crack test; ~ **de fixité** m CINEMAT steadiness test; ~ **de flexion au choc** m CONS MECA blow bending test; ~ **de flexion rotative** m METALL rotating bending test; ~ **à la flexion sur éprouvette entaillée** m CONS MECA notch bending test; ~ **de fluage** m RESSORTS creep test; ~ **fonctionnel** m TELECOM functional test; ~ **de fonctionnement** m CONS MECA running test, ELECTR performance test, METROLOGIE, PRODUCTION operational test, QUALITE performance testing, TELECOM functional test; ~ **de fonctionnement hydraulique** m CONS MECA hydraulic performance test; ~ **de force d'arrachement** m ESSAIS peel strength test; ~ **de formation** m PETROLE DST, drill stem test, *géologie* formation test; ~ **de formation de boue** m ELECTR *huile de transformateur* sludge formation test; ~ **de freinage** m CONS MECA brake test, CONSTR brake testing; ~ **de fréquence** m PHYS RAYON frequency test; ~ **frigorifique** m REFRIG refrigeration test; ~ **de fusion** m THERMODYN melting test;

■**g** ~ **gammamétrique** m NUCLEAIRE gammametric ore assay;

■**h** ~ **d'homologation** m ESPACE, ESSAIS approval test, QUALITE approval test, approval testing; ~ **d'homologation de type** m AERONAUT *turbomachines* type test;

■**i** ~ **image** m CINEMAT test strip; ~ **à impulsion hydraulique** m CONS MECA *avec flexion* hydraulic impulse test; ~ **d'inclinaison** m NAUT inclining test; ~ **d'investigation** m ESPACE investigation test; ~ **isotherme** m METALL isothermal test;

■**j** ~ **Jominy** m MECANIQUE *matériaux* Jominy test;

■**l** ~ **Los Angeles** m CONSTR Los Angeles abrasion test;

■**m** ~ **Marshall** m CONSTR Marshall test; ~ **de Martens** m PLAST CAOU Martens test; ~ **des matériaux** m CONS MECA material testing; ~ **de la maturation** m EMBALLAGE ageing test (BrE), aging test (AmE); ~

mécanique m CONS MECA mechanical testing; ~ **à la mer** m NAUT sea trial; ~ **des minerais** m NUCLEAIRE ore assaying, ore testing; ~ **de mise en régime** m REFRIG pull down test; ~ **de mise en service** m TELECOM commissioning test; ~ **de mise à fin** m ESPACE firing test, test firing; ~ **de mise au point** m ESPACE development test; ~ **de moussage** m AERONAUT foaming test;

■**n** ~ **de netteté des syllabes** m TELECOM syllable articulation test; ~ **de niveau pour la voix** m ENREGISTR voice level test; ~ **de non-combustibilité** m SECURITE noncombustibility test; ~ **non destructif** m CONS MECA nondestructive test, ESPACE NDT, nondestructive testing, PHYSIQUE nondestructive test; ~ **nucléaire** m ESSAIS nuclear test, MILITAIRE atomic test, nuclear test;

■**o** ~ **de l'ouïe** m SECURITE hearing test; ~ **d'outillage** m CONS MECA tool trias;

■**p** ~ **par lots** m PRODUCTION batch test; ~ **par rupture** m CONS MECA fracture test; ~ **par voie humide** m CHIMIE wet assay; ~ **de pelage angulaire** m PLAST CAOU T-peel test, *pour adhésifs* angle peeling test; ~ **de pénétration** m CHARBON penetration test; ~ **de perforation** m ELECTR *appareil de haute tension* puncture test; ~ **pilote** m CHARBON pilot test, INFORMAT, ORDINAT beta test; ~ **de pliage** m EMBALLAGE folding test, IMPRIM *papier* bending test; ~ **de poinçonnement** m CONSTR CBR, California Bearing Ratio; ~ **au point fixe** m ESPACE static test; ~ **de pompage** m CHARBON, DISTRI EAU pumping test; ~ **de porosité à l'encre** m IMPRIM absorption ink test; ~ **au porter** m TEXTILE wearer trial; ~ **de pose** m CINEMAT exposure test; ~ **pour l'environnement** m QUALITE environmental testing; ~ **de précision** m CONS MECA accuracy test, test for accuracy; ~ **de pression** m PETROLE LOT, leak-off test, *du forage* leak-off test; ~ **Proctor** m CONSTR Proctor test; ~ **de production** m PETR production test; ~ **de programme** m INFORMAT, ORDINAT program testing; ~ **à puissance nulle** m NUCLEAIRE startup zero power test, zero power test;

■**q** ~ **de qualification** m ESPACE, NUCLEAIRE, QUALITE qualification test, TELECOM acceptance test; ~ **de qualification en fonctionnement** m NUCLEAIRE ongoing qualification test;

■**r** ~ **de rabattement** m PRODUCTION *des collerettes* flanging test; ~ **rapide** m ESSAIS accelerated testing; ~ **rapide de fatigue** m METALL rapid fatigue test; ~ **aux rayons X** m NUCLEAIRE X-ray inspection, X-ray testing; ~ **de réception** m CHARBON, ESPACE, ORDINAT, TELECOM acceptance test; ~ **de réception à chaud** m ESPACE acceptance firing test; ~ **de recette** m MECANIQUE *contrats* acceptance testing, NAUT acceptance test, acceptance trial, TELECOM acceptance test; ~ **de résilience** m METALL impact test, NUCLEAIRE notch impact test, PHYSIQUE impact test; ~ **de résilience Charpy** m MECANIQUE *matériaux* Charpy impact test; ~ **de résilience au mouton de Charpy** m METALL Charpy impact test; ~ **de résilience sur éprouvette entaillée** m MECANIQUE *matériaux* notched bar impact test; ~ **de résistance au cheminement** m ESSAIS creep resistance test; ~ **de résistance au choc** m MATERIAUX drop test; ~ **de résistance au frottement** m IMPRIM abrasion test; ~ **de ressuage** m MECANIQUE dye penetrant test; ~ **de rigidité diélectrique** m ELECTROTEC dielectric rigidity test; ~ **de roulis** m NAUT roll test; ~ **de rupture** m MECANIQUE *matériaux* breaking test;

■**s** ~ **de secousses** m EMBALLAGE jarring test; ~ **de sédimentation** m CONSTR sedimentation test; ~ **sélectif** *m* QUALITE screening test; **~ de sélection** *m* ESPACE, QUALITE screening test; **~ séquentiel** *m* TELECOM sequential test; **~ de seuil de décharge partielle** *m* ELECTR partial discharge inception test; **~ au sol** *m* AERONAUT, ESPACE ground test; **~ de soudabilité** *m* ESSAIS weldability test; **~ de souplesse à température inférieure à l'ambiante** *m* CONS MECA subambient temperature flexibility test; **~ sous amplitude variable** *m* METALL variable amplitude test; **~ sous pression** *m* INST HYDR pressure test; **~ sous tension de choc** *m* ELECTROTEC impulse test; **~ sous vide** *m* REFRIG vacuum test; **~ de stabilité** *m* NAUT inclining test; **~ statique** *m* ESPACE static test; **~ statique de charge** *m* CHARBON weight penetration test; **~ statistique** *m* ESSAIS statistical test; **~ subjectif** *m* TELECOM subjective test; **~ de surcharge** *m* ELECTR overload test, proof test; **~ sur modèle réduit** *m* NAUT model test; **~ sur produit** *m* QUALITE product test; **~ de surtension** *m* PRODUCTION overpressure test; **~ à surtension induite** *m* ELECTR *transformateur* induced overvoltage test; **~ sur le terrain** *m* POLLU MER field trial; **~ du système** *m* INFORMAT, ORDINAT system testing;

~ t **~ de tension de tenue** *m* ELECTR *installation* withstand voltage test; **~ aux tiges** *m* EN RENOUV, PETROLE drill stem test; **~ de torsion** *m* METALL torsion test; **~ à la torsion** *m* CONS MECA torsional test; **~ au touchau** *m* CONS MECA touch needle test; **~ de traçage** *m* CINEMAT pencil test; **~ de traction** *m* MATERIAUX, METALL, PHYSIQUE tensile test; **~ à la traction** *m* CONS MECA tensile test; **~ de traction longitudinale** *m* CONS MECA longitudinal traction test; **~ de traction par choc** *m* METALL tensile impact test; **~ de transmission** *m* TV test transmission; **~ de trempabilité** *m* MECANIQUE *matériaux* Jominy test; **~ triaxial** *m* CONSTR triaxial test; **~ tronqué** *m* ESPACE truncated test;

~ u **~ aux ultrasons** *m* COMMANDE, ESSAIS, MATERIAUX, NUCLEAIRE ultrasonic testing, RESSORTS ultrasonic inspection;

~ v **~ de vérification** *m* QUALITE verification testing; **~ de vibration** *m* AERONAUT, ESSAIS, METROLOGIE vibration test; **~ à vide** *m* ELECTR no-load test, PRODUCTION dry run; **~ de vieillissement accéléré** *m* PLAST CAOU accelerated ageing test (BrE), accelerated aging test (AmE); **~ de vieillissement accéléré aux intempéries** *m* PLAST CAOU accelerated weathering test

essaim: ~ d'ions *m* PHYS RAYON ion cluster; **~ de météore** *m* ASTRONOMIE meteor swarm

essayage *m* CHIMIE testing

essayé: ~ en premier *adj* TELECOM tested first

essayer[1] *vt* CHIMIE analyze, test, CONS MECA, ESSAIS, TELECOM test

essayer:[2] **~ au pliage et à la compression** *vi* CONS MECA test for bending and for compression

essayeur *m* CHIMIE analyst, assayer; **~ à haute tension** *m* ELECTR high-voltage tester

esse *f* AGRO ALIM meat hook, CONS MECA S-hook, S-shaped hook

essence *f* AUTO gasoline (AmE), petrol (BrE), BREVETS *de la solution* gist, CHIMIE spirit, PETROLE gas (AmE), gasoline (AmE), petrol (BrE), motor spirit, THERMODYN gasoline (AmE), petrol, VEHICULES *carburant* gas (AmE), gasoline (AmE), petrol (BrE); **~ aviation** *f* PETROLE aviation fuel; **~ de cannelle de Chine** *f* AGRO ALIM cassia oil; **~ de cardamome** *f* AGRO ALIM cardamom oil; **~ de citronelle** *f* AGRO ALIM citronella, citronella oil; **~ de dégasolinage** *f* PETROLE casing

head gasoline; **~ à faible teneur en plomb** *f* AUTO low lead gasoline (AmE), low lead petrol (BrE); **~ légère** *f* AUTO high-gravity gasoline (AmE), high-gravity petrol (BrE), light gasoline (AmE), light petrol (BrE); **~ lourde** *f* AUTO low gravity gasoline (AmE), low gravity petrol (BrE), low test gasoline (AmE), low test petrol (BrE); **~ de moutarde** *f* AGRO ALIM mustard oil; **~ ordinaire** *f* AUTO regular gas (AmE), regular petrol (BrE), regular gasoline (AmE), regular petrol (BrE), VEHICULES *carburant* regular gas (AmE), regular gasoline (AmE), regular petrol (BrE); **~ de pin** *f* LESSIVES pine oil; **~ sans plomb** *f* PETROLE, POLLUTION lead-free gasoline (AmE), lead-free petrol (BrE), unleaded gasoline (AmE), unleaded petrol (BrE), VEHICULES *carburant* unleaded gas (AmE), unleaded gasoline (AmE), unleaded petrol (BrE); **~ super** *f* AUTO four-star petrol; **~ synthétique** *f* AUTO synthetic gasoline; **~ de térébenthine** *f* CHIMIE spirit of turpentine; **~ de verveine** *f* CHIMIE verbena oil, vervein oil

essieu *m* CONSTR, VEHICULES axle; **~ arrière** *m* MECANIQUE *véhicules*, VEHICULES rear axle; **~ avant** *m* VEHICULES front axle; **~ balancier** *m* VEHICULES pivot axle; **~ brisé** *m* AUTO swing axle; **~ à chapes** *m* VEHICULES *roue* stub axle; **~ coudé** *m* VEHICULES dropped axle; **~ de direction** *m* VEHICULES steering axle; **~ en tandem** *m* VEHICULES tandem axle; **~ fixe** *m* CONS MECA dead axle; **~ flottant** *m* VEHICULES floating axle; **~ mobile** *m* CH DE FER adjustable axle; **~ moteur** *m* AUTO driving axle, VEHICULES driving axle, live axle; **~ porteur** *m* CONS MECA carrying axle; **~ porteur d'avant** *m* CH DE FER *véhicules* carrying axle, idler; **~ rigide** *m* AUTO, VEHICULES rigid axle; **~ surbaissé** *m* VEHICULES dropped axle; **~ tournant** *m* CONS MECA live axle; **~ traîné** *m* VEHICULES trailing axle

essonite *f* MINERAUX essonite, hessonite

essorage *m* GENIE CHIM centrifugation; **~ de la mousse** *m* GENIE CHIM foam drainage; **~ par pression** *m* PAPIER squeezing; **~ par torsion** *m* PAPIER wringing

essorer *vt* CHIMIE *un liquide* drain, PAPIER squeeze, wring, PHOTO squeegee, POLLU MER, TEXTILE wring; **~ à la machine centrifuge** *vt* GENIE CHIM centrifuge

essoreuse *f* CINEMAT squeegee, PLAST CAOU centrifuge, POLLUTION wringer; **~ centrifuge** *f* CHARBON centrifugal dryer; **~ par succion** *f* CINEMAT air squeegee; **~ à rouleaux** *f* TEXTILE hydroextractor, roll wringer; **~ séparatrice** *f* GENIE CHIM centrifugal, centrifugal separator; **~ à tambour** *f* TEXTILE hydroextractor

essuie-glace *m* VEHICULES windscreen wiper (BrE), windshield wiper (AmE), wiper

essuyage *m* IMPRIM wiping; **~ inversé** *m* IMPRIM reverse wipe

essuyer: ~ un grain *vi* NAUT weather a squall

est: d'~ *adj* NAUT *vent* easterly; **de l'~** *adj* NAUT east

estacade *f* CH DE FER elevated track, CONSTR elevated runway, INST HYDR stockade; **~ flottante** *f* NAUT *l'entrée du port* boom

estampage *m* IMPRIM blind blocking, stamping, *finition, façonnage* blind embossing, MECANIQUE die-stamping, PRODUCTION drop forging, stamping, swaging; **~ à chaud** *m* EMBALLAGE hot pressing, IMPRIM *finition* hot-stamping; **~ à pression** *m* PLAST CAOU pressure forming

estampé: ~ à chaud *adj* IMPRIM *façonnage* hot-stamped

estamper *vt* PRODUCTION drop-forge, stamp

estampeur *m* PRODUCTION stamper

estampeuse *f* EMBALLAGE embossing press, PRODUC-

TION stamp, stamping machine, stamping press
estampillage *m* GAZ type approval
estarie *f* PETROLE *commerce, transport maritime* lay day
estau *m* MINES arch, support pillar
ester *m* CHIMIE, LESSIVES ester; ~ **adipique** *m* PLAST CAOU adipic ester; ~ **maléique** *m* LESSIVES maleic ester; ~ **méthylique** *m* LESSIVES methyl ester; ~ **phosphorique** *m* LESSIVES phosphate ester
estérification *f* AGRO ALIM esterification
estérifier *vt* CHIMIE esterify
estibois *m* CONS MECA vice cap (BrE), vise cap (AmE)
estimateur *m* MATH estimator
estimation *f* CONS MECA assessment, MATH estimation, QUALITE assessment; ~ **du nombre de mots dans un texte** *f* IMPRIM wordage; ~ **de l'ordre de grandeur de l'erreur** *f* MATH error estimation; ~ **prudente** *f* PRODUCTION conservative estimate; ~ **du risque** *f* QUALITE risk assessment; ~ **du temps d'exécution** *f* PRODUCTION *automatisme industriel* approximate execution time
estime *f* OCEANO dead reckoning
estimer *vt* QUALITE assess
estomac *m* CONS MECA sheave, *d'excentrique* disc (BrE), disk (AmE), MINES *d'une bobine pour câble plat d'extraction* hub, PRODUCTION conscience; ~ **d'excentrique** *m* CONS MECA eccentric disc (BrE), eccentric disk (AmE), eccentric sheave
estompage: ~ **de ligne** *m* TV line diffusion
estouffée *f* MINES *dans une galerie de mine* dam
estran *m* GEOLOGIE foreshore, OCEANO foreshore, strand, POLLU MER intertidal zone
estrope *f* CONS MECA strop, CONSTR strap
estuaire *m* EN RENOUV, HYDROLOGIE, NAUT estuary
estuarien *adj* GEOLOGIE estuarine
établi *m* CONSTR bench; ~ **de charpentier** *m* CONSTR carpenters' bench; ~ **de menuisier** *m* CONSTR joiner's bench; ~ **d'outillage** *m* PRODUCTION workbench unit; ~ **roulant pour étaux** *m* CONSTR portable vice bench (BrE), portable vice stand (BrE), portable vise bench (AmE), portable vise stand (AmE), PRODUCTION vice bench (BrE), vise bench (AmE); ~ **à scier** *m* CONSTR saw bench
établir[1] *vt* CONSTR construct, INFORMAT, ORDINAT, TELECOM *une communication* set up
établir:[2] ~ **une canalisation dans** *vi* CONSTR pipe; ~ **une liaison** *vi* INFORMAT connect; ~ **les voiles** *vi* NAUT trim
établissement *m* BREVETS *d'un rapport* drawing up, CONSTR laying; ~ **d'attache** *m* CH DE FER home depot; ~ **de communication** *m* INFORMAT, ORDINAT handshaking; ~ **des communications** *m* TELECOM call setup; ~ **de connexion** *m* INFORMAT, ORDINAT handshake; ~ **d'une connexion sans émission** *m* TELECOM off-air call setup; ~ **de liaison** *m* INFORMAT, ORDINAT handshake, handshaking; ~ **d'une liaison entre satellites** *m* ESPACE *communications* intersatellite link acquisition; ~ **d'une machine** *m* CONS MECA setting up; ~ **d'organigramme** *m* INFORMAT flowcharting; ~ **de la pression** *m* AERONAUT pressure build-up
établissement-coupure *m* ELECTROTEC make-and-break
étage *m* CONS MECA *d'un cône, d'un cône-poulie* lift, CONSTR floor, GEOLOGIE stage, MINES deck, level, lift, *niveau* stage; ~ **amplificateur** *m* ELECTRON amplifier stage; ~ **d'amplification** *m* ENREGISTR amplifying stage; ~ **d'attaque du modulateur** *m* ELECTRON modulator driver; ~ **de brassage** *m* TELECOM distribution stage; ~ **changeur de fréquence** *m* ELECTRON mixer

stage; ~ **de commande** *m* AERONAUT control stage; ~ **de commutation** *m* TELECOM switching stage; ~ **de commutation distante** *m* TELECOM remote switching stage; ~ **de compression** *m* CONS MECA compression stage; ~ **de concentration** *m* TELECOM concentration stage; ~ **des crêtes** *m* OCEANO crest province; ~ **cryotechnique** *m* ESPACE *propulsion* cryogenic stage; ~ **destiné à échapper à l'attraction terrestre** *m* ESPACE *propulsion* Earth escape stage; ~ **d'entrée** *m* ELECTRON input stage; ~ **d'excitation** *m* ESPACE *communications* driver stage; ~ **exciteur** *m* AUTO driver stage; ~ **d'expansion** . *m* TELECOM expansion stage; ~ **FI** *m* ELECTRON, TELECOM IF stage; ~ **du fond** *m* MINES bottom level; ~ **à fréquence intermédiaire** *m* ELECTRON, TELECOM intermediate frequency stage; ~ **haute fréquence** *m* ELECTRON RF stage; ~ **HF** *m* ELECTRON RF stage; ~ **houiller** *m* MINES coal measures, coal-bearing rock; ~ **d'impulsion** *m* ESPACE kick stage; ~ **incite** *m* ESPACE dummy stage; ~ **de libération** *m* ESPACE *propulsion* escape rocket stage; ~ **mélangeur** *m* ELECTRON mixer stage; ~ **modulateur** *m* TV modulator; ~ **de montée** *m* ESPACE *propulsion* ascent stage; ~ **orbital** *m* ESPACE orbiter stage; ~ **de périgée** *m* ESPACE perigee stage; ~ **de pression** *m* INST HYDR *d'une turbine* pressure stage; ~ **S** *m* TELECOM S-stage; ~ **de sélection** *m* TELECOM selection stage; ~ **de sortie de la base de temps trames** *m* ELECTRON vertical output stage; ~ **de sortie sans transformateur** *m* ENREGISTR transformerless output stage; ~ **de sortie trames** *m* ELECTRON vertical output stage; ~ **spatial** *m* TELECOM S-stage, space stage; ~ **supérieur** *m* ESPACE upper stage; ~ **supérieur inertiel** *m* ESPACE *propulsion* IUS, Inertial Upper Stage; ~ **supérieur stabilisé par rotation** *m* ESPACE *véhicules* SSUS, solid spinning upper stage; ~ **T** *m* TELECOM T-stage; ~ **temporel** *m* TELECOM T-stage, time stage; ~ **terminal** *m* TELECOM terminating stage; ~ **de transfert** *m* ESPACE transfer stage
étagé *adj* MATERIAUX staged
étagement *m* RESSORTS stepping
étagère *f* EQUIP LAB *meuble* shelf; ~ **à câbles** *f* ELECTROTEC cable rack
étages: **à ~** *adj* CONS MECA stepped, EMBALLAGE *palette* double-decked
étagiste *m* ESPACE stage integrator
étai *m* CHARBON brace, prop, strut, CONSTR prop, shore, stay, support, MINES post, prop, shore, tree, NAUT stay; ~ **arrière** *m* NAUT aft stay; ~ **avant** *m* NAUT forestay; ~ **de grand mât** *m* NAUT mainstay; ~ **de guignol** *m* NAUT jumper stay; ~ **incliné** *m* CONSTR raker, raking shore; ~ **de mine** *m* MINES pit prop; ~ **vertical** *m* CONSTR vertical shore
étaiement *m* CHARBON shoring up, CONSTR shoring
étain *m* *(Sn)* CHIMIE tin *(Sn)*; ~ **de bois** *m* MINERAUX wood tin; ~ **en saumon** *m* PRODUCTION block tin; ~ **oxydé** *m* MINERAUX tin stone; ~ **de roche** *m* MINES lode tin, mine tin
étais *m pl* CONSTR shoring
étalage *m* EMBALLAGE display; ~ **au point de vente** *m* EMBALLAGE point of sale display
étale *m* OCEANO slack tide, stand of tide, tidal stand; ~ **de courant** *m* OCEANO dead tide, slack tide, slack water; ~ **du flot** *m* NAUT slack water; ~ **de marée** *m* NAUT stand of tide
étalement *m* ESPACE, INFORMAT spread, PLAST CAOU *mélange* extender, POLLU MER spreading, REFRIG spread; ~ **de bande** *m* PHYS RAYON bandspread; ~

d'impulsion *m* OPTIQUE pulse broadening, pulse dispersion, TELECOM pulse broadening, pulse dispersion, pulse spreading; ~ **des noirs** *m* TV black stretch

étaler[1] *vt* DISTRI EAU *un jet d'eau* spread

étaler:[2] ~ **une tempête** *vi* NAUT weather a storm

étaler:[3] **s'~** *v réfl* POLLU MER spread

étalinguer *vt* NAUT bend, clinch

étalingure *f* NAUT anchor cable attachment, cable clinch

étalon[1] *adj* CONS MECA, PHYSIQUE standard

étalon[2] *m* CONS MECA standard, METROLOGIE *pour comparaison avec d'autres instruments de mesure* measurement standard, PETR caliber (AmE), calibre (BrE), PHYSIQUE etalon, standard, RESSORTS duplicate standard, TEXTILE yardstick; ~ **de fréquence** *m* ELECTRON frequency standard; ~ **de fréquence atomique** *m* NUCLEAIRE atomic beam frequency standard; ~ **industriel** *m* PRODUCTION commercial standard; ~ **primaire** *m* PHYSIQUE primary standard; ~ **radioactif** *m* PHYS RAYON radioactive standard; ~ **de rayonnement à large surface** *m* NUCLEAIRE large area radiation standard; ~ **de référence** *m* METROLOGIE reference standard; ~ **de réglage** *m* CONS MECA setting master; ~ **secondaire** *m* PHYSIQUE secondary standard; ~ **de travail** *m* PHYSIQUE working standard

étalonnage *m* CINEMAT grading, timing, CONS MECA, ELECTR, ELECTRON, ENREGISTR, EQUIP LAB *instrument, verrerie,* ESPACE, MATERIAUX, METROLOGIE, NUCLEAIRE, ORDINAT, PAPIER, PETROLE *métrologie, forage* calibration, PHYSIQUE standardization, PRODUCTION *automatisme industriel* scaling, *thermocouple* calibration; ~ **couleur** *m* CINEMAT color matching (AmE), colour matching (BrE); ~ **couleur plan par plan** *m* CINEMAT scene-to-scene color grading (AmE), scene-to-scene colour grading (BrE); ~ **des couleurs** *m* COULEURS color gradation (AmE), colour gradation (BrE); ~ **dynamique** *m* CONS MECA dynamic force calibration; ~ **de générateurs de signaux** *m* ELECTRON signal generator calibration; ~ **géométrique** *m* TV geometric calibration; ~ **de modèle** *m* POLLUTION model calibration; ~ **de la vitesse de son** *m* EN RENOUV acoustic velocity log

étalonnement *m* PHYS RAYON calibration

étalonner *vt* CINEMAT grade, time, CONS MECA caliper gage (AmE), calliper gauge (BrE), PHYSIQUE calibrate

étalonneur *m* CINEMAT grader, timer, print grader; ~ **couleur** *m* CINEMAT color timer (AmE), colour timer (BrE)

étamage *m* CERAM VER, CONSTR, ELECTR *conducteur d'un câble* tinning

étambot *m* NAUT rudder post, stern post

étamé *adj* CHIMIE tinned; ~ **par électrolyse** *adj* REVETEMENT electroplated with tin

étampage *m* PRODUCTION stamping, swaging

étampe *f* PRODUCTION swage; ~ **de dessous** *f* PRODUCTION bottom swage; ~ **de dessus** *f* CONS MECA top rounding-tool, top swage; ~ **de dessus pour fers ronds** *f* CONS MECA top swage

étamper *vt* PRODUCTION drop-forge, stamp

étampeur *m* PRODUCTION stamper

étampeuse *f* PRODUCTION stamp, stamping machine, stamping press; ~ **à main** *f* PRODUCTION hand stamp

étanche *adj* CONSTR impermeable, impervious, DISTRI EAU impermeable, EMBALLAGE impervious, GAZ, GEOLOGIE impermeable, HYDROLOGIE impermeable, impervious, MATERIAUX, PAPIER impervious, PETR impermeable, impervious, PRODUCTION gas tight, staunch, REFRIG leak-free; ~ **à l'air** *adj* CONS MECA, MECANIQUE, NAUT, PETROLE, PHYSIQUE airtight; ~ **à l'eau** *adj* CHAUFFAGE, CONSTR, EMBALLAGE, NAUT, PHYSIQUE, TEXTILE watertight; ~ **aux fuites** *adj* MECANIQUE leak-tight; ~ **au gaz** *adj* CONS MECA gas-proof, MECANIQUE gastight, THERMODYN gas-proof, gastight; ~ **à la graisse** *adj* EMBALLAGE greaseproof; ~ **à l'huile** *adj* PRODUCTION oiltight; ~ **à la lumière** *adj* CINEMAT light-tight, EMBALLAGE lightproof; ~ **aux poussières** *adj* ELECTR *matériel* dustproof, EMBALLAGE dust-tight, dustproof; ~ **à la vapeur** *adj* CHAUFFAGE, INST HYDR steamtight; ~ **aux vapeurs** *adj* SECURITE vapor-proof (AmE), vapour-proof (BrE)

étanchéisation *f* CONSTR waterproofing

étanchéité *f* CH DE FER *véhicules* sealing, tightness, CONS MECA *d'un joint* tightness, GAZ leakage, PETROLE seal, sealing, PRODUCTION staunchness, *d'un joint* imperviousness; ~ **à l'eau** *f* CONSTR watertightness; ~ **aux fuites** *f* NUCLEAIRE leak tightness; ~ **limitée** *f* CONS MECA *tuyauterie* limited tightness

étanchement: ~ **avec laque** *m* EMBALLAGE lacquer sealing

étancher *vt* DISTRI EAU *une voie d'eau* stop, PRODUCTION stop, stop up

étançon *m* CONSTR prop, shore, shoring, stanchion, EMBALLAGE *partie d'un conteneur* strut; ~ **hydraulique** *m* MINES hydraulic prop; ~ **hydraulique simple** *m* MINES pack system

étançonnement *m* CONSTR propping, shoring

étang: ~ **à boues** *m* CERAM VER grader waste pond (AmE), silt field (BrE); ~ **de décantation** *m* CONSTR settling pit; ~ **d'oxydation** *m* DISTRI EAU oxidation ponds; ~ **de refroidissement** *m* DISTRI EAU cooling pond

étape *f* INFORMAT step, MECANIQUE *d'un projet* milestone, ORDINAT step, PRODUCTION stage, step; ~ **de découpe** *f* ELECTRON scribing step; ~ **de travail** *f* INFORMAT, ORDINAT job step

état:[1] **à l'~ libre** *adj* CHIMIE free; **à l'~ natif** *adj* MINERAUX native; **en ~ de navigabilité** *adj* AERONAUT airworthy, NAUT seaworthy; **en ~ de prendre la mer** *adj* NAUT in navigable condition; **à l'~ brut** *adj* PRODUCTION in its crude state, untreated; **à l'~ de repos** *adj* ELECTROTEC, ORDINAT, INFORMAT quiescent

état[2] *m* INFORMAT report, state, status, NAUT *du temps* state, ORDINAT report, state, status, TELECOM status data; ~ **activé** *m* METALL activated state; ~ **actuel de la technique** *m* TELECOM current state of the art; ~ **atmosphérique** *m* MATERIAUX atmospheric conditions; ~ **atomique** *m* NUCLEAIRE *énergétique d'un atome* atomic state; ~ **d'attente** *m* INFORMAT, ORDINAT wait state; ~ **d'avancement** *m* PRODUCTION progress; ~ **des batteries** *m* TELECOM battery condition; ~ **bloqué** *m* ELECTRON blocking state, ELECTROTEC off state; ~ **composé** *m* NUCLEAIRE compound state; ~ **conducteur** *m* ELECTRON conducting state, ELECTROTEC on state; ~ **de conduction** *m* ELECTROTEC on state; ~ **des connaissances et des techniques** *m* PRODUCTION state of the art; ~ **contractant** *m* BREVETS contracting state; ~ **de contrainte triaxial** *m* METALL triaxial state of stress; ~ **contrôlé** *m* MATERIAUX controlled conditions; ~ **cristallin** *m* MATERIAUX crystal state; ~ **débloqué** *m* ELECTROTEC on state; ~ **dépressurisé** *m* PRODUCTION *système hydraulique* depressurized condition; ~ **désordonné** *m* MATERIAUX disordered state; ~ **de disponibilité** *m* TELECOM idle state; ~ **des E/S physiques** *m*

PRODUCTION *automatisme industriel* I/O device status; ~ **écrit** m ELECTRON written state; ~ **écroui** m RESSORTS work hardened state; ~ **d'équilibre** m TELECOM steady-state, THERMODYN state of equilibrium; ~ **estimatif** m PRODUCTION estimate; ~ **excité** m CHIMIE *d'un atome*, METALL, PHYSIQUE excited state; ~ **de fonctionnement** m METROLOGIE *d'une machine* operating condition; ~ **fondamental** m PHYS PART *de l'atome*, PHYSIQUE ground state; ~ **gazeux** m GAZ gaseous state; ~ **haut** m ELECTRON ONE state; ~ **à haute fréquence** m ELECTROTEC high impedance state; ~ **hydrométrique** m METEO hydrometric state; ~ **hygrométrique** m HYDROLOGIE hydrometric state; ~ **initial** m INFORMAT, ORDINAT initial state; ~ **instable** m COMMANDE unstable state; ~ **intermédiaire** m NUCLEAIRE compound state, PRODUCTION buffer stage; ~ **ionisé** m PHYS PART ionized state; ~ **K** m NUCLEAIRE K-state; ~ **logique** m ELECTRON logic state; ~ **de la machine** m CONS MECA machine status; ~ **de la mer** m NAUT sea state; ~ **métastable** m METALL, PHYSIQUE metastable state; ~ **microscopique** m PHYS RAYON microscopic state; ~ **de navigabilité** m NAUT seaworthiness; ~ **neutre** m PHYS PART neutral state; ~ **non conducteur** m ELECTROTEC off state; ~ **non passant** m ELECTROTEC off state; ~ **normal d'énergie** m CHIMIE *d'un atome* ground state; ~ **d'occupation** m TELECOM busy state, busy status; ~ **passant** m ELECTROTEC on state; ~ **permanent** m COMMANDE steady state; ~ **de préusinage** m CONS MECA premachined condition; ~ **de processus** m INFORMAT, ORDINAT process state; ~ **quantique** m ESPACE, PHYS PART quantum state; ~ **de raccrochage** m TELECOM on-hook condition; ~ **récapitulatif** m PRODUCTION summary report; ~ **réel** m NUCLEAIRE actual state; ~ **de repos** m PHYSIQUE state of rest, PRODUCTION *système hydraulique* de-energized position; ~ **de réservoir** m PETR reservoir conditions; ~ **séparateur** m PRODUCTION buffer stage; ~ **solide** m ELECTR, ELECTRON, INFORMAT, PHYS PART, PHYS RAYON solid state; ~ **de sortie à la saturation** m ELECTRON saturation output state; ~ **stable** m COMMANDE stable state; ~ **stationnaire** m ELECTR steady-state, PHYS RAYON, PHYSIQUE, THERMODYN stationary state; ~ **de surface** m CONS MECA *de produit* surface texture, PAPIER surface finish; ~ **de la technique** m BREVETS prior art, state of the art; ~ **de la technique antérieure** m BREVETS background art; ~ **UN** m ELECTRON ONE state; ~ **1-0** m PRODUCTION *automatisme industriel* set versus reset; ~ **de valence** m NUCLEAIRE valence state; ~ **de vapeur** m GENIE CHIM vapor state (AmE), vapour state (BrE); ~ **vitreux** m CERAM VER glassy state, vitreous state; ~ **zéro** m MECANIQUE baseline inspection

état:[3] **en ~ de fonctionner** *loc* CONS MECA in working order

étau m CONS MECA, MECANIQUE *outillage* vice (BrE), vise (AmE); ~ **à agrafes** m CONS MECA vice with clamp (BrE), vise with clamp (AmE); ~ **à agrafes d'établi** m CONS MECA table vice with clamp (BrE), table vise with clamp (AmE), CONSTR bench vice with clamp (BrE), bench vise with clamp (AmE); ~ **à barres parallèles** m CONS MECA vice sliding between parallel bars (BrE), vise sliding between parallel bars (AmE); ~ **à base tournante** m CONS MECA swivel vice (BrE), swivel vise (AmE); ~ **à base tournante pour établis à serrage instantané** m CONS MECA sudden-grip rotary bench vice (BrE), sudden-grip rotary bench vise (AmE); ~ **à chaîne** m CONS MECA chain vice (BrE), chain vise

(AmE); ~ **à enclumette** m CONS MECA anvil vice (BrE), anvil vise (AmE); ~ **à griffes** m CONS MECA vice with clamp (BrE), vise with clamp (AmE); ~ **à griffes pour établi** m CONS MECA table vice with clamp (BrE), table vise with clamp (AmE), CONSTR bench vice with clamp (BrE), bench vise with clamp (AmE); ~ **à mâchoires rapportées** m CONS MECA vice with detachable jaws (BrE), vice with inserted jaws (BrE), vise with detachable jaws (AmE), vise with inserted jaws (AmE); ~ **à main** m CONS MECA hand vice (BrE), tail vice (BrE), tail vise (AmE), CONSTR pin vice (BrE), pin vise (AmE), MECANIQUE *outillage* hand vice (BrE), hand vise (AmE); ~ **parallèle** m CONS MECA parallel vice (BrE), parallel vise (AmE); ~ **à pied** m PRODUCTION leg vice (BrE), leg vise (AmE), staple vice (BrE), staple vise (AmE); ~ **à pied roulant** m CONSTR portable vice stand with leg vice (BrE), portable vise stand with leg vise (AmE); ~ **pour aléseuse-pointeuse** m CONS MECA jig-boring vice (BrE), jig-boring vise (AmE); ~ **à queue** m CONS MECA tail vice (BrE), tail vise (AmE), CONSTR pin vice (BrE), pin vise (AmE); ~ **roulant** m CONSTR portable vice bench (BrE), portable vice stand (BrE), portable vice bench (AmE), portable vise stand (AmE), PRODUCTION vice bench (BrE), vise bench (AmE); ~ **à serrage concentrique** m CONS MECA self-centering vice (AmE), self-centring vice (BrE); ~ **à table** m PRODUCTION standing vice (BrE), standing vise (AmE); ~ **tournant** m CONS MECA swivel vice (BrE), swivel vise (AmE); ~ **à tubes** m CONS MECA tube vice (BrE), tube vise (AmE), CONSTR pipe vice (BrE), pipe vise (AmE); ~ **de tuyauteur** m CONSTR pipe vice (BrE), pipe vise (AmE); ~ **à vis** m CONS MECA hand vice (BrE); ~ **à vis cachée** m CONS MECA vice with protected screw (BrE), vise with protected screw (AmE)

étau-limeur m CONS MECA shaping machine, shaping planer, MECANIQUE shaper; ~ **à commande par bielle** m CONS MECA crank shaping machine; ~ **double** m CONS MECA double-headed shaping machine; ~ **d'établi** m CONS MECA bench-type shaping machine; ~ **à outil mobile** m CONS MECA traverse shaper, traversing-head shaping machine

étau-plateau m CONS MECA combined parallel vice (BrE), combined parallel vise (AmE), vice plate (BrE), vise plate (AmE)

étau-tiroir m CONS MECA machine vice (BrE), machine vise (AmE), sliding parallel vice (BrE), sliding parallel vise (AmE)

étayage m CONSTR buttressing, propping, shoring

étayé *adj* PRODUCTION supported

étayement m CONSTR propping, shoring

étayer *vt* CHARBON shore up

ETCD *abrév* (*équipement terminal de circuit de données*) TELECOM DCE (*data circuit terminal equipment*)

ETD *abrév* (*équipement terminal de données*) AERONAUT, ORDINAT, TELECOM DTE (*data terminal equipment*)

éteindre[1] *vt* CHIMIE quench, CINEMAT kill, turn off, ELECTROTEC turn off, SECURITE *incendie* put out, THERMODYN quench, smother, TV switch off

éteindre:[2] **~ de la chaux** *vi* CHIMIE slake

éteindre:[3] **s'~** *v réfl* ELECTROTEC go out

étendage m CERAM VER *cylindre* flattening

étenderie: ~ **à rouleaux** f CERAM VER annealing lehr with rollers

étendre *vt* INFORMAT unpack, ORDINAT extend, unpack

étendue f BREVETS *de la protection* extent, scope, CONSTR area, MINES *des dégâts* extent; ~ **d'échelle** *f* METRO-LOGIE scale range; ~ **de fréquence** *f* ENREGISTR frequency range; ~ **de mesure** *f* INSTRUMENT instrument range; ~ **à mi-crête** *f* OPTIQUE FWHM, full-width half-maximum, TELECOM full-width half-maximum; ~ **de prises** *f* ELECTR tapping range; ~ **de sensibilité auditive** *f* ENREGISTR range of audibility; ~ **superficielle** *f* CONSTR area; ~ **de volume** *f* ENREGISTR volume range

éthal *m* CHIMIE ethal

éthanal *m* CHIMIE ethanal

éthane *m* CHIMIE, PETROLE ethane

éthanethiol *m* CHIMIE ethanethiol

éthanol *m* AGRO ALIM, CHIMIE, PETROLE ethanol

éthanolamine *f* CHIMIE, LESSIVES ethanolamine

éthanolyse *f* CHIMIE ethanolysis

éthène *m* CHIMIE, PETROLE ethene

éther *m* CHIMIE ether; ~ **allylglycidique** *m* PLAST CAOU *résine époxyde* AGE, allyl glycidyl ether; ~ **butylique** *m* AGRO ALIM butyl ether; ~ **diéthylique** *m* LESSIVES diethyl ether; ~ **glycidique** *m* PLAST CAOU *résine époxyde* diglycidyl ether; ~ **méthyltributylique** *m* PETROLE methyl tertiary-butyl ether; ~ **de pétrole** *m* REVETEMENT varnish maker's naphtha

éthéré *adj* CHIMIE ethereal

éthionique *adj* CHIMIE *acide* ethionic

éthogène *m* CHIMIE aethogen

éthoxylation *f* LESSIVES ethoxylation

éthylamine *f* CHIMIE ethylamine

éthylaniline *f* CHIMIE ethylaniline

éthylate *m* CHIMIE ethylate

éthylation *f* CHIMIE ethylation

éthylcellulose *f* PLAST CAOU ethyl cellulose

éthyle *m* PETROLE ethyl

éthylène *m* AGRO ALIM, CHIMIE, GAZ, LESSIVES, PETROLE, PLAST CAOU *matière première* ethylene; ~ **glycol** *m* LESSIVES ethylene glycol, glycol ether

éthylène-acétate: ~ **de vinyle** *m* PLAST CAOU *type de polymère* EVA, ethylene vinyl acetate

éthylénique *adj* CHIMIE ethylenic

éthyler *vt* CHIMIE ethylate

éthylidène *m* CHIMIE ethylidene

éthylique *adj* CHIMIE ethylic

éthylmorphine *f* CHIMIE ethylmorphine

éthylsulfurique *adj* CHIMIE ethylsulfuric (AmE), ethylsulphuric (BrE)

éthylthioéthanol *m* PETROLE ethylthioethanol

éthyluréthanne *m* CHIMIE ethylurethane

éthyl-vanilline *f* AGRO ALIM ethyl vanillin

éthyne *m* CHIMIE ethyne

étiage *m* DISTRI EAU minimum low water, HYDROLOGIE low water, low-water mark, period of lowest flow

étier *m* OCEANO tidal creek

étinceleur *m* GEOPHYS sparker

étincelle *f* AUTO, ELECTR, ELECTROTEC, PHYSIQUE, PRODUCTION spark; ~ **d'amorçage** *f* ELECTROTEC initiating spark; ~ **électrique** *f* ELECTR electric spark

étincellement *m* PRODUCTION sparkling

étincelles: ~ **volantes** *f pl* SECURITE flying sparks

étiquetage *m* EMBALLAGE, INFORMAT, ORDINAT, PHYS RAYON, TEXTILE labeling (AmE), labelling (BrE); ~ **avec vignette attachée** *m* TEXTILE tagging; ~ **à chaud** *m* IMPRIM *emballage* heat-set labeling (AmE), heat-set labelling (BrE); ~ **d'entretien** *m* TEXTILE care labeling (AmE), care labelling (BrE); ~ **par air soufflé** *m* EMBALLAGE air blast labeling (AmE), air blast labelling

(BrE); ~ **par jet d'air** *m* EMBALLAGE air jet labeling (AmE), air jet labelling (BrE); ~ **textile** *m* TEXTILE textile labeling (AmE), textile labelling (BrE)

étiqueter *vt* INFORMAT, ORDINAT label, tag, PRODUCTION tag, TEXTILE label, tag

étiqueteur *m* PRODUCTION label stamper

étiqueteuse *f* EMBALLAGE labeling machine (AmE), labelling machine (BrE); ~ **autocollante** *f* EMBALLAGE pressure-sensitive labeler (AmE), pressure-sensitive labeller (BrE); ~ **autocollante entièrement automatique** *f* EMBALLAGE fully-automatic self-adhesive labeling machine (AmE), fully-automatic self-adhesive labelling machine (BrE); ~ **intelligente** *f* EMBALLAGE intelligent labeling machine (AmE), intelligent labelling machine (BrE); ~ **manuelle** *f* EMBALLAGE hand labeler (AmE), hand labeller (BrE); ~ **pour le devant de l'emballage** *f* EMBALLAGE front of pack labeler (AmE), front of pack labeller (BrE); ~ **semiautomatique** *f* EMBALLAGE semiautomatic labeling machine (AmE), semiautomatic labelling machine (BrE)

étiquette *f* EMBALLAGE label, IMPRIM *façonnage* tag, INFORMAT, ORDINAT label, tag, PRODUCTION docket, TEXTILE label, tag; ~ **activable à chaleur** *f* EMBALLAGE heat-activated label; ~ **autocollante** *f* EMBALLAGE self-adhesive label; ~ **autocollante facile à peler** *f* EMBALLAGE easy peel off self-adhesive label; ~ **avec prix** *f* EMBALLAGE price tag; ~ **d'avertissement** *f* EMBALLAGE caution label; ~ **de bande** *f* INFORMAT, ORDINAT tape label; ~ **d'un champ** *f* INFORMAT, ORDINAT field label; ~ **de contrôle** *f* EMBALLAGE control tag; ~ **cousue sur le vêtement** *f* TEXTILE sewn-in label; ~ **décalquée à chaud** *f* EMBALLAGE hot transfer label; ~ **à encoller** *f* EMBALLAGE wet glue label; ~ **en polyprène étiré** *f* EMBALLAGE orientated polypropylene label; ~ **en relief** *f* EMBALLAGE embossed label; ~ **d'en-tête** *f* INFORMAT, ORDINAT header label; ~ **enveloppante** *f* EMBALLAGE wraparound label; ~ **de fichier** *f* INFORMAT, ORDINAT file label; ~ **film** *f* EMBALLAGE label film; ~ **gommée** *f* EMBALLAGE gummed label; ~ **imprimée par transfert thermique** *f* EMBALLAGE heat transfer label; ~ **d'instruction** *f* ORDINAT statement label; ~ **moulée en polystyrène** *f* EMBALLAGE polystyrene injection in-mold label (AmE), polystyrene injection in-mould label (BrE); ~ **d'opérateur** *f* INFORMAT statement label; ~ **pour l'adresse** *f* EMBALLAGE address label; ~ **pour le renvoi** *f* EMBALLAGE return label; ~ **préimprimée** *f* EMBALLAGE preprinted label; ~ **de qualité** *f* EMBALLAGE quality label; ~ **de repérage** *f* EMBALLAGE marking label; ~ **de sécurité** *f* TELECOM security label; ~ **sur panneau** *f* CONS MECA placard; ~ **thermocollante** *f* EMBALLAGE heat seal label; ~ **au verso** *f* EMBALLAGE back label; ~ **verte** *f* TELECOM application appliance label; ~ **vierge** *f* EMBALLAGE blank ticket; ~ **vitrifiée** *f* CERAM VER vitreous enamel label; ~ **volante** *f* EMBALLAGE hangtag, swing ticket (BrE); ~ **de volume** *f* INFORMAT, ORDINAT volume label

étiquette-bande *f* EMBALLAGE band label

étirage *m* CHIMIE stretching, PAPIER pull, stretching, PRODUCTION drawing, wire drawing, TEXTILE drafting, drawing; ~ **centrifuge** *m* CERAM VER centrifugal drawing; ~ **à chaud** *m* THERMODYN hot drawing; ~ **continu** *m* CERAM VER continuous drawing process; ~ **à froid** *m* MECANIQUE cold drawing; ~ **mécanique en cylindres** *m* CERAM VER cylinder-drawing process; ~ **par la flamme** *m* CERAM VER flame attenuation; ~ **par**

soufflage *m* CERAM VER steam blowing

étiré *adj* CERAM VER *verre*, PRODUCTION *tube* drawn; ~ **à chaud** *adj* THERMODYN hot-drawn; ~ **à froid** *adj* THERMODYN cold-drawn

étirement *m* CHIMIE stretching

étirer[1] *vt* PAPIER pull, stretch, PRODUCTION draw, TEXTILE draft, draw

étirer:[2] ~ **à chaud** *vi* THERMODYN hot draw; ~ **à froid** *vi* THERMODYN cold draw

étireur *m* CERAM VER drawing machine, PRODUCTION draw bench, drawing bench, wiredrawing bench

étoffe *f* ESPACE fabric; ~ **à filtrer** *f* CERAM VER filter cloth

étoile *f* INFORMAT, ORDINAT star, PETR spider; ~ **active** *f* INFORMAT *réseaux* active star; ~ **B** *f* ASTRONOMIE B-star; ~ **Barnard** *f* ASTRONOMIE Barnard's star; ~ **du berger** *f* ASTRONOMIE evening star; ~ **binaire** *f* ASTRONOMIE binary star; ~ **binaire photométrique** *f* ASTRONOMIE photometric binary star; ~ **binaire visuelle** *f* ASTRONOMIE visual binary; ~ **C** *f* ASTRONOMIE carbon star; ~ **double optique** *f* ASTRONOMIE optical double star; ~ **éruptive** *f* ASTRONOMIE eruptive star; ~ **F** *f* ASTRONOMIE F-star; ~ **filante** *f* ASTRONOMIE shooting star; ~ **G** *f* ASTRONOMIE G-star; ~ **d'induit** *f* ELECTR *machine* armature spider; ~ **K** *f* ASTRONOMIE K-star; ~ **M** *f* ASTRONOMIE M-star; ~ **massive** *f* ASTRONOMIE massive star; ~ **du matin** *f* ASTRONOMIE morning star; ~ **multiple** *f* ASTRONOMIE multiple star; ~ **naine** *f* ASTRONOMIE dwarf, dwarf star, ESPACE dwarf star, dwarf; ~ **de neutrons** *f* ASTRONOMIE neutron star; ~ **O** *f* ASTRONOMIE O-star; ~ **passive** *f* INFORMAT, ORDINAT passive star; ~ **polaire** *f* ASTRONOMIE North Star, Pole Star; ~ **préséquence dominante** *f* ASTRONOMIE pre-main sequence star; ~ **R** *f* ASTRONOMIE R-star; ~ **de référence** *f* ASTRONOMIE reference star; ~ **supergéante** *f* ASTRONOMIE supergiant; ~ **supergéante rouge** *f* ASTRONOMIE red supergiant; ~ **à sursauts** *f* ASTRONOMIE flare star; ~ **symbiotique** *f* ASTRONOMIE symbiotic star; ~ **T Tauri** *f* ASTRONOMIE T-Tauri star; ~ **variable** *f* ASTRONOMIE variable star; ~ **variable éclipsante** *f* ASTRONOMIE eclipsing variable star

étoiles: ~ **binaires éclipsantes** *f pl* ASTRONOMIE eclipsing binaries; ~ **binaires émettant des rayons X** *f pl* ASTRONOMIE X-ray emitting binary stars; ~ **bleues** *f pl* ASTRONOMIE blue stars; ~ **circumpolaires** *f pl* ASTRONOMIE circumpolar stars; ~ **RR Lyrae** *f pl* ASTRONOMIE RR Lyrae stars; ~ **ultra rapides** *f pl* ASTRONOMIE high-velocity stars; ~ **vibrantes** *f pl* ASTRONOMIE pulsating stars; ~ **visibles** *f pl* ASTRONOMIE visible stars

étonner *vt* CERAM VER start, CHARBON blast by heating

étoquiau *m* RESSORTS steadying pin

étouffement: ~ **d'étincelles** *m* ELECTROTEC spark quenching

étouffer *vt* THERMODYN quench, smother

étouffoir *m* PRODUCTION damper; ~ **de surchauffeur** *m* PRODUCTION superheater damper

étoupage *m* NUCLEAIRE *d'une boîte à étoupe* packing seal

étoupe *f* NAUT oakum, PRODUCTION junk, tow; ~ **de chanvre** *f* NAUT *corde* tow

étoupille *f* ESPACE squib, MINES fuse; ~ **à friction** *f* MINES friction fuse; ~ **à percussion** *f* MINES percussion fuse; ~ **de sûreté** *f* MINES common fuse, ordinary fuse, safety fuse

étourdir *vt* AGRO ALIM stun

étrainage *m* METALL drag

étranger: ~ **au sujet** *adj* BREVETS irrelevant

étrangeté *f* PHYSIQUE strangeness

étranglement *m* CONS MECA throttling, METALL necking, MINES contraction, nip, pinch; ~ **de terre** *m* MINES contraction, nip, pinch

étrangler *vt* GENIE CHIM baffle

étrangleur *m* INST HYDR, VEHICULES *carburateur* throttle

étrave *f* NAUT bow, stem; ~ **à bulbe** *f* NAUT bulbous bow; ~ **droite** *f* NAUT straight stem; ~ **élancée** *f* NAUT raking stem; ~ **en cuiller** *f* NAUT spoon bow

étreinte *f* MINES contraction, nip, pinch

étrésillon *m* AERONAUT drag link, CONSTR bridging piece, flying shore, strut, strut, MINES spreader

étrésillonnement *m* CONSTR bracing, strutting

étrésillonner *vt* CONS MECA, CONSTR *les berges d'une fouille* brace

étrésillons *m pl* CONSTR bridging, stiffening, strutting

étrier *m* AUTO brake caliper, caliper (AmE), calliper (BrE), rebound clip, CINEMAT stirrup hanger, CONS MECA bracket, link, stirrup, stirrup bolt, stirrup piece, stirrup strap, strap, *d'un tour, d'un étau-limeur, d'une raboteuse* tool post, CONSTR U-bolt, fastening, stirrup, strap, strap hinge, MECANIQUE clevis, NAUT U-bolt, crossbrace, VEHICULES *frein* caliper (AmE), calliper (BrE); ~ **capitonné** *m* ENREGISTR *de casque* padded headband; ~ **d'échafaudage** *m* CONSTR cradle iron, cradle stirrup; ~ **fixe** *m* AUTO fixed caliper; ~ **flottant** *m* AUTO floating caliper (AmE), floating calliper (BrE); ~ **de frein** *m* MECANIQUE brake caliper (AmE), brake calliper (BrE), *véhicules* caliper (AmE), calliper (BrE); ~ **à touret** *m* CONS MECA swivel stirrup

étriper *vt* OCEANO gut

ETTD *abrév* (*équipement terminal de traitement de données*) AERONAUT, ORDINAT, TELECOM DTE (*data terminal equipment*)

ETTD-F *abrév* (*équipement terminal de traitement de données fixe*) TELECOM fixed data processing terminal equipment

ETTD-MT *abrév* (*équipement terminal mobile terrestre de traitement de données*) TELECOM mobile data processing terminal equipment

étude *f* CONS MECA analysis, study, CONSTR design, survey, surveying, INFORMAT, ORDINAT design, PHYS RAYON study, PRODUCTION design; ~ **acoustique** *f* ENREGISTR acoustical design; ~ **de l'aptitude au brasage** *f* CONS MECA investigation of brazability; ~ **avant-après** *f* TRANSPORT before and after study; ~ **de la charge de réseau** *f* INFORMAT, ORDINAT network load analysis; ~ **de composition** *f* CONSTR *de béton* mix design; ~ **et suivi de fabrication** *f* CONS MECA development and subsequent manufacture; ~ **d'exploitation** *f* PRODUCTION operation analysis; ~ **de faisabilité** *f* CONSTR, INFORMAT feasibility study; ~ **de fiabilité** *f* ESPACE *qualité* reliability analysis; ~ **fonctionnelle** *f* INFORMAT, ORDINAT functional design; ~ **géologique** *f* CHARBON, PETROLE geological survey; ~ **géophysique** *f* GEOLOGIE, PETROLE geophysical survey; ~ **granulométrique** *f* MATERIAUX *métallurgie* grain size classification; ~ **haute-résolution des profils des raies** *f* PHYS RAYON *raies spectrales* high-resolution study of line profiles; ~ **hydrogéologique** *f* HYDROLOGIE ground water investigation; ~ **hydrologique** *f* CONSTR hydrologic study, HYDROLOGIE hydrologic investigation; ~ **d'impact** *f* DISTRI EAU, GAZ impact study; ~ **d'incendie** *f* SECURITE fire research; ~ **logique** *f* INFORMAT, ORDINAT logic design; ~ **des machines-outils** *f* CONS MECA *ergonomie* machine tool design; ~ **de marché** *f* TEXTILE market research; ~ **de la microstructure**

par rayons X *f* NUCLEAIRE X-ray microstructure investigation; **~ origine-destination** *f* TRANSPORT O-D survey, origin and destination survey; **~ par photographies aériennes** *f* TRANSPORT aerial survey; **~ par procédé aérocinématographique** *f* TRANSPORT aerial motion picture survey; **~ de pavé** *f* CONSTR pavement design; **~ des rayons gamma** *f* NUCLEAIRE gamma ray survey; **~ des ressources en eau** *f* HYDROLOGIE water resources study; **~ sismique** *f* CONSTR seismic design, PETROLE seismic survey; **~ sur la pollution** *f* POLLUTION pollution research; **~ du travail avec bruit réduit** *f* CONS MECA low-noise engineering; **~ de vieillissement** *f* ESPACE *qualité* ageing study (BrE), aging study (AmE)

études: **~ et méthodes** *f pl* PRODUCTION engineering and methods

étudier *vt* CONSTR, MECANIQUE design

étui *m* MECANIQUE case; **~ de cuir** *m* PHOTO leather case; **~ de latte** *m* NAUT batten pocket; **~ d'objectif** *m* PHOTO lens case

étuvage *m* PAPIER steaming, PRODUCTION stoving, *des noyaux* baking, REFRIG oven dehydration; **~ par faisceau d'électrons** *m* NUCLEAIRE electron beam curing

étuve *f* CHARBON drying oven, CONS MECA drying furnace, CONSTR kiln, EQUIP LAB *chauffage* oven, PAPIER drying oven, PLAST CAOU *cuisson de peintures et plastiques* cabinet, PRODUCTION drying chamber, drying house, drying room, oven, stove, TEXTILE oven, THERMODYN heating chamber; **~ à l'air chaud** *f* PLAST CAOU *matériel* air oven; **~ bactériologique** *f* EQUIP LAB bacteriological oven; **~ à convection forcée** *f* EQUIP LAB *chauffage* oven with forced convection; **~ à convection naturelle** *f* EQUIP LAB *chauffage* oven with natural convection; **~ de dessiccation** *f* AGRO ALIM drying oven; **~ à fermentation** *f* AGRO ALIM proving cabinet; **~ industrielle** *f* CONS MECA industrial oven; **~ à noyaux** *f* PRODUCTION core stove, *chauffée au coke* core oven; **~ de préchauffage** *f* PLAST CAOU preheating oven; **~ réfrigérée** *f* EQUIP LAB refrigerated incubator; **~ de séchage** *f* PRODUCTION drying stove; **~ de séchage à infrarouge** *f* PRODUCTION infrared oven; **~ sèche** *f* AGRO ALIM drying cupboard; **~ à température constante** *f* EQUIP LAB *chauffage*, MAT CHAUFF constant temperature oven; **~ à vide** *f* AGRO ALIM vacuum dryer, EQUIP LAB vacuum oven

étuvé *adj* THERMODYN oven-dried

étuvement *m* PRODUCTION stoving, *des noyaux* baking

étuver *vt* PRODUCTION bake, THERMODYN bake, kiln dry

Eu *(europium)* CHIMIE Eu *(europium)*

eucaïrite *f* MINERAUX eucairite, eukairite

eucalyptol *m* CHIMIE eucalyptol

euchroïte *f* MINERAUX euchroite

euclase *f* MINERAUX euclase

euclidien *adj* GEOMETRIE euclidean

eucolite *f* MINERAUX eucolite

eudialyte *f* MINERAUX eudialite, eudialyte

eudiomètre *m* CHIMIE eudiometer

eudiométrie *f* CHIMIE eudiometry

eudnophite *f* MINERAUX eudnophite

eugénol *m* CHIMIE eugenol

eugéosynclinal *m* GEOLOGIE eugeosyncline

eukaïrite *f* MINERAUX eucairite, eukairite

eulytine *f* MINERAUX eulytine, eulytite

euosmite *f* MINERAUX euosmite

eurofente *f* EMBALLAGE euroslot

europeux *adj* CHIMIE europous

europique *adj* CHIMIE europic

europium *m (Eu)* CHIMIE europium *(Eu)*

eustasie *f* OCEANO eustatic movement

eustatique *adj* EN RENOUV, GEOLOGIE *variations du niveau de la mer*, GEOPHYS eustatic

eusynchite *f* MINERAUX eusynchite

eutectique *m* CERAM VER, CHIMIE *alliage* eutectic

eutectoïde *m* METALL eutectoid

eutétique *adj* CHIMIE eutetic

eutexie *f* CHIMIE eutexia

eutrophe *adj* RECYCLAGE eutrophic

eutrophie *f* RECYCLAGE eutrophy

eutrophisation *f* LESSIVES, POLLUTION, RECYCLAGE eutrophication

euxénite *f* MINERAUX euxenite

euxinique *adj* GEOLOGIE euxinic

eV *abrév (électron-volt)* ELECTROTEC, METROLOGIE, PHYS PART, PHYSIQUE eV *(electronvolt)*

évacuateur *m* DISTRI EAU spillway; **~ avec vanne** *m* DISTRI EAU controlled spillway; **~ de crue** *m* DISTRI EAU flood spillway; **~ de crues** *m* DISTRI EAU high water overflow; **~ de secours** *m* DISTRI EAU emergency spillway

évacuation *f* ESPACE escape, *véhicules* emergency, INST HYDR *par opposition à source ou alimentation* sink, NAUT drain, POLLU MER discharge, PRODUCTION *système hydraulique* drain, SECURITE evacuation; **~ d'air** *f* CONS MECA air outlet; **~ des boues** *f* DISTRI EAU sludge disposal; **~ dans la mer** *f* RECYCLAGE marine disposal; **~ des déblais** *f* CONSTR spoil disposal, PETROLE cuttings removal; **~ des déchets** *f* DISTRI EAU, RECYCLAGE waste disposal; **~ des eaux d'égout** *f* RECYCLAGE sewage disposal; **~ d'eaux superficielles** *f* CONSTR surface water drainage; **~ de frigorigène** *f* REFRIG pumpdown; **~ des résidus** *f* CHARBON reject disposal, tail disposal; **~ d'urgence** *f* ESPACE *véhicules* emergency escape; **~ d'urgence des lieux** *f* SECURITE emergency evacuation of buildings

évacué *adj* CHARBON dumped, DISTRI EAU *eau* discharged

évacuer[1] *vt* CONS MECA dissipate, CONSTR clear out, DISTRI EAU, HYDROLOGIE *l'eau d'un fossé au moyen d'un canal* drain, NAUT *de l'eau*, RECYCLAGE discharge

évacuer:[2] **~ les eaux** *vi* DISTRI EAU drain off; **~ le navire** *vi* NAUT abandon ship

évaluation *f* CONS MECA assessment, QUALITE, SECURITE *d'intensité vibratoire* evaluation; **~ de la fiabilité** *f* QUALITE assessment of reliability; **~ des formations traversées** *f* PETROLE *géologie* formation evaluation; **~ des performances** *f* INFORMAT, ORDINAT benchmarking; **~ prudente** *f* PRODUCTION conservative estimate; **~ de qualité** *f* METROLOGIE *d'un processus de fabrication ou de contrôle* quality assessment; **~ du risque** *f* POLLU MER risk assessment, QUALITE risk evaluation; **~ de stock** *f* PRODUCTION stock valuation

évaluer *vt* QUALITE, SECURITE evaluate, TEXTILE assess; **~ les performances de** *vt* INFORMAT, ORDINAT benchmark; **~ la répartition** *vt* CONS MECA *des carbures dans les aciers pour outils* assess the distribution

évanescence *f* ELECTRON fading

évanouissement *m* ELECTRON decay, fading, ESPACE, PHYSIQUE, TELECOM fading; **~ dû à la propagation par trajets multiples** *m* TELECOM multipath fading; **~ lent** *m* TELECOM log normal shadowing; **~ prononcé** *m* ELECTRON deep fading; **~ de Rayleigh** *m* TELECOM Rayleigh fading; **~ sélectif** *m* TELECOM selective fading

évaporable *adj* MAT CHAUFF evaporable

évaporateur *m* CHIMIE, EQUIP LAB *verrerie* evaporator, GENIE CHIM evaporating apparatus, evaporator, MAT CHAUFF evaporator, REFRIG cooler, evaporator, THERMODYN vaporizer, VEHICULES *climatiseur* evaporator; **~ accumulateur de glace** *m* REFRIG ice bank evaporator; **~ alimenté par pompe** *m* REFRIG pump-fed evaporator; **~ à aspersion interne** *m* REFRIG spray-type evaporator; **~ à bain-marie** *m* NUCLEAIRE water bath evaporator; **~ à calandre et serpentin** *m* REFRIG shell and tube evaporator; **~ des déchets liquides** *m* NUCLEAIRE radioactive waste evaporator, waste evaporator; **~ à détente sec** *m* REFRIG dry expansion evaporator; **~ à effet simple** *m* AGRO ALIM single effect evaporator; **~ enveloppant** *m* REFRIG wraparound evaporator; **~ noyé** *m* REFRIG flooded evaporator; **~ rotatif** *m* EQUIP LAB *verrerie* rotary evaporator; **~ sous vide** *m* AGRO ALIM vacuum evaporator; **~ à tubes verticaux** *m* REFRIG vertical-type evaporator; **~ ventilé** *m* REFRIG ventilated froster

évaporation *f* GAZ evaporation, GENIE CHIM vaporization, HYDROLOGIE, IMPRIM, MAT CHAUFF, MATERIAUX, PETROLE *raffinage*, PHYSIQUE evaporation, POLLUTION steam emission, THERMODYN evaporation; **~ annuelle** *f* DISTRI EAU annual evaporation; **~ éclair** *f* AGRO ALIM, NUCLEAIRE flash evaporation; **~ efficace** *f* DISTRI EAU effective evaporation; **~ flash** *f* AGRO ALIM flash evaporation; **~ instantanée** *f* AGRO ALIM flash evaporation; **~ latente** *f* HYDROLOGIE latent evaporation; **~ par détente** *f* NUCLEAIRE flash evaporation; **~ relative** *f* HYDROLOGIE relative evaporation; **~ des solvants à la limite de l'ignition** *f* IMPRIM flash-off; **~ sous vide** *f* ELECTRON vapor deposition (AmE), vapour deposition (BrE); **~ thermique** *f* METALL thermal evaporation; **~ totale** *f* HYDROLOGIE fly-off, total evaporation, total losses

évaporé *adj* THERMODYN vaporized

évaporer[1] *vt* AGRO ALIM boil down, CHIMIE volatilize, GENIE CHIM evaporate, vaporize, MAT CHAUFF evaporate, THERMODYN vaporize; **~ jusqu'à sec** *vt* GENIE CHIM evaporate dry; **~ jusqu'à siccité** *vt* GENIE CHIM evaporate dry

évaporer:[2] **s'~** *v réfl* CHIMIE, MAT CHAUFF evaporate, TEXTILE volatilize

évaporite *f* EN RENOUV, GEOLOGIE, PETR evaporite

évaporomètre *m* GENIE CHIM evaporation meter, evaporimeter, porometer, HYDROLOGIE evaporimeter

évapotranspiration *f* HYDROLOGIE fly-off, total evaporation, total losses; **~ potentielle** *f* DISTRI EAU potential evapotranspiration; **~ réelle** *f* HYDROLOGIE actual evapotranspiration; **~ relative** *f* HYDROLOGIE relative evapotranspiration

évasé *adj* MECANIQUE flared, PRODUCTION flaring, TEXTILE flared

évasement *m* CERAM VER flaring, PRODUCTION flare, flaring; **~ du col** *m* CERAM VER flared neck

évaser *vt* TEXTILE flare

évection *f* ASTRONOMIE evection

événement *m* GEOLOGIE, INFORMAT, MATH, ORDINAT event, PHYS PART *relativité* event, *technique de détection* event, PHYSIQUE event; **~ aléatoire** *m* ELECTRON random event; **~ de justification de pointeur** *m* TELECOM PJE, pointer justification event; **~ de précipitation** *m* POLLUTION precipitation event; **~ de référence** *m* NUCLEAIRE design basis event; **~ simulé** *m* PHYS RAYON simulated event; **~ téléphonique d'interfonctionnement vers l'arrière** *m* TELECOM backward

interworking telephony event; **~ téléphonique d'interfonctionnement vers l'avant** *m* TELECOM *maritime mobile* FITE, forward interworking telephony event; **~ téléphonique de traitement des opérations de commutation** *m* TELECOM SPITE, switching process interworking telephony event; **~ de vol** *m* ESPACE *véhicules* flight occurrence

évent *m* CERAM VER vent, CONS MECA air vent, CONSTR, ESPACE vent, vent hole, GEOLOGIE *volcanique* vent, INST HYDR pet-valve, MECANIQUE, PLAST CAOU *presse* vent, PRODUCTION air hole, riser, riser pin; **~ de gaz** *m* NUCLEAIRE gas vent, issue; **~ volcanique** *m* OCEANO volcanic vent

éventé *adj* AGRO ALIM stale

éventer *vt* MINES *une carrière* open up

évidage *m* CERAM VER *des pièces céramiques moulées* fettling, CONSTR fluting, hollowing, hollowing out, PRODUCTION grooving

évidement *m* CONS MECA cutout, CONSTR hollowing, hollowing out, NUCLEAIRE dishing shallow depression, PRODUCTION grooving; **~ de noyautage** *m* CONS MECA cored passage

évider *vt* PRODUCTION channel out, hollow, hollow out

évier *m* EQUIP LAB *services* sink

évité: ~ au vent *adj* NAUT wind-rode

évite-molettes *m pl* MINES overwind gear, overwinder, overwinding gear; **~ modérateur de vitesse** *m* MINES overwinder and overspeeder

éviter[1] *vt* SECURITE *accidents* prevent

éviter[2] *vti* NAUT swing away

évolué *adj* GEOLOGIE *roches ou séries magmatiques* differentiated

évolutif *adj* INFORMAT expandable, ORDINAT expandable, upgradable, TELECOM expandable

évolution *f* ASTRONOMIE *galaxies, étoiles*, MATH, PHYSIQUE evolution; **~ chimique** *f* ASTRONOMIE *d'une galaxie ou d'une étoile* chemical evolution; **~ des hydrocarbures** *f* POLLU MER fate of oil; **~ matérielle** *f* INFORMAT hardware upgrade; **~ de pression** *f* GAZ pressure change; **~ stellaire** *f* ASTRONOMIE stellar evolution

exa- *préf (E)* METROLOGIE exa- *(E)*

exact *adj* MECANIQUE, METROLOGIE, PHYSIQUE accurate

exactement *adv* METROLOGIE accurately

exactitude *f* MATERIAUX soundness, MECANIQUE *physique*, METROLOGIE, ORDINAT, PHYSIQUE accuracy, PRODUCTION exactitude, exactness; **~ de mesure** *f* METROLOGIE accuracy of measurement

exalteur: ~ de mousse *m* AGRO ALIM foam booster, lather booster

examen *m* BREVETS, ESSAIS, MECANIQUE examination; **~ de l'assurance de la qualité** *m* NUCLEAIRE quality assurance examination; **~ médical avant embauche** *m* SECURITE pre-employment health screening; **~ de la microstructure par rayons X** *m* NUCLEAIRE X-ray microstructure investigation; **~ périodique** *m* PETR scan; **~ préliminaire** *m* BREVETS preliminary examination; **~ radiographique** *m* CONS MECA, ESSAIS radiographic examination; **~ aux rayons X** *m* COMMANDE, MECANIQUE X-ray examination, NUCLEAIRE X-ray inspection, X-ray testing; **~ aux ultrasons** *m* MATERIAUX, MECANIQUE, NUCLEAIRE ultrasonic examination; **~ visuel** *m* METROLOGIE visual inspection

examinateur *m* BREVETS examiner

examiner *vt* SECURITE *plainte* investigate

excavateur *m* CONSTR digging machine, mechanical

grab, excavator, power shovel, MINES heading machine, TRANSPORT excavator; **~ dragline** *m* CONSTR dragline excavator; **~ à godets** *m* CONSTR bucket excavator, DISTRI EAU bucket dredger; **~ à section entière** *m* MINES full-face tunnel borer; **~ de tranchées** *m* CONSTR trench cutter

excavation *f* CHARBON excavation, CONSTR cut, cutting, digging, excavating, excavation, pit, MINES excavation, *d'un puits* excavating, excavation, sinking

excavatrice *f* PETR mechanical cutter, mechanical trencher; **~ à godets** *f* MINES bucket chain excavator; **~ à roue** *f* MINES bucket wheel excavator

excédent *m* CHIMIE overflow; **~ d'eau** *m* DISTRI EAU surplus water; **~ d'énergie** *m* THERMODYN excess energy

excédentaire *m* IMPRIM overrun

excéder: **~ le temps prévu** *vi* TV overrun

excentrage *m* CONS MECA offsetting

excentration *f* CONS MECA setting-over

excentré *adj* CONS MECA offset, ESPACE, PAPIER off-center (AmE), off-centre (BrE)

excentrer[1] *vt* CONS MECA set over, throw off center (AmE), throw off centre (BrE)

excentrer:[2] **s'~** *v réfl* CONS MECA set over

excentricité *f* ACOUSTIQUE, ASTRONOMIE eccentricity, CONS MECA throw, ESPACE eccentricity, MATERIAUX radial deviation, MECANIQUE eccentricity

excentrique *m* CINEMAT cam, CONS MECA cam, eccentric, eccentric chuck, INST HYDR *de commande de tiroir* valve eccentric, MECANIQUE eccentric; **~ à développement** *m* CONS MECA involute cam; **~ en triangle** *m* CONS MECA triangular cam; **~ évidé** *m* CONS MECA chambered eccentric; **~ triangulaire** *m* CONS MECA triangular cam

exception *f* INFORMAT, ORDINAT exception

excès: **~ de fluide** *m* REFRIG overcharge; **~ de masse** *m* PHYSIQUE mass excess; **~ de neutrons** *m* PHYSIQUE isotopic number, neutron excess; **~ de pose** *m* PHOTO overexposure; **~ de pression** *m* PRODUCTION overpressure

excitance *f* OPTIQUE radiant emittance, radiant excitance, TELECOM radiant emittance, radiant excitance; **~ énergétique** *f* OPTIQUE energy excitance, radiant emittance, radiant excitance, PHYS RAYON, PHYSIQUE radiant excitance, TELECOM radiant emittance, radiant excitance; **~ radiante** *f* PHYS RAYON radiant excitance

excitateur *m* ELECTROTEC exciter; **~ électrostatique** *m* ACOUSTIQUE electrostatic exciter; **~ de ligne** *m* INFORMAT, ORDINAT line driver

excitation *f* ELECTR *atome, rayonnement* excitation, ELECTROTEC energization, excitation, GEOPHYS, PART PHYS excitation, PHYS RAYON energization, excitation, TELECOM excitation; **~ aléatoire** *f* TELECOM random excitation; **~ de champ** *f* ELECTR *machine* field excitation; **~ collective** *f* PHYS RAYON *interaction des particules* collective excitation; **~ électrique** *f* PHYSIQUE E-field, electric field; **~ en dérivation** *f* ELECTROTEC shunt excitation, separate excitation; **~ en série** *f* ELECTROTEC series excitation; **~ indépendante** *f* ELECTROTEC independent excitation, separate excitation; **~ laser** *f* PHYS RAYON laser excitation; **~ par choc** *f* PHYS RAYON impact excitation, impulse excitation, TELECOM impulse excitation, shock excitation; **~ par un courant alternatif** *f* ELECTROTEC AC excitation; **~ par une impulsion** *f* ELECTRON firing; **~ par rayonnement** *f*

ELECTRON radiation excitation; **~ du satellite par le lanceur** *f* ESPACE *véhicules* POGO effect; **~ séparée** *f* ELECTROTEC independent excitation, separate excitation; **~ shunt** *f* ELECTROTEC shunt excitation

excitatrice *f* ELECTROTEC, EN RENOUV *turbines* exciter

excité *adj* PHYS RAYON *atome ou molécule* excited, PRODUCTION energized, TELECOM illuminated

exciter *vt* PHYSIQUE supply

exciton *m* PHYSIQUE exciton

excitron *m* ELECTROTEC excitron

excreta *m pl* RECYCLAGE faeces (BrE), feces (AmE)

excursion *f* ESPACE *communications*, TV deviation; **~ de fréquence** *f* ELECTRON frequency deviation; **~ de fréquence crête** *f* ESPACE *communications* peak frequency deviation; **~ de fréquence efficace** *f* ESPACE *communications* RMS frequency deviation; **~ de fréquence maximale** *f* TELECOM peak frequency deviation

exécuter[1] *vt* INFORMAT, ORDINAT execute, TEXTILE implement

exécuter:[2] **~ un freinage aérodynamique** *vi* ESPACE *véhicules* aerobrake

exécution *f* INFORMAT, ORDINAT execution, run, running, PRODUCTION design, QUALITE performance, TEXTILE implementation; **~ concurrente** *f* ORDINAT concurrent execution; **~ d'instruction** *f* INFORMAT, ORDINAT instruction execution; **~ pas à pas** *f* INFORMAT, ORDINAT single step operation; **~ de programme** *f* INFORMAT, ORDINAT program execution

exemplaire *m* CHIMIE specimen, IMPRIM copy; **~ forcé hors de l'alignement** *m* IMPRIM *sortie rotatives* kick copy; **~ numéroté** *m* IMPRIM numbered copy

exemplaires *m pl* IMPRIM *produits imprimés* section; **~ devant obligatoirement être déposés** *m pl* IMPRIM *dépôt légal, presse et livre* deposit copies; **~ en supplément de la commande** *m pl* IMPRIM *tirage* overrun; **~ imprimés en excès** *m pl* IMPRIM *tirage* overs

exempt *adj* MATERIAUX free; **~ de carbone** *adj* MATERIAUX, METALL carbon-free; **~ de précipités** *adj* MATERIAUX precipitation-free; **~ de scintillement** *adj* CINEMAT flicker free; **~ de soufre** *adj* CHIMIE sulfa-free (AmE), sulpha-free (BrE)

exercer *vt* PHYSIQUE exert

exercice: **~ d'embarcation** *m* NAUT boat drill; **~ d'évacuation** *m* NAUT emergency drill, THERMODYN *en cas d'incendie* fire drill; **~ de sauvetage anti-incendie** *m* SECURITE fire drill

exfoliation *f* GEOLOGIE, PHYSIQUE exfoliation

exhaure *f* CONSTR dewatering, DISTRI EAU pumping, pumping out, MINES dewatering, draining, drainage, mine pumping

exhaussement *m* CONSTR *d'un mur* raising, HYDROLOGIE raising of the bed level

exhausteur *m* AGRO ALIM, CONS MECA exhauster, GENIE CHIM extractor fan, OCEANO air exhauster; **~ d'arôme** *m* AGRO ALIM flavor potentiator (AmE), flavour potentiator (BrE)

exigence *f* ESSAIS, SECURITE requirement

exigences: **~ pour les essais** *f pl* ESSAIS, SECURITE test requirements

existant *adj* CONSTR existing

exitance *f* PHYSIQUE luminous exitance

ex-libris *m* IMPRIM bookplate

exoatmosphérique *adj* ESPACE exoatmospheric

exobase *f* ESPACE *thermique* exobase

exobiologie *f* ASTRONOMIE exobiology

exosphère *f* ESPACE exosphere

exothermique *adj* CHIMIE, ESPACE exothermic, THERMO-DYN exothermal, exothermic

expansé: ~ **sous forme de vapeur** *adj* GENIE CHIM vapor-expanded (AmE), vapour-expanded (BrE)

expanseur *m* ENREGISTR, PRODUCTION expander

expansibilité *f* THERMODYN *des gaz* expansibility

expansion *f* ASTRONOMIE *de l'Univers*, ELECTRON *de dynamique*, ENREGISTR, ESPACE, INST HYDR, MECANIQUE, PHYSIQUE, PLAST CAOU expansion, THERMODYN expansion, heat expansion, *dilatation thermique* heat dilatation; ~ **de bande** *f* ELECTRON bandwidth expansion; ~ **cosmologique** *f* ASTRONOMIE cosmological expansion; ~ **de douille par frappe** *f* CONSTR shield-driven anchor; ~ **des fonds océaniques** *f* GEOLOGIE, OCEANO ocean floor spreading; ~ **océanique** *f* GEOPHYS seafloor spreading; ~ **thermique** *f* PETROLE, PLAST CAOU thermal expansion

expédier *vt* NAUT ship

expéditeur *m* NAUT shipper, PRODUCTION consignor, TELECOM originator, sender, transmission sender; ~ **de l'échange** *m* TELECOM interchange sender

expédition *f* NAUT shipment, *des marchandises* shipping, PRODUCTION shipment, shipping

expéditionnaire *m* NAUT shipping clerk

expérience *f* CHIMIE experiment, test, ESPACE, PHYSIQUE experiment; ~ **ALEPH** *f* PHYS PART ALEPH experiment; ~ **avec cible fixe** *f* PHYS PART fixed target experiment; ~ **de Cavendish** *f* PHYSIQUE Cavendish experiment; ~ **de collision** *f* PHYS PART collision experiment; ~ **de durée de trajectoire à faisceau thermique** *f* PHYS RAYON thermal beam time-of-flight experiment; ~ **en pile** *f* NUCLEAIRE in-pile experiment, in-reactor experiment; ~ **à faisceau de haute énergie** *f* PHYS RAYON high-energy beam experiment; ~ **à faisceau surgénéré** *f* PHYS RAYON fast beam experiment; ~ **de Franck et Hertz** *f* PHYSIQUE Franck-Hertz experiment; ~ **d'ignition** *f* NUCLEAIRE ignition experiment; ~ **de Melde** *f* PHYSIQUE Melde's experiment; ~ **de Michelson** *f* PHYSIQUE Michelson-Morley experiment; ~ **de Millikan** *f* PHYSIQUE Millikan's experiment; ~ **radiative** *f* PHYS RAYON radiative experiment; ~ **de rétroflecteur laser** *f* PHYS RAYON laser retroflector experiment; ~ **de Rowland** *f* PHYSIQUE Rowland experiment; ~ **de Stern et Gerlach** *f* PHYSIQUE Stern-Gerlach experiment; ~ **de striction triaxiale** *f* NUCLEAIRE triaxial pinch experiment

expérimental *adj* CHIMIE, NUCLEAIRE, PHYS PART, PHYS RAYON, PHYSIQUE experimental

expérimenter *vt* CHIMIE, ESSAIS test

expert: ~ **en réseaux informatiques** *m* ORDINAT network specialist; ~ **maritime** *m* NAUT surveyor

expertise *f* CONS MECA assessment, CONSTR survey

expiration: ~ **de la temporisation** *f* TELECOM expiration of timer (AmE), expiry of timer (BrE)

exploitabilité *f* MINES feasibility, mineability, workability

exploitable *adj* MINES mineable, workable

exploitant *m* MINES operator; ~ **de télécommunications** *m* TELECOM telecommunications operator

exploitation[1] *f* CHARBON mining, ESPACE *communications* operation, HYDROLOGIE *des réserves d'eau souterraine* mining, MINES diggings, mine, TELECOM operation; ~ **administration maintenance et mise en service** *f* TELECOM OAMP, operation, administration, maintenance and provisioning; ~ **des alluvions au** moyen de drague *f* MINES dredge mining; ~ **de l'argile** *f* MINES clay mining; ~ **aurifère** *f* MINES gold mine; ~ **des bois** *f* PRODUCTION logging; ~ **de carrière** *f* MINES quarrying; ~ **du charbon** *f* CHARBON coal mining; ~ **d'un chemin de fer** *f* TRANSPORT railroad operation (AmE), railway operation (BrE); ~ **à ciel ouvert** *f* MINES open cast mining, open-cut mining, openwork, surface mining, NUCLEAIRE open pit mining; ~ **à distance** *f* TELECOM remote operation; ~ **en allongement de cycle** *f* PRODUCTION stretch-out operation; ~ **en autonome** *f* TELECOM off-line working; ~ **en avant** *f* MINES advance mining; ~ **d'énergie géothermique** *f* POLLUTION geothermal energy exploitation; ~ **en gradins** *f* MINES stoping; ~ **en gradins renversés** *f* MINES overhand stoping; ~ **en multiplex** *f* ELECTRON multiplex operation; ~ **en multitâche** *f* INFORMAT, ORDINAT multitasking; ~ **en retour** *f* MINES retreat mining; ~ **et maintenance** *f* TELECOM OAM, operations and maintenance, organization and maintenance; ~ **filonienne** *f* MINES lode mining; ~ **des filons** *f* MINES lode mining; ~ **au fond** *f* MINES drift mining, underground working; ~ **de la houille** *f* CHARBON coal mining; ~ **hydraulique** *f* MINES spatter work; ~ **interurbaine automatique** *f* TELECOM automatic trunk working; ~ **au jour** *f* MINES open cast mining, open-cut mining, openwork, surface mining; ~ **locale** *f* TELECOM local operation; ~ **des minerais** *f* MINES ore mining; ~ **de mines** *f* CHARBON mining; ~ **des mines de diamants** *f* MINES diamond mining; ~ **des mines des métaux** *f* MINES metal mining; ~ **minière** *f* CHARBON mining; ~ **minière de métaux** *f* MINES metal mining; ~ **modulable** *f* GAZ adaptable operation; ~ **par grandes tailles** *f* CHARBON straining work, thick-seam winning; ~ **par ouvrages en travers** *f* MINES crosscutting; ~ **placérienne** *f* MINES placer mine, placer workings; ~ **de placers** *f* MINES placer mine, placer workings; ~ **privée reconnue** *f (EPR)* TELECOM recognized private operating agency; ~ **sans surveillance** *f* INFORMAT, ORDINAT unattended operation; ~ **semi-automatique interurbaine** *f* TELECOM semiautomatic trunk working; ~ **sous surveillance** *f* INFORMAT, ORDINAT attended operation; ~ **souterraine** *f* MINES closed work, underground operation, underground working; ~ **tous-temps** *f* AERONAUT all-weather operations

exploitation:[2] **en ~ normale** *loc* PRODUCTION in working order

exploité *adj* GEOLOGIE quarried

exploiter *vt* MINES mine, operate, NUCLEAIRE, PRODUCTION operate

explorateur: ~ **radar** *m* TRANSPORT radar scanner

exploration *f* INFORMAT, ORDINAT scanning, PETROLE exploration, prospecting, TV scan; ~ **du champ proche** *f* TELECOM near field scanning technique; ~ **en champ proche** *f* OPTIQUE near field scanning technique; ~ **géophysique** *f* GEOPHYS geophysical exploration; ~ **pétrolière** *f* PETROLE oil exploration; ~ **sismique** *f* CHARBON seismic exploration, GEOPHYS seismic exploration method, PETROLE seismic exploration; ~ **du sous-sol** *f* GAZ underground exploration

explorer *vt* TV scan

exploser[1] *vt* THERMODYN detonate

exploser[2] *vi* ESPACE blow up; ~ **violemment** *vi* SECURITE deflagrate

exploseur *m* MINES blaster, blasting machine, exploder; ~ **à condensateur** *m* MINES condenser discharge exploder; ~ **à dynamo** *m* MINES dynamo blaster, dynamo exploder; ~ **électrique** *m* MINES electric blasting machine, electric shotfirer; ~ **à manivelle** *m* MINES crank blasting machine; ~ **à poignée** *m* MINES push-down blasting machine

explosible *adj* MINES capable of detonation, THERMODYN detonatable

explosif[1] *adj* SECURITE, THERMODYN explosive

explosif[2] *m* CHIMIE, ESPACE explosive, MINES detonating explosive, high explosive, SECURITE explosive; ~ **agréé** *m* MINES permissible explosive (AmE), permitted explosive (BrE); ~ **d'amorçage** *m* MINES initiating explosive, primary explosive; ~ **d'amorce** *m* MINES priming explosive; ~ **antigrisouteux** *m* MINES permissible explosive (AmE), permitted explosive (BrE); ~ **à base de coton nitré** *m* MINES nitrocotton explosive; ~ **à basse vitesse de détonation** *m* MINES low explosive; ~ **brisant** *m* MINES high explosive; ~ **de chargement** *m* MINES SBA, slurry-blasting agent, SE, slurry explosive, secondary explosive, secondary high explosive; ~ **chloraté** *m* MINES chlorate explosive; ~ **au coton nitré** *m* MINES nitrocotton explosive; ~ **couche** *m* CHARBON coal mining explosive; ~ **déflagrant** *m* MINES deflagrating explosive; ~ **détonant** *m* MINES detonating explosive, high explosive; ~ **en bouillie** *m* MINES SBA, slurry-blasting agent, SE, slurry explosive, slurry; ~ **de grande puissance** *m* MINES high explosive; ~ **à grande vitesse de détonation** *m* MINES high explosive; ~ **lent** *m* MINES low explosive; ~ **nitraté** *m* MINES ammonia dynamite, extradynamite, nitrate-based explosive; ~ **à l'oxygène liquide** *m* MINES liquid oxygen explosive; ~ **au perchlorate** *m* MINES perchlorate explosive; ~ **primaire** *m* MINES initiating explosive, primary explosive; ~ **puissant** *m* MILITAIRE high explosive; ~ **pulvérulent** *m* MINES powder explosive; ~ **roche** *m* MINES rock work explosive; ~ **rocher** *m* MINES rock work explosive; ~ **secondaire** *m* MINES secondary explosive, secondary high explosive; ~ **de sécurité** *m* MINES permissible explosive (AmE), permitted explosive (BrE); ~ **de sécurité grisou poussière** *m* (Bel) MINES permissible explosive (AmE), permitted explosive (BrE); ~ **SGP** *m* (Bel) MINES permissible explosive (AmE), permitted explosive (BrE); ~ **de sûreté** *m* MINES safety explosive

explosimètre *m* EQUIP LAB *gaz inflammables* explosimeter

explosion *f* ESPACE explosion, MINES detonation, report, PETROLE *gaz, puits, raffinerie, etc* explosion, SECURITE detonation, explosion, THERMODYN detonation; ~ **au carburateur** *f* AUTO blowback; ~ **de chaudière** *f* INST HYDR, SECURITE boiler explosion; ~ **cosmologique initiale** *f* ESPACE *astronomie* Big Bang; ~ **nucléaire** *f* MILITAIRE nuclear explosion; ~ **primordiale** *f* ESPACE Big Bang; ~ **retardée** *f* MINES delayed explosion; ~ **superficielle** *f* MILITAIRE *guerre nucléaire* surface burst; ~ **de supernova** *f* ASTRONOMIE supernova explosion

exponentiel *adj* ELECTR, MATH exponential

exponentielle *f* ELECTR *mathématique*, MATH exponential curve

exportateur: ~ **net** *m* POLLUTION net donator

exposant *m* IMPRIM *composition* superscript, INFORMAT exponent, superscript, MATH, ORDINAT exponent; ~ **d'affaiblissement sur images** *m* ACOUSTIQUE image transfer exponent; ~ **de charge** *m* NAUT boot topping; ~ **du durcissement par écrouissage** *m* MATERIAUX strain-hardening exponent; ~ **linéique de propagation**

m ACOUSTIQUE propagation coefficient, OPTIQUE propagation constant, TELECOM propagation coefficient, propagation constant; ~ **linéique de propagation longitudinale** *m* OPTIQUE, TELECOM axial propagation coefficient; ~ **de la sensibilité de la vitesse à la contrainte** *m* MATERIAUX strain rate sensitivity exponent; ~ **de transfert sur images** *m* ELECTRON image transfer coefficient

exposé: ~ **de l'invention** *m* BREVETS disclosure of the invention

exposer *vt* CINEMAT, PHOTO *une émulsion* expose, TEXTILE display

exposition *f* BREVETS exhibition, IMPRIM *photogravure*, PHOTO, PHYSIQUE, POLLUTION exposure, TEXTILE display; ~ **au bruit durant le travail** *f* SECURITE occupational noise exposure; ~ **énergétique** *f* PHYSIQUE radiant exposure; ~ **au flash** *f* IMPRIM *photogravure* flash exposure; ~ **humaine aux vibrations mécaniques** *f* SECURITE human exposure to mechanical vibrations; ~ **aux intempéries** *f* PLAST CAOU weathering, *revêtements, plastiques* weathering; ~ **aux intempéries artificielles** *f* PLAST CAOU *essai* artificial weathering; ~ **intermédiaire** *f* IMPRIM *insolation* intermediate exposure; ~ **lumineuse** *f* PHYSIQUE *quantité d'éclairement* light exposure; ~ **multiple** *f* CINEMAT multiple exposure; ~ **partielle** *f* IMPRIM *photogravure* partial exposure; ~ **principale** *f* IMPRIM *photogravure* main exposure; ~ **aux radiations** *f* PLAST CAOU exposure to radiation; ~ **secondaire** *f* IMPRIM flash exposure, *photogravure* bump exposure; ~ **aux vapeurs** *f* SECURITE exposure to fumes

expression *f* INFORMAT, ORDINAT expression; ~ **conditionnelle** *f* INFORMAT, ORDINAT conditional expression; ~ **de la sensation d'intensité** *f* ENREGISTR loudness function

exprimer *vt* PRODUCTION squeeze out

expulsion *f* MECANIQUE ejection, PETROLE expulsion

exsudat *m* REFRIG drip

exsudation *f* CHIMIE exudation, MINES sweat, PLAST CAOU exudation

exsuder *vt* CHIMIE, PLAST CAOU exude

extendeur *m* CONSTR tube expander

extenseur: ~ **de ligne** *m* PHYSIQUE line stretcher

extensibilité *f* CONS MECA, INFORMAT, MATERIAUX, ORDINAT, PLAST CAOU extensibility; ~ **de gluten** *f* AGRO ALIM gluten extensibility

extensible *adj* CONS MECA, ELECTR tensile, PAPIER stretchable, TEXTILE stretchy; ~ **sur le site** *adj* PRODUCTION field-expandable

extensif *adj* INFORMAT, ORDINAT, TELECOM expandable

extensiomètre *m* METROLOGIE, PAPIER extensometer

extension *f* CONS MECA extension, CONSTR development, ESPACE expansion, GAZ spread, GEOLOGIE extension, INFORMAT, ORDINAT upgrade, TELECOM telephone extension; ~ **matérielle** *f* INFORMAT hardware upgrade; ~ **mémoire** *f* ORDINAT add-on memory; ~ **de nom de fichier** *f* INFORMAT, ORDINAT filename extension; ~ **de signal** *f* TELECOM signal expansion, signal extension

extensomètre *m* CONSTR extensometer, PHYSIQUE strain gauge (BrE); ~ **à lames** *m* METALL clip gage (AmE), clip gauge (BrE)

extérieur[1] *adj* NAUT outboard

extérieur[2] *m* CINEMAT exterior, location, CONS MECA outboard); ~ **jour** *m* CINEMAT day exterior

externe *adj* POLLUTION external

extincteur *m* CONS MECA extinguisher, SECURITE, THER-

MODYN *d'incendie* fire extinguisher; ~ **automatique d'incendie** *m* NAUT automatic fire sprinkler; ~ **d'incendie** *m* CONSTR, NAUT, SECURITE fire extinguisher; ~ **d'incendie à acide carbonique** *m* SECURITE soda acid fire extinguisher; ~ **d'incendie à dioxyde de carbone** *m* SECURITE carbon dioxide fire extinguisher; ~ **d'incendie à eau** *m* SECURITE water fire extinguisher; ~ **d'incendie encastré** *m* SECURITE fixed fire extinguisher; ~ **d'incendie à halon** *m* SECURITE halon fire extinguisher; ~ **d'incendie à mousse** *m* SECURITE foam fire extinguisher; ~ **d'incendie à neige carbonique** *m* SECURITE soda acid fire extinguisher; ~ **d'incendie à poudre** *m* SECURITE dry powder fire extinguisher; ~ **à liquide dit "ignifuge"** *m* SECURITE nonflammable liquid extinguisher; ~ **mobile** *m* SECURITE mobile fire-extinguisher; ~ **à mousse** *m* AERONAUT, SECURITE foam extinguisher; ~ **à mousse carbonique** *m* THERMODYN foam; ~ **à mousse chimique** *m* THERMODYN foam; ~ **portatif** *m* SECURITE portable fire extinguisher

extinction *f* ASTRONOMIE extinction, CRISTALL absent reflection, extinction, ELECTROTEC turn-off, ESPACE *communications* blowout, flameout, *propulsion* shutdown, GAZ extinction; ~ **accidentelle** *f* ESPACE *communications* flameout; ~ **accidentelle du moteur** *f* ESPACE *propulsion* engine flameout; ~ **d'arc** *f* ELECTR arc extinction, ELECTROTEC arc quenching; ~ **commandée** *f* ESPACE *propulsion* thrust cutoff; ~ **de flamme** *f* THERMODYN flame failure, *dans la chambre de combustion* flameout; ~ **de la flamme dans la chambre de combustion** *f* THERMODYN burnout; ~ **de luminescence** *f* PHYS RAYON quenching of luminescence; ~ **par épuisement** *f* ESPACE *propulsion* burnout; ~ **par excès d'air** *f* AERONAUT *à la décélération* lean die out; ~ **primaire** *f* CRISTALL primary extinction; ~ **du réacteur** *f* AERONAUT engine flameout; ~ **secondaire** *f* CRISTALL secondary extinction; ~ **sélective** *f* PHYS RAYON *des ions* selective quenching; ~ **systématique** *f* CRISTALL systematic absence

extirpateur *m* CONSTR cultivator

extracourant: ~ **de rupture** *m* ELECTROTEC break-induced current

extracteur *m* CERAM VER takeout, CONS MECA ejector pin, CONSTR extractor, MINES core breaker, core catcher, core extractor, core lifter, core plunger, core pusher, PAPIER, PLAST CAOU *moulage* extractor; ~ **2 griffes** *m* CONS MECA two-leg puller; ~ **centrifuge** *m* NUCLEAIRE centrifugal extractor; ~ **de débris** *m* PAPIER junk remover; ~ **de dévasement** *m* NAUT pump dredger; ~ **de fusible** *m* PRODUCTION *électricité* fuse puller; ~ **de goujons cassés** *m* CONS MECA stud extractor; ~ **de modes de gaine** *m* OPTIQUE cladding mode stripper, TELECOM cladding mode stripper, mode stripper; ~ **des pieux** *m* CONSTR pile extractor; ~ **Soxhlet** *m* EQUIP LAB *verrerie* Soxhlet extraction equipment; ~ **à vis** *m* CONS MECA jack off screw

extraction *f* CHARBON extraction, stripping, CINEMAT color separation (AmE), colour separation (BrE), CONS MECA *d'un clou* pulling out, CONSTR extraction, *d'un clou* pulling out, *des clous* drawing, INFORMAT read-out, retrieval, MINES drawing, hoisting, raising, ORDINAT fetch, read-out, retrieval, PAPIER extrusion, PETROLE *forage, raffinage, etc* extraction, PRODUCTION hoisting, off-load, TEXTILE retrieval; ~ **de l'argile** *f* MINES clay mining; ~ **de caractéristiques** *f* INFORMAT, ORDINAT feature extraction; ~ **d'une carrière** *f* MINES quarrying; ~ **de charbon de la houille** *f* CHARBON coal extraction; ~ **des données** *f* INFORMAT data retrieval; ~ **électrolytique** *f* CHIMIE electrowinning; ~ **en discontinu** *f* NUCLEAIRE batch extraction; ~ **d'énergie** *f* EN RENOUV energy extraction; ~ **en va-et-vient** *f* CHARBON shuttle haulage; ~ **de fumée** *f* GENIE CHIM fume extraction; ~ **de gaz** *f* GENIE CHIM degasifying; ~ **d'information** *f* ELECTRON data extraction; ~ **d'instruction** *f* ORDINAT instruction fetching; ~ **du mercure** *f* CHIMIE mercurification; ~ **de message** *f* INFORMAT, ORDINAT message retrieval; ~ **d'une mine** *f* CHARBON mine yield; ~ **monochrome** *f* CINEMAT separation negative; ~ **non planifiée** *f* NUCLEAIRE unscheduled withdrawal; ~ **par câble** *f* CHARBON rope hauling; ~ **par chaîne** *f* CHARBON chain haulage; ~ **par cuffat** *f* CHARBON skip extraction; ~ **par solvant** *f* AGRO ALIM solvent extraction; ~ **positive monochrome** *f* CINEMAT positive separation; ~ **de terre à poterie** *f* CERAM VER potter's clay extraction; ~ **à la vapeur** *f* AGRO ALIM steam extraction

extrados *m* AERONAUT *d'aile* upper surface, CONSTR extrados, *d'une voûte* back, PHYSIQUE upper surface; ~ **de la pale** *m* AERONAUT blade upper surface

extra-fin *adj* TEXTILE sheer

extragalactique *adj* ASTRONOMIE, ESPACE extragalactic

extraire[1] *vt* CHIMIE abstract, extract, CONS MECA *un clou* pull out, CONSTR extract, *un clou* pull out, GAZ extract, INFORMAT, ORDINAT fetch, read out, retrieve, PAPIER extract, PRODUCTION hoist, TEXTILE retrieve

extraire:[2] ~ **en dissolvant** *vi* GENIE CHIM dissolve away, dissolve out; ~ **par distillation** *vi* THERMODYN distil (BrE), distill (AmE); ~ **à la vapeur** *vi* CHIMIE steam distil (BrE), steam distill (AmE)

extrait:[1] ~ **d'une carrière** *adj* GEOLOGIE quarried

extrait[2] *m* CHIMIE, GAZ, PAPIER extract; ~ **à l'acétone** *m* PLAST CAOU *essai* acetone extract; ~ **de levure** *m* AGRO ALIM yeast extract; ~ **de registre** *m* BREVETS extract from the register

extrait-sec *m* PLAST CAOU nonvolatile content

extrapolation *f* QUALITE extrapolation

extrapoler *vt* QUALITE extrapolate

extra-terrestre *adj* ESPACE extraterrestrial

extraterrestre *adj* ASTRONOMIE extraterrestrial

extrême[1] *adj* CONS MECA outer

extrême:[2] ~ **gros-plan** *m* CINEMAT close-up

extrémité *f* ELECTR termination, NAUT *de câble* bitter end, NUCLEAIRE end fitting, end section; ~ **acérée de pointure** *f* IMPRIM *impression sur rotative* chip; ~ **d'aile** *f* AERONAUT *aéronef* wing tip; ~ **amincie** *f* RESSORTS tapered end; ~ **de câble** *f* ELECTR cable end, *liaison* cable termination, ELECTROTEC cable end; ~ **d'une chaîne** *f* CHIMIE end group; ~ **de connexion de canal virtuel** *f* TELECOM VCCE, virtual channel connection endpoint; ~ **de connexion de trajet virtuel** *f* TELECOM VPCE, virtual path connection endpoint; ~ **découpée** *f* RESSORTS trimmed end; ~ **à double fonction** *f* PRODUCTION double-ended; ~ **ébavurée** *f* RESSORTS deburred end; ~ **embrochable** *f* ELECTR *accessoire de câble* plug-in termination; ~ **enfichable** *f* ELECTR *accessoire de câble* plug-in termination; ~ **fermée meulée** *f* RESSORTS closed and ground end; ~ **d'un fil** *f* ELECTROTEC wire end; ~ **forgée** *f* RESSORTS forged end; ~ **meulée** *f* RESSORTS ground end; ~ **motrice** *f* MECANIQUE driving end; ~ **non rapprochée** *f* RESSORTS open end; ~ **de pied de pale** *f* AERONAUT blade shank; ~ **queue de cochon meulée** *f* RESSORTS coned end, ground pigtail end; ~ **rapprochée** *f* RESSORTS squared end; ~ **rapprochée et meulée** *f* RESSORTS squared and ground end; ~ **réduite** *f* RESSORTS coned end; ~ **du réseau** *f* ELECTROTEC network spur; ~ **de trajet de transmission** *f* TELECOM TPE, transmission path endpoint

extruder *vi* PLAST CAOU *caoutchouc, plastiques* extrude

extrudeur: ~ **hélicoïdal** *m* AGRO ALIM screw extruder; ~ **à vis** *m* AGRO ALIM screw extruder

extrudeuse *f* PAPIER extruder, PLAST CAOU extruder, *plastiques* extrusion machine; ~ **pour caoutchouc** *f* CONS MECA rubber extruder

extrusion *f* AGRO ALIM, CONS MECA, MECANIQUE, PAPIER extrusion, PLAST CAOU extrudability; ~ **de feuille** *f* PLAST CAOU *procédé* film extrusion; ~ **par soufflage** *f* EMBALLAGE blow moulding

extrusion-soufflage *f* EMBALLAGE extrusion blow molding (AmE), extrusion blow moulding (BrE)

exutoire *m* DISTRI EAU outlet, HYDROLOGIE outfall, outlet

F

f *abrév (femto-)* METROLOGIE f *(femto-)*
F[1] *(fluor)* CHIMIE F *(fluorine)*
F[2] *abrév (farad)* METROLOGIE F *(farad)*

fabricant *m* CONSTR fabricator, PRODUCTION maker; ~ **d'encre** *m* IMPRIM ink maker; ~ **d'encre d'impression** *m* IMPRIM ink maker; ~ **d'équipement** *m* NAUT equipment manufacturer; ~ **de sacs** *m* EMBALLAGE bagmaker

fabricateur *m* CONSTR fabricator

fabrication *f* CINEMAT batch, PRODUCTION make, manufacture, manufacturing; ~ **assistée par ordinateur** *f* *(FAO)* ELECTR, ORDINAT, TELECOM computer-aided manufacturing *(CAM)*; ~ **de circuits intégrés** *f* ELECTRON integrated circuit fabrication; ~ **de clichés pour la reliure** *f* IMPRIM blockmaking; ~ **à la commande** *f* PRODUCTION custom manufacture, custom production, job shop, order shop; ~ **d'encarts** *f* IMPRIM *impression, façonnage* insert production; ~ **en ligne** *f* PRODUCTION *production en grande série* flow shop; ~ **en petite quantité** *f* EMBALLAGE short run; ~ **en série** *f* PRODUCTION gang work, mass production, repetitive work; ~ **de masques** *f* ELECTRON mask generation; ~ **de matrices et poinçons en forgeage à froid** *f* CONS MECA manufacture of forging dies and punches; ~ **de papier** *f* PAPIER paper making; ~ **par lots** *f* PRODUCTION job shop; ~ **de petits lots** *f* CONS MECA small batch production; ~ **de plaques** *f* IMPRIM *copie* plate making; ~ **de plaquettes** *f* ELECTRON wafer fabrication; ~ **de précision** *f* CONS MECA precision engineering; ~ **de semi-conducteur** *f* ELECTRON semiconductor fabrication; ~ **de tickets** *f* IMPRIM *continu* ticketing

fabrique *f* PETR fabric; ~ **de ciment** *f* CERAM VER cement works

façade *f* CONSTR front, *d'un édifice* façade, PRODUCTION *d'une chaudière, d'un foyer* front; ~ **borgne** *f* CONSTR blind wall; ~ **de chaudière** *f* INST HYDR boiler front; ~ **maritime** *f* NAUT waterfront

face:[1] ~ **texte** *adv* IMPRIM *composition, préparation de copie, maquette* against text; ~ **au vent** *adv* AERONAUT into the wind

face[2] *f* CONSTR front, GEOMETRIE, PRODUCTION *d'un marteau*, PHYSIQUE face; ~ **d'appui** *f* CONS MECA chuck face; ~ **arrière** *f* ORDINAT backplane; ~ **avant** *f* CONS MECA front face, front panel; ~ **comprimée** *f* RESSORTS compression side; ~ **concave** *f* RESSORTS concave side; ~ **convexe** *f* RESSORTS convex side; ~ **couchée** *f* IMPRIM *papier autocopiant* coated front; ~ **cristalline** *f* CRISTALL crystal face; ~ **jointive** *f* PRODUCTION flange face; ~ **magnétique** *f* CONS MECA magnetic face; ~ **polaire** *f* TV pole face; ~ **de soupape** *f* VEHICULES *moteur* valve face; ~ **de taille** *f* CONSTR *tunnel* face; ~ **tendue** *f* RESSORTS tension side; ~ **texte** *f* IMPRIM *composition, montage* opposite text, *mise en page* facing matter

faces:[1] **à ~ bien cristallisées** *adj* GEOLOGIE *roche métamorphique* idioblastic

faces:[2] ~ **de mesure extérieure** *f pl* CONS MECA *pied à coulisse* outside measuring faces; ~ **de mesure intérieure** *f pl* CONS MECA inside measuring faces

facette: ~ **de brunissage** *f* ACOUSTIQUE surface burnishing facet; ~ **de clivage** *f* METALL cleavage facet; ~ **plate** *f* INSTRUMENT flat surface; ~ **spéciale** *f* INSTRUMENT special surface

faciès *m* GEOLOGIE *métamorphique et sédimentaire*, PETR facies; ~ **métamorphique** *m* GEOLOGIE metamorphic facies; ~ **de métamorphisme** *m* GEOLOGIE metamorphic facies; ~ **de rupture** *m* MECANIQUE *matériaux* breaking pattern

facilité: ~ **d'accès** *f* MECANIQUE ease of access; ~ **d'entretien** *f* PRODUCTION maintainability; ~ **de manipulation** *f* MATERIAUX ease of operation; ~ **N** *f* TELECOM N-facility; ~ **d'utilisation** *f* MECANIQUE ease of operation

façon *f* PRODUCTION pattern, workmanship

façonnage *m* IMPRIM finishing, MECANIQUE *matériaux* forming, PAPIER finishing, PETROLE processing, PRODUCTION manufacturing; ~ **de brides** *m* PRODUCTION flanging; ~ **à chaud** *m* MECANIQUE hot forming, THERMODYN heat forming; ~ **dos collé** *m* IMPRIM tightback binding; ~ **à froid** *m* MECANIQUE cold forming; ~ **des joints** *m* CERAM VER pencil edging

façonné: ~ **à chaud** *adj* RESSORTS hot-formed; ~ **à froid** *adj* RESSORTS cold-formed

façonner *vt* PRODUCTION shape; ~ **à chaud** *vt* THERMODYN heat-form

fac-similé *m* IMPRIM *télétransmissions*, INFORMAT, ORDINAT, TELECOM facsimile; ~ **à éléments d'intensité constante** *m* IMPRIM A-type facsimile

facteur *m* INFORMAT, ORDINAT factor; ~ **d'absorption** *m* ACOUSTIQUE absorption factor, PHYSIQUE absorptance, TELECOM absorption factor; ~ **d'absorption acoustique** *m* PHYSIQUE acoustic absorption coefficient; ~ **d'accommodation thermique** *m* ESPACE thermal accommodation coefficient; ~ **d'activité** *m* ESPACE *communications* activity factor, PHYSIQUE activity coefficient; ~ **d'activité des signaux vocaux** *m* TELECOM speech activity factor; ~ **d'amélioration par préaccentuation** *m* ESPACE *communications* pre-emphasis improvement factor; ~ **d'amortissement** *m* ELECTR *oscillation* damping factor, ELECTROTEC decay factor; ~ **d'amortissement hydrodynamique** *m* EN RENOUV hydrodynamic damping factor; ~ **d'amplification** *m* ENREGISTR amplification factor; ~ **d'amplitude** *m* ENREGISTR gain; ~ **d'anisoélasticité** *m* ESPACE *mécanique* anisoelasticity factor; ~ **d'atténuation** *m* AERONAUT alleviation factor; ~ **Atwater** *m* AGRO ALIM Atwater factor; ~ **d'autoserrage** *m* ESPACE port to throat area ratio; ~ **d'avantage** *m* NUCLEAIRE advantage factor; ~ **de bruit** *m* ELECTRON noise factor, noise figure, ESPACE, IMPRIM *ergonomie*, PHYSIQUE noise factor; ~ **de cadrage** *m* ORDINAT scale factor; ~ **camions** *m* TRANSPORT truck factor (AmE); ~ **de capacité de rendement annuelle** *m* EN RENOUV annual capacity factor; ~ **de charge** *m* AERONAUT, ELECTROTEC load factor, ESPACE *communications* loading factor, MECANIQUE load factor, PRODUCTION *automatisme industriel* power factor, REFRIG load factor; ~ **de charge d'entrée** *m* PRODUCTION input power factor; ~ **de charge limite** *m* AERONAUT limit load factor; ~ **de charge de rafale** *m* AERONAUT gust load factor; ~ **de cimentation** *m* PETR cementation factor; ~ **de compressibilité** *m* PETR, THERMODYN compressibility factor; ~ **de compression** *m* ENREGISTR compression ratio; ~ **de confiance** *m* CRISTALL R-factor, reliability index; ~ **de contraste** *m* CINEMAT contrast, contrast ratio, gamma; ~ **de conversion d'énergie** *m* PHYS RAYON energy conversion factor; ~ **de correction** *m* METROLOGIE correction factor; ~ **de correction de la contrainte** *m* RESSORTS stress correction factor; ~ **de correction de flèche de la contrainte** *m* RESSORTS curvature correction factor, stress correction factor; ~ **de correction de la traînée induite** *m* AERONAUT correction factor for induced drag; ~ **de courbe** *m* EN RENOUV curve factor; ~ **de crête** *m* ELECTRON peak factor, ELECTROTEC crest factor, ESPACE *communications* peak factor; ~ **de Debye-Waller** *m* CRISTALL Debye-Waller factor; ~ **de décontamination** *m* PHYS RAYON decontamination factor; ~ **de décroissance** *m* ENREGISTR decay factor; ~ **de déviation** *m* ELECTRON deflection factor; ~ **de diffusion** *m* CRISTALL scattering factor; ~ **de diffusion atomique** *m* CRISTALL atomic scattering factor; ~ **de diffusion thermique** *m* PHYSIQUE thermal diffusion factor; ~ **directionnel** *m* EN RENOUV directionality factor; ~ **de directivité** *m* ACOUSTIQUE directivity factor, EN RENOUV directionality factor; ~ **de dispersion de profil** *m* OPTIQUE profile dispersion factor, TELECOM profile dispersion parameter; ~ **de dissipation** *m* ELECTR, PHYSIQUE dissipation factor; ~ **d'échelle** *m* ELECTRON scaling factor, INFORMAT scale factor; ~ **écologique** *m* POLLUTION ecological factor; ~ **d'écran** *m* NUCLEAIRE screen factor; ~ **d'efficacité lumineuse** *m* PHYS RAYON luminosity coefficient; ~ **d'efficacité de la pale** *m* AERONAUT blade efficiency factor; ~ **d'encrassement** *m* REFRIG fouling factor; ~ **d'enrichissement unitaire** *m* NUCLEAIRE elementary enrichment factor; ~ **d'entrance** *m* ELECTROTEC fan-in factor; ~ **d'entrecroisement** *m* TRANSPORT weaving factor; ~ **êta** *m* PHYSIQUE eta factor, neutron yield; ~ **de fission rapide** *m* PHYSIQUE fast-fission factor; ~ **de fission thermique** *m* PHYSIQUE thermal fission factor; ~ **de flexibilité** *m* CONS MECA flexibility factor; ~ **de formation** *m* PETR formation factor, formation resistivity; ~ **de formation d'énergie** *m* EN RENOUV energy pattern factor; ~ **de forme de particules** *m* GENIE CHIM particle form factor; ~ **de frottement** *m* METROLOGIE coefficient of friction; ~ **g** *m* PHYSIQUE g-factor; ~ **géométrique** *m* PHYSIQUE geometric factor; ~ **d'induction mutuelle** *m* ELECTROTEC mutual inductance; ~ **de Landé** *m* PHYSIQUE Landé factor; ~ **de lissage** *m* PRODUCTION smoothing factor; ~ **de lissage de tendance** *m* PRODUCTION smoothing factor for trend; ~ **de luminosité** *m* PHYS RAYON luminosity factor, TV brightness value; ~ **majeur** *m* PRODUCTION chief factor; ~ **de mérite** *m* ELECTRON, ESPACE figure of merit; ~ **de modulation** *m* ELECTRON modulation factor; ~ **multiplicateur** *m* PRODUCTION coefficient; ~ **de multiplication de gaz** *m* ELECTRON gas multiplication factor; ~ **nu** *m* PHYSIQUE neutron yield; ~ **d'orientation** *m* METALL orientation factor; ~ **de pente** *m* ENREGISTR selectivity Q; ~ **de perte** *m* ELECTR *d'éner-*

gie loss factor; ~ **de perte en bout de pale** *m* AERONAUT blade tip loss factor; ~ **de perte transductique** *m* ACOUSTIQUE transducer loss factor; ~ **de phase** *m* ESPACE phase integral; ~ **de pleurage** *m* ENREGISTR flutter factor; ~ **de pointe** *m* TRANSPORT PHF, peak hour factor, rush hour factor; ~ **de pondération** *m* ESPACE *communications* weighting factor; ~ **de pondération psophométrique** *m* ESPACE *communications* psophometric weighting factor; ~ **de poussée** *m* ESPACE thrust coefficient; ~ **premier** *m* MATH prime factor; ~ **de prise** *m* ELECTR tapping factor; ~ **de prolongation de temps de pose** *m* PHOTO *d'un filtre* filter factor; ~ **de puissance** *m* ELECTR, ELECTROTEC, PHYSIQUE, PLAST CAOU power factor; ~ **de puissance au maintien** *m* PRODUCTION *contact* sealed power factor; ~ **Q** *m* ESSAIS, PHYSIQUE Q-factor, quality factor; ~ **Q de bobine** *m* ELECTR coil Q-factor; ~ **de qualité** *m* PHYSIQUE, POLLUTION Q-factor, quality factor; ~ **R** *m* CRISTALL R-factor, reliability index, NUCLEAIRE agreement residual; ~ **de récupération** *m* PETR, PETROLE recovery factor; ~ **de récupération d'énergie** *m* EN RENOUV energy recovery factor; ~ **de réduction du brouillage** *m* ESPACE *communications* interference reduction factor; ~ **de réduction du temps de transit** *m* PRODUCTION transit-time reduction factor; ~ **de réflectance** *m* PAPIER reflectance factor; ~ **de réflectance dans le bleu** *m* PAPIER blue reflectance factor; ~ **de réflectance diffuse dans le bleu** *m* PAPIER diffuse blue reflectance factor; ~ **de réflectance directionnelle dans le bleu** *m* PAPIER directional blue reflectance factor; ~ **de réflexion** *m* ELECTRON reflection factor, OPTIQUE reflectance energy factor, reflection coefficient, PHYS RAYON reflectance factor, PHYSIQUE reflectance, reflectance factor, reflection factor, TELECOM reflectance; ~ **de réflexion énergétique** *m* OPTIQUE power reflection coefficient, reflectance energy factor; ~ **de réflexion en pression** *m* ACOUSTIQUE pressure reflection coefficient; ~ **de remplissage** *m* OPTIQUE *d'un faisceau de fibres*, TELECOM packing fraction; ~ **de retour** *m* ESPACE return factor; ~ **de rétrodiffusion** *m* ESPACE backscattering factor; ~ **de Sabine** *m* ACOUSTIQUE Sabine coefficient; ~ **de saisonnalité** *m* PRODUCTION season factor; ~ **de saturation** *m* TRANSPORT load factor; ~ **de sécurité** *m* ELECTR safety factor, PRODUCTION coefficient of safety, SECURITE safety factor; ~ **de serrage** *m* ESPACE burning surface-to-throat area ratio; ~ **spectral de réflexion** *m* PHYSIQUE spectral reflectance; ~ **de structure** *m* CRISTALL structure factor; ~ **de suppression** *m* ESPACE *communications* suppression factor; ~ **de surcharge** *m* ELECTR *réseau* overload factor; ~ **de surtension** *m* PHYSIQUE Q-factor, quality factor; ~ **de taille volumétrique** *m* METALL volume size factor; ~ **de tassement** *m* PHYSIQUE packing fraction; ~ **de température** *m* CRISTALL temperature factor; ~ **de transmission** *m* OPTIQUE, PHYSIQUE, TELECOM transmittance; ~ **d'utilisation** *m* ELECTROTEC load factor; ~ **d'utilisation thermique** *m* PHYSIQUE thermal resistivity, thermal utilization factor; ~ **de vide** *m* NUCLEAIRE vacuum factor; ~ **volumétrique de formation** *m* PETR formation volume factor; ~ **volumétrique de gaz** *m* PETR gas formation volume factor; ~ **volumétrique d'huile** *m* PETR oil formation volume factor

factice *adj* EMBALLAGE dummy

faction: ~ **densimétrique** *f* CHARBON specific gravity fraction

factoriel *adj* MATH factorial
factorielle *f* MATH, ORDINAT factorial
factorisation *f* MATH factorization
factoriser *vt* MATH factorize
facturation *f* TELECOM billing; ~ **détaillée** *f* TELECOM detailed billing
facule *f* ASTRONOMIE facula; ~ **solaire** *f* ASTRONOMIE solar flare
facultatif *adj* TELECOM nonmandatory, optional
faculté: ~ **de conservation** *f* AGRO ALIM keeping quality
fading *m* ELECTRON fading; ~ **des freins** *m* VEHICULES *plaquette, garniture* brake fade
fahlerz *m* MINERAUX fahl ore, fahlerz
fahlunite *f* MINERAUX fahlunite
faible[1] *adj* PRODUCTION thin; **à** ~ **consommation d'énergie** *adj* THERMODYN energy-saving; ~ **consommatrice d'énergie** *adj* THERMODYN energy-saving; **de** ~ **encombrement** *adj* CONS MECA compact; **de** ~ **puissance** *adj* ELECTROTEC low-power; **à** ~ **teneur en matière grasse** *adj* AGRO ALIM low-fat
faible:[2] ~ **tirant d'eau** *m* NAUT shallow draft
faible[3] *f* ASTRONOMIE fading comet; ~ **capacité** *f* ELECTROTEC low capacitance; ~ **charge** *f* ELECTROTEC light loading; ~ **concentration** *f* ELECTRON low concentration; ~ **densité** *f* MATERIAUX low density; ~ **densité de xénon dans l'atmosphère terrestre** *f* ASTRONOMIE low density xenon in the Earth's atmosphere; ~ **dépression** *f* METEO low depression, shallow depression; ~ **épaisseur** *f* PRODUCTION thinness; ~ **inversion** *f* ELECTRON weak inversion; ~ **résistance** *f* TELECOM low resistance; ~ **surchauffe** *f* REFRIG low superheat; ~ **teneur** *f* MINES baseness, low grade, poor grade; ~ **teneur en soufre** *f* PETROLE *brut* low sulfur content (AmE), low sulphur content (BrE); ~ **torsion** *f* TEXTILE low level of twist; ~ **vitesse** *f* CONS MECA low-speed
faiblisseur *m* PHOTO reducer
faïence *f* CERAM VER glazed earthenware
faïencier *m* CERAM VER crockery maker, pottery maker
faille *f* CHARBON fault, stone wall, CONSTR crack, GEOLOGIE crack, fault, METALL failure, MINES, PETROLE, PRODUCTION fault; ~ **antithétique** *f* GEOLOGIE antithetic fault; ~ **de bloc** *f* GEOLOGIE block faulting; ~ **bordière** *f* GEOLOGIE boundary fault; ~ **de charriage** *f* GEOLOGIE lag fault; ~ **courbe** *f* GEOLOGIE *en forme de cuiller* listric fault; ~ **de croissance** *f* GEOLOGIE growth fault, synsedimentary fault; ~ **de déchirement** *f* GEOLOGIE tear fault; ~ **décrochante** *f* GEOLOGIE tear fault; ~ **de distension** *f* GEOLOGIE distensional fault; ~ **en gradins** *f* GEOLOGIE distributive fault; ~ **de Griffith** *f* CERAM VER Griffith flaw; ~ **inverse** *f* GEOLOGIE reverse fault; ~ **inverse sur un flanc de pli** *f* GEOLOGIE break thrust; ~ **listrique** *f* GEOLOGIE *en forme de cuiller* listric fault; ~ **normale** *f* GEOLOGIE normal fault; ~ **oblique** *f* GEOLOGIE dip fault; ~ **parallèle à la direction du pendage** *f* GEOLOGIE dip fault; ~ **par fatigue** *f* METALL fatigue failure; ~ **pentée** *f* PETR dip fault; ~ **radiale** *f* MATERIAUX failure, radial fault; ~ **senestre** *f* PETR sinistral fault; ~ **syngénétique** *f* GEOLOGIE contemporaneous fault, depositional fault; ~ **synsédimentaire** *f* GEOLOGIE growth fault, synsedimental fault; ~ **synthétique** *f* GEOLOGIE synthetic fault; ~ **transformante** *f* GEOLOGIE transform fault; ~ **transversale** *f* GEOLOGIE dip fault, strike slip; ~ **verticale de décrochement** *f* GEOLOGIE wrench fault
faillir *vi* PRODUCTION give out

faire:[1] ~ **abattre** *vt* NAUT cant; ~ **apparaître lentement** *vt* ENREGISTR fade in; ~ **avancer** *vt* IMPRIM forward; ~ **avorter** *vt* ORDINAT abort; ~ **baisser** *vt* CONSTR cause to subside; ~ **balancer** *vt* CONSTR *marche* dance; ~ **basculer** *vt* CONS MECA swing, CONSTR tip, tip up, PHYSIQUE trip; ~ **du bois** *vt* CONSTR timber; ~ **bouillir** *vt* AGRO ALIM parboil, THERMODYN boil; ~ **breveter** *vt* BREVETS patent; ~ **cailler** *vt* GENIE CHIM coagulate; ~ **chevaucher** *vt* PRODUCTION *un module* straddle; ~ **coïncider** *vt* CONS MECA align, PRODUCTION match; ~ **une collure** *vt* CINEMAT, TV splice; ~ **la copie originale de** *vt* ENREGISTR master; ~ **correspondre à** *vt* PHOTO register; ~ **couler du texte** *vt* IMPRIM *composition électronique* pour; ~ **crever** *vt* CONSTR burst; ~ **cuire à demi** *vt* AGRO ALIM blanch, parboil; ~ **cuire à l'étuvée** *vt* AGRO ALIM braise; ~ **dégeler** *vt* METEO thaw; ~ **démarrer** *vt* CONS MECA start, start up; ~ **dérailler** *vt* CH DE FER derail; ~ **détoner** *vt* MINES detonate, THERMODYN detonate, explode; ~ **disparaître au fer** *vt* TEXTILE iron out; ~ **disparaître lentement** *vt* ENREGISTR fade out; ~ **éclater** *vt* CONSTR burst, THERMODYN explode; ~ **écouler** *vt* DISTRI EAU drain, *eau d'un réservoir* run off; ~ **effondrer** *vt* CONSTR cause to subside; ~ **égoutter** *vt* DISTRI EAU drain; ~ **entrer au bassin** *vt* NAUT dock; ~ **entrer au dock** *vt* NAUT dock; ~ **l'estimation de** *vt* SECURITE make a valuation of; ~ **éviter** *vt* NAUT cant; ~ **l'expertise de l'état de** *vt* NAUT *navire* survey; ~ **exploser** *vt* THERMODYN detonate; ~ **flotter** *vt* PHYSIQUE float; ~ **fonctionner** *vt* CONS MECA run; ~ **fondre** *vt* CHIMIE *substance*, PRODUCTION melt, THERMODYN melt down, melt; ~ **frémir** *vt* CHIMIE simmer; ~ **gonfler** *vt* AGRO ALIM puff; ~ **gouverner** *vt* NAUT conn; ~ **l'hydrographie de** *vt* NAUT *côte* survey; ~ **jaillir** *vt* PHYS FLUID jet; ~ **joint étanche** *vt* PRODUCTION make a tight joint; ~ **macérer** *vt* AGRO ALIM steep; ~ **marcher** *vt* CINEMAT run; ~ **marcher par à-coups** *vt* IMPRIM jog; ~ **un mixage de** *vt* TV mix; ~ **passer à l'antenne** *vt* TV air; ~ **pénétrer les dents dans** *vt* CONS MECA bite, bite into; ~ **pivoter** *vt* INFORMAT, ORDINAT rotate; ~ **des plis** *vt* TEXTILE pleat; ~ **une prise à** *vt* PRODUCTION tap; ~ **prise sur** *vt* PRODUCTION tap; ~ **le rapport de scripte** *vt* CINEMAT log; ~ **un recuit** *vt* THERMODYN anneal, stress relief; ~ **le relevé de** *vt* CONSTR plot; ~ **sauter** *vt* THERMODYN detonate; ~ **une séchée** *vt* CERAM VER polish till dry; ~ **sortir par pression** *vt* GENIE CHIM separate by pressing; ~ **sur mesure** *vt* TEXTILE customize; ~ **la tare d'un ressort** *vt* CONS MECA scale; ~ **travailler** *vt* CONS MECA, *moteur* run; ~ **tremper** *vt* TEXTILE soak; ~ **venir de fonte** *vt* PRODUCTION cast
faire:[2] ~ **un aller-retour** *vi* PETROLE make a round trip; ~ **l'aperçu** *vi* NAUT acknowledge a signal; ~ **bip-bip** *vi* NAUT bleep; ~ **des bulles** *vi* PAPIER bubble; ~ **la cargaison** *vi* NAUT load a ship; ~ **du charbon** *vi* CHARBON break coal, coal; ~ **une copie de sauvegarde** *vi* ORDINAT back up; ~ **coulisser d'avant en arrière** *vi* PRODUCTION slide back and forth; ~ **défaut** *vi* PRODUCTION give out; ~ **défiler** *vi* INFORMAT, ORDINAT scroll; ~ **de l'eau** *vi* DISTRI EAU water; ~ **eau** *vi* CONSTR leak, NAUT leak; ~ **écouler** *vi* DISTRI EAU *les eaux* drain off; ~ **une embardée** *vi* ESPACE *véhicules* yaw, NAUT lurch, sheer off, yaw; ~ **explosion** *vi* THERMODYN explode; ~ **des forages** *vi* MINES bore, drill; ~ **un joint** *vi* CONSTR make a joint; ~ **des lacets** *vi* EN RENOUV yaw; ~ **un levé de plans** *vi* CONSTR do a survey; ~ **long feu** *vi* ESPACE abort; ~ **machine arrière** *vi* NAUT go

astern; ~ **une manoeuvre** *vi* PETROLE make a round trip; ~ **marche arrière** *vi* NAUT go astern; ~ **des méandres** *vi* HYDROLOGIE invert; ~ **la mise au point** *vi* CINEMAT adjust focus, rack focus, focus, pull focus; ~ **un montage papier** *vi* IMPRIM paste up; ~ **monter la température** *vi* THERMODYN heat up; ~ **un mouvement de lacet** *vi* ESPACE *véhicules* yaw; ~ **des moyennes sur les écoulements turbulents** *vi* PHYS FLUID average in turbulent flow; ~ **naufrage** *vi* NAUT be wrecked, go down, suffer shipwreck; ~ **un panoramique vers le bas** *vi* CINEMAT pan down; ~ **le point** *vi* NAUT take a bearing, *sur la carte* plot the position; ~ **le point fixe** *vi* AERONAUT *moteur* run-up; ~ **prise** *vi* CONSTR set; ~ **des prises de vues** *vi* CINEMAT shoot; ~ **le quart** *vi* NAUT keep watch; ~ **route** *vi* NAUT run, sail; ~ **des sondages** *vi* CONSTR bore, drill a borehole, MINES bore, drill; ~ **des sondages pour trouver de l'eau** *vi* DISTRI EAU bore for water; ~ **surface** *vi* NAUT *sous-marin* shelter; ~ **un tour mort** *vi* NAUT make a turn round winch with line; ~ **des travaux miniers** *vi* MINES mine; ~ **un travelling** *vi* CINEMAT dolly, track; ~ **un travelling arrière** *vi* CINEMAT dolly back, pull back; ~ **un travelling avant** *vi* CINEMAT dolly in; ~ **un travelling optique** *vi* CINEMAT zoom; ~ **un trou de sondage** *vi* CONSTR bore; ~ **de l'usage** *vi* TEXTILE wear; ~ **ventre** *vi* CONSTR bulge; ~ **une vérification orthographique** *vi* INFORMAT run a spellcheck; ~ **le vide** *vi* MECANIQUE evacuate, PAPIER apply vacuum, PHYSIQUE evacuate; ~ **voile** *vi* NAUT sail

faisceau *m* CH DE FER group, sidings, CINEMAT beam, CONS MECA *de ressorts* cluster, cluster spring, nest, CRISTALL, ELECTRON, ESPACE *communications* beam, GEOLOGIE sequence, set, NAUT *phare* beam, OPTIQUE bundle, PHYS RAYON *physique nucléaire*, PHYSIQUE beam, PRODUCTION cluster, sheaf, TELECOM beam, bundle, group, TRANSPORT cluster, TV beam; ~ **aimanté** *m* PHYSIQUE compound magnet; ~ **analyseur** *m* TV scanning beam; ~ **analyseur reconduit à la cathode** *m* TV return-scanning beam; ~ **atomique** *m* NUCLEAIRE *jet* atomic beam; ~ **d'attente** *m* CH DE FER locomotive-holding siding; ~ **de balayage** *m* ELECTRON scanning beam; ~ **à balayage cavalier** *m* ELECTRON vector-scanned beam; ~ **à balayage tramé** *m* ELECTRON raster scanned beam; ~ **bleu** *m* ELECTRON blue beam; ~ **à bouts compactés** *m* CERAM VER fused bundle; ~ **de câbles** *m* ELECTROTEC cable bundle, MECANIQUE harness cable; ~ **cathodique** *m* ELECTR TRC cathode ray pencil, ELECTRON cathode beam; ~ **de circuits** *m* TELECOM circuit group, route; ~ **à cohérence temporelle** *m* ELECTRON temporally-coherent beam; ~ **collimaté** *m* ELECTRON collimated beam; ~ **continu** *m* ELECTRON continuous beam; ~ **convergent** *m* OPTIQUE convergent beam; ~ **à couverture totale** *m* ESPACE *communications* full coverage beam, global beam; ~ **de dernier choix** *m* TELECOM last-choice circuit group, last-choice group; ~ **de détection incendie** *m* AERONAUT fire detecting wire; ~ **dévié** *m* TV deflected beam; ~ **diffracté** *m* CRISTALL diffracted beam; ~ **directionnel** *m* TELECOM directional beam; ~ **dirigé** *m* ELECTRON directional beam; ~ **à double sens** *m* TELECOM both-way group; ~ **d'éjection** *m* NUCLEAIRE ejected beam; ~ **élargi** *m* CINEMAT flooded beam; ~ **électronique** *m* ELECTR *microscope*, METALL, ORDINAT, TELECOM, TV EB, electron beam; ~ **électronique analyseur** *m* TV electron scanning beam; ~ **d'électrons** *m* ELECTRON, NUCLEAIRE, PHYS ONDES, PHYS PART EB,

electron beam; ~ **d'électrons de balayage** *m* ELECTRON scanning electron beam; ~ **d'électrons à gravure directe** *m* ELECTRON direct write electron beam; ~ **d'éléments absorbants** *m* NUCLEAIRE absorber element bundle; ~ **d'éloignement** *m* AERONAUT outbound beam; ~ **en éventail** *m* ELECTRON fan beam; ~ **de l'énième choix** *m* TELECOM nth choice group; ~ **entrant** *m* TELECOM incoming group; ~ **d'entretien** *m* ELECTRON holding beam; ~ **étroit** *m* ESPACE *communications* spot beam, PHYS RAYON *de lumière* pencil beam; ~ **explorateur** *m* TV scanning beam; ~ **à faible énergie** *m* ELECTRON low-energy beam; ~ **de failles** *m* GEOLOGIE fault bundle; ~ **de fibres** *m* OPTIQUE, TELECOM fiber bundle (AmE), fibre bundle (BrE); ~ **de fils** *m* ELECTROTEC wire bundle; ~ **à fort trafic** *m* TELECOM high-usage circuit group; ~ **gaussien** *m* TELECOM Gaussian beam; ~ **à haute énergie** *m* ELECTRON high-energy beam; ~ **hertzien** *m* PHYS RAYON electromagnetic wave, TELECOM microwave beam, TV Hertzian beam, radio link; ~ **hertzien numérique** *m* ESPACE DRS, digital radio system; ~ **ILS** *m* ESPACE *véhicules* ILS beam; ~ **incident** *m* CRISTALL, PHYSIQUE incident beam; ~ **d'ions** *m* ELECTRON, PHYS RAYON ion beam; ~ **d'ions mis au point** *m* PHYS RAYON focused ion beam; ~ **d'ions mis au point de faible énergie** *m* PHYS RAYON low-energy focused ion beam; ~ **isogène** *m* PHYSIQUE homocentric beam; ~ **de lames constituant la barre de torsion** *m* AERONAUT laminated torsion bar; ~ **laser** *m* ELECTRON, NUCLEAIRE, TELECOM laser beam; ~ **laser continu** *m* ELECTRON continuous laser beam; ~ **laser diode** *m* ELECTRON CW laser beam; ~ **laser à grande densité de puissance** *m* ELECTRON high-irradiance laser beam; ~ **de lecture** *m* ELECTRON reading beam, OPTIQUE scanning laser beam; ~ **de lignes** *m* TELECOM line group; ~ **de lumière** *m* PHYSIQUE light beam; ~ **de lumière laser** *m* PHYS RAYON laser light beam; ~ **à lumière rouge** *m* ELECTRON red beam; ~ **lumineux** *m* CINEMAT light beam, ENREGISTR scanning light beam, IMPRIM *photo, laser, optique* beam, PHOTO light beam; ~ **mis en forme** *m* ELECTRON shaped beam; ~ **mixte** *m* TELECOM both-way group; ~ **modulé** *m* ELECTRON modulated beam; ~ **modulé en vitesse** *m* ELECTRON velocity-modulated beam; ~ **moléculaire** *m* TELECOM molecule beam; ~ **monochromatique cohérent** *m* PHYS RAYON coherent monochromatic beam; ~ **multiple** *m* TELECOM multiple beam; ~ **de neutrons** *m* PHYS PART neutron beam; ~ **optique** *m* TELECOM light beam; ~ **parallèle** *m* PHYSIQUE parallel beam; ~ **de particules** *m* ELECTRON particle beam, PHYS PART beam; ~ **de particules chargées** *m* ELECTRON charged particle beam; ~ **de pieux** *m* CHARBON pile group; ~ **pour le bleu** *m* TV blue beam; ~ **pour le rouge** *m* TV red beam; ~ **pour le vert** *m* TV green beam; ~ **de premier choix** *m* TELECOM first choice group; ~ **principal** *m* ESPACE *communications* main beam; ~ **de protons** *m* PHYS PART proton beam; ~ **radar** *m* NAUT radar beam; ~ **de radiateur** *m* AUTO, VEHICULES *refroidissement* radiator core; ~ **radio** *m* PHYS RAYON radio beam; ~ **de radioalignement de descente** *m* TRANSPORT glide path beam; ~ **de radiophare de balisage** *m* AERONAUT localizer beam; ~ **de rayonnement** *m* PHYS RAYON beam; ~ **de rayons cathodiques** *m* TV cathode ray beam; ~ **de rayons gamma** *m* PHYS PART gamma ray beam; ~ **de rayons parallèles** *m* ELECTRON parallel beam; ~ **de rayons X** *m* ELECTRON X-ray beam; ~ **réfléchi** *m*

PHYSIQUE reflected beam; ~ **de régénération** m ELECTRON holding beam; ~ **de rétrofusées** m ESPACE *véhicules* retropack; ~ **rouge** m ELECTRON red beam; ~ **sortant** m TELECOM outgoing group; ~ **sorti** m NUCLEAIRE *d'un accélérateur, d'un réacteur* ejected beam; ~ **supprimé** m ELECTRON blanked beam; ~ **de surfaces chauffantes** m NUCLEAIRE heating surface bundle; ~ **de trajectoire d'atterrissage** m AERONAUT glide path beam; ~ **transmis** m PHYSIQUE transmitted beam; ~ **très étroit** m ELECTRON pencil beam; ~ **tubulaire** m NUCLEAIRE tube bundle, tube nest

faisceaux: ~ **à bande large** m pl PHYS RAYON *rayonnement* wide band beams; ~ **d'électrons et de positrons de haute énergie** m pl PHYS PART high-energy electron-positron beams; ~ **hertziens** m pl TELECOM microwave systems; ~ **d'ions à forte intensité** m pl PHYS RAYON high-intensity ion beams; ~ **de kaons de haute énergie** m pl PHYS PART high-energy kaon beams; ~ **de muons de haute énergie** m pl PHYS PART high-energy muon beams

fait: ~ **à la main** adj PRODUCTION made by hand; ~ **mécaniquement** adj PRODUCTION made by machine, made by machinery; ~ **sur demande** adj EMBALLAGE custom-made, purpose-designed

faîtage m CONSTR ridge, ridge beam, ridge piece, ridge plate, ridge capping, ridge tile, *d'un comble* crest

faîte m CONSTR crest, ridge beam, ridge piece, ridge plate, *d'un comble* ridge, MINES *d'un filon* apex

faîtière f CONSTR ridge beam, ridge piece, ridge plate, ridge tile

falaise f NAUT cliff; ~ **à pic** f NAUT bluff

falsifié adj AGRO ALIM adulterated

famatinite f MINERAUX famatinite

famennien adj GEOLOGIE Famennian

familiale f TRANSPORT estate car (BrE), station wagon (AmE)

famille f INFORMAT, ORDINAT suite; ~ **de l'actinium** f PHYS RAYON actinium series; ~ **de caractère** f IMPRIM *typographie* font (BrE), fount (AmE); ~ **de caractères** f IMPRIM type family; ~ **de curium** f PHYS RAYON curium series; ~ **des éléments** f PHYS RAYON family of elements; ~ **logique** f ELECTRON, INFORMAT, ORDINAT logic family; ~ **logique TTL** f ELECTRON TTL logic family; ~ **d'ordinateurs** f INFORMAT, ORDINAT computer family; ~ **de particules** f PHYS PART family of particles; ~ **de produits** f PRODUCTION product family; ~ **radioactive** f PHYSIQUE radioactive series; ~ **de segments emboîtés** f MATH nested intervals; ~ **du thorium** f PHYS RAYON thorium series

fanal m COMMANDE signal beacon, NAUT beacon

faner: se ~ v réfl TEXTILE fade

fanion m NAUT pennant; ~ **de courtoisie** m NAUT courtesy flag; ~ **de nouvelles données** m TELECOM NDF, new data flag

fanion-signal m COMMANDE signaling flag (AmE), signalling flag (BrE)

FAO abrév *(fabrication assistée par ordinateur)* ELECTR, ORDINAT, TELECOM CAM *(computer-aided manufacture)*

farad m ELECTR, ELECTROTEC, METROLOGIE, PHYSIQUE farad

faraday m PHYSIQUE faraday

fardeleuse f IMPRIM bundle-type machine

fardeleuse-ficeleuse f IMPRIM bundle tier

farinacé adj AGRO ALIM farinaceous

farinage m PLAST CAOU *plastiques, revêtements* chalking

farine f CONSTR filler, MINES drillings; ~ **blanche** f AGRO ALIM bleached flour; ~ **blanchie** f AGRO ALIM bleached flour; ~ **de bois** f PLAST CAOU *charge* wood flour; ~ **fossile** f MINERAUX infusorial earth, rock meal; ~ **grossière** f AGRO ALIM wheatmeal; ~ **de poisson** f OCEANO fish meal; ~ **de première qualité** f AGRO ALIM patent flour; ~ **de qualité** f AGRO ALIM patent flour

farineux adj AGRO ALIM amylaceous, farinaceous

farinographe m AGRO ALIM farinograph

farnésol m CHIMIE farnesol

fascicule m BREVETS specification; ~ **de brevet** m BREVETS patent specification

fassaïte f MINERAUX fassaite, pyrgom

fathom m METROLOGIE fathom

fatigue f CONS MECA strain, stress, CRISTALL fatigue, GEOLOGIE strain, MECANIQUE *matériaux* fatigue, NAUT strain, PLAST CAOU fatigue; ~ **auditive** f ACOUSTIQUE hearing fatigue; ~ **de corrosion** f METALL corrosion fatigue; ~ **due au débit** f CONS MECA flow fatigue; ~ **de matériel** f MATERIAUX fatigue; ~ **des métaux** f MATERIAUX metal fatigue; ~ **oculaire** f SECURITE eye strain; ~ **oligocyclique** f CRISTALL, METALL low-cycle fatigue; ~ **sonique** f METALL sonic fatigue; ~ **thermique** f AERONAUT, ESPACE, THERMODYN thermal fatigue; ~ **d'usure** f METALL fretting fatigue

faujasite f MINERAUX faujasite

faune: ~ **exotique** m GEOLOGIE exotic fauna; ~ **introduite** m GEOLOGIE exotic fauna

fausérite f MINERAUX fauserite

fausse: ~ **alarme** f AERONAUT false warning, TELECOM false alarm; ~ **arche** f CONSTR *architecture* blind arch; ~ **bague de roulement** f CONS MECA dummy bearing race; ~ **cartouche** f MINES dummy cartridge; ~ **couleur** f INFORMAT false color (AmE), false colour (BrE); ~ **crémaillère** f CONSTR cut wall string, open wall string; ~ **équerre** f METROLOGIE bevel square; ~ **fenêtre** f CONSTR blind window; ~ **glaise** f GEOLOGIE marly loam; ~ **languette** f CONSTR feather, feather tongue, fillet, loose tongue; ~ **maille** f CONS MECA connecting link, mending link, repair link; ~ **manoeuvre** f POLLUTION operational error; ~ **nervure** f AERONAUT false rib; ~ **porte** f CONSTR blind door; ~ **turquoise** f MINERAUX odontolite; ~ **voûte** f CONSTR blind arch

faussé adj CONS MECA out-of-true, MECANIQUE warped

fausser[1] vt CONS MECA buckle, foul, PRODUCTION kink out of line, *filet de vis* cross

fausser:[2] **se** ~ v réfl PRODUCTION fall out of order

fausses-doubles f pl IMPRIM bastard double

fausset m CONSTR spigot, vent peg, vent plug

faute: ~ **humaine** f QUALITE, SECURITE human error

fauteuil: ~ **volant** m ESPACE manned maneuvring unit (AmE), manned manoeuvring unit (BrE)

faux[1] adj INFORMAT, ORDINAT false; ~ **équerrage** adj CONS MECA out-of-square; ~ **rond** adj IMPRIM *machines* out-of-true

faux:[2] ~ **alignement** m CONS MECA mismatch; ~ **char d'assaut** m MILITAIRE decoy tank; ~ **chenal** m OCEANO side channel; ~ **contact** m ELECTROTEC bad contact; ~ **couple** m AERONAUT false frame; ~ **décalque bleu** m IMPRIM *préimpression* blue key; ~ **écho** m OCEANO false echo; ~ **entrait** m CONS MECA collar, collar beam, collar tie, CONSTR needle, span piece, straining beam, straining piece; ~ **essieu** m AUTO deadbeam axle; ~ **étambrai** m NAUT king plank; ~ **filigrane** m PAPIER simulated watermark; ~ **fond** m PRODUCTION false bottom; ~ **fret** m PETROLE dead freight; ~ **fuyant** m

CONSTR bypath, byway, byroad; ~ **limon** *m* CONSTR
wall string; ~ **limon à crémaillère** *m* CONSTR cut wall
string; ~ **longeron** *m* AERONAUT false spar; ~ **numéro**
m TELECOM wrong number; ~ **parallélisme** *m* CONS
MECA out-of-parallelism; ~ **plafond** *m* REFRIG false
ceiling; ~ **plancher** *m* REFRIG false floor; ~ **plateau** *m*
CONS MECA backplate, *pour monter un mandrin sur la
broche d'une machine-outil* adaptor plate; ~ **plateau
de montage des mandrins** *m* CONS MECA chuck back;
~ **pli** *m* PAPIER crease, wrinkle; ~ **plis** *m pl* CERAM VER
laps; ~ **poisson** *m* OCEANO trash fish; ~ **pont** *m* NAUT
orlop deck; ~ **pont inférieur** *m* NAUT orlop deck; ~
puits *m* MINES staple, staple pit, staple shaft; ~ **raccord** *m* CINEMAT, TV jump cut; ~ **rond** *m* CONS MECA
out-of-round, MECANIQUE eccentricity; ~ **signal** *m*
ELECTRON false signal; ~ **titre** *m* IMPRIM bastard title;
~ **uni** *m* TEXTILE false plain
fayalite *f* CERAM VER, MINERAUX fayalite
fcém *abrév (force contre-électromotrice)* ELECTR, ELEC-
TROTEC, PHYSIQUE bemf *(back electromotive force,
back emf)*, cemf *(counter-electromotive force,
counter emf)*
Fe *(fer)* CHIMIE Fe *(iron)*
fécal *adj* HYDROLOGIE *égout*, RECYCLAGE faecal (BrE),
fecal (AmE)
fèces *f* HYDROLOGIE, RECYCLAGE faeces (BrE), feces
(AmE)
fécule *f* IMPRIM *colles et papiers* starch; ~ **de marante** *f*
AGRO ALIM arrowroot
féculence *f* CHIMIE turbidity, *d'une solution* thickness
féculent *adj* CHIMIE starchy, thick
feedback *m* ACOUSTIQUE, CINEMAT, TV larsen effect
feeder: ~ **égalisateur** *m* ELECTR *alimentation* equalizing
feeder; ~ **final** *m* ELECTR independent feeder, *alimentation* dead end feeder, dead ended feeder, radial
feeder; ~ **à impasse** *m* ELECTR *alimentation* dead end
feeder, dead ended feeder; ~ **multiple** *m* ELECTR
alimentation multiple feeder; ~ **principal** *m* ELECTR
trunk main, *alimentation* trunk feeder; ~ **de retour** *m*
ELECTR *alimentation* negative feeder; ~ **secondaire** *m*
ELECTR duplicate feeder
feldspath *m* CERAM VER, CHIMIE, MINERAUX feldspar; ~
alcalin *m* PETR alkali feldspar; ~ **aventurine** *m* MINE-
RAUX aventurine feldspar; ~ **vert** *m* MINERAUX green
feldspar; ~ **vitreux** *m* CERAM VER glassy feldspar
fêlé *adj* MECANIQUE *matériaux* cracked
fém *abrév (force électromotrice)* ELECTR, ELECTROTEC,
PHYSIQUE emf *(electromotive force)*
femto- *préf (f)* METROLOGIE femto-*(f)*
fenchène *m* CHIMIE fenchene
fenchone *f* CHIMIE fenchone
fenchyle *m* CHIMIE fenchyl
fendage *m* CERAM VER *du cylindre* splitting, CONS MECA
slotting, CONSTR cleaving, splitting, PRODUCTION
nicking, slitting; ~ **du diamant** *m* PRODUCTION diamond cleaving
fendante *f* CONS MECA cotter file, slot file, slotting file
fendillement *m* PLAST CAOU *défaut de surface* crazing
fendiller: **se** ~ *v réfl* CERAM VER craze
fendre[1] *vt* TEXTILE split
fendre:[2] ~ **avec des coins** *vi* CONSTR *bois* split with
wedges
fendre:[3] **se** ~ *v réfl* CONSTR split
fendu *adj* CERAM VER split, MECANIQUE *matériaux*
cracked
fendue *f* CHARBON coal drift, MINES chimney, chute, day

drift, day level, slope, surface drive
fenêtrage *m* INFORMAT, ORDINAT windowing
fenêtre *f* CONS MECA *d'un vernier*, CONSTR window, GEO-
LOGIE *dans une nappe de charriage* inlier, IMPRIM,
INFORMAT, ORDINAT window, TELECOM spectral window, TV faceplate, VEHICULES *carrosserie* window; ~
atmosphérique *f* ASTRONOMIE, PHYS RAYON, PHYSIQUE
atmospheric window; ~ **aveugle** *f* CONSTR blank window; ~ **basculante** *f* CONSTR center hung window
(AmE), centre hung window (BrE), pivot-hung window; ~ **à bascule** *f* CONSTR center hung window
(AmE), centre hung window (BrE), pivot-hung window; ~ **à battants** *f* CONSTR casement; ~ **blindée** *f*
SECURITE security window; ~ **de commande** *f* ORDI-
NAT command window; ~ **de contact** *f* ELECTROTEC
contact window; ~ **à coulisses** *f* CONSTR sash window; ~ **en cascade** *f* ORDINAT pop-up window; ~ **en
silice fondue** *f* ESPACE *véhicules* fused silica window; ~
d'exposition *f* CINEMAT camera gate, gate, ENREGISTR
scanning slit; ~ **glissante** *f* CONSTR sliding window; ~
à guillotine *f* CONSTR sash window; ~ **d'image** *f* CINE-
MAT picture gate; ~ **d'impression** *f* CINEMAT printing
gate; ~ **de lancement** *f* ESPACE launch window, *véhicules* firing window; ~ **météorologique** *f* PETROLE
weather window; ~ **de mise au point automatique** *f*
PHOTO autofocus window; ~ **d'observation** *f* INSTRU-
MENT viewing window; ~ **d'observation de l'image
finale** *f* INSTRUMENT final image tube; ~ **d'observation
de la première image** *f* INSTRUMENT intermediate-
image screen; ~ **ordinaire** *f* CONSTR casement,
casement window; ~ **à pivot** *f* CONSTR pivot-hung
window; ~ **pivotante** *f* CONSTR pivot-hung window; ~
de projection *f* CINEMAT gate, projection port; ~
radioélectrique *f* PHYSIQUE radio window; ~ **roulante** *f*
CONSTR sliding window; ~ **spectrale** *f* OPTIQUE optical
window, spectral window, transmission window,
TELECOM transmission window; ~ **standard** *f* CINEMAT
academy aperture; ~ **sur instruments** *f* AERONAUT
flag window; ~ **de synchronisation** *f* ESPACE *communications* synchronization window; ~ **de télémètre**
f PHOTO rangefinder window; ~ **de tirage** *f* CINEMAT
printer aperture, printing gate; ~ **à tirage humide** *f*
CINEMAT liquid gate; ~ **du tube X** *f* INSTRUMENT X-ray
gate; ~ **de viseur** *f* PHOTO viewfinder eyepiece; ~ **de
visualisation** *f* INFORMAT, ORDINAT viewing window
fenêtres: ~ **en mosaïque** *f pl* ORDINAT tiled windows; ~
juxtaposées *f pl* INFORMAT tiled windows
fente *f* CONS MECA slot, *tête de vis* slot, CONSTR split,
ELECTROTEC slot, ESPACE *communications* gap, slit,
MECANIQUE crack, PHYSIQUE slit, PRODUCTION slit,
dans une tête de vis nick, TELECOM slot; ~ **d'aile** *f*
AERONAUT *d'un aéronef* wing slot; ~ **de chargement** *f*
CINEMAT threading slot, TV loading slot; ~ **de la
débiteuse** *f* CERAM VER slot; ~ **de dessiccation** *f* GEO-
LOGIE desiccation crack; ~ **en haricot** *f* CONS MECA
kidney-shaped slot; ~ **d'enregistrement** *f* ENREGISTR
recording slit; ~ **frontale** *f* NUCLEAIRE face gap; ~
imperceptible *f* IMPRIM *papier* hairline; ~ **de lecture** *f*
TV scanning gap, scanning gate; ~ **longitudinale** *f*
TELECOM longitudinal slot; ~ **pour filtre** *f* CINEMAT
filter slot; ~ **de réduction de bruit** *f* ENREGISTR noise
reduction slit; ~ **de retrait** *f* GEOLOGIE mud crack,
shrinkage crack; ~ **de tension** *f* GEOLOGIE tension
gash; ~ **tournevis** *f* ELECTROTEC screwdriver slot; ~
transversale *f* TELECOM transverse slot
fentes *f pl* PHYS ONDES *sur le disque du stroboscope* slits;

~ **de Young** *f pl* PHYSIQUE Young's slits

fer:[1] **au ~ à droite** *adj* IMPRIM *composition* flush right, rag-left (AmE), ragged left (BrE), right-justified; **au ~ à gauche** *adj* IMPRIM flush left, *composition* ragged right (BrE)

fer:[2] **au ~ à droite** *adv* IMPRIM *composition* flush right; **au ~ à gauche** *adv* IMPRIM flush left

fer[3] *m* CHARBON, CHIMIE *(Fe)* iron *(Fe)*; ~ **d'angle** *m* CONSTR L-iron, angle iron; ~ **à barreaux de grille** *m* CONSTR screen bar, PRODUCTION grate bar, grid bar; ~ **Bessemer** *m* PRODUCTION Bessemer iron; ~ **biseauté** *m* CONS MECA bevel-edged flat; ~ **de bouvet double** *m* CONSTR tonguing iron; ~ **de bouvet simple** *m* CONSTR grooving iron; ~ **à braser** *m* CONSTR soldering iron; ~ **brut** *m* PRODUCTION puddle bar; ~ **carrelé** *m* CONSTR channel iron; ~ **cavalier** *m* CONSTR shoeing bar; ~ **de construction** *m* CONSTR structural iron; ~ **cornière** *m* CONSTR L-iron, angle iron; ~ **à détacher** *m* CERAM VER crack-off iron (AmE), wetting-off iron (BrE); ~ **double T** *m* CONSTR H-bar, H-iron; ~ **à double T** *m* CONSTR H-bar, H-iron; ~ **doux** *m* ELECTROTEC, PHYSIQUE soft iron; ~ **ductile** *m* CONSTR wrought iron; ~ **ébauché** *m* PRODUCTION puddle bar; ~ **en croix** *m* PRODUCTION cross section iron; ~ **en équerre** *m* CONSTR L-iron, angle iron; ~ **en H** *m* CONSTR H-bar, H-iron; ~ **en L** *m* CONSTR L-iron, angle iron; ~ **en U** *m* CONSTR channel, channel iron, MECANIQUE channel; ~ **feuillard** *m* CONSTR hoop iron; ~ **forgé** *m* CONSTR wrought iron; ~ **de guillaume** *m* CONSTR rabbet iron; ~ **à I** *m* CONSTR H-bar, H-iron; ~ **d'induit** *m* ELECTROTEC armature iron; ~ **des marais** *m* MINES meadow ore; ~ **à marquer à chaud** *m* EMBALLAGE branding iron; ~ **micacé** *m* MINERAUX micaceous iron ore; ~ **de rabot** *m* CONSTR plane bit, plane iron; ~ **à raboter** *m* CONSTR plane bit, plane iron; ~ **de rabot simple** *m* CONSTR single plane iron; ~ **à souder** *m* CONS MECA soldering bit, CONSTR bit, soldering iron, ELECTR soldering gun, soldering iron, PRODUCTION soldering bit, soldering copper, soldering iron; ~ **sulfaté rouge** *m* MINERAUX red iron vitriol; ~ **de suspension** *m* CONSTR stirrup; ~ **à vitrage** *m* CONSTR sash bar, sash bar iron, sash iron; ~ **de vitrage en treillis** *m* CONSTR window bar

ferblanterie *f* PRODUCTION tin plate working

ferblantier *m* PRODUCTION tin plate worker, tinsmith

ferler *vt* NAUT *voile* furl

ferme[1] *adj* TEXTILE firm

ferme[2] *f* CONSTR girder, solid, truss; ~ **de comble** *f* CONSTR roof truss; ~ **en bois à armature en fer** *f* CONSTR timber truss with iron bracing; ~ **à faux entrait** *f* CONSTR collar beam truss, collar truss; ~ **marine** *f* OCEANO marine farm, sea ranch, shellfish farm; ~ **métallique** *f* CONSTR girder; ~ **de pont** *f* CONSTR bridge truss; ~ **solaire** *f* ELECTROTEC solar power farm; ~ **à tirant** *f* CONSTR close couple truss, close couple

fermé *adj* ELECTROTEC *électricité* off, MATH closed; ~ **par les glaces** *adj* NAUT *port* icebound

fermentation *f* AGRO ALIM, CHIMIE, HYDROLOGIE *égout* fermentation; ~ **acétique** *f* AGRO ALIM acetic fermentation; ~ **aérobie** *f* AGRO ALIM aerobic fermentation; ~ **alcoolique** *f* AGRO ALIM alcoholic fermentation; ~ **méthanique** *f* HYDROLOGIE, METEO methane fermentation; ~ **panaire** *f* AGRO ALIM panary fermentation; ~ **par ébullition** *f* GENIE CHIM boiling fermentation

fermenter *vi* CHIMIE ferment

fermenteur *m* AGRO ALIM fermenter

fermer *vt* DISTRI EAU *l'eau* turn off, ELECTROTEC make, *circuit* close, close, PRODUCTION stop, stop up, *moule* close, *tube* close; ~ **avec une fermeture éclair** *vt* TEXTILE zip (BrE), zipper (AmE); ~ **le circuit** *vt* ELECTROTEC turn on; ~ **à clef** *vt* CONSTR lock; ~ **dans un fondu** *vt* CINEMAT black out, fade out; ~ **l'objectif** *vt* CINEMAT stop down; ~ **par un volet** *vt* CINEMAT wipe off

fermeté: ~ **de la mie** *f* AGRO ALIM crumb firmness

fermeture:[1] **à ~ automatique** *adj* COMMANDE automatically-closing

fermeture[2] *f* CHIMIE closure, CONS MECA make, CONSTR locking, *à l'orifice du puits* covering, ELECTR *relais* closing operation, ELECTROTEC closure, make, EMBALLAGE, GEOLOGIE closure, INST HYDR *de l'arrivée de vapeur* cutoff, *de la vapeur* shutting-off, NAUT lock, ORDINAT close down, PRODUCTION fastening, *d'une usine* closing; ~ **antivol** *f* EMBALLAGE pilferproof; ~ **arrachable** *f* EMBALLAGE tear-off closure; ~ **avec bande métallique** *f* EMBALLAGE metal strip closure; ~ **avec bec pour verser** *f* EMBALLAGE pour spout seal; ~ **avec bec verseur** *f* EMBALLAGE pour spout closure; ~ **avec capsule** *f* EMBALLAGE cap sealing; ~ **avec charnière à enclenchement** *f* EMBALLAGE snap hinge closure; ~ **avec lame chauffée** *f* EMBALLAGE hot-blade-sealing; ~ **avec ligature** *f* EMBALLAGE binding closure; ~ **avec ruban** *f* EMBALLAGE tape sealer, taped closure; ~ **de bouteille** *f* EMBALLAGE bottle closure, bottle stopper; ~ **de branche** *f* PRODUCTION *automatisme industriel* branch close; ~ **de cerclage** *f* EMBALLAGE strapping seal; ~ **du circuit** *f* ELECTROTEC turn-on; ~ **à la clef** *f* CONSTR locking; ~ **collée** *f* EMBALLAGE glued seal; ~ **à détente** *f* EMBALLAGE snap-off closure; ~ **de l'eau** *f* DISTRI EAU shutting-off water; ~ **éclair** *f* TEXTILE zip fastener (BrE); ~ **à encliquetage** *f* EMBALLAGE snap-on closure; ~ **en fondu** *f* CINEMAT fade out; ~ **en polypropylène** *f* EMBALLAGE polypropylene closure; ~ **estampée** *f* EMBALLAGE embossing closure; ~ **de garantie** *f* EMBALLAGE guarantee closure; ~ **hermétique** *f* EMBALLAGE hermetic closure; ~ **hermétique collée** *f* EMBALLAGE bonded seal; ~ **intempestive** *f* ELECTROTEC false closure; ~ **inviolable** *f* EMBALLAGE tamper-evident closure, tamperproof closure; ~ **à l'iris** *f* CINEMAT iris-out; ~ **nouée** *f* EMBALLAGE tying closure; ~ **pour emballage thermoformé** *f* EMBALLAGE blister sealer; ~ **pour sachets et sacs en papier** *f* EMBALLAGE paper bag and sack closure; ~ **de protection pour enfants** *f* EMBALLAGE child-resistant closure; ~ **rentrante** *f* EMBALLAGE tuck-in closure; ~ **de sécurité** *f* EMBALLAGE safety closure; ~ **sertie** *f* EMBALLAGE crimp-on closure; ~ **de session** *f* INFORMAT log-off; ~ **simple** *f* CONSTR casement fastener; ~ **à torsion** *f* EMBALLAGE twisting closure; ~ **totalement étanche** *f* EMBALLAGE hermetic seal; ~ **à traction** *f* EMBALLAGE pull-off closure; ~ **d'une vanne** *f* NUCLEAIRE valve off, valving out; ~ **vissée** *f* EMBALLAGE screw closure; ~ **de volet** *f* EMBALLAGE flap snap

fermion *m* PHYS PART, PHYSIQUE fermion

fermium *m* *(Fm)* CHIMIE fermium *(Fm)*

fermoir *m* CONS MECA clasp, CONSTR double-beveled chisel (AmE), double-bevelled chisel (BrE), PRODUCTION fastener; ~ **de tour** *m* CONSTR double-beveled turning chisel (AmE), double-bevelled turning chisel (BrE); ~ **de tour nez rond** *m* CONSTR side chisel

fernure *f* CONSTR *acte* reinforcement

féroélite *f* MINERAUX faröelite

ferraillage *m* CONSTR reinforcement; **~ longitudinal** *m* CONSTR longitudinal reinforcement

ferraille *f* CHARBON, MATERIAUX scrap, MECANIQUE junk, *matériaux* scrap, METALL scrap, PRODUCTION scrap iron

ferrailleur *m* CONSTR steel fixer

ferrasse *f* CERAM VER nog plate, pan; **~ à aubes** *f* CERAM VER nog plate with spiral runner bars; **~ à chevrons** *f* CERAM VER nog plate with chevron runner bars; **~ à pavés** *f* CERAM VER shoe nog plate

ferrate *m* CHIMIE ferrate

ferré *adj* PRODUCTION iron-shod

ferredoxine *f* CHIMIE ferredoxin

ferrer *vt* CONSTR metal, OCEANO strike, PRODUCTION tip

ferrerie *f* CONSTR ironwork

ferret *m* CERAM VER gathering iron; **~ à mors en terre** *m* CERAM VER dolly

ferreux *adj* CHIMIE ferrous

ferricyanogène *m* CHIMIE ferricyanogen

ferricyanure *m* CHIMIE ferricyanide

ferrimagnétique *adj* PHYSIQUE ferrimagnetic

ferrimagnétisme *m* PHYSIQUE ferrimagnetism

ferrioxalique *adj* CHIMIE ferrioxalic

ferrique *adj* CHIMIE ferric

ferrite *f* CHIMIE, ELECTR *noyau*, ELECTROTEC, PHYSIQUE ferrite; **~ bainitique** *f* METALL bainitic ferrite; **~ à cycle rectangulaire** *f* ELECTROTEC *hystérésis* square loop ferrite

ferritine *f* CHIMIE ferritin

ferritique *adj* MECANIQUE *matériaux*, METALL ferritic

ferritisation *f* MATERIAUX *métallurgie*, METALL ferritizing annealing

ferro-alliage *m* MATERIAUX ferroalloy

ferrocyanogène *m* CHIMIE ferrocyanogen

ferroélectricité *f* ELECTROTEC, PHYSIQUE ferroelectricity

ferroélectrique *adj* PHYSIQUE ferroelectric

ferromagnétique *adj* ESSAIS, MATERIAUX, PHYSIQUE ferromagnetic

ferromagnétisme *m* ELECTR, ENREGISTR, PHYSIQUE ferromagnetism

ferromolybdène *m* MATERIAUX, METALL ferromolybdenum

ferronickel *m* MATERIAUX, METALL ferronickel

ferroprussiate *m* CHIMIE ferroprussiate

ferrorésonance *f* ELECTROTEC ferroresonance

ferrosoferrique *adj* CHIMIE ferrosoferric

ferroutage *m* CH DE FER piggyback traffic, TRANSPORT TOFC, trailer on flatcar, piggyback, piggyback traffic, piggyback transport, rail transport of road trailers, railroad transport (AmE), railway transport (BrE)

ferrouter *vt* TRANSPORT transport by rail and road

ferrugineux *adj* GEOLOGIE ferruginous

ferrule *f* OPTIQUE, TELECOM ferrule; **~ de fixation** *f* CONS MECA attachment fitting

ferrure *f* CONSTR ironwork; **~ d'articulation** *f* CONS MECA hinge fitting; **~ d'attache de la pale** *f* AERONAUT blade attachment fitting; **~ d'élingage** *f* NAUT lifting eye; **~ en delta** *f* CONS MECA delta fitting; **~ d'étrave** *f* NAUT stem fitting; **~ forgée d'attache voilure-fuselage** *f* AERONAUT forged wing attachment; **~ de gouvernail** *f* NAUT rudder brace; **~ de hissage** *f* AERONAUT hoist fitting; **~ d'isolateur** *f* PRODUCTION insulator pin; **~ de pied de pale** *f* AERONAUT blade cuff; **~ de reprise** *f* CONS MECA pick-up fitting; **~ de verrouillage** *f* CONSTR lock fitting

ferrures *f pl* CONS MECA fittings, CONSTR ironwork, PRODUCTION mounting

ferry-boat *m* NAUT, TRANSPORT ferryboat; **~ pour voitures** *m* NAUT car ferry

fers: **~ d'angle** *m pl* CONSTR angle; **~ d'armature** *m pl* CONSTR reinforcement; **~ à barreaux de grille** *m pl* PRODUCTION grate bar, grid bar; **~ à boutons** *m pl* CERAM VER knob tools; **~ à bouveter** *m pl* CONSTR tonguing-and-grooving irons; **~ cavaliers** *m pl* CONS MECA horseshoe sections; **~ cornières** *m pl* CONSTR angle; **~ à étrangler** *m pl* CERAM VER pinching tools; **~ à goulot** *m pl* CERAM VER mouth tools; **~ à lames de bois** *m pl* CERAM VER woods; **~ spéciaux** *m pl* CONS MECA *perçage* special sections

férulique *adj* CHIMIE ferulic

feston *m* GEOLOGIE festoon, TV scallop

festonnage *m (cf serpentage)* CERAM VER curled edge, TV scalloping

fétu *m* CONSTR squib

feu:[1] **en ~** *adj* THERMODYN ablaze; **~ en veilleuse** *adj* THERMODYN banked up; **~ four** *adj* THERMODYN banked up; **~ fourneau** *adj* THERMODYN banked up

feu[2] *m* THERMODYN blaze, fire, VEHICULES *éclairage, témoins* lamp, *éclairage* light; **~ d'aéronef** *m* AERONAUT aircraft light; **~ d'alignement** *m* NAUT leading light; **~ anticollision** *m* AERONAUT anticollision light; **~ arrière** *m* CONSTR rear light, NAUT stern light, VEHICULES *éclairage* rear lamp, tail lamp; **~ d'avertissement** *m* SECURITE warning light; **~ d'axe de piste** *m* AERONAUT runway centerline light (AmE), runway centreline light (BrE); **~ axial de voie de circulation** *m* AERONAUT taxiway centerline light (AmE), taxiway centreline light (BrE); **~ de barre de flanc** *m* AERONAUT wing bar light; **~ de bord** *m* AERONAUT navigation light; **~ brisou** *m* MINES gas, pit gas; **~ clignotant** *m* ESPACE blinking light; **~ de cockpit** *m* AERONAUT cockpit light; **~ commandé par les piétons** *m* TRANSPORT pedestrian-actuated signal; **~ commandé partiellement par les véhicules** *m* TRANSPORT semitraffic actuated signal; **~ de côté** *m* VEHICULES *éclairage* side marker light (AmE), sidelight (BrE); **~ court** *m* CERAM VER sharp fire; **~ couvant** *m* THERMODYN smoldering fire (AmE), smouldering fire (BrE); **~ croisé** *m* MILITAIRE crossfire; **~ de croisement** *m* VEHICULES *éclairage* passing light; **~ à cycle fixe** *m* TRANSPORT pretimed signal; **~ de détresse** *m* NAUT distress flare; **~ d'éclairage** *m* VEHICULES light; **~ à éclat** *m* NAUT flashing light; **~ d'encombrement** *m* VEHICULES *éclairage* marker lamp, side marker light (AmE); **~ d'enfer** *m* CONSTR blazing fire; **~ d'extrémité de piste** *m* AERONAUT runway end light; **~ fixe** *m* NAUT fixed light; **~ de freinage** *m* VEHICULES *éclairage* stop lamp; **~ grieux** *m* MINES gas, pit gas; **~ de guidage sur circuit** *m* AERONAUT circling guidance light; **~ d'horizon** *m* NAUT all-round light; **~ de hune** *m* NAUT steaming light; **~ d'hydrocarbure** *m* SECURITE hydrocarbon fire; **~ d'identification** *m* AERONAUT identification light; **~ à main** *m* NAUT hand flare; **~ de marche arrière** *m* VEHICULES *éclairage* reverse light (AmE), reversing light (BrE); **~ de mouillage** *m* NAUT anchor light, riding light; **~ de navigation** *m* AERONAUT, NAUT navigation light; **~ à occultation** *m* NAUT occulting light; **~ à occultation groupée** *m* NAUT group occulting light; **~ de position** *m* AERONAUT navigation light, ESPACE *véhicules* position light,

NAUT navigation light, position light, VEHICULES *éclairage* position light, side marker light (AmE), sidelight (BrE); ~ **de poupe** *m* NAUT stern light; ~ **poussé** *m* PRODUCTION blown fire; ~ **de prolongement d'arrêt** *m* AERONAUT *piste* stopway light; ~ **de recul** *m* VEHICULES *éclairage* backup light, reverse light (AmE), reversing light (BrE); ~ **de réverbère** *m* PRODUCTION reverberatory flame; ~ **rouge** *m* COMMANDE red light, traffic signals; ~ **de route** *m* NAUT navigation light, VEHICULES *éclairage* headlamp; ~ **scintillant** *m* NAUT quick-flashing light; ~ **à secteur** *m* NAUT sector light; ~ **de stop** *m* COMMANDE stop light, VEHICULES *éclairage* stop lamp; ~ **terrou** *m* MINES pit gas; ~ **de tête de mât** *m* NAUT masthead light; ~ **de traversée de piste** *m* AERONAUT runway crossing light; ~ **tricolore de circulation** *m* COMMANDE traffic signals; ~ **de voie de circulation** *m* AERONAUT taxiway light; ~ **de zone de toucher des roues** *m* AERONAUT runway touchdown zone light

feuillard: ~ **de fer** *m* CONSTR hoop iron, strip; ~ **pour cerclage** *m* EMBALLAGE strapping steel; ~ **pour cercler les emballages** *m* EMBALLAGE hoop iron

feuille *f* BREVETS sheet, CERAM VER ribbon, CRISTALL foil, IMPRIM sheet, INFORMAT leaf, MECANIQUE *matériaux* sheet, ORDINAT leaf, PLAST CAOU *plastiques* film, sheet, PRODUCTION foil; ~ **abrasive** *f* CONS MECA abrasive sheet; ~ **d'acier** *f* MATERIAUX steel sheet; ~ **adhésive** *f* PHOTO dry-mounting tissue; ~ **d'aluminium** *f* AGRO ALIM, CHAUFFAGE aluminium foil (BrE), aluminum foil (AmE), EMBALLAGE aluminium sheet (BrE), aluminum sheet (AmE); ~ **d'amiante** *f* PAPIER asbestos sheet; ~ **d'arrêt métallique** *f* ENREGISTR metallic stop foil; ~ **calandrée** *f* PLAST CAOU *plastiques* calendered film; ~ **continue** *f* PAPIER web; ~ **de couverture** *f* PLAST CAOU *fibre de verre* surfacing sheet; ~ **de dessus** *f* IMPRIM upper sheet; ~ **de diffusion** *f* NUCLEAIRE scattering foil; ~ **échantillon type** *f* PAPIER outturn sheet; ~ **d'emballage à enfoncer** *f* EMBALLAGE press-through packaging sheet; ~ **d'étalonnage** *f* CINEMAT grading sheet; ~ **extrudée** *f* PLAST CAOU *plastiques* extruded film; ~ **fondue de fermeture** *f* EMBALLAGE fuse seal sheet; ~ **gabarit** *f* NAUT construction sheet; ~ **de garde** *f* IMPRIM end sheet, *reliure* outer end paper; ~ **à grille** *f* PRODUCTION grid sheet; ~ **d'habillage** *f* IMPRIM backing sheet, plate backing; ~ **d'impression** *f* IMPRIM printing sheet; ~ **imprimée** *f* IMPRIM printed sheet; ~ **à intensifier les radiographies** *f* INSTRUMENT X-ray image amplifier; ~ **isolante** *f* EMBALLAGE insulating sheet; ~ **laminée** *f* REVETEMENT lamination sheet; ~ **de métal à faisceau** *f* PHYS RAYON metal beam foil; ~ **métallique mince** *f* EMBALLAGE metal foil; ~ **mince** *f* MECANIQUE, REVETEMENT film; ~ **mince d'aluminium** *f* EMBALLAGE aluminium foil (BrE), aluminum foil (AmE); ~ **mince coulée** *f* PLAST CAOU *plastiques* cast film; ~ **de minutage** *f* TV cue sheet; ~ **de mise en train** *f* IMPRIM make-ready sheet; ~ **de mixage** *f* CINEMAT dubbing chart, ENREGISTR dubbing cue sheet, mixing sheet; ~ **d'or** *f* IMPRIM gold foil; ~ **à orientation biaxiale** *f* PLAST CAOU *feuille plastique* biaxially-oriented film; ~ **de papier** *f* IMPRIM, PAPIER sheet; ~ **de placage** *f* CONSTR veneer; ~ **de plastique** *f* EMBALLAGE plastic sheeting; ~ **plein format** *f* IMPRIM broadsheet; ~ **de présence** *f* PRODUCTION time sheet; ~ **rétractile** *f* EMBALLAGE shrink film, shrink wrap; ~ **de route** *f* NAUT waybill; ~ **de scie** *f* CONS MECA saw blade; ~ **de sécurité** *f* CONSTR safety record; ~ **de**

service *f* TV cue sheet; ~ **soufflée** *f* PLAST CAOU *plastiques* blown film; ~ **de tête** *f* IMPRIM *impression* apron; ~ **volante** *f* PAPIER fly sheet; ~ **zapon** *f* NUCLEAIRE zapon foil

feuille-de-sauge *f* PRODUCTION cross file, double half-round file

feuilleret *m* CONSTR fillister, fillister plane, rabbet plane

feuilles:[1] **à ~** *adj* IMPRIM sheet fed

feuilles:[2] ~ **d'amiante** *f pl* CONSTR asbestos sheeting; ~ **d'asbeste** *f pl* CONSTR asbestos sheeting; ~ **de cuivre** *f pl* CONSTR copper sheets; ~ **échantillons** *f pl* PAPIER specimen; ~ **sortant de la machine** *f pl* IMPRIM *tirage* pull; ~ **de suite** *f pl* IMPRIM continuation sheets

feuillet *m* CHIMIE lamina, IMPRIM leaf; ~ **magnétique** *m* PHYSIQUE magnetic shell; ~ **mince pour estampage à chaud** *m* EMBALLAGE hot-stamping foil; ~ **mobile** *m* IMPRIM, PAPIER loose-leaf

feuilletage *m* GEOLOGIE foliation, sheeting

feuilleté *adj* GEOLOGIE, PRODUCTION laminated

feuillure *f* CONS MECA rebate, CONSTR feather edge, rabbet, *d'un châssis de fenêtre* fillister, window rabbet

feutrage *m* PAPIER felting

feutre *m* PAPIER, TEXTILE felt; ~ **aiguilleté** *m* PAPIER needled felt; ~ **de carbone** *m* ESPACE *véhicules* carbon fiber felt (AmE), carbon fibre felt (BrE); ~ **empâté** *m* CERAM VER clogged felt; ~ **marqueur** *m* PAPIER marking felt, ribbing felt; ~ **montant** *m* PAPIER reverse press felt; ~ **non polymérisé** *m* CERAM VER uncured mat; ~ **pour toiture** *m* CONSTR roofing felt; ~ **preneur** *m* PAPIER pick-up, pick-up roll; ~ **preneur pour carton** *m* PAPIER board felt; ~ **preneur pour prise automatique** *m* PAPIER lick-up overfelt; ~ **de rouleau aspirant** *m* PAPIER suction roll felt; ~ **de séchage** *m* IMPRIM drying felt; ~ **sécheur** *m* PAPIER dryer felt

feux: ~ **alternatifs** *m pl* NAUT alternating colored lights (AmE), alternating coloured lights (BrE); ~ **de détresse** *m* AUTO hazard warning system; ~ **de distance constante** *m pl* AERONAUT *aéroport* fixed distance lights; ~ **d'impossibilité de manoeuvre** *m pl* NAUT not-under-command lights; ~ **mixtes** *m pl* NAUT alternating colored lights (AmE), alternating coloured lights (BrE)

FI *abrév (fréquence intermédiaire)* ELECTRON, TELECOM IF *(intermediate frequency)*

fiabilité *f* CONS MECA, ELECTROTEC reliability, IMPRIM *photogravure et impression* consistency, INFORMAT, MATERIAUX, METROLOGIE, ORDINAT, PRODUCTION, QUALITE, TELECOM reliability; ~ **humaine** *f* QUALITE human reliability; ~ **de l'installation** *f* AERONAUT facility reliability; ~ **du matériel** *f* INFORMAT, ORDINAT hardware reliability; ~ **prévisionnelle** *f* ESPACE *véhicules* predicted reliability; ~ **de signalisation** *f* TELECOM signaling reliability (AmE), signalling reliability (BrE)

fibrage *m* TELECOM drawing process

fibre *f* CERAM VER, PAPIER, TELECOM, TEXTILE fiber (AmE), fibre (BrE); ~ **à 0,85mm** *f* OPTIQUE FWF, first window fiber (AmE), first window fibre (BrE); ~ **à 113μm** *f* OPTIQUE second window fiber (AmE), second window fibre (BrE); ~ **acrylique** *f* MATERIAUX acrylic fiber (AmE), acrylic fibre (BrE); ~ **alimentaire** *f* AGRO ALIM dietary fiber (AmE), dietary fibre (BrE); ~ **amorce** *f* OPTIQUE fiber pigtail (AmE), fibre pigtail (BrE), launching fiber (AmE), launching fibre (BrE), TELECOM dummy fiber (AmE), dummy fibre (BrE); ~ **artificielle** *f* MATERIAUX artificial fiber (AmE), artificial fibre (BrE); ~ **de base** *f* CERAM VER basic fiber (AmE), basic fibre (BrE), strand; ~ **de bois** *f* EMBALLAGE wood wool; ~ **de bore** *f* MATERIAUX *matières plastiques* boron fiber (AmE), boron fibre (BrE);~ **de carbone** *f* ESPACE *véhicules,* MATERIAUX, PLAST CAOU *charge renforçante* carbon fiber (AmE), carbon fibre (BrE); ~ **de cellulose** *f* AGRO ALIM crude fiber (AmE), crude fibre (BrE); ~ **céramique** *f* MAT CHAUFF ceramic fiber (AmE), ceramic fibre (BrE); ~ **chimique** *f* CHAUFFAGE man-made fiber (AmE), man-made fibre (BrE); ~ **continue** *f* METALL continuous fiber (AmE), continuous fibre (BrE); ~ **coupée** *f* CERAM VER chopped strand; ~ **courte** *f* CERAM VER wool; ~ **courte en vrac** *f* CERAM VER loose wool; ~ **détendue** *f* TEXTILE relaxed fiber (AmE), relaxed fibre (BrE); ~ **à deux fenêtres** *f* OPTIQUE double-window fiber (AmE), double-window fibre (BrE), dual-window fiber (AmE), dual-window fibre (BrE); ~ **ductile** *f* MATERIAUX ductile fiber (AmE), ductile fibre (BrE); ~ **à échelon d'indice** *f* PHYSIQUE step index fiber (AmE), step index fibre (BrE); ~ **enrobée** *f* MATERIAUX coated fiber (AmE), coated fibre (BrE); ~ **étirée à la chaleur** *f* TEXTILE heat-stretched fiber (AmE), heat-stretched fibre (BrE); ~ **de faible atténuation** *f* OPTIQUE low-loss fiber (AmE), low-loss fibre (BrE); ~ **à faible perte** *f* OPTIQUE low-loss fiber (AmE), low-loss fibre (BrE); ~ **fragile** *f* MATERIAUX brittle fiber (AmE), brittle fibre (BrE); ~ **frisée** *f* TEXTILE crimped fiber (AmE), crimped fibre (BrE); ~ **fusible** *f* TEXTILE thermobonding fiber (AmE), thermobonding fibre (BrE); ~ **gainée** *f* OPTIQUE buffered fiber (AmE), buffered fibre (BrE); ~ **à gradient exponentiel** *f* OPTIQUE, PHYSIQUE power law index fiber (AmE), power law index fibre (BrE); ~ **à gradient d'indice** *f* OPTIQUE graded index fiber (AmE), graded index fibre (BrE), parabolic index fiber (AmE), parabolic index fibre (BrE), PHYSIQUE graded index fiber (AmE), graded index fibre (BrE), TELECOM grading index fiber (AmE), grading index fibre (BrE); ~ **à gradient linéaire** *f* OPTIQUE uniform index fiber (AmE), uniform-index fibre (BrE), uniform-index profile fiber (AmE), uniform-index profile fibre (BrE); ~ **à gradient parabolique** *f* OPTIQUE, PHYSIQUE parabolic index fiber (AmE), parabolic index fibre (BrE); ~ **à guidage faible** *f* TELECOM weakly-guiding fiber (AmE), weakly-guiding fibre (BrE); ~ **de guipage** *f* TEXTILE wrapper fiber (AmE), wrapper fibre (BrE); ~ **haute ténacité** *f* TEXTILE high-tenacity fiber (AmE), high-tenacity fibre (BrE); ~ **d'injection** *f* OPTIQUE launching fiber (AmE), launching fibre (BrE), optical fiber pigtail (AmE), optical fibre pigtail (BrE), TELECOM launching fiber (AmE), launching fibre (BrE); ~ **jusqu'à l'immeuble** *f* TELECOM FTTB, fiber to the building (AmE), fibre to the building (BrE); ~ **jusqu'au bureau** *f* TELECOM FTTO, fiber to the office (AmE), fibre to the office (BrE); ~ **jusqu'au logement** *f* TELECOM FTTH, fiber to the home (AmE), fibre to the home (BrE); ~ **jusqu'au trottoir** *f* TELECOM FTTC, fiber to the kerb (AmE), fibre to the curb (BrE); ~ **à loi parabolique** *f* PHYSIQUE parabolic index fiber (AmE), parabolic index fibre (BrE); ~ **longue** *f* CERAM VER silk; ~ **minérale** *f* CHAUFFAGE mineral fiber (AmE), mineral fibre (BrE); ~ **monomode** *f* ELECTROTEC single-mode optical fiber (AmE), single-mode optical fibre (BrE), OPTIQUE monomode fiber (AmE), monomode fibre (BrE), single-mode optical fiber (AmE), single-mode optical fibre (BrE), PHYSIQUE monomode fiber (AmE), monomode fibre (BrE), TELECOM monolithic integrated circuit, single-mode fiber (AmE), single-mode fibre (BrE); ~ **multicomposant** *f* OPTIQUE multicomponent glass fiber (AmE), multicomponent glass fibre (BrE); ~ **multimode** *f* OPTIQUE, PHYSIQUE multimode fiber (AmE), multimode fibre (BrE); ~ **naturelle** *f* TEXTILE natural fiber (AmE), natural fibre (BrE); ~ **optique** *f* CERAM VER optical fiber (AmE), optical fibre (BrE), CINEMAT fiber optics (AmE), fibre optics (BrE), ELECTROTEC, ESPACE, OPTIQUE, ORDINAT, PHYSIQUE optical fiber (AmE), optical fibre (BrE); ~ **optique monomode** *f* OPTIQUE single-mode optical fiber (AmE), single-mode optical fibre (BrE), TELECOM single-mode fiber (AmE), single-mode fibre (BrE); ~ **optique multimode** *f* ELECTROTEC multimode optical fiber (AmE), multimode optical fibre (BrE); ~ **optique multimode à gradient d'indice** *f* ELECTROTEC graded-index multimode-optical fiber (AmE), graded-index multimode-optical fibre (BrE); ~ **optique plastique-plastique** *f* ELECTROTEC all-plastic optical fiber (AmE), all-plastic optical fibre (BrE); ~ **optique unimodale** *f* OPTIQUE single-mode optical fiber (AmE), single-mode optical fibre (BrE); ~ **optique verre-verre** *f* ELECTROTEC all-glass optical fiber (AmE), all-glass optical fibre (BrE); ~ **de papier** *f* EMBALLAGE paper fiber (AmE), paper fibre (BrE); ~ **plastique** *f* ELECTROTEC, OPTIQUE plastic fiber (AmE), plastic fibre (BrE), TELECOM all-plastic fiber (AmE), all-plastic fibre (BrE); ~ **polymère** *f* MATERIAUX polymer fiber (AmE), polymer fibre (BrE); ~ **primaire** *f* CERAM VER primary fiber (AmE), primary fibre (BrE); ~ **à profil parabolique** *f* OPTIQUE, PHYSIQUE parabolic index fiber (AmE), parabolic index fibre (BrE); ~ **récupérée** *f* EMBALLAGE secondary fiber (AmE), secondary fibre (BrE); ~ **à saut d'indice** *f* OPTIQUE, PHYSIQUE, TELECOM step index fiber (AmE), step index fibre (BrE); ~ **de silicate d'aluminium** *f* CHAUFFAGE aluminium silicate fibre (BrE), aluminum silicate fiber (AmE); ~ **de silice** *f* CHAUFFAGE silica fiber (AmE), silica fibre (BrE), OPTIQUE doped fiber (AmE), doped fibre (BrE), silica fiber (AmE), silica fibre (BrE), TELECOM all-silica fiber (AmE), all-silica fibre (BrE), silica fiber (AmE), silica fibre (BrE); ~ **de silice dopée** *f* OPTIQUE doped silica fiber (AmE), doped silica fibre (BrE); ~ **de silice gainée de plastique** *f* OPTIQUE PCS-fiber (AmE), PCS-fibre (BrE), plastic-clad silica fiber (AmE), plastic-clad silica fibre (BrE), TELECOM PCS-fiber (AmE), PCS-fibre (BrE), plastic-clad silica fiber (AmE), plastic-clad silica fibre (BrE); ~ **silice-plastique** *f* OPTIQUE PCS-fiber (AmE), PCS-fibre (BrE), plastic-clad silica fiber (AmE), plastic-clad silica fibre (BrE), TELECOM PCS-fiber (AmE), PCS-fibre (BrE); ~ **synthétique** *f* CHAUFFAGE synthetic fiber (AmE), synthetic fibre (BrE), EMBALLAGE man-made fiber (AmE), man-made fibre (BrE), TEXTILE synthetic fiber (AmE), synthetic fibre (BrE); ~ **textile continue** *f* CERAM VER continuous filament; ~ **unimodale** *f* OPTIQUE single-mode optical fiber (AmE), single-mode optical fibre (BrE);~ **de verre** *f* CONSTR fiberglass (AmE), fibreglass (BrE), ELECTROTEC glass fiber (AmE), glass fibre (BrE), NAUT fiberglass (AmE), fibreglass (BrE), glass fiber (AmE), glass fibre (BrE), OPTIQUE glass fiber (AmE), glass fibre (BrE), PLAST CAOU *charge* glass fiber (AmE), glass fibre (BrE), *matière première* glass wool, *plastiques* fiberglass (AmE), fibreglass (BrE), PRODUCTION fiberglass (AmE), fibreglass (BrE), REFRIG glass fiber (AmE), glass fibre (BrE), TELECOM all-glass fiber (AmE), all-glass fibre (BrE), glass fiber (AmE), glass fibre (BrE), TEXTILE glass fiber (AmE), glass fibre (BrE); **~ de verre à coeur de grand diamètre** *f* ELECTROTEC large core glass fiber (AmE), large core glass fibre (BrE); **~ de verre à composants multiples** *f* OPTIQUE multicomponent glass fiber (AmE), multicomponent glass fibre (BrE); **~ de verre textile** *f* CERAM VER textile glass fiber (AmE), textile glass fibre (BrE); **~ vierge** *f* CERAM VER pristine fiber (AmE), pristine fibre (BrE); **~ de viscose** *f* PRODUCTION viscose fiber (AmE), viscose fibre (BrE); **~ vulcanisée** *f* ELECTROTEC fish paper

fibrer *vi* TELECOM form the fiber (AmE), form the fibre (BrE)

fibres: ~ anisotropes *f pl* MATERIAUX anisotropic fibers (AmE), anisotropic fibres (BrE); **~ courtes** *f pl* MATERIAUX short fibers (AmE), short fibres (BrE); **~ protéiques** *f pl* TEXTILE protein fibers (AmE), protein fibres (BrE); **~ de tungstène-rhénium** *f pl* MATERIAUX tungsten-rhenium fibers (AmE), tungsten-rhenium fibres (BrE)

fibreux *adj* PAPIER fibrous

fibrillation *f* PAPIER fibrillating, fibrillation

fibrille *f* ASTRONOMIE fibril

fibroïne *f* CHIMIE fibroin

ficeleuse *f* EMBALLAGE binder, binding machine

ficelle: ~ d'amiante *f* CONSTR asbestos string, asbestos thread, asbestos twine; **~ d'asbeste** *f* CONSTR asbestos string

fiche *f* CINEMAT jack, jack plug, plug, CONSTR arrow, hinge, peg, stake, ELECTR *raccordement* plug, ELECTROTEC pin, plug, ENREGISTR jack, MINES chain pin, ORDINAT jack, PAPIER index card, PHYSIQUE, TELECOM, TV plug, VEHICULES data sheet; **~ aller-retour** *f* PRODUCTION turnaround card; **~ banane** *f* CINEMAT, ELECTROTEC banana plug; **~ à barrages** *f* CONSTR line pin; **~ à bouton** *f* CONSTR hinge with knobbed pin; **~ Canon** *f* CINEMAT, TV XLR connector; **~ CINCH** *f* ENREGISTR phono plug **~ de contrôle** *f* PRODUCTION acceptance test sheet, inspection card; **~ d'entretien élémentaire** *f* PRODUCTION elementary servicing sheet; **~ d'étalonnage** *f* CINEMAT timing card; **~ femelle** *f* CINEMAT jack socket, plug socket, ELECTR *raccordement* female connector, ELECTRON, PHYSIQUE socket; **~ de jack** *f* ELECTROTEC jack plug; **~ de laboratoire** *f* CINEMAT lab data sheet; **~ mâle** *f* TELECOM male plug; **~ de mesure** *f* COMMANDE test sheet; **~ à noeud** *f* CONSTR loose pin hinge; **~ d'opérations** *f* PRODUCTION route sheet; **~ plombée** *f* CONSTR drop arrow; **~ polaire** *f* ELECTROTEC two-pin plug; **~ polarisée** *f* ELECTROTEC polarized plug; **~ de prélèvement** *f* PRODUCTION parts requisition; **~ de prélèvement de stock** *f* PRODUCTION parts requisition; **~ de présence** *f* PRODUCTION time card; **~ de prévision de tournage** *f* CINEMAT call sheet; **~ de prise de courant** *f* ELECTROTEC electrical plug (AmE), plug (AmE); **~ à prises multiples** *f* ELECTROTEC multiplug adaptor; **~ de ramassage** *f* PRODUCTION parts requisition; **~ de rapport de tournage** *f* CINEMAT dope sheet, report sheet; **~ RCA** *f* (MD) ENREGISTR phono plug; **~ à ressort** *f* PHOTO banana plug; **~ secteur** *f* ELECTROTEC electrical plug (AmE), mains plug (BrE), power

plug; **~ de stock** *f* PRODUCTION stock record, stock record card; **~ technique** *f* TV specification sheet, technical report; **~ technique d'information** *f* PRODUCTION information product data; **~ téléphonique** *f* TELECOM switchboard plug; **~ Tuchel** *f* CINEMAT Tuchel connector; **~ UIC** *f* CH DE FER UIC leaflet; **~ verrouillable** *f* CINEMAT twist lock plug; **~ XLR** *f* TV XLR connector

ficher *vt* CONS MECA drive, drive in, drive into

fichier *m* IMPRIM, INFORMAT, ORDINAT, TELECOM file; **~ d'abonnés** *m* TELECOM directory store, subscriber's store; **~ à accès direct** *m* INFORMAT, ORDINAT random access file; **~ à accès sélectif** *m* INFORMAT, ORDINAT random file; **~ altéré** *m* ORDINAT corrupt file; **~ archive** *m* INFORMAT archived file; **~ article** *m* PRODUCTION material item file; **~ brut non paginé** *m* IMPRIM galley; **~ chaîné** *m* ORDINAT chained file; **~ de commandes** *m* ORDINAT batch file; **~ créateur** *m* INFORMAT father file; **~ direct** *m* INFORMAT, ORDINAT direct data entry, direct file; **~ disque** *m* INFORMAT disk file; **~ de données** *m* INFORMAT, ORDINAT data file; **~ en séquentiel indexé** *m* INFORMAT indexed sequential file; **~ d'entrée** *m* INFORMAT, ORDINAT input file; **~ d'entrée/sortie** *m* INFORMAT, ORDINAT input/output file; **~ générateur** *m* INFORMAT, ORDINAT father file; **~ indexé** *m* INFORMAT, ORDINAT indexed file; **~ inversé** *m* INFORMAT, ORDINAT inverted file; **~ logique** *m* INFORMAT, ORDINAT logical file; **~ maître** *m* INFORMAT master file; **~ des mouvements** *m* ORDINAT amendment file, change file, movement file, transaction file; **~ partagé** *m* INFORMAT, ORDINAT shared file; **~ physique** *m* INFORMAT, ORDINAT physical file; **~ de plans** *m* PRODUCTION drawing file; **~ principal** *m* ORDINAT master file; **~ de programme** *m* INFORMAT, ORDINAT program file; **~ séquentiel** *m* INFORMAT sequential file, ORDINAT batch file, sequential file; **~ séquentiel indexé** *m* ORDINAT indexed sequential file; **~ de sortie** *m* IMPRIM, INFORMAT, ORDINAT output file; **~ de statistiques** *m* ORDINAT accounting file; **~ sur bande** *m* INFORMAT, ORDINAT tape file; **~ sur disque** *m* ORDINAT disk file; **~ temporaire** *m* INFORMAT, ORDINAT temporary file; **~ texte** *m* INFORMAT, ORDINAT text file; **~ des transactions** *m* INFORMAT transaction file; **~ de travail** *m* INFORMAT, ORDINAT scratch file, work file; **~ des travaux réalisés** *m* PRODUCTION unload file; **~ vidéo** *m* ELECTRON image file

ficine *f* CHIMIE ficin

fidèle *adj* ENREGISTR *reproduction* faithful

fidélité *f* ACOUSTIQUE fidelity; **~ de la couleur** *f* IMPRIM *photogravure et impression* color consistency (AmE), colour consistency (BrE)

figer *vt* CINEMAT *image* freeze, MATERIAUX congeal

figure *f* BREVETS figure; **~ d'attaque à fond plat** *f* METALL flat-bottomed etch pit; **~ de charge** *f* GEOLOGIE load cast; **~ d'interférence** *f* CRISTALL interference figure, PHYS ONDES interference pattern, TV beam pattern; **~ d'onde stationnaire** *f* PHYS ONDES stationary wave pattern; **~ de pôle** *f* CRISTALL pole figure; **~ sédimentaire** *f* GEOLOGIE sedimentary structure; **~ de Widmannstätten** *f* ASTRONOMIE Widmannstätten figure

figurer: ~ en coupe *vt* CONS MECA show in section

figures: ~ de Bitter *f pl* PHYSIQUE Bitter pattern; **~ de croissance** *f pl* METALL growth pattern; **~ planes** *f pl* GEOMETRIE plane figures; **~ semblables** *f pl* GEOMETRIE similar figures

fil *m* CERAM VER yarn, CONS MECA cutting edge, edge, ELECTROTEC wire, IMPRIM *reliure* thread, MATERIAUX, NAUT *du bois* grain, PAPIER thread, PLAST CAOU *produit* yarn, TELECOM leg, TEXTILE end, thread, yarn end, yarn; ~ **abrasé** *m* TEXTILE abraded yarn; ~ **d'acier pour électrodes de soudure** *m* MATERIAUX welding steel wire; ~ **d'alimentation** *m* TEXTILE feeder yarn; ~ **à âme d'acier** *m* ELECTROTEC bimetallic wire; ~ **d'amenée** *m* ELECTROTEC lead, lead-in wire; ~ **d'âme tordu** *m* TEXTILE twisted core; ~ **d'apport** *m* MECANIQUE *soudage* filler wire; ~ **d'armure** *m* OPTIQUE armor wire (AmE), armour wire (BrE); ~ **artificiel** *m* MATERIAUX artificial filament; ~ **assemblé sans torsion** *m* TEXTILE parallel-wound yarn; ~ **d'attache pour sac** *m* EMBALLAGE wire bag tie; ~ **de base** *m* CERAM VER strand; ~ **de blindage** *m* ELECTR drain wire, shield drain wire, PRODUCTION drain wire, shield drain wire; ~ **blindé** *m* ELECTROTEC shielded wire; ~ **bouclé** *m* TEXTILE looped yarn; ~ **de bougie** *m* AUTO spark plug wire; ~ **bouillonneux** *m* CERAM VER train of bubbles; ~ **à brocher** *m* EMBALLAGE stitching wire, IMPRIM binding thread; ~ **de campagne** *m* ELECTROTEC field wire; ~ **de caret** *m* TEXTILE rope wire; ~ **de chaîne** *m* PAPIER warp yarn; ~ **de chaîne du continu** *m* TEXTILE ring-spun yarn; ~ **chenillé** *m* TEXTILE chenille yarn, spiral corkscrew; ~ **chiné** *m* TEXTILE marked yarn; ~ **conducteur** *m* ELECTROTEC conductor wire, lead; ~ **à conducteur unique** *m* PRODUCTION single conductor wire; ~ **de connexion** *m* ELECTROTEC connecting wire, jumper, plug wire, tie wire; ~ **continu** *m* TEXTILE continuous yarn; ~ **de coton** *m* TEXTILE cotton yarn; ~ **de coupage** *m* PAPIER tearing wire; ~ **cuivré** *m* CONSTR coppered wire; ~ **de cuivre** *m* CONSTR, ELECTR *conducteur* copper wire; ~ **de détonateur** *m* MINES leg wire; ~ **de l'eau** *m* HYDROLOGIE streamline; ~ **éboulé** *m* CERAM VER sloughed yarn; ~ **émaillé** *m* ELECTR *conducteur*, ELECTROTEC, REVETEMENT enameled wire (AmE), enamelled wire (BrE); ~ **émaillé en cuir** *m* ELECTROTEC enameled copper wire (AmE), enamelled copper wire (BrE); ~ **en cuivre émaillé** *m* REVETEMENT enameled copper wire (AmE), enamelled copper wire (BrE); ~ **endommagé** *m* CERAM VER damaged yarn; ~ **enrobé** *m* REVETEMENT coated wire; ~ **ensimé** *m* TEXTILE bonded thread; ~ **étamé** *m* ELECTROTEC tinned wire; ~ **étiré dur** *m* CONS MECA bright hard-drawn wire; ~ **à facettes** *m* TEXTILE spinning figures; ~ **fantaisie** *m* TEXTILE fancy yarn; ~ **de fer** *m* PRODUCTION iron wire; ~ **de fer barbelé** *m* CONSTR, MILITAIRE barbed wire; ~ **de fer barbelé coupant** *m* MILITAIRE razor wire; ~ **filé sur système centrifuge** *m* TEXTILE box-spun yarn; ~ **filé sur système continu** *m* TEXTILE continuous spun yarn; ~ **flammé** *m* TEXTILE flammé yarn, thick-and-thin yarn; ~ **flammé irrégulier** *m* TEXTILE stripe; ~ **à flux incorporé** *m* CONSTR flux-cored wire; ~ **à freiner** *m* CONS MECA lock wire; ~ **fusible** *m* ELECTR fuse link, fuse wire, wire fuse; ~ **à fusible** *m* ELECTROTEC fuse wire; ~ **galvanisé** *m* ELECTROTEC zinc wire; ~ **de garde** *m* ELECTR *ligne aérienne* guard wire; ~ **gazé** *m* TEXTILE gassed yarn; ~ **glacé** *m* TEXTILE glazed yarn; ~ **de glissement** *m* ELECTR *câble* skid wire; ~ **grossier** *m* TEXTILE coarse yarn; ~ **guipé** *m* TEXTILE covered yarn, wrapped yarn; ~ **guipé de métal** *m* REVETEMENT metal-coated thread; ~ **irrégulier** *m* TEXTILE irregular yarn; ~ **isolé** *m* ELECTROTEC insulated wire, TELECOM insulated conductor;

~ **jarretière** *m* TELECOM jumper wire; ~ **jaspé** *m* TEXTILE jaspé yarn; ~ **de jute** *m* TEXTILE jute yarn; ~ **de laiton** *m* CONSTR brass wire; ~ **à ligaturer** *m* AERONAUT lacing cord; ~ **de lisse** *m* TEXTILE heald wire; ~ **magnétique** *m* ACOUSTIQUE magnetic wire; ~ **de masse** *m* ELECTROTEC earth wire (BrE), ground wire (AmE); ~ **de masse nu** *m* ELECTR, PRODUCTION bare drain wire; ~ **méplat** *m* ELECTROTEC flat wire; ~ **de mesure** *m* ELECTROTEC sensing lead; ~ **de métallisation** *m* AERONAUT airframe bonding lead; ~ **métallisé** *m* REVETEMENT metal-coated thread; ~ **monobrin** *m* TEXTILE monofilament yarn; ~ **monocristallin** *m* CRISTALL whisker; ~ **monocristallin cylindrique** *m* MATERIAUX cylindrical whisker; ~ **moussé** *m* TEXTILE crimped yarn; ~ **multifilament** *m* TEXTILE multifilament yarn; ~ **de neutre** *m* PRODUCTION *électricité* common wire; ~ **neutre** *m* ELECTR *circuit* neutral wire, ELECTROTEC neutral conductor, protective conductor; ~ **de neutre de terre** *m* PRODUCTION common wire; ~ **non coupé** *m* TEXTILE hanging thread; ~ **non isolé** *m* ELECTROTEC bare wire; ~ **nu** *m* ELECTROTEC, TELECOM bare wire; ~ **de nuque** *m* TELECOM B-leg, ring; ~ **de nylon** *m* PLAST CAOU *textiles* nylon thread; ~ **ondé** *m* TEXTILE eccentric; ~ **peigné** *m* TEXTILE combed yarn; ~ **de pierre** *m* MINES grain; ~ **pilote** *m* ELECTROTEC pilot wire; ~ **plat** *m* TEXTILE flat yarn; ~ **de platine** *m* EQUIP LAB *analyse* platinum wire; ~ **plein** *m* ELECTR *conducteur* solid wire; ~ **à plomb** *m* CONSTR plumb line, plummet; ~ **plombé** *m* PRODUCTION lead seal wire; ~ **de pneu** *m* TEXTILE tire yarn (AmE), tyre yarn (BrE); ~ **de pointe** *m* TELECOM A-leg, tip; ~ **porte-câble** *m* ELECTROTEC cable suspension wire; ~ **pour agrafes** *m* EMBALLAGE stapling wire; ~ **protecteur** *m* ELECTROTEC guard wire; ~ **de puissance** *m* ELECTR, PRODUCTION power lead; ~ **rapporté** *m* CERAM VER applied thread; ~ **recuit blanc** *m* CONS MECA bright annealed wire; ~ **à résistances** *m* ELECTROTEC resistance wire; ~ **résistant** *m* ELECTR, ELECTROTEC, METALL resistance wire; ~ **à ressort** *m* RESSORTS spring wire; ~ **retors** *m* TEXTILE plied yarn; ~ **de retour** *m* ELECTROTEC return wire; ~ **rosette** *m* ELECTR *conducteur d'un câble* tinsel conductor; ~ **de silionne** *m* CERAM VER glass continuous filament yarn; ~ **de soie** *m* TEXTILE silk yarn; ~ **de sonnerie** *m* ELECTROTEC bell wire; ~ **souple** *m* ELECTROTEC flex, flexible wire; ~ **sous tension** *m* ELECTROTEC live wire; ~ **sur ensouple** *m* CERAM VER beamed yarn; ~ **de synchro** *m* CINEMAT sync pulse cable; ~ **de tapis** *m* TEXTILE carpet yarn; ~ **teint** *m* TEXTILE dyed yarn; ~ **téléphonique** *m* ELECTROTEC telephone wire; ~ **de terre** *m* ELECTROTEC earth conductor (BrE), ground conductor (AmE), earth wire (BrE), ground wire (AmE), TV earth wire (BrE), ground wire (AmE); ~ **textile** *m* PAPIER, PLAST CAOU *produit* yarn; ~ **texturé** *m* CERAM VER textured yarn; ~ **texturé par assemblage** *m* TEXTILE comingled yarn, intermingled yarn; ~ **tirant en chaîne** *m* TEXTILE tight end; ~ **tirant en trame** *m* TEXTILE tight pick; ~ **torsadé** *m* PRODUCTION stranded wire, RESSORTS twisted wire; ~ **de torsion** *m* ELECTROTEC torsion string; ~ **de trame** *m* PAPIER weft yarn; ~ **tranchant** *m* CONSTR *d'un outil* cutting edge (AmE), keen edge (BrE); ~ **de traversée** *m* ELECTROTEC lead-wire; ~ **tréfilé** *m* CONS MECA drawn wire; ~ **tréfilé dur** *m* RESSORTS hard drawn wire; ~ **trempé en étages** *m* RESSORTS marquenched wire, step-hardened wire; ~ **tressé** *m* PLAST CAOU *matériel* wire mesh;

~ **verni** *m* ELECTR *conducteur*, ELECTROTEC enameled wire (AmE), enamelled wire (BrE); ~ **de verranne** *m* CERAM VER glass staple fiber yarn (AmE), glass staple fibre yarn (BrE); ~ **de verre** *m* EMBALLAGE glass fiber (AmE), glass fibre (BrE); ~ **volant** *m* ELECTROTEC jumper; ~ **vrillé** *m* TEXTILE snarl; ~ **de zinc** *m* ELECTROTEC zinc wire

filage *m* CERAM VER spinning, CINEMAT ghost image, streaking, TV bearding, crawling, smearing; ~ **image** *m* TV ghost image

filament *m* ASTRONOMIE *structure de l'univers*, CONSTR, ELECTR *ampoule*, ELECTROTEC, INSTRUMENT, PHYSIQUE, PLAST CAOU *textiles*, TEXTILE filament; ~ **bispiral** *m* ELECTR *ampoule* coiled coil filament; ~ **de chauffage** *m* ELECTROTEC heater; ~ **chauffant** *m* ELECTROTEC heater; ~ **luisant de tungstène** *m* PHYS RAYON glowing tungsten filament; ~ **lumineux** *m* CONSTR filament; ~ **métallique** *m* ELECTROTEC metal filament; ~ **de tube électronique** *m* ELECTRON electron tube heater; ~ **au tungstène** *m* ELECTR *lampe* tungsten filament

filaments: ~ **d'alimentation** *m pl* ELECTROTEC heater power supply

filasse *f* CERAM VER sleek; ~ **taillée** *f* CERAM VER deep sleek

filature: ~ **à anneaux** *f* TEXTILE ring spinning; ~ **commerciale** *f* TEXTILE sales yarn spinning; ~ **de coton** *f* TEXTILE cotton spinning; ~ **de coton condenseur** *f* TEXTILE cotton condenser spinning; ~ **de jute** *f* TEXTILE jute spinning; ~ **de laine cardée** *f* TEXTILE woollen spinning; ~ **de laine peignée** *f* TEXTILE worsted spinning; ~ **de soie** *f* TEXTILE silk spinning

file *f* TRANSPORT lane; ~ **d'attente** *f* INFORMAT, ORDINAT, TELECOM queue, TRANSPORT *circulation* line of cars (AmE), line of traffic (AmE), traffic queue (BrE); ~ **d'attente d'un dispositif** *f* INFORMAT, ORDINAT device queue; ~ **d'attente en entrée** *f* ORDINAT input queue; ~ **d'attente en sortie** *f* ORDINAT output queue; ~ **d'attente d'entrée** *f* INFORMAT entry queue, input queue, ORDINAT entry queue; ~ **d'attente limitée** *f* TELECOM limited waiting queue; ~ **d'attente par priorités** *f* ORDINAT priority queue; ~ **d'attente d'un périphérique** *f* INFORMAT, ORDINAT device queue; ~ **d'attente prioritaire** *f* INFORMAT priority queue; ~ **d'attente à serveurs multiples** *f* TELECOM multiple-server queue; ~ **d'attente de sortie** *f* INFORMAT output queue; ~ **à un seul serveur** *f* TELECOM single server queue; ~ **de travaux** *f* INFORMAT, ORDINAT job stack

filé:[1] ~ **de fibres coupées** *adj* TEXTILE cut-staple spun

filé[2] *m* TEXTILE staple fiber yarn (AmE), staple fibre yarn (BrE); ~ **fondu non tissé** *m* TEXTILE spunbond; ~ **à gonflant élevé** *m* TEXTILE high-bulk spun yarn; ~ **de trame en produit de récupération** *m* TEXTILE shoddy-type filling (AmE), shoddy-type weft (BrE); ~ **de verranne** *m* CERAM VER single staple fiber yarn (AmE), single staple fibre yarn (BrE)

filer[1] *vt* NAUT *câble* pay out, PRODUCTION draw, TEXTILE spin; ~ **son câble par le bout** *vt* NAUT slip one's cable

filer[2] *vi* NAUT run; ~ **une aussière** *vi* NAUT stream a warp

filés: ~ **fins** *m pl* TEXTILE fine counts yarns

filet *m* CERAM VER string (AmE), thread (BrE), CONS MECA thread, worm, *d'un écrou* thread, HYDROLOGIE stream, IMPRIM rule, *composition, photogravure* line, *visserie* thread, MECANIQUE thread, MINES stringer, thread, NAUT net, OCEANO fishing net, net, PHYSIQUE filament, PRODUCTION *d'une vis* fillet; ~ **d'amarrage** *m*

AERONAUT mooring harness; ~ **aminci** *m* CERAM VER depressed thread; ~ **de camouflage avec feuilles découpées** *m* MILITAIRE incised-leaf-type camouflage net; ~ **carré** *m* CONS MECA square thread; ~ **de chargement** *m* NAUT net sling; ~ **décolleté** *m* CONS MECA undercut; ~ **dérivant** *m* NAUT drift net; ~ **de drague** *m* NAUT dredge net; ~ **à droite** *m* CONS MECA right-hand thread; ~ **d'embase** *m* CONSTR *charpenterie* baseboard (AmE), mopboard (AmE), skirt board, skirting, skirting board (BrE); ~ **extérieur** *m* CONS MECA external thread, male thread, outside thread; ~ **intérieur** *m* CONS MECA inside thread; ~ **orné** *m* IMPRIM ornamental rule; ~ **pare-torpilles** *m* MILITAIRE torpedo net; ~ **de pêche** *m* OCEANO fishing net, TEXTILE fishnet; ~ **rentré** *m* CERAM VER pinched thread; ~ **de sécurité** *m* SECURITE safety net; ~ **traînant** *m* NAUT fishing drift, fishing drift net; ~ **trapézoïdal** *m* CONS MECA trapezoidal thread; ~ **de vis** *m* CONS MECA screw thread; ~ **de vis trapézoïdal** *m* CONSTR buttress thread

filetage *m* CONS MECA screw cutting, screwing, thread, threading, *d'une vis* pitch, MECANIQUE thread, OCEANO fish filleting, net making, PRODUCTION drawing, thread, wire drawing; ~ **Acmé** *m* CONS MECA Acme thread; ~ **à ajustement serré** *m* CONS MECA close-fit thread; ~ **British Association** *m* CONS MECA BA screw thread, British Association screw thread; ~ **conique NPT** *m* CONS MECA NPT screwthread; ~ **conique de tuyauterie à norme américaine** *m* CONS MECA American NPT, American National Pipe Taper; ~ **conique de tuyauterie à norme britannique** *m* CONS MECA BSPT, British Standard Pipe Taper, British Standard Pipe Taper; ~ **cylindrique de tuyauterie** *m* CONS MECA parallel pipe thread; ~ **cylindrique de tuyauterie à norme britannique** *m* CONS MECA BSP, British Standard parallel pipe thread; ~ **en pouces** *m* CONS MECA inch screw thread; ~ **extérieur** *m* CONS MECA external thread; ~ **femelle** *m* CONS MECA female thread; ~ **fin norme britannique** *m* CONS MECA BSF screw thread, British Standard fine screw thread; ~ **mâle** *m* CONS MECA male thread; ~ **métrique ISO** *m* CONS MECA ISO metric thread; ~ **métrique à pas fin** *m* CONS MECA metric fine-pitch thread; ~ **métrique trapézoïdal** *m* CONS MECA metric trapezoidal screw thread; ~ **miniature** *m* CONS MECA miniature screw thread; ~ **miniature métrique ISO** *m* CONS MECA ISO miniature metric thread; ~ **normal anglais** *m* CONS MECA BSW thread, British Standard Whitworth thread, Whitworth screw thread, Whitworth thread; ~ **NPT** *m* CONS MECA NPT, National Pipe Taper; ~ **trapézoïdal** *m* CONS MECA trapezoidal thread, *filetage asymétrique* buttress screw thread; ~ **trapézoïdal asymétrique** *m* CONS MECA asymmetrical trapezoidal screw thread; ~ **trapézoïdal symétrique** *m* CONS MECA symmetrical trapezoidal screw thread; ~ **de tube au pas Briggs** *m* CONS MECA Brigg's pipe thread; ~ **de tube au pas standard américain** *m* CONS MECA Brigg's pipe thread; ~ **de tuyau** *m* CONSTR pipe screwing, pipe threading; ~ **de tuyauterie** *m* CONS MECA pipe thread; ~ **unifié** *m* CONS MECA unified screw thread; ~ **unifié fin** *m* CONS MECA UNF, unified fine thread; ~ **unifié gros** *m* CONS MECA UNC, unified coarse thread; ~ **à usage général** *m* CONS MECA general-purpose screw thread; ~ **de vis à tôle** *m* CONS MECA tapping screws thread; ~ **Whitworth** *m* CONS MECA BSW thread, British Standard Whitworth thread, Whitworth screw thread, Whitworth thread; ~ **Whitworth norme britannique** *m*

CONS MECA British Standard Whitworth thread
fileté *adj* MECANIQUE threaded
fileter *vt* CONS MECA screw, PRODUCTION draw
fileteuse *f* OCEANO filleting machine
filets: ~ **doubles** *m pl* IMPRIM *mise en page* double ruling; ~ **de guidage** *m pl* IMPRIM feint rules; ~ **incomplets pour éléments de fixation** *m pl* CONS MECA thread run-outs for fasteners; ~ **de protection d'échafaudage** *m pl* SECURITE scaffolding protective nets
fileur *m* CERAM VER yarn applicator
filicique *adj* CHIMIE filicic
filière *f* CERAM VER bushing, CERAM VER bushing assembly, CONS MECA screw plate, screw stock, screwing die, stock, tap plate, *d'une machine à tarauder les tiges, les tubes* screwing chuck, screwing head, CONSTR ledger, purlin, MECANIQUE *filetage, étirage* die, NAUT guardrail, *accastillage de pont* lifeline, ORDINAT path, PRODUCTION die, die head, die plate, die plate, die-stock, drawplate, *d'une machine à tarauder les tiges, les tubes* die-head; ~ **annulaire** *f* CERAM VER annular bushing; ~ **de bijouterie** *f* CONS MECA *pas très fin* watch screw plate; ~ **à billes** *f* CERAM VER marble bushing; ~ **à bois** *f* CONSTR box screw; ~ **de boudineuse** *f* PLAST CAOU *presse à extrusion* extrusion die; ~ **à cage** *f* CONS MECA screw plate, screw stock, stock; ~ **à cliquet** *f* CONS MECA ratchet screwing stock; ~ **à coussinets** *f* CONS MECA screw plate, screw stock, stock, PRODUCTION die-stock; ~ **à coussinets-lunettes** *f* CONS MECA solid die stock; ~ **à déclenchement automatique** *f* CONS MECA self-opening die head, self-opening screwing head; ~ **double** *f* CONS MECA two-part screw plate; ~ **en métal dur pour le tréfilage de fils** *f* CONS MECA tungsten-carbide wiredrawing die; ~ **d'étirage et de tréfilage** *f* CONS MECA die; ~ **à étirer** *f* PRODUCTION die, die plate, drawplate; ~ **de filetage** *f* CONS MECA die; ~ **garnie** *f* CONS MECA stock and dies; ~ **garnie de coussinets** *f* CONS MECA stock and dies; ~ **à gaz** *f* PRODUCTION gas stock; ~ **à guide** *f* PRODUCTION guide stock; ~ **hexagonale pour filetage à la main** *f* CONS MECA hexagonal die nut; ~ **d'horlogerie** *f* PRODUCTION clock screw plate; ~ **à lunettes** *f* CONS MECA solid die stock; ~ **à la machine** *f* CONS MECA machine die plate; ~ **à palette** *f* CONS MECA screw plate, tap plate; ~ **à peignes** *f* CONS MECA chaser die screwing stock; ~ **plate** *f* CONS MECA screw plate, tap plate; ~ **pour tubes en fer pas de gaz** *f* PRODUCTION gas thread pipe stock; ~ **de préfusion** *f* CERAM VER foremelter; ~ **à propulseurs liquides** *f* ESPACE *propulsion* liquid propellant system; ~ **à propulseurs solides** *f* ESPACE *propulsion* solid propellant system; ~ **ronde de filetage** *f* CONS MECA circular screwing die; ~ **simple** *f* CONS MECA one-part screw plate, screw plate, tap plate; ~ **de tréfilage de fils métalliques** *f* CONS MECA wiredrawing die; ~ **à truelle** *f* CONS MECA screw plate, tap plate
filigrane *m* IMPRIM, PAPIER watermark
filigraneur *m* EMBALLAGE dandy roll
filin *m* NAUT cordage, small stuff; ~ **flottant** *m* NAUT floating line, heaving line; ~ **flottant de sauvetage** *m* NAUT heaving line
film *m* CINEMAT film, motion picture, movie, PETR record, PHOTO, REVETEMENT film; ~ **d'acétate** *m* EMBALLAGE acetate film; ~ **adhésif** *m* REVETEMENT adhesive film; ~ **d'animation** *m* CINEMAT animated film; ~ **antibuée** *m* EMBALLAGE antifog film; ~ **d'archives** *m* CINEMAT archival film; ~ **autocollant** *m*

EMBALLAGE self-adhesive film; ~ **barrière en polyoléfine** *m* EMBALLAGE polyolefin barrier film; ~ **barrière stratifié en cinq couches** *m* EMBALLAGE five-layer barrier film laminate; ~ **du bleu** *m* IMPRIM *préimpression* blue printer; ~ **à bulles** *m* EMBALLAGE bubble film; ~ **de cellophane** *m* EMBALLAGE cellophane film; ~ **de contrôle** *m* PETR monitor record; ~ **couleur à couches multiples** *m* IMPRIM multiple layer color film (AmE), multiple layer colour film (BrE); ~ **couleur lumière artificielle** *m* PHOTO artificial light color film (AmE), artificial light colour film (BrE); ~ **couleur lumière du jour** *m* PHOTO daylight color film (AmE), daylight colour film (BrE); ~ **couleur pour prise de vue en lumière artificielle** *m* IMPRIM tungsten film; ~ **couleur type lumière artificielle** *m* CINEMAT artificial light color film (AmE), artificial light colour film (BrE); ~ **coupé au format** *m* PHOTO cut film; ~ **du cyan** *m* IMPRIM *photogravure* blue key; ~ **en 3-D** *m* CINEMAT stereoscopic film; ~ **en couleur inversible** *m* PHOTO color reversal film (AmE), colour reversal film (BrE), reversal-type color film (AmE), reversal-type colour film (BrE); ~ **d'enduit** *m* REVETEMENT coating film; ~ **en polyprène étiré** *m* EMBALLAGE orientated polypropylene film; ~ **en relief** *m* CINEMAT stereoscopic film; ~ **en rouleau** *m* IMPRIM roll film; ~ **en trois dimensions** *m* CINEMAT stereoscopic film; ~ **en vrac** *m* PHOTO bulk film; ~ **étirable** *m* EMBALLAGE stretch film; ~ **format réduit** *m* CINEMAT narrow gage film (AmE), narrow gauge film (BrE); ~ **de format standard** *m* CINEMAT standard gage film (AmE), standard gauge film (BrE); ~ **gamma** *m* PHYS RAYON *détection de radiation* gamma film; ~ **grand format** *m* PHOTO sheet film; ~ **infrarouge** *m* PHOTO infrared film; ~ **isolant** *m* REVETEMENT insulating film; ~ **métallisé** *m* EMBALLAGE metalized film (AmE), metallized film (BrE); ~ **au mètre** *m* PHOTO bulk film; ~ **monté** *m* IMPRIM *copie* film flat, *montage* flat; ~ **muet** *m* CINEMAT silent film; ~ **noir** *m* IMPRIM *photogravure* skeleton black, *préimpression* black printer; ~ **noir imprimant sur toute la surface de l'illustration** *m* IMPRIM *impression* full case black; ~ **non glissant** *m* IMPRIM *photogravure* low-slip film; ~ **de peinture rétroréfléchissant** *m* REVETEMENT reflective coat; ~ **pelable** *m* REVETEMENT protective film; ~ **de petit format** *m* PHOTO miniature film; ~ **plastique rétractile** *m* EMBALLAGE shrink film, shrink wrap; ~ **de polyéthylène** *m* EMBALLAGE PET film; ~ **pour emballage alimentaire** *m* EMBALLAGE food grade packaging film; ~ **pour emboutissage profond** *m* EMBALLAGE deep drawing film; ~ **pour pelliplacage** *m* EMBALLAGE skin film; ~ **protecteur** *m* EMBALLAGE protective film; ~ **réalisé par animation de diapositives** *m* CINEMAT slide motion film; ~ **de rouille** *m* REVETEMENT rust film; ~ **ruisselant** *m* LESSIVES falling film; ~ **sans fin** *m* CINEMAT loop; ~ **de sélection** *m* IMPRIM *photogravure* color key (AmE), colour key (BrE); ~ **spécial pour l'alimentation** *m* EMBALLAGE food grade film; ~ **stéréoscopique** *m* CINEMAT stereoscopic film; ~ **de sûreté** *m* IMPRIM, PHOTO safety film; ~ **surexposé** *m* PHOTO overexposed film; ~ **thermorétractable** *m* EMBALLAGE shrink film; ~ **tombant** *m* LESSIVES falling film; ~ **transparent** *m* EMBALLAGE transparent film; ~ **au tungstène** *m* IMPRIM *photographie* tungsten film; ~ **vierge** *m* PHOTO unexposed film
filmer *vt* CINEMAT film, film shoot
filmogène *adj* PLAST CAOU *liant de peinture* film-forming

filon[1] *m* MINES lead, lode; **~ croiseur** *m* GEOLOGIE cross vein, intersecting vein, MINES contralode, counterlode, counter, cross vein, crosslode; **~ en gradins** *m* MINES lob; **~ épuisé** *m* MINES exhausted vein, worked-out lode, worked-out vein; **~ de granite** *m* GEOLOGIE elvan; **~ horizontalement allongé** *m* MINES course of ore; **~ intrusif annulaire** *m* GEOLOGIE concentric dike (AmE), concentric dyke (BrE); **~ intrusif composite** *m* GEOLOGIE composite dike (AmE), composite dyke (BrE); **~ mère** *m* MINES main lode, master lode, mother lode; **~ nodulaire** *m* MINES ball vein; **~ à nodules** *m* MINES ball vein; **~ nourricier** *m* GEOLOGIE *magmatique* feeder; **~ principal** *m* MINES main lode, master lode, mother lode; **~ de quartz** *m* GEOLOGIE quartz vein; **~ superficiel** *m* GEOLOGIE ripple mark

filon:[2] **être dans le ~** *vi* MINES to be in ore

filon-couche *m* GEOLOGIE *corps intrusif* intrusive sheet; **~ composé** *m* GEOLOGIE composite sill

filonnet *m* GEOLOGIE veinlet

filons: ~ de calcite fibreux *m pl* GEOLOGIE beef

fil-R *m* TELECOM R-wire

fils: ~ croisés *m pl* TEXTILE crossed ends; **~ entièrement étirés** *m pl* TEXTILE fully drawn yarns; **~ perdus** *m pl* TEXTILE lost ends; **~ de réserve** *m pl* TEXTILE spare ends; **~ du réticule** *m pl* ASTRONOMIE *de l'oculaire d'un télescope* cross wires

fil-T *m* TELECOM T-wire

filtrabilité *f* CHARBON filterability

filtrage *m* CHIMIE filtering, filtration, straining, CONSTR filtration, ELECTRON, GEOLOGIE, INFORMAT, ORDINAT filtering, POLLU MER screening, RECYCLAGE filtration, TELECOM filtering; **~ actif** *m* ELECTRON active filtering; **~ adaptatif** *m* ORDINAT, TELECOM adaptive filtering; **~ adapté** *m* ELECTRON matched filtering; **~ des aigus** *m* ENREGISTR treble roll-off; **~ analogique** *m* ELECTRON analog filtering (AmE), analogue filtering (BrE); **~ à bande étroite** *m* ELECTRON narrow band filtering; **~ Doppler** *m* ELECTRON Doppler filtering; **~ à l'entrée** *m* ELECTRON input filtering; **~ des fréquences hors bande** *m* ELECTRON out-of-band filtering; **~ de Kalman** *m* ELECTRON Kalman filtering; **~ à large bande** *m* ELECTRON wide band filtering; **~ linéaire** *m* TELECOM linear filtering; **~ multidimensionnel** *m* TELECOM multidimensional filtering; **~ non linéaire** *m* TELECOM nonlinear filtering; **~ numérique** *m* ELECTRON, INFORMAT, ORDINAT, TELECOM digital filtering; **~ par absorption** *m* ENREGISTR absorption filtering; **~ des parasites** *m* ELECTRON electromagnetic interference filtering; **~ par capacité seule** *m* ELECTRON all-capacitor filtering; **~ par convolution** *m* ELECTRON convolutional filtering; **~ par filtre antirepliement de spectre** *m* ELECTRON anti-aliasing filtering; **~ par filtre coupe-bande** *m* ELECTRON bandstop filtering; **~ par filtre en peigne** *m* ELECTRON comb filtering; **~ par filtre à gain fixe** *m* ELECTRON fixed gain filtering; **~ par filtre à ondes acoustiques de surface** *m* ELECTRON SAW filtering; **~ par filtre passe-bande** *m* *(cf filtrage passe-haut, filtrage passe-bas)* ELECTRON band-pass filtering; **~ par filtre passe-bas à bande étroite** *m* ELECTRON narrow band low-pass filtering; **~ par filtre transversal** *m* ELECTRON transversal filtering; **~ passe-bas** *m* *(cf filtrage passe-haut, filtrage par filtre passe-bande)* ELECTRON low-pass filtering; **~ passe-haut** *m* *(cf filtrage par filtre passe-bande, filtrage passe-bas)* ELECTRON high-pass filtering; **~ passif** *m* ELECTRON passive filtering; **~ préalable** *m* ELECTRON

prefiltering; **~ récursif** *m* ELECTRON recursive filtering; **~ de signaux échantillonnés** *m* ELECTRON sampled data filtering; **~ à temps variable** *m* GEOPHYS time-variable filtering

filtramètre *m* PAPIER filtration tester

filtrat *m* CHARBON, CHIMIE, GENIE CHIM, RECYCLAGE filtrate; **~ de boue** *m* PETR mud filtrate; **~ en eau libre** *m* PETR filtrate loss

filtration *f* CHIMIE filtering, filtration, leaching, straining, CONSTR filtration, GENIE CHIM filtering, HYDROLOGIE percolation, PAPIER, PETROLE *raffinage, géologie*, PRODUCTION *système hydraulique*, RECYCLAGE filtration; **~ accélérée** *f* AGRO ALIM, GENIE CHIM accelerated filtration; **~ dans la canalisation de retour** *f* PRODUCTION *système hydraulique* return line filtration; **~ lente sur sable** *f* DISTRI EAU slow sand filtration; **~ sous vide** *f* AGRO ALIM, CHARBON, EQUIP LAB vacuum filtration; **~ sur couches multiples** *f* DISTRI EAU multilayer filtration

filtre *m* ASTRONOMIE, CHARBON, CONSTR, ELECTR *réseau*, ELECTRON, EQUIP LAB, ESPACE *véhicules*, GENIE CHIM filter, IMPRIM light filter, INFORMAT, MECANIQUE, ORDINAT, PAPIER filter, PETROLE strainer, *géologie, levé sismique, raffinerie* filter, PHOTO, PHYSIQUE, TELECOM, VEHICULES *carburateur, huile* filter;

~ a **~ absorbant le rouge** *m* INSTRUMENT red-abstracting filter; **~ d'absorption** *m* CINEMAT, INSTRUMENT absorption filter; **~ accordable hyper-fréquence** *m* ELECTRON microwave tunable filter; **~ accordable multioctave** *m* ELECTRON multioctave tunable filter; **~ à accord continu** *m* ENREGISTR continuously-tunable filter; **~ accordé** *m* ELECTRON narrow band filter, tuned filter; **~ à accord électronique** *m* ELECTRON electronically-tuned filter; **~ à accord rapide** *m* ELECTRON fast-tuned filter; **~ acoustique** *m* ACOUSTIQUE, CONS MECA, ELECTRON, ENREGISTR acoustic filter; **~ actif** *m* ELECTRON active filter; **~ actif du troisième ordre** *m* ELECTRON third-order active filter; **~ adaptatif** *m* ELECTRON adaptive filter; **~ adapté** *m* ELECTRON matched filter; **~ adapté numérique** *m* ELECTRON digital matched filter; **~ additionnel** *m* INSTRUMENT front lens-filter; **~ d'aiguillage** *m* ELECTRON branching filter; **~ à air** *m* AUTO, CHARBON, CHAUFFAGE air filter, CONS MECA air cleaner, GENIE CHIM, MECANIQUE air filter, VEHICULES *carburateur* air cleaner, air filter; **~ à air autonettoyant** *m* CHAUFFAGE self-cleaning air filter; **~ à air à bain d'huile** *m* AUTO oil bath air cleaner, oil bath air filter; **~ à air électrostatique** *m* CHAUFFAGE, SECURITE electrostatic air filter; **~ à air mécanique** *m* CHAUFFAGE mechanical air filter; **~ à air nettoyable** *m* CHAUFFAGE cleanable air filter; **~ à air perdu** *m* CHAUFFAGE wet-air filter; **~ à air sec** *m* CHAUFFAGE dry-air filter; **~ d'alimentation** *m* CONSTR ripple filter, ELECTRON power supply filter; **~ analogique** *m* ELECTRON analog filter (AmE), analogue filter (BrE); **~ antibrouillard** *m* CINEMAT haze filter; **~ antibruit** *m* ENREGISTR scratch filter; **~ anticalcaire** *m* DISTRI EAU hard water filter; **~ anticalorifique** *m* PHOTO heat-absorbing filter; **~ anticalorique** *m* CINEMAT heat filter; **~ antifouillis** *m* ELECTRON clutter filter; **~ antiparasite** *m* ELECTR *circuit* interference filter, ELECTRON electromagnetic interference filter, interference filter, line filter, parasitic suppressor, ELECTROTEC spark suppressor, PRODUCTION suppressor, TV interference eliminator, interference filter; **~ antirepliement du spectre** *m*

ELECTRON anti-aliasing filter; ~ **antirepliement de spectre à trois zéros** m ELECTRON three-zeros anti-aliasing filter; ~ **antiultraviolet** m PHOTO ultraviolet filter; ~ **d'arrêt** m ORDINAT band-rejection filter, bandstop filter; ~ **d'aspiration** m DISTRI EAU, PRODUCTION *système hydraulique* suction filter, REFRIG suction strainer; ~ **atténuateur** m ENREGISTR attenuating filter; ~ **audiofréquence** m ELECTRON audio filter; **~ b** ~ **bactérien** m POLLUTION trickling filter; ~ **bande** m ESSAIS bandstop filter; ~ **de bande** m ELECTRON vestigial sideband filter, ESPACE *communications* band-rejection filter; ~ **à bande étroite** m ELECTRON frequency selective filter, narrow band filter, IMPRIM *électronique* narrow band filter; ~ **à bande étroite accordable** m ELECTRON window filter; ~ **à bande d'un octave** m ELECTRON octave band filter; ~ **à bande passante relative constante** m ELECTRON constant percentage band width filter; ~ **de bande latérale inférieure** m ELECTRON lower sideband filter; ~ **de bande latérale unique** m ELECTRON single sideband filter; ~ **basse fréquence** m ELECTRON low-frequency filter, ENREGISTR low-frequency filter, low-pass filter; ~ **basse pression** m PRODUCTION *système hydraulique* low-pressure filter; ~ **BF** m ELECTRON, ENREGISTR low-frequency filter; ~ **biréfringent** m ASTRONOMIE birefringent filter; ~ **bouchon** m ENREGISTR bandstop filter; ~ **de bruit** m ENREGISTR noise filter; ~ **de Butterworth** m ELECTRON, PHYSIQUE Butterworth filter; **~ c** ~ **carburant basse pression** m AERONAUT low-pressure fuel filter; ~ **à cartouche** m CONS MECA cartridge filter; ~ **de Cauer** m PHYSIQUE Cauer filter; ~ **à cavités** m ELECTRON cavity filter; ~ **à CCD** m ELECTRON CCD filter; ~ **à une cellule** m ELECTRON single section filter; ~ **à cellules RC** m ELECTRON RC ladder filter; ~ **central** m CINEMAT between-the-lens filter; ~ **centrifuge** m CHARBON, CONS MECA centrifugal filter; ~ **centripète** m CONS MECA centripetal filter; ~ **à charbon** m NUCLEAIRE activated carbon filter; ~ **à charbon actif** m HYDROLOGIE activated carbon filter; ~ **à charbon activé** m MATERIAUX activated charcoal filter; ~ **à charbon de bois** m EQUIP LAB *filtration* charcoal filter; ~ **de Chebychev** m ELECTRON, PHYSIQUE Chebyshev filter; ~ **de Chebychev du huitième ordre** m ELECTRON eighth-order Chebyshev filter; ~ **du circuit intermédiaire** m NUCLEAIRE component cooling filter; ~ **à circuits couplés** m ELECTRON double-tuned filter; ~ **clarificateur** m GENIE CHIM water purification filter; ~ **coaxial** m ELECTRON coaxial filter; ~ **coloré** m INSTRUMENT light filter; ~ **de combustible** m AERONAUT fuel filter; ~ **à combustible double** m AUTO two-stage fuel filter; ~ **compensateur** m PHOTO compensating filter, correction filter; ~ **compensateur de couleurs** m CINEMAT CC filter, color compensating filter (AmE), colour compensating filter (BrE); ~ **composé** m ENREGISTR composite filter; ~ **compresseur d'impulsions à ondes accoustiques de surface** m ELECTRON SAW compression filter; ~ **de compression d'impulsions** m ELECTRON compression filter; ~ **contre les microparticules en suspension dans l'air** m SECURITE submicron particulate airfilter; ~ **de contre-réaction** m ELECTRON inverse feedback filter; ~ **de conversion** m CINEMAT conversion filter; ~ **de conversion de couleur** m CINEMAT color conversion filter (AmE), colour conversion filter (BrE); ~ **à convolution** m ELECTRON convolutional filter; ~ **correcteur** m CINEMAT color correction filter (AmE), colour correction filter (BrE), light-balancing filter, ENREGISTR equalizer; ~ **de correction de chrominance** m ELECTRON color correction filter (AmE), colour correction filter (BrE); ~ **coupe-bande** m ELECTRON bandstop filter, rejection filter, ORDINAT band-rejection filter, bandstop filter; ~ **coupe-bande actif** m ELECTRON active bandstop filter; ~ **coupe-bande à bande étroite** m ELECTRON narrow band rejection filter, notch filter; ~ **coupe-bande à bande étroite actif** m ELECTRON active notch filter; ~ **coupe-bande à flancs raides** m ELECTRON deep rejection trap; ~ **coupe-bande hyperfréquence** m ELECTRON microwave band-stop filter; ~ **coupe-bande passif** m ELECTRON passive band stop filter; ~ **coupe-bande du second ordre** m ELECTRON second order bandstop filter; ~ **coupe-bande du troisième ordre** m ELECTRON third-order bandstop filter; ~ **coupe-basses** m ENREGISTR bass cut filter; ~ **coupe-fréquences** m TELECOM notch filter; ~ **à coupure brusque** m TELECOM notch filter; ~ **à cristal** m TELECOM crystal filter; **~ d** ~ **de découplage** m ELECTRON decoupling filter; ~ **dégradé** m CINEMAT, PHOTO grad, graduated filter; ~ **dépoussiéreur** m GAZ antidust filter; ~ **de dessus du réservoir** m PRODUCTION *système hydraulique* tank top filter; ~ **à diaphragme** m GENIE CHIM membrane filtre; ~ **dichroïque** m CINEMAT, ELECTRON, OPTIQUE, TELECOM dichroic filter; ~ **discret** m ELECTRON discrete filter; ~ **à disque** m CHARBON disc filter (BrE), disk filter (AmE); ~ **à disque résonnant** m ELECTRON disc resonator filter (BrE), disk resonator filter (AmE); ~ **dissymétrique** m ENREGISTR unbalanced filter; ~ **à dix pôles** m ELECTRON ten-pole filter; ~ **Doppler** m ELECTRON Doppler filter; ~ **duplex** m PRODUCTION *système hydraulique* duplex filter; **~ e** ~ **à eau** m DISTRI EAU, NAUT water filter; ~ **à effet** m CINEMAT effect filter; ~ **élargisseur d'impulsions** m ELECTRON expansion filter; ~ **élargisseur d'impulsions à ondes accoustiques de surface** m ELECTRON SAW expansion filter; ~ **électrique** m ELECTRON electric filter, electrical filter; ~ **électromécanique** m ELECTRON electromechanical filter; ~ **électrostatique** m ELECTRON electrostatic filter; ~ **elliptique** m ELECTRON elliptic filter; ~ **à encoches** m TELECOM notch filter; ~ **en échelle** m ELECTRON ladder filter; ~ **en échelle à quartz** m ELECTRON crystal ladder filter; ~ **d'énergie électronique** m PHYS RAYON electron energy filter; ~ **en guide d'ondes** m ELECTRON waveguide filter; ~ **d'énième ordre** m ELECTRON nth order filter; ~ **en laine de verre** m CERAM VER glass wool filter; ~ **en peigne** m ELECTRON comb filter; ~ **en ruban** m NUCLEAIRE TBF, traveling belt filter (AmE), travelling belt filter (BrE); ~ **d'entrée** m ELECTRON, ESPACE *communications* input filter; ~ **d'entrée de retardement** m PRODUCTION input filter time delay; ~ **en treillis** m ELECTRON lattice filter; ~ **épaississeur** m CHARBON filter thickener; ~ **escamotable** m PHOTO retractable filter, swing-in filter; ~ **à essence** m AUTO fuel filter, VEHICULES *carburant* gas filter (AmE), gasoline filter (AmE), petrolfilter (BrE), gas filter (AmE), gasoline filter (AmE); ~ **étoile** m CINEMAT star filter; ~ **d'expansion** m ELECTRON expansion filter; **~ f** ~ **à faible temps de réponse** m PRODUCTION short-time constant filter; ~ **FI** m ELECTRON, TELECOM

IF filter; ~ **à flancs raides** m ELECTRON sharp cutoff filter; ~ **à fréquence intermédiaire** m ELECTRON, TELECOM intermediate frequency filter;

~ g ~ **à gain fixe** m ELECTRON fixed gain filter; ~ **gris neutre** m CINEMAT neutral density filter; ~ **gros** m DISTRI EAU coarse filter;

~ h ~ **d'harmonique** m ELECTRON, ESPACE *communications* harmonic filter, PHYS RAYON harmonic suppressor; ~ **à huile** m AUTO, CONS MECA, MECANIQUE, VEHICULES *lubrification* oil filter; ~ **à huile à cartouche jetable** m AUTO replaceable element oil filter; ~ **à huile en dérivation** m AUTO bypass oil cleaner; ~ **à huile jetable** m AUTO screw-type oil filter, throwaway oil filter; ~ **à huile à passage total** m VEHICULES *lubrification* full-flow oil filter; ~ **humide** m AUTO oil-moistened air filter cartridge; ~ **hyperfréquence** m ELECTRON microwave filter;

~ i ~ **idéal** m ELECTRON ideal filter; ~ **d'impulsions** m PHYS RAYON impulse regenerator, pulse generator; ~ **incorporé** m CINEMAT built-in filter, ELECTRON on-chip filter; ~ **à inductance en tête** m ELECTROTEC choke input filter; ~ **à inductance et capacité** m ELECTRON inductance-capacitance filter; ~ **infrarouge** m PHYS RAYON infrared filter; ~ **intégré** m ELECTRON integrated filter; ~ **intégré à CCD** m ELECTRON CCD filter; ~ **d'interférence** m ENREGISTR interference filter; ~ **interférentiel** m ESPACE *véhicules*, OPTIQUE, PHYSIQUE, TELECOM interference filter;

~ k ~ **de Kalman** m ELECTRON Kalman filter;

~ l ~ **à large bande** m ELECTRON flatband pass filter, wide band filter; ~ **LC** m ELECTRON LC filter; ~ **lent** m HYDROLOGIE slow sand filter; ~ **lent au sable** m DISTRI EAU slow sand filter; ~ **linéaire** m TELECOM linear filter; ~ **de lissage** m CONSTR ripple filter, ELECTRON smoothing filter; ~ **longitudinal** m ELECTRON longitudinal filter;

~ m ~ **magnétique** m CONS MECA magnetic filter; ~ **à manche** m CHARBON bag filter, GENIE CHIM filter bag; ~ **mécanique** m ELECTRON mechanical filter; ~ **mécanique à disques et à fils** m ENREGISTR disc-wire-type mechanical filter (BrE), disk-wire-type mechanical filter (AmE); ~ **MIC** m ELECTRON PCM filter; ~ **microporeux** m GENIE CHIM membrane filtre; ~ **miroir en quadrature** m TELECOM quadrature mirror filter; ~ **de mise en forme du signal** m TELECOM signal-shaping filter; ~ **de mode** m ELECTRON, OPTIQUE, TELECOM mode filter; ~ **moléculaire** m GENIE CHIM membrane filtre; ~ **monolithique** m ELECTRON, TELECOM monolithic filter; ~ **multibande** m TELECOM multiband filter; ~ **multicouche** m HYDROLOGIE multimedia filter; ~ **multiple passe-bande** m ENREGISTR multiple band-pass filter; ~ **multipôle** m ELECTRON multipole filter; ~ **multivoie** m TELECOM multichannel filter;

~ n ~ **neutre** m PHOTO neutral density filter; ~ **non récursif** m ELECTRON nonrecursive pulse, TELECOM nonrecursive filter; ~ **nuancé** m PHOTO graduated filter; ~ **numérique** m ELECTRON, TELECOM digital filter;

~ o ~ **à octave** m ENREGISTR octave filter; ~ **à ondes** m PHYS ONDES wave filter; ~ **à ondes accoustiques de surface** m ELECTRON SAW filter; ~ **à ondes acoustiques** m ELECTRON acoustic wave filter; ~ **d'ondulation** m PHYS RAYON ripple filter; ~ **optique** m CINEMAT optical flat filter, ELECTRON, IMPRIM optical filter, INSTRUMENT gray glass filter (AmE), grey glass

filter (BrE), OPTIQUE, TELECOM optical filter; ~ **optique encadrant** m INSTRUMENT stray light filter; ~ **d'ordre 2** m ELECTRON second order filter; ~ **d'ordre 3** m ELECTRON third-order filter; ~ **d'ordre élevé** m ELECTRON high-order filter; ~ **d'ordre impair** m ELECTRON odd-order filter; ~ **d'ordre multiple** m ELECTRON multiple order filter; ~ **d'ordre n** m ELECTRON nth order filter; ~ **d'ordre pair** m ELECTRON even-order filter; ~ **d'ordre peu élevé** m ELECTRON low-order filter; ~ **à oxyde de carbone** m SECURITE carbon monoxide filter;

~ p ~ **panchromatique** m INSTRUMENT pan filter; ~ **de parole** m ENREGISTR speech filter; ~ **passe-bande** m *(FPB, filtre passe-bas, filtre passe-haut)* ELECTR, ELECTRON, ENREGISTR, INFORMAT, ORDINAT, PHYSIQUE, TELECOM, TV band-pass filter *(BPF)*; ~ **passe-bande actif** m ELECTRON active band-pass filter; ~ **passe-bande autocentré** m ELECTRON self-tracking band-pass filter; ~ **passe-bande à bande étroite** m ELECTRON narrow band low-pass filter; ~ **passe-bande hyperfréquence** m ELECTRON microwave band-pass filter; ~ **passe-bande à large bande** m ELECTRON wide band band-pass filter; ~ **passe-bande d'ordre 2** m ELECTRON second order band-pass filter; ~ **passe-bande passif** m ELECTRON passive band pass filter; ~ **passe-bande du second ordre** m ELECTRON second order band-pass filter; ~ **passe-bande YIG** m ELECTRON YIG band pass filter; ~ **passe-bande de récepteur** m TV receiver band pass; ~ **passe-bas** m *(cf filtre passe-haut, filtre passe-bande)* CONS MECA high-stop filter, ELECTR, ELECTRON, ENREGISTR, INFORMAT, ORDINAT, PHYSIQUE, TELECOM, TV low-pass filter; ~ **passe-bas hyperfréquence** m ELECTRON microwave low-pass filter; ~ **passe-bas à large bande** m ELECTRON wide band low-pass filter; ~ **passe-bas d'ordre 2** m ELECTRON second order low-pass filter; ~ **passe-bas pour signaux échantillonnés** m ELECTRON low-pass sampled data filter; ~ **passe-bas du second ordre** m ELECTRON second order low-pass filter; ~ **passe-haut** m *(cf filtre passe-bas, filtre passe-bande)* CONS MECA low-stop filter, ELECTR, ELECTRON, ENREGISTR, INFORMAT, ORDINAT, PHYSIQUE, TELECOM, TV high-pass filter; ~ **passe-haut à large bande** m ELECTRON wide band high-pass filter; ~ **passe-haut d'ordre 2** m ELECTRON second order high-pass filter; ~ **passe-haut du second ordre** m ELECTRON second order high-pass filter; ~ **passe-tout** m ELECTRON all-pass filter; ~ **passif** m ELECTRON, TELECOM passive filter; ~ **piézo-électrique** m PHYS RAYON piezoelectric crystal filter; ~ **à plomb** m TRANSPORT lead filter; ~ **à plusieurs cellules** m ELECTRON multisection filter; ~ **polarisant** m CINEMAT polarization filter, INSTRUMENT polarizing filter; ~ **polynomial** m ELECTRON polynomial filter; ~ **pour hautes fréquences** m ENREGISTR high-frequency filter; ~ **pour signaux échantillonnés** m ELECTRON sampled data size filter; ~ **pour les yeux** m SECURITE eye filter; ~ **préalable** m ELECTRON prefilter; ~ **du premier ordre** m ELECTRON first order filter; ~ **presse** m CERAM VER, CHARBON, EQUIP LAB, GENIE CHIM, PAPIER filter press; ~ **programmé par masquage** m ELECTRON mask-programmable filter; ~ **protecteur contre le rayonnement du soleil** m INSTRUMENT dark filter; ~ **de protection des yeux** m SECURITE *soudure* eye protection filter; ~ **pseudo-elliptique** m ESPACE *communications* pseudoelliptic filter;

~ q ~ **à quartz** m ELECTRON crystal filter, quartz

crystal filter; ~ **à quartz en treillis** *m* ELECTRON crystal lattice filter; ~ **à quatre pôles** *m* ELECTRON four-pole filter;

~ r ~ **de réception** *m* ELECTRON receive filter; ~ **de rechange** *m* GENIE CHIM filter cartridge; ~ **récursif** *m* ELECTRON, TELECOM recursive filter; ~ **de redressement** *m* ENREGISTR rectifier filter; ~ **réjecteur** *m* GEOPHYS, TELECOM notch filter; ~ **à réponse impulsionnelle** *m (filtre RIF)* TELECOM finite impulse response filter; ~ **à réponse impulsionnelle finie** *m* ELECTRON finite impulse response filter; ~ **à réponse impulsionnelle infinie** *m* ELECTRON infinite impulse response filter; ~ **à réponse infinie à une impulsion** *m* TELECOM IIR filter, infinite impulse response digital filter, TELECOM *(filtre RIF)* finite impulse response filter; ~ **à résonateur diélectrique** *m* ESPACE *communications* dielectric resonator filter; ~ **résonnant** *m* ENREGISTR, PHYS RAYON resonance filter; ~ **respiratoire** *m* SECURITE respiratory filter; ~ **de retour** *m* PRODUCTION *système hydraulique* return filter; ~ **RIF** *m (filtre à réponse infinie à une impulsion, filtre à réponse impulsionnelle)* TELECOM FIR filter; ~ **rotatif** *m* CHARBON, DISTRI EAU rotary filter, HYDROLOGIE drum filter; ~ **de roulement** *m* ENREGISTR rumble filter;

~ s ~ **à sable** *m* CHARBON sand filter; ~ **à sacs** *m* GENIE CHIM filter bag; ~ **du second ordre** *m* ELECTRON second order filter; ~ **de sélection** *m* CINEMAT, PHOTO *sélection trichrome* color separation filter (AmE), colour separation filter (BrE); ~ **de sens de transmission** *m* ELECTRON directional filter; ~ **serti** *m* PHOTO mounted filter; ~ **de sifflement** *m* ENREGISTR hiss filter; ~ **de sortie** *m* CONSTR ripple filter; ~ **de sortie d'alimentation** *m* CONSTR ripple filter; ~ **sous pression** *m* CHARBON, DISTRI EAU, GENIE CHIM pressure filter; ~ **sous vide** *m* CHARBON vacuum filter; ~ **statique** *m* CHARBON pan filter; ~ **stop-bande** *m* ORDINAT band-rejection filter, bandstop filter; ~ **de succion** *m* GENIE CHIM suction strainer; ~ **suiveur** *m* ELECTRON tracking filter; ~ **sur conduite** *m* PLAST CAOU *matériel* supply line filter;

~ t ~ **à tambour** *m* CHARBON drum filter, rotary filter, DISTRI EAU rotary filter, HYDROLOGIE drum filter; ~ **tamis** *m* GENIE CHIM filtering screen; ~ **de télécommunications** *m* ELECTRON communications filter; ~ **à tige résonnante** *m* ELECTRON free bar filter; ~ **transversal** *m* ELECTRON, TELECOM transversal filter; ~ **tressé** *m* PLAST CAOU *matériel, peintures* filter screen; ~ **du troisième ordre** *m* ELECTRON third-order filter; ~ **à trois pôles** *m* ELECTRON three-pole filter; ~ **à trois zéros** *m* ELECTRON three-zeros filter;

~ u ~ **ultraviolet** *m* CINEMAT, SECURITE ultraviolet filter;

~ v ~ **à variation temporelle** *m* ELECTRON time-varying filter; ~ **à vide** *m* CHARBON vacuum filter, DISTRI EAU suction filter; ~ **à vis** *m* CINEMAT screw-in filter; ~ **de voie** *m* ELECTRON channel filter, separation filter;

~ w ~ **Wratten** *m* CINEMAT Wratten filter;

~ y ~ **à YIG** *m* ELECTRON YIG filter

filtrer *vt* CHIMIE leach, strain, CONSTR, ELECTRON, GENIE CHIM, PHOTO filter, POLLU MER leach, screen, RECYCLAGE filter; ~ **par aspiration** *vt* GENIE CHIM filter by suction; ~ **à la trompe** *vt* GENIE CHIM filter by suction

filtres: ~ **pour l'observation visuelle et la photographie** *m pl* ASTRONOMIE filters for photographic and visual operation

filtre-tamis *m* GENIE CHIM sieving filter, PRODUCTION *système hydraulique* strainer

fin[1] *adj* CERAM VER seed-free, MATERIAUX fine, PRODUCTION thin

fin:[2] **par la** ~ *adv* CINEMAT tailout

fin[3] *f* (Fra) *(cf filet)* CERAM VER string (AmE), thread (BrE), CHIMIE *d'une réaction* end point, INFORMAT, ORDINAT end, tail; ~ **d'adresse** *f* INFORMAT, ORDINAT end of address; ~ **d'alinéa** *f* IMPRIM *composition* break line; ~ **anormale** *f* ORDINAT abnormal termination; ~ **avancée** *f* TV early finish; ~ **de bande** *f* ORDINAT EOT, end of tape; ~ **de bloc** *f* INFORMAT end of block, ORDINAT EOB, end of block; ~ **de bloc de transmission** *f* ORDINAT ETB, end of transmission block; ~ **de bobine** *f* CINEMAT reel end, tail, INFORMAT, ORDINAT end of reel; ~ **de branche** *f* PRODUCTION *automatisme industriel* branch end; ~ **de communication** *f* TELECOM EOC, end of communication; ~ **de connexion** *f* INFORMAT log-off; ~ **de course** *f* NUCLEAIRE final position setting, limit setting; ~ **de course mécanique** *f* ELECTR *changeur de prises* mechanical end stop; ~ **de données** *f* INFORMAT DP end of data, EOD, end of data, ORDINAT EOD, end of data; ~ **d'exercice** *f* PRODUCTION cutoff; ~ **de fichier** *f* INFORMAT end of file, ORDINAT EOF, end of file; ~ **image avancée** *f* TV early finish video; ~ **de message** *f* INFORMAT end of message, ORDINAT, TELECOM EOM, end of message; ~ **de papier imminente** *f* INFORMAT paper low; ~ **de période** *f* PRODUCTION cutoff; ~ **serré** *f* CERAM VER heavy seed; ~ **de session** *f* INFORMAT log-off, ORDINAT log-off, log-out; ~ **son avancée** *f* TV early finish audio; ~ **de support** *f* INFORMAT end of medium, ORDINAT EM, end of medium; ~ **de texte** *f* ORDINAT ETX, end of text; ~ **de transaction** *f* TELECOM EOT, end of transaction; ~ **de transmission** *f* ORDINAT EOT, end of transmission; ~ **de travail** *f* INFORMAT end of job, ORDINAT EOJ, end of job; ~ **de vol** *f* ESPACE *véhicules* end of flight

financement *m* PETROLE *commerce* financing

finement: ~ **grenu** *adj* GEOLOGIE fine-grained; ~ **stratifié** *adj* GEOLOGIE thin-bedded, thinly-bedded

fines:[1] **à** ~ **rainures** *adj* CONS MECA *alésoir* fine-fluted

fines[2] *f pl* CHARBON smalls, CONSTR filler, fines, MINES fines; ~ **dans la pâte** *f pl* PAPIER fines

finesse *f* AERONAUT *rendement d'aéronef* L-D ratio, lift-drag ratio, CONS MECA *du tranchant d'un outil* sharpness, CONSTR *de sable* fineness, *du tranchant d'un outil* keenness, NAUT *d'un navire* fineness, OPTIQUE finesse, PAPIER fineness, PHYSIQUE finesse, lift-drag ratio, PRODUCTION thinness; ~ **aérodynamique** *f* AERONAUT aerodynamic efficiency; ~ **d'ajustage** *f* ELECTROTEC trimming resolution

fini:[1] ~ **machine** *adj* IMPRIM *papiers* machine-finished

fini[2] *m* IMPRIM, PAPIER, PRODUCTION finish; ~ **à l'anglaise** *m* IMPRIM English finish; ~ **brut** *m* IMPRIM antique finish; ~ **crispé** *m* PAPIER cockle finish; ~ **satiné** *m* MATERIAUX satin finish; ~ **sec** *m* TEXTILE crisp paper-like finish; ~ **de surface** *m* IMPRIM surface finish; ~ **vélin** *m* PRODUCTION vellum finish; ~ **vermiculé** *m* PRODUCTION crackled finish

finir *vt* IMPRIM *reliure* pare, MECANIQUE trim, PRODUCTION, TEXTILE finish

finissage *m* CERAM VER, PAPIER finishing; ~ **antistatique** *m* MATERIAUX antistatic finishing; ~ **mécanique** *m* CONS MECA machine finishing

finisseur *m* CONSTR finisher, TRANSPORT road finishing

machine

finition f COULEURS final coat, top coat, finish, IMPRIM finishing, *façonnage* trim, MECANIQUE, PRODUCTION finish; ~ **brillante** f COULEURS gloss finish; ~ **chromée dure** f CONS MECA hard chrome finish; ~ **coquille d'oeuf** f COULEURS eggshell finish; ~ **électrolytique** f REVETEMENT galvanic deposition, galvanic plating; ~ **galvanique** f REVETEMENT galvanic deposition, galvanic plating; ~ **mate** f COULEURS matt finish, TEXTILE dull finish; ~ **par électro-érosion** f CONS MECA spark erosion finish; ~ **raide** f TEXTILE stiff finish; ~ **satinée** f COULEURS satin finish; ~ **terne** f COULEURS dull finish

fins m pl CHARBON fines, screenings, MINES fines

fiole f CERAM VER phial (BrE), vial (AmE), CHIMIE flask, phial (BrE), vial, CONSTR bubble tube, EQUIP LAB *verrerie* phial (BrE), vial (AmE); ~ **d'arpentage** f CONSTR bubble tube; ~ **bouchée à rodage** f EQUIP LAB *verrerie* stoppered flask; ~ **conique** f EQUIP LAB Erlenmeyer flask, *verrerie* conical flask; ~ **Erlenmeyer** f EQUIP LAB *verrerie* Erlenmeyer flask; ~ **à filtre** f GENIE CHIM filter flask; ~ **à iode** f EQUIP LAB *analyse, verrerie* iodine flask; ~ **jaugée** f EQUIP LAB volumetric flask, *verrerie, analyse* graduated flask; ~ **à vide** f EQUIP LAB *filtration* Buchner flask, *matériel général* vacuum flask

fiord m NAUT, OCEANO fjord

fisétin m CHIMIE fisetin

fissile[1] *adj* PHYSIQUE *par neutrons lents* fissile

fissile[2] m NUCLEAIRE fissile

fission: ~ **nucléaire** f PHYS PART, PHYSIQUE nuclear fission; ~ **quaternaire** f NUCLEAIRE quaternary fission; ~ **spontanée** f PHYS RAYON, PHYSIQUE spontaneous fission; ~ **thermique** f NUCLEAIRE *provoquée par des neutrons thermiques* thermal neutron fission; ~ **tout près de la barrière** f NUCLEAIRE near barrier fission

fissionnable *adj* PHYSIQUE fissionable

fissium m NUCLEAIRE fissium

fissuration f CONSTR *béton* cracking, GEOLOGIE fracturing, jointing, MECANIQUE *matériaux* cracking, NUCLEAIRE jointing, QUALITE cracking; ~ **des carbures** f METALL carbide cracking; ~ **à chaud** f MECANIQUE *matériaux* hot tear; ~ **hydraulique** f EN RENOUV hydraulic fracturing; ~ **de retrait** f CONSTR shrinkage cracking; ~ **transgranulaire** f MATERIAUX transgranular cracking

fissure f ASTRONOMIE rille, CONSTR fissure, CRISTALL crack, GEOLOGIE joint, GEOPHYS fissure, MECANIQUE *matériaux*, METALL, TEXTILE crack, THERMODYN *crique de trempe* heat treatment crack; ~ **circulaire** f METALL penny-shaped crack; ~ **de clivage** f METALL cleavage crack; ~ **de dessication** f GEOLOGIE desiccation crack; ~ **ductile** f METALL ductile crack; ~ **en coin** f METALL wedge crack; ~ **de fatigue** f ESPACE *véhicules*, METALL fatigue crack; ~ **de fatigue due à la corrosion** f NUCLEAIRE corrosion fatigue crack; ~ **fragile** f NUCLEAIRE brittle crack; ~ **interne** f METALL internal crack; ~ **lenticulaire** f NUCLEAIRE penny-shaped crack; ~ **principale** f METALL main crack; ~ **de retrait** f CONSTR shrinkage crack; ~ **semi-infinie** f NUCLEAIRE semi-infinite crack; ~ **sous cordon** f NUCLEAIRE underbead crack

fissuré *adj* MECANIQUE *matériaux* cracked

fixage m CONS MECA fixing; ~ **acide** m GENIE CHIM acid fixing bath

fixateur m CINEMAT fixer; ~ **de gaz** m ELECTROTEC getter

fixatif m PAPIER fixing agent

fixation f CHARBON attachment, landing, pit bottom, CHIMIE retention, CONS MECA attachment, pick-up, ESPACE *véhicules* anchoring, attachment, GAZ fixing, MECANIQUE fastening, NAUT fitting, PHOTO *d'une caméra, d'une lampe* mounting, PLAST CAOU scorch; ~ **de la barrette de masse** f PRODUCTION *électricité* ground bus mounting; ~ **à boulon unique** f PRODUCTION single bolt clamping; ~ **d'un électron** f NUCLEAIRE electron attachment; ~ **des frais** f BREVETS awarding of costs; ~ **de niveau** f ELECTRON clamping; ~ **d'un seuil** f ELECTRON thresholding; ~ **à vis** f CONS MECA screw fixing

fixations f pl CONS MECA fixtures; ~ **du moteur** f pl ESPACE *véhicules, propulsion* engine mountings

fixe *adj* MECANIQUE fixed; **qui se ~ à la chaleur** *adj* IMPRIM *encres* heat-set

fixer vt CONS MECA attach, CONSTR fix, secure, set, ESPACE *véhicules* anchor, attach, INFORMAT set, MECANIQUE fasten, MINES *l'emplacement d'un puits* select, ORDINAT set, *une variable* bind, PAPIER attach, fix, set, PRODUCTION bed in; ~ **à demeure** vt CONSTR set, *rivet* set; ~ **sur** vt GENIE CHIM settle on; ~ **à la vapeur** vt TEXTILE steam set

fjord m NAUT fjord, sea loch, OCEANO fjord

flabage m NUCLEAIRE buckling

flache f CONSTR slab, wane

flacon m AGRO ALIM, CERAM VER flask, CHIMIE flask, phial (BrE), vial, EQUIP LAB bottle, *récipient* reagent bottle, *à col étroit* flask, *à large ouverture* flask; ~ **bouché à rodage** m EQUIP LAB *récipient* stoppered bottle; ~ **de Claisen** m GENIE CHIM Claisen flask; ~ **à col étroit** m EQUIP LAB *verrerie* narrow-necked bottle, narrow-necked flask; ~ **à col large** m EQUIP LAB *récipient* wide-mouth bottle; ~ **de collyre** m CERAM VER eye drop bottle; ~ **à col moulé** m EQUIP LAB flask with molded neck (AmE), flask with moulded neck (BrE), *verrerie* bottle with molded neck (AmE), bottle with moulded neck (BrE); ~ **compte-gouttes** m EQUIP LAB *verrerie* dropping bottle; ~ **à filtrer** m GENIE CHIM filtering flask; ~ **à large ouverture** m EQUIP LAB *verrerie* wide-mouth bottle; ~ **de lavage** m CHIMIE impinger; ~ **laveur de Durand** m EQUIP LAB *verrerie* Dreschel bottle; ~ **à peser** m CHIMIE weighing bottle; ~ **pour lyophilisation** m CERAM VER lyophilization flask; ~ **pour transfusion** m CERAM VER transfusion bottle; ~ **soluté** m CERAM VER infusion bottle; ~ **souple** m PHOTO *révélateur* collapsible bottle; ~ **à tare** m CHIMIE, EQUIP LAB *verrerie* weighing bottle; ~ **tubulé** m EQUIP LAB *verrerie* aspirator

flaconnage m CERAM VER manufacture of small bottles

flacons: ~ **pour douche oculaire** m pl SECURITE eye rinse bottles

flambage m CONS MECA buckle, buckling, CONSTR charring, PRODUCTION skin drying, torching, RESSORTS lateral buckling, TEXTILE singeing

flambant *adj* THERMODYN flaming

flambée f THERMODYN blaze

flambement m MATERIAUX buckle, buckling, MECANIQUE *matériaux* buckling, PETR buckle

flamber[1] vt TEXTILE singe, THERMODYN set ablaze

flamber[2] vi MECANIQUE *matériaux*, RESSORTS buckle

flamboyant *adj* TEXTILE blazing

flamme f CHIMIE flame, NAUT pennant, SECURITE flame, THERMODYN blaze, flame; ~ **aperçue** f NAUT answering pennant; ~ **molle** f CERAM VER easy fire, soft fire; ~

normale f CONSTR neutral flame; ~ **oxydante** f CHIMIE, CONSTR oxidizing flame; ~ **d'oxydation** f CONSTR oxidizing flame; ~ **réductrice** f THERMODYN reducing flame; ~ **de tuyère** f MILITAIRE rocket plume

flammèche f PRODUCTION spark

flammes:[1] **en** ~ adj THERMODYN burning, flaming

flammes:[2] ~ **perdues** f pl PRODUCTION waste gases

flammes:[3] **être en** ~ vi THERMODYN burn

flan m IMPRIM stéréo mat, MECANIQUE, PRODUCTION blank

flanc m GEOLOGIE d'un pli limb, MECANIQUE engrenage flank, OPTIQUE d'une microcuvette side; ~ **arrière** m ELECTRON falling edge, TV trailing edge; ~ **avant** m ELECTRON leading edge; ~ **de brûleur** m CERAM VER port side wall; ~ **inverse** m GEOLOGIE overturned limb; ~ **d'un pli** m GEOLOGIE fold limb; ~ **de saillie** m CONS MECA engrenages addendum flank; ~ **de signal** m ELECTRON signal edge

flancs: ~ **parallèles** f pl CONS MECA à cannelures cylindriques straight-sided splines

flandre f MINES crown tree

flaque f DISTRI EAU, HYDROLOGIE puddle, POLLU MER patch

flash m CINEMAT, IMPRIM photogravure, MINES, PHOTO flash; ~ **annulaire** m PHOTO ring flash; ~ **électronique à accumulateur** m PHOTO battery-powered flash unit; ~ **thermique** m NUCLEAIRE thermal flash, thermal radiation

flashage m CINEMAT flashing; ~ **de page** m IMPRIM page bursting

flasque m ACOUSTIQUE, AUTO flange, CONS MECA flange, d'un tour side, ESPACE, MECANIQUE flange, PRODUCTION d'un soufflet board, d'un treuil à main side, des maillons d'une chaîne à rouleaux side bar, side plates; ~ **d'arbre d'attaque** m VEHICULES transmission pinion shaft flange; ~ **d'arbre du pignon** m AUTO pinion shaft flange; ~ **de coulisse** m CONS MECA link plate; ~ **de l'essieu** m VEHICULES roues axle flange; ~ **de frein** m CH DE FER véhicules brake flange; ~ **de moyeu** m AUTO hub flange; ~ **de roue** m CH DE FER véhicules wheel web

flasques m pl CONS MECA shears, d'un tour cheeks, PRODUCTION guide plates

flavane m CHIMIE flavan

flavanone f CHIMIE flavanone

flavine f CHIMIE flavin

flavone f AGRO ALIM, CHIMIE flavone

flavonoïde f AGRO ALIM flavonoid

flavonol m CHIMIE flavonol

flavoprotéine f AGRO ALIM flavoprotein

flavopurpurine f CHIMIE flavopurpurin

fléau m METROLOGIE beam; ~ **de balance** m CONS MECA balance beam, scale beam, METROLOGIE balance beam

Flèche f ASTRONOMIE Sagitta

flèche f CINEMAT boom arm, CONS MECA d'un ressort compression, résistance des ressorts set, CONSTR deflection, rise, d'une grue boom, d'une ligne aérienne dip, d'une voûte height above impost level, d'une grue jib, DISTRI EAU d'une porte d'écluse balance bar, EMBALLAGE pour dispositif de fermeture arrowhead, ESPACE véhicules boom, sweep, MECANIQUE deflection, matériel de levage boom, NUCLEAIRE boom, jib, deflection, sag, OCEANO harpoon, TRANSPORT derrick boom; ~ **abyssale** f OCEANO abyssal spit; ~ **de direction de marche sur le feutre** f PAPIER felt direction

mark; ~ **en place** f RESSORTS deflection when assembled; ~ **de grue** f MECANIQUE matériel de levage crane jib; ~ **libre** f RESSORTS free deflection; ~ **littorale** f OCEANO spit; ~ **de pilon** f PRODUCTION stamp stem; ~ **sous charge** f RESSORTS deflection under load; ~ **à spires jointives** f RESSORTS deflection to solid; ~ **de travail** f RESSORTS working deflection; ~ **de vent** f METEO wind arrow

fléchir[1] vt CONSTR, PAPIER bend

fléchir[2] vi CONS MECA yield

fléchissement m GEOLOGIE downwarp, MECANIQUE deflection

flector m AERONAUT coupling

flegmatisant m MINES desensitizer

flegmatisation f MINES desensitization

flegmatiser vt MINES desensitize, phlegmatize

flétri adj AGRO ALIM withered

flettage m CERAM VER flatting

fletteur m CERAM VER crimper, flatter; ~ **d'équilibrage** m AERONAUT balance tab

fleur:[1] **à** ~ **de sol** adj CONSTR even with the ground, level with the ground

fleur:[2] **à** ~ **d'eau** adv DISTRI EAU at water level, NAUT awash

fleur[3] f CONSTR flower; ~ **de farine** f AGRO ALIM patent flour

fleur:[4] **être à** ~ **de** vi PRODUCTION be flush with

fleuret m CHARBON cutting bit, rock drill, CONSTR bit, drill, rock drill, breaker point, MINES borer, drill, jackhammer, rock drill, chisel, d'une perforatrice, d'un marteau perforateur drill bit, d'une haveuse à pic pick

fleuve m HYDROLOGIE, NAUT river

flexibilité f NAUT elasticity, flexibility, PLAST CAOU, TEXTILE flexibility

flexible[1] adj TEXTILE flexible

flexible[2] m CH DE FER véhicules flexible connection, CONS MECA flexible shaft, POLLU MER flexible hose; ~ **d'air** m MINES air hose; ~ **à air comprimé** m MECANIQUE air hose; ~ **à boue** m PETR mud hose; ~ **à dépression** m CONS MECA vacuum hose; ~ **d'eau** m MINES water hose; ~ **d'entraînement** m CONS MECA flexible drive shaft; ~ **de frein** m VEHICULES brake hose; ~ **de rotary** m PETROLE rotary hose; ~ **de tachymètre** m AUTO speedometer cable

flexiomètre m PAPIER bending stiffness tester

flexion f CH DE FER flexion, sagging, CONSTR flexion, ESPACE véhicules bending, deflection, MECANIQUE bending, deflection, METALL yielding, PAPIER bending, PRODUCTION buckling, des pièces coulées warping; ~ **en trois points** f METALL three-point bending

flexographie f EMBALLAGE aniline printing, IMPRIM, PLAST CAOU imprimerie flexographic printing, flexography

flexure f GEOLOGIE downbending; ~ **synclinale** f CONS MECA synclinal flexure, synclinal fold

flint: ~ **dense** m CERAM VER dense flint; ~ **léger** m CERAM VER light flint

flockage m GAZ flocking

flocon m IMPRIM impression flake, PLAST CAOU enduit flock

floconner vi CHIMIE flocculate

floculant m CHARBON flocculant, GENIE CHIM flocculant, flocculator, PLAST CAOU caoutchouc flocculant

floculat m GENIE CHIM flocculate

floculation f AGRO ALIM, CHARBON flocculation,

CHAUFFAGE coagulation, CHIMIE clotting, flocculation, GENIE CHIM coagulation, flocculation, flocculence, PETROLE *comportement des solides dans un liquide*, PLAST CAOU *imperfection de peinture* flocculation

floculer *vi* CHIMIE flocculate

floculeux *adj* GENIE CHIM flocculent

floe *m* OCEANO floe

flop *m* PLAST CAOU *peinture* flop

flos: ~ **ferri** *m* MINERAUX flos ferri

flot[1] *m* HYDROLOGIE flood tide, flow, INFORMAT stream, NAUT flood tide, *marée* flood, OCEANO flood tide, rising tide, ORDINAT stream, PRODUCTION throughput; ~ **binaire** *m* INFORMAT bit stream; ~ **de données** *m* INFORMAT, ORDINAT, TELECOM data stream; ~ **d'instructions** *m* INFORMAT, ORDINAT instruction stream; ~ **de retour** *m* OCEANO backrush, backwash; ~ **de travaux** *m* INFORMAT job stack, job stream, ORDINAT job stream

flot[2] **être à** ~ *vi* NAUT *navire* float

flotille *f* NAUT flotilla

flottabilité *f* AERONAUT, INST HYDR, NAUT, PHYS FLUID, PHYSIQUE buoyancy

flottable *adj* NAUT buoyant

flottage *m* MINES flotation

flottaison *f* CERAM VER top course of tank blocks, NAUT flotation, POLLUTION air flotation; ~ **à la construction** *f* NAUT construction waterline; ~ **en charge** *f* NAUT load line, load waterline; ~ **lège** *f* NAUT light waterline; ~ **de tracé** *f* NAUT design waterline, design waterplane

flottant *adj* MECANIQUE floating

flottation *f* CHARBON, CHIMIE flotation; ~ **collective** *f* CHARBON bulk flotation; ~ **due à l'énergie cinétique** *f* POLLUTION kinetically-induced buoyancy; ~ **due au gradient thermique** *f* POLLUTION thermally-induced buoyancy; ~ **à la mousse** *f* GENIE CHIM froth flotation; ~ **par écumage** *f* GENIE CHIM froth flotation; ~ **simple** *f* CHARBON single flotation

flottations: ~ **de mousses** *f pl* MINES froth flotation plant

flotte *f* NAUT, TRANSPORT *avions, navires* fleet; ~ **de commerce** *f* NAUT merchant fleet; ~ **de haute mer** *f* TRANSPORT sea fleet; ~ **marchande** *f* NAUT merchant fleet

flottement *m* AERONAUT buffeting, *aérodynamique* flutter, ENREGISTR flutter, ESPACE buffeting; ~ **magnétique** *m* NUCLEAIRE field flutter; ~ **de ruban** *m* ENREGISTR tape scrape

flotter[1] *vt* CONSTR *bois* run

flotter[2] *vi* NAUT, PHYSIQUE float

flotteur *m* AGRO ALIM swimmer, AUTO float, CERAM VER floater, CHARBON float, CONSTR ball, DISTRI EAU, MECANIQUE, NAUT, PETR float, PRODUCTION floater, TRANSPORT, VEHICULES *carburateur* float; ~ **d'alarme** *m* PAPIER level indicator; ~ **d'alarme de chaudière** *m* INST HYDR boiler emergency float; ~ **de carburateur** *m* VEHICULES carburetor float (AmE), carburettor float (BrE); ~ **de chaudière** *m* INST HYDR boiler float; ~ **dérivant** *m* OCEANO drifting float; ~ **d'embase** *m* PETROLE *exploitation en mer* flotation collar; ~ **lagrangien** *m* NAUT Lagrangian drifter; ~ **de relevage** *m* NAUT caisson, camel; ~ **sphérique** *m* CONSTR ball cock; ~ **de surface** *m* NAUT, OCEANO surface float

flottille: ~ **de pêche** *f* NAUT fishing fleet

flou[1] *adj* CINEMAT out-of-focus, soft focus, TEXTILE hazy

flou:[2] ~ **artistique** *m* CINEMAT defocus effect, soft focus; ~ **de bougé** *m* PHOTO motion blur; ~ **du fond de l'image** *m* PHOTO background blur; ~ **d'image** *m* CINEMAT blurring; ~ **de mouvement** *m* CINEMAT motion unsharpness; ~ **d'obturateur** *m* CINEMAT shutter blur

fluage *m* CERAM VER washing, CHARBON, CHAUFFAGE, CONSTR, CRISTALL, GAZ, MATERIAUX, MECANIQUE *matériaux* creep, NUCLEAIRE plastic yield, yielding, PLAST CAOU creep, *plastiques, peintures* flow; ~ **accéléré** *m* METALL accelerated creep; ~ **à chaud** *m* THERMODYN hot bonding, hot creep; ~ **à froid** *m* MECANIQUE, PLAST CAOU cold flow, THERMODYN cold creep; ~ **à haute température** *m* METALL high-temperature creep; ~ **logarithmique** *m* METALL logarithmic creep; ~ **nul** *m* METALL zero creep; ~ **parabolique** *m* METALL parabolic creep; ~ **par épuisement** *m* METALL exhaustion creep; ~ **par restauration** *m* METALL recovery creep; ~ **plastique** *m* NUCLEAIRE plastic yield, yielding; ~ **primaire** *m* METALL primary creep; ~ **primaire inverse** *m* METALL inverse primary creep; ~ **secondaire** *m* METALL secondary creep; ~ **stationnaire** *m* METALL steady-state creep; ~ **tertiaire** *m* METALL tertiary creep; ~ **transitoire** *m* METALL transient creep

fluate *m* CHIMIE fluate

fluctuation: ~ **de charge** *f* ELECTR load fluctuation; ~ **du faisceau** *f* TV beam jitter; ~ **de longueur d'onde** *f* OPTIQUE wavelength fluctuation, TELECOM chirping; ~ **de la nappe phréatique** *f* HYDROLOGIE water table fluctuation; ~ **de phase** *f* ESPACE phase jitter, TV *du signal* jitter; ~ **saisonnière** *f* PRODUCTION seasonal pattern, seasonal pattern code, *du stock de sécurité* season pattern code; ~ **de température** *f* REFRIG temperature fluctuation; ~ **de tension** *f* ELECTR *alimentation* voltage fluctuation; ~ **de vitesse** *f* ENREGISTR wow and flutter

fluctuations: ~ **à point zéro** *f pl* PHYS RAYON zero point fluctuations; ~ **de vitesse** *f* TV wow and flutter

fluellite *f* MINERAUX fluellite

fluence *f* PHYSIQUE fluence; ~ **énergétique** *f* PHYSIQUE energy fluence; ~ **de particules** *f* PHYSIQUE particle fluence

fluide[1] *adj* PHYS FLUID fluid

fluide[2] *m* CHIMIE *liquide, gaz*, PETR, PHYS FLUID, PHYSIQUE fluid; ~ **ambiant** *m* PHYS FLUID ambient fluid; ~ **caloporteur** *m* CONSTR coolant; ~ **cryogénique** *m* REFRIG cryogenic fluid; ~ **de formation** *m* PETROLE *géologie* formation fluid; ~ **des freins** *m* VEHICULES brake fluid; ~ **frigoporteur** *m* REFRIG coolant; ~ **frigorifique** *m* AUTO refrigerant; ~ **frigorigène** *m* REFRIG, VEHICULES *refroidissement* refrigerant; ~ **frigorigène organique** *m* CONS MECA organic refrigerant; ~ **monoatomique** *m* GAZ monoatomic fluid; ~ **parfait** *m* PHYSIQUE perfect fluid; ~ **réfrigérant** *m* POLLUTION cooling medium; ~ **de refroidissement** *m* CONS MECA, PHYSIQUE coolant; ~ **silicone** *m* ELECTR *isolateur* silicone fluid

fluides: ~ **tournants** *m pl* PHYS FLUID rotating fluids

fluidifiant *m* CONSTR plasticizer, plasticizer admixture, plastifying admixture, MATERIAUX plasticizer

fluidifiants *m pl* PETR thinners

fluidification *f* THERMODYN liquefaction

fluidifier *vt* PAPIER fluidify, fluidize, THERMODYN liquefy

fluidique *f* PHYS FLUID fluidics

fluidisation *f* CHARBON fluidization, sintering, PETR

fluidization

fluidité *f* PHYS FLUID, PHYSIQUE fluidity, PLAST CAOU *plastiques, peintures* flow

fluoanthène *m* CHIMIE fluoanthene

fluoanthrène *m* CHIMIE fluoanthrene

fluocérine *f* MINERAUX fluocerine, fluocerite

fluocérite *f* MINERAUX fluocerine, fluocerite

Fluon *m* (MD) PLAST CAOU Fluon (TM)

fluor *m* (*F*) CHIMIE fluorine (*F*)

fluoration *f* CHIMIE fluoridation, PHOTO blooming, lens coating

fluorène *m* CHIMIE fluorene

fluorénone *f* CHIMIE fluorenone

fluoroscéine *f* CHIMIE fluorescein

fluorescence *f* CHIMIE, PHYS ONDES, PHYS RAYON, PHYSIQUE fluorescence; **~ par impact** *f* TV impact fluorescence; **~ sensibilisée** *f* PHYS RAYON sensitized fluorescence; **~ X** *f* PHYS RAYON X-ray fluorescence

fluorescent *adj* CHIMIE, COULEURS, IMPRIM, MATERIAUX fluorescent

fluorhydrate *m* CHIMIE hydrofluoride

fluorhydrique *adj* CHIMIE *acide* hydrofluoric

fluorine *f* (*cf fluorite*) MINERAUX fluorite (BrE), fluorspar (AmE)

fluorite *f* MINERAUX fluorite (BrE), fluorspar (AmE)

fluoroborate *m* CHIMIE fluoroborate

fluoroborique *adj* CHIMIE fluoroboric

fluoroforme *m* CHIMIE fluoroform

fluorophosphate *m* CHIMIE fluorophosphate

fluoroscopie *f* ELECTROTEC fluoroscopy

fluoroscopique *adj* MATERIAUX *examen* fluoroscopic

fluorosilicate *m* CHIMIE fluorosilicate

fluorosilicique *adj* CHIMIE fluorosilicic

fluorosulphonique *adj* CHIMIE fluosulfonic (AmE), fluosulphonic (BrE)

fluoruration *f* CHIMIE fluoridation

fluorure *m* CHIMIE fluoride; **~ d'argent** *m* CHIMIE silver fluoride; **~ de polyvinyle** *m* PLAST CAOU polyvinyl fluoride

fluosilicate *m* CHIMIE silicofluoride

fluotournage *m* CONS MECA flow spinning

fluroaluminate *m* CHIMIE fluroaluminate

flûte *f* IMPRIM *transformation* flute

flute-mark *m* GEOLOGIE flute mark

flutter *m* AERONAUT *aérodynamique* flutter

fluviatile *adj* GEOLOGIE fluviatile

fluvio-glaciaire *adj* GEOLOGIE fluvio-glacial

fluvio-marin *adj* GEOLOGIE fluvio-marine

flux *m* CONSTR, ELECTR *magnétisme*, ELECTROTEC flux, HYDROLOGIE *de la marée* flow, INFORMAT flow, stream, MECANIQUE *soudage* flux, NAUT flood tide, rise, OCEANO flood tide, rising tide, tide flow, ORDINAT flow, stream, PHYSIQUE flux, PLAST CAOU *plastiques, peintures* flow, PRODUCTION throughput; **~ d'accrétion** *m* ASTRONOMIE accretion flow; **~ d'air** *m* CONSTR airflow; **~ alternatif** *m* ELECTR *électromagnétisme* alternating flux; **~ alterné** *m* ELECTR *électromagnétisme* alternating flux; **~ axial** *m* AERONAUT, VEHICULES *moteur* axial flow; **~ de brasage** *m* CONSTR brazing flux; **~ de chaleur** *m* CHAUFFAGE, GEOLOGIE, THERMODYN heat flow; **~ de chaleur maximum** *m* NUCLEAIRE maximum flux heat, peak heat flux; **~ de circulation en conflit** *m pl* TRANSPORT conflicting traffic flows; **~ de commande** *m* INFORMAT, ORDINAT control flow; **~ de court-circuit** *m* ACOUSTIQUE, TV short circuit flux; **~ décapant** *m* ELECTR *raccordement* soldering flux; **~ de**

déplacement électrique *m* ELECTROTEC electric flux; **~ de données** *m* ORDINAT data path; **~ électrique** *m* PHYSIQUE electric flux; **~ électronique** *m* TV electron stream; **~ électrostatique** *m* ELECTR electrostatic flux; **~ embrassé** *m* ELECTROTEC flux linkage; **~ énergétique** *m* OPTIQUE energy flux, optical flux, radiant power, PHYS RAYON energy flux, radiant flux, PHYSIQUE radiant flux, radiant power, TELECOM radiant flux; **~ d'énergie acoustique** *m* PHYSIQUE sound energy flux; **~ entrant** *m* PHYSIQUE inward flux; **~ d'entropie** *m* THERMODYN entropic flux; **~ équilibré** *m* REFRIG balanced flow; **~ de fuite** *m* ELECTROTEC, PHYSIQUE leakage flux; **~ hydrosoluble** *m* CONSTR water-soluble flux; **~ inducteur** *m* ELECTROTEC induction flux; **~ d'induction magnétique** *m* ELECTROTEC magnetic flux, magnetic induction flux, PHYS RAYON, PHYSIQUE magnetic flux; **~ induit** *m* AERONAUT inflow; **~ d'informations** *m* ELECTROTEC data stream; **~ lumineux** *m* ELECTROTEC, PHYSIQUE luminous flux; **~ magnétique** *m* ELECTR, ELECTROTEC, ENREGISTR, ESSAIS, PHYSIQUE, TV magnetic flux; **~ de marée** *m* HYDROLOGIE tidal flow; **~ massique** *m* PHYS FLUID *par tuyau* mass flux; **~ de météore** *m* ASTRONOMIE meteor shower; **~ neutronique radial** *m* NUCLEAIRE radial neutron flux; **~ de production** *m* TEXTILE production flow; **~ propre** *m* PHYSIQUE self-flux; **~ de radiation** *m* PHYS RAYON radiant flux; **~ de rayonnement** *m* PHYS RAYON flux of radiation; **~ secondaire** *m* AERONAUT engine bypass air; **~ secondaire réacteur** *m* AERONAUT engine bypass air; **~ sortant** *m* PHYSIQUE outward flux; **~ à souder** *m* ELECTROTEC soldering flux; **~ thermique** *m* ESPACE heat flux, GEOLOGIE heat flow, MATERIAUX thermal flow, PHYSIQUE heat flow rate, THERMODYN flow of heat; **~ du trafic** *m* TELECOM call flow, traffic flow; **~ transversal** *m* VEHICULES *moteur* crossflow; **~ de travaux** *m* INFORMAT, ORDINAT job stream; **~ à travers un rotor** *m* AERONAUT *hélicoptère* rotor inflow; **~ de vitesse acoustique** *m* ACOUSTIQUE *à travers un élément de surface* volume velocity

fluxage *m* CONSTR fluxing

fluxmètre *m* ELECTR *magnétisme*, ELECTROTEC fluxmeter, GEOPHYS magnetic flux density meter, PHYSIQUE fluxmeter

fluxoïde *m* PHYSIQUE flux quantum

flysch *m* GEOLOGIE flysch

Fm (*fermium*) CHIMIE Fm (*fermium*)

fmm *abrév* (*force magnétomotrice*) ELECTR, PHYSIQUE mmf (*magnetomotive force*)

FNE *abrév* (*fumée normalisée équivalente*) POLLUTION equivalent standard smoke

FOB *abrév* (*franco à bord*) NAUT *commerce, transport maritime* FOB (*free on board*)

foc *m* NAUT jib

focale *f* ASTRONOMIE *téléscope* focal length; **~ sagitalle** *f* PHYSIQUE sagittal focal line; **~ tangentielle** *f* PHYSIQUE tangential focal line; **~ variable** *f* PHOTO variable focal length

focalisation *f* ELECTRON focusing; **~ électromagnétique** *f* ELECTROTEC electromagnetic focusing; **~ électrostatique** *f* ELECTROTEC electrostatic focusing; **~ du faisceau** *f* ELECTRON beam focusing; **~ magnétique** *f* ELECTROTEC magnetic focusing; **~ par aimant permanent** *f* ELECTROTEC permanent magnet focusing

focaliser *vt* ELECTRON, PHYS ONDES focus

focomètre: ~ universel *m* INSTRUMENT universal centering apparatus (AmE), universal centring apparatus

(BrE)

foehn *m* METEO foehn, föhn

foène *f* OCEANO clamp, fish gig

foisonnement *m* CONSTR bulking; ~ **dû au gel** *m* METEO frost heaving; ~ **par le gel** *m* METEO frost heave

foisonner *vt* AGRO ALIM aerate

foliaire *adj* POLLUTION *surface* foliar

foliation *m* GEOLOGIE foliation, sheeting

folié *adj* GEOLOGIE foliated

folinique *adj* CHIMIE folinic

folio *m* IMPRIM folio, page number

foliotage *m* IMPRIM pagination; ~ **automatique** *m* IMPRIM *mise en page ou imposition* automatic pagination, ORDINAT automatic page numbering

folioter *vt* IMPRIM paginate

folle *f* OCEANO entangling net, tangle net

fonçage *m* MINES sinking; ~ **des noirs** *m* TV batting down; ~ **par congélation** *m* THERMODYN low-temperature sinking

foncé *adj* TEXTILE deep

foncée *f* MINES lift

foncement *m* MINES sinking

foncer[1] *vt* CONSTR sink

foncer[2] *vi* NAUT bear down

fonction:[1] **à ~ double** *adj* COMMANDE dual-purpose; **à ~ multiple** *adj* COMMANDE multipurpose function, multipurpose; **en ~ du temps** *adj* COMMANDE time-dependent

fonction[2] *f* ELECTRON function, INFORMAT feature, function, MATH, ORDINAT, PHYSIQUE *d'état* function; ~ **d'alarme** *f* TELECOM alarm function; ~ **d'application de gestion** *f* TELECOM MAF, management applications function; ~ **d'autocorrélation** *f* PETR autocorrelation function; ~ **caractéristique de filtre** *f* ELECTRON filter characteristic function; ~ **de charge** *f* METALL loading function; ~ **de commande** *f* TELECOM CF, control function; ~ **de communication de messages** *f* TELECOM MCF, message communication function; ~ **de convergence dépendant du sous-réseau** *f* TELECOM SNDCF, subnetwork dependent convergence function; ~ **de corrélation** *f* ELECTRON correlation function; ~ **de couche supérieure** *f* TELECOM HLF, higher-layer function; ~ **de courant** *f* PHYS FLUID stream function; ~ **de crosscorrélation** *f* PETR cross-correlation function; ~ **delta** *f* PETR delta function; ~ **de densité de probabilité** *f* MATH PDF, probability density function; ~ **Dirac** *f* PETR Dirac function; ~ **discriminante** *f* MATH discriminant function; ~ **double** *f* COMMANDE dual-purpose function; ~ **EMCN** *f* TELECOM DCME function; ~ **en échelon** *f* ELECTRON, INFORMAT, ORDINAT step function; ~ **d'excès** *f* METALL excess function; ~ **d'excitation** *f* PHYS RAYON excitation function; ~ **de gain** *f* ELECTRON gain function; ~ **de gestion d'équipement synchrone** *f* TELECOM SEMF, synchronous equipment management function; ~ **de Gibbs** *f* PHYSIQUE Gibbs free energy; ~ **harmonique** *f* ELECTRON harmonic function; ~ **hash** *f* INFORMAT, ORDINAT hash function; ~ **de Helmholtz** *f* PHYSIQUE Helmholtz free energy; ~ **implicite** *f* MATH implicit function; ~ **impulsion** *f* ELECTRON impulse function; ~ **d'impulsion mathématique** *f* COMMANDE unit impulse function; ~ **impulsionnelle** *f* COMMANDE impulse function, pulse function; ~ **intégrée** *f* ELECTRON integrated function; ~ **d'intercorrélation** *f* ELECTRON cross-correlation function; ~ **d'interfonctionnement télécopie** *f* TELE-COM FAXFIF, facsimile interworking function; ~ **intrinsèque** *f* ORDINAT built-in function; ~ **de Jost** *f* NUCLEAIRE Jost function; ~ **liée à la connexion** *f* TELECOM CRF, connection-related function; ~ **liée à la connexion sur les VC** *f* TELECOM CRF, virtual channel connection-related function; ~ **liée à la connexion sur les VP** *f* TELECOM CRF, virtual path connection-related function; ~ **liée à une connexion de transit** *f* TELECOM TCRF, transit connection-related function; ~ **de linéarisation** *f* PRODUCTION *automatisme industriel* linearization function; ~ **de maintenance** *f* TELECOM maintenance function; ~ **mathématique** *f* PRODUCTION arithmetic function; ~ **de médiation** *f* TELECOM MF, mediation function; ~ **de mise à poste** *f* ESPACE *véhicules* station acquisition function; ~ **d'onde** *f* PHYS ONDES, PHYSIQUE wave function; ~ **d'onde antisymétrique** *f* PHYSIQUE antisymmetric wave function; ~ **d'onde symétrique** *f* PHYSIQUE symmetric wave function; ~ **d'orientation de cohérence** *f* MATERIAUX *cristallographie* orientation coherence function; ~ **de partition** *f* PHYSIQUE partition function; ~ **périodique** *f* ELECTRON periodic function; ~ **pipeline** *f* ORDINAT pipelining; ~ **du potentiel** *f* PHYSIQUE potential function; ~ **propre** *f* PHYSIQUE eigenfunction; ~ **radiale de distribution** *f* PHYS RAYON radial distribution function; ~ **de recherche et remplacement** *f* INFORMAT, ORDINAT search and replace function; ~ **récurrente** *f* INFORMAT, ORDINAT recursive function; ~ **de relais et de routage** *f* TELECOM relaying and routing function; ~ **de répartition** *f* MATH CDF, cumulative distribution function, distribution function; ~ **de réponse en bande de base** *f* OPTIQUE, TELECOM baseband response function; ~ **de service sans connexion** *f* TELECOM CLSF, connectionless service function; ~ **sinusoïdale** *f* ELECTROTEC sinusoidal function; ~ **de système d'exploitation** *f* TELECOM OSF, operating system function; ~ **de temps** *f* COMMANDE time response, time-based function; ~ **de traitement de texte** *f* INFORMAT text editing function; ~ **de transfert** *f* COMMANDE, OPTIQUE, TELECOM transfer function; ~ **de transfert de commande** *f* COMMANDE actuating transfer function; ~ **de transfert en bande de base** *f* OPTIQUE, TELECOM baseband transfer function; ~ **de transfert en boucle ouverte** *f* NUCLEAIRE open loop transfer function; ~ **de transfert de modulation** *f* ELECTRON modulation transfer function; ~ **de transfert de réaction** *f* COMMANDE feedback transfer function; ~ **de transmission** *f* NUCLEAIRE transmission function; ~ **unitaire** *f* COMMANDE unit impulse function

fonctionnalité: ~ **de confiance** *f* TELECOM trusted functionality

fonctionnel *adj* INFORMAT, ORDINAT functional

fonctionnement *m* CONS MECA running, working, ELECTROTEC operation, MECANIQUE action, PAPIER operating, *d'une machine* running, TEXTILE *d'une machine* running; ~ **asynchrone** *m* ELECTR asynchronous operation; ~ **automatique** *m* INFORMAT unattended operation; ~ **autoprotégé** *m* INFORMAT fail-safe operation; ~ **avec bouclage** *m* PRODUCTION loop-through operation; ~ **à couple bas** *m* PRODUCTION low-torque operation; ~ **défectueux** *m* CONS MECA faulty operation; ~ **à deux fréquences avec relais automatique** *m* TELECOM two-frequency operation automatic repeater mode; ~ **à deux fréquences sans relais** *m* TELECOM two-frequency operation non-repeater mode; **~ à deux niveaux** *m* ELECTROTEC bilevel operation; **~ à deux niveaux de puissance** *m* ELECTROTEC bilevel operation; **~ en autogyre** *m* AERONAUT autorotative flight; **~ en continu** *m* CINEMAT continuous run; **~ en courant alternatif** *m* ELECTROTEC AC operation; **~ en grands signaux** *m* ELECTRON large-signal operation; **~ en impulsion** *m* ELECTRON pulsed operation; **~ en mode déclenché** *m* ELECTRON Q-switching; **~ en mode dégradé** *m* ESPACE *véhicules* degraded operating conditions, ORDINAT degradation; **~ en mode duplex** *m* INFORMAT duplex operation; **~ en mode simplex** *m* INFORMAT simplex operation; **~ en parallèle** *m* IMPRIM parallel operation; **~ en régime humide** *m* REFRIG wet compression; **~ en régime d'impulsion** *m* ELECTRON pulsed operation; **~ en régime de surchauffe** *m* REFRIG dry compression; **~ en sauts de fréquence** *m* ELECTRON frequency hopping; **~ en sortie simple** *m* PRODUCTION singled-ended operation; **~ en sous-tension** *m* ELECTRON underbunching; **~ équilibré triphasé** *m* PRODUCTION *automatisme industriel* three-phase balanced condition; **~ à forte intensité** *m* PHYS RAYON high-intensity operation; **~ limité par l'affaiblissement** *m* OPTIQUE, TELECOM attenuation-limited operation; **~ limité par le bruit quantique** *m* OPTIQUE quantum-limited operation, quantum-noise-limited operation, TELECOM quantum-limited operation, quantum-noise-limited operation; **~ limité par la distorsion** *m* TELECOM distortion-limited operation; **~ limité par la largeur de bande** *m* OPTIQUE, TELECOM bandwidth-limited operation; **~ linéaire** *m* ELECTROTEC linear operation; **~ nominal** *m* ESPACE *véhicules* nominal operating conditions; **~ optimal** *m* GAZ optimal operating method; **~ à pression constante** *m* ESPACE *véhicules* constant pressure operation; **~ sans à-coups** *m* PRODUCTION smooth operation; **~ sans surveillance** *m* INFORMAT unattended operation; **~ à sécurité intégrée** *m* INFORMAT, ORDINAT fail-safe operation; **~ à une seule fréquence** *m* TELECOM single frequency operation; **~ silencieux** *m* AUTO noiseless running; **~ sous surveillance** *m* INFORMAT attended operation; **~ statique** *m* ELECTROTEC static operation; **~ sur pile** *m* ELECTROTEC battery operation; **~ à vide** *m* ELECTR no-load operation, *matériel* open circuit operation

fonctionner *vi* CONS MECA operate, run
fonctions: **~ automatiques de contrôle** *f pl* COMMANDE automatic control functions; **~ thermodynamiques** *f pl* THERMODYN thermodynamic functions; **~ trigonométriques** *f pl* GEOMETRIE trigonometrical functions
fond:[1] **au ~** *adj* MINES underground; **de ~ en comble** *adj* CONSTR from top-to-bottom; **à ~ plat** *adj* NAUT flat-bottomed; **au ~ d'un puits** *adj* PETROLE bottom-hole; **à ~ sableux** *adj* HYDROLOGIE sandy-bedded
fond:[2] **de ~ en comble** *adv* CONSTR from top-to-bottom
fond[3] *m* CERAM VER punt, CONS MECA *d'un cylindre* cylinder head, head, CONSTR *d'une vallée* bottom, *d'une serrure* plate, HYDROLOGIE *d'un bassin, d'un réservoir* bottom, IMPRIM background, bottom, *photogravure* base tint, INST HYDR *de cylindre plateau* cylinder head, MINES *d'un puits de mine, d'un trou de sonde* bottom, OCEANO diving depth, TEXTILE *du tissu* body, TV faceplate; **~ de bobine** *m* PAPIER header, roll end, roll head; **~ bombé** *m* NUCLEAIRE dished bottom; **~ de bonne tenue** *m* NAUT safe ground; **~ de boue** *m* MINES mud bottom; **~ de cale** *m* NAUT bilge; **~ cellulaire** *m* NAUT cellular bottom; **~ clair** *m* METALL bright

field; **~ coloré** *m* IMPRIM *photogravure* base tint; **~ Compton** *m* PHYS RAYON Compton continuum; **~ continu** *m* CRISTALL *de rayons X* background intensity; **~ de cylindre** *m* CONS MECA *de machine horizontale fixe* back cylinder cover, PRODUCTION cylinder cover, cylinder head; **~ de cylindre à vapeur** *m* INST HYDR cover; **~ ébaucheur** *m* CERAM VER baffle plate; **~ embouti** *m* MECANIQUE dished head; **~ en coin** *m* CERAM VER slugged bottom; **~ en dos d'âne** *m* TRANSPORT saddle-bottomed car; **~ en dos d'âne pour autodéchargeur** *m* TRANSPORT saddle-bottomed self-discharging car; **~ gazeux** *m* PETROLE BG, background gas; **~ hémi-ellipsoïdal** *m* NUCLEAIRE hemiellipsoidal bottom, hemiellipsoidal head; **~ d'impression** *m* TEXTILE body of the print, ground fabric, ground cloth; **~ marin** *m* CONSTR, EN RENOUV sea bed, OCEANO sea bed, sea bottom; **~ marin durci** *m* GEOLOGIE hard ground; **~ de mauvaise tenue** *m* NAUT foul bottom; **~ de mer** *m* PETROLE mud line; **~ mobile** *m* CINEMAT moving background, EMBALLAGE sliding bottom; **~ du navire** *m* NAUT ship's bottom; **~ océanique** *m* GEOPHYS abyssal plain, deep-sea floor, ocean bottom, OCEANO ocean floor; **~ de panier** *m* ELECTRON backplane, motherboard, ELECTROTEC socket board, ORDINAT motherboard, PRODUCTION backplane; **~ perdu** *m* IMPRIM bleed; **~ perforé** *m* GENIE CHIM sieve plate, sieve tray; **~ pierreux** *m* HYDROLOGIE stony bottom; **~ piqué** *m* CERAM VER pushed punt; **~ de piston** *m* AUTO piston top; **~ de poche** *m* PRODUCTION scull, skull; **~ projeté** *m* CINEMAT projected background; **~ du puits** *m* MINES pit bottom, pit eye, PETROLE bottom hole; **~ de rayons cosmiques** *m* PHYS RAYON cosmic ray background; **~ retombé** *m* CERAM VER rocker; **~ de sable** *m* NAUT sandy bottom; **~ sale** *m* NAUT foul bottom; **~ de sondage** *m* PETROLE bottom hole; **~ spectral** *m* PHYS RAYON background absorption; **~ à tamis** *m* GENIE CHIM sieve bottom, sieve diaphragm; **~ tramé** *m* IMPRIM mechanical tint, tint, *photogravure* Ben Day; **~ tramé en dégradé** *m* IMPRIM *photogravure* vignette; **~ tramé régulier** *m* IMPRIM *photogravure* screen tint; **~ tramé simple sans dégradé** *m* IMPRIM *photogravure* flat screening; **~ tramé uniforme** *m* IMPRIM tint; **~ de trou** *m* PETROLE bottom hole

fond:[4] **à ~ de course** *loc* PRODUCTION fully-compressed
fondamental[1] *adj* PHYS PART *principe* fundamental
fondamental[2] *m* PHYS ONDES fundamental tone
fondamentale *f* ELECTRON fundamental frequency
fondant[1] *adj* METEO melting
fondant[2] *m* CERAM VER flux, CHARBON flux powder, slag, MATERIAUX *soudage* flux, fluxing agent; **~ incolore** *m* CERAM VER colorless flux (AmE), colourless flux (BrE)
fondation *f* CHARBON foundation, CONSTR bed, foundation, sub-base; **~ compensée** *f* CHARBON compensated foundation; **~ d'élément de réseau** *f* TELECOM NERF, network element function; **~ isolée** *f* CHARBON spot footing; **~ du mortier** *f* CONSTR bocard, PRODUCTION mortar bed; **~ profonde** *f* CHARBON deep foundation
fondement *m* CONSTR base, foundation
fonderie *f* CHARBON, MAT CHAUFF foundry, PRODUCTION founding, foundry; **~ de cuivre** *f* CONSTR brass foundry, PRODUCTION copper works; **~ de fer** *f* PRODUCTION iron founding, iron foundry, ironworks; **~ de fonte** *f* PRODUCTION iron founding, iron foundry,

ironworks; ~ **de plomb** *f* PRODUCTION lead-smelting works; ~ **de silicium** *f* ELECTRON silicon foundry

fondeur *m* CERAM VER teaser, PRODUCTION caster, founder, smelter

fondeuse *f* IMPRIM caster, PAPIER casting machine

fondis *m* CONSTR *de la surface* subsidence; ~ **à jour** *m* MINES day hole

fondoir-réchauffeur *m* CONSTR heating melter

fondre[1] *vt* CINEMAT fade, CONS MECA cast, PAPIER cast, smelt, melt, PRODUCTION melt, *banc de tour* cast, TEXTILE melt, THERMODYN fuse, melt, melt down

fondre[2] *vi* MAT CHAUFF smelt

fondre[3] *vti* METEO melt

fondrière *f* CONSTR hollow, MINES daylight mine

fonds *m pl* NAUT soundings; ~ **marins** *m pl* CONSTR, EN RENOUV sea bed, OCEANO sea bed, sea bottom, seafloor; ~ **mousse** *m pl* TEXTILE foam backing

fondu[1] *adj* CERAM VER batch-free, METEO melted, PRODUCTION cast, THERMODYN fused, melted, molten

fondu[2] *m* ACOUSTIQUE fade, CINEMAT dissolve, fade, ENREGISTR shunt; ~ **analogique** *m* TV match dissolve; ~ **avec filtre polarisant** *m* CINEMAT Polaroid fade; ~ **au blanc** *m* CINEMAT fade-to-white; ~ **au diaphragme** *m* CINEMAT iris fade; ~ **enchaîné** *m* ACOUSTIQUE cross-fade, CINEMAT cross-fade, lap dissolve, dissolve, ENREGISTR cross-fade, TV mix dissolve, wipe; ~ **en iris** *m* CINEMAT circle wipe; ~ **au noir** *m* CINEMAT fade out, fade-to-black; ~ **sonore** *m* ENREGISTR sound dissolve; ~ **très court** *m* CINEMAT soft cut

fondu:[3] **être ~** *vi* PRODUCTION be cast

fongicide *m* CHIMIE, PLAST CAOU *additif* fungicide

fongistat *m* AGRO ALIM fungistat

fongistatique *m* AGRO ALIM fugistat

fontaine *f* CERAM VER glass pocket, HYDROLOGIE spring; ~ **d'arrosage** *f* PRODUCTION water can; ~ **jaillissante** *f* HYDROLOGIE artesian well, geyser; ~ **réfrigérée** *f* REFRIG drinking water cooler

fonte *f* CHIMIE fusion, CONS MECA cast iron, INFORMAT font (BrE), fount (AmE), MAT CHAUFF smelting, MECANIQUE *matériaux*, PAPIER cast iron, PRODUCTION casting, founding, pig, melt, melting, metal, pig iron; ~ **d'affinage** *f* PRODUCTION conversion pig, converter pig; ~ **Bessemer** *f* PRODUCTION Bessemer pig; ~ **de caractères** *f* IMPRIM *fonderie* font (BrE), fount (AmE); ~ **en coquille** *f* PRODUCTION chill casting; ~ **en cuivre au béryllium** *f* CONS MECA beryllium copper casting; ~ **en gueuse** *f* PRODUCTION pig, pig iron; ~ **en saumon** *f* PRODUCTION pig, pig iron; ~ **ferritique** *f* MATERIAUX ferritic cast iron; ~ **à graphite lamellaire** *f* MECANIQUE *matériaux* lamellar graphite cast iron; ~ **à graphite sphéroïdal** *f* MATERIAUX spheroidal graphite cast iron; ~ **grise** *f* MECANIQUE *matériaux* gray cast iron (AmE), grey cast iron (BrE); ~ **hématite** *f* MATERIAUX haematite pig iron (BrE), hematite pig iron (AmE); ~ **malléable** *f* MATERIAUX, MECANIQUE malleable cast iron; ~ **matricielle** *f* INFORMAT bit-mapped font; ~ **de moulage** *f* PRODUCTION foundry iron; ~ **phosphore** *f* MATERIAUX basic pig iron; ~ **trempée** *f* PRODUCTION chilled cast iron, chilled iron

fontis *m* CONSTR *de la surface* subsidence

fonture *f* TEXTILE needle bed

foolscap *m* IMPRIM foolscap

forabilité *f* PETROLE drillability

forable *adj* PETROLE *bouchon* drillable

forage *m* CHARBON boring, drilling, CONS MECA drilling, CONSTR borehole, boreholing, hole, GAZ drilling, MINES blast hole, borehole, drill hole, bore, drilling, boring, PETROLE hole, well bore, well; ~ **à l'air** *m* PETR air drilling; ~ **à l'air comprimé** *m* PETROLE air drilling; ~ **à la barre** *m* CONSTR jump drilling; ~ **au câble** *m* PETR cable drilling; ~ **de captage** *m* HYDROLOGIE borehole; ~ **à chute libre** *m* CONSTR free fall boring, free fall drilling; ~ **à découvert** *m* PETR open hole, PETROLE open hole drilling; ~ **de délinéation** *m* PETROLE appraisal drilling; ~ **dévié** *m* PETROLE deviated drilling, directional drilling, sidetrack drilling; ~ **au diamant** *m* MINES, PETROLE diamond drilling; ~ **à diamètre réduit** *m* PETROLE slim hole; ~ **directionnel** *m* PETR directional drilling; ~ **dirigé** *m* PETR directional drilling, PETROLE deviated drilling, directional drilling; ~ **électro-hydraulique** *m* CHARBON electrodrilling; ~ **en diamètre réduit** *m* PETROLE slim hole; ~ **en éruption non contrôlée** *m* PETROLE wild well; ~ **en grand diamètre** *m* PETROLE big hole; ~ **en mer** *m* PETROLE offshore drilling; ~ **à l'entreprise** *m* MINES contract boring, contract drilling; ~ **d'exploration** *m* GAZ exploratory drilling, PETROLE exploration drilling, exploratory drilling, wildcat drilling; ~ **à faible diamètre** *m* PETR slim hole; ~ **au gabarit** *m* PETR template drilling; ~ **à grande profondeur** *m* MINES deep boring, deep drilling; ~ **à la grenaille** *m* PETROLE shot drilling; ~ **à la grenaille d'acier** *m* MINES shot boring, shot drilling; ~ **d'injection** *m* NUCLEAIRE injection borehole, injection well; ~ **à injection** *m* PETROLE hydraulic circulation system, wash boring; ~ **à jet** *m* CHARBON jet piercing; ~ **à la lance** *m* CONSTR oxygen lancing; ~ **mécanique** *m* MINES machine drilling; ~ **par battage** *m* PETROLE percussion drilling; ~ **par injection** *m* CHARBON wash boring; ~ **par jet de flammes** *m* CHARBON jet drilling; ~ **par rodage** *m* CONSTR boring by rotation, MINES rotary drilling; ~ **à percussion** *m* CHARBON jumper boring, percussion drilling, percussive drilling, percussive rope boring, percussive rope drilling; ~ **pour le captage du grisou** *m* CHARBON methane draining boring; ~ **de production** *m* PETROLE production drilling; ~ **profond** *m* CHARBON well drill hole; ~ **de recherche** *m* PETROLE wildcat drilling; ~ **rotary** *m* CHARBON, PETR, PETROLE rotary drilling; ~ **sismique** *m* PETROLE shot hole drilling; ~ **thermique** *m* CHARBON fusion drilling, CONSTR oxygen lancing; ~ **au trépan à jet** *m* PETROLE jet bit drilling; ~ **de trou à grand diamètre** *m* CHARBON large-hole boring

foraminifère: à ~ *adj* GEOLOGIE foraminiferal

forçage *m* PRODUCTION hobbing, *automatisme industriel* forced ventilation; ~ **par matrice** *m* CONS MECA die-sinking

force:[1] **à ~ de bras** *adv* PRODUCTION by hand, by hand power

force[2] *f* CHIMIE *d'un acide* strength, CONS MECA power, CONSTR strut, HYDROLOGIE *d'une chute d'eau* force, MINES deoxidation, oxygen depletion of air, PAPIER strength, PHYSIQUE force, load, PRODUCTION strength; ~ **d'accélération** *f* ESPACE *véhicules* accelerating force, g-force, PHYSIQUE accelerating force; ~ **d'un acide** *f* CHIMIE acid strength; ~ **d'action** *f* PRODUCTION *automatisme industriel* operating force; ~ **d'adhérence** *f* PLAST CAOU *adhésifs, caoutchouc* bond strength; ~ **d'adhésion** *f* PLAST CAOU adhesive strength; ~ **antagoniste** *f* CONS MECA counteracting force; ~ **d'appui** *f* ACOUSTIQUE stylus force; ~ **d'appui de la pointe de lecture** *f* ENREGISTR vertical tracking force; ~ **d'Archimède** *f* PHYS FLUID buoyancy force; ~

d'attraction f ELECTR *électromagnétisme* attractive force, PHYSIQUE attractive force, force of attraction, force of attraction; **~ à balourd** f CONS MECA out-of-balance forces; **~ de Bartlett** f NUCLEAIRE Bartlett force; **~ boulangère** f AGRO ALIM baking quality; **~ centrale** f PHYSIQUE central force; **~ centrifuge** f ESPACE *véhicules*, PHYS FLUID, PHYSIQUE, POLLUTION centrifugal force; **~ centripète** f CONS MECA side thrust, PHYSIQUE centripetal force; **~ de cisaillement** f CONS MECA shear force, MATERIAUX, PHYSIQUE shearing force; **~ coercitive** f ELECTR coercive force, coercive intensity, *magnétisme* coercive field strength, ENREGISTR, MATERIAUX coercivity, METALL, PHYSIQUE coercive force; **~ de cohésion** f PHYSIQUE cohesive force; **~ conservatrice** f PHYSIQUE conservative force; **~ contre-électromotrice** f *(fcém)* ELECTR, ELECTROTEC, PHYSIQUE back electromotive force, back emf, counter emf, counter-electromotive force *(cemf)*; **~ de Coriolis** f METEO, PHYS FLUID, PHYSIQUE Coriolis force; **~ de dilatation** f INST HYDR expansion stress; **~ d'échange de position opérateur** f NUCLEAIRE Majorana force, position exchange force; **~ d'échange de spin** f NUCLEAIRE spin exchange; **~ d'écrasement** f SECURITE *d'une machine* crushing power; **~ d'éjection** f ESPACE *véhicules* ejection force; **~ électrique** f ELECTROTEC electric force; **~ électromagnétique** f ELECTR, ELECTROTEC, PHYS PART electromagnetic force; **~ électromotrice** f *(fém)* ELECTR, ELECTROTEC, PHYSIQUE electromotive force *(emf)*; **~ électromotrice alternative** f ELECTROTEC AC electromotive force; **~ électromotrice appliquée** f ELECTR alternating electromotive force, *tension* impressed electromotive force, PHYSIQUE applied electromagnetic force, applied emf; **~ électromotrice de contact** f ELECTR *entre deux métaux* contact emf, contact potential, PHYSIQUE contact emf; **~ électromotrice effective** f ELECTR effective electromotive force; **~ électromotrice efficace** f ELECTR effective electromotive force; **~ électromotrice induite** f ELECTR, ELECTROTEC induced electromotive force, PHYSIQUE induced emf; **~ électromotrice d'origine thermique** f ELECTROTEC thermoelectromotive force; **~ électromotrice subtransitoire longitudinale** f ELECTR *machine* direct axis subtransient emf; **~ électromotrice de transformation** f ELECTR, PHYSIQUE transformer emf; **~ électromotrice transitoire longitudinale** f ELECTR *machine* direct axis transient emf; **~ électrostatique** f ELECTROTEC electrostatic force; **~ élévatoire** f CONS MECA lifting power; **~ extérieure** f METALL external force; **~ faible** f PHYS PART weak force; **~ de freinage** f TRANSPORT brake effort; **~ de frottement** f CONS MECA force of friction, frictional force, METALL friction force, PHYSIQUE frictional force; **~ gravitationnelle** f POLLUTION gravitational force; **~ de gravité** f ASTRONOMIE force of gravity; **~ hydraulique** f DISTRI EAU water power; **~ d'impulsion** f CONS MECA impetus; **~ d'inertie** f CONS MECA inertia, MECANIQUE inertial force, PHYSIQUE force, inertial force; **~ ionique** f PHYS RAYON ionic strength; **~ latérale** f TRANSPORT lateral force; **~ de levage** f CONS MECA lifting power; **~ de levier** f CONS MECA leverage; **~ de lévitation** f PHYSIQUE lifting force; **~ de liaison** f CRISTALL bond strength; **~ de Lorentz** f ELECTROTEC, PHYSIQUE Lorentz force; **~ magnétique** f ELECTR, GEOPHYS magnetic force, PETR magnetic field strength, magnetic force, PHYS RAYON magnetic in-

tensity; **~ magnétomotrice** f *(fmm)* ELECTR *électromagnétisme*, PHYSIQUE magnetomotive force *(mmf)*; **~ majeure** f CONSTR force majeure; **~ de Majorana** f NUCLEAIRE Majorana force, position exchange force; **~ de marée** f ASTRONOMIE tidal force; **~ mobile** f CONSTR *personnel* flying squad; **~ motrice** f CONS MECA mover, power, METALL driving force, NAUT motive force, PAPIER power, TEXTILE driving force; **~ motrice de la vapeur** f INST HYDR steam power; **~ navale opérationnelle** f NAUT task force; **~ navale tactique** f NAUT task force; **~ nucléaire forte** f PHYS PART strong nuclear force; **~ opérationnelle** f NAUT task force; **~ de pénétration** f MILITAIRE percussion pressure; **~ de percussion** f CONS MECA percussive force; **~ percutante** f CONS MECA percussive force; **~ portante** f CHARBON load-bearing capacity, PHYSIQUE lifting force; **~ d'un projectile** f MILITAIRE projectile energy; **~ de propulsion** f MILITAIRE *d'une fusée* propellant force; **~ propulsive** f CONS MECA propelling force, propulsive force; **~ de rappel** f MECANIQUE, PHYSIQUE restoring force; **~ de rappel à ressort** f PRODUCTION *commutateur de sélection* spring return force; **~ de réaction de radiation** f PHYS RAYON radiation reaction force; **~ de recul** f MILITAIRE recoil energy; **~ de répulsion** f ELECTR *électrostatique, magnétisme*, ELECTROTEC repulsive force, PHYSIQUE force, repulsive force; **~ de serrage** f EMBALLAGE clamping force; **~ tactique** f NAUT task force; **~ tangentielle** f CONS MECA tangential force; **~ de tension** f PHYSIQUE tensile force; **~ de torsion** f RESSORTS torque; **~ de traction** f CONS MECA tensile force, METROLOGIE tractive force, PHYSIQUE tensile force; **~ des vagues** f OCEANO wave velocity; **~ à vide** f NUCLEAIRE no-load force; **~ de viscosité** f PHYS FLUID viscous force; **~ vive** f CONS MECA momentum, GEOPHYS kinetic energy; **~ volumique** f METALL body force

forcement m CONSTR *d'une serrure* forcing

forcer vt POLLU MER wring; **~ à un** vt PRODUCTION *automatisme industriel* force on; **~ à zéro** vt PRODUCTION *automatisme industriel* force off

forces: ~ attractives de très courte portée f pl PHYS PART very short-range attractive forces; **~ coplanaires** f pl PHYSIQUE coplanar forces; **~ interatomiques** f pl PHYS RAYON interatomic forces

forer[1] vt CONS MECA drill, CONSTR bore, MECANIQUE bore, drill, MINES bore, drill; **~ à la barre** vt MINES jump

forer:[2] **~ au large** vi NAUT drill offshore

forerie: ~ à colonne f CONS MECA *pour percer au vilebrequin* drilling pillar

foret m CHARBON drill bit, CONS MECA drill, *de vilebrequin, de perceuse* bit, CONSTR auger gimlet, bore bit, MECANIQUE drill; **~ à archet** m CONS MECA bow drill, fiddle drill; **~ à arçon** m CONS MECA piercer; **~ avec plaquette à jeter en métal dur** m CONS MECA throw-away carbide drill; **~ à centre** m CONS MECA center bit for bit stock (AmE), center brace bit (AmE), centre bit for bit stock (BrE), centre brace bit(BrE); **~ à centrer** m CONS MECA center drill (AmE), centre drill (BrE), combined drill and countersink; **~ conique** m CONS MECA cone bit, tube-and-steel drill; **~ creux** m CONS MECA shell drill; **~ en acier rapide** m MECANIQUE *outillage* high-speed drill; **~ étagé** m CONS MECA step drill, subland twist drill; **~ hélicoïdal** m CONS MECA, MECANIQUE twist drill; **~ hélicoïdal à queue carrée conique** m CONS MECA twist drill with taper square shank; ~ **hélicoïdal à queue conique au cône Morse** *m* CONS MECA Morse taper shank twist drill; ~ **hélicoïdal à queue cylindrique** *m* CONS MECA parallel shank twist drill, straight-shank twist drill, twist drill with parallel shank, twist drill with straight shank; ~ **à langue d'aspic** *m* CONS MECA arrowhead drill, flat drill; ~ **marteau** *m* CONS MECA hammer drill; ~ **pour avant-trou de taraudage** *m* CONS MECA tapping drill; ~ **pour bâtiment** *m* CONS MECA masonry drill; ~ **pour bâtiment à rotation et percussion** *m* CONS MECA rotary percussive masonry drill; ~ **à queue carrée** *m* CONS MECA center bit for bit stock (AmE), center brace bit (AmE), centre bit for bit stock (BrE), centre brace bit (BrE), square shank drill; ~ **à queue cylindrique court** *m* CONS MECA jobber drill; ~ **à queue cylindrique extra-court** *m* CONS MECA stub drill; ~ **à rainures droites** *m* CONS MECA straight-fluted drill; ~ **à roche** *m* CHARBON rock drill; ~ **à téton cylindrique** *m* CONS MECA counterbore, pin drill, plug center bit (AmE), plug centre bit (BrE); ~ **de vilebrequin** *m* CONS MECA bit stock drill

foret-aléseur *m* CONS MECA core drill; ~ **en bout** *m* CONS MECA spotface cutter

foreuse *f* CH DE FER sleeper-drilling machine (BrE), tie-drilling machine (AmE), CONS MECA drilling machine, CONSTR rock borer, rock drill, MINES borer, drill, jackhammer, rock drill, boring machine, drilling machine, rock drill; ~ **à colonne** *f* CONS MECA drill press; ~ **mécanique** *f* CONS MECA drilling machine; ~ **à pointes de diamant** *f* PRODUCTION diamond drill; ~ **pour dégazage** *f* PETROLE methane borehole rig; ~ **à témoins** *f* MINES core borer, core drill

forge *f* CONSTR smithy, PRODUCTION forge; ~ **artisanale** *f* CONS MECA blacksmith's forge; ~ **portative** *f* PRODUCTION portable forge

forgé *adj* MECANIQUE wrought, *matériaux* forged, PRODUCTION forged; ~ **à chaud** *adj* THERMODYN hot-forged; ~ **à froid** *adj* THERMODYN cold-forged

forgeage *m* MECANIQUE *matériaux* forging; ~ **à chaud** *m* THERMODYN hot forging; ~ **à froid** *m* THERMODYN cold forging; ~ **mécanique** *m* PRODUCTION drop forging

forger: ~ **à chaud** *vt* THERMODYN hot-forge; ~ **à froid** *vt* THERMODYN cold-forge

forgeron *m* CONS MECA blacksmith, CONSTR smith

formage *m* MECANIQUE *matériaux*, PLAST CAOU *procédé*, PRODUCTION forming; ~ **automatique** *m* CERAM VER automatic forming; ~ **à chaud** *m* PRODUCTION hot forming, THERMODYN heat forming; ~ **par explosion** *m* MECANIQUE, THERMODYN explosive forming; ~ **par fluage** *m* CONS MECA extrusion diecasting; ~ **par soufflage** *m* PLAST CAOU blast forming; ~ **à pression** *m* PLAST CAOU pressure forming; ~ **sous vide** *m* PLAST CAOU *procédé* vacuum forming

formaldéhyde *m* CHIMIE formaldehyde, methanal, MATERIAUX, PLAST CAOU *matière première*, TEXTILE formaldehyde

formaldéhyde-sulfoxylate *m* AGRO ALIM formaldehyde sulfoxylate (AmE), formaldehyde sulphoxylate (BrE)

formamide *m* CHIMIE formamide

format *m* CINEMAT gage (AmE), gauge (BrE), size, IMPRIM dimension, size, format, INFORMAT, ORDINAT format, PAPIER size, TV format; ~ **A4** *m* IMPRIM A4 size; ~ **d'adresse** *m* ORDINAT address format; ~ **d'affichage** *m* NUCLEAIRE display format; ~ **atlas** *m* IMPRIM oblong size; ~ **bâtard** *m* PAPIER bastard size; ~

brut *m* PAPIER untrimmed size; ~ **de données** *m* INFORMAT data format; ~ **d'écran** *m* INFORMAT, ORDINAT display setting; ~ **d'enregistrement** *m* INFORMAT, ORDINAT record format; ~ **fini** *m* EMBALLAGE, IMPRIM, PAPIER trimmed size; ~ **fixe** *m* INFORMAT, ORDINAT fixed format; ~ **à la française** *m* IMPRIM *imposition, maquette* portrait, INFORMAT portrait format; ~ **graphique** *m* PRODUCTION *automatisme industriel* display format; ~ **horizontal** *m* IMPRIM broadside; ~ **hors norme** *m* PAPIER bastard size; ~ **de l'image** *m* CINEMAT picture ratio, ELECTROTEC aspect ratio, PHOTO picture size; ~ **d'impression** *m* INFORMAT, ORDINAT print format; ~ **d'instruction** *m* INFORMAT, ORDINAT instruction format; ~ **international** *m* IMPRIM DIN size; ~ **à l'italienne** *m* IMPRIM landscape size, INFORMAT landscape format; ~ **libre** *m* INFORMAT, ORDINAT free format; ~ **oblong** *m* IMPRIM landscape size; ~ **de papier** *m* IMPRIM paper size; ~ **paysage** *m* INFORMAT landscape format; ~ **de pellicule** *m* CINEMAT film gage (AmE), film gauge (BrE); ~ **portrait** *m* INFORMAT portrait format; ~ **réduit** *m* CINEMAT substandard gage (AmE), substandard gauge (BrE); ~ **rogné** *m* IMPRIM trimmed size; ~ **vertical** *m* INFORMAT, ORDINAT vertical format

formatage *m* INFORMAT, ORDINAT, TELECOM formatting

formater *vt* IMPRIM, INFORMAT, ORDINAT format

formateur *m* INFORMAT, ORDINAT formatter; ~ **de réseau** *m* CERAM VER network former; ~ **de texte** *m* INFORMAT, ORDINAT text formatter

formation *f* CONS MECA, CONSTR training, GEOLOGIE formation, PAPIER *de la feuille* formation, sheet formation; ~ **absorbante** *f* PETR thief formation; ~ **d'amas** *f* MATERIAUX *cinétique* clustering, METALL cluster formation, clustering; ~ **d'un anticyclone** *f* METEO anticyclonic generation, anticyclonic growth; ~ **aquifuge** *f* GEOLOGIE aquifuge; ~ **d'un arc** *f* ELECTROTEC flashing; ~ **carbonifère** *f* MINES coal measures, coal-bearing rock; ~ **de carbures** *f* METALL carbide formation; ~ **de cavités** *f* MATERIAUX, METALL void formation; ~ **de cluster** *f* MATERIAUX cluster formation; ~ **d'une couche** *f* ELECTRON layer deposition; ~ **de la couche limite** *f* PHYS FLUID boundary layer formation; ~ **de cratères** *f* ASTRONOMIE cratering, PLAST CAOU *défaut de revêtement* cissing; ~ **dendritique** *f* GEOLOGIE, MATERIAUX dendritic form; ~ **du faisceau** *f* ELECTRON beam forming; ~ **de files d'attente** *f* TELECOM queueing; ~ **de fissure** *f* METALL crack formation; ~ **de fissures** *f* GEOLOGIE fracturing; ~ **de frisures** *f* AERONAUT alligatoring; ~ **de germes cristallins** *f* MATERIAUX nucleation; ~ **de glace** *f* NAUT *sur navire* icing; ~ **de gouttelettes d'eau** *f* IMPRIM sweating; ~ **de gouttes** *f* PHYS FLUID drop formation; ~ **de greisen** *f* GEOLOGIE greisening, greisenization; ~ **houillère** *f* CHARBON coal formation, MINES coal measures, coal-bearing rock; ~ **hydrophobe** *f* GEOLOGIE aquifuge; ~ **du matelas de verre** *f* CERAM VER mat formation; ~ **métallifère** *f* MINES ore formation; ~ **de la mie** *f* AGRO ALIM crumb formation; ~ **de motifs** *f* ELECTRON patterning; ~ **de nuages** *f* METEO cloud formation; ~ **peu perméable** *f* PETR tight formation; ~ **de rayures** *f* TV crawling; ~ **de rifts** *f* GEOLOGIE rift tectonics, taphrogenesis; ~ **sédimentaire** *f* RECYCLAGE sedimentary deposit; ~ **de spires terminales** *f* RESSORTS end forming; ~ **sur la sécurité** *f* SECURITE safety education; ~ **de zones** *f* METALL zone formation

formations: ~ **rouges** *f pl* GEOLOGIE red beds

formats: ~ **B** *m pl* IMPRIM B-sizes

formazyle *m* CHIMIE formazyl

forme:[1] **de** ~ **conique** *adj* TEXTILE conic; **en** ~ **de crois-sant** *adj* GEOMETRIE crescent-shaped; **en** ~ **de langue** *adj* GEOLOGIE lingoid, linguiform; **en** ~ **de V** *adj* CONS MECA V-shaped

forme[2] *f* BREVETS *de l'abrégé*, CONSTR form, ELECTRON pattern, INFORMAT pattern, schema, ORDINAT pattern, PAPIER mold (AmE), mould (BrE), PRODUCTION pattern, TEXTILE shape, styling; ~ **aérodynamique** *f* VEHICULES *carrosserie* aerodynamic form, aerodynamic shape; ~ **allotropique** *f* CHIMIE allotrope; ~ **de l'alvéole** *f* IMPRIM cell shape; ~ **de l'alvéole du rouleau anilox** *f* IMPRIM *flexographie* screen shape; ~ **de câble** *f* ELECTROTEC cable form; ~ **cétonique** *f* CHIMIE keto-form; ~ **de découpe** *f* IMPRIM die cut, *transformation* die; ~ **en béton** *f* CONSTR blinding concrete, lean concrete; ~ **en couleur** *f* IMPRIM color form (AmE), colour form (BrE); ~ **en saillie** *f* CONSTR projection; ~ **de grain** *f* CHARBON grain shape; ~ **d'impression** *f* IMPRIM printing form; ~ **imprimante** *f* IMPRIM form, printing form; ~ **d'impulsion** *f* ELECTRON pulse shape; ~ **intérieure** *f* IMPRIM inner form, inside form; ~ **normale** *f* INFORMAT, ORDINAT normal form; ~ **normale de Backus** *f* ORDINAT Backus normal form; ~ **d'onde** *f* ELECTR *courant alternatif*, ELECTROTEC, INFORMAT, ORDINAT, PHYS ONDES, PHYSIQUE waveform; ~ **d'onde complexe** *f* ELECTR *courant alternatif* complex waveform; ~ **parallèle** *f* ELECTROTEC parallel form; ~ **pour impression en couleur** *f* IMPRIM color form (AmE), colour form (BrE); ~ **du premier côté** *f* IMPRIM outer form (AmE), outer forme (BrE); ~ **de radoub** *f* NAUT dry dock, graving dock; ~ **ronde** *f* PAPIER cylinder, cylinder mold (AmE), cylinder mould (BrE); ~ **du second côté** *f* IMPRIM inner form, inside form; ~ **série** *f* ELECTROTEC serial form; ~ **tautomère** *f* CHIMIE *d'un composé* tautomer; ~ **trans** *f* CHIMIE transform

formé: ~ **à chaud** *adj* RESSORTS hot-formed, THERMODYN heat-formed; ~ **à froid** *adj* RESSORTS cold-formed

formel *adj* CHIMIE formal

former:[1] ~ **à chaud** *vt* THERMODYN heat-form; ~ **à froid** *vt* THERMODYN cold-form; ~ **remplir et sceller** *vt* IMPRIM *trilogie de l'emballage* form fill and seal

former:[2] ~ **des matons** *vi* PAPIER clot

formes: ~ **de l'avant** *f pl* NAUT bow entrance

formette *f* IMPRIM handsheet machine, PAPIER handsheet

formeur *m* PAPIER former

formeuse: ~ **de barquettes** *f* EMBALLAGE tray erector

formeuse-remplisseuse-scelleuse *f* EMBALLAGE form fill and seal machine

formiamide *m* CHIMIE formamide

formiate *m* CHIMIE formate

formique *adj* CHIMIE formic, methanoic

formulaire *m* BREVETS *imprimé* form; ~ **avec bande ad-hésive sur le premier feuillet** *m* IMPRIM *continu* tip-on-form; ~ **avec tableau** *m* IMPRIM *continu* tab form; ~ **de message** *m* PRODUCTION *automatisme industriel* message slip; ~ **personnalisé** *m* IMPRIM custom form; ~ **à plusieurs formes encollées pour constituer des poches** *m* IMPRIM patch pocket form

formulaires: ~ **à copies multiples** *m pl* PAPIER multicopy business forms; ~ **non carbonés** *m pl* PAPIER carbonless copy paper forms

formulation *f* PLAST CAOU *procédé* formulation; ~ **de couleur** *f* COULEURS color formulation (AmE), colour formulation (BrE)

formule *f* CERAM VER *verre* percentage composition, CHIMIE, PHOTO *développeur* formula; ~ **d'aiguilletage** *f* TEXTILE needling code; ~ **d'Archie** *f* PETR Archie's formula; ~ **de Balmer** *f* PHYSIQUE Balmer's formula; ~ **de battage** *f* CHARBON pile-driving formula; ~ **de Bayes** *f* MATH Bayes' theorem; ~ **de Bazin** *f* INST HYDR Bazin's formula; ~ **du binôme de Newton** *f* MATH binomial theorem; ~ **de Chézy** *f* HYDROLOGIE Chezy's formula; ~ **de Clapeyron** *f* PHYSIQUE Clapeyron's equation; ~ **de Clausius-Mosotti** *f* PHYSIQUE Clausius-Mosotti formula; ~ **de composition** *f* CERAM VER batch composition, batch formula; ~ **de constitution** *f* CHIMIE structural formula; ~ **empirique** *f* CHIMIE empirical formula; ~ **d'Euler** *f* GEOMETRIE *géométrie à trois dimensions* Euler's formula; ~ **de Kutter** *f* HYDROLOGIE Kutter's formula; ~ **de Lacey** *f* HYDROLOGIE Lacey's formula; ~ **de Lorentz-Lorenz** *f* PHYSIQUE Lorentz-Lorenz formula; ~ **de Manning** *f* HYDROLOGIE Manning's formula; ~ **de Newton** *f* MATH binomial theorem; ~ **de Planck** *f* PHYSIQUE Planck's formula; ~ **de Poisson** *f* PETR Poisson's ratio; ~ **de la probabilité des causes** *f* MATH Bayes' theorem; ~ **de radiation de Planck** *f* PHYS RAYON *énergie d'un corps noir* Planck's radiation formula; ~ **de Rayleigh et Jeans** *f* PHYSIQUE Rayleigh-Jeans formula; ~ **de Steinmetz** *f* PHYSIQUE Steinmetz's law; ~ **de Strickler** *f* HYDROLOGIE Strickler's formula

formules: ~ **de Fresnel** *f pl* PHYSIQUE Fresnel's formulae

formyle *m* CHIMIE formyl

forstérite *f* MINERAUX forsterite

fort[1] *adj* MECANIQUE heavy

fort:[2] ~ **couplage** *m* ELECTROTEC tight coupling; ~ **courant** *m* NAUT race; ~ **du courant** *m* NAUT tideway

forte:[1] **à** ~ **teneur** *adj* CHARBON high-grade; **à** ~ **viscosité** *adj* IMPRIM *encre* full-bodied

forte:[2] ~ **concentration** *f* POLLUTION high concentration; ~ **dépression** *f* METEO deep depression; ~ **inversion** *f* ELECTRON strong inversion; ~ **passe** *f* CONS MECA heavy cut; ~ **pente** *f* CONSTR high gradient, steep gradient, steep slope; ~ **pièce de bois équarri** *f* CONSTR balk (AmE), baulk (BrE); ~ **pièce équarrie** *f* CONSTR balk (AmE), baulk (BrE); ~ **production d'énergie turbulente** *f* PHYS FLUID strong turbulent energy production; ~ **teneur en soufre** *f* PETROLE high sulfur content (AmE), high sulphur content (BrE)

fortement: ~ **sollicité** *adj* PRODUCTION *système hydraulique* highly-loaded

fortes: ~ **radiations ultraviolettes** *f pl* SECURITE strong ultraviolet rays

fortifié *adj* AGRO ALIM fortified

fortin *m* MILITAIRE pillbox

forts: ~ **coups de vent** *m pl* METEO strong gale

fortune:[1] **de** ~ *adv* ESPACE makeshift

fortune:[2] **de mer** *f* NAUT maritime peril, sea damage

fosse *f* CHARBON coal pit, pit, CONS MECA hole, CONSTR, DISTRI EAU pit, GEOLOGIE furrow, trough, OCEANO deep, hole, trench, POLLU MER pit, PRODUCTION hole; ~ **d'aisance** *f* DISTRI EAU cesspit, cesspool; ~ **de bâti** *f* AERONAUT jig pit; ~ **à ciel ouvert** *f* MINES open pit; ~ **de coulée** *f* CERAM VER running out pit, PRODUCTION casting pit; ~ **creusée en terre** *f* PETR burn pit; ~ **de moulage** *f* PRODUCTION molding hole (AmE), moulding hole (BrE); ~ **océanique** *f* GEOLOGIE ocean trench, *de la marge continentale* marginal trench; ~ **à piquer**

le feu *f* PRODUCTION cleaning pit, engine pit; ~ de remmoulage *f* PRODUCTION setting-up pit; ~ de remplissage *f* MINES pocket; ~ de repos *f* CONSTR settling pit; ~ de sédimentation *f* GENIE CHIM settling basin, settling cistern, settling sump; ~ septique *f* DISTRI EAU, HYDROLOGIE, RECYCLAGE septic tank; ~ septique à compartiments *f* HYDROLOGIE septic tank; ~ sous défibreur *f* PAPIER defibrer pit, grinder pit; ~ sous-marine *f* GEOPHYS deep-sea trench; ~ à visiter *f* PRODUCTION cleaning pit, engine pit, inspection pit

fossé *m* CHARBON ditch, trench, CONSTR ditch, trench, DISTRI EAU ditch, GEOLOGIE downbuckle, HYDROLOGIE ditch, OCEANO deep, sea moat, trench, PETROLE trench; ~ de berge *m* DISTRI EAU berm ditch; ~ central *m* MINES center cut (AmE), centre cut (BrE); ~ collecteur *m* DISTRI EAU collecting ditch; ~ de crête *m* CONSTR cutoff ditch; ~ de drainage *m* DISTRI EAU open drain, HYDROLOGIE drainage ditch; ~ d'infiltration *m* DISTRI EAU leaching trench; ~ médian *m* GEOLOGIE *d'une ride océanique, d'un graben intracontinental* axial rift zone; ~ norvégien *m* PETROLE *géologie* Norwegian trench; ~ d'oxydation *m* DISTRI EAU oxidation ditches, HYDROLOGIE bio-oxidation ditch, oxidation ditch; ~ serpent *m* HYDROLOGIE bio-oxidation ditch

fossette *f* CERAM VER dimple

fossile *m* GEOLOGIE fossil; ~ caractéristique *m* GEOLOGIE index fossil; ~ remanié *m* GEOLOGIE derived fossil

fossilifère *adj* GEOLOGIE fossil-bearing, fossiliferous

fossiliser *vt* GEOLOGIE fossilize

fou *adj* CONS MECA *poulie, bobine, manchon, roue*, PRODUCTION loose

foudre *f* ELECTR *phénomène*, ELECTROTEC lightning

fouettement *m* MINES *des tiges dans le sondage* lashing, NUCLEAIRE *d'une conduite* hammering, whipping

fouille *f* CHARBON borrow pit, excavation, CONS MECA *d'une plaque tournante* pit, CONSTR cut, digging, excavating, excavation, pit, trench, trenching, MINES excavation, PRODUCTION hole; ~ à ciel ouvert *f* MINES open pit; ~ en surface *f* MINES surface cut; ~ de remmoulage *f* PRODUCTION setting-up pit

fouiller *vt* MINES mine; ~ la terre *vt* MINES mine

fouillis *m* ELECTRON clutter; ~ d'écho *m* ESPACE clutter

foulage *m* TEXTILE fulling, milling

foulard *m* TEXTILE pad mangle

foule *f* TEXTILE shed

foulée *f* CONSTR *d'une marche d'escalier* tread

foulement *m* PRODUCTION ramming

fouler *vt* PRODUCTION ram

fouloir *m* PRODUCTION rammer; ~ à air comprimé *m* PRODUCTION pneumatic rammer; ~ d'établi *m* PRODUCTION *de mouleur* bench rammer; ~ à main *m* PRODUCTION hand rammer; ~ pneumatique *m* PRODUCTION pneumatic rammer

foulon *m* PAPIER wringer roll

foulonnage *m* TEXTILE dewatering under load

four *m* CONSTR kiln, EQUIP LAB *chauffage* furnace, MAT CHAUFF kiln, oven, PAPIER furnace, kiln, oven, PRODUCTION furnace, kiln, oven, TEXTILE oven, THERMODYN kiln, oven; ~ d'aciérie *m* CHARBON open hearth furnace; ~ d'affinage *m* MAT CHAUFF, PRODUCTION, THERMODYN refining furnace; ~ à air chaud *m* MAT CHAUFF, THERMODYN convection oven; ~ à air forcé *m* PRODUCTION forced draft furnace (AmE), forced draught furnace (BrE); ~ à air soufflé *m* PRODUCTION forced draft furnace (AmE), forced draught furnace (BrE); ~ annulaire *m* CERAM VER annular kiln;

~ annulaire à sole tournante *m* MAT CHAUFF rotary hearth kiln; ~ à arc *m* CONS MECA, MAT CHAUFF arc furnace, THERMODYN electric arc furnace; ~ à arc direct *m* MAT CHAUFF arc furnace direct; ~ à arc électrique *m* CHARBON EAF, electric arc furnace, ELECTR *chauffage* electric arc furnace; ~ à arc de fusion d'acier *m* CONS MECA arc furnace for steel melting, electric arc furnace; ~ à arc sous vide *m* MAT CHAUFF vacuum arc furnace; ~ armoire *m* MAT CHAUFF box furnace, box kiln; ~ à bain de sel *m* MAT CHAUFF salt bath furnace; ~ à basse fréquence *m* ELECTROTEC low-frequency furnace; ~ à bassin *m* CERAM VER tank furnace; ~ BF *m* ELECTROTEC low-frequency furnace; ~ à billes *m* CERAM VER marble furnace; ~ à boucle *m* CERAM VER horseshoe-fired furnace; ~ de braise *m* CERAM VER soaking pit; ~ à briques *m* CONSTR brick kiln; ~ à brûleurs dans les pignons *m* CERAM VER top-flame furnace; ~ à brûleurs dans le siège *m* CERAM VER under fired furnace; ~ à brûleurs transversaux *m* CERAM VER cross-fired furnace; ~ à cascade *m* MAT CHAUFF cascade furnace; ~ de cémentation *m* CONS MECA carburizing furnace; ~ céramique *m* CERAM VER ceramic kiln; ~ de chauffage *m* THERMODYN heating furnace; ~ chauffé au gaz *m* CHAUFFAGE gas-fired furnace, PRODUCTION gas furnace; ~ à chaux *m* MAT CHAUFF lime kiln, MATERIAUX limeburning kiln, PRODUCTION lime kiln, lime pit; ~ à chaux vertical *m* MAT CHAUFF vertical lime kiln; ~ à ciment *m* CERAM VER cement kiln; ~ de cimentation *m* MAT CHAUFF cementation furnace; ~ circulaire *m* CERAM VER rotary kiln; ~ à cloche *m* PRODUCTION bell furnace; ~ à coke *m* CERAM VER, MAT CHAUFF, MINES, PRODUCTION coke oven; ~ continu *m* MAT CHAUFF continuous kiln; ~ crématoire *m* MAT CHAUFF cremator; ~ à creuset *m* EQUIP LAB *chauffage* crucible furnace, PRODUCTION crucible furnace, open hearth furnace, THERMODYN crucible furnace, pot furnace; ~ à cuire la laque *m* REVETEMENT enameling furnace (AmE), enamelling stove (BrE); ~ à cuire la peinture *m* REVETEMENT enameling stove (AmE), enamelling stove (BrE); ~ à cuire la porcelaine *m* CERAM VER porcelain calcining furnace; ~ à cuve *m* CHARBON shaft kiln, PRODUCTION shaft furnace; ~ cyclone *m* CERAM VER, MAT CHAUFF cyclone furnace; ~ à décorer *m* CERAM VER decorating kiln; ~ à diffusion *m* ELECTRON, GENIE CHIM diffusion oven; ~ discontinu *m* THERMODYN batch furnace; ~ à double voûte *m* CERAM VER double-deck crown furnace; ~ à effusion *m* ELECTRON effusion oven; ~ électrique *m* CHARBON, ELECTR electric furnace, THERMODYN electric oven; ~ électrique à induction *m* ELECTROTEC electric induction furnace; ~ électrique à résistance *m* ELECTROTEC electric resistance furnace; ~ élévateur *m* MAT CHAUFF lift-up furnace; ~ à émailler *m* REVETEMENT enameling furnace, enameling kiln (AmE), enamelling furnace (BrE), enamelling kiln (BrE); ~ en taille de guêpe *m* CERAM VER wasp-waisted tank; ~ d'essai *m* CHIMIE assay furnace; ~ à étendre *m* CERAM VER flattening kiln; ~ de fabrication de l'acier *m* PRODUCTION steel furnace; ~ à faisceau d'électrons *m* NUCLEAIRE electron beam bombardment furnace; ~ à fritte *m* CERAM VER, MAT CHAUFF *verrerie* fritting furnace; ~ de fusion *m* CHARBON melting furnace, ELECTROTEC smelting furnace, PLAST CAOU *matériel* fusing oven, THERMODYN melting furnace; ~ de galère *m* PRODUCTION gallery furnace; ~ à galeries parallèles *m* MAT CHAUFF longitudinal arch kiln; ~ **à gaz** *m* CHAUFFAGE gas-fired furnace, PRODUCTION gas furnace, THERMODYN gas-fired furnace; ~ **à glaçure** *m* CERAM VER glaze kiln; ~ **de grillage** *m* CHARBON calcining kiln, PRODUCTION burning house, roasting kiln, roasting oven, roaster, roasting furnace; ~ **à griller** *m* PRODUCTION burning house, roasting kiln, roasting oven, roaster, roasting furnace; ~ **à haute fréquence** *m* ELECTROTEC high-frequency furnace; ~ **à incinération d'ordures ménagères** *m* THERMODYN destructor; ~ **à induction** *m* ELECTROTEC, PHYSIQUE, PRODUCTION induction furnace; ~ **à induction à canal** *m* MAT CHAUFF channel induction furnace; ~ **à induction à creuset** *m* MAT CHAUFF coreless induction furnace; ~ **à induction sans noyau** *m* MAT CHAUFF coreless induction furnace; ~ **industriel** *m* CONS MECA industrial oven, GAZ industrial furnace; ~ **intermittent** *m* GENIE CHIM batch furnace; ~ **journalier** *m* CERAM VER day tank; ~ **de liquidation** *m* PRODUCTION sweating furnace; ~ **à lit fluidisé** *m* GENIE CHIM fluidized bed kiln, NUCLEAIRE *de recuit* fluid-bed furnace; ~ **à manche** *m* PRODUCTION shaft furnace; ~ **Martin** *m* CHARBON open hearth furnace, oxygen furnace, PRODUCTION open hearth furnace; ~ **Martin basique** *m* CERAM VER basic open-hearth furnace; ~ **Martin-Siemens** *m* PRODUCTION open hearth furnace; ~ **métallurgique** *m* CONS MECA metallurgical furnace; ~ **MF** *m (four à moyenne fréquence)* ELECTROTEC medium-frequency furnace; ~ **à micro-ondes** *m* AGRO ALIM, ELECTROTEC microwave oven; ~ **à moufle** *m* EQUIP LAB *chauffage*, MAT CHAUFF muffle furnace, PRODUCTION blind roaster, muffle furnace; ~ **à moyenne fréquence** *m (four MF)* ELECTROTEC medium-frequency furnace; ~ **oscillant** *m* MAT CHAUFF tilting furnace, PRODUCTION rolling furnace; ~ **à paquets** *m* THERMODYN batch furnace; ~ **passant** *m* MAT CHAUFF pusher furnace; ~ **de polymérisation** *m* TEXTILE curing oven; ~ **à postcombustion** *m* NUCLEAIRE afterburner; ~ **potager** *m* PRODUCTION crucible furnace; ~ **pour céramique** *m* CERAM VER, THERMODYN pottery kiln; ~ **à pyrite** *m* PRODUCTION desulfurizing furnace (AmE), desulphurizing furnace (BrE); ~ **de ramollissement** *m* CERAM VER softening furnace; ~ **à réchauffer** *m* THERMODYN heating furnace; ~ **de recuisson** *m* CERAM VER, THERMODYN annealing furnace; ~ **de recuit** *m* MECANIQUE *procédé*, NUCLEAIRE, THERMODYN annealing furnace; ~ **de recuit à lit fluidisé** *m* GENIE CHIM fluid bed furnace; ~ **à récupération** *m* CERAM VER recuperative furnace; ~ **à réduction** *m* PRODUCTION reducing furnace, THERMODYN reduction furnace; ~ **à refroidissement l'eau** *m* MAT CHAUFF *chaudière marine* water-cooled furnace; ~ **à régénération** *m* CERAM VER regenerative furnace; ~ **à résistance** *m* ELECTROTEC resistance furnace; ~ **à réverbère** *m* MAT CHAUFF air furnace, PRODUCTION reverberatory, reverberatory furnace; ~ **rotatif** *m* CHARBON, MAT CHAUFF rotary kiln, PRODUCTION rotary furnace, THERMODYN drum furnace; ~ **rotatif à ciment** *m* MAT CHAUFF rotary kiln for cement manufacture; ~ **rotatoire** *m* PRODUCTION rotary furnace; ~ **à ruche** *m* CERAM VER beehive kiln, PRODUCTION beehive oven; ~ **de séchage** *m* PRODUCTION drying furnace, drying kiln, TEXTILE drying oven; ~ **de séchage des moules** *m* PRODUCTION mould dryer (BrE); ~ **à sécher sous vide** *m* AGRO ALIM vacuum drying oven; ~ **sécheur** *m* PRODUCTION drying furnace, drying kiln; ~ **séchoir** *m* CHARBON

drying kiln, TEXTILE drying stove; ~ **solaire** *m* EN RENOUV solar furnace; ~ **à sole** *m* PRODUCTION open hearth furnace; ~ **à sole mobile** *m* MAT CHAUFF bogie kiln; ~ **à sole multiple** *m* MAT CHAUFF multiple hearth furnace; ~ **à soufre pulvérisé** *m* PAPIER jet sulfur burner (AmE), jet sulphur burner (BrE); ~ **à tambour** *m* THERMODYN drum furnace, drum kiln; ~ **tournant** *m* PRODUCTION rotary furnace, THERMODYN drum furnace; ~ **de trempe au gaz** *m* MAT CHAUFF gas quench; ~ **de trempe à mazout** *m* MAT CHAUFF oil quench; ~ **de trempe scellé** *m* MAT CHAUFF sealed quench furnace; ~ **trommel** *m* THERMODYN drum kiln; ~ **à tunnel** *m* MAT CHAUFF *céramique* tunnel kiln; ~ **à tuyère et courant d'air forcé** *m* PRODUCTION forced draft furnace (AmE), forced draught furnace (BrE); ~ **de type bas** *m* CHARBON low-shaft furnace; ~ **à vent chaud** *m* PRODUCTION hot blast furnace; ~ **à vide** *m* CONS MECA vacuum furnace; ~ **à vide poussé** *m* CONS MECA high-vacuum furnace

fourche *f* AUTO knuckle, CERAM VER fork, INSTRUMENT fork mounting, VEHICULES *d'une motocyclette, boîte de vitesse, d'un embrayage* fork, *joint universel* yoke; ~ **antiplongée** *f* VEHICULES *motocyclette* antidive fork; ~ **d'articulation** *f* AERONAUT hinge fork; ~ **à coke** *f* CHARBON coke fork; ~ **de débrayage** *f* CONS MECA strap fork, PRODUCTION belt fork; ~ **de direction** *f* AERONAUT nose wheel steering bar; ~ **de manoeuvre de courroie** *f* CONS MECA strap fork, PRODUCTION belt fork; ~ **pour mise à l'arche** *f* CERAM VER carrying-in fork

fourches: ~ **télescopiques** *f pl* VEHICULES *suspension d'une motocyclette* telescopic forks

fourchette *f* CONS MECA fork arm, *d'un manchon d'embrayage* fork, METROLOGIE beam support; ~ **de débrayage** *f* PAPIER belt conveyor, VEHICULES *embrayage* clutch release fork; ~ **d'embrayage** *f* AUTO clutch fork; ~ **de sélection** *f* VEHICULES *d'une boîte de vitesse* gearbox selector fork

fourchon *m* CONSTR prong

four-filière *m* (Fra) *(cf filière)* CERAM VER bushing assembly

fourgon *m* CH DE FER caboose (AmE), guard's van (BrE), PRODUCTION poker, prick bar, pricker; ~ **à bagages** *m* CH DE FER *véhicules*, TRANSPORT baggage car (AmE), luggage van (BrE); ~ **de queue** *m* CH DE FER *véhicules* rear brake van; ~ **surélevé** *m* VEHICULES raised-roof van

fourgonnette: ~ **électrique** *f* TRANSPORT electric pick-up

fourgon-pompe *f* THERMODYN fire engine

fourneau *m* CHARBON kiln, MAT CHAUFF, PRODUCTION furnace, THERMODYN kiln; ~ **à chauffer les rivets** *m* CONSTR rivet-heating furnace; ~ **à creuset** *m* THERMODYN pot furnace; ~ **à cuve** *m* MAT CHAUFF vertical-shaft furnace; ~ **d'essai** *m* MAT CHAUFF assay furnace, PRODUCTION test furnace; ~ **de mine** *m* MINES blast hole, borehole, mining hole, chamber, mine chamber; ~ **à réverbère** *m* MAT CHAUFF open hearth furnace

Fourneau *m* ASTRONOMIE Fornax

fournée *f* AGRO ALIM, PLAST CAOU batch

fournir[1] *vt* PHYS RAYON *rayonnement thermique* emit; ~ **de** *vt* PRODUCTION provide with, supply with

fournir:[2] ~ **une réserve d'oxygène** *vi* ESPACE provide an oxygen supply

fournisseur *m* PRODUCTION, QUALITE supplier; ~ **de lignes de couchage** *m* IMPRIM *industrie* coating line supplier; ~ **maritime** *m* NAUT ship chandler; ~ **de service** *m* TELECOM service provider; ~ **du service CMISE** *m* TELECOM CMISE service provider; ~ **de systèmes** *m* TELECOM system provider

fourniture *f* PRODUCTION supplying, TELECOM provision; ~ **d'énergie** *f* EN RENOUV energy supply; ~ **au réseau** *f* NUCLEAIRE delivery into the mains (BrE), delivery into the utility network (AmE), output

fournitures: ~ **pour usines** *f pl* PRODUCTION engineer's stores

fourreau *m* CONS MECA *d'une contre-poupée de tour* barrel, *d'une poupée de tour* barrel, DISTRI EAU priming pipe, MECANIQUE sheath, MILITAIRE scabbard; ~ **d'avance** *m* CONS MECA feed sleeve; ~ **de carbone** *m* CHIMIE tamped carbon; ~ **de traversée** *m* NUCLEAIRE penetration sleeve

fourrure *f* AERONAUT liner, CH DE FER bushing, *pour joint de rail* shim, CONSTR cover, PRODUCTION covering plate, welt, TEXTILE fur; ~ **de frein** *f* CERAM VER brake lining; ~ **mécanique** *f* CH DE FER bushing

fowlérite *f* MINERAUX fowlerite

foyer *m* ASTRONOMIE *du télescope* focus, CH DE FER *véhicules* firebox, CINEMAT focal point, focus, CONSTR hearth, GEOLOGIE hypocenter (AmE), hypocentre (BrE), GEOMETRIE focus, GEOPHYS earthquake focus, focus, seismic focus, MAT CHAUFF *four* vestibule, PHOTO focal point, PHYSIQUE focus, PRODUCTION furnace, THERMODYN firebox; ~ **d'aérage** *m* MINES dumb furnace; ~ **câblé** *m* TV cabled home; ~ **à cendres fondues** *m* CHAUFFAGE slag tap furnace; ~ **de chaudière** *m* INST HYDR boiler furnace; ~ **fixe** *m* PHOTO fixed focus; ~ **intérieur cylindrique** *m* PRODUCTION *d'une chaudière* flue; ~ **linéaire** *m* TV line focus; ~ **lumineux** *m* CINEMAT light center (AmE), light centre (BrE), PHOTO hot spot; ~ **à mazout** *m* CHAUFFAGE oil-fired furnace, CONS MECA oil-fired installation; ~ **mécanique** *m* PRODUCTION stoker; ~ **mécanique à alimentation par le dessus** *m* CONS MECA overfeed stoker; ~ **de la pale** *m* AERONAUT blade aerodynamic center (AmE), blade aerodynamic centre (BrE); ~ **postérieur** *m* PHOTO rear focus; ~ **primaire** *m* ASTRONOMIE prime focus, *d'un télescope* primary focus; ~ **d'un profil aérodynamique** *m* AERONAUT aerodynamic center (AmE), aerodynamic centre (BrE); ~ **raccordé** *m* TV cabled home; ~ **de sédimentation maximum** *m* GEOLOGIE depocenter (AmE), depocentre (BrE); ~ **du séisme** *m* GEOPHYS earthquake focus, focus, hypocenter (AmE), hypocentre (BrE), seismic focus; ~ **statique** *m* TV static focus; ~ **du tremblement de terre** *m* GEOPHYS seismic focus; ~ **ultrafin** *m* NUCLEAIRE ultrafine focus

FPB *abrév (filtre passe-bande)* ELECTR, ELECTRON, ENREGISTR, INFORMAT, ORDINAT, PHYSIQUE, TELECOM, TV BPF *(band-pass filter)*

Fr *(francium)* CHIMIE Fr *(francium)*

fraçage: ~ **supplémentaire** *f* CHARBON redriving

fractale *f* INFORMAT, ORDINAT fractal

fraction *f* CHIMIE moiety, IMPRIM, PETROLE fraction; ~ **commune** *f* MATH simple fraction; ~ **de gel** *f* TELECOM FOF, freeze-out fraction; ~ **granulométrique** *f* CERAM VER sieve fraction, CHARBON grain fraction, size fraction; ~ **irréductible** *f* MATH reduced fraction; ~ **massique** *f* NUCLEAIRE mass fraction, weight fraction; ~ **mère** *f* NUCLEAIRE parent fraction; ~ **molaire** *f* METALL, REFRIG mole fraction; ~ **périodique** *f* MATH nonterminating decimal, recurring decimal, repeat-

ing decimal; ~ **de recyclage** *f* NUCLEAIRE rabbit fraction; ~ **volumétrique** *f* METALL *des particules* volume fraction; ~ **volumique** *f* MATERIAUX, METALL volume fraction

fractionnaire *adj* MATH fractional

fractionnement *m* CHIMIE *d'huile*, MATERIAUX *chimie* fractionation, PETROLE fractional distillation, PRODUCTION split, splitting; ~ **des lots** *m* PRODUCTION lot splitting

fractions: ~ **légères** *f pl* PETROLE light fractions; ~ **légères d'hydrocarbures** *f pl* PETROLE light hydrocarbon fractions; ~ **lourdes** *f pl* PETROLE heavy fractions, *raffinage* heavy ends; ~ **lourdes d'hydrocarbures** *f pl* PETROLE heavy hydrocarbon fractions

fracturation *f* GEOLOGIE, PETROLE fracturing; ~ **hydraulique** *f* PETR hydraulic fracturing

fracture *f* CONSTR *d'une serrure* breaking, MECANIQUE *matériaux* fracture; ~ **de base** *f* CONSTR base failure; ~ **conchoïdale** *f* CERAM VER conchoidal fracture; ~ **décrochante** *f* GEOLOGIE tear fault; ~ **en lancette** *f* CERAM VER hackle (AmE), hackle mark (BrE)

fracturer[1] *vt* CONSTR *une serrure* break, MATERIAUX fracture; **se** ~ *vt* MATERIAUX fracture

fracturer:[2] **se** ~ *v réfl* CONSTR break, GEOPHYS fracture

fragile *adj* CRISTALL brittle, EMBALLAGE fragile, MECANIQUE *matériaux*, METALL, PLAST CAOU brittle

fragilisation *f* MATERIAUX, METALL, NUCLEAIRE embrittlement

fragilité *f* CERAM VER, CRISTALL, MATERIAUX, METALL, PLAST CAOU brittleness; ~ **au bleu** *f* METALL blue brittleness; ~ **au froid** *f* REFRIG, THERMODYN cold brittleness; ~ **de trempe** *f* METALL temper brittleness

fragment *m* PRODUCTION scrap

fragmentation *f* CONSTR breaking-up, GENIE CHIM comminution, milling, size reduction, INFORMAT, METALL fragmentation, MINES breakage, shatter, ORDINAT fragmentation; ~ **de gros blocs de minerai au moyen de petits** *f* CONSTR bulldozing; ~ **mémoire** *f* INFORMAT, ORDINAT storage fragmentation

fragmenter[1] *vt* CHARBON fragment, CONSTR break, break up; ~ **par explosif** *vt* CHARBON, CONSTR blast

fragmenter:[2] **se** ~ *v réfl* CONSTR break, break up

fragments: ~ **de fission** *m pl* PHYSIQUE fission fragments; ~ **d'outils abîmés** *m pl* SECURITE fragments from worn tools

fraîcheur *f* MAT CHAUFF *ventilation* freshness, NAUT *vent* cat's paw

frais[1] *adj* GEOLOGIE fresh, unaltered, MATERIAUX fresh

frais[2] *m pl* BREVETS costs; ~ **de base** *m pl* TELECOM basic call charge; ~ **de batelage** *m pl* NAUT lighterage charges; ~ **de communication** *m pl* TELECOM call charge; ~ **de débarquement** *m pl* NAUT landing charges; ~ **engagés** *m pl* POLLU MER out-of-pocket expenses; ~ **d'expédition** *m pl* NAUT shipping charges; ~ **d'exploitation** *m pl* TEXTILE running costs; ~ **d'exploitation et de maintenance** *m pl* QUALITE life-cycle cost; ~ **généraux de production** *m pl* CINEMAT production overhead; ~ **de mise à terre** *m pl* NAUT landing charges; ~ **payés à l'avance** *m pl* PRODUCTION deferred charges; ~ **de production** *m pl* CINEMAT production expenses; ~ **relatifs à la qualité** *m pl* QUALITE quality-related cost; ~ **de remorquage** *m pl* NAUT towage charges; ~ **de temps d'arrêt** *m* EMBALLAGE downtime cost

fraisage *m* CONS MECA countersinking, PRODUCTION milling; ~ **d'après calibre** *m* CONS MECA jig milling; ~

en opposition *m* CONS MECA down-cut milling; ~ **en plan** *m* CONS MECA plane milling, surface milling; ~ **en roulant** *m* CONS MECA out-milling; ~ **de forme** *m* PRODUCTION form milling; ~ **normal** *m* CONS MECA conventional milling; ~ **par contourage** *m* MATERIAUX contouring; ~ **par reproduction** *m* CONS MECA copy milling; ~ **de pièces en série** *m* PRODUCTION gang milling, multiple milling; ~ **de précision** *m* CONS MECA precision milling; ~ **de rainures** *m* CONS MECA slot milling; ~ **à la vis-mère** *m* CONS MECA hobbing

fraise *f* CONS MECA countersink, countersink bit, milling cutter; ~ **d'angle** *f* CONS MECA angle cutter, bevel cutter; ~ **d'angle avec l'une des faces en bout** *f* CONS MECA single angle cutter, single angular cutter; ~ **angulaire** *f* CONS MECA cone countersink; ~ **avec denture à droite** *f* CONS MECA right-hand milling cutter; ~ **axiale** *f* CONS MECA face cutter; ~ **de bout** *f* CONS MECA end mill; ~ **à champ rond** *f* CONS MECA round-edge milling cutter; ~ **à chanfreiner** *f* CONS MECA angle cutter; ~ **composée** *f* CONS MECA interlocking milling cutter; ~ **conique** *f* CONS MECA dovetail cutter, MECANIQUE *outillage* angular milling cutter, PRODUCTION dovetail cutter; ~ **conique à cône renversé** *f* CONS MECA inverse dovetail cutter; ~ **conique à ébavurer** *f* CONS MECA deburring tool; ~ **de côté** *f* CONS MECA side mill; ~ **creuse** *f* CONS MECA running down cutter, shell mill; ~ **cylindrique** *f* CONS MECA parallel milling cutter; ~ **cylindrique à deux tailles** *f* CONS MECA shell end mill; ~ **à défoncer** *f* CONS MECA side-and-face milling cutter; ~ **dégagée** *f* CONS MECA backed-off cutter; ~ **à dégrossir les rainures** *f* CONS MECA roughing slot mill; ~ **demi-lune** *f* CONS MECA Woodruff cutter; ~ **à dents dégagées** *f* CONS MECA relieved milling cutter; ~ **à dents rapportées** *f* CONS MECA inserted-blade milling cutter, milling cutter with inserted teeth; ~ **à denture à dépouille** *f* CONS MECA relieved milling cutter; ~ **à denture droite** *f* CONS MECA milling cutter with straight teeth; ~ **à denture hélicoïdale** *f* CONS MECA milling cutter with spiral teeth, spiral milling cutter; ~ **à denture interrompue** *f* CONS MECA nicked tooth milling cutter; ~ **à denture recoupée** *f* CONS MECA nicked tooth milling cutter; ~ **à dresser** *f* CONS MECA face milling cutter; ~ **ébarbeuse** *f* CONS MECA burring reamer, CONSTR pipe-coning tool; ~ **ébarbeuse femelle** *f* CONS MECA coning tool female; ~ **ébarbeuse mâle** *f* CONS MECA coning tool male; ~ **en bout** *f* CONS MECA end mill; ~ **en bout à plaquettes amovibles** *f* CONS MECA end mill with indexable inserts; ~ **de face** *f* CONS MECA face cutter; ~ **à fileter** *f* CONS MECA thread milling cutter; ~ **de forme** *f* CONS MECA form milling cutter, formed cutter, formed milling cutter; ~ **de forme à profil constant** *f* CONS MECA form milling cutter with constant profile; ~ **à fraiser les trous** *f* CONS MECA countersink, countersink bit; ~ **genre raboteuse** *f* CONS MECA plano-miller; ~ **isocèle** *f* CONS MECA double equal angle cutter; ~ **à lames amovibles** *f* CONS MECA inserted-tooth milling cutter, milling cutter with inserted teeth; ~ **à lames rapportées** *f* CONS MECA inserted-blade milling cutter, milling cutter with inserted teeth; ~ **à manche** *f* CONS MECA cutter with shank; ~ **mère** *f* CONS MECA gear hob, hob, MECANIQUE hob; ~ **mère monobloc à entrée** *f* CONS MECA single start solid gear hob; ~ **à moyeu** *f* CONS MECA cutter with hub; ~ **pour alésoir** *f* CONS MECA reamer cutter; ~ **pour peigne** *f* CONS MECA hob; ~ **pour profil courbe** *f* CONS MECA arc cutter; ~ **pour rainure** *f* CONS MECA slotting cutter; ~ **pour rainure à T** *f* CONS MECA T-slot cutter; ~ **à quart de rond** *f* CONS MECA quarter round milling cutter; ~ **radiale** *f* CONS MECA end mill; ~ **à rainurer** *f* CONS MECA slot drill; ~ **à rouler** *f* CONS MECA plain milling cutter; ~ **à surfacer** *f* CONS MECA face milling cutter, face milling grinder; ~ **à tailler les engrenages** *f* CONS MECA gear cutter; ~ **à tailler les queues-d'aronde** *f* PRODUCTION dovetail cutter; ~ **à trois tailles** *f* CONS MECA side-and-face milling cutter; ~ **de trois tailles à alésage lisse** *f* CONS MECA side-and-face milling cutter with plain; ~ **à trou taraudé** *f* CONS MECA cutter with tapped hole

fraise-lime *f* CONS MECA burr; ~ **en métal dur** *f* CONS MECA hard metal burr

fraisement *m* PRODUCTION milling

fraiser[1] *vt* MECANIQUE mill, *trou* countersink, PRODUCTION mill

fraiser:[2] ~ **entre pointes** *vi* PRODUCTION mill between centers (AmE), mill between centres (BrE)

fraises: ~ **à lames amovibles** *f pl* CONS MECA inserted-blade milling cutter; ~ **pour congés** *f pl* CONS MECA corner-rounding cutters; ~ **à tailler les engrenages à développante** *f pl* CONS MECA involute gear cutters

fraise-scie *f* CONS MECA metal slitting saw; ~ **à denture fine** *f* CONS MECA metal slitting saw with fine teeth

fraises-limes: ~ **ovales** *f pl* CONS MECA oval burrs; ~ **sphériques** *f pl* CONS MECA spherical burrs

fraiseuse *f* MECANIQUE milling machine, PRODUCTION miller, milling machine, SECURITE milling machine; ~ **à console** *f* CONS MECA knee-type milling machine; ~ **genre raboteuse** *f* PRODUCTION slabber, slabbing miller; ~ **par copiage** *f* CONS MECA copy milling machine; ~ **par reproduction** *f* CONS MECA copy milling machine; ~ **à reproduire** *f* CONS MECA copy milling machine; ~ **à surface longitudinale** *f* CONS MECA plane milling machine; ~ **à surface plane** *f* CONS MECA surface milling machine; ~ **universelle** *f* CONS MECA universal milling machine

fraisil *m* CERAM VER culm

fraisure *f* CONS MECA countersunk hole, PRODUCTION countersink

franc-bord *m* NAUT freeboard

franchir *vt* CH DE FER *les aiguilles* cross-over, *un signal d'arrêt* pass, *un signal fermé* pass, *une courbe* negotiate, CONSTR cross, *vallée* bridge, bridge over; ~ **une courbe** *vt* CH DE FER negotiate a curve

franchissement: ~ **par effet tunnel** *m* ELECTRON tunneling (AmE), tunnelling (BrE)

francium *m (Fr)* CHIMIE francium *(Fr)*

franco:[1] ~ **à bord** *adj (FOB)* NAUT *commerce, transport maritime* free on board *(FOB)*; ~ **long du bord** *adj* NAUT free alongside ship; ~ **à pied d'oeuvre** *adj* CONSTR delivered site; ~ **sous palan** *adj* NAUT free alongside ship

franco:[2] ~ **à bord** *adv (FOB)* NAUT *commerce, transport maritime* free on board *(FOB)*; ~ **long du bord** *adv* NAUT free alongside ship; ~ **à quai** *adv* NAUT free on quay; ~ **sous palan** *adv* NAUT free alongside ship

frange *f* PHYSIQUE fringe; ~ **brillante** *f* PHYSIQUE bright fringe; ~ **capillaire** *f* HYDROLOGIE capillary fringe; ~ **couleur** *f* TV color fringing (AmE), colour fringing (BrE); ~ **de lumière blanche** *f* PHYSIQUE white-light fringe; ~ **sombre** *f* PHYSIQUE dark fringe

franger *vt* CINEMAT bleed

franges: ~ **achromatiques** *f pl* PHYSIQUE achromatic

fringes; **~ de contour** *f pl* PHYSIQUE contour fringes, fringes; **~ d'égale inclinaison** *f pl* PHYSIQUE fringes; **~ de Fizeau** *f pl* PHYSIQUE Fizeau fringes; **~ de Haidinger** *f pl* PHYSIQUE Haidinger fringes; **~ d'interférence** *f pl* PHYS ONDES bands, fringes, interference bands, interference fringes, PHYSIQUE interference fringes; **~ localisées** *f pl* PHYSIQUE localized fringes; **~ moirées** *f pl* PHYSIQUE moiré fringes; **~ non localisées** *f pl* PHYSIQUE nonlocalized fringes

frangeux *adj* EMBALLAGE *papier* deckled

frangibilité *f* MATERIAUX brittleness

franguline *f* CHIMIE frangulin

franklinite *f* MINERAUX franklinite

frappage *m* POLLUTION rapping, PRODUCTION stamping

frappe *f* INFORMAT, ORDINAT hit, PRODUCTION die, tup die, pallet for tup, top die, tup pallet, top pallet; **~ supérieure** *f* PRODUCTION top die, top die, tup die, pallet for tup, top pallet, tup pallet

frapper *vt* INFORMAT hit, NAUT bend, lash, ORDINAT hit, PRODUCTION stamp, tap; **~ un coup sur** *vt* PRODUCTION tap

frappeuse *f* PRODUCTION *boulon, rivet, crampon* bolt forging machine

frasnien *adj* GEOLOGIE Frasnian

frayère *f* OCEANO spawning ground

frégatage *m* NAUT tumblehome

frégate *f* NAUT frigate

freibergite *f* MINERAUX freibergite

freieslébenite *f* MINERAUX freieslebenite

frein *m* AUTO, CONS MECA, MECANIQUE, PAPIER, VEHICULES brake; **~ à air comprimé** *m* AUTO air pressure brake, CONS MECA air brake, atmospheric brake, MECANIQUE *véhicules* air brake, VEHICULES pneumatic brake; **~ assisté** *m* AUTO power brake, VEHICULES power-assisted brake; **~ assisté par servofrein à dépression** *m* AUTO vacuum-assisted power brake; **~ automatique** *m* VEHICULES automatic brake, self-acting brake; **~ d'axe** *m* CONS MECA circlip; **~ à bande** *m* CONS MECA band brake, ribbon brake, strap brake, MECANIQUE band brake; **~ à courant de Foucault** *m* CH DE FER, ELECTROTEC, MECANIQUE eddy current brake; **~ à dépression** *m* CH DE FER, CONS MECA, VEHICULES vacuum brake; **~ de détresse** *m* AERONAUT emergency brake; **~ à dilatation interne** *m* CONS MECA internal expanding brake; **~ à disque** *m* AUTO, MECANIQUE, VEHICULES disc brake (BrE), disk brake (AmE); **~ à double circuit** *m* AUTO twin-line brake; **~ d'écrou** *m* CONS MECA nut lock; **~ électromagnétique** *m* CH DE FER *véhicules*, TRANSPORT electromagnetic brake; **~ électropneumatique** *m* TRANSPORT electropneumatic brake; **~ à enroulement** *m* CONS MECA strap brake; **~ EP** *m* CH DE FER EP brake; **~ à friction** *m* VEHICULES friction brake; **~ fritté** *m* CH DE FER *véhicules* sintered brake; **~ de gouverne** *m* AERONAUT gust lock; **~ à huile** *m* CONS MECA oil dashpot; **~ hydrocinétique** *m* TRANSPORT hydrokinetic brake; **~ hydropneumatique** *m* TRANSPORT hydropneumatic brake; **~ à levier** *m* CONS MECA lever brake; **~ linéaire à courant de Foucault** *m* TRANSPORT eddy rail brake; **~ de machine-outil** *m* CONS MECA machine tool brake; **~ à mâchoire** *m* VEHICULES shoe brake; **~ à mâchoires** *m* TRANSPORT clasp brake; **~ magnétique** *m* TV eddy brake (BrE), eddy current brake; **~ à main** *m* CONS MECA, VEHICULES handbrake; **~ modérable** *m* CONS MECA overspeed brake; **~ moteur** *m* VEHICULES engine brake; **~ à palettes** *m* CONS MECA fan brake; **~ de parc** *m* AERONAUT parking brake; **~ par coinçage** *m* CONS MECA wedge brake; **~ à pied** *m* VEHICULES foot brake; **~ de piqué** *m* AERONAUT diving brake; **~ plat** *m* CONS MECA lockplate; **~ pneumatique** *m* CONS MECA air brake, VEHICULES air brake, pneumatic brake; **~ de Prony** *m* AUTO Prony brake; **~ à rattrapage automatique de jeu** *m* AUTO self-adjusting brake; **~ de recul** *m* MILITAIRE recoil brake; **~ de remorque** *m* VEHICULES trailer brake; **~ de retenue** *m* CONSTR *pour la descente des tubages de puits* casing clamp, MINES *pour la descente des tubages de puits* pipe clamp; **~ rhéostatique** *m* CH DE FER *véhicules* dynamic brake, TRANSPORT rheostatic brake; **~ à ruban** *m* CONS MECA ribbon brake, strap brake; **~ à sangle** *m* CONS MECA band brake, ribbon brake, strap brake; **~ de secours** *m* TRANSPORT emergency brake; **~ de service** *m* VEHICULES service brake; **~ de stationnement** *m* AUTO, MECANIQUE *véhicules* parking brake, VEHICULES handbrake, parking brake; **~ à tambour** *m* AUTO drum brake; **~ à vapeur** *m* INST HYDR steam brake; **~ à vide** *m* CH DE FER *véhicules*, CONS MECA, VEHICULES vacuum brake; **~ à vide automatique** *m* CONS MECA automatic vacuum brake; **~ à vide duplex automatique** *m* CONS MECA duplex automatic vacuum brake; **~ à vis** *m* CH DE FER *véhicules*, CONS MECA screw brake, EMBALLAGE screw locking device, VEHICULES screw brake; **~ à vis manivelle** *m* CH DE FER screw brake with crank handle; **~ de voie** *m* TRANSPORT rail brake

freinage *m* CH DE FER, MECANIQUE braking; **~ aérodynamique** *m* ESPACE *véhicules* aerodynamic braking; **~ d'arrêt** *m* TRANSPORT braking to a stop; **~ autovariable** *m* TRANSPORT load-sensitive braking; **~ à contrecourant** *m* TRANSPORT reverse braking; **~ à courant de Foucault** *m* ELECTR *moteur*, ELECTROTEC eddy current braking; **~ différentiel** *m* AERONAUT differential braking; **~ dynamique** *m* TRANSPORT dynamic braking; **~ électrique** *m* ELECTR *moteur, générateur* electric braking; **~ électronique** *m* TRANSPORT electronic braking control; **~ gradué** *m* CH DE FER *véhicules* graduated braking; **~ d'immobilisation** *m* CH DE FER *véhicules* parking brake, stop brake; **~ intempestif** *m* CH DE FER *véhicules* accidental braking, unexpected braking; **~ mixte** *m* CH DE FER combined braking; **~ modéré en fin de cordée** *m* MINES overspeed braking at end of hoist; **~ par récupération** *m* CH DE FER *véhicules*, TRANSPORT regenerative braking; **~ rhéostatique** *m* CH DE FER *véhicules* rheostatic braking; **~ sans à-coups** *m* CH DE FER *véhicules* smooth braking; **~ de secours** *m* VEHICULES emergency brake system; **~ de service** *m* CH DE FER *véhicules* spontaneous brake application

freiner[1] *vt* ESPACE *véhicules* retard

freiner[2] *vi* VEHICULES apply the brake, brake

freineur *m* CH DE FER brakeman

frémir *vi* CHIMIE simmer

fréon *m* CHIMIE freon

fréquence:[1] **à ~ élevée** *adj* TV high band; **à ~ radioélectrique** *adj* ELECTRON radio frequency; **à ~ télécommandée** *adj* ELECTRON *oscillateur* labile

fréquence[2] *f* ACOUSTIQUE, ELECTR *d'une onde*, ELECTRON frequency, ENREGISTR frequency, tonality, INFORMAT, ORDINAT, PETR, PHYS ONDES, PHYSIQUE frequency; **~ d'accord normale** *f* ACOUSTIQUE standard tuning frequency; **~ acoustique** *f* ELECTRON, ENREGISTR acoustic frequency; **~ affectée** *f* TV allocated frequency; **~ d'alignement** *f* ELECTRON tie-down point; **~ d'analyse**

horizontale *f* TV horizontal scanning frequency; ~ **angulaire** *f* ELECTR, ELECTROTEC, PHYS ONDES, PHYS RAYON, PHYSIQUE angular frequency; ~ **assignée** *f* ELECTR rated frequency; ~ **audible** *f* ACOUSTIQUE, ELECTRON, ENREGISTR, PHYS ONDES, TELECOM AF, audio frequency; ~ **de balayage** *f* ELECTR *oscilloscope* time-base frequency, ELECTRON sweep frequency, TV line frequency, sweep frequency; ~ **de balayage vertical** *f* TV field frequency; ~ **d'une bande latérale** *f* ELECTRON sideband frequency; ~ **de base** *f* ELECTRON basic frequency, ORDINAT clock rate; ~ **de battement** *f* ELECTRON, ENREGISTR, PHYSIQUE beat frequency; ~ **du blanc** *f* COMMANDE white signal frequency; ~ **caractéristique** *f* PHYS RAYON characteristic frequency; ~ **centrale** *f* ELECTRON center frequency (AmE), centre frequency (BrE); ~ **centrale de filtre** *f* ELECTRON filter frequency; ~ **commandée** *f* ELECTRON controlled frequency; ~ **de commutation** *f* PRODUCTION *automatisme industriel* switching frequency; ~ **de commutation de couleurs** *f* TV color sampling rate (AmE), colour sampling rate (BrE); ~ **de commutation des couleurs** *f* PHYS RAYON color sampling frequency (AmE), colour sampling frequency (BrE); ~ **de coupure** *f* ACOUSTIQUE, ELECTR, ELECTRON, ENREGISTR, PHYSIQUE, TELECOM cutoff frequency; ~ **de coupure de filtre** *f* ELECTRON filter cutoff frequency; ~ **de coupure théorique** *f* ELECTRON theoretical cutoff frequency; ~ **critique** *f* ESPACE *communications*, TELECOM critical frequency; ~ **critique de scintillement** *f* TV critical flicker frequency; ~ **de cyclotron** *f* PHYSIQUE cyclotron frequency; ~ **de Debye** *f* PHYSIQUE Debye frequency; ~ **désignée** *f* TELECOM designated frequency; ~ **de différence** *f* ELECTRON difference frequency; ~ **différentielle** *f* ELECTRON difference frequency; ~ **discrète** *f* ELECTRON discrete frequency; ~ **Doppler** *f* ELECTRON Doppler frequency; ~ **d'échantillonnage** *f* TELECOM sampling frequency; ~ **d'effacement** *f* ENREGISTR erase frequency; ~ **éliminée** *f* ELECTRON rejected frequency; ~ **d'émission** *f* TV transmitting frequency; ~ **en dehors de l'accord** *f* ELECTRON off-tune frequency; ~ **d'essai** *f* ELECTRON test frequency; ~ **d'excitation** *f* ESSAIS excitation frequency; ~ **de fluctuation** *f* ACOUSTIQUE speed variation frequency; ~ **fondamentale** *f* ACOUSTIQUE fundamental frequency, ELECTRON basic frequency, fundamental frequency, PHYS RAYON ground state frequency, TELECOM fundamental frequency, TV basic frequency; ~ **du fond de synchronisation** *f* TV sync tip frequency; ~ **glissante** *f* TV sliding frequency; ~ **gyromagnétique** *f* NUCLEAIRE electron cyclotron frequency; ~ **harmonique** *f* ELECTRON harmonic; ~ **d'horloge** *f* ELECTRON clock frequency, INFORMAT clock rate; ~ **hors accord** *f* ELECTRON off-tune frequency; ~ **idler** *f* ELECTRON idler frequency; ~ **image** *f* ELECTRON image frequency, second channel frequency, TV frame frequency, frame rate; ~ **d'images** *f* CINEMAT frame rate, motion picture speed; ~ **d'impulsion** *f* ELECTRON pulse frequency; ~ **industrielle** *f* ELECTR *réseau* power frequency, ELECTROTEC commercial power frequency, power frequency; ~ **infrasonore** *f* ACOUSTIQUE, PHYSIQUE infrasonic frequency; ~ **instantanée** *f* ELECTRON instantaneous frequency, ESPACE pump frequency, *communications* instantaneous frequency; ~ **intermédiaire** *f* (FI) ELECTRON, TELECOM intermediate frequency (IF); ~ **de Larmor** *f* PHYSIQUE Larmor frequency; ~ **latérale** *f*

ELECTRON side frequency; ~ **de la liaison montante** *f* ESPACE *communications* uplink frequency; ~ **de ligne** *f* TV line frequency; ~ **maximale utilisable** *f* ELECTROTEC MUF, maximum usable frequency; ~ **à mi-bande** *f* ELECTRON midband frequency; ~ **minimale utilisable** *f* ESPACE LUF, lowest usable frequency; ~ **de modulation** *f* ELECTR *courant alternatif*, ELECTRON MF, modulation frequency; ~ **moyenne de passage à zéro** *f* TELECOM average crossing rate; ~ **multiple** *f* TELECOM MF, multiple frequency; ~ **de multiplexage** *f* ELECTRON multiplexing frequency; ~ **naturelle** *f* CONS MECA *de vibration*, ELECTRON, PHYS ONDES *de vibration* natural frequency; ~ **du niveau de blanc** *f* TV white-level frequency; ~ **du niveau de noir** *f* TV black level frequency; ~ **nominale** *f* ELECTR rated frequency; ~ **normalisée** *f* TELECOM normalized frequency; ~ **normée** *f* OPTIQUE normalized frequency; ~ **Nyquist** *f* PETR Nyquist frequency, folding frequency; ~ **d'onde porteuse** *f* INFORMAT carrier frequency; ~ **d'ondulation** *f* CONSTR ripple frequency, PHYS RAYON ripple frequency, wave frequency; ~ **d'ondulation résiduelle** *f* CONSTR ripple frequency; ~ **optique** *f* ELECTRON optical frequency; ~ **de l'oscillateur local** *f* ELECTRON conversion frequency, local oscillator frequency; ~ **d'oscillation** *f* ELECTRON, TELECOM oscillation frequency; ~ **d'oscillation libre** *f* ELECTRON free-running frequency; ~ **d'oscillation du quartz** *f* ELECTRON crystal frequency; ~ **de papillotement** *f* TV flicker frequency; ~ **de papillotement critique** *f* TV critical flicker frequency; ~ **passante** *f* PHYS RAYON filter frequency; ~ **perturbée** *f* PHYS RAYON *énergie spectrale* perturbed frequency; ~ **pilote** *f* CINEMAT pilot frequency, pilotone, ELECTRON master frequency, TV *sous-porteuse de chrominance* control frequency, pilot tone; ~ **pilote de sous-porteuse de chrominance** *f* TV chroma pilot; ~ **de planification** *f* PRODUCTION planning interval; ~ **de polarisation** *f* ENREGISTR bias frequency; ~ **porteuse** *f* ELECTRON, INFORMAT, ORDINAT, TELECOM, TV carrier frequency; ~ **préréglée** *f* ELECTRON preset frequency; ~ **propre** *f* ACOUSTIQUE, ELECTR *oscillations*, ELECTRON natural frequency, ESPACE *véhicules* eigenfrequency, natural frequency, PETR natural frequency, PHYS RAYON eigenfrequency, PHYSIQUE, RESSORTS natural frequency; ~ **radio** *f* ELECTRON, ELECTROTEC, ENREGISTR, TV, TELECOM, TRANSPORT radio frequency; ~ **de rayonnement** *f* PHYS RAYON *émis par un atome* frequency of radiation, radiation frequency; ~ **de réception** *f* ELECTRON reception frequency; ~ **de recoupement** *f* ENREGISTR crossover frequency; ~ **de récurrence** *f* ELECTRON pulse rate, repetition rate; ~ **de récurrence des impulsions** *f* ELECTRON PRF, pulse repetition frequency, pulse rate; ~ **de référence** *f* TELECOM reference frequency; ~ **relative** *f* INFORMAT, ORDINAT relative frequency; ~ **de répétition** *f* ASTRONOMIE frequency of recurrence; ~ **de répétition des impulsions** *f* ELECTRON, INFORMAT, ORDINAT PRF, pulse repetition frequency, PHYSIQUE pulse repetition frequency, TELECOM PRF, pulse repetition frequency; ~ **de repliement** *f* ELECTRON aliased frequency; ~ **requise** *f* EN RENOUV required frequency; ~ **de réseau** *f* ELECTR *alimentation*, ELECTROTEC current frequency (AmE), mains frequency (BrE); ~ **réservée** *f* TELECOM dedicated frequency; ~ **de résonance** *f* ACOUSTIQUE, ELECTRON, PHYS ONDES resonant frequency, PHYS RAYON resonance frequency, PHYSIQUE, TELECOM resonant frequency; ~ **de**

scintillement f CINEMAT flicker frequency; ~ **du secteur** f ELECTROTEC power frequency; ~ **de seuil** f ELECTRON, PHYS ONDES *d'un électron libre*, PHYSIQUE threshold frequency; ~ **du signal** f ELECTRON signal frequency; ~ **sous-porteuse** f TV subcarrier frequency; ~ **de la sous-porteuse** f TELECOM subcarrier frequency; ~ **spatiale** f ELECTROTEC, PHYSIQUE spatial frequency; ~ **standard** f ENREGISTR standard tone; ~ **subsonique** f PHYS RAYON subsonic frequency; ~ **supersonique** f PHYS RAYON supersonic frequency; ~ **téléphonique** f TELECOM telephone frequency; ~ **temporelle** f ELECTRON time frequency; ~ **de trame** f TV field frequency; ~ **de travail** f CONS MECA, RESSORTS operating frequency; ~ **ultrabasse** f ELECTR *courant alternatif* extremely low frequency; ~ **ultrasonique** f ACOUSTIQUE, PHYS RAYON, PHYSIQUE ultrasonic frequency; ~ **vidéo** f ELECTRON video frequency; ~ **vocale** f ELECTRON VF, voice frequency, ENREGISTR vocal frequency, PHYS RAYON VF, voice frequency, PHYSIQUE vocal frequency, TELECOM VF, vocal frequency, voice frequency

fréquencemètre m ELECTROTEC, TELECOM frequency meter; ~ **à comptage d'impulsions** m ELECTRON frequency counter; ~ **à lames vibrantes** m ELECTROTEC vibrating reed frequency meter

fréquences: ~ **conversationnelles** f pl ACOUSTIQUE conversational frequencies

fret m AERONAUT cargo, NAUT freight, PETROLE freight rate, freight; ~ **aérien** m AERONAUT, EMBALLAGE air freight; ~ **de retour** m NAUT back freight, home freight, return cargo; ~ **sur le vide** m PETROLE dead freight

fréter[1] vt AERONAUT, NAUT charter

fréter[2] vi NAUT freight

frettage m CONS MECA shrinking on, ELECTR *d'un câble* reinforcement, PRODUCTION hooping

frette f CONS MECA collar, *autour d'un manchon* collar, CONSTR band, hoop, MECANIQUE, PRODUCTION hoop; ~ **de pieu** f CONSTR pile ferrule, pile hoop

fretté: ~ **de fer** adj PRODUCTION ironbound

fretter vt CONS MECA band, collar, MECANIQUE hoop

friable adj MATERIAUX brittle, PLAST CAOU friable

friction f PAPIER, PHYSIQUE, PLAST CAOU friction; ~ **de courroie de transmission** f CONS MECA belt friction; ~ **liée à la distribution de la couche** f IMPRIM *papier* metering friction

frictionnel adj CONSTR frictional

frictionneur m PAPIER MG cylinder, machine-glazed cylinder; ~ **sécheur** m PAPIER MG cylinder, machine-glazed cylinder

friedélite f MINERAUX friedelite

frieséite f MINERAUX frieseïte

frigélisation f REFRIG winterization

frigorifier vt REFRIG, THERMODYN refrigerate

frigorifique adj CONS MECA refrigerating, PHYSIQUE freezing, REFRIG frigorific, refrigerating, refrigerated

frigorigène m REFRIG refrigerant; ~ **fluorocarboné** m REFRIG fluorocarbon refrigerant; ~ **hydrocarbure halogéné** m REFRIG halocarbon refrigerant; ~ **primaire** m REFRIG primary refrigerant; ~ **secondaire** m REFRIG secondary refrigerant

frigoriste m THERMODYN refrigerating engineer

fripé m (Bel) CERAM VER washboard

fripées f pl CERAM VER washboard

frisage m PLAST CAOU *peinture* curtaining

friser vt TEXTILE crimp

frisure f CERAM VER chill mark (BrE), chill wrinkle (AmE), ENREGISTR *de la bande* curl, TEXTILE crimp

friteuse f AGRO ALIM deep-fryer

frittage m CERAM VER *de la composition* fritting, sintering, CH DE FER *véhicules* sintering, CHIMIE calcination, calcining, GENIE CHIM, MAT CHAUFF, METALL sintering, PRODUCTION roasting, TELECOM sintering; ~ **en turbulence** m GENIE CHIM fluidized bed sintering; ~ **sous pression** m GENIE CHIM sintering under pressure; ~ **sous vide** m METALL vacuum sintering

fritte f CERAM VER frit; ~ **transparente** f CERAM VER clear frit; ~ **de verre** f CERAM VER glass frit

fritté adj GENIE CHIM, MECANIQUE *matériaux* sintered

fritter[1] vt CHIMIE, GENIE CHIM sinter

fritter:[2] **se** ~ v réfl CHIMIE sinter

froid[1] adj REFRIG cold, THERMODYN cold, cool

froid[2] m REFRIG, THERMODYN cold; ~ **dû à l'évaporation** m THERMODYN latent heat of evaporation; ~ **industriel** m THERMODYN refrigeration

froideur f THERMODYN cold, coolness

froissement m PAPIER crumpling, rumpling

froisser[1] vt PAPIER crumple, rumple

froisser:[2] **se** ~ v réfl TEXTILE crease

frôlure f CERAM VER transit rub

fromage: ~ **à 0 % de matière grasse** m AGRO ALIM skimmed milk cheese; ~ **à 50 % de matière grasse** m AGRO ALIM full-fat cheese; ~ **blanc** m AGRO ALIM curd cheese; ~ **extra-gras** m AGRO ALIM full-fat cheese; ~ **au lait entier** m AGRO ALIM full-fat cheese; ~ **maigre** m AGRO ALIM skimmed milk cheese

froment: ~ **vitreux** m AGRO ALIM durum wheat

froncé adj TEXTILE gathered

froncer vt TEXTILE gather

fronces f pl TEXTILE gathering

fronde f ESPACE *véhicules* slingshot

front:[1] **sur** ~ **de descente** adj PRODUCTION *automatisme industriel* trailing edge; **sur** ~ **de montée** adj PRODUCTION leading-edge

front[2] m CONSTR *d'une colline* brow, ELECTRON leading edge, METEO front, MINES bank, stope face, breast face, face; ~ **d'abattage** m MINES bank, stope face, working face, breast face, face; ~ **anabatique** m METEO anabatic front; ~ **arrière d'impulsion** m TELECOM pulse trailing edge; ~ **d'attaque** m MINES bank, breast face, face, stope face, working face; ~ **d'avancement** m CHARBON advancing face, road head, MINES heading face; ~ **avant d'impulsion** m TELECOM pulse leading edge; ~ **chaud** m METEO warm front; ~ **de choc** m MILITAIRE *d'une explosion* pressure front; ~ **de choc arrière** m AERONAUT tail shock wave; ~ **de dragage** m MINES digging face, dredging face; ~ **froid** m METEO cold front; ~ **katabatique** m METEO katabatic front; ~ **de Mach** m NUCLEAIRE head wave; ~ **non occlus** m METEO nonoccluded front; ~ **occlus** m METEO occluded front; ~ **d'onde** m ACOUSTIQUE, ELECTROTEC, PETR, PHYS ONDES, PHYSIQUE wavefront, TELECOM leading edge; ~ **d'onde de choc** m ASTRONOMIE bow shock; ~ **polaire** m METEO polar front; ~ **récifal** m OCEANO reef front; ~ **de solidification** m MATERIAUX solid-liquid interface; ~ **stationnaire** m METEO stationary front; ~ **de taille** m MINES bank, breast face, stope face, working face, face; ~ **de taille du charbon** m CHARBON coal wall, coalface; ~ **de taille en porte-à-faux** m MINES overhanging face; ~ **de taille en surplomb** m MINES overhanging face

frontal[1] adj ESPACE ahead, *véhicules* head-on, INFOR-

MAT, ORDINAT front-end, TRANSPORT head-on

frontal[2] *m* ORDINAT front-end computer, TELECOM front-end processor

frontière *f* CONSTR boundary; **~ d'une cellule** *f* TELECOM cell boundary; **~ d'une plaque** *f* GEOLOGIE plate boundary; **~ de plaques divergentes** *f* GEOLOGIE divergent plate boundary

frontispice *m* IMPRIM frontispiece

fronto-focomètre *m* INSTRUMENT focimeter, vertex refractionometer

frottement *m* CHARBON, CONS MECA, MECANIQUE friction, PAPIER friction, scuffing, PHYSIQUE, PLAST CAOU, PRODUCTION *système hydraulique*, TEXTILE, TV *du disque de têtes sur la bande* friction; **~ de l'air** *m* ESPACE *véhicules* air friction; **~ au départ** *m* CONS MECA starting friction, static friction; **~ dynamique** *m* PHYSIQUE dynamic friction; **~ intérieur** *m* CONS MECA, MATERIAUX internal friction; **~ interne** *m* CERAM VER, MATERIAUX, METALL internal friction; **~ latéral négatif** *m* CHARBON negative skin friction; **~ par glissement** *m* PHYSIQUE sliding friction; **~ pariétal** *m* PHYSIQUE skin friction; **~ de roulement** *m* PHYSIQUE rolling friction; **~ statique** *m* PHYSIQUE static friction; **~ du train de tiges** *m* PETROLE *forage* drill string drag

frotter *vt* CONSTR *les deux extrémités d'une planche d'échafaudage* bind

frotteur *m* ELECTR *commutateur* collector shoe, ELECTROTEC brush, collector shoe; **~ de pantographe** *m* CH DE FER pantograph slipper

fructosane *m* CHIMIE fructan, fructosan

fructose *m* AGRO ALIM fructose, fruit sugar, laevulose (BrE), levulose (AmE), CHIMIE fructose, fruit sugar

fruit *m* CONSTR *d'un mur* batter; **~ à noyau** *m* AGRO ALIM stone fruit

fruitier *m* NAUT fruit carrier

fruits: **~ à pépins** *m pl* AGRO ALIM pomaceous fruit, pome fruit; **~ rouges** *m pl* AGRO ALIM soft fruit

frusemide *m* CHIMIE frusemide

fuchsine *f* CHIMIE fuchsin, rubin

fuchsite *f* MINERAUX fuchsite

fuchsone *f* CHIMIE fuchsone

fucose *m* CHIMIE fucose

fucostérol *m* CHIMIE fucosterol

fucoxanthine *f* CHIMIE fucoxanthin

fuel *m* PETROLE fuel oil, THERMODYN fuel, heating oil; **~ gaz** *m* GAZ diesel gas; **~ lourd pour soutes** *m* POLLU MER bunker C fuel; **~ résiduel** *m* PETROLE residual fuel oil; **~ de soute** *m* AERONAUT bunker C

fuel-oil *m* PETROLE fuel oil; **~ domestique** *m* PETROLE domestic fuel oil

fuels: **~ de soutes** *m pl* POLLU MER bunker fuels

fugacité *f* CHIMIE *de gaz*, THERMODYN *de gaz* fugacity

fugitive *adj* POLLUTION *émissions* fugitive

fuir *vi* CONSTR leak

fuite:[1] **en ~** *adj* NAUT *par mauvais temps* running before wind

fuite[2] *f* DISTRI EAU leakage, ELECTR *courant, charge* leak, leakage, ELECTROTEC, EN RENOUV leakage, GAZ leak, PHYSIQUE leak, leakage, POLLU MER leakage, SECURITE leak, TELECOM leakage; **~ de l'assemblage combustible** *f* NUCLEAIRE leaking fuel assembly; **~ électrique** *f* ELECTR *condensateur* charge leakage; **~ des galaxies** *f* ASTRONOMIE recession of the galaxies; **~ de gaz** *f* THERMODYN gas leak; **~ par la terre** *f* ELECTROTEC earth leakage (BrE), ground leakage (AmE); **~ de particules** *f* NUCLEAIRE particle leakage;

~ totale intérieure *f* SECURITE *appareils de protection respiratoire* total inward leakage

fuites: **~ de flux** *f pl* ELECTROTEC flux leakage; **~ de fonte** *f pl* PRODUCTION spillings; **~ de la jonction** *f pl* ELECTROTEC junction leakage; **~ magnétiques** *f pl* ELECTROTEC magnetic leakage

fulgurite *f* GEOLOGIE, PRODUCTION fulgurite

fulmicoton *m* MINES guncotton

fulminate *m* CHIMIE fulminate; **~ de mercure** *m* CHIMIE mercury fulminate

fulmination *f* CHIMIE fulmination

fulminer *vi* CHIMIE fulminate

fulminique *adj* CHIMIE fulminic

fulvène *m* CHIMIE fulvene

fumage *m* AGRO ALIM smoking; **~ de poisson** *m* OCEANO fish smoking

fumaison *f* AGRO ALIM smoking

fumarique *adj* CHIMIE *acide* fumaric

fumé: **~ à chaud** *adj* AGRO ALIM hot-smoked; **~ à froid** *adj* AGRO ALIM cold-smoked

fumée *f* CHAUFFAGE smoke, CHIMIE fume, POLLUTION, SECURITE smoke; **~ de convertisseurs** *f* LESSIVES converter gas; **~ normalisée équivalente** *f (FNE)* POLLUTION equivalent standard smoke

fumées *f pl* MATERIAUX fumes, POLLUTION flue gas, fumes, SECURITE fumes; **~ d'usine** *f pl* SECURITE factory fumes

fumerolle *f* GEOLOGIE fumarole

fumidôme *m* GENIE CHIM fume extraction cupola

fumier: **~ humain** *m* RECYCLAGE night soil

fumigation *f* POLLUTION fumigation

fumigène *m* NAUT *de l'étrave* flare

fumivore *adj* CHARBON fumivorous

fumivorité *f* CHARBON consumption of smoke

fune *f* OCEANO dragrope, trawl warp

funiculaire *m* TRANSPORT funicular, funicular railway; **~ fixe à câble** *m* CONS MECA, TRANSPORT cable railway; **~ souterrain** *m* TRANSPORT underground cable railway

furaldéhyde *f* PLAST CAOU *matière première* furfuraldehyde

furanne *m* CHIMIE furon

furfural *m* PLAST CAOU *matière première* furfural

furfurane *m* CHIMIE furon

furfuryle *adj* CHIMIE furfuryl

furile *m* CHIMIE furile

furilique *adj* CHIMIE *acide* furilic

furlong *m* METROLOGIE furlong

furtif *adj* MILITAIRE stealthy

fusé *adj* THERMODYN melted

fuseau: **~ horaire** *m* AERONAUT, NAUT time zone; **~ réacteur** *m* AERONAUT engine nacelle

fusée *f* AUTO spindle, ESPACE rocket, MINES fuse, NAUT rocket, VEHICULES *d'une roue* spindle; **~ air-air à charge atomique** *f* MILITAIRE atomic air-to-air rocket; **~ d'appoint** *f* ESPACE kick rocket; **~ atomique** *f* NUCLEAIRE atomic rocket; **~ à combustion lente** *f* MINES slow match, slow-burning fuse; **~ de déclenchement** *f* MILITAIRE fuse; **~ de détresse** *f* NAUT distress flare, emergency rocket; **~ éclairante** *f* AERONAUT, MILITAIRE flare, NAUT distress flare; **~ éclairante à parachute** *f* NAUT, MILITAIRE parachute flare; **~ d'essieu** *f* VEHICULES steering knuckle; **~ à fumée** *f* CINEMAT smoke candle; **~ de mise en rotation** *f* ESPACE spin rocket, spin thruster; **~ multiétage** *f* ESPACE *véhicules* multistage rocket; **~ orbitale** *f* ES-

PACE *véhicules* orbital rocket; ~ **de pale** *f* AERONAUT blade spindle; ~ **percutante** *f* MILITAIRE, MINES percussion fuse; ~ **de pilotage** *f* ESPACE *véhicules* control rocket; ~ **à poudre** *f* ESPACE *véhicules* solid propellant rocket; ~ **à propergol liquide** *f* ESPACE liquid propellant rocket, THERMODYN liquid fuel rocket; ~ **de séparation** *f* ESPACE *véhicules* separation rocket; ~ **de signaux** *f* MILITAIRE rocket signal; ~ **spatiale** *f* ASTRONOMIE space rocket; ~ **de sûreté** *f* MINES common fuse, ordinary fuse

fusée-détonateur: ~ **à fusion rapide** *f* MILITAIRE quickacting fuse

fusée-sonde *f* ESPACE, MILITAIRE sounding rocket

fuselage *m* TRANSPORT fuselage

fuselé *adj* AERONAUT streamlined

fuser[1] *vt* THERMODYN melt

fuser[2] *vi* CHIMIE crackle

fusible[1] *adj* MATERIAUX fusible, meltable, THERMODYN fusible, meltable

fusible[2] *m* ELECTR *circuit*, ELECTROTEC fuse, INST HYDR safety plug, TV fuse; ~ **à action retardée** *m* ELECTROTEC slow-blow fuse, PRODUCTION slow-acting fuse; ~ **d'alimentation** *m* PRODUCTION power supply input fuse; ~ **à cartouche** *m* ELECTR, ELECTROTEC cartridge fuse; ~ **d'éclatement sur roue de train** *m* AERONAUT *d'un bouchon fusible* landing gear wheel rim fusible plug; ~ **enfermé** *m* ELECTROTEC enclosed fuse; ~ **à expulsion** *m* ELECTR expulsion fuse; ~ **fondu** *m* ELECTROTEC blown fuse; ~ **à fusion lente** *m* CINEMAT, PRODUCTION slow-blow fuse; ~ **de liaison** *m* ELECTROTEC link fuse; ~ **limiteur de courant** *m* ELECTR current-limiting fuse link; ~ **non protégé** *m* ELECTR open fuse; ~ **non renouvable** *m* ELECTR nonrenewable fuse; ~ **parafoudre** *m* NAUT lightning arrester; ~ **principal d'alimentation** *m* PRODUCTION *électricité* input power fuse; ~ **de protection** *m* PRODUCTION *électricité* control fuse; ~ **retardé** *m* ELECTROTEC slow-blow fuse; ~ **sauté** *m* ELECTROTEC blown fuse; ~ **sec contre le retour de flamme** *m* SECURITE flashback preventer; ~ **sec contre le retour de gaz** *m* SECURITE gas return safety device; ~ **de signalisation** *m* ELECTR alarm fuse; ~ **temporisé** *m* ELECTROTEC delayed-action fuse; ~ **tubulaire** *m* ELECTR enclosed fuse

fusil *m* AGRO ALIM sharpening steel, MILITAIRE rifle; ~ **à aiguiser** *m* AGRO ALIM sharpening steel; ~ **d'assaut** *m*

MILITAIRE assault rifle; ~ **à canon rayé** *m* MILITAIRE rifled gun; ~ **non rayé** *m* MILITAIRE smoothbore gun

fusion:[1] **en** ~ *adj* METEO melting, THERMODYN molten

fusion[2] *f* CHIMIE, GAZ fusion, INFORMAT merge, MATERIAUX melting, smelting, *métallurgie* fusion, NUCLEAIRE meltdown, ORDINAT merge, merging, PAPIER melting, PHYSIQUE fusion, melting, PLAST CAOU *opération* fusion, PRODUCTION melting, REFRIG *du plateau de glace* de-icing, TEXTILE melting, THERMODYN fusing, fusion, liquefaction, melting; ~ **capillaire** *f* NUCLEAIRE capillary fusion; ~ **électrique** *f* ELECTROTEC electric smelting; ~ **en zones** *f* METALL zone melting; ~ **à haute énergie** *f* NUCLEAIRE high-energy fusion; ~ **d'ions lourds** *f* NUCLEAIRE heavy-ion fusion; ~ **au laser** *f* ELECTRON laser melting; ~ **nucléaire** *f* ASTRONOMIE, PHYS PART, PHYSIQUE nuclear fusion; ~ **par faisceau d'électrons** *f* NUCLEAIRE electron beam melting; ~ **par laser** *f* NUCLEAIRE laser fusion, laser-driven fusion; ~ **sous vide** *f* METALL vacuum melting; ~ **de zone** *f* NUCLEAIRE zone melting; ~ **de zone sans creuset** *f* NUCLEAIRE floating zone melting method

fusionnement *m* CHIMIE fusion

fusionner[1] *vti* INFORMAT, ORDINAT merge

fusionner:[2] **se** ~ *v réfl* CHIMIE coalesce

fusion-réduction *f* CHARBON smelting

fût:[1] **en** ~ *adj* AGRO ALIM drawn from the wood

fût[2] *m* AGRO ALIM barrel, CHARBON drum, CONS MECA *d'un rabot* stock, CONSTR post, *d'une grue* jib post, *d'une colonne* shaft, *d'un rivet* shank, EMBALLAGE, MECANIQUE drum, NUCLEAIRE *déchets radioactifs* waste drum, PLAST CAOU *récipient*, POLLU MER, PRODUCTION *système hydraulique* drum, TRANSPORT barrel; ~ **allégé** *m* NUCLEAIRE *en contre-plaqué* fiber drum (AmE), fibre drum (BrE); ~ **de l'atterrisseur** *m* AERONAUT landing gear leg; ~ **de canon** *m* MILITAIRE gun barrel; ~ **contre-plaqué** *m* EMBALLAGE fiber drum (AmE), fibre drum (BrE); ~ **de cylindre** *m* CONS MECA cylinder barrel; ~ **en contre-plaqué** *m* EMBALLAGE plywood drum; ~ **de fusil** *m* MILITAIRE rifle butt, rifle stock; ~ **d'huile** *m* MECANIQUE drum; ~ **métallique** *m* EMBALLAGE metal drum; ~ **de rabot** *m* CONSTR plane stock

fût-pylône *m* CONSTR trellis post

G

G *abrév (giga-)* METROLOGIE G *(giga-)*

Ga *(gallium)* CHIMIE Ga *(gallium)*

gabare *f* NAUT lighter, *voilée* barge, TRANSPORT barge, dumb barge

gabariage *m* METROLOGIE gaging (AmE), gauging (BrE), NAUT molding (AmE), moulding (BrE)

gabarier *vt* PRODUCTION *plaque métallique* gage (AmE), gauge (BrE)

gabarit *m* CH DE FER gage (AmE), gauge (BrE), CONS MECA gage (AmE), gauge (BrE), jig, template, templet, ELECTR template, templet, *mesure, fabrication* gage (AmE), gauge (BrE), INFORMAT, MECANIQUE template, NAUT mold (AmE), mould (BrE), template, ORDINAT template, PRODUCTION former, patron, pattern, strickle, sweep, template, templet, SECURITE *détoureuse* jig, TEXTILE template, templet, VEHICULES *outil* gage (AmE), gauge (BrE), template, templet; ~ de charge *m* CH DE FER *véhicules* loading gage (AmE), loading gauge (BrE); ~ cinématique *m* CH DE FER *véhicules* kinematic gage (AmE), kinematic gauge (BrE); ~ à cire *m* PAPIER casting template; ~ de collage *m* CINEMAT splicing block; ~ d'écartement *m* CH DE FER rail gage (AmE), rail gauge (BrE); ~ d'écartement de voie *m* CH DE FER rail gage (AmE), rail gauge (BrE); ~ d'estimation *m* CERAM VER test plate; ~ de filtrage *m* ELECTRON attenuation contour, ESPACE *communications* filter jig, filter mask, filter template; ~ de filtre *m* ELECTRON attenuation contour, ESPACE *communications* filter template; ~ de fluctuation des charges *m* ESPACE *véhicules* load fluctuation pattern; ~ de fraisage *m* CONS MECA milling jig; ~ d'indice de réfraction à quatre cercles concentriques *m* OPTIQUE four-concentric-circle refractive index template, TELECOM four-concentric circle refractive index template; ~ d'installation *m* PRODUCTION back panel layout; ~ d'installation de l'automate *m* PRODUCTION *automatisme industriel* controller layout; ~ de Mercator *m* OCEANO Mercator plotting chart; ~ de montage *m* CONS MECA assembly jig; ~ de perçage *m* CONS MECA drilling jig; ~ à quatre cercles concentriques en champ proche *m* OPTIQUE, TELECOM four-concentric-circle near-field template; ~ type *m* CONS MECA standard gage (AmE), standard gauge (BrE); ~ de vérification *m* CONS MECA inspection gage (AmE), inspection gauge (BrE)

gabion *m* CONSTR gabion

gâche *f* CONSTR box, box staple, keeper, lock staple, nosing, staple, striking plate, IMPRIM waste sheets

gâchée *f* PRODUCTION batch

gâcher *vt* CONSTR *mortier* mix

gâchette *f* CONS MECA trigger, ELECTROTEC gate, MILITAIRE *d'une arme à feu*, PHOTO trigger, PHYSIQUE gate; ~ de déclenchement *f* PHOTO shutter release

gâchis *m* CONSTR mortar; ~ à centrale *m* CONSTR batch mix

gadolinite *f* MINERAUX gadolinite

gadolinium *m (Gd)* CHIMIE gadolinium *(Gd)*

gaffe *f* NAUT gaff, *pêche* boat hook

gage *m* CH DE FER single line token

gagner *vt* IMPRIM close up, NAUT *au vent* fetch

gaïac *m* NAUT lignum vitae

gaïacol *m* CHIMIE guaiacol

gaïaconique *adj* CHIMIE guaiaconic

gaïarétique *adj* CHIMIE guaiaretic

gaillard: ~ arrière *m* NAUT afterdeck; ~ d'avant *m* NAUT forecastle

gaillet *m* AGRO ALIM lady's bedstraw; ~ jaune *m* AGRO ALIM lady's bedstraw; ~ vrai *m* AGRO ALIM lady's bedstraw

gailleterie *f* CHARBON cob coal, cobbles

gaillette *f* CHARBON cob coal, cobbles

gain *m* ELECTR *signal*, ELECTRON, ENREGISTR, INFORMAT, NAUT, ORDINAT, TELECOM, TV gain; ~ d'un amplificateur *m* ELECTRON, PHYSIQUE amplifier gain; ~ d'antenne *m* ESPACE *communications* antenna gain, PHYSIQUE, TV aerial gain; ~ d'avalanche *m* ELECTRON avalanche gain; ~ de la boucle *m* ELECTRON loop gain; ~ de concentration *m* TELECOM IG, interpolation gain; ~ de conversion *m* ELECTRON conversion gain; ~ différentiel *m* ELECTRON, TV differential gain; ~ de l'EMCN *m* TELECOM DCME gain; ~ en boucle fermée *m* ELECTRON closed-loop gain; ~ en courant *m* ELECTRON, PHYSIQUE current gain; ~ en courant continu *m* ELECTRON DC current gain; ~ en mode commun *m* ELECTRON common mode gain; ~ en puissance *m* ELECTRON, ENREGISTR, PHYSIQUE power gain; ~ en puissance disponible *m* ENREGISTR available power gain; ~ en puissance du transistor *m* ENREGISTR transistor power gain; ~ en tension du changeur de fréquence *m* ELECTROTEC conversion voltage gain; ~ de l'équipement de multiplication de circuit numérique *m (GMCN)* TELECOM digital circuit multiplication gain *(DCMG)*; ~ de l'étage d'entrée *m* ELECTRON input stage gain; ~ d'insertion *m* PHYSIQUE insertion gain; ~ d'intégration *m* ELECTRON integration gain; ~ interne *m* ELECTRON internal gain; ~ inverse *m* ELECTRON inverse gain; ~ isotrope *m* ESPACE *communications* absolute gain, isotropic gain; ~ maximal d'un circuit *m* ELECTRON singing point; ~ à mi-bande *m* ELECTRON midband gain; ~ au minimum du bruit *m* ELECTRON associated gain; ~ d'obstacle *m* ELECTRON obstacle gain; ~ optique *m* ELECTRON optical gain; ~ de photoconduction *m* ELECTRON photoconductive gain; ~ du récepteur *m* ELECTRON receiver gain; ~ relatif de déviation angulaire *m* ACOUSTIQUE relative angular deviation gain; ~ de tension *m* ELECTROTEC voltage gain; ~ de transcodage *m* TELECOM TG, transcoding gain; ~ de transmission *m* ACOUSTIQUE transmission gain; ~ d'unité *m* ELECTRON unity gain

gainage *m* ESPACE *véhicules* cladding, OPTIQUE buffering, fiber buffer (AmE), fibre buffer (BrE), PHOTO *d'un appareil photographique* covering, TV *de câble* screening; ~ lâche *m* OPTIQUE loose buffer, loose buffering; ~ serré *m* OPTIQUE tight buffer, tight buffering

gaine *f* ELECTR *câble* jacket (AmE), sheath (BrE), MECANIQUE casing, sheath, OPTIQUE cladding, fiber cladding (AmE), fibre cladding (BrE), PHYSIQUE jacket, PRODUCTION guard, sheath, sleeve, REFRIG duct, SECURITE cover, guard, TELECOM cladding; ~ **adaptée** *f* TELECOM matched cladding; ~ **à ailettes** *f* NUCLEAIRE finned can; ~ **d'air** *f* REFRIG air duct; ~ **de dégivrage** *f* AERONAUT de-icing duct; ~ **déprimée** *f* TELECOM depressed cladding; ~ **en alumine** *f* NUCLEAIRE aluminium can (BrE), aluminum can (AmE); ~ **en caoutchouc aux silicones** *f* ELECTROTEC silicone cladding; ~ **en plastique** *f* ELECTROTEC plastic cladding; ~ **en plastique thermorétractable** *f* PRODUCTION shrink tubing; ~ **en PVC** *f* ELECTROTEC PVC sheath; ~ **en verre** *f* ELECTROTEC glass cladding; ~ **en zircalloy** *f* NUCLEAIRE zircaloy cladding; ~ **époxy** *f* TELECOM epoxy buffer; ~ **d'étirage** *f* CERAM VER drawing tower; ~ **extérieure** *f* ELECTROTEC sheath; ~ **externe** *f* ELECTR *câble* overSheath; ~ **de fibre optique** *f* TELECOM fiberoptic cladding (AmE), fibreoptic cladding (BrE); ~ **homogène** *f* TELECOM homogeneous cladding; ~ **isolante** *f* ELECTROTEC insulating sheath, PRODUCTION insulating sleeve; ~ **de latte** *f* NAUT batten pocket; ~ **métallique** *f* ELECTR *d'un câble* metallic sheath, ELECTROTEC metal sheath; ~ **métallique souple** *f* CONS MECA flexible metal conduit; ~ **optique** *f* OPTIQUE cladding, fiber cladding (AmE), fibre cladding (BrE), PHYSIQUE cladding; ~ **optique compensée** *f* OPTIQUE matched cladding; ~ **optique déprimée** *f* OPTIQUE depressed cladding; ~ **optique homogène** *f* OPTIQUE homogeneous cladding; ~ **de parachute de queue** *f* AERONAUT drag chute cover; ~ **de PCV** *f* PRODUCTION PVC sleeve; ~ **de plomb** *f* ELECTR *câble*, ELECTROTEC lead sheath; ~ **pour bouteille** *f* EMBALLAGE bottle jacket; ~ **protectrice contre les accidents** *f* CONS MECA case, casing, cover, guard; ~ **rétrécissable par la chaleur** *f* REVETEMENT heat-shrinkable sleeve; ~ **de soufflet** *f* PHOTO bellows covering; ~ **thermorétractable** *f* PRODUCTION shrink tubing, REVETEMENT heat-shrinkable sleeve

gainerie *f* PHOTO *d'un appareil photographique* covering

gaines: ~ **souples** *f pl* CONSTR flexible ducting

galactique *adj* ASTRONOMIE galactic

galactomètre *m* AGRO ALIM lactometer

galactonique *adj* CHIMIE *acide* galactonic

galactosamine *f* CHIMIE galactosamine

galactose *m* AGRO ALIM galactose

galaxie *f* ASTRONOMIE galaxy; ~ **active** *f* ASTRONOMIE active galaxy; ~ **d'Andromède** *f* ASTRONOMIE Andromeda galaxy; ~ **annuaire** *f* ASTRONOMIE ring galaxy; ~ **des Chiens de Chasse** *f* ASTRONOMIE Whirlpool galaxy; ~ **à disque** *f* ASTRONOMIE disc galaxy (BrE), disk galaxy (AmE); ~ **double** *f* ASTRONOMIE double galaxy; ~ **elliptique** *f* ASTRONOMIE elliptical galaxy; ~ **à flambée** *f* ASTRONOMIE starburst galaxy; ~ **naine** *f* ASTRONOMIE dwarf galaxy; ~ **quasi-stellaire** *f* ESPACE QSG, quasi-stellar galaxy; ~ **spirale** *f* ASTRONOMIE spiral galaxy

galaxies: ~ **irrégulières** *f pl* ASTRONOMIE irregular galaxies; ~ **de Seyfert** *f pl* ASTRONOMIE Seyfert galaxies; ~ **spirales barrées** *f pl* ASTRONOMIE barred spiral galaxies

galbe *m* CERAM VER principal curvature

galber *vt* PRODUCTION curve

galbord *m* NAUT garboard

galée *f* IMPRIM galley

galène *f* CHIMIE galena, MINERAUX galena, galenite

galénobismuthite *f* MINERAUX galenobismuthite, galenobismutite

galerie *f* AERONAUT *conditionnement d'air* manifold, MINES drift, drive, tunnel, level, passageway, roadway; ~ **d'accès** *f* CONSTR *tunnel, barrage* mine access, NUCLEAIRE catwalk, gallery, gangway; ~ **d'aérage** *f* MINES airhead, airheading, airway, ventilation drive; ~ **d'allongement** *f* MINES drift, level, strike drive, drifting level, driving level, drivage, drive, level running along the strike; ~ **d'assèchement** *f* DISTRI EAU water adit, MINES drainage level; ~ **d'avancement** *f* CONS MECA heading, MINES head; ~ **à boisage jointif** *f* MINES close-timbered level; ~ **à boisage serré** *f* MINES close-timbered level; ~ **au charbon** *f* CHARBON coal road; ~ **de chassage** *f* MINES drifting level, driving level, drivage, drive, level running along the strike; ~ **chassante** *f* MINES drift, level, strike drive, drifting level, driving level, drivage, drive, level running along the strike; ~ **de circulation** *f* MINES manway; ~ **costresse** *f* MINES counter, counter gangway, counter level, subdrift; ~ **de décharge** *f* HYDROLOGIE *barrage* tailrace tunnel; ~ **de dérivation** *f* HYDROLOGIE diversion tunnel; ~ **de desserte** *f* MINES stall road; ~ **desservant la taille** *f* CHARBON gate road, MINES stall road; ~ **de direction** *f* MINES drift, level, strike drive, drifting level, driving level, drivage, drive, level running along the strike; ~ **de drainage** *f* DISTRI EAU water adit, HYDROLOGIE *tunnel* drainage gallery, MINES drainage level; ~ **d'écoulement** *f* DISTRI EAU deep adit, water adit, MINES drainage level, offset, offtake; ~ **en couche** *f* MINES level in the seam; ~ **en cul-de-sac** *f* MINES blind level, dumb drift; ~ **en direction** *f* MINES drift, level, strike drive, drifting level, driving level, drivage, drive, lateral, level running along the strike; ~ **en pression** *f* EN RENOUV *hydro-électricité* pressure tunnel; ~ **d'évacuation** *f* HYDROLOGIE *barrage* tailrace tunnel; ~ **d'évacuation d'air** *f* MINES return airway; ~ **d'évacuation d'eau** *f* MINES offset, offtake; ~ **filtrante** *f* DISTRI EAU filter gallery, infiltration gallery; ~ **à flanc de coteau** *f* CHARBON, MINES adit; ~ **de fond** *f* MINES bottom level; ~ **latérale** *f* MINES side entry; ~ **maîtresse** *f* CHARBON entry, MINES mainway; ~ **de mine** *f* MINES mine level; ~ **de niveau** *f* MINES level; ~ **de niveau de mine** *f* MINES mine level; ~ **de niveau débouchant au jour** *f* MINES day drift, day level; ~ **principale** *f* CHARBON entry, main roadway, gangway, MINES level road, mainway; ~ **de prospection** *f* MINES prospecting level; ~ **de recherches** *f* MINES drift, exploration drive, exploration level, prospecting level; ~ **de recuisson** *f* CERAM VER annealing lehr; ~ **de retour d'air** *f* MINES return airway; ~ **au rocher** *f* CHARBON metal drift, stone drift, MINES crosscut, rock drift, gallery in dead ground, stone drift; ~ **de roulage** *f* MINES haulage way; ~ **de taille** *f* MINES lode drive, reef drive; ~ **de toit** *f* VEHICULES *carrosserie* roof rack; ~ **de traçage** *f* MINES development heading, tunneling (AmE), tunnelling (BrE), forewinning heading; ~ **transversale** *f* MINES crossheading; ~ **de ventilateur** *f* MINES fan drift

galeries: ~ **jumelles doubles** *f pl* MINES double entries

galet *m* CINEMAT roller, CONS MECA follower, guide, guide pulley, idler, leading-on pulley, runner, wheel, CONSTR boulder, shingle, GEOLOGIE cobble, IMPRIM puck, MECANIQUE *roulette* roller, PETR pebble, PRODUCTION friction roller, TRANSPORT roller; ~ **à bille** *m* PRODUCTION ball bearing roller; ~ **de calibrage** *m*

CERAM VER calipers (AmE), callipers (BrE), roller gage (AmE), roller gauge (BrE); ~ **de came** *m* CONS MECA *roulement à aiguille* track roller; ~ **décalé** *m* PRODUCTION *automatisme industriel* offset roller; ~ **à deux joues** *m* PRODUCTION *pour chariot de pont roulant* double-flanged traveling wheel (AmE), double-flanged travelling wheel (BrE); ~ **d'entraînement de la bande** *m* ENREGISTR, TV tape roller; ~ **fou** *m* CINEMAT idler; ~ **de friction** *m* PRODUCTION friction roller; ~ **de guidage de la bande** *m* TV tape alignment guide; ~ **guide** *m* CINEMAT drag roller, guide roller, CONS MECA guide, guide pulley, idler, leading-on pulley, runner, ENREGISTR ribbon guide, PRODUCTION belt idler, TV ribbon guide; ~ **à une joue** *m* CONS MECA single-flanged traveling wheel (AmE), single-flanged travelling wheel (BrE); ~ **libre** *m* CINEMAT idler, TV idle roller, idler; ~ **mécanique** *m* CONS MECA wheel; ~ **orienté vers l'arrière** *m* PRODUCTION rear-facing roller; ~ **orienté vers l'avant** *m* PRODUCTION front-facing roller; ~ **du passage papier** *m* IMPRIM *rotatives* lead roll; ~ **pivotant** *m* PRODUCTION caster; ~ **plein** *m* CONS MECA flat running wheel, plain traveling wheel (AmE), plain travelling wheel (BrE); ~ **presseur** *m* ACOUSTIQUE pressure roller, CINEMAT pad roller, pressure roller, pinch roller, CONS MECA, ENREGISTR pressure roller; ~ **de renvoi** *m* CONS MECA guide, guide pulley, idler, leading-on pulley, runner, PRODUCTION belt idler; ~ **de roulement** *m* CONS MECA runner, running wheel, *chariot de pont roulant* rail wheel, PRODUCTION traveling wheel (AmE), travelling wheel (BrE); ~ **suiveur** *m* AERONAUT, CONS MECA cam follower; ~ **tendeur** *m* CINEMAT tension roller, CONS MECA binding pulley, idler, jockey, jockeyroller, jockey wheel, tension pulley, tension roller, tightening pulley, MECANIQUE idler, PRODUCTION belt idler; ~ **de tension** *m* MECANIQUE jockey pulley; ~ **unidirectionnel** *m* PRODUCTION *automatisme industriel* one-way roller; ~ **usiné** *m* CONS MECA machined circular plate

galets *m pl* NAUT shingle; ~ **à boudins** *m pl* CONS MECA wheel flange rollers; ~ **d'entraînement** *m pl* IMPRIM pull-in wheel, trolley

galette *f* CINEMAT roll, CONS MECA plate, ELECTR pancake coil, ELECTROTEC *de commutateur* wafer, ESSAIS pancake coil, INFORMAT wafer; ~ **élémentaire** *f* ELECTROTEC pie section; ~ **de microcanaux** *f* ELECTRON microchannel plate; ~ **de papier** *f* PAPIER coil

galhauban *m* NAUT backstay, main shroud

gallate *m* CHIMIE gallate

galle *f* CERAM VER gall

galléine *f* CHIMIE gallein

gallique *adj* CHIMIE *acide* gallic

gallium *m* (*Ga*) CHIMIE gallium (*Ga*)

gallon *m* METROLOGIE, PETR gallon; ~ **à anse** *m* CERAM VER gallon jug

galoche *f* CONS MECA return block, NAUT cheek block, PRODUCTION bearer bracket, bearer cradle; ~ **d'avant** *f* NAUT bow chock

galopin: ~ **de tension** *m* CONS MECA jockey pulley

galvanique *adj* CHIMIE, ELECTR *métaux, pile* galvanic

galvanisation *f* CHIMIE zincking, ELECTR *procédé* electroplating, MATERIAUX galvanizing, PRODUCTION galvanization, REVETEMENT zinc coating; ~ **à chaud** *f* REVETEMENT hot-dip galvanizing

galvanisé *adj* ELECTR *procédé* electroplated, MECANIQUE *matériaux* galvanized, REVETEMENT electroplated, zinc-coated

galvaniser *vt* CONSTR zinc, ELECTR electroplate, PRODUCTION galvanize

galvano *m* REVETEMENT electroplate

galvanomètre *m* CINEMAT, ELECTR, ELECTROTEC, EQUIP LAB, PETR, PHYSIQUE galvanometer; ~ **à aiguille mobile** *m* ELECTR moving magnet galvanometer, needle galvanometer; ~ **à aimant mobile** *m* ELECTROTEC moving magnet galvanometer, tangent galvanometer; ~ **astatique** *m* ELECTROTEC, PHYSIQUE astatic galvanometer; ~ **balistique** *m* ELECTR, PHYSIQUE ballistic galvanometer; ~ **à cadre** *m* ELECTROTEC loop galvanometer; ~ **à cadre mobile** *m* ELECTR, ELECTROTEC, PHYSIQUE moving coil galvanometer; ~ **à corde** *m* ELECTR loop galvanometer, torsion-string galvanometer; ~ **de Desprez et d'Arsonval** *m* ELECTROTEC d'Arsonval galvanometer; ~ **différentiel** *m* ELECTR, ELECTROTEC differential galvanometer; ~ **Einthoven** *m* ELECTR Einthoven galvanometer, torsion-string galvanometer; ~ **enregistreur** *m* GEOPHYS galvanometer; ~ **à faisceau de lumière** *m* PHYS RAYON light beam galvanometer; ~ **de Helmholtz** *m* ELECTR Helmholtz galvanometer; ~ **à index lumineux** *m* ELECTR light spot galvanometer; ~ **magnéto-électrique** *m* ELECTROTEC moving coil galvanometer; ~ **à miroir** *m* ELECTR mirror galvanometer, reflecting mirror galvanometer; ~ **de résonance** *m* PHYSIQUE vibration galvanometer; ~ **du sinus** *m* ELECTR, PHYSIQUE sine galvanometer; ~ **à spot lumineux** *m* ELECTR light spot galvanometer; ~ **à la tangente** *m* ELECTR tangent galvanometer; ~ **à vibrations** *m* ELECTR, PHYSIQUE vibration galvanometer

galvanoplastie *f* ELECTROTEC electrodeposition, electroplating, IMPRIM galvanics, PRODUCTION galvanoplastics, REVETEMENT electroplating, galvanoplastics; ~ **au tampon** *f* REVETEMENT brush plating

gambir *m* CHIMIE gambier

gamelle *f* MINES pan

gamma *m* CINEMAT, PETR, TV gamma

gammagraphie *f* PHYS RAYON gamma radiography

gamme *f* ACOUSTIQUE gamut, *de fréquences* scale, ELECTRON, INFORMAT, ORDINAT, TV range; ~ **d'Aristoxène-Zarlin** *f* ACOUSTIQUE Aristoxene-Zarlin scale; ~ **des avances** *f* CONS MECA feed range; ~ **de capteurs** *f* CONS MECA range of transducers; ~ **chromatique** *f* ACOUSTIQUE chromatic scale; ~ **défective** *f* ACOUSTIQUE defective scale; ~ **de Delezenne** *f* ACOUSTIQUE Delezenne scale; ~ **de la demi-vie** *f* PHYS RAYON range of half life; ~ **dynamique** *f* PHYS RAYON dynamic range; ~ **d'énergie** *f* PHYS RAYON *des particules émises* energy range; ~ **d'épreuves progressives** *f* IMPRIM progressive; ~ **de fabrication** *f* PRODUCTION route sheet, *un ensemble d'opérations* routing; ~ **des focales** *f* CINEMAT focal range, zoom range; ~ **de fréquences** *f* ELECTR *courant alternatif*, ENREGISTR, TV frequency range; ~ **de fréquences acoustiques** *f* ENREGISTR audio band; ~ **des fréquences audibles** *f* PHYS RAYON audio frequency range; ~ **de fréquences couvertes** *f* ELECTRON frequency coverage; ~ **de gris** *f* CINEMAT gray scale (AmE), grey scale (BrE), neutral test card, PHOTO, TV gray scale (AmE), grey scale (BrE); ~ **heptatonique** *f* ACOUSTIQUE heptatonic scale; ~ **hexatonique** *f* ACOUSTIQUE hexatonic scale; ~ **des lumières** *f* CINEMAT printer scale; ~ **majeure** *f* ACOUSTIQUE major scale; ~ **de Mercator-Holder** *f* ACOUSTIQUE Mercator-Holder scale; ~ **mineure dite harmonique** *f* ACOUSTIQUE harmonic minor scale; ~ **mineure réelle** *f*

ACOUSTIQUE real minor scale; ~ **d'ondes** *f* NAUT, PHYS RAYON waveband; ~ **opératoire** *f* PRODUCTION route sheet, routing; ~ **pantonale** *f* ACOUSTIQUE pantonal scale; ~ **pentatonique** *f* ACOUSTIQUE pentatonic scale; ~ **de poids** *f* PAPIER weight range; ~ **préheptatonique** *f* ACOUSTIQUE preheptatonic scale; ~ **de produits** *f* PRODUCTION product range; ~ **de Pythagore** *f* ACOUSTIQUE Pythagorean scale; ~ **de Rameau-Bach** *f* ACOUSTIQUE Rameau-Bach scale, major scale of equal temperament; ~ **de réception** *f* TV receiving range; ~ **de remplacement** *f* PRODUCTION alternate routing; ~ **de retouche** *f* PRODUCTION rework routing; ~ **à tempérament égal** *f* ACOUSTIQUE major scale of equal temperament; ~ **tempérée** *f* ACOUSTIQUE major scale of equal temperament; ~ **de temporisation** *f* PRODUCTION *automatisme industriel* timing range; ~ **de traitement de thermique** *f* RESSORTS heat treatment range; ~ **de vitesses** *f* CONS MECA range of speeds, set of speeds

gammes: ~ **de réglage** *f pl* PHYS RAYON *des teintures laser* tuning ranges

gammexane *m* CHIMIE gammexane

gangue: ~ **stérile** *f* CHARBON barren gangue, dirt

ganse *f* NAUT becket

gants: ~ **calorifuges** *m pl* SECURITE heat-resistant gloves; ~ **à crispin en cuir** *m pl* SECURITE leather gauntlets; ~ **isolants** *m pl* SECURITE insulating gloves; ~ **pour l'industrie** *m pl* SECURITE industrial gloves; ~ **protecteurs antiacides** *m pl* SECURITE acid-proof protective gloves; ~ **de protection** *m pl* SECURITE protective gloves; ~ **de protection antichaleur** *m pl* EQUIP LAB *sécurité* heat-resistant gloves; ~ **thermoisolants** *m pl* SECURITE oven gloves; ~ **de travail** *m pl* SECURITE working gloves; ~ **de travail résistants à l'huile** *m pl* SECURITE oilproof protective gloves

gap *m* PHYSIQUE gap

garage *m* CH DE FER stabling

garant *m* CONS MECA *d'un palan* running end; ~ **de bossoir** *m* NAUT boat fall, boat tackle, davit fall

garantie *f* PRODUCTION warranty; ~ **de qualité** *f* EMBALLAGE quality guarantee

garantir *vt* PRODUCTION warrant

garcette: ~ **de ris** *f* NAUT reefing pennant

garde:[1] **en** ~ *adv* TELECOM on hold

garde[2] *f* AERONAUT *d'hélice, d'aile* clearance, CONS MECA clearance, guard, CONSTR *d'une serrure* ward, SECURITE guard; ~ **de côtes** *f* NAUT coastguard; ~ **de déclenche** *f* SECURITE trip guard; ~ **d'embrayage** *f* AUTO clutch clearance; ~ **montante** *f* NAUT spring; ~ **de pare-chocs** *f* VEHICULES *carrosserie* overrider; ~ **à la pédale d'embrayage** *f* AUTO clutch pedal clearance; ~ **du sillon** *f* ACOUSTIQUE groove guard; ~ **au sol** *f* AUTO road clearance, VEHICULES *carrosserie* ground clearance, road clearance

garde-boue *m* VEHICULES *carrosserie* fender (AmE), mudguard (BrE), wing (BrE)

garde-chaîne *m* VEHICULES *transmission, motocyclette* chain guard

garde-corps *m* CONSTR balustrade, rail, railing, guardrail, hand railing, handrail, MECANIQUE handrail, NAUT guardrail, *accastillage de pont* lifeline, SECURITE guardrail

garde-feu *f* THERMODYN fireguard

garde-fou *m* CONSTR guardrail, hand railing, handrail, railing, SECURITE guardrail

garde-pêche *m* NAUT fishery protection vessel

garder:[1] ~ **en attente** *vt* TV *magnétoscope* park

garder:[2] ~ **au frais** *loc* EMBALLAGE keep cool

gardes: ~ **de machine** *f pl* SECURITE machine guard

Gardes *m pl* ASTRONOMIE Pointers

gardien: ~ **d'écluse** *m* NAUT lock keeper; ~ **de phare** *m* NAUT lighthouse keeper

gare *f* TRANSPORT railroad station (AmE), railway station (BrE), station; ~ **d'aéroglisseur** *f* NAUT hoverport; ~ **d'attache** *f* CH DE FER home station; ~ **de bifurcation** *f* CH DE FER junction station; ~ **centre** *f* CH DE FER railhead; ~ **centre d'informations** *f* CH DE FER passenger information center (AmE), passenger information centre (BrE); ~ **commutable** *f* CH DE FER traction supply-voltage changeover station; ~ **de contact entre lignes d'écartement différent** *f* CH DE FER change-of-gage station (AmE), change-of-gauge station (BrE); ~ **à conteneurs** *f* TRANSPORT container station; ~ **directe** *f* TRANSPORT through station; ~ **d'embranchement** *f* CH DE FER junction station; ~ **en cul-de-sac** *f* TRANSPORT dead end station, terminal station; ~ **de fret** *f* TRANSPORT cargo terminal; ~ **kangourou** *f* TRANSPORT railroad freight terminal (AmE), railway freight terminal (BrE); ~ **de marchandises** *f* EMBALLAGE freight terminal, TRANSPORT freight depot, freight station (AmE), goods station (BrE); ~ **maritime** *f* NAUT harbor station (AmE), harbour station (BrE), TRANSPORT maritime terminal; ~ **de messagerie** *f* TRANSPORT parcels depot; ~ **racleur** *f* PETR launching trap, receiving trap; ~ **tête de ligne** *f* TRANSPORT railroad terminus (AmE), railway terminus (BrE); ~ **de triage** *f* CH DE FER marshalling yard (BrE), switching yard (AmE), TRANSPORT shunting yard

garer *vt* CH DE FER shunt, *véhicules* stable

gargouille *f* MINES curb ring, garland curb, water ring

garni: ~ **de caoutchouc** *adj* REVETEMENT rubber-lined

garniérite *f* MINERAUX garnierite

garnir *vt* IMPRIM *texte* fill, MECANIQUE *de graisse* pack, PRODUCTION jacket, line, *palier* daub; ~ **de briques** *vt* CONSTR brick, brick up; ~ **d'une couverture** *vt* NUCLEAIRE blanket; ~ **de** *vt* CONS MECA fit with; ~ **de planches** *vt* CONSTR board

garnissage *m* CONS MECA packing, MECANIQUE lining, MINES lagging, ORDINAT padding, PRODUCTION daubing, gasket, lining, stuffing, VEHICULES *sièges* upholstery; ~ **basique** *m* MATERIAUX, METALL basic lining; ~ **au dos** *m* IMPRIM backing up; ~ **du dos** *m* IMPRIM *d'un livre* backing; ~ **de pavillon** *m* VEHICULES *habitacle* head lining; ~ **réfractaire** *m* MATERIAUX refractory lining; ~ **de siège** *m* VEHICULES seat upholstery

garniture *f* AGRO ALIM topping, CONS MECA fitments, fittings, packing, CONSTR *d'une serrure* ward, IMPRIM *reliure, emballage* lining, INST HYDR clothing, lagging, NAUT gasket, NUCLEAIRE *d'une boîte à étoupe* packing seal, *plate* flat gasket, flat packing gasket, PRODUCTION deading, gasket, jacket, lining, mounting, sheathing, stuffing, VEHICULES *frein, embrayage* lining; ~ **antifriction** *f* CONS MECA antifriction lining; ~ **antivol** *f* EMBALLAGE pilferproof seal; ~ **de câble** *f* ELECTROTEC cable fitting; ~ **de chanvre** *f* PRODUCTION hemp packing; ~ **de coussinet** *f* MECANIQUE bearing lining; ~ **de disque d'embrayage** *f* CONS MECA clutch lining; ~ **d'embrayage** *f* AUTO, MECANIQUE clutch lining; ~ **en cuir** *f* PRODUCTION leather gasket, leather packer; ~ **en métal blanc** *f* CH DE FER *véhicules* white metal packing; ~ **en velours** *f* PHOTO velvet light trap; ~ **étanche** *f* CONS MECA packer, PRODUCTION fluid-tight packing; ~ **d'étanchéité** *f* MECANIQUE packing; ~ **d'étanchéité d'un cylindre à vapeur** *f* INST HYDR steam packing; ~ **d'étanchéité hydraulique** *f* CONS MECA hydraulic packing seal; ~ **d'étanchéité de piston** *f* INST HYDR ring; ~ **d'étanchéité sous pression** *f* INST HYDR pressure seal; ~ **étanche pour tubage** *f* CONSTR casing packer; ~ **d'étoupe** *f* PRODUCTION junk packing; ~ **flexible** *f* CONS MECA flexible gasket; ~ **de forage** *f* PETROLE drill string; ~ **de frein** *f* CONS MECA, MECANIQUE, VEHICULES brake lining; ~ **de friction** *f* AUTO friction facing, lining, VEHICULES *embrayage* clutch lining; ~ **isolante** *f* INST HYDR lagging; ~ **de joint** *f* NAUT gasket; ~ **à labyrinthe** *f* PRODUCTION labyrinth packing; ~ **de mâchoires** *f* CHARBON jaw plate; ~ **de molettes** *f* PRODUCTION *pour décrasse-meule* set of cutters; ~ **de piston** *f* CONS MECA piston packing, piston ring; ~ **de planches** *f* CONSTR boarding; ~ **de porte** *f* VEHICULES door casing; ~ **rotative** *f* REFRIG rotative seal; ~ **soudée** *f* CONS MECA soldered fitting; ~ **à tresse** *f* CONS MECA soft packing seal; ~ **de velours** *f* CINEMAT *sur l'ouverture d'un chargeur* velvet trap

garnitures *f pl* CONS MECA fitments, fittings

gas: ~ **cap** *m* PETR, PETROLE gas cap; ~ **aux terres rares** *m* CHIMIE, MATERIAUX rare earths

gas-lift *m* PETROLE gas lift

gas-oil *m* PETROLE *combustible*, THERMODYN gas oil, VEHICULES *carburant* diesel fuel

gaspillage *m* PRODUCTION wastage, waste, RECYCLAGE wastage; ~ **d'énergie** *m* GAZ energy waste, THERMODYN waste of energy

gaspiller *vt* PRODUCTION, RECYCLAGE waste

gastéropode *m* GEOLOGIE gastropod

gâteau *m* CERAM VER cake, CHARBON filter cake; ~ **de filtre** *m* CHARBON, GENIE CHIM filter cake; ~ **de filtre-presse** *m* GENIE CHIM, PAPIER filter cake; ~ **pour teinture** *m* TEXTILE mock cake

gâter *vt* AGRO ALIM spoil, taint

gauche:[1] **à** ~ *adj* PHYSIQUE left-handed

gauche[2] *f* AERONAUT port

gauchi *adj* CONS MECA out-of-true, MECANIQUE warped

gauchir[1] *vt* CONS MECA buckle

gauchir[2] *vi* CONSTR wind

gauchir:[3] **se** ~ *v réfl* CONSTR wind

gauchissement *m* CERAM VER sag, warpage, CH DE FER distortion, *d'une roue* warping, CONS MECA buckle, buckling, CONSTR winding, *du bois* warping, GEOLOGIE, NUCLEAIRE buckling, PRODUCTION warping, *de pièce coulée* buckling

gaufrage *m* CONS MECA embossment, IMPRIM blind blocking, *façonnage* embossing, PAPIER, PLAST CAOU *procédé* embossing; ~ **à pression** *m* PLAST CAOU pressure forming; ~ **à sec** *m* IMPRIM blind embossing, *finition, façonnage* blind blocking

gaufré *adj* CONS MECA embossed

gaufrer *vt* IMPRIM *liasse en continu* crimp, PAPIER emboss

gaufreuse *f* PAPIER embossing calender

gault *m* GEOLOGIE gault

gauss *m* ELECTR *unité*, ENREGISTR, GEOLOGIE gauss

gaussien *adj* OPTIQUE Gaussian

gaussmètre *m* ELECTR gaussmeter, GEOPHYS magnetic flux density meter

gave *m* HYDROLOGIE torrent

gaver *vt* MECANIQUE boost

gaylussite *f* MINERAUX gaylussite

gaz:[1] **à** ~ **pauvre** *adj* AUTO, THERMODYN *moteur* lean-burn

gaz[2] *m* CHAUFFAGE gas, CHIMIE fume, gas, GEOLOGIE volatile, PHYSIQUE, REFRIG, THERMODYN gas; ~ **acide** *m* GAZ, PETROLE sour gas; ~ **d'air** *m* GAZ air gas; ~ **à l'air** *m* GAZ producer gas; ~ **ammoniac** *m* HYDROLOGIE, LESSIVES ammonia gas; ~ **d'appoint** *m* GAZ make-up gas; ~ **d'arrêt** *m* NUCLEAIRE seal gas; ~ **associé** *m* GAZ, PETROLE associated gas; ~ **azote** *m* CHIMIE nitrogen gas; ~ **brûlé** *m* AUTO exhaust gas, GAZ waste gas, POLLUTION, THERMODYN exhaust gas, flue gas; ~ **brut** *m* GAZ raw gas; ~ **captif** *m* GAZ entrapped gas; ~ **carbonique** *m* CHIMIE, CONS MECA carbon dioxide; ~ **carburant** *m* GAZ power gas; ~ **de carneau** *m* GAZ, PHYSIQUE flue gas; ~ **de chasse** *m* ESPACE *véhicules* pressurizing gas; ~ **de chauffage** *m* GAZ fuel gas, heating gas, PRODUCTION furnace gas; ~ **combustible** *m* GAZ combustible gas, power gas; ~ **de combustion** *m* ESPACE *véhicules* combustion gas, POLLUTION flue gas, gaseous combustion product, THERMODYN flue gas; ~ **complétion** *m* GAZ gas completion unit; ~ **condensable** *m* GAZ condensable gas; ~ **à condensat** *m* GAZ condensate, condensate gas; ~ **corrosif** *m* PETR sour gas; ~ **coussin** *m* GAZ cushion gas; ~ **de couverture** *m* NUCLEAIRE *servant* blanket gas, cover gas; ~ **de curage** *m* THERMODYN digester gas; ~ **de dégagement** *m* GAZ off-gas; ~ **diatomique** *m* GAZ biatomic gas, PHYSIQUE diatomic gas; ~ **de digestion** *m* HYDROLOGIE *égouts* digester gas, sludge digestion gas, RECYCLAGE digester gas, sludge gas; ~ **dissous** *m* GAZ dissolved gas; ~ **de distillation** *m* GENIE CHIM, THERMODYN distillation gas; ~ **de dôme** *m* GAZ dome gas; ~ **domestique** *m* GAZ domestic gas; ~ **à l'eau** *m* GAZ water gas; ~ **d'eaux résiduaires** *m* GAZ sewage gas; ~ **d'échappement** *m* AUTO exhaust gases, CHIMIE off-gas, waste gas, MECANIQUE exhaust gas, NUCLEAIRE off-gas, stack gas, waste gas, POLLUTION exhaust gas, waste gas, THERMODYN exhaust gas, VEHICULES emission; ~ **d'éclairage** *m* GAZ coal gas; ~ **d'égout** *m* RECYCLAGE sewage gas; ~ **électronique** *m* PHYSIQUE electron gas; ~ **électronique dégénéré** *m* PHYS RAYON degenerate electron gas; ~ **en bouteille** *m* GAZ bottled gas, PETROLE camping gas, THERMODYN bottled gas; ~ **en place** *m* PETR gas in place; ~ **épuré** *m* GAZ cleaned gas, purified gas; ~ **et poussière cosmiques** *m* ASTRONOMIE cosmic gas and dust; ~ **et vapeurs** *m pl* SECURITE *risques pour la sécurité* gases and fumes; ~ **d'évacuation** *m* GAZ off-gas; ~ **de four à coke** *m* GAZ by-product gas; ~ **de fumée** *m* CHAUFFAGE flue gas, fumes, THERMODYN flue gas; ~ **de gadoues** *m* GAZ sewage gas; ~ **de gazogène** *m* GAZ power gas, PRODUCTION generator gas; ~ **de gueulard** *m* GAZ top gas; ~ **de haut-fourneau** *m* PRODUCTION blast furnace gas; ~ **de houille** *m* CHARBON, GAZ coal gas; ~ **humide** *m* PETR wet gas, PETROLE wet natural gas, PHYSIQUE wet gas; ~ **hydrogène** *m* CHIMIE hydrogen gas; ~ **idéal** *m* PHYSIQUE ideal gas, perfect gas; ~ **inerte** *m* GAZ inert gas; ~ **initialement en place** *m* PETR gas originally in place; ~ **injecté** *m* GAZ input gas, PETR injected gas; ~ **d'injection** *m* PETR input gas; ~ **interplanétaire** *m* ASTRONOMIE interplanetary gas; ~ **lacrymogène** *m* CHIMIE lachrymator, MILITAIRE tear gas; ~ **de lignite** *m* GAZ brown coal gas; ~ **liquéfié** *m* GAZ liquefied gas, liquid gas; ~ **liquéfié conditionné** *m* GAZ bottled liquefied petroleum gas; ~ **liquides** *m pl* THERMODYN liquid gases; ~

manufacturé *m* GAZ manufactured gas; ~ **marchand** *m* GAZ marketable gas; ~ ~ **de mines** *m* THERMODYN firedamp; ~ **mixte** *m* GAZ conventional gas, mixed gas; ~ **monoatomique** *m* PHYSIQUE monatomic gas; ~ **moutarde** *m* CHIMIE mustard gas; ~ **naturel** *m* CHAUFF-AGE natural gas, GAZ natural gas, rock gas, PETROLE, POLLUTION, THERMODYN natural gas; ~ **naturel comprimé** *m* TRANSPORT pressurized natural gas; ~ **naturel liquéfié** *m (GNL)* GAZ, PETROLE liquefied natural gas *(LNG)*, THERMODYN liquid natural gas *(LNG)*; ~ **naturel de synthèse** *m (GNS)* GAZ substitute natural gas, synthetic natural gas *(SNG)*, PETROLE substitute natural gas, synthetic natural gas *(SNG)*; ~ **nettoyant** *m* MILITAIRE *guerre nucléaire* sweep gas; ~ **neutre** *m* ESPACE neutral gas, NUCLEAIRE inert gas; ~ **non acide** *m* PETR sweet gas; ~ **non associé** *m* PETROLE *découverte de pétrole* nonassociated gas; ~ **non corrosif** *m* GAZ sweet natural gas; ~ **non purifié** *m* GAZ foul gas; ~ **occlus** *m* PETROLE cuttings gas; ~ **oléfiant** *m* GAZ ethylene; ~ **parfait** *m* PHYSIQUE ideal gas, perfect gas, THERMODYN perfect gas; ~ **pauvre** *m* GAZ dry gas, gas producer gas, generator gas, lean gas, poor gas, producer gas, PETR lean gas, PETROLE dry natural gas, PRODUCTION generator gas; ~ **pauvre en gazogène** *m* PRODUCTION generator gas; ~ **pauvre de haut-fourneau** *m* PRODUCTION blast furnace gas; ~ **perdus** *m pl* PRODUCTION waste gases; ~ **périphérique** *m* NUCLEAIRE peripheral gas; ~ **de pétrole** *m* PETR petroleum gas; ~ **de pétrole liquéfié** *m (GPL)* AUTO, CHAUFFAGE, GAZ, PETROLE, THERMODYN, TRANSPORT *(GPL)* liquefied petroleum gas *(LPG)*; ~ **plasmagène** *m* GAZ plasmagene gas; ~ **porteur** *m* GAZ, MATERIAUX, POLLUTION carrier gas; ~ **de pressurisation** *m* ESPACE *véhicules* pressurizing gas; ~ **de process** *m* CHARBON process gas; ~ **propulseur** *m* PETROLE aerosol propellant, hydrocarbon aerosol propellant; ~ **protecteur** *m* CERAM VER bath atmosphere; ~ **q** *m* THERMODYN q-gas; ~ **de raffinerie** *m* PETROLE, THERMODYN refinery gas; ~ **de récupération** *m* GAZ waste gas; ~ **réducteur** *m* THERMODYN reducing gas; ~ **rejeté** *m* NUCLEAIRE off-gas, stack gas, waste gas; ~ **résiduaire** *m* POLLUTION residual gas; ~ **résiduel** *m* CHIMIE off-gas, ELECTRON, POLLUTION residual gas; ~ **riche** *m* GAZ rich gas, wet gas, PETR rich gas, PETROLE wet natural gas; ~ **sec** *m* GAZ, PETR dry gas; ~ **sec naturel** *m* GAZ natural dry gas, PETROLE dry natural gas; ~ **synthétique** *m* GAZ synthetic gas; ~ **toxiques** *m pl* SECURITE toxic gases; ~ **vecteur** *m* NUCLEAIRE *porteur* carrier gas; ~ **de ville** *m* GAZ city gas, manufactured gas, town gas, PETROLE town gas

gaze *f* IMPRIM canvas; ~ **de cible** *f* TV target mesh; ~ **métallique** *f* PRODUCTION gauze, wire gauze, wire screen, wire sieve

gazéifiable *adj* CHIMIE volatile

gazéification *f* CHIMIE, MATERIAUX, PETROLE *raffinage*, PHYSIQUE, THERMODYN gasification; ~ **de la bouteille** *f* PETROLE coal gasification; ~ **en lit fluidisé** *f* GENIE CHIM fluidized bed gasification; ~ **du pétrole** *f* PETROLE oil gasification; ~ **souterraine** *f* THERMODYN underground gasification

gazéifier *vt* CHIMIE gasify, vaporize, GAZ, PHYSIQUE gasify

gazeux *adj* AGRO ALIM carbonated, effervescent, CHIMIE, PHYSIQUE gaseous, THERMODYN gaseous, gassy

gazier *m* CERAM VER top man, NAUT gas tanker, PRODUCTION gas fitter

gazoduc *m* GAZ gas pipeline, gas transmission line, PETR, PETROLE, THERMODYN gas pipeline, TRANSPORT gas outlet

gazofacteur *m* PRODUCTION gas generator, gas producer

gazogène *m* GAZ producer, PRODUCTION gas generator, gas producer, gasogene, gazogene, generator, THERMODYN gas generator; ~ **à aspiration** *m* PRODUCTION suction gas producer

gazole *m* AUTO diesel fuel, PETROLE, THERMODYN gas oil, TRANSPORT, VEHICULES *carburant* diesel fuel

gazomètre *m* GAZ gas tank, MINES gasometer, PRODUCTION gas tank, gasholder, gasometer, THERMODYN gas holder

gazométrie *f* THERMODYN gasometry

gazométrique *adj* CHIMIE gasometric

GBD *abrév (gestion de base de données)* INFORMAT, ORDINAT DBM *(database management)*

Gd *(gadolinium)* CHIMIE Gd *(gadolinium)*

Ge *(germanium)* CHIMIE Ge *(germanium)*

géant[1] *adj* PRODUCTION jumbo-size

géant[2] *m* ASTRONOMIE *astre* giant; ~ **rouge** *m* ASTRONOMIE red giant

gedinnien *adj* GEOLOGIE Gedinnian

gédrite *f* MINERAUX gedrite

gegenschein *m* ASTRONOMIE gegenschein

gehlénite *f* MINERAUX gehlenite

gel *m* CHIMIE *coagulé* gel, METEO frost, PAPIER freezing, PETROLE, PLAST CAOU *état physique* gel, TELECOM freeze-out, THERMODYN freeze-up; ~ **aérobie de silice opacifié** *m* REFRIG opacified silica aerogel; ~ **coat** *m* NAUT, PLAST CAOU *polyesters*, REVETEMENT gel coat; ~ **de l'image** *m* TELECOM freeze-picture; ~ **de silice** *m* AGRO ALIM, CHIMIE, MATERIAUX silica gel; ~ **de silice bleue** *m* EMBALLAGE blue silica gel; ~ **du sol** *m* REFRIG soil freezing

gélatine *f* CHIMIE gelatin, gelatine, CINEMAT gel, EMBALLAGE gelatin, gelatine; ~ **d'esturgeon** *f* AGRO ALIM isinglass; ~ **explosive** *f* MINES blasting gelatine; ~ **de poisson** *f* AGRO ALIM isinglass

gélatine-dynamite *f* MINES gelatin dynamite, gelatine dynamite, nitrogelatine

gélatino-bromure *m* CHIMIE gelatino-bromide

gélatino-chlorure *m* CHIMIE gelatino-chloride

gélation *f* METALL freezing

gelé *adj* REFRIG, THERMODYN frozen

gelée *f* METEO frost, REFRIG gel; ~ **blanche** *f* METEO hoar frost, white frost, REFRIG hoar frost; ~ **de pectine** *f* AGRO ALIM pectin jelly

geler[1] *vt* PAPIER, REFRIG, THERMODYN freeze

geler[2] *vi* METEO, PHYSIQUE freeze

gélifiant *m* AGRO ALIM gelling agent, POLLU MER gelling agent, solidifier

gélification *f* CHIMIE gelation, GENIE CHIM gelation, jellification, PLAST CAOU *procédé* gelation

gélifier: se ~ *v réfl* CHIMIE gel

gélignite *f* CHIMIE, MINES gelignite

gélivation *f* GEOLOGIE frost action, frostwork

gélivité *f* CHARBON frost susceptibility

gélose *f* AGRO ALIM agar-agar, CHIMIE gelose; ~ **inclinée** *f* AGRO ALIM agar slant

gelsémine *f* CHIMIE gelsemine

gelure *f* REFRIG frostbite

Gémeaux *m pl* ASTRONOMIE Gemini, the Twins

Géminides *m pl* ASTRONOMIE Geminids

gemme *f* CERAM VER cameo

gêne *f* SECURITE hindrance

générateur[1] *adj* ELECTROTEC generating

générateur[2] *m* CINEMAT generator, genny, ELECTR *alimentation*, ELECTROTEC, INFORMAT generator, INST HYDR generator, hydraulic pressure source, NAUT, ORDINAT generator, PHYSIQUE source, PRODUCTION generator, REFRIG boiler, TELECOM generator, TV electric generator; ~ **d'acétylène** *m* CONSTR, GAZ, GENIE CHIM acetylene generator; ~ **d'air chaud pulsé** *m* SECURITE fan-assisted air heater; ~ **d'allumage** *m* AERONAUT ignition generator; ~ **asservi** *m* ELECTRON tracking generator; ~ **asynchrone** *m* ELECTROTEC induction generator; ~ **audiofréquence** *m* ELECTRON audio frequency signal generator, tone generator; ~ **auxiliaire** *m* ELECTRON companion source; ~ **auxiliaire de bord** *m* AERONAUT auxiliary power unit; ~ **de balayage de fréquence** *m* ENREGISTR sliding-frequency generator; ~ **de balise** *m* ESPACE *communications* beacon generator; ~ **de barres couleurs** *m* TV color bar generator (AmE), colour bar generator (BrE); ~ **de base de temps** *m* ELECTRON, TV time-base generator; ~ **à basse fréquence** *m* ELECTR, ELECTRON low-frequency generator, PHYS RAYON audio oscillator; ~ **de bruit** *m* ELECTRON, TELECOM noise generator; ~ **de bruit aléatoire** *m* ELECTRON random noise generator; ~ **de bruit blanc** *m* ELECTRON white noise generator; ~ **de bruit diffus** *m* ENREGISTR random noise generator; ~ **de bruit thermique** *m* ELECTRON thermal noise generator; ~ **bulbe** *m* ELECTR bulb alternator, bulb generator; ~ **de cadre** *m* TV safe area generator; ~ **de caractères** *m* ELECTRON, INFORMAT, ORDINAT character generator; ~ **de choc** *m* ELECTR high-voltage impulse generator; ~ **de code temporel** *m* CINEMAT, TV time code generator; ~ **de couleur** *m* TV color synthesizer (AmE), colour synthesizer (BrE); ~ **de courant** *m* ELECTROTEC current generator, current source, PHYSIQUE current generator; ~ **de courant alternatif** *m* ELECTROTEC AC generator; ~ **de courant continu** *m* ELECTR direct current generator; ~ **de courant de sonnerie** *m* TELECOM ringer, ringing machine; ~ **de dents de scie** *m* TV sawtooth generator; ~ **de diagramme** *m* ORDINAT autochart; ~ **de données** *m* INFORMAT test-data generator; ~ **de données d'essai** *m* ORDINAT test-data generator; ~ **d'effets** *m* TV effects generator; ~ **d'effets spéciaux** *m* TV special effects generator; ~ **électrique** *m* ELECTROTEC electric generator; ~ **électrochimique secondaire** *m* TRANSPORT secondary electrochemical generator; ~ **électronique de points** *m* IMPRIM *scanner* electronic dot generator; ~ **électrostatique** *m* ELECTR Van de Graaff generator, ELECTROTEC electrostatic generator; ~ **fixe** *m* ESPACE *véhicules* fixed generator; ~ **de fonctions** *m* ELECTRON function generator; ~ **de fonctions en échelon** *m* ELECTRON step function generator; ~ **de fond coloré** *m* TV color background generator (AmE), colour background generator (BrE); ~ **de fréquence pilote** *m* CINEMAT pilot tone generator, sound sync generator, sync generator; ~ **de fréquences étalons** *m* ELECTRON frequency calibrator; ~ **de fréquence standard** *m* ENREGISTR standard tone generator; ~ **de fréquences vocales** *m* ELECTRON tone generator; ~ **de gaz** *m* ESPACE gas generator, PRODUCTION gas generator, gas producer; ~ **de gaz inerte** *m* GAZ inert-gas generator; ~ **de glace** *m* REFRIG ice maker; ~ **d'harmoniques** *m* ELECTRON, PHYSIQUE, TELECOM harmonic generator; ~ **à haute fréquence** *m* ELECTR high-frequency generator; ~ **à haute tension** *m* ELECTR high-voltage impulse generator; ~ **HF** *m* ELECTRON service oscillator, ELECTROTEC RF generator; ~ **hydraulique** *m* ELECTR, ELECTROTEC hydroelectric generator; ~ **hydroélectrique** *m* ELECTR hydroelectric generator; ~ **hyperfréquence** *m* ELECTRON microwave generator, microwave signal generator; ~ **d'impulsions** *m* ELECTR pulse generator, *équipement d'essais* impulse generator, ELECTRON, INFORMAT, ORDINAT, PHYSIQUE, TELECOM pulse generator; ~ **d'impulsions de clamp** *m* TV clamp pulse generator; ~ **d'impulsions codées** *m* PHYS RAYON pulse coder; ~ **d'impulsions sous-marines** *m* OCEANO pinger; ~ **d'impulsions de suppression** *m* ELECTRON blanking generator; ~ **d'impulsions de synchronisation** *m* TV sync pulse generator; ~ **d'impulsions de verrouillage** *m* TV clamp pulse generator; ~ **magnéto-électrique** *m* ELECTROTEC magnetoelectric generator; ~ **magnéto-hydrodynamique** *m* *(générateur MHD)* ELECTROTEC magnetohydrodynamic generator; ~ **de Marx** *m* NUCLEAIRE Marx generator, surge generator; ~ **MHD** *m* *(générateur magnéto-hydrodynamique)* ELECTROTEC MHD generator; ~ **de mire** *m* TV pattern generator; ~ **de mire de barres** *m* TV bar generator; ~ **de mots** *m* ELECTRON word generator; ~ **multifréquence** *m* TELECOM MF generator, multifrequency generator; ~ **de nombres aléatoires** *m* INFORMAT, ORDINAT random number generator; ~ **d'ondes** *m* PHYS ONDES wave generator; ~ **d'ondes rectangulaires** *m* TV square wave generator; ~ **orientable** *m* ESPACE *véhicules* pointable generator; ~ **d'oxygène** *m* CONSTR oxygen generator; ~ **de parasites** *m* ELECTRON interference generator; ~ **de phases** *m* ELECTRON phase generator; ~ **photoélectrique** *m* ELECTROTEC photogenerator; ~ **photovoltaïque** *m* ELECTROTEC photovoltaic generator; ~ **de polarisation** *m* ELECTROTEC bias generator; ~ **de pression hydraulique** *m* INST HYDR hydraulic generator; ~ **de programme d'états** *m* INFORMAT, ORDINAT report program generator; ~ **pulseur d'air chaud** *m* CHAUFFAGE fan-assisted air heater; ~ **radio-isotopique** *m* ESPACE radioisotope power generator, *véhicules* isotopic generator; ~ **de rampe** *m* ELECTROTEC ramp generator; ~ **de rayons X** *m* INSTRUMENT X-ray tube; ~ **à retard** *m* ELECTRON delay generator; ~ **de retard** *m* ELECTRON time synthesizer; ~ **de rythme de multiplexeur** *m* TELECOM multiplex timing generator; ~ **de rythme de régénérateur** *m* TELECOM RTG, regenerator timing generator; ~ **SHF** *m* ELECTRON SHF signal generator; ~ **de signal** *m* TELECOM signal generator; ~ **de signalisation multifréquence** *m* TELECOM MF generator, multifrequency generator; ~ **de signaux** *m* ELECTRON, PHYSIQUE signal generator; ~ **de signaux d'alignement** *m* TV tracking generator; ~ **de signaux analogiques** *m* ELECTRON analog signal generator (AmE), analogue signal generator (BrE); ~ **de signaux à audiofréquence** *m* ELECTRON audio frequency signal generator; ~ **de signaux carrés** *m* ELECTRON, ENREGISTR square wave generator; ~ **de signaux d'essai** *m* ELECTRON test signal generator; ~ **de signaux à haute fréquence** *m* ELECTRON RF section generator; ~ **de signaux HF** *m* ELECTRON HF signal generator, RF section generator; ~ **de signaux hyperfréquence** *m* ELECTRON microwave signal generator; ~ **de signaux SHF** *m* ELECTRON SHF signal generator; ~ **de signaux sinusoïdaux** *m* ELECTRON sinusoidal signal generator; ~ **de** signaux synthétisés *m* ELECTRON synthesized signal generator; ~ **de signaux UHF** *m* ELECTRON UHF signal generator; ~ **de signaux VHF** *m* ELECTRON VHF signal generator; ~ **solaire** *m* ELECTROTEC, ESPACE *véhicules* solar generator; ~ **solaire principal** *m* ESPACE main solar generator; ~ **de la sous-porteuse** *m* TV subcarrier oscillator; ~ **de synchro** *m* CINEMAT sync pulse generator, TV sync generator; ~ **de synchro général** *m* TV station sync generator; ~ **synchrone** *m* ELECTROTEC synchronous generator; ~ **de synchronisation** *m* ELECTRON timing generator; ~ **synthétisé** *m* ELECTRON synthesized signal generator; ~ **tachymétrique** *m* CONS MECA tachogenerator; ~ **de tension** *m* PHYSIQUE voltage generator; ~ **de tension de choc** *m* ELECTROTEC impulse generator; ~ **de tension d'impulsions** *m* ELECTR surge generator; ~ **thermo-électrique** *m* ELECTROTEC thermoelectric generator; ~ **thermoionique** *m* ELECTROTEC thermionic generator; ~ **de titres** *m* TV caption generator; ~ **de tonalité** *m* ENREGISTR, TELECOM tone generator; ~ **de tourbillons** *m* TRANSPORT vortex generator; ~ **de trame** *m* TELECOM frame generator, TV raster generator; ~ **de tri** *m* INFORMAT, ORDINAT sort generator; ~ **triphasé** *m* ELECTR three-phase generator; ~ **à trois fils** *m* ELECTR three-wire generator; ~ **de trucages** *m* TV effects generator; ~ **UHF** *m* ELECTRON UHF signal generator; ~ **ultrasonique** *m* PHYS RAYON ultrasonic generator; ~ **de Van de Graaff** *m* ELECTROTEC, PHYSIQUE Van de Graaff generator; ~ **de vapeur** *m* INST HYDR steam-boiler, MAT CHAUFF steam generator, NUCLEAIRE vapor generator (AmE), vapour generator (BrE); ~ **de vapeur macromodulaire** *m* NUCLEAIRE macromodular steam generator; ~ **de vapeur à passage unique** *m* NUCLEAIRE OTSG, once-through steam generator; ~ **VHF** *m* ELECTRON VHF signal generator; ~ **de vibrations** *m* ESPACE vibration generator, vibrator

génération *f* ELECTR *alimentation*, INFORMAT, ORDINAT generation, TV *numéro de copie* generation copy; ~ **d'adresses** *f* ORDINAT address generation; ~ **automatique de messages** *f* PRODUCTION *automatisme industriel* automatic report generation; ~ **continue** *f* ELECTROTEC DC generation; ~ **de contours** *f* PRODUCTION contour generation; ~ **de courant alternatif** *f* ELECTROTEC AC generation; ~ **d'électricité** *f* ELECTROTEC electricity generation; ~ **électrostatique** *f* ELECTR electrostatic generator; ~ **d'états** *f* INFORMAT, ORDINAT report generation; ~ **d'harmoniques** *f* ELECTRON harmonic generation; ~ **d'impulsion** *f* ELECTRON pulse generation; ~ **magnétohydrodynamique** *f (génération MHD)* ELECTROTEC magnetohydrodynamic generation; ~ **MHD** *f (génération magnétohydrodynamique)* ELECTROTEC MHD generation; ~ **de mots** *f* ELECTRON word generation; ~ **de nombres aléatoires** *f* TELECOM random number generation; ~ **d'ondes** *f* TELECOM wave generation; ~ **de parole** *f* TELECOM speech generation; ~ **de la porteuse** *f* ELECTRON carrier generation; ~ **de reflux** *f* EN RENOUV ebb generation; ~ **de retard** *f* ELECTRON time synthesis, time-delay generation; ~ **de signaux** *f* ELECTRON signal generation; ~ **de signaux carrés** *f* ELECTRON square wave generation; ~ **de système** *f* INFORMAT, ORDINAT system generation

génératrice *f* CINEMAT, CONSTR, ELECTROTEC generator, NUCLEAIRE electric generator, generator, PHYSIQUE generator, VEHICULES *système électrique* generator; ~ **à aimants permanents** *f* ELECTROTEC, EN RENOUV permanent magnet generator; ~ **asynchrone** *f* ELECTROTEC induction generator; ~ **continue** *f* ELECTROTEC DC generator; ~ **à courant alternatif** *f* PHYSIQUE alternative current generator, alternator; ~ **à courant continu** *f* ELECTR, ELECTROTEC, PHYSIQUE DC generator, direct current generator; ~ **électrique à vapeur** *f* ELECTROTEC steam-electric generator; ~ **éolienne** *f* ELECTR wind-powered generator; ~ **à excitation séparée** *f* ELECTROTEC separate excited generator; ~ **homopolaire** *f* ELECTR, ELECTROTEC homopolar generator; ~ **d'impulsion** *f* ELECTR *équipement d'essais* impulse generator; ~ **de l'onde porteuse** *f* PHYS ONDES carrier wave generator; ~ **à pôles saillants** *f* ELECTR *machine* salient pole generator; ~ **polymorphique** *f* ELECTROTEC multiple current generator; ~ **pour énergie éolienne** *f* ELECTROTEC wind-driven generator; ~ **de pression hydraulique** *f* INST HYDR hydraulic pressure source; ~ **sans balais** *f* ELECTR *machine* brushless generator; ~ **de signaux acoustiques** *f* CONS MECA acoustic generator, acoustic signal generator

générer *vt* PHYS RAYON generate

générique[1] *adj* INFORMAT, ORDINAT generic

générique[2] *m* CINEMAT credits, titles; ~ **déroulant** *m* CINEMAT crawl

génériques: ~ de fin *m pl* CINEMAT closing credits, end credits

génétique *adj* PHYS RAYON *dégât* genetic

génie *m* MECANIQUE engineering; ~ **civil** *m* CONSTR civil engineering, engineering; ~ **des écoulements** *m* PHYS FLUID fluid engineering; ~ **industriel** *m* PRODUCTION industrial engineering; ~ **maritime** *m* NAUT naval architecture; ~ **sismique** *m* GEOPHYS seismic engineering

genistéine *f* CHIMIE genistein

genou *m* CONS MECA elbow joint, knee; ~ **de Cardan** *m* CONS MECA universal joint

genouillère *f* CONS MECA knuckle, knuckle joint, MECANIQUE knuckle; ~ **de train avant** *f* AERONAUT drag brace

genouillères *f pl* SECURITE knee pads

genre *m* GEOMETRIE *d'une surface* genus

genthite *f* MINERAUX genthite

gentianine *f* CHIMIE gentianin

gentilhomme *m* PRODUCTION dam plate

gentiobiose *m* CHIMIE gentiobiose

gentiopicrine *f* CHIMIE gentiopicrin

gentisate *m* CHIMIE gentisate

gentisine *f* CHIMIE gentisin

gentisique *adj* CHIMIE gentisic

géobaromètre *m* GEOLOGIE geobarometer

géocentrique *adj* ASTRONOMIE geocentric

géochimie *f* CHIMIE, GEOLOGIE, PETROLE geochemistry; ~ **de l'eau** *f* GEOLOGIE hydrogeochemistry; ~ **isotopique** *f* GEOLOGIE isotope geology

géochronologie *f* GEOLOGIE, PETR geochronology

géode *f* GEOLOGIE druse, vug

géodésie *f* GEOMETRIE geodesy

géodésique[1] *adj* CONSTR geodetic

géodésique[2] *f* GEOMETRIE geodesic

géodimètre *m* CONSTR geodimeter

géodynamique *f* ASTRONOMIE, ESPACE geodynamics

géohydrologie *f* CHARBON geohydrology

géoïde *m* GEOLOGIE, OCEANO geoid

géologie *f* CHARBON, MINES, PETROLE geology; ~ **du pétrole** *f* PETROLE petroleum geology; ~ **pétrolière** *f* PETROLE petroleum geology

géologue: ~ **de subsurface** *m* PETROLE subsurface geologist

géomagnétique *adj* ESPACE *géophysique* geomagnetic

géomagnétisme *m* ASTRONOMIE, ESPACE *géophysique*, GEOLOGIE, PHYSIQUE geomagnetism

géomètre *m* GEOMETRIE geometer, geometrician; ~ **du cadastre** *m* CONSTR ordnance surveyor

géométrie: ~ **de l'absorption** *f* PHYS RAYON *de la radiation ionisante* geometry of absorption; ~ **affine** *f* GEOMETRIE affine geometry; ~ **algébrique** *f* GEOMETRIE algebraic geometry; ~ **analytique** *f* GEOMETRIE analytical geometry; ~ **cartésienne** *f* GEOMETRIE Cartesian geometry; ~ **des coordonnées** *f* GEOMETRIE coordinate geometry; ~ **dans l'espace** *f* GEOMETRIE solid geometry; ~ **différentielle** *f* GEOMETRIE differential geometry; ~ **elliptique** *f* GEOMETRIE elliptical geometry; ~ **euclidienne** *f* GEOMETRIE Euclidean geometry; ~ **du glissement** *f* METALL geometry of glide; ~ **hyperbolique** *f* GEOMETRIE hyperbolic geometry; ~ **de l'irradiation** *f* NUCLEAIRE geometry of irradiation; ~ **localement homogène** *f* GEOMETRIE locally homogeneous geometry; ~ **métrique** *f* GEOMETRIE metrical geometry; ~ **non euclidienne** *f* GEOMETRIE non-Euclidean geometry; ~ **des pistes** *f* ENREGISTR tracking configuration, TV track configuration; ~ **plane** *f* GEOMETRIE plane geometry; ~ **des points d'ensemble** *f* GEOMETRIE point set geometry; ~ **projective** *f* GEOMETRIE graphic geometry, projective geometry; ~ **riemannienne** *f* GEOMETRIE Riemannian geometry; ~ **sphérique** *f* GEOMETRIE spherical geometry; ~ **du train** *f* AUTO tracking; ~ **du train avant** *f* AUTO front-wheel alignment, steering geometry; ~ **à trois dimensions** *f* GEOMETRIE solid geometry

géométrique *adj* GEOMETRIE geometric

géon *m* GEOPHYS geon

géopétale *adj* PETR geopetal

géophone *m* CHARBON, GAZ, GEOLOGIE, GEOPHYS, PETROLE *levé sismique* geophone

géophysique *f* CHARBON, PETR, PETROLE, PHYSIQUE geophysics

géopotentiel *adj* GEOPHYS geopotential

géosynchrone *adj* ASTRONOMIE *satellite artificiel* geosynchronous

géosynclinal[1] *adj* GEOLOGIE, GEOPHYS geosynclinal

géosynclinal[2] *m* GEOLOGIE, GEOPHYS, PETROLE geosyncline

géotechnique *f* CHARBON geotechnics

géotectoclinal *m* GEOPHYS geotectocline

géotectonique[1] *adj* GEOLOGIE geotectonic

géotectonique[2] *f* GEOPHYS geotectonic

géothermie *f* EN RENOUV geothermal power, GEOLOGIE, PETROLE *température des formations* geothermics

géothermique *adj* EN RENOUV, GEOPHYS geothermal

géothermomètre *m* GEOLOGIE, GEOPHYS geothermometer

géraniol *m* CHIMIE geraniol

géranyle *m* CHIMIE geranyl

gerbage *m* IMPRIM *de bobine* stacking, PETROLE racking pipe

gerbe *f* CONSTR *d'étincelles* shower; ~ **électronique** *f* NUCLEAIRE electron cascade, electron shower; ~ **de rayons cosmiques** *f* ASTRONOMIE air shower

gerbeur *m* EMBALLAGE stacking truck

gerçure *f* CHARBON crack, crevice, PRODUCTION surface crack

germanium *m* (*Ge*) CHIMIE germanium (*Ge*)

germe *m* CERAM VER nucleus, MATERIAUX germ; ~ **cristallin** *m* CRISTALL seed crystal

germination *f* CRISTALL, MATERIAUX nucleation; ~ **spontanée** *f* METALL spontaneous nucleation

gersdorffite *f* MINERAUX gersdorffite

gestion: ~ **à l'affaire** *f* PRODUCTION contract pegging; ~ **d'atelier** *f* PRODUCTION production scheduling and control; ~ **de base de données** *f* (*GBD*) INFORMAT, ORDINAT database management (*DBM*); ~ **des besoins** *f* PRODUCTION demand management; ~ **du brouillage** *f* TELECOM scrambling control; ~ **des clés** *f* TELECOM key management; ~ **des commandes de clients** *f* PRODUCTION customer order servicing; ~ **de crue** *f* EN RENOUV flood control; ~ **des déchets** *f* RECYCLAGE waste management; ~ **des demandes** *f* PRODUCTION demand management; ~ **de données** *f* ORDINAT, TELECOM DM, data management; ~ **des données techniques** *f* PRODUCTION technical data management; ~ **des eaux superficielles** *f* DISTRI EAU surface water management; ~ **des eaux urbaines** *f* DISTRI EAU urban water management; ~ **des emplacements** *f* PRODUCTION location management; ~ **de l'en-cours de fabrication** *f* PRODUCTION work-in-progress control; ~ **d'erreurs** *f* INFORMAT, ORDINAT error management; ~ **de l'exécution d'un programme** *f* ORDINAT program control; ~ **de fichier** *f* INFORMAT, ORDINAT file management; ~ **de file d'attente** *f* INFORMAT, ORDINAT queue management; ~ **informatisée** *f* COMMANDE computerized management; ~ **intégrale des eaux** *f* DISTRI EAU integral water management; ~ **intégrée automatisée** *f* COMMANDE computerized integrated management; ~ **de magasin** *f* PRODUCTION stores control, warehouse management, warehousing; ~ **de mémoire** *f* INFORMAT, ORDINAT memory management; ~ **opérative** *f* NUCLEAIRE operative management; ~ **par projets** *f* PRODUCTION project production; ~ **périphérique** *f* TELECOM peripheral management; ~ **des périphériques** *f* INFORMAT, ORDINAT DC, device control; ~ **de la production** *f* COMMANDE, PRODUCTION production control; ~ **de la production assistée par ordinateur** *f* PRODUCTION manufacturing resource planning; ~ **de la qualité** *f* CONSTR quality management; ~ **rationnelle des stocks** *f* OCEANO rational fish-stock management, rational fishery management; ~ **des requêtes** *f* ORDINAT inquiry control; ~ **de réseaux** *f* INFORMAT, ORDINAT network management; ~ **des risques** *f* QUALITE risk management; ~ **de la sécurité** *f* QUALITE safety management; ~ **des stocks** *f* PRODUCTION inventory control, stock control; ~ **des systèmes** *f* TELECOM systems management; ~ **totale de la qualité** *f* PRODUCTION total quality control; ~ **de la transmission** *f* ORDINAT transmission control; ~ **des travaux** *f* INFORMAT, ORDINAT job control

gestionnaire *m* INFORMAT, ORDINAT driver; ~ **d'anomalies** *m* INFORMAT, ORDINAT exception handler; ~ **de base de données** *m* INFORMAT, ORDINAT database manager; ~ **d'écran** *m* INFORMAT, ORDINAT display driver; ~ **de mémoire étendue** *m* INFORMAT, ORDINAT expanded memory manager; ~ **de périphérique** *m* INFORMAT, ORDINAT device driver

getter *m* ELECTR, ELECTROTEC getter

geyser *m* EN RENOUV, GEOPHYS, HYDROLOGIE geyser

geysérite *f* MINERAUX geyserite

GFU *abrév* (*groupe fermé d'usagers*) INFORMAT, ORDINAT, TELECOM CUG (*closed user group*)

gibbsite *f* MINERAUX gibbsite

giclée *f* PHYS FLUID jet

gicler *vt* PHYS FLUID jet

gicleur *m* AERONAUT jet, AUTO jet, nozzle, windscreen washer jet (BrE), windshield washer jet (AmE); ~ **d'accélération** *m* VEHICULES *carburateur* accelerator jet; ~ **à aiguille** *m* VEHICULES *carburateur* needle jet; ~ **auxiliaire** *m* VEHICULES *carburateur* auxiliary jet; ~ **auxiliaire de puissance** *m* AUTO high-speed auxiliary jet; ~ **calibré** *m* CONS MECA metering jet; ~ **compensateur** *m* VEHICULES *carburateur* compensating jet; ~ **de départ** *m* AUTO starter jet, starting jet; ~ **d'économie** *m* VEHICULES *carburateur* economizer jet; ~ **d'incendie** *m* CONSTR, SECURITE sprinkler; ~ **noyé** *m* AUTO flooded jet; ~ **de pompe** *m* AUTO acceleration jet; ~ **principal** *m* AUTO, VEHICULES *carburateur* main jet; ~ **de ralenti** *m* AUTO, VEHICULES *carburateur* idle jet; ~ **de reprise** *m* VEHICULES *carburateur* accelerator jet

gieseckite *f* MINERAUX gieseckite

giga- *préf (G)* METROLOGIE giga-*(G)*

gigadisc *m* OPTIQUE gigadisc (BrE), gigadisk (AmE)

gigantolite *f* MINERAUX gigantolite

gigaoctet *m* INFORMAT, OPTIQUE, ORDINAT gigabyte

gigue *f* ELECTRON, ORDINAT, TELECOM, TV jitter; ~ **de largeur** *f* ELECTRON width jitter; ~ **de phase** *f* ESPACE *communications* phase jitter; ~ **temporelle** *f* ELECTRON time jitter

gilbert *m* ELECTROTEC gilbert

gilbertite *f* MINERAUX gilbertite

gilet: ~ **de protection pare-balles** *m* MILITAIRE bulletproof jacket, bulletproof vest; ~ **de sauvetage** *m* AERONAUT life jacket, life preserver

gill *m* METROLOGIE gill

giobertite *f* CHIMIE magnesite, MINERAUX giobertite

Girafe *f* ASTRONOMIE Camelopardalis

girasol *m* MINERAUX girasol, girasole

giravion *m* TRANSPORT rotor aircraft

giron *m* CONSTR *d'une marche d'escalier* tread

girouette *f* NAUT wind telltale

gisement *m* AERONAUT relative bearing, CONSTR bed, deposit, MINES ore deposit, OCEANO relative bearing, PETR, PETROLE field; ~ **alluvionnaire** *m* MINES placer, placer deposit; ~ **azimutal** *m* OCEANO azimuth bearing; ~ **de gaz** *m* GAZ gas field; ~ **de gaz à condensat** *m* MATERIAUX gas condensate deposit; ~ **de gaz naturel** *m* THERMODYN gas field; ~ **houiller** *m* CHARBON coal bed, coal deposit, coal seam, MINES coal measure; ~ **d'interception** *m* AERONAUT intercept bearing; ~ **marginal** *m* PETROLE marginal field; ~ **marin** *m* PETROLE offshore field; ~ **de minerai** *m* MINES deposit of ore, mineral deposit, ore deposit, NUCLEAIRE ore deposit; ~ **minéral** *m* MINES mineral deposit; ~ **minéral hydrothermal** *m* GEOLOGIE hydrothermal deposit; ~ **minier** *m* MINES mineral deposit; ~ **naturel de gaz** *m* GAZ natural gas deposit; ~ **de pétrole** *m* PETROLE oilfield; ~ **polymétallique** *m* MATERIAUX polymetallic deposit; ~ **prouvé** *m* PETROLE proven area; ~ **rentable** *m* PETROLE commercial field

gisements: ~ **alluvionnaires** *m pl* MINES alluvial mining, diggings

gismondite *f* MINERAUX gismondine, gismondite

gîte[1] *m* CONSTR bed, deposit; ~ **alluvionnaire** *m* GEOLOGIE placer deposit; ~ **en aval pendage** *m* CONSTR foot wall seam; ~ **de fer** *m* MINES iron deposit; ~ **filonien** *m* MINES lode; ~ **houiller** *m* CHARBON coal bed, coal deposit, coal seam; ~ **métallifère** *m* MINES deposit

of ore, mineral deposit, ore deposit; ~ **minéral** *m* MINES mineral deposit; ~ **de plomb** *m* MINES lead deposit

gîte[2] *f* NAUT heel

gîter *vi* NAUT cant over, heel

givétien *adj* GEOLOGIE *stratigraphie* Givetian

givrage *m* CERAM VER frosting, DISTRI EAU ice accretion, NAUT *sur navire* icing, REFRIG frost formation; ~ **à l'aspiration** *m* REFRIG frost back; ~ **à la colle** *m* CERAM VER glue etching

givre *m* AGRO ALIM bloom, REFRIG freezing trawler, frost; ~ **blanc** *m* METEO silver frost, REFRIG rime; ~ **transparent** *m* REFRIG glaze

givré *adj* AGRO ALIM, REFRIG frosted

glaçage *m* IMPRIM *d'un blanchet* piling, *finition* glazing, PAPIER glazing, PRODUCTION glazing, glossing, REFRIG icing, TEXTILE glazing; ~ **à la calandre à friction** *m* PAPIER friction glazing; ~ **direct** *m* REFRIG contact icing; ~ **direct sur le chargement** *m* REFRIG top icing; ~ **au laminoir à plaque** *m* PAPIER plate glazing; ~ **au sein du chargement** *m* REFRIG body icing

glace *f* ACOUSTIQUE label area, CERAM VER plate glass; ~ **d'appui** *f* PHOTO glass pressure plate; ~ **armée** *f* CERAM VER polished wired glass; ~ **de banquise** *f* NAUT pack ice; ~ **broyée** *f* REFRIG crushed ice; ~ **brute coulée** *f* CERAM VER rough cast plate; ~ **calibrée** *f* REFRIG sized ice; ~ **carbonique** *f* AGRO ALIM, REFRIG dry ice; ~ **chauffante** *f* AERONAUT heated windshield pane; ~ **concassée** *f* REFRIG broken ice; ~ **cristalline** *f* REFRIG crystal ice; ~ **de cylindre** *f* INST HYDR valve seat; ~ **de distribution** *f* INST HYDR valve seat; ~ **d'eau de mer** *f* REFRIG sea water ice; ~ **en copeaux** *f* REFRIG chipped ice; ~ **en mer** *f* NAUT sea ice; ~ **en plaque** *f* REFRIG plate ice; ~ **en ruban** *f* REFRIG ribbon ice; ~ **en tube** *f* REFRIG shell ice; ~ **d'évaporation** *f* GENIE CHIM evaporative ice; ~ **de fond** *f* OCEANO anchor ice, bottom ice; ~ **fractionnée** *f* REFRIG processed ice; ~ **navigable** *f* OCEANO ice-free water, open water; ~ **noire** *f* METEO black ice; ~ **opaque** *f* REFRIG white ice; ~ **de phare** *f* AUTO headlamp lens; ~ **sèche** *f* REFRIG dry ice; ~ **Sécurit** *f* (MD) SECURITE safety glass; ~ **Sécurit à une et à plusieurs couches de verre** *f* (MD) SECURITE single and multilayer glass; ~ **Sécurit à une et à plusieurs plaques de verre** *f* (MD) SECURITE single and multilayer glass; ~ **de tiroir** *f* INST HYDR valve seat; ~ **transparente** *f* REFRIG clear ice; ~ **twinée** *f* CERAM VER twin-ground plate; ~ **de vitrage** *f* CONSTR plate glass

glacé[1] *adj* AGRO ALIM frosted, REFRIG iced, THERMODYN icy; ~ **par friction** *adj* PAPIER friction-glazed

glacé[2] *m* PRODUCTION gloss

glace-neige *f* REFRIG snow-ice; ~ **mouillée** *f* REFRIG slush ice

glacer[1] *vt* AGRO ALIM, EMBALLAGE, PHOTO, PRODUCTION glaze

glacer[2] *vi* REFRIG ice

glacer:[3] **se** ~ *v réfl* PRODUCTION glaze

glaces: ~ **flottantes** *f pl* NAUT drift ice

glaceuse *f* PHOTO glazing machine

glaciaire *adj* GEOLOGIE glacial

glacial *adj* THERMODYN ice-cold, icy

glacière *f* REFRIG ice cellar, THERMODYN ice-making machine, ice-making plant

glacio-eustatisme *m* OCEANO glacial eustasy, glacial eustatism

glacis *m* IMPRIM *finition* glazing; ~ **continental** *m* GEOLOGIE *sous-marin*, OCEANO continental rise; ~

désertique *m* GEOLOGIE desert pediment; ~ **récifal** *m* OCEANO reef glacis, reef pediment

glaçon: ~ **stationnaire** *m* REFRIG ice cake

glaçure *f* CERAM VER check, glaze, split, REVETEMENT glass glazing; ~ **brute** *f* CERAM VER rough rolled glazing; ~ **céramique** *f* CERAM VER ceramic glaze; ~ **de faïence** *f* CERAM VER earthenware glazing; ~ **frittée** *f* CERAM VER fritted glaze; ~ **mate** *f* CERAM VER matt glaze; ~ **de porcelaine** *f* REVETEMENT glass glazing; ~ **de soufflage** *f* CERAM VER pressure check; ~ **transparente** *f* CERAM VER transparent glaze

glairine *f* CHIMIE glairin

glaise *f* DISTRI EAU loam, INST HYDR pug; ~ **végétale** *f* GEOLOGIE loam

glaisière *f* MINES clay pit

gland *m* CERAM VER mallet, CONS MECA nipple

glasérite *f* MINERAUX glaserite

glaubérite *f* MINERAUX glauberite

glaucolite *f* MINERAUX glaucolite

glauconie *f* GEOLOGIE glauconite, glaucony

glauconieux *adj* GEOLOGIE glauconitic

glauconite *f* MINERAUX glauconite

glaucophane *f* MINERAUX glaucophane

glèbe *f* MINES glebe

glène *f* NAUT coil

gléner *vt* NAUT coil

glissance *f* TRANSPORT skidding conditions, slipperiness

glissement *m* AERONAUT *d'une hélice* slip, CERAM VER letter sag, letter slip, CHARBON slide, CONS MECA shear, slide, sliding, CONSTR slippage, CRISTALL glide, gliding, slip, ELECTR *machine*, ELECTROTEC slip, IMPRIM *photogravure et impression* color shift (AmE), colour shift (BrE), MATERIAUX slip, METALL sliding, PRODUCTION *d'une courroie* creep; ~ **amont** *m* ELECTRON frequency pushing; ~ **amont de fréquence** *m* ELECTRON frequency pushing; ~ **aval** *m* ELECTRON frequency pulling; ~ **aval de fréquence** *m* ELECTRON frequency pulling; ~ **de la bande** *m* ENREGISTR, TV tape slippage; ~ **basal** *m* METALL basal slip; ~ **conjugué** *m* METALL conjugate slip; ~ **cristallographique** *m* MATERIAUX, METALL crystallographic slip; ~ **croisé** *m* METALL cross-slip; ~ **de décrochage** *m* CRISTALL, MATERIAUX prismatic slip; ~ **dévié** *m* MATERIAUX cross-slip; ~ **discontinu** *m* METALL discontinuous glide; ~ **de l'embrayage** *m* VEHICULES clutch slip; ~ **en barreaux** *m* METALL pencil glide; ~ **facile** *m* CRISTALL easy glide; ~ **fin** *m* METALL fine slip; ~ **de fréquence** *m* ELECTRON frequency departure, INFORMAT frequency shift, TV shift; ~ **de fréquence Doppler** *m* ENREGISTR Doppler shift; ~ **gravitaire** *m* GEOLOGIE gravity gliding; ~ **horizontal** *m* TV line slip; ~ **par gravité** *m* GEOLOGIE gravity gliding; ~ **de pôle** *m* ELECTR *machine* pole slip; ~ **pyramidal** *m* METALL pyramidal slip; ~ **quasi-constant** *m* NUCLEAIRE quasi-constant slip; ~ **relatif** *m* ELECTR *machine* relative slip; ~ **des spires de bande** *m* TV cinch, cinching; ~ **de terrain** *m* GEOLOGIE landslide, landslip, rock slip, rockslide; ~ **de terre** *m* CONSTR earth fall, landslide; ~ **transversal** *m* CRISTALL cross-slip, MATERIAUX cross-banding; ~ **unitaire** *m* PHYSIQUE shear strain

glisser *vi* CONS MECA, MECANIQUE slide, VEHICULES *circulation* skid

glissière *f* CINEMAT *de parasoleil, soufflet* slide bar, CONS MECA guide bar, slide bar, slide, slider, *de moule d'injection* guide block, IMPRIM *mécanique*, MECANIQUE slide, PHOTO *de cassette* slit; ~ **à billes** *f* CONS MECA ball bearing guideway; ~ **de chenilles** *f* CONSTR track strip; ~ **de crosse** *f* CONS MECA crosshead guide, guide bar, slide bar; ~ **de détente** *f* INST HYDR expansion slide; ~ **d'évacuation d'urgence** *f* AERONAUT emergency slide; ~ **de fixation** *f* INSTRUMENT dovetail; ~ **de recul** *f* MILITAIRE recoil slide; ~ **de réglage** *f* PHOTO focusing stage; ~ **des roues** *f* PRODUCTION wheel slide; ~ **de sauvetage** *f* SECURITE rescue chute; ~ **de sécurité** *f* CONSTR guardrail, SECURITE crash barrier

glissières: ~ **à coussin d'air** *f pl* CONS MECA aeroslides; ~ **pneumatiques** *f pl* CONS MECA aeroslides; ~ **de tour** *f pl* CONS MECA lathe bed

glissoir *m* RESSORTS hook end

glitches: ~ **de pulsar** *m pl* ASTRONOMIE pulsar glitches

global *adj* INFORMAT, ORDINAT global

globe: ~ **de pendule** *m* CERAM VER bell jar

globulaire *adj* METALL globular

globule *m* CHIMIE globule; ~ **de Bok** *m* ASTRONOMIE Bok globule; ~ **éphémère** *m* PHYS PART transient globule

glossecollite *f* MINERAUX glossecolite

gluant *adj* CHIMIE, PHYS FLUID viscid

glucagon *m* CHIMIE glucagon

glucamine *f* CHIMIE glucamine

glucaronique *adj* CHIMIE glucaronic

glucide *m* AGRO ALIM carbohydrate, CHIMIE glucide

glucine *f* CERAM VER beryllia

gluconique *adj* CHIMIE gluconic

glucoprotéine *f* CHIMIE glucoprotein

glucopyrannose *m* CHIMIE glucopyranose

glucosamine *f* CHIMIE glucosamine

glucosane *m* CHIMIE glucosan

glucose *m* CHIMIE glucose

glucoside *m* CHIMIE glucoside

glume *f* AGRO ALIM chaff

gluon *m* PHYSIQUE gluon

glutaconique *adj* CHIMIE glutaconic

glutamate *m* CHIMIE glutamate; ~ **monosodique** *m* AGRO ALIM MSG, monosodium glutamate; ~ **de sodium** *m* AGRO ALIM MSG, monosodium glutamate

glutamine *f* CHIMIE glutamine

glutamique *adj* CHIMIE glutamic

glutaraldéhyde *m* CHIMIE glutaraldehyde

glutarique *adj* CHIMIE glutaric

glutathion *m* CHIMIE glutathione

gluten *m* AGRO ALIM gluten

glycéraldéhyde *m* CHIMIE glyceraldehyde

glycéride *f* AGRO ALIM, CHIMIE glyceride

glycérique *adj* CHIMIE glyceric

glycérol *m* CHIMIE glycerin, glycerine, glycerol

glycérophosphate *m* CHIMIE glycerophosphate

glycérophosphorique *adj* CHIMIE glycerophosphoric

glycéryle *m* CHIMIE glyceryl; ~ **margarate** *m* CHIMIE margarine

glycine *f* AGRO ALIM, CHIMIE glycine

glycocide *f* CHIMIE glycocide

glycogène *m* AGRO ALIM animal starch, glycogen, CHIMIE glycogen

glycol *m* CHIMIE glycol, LESSIVES ethylene glycol, glycol, REFRIG glycol

glycoline *f* CHIMIE glycoline

glycolipide *m* CHIMIE glycolipid

glycollique *adj* CHIMIE *acide* glycolic, glycollic

glycolyse *f* AGRO ALIM glycolysis

glycoprotéine *f* CHIMIE glucoprotein

glycosamine *f* CHIMIE glucosamine

glycoside *m* AGRO ALIM glycoside
glycuronique *adj* CHIMIE glycuronic
glycylglycine *f* CHIMIE glycylglycine
glycyrrhizine *f* CHIMIE glycyrrhizine
glyoxal *m* CHIMIE glyoxal
glyoxalidine *f* CHIMIE glyoxalidine
glyoxaline *f* CHIMIE glyoxaline
glyoxime *f* CHIMIE glyoxime
glyoxylique *adj* CHIMIE glyoxylic
GMCN *abrév (gain de l'équipement de multiplication de circuit numérique)* TELECOM DCMG *(digital circuit multiplication gain)*
gmélinite *f* MINERAUX gmelinite
gneiss *m* CONSTR, GEOLOGIE, MATERIAUX gneiss; ~ à injection *m* GEOLOGIE injection gneiss
gneissique *adj* GEOLOGIE gneissic
GNL *abrév (gaz naturel liquéfié)* GAZ, PETROLE, THERMODYN LNG *(liquefied natural gas)*
gnomon *m* ASTRONOMIE gnomon
GNS *abrév (gaz naturel de synthèse)* GAZ, PETROLE SNG *(synthetic natural gas)*
gobelet: ~ en papier froncé *m* EMBALLAGE crimp paper cup; ~ gradué *m* PHOTO measuring cylinder
gode *m* IMPRIM *papier* curl
godet *m* CONSTR *d'un élévateur, d'une drague* bucket, PLAST CAOU *peinture, instrument* cup, flow cup; ~ de centrifugeur *m* EQUIP LAB *séparation* centrifuge bucket; ~ de dragage *m* TRANSPORT dredger bucket; ~ de drague *m* MINES, NAUT dredge bucket; ~ d'élévateur *m* PRODUCTION elevator bucket, elevator cup; ~ embouti *m* CONSTR stamped bucket; ~ en tôle d'acier embouti *m* PRODUCTION pressed-steel bucket; ~ en verre à tige *m* PRODUCTION needle lubricator; ~ graisseur *m* CONS MECA oil cup, PRODUCTION grease cup, greaser, grease lubricator, oiler; ~ à huile *m* CONS MECA oil cup, PRODUCTION oiler; ~ de la pelle *m* TRANSPORT digging bucket
godille *f* NAUT *à l'arrière du bateau* scull
godiller *vi* NAUT *à l'arrière du bateau* scull
godronnage *m* CONS MECA knurling, nurling, PRODUCTION milling
godronner *vt* PRODUCTION mill
godronnoir *m* CONS MECA knurling tool, nurl, *de tourneur* knurl, PRODUCTION nurling tool, *de tourneur* milling tool
goélette *f* NAUT schooner
goémon *m* POLLU MER seaweed; ~ d'épave *m* OCEANO algal mat
goethite *f* MINERAUX goethite
golfe *m* NAUT, OCEANO gulf
gommage *m* PAPIER gumming, PLAST CAOU *défaut de couleur de peinture* rub-up, REVETEMENT rubber coating
gomme *f* CHIMIE gum, rubber, IMPRIM gum, MINES blasting gelatine; ~ adragante *f* AGRO ALIM gum tragacanth, tragacanth; ~ élastique *f* CHIMIE caoutchouc; ~ ester *f* PLAST CAOU *caoutchouc* ester gum; ~ gélifiante *f* IMPRIM *plaques* jelly gum; ~ de karaya *f* AGRO ALIM, CHIMIE karaya gum; ~ laque *f* COULEURS lacca, shellac, shellack, ELECTR *isolation* shellac, PRODUCTION lac, REVETEMENT rubber varnish
gommé *adj* REVETEMENT rubber-coated, rubber-covered
gommes: ~ spéciales pour le revêtement anticorrosion *f pl* SECURITE special rubber-lining protecting against corrosion

gond *m* CONSTR gate hook, hook; ~ et penture *m* CONSTR hook and hinge; ~ de porte *m* CONSTR gate hook
gondolage *m* CINEMAT buckle, PAPIER waviness
gondwanien *adj* GEOLOGIE Gondwanan
gonflable *adj* POLLU MER inflatable
gonflage *m* CINEMAT *tirage optique par agrandissement* blowup, optical enlargement, POLLU MER inflation; ~ cabine *m* AERONAUT cabin pressurization
gonflant *m* TEXTILE bulk
gonflé *adj* VEHICULES *moteur* hotted-up (BrE), souped-up (AmE)
gonflement *m* CONSTR bulking, MINES creep, floor heave, PLAST CAOU swelling, RECYCLAGE *des boues* bulking, TEXTILE swelling; ~ des boues *m* DISTRI EAU, HYDROLOGIE sludge bulking; ~ diélectrique *m* NUCLEAIRE dielectric swelling; ~ dû au gel *m* CHARBON frost heave; ~ des fibres *m* IMPRIM *papier* fiber puffing (AmE), fibre puffing (BrE); ~ de la fonte *m* MATERIAUX, METALL growth; ~ secondaire *m* NUCLEAIRE secondary swelling
gonfler[1] *vt* CINEMAT blow up, bump up, print up, DISTRI EAU bulk, PHYSIQUE inflate, TEXTILE swell, TV bump up
gonfler[2] *vi* CONS MECA bulge, MINES creep, PHYSIQUE swell
gonio *m* OCEANO position finder
goniomètre *m* AERONAUT direction finder, CRISTALL, GEOMETRIE goniometer, OCEANO goniometer, position finder, radiogoniometer; ~ à réflexion *m* GEOMETRIE reflecting goniometer
goniométrie *f* PHYSIQUE direction finding, TELECOM DF, direction finding
GOR: ~ de dissolution *m* PETR solution gas-oil ratio
gore *m* MINES clay parting
gorge:[1] à ~ *adj* PRODUCTION grooved
gorge[2] *f* ACOUSTIQUE, CERAM VER throat, CONS MECA *d'une poulie* groove, CONSTR *d'une serrure* tumbler, MECANIQUE groove, PAPIER *d'un essieu* neck, PRODUCTION groove; ~ au-dessus du niveau de la sole *f* CERAM VER lifted throat; ~ de brûleur *f* CERAM VER port neck; ~ mobile *f* CONSTR *d'une serrure* tumbler; ~ au niveau de la sole *f* CERAM VER straight throat; ~ pare-chaleur *f* AUTO heat dam; ~ du planétaire *f* AUTO sun gear lever collar (BrE), sun gearshift collar (AmE); ~ de segment de piston *f* VEHICULES *moteur* piston ring groove
gorges:[1] à ~ *adj* PRODUCTION grooved
gorges:[2] ~ de dégagement *f pl* CONS MECA thread undercuts
goslarite *f* MINERAUX goslarite
gouachage *m* CINEMAT opaquing
goudron *m* CHIMIE, CONSTR, NAUT tar, PETROLE bitumen, PLAST CAOU tar, POLLU MER tar ball; ~ de gaz *m* CHARBON coal tar, gas tar; ~ de houille *m* CHARBON coal tar, gas tar; ~ minéral *m* CONSTR mineral tar
goudronnage *m* CONSTR tarring
goudronner *vt* NAUT tar
goudronneuse *f* CONSTR tar sprayer, tar sprinkler
gouge *f* CONSTR gouge, PRODUCTION bead, bead tool; ~ pleine *f* CONS MECA chisel, round-nosed chisel, round-nosed cold chisel, PRODUCTION chipping chisel; ~ de sculpteur *f* CONS MECA firmer gouge; ~ de tour *f* CONS MECA turning gouge; ~ de tourneur *f* CONS MECA turning gouge
gougeage *m* CONSTR flame gouging, PRODUCTION gouging

goujon *m* AUTO stud, CONS MECA gudgeon, set pin, stub, stud, stud bolt, CONSTR gudgeon, joggle, pin, *d'une charnière* dowel, dowel pin, MECANIQUE stud, PRODUCTION stud, *d'un châssis de fonderie* pin, *d'un châssis de moulage* steady pin, *de boîte à noyaux* dowel, dowel pin, VEHICULES bolt, stud; **~ d'assemblage** *m* MECANIQUE alignment pin; **~ de centrage** *m* CONS MECA box pin; **~ de châssis** *m* CONS MECA flask pin; **~ prisonnier** *m* CONS MECA set pin, standing bolt, stud, stud bolt, CONSTR dowel, dowel pin, gudgeon, joggle; **~ repère** *m* CONS MECA locating pin

goujonner *vt* CONSTR dowel, joggle

goujure *f* CONS MECA gash; **~ d'usure** *f* PRODUCTION gouging

goulet *m* NAUT *d'un port* narrows, OCEANO gut, narrows, sound; **~ abyssal** *m* OCEANO abyssal pass; **~ d'étranglement** *m* PRODUCTION bottleneck; **~ de marée** *m* OCEANO tidal inlet

goulot **~ d'étranglement** *m* IMPRIM, MECANIQUE, PRODUCTION, TRANSPORT bottleneck; **~ large** *m* EMBALLAGE wide-mouth neck; **~ de remplissage** *m* AUTO neck

goulotte *f* CERAM VER spout, trough, MECANIQUE chute, PETROLE *canalisations des boues* feed hose union, PRODUCTION conduit, spout; **~ d'amenée des billes** *f* CERAM VER chute; **~ à boue** *f* PETROLE mud return line; **~ à calcin** *f* CERAM VER cullet chute; **~ à coussin d'air** *f* TRANSPORT aeroglide; **~ froide** *f* PRODUCTION *moulage* cold shot; **~ orientable** *f* CONSTR swinging chute; **~ pour câble** *f* PRODUCTION wiring duct; **~ pour fil** *f* PRODUCTION wiring duct

goulottes *f pl* PRODUCTION duct work

goupille *f* CONS MECA cotter pin, pin, CONSTR brad, MECANIQUE pin, NAUT cotter pin; **~ antidérapante du levier de commande** *f* PRODUCTION antislip operating lever clamp; **~ d'arrêt** *f* PHOTO locating pin; **~ de blocage** *f* PRODUCTION clamp pin; **~ de calage** *f* CONS MECA set pin; **~ cannelée** *f* CONS MECA grooved pin; **~ au cône Morse** *f* CONS MECA Morse taper pin; **~ conique** *f* MECANIQUE taper pin; **~ conique de positionnement** *f* CONS MECA taper dowel; **~ conique de positionnement à trou taraudé** *f* CONS MECA taper dowel with extracting thread; **~ cylindrique** *f* CONS MECA cylindrical pin, parallel dowel pin; **~ cylindrique trempée** *f* CONS MECA hardened dowel pin; **~ cylindrique à trou taraudé** *f* CONS MECA parallel pin with internal thread; **~ à demeure** *f* CONS MECA set pin; **~ élastique spiralée** *f* CONS MECA coiled spring-type straight pin; **~ fendue** *f* CONS MECA split pin, MECANIQUE cotter pin; **~ filetée** *f* CONS MECA bolt; **~ de galet** *f* PRODUCTION roller pin; **~ pleine** *f* CONS MECA solid cotter pin, solid pin; **~ de position conique** *f* CONS MECA taper pin; **~ de position conique à longueur filetée** *f* CONS MECA taper pin with external thread; **~ de position conique à trou taraudé** *f* CONS MECA taper pin with internal thread; **~ de sécurité** *f* CINEMAT safety pin, IMPRIM *mécanique* shearing pin, NAUT safety pin; **~ de sûreté** *f* MILITAIRE fuse safety pin

goupille-frein *f* CONS MECA locking pin

goupillon *m* EQUIP LAB *nettoyage de tubes* brush, *nettoyage* tube brush

gousset *m* IMPRIM *plieuse* gusset, NAUT bracket, gusset; **~ de barrot** *m* NAUT beam bracket, beam knee; **~ de contreventement** *m* NAUT tripping bracket; **~ de pont** *m* NAUT beam bracket, beam knee

goût **~ défectueux** *m* AGRO ALIM off-flavor (AmE), off-flavour (BrE)

goutte *f* AGRO ALIM drop, CERAM VER bead, gob, PAPIER drop; **~ d'étain en cratère** *f* CERAM VER crater drip (BrE), top tin (AmE); **~ de verre** *f* CERAM VER Dutch drop; **~ de voûte** *f* CERAM VER crown drop, shear alignment

gouttelette *f* METEO, POLLUTION droplet; **~ d'huile** *f* PHYSIQUE oil drop; **~ de saumure** *f* NUCLEAIRE brine droplet

gouttelettes **~ liquides** *f pl* POLLUTION liquid droplets; **~ liquides suspendues** *f pl* POLLUTION suspended liquid droplets

goutter *vi* PAPIER drop

gouttes **~ froides** *f pl* PRODUCTION *moulage* cold shot

gouttière *f* CONS MECA gutter, CONSTR box gutter, gutter, trough gutter, IMPRIM *imposition* gutter, NAUT stringer; **~ en dessus** *f* CONSTR parapet gutter; **~ pendante** *f* CONSTR eaves gutter, eaves trough

gouvernail *m* NAUT rudder; **~ compensé** *m* NAUT balanced rudder; **~ de direction** *m* PHYSIQUE rudder; **~ de fortune** *m* NAUT jury rudder; **~ non compensé** *m* NAUT unbalanced rudder; **~ plat** *m* NAUT single plate rudder; **~ de profondeur** *m* NAUT diving rudder; **~ suspendu** *m* NAUT spade rudder, underhung rudder

gouverne *f* AERONAUT, PHYSIQUE control surface; **~ aérodynamique** *f* ESPACE aerodynamic control surface; **~ compensée** *f* AERONAUT balanced control surface; **~ de direction** *f* AERONAUT, PHYSIQUE rudder; **~ de direction par effet de frein** *f* AERONAUT drag rudder; **~ de profondeur** *f* AERONAUT elevator

gouverner *vt* NAUT navigate, *navire* handle; **~ à un cap** *vt* NAUT steer; **~ sur** *vt* NAUT stand for, steer for

gouvernes **~ en série** *f pl* AERONAUT *d'un aéronef* serial rudders

gouverneur *m* PRODUCTION checker

GPL *abrév* (*gaz de pétrole liquéfié*) CHAUFFAGE, GAZ, PETROLE, THERMODYN, TRANSPORT LPG (*liquefied petroleum gas*)

graben **~ intracratonique** *m* GEOLOGIE rift valley; **~ médio-océanique** *m* GEOLOGIE rift valley

gradateur *m* CINEMAT dimmer

gradation *f* COULEURS gradation, IMPRIM graduation, *photogravure* gradation, TELECOM grading; **~ des teintes** *f* PHOTO tonal gradation

grade *m* PHYSIQUE grade; **~ de papier** *m* PHOTO paper grade

gradient *m* ELECTROTEC gradient, GEOMETRIE grade, *d'une courbe, spécifié à un point donné* gradient, PHYS FLUID *température, pression* gradient, PHYSIQUE gradient, slope; **~ adiabatique** *m* AERONAUT adiabatic lapse rate; **~ adiabatique sec** *m* POLLUTION dry adiabatic lapse rate; **~ de champ électrique** *m* ELECTROTEC electric field gradient; **~ de champ magnétique** *m* ELECTROTEC magnetic field gradient; **~ de la contrainte de Reynolds** *m* PHYS FLUID gradient of Reynolds stress; **~ de fracturation** *m* GEOLOGIE, PETROLE fracture gradient; **~ géostatique** *m* GEOLOGIE, PETROLE overburden gradient; **~ géothermique** *m* EN RENOUV, GEOLOGIE, GEOPHYS, PETROLE geothermal gradient; **~ hydraulique** *m* HYDROLOGIE hydraulic gradient; **~ d'indice** *m* ELECTROTEC, OPTIQUE graded index; **~ de potentiel** *m* ELECTR, PHYSIQUE potential gradient; **~ de pression** *m* PETROLE, PHYS FLUID pressure gradient; **~ de pression de formation** *m* GEOLOGIE, PETROLE formation pressure gradient; **~ de pression**

de fracturation *m* PETROLE fracture gradient; ~ **de pression imposés** *m* PHYS FLUID imposed pressure gradient – **de pression nul** *m* PHYS FLUID zero pressure gradient; ~ **de température** *m* MAT CHAUFF, REFRIG, THERMODYN temperature gradient, thermal gradient; ~ **de température adiabatique** *m* PHYS FLUID adiabatic temperature gradient; ~ **de tension** *m* ELECTR voltage gradient; ~ **thermique** *m* MAT CHAUFF, REFRIG, THERMODYN temperature gradient, thermal gradient; ~ **vertical de température** *m* METEO vertical temperature gradient

gradin *m* CONS MECA step, *d'un cône, d'un cône-poulie* lift, CRISTALL step, MINES lift, stope; ~ **chassant** *m* MINES drift stope; ~ **de plage** *m* GEOLOGIE, OCEANO beach berm; ~ **renversé** *m* CONSTR back stope, MINES overhand stope

gradins: **à ~** *adj* CONS MECA stepped; **en ~** *adj* CONS MECA stepped

gradiomanomètre *m* PETR gradiomanometer

graduation *f* EQUIP LAB graduation, GEOMETRIE scale, INSTRUMENT compass card; ~ **chiffrée** *f* METROLOGIE scale mark

graduer *vt* PHYSIQUE calibrate

grain:[1] **à ~ fin** *adj* CINEMAT *pellicule, révélateur* fine-grained, GEOLOGIE fine-grained, fine-textured, MATERIAUX, METALL fine-grained; **à ~ gros** *adj* CONSTR rough-grained; **à ~ grossier** *adj* CONSTR rough-grained; **à ~ moyen** *adj* GEOLOGIE medium-grained

grain[2] *m* ACOUSTIQUE, CHARBON, CINEMAT grain, IMPRIM photographic grain, MATERIAUX grain, METEO shower, squall, METROLOGIE grain, NAUT gust, *du bois* grain, PRODUCTION grain; ~ **abrasif** *m* PRODUCTION grit; ~ **d'acier** *m* CONS MECA center bearing plate (AmE), centre bearing plate (BrE); ~ **allongé** *m* METALL elongated grain; ~ **blanc** *m* OCEANO white squall; ~ **du chapeau** *m* PRODUCTION follower bush; ~ **court** *m* IMPRIM *papier* short grain; ~ **équiaxe** *m* METALL equiaxed grain; ~ **fin** *m* METALL fine-grain; ~ **flottant** *m* AGRO ALIM swimmer; ~ **grossier** *m* MINES coarse grain; ~ **limite** *m* CHARBON near mesh; ~ **noir** *m* OCEANO black squall; ~ **d'orge** *m* CONS MECA round-nose tool, round-nosed chisel, round-nosed cold chisel; ~ **d'un papier** *m* PAPIER paper grain; ~ **de la photo** *m* IMPRIM *photogravure* graininess; ~ **plongeur** *m* AGRO ALIM sinker

grainage *m* PAPIER graining

graine: **oléagineuse** *f* AGRO ALIM oil seed

grainette *f* CERAM VER breezing

grainoir *m* PAPIER graining machine

grains:[1] **en ~** *adj* MATERIAUX in grains

grains[2] *m pl* CERAM VER specking; ~ **bien classés** *m pl* GEOLOGIE well-sorted grains; ~ **de carbure** *m pl* MATERIAUX carbide grains

graissage *m* AUTO lubrication, IMPRIM *impression* plugging, MATERIAUX lubrification, PAPIER greasing, lubrication, PRODUCTION greasing, lubricating, lubrification, oiling, REFRIG, VEHICULES lubrification; ~ **à carter** *m* VEHICULES *lubrification du moteur* sump-type lubrication; ~ **à carter sec** *m* AUTO dry sump lubrication; ~ **à compte-gouttes** *m* CONS MECA drip-feed lubrication; ~ **à film d'huile** *m* AERONAUT boundary lubrication; ~ **à l'huile** *m* PRODUCTION oiling; ~ **du moule** *m* CERAM VER doping, swabbing; ~ **par barbotage** *m* AUTO, CH DE FER splash lubrication, REFRIG splash lubrication; ~ **sous pression** *m* AUTO forced feed lubrication, pressure feed, pressure lubri-

cation, CONS MECA, PRODUCTION force-feed lubrication, REFRIG forced lubrification

graisse *f* AGRO ALIM fat, shortening, AUTO grease, CHIMIE tallow, IMPRIM *composition* weight, MECANIQUE *matériaux* grease, PAPIER fat, grease; ~ **animale** *f* AGRO ALIM animal fat; ~ **à câble** *f* ELECTROTEC cable grease; ~ **de caractère** *f* IMPRIM weight of face, weight of type; ~ **comestible artificielle** *f* AGRO ALIM manufactured edible fat; ~ **conductrice** *f* ESPACE *véhicules* conductive grease; ~ **consistante** *f* CONS MECA block grease; ~ **de copra** *f* AGRO ALIM coconut oil; ~ **durcie** *f* AGRO ALIM solidified fat; ~ **fondue** *f* AGRO ALIM rendered fat; ~ **graphitée** *f* MECANIQUE *matériaux* graphite grease; ~ **hydrogénée** *f* AGRO ALIM hydrogenated fat; ~ **de laine** *f* CHIMIE lanolin, lanoline; ~ **pour hautes températures** *f* MECANIQUE *matériaux* high-temperature grease; ~ **solidifiée** *f* AGRO ALIM solidified fat; ~ **végétale** *f* AGRO ALIM vegetable fat

graisser *vt* PRODUCTION grease, lubricate, oil; ~ **à l'huile** *vt* PRODUCTION oil

graisseur *m* MECANIQUE lubricating nipple, MINES oiler, PRODUCTION grease cup, grease lubricator, greaser, lubricator, oiler, TEXTILE oiler, VEHICULES grease cap; ~ **à casque** *m* PRODUCTION helmet cap lubricator; ~ **à chapeau mobile** *m* PRODUCTION helmet cap lubricator; ~ **à compression** *m* PRODUCTION spring grease lubricator; ~ **compte-gouttes** *m* CONS MECA drip-feed lubricator; ~ **à débit visible** *m* CONS MECA sight-feed lubricator; ~ **à épinglette** *m* PRODUCTION needle lubricator; ~ **à graisse consistante** *m* CONS MECA set grease cup; ~ **à ressort** *m* PRODUCTION spring grease lubricator; ~ **à tige** *m* PRODUCTION needle lubricator; ~ **verse-gouttes** *m* CONS MECA drip-feed lubricator

graisseux *adj* AGRO ALIM tallowy

grammage *m* IMPRIM paper substance, paper weight, PAPIER basis weight, grammage, substance; ~ **de la couche** *m* IMPRIM *papier* coating weight; ~ **réel** *m* IMPRIM actual weight

grammaire *f* INFORMAT, ORDINAT grammar

grammatite *f* MINERAUX grammatite

gramme *m* CHIMIE, METROLOGIE, PHYSIQUE gram (AmE), gramme (BrE); ~ **au mètre carré** *m* IMPRIM gram per square meter (AmE), gramme per square metre (BrE)

gramme-équivalent *m* CHIMIE gram equivalent (AmE), gramme equivalent (BrE)

gramme-masse *m* METROLOGIE gram in mass (AmE), gramme in mass (BrE)

gramophone *m* ENREGISTR gramophone

gran: ~ **de pêche** *f* OCEANO deep-sea fishery, offshore fishery

grand:[1] **à ~ rendement** *adj* CONS MECA heavy duty; ~ **teint** *adj* COULEURS *textiles*, TEXTILE colorfast (AmE), colourfast (BrE)

grand:[2] **au ~ largue** *adv* NAUT on a broad reach

grand:[3] ~ **air** *m* CONSTR open air; ~ **angulaire** *m* CINEMAT wide-angle lens; ~ **axe** *m* GEOMETRIE *d'une ellipse* major axis, TRANSPORT arterial highway; ~ **bras de vergue** *m* NAUT mainbrace; ~ **cercle** *m* PHYSIQUE great circle; ~ **collisionneur électron-positron** *m (LEP)* PHYS PART large electron-positron collider *(LEP)*; ~ **collisionneur de hadrons** *m* PHYS PART LHC, large hadron collider; ~ **escorteur** *m* NAUT destroyer; ~ **format journal** *m* IMPRIM broadside page; ~ **fragment dans une mylonite** *m* GEOLOGIE porphyroclast; ~ **frag-**

ment détritique *m* GEOLOGIE *dans une matrice plus fine*, PETR phenoclast; ~ **frais** *m* METEO moderate gale; ~ **mât** *m* NAUT mainmast; ~ **pas** *m* AERONAUT high pitch, *d'une hélice* coarse pitch; ~ **pas taraudage** *m* CONS MECA coarse pitch; **très** ~ **réseau d'antennes** *m* (*VLA*) ASTRONOMIE Very Large Array (*VLA*); ~ **ressort** *m* CONS MECA main spring; ~ **routier transocéanique** *m* NAUT oceanic routing chart; ~ **schelem** *m* PETR grand slam; ~ **signal** *m* ELECTRON large signal; ~ **teint** *m* PLAST CAOU *matière première pour peinture* lasting color (AmE), lasting colour (BrE), lasting pigment

Grand: ~ **Chariot** *m* ASTRONOMIE Big Dipper (AmE), Plough (BrE); ~ **nuage de magellan** *m* ASTRONOMIE Large Magellanic Cloud

grande:[1] **à** ~ **consommation d'énergie** *adj* THERMODYN energy-intensive; ~ **consommatrice d'énergie** *adj* THERMODYN energy-intensive; **à** ~ **échelle** *adj* GEOLOGIE large-scale, megascale, GEOPHYS *carte* large-scale; **à** ~ **vitesse** *adj* MECANIQUE high-speed; **de** ~ **puissance** *adj* CONS MECA heavy duty

grande:[2] ~ **aiguille** *f* METROLOGIE *d'une horloge, d'une montre* minute hand; ~ **constante de temps** *f* ELECTRON longtime constant; ~ **couronne** *f* AUTO crown wheel, ring gear; ~ **écoute** *f* NAUT mainsheet; ~ **informatique** *f* ORDINAT high end computing; ~ **ligne** *f* CH DE FER main line; ~ **ligne de chemin de fer** *f* TRANSPORT arterial railroad (AmE), arterial railway (BrE); ~ **marée** *f* HYDROLOGIE spring tide, NAUT equinoctial tide, OCEANO spring tide; ~ **multiplication** *f* CONS MECA high gear; ~ **normale** *f* GEOPHYS long normal; ~ **onde** *f* ELECTR *rayonnement* long wave; ~ **route** *f* CONSTR main road, TRANSPORT arterial highway; ~ **visite** *f* AERONAUT major inspection; ~ **vitesse** *f* CONS MECA high-speed

Grande: ~ **Ourse** *f* ASTRONOMIE Great Bear, Ursa Major

grandes: ~ **eaux** *f pl* NAUT high water; ~ **lumières** *f pl* IMPRIM *photogravure* highlights; ~ **ondes** *f pl* PHYS ONDES *radio* long waves

grandeur *f* ELECTRON quantity, PHYSIQUE bulk, magnitude; ~ **alternative** *f* ESSAIS alternating quantity; ~ **électrique** *f* ELECTR electric variable; ~ **extensive** *f* PHYSIQUE extensive quantity; ~ **intensive** *f* PHYSIQUE intensive quantity; ~ **mesurée** *f* ELECTRON measurand, measured quantity; ~ **nature** *f* CONS MECA full scale; ~ **normale** *f* PRODUCTION standard size; ~ **oscillante** *f* ELECTRON oscillating quantity; ~ **périodique** *f* ACOUSTIQUE, ELECTRON periodic quantity; ~ **quantifiée** *f* ELECTRON quantized quantity; ~ **réglée** *f* ELECTROTEC controlled variable; ~ **sinusoïdale** *f* ELECTRON, ELECTROTEC sinusoidal quantity; ~ **sinusoïdale amortie** *f* ELECTROTEC damped sinusoidal quantity; ~ **de sortie** *f* ELECTROTEC output quantity; ~ **variable** *f* ELECTROTEC variable quantity

grandeurs: ~ **de prises** *f pl* ELECTR tapping quantities

grandissement *m* INSTRUMENT magnification scale, PHYSIQUE magnification; ~ **angulaire** *m* PHYSIQUE angular magnification; ~ **axial** *m* PHYSIQUE axial magnification; ~ **latéral** *m* PHYSIQUE lateral magnification; ~ **linéaire** *m* PHYSIQUE linear magnification; ~ **longitudinal** *m* PHYSIQUE longitudinal magnification; ~ **transversal** *m* PHYSIQUE transverse magnification

grands: ~ **blancs** *m pl* IMPRIM *photogravure* highlights; ~ **ciseaux** *m pl* TEXTILE shears; ~ **fonds** *m pl* NAUT ocean deeps, ocean depths; ~ **tourbillons** *m pl* PHYS FLUID large eddies

grand-voile *f* NAUT mainsail

granit *m* CONSTR, GEOLOGIE, MATERIAUX granite

granitage *m* CERAM VER knurling

granite *m* CONSTR, GEOLOGIE, MATERIAUX granite

granité *adj* PRODUCTION crinkled

granitelle *m* PETR granitell, granitelle

granitisation *f* GEOLOGIE, MATERIAUX granitization

granitite *f* PETR granitite

granitoïde[1] *adj* MATERIAUX *structure* granitoid

granitoïde[2] *m* GEOLOGIE granitoid

granoclassement: ~ **vertical progressif** *m* GEOLOGIE graded bedding

granophyre *m* PETR granophyre

granulaire *adj* CONSTR granular

granularité *f* INFORMAT, ORDINAT granularity

granulateur *m* GENIE CHIM granulator; ~ **en lit fluidisé** *m* GENIE CHIM fluid-bed granulator

granulation *f* CERAM VER *de la composition*, CHARBON, GENIE CHIM, MATERIAUX granulation, PHOTO graining, *d'une émulsion* granularity; ~ **de la surface solaire** *f* ASTRONOMIE solar granulation

granulatoire *m* GENIE CHIM granulating machine

granulats: ~ **marins** *m pl* OCEANO marine aggregates

granule *m* EMBALLAGE granule

granulé *m* PLAST CAOU *plastiques* pellet

granuler *vt* EMBALLAGE, GENIE CHIM granulate

granulés *m pl* GENIE CHIM granulates

granuleux *adj* GEOLOGIE granulated

granulomètre *m* NUCLEAIRE PSA, particle size analyzer

granulométrie *f* CERAM VER grading, CHARBON granulometry, size analysis, size distribution, size grading, CHIMIE particle size distribution, CONS MECA *abrasifs agglomérés* grain size analysis, CONSTR grading, GENIE CHIM particle size analysis, GEOLOGIE grain size distribution, MATERIAUX particle size analysis, NUCLEAIRE sieve analysis, PLAST CAOU *pigment, charge* particle size, RESSORTS grain size distribution; ~ **discontinue** *f* CERAM VER gap sizing; ~ **grossière** *f* GEOLOGIE coarse texture

granulométrique *adj* CHARBON granulometric

graphe *m* INFORMAT, ORDINAT graph; ~ **d'utilisation** *m* EN RENOUV utilization curve

graphes: ~ **de puissance** *m pl* EN RENOUV power curves

graphique *m* IMPRIM graphic, *tableautage* chart, INFORMAT, ORDINAT graphics, PHYSIQUE chart, PRODUCTION diagram; ~ **à barres** *m* ORDINAT bar chart; ~ **circulaire** *m* INFORMAT, MATH pie chart; ~ **couleur** *m* ORDINAT color display (AmE), colour display (BrE); ~ **du flux thermique** *m* THERMODYN heat flow chart; ~ **de fumée** *m* SECURITE *classification* smoke chart; ~ **linéaire** *m* INFORMAT line graph; ~ **PERT** *m* INFORMAT PERT chart; ~ **de présentation** *m* INFORMAT, ORDINAT presentation graphics; ~ **de la production** *m* PRODUCTION output diagram; ~ **de répartition des vitesses** *m* CONS MECA velocity diagram; ~ **à secteurs** *m* INFORMAT pie chart; ~ **tramé** *m* INFORMAT, ORDINAT raster graphics; ~ **tridimensionnel** *m* INFORMAT three-dimensional graphics; ~ **vectoriel** *m* INFORMAT, ORDINAT vector graphics

graphiques: ~ **coordonnés avec étiquettes pour bouteilles** *m pl* EMBALLAGE graphics coordinated with bottle labels; ~ **couleurs** *m* ORDINAT color graphics (AmE), colour graphics (BrE); ~ **haute définition** *m pl* ORDINAT high-resolution graphics

graphisme: ~ **informatique** *m* ORDINAT computer art

graphiste *m* IMPRIM draftsman (AmE), draughtsman

(BrE)

graphite *m* CHIMIE graphite, plumbago, COULEURS black lead, MINERAUX graphite; **~ sphéroïdal** *m* MATERIAUX *minéralogie*, MINERAUX spheroidal graphite

graphitisation *f* METALL graphitization

graphomètre *m* CONSTR demi circle, INSTRUMENT alidade

grappe:[1] **en ~** *adj* TRANSPORT clustered

grappe[2] *f* INFORMAT, ORDINAT, PRODUCTION cluster; **~ de compensation** *f* NUCLEAIRE shim rod bank; **~ de parachutes** *f* MILITAIRE parachute cluster

grappin *m* CONS MECA grapnel, NAUT grab, grapnel, grapple, grappling hook, NUCLEAIRE grab, grapple, TRANSPORT grapple

gras *adj* IMPRIM bold

graticule *m* ELECTRON graticule; **~ extérieur** *m* ELECTRON external graticule; **~ intérieur** *m* ELECTRON internal graticule

grattage *m* PRODUCTION scraping, TEXTILE brushing, napping; **~ de l'émulsion** *m* IMPRIM emulsion stripping

gratte-brosse *f* CONSTR scratch brush

gratter[1] *vt* POLLU MER scrape, TEXTILE nap

gratter[2] *vi* CONSTR *lime ou sable sur une surface* bite

gratteur *m* POLLU MER scraper

grattoir *m* CONS MECA, CONSTR, MECANIQUE *outillage*, POLLU MER scraper; **~ triangulaire** *m* CONSTR shave hook

grau *m* OCEANO inlet, lagoon channel

grauwacke *f* GEOLOGIE graywacke (AmE), greywacke (BrE); **~ sans feldspath** *f* GEOLOGIE low-rank graywacke (AmE), low-rank greywacke (BrE)

gravé: ~ par le client *adj* PRODUCTION field-engraved

graver *vt* ENREGISTR *disques* record, IMPRIM engrave

graves *m pl* ENREGISTR bass

graveur *m* CERAM VER engraver; **~ à faisceau dirigé** *m* ELECTRON scanning electron beam system; **~ à faisceau d'électrons** *m* ELECTRON electron beam lithography machine; **~ à faisceau d'électrons réparti** *m* ELECTRON electron beam projection printer; **~ sur bois** *m* IMPRIM print cutter

gravicélération *f* ESPACE *orbitographie* swing-by, swing-by effect

gravidéviation *f* ESPACE swing-by effect, *orbitographie* swing-by

gravier *m* CHARBON gravel, CONSTR aggregate, gravel, GEOLOGIE, PETR gravel; **~ à béton** *m* CONSTR aggregate, coarse aggregate; **~ de filtrage** *m* GENIE CHIM filter gravel; **~ filtrant** *m* DISTRI EAU, GENIE CHIM filter gravel; **~ fin** *m* CONSTR fine aggregate; **~ à grains fins** *m* CONSTR fine aggregate, grit; **~ de grosseur unique** *m* CONSTR single size gravel aggregate; **~ grossier** *m* CONSTR coarse aggregate; **~ à haute teneur d'or** *m* MINES highly-auriferous gravel; **~ serré** *m* CONSTR tight gravel

gravière *f* CONSTR, DISTRI EAU gravel pit

graviers *m pl* CONSTR gravel, grit; **~ aurifères** *m pl* MINES pay dirt, placer dirt

gravillon *m* CONSTR grit

gravillonnage *m* CONSTR gritting, sanding

gravillonneuse *f* TRANSPORT grit spreader, gritter

gravillons *m pl* CONSTR fine gravel

gravimètre *m* GEOPHYS gravimeter, gravity meter, PHYSIQUE gravimeter, gravity meter

gravimétrie *f* GEOLOGIE, GEOPHYS gravimetry, PETROLE gravimetric survey, gravimetry, PHYSIQUE gravimetry

gravimétrique *adj* CHARBON, GEOPHYS gravimetric

gravitation:[1] **de ~** *adj* ASTRONOMIE gravitational

gravitation[2] *f* ASTRONOMIE gravitation, ESPACE attraction, pull, gravitation, PHYSIQUE attraction, gravitation

gravitationnel *adj* ASTRONOMIE gravitational

gravité *f* ASTRONOMIE, ESPACE, MECANIQUE, PHYSIQUE gravity, QUALITE *d'une défaillance* criticality; **~ artificielle** *f* ESPACE artificial gravity

graviter:[1] **~ autour de** *vt* ESPACE orbit

graviter[2] *vi* ESPACE orbit

graviton *m* PHYSIQUE graviton

gravure *f* CHIMIE etching, ELECTRON engraving, lithography, IMPRIM engraving, PRODUCTION marking; **~ à l'acide** *f* CERAM VER acid etching; **~ avec masque** *f* ELECTRON masked lithography; **~ avec masque en contact** *f* ELECTRON contact lithography; **~ à balayage cavalier** *f* ELECTRON vector-scan electron beam lithography; **~ à balayage tramé** *f* ELECTRON raster scan electron beam lithography; **~ au cachet** *f* CERAM VER acid badging; **~ chimique du point** *f* IMPRIM *sur la totalité de l'illustration* flat etching; **~ au diamant** *f* CERAM VER diamond point engraving; **~ directe** *f* ELECTRON direct writing, IMPRIM *héliogravure* direct gravure; **~ directe par faisceau d'électrons** *f* ELECTRON direct electron beam writing; **~ directe sur métal** *f* ENREGISTR DMM, PRODUCTION direct metal mastering; **~ double offset** *f* IMPRIM double offset gravure; **~ à double transfert** *f* IMPRIM double offset gravure; **~ électronique** *f* ELECTRON electron beam lithography, IMPRIM electronic engraving; **~ électronique répartie** *f* ELECTRON projection electron beam lithography; **~ en contact** *f* ELECTRON contact lithography; **~ en proximité aux rayons X** *f* ELECTRON X-ray proximity printing; **~ au jet de sable** *f* CERAM VER sandblasting; **~ linoléum** *f* IMPRIM linocut; **~ lisse** *f* CERAM VER bright etching, clear etching; **~ lithographique** *f* IMPRIM lithographic print; **~ des moules** *f* CONS MECA mold engraving (AmE), mould engraving (BrE); **~ nuancée** *f* CERAM VER French embossing; **~ optique** *f* ELECTRON optical engraving; **~ à l'outil** *f* IMPRIM line engraving; **~ par faisceau d'électrons** *f* ELECTRON electron beam lithography; **~ par faisceau d'électrons à balayage** *f* ELECTRON scanning electron beam lithography; **~ par faisceau d'électrons à balayage cavalier** *f* ELECTRON vector-scan electron beam lithography; **~ par faisceau d'électrons à balayage tramé** *f* ELECTRON raster scan electron beam lithography; **~ par faisceau d'électrons dirigé** *f* ELECTRON direct writing, electron beam direct writing; **~ par faisceau d'électrons réparti** *f* ELECTRON electron beam projection lithography, projection electron beam lithography; **~ par faisceau d'ions** *f* ELECTRON ion beam lithography; **~ par flux d'électrons** *f* ELECTRON electron flood lithography; **~ par pressage** *f* OPTIQUE disc mastering (BrE), disk mastering (AmE), mastering; **~ par projection** *f* ELECTRON image projection, projection lithography; **~ du point** *f* IMPRIM *photogravure* dot etching; **~ profonde** *f* CERAM VER deep etching, rotting; **~ à proximité** *f* ELECTRON proximity lithography; **~ à quatre rouleaux inversés** *f* IMPRIM *héliogravure* four-roll reverse pan feed; **~ de la rainure en V** *f* ELECTRON V-groove etching; **~ aux rayons X** *f* ELECTRON X-ray lithography; **~ à relief prononcé** *f* CERAM VER embossing, engraving in relief; **~ à la roue** *f* CERAM VER engraving; **~ sans masque** *f*

ELECTRON maskless lithography; ~ **sans masque ni réticule** *f* ELECTRON direct pattern generation; ~ **universelle** *f* ACOUSTIQUE compatible groove modulation

gray *m (Gy)* METROLOGIE, PHYS RAYON, PHYSIQUE gray *(Gy)*

gréage *m* NAUT rigging

gréement *m* NAUT rigging, rig, OCEANO rig, rigging, vessel equipment, PETROLE rigging up; ~ **courant** *m* NAUT running rigging; ~ **dormant** *m* NAUT standing rigging

greenockite *f* MINERAUX cadmium blende, cadmium ocher (AmE), cadmium ochre (BrE), greenockite

greenovite *f* MINERAUX greenovite

gréer *vt* NAUT rig

gréeur *m* NAUT rigger

greffe: ~ **en phase gazeuse** *f* NUCLEAIRE gas phase grafting

greffons *m pl* IMPRIM *infographie* traps

grêle *f* METEO, NAUT, PHYSIQUE hail; ~ **de météore** *f* ASTRONOMIE meteor storm, meteor swarm

grêler *vi* METEO hail

grêlon *m* METEO, PHYSIQUE hailstone

grenade *f* MILITAIRE grenade; ~ **active** *f* MILITAIRE live grenade; ~ **antichar** *f* MILITAIRE antitank grenade; ~ **d'exercice** *f* MILITAIRE dummy grenade; ~ **fumigène** *f* MILITAIRE smoke grenade; ~ **à fusil** *f* MILITAIRE rifle grenade; ~ **lacrymogène** *f* MILITAIRE *guerre chimique* tear grenade; ~ **à main** *f* MILITAIRE hand grenade; ~ **à retardement** *f* MILITAIRE time grenade

grenaillage *m* CERAM VER shot peening, CONSTR shot-blasting

grenaille: ~ **abrasive** *f* MECANIQUE *traitement de surface* abrasive shot; ~ **d'acier trempé** *f* PRODUCTION chilled shot; ~ **de plomb** *f* PRODUCTION lead shot

grenaillé *adj* RESSORTS shot-peened

grenaillement *m* MINES shotting

grenailler *vt* GENIE CHIM granulate, PRODUCTION shot

grenailles *f pl* MINES coarse sand middlings

grenat *m* MATERIAUX, MINERAUX garnet; ~ **alumineux** *m* MINERAUX aluminium garnet (BrE), aluminum garnet (AmE); ~ **ferreux** *m* MINERAUX iron garnet; ~ **d'yttrium et d'aluminium** *m (YAG)* ELECTRON yttrium aluminium garnet (BrE), yttrium aluminum garnet (AmE) *(YAG)*; ~ **d'yttrium ferreux** *m (YIG)* ELECTRON yttrium iron garnet *(YIG)*

grener *vt* PRODUCTION grain

grenier *m* AGRO ALIM granary

grenouillère *f* DISTRI EAU rose, strainer, tailpiece, wind bore

grenu[1] *adj* GEOLOGIE, MATERIAUX granular

grenu[2] *m* MATERIAUX granularity

grès *m* CERAM VER grinding sand, CONSTR, GEOLOGIE sandstone, PETR grit, PETROLE sandstone; ~ **calcaire** *m* GEOLOGIE calcareous sandstone; ~ **coquillier** *m* GEOLOGIE shelly sandstone; ~ **feldspathique** *m* CERAM VER arkose, PETR graywacke (AmE), greywacke (BrE); ~ **meulier** *m* PRODUCTION millstone grit; ~ **meulière** *f* GEOLOGIE millstone grit (BrE); ~ **molaire** *m* PRODUCTION millstone grit; ~ **à pavés** *m* CONSTR paving stone; ~ **de plage** *m* OCEANO beach rock, sandstone; ~ **pur** *m* GEOLOGIE *très riche en quartz* orthoquartzite; ~ **quartzeux** *m* MATERIAUX, MINERAUX quartz sandstone; ~ **quartzite** *m* GEOLOGIE quartzitic sandstone

grésil *m* METEO graupel

grésillement *m* ACOUSTIQUE crackle

grésillon *m* MINES small, small coal

grève *f* HYDROLOGIE shoreline, OCEANO shingle beach, strand

griffage *m* IMPRIM *continu* crimping, *façonnage* crimp lock

griffe *f* CERAM VER scratch, CINEMAT claw, pin, CONS MECA clip, clutch, dog, fork chuck, prong chuck, three-pronged chuck, PRODUCTION clamping dog, gripping dog, grip, *d'une agrafe* dog; ~ **à accessoires** *f* PHOTO accessory shoe; ~ **de blocage** *f* CONS MECA clamping handle; ~ **centrale** *f* CINEMAT central claw; ~ **d'entraînement** *f* CINEMAT feed claw, film feeder pin, intermittent claw, pull down claw; ~ **de fixité** *f* CINEMAT register pin; ~ **de guidage** *f* MINES guide shoe; ~ **latérale unique** *f* CINEMAT single side claw; ~ **de serrage** *f* CONS MECA clip, clutch

griffer *vt* IMPRIM crimp

griffe-support *f* PHOTO accessory shoe; ~ **pour lampe flash** *f* PHOTO flash shoe

griffure *f* IMPRIM *surface* scratch

grignoteuse *f* CONS MECA nibbling machine (AmE), power nibbler (BrE)

grillage *m* CHARBON roasting, CONSTR netting, network, wire netting, MECANIQUE screen, PLAST CAOU *caoutchouc* scorch, PRODUCTION grating, roasting, TEXTILE grid, THERMODYN burning; ~ **du crible** *m* GENIE CHIM sieve netting; ~ **métallique** *m* CONSTR wire mesh reinforcement; ~ **Mooney** *m* PLAST CAOU *caoutchouc* Mooney scorch; ~ **par fluidisation** *m* GENIE CHIM fluid-bed roasting

grille *f* AUTO grille, CHARBON grid, CONSTR railing, ELECTR *électrode* grid, ELECTRON grid, mesh, ELECTROTEC gate, HYDROLOGIE bar screen, screen, INFORMAT raster, MAT CHAUFF grate, NUCLEAIRE grid, ORDINAT raster, PHYSIQUE gate, grid, PRODUCTION grate, grating, grid, grizzly, *séparation des minerais bruts* screen, SECURITE guard, TV schedule, VEHICULES *commande de boîte de vitesses* range indicator; ~ **antigivre** *f* AERONAUT ice guard; ~ **d'arrêt** *f* ELECTRON barrier grid, suppressor grid, ELECTROTEC suppression grid, TV ion trap; ~ **d'assemblage combustible** *f* NUCLEAIRE grid-spaced fuel assembly; ~ **d'attaque** *f* AERONAUT injection grid; ~ **à aube** *f* AERONAUT deflector; ~ **d'aubes** *f* AERONAUT cascade blades, cascade vanes; ~ **autoalignée** *f* ELECTRON self-aligned gate; ~ **à barreaux** *f* CONS MECA bar screen, GENIE CHIM sieve grate, PRODUCTION grizzly; ~ **à barreaux mobiles** *f* PRODUCTION shaking grate; ~ **de carénage** *f* NAUT careening grid; ~ **à chaîne** *f* CONS MECA chain grate; ~ **de chaudière** *f* MAT CHAUFF boiler grate; ~ **de clavier** *f* INFORMAT keyboard template; ~ **du coeur** *f* NUCLEAIRE core grid structure; ~ **de commande** *f* ELECTROTEC control grid; ~ **de commutation** *f* TV switching matrix; ~ **de commutation à chevilles** *f* CINEMAT peg board; ~ **de commutation vidéo** *f* TV video switching matrix; ~ **de connexion** *f* ELECTROTEC lead frame; ~ **de couplage** *f* ELECTRON resonator grid; ~ **de crible** *f* GENIE CHIM sieve grate; ~ **démontable** *f* CONSTR collapsible gate; ~ **de désionisation** *f* ELECTRON deionizing grid; ~ **directrice d'entrée** *f* AERONAUT inducer; ~ **directrice de sortie** *f* AERONAUT exducer; ~ **en l'air** *f* ELECTRON floating gate, free grid, ELECTROTEC floating grid; ~ **en aluminium** *f* ELECTRON aluminium gate (BrE), aluminum gate (AmE); ~ **en polysilicium** *f* ELECTRON polysilicon gate; ~ **en silicium** *f* ELECTRON silicon gate; ~ **à étages** *f* PRODUCTION stepped grate; ~ **extensible** *f*

CONSTR collapsible gate; ~ **fixe** *f* MAT CHAUFF fixed grate; ~ **de foyer** *f* PRODUCTION fire grate, furnace grate; ~ **génératrice** *f* PHYS FLUID generating grid; ~ **génératrice de turbulence** *f* PHYS FLUID turbulence-generating grid; ~ **à gradins** *f* PRODUCTION stepped grate; ~ **à granuler** *f* GENIE CHIM granulating grate; ~ **internationale** *f* ELECTRON *fabrication des circuits imprimés* grid; ~ **de lavage** *f* CHARBON jig sieve; ~ **métallique** *f* ELECTRON metal gate; ~ **mobile** *f* MAT CHAUFF moving grate; ~ **de modulation** *f* TV modulation grid; ~ **non tissée** *f* CERAM VER nonwoven scrim; ~ **oscillante** *f* PRODUCTION shaking grate; ~ **de l'oscillateur local** *f* ELECTRON injection grid; ~ **de partage** *f* ELECTROTEC partition gate; ~ **de points fixes** *f* NUCLEAIRE fixed point net, observation grid; ~ **de polarisation** *f* ESPACE *communications* polarization grid; ~ **porte-objet** *f* INSTRUMENT specimen stage; ~ **à potentiel flottant** *f* ELECTRON floating gate, ELECTROTEC floating grid; ~ **de protection** *f* REFRIG fan guard; ~ **de protection en fil de fer** *f* PRODUCTION wire guard; ~ **de protection d'entrée** *f* CONS MECA guard against debris; ~ **rapide** *f* ELECTRON high-speed mesh; ~ **de réfraction** *f* EQUIP LAB *analyse*, OPTIQUE refraction grating; ~ **régulatrice** *f* COMMANDE regulating grid; ~ **rotative** *f* PRODUCTION rotary grate; ~ **de saisie** *f* PRODUCTION data form; ~ **de saisie pour séquenceur** *f* PRODUCTION *automatisme industriel* sequencer instruction data form; ~ **à secousses** *f* PRODUCTION shaking grate; ~ **de sécurité soudée à pression** *f* SECURITE pressure-welded safety grating; ~ **de stabilisation** *f* CINEMAT register pin; ~ **supérieure** *f* NUCLEAIRE upper grid; ~ **suppresseuse** *f* ELECTRON suppressor grid, ELECTROTEC suppression grid; ~ **de tube électronique** *f* ELECTRON electron tube grid; ~ **vibrante** *f* CHARBON vibrating grizzly

grille-cadre *f* ELECTRON frame grid

grille-écran *f* CONS MECA louver (AmE), ELECTRON screen grid; ~ **bleue** *f* TV blue screen grid; ~ **rouge** *f* TV red screen grid; ~ **verte** *f* TV green screen grid

grille-mémoire *f* ELECTRON storage mesh

griller *vt* THERMODYN burn

grimpement *m* CHIMIE *des liquides* creep

grippage *m* AERONAUT *d'un moteur* binding, AUTO jamming, seizing, CONS MECA seizing, NUCLEAIRE galling, VEHICULES *palier, piston* seizing; ~ **du piston** *m* AUTO piston freezing

grippement *m* CONS MECA seizing

gripper[1] *vi* CONS MECA seize

gripper:[2] **se ~** *v réfl* CONSTR bind, PRODUCTION *machine* stick

gris: ~ **neutre** *m* IMPRIM *photogravure, impression* neutral grey

grisé *m* IMPRIM *photogravure* base tint; ~ **mécanique** *m* IMPRIM *photogravure* flat tint

grisou *m* CHARBON firedamp, MINES firedamp, gas, marsh gas, pit gas, THERMODYN firedamp

grisoumètre *m* MINES methane detector, methane indicator, pit gas indicator

grisouteux *adj* MINES gaseous, gassy

grondements *m pl* MINES rumblings

groroïlite *f* MINERAUX groroilite

gros[1] *adj* GEOLOGIE *granulométrie* coarse; **à ~ grain** *adj* CONSTR rough-grained, GEOLOGIE, METALL coarse-grained

gros[2] *m* MINES coarse ore, lump ore; ~ **ballon** *m* CHIMIE kettle; ~ **béton** *m* CONSTR mass concrete; ~ **fil pour**

contours *m* TEXTILE gimp; ~ **galet** *m* CONSTR boulder; ~ **grain** *m* CINEMAT, METALL, MINES coarse grain; ~ **morceau** *m* CONSTR lump; ~ **murs** *m pl* CONSTR *d'un bâtiment* main walls; ~ **ordinateur** *m* ORDINAT mainframe; ~ **plan** *m* CINEMAT close-up; **très ~ plan** *m* CINEMAT BCU, big close up, extreme close-up; ~ **plan de tête** *m* CINEMAT head shot; ~ **porteur** *m* AERONAUT jumbo jet, TRANSPORT heavy jet, jumbo jet; ~ **sables** *m pl* MINES coarse sand, coarse sands; ~ **sel** *m* AGRO ALIM kitchen salt; ~ **temps** *m* NAUT *météorologie* heavy weather; ~ **titre** *m* IMPRIM bank, TEXTILE coarse count; ~ **tourbillons** *m pl* PHYS FLUID large eddies; **très ~ transporteur de brut** *m* (*TGTB*) PETROLE very large crude carrier (*VLCC*)

grosse *f* METROLOGIE gross; ~ **céramique** *f* CERAM VER ordinary ceramic, thick ware; ~ **chaudronnerie** *f* MAT CHAUFF boilermaking; ~ **étoile** *f* ASTRONOMIE huge star; ~ **houle** *f* NAUT heavy swell; ~ **jauge** *f* TEXTILE heavy gage (AmE), heavy gauge (BrE); ~ **mer** *f* NAUT heavy seas, OCEANO green sea; ~ **serrurerie** *f* CONSTR heavy ironwork; ~ **tête** *f* CONS MECA *de bielle* stub end; ~ **tête de bielle** *f* CONS MECA connecting rod big end, large end of connecting rod; ~ **trame** *f* IMPRIM coarse screen

grosses: ~ **pièces** *f pl* PRODUCTION heavy castings

grosseur *f* PHYSIQUE bulk; ~ **de grain** *f* CHIMIE particle size; ~ **du grain** *f* MATERIAUX, METALL grain size; ~ **de particule** *f* PLAST CAOU *pigment, charge* particle size

grossier *adj* CONSTR rough-hewn, GEOLOGIE *granulométrie* coarse

grossir[1] *vt* PHYSIQUE magnify

grossir[2] *vi* GEOMETRIE expand, HYDROLOGIE rise

grossissant *adj* INSTRUMENT magnifying

grossissement *m* INSTRUMENT enlargement, magnification, enlarging, magnifying, MATERIAUX, METALL coarsening, PHYSIQUE magnifying power; ~ **latéral** *m* INSTRUMENT lateral magnification; ~ **longitudinal** *m* INSTRUMENT longitudinal magnification; ~ **de loupe** *m* INSTRUMENT factorial magnification, lens magnification, magnifier enlargement; ~ **ultime** *m* METALL ultimate magnification; ~ **utile** *m* INSTRUMENT *de la loupe* magnification effectiveness

grossulaire *f* MINERAUX grossular, grossularite

grossularite *f* MINERAUX grossular, grossularite

groupage *m* ORDINAT blocking, TRANSPORT consolidation; ~ **des positifs pour les analyser ensemble** *m* IMPRIM *photogravure* ganging

groupe *m* ASTRONOMIE *de galaxies, d'étoiles* cluster, CHIMIE group, CONS MECA cluster, ELECTROTEC set, IMPRIM batch, INFORMAT, MATH, ORDINAT group, VEHICULES unit; ~ **acétoxyle** *m* AGRO ALIM acetoxyl; ~ **acétyle** *m* CHIMIE acetyl group; ~ **acyle** *m* MATERIAUX acyl group; ~ **d'articles de commerce** *m* EMBALLAGE commodity group; ~ **auxiliaire de puissance** *m* AERONAUT auxiliary power unit; ~ **auxiliaire au sol** *m* AERONAUT GPU, ground power unit; ~ **de base** *m* ELECTROTEC basic group; ~ **de caractères** *m* INFORMAT zone; ~ **de compresseur d'air** *m* CONS MECA air compressor set; ~ **compresseur-condenseur** *m* REFRIG condensing unit; ~ **convertisseur** *m* ELECTROTEC converter set; ~ **convertisseur Ward-Leonard** *m* ELECTROTEC Ward-Leonard set; ~ **de couchage** *m* IMPRIM *papier et finition* coating unit; ~ **de couplage** *m* ELECTR *transformateur* vector group; ~ **de démarrage au sol** *m* AERONAUT GPU, ground power unit; ~ **désherbeur** *m* CH DE FER *véhicules* weed-killing train;

~ **électrogène** m CINEMAT generator, jenny, CONSTR generator, ELECTR *alimentation* generating set, ELECTROTEC generating set, generator set; ~ **électrogène diesel** m ELECTROTEC diesel-driven generating set; ~ **électrogène de secours** m NUCLEAIRE diesel generator standby power plant; ~ **en cascade** m ELECTROTEC cascade set; ~ **encombrant** m CHIMIE bulky group; ~ **d'espace** m CRISTALL space group; ~ **d'essais** m ESSAIS test group; ~ **fermé d'abonnés** m TELECOM closed user group; ~ **fermé d'usagers** m *(GFU)* ORDINAT, TELECOM closed user group *(CUG)*; ~ **de fonction** m CHIMIE functional group; ~ **fonctionnel** m CHIMIE functional group; ~ **frigorifique** m REFRIG refrigerating unit; ~ **frigorifique amovible** m REFRIG clip-on refrigerating unit; ~ **frigorifique cavalier** m REFRIG saddle unit; ~ **frigorifique commercial** m REFRIG commercial condensing unit; ~ **frigorifique à faible puissance** m REFRIG fractional low-power condensing unit; ~ **générateur** m ELECTROTEC generating set; ~ **imprimant** m IMPRIM unit; ~ **imprimant en retiration** m IMPRIM *machine* perfecting unit; ~ **d'injecteurs** m AERONAUT engine nozzle cluster; ~ **de liquéfaction pour réfrigérant** m CONS MECA refrigerant liquifying set; ~ **lourd** m NUCLEAIRE heavy group; ~ **de marchandises** m EMBALLAGE group of commodities; ~ **de microcommutateurs** m PRODUCTION switch group assembly; ~ **de modules d'E/S** m PRODUCTION *automatisme industriel* I/O module group; ~ **de modules d'E/S à communication bidirectionnelle** m PRODUCTION *automatisme industriel* bidirectional I/O module group; ~ **moteur** m AERONAUT power plant, PRODUCTION *système hydraulique* power unit; ~ **moteur-générateur** m CONS MECA, ELECTROTEC motor-generator set; ~ **motopropulseur** m VEHICULES *moteur* power unit; ~ **motopropulseur critique** m AERONAUT critical power unit; ~ **motopropulseur le plus défavorable** m AERONAUT *navigabilité* critical power unit; ~ **d'ondes** m PHYSIQUE wave group; ~ **de pelliculage** m IMPRIM *papier et finition* coating unit; ~ **pendant** m CHIMIE pendant group; ~ **de pieux** m CHARBON pile group; ~ **ponctuel** m CRISTALL point group; ~ **primaire** m TELECOM basic group, group; ~ **propulseur** m NAUT power plant; ~ **propulsif** m ESPACE *propulsion* thrust subsystem; ~ **de puissance** m POLLU MER power pack; ~ **de purge** m REFRIG purge recovery system; ~ **quaternaire** m TELECOM line system, system; ~ **de répartition** m CH DE FER car distributor's office, stock control; ~ **secondaire** m TELECOM supergroup; ~ **de secours** m ELECTROTEC stand-by set, stand-by unit, MECANIQUE emergency power generator; ~ **de soudage à postes multiples** m PRODUCTION multiple operator welding set; ~ **de soutien spécialisé** m PHYS RAYON *recherche-développement* specialized support group; ~ **spatial** m CRISTALL space group; ~ **tertiaire** m TELECOM hypergroup, master group; ~ **des Troyens** m ASTRONOMIE Trojan group; ~ **turbo-réacteur** m AERONAUT power plant; ~ **d'unité d'affluents** m TELECOM TUG, tributary-unit group; ~ **d'unités administratives** m *(GUA)* TELECOM administrative unit group; ~ **d'utilisateurs** m INFORMAT, ORDINAT user group; ~ **de vernissage** m IMPRIM *papier et finition* coating unit; ~ **à vide** m POLLU MER vacuum unit

Groupe: ~ **local** m ASTRONOMIE Local Group

groupe-capteur m ESPACE sensor system

groupement m CHIMIE group, ELECTROTEC grouping, TELECOM group; ~ **d'antennes** m ESPACE antenna array, antenna system; ~ **après réflexion** m ELECTRON reflex bunching; ~ **des électrons en paquets** m ELECTRON bunching; ~ **en quarte** m ELECTROTEC quadding; ~ **excessif** m ELECTRON overbunching; ~ **de lignes à trafic équilibré** m TELECOM balanced grading group; ~ **monolithique** m ELECTRON monolithic array; ~ **optimal** m ELECTRON optimum bunching; ~ **parfait** m ELECTRON ideal bunching; ~ **de photodétecteurs** m ELECTRON imaging array; ~ **de photodiodes** m ELECTRON photodiode array

grouper vt ELECTRON *des signaux* multiplex, ELECTROTEC group, PRODUCTION bundle

groupes: ~ **de quasars** m ASTRONOMIE quasar group

groupeur m CH DE FER *véhicules* groupage traffic forwarder

grue f CINEMAT boom dolly, crane, CONSTR, MECANIQUE *matériel de levage*, NAUT crane; ~ **d'applique** f CONSTR wall crane; ~ **d'atelier** f PRODUCTION shop crane; ~ **automatique** f NUCLEAIRE self-propelled crane; ~ **de bord** f NAUT deck crane; ~ **de caméra** f CINEMAT camera boom; ~ **camion** f CONSTR mobile crane; ~ **centrale** f CONSTR independent crane; ~ **de chargement** f CH DE FER loading crane, NAUT cargo crane; ~ **à chevalet** f CH DE FER gantry crane; ~ **à colonne** f CONSTR postcrane, tower crane; ~ **à demi-portique** f CONSTR semigantry crane; ~ **dépanneuse** f TRANSPORT salvage crane; ~ **derrick** f CONSTR derrick, derrick crane; ~ **dragline** f CONSTR dragline excavator; ~ **à flèche** f CONSTR jib crane, NUCLEAIRE jib crane, slewing crane; ~ **flottante** f NAUT pontoon crane; ~ **à grappin** f CONSTR grab crane; ~ **de manutention de matériaux** f EMBALLAGE material handling crane; ~ **de milieu** f CONSTR independent crane; ~ **mobile** f CONSTR mobile crane; ~ **murale** f CONSTR wall crane; ~ **pivotante** f CONSTR all-around swing crane (AmE), all-round swing crane (BrE), rotary crane, swing crane, NUCLEAIRE jib crane, slewing crane; ~ **pivotante murale** f CONSTR rotary wall crane; ~ **à pont roulant** f EMBALLAGE overhead traveling crane (AmE), overhead travelling crane (BrE); ~ **à portique** f CONSTR gantry crane, portal crane, NAUT gantry crane, traveling-gantry crane (AmE), travelling gantry crane (BrE), NUCLEAIRE gantry crane; ~ **à potence** f CONSTR wall crane; ~ **à potence murale** f CONSTR wall crane; ~ **pour poids lourds** f CONSTR heavy-duty lift; ~ **de quai** f TRANSPORT quay crane; ~ **de relevage** f CH DE FER heavy breakdown crane (BrE), wrecking crane (AmE); ~ **à rotation complète** f CONSTR all-around swing crane (AmE), all-round swing crane (BrE); ~ **roulante** f PRODUCTION traveler (AmE), traveller (BrE), traveling crane (AmE), travelling crane (BrE); ~ **roulante aérienne** f PRODUCTION overhead crane; ~ **roulante à portique** f PRODUCTION traveling-gantry crane (AmE), travelling-gantry crane (BrE); ~ **sur voie ferrée** f TRANSPORT rail crane; ~ **à tour** f CONSTR tower crane; ~ **tournante** f CONSTR rotary crane; ~ **Vinten** f CINEMAT Vinten crane; ~ **à volée** f CONSTR jib crane; ~ **à volée basculante** f CONSTR derricking crane, luffing crane; ~ **à volée variable** f CONSTR derricking crane, luffing crane

Grue f ASTRONOMIE Grus

grue-chevalet f CONSTR goliath crane

grue-tour f CONSTR overhead crane

grugeoir m CERAM VER cracking tool

grumelage m AGRO ALIM clotting, coagulating

grumeler[1] *vt* GENIE CHIM cake

grumeler:[2] **se ~** *v réfl* AGRO ALIM cake

grumeleux *adj* IMPRIM *impression* mottled

grunauite *f* MINERAUX grünauite

grunérite *f* MINERAUX grunerite

grutier *m* CINEMAT crane operator, CONSTR craneman, NAUT crane operator

G-T *abrév (rapport gain-température de bruit)* ESPACE *facteur de qualité* G-T *(gain-to-noise temperature ratio)*

GUA *abrév (groupe d'unités administratives)* TELECOM administrative unit group

guanidine *f* CHIMIE guanidine

guanine *f* CHIMIE guanine

guano *m* CHIMIE guano

guanosine *f* CHIMIE guanosine

guanyle *m* CHIMIE guanyl

gué *m* CONSTR ford, fording

guérite *f* CH DE FER *véhicules* brakeman's cabin, cupola, CONSTR house, *d'une grue* cabin; **~ de frein** *f* CH DE FER *véhicules* brakeman's cabin, cupola

guerre: **~ bactériologique** *f* MILITAIRE bacteriological warfare; **~ électronique** *f* ELECTRON EW, electronic warfare

guêtres: **~ de protection** *f pl* SECURITE protective gaiters

gueulard *m* PRODUCTION throat, *d'un cubilot* charging hole, *d'un haut fourneau* mouth

gueule *f* CONSTR *d'un concasseur* mouth, OCEANO net mouth, PRODUCTION *d'un four, d'un convertisseur* mouth; **~ du pot** *f* CERAM VER pot mouth

gueule-bée *f* INST HYDR open front, opening in thick wall

gueule-de-loup *f* CONSTR groove, NAUT blackwall hitch; **~ double** *f* NAUT double blackwall hitch; **~ simple** *f* NAUT single blackwall hitch

gueule-de-raie *f* NAUT *noeud* cat's paw

gueuse *f* PRODUCTION iron pig, pig, pig mold (AmE), pig mould (BrE); **~ de fonte** *f* PRODUCTION pig, pig iron; **~ de mère** *f* PRODUCTION sow

guichet *m* MINES *d'une porte* shutter; **~ automatique de banque** *m* ORDINAT ATM, automatic teller machine; **~ des colis** *m* TRANSPORT parcels counter; **~ libre-service** *m* COMMANDE automatic teller, self-service teller; **~ mobile** *m* MINES *d'une porte* sliding shutter; **~ unique** *m* TELECOM one-stop shopping

guidage *m* CONS MECA guiding, ESPACE *pilotage* guidance, MINES cage guides, cage slides, guide, pit guides, PETROLE stabbing; **~ actif** *m* ESPACE *pilotage* active guidance; **~ alpha** *m* TV *trajet de la bande* alpha wrap; **~ de câbles** *m* VEHICULES *système électrique, commande* cable guide; **~ en azimut arrière** *m* AERONAUT *navigation* back azimuth guidance; **~ en phase d'approche** *m* ESPACE *pilotage* approach guidance; **~ en site d'approche** *m* AERONAUT approach elevation guidance; **~ extérieur** *m* RESSORTS outside guide; **~ inertiel** *m* ESPACE *pilotage* inertial guidance; **~ laser** *m* ELECTRON laser guidance; **~ latéral** *m* TRANSPORT lateral guidance; **~ magnétique latéral** *m* TRANSPORT electromagnetic lateral guidance system; **~ par inertie** *m* ESPACE *pilotage* inertial guidance; **~ par itération** *m* ESPACE path correction, *pilotage* iterative guidance; **~ par radar** *m* AERONAUT, TRANSPORT radar vectoring; **~ routier automatique** *m* TRANSPORT guidance by automatic road signs; **~ stellaire** *m* ESPACE stellar guidance, *pilotage* celestial guidance; **~ vertical** *m* AERONAUT elevation guidance

guidages *m pl* CONS MECA *d'un tour* track

guide *m* CONS MECA guide bar, *pour filière à lunettes* guide, MINES, PAPIER guide, PRODUCTION track; **~ d'affûtage** *m* CONS MECA honing guide; **~ de bande** *m* ENREGISTR, TV tape guide; **~ de bord** *m* CERAM VER edge guide; **~ circulaire** *m* PHYSIQUE circular waveguide; **~ de coulisseau** *m* CH DE FER link block guide, sliding-f-guide; **~ de crochet de traction** *m* CH DE FER *véhicules* drawbar guide; **~ à dépression** *m* TV female guide, shoe, vacuum guide; **~ d'entrée de bande** *m* TV tape input guide; **~ d'exploitation des liaisons par satellite** *m* ESPACE *communications* SSOG, Satellite System Operation Guide; **~ d'exposition** *m* CINEMAT exposure calculator; **~ à fente** *m* ELECTROTEC slotted waveguide; **~ de front** *m* IMPRIM *machines* front lay; **~ latéral** *m* IMPRIM *machines* lay edge; **~ de lumière** *m* PHYSIQUE light guide; **~ d'ondes** *m* ELECTROTEC, NAUT, PHYS ONDES, PHYSIQUE, TELECOM waveguide; **~ d'ondes adapté** *m* ELECTROTEC matched waveguide; **~ d'ondes d'alimentation** *m* ELECTROTEC feed waveguide; **~ d'ondes circulaire** *m* ELECTROTEC circular waveguide; **~ d'ondes à un conducteur** *m* ELECTROTEC uniconductor waveguide; **~ d'ondes à double nervure** *m* ELECTROTEC double ridge waveguide; **~ d'ondes en couches minces** *m* TELECOM thin-film waveguide; **~ d'ondes à fentes** *m* ELECTROTEC slotted waveguide; **~ d'ondes flexible** *m* ELECTROTEC, ESPACE *communications* flexible waveguide; **~ d'ondes hélicoïdal** *m* ELECTROTEC helix waveguide, TELECOM spiral waveguide; **~ d'ondes nervuré** *m* ELECTROTEC ridge waveguide; **~ d'ondes non réciproque** *m* TELECOM nonreciprocal wave guide; **~ d'ondes optiques** *m* ELECTROTEC, OPTIQUE, TELECOM optical waveguide; **~ d'ondes optiques en couches minces** *m* OPTIQUE thin-film optical waveguide; **~ d'ondes planes** *m* ELECTROTEC planar waveguide; **~ d'ondes rectangulaire** *m* ELECTROTEC rectangular waveguide; **~ d'ondes torsadé** *m* ELECTROTEC twisted waveguide; **~ d'onglet** *m* CONSTR miter fence (AmE), mitre fence (BrE); **~ opérateur** *m* INFORMAT, ORDINAT prompt; **~ optique** *m* ELECTROTEC optical waveguide; **~ parlant** *m* TELECOM intercept announcer; **~ de perçage** *m* CONS MECA jig bush; **~ de pilon** *m* PRODUCTION stamp guide; **~ du pointeau** *m* AUTO needle valve guide; **~ rectangulaire** *m* ELECTROTEC, PHYSIQUE rectangular waveguide; **~ rectiligne** *m* CONS MECA straight fence, PRODUCTION parallel fence; **~ de ressort** *m* PRODUCTION spring guide; **~ de sortie de bande** *m* TV tape output guide; **~ de soupape** *m* AUTO, INST HYDR, VEHICULES *moteur* valve guide; **~ de la tête de piston** *m* CONS MECA crosshead guide, guide bar, slide bar; **~ de tige** *m* PRODUCTION rod guide

guidé: **~ par infrarouge** *adj* ESPACE *véhicules*, THERMODYN heat-seeking; **~ par laser** *adj* ELECTRON laser-guided; **~ par menu** *adj* INFORMAT, ORDINAT menu-driven

guide-bande *m* IMPRIM *impression, rotatives* web guide; **~ à effet de vide** *m* ENREGISTR vacuum guide system

guide-câble *m* AERONAUT fairlead

guide-chaîne *m* CONS MECA *d'un palan*, VEHICULES *moteur* chain guide

guide-coussinets *m* PRODUCTION die guide

guide-fil *m* CERAM VER wire guide; **~ en porcelaine** *m* CERAM VER porcelain thread guide

guide-lame *m* CONS MECA saw guide

guider *vt* INFORMAT, ORDINAT prompt

guides *m pl* MINES cage guides, cage slides, pit guides; ~ **de marge** *m pl* IMPRIM feed guides, *machine* feedlays, feedlays

guide-toile *m* PAPIER wire guide

guidon *m* MILITAIRE *d'un fusil* foresight, NAUT burgee; ~ **d'arrêt** *m* CH DE FER stop board

guidonnage *m* CONS MECA guiding, MINES cage guides, cage slides, guide, pit guides

guignol *m* AERONAUT bell crank, NAUT jumper struts, PETROLE traveling block (AmE), travelling block (BrE); ~ **additionneur** *m* AERONAUT collective bell crank; ~ **d'angle** *m* AERONAUT bell crank; ~ **droit** *m* AERONAUT lever; ~ **de gouvernes** *m* AERONAUT horn; ~ **de pas général** *m* AERONAUT collective bell crank

guillaume *m* CONSTR rabbet, rabbet plane, rebate plane; ~ **de bout** *m* CONSTR square rabbet plane, square-mouthed rabbet; ~ **de côté** *m* CONSTR side rabbet plane; ~ **en navette** *m* CONSTR rabbet plane; ~ **de fil** *m* CONSTR square rabbet plane, square-mouthed rabbet

guillemets *m pl* IMPRIM inverted commas, quotes, pull-quotes

guillochage *m* CERAM VER needle etching

guillocher *vt* PRODUCTION checker (AmE), chequer (BrE)

guillochure *f* PRODUCTION checkering (AmE), chequering (BrE)

guillotine *f* EMBALLAGE guillotine

guinand *m* CERAM VER thimble

guinandage *m* CERAM VER stirring

guindant *m* NAUT luff, *du pavillon* hoist

guindeau *m* NAUT windlass

guipage *m* ELECTROTEC braiding

guipé *adj* ELECTR *conducteur*, ELECTROTEC covered; ~ **de coton** *adj* ELECTROTEC cotton-covered; ~ **au coton double** *adj* ELECTR *conducteur* DCC, double-cotton-covered; ~ **une couche caoutchouc** *adj* ELECTR *conducteur* SRC, single-rubber-covered; ~ **une couche coton** *adj* ELECTR *conducteur* SCC, single-cotton-covered; ~ **une couche papier** *adj* ELECTR *conducteur* SPC, single-paper-covered; ~ **deux couches caoutchouc** *adj* ELECTR *conducteur* DPRC, double-pure-rubber-covered; ~ **deux couches coton** *adj* ELECTR *conducteur* double-cotton-covered

gulonique *adj* CHIMIE gulonic

gulose *m* CHIMIE gulose

gumbo *m* PETR gumbo

gummite *f* MINERAUX gummite

gunitage *m* CERAM VER guniting, CONSTR guniting, gun-ning

gunite *f* CONSTR gunite

gustation *f* AGRO ALIM tasting

gutta-percha *f* CHIMIE, PLAST CAOU *caoutchouc* gutta-percha

guyot *m* GEOLOGIE guyot, seamount, OCEANO guyot, tablemount

Gy *abrév (gray)* METROLOGIE, PHYS RAYON, PHYSIQUE Gy *(gray)*

gymnite *f* MINERAUX gymnite

gynocardique *adj* CHIMIE gynocardic

gypse *m* CHIMIE gypsum, CONSTR plaster rock, plaster stone, MATERIAUX, MINERAUX, PETR, PETROLE gypsum; ~ **flocculeux** *m* CHAUFFAGE flocculent gypsum

gypseux *adj* CHIMIE gypseous

gypsifère *adj* GEOLOGIE gypsiferous, gypsum-bearing

gyrateur *m* PHYSIQUE gyrator; ~ **à ferrite** *m* ELECTROTEC ferrite rotator

gyro: ~ **d'azimut** *m* ESPACE *pilotage* azimuth gyro; ~ **directionnel** *m* AERONAUT directional gyro

gyrobus *m* TRANSPORT gyrobus

gyroclinomètre *m* ESPACE *pilotage* gyroclinometer

gyrocompas *m* AERONAUT gyrocompass, gyroscopic compass, NAUT gyrocompass

gyrodyne *m* AERONAUT compound helicopter

gyrofréquence *f* PHYSIQUE cyclotron frequency, frequency

gyrolaser *m* ESPACE *pilotage* gyro laser, laser gyro

gyromètre *m* ESPACE *pilotage* gyrometer, PHYSIQUE rate gyro; ~ **à fibre optique** *m* ESPACE *pilotage* optical fiber gyrometer (AmE), optical fibre gyrometer (BrE); ~ **longitudinal** *m* AERONAUT pitch rate gyro; ~ **de roulis** *m* ESPACE *pilotage* roll rate gyro; ~ **de tangage** *m* AERONAUT pitch rate gyro, ESPACE *pilotage* pitch gyro

gyropilote *m* NAUT gyropilot

gyroscope *m* ESPACE *pilotage*, MECANIQUE, PHYSIQUE gyroscope; ~ **de commande** *m* AERONAUT control gyro; ~ **directionnel** *m* TRANSPORT directional gyro; ~ **libre** *m* AERONAUT free gyroscope, *pilotage* free gyro; ~ **méridien** *m* ESPACE *pilotage* meridian gyro; ~ **vertical** *m* ESPACE *pilotage*, TRANSPORT vertical gyro

gyroscopique *adj* AERONAUT, ESPACE, MECANIQUE, PHYSIQUE, TRANSPORT gyroscopic

gyrostat *m* CHIMIE, PHYSIQUE gyrostat

gyrostatique *adj* CHIMIE gyrostatic

gyrotron *m* TELECOM gyrotron

gyttja *f* CHARBON gyttja

H

h *abrév (hecto-)* METROLOGIE h *(hecto-)*

H[1] *(hydrogène)* CHIMIE H *(hydrogen)*

H[2] *abrév (henry)* ELECTR *unité d'inductance*, ELECTRO-TEC, METROLOGIE, PHYSIQUE H *(henry)*

Ha[1] *(hahnium)* CHIMIE Ha *(hahnium)*

Ha[2] *abrév (humidité relative de l'air)* METEO relative humidity of the air

habilitation *f* INFORMAT *sécurité*, ORDINAT *sécurité* clearance

habillage *m* IMPRIM pad, *plaque, blanchet* lining, MAT CHAUFF *chaudière* jacket, MECANIQUE cabinet, PAPIER *machine* clothing; **~ de carde** *m* TEXTILE card clothing; **~ transparent** *m* EMBALLAGE blister pack

habillement *m* TEXTILE apparel

habiller *vt* IMPRIM back up

habit: **~ de plongée** *m* OCEANO diving suit, wetsuit

habitacle *m* AERONAUT cockpit, crew compartment, ESPACE cabin, manned module, *véhicules* habitation module, NAUT binnacle, TRANSPORT cockpit, VE-HICULES *d'une voiture* interior; **~ de sécurité** *m* TRANSPORT strengthened passenger compartment

habitat *m* PETR habitat; **~ sous-marin** *m* OCEANO undersea habitat, underwater habitat

habitus *m* METALL habit

hachage *m* INFORMAT, ORDINAT hashing

hachard *m* CONS MECA shears, CONSTR bolster, PRODUCTION hand shears

hache *f* CONSTR ax (AmE), axe (BrE); **~ à fendre** *f* CONSTR splitting ax (AmE), splitting axe (BrE); **~ à main** *f* PRODUCTION hatchet; **~ pour combattre l'incendie** *f* SECURITE firefighting axe

hachette *f* CONSTR slate ax (AmE), slate axe (BrE), PRODUCTION hatchet

hacheur: **~ de faisceau** *m* NUCLEAIRE beam pulser, mechanical chopper

hachoir *m* AERONAUT chopper, AGRO ALIM mincer; **~ à viande** *m* AGRO ALIM grinder

hachure *f* CONS MECA cross hatching, hatching

hachurer *vt* PRODUCTION cross hatch

hadron *m* PHYS PART, PHYSIQUE hadron

hafnium *m (Hf)* CHIMIE hafnium *(Hf)*

hahnium *m (Ha)* CHIMIE hahnium *(Ha)*

halage *m* NAUT *chemin* towage

halde *f* MINES barrow, dump heap, waste dump, pit heap, spoil bank, spoil heap; **~ de déblais** *f* CONSTR waste heap, MINES barrow, dump heap, waste dump, pit heap, spoil bank, spoil heap; **~ de déchets** *f* CONSTR waste heap, MINES barrow, dump heap, waste dump, pit heap, spoil bank, spoil heap; **~ de minerai** *f* MINES ore dump; **~ de scories** *f* PRODUCTION slag dump, slag heap, slag tip

hale-à-bord *m* OCEANO inhaul, inhauler

hale-bas *m* NAUT downhaul; **~ de bôme** *m* NAUT boom vang, kicking strap

hale-dehors *m* NAUT outhaul

haler[1] *vt* NAUT warp, *chaland* tow; **~ à bord** *vt* NAUT haul in, OCEANO haul on board; **~ à sec** *vt* NAUT *bateau* haul up

haler[2] *vi* NAUT *sur une manoeuvre* haul

halètement *m* ESPACE *véhicules* chuffing

halieutique *f* OCEANO fisher science, fishery science

halieutiste *m* OCEANO fishing expert

halite *f* CHIMIE rock salt, GEOLOGIE salt rock, MATERIAUX, MINERAUX halite

hall: **~ de gare** *m* TRANSPORT concourse, passenger hall; **~ du réacteur** *m* NUCLEAIRE reactor hall

halle: **~ d'assemblage** *f* ESPACE assembly building; **~ des chaudières** *f* MAT CHAUFF boiler house; **~ de coulée** *f* PRODUCTION cast house; **~ aux marchandises** *f* TRANSPORT freight house (AmE), freight shed (AmE), goods shed (BrE); **~ de montage** *f* PRODUCTION erecting shop

hallig *m* OCEANO marsh island

halloysite *f* MINERAUX halloysite

halmyrolyse *f* GEOLOGIE halmyrolysis

halo *m* ASTRONOMIE halo, ELECTRON halation, halo, ESPACE, IMPRIM *photogravure* halo; **~ de contrainte** *m* CERAM VER stressed zone; **~ noir** *m* ASTRONOMIE dark halo; **~ de réflexion** *m* PHOTO halation

halocinèse *f* GEOLOGIE halokinesis, salt diapirism, salt tectonics, PETROLE halokinesis, salt diapirism, salt tectonics

halogénation *f* CHIMIE halogenation

halogène[1] *adj* CHIMIE *composé* halogenous

halogène[2] *m* CHIMIE halide, halogen, CINEMAT halogen

halogénure *m* CHIMIE, IMPRIM *photogravure* halide; **~ alcalin** *m* CRISTALL alkali halide; **~ d'alcoyle** *m* MATERIAUX alkyl halide; **~ d'alkyle** *m* MATERIAUX alkyl halide; **~ d'argent** *m* PHOTO silver halide; photohalides

halographie *f* CHIMIE halography

haloïdation *f* CHIMIE halogenation

haloïde[1] *adj* CHIMIE haloid

haloïde[2] *m* CHIMIE haloid

hâloir: **~ à fromage** *m* REFRIG cheese drying room

halon *m* ESPACE *véhicules* halon

halophyte *f* DISTRI EAU saltwater plant

halos: **~ gazeux** *m pl* ASTRONOMIE *autour de galaxies* gaseous haloes

halosel *m* CHIMIE haloid

halotechnie *f* CHIMIE halotechny

halotrichite *f* MINERAUX halotrichite

halte *f* INFORMAT halt

hamiltonien *adj* PHYSIQUE Hamiltonian

hampe *f* IMPRIM *typographie* ascender; **~ de vent** *f* METEO wind shaft

hanche *f* NAUT quarter

hanches *f pl* CONSTR shear legs

hangar *m* AERONAUT hangar, CONSTR shed; **~ à bateaux** *m* TRANSPORT boat house

happe *f* CONS MECA G-clamp, G-cramp, clamp, cramp, CONSTR cramp, cramp iron, joint cramp, PRODUCTION dog iron; **~ à gros ventre** *f* CONSTR deep-pattern G cramp; **~ à nervure** *f* CONS MECA ribbed G cramp

happement *m* SECURITE entanglement

hardware *m* PETR hardware

harenguier *m* OCEANO herring boat
harenguière *f* OCEANO herring net
harmaline *f* CHIMIE harmaline
harmine *f* CHIMIE harmine
harmonie *f* ACOUSTIQUE harmony
harmonique[1] *adj* GEOMETRIE harmonic
harmonique[2] *m* ACOUSTIQUE, ELECTRON, MECANIQUE, PHYS ONDES, PHYSIQUE, PRODUCTION harmonic, harmonics; ~ **1** *m* ELECTRON first harmonic; ~ **2** *m* ELECTRON second harmonic; ~ **3** *m* ELECTRON third harmonic; ~ **impair** *m* ELECTRON, PHYSIQUE *d'ordre* odd harmonic; ~ **inférieur** *m* ELECTRON lower harmonic, subharmonic; ~ **pair** *m* ELECTRON, PHYSIQUE *d'ordre* even harmonic; ~ **de rang élevé** *m* ELECTRON high-order harmonic; ~ **de rang peu élevé** *m* ELECTRON low-order harmonic; ~ **sphérique** *m* ESPACE spherical harmonic; ~ **subjectif** *m* ACOUSTIQUE aural harmonic; ~ **supérieur** *m* ELECTRON overtone; ~ **tesseral** *m* ESPACE tesseral harmonic; ~ **zonal** *m* ESPACE zonal harmonic
harmoniques: ~ **naturels** *m pl* PHYS ONDES natural harmonics
harmonisation: ~ **des couleurs** *f* PHOTO color balance (AmE), colour balance (BrE)
harmotome *m* MINERAUX harmotome
harnais *m* ESPACE *véhicules*, MILITAIRE *d'un parachute* harness; ~ **de câbles** *m* ELECTR harness cable, ESPACE *véhicules* wiring harness, MECANIQUE harness cable; ~ **d'engrenages** *m* CONS MECA gear, gearing; ~ **pyrométrique** *m* AERONAUT fire detection harness; ~ **de sécurité** *m* AERONAUT, CINEMAT, NAUT safety harness, PETROLE safety belt, SECURITE safety harness
harpe *f* CONSTR toothing stone, PRODUCTION grizzly
harpon *m* OCEANO harpoon
hartine *f* MINERAUX hartine
hartite *f* MINERAUX hartite
hasard:[1] **au ~** *adj* METROLOGIE random; **par ~** *adj* METROLOGIE random
hasard:[2] **par ~** *adv* SECURITE accidentally
hasards: ~ **climatiques** *m pl* SECURITE climatic hazards
hash *m* INFORMAT, ORDINAT hash
hatchettine *f* MINERAUX hatchetine, hatchettite
hatchite *f* NUCLEAIRE hatchite
hauban *m* CONS MECA tieback, CONSTR guy, ELECTROTEC guy wire, MECANIQUE guy, NAUT shroud
haubanage *m* CONSTR guying
hauérite *f* MINERAUX hauerite
hausmannite *f* MINERAUX hausmannite
hausse *f* DISTRI EAU flashboard, flushboard, stop plank; ~ **de ceinture** *f* TEXTILE waistband; ~ **circulaire** *f* MILITAIRE dial sight; ~ **de combat** *f* MILITAIRE *sur un canon* battle sight; ~ **de température** *f* PHYSIQUE, THERMODYN temperature rise
hausser *vi* HYDROLOGIE rise
hausses: ~ **combinées** *f pl* MILITAIRE *sur un canon* combined sights
haussière *f* CONS MECA, NAUT hawser; ~ **de déhalage** *f* NAUT warp
haut:[1] **de ~** *adj* CONS MECA high CONS MECA, PAPIER high; ~ **le pied** *adj (hlp)* CH DE FER *véhicules* running light
haut[2] *m* EMBALLAGE *inscription ou étiquette de manutention* this side up, ENREGISTR treble, HYDROLOGIE *d'une rivière* upper part; ~ **de course** *m* CONS MECA *d'un piston* top of stroke; ~ **de l'eau** *m* HYDROLOGIE high water; ~ **logique** *m* ELECTRON logic high; ~ **rendement** *m* PAPIER high yield

haute:[1] **à ~ fréquence** *adj* ELECTRON radio frequency; **à ~ pression** *adj* PHYSIQUE high-pressure; **de ~ qualité** *adj* CHARBON high-grade; **à ~ résistance** *adj* MATERIAUX high-tensile; **à ~ résistance à la traction** *adj* MECANIQUE *matériaux* high-tensile; **à ~ température** *adj* PHYSIQUE high-temperature; **à ~ teneur** *adj* CHARBON high-grade; **à ~ teneur en cellulose** *adj* AGRO ALIM high-fiber (AmE), high-fibre (BrE); **à ~ tension** *adj* PHYSIQUE high-voltage
haute:[2] ~ **barrière** *f* EMBALLAGE, IMPRIM high barrier; ~ **définition** *f* ORDINAT high resolution; ~ **fréquence** *f (HF)* AERONAUT, ELECTR *alimentation en courant alternatif*, ELECTRON, ELECTROTEC high-frequency *(HF)*; **très ~ fréquence** *f (VHF)* ELECTRON, ESPACE, PHYS ONDES, TELECOM, TV very high-frequency *(VHF)*; ~ **intégration personnalisée** *f* ELECTRON custom large-scale integration; ~ **lumière** *f* CINEMAT high key; ~ **mer** *f* HYDROLOGIE high water, OCEANO high seas; ~ **performance** *f* ENREGISTR high performance; ~ **pression** *f* GAZ, PHYSIQUE high-pressure; ~ **résistance** *f* TELECOM HR, high resistance; ~ **résolution** *f* INFORMAT high resolution; ~ **température** *f* PHYSIQUE high-temperature; ~ **teneur** *f* CHIMIE high-grade; ~ **teneur en soufre** *f* CHIMIE high sulfur content (AmE), high sulphur content (BrE); ~ **tension** *f (HT)* ELECTR *alimentation*, ELECTROTEC, PHYSIQUE high-tension *(HT)*, high-voltage *(HV)*; **très ~ tension** *f (THT)* ELECTROTEC, TV extra high tension *(EHT)*
haute-fidélité *adj* ENREGISTR high fidelity
hautement: ~ **polyvalent** *adj* PRODUCTION highly-flexible
hauterivien *adj* GEOPHYS Hauterivian
hautes: ~ **eaux** *f pl* HYDROLOGIE, NAUT high water; ~ **lumières** *f pl* IMPRIM, PHOTO highlights
hauteur:[1] **à ~ d'appui** *adj* CONSTR elbow-high; **de ~** *adj* CONS MECA high; **en ~** *adj* CONS MECA high
hauteur[2] *f* ACOUSTIQUE *du son* pitch, CONS MECA height, CONSTR elevation, DISTRI EAU lift, static head, static lift, EN RENOUV *d'une vague* height, ESPACE altitude, elevation angle, GEOMETRIE altitude, IMPRIM *des capitales*, INFORMAT height, MECANIQUE elevation, NAUT headroom, height, *d'un astre* altitude, *navigation* elevation, ORDINAT height, PHYS ONDES *de l'onde sonore* pitch, PHYSIQUE altitude, height, *de son* pitch; ~ **d'alimentation requise** *f* NUCLEAIRE net positive suction head; ~ **apparente** *f* NAUT apparent altitude; ~ **d'aspiration** *f* DISTRI EAU static suction lift, suction head, suction lift, MAT CHAUFF pump head; ~ **au-dessous du primitif** *f* CONS MECA depth below pitch line; ~ **au-dessus du niveau de la mer** *f* METEO elevation above sea level; ~ **au-dessus du primitif** *f* CONS MECA height above pinch line; ~ **axiale** *f* RESSORTS axial height; ~ **barométrique** *f* METEO barometric height of pressure, NAUT barometer reading; ~ **à bloc** *f* RESSORTS solid height; ~ **du caractère** *f* IMPRIM height of type, height-to-paper, type height; ~ **de centre d'arbre** *f* CONS MECA shaft center height (AmE), shaft centre height (AmE); ~ **de charge** *f* CONSTR head of water; ~ **de chute** *f* CHARBON drop height, DISTRI EAU fall, EMBALLAGE height of fall, INST HYDR head, head of water, water fall height; ~ **de chute libre** *f* AERONAUT free drop height; ~ **du couronnement** *f* EN RENOUV crest height; ~ **de décision** *f* AERONAUT decision height; ~ **de démoulage** *f* PRODUCTION draft (AmE), draught (BrE), *d'une machine à démouler* drop; ~ **de la dent** *f* CONS MECA working depth of tooth; ~ **d'eau** *f*

HYDROLOGIE depth of water, INST HYDR head of water pressure, head, head of water; ~ **d'eau limite** *f* INST HYDR head limit; ~ **d'eau moyenne quadratique** *f* EN RENOUV root mean square water level; ~ **d'échappée** *f* CONSTR headroom; ~ **effective de chute** *f* CHARBON effective drop height; ~ **d'élévation** *f* DISTRI EAU lift, static head, static lift; ~ **d'empilage** *f* EMBALLAGE stacking height; ~ **en sustentation** *f* TRANSPORT height hovering; ~ **à flot** *f* TRANSPORT height-off cushion; ~ **géométrique** *f* NUCLEAIRE elevation head, potential geodesic head; ~ **géométrique de refoulement** *f* HYDROLOGIE discharge head; ~ **du gradin** *f* MINES bench height; ~ **de la houle** *f* NAUT, OCEANO wave height; ~ **d'inclinaison** *f* GEOMETRIE *d'un cône circulaire droit* slant height; ~ **instrumentale** *f* NAUT sextant altitude; ~ **de l'instrument en station** *f* CONSTR height of instrument; ~ **de levage** *f* CONSTR *d'une grue* lift; ~ **manométrique** *f* DISTRI EAU lift, static head, static lift, INST HYDR pressure head, static head, NUCLEAIRE delivery head, discharge head, PETROLE *écoulement des fluides* head; ~ **de marche** *f* CONSTR rise; ~ **de marche de glissement** *f* METALL slip step height; ~ **de la marée** *f* OCEANO tidal height; ~ **maximum à scier** *f* PRODUCTION depth of cut; ~ **maximum du trait de scie** *f* PRODUCTION depth of cut; ~ **métacentrique** *f* NAUT metacentric height; ~ **minimale de descente** *f* AERONAUT minimum descent height; ~ **observée** *f* NAUT observed altitude; ~ **de l'oeil** *f* CONSTR eyelevel; ~ **de l'oeil du caractère** *f* IMPRIM X-height; ~ **de page** *f* IMPRIM page depth; ~ **du pas** *f* CONS MECA *d'une vis* lead; ~ **de passage** *f* CONSTR headroom; ~ **piézométrique** *f* INST HYDR pressure head; ~ **de poil** *f* TEXTILE pile height; ~ **des pointes** *f (HDP)* CONS MECA height of centers (AmE), height of centres (BrE); ~ **de pompage** *f* INST HYDR *hauteur manométrique* head; ~ **du portail** *f* CONSTR *architecture* spandrel; ~ **de préconformation** *f* RESSORTS preset height; ~ **de refoulement** *f* DISTRI EAU delivery head, delivery lift, discharge head, discharge lift, static discharge head, NUCLEAIRE delivery head, discharge head; ~ **de la règle** *f* CONSTR screed height; ~ **de sécurité** *f* MINES clearance, overwinding allowance; ~ **du soleil au-dessus de l'horizon** *f* EN RENOUV solar altitude; ~ **du soleil sur l'horizon** *f* EN RENOUV solar altitude angle; ~ **de la solution de couchage sur le papier** *f* PAPIER pond depth; ~ **du son** *f* PHYS ONDES *d'une onde sonore* pitch; ~ **du son de battement** *f* PHYS ONDES beat note pitch; ~ **sous barrots** *f* NAUT cabin headroom; ~ **sous clef** *f* CONSTR height above impost level, *d'une voûte* rise; ~ **totale** *f* NUCLEAIRE total height; ~ **totale de dragage** *f* DISTRI EAU full dredging depth; ~ **typographique** *f* IMPRIM height of type, height-to-paper, type height; ~ **des vagues** *f* EN RENOUV, OCEANO wave height; ~ **de verre** *f* CERAM VER glass depth, metal depth; ~ **verticale** *f* MINES lift; ~ **de vol** *f* TRANSPORT height-on cushion, hoverheight; ~ **des yeux** *f* CONSTR eyelevel

haut-fond *m* GEOLOGIE shallows, shoal, NAUT bank, shallows, shoal, OCEANO shallow, shelf, shoal, PRODUCTION shoal; ~ **sableux** *m* HYDROLOGIE sandbank

haut-fourneau *m* CERAM VER, CONS MECA, MAT CHAUFF, PRODUCTION, THERMODYN blast furnace; ~ **au coke** *m* PRODUCTION coke blast furnace; ~ **conventionnel** *m* CHARBON blast furnace

haut-parc *m* OCEANO stake net, tide net

haut-parleur *m* ACOUSTIQUE, ELECTR *radio*, ENREGISTR, PHYSIQUE, TELECOM loudspeaker; ~ **d'aigus** *m* ENREG-

ISTR tweeter; ~ **à aimant permanent** *m* ACOUSTIQUE permanent magnet loudspeaker; ~ **d'angle** *m* ENREGISTR corner loudspeaker; ~ **à armature équilibrée** *m* ENREGISTR balanced armature loudspeaker; ~ **à armature magnétique** *m* ENREGISTR magnetic armature loudspeaker; ~ **à baffle infini** *m* ENREGISTR infinite baffle loudspeaker; ~ **à bobine mobile** *m* ACOUSTIQUE dynamic loudspeaker, ENREGISTR moving coil loudspeaker; ~ **de cabine** *m* CINEMAT monitoring loudspeaker; ~ **coaxial** *m* ACOUSTIQUE, ENREGISTR coaxial loudspeaker; ~ **à colonne** *m* ENREGISTR column loudspeaker; ~ **à colonne d'air** *m* ENREGISTR air column loudspeaker; ~ **composé** *m* ENREGISTR composite loudspeaker; ~ **conique** *m* ENREGISTR cone loudspeaker; ~ **de contrôle** *m* ENREGISTR control loudspeaker, monitoring loudspeaker; ~ **à double cône** *m* ENREGISTR dual cone loudspeaker; ~ **d'effets spéciaux** *m* ENREGISTR effects loudspeaker; ~ **à électro-aimant** *m* ACOUSTIQUE electromagnet loudspeaker; ~ **électrodynamique** *m* ACOUSTIQUE, ENREGISTR electrodynamic loudspeaker; ~ **électromagnétique** *m* ACOUSTIQUE, ENREGISTR electromagnetic loudspeaker; ~ **électrostatique** *m* ACOUSTIQUE, ENREGISTR electrostatic loudspeaker; ~ **électrostatique à basse tension** *m* ENREGISTR low-voltage electrostatic loudspeaker; ~ **élémentaire** *m* ACOUSTIQUE elementary loudspeaker; ~ **élémentaire à voies multiples** *m* ACOUSTIQUE multichannel elementary loudspeaker; ~ **à excitation** *m* ENREGISTR excited field loudspeaker; ~ **fantôme de canal central** *m* ENREGISTR phantom-center-channel loudspeaker (AmE), phantom-centre-channel loudspeaker (BrE); ~ **de graves** *m* ENREGISTR boomer; ~ **ionique** *m* ACOUSTIQUE, ENREGISTR ionic loudspeaker; ~ **à large bande** *m* ENREGISTR full-range loudspeaker; ~ **à magnétostriction** *m* ACOUSTIQUE magnetostriction loudspeaker; ~ **à membrane** *m* ACOUSTIQUE membrane loudspeaker; ~ **à membrane multiple** *m* ENREGISTR multiple cone loudspeaker; ~ **multicanal** *m* ENREGISTR multichannel loudspeaker; ~ **à pavillon** *m* ACOUSTIQUE, ENREGISTR horn loudspeaker; ~ **à pavillon pour basse fréquence** *m* ENREGISTR low-frequency horn loudspeaker; ~ **à pavillon pour haute fréquence** *m* ENREGISTR high-frequency horn loudspeaker; ~ **piézoélectrique** *m* ENREGISTR piezoelectric loudspeaker; ~ **pneumatique** *m* ACOUSTIQUE pneumatic loudspeaker; ~ **pour fréquences moyennes** *m* ENREGISTR midrange loudspeaker; ~ **à rayonnement direct** *m* ACOUSTIQUE direct loudspeaker; ~ **à réponse étendue** *m* ENREGISTR extended range loudspeaker; ~ **à ruban** *m* ACOUSTIQUE, ENREGISTR ribbon loudspeaker; ~ **super-tweeter** *m* ENREGISTR super-tweeter loudspeaker; ~ **témoin** *m* ENREGISTR monitoring loudspeaker

haüyne *f* MINERAUX hauyne, hauynite

havage *m* CHARBON cutting, kerf, MINES cutting, cut, holing, jad, kerving, kirving

havé *adj* MINES holed

haveneau *m* OCEANO brailer, dip net, scoop net, hand lift net, push net, shrimping net

haver *vt* MINES hole

haveur *m* MINES coal cutter, cutting machine, cutter

haveuse *f* CHARBON coal cutter, MINES coal cutter, coal-cutting machine; ~ **à barre coupante** *f* MINES bar coal-cutting machine; ~ **à chaîne** *f* MINES chain coal-cutting machine; ~ **ripante** *f* CHARBON cutter loader, short-wall coal-cutting machine

haveuse-rouilleuse *f* CHARBON holing and shearing machine

havrits *m pl* CHARBON fakes

hayésine *f* MINERAUX hayesine

hayon *m* AUTO lift gate, MECANIQUE *véhicules* tailgate, TRANSPORT hatchback, rear door

HC *abrév (conteneur hors-cotes)* TRANSPORT HC *(high-cube container)*

HDP *abrév (hauteur des pointes)* CONS MECA height of centers (AmE), height of centres (BrE)

He *(hélium)* CHIMIE He *(helium)*

hébronite *f* MINERAUX hebronite

hectare *m* METROLOGIE hectare

hecto- *préf (h)* METROLOGIE hecto-*(h)*

hectogramme *m* METROLOGIE hectogram (AmE), hectogramme (BrE)

hectolitre *m* METROLOGIE hectoliter (AmE), hectolitre (BrE)

hectomètre *m* METROLOGIE hectometer (AmE), hectometre (BrE)

hectowatt *m* ELECTROTEC hectowatt

hédenbergite *f* MINERAUX hedenbergite

hédyphane *m* MINERAUX hedyphane

héler *vt* NAUT *navire* hail

hélianthine *f* CHIMIE helianthin, helianthine

héliaque *adj* ASTRONOMIE *relatif au soleil* heliacal

hélice:[1] **à ~** *adj* CONS MECA helical, spiral; **en ~** *adj* CONS MECA helical, spiral

hélice[2] *f* AERONAUT *d'avion* propeller, CHIMIE helix, CONS MECA helix, propeller, spiral, GEOMETRIE helix, NAUT propeller, screw, POLLU MER, TRANSPORT propeller; **~ aérienne** *f* TRANSPORT air propeller, airscrew; **~ aérienne à pas variable** *f* TRANSPORT variable pitch air propeller; **~ anticouple** *f* AERONAUT antitorque propeller; **~ bec-de-canard** *f* NAUT folding propeller; **~ carénée** *f* AERONAUT shrouded propeller, TRANSPORT Schottel propeller, ducted propeller, carinated propeller, shrouded propeller; **~ coaxiale** *f* TRANSPORT coaxial propeller; **~ à droite** *f* CONS MECA right-handed spiral; **~ en arrière** *f* TRANSPORT rear propeller; **~ en moulinet** *f* AERONAUT windmilling propeller; **~ de freinage** *f* TRANSPORT braking airscrew; **~ libre** *f* TRANSPORT open propeller; **~ marine** *f* TRANSPORT marine propeller, water propeller (BrE), water screw (AmE); **~ à pas fixe** *f* AERONAUT fixed pitch propeller; **~ à pas nul** *f* POLLU MER zero-pitch propeller; **~ à pas réglable** *f* AERONAUT adjustable pitch propeller; **~ à pas réversible** *f* AERONAUT reversible pitch propeller, NAUT reversible-pitch propeller, TRANSPORT reversible pitch propeller; **~ à pas variable** *f* AERONAUT variable pitch propeller, NAUT controllable-pitch propeller, variable pitch propeller, POLLU MER variable pitch propeller; **~ à prise directe** *f* AERONAUT direct-drive propeller; **~ à prise directe sans réducteur** *f* AERONAUT direct-drive propeller; **~ propulsive** *f* AERONAUT pusher propeller; **~ de queue** *f* TRANSPORT tail propeller; **~ sans réducteur** *f* AERONAUT direct-drive propeller; **~ à supercavitation** *f* TRANSPORT supercavitating propeller; **~ tractive** *f* AERONAUT tractor propeller, TRANSPORT driving propeller; **~ transsonique** *f* AERONAUT propfan; **~ ventilée** *f* TRANSPORT ventilated propeller; **~ à vitesse constante** *f* AERONAUT constant speed propeller

hélices: **~ contrarotatives** *f pl* TRANSPORT counter-rotating propellers; **~ Fenske** *f pl* EQUIP LAB *distillation*

Fenske helices

hélicine *f* CHIMIE helicin

hélicoïdal *adj* CONS MECA helical, helicoid, helicoidal, GEOMETRIE helical, helicoid, MATERIAUX helicoidal

hélicoïde[1] *adj* CONS MECA helical, spiral, helicoid, helicoidal, TV helical

hélicoïde[2] *m* GEOMETRIE helicoid

hélicoplane *m* AERONAUT cyclogyro

hélicoptère *m* AERONAUT helicopter; **~ ABC** *m* TRANSPORT advancing blade concept helicopter; **~ d'affaires** *m* AERONAUT executive helicopter; **~ antichar** *m* AERONAUT antitank helicopter; **~ anti-sous-marin** *m* AERONAUT antisubmarine helicopter; **~ armé** *m* AERONAUT combat helicopter; **~ avec armement lourd** *m* MILITAIRE attack helicopter, helicopter gunship; **~ birotor** *m* AERONAUT dual-rotor helicopter; **~ combiné** *m* AERONAUT compound helicopter, gyrodyne, TRANSPORT compound helicopter; **~ embarqué** *m* AERONAUT carrier shipborne helicopter; **~ expérimental** *m* AERONAUT experimental helicopter; **~ grue** *m* AERONAUT crane helicopter; **~ léger** *m* TRANSPORT light multi-role helicopter; **~ léger d'observation** *m* AERONAUT light observation helicopter; **~ léger de transport et de secours** *m* TRANSPORT transport and rescue helicopter; **~ à missions multiples** *m* AERONAUT multipurpose helicopter; **~ multimoteur** *m* AERONAUT multiengine helicopter; **~ navette** *m* PETROLE shuttle helicopter; **~ piloté** *m* AERONAUT manned helicopter; **~ polyvalent** *m* AERONAUT multipurpose helicopter; **~ à réaction** *m* AERONAUT jet helicopter; **~ à rotors basculants** *m* TRANSPORT tilting rotor helicopter; **~ à rotors coaxiaux** *m* AERONAUT, TRANSPORT coaxial helicopter; **~ à rotors en tandem** *m* TRANSPORT dual tandem helicopter, tandem rotor helicopter; **~ de sauvetage** *m* MILITAIRE, TRANSPORT rescue helicopter; **~ téléguidé** *m* AERONAUT drone helicopter; **~ tous-temps** *m* AERONAUT all-weather helicopter; **~ de transport** *m* TRANSPORT cargo helicopter, transport helicopter; **~ de transport lourd** *m* AERONAUT heavy-lift helicopter

héligare *f* TRANSPORT helicopter station, heliport; **~ sur immeuble** *f* AERONAUT rooftop heliport

héligyre *m* TRANSPORT heligyro

hélimagnétisme *m* PHYSIQUE helimagnetism

hélioalimenté *adj* ELECTROTEC solar-powered

héliocentrique *adj* ASTRONOMIE heliocentric

héliodore *m* MINERAUX heliodor

héliodynamique *f* EN RENOUV solar dynamics

héliogénérateur *m* ELECTROTEC solar generator

héliographe: **~ radio** *m* ASTRONOMIE radio heliograph

héliogravure *f* IMPRIM *impression* gravure, *technique* gravure printing, PLAST CAOU rotogravure printing

héliomètre *m* ASTRONOMIE heliometer

héliostat *m* ASTRONOMIE heliostat, EN RENOUV heat mirror, heliostat

héliotechnique *f* EN RENOUV solar technology

héliotrope *m* MINERAUX heliotrope

héliotropine *f* CHIMIE heliotropin, piperonal

héliotropique *adj* EN RENOUV heliotropic

héliox *m* OCEANO heliox, oxygen-helium mixture

héliport *m* AERONAUT, PETROLE *installation à terre*, POLLU MER heliport, TRANSPORT heliport deck, heliport; **~ sur immeuble** *m* AERONAUT rooftop heliport

héliportage *m* AERONAUT, NAUT, TRANSPORT transport by helicopter

héliporté *adj* AERONAUT, POLLU MER, TRANSPORT helicopter-lifted

héliporter[1] *m* TRANSPORT helicopter

héliporter[2] *vt* AERONAUT helicopter

hélistation *f* AERONAUT helistop, TRANSPORT helipad, helistop; **~ sur immeuble** *f* AERONAUT rooftop heliport

hélisurface *f* PETROLE *plate-forme en mer* helipad, TRANSPORT helicopter landing platform, helicopter landing surface

hélitreuiller *vt* AERONAUT, NAUT, TRANSPORT winch into helicopter

hélium *m (He)* CHIMIE helium *(He)*; **~ liquide** *m* THERMODYN liquid helium

hélix: ~ cylindrique *m* RESSORTS cylindrical helix

helvine *f* MINERAUX helvine, helvite

helvite *f* MINERAUX helvine, helvite

hématéine *f* CHIMIE haematein (BrE), hematein (AmE)

hématine *f* CHIMIE haematin (BrE), hematin (AmE)

hématique *adj* CHIMIE haematic (BrE), hematic (AmE)

hématite *f* CHIMIE, MATERIAUX, MINERAUX haematite (BrE), hematite (AmE); **~ brune** *f* CHIMIE brown haematite (BrE), brown hematite (AmE), brown iron ore

hématolite *f* MINERAUX haematolite (BrE), hematolite (AmE)

hématoporphyrine *f* CHIMIE haematoporphyrin (BrE), hematoporphyrin (AmE)

hématoxyline *f* CHIMIE haematoxylin (BrE), hematoxylin (AmE)

hémiacétal *m* CHIMIE hemi-acetal

hémicellulose *f* CHIMIE hemicellulose

hémimétallique *adj* CHIMIE hemimetallic

hémimorphite *f* MINERAUX electric calamine, hemimorphite

hémioxyde: ~ d'azote *m* POLLUTION nitrous oxide

hémipinique *adj* CHIMIE hemipinic

hémisphère *m* GEOMETRIE hemisphere

hémitropie *f* CRISTALL twin formation, twinning

hémoglobine *f* CHIMIE haemoglobin (BrE), hemoglobin (AmE)

hémolyse *f* CHIMIE haemolysis (BrE), hemolysis (AmE)

hémolysine *f* CHIMIE haemolysin (BrE), hemolysin (AmE)

hémolytique *adj* CHIMIE haemolytic (BrE), hemolytic (AmE)

hémopyrrol *m* CHIMIE haemopyrrole (BrE), hemopyrrole (AmE)

hémosidérine *f* CHIMIE haemosiderin (BrE), hemosiderin (AmE)

hémotoxine *f* CHIMIE haemotoxin (BrE), hemotoxin (AmE)

henry *m (H)* ELECTR, ELECTROTEC, METROLOGIE, PHYSIQUE henry *(H)*

henrymètre *m* ELECTR inductance meter

héparine *f* CHIMIE heparin

hépatite *f* MINERAUX hepatite

heptade *f* CHIMIE heptad

heptaèdre *m* GEOMETRIE heptahedron

heptagonal *adj* GEOMETRIE heptagonal

heptagone *m* GEOMETRIE heptagon

heptane *m* CHIMIE, PETROLE heptane

heptavalent *adj* CHIMIE heptavalent

heptène *m* CHIMIE heptene

heptode *f* ELECTRON heptode

heptose *m* CHIMIE heptose

héptyle *m* CHIMIE heptyl

heptylène *m* CHIMIE heptylene

heptylique *adj* CHIMIE heptylic

heptyne *m* CHIMIE heptyne

herbe *f* ELECTRON, NUCLEAIRE grass

herchage *m* MINES drawing

Hercule *m* ASTRONOMIE Hercules

hercynite *f* MINERAUX hercynite

hérisson *m* CONS MECA rag wheel, REFRIG manifold drying apparatus

héritage *m* INFORMAT, ORDINAT inheritance

herméticité *f* CONS MECA *d'un joint* tightness, PRODUCTION *d'un joint* imperviousness

hermétique *adj* CONS MECA, EMBALLAGE, NAUT, PHYSIQUE airtight, TV *d'un relais* solid-state

hermétiquement: ~ clos *adj* MECANIQUE hermetically-sealed

herminette *f* CONSTR adze; **~ à tête** *f* CONSTR poll adze

héroïne *f* CHIMIE heroin

herschage *m* MINES drawing

herse *f* IMPRIM web severer

hertz *m (Hz)* ELECTR *unité de fréquence*, ELECTROTEC, METROLOGIE, PETR, PHYSIQUE, TV hertz *(Hz)*

hertzien *adj* ELECTR *oscillateur* Hertzian

hespéridine *f* AGRO ALIM, CHIMIE hesperidin

hespéritine *f* CHIMIE hesperitin

hessite *f* MINERAUX hessite

hessonite *f* MINERAUX essonite, hessonite

hétéroatome *m* CHIMIE heteroatom

hétéroatomique *adj* CHIMIE heteroatomic

hétéroauxine *f* CHIMIE heteroauxin

hétérocyclique *adj* CHIMIE heterocyclic

hétérodynation *f* TV heterodyning

hétérodyne *m* ELECTRON service oscillator; **~ de service** *m* ELECTRON test oscillator

hétérogène *adj* METALL heterogeneous

hétérogénéité *f* GAZ movement

hétérogénite *f* MINERAUX heterogenite

hétérojonction *f* ELECTRON, OPTIQUE, TELECOM heterojunction

hétéromarquage *m* NUCLEAIRE heterolabeling (AmE), heterolabelling (BrE)

hétérométrique *adj* GEOLOGIE *cristaux de taille différente* heterometric

hétéromorphite *f* MINERAUX heteromorphite

hétéropolaire *adj* CHIMIE heteropolar

hétéroside *m* CHIMIE heteroside

hétérosite *f* MINERAUX heterosite

hétéroxanthine *f* CHIMIE heteroxanthine

Hettangien *adj* GEOPHYS Hettangian

heulandite *f* MINERAUX heulandite

heure *f* PHYSIQUE hour; **~ d'approche prévue** *f* AERONAUT expected approach time; **~ chargée** *f* TELECOM busy hour; **~ chargée moyenne** *f* TELECOM mean busy hour, time-consistent busy hour; **~ creuse** *f* TRANSPORT lowest hourly traffic; **~ de déblocage** *f* AERONAUT *circulation aérienne* release time; **~ de début** *f* ORDINAT start time; **~ de départ prévue** *f* AERONAUT, NAUT estimated time of departure; **~ de l'échange** *f* TELECOM interchange time; **~ d'émission** *f* TV airtime; **~ estimée de départ du poste de stationnement** *f* AERONAUT estimated off-block time; **~ de feu vert** *f* TRANSPORT hour of green signal indication; **~ du fuseau** *f* NAUT standard time; **~ légale** *f* NAUT standard time; **~ de pointe** *f* CH DE FER peak hour, rush hour, TELECOM peak busy hour, TRANSPORT peak hour, rush hour; **~ prévue d'arrivée** *f (HPA)* AERONAUT, NAUT estimated time of arrival *(ETA)*; **~ de la**

station *f* TV station time; ~ **TU** *f* TELECOM *temps universel* universal time coordinated; ~ **universelle** *f* TELECOM universal time coordinated

heures: ~ **d'antenne** *f pl* TV broadcasting times; ~ **effectives de production** *f pl* PRODUCTION realized production time; ~ **de fonctionnement** *f pl* PRODUCTION operating hours; ~ **de grande écoute** *f pl* TV peak time; ~ **opératoires** *f pl* PRODUCTION operating hours; ~ **passées** *f pl* PRODUCTION spent capacity; ~ **de vol** *f pl* AERONAUT flying hours

heuristique *adj* INFORMAT, ORDINAT heuristic

heurtequin *m* CONS MECA *d'un essieu* collar

heurter: **se ~ à** *v réfl* MECANIQUE impinge on; **se ~ contre** *v réfl* NAUT *navire* foul

heurtoir *m* CH DE FER buffer, buffer stop; ~ **glissant** *m* (Fra) *(cf heurtoir patinant)* CH DE FER *véhicules* buffer stop block; ~ **patinant** *m* (Bel) *(cf heurtoir glissant)* CH DE FER *véhicules* buffer stop block

heurtoir-frein *m* CH DE FER *véhicules* buffer stop block

hexachlorure: ~ **de benzène** *m* AGRO ALIM benzene hexachloride

hexacontane *m* CHIMIE hexacontane

hexacosane *m* CHIMIE hexacosane

hexadécane *m* CHIMIE hexadecane

hexadécimal *adj* INFORMAT hexadecimal, ORDINAT hex, hexadecimal

hexadiène *m* CHIMIE hexadiene

hexaèdre[1] *adj* GEOMETRIE hexahedral

hexaèdre[2] *m* GEOMETRIE hexahedron

hexafluorure: ~ **d'uranium** *m* NUCLEAIRE hex, uranic fluoride, uranium hexafluoride

hexagonal *adj* CRISTALL, GEOMETRIE, MATERIAUX hexagonal

hexagone *m* GEOMETRIE hexagon

hexahydrobenzène *m* CHIMIE hexahydrobenzene

hexahydrobenzoïque *adj* CHIMIE *acide* hexahydrobenzoic

hexahydrophénol *m* CHIMIE hexahydrophenol

hexahydropyridine *f* CHIMIE hexahydropyridine

hexaméthylène: ~ **tétramine** *m* PLAST CAOU hexamethylene diisocyanate

hexane *m* CHIMIE, PETROLE hexane

hexanol *m* CHIMIE hexanol

hexavalent[1] *adj* CHIMIE hexadic, hexavalent

hexavalent[2] *m* CHIMIE hexad

hexène *m* CHIMIE hexene

hexode *f* ELECTRON hexode

hexogène *m* CHIMIE hexogen

hexosane *m* CHIMIE hexosan

hexose *m* CHIMIE hexose

hexyl *m* CHIMIE hexyl

hexylène *m* CHIMIE hexylene

hexylique *adj* CHIMIE hexylic

hexyne *m* CHIMIE hexyne

Hf *(hafnium)* CHIMIE Hf *(hafnium)*

HF *abrév (haute fréquence)* AERONAUT, ELECTR, ELECTRON, ELECTROTEC HF *(high-frequency)*

Hg *(mercure)* CHIMIE Hg *(mercury)*

HI: ~ **type de nébuleuse** *m* ASTRONOMIE HI type region

hiatus *m* PETR hiatus

hiddénite *f* MINERAUX hiddenite

hie *f* CONSTR earth rammer, gin, pile driver, postdriver, rammer, rammer

hiérarchie *f* INFORMAT, ORDINAT hierarchy; ~ **de données** *f* INFORMAT, ORDINAT data hierarchy; ~ **de mémoire** *f* INFORMAT, ORDINAT memory hierarchy,

storage hierarchy; ~ **numérique** *f* TELECOM digital hierarchy; ~ **numérique plésiochrone** *f* TELECOM PDH, plesiochronous digital hierarchy; ~ **numérique synchrone** *f (HNS)* TELECOM synchronous digital hierarchy *(SDH)*

high: ~ **band** *adj* TV high band

hiloire *f* NAUT coaming, girder, stringer; ~ **d'écoutille** *f* NAUT hatch coaming; ~ **de protection** *f* AERONAUT coaming; ~ **sous barrots** *f* NAUT deck girder

hissage *m* MINES raising, PRODUCTION hoisting

hisser *vt* AERONAUT, MECANIQUE hoist, NAUT *drapeau* break, PRODUCTION hoist; ~ **les couleurs** *vt* NAUT hoist the colors (AmE), hoist the colours (BrE)

histamine *f* CHIMIE histamine

histogramme *m* INFORMAT, MATH histogram, ORDINAT bar chart, PHYSIQUE, TELECOM histogram; ~ **d'état des contacts** *m* ELECTR, PRODUCTION contact histogram

histone *f* CHIMIE histone

historique *m* IMPRIM background

hivernage *m* METEO rainy season, NAUT winter storage

hiverniser *vt* AUTO winterize

hlp *abrév (haut le pied)* CH DE FER *véhicules* running light

HNS *abrév (hiérarchie numérique synchrone)* TELECOM SDH *(synchronous digital hierarchy)*

Ho *(holmium)* CHIMIE Ho *(holmium)*

holmium *m (Ho)* CHIMIE holmium *(Ho)*

holocène *m* GEOLOGIE *stratigraphie* Holocene

hologramme *m* PHYS ONDES, PHYSIQUE hologram

holographie *f* ESPACE *véhicules*, INFORMAT, ORDINAT, PHYS ONDES, PHYS RAYON, PHYSIQUE holography

homilite *f* MINERAUX homilite

homme: ~ **de barre** *m* NAUT helmsman; ~ **de cabestan** *m* PETROLE motorman

homme-an *m* PRODUCTION man-year

homme-heure *m* CONSTR, PRODUCTION man-hour; ~ **indirect** *m* CONS MECA indirect man-hour

homme-jour *m* PRODUCTION man-day

homme-semaine *m* PRODUCTION man-week

homocyclique *adj* CHIMIE homocyclic

homogène *adj* CHIMIE homogeneous, uniform, GEOLOGIE massive, MATERIAUX, METALL homogeneous

homogénéisateur *m* EQUIP LAB *préparation* homogenizer

homogénéisation *f* GENIE CHIM diffusion annealing, MAT CHAUFF homogenizing, METALL, PLAST CAOU homogenization

homogénéité *f* MATERIAUX homogeneity

homographie *f* GEOMETRIE homograph

homographique *adj* GEOMETRIE homographic

homojonction *f* ELECTRON, OPTIQUE, TELECOM homojunction

homologation *f* AERONAUT approval, ESPACE *qualité* type approval, PRODUCTION, QUALITE approval, VEHICULES *réglementation* approval, certification, homologation; ~ **d'aptitude** *f* QUALITE capability approval; ~ **de qualification** *f* QUALITE qualification approval; ~ **de type** *f* QUALITE type approval

homologue *adj* CHIMIE, MATERIAUX, METALL homologous

homologuer *vt* AERONAUT, QUALITE approve

homopolymère *m* PLAST CAOU homopolymer

homopolymérisation *f* PLAST CAOU *procédé* homopolymerization

homopyrrole *m* CHIMIE homopyrrole

homotéréphtalique *adj* CHIMIE homoterephthalic

homothétique *adj* IMPRIM *reproduction* homothetical
hopcalite *f* CHIMIE hopcalite
hopéite *f* MINERAUX hopeite
hordéine *f* CHIMIE hordein
horizon *m* ASTRONOMIE, GEOLOGIE, NAUT, PETROLE *des couches stratigraphiques* horizon; ~ apparent *m* ASTRONOMIE apparent horizon; ~ artificiel *m* AERONAUT artificial horizon, ESPACE *véhicules* artificial horizon, gyro horizon, TRANSPORT artificial horizon, gyro horizon; ~ céleste *m* ASTRONOMIE celestial horizon; ~ des évènements *m* ASTRONOMIE event horizon; ~ fantôme *m* GEOPHYS phantom horizon; ~ gyroscopique *m* AERONAUT gyro horizon; ~ de lancement *m* PRODUCTION release horizon; ~ pédologique induré *m* GEOLOGIE hardpan; ~ de planification *m* PRODUCTION forecast horizon, planning horizon, time fence; ~ de prévision *m* PRODUCTION forecast horizon; ~ producteur *m* PETROLE producing horizon; ~ productif *m* PETROLE producing horizon; ~ repère *m* GEOLOGIE datum horizon, marker bed; ~ sismique *m* GEOLOGIE event, marker; ~ visible *m* ASTRONOMIE apparent horizon; ~ visuel *m* NAUT visible horizon
horizontal *adj* GEOMETRIE horizontal
horizontale *f* GEOMETRIE horizontal
horloge *f* INFORMAT clock, timer, ORDINAT clock, watchdog timer; ~ atomique *f* PHYSIQUE, TELECOM atomic clock; ~ au césium 133 *f* ESPACE caesium clock (BrE), cesium clock (AmE); ~ chien de garde *f* INFORMAT, PRODUCTION watchdog timer; ~ électrique synchrone *f* ELECTR synchronous electric clock; ~ électronique *f* ELECTRON, TELECOM electronic clock; ~ interne *f* TELECOM internal clock; ~ mère *f* INFORMAT, ORDINAT, TELECOM master clock; ~ numérique *f* INFORMAT, ORDINAT digital clock; ~ parlante *f* TELECOM speaking clock; ~ pilote *f* TELECOM master clock; ~ principale *f* INFORMAT, ORDINAT master clock; ~ à quartz *f* ELECTR quartz crystal clock; ~ de référence *f* TELECOM reference clock; ~ sidérale *f* ASTRONOMIE sidereal clock; ~ de surveillance *f* INFORMAT, ORDINAT watchdog timer; ~ temps réel *f* INFORMAT, ORDINAT real-time clock
Horloge *f* ASTRONOMIE Horologium
hornblende *f* MATERIAUX *géologie* blende, MINERAUX hornblende
hornblendite *f* PETR hornblendite
horodateur *m* INFORMAT, ORDINAT dater, TELECOM time stamp, TRANSPORT parking meter
hors: ~ d'aplomb *adj* CONS MECA out-of-plumb, CONSTR off plumb, out-of-plumb; ~ carte *adj* ELECTRON off board; ~ champ *adj* CINEMAT off-camera, off-screen; ~ émission *adj* TELECOM off-air; ~ d'équerre *adj* CONS MECA, IMPRIM *papier, machine* out-of-square; ~ d'équilibre *adj* PHYSIQUE not in equilibrium; ~ ligne *adj* INFORMAT, ORDINAT, TELECOM off-line; ~ micro *adj* ENREGISTR off-mike; ~ d'oeuvre *adj* CONSTR overall; ~ de portée *adj* MILITAIRE *artillerie* out-of-range; ~ puce *adj* ELECTRON off chip; ~ service *adj* CONS MECA out-of-action, out-of-use; ~ tolérance *adj* CONS MECA out-of-tolerance; ~ tout *adj* CONS MECA, CONSTR *dimensions* overall; ~ trim *adj* AERONAUT out-of-trim; ~ d'usage *adj* CONS MECA out-of-action, out-of-use
hors-bord *adj* NAUT outboard
hors-profil *m* MINES overbreak
hôte *m* INFORMAT host, ORDINAT host
hotte *f* CONSTR head, hopper head, rainwater head, EQUIP LAB extraction hood, fume cupboard, PAPIER *de machine*, PRODUCTION *d'une forge, d'un laboratoire* hood; ~ d'aspiration *f* EQUIP LAB fume hood, GENIE CHIM fume cupboard, fume hood; ~ de drague *f* NAUT dredge bucket; ~ fermée *f* EQUIP LAB fume cupboard, GENIE CHIM fume cupboard, fume hood; ~ ouverte *f* PAPIER open hood
houache *f* OCEANO track
houage *m* CHARBON cubage
houe *f* CONSTR hoe
houille *f* CHARBON, GEOLOGIE coal; ~ anthraciteuse *f* CHARBON semianthracite; ~ blanche *f* DISTRI EAU water power, EN RENOUV hydroelectric power, water power; ~ bleue *f* EN RENOUV tidal power, wave power; ~ demi-grasse *f* CHARBON cherry coal; ~ à gaz *f* CHARBON gas coal; ~ grasse *f* CHARBON fat coal, gas coal, flaming coal; ~ tout-venant *f* MINES run-of-mine, run-of-mine coal
houillère *f* CHARBON coal mine, colliery, MINES coal mine, colliery, pit; ~ à ciel ouvert *f* CHARBON daylight colliery, open cast mine
houilleur *m* CHARBON collier
houilleuse *f* CHARBON coal cutter, MINES coal cutter, coal-cutting machine
houillification *f* CHARBON carbonization, coalification
houillifier *vt* CHARBON carbonize
houle *f* NAUT, OCEANO swell; ~ déferlante *f* OCEANO breaker, breaking wave; ~ par le travers *f* NAUT beam sea
houlographe *m* OCEANO wave recorder
housse *f* CONS MECA cover; ~ de protection du clavier *f* ORDINAT keyboard mask
HPA *abrév (heure prévue d'arrivée)* AERONAUT, NAUT ETA *(estimated time of arrival)*
HT *abrév (haute tension)* ELECTR *alimentation*, ELECTROTEC, PHYSIQUE HT *(high-tension)*, HV *(high-voltage)*
hublot *m* CERAM VER porthole, NAUT port, porthole, window; ~ d'aération *m* NAUT air vent; ~ éjectable *m* AERONAUT jettisonable window; ~ d'observation *m* ESPACE *véhicules* viewing port; ~ de projection *m* CINEMAT projection port; ~ tournant *m* NAUT clearview screen
hubnérite *f* MINERAUX hubnerite
huche *f* INST HYDR closed turbine chamber, enclosed casing, MINES hutch, PRODUCTION closed turbine chamber
huilage *m* PRODUCTION oiling
huile *f* PAPIER, PETROLE oil, POLLU MER hydrocarbon, REFRIG oil; ~ absolue *f* CHIMIE *de Braconnot* olein; ~ d'acajou *f* PLAST CAOU *liant de peinture* cashew nut oil; ~ d'ambre blanc *f* LESSIVES sperm oil, spermaceti oil; ~ anthracénique *f* CHIMIE anthracene oil; ~ d'arachide *f* AGRO ALIM arachis oil, groundnut oil, CHIMIE peanut oil; ~ de beurre *f* AGRO ALIM butter oil; ~ de blanc de baleine *f* LESSIVES sperm oil, spermaceti oil; ~ camphrée *f* CHIMIE camphor oil; ~ de carthame *f* AGRO ALIM safflower oil; ~ chimiquement neutre *f* PETROLE chemically neutral oil; ~ de coffrage *f* CONSTR formwork oil, mold oil (AmE), mould oil (BrE); ~ de colza *f* AGRO ALIM canola oil, rapeseed oil; ~ compoundée *f* PRODUCTION compound oil; ~ contenant de l'eau *f* PETROLE cut oil; ~ de conversion *f* PETROLE conversion oil; ~ de copra *f* AGRO ALIM coconut oil; ~ de coton *f* AGRO ALIM cottonseed oil; ~ de coupe *f* CONS MECA coolant, cutting oil; ~ désasphaltée *f* PETROLE DAO, deasphalted oil; ~ détergente *f* LESSIVES, VE-

HICULES *lubrication* detergent oil; ~ **diesel pour les machines marines** *f* NAUT marine diesel oil; ~ **en place** *f* PETR oil in place; ~ **époxidique** *f* PLAST CAOU *liant de peinture* epoxidized oil; ~ **essentielle** *f* AGRO ALIM essential oil; ~ **d'extension** *f* PETROLE *raffinage* extender oil; ~ **fixe** *f* CHIMIE fixed oil; ~ **de foie de morue** *f* AGRO ALIM cod liver oil; ~ **de fusel** *f* AGRO ALIM fusel oil; ~ **de graine de coton** *f* AGRO ALIM cottonseed oil; ~ **de graine de lin** *f* CHIMIE linseed oil; ~ **de graissage** *f* AUTO lubricating oil, PRODUCTION lubricant, lubricating oil, *système hydraulique* lubrication oil; ~ **à graisser** *f* PRODUCTION lubricating oil; ~ **à haute tenue** *f* PETROLE HD, heavy-duty oil; ~ **de houille** *f* CHARBON coal oil, coal tar naphtha; ~ **hydrogénée** *f* PRODUCTION hardened oil; ~ **à immersion** *f* METALL immersion oil; ~ **isolante** *f* ELECTR, ELECTROTEC, PETROLE insulating oil; ~ **de kapok** *f* CHIMIE kapok oil; ~ **de lin** *f* CHIMIE, CONSTR, NAUT linseed oil; ~ **de lin cuite** *f* CHIMIE boiled linseed oil; ~ **lubrifiante** *f* VEHICULES lubricating oil; ~ **de macis** *f* AGRO ALIM *épice* mace oil; ~ **minérale** *f* AUTO, PLAST CAOU *matière première* mineral oil; ~ **morte** *f* PETROLE dead oil; ~ **de moutarde** *f* AGRO ALIM *épice* mustard-seed oil; ~ **multigrade** *f* AUTO, VEHICULES *lubrification* multigrade oil; ~ **de muscade** *f* AGRO ALIM *épice* mace oil; ~ **de noix** *f* AGRO ALIM walnut oil; ~ **de palme** *f* CHIMIE palm oil; ~ **de palmiste** *f* AGRO ALIM palm kernel oil, CHIMIE palm nut oil; ~ **de paraffine** *f* CHIMIE, THERMODYN liquid paraffin; ~ **paraffinée** *f* CHIMIE paraffin oil; ~ **partiellement émulsionnée** *f* PETROLE cut oil; ~ **de perilla** *f* CHIMIE perilla seed oil; ~ **de pied de boeuf** *f* AGRO ALIM neat's-foot oil; ~ **de pierre** *f* CHARBON coal oil, stone oil, PETR earth oil, stone oil; ~ **de poisson** *f* CHIMIE fish oil; ~ **pour mécanisme** *f* CONS MECA machine oil; ~ **pour moteur** *f* VEHICULES engine oil; ~ **pour moteurs 2 temps** *f* AUTO two-stroke oil; ~ **pour mouvement** *f* CONS MECA machine oil; ~ **pour organe de machine** *f* CONS MECA engine oil; ~ **pour transformateur** *f* ELECTR, ELECTROTEC transformer oil; ~ **de protection** *f* PRODUCTION anticorrosion oil; ~ **de ricin** *f* PLAST CAOU *liant de peinture* castor oil; ~ **de roche** *f* CHARBON coal oil, rock oil, PETR earth oil, rock oil; ~ **siccative** *f* AGRO ALIM, PLAST CAOU *liant de peinture*, PRODUCTION drying oil; ~ **de spermaceti** *f* LESSIVES sperm oil, spermaceti oil; ~ **de suif** *f* CHIMIE olein, oleo oil, tallow oil; ~ **sulfatée** *f* LESSIVES sulfated oil (AmE), sulphated oil (BrE); ~ **de tall** *f* PLAST CAOU *matière première pour peinture* tall oil; ~ **végétale** *f* AGRO ALIM vegetable oil; ~ **de vitriol** *f* CHIMIE oil of vitriol

huilement *m* PRODUCTION oiling
huiler *vt* PRODUCTION lubricate, oil
huisserie *f* CONSTR casing, door framing
huîtrière *f* OCEANO oyster bed, oyster farm
hululement *m* TELECOM warble
humboldtilite *f* MINERAUX humboldtilite
humboldtine *f* MINERAUX humboldtine
humectage *m* PAPIER dampening, damping
humectant *m* CHIMIE humectant
humecté *adj* THERMODYN humid, moist
humecter *vt* AGRO ALIM moisten, CHIMIE wet, THERMODYN moisten
humecteur *m* THERMODYN humidifier
humecteuse *f* PAPIER dampener, humidifier, moistener
humide *adj* PAPIER damp, moist, wet, TEXTILE wet, THERMODYN humid, moist

humidificateur *m* AERONAUT humidifier, EMBALLAGE moistening equipment, REFRIG, THERMODYN humidifier; ~ **d'air** *m* SECURITE air humidifier; ~ **à disque tournant** *m* REFRIG spinning disc humidifier (BrE), spinning disk humidifier (AmE); ~ **à injection de vapeur** *m* REFRIG steam humidifier
humidification *f* CHIMIE moistening, wetting, CONS MECA wetting, CONSTR *béton* tempering, THERMODYN humidification; ~ **de la composition** *f* CERAM VER batch wetting
humidifier *vt* PAPIER humidify, PHYSIQUE wet, REFRIG humidify, THERMODYN humidify, moisten
humidifuge *adj* EMBALLAGE moisture-repellent
humidiostat *m* REFRIG humidistat
humidité *f* CHIMIE moistness, moisture, MAT CHAUFF, METEO humidity, PAPIER dampness, humidity, moisture content, PHYSIQUE, REFRIG, THERMODYN humidity; ~ **absolue** *f* CHAUFFAGE, HYDROLOGIE *du sol*, METEO *de l'air*, PHYSIQUE absolute humidity; ~ **d'air** *f* CHARBON air moisture; ~ **atmosphérique** *f* EMBALLAGE humidity of the air, THERMODYN air humidity; ~ **relative** *f* CHAUFFAGE, DISTRI EAU, MAT CHAUFF, MATERIAUX, PHYSIQUE, PLAST CAOU, REFRIG, TEXTILE relative humidity; ~ **relative de l'air** *f (Ha)* METEO relative humidity of the air; ~ **relative du sol** *f* HYDROLOGIE relative humidity of the ground; ~ **résiduelle** *f* EMBALLAGE, REFRIG residual moisture; ~ **spécifique** *f* METEO specific humidity
humique *adj* CHIMIE humic
humite *f* MINERAUX humite
humulène *m* CHIMIE humulene
humus *m* CHARBON, CHIMIE, CONSTR humus
hureaulite *f* MINERAUX hureaulite
hurleur *m* TELECOM howler
hyacinthe *f* MINERAUX hyacinth
hyalin *adj* CHIMIE vitreous, GEOLOGIE hyaline
hyalite *f* MINERAUX hyalite
hyaloclastite *f* GEOLOGIE hyaloclastic rock, hyaloclastite
hyalogène *m* CHIMIE hyalogen
hyalophane *f* MINERAUX hyalophane
hybridisation *f* CHIMIE hybridization
hydantoïne *f* CHIMIE hydantoin
hydracrylique *adj* CHIMIE *acide* hydracrylic
hydrante *m* DISTRI EAU plug, water hydrant, water plug
hydrargillite *f* MINERAUX hydrargillite
hydrastine *f* CHIMIE hydrastine
hydrastique *adj* CHIMIE *acide* hydrastic
hydratation *f* CHIMIE, CONSTR *du ciment*, GEOLOGIE hydration
hydrate *m* CHIMIE hydrate; ~ **de carbone** *m* AGRO ALIM, CHIMIE carbohydrate; ~ **de chloral** *m* CHIMIE chloralhydrate; ~ **de chlorure d'aluminium** *m* HYDROLOGIE aluminium chlorohydrate (BrE), aluminum chlorohydrate (AmE)
hydraté *adj* CHIMIE hydrous, GEOLOGIE *minéraux* hydrated, hydrous
hydrater *vt* CHIMIE, GEOLOGIE hydrate
hydrateur *m* AGRO ALIM masher
hydratropique *adj* CHIMIE *acide* hydratropic
hydrauliquage *m* MINES spatter work
hydraulique[1] *adj* MECANIQUE, REFRIG hydraulic
hydraulique[2] *f* INST HYDR, MECANIQUE hydraulics, NAUT hydraulic system, PETROLE hydraulics; ~ **fluviale** *f* DISTRI EAU fluvial hydraulics
hydravion *m* AERONAUT seaplane, NAUT hydroplane,

TRANSPORT flying boat; ~ **à coque** *m* AERONAUT flying boat; ~ **monocoque** *m* AERONAUT flying boat; ~ **monomoteur** *m* TRANSPORT float seaplane, floatplane

hydrazide *f* CHIMIE hydrazide

hydrazine *f* CHIMIE, ESPACE *matière de propulsion* hydrazine

hydrazoïque *adj* CHIMIE hydrazoic

Hydre *f* ASTRONOMIE Hydra, The Sea Serpent; ~ **mâle** *f* ASTRONOMIE Hydrus

hydrindène *f* CHIMIE hydrindene, indan

hydriodique *adj* CHIMIE hydriodic

hydrique *adj* CHIMIE hydric

hydroaromatique *adj* CHIMIE hydroaromatic

hydrobase *f* AERONAUT seaplane base

hydrobilirubine *f* CHIMIE hydrobilirubin

hydrocarbonate *m* CHIMIE hydrocarbonate

hydrocarboné *adj* CHIMIE hydrocarbonic

hydrocarbure *m* CHIMIE, GEOLOGIE, PETROLE *composé pétrolier de base* hydrocarbon, POLLU MER hydrocarbon, oil, POLLUTION, VEHICULES *carburant* hydrocarbon; ~ **aliphatique** *m* CHIMIE, PLAST CAOU aliphatic hydrocarbon; ~ **aromatique** *m* CHIMIE, PLAST CAOU *composé chimique* aromatic hydrocarbon; ~ **chlorofluoré** *m* (*CFC*) POLLUTION chlorofluorocarbon (*CFC*); ~ **éthylénique** *m* LESSIVES alkene, alkylene; ~ **gazeux** *m* GAZ gas hydrocarbon; ~ **liquide** *m* GAZ liquid hydrocarbon; ~ **polycyclique aromatique** *m* POLLUTION polycyclic aromatic hydrocarbon; ~ **polynucléaire aromatique** *m* POLLUTION polycyclic aromatic hydrocarbon; ~ **saturé** *m* PETROLE saturated hydrocarbon; ~ **vieilli** *m* POLLU MER weathered oil

hydrocarbures: ~ **de base** *m pl* PETROLE hydrocarbon feedstocks; ~ **solides** *m pl* CHIMIE solid hydrocarbons

hydrocellulose *f* CHIMIE hydrocellulose

hydrocinnamique *adj* CHIMIE hydrocinnamic

hydroclone *m* GENIE CHIM hydroclone

hydrocortisone *f* CHIMIE hydrocortisone

hydrocotarnine *f* CHIMIE hydrocotarnine

hydrocraquage *m* MATERIAUX *catalyse*, PETROLE *procédé de raffinage* hydrocracking

hydrocraqueur *m* PETROLE hydrocracker

hydrocyanite *f* MINERAUX hydrocyanite

hydrocyclone *m* CHARBON, PETROLE *piège à sable* hydrocyclone

hydrodésulfuration *f* POLLUTION hydrodesulfurization (AmE), hydrodesulphurization (BrE)

hydrodolomite *f* MINERAUX hydrodolomite

hydrodynamique[1] *adj* CHIMIE, GEOLOGIE, NAUT, PETROLE, PHYSIQUE hydrodynamic

hydrodynamique[2] *f* NAUT, PHYS FLUID, PHYSIQUE hydrodynamics

hydrodynamisme *m* PETROLE hydrodynamics

hydroéjecteur *m* DISTRI EAU jet pump

hydro-électricité *f* ELECTR *alimentation* hydroelectricity, EN RENOUV hydroelectric power

hydroextracteur *m* GENIE CHIM centrifugal dryer, centrifugal hydroextrator

hydroextraction *f* GENIE CHIM dehydration

hydrofoil *m* NAUT hydrofoil

hydroformage *m* MATERIAUX hydroforming

hydroformulation *f* MATERIAUX hydroformulation

hydrofuge *adj* MATERIAUX water-repellent, water-resisting, REVETEMENT, TEXTILE water-repellent

hydrofuger *vt* REVETEMENT waterproof

hydrogénateur *m* AGRO ALIM hydrogenator

hydrogénation *f* AGRO ALIM, CHIMIE, LESSIVES, MATERIAUX, PETROLE *raffinage* hydrogenation

hydrogéné *adj* AGRO ALIM, CHIMIE *gaz, atome* hydrogenated

hydrogène *m* (*H*) CHIMIE hydrogen (*H*); ~ **d'appoint** *m* CHIMIE make-up hydrogen; ~ **hyperlourd** *m* CHIMIE tritium; ~ **libre** *m* MATERIAUX free hydrogen; ~ **liquide** *m* ESPACE liquid hydrogen, THERMODYN hydrogen liquid; ~ **lourd** *m* CHIMIE heavy hydrogen, NUCLEAIRE deuterium, heavy hydrogen, PHYSIQUE heavy hydrogen; ~ **sulfuré** *m* AGRO ALIM hydrogen sulfide (AmE), hydrogen sulphide (BrE), sulfuretted hydrogen (AmE), sulphurettedhydrogen (BrE), CHIMIE, POLLUTION hydrogen sulfide (AmE), hydrogen sulphide (BrE)

hydrogéner *vt* AGRO ALIM, CHIMIE *gaz, atome* hydrogenate

hydrogéologie *f* DISTRI EAU, HYDROLOGIE hydrogeology

hydroglisseur *m* NAUT jetfoil, *bateau* hydroplane, OCEANO aquaplane, hydroplane, TRANSPORT gliding boat, hydroplane, hydroskimmer

hydrogramme *m* DISTRI EAU hydrograph

hydrographie *f* EN RENOUV, HYDROLOGIE hydrography, NAUT hydrography, surveying, OCEANO hydrography

hydrographier *vt* NAUT chart, *côte* survey

hydrographique *adj* NAUT hydrographic, hydrographical

hydroisohypse: ~ **de la nappe phréatique** *m* HYDROLOGIE ground water contour

hydrojet *m* TRANSPORT hydrojet

hydrologie *f* CHARBON, CONSTR, DISTRI EAU, OCEANO hydrology; ~ **karstique** *f* DISTRI EAU karst hydrology

hydrologiste *m* CONSTR hydrologist

hydrologue *m* CONSTR hydrologist

hydrolysat: ~ **de caséine** *m* AGRO ALIM casein hydrolysate

hydrolyse *f* AGRO ALIM, CHIMIE, GEOLOGIE, MATERIAUX, PLAST CAOU hydrolysis; ~ **à la flamme** *f* OPTIQUE flame hydrolysis

hydromagnésite *f* MINERAUX hydromagnesite

hydromécanique *f* PHYS FLUID hydromechanics

hydrométallurgie *f* CHARBON hydrometallurgy

hydromètre *m* AGRO ALIM, HYDROLOGIE, PETROLE *prospection, raffinage*, PHYSIQUE hydrometer

hydrométrie *f* CHIMIE, DISTRI EAU, HYDROLOGIE, PHYSIQUE hydrometry

hydronomie *f* OCEANO hydronomy

hydrophane *f* MINERAUX hydrophane

hydrophile *adj* CHARBON, CHIMIE hydrophilic

hydrophobe *adj* CHARBON, CHIMIE hydrophobic, REVETEMENT water-repellent

hydrophobicité *f* REVETEMENT water repellency

hydrophobique *adj* CHIMIE hydrophobic

hydrophone *m* OCEANO, PETROLE *levé sismique*, TELECOM hydrophone

hydroplanage *m* AERONAUT aquaplaning

hydroptère *m* AERONAUT, TRANSPORT hydrofoil; ~ **à ailes émergentes** *m* TRANSPORT emerging-foil craft; ~ **à ailes en V** *m* TRANSPORT VEE foil craft, surface-piercing craft; ~ **hybride** *m* TRANSPORT hybrid foil craft

hydroquinone *f* CHIMIE hydroquinone, quinol

hydroraffinage *m* MATERIAUX hydrorefining

hydrosilicate *m* CHIMIE hydrosilicate

hydrosol *m* CHIMIE hydrosol

hydrosoluble *adj* AGRO ALIM, CHIMIE water-soluble

hydrosopoline f CHIMIE hydrosopoline
hydrosphère f HYDROLOGIE, OCEANO, POLLUTION hydrosphere
hydrostatique[1] *adj* MECANIQUE, PHYSIQUE hydrostatic
hydrostatique[2] f CONSTR, DISTRI EAU, PHYS FLUID, PHYSIQUE hydrostatics
hydrosulfite m CHIMIE hydrosulfite (AmE), hydrosulphite (BrE)
hydrotamis m MINES jig
hydrothermal *adj* GEOLOGIE hydrothermal
hydrox m OCEANO hydrogen-oxygen mixture, hydrox
hydroxyanisol: ~ **butylé** m *(BHA)* AGRO ALIM butylated hydroxyanisole *(BHA)*
hydroxyde: ~ **d'aluminium** m HYDROLOGIE, PLAST CAOU *charge* aluminium hydroxide (BrE), aluminum hydroxide (AmE); ~ **de nickel** m ESPACE *véhicules* nickel hydroxide; ~ **de potassium** m CHIMIE potassium hydroxide
hydroxyéthylcellulose f CHIMIE, PETROLE hydroxyethylcellulose
hydroxyle m CHIMIE hydroxyl
hydroxylé *adj* AGRO ALIM, CHIMIE hydroxylated
hydroxytoluène: ~ **butylé** m *(BHT)* AGRO ALIM butylated hydroxytoluene *(BHT)*
hydrozincite f MINERAUX hydrozincite
hydrure m CHIMIE hydride, tetrahydride, METALL hydride; ~ **lourd** m CHIMIE deuteride
hygiène: ~ **publique** f DISTRI EAU public health; ~ **du travail** f SECURITE industrial hygiene
hygromètre m EQUIP LAB, METEO, PETROLE *raffinage*, PHYSIQUE, REFRIG hygrometer; ~ **à cheveu** m EQUIP LAB, PHYSIQUE, REFRIG hair hygrometer; ~ **à condensation** m GENIE CHIM condensation hygrometer; ~ **électrique** m REFRIG electrical hygrometer; ~ **électrolytique** m REFRIG electrolytic hygrometer; ~ **fronde** m REFRIG sling hygrometer; ~ **organique** m REFRIG organic hygrometer; ~ **à point de rosée** m REFRIG dew point hygrometer
hygrométrie f DISTRI EAU, METEO hygrometry, NAUT humidity measurement, REFRIG hygrometry
hygroscope m PHYSIQUE hygroscope
hygroscopique *adj* CHIMIE, CONSTR, HYDROLOGIE, MECANIQUE *matériaux*, PHYSIQUE hygroscopic
hyocholanique *adj* CHIMIE hyocholanic
hyoscine f CHIMIE hyoscine
hyper: ~ **petit** *adj* PRODUCTION ultrasmall
hyperalcalin *adj* GEOLOGIE peralkaline
hyperalumineux *adj* GEOLOGIE peraluminous
hyperapnée f OCEANO hyperapnea, panting
hyperbalistique[1] *adj* ESPACE hyperballistic
hyperbalistique[2] f ESPACE hyperballistics
hyperbarie f OCEANO hyperbary
hyperbole f GEOMETRIE hyperbola
hyperbolique *adj* GEOMETRIE hyperbolic
hyperboloïde m GEOMETRIE hyperboloid
hypercapnie f OCEANO hyperkapnia
hypercharge f PHYSIQUE hypercharge
hypereutectique *adj* METALL hypereutectic
hyperfréquence f ELECTRON, ENREGISTR, PHYSIQUE, TELECOM, TV microwave frequency

hypergol m ESPACE *propulsion* hypergol
hypergolicité f ESPACE hypergolic property
hypergolique *adj* ESPACE hypergolic
hyperluminosité: ~ **d'aire réduite** f TV peak brightness
hypéron m PHYS PART, PHYSIQUE hyperon
hypéroxie f OCEANO hyperoxia, hyperoxie
hyperoxyde m CHIMIE hyperoxide
hyperplan m GEOMETRIE hyperplane
hypersaturé *adj* GEOLOGIE oversaturated
hypersonique *adj* ESPACE hypersonic
hypersthène m MINERAUX hypersthene
hypersurface f GEOMETRIE hypersurface
hypersustentateurs m pl AERONAUT high lift devices
hypertexte m INFORMAT, ORDINAT hypertext
hypertrempe f CERAM VER splat cooling
hyperventilation f OCEANO hyperventilation, oxygen poisoning
hypidiomorphe *adj* GEOLOGIE *texture* hypautomorphic, hypidiomorphic
hypocalorique *adj* AGRO ALIM low-calorie
hypocentre m GEOLOGIE hypocenter (AmE), hypocentre (BrE), GEOPHYS earthquake focus, focus, hypocenter (AmE), hypocentre (BrE), seismic focus
hypochlorate m CHIMIE hypochlorate
hypochlorique *adj* CHIMIE hypochloric
hypochlorite m CHIMIE hypochlorite; ~ **de chaux** m LESSIVES bleaching lime, bleaching powder, chlorinated lime
hypoeutectique *adj* METALL hypoeutectic
hypoïde *adj* MECANIQUE *engrenage* hypoid
hypomagma m PETR plutonic magma
hyponeuston m OCEANO hyponeuston
hypophosphate m CHIMIE hypophosphate
hypophosphite m CHIMIE hypophosphite
hypophosphoreux *adj* CHIMIE hypophosphorous
hypophosphorique *adj* CHIMIE hypophosphoric
hyposulfite m CHIMIE hyposulfite (AmE), hyposulphite (BrE), thiosulfate (AmE), thiosulphate (BrE), CINEMAT hyposulfite (AmE), hyposulphite (BrE); ~ **de soude** m CHIMIE sodium thiosulfate (AmE), sodium thiosulphate (BrE)
hyposulfureux *adj* CHIMIE thiosulfuric (AmE), thiosulphuric (BrE)
hypoténuse f GEOMETRIE hypotenuse
hypothermal *adj* GEOLOGIE *minéralisation* hypothermal
hypothermie f NAUT hypothermia
hypothèse f CHIMIE hypothesis
hypotonique *adj* CHIMIE hypotonic
hypsomètre m PHYSIQUE hypsometer
hypsométrique *adj* PETR hypsometric
hystarazine f CHIMIE hystarazin
hystérésis f CONS MECA magnetic lag, ELECTR *courbe*, ELECTROTEC, ENREGISTR, MECANIQUE, METALL, PETR, PHYSIQUE, PLAST CAOU hysteresis; ~ **diélectrique** f ELECTR, ELECTROTEC dielectric hysteresis; ~ **électrique** f ENREGISTR electric hysteresis; ~ **magnétique** f ELECTR, ELECTROTEC magnetic hysteresis
Hz *abrév (hertz)* ELECTR, ELECTROTEC, METROLOGIE, PETR, PHYSIQUE, TV Hz *(hertz)*

I

I *(iode)* CHIMIE I *(iodine)*

IA *abrév (intelligence artificielle)* ORDINAT, TELECOM AI *(artificial intelligence)*

IAO *abrév (instruction assistée par ordinateur)* ORDINAT CAI *(computer-assisted instruction)*

ichtyocolle *f* AGRO ALIM isinglass

icône *f* INFORMAT icon

iconoscope *m* ELECTRON iconoscope

iconoscope-image *m* ELECTRON image iconoscope

icosaèdre[1] *adj* GEOMETRIE icosahedral

icosaèdre[2] *m* GEOMETRIE icosahedron

ID *abrév (identification)* INFORMAT, ORDINAT ID *(identification)*

identificateur *m* INFORMAT, ORDINAT, TELECOM ID, identifier; **~ d'autorité et de format** *m* TELECOM AFI, authority and format identifier; **~ de canal virtuel** *m* TELECOM VCI, virtual channel identifier; **~ de conduit virtuel** *m* TELECOM VPI, virtual path identifier; **~ de connexion de liaison consolidée** *m* TELECOM DLCI, data link connection identifier; **~ de dépôt** *m* TELECOM submission identifier; **~ du domaine initial** *m (IDI)* TELECOM initial domain identifier *(IDI)*; **~ de fichier** *m* INFORMAT, ORDINAT file identifier; **~ de modem** *m* TELECOM DSI, data set identifier; **~ de point d'accès au réseau** *m* TELECOM SAPI, service access point identifier; **~ de point d'extrémité de terminal** *m* TELECOM TEI, terminal end-point identifier; **~ de syntaxe** *m* TELECOM syntax identifier; **~ de trajet virtuel** *m* TELECOM VPI, virtual path identifier; **~ de voie virtuelle** *m* TELECOM VCI, virtual channel identifier

identification *f* ACOUSTIQUE, CONS MECA, INFORMAT, ORDINAT, PHYS PART *particules* , SECURITE *risques, dangers* identification; **~ de l'abonné demandé** *f* TELECOM CSI, called subscriber identification; **~ d'un aéronef** *f* AERONAUT aircraft identification; **~ d'appel** *f* TELECOM call identification, call trace; **~ d'appels malveillants** *f* TELECOM malicious call tracing; **~ automatique des véhicules** *f* TRANSPORT AVI, automatic vehicle identification; **~ automatique des wagons** *f* TRANSPORT ACI (AmE), automatic car identification (AmE), automatic wagon identification (BrE); **~ avec code à barres masqué** *f* EMBALLAGE hidden bar code identification; **~ des besoins** *f* PRODUCTION pegging; **~ du destinataire de l'échange** *f* TELECOM interchange receiver identification; **~ de l'expéditeur** *f* TELECOM sender identification; **~ de l'expéditeur de l'échange** *f* TELECOM interchange sender identification; **~ de la ligne appelante** *f (ILA)* TELECOM calling line identification *(CLI)*; **~ de la ligne appelée** *f* TELECOM called line identification; **~ de la ligne connectée** *f* TELECOM COLI, connected line identification; **~ de la ligne du demandé** *f* TELECOM CDLI, called line identification; **~ d'un lot** *f* EMBALLAGE batch tabbing; **~ de multiplexage** *f* TELECOM multiplexing identification; **~ de l'octet** *f* PRODUCTION *automatisme industriel* byte designation; **~ par radar** *f* TRANSPORT radar identification; **~ du plan de numérotage** *f* TELECOM NPI, numbering plan identification; **~ radar** *f* AERONAUT radar identification

identifier *vt* CHIMIE, INFORMAT, ORDINAT identify

identique: ~ au produit naturel *adj* AGRO ALIM nature-identical

identité *f* INFORMAT, MATH, ORDINAT identity; **~ d'appel** *f* TELECOM call identity; **~ d'appel de groupe** *f* TELECOM group call identity; **~ de station côtière** *f* TELECOM coastal station identity; **~ de la station demandée** *f* TELECOM CSI, called station identity; **~ de station de navire** *f* TELECOM ship station identity

idéogramme *m* INFORMAT ideogram

IDI *abrév (identificateur du domaine initial)* TELECOM IDI *(initial domain identifier)*

idiomorphe *adj* GEOLOGIE *texture* automorphic, euhedral, PETR idiomorphic, idiomorphous

iditol *m* CHIMIE iditol

idocrase *f* MINERAUX idocrase

idonique *adj* CHIMIE *acide* idonic

idosaccharique *adj* CHIMIE idosaccharic

idose *m* CHIMIE idose

idranal *m* CHIMIE idranal

idrialite *f* MINERAUX idrialite

IGD *abrév (message d'interrogation de groupe de circuits demande)* TELECOM CQM *(circuit group query message)*

igloo *m* TRANSPORT igloo container

ignifugation *f* SECURITE fire prevention; **~ préventive** *f* SECURITE preventive fire protection

ignifuge[1] *adj* AERONAUT flame-resistant, ELECTR *matériel* fireproof, PLAST CAOU *peinture, plastiques* fire-retardant, PRODUCTION fire-resistant, fire-retardant, fireproof, THERMODYN fire-resistant, fire-resisting, fire-retarding, refractory

ignifuge[2] *m* PLAST CAOU flame-retardant

ignifugé *adj* PRODUCTION fire-resistant, SECURITE fire-resistant, fireproof, THERMODYN fireproofed

ignifugeage *m* THERMODYN fireproofing

ignifuger *vt* SECURITE, THERMODYN fireproof

ignimbrite *f* GEOLOGIE ignimbrite

igniteur *m* ELECTROTEC igniter

ignition *f* CHIMIE, PLAST CAOU *opération*, SECURITE ignition

ignitron *m* ELECTR *redresseur à vapeur de mercure*, ELECTROTEC ignitron

IGR *abrév (message d'interrogation de groupe de circuits réponse)* TELECOM CQR *(circuit group query response message)*

I²L *abrév (logique intégrée à injection)* ELECTRON I²L *(integrated injection logic)*

ILA *abrév (identification de la ligne appelante)* TELECOM CLI *(calling line identification)*

île: ~ de glace *f* OCEANO ice island

iliaque *adj* CHIMIE *crête* iliac

illisible *adj* IMPRIM illegible

illite *f* CHARBON, MINERAUX, PETROLE illite

illumination *f* ELECTROTEC, METALL illumination; **~ laser** *f* ELECTRON laser illumination

illustrateur *m* IMPRIM draftsman (AmE), draughtsman (BrE)

illustration *f* IMPRIM figure, illustration; ~ **au trait** *f* IMPRIM *photogravure* line work

illustrations: ~ **et maquette** *f pl* IMPRIM *avant la photogravure* artwork

illustrer *vt* IMPRIM illustrate

ilménite *f* MATERIAUX ilmenite, titanium iron oxide, MINERAUX ilmenite, titanium iron oxide

îlot *m* HYDROLOGIE, NAUT islet; ~ **de canalisation** *m* CONSTR traffic island; ~ **de fabrication** *m* PRODUCTION facility; ~ **de stabilité bêta** *m* NUCLEAIRE beta stability island

ilsemannite *f* MINERAUX ilsemannite

ivaïte *f* MINERAUX ivaite

image *f* CINEMAT, IMPRIM image, INFORMAT, ORDINAT image, picture, PHOTO image, picture, PHYSIQUE image, TV frame, picture; ~ **agrandie** *f* PHYSIQUE enlarged image; ~ **arrêtée** *f* CINEMAT frozen frame, still frame; ~ **de basse fréquence** *f* ESPACE low-frequency image; ~ **binaire** *f* ESPACE, TELECOM binary image; ~ **blanche** *f* CINEMAT flash frame; ~ **clip art** *f* IMPRIM clip art; ~ **côtière par radar** *f* TRANSPORT radar coast image; ~ **découpée** *f* PHOTO cutout photograph; ~ **défocalisée** *f* PHOTO fuzzy image, out-of-focus image; ~ **de départ** *f* CINEMAT zero frame; ~ **de diffraction** *f* MATERIAUX diffraction pattern; ~ **d'écoulement** *f* DISTRI EAU flow pattern; ~ **d'écran** *f* INFORMAT screen image, soft copy, ORDINAT soft copy; ~ **électrique** *f* ELECTROTEC electric image, *charge* image charge; ~ **électronique** *f* ELECTRON electron image; ~ **en champ clair** *f* CRISTALL bright field image; ~ **en champ sombre** *f* CRISTALL dark field image; ~ **en couleur** *f* PHOTO color picture (AmE), colour picture (BrE); ~ **à faible granulation** *f* PHOTO fine-grain image; ~ **fantôme** *f* CINEMAT double-image, ghost image, IMPRIM *écran, informatique* echo image, TV ghost image; ~ **fantôme négative** *f* TV negative echo; ~ **figée** *f* CINEMAT frozen frame; ~ **fixe** *f* CINEMAT frozen frame, still frame, TV freeze-frame, still frame; ~ **floue** *f* CINEMAT out-of-focus image, PHYSIQUE blurred image; ~ **à forte granulation** *f* PHOTO coarse grain image; ~ **intermédiaire** *f* PHYSIQUE intermediate image; ~ **inversée** *f* CHIMIE mirror image, CINEMAT reversed image; ~ **inverse latérale** *f* CINEMAT laterally inverted image; ~ **latente** *f* CINEMAT, IMPRIM *écran, développement, impression*, OPTIQUE, PHOTO, PHYSIQUE latent image; ~ **de Lichtenberg** *f* PHYSIQUE Lichtenberg figure; ~ **ligne par ligne** *f* ORDINAT raster display; ~ **lithographie** *f* IMPRIM lithograph; ~ **multicapteur** *f* ESPACE multisensor image; ~ **négative** *f* PHOTO negative image; ~ **numérique** *f* ELECTRON digital image; ~ **numérisée** *f* ELECTRON digitized image; ~ **obtenue par rayonnement thermique** *f* THERMODYN heat image; ~ **optique** *f* ELECTRON optical image; ~ **orthicon** *f* ELECTRON image orthicon; ~ **panoramique** *f* CINEMAT wide-screen picture; ~ **par image** *f* CINEMAT frame by frame, single frame, TV frame by frame; ~ **positive** *f* PHOTO positive image; ~ **rafraîchie** *f* ELECTRON refreshed image; ~ **réelle** *f* PHYSIQUE real image; ~ **réfléchie** *f* CINEMAT mirror image; ~ **renversée** *f* PHYSIQUE inverted image; ~ **renversée de haut en bas** *f* PHOTO inverted image; ~ **du réseau** *f* TELECOM network map; ~ **à trois dimensions** *f* TELECOM three-dimensional image; ~ **vidéo** *f* ORDINAT soft copy; ~ **virtuelle** *f* CINEMAT aerial image, virtual image, PHOTO, PHYS ONDES *hologramme*,

PHYSIQUE virtual image; ~ **de viseur grossie** *f* PHOTO magnified viewfinder image

imagerie: ~ **électronique** *f* ELECTRON electronic imaging

images: ~ **première équipe** *f pl* CINEMAT principal photography

imageur *m* INFORMAT, ORDINAT imager

imbibition *f* HYDROLOGIE absorption, imbibition, PRODUCTION *bois* impregnation

imbrication *f* ELECTRON interleaving, INFORMAT interleaving, nesting, ORDINAT interleaving

imbrifuge *adj* MATERIAUX waterproof

imbriqué *adj* GEOLOGIE imbricate, imbricated, INFORMAT nested, ORDINAT embedded, PRODUCTION *automatisme industriel* interwoven

imbriquer[1] *vt* CONS MECA *activités industrielles et zones résidentielles* blend, ELECTRON, INFORMAT, ORDINAT interleave

imbriquer:[2] **s'~** *v réfl* TEXTILE interlock

imbrûlés *m pl* POLLUTION combustion residue

imide *m* CHIMIE imide, imido

imidogène *m* CHIMIE imidogen

imine *f* CHIMIE, VEHICULES imine

immatriculation *f* AERONAUT registration

immature *adj* GEOLOGIE *élément feldspathique, argilomicacé* immature sandstone

immerger *vt* CHIMIE immerse, PAPIER dip, immerse

immersion *f* ASTRONOMIE, CHIMIE, GEOMETRIE *sphère*, PAPIER immersion; ~ **à chaud** *f* EMBALLAGE hot dipping, IMPRIM *collure* hot dip

immersions: ~ **convexes des surfaces fermées** *f pl* GEOMETRIE convex immersions of closed surfaces

immiscible *adj* CHIMIE, PETROLE immiscible

immobiliser *vt* AERONAUT ground

immunité: ~ **aux bruits** *f* INFORMAT, ORDINAT noise immunity

impact *m* CONS MECA impingement, shock, CONSTR impact, ESPACE *véhicules* touchdown, MECANIQUE impact, NUCLEAIRE knock-on, PHYSIQUE impact, POLLUTION impaction; ~ **de l'air sur la bande** *m* IMPRIM *sécheurs* impingement; ~ **sur l'environnement** *m* POLLUTION environmental impact

impair *adj* PAPIER odd

imparité *f* INFORMAT, ORDINAT odd parity

impédance *f* ELECTR, ELECTROTEC, ENREGISTR, ESSAIS, PHYSIQUE *du vide*, TELECOM impedance; ~ **acoustique** *f* ACOUSTIQUE, ELECTROTEC, ENREGISTR acoustic impedance, PETR acoustic impedance, elastic impedance, PHYSIQUE acoustic impedance; ~ **acoustique spécifique** *f* ACOUSTIQUE, PHYSIQUE specific acoustic impedance; ~ **acoustique de transfert** *f* ACOUSTIQUE transfer acoustic impedance; ~ **adaptée** *f* ELECTROTEC matched impedance; ~ **de bouclage** *f* ELECTROTEC terminating impedance; ~ **caractéristique** *f* ELECTR *câble* surge impedance, ELECTROTEC, PHYSIQUE characteristic impedance; ~ **de charge** *f* ELECTROTEC load impedance, ENREGISTR loading, PHYSIQUE, TELECOM load impedance; ~ **complexe** *f* ELECTR *circuit à courant alternatif*, ELECTROTEC, PHYSIQUE complex impedance; ~ **de couplage** *f* ELECTR coupling impedance; ~ **de court-circuit** *f* ELECTR *enroulement* short circuit impedance; ~ **électrique** *f* ENREGISTR electrical impedance; ~ **électrique cinétique** *f* ACOUSTIQUE electrical kinetic impedance; ~ **électrique cinétique en vibration libre** *f* ACOUSTIQUE free electrical motional impedance; ~ **électrique en blocage mécanique** *f* ACOUSTIQUE mechanically-blocked electrical imped-

ance; ~ **électrique en vibration libre** f ACOUSTIQUE free electrical vibration impedance; ~ **en charge normale** f ACOUSTIQUE loaded impedance; ~ **en circuit ouvert** f ELECTR, ELECTROTEC open circuit impedance; ~ **en court-circuit** f ELECTROTEC short circuit impedance; ~ **d'entrée** f ELECTROTEC, PHYSIQUE, TELECOM, TV input impedance; ~ **de haut-parleur** f ENREGISTR loudspeaker impedance; ~ **homopolaire** f ELECTR *enroulement polyphasé* zero sequence impedance; ~ **image** f ACOUSTIQUE, ELECTROTEC, PHYSIQUE image impedance; ~ **intrinsèque** f ELECTR *électromagnétisme* intrinsic impedance; ~ **itérative** f ACOUSTIQUE, ELECTR *d'un quadripole*, ELECTROTEC, PHYSIQUE iterative impedance; ~ **de la ligne** f ELECTROTEC line impedance; ~ **mécanique** f ACOUSTIQUE, ELECTROTEC mechanical impedance; ~ **mécanique libre** f ACOUSTIQUE free mechanical impedance; ~ **mécanique de transfert** f ACOUSTIQUE transfer mechanical impedance; ~ **mutuelle** f TELECOM mutual impedance; ~ **négative** f ELECTROTEC negative impedance; ~ **nominale de court-circuit** f ELECTROTEC impedance voltage; ~ **de passage** f ELECTR *résistance, bobine* transition impedance; ~ **ramenée à l'entrée** f ELECTROTEC reflected impedance; ~ **de sortie** f ELECTR, ELECTROTEC, PHYSIQUE, TELECOM, TV output impedance; ~ **de la source** f ELECTROTEC source impedance; ~ **statique** f ELECTROTEC blocked impedance; ~ **de transfert** f ELECTR *réseau*, TELECOM transfer impedance; ~ **vue de l'entrée** f ELECTROTEC reflected impedance
impédances: ~ **conjuguées** f pl ACOUSTIQUE conjugate impedances
impératif adj INFORMAT, ORDINAT imperative
impératifs: ~ **des essais** m pl PRODUCTION test requirements; ~ **globaux** m pl PRODUCTION total requirement
imperdable adj MECANIQUE captive
imperfection: ~ **cristalline** f QUALITE crystal defect; ~ **de surface** f QUALITE surface defect
imperméabilisant m PETROLE sealant polymer, REVETEMENT waterproofing agent
imperméabilisation f REVETEMENT water-repellent finishing, waterproofing, TEXTILE waterproofing; ~ **à l'eau** f CONSTR waterproofing
imperméabiliser vt CONSTR make impermeable, REVETEMENT waterproof
imperméabilité f CONSTR, MATERIAUX, PAPIER, TELECOM impermeability
imperméable adj CONSTR impermeable, impervious, DISTRI EAU, EMBALLAGE, GAZ, GEOLOGIE impermeable, HYDROLOGIE impermeable, impervious, MATERIAUX impervious, PAPIER waterproof, PETR impermeable, impervious, PLAST CAOU, TEXTILE waterproof; ~ **à l'air** adj PAPIER airproof, airtight, PHYSIQUE airtight; ~ **aux corps gras** adj PAPIER greaseproof; ~ **à l'eau** adj CONSTR, MATERIAUX watertight
implant m ELECTRON implant
implantation f CONS MECA layout, location, CONSTR setting out, ELECTRON implant, implantation, INFORMAT, MECANIQUE layout; ~ **d'arsenic** f ELECTRON arsenic implantation; ~ **et recuit** f ELECTRON implant and anneal; ~ **d'ions** f ELECTRON, PHYS PART ion implantation; ~ **d'ions radioactifs** f PHYS PART radioactive ion implantation; ~ **des modules d'E/S** f PRODUCTION *automatisme industriel* I/O module placement
implanté adj ELECTRON *base, diode, transistor* implanted
implanter vt PRODUCTION implant

implication f PRODUCTION commitment
imploser vi ELECTRON implode
implosion f CHIMIE, ELECTRON, NUCLEAIRE *corps noir*, PRODUCTION implosion
impluvium m DISTRI EAU precipitation area, rain area, HYDROLOGIE catchment basin
imporosité f MATERIAUX imporosity
importateur: ~ **net** m POLLUTION net receiver
importation f INFORMAT importation
importer vt INFORMAT *données*, TELECOM *données* import
imposer vt IMPRIM impose
imposition f IMPRIM imposition, in-line position, *tirage* pagination; ~ **en demi-feuille** f IMPRIM half sheetwork; ~ **en feuille** f IMPRIM sheetwise form (AmE), sheetwise forme (BrE); ~ **des formes** f IMPRIM *finition, emballage* nest
imposte f CONSTR impost
imprécis adj IMPRIM *photogravure, impression, documents* washed
imprégnant m EMBALLAGE impregnating agent
imprégnation f CONSTR prime coat, *génie civil* impregnation, IMPRIM impregnating, PAPIER impregnation, saturation, PLAST CAOU *procédé*, PRODUCTION *des bois*, TEXTILE impregnation; ~ **galvanostatique** f MATERIAUX galvanostatic permeation
imprégné adj PAPIER impregnated
imprégner vt CHIMIE, TEXTILE impregnate
impression f CERAM VER bloom, printing, IMPRIM impression, *brochure* printing, INFORMAT, ORDINAT printing, print, PAPIER printing, PRODUCTION impression, priming, TEXTILE impression, printing; ~ **ailes de moulin** f IMPRIM work-and-whirl; ~ **avec formes en relief et forte pression** f IMPRIM *typographie* crash printing; ~ **au cadre automatique** f TEXTILE automatic screen printing; ~ **au cadre manuel** f TEXTILE hand screen printing; ~ **à l'écran** f (Fra) (*cf impression au tamis de soie*) CERAM VER screen printing; ~ **en blanc** f IMPRIM *seul côté* blank printing; ~ **en caractères gras** f INFORMAT bold face print; ~ **en continu** f IMPRIM business forms printing, endless printing; ~ **en creux** f IMPRIM plate printing; ~ **en deux couleurs** f IMPRIM two-color printing (AmE), two-colour printing (BrE); ~ **en gravure** f IMPRIM gravure printing; ~ **en noir** f IMPRIM printing in black; ~ **en plusieurs couleurs** f EMBALLAGE multicolor printing (AmE), multicolour printing (BrE); ~ **en quadrichromie** f IMPRIM process printing; ~ **en quatre couleurs** f IMPRIM four-color printing (AmE), four-color process (AmE), four-colour printing (BrE), four-colour process (BrE), printing with four colors (AmE), printing with four colours (BrE), process printing; ~ **en relief** f IMPRIM relief printing; ~ **en retiration** f IMPRIM back printing; ~ **en taille-douce** f EMBALLAGE gravure printing, intaglio printing, IMPRIM intaglio printing; ~ **en timbrage-relief** f IMPRIM die-stamping; ~ **à fonds perdus** f IMPRIM bleed, bleed off, bleed printing; ~ **grainée** f IMPRIM speckle; ~ **groupée** f IMPRIM gang printing; ~ **hors chaîne** f EMBALLAGE printing off-line; ~ **au laser** f OPTIQUE laser printing; ~ **à la machine** f IMPRIM printing by machine; ~ **manuelle** f IMPRIM hand printing; ~ **manuelle au pochoir** f TEXTILE hand block printing; ~ **offset** f EMBALLAGE, PAPIER offset printing; ~ **optique** f IMPRIM *reproduction* optical printing; ~ **de papier** f CERAM VER paper hum (AmE), paper stain (BrE); ~ **à**

la planche *f* TEXTILE block printing; ~ **planographique** *f* PAPIER offset printing; ~ **polychrome** *f* IMPRIM multicolor printing (AmE), multicolour printing (BrE); ~ **poudreuse** *f* IMPRIM chalking; ~ **recto-verso** *f* IMPRIM perfect printing, perfecting; ~ **résistant à l'alcool** *f* IMPRIM alcohol-proof printing; ~ **au rongeant** *f* TEXTILE discharge printing; ~ **au rouleau** *f* IMPRIM, TEXTILE roller printing; ~ **sans couture** *f* IMPRIM seamless printing; ~ **sans marge** *f* IMPRIM seamless printing; ~ **sérigraphique** *f* IMPRIM serigraphy; ~ **sérigraphique sur rotative** *f* IMPRIM rotary screen printing; ~ **située en dessous** *f* IMPRIM lower printing; ~ **située au verso** *f* IMPRIM lower printing; ~ **sur chaîne** *f* EMBALLAGE printing on-line; ~ **sur étiquettes en rouleau** *f* EMBALLAGE roll label printing; ~ **d'une surface gravée** *f* IMPRIM etched surface printing; ~ **sur place** *f* EMBALLAGE printing onsite; ~ **au tamis de soie** *f* (Bel) *(cf impression à l'écran)* CERAM VER screen printing; ~ **tête-à-queue** *f* IMPRIM twelve ways back up; ~ **de titres par dorure à chaud** *f* IMPRIM *reliure* block printing; ~ **typographique** *f* IMPRIM block printing; ~ **au verso** *f* EMBALLAGE reverse side printing; ~ **de zones** *f* IMPRIM zoning
imprévu *adj* PRODUCTION unplanned
imprimabilité *f* IMPRIM printability
imprimante *f* EMBALLAGE imprinter, IMPRIM, ORDINAT, TELECOM printer; ~ **à bande** *f* INFORMAT band printer, ORDINAT belt printer; ~ **à bulle** *f* IMPRIM bubble jet printer; ~ **caractère par caractère** *f* ORDINAT character printer; ~ **à chaîne** *f* ORDINAT chain printer (AmE), train printer (BrE); ~ **à courroie** *f* INFORMAT belt printer, ORDINAT band printer; ~ **électrographique** *f* INFORMAT electrographic printer, ORDINAT electrographic printer; ~ **électrophotographique** *f* INFORMAT, ORDINAT electrophotographic printer; ~ **électrosensible** *f* INFORMAT, ORDINAT electrosensitive printer; ~ **électrostatique** *f* INFORMAT, ORDINAT electrostatic printer; ~ **électrothermique** *f* INFORMAT, ORDINAT electrothermal printer; ~ **en série** *f* IMPRIM serial printer; ~ **à impact** *f* ORDINAT impact printer; ~ **à jet d'encre** *f* EMBALLAGE, IMPRIM, ORDINAT ink jet printer; ~ **à laser** *f* IMPRIM, OPTIQUE, ORDINAT laser printer; ~ **ligne par ligne** *f* ORDINAT line printer; ~ **magnétographique** *f* ORDINAT magnetographic printer; ~ **à marguerite** *f* IMPRIM, INFORMAT, ORDINAT daisywheel printer; ~ **matricielle** *f* IMPRIM dot printer, dot-matrix printer, matrix printer, INFORMAT dot printer, dot-matrix printer, ORDINAT dot printer, dot-matrix printer, matrix printer; ~ **page par page** *f* ORDINAT page printer; ~ **sans impact** *f* ORDINAT non-impact printer; ~ **sérielle** *f* ORDINAT serial printer; ~ **à tambour** *f* INFORMAT, ORDINAT barrel printer (BrE), drum printer (AmE); ~ **thermique** *f* ORDINAT thermal printer; ~ **à train de caractères** *f* ORDINAT chain printer; ~ **ultrarapide** *f* IMPRIM high-speed printer; ~ **à la volée** *f* INFORMAT, ORDINAT hit-on-the-fly printer
imprimante-copieur: ~ **à laser** *f* OPTIQUE laser printer-copier
imprimé[1] *adj* BREVETS printed
imprimé[2] *m* IMPRIM printed matter, INFORMAT form, ORDINAT form, hard copy, printout
imprimer *vt* CONS MECA *mouvement de rotation* impart, INFORMAT, ORDINAT, PAPIER print, PRODUCTION prime, TEXTILE impress, print; ~ **en deux poses** *vt* IMPRIM *impression, imposition* double-print; ~ **au verso** *vt* IMPRIM back up, perfect

imprimerie *f* IMPRIM printing works; ~ **par offset sèche** *f* EMBALLAGE dry offset printing
imprimeur *m* IMPRIM printer; ~ **d'étiquettes code à barres** *m* EMBALLAGE bar code label printer
imprimeur-applicateur *m* EMBALLAGE printer applicator
imprimeuse: ~ **et fendeuse pour carton ondulé** *f* EMBALLAGE printer slotter for corrugated board
imprimure *f* PRODUCTION priming
impropre: ~ **à la consommation humaine** *loc* AGRO ALIM unfit for human consumption
impulseur *m* MECANIQUE impeller
impulsif *adj* CONS MECA impulsive
impulsion *f* CONS MECA impetus, impulse, impulsion, propulsion, *force* impulse, ELECTR pulse, surge, ELECTRON, ENREGISTR, ESPACE *communications*, INFORMAT pulse, MECANIQUE impulse, OPTIQUE, ORDINAT pulse, PAPIER, PETR impulse, PHYS ONDES pulse, PHYSIQUE impulse, pulse, TELECOM impulse; ~ **d'ablation** *f* NUCLEAIRE ablating momentum, deconfining momentum; ~ **d'Abraham** *f* NUCLEAIRE Abraham momentum; ~ **acoustique** *f* ELECTRON acoustic pulse; ~ **aléatoire** *f* ELECTRON, TELECOM random pulse; ~ **d'amorçage** *f* ELECTROTEC firing pulse; ~ **de blocage** *f* ELECTRON turn-off pulse; ~ **de cadencement** *f* ELECTRON timing pulse; ~ **de charge d'espace** *f* ELECTROTEC cloud pulse; ~ **de comptage** *f* TV tach pulse; ~ **de courant** *f* ELECTROTEC current pulse; ~ **courte** *f* ELECTRON, NAUT short pulse; ~ **à court temps de montée** *f* ELECTRON fast rise pulse; ~ **à crête fractionnée** *f* TV serrated pulse; ~ **de déblocage** *f* ELECTRON gating pulse, turn-on pulse; ~ **de décalage** *f* ELECTRON shift pulse; ~ **décimale** *f* TELECOM DP, dial impulse; ~ **de déclenchement** *f* ELECTRON trigger pulse, TELECOM triggering lead pulse, TV gating pulse, triggering pulse; ~ **de décomptage** *f* ELECTRON down pulse; ~ **de demi-ligne** *f* TV broad pulse; ~ **d'une durée de l'ordre de la picoseconde** *f* PHYS PART picosecond pulse; ~ **d'écriture** *f* INFORMAT, ORDINAT write pulse; ~ **d'égalisation** *f* TV equalizing pulse; ~ **électrique** *f* ELECTROTEC electric pulse; ~ **électromagnétique** *f* ELECTROTEC, TELECOM electromagnetic pulse; ~ **d'énergie électromagnétique** *f* ELECTROTEC electromagnetic energy pulse; ~ **d'entrée** *f* ELECTRON input pulse; ~ **étroite** *f* ELECTRON narrow pulse; ~ **excitatrice** *f* TV driving pulse; ~ **de fermeture** *f* ELECTROTEC make pulse; ~ **formant signal** *f* ELECTRON signal pulse; ~ **à fréquence vocale** *f* ELECTRON tone pulse; ~ **gaussienne** *f* TELECOM Gaussian pulse; ~ **de grande amplitude** *f* ELECTRON high-amplitude pulse; ~ **d'horloge** *f* ELECTRON, INFORMAT, ORDINAT clock pulse; ~ **image** *f* TV frame pulse; ~ **d'interdiction** *f* ELECTRON inhibiting pulse; ~ **isolée** *f* ELECTRON nonrecurrent pulse, single pulse; ~ **laser** *f* ELECTRON laser pulse; ~ **longue** *f* ELECTRON boxcar pulse, NAUT long pulse; ~ **de lumière** *f* ELECTRON light pulse; ~ **de marquage** *f* ELECTRON marker pulse, TV timing pulse; ~ **mise en forme** *f* ELECTRON shaped pulse; ~ **de montage** *f* TV edit pulse; ~ **non récurrente** *f* ELECTRON nonrecurrent pulse; ~ **optique** *f* ELECTRON optical pulse; ~ **d'ouverture de porte** *f* ELECTRON gating pulse; ~ **parasite** *f* ELECTR *tension* pulse spike, TV spike; ~ **périodique** *f* ELECTRON period pulse; ~ **pilote** *f* ELECTRON master pulse; ~ **pointue** *f* ELECTRON hard pulse; ~ **de position de tête** *f* TV head position pulse; ~ **de radiofréquence** *f* TV RF pulse; ~ **de rayon X** *f* ELECTRON X-ray pulse; ~ **rectangulaire** *f* ELECTRON rectangular pulse; ~ **rectan-**

gulaire allongée *f* ELECTRON boxcar pulse; **~ récurrente** *f* ELECTRON period pulse, periodic pulse; **~ régénérée** *f* ELECTRON regenerated pulse; **~ de repérage de cap** *f* TELECOM course blip pulse; **~ spécifique** *f* ESPACE *propulsion* specific impulse; **~ stroboscopique** *f* TELECOM strobe pulse; **~ de suppression** *f* TV blanking pulse; **~ de suppression de trame** *f* TV vertical blanking pulse; **~ de synchronisation** *f* TV burst, synchronization pulse; **~ de synchronisation couleur** *f* TV color burst (AmE), colour burst (BrE); **~ de synchronisation d'image** *f* TV frame sync pulse; **~ technique** *f* ESSAIS gating technique; **~ de tension** *f* ELECTR voltage pulse; **~ très courte** *f* ELECTRON sharp pulse; **~ très étroite** *f* ELECTRON sharp pulse; **~ de très grande amplitude** *f* ELECTRON giant pulse; **~ de validation** *f* ELECTRON, INFORMAT, ORDINAT enable pulse; **~ vidéo** *f* TV video signal pulse; **~ vocale** *f* ESPACE *communications* spurt

impulsions: **~ d'annulation** *f pl* TV unblanking pulses; **~ de clamp** *f pl* TV clamping pulses; **~ codées** *f pl* TV encoded pulses; **~ par seconde** *f pl* TELECOM pps, pulses per second; **~ récurrentes** *f pl* ELECTRON recurrent pulses; **~ de verrouillage** *f pl* TV clamping pulses

impureté *f* CHIMIE impureness, impurity, CRISTALL impurity atom, ELECTRON dopant, impurity, METALL, QUALITE impurity; **~ acceptrice** *f* ELECTRON acceptor impurity; **~ donneuse** *f* ELECTRON donor impurity; **~ implantée à haute dose** *f* ELECTRON high-dose implant; **~ du type donneur** *f* ELECTRON donor impurity; **~ de type N** *f* ELECTRON n-type impurity; **~ de type P** *f* ELECTRON p-type impurity

impuretés *f pl* AGRO ALIM dockage, PRODUCTION foreign matter; **~ de la base** *f pl* ELECTRON base impurities; **~ dans la pâte et le papier** *f pl* PAPIER pulp and paper contraries

imputabilité *f* TELECOM accountability

imputation *f* PRODUCTION posting

imputer: **~ des heures** *vt* PRODUCTION post hours; **~ les taxes à** *vt* TELECOM *de la communication* charge the call to

imputrescible *adj* PAPIER rot-proof

in: **~ situ** *adv* CONSTR, MECANIQUE in situ

In *(indium)* CHIMIE In *(indium)*

IN *abrév (indice de netteté)* TELECOM AI *(articulation index)*

inactif *adj* CHIMIE inactive, inert, ELECTRON, INFORMAT, ORDINAT inactive, PRODUCTION idle

inactinique *adj* CERAM VER *verre* inactinic

inaction: être dans l'~ *vi* CONS MECA lie idle

inactivation *f* CHIMIE inactivation

inattaquable: **~ par les acides** *adj* CHIMIE incorrodible

incandescence *f* CHIMIE glow, incandescence; **~ résiduelle** *f* PAPIER, THERMODYN afterglow

incandescent[1] *adj* CHIMIE, MATERIAUX glowing, PHYS RAYON *solide* incandescent, THERMODYN glowing, white-hot

incandescent:[2] **être ~** *vi* THERMODYN glow

incapacité: **~ permanente** *f* SECURITE permanent disability

incendiaire *adj* MILITAIRE *bombe* incendiary

incendie *m* SECURITE, THERMODYN blaze, fire; **~ criminel** *m* SECURITE arson; **~ instantané** *m* THERMODYN flash fire

incertitude *f* INFORMAT, ORDINAT uncertainty; **~ de mesurage** *f* METROLOGIE inaccuracy of measurement; **~ de mesure** *f* METROLOGIE uncertainty of measurement

inchavirable *adj* NAUT self-righting

incidence *f* AERONAUT attack angle, OPTIQUE, PHYSIQUE incidence; **~ brewstérienne** *f* PHYSIQUE Brewster incidence; **~ de la pale** *f* AERONAUT blade angle of attack; **~ de portance nulle** *f* AERONAUT zero lift angle; **~ rasante** *f* PHYSIQUE grazing incidence

incident *m* INFORMAT crash, incident, ORDINAT crash, TRANSPORT incident; **~ de fonctionnement** *m* CONS MECA breakdown; **~ de frein** *m* TRANSPORT brake failure; **~ de pollution atmosphérique** *m* POLLUTION air pollution incident

incinérateur *m* MAT CHAUFF, POLLUTION, THERMODYN incinerator; **~ pour détritus** *m* EMBALLAGE garbage incinerator (AmE); **~ pour les gaz de fumée** *m* GENIE CHIM fume incinerator

incinération *f* THERMODYN burning; **~ des boues** *f* DISTRI EAU sludge incineration

incinéré *adj* THERMODYN burnt, incinerated

incinérer *vt* THERMODYN burn, incinerate

incitation: **~ d'adressage** *f* TELECOM ADD, address prompt

inclinaison *f* ASTRONOMIE inclination, CINEMAT rake, tilt, CONSTR cant, grade, gradient, pitch, slant, GEOMETRIE inclination, slant, IMPRIM *italique, plaque* slant, MINES dip, NAUT rake, PETR dip, PHYSIQUE angle of dip, inclination, PRODUCTION angle of inclination, REFRIG pitch, TV tilt; **~ de comble** *f* CONSTR pitch of roof, roof pitch; **~ des cylindres** *f* AUTO cylinder bank angling; **~ du diagramme** *f* TV beam tilt; **~ latérale** *f* ACOUSTIQUE camber; **~ de ligne** *f* TV line tilt; **~ longitudinale** *f* ACOUSTIQUE rake, AERONAUT pitch; **~ magnétique** *f* GEOPHYS magnetic dip, magnetic inclination, magnetic latitude, PETR magnetic dip, PHYSIQUE angle of dip, angle of magnetic inclination; **~ du mât** *f* NAUT mast rake; **~ d'orbite** *f* ESPACE orbit inclination; **~ du pivot** *f* AUTO kingpin inclination, steering axis inclination; **~ du sommet** *f* ELECTRON pulse tilt; **~ du sommet d'impulsion** *f* ELECTRON pulse tilt; **~ de trame** *f* TV field tilt; **~ transversale** *f* AERONAUT bank; **~ variable** *f* REFRIG variable pitch

inclination *f* CONSTR *câble* dip

inclinatoire: **~ magnétique** *m* GEOPHYS dip needle, magnetic inclinometer

incliné *adj* CONSTR slanting, GEOLOGIE, GEOMETRIE inclined

incliner[1] *vt* CINEMAT tilt

incliner:[2] **s'~ par rapport à la verticale** *v réfl* GEOLOGIE hade

inclinomètre *m* CONSTR clinometer, GEOPHYS, PETR inclinometer; **~ à câble tendu** *m* OCEANO taut-wire angle indicator, taut-wire indicator

inclus *adj* EMBALLAGE enclosed

inclusion *f* CRISTALL, ESSAIS, METALL, MINERAUX, NUCLEAIRE, PETR, QUALITE inclusion; **~ fluide** *f* GEOLOGIE fluid inclusion; **~ gazeuse** *f* NUCLEAIRE gas cavity; **~ nonmétallique** *f* METALL, QUALITE nonmetallic inclusion

incohérence *f* OPTIQUE, TELECOM incoherence

incohérent *adj* METALL, OPTIQUE incoherent

incolore *adj* AGRO ALIM, COULEURS colorless (AmE), colourless (BrE)

incombustibilité *f* MATERIAUX incombustibility, nonflammability

incombustible *adj* AERONAUT flame-resistant, EMBALLAGE fireproof, incombustible, MATERIAUX incombustible, PRODUCTION fireproof, SECURITE flame-resistant, THERMODYN fireproof, flameproof

incompétent *adj* GEOLOGIE *couche* incompetent

incompressibilité *f* MATERIAUX incompressibility, PHYS FLUID incompressibilty

incompressible *adj* CHIMIE incompressible

inconditionnel *adj* INFORMAT, ORDINAT unconditional

incongelable *adj* AERONAUT antifreezing

inconnue: ~ **de déplacement** *f* ESPACE *véhicules* displacement variable

inconsommable *adj* AGRO ALIM inedible

incorporation *f* IMPRIM *photogravure, composition, montage* melding

incorporé *adj* CONS MECA, ELECTROTEC built-in, INFORMAT embedded, MECANIQUE built-in; ~ **à la carte** *adj* ELECTRON on-board; ~ **à la puce** *adj* ELECTRON on chip

incrément *m* ELECTRON increment; ~ **de vitesse** *m* ESPACE *propulsion* velocity increment

incrémenter *vt* ELECTRON increment

incrustateur *m* TV keyer; ~ **aval** *m* TV downstream keyer; ~ **de titres** *m* TV title keyer

incrustation *f* CINEMAT key, INST HYDR boiler scale, PRODUCTION fur, scale, TV inlay, key, overlay; ~ **avec ombre** *f* CINEMAT shadow key; ~ **couleur** *f* TV chromakey; ~ **électronique** *f* TV chromakey; ~ **noir et blanc** *f* TV mono key

incruster *vt* CINEMAT burn in, key in, PRODUCTION fur, scale, TV burn in, key, overlay

incrusteur *m* TV matting amplifier

incubateur *m* MAT CHAUFF incubator

incunable *m* IMPRIM *livre* incunabulum

IND *abrév (message de demande d'information)* TELECOM INR *(information request message)*

indamine *f* CHIMIE indamine

indane *f* CHIMIE hydrindene, indan

indanthrène *m* CHIMIE indanthrene

indanthrone *m* CHIMIE indanthrone

indazine *f* CHIMIE indazine

indazole *m* CHIMIE indazole

indécomposé *adj* CHIMIE undecomposed

indéformable *adj* CH DE FER unsplittable

indemnité: ~ **d'accident du travail** *f* SECURITE industrial injury benefit; ~ **de remorquage** *f* NAUT salvage; ~ **de sauvetage** *f* NAUT salvage award

indène *m* CHIMIE indene

indénone *f* CHIMIE indone

indentation *f* CONS MECA dent, PRODUCTION indentation

indenture *f* PRODUCTION indentation

indépendance: ~ **pétrolière** *f* PETROLE oil self-sufficiency

indépendant *adj* EMBALLAGE freestanding, ESPACE *véhicules* self-contained; ~ **du contexte** *adj* INFORMAT, ORDINAT context-free; ~ **de la machine** *adj* INFORMAT, ORDINAT machine-independent

indéplissable *adj* TEXTILE permanently pleated

indétonant *m* AUTO no-knock mixture

index *m* CONS MECA index, IMPRIM *cadrans* pointer, *signe de composition* pointer, INFORMAT, ORDINAT index; ~ **d'efficacité** *m* CHIMIE performance index; ~ **d'instrument** *m* CONS MECA marker; ~ **primaire** *m* INFORMAT, ORDINAT primary index; ~ **secondaire** *m* INFORMAT, ORDINAT secondary index; ~ **vitellinique** *m* AGRO ALIM egg yolk index

indexation *f* CRISTALL, INFORMAT, ORDINAT indexing

indexer *vt* INFORMAT, ORDINAT index

indican *m* CHIMIE indican

indicateur *m* CONS MECA gage (AmE), gauge (BrE), DISTRI EAU indicator, INFORMAT indicator, tag, INST HYDR indicator, MECANIQUE gage (AmE), gauge (BrE), ORDINAT indicator, tag; ~ **d'abandon de bloc** *m* TELECOM block dropping indicator; ~ **d'accord** *m* ELECTRON tuning indicator; ~ **d'alignement de piste** *m* AERONAUT runway alignment indicator; ~ **d'angle de barre** *m* NAUT helm indicator, rudder angle indicator; ~ **d'angle de câble** *m* NAUT cable angle indicator; ~ **d'appel** *m* TELECOM calling indicator; ~ **biologique** *m* HYDROLOGIE biological indicator, POLLUTION bioindicator, biological indicator; ~ **de bourrage** *m* CINEMAT trip indicator; ~ **de cap** *m* ESPACE *véhicules* heading indicator, NAUT course indicator; ~ **de charge** *m* NAUT charge indicator; ~ **de charge admissible** *m* SECURITE safe load indicator; ~ **des chemins de fer** *m* TRANSPORT time indicator; ~ **de chute de pression** *m* AUTO pressure differential warning valve; ~ **de commande manuelle** *m* PHOTO manual control indicator; ~ **de commande de protocole** *m* TELECOM protocol control indicator; ~ **de communication** *m* PRODUCTION switch indicator; ~ **de compensation du temps réel** *m* TV drop frame indicator; ~ **de contrôle** *m* TELECOM SI, screening indicator; ~ **de crédit** *m* TELECOM credit indicator; ~ **de crête** *m* ELECTRON peak indicator, TV peak meter; ~ **de défaut du programme** *m* PRODUCTION *automatisme industriel* program error flag (AmE), programme error flag (BrE); ~ **de demande d'adresse du demandeur** *m* TELECOM calling party address request indicator; ~ **de demande de catégorie du demandeur** *m* TELECOM calling party category request indicator; ~ **de demande d'identité de la ligne connectée** *m* TELECOM connected line identity request indicator; ~ **de dérive** *m* AERONAUT drift indicator; ~ **de déviation** *m* AERONAUT deviation indicator; ~ **de direction** *m* ESPACE heading indicator, VEHICULES *accessoire* direction indicator; ~ **de direction d'atterrissage** *m* AERONAUT landing direction indicator; ~ **double** *m* CONS MECA dual indicator; ~ **dynamométrique** *m* INST HYDR steam-engine indicator; ~ **écologique** *m* POLLUTION indicator species; ~ **d'épaisseur de tuyau** *m* NUCLEAIRE tube thickness gage (AmE), tube thickness gauge (BrE); ~ **d'erreur de programme** *m* PRODUCTION internal program error flag (AmE), internal programme error flag (BrE); ~ **d'essai** *m* TELECOM test indicator; ~ **d'état de circuit** *m* TELECOM circuit state indicator; ~ **d'état à DEL verte pour présence tension CC** *m* PRODUCTION *électricité* green LED status indicator DC power ON; ~ **d'état en/hors service** *m* PRODUCTION *automatisme* on/off service indicator, on/off switch indicator; ~ **de film** *m* PHOTO film type indicator; ~ **de frein** *m* CH DE FER brake valve; ~ **de fuite** *m* EMBALLAGE leak detector; ~ **de fuite sur bouteille** *m* EMBALLAGE bottle leak detector; ~ **de gaz** *m* MINES gas detector, methanometer; ~ **de givrage d'aéronef** *m* AERONAUT aircraft icing indicator; ~ **gyro compas** *m* AERONAUT gyrosyn compass indicator; ~ **d'humidité** *m* EMBALLAGE humidity indicator, TV dew indicator; ~ **d'incidence** *m* AERONAUT angle of attack indicator; ~ **d'inclinaison longitudinale et latérale** *m* AERONAUT bank-and-pitch indicator (BrE), turn-and-bank indicator (AmE); ~ **d'information de bout en bout** *m* TELECOM end-to-end information indicator; ~ **d'information demandée** *m* TELECOM solicited information indicator; ~ **isotopique** *m* NUCLEAIRE isotopic tracer, tracer; ~ **de jaugeur de carburant** *m* AERONAUT fuel gage indicator (AmE), fuel gauge indicator (BrE); ~

de libération *m* TELECOM release indicator; ~ **de ligne sous tension** *m* ELECTR *sécurité, ligne aérienne* live line indicator; ~ **de longueur** *m* TELECOM LI, length indicator; ~ **de longueur de bande** *m* TV tape length indicator; ~ **magnétique** *m* CONS MECA magnetic indicator; ~ **des marées** *m* NAUT tide table; ~ **de méthode de bout en bout** *m* TELECOM end-to-end method indicator; ~ **de méthode SSCS** *m* TELECOM SCCP method indicator; ~ **de modification** *m* TELECOM modification indicator; ~ **au néon** *m* ELECTR *lampe* neon glow lamp, ELECTROTEC neon indicator; ~ **de niveau** *m* CINEMAT level meter, CONS MECA, ENREGISTR level indicator, NUCLEAIRE level indicator, level meter; ~ **de niveau des cages** *m* MINES depth indicator; ~ **de niveau d'eau** *m* DISTRI EAU water gage (AmE), water gauge (BrE), water indicator, water level indicator; ~ **de niveau d'essence** *m* AUTO fuel indicator; ~ **du niveau d'un liquide** *m* EMBALLAGE liquid level indicator; ~ **du niveau sonore** *m* SECURITE sound level meter; ~ **du niveau vidéo** *m* TV video level indicator; ~ **de nouvelles données** *m* TELECOM NDF, new data flag; ~ **de numéro du demandeur incomplet** *m* TELECOM calling party number incomplete indicator; ~ **d'objectif à laser** *m* MILITAIRE laser target marker; ~ **omnidirectionnel** *m* AERONAUT omnirange indicator; ~ **optique d'arrêt du train d'atterrissage** *m* AERONAUT landing gear optical inspection system; ~ **panoramique** *m* PHYSIQUE plan position indicator; ~ **de pas général** *m* AERONAUT collective pitch indicator; ~ **de pas des pales** *m* AERONAUT blade pitch indicator; ~ **de passage de liquide** *m* REFRIG liquid flow indicator; ~ **de pente** *m* AERONAUT glide path localizer, GEOPHYS clinometer, inclinometer; ~ **du plan de numérotage** *m* TELECOM numbering plan indicator; ~ **de pointe de programme** *m* ENREGISTR peak program meter (AmE), peak programme metre (BrE); ~ **de position** *m* PRODUCTION *automatisme industriel* position indicator; ~ **de position de gauchissement** *m* AERONAUT aileron position indicator; ~ **de position de prise** *m* ELECTR *changeur de prises* tap position indicator; ~ **de position du train** *m* AERONAUT landing gear position indicator; ~ **de présentation** *m* TELECOM PI, presentation indicator; ~ **de pression** *m* CONSTR pressure gage (AmE), pressure gauge (BrE); ~ **de pression d'huile** *m* COMMANDE oil pressure gage (AmE), oil pressure gauge (BrE); ~ **de pression de vapeur** *m* INST HYDR steam-engine indicator; ~ **de pression de vent** *m* PRODUCTION blast gage (AmE), blast gauge (BrE); ~ **principal** *m* CONS MECA master indicator; ~ **de prolongement d'appel possible** *m* TELECOM call forwarding may occur indicator; ~ **à radioélément à rétrodiffusion bêta** *m* NUCLEAIRE *réflexion* beta backscatter gage (AmE), beta backscatter gauge (BrE); ~ **de raison du renvoi initial** *m* TELECOM original redirection reason; ~ **de recommandation** *m* TELECOM recommendation indicator; ~ **de recopie de cap** *m* AERONAUT heading remote indicator; ~ **de rejet par le réseau** *m* TELECOM network discard indicator; ~ **de relèvement** *m* AERONAUT omnibearing indicator; ~ **de renvoi** *m* TELECOM redirecting indicator; ~ **de réponse à une demande d'adresse du demandeur** *m* TELECOM calling party address response indicator; ~ **de réponse à une demande de catégorie du demandeur** *m* TELECOM calling party category response indicator; ~ **de restriction de divulgation d'adresse** *m* TELECOM address presentation restricted indicator; ~ **de restriction de divulgation d'événement** *m* TELECOM event presentation restriction indicator; ~ **de routage** *m* INFORMAT, ORDINAT routing indicator; ~ **de segmentation permise** *m* TELECOM SPF, segmentation permitted flag; ~ **sélecteur de course** *m* AERONAUT course indicator selector; ~ **de service supplémentaire** *m* TELECOM facility indicator; ~ **à sifflet d'alarme** *m* INST HYDR alarm whistle signal; ~ **de signalisation d'usager à usager** *m* TELECOM user-to-user indicator; ~ **de situation horizontale** *m* AERONAUT horizontal situation indicator; ~ **sonore de fin de bobine** *m* CINEMAT audible runout indicator; ~ **de tassement** *m* GENIE CHIM settlement reference marker; ~ **de température de l'air de dégivrage** *m* AERONAUT de-icing air temperature indicator; ~ **de température de cabine** *m* AERONAUT cabin temperature indicator; ~ **de température de l'eau** *m* AUTO *gaz d'échappement* water temperature gage (AmE), water temperature gauge (BrE); ~ **de température extérieure** *m* AERONAUT outside air temperature indicator; ~ **de température de gaz** *m* AUTO exhaust gas indicator; ~ **de température d'huile** *m* AERONAUT oil temperature indicator; ~ **de température du poste pilote** *m* AERONAUT cockpit temperature indicator; ~ **de température de tuyère** *m* AERONAUT nozzle temperature indicator; ~ **de tension** *m* ELECTROTEC voltage indicator; ~ **de terre** *m* ELECTROTEC earth indicator (BrE), ground indicator (AmE), leakage indicator; ~ **de tirage** *m* PRODUCTION draft gage (AmE), draught gauge (BrE); ~ **de trajectoire d'approche de précision simplifié** *m* AERONAUT abbreviated precision approach path indicator; ~ **trois axes** *m* ESPACE *véhicules* three-axis indicator; ~ **de vide** *m* AGRO ALIM vacuum gage (AmE), vacuum gauge (BrE); ~ **du vide** *m* INSTRUMENT vacuum gage (AmE), vacuum gauge (BrE); ~ **visuel de pente d'approche simplifié** *m* AERONAUT abbreviated visual approach slope indicator system; ~ **de vitesse** *m* CONS MECA motion indicator, revolution indication, NAUT speedometer, PAPIER speed indicator; ~ **de vitesse ascensionnelle** *m* AERONAUT rate-of-climb indicator; ~ **de vitesse relative** *m* AERONAUT airspeed indicator; ~ **de volume standard** *m* ENREGISTR standard volume indicator

indicateurs: ~ **de dose à couleurs** *m pl* PHYS RAYON *radioactivité* color indicators of dose (AmE), colour indicators of dose (BrE)

indicatif *m* TELECOM answerback, code, dialing code (AmE), dialling code (BrE); ~ **d'appel** *m* NAUT call sign, TELECOM calling signal; ~ **d'appel d'aéronef** *m* AERONAUT aircraft call sign; ~ **de décrochage** *m* TV network cue; ~ **d'émetteur** *m* TV station identification; ~ **interurbain** *m* TELECOM TC, trunk code, area code; ~ **national de destination** *m* TELECOM NDC, national destination code; ~ **du pays** *m* TELECOM CC, country code, national code; ~ **de piste** *m* AERONAUT runway designator; ~ **réseau** *m* TV network identification; ~ **sonore** *m* ENREGISTR sound code; ~ **de zone** *m* TELECOM area code

indication *f* TELECOM Ind, indication; ~ **d'alarme distante** *f* TELECOM RAI, remote alarm indication; ~ **d'appel en instance** *f* TELECOM call waiting signal; ~ **audio active** *f* TELECOM AIA, audio indicate active; ~ **audio muette** *f* TELECOM AIM, audio indicate muted; ~ **automatique verbale des éléments de taxation** *f* TELECOM automatic ADC; ~ **de concaténation** *f* TELECOM CI, concatenation indication; ~ **de coût en**

temps réel *f* TELECOM call-in-progress cost information; ~ **de départ** *f* CINEMAT roll cue, TV cue; ~ **d'élévation maximale** *f* IMPRIM maximum elevation figure; ~ **d'état** *f* TELECOM status indication; ~ **multipoint de boucle** *f* TELECOM MIL, multipoint indication loop; ~ **multipoint d'état secondaire** *f* TELECOM MIS, multipoint indication secondary status; ~ **multipoint de non-communication** *f* TELECOM MIZ, multipoint indication zero communication; ~ **multipoint de visualisation** *f* TELECOM MIV, multipoint indication visualization; ~ **de pointeur zéro** *f* TELECOM NPI, null pointer indication; ~ **de provenance** *f* BREVETS indication of source; ~ **sur le contenu de la page** *f* IMPRIM telltale; ~ **verbale des éléments de taxation** *f* TELECOM advise duration and charge; ~ **vidéo active** *f* TELECOM VIA, video indicate active; ~ **vidéo prête à être activée** *f* TELECOM VIR, video indicate ready-to-activate; ~ **vidéo supprimée** *f* TELECOM VIS, video indicate suppressed

indicatrice *f* CRISTALL indicatrix

indice *m* CHIMIE index, IMPRIM inferior characters, inferior figures, inferior letters, *de caractères au-dessous de la ligne normale de texte* subscript, INFORMAT index, subscript, ORDINAT index, PETROLE show, *exploration* gas show, *prospection* oil show; ~ **d'abrasion** *m* PLAST CAOU abrasion resistance index; ~ **d'abrasion de Taber** *m* PLAST CAOU abrasion resistance index; ~ **d'acétyle** *m* PLAST CAOU acetyl value; ~ **d'acide** *m* AGRO ALIM, PAPIER, PLAST CAOU acid value; ~ **d'acidité** *m* CHIMIE TAN, total acid number, PETROLE acid number; ~ **d'activité biologique** *m* GEOLOGIE *empreinte ou bioturbation* trace fossil; ~ **d'affaiblissement acoustique** *m* ACOUSTIQUE transition loss index, PHYSIQUE sound reduction index; ~ **d'articulation** *m* ACOUSTIQUE articulation index; ~ **du bouchage de filtre** *m* GENIE CHIM filter plugging value; ~ **de bouffant** *m* IMPRIM bulk (BrE), bulk index (BrE), bulking index (BrE), specific index (AmE), specific volume (AmE); ~ **de bullage** *m* CERAM VER outgassing index; ~ **de calorifugeage** *m* THERMODYN thermal insulation index; ~ **de capture** *m* OCEANO catch index, catchability coefficient; ~ **de coloration** *m* AGRO ALIM egg yolk index; ~ **de combustion** *m* THERMODYN combustion index; ~ **de compression** *m* CHARBON compression index; ~ **de confiance** *m* CRISTALL R-factor, reliability index; ~ **de consistance** *m* CHARBON consistency index; ~ **de construction** *m* ESPACE construction nozzle; ~ **de coordination** *m* CHIMIE coordination number; ~ **de correspondence spectrale** *m* TELECOM PCI, pattern correspondence index; ~ **de couleur** *m* ASTRONOMIE color index (AmE), colour index (BrE); ~ **de densité** *m* CHARBON relative density; ~ **de directivité** *m* ACOUSTIQUE directivity index; ~ **d'éclatement** *m* PAPIER burst factor, burst index, burst ratio, burst value; ~ **d'écoute** *m* TV audience rating; ~ **d'égouttage** *m* PAPIER freeness value; ~ **élevé de protection** *m* PRODUCTION high degree of protection; ~ **d'enroulement faible** *m* RESSORTS low coiling index; ~ **d'ester** *m* LESSIVES ester number, ester value; ~ **d'évaluation du bruit** *m* POLLUTION weighted noise level indicator; ~ **foliaire** *m* POLLUTION leaf area index; ~ **de groupe** *m* OPTIQUE, TELECOM group index; ~ **d'humidité** *m* METEO humidity index, moisture index; ~ **d'hydrogène** *m* PETR hydrogen index; ~ **inférieur** *m* ORDINAT subscript; ~ **d'intelligibilité** *m* ACOUSTIQUE intelligibility index; ~ **d'iode** *m* AGRO ALIM iodine number, iodine value, PLAST CAOU iodine value; ~ **de jaune d'oeuf** *m* AGRO ALIM egg yolk index; ~ **de liquidité** *m* CHARBON liquidity index; ~ **de lumination** *m* CINEMAT exposure value, PHOTO light value; ~ **de main** *m* IMPRIM bulk (BrE), bulk index (BrE), bulking index (BrE), specific index (AmE), specific volume (AmE); ~ **de modulation** *m* ELECTRON deviation ratio, modulation index; ~ **de netteté** *m (IN)* TELECOM *d'un circuit téléphonique* articulation index *(AI)*; ~ **de netteté des logatomes** *m* TELECOM logatom articulation; ~ **de noircissement** *m* CERAM VER darkening index; ~ **d'octane** *m* AERONAUT fuel grade, AUTO ONR, octane number rating, PETROLE ON, octane number, VEHICULES *essence* octane index, octane number, octane rating; ~ **d'oxygène** *m* AERONAUT oxygen index; ~ **de perte d'audition** *m* ACOUSTIQUE impairment of hearing index; ~ **de plasticité** *m* CHARBON, CONSTR plasticity index; ~ **de pollution gazeuse acide de l'air** *m* SECURITE gaseous acid air pollution index; ~ **de popularité** *m* TV rating; ~ **de porosité secondaire** *m* PETR SPI, secondary porosity index; ~ **de pose** *m* PHOTO exposure index; ~ **de productivité** *m* PETR productivity index; ~ **de protection** *m* PRODUCTION degree of protection; ~ **de pureté** *m* RESSORTS cleanness value; ~ **de qualité d'une tuyère** *m* ESPACE nozzle efficiency; ~ **de réfraction** *m* CINEMAT, ESPACE *communications* refractive index, OPTIQUE index of refraction, refractive index, PHOTO, PHYS ONDES, PHYSIQUE, TELECOM refractive index; ~ **de réfraction absolu** *m* PHYS RAYON absolute refractive index; ~ **de réfraction de l'air** *m* PHYS ONDES air refractive index; ~ **de réfraction complexe** *m* PHYSIQUE complex refractive index; ~ **de résistance à l'état humide** *m* PAPIER wet strength retention; ~ **de résistance par friction** *m* HYDROLOGIE flow resistance coefficient; ~ **de résistivité** *m* PETR resistivity index; ~ **de reste d'audition** *m* ACOUSTIQUE hearing loss factor index; ~ **de saisonnalité** *m* PRODUCTION seasonal index; ~ **de saturation Langelier** *m* HYDROLOGIE Langelier's index; ~ **à saut équivalent** *m* TELECOM ESI, equivalent step index; ~ **de structure** *m* ESPACE *véhicules* structure index; ~ **supérieur** *m* ORDINAT superscript; ~ **des vides** *m* CHARBON void ratio; ~ **de viscosité** *m* PETROLE, PHYS FLUID, THERMODYN, VEHICULES *huile* viscosity index; ~ **de viscosité limite** *m* PHYS FLUID limiting viscosity number; ~ **de wagonnage** *m* CH DE FER *véhicules* routing code for part-load traffic

indices *m pl* CRISTALL indices; ~ **de Bragg** *m pl* CRISTALL Bragg indices; ~ **de collationnement** *m pl* IMPRIM back marks, collating marks; ~ **de Miller** *m pl* CRISTALL, METALL Miller indices

indicolite *f* MINERAUX indicolite, indigolite

Indien *m* ASTRONOMIE Indus

indifférence *f* CHIMIE indifference

indifférent *adj* CHIMIE inert, *sel* neutral

indigo *m* CHIMIE indigo

indigolite *f* MINERAUX indicolite, indigolite

indigotine *f* CHIMIE indigo

indique *adj* CHIMIE indic

indiquer *vt* IMPRIM *couleurs* key, SECURITE *sur une plaque* show

indirubine *f* CHIMIE indirubin, indirubine

indiscernabilité *f* PHYSIQUE indistinguishability

indisponible *adj* QUALITE unavailable

indissoluble *adj* MATERIAUX indissoluble

indium *m (In)* CHIMIE indium *(In)*
individu *m* ESSAIS item
indogène *m* CHIMIE indogen
indogénide *m* CHIMIE indogenide
indole *m* CHIMIE indole, ketol
indoléacétique *adj* CHIMIE indoleacetic
indoline *f* CHIMIE indolin, indoline
indone *f* CHIMIE indone
indophénine *f* CHIMIE indophenin
indophénol *m* CHIMIE indophenol
in-douze *m* IMPRIM duodecimo
indoxyle *m* CHIMIE indoxyl
indoxylesulfurique *adj* CHIMIE indoxylsulfuric (AmE), indoxylsulphuric (BrE)
indoxylique *adj* CHIMIE indoxylic
inductance *f* ELECTR *électromagnétisme* inductance, ELECTROTEC inductance, inductor, ENREGISTR, PHYSIQUE, TELECOM inductance; ~ **à air** *f* ELECTR *réactance* air reactor; ~ **de la charge** *f* ELECTROTEC load inductance; ~ **différentielle** *f* ELECTR incremental inductance; ~ **extérieure** *f* ELECTR external inductance; ~ **limiteuse de courant** *f* ELECTR current-limiting inductor; ~ **de lissage de bus** *f* PRODUCTION bus choke; ~ **mutuelle** *f* ELECTR *d'une bobine*, ELECTROTEC, PHYSIQUE mutual inductance; ~ **parasite** *f* ELECTROTEC parasitic inductance; ~ **primaire** *f* ELECTR *transformateur* primary inductance; ~ **propre** *f* ELECTR *bobine* self-inductance, ELECTROTEC self-induction, PHYSIQUE self-inductance; ~ **de protection** *f* ELECTROTEC current-limiting reactor; ~ **de puissance** *f* ELECTROTEC power inductor; ~ **réglable** *f* ELECTR adjustable inductance; ~ **de réglage** *f* COMMANDE regulating choke coil; ~ **répartie** *f* ELECTROTEC distributed inductance; ~ **saturable** *f* ELECTROTEC saturable reactor, PHYSIQUE magnetic amplifier, transductor, saturable reactor; ~ **secondaire** *f* ELECTROTEC secondary inductance; ~ **série** *f* ELECTR series inductor; ~ **variable** *f* ELECTR, ELECTROTEC variable inductance
inducteur *m* TRANSPORT primary winding; ~ **auxiliaire** *m* ELECTR *bobine* mutual inductor; ~ **à basse fréquence** *m* ELECTROTEC *chauffage* low-frequency induction heater; ~ **de chauffage** *m* ELECTROTEC induction heater; ~ **de démarreur** *m* AUTO starter field coil, starter field winding; ~ **terrestre** *m* GEOPHYS earth inductor
inductilité *f* MATERIAUX inductility
induction *f* ELECTR, ELECTROTEC, MATH, PHYSIQUE, TELECOM induction; ~ **critique** *f* ELECTROTEC critical field; ~ **dans l'entrefer** *f* ELECTR *bobine* air gap induction; ~ **dans l'induit** *f* ELECTR *machine* armature induction; ~ **électrique** *f* PHYSIQUE electric displacement; ~ **électromagnétique** *f* ELECTROTEC, ESSAIS, PHYSIQUE electromagnetic induction, PRODUCTION *électricité* EMI, electromagnetic induction; ~ **électrostatique** *f* ELECTR electrostatic induction; ~ **magnétique** *f* ELECTR flux density, magnetic flux density, ELECTROTEC, ENREGISTR, PETR magnetic induction, PHYSIQUE magnetic flux density, magneticinduction, TELECOM magnetic induction; ~ **mutuelle** *f* ELECTR mutual induction, *bobine* common reactance, ELECTROTEC, PHYSIQUE mutual induction; ~ **propre** *f* ELECTROTEC self-induction; ~ **rémanente** *f* ELECTR residual flux density, *magnétisation* remanent flux density, ELECTROTEC remanent induction; ~ **rémanente après induction** *f* TV retentivity; ~ **à saturation** *f* ELECTROTEC

saturation induction; ~ **superficielle** *f* TV surface induction
inductomètre *m* ELECTR inductometer
induire *vt* ELECTR *induction*, PHYSIQUE induce
induit[1] *adj* CHIMIE, ELECTR *courant, tension, charge*, PHYSIQUE induced
induit[2] *m* ELECTR *machine*, ELECTROTEC armature; ~ **axial** *m* ELECTR *machine* axial armature; ~ **à bagues collectrices** *m* ELECTR *générateur, moteur* slip-ring rotor; ~ **à barres** *m* ELECTR *générateur, moteur* cage armature, *machine* bar armature; ~ **à canaux fermés** *m* ELECTR *générateur, moteur* closed slot armature; ~ **à canaux ouverts** *m* ELECTR *générateur, moteur* open slot armature; ~ **à circuit fermé** *m* ELECTR *générateur, moteur* closed coil armature; ~ **à circuit ouvert** *m* ELECTR *machine* open coil armature; ~ **à courant triphasé** *m* ELECTR three-phase current armature, *générateur, moteur* rotary current armature; ~ **à court-circuit** *m* ELECTR *générateur, moteur* short circuit armature, short circuit rotor; ~ **à croisillons** *m* ELECTR *générateur, moteur* spider-type armature; ~ **denté** *m* ELECTROTEC slotted armature; ~ **à dents** *m* ELECTR *générateur, moteur* toothed ring armature; ~ **à disque** *m* ELECTR *machine*, ELECTROTEC disc armature (BrE), disk armature (AmE); ~ **en anneau** *m* ELECTR *générateur, moteur* ring armature; ~ **en cloche** *m* ELECTR *générateur, moteur* bell-type armature; ~ **à encoches** *m* ELECTR *générateur, moteur* slotted armature; ~ **en court-circuit** *m* ELECTROTEC short-circuited armature; ~ **en court-circuit à bagues collectrices** *m* ELECTR *générateur, moteur* short-circuited slip ring rotor; ~ **en double T** *m* ELECTR *générateur, moteur* shuttle armature, *machine* H-armature; ~ **en I** *m* ELECTR *générateur, moteur* shuttle armature, *machine* H-armature; ~ **à enroulement** *m* ELECTR *générateur, moteur* wire-wound armature; ~ **à enroulement double** *m* ELECTR *machine* double-winding armature, double-wound armature; ~ **en tambour** *m* ELECTR *machine*, ELECTROTEC drum armature; ~ **étoilé** *m* ELECTR *générateur, moteur* star-connected armature; ~ **feuilleté** *m* ELECTR *moteur* laminated armature; ~ **à fils** *m* ELECTR *générateur, moteur* wire-wound armature; ~ **fixe** *m* ELECTR *générateur, moteur* fixed armature, stationary armature, ELECTROTEC stationary armature; ~ **inverse** *m* ELECTR *générateur, moteur* inverse induced armature; ~ **lisse** *m* ELECTR *générateur, moteur* smooth core armature; ~ **mobile** *m* ELECTROTEC revolving armature; ~ **moteur** *m* ELECTR motor armature; ~ **multipolaire** *m* ELECTR *générateur, moteur* multipolar armature; ~ **de primaire** *m* ELECTR *générateur, moteur* primary armature; ~ **à résistance élevée** *m* ELECTR *générateur, moteur* increased resistance rotor; ~ **rotatif** *m* ELECTR *générateur, moteur* rotating armature; ~ **sans noyau** *m* ELECTR coreless armature; ~ **stationnaire** *m* ELECTR *générateur, moteur* stationary armature; ~ **à trous** *m* ELECTR *générateur, moteur* closed slot armature
induline *f* CHIMIE indulin
induration *f* GEOLOGIE induration
industrie: ~ **aurifère** *f* MINES gold-mining industry; ~ **de l'automobile** *f* PRODUCTION automotive industry; ~ **du bâtiment** *f* CONSTR building trade; ~ **céramique** *f* CERAM VER ceramic industry, clay industry; ~ **graphique** *f* IMPRIM printing trade; ~ **lourde** *f* CONSTR heavy engineering; ~ **meunière** *f* AGRO ALIM milling, milling industry; ~ **de l'or** *f* MINES gold-mining indus-

try; ~ **de la porcelaine** *f* CERAM VER porcelain industry; ~ **sucrière** *f* AGRO ALIM sugar industry; ~ **de transformation** *f* PRODUCTION process industry; ~ **de la transformation du papier** *f* EMBALLAGE paper-converting industry; ~ **du verre d'emballage** *f* CERAM VER bottle industry

industries: ~ **graphiques** *f pl* IMPRIM graphic arts

inefficace *adj* MATERIAUX ineffective, ineffectual, inefficient

inefficacité: ~ **de transfert** *f* ELECTROTEC transfer inefficiency

inégalité *f* ORDINAT inequality

inélasticité *f* MATERIAUX inelasticity

inertage *m* PETROLE inerting, *sécurité de production* blanketing

inertance: ~ **acoustique** *f* PHYSIQUE acoustic inertance

inerte *adj* CHIMIE inactive, inert, MATERIAUX, PETROLE inert

inertie *f* CONS MECA, MECANIQUE, PHYSIQUE, POLLUTION inertia; ~ **à l'eau** *f* PAPIER hygrostability; ~ **thermique** *f* GAZ thermal inertia, thermic inertia, REFRIG thermal inertia, THERMODYN temperature lag, thermal inertia

inertiel *adj* MECANIQUE, PHYSIQUE inertial

inexplosible *adj* MATERIAUX explosion-proof, inexplosive, nonexplosive

inextensible *adj* MATERIAUX inextensible

inférence *f* INFORMAT, ORDINAT inference

inférieur *adj* GEOLOGIE lower

infiltration *f* CHARBON infiltration, CHIMIE percolation, seepage, DISTRI EAU infiltration, HYDROLOGIE infiltration, ooze, oozing, percolation, POLLU MER seepage

infiltrer: **s'~** *v réfl* CHIMIE seep, HYDROLOGIE percolate TEXTILE seep through

infinitésimal *adj* GEOMETRIE infinitesimal

inflammabilité *f* AERONAUT, EMBALLAGE flammability, MATERIAUX inflammability, PLAST CAOU, SECURITE flammability, THERMODYN combustibility, flammability, inflammability

inflammable *adj* EMBALLAGE, MATERIAUX inflammable, PLAST CAOU, SECURITE flammable, THERMODYN combustible, flammable, inflammable; **très** ~ *adj* SECURITE highly-flammable

inflammation *f* CHIMIE ignition, GAZ fire; ~ **par frottement** *f* MINES frictional ignition; ~ **spontanée** *f* ESPACE *propulsion* spontaneous ignition

inflexibilité *f* MATERIAUX inflexibility

inflexion *f* MATERIAUX inflection

influence *f* CHIMIE influence; ~ **électrostatique** *f* PHYSIQUE electrostatic induction

influx *m* DISTRI EAU inflow; ~ **d'eau** *m* DISTRI EAU inflow of water

infographie *f* INFORMAT, ORDINAT, TV computer graphics; ~ **d'entreprise** *f* IMPRIM business graphics; ~ **de gestion** *f* IMPRIM business graphics; ~ **interactive** *f* INFORMAT interactive graphics

in-folio *m* IMPRIM folio

infondu *m* CERAM VER batch stone

informathèque *f* ELECTRON, ORDINAT databank, database

information *f* ELECTRON, INFORMAT, ORDINAT information; ~ **d'acheminement** *f* INFORMAT, ORDINAT routing information; ~ **d'amplitude** *f* ELECTRON amplitude information; ~ **analogique** *f* ELECTRON analog information (AmE), analogue information (BrE); ~ **d'authentification** *f* TELECOM authentication information; ~ **avant le vol** *f* AERONAUT preflight information;

~ **de cap** *f* AERONAUT heading information; ~ **de contrôle du protocole AAL** *f* TELECOM AAL protocol control information, AAL-PCI; ~ **disponible immédiatement** *f* EMBALLAGE off-the-shelf information; ~ **de gestion** *f* TELECOM management information; ~ **non numérotée** *f* TELECOM UI, unnumbered information; ~ **parasite** *f* ELECTROTEC, INFORMAT drop-in; ~ **prédictive** *f* TRANSPORT advance information; ~ **routière** *f* TRANSPORT traffic information; ~ **routière locale** *f* TRANSPORT local traffic information; ~ **routière régionale** *f* TRANSPORT area traffic information; ~ **de tangage** *f* AERONAUT pitch information; ~ **de taxation** *f* TELECOM charging information; ~ **d'usager à usager** *f* TELECOM UUI, user-to-user information; ~ **de vol** *f* AERONAUT flight information

informations *f pl* ELECTRON, INFORMAT, ORDINAT data; ~ **d'autorisation** *f pl* TELECOM authorization information; ~ **brutes** *f pl* ELECTRON raw data; ~ **éparses** *f* INFORMAT garbage; ~ **de fonctionnement** *f pl* TELECOM performance data; ~ **numériques** *f pl* ELECTRON digital data; ~ **numérisées** *f pl* ELECTRON, TELECOM digitized data; ~ **parasites** *f pl* ORDINAT garbage, meaningless data; ~ **de signalisation** *f pl* TELECOM signaling information (AmE), signalling information (BrE)

informatique *f* ELECTRON EDP, electronic data processing, INFORMAT EDP, electronic data processing, computer science, informatics, ORDINAT EDP, electronic data processing, IT, information technology, computer science, informatics, TELECOM IT, information technology; ~ **distribuée** *f* ORDINAT DDP, distributed data processing; ~ **de gestion** *f* INFORMAT commercial computing; ~ **répartie** *f* ORDINAT distributed data processing

infraction: ~ **aux règles de sécurité** *f* SECURITE breach of the safety rules

infraprotéines *f pl* CHIMIE infraproteins

infrarouge[1] *adj* (*IR*) ASTRONOMIE, OPTIQUE, PAPIER, PHYS RAYON, PLAST CAOU *rayonnement* infrared (*IR*)

infrarouge[2] *m* (*IR*) ASTRONOMIE, OPTIQUE, PAPIER, PHYSIQUE, PHYS RAYON, PLAST CAOU infrared (*IR*); ~ **lointain** *m* PHYS RAYON far infrared; ~ **moyen** *m* PHYS RAYON middle infrared; ~ **proche** *m* PHYS RAYON near infrared

infrason *m* ACOUSTIQUE, PHYSIQUE infrasound

infrastructure *f* AERONAUT ground installation, CONS MECA underframe, INFORMAT, ORDINAT infrastructure; ~ **portuaire** *f* NAUT port facilities

infrastructures *f pl* ESPACE ground facilities

infroissabilité *f* TEXTILE crease resistance

infroissable *adj* TEXTILE crush-resistant

infusibilité *f* MATERIAUX infusibility

infusible *adj* MATERIAUX infusible

ingénierie *f* CONS MECA engineering, CONSTR structural analysis, MECANIQUE engineering; ~ **de la chaleur** *f* CONS MECA heat engineering; ~ **de la circulation** *f* TRANSPORT traffic engineering; ~ **électronique** *f* ELECTRON electronic engineering; ~ **de l'environnement et de la sécurité** *f* SECURITE environmental and safety engineering; ~ **logicielle** *f* INFORMAT, ORDINAT software engineering; ~ **logicielle assistée par ordinateur** *f* ORDINAT CASE, computer-aided software engineering; ~ **des procédés** *f* PETROLE process engineering; ~ **de la sécurité** *f* ESSAIS safety engineering; ~ **solaire** *f* EN RENOUV solar engineering; ~ **spatiale** *f* ESPACE space engineering; ~ **des systèmes** *f* INFORMAT systems engineering; ~ **de la transmission de chaleur** *f* CONS MECA heat transfer engineering; ~ **ultrasonique** *f* CONS MECA ultrasonic engineering; ~ **de la vapeur** *f* CONS MECA steam engineering; ~ **du vide** *f* CONS MECA vacuum engineering

ingénieur *m* MECANIQUE engineer; ~ **des boues** *m* PETROLE mud engineer; ~ **civil** *m* CONSTR civil engineer; ~ **civil des mines** *m* MINES mining engineer; ~ **commercial** *m* PRODUCTION sales engineer; ~ **éclairagiste** *m* CINEMAT lighting engineer; ~ **en chef** *m* CONSTR chief engineer; ~ **en construction navale** *m* NAUT marine architect, naval architect, ship designer; ~ **en recherche-développement** *m* CONS MECA research development engineer; ~ **de forage** *m* PETR, PETROLE drilling engineer; ~ **frigoriste** *m* REFRIG refrigeration engineer; ~ **mécanicien** *m* NAUT engineer, engineer officer, marine engineer, PRODUCTION mechanical engineer; ~ **des mines** *m* MINES mining engineer; ~ **pétrolier** *m* PETROLE petroleum engineer; ~ **radio** *m* NAUT radio engineer; ~ **du son** *m* ENREGISTR audio control engineer, balance engineer; ~ **de terrain** *m* MECANIQUE field engineer

ingénieur-conseil *m* PRODUCTION consulting engineer

ingénieur-technicien: ~ **de montage** *m* CONSTR chief erecting engineer

ingérer *vt* POLLUTION ingest

ingrédients *m pl* CONS MECA products

inguéable *adj* HYDROLOGIE unfordable

inhalateur: ~ **d'oxygène** *m* ESPACE *véhicules* oxygen respirator, SECURITE oxygen breathing apparatus; ~ **d'oxygène d'application rapide** *m* AERONAUT quick-donning oxygen mask

inhiber *vt* CHIMIE inhibit, *réaction* retard, ELECTRON, INFORMAT, ORDINAT inhibit

inhibiteur:[1] ~ **de frittage** *adj* GENIE CHIM sinter-inhibiting

inhibiteur[2] *m* AGRO ALIM, CHIMIE, DISTRI EAU, IMPRIM *chimie*, LESSIVES, MATERIAUX, PLAST CAOU *ingrédient de mélange* inhibitor; ~ **catalytique** *m* GENIE CHIM catalytic poison; ~ **de corrosion** *m* ESPACE *véhicules* corrosion inhibitor; ~ **de frittage** *m* GENIE CHIM sinter inhibiter

inhibition *f* CHIMIE *réaction*, ELECTRON inhibition

inhomogénéité *f* CERAM VER, MATERIAUX inhomogeneity

ininflammabilité *f* ESSAIS nonflammability, MATERIAUX uninflammability

ininflammable *adj* CHIMIE nonflammable, MATERIAUX uninflammable, SECURITE fireproof, nonflammable, THERMODYN fireproof, flameproof

initial *adj* ESPACE initial

initiale *f* IMPRIM *composition, maquette* initial

initialisation *f* ORDINAT initialization; ~ **de la fissure** *f* METALL crack initiation

initialiser *vt* ELECTRON initialize, IMPRIM format, ORDINAT initialize

initiateur *m* AGRO ALIM, CHIMIE initiator; ~ **d'onde de choc** *m* ESPACE *véhicules* shock wave initiator

initiation *f* CHIMIE *d'une réaction* initiation

initiative: ~ **du fabricant** *f* CONS MECA manufacturer's discretion

injecter *vt* ESPACE *véhicules*, GAZ, PRODUCTION inject; ~ **sur orbite** *vt* ESPACE *véhicules* inject

injecteur *m* AUTO fuel nozzle, injection nozzle, injector, ELECTRON injector, EN RENOUV nozzle, GAZ, INST HYDR, MECANIQUE injector, VEHICULES *carburant* injection nozzle, injector; ~ **d'air** *m* CONS MECA air

injector; ~ **aspirant** *m* CONS MECA inspirator, lifting injector; ~ **de carburant** *m* CONS MECA fuel injector; ~ **à deux trous** *m* AUTO twin-jet injection nozzle; ~ **d'essence à dosage électronique** *m* TRANSPORT electronic metering of fuel injection; ~ **à étranglement** *m* AUTO throttle pintle nozzle; ~ **à jeton** *m* AUTO pintle injection nozzle; ~ **à jet unique** *m* AUTO single jet injection nozzle; ~ **à mise en marche automatique** *m* CONS MECA restarting injector, self-acting injector; ~ **pompe** *m* AUTO united injector; ~ **pompe à jet** *m* CHAUFFAGE steam injector; ~ **à un trou** *m* AUTO single jet injection nozzle; ~ **de vapeur vive** *m* INST HYDR live steam injector

injection *f* AERONAUT priming, AUTO injection, CHARBON grouting, ELECTRON, ESPACE, GAZ injection, PRODUCTION injection, *du bois* impregnation, VEHICULES *carburant* injection; ~ **d'air comprimé** *f* PETROLE air flooding; ~ **à bas niveau** *f* ELECTRON low-level injection; ~ **de carburant** *f* CHAUFFAGE *automobile*, THERMODYN, VEHICULES fuel injection; ~ **de ciment** *f* CONSTR grouting, NUCLEAIRE cementation, grouting; ~ **de combustible** *f* VEHICULES fuel injection; ~ **directe** *f* AUTO direct injection, integral injection; ~ **d'eau** *f* DISTRI EAU flushing, PETR water flooding, PETROLE *puits* water injection; ~ **électronique** *f* AUTO electronic injection; ~ **de faisceau** *f* NUCLEAIRE beam injection; ~ **de faisceau d'atomes neutres** *f* NUCLEAIRE neutral atom beam injection; ~ **à la flamme** *f* REVETEMENT plast spraying; ~ **de gaz** *f* PETROLE *récupération du pétrole* gas injection; ~ **d'harmonique deux** *f* ELECTRON second harmonic injection; ~ **à haut niveau** *f* ELECTRON high-level injection; ~ **indirecte** *f* AUTO external injection; ~ **sur orbite** *f* ESPACE *véhicules* orbital injection; ~ **tourbillonnaire** *f* GAZ swirling injection

injonction: ~ **provisoire** *f* BREVETS interim injunction, interlocutory injunction

inlandsis *m* OCEANO ice sheet, inlandsis

innavigable *adj* HYDROLOGIE unnavigable

innovations: ~ **d'ennoblissement** *f pl* TEXTILE innovative finishes

inoccupé *adj* PRODUCTION idle

in-octavo *m* IMPRIM octavo

inoculation *f* MATERIAUX inoculation, *métallurgie* injection

inoculum *m* AGRO ALIM starter

inodore *adj* CHIMIE, EMBALLAGE, GENIE CHIM odorless (AmE), odourless (BrE)

inoffensif *adj* MATERIAUX innoxious

inondation *f* HYDROLOGIE flood, inundation, IMPRIM *encrier, réservoir*, NAUT flood

inondé *adj* HYDROLOGIE flooded

inonder *vt* NAUT flood

inorganique *adj* MATERIAUX inorganic, inorganical

inosine *f* AGRO ALIM, CHIMIE inosine

inositol *m* AGRO ALIM, CHIMIE inositol

inoxydable *adj* CHIMIE inoxidizable, unoxidizable, MATERIAUX incorrodible, inoxidizable, noncorrodible, rustless, METALL, PAPIER, PHOTO stainless, PRODUCTION rustproof

inoxydant *adj* CHIMIE nonoxidizing

inoxyde *adj* CHIMIE unoxidized

in-quarto *m* IMPRIM quarto

insaturable *adj* CHIMIE unsaturable

insaturation *f* CHIMIE nonsaturation

insaturé[1] *adj* CHIMIE unsaturated

insaturé[2] *m* CHIMIE unsaturate

inscription *f* BREVETS registration, PRODUCTION marking; ~ **des bornes** *f* PRODUCTION terminal marking; ~ **maritime** *f* NAUT shipping office

inscrire:[1] ~ **au journal de bord** *vt* NAUT log; ~ **au registre** *vt* BREVETS record in the register

inscrire[2] *vi* ORDINAT enter

inscrire:[3] **s'~ en courbe** *v réfl* CH DE FER *véhicules* negotiate a curve

insecte *m* IMPRIM *typographie* bug

in-seize *m* IMPRIM sixteenmo

insensible: ~ **aux fautes** *adj* ORDINAT fault-tolerant

insérer[1] *vt* CINEMAT, INFORMAT, ORDINAT, PRODUCTION insert, TV play in

insérer:[2] ~ **dans un courant de circulation** *vi* TRANSPORT join a traffic stream

insert *m* CINEMAT insert shot, MECANIQUE, PLAST CAOU *plastiques* insert; ~ **de moule** *m* PLAST CAOU *matériel* mold insert (AmE), mould insert (BrE)

insertion *f* IMPRIM insertion, inset-insert, INFORMAT insert, pasting, ORDINAT, PLAST CAOU insert, PRODUCTION insertion; ~ **de bits** *f* ORDINAT bit stuffing; ~ **de la composante continue** *f* TV DC insertion

in-six *m* IMPRIM sixmo

insolation *f* ASTRONOMIE, GEOPHYS insolation, IMPRIM insolation, *de la plaque* burn, *photogravure* exposure, PHYSIQUE, REFRIG insolation; ~ **des demi-teintes** *f* IMPRIM *photogravure* halftone exposure

insolubilité *f* MATERIAUX, TEXTILE insolubility

insoluble *adj* CHIMIE lyophobic, MATERIAUX, PETROLE insoluble; ~ **à l'eau** *adj* TEXTILE insoluble in water

insonore *adj* MATERIAUX insonorous

insonorisation *f* CINEMAT soundproofing, ENREGISTR sound insulation, SECURITE noise protection, soundproofing

insonoriser *vt* CINEMAT blimp

inspecter *vt* NAUT survey

inspecteur *m* CONSTR surveyor, MECANIQUE, QUALITE inspector; ~ **chargé de la sécurité** *m* SECURITE security officer; ~ **du travail** *m* SECURITE factory inspector

inspection *f* MECANIQUE examination, inspection, NAUT surveying, PRODUCTION, QUALITE, SECURITE *lieu du travail* inspection; ~ **du dossier** *f* BREVETS inspection of files; ~ **électrique** *f* PETR electrical survey; ~ **externe** *f* ESPACE *véhicules* walkaround inspection; ~ **minutieuse** *f* CONSTR meticulous inspection, PRODUCTION minute examination; ~ **périodique** *f* CONS MECA periodic inspection; ~ **radiographique** *f* ESPACE *véhicules* X-ray inspection; ~ **rapide** *f* EMBALLAGE high-speed inspection; ~ **aux rayons X** *f* NUCLEAIRE X-ray inspection, X-ray testing; ~ **volante** *f* QUALITE patrol inspection

instabilité *f* CHIMIE instability, ELECTRON jitter, ELECTROTEC, EMBALLAGE instability, IMPRIM flutter, INFORMAT jitter; ~ **de ballonnement** *f* NUCLEAIRE ballooning instability; ~ **capillaire** *f* PHYS FLUID *jet fluide* capillary instability; ~ **de combustion** *f* ESPACE *propulsion* chuffing, THERMODYN combustion instability; ~ **conditionnelle** *f* METEO conditional instability; ~ **à coques** *f* NUCLEAIRE kink instability; ~ **dans les écoulements tournants de Couette** *f* PHYS FLUID instability of rotating Couette flow; ~ **de double faisceau** *f* NUCLEAIRE two-stream instability; ~ **des écoulements** *f* PHYS FLUID flow instability; ~ **des écoulements cisaillés** *f* PHYS FLUID shear flow instability; ~ **en hélice** *f* NUCLEAIRE helical instability; ~

hydrodynamique *f* GAZ hydrodynamic instability; ~ **d'un jet** *f* PHYS FLUID jet instability; ~ **de largeur** *f* ELECTRON width jitter; ~ **magnétohydrodynamique** *f* (*instabilité MHD*) GEOPHYS magnetohydrodynamic instability; ~ **de marche** *f* CH DE FER uneven running; ~ **mécanique** *f* METALL mechanical instability; ~ **MHD** *f* (*instabilité magnétohydrodynamique*) GEOPHYS MHD instability; ~ **de mode** *f* ELECTRON moding; ~ **de mode d'oscillation** *f* ELECTRON double moding; ~ **périodique** *f* MATERIAUX periodic instability; ~ **plastique** *f* METALL plastic instability; ~ **temporelle** *f* ELECTRON time jitter; ~ **de tension superficielle** *f* PHYS FLUID surface tension instabilities; ~ **thermique** *f* TELECOM, THERMODYN thermal instability

instable *adj* ELECTR, PHYSIQUE unstable

installateur: ~ **de chaufferie à gaz** *m* PRODUCTION gas fitter; ~ **frigoriste** *m* REFRIG refrigeration contractor

installation *f* CONSTR, INFORMAT, ORDINAT installation, PRODUCTION installation, plant, REFRIG plant, TELECOM installation, TV setup; ~ **d'absorption** *f* SECURITE *séparation sèche de gaz nocifs* absorption plant; ~ **d'agglomération** *f* GENIE CHIM agglomerating plant; ~ **d'alarme antivol** *f* SECURITE theft alarm installation; ~ **d'alarme pour le grisou** *f* MINES gas alarm system; ~ **d'alkylation** *f* LESSIVES alkylation plant, alkylation unit; ~ **d'aspiration** *f* SECURITE exhaust vent installation; ~ **d'aspiration concentrée** *f* SECURITE point vacuum cleaning system; ~ **d'aspiration de copeaux** *f* SECURITE chips exhaust installation; ~ **d'aspiration et de filtration** *f* SECURITE suction-and-filter installation; ~ **d'assainissement** *f* HYDROLOGIE sewage treatment plant, sewerage system; ~ **à basse tension** *f* ELECTROTEC low-voltage instalation (AmE), low-voltage installation (BrE); ~ **booster** *f* EN RENOUV booster mill; ~ **de broyage primaire** *f* GENIE CHIM crushing plant; ~ **de calcul** *f* ORDINAT computing facility; ~ **centrale de froid** *f* REFRIG central refrigerating plant; ~ **de chargement** *f* MINES loading system; ~ **de chauffage** *f* THERMODYN heating installation; ~ **de chauffage à air chaud** *f* MAT CHAUFF warm air heating system; ~ **de chauffage d'eau à basse pression** *f* MAT CHAUFF low-pressure hot water system; ~ **de chauffage d'eau à haute pression** *f* MAT CHAUFF high-pressure hot water system; ~ **de chauffage à vapeur** *f* MAT CHAUFF steam heating system; ~ **de clarification** *f* DISTRI EAU clarification plant; ~ **clef en main** *f* CONS MECA turnkey installation; ~ **de commande par radio** *f* TELECOM radio control system; ~ **de communication d'entreprises** *f* TELECOM business communication system, business system; ~ **complète** *f* NUCLEAIRE ultimate installation; ~ **comportant des gicleurs et pulvérisateurs anti-incendie** *f* SECURITE sprinkler and water spray fire-extinguishing installations; ~ **de compression** *f* GAZ compression installation; ~ **de concassage** *f* CHARBON crushing plant; ~ **de concassage grossier** *f* GENIE CHIM coarse crushing mill; ~ **de condensation** *f* GENIE CHIM condensing plant; ~ **de conditionnement d'air** *f* MAT CHAUFF, REFRIG air conditioning installation, air conditioning plant; ~ **de congélation** *f* REFRIG freezing plant; ~ **de congélation rapide** *f* CONS MECA quick-freezing installation, REFRIG quick-freezing plant; ~ **de conversion d'uranium** *f* NUCLEAIRE uranium conversion plant; ~ **de craquage** *f* PETROLE cracking plant; ~ **de criblage** *f* CHARBON screening plant; ~ **de décharge des eaux résiduaires** *f* DISTRI EAU sewage disposal plant; ~ **de**

décontamination *f* MATERIAUX decontamination plant; ~ **de dépoussiérage** *f* SECURITE dust removal plant; ~ **de dépoussiérage à l'électricité** *f* SECURITE electrical dust removal installation; ~ **de dépoussiérage à l'humidité** *f* SECURITE wet dust removal installation; ~ **de dessalement** *f* DISTRI EAU desalination plant, GENIE CHIM desalination plant, desalinization plant; ~ **de désulfuration de gaz de fumée** *f* SECURITE installation for reducing sulfur emissions (AmE), installation for reducing sulphur emissions (BrE), smoke gas desulfuration installation (AmE), smoke gas desulphuration installation (BrE); ~ **de détrompeurs** *f* PRODUCTION *automatisme industriel* keying; ~ **de diffusion à travers un gaz** *f* NUCLEAIRE countercurrent diffusion plant; ~ **de distribution à haute tension** *f* ELECTR *commutateur* high-voltage switch gear; ~ **domestique** *f* ELECTROTEC domestic electric installation (BrE), home electric installation (AmE); ~ **électrique** *f* ELECTR, ELECTROTEC, NAUT electrical installation; ~ **d'épuration d'air d'échappement** *f* SECURITE *fonctionnement mécanique* mechanical exhaust air installation; ~ **d'épuration de gaz brûlés** *f* SECURITE flue gas cleaning installation; ~ **d'évacuation de fumée et de chaleur** *f* SECURITE smoke and heat exhaust installation, smoke and heat extraction system; ~ **d'extinction à halon à mousse et à poudre** *f* SECURITE halon foam and powder firefighting installation; ~ **d'extraction par cages** *f* MINES cage winding system, hoisting system; ~ **d'extraction par cages à berlines** *f* MINES cage winding system, hoisting system; ~ **d'extraction par skip** *f* MINES skip-winding system; ~ **au fil de l'eau** *f* EN RENOUV *hydro-électricité* run-of-river scheme; ~ **de filtrage** *f* DISTRI EAU filter plant; ~ **fixe d'extinction automatique** *f* SECURITE automatic fire-fighting system; ~ **de force motrice hydraulique** *f* ELECTROTEC water power station; ~ **de formage de feuille** *f* PRODUCTION foil-forming plant; ~ **de formage de feuille d'aluminium intégrée** *f* PRODUCTION integral aluminium foil forming plant (BrE), integral aluminum foil forming plant (AmE); ~ **frigorifique** *f* CONS MECA, REFRIG, THERMODYN refrigerating plant; ~ **frigorifique à absorption** *f* CONS MECA absorption refrigerating installation; ~ **frigorifique à basse température** *f* CONS MECA low-temperature cooling installation; ~ **frigorifique étagée** *f* REFRIG multistage refrigerating plant; ~ **frigorifique marine** *f* REFRIG marine refrigeration plant; ~ **géothermique** *f* EN RENOUV geothermal plant; ~ **à guidage forcé** *f* MINES trapped rail system; ~ **à haute tension** *f* ELECTROTEC high-tension power supply; ~ **informatique** *f* INFORMAT computing facility; ~ **intérieure** *f* ELECTR indoor installation, ELECTROTEC indoor wiring; ~ **d'irradiation au cobalt 60** *f* NUCLEAIRE cobalt 60 irradiation plant; ~ **d'irradiation des laques** *f* NUCLEAIRE lacquer irradiation facility; ~ **de lixiviation** *f* CHARBON leaching plant; ~ **de manutention horizontale** *f* TRANSPORT ro-ro depot; ~ **de manutention de marchandises** *f* TRANSPORT cargo handling berth; ~ **de mélange** *f* PETROLE blending plant; ~ **mixte** *f* TELECOM hybrid system; ~ **mobile** *f* TELECOM mobile installation; ~ **motrice** *f* NAUT power plant; ~ **d'ozonation** *f* HYDROLOGIE ozonization plant; ~ **de pompage** *f* POLLU MER pumping unit; ~ **pour l'épuration d'air d'échappement** *f* SECURITE exhaust cleaning installation; ~ **de production** *f* PETR production facilities; ~ **de production de vapeur** *f* CONS MECA

steam plant; ~ **de protection contre la foudre et mise à la terre** *f* SECURITE lightning protection and earthing installation (BrE), lightning protection and grounding installation (AmE); ~ **de pulvérisation** *f* GENIE CHIM pulverizing equipment; ~ **de purification d'air évacué** *f* SECURITE exhaust cleaning installation; ~ **radio** *f* AERONAUT radio facility; ~ **radio d'appel du personnel** *f* SECURITE staff-calling installation; ~ **de raffinage** *f* PAPIER refining plant; ~ **de réception terrestre** *f* POLLU MER shore reception facility; ~ **de récupération de l'acide** *f* PETROLE acid recovery plant; ~ **de récupération de l'essence** *f* PETROLE *contenue dans les gaz* absorption plant; ~ **de refroidissement d'air** *f* CONS MECA air-cooling installation; ~ **de régulation de la circulation** *f* TRANSPORT traffic control installation; ~ **de répétition des signaux en cabine** *f* TRANSPORT cab signaling (AmE), cab signalling (BrE); ~ **de retraitement chimique** *f* NUCLEAIRE chemical reprocessing plant; ~ **de rideaux d'air chaud** *f* SECURITE *entrée ouverte* air curtain installation; ~ **de roulage** *f* MINES tram system; ~ **de secours** *f* TELECOM emergency installation; ~ **de séparation des matières fertiles** *f* NUCLEAIRE blanket separation plant; ~ **de signalisation lumineuse** *f* TRANSPORT signal installation; ~ **de sondage** *f* CONSTR boreholing plant, MINES boring plant, drilling equipment, drilling plant; ~ **de stockage** *f* POLLU MER storage facility; ~ **de stockage par pompage** *f* EN RENOUV *hydro-électricité* pumped storage scheme; ~ **de surface** *f* MINES surface equipment; ~ **télégraphique** *f* TELECOM telegraph installation; ~ **de traitement** *f* GAZ processing facility, processing installation; ~ **de traitement des eaux usées** *f* DISTRI EAU effluent treatment plant; ~ **de transbordement en mer** *f* TRANSPORT offshore floating terminal; ~ **de transmission de données** *f* TELECOM DCE, data communications equipment; ~ **de transport sanitaire** *f* AERONAUT ambulance installation; ~ **à trémies doseuses** *f* CONSTR batch plant; ~ **de triage** *f* CH DE FER shunting yard; ~ **à vapeur** *f* MAT CHAUFF steam plant

installations *f pl* TV facilities; ~ **et services** *f pl* AERONAUT facilities; ~ **et services de route aérienne** *f pl* AERONAUT air route facilities; ~ **portuaires** *f pl* NAUT port facilities; ~ **de sécurité** *f pl* SECURITE safety fittings, *bâtiment* safety facility

installer *vt* CINEMAT set up, IMPRIM, INFORMAT install, NAUT fit, ORDINAT install, PRODUCTION rig, rig up, TV set up; ~ **l'électricité** *vt* ELECTR put in electricity; ~ **un tir** *vt* MILITAIRE *artillerie* register

instance: en ~ *adj* PRODUCTION outstanding, pending

instant *m* ELECTRON, PHYSIQUE time; ~ **d'amorçage** *m* ELECTROTEC firing time; ~ **de courbure maximale** *m* ESPACE *véhicules* maximum bending moment; ~ **de démarrage** *m* INFORMAT start time; ~ **d'explosion** *m* GEOPHYS time break; ~ **d'impulsion** *m* ELECTRON pulse time; ~ **d'inclinaison maximale** *m* ESPACE *véhicules* maximum bending moment; ~ **d'ouverture** *m* ELECTROTEC break time; ~ **zéro** *m* GEOPHYS time break

instantané[1] *adj* ELECTROTEC *fusible* fast-acting, PRODUCTION snap-on

instantané[2] *m* INFORMAT, ORDINAT snapshot, PHOTO instantaneous exposure; ~ **photogravure** *m* IMPRIM shot

Institut: ~ américain de normalisation *m (ANSI)* TELECOM American National Standards Institute *(ANSI)*; ~ **européen de normalisation des télécommunications** *m* TELECOM ETSI, European

Telecommunication Standardization Institute

instruction *f* CONS MECA instruction book, INFORMAT instruction, statement, ORDINAT command, instruction, language statement, statement, PRODUCTION *automatisme industriel* statement; **~ à une adresse** *f* INFORMAT, ORDINAT one-address instruction, single address instruction; **~ à une adresse plus une** *f* INFORMAT one-plus-one address instruction; **~ d'affectation** *f* INFORMAT, ORDINAT assignment statement; **~ d'appel** *f* ORDINAT call instruction; **~ arithmétique** *f* ORDINAT arithmetic instruction; **~ d'arrêt** *f* INFORMAT stop instruction, ORDINAT halt instruction, stop instruction; **~ d'asservissement de sortie** *f* PRODUCTION *automatisme industriel* output override instruction; **~ assistée par ordinateur** *f (IAO)* ORDINAT computer-assisted instruction *(CAI)*; **~ de bouclage** *f* INFORMAT loop statement; **~ de boucle** *f* ORDINAT loop statement; **~ de branchement** *f* ORDINAT branch instruction; **~ de branches** *f* PRODUCTION *automatisme industriel* branching instruction; **~ de cas** *f* ORDINAT case statement; **~ composée** *f* INFORMAT, ORDINAT compound statement; **~ de comptage** *f* PRODUCTION *automatisme industriel* counter address; **~ conditionnelle** *f* ORDINAT conditional instruction, PRODUCTION *automatisme industriel* condition instruction; **~ des conditions d'entrée** *f* PRODUCTION *automatisme industriel* conditioning instruction; **~ de début** *f* PRODUCTION *automatisme industriel* start statement; **~ déclarative** *f* INFORMAT, ORDINAT declarative statement; **~ à deux adresses** *f* INFORMAT, ORDINAT two-address instruction; **~ à deux adresses plus une** *f* INFORMAT, ORDINAT two-plus-one address instruction; **~ de déverrouillage** *f* PRODUCTION *automatisme industriel* unlatch instruction; **~ d'écriture** *f* INFORMAT, ORDINAT write instruction; **~ d'entrée** *f* INFORMAT, ORDINAT entry instruction; **~ d'entrée/sortie** *f* INFORMAT, ORDINAT input/output instruction; **~ exécutable** *f* INFORMAT, ORDINAT executable instruction, executable statement; **~ d'extraction** *f* ORDINAT fetch instruction; **~ de fermeture de branche** *f* PRODUCTION *automatisme industriel* branch close instruction; **~ fictive** *f* ORDINAT do-nothing instruction, dummy instruction; **~ de fin temporaire** *f* PRODUCTION *automatisme industriel* temporary end instruction; **~ illégale** *f* INFORMAT, ORDINAT illegal instruction; **~ indéfinie** *f* INFORMAT, ORDINAT undefined statement; **~ ineffective** *f* INFORMAT, ORDINAT no-op, no-operation no-instruction; **~ d'interruption** *f* INFORMAT halt instruction; **~ de lecture** *f* INFORMAT fetch instruction; **~ logique** *f* INFORMAT, ORDINAT logic instruction; **~ machine** *f* INFORMAT, ORDINAT machine instruction; **~ multi-adresse** *f* INFORMAT, ORDINAT multi-address instruction; **~ nulle** *f* INFORMAT, ORDINAT null instruction; **~ d'ouverture de branche** *f* PRODUCTION *automatisme industriel* branch open instruction; **~ de positionnement de bit** *f* PRODUCTION *automatisme industriel* bit controlling instruction; **~ privilégiée** *f* INFORMAT, ORDINAT privileged instruction; **~ de programme** *f* INFORMAT, ORDINAT program instruction; **~ de rafraîchissement prioritaire des E/S** *f* PRODUCTION immediate I/O update instruction; **~ de retour** *f* INFORMAT, ORDINAT return instruction; **~ sans adresse** *f* INFORMAT, ORDINAT zero address instruction; **~ de saut** *f* INFORMAT, ORDINAT jump instruction; **~ de saut dans un séquenceur** *f* PRODUCTION *automatisme industriel* sequencer jump operation; **~ de**

sécurité *f* SECURITE safety first training; **~ de séquenceur sur entrées** *f* PRODUCTION *automatisme industriel* sequencer input instruction; **~ de séquenceur sur sorties** *f* PRODUCTION *automatisme industriel* sequencer output instruction; **~ de temporisateur ultrarapide** *f* PRODUCTION *automatisme industriel* fine-time based instruction; **~ de temporisation** *f* PRODUCTION *automatisme industriel* timer instruction; **~ de temporisation à mémoire** *f* PRODUCTION *automatisme industriel* retentive timer-on; **~ de test de bits** *f* PRODUCTION bit examining instruction; **~ à trois adresses** *f* INFORMAT, ORDINAT three-address instruction; **~ de verrouillage** *f* PRODUCTION *automatisme industriel* latch instruction; **~ vide** *f* ORDINAT do-nothing instruction

instructions: **~ de lavage** *f pl* TEXTILE washing instructions; **~ nautiques** *f pl* NAUT sailing directions; **~ pour ouvrir** *f pl* EMBALLAGE instructions for opening, opening instructions; **~ de réglage** *f pl* COMMANDE adjustment instructions

instrument *m* AERONAUT instrument, CONS MECA implement, instrument, ELECTR *de mesure*, INFORMAT, NAUT, ORDINAT instrument; **~ à aiguille** *m* INSTRUMENT indicating instrument, pointer instrument; **~ à aimant mobile** *m* INSTRUMENT moving magnet instrument; **~ à aimant tournant** *m* INSTRUMENT moving magnet instrument; **~ auxiliaire** *m* INSTRUMENT attachment; **~ à cadran** *m* INSTRUMENT indicating instrument, pointer instrument; **~ à champ magnétique rotatif** *m* INSTRUMENT rotating field instrument; **~ à éclairage intérieur** *m* INSTRUMENT illuminated dial instrument; **~ étalon** *m* INSTRUMENT calibration instrument; **~ d'étalonnage** *m* INSTRUMENT calibration instrument; **~ à fer mobile** *m* ELECTR moving iron instrument, moving iron meter, ELECTROTEC moving iron instrument, INSTRUMENT moving iron instrument, moving iron meter; **~ ferromagnétique** *m* ELECTR moving iron instrument, moving iron meter, ELECTROTEC moving iron instrument, INSTRUMENT ferromagnetic instrument, moving iron instrument, moving iron meter; **~ à grand angle** *m* INSTRUMENT wide-angle instrument; **~ grand-angulaire** *m* INSTRUMENT wide-angle instrument; **~ à lecture directe** *m* INSTRUMENT direct reading instrument; **~ de mesurage de longueur** *m* CONS MECA length measuring instrument; **~ de mesure** *m* ELECTROTEC current testing meter, METROLOGIE measuring instrument; **~ de mesure analogique** *m* ELECTR analog measuring instrument (AmE), analogue measuring instrument (BrE); **~ de mesure à avertisseur** *m* CONS MECA alarm gage (AmE), alarm gauge (BrE); **~ de mesure différentiel** *m* INSTRUMENT differential measuring instrument; **~ de mesure dimensionnelle** *m* METROLOGIE dimensional measuring instrument; **~ de mesure de la droiture** *m* METROLOGIE straightness-measuring instrument; **~ de mesure de précision** *m* INSTRUMENT precision instrument; **~ de mesure de la rondeur** *m* METROLOGIE roundness-measuring instrument; **~ à mesurer la visibilité** *m* INSTRUMENT visual range meter; **~ de mesure des surfaces** *m* METROLOGIE surface-measuring instrument; **~ de mesure thermique** *m* INSTRUMENT thermal instrument; **~ de mesure thermoélectrique** *m* INSTRUMENT thermocouple instrument; **~ de mesure des vibrations** *m* INSTRUMENT NAUT vibration measurer; **~ à miroir** *m* INSTRUMENT reflecting instrument; **~ d'optique** *m* INSTRUMENT, PHYSIQUE optical instrument; **~**

à palpeur *m* INSTRUMENT stylus instrument; **~ de précision** *m* INSTRUMENT, PHYSIQUE precision instrument; **~ de transposition** *m* ACOUSTIQUE transposing instrument; **~ de vérification** *m* INSTRUMENT monitor

instrumentation *f* INFORMAT, ORDINAT instrumentation, PETROLE *forage, raffinerie* instruments; **~ interne du coeur** *f* NUCLEAIRE in-core instrument assembly

instruments: **~ gyroscopiques** *m pl* AERONAUT gyro instruments; **~ horaires** *m pl* INSTRUMENT horological instruments; **~ de métrologie** *m pl* INSTRUMENT measuring apparatus; **~ moteur** *m pl* AERONAUT engine instruments; **~ optiques pour mesure dimensionnelle** *m pl* METROLOGIE optical instruments for dimensional measurement; **~ de vol** *m pl* AERONAUT flight instruments

insuffisamment: **~ développé** *adv* IMPRIM *photographie* underdeveloped; **~ sensibilisé** *adv* IMPRIM *surface sensible* undersensitized

insulaire *adj* OCEANO *arc* insular

insulfoné *m* LESSIVES unsulfonated matter (AmE), unsulphonated matter (BrE)

insuline *f* CHIMIE insulin

intégrale *f* MATH *fonction* integral; **~ des collisions** *f* PHYS RAYON *équation de Boltzmann* collision integral; **~ curviligne** *f* PHYSIQUE line integral; **~ définie** *f* MATH Riemann integral, definite integral; **~ de Fourier** *f* PHYSIQUE Fourier integral; **~ de ligne** *f* PHYSIQUE line integral; **~ primitive** *f* MATH indefinite integral; **~ au sens de Riemann** *f* MATH Riemann integral, definite integral; **~ de surface** *f* PHYSIQUE surface integral; **~ de volume** *f* PHYSIQUE volume integral

intégrateur *m* AERONAUT heading synchronizer and lateral path integrator, CHIMIE, ELECTRON integrator, ELECTROTEC integrating circuit, integrator, PHOTO incident light attachment, TRANSPORT integrator; **~ actif** *m* ELECTRON active integrator; **~ d'erreur de cap** *m* AERONAUT heading error integrator; **~ numérique** *m* ELECTRON digital integrator; **~ de trajectoire transversale** *m* AERONAUT lateral path integrator

intégration *f* ELECTRON, ESPACE *satellite*, MATH, TELECOM integration; **~ des circuits** *f* ELECTRON circuit integration; **~ des circuits électroniques** *f* ELECTRON electronic circuit integration; **~ à l'échelle d'une tranche** *f* ELECTRON, ORDINAT wafer scale integration; **~ à faible échelle** *f* INFORMAT SSI, small-scale integration; **~ à forte densité** *f* *(LSI)* PHYSIQUE large-scale integration *(LSI)*; **~ à grande échelle** *f* *(LSI)* ELECTRON, INFORMAT, NAUT, ORDINAT, PHYSIQUE, TELECOM large-scale integration *(LSI)*; **~ à moyenne échelle** *f* ELECTRON, INFORMAT, ORDINAT, TELECOM MSI, medium-scale integration; **~ numérique** *f* ELECTRON digital integration; **~ à petite échelle** *f* ELECTRON, ORDINAT SSI, small-scale integration; **~ sur plaquette** *f* ELECTRON, INFORMAT wafer scale integration; **~ du temps de trajet** *f* PETROLE *levé sismique, son* ITT, integrated transit time; **~ de la trace** *f* ELECTRON trace integration; **~ à très grande échelle** *f* ELECTRON, INFORMAT, ORDINAT, TELECOM VLSI, very large-scale integration; **~ tridimensionnelle** *f* ELECTRON three-dimensional integration

intégré *adj* CONS MECA built-in, ELECTRON integrated, MECANIQUE built-in

intégrer *vt* ELECTROTEC ramp, INFORMAT, ORDINAT integrate, POLLUTION ingest

intégrité *f* INFORMAT, ORDINAT, TELECOM integrity; **~ de données** *f* TELECOM data integrity

intelligence: **~ artificielle** *f* *(IA)* ORDINAT, TELECOM artificial intelligence *(AI)*

intelligent *adj* INFORMAT, ORDINAT intelligent

intelligibilité *f* ACOUSTIQUE, ENREGISTR intelligibility

intensificateur: **~ d'image** *m* ASTRONOMIE, ELECTRON, INSTRUMENT image intensifier tube, image intensifier

intensification *f* ELECTRON intensification; **~ de la trace** *f* ELECTRON trace intensification

intensifier *vt* ELECTRON intensify

intensimètre *m* ELECTR field strength meter

intensité *f* CHIMIE, ELECTR *d'un courant, d'un champ magnétique*, ELECTRON intensity, ELECTROTEC current, GAZ, OPTIQUE intensity, PHYSIQUE current; **~ absorbée** *f* ELECTROTEC current input; **~ acoustique** *f* ACOUSTIQUE sound intensity, ENREGISTR loudness, PHYSIQUE sound intensity; **~ acoustique de référence** *f* ACOUSTIQUE reference sound intensity; **~ admissible** *f* ELECTROTEC permissible current; **~ admissible de courant** *f* ELECTR *ligne* current-carrying capacity; **~ de champ** *f* ELECTR field intensity, *électromagnétisme* field strength, ELECTROTEC field strength; **~ du champ électrique** *f* ELECTROTEC, PHYSIQUE electric field strength; **~ du champ magnétique** *f* ELECTR magnetic field intensity, magnetic field strength, ELECTROTEC, PHYSIQUE magnetic field strength; **~ de cisaillement** *f* METALL shear strength; **~ du coloris** *f* TEXTILE depth of shade; **~ de la couleur** *f* IMPRIM tinting strength; **~ du courant** *f* ELECTR amperage, ELECTROTEC current intensity, current strength; **~ du courant d'appel** *f* ELECTROTEC operate current; **~ du courant débité** *f* ELECTROTEC current output; **~ du courant d'obscurité** *f* ELECTROTEC dark current; **~ de déclenchement** *f* ELECTROTEC release current; **~ d'échec instantanée** *f* QUALITE instantaneous failure intensity; **~ efficace** *f* ELECTROTEC RMS current, effective current; **~ en champ éloigné** *f* ESPACE *communications* far-field intensity; **~ en champ proche** *f* ESPACE *communications* near field intensity; **~ en charge** *f* ELECTROTEC *courant* on-load current; **~ énergétique** *f* OPTIQUE, PHYS RAYON, PHYSIQUE, TELECOM radiant intensity; **~ instantanée du courant** *f* ELECTROTEC instantaneous current; **~ de lumière** *f* PHYS RAYON intensity of light; **~ lumineuse** *f* ELECTROTEC, PHYS RAYON, PHYSIQUE luminous intensity; **~ lumineuse mesurée en bougies** *f* PHOTO candle power; **~ magnétique** *f* GEOPHYS magnetic intensity, PETR magnetic field strength, PHYS RAYON magnetic intensity; **~ maximale admissible** *f* ELECTROTEC maximum current rating; **~ nominale** *f* ELECTROTEC rated current, PRODUCTION amp rating; **~ de la pluie** *f* METEO rainfall intensity; **~ de pôle** *f* PHYSIQUE pole strength; **~ du pôle magnétique** *f* GEOPHYS magnetic pole strength; **~ de rafale** *f* AERONAUT gust intensity; **~ de rayonnement** *f* ESPACE *communications* radiation intensity, OPTIQUE, PHYS RAYON, PHYSIQUE, TELECOM radiant intensity; **~ de référence standard** *f* ENREGISTR standard reference intensity; **~ du relâchement** *f* ELECTROTEC release current; **~ de rupture instantanée** *f* QUALITE instantaneous failure intensity; **~ du signal** *f* COMMANDE signal strength; **~ du sillage** *f* PHYS FLUID wake intensity; **~ sismique** *f* GEOPHYS earthquake intensity; **~ subjective** *f* ACOUSTIQUE *son* subjective loudness; **~ du trafic** *f* COMMANDE traffic flow; **~ de trafic équivalent** *f* TELECOM equivalent random traffic intensity; **~ vibratoire** *f* SECURITE vibration severity

interactif *adj* INFORMAT, ORDINAT interactive, on-line

interaction *f* CHIMIE, INFORMAT, METALL, ORDINAT inter-action; **~ chimique pastille-gaine** *f* NUCLEAIRE pellet-clad chemical interaction; **~ dipolaire** *f* PHYS RAYON dipole-dipole interaction; **~ dynamique** *f* METALL dynamic interaction; **~ électromagnétique** *f* PHYS RAYON electromagnetic interaction; **~ faible** *f* PHYSIQUE *nucléaire* weak interaction; **~ faisceau-plasma** *f* NUCLEAIRE beam plasma interaction; **~ forte** *f* NUCLEAIRE, PHYSIQUE strong interaction; **~ mécanique gaine-pastille** *f* NUCLEAIRE pellet-clad mechanical interaction; **~ à portée finie** *f* NUCLEAIRE finite range interaction; **~ de premiers voisins** *f* CRISTALL nearest neighbor interaction (AmE), nearest neighbour interaction (BrE)

interagir *vi* CHIMIE, PHYS RAYON interact

interateliers *adj* PRODUCTION interplant

interatomique *adj* CRISTALL *distance* interatomic

intercalage *m* PAPIER *feuille entre deux autres* interleaving

intercalaire *m* CERAM VER spacer, CONS MECA divider, IMPRIM *brochure, reliure* interleaf, PRODUCTION spacer

intercalation *f* PRODUCTION insertion; **~ marine** *f* GEOLOGIE marine band; **~ de roches** *f* CHARBON stone band

intercalé *adj* GEOLOGIE *entre les feuillets d'une roche métamorphique* interfoliated

intercaler *vt* PRODUCTION insert

intercepteur: **~ d'électrons** *m* NUCLEAIRE electron scavenger

interception *f* ESPACE, GEOMETRIE intercept, NUCLEAIRE scavenging, ORDINAT trap; **~ d'appel** *f* TELECOM call interception; **~ directe** *f* POLLUTION direct interception; **~ d'erreurs** *f* INFORMAT, ORDINAT error trapping

interchangeabilité *f* CONS MECA interchangeability

interchangeable *adj* PHOTO interchangeable

intercirculation *f* CH DE FER *véhicules* gangway

interclassement *m* INFORMAT, ORDINAT collation

interclasser *vt* IMPRIM interpolate, INFORMAT, ORDINAT collate

interclasseuse *f* INFORMAT, ORDINAT collator

interconnexion *f* AERONAUT, ELECTR *réseau*, ELECTROTEC interconnection, ENREGISTR cross-plugging, INFORMAT interblock gap, interconnection, ORDINAT interconnection, TELECOM configuration; **~ en boucle** *f* TELECOM ring configuration; **~ en étoile** *f* TELECOM star configuration; **~ en matrice** *f* TELECOM matrix configuration; **~ matricielle** *f* INFORMAT, ORDINAT array interconnection; **~ de réseaux** *f* INFORMAT, ORDINAT internetting, network interconnection; **~ sélective** *f* ELECTRON discretionary wiring; **~ de systèmes ouverts** *f* (ISO) INFORMAT, ORDINAT, TELECOM open systems interconnection *(OSI)*; **~ totale** *f* TELECOM total configuration; **~ des travées** *f* ELECTROTEC trunking

intercorrélateur *m* ELECTRON cross-correlator

intercorrélation *f* ELECTRON cross-correlation

interdiction *f* ELECTRON inhibition; **~ d'appel** *f* TELECOM call barring; **~ des appels à l'arrivée** *f* TELECOM ICB, incoming calls barred; **~ des appels au départ** *f* TELECOM OCB, outgoing calls barred; **~ de vol** *f* AERONAUT grounding

interdiffusion *f* MATERIAUX interdiffusion

interdigitation *f* GEOLOGIE interdigitation, interfingering

interdire *vt* ELECTRON inhibit

interfaçage *m* ESPACE interfacing

interface *f* CONS MECA, ELECTRON interface, INFORMAT interface unit, interface, MATERIAUX, METALL interface, ORDINAT interface unit, interface, TELECOM I/F, interface; **~ analogique** *f* TELECOM analog interface (AmE), analogue interface (BrE); **~ de bus** *f* INFORMAT, ORDINAT bus interface; **~ Centronics** *f* (MD) IMPRIM Centronics interface (TM); **~ coeur-gaine** *f* OPTIQUE core-cladding interface; **~ cohérente** *f* METALL coherent boundary, coherent interface; **~ à déclenchement par commande** *f* ORDINAT command-driven interface; **~ de données avec distribution par fibre** *f* TELECOM FDDI, fiber-distributed data interface (AmE), fibre-distributed data interface (BrE); **~ eau douce** *f* HYDROLOGIE freshwater interface; **~ eau salée** *f* HYDROLOGIE sea water interface; **~ externe** *f* ESPACE *véhicules* external interface; **~ gaz-eau** *f* PETR gas-water contact; **~ gaz-huile** *f* PETR gas-oil contact; **~ homme-machine** *f* ESPACE *véhicules*, INFORMAT, ORDINAT MMI, man-machine interface; **~ informatique** *f* TELECOM computer interface; **~ matrice-fibre** *f* MATERIAUX matrix fiber interface (AmE), matrix fibre interface (BrE); **~ modem** *f* ELECTRON, INFORMAT, ORDINAT modem interface; **~ de noeuds de réseau** *f* TELECOM NNI, network node interface; **~ normalisée** *f* TELECOM standard interface; **~ numérique** *f* TELECOM digital interface; **~ ordre-désordre** *f* MATERIAUX order-disorder interface; **~ PABX-serveur** *f* TELECOM CPI, computer-PABX interface; **~ parallèle** *f* IMPRIM parallel interface; **~ physique** *f* TELECOM PI, physical interface; **~ physique de rythme de multiplexeur** *f* TELECOM MTPI, multiplexer timing physical interface; **~ de poste d'affichage** *f* TELECOM DSI, display station interface; **~ série** *f* IMPRIM, INFORMAT, ORDINAT, TELECOM serial interface; **~ série programmable** *f* TELECOM serial programmable interface; **~ de souris-bus** *f* INFORMAT, ORDINAT bus-mouse adaptor; **~ de souris parallèle** *f* INFORMAT, ORDINAT parallel mouse adaptor; **~ standard** *f* INFORMAT, ORDINAT standard interface; **~ de transmission** *f* ELECTROTEC line interface; **~ usager-réseau** *f* TELECOM UNI, user-network interface; **~ utilisateur** *f* INFORMAT, ORDINAT, TELECOM user interface

interfacer *vt* ESPACE, ORDINAT interface

interférence *f* ACOUSTIQUE, ELECTRON, ENREGISTR, INFORMAT, OPTIQUE, ORDINAT, PHYS ONDES, PHYSIQUE, TELECOM, TV interference; **~ de canal adjacent** *f* ENREGISTR adjacent channel interference; **~ constructive** *f* PHYS ONDES, PHYSIQUE constructive interference; **~ destructive** *f* ELECTROTEC, PHYS ONDES, PHYSIQUE destructive interference; **~ électromagnétique** *f* ORDINAT EMI, electromagnetic interference; **~ entre canaux** *f* ENREGISTR co-channel interference; **~ entre fréquences d'émissions** *f* ELECTROTEC interchannel interference; **~ extérieure négative du tiroir** *f* INST HYDR outside clearance; **~ intersymbole** *f* ELECTRON intersymbol interference; **~ longitudinale** *f* ELECTRON intersymbol interference; **~ magnétique** *f* GEOPHYS magnetic interference; **~ d'onde** *f* TELECOM wave interference; **~ à ondes multiples** *f* PHYSIQUE multiple beam interference; **~ optique** *f* TELECOM optical interference; **~ par bandes latérales** *f* ELECTRON sideband interference; **~ par canal commun** *f* TV co-channel interference

interférences: **~ radio** *f pl* PHYS ONDES radio interference

interférer *vi* PHYSIQUE interfere
interféromètre *m* METROLOGIE, OPTIQUE, PHYSIQUE, TELECOM interferometer; **~ acoustique** *m* ACOUSTIQUE acoustic interferometer; **~ de Fabry-Pérot** *m* ESPACE, PHYSIQUE Fabry-Pérot interferometer; **~ à laser** *m* CONS MECA, ELECTRON laser interferometer; **~ de Michelson** *m* PHYSIQUE Michelson interferometer; **~ quantique** *m (squid)* PHYSIQUE superconduting quantum interference device *(squid)*; **~ de Rayleigh** *m* PHYSIQUE Rayleigh interferometer
interférométrie: **~ axiale** *f* OPTIQUE axial interference, axial interferometry, slab interferometry, TELECOM axial slab interferometry, slab interferometry; **~ transversale** *f* OPTIQUE, TELECOM transverse interferometry
interfoliaire *adj* PETROLE *géologie* interlayer
interfonctionnement *m* TELECOM interworking
interfrange *f* PHYSIQUE fringe separation
intergranulaire *adj* MATERIAUX, METALL intergranular
intérieur[1] *adj* AERONAUT inboard, PAPIER *carton* middle; **à l'~ du navire** *adj* NAUT below decks
intérieur:[2] **à l'~ du navire** *adv* NAUT below
interionique *adj* CHIMIE *distance* interionic
interlignage *m* IMPRIM lead, leading, line space, line spacing, *composition* leading matter, INFORMAT *composition* leading
interligner *vti* IMPRIM lead
interlock *m* CINEMAT interlock
intermédiaire *m* PETROLE *raffinage* intermediate chemical; **~ monture C** *m* CINEMAT C-mount adaptor
intermodulation *f* ELECTRON intermodulation, ENREGISTR crosstalk, intermodulation, ESPACE *communications*, TELECOM intermodulation, TV cross modulation, intermodulation; **~ d'aiguille** *f* ENREGISTR stylus crosstalk; **~ d'enregistrement** *f* ENREGISTR record crosstalk; **~ de positionnement** *f* TV positional crosstalk
intermoléculaire *adj* CHIMIE intermolecular
internégatif *m* CINEMAT intermediate reversal negative, internegative; **~ couleur** *m* CINEMAT color reversal intermediate (AmE), colour reversal intermediate (BrE)
internes: **~ supérieurs** *m pl* NUCLEAIRE upper core, upper internals
Internet *m* TELECOM Internet
interpénétration *f* CH DE FER *voies* crossover
interphone *m* ENREGISTR intercom, squawkbox, talkback, TELECOM intercom
interplanétaire *adj* ESPACE interplanetary
interpolateur[1] *adj* ELECTRON *filtre* interpolating
interpolateur[2] *m* TELECOM interpolator
interpolation *f* INFORMAT, MATH, ORDINAT, TELECOM interpolation; **~ linéaire** *f* TELECOM linear interpolation; **~ non linéaire** *f* TELECOM nonlinear interpolation
interpositif *m* CINEMAT intermediate positive; **~ de sélection** *m* CINEMAT separation master
interprétation *f* INFORMAT, ORDINAT interpretation; **~ photographique aérienne** *f* CHARBON air photo interpretation
interpréter *vt* INFORMAT, ORDINAT interpret
interpréteur *m* INFORMAT, ORDINAT interpreter
interrogateur: **~ de distance** *m* AERONAUT DME, distance-measuring equipment
interrogateur-répondeur *m* TELECOM interrogator transponder
interrogation *f* INFORMAT data query, polling, query,

inquiry, interrogation, ORDINAT inquiry, interrogation, polling, query; **~ de base de données** *f* INFORMAT, ORDINAT database query; **~ de données** *f* ORDINAT data query; **~ des navires** *f* TELECOM ship polling; **~ préalable** *f* TELECOM polling; **~ de table** *f* ORDINAT table lookup; **~ d'utilisateur** *f* ORDINAT user query; **~ de l'utilisateur** *f* INFORMAT user query
interrogation-sélection *f* INFORMAT, ORDINAT polling selection
interroger *vt* INFORMAT, ORDINAT interrogate, poll
interrompre *vt* COMMANDE cutout, discontinue, interrupt, truncate, shut down, ELECTROTEC turn-off, ESPACE abort, INFORMAT halt, interrupt, ORDINAT break, interrupt
interrompu *adj* TELECOM broken
interrupteur *m* CINEMAT cutoff switch, on/off switch, switch, ELECTR interrupter, make-and-break device, on/off switch, switch, *commutateur* circuit breaker, *disjoncteur* cutout switch, ELECTROTEC circuit breaker, single throw switch, switch, INFORMAT switch, NAUT contact breaker, PHOTO on/off switch, PHYSIQUE switch, TELECOM interrupter, THERMODYN, TV switch;
~ a **~ à action momentanée** *m* ELECTROTEC momentary action switch; **~ actionné par tige** *m* COMMANDE flag switch; **~ à action rapide** *m* ELECTR quick break switch; **~ d'alarme** *m* COMMANDE alarm switch; **~ d'alimentation** *m* COMMANDE, ELECTR, ELECTROTEC current switch (AmE), mains switch (BrE); **~ d'allumage** *m* AUTO ignition starter switch, COMMANDE, VEHICULES ignition switch; **~ antidéflagrant** *m* ELECTR *sécurité* flameproof switch; **~ antigrisouteux** *m* ELECTR flameproof switch; **~ d'arrêt** *m* PRODUCTION stopbutton switch; **~ automatique** *m* CINEMAT buckle trip, ELECTR, SECURITE automatic cutout switch; **~ auxiliaire** *m* ELECTR auxiliary switch;
~ b **~ basculant** *m* CINEMAT toggle switch, COMMANDE toggle switch, tumbler switch, ELECTR toggle switch, ELECTROTEC rocker switch; **~ basculant à mercure** *m* COMMANDE mercury switch, wet reed relay, ELECTR mercury switch; **~ de batterie** *m* PHOTO battery switch; **~ bidirectionnel** *m* ELECTROTEC bidirectional switch; **~ bimétallique** *m* ELECTR bimetallic switch; **~ bipolaire** *m* CINEMAT double-pole switch, COMMANDE bipolar cutout switch, ELECTR DPS, double-pole switch, ELECTROTEC DPST switch, double-pole switch, two-pole switch; **~ bipolaire à une direction** *m* ELECTROTEC DPST, DPST switch, double-pole single-throw switch; **~ à boîte** *m* ELECTR box switch; **~ à bouton-poussoir** *m* COMMANDE pressbutton switch, ELECTROTEC push-button switch;
~ c **~ centrifuge** *m* COMMANDE centrifuge switch; **~ de champ magnétique** *m* NUCLEAIRE field discharge switch, field-breaking switch; **~ de chantier** *m* MINES dead end switch; **~ de charge** *m* COMMANDE battery load switch, battery switch; **~ de clavier à membrane** *m* ELECTROTEC membrane keyswitch; **~ à clef** *m* COMMANDE key-operated switch; **~ à clef amovible** *m* ELECTR key-operated switch; **~ à commande à distance** *m* COMMANDE remote control switch; **~ à commande au pied** *m* COMMANDE foot switch, pedal switch, treadle switch, ELECTR floor contact switch; **~ commandé au silicium** *m* ELECTROTEC silicon-controlled switch; **~ de commande électrique de compensation de régime** *m* AERONAUT trim control switch; **~ de contact à pendule** *m* COMMANDE pendu-

lum circuit breaker; ~ **à cordon** *m* COMMANDE pull-cord switch, ELECTR pull switch; ~ **à coulisse** *m* COMMANDE, ELECTR slide switch; ~ **à coupure** *m* COMMANDE circuit breaker; ~ **à couteaux** *m* COMMANDE knife-blade switch, ELECTR knife switch; ~ **de crash** *m* AERONAUT crash switch;

~ **d** ~ **de démarrage** *m* COMMANDE start switch, starter, ELECTR line starter (AmE), starter (BrE); ~ **de démarrage à pédale** *m* COMMANDE foot-activated starter switch; ~ **de dérivation** *m* COMMANDE, ELECTR override switch; ~ **à deux directions** *m* COMMANDE, ELECTR two-way switch; ~ **à distance** *m* COMMANDE remote-controlled switch, ELECTR distance switch; ~ **à double rupture** *m* ELECTR double break switch;

~ **e** ~ **électrosensible** *m* ELECTR proximity switch; ~ **embrochable** *m* PRODUCTION plug-in switch; ~ **à encliqueter** *m* ELECTROTEC snap-in switch; ~ **enfichable** *m* COMMANDE plug switch;

~ **f** ~ **à faible course** *m* ELECTROTEC sensing switch; ~ **à fil souple** *m* ELECTR cord switch; ~ **de fin de course** *m* ELECTR *interrupteur*, ELECTROTEC, MECANIQUE limit switch; ~ **à flotteur** *m* ELECTROTEC float switch, IMPRIM *montage* floating switch, REFRIG float switch; ~ **à fonctionnement retardé** *m* COMMANDE, ELECTR delay switch; ~ **de Foucault** *m* COMMANDE mercury circuit breaker, ELECTR mercury switch;

~ **g** ~ **à garrot** *m* COMMANDE rotary light switch; ~ **général** *m* COMMANDE main switch, master switch, ELECTR master switch, ELECTROTEC main switch, master switch, on/off switch, PRODUCTION power switch, TV master switch; ~ **à glissière** *m* ELECTROTEC slide switch; ~ **à gradation de lumière rhéostatique** *m* COMMANDE, ELECTR dimmer switch; ~ **à graduation de lumière** *m* ELECTROTEC dimmer switch; ~ **de groupe** *m* ELECTROTEC grouping switch;

~ **h** ~ **à haute tension** *m* ELECTR high-voltage circuit breaker; ~ **horaire** *m* COMMANDE time switch, timer, ELECTR switch clock, time switch; ~ **à huile** *m* ELECTR oil switch, ELECTROTEC oil circuit breaker, PRODUCTION oil break switch, oil interrupter;

~ **i** ~ **à inertie** *m* COMMANDE, ELECTROTEC inertia switch; ~ **d'installation** *m* ELECTR house wiring switch, installation switch; ~ **instantané** *m* COMMANDE break-free switch, quick switch; ~ **inverseur** *m* COMMANDE reversible switch, ELECTROTEC grouping switch;

~ **j** ~ **à jack** *m* ELECTR toggle switch;

~ **l** ~ **à lame** *m* COMMANDE knife-blade switch, NUCLEAIRE knife-edge switch; ~ **à lames souples** *m* PHYSIQUE reed switch; ~ **à levier** *m* COMMANDE lever switch, ELECTR lever on-off switch, ELECTROTEC lever switch, toggle switch, NUCLEAIRE lever switch; ~ **limiteur** *m* COMMANDE, ELECTR *commutateur* limit switch; ~ **de lumière réduite** *m* AUTO dip switch, COMMANDE dimmer switch;

~ **m** ~ **à main** *m* ELECTR hand-operated switch; ~ **manométrique** *m* COMMANDE manometric switch; ~ **manométrique à membrane** *m* COMMANDE pressure-sensitive manometric switch; ~ **manuel** *m* ELECTR hand-operated switch; ~ **marche-arrêt à bascule** *m* PRODUCTION toggle on-off switch; ~ **à maximum de courant** *m* COMMANDE current overload switch, overload switch; ~ **à mercure** *m* COMMANDE mercury circuit breaker, ELECTROTEC mercury interrupter, mercury interruptor, mercury switch; ~ **à minimum** *m* ELECTROTEC minimum circuit breaker; ~ **à minuterie** *m* COMMANDE time switch, timer; ~ **de mise en court-**

circuit *m* ELECTROTEC shorting switch; ~ **de mise à la terre** *m* COMMANDE earthing switch (BrE), grounding switch (AmE), ELECTR earth switch (BrE), ground switch (AmE); ~ **modèle tumbler** *m* ELECTROTEC tumbler switch; ~ **monostable** *m* ELECTROTEC momentary action switch;

~ **n** ~ **non embrochable** *m* PRODUCTION non-plug-in switch;

~ **o** ~ **optique** *m* ELECTROTEC optical switch; ~ **optoélectronique** *m* ELECTROTEC optoelectronic switch;

~ **p** ~ **pas-à-pas** *m* AERONAUT *manche cyclique* beep switch; ~ **de pas général** *m* AERONAUT collective pitch switch; ~ **à passage de point mort** *m* ELECTROTEC snap-action switch; ~ **à pédale** *m* COMMANDE foot switch, pedal switch, treadle switch, INSTRUMENT foot switch; ~ **de plafond** *m* COMMANDE ceiling switch; ~ **à plusieurs contacts** *m* ELECTROTEC multiple contact switch; ~ **pneumatique** *m* COMMANDE pneumatic switch, ELECTR pneumatically-operated switch; ~ **à pompe de puits** *m* COMMANDE well-pump switch; ~ **de porte** *m* ELECTR gate switch; ~ **de position** *m* COMMANDE, ELECTROTEC, PRODUCTION *automatisme industriel* position switch; ~ **de position avec boîtier métallique** *m* PRODUCTION metal position switch; ~ **de position avec boîtier thermoplastique** *m* PRODUCTION *automatisme industriel* thermoplastic position switch; ~ **de position à base de codeur programmable** *m* PRODUCTION programmable encoder position switch; ~ **de position non embrochable** *m* PRODUCTION *automatisme industriel* non-plug-in position switch; ~ **de position pneumatique** *m* PRODUCTION *électricité* air-operated position switch; ~ **de position de sécurité** *m* PRODUCTION *automatisme industriel* extreme overtravel limit switch; ~ **de position de surcourse extrême** *m* PRODUCTION *automatisme industriel* extreme overtravel limit switch; ~ **de position temporisé** *m* PRODUCTION *automatisme industriel* time-delay position switch; ~ **de position à tête à tourelle** *m* PRODUCTION turret-head position switch; ~ **de position à tige à ressort** *m* PRODUCTION wobble stick position stick; ~ **à poussoir** *m* COMMANDE press switch, push switch, PRODUCTION push rod switch; ~ **à pression** *m* COMMANDE manometric switch; ~ **à pression d'air** *m* COMMANDE air pressure switch; ~ **à pression différentielle** *m* COMMANDE pressure differential switch; ~ **à pression d'huile** *m* COMMANDE oil pressure switch; ~ **principal** *m* COMMANDE main switch, master switch, ELECTR line breaker, main switch, master switch; ~ **profilé** *m* ELECTR *commutateur* rocker switch; ~ **de proximité** *m* ELECTROTEC, PRODUCTION proximity switch;

~ **r** ~ **à rappel automatique** *m* COMMANDE self-canceling switch (AmE), self-cancelling switch (BrE); ~ **de redondance** *m* PRODUCTION *électricité* backup switch; ~ **de relais** *m* ELECTR relay interruptor; ~ **à ressort de rappel** *m* ELECTR spring return switch; ~ **à ressorts** *m* ELECTR spring switch; ~ **à retard thermique** *m* COMMANDE thermal delay switch; ~ **de retour** *m* COMMANDE cutout relay; ~ **à retour de courant** *m* ELECTR discriminating circuit breaker, discriminating protective system, reverse current circuit breaking; ~ **rotatif** *m* COMMANDE, ELECTR, ELECTROTEC rotary switch; ~ **rotatif à gaufres** *m* COMMANDE wafer switch; ~ **à rupture brusque** *m* COMMANDE break-free switch, quick switch, ELECTROTEC quick break switch; ~ **à rupture lente** *m* COMMANDE, ELECTR slow-break switch;

~ s ~ **de secours** *m* COMMANDE backup switch, emergency switch; ~ **de sécurité** *m* ELECTR, ELECTROTEC safety switch, REFRIG safety cutout; ~ **de sélection de la vitesse de transmission de données** *m* PRODUCTION *automatisme industriel* data transmission rate switch; ~ **à semi-conducteur** *m* ELECTROTEC semiconductor switch; ~ **séparateur** *m* COMMANDE, ELECTR isolating switch, ELECTROTEC disconnecting switch; ~ **de service** *m* ELECTR operating switch; ~ **shunt** *m* ELECTR shunt switch; ~ **de surcharge** *m* COMMANDE overload cutout, ELECTR excess current switch, overcurrent switch;

~ t ~ **tachymétrique** *m* PRODUCTION speed switch; ~ **terminal** *m* ELECTR pilot switch; ~ **à tiges** *m* ELECTROTEC reed switch; ~ **à touche** *m* ELECTROTEC keyswitch; ~ **tripolaire** *m* ELECTROTEC three-pole switch; ~ **tumbler** *m* COMMANDE tumbler switch;

~ u ~ **unipolaire** *m* ELECTR single-pole switch, ELECTROTEC SPST switch, single-pole single-throw switch, single-pole switch; ~ **d'urgence** *m* COMMANDE emergency switch;

~ v ~ **va-et-vient** *m* COMMANDE push-pull switch, ELECTR push-pull switch, two-way switch; ~ **à vanne** *m* CH DE FER vane circuit breaker; ~ **à vide** *m* ELECTR vacuum switch

interruption *f* COMMANDE breakdown, failure, ELECTROTEC interruption, turn-off, INFORMAT interrupt, ORDINAT break, interrupt; ~ **d'entrée/sortie** *f* INFORMAT, ORDINAT input/output interrupt; ~ **externe** *f* INFORMAT, ORDINAT external interrupt; ~ **de fabrication** *f* COMMANDE shutdown; ~ **imprévisible** *f* TELECOM unforeseen interruption; ~ **de marche** *f* COMMANDE breakdown, failure; ~ **prioritaire** *f* INFORMAT, ORDINAT priority interrupt; ~ **de processus** *f* INFORMAT, ORDINAT process suspension; ~ **de programme** *f* COMMANDE program interrupt (AmE), programme interrupt (BrE); ~ **programmée** *f* INFORMAT, ORDINAT software interrupt; ~ **de service** *f* COMMANDE breakdown, failure; ~ **de transmission** *f* TELECOM transmission breakdown; ~ **vectorisée** *f* INFORMAT, ORDINAT vectored interrupt; ~ **de voyage** *f* AERONAUT stopover

intersecté *adj* GEOMETRIE intersecting

intersecter *vt* GEOLOGIE, GEOMETRIE intersect

intersection *f* CHIMIE, GEOMETRIE, INFORMAT, ORDINAT intersection; ~ **avec le plan de l'équateur** *f* ESPACE *astronomie, orbitographie* equatorial crossing

intersidéral *adj* ESPACE *astronomie* interstellar

interstellaire *adj* ASTRONOMIE, ESPACE *astronomie* interstellar

interstice *m* CONSTR, HYDROLOGIE interstice

interstitiel: ~ **dissocié** *m* METALL dumb-bell

interurbain: ~ **automatique** *m* TELECOM, direct distance dialing (AmE), DDD (AmE), subscriber trunk dialling (BrE), STD (BrE)

inter-usines *adj* PRODUCTION interplant

intervalle *m* ACOUSTIQUE interval, CH DE FER *voie* possession, CONS MECA gap, ELECTROTEC clearance, GEOLOGIE *entre deux niveaux repères* interval, INFORMAT, MECANIQUE, ORDINAT gap; ~ **d'air** *m* ELECTR *condensateur, transformateur*, ELECTROTEC, PETROLE air gap; ~ **augmenté** *m* ACOUSTIQUE augmented interval; ~ **de confiance** *m* MATH *statistique*, ORDINAT confidence interval; ~ **de cuisson** *m* CERAM VER firing range; ~ **de dégagement** *m* TRANSPORT clearance

period; ~ **diminué** *m* ACOUSTIQUE diminished interval; ~ **de distillation** *m* THERMODYN distillation range; ~ **d'ébullition** *m* PLAST CAOU *d'un solvant* boiling range; ~ **d'échantillon** *m* PETR sample period; ~ **entre impulsions** *m* ELECTRON pulse interval, pulse spacing; ~ **entre véhicules** *m* TRANSPORT time headway; ~ **fermé** *m* MATH closed interval; ~ **de fuite d'air** *m* TRANSPORT air gap; ~ **de garde** *m* TV preroll time; ~ **de luminosité** *m* PHOTO brightness range; ~ **de mesure** *m* METROLOGIE span; ~ **moyen entre véhicules** *m* TRANSPORT average time interval; ~ **musical** *m* PHYS ONDES *entre deux notes* musical interval; ~ **de ramollissement** *m* CERAM VER softening range; ~ **de recuisson** *m* CERAM VER annealing range; ~ **de séparation entre impulsions** *m* ELECTRON pulse separation; ~ **spectral** *m* PHYSIQUE spectral range; ~ **de suppression** *m* TV blanking interval; ~ **de suppression horizontale** *m* TV horizontal blanking interval; ~ **de suppression de trame** *m* TV vertical blanking interval; ~ **de suppression de trame après synchronisation** *m* TV postsync field-blanking interval; ~ **de suppression verticale** *m* TV vertical blanking interval; ~ **de temps** *m* ELECTRON time slice, ESPACE time slot, *communications* time slot, PRODUCTION time interval, *automatisme industriel* timed interval, TELECOM time slot; ~ **de temps entre véhicules** *m* TRANSPORT overall time interval; ~ **de temps net entre véhicules** *m* TRANSPORT net time interval; ~ **de tolérance** *m* QUALITE tolerance interval; ~ **de trame** *m* TV vertical interval; ~ **travaux** *m* CH DE FER possession; ~ **unitaire** *m* TELECOM UI, unit interval; ~ **vertical** *m* TV vertical interval

intervalliste *m* CINEMAT animator, in-betweener

intervention *f* CONS MECA action, INFORMAT, ORDINAT intervention; ~ **en cas de déversement** *f* POLLU MER oilspill response; ~ **ligne-réseau** *f* TELECOM TKO, trunk offer; ~ **non autorisée** *f* PRODUCTION unauthorized operation; ~ **sous-marine** *f* OCEANO diving operation

interverrouillage: ~ **de sécurité** *m* CONS MECA safety interlock

intonation *f* ACOUSTIQUE intonation

intoxication *f* POLLUTION poisoning; ~ **alimentaire** *f* AGRO ALIM food poisoning; ~ **directe** *f* POLLUTION direct poisoning

intraclaste *f* GEOLOGIE intraclast

intracratonique *adj* GEOLOGIE *bassin* intracratonic

intrados *m* AERONAUT lower surface, CONSTR soffit, *voûte* intrados, PHYSIQUE lower surface; ~ **de la pale** *m* AERONAUT blade lower surface

intragranulaire *adj* METALL intragranular

intramoléculaire *adj* CHIMIE intramolecular

intraplaque *adj* GEOLOGIE *cadre géotectonique* intraplate, within-plate

in-trente-six *m* IMPRIM thirty-sixmo

intrinsèque *adj* CHIMIE intrinsic

intrinsèquement: ~ **sûr** *adj* ELECTROTEC, SECURITE *appareillage et circuits électriques* intrinsically safe

introduction *f* PRODUCTION insertion; ~ **pratique** *f* PRODUCTION hands-on introduction

introduire *vt* ELECTRON input, PRODUCTION insert; ~ **un délai** *vt* ELECTRON delay

intrusif *adj* EN RENOUV intrusive

intrusion *f* GEOLOGIE, PETR intrusion; ~ **d'eau de mer** *f* DISTRI EAU sea water intrusion

intumescent *adj* PLAST CAOU *peinture* intumescent

inuline *f* AGRO ALIM, CHIMIE inulin

invariance: ~ **de jauge** *f* PHYSIQUE gage invariance (AmE), gauge invariance (BrE)

invariant[1] *adj* GEOMETRIE invariant

invariant[2] *m* GEOMETRIE invariant; ~ **adiabatique** *m* PHYSIQUE adiabatic invariant

invasion *f* HYDROLOGIE inrush; ~ **d'eau salée** *f* HYDROLOGIE saltwater infiltration, saltwater invasion

inventaire *m* EMBALLAGE inventory, PRODUCTION inventory, stock taking; ~ **cyclique** *m* PRODUCTION cycle counting; ~ **des émissions** *m* POLLUTION emission inventory; ~ **en radioactivité** *m* NUCLEAIRE activity inventory; ~ **des machines** *m* PRODUCTION schedule of machinery; ~ **permanent** *m* PRODUCTION perpetual inventory; ~ **tournant** *m* PRODUCTION cycle counting, cyclic inventory

inventeur *m* BREVETS inventor

invention *f* BREVETS invention; ~ **brevetable** *f* BREVETS patentable invention

inventorier *vi* PRODUCTION take stock of

inverse[1] *adj* CONS MECA, MATH inverse

inverse[2] *m* CONS MECA inverse, MATH inverse, reciprocal

inversé *adj* CINEMAT inverted

inverser *vt* ELECTRON reverse, INFORMAT, ORDINAT invert

inverseur *m* CONS MECA *tour* reversing gear, ELECTRON reverser, ELECTROTEC changeover switch, double-throw switch, inverter, switch, *polarité* reversing switch, INFORMAT inverter, negator, switch, NAUT changeover switch, ORDINAT inverter, PHYSIQUE inverter, TELECOM inverter; ~ **bipolaire** *m* ELECTROTEC DPDT switch; ~ **de courant** *m* ELECTR *commutateur* pole changer switch; ~ **démarrage/ventilation** *m* AERONAUT engine starter/crank switch; ~ **à galette** *m* ELECTROTEC wafer switch; ~ **à glissière** *m* ELECTROTEC slide switch; ~ **d'image** *m* IMPRIM straight-line image reverser; ~ **de jet** *m* TRANSPORT thrust reverser; ~ **à levier** *m* ELECTROTEC lever switch; ~ **de marche** *m* CINEMAT reversing gear; ~ **de marche électronique** *m* TRANSPORT electronic direction reverser; ~ **à mercure** *m* ELECTROTEC mercury switch; ~ **de phase** *m* ELECTROTEC phase reversal switch; ~ **à point milieu** *m* ELECTROTEC alternate action switch; ~ **de polarité** *m* ELECTR *commutateur* polarity reverser, ELECTROTEC polarity-reversing switch, TV reverse image switch; ~ **de pôles** *m* ELECTR current reverser; ~ **de poussée** *m* AERONAUT *véhicules*, TRANSPORT thrust reverser; ~ **de sélection réservoir** *m* AERONAUT fuel tank selector switch; ~ **statique** *m* ESPACE *véhicules* static inverter; ~ **unipolaire** *m* ELECTROTEC SPDT switch

inversible *m* CINEMAT reversal

inversion *f* CONS MECA reversing, *sens de la marche* reversing, *sens de rotation* reversing, ELECTRON inversion, reversing, IMPRIM reversal, PETR inversion, TRANSPORT *pas de l'hélice* reversal; ~ **atmosphérique** *f* POLLUTION atmospheric inversion; ~ **de batterie** *f* TELECOM line reversal, reversal; ~ **champ** *f* GEOPHYS geomagnetic reversal; ~ **de champ magnétique** *f* GEOLOGIE field reversal; ~ **de charge en ligne** *f* TELECOM line reversal, reversal; ~ **chiffres** *f* ORDINAT figures shift, TELECOM figure shift; ~ **de commande** *f* AERONAUT control reversal; ~ **de déroulement des pas du séquenceur** *f* PRODUCTION *automatisme industriel* reversing sequencer step operation; ~ **d'état continu** *f* PHYS RAYON *création laser* steady-state inversion; ~ **de fréquence** *f* TELECOM frequency inversion; ~

gauche-droite *f* TV flopover; ~ **latérale** *f* TV lateral inversion; ~ **de lettres** *f* INFORMAT, ORDINAT letters shift, TELECOM letter shift; ~ **magnétique** *f* GEOLOGIE magnetic reversal; ~ **de marche** *f* MECANIQUE, VEHICULES reverse; ~ **météorologique** *f* POLLUTION meteorological inversion; ~ **de micro-onde** *f* PHYS RAYON microwave inversion; ~ **de pas** *f* AERONAUT *hélice*, TRANSPORT pitch reversing; ~ **du pas de l'hélice** *f* TRANSPORT blade pitch reversal; ~ **périodique de polarité** *f* TV periodic polarity inversion; ~ **de phase** *f* CHARBON phase inversion, ELECTR *courant alternatif* phase reversal, ENREGISTR phase inversion, PETR phase inversion, phase reversal, PRODUCTION *automatisme industriel*, TV phase reversal; ~ **de polarité** *f* ELECTR *machine*, ELECTROTEC, ESPACE *véhicules* polarity reversal; ~ **de polarité vidéo** *f* TV video phase reversal; ~ **de population** *f* ELECTRON, PHYS RAYON *laser*, PHYSIQUE population inversion; ~ **de température** *f* POLLUTION, THERMODYN temperature inversion; ~ **des tonalités** *f* IMPRIM *photogravure* tonal inversion; ~ **de vitesse** *f* PETR velocity inversion; ~ **de Walden** *f* CHIMIE Walden inversion

invertase *f* AGRO ALIM invertase, saccharase, sucrase, CHIMIE invertase

investison *m* MINES boundary pillar

invitation: ~ **à continuer** *f* TELECOM GA, go ahead; ~ **à émettre** *f* INFORMAT polling, ORDINAT invitation to send, polling, TELECOM invitation to transmit, polling; ~ **à émettre de proche en proche** *f* INFORMAT hub polling; ~ **à recevoir** *f* TELECOM selecting; ~ **à transmettre** *f* INFORMAT invitation to send

invite *f* PRODUCTION *informatique* prompt

involution *f* GEOMETRIE, MATH involution

iodargyrite *f* MINERAUX iodargyrite, iodyrite

iodate *m* CHIMIE iodate

iode *m (I)* CHIMIE iodine *(I)*; ~ **radioactif** *m* CHIMIE radioiodine

iodeux *adj* CHIMIE *acide* iodous

iodhydrate *m* CHIMIE hydriodide

iodique *adj* CHIMIE iodic

iodo-aurate *m* CHIMIE iodoaurate

iodobenzène *m* CHIMIE iodobenzene

iodobromite *f* MINERAUX iodembolite, iodobromite

iodoforme *m* CHIMIE iodoform

iodohydrine *f* CHIMIE iodohydrin

iodomercurate *m* CHIMIE iodomercurate

iodométrie *f* CHIMIE iodometry

iodométrique *adj* CHIMIE iodometric

iodonium *m* CHIMIE iodonium

iodopsine *f* CHIMIE iodopsin

iodosé- *préf* CHIMIE iodoso-

iodosobenzène *m* CHIMIE iodosobenzene

iodure *m* CHIMIE iodide; ~ **d'acétyle** *m* CHIMIE acetyl iodide; ~ **d'argent** *m* PHOTO silver iodide; ~ **de méthyle** *m* CHIMIE methyl iodide; ~ **de méthylène** *m* CHIMIE methylene iodide

iodurer *vt* CHIMIE iodize

iolite *f* MINERAUX iolite

ion *m* CHIMIE hexad, ion, ELECTR, ELECTRON, GAZ, PETROLE, PHYS PART, PHYSIQUE ion; ~ **ablati** *m* NUCLEAIRE ablated ion; ~ **à haute énergie** *m* ELECTRON high-energy ion; ~ **hybride** *m* CHIMIE zwitter ion; ~ **négatif** *m* ELECTR, PHYS PART, PHYSIQUE negative ion; ~ **positif** *m* ELECTR, PHYS PART, PHYSIQUE positive ion

ion-gramme *m* METROLOGIE gram ion (AmE), gramme ion (BrE)

ionique *adj* HYDROLOGIE, PHYS RAYON ionic
ionisation *f* ASTRONOMIE, ELECTR *charge d'atomes*, ELEC-
TROTEC, GAZ, GEOPHYS, MATERIAUX, PHYS PART,
PHYSIQUE ionization; ~ **linéique** *f* PHYSIQUE linear
ionization; ~ **par choc** *f* PHYS RAYON collision ionization, impact ionization, PHYSIQUE ionization by
collision; ~ **par impact** *f* PHYSIQUE ionization by collision; ~ **par rayonnement** *f* GEOPHYS radiation
ionization; ~ **primaire** *f* PHYS RAYON primary ionization; ~ **secondaire** *f* PHYS RAYON secondary
ionization; ~ **superficielle par impact laser** *f* NU-
CLEAIRE laser impact surface ionization
ionisé *adj* GAZ, GEOPHYS, PHYSIQUE ionized
ioniser *vt* GEOPHYS, PHYSIQUE ionize
ionographique *adj* ORDINAT *imprimante* ionographic
ionone *f* CHIMIE ionone
ionosphère *f* ASTRONOMIE, GEOPHYS, PHYS ONDES,
PHYSIQUE ionosphere; ~ **supérieure** *f* TELECOM upper
ionosphere
ionotropie *f* CHIMIE ionotropy
ions: ~ **positifs d'anode** *m pl* ELECTROTEC anode rays
ipéca *m* AGRO ALIM ipecac, ipecacuanha
ipécacuana *m* AGRO ALIM ipecac, ipecacuanha
ipécacuanique *adj* CHIMIE ipecacuanic
Ir *(iridium)* CHIMIE Ir *(iridium)*
IR *abrév (infrarouge)* OPTIQUE, PHYS RAYON, PHYSIQUE
IR *(infrared)*
IRAS *abrév (satellite astronomique infrarouge)* ASTRON-
OMIE IRAS *(infrared astronomical satellite)*
iraser *m* ELECTRON iraser
iridique *adj* CHIMIE iridic
iridite *f* CHIMIE iridite
iridium *m (Ir)* CHIMIE iridium *(Ir)*
iridosmine *f* MINERAUX iridium osmine, iridosmine
iris *m* CINEMAT diaphragm, iris, PHYSIQUE iris
irisation *f* CERAM VER iridizing, POLLU MER iridescence
irisé *adj* CERAM VER *verre* iridescent
irone *f* CHIMIE irone
irradiateur: ~ **cylindrique** *m* NUCLEAIRE cylindrical irradiator; ~ **industriel** *m* NUCLEAIRE industrial
irradiator
irradiation *f* EN RENOUV irradiance, PHYS RAYON, POLLU-
TION irradiation; ~ **alimentaire** *f* AGRO ALIM food
irradiation, EMBALLAGE irradiation of food; ~ **d'une
cible** *f* PHYS PART target irradiation; ~ **en électrons** *f*
ESPACE electron irradiation; ~ **en protons** *f* ESPACE
proton irradiation; ~ **gamma au cobalt 60** *f* NU-
CLEAIRE cobalt 60 gamma irradiation; ~ **minimale** *f*
PHYS RAYON *échantillon* minimum irradiation; ~ **aux
rayons X** *f* NUCLEAIRE X-ray irradiation
irradié *adj* PHYSIQUE irradiated
irradier *vt* THERMODYN radiate
irrationnel *adj* MATH irrational
irrécupérable *adj* INFORMAT, ORDINAT irrecoverable
irréductible *adj* ORDINAT irreducible
irrégularité: ~ **parabolique** *f* TV parabolic shading
irrégulier *adj* CHIMIE *caractère* paratypical
irréparable *adj* CONS MECA beyond repair
irréprochable *adj* TEXTILE faultless
irrésorbable *adj* CHIMIE nonabsorbable
irrétrécissable *adj* PAPIER nonshrink, unshrinkable
irréversible *adj* CHIMIE nonreversible, MATERIAUX *cristallographie*, PHYSIQUE irreversible
irrigation *f* DISTRI EAU, HYDROLOGIE irrigation; ~ **directe**
f HYDROLOGIE direct irrigation; ~ **en sous-sol** *f* DISTRI
EAU subsurface irrigation; ~ **par aspersion** *f* DISTRI

EAU broad irrigation, HYDROLOGIE spray irrigation; ~
par infiltration *f* HYDROLOGIE flood irrigation; ~ **par
ruissellement** *f* DISTRI EAU irrigation by surface flooding, HYDROLOGIE broad irrigation, irrigation by
surface flooding; ~ **par submersion** *f* DISTRI EAU flood
irrigation; ~ **par surverse** *f* DISTRI EAU border irrigation; ~ **à la raie** *f* DISTRI EAU ditch irrigation
irriguer *vt* HYDROLOGIE irrigate
irritant[1] *adj* SECURITE irritant
irritant[2] *m* SECURITE irritant
irrotationnel *adj* PHYS FLUID, PHYSIQUE irrotational
irruption *f* DISTRI EAU *d'eau* irruption, HYDROLOGIE
d'eau, PHYS FLUID inrush
isallobare *f* METEO isallobar
isanomales *f pl* GEOLOGIE isanomals
isatine *f* CHIMIE isatin
isatique *adj* CHIMIE isatic
isatogénique *adj* CHIMIE isatogenic
isatropique *adj* CHIMIE isatropic
isentrope *adj* THERMODYN isentropic
isentropique *adj* PHYSIQUE, THERMODYN isentropic
iséthionate *m* CHIMIE isethionate
iséthionique *adj* CHIMIE isethionic
isinglass *m* AGRO ALIM isinglass
ISO *abrév* CONS MECA *(Organisation internationale de
normalisation)* ISO *(International Standards Organization)*, INFORMAT *(interconnexion de systèmes
ouverts)*, ORDINAT *(interconnexion de systèmes ouverts)* OSI *(open systems interconnection)*, TELECOM
(Organisation internationale de normalisation) ISO
(International Standards Organization), TELECOM
(interconnexion de systèmes ouverts) OSI *(open systems interconnection)*
isoallyle *m* CHIMIE isoallyl
isoamyle *m* CHIMIE isoamyl
isoamylique *adj* CHIMIE isoamylic
isoapiol *m* CHIMIE isoapiol, isoapiole
isobare *f* METEO, NAUT, PETR *atome*, PHYSIQUE *atome*
isobar
isobathe *f* GEOLOGIE, NAUT isobath, OCEANO depth
curve, isobath, PETR isobath
isobornéol *m* CHIMIE isoborneol
isobutane *m* CHIMIE, PETROLE isobutane
isobutène *m* CHIMIE isobutylene
isobutyle *m* CHIMIE isobutyl
isobutylène *m* CHIMIE isobutylene
isobutylique *adj* CHIMIE isobutylic
isobutyrique *adj* CHIMIE isobutyric
isochimène *f* METEO isocheim, isochime
isochore *f* GEOLOGIE *inclusion fluide* isochor, isochore,
METEO isocheim core, PHYSIQUE isochor, isochore
isochrone[1] *adj* INFORMAT, ORDINAT isochronous
isochrone[2] *f* GEOLOGIE isochronal surface, isochronal
time line, isochrone, isochrone diagram; ~ **roches
totales** *f* GEOLOGIE whole rock isochrone; ~ **sur minéraux** *f* GEOLOGIE mineral isochrone
isochronisme *m* PETR isochronism
isocinchoméronique *adj* CHIMIE isocinchomeronic
isoclinal[1] *adj* GEOPHYS isoclinal
isoclinal[2] *m* GEOPHYS isocline
isocline *f* PHYSIQUE isoclinal line
isocontrainte *f* AERONAUT isostress
isocraquage *m* PETR isocracking
isocrotonique *adj* CHIMIE isocrotonic
isocyanate *m* CHIMIE, MATERIAUX, PLAST CAOU isocyanate

isocyanique *adj* CHIMIE isocyanic
isocyanure *m* CHIMIE isocyanide
isocyclique *adj* CHIMIE isocyclic
isodulcite *f* CHIMIE isodulcital
isoélectrique *adj* CHIMIE isoelectric
isofaciès *m* GEOLOGIE isofacies
isofenchol *m* CHIMIE isofenchol
isoflavone *f* CHIMIE isoflavone
isoformat *m* CHIMIE isoformate
isogal *m* GEOLOGIE isogal
isogamme *f* GEOLOGIE isogam
isogone[1] *adj* GEOMETRIE isogonal
isogone[2] *f* GEOPHYS agonic line, isogonal
isograde *f* GEOLOGIE isograd
isogramme *m* METEO, PETR isogram
isogranulaire *adj* GEOLOGIE *minéraux* equigranular, homometric
isohaline *f* GEOLOGIE *des eaux* isohaline
isohèle *f* METEO isohel
isohypse *f* GEOLOGIE isohypse
isolable *adj* CHIMIE isolable
isolant[1] *adj* ELECTROTEC, MATERIAUX, REFRIG insulating
isolant[2] *m* AERONAUT liner, CHIMIE, CONSTR, ELECTR, ELECTROTEC, PHYSIQUE, PRODUCTION insulator, REFRIG insulant, TELECOM insulation, insulator; ~ **en matelas souple** *m* REFRIG blanket-type insulant; ~ **en panneau** *m* REFRIG board-type insulant; ~ **en poudre** *m* REFRIG powdered insulant; ~ **à faibles pertes** *m* ELECTROTEC low-loss insulator; ~ **réfléchissant** *m* REFRIG reflective insulant; ~ **thermique** *m* CONSTR insulating material
isolateur[1] *adj* MATERIAUX insulating
isolateur[2] *m* ELECTR, ELECTROTEC insulator, PHYSIQUE isolator, PRODUCTION insulator, TELECOM isolator; ~ **affaiblisseur** *m* OPTIQUE isolator; ~ **d'angle** *m* ELECTROTEC shackle insulator; ~ **d'arrêt** *m* ELECTROTEC guy insulator, terminal insulator; ~ **capot et tige** *m* ELECTROTEC cap and rod insulator; ~ **céramique** *m* ELECTR ceramic insulator, ELECTROTEC ceramic insulating material; ~ **à cloche** *m* ELECTROTEC bell-shaped insulator, petticoat insulator; ~ **double** *m* ELECTROTEC double insulator; ~ **élastique** *m* SECURITE *contre vibrations* resilient isolator; ~ **en champignon** *m* ELECTROTEC mushroom insulator; ~ **en guide d'ondes** *m* ELECTROTEC waveguide isolator; ~ **en porcelaine** *m* CERAM VER china insulator, porcelain insulator, ELECTR, ELECTROTEC porcelain insulator; ~ **en pot** *m* ELECTR pot insulator; ~ **d'entrée** *m* ELECTROTEC wall-entrance insulator; ~ **en verre** *m* CERAM VER, ELECTR *isolation* glass insulator; ~ **à ferrite** *m* ELECTROTEC ferrite isolator; ~ **à fût massif** *m* ELECTROTEC solid-core-type insulator; ~ **à l'huile** *m* ELECTROTEC oil insulator; ~ **de ligne** *m* ELECTROTEC line insulator; ~ **multiple** *m* PRODUCTION *système hydraulique* multi-gage isolator (AmE), multigauge isolator (BrE); ~ **optique** *m* TELECOM optical isolator; ~ **pour câble** *m* ELECTROTEC cable insulator; ~ **rigide** *m* ELECTROTEC pin insulator; ~ **de soutien** *m* ELECTROTEC post insulator; ~ **support** *m* ELECTROTEC pin insulator, post insulator; ~ **de suspension** *m* ELECTROTEC suspension insulator; ~ **tige** *m* ELECTR pin insulator; ~ **de vibration** *m* GEOPHYS vibration isolator
isolation *f* CERAM VER, CONSTR, ELECTR *de conducteur*, ELECTROTEC *conducteur* insulation, INFORMAT isolation, MATERIAUX, MECANIQUE *matériaux*, NAUT insulation, ORDINAT isolation, PHYSIQUE, PLAST CAOU

chaleur, électricité, REFRIG, SECURITE *contre les bruits, vibrations*, TELECOM insulation; ~ **acoustique** *f* ACOUSTIQUE acoustic isolation, sound isolation; ~ **à l'air** *f* ELECTR air insulation; ~ **antibruit** *f* VEHICULES *carrosserie* sound insulation; ~ **de câble** *f* ELECTR, ELECTROTEC cable insulation; ~ **au caoutchouc** *f* REVETEMENT rubber insulation; ~ **contre la chaleur et le froid** *f* SECURITE insulation against heat and cold; ~ **défectueuse** *f* ELECTR faulty insulation; ~ **double** *f* ELECTROTEC double insulation; ~ **en bas de page** *f* IMPRIM *composition, mise en page* widow; ~ **en coton** *f* ELECTR cotton insulation; ~ **en porcelaine** *f* ELECTROTEC porcelain insulation; ~ **d'enroulement** *f* ELECTR *bobine* winding insulation; ~ **entre bobines** *f* ELECTR *transformateur* coil-to-coil insulation; ~ **entre couches** *f* ELECTR layer insulation; ~ **entre phases** *f* ELECTR phase insulation; ~ **entre spires** *f* ELECTR *bobine* interturn insulation; ~ **externe** *f* ELECTR external insulation, outer insulation; ~ **extrudée** *f* ELECTR *conducteur d'un câble* extruded insulation; ~ **fibreuse** *f* CHAUFFAGE fibrous insulation; ~ **à haute température** *f* ELECTR high-temperature insulation; ~ **à haute tension** *f* ELECTR high-voltage insulation; ~ **d'intérieur** *f* ELECTR indoor insulation; ~ **mécanique** *f* SECURITE *contre les vibrations* mechanical isolation; ~ **minérale** *f* ELECTR *conducteur d'un câble* mineral insulation; ~ **optique** *f* ELECTROTEC optical isolation; ~ **opto-électrique** *f* PRODUCTION *électricité* electrical-optical isolation; ~ **au papier** *f* ELECTR paper insulation; ~ **au papier préimprégné** *f* ELECTR *conducteur d'un câble* impregnated paper insulation; ~ **par air** *f* ELECTROTEC air insulation; ~ **par lame d'air** *f* CHAUFFAGE airspace insulation; ~ **par panneau sandwich** *f* REFRIG sandwich panel insulation; ~ **par panneau stratifié isolant** *f* REFRIG sandwich panel insulation; ~ **phonique** *f* NAUT sound insulation; ~ **primaire** *f* MATERIAUX primary insulation; ~ **PVC** *f* ELECTR PVC insulation; ~ **réflective** *f* CHAUFFAGE reflective insulation; ~ **rubanée** *f* ELECTR *conducteur d'un câble* lapped insulation; ~ **thermique** *f* CH DE FER, CHAUFFAGE, CONSTR, MATERIAUX thermal insulation, NAUT insulation against heat and cold, THERMODYN *tuyau, chaudière* lagging; ~ **thermique en bois** *f* INST HYDR wood lagging
isolé *adj* CONSTR, ELECTROTEC, REFRIG, SECURITE *outil* insulated; ~ **au caoutchouc** *adj* REVETEMENT rubber-insulated; ~ **par le vide** *adj* ELECTROTEC vacuum-insulated
isolement *m* CONSTR insulation, DISTRI EAU shutting-off, ELECTR *conducteur*, ELECTROTEC *conducteur* insulation, ESPACE *communications* isolation, PRODUCTION isolating, isolation, TELECOM insulation; ~ **acoustique** *m* ACOUSTIQUE sound insulation; ~ **acoustique brut** *m* ACOUSTIQUE level difference; ~ **acoustique normalisé** *m* ACOUSTIQUE standardized sound insulation; ~ **calorifuge** *m* THERMODYN heat insulation, thermal insulation; ~ **diélectrique** *m* ELECTROTEC dielectric isolation; ~ **électrique** *m* ELECTROTEC electrical insulation; ~ **électromagnétique** *m* ELECTROTEC electromagnetic isolation; ~ **en courant continu** *m* ELECTROTEC DC isolation; ~ **galvanique** *m* ELECTROTEC galvanic isolation; ~ **optique** *m* ELECTROTEC optical isolation; ~ **par transformateur** *m* ELECTROTEC transformer isolation; ~ **par le vide** *m* ELECTROTEC vacuum insulation; ~ **sonore** *m* ENREGISTR sound insulation; ~ **sous vide** *m* CONS MECA vacuum insulation; ~ **thermique** *m* CHAUFFAGE

thermal insulation

isoler *vt* CHIMIE isolate, CONS MECA cutout, CONSTR fence in, insulate, DISTRI EAU *nappe aquifère* shut off, ELECTR insulate, ELECTROTEC isolate, MATERIAUX, PHYSIQUE insulate, PRODUCTION de-energize, SECURITE isolate; ~ **les sources d'alimentation** *vt* PRODUCTION lock out power sources

isoleucine *f* CHIMIE isoleucine

isologue[1] *adj* CHIMIE *corps* isologous

isologue[2] *m* CHIMIE isolog (AmE), isologue (BrE)

isomère[1] *adj* MATERIAUX isomeric

isomère[2] *m* CHIMIE isomeride, MATERIAUX, PETROLE, PHYS RAYON isomer; ~ **géométrique** *m* CHIMIE geometric isomer; ~ **optique** *m* CHIMIE optical isomer

isomérie *f* CHIMIE, PHYSIQUE isomerism; ~ **nucléaire** *f* PHYSIQUE nuclear isomerism; ~ **structurelle** *f* CHIMIE structural isomerism

isomérisation *f* CHIMIE, PETROLE isomerization

isomérisme *m* PHYSIQUE isomerism

isomorphe *adj* GEOLOGIE isomorphous

isomorphisme *m* CHIMIE, CRISTALL isomorphism

isonicotinique *adj* CHIMIE isonicotinic

isonitrile *m* CHIMIE isonitrile

isooctane *m* CHIMIE isooctane

isopaque *m* GEOLOGIE isopach, PETROLE *levé géophysique* isopach map

isoparaffines *f pl* CHIMIE isoparaffins

isopellétiérine *f* CHIMIE isopelletierine

isopentane *m* CHIMIE isopentane

isophorone: ~ **diamine** *f* PLAST CAOU isophorone diamine

isoplèthe *f* CHIMIE, GEOLOGIE *courbe d'égale composition* isopleth

isopolyacide *m* CHIMIE isopoly acid

isoprène *m* CHIMIE isoprene

isoprénoïde *m* CHIMIE isoprenoid

isopropanol *m* CHIMIE isopropanol, LESSIVES IPA, isopropanol, isopropyl acid

isopropényle *m* CHIMIE isopropenyl

isopropylbenzène *m* CHIMIE isopropylbenzene

isopropylcarbinol *m* CHIMIE isopropylcarbinol

isopropyle *m* CHIMIE isopropyl

isopropylique *adj* CHIMIE isopropyl

isoquinoléine *f* CHIMIE isoquinoline

isosiste *adj* GEOPHYS isoseismal

isospin *m* PHYSIQUE isobaric spin, isotopic spin, isospin

isostasie *f* EN RENOUV isostacy, isostasy, GEOLOGIE isostacy, isostasy

isostère *adj* CHIMIE isosteric

isostérie *f* CHIMIE isosterism

isostérique *adj* CHIMIE isosteric

isosurpression *f* AERONAUT constant differential pressure

isotactique *adj* CHIMIE *polymère* isotactic

isotherme[1] *adj* MECANIQUE *thermodynamique*, PHYSIQUE isothermal, REFRIG insulated

isotherme[2] *f* AERONAUT, GEOLOGIE, METEO, NAUT, PETR, PHYSIQUE isotherm; ~ **d'adsorption** *f* NUCLEAIRE adsorption isotherm; ~ **critique** *f* CHIMIE critical isotherm; ~ **d'échange** *f* PHYS RAYON ion exchange isotherm

isotone *m* PHYSIQUE isotone

isotope *m* CHIMIE, GEOLOGIE, NUCLEAIRE, PHYS PART, PHYSIQUE isotope; ~ **fertile** *m* PHYSIQUE fertile isotope; ~ **fille** *m* GEOLOGIE daughter isotope; ~ **fissile** *m* PHYSIQUE fissile isotope; ~ **industriel** *m* NUCLEAIRE industrial isotope; ~ **radioactif** *m* CHIMIE radioisotope, PHYS PART, PHYS RAYON, PHYSIQUE radioactive isotope; ~ **radiogénique** *m* GEOLOGIE daughter isotope, radiogenic isotope; ~ **stable** *m* PHYSIQUE stable isotope

isotopie *f* CHIMIE isotopy

isotrope *adj* CRISTALL, ESPACE *communications*, GEOLOGIE *du milieu*, OPTIQUE *onde électromagnétique*, TELECOM isotropic

isotropie *f* CRISTALL, GEOLOGIE isotropy

isotropique *adj* ASTRONOMIE isotropic

isovalérone *m* CHIMIE isovalerone

isovanilline *f* CHIMIE isovanilline

isoxazole *m* CHIMIE isoxazole

issue *f* PRODUCTION outlet; ~ **de secours** *f* AERONAUT emergency exit

issues *f pl* AGRO ALIM offal; ~ **de blé** *f pl* AGRO ALIM middlings

isthme *m* NAUT isthmus

itaconique *adj* CHIMIE, *anhydride, acide* itaconic

itague *f* NAUT *bastaque* runner, *ris* reefing pennant

italiciser *vt* IMPRIM italicize

italique *adj* IMPRIM italic

italiques *m pl* IMPRIM italics, slanted letters

italiser *vti* IMPRIM *police de caractères* tilt

itératif *adj* INFORMAT, ORDINAT iterative

itération *f* INFORMAT, ORDINAT iteration

itérer *vt* INFORMAT, ORDINAT iterate

itinéraire *m* AERONAUT, CH DE FER route, NAUT itinerary, route, ORDINAT, TRANSPORT route; ~ **de dégagement** *m* TRANSPORT bypass line; ~ **enclenché à l'approche** *m* CH DE FER approach-locked route

J

J *abrév (joule)* AGRO ALIM, ELECTR, MECANIQUE, METROLOGIE, PHYSIQUE, THERMODYN J *(joule)*

jable *m* CERAM VER insweep

jacinthe *f* MINERAUX jacinth

jack *m* CINEMAT jack, jack plug, ELECTR *raccordement*, ELECTROTEC, ENREGISTR, TELECOM jack; **~ à ressort** *m* ELECTROTEC spring jack

jacket *m* PETROLE jacket

jade: **~ de Saussure** *m* PETR saussurite

jadéite *f* MINERAUX jadeite

jaillir *vi* ELECTR *arc* jump

jaillissement *m* HYDROLOGIE spouting, spurting out; **~ d'étincelles** *m* ELECTROTEC sparking

jais *m* GEOLOGIE *variété de lignite*, MINERAUX jet

jalapine *f* CHIMIE jalapin

jalapique *adj* CHIMIE *acide* jalapic

jalon *m* CONSTR picket, range pole, ranging pole, ranging rod, stake

jalon-mire *m* CONSTR target levelling rod, target levelling-staff

jalonnement *m* CONSTR staking; **~ amont** *m* PRODUCTION backward scheduling; **~ aval** *m* PRODUCTION forward scheduling; **~ au plus tard** *m* PRODUCTION backward scheduling; **~ au plus tôt** *m* PRODUCTION forward scheduling

jalonner *vt* PRODUCTION schedule

jalousie *f (cf louvre)* CERAM VER jalousie, louver (AmE), louvre (BrE), MECANIQUE louver (AmE), louvre (BrE)

jalpaïte *f* MINERAUX jalpaite

jambage *m* CONSTR *baie de porte* jamb, jamb post, *baie de fenêtre* jamb, jamb post, *cheminée* jamb, IMPRIM descender, PRODUCTION *marteau-pilon* standard; **~ de brûleur** *m* CERAM VER jamb; **~ en pierre** *m* CONSTR jamb stone

jambe *f* CERAM VER stem, CHARBON entry pillar, entry stump, CONS MECA leg; **~ d'atterrisseur** *f* AERONAUT landing gear leg; **~ creuse** *f* CERAM VER straw stem; **~ de force** *f* AUTO, CONSTR strut, VEHICULES *suspension* MacPherson strut; **~ rapportée** *f* CERAM VER stuck shank; **~ de suspension** *f* AUTO, VEHICULES MacPherson strut; **~ du train avant** *f* AERONAUT nose gear leg

jambette *f* CONSTR purlin post

jamesonite *f* MINERAUX feather ore, jamesonite

jante *f* VEHICULES *roue* rim; **~ à base creuse** *f* AUTO, VEHICULES *roue* drop center rim (AmE), drop centre rim (BrE)

jantille *f* CONS MECA *ventilateur, roue hydraulique* paddle, paddle board, DISTRI EAU float, floatboard

japanique *adj* CHIMIE *acide* japanic

jargon *m* MINERAUX jargon, jargoon

jarosite *f* MINERAUX jarosite

jarret *m* CONS MECA *courbe* knee

jarretière *f* ELECTR *raccordement* jump lead, jumper, TELECOM jumper, VEHICULES *système électrique* jump lead, jumper; **~ de masse** *f* PRODUCTION bonding strip

jas: **~ d'ancre** *m* NAUT anchor stock

jaspage *m* PAPIER marbling; **~ des tranches** *m* IMPRIM marbling

jaspe *m* GEOLOGIE *roche* jasper, jasperite, MINERAUX jasper; **~ porcelaine** *m* CERAM VER porcelain jasper; **~ sanguin** *m* MINERAUX bloodstone

jasper *vt* PAPIER marble

jaspilite *f* GEOLOGIE jaspilite

jauge *f* EQUIP LAB, MECANIQUE, METROLOGIE gage (AmE), gauge (BrE), NAUT tonnage, PAPIER, PRODUCTION, TEXTILE gage (AmE), gauge (BrE); **~ d'alignement pour vilebrequin** *f* CONS MECA crankshaft alignment gage (AmE), crankshaft alignment gauge (BrE); **~ d'allongement** *f* PHYSIQUE, PLAST CAOU *essai* strain gage (AmE), strain gauge (BrE); **~ à billes** *f* METROLOGIE ball gage (AmE), ball gauge (BrE); **~ de broyage Hegman** *f* PLAST CAOU *instrument* Hegman fineness-of-grind gage (AmE), Hegman fineness-of-grind gauge (BrE); **~ brute** *f* NAUT gross register, gross tonnage, PETROLE *transport maritime* gross tonnage; **~ de carburant** *f* AUTO fuel gage (AmE), fuel gauge (BrE); **~ de contrainte** *f* EQUIP LAB *instrument* strain gage (AmE), strain gauge (BrE), MECANIQUE extensometer, strain gage (AmE), strain gauge (BrE), PLAST CAOU strain gage (AmE), strain gauge (BrE); **~ de Coulomb** *f* PHYSIQUE Coulomb gage (AmE), Coulomb gauge (BrE); **~ d'écrasement** *f* MECANIQUE crusher gage (AmE), crusher gauge (BrE); **~ d'enfoncement** *f* AERONAUT bottoming indicator; **~ d'épaisseur** *f* CONS MECA, EQUIP LAB thickness gage (AmE), thickness gauge (BrE), IMPRIM *impression* feeler, MECANIQUE thickness gage (AmE), thickness gauge (BrE), METROLOGIE, NUCLEAIRE, VEHICULES feeler gage (AmE), feeler gauge (BrE); **~ d'épaisseur Elcometer** *f* PLAST CAOU *instrument* Elcometer thickness gage (AmE), Elcometer thickness gauge (BrE); **~ d'ergol** *f* ESPACE *propulsion* fuel measuring unit; **~ d'essence** *f* AUTO fuel gage (AmE), fuel gauge (BrE); **~ étalon** *f* CONS MECA standard gage (AmE), standard gauge (BrE); **~ d'extension** *f* ELECTROTEC strain gage (AmE), strain gauge (BrE); **~ extensométrique** *f* PHYSIQUE strain gage (AmE), strain gauge (BrE); **~ de filetage** *f* CONS MECA thread pitch gage (AmE), thread pitch gauge (BrE); **~ fine** *f* TEXTILE fine gage (AmE), fine gauge (BrE); **~ d'huile** *f* AUTO dipstick, oil dipstick, oil level stick, VEHICULES *lubrification* dipstick; **~ à ionisation** *f* PHYSIQUE ionization gage (AmE), ionization gauge (BrE); **~ de Lorentz** *f* PHYSIQUE Lorentz gage (AmE), Lorentz gauge (BrE); **~ magnétique d'épaisseur** *f* EQUIP LAB *peinture, revêtements* magnetic thickness gage (AmE), magnetic thickness gauge (BrE); **~ nette** *f* NAUT net register, PETROLE *navigation* net, net tonnage; **~ de pas** *f* CONS MECA screw pitch gage (AmE), screw pitch gauge (BrE); **~ passe** *f* CONS MECA go gage (AmE), go gauge (BrE); **~ passe pas** *f* CONS MECA no-go gage (AmE), no-go gauge (BrE); **~ de Pirani** *f* PHYSIQUE Pirani gage (AmE), Pirani gauge (BrE); **~ pour câble** *f* ELECTROTEC cable gage (AmE), cable gauge (BrE); **~ pour filetage** *f* METROLOGIE screw thread gage (AmE), screw thread gauge (BrE); **~ pour fil métallique** *f*

METROLOGIE wire gage (AmE), wire gauge (BrE); ~ pour mèche f CONS MECA drill gage (AmE), drill gauge (BrE); ~ pour tôle f CONS MECA plate gage (AmE), plate gauge (BrE), sheet gage (AmE), sheet gauge (BrE), sheet iron gage (AmE), sheet iron gauge (BrE); ~ pour tôle fine f CONS MECA sheet gage (AmE), sheet gauge (BrE), sheet iron gage (AmE), sheet iron gauge (BrE); ~ pour tôle forte f CONS MECA plate gage (AmE), plate gauge (BrE); ~ de pression f CH DE FER, CONSTR, REFRIG pressure gage (AmE), pressure gauge (BrE); ~ de profondeur f MECANIQUE outillage depth gage (AmE), depth gauge (BrE); ~ de profondeur de sculpture f VEHICULES pneu tread depth gage (AmE), tread depth gauge (BrE); ~ à réservoir f METROLOGIE receiver gage (AmE), receiver gauge (BrE); ~ thermique f REFRIG thermal conductivity vacuum gage (AmE), thermal conductivity vacuum gauge (BrE); ~ à vide f PHYSIQUE, PRODUCTION vacuum gage (AmE), vacuum gauge (BrE), REFRIG ionization vacuum gage (AmE), ionization vacuum gauge (BrE), vacuum gage (AmE), vacuum gauge (BrE); ~ de vide Pirani f EQUIP LAB instrument Pirani vacuum gage (AmE), Pirani vacuum gauge (BrE)

jaugeage m METROLOGIE gaging (AmE), gauging (BrE), NUCLEAIRE calibration, PETROLE gaging (AmE), gauging (BrE); ~ en déversoir m INST HYDR notch gaging (AmE), notch gauging (BrE); ~ à rétrodiffusion m NUCLEAIRE densité ou épaisseur backscatter gage (AmE), backscatter gauge (BrE)

jauger vt DISTRI EAU débit d'une pompe PRODUCTION tonneau gage (AmE), gauge (BrE)

jaugeur: ~ à canne m CONS MECA dipstick; ~ d'huile m CONS MECA oil gage (AmE), oil gauge (BrE); ~ de réservoir de carburant m AERONAUT fuel gage transmitter (AmE), fuel gauge transmitter (BrE)

jaumière f NAUT rudder trunk

jaune[1] adj CHIMIE xanthous

jaune:[2] ~ de métanile m CHIMIE metanil

jaunir vt TEXTILE yellow

jaunissement m PAPIER yellowing

javellisation f CHIMIE javellization

jayet m MINERAUX jet

jenkinsite f MINERAUX jenkinsite

jéréméiéwite f MINERAUX jeremejevite

jeroboam m CERAM VER jeroboam

jerrican m MILITAIRE, TRANSPORT jerry can

jervine f CHIMIE jervine

jet m ASTRONOMIE jet, CONS MECA nozzle, DISTRI EAU jet, pompe spout, ESPACE propulsion jet, HYDROLOGIE stream, MECANIQUE outillage drift, METALL jet, MINES lift, stage, NUCLEAIRE jet, PAPIER squirt, PETROLE trépan, PHYS FLUID, PHYSIQUE jet, PRODUCTION casting, gate, header, jet, pouring, runner, sprue, teeming; ~ d'abrasif m CONSTR grit blasting; ~ d'air m MATERIAUX air blast; ~ d'air chaud m TEXTILE hot air stream; ~ de bordure m PAPIER edge cutter; ~ de coulée m CONS MECA knuckle, PRODUCTION cast gate, down runner, pouring hole, sprue hole, funnel, gate, header, jet, pouring gate, runner, running gate; ~ d'eau m CONSTR wash, weathering, DISTRI EAU water jet; ~ d'eau chaude m GEOPHYS hot water jet; ~ à éventail m DISTRI EAU spreader jet; ~ d'extraction m CONS MECA drift; ~ de faible énergie transversal m PHYS RAYON low-energy transverse jet; ~ de gaz m PRODUCTION gas jet; ~ à la mer m OCEANO jetsam, jettison; ~ des moules m PRODUCTION running molds (AmE), running moulds

(BrE); ~ des réacteurs m AERONAUT jet wash; ~ de rive m OCEANO swash, uprush; ~ de sable m CONSTR sandblasting, PRODUCTION sand jet, sandblast; ~ sous pression m CHAUFFAGE pressure jet; ~ de vapeur m GEOPHYS, INST HYDR steam jet

JET:[1] abrév (tore européen conjoint) NUCLEAIRE, PHYS RAYON recherche de fusion JET (Joint European Torus)

JET:[2] ~ Tokamac m NUCLEAIRE, PHYS RAYON JET Tokamac

jetable adj MECANIQUE expendable

jetée f AERONAUT finger, CONSTR jetty, NAUT jetty, pier

jeter[1] vt PRODUCTION cast, teem, run, THERMODYN give off; ~ à la mer vt NAUT jettison; ~ par-dessus bord vt NAUT jettison

jeter:[2] ~ l'ancre vi NAUT cast anchor; ~ les fondations vi CONSTR maison lay the foundations; ~ un pont sur une rivière vi CONSTR throw a bridge over a river

jeton m INFORMAT, ORDINAT token

jets: ~ d'air m pl MATERIAUX métallurgie air blasting; ~ et débris provenant de la coulée m pl PRODUCTION returns

jet-stream m AERONAUT jet stream

jette-feu m PRODUCTION drop grate, dump grate

jeu m CINEMAT mécanique backlash, play, CONS MECA backlash, kit, play, lash, slack, working, cylindres battery, d'écart gap, engrenages clearance, piston stroke, DISTRI EAU, INFORMAT set, INST HYDR clearance, clearance space, MATERIAUX clearance, MECANIQUE backlash, clearance, play, MINES lift, NUCLEAIRE end float, kit, ORDINAT set, PRODUCTION dégagement, système hydraulique clearance; ~ axial m CONS MECA end play, MECANIQUE axial clearance, end play; ~ de barres m ELECTR connexion busbar, raccordement busbar system; ~ de barres de distribution m ELECTR distribution bus; ~ du bloc de balayage m TV deflection yoke pullback; ~ de boudins m CH DE FER flange-to-rail clearance; ~ de caméra m CINEMAT camera movement; ~ de caractères m IMPRIM type family, INFORMAT character set; ~ de cartes m INFORMAT card deck, deck; ~ combustible-gaine m NUCLEAIRE clad fuel clearance; ~ de connexions puissance m PRODUCTION automatisme industriel power wiring kit; ~ de contacts m ELECTR relais set of contacts, VEHICULES allumage contact set; ~ de cylindres m CONS MECA train of rolls, PRODUCTION set of rolls; ~ dans la direction m VEHICULES steering play; ~ de denture m ESPACE backlash; ~ de données m GAZ data set; ~ d'éléments de montage m PRODUCTION mounting hardware set; ~ d'engrènement m VEHICULES transmission backlash; ~ d'entraînement m ESPACE communications backlash; ~ entre les dents m CONS MECA side clearance; ~ de filtres m CINEMAT filter kit, PHOTO filter set; ~ de filtres à octave m ENREGISTR octave filter set; ~ fixe m MINES fixed lift, fixed set; ~ au fond des dents m CONS MECA top and bottom clearance; ~ foulant m MINES plunger lift, plunger set; ~ d'instructions m INFORMAT, ORDINAT, PRODUCTION automatisme industriel instruction set; ~ interne radial m CONS MECA roulements radial internal clearance; ~ à l'inversion du mouvement m CONS MECA backlash; ~ latéral m CONS MECA side clearance, side lash, side play; ~ de lumière m CINEMAT lighting effect; ~ de masques m ELECTRON mask set; ~ mécanique m IMPRIM backlash; ~ de microprogrammes m PRODUCTION firmware chip set; ~ de modification m

PRODUCTION modification kit; ~ **de modules** m ELEC-TRON module set; ~ **d'objectifs** m PHOTO set of lenses; ~ **partiel de caractères** m INFORMAT character subset; ~ **de pièces de rechange** m PRODUCTION set of spare parts; ~ **du piston** m AUTO piston clearance, CONS MECA piston stroke, CONSTR length of piston stroke, VEHICULES *moteur* piston clearance; ~ **de poids** m EQUIP LAB *analyse* set of weights; ~ **posé** m MINES fixed lift, fixed set; ~ **de puces** m ELECTRON chip set; ~ **de réglage des culbuteurs** m AUTO camshaft clearance; ~ **de relais** m TELECOM relay set; ~ **de revendications** m BREVETS set of claims; ~ **de roues** m CH DE FER *véhicules* wheel clearance; ~ **de roues à fileter** m CONS MECA set of change wheels; ~ **des soupapes** m AUTO, CONS MECA valve clearance; ~ **de symboles** m INFORMAT symbol set; ~ **de tamis** m GENIE CHIM sieve set; ~ **de tolérance** m CONS MECA clearance; ~ **de transmission d'un engrenage** m CONS MECA backlash; ~ **universel** m INFORMAT universal set; ~ **universel des caractères** m INFORMAT universal character set; ~ **d'usure** m CONS MECA play; ~ **de vannes** m GAZ set of valves; ~ **de la voie** m CH DE FER gage clearance (AmE), gauge clearance (BrE); ~ **volant** m MINES suspended lift, suspended set

jeune *adj* CERAM VER shallow

jeux: ~ **de montage** m *pl* CONS MECA fits and clearances; ~ **d'orgues** m *pl* CERAM VER organ stop

jig m MINES jig; ~ **à air** m CONS MECA pneumatic jig; ~ **de montage** m NAUT erection jig; ~ **pneumatique** m CHARBON air jig, pneumatic jig, CONS MECA pneumatic jig

jiningite f NUCLEAIRE jiningite

johannite f MINERAUX, NUCLEAIRE Johannite

joindre *vt* CONSTR join, PRODUCTION connect, TELECOM reach, *abonné* obtain; ~ **avec de la colle** *vt* GENIE CHIM agglutinate; ~ **par des chevilles** *vt* PRODUCTION dowel

joint m CONS MECA coupling, CONSTR connection, *charnière* joint, IMPRIM *rotatif* union, METALL boundary, NUCLEAIRE bond, joint, *d'une boîte à étoupe* packing seal, *grain* grain boundary, PETR joint, PRODUCTION *moule* parting, TELECOM jointing; ~ **d'about** m PRODUCTION butt joint; ~ **d'about sans espace** m PRODUCTION closed butt joint; ~ **d'amenée de vapeur** m PAPIER steam joint; ~ **anglais** m CONSTR bridle joint; ~ **annulaire** m VEHICULES sealing ring; ~ **arête abattue** m CERAM VER arrissed edge; ~ **arête abattue et arête arrondie** m CERAM VER half round edge; ~ **articulé** m CONS MECA elbow joint; ~ **d'assise** m CONSTR bedding mortar; ~ **à baïonnette** m ELECTR *jonction* bayonet joint; ~ **biseauté** m CONS MECA bevel joint; ~ **à boudin** m CONS MECA flange joint; ~ **de bougie** m AUTO spark plug gasket; ~ **de bout** m CONSTR heading joint; ~ **bout à bout** m PRODUCTION butt joint; ~ **à bride** m CONS MECA flange joint; ~ **brisé** m CONS MECA universal joint, CONSTR break joint; ~ **calfaté** m NAUT caulked joint; ~ **à calotte sphérique** m CONS MECA globe joint, socket joint, PRODUCTION cup joint, cup-and-ball joint; ~ **de Cardan** m CONS MECA, MECANIQUE cardan joint; ~ **carré** m CONSTR square joint; ~ **de carter** m AUTO oil pan gasket; ~ **de chambre** m CONS MECA gasket; ~ **à chanfrein** m CONSTR chamfered joint; ~ **chevauché** m CONSTR overlap joint; ~ **à chute libre** m MINES free fall; ~ **circonférentiel** m MECANIQUE *soudage* girth weld; ~ **cloison** m CONS MECA *raccord pour tubes* bulkhead coupling; ~ **collé** m EMBALLAGE glue joint; ~ **collé à froid** m THERMODYN cold bond; ~ **du conducteur électrique** m NUCLEAIRE *étanchéité* electrical conductor seal; ~ **de construction** m CONSTR construc-

tion joint; ~ **de contraction** m CONSTR contraction joint; ~ **coulissant** m AUTO slip joint; ~ **à croisillon** m MECANIQUE universal joint; ~ **de culasse** m AUTO cylinder head gasket, REFRIG cylinder gasket, VEHICULES *moteur* cylinder head gasket, head gasket; ~ **de dilatation** m CONS MECA slip joint, CONSTR, INST HYDR expansion joint; ~ **de dilatation thermique** m THERMODYN thermal expansion joint; ~ **à dos d'âne** m CERAM VER full round edge; ~ **douci** m CERAM VER smoothed edge; ~ **à emboîtement** m CONSTR faucet joint, spigot joint, spigot-and-faucet joint, spigot-and-faucet joint pipes; ~ **en about** m CONSTR abutting joint; ~ **en biseau** m CONSTR bevel joint; ~ **en bout** m PRODUCTION butt seal; ~ **en fibre** m MECANIQUE fiber gasket (AmE), fibre gasket (BrE); ~ **en labyrinthe** m EMBALLAGE, NUCLEAIRE labyrinth seal; ~ **étanche** m MECANIQUE seal, NAUT gasket, seal, PRODUCTION close joint; ~ **étanche à l'huile** m MECANIQUE oil seal; ~ **d'étanchéité** m AUTO gasket, CONS MECA gasket, *application dynamique* seal, ELECTR *protection* seal, MECANIQUE gasket, NUCLEAIRE seal assembly, seal unit, PRODUCTION body gasket, gasket, VEHICULES gasket; ~ **d'étanchéité en caoutchouc** m VEHICULES *moteur* rubber weather seal; ~ **d'étanchéité en élastomère** m PRODUCTION elastomer seal; ~ **d'étanchéité en Viton** m PRODUCTION seal of Viton; ~ **d'étanchéité gonflable** m NUCLEAIRE inflatable seal; ~ **d'étanchéité pour arbres à mouvement alternatif** m CONS MECA reciprocating shaft seal; ~ **d'étanchéité pour arbres tournants** m CONS MECA rotary shaft seal; ~ **d'étanchéité de soupape** m AUTO valve shaft seal; ~ **d'étanchéité de vitre** m VEHICULES *carrosserie* window seal; ~ **étanche sous pression** m INST HYDR pressure seal; ~ **feutre et mousse** m CONSTR felt and foam joint; ~ **fileté** m NUCLEAIRE screwed joint, threaded joint; ~ **flexible** m CONS MECA flexible joint; ~ **à franc-bord** m PRODUCTION butt joint; ~ **à genou** m CONS MECA globe joint, socket joint, PRODUCTION cup joint, cup-and-ball joint; ~ **glissant** m CONS MECA bellow expansion joint; ~ **glissant à tube ondulé** m NUCLEAIRE corrugated expansion joint, corrugated tube compensator; ~ **de grain** m CRISTALL, MATERIAUX, METALL grain boundary; ~ **hermétique** m NUCLEAIRE hermetic sealing; ~ **hollandais** m CONS MECA universal joint; ~ **homocinétique** m VEHICULES *arbre de transmission* constant velocity universal joint; ~ **d'huile** m CONS MECA oil seal; ~ **ignifuge** m AERONAUT fireseal; ~ **à insertion** m PRODUCTION inserted joint; ~ **d'interphase** m METALL phase boundary; ~ **labyrinthe** m CONS MECA labyrinth seal; ~ **à lèvres** m CONS MECA, MECANIQUE lip seal; ~ **lisse** m PRODUCTION flush joint; ~ **de macles** m METALL twin boundary; ~ **métalloplastique** m AUTO, CONS MECA copper asbestos gasket; ~ **au minium** m CONSTR putty joint; ~ **moulé en néoprène** m PLAST CAOU *caoutchouc synthétique* neoprene molded seal (AmE), neoprene moulded seal (BrE); ~ **papier** m CONS MECA paper gasket; ~ **par torsade** m PRODUCTION twist joint; ~ **de pieu** m CHARBON pile joint, pile splice; ~ **plan** m MECANIQUE gasket; ~ **plat** m CERAM VER flat edge, CONS MECA gasket; ~ **à plat** m CONS MECA straight joint, CONSTR butt joint, square joint; ~ **de plomb** m CONSTR lead joint, PRODUCTION solder joint, soldering joint; ~ **poli** m CERAM VER polished edge; ~ **de pompe à l'huile** m REFRIG oil pump gasket; ~ **à porte-à-faux** m CONSTR *charpenterie* suspended joint; ~ **pour tube** m CONS MECA pipe joint; ~ **de protection au nitrile** *m* PRODUCTION nitrile seal; ~ **quart-de-rond** *m* CERAM VER rounded edge; ~ **de raccord de vanne** *m* REFRIG valve adaptor gasket; ~ **de rail** *m* CH DE FER rail joint; ~ **à recouvrement** *m* CONS MECA step joint, CONSTR lap joint, overlap joint; ~ **à recouvrement rivé** *m* CONS MECA riveted lap joint; ~ **refeuillé** *m* CONSTR angular grooved-and-tongued joint; ~ **rotatif** *m* IMPRIM *machines* rotary unit; ~ **de rotation** *m* PETR swivel; ~ **à rotule** *m* CONS MECA globe joint, socket joint, swivel joint, IMPRIM *mécanique* ball and socket joint, MECANIQUE universal joint, PRODUCTION cup joint, cup-and-ball joint, VEHICULES *direction* ball joint; ~ **à rotule sphérique** *m* CONS MECA ball and socket joint, globe joint, socket joint, PRODUCTION cup joint, cup-and-ball joint; ~ **à sifflet** *m* CONSTR splayed joint; ~ **soudé bout à bout par fusion** *m* CONS MECA fusion-welded butt joint; ~ **soudé par fusion** *m* CONS MECA fusion-welded joint; ~ **à soufflet** *m* CONS MECA bellow expansion joint, ESPACE *véhicules* bellows seal; ~ **sphérique** *m* PAPIER ball joint, socket joint; ~ **télescopique** *m* CONS MECA telescopic joint; ~ **de tige** *m* CONS MECA rod seal; ~ **torique** *m* CONS MECA O-ring, toroidal sealing ring, MECANIQUE, PLAST CAOU O-ring; ~ **torique à voyant d'huile** *m* REFRIG oil-sight o-ring; ~ **tournant** *m* ELECTROTEC rotary joint; ~ **de transmission** *m* PRODUCTION transmission joint; ~ **de trou d'homme** *m* MECANIQUE manhole gasket; ~ **universel** *m* CONS MECA, VEHICULES *transmission* universal joint; ~ **venture** *m* CONSTR joint venture; ~ **à vis** *m* CONS MECA screw joint

jointoiement *m* CONSTR pointing
jointoyage *m* CONSTR pointing
jointure *f* CONSTR joining, joint; ~ **cohérente** *f* METALL coherent boundary; ~ **sphérique** *f* CONS MECA globe joint, socket joint, PRODUCTION cup joint, cup-and-ball joint
jonc *m* CONSTR rush, MECANIQUE retaining ring, OPTIQUE core, element; ~ **de manivelle** *m* CONS MECA crankshaft
joncteur *m* TELECOM junctor, trunk; ~ **d'abonné** *m* TELECOM SLC, subscriber line circuit; ~ **d'arrivée** *m* TELECOM incoming trunk circuit, terminating junctor; ~ **de départ** *m* TELECOM originating junctor, outgoing trunk circuit; ~ **entrant** *m* TELECOM incoming trunk circuit; ~ **sortant** *m* TELECOM outgoing trunk circuit
jonction *f* CH DE FER rail junction, track connection, CONS MECA joint, CONSTR joining, junction, ELECTR *raccordement* junction, GAZ connection, INFORMAT junction, ORDINAT interface, junction, PAPIER seam, PETR tie-in, PRODUCTION, TELECOM junction; ~ **abrupte** *f* ELECTRON abrupt junction; ~ **bout à bout** *f* CONS MECA butt joint; ~ **de câbles** *f* ELECTR *raccordement* cable joint, ELECTROTEC cable junction; ~ **de dislocation** *f* METALL dislocation junction; ~ **double** *f* CH DE FER double crossover; ~ **émetteur-base** *f* ELECTRON emitter base junction; ~ **formée au tirage** *f* ELECTRON grown junction; ~ **hybride** *f* ELECTRON hybrid junction; ~ **hyperabrupte** *f* ELECTRON hyperabrupt junction; ~ **de Josephson** *f* ELECTRON, NUCLEAIRE, PHYSIQUE Josephson junction; ~ **métal-semi-conducteur** *f* ELECTRON metal-semiconductor junction; ~ **mixte** *f* ELECTR transition joint; ~ **à oxydation sélective** *f* ELECTRON locally oxided junction; ~ **par alliage** *f* ELECTRON alloy junction; ~ **par diffusion** *f* ELECTRON diffused junction; ~ **PN** *f* ELECTRON, PHYSIQUE p-n junction; ~ **à point d'arrêt** *f* ELECTR stop joint; ~ **redresseuse** *f* ELECTROTEC rectifying junction; ~ **de**

référence *f* ELECTROTEC cold junction; ~ **répulsive** *f* METALL repulsive junction; ~ **de sectionnement** *f* ELECTR sectionalizing joint; ~ **simple** *f* ELECTR straight joint; ~ **tirée** *f* ELECTRON grown junction; ~ **tri-mono** *f* ELECTR *liaison de câble* trifurcating joint; ~ **triple** *f* METALL triple junction; ~ **de tuyaux** *f* CONS MECA pipe junction; ~ **urbaine** *f* TELECOM local junction; ~ **de voies** *f* CH DE FER rail junction, track connection
jonctionnement *m* TEXTILE seaming
jonctionner *vt* TEXTILE seam
jottereaux *m pl* NAUT hounds
joue *f* CONS MECA *poulie, mortaise* cheek, *tambour d'un treuil* flange, NAUT *poulie* cheek, PRODUCTION *galet à joues pour chariot de pont roulant* flange; ~ **de jante** *f* VEHICULES *roue* rim flange; ~ **de manutention** *f* CONS MECA handling lugs (AmE), lifting lugs (BrE)
jouée *f* CONSTR reveal
joug *m* CONS MECA yoke
joule *m (J)* AGRO ALIM, ELECTR *unité d'énergie*, MECANIQUE, METROLOGIE, PHYSIQUE, THERMODYN joule *(J)*
jour:[1] **au ~** *adj* MINES above ground, surface; **du ~** *adj* MINES above ground, surface
jour[2] *m* CONSTR well, MINES grass, PHYSIQUE day; ~ **de l'escalier** *m* CONSTR well; ~ **de planche** *m* PETROLE lay day; ~ **de porte** *m* CONSTR door opening; ~ **de production** *m* PRODUCTION production day; ~ **sidéral** *m* ASTRONOMIE, PHYSIQUE sidereal day; ~ **sidéral moyen** *m* ASTRONOMIE mean sidereal day; ~ **solaire** *m* METROLOGIE solar day; ~ **de travail** *m* CONSTR workday
journal *m* INFORMAT, ORDINAT log; ~ **d'audit de sécurité** *m* TELECOM security audit trail; ~ **de bord** *m* AERONAUT flight log, NAUT ship's log, TELECOM log, TRANSPORT logbook; ~ **d'entreprise** *m* IMPRIM house organ; ~ **des machines** *m* NAUT engine room log; ~ **télévisé** *m* TV newscast; ~ **de vérification** *m* PRODUCTION audit trail
journalisme: ~ **électronique** *m* TV ENG, electronic news gathering
jovien *adj* ASTRONOMIE Jovian
joystick *m* ORDINAT joystick
juglon *m* CHIMIE juglone
juke-box *m* OPTIQUE jukebox, optical disc library (BrE), optical disk library (AmE)
jumbo: ~ **avec flèche** *m* MINES jumbo including boom
jumelage *m* ELECTROTEC ganging
jumelé *adj* ELECTR *potentiomètre* dual-ganged
jumelle *f* AUTO *suspension* shackle, CONS MECA upright, *machine à raboter* housing, PRODUCTION *machine à raboter* standard, RESSORTS double shackle, VEHICULES *ressort à lames* shackle; ~ **de liaison** *f* AERONAUT connecting twin yoke
jumelle-loupe *f* CERAM VER field glass magnifier
jumelles *f pl* ASTRONOMIE binoculars, CONSTR *sonnette* guidepoles, INSTRUMENT binoculars, field glasses, MILITAIRE, NAUT, PHYSIQUE binoculars; ~ **à fort grossissement** *f pl* INSTRUMENT high-power field glasses; ~ **à intensificateur de lumière** *f pl* ASTRONOMIE binoculars with light intensification; ~ **périscopiques** *f pl* INSTRUMENT shear-jointed telescope; ~ **de poche** *f pl* INSTRUMENT miniature binoculars; ~ **à prismes** *f pl* INSTRUMENT prism binoculars, prismatic binoculars
jupe *f* CONSTR, MILITAIRE *lanceur* skirt, OCEANO diving bell, POLLU MER skirt, TRANSPORT skirt, spoiler; ~ **de cloche** *f* AERONAUT drag cup skirt; ~ **à géométrie variable** *f* TRANSPORT variable geometry skirt; ~ **de liaison** *f* ESPACE *véhicules* connecting skirt; ~ **périph-**

érique *f* TRANSPORT peripheral skirt; ~ **de piston** *f* AUTO, VEHICULES *moteur* piston skirt; ~ **de piston fendue** *f* AUTO split piston skirt; ~ **rigide** *f* TRANSPORT rigid skirt; ~ **de stabilité** *f* TRANSPORT stability skirt

jurassique[1] *adj* GEOLOGIE *stratigraphie* Jurassic

jurassique[2] *m* GEOLOGIE, PETROLE Jurassic period

jurisprudence *f* BREVETS case law

jus: ~ **de décongélation** *m* AGRO ALIM drip; ~ **stérile** *m* CHARBON barren solution; ~ **sucré** *m* AGRO ALIM cane juice

jusant *m* HYDROLOGIE ebb tide, NAUT, OCEANO ebb

juste[1] *adj* METROLOGIE, PHYSIQUE accurate

juste:[2] ~ **à temps** *m* EMBALLAGE, TEXTILE JIT, just-in-time

justement *adv* METROLOGIE accurately

justesse *f* MATERIAUX soundness, METROLOGIE accuracy, *balance* correctness, PHYSIQUE accuracy, PRODUCTION exactitude, exactness

justificatif: ~ **d'identité** *m* TELECOM credentials

justification *f* IMPRIM justification, measure, INFORMAT, TELECOM justification; ~ **à droite** *f* INFORMAT, ORDINAT right justification; ~ **à gauche** *f* INFORMAT left justification; ~ **verticale** *f* IMPRIM *composition* page depth

justifié: ~ **à droite et à gauche** *adj* IMPRIM *composition* BT, both justified

justifier *vt* INFORMAT justify; ~ **à droite** *vt* INFORMAT, ORDINAT right justify; ~ **à gauche** *vt* INFORMAT left justify

jute *m* TEXTILE jute

juvénile *adj* GEOLOGIE juvenile

juxtaposition: ~ **de points** *f* INFORMAT *graphique* dithering

K

k *abrév (kilo-)* METROLOGIE k *(kilo-)*
K[1] *(potassium)* CHIMIE K *(potassium)*
K[2] *abrév (kelvin)* METROLOGIE, PHYSIQUE, THERMODYN K *(kelvin)*
kaempférol *m* CHIMIE kaempferol
kahlerite *f* NUCLEAIRE kahlerite
kaïnite *f* MINERAUX kainite
kali *m* CHIMIE kali
kammerérite *f* MINERAUX kämmererite
kaolin *m* CHIMIE kaolin, GEOLOGIE china clay, IMPRIM kaolin, MINERAUX, PLAST CAOU *pigment, charge* china clay, kaolin
kaolinisation *f* EN RENOUV, GEOLOGIE kaolinization
kaolinite *f* CHARBON, MATERIAUX, MINERAUX, PETROLE kaolinite
kaon *m* PHYS PART, PHYSIQUE kaon
kapok *m* CHAUFFAGE kapok
karman *m* AERONAUT fillet
karst *m* DISTRI EAU chalk formation, GEOLOGIE karst
karsténite *f* MINERAUX karstenite
karyocérite *f* NUCLEAIRE karyocerite
kauri-butanol *m* CHIMIE kauri-butanol
kazanien *m* GEOLOGIE *stratigraphie* Kazanian
Kcal *abrév (kilocalorie)* AGRO ALIM Kcal *(kilocalorie)*
kCi *abrév (kilocurie)* CHIMIE kCi *(kilocurie)*
keilhauite *f* MINERAUX keilhauite
kelly *m* PETROLE *forage* kelly
kelvin *m (K)* METROLOGIE, PHYSIQUE, THERMODYN kelvin *(K)*
kelvinomètre *m* CINEMAT kelvinometer
kempféride *f* CHIMIE kaempferide
kemsolène *m* CHIMIE kemsolene
kératine *f* CHIMIE keratin
kératinique *adj* CHIMIE keratinous
kératinisation *f* CHIMIE keratinization
kératogène *adj* CHIMIE keratogenous
kerma *m* PHYSIQUE kerma
kermès: **~ minéral** *m* MINERAUX kermes mineral, kermesite
kermésite *f* MINERAUX kermes mineral, kermesite
kermet *m* CHARBON flume, water channel
kérogène *m* CHIMIE, GEOLOGIE, PETR, PETROLE *formation des hydrocarbures* kerogen
kérolite *f* MINERAUX cerolite
kérosène *m* CHIMIE, PETR, PETROLE *raffinage*, TRANSPORT kerosene, kerosine, paraffin; **~ chloré** *m* CHIMIE keryl
kersantite *f* PETR kersantite
ketch *m* NAUT ketch
keV *abrév (kilo-électronvolt)* CHIMIE keV *(kilo-electronvolt)*
kevlar *m* NAUT Kevlar
kg *abrév (kilogramme)* METROLOGIE kg *(kilogram, kilogramme)*
khlopinite *f* NUCLEAIRE khlopinite
kick-down *m* VEHICULES *boîte de vitesses automatique* kick down
kick-starter *m* VEHICULES *moteur de motocyclette* kick-starter

kiesérite *f* MINERAUX kieserite
kilo- *préf (k)* METROLOGIE kilo-*(k)*
kilocalorie *f (Kcal)* AGRO ALIM kilocalorie *(Kcal)*
kilocurie *m (kCi)* CHIMIE kilocurie *(kCi)*
kilo-électronvolt *m (keV)* CHIMIE kilo-electronvolt *(keV)*
kilogramme *m (kg)* METROLOGIE kilogram (AmE), kilogramme (BrE) *(kg)*
kilogrammètre *m* METROLOGIE kilogram meter (AmE), kilogramme meter (BrE)
kilohertz *m* ELECTR *unité* kHz, kilohertz
kiloline *m* METROLOGIE kiloline
kilométrage *m* TRANSPORT mileage
kilomètre *m (km)* METROLOGIE kilometer (AmE), kilometre (BrE)
kilonème *m (kn)* CHIMIE kilonem *(kn)*
kilo-octet *m (ko)* INFORMAT, ORDINAT kilobyte *(kb)*
kiloparsec *m* ASTRONOMIE kiloparsec
kilovolt *m (kV)* ELECTROTEC kilovolt *(kV)*
kilowatt *m (kW)* ELECTR *unité*, ELECTROTEC kilowatt *(kW)*
kilowatt-heure *m* ELECTR *unité*, ELECTROTEC, PHYSIQUE kilowatt-hour
kimberlite *f* GEOLOGIE, PETR kimberlite
kimmeridgien *m* GEOLOGIE *stratigraphie*, PETROLE Kimmeridgian
kinescopage *m* CINEMAT telerecording, TV film transfer, tape-to-film transfer, telerecording
kinescope *m* ELECTRON kinescope, TV telerecorder
kink-bands *m pl* GEOLOGIE kink bands
kiosque *m* CONSTR kiosk, NAUT conning tower
kit *m* PRODUCTION kit; **~ de conversion double entrée** *m* PRODUCTION *automatisme industriel* dual input conversion kit; **~ de cosses** *m* PRODUCTION *automatisme industriel* lug kit; **~ de cosses de raccordement** *m* PRODUCTION terminal lug kit
klaubés *m pl* MINES picked ore
klaubeur *m* MINES picker
klippe *f* GEOLOGIE klippe
klystron *m* ELECTRON, ESPACE *communications*, PHYS RAYON, PHYSIQUE, TELECOM klystron; **~ accordable** *m* ESPACE *communications* tunable klystron; **~ amplificateur** *m* ELECTRON klystron amplifier; **~ multicavité** *m* ELECTRON, PHYSIQUE multicavity klystron; **~ multiplicateur de fréquence** *m* ELECTRON frequency multiplier klystron, klystron frequency multiplier; **~ oscillateur** *m* ELECTRON klystron oscillator; **~ reflex** *m* ELECTRON, PHYSIQUE reflex klystron; **~ à trois cavités** *m* ELECTRON three-cavity klystron
km *abrév (kilomètre)* METROLOGIE km *(kilometer, kilometre)*
kn *abrév (kilonème)* CHIMIE kn *(kilonem)*
knébélite *f* MINERAUX knebelite
ko *abrév (kilo-octet)* INFORMAT, ORDINAT kb *(kilobyte)*
koninckite *f* MINERAUX koninckite
konléinite *f* MINERAUX konleinite, könlite
konlite *f* MINERAUX konleinite, könlite

koréite f MINERAUX agalmatolite
kotschubéite f MINERAUX kochubeïte, kotschubeite
köttigite f MINERAUX koettigite, köttigite
Kr *(krypton)* CHIMIE Kr *(krypton)*
krarupisation f ELECTROTEC continuous loading, krarup loading
krémersite f MINERAUX kremersite
krennérite f MINERAUX krennerite
krigeage m DISTRI EAU kriging

krohnkite f MINERAUX kröhnkite
krypton m *(Kr)* CHIMIE krypton *(Kr)*
kryptonate: ~ **de l'amalgame de cadmium** m NUCLEAIRE kryptonate of cadmium amalgam
kupfernickel m MINERAUX kupfernickel
kV *abrév (kilovolt)* ELECTROTEC kV *(kilovolt)*
kW *abrév (kilowatt)* ELECTR, ELECTROTEC kW *(kilowatt)*

L

l *abrév (litre)* METROLOGIE l *(litre)*

La *(lanthane)* CHIMIE La *(lanthanum)*

label *m* INFORMAT label record; **~ fin** *m* INFORMAT, ORDINAT trailer label

labeur *m* IMPRIM commercial printing

labile *adj* CHIMIE, GEOLOGIE labile

labo *m* CINEMAT darkroom, PHOTO lab

laboratoire *m* CHIMIE, CINEMAT, PHOTO laboratory, PRODUCTION charge chamber, laboratory, reverberatory chamber; **~ d'analyse** *m* CHARBON analysis laboratory, assay office; **~ en orbite** *m* ESPACE *véhicules* orbiting laboratory; **d'essai** *m* QUALITE test laboratory; **~ indépendant** *m* CINEMAT outside lab; **~ marin** *m* OCEANO marine laboratory; **~ maritime** *m* OCEANO marine laboratory, oceanographic laboratory; **~ obscur** *m* PHOTO darkroom; **~ océanographique** *m* OCEANO marine laboratory, oceanographic laboratory; **~ orbital** *m* ESPACE *véhicules* orbiting laboratory; **~ orbital habité** *m* ESPACE *véhicules* MOL, manned orbiting laboratory; **~ semi-chaud** *m* NUCLEAIRE semihot laboratory, warm laboratory; **~ spatial** *m* ESPACE *véhicules*, space laboratory, spacelab; **~ de tirage** *m* CINEMAT printing lab, processing laboratory; **~ de trucages** *m* CINEMAT optical house

labradorite *f* MINERAUX labradorite

labyrinthe: **~ d'étanchéité** *m* CONS MECA labyrinth seal

lac *m* DISTRI EAU, HYDROLOGIE lake; **~ acide** *m* POLLUTION acid lake; **~ acide naturel** *m* POLLUTION naturally acid lake; **~ acidifié** *m* POLLUTION acid lake, acidified lake; **~ de barrage** *m* DISTRI EAU artificial lake, HYDROLOGIE storage lake; **~ de barrage glaciaire** *m* HYDROLOGIE glacier lake; **~ borique** *m* LESSIVES borax lake; **~ en transition** *m* POLLUTION transition lake; **~ eutrophe** *m* RECYCLAGE eutrophic lake; **~ de glacier** *m* HYDROLOGIE glacier lake; **~ non acide** *m* POLLUTION nonacidic lake; **~ non acidifié** *m* POLLUTION nonacidic lake

laçage *m* ENREGISTR lacing

laccaïque *adj* CHIMIE laccaic

laccol *m* CHIMIE laccol

laccolite *m* GEOLOGIE, GEOPHYS, PETR laccolith

lacer *vt* PRODUCTION *courroie* lace

laceret *m* CONSTR auger, screw eye; **~ à cuiller** *m* CONSTR spoon auger; **~ à vrille** *m* CONSTR gimlet

lacet *m* AERONAUT yaw, CONSTR *charnière* pin, EN RENOUV, ESPACE *pilotage* yaw, GEOMETRIE *topologie* loop, PHYSIQUE yaw, yawing

lâche *adj* PAPIER loose

lâcher *vt* DISTRI EAU *robinet* turn on, NAUT *corde* loosen

lacis *m* PRODUCTION network, *de fils* network

lactame *f* CHIMIE lactam

lactamide *f* CHIMIE lactamide

lactate *m* CHIMIE lactate

lacténine *f* CHIMIE lactenin

lactide *m* CHIMIE lactide

lactique *adj* CHIMIE lactic

lactobutyromètre *m* AGRO ALIM lactobutyrometer

lactodensimètre *m* AGRO ALIM lactometer

lactone *f* CHIMIE lactone

lactonique *adj* CHIMIE lactonic

lactonisation *f* CHIMIE lactonization

lactonitrile *m* CHIMIE lactonitrile

lactose *m* CHIMIE lactose

lactosérum *m* AGRO ALIM whey

lacune *f* CRISTALL vacancy, ELECTROTEC hole, GEOLOGIE disconformity, *érosion, sédimentation* gap, hiatus, METALL vacancy; **~ granulométrique** *f* CERAM VER gap; **~ de miscibilité** *f* METALL miscibility gap; **~ de sédimentation** *f* GEOLOGIE nondepositional gap, nonsequence

lacustre *adj* GEOLOGIE lacustrine

lagon *m* GEOLOGIE, OCEANO lagoon

lagrangien *adj* PHYSIQUE Lagrangian

lagre *m* CERAM VER flattening table

lagunage *m* POLLUTION lagooning

lagune *f* CONSTR, DISTRI EAU, GEOLOGIE, HYDROLOGIE, OCEANO lagoon; **~ côtière** *f* GEOLOGIE lagoon

lahar *m* GEOLOGIE *débris volcaniques* lahar

laine *f* PAPIER, TEXTILE wool; **~ d'amiante** *f* NUCLEAIRE asbestos wool, cotton asbestos; **~ minérale** *f* CHAUFFAGE slag wool; **~ à repriser** *f* TEXTILE darning wool; **~ de roche** *f* CHAUFFAGE rock wool, REFRIG mineral wool; **~ de la salamandre** *f* PRODUCTION cinder wool; **~ de scorie** *f* PRODUCTION cinder wool; **~ de verre** *f* CHAUFFAGE glass wool, PLAST CAOU glass wool, *plastiques* fiberglass (AmE), fibreglass (BrE), REFRIG glass wool

laineux *adj* PAPIER woolen, TEXTILE woolly

lainière *f* PRODUCTION *courroies* lace

lais *m* HYDROLOGIE silt, OCEANO alluvium, silt; **~ de la mer** *m* OCEANO alluvium, silt

laisse:[1] **en ~** *adv* ESPACE *véhicules* tethered

laisse:[2] **~ de basse mer** *f* NAUT, OCEANO low water mark; **~ de haute mer** *f* GEOPHYS tidemark, HYDROLOGIE high water mark, tidemark, OCEANO high water mark; **~ de pleine mer** *f* NAUT high water mark

laisser:[1] **~ couver** *vt* PRODUCTION allow to breed; **~ échapper** *vt* CHIMIE *gaz* release; **~ ouvert** *vt* ORDINAT *fichier* leave open; **~ rasseoir** *vt* GENIE CHIM settle; **~ reposer** *vt* GENIE CHIM settle; **~ tremper** *vt* TEXTILE soak

laisser:[2] **~ arriver** *vi* NAUT *sur un cap* bear away; **~ porter** *vi* NAUT *sur un cap* bear away

laisses: **~ de crue** *m pl* HYDROLOGIE flood deposits

lait: **~ certifié** *m* AGRO ALIM TT milk, tuberculin-tested milk; **~ de chaux** *m* CONSTR limewash, whitewash; **~ de couchage** *m* PAPIER slurry; **~ de couche** *m* PAPIER slip; **~ entier concentré** *m* AGRO ALIM evaporated whole milk; **~ garanti** *m* AGRO ALIM TT milk, tuberculin-tested milk; **~ de kaolin** *m* PAPIER clay slip; **~ de roche** *m* MINERAUX rock milk

laitance *f* CONSTR laitance

laiterie *f* AGRO ALIM dairy plant

laitier *m* CHARBON, CHAUFFAGE, CONSTR slag, PRODUCTION cinder; **~ de ciment** *m* CERAM VER clinker cement; **~ de haut fourneau** *m* PRODUCTION blast furnace slag; **~ mousseux** *m* MATERIAUX *métallurgie* foamed slag; **~ ultra-acide** *m* PRODUCTION highly-acid slag; **~ ultra-basique** *m* PRODUCTION highly-basic slag

laiton *m* CONS MECA, ELECTR, MATERIAUX, MECANIQUE, PRODUCTION brass; **~ à cartouches** *m* CONS MECA cartridge brass; **~ qualité marine** *m* MECANIQUE naval brass

laitonnage *m* CONSTR brassing

laize *f* IMPRIM *impression* web width, NAUT sailcloth, PAPIER width

lamage: **~ arrière** *m* CONS MECA back spotfacing

lamanage *m* NAUT inshore pilotage

lamaneur *m* NAUT inshore pilot

lambda *m* IMPRIM caret

lambeau: **~ de charriage** *m* GEOLOGIE klippe

lambert *m* METROLOGIE lambert

lambert-pied *m* CINEMAT foot lambert

lambourde *f* CONSTR wall plate, MINES lagging

lame *f* CHIMIE lamina, CONS MECA cutter, *outil* blade, CONSTR blade, ELECTR *condensateur* plate, MECANIQUE blade, *outillage* knife, NAUT billow, wave, NUCLEAIRE *métal* sheet, PAPIER bar, blade, RESSORTS leaf; **~ d'aiguille** *f* CH DE FER switch blade, switch tongue; **~ d'air** *f* EMBALLAGE airbrush, IMPRIM *séchage* air knife, PAPIER air blade, air knife, airbrush, PLAST CAOU air knife, *matériel pour revêtement* airbrush; **~ d'attaque** *f* POLLU MER front blade; **~ bimétallique** *f* ELECTR *thermostat, thermomètre* bimetallic strip; **~ de bistouri** *f* EQUIP LAB scalpel blade; **~ à cisailler** *f* CONS MECA shear blade; **~ de cisailles** *f* CONS MECA shear blade; **~ à cisailles à rouleaux** *f* CONS MECA rotary shear blade; **~ de ciseaux** *f* CERAM VER shear blade; **~ de collecteur** *f* ELECTR commutator segment, *machine* commutator bar, ELECTROTEC commutator bar; **~ complète** *f* ELECTRON finished quartz; **~ coudée de platine** *f* PAPIER angle bar; **~ de coupe** *f* IMPRIM *façonnage* cutter; **~ déchiquetée** *f* SECURITE jagged edge of a blade; **~ demi-onde** *f* PHYSIQUE half-wave plate; **~ déversante** *f* HYDROLOGIE overflow; **~ dissymétrique** *f* RESSORTS asymmetrical leaf; **~ d'encrier** *f* IMPRIM ink blade, ink knife, *machine* fountain blade; **~ engageante** *f* IMPRIM *plieuse* tucking blade; **~ d'étrave** *f* NAUT bow wave; **~ à faces parallèles** *f* CINEMAT optical flat; **~ fixe** *f* ELECTROTEC stator plate; **~ de fond** *f* NAUT ground swell, OCEANO bottom surge, ground swell; **~ fusible** *f* ELECTR link fuse, *sécurité* fuse strip; **~ de gaz** *f* NUCLEAIRE gas discharge gap; **~ de houle** *f* NAUT roller; **~ maîtresse** *f* AUTO master leaf, RESSORTS main leaf; **~ mince** *f* CRISTALL thin section; **~ mobile** *f* ELECTROTEC rotor plate; **~ niveleuse** *f* TRANSPORT grader leveling blade (AmE), grader levelling blade (BrE); **~ de perforation** *f* IMPRIM *façonnage* perforation blade; **~ de pile** *f* PAPIER beater bar, refiner bar; **~ du pli d'équerre** *f* IMPRIM *rotative* chopper fold blade; **~ porte-objet** *f* EQUIP LAB *microscope* slide, INSTRUMENT glass slide; **~ pour microscope** *f* EQUIP LAB microscope slide; **~ pour scie sauteuse** *f* CONS MECA jig saw blade; **~ quart d'onde** *f* PHYSIQUE quarter wave plate; **~ de rabot** *f* CONSTR plane bit; **~ de raboteuse** *f* CONS MECA plane iron; **~ de racle** *f* PAPIER doctor blade; **~ de retenue de pale** *f* AERONAUT blade retention strap; **~ de rotor** *f* ELECTROTEC rotor plate; **~ de scie** *f* CONS MECA saw blade; **~ de scie circulaire** *f* CONS MECA circular saw; **~ de scie circulaire à bois** *f* CONS MECA woodsawing circular saw blade; **~ de scie à métaux** *f* CONS MECA hacksaw blade, metal-cutting saw blade; **~ de scie à ruban à métaux** *f* CONS MECA metal-cutting band-saw

blade; **~ de scie sabre** *f* CONS MECA reciprocating saw blade; **~ de sécurité** *f* RESSORTS safety leaf; **~ semi-réfléchissante** *f* PHYSIQUE semireflecting plate; **~ significative** *f* OCEANO significant wave; **~ sous-maîtresse** *f* RESSORTS second leaf; **~ du stator** *f* ELECTROTEC stator plate; **~ de support** *f* CONS MECA *rectification sans centre* work rest blade; **~ teinte sensible** *f* CERAM VER tint plate; **~ de tournevis pour vilebrequin** *f* CONS MECA screwdriver bit, turnscrew bit; **~ trapézoïdale** *f* CONS MECA trapezoidal blade

lamellaire *adj* GEOLOGIE, MECANIQUE *matériaux*, METALL lamellar

lamelle *f* CHIMIE, GEOLOGIE lamina, METALL lamella; **~ couvre-objet** *f* EQUIP LAB cover glass, cover slip, INSTRUMENT cover slip; **~ maclée** *f* METALL twin lamella; **~ de masse** *f* PRODUCTION earth pin (BrE), ground pin (AmE); **~ porte-courant** *f* PRODUCTION *électricité* current-conducting pin; **~ pour condensateur** *f* ELECTR capacitor film; **~ pour microscope** *f* EQUIP LAB microscope slide cover slip

lamelliforme *adj* GEOLOGIE laminar

lames:[1] **à ~** *adj* PRODUCTION laminated

lames:[2] **~ galvanométriques** *f pl* PHYSIQUE *laser* galvo-plates

laminage *m* GEOLOGIE lamination, PAPIER rolling, PLAST CAOU *plastiques* lamination, PRODUCTION lamination, rolling, REFRIG wire drawing; **~ à chaud** *m* THERMODYN hot rolling; **~ à froid** *m* THERMODYN cold rolling; **~ à pellicule brillante** *m* EMBALLAGE high gloss foil; **~ de la vapeur** *m* CH DE FER *véhicules* throttling

laminaire *adj* CHIMIE, MATERIAUX, PHYS FLUID laminar

lamination *f* GEOLOGIE, PLAST CAOU *plastiques* lamination; **~ contournée** *f* GEOLOGIE convolute lamination

lamine *m* GEOLOGIE lamina

laminé[1] *adj* ELECTR *capaciteur*, GEOLOGIE, NAUT *bois* laminated, PAPIER laminated, rolled, PLAST CAOU, PRODUCTION laminated; **~ à chaud** *adj* MECANIQUE *matériaux*, THERMODYN hot-rolled; **~ à froid** *adj* THERMODYN cold-rolled; **~ à la plaque** *adj* PAPIER *carton* plate-glazed

laminé[2] *m* IMPRIM, PLAST CAOU laminate; **~ d'acétate** *m* EMBALLAGE acetate laminate

laminer *vt* PRODUCTION laminate; **~ à chaud** *vt* THERMODYN hot roll; **~ à froid** *vt* THERMODYN cold roll

laminerie *f* PRODUCTION flatting mill, flatting works, rolling mill

lamineuse *f* CERAM VER casting unit

laminoir *m* CH DE FER flatting mill, rolling mill, CONS MECA rolling mill, PAPIER caliper calender (AmE), calliper calender (BrE), thickness calender, PRODUCTION mill, rolling mill, rolls; **~ à l'argile** *m* CERAM VER clay rollers; **~ à barres** *m* CONS MECA bar mill; **~ à billettes** *m* CONS MECA billetting rolls; **~ à blindage** *m* PRODUCTION armor plate mill (AmE), armour plate mill (BrE); **~ à blooms** *m* CONS MECA blooming mill, PRODUCTION cogging mill; **~ double duo** *m* PRODUCTION four-high rod mill; **~ duo** *m* PRODUCTION two-high mill, two-high rolls, two-high train; **~ ébaucheur** *m* PRODUCTION puddle bar train, puddle train, roughing rolls, puddle rolls; **~ à grosses sections** *m* PRODUCTION cogging mill; **~ à guides** *m* PRODUCTION guide mill; **~ à mouvement alternatif** *m* PRODUCTION reciprocating mill; **~ à plaque** *m* PAPIER plate glazing calender; **~ à profilés** *m* PRODUCTION section mill; **~ de puddlage** *m* PRODUCTION puddle bar train, puddle rolls, puddle train; **~ à rails** *m* CH DE FER rolling mill; **~**

réversible *m* PRODUCTION reversing mill; ~ **à tôles fines** *m* PRODUCTION sheet mill; ~ **trio** *m* CONS MECA three-high mill, three-high rolls, three-high train; ~ **universel** *m* PRODUCTION slabbing mill

lampadite *f* MINERAUX lampadite

lampara *m* OCEANO beach seine, lampara net

lampe *f* CINEMAT, ELECTROTEC bulb, lamp, PHOTO lamp, PHYSIQUE valve, VEHICULES *éclairage, témoins* lamp; ~ **à acétylène** *f* CONSTR acetylene lamp; ~ **d'alarme clignotante** *f* SECURITE alarm flashing light, flashing light; ~ **à alcool** *f* EQUIP LAB *chauffage* spirit lamp; ~ **à amorçage à froid** *f* ELECTR cold start lamp; ~ **à ampoule métallisée** *f* PHOTO mirror-coated lamp; ~ **d'appel** *f* TELECOM calling lamp; ~ **à arc** *f* CINEMAT arc, ELECTR *éclairage* arc lamp; ~ **à arc de charbon** *f* ELECTR *éclairage* carbon arc lamp; ~ **à arc à mercure** *f* PHYS RAYON mercury arc lamp; ~ **à arc de xénon** *f* CINEMAT xenon arc lamp; ~ **avec chapeau** *f* CONSTR bonneted lamp; ~ **baladeuse** *f* ELECTROTEC inspection lamp; ~ **à braser** *f* CONSTR blowlamp, PRODUCTION brazing lamp; ~ **clignotante** *f* ELECTR *automobile* flasher; ~ **à condensateur** *f* PHOTO condenser lamp; ~ **de contrôle** *f* ELECTROTEC inspection lamp; ~ **de côté** *f* VEHICULES *éclairage* side marker light (AmE), side-light (BrE); ~ **Davy** *f* CHARBON Davy lamp; ~ **à décharge** *f* ELECTROTEC discharge lamp; ~ **à décharge haute intensité** *f* CINEMAT high-intensity discharge lamp; ~ **à double boudinage** *f* ELECTR *ampoule* coiled coil lamp; ~ **d'éclairage du champ de l'objet** *f* INSTRUMENT field illumination; ~ **d'effaçage du raccord de la piste sonore** *f* ENREGISTR bloop lamp; ~ **étalon** *f* ELECTROTEC standard light source; ~ **excitatrice** *f* CINEMAT exciter lamp, sound film lamp; ~ **à filament de charbon** *f* ELECTROTEC carbon filament lamp; ~ **flash** *f* PHOTO flash; ~ **fluorescente** *f* ELECTROTEC, PHYSIQUE fluorescent lamp; ~ **halogène** *f* CINEMAT quartz iodine lamp; ~ **à halogène** *f* ELECTR *éclairage* halogen lamp; ~ **HMI** *f* CINEMAT HMI lamp; ~ **800 watts sur batterie** *f* CINEMAT hand basher; ~ **à incandescence** *f* ELECTR *éclairage* incandescent lamp, ELECTROTEC glow lamp, incandescent lamp, PHOTO photoflood bulb; ~ **incandescente** *f* ELECTROTEC glow lamp, incandescent lamp; ~ **de laboratoire** *f* PHOTO *chambre noire* safelight; ~ **Lowell** *f* CINEMAT Lowell light; ~ **lumière de jour** *f* CINEMAT daylight lamp; ~ **luminescente à gaz** *f* ELECTR *éclairage* gas discharge lamp; ~ **de marquage** *f* CINEMAT marker light; ~ **à mercure** *f* ELECTR *éclairage* mercury arc lamp; ~ **à mercure à haute pression** *f* ELECTR high-pressure mercury lamp; ~ **à miroir incorporé** *f* CINEMAT mirror condenser lamp, reflector lamp; ~ **au néon** *f* ELECTROTEC neon lamp; ~ **de peintre en bâtiment** *f* CONSTR paint-burning lamp; ~ **de phare** *f* AUTO headlamp bulb; ~ **phare** *f* ELECTRON disc seal tube (BrE), disk seal tube (AmE); ~ **phonique** *f* CINEMAT exciter lamp, sound film lamp; ~ **de poche** *f* ELECTR *éclairage* flashlight, pocket lamp, ELECTROTEC flashlight; ~ **à pointe de tungstène** *f* CHIMIE pointolite; ~ **pour projecteur** *f* PHOTO projector lamp; ~ **de projection** *f* CINEMAT projection lamp; ~ **pulsée** *f* CINEMAT pulsed lamp; ~ **à quartz** *f* CINEMAT quartz halogen lamp; ~ **de rechange** *f* PHOTO spare bulb; ~ **à réflecteur incorporé** *f* CINEMAT internal mirror lamp; ~ **de signal** *f* COMMANDE signal lamp; ~ **de signalisation** *f* IMPRIM *machines* indicating lamp, TV cue light; ~ **au sodium** *f* CINEMAT sodium-vapor lamp (AmE), sodium-

vapour lamp (BrE); ~ **à sodium** *f* ELECTR *éclairage* sodium lamp; ~ **à souder** *f* CONSTR blowlamp; ~ **stylo** *f* ELECTROTEC pen light; ~ **de sûreté agréée** *f* CHARBON approved safety lamp; ~ **survoltée** *f* CINEMAT photoflood; ~ **à suspension** *f* ELECTROTEC hanging lamp; ~ **de tachymètre du cabestan** *f* CINEMAT capstan tach lamp; ~ **témoin** *f* CINEMAT control light, pilot lamp (AmE), pilot light (BrE), ELECTR indicator lamp, VEHICULES *accessoire* pilot lamp (AmE), pilot light (BrE); ~ **témoin clignotante** *f* AUTO flashing warning light; ~ **tubulaire** *f* ELECTR *éclairage* tubular lamp; ~ **à vapeur** *f* THERMODYN vapor discharge lamp (AmE), vapour discharge lamp (BrE); ~ **à vapeur de mercure** *f* ELECTROTEC mercury vapor lamp (AmE), mercury vapor lamp (BrE); ~ **à vapeur de mercure à basse pression** *f* ELECTR low-pressure mercury lamp; ~ **à vapeur de sodium** *f* PHYS RAYON sodium-vapor lamp (AmE), sodium-vapour lamp (BrE); ~ **à vide** *f* TV vacuum tube

lampe-éclair: ~ **électronique** *f* PHOTO flash

lampe-tempête *f* CONSTR, NAUT hurricane lamp

lampe-torche *f* MECANIQUE flashlight

lampe-UV *f* EQUIP LAB ultraviolet lamp

lampisterie *f* MINES lamp room

lamprophyre *m* PETR lamprophyre

lanarkite *f* MINERAUX lanarkite

lance *f* CONSTR branch, branch pipe, PRODUCTION nozzle, prick bar, pricker; ~ **anti-incendie** *f* SECURITE fire hose nozzle; ~ **d'arrosage** *f* DISTRI EAU branch pipe; ~ **canon** *f* POLLU MER fire monitor; ~ **à eau** *f* CONSTR branch, branch pipe, PRODUCTION nozzle; ~ **d'incendie** *f* DISTRI EAU branch pipe; ~ **à incendie** *f* DISTRI EAU branch pipe; ~ **monitor** *f* POLLU MER fire monitor; ~ **à oxygène** *f* CONSTR oxygen lancing; ~ **portable antichar** *f* MILITAIRE LAW, light anti-armor weapon (AmE); light anti-armour weapon (BrE); ~ **de sonde** *f* MINES pricker, probe; ~ **thermique** *f* THERMODYN thermic lance; ~ **tourelle** *f* POLLU MER fire monitor

lance-amarre *m* NAUT line thrower

lance-bombes *m* MILITAIRE bomb rack

lance-flammes *m* MILITAIRE flame projector, flame-thrower, THERMODYN flame thrower

lance-fusées *m* MILITAIRE rocket launcher

lance-glace *m* REFRIG ice blower

lance-grenades *m* MILITAIRE grenade launcher

lancement *m* CONS MECA launch, ESPACE liftoff, *véhicules* launch, INFORMAT start, NAUT *torpille* launching, ORDINAT start, PETROLE *chaîne* throwing, TELECOM launching; ~ **à froid** *m* ORDINAT cold start; ~ **spatial** *m* ESPACE space shot, *véhicules* space launch

lancer:[1] ~ **de rayons** *m* TV ray tracing

lancer[2] *vt* AERONAUT *réacteur* crank, CINEMAT release, IMPRIM *machine* actuate, INFORMAT start, NAUT *navire, torpille* launch, ORDINAT start, PRODUCTION inject; ~ **en fabrication** *vt* PRODUCTION release for manufacturing; ~ **un pont sur une rivière** *vt* CONSTR throw a bridge over a river

lance-roquettes *m* MILITAIRE rocket launcher

lanceur *m* AUTO starter drive assembly, ESPACE *véhicules* launch vehicle, launcher, MILITAIRE launch vehicle; ~ **Bendix** *m* MECANIQUE inertial starter; ~ **à inertie** *m* AUTO inertia drive; ~ **lourd** *m* ESPACE *véhicules* HLLV, heavy-lift launch vehicle; ~ **à pignon poussé** *m* AUTO positive drive

langage *m* ORDINAT language; ~ **algorithmique** *m*

ORDINAT algorithmic language, procedural language; **~ d'analyse** m ORDINAT design language; **~ d'assemblage** m ORDINAT assembly language; **~ bas de gamme** m ORDINAT low-level language; **~ de contrôle** m ORDINAT command language; **~ de contrôle des travaux** m ORDINAT JCL, job control language; **~ de description de données** m ORDINAT DDL, data description language; **~ de description et de spécification** m TELECOM specification and description language; **~ évolué** m ORDINAT high-level language; **~ extensible** m INFORMAT, ORDINAT extensible language; **~ fonctionnel** m ORDINAT applicative language, functional language; **~ formel** m ORDINAT formal language; **~ de gestion** m ORDINAT commercial language; **~ de gestion binaire** m PRODUCTION binary command language; **~ informatique de description d'image** m IMPRIM tag image file format; **~ interprétatif** m ORDINAT interpretative language; **~ d'interrogation** m INFORMAT, ORDINAT QL, query language; **~ machine** m ORDINAT machine language; **~ de manipulation de données** m ORDINAT DML, data manipulation language; **~ naturel** m INFORMAT, ORDINAT natural language; **~ non algorithmique** m ORDINAT nonprocedural language; **~ orienté application** m ORDINAT application-oriented language; **~ orienté machine** m ORDINAT low-level language; **~ orienté problème** m ORDINAT problem-oriented language; **~ orienté vers le traitement** m ORDINAT procedure-oriented language; **~ par signes** m COMMANDE sign language; **~ de programmation** m INFORMAT, ORDINAT programming language; **~ de représentation des connaissances** m ORDINAT KRL, knowledge representation language; **~ résultant** m INFORMAT, ORDINAT object language; **~ scientifique** m ORDINAT scientific language; **~ de simulation** m ORDINAT simulation language; **~ source** m ORDINAT source language; **~ de spécification** m ORDINAT specification language; **~ à structure de blocs** m ORDINAT block-structured language; **~ temps réel** m ORDINAT real-time language; **~ de traitement de listes** m ORDINAT LISP, list processing language; **~ universel** m ORDINAT general-purpose language

langage: **~ standard généralisé de balisage** m (SGML) IMPRIM, INFORMAT Standard Generalized Mark-up Language (SGML)

langelotte m MINES puddling trough, trough washer

langite f MINERAUX langite

langue f CERAM VER settle ring, CONS MECA index, balance tongue; **~ d'aspic** f CONSTR arrowhead

languette f CONS MECA feather, index, spline, balance tongue, CONSTR feather, feather tongue, fillet, loose tongue, strip, tongue, bois cleat, TEXTILE tongue; **~ d'ajustage** f ELECTROTEC trim tab; **~ de brûleur** f CERAM VER tongue; **~ collée** f EMBALLAGE glued tab; **~ empêchant l'enregistrement** f ENREGISTR, TV record defeat tab; **~ d'entraînement du plateau de pression** f AUTO pressure plate drive strap; **~ pour ouverture facile** f EMBALLAGE easy opening tag; **~ de protection** f PRODUCTION protective strip; **~ rapportée** f CONSTR feather, feather tongue, fillet, loose tongue; **~ venue de bois** f CONSTR feather, tongue; **~ de verrouillage des cartes** f PRODUCTION automatisme industriel board locking tab

lanière f CONS MECA cord, IMPRIM mécanique strip; **~ pour courroie** f PRODUCTION belt lace

lanoléine f CHIMIE lanolin, lanoline

lanoline f CHIMIE lanolin, lanoline

lanostérine f CHIMIE lanosterol

lanterne f CINEMAT lamphouse, CONS MECA right-and-left coupling, right-and-left screw link, turnbuckle, DISTRI EAU rose, strainer, tailpiece, wind bore, PRODUCTION core barrel, lantern, VEHICULES éclairage, témoins lamp; **~ d'aiguille** f CH DE FER switchpoint light; **~ murale** f ELECTR éclairage wall lamp; **~ de queue** f CH DE FER véhicules signal lamp; **~ de serrage** f CONS MECA right-and-left coupling, right-and-left screw link, turnbuckle; **~ de signal** f CH DE FER signal lamp, véhicules signal lamp; **~ de tireuse additive** f CINEMAT additive lamphouse

lanterne-signal f COMMANDE signalling lamp (BrE), signalling lantern (BrE)

lanthane m (La) CHIMIE lanthanide, lanthanum (La)

lanthanide m CHIMIE lanthanide

lanthanite f MINERAUX lanthanite

lapidaire m CERAM VER disc grinder (BrE), disk grinder (AmE), MECANIQUE lapping machine, PRODUCTION face wheel

lapilli m pl GEOLOGIE lapilli

laplacien m PHYSIQUE laplacian; **~ géométrique** m NUCLEAIRE geometric buckling; **~ matière** m NUCLEAIRE material buckling

lappaconitine f CHIMIE lappaconitine

laps: **~ de temps écoulé** m MECANIQUE elapsed time

laquage m CINEMAT copie lacquering, COULEURS enameling (AmE), enamelling (BrE), lacquering, varnishing, japan work, lacquered work, MATERIAUX lacquering, REVETEMENT enameling (AmE), enamelling (BrE); **~ électrostatique** m COULEURS electrostatic enamelling; **~ électrostatique de couleurs en poudre** m COULEURS electrostatic powder coating; **~ de moule** m CERAM VER mold coating (AmE), mould coating (BrE)

laque f CHIMIE varnish, CONSTR lacquer, COULEURS lacquer, lake, shellac, MECANIQUE matériaux lacquer, PRODUCTION lac, lacquer, REVETEMENT coat of varnish; **~ alcoolique** f CONSTR spirit lacquer; **~ à l'asphalte** f COULEURS asphalt varnish, black japan; **~ carmine** f COULEURS carmine lacquer; **~ cellulosique** f COULEURS nitrocellulose lacquer, pyroxyline lacquer; **~ de cochenille** f COULEURS crimson lake; **~ colorée** f COULEURS colored lake (AmE), coloured lake (BrE); **~ écarlate** f COULEURS scarlet lake; **~ en écailles** f CONSTR shellac; **~ en feuilles** f CONSTR shellac; **~ en grains** f COULEURS seed lac; **~ en masse** f COULEURS stick lack; **~ en plaques** f CONSTR shellac; **~ au four** f COULEURS baked enamel, baking enamel, stove enamel; **~ d'impression** f COULEURS printing lake, printing varnish; **~ du Japon** f COULEURS japan; **~ martelée** f COULEURS hammer enamel, hammer tone finish; **~ nitrocellulosique** f CONSTR nitrocellulose lacquer; **~ noire** f COULEURS black varnish; **~ d'orient** f COULEURS Chinese lacquer, Japanese lacquer; **~ photosensible** f COULEURS photoresist, photosensitive resist; **~ plate** f CONSTR shellac; **~ polymérisée** f CONS MECA polymerized enamel; **~ pour cache** f COULEURS masking lacquer; **~ pourpre** f COULEURS crimson lake; **~ synthétique** f COULEURS synthetic enamel; **~ de teinturier** f COULEURS lac dye; **~ vinylique** f CONSTR vinyl lacquer

laqué adj COULEURS, MECANIQUE matériaux lacquered, REVETEMENT enamel-covered

laque-émail f COULEURS, REVETEMENT enamel paint, enamel varnish

laquer *vt* COULEURS lacquer; ~ **à la laque à cuire** *vt* COULEURS enamel bake, stove enamel; ~ **au vernis à cuire** *vt* REVETEMENT enamel

lardite *f* MINERAUX lardite

lardon: ~ **de guidage** *m* CONS MECA gib; ~ **réglable** *m* CONS MECA adjustable gib; ~ **de réglage** *m* CONS MECA adjusting gib

largable *adj* ESPACE *véhicules* jettisonable

largage *m* ESPACE *véhicules* drop; ~ **de carburant** *m* AERONAUT dumping; ~ **de la charge** *m* AERONAUT load release

large:[1] **au** ~ *adj* NAUT in the offing, offshore, PETROLE offshore; ~ **bande** *adj* TV broadband

large:[2] **au** ~ *adv* NAUT, PETROLE offshore

large[3] *m* NAUT offing, open sea, OCEANO offshore, open sea

largeur *f* INFORMAT width, NAUT breadth, *navire* beam, ORDINAT width, PAPIER breadth, width, TEXTILE width; ~ **de bande** *f* ELECTRON bandwidth, ENREGISTR bandwidth, tape width, ESPACE *communications* bandwidth, IMPRIM *impression* web width, OPTIQUE, ORDINAT, PHYS RAYON, PHYSIQUE, TELECOM, TV bandwidth; ~ **de bande de canal** *f* TV channel bandwidth; ~ **de bande de cohérence** *f* TELECOM coherence bandwidth; ~ **de bande effective** *f* ENREGISTR effective bandwidth; ~ **de bande de la porteuse** *f* ELECTRON carrier bandwidth; ~ **de bande d'un rayonnement laser** *f* ELECTRON laser bandwidth; ~ **de bande du signal** *f* ELECTRON signal bandwidth; ~ **de bande spectrale** *f* TELECOM spectral bandwidth; ~ **de bande vidéo** *f* INFORMAT, ORDINAT, TV video bandwidth; ~ **de chaîne** *f* TEXTILE dressed width of warp; ~ **de chaîne maximum** *f* TEXTILE maximum dressed width of warp; ~ **de chaîne minimum** *f* TEXTILE minimum-dressed width of warp; ~ **Doppler** *f* PHYS RAYON Doppler width; ~ **en drap à plat et en contours** *f* TEXTILE flat and fitted width; ~ **d'entrefer** *f* ELECTROTEC gap length, ENREGISTR gap depth, TV gap width; ~ **de l'escalier** *f* CONSTR length of step; ~ **du faisceau** *f* ELECTRON, OPTIQUE beam width; ~ **de faisceau à demi-puissance** *f* ELECTRON half-power width, ESPACE *communications* half-power beam width; ~ **de fendage** *f* METALL width of splitting; ~ **de fente optimum** *f* TV effective slit width; ~ **finie** *f* TEXTILE finished width of cloth; ~ **de giron** *f* CONSTR going; ~ **hors membres** *f* NAUT molded breadth (AmE), moulded breadth (BrE); ~ **hors tout** *f* CONS MECA overall width, NAUT extreme breadth, maximum beam; ~ **d'impulsion** *f* ELECTRON, INFORMAT, ORDINAT, PHYSIQUE, TELECOM, TV pulse width; ~ **de l'impulsion comprimée** *f* ELECTRON compressed pulse width; ~ **de justification** *f* IMPRIM justifying scale; ~ **de lame** *f* SECURITE width of blade; ~ **de lumière** *f* CONS MECA port width; ~ **de machine** *f* IMPRIM machine width; ~ **de marche** *f* CONSTR going; ~ **maximum de coupe d'une machine** *f* EMBALLAGE maximum trimmed machine width; ~ **à mi-crête** *f* OPTIQUE FWHM, full-width half-maximum, TELECOM full-duration half-maximum, full-width half-maximum; ~ **à mi-hauteur** *f* PHYSIQUE half-width; ~ **moyenne des caractères** *f* IMPRIM en space; ~ **naturelle** *f* NUCLEAIRE *niveau d'énergie* natural width; ~ **non rognée de la machine** *f* PAPIER untrimmed machine width; ~ **au peigne** *f* TEXTILE width in reed; ~ **de la piste** *f* ENREGISTR track width; ~ **propre de raie spectrale** *f* PHYS RAYON natural line width; ~ **radiale** *f* RESSORTS radial width; ~ **de raie** *f* CRISTALL line breadth, OPTIQUE spectral line width, PHYS RAYON line width; ~ **de raie atomique** *f* PHYS PART atomic line width; ~ **de la raie spectrale** *f* PHYS RAYON, TELECOM spectral line width; ~ **rognée maximale de la machine** *f* PAPIER maximum trimmed machine width; ~ **de rouleau** *f* PAPIER face roll; ~ **spectrale** *f* TELECOM spectral width; ~ **du tissu** *f* TEXTILE fabric width; ~ **de toile utile** *f* PAPIER maximum deckle; ~ **de toile utilisée** *f* PAPIER machine deckle, machine direction; ~ **totale** *f* PAPIER deckle, total width; ~ **utile** *f* PAPIER machine fill; ~ **vraie à mi-absorption** *f* PHYS RAYON *raie* true half-width

larguer *vt* AERONAUT jettison, ESPACE jettison, *véhicules* drop, NAUT *amarres* cast off

larme *f* CERAM VER knot, PLAST CAOU *imperfection* fat edge; ~ **batavique** *f* CERAM VER Prince Rupert drop

larmier *m* AERONAUT gutter, CONSTR eaves

laryngophone *m* ACOUSTIQUE, ENREGISTR throat microphone

laser *m* ELECTRON, IMPRIM, INFORMAT, MATERIAUX, OPTIQUE, ORDINAT, PHYS ONDES, PHYSIQUE laser; ~ **antisatellite** *m* ELECTRON antisatellite laser; ~ **à argon** *m* ELECTRON argon laser, PHYS RAYON argon gas laser; ~ **à argon ionisé** *m* ELECTRON ionized argon laser; ~ **à l'arsinure de gallium** *m* PHYS RAYON GaAs laser, gallium arsenide laser; ~ **atomique** *m* ELECTRON atomic gas laser; ~ **bleu-vert** *m* ELECTRON blue-green laser; ~ **à bromure de mercure** *m* ELECTRON mercury bromide laser; ~ **chimique** *m* ELECTRON chemical laser; ~ **au chlorure de xénon** *m* ELECTRON xenon chloride laser; ~ **à CO2** *m* ELECTRON CO_2 laser; ~ **à colorant** *m* PHYSIQUE dye laser; ~ **à commutation-Q** *m* NUCLEAIRE Q-switched laser; ~ **continu** *m* ELECTRON CW laser, continuous laser; ~ **à courte longueur d'onde** *m* ELECTRON short wavelength laser; ~ **à cristal** *m* ELECTRON crystal laser; ~ **à cristal de rubis** *m* ELECTRON, PHYS RAYON ruby crystal laser; ~ **à décharge électrique** *m* ELECTRON electric discharge laser; ~ **déclenché** *m* ELECTRON Q-switched laser; ~ **à détente** *m* ELECTRON gas dynamic laser; ~ **à diode** *m* ELECTRON diode laser; ~ **disc** *m* TV laser disc (BrE), laser disk (AmE); ~ **éclairant la cible** *m* ELECTRON target illuminating laser; ~ **embarqué** *m* ELECTRON airborne laser; ~ **à émission continue** *m* ELECTRON CW laser; ~ **à émission par impulsion** *m* ELECTRON pulsed laser; ~ **en anneau** *m* PHYSIQUE ring laser; ~ **à faible énergie** *m* ELECTRON low-energy laser; ~ **à faisceau continu** *m* ELECTRON CW laser; ~ **à faisceau d'électrons** *m* ELECTRON electron beam laser; ~ **à faisceau pulsé** *m* ELECTRON pulsed laser; ~ **à faisceau vert** *m* ELECTRON green beam laser; ~ **à gaz** *m* ELECTRON, PHYS RAYON gas laser; ~ **à gaz atomique** *m* ELECTRON atomic gas laser; ~ **à gaz carbonique** *m* ELECTRON carbon dioxide laser; ~ **à gaz à émission continue** *m* ELECTRON CW gas laser; ~ **à gaz moléculaire** *m* ELECTRON molecular gas laser; ~ **à hélium-néon** *m* PHYS RAYON helium-neon laser, PHYSIQUE He-Ne laser; ~ **illuminant la cible** *m* ELECTRON target illuminating laser; ~ **à impulsions courtes** *m* PHYS ONDES short-pulsed laser; ~ **infrarouge** *m* ELECTRON infrared laser; ~ **à injection** *m* ELECTRON injection laser, OPTIQUE ILD, diode laser, injection laser diode, TELECOM ILD, injection laser diode; ~ **à iode** *m* ELECTRON iodine laser; ~ **ionique** *m* ELECTRON ion laser; ~ **à ions** *m* CONS MECA ion laser; ~ **de lecture** *m* ELECTRON, OPTIQUE read laser; ~ **à liquide** *m* ELECTRON liquid laser; ~ **à liquide inorganique** *m*

ELECTRON inorganic liquid laser; **~ à liquide organique** *m* ELECTRON organic liquid laser; **~ à lumière rouge** *m* ELECTRON red laser; **~ marqueur de cible** *m* ELECTRON target designation laser; **~ à mercure** *m* ELECTRON mercury laser; **~ à modes synchronisés** *m* ELECTRON mode-locked laser; **~ moléculaire** *m* ELECTRON molecular laser; **~ monofréquence** *m* TELECOM single frequency laser; **~ monofréquence de faible énergie** *m* PHYS RAYON low-energy single-frequency laser; **~ multikilowatt** *m* NUCLEAIRE high-power laser; **~ multimodal** *m* OPTIQUE, TELECOM multimode laser; **~ au néodyme** *m* ELECTRON neodymium laser; **~ à onde continue** *m* PHYS ONDES continuous wave laser; **~ à oxyde de carbone** *m* ELECTRON carbon monoxide laser; **~ paramétrique** *m* ELECTRON parametric laser; **~ à pompage chimique** *m* ELECTRON chemical laser; **~ à pompage électrique** *m* ELECTRON electrically-pumped laser; **~ à pompage optique** *m* ELECTRON optically-pumped laser; **~ à pompage thermique** *m* ELECTRON thermally-pumped laser; **~ de poursuite** *m* ELECTRON laser tracker; **~ de puissance** *m* ELECTRON high-energy laser, NUCLEAIRE high-power laser; **~ pulsé** *m* ELECTRON, PHYS RAYON pulsed laser; **~ à rayons X** *m* ELECTRON, NUCLEAIRE, PHYS RAYON X-ray laser; **~ à rayon vert** *m* ELECTRON green beam laser; **~ à semi-conducteur** *m* ELECTRON semiconductor laser, OPTIQUE ILD, diode laser, semiconductor laser, PHYS RAYON semiconductor laser, PHYSIQUE diode laser, laser diode, TELECOM semiconductor laser; **~ à solide** *m* ELECTRON solid-state laser; **~ à teinture organique** *m* PHYS RAYON organic dye laser; **~ à trois niveaux** *m* ELECTRON three-level laser; **~ à vapeur métallique** *m* ELECTRON metal vapor laser (AmE), metal vapour laser (BrE); **~ à verre** *m* ELECTRON glass laser; **~ verrouillé par injection** *m* OPTIQUE, TELECOM injection-locked laser; **~ YAG** *m* ELECTRON YAG laser

lasercard *m* OPTIQUE lasercard; **~ drexon** *m* OPTIQUE drexon card

Laserjet *m* (MD) OPTIQUE Laserjet (TM)

laservision *f* OPTIQUE LV, laser vision

lasure *f* COULEURS wood stain

latence *f* INFORMAT, ORDINAT latency

latensification *f* CINEMAT flashing, latensification

latensifier *vt* CINEMAT hypersensitize

latérale *f* PETR lateral

latérite *f* CONSTR laterite

latex *m* PLAST CAOU, TEXTILE latex; **~ de caoutchouc** *m* PLAST CAOU rubber latex; **~ centrifugé** *m* PLAST CAOU centrifuged latex; **~ crémé** *m* PLAST CAOU creamed latex; **~ évaporé** *m* PLAST CAOU evaporated latex; **~ pauvre** *m* PLAST CAOU skimmed latex; **~ plantation** *m* PLAST CAOU field latex; **~ préservé** *m* PLAST CAOU preserved latex; **~ prévulcanisé** *m* PLAST CAOU prevulcanized latex; **~ stabilisé** *m* PLAST CAOU stabilized latex; **~ synthétique** *m* PLAST CAOU synthetic latex

latitude *f* NAUT latitude; **~ australe** *f* NAUT southern latitude; **~ boréale** *f* NAUT northern latitude; **~ d'exposition** *f* CINEMAT, PHOTO exposure latitude; **~ géocentrique** *f* ASTRONOMIE geocentric latitude; **~ géomagnétique** *f* GEOPHYS geomagnetic latitude; **~ magnétique** *f* PHYSIQUE magnetic latitude; **~ de mise au point** *f* PHOTO focusing range; **~ de pose** *f* CINEMAT, PHOTO exposure latitude

latitudinal *adj* NAUT transverse

lattage *m* CONSTR lathing, PRODUCTION lagging; **~ espacé** *m* CONS MECA spaced lathing; **~ jointif** *m*

PRODUCTION close lathing

latte:[1] **à ~ double** *adj* EMBALLAGE *caisse* double-battened

latte[2] *f* CINEMAT batten, CONSTR lath, NAUT batten; **~ à ardoises** *f* CONSTR lath, slate lath; **~ volige** *f* CONSTR batten, lath, slate lath; **~ volisse** *f* CONSTR lath

lattis *m* CONSTR lathing, PRODUCTION lagging; **~ espacé** *m* CONS MECA spaced lathing; **~ jointif** *m* PRODUCTION close lathing

laudanine *f* CHIMIE laudanine

laudanosine *f* CHIMIE laudanosine

laumonite *f* MINERAUX laumonite, laumontite

laumontite *f* MINERAUX laumonite, laumontite

laurionite *f* MINERAUX laurionite

laurique *adj* CHIMIE lauric

laurylique *adj* CHIMIE lauryl

lavabilité *f* PAPIER, TEXTILE washability

lavable *adj* PAPIER washable

lavage *m* CHIMIE panning, wash, CINEMAT wash, GENIE CHIM elutriation, scrubbing, washing out, washing, IMPRIM *blanchets* washing, *impression* washup, PAPIER washup, PETROLE scrubbing, POLLUTION rainout, scrubbing, washout, PRODUCTION, TEXTILE washing, THERMODYN *gaz* scrubbing; **~ à l'acide** *m* PAPIER acid washing; **~ alcalin** *m* LESSIVES alkali treatment; **~ atmosphérique** *m* POLLUTION atmospheric scrubbing; **~ au bac à piston** *m* MINES jigging; **~ basse pression** *m* POLLU MER low-pressure flushing; **~ au brut des citernes** *m* PETROLE COW, crude oil washing; **~ à l'eau acidulée** *m* PAPIER acid wash; **~ à l'eau chaude** *m* POLLU MER hot water washing; **~ en cascade** *m* PHOTO cascade washing; **~ à fond** *m* TEXTILE scouring; **~ des gaz de fumée** *m* THERMODYN fluc gas scrubbing; **~ haute pression** *m* POLLU MER high-pressure flushing; **~ au jig** *m* MINES jigging; **~ à la main** *m* PRODUCTION hand washing; **~ par retour de courant** *m* HYDROLOGIE backwashing; **~ aux sluices** *m* DISTRI EAU sluicing

lavande *f* CINEMAT fine-grain master, lavender

lave: **~ blocailleuse** *f* GEOLOGIE block lava; **~ en coussins** *f* GEOLOGIE pillow lava

lave-glace *m* VEHICULES *vitrage* washer; **~ de pare-brise** *m* VEHICULES *accessoire* windscreen washer (BrE), windshield washer (AmE)

laver *vt* CHIMIE wash, GENIE CHIM purify, PAPIER, TEXTILE wash; **~ avec de l'eau acidulée** *vt* PAPIER sour; **~ à l'eau chaude** *vt* POLLU MER wash with hot water

laverie *f* PRODUCTION wash house; **~ de kaolin** *f* CERAM VER china clay washing

lavé-séché *adj* TEXTILE drip-dry

laveur *m* CHARBON scrubber, washer, GAZ gas cleaner, GENIE CHIM washer, MINES scrubber, PRODUCTION washer, washing machine, TEXTILE washer; **~ d'air** *m* MINES air scrubber; **~ à la brosse** *m* TEXTILE brush washer; **~ de gaz** *m* NUCLEAIRE gas scrubber, gas washer; **~ humide ionisant** *m* SECURITE ionizing wet washer; **~ mécanique** *m* PRODUCTION washing machine; **~ à minerai** *m* MINES ore washer; **~ rotatif** *m* PRODUCTION rotary washer, rotary washing machine; **~ à tambour** *m* CONSTR drum washer; **~ venturi** *m* CHARBON venturi scrubber

laveuse: **~ de bouteille** *f* AGRO ALIM bottle washer

lave-verrerie *f* EQUIP LAB *nettoyage* glass washer

lavique *adj* GEOLOGIE *structure* lava-like

lavis *m* CONS MECA wash

lavoir *m* MINES washery, PRODUCTION washer, washing

machine; ~ **à charbon** *m* CHARBON coal washer, coal washery

lawrencium *m (Lr)* CHIMIE lawrencium *(Lr)*

lawsone *f* CHIMIE lawsone

lawsonite *f* MINERAUX lawsonite

laxmannite *f* MINERAUX laxmannite

lazulite *f* MINERAUX blue spar, lazulite

lazurite *f* MINERAUX lazurite

leader *m* NUCLEAIRE leader

leadhillite *f* MINERAUX leadhillite

LEAR *abrév (anneau d'antiprotons de basse énergie)* PHYS PART LEAR *(low-energy antiproton ring)*

lecam *m* TELECOM card reader

lécheur *m* CONS MECA licker

lécithine *f* AGRO ALIM lecithin

lecteur *m* ENREGISTR pick-up, INFORMAT, ORDINAT reader; ~ **acoustique** *m* ENREGISTR acoustic pick-up; ~ **audionumérique** *m* OPTIQUE CD audio player, audio CD player, audio compact disc player (BrE), audio compact disk player (AmE), compact music disc drive (BrE), compact music disc player (BrE), compact music disk drive (AmE), compact music disk player (AmE); ~ **de badge** *m* INFORMAT badge reader; ~ **de bande** *m* ENREGISTR tape player, INFORMAT tape drive, tape reader; ~ **de bande perforée** *m* INFORMAT paper tape reader, punched tape reader, ORDINAT punch tape reader (AmE), punched tape reader (BrE); ~ **à bobine mobile** *m* ENREGISTR moving coil pick-up; ~ **de caractères** *m* ORDINAT character reader; ~ **de caractères magnétiques** *m* ORDINAT magnetic ink character recognition; ~ **de cartes** *m* INFORMAT card reader, punched card reader, ORDINAT punched card reader, TELECOM card reader; ~ **de cartes magnétiques** *m* INFORMAT, ORDINAT magnetic card reader; ~ **de cartes perforées** *m* INFORMAT, ORDINAT punched card reader; ~ **de cartouche magnétique** *m* INFORMAT streamer, streaming tape drive; ~ **de CD-ROM** *m* OPTIQUE CD-ROM player; ~ **de code à barres** *m* EMBALLAGE bar code reader, INFORMAT bar code scanner; ~ **de disque** *m* OPTIQUE disc player (BrE), disk player (AmE); ~ **de disque audionumérique** *m* OPTIQUE CD audio player, audio CD player, audio compact disc player (BrE), audio compact disk player (AmE), compact music disc player (BrE), compact music disc drive (BrE), compact music disk drive (AmE), compact music disk player (AmE); ~ **de disque compact** *m* OPTIQUE CD drive; ~ **de disque optique** *m* OPTIQUE optical disc drive (BrE), optical disc player (BrE), optical disc reader (BrE), optical disk drive (AmE), optical disk player (AmE), optical disk reader (AmE); ~ **de disquettes** *m* INFORMAT floppy disk drive, floppy disk reader; ~ **de document** *m* INFORMAT, ORDINAT document reader; ~ **électronique de mesure micrométrique** *m* METROLOGIE electronic display micrometric head; ~ **et dérouleur de bande magnétique** *m* IMPRIM streamer; ~ **à faisceau lumineux** *m* ENREGISTR light beam pick-up; ~ **holographique** *m* INFORMAT holographic scanner; ~ **laservision** *m* OPTIQUE LV player, laservision player; ~ **magnétique** *m* ENREGISTR magnetic pick-up, TV magnetic reproducer; ~ **de marques** *m* INFORMAT, ORDINAT mark reader; ~ **de microfiche** *m* IMPRIM, INFORMAT, ORDINAT microfiche reader; ~ **de microfilm** *m* INFORMAT, ORDINAT microfilm reader; ~ **optique** *m* INFORMAT optical scanner, METROLOGIE *machine-outil* optical reader; ~ **optique de caractères** *m* IMPRIM,

INFORMAT, ORDINAT OCR, optical character reader; ~ **optique de marques** *m* INFORMAT, ORDINAT optical mark reader; ~ **phonographique photoélectrique** *m* ENREGISTR photoelectric pick-up; ~ **pour piste magnétique couchée** *m* CINEMAT magnetic stripe sound head; ~ **de son** *m* CINEMAT sound film head, ENREGISTR sound reader; ~ **de son optique** *m* CINEMAT optical sound head; ~ **de vidéodisque** *m* OPTIQUE, TV videodisc player (BrE), videodisk player (AmE)

lecture:[1] **à ~ seule** *adj* INFORMAT, ORDINAT read only

lecture[2] *f* ACOUSTIQUE reproducing, CHIMIE read-out, reading, CONSTR reading, INFORMAT fetch, read, read-out, ORDINAT read-out, read, TV playback, replay; ~ **accélérée** *f* TV fast playback; ~ **après écriture** *f* INFORMAT, ORDINAT read after write; ~ **avec éclatement** *f* INFORMAT, ORDINAT scatter read; ~ **capacitive** *f* OPTIQUE capacitance sensing; ~ **de carte à mémoire** *f* TELECOM smart card reader; ~ **densitométrique d'une zone de document au hasard** *f* IMPRIM *photogravure* random sample reading; ~ **destructive** *f* INFORMAT, ORDINAT destructive read; ~ **différentielle** *f* OPTIQUE push-pull scanning; ~ **digitale** *f* ELECTR digital readout; ~ **directe** *f* CONS MECA direct reading; ~ **de documents** *f* INFORMAT, ORDINAT document reading; ~ **hélicoïdale** *f* TV helical scan; ~ **d'instruction** *f* INFORMAT instruction fetching; ~ **labiale** *f* ACOUSTIQUE lip reading; ~ **de marques** *f* INFORMAT, ORDINAT mark reading, mark scanning, mark sensing; ~ **non destructive** *f* INFORMAT, ORDINAT nondestructive read; ~ **numérique** *f* ELECTR, TELECOM digital readout; ~ **optique** *f* IMPRIM optical character recognition; ~ **optique de marques** *f* INFORMAT, ORDINAT OMR, optical mark reading, mark scanning, mark sensing; ~ **de parasite** *f* ORDINAT drop-in; ~ **par la tache centrale** *f* OPTIQUE axial scanning; ~ **au scanner** *f* IMPRIM electronic scanning; ~ **stéréophonique** *f* ENREGISTR stereophonic reproduction

lecture:[3] **~ et écriture simultanées** *loc* INFORMAT, ORDINAT read while write

lecture-écriture *f* INFORMAT, ORDINAT read-write

lédéburite *f* METALL ledeburite

lège *adj* POLLU MER unladen

légende *f* CINEMAT, EMBALLAGE caption, IMPRIM caption, *schéma, illustration* callout; ~ **d'organigramme** *f* INFORMAT flowchart text

léger *adj* MECANIQUE lightweight

légèreté *f* IMPRIM *papier, photogravure*, MATERIAUX lightness

législation: ~ des eaux *f* DISTRI EAU water law; ~ **de fond** *f* SECURITE basic legislation; ~ **industrielle** *f* SECURITE Factory Act (BrE)

lenticulaire *adj* GEOLOGIE lenticular

lenticulé *adj* PHOTO lens-shaped

lentille *f* CINEMAT, EQUIP LAB *optique*, ESPACE *communications*, HYDROLOGIE lens, INSTRUMENT lens, telescope objective, PHOTO, PHYSIQUE lens; ~ **achromatique** *f* PHYSIQUE achromatic lens; ~ **achromatique en quartz-fluorine** *f* INSTRUMENT achromatic quartz fluoride lens; ~ **additionnelle** *f* INSTRUMENT supplementary lens; ~ **anamorphosique** *f* INSTRUMENT anamorphic lens; ~ **antérieure** *f* INSTRUMENT condensing lens, field lens, front lens; ~ **antireflet** *f* INSTRUMENT coated lens, lumenized lens; ~ **d'approche** *f* INSTRUMENT close-up lens, portrait lens; ~ **arrière** *f* INSTRUMENT back lens; ~ **asphérique correctrice** *f* TV aspheric corrector plate; ~ **de balancier** *f* CONS MECA ball; ~ **biconcave** *f* INSTRU-

MENT, PHYSIQUE biconcave lens; ~ **biconvexe** f INSTRUMENT, PHYSIQUE biconvex lens; ~ **bifocale** f CINEMAT split field lens, INSTRUMENT bifocal lens; ~ **à bord épais** f INSTRUMENT concave lens, divergent lens, diverging lens, negative lens; ~ **à bord mince** f INSTRUMENT convergent lens, converging lens, convex lens, positive lens; ~ **de champ** f INSTRUMENT condensing lens, field lens, front lens, PHOTO field lens; ~ **collimatée** f PHOTO collimated lens; ~ **collimatrice** f OPTIQUE correcting optics; ~ **concave** f CINEMAT concave lens, INSTRUMENT concave lens, divergent lens, diverging lens, negative lens, PHOTO concave lens; ~ **condensatrice** f CINEMAT condenser lens; ~ **de condenseur** f INSTRUMENT first condenser lens; ~ **de contact** f INSTRUMENT, OPTIQUE contact lens; ~ **convergente** f CINEMAT converging lens, INSTRUMENT convergent lens, converging lens, convex lens, positive lens, eye lens, focusing lens, objective lens, PHYSIQUE converging lens; ~ **convexe** f INSTRUMENT convergent lens, converging lens, convex lens, positive lens, PHOTO convex lens; ~ **correctrice** f PHOTO correcting lens, correction lens; ~ **à couche antireflet** f INSTRUMENT coated lens, lumenized lens; ~ **cylindrique** f INSTRUMENT cylindrical lens; ~ **cylindrique de Fresnel** f INSTRUMENT Fresnel lens; ~ **déformante** f CINEMAT distortion lens; ~ **demi-boule** f INSTRUMENT semicircular lens; ~ **diaphragmée** f PHYSIQUE stopped lens; ~ **de diffraction** f INSTRUMENT intermediate lens; ~ **diffusante** f INSTRUMENT diffuser lens, soft-focus lens; ~ **dioptrique** f CINEMAT plus diopter (AmE), plus dioptre (BrE), PHOTO eyepiece; ~ **divergente** f CINEMAT diverging lens, INSTRUMENT concave lens, divergent lens, diverging lens, negative lens, PHYSIQUE diverging lens; ~ **à double focale** f CINEMAT split field lens; ~ **à échelons** f INSTRUMENT drum lens; ~ **électromagnétique** f ELECTROTEC electromagnetic lens; ~ **électronique** f ELECTRON electron lens, INSTRUMENT electron lens, focusing diode, PHYSIQUE electron lens, TV electromagnetic lens, electron lens; ~ **électronique à immersion** f TV immersion electron lens; ~ **électrostatique** f ELECTROTEC, PHYS RAYON, PHYSIQUE electrostatic lens; ~ **en crown-glass** f CERAM VER crown glass lens; ~ **fendue** f INSTRUMENT split lens; ~ **filtre** f INSTRUMENT filter lens; ~ **de flou** f CINEMAT soft-focus lens, INSTRUMENT diffuser lens, soft-focus lens, PHOTO soft-focus lens; ~ **fluorurée** f INSTRUMENT fluorite lens (BrE), fluorspar lens (AmE); ~ **à focale variable** f INSTRUMENT zoom lens; ~ **de Fresnel** f CINEMAT Fresnel lens, step lens, INSTRUMENT zoned lens, PHOTO, PHYSIQUE Fresnel lens; ~ **Fresnel plane** f INSTRUMENT concentric Fresnel lens, echelon lens; ~ **frontale** f INSTRUMENT condensing lens, field lens, front lens, PHOTO front element; ~ **de glace** f CHARBON ice lens; ~ **gravitationnelle** f ASTRONOMIE gravitational lens; ~ **grossissante** f INSTRUMENT magnifying lens; ~ **à immersion** f INSTRUMENT immersion lens, immersion objective; ~ **magnétique** f ELECTROTEC magnetic lens, INSTRUMENT magnetic lens, magnetic objective, *microscope* second condenser lens, PHYS RAYON, PHYSIQUE magnetic lens; ~ **ménisque** f INSTRUMENT meniscus lens; ~ **ménisque convergente** f INSTRUMENT positive meniscus lens; ~ **ménisque divergent** f INSTRUMENT negative meniscus lens; ~ **ménisquée** f PHYSIQUE meniscus lens; ~ **mince** f PHYSIQUE thin lens; ~ **monochromatique** f INSTRUMENT monochromatic lens; ~ **d'objectif** f EQUIP LAB, INSTRUMENT objective lens; ~ **objective** f EQUIP LAB, INSTRUMENT, METALL objective lens; ~ **de pendule** f CONS MECA ball, PHYSIQUE pendulum bob; ~ **plan-concave** f PHYSIQUE planoconcave lens; ~ **plan-convexe** f INSTRUMENT, PHYSIQUE planoconvex lens; ~ **de pont** f NAUT deck light; ~ **de projection** f INSTRUMENT projection lens, projector lens; ~ **de redressement** f INSTRUMENT erecting lens, rectification lens, spreading lens; ~ **sphérique** f PHYSIQUE spherical lens; ~ **supplémentaire** f PHOTO supplementary lens; ~ **traitée** f PHOTO bloomed lens, coated lens; ~ **unipotentielle** f NUCLEAIRE Einzel lens, unipotential lens; ~ **de visée** f ASTRONOMIE viewing lens

lentilles: ~ **collées** f pl CERAM VER cemented lenses; ~ **d'éclairage** f pl INSTRUMENT illumination optics; ~ **à foyer progressif** f pl INSTRUMENT multifocal glasses; ~ **multifocales** f pl INSTRUMENT multifocal glasses; ~ **de Schmidt** f pl INSTRUMENT Schmidt system

lenzinite f MINERAUX lenzinite

léonhardite f NUCLEAIRE leonhardite

Léonides m pl ASTRONOMIE Leonids

LEP abrév (*grand collisionneur électron-positron*) PHYS PART LEP (*large electron-positron collider*)

lépidolite f MINERAUX lepidolite

lépidomélane m MINERAUX lepidomelane

leptochlorite f MINERAUX leptochlorite

lepton m PHYS PART, PHYSIQUE lepton

lésion f SECURITE injury

lessivage m AGRO ALIM leaching, CHIMIE leaching, lixiviation, GAZ, HYDROLOGIE leaching, PAPIER boiling, cooking, digestion, PETR washover, wave delta, POLLUTION below-cloud scavenging, washout; ~ **atmosphérique** m POLLUTION washout; ~ **à basse pression** m POLLU MER low-pressure flushing; ~ **direct** m GAZ direct leaching; ~ **à haute pression** m POLLU MER high-pressure flushing; ~ **inverse** m GAZ indirect leaching; ~ **rapide** m POLLU MER, POLLUTION flushing

lessive f CHIMIE lye, LESSIVES scouring liquid, scouring liquor; ~ **alcaline** f LESSIVES alkaline solution; ~ **en poudre** f LESSIVES washing powder

lessiver vt CHIMIE, GEOLOGIE, HYDROLOGIE leach, LESSIVES scour, POLLU MER leach, THERMODYN *papier* cook

lessiveur m PAPIER boiler, cooker, digester, kier; ~ **en continu** m PAPIER continuous digester; ~ **en discontinu** m PAPIER batch digester; ~ **vertical** m PRODUCTION *industrie du papier* vertical digester

lessiviel adj GENIE CHIM detergent

lest:[1] **sur** ~ adv NAUT in ballast

lest[2] m AERONAUT, ELECTROTEC ballast, NAUT ballast keel

lestage: ~ **de talus** m CONSTR toe weighting

léthargie f PHYS RAYON lethargy

lettrage m IMPRIM lettering

lettre f IMPRIM, INFORMAT letter; ~ **accentuée** f IMPRIM accented letter; ~ **de code correspondant à la tension de la bobine** f PRODUCTION coil voltage code; ~ **de code de couleur** f PRODUCTION color code letter (AmE), colour code letter (BrE); ~ **gothique** f IMPRIM *typographie* black letter; ~ **longue** f IMPRIM long descender; ~ **de mer** f NAUT certificate of registry; ~ **montante** f IMPRIM ascending letter; ~ **ornée** f IMPRIM swash letter; ~ **pleine** f IMPRIM solid letter; ~ **de stock** f PRODUCTION stock record; ~ **de transport aérien** f AERONAUT, TRANSPORT airway bill; ~ **de transport maritime** f NAUT waybill

lettres: ~ **capitales bâton** *f pl* IMPRIM block capitals; ~ **majuscules écrites à la main** *f pl* IMPRIM *document administratif* block letters; ~ **de titrage** *f pl* IMPRIM *typographie* block letters; ~ **de transfert sec** *f pl* IMPRIM *maquette* dry transfer

lettrine *f* IMPRIM *composition, maquette* initial; ~ **encastrée** *f* IMPRIM *mise en page, maquette* factotum initial; ~ **habillée** *f* IMPRIM versals

lettsomite *f* MINERAUX lettsomite

leuchtenbergite *f* MINERAUX leuchtenbergite

leucite *f* MINERAUX leucite

leucobase *f* CHIMIE leuco compound

leucocrate *adj* GEOLOGIE leucocratic, light-colored (AmE), light-coloured (BrE)

leucophane *m* MINERAUX leucophane, leucophanite

leucopyrite *f* MINERAUX leucopyrite

leucosome *m* GEOLOGIE leucosome

leucoxène *m* MINERAUX leucoxene

leurre *m* OCEANO artificial bait, jig, lure

levage[1] *m* CONS MECA lifting, PRODUCTION hoisting, SECURITE lifting; ~ **par hélicoptère** *m* AERONAUT helilifting

levage:[2] ~ **et déplacement des charges lourdes** *loc* SECURITE lifting and moving heavy loads

levain *m* AGRO ALIM leaven, starter

lévane *m* CHIMIE levan

levé *m* CONSTR survey, surveying; ~ **aérien** *m* AERONAUT aerial survey; ~ **aéromagnétique** *m* GEOLOGIE aeromagnetic survey; ~ **à la boussole** *m* MINES compass survey; ~ **de détail** *m* CONSTR detailed survey; ~ **gamma** *m* NUCLEAIRE gamma ray survey; ~ **géophysique** *m* CONSTR geophysical survey; ~ **gravimétrique** *m* GEOLOGIE gravimetric survey; ~ **hydrographique** *m* OCEANO hydrographic survey; ~ **de plan à la boussole** *m* MINES compass survey, dialing (AmE), dialling (BrE); ~ **de plans** *m* CONSTR survey, surveying; ~ **de plans au stadia** *m* CONSTR stadia surveying; ~ **sismique** *m* GEOPHYS, PETROLE seismic survey; ~ **de terrains** *m* CONSTR land survey, land surveying; ~ **topographique** *m* CONSTR topographical survey

lève-balai *m* ELECTR *machine* brush lifting device

levée *f* AGRO ALIM raising power, CERAM VER doff, laying, CONS MECA play, *piston* stroke, CONSTR causeway, *pilons* lift, NUCLEAIRE length of stroke, lift, stroke, travel, OCEANO *plage* shingle spit, TEXTILE doffing; ~ **d'ambiguïté** *f* ESPACE *communications* ambiguity resolution; ~ **d'ambiguïté sur la phase** *f* ESPACE *communications* phase ambiguity resolution; ~ **de came** *f* CONS MECA cam action; ~ **d'un clapet** *f* INST HYDR lift; ~ **du levier de battage** *f* MINES stroke of the walking beam; ~ **de pâte par agents chimiques** *f* AGRO ALIM chemical leavening; ~ **du piston** *f* CONS MECA piston stroke; ~ **de plage** *f* OCEANO beach ridge; ~ **de la production** *f* MINES gold cleanup

lève-glace *m* VEHICULES *carrosserie* winding mechanism, window crank (AmE), window regulator (BrE)

lever:[1] ~ **héliaque** *m* ASTRONOMIE heliacal rising; ~ **de lune** *m* ASTRONOMIE moonrise

lever[2] *vt* AERONAUT hoist, CONSTR plot, MECANIQUE lift, NAUT weigh, *l'ancre* heave, PRODUCTION hoist, *litige* settle

lève-tôles *m* PRODUCTION plate hoist

levier *m* CONS MECA handspike, lever, CONSTR crow, crowbar, PHYSIQUE lever; ~ **d'armement** *m* PHOTO cocking lever; ~ **d'avance et de retard** *m* INST HYDR *distribution Walchaerts* lap and lead lever;

~ **d'avancement de film** *m* PHOTO film transport lever; ~ **d'avancement de pellicule** *m* PHOTO film advance lever; ~ **à bascule** *m* CONS MECA balance lever; ~ **de battage** *m* MINES walking beam; ~ **à boucle** *m* PRODUCTION *automatisme industriel* loop lever; ~ **à chaîne** *m* CONS MECA chain lever; ~ **de changement de marche** *m* CONS MECA reversing lever; ~ **de changement de vitesse** *m* AUTO, VEHICULES gear change lever (BrE), gearshift lever (AmE); ~ **à cliquet** *m* CONS MECA ratchet lever; ~ **de commande** *m* AERONAUT control column, control stick, control lever, drop arm, CINEMAT control arm, CONS MECA arm rocker, ESPACE *véhicules* joystick, MINES control lever; ~ **de commande de direction** *m* VEHICULES drop arm; ~ **de commande de papillons** *m* AUTO throttle control lever; ~ **de commande de pas** *m* AERONAUT pitch control lever; ~ **de commande de vitesse** *m* VEHICULES gear change lever (BrE), gearshift lever (AmE); ~ **à contrepoids** *m* CONS MECA swing bob lever; ~ **coudé** *m* CONS MECA bell crank; ~ **de débrayage** *m* AUTO clutch pedal release lever, pressure plate release lever, CONS MECA disengaging lever, VEHICULES *embrayage* pressure plate release lever; ~ **du deuxième genre** *m* CONS MECA lever of the second kind; ~ **double** *m* CONS MECA compound lever; ~ **d'équilibrage** *m* CONS MECA balance lever; ~ **équilibré par contrepoids** *m* CONS MECA counterbalanced lever; ~ **de frein** *m* CH DE FER *véhicules* brake lever; ~ **de freinage** *m* CONS MECA brake lever; ~ **de frein à main** *m* AUTO handbrake lever; ~ **du frein de stationnement** *m* VEHICULES parking brake lever; ~ **de fusée** *m* AUTO spindle arm, steering arm; ~ **à galet** *m* PRODUCTION roller lever; ~ **interappui** *m* CONS MECA lever of the first kind; ~ **interpuissant** *m* CONS MECA lever of the third kind; ~ **interrésistant** *m* CONS MECA lever of the second kind; ~ **d'interrupteur** *m* ELECTROTEC switch lever; ~ **inverseur** *m* CONS MECA reversing lever; ~ **à main** *m* CONS MECA hand lever; ~ **de manoeuvre** *m* CINEMAT pan and tilt handle, COMMANDE adjusting lever, CONS MECA operating lever; ~ **de manoeuvre des aiguilles** *m* CH DE FER pointer, switch lever; ~ **de mise en marche** *m* CONS MECA starting handle, starting lever; ~ **de mise au point** *m* CINEMAT focusing lever; ~ **pas-gaz** *m* AERONAUT pitch throttle synchronizer; ~ **de pas général** *m* AERONAUT collective pitch lever; ~ **à pied-de-biche et à pointe** *m* CONSTR pick-and-claw crowbar; ~ **pivotant** *m* CONS MECA pivoted lever; ~ **à poignée** *m* CONS MECA handle lever; ~ **porte-train d'un système d'engrenage épicycloïdal** *m* CONS MECA arm of an epicyclic train; ~ **de pose** *m* COMMANDE position lever, regulating lever; ~ **de positionnement** *m* CINEMAT positioner; ~ **à poussoir** *m* CONS MECA latched lever; ~ **du premier genre** *m* CONS MECA lever of the first kind; ~ **de pression à ressort** *m* PHOTO spring-tensioned pressure lever; ~ **à rappel** *m* PRODUCTION spring return lever; ~ **de régulateur** *m* INST HYDR throttle lever; ~ **de renvoi de direction** *m* AUTO steering idler arm; ~ **sélecteur** *m* AUTO, VEHICULES *transmission* selector lever; ~ **de serrage** *m* CONS MECA clamping lever; ~ **à tige rigide** *m* PRODUCTION rod lever; ~ **du troisième genre** *m* CONS MECA lever of the third kind; ~ **de zoom** *m* CINEMAT, TV zoom lever

levier-fourche: ~ **à galets** *m* PRODUCTION fork-lever roller

levier-gachette *m* PHOTO rapid film-advance lever, single stroke lever lévigation *f* PRODUCTION levigation

lévitation *f* ESPACE, PHYSIQUE levitation; ~ **magnétique** *f* PHYSIQUE magnetic levitation

lévogyre *adj* PHYSIQUE laevorotatory

lévorotatoire *adj* CHIMIE laevorotatory, levorotatory

lèvre *f* CONS MECA *foret, mèche*, CONSTR *godet* lip; ~ **de la caisse de tête** *f* PAPIER slice, slice lip; ~ **de cisaillement** *f* ELECTRON resonator grid, METALL shear lip; ~ **de coulée** *f* CERAM VER casting lip, spout; ~ **de la débiteuse** *f* CERAM VER slot lip; ~ **de fracture** *f* CERAM VER edge fracture; ~ **supérieure d'une faille** *f* GEOLOGIE hanging wall

lévuline *f* CHIMIE levulin, synanthrose

lévulique *adj* CHIMIE levulinic

lévulose *m* AGRO ALIM, CHIME fructose, fruit sugar, laevulose (BrE), levulose (AmE)

levure *f* AGRO ALIM raising agent; ~ **basse** *f* AGRO ALIM bottom yeast; ~ **chimique** *f* AGRO ALIM chemical leavening

lévyne *f* MINERAUX levyne, levynite

Lézard *m* ASTRONOMIE Lacerta

LGN *abrév (liquide de gaz naturel)* GAZ, PETROLE NGL *(natural gas liquid)*

Li *(lithium)* CHIMIE Li *(lithium)*

liaison *f* CH DE FER *voies* rail junction, CHIMIE bond, linkage, linking, CONSTR bonding, CRISTALL bond, ELECTROTEC coupling, ESPACE *véhicules* bus, INFORMAT linkage, link, MATERIAUX bonding, MECANIQUE linkage, METALL binding, NAUT bonding, NUCLEAIRE bond, bonding material, ORDINAT communication link, linkage, link, PLAST CAOU bond, TELECOM link; ~ **d'accès** *f* TELECOM AL, access link; ~ **aller** *f* ESPACE *communications* forward link; ~ **asynchrone** *f* ELECTR *deux réseaux en courant alternatif* asynchronous link; ~ **de base** *f* INFORMAT, ORDINAT basic linkage; ~ **chimique** *f* CRISTALL chemical bond, PETROLE bond, chemical bond; ~ **de communication** *f* INFORMAT communication link; ~ **de connexion** *f* ESPACE *communications* feeder link; ~ **covalente** *f* CRISTALL, METALL covalent bond; ~ **croisée** *f* CHIMIE cross-link; ~ **dans un réseau** *f* ELECTR link; ~ **dative** *f* CHIMIE dative bond; ~ **delta** *f* CHIMIE delta bonding; ~ **descendante** *f* ESPACE *communications* down link; ~ **directe** *f* ELECTRON, ELECTROTEC direct coupling; ~ **dirigée** *f* CRISTALL directed bond; ~ **de données** *f* ESPACE *communications*, INFORMAT, ORDINAT data link, TELECOM DL, data link; ~ **double** *f* CHIMIE double bond; ~ **en courant continu** *f* ELECTROTEC direct coupling; ~ **entre étages** *f* ELECTRON coupling between stages, ELECTROTEC stage coupling; ~ **éther** *f* LESSIVES ether linkage, etherlene linkage; ~ **des fibres** *f* MATERIAUX fiber bonding (AmE), fibre bonding (BrE); ~ **fusible** *f* ELECTROTEC fuse link; ~ **hertzienne** *f* PHYSIQUE microwave link, TV radio link; ~ **hétéropolaire** *f* CRISTALL ionic bond; ~ **homopolaire** *f* CRISTALL covalent bond, METALL coordinate linkage; ~ **hydrogène** *f* CHIMIE, CRISTALL hydrogen bond; ~ **informatique** *f* ELECTRON data link; ~ **intercalculateur** *f* TELECOM interprocessor link; ~ **intermoléculaire** *f* MATERIAUX intermolecular bond; ~ **intersatellite** *f* ESPACE *communications* intersatellite link; ~ **ionique** *f* CHIMIE, CRISTALL, PHYS RAYON ionic bond; ~ **maritime** *f* NAUT sea link; ~ **mécanique** *f* NUCLEAIRE mechanical bond; ~ **métal-céramique** *f* MATERIAUX metal-ceramic bond; ~ **métallique** *f* METALL metallic bond; ~ **modulateur-démodulateur** *f* PRODUCTION *automatisme industriel* modem link; ~ **à modulateur-démodulateur multipoint** *f* PRODUCTION *automatisme industriel* multipoint modem link; ~ **montante** *f* ESPACE *communications* uplink; ~ **multipoint** *f* INFORMAT, ORDINAT multidrop link, multipoint link; ~ **navette par hélicoptère** *f* AERONAUT helicopter shuttle service; ~ **non saturée entre carbones** *f* PETROLE unsaturated carbon-to-carbon bond; ~ **numérique** *f* TELECOM digital modulation link; ~ **optique** *f* OPTIQUE optical fiber link (AmE), optical fibre link (BrE), optical link; ~ **par câble** *f* TV cable link; ~ **par capacité** *f* ELECTROTEC capacitance coupling; ~ **par double transformateur** *f* ELECTROTEC link coupling; ~ **par fibre optique** *f* OPTIQUE, TELECOM optical fiber link (AmE), optical fibre link (BrE); ~ **par inductance et capacité** *f* ELECTROTEC impedance coupling; ~ **par infrarouges** *f* TV infrared link; ~ **par rafales météoriques** *f* ESPACE *communications* meteor burst link; ~ **par résistance et capacitance** *f* ELECTROTEC RC coupling, resistance-capacitance coupling; ~ **par satellite** *f* ESPACE *communications*, TV satellite link; ~ **par transformateur** *f* ELECTROTEC transformer coupling; ~ **pi** *f* CHIMIE pi bond; ~ **de point à point** *f* ELECTROTEC point-to-point link; ~ **pont-coque** *f* NAUT deck-hull bonding; ~ **de prestataire de service** *f* TELECOM SPL, service provider link; ~ **primaire** *f* TELECOM primary link; ~ **primaire pour les services de distribution** *f* TELECOM DPL, distribution primary link; ~ **primaire pour les services interactifs** *f* TELECOM IPL, interactive primary link; ~ **radio** *f* AERONAUT, NAUT radio link; ~ **radio navire-sol** *f* NAUT ship-to-shore radio; ~ **radiotéléphone** *f* NAUT radiotelephone link; ~ **sigma** *f* CHIMIE sigma bond; ~ **simple** *f* CHIMIE single bond; ~ **spatiale** *f* TV satellite link; ~ **spécialisée** *f* TELECOM PW, leased line, direct line, private wire; ~ **spécialisée tous-usages** *f* TELECOM analog private wire (AmE), analogue private wire (BrE); ~ **spécialisée tous usages** *f* TELECOM speech-grade private wire; ~ **spécialisée transmission de données** *f* TELECOM data private wire; ~ **thermique** *f* THERMODYN thermal link; ~ **de transmission de données** *f* ELECTRON data link; ~ **transversale** *f* NAUT transverse member; ~ **triple** *f* CHIMIE triple bond; ~ **de Van der Waals** *f* CRISTALL Van der Waals bond; ~ **de voies** *f* CH DE FER rail junction; ~ **de voies en courbe** *f* CH DE FER crossover between curved tracks

liaisonner *vt* CONSTR bond, *maçonnerie* bond

liant *m* AGRO ALIM binding agent, CERAM VER binder, bond, CONSTR, ENREGISTR, ESPACE *véhicules*, GEOLOGIE binder, IMPRIM bond, carrying medium, *encre* binder, MATERIAUX bonding material, pliability, pliableness, pliancy, *revêtement* binder agent, PLAST CAOU linkage, *adhésif* bonding agent, *peinture* binder, PRODUCTION bond, TV binder; ~ **du carbone** *m* IMPRIM vehicle; ~ **clair** *m* TV clear binder; ~ **à émulsion** *m* GENIE CHIM emulsion binder; ~ **de l'encre** *m* IMPRIM vehicle; ~ **fillerisé** *m* CONSTR filled binder; ~ **véhicule** *m* IMPRIM *encre* medium

liasse *f* IMPRIM *continu* formset; ~ **pliée en zigzag** *f* IMPRIM *continu* flat pack form; ~ **sans papier carbone** *f* IMPRIM *continu* flat form

LIB *abrév (message de libération)* TELECOM REL *(release message)*

libération *f* ELECTROTEC, INFORMAT, ORDINAT, TELECOM release; ~ **de chaleur** *f* NUCLEAIRE heat release; ~ **de pierres** *f* CERAM VER stoning

libérer *vt* MECANIQUE release, PHYSIQUE liberate

libéthénite *f* MINERAUX libethenite

libration *f* ASTRONOMIE libration; **~ diurne** *f* ASTRONOMIE diurnal libration

libre[1] *adj* CHIMIE free, *électron* unpaired, TELECOM idle

libre:[2] **~ parcours moyen** *m* ACOUSTIQUE, PHYSIQUE mean free path; **~ parcours moyen de diffusion** *m* NUCLEAIRE diffusion mean free path; **~ parcours moyen total** *m* NUCLEAIRE total mean free path; **~ pratique** *m* NAUT free pratique

librement: ~ réglable *adj* CONS MECA adjustable at will

libre-pratique *m* NAUT pratique

licaréol *m* CHIMIE licareol

licence *f* BREVETS, QUALITE licence (BrE), license (AmE); **~ exclusive** *f* BREVETS exclusive licence (BrE), exclusive license (AmE); **~ d'exploitation** *f* AERONAUT operating permit; **~ d'exportation** *f* NAUT export licence (BrE), export license (AmE); **~ d'importation** *f* NAUT import licence (BrE), import license (AmE); **~ obligatoire** *f* BREVETS compulsory licence (BrE), compulsory license (AmE)

licencier *vt* NAUT *membre de l'équipage* discharge

Licorne *f* ASTRONOMIE Monoceros

lidar *m* ESPACE *véhicules* lidar; **~ de sondage** *m* ESPACE *véhicules* sounding lidar

lié *adj* CONS MECA connected, ESPACE *véhicules* strap-down-mounted; **~ à l'environnement** *adj* POLLUTION environmental

liebénérite *f* MINERAUX liebenerite

liège *m* CONSTR, REFRIG cork; **~ expansé** *m* REFRIG expanded cork; **~ de fossile** *m* MINERAUX mountain cork; **~ granulé** *m* REFRIG granulated cork; **~ de montagne** *m* MINERAUX mountain cork

lien *m* CONS MECA link, strap, tie, CONSTR bond, strut, fastening, strap, strap bolt, IMPRIM *emballage* bond, INFORMAT, ORDINAT link, PRODUCTION fastening, strap, TELECOM link; **~ en bout** *m* CHIMIE *polymère* endlink; **~ en fer à U** *m* CONS MECA stirrup, stirrup bolt, stirrup piece, stirrup strap, CONSTR U-bolt, strap, strap bolt; **~ peptidique** *m* CHIMIE peptide link; **~ réticulé** *m* PLAST CAOU *polymérisation* cross-link

lier *vt* CONSTR *pierre* bind, EMBALLAGE bond

lierne *f* CONSTR bridging piece, rail, strut

liernes *f pl* CONSTR bridging, stiffening, strutting

lieu *m* CONS MECA location; **~ destinataire** *m* PRODUCTION destination bin; **~ d'émission** *m* POLLUTION emission point, point source; **~ géométrique** *m* GEOMETRIE *point mobile* locus; **~ de naissance du tremblement de terre** *m* GEOPHYS seismic focus; **~ de pêche** *m* NAUT fishery, fishing ground; **~ de refuge** *m* CONSTR refuge hole, shelter; **~ de travail** *m* SECURITE workplace

lieux: sur les ~ *adv* CONSTR on the spot

Lièvre *m* ASTRONOMIE Lepus

liévrite *f* MINERAUX lievrite

lift *m* PRODUCTION elevator

ligand *m* CHIMIE, MATERIAUX, METALL ligand

ligature *f* IMPRIM double letter, *composition* tied letter, *typographie* ligature, PRODUCTION *fil, câble* lashing; **~ de fil-frein** *f* CONS MECA lock wire twist

ligaturer *vt* CONSTR *fil* bind

lignage *m* MECANIQUE alignment

lignane *f* CHIMIE lignan

ligne:[1] **en ~** *adj* INFORMAT, ORDINAT on-line

ligne:[2] **en ~** *adv* IMPRIM in-line, INFORMAT on-line, MECANIQUE in-line, ORDINAT, TELECOM on-line

ligne[3] *f* CONSTR, ELECTR *réseau d'alimentation*, ELECTROTEC line, ENREGISTR line, nodal line, GEOMETRIE line, *de raccord* join, IMPRIM *composition, photogravure* line, INFORMAT line, row, NAUT *équatoriale* line, NUCLEAIRE line, maximum, peak, ORDINAT line, row, PRODUCTION *automatisme industriel* rung, TELECOM, TV line;

~ a **~ d'abonné** *f* TELECOM subscriber's line; **~ d'accès** *f* ELECTR bus line, ORDINAT access line; **~ accordée** *f* ELECTRON resonant line; **~ aclinique** *f* GEOPHYS aclinic line; **~ d'action** *f* CONS MECA line of contact; **~ active** *f* TV active line, line, scanning line; **~ aérienne** *f* CONSTR overhead line, ELECTR overhead line, *réseau* aerial line, ELECTROTEC overhead line, TELECOM overhead line, pole route, TRANSPORT airline; **~ aérienne à courant** *f* ELECTROTEC overhead power line; **~ affluente d'apport** *f* CH DE FER feeder line; **~ affluente de ramassage** *f* CH DE FER feeder line; **~ agate** *f* IMPRIM *composition* agate line; **~ agonique** *f* GEOPHYS agonic line; **~ à ailette** *f* PHYSIQUE fin line; **~ d'alimentation** *f* ELECTR independent feeder, *réseau* feeder, feeder cable, ELECTROTEC feeder, supply main, ESPACE *communications* feeder; **~ d'alimentation en fils nus** *f* ELECTROTEC open wire feeder; **~ d'alternance de phase** *f* TV PAL, phase alternation line; **~ d'analyse** *f* IMPRIM *curseur sur écran* picture strip; **~ appelante** *f* TELECOM calling line; **~ d'apport intérieur** *f* AERONAUT feeder line; **~ des apsides** *f* ESPACE *communications* line of apsides; **~ d'arbres** *f* CONS MECA line of shafting; **~ d'artère** *f* CH DE FER *voie* main line; **~ atmosphérique** *f* PHYSIQUE atmospheric line; **~ d'attrape** *f* NAUT heaving line; **~ avec pertes** *f* PHYSIQUE lossy line; **~ d'axe** *f* PAPIER axis;

~ b **~ de bac** *f* NAUT, TRANSPORT ferry service; **~ de balayage** *f* ELECTRON active line, scanning line, ESPACE scanning line, IMPRIM *curseur sur écran* picture strip; **~ à bande** *f* PHYSIQUE strip line; **~ de base** *f* IMPRIM, NAUT baseline; **~ de base des argiles** *f* PETR shale base line; **~ bipolaire** *f* ELECTR *alimentation* bipolar line; **~ blanche discontinue** *f* CONSTR broken white line; **~ blindée** *f* ELECTROTEC *transmission* shielded transmission line; **~ brisée** *f* GEOMETRIE broken line;

~ c **~ de cadrage** *f* CINEMAT frame line; **~ de carte** *f* INFORMAT card row; **~ des centres** *f* CONS MECA line of centers (AmE), line of centres (BrE); **~ de champ** *f* ELECTROTEC, PHYSIQUE field line; **~ de changement de date** *f* NAUT date line, international date line; **~ de charge** *f* AERONAUT, NAUT load line; **~ chargée** *f* ELECTROTEC loaded line; **~ coaxiale** *f* ELECTROTEC, ENREGISTR, PHYSIQUE, TELECOM coaxial line; **~ coaxiale rigide** *f* ELECTROTEC rigid coaxial line; **~ cofluctuale** *f* OCEANO co-current line; **~ de commande d'ascenseur** *f* ELECTROTEC trailing cable; **~ de communication** *f* ORDINAT communication link; **~ de comptage temps** *f* PETR timing line; **~ de compteur incrémentiel** *f* PRODUCTION *automatisme industriel* up counter rung; **~ de construction** *f* CONSTR building line; **~ de contact** *f* IMPRIM *machines, rouleaux* line of contact; **~ de contact entre deux rouleaux** *f* IMPRIM *machines* nip; **~ de contact gaz-eau** *f* PETR gas-water contact; **~ de contact gaz-huile** *f* PETR gas-oil contact; **~ de contact huile-eau** *f* PETR oil-water contact; **~ continue** *f* CONSTR continuous white line; **~ coplanaire** *f* PHYSIQUE coplanar waveguide; **~ de corde** *f* EN RENOUV chord line; **~ cordon** *f* TRANSPORT cordon line; ~ **de cote** *f* CONS MECA dimension line; ~ **de côte** *f* GEOLOGIE coastline; ~ **cotidale** *f* GEOPHYS cotidal line; ~ **coupée à longueur** *f* PRODUCTION cut-to-length line; ~ **de coupure** *f* IMPRIM *composition* break line; ~ **de courant** *f* HYDROLOGIE current, PHYS FLUID *écoulement de fluide ou de gaz* stream line, PHYSIQUE streamline; ~ **à courant alternatif** *f* ELECTROTEC AC line; ~ **courbe** *f* GEOMETRIE curved line; ~ **de couronnement** *f* CONSTR *comble* ridge line; ~ **de crête** *f* OCEANO crest line;

~ d ~ **de début** *f* PRODUCTION *automatisme industriel* start rung; ~ **de décompteur** *f* PRODUCTION *automatisme industriel* down counter rung; ~ **dédiée** *f* INFORMAT, ORDINAT dedicated line; ~ **défectueuse** *f* ELECTROTEC faulty line; ~ **demi-onde** *f* PHYSIQUE half-wave line; ~ **de départ de cote** *f* CONS MECA extension line; ~ **de désir** *f* TRANSPORT desire line; ~ **directe** *f* TELECOM DL, direct line; ~ **de direction** *f* GEOLOGIE, MINES line of strike; ~ **directrice** *f* BREVETS leading line, reference line; ~ **de dislocation** *f* CRISTALL, MATERIAUX *cristallographie* dislocation line; ~ **de division** *f* CONS MECA pitch line; ~ **à double sens** *f* TELECOM both-way line;

~ e ~ **d'eau** *f* CERAM VER shoreline, HYDROLOGIE hydraulic grade line; ~ **d'eau à la flottaison d'été** *f* NAUT summer load waterline; ~ **d'échantillonnage** *f* QUALITE *qualité d'eau* sampling line; ~ **d'égale salinité** *f* GEOLOGIE *eaux* isohaline; ~ **électrique** *f* THERMODYN electric power line; ~ **d'emmarchement** *f* CONSTR walking line; ~ **en antenne** *f* ELECTR single feeder, *alimentation* radial feeder; ~ **en câble monofibre** *f* ELECTROTEC single fiber line (AmE), single fibre line (BrE); ~ **en crosse** *f* CERAM VER rib mark; ~ **en faux appel** *f* TELECOM parked line; ~ **en fils nus** *f* ELECTROTEC open wire line; ~ **d'engrènement** *f* CONS MECA pitch line; ~ **en haute fréquence** *f* PHYSIQUE high-frequency line; ~ **en quart d'onde** *f* PHYSIQUE quarter wave line; ~ **en sommaire** *f* IMPRIM *composition* hanging indent; ~ **entrante** *f* TELECOM incoming line; ~ **équilibrée** *f* ELECTR *moteur*, ELECTROTEC balanced line; ~ **équipotentielle** *f* ESPACE equipotential line; ~ **d'E-S à tension continue bas niveau** *f* PRODUCTION *automatisme industriel* low-level DC I-O line; ~ **expérimentale** *f* TRANSPORT test track; ~ **exploitée** *f* CH DE FER line in service;

~ f ~ **de fabrication** *f* CONS MECA production line; ~ **de faille** *f* GEOLOGIE fault trace; ~ **de faîte** *f* CONSTR *comble* ridge line, HYDROLOGIE watershed; ~ **à fente** *f* PHYSIQUE slot line; ~ **de fer** *f* PETR guide line; ~ **de ferrasse** *f* CERAM VER runner cut; ~ **de feu** *f* CERAM VER spark; ~ **à fils parallèles** *f* ELECTROTEC parallel wire line; ~ **de fin** *f* PRODUCTION *automatisme industriel* end rung; ~ **de fin inconditionnelle** *f* PRODUCTION *automatisme industriel* unconditional end rung; ~ **de flottaison** *f* CERAM VER flux line, NAUT, POLLU MER, TRANSPORT water line; ~ **de flottaison en charge** *f* NAUT deep-water line; ~ **de flux** *f* ELECTROTEC flux line, line of flux, INFORMAT, PETR, PETROLE flow line; ~ **de flux thermique** *f* THERMODYN heat flow line; ~ **de foi** *f* AERONAUT *compas*, ESPACE lubber line, NAUT boat's heading, lubber line, OCEANO lubber line; ~ **de force** *f* CONS MECA force line, ELECTR *magnétisme*, ELECTROTEC line of force, GEOPHYS force line, PHYSIQUE line of force; ~ **de force magnétique** *f* ELECTROTEC magnetic line of force; ~ **de foulée** *f* CONSTR walking line; ~ **frontière** *f* CONSTR boundary line; ~ **de fuite** *f* ELECTR *isolateur*, ELECTROTEC leakage path; ~ **de fusible entrante** *f* PRODUCTION incoming line fuse;

~ g ~ **de giron** *f* CONSTR walking line; ~ **de glissement** *f* CRISTALL slip line; ~ **à grande distance** *f* ELECTROTEC, TELECOM long-distance line; ~ **de guidage d'entrée** *f* AERONAUT *marque d'aire de trafic* hold-short line (AmE), lead-in line (BrE); ~ **de guidage de sortie** *f* AERONAUT *marque d'aire de trafic* hold-short line (AmE), lead-out line (BrE); ~ **guide** *f* PETR guide line;

~ h ~ **des hautes eaux** *f* HYDROLOGIE high water line, tidemark; ~ **à haute tension** *f* ELECTR *distribution* high-voltage transmission line; ~ **hyperfréquence** *f* ELECTROTEC microwave transmission line;

~ i ~ **à impasse** *f* ELECTR *alimentation* dead end feeder, dead ended feeder; ~ **d'impression** *f* IMPRIM line of impression; ~ **d'influence** *f* CONSTR influence line; ~ **interautomatique** *f* (*cf ligne de jonction*) TELECOM inter-PABX tie circuit, tie line; ~ **interdigitale** *f* PHYSIQUE interdigital line; ~ **interstandard** *f* TELECOM interswitchboard tie-circuit; ~ **interurbaine** *f* ELECTROTEC, TELECOM long-distance line; ~ **isobare** *f* METEO isobar; ~ **isobarique** *f* METEO isobar; ~ **isocline** *f* GEOPHYS isoclinic line; ~ **isogone** *f* GEOPHYS isogonic line; ~ **à isolation gazeuse** *f* ELECTR *réseau* gas-insulated line; ~ **isosonique** *f* ACOUSTIQUE equal loudness contour;

~ j ~ **de jonction** *f* (Can) (*cf ligne interautomatique*) TELECOM tie line, inter-PABX tie circuit;

~ l ~ **de liaison** *f* ORDINAT, TELECOM flow line; ~ **limite** *f* CONS MECA clearance line; ~ **liquidus** *f* METALL liquidus line; ~ **de loch** *f* NAUT log line; ~ **louée** *f* INFORMAT, ORDINAT leased line;

~ m ~ **de marquage** *f* PETR timing line; ~ **de masse** *f* ELECTROTEC earth line (BrE), ground line (AmE); ~ **médiane** *f* MECANIQUE center line (AmE), centre line (BrE), PETROLE *entre secteurs* median line; ~ **mère** *f* NUCLEAIRE parent mass peak, parent peak; ~ **méridienne** *f* INSTRUMENT compass meridian line; ~ **de mesure** *f* ELECTROTEC slotted line; ~ **microruban** *f* ELECTRON microstrip; ~ **de mire** *f* MILITAIRE *arme à feu* sighting line; ~ **mixte** *f* TELECOM both-way line; ~ **mixte ordinaire** *f* TELECOM ordinary bothway line, ordinary line; ~ **du monde** *f* ASTRONOMIE world line; ~ **monopolaire** *f* ELECTR *alimentation* monopolar line; ~ **de montage** *f* NAUT assembly line; ~ **de mousse** *f* CERAM VER foam line;

~ n ~ **des naissances** *f* CONSTR springing line; ~ **du nez de marche** *f* CONSTR nosing line; ~ **de niveau** *f* CONSTR line of level; ~ **nodale** *f* ACOUSTIQUE nodal line; ~ **de noeuds** *f* ESPACE *communications* line of nodes; ~ **non attribuée** *f* TELECOM spare line; ~ **non équilibrée** *f* ELECTROTEC unbalanced line; ~ **non résonnante** *f* ELECTRON nonresonant line;

~ o ~ **d'observations** *f* PRODUCTION comment line; ~ **omnibus** *f* ELECTR bus line; ~ **à onde lente** *f* ELECTROTEC slow-wave structure; ~ **d'opérations** *f* CONSTR base, baseline, datum, datum line; ~ **optique** *f* ELECTROTEC optical transmission line; ~ **d'ordre technique** *f* TELECOM EOW, engineering order wire; ~ **d'ouverture du filet** *f* TEXTILE head line;

~ p ~ **de partage** *f* HYDROLOGIE watershed; ~ **partagée** *f* TELECOM shared service line; ~ **de partage des eaux** *f* DISTRI EAU, HYDROLOGIE watershed; ~ **de perforations** *f* IMPRIM *continu, façonnage* tear line; ~ **perforée** *f* IMPRIM perforated line; ~ **à pertes** *f* ELEC-

TROTEC lossy line; ~ **point à point** *f* INFORMAT, ORDINAT point-to-point line; ~ **de pont** *f* NAUT deck line; ~ **de poussée** *f* CONS MECA common normal, line of action, train of action; ~ **de pression** *f* CONS MECA line of action, train of action, *engrenages* common normal; ~ **primitive** *f* CONS MECA pitch line; ~ **principale** *f* ELECTR *alimentation* trunk line, ELECTROTEC main conductor; ~ **principale de chemin de fer** *f* CH DE FER trunk line, TRANSPORT main line railroad (AmE), main line railway (BrE); ~ **privée** *f* TELECOM DL, direct line; ~ **de production** *f* NAUT production line; ~ **de produits** *f* TEXTILE range; ~ **de programme** *f* PRODUCTION *automatisme industriel* program rung (AmE), programme rung (BrE);

~ **r** ~ **de raccordement** *f* TELECOM subscriber's line; ~ **de racine** *f* CONS MECA dedendum line; ~ **de rappel de cote** *f* CONS MECA leader line; ~ **de rattachement** *f* TELECOM subscriber's line; ~ **à refendre** *f* PRODUCTION slitting time; ~ **de référence** *f* CONS MECA, ESPACE *communications* datum line, GEOMETRIE reference line, MECANIQUE datum line; ~ **de remise à zéro** *f* PRODUCTION *automatisme industriel* reset rung; ~ **de réseau** *f* ELECTROTEC supply main; ~ **réseau** *f* TELECOM central exchange trunk (BrE), central office trunk (AmE), exchange line; ~ **à retard** *f* ELECTRON, ORDINAT, PHYSIQUE delay line, TELECOM delay circuit, TV delay line; ~ **à retard acoustique** *f* ELECTRON, ORDINAT acoustic delay line; ~ **à retard analogique** *f* TV analog delay line (AmE), analogue delay line (BrE); ~ **à retard binaire** *f* TV binary delay line; ~ **à retard constant** *f* ELECTRON constant delay line; ~ **à retard dispersive** *f* ELECTRON dispersive delay line; ~ **à retard électrique** *f* ELECTRON electric delay line; ~ **à retard hyperfréquence** *f* ELECTRON microwave delay line; ~ **à retard au mercure** *f* ELECTRON mercury delay line; ~ **à retard MOS** *f* ELECTRON MOS delay line, metal-oxide semi-conductor delay line; ~ **à retard à ondes accoustiques de surface** *f* ELECTRON SAW delay line; ~ **à retard polygonale** *f* ELECTRON polygonal delay line; ~ **à retard à prises** *f* ELECTRON tapped delay line; ~ **à retard quantifié** *f* TV quantized delay line; ~ **à retard à quartz** *f* ELECTRON, TV quartz delay line; ~ **rigide** *f* ELECTROTEC rigid coaxial line;

~ **s** ~ **de sable** *f* PETR sand line; ~ **de sauvetage** *f* NAUT lifeline; ~ **de schéma à relais** *f* PRODUCTION *automatisme industriel* ladder diagram rung, relay ladder rung; ~ **secondaire** *f* CH DE FER branch line, TRANSPORT secondary line; ~ **secteur** *f* PRODUCTION *électricité* power line; ~ **de service** *f* ELECTROTEC service line; ~ **de signaux** *f* ELECTROTEC *transmission* signal line; ~ **de sonde** *f* NAUT lead line, sounding line; ~ **de sortie** *f* TELECOM, TV outgoing line; ~ **de sortie déverrouillée** *f* PRODUCTION *automatisme industriel* unlatch rung; ~ **de sortie verrouillée** *f* PRODUCTION *automatisme industriel* latch rung; ~ **sous tension** *f* ELECTR *alimentation* live line; ~ **souterraine** *f* ELECTR *réseau* underground cable, ELECTROTEC, TELECOM underground line; ~ **spécialisée** *f* INFORMAT dedicated line, leased line, ORDINAT, TELECOM dedicated line; ~ **spécialisée arrivée** *f* TELECOM outgoing calls barred line; ~ **spécialisée départ** *f* TELECOM incoming-calls-barred line; ~ **supraconductrice** *f* TELECOM superconductor line; ~ **symétrique** *f* ENREGISTR balanced line;

~ **t** ~ **de tangence** *f* IMPRIM *machines* nip; ~ **de télécommunications** *f* ELECTROTEC communications line;

~ **téléphonique** *f* ELECTROTEC telephone line; ~ **téléphonique d'abonné** *f* TELECOM subscriber's line; ~ **téléphonique principale** *f* TELECOM main line; ~ **de temporisation** *f* PRODUCTION *automatisme industriel* timer rung; ~ **terminée par une impédance** *f* PHYSIQUE line terminated by an impedance; ~ **de terre** *f* ELECTROTEC earth line (BrE), ground line (AmE); ~ **terrestre** *f* TELECOM land line; ~ **de tir** *f* MINES leading wire; ~ **de tonture** *f* NAUT sheer line; ~ **de transfert** *f* CONS MECA transfer line, TELECOM throughline; ~ **de transmission** *f* CONS MECA line of shafting, CONSTR, ELECTRON, ELECTROTEC, PHYSIQUE, TELECOM transmission line; ~ **de transmission accordée** *f* ELECTRON resonant line; ~ **de transmission acoustique** *f* ELECTROTEC acoustic transmission line; ~ **de transmission demi-onde** *f* ELECTR *alimentation* half-wave transmission line; ~ **de transmission électrique** *f* ELECTROTEC electrical transmission line; ~ **de transmission en fils nus** *f* ELECTROTEC open wire transmission line; ~ **de transmission en série** *f* ELECTROTEC serial line; ~ **de transmission équilibrée** *f* ELECTROTEC balanced line; ~ **de transmission hyperfréquence** *f* ELECTROTEC microwave transmission line; ~ **de transmission optique** *f* ELECTROTEC optical transmission line; ~ **de transport de courant** *f* ELECTROTEC power transmission line; ~ **de transport à courant alternatif** *f* ELECTR *réseau* alternating current transmission line; ~ **de transport de courant HT** *f* ELECTROTEC power transmission line; ~ **de transport de l'électricité** *f* THERMODYN electric power line; ~ **de transport d'énergie** *f* ELECTROTEC power line; ~ **de transport d'énergie à courant alternatif** *f* ELECTROTEC AC power line; ~ **de transport d'énergie électrique** *f* ELECTROTEC power transmission line; ~ **de transport d'énergie résistant à la tenue à la foudre** *f* ELECTR *alimentation* lightning-resistant power line; ~ **triplaque** *f* ELECTRON planar line, ELECTROTEC strip line;

~ **u** ~ **uniforme** *f* ELECTROTEC *transmission* uniform line;

~ **v** ~ **ventrale** *f* ACOUSTIQUE antinodal line; ~ **de visée** *f* ASTRONOMIE line of sight, INSTRUMENT sighting line; ~ **à voie unique** *f* CH DE FER single track line

lignes: ~ **des champs magnétiques** *f pl* PHYS RAYON magnetic field lines; ~ **concourantes** *f pl* GEOMETRIE concurrent lines; ~ **convergentes** *f pl* GEOMETRIE convergent lines; ~ **d'eau** *f pl* NAUT water lines; ~ **d'émission** *f pl* PHYS FLUID *cylindre traversant un fluide* streaklines; ~ **intersectées** *f pl* GEOMETRIE intersecting lines; ~ **à la minute** *f pl* IMPRIM *imprimante* lines per minute; ~ **parallèles** *f pl* GEOMETRIE parallel lines; ~ **par minute** *f pl* (*LPM*) INFORMAT, ORDINAT lines per minute (*LPM*); ~ **perpendiculaires** *f pl* GEOMETRIE perpendicular lines; ~ **pointillées** *f pl* IMPRIM *composition* leaders; ~ **de série Paschen** *f pl* PHYS RAYON Paschen series lines

ligneur *m* OCEANO troller, PETR alignment frame

ligneux *adj* PAPIER ligneous, woody

lignine *f* CHIMIE, PLAST CAOU lignin

lignite *m* CHARBON brown coal, lignite, MINERAUX, THERMODYN lignite

ligroïne *f* CHIMIE ligroin, REVETEMENT varnish maker's naphtha

ligurite *f* MINERAUX ligurite

limace: ~ **au col** *f* CERAM VER slug in neck

limage *m* PRODUCTION filing

limaille *f* PRODUCTION filings, metal particles; ~ **de fer** *f*

CHIMIE, PHYSIQUE iron filings

limbe *m* ASTRONOMIE limb; **~ vertical de calage** *m* INSTRUMENT divided circle, graduated circle

lime *f* MECANIQUE, PRODUCTION, VEHICULES file; **~ d'affûtage des scies** *f* CONS MECA saw file; **~ à aiguille** *f* CONS MECA needle file; **~ à barrettes** *f* CONS MECA barrette file; **~ bâtarde** *f* CONS MECA rough file, MECANIQUE bastard file; **~ à biseau** *f* CONS MECA barrette file; **~ biseautée** *f* CONS MECA cant file; **~ à bords arrondis** *f* CONS MECA round-edge file; **~ à bouter** *f* CONS MECA key file, warding file; **~ carrée** *f* CONS MECA square file; **~ à champs ronds** *f* CONS MECA round-edge file; **~ contact** *f* CONS MECA contact point file; **~ à côté lisse** *f* CONS MECA safe edge file; **~ à couteau** *f* CONS MECA knife file, knife-edge file; **~ à deux queues** *f* CONS MECA two-tanged file; **~ à deux soies** *f* CONS MECA two-tanged file; **~ à dossière** *f* CONS MECA screw-head file, slitting file, PRODUCTION feather-edge file; **~ double demi-ronde** *f* PRODUCTION cross file; **~ à double taille** *f* PRODUCTION crosscut file; **~ à égaliser** *f* PRODUCTION equalizing file; **~ d'entrée** *f* PRODUCTION entering file; **~ à fendre** *f* CONS MECA screw-head file, slitting file, PRODUCTION feather-edge file; **~ feuille-de-sauge** *f* PRODUCTION cross file, double half-round file; **~ à garnir** *f* CONS MECA key file, warding file; **~ grosse** *f* CONS MECA rough file; **~ à lanterne** *f* CONS MECA frame saw file; **~ à losange** *f* CONS MECA screw-head file, slitting file, PRODUCTION feather-edge file; **~ olive** *f* CONS MECA oval file; **~ parallèle** *f* CONS MECA parallel file; **~ plate à main** *f* PRODUCTION hand file; **~ queue-de-rat** *f* CONS MECA rat-tail file; **~ queue-de-rat ovale** *f* CONS MECA oval file, rat-tail file; **~ ronde** *f* CONS MECA round file; **~ ronde à scies** *f* PRODUCTION gulleting saw file; **~ à scies** *f* CONS MECA saw file; **~ à simple taille** *f* CONS MECA float, float-cut file, single-cut file; **~ à taille croisée** *f* PRODUCTION crosscut file; **~ tiers-point** *f* CONS MECA three-square file, tri-square file; **~ très douce** *f* PRODUCTION extrasmooth file; **~ triangulaire** *f* CONS MECA three-square file, tri-square file; **~ trois-quarts** *f* CONS MECA three-square file

lime-couteau *f* CONS MECA knife file, knife-edge file

lime-fraiseuse: **~ à main** *f* CONS MECA circular cut file, PRODUCTION milling file

limet: **~ parallèle à la direction** *m* CHARBON face cleat; **~ parallèle à l'inclinaison** *m* CHARBON end cleat

limeuse *f* CONS MECA shaping machine, shaping planer

limitateur: **~ de crêtes** *m* TV peak limiter

limitation *f* ENREGISTR limiting; **~ d'amplitude** *f* ELECTRON limiting; **~ d'amplitude à niveau constant** *f* ELECTRON hard limiting; **~ de la charge** *f* ELECTROTEC load limiting; **~ des collisions** *f* TELECOM contention control; **~ de courant** *f* ELECTROTEC current limiting; **~ d'entrée** *f* ELECTRON input control; **~ de l'intensité du courant** *f* ELECTROTEC current limiting; **~ des parasites transitoires** *f* PRODUCTION transient voltage limitation; **~ de pointe** *f* ENREGISTR peak limitation; **~ réglementaire de vitesse** *f* TRANSPORT speed limit; **~ de vitesse** *f* TRANSPORT *véhicules* speed restriction

limite *f* CONS MECA limit, margin, tolerance, CONSTR boundary, GEOLOGIE boundary, margin, HYDROLOGIE margin, MATH limit, METALL boundary, METROLOGIE *mécanique* tolerance; **~ d'absorption** *f* CRISTALL absorption edge; **~ d'accrochage** *f* ELECTRON singing point; **~ d'allongement** *f* MATERIAUX yield point; **~ d'antiphase** *f* CRISTALL antiphase boundary; **~ de**

Chandrasekhar *f* ASTRONOMIE Chandrasekhar limit; **~ de consistance** *f* CHARBON limit of consistency; **~ de contrôle** *f* QUALITE control limit; **~ de couleur** *f* COULEURS color limit (AmE), colour limit (BrE); **~ de déshydratation** *f* TEXTILE dewatering point; **~ de détection** *f* POLLUTION lower limit of detectability; **~ d'écoulement** *f* ELECTROTEC flow limit, PHYSIQUE *plastique* yield point; **~ d'élasticité** *f* CONSTR, EMBALLAGE, MATERIAUX, PHYSIQUE, PLAST CAOU elastic limit; **~ élastique** *f* CONSTR elastic limit, MECANIQUE elastic limit, yield strength, METALL yield strength, NUCLEAIRE *déformation* yield point, yield strength, PHYSIQUE, PLAST CAOU elastic limit, RESSORTS elastic limit, yield point; **~ élastique inférieure** *f* METALL lower yield point; **~ d'émission** *f* POLLUTION emission standard; **~ d'emploi** *f* PHOTO working life; **~ d'endurance** *f* CRISTALL, METALL endurance limit; **~ d'exposition** *f* SECURITE exposure limit; **~ de filtrabilité** *f* GENIE CHIM filtering limit; **~ du gel** *f* CHARBON frost limit; **~ inférieure** *f* TELECOM lower limit; **~ inférieure de contrôle** *f* QUALITE lower control limit; **~ inférieure de détection** *f* POLLUTION lower limit of detectability; **~ interfaciale** *f* METALL interface boundary; **~ de Kruskal** *f* NUCLEAIRE Kruskal limit; **~ de liquidité** *f* CHARBON, CONSTR liquid limit; **~ de la marée** *f* HYDROLOGIE high water mark, tidemark; **~ maximale d'exposition** *f* SECURITE maximum exposure limit; **~ des neiges** *f* METEO snow line; **~ des neiges éternelles** *f* METEO snow line; **~ de nuisance** *f* POLLUTION ambient emission standard, ambient quality standard; **~ de phase** *f* METALL phase boundary; **~ d'une plaque** *f* GEOLOGIE plate boundary; **~ de plaques lithosphériques divergentes** *f* GEOLOGIE divergent plate boundary; **~ de plasticité** *f* CHARBON plastic limit; **~ plastique** *f* CONSTR plastic limit; **~ de qualité moyenne après contrôle** *f* (*LQMAC*) QUALITE average outgoing quality limit (*AOQL*); **~ à quatre masses solaires** *f* ASTRONOMIE *étoiles à neutrons* four-solar mass limit; **~ de résistance** *f* CRISTALL endurance limit; **~ de résolution en portée** *f* ESPACE range resolution; **~ de retrait** *f* CHARBON shrinkage limit; **~ de Roche** *f* ASTRONOMIE Roche limit; **~ de rupture** *f* MECANIQUE breaking point; **~ de sécurité** *f* SECURITE safe limit; **~ supérieure** *f* TELECOM upper limit; **~ supérieure de contrôle** *f* QUALITE upper control limit; **~ supérieure de l'ozonosphère** *f* METEO upper limit of ozone layer; **~ de teinte** *f* COULEURS color limit (AmE), colour limit (BrE); **~ de tolérance** *f* METROLOGIE *mécanique* limit of tolerance, QUALITE tolerance limit; **~ d'usure** *f* CONS MECA wear limit; **~ d'utilisation** *f* PRODUCTION operating limitations

limité: **~ par les entrées/sorties** *adj* ORDINAT input/output-limited; **~ par le périphérique** *adj* ORDINAT peripheral-limited; **~ par le processeur** *adj* INFORMAT, ORDINAT processor-limited; **~ par la vitesse du périphérique** *adj* INFORMAT peripheral-limited; **~ par la vitesse des périphériques d'entrée** *adj* ORDINAT input-limited; **~ par la vitesse des périphériques de sortie** *adj* ORDINAT output-limited

limiter *vt* ELECTRON *amplitude* limit

limites: **~ de spécification** *f pl* QUALITE specification limits

limiteur *m* CONS MECA, ELECTRON, ELECTROTEC, ENREGISTR, ESPACE *communications*, TELECOM limiter, TV amplitude limiter circuit, limiter; **~ d'amplitude** *m* CINEMAT peak limiter, ELECTRON amplitude limiter, clipper; ~ **d'amplitude à diode** m ELECTRON diode limiter; ~ **d'appel de courant** m ELECTROTEC inrush current limiter; ~ **automatique de crête** m TV automatic peak limiter; ~ **automatique de crête du blanc** m TV automatic peak limiter; ~ **d'avance** m CONS MECA feed limiter; ~ **de bruit** m ENREGISTR noise limiter; ~ **de bruit dynamique** m ENREGISTR dynamic noise suppressor; ~ **central** m ENREGISTR center clipping (AmE), centre clipping (BrE); ~ **de courant** m ELECTR, ELECTROTEC current limiter; ~ **de débit** m CONS MECA flow rate controller, NUCLEAIRE gag; ~ **à ferrite** m ELECTROTEC ferrite limiter; ~ **de flambement** m PETR buckle arrester; ~ **de freinage** m AUTO metering valve; ~ **hyperfréquence** m ELECTRON microwave limiter; ~ **d'intensité** m ELECTROTEC current limiter; ~ **de pression** m PRODUCTION *système hydraulique* pressure relief valve; ~ **de pression à cartouche** m PRODUCTION *système hydraulique* cartridge relief valve; ~ **de pression de défibrage** m PAPIER grinding pressure limiter; ~ **de puissance** m CONS MECA power limiter; ~ **à seuil** m ELECTRON inverse limiter; ~ **de surtension** m ELECTROTEC arrester, surge arrester; ~ **de surtension à semi-conducteur** m ELECTROTEC solid-state surge arrester; ~ **de tension** m ELECTR voltage limiter, ELECTROTEC overpotential protection; ~ **de vitesse** m AUTO speed limiter; ~ **de vitesse automatique** m CONS MECA automatic speed checker

limiteur-régleur: ~ **de freinage** m CONS MECA brake pressure regulator

limma m ACOUSTIQUE limma

limnimètre m HYDROLOGIE level gage (AmE), level gauge (BrE), limnimeter, NUCLEAIRE level indicator, level meter

limon m CERAM VER common clay, CHARBON silt, CONSTR face string, outside string, string, string board, string piece, stringer, DISTRI EAU silt, slime, HYDROLOGIE ooze, silt, slime, sludge, MINES mud; ~ **à l'anglaise** m CONSTR cut string, open string; ~ **argileux** m DISTRI EAU clay silt; ~ **à crémaillère** m CONSTR cut string, open string, housed string; ~ **droit** m CONSTR close string, housed string; ~ **à l'escalier** m CONSTR close string; ~ **fin** m GEOLOGIE fine silt; ~ **à la française** m CONSTR housed string; ~ **à gradin** m CONSTR open string; ~ **grossier** m GEOLOGIE coarse silt; ~ **sableux** m GEOLOGIE sandy loam

limonite f CHIMIE brown haematite (BrE), brown hematite (AmE), brown iron ore, MINERAUX limonite

limpidité f DISTRI EAU *eau* clearness, MATERIAUX transparency

lin: ~ **teillé** m TEXTILE line flax

linalol m CHIMIE licareol, linalool

linarite f MINERAUX linarite

lindane m CHIMIE lindane

linéaire adj PAPIER, PHYSIQUE linear

linéales f pl IMPRIM lineals

linéament m GEOLOGIE lineament

linéarisateur m ESPACE *communications* linearizer

linéariser vt CHIMIE linearize

linéarité f ELECTR, ELECTRON, ENREGISTR, TELECOM linearity; ~ **défectueuse** f TV linearity error

linéation f GEOLOGIE *minéraux* lineation

linéature f IMPRIM screen ruling, *photogravure* screen count

linéique adj PHYSIQUE per unit length

liner m PETR liner

lingot m CHARBON, MECANIQUE, PRODUCTION ingot;

~ **d'uranium** m NUCLEAIRE uranium ingot

lingotière f MECANIQUE *matériaux*, PRODUCTION ingot mold (AmE), ingot mould (BrE)

lingots: ~ **d'interlignage** m pl IMPRIM *composition* leading matter

linguet m CONS MECA pawl

linnéite f MINERAUX linnaeite

linoléate m CHIMIE linoleate

linoléine f CHIMIE linoleine

linoléique adj CHIMIE linoleic

linolénate m CHIMIE linolenate

linolénique adj CHIMIE linolenic

Linotype f (MD) IMPRIM Linotype (TM)

linotypie f IMPRIM Linotype (TM) setting

linteau m CONSTR breast summer, bressummer, lintel, transom; ~ **de niche d'enfournement** m CERAM VER mantle block

Lion m ASTRONOMIE Leo, The Lion

lipase f CHIMIE lipase

lipide m AGRO ALIM fat, CHIMIE lipid

lipoïde adj CHIMIE lipoid

lipophile m CHIMIE lipophile, lipophilic

lipopolysaccharide m CHIMIE lipopolysaccharide

liposite f CHIMIE lipositol

liposoluble adj CHIMIE liposoluble

liquation f CHIMIE liquation

liquéfacteur m REFRIG liquefier

liquéfaction f CHIMIE, GAZ, PHYSIQUE *gaz*, THERMODYN liquefaction; ~ **du charbon** f PETROLE coal liquefaction; ~ **de la houille** f PETROLE coal liquefaction

liquéfié adj THERMODYN liquefied

liquéfier vt CHIMIE *gaz* liquefy, THERMODYN liquefy, melt down

liquescence f CHIMIE liquescence

liquescent adj CHIMIE liquescent

liqueur f CHIMIE liquor, solution; ~ **mixte** f DISTRI EAU mixed liquor; ~ **noire** f PAPIER black liquor; ~ **de teinture** f TEXTILE dye liquor; ~ **titrée** f CHIMIE standard solution

liquide[1] adj CHIMIE, THERMODYN liquid

liquide[2] m PHYSIQUE, REFRIG, THERMODYN liquid; ~ **anti-corrosion** m AUTO corrosion inhibitor; ~ **associé** m PETROLE associated liquid; ~ **de broyage** m GENIE CHIM milling liquid; ~ **chargé** m CONS MECA slurry; ~ **de circuit hydraulique** m INST HYDR hydraulic fluid; ~ **de coagulation** m GENIE CHIM coagulation liquid; ~ **de coupure** m PRODUCTION cutting fluid; ~ **cryogénique** m CONS MECA cryogenic liquid; ~ **de dégraissage** m INSTRUMENT cleaning fluid; ~ **dense** m CHARBON dense liquid; ~ **émulseur** m SECURITE emulsifying liquid; ~ **émulsionnant** m GENIE CHIM emulsifying liquid; ~ **d'ensilage** m HYDROLOGIE silage effluent; ~ **de frein** m AUTO, CONS MECA, VEHICULES brake fluid; ~ **de gaz naturel** m *(LGN)* GAZ, PETROLE natural gas liquid *(NGL)*; ~ **incongelable** m REFRIG nonfreeze liquid; ~ **inflammable** m SECURITE flammable liquid; ~ **laveur** m LESSIVES scouring solution; ~ **réfrigérant** m CHIMIE freezing liquid, CONS MECA coolant; ~ **de refroidissement** m THERMODYN liquid coolant; ~ **séparateur** m GENIE CHIM separation liquid; ~ **surnageant** m DISTRI EAU, HYDROLOGIE sludge liquor; ~ **toxique** m SECURITE toxic liquid; ~ **triergol** m THERMODYN liquid tripropellant

liquidus m CHIMIE liquidus

lire vt INFORMAT, ORDINAT fetch, read, read out

liroconite f MINERAUX liroconite

lise *f* HYDROLOGIE quicksand
liser *f* TEXTILE heald
liséré *m* CERAM VER irregular edge
lisible: ~ **par machine** *adj* INFORMAT, ORDINAT machine-readable
lisière *f* HYDROLOGIE margin, MINES gouge, pug, selvage, selvedge, PAPIER *toile* selvage, selvedge, TEXTILE edge, *tissu* selvage, selvedge; ~ **rentrée** *f* TEXTILE pulled-in selvage, pulled-in selvedge; ~ **tendue** *f* TEXTILE tight selvage, tight selvedge
lissage *m* ELECTRON, INFORMAT, ORDINAT smoothing, PRODUCTION leveling (AmE), levelling (BrE), smoothing; ~ **de charge** *m* PRODUCTION production smoothing
lisse[1] *adj* GEOLOGIE even, NAUT longitudinal, PAPIER smooth, PRODUCTION safe, *surface* even, TEXTILE sleek
lisse[2] *f* CHARBON wale, CONSTR hand railing, handrail, ESPACE *véhicules* stringer, NAUT bulwark rail, rail, ribband, strake, PAPIER breaker stack, calender stack, smoothing roll; ~ **de couronnement** *f* NAUT taffrail; ~ **intermédiaire** *f* PAPIER breaker stack; ~ **longitudinale** *f* NAUT longitudinal framing; ~ **de plafond de double fond** *f* NAUT inner bottom longitudinal; ~ **de plat-bord** *f* NAUT gunnel, gunwale; ~ **de pont** *f* NAUT deck longitudinal
lissé *m* PAPIER smoothness
lisses: ~ **planes** *f pl* NAUT diagonal lines
lissoir *m* PRODUCTION slick, slicker; ~ **à bride** *m* PRODUCTION flange smoother; ~ **à champignon** *m* CONS MECA *mouleur* bacca box smoother; ~ **à congé** *m* PRODUCTION fillet slick; ~ **équerre** *f* PRODUCTION corner slick, corner smoother; ~ **équerre à congé** *f* PRODUCTION round edge corner smoother; ~ **à tuyau** *m* PRODUCTION pipe slick, pipe smoother
listage *m* INFORMAT listing, ORDINAT listing, printout; ~ **de programmes** *m* INFORMAT, ORDINAT program listing
liste *f* INFORMAT, ORDINAT list; ~ **d'activités** *f* PRODUCTION job sequence list; ~ **de cadrages** *f* CINEMAT shot list; ~ **chaînée** *f* ORDINAT chained list; ~ **de colisage** *f* PRODUCTION delivery sheet; ~ **de contrôle d'accès** *f* TELECOM access control list; ~ **de découpe** *f* PRODUCTION sawing list; ~ **directe** *f* INFORMAT, ORDINAT push-up list; ~ **d'erreurs** *f* INFORMAT error list, ORDINAT error list, error report; ~ **d'exécution** *f* CONSTR construction schedule; ~ **du fret** *f* AERONAUT cargo manifest; ~ **des habilitations** *f* ORDINAT access list; ~ **des heures** *f* PRODUCTION taking-off sheets hours; ~ **inversée** *f* INFORMAT push-down list; ~ **libre** *f* INFORMAT free list, ORDINAT available list, free list; ~ **linéaire** *f* INFORMAT linear list; ~ **des matières** *f* PRODUCTION taking-off sheets materials; ~ **de phases opératoires** *f* PRODUCTION routing list; ~ **des pièces** *f* PRODUCTION drawing list; ~ **des pièces de rechange** *f* PRODUCTION renewal parts list; ~ **des plans tournés** *f* CINEMAT shot list; ~ **des produits** *f* BREVETS specification of goods; ~ **des produits services** *f* BREVETS specification of goods, specification of services; ~ **refoulée** *f* ORDINAT push-down list; ~ **de sciage** *f* PRODUCTION sawing list; ~ **séquentielle** *f* INFORMAT, ORDINAT linear list; ~ **à servir** *f* PRODUCTION pick list, picking list; ~ **de stock** *f* PRODUCTION inventory reporting; ~ **de vérification** *f* CONS MECA checklist
lister *vt* INFORMAT, ORDINAT list
liston *m* NAUT rail, rubbing strake
lit *m* CONSTR bed, layer, DISTRI EAU river bed, HYDRO-
LOGIE, IMPRIM *impression typo* bed, OCEANO bottom; ~ **alluvial** *m* DISTRI EAU alluvial bed; ~ **bactérien** *m* DISTRI EAU bacteria bed, GENIE CHIM biological filter, HYDROLOGIE, RECYCLAGE bacterial bed, bacteria bed; ~ **bouillant** *m* NUCLEAIRE boiling bed; ~ **de boulets** *m* NUCLEAIRE pebble bed; ~ **de carrière** *m* MINES quarry face; ~ **catalytique** *m* NUCLEAIRE catalyst bed; ~ **de charbon de bois activé** *m* NUCLEAIRE activated charcoal bed; ~ **de coke** *m* CHARBON coke bed; ~ **continu** *m* MINES bank; ~ **de coulée** *m* PRODUCTION pig mold (AmE), pig mould (BrE); ~ **de cours d'eau** *m* HYDROLOGIE stream bed; ~ **filtrant** *m* GENIE CHIM filter bed, filtering layer, NUCLEAIRE filter bed; ~ **de filtration** *m* RECYCLAGE filter bed; ~ **fluidifié** *m* GENIE CHIM fluid bed, fluidized bed; ~ **fluidifié à grains** *m* GENIE CHIM particle-operated fluidized bed; ~ **fluidifié homogène** *m* GENIE CHIM particulate fluidized bed; ~ **fluidisé** *m* GENIE CHIM fluid bed, fluidized bed, MAT CHAUFF *combustion*, POLLUTION fluidized bed; ~ **de gueuse** *m* PRODUCTION pig bed, pig mold (AmE), pig mould (BrE); ~ **de hautes eaux** *m* HYDROLOGIE flood plain; ~ **de houille** *m* CHARBON coal bed; ~ **isolant** *m* CONSTR damp-proof course; ~ **de lavage** *m* CHARBON jig bed; ~ **de mâchefer** *m* PRODUCTION cinder bed; ~ **majeur** *m* HYDROLOGIE flood plain, *rivière* flood bed; ~ **mineur** *m* HYDROLOGIE *rivière* normal bed; ~ **percolateur** *m* GENIE CHIM biological filter; ~ **de rivière** *m* DISTRI EAU, HYDROLOGIE river bed; ~ **de séchage des boues** *m* HYDROLOGIE sludge-drying bed
litage *m* GEOLOGIE layering, PETROLE *géologie* bed; ~ **de flux** *m* GEOLOGIE *roche magmatique* flow banding
lité *adj* GEOLOGIE banded
liteau *m* CONSTR batten
litharge *f* CHIMIE, PLAST CAOU *caoutchouc* litharge
lithergol *m* ESPACE *propulsion*, THERMODYN lithergol
lithification *f* GEOLOGIE induration, lithification
lithionite *f* MINERAUX lithionite
lithique *adj* GEOLOGIE lithic
lithium *m* (*Li*) CHIMIE lithium (*Li*)
lithoclase *f* GEOLOGIE rock fracture
lithofaciès *m* GEOLOGIE lithofacies
lithogénétique *adj* GEOLOGIE lithogenous
lithographie *f* IMPRIM lithography; ~ **offset** *f* IMPRIM lithography
lithologique *adj* GEOLOGIE lithological, lithologic
lithomarge *f* MINERAUX lithomarge
lithopone *m* CHIMIE lithopone
lithosphère *f* EN RENOUV, GEOLOGIE, GEOPHYS, POLLUTION lithosphere
litophile *f* GEOLOGIE lithophile element
litre *m* METROLOGIE, PHYSIQUE liter (AmE), litre (BrE)
lits: **à** ~ **épais** *adj* GEOLOGIE thick-bedded; **à** ~ **minces** *adj* GEOLOGIE thin-bedded
littéral *m* INFORMAT literal; ~ **chaîne** *m* INFORMAT string literal
littoral[1] *adj* GEOLOGIE coastal, nearshore, OCEANO littoral
littoral[2] *m* GEOLOGIE coast, coastline, shore, NAUT coastline, seaboard, shore, shoreline
liure *f* NAUT lashing
livet: ~ **de pont** *m* NAUT deck line
livraison *f* IMPRIM delivery; ~ **client** *f* PRODUCTION shipment, shipping; ~ **directe** *f* PRODUCTION direct delivery, drop shipment; ~ **échéancée** *f* PRODUCTION time phased delivery; ~ **échelonnée** *f* PRODUCTION time phased delivery; ~ **excédentaire** *f* PRODUCTION

overshipment; ~ **fournisseur** *f* PRODUCTION delivery, reception; ~ **magasin** *f* PRODUCTION warehouse delivery; ~ **multiple** *f* PRODUCTION time phased delivery; ~ **ponctuelle** *f* PRODUCTION single delivery; ~ **unique** *f* PRODUCTION single delivery

livre:[1] ~ **de bord** *m* NAUT ship's log; ~ **broché** *m* IMPRIM paperback; ~ **cartonné** *m* IMPRIM cased book; ~ **du concepteur** *m* TELECOM designer handbook; ~ **d'images** *m* IMPRIM picture book; ~ **imprimé** *m* IMPRIM printed book; ~ **des phares** *m* NAUT list of lights; ~ **de poche** *m* IMPRIM pocket book; ~ **princeps** *m* IMPRIM original edition; ~ **relié** *m* IMPRIM bound book; ~ **routier** *m* NAUT track chart; ~ **des signaux** *m* NAUT signal book; ~ **de topographie** *m* CONSTR field book

livre[2] *f* METROLOGIE pound, pound avoirdupois; ~ **avoirdupois** *f* METROLOGIE pound, pound avoirdupois; ~ **poids** *f* METROLOGIE pound force

livres:[1] ~ **de bord** *m pl* NAUT ship's books

livres:[2] ~ **par heure** *f pl* METROLOGIE pounds per hour; ~ **par pouce carré** *f pl* METROLOGIE PETROLE pounds per square inch, psi

livreur *m* EMBALLAGE deliverer

lixiviation *f* CERAM VER leaching, CHARBON leachability, leaching, CHIMIE leaching, lixiviation, MATERIAUX *métallurgie* leaching, POLLUTION leaching, lixiviation; ~ **par solvant** *f* CHARBON solvent leaching

lixivier *vt* GEOLOGIE, POLLU MER leach

lm *abrév (lumen)* METROLOGIE lm *(lumen)*

lobe *m* ESPACE *communications* lobe; ~ **latéral** *m* ELECTRON sidelobe, PHYSIQUE side lobe; ~ **radioélectrique** *m* ESPACE *communications* lobe; ~ **secondaire** *m* ELECTRON, ESPACE *communications*, NAUT, PHYSIQUE side lobe; ~ **secondaire de grande amplitude** *m* ELECTRON high side lobe

lobéline *f* CHIMIE lobeline

lobinine *f* CHIMIE lobinine

local[1] *adj* INFORMAT, ORDINAT local

local[2] *m* CONSTR room; ~ **dépoussiéré** *m* EMBALLAGE clean room; ~ **de stockage de films** *m* CINEMAT vault

localisateur: ~ **de défaut** *m* ELECTR *câble* fault detector

localisation *f* CONSTR locating, location, MILITAIRE position fixing, NAUT positioning, PETR habitat; ~ **automatique des véhicules** *f* TELECOM AVL, automatic vehicle location; ~ **horaire** *f* AERONAUT clock face reference; ~ **du navire** *f* NAUT vessel location; ~ **par radar** *f* TRANSPORT RT, radar tracking; ~ **par radio** *f* MILITAIRE radio tracking; ~ **sommaire** *f* TELECOM general localization

localisé *adj* PHYSIQUE lumped

localiser *vt* CONS MECA pinpoint, ELECTROTEC isolate, locate, INFORMAT, ORDINAT localize, PRODUCTION locate

locaux: ~ **d'habitation** *m pl* NAUT *équipage* accommodation

loch: ~ **à hélice** *m* NAUT patent log

locomobile *f* TRANSPORT steam car

locomotive *f* CH DE FER locomotive; ~ **à adhérence mixte** *f* CH DE FER rack-rail locomotive; ~ **bicourant** *f* CH DE FER dual-current locomotive; ~ **à convertisseur statique** *f* TRANSPORT thyristor-controlled locomotive; ~ **à crémaillère** *f* TRANSPORT rack engine, rack locomotive; ~ **diesel-électrique** *f* CH DE FER diesel-electric locomotive; ~ **diesel-hydraulique** *f* CH DE FER, TRANSPORT diesel-hydraulic locomotive; ~ **diesel à transmission hydromécanique** *f* CH DE FER diesel-hydromechanical locomotive; ~ **diesel à voie étroite** *f* TRANSPORT narrow gage diesel locomotive (AmE), narrow gauge diesel locomotive (BrE); ~ **électrique** *f* CH DE FER electric locomotive; ~ **à groupe monocontinu** *f* CH DE FER locomotive with ac/dc motor converter set; ~ **haut-le-pied** *f* CH DE FER light engine, light locomotive; ~ **à ignitrons** *f* CH DE FER ignitron locomotive; ~ **de manoeuvre** *f* CH DE FER, CONSTR shunting engine, TRANSPORT shunter, shunting engine, shunting locomotive, switch engine (AmE), switcher (AmE); ~ **à marchandises** *f* CH DE FER freight locomotive; ~ **monocontinue** *f* CH DE FER locomotive with ac/dc motor converter set; ~ **de pousse** *f* CH DE FER banking locomotive (BrE), pusher locomotive (AmE); ~ **à redresseurs** *f* CH DE FER rectifier locomotive; ~ **de renfort en queue** *f* CH DE FER banking locomotive (BrE), pusher locomotive (AmE); ~ **de route** *f* TRANSPORT road locomotive; ~ **de traction** *f* CH DE FER traction locomotive

locomotive-tender *f* CH DE FER, MINES tank engine, tank locomotive

locotracteur *m* CH DE FER light rail motor tractor, TRANSPORT rail motor tractor; ~ **diesel-électrique de manoeuvre** *m* CH DE FER diesel-electric shunting motor tractor

lofer *vi* NAUT come to, luff

log *m (logarithme)* MATH log *(logarithm)*; ~ **de chantier** *m* PETR mud log; ~ **de fracturation** *m* PETR fracture log; ~ **d'induction** *m* PETR induction log; ~ **d'interprétation géologique** *m* PETR synergetic log; ~ **lithostratigraphique** *m* GEOLOGIE geological column; ~ **nucléaire de cimentation** *m* PETR nuclear cement log; ~ **de proximité** *m* PETR proximity log; ~ **renseigné** *m* PETR strip log

logarithme *m (log)* MATH, ORDINAT logarithm *(log)*; ~ **à base 10** *m* MATH common logarithm; ~ **naturel** *m* MATH Naperian logarithm, natural logarithm; ~ **népérien** *m* MATH Naperian logarithm, natural logarithm

logarithmique *adj* MATH logarithmic

logatome *f* ACOUSTIQUE logatom

loge: ~ **de coupeur** *f* CERAM VER cutter's bay; ~ **d'emballeur** *f* (Fra) *(cf baie d'emballeur)* CERAM VER packer's bay

logement *m* CONS MECA compartment, groove, CONSTR housing, MECANIQUE socket, *chantier* accommodation, NAUT accommodation, PRODUCTION receptacle, *module* slot; ~ **de barre** *m* CONS MECA socket, *d'un cabestan* bar holes; ~ **de bloc porte-empreinte** *m* CONS MECA *fonderie* insert cavity; ~ **de cassette** *m* ENREGISTR cassette compartment; ~ **de clavette** *m* AUTO lock groove, NUCLEAIRE key bed, key groove, keyway, PAPIER keyseat; ~ **de filtre** *m* INSTRUMENT filter pickup; ~ **de joints de piston** *m* CONS MECA piston seal housings; ~ **de joint de tige** *m* CONS MECA rod seal housing; ~ **de palier** *m* PAPIER bearing housing; ~ **de pile** *m* PHOTO battery chamber, PRODUCTION battery holder; ~ **des roues** *m* AERONAUT wheel well; ~ **de train** *m* AERONAUT wheel well; ~ **du train** *m* AERONAUT landing gear bay, landing gear well

logements: ~ **des barres** *m pl* CONS MECA poppet holes

loger *vt* ESPACE *véhicules* stow

loggia *f* CONSTR loggia

logiciel *m* ELECTR, INFORMAT, ORDINAT, PHYSIQUE, TV software; ~ **d'aide à la programmation** *m* ORDINAT support program; ~ **d'analyse de structures** *m* ESPACE *véhicules* structural analysis software; ~ **d'application**

m ORDINAT application software; **~ de base** *m* INFOR-MAT systems software; **~ de communications** *m* ORDINAT communication software; **~ d'exploitation** *m* ORDINAT systems software; **~ fourni en bundle** *m* ORDINAT bundled software; **~ de gestion transaction-nelle** *m* INFORMAT, ORDINAT transaction management software; **~ maison** *m* ORDINAT in-house software; **~ pour lequel une contribution volontaire est demandée** *m* INFORMAT, ORDINAT shareware; **~ de problématique** *m* ORDINAT problem-oriented software; **~ de recon-naissance de la parole** *m* ORDINAT speechware; **~ de réseau** *m* ORDINAT network software; **~ souris** *m* ORDINAT mouse software

logique[1] *adj* INFORMAT, ORDINAT logical

logique[2] *f* ELECTRON, INFORMAT, ORDINAT logic; **~ à l'arséniure de gallium** *f* ELECTRON gallium arsenide logic; **~ binaire** *f* ORDINAT binary logic; **~ bipolaire** *f* ELECTRON bipolar logic; **~ câblée** *f* INFORMAT, ORDI-NAT hardwired logic; **~ de calculateur** *f* INFORMAT, ORDINAT computer logic; **~ cellulaire** *f* ELECTRON cel-lular logic; **~ CMOS** *f* ELECTRON CMOS logic; **~ combinatoire** *f* ELECTRON combinatorial logic; **~ com-patible** *f* ELECTRON compatible logic; **~ à couplage en courant** *f* ELECTROTEC current-mode logic; **~ à coup-lage par émetteurs** *f* ELECTRON, ORDINAT ECL, emitter-coupled logic; **~ à diodes** *f* ELECTRON diode logic; **~ à diodes et transistors** *f* ELECTRON, ORDINAT DTL, diode-transistor logic; **~ ECL** *f* ELECTRON, ORDI-NAT *(logique à couplage par émetteurs)* emitter-coupled logic *(ECL)*; **~ floue** *f* ORDINAT fuzzy logic; **~ formelle** *f* INFORMAT, ORDINAT formal logic; **~ à haute densité** *f* ELECTRON high-density logic; **~ à haut niveau** *f* ELECTRON high-level logic; **~ à injection** *f* ELECTRON injection logic; **~ intégrée à injection** *f (IL)* ELECTRON integrated injection logic *(IL)*; **~ d'interface** *f* ELECTRON interface logic; **~ de lecture d'étiquetage avec code à barres** *f* EMBALLAGE bar code scanner and decoder logic; **~ majoritaire** *f* ELECTRON majority logic; **~ négative** *f* ELECTRON ne-gative logic; **~ NMOS** *f* ELECTRON NMOS logic; **~ non saturée** *f* ELECTRON nonsaturated logic; **~ numérique** *f* ELECTRON digital logic; **~ par les fluides** *f* CONS MECA *transmission hydraulique* fluid logic circuit; **~ positive** *f* ELECTRON positive logic; **~ programmable** *f* ELEC-TRON random logic; **~ de programmation** *f* PRODUCTION *automatisme industriel* programming logic; **~ rapide** *f* ELECTRON fast logic, high-speed logic; **~ RCTL** *f* ELECTRON RCTL logic; **~ à relais** *f* PRODUC-TION *automatisme industriel* relay logic; **~ saturée** *f* ELECTRON saturated logic; **~ à transistor et transistors** *f* ELECTRON TTL, transistor-transistor logic; **~ à tran-sistors fusionnés** *f* ELECTRON MTL, merged transistor logic; **~ transistor-transistor** *f* INFORMAT, ORDINAT TTL, transistor-transistor logic; **~ à trois états** *f* ELECTRON three-state logic; **~ TTL Schottky** *f* ELEC-TRON Schottky TTL

logistique *f* INFORMAT, ORDINAT logistics; **~ vitale** *f* OCEANO life support system

logo *m* CONSTR logo; **~ type** *m* CONSTR logo

loi *f* BREVETS statute law, SECURITE Act; **~ d'action de masse** *f* CHIMIE mass action law, PHYSIQUE law of mass action; **~ des aires** *f* AERONAUT area rule; **~ des aires de Kepler** *f* ESPACE Kepler's law of areas; **~ binomiale** *f* MATH binomial distribution; **~ de Biot et Savart** *f* PHYSIQUE Biot-Savart law; **~ de Boyle-Mariotte** *f* PHYSIQUE Boyle's law; **~ de Charles** *f* PHYSIQUE Charles's law; **~ de la conservation du nom-bre des particules** *f* NUCLEAIRE particle number conservation law; **~ de conservation de la parité** *f* PHYS RAYON parity conservation law; **~ de correction biquadratique** *f* TV fourth-power law; **~ du cosinus de Lambert** *f* OPTIQUE Lambert's cosine law, cosine emission law; **~ de Coulomb** *f* ELECTR, PHYS RAYON Cou-lomb's law; **~ de Curie** *f* PETR, PHYS RAYON, PHYSIQUE Curie's law; **~ de Curie-Weiss** *f* PHYS RAYON, PHYSIQUE Curie-Weiss law; **~ de Dalton** *f* PHYSIQUE Dalton's law; **~ de décroissance radioactive** *f* PHYS RAYON law of radioactive decay; **~ de déplacement de Wien** *f* PHYSIQUE Wien displacement law; **~ de Des-cartes-Snell** *f* PHYSIQUE Snell's law; **~ de dilution d'Ostwald** *f* CHIMIE Ostwald's dilution law; **~ de Du-long et Petit** *f* PHYSIQUE Dulong and Petit's law; **~ des états correspondants** *f* PHYSIQUE law of correspond-ing states; **~ de Fick** *f* PHYSIQUE Fick's law; **~ de Gay-Lussac** *f* PHYSIQUE Gay-Lussac's law; **~ géomé-trique** *f* MATH *statistique* geometric distribution; **~ de Graham** *f* PHYSIQUE Graham's law; **~ de Hooke** *f* CONSTR, PHYSIQUE Hooke's law; **~ de Hubble** *f* AS-TRONOMIE Hubble's law; **~ hypergéométrique** *f* MATH *statistique* hypergeometric distribution; **~ de l'inverse du carré** *f* PHYSIQUE inverse square law; **~ de Joule** *f* PHYSIQUE Joule's law; **~ de Kirchhoff** *f* ELECTR, ELEC-TROTEC, PHYS RAYON *coefficient de la température* Kirchhoff's law; **~ de Lambert** *f* OPTIQUE Lambert's cosine law, cosine emission law, PHYSIQUE Lambert's law; **~ de Lenz** *f* ELECTR *induction*, PHYSIQUE Lenz's law; **~ log-normale** *f* MATH log normal distribution; **~ de Malus** *f* PHYSIQUE Malus law; **~ de Mariotte** *f* PHYSIQUE Boyle's law; **~ du mélange des gaz** *f* PHYSIQUE Dalton's law; **~ de Moseley** *f* PHYSIQUE Moseley's law; **~ de Newton de refroidissement** *f* PHYSIQUE Newton's law of cooling; **~ d'Ohm** *f* ELECTR, PHYSIQUE Ohm's law; **~ de Paschen** *f* PHYSIQUE Pa-schen's law; **~ de Planck** *f* PHYS RAYON *rayonnement* Planck's law, PHYSIQUE Planck's formula; **~ de Poi-seuille** *f* PHYSIQUE Poiseuille's law; **~ de Poisson** *f* ESPACE *véhicules* Poisson's law, MATH Poisson dis-tribution; **~ des probabilités** *f* INFORMAT probability distribution; **~ de réciprocité** *f* CINEMAT reciprocity law; **~ de sélection** *f* NUCLEAIRE selection rule; **~ de Stefan** *f* PHYS RAYON Planck's law, Stefan's law; **~ de Stefan-Boltzmann** *f* PHYS RAYON, PHYSIQUE Stefan-Boltzmann law; **~ de Stokes** *f* PHYSIQUE Stokes' law; **~ sur la lutte contre la pollution atmosphérique** *f* POLLU-TION clean air act; **~ de t** *f* MATH t-distribution; **~ de terre** *f* ELECTROTEC Ohm's law; **~ de Wiedemann et Franz** *f* PHYSIQUE Wiedemann-Franz law; **~ de Wien** *f* PHYSIQUE Wien law

lois: **~ de Faraday** *f pl* ELECTR *électrolyse, induction*, PHYSIQUE Faraday's laws; **~ de Kepler** *f pl* PHYSIQUE Kepler's laws; **~ de Kepler des mouvements des planètes** *f pl* ASTRONOMIE Kepler's laws of planetary motion; **~ de Newton des mouvements des planètes** *f pl* ASTRONOMIE Newton's laws of motion; **~ de la radiation** *f pl* PHYS RAYON radiation laws; **~ de la réflexion** *f pl* PHYSIQUE laws of reflection; **~ de la réfraction** *f pl* PHYSIQUE laws of refraction; **~ de la thermodynamique** *f pl* THERMODYN laws of thermody-namics; **~ thermodynamiques** *f pl* THERMODYN thermodynamic laws; **~ de vibration d'une corde fixe** *f pl* PHYS ONDES laws of vibration of a fixed string

löllingite *f* MINERAUX löllingite

long:[1] **de ~** *adv* CONS MECA lengthways, lengthwise; **en ~** *adv* CONS MECA lengthways, lengthwise; **le ~ de la côte** *adv* NAUT alongshore

long:[2] **~ métrage** *m* CINEMAT feature; **~ rail soudé** *m* CH DE FER long welded rail (BrE), ribbon rail (AmE), CH DE FER continuous welded rail

long:[3] **le ~ de** *prép* NAUT alongside; **le ~ du bord de** *prép* NAUT alongside

long-courrier *m* AERONAUT long distance aircraft, NAUT ocean going ship

longeage *m* CERAM VER swinging pit; **~ du cylindre** *m* CERAM VER elongation of the cylinder

longer *vt* HYDROLOGIE run alongside

longeron *m* AERONAUT *aéronef* spar, *treillis* chord member, CERAM VER throat cheek, CONSTR main beam, main girder, stringer, ESPACE spar, VEHICULES *châssis* side member; **~ de châssis** *m* VEHICULES *carrosserie* chassis member; **~ de gouverne de direction** *m* AERONAUT rudder post

longévité *f* CONS MECA durability, MATERIAUX longevity, MINES life, lifetime; **~ de la tête magnétique** *f* TV head life

longifolène *m* CHIMIE longifolene

longitude *f* ESPACE, NAUT longitude; **~ astronomique** *f* ESPACE astronomic longitude; **~ céleste** *f* ESPACE celestial longitude; **~ solaire** *f* ASTRONOMIE solar longitude

longitudinal[1] *adj* ELECTRON, NAUT longitudinal

longitudinal:[2] **~ de pont** *m* NAUT deck longitudinal

longrinage *m* MINES double timbering, reinforced timbering, herringbone timbering

longrine *f* CH DE FER, CONSTR stringer

longue: à ~ portée *adj* MILITAIRE long-range

longue-conservation *adj* (UHT) AGRO ALIM long-life, ultra heat treated (UHT)

longue-durée: ~ de service *f* PRODUCTION long life

longue-période *f* OCEANO *onde* long period

longue-taille *f* MINES longwall extraction, longwall face

longueur:[1] **en ~** *adv* CONS MECA lengthways, lengthwise

longueur[2] *f* CINEMAT footage, IMPRIM *document* extent, INFORMAT, ORDINAT, PAPIER *bobine, rouleau*, PHYSIQUE length; **~ active** *f* NUCLEAIRE *partie* active length; **~ de l'âme** *f* MILITAIRE *canon* length of bore; **~ d'aplatissement** *f* RESSORTS solid length; **~ de base d'une piste** *f* AERONAUT runway basic length; **~ à bloc** *f* RESSORTS solid length; **~ de bloc** *f* ORDINAT block length, block size; **~ de bobine** *f* ESSAIS coil length; **~ de boucle** *f* RESSORTS hook length; **~ de bridage** *f* RESSORTS seat length; **~ de chaîne** *f* INFORMAT, ORDINAT string length, PLAST CAOU chain length; **~ de chenal** *f* EN RENOUV length of channel; **~ de cohérence** *f* OPTIQUE, PHYSIQUE, TELECOM coherence length; **~ de coupe** *f* TEXTILE staple length; **~ de course du piston** *f* CONSTR length of piston stroke; **~ critique de fissure** *f* METALL critical crack length; **~ de décohésion** *f* MATERIAUX debond length; **~ de décollage** *f* AERONAUT takeoff run; **~ dépassante** *f* CONSTR projection length; **~ développée** *f* RESSORTS extended length; **~ de diffusion** *f* ELECTRON diffusion length; **~ d'une division** *f* METROLOGIE scale spacing; **~ d'échelle** *f* METROLOGIE scale length; **~ de l'échelon** *f* METROLOGIE length of the interval; **~ efficace d'entrefer** *f* ACOUSTIQUE, TV effective gap length; **~ d'emmarchement** *f* CONSTR length of step; **~ en place** *f* RESSORTS working length; **~ d'enregistrement** *f* INFORMAT, ORDINAT record length; **~ d'entrefer** *f* ENREGISTR gap length; **~ entre**

perpendiculaires *f* NAUT length between perpendiculars; **~ entre pointes** *f* CONS MECA distance between centers (AmE), distance between centres (BrE); **~ d'équilibrage** *f* TELECOM equilibrium length, equilibrium mode distribution length; **~ d'équilibre** *f* OPTIQUE equilibrium length, equilibrium mode distribution length; **~ d'essai** *f* RESSORTS test length; **~ de fil** *f* TEXTILE knotless yarn length; **~ de film** *f* CINEMAT film length; **~ fixe** *f* INFORMAT, ORDINAT fixed length; **~ focale** *f* ASTRONOMIE *téléscope*, CINEMAT, PHYS RAYON *lentille électrostatique* focal length; **~ hors tout** *f* CONS MECA, NAUT, TEXTILE overall length; **~ d'instruction** *f* INFORMAT, ORDINAT instruction length; **~ de liaison** *f* CRISTALL bond length; **~ libre** *f* CONS MECA *ressort*, RESSORTS free length; **~ libre du corps** *f* RESSORTS body free length; **~ de mot** *f* INFORMAT, ORDINAT word length, word size; **~ de mot fixe** *f* INFORMAT, ORDINAT fixed word length; **~ moyenne des véhicules** *f* TRANSPORT average vehicle length; **~ non coupée** *f* TELECOM uncut length; **~ d'onde de coupure** *f* OPTIQUE cutoff wavelength, PHYSIQUE critical wavelength, cutoff wavelength, TELECOM cutoff wavelength; **~ d'onde** *f* ACOUSTIQUE, CHIMIE, ELECTR, ELECTRON, METALL, OPTIQUE, PETR, PHYS ONDES, PHYSIQUE, TELECOM wavelength; **~ d'onde Compton** *f* NUCLEAIRE, PHYSIQUE, PHYS RAYON Compton wavelength; **~ d'onde critique** *f* TELECOM cutoff wavelength; **~ d'onde dans le guide** *f* PHYSIQUE guide wavelength; **~ d'onde enregistrée** *f* ACOUSTIQUE recorded wavelength; **~ d'onde du maximum d'intensité de rayonnement** *f* OPTIQUE, TELECOM peak intensity wavelength; **~ d'onde de seuil** *f* ELECTRON threshold wavelength; **~ de page** *f* IMPRIM length of page; **~ de page logique** *f* IMPRIM logical page length; **~ de pieu** *f* CHARBON pile length; **~ de piste équivalente** *f* AERONAUT balanced field length; **~ préréglée** *f* RESSORTS preset length; **~ de ralentissement** *f* NUCLEAIRE, PHYSIQUE slowing-down length; **~ réelle d'entrefer** *f* ACOUSTIQUE gap length, TV real gap length; **~ de registre** *f* INFORMAT, ORDINAT register length; **~ de résolution géométrique** *f* NUCLEAIRE geometric resolution length; **~ retirée** *f* MATERIAUX pullout length; **~ de roulement à l'atterrissage** *f* AERONAUT landing run; **~ de rupture** *f* PAPIER tensile length, tensile strength; **~ sous tête** *f* CONS MECA length under head to point; **~ à spires jointives** *f* RESSORTS solid length; **~ tête comprise** *f* CONS MECA length overall; **~ tête non comprise** *f* CONS MECA length under head to point; **~ de tige** *f* PETROLE stand of pipe; **~ de tissu sur rouleau** *f* TEXTILE roll length; **~ totale** *f* METROLOGIE overall length; **~ de trajectoire** *f* NUCLEAIRE path length; **~ de trame** *f* ESPACE *communications* frame length; **~ utile de pieu** *f* CHARBON effective pile length; **~ variable** *f* INFORMAT, ORDINAT variable length

longue-vis *f* CONS MECA *tube* long screw

longue-vue *f* INSTRUMENT monocular telescope, NAUT telescope

lophine *m* CHIMIE lophine

lopin *m* MINES pillar

lopolite *m* GEOLOGIE lopolith

loquet *m* CONSTR latch, MECANIQUE catch; **~ à bouton** *m* CONSTR lift-latch; **~ à bouton simple** *m* CONSTR lift-latch; **~ de porte** *m* CONSTR gate latch; **~ à poucier** *m* CONSTR thumb latch; **~ à ressort** *m* PRODUCTION spring latch; **~ de verrouillage** *m* PRODUCTION locking latch

loqueteau *m* CONS MECA latch, CONSTR catch; ~ **de fermeture** *m* CONSTR lock

lot *m* AGRO ALIM, CINEMAT, IMPRIM, INFORMAT, MECANIQUE, ORDINAT, PETROLE, PRODUCTION, TELECOM *fabrication*, TRANSPORT batch; ~ **de contrôle** *m* QUALITE inspection lot; ~ **économique** *m* PRODUCTION economic order quantity; ~ **de fabrication** *m* CINEMAT emulsion batch; ~ **fractionné** *m* PRODUCTION split; ~ **de minerai** *m* MINES parcel of ore; ~ **de modification** *m* PRODUCTION modification kit; ~ **de production** *m* QUALITE production batch; ~ **technique** *m* PRODUCTION lot size; ~ **de travaux** *m* INFORMAT, ORDINAT job batch

lotionnage: ~ **d'émeri** *m* CERAM VER emery washing

lotissement *m* PRODUCTION lot sizing

loup *m* CERAM VER bear, PRODUCTION bear, horse, sow

Loup *m* ASTRONOMIE Lupus

loupe *f* EQUIP LAB *optique* magnifying glass, IMPRIM *contrôle qualité* magnifying glass, magnifying lens, INSTRUMENT magnifier, magnifying glass, multiplying glass, MECANIQUE *outillage*, PHYSIQUE magnifying glass; ~ **éclairante de poche** *f* INSTRUMENT illuminated folding lens; ~ **d'écoulement** *f* GEOLOGIE gravity slide; ~ **de glissement** *f* GEOLOGIE flow lobe, solifluction lobe; ~ **de lapidaire** *f* INSTRUMENT gem magnifier, jeweler's eyepiece (AmE), jeweller's eyepiece (BrE); ~ **de lecture** *f* INSTRUMENT measuring microscope, reading microscope; ~ **à manche pliante** *f* INSTRUMENT folding lens, folding pocket magnifier; ~ **de mise au point** *f* INSTRUMENT focusing magnifier, focusing magnifying glass; ~ **photoscopique** *f* INSTRUMENT magnifying picture viewer; ~ **pliante** *f* INSTRUMENT folding lens, folding pocket magnifier; ~ **à poisson** *f* OCEANO fish finder, fish scope; ~ **de puddlage** *f* PRODUCTION puddle ball; ~ **serre-tête** *f* INSTRUMENT headset magnifier; ~ **de visée** *f* INSTRUMENT ranging magnifier, PHOTO viewing magnifier

loupes-lunettes *f pl* INSTRUMENT spectacle magnifier

lourd *adj* IMPRIM *papier* heavyweight

louve: ~ **à genouillère** *f* PRODUCTION lever grip tongs; ~ **à pince** *f* PRODUCTION lever grip tongs

louvoyage *m* NAUT tacking

louvoyer *vi* NAUT beat, tack

louvre *m* (Bel) *(cf jalousie)* CERAM VER jalousie, louver (AmE), louvre (BrE)

lover *vt* NAUT flake, *cordage* coil

lowéite *f* MINERAUX loeweite

loxodromie *f* NAUT rhumb line

LPM *abrév (lignes par minute)* INFORMAT, ORDINAT LPM *(lines per minute)*

LQMAC *abrév (limite de qualité moyenne après contrôle)* QUALITE AOQL *(average outgoing quality limit)*

Lr *(lawrencium)* CHIMIE Lr *(lawrencium)*

LRS *abrév (long rail soudé)* CH DE FER CWR *(continuous welded rail)*

LSI *abrév (intégration à grande échelle)* ELECTRON, INFORMAT, NAUT, ORDINAT, PHYSIQUE, TELECOM LSI *(large-scale integration)*

Lu *(lutétium)* CHIMIE Lu *(lutetium)*

lubrifiant *m* AUTO, CERAM VER, CONSTR, MECANIQUE lubricant, PETR dope, PETROLE, PLAST CAOU, PRODUCTION, TEXTILE lubricant; ~ **de boudin** *m* CH DE FER *véhicules* wheel flange lubricant

lubrificateur: ~ **à air comprimé** *m* CONS MECA compressed air lubricator; ~ **de pompe à air** *m* CONS MECA air pump lubricator

lubrification *f* MATERIAUX lubrification, PRODUCTION greasing, lubricating, lubrifaction, lubrification, REFRIG, VEHICULES lubrification

lubrifié *adj* GAZ lubricated

lubrifier *vt* MECANIQUE lubricate, PRODUCTION grease, lubricate, TEXTILE lubricate; ~ **pour le froid** *vt* CINEMAT winterize

lucarne *f* CONSTR dormer

lucidol *m* PLAST CAOU benzoyl peroxide

lueur *f* MATERIAUX glow, NAUT loom; ~ **de l'atmosphère** *f* ASTRONOMIE airglow; ~ **cathodique** *f* PHYSIQUE cathode glow; ~ **du feu** *f* THERMODYN firelight; ~ **nocturne** *f* ASTRONOMIE nightglow; ~ **propre** *f* ESPACE self-luminosity

lumachelle *f* GEOLOGIE coquina limestone, shell breccia, shelly limestone

lumen *m* METROLOGIE, PHYSIQUE lumen

lumenmètre *m* PHYSIQUE lumenmeter

lumière *f* CONS MECA aperture, oil hole, opening, porthole, CONSTR throat, *rabot* mouth, DISTRI EAU *pompe* spout hole, OPTIQUE light, visible radiation, PHOTO, PHYSIQUE light, VEHICULES *moteur* port; ~ **actinique** *f* CINEMAT actinic light; ~ **d'admission** *f* INST HYDR induction port, steam port, VEHICULES *moteur* inlet port (BrE), intake port (AmE); ~ **ambiante** *f* CINEMAT ambient light, available light, existing light; ~ **d'appoint** *f* CINEMAT booster light, fill-in light, PHOTO fill-in light; ~ **à arc** *f* ELECTR arc light; ~ **à l'aurore** *f* ASTRONOMIE auroral light; ~ **blanche** *f* IMPRIM *photogravure*, PHYSIQUE white light; ~ **cendrée** *f* ASTRONOMIE ashen light; ~ **clignotante** *f* IMPRIM *contrôle* blinking light; ~ **cohérente** *f* ELECTRON, PHYS ONDES, TELECOM coherent light; ~ **collimatée** *f* EN RENOUV collimated light; ~ **de cylindre à vapeur** *f* INST HYDR port; ~ **de décrochement** *f* CINEMAT backlight, counter key light, hair light; ~ **diffuse** *f* CINEMAT diffused light; ~ **diffusée** *f* PHYS RAYON scattered light; ~ **directe** *f* PHOTO direct light; ~ **douce** *f* CINEMAT soft light; ~ **éblouissante** *f* SECURITE dazzle, glare; ~ **d'échappement** *f* INST HYDR, VEHICULES exhaust port; ~ **d'entrée** *f* INST HYDR induction port, steam port; ~ **des étoiles** *f* ASTRONOMIE starlight; ~ **froide** *f* CINEMAT cold light; ~ **halogène** *f* CINEMAT quartz light; ~ **inactinique** *f* CINEMAT safelight; ~ **incidente** *f* CINEMAT, PHOTO, PHYS RAYON incident light; ~ **incohérente** *f* PHYS ONDES, TELECOM incoherent light; ~ **intense** *f* PHYS ONDES intense light; ~ **du jour** *f* CINEMAT natural light; ~ **monochromatique** *f* METALL monochromatic light; ~ **monochrome** *f* PHYS ONDES monochromatic light; ~ **négative** *f* PHYSIQUE negative glow; ~ **noire** *f* GEOPHYS ultraviolet radiation, IMPRIM black light; ~ **non tamisée** *f* CINEMAT bare light; ~ **non tramée** *f* CINEMAT bare light; ~ **parasite** *f* CINEMAT flare, leak light, spill light, stray light; ~ **polarisée** *f* CINEMAT, PHOTO, PHYS ONDES, PHYS RAYON, PHYSIQUE polarized light; ~ **de pompage** *f* ELECTRON pumping light; ~ **pour éclairer les yeux** *f* CINEMAT catch light; ~ **pour fixation** *f* CONS MECA cotter slot; ~ **principale** *f* CINEMAT keylight; ~ **pulsée** *f* CINEMAT intermittent light; ~ **quartz** *f* CINEMAT quartz light; ~ **réfléchie** *f* PHOTO reflected light; ~ **d'une source ponctuelle** *f* PHOTO point source light; ~ **spéculaire** *f* IMPRIM *optique, photogravure* scattered light; ~ **stroboscopée** *f* ESPACE strobe light; ~ **stroboscopique** *f* CINEMAT strobe light; ~ **tamisée** *f* CINEMAT soft light; ~ **de tirage**

f CINEMAT printer light; ~ **de transfert** *f* VEHICULES *moteur à deux temps* transfer port; ~ **transmise** *f* PHOTO, PHYS RAYON transmitted light; ~ **ultraviolette** *f* PHYS RAYON, PLAST CAOU ultraviolet light; ~ **zodiacale** *f* ASTRONOMIE zodiacal light

lumière-éclair *f* PHOTO flashlight

luminaire *m* ELECTR luminaire, ELECTROTEC light fitting, EQUIP LAB *éclairage* light source; ~ **antidéflagrant** *m* ELECTR fireproof lighting installation (AmE), flameproof lighting installation (BrE)

luminance *f* ELECTRON, ELECTROTEC, ESPACE *communications* luminance, OPTIQUE brightness, radiance, PHYSIQUE luminance, TELECOM luminance, radiance, TV luminance; ~ **élevée** *f* TV high picture level; ~ **énergétique** *f* ESPACE radiance, OPTIQUE brightness, radiance, PHYSIQUE, TELECOM, TV radiance; ~ **énergétique spectrique** *f* TELECOM spectral radiance; ~ **spectrale** *f* PHYSIQUE spectral luminance; ~ **spectrique** *f* TELECOM spectral radiance; ~ **zéro** *f* TV zero luminance

lumination *f* ACOUSTIQUE photographic exposure

luminescence *f* CHIMIE, ELECTROTEC, PHYS RAYON, PHYSIQUE, TV luminescence; ~ **aux rayons X** *f* NUCLEAIRE X-ray luminescence, roentgenoluminescence

luminescent *adj* CHIMIE, ELECTROTEC luminescent

lumineuse *f* PHYSIQUE *émittance* luminous exitance, TV luminance

lumineux[1] *adj* OPTIQUE bright

lumineux:[2] ~ **rectiligne** *m* PETR ray path

luminombre *m* PHOTO light value

luminophore *m* ELECTRON phosphor

luminosité *f* ASTRONOMIE luminosity, ELECTRON brightness, PHYS PART luminosity, PHYSIQUE brightness, luminosity, TV brightness; ~ **accrue** *f* PHYS RAYON developed luminosity; ~ **de crête** *f* PHYS RAYON peak luminosity; ~ **de l'écran** *f* CINEMAT screen brightness; ~ **équivalente** *f* TV gray scale value (AmE), grey scale value (BrE); ~ **réelle** *f* PHOTO effective candle power

lunaire *adj* ASTRONOMIE lunar

lunaison *f* ASTRONOMIE lunation, synodic month

lune *f* ASTRONOMIE moon; ~ **bleue** *f* ASTRONOMIE blue moon; ~ **dans le deuxième ou le troisième quartier** *f* ASTRONOMIE gibbous moon; ~ **de la moisson** *f* ASTRONOMIE harvest moon; ~ **de septembre** *f* ASTRONOMIE harvest moon

lunette *f* CONS MECA center rest (AmE), centre rest (BrE), collar plate, solid die, steady, steady rest, CONSTR pipe connection, pipe coupling, INSTRUMENT spyglass, telescope, PRODUCTION die, RESSORTS oblong hole; ~ **d'alignement** *f* INSTRUMENT alignment telescope; ~ **d'approche** *f* ASTRONOMIE refracting telescope; ~ **d'approche de mise au point** *f* INSTRUMENT adjusting telescope; ~ **arrière** *f* VEHICULES *carrosserie* rear window; ~ **astromique** *f* PHYSIQUE refractor; ~ **astronomique** *f* INSTRUMENT astronomical telescope, refracting telescope, refractor, refractor telescope, PHYSIQUE astronomical telescope, refracting telescope; ~ **à autocollimation** *f* INSTRUMENT autocollimator; ~ **de calfat** *f* OCEANO observation chamber; ~ **à coussinets** *f* CONS MECA jaw steady rest; ~ **de custode** *f* VEHICULES *carrosserie* rear window; ~ **à fileter** *f* CONS MECA solid die, PRODUCTION die; ~ **fixe** *f* CONS MECA *tour* fixed steady rest; ~ **de Galilée** *f* PHYSIQUE Galilean telescope; ~ **méridienne** *f* ASTRONOMIE transit telescope, INSTRUMENT meridian

telescope; ~ **de nuit** *f* INSTRUMENT night telescope; ~ **d'observation** *f* INSTRUMENT telescope magnifier; ~ **panoramique** *f* INSTRUMENT panoramic telescope; ~ **de pointage** *f* INSTRUMENT rifle telescope, sighting telescope; ~ **à prismes redresseurs** *f* INSTRUMENT erecting prism telescope; ~ **de regard** *f* PRODUCTION eyepiece; ~ **d'une seule pièce** *f* PRODUCTION die in one piece; ~ **à suivre** *f* CONS MECA follow rest, traveling stay (AmE), travelling stay (BrE); ~ **à tarauder** *f* CONS MECA solid die, PRODUCTION die; ~ **terrestre** *f* INSTRUMENT terrestrial telescope; ~ **de tour** *f* CONS MECA backrest; ~ **à trois touches réglables** *f* CONS MECA three-jaw steady, three-jaw steady rest; ~ **de visée** *f* ASTRONOMIE magnifying sight, INSTRUMENT panoramic sight, telescopic sight; ~ **de visée d'un fusil** *f* MILITAIRE rifle telescope; ~ **viseur** *f* CONSTR sighting telescope; ~ **zénithale** *f* INSTRUMENT zenith telescope

lunette-loupe *f* INSTRUMENT telescope magnifier, telescopic spectacles

lunettes *f pl* PRODUCTION goggles; ~ **bifocales** *f pl* INSTRUMENT bifocal glasses; ~ **à branches** *f pl* INSTRUMENT temple spectacles; ~ **à coques latérales** *f pl* INSTRUMENT safety glasses, safety goggles; ~ **à double foyer** *f pl* INSTRUMENT bifocal glasses; ~ **grossissantes** *f pl* INSTRUMENT telescopic spectacles; ~ **de nuit** *f pl* MILITAIRE night vision goggles; ~ **de nuit à hautes performances** *f pl* MILITAIRE high-performance night vision goggles; ~ **de protection** *f pl* EQUIP LAB safety glasses, *sécurité* protective glasses, protective spectacles, SECURITE eye protectors, goggles, protective goggles, safety goggles, safety spectacles; ~ **de protection pour le travail** *f pl* SECURITE protective goggles for occupational safety; ~ **protectrices** *f pl* INSTRUMENT X-ray protective glasses, eye protectors, eye shields, safety glasses, SECURITE goggles; ~ **protectrices contre l'éblouissement** *f pl* INSTRUMENT antidazzle glasses, antiglare glasses; ~ **de soudure** *f pl* INSTRUMENT welder's goggles; ~ **de sûreté** *f pl* INSTRUMENT X-ray protective glasses, eye protectors, eye shields, safety glasses; ~ **à tempes** *f pl* INSTRUMENT temple spectacles; ~ **à verres polarisés** *f pl* PHOTO polarizing spectacles

lunnite *f* MINERAUX lunnite

lupuline *f* CHIMIE lupuline

lussatite *f* MINERAUX lussatite

lustrage *m* PRODUCTION buffing, glazing, glossing, TEXTILE glazing; ~ **par brosse** *m* PAPIER brush glazing, brush polishing

lustre *m* CERAM VER, ELECTR *éclairage* chandelier, PAPIER gloss, polish, *surface* glaze, PLAST CAOU gloss, PRODUCTION glossiness, gloss

lustré *adj* MATERIAUX lustrous, TEXTILE glossy

lustrer *vt* PRODUCTION, TEXTILE glaze

lustromètre *m* PAPIER gloss meter, lustrometer

lut *m* PRODUCTION lute

lutage *m* CERAM VER making-up

lutation *f* PRODUCTION lutation

lutéine *f* CHIMIE lutein

lutéocobaltique *adj* CHIMIE luteocobaltic

lutéol *m* CHIMIE luteol

lutéoline *f* CHIMIE luteolin, luteoline

lutétium *m (Lu)* CHIMIE lutecium, lutetium *(Lu)*

lutidine *f* CHIMIE lutidine

lutidinique *adj* CHIMIE lutidinic

lutidone *f* CHIMIE lutidone

lutite *f* GEOLOGIE lutite

lutte: ~ **antibruit** *f* SECURITE noise abatement, sound-absorbing machines; ~ **anti-incendie** *f* CONSTR firefighting; ~ **contre les algues** *f* HYDROLOGIE algal destruction; ~ **contre le bruit** *f* POLLUTION prevention of noise pollution; ~ **contre l'incendie** *f* SECURITE, THERMODYN firefighting; ~ **contre les inondations** *f* DISTRI EAU flood control; ~ **contre les odeurs** *f* POLLUTION odor control (AmE), odour control (BrE); ~ **contre la pollution** *f* POLLUTION pollution control; ~ **contre la pollution atmosphérique** *f* POLLUTION prevention of atmospheric pollution; ~ **contre la pollution des eaux** *f* POLLUTION prevention of water pollution

lux *m* METROLOGIE, PHOTO, PHYSIQUE lux

lx *abrév (lux)* METROLOGIE lx *(lux)*

Lynx *m* ASTRONOMIE Lynx

lyogel *m* CHIMIE lyogel

lyophile *adj* CHIMIE lyophilic

lyophilisat *m* REFRIG lyophilizate

lyophilisateur *m* REFRIG freeze-dryer; ~ **à tambour** *m* REFRIG drum freeze dryer

lyophilisation *f* AGRO ALIM freeze-drying, EMBALLAGE dry freeze, freeze-drying, GENIE CHIM freeze-drying, lyophilization, REFRIG, THERMODYN freeze-drying; ~ **accélérée** *f* AGRO ALIM AFD, accelerated freeze-drying; ~ **continue** *f* REFRIG continuous freeze-drying

lyophilisé *adj* AGRO ALIM, REFRIG freeze-dried

lyophiliser *vt* AGRO ALIM, THERMODYN freeze-dry

lyophillie *f* CHIMIE lyophily

lyophobe *adj* CHIMIE lyophobic

lyosol *m* CHIMIE lyosol

lyosolécithine *f* CHIMIE lysolecithin

lyre *f* AERONAUT *commande de vol* lyre-shaped bell-crank, CONS MECA quadrant, quadrant plate, *tour à fileter* swing frame, tangent plate; ~ **d'accrochage** *f* AERONAUT finger grip clip; ~ **de dilatation** *f* REFRIG expansion bend

Lyre *f* ASTRONOMIE Lyra

lysergique *adj* CHIMIE lysergic

lysine *f* CHIMIE lysine

lysophosphatide *m* CHIMIE lysophosphatide

lyxonique *adj* CHIMIE lyxonic

lyxose *m* CHIMIE lyxose

M

m *abrév (milli-)* METROLOGIE m *(milli-)*

M *abrév (méga-)* METROLOGIE M *(mega-)*

mA *abrév (milliampère)* ELECTR, ELECTROTEC mA *(milliampere)*

MA *abrév* ELECTRON *(modulation d'amplitude)*, ENREGISTR *(modulation d'amplitude)*, ORDINAT *(modulation d'amplitude)* AM *(amplitude modulation)*, PHYSIQUE *(multiplexage analogique)* FDM *(frequency-division multiplexing)*, TV *(modulation d'amplitude)* AM *(amplitude modulation)*

maar *m* GEOLOGIE *cratère d'explosion volcanique* maar

macadam *m* CONSTR macadam

macadamisage *m* CONSTR macadamization

macadamisation *f* CONSTR macadamization

macérateur *m* CHIMIE macerator

macération *f* CHIMIE maceration

macérer *vt* AGRO ALIM, CHIMIE macerate

Mach: ~ **à ne jamais dépasser** *m* AERONAUT never exceed Mach number

mâchefer *m* PRODUCTION *système hydraulique* clinker

machine *f* AUTO machine, CONS MECA engine, machine, motor, ELECTROTEC, INFORMAT machine, NAUT *navire* engine, ORDINAT, PAPIER, PRODUCTION machine; **~ a** ~ **à additionner** *f* ORDINAT calculator; ~ **à adresser** *f* IMPRIM Addressograph (TM); ~ **à affûter** *f* CONS MECA grinding machine, sharpener, sharpening machine, *lames de scie* saw-sharpening machine, PAPIER sharpening machine; ~ **à affûter les forets** *f* CONS MECA drill grinder, drill sharpener; ~ **à affûter les forets hélicoïdaux** *f* CONS MECA twist drill grinder; ~ **à affûter les fraises** *f* PRODUCTION milling cutter sharpening machine; ~ **à affûter les lames de couteaux** *f* PRODUCTION knife grinding machine; ~ **à affûter les mèches** *f* CONS MECA drill grinder, drill sharpener; ~ **à affûter les outils** *f* CONS MECA tool grinder, tool sharpener; ~ **à affûter universelle** *f* CONS MECA universal tool-and-cutter sharpener; ~ **agricole** *f* MECANIQUE agricultural machine; ~ **à air comprimé** *f* CONS MECA compressed air engine; ~ **à aléser** *f* CONS MECA cutter bar; ~ **à aléser les boîtes à noyaux** *f* PRODUCTION core box-boring machine; ~ **à aléser à deux broches opposées** *f* CONS MECA duplex boring machine; ~ **d'alimentation** *f* INST HYDR auxiliary boiler feeder; ~ **alternative** *f* NAUT reciprocating engine; ~ **analytique** *f* ORDINAT analytical engine; ~ **arroseuse de goudron** *f* CONSTR tar sprayer, tar sprinkler; ~ **aspirante** *f* DISTRI EAU suction pump; ~ **à aspiration** *f* CERAM VER suction machine; ~ **à assembler** *f* IMPRIM gatherer, gathering machine; ~ **asservie au laser** *f* CONSTR laser-controlled machine; ~ **asynchrone** *f* ELECTROTEC asynchronous machine; ~ **d'Atwood** *f* PHYSIQUE Atwood's machine; ~ **auto-adaptative** *f* ELECTRON learning machine; ~ **d'auto-apprentissage** *f* INFORMAT, ORDINAT self-learning machine; ~ **automatique pour chargement latéral et par le fond** *f* EMBALLAGE automatic side and bottom loading machine; ~ **automatique pour remplir les sacs flexibles** *f* EMBALLAGE automatic flexible bag filling machine; ~ **automat-**

ique à tailler les engrenages à denture droite *f* CONS MECA automatic spur gear cutting machine; ~ **auxiliaire** *f* CONS MECA auxiliary motor, NAUT auxiliary engine; ~ **à avoyer** *f* CONS MECA *lames de scie à ruban* setting machine; **~ b** ~ **à balancier** *f* CONS MECA beam engine; ~ **bicylindrique** *f* CONS MECA double cylinder engine, double engine, duplex engine, duplex cylinder engine, twin-cylinder engine; ~ **bipolaire** *f* ELECTR bipolar machine; ~ **à biseauter** *f* CONS MECA beveling machine (AmE), bevelling machine (BrE); ~ **à biseaux** *f* CERAM VER miter grinding machine (AmE), mitre grinding machine (BrE); ~ **à border** *f* PRODUCTION flanger, flanging machine; ~ **à boucher les bouteilles** *f* EMBALLAGE bottle-closing machine, bottle-sealing machine; ~ **à boulonner au toit** *f* MINES roof bolting drilling machine; ~ **à bouveter** *f* CONSTR matching machine; ~ **à braser à affûter et à avoyer les lames de scies à ruban** *f* CONS MECA band-saw brazing sharpening and setting machine; ~ **à brocher** *f* CONS MECA, MECANIQUE broaching machine; ~ **à brocher à plusieurs coulisseaux** *f* CONS MECA multiple-ram broaching machine; ~ **à brocher verticale type presse** *f* CONS MECA press-type vertical broaching machine; ~ **à brouillard** *f* CINEMAT fog gun; ~ **broyeuse** *f* CONS MECA grinding machine; ~ **de bureau pour l'impression** *f* IMPRIM office printing machine; **~ c** ~ **à calculer** *f* MATH calculator, ORDINAT calculating machine; ~ **à canneler portative** *f* PRODUCTION keyway cutting tool; ~ **à capsuler** *f* EMBALLAGE capper (AmE); ~ **de Carnot** *f* PHYSIQUE Carnot engine; ~ **carrousel** *f* CERAM VER rotating machine; ~ **à carton** *f* PAPIER board machine; ~ **à carton multiforme** *f* PAPIER multivat board machine; ~ **à centrer** *f* CONS MECA centering machine (AmE), centring machine (BrE); ~ **à chanfreiner** *f* CONS MECA plate edge planing machine; ~ **à charger** *f* PRODUCTION charging machine; ~ **chasse-clou** *f* EMBALLAGE nailing machine; ~ **à cintrer** *f* MECANIQUE bending machine; ~ **à cintrer les tôles** *f* CONS MECA plate bending rollers, plate bending rolls; ~ **à cintrer les tuyaux** *f* CONSTR pipe bender; ~ **à cisailler** *f* CONS MECA shear, shearing machine, shears; ~ **à cisailler les barres** *f* CONS MECA bar shearing machine; ~ **à CN** *f (machine à commande numérique)* CONS MECA NC machine, NC machine tool; ~ **CNC à rectifier les surfaces planes** *f* CONS MECA CNC surface grinder; ~ **à coller les bords** *f* EMBALLAGE edge gumming machine; ~ **combinée à dégauchir raboter mouluer et mortaiser** *f* CONS MECA combined surfacing planing molding and slot-mortising machine (AmE), combined surfacing planing moulding and slot-mortising machine (BrE); ~ **à commande automatique** *f* CONS MECA push-button machine; ~ **à commande numérique** *f (machine à CN)* CONS MECA numerical control machine, numerical control machine tool; ~ **à composer** *f* IMPRIM composing machine, typesetting machine; ~ **compound** *f* CONS MECA compound engine; ~ **à compression** *f* PRODUC-

TION press, squeezer; ~ **comptable** *f* ORDINAT accounting machine; ~ **de concassage** *f* GENIE CHIM crushing machine; ~ **à contrecoller** *f* EMBALLAGE laminating machine; ~ **de contrôle des engrenages** *f* METROLOGIE gear testing machine; ~ **à côtes plates** *f* CERAM VER flat-grinding machine; ~ **à coudre** *f* IMPRIM, TEXTILE sewing machine; ~ **à coudre les sacs** *f* EMBALLAGE bag stitching machine, IMPRIM *sacherie* bag stitcher; ~ **à couper les coulées** *f* CONS MECA gate cutter, PRODUCTION git cutter, sprue cutter; ~ **à couper d'onglet** *f* CONSTR miter cutting machine (AmE), miter machine (AmE), mitre cutting machine (BrE), mitre machine (BrE); ~ **à courant alternatif** *f* ELECTR alternating current machine, ELECTROTEC AC machine, alternating current machine; ~ **à courant continu** *f* ELECTROTEC DC machine, direct current machine; ~ **à courroie émerisée** *f* PRODUCTION emery belt polishing machine; ~ **à cylindre renversé** *f* PRODUCTION inverted cylinder engine; ~ **à cylindre unique** *f* CONS MECA one-cylinder engine, single cylinder engine;

~ d ~ **dans l'inaction** *f* CONS MECA machine lying idle; ~ **de déboîtage de remplissage et de recouvrement de bac** *f* EMBALLAGE tray denesting filling and lidding machine; ~ **à décanter** *f* GENIE CHIM decanting machine, elutriating machine; ~ **de découpe à gabarit** *f* CERAM VER shape cutting machine; ~ **à défoncer** *f* CONS MECA routing machine, CONSTR recessing machine; ~ **à dégauchir** *f* CONS MECA surface planer, surface-planing machine; ~ **à démouler** *f* PRODUCTION draft machine (AmE), draught machine (BrE); ~ **à démouler à levier** *f* PRODUCTION lever draft machine (AmE), lever draught machine (BrE); ~ **à démouler à renversement** *f* PRODUCTION roll-over draft machine (AmE), roll-over draught machine (BrE), roll-over drop machine; ~ **démouleuse** *f* PRODUCTION stripping machine; ~ **à dessabler à table rotative** *f* PRODUCTION rotary table sandblast machine; ~ **à détente** *f* CONS MECA expansion engine; ~ **à détente simple** *f* CONS MECA simple expansion engine; ~ **à deux plateaux** *f* CERAM VER two-table machine; ~ **de développement continu** *f* PHOTO continuous processing machine; ~ **à développer** *f* IMPRIM *films et plaques* processing machine, processor, PHOTO processing machine; ~ **à développer les plaques** *f* IMPRIM *copie* plate processor; ~ **diphasée** *f* ELECTROTEC two-phase machine; ~ **à disque émerisé** *f* PRODUCTION disc grinder (BrE), disk grinder (AmE); ~ **à diviser** *f* CONS MECA graduating engine; ~ **à doser les cartons** *f* EMBALLAGE carton dosing machine; ~ **à draguer** *f* MINES dredge, dredger; **~ e** ~ **à ébarber** *f* CONS MECA grinding machine, trimming machine; ~ **à ébavurer** *f* CONS MECA deburring machine; ~ **électrique** *f* ELECTROTEC electric machine, electrical machine; ~ **électrique à courant alternatif** *f* ELECTROTEC AC machine, alternating current machine; ~ **électrique statique** *f* ELECTROTEC static electrical machine; ~ **électrique tournante** *f* ELECTROTEC rotating electrical machine; ~ **à électro-érosion** *f* CONS MECA wire spark machine; ~ **d'emballage de boîtes** *f* EMBALLAGE can packing machine (AmE), tin packing machine (BrE); ~ **d'emballage en portion unique** *f* EMBALLAGE single portion packaging machine; ~ **d'emballage entièrement automatique pour film étirable** *f* EMBALLAGE fully-automatic stretch wrapper; ~ **d'emballage pour bouteilles** *f* EMBALLAGE bottle-packing machine; ~ **à**

emboîter *f* IMPRIM casing-in machine; ~ **émettrice** *f* TELECOM transmit machine; ~ **à émulsionner** *f* GENIE CHIM emulsifying machine; ~ **à encaisser** *f* EMBALLAGE case loader; ~ **à encoder les étiquettes** *f* EMBALLAGE label coding machine; ~ **d'encollage** *f* EMBALLAGE adhesive machine, glue gumming machine; ~ **d'encollage à points multiples** *f* EMBALLAGE multipoint gluing machine; ~ **à encoller** *f* IMPRIM gluer; ~ **en continu à laver les bidons** *f* AGRO ALIM straight-through can washer; ~ **à enduire** *f* EMBALLAGE, PLAST CAOU *matériel* coating machine, REVETEMENT coater, coating machine; ~ **à engommer** *f* EMBALLAGE gumming machine; ~ **à enrober le chocolat** *f* AGRO ALIM chocolate coating machine; ~ **à enrober les fils** *f* PRODUCTION wire coating machine; ~ **à enrouler** *f* RESSORTS coiling machine; ~ **à enrouler les ressorts** *f* RESSORTS spring-coiling machine; ~ **d'ensouplage** *f* TEXTILE beamer; ~ **enveloppeuse** *f* EMBALLAGE wrapping machine; ~ **d'épuisement** *f* DISTRI EAU draining engine, pumping engine; ~ **à équilibrer** *f* CONS MECA balancing machine; ~ **d'essai** *f* CONS MECA testing machine; ~ **d'essai de charge de ressorts** *f* RESSORTS spring load testing machine; ~ **d'essai de dureté Rockwell** *f* CONS MECA Rockwell hardness testing machine; ~ **d'essai de fatigue** *f* RESSORTS fatigue testing machine; ~ **d'essai des ressorts de torsion** *f* RESSORTS torsion-spring testing machine; ~ **à essais de compression** *f* EMBALLAGE compression test machine; ~ **d'essais de dureté Brinell** *f* CONS MECA Brinell hardness testing machine; ~ **d'essais de dureté Vickers** *f* CONS MECA Vickers hardness testing machine; ~ **d'estampage pour feuilles minces** *f* EMBALLAGE foil backing machine; ~ **à étalonner à lecture vidéo** *f* CINEMAT video color analyser (AmE), video colour analyser (BrE); ~ **à étamper forger cisailler et poinçonner** *f* CONS MECA combined stamping forging shearing and punching machine; ~ **à excitation en série** *f* ELECTR series excited machine, *générateur* series-wound machine; ~ **d'exécution** *f* INFORMAT, ORDINAT object machine; ~ **d'exhaure** *f* DISTRI EAU draining engine, pumping engine; ~ **à expansion** *f* CONS MECA expansion engine; ~ **d'extraction** *f* MINES draft engine (AmE), draught engine (BrE), mine hoist, drawing engine, winding engine, hoist, hoisting engine; ~ **d'extraction compound bicylindrique** *f* CONS MECA duplex compound winding engine;

~ f ~ **à façonner des blocs** *f* IMPRIM *façonnage* padding press; ~ **à faire les emboîtages** *f* IMPRIM case maker; ~ **à faire les joints** *f* PRODUCTION jointer, jointing machine; ~ **à faire les moulures** *f* CONSTR molding machine (AmE), moulding machine (BrE); ~ **à faire des poignées** *f* CERAM VER machine for making handles; ~ **à faire des portions** *f* EMBALLAGE portioning machine; ~ **à faire les rainures et les languettes** *f* CONSTR tonguing-and-grooving machine; ~ **à fermer** *f* EMBALLAGE sealing machine; ~ **à fermer les tubes** *f* EMBALLAGE tube-closing machine; ~ **de fermeture** *f* EMBALLAGE closing machine; ~ **de fermeture thermosoudable** *f* EMBALLAGE heat-sealing and welding machine; ~ **à fer tournant** *f* ELECTROTEC inductor machine; ~ **à feuilles** *f* IMPRIM sheet-fed machine; ~ **à fileter à la filière** *f* CONS MECA die-threading machine; ~ **à fileter au peigne** *f* CONS MECA chasing machine; ~ **de flambage** *f* TEXTILE singeing machine; ~ **fonctionnant en mode caractère** *f* INFORMAT character-oriented machine; ~ **fonctionnant manuellement** *f* EMBALLAGE hand-operated machine; ~ **à forme ronde** *f* PAPIER cylinder machine; ~ **à fraiser** *f* PRODUCTION miller, milling machine; ~ **à fraiser horizontale** *f* SECURITE horizontal milling machine; ~ **à fraiser les matrices et les moules** *f* CONS MECA die-sinking machine; ~ **à fraiser à portique** *f* CONS MECA plane milling machine; ~ **à fraiser les rainures de cales** *f* PRODUCTION keyway cutting machine; ~ **à fraiser universelle** *f* CONS MECA universal milling machine; ~ **à frapper** *f* PRODUCTION *boulon, rivet, crampon, etc* bolt forging machine; ~ **frictionneuse** *f* PAPIER MG machine; ~ **frigorifique** *f* CONS MECA refrigerating system, PRODUCTION freezing machine, REFRIG refrigerating machine, refrigeration machine; ~ **frigorifique à absorption** *f* REFRIG absorption refrigeration machine; ~ **frigorifique à air** *f* REFRIG air cycle refrigeration machine;

~ **g** ~ **à gaz** *f* PRODUCTION gas engine, gas motor; ~ **à glacer** *f* CERAM VER, PHOTO glazing machine; ~ **à gommer** *f* EMBALLAGE glue spreading machine; ~ **à granuler** *f* EMBALLAGE granulating machine; ~ **à gratter** *f* TEXTILE raising machine; ~ **à graver** *f* IMPRIM *eau-forte* etching machine; ~ **à graver les disques** *f* ACOUSTIQUE disc recorder (BrE), disk recorder (AmE); ~ **guidée à la main** *f* SECURITE hand-guided machine;

~ **h** ~ **homopolaire** *f* ELECTROTEC homopolar generator, homopolar machine; ~ **à huit postes** *f* RESSORTS eight-station machine; ~ **hydraulique de reproduction** *f* CONS MECA hydraulic copy mill;

~ **i** ~ **à imprégner** *f* EMBALLAGE impregnating machine; ~ **à impression** *f* IMPRIM printing machine; ~ **d'impression sérigraphique** *f* EMBALLAGE silk-screen printing machine; ~ **à impression sur métal** *f* IMPRIM metal decorating machine; ~ **à imprimer** *f* TEXTILE printing machine; ~ **à imprimer les cartons en feuilles** *f* EMBALLAGE sheet-fed carton printer; ~ **à imprimer conçue pour tissu adroit** *f* TEXTILE printer designed for narrow fabric; ~ **à imprimer à cylindre** *f* IMPRIM cylinder printing machine; ~ **à imprimer en creux** *f* IMPRIM plate printing machine; ~ **à imprimer à rouleaux** *f* EMBALLAGE rotary printing press;

~ **j** ~ **au jet de sable** *f* PRODUCTION sand jet, sandblast; ~ **à jointer les placages** *f* CONS MECA veneer splicing machine; ~ **à jointer les placages transversalement** *f* CONS MECA crosswise veneer splicing machine;

~ **l** ~ **de labeur** *f* IMPRIM commercial press; ~ **de laquage** *f* EMBALLAGE lacquering machine; ~ **à laver** *f* TEXTILE washing machine; ~ **de lecture à bobines** *f* ENREGISTR reel-to-reel player; ~ **à lier les bottes** *f* EMBALLAGE bundle-tying machine;

~ **m** ~ **marchant à blanc** *f* CONS MECA machine running light, machine running on no load, PRODUCTION empty machine, machine running empty; ~ **marchant chargée** *f* CONS MECA machine running under load; ~ **marchant à vide** *f* CONS MECA machine running light, machine running on no load, PRODUCTION empty machine, machine running empty; ~ **à marquer** *f* EMBALLAGE marking equipment, marking machine; ~ **à matelasser** *f* TEXTILE quilter; ~ **à mélanger la glaise** *f* CERAM VER clay mixing machine; ~ **de mesure** *f* METROLOGIE *filet de vis* measuring machine; ~ **de mesure au laser** *f* METROLOGIE laser measuring instrument; ~ **de mesure des profils** *f* METROLOGIE contour measuring equipment; ~ **à mesurer en coordonnées** *f* METROLOGIE coordinate measuring machine; ~ **à meule d'émeri** *f* PRODUCTION emery grinder, emery grinding machine, emery machine; ~ **à meuler** *f* CONS MECA, RESSORTS grinding machine; ~ **à meuler double** *f* CONS MECA two-wheel grinding machine; ~ **à meuler les surfaces planes extérieures** *f* CONS MECA surface grinder, surface-grinding machine; ~ **à meule travaillant sur périphérie** *f* PRODUCTION edge wheel grinding machine; ~ **à molettes** *f* MINES headgear, pithead gear; ~ **monophasée** *f* ELECTROTEC single-phase machine; ~ **à monter les plaques et tirer des épreuves** *f* IMPRIM *flexographie* mounter-proofer; ~ **à mortaiser** *f* CONS MECA slotting machine, PRODUCTION mortising machine; ~ **à mortaiser et percer** *f* PRODUCTION mortising and boring machine; ~ **à mortaiser les rainures de cales** *f* PRODUCTION keyway cutting machine; ~ **à mortaises** *f* CONS MECA slotter; ~ **mortaiseuse** *f* PRODUCTION mortising machine; ~ **à mouiller** *f* CERAM VER mechanical boy; ~ **de moulage par soufflage** *f* EMBALLAGE injection blow molding machine (AmE), injection blow moulding machine (BrE); ~ **à mouler** *f* PRODUCTION molding machine (AmE), moulding machine (BrE); ~ **à mouler en coquille** *f* CONS MECA die casting machine; ~ **à mouler d'établi** *f* PRODUCTION bench molding machine (AmE), bench moulding machine (BrE); ~ **à mouler par compression** *f* PLAST CAOU *plastiques* compression molding machine (AmE), compression moulding machine (BrE); ~ **à mouler le polystyrène et le polyéthylène mousse** *f* EMBALLAGE foamed polystyrene and polyethylene molder (AmE), foamed polystyrene and polyethylene moulder (BrE); ~ **à moulurer** *f* CONSTR molding machine (AmE), moulding machine (BrE); ~ **à moulurer dite toupie** *f* CONSTR spindle molding machine (AmE), spindle moulding machine (BrE); ~ **à multiple expansion** *f* PRODUCTION multiple expansion engine;

~ **n** ~ **à nettoyer** *f* PRODUCTION cleaning machine; ~ **à noyauter** *f* PRODUCTION coring machine; ~ **à numéroter** *f* IMPRIM numbering machine;

~ **o** ~ **octale** *f* ORDINAT byte machine; ~ **à onduler** *f* PAPIER corrugator, vat machine; ~ **à ouate** *f* PAPIER tissue machine;

~ **p** ~ **à papier** *f* IMPRIM, PAPIER paper machine; ~ **à papier à table inversée** *f* PAPIER harper machine; ~ **à papier à table plate** *f* PAPIER Fourdrinier paper machine; ~ **parlante** *f* TELECOM announcement machine, recorded announcement machine; ~ **peigneuse circulaire** *f* TEXTILE circular combing machine; ~ **à pelliculer** *f* IMPRIM *façonnage, flexographie* laminator; ~ **à percer** *f* CONS MECA drilling machine; ~ **à percer avec pression du porte-foret à la main par levier** *f* CONS MECA lever-feed drilling machine; ~ **à percer grande vitesse à monopoulie** *f* CONS MECA single pulley high-speed drilling machine; ~ **à percer montée sur colonne** *f* CONS MECA drill press, pillar drill, pillar drilling machine; ~ **à percer multiple** *f* PRODUCTION gang drill, multiple-spindle drill; ~ **à percer portative** *f* CONS MECA portable drilling machine; ~ **à percer quatre forets** *f* PRODUCTION four-spindle drilling machine; ~ **à percer radiale à potence** *f* CONS MECA swing-jib radial drill; ~ **à percer sensitive multiple** *f* CONS MECA sensitive gang drill; ~ **à percer sensitive à plateaux de friction** *f* CONS MECA sensitive friction drill; ~ **à percer sur colonne** *f* CONS MECA column-type drilling machine; ~ **à perforer** *f* IMPRIM perforating machine; ~ **à peser** ƒ IMPRIM weighing machine; ~ **à pétrir la glaise** ƒ CERAM VER clay kneading machine; ~ **à piéter** ƒ CINEMAT edge numbering machine; ~ **à planer** ƒ CONS MECA planisher; ~ **à plat** ƒ IMPRIM flat-bed press; ~ **de pliage** ƒ PRODUCTION folding machine; ~ **à plier** ƒ PRODUCTION folding machine; ~ **à plier et à agrafer les boîtes** ƒ EMBALLAGE folding and seaming machine; ~ **à plier et à coller** ƒ EMBALLAGE crease and glueing machine, folder-gluer; ~ **à plier et à couder les tôles** ƒ CONS MECA plate folding and bending machine; ~ **à plier et à entailler** ƒ EMBALLAGE creasing and scoring machine; ~ **à plier et à jointurer** ƒ EMBALLAGE bottom-folding and seaming machine; ~ **à plisser** ƒ TEXTILE pleating machine; ~ **pneumatique** ƒ CONS MECA air engine, air motor, pneumatic motor, aspiring pump, pneumatic pump; ~ **à poinçonner** ƒ CONS MECA punching machine; ~ **à poinçonner et à cisailler** ƒ CONS MECA punching and shearing machine; ~ **à pointer** ƒ MECANIQUE jig borer; ~ **à pointer et à aléser** ƒ CONS MECA jig boring machine; ~ **à pôle intermédiaire** ƒ ELECTR interpole machine; ~ **à polir** ƒ PRODUCTION polishing machine; ~ **à poncer** ƒ PRODUCTION sandpapering machine; ~ **à poncer à deux plateaux** ƒ PRODUCTION double disc sandpapering machine (BrE), double disk sandpapering machine (AmE); ~ **à poncer à plateau** ƒ PRODUCTION disc sandpapering machine (BrE), disk sandpapering machine (AmE); ~ **portative** ƒ SECURITE portable machine; ~ **à poser les agrafes pour jonction** ƒ TEXTILE clipper dryerfelt; ~ **à poste unique** ƒ RESSORTS single station machine; ~ **pour appliquer un opercule et sceller à chaud** ƒ EMBALLAGE film-applying lid and heat-sealing machine; ~ **pour appliquer le papier métallisé** ƒ EMBALLAGE tin-foiling machine; ~ **pour l'art graphique** ƒ IMPRIM printer's machine; ~ **pour assemblage automatique** ƒ CONS MECA automatic assembly machine; ~ **pour assembler les boîtes** ƒ EMBALLAGE box-erecting machine; ~ **pour atmosphère grisouteuse** ƒ CHARBON firedamp-proof machine, machine for potentially explosive atmosphere; ~ **pour bander avec du papier** ƒ EMBALLAGE paper banding machine; ~ **pour la céramique** ƒ CERAM VER ceramic machine; ~ **pour charger les sacs** ƒ EMBALLAGE bag loading machine; ~ **pour coudre les sacs** ƒ EMBALLAGE sack sewing machine; ~ **pour doser** ƒ EMBALLAGE dosing machine; ~ **pour doser et remplir** ƒ EMBALLAGE filling and dosing machine; ~ **pour dresser et fermer les cartons** ƒ EMBALLAGE carton erector and closer; ~ **pour dresser remplir et fermer les cartons** ƒ EMBALLAGE case erecting filling and closing machine; ~ **pour emballage alimentaire** ƒ EMBALLAGE food-wrapping machinery; ~ **pour emballage en manchons thermorétractables** ƒ EMBALLAGE shrink sleeve wrapping machine; ~ **pour emballage extérieur** ƒ EMBALLAGE overwrapping machinery; ~ **pour emballage flexible** ƒ EMBALLAGE flexible packaging machine; ~ **pour emballage de palettes sous tension** ƒ EMBALLAGE pallet stretch-wrapping machine; ~ **pour emballage thermoformé** ƒ EMBALLAGE blister packaging machine; ~ **pour emballage thermoformé avec aluminium mince** ƒ EMBALLAGE blister edge and foil machine; ~ **pour emballer et déballer les ampoules** ƒ EMBALLAGE case packing and unpacking of ampoules machine; ~ **pour emboutissage profond** ƒ EMBALLAGE deep drawing machine; ~ **pour empiler les fils** ƒ EMBALLAGE wire stacking machine; ~ **pour encapsuler les bouteilles** ƒ EMBALLAGE bottle-capping machine; ~ **pour enveloppement thermorétractable** ƒ EMBALLAGE shrink overwrapping machine; ~ **pour envelopper** ƒ EMBALLAGE enveloping machine; ~ **pour envelopper avec film** ƒ EMBALLAGE film wrapping machine; ~ **pour essais de flexion** ƒ PLAST CAOU *instrument d'essai* bending tester; ~ **pour estamper** ƒ EMBALLAGE embossing machine; ~ **pour la fabrication des briques et des tuiles** ƒ CERAM VER brick and tile machine; ~ **pour la fabrication de céramique fine** ƒ CERAM VER machine for fine ceramics; ~ **pour fabriquer les boîtes** ƒ EMBALLAGE box-making machine; ~ **pour fabriquer les sacs** ƒ EMBALLAGE bag-making machine; ~ **pour faire les paquets** ƒ EMBALLAGE parcelling machine; ~ **pour faire les sachets** ƒ EMBALLAGE pouch-making machine; ~ **pour fermer les boîtes** ƒ EMBALLAGE can closing machine (AmE), tin closing machine (BrE); ~ **pour fermer les caisses** ƒ EMBALLAGE case-sealing machine; ~ **pour fermer les sacs** ƒ EMBALLAGE sack sealer, sack-closing machine; ~ **pour fermeture sous vide** ƒ EMBALLAGE vacuum-closing machine, vacuum-sealing machine; ~ **pour fermeture verticale sous vide** ƒ EMBALLAGE vertical vacuum sealer; ~ **pour formage à chaud** ƒ EMBALLAGE thermoform machinery; ~ **pour former sous pression** ƒ EMBALLAGE pressure-forming machine; ~ **pour l'impression en couleurs** ƒ IMPRIM color printing machine (AmE), colour printing machine (BrE); ~ **pour imprimer et coller les étiquettes** ƒ EMBALLAGE print-and-apply labeling machine (AmE), print-and-apply labelling machine (BrE); ~ **pour lyophilisation sous vide** ƒ EMBALLAGE vacuum freeze dryer; ~ **pour mettre en bottes** ƒ EMBALLAGE bundling machine; ~ **pour la mise en boîtes** ƒ EMBALLAGE boxing machine; ~ **pour la mise en bouteilles** ƒ EMBALLAGE bottling machine; ~ **pour palettiser** ƒ EMBALLAGE palletizing machine; ~ **pour remplir les boîtes** ƒ EMBALLAGE box-filling machine, can-filling machine (AmE), tin-filling machine (BrE); ~ **pour remplir et encapsuler** ƒ EMBALLAGE filling and capping machine; ~ **pour remplir et fermer** ƒ EMBALLAGE fill-and-seal machine; ~ **pour remplir les sacs** ƒ EMBALLAGE bag filling machine; ~ **pour le remplissage sous vide** ƒ EMBALLAGE vacuum filling machine; ~ **pour le soudage des plastiques** ƒ CONS MECA plastic welding machine; ~ **pour le taraudage des tiges et des écrous** ƒ PRODUCTION bolt-screwing and nut-tapping machine; ~ **pour utilisation sur comptoir** ƒ EMBALLAGE countertop machine; ~ **à produire des toiles d'araignée** ƒ CINEMAT cobweb gun; ~ **à produire du vent** ƒ CINEMAT wind machine; ~ **du protocole commun de transfert d'informations de gestion** ƒ TELECOM CMIPM, common management information protocol machine;

~ r ~ **à raboter** ƒ CH DE FER rail-planing machine, CONSTR planer (AmE), planing machine (BrE); ~ **à raboter latérale** ƒ PRODUCTION side planing machine; ~ **à raboter ouverte sur le côté** ƒ PRODUCTION open-side planing machine; ~ **à raboter tirant des bois d'épaisseur** ƒ CONSTR planing and thicknessing machine; ~ **à rainer** ƒ CONS MECA grooving machine; ~ **à rainurer les poulies** ƒ CONS MECA pulley key-seating machine; ~ **rangeuse de bouteilles** ƒ EMBALLAGE bottle unscrambler; ~ **à raser les engrenages** ƒ CONS MECA gear shaving machine; ~ **réceptrice** ƒ TELECOM receive machine; ~ **à rectifier** ƒ CONS MECA grinder, grinding machine; ~ **à rectifier les arbres à cames** ƒ

CONS MECA camshaft grinding machine; ~ **à rectifier les coulisses de changement de marche** *f* PRODUCTION link grinder; ~ **à rectifier cylindriquement CNC** *f* CONS MECA CNC cylindrical grinder; ~ **à rectifier en l'air les surfaces cylindriques** *f* CONS MECA vertical cylinder-grinding machine; ~ **à rectifier les intérieurs à CNC pour travaux de série** *f* CONS MECA CNC production internal grinding machine; ~ **à rectifier à meule à 90** *f* CONS MECA face grinder; ~ **à rectifier les surfaces cylindriques extérieures** *f* CONS MECA plain grinder; ~ **à rectifier les surfaces intérieures** *f* CONS MECA internal grinder; ~ **à rectifier les surfaces planes extérieures** *f* CONS MECA surface grinder, surface-grinding machine; ~ **à rectifier les surfaces profilées** *f* CONS MECA profile grinder; ~ **à redresser** *f* CONS MECA straightener, straightening machine; ~ **à refouler et à souder** *f* CONS MECA shrinking and welding machine; ~ **à refouler souder couder et contrecouder** *f* CONS MECA combined bending shrinking and welding machine; ~ **de remblayage** *f* MINES dirt packing machine; ~ **à remouler** *f* PRODUCTION setting-up machine; ~ **à remplir et à fermer les tubes** *f* EMBALLAGE tube filling and closing machine; ~ **de remplissage** *f* EMBALLAGE filling machine; ~ **de remplissage par gravité** *f* EMBALLAGE gravity filling machine; ~ **de remplissage volumétrique** *f* EMBALLAGE density filling machine; ~ **de réserve tournant à vide** *f* EN RENOUV spinning reserves; ~ **à ressort-moteur** *f* RESSORTS clock spring machine; ~ **à revêtir** *f* REVETEMENT coating machine; ~ **à rincer les bouteilles** *f* AGRO ALIM bottle washer, EMBALLAGE bottle-rinsing machine, bottle-washing machine; ~ **à river** *f* CONSTR riveter, riveting machine; ~ **à river hydraulique fixe** *f* PRODUCTION stationary hydraulic riveter (AmE), stationary hydraulic rivetter (BrE); ~ **à riveter** *f* CONSTR riveter, riveting machine; ~ **à roder** *f* CONS MECA, MECANIQUE honing machine, PAPIER sander, PRODUCTION lapping machine; ~ **rotative pneumatique** *f* CONS MECA rotary pneumatic engine; ~ **à rotor cylindrique** *f* ELECTR cylindrical rotor machine; ~ **à rouler** *f* CONS MECA bending press; ~ **à rouler et à cintrer les tôles** *f* CONS MECA plate flattening and bending machine;

~ **s** ~ **sans détente** *f* CONS MECA nonexpansion engine; ~ **à satiner** *f* EMBALLAGE glazing machine; ~ **à scier** *f* CONS MECA, CONSTR sawing machine; ~ **à scier alternative** *f* CONS MECA power hacksaw; ~ **à scier circulaire monolame** *f* CONS MECA single blade circular sawing machine; ~ **à scier les métaux** *f* PRODUCTION metal-sawing machine; ~ **à sculpter** *f* PRODUCTION carving machine; ~ **sectionnelle** *f* CERAM VER IS machine; ~ **sérigraphique** *f* EMBALLAGE screen printing machine; ~ **à simple extension** *f* CONS MECA single expansion engine; ~ **de soudage à l'arc** *f* MECANIQUE arc welding machine; ~ **de soudage en atmosphère inerte** *f* SECURITE protective gas welding machine; ~ **à souder** *f* PRODUCTION welding machine; ~ **à souder les anses** *f* PRODUCTION handle welding machine; ~ **à souder par rapprochement** *f* PRODUCTION butt welding machine; ~ **soufflante** *f* CONS MECA piston blower, PRODUCTION blower, blowing engine; ~ **à souffler les noyaux** *f* CONS MECA core-blowing machine; ~ **spéciale** *f* CONS MECA *produit à fabrication unique* special purpose machine; ~ **synchrone** *f* ELECTROTEC synchronous machine;

~ **t** ~ **à tailler les engrenages** *f* CONS MECA gear cutter, gear cutting machine; ~ **à tailler les engrenages**

par couteau *f* CONS MECA gear shaping machine; ~ **à tailler les engrenages par fraise-disque** *f* CONS MECA gear milling machine; ~ **à tailler les engrenages par fraise-mère** *f* CONS MECA gear hobbing machine; ~ **à tailler les pignons** *f* CONS MECA pinion-cutting machine; ~ **à tambour** *f* TEXTILE cylinder drying machine; ~ **à tarauder** *f* CONS MECA screw machine, screwing and tapping machine, screwing machine, tapping machine; ~ **à tarauder les tiges et les écrous** *f* PRODUCTION bolt-screwing and nut-tapping machine; ~ **à tarauder les tubes** *f* CONS MECA tube-screwing machine; ~ **à tarauder les tuyaux** *f* CONSTR pipe threader; ~ **tenue à main** *f* SECURITE hand-held machine; ~ **thermique** *f* CONS MECA heat engine, THERMODYN thermal engine; ~ **thermique combinée** *f* CONS MECA binary heat engine, binary heat engine; ~ **de thermosoudage** *f* EMBALLAGE heat-sealing machine; ~ **de tondage** *f* TEXTILE shearing machine; ~ **tournante amplificatrice** *f* ELECTROTEC rotary amplifier; ~ **de traçage** *f* MINES ripper, tunneling machine (AmE), tunnelling machine (BrE); ~ **à tracer les voies à travers les rochers** *f* MINES tunneling machine (AmE), tunnelling machine (BrE); ~ **de traitement de texte** *f* ORDINAT word processor; ~ **à trancher et dresser les bois en bout** *f* CONS MECA trimmer, CONSTR paring machine; ~ **de transfert** *f* MECANIQUE transfer machine; ~ **à travailler la terre glaise** *f* CERAM VER clay working machine; ~ **à travers les voies** *f* MINES roadheader; ~ **de triage et d'inspection pour pastilles** *f* EMBALLAGE tablet sorting and inspection machine; ~ **triphasée** *f* ELECTROTEC three-phase machine; ~ **à triple détente** *f* NAUT triple-expansion engine; ~ **à trois cylindres** *f* CONS MECA three-cylinder engine, triplex engine; ~ **à tunnels** *f* CONSTR tunneling machine (AmE), tunnelling machine (BrE); ~ **à turbines** *f* NAUT turbine engine; ~ **de Turing** *f* INFORMAT, ORDINAT Turing machine; ~ **de type SIMD** *f* ORDINAT *à flots d'instructions uniques et de données multiples* SIMD machine, single-instruction multiple-data machine; ~ **de type SISD** *f* ORDINAT *flots d'instructions et de données unique* single-instruction single-data machine;

~ **u** ~ **universelle à tailler** *f* CERAM VER universal grinder;

~ **v** ~ **à vapeur** *f* CONS MECA steam engine, INST HYDR, PHYSIQUE steam engine; ~ **ventilée en circuit fermé** *f* CONS MECA machine with closed-circuit ventilation; ~ **ventilée en circuit ouvert** *f* CONS MECA machine with open-circuit ventilation; ~ **à vernir** *f* REVETEMENT varnishing machine; ~ **à vernir par rideaux** *f* CONS MECA curtain coating machine; ~ **verticale à brocher les extérieurs** *f* CONS MECA vertical surface-type broaching machine; ~ **verticale et horizontale pour former remplir et fermer** *f* EMBALLAGE vertical and horizontal form fill seal machine; ~ **virtuelle** *f* INFORMAT, ORDINAT virtual machine; ~ **à voies multiples** *f* EMBALLAGE multilane machine; ~ **de von Neumann** *f* INFORMAT, ORDINAT von Neumann machine;

~ **w** ~ **de Wimshurst** *f* ELECTROTEC Wimshurst machine;

~ **x** ~ **à x têtes** *f* CERAM VER x-arm machine

Machine: ~ **pneumatique** *f* ASTRONOMIE Antlia

machine-outil *f* CONS MECA, MECANIQUE machine tool; ~ **à usage général** *f* PRODUCTION general-purpose machine tool

machine-pilon *f* PRODUCTION overhead engine

machinerie *f* CONS MECA machinery, PRODUCTION engine house, engine room; **~ de conversion** *f* EMBALLAGE conversion machinery; **~ hydraulique** *f* CONS MECA hydraulic machinery

machine-ruban *f* CERAM VER ribbon machine

machines *f pl* CONS MECA machinery; **~ acrobatiques** *f pl* CONS MECA lifting machinery; **~ conjuguées** *f pl* CONS MECA twin engines; **~ couplées** *f pl* CONS MECA coupled engines; **~ économisant la main-d'oeuvre** *f pl* PRODUCTION labor-saving machinery (AmE), labour-saving machinery (BrE); **~ élévatoires** *f pl* CONS MECA elevating machinery, lifting machinery; **~ jumelles** *f pl* CONS MECA twin engines; **~ de propulsion** *f pl* NAUT power plant

machines-outils: **~ de précision** *f pl* CONS MECA precision machine tools

machine-tender *f* MINES tank engine, tank locomotive

machiniste *m* PRODUCTION machinist; **~ de grue** *m* CINEMAT arm swinger, CONSTR craneman; **~ de plateau** *m* CINEMAT grip

machmètre *m* AERONAUT machmeter; **~ audible** *m* AERONAUT audible machmeter

mâchoire *f* CHARBON, CONS MECA, MECANIQUE, NUCLEAIRE *grappin*, PAPIER jaw, PRODUCTION *poulie à gorge* flange, VEHICULES *frein* shoe, yoke; **~ de concasseur** *f* GENIE CHIM crusher jaw; **~ étau** *f* CINEMAT set clamp; **~ de fixation** *f* CINEMAT set clamp; **~ de frein** *f* CONS MECA brake jaw, MECANIQUE shoe, VEHICULES *frein à tambour* brake shoe; **~ de frein à disque** *f* CH DE FER *véhicules* disc brake calliper (BrE), disk brake calliper (AmE); **~ à ressort** *f* CONS MECA saw clamp; **~ tendue** *f* VEHICULES *d'un frein* trailing shoe

mâchoires *f pl* CONS MECA cheeks, *d'un étau* chaps, *d'un étau de menuisier* chops, IMPRIM *d'un étau* vice jaws (BrE), vise jaws (AmE); **~ cannelées** *f pl* MINES corrugated jaws; **~ rapportées** *f pl* CONS MECA inserted jaws, *étau* detachable jaws; **~ de serrage** *f pl* PRODUCTION gripping jaws

maclage *m* CRISTALL twin formation, METALL twinning; **~ composé** *m* METALL compound twinning; **~ mécanique continu** *m* METALL continual mechanical twinning

macle *f* CRISTALL, MATERIAUX, METALL twin, MINERAUX macle; **~ de contact** *f* CRISTALL contact twin, juxtaposition twin; **~ de croissance** *f* METALL growth twin; **~ de juxtaposition** *f* CRISTALL contact twin, juxtaposition twin; **~ lenticulaire** *f* METALL lenticular twin; **~ non cohérente** *f* METALL incoherent twin; **~ par pénétration** *f* CRISTALL interpenetration twin

maclé *adj* CRISTALL twinned

maclurine *f* CHIMIE maclurin

maçon *m* CONSTR stonemason, *artisan* mason, *ouvrier* bricklayer

maçonnage *m* CONSTR brickwork, masonry, masonry work, stonework

maçonner *vt* CONSTR bed out, brick, brick up

maçonnerie *f* CERAM VER brickwork, masonry, CONSTR brickwork, masonry, masonry work, stonework; **~ de béton** *f* CONSTR concrete masonry; **~ de brique** *f* CONSTR brickwork; **~ en liaison** *f* CONSTR bonded masonry; **~ en moellons** *f* CONSTR rubble masonry; **~ de pierres** *f* CONSTR building stone

macque *f* PRODUCTION crocodile squeezer

macro *m* INFORMAT, ORDINAT macro

macroassembleur *m* INFORMAT, ORDINAT macro-assembler

macroclimat *m* METEO macroclimate

macroconstituant *m* MATERIAUX macrocomponent

macrocourbure *f* ELECTROTEC macrobend

macrocourbures *f pl* OPTIQUE, TELECOM macrobending

macrocyclique *adj* CHIMIE macrocyclic

macrodéchet *m* POLLUTION macrowaste

macrodureté *f* CONS MECA macro hardness

macroinstruction *f* INFORMAT, ORDINAT macroinstruction

macrolimite: **~ élastique critique** *f* MATERIAUX critical resolved shear stress

macromoléculaire *adj* CHIMIE macromolecular

macromolécule *f* CHIMIE, PLAST CAOU macromolecule

macronomenclature *f* PRODUCTION planning bill of material

macropolymère *m* CHIMIE macropolymer

macroprocesseur *m* INFORMAT, ORDINAT macroprocessor

macroprogramme: **~ de régulation** *m* TRANSPORT master program (AmE), master programme (BrE)

macroradiographie *f* NUCLEAIRE macroradiography

macrorégulation *f* TRANSPORT area control, macro control

macrosismique *adj* GEOPHYS macroseismic

macrosismologie *f* GEOPHYS effects of earthquakes

macrostructural *adj* CHIMIE macrostructural

macrostructure *f* CHIMIE macrostructure

maculage *m* IMPRIM marring, set-off, smearing, smudging

macule *f* ASTRONOMIE macula, IMPRIM, PAPIER offset paper

maculer *vt* IMPRIM set-off

macules *f pl* IMPRIM spoils

MAD *abrév (demande de modification d'appel)* TELECOM CMR *(call modification request message)*

madrague *f* CONSTR all-in ballast

madrier *m* CONSTR deal, plank, PRODUCTION *système hydraulique* runner

madriers *m pl* CHARBON, CONSTR planking

MAE *abrév (message de modification d'appel effectuée)* TELECOM CMC *(call modification completed message)*

mafique *adj* GEOLOGIE *ferromagnésien* mafic

magasin *m* CINEMAT magazine, CONS MECA hopper, magazine, EMBALLAGE storage space, storeroom, IMPRIM storage area, INFORMAT repository, PRODUCTION storeroom, stores, warehouse; **~ d'alimentation de cartes** *m* INFORMAT card hopper; **~ de découpe** *m* (Bel) *(cf atelier de découpe)* CERAM VER cutting shop; **~ d'emboîtement** *m* EMBALLAGE nesting magazine; **~ de film photographique** *m* INSTRUMENT film cassette; **~ d'outillage** *m* PRODUCTION tool crib; **~ petit format** *m* INSTRUMENT miniature film cassette; **~ plein jour** *m* CINEMAT daylight magazine; **~ pour produits finis** *m* EMBALLAGE finished goods store; **~ récepteur** *m* CINEMAT *pellicule exposée* take-up magazine

magasinage *m* PRODUCTION storage

magasinier *m* PRODUCTION storeman, warehouseman

magenta *m* IMPRIM magenta

magma: **~ des profondeurs** *m* PETR plutonic magma

magnésie *f* CHAUFFAGE, CHIMIE magnesia, PLAST CAOU *matière première pour peinture* magnesite; **~ calcinée** *f* PLAST CAOU *ingrédient de mélange* calcined magnesia

magnésien *adj* CHIMIE, GEOLOGIE magnesian

magnésioferrite *f* MINERAUX magnesioferrite

magnésique *adj* CHIMIE magnesic

magnésite *f* CHIMIE, MINERAUX magnesite

magnésium *m (Mg)* CHIMIE magnesium *(Mg)*

magnésol *m* CHIMIE *silicate acide de magnésium* magnesol

magnétique *adj* ELECTR, ENREGISTR, ESPACE, NAUT, PHYSIQUE magnetic; ~ **aéroporté** *adj* PETR aeromagnetic; ~ **transversal** *adj* ELECTROTEC, OPTIQUE, TELECOM TM, transverse magnetic

magnétisation *f* ELECTR, ELECTROTEC, ENREGISTR, GEOLOGIE, PETR, PHYSIQUE, TELECOM, TV magnetization; ~ **rémanente** *f* PETR remanent magnetization

magnétiser *vt* ELECTROTEC magnetize

magnétisme *m* ELECTR, PHYSIQUE magnetism; ~ **terrestre** *m* GEOPHYS geomagnetism, terrestrial magnetism, PHYSIQUE terrestrial magnetism

magnétite *f* MATERIAUX, MINERAUX, NUCLEAIRE magnetite

magnéto *f* ELECTR *automoteur*, ELECTROTEC, NAUT, VEHICULES *allumage* magneto; ~ **d'allumage** *f* VEHICULES ignition magneto; ~ **d'appel** *f* ELECTROTEC signaling generator (AmE), signalling generator (BrE)

magnétoconductivité *f* TELECOM magnetoconductivity

magnétodiode *f* ELECTRON magnetodiode

magnétodynamique: ~ **des gaz** *f* NUCLEAIRE MGD, magnetogasdynamics

magnéto-électricité *f* ELECTROTEC magnetoelectricity

magnétogramme *m* GEOPHYS magnetogram

magnétographe *m* GEOPHYS magnetograph

magnétohydrodynamique[1] *adj (MHD)* ELECTROTEC, ESPACE, GEOPHYS magnetohydrodynamic *(MHD)*

magnétohydrodynamique[2] *f* GEOPHYS, PHYS FLUID, PHYSIQUE magnetohydrodynamics

magnétomètre *m* AERONAUT, ELECTR, GEOPHYS magnetometer, NUCLEAIRE electron spin resonance magnetometer, PETR, PHYSIQUE magnetometer; ~ **à déviation** *m* PHYS RAYON deflection magnetometer; ~ **différentiel** *m* ELECTR differential magnetometer; ~ **à échantillon vibrant** *m* NUCLEAIRE vibrating sample magnetometer; ~ **de Hall** *m* PHYSIQUE Hall magnetometer; ~ **à induction** *m* PETR flux gate magnetometer (AmE), flux valve magnetometer (BrE); ~ **à noyau saturable** *m* ELECTROTEC flux gate magnetometer (AmE), flux valve magnetometer (BrE); ~ **à protons** *m* PETR proton resonance magnetometer

magnétométrie *f* PETROLE magnetometer survey, magnetometry

magnéton *m* PHYSIQUE magneton; ~ **de Bohr** *m* PHYS RAYON, PHYSIQUE Bohr magneton

magnétophone *m* ACOUSTIQUE tape recorder, ENREGISTR magnetic tape recorder, tape recorder, GEOPHYS magnetophone, tape recorder, TV audio tape machine; ~ **à bobines** *m* ENREGISTR reel-to-reel tape recorder; ~ **à cassette** *m* ENREGISTR cartridge tape recorder, cassette tape recorder; ~ **à cassette portatif** *m* ENREGISTR portable cassette recorder; ~ **à double piste** *m* ENREGISTR twin-track recorder; ~ **huit pistes** *m* ENREGISTR eight-track recorder; ~ **de lecture** *m* ENREGISTR play-only recorder; ~ **pleine piste** *m* ENREGISTR full track recorder; ~ **quatre pistes** *m* ENREGISTR four-track recorder; ~ **stéréo** *m* ENREGISTR stereo tape recorder

magnétoplasma *m* NUCLEAIRE magnetized plasma, magnetoplasma

magnétorésistance *f* PHYSIQUE magnetoresistance

magnétoscope *m* GEOPHYS, TELECOM magnetoscope, TV VTR, video recorder, videotape recorder; ~ **à balayage transversal** *m* TV transverse scanning recorder; ~ **à cassette** *m* TV videocassette recorder; ~ **à cassette asservi** *m* TV slave videocassette recorder; ~ **à défilement hélicoïdal** *m* TV helical-scan videotape recorder; ~ **enregistreur format un pouce C** *m* TV C-format videotape recorder; ~ **de lecture** *m* TV playback videotape recorder, videotape player; ~ **numérique** *m* TV DVTR, digital videotape recorder; ~ **à pistes transversales** *m* TV quadruplex videotape recorder; ~ **un pouce B** *m* TV *fabrication Bosch* B-format video recorder; ~ **de prise de vues image par image** *m* PRODUCTION time lapse videotape recorder; ~ **à quatre têtes** *m* TV quadruplex videotape recorder; ~ **stéréo à cassette** *m* TV stereo videocassette recorder

magnétoscopie *f* MECANIQUE magnetic particle examination

magnétosphère *f* ASTRONOMIE, ESPACE, GEOPHYS magnetosphere; ~ **externe** *f* GEOPHYS external magnetosphere; ~ **interne** *f* GEOPHYS internal magnetosphere

magnétostatique *adj* NUCLEAIRE, PHYSIQUE magnetostatic

magnétostriction *f* ELECTROTEC, PHYSIQUE magnetostriction; ~ **négative** *f* ELECTROTEC negative magnetostriction; ~ **positive** *f* ELECTROTEC positive magnetostriction

magnétron *m* CONS MECA magnetron, ELECTRON magnetron, traveling-wave magnetron (AmE), travelling-wave magnetron (BrE), PHYSIQUE magnetron; ~ **accordable** *m* ELECTRON tunable magnetron; ~ **à accord mécanique** *m* ELECTRON mechanically-tuned magnetron; ~ **à accord piézo-électrique** *m* ELECTROTEC piezoelectric-tuned magnetron; ~ **amplificateur** *m* ELECTRON magnetron amplifier; ~ **à anode en deux parties** *m* ELECTRON split anode magnetron; ~ **à anode à segments multiples** *m* ELECTRON multisegment magnetron; ~ **à cavités** *m* ELECTRON cavity magnetron, multicavity magnetron, PHYSIQUE cavity magnetron; ~ **à cavités alternées** *m* CONSTR rising sun magnetron; ~ **coaxial** *m* ELECTRON coaxial magnetron; ~ **en bande X** *m* ELECTRON X-band magnetrons; ~ **à fréquence fixe** *m* ELECTRON fixed frequency magnetron; ~ **à impulsion** *m* ELECTRON pulsed magnetron; ~ **industriel** *m* ELECTRON industrial magnetron; ~ **à ligne interdigitée** *m* ELECTRON interdigital magnetron; ~ **miniature** *m* ELECTRON miniature magnetron; ~ **non accordable** *m* ELECTRON fixed frequency magnetron; ~ **à ondes électroniques** *m* ELECTRON electron wave magnetron; ~ **à ondes millimétriques** *m* ELECTRON millimeter wave magnetron (AmE), millimetre wave magnetron (BrE); ~ **oscillateur** *m* ELECTRON magnetron oscillator

magnitude *f* ASTRONOMIE, PHYSIQUE magnitude; ~ **absolue** *f* ASTRONOMIE absolute magnitude; ~ **apparente** *f* ASTRONOMIE apparent magnitude; ~ **stellaire** *f* ASTRONOMIE magnitude class; ~ **visuelle** *f* ASTRONOMIE visual magnitude

magnon *m* PHYSIQUE magnon

maie *f* CERAM VER mixing box, mixing trough

maillage *m* OCEANO mesh size, TELECOM linking

maille *f* AGRO ALIM mesh, CHARBON mesh, sieve mesh, CONS MECA *câble-chaîne* link, DISTRI EAU, ELECTR *réseau*, ELECTROTEC, ESPACE *véhicules* mesh, NAUT link, OCEANO, PAPIER *toile de machine*, PHYSIQUE, PRODUCTION mesh, TEXTILE mesh, stitch; ~ **de contrôle** *f*

CHARBON control size; ~ **à étai** *f* CONSTR stud link; ~ **étançonnée** *f* CONSTR stud link; ~ **folle** *f* OCEANO flying mesh, flymesh; ~ **de libération** *f* CHARBON release mesh; ~ **optimale de libération** *f* CHARBON optimal crushing size, optimum grind; ~ **de partage** *f* CHARBON partition size; ~ **de prévision** *f* PRODUCTION forecast interval; ~ **de séparation** *f* GENIE CHIM separation size; ~ **de tamisage** *f* CHARBON screening mesh

maillé *adj* TELECOM linked together

maillechort *m* ELECTROTEC nickel silver

mailler *vt* OCEANO *filet de pêche* lace

maillet *m* CERAM VER swinging brick, CONSTR maul, MECANIQUE *outillage*, PRODUCTION mallet; ~ **de cuir** *m* CONS MECA hide-faced mallet; ~ **à déglanter** *m* CERAM VER knocker-off

mailloche *f* CERAM VER shaping block, CONSTR maul, PRODUCTION mallet

maillon *m* CONS MECA *chaîne, câble-chaîne* link, TELECOM link; ~ **d'attache** *m* CONS MECA clevis; ~ **de chaîne** *m* MECANIQUE link, VEHICULES *transmission de motocyclette* chain link; ~ **à crémaillère** *m* CONS MECA cranked link; ~ **de jonction** *m* CONS MECA clevis

maillure: ~ **encastrée** *f* CONS MECA inset joint; ~ **superposée** *f* CONS MECA scissor joint

main:[1] **à la** ~ *adv* PRODUCTION by hand, by hand power

main[2] *f* IMPRIM *papier* bulk, PAPIER quire; ~ **d'arrêt** *f* CONS MECA latch; ~ **de coulée** *f* CERAM VER guide; ~ **courante** *f* CONSTR hand railing, handrail, MECANIQUE handrail, MINES guide shoe, NAUT handrail, NUCLEAIRE hand railing, TRANSPORT handrail; ~ **courante de garde** *f* CONSTR guardrail; ~ **de guidage** *f* MINES guide shoe; ~ **de papier** *f* IMPRIM quire; ~ **du papier** *f* IMPRIM paper substance, PAPIER quire

main-d'oeuvre *f*; ~ *f* PRODUCTION manpower, manual labor (AmE), manual labour (BrE), workmanship

mains: ~ **libres** *adj* TELECOM hands-free

maintenabilité *f* ESPACE maintainability, MECANIQUE ease of maintenance, PRODUCTION, QUALITE maintainability

maintenage *m* CONSTR back stope, MINES overhand stope

maintenance *f* ESPACE, INFORMAT, MECANIQUE, ORDINAT, TV maintenance; ~ **corrective** *f* INFORMAT, ORDINAT remedial maintenance, TELECOM fault maintenance; ~ **imprévue** *f* QUALITE unplanned maintenance; ~ **locale** *f* TELECOM local maintenance; ~ **de matériel** *f* INFORMAT, ORDINAT hardware maintenance; ~ **périodique** *f* ORDINAT scheduled maintenance; ~ **préventive** *f* INFORMAT, ORDINAT, TELECOM preventive maintenance; ~ **programmée** *f* NUCLEAIRE scheduled maintenance, QUALITE planned maintenance; ~ **de secours** *f* ORDINAT emergency maintenance; ~ **systématique** *f* INFORMAT scheduled maintenance; ~ **d'urgence** *f* INFORMAT, ORDINAT emergency maintenance

maintenir[1] *vt* INFORMAT hold, MECANIQUE maintain, ORDINAT hold

maintenir:[2] ~ **les locaux dans des conditions aseptiques** *vi* SECURITE maintain aseptic area conditions; ~ **route et vitesse** *vi* NAUT maintain course and speed; ~ **la zone de travail en bon ordre** *vi* SECURITE keep the work area tidy

maintien *m* ELECTROTEC holding, PRODUCTION maintenance; ~ **en orbite** *m* ESPACE orbit support; ~ **en séquence** *m* TELECOM sequencing; ~ **de niveau** *m* NUCLEAIRE level holding; ~ **à poste** *m* ESPACE

véhicules, orbitographie station-keeping; ~ **de pression** *m* PETR pressure maintenance

maison: ~ **éclusière** *f* DISTRI EAU lock house; ~ **en pans de bois** *f* CONSTR frame house; ~ **sous la mer** *f* OCEANO undersea habitat

maître *m* INFORMAT, ORDINAT master; ~ **bau** *m* NAUT main beam, midship beam; ~ **de chantier** *m* CONSTR chief superintendent engineer; ~ **de conférence** *m* TELECOM conference call chairman, conference call chairperson; ~ **couloir** *m* MINES main chute; ~ **couple** *m* AERONAUT *structural* main shaft, NAUT midship frame, transverse section; ~ **drain** *m* CONSTR main drain; ~ **d'égal à égal** *m* PRODUCTION *automatisme industriel* peer-to-peer master; ~ **d'équipage** *m* NAUT boatswain; ~ **d'oeuvre** *m* CONSTR chief engineer, project manager; ~ **oscillateur** *m* ELECTRON, PHYSIQUE master oscillator; ~ **oscillateur thermostaté** *m* ELECTRON temperature-controlled crystal oscillator

maître-à-danser *m* CONS MECA in-and-out calipers (AmE), in-and-out callipers (BrE), inside-and-outside calipers (AmE), inside-and-outside callipers (BrE), outside-and-inside calipers (AmE), outside-and-inside callipers (BrE), CONSTR double calipers (AmE), double callipers (BrE)

maître-cylindre *m* AERONAUT master cylinder, AUTO master cylinder, VEHICULES *frein, embrayage* master cylinder; ~ **d'embrayage** *m* AUTO clutch master cylinder; ~ **de frein** *m* VEHICULES, AUTO brake master cylinder

maître-sondeur *m* PETROLE driller

maîtresse: ~ **partie** *f* NAUT midship section; ~ **pièce** *f* CONSTR *charpente* principal member; ~ **poutre** *f* CONSTR main beam, main girder

maîtresse-feuille *f* CONS MECA *ressort à lames superposées* top plate

maîtresse-lame *f* CONS MECA *ressort à lames superposées* top plate

maîtresse-tige *f* MINES *pompe de mine* spear rod

maîtrise: ~ **de crue** *f* HYDROLOGIE flood control; ~ **d'éruption** *f* PETROLE killing a well; ~ **des processus** *f* QUALITE process control; ~ **de la qualité** *f* COMMANDE, ESSAIS, IMPRIM, MECANIQUE, METROLOGIE, NUCLEAIRE, QUALITE QC, quality control; ~ **de la qualité en cours de fabrication** *f* QUALITE process quality control; ~ **statistique de la qualité** *f* COMMANDE, QUALITE statistical quality control; ~ **totale de la qualité** *f* QUALITE TQC, total quality control

maîtriser *vt* DISTRI EAU overpower

majolique *f* CERAM VER majolica

majuscule *f* IMPRIM capital letter, upper case

mal:[1] ~ **centré** *adj* CERAM VER siding; ~ **équerré** *adj* IMPRIM *papier, machine* out-of-square; ~ **rendu** *adj* (Fra) (*cf non moulé*) CERAM VER not blown up; ~ **trié** *adj* GEOLOGIE ill-sorted

mal:[2] ~ **des caissons** *m* PETROLE *sécurité du personnel* bends; ~ **de l'espace** *m* ESPACE space sickness; ~ **des rayons** *m* SECURITE radiation sickness

malachite *f* MINERAUX malachite

malacolite *f* MINERAUX malacolite

malacon *m* MINERAUX malacon, malakon, NUCLEAIRE malacon

maladie: ~ **de décompression** *f* NAUT caisson disease, OCEANO bends, caisson disease, decompression sickness; ~ **des plongeurs** *f* NAUT bends

malakon *m* MINERAUX malacon, malakon

malate *m* CHIMIE malate

malaxage *m* CONS MECA malaxage, CONSTR, PETROLE *des boues*, PRODUCTION mixing; **~ à tambour** *m* CONSTR drum mix

malaxation *f* PRODUCTION mixing

malaxer *vt* CONSTR *mortier* mix

malaxeur *m* CONS MECA malaxator, mixer, CONSTR mixer, PLAST CAOU *matériel pour caoutchouc* open mill; **~ d'argile** *m* CERAM VER clay kneader, clay mixer; **~ à dispersion** *m* GENIE CHIM dispersion kneader; **~ à glaise** *m* INST HYDR pug mill; **~ à mortier** *m* CONSTR mortar mixer

maldonite *f* MINERAUX maldonite

maléimide *m* CHIMIE maleimide

malfaçon *f* PRODUCTION bad work, bad workmanship

malique *adj* CHIMIE malic

mallardite *f* MINERAUX mallardite

malle *f* NAUT ferry, ferryboat

malléabilisation *f* MAT CHAUFF malleablizing

malléabilité *f* MATERIAUX, METALL malleability

malléable *adj* MECANIQUE malleable

malléine *f* CHIMIE morvin

malonamide *m* CHIMIE malonamide

malonate *m* CHIMIE malonate

malonique *adj* CHIMIE malonic

malonitrile *m* CHIMIE malonitrile

malt *m* AGRO ALIM, CHIMIE malt; **~ touraillé** *m* AGRO ALIM cured malt, kiln malt

maltase *f* AGRO ALIM, CHIMIE maltase

malter *vt* AGRO ALIM malt

malterie *f* AGRO ALIM malt house (AmE), maltings (BrE)

malthacite *f* MINERAUX malthacite

malthe *m* MINERAUX maltha

maltose *m* CHIMIE maltose

mamelon *m* CONS MECA, CONSTR nipple

mamelonné *adj* GEOLOGIE mammillated

management: **~ de la qualité** *m* QUALITE QM quality management; **~ total de la qualité** *m* QUALITE TQM, total quality management

manche[1] *m* CONS MECA shaft, CONSTR *pelle* D-handle, MECANIQUE *outils* handle, PRODUCTION helve, helver, *d'un outil* handle, *pioche* hilt; **~ d'accouplement** *m* CONS MECA coupling sleeve; **~ à balai** *m* AERONAUT control column, control stick, CINEMAT, ESPACE *véhicules*, INFORMAT, ORDINAT joystick; **~ à béquille** *m* PRODUCTION crutch handle; **~ de commande de pas** *m* AERONAUT cyclic pitch control stick, cyclic pitch stick, cyclic stick; **~ cyclique** *m* AERONAUT cyclic pitch stick, cyclic stick; **~ de manoeuvre** *m* MINES brace head, brace key, rod-turning tool, tiller; **~ à oeil** *m* CONSTR *pelle* D-handle, eyehandle; **~ de pas général** *f* AERONAUT *hélicoptère* collective pitch lever; **~ de pic** *m* PRODUCTION pick handle; **~ pour tête panoramique** *m* CINEMAT pan handle; **~ treuilliste** *m* AERONAUT hoist lever

manche[2] *f* CHARBON filter bag, PRODUCTION hose; **~ à air** *f* AERONAUT wind cone, wind sock, CONS MECA air duct, air scoop, NAUT *accastillage de pont* ventilator; **~ en toile à voile** *f* MINES canvas filter; **~ d'évacuation** *f* AERONAUT, ESPACE escape chute; **~ d'évacuation sur toboggan** *f* AERONAUT escape chute; **~ à gonfler** *f* POLLU MER inflation cuff; **~ à vent** *f* AERONAUT wind cone, wind sock, NAUT wind sail

manches: **~ de sécurité** *m pl* SECURITE *ciseaux, burin* safety handles

manchette: **~ de raccordement** *f* PETR spool piece; **~ de traversée** *f* NUCLEAIRE penetration sleeve

manchon *m* CERAM VER sleeve, CHARBON skin, CONS MECA bushing, bush, coupling, coupling box, muff, sleeve, socket, EMBALLAGE, IMPRIM *flexographie* sleeve, MECANIQUE ferrule, sheath, sleeve, PETR collar; **~ abrasif cylindrique** *m* CONS MECA cylindrical abrasive sheet; **~ abrasif tronconique** *m* CONS MECA truncated cone-abrasive sheet; **~ d'accouplement** *m* CONS MECA coupling box, coupling sleeve; **~ d'accouplement d'arbres** *m* CONS MECA shaft coupling; **~ d'accouplement élastique** *m* CONS MECA compensating coupling, flexible coupling; **~ d'assemblage** *m* CONS MECA coupling box; **~ d'assemblage d'arbres** *m* CONS MECA shaft coupling; **~ Auer** *m* THERMODYN gas mantle; **~ avec boulons à têtes noyées** *m* CONS MECA shrouded coupling; **~ à boulons noyés** *m* CONS MECA shrouded coupling; **~ de câble** *m* ELECTR *raccordement* cable box; **~ de centrage** *m* CONS MECA cathead; **~ chargeur** *m* PHOTO changing bag; **~ de couplage** *m* CONS MECA coupling box; **~ cylindrique** *m* CONS MECA muff coupling; **~ cylindrique avec boulons à têtes noyées** *m* CONS MECA shrouding muff coupling; **~ de dilatation** *m* INST HYDR expansion coupling; **~ d'écubier** *m* NAUT hawse pipe; **~ élastique** *m* CONS MECA compensating coupling, flexible coupling; **~ d'emballage** *m* IMPRIM wraparound; **~ d'embrayage** *m* CONS MECA clutch; **~ d'embrayage à dents** *m* CONS MECA claw clutch; **~ fileté** *m* CONS MECA screw ferrule, sleeve nut, PAPIER nipple; **~ fou** *m* CONS MECA loose sleeve; **~ à frettes** *m* CONS MECA collared coupling; **~ à friction** *m* CONS MECA friction coupling; **~ incombustible** *m* AERONAUT heat shield; **~ isolant** *m* ELECTROTEC insulating joint, insulating sleeve; **~ noir** *m* CINEMAT changing bag; **~ de pale** *m* AERONAUT blade sleeve; **~ à plateaux** *m* CONS MECA faceplate coupling, flange coupling, plate coupling; **~ à plateaux à boulons noyés** *m* CONS MECA pulley coupling, recessed flange coupling, shrouded flange coupling; **~ de pliage** *m* MILITAIRE *sur un parachute* sleeve; **~ pour bouteille** *m* EMBALLAGE bottle sleeve; **~ pour expédition postale** *m* EMBALLAGE mailing sleeve; **~ pour foret** *m* CONS MECA drill socket; **~ pour tuyau** *m* CONSTR pipe connection, pipe coupling; **~ pour tuyau d'incendie** *m* SECURITE fire hose coupling; **~ de presse humide** *m* PAPIER couch roll jacket; **~ de protection** *m* CONS MECA protection sleeve; **~ de raccordement** *m* CONS MECA coupling sleeve; **~ de refroidissement** *m* PRODUCTION cooler, jumbo; **~ de réglage** *m* AUTO adjusting sleeve; **~ repère** *m* CONS MECA identification sleeve; **~ rétractable** *m* PAPIER shrink sleeve; **~ de sécurité** *m* PRODUCTION guard ring; **~ taraudé** *m* CONS MECA screw ferrule, sleeve nut; **~ à toc** *m* CONS MECA pin coupling; **~ à vis** *m* CONS MECA screw box, screw coupling

manchon-bride *m* PRODUCTION wire-rope clamp

manchonnage *m* CONS MECA coupling box, *deux arbres* coupling

mandarine *f* CINEMAT redhead

mandataire *f* BREVETS representative

mandélique *adj* CHIMIE *acide* mandelic

mandrin *m* CERAM VER mandrel, mandril, plug, CONS MECA arbor, drift, drift pin, driver, mandrel, mandril, spindle, *tour* chuck, ELECTROTEC former, EMBALLAGE center (AmE), centre (BrE), PAPIER core, PLAST CAOU *boudineuse* mandrel, mandril; **~ à arrondir les tubes de chaudières** *m* CONSTR boiler tube expander; **~ de bobine** *m* IMPRIM reelcore; **~ de bobine mère** *m* PAPIER reel spool; **~ carré** *m* CONS MECA square drift, square driftpin; ~ **à combinaisons** *m* CONS MECA combination chuck; ~ **conformateur de tubes de chaudière** *m* INST HYDR boiler pipe shaping mandrel; ~ **de coulée** *m* PRODUCTION gate pin, gate stick, runner stick, runner pin; ~ **à coussinets** *m* PRODUCTION die chuck; ~ **électromagnétique** *m* CONS MECA electromagnetic chuck; ~ **d'étirage de tubes** *m* CONS MECA tube-drawing mandrel; ~ **d'évent** *m* PRODUCTION riser pin, riser stick; ~ **excentrique** *m* CONS MECA eccentric chuck; ~ **extensible** *m* CONS MECA expanding mandrel; ~ **à gobelet** *m* CONS MECA cup chuck; ~ **lisse** *m* CONS MECA smooth drift; ~ **à mors** *m* CONS MECA jaw chuck; ~ **à mors étagés** *m* CONS MECA *tour* bell chuck; ~ **oscillant** *m* CONS MECA floating tool holder; ~ **de perceuse** *m* CONS MECA bit holder; ~ **à pince pour la prise de barres** *m* CONS MECA bar chuck; ~ **pneumatique** *m* CONS MECA air chuck, air-operated chuck, IMPRIM *mécanique* air chuck; ~ **porte-foret** *m* CONS MECA drill chuck; ~ **porte-fraise** *m* CONS MECA milling cutting arbor, milling machine arbor, PRODUCTION milling machine cutter arbor; ~ **porte-mèche** *m* CONS MECA drill chuck; ~ **porte-outil** *m* CONS MECA cutter mandrel, cutter spindle; ~ **porte-taraud** *m* CONS MECA tapping chuck; ~ **pour rainures** *m* PRODUCTION groove drift; ~ **principal** *m* CONS MECA live spindle; ~ **à quatre vis** *m* CONS MECA four-screw bell chuck; ~ **à queue-de-cochon** *m* CONS MECA screw chuck; ~ **de serrage** *m* MECANIQUE *outillage* chuck; ~ **à serrage concentrique** *m* CONS MECA self-centering chuck (AmE), self-centring chuck (BrE); ~ **de serrage élastique** *m* CONS MECA draw-in spring chuck; ~ **à serrage mécanique pour tour** *m* CONS MECA power-operated lathe chuck; ~ **à serrage rapide** *m* CONS MECA quick action chuck; ~ **à spirale** *m* CONS MECA scroll chuck; ~ **taillé** *m* CONS MECA cutting drift, cutting driftpin; ~ **à toc** *m* CONS MECA catch plate, dog chuck, driver chuck, driver plate, point chuck, take-about chuck; ~ **de tour** *m* MECANIQUE lathe chuck; ~ **tournant dans des coussinets** *m* CONS MECA mandrel running in bearings, mandril running in bearings; ~ **à trois mâchoires** *m* CONS MECA three-jaw chuck; ~ **à trcis pointes** *m* CONS MECA fork chuck, prong chuck, spur chuck, three-pronged chuck; ~ **à tulipe** *m* CONS MECA fork chuck, prong chuck, three-pronged chuck; ~ **type rentrant** *m* CONS MECA draw-in chuck; ~ **type sans retrait** *m* CONS MECA dead-length-type chuck; ~ **à vis** *m* CONS MECA shell chuck

mandrinage *m* CONS MECA drifting, MECANIQUE *outillage* chucking

mandriner *vt* CONS MECA *pièce* chuck

maneton *m* AUTO crankpin, CONS MECA *manivelle à main* handle, MECANIQUE, VEHICULES *moteur* crankpin; ~ **de manivelle** *m* CONS MECA crankpin

manette *f* CONS MECA handle, ELECTROTEC lever, ESPACE *véhicules*, MECANIQUE handle, PHYSIQUE lever, VEHICULES handle, lever; ~ **de commande** *f* TV control arm; ~ **de commande d'éclairage** *f* CINEMAT dimmer quadrant; ~ **de gaz** *f* AERONAUT throttle, ESPACE *véhicules* throttle control; ~ **de guidage** *f* TV control arm; ~ **de jeux** *f* INFORMAT joystick; ~ **de mise en marche** *f* CONS MECA starting handle, starting lever; ~ **tous azimuts** *f* CINEMAT joystick

manganate *m* CHIMIE manganate

manganèse *m (Mn)* CHIMIE manganese *(Mn)*

manganésifère *adj* GEOLOGIE manganiferous

manganeux *adj* CHIMIE manganous

manganique *adj* CHIMIE manganic

manganite *f* CHIMIE manganite, MINERAUX gray manganese ore (AmE), grey manganese ore (BrE), manganite

manganocalcite *f* MINERAUX manganocalcite

maniabilité *f* AERONAUT controllability, CONS MECA maneuverability (AmE), manoeuvrability (BrE), CONSTR workability, TRANSPORT maneuverability (AmE), manoeuvrability (BrE)

maniable *adj* CONSTR workable

maniement *m* ESPACE *véhicules*, PRODUCTION handling

manier *vt* MECANIQUE handle, PRODUCTION handle, *outil* handle

manière: ~ **d'exécuter l'invention** *f* BREVETS way of carrying out the invention

manifeste: ~ **de cargaison** *m* NAUT cargo manifest; ~ **de marchandises** *m* AERONAUT cargo manifest

manille *f* IMPRIM *impression* backing sheet, MECANIQUE *matériel de levage*, NAUT, POLLU MER shackle; ~ **d'assemblage** *f* CONS MECA clevis, connecting link; ~ **d'attelage** *f* CONS MECA attachment link, coupling link; ~ **droite** *f* NAUT D-shackle; ~ **forgée** *f* CONS MECA *levage* forged shackle; ~ **mobile** *f* CH DE FER *véhicules* removable coupling link; ~ **rapide** *f* NAUT snap shackle; ~ **de tendeur** *f* CH DE FER *véhicules* D-link

maniller *vt* NAUT shackle

manipulation *f* PRODUCTION handling, manipulating, manipulation, SECURITE, TEXTILE handling; ~ **corrélative par déplacement de phase** *f* TELECOM correlative phase shift keying; ~ **par commande à distance** *f* SECURITE remote handling device; ~ **par déplacement de fréquence** *f* TELECOM frequency shift keying; ~ **par déplacement de fréquence rapide** *f* TELECOM fast frequency-shift keying; ~ **par déplacement minimal** *f* TELECOM MSK, minimum-shift keying; ~ **par déplacement de phase à bande étroite** *f* TELECOM NBPSK, narrow band phase shift keying

manipuler *vt* MECANIQUE, PRODUCTION, TEXTILE handle

manique *f* CERAM VER hook

manivelle *f* CH DE FER *véhicules* crank handle, CONS MECA handle, *essieu d'une locomotive* crank, CONSTR winch, MECANIQUE crank, MINES brace head, brace key, rod-turning tool, tiller, POLLU MER winch, VEHICULES *moteur* crank; ~ **à contrepoids** *f* CONS MECA balance crank; ~ **de démarreur** *f* VEHICULES *moteur* starting crank; ~ **double** *f* CONS MECA duplex crank; ~ **en plusieurs pièces** *f* CONS MECA built-up crank; ~ **en porte-à-faux** *f* CONS MECA overhanging crank; ~ **d'équilibrage** *f* CONS MECA balance crank; ~ **d'essieu** *f* CONS MECA axle crank; ~ **de frein à vis** *f* CH DE FER *véhicules* brake screw handle, CONS MECA brake crank; ~ **lève-glace** *f* AUTO window winder; ~ **de machine** *f* CONS MECA engine crank; ~ **à plateau** *f* CONS MECA wheel crank, PRODUCTION disc crank (BrE), disk crank (AmE); ~ **de rebobinage** *f* CINEMAT backwind handle; ~ **de réembobinage** *f* PHOTO film rewind handle, rewind handle; ~ **triple** *f* CONS MECA three-throw crank; ~ **un-tour-une-image** *f* CINEMAT single picture crank

manivelle-glisseur *f* CONS MECA slider crank

manne: ~ **à charbon** *m* CHARBON coal basket

mannide *m* CHIMIE mannide

mannitane *m* CHIMIE mannitan

mannite *f* CHIMIE mannite

mannitol *m* CHIMIE mannitol

mannonique *adj* CHIMIE *acide* mannonic

mannose *m* CHIMIE mannose

manocontact *m* AERONAUT oil pressure switch, ELEC-TROTEC pressure switch

manodétendeur *m* INST HYDR pressure-reducing valve; **~ pour gaz** *m* EQUIP LAB *régulateur* reducing valve

manoeuvrabilité *f* AERONAUT maneuverability (AmE), manoeuvrability (BrE), *aéronefs* controllability, NAUT, NUCLEAIRE *de la puissance* maneuverability (AmE), manoeuvrability (BrE)

manoeuvrable *adj* NAUT maneuverable (AmE), manoeuvrable (BrE)

manoeuvre *f* CH DE FER shunting, *véhicules* switching, CONS MECA handling, maneuver (AmE), manoeuvre (BrE), operation, NAUT maneuver (AmE), manoeuvre (BrE), ship handling, PETROLE round trip, trip, PRODUCTION manipulating, manipulation, TRANSPORT shunting; **~ d'abordage** *f* NAUT docking maneuver (AmE), docking manoeuvre (BrE); **~ d'apogée** *f* ESPACE *orbitographie* apogee maneuver (AmE), apogee manoeuvre (BrE); **~ de correction** *f* ESPACE *orbitographie* correction maneuver (AmE), correction manoeuvre (BrE); **~ du curseur** *f* PRODUCTION cursor hit; **~ à distance** *f* COMMANDE remote actuation; **~ d'entrecroisement** *f* TRANSPORT weaving maneuver (AmE), weaving manoeuvre (BrE); **~ en vol** *f* AERONAUT flight maneuver (AmE), flight manoeuvre (BrE); **~ au lancer** *f* CH DE FER *véhicules* fly shunting; **~ par gravité** *f* CH DE FER *véhicules* hump shunting; **~ de rebroussement** *f* CH DE FER *véhicules* backing movement; **~ de refoulement** *f* CH DE FER *véhicules* backing movement; **~ de séparation** *f* ESPACE *véhicules* separation maneuver (AmE), separation manoeuvre (BrE); **~ au sol** *f* AERONAUT ground operation; **~ de vol** *f* AERONAUT flight maneuver (AmE), flight manoeuvre (BrE)

manoeuvrer *vt* CH DE FER shunt, NAUT maneuver (AmE), manoeuvre (BrE), *voiles, navire* handle, *voilier* sail, PRODUCTION operate

manoeuvres: ~ courantes *f pl* NAUT running rigging, standing rigging; **~ des embarcations** *f pl* NAUT boat drill

manomètre *m* AGRO ALIM vacuum gage (AmE), vacuum gauge (BrE), CH DE FER, CHARBON, COMMANDE, CONS MECA, CONSTR pressure gage (AmE), pressure gauge (BrE), EQUIP LAB manometer, pressure gage (AmE), pressure gauge (BrE), INST HYDR pressure gage (AmE), pressure gauge (BrE), *de machine à vapeur* indicator, PAPIER, PETROLE, PHYSIQUE manometer, pressure gage (AmE), pressure gauge (BrE), PRODUCTION *système hydraulique*, REFRIG pressure gage (AmE), pressure gauge (BrE); **~ à air** *m* CONS MECA, METROLOGIE air gage (AmE), air gauge (BrE), PETROLE air pressure gage (AmE), air pressure gauge (BrE); **~ d'aspiration** *m* REFRIG suction gage (AmE), suction gauge (BrE); **~ de Bourdon** *m* PHYSIQUE Bourdon gage (AmE), Bourdon gauge (BrE); **~ à chambre d'ionisation** *m* REFRIG ionization vacuum gage (AmE), ionization vacuum gauge (BrE); **~ différentiel** *m* MECANIQUE differential pressure gage (AmE), differential pressure gauge (BrE); **~ double de pression kérosène** *m* AERONAUT dual fuel pressure gage (AmE), dual fuel pressure gauge (BrE); **~ à huile** *m* AUTO, VEHICULES *lubrification* oil pressure gage (AmE), oil pressure gauge (BrE); **~ à ionisation Bayard-Alpert** *m* NUCLEAIRE Bayard-Alpert ionization gage (AmE), Bayard-Alpert ionization gauge (BrE);

~ métallique indicateur *m* CONS MECA dial-type metallic pressure gage (AmE), dial-type metallic pressure gauge (BrE); **~ de monteur** *m* REFRIG service gage (AmE), service gauge (BrE); **~ à piston** *m* PHYSIQUE dead-weight pressure gage (AmE), dead-weight pressure gauge (BrE); **~ de pression différentielle de cabine** *m* AERONAUT cabin differential pressure gage (AmE), cabin differential pressure gauge (BrE); **~ de pression de vapeur** *m* INST HYDR steam gage (AmE), steam gauge (BrE); **~ de refoulement** *m* REFRIG high-pressure gage (AmE), high-pressure gauge (BrE); **~ à ressort** *m* PHYSIQUE spring manometer; **~ thermique** *m* REFRIG thermal conductivity vacuum gage (AmE), thermal conductivity vacuum gauge (BrE); **~ à vapeur** *m* COMMANDE steam pressure gage (AmE), steam pressure gauge (BrE), PHYSIQUE steam gage (AmE), steam gauge (BrE); **~ à vide** *m* CONS MECA, PRODUCTION vacuum gage (AmE), vacuum gauge (BrE)

manovacuomètre *m* REFRIG compound gage (AmE), compound gauge (BrE)

manquant:[1] ~ de contraste *adj* CINEMAT flat

manquant[2] *m* PRODUCTION out-of-stock situation, runout, stock-out

manque *m* IMPRIM starvation; **~ de carburant** *m* THERMODYN lack of fuel; **~ de définition** *m* CINEMAT poor resolution; **~ d'impression** *m* ACOUSTIQUE unfill; **~ de netteté** *m* IMPRIM *impression* fog; **~ de pénétration** *m* NUCLEAIRE incomplete roof penetration; **~ de phase** *m* TV phase failure; **~ de signal** *m* TV drop-out

manquer *vi* PRODUCTION fail

manteau *m* GEOLOGIE mantel, GEOPHYS mantle; **~ terrestre** *m* GEOPHYS mantle

mantisse *f* INFORMAT fixed point part, mantissa, MATH, ORDINAT mantissa

manuel[1] *adj* MECANIQUE manual

manuel[2] *m* CONS MECA handbook, PRODUCTION handbook, manual; **~ d'autoformation** *m* PRODUCTION self-teach manual; **~ d'entretien** *m* AERONAUT, PRODUCTION maintenance manual; **~ de l'équipage** *m* AERONAUT crew operating manual; **~ des études** *m* CONS MECA engineering standards; **~ d'exploitation** *m* AERONAUT operations manual; **~ d'instructions** *m* CONS MECA instruction book, operating instructions, operating manual, PRODUCTION instruction book, instruction manual; **~ de qualité** *m* ESPACE, QUALITE quality manual; **~ de l'utilisateur** *m* INFORMAT, ORDINAT user manual, TELECOM user guide; **~ de vol** *m* AERONAUT flight manual

manuelle *f* NUCLEAIRE manual handling

manuellement *adv* PRODUCTION by hand, by hand power

manufacturé *adj* MATERIAUX manufactured, mfd

manuscrit *m* IMPRIM copy, manuscript, matter

manutention *f* CONS MECA handling, EMBALLAGE work handling, *consigné* handling, *marchandises* handling, PAPIER, PRODUCTION, SECURITE *matières dangereuses* handling; **~ de la cargaison** *f* NAUT cargo handling; **~ du fret** *f* AERONAUT cargo handling; **~ horizontale** *f* TRANSPORT ro-ro system, roll-on/roll-off system, truck-to-truck handling; **~ manuelle** *f* NUCLEAIRE manual handling; **~ de matériaux** *f* NUCLEAIRE materials handling; **~ portuaire** *f* PRODUCTION dock work; **~ verticale** *f* TRANSPORT lift on-off system

manutentionner *vt* PRODUCTION handle

MAQ *abrév (modulation d'amplitude en quadrature)*

ELECTRON, INFORMAT, ORDINAT, TELECOM QAM *(quadrature amplitude modulation)*

maque *f* PRODUCTION crocodile squeezer

maquette *f* CINEMAT miniature, ESPACE *essais* mock-up, model, IMPRIM design, layout, *livre* mock-up, *préparation* mechanicals, MECANIQUE experimental model, NAUT mock-up, model, scale model, ORDINAT breadboard, PRODUCTION mock-up; **~ d'agencement** *f* ESPACE *essais* soft mock-up; **~ du client** *f* CONS MECA customer's model; **~ de composition des annonces** *f* IMPRIM advertisement layout; **~ à l'échelle** *f* CINEMAT scale model; **~ d'entraînement au sol** *f* AERONAUT link trainer; **~ en volume** *f* IMPRIM *livre* dummy; **~ fixe sur instruments** *f* AERONAUT miniature aircraft index; **~ de premier plan** *f* CINEMAT foreground miniature; **~ de structure** *f* ESPACE *essais* structural model; **~ thermique** *f* ESPACE *essais* thermal model

MAR *abrév (message de refus de modification d'appel)* TELECOM CMRJ *(call modification reject message)*

marais *m* DISTRI EAU marsh, swamp; **~ maritime** *m* OCEANO saltern, sea marsh; **~ salant** *m* AGRO ALIM saltern, DISTRI EAU salt swamp, OCEANO salt marsh

marbrage *m* CERAM VER marvering

marbre *m* CERAM VER marver mark, marver, CONS MECA plane, surface plate, GEOLOGIE marble, IMPRIM bed, slab, type plate, MECANIQUE *outillage* surface plate, PRODUCTION engineer's surface plate; **~ d'ajusteur** *m* CONS MECA plane, surface plate, PRODUCTION engineer's surface plate; **~ de contrôle** *m* METROLOGIE surface plate; **~ de contrôle en granite** *m* CONS MECA granite surface plate; **~ à dresser** *m* CONS MECA plane, surface plate, PRODUCTION engineer's surface plate; **~ d'imposition** *m* IMPRIM imposing table; **~ phylliteux** *m* GEOLOGIE phyllitic marble

marbré *adj* IMPRIM *impression* mottled

marbrière *f* MINES marble quarry

marcassite *f* MINERAUX marcasite, spear pyrites

marchage *m* CERAM VER tramping

marchandises *f pl* EMBALLAGE goods; **~ dangereuses** *f pl* AERONAUT, EMBALLAGE dangerous goods; **~ de détail** *f pl* CH DE FER less-than-carload freight (AmE), part-load traffic (BrE), TRANSPORT part-load freight (AmE), part-load goods (BrE); **~ empaquetées** *f pl* EMBALLAGE parcelled goods; **~ en vrac** *f pl* EMBALLAGE bulk goods; **~ de groupage** *f pl* TRANSPORT package freight, part loads; **~ non unitisées** *f pl* TRANSPORT break bulk; **~ à la réception** *f pl* PRODUCTION goods inward; **~ rejetées** *f pl* PRODUCTION rejects; **~ sous douane** *f pl* PETROLE *commerce* bonded goods

marchant: ~ au moteur *adj* PRODUCTION engine-driven

marche:[1] **en ~** *adj* CONS MECA operating, ELECTROTEC on CONS MECA on

marche[2] *f* CONS MECA movement, running, run, working, *vis d'Archimède* flange, CONSTR step, *escalier* stair, staircase, stairs, stairway, *échelle* step, CRISTALL, METALL step, PAPIER *machine* running, PHYSIQUE *expérience* course, PRODUCTION working, TEXTILE *machine* running; **~ altimétrique** *f* AERONAUT fixed error on radio altimeter; **~ arrière** *f* CH DE FER *véhicules* reversing, CINEMAT back run, reverse, reverse action, CONS MECA back gear, back speed, MECANIQUE *véhicules* reverse, TV back run, reverse action, reverse motion, VEHICULES reverse; **~ asynchrone** *f* ELECTR *moteur* asynchronous running; **~ automatique** *f* CONSTR automatic operation; **~ balançante** *f* CONSTR balance step, dancing step; **~ balancée**

f CONSTR balance step, dancing step; **~ à blanc** *f* CONS MECA running light, running on no load; **~ carrée** *f* CONSTR flier, flyer; **~ du chronomètre** *f* NAUT chronometer rate; **~ cintrée** *f* CONSTR curved step; **~ continue** *f* CINEMAT continuous run, ELECTR *matériel* constant duty; **~ courbe** *f* CONSTR curved step; **~ de croissance** *f* METALL growth step; **~ dansante** *f* CONSTR winder; **~ dans l'espace** *f* ESPACE spacewalk; **~ droite** *f* CONSTR flier, flyer; **~ en charge** *f* CONS MECA running under load; **~ en continu** *f* CINEMAT auto-reverse; **~ en pousse** *f* CH DE FER pusher operation (AmE), banking (BrE); **~ en régime humide** *f* REFRIG wet compression; **~ en régime de surchauffe** *f* REFRIG dry compression; **~ en surcharge** *f* CONS MECA running an overload, PRODUCTION overload running; **~ d'essai** *f* CONS MECA test run, NUCLEAIRE precommissioning checks, proving run, trial run; **~ gironnée** *f* CONSTR winder; **~ image par image** *f* CINEMAT stop motion; **~ des opérations** *f* CONS MECA procedure; **~ optique** *f* PHYSIQUE optical path; **~ palière** *f* CONSTR landing step; **~ par à-coups** *f* PRODUCTION inching; **~ par à-coups et freinage par contre-courant** *f* PRODUCTION *automatisme industriel* inching and plugging service; **~ par engrenages** *f* CONS MECA gear drive; **~ au ralenti** *f* VEHICULES *moteur* idling; **~ rapide** *f* CONS MECA high-speed; **~ rayonnante** *f* CONSTR winder; **~ rétrograde** *f* CONS MECA backward motion, backward movement; **~ séculaire** *f* GEOPHYS secular change; **~ silencieuse** *f* AUTO noiseless running, CONS MECA quiet running; **~ à suivre** *f* CONS MECA, PRODUCTION procedure; **~ de tension** *f* PHYSIQUE voltage step; **~ tournante** *f* CONSTR winder; **~ à vide** *f* AERONAUT no-load operation, CONS MECA running light, running on no load, ELECTR *moteur* idling; **~ à la volée** *f* CONS MECA belt drive

marche/arrêt *f* CINEMAT, CONS MECH on/off

marche-palier *f* CONSTR landing step

marchepied *m* CH DE FER *véhicules* step, CONSTR stepladder, steps

marcher *vi* CONS MECA run; **~ à blanc** *vi* CONS MECA run light, run on no load; **~ en charge** *vi* CONS MECA run under load; **~ en surcharge** *vi* CONS MECA run on overload; **~ au ralenti** *vi* VEHICULES *moteur* idle; **~ à vide** *vi* CONS MECA run light, run on no load

mare *f* ASTRONOMIE mare

marécage *m* DISTRI EAU marsh, HYDROLOGIE intake

marécageux *adj* CHARBON boggy, HYDROLOGIE marshy

maréchal *m* CONSTR smith

maréchalerie *f* CONSTR smithy

maréchal-ferrant *m* CONS MECA blacksmith, CONSTR smith

marée *f* EN RENOUV, NAUT, OCEANO tide; **~ astronomique** *f* OCEANO astronomical tide; **~ atmosphérique** *f* GEOPHYS atmospheric tide; **~ atmosphérique solaire** *f* GEOPHYS solar tide; **~ basse** *f* EN RENOUV low tide, HYDROLOGIE, NAUT low tide, low water; **~ descendante** *f* EN RENOUV ebb current, ebb tide, falling tide, HYDROLOGIE ebb tide, NAUT ebb tide, falling tide, OCEANO ebb tide, falling tide; **~ diurne** *f* NAUT diurnal tide, single day tide, OCEANO diurnal tide; **~ dynamique** *f* OCEANO dynamic tide; **~ d'équilibre** *f* EN RENOUV equilibrium tide; **~ d'équinoxe** *f* EN RENOUV, NAUT equinoctial tide; **~ haute** *f* EN RENOUV high tide, HYDROLOGIE high tide, high water, NAUT high tide; **~ de jusant** *f* NAUT ebb tide; **~ météorologique** *f* OCEANO meteorological tide; **~ mixte** *f* OCEANO mixed tide; **~**

montante *f* EN RENOUV flowing tide, rising tide, HYDROLOGIE flood tide, NAUT flood tide, rising tide, OCEANO flood tide; **~ de morte-eau** *f* EN RENOUV, HYDROLOGIE, OCEANO neap tide; **~ noire** *f* POLLU MER black tide, POLLUTION black tide, oil slick; **~ de quadrature** *f* HYDROLOGIE neap tide; **~ rouge** *f* OCEANO red tide; **~ semi-diurne** *f* NAUT, OCEANO semidiurnal tide; **~ statique** *f* OCEANO equilibrium tide; **~ de tempête** *f* OCEANO storm surge, storm tide; **~ terrestre** *f* OCEANO earth tide, terrestrial tide; **~ de vive eau** *f* EN RENOUV, HYDROLOGIE spring tide

marégramme *m* EN RENOUV marigram, GEOPHYS tide record

marégraphe *m* GEOPHYS recording tide gage (AmE), recording tide gauge (BrE), tide gage (AmE), tide gauge (BrE), tide pole, OCEANO marigraph, tide gage (AmE), tide gauge (BrE), tide recorder

marémètre *m* GEOPHYS tide gage (AmE), tide gauge (BrE), recording tide gage (AmE), recording tide gauge (BrE), tide pole, OCEANO tide recorder

maréomètre *m* EN RENOUV, GEOPHYS, OCEANO tide gage (AmE), tide gauge (BrE), recording tide gage (AmE), recording tide gauge (BrE)

mareyage *m* NAUT, OCEANO fish trade, fresh fish trade

margarate *m* CHIMIE margarate

margarine *f* CHIMIE margarine

margarique *adj* CHIMIE *acide* margaric

margarite *f* MINERAUX margarite

margarodite *f* MINERAUX margarodite

marge *f* BREVETS, GEOLOGIE, HYDROLOGIE, IMPRIM, INFORMAT, ORDINAT margin **~ active** *f* GEOLOGIE constructive plate margin, convergent margin, *bordure continentale ou arc insulaire* active margin; **~ brute** *f* PRODUCTION gross margin; **~ centrale** *f* IMPRIM back edge margin; **~ continentale** *f* GEOPHYS continental shelf, OCEANO continental margin; **~ de droite** *f* IMPRIM right margin; **~ extérieure** *f* IMPRIM fore edge; **~ de gauche** *f* IMPRIM left margin; **~ longitudinale en rotative** *f* IMPRIM gutter; **~ passive** *f* GEOLOGIE conservative plate-margin; **~ de petit fond** *f* IMPRIM inner margin; **~ de phase** *f* ELECTRON phase margin; **~ d'une plaque** *f* GEOLOGIE plate margin; **~ de plaque en subduction** *f* GEOLOGIE destructive plate-margin; **~ plaque lithosphérique en accrétion** *f* GEOLOGIE constructive plate margin; **~ de prise** *f* IMPRIM grasping margin; **~ de sécurité** *f* PRODUCTION protection time, SECURITE safety margin; **~ de tête** *f* IMPRIM head margin; **~ totale** *f* PRODUCTION total float; **~ transversale en feuilles** *f* IMPRIM gutter

marges: ~ applicables à une liaison *f pl* TELECOM link margins

margeur *m* IMPRIM feed table, feedboard, feeder, PHOTO masking frame; **~ d'agrandisseur** *m* PHOTO baseboard; **~ à feuilles** *m* IMPRIM sheet feeder

marguerite *f* IMPRIM, INFORMAT daisywheel, ORDINAT daisywheel, print wheel

marialite *f* MINERAUX marialite

mariculture *f* OCEANO marine aquaculture, marine fish farming

marin[1] *adj* GEOLOGIE marine, NAUT marine, nautical, PETROLE offshore

marin[2] *adv* PETROLE offshore

marina *m* NAUT marina

marinade *f* OCEANO marinade, souse

marinage *m* CONSTR removal

marine *f* NAUT navy, OCEANO seascape; **~ de guerre** *f*
NAUT national navy, naval forces, navy; **~ marchande** *f* NAUT mercantile marine, merchant marine, merchant navy; **~ militaire** *f* NAUT navy; **~ nationale** *f* NAUT national navy

marinier *m* NAUT waterman; **~ de chaland** *m* NAUT, TRANSPORT bargee (BrE), bargeman (AmE)

marin-paysan *m* OCEANO coastal fisherman-farmer

maritime *adj* NAUT marine, maritime, *commerce* seaborne

marmite *f* CHIMIE kettle, HYDROLOGIE pothole; **~ torrentielle** *f* HYDROLOGIE pothole

marmolite *f* MINERAUX marmolite

marnage *m* EN RENOUV, GEOPHYS, HYDROLOGIE tidal range, NAUT tidal range, *marée* range; **~ moyen** *m* EN RENOUV mean tidal range

marne *f* DISTRI EAU marl; **~ argileuse** *f* DISTRI EAU clay marl; **~ calcaire** *f* GEOLOGIE chalk marl; **~ à ciment** *f* CONSTR cement marl; **~ à rognons** *f* GEOLOGIE nodular marl; **~ à silex** *f* GEOLOGIE cherty marl

marneux *adj* GEOLOGIE marlaceous, marly

maroquin *m* NAUT jumper stay

marquage *m* CERAM VER badging, ESSAIS *échantillon* marking, IMPRIM *façonnage, emballage, transformation* scoring, PAPIER, PRODUCTION, TELECOM, TEXTILE marking; **~ au burin** *m* CONS MECA chisel marking; **~ à chaud** *m* EMBALLAGE hot-stamping, IMPRIM *film portant une poudre ou un toner* hot foil; **~ électrolytique** *m* CONS MECA *métaux conducteurs* electrolytic marking, NUCLEAIRE electrolytic etching; **~ laser** *m* ELECTRON laser designation; **~ à la molette** *m* PAPIER rubber mark; **~ par échange** *m* CHIMIQUE, NUCLEAIRE labeling by chemical exchange (AmE), labelling by chemical exchange (BrE); **~ par roulement** *m* CONS MECA roll marking; **~ pour l'identification du contenu** *m* SECURITE *bouteilles à gaz industriel* identification of contents; **~ de prix** *m* EMBALLAGE price marking; **~ radioactif** *m* CHIMIE radio labeling (AmE), radio labelling (BrE)

marque *f* BREVETS mark, trademark, CINEMAT cue, IMPRIM *blanchet, cylindre, bobine, carrosserie, ou début d'un alinéa* indent, INFORMAT, NAUT, ORDINAT mark, PRODUCTION mark, trademark; **~ d'alignement** *f* NAUT leading mark; **~ associée** *f* BREVETS associated mark; **~ d'axe de piste** *f* AERONAUT runway centerline marking (AmE), runway centreline marking (BrE); **~ axiale de voie de circulation** *f* AERONAUT taxiway centerline marking (AmE), taxiway centreline marking (BrE); **~ de bande** *f* INFORMAT, ORDINAT tape mark; **~ des basses eaux** *f* CONSTR low-water mark; **~ de bifurcation** *f* TRANSPORT bifurcation; **~ de certification** *f* BREVETS certification mark; **~ de charge** *f* GEOLOGIE load cast; **~ de ciseaux** *f* CERAM VER shear mark; **~ collective** *f* BREVETS collective mark; **~ combinée** *f* BREVETS combined mark, composite mark, figurative device, word-and-device mark; **~ de courant en forme de flûte** *f* GEOLOGIE flute mark; **~ au crayon gras** *f* CINEMAT *pour indiquer les trucages* streamer; **~ de danger isolé** *f* NAUT isolated danger mark; **~ dénominative** *f* BREVETS work mark; **~ de départ** *f* CINEMAT start mark; **~ déposée** *f* BREVETS registered mark; **~ d'eau saine** *f* NAUT safe water mark; **~ d'éditeur** *f* IMPRIM imprint; **~ en fer à cheval** *f* CERAM VER hoof mark, hook mark; **~ de fabrication** *f* BREVETS, PRODUCTION trademark; **~ de fabrique** *f* BREVETS, PRODUCTION trademark; **~ de feutre** *f* PAPIER felt mark; **~ de fichier** *f* INFORMAT, ORDINAT file mark;

~ **figurative** *f* BREVETS device mark; ~ **de fin** *f* INFORMAT, ORDINAT end mark; ~ **de fin de bobine** *f* CINEMAT changeover cue; ~ **de fond ébaucheur déportée** *f* CERAM VER swung baffle; ~ **de franc-bord** *f* NAUT plimsoll line; ~ **de groupe** *f* INFORMAT group code recording, group mark, ORDINAT group mark; ~ **de haute renommée** *f* BREVETS mark with high reputation; ~ **d'imprimeur** *f* IMPRIM printer's mark, *typographie* imprint; ~ **de l'imprimeur** *f* IMPRIM *typographie* fleuron; ~ **d'intersection de voies de circulation** *f* AERONAUT taxiway intersection marking; ~ **de mixage sur copie** *f* CINEMAT picture-cueing mark; ~ **de moule** *f* CERAM VER mold mark (AmE), mould mark (BrE); ~ **non déposée** *f* BREVETS unregistered mark; ~ **notoire** *f* BREVETS well-known mark; ~ **de passage** *f* CINEMAT changeover cue, cue mark, ENREGISTR cue mark, TV changeover cue; ~ **de remplissage** *f* CERAM VER settle mark; ~ **de rouleau** *f* CERAM VER roll mark (AmE), roller mark (BrE); ~ **de séchage** *f* CINEMAT drying mark; ~ **de service** *f* BREVETS service mark; ~ **de seuil de piste** *f* AERONAUT runway threshold marking; ~ **sur fond** *f* CERAM VER lettering on bottom; ~ **de synchronisation** *f* CINEMAT sync mark; ~ **de toile** *f* IMPRIM, PAPIER wire mark; ~ **verbale** *f* BREVETS work mark

marqué *adj* CHIMIE labeled (AmE), labelled (BrE)

marquer *vt* IMPRIM *blanchet* indent, NAUT *épave* buoy

marques: ~ **d'arrêt** *f pl* TEXTILE stopping marks; ~ **de balisage** *f pl* TRANSPORT channel marks; ~ **de correction de copie** *f pl* IMPRIM *contrôle de qualité, composition* proof marks; ~ **de développement** *f pl* CINEMAT developer streaks; ~ **de feu** *f pl* CERAM VER fire marks; ~ **de pinces** *f pl* CERAM VER tong marks; ~ **de repérage** *f pl* IMPRIM *coupe, couleur, fabrication* lay marks; ~ **de tapis** *f pl* CERAM VER belt marks

marqueterie: ~ **en verre** *f* CERAM VER marquetry

marqueur *m* ELECTRON marker pulse, GEOLOGIE, INFORMAT, ORDINAT marker, PRODUCTION checker, TELECOM, TRANSPORT marker; ~ **anticollision** *m* NAUT AC marker, anticollision marker; ~ **de début de bande** *m* INFORMAT, ORDINAT BOT marker, beginning-of-tape marker; ~ **de temps** *m* ELECTRON time marker

marquise *f* CH DE FER platform awning

marron *m* CINEMAT fine-grain master, lavender; ~ **pour trucages** *m* CINEMAT optical fine grain; ~ **de sécurité** *m* CINEMAT protection master

Mars *m* ASTRONOMIE Mars

marteau *m* CHARBON hammer, CONSTR beetle, MECANIQUE *outillage*, PRODUCTION hammer; ~ **d'ajusteur** *m* CONS MECA fitter's hammer; ~ **à ardoise** *m* CONSTR slater's hammer; ~ **à bascule** *m* PRODUCTION tilt hammer, tilting hammer; ~ **de battage** *m* CONSTR piling hammer; ~ **brise-béton** *m* CONSTR concrete breaker; ~ **à buriner** *m* PRODUCTION chipping hammer; ~ **chasse-coins** *m* PRODUCTION keying hammer; ~ **à chute libre** *m* CONS MECA drop hammer; ~ **de coffreur** *m* CONS MECA formwork hammer; ~ **de couvreur** *m* CONSTR roofer's hammer; ~ **à découper les rivets** *m* CONS MECA rivet knocking-off hammer; ~ **à dent** *m* CONSTR claw hammer; ~ **à détartrer les chaudières** *m* INST HYDR boiler scaling hammer; ~ **à deux têtes** *m* CONSTR double-faced sledgehammer; ~ **à devant** *m* CONSTR double-faced sledgehammer; ~ **à devant panne en travers** *m* CONSTR cross-peen sledgehammer; ~ **en métal tendre** *m* PRODUCTION soft metal hammer; ~ **à forger** *m* PRODUCTION forge hammer, power hammer; ~ **de forgeron** *m* CONS MECA blacksmith's hammer, PRODUCTION forge hammer; ~ **à garnir** *m* CONS MECA dinging hammer; ~ **à granuler** *m* GENIE CHIM granulating hammer; ~ **à main** *m* PRODUCTION hand hammer; ~ **à mater** *m* CONS MECA caulking hammer, caulking mallet, PRODUCTION caulking hammer; ~ **à panne** *m* PRODUCTION pean hammer, peen hammer; ~ **à panne en long** *m* CONSTR straight pane hammer, straight peen hammer; ~ **à panne en travers** *m* CONSTR cross-pane hammer, cross-peen hammer; ~ **de paveur** *m* CONSTR paviour's hammer; ~ **perforateur** *m* CONS MECA percussion drill, CONSTR, MINES hammer drill; ~ **perforateur pneumatique** *m* CONSTR pneumatic hammer drill; ~ **perforateur à poussoir pneumatique** *m* MINES jackleg drill; ~ **à pioche** *m* PRODUCTION pick hammer; ~ **de piquage** *m* PRODUCTION scaling hammer; ~ **à piquer** *m* PRODUCTION scaling hammer; ~ **à piquer les soudures** *m* PRODUCTION chipping hammer; ~ **piqueur** *m* PRODUCTION pick hammer; ~ **pneumatique** *m* MECANIQUE air hammer, MINES pneumatic hammer; ~ **pour piquer les chaudières** *m* PRODUCTION scaling hammer; ~ **à rétreindre** *m* CONS MECA shrinking hammer; ~ **à river** *m* CONSTR riveting hammer; ~ **à soulèvement** *m* PRODUCTION tilt hammer; ~ **à têtes rapportées** *m* PRODUCTION ironbound mallet, metal-bound mallet; ~ **à trous de coins** *m* CHARBON stone-splitting hammer

marteau-batte *m* CONS MECA beating hammer

marteau-matoir *m* PRODUCTION caulking hammer

marteau-pilon *m* PRODUCTION forge hammer, hammer, power hammer; ~ **atmosphérique** *m* CONSTR pneumatic power hammer; ~ **à friction** *m* PRODUCTION drop hammer, friction hammer; ~ **à ressort** *m* PRODUCTION spring power hammer

marteau-piqueur *m* MINES pneumatic pick

marteau-rivoir *m* CONSTR riveting hammer

martelage *m* CERAM VER hammer, CONSTR hammering, PRODUCTION hammering, malleation, peening; ~ **d'une surface** *m* MATERIAUX surface hammering

martèlement *m* NAUT slamming, PRODUCTION hammering

martelet *f* CONSTR slate ax (AmE), slate axe (BrE)

martelures *f pl* PRODUCTION cinder, forge scale, hammer slag, hammer scale, iron scale, nill, scale

martensite *f* CRISTALL, MATERIAUX martensite; ~ **thermoélastique** *f* METALL thermoelastic martensite

martensitique *adj* MATERIAUX, METALL martensitic

martien *adj* ASTRONOMIE Martian

martinet *m* CONS MECA power hammer, PRODUCTION tilt hammer, tilting hammer

martite *f* MINERAUX martite

mascaret *m* EN RENOUV *houille bleue*, HYDROLOGIE, NAUT bore, OCEANO bore, seiche, tidal wave

maser *m* ELECTRON, PHYSIQUE, TELECOM maser; ~ **à l'ammoniaque** *m* ELECTRON ammonia maser; ~ **à gaz** *m* ELECTRON gas maser; ~ **à hydrogène atomique** *m* ELECTRON atomic hydrogen maser; ~ **à impulsion** *m* ELECTRON pulsed maser; ~ **à ondes progressives** *m* ELECTRON traveling-wave maser (AmE), travelling-wave maser (BrE); ~ **optique** *m* ELECTRON optical maser; ~ **à quatre niveaux** *m* ELECTRON four-level maser; ~ **à solide** *m* ELECTRON solid-state maser; ~ **à trois niveaux** *m* ELECTRON three-level maser

masonite *f* MINERAUX masonite

masquage *m* ELECTRON, ENREGISTR *son*, IMPRIM *photogravure* masking, INFORMAT, ORDINAT masking, reverse clipping, TV shadowing; ~ **d'information** *m* INFORMAT information-hiding; ~ **par le bruit** *m* TELECOM noise masking; ~ **par contact** *m* ELECTRON contact masking

masque *m* CINEMAT mask, vignette, CONSTR facing, ELECTRON, INFORMAT, ORDINAT mask, SECURITE mask, *soudure* face shield; ~ **antifumée** *m* AERONAUT smoke mask; ~ **antipoussière** *m* SECURITE dust mask; ~ **appris par la caméra** *m* PRODUCTION train-through-the-lens mask; ~ **du cadrage** *m* TV framing mask; ~ **de clavier** *m* INFORMAT keyboard mask, ORDINAT keytop overlay; ~ **complet** *m* SECURITE full-face mask; ~ **en contact** *m* ELECTRON contact mask; ~ **à fentes** *m* ELECTRON aperture grill (AmE), aperture grille (BrE); ~ **de filtrage** *m* ESPACE *communications* filter jig, filter mask, filter template; ~ **à gaz** *m* MILITAIRE gas mask; ~ **de gravure** *m* ELECTRON lithographic mask; ~ **d'interruption** *m* INFORMAT, ORDINAT interrupt mask; ~ **lithographique** *m* PHYS RAYON *production des circuits intégrés* lithographic mask; ~ **à main** *m* CONSTR welding handshield; ~ **de métallisation** *m* ELECTRON metalization mask (AmE), metallization mask (BrE); ~ **d'ombre** *m* TV aperture mask, shadow mask; ~ **optique** *m* ELECTRON optical mask; ~ **à oxygène** *m* ESPACE *véhicules* oxygen mask, SECURITE oxygen breathing apparatus, oxygen mask; ~ **perforé** *m* ELECTRON aperture mask, shadow mask; ~ **de photogravure** *m* ELECTRON photomask; ~ **à plaquette** *m* ELECTRON wafer mask; ~ **de plongée** *m* OCEANO diving mask; ~ **pour circuits intégrés** *m* ELECTRON integrated circuit mask; ~ **pour gravure par faisceau d'électrons réparti** *m* ELECTRON electron beam mask; ~ **pour rayons X** *m* ELECTRON X-ray mask; ~ **à poussière** *m* SECURITE dust mask; ~ **primaire** *m* ELECTRON master mask; ~ **de proximité** *m* ELECTRON proximity mask; ~ **à serre-tête** *m* CONSTR welding helmet; ~ **sonore** *m* ENREGISTR sound blanket; ~ **de soudure** *m* PRODUCTION face shield

masqué *adj* GEOLOGIE concealed

masquer *vt* IMPRIM *photogravure* block out, NAUT *navire* darken, *voiles* back, lay aback, PRODUCTION blank

masse *f* CHIMIE mass, CONSTR bed, heap, lump, sledge, sledgehammer, ELECTR *raccordement*, ELECTROTEC earth (BrE), ground (AmE), GEOPHYS mass, PHYSIQUE earth (BrE), ground (AmE), mass, PRODUCTION hammer, solid, solid blank, *électricité* common, VEHICULES *système électrique* earth (BrE), ground (AmE); ~ **d'acier** *f* MATERIAUX steel weight; ~ **acoustique** *f* ACOUSTIQUE acoustic mass; ~ **admissible à l'atterrissage** *f* AERONAUT allowable landing mass; ~ **admissible au décollage** *f* AERONAUT allowable takeoff mass; ~ **d'air** *f* EN RENOUV *énergie solaire* air mass; ~ **atomique** *f* CHIMIE, PHYS PART atomic mass; ~ **atomique relative** *f* CHIMIE, PHYS PART atomic weight, PHYSIQUE atomic weight, relative atomic mass; ~ **à l'atterrissage** *f* AERONAUT landing weight; ~ **brute** *f* AERONAUT gross weight; ~ **brute initiale** *f* AERONAUT initial gross weight; ~ **de câblage** *f* AERONAUT cable weight; ~ **de cacao** *f* AGRO ALIM cocoa mass; ~ **cachée** *f* ASTRONOMIE missing mass; ~ **de calcul** *f* AERONAUT design weight; ~ **de calcul à l'atterrissage** *f* AERONAUT design landing weight; ~ **de calcul de l'avion en vol** *f* AERONAUT design flight weight; ~ **de calcul au décol-**

lage *f* AERONAUT design takeoff mass; ~ **de calcul pour le roulement au sol** *f* AERONAUT design taxi weight; ~ **de calcul de roulage** *f* AERONAUT design taxi weight; ~ **au cheval** *f* METROLOGIE power loading; ~ **commerciale** *f* ESSAIS, TEXTILE commercial mass; ~ **critique** *f* PHYSIQUE critical mass; ~ **efficace** *f* ACOUSTIQUE effective mass; ~ **éjectable** *f* ESPACE *propulsion* propellant mass; ~ **de l'électron** *f* PHYS PART electron mass; ~ **électronique** *f* CHIMIE electron mass, em, PHYS PART electron mass; ~ **d'équilibrage** *f* AERONAUT balance weight, AUTO crankweb; ~ **d'équilibrage de pale** *f* AERONAUT blade balance weight; ~ **facturée** *f* ESSAIS invoice mass, PAPIER *pâte* invoiced mass, TEXTILE invoice mass; ~ **filtrante** *f* GENIE CHIM filter pulp, filter stuff, PAPIER filter mass; ~ **flotille** *f* AERONAUT fleet weight; ~ **garantie** *f* AERONAUT guaranteed weight; ~ **gravitationnelle** *f* PHYSIQUE gravitational mass; ~ **d'inertie** *f* MECANIQUE centrifugal mass, gyrating mass, PHYSIQUE inertial mass; ~ **linéique** *f* PHYSIQUE mass per unit length; ~ **manquante** *f* ASTRONOMIE missing mass; ~ **marchande** *f* PAPIER *pâte* saleable mass; ~ **maximale** *f* AERONAUT gross weight; ~ **du mobile** *f* GEOPHYS mass; ~ **moléculaire relative** *f* PHYSIQUE relative molecular mass; ~ **moyenne** *f* AERONAUT fleet weight; ~ **du neutron** *f* PHYS RAYON neutron mass; ~ **au parking** *f* AERONAUT ramp weight; ~ **polaire** *f* CONS MECA pole piece, TV pole shoe; ~ **polaire de démarreur** *f* AUTO starter pole shoe; ~ **de port** *f* CONSTR *pont* pier; ~ **réduite** *f* PHYSIQUE reduced mass; ~ **au repos** *f* PHYS PART *atome*, PHYSIQUE rest mass; ~ **sèche** *f* AERONAUT dry weight, ESPACE *propulsion* dry mass, dry weight; ~ **sèche à l'air** *f* PAPIER *pâte* air-dry mass; ~ **sismique** *f* GEOPHYS seismic mass; ~ **solaire** *f* ASTRONOMIE solar mass; ~ **spécifique** *f* GEOLOGIE density; ~ **au stationnement** *f* AERONAUT ramp weight; ~ **surface** *f* CONSTR *terrain* total area; ~ **tenue par un ressort vertical** *f* CONS MECA mass on a vertical spring; ~ **thermique** *f* THERMODYN thermal mass; ~ **de tierçage** *f* AERONAUT cable weight; ~ **totale** *f* AERONAUT certification weight; ~ **à vide** *f* AERONAUT empty weight; ~ **volumique** *f* CHARBON, GEOLOGIE, PETROLE, PHYSIQUE, PRODUCTION density; ~ **volumique apparente** *f* CHARBON apparent density, bulk density, GENIE CHIM settled apparent density, PAPIER *carton*, *papier* apparent density; ~ **volumique après tassement** *f* GENIE CHIM compacted apparent density; ~ **volumique effective** *f* NUCLEAIRE effective particle density; ~ **volumique frittée** *f* GENIE CHIM sintered density; ~ **volumique sèche** *f* CHARBON dry density; ~ **volumique théorique** *f* NUCLEAIRE theoretical density, true density

masselotte *f* CONS MECA flyweight, PRODUCTION deadhead, feed head, feeder, head metal, head, shrink head, sinking head, sullage head, sullage piece; ~ **d'équilibrage** *f* MECANIQUE balancing weight

masse-tampon *f* CERAM VER pool block (BrE), pool tablet (AmE)

masse-tige *f* PETR, PETROLE drill collar

massette *f* CONSTR sledge, sledgehammer, PRODUCTION hammer

massicot *m* CHIMIE massicot, IMPRIM paper cutter, *façonnage* cutter, MINERAUX massicot; ~ **trilame** *m* IMPRIM three-sided cutting machine, tri-blade cutting machine

massicotage *m* PAPIER guillotining; ~ **refente de feuilles** *m* PAPIER guillotining

massicotage-rognage *m* PAPIER guillotining-trimming
massicoter *vt* IMPRIM cut, trim
massif[1] *adj* GEOLOGIE massive
massif[2] *m* HYDROLOGIE *minerai* body, MINES *charbon, minerai, stérile* pillar, *de minerai* largebody,   NAUT deadwood; ~ **d'ancrage** *m* CONSTR anchorage block; ~ **de fondation** *m* CONSTR foundation block; ~ **de minerai** *m* MINES overburden; ~ **de protection** *m* MINES boundary pillar, support pillar, cranch, craunch (BrE); ~ **de protection de puits** *m* MINES bottom pillar, shaft safety pillar; ~ **salifère** *m* GAZ salt deposit
massique *adj* PHYSIQUE per unit mass
master: ~ **disque** *m* OPTIQUE master disc (BrE), master disk (AmE); ~ **gravure vinyle** *m* ENREGISTR wax master
mastic *m* CONSTR mastic, putty, NAUT mastic, resin, PETR mastic; ~ **d'étanchéité** *m* PLAST CAOU *composé polymérique* sealant; ~ **de fonte** *m* PRODUCTION beaumontage, fake; ~ **isolant** *m* REFRIG insulating mastic; ~ **pour carrosserie** *m* VEHICULES body filler; ~ **silicone** *m* NAUT silicone compound; ~ **de vitrier** *m* CONSTR putty
masticage *m* CONSTR puttying
mastication *f* PLAST CAOU mastication
mastiquer *vt* CONSTR putty, *trou* stop with putty
mastoïde: ~ **artificiel** *m* ACOUSTIQUE artificial mastoid
mat[1] *adj* MATERIAUX mat, matt, tarnished, MECANIQUE *traitement de surface* brushed, TEXTILE matt, mat
mat[2] *m* MATERIAUX mat; ~ **en fibre de verre à fils coupés** *m* PLAST CAOU *résine renforcée de fibre de verre* chopped strand mat; ~ **à fils continus** *m* CERAM VER continuous strand mat; ~ **à fils coupés** *m* CERAM VER chopped strand mat; ~ **à fils de verre** *m* PLAST CAOU *fibre de verre* continuous strand mat; ~ **non tissé** *m* PLAST CAOU *fibre de verre* nonwoven mat; ~ **overlay** *m* CERAM VER bonded mat, overlay mat; ~ **de verre** *m* NAUT chopped strand mat
mât *m* AERONAUT *support rigide de moteur* pylon, CONSTR pole, ELECTR *réseau*, ELECTROTEC pylon, NAUT, PETR mast; ~ **d'antenne** *m* TELECOM, TV aerial mast; ~ **d'artimon** *m* NAUT mizzen mast; ~ **de charge** *m* NAUT cargo derrick, derrick boom, derrick, TRANSPORT derrick mast; ~ **de forage** *m* PETR drilling mast; ~ **de liaison** *m* AERONAUT engine nacelle stub; ~ **de misaine** *m* NAUT foremast; ~ **ombilical** *m* ESPACE *véhicules* umbilical mast; ~ **de pavillon** *m* NAUT flagstaff; ~ **portique** *m* NAUT portal mast; ~ **profilé** *m* NAUT aerodynamic mast; ~ **radar** *m* TRANSPORT radar mast; ~ **réacteur** *m* AERONAUT engine nacelle stub; ~ **rotor** *m* AERONAUT *hélicoptère* rotor mast, main rotor shaft; ~ **de signaux** *m* NAUT signal mast
matage *m* CERAM VER sandblast obscuring, MECANIQUE caulking, PRODUCTION caulking, jagging, peening; ~ **à l'acide** *m* CERAM VER acid embossing
maté *adj* IMPRIM matted
matelas *m* CHAUFFAGE *isolement thermique* mattress, ELECTR *câble* bedding, ELECTROTEC filler, ESPACE *véhicules* blanket, TEXTILE mattress; ~ **d'air** *m* AERONAUT air cushion; ~ **d'azote** *m* NUCLEAIRE nitrogen cover gas; ~ **de calorifugeage** *m* THERMODYN heat-insulating jacket; ~ **en fibre de verre** *m* CERAM VER glass fiber mat (AmE), glass fibre mat (BrE); ~ **extérieur** *m* ELECTR *câble* serving; ~ **de fibres** *m* PAPIER mat; ~ **de gaz** *m* NUCLEAIRE gas cushion; ~ **protecteur** *m* TELECOM fiber buffer (AmE), fibre buffer (BrE)
matelasser *vt* TEXTILE quilt

mater *vt* CINEMAT mat down, spray down, CONS MECA batter, PRODUCTION caulk, jag
mâter *vt* NAUT step
mâtereau *m* NAUT king post
matériau *m* CONSTR material; ~ **absorbant** *m* ACOUSTIQUE sound absorber, CONSTR blotter material; ~ **alvéolaire** *m* CONSTR foam material; ~ **d'apport** *m* NUCLEAIRE filler, filling material; ~ **combustible** *m* POLLUTION combustible material; ~ **composite** *m* ESPACE *véhicules* composite material, PLAST CAOU composite; ~ **en vrac** *m* CHARBON bulk material; ~ **ferromagnétique** *m* PETR ferromagnetic material; ~ **fibreux** *m* CONSTR fiber-like material (AmE), fibre-like material (BrE); ~ **de gainage** *m* NUCLEAIRE cladding material, fuel cladding; ~ **granulaire** *m* CONSTR granular material; ~ **grenu** *m* CONSTR granular material; ~ **insonore** *m* ACOUSTIQUE impact-sound reducing material, soundproofing material; ~ **isolant** *m* CONSTR, MECANIQUE insulating material; ~ **magnétique doux** *m* ELECTROTEC, PHYSIQUE soft magnetic material; ~ **magnétique dur** *m* MECANIQUE, PHYSIQUE hard magnetic material; ~ **paramagnétique** *m* PETR paramagnetic material; ~ **polymère** *m* MATERIAUX polymeric material; ~ **pour couches épaisses** *m* ELECTRON thick-film material; ~ **pour couches minces** *m* ELECTRON thin-film material; ~ **pour scellement** *m* NUCLEAIRE sealing material; ~ **de recouvrement** *m* REVETEMENT coating material; ~ **recyclé** *m* CONSTR recycled material; ~ **réfractaire** *m* CHARBON, GAZ refractory material, THERMODYN refractory; ~ **de remblai** *m* CHARBON backfill, stowing material, landfill; ~ **de remplissage** *m* CONSTR core; ~ **semi-conducteur** *m* ELECTRON semiconductor material; ~ **stabilisé** *m* CONSTR stabilized material
matériaux *m pl* CONSTR materials, PRODUCTION stuff, SECURITE, TEXTILE materials; ~ **antidérapants pour revêtement de sol** *m pl* SECURITE antislip material floor covering; ~ **antistatiques** *m pl* SECURITE antistatic materials; ~ **combustibles** *m pl* POLLUTION, SECURITE combustible material; ~ **composant des ailes** *m pl* EN RENOUV blade materials; ~ **composant des pales** *m pl* EN RENOUV blade materials; ~ **composites** *m pl* MATERIAUX composites; ~ **de concassage** *m pl* CONSTR crushed material; ~ **de construction** *m pl* CONSTR building materials; ~ **denses** *m pl* PETR weighting material; ~ **d'empierrement** *m pl* CONSTR metal; ~ **d'empierrement pour route** *m pl* CONSTR paving material (AmE), road metal (BrE); ~ **en fusion** *m pl* SECURITE molten materials; ~ **feuilletés** *m pl* MATERIAUX laminated materials; ~ **d'isolation acoustique** *m pl* POLLUTION acoustic insulating materials; ~ **non isotropes** *m pl* CONS MECA nonisotropic materials; ~ **orthotropiques** *m pl* CONS MECA orthotropic materials; ~ **plastiques** *m pl* SECURITE plastic materials; ~ **pour paliers** *m pl* CONS MECA bearing materials; ~ **de ressorts** *m pl* RESSORTS spring materials; ~ **toxiques** *m pl* SECURITE toxic materials
matériel *m* CONS MECA outfit, CONSTR equipment, plant, INFORMAT, ORDINAT hardware, PRODUCTION equipment, plant, TELECOM hardware; ~ **absorbant le son** *m* ENREGISTR sound-absorbing material; ~ **alvéolé** *m* EMBALLAGE honeycomb material; ~ **auxiliaire** *m* MECANIQUE ancillary equipment; ~ **avec marche avant-arrière** *m* ENREGISTR rock and roll equipment; ~ **barrière** *m* EMBALLAGE barrier material; ~ **de bord** *m* ESPACE *véhicules* on-board equipment, strapdown

equipment; ~ **de canaux** *m* TELECOM CE, channel equipment; ~ **de chemin de fer** *m* CONSTR rolling stock; ~ **commun** *m* TELECOM CE, common equipment; ~ **de commutation numérique** *m* ELECTROTEC digital switching equipment; ~ **de commutation téléphonique** *m* ELECTROTEC telephone switchgear; ~ **de contrôle** *m* QUALITE inspection equipment; ~ **d'éclairage** *m* PHOTO lighting equipment; ~ **électrique** *m* ELECTROTEC electrical equipment; ~ **électronique** *m* ELECTRON electronic equipment; ~ **électronique grand public** *m* ELECTROTEC consumer electronic equipment, domestic electronic equipment (BrE), home electronic equipment (AmE); ~ **électronique industriel** *m* ELECTROTEC industrial electronic equipment; ~ **d'emballage en plastique renforcé** *m* EMBALLAGE reinforced plastic packaging material; ~ **embarqué** *m* ESPACE on-board equipment; ~ **d'enregistrement feuilleté** *m* ENREGISTR laminated record; ~ **en taille** *m* MINES coalface system; ~ **d'épuisement** *m* DISTRI EAU pumping equipment, pumping plant; ~ **d'exhaure** *m* DISTRI EAU pumping equipment, pumping plant; ~ **ferroviaire** *m* TRANSPORT railroad material (AmE), railway material (BrE), railroad stock (AmE), railway stock (BrE); ~ **fixe** *m* PRODUCTION fixed plant; ~ **de forage** *m* CONSTR boreholing plant, MINES boring plant, drilling equipment, drilling plant; ~ **de graissage à main** *m* CONS MECA manual lubricating equipment; ~ **de guerre** *m* MILITAIRE ordnance material; ~ **hydraulique** *m* CONS MECA hydraulic equipment; ~ **hydrostatique** *m* CONS MECA hydrostatic equipment; ~ **inflammable** *m* SECURITE flammable material; ~ **d'injection** *m* CONSTR grouting equipment; ~ **isolant** *m* EMBALLAGE insulating material; ~ **du jour** *m* MINES surface equipment; ~ **de laboratoire** *m* CINEMAT processing equipment; ~ **de levage** *m* MECANIQUE lifting gear; ~ **de manutention de combustible** *m* MAT CHAUFF fuel handling plant; ~ **métallique fritté** *m* CONS MECA sintered metal material; ~ **de mines** *m* MINES mining appliances; ~ **mobile** *m* CONS MECA loose plant, portable plant; ~ **de modules de lignes** *m* TELECOM LME, line module equipment; ~ **de parafoudre** *m* SECURITE lightning conductor material; ~ **photographique** *m* MATERIAUX photographic equipment, PHOTO photographic apparatus; ~ **pneumatique** *m* CONS MECA pneumatic equipment; ~ **pour le cerclage de palettes** *m* EMBALLAGE pallet-strapping material; ~ **pour lignes aériennes** *m* ELECTROTEC overhead power line fittings; ~ **pour vide élevé** *m* CONS MECA vacuum equipment; ~ **de prise de vues** *m* CINEMAT camera equipment; ~ **de profilage de feuillard** *m* PRODUCTION roll forming equipment; ~ **de protection contre le bruit** *m* SECURITE noise-insulating equipment; ~ **de radar** *m* TRANSPORT radar equipment; ~ **rebuté** *m* EMBALLAGE scrap material; ~ **récupéré** *m* NAUT *après un naufrage* salvage, RECYCLAGE salvaged material; ~ **résistant aux produits chimiques** *m* MILITAIRE CARM, chemical agent resisting material; ~ **de rhabillage de meules** *m* CONS MECA grinding wheel dressing equipment; ~ **roulant** *m* CH DE FER *véhicules*, CONSTR rolling stock, TRANSPORT railroad vehicles (AmE), railway vehicles (BrE); ~ **sauvé** *m* RECYCLAGE salvaged material; ~ **de sauvetage** *m* NAUT rescue apparatus, SECURITE rescue equipment; ~ **de secours** *m* SECURITE rescue equipment; ~ **son** *m* ENREGISTR sound equipment; ~ **de soudage par résistance** *m* CONS MECA resistance welding equipment; ~ **de test automatique** *m* ORDINAT ATE, automatic test equipment; ~ **thermosensible** *m* EMBALLAGE heat-sensitive material; ~ **de transfusion du sang** *m* SECURITE blood transfusion equipment; ~ **de voies** *m* TELECOM CE, channel equipment

mathématiques *f pl* INFORMAT, ORDINAT mathematics

mathusalem *m* CERAM VER methuselah

matière *f* CHIMIE, CONS MECA material, PRODUCTION stuff; ~ **active** *f* ELECTROTEC active material; ~ **allochtone** *f* POLLUTION allochthonous matter; ~ **anisotrope** *f* MATERIAUX, TEXTILE anisotropic material; ~ **autochtone** *f* POLLUTION autochtonous matter; ~ **brute secondaire plastique** *f* MATERIAUX secondary raw plastic material; ~ **cellulosique** *f* AGRO ALIM crude fiber (AmE), crude fibre (BrE); ~ **de charge** *f* COULEURS extender; ~ **cimentaire** *f* CONSTR cementing material; ~ **de cimentation** *f* CONSTR cementing material; ~ **colorante** *f* COULEURS coloring agent (AmE), coloring matter (AmE), coloring substance (AmE), colouring agent (BrE), colouring matter(BrE), colouring substance (BrE); ~ **combustible** *f* SECURITE combustible material; ~ **de contact** *f* ELECTR, PRODUCTION contact material; ~ **dégénérée** *f* ASTRONOMIE, CHIMIE degenerate matter; ~ **déposée** *f* POLLUTION deposited matter; ~ **dispersée** *f* GENIE CHIM dispersoid; ~ **effondrée** *f* ASTRONOMIE collapsed matter; ~ **enrichie** *f* PHYS RAYON *chimie radioactive* enriched material; ~ **épaississante** *f* GENIE CHIM thickener; ~ **explosive** *f* THERMODYN explosive; ~ **extractible** *f* ESSAIS extractable component; ~ **fissile** *f* PHYS RAYON fissile material; ~ **de gaine** *f* NUCLEAIRE cladding material, fuel cladding; ~ **granulée** *f* GENIE CHIM granule material; ~ **grasse** *f* AGRO ALIM fat, greasing agent, shortening; ~ **grasse de lait** *f* AGRO ALIM milk fat; ~ **imparfaite** *f* ELECTR *diélectrique, ligne, etc* lossy material; ~ **interstellaire** *f* ASTRONOMIE, ESPACE interstellar matter; ~ **isolante** *f* ELECTROTEC insulating compound, insulating material; ~ **à mouler par injection** *f* EMBALLAGE, PRODUCTION injection molding compound (AmE), injection moulding compound (BrE); ~ **noire** *f* ASTRONOMIE dark matter; ~ **noire chaude** *f* ASTRONOMIE hot dark matter; ~ **noire froide** *f* ASTRONOMIE *non relativiste* cold dark matter; ~ **non réfractaire** *f* PHYSIQUE nonrefractory material; ~ **nucléaire comprimée** *f* NUCLEAIRE compressed nuclear matter; ~ **odorante** *f* CHIMIE *molécule* odoriphore; ~ **organique** *f* GEOLOGIE *sédimentaire*, HYDROLOGIE, PETROLE *sédimentaire* organic matter; ~ **organique allochtone** *f* POLLUTION allochthonous matter; ~ **organique autochtone** *f* POLLUTION autochtonous matter; ~ **organique digestible** *f* *(MOD)* RECYCLAGE digestible organic matter *(DOM)*; ~ **organique dissoute** *f* POLLUTION dissolved organic matter; ~ **particulaire** *f* GENIE CHIM, MATERIAUX particulate; ~ **plastique** *f pl* CHIMIE plastics, PETROLE, PLAST CAOU plastic; ~ **plastique armée de fibre de verre** *f* NAUT GRP, glass-refined plastic; ~ **plastique renforcée par fibre de carbone** *f* PLAST CAOU carbon fiber reinforced plastic (AmE), carbon fibre reinforced plastic (BrE); ~ **pour résistance** *f* ELECTROTEC resistance material; ~ **première** *f* CERAM VER, CHARBON raw material, ELECTROTEC feedstock, PAPIER, PETROLE, PLAST CAOU, PRODUCTION, TEXTILE raw material; ~ **de remplissage** *f* MATERIAUX, PLAST CAOU filler; ~ **rétrodiffusante** *f* NUCLEAIRE backscatterer; ~ **sèche** *f* HYDROLOGIE dry matter, solid matter; ~ **solide** *f* PETR propping agent;

~ **tinctoriale** *f* COULEURS coloring agent (AmE), coloring matter (AmE), coloring substance (AmE), colouring agent (BrE), colouring matter (BrE), colouring substance (BrE)

matières: ~ **consommables** *f pl* PRODUCTION factory supplies; ~ **dangereuses** *f pl* SECURITE dangerous materials; ~ **denses** *f* PETR weighting material; ~ **en suspension décantables** *f pl* HYDROLOGIE settleable solids; ~ **fécales** *f pl* HYDROLOGIE, RECYCLAGE faecal matter (BrE), fecal matter (AmE); ~ **indésirables contenues dans les vieux papiers** *f* PAPIER waste paper contraries; ~ **inflammables** *f pl* MATERIAUX inflammable materials; ~ **minérales exclues** *f pl* POLLUTION mineral-matter-free; ~ **organiques** *f pl* POLLUTION organic matter; ~ **particulaires** *f pl* POLLUTION particulate materials, particulate matter; ~ **plastiques moulées** *f pl* PLAST CAOU molded plastics (AmE), moulded plastics (BrE); ~ **plastiques renforcées aux fibres de verre** *f pl* SECURITE glass fiber reinforced plastic (AmE), glass fibre reinforced plastic (BrE); ~ **refusées** *f pl* MINES *crible* oversize, PRODUCTION *crible* riddlings; ~ **de remplissage des extincteurs** *f pl* SECURITE fire extinguisher fillings; ~ **tamisées** *f pl* PRODUCTION siftings; ~ **de vidange** *f pl* HYDROLOGIE night soil

matipo *f* CINEMAT contact printer

matir *vt* PRODUCTION caulk, jag

matlockite *f* MINERAUX matlockite

matoir *m* PRODUCTION caulking chisel, caulking iron

maton *m* PAPIER lump

matras *m* EQUIP LAB bolthead, GENIE CHIM distillation flask, distilling flask, still, THERMODYN distillation flask, distillation retort

matriçage *m* CONS MECA dying, MECANIQUE die stamping, PRODUCTION die forging, TV matrixing; ~ **à froid** *m* CONS MECA cold hobbing

matrice *f* ACOUSTIQUE stamper, CERAM VER, CINEMAT die, CONS MECA hob, hob tap, master tap, *conjointement avec poinçon* die, ENREGISTR master, GEOLOGIE matrix, IMPRIM *clicherie typographique* mat, INFORMAT, MATH matrix, MECANIQUE *emboutissage* die, METALL matrix, NAUT plug, wooden plug, ORDINAT matrix, PRODUCTION die, TELECOM array, TV matrix; ~ **cellulaire** *f* ELECTRON cellular array; ~ **de céramique** *f* CERAM VER, MATERIAUX ceramic matrix; ~ **de commutation** *f* ESPACE *communications*, TELECOM switching matrix; ~ **de commutation optique** *f* TELECOM optical switching matrix; ~ **de commutation optique intégrée** *f* TELECOM integrated optical switching matrix; ~ **de commutation optoélectronique** *f* TELECOM optoelectronic switching matrix; ~ **de connexion** *f* TELECOM CM, connection matrix; ~ **creuse** *f* INFORMAT, ORDINAT sparse matrix; ~ **de décodage** *f* TV decoding matrix; ~ **à découper** *f* PRODUCTION die; ~ **à démontage rapide** *f* CONS MECA quick-release die; ~ **en cuivre au béryllium** *f* CONS MECA beryllium copper die; ~ **époxyde** *f* ESPACE *véhicules* epoxy matrix; ~ **de fabrication** *f* OPTIQUE master disc (BrE), master disk (AmE); ~ **de frappe à froid** *f* CONS MECA heading die; ~ **inférieure** *f* CONS MECA *de marteau-pilon* anvil die; ~ **intermétallique** *f* MATERIAUX intermetallic matrix; ~ **linéaire** *f* TV linear matrix; ~ **logique** *f* ELECTRON logic array; ~ **monolithique** *f* ELECTRON monolithic array; ~ **de moulage en coquille** *f* CONS MECA gravity diecasting die; ~ **de moulage à ligne perdue** *f* CONS MECA investment casting die; ~ **de moulage sous pression** *f*

CONS MECA pressure diecasting die; ~ **optique** *f* TELECOM optical switching matrix; ~ **de photodétecteurs** *f* ELECTRON imaging array; ~ **de photodiodes** *f* ELECTRON photodiode array; ~ **de poinçonnage** *f* CONS MECA *petit procédé* blanking die; ~ **de points** *f* ELECTRON, INFORMAT, ORDINAT dot matrix; ~ **de portes** *f* ELECTRON, INFORMAT gate array; ~ **de portes programmable par masquage** *f* ELECTRON mask-programmable array; ~ **positive** *f* PHOTO lavender print; ~ **prédiffusée** *f* ELECTRON gate array; ~ **prédiffusée ECL** *f* ELECTRON ECL gate array, emitter-coupled logic gate array; ~ **de pressage** *f* OPTIQUE stamper; ~ **de programmation** *f* ELECTROTEC pinboard; ~ **des roches** *f* GEOLOGIE matrix; ~ **R-Y** *f* TV R-Y matrix; ~ **symétrique** *f* INFORMAT, ORDINAT symmetric matrix; ~ **temporelle symétrique** *f* TELECOM digital switching matrix, symmetrical time matrix; ~ **de transfert** *f* PHYSIQUE transfer matrix; ~ **triangulaire** *f* INFORMAT, ORDINAT triangular matrix; ~ **à vague** *f* INFORMAT, ORDINAT wavefront array; ~ **V-Y** *f* TV G-Y matrix

matricé *adj* PRODUCTION drop-forged

matronite *f* CHIMIE nitratine

mattage *m* PLAST CAOU *peinture* matting

matte *f* GAZ, MATERIAUX, METALL matte; ~ **de plomb** *f* PRODUCTION lead matte; ~ **plombeuse** *f* PRODUCTION lead matte

matter *vt* PRODUCTION caulk, jag

mattoir *m* PRODUCTION caulking chisel, caulking iron

maturation *f* AGRO ALIM, EMBALLAGE ageing (BrE), aging (AmE), IMPRIM ripening, PAPIER maturing, PETROLE maturation, PLAST CAOU *peintures*, REFRIG ageing (BrE), aging (AmE), THERMODYN *à température ambiante* precipitation hardening; ~ **artificielle** *f* THERMODYN artificial ageing (BrE), artificial aging (AmE); ~ **des boues** *f* DISTRI EAU sludge ripening; ~ **chimique** *f* PHOTO ripening

maturer *vt* AGRO ALIM cure

mauvais:[1] **en ~ état** *adj* CONS MECA out-of-repair; **en ~ état de navigabilité** *adj* NAUT unseaworthy

mauvais:[2] ~ **air** *m* MINES bad air; ~ **alignement** *m* IMPRIM misalignment; ~ **conducteur** *m* ELECTROTEC poor conductor; ~ **fonctionnement** *m* CONS MECA faulty operation, malfunctioning, ESPACE *véhicules* malfunction; ~ **fonctionnement du système de commande** *m* PRODUCTION *automatisme industriel* control malfunction; ~ **fond** *m* NAUT foul ground; ~ **goût** *m* AGRO ALIM off-flavor (AmE), off-flavour (BrE); ~ **isolant** *m* ELECTROTEC poor insulant; ~ **isolement** *m* ELECTROTEC poor insulation; ~ **nappage** *m* CERAM VER dry spray; ~ **poli** *m* CERAM VER short finish; ~ **recuit** *m* CERAM VER bad annealing; ~ **rendu des couleurs** *m* IMPRIM wrong color rendering (AmE), wrong colour rendering (BrE); ~ **repérage** *m* IMPRIM *contrôle de qualité* misregistration; ~ **terrain** *m* CONSTR bad ground

mauvaise: ~ **adaptation** *f* ELECTROTEC mismatch; ~ **adaptation d'impédance** *f* ELECTROTEC impedance mismatch; ~ **césure** *f* IMPRIM *composition* bad break; ~ **condition de terrain** *f* CONSTR bad ground; ~ **contenance** *f* CERAM VER off-content, wrong capacity; ~ **coupe** *f* CERAM VER sugary cut; ~ **coupure de ligne** *f* IMPRIM *composition* bad break

mauvéine *f* CHIMIE mauveine

maxima: ~ **principaux** *m pl* PHYSIQUE principal maxima; ~ **secondaires** *m pl* OPTIQUE secondary maxima

maximisation f TELECOM maximization

maximum m NUCLEAIRE line, maximum, peak; ~ **et minimum** m CONS MECA *calibre de tolérance* go and not go, go-no-go; ~ **de vraisemblance** m MATH maximum likelihood

maxite f MINERAUX maxite

maxwell m *(Mx)* ELECTR, ELECTROTEC *flux magnétique* maxwell *(Mx)*

mayday m AERONAUT, NAUT Mayday

mazerie f PRODUCTION finery, finery furnace, refinery

mazout m CHIMIE, CONSTR, MAT CHAUFF, PETROLE fuel oil, THERMODYN fuel, heating oil

mazoutage m NAUT bunkering

mazouteur m POLLU MER tender

Md *(mendélévium)* CHIMIE Md *(mendelevium)*

MDF *abrév (modulation par déplacement de fréquence)* ELECTRON, INFORMAT, ORDINAT, TELECOM, TV FSK *(frequency shift keying)*

MDP *abrév (modulation par déplacement de phase)* ELECTRON, ESPACE *communications*, INFORMAT, ORDINAT PSK *(phase shift keying)*

MDPB *abrév (modulation par déplacement de phase bivalente)* TELECOM BPSK *(binary phase shift keying)*

MDPC *abrév (modulation par déplacement de phase cohérente)* TELECOM CPSK *(coherent phase shift keying)*

MDPQ:[1] *abrév (modulation par déplacement de phase quadrivalente)* ELECTRON, TELECOM QPSK *(quadriphase shift keying, quatenary phase-shift keying)*

MDPQ[2] ~ **avec filtrage** f TELECOM filtered QPSK; ~ **avec mise en forme de phase** f TELECOM phase-shaped QPSK

méandre m HYDROLOGIE bend, meander; ~ **recoupé** m DISTRI EAU cutoff

mécanicien m CH DE FER *véhicules* driver (BrE), engineer (AmE), MECANIQUE, NAUT engineer, PRODUCTION mechanic; ~ **ajusteur** m CONS MECA artificer, fitter; ~ **constructeur** m CONS MECA fitter; ~ **d'entretien d'aéronefs** m AERONAUT aircraft maintenance engineer, aircraft maintenance mechanic; ~ **d'entretien avions** m AERONAUT aircraft maintenance engineer, aircraft maintenance mechanic; ~ **de la marine** m NAUT naval engineer; ~ **navigant** m AERONAUT flight engineer; ~ **de précision** m INSTRUMENT instrument maker

mécanique f CONS MECA mechanics, mechanism, PHYSIQUE mechanics; ~ **analytique** f PHYSIQUE analytical mechanics; ~ **céleste** f ASTRONOMIE, ESPACE celestial mechanics; ~ **des fluides** f PHYS FLUID fluid mechanics; ~ **de fracture** f MATERIAUX, MECANIQUE *matériaux* fracture mechanics; ~ **des matrices** f PHYSIQUE matrix mechanics; ~ **navale** f NAUT marine engineering; ~ **de Newton** f ASTRONOMIE, PHYSIQUE Newtonian mechanics; ~ **newtonienne** f ASTRONOMIE, PHYSIQUE Newtonian mechanics; ~ **ondulatoire** f CHIMIE, ELECTROTEC, PHYS ONDES, PHYSIQUE wave mechanics; ~ **quantique** f PHYS PART, PHYSIQUE quantum mechanics; ~ **rationnelle** f CONS MECA rational mechanics; ~ **relativiste** f ESPACE, PHYSIQUE relativistic mechanics; ~ **des roches** f CHARBON rock mechanics; ~ **des sols** f CHARBON, CONSTR, GEOLOGIE soil mechanics

mécanisme m CONS MECA gear, mechanism, MECANIQUE gear; ~ **d'action** m CONS MECA working mechanism; ~ **d'alimentation** m CONS MECA feed magazine, INFORMAT card feed; ~ **d'alimentation en cartes** m INFORMAT card feed; ~ **d'armure** m TEXTILE fashioning mechanism; ~ **asservi** m INFORMAT servomechanism; ~ **d'avance centrifuge** m AUTO centrifugal advance mechanism; ~ **de bande asservi** m TV servo-controlled tape mechanism; ~ **à bascule et à ressort** m PRODUCTION spring and toggle mechanism; ~ **de blocage** m CINEMAT locking mechanism; ~ **casse-fil** m TEXTILE stop motion; ~ **de commande** m INFORMAT actuator, INST HYDR *tiroir ou distributeur de vapeur* valve gear, *vanne* gate gear; ~ **de commande à crémaillère** m NUCLEAIRE rack-and-pinion drive gear; ~ **de commande principal** m INSTRUMENT main drive unit; ~ **de contact** m ESPACE feel mechanism; ~ **de décharge** m EMBALLAGE dumping mechanism; ~ **de déclinaison** m INSTRUMENT declination gear; ~ **de défaillance** m QUALITE failure mechanism; ~ **de déroulement** m TEXTILE let-off motion; ~ **de détente** m TEXTILE let-off motion; ~ **de direction** m VEHICULES steering gear; ~ **de dislocation** m CRISTALL, MATERIAUX dislocation mechanism; ~ **de distribution** m AUTO valve-gear mechanism; ~ **d'élimination alpha** m PHYS RAYON *radiation ionisante* alpha elimination mechanism; ~ **d'enroulement** m TEXTILE take-up motion; ~ **d'entraînement** m CINEMAT drive mechanism, TEXTILE take-away mechanism; ~ **d'entraînement de la bande** m ENREGISTR tape transport; ~ **d'entraînement de bande magnétique** m INFORMAT, ORDINAT tape drive; ~ **d'entraînement du générateur solaire** m ESPACE *véhicules* bearing and power transfer assembly; ~ **d'entraînement à moteur** m ELECTR *réglage* motor-drive mechanism; ~ **de glissement dévié** m MATERIAUX cross-slip mechanism; ~ **d'impression** m IMPRIM printer machine; ~ **indicateur de réglage** m COMMANDE adjustment indicator; ~ **d'inversion de population** m PHYS RAYON *laser à gaz* population inversion mechanism; ~ **de levage** m NUCLEAIRE hogging-ejector hoist; ~ **de manoeuvre** m CONS MECA rig, rigging; ~ **de manoeuvre de la grille** m PRODUCTION grate-shaking rig; ~ **de montée** m CRISTALL, MATERIAUX climb mechanism; ~ **d'ouverture** m EMBALLAGE opening mechanism; ~ **de population laser** m PHYS RAYON laser population mechanism; ~ **de positionnement** m INFORMAT actuator; ~ **pour circulation de colle** m TEXTILE size circulator unit; ~ **régulateur** m CINEMAT governor; ~ **de roue libre** m CONS MECA freewheel mechanism; ~ **à roue libre** m MECANIQUE freewheel mechanism; ~ **de séparation** m ESPACE *véhicules* kick-off mechanism, separation mechanism; ~ **à sûreté intégrée** m SECURITE fail-safe device, fail-to-safety device; ~ **de temporisation interne** m PRODUCTION internal timing mechanism; ~ **de translation** m NUCLEAIRE traversing mechanism; ~ **de transport** m TV transport mechanism; ~ **vireur** m NUCLEAIRE slewing gear, turning gear

mèche f CERAM VER sliver, CINEMAT core, CONS MECA core driver, drill, *cabestan* spindle, *vilebrequin ou perceuse* bit, ESPACE *pyrotechnie* wick, MINES fuse, squib, NAUT *corde* core, TEXTILE rove; ~ **absorbante** f POLLU MER sorbent wick; ~ **de banc à broches** f TEXTILE roving; ~ **à bois** f CONS MECA wood bit; ~ **à centre** f CONS MECA center bit (AmE), centre bit (BrE), center bit for bit stock (AmE), center brace bit (AmE), centre bit for bit stock(BrE), centre brace bit (BrE); ~ **à centrer** f CONS MECA center drill (AmE), centre drill (BrE); ~ **à combustion lente** f MINES slow match, slow-burning fuse; ~ **évidée** f CONS MECA straight-fluted drill; ~ **extensible** f CONS MECA extension bit; ~

de gouvernail *f* NAUT rudder stock; **~ hélicoïdale** *f* CONS MECA twist drill; **~ hélicoïdale à tube d'huile** *f* CONS MECA oil tube twist drill; **~ lente** *f* MINES blasting fuse, safety fuse, slow-burning fuse; **~ de mineur** *f* MINES safety fuse; **~ ordinaire** *f* MINES common fuse, ordinary fuse, safety fuse, ordinary fuse; **~ plate** *f* CONS MECA arrowhead drill, flat drill; **~ pour rocher** *f* CONSTR rock dowel; **~ à queue carrée** *f* CONS MECA center bit for bit stock (AmE), center brace bit (AmE), centre bit for bit stock (BrE), centre brace bit (BrE); **~ de sûreté** *f* MINES blasting fuse, common fuse, ordinary fuse, safety fuse, slow-burning fuse; **~ à trois pointes** *f* CONS MECA center bit (AmE), centre bit (BrE); **~ à verre** *f* CONS MECA glass bit, glass drill; **~ de vilebrequin** *f* CONS MECA bit stock drill, brace bit

méconate *m* CHIMIE meconate

méconine *f* CHIMIE meconin

méconique *adj* CHIMIE meconic

médecine: **~ aérospatiale** *f* ESPACE aerospace medicine

média *m* TV media; **~ physique** *m* TELECOM physical medium

médiane *f* GEOMETRIE, INFORMAT, MATH *statistiques*, ORDINAT median

médiante *f* ACOUSTIQUE mediant

médiatrice *f* PHYS PART *force électromagnétique* mediator

médicamenteux *adj* CHIMIE medicinal

médicinal *adj* CHIMIE medicinal

médimarémètre *m* OCEANO mediamarimeter

médiolittoral *m* OCEANO eulittoral, mesolittoral

médium *m* IMPRIM *encre* medium

méga- *préf (M)* METROLOGIE mega-*(M)*

mégacycle *m* ELECTR *fréquence* megacycle

mégadoc *m* OPTIQUE megadoc

mégadyne *f* METROLOGIE megadyne

mégahertz *m* ELECTR *fréquence*, PETR, TV megahertz

méga-octet *m (Mo)* INFORMAT, ORDINAT megabyte *(Mb)*

mégaparsec *m* ASTRONOMIE megaparsec

mégapuce *f* ELECTRON megachip

mégaride *f* OCEANO sand wave

mégawatt *m (MW)* ELECTR *puissance* megawatt *(MW)*

megger *m* (MD) GEOPHYS Megger (TM)

mégohm *m* ELECTR *unité de résistance*, ELECTROTEC megohm

mégohmmètre *m* ELECTR, ELECTROTEC Megger (TM)

méionite *f* MINERAUX meionite, mionite

mel *m* ACOUSTIQUE, ENREGISTR mel

mélaconite *f* MINERAUX melaconite

mélamine *f* CHIMIE, TEXTILE melamine

mélampyrite *f* CHIMIE melampyrite

mélange:[1] **à ~ pauvre** *adj* AUTO, THERMODYN *moteur* lean-burn

mélange[2] *m* ACOUSTIQUE mixing, AGRO ALIM mixture, mix, CHIMIE mixture, GENIE CHIM mixing technique, IMPRIM melding, PAPIER blend, mixing, PETROLE mixture, PLAST CAOU blend, compound, mix, PRODUCTION compound, mixing, TEXTILE admixture, blend; **~ additionnel** *m* PLAST CAOU *ingrédient* admixture; **~ d'air et de carburant** *m* THERMODYN fuel-air mixture; **~ air-gaz** *m* THERMODYN gas-air mixture; **~ azéotrope** *m* CHIMIE azeotrope; **~ azéotropique** *m* REFRIG azeotropic mixture; **~ colorant** *m* CERAM VER color mix (AmE), colour mix (BrE); **~ de la composition** *m* CERAM VER batch mixing; **~ congélateur** *m*

REFRIG freezing mixture; **~ de couchage** *m* IMPRIM *papier* coating mix; **~ de couleurs** *m* COULEURS color mix (AmE), colour mix (BrE), *opération* color mixing (AmE), colour mixing (BrE), coloring (AmE), colouring (BrE), *résultat* color mixture (AmE), colour mixture (BrE); **~ des couleurs par addition de lumière** *m* PHOTO additive synthesis; **~ des couleurs par soustraction de lumière** *m* PHOTO subtractive synthesis; **~ détonant** *m* AUTO explosive mixture; **~ à dosage variable** *m* AUTO variable mixture; **~ encre-eau provoquant de la mousse sur la plaque** *m* IMPRIM *impression* foaming; **~ frigorifique** *m* PHYSIQUE freezing mixture; **~ à froid** *m* CONSTR asphaltage cold mix; **~ huile-essence** *m* VEHICULES *moteur à deux-temps* gas-oil mixture (AmE), gasoline mixture (AmE), gasoline-oil mixture (AmE), petrol mixture (BrE), petrol-oil mixture (BrE); **~ de matières premières** *m* PAPIER batch; **~ de méthanol** *m* CHIMIE methylated spirits; **~ pauvre** *m* AERONAUT *moteur* lean mixture, AUTO poor mixture, VEHICULES *carburation* lean mixture; **~ à point d'ébullition constante** *m* CHIMIE constant boiling mixture; **~ réfrigérant** *m* REFRIG cooling mixture; **~ respiratoire** *m* OCEANO breathing mixture; **~ riche** *m* AUTO, VEHICULES *carburation* rich mixture; **~ thermique** *m* NUCLEAIRE thermal mixing

mélangeage: **~ sur le chantier** *m* CONSTR mix-in-place; **~ sur place** *m* CONSTR mix-in-place

mélanger *vt* CHIMIE, CONSTR *mortier*, ENREGISTR mix, PAPIER blend, mix, PLAST CAOU, TEXTILE blend

mélangeur[1] *adj* GENIE CHIM mixing

mélangeur[2] *m* CERAM VER batch mixer, blender, CONS MECA chamber, mixer, ELECTRON, ENREGISTR, ESPACE *communications*, GENIE CHIM mixer, PAPIER blender, mixer, PHYSIQUE mixer, PLAST CAOU *matériel* mixer, blender, PRODUCTION mixing plant; **~ actif** *m* CONS MECA active mixer; **~ agitateur** *m* GENIE CHIM agitating mixer; **~ à auge** *m* CERAM VER trough mixer; **~ Banbury** *m* PLAST CAOU *matériel* Banbury mixer; **~ brasseur** *m* GENIE CHIM agitating mixer; **~ à cristal non équilibré** *m* ELECTRON single-ended crystal mixer; **~ à cristal de silicium** *m* ELECTRON silicon crystal mixer; **~ à cylindres** *m* PLAST CAOU *matériel pour fabriquer le caoutchouc* open mill; **~ à diode** *m* ELECTRON diode mixer; **~ discontinu** *m* AGRO ALIM batch mixer; **~ dissolution** *m* PLAST CAOU *matériel pour fabriquer le caoutchouc* solution mixer; **~ d'encre** *m* IMPRIM ink mixer; **~ en discontinu** *m* GENIE CHIM batch mixer; **~ équilibré** *m* ELECTROTEC balanced mixer; **~ harmonique** *m* ELECTRON harmonic mixer; **~ hyperfréquence** *m* ELECTRON microwave mixer; **~ de mesure** *m* TV blanking and sync signal mixer; **~ à meules** *m* PLAST CAOU *peinture, matériel* edge mill; **~ à meules verticales** *m* GENIE CHIM mixing pan mill; **~ de modes** *m* TELECOM mode mixer; **~ ouvert** *m* PLAST CAOU *matériel pour fabriquer le caoutchouc* open mill; **~ à palettes** *m* MINES paddle mixer; **~ de pâte** *m* PLAST CAOU dough mixer; **~ symétrique** *m* ELECTRON, ELECTROTEC balanced mixer; **~ symétrique double** *m* ELECTRON DBM, double-balanced mixer; **~ symétrique simple** *m* ELECTRON single-balanced mixer; **~ à tonneau** *m* AGRO ALIM barrel mixer; **~ vidéo** *m* TV vision mixer

mélangeur-préamplificateur *m* ELECTRON mixer preamplifier

mélangeuse *f* GENIE CHIM mixer

mélanine *f* CHIMIE melanin

mélanite f MINERAUX andradite, melanite

mélanocrate adj GEOLOGIE dark-colored (AmE), dark-coloured (BrE), melanocratic

mélanosome m GEOLOGIE melanosome

mélantérite f MINERAUX melanterite

mélasse f CHIMIE treacle

mélibiose m CHIMIE melibiose

mélilite f MINERAUX melilite

mélinite f MINERAUX melinite

mélinophane f MINERAUX meliphane, meliphanite

méliphanite f MINERAUX meliphane, meliphanite

mélitose m CHIMIE mellitose

mellite m MINERAUX mellite

mellitique adj CHIMIE mellitic

mellon m CHIMIE mellon

membrane f CONS MECA diaphragm, ENREGISTR diaphragm, *haut-parleur* cone, ESPACE *véhicules* membrane; ~ **bitumineuse** f CONSTR bituminous membrane; ~ **de cure** f CONSTR curing membrane; ~ **filtrante** f EQUIP LAB filter membrane, membrane filter (AmE), membrane filtre (BrE); ~ **inférieure** f CONSTR bottom flange; ~ **semiperméable** f PHYSIQUE semipermeable membrane; ~ **synthétique** f CONSTR synthetic membrane

membre m CONS MECA, GEOLOGIE *subdivision d'une formation*, INFORMAT, MATH *équation* member, NAUT rib, timber, ORDINAT member; ~ **de précontrainte** m NUCLEAIRE steel tendon, prestressed tendon

membrure f CONS MECA bracing truss, member, NAUT frame, rib, timber, *de la coque* hull girder

mémo: ~ **rappel** m TELECOM reminder call

mémoire f ELECTROTEC memory, store, INFORMAT storage device, ORDINAT memory, storage (AmE), store (BrE), storagedevice, storage memory; ~ **à accès aléatoire** f ELECTRON, INFORMAT, ORDINAT RAM, random access memory; ~ **à accès direct** f ELECTROTEC direct access memory, INFORMAT, ORDINAT direct access storage; ~ **à accès immédiat** f ORDINAT IAS, immediate access store; ~ **à accès sélectif** f ELECTRON, INFORMAT, ORDINAT RAM, random access memory; ~ **à accès séquentiel** f ORDINAT serial access storage; ~ **associative** f ORDINAT associative memory, associative storage (AmE), associative store (BrE), content-addressable memory, content-addressable storage (AmE), content-addressable store (BrE), parallel search storage (AmE), parallel search store (BrE); ~ **auxiliaire** f ORDINAT auxiliary memory, auxiliary storage (AmE), auxiliary store (BrE), backing storage (AmE), backing store (BrE), secondary memory; ~ **à bulles** f ORDINAT magnetic bubble memory; ~ **à bulles magnétiques** f ELECTROTEC bubble memory, magnetic bubble memory, ORDINAT magnetic bubble memory; ~ **cache** f ORDINAT cache, cache memory; ~ **de commande** f TELECOM control memory; ~ **commune** f ORDINAT shared memory, TELECOM common store; ~ **à condensateur** f ORDINAT capacitor store; ~ **à couche mince** f INFORMAT, ORDINAT thin-film memory; ~ **cryogénique** f ORDINAT cryogenic memory; ~ **descriptive** f BREVETS specification; ~ **à disque** f TELECOM disk store (AmE); ~ **de données** f INFORMAT DM, data memory, ORDINAT DS, data store; ~ **à double accès** f INFORMAT, ORDINAT dual-port memory; ~ **dynamique** f INFORMAT, ORDINAT DRAM, dynamic memory, dynamic random access memory; ~ **effaçable** f INFORMAT, ORDINAT erasable PROM, erasable storage; ~ **électronique** f ELECTROTEC electronic memory; ~ **étendue** f INFORMAT, ORDINAT expanded memory; ~ **externe** f ELECTROTEC external memory, INFORMAT, ORDINAT external memory, external storage; ~ **fixe** f ELECTRON *ordinateur*, ELECTROTEC, INFORMAT, ORDINAT ROM, read-only memory; ~ **de grande capacité** f ORDINAT bulk memory, mass storage; ~ **d'images** f TV frame store; ~ **individuelle** f TELECOM individual store; ~ **ineffaçable** f ORDINAT nonerasable storage; ~ **intégrée** f ELECTROTEC solid-state memory; ~ **intermédiaire** f ELECTROTEC temporary memory, ORDINAT intermediate storage, TELECOM buffer memory; ~ **interne** f ELECTROTEC internal memory, ORDINAT internal memory, internal storage (AmE), internal store (BrE), PRODUCTION internal storage; ~ **des itinéraires** f TELECOM path memory; ~ **de lecture-écriture** f ORDINAT read-write memory; ~ **à lecture majoritaire** f ORDINAT read-mostly memory; ~ **à lecture par laser** f OPTIQUE LO-M, laser-optic memory; ~ **à lignes de retard** f NUCLEAIRE delay-line storage; ~ **magnéto-optique** f OPTIQUE magneto-optic memory; ~ **de masse** f INFORMAT file store, ORDINAT bulk memory, file store, mass storage; ~ **de messages** f TELECOM MS, message store; ~ **de messages EDI** f TELECOM EDI message store, EDI-MS; ~ **morte** f ELECTRON *ordinateur*, ELECTROTEC, INFORMAT, ORDINAT ROM, read-only memory; ~ **morte effaçable électriquement** f ORDINAT EEROM, electrically-erasable ROM; ~ **morte optique** f OPTIQUE optical read-only memory; ~ **nécessaire** f INFORMAT storage requirement; ~ **non rémanente** f ORDINAT volatile memory; ~ **non volatile** f ELECTRON nonvolatile memory; ~ **optique** f ELECTROTEC, OPTIQUE optical memory, ORDINAT optical storage; ~ **optique d'archivage** f OPTIQUE optical storage medium; ~ **optique effaçable** f OPTIQUE alterable optical memory, erasable optical memory, erasable optical storage; ~ **optique inscriptible une seule fois** f OPTIQUE write-once optical storage; ~ **de parole** f TELECOM speech memory; ~ **partagée** f ORDINAT shared memory; ~ **permanente** f ELECTROTEC, ORDINAT permanent memory; ~ **physique** f ELECTROTEC physical memory; ~ **principale** f ORDINAT main memory, main storage (AmE), main store (BrE), primary memory, primary storage (AmE), primary store (BrE); ~ **à propagation** f NUCLEAIRE delay-line storage; ~ **réelle** f ORDINAT real memory; ~ **rémanente** f ORDINAT nonvolatile memory; ~ **de sauvegarde** f ORDINAT auxiliary storage (AmE), auxiliary store (BrE), backing storage (AmE), backing store (BrE), PRODUCTION *automatisme industriel* memory backup; ~ **secondaire** f ORDINAT secondary memory, secondary storage (AmE), secondary store (BrE); ~ **à semi-conducteurs** f ELECTROTEC, ORDINAT semiconductor memory; ~ **série** f ELECTROTEC serial memory, ORDINAT serial storage; ~ **statique** f ELECTROTEC, ORDINAT static memory; ~ **de stockage** f TV memory store; ~ **supraconductrice** f ORDINAT superconducting memory; ~ **à tambour** f TELECOM drum store; ~ **à tambour magnétique** f ELECTROTEC magnetic drum memory; ~ **tampon** f ELECTROTEC buffer memory, IMPRIM, ORDINAT buffer; ~ **temporaire** f TELECOM call store; ~ **à tores** f ELECTROTEC magnetic core memory, ORDINAT core storage (AmE), core store (BrE); ~ **de traduction** f TELECOM translation store; ~ **de trame** f TELECOM speech memory; ~ **de transit** f ORDINAT temporary storage; ~ **de travail** f ORDINAT scratch pad memory, working storage; ~ **utilisable** *f* INFORMAT, ORDINAT usable memory; ~ **virtuelle** *f* ORDINAT virtual memory, virtual storage; ~ **vive** *f (MEV)* ELECTRON, INFORMAT, ORDINAT random access memory *(RAM)*; ~ **volatile** *f* ELECTROTEC, ORDINAT volatile memory

mémorisation *f* INFORMAT, ORDINAT storage; ~ **de don-nées** *f* INFORMAT, ORDINAT data storage; ~ **en parallèle** *f* ELECTROTEC parallel storage; ~ **et retransmission** *f* INFORMAT store and forward; ~ **et retransmission en différé** *f* ORDINAT store and forward; ~ **d'images** *f* ELECTRON, ELECTROTEC image storage; ~ **d'informa-tion** *f* ELECTROTEC data storage, INFORMAT, ORDINAT information storage; ~ **à persistance variable** *f* ELEC-TRON variable persistence storage

mémoriser *vt* ELECTROTEC, INFORMAT, ORDINAT store; ~ **par dessus** *vt* IMPRIM overwrite

menace *f* INFORMAT, ORDINAT threat; ~ **active** *f* TELE-COM active threat; ~ **passive** *f* TELECOM passive threat

ménagement: ~ **de pente** *m* CONSTR grading

ménager: ~ **la pente de** *vt* CONSTR grade

mendélévium *m (Md)* CHIMIE mendelevium *(Md)*

mendipite *f* MINERAUX mendipite

mendozite *f* MINERAUX mendozite

meneau *m* CERAM VER mullion

mener: ~ **à bonne fin** *vt* CONSTR successfully complete

meneur *m* CONS MECA cutter bar

ménilite *f* MINERAUX menilite

ménisque *m* CONSTR, GEOMETRIE meniscus, PHYSIQUE lens, meniscus; ~ **divergent** *m* PHOTO divergent me-niscus

menthane *m* CHIMIE menthane

menthanédiamine *f* CHIMIE menthanediamine

menthanol *m* CHIMIE menthanol

menthanone *f* CHIMIE menthanone

menthène *m* CHIMIE menthene

menthénol *m* CHIMIE menthenol

menthénone *f* CHIMIE menthenone

menthofurane *m* CHIMIE menthofuran

menthol *m* CHIMIE menthol

menthone *f* CHIMIE menthone

menthyle *m* CHIMIE menthyl

mentonnet *m* CONS MECA catch pin, tappet, CONSTR latch catch, latch pin, nosing, *loquet* keeper, *pêne d'une serrure à gorge* stub, stump

menu *m* CHARBON coal slack, coal slake, INFORMAT menu, MINES slack, slack coal, small, small coal, ORDINAT menu; ~ **brut** *m* CHARBON rough pea coal, unwashed small, slack coal, small coal, untreated small; ~ **de charbon** *m* CHARBON culm; ~ **de charbon de bois** *m* CHARBON charcoal duff; ~ **coke** *m* CHARBON coking duff; ~ **de concassage** *m* CHARBON broken rock, crushed material; ~ **déroulant** *m* IMPRIM pull-down menu, INFORMAT, ORDINAT drop-down menu, pulldown menu; ~ **d'écran** *m* INFORMAT, ORDINAT display menu; ~ **en cascade** *m* ORDINAT pop-up menu; ~ **en mode fenêtre** *m* INFORMAT pop-up menu; ~ **des états du système** *m* PRODUCTION *automatisme industriel* system status menu; ~ **de forage** *m* CHAR-BON drilling; ~ **gravier** *m* CONSTR fine gravel; ~ **grenu** *m* CHARBON small coal without fines; ~ **de houille** *m* MINES slack, slack coal, small, small coal; ~ **de houille brut** *m* CHARBON coal bean, untreated small; ~ **lavé** *m* CHARBON washed small; ~ **sortant** *m* CHARBON lump-less small coal

menuiserie *f* CONSTR joinery

menuiseries: ~ **isolantes** *f pl* REFRIG insulated openings

menuisier *m* CONSTR cabinetmaker, joiner

mépacrine *f* CHIMIE mepacrine, quinacrine

méplat[1] *adj* CONSTR flat

méplat[2] *m* ELECTR flat cable, MECANIQUE flat

méplats *m pl* CERAM VER flats

méprobamate *m* CHIMIE meprobamate

mer:[1] **de la** ~ *adj* NAUT maritime; **sur** ~ *adj* NAUT at sea

mer:[2] **en** ~ *adv* NAUT at sea, PETROLE offshore; **par** ~ *adv* NAUT by sea

mer:[3] ~ **agitée** *f* NAUT confused sea, rough sea; ~ **creuse** *f* NAUT rough sea; ~ **croisée** *f* OCEANO confused sea; ~ **debout** *f* NAUT head sea; ~ **épicontinentale** *f* GEOLOGIE epeiric sea, epicontinental sea; ~ **étale** *f* NAUT slack water; ~ **fermée** *f* HYDROLOGIE inland sea, OCEANO closed sea, enclosed sea; ~ **grosse** *f* NAUT rough sea; ~ **houleuse** *f* OCEANO green sea; ~ **libre** *f* NAUT open water; ~ **marginale** *f* GEOLOGIE epicontinental sea, marginal sea, OCEANO marginal sea; ~ **patrimoniale** *f* OCEANO patrimonial sea; ~ **de travers** *f* NAUT beam sea; ~ **du vent** *f* OCEANO wind stress sea, wind-driven sea

merbromine *f* CHIMIE merbromin

mercaptal *m* CHIMIE mercaptal

mercaptan *m* CHIMIE mercaptan, thioalcohol, thiol, PETROLE, PLAST CAOU *additif pour caoutchouc*, POLLU-TION mercaptan

mercaptide *m* CHIMIE mercaptide

mercaptoacétique *adj* CHIMIE mercaptoacetic

mercaptomérine *f* CHIMIE mercaptomerin

mercerisation *f* CHIMIE mercerization

mercuration *f* CHIMIE mercuration

mercure *m* CHIMIE quicksilver, CHIMIE *(Hg)* mercury *(Hg)*; ~ **sulfuré** *m* CHIMIE cinnabar

mercuriel *adj* CHIMIE *onguent* mercurial

mercurification *f* CHIMIE mercurification

mercurique *adj* CHIMIE mercuric

mère *f* ACOUSTIQUE mother, PRODUCTION sow

mère-galerie *f* CHARBON entry, MINES mainway

mère-gueuse *f* PRODUCTION sow

méridien[1] *adj* ESPACE, TELECOM *rayon* meridional

méridien[2] *m* ASTRONOMIE *observatoire* meridian, *planète* meridian, ESPACE meridian; ~ **géomagnétique** *m* GEOPHYS geomagnetic meridian; ~ **magnétique** *m* GEOPHYS, PHYSIQUE magnetic meridian; ~ **origine** *m* ASTRONOMIE prime meridian

méridienne *f* NAUT noon sight

merlin *m* CONSTR *bois* cleaver

merlon *m* ESPACE barricade

méroxène *m* MINERAUX meroxene

mers: ~ **lunaires** *f pl* ASTRONOMIE lunar maria; ~ **du sud** *f pl* OCEANO south seas

mésaconique *adj* CHIMIE mesaconic

mésidine *f* CHIMIE mesidine

mésitylène *m* CHIMIE mesitylene

mésitylénique *adj* CHIMIE mesitylenic

mésolite *f* MINERAUX mesolite

mésomère *adj* CHIMIE mesomeric

mésomérie *f* CHIMIE mesomerism

mésomérique *adj* CHIMIE mesomeric

mésométamorphisme *m* GEOLOGIE *température et pression moyennes* medium-grade metamorphism

méson *m* CHIMIE, PHYS PART, PHYSIQUE meson; ~ **êta** *m* PHYSIQUE eta meson; ~ **êta neutre** *m* PHYS PART eta neutral meson; ~ **K** *m* PHYS PART K-meson; ~ **négatif** *m* PHYS PART negative meson; ~ **pi** *m (pion)* PHYS

PART pi-meson *(pion)*; ~ **positif** *m* PHYS PART positive meson

mésorcine *f* CHIMIE mesorcinol

mésosphère *f* ASTRONOMIE, ESPACE, GEOPHYS mesosphere

mésostructure *f* CRISTALL, MATERIAUX mesostructure

mésotartrique *adj* CHIMIE *acide* mesotartaric

mésothorium *m* CHIMIE mesothorium

mésotype *m* MINERAUX mesotype

mésoxalique *adj* CHIMIE mesoxalic

mésozoïque *m* PETROLE mesozoic

message *m* INFORMAT, ORDINAT, TELECOM message; ~ **d'acceptation de service supplémentaire** *m (SUAC)* TELECOM facility accepted message *(FAA)*; ~ **d'aide** *m* INFORMAT, ORDINAT help message; ~ **d'assignation** *m* TELECOM assignment message; ~ **d'attente d'une commande** *m* INFORMAT, ORDINAT command prompt; ~ **d'avertissement** *m* TRANSPORT warning message; ~ **de contrôle** *m* TELECOM supervisory announcement, supervisory tone; ~ **de demande d'information** *m (IND)* TELECOM information request message *(INR)*; ~ **de demande de service supplémentaire** *m (SUDM)* TELECOM facility request message *(FAR)*; ~ **de diagnostique d'erreur** *m* INFORMAT, ORDINAT diagnostic error message; ~ **EDI** *m* TELECOM EDI message, EDIM; ~ **en réception** *m* ORDINAT incoming message; ~ **entrant** *m* ORDINAT incoming message; ~ **d'erreurs** *m* INFORMAT, ORDINAT, TELECOM error message; ~ **à faire passer** *m* TELECOM PAM, pass-along message; ~ **de gestion de couche liaison consolidé** *m* TELECOM CLLM, consolidated link-layer management message; ~ **d'incohérence** *m* TELECOM confusion message; ~ **inconnu** *m* TELECOM unknown message; ~ **d'information** *m* TELECOM INF, information message; ~ **d'information d'usager à usager** *m* TELECOM user-to-user information message; ~ **intéressant la régularité des vols** *m* AERONAUT flight regularity message; ~ **d'interrogation de groupe de circuits** *m (IGD)* TELECOM circuit group query message *(CQM)*; ~ **de libération** *m (LIB)* TELECOM release message *(REL)*; ~ **de modification d'appel effectuée** *m (MAE)* TELECOM call modification completed message *(CMC)*; ~ **neutralisation-salve** *m* TELECOM blank-and-burst message; ~ **opérateur** *m* INFORMAT, ORDINAT operator message; ~ **par télécopieur** *m* TELECOM facsimile message; ~ **préenregistré** *m* TELECOM prerecorded message; ~ **recommandé** *m* TRANSPORT advisory message; ~ **de refus de modification d'appel** *m (MAR)* TELECOM call modification reject message *(CMRJ)*; ~ **de refus de service supplémentaire** *m (SURF)* TELECOM facility rejected message *(FRJ)*; ~ **de réponse à une interrogation de groupe de circuits** *m (IGR)* TELECOM circuit group query response message *(CQR)*; ~ **routier** *m* TRANSPORT road message; ~ **à segment unique** *m* TELECOM SSM, single segment message; ~ **à un seul segment** *m* TELECOM SSM, single segment message; ~ **de supervision** *m* TELECOM supervisory message

messagerie *f* INFORMAT, ORDINAT messaging, TELECOM MH, message handling, MHS, message handling system; ~ **accélérée** *f* CH DE FER express parcel service; ~ **EDI** *f* TELECOM EDI messaging, EDIMG; ~ **électronique** *f* ELECTRON, INFORMAT EM, electronic mail, electronic messaging, ORDINAT E-mail, EM, electronic mail, electronic messaging, TELECOM E-mail, EM, electronic mail; ~ **vocale** *f* TELECOM voice

messaging

messageries *f pl* CH DE FER small parcels; ~ **maritimes** *f pl* NAUT sea transport, shipping company

messages: ~ **de signalisation** *m pl* TELECOM signaling information (AmE), signalling information (BrE)

mesurage *m* GEOMETRIE mensuration, IMPRIM measuring, METROLOGIE *action* measurement, *terrain* measurement, measuring SECURITE measuring; ~ **et évaluation de l'intensité vibratoire** *m* SECURITE measurement and evaluation of vibration severity; ~ **non répétable** *m* METROLOGIE nonrepeatable measurement; ~ **de la pollution** *m* SECURITE pollution measurement; ~ **répétable** *m* METROLOGIE repeatable measurement; ~ **des vibrations émises par les machines portatives** *m* SECURITE measurement of the vibration produced by portable machines

mesurande *f* METROLOGIE measurand

mesure:[1] **sur** ~ *adj* IMPRIM custom-made, tailor made

mesure[2] *f* ACOUSTIQUE tempo, time, CHIMIE measurement, measuring, ELECTRON measurement, INFORMAT measure, METROLOGIE measure, *action* measurement, ORDINAT measure, PHYS ONDES *longueur d'onde*, PHYS RAYON, SECURITE *bruit ambiant* measurement, TEXTILE yardstick; ~ **agraire** *f* CONSTR land measure; ~ **d'angle** *f* METROLOGIE angle measurement; ~ **à bouts** *f* METROLOGIE end measure; ~ **de capacité pour les liquides** *f* METROLOGIE liquid measure; ~ **à charbon** *f* METROLOGIE *capacité variable* chaldron; ~ **circulaire** *f* GEOMETRIE circular measure; ~ **à coke** *f* METROLOGIE *capacité variable* chaldron; ~ **à coulisse** *f* CONS MECA sliding caliper gage (AmE), sliding calipers (AmE), sliding calliper gauge (BrE), sliding callipers (BrE), METROLOGIE beam caliper (AmE), beam caliper gage (AmE), beam calliper (BrE), beam calliper gauge (BrE); ~ **de distance** *f* ESPACE range finding, ranging; ~ **de dureté Brinell par empreinte de bille** *f* CONS MECA Brinell ball test; ~ **en liaison directe** *f* NUCLEAIRE on-line measurement; ~ **de l'épaisseur des couches** *f* NUCLEAIRE *revêtements* layer thickness gaging (AmE), layer thickness gauging (BrE); ~ **de l'épaisseur de paroi** *f* NUCLEAIRE wall thickness gaging (AmE), wall thickness gauging (BrE); ~ **de l'épaisseur des revêtements** *f* CONS MECA coated thickness measurement; ~ **étalon** *f* METROLOGIE standard measure; ~ **de fréquence instantanée** *f* ELECTRON IFM, instantaneous frequency measurement; ~ **de géodésie** *f* CONSTR geodesic survey, geodetic survey; ~ **géophysique** *f* GAZ geophysical measurement; ~ **d'une grandeur dépassant sa valeur de référence** *f* INST HYDR effective head; ~ **de la grosseur des particules** *f* PLAST CAOU *charges, pigments* particle size measurement; ~ **à large bande** *f* ELECTRON wide band measurement; ~ **linéaire** *f* METROLOGIE long measure; ~ **de longueur** *f* METROLOGIE long measure; ~ **de lumière réfléchie** *f* CINEMAT reflected light reading; ~ **numérique de la fréquence instantanée** *f* ELECTRON digital instantaneous frequency measurement; ~ **d'une once et demie** *f* TEXTILE jigger; ~ **des paramètres géométriques d'état de surface** *f* CONS MECA surface texture measurement; ~ **de poids** *f* METROLOGIE weight; ~ **du point de rosée** *f* CERAM VER dew point measurement; ~ **pondérale** *f* METROLOGIE weight; ~ **du pouvoir absorbant** *f* PRODUCTION zone test; ~ **de précaution** *f* SECURITE precautionary measure; ~ **de pression** *f* ESPACE *véhicules* pressure measurement; ~ **aux radionucléides** *f* CHARBON isotope measurement; ~ **de rayonnement** *f* PHYS RAYON radiation measurement; ~ **à rétrodiffusion** *f* NUCLEAIRE backscatter gage (AmE), backscatter gauge (BrE); ~ **roulante** *f* METEO spring tape rule; ~ **à ruban** *f* METEO spring tape rule, METROLOGIE measure, measuring tape, tape measure; ~ **à ruban d'arpenteur** *f* CONSTR surveyor's tape; ~ **scalaire** *f* ELECTROTEC scalar measurement; ~ **de sécurité contre la propagation d'incendie** *f* SECURITE fire spread prevention; ~ **de superficie** *f* METROLOGIE square measure; ~ **de surface** *f* METROLOGIE square measure; ~ **de taux d'erreurs** *f* TELECOM error rate measurement; ~ **de volume** *f* METROLOGIE cubic measure, solid measure

mesure:[3] **être de ~** *vi* CONSTR be to size

mesurer *vt* CHIMIE, METROLOGIE measure, TEXTILE gage (AmE), gauge (BrE); ~ **au mètre** *vt* METROLOGIE measure

mesures: ~ **anticorrosives** *f pl* EMBALLAGE corrosion prevention; ~ **différentielles de correction** *f pl* NAUT differential corrections; ~ **en cours de forage** *f pl* PETROLE MWD, measurements while drilling; ~ **fixes** *f pl* CERAM VER cut sizes; ~ **de fond** *f pl* PETROLE downhole measurements; ~ **libres** *f pl* CERAM VER stock sheets (AmE), stock sizes (BrE); ~ **magnétiques** *f pl* ASTRONOMIE magnetic measurements; ~ **de profil des raies** *f pl* PHYS RAYON *raies spectrales* line profile measurements; ~ **de secours** *f pl* SECURITE emergency measures; ~ **de sécurité** *f pl* COMMANDE, QUALITE, SECURITE safety measures; ~ **de sécurité contre l'incendie** *f pl* SECURITE fire prevention

mesureur *m* AERONAUT distance-measuring equipment, ELECTR instrument; ~ **de distorsion** *m* ENREGISTR distortion meter; ~ **d'isolation** *m* ELECTR insulation tester; ~ **du niveau sonore** *m* ENREGISTR sound level meter; ~ **de résistance** *m* ELECTR resistance meter; ~ **de terre** *m* ELECTR earth leakage meter (BrE), ground leakage meter (AmE)

métabasite *f* GEOLOGIE *roche basique métamorphisée* metabasic rock, metabasite

métabisulfite *m* CHIMIE metabisulfite (AmE), metabisulphite (BrE)

métaborate *m* CHIMIE metaborate

métaborique *adj* CHIMIE metaboric

métacentre *m* NAUT, PHYSIQUE metacenter (AmE), metacentre (BrE); ~ **latitudinal** *m* NAUT transverse metacenter (AmE), transverse metacentre (BrE); ~ **longitudinal** *m* NAUT longitudinal metacenter (AmE), longitudinal metacentre (BrE); ~ **transversal** *m* NAUT transverse metacenter (AmE), transverse metacentre (BrE)

métachlorite *f* MINERAUX metachlorite

métachlorotoluène *m* CHIMIE metachlorotoluene

métacrésol *m* CHIMIE metacresol

métacrylique *adj* CHIMIE metacrylic

métadyne *f* ELECTRON metadyne

métal *m* PRODUCTION metal; ~ **alcalin** *m* METALL alkali metal; ~ **alcalino-terreux** *m* MATERIAUX, METALL alkaline-earth metal; ~ **d'alliage** *m* CONSTR filler alloy, filler metal; ~ **d'apport** *m* CONSTR, MECANIQUE, PRODUCTION *soudage* filler metal; ~ **Babbitt** *m* METALL Babbitt's metal;~ **de base** *m* METALL bare metal; ~ **cassant** *m* MATERIAUX brittle metal; ~ **déployé** *m* MECANIQUE expanded metal; ~ **dumet** *m* MATERIAUX duplex metal; ~ **en fusion** *m* SECURITE molten metal; ~ **en gueuse** *m* PRODUCTION pig metal; ~ **en saumon** *m* PRODUCTION pig metal; ~ **fondu** *m* MATERIAUX molten

metal; ~ **hexagonal** *m* MATERIAUX hexagonal metal; ~ **liquide** *m* CHARBON, MATERIAUX liquid metal; ~ **lourd** *m* CHARBON, PHYS RAYON, RECYCLAGE heavy metal; ~ **mort** *m* IMPRIM *clicherie stéréo* bearers; ~ **noble** *m* METALL, POLLUTION noble metal; ~ **précieux en barres** *m* METALL bullion; ~ **précieux en lingots** *m* METALL bullion; ~ **récupéré** *m* MATERIAUX secondary metal; ~ **réfractaire** *m* METALL refractory metal; ~ **de soudure** *m* METALL weld metal; ~ **de transition** *m* METALL transition metal

métalangage *m* ORDINAT metalanguage

métaldéhyde *m* CHIMIE metaldehyde

métallation *f* CHIMIE metalation (AmE), metallation (BrE)

métallifère *adj* CHIMIE metaliferous (AmE), metalliferous (BrE), MINES ore-bearing

métallin *adj* CHIMIE metaline (AmE), metalline (BrE)

métallisable *adj* REVETEMENT electroplatable; ~ **par galvanisation** *adj* REVETEMENT electroplatable

métallisage *m* PRODUCTION metalization (AmE), metallization (BrE)

métallisation *f* CERAM VER metalizing (AmE), metallizing (BrE), CONS MECA metal coating, CONSTR, ELECTRON metalization (AmE), metallization (BrE), ESPACE *véhicules* bonding, metalization (AmE), metallization (BrE), MATERIAUX, PHYSIQUE metalization (AmE), metallization (BrE), PRODUCTION bonding, metal coating, metalization (AmE), metallization (BrE), REVETEMENT metal coating; ~ **électrolytique** *f* ELECTR *procédé* electroplating; ~ **sous vide** *f* CERAM VER vacuum metallizing, ELECTRON vacuum metallization, THERMODYN vapor deposition (AmE), vapour deposition (BrE); ~ **spéculaire** *f* CERAM VER mirror-plating

métallisé *adj* PRODUCTION metal-coated, REVETEMENT electroplated, metal-faced

métalliser *vt* MECANIQUE plate, REVETEMENT metal-coat; ~ **par galvanisation** *vt* REVETEMENT electroplate

métallochimie *f* CHIMIE chemicometallurgy

métallochimique *adj* CHIMIE chemicometallurgical

métallogénétique *adj* MATERIAUX metallogenetic (BrE), metalogenetic (AmE)

métallographie *f* METALL metallography (BrE), metalography (AmE); ~ **en couleurs** *f* METALL color metallography (AmE), colour metallography (BrE); ~ **par rayons X** *f* NUCLEAIRE X-ray metallography, roentgenometallography

métalloïde *m* CHIMIE metalloid (BrE), metaloid (AmE)

métalloïdique *adj* CHIMIE metalloidal (BrE), metaloidal (AmE)

métalloscope *m* CONS MECA magnetic crack detector

métamère *adj* CHIMIE metameric

métamérie *f* CHIMIE metamerism

métamicte *adj* GEOLOGIE metamict

métamorphisme: ~ **de contact** *m* GEOLOGIE contact metamorphism; ~ **dynamique** *m* EN RENOUV dynamic metamorphism; ~ **général** *m* GEOLOGIE burial metamorphism, load metamorphism; ~ **isochimique** *m* GEOLOGIE isochemical metamorphism; ~ **prograde** *m* GEOLOGIE prograde metamorphism; ~ **régional** *m* EN RENOUV regional metamorphism; ~ **rétrograde** *m* EN RENOUV retrograde metamorphism; ~ **topochimique** *m* GEOLOGIE *sans changement de composition* isochemical metamorphism

métanilique *adj* CHIMIE *acide* metanilic

métaphosphate *m* CHIMIE metaphosphate

métaphosphorique *adj* CHIMIE metaphosphoric

métarsénieux *adj* CHIMIE metarsenious

métasédiment *m* GEOLOGIE metasediment

métasilicate *m* CHIMIE bisilicate; **~ de plomb** *m* CERAM VER lead silicate

métasilicique *adj* CHIMIE metasilicic

métasomatose *f* GEOLOGIE metasomatism; **~ de contact** *f* GEOLOGIE contact metasomatism

métastabilité *f* MATERIAUX metastability

métastable *adj* PHYS RAYON metastable

métastannique *adj* CHIMIE metastannic

métaux: **~ lourds** *m pl* POLLUTION heavy metal

métaxite *f* MINERAUX metaxite

météore *m* ASTRONOMIE, ESPACE, METEO meteor; **~ radioélectrique** *m* GEOPHYS electrometeor

météorite *f* ASTRONOMIE meteorite, ESPACE meteorite, meteoroid; **~ Allende** *f* ASTRONOMIE Allende meteorite; **~ ferreuse** *f* ASTRONOMIE iron meteorite; **~ pierreuse** *f* ASTRONOMIE stony meteorite, ESPACE aerolite

météoroïde *m* ASTRONOMIE meteoroid

météorologie *f* AERONAUT, NAUT meteorology; **~ spatiale** *f* ESPACE satellite meteorology

méthacrylate *m* PLAST CAOU methacrylate

méthacrylique *adj* CHIMIE methacrylic

méthadone *f* CHIMIE methadone, phenadone

méthanal *m* CHIMIE methanal

méthanation *f* GAZ methanation

méthane *m* CHIMIE methane, methane gas, GAZ, METEO, PETROLE, SECURITE methane, THERMODYN firedamp

méthanier *m* NAUT methane carrier, PETROLE NGL tanker, natural gas liquids tanker, methane tanker, THERMODYN LNG-LPG carrier, liquefied natural gas and liquefied petroleum gas carrier, TRANSPORT LNG carrier, liquid natural gas carrier, methane carrier; **~ à cuve autoporteuse** *m* TRANSPORT methane carrier with self-supporting tank

méthanol:[1] **dans le ~** *adj* CHIMIE methanolic

méthanol[2] *m* CHIMIE, GAZ methanol

méthénamine *f* CHIMIE methenamine

méthimazole *m* CHIMIE methimazol

méthionique *adj* CHIMIE methionic

méthode *f* CHIMIE method, CONSTR way, IMPRIM, PHYSIQUE method, PRODUCTION mode, procedure, way; **~ d'accès** *f* ORDINAT access method; **~ d'accès avec file d'attente** *f* INFORMAT queued access method; **~ d'acheminement** *f* CH DE FER method of routing; **~ additive** *f* CINEMAT, ELECTRON additive method; **~ d'alignement en gravure par faisceau d'électrons** *f* ELECTRON electron beam alignment method; **~ d'alliage** *f* ELECTRON alloying method; **~ du bain de sulfate de manganèse** *f* NUCLEAIRE manganous sulfate bath method (AmE), manganous sulphate bath method (BrE); **~ de calcul par éléments finis** *f* MECANIQUE finite element calculation method; **~ du canon à air** *f* GEOPHYS air gun exploration method; **~ du champ réfracté proche** *f* OPTIQUE refracted near-field method, TELECOM refracted near-end method, refracted ray method; **~ du chemin critique** *f* ORDINAT CPM, critical path method; **~ de compensation** *f* PHYSIQUE null method; **~ de coupe et de couverture** *f* CONSTR cut and cover method; **~ du cristal rotatif** *f* PHYS RAYON rotating crystal method; **~ à deux bains** *f* NUCLEAIRE *décontamination* two-bath method; **~ de développement nodal** *f* NUCLEAIRE nodal expansion method; **~ de diffusion diffuse** *f* NUCLEAIRE diffuse scattering method; **~ en champ diffus** *f* ENREGISTR diffuse field method; **~ en long** *f* MINES flat back stoping method, longwall stoping; **~ essai-erreur** *f* CRISTALL trial and error method; **~ d'essai à pénétration** *f* NUCLEAIRE penetration test method; **~ d'estimation du prix de revient** *f* CONS MECA method of costing; **~ d'exploration du champ réfracté proche** *f* OPTIQUE refracted near-field method, TELECOM refracted near-end method, refracted ray method; **~ d'exploration magnétique** *f* GEOPHYS magnetic method; **~ de fabrication** *f* ELECTRON fabrication technique; **~ du faisceau lumineux réfléchi** *f* ACOUSTIQUE Buchmann and Meyer pattern, backscattered light beam method; **~ de la fibre coupée** *f* OPTIQUE cutback fiber technique (AmE), cutback fibre technique (BrE), TELECOM cutback technique; **~ de flottation** *f* PETR flotation method; **~ d'intégrale de Rice** *f* NUCLEAIRE J-integral method, Rice integral method; **~ interférentielle** *f* CONS MECA *mesure* interference method; **~ itérative** *f* INFORMAT, ORDINAT iterative method; **~ de Kjeldahl** *f* NUCLEAIRE Kjeldahl method; **~ de Laue** *f* CRISTALL Laue method; **~ de longwall** *f* CHARBON longwall system; **~ de mesure par zéro** *f* ELECTR null method; **~ de mesure de référence** *f* OPTIQUE, TELECOM RTM, reference test method; **~ de mesure de remplacement** *f* OPTIQUE practical test method, *optique des fibres* ATM, RTM, alternative testmethod, reference test method, TELECOM practical test method; **~ de métrage** *f* CONSTR method of measurement; **~ micrographique** *f* CONS MECA *analyse des matériaux* micrographic method; **~ de minéralisation Kjeldahl** *f* CHIMIE Kjeldahl method; **~ des moindres carrés** *f* CRISTALL, MATH, PHYSIQUE least squares method; **~ de Monte-Carlo** *f* ORDINAT Monte Carlo method; **~ des ondes déformées** *f* NUCLEAIRE distorted wave method; **~ d'oscillation du cristal** *f* PHYS RAYON *diffraction de rayons X* oscillating crystal method; **~ d'oxydation par le minerai** *f* PRODUCTION ore process; **~ par dilution** *f* PRODUCTION ore process, scrap process; **~ par transmission** *f* ESSAIS, NUCLEAIRE transmission technique; **~ planar** *f* ELECTRON planar process; **~ du planning PERT** *f* COMMANDE, PRODUCTION PERT, program evaluation and review technique; **~ possible pour les mesures** *f* OPTIQUE alternative test method; **~ quasi albédo** *f* NUCLEAIRE quasi-albedo approach; **~ de recyclage** *f* RECYCLAGE recycling method; **~ de réduction au zéro** *f* PHYSIQUE null method; **~ de réflexion en retour** *f* CRISTALL back reflection method; **~ de réflexion de Fresnel** *f* TELECOM Fresnel reflection method; **~ de rétrodiffusion** *f* TELECOM backscattering technique; **~ de rétrodiffusion gamma** *f* NUCLEAIRE gamma backscatter method, reflection method; **~ de rétroréflexion** *f* CRISTALL back reflection method; **~ de sectionnement** *f* NUCLEAIRE *couches minces* sectioning technique; **~ de la sonde d'or** *f* NUCLEAIRE gold probe method; **~ soustractive** *f* ELECTRON subtractive method; **~ des sphères d'action d'influence** *f* ESPACE *mécanique* matched conics technique; **~ sur poudre calibrée** *f* CERAM VER grain test; **~ tir au but** *f* CH DE FER *véhicules* fly shunting; **~ de transmission** *f* ESSAIS, NUCLEAIRE *analyse par radiocristallographie* transmission technique; **~ triangulaire** *f* AGRO ALIM triangle test, triangle testing; **~ de vapeur atomique** *f* NUCLEAIRE atomic vapor method (AmE), atomic vapour method (BrE)

méthodes: ~ **d'échantillonnage** *f pl* QUALITE sampling methods; ~ **des éléments finis** *f pl* CONS MECA *dynamique structurale* finite elements methods; ~ **de travail sûres** *f pl* SECURITE safe methods of working, safe working practices

méthodologie: ~ **ascendante** *f* INFORMAT, ORDINAT bottom-up methodology; ~ **descendante** *f* INFORMAT, ORDINAT top-down methodology

méthol *m* CHIMIE methol

méthoxyle *m* CHIMIE methoxyl

méthylal *m* CHIMIE methylal

méthylamine *f* CHIMIE methylamine

méthylaniline *f* CHIMIE methylaniline

méthylate *m* CHIMIE methylate

méthylation *f* CHIMIE methylation

méthylcellosolve *m* CHIMIE methoxyethanol

méthyle *m* CHIMIE methyl

méthyler *vt* CHIMIE *dénaturer l'alcool* methylate

méthyléthylcétone *m* CHIMIE methyl ethyl ketone

méthyléthylcétoxime *m* PLAST CAOU *additif de peinture* methyl ethyl ketoxime

méthylique *adj* CHIMIE methylic

méthylnaphtalène *m* CHIMIE methylnaphthalene

méthylpentose *m* CHIMIE methylpentose

méthylpropane *m* CHIMIE methylpropane

métier *m* TEXTILE loom; ~ **chaîne** *m* TEXTILE warp-knitting machine; ~ **continu à ailettes** *m* TEXTILE flyer-spinning frame; ~ **continu à anneaux** *m* TEXTILE ring-spinning frame; ~ **à filer à cloches** *m* TEXTILE cap spinning frame; ~ **à filet** *m* OCEANO netting frame; ~ **jacquard** *m* TEXTILE Jacquard loom; ~ **à navette** *m* TEXTILE fly shuttle loom; ~ **non automatique** *m* TEXTILE nonautomatic loom; ~ **Raschel** *m* TEXTILE Raschel knitting machine; ~ **rectiligne** *m* TEXTILE flat knitting machine

métol *m* CHIMIE metol

métrage *m* CINEMAT film length, footage, CONSTR measurement of quantities, METROLOGIE measurement, measuring, survey, surveying, TEXTILE yardage

métré *m* CONSTR measurement of quantities

mètre *m* METROLOGIE measure, meter (AmE), metre (BrE); ~ **carré** *m* METROLOGIE square meter (AmE), square metre (BrE); ~ **cube** *m* MATH, METROLOGIE cubic meter (AmE), cubic metre (BrE); ~ **cube normal** *m* PETR normal cubic meter (AmE), normal cubic metre (BrE); ~ **géopotentiel** *m* GEOPHYS geopotential meter; ~ **pliant** *m* METEO folding rule; ~ **à retrait** *m* PRODUCTION contraction rule, shrink rule; ~ **à ruban** *m* MECANIQUE *outillage* tape measure, METROLOGIE measure, measuring tape, tape measure

mètre-étalon *m* PHYSIQUE standard meter (AmE), standard metre (BrE)

métrer *vt* METROLOGIE measure

métreur *m* CONSTR quantity surveyor, METROLOGIE surveyor

métreuse *f* CINEMAT footage counter

métrique *adj* INFORMAT metric, METROLOGIE metric, metrical, ORDINAT metric

métro *m* CH DE FER subway (AmE), underground (BrE); ~ **aérien** *m* TRANSPORT EL, elevated line, overhead railway, elevated rapid transit system; ~ **avec stabilisation au-dessus du véhicule** *m* TRANSPORT top-stabilized rapid transit system; ~ **léger** *m* CH DE FER LRT, light rail transport (BrE), light rail transit (AmE); ~ **urbain et régional** *m* TRANSPORT rapid transit railroad (AmE), rapid transit railway (BrE),

urban and regional metropolitan railroad (AmE), urban and regional metropolitan railway (BrE)

métrologie *f* ESSAIS metrology

métropolitain *m* TRANSPORT metropolitan railroad (AmE), metropolitan railway (BrE); ~ **sur pneumatiques** *m* TRANSPORT pneumatic-tired metropolitan railroad (AmE), pneumatic-tyred metropolitan railway (BrE)

metteur: ~ **en scène** *m* CINEMAT film director

mettre[1] *vt* MECANIQUE adjust; ~ **à l'abri** *vt* CONSTR put under cover; ~ **à la bande** *vt* NAUT *navire* cant; ~ **à bord** *vt* NAUT put on board; ~ **le cap sur** *vt* NAUT head for; ~ **la dernière main à** *vt* PRODUCTION give the finishing touches to; ~ **un diffuseur sur** *vt* CINEMAT *lumières* trim; ~ **une doublure à** *vt* TEXTILE interline; ~ **une doublure intermédiaire à** *vt* TEXTILE interline; ~ **à l'eau** *vt* NAUT *navire* launch; ~ **à l'échelle** *vt* INFORMAT, ORDINAT scale; ~ **en alerte** *vt* POLLU MER *navire* put on standby; ~ **en attente** *vt* TELECOM put on hold; ~ **en balle** *vt* EMBALLAGE bale; ~ **en boîte** *vt* CINEMAT *pellicule* can; ~ **en botte** *vt* PAPIER bundle; ~ **en cale sèche** *vt* NAUT *navire* dry-dock; ~ **en caractères gras** *vt* IMPRIM embolden; ~ **en carène** *vt* NAUT *navire* careen; ~ **en circuit** *vt* ELECTROTEC close, switch in, switch on, turn on, TV switch on; ~ **en communication** *vt* ELECTROTEC connect, TELECOM put through; ~ **en conduction** *vt* ELECTROTEC turn on; ~ **en conserve** *vt* AGRO ALIM preserve, EMBALLAGE can; ~ **en conteneur** *vt* EMBALLAGE containerize; ~ **en court-circuit** *vt* ELECTROTEC short, PRODUCTION short out; ~ **en dépôt** *vt* CONSTR stockpile; ~ **en feu** *vt* PRODUCTION *haut fourneau* blow in; ~ **en flamme** *vt* THERMODYN burn; ~ **en forme** *vt* INFORMAT, ORDINAT edit; ~ **en garde** *vt* TELECOM *appel* put on hold; ~ **en interface** *vt* PRODUCTION interface; ~ **en large** *vt* TEXTILE *tissu* keep at open width; ~ **en marche** *vt* CONS MECA set in motion, start, start up, ELECTROTEC turn on, TV play; ~ **en mémoire** *vt* ELECTROTEC store; ~ **en mémoire tampon** *vt* ORDINAT buffer; ~ **en mouvement** *vt* CONS MECA set in motion; ~ **en oeuvre** *vt* BREVETS work, CONS MECA implement, *machine* set to work, IMPRIM actuate; ~ **en opération** *vt* PRODUCTION put into operation; ~ **en page** *vt* IMPRIM make up; ~ **en palier** *vt* AERONAUT level out; ~ **en perce** *vt* AGRO ALIM tap; ~ **en place** *vt* CINEMAT *caméra* set up, CONSTR lay, *béton pour, canalisation* lay; ~ **en pression** *vt* PRODUCTION get up steam; ~ **en quarantaine** *vt* TRANSPORT quarantine; ~ **en rade** *vt* NAUT lay up; ~ **en relief** *vt* IMPRIM accentuate, enhance; ~ **en repérage** *vt* IMPRIM *impression* line up; ~ **en route** *vt* CONS MECA set in motion, start, start up; ~ **en scène** *vt* CINEMAT direct; ~ **en service** *vt* CONSTR commission, INST HYDR *machine à vapeur* bar; ~ **en tablette** *vt* IMPRIM pad; ~ **en tas** *vt* CONSTR bank, PRODUCTION stack; ~ **en température** *vt* THERMODYN heat up; ~ **en train** *vt* CONS MECA set in motion, start, start up; ~ **entre crochets** *vt* IMPRIM bracket; ~ **en valeur** *vt* AGRO ALIM enhance, IMPRIM *composition* outline, *mise en page* bring up; ~ **en vedette** *vt* IMPRIM highlight; ~ **en veilleuse** *vt* ELECTROTEC power down; ~ **à l'état initial** *vt* ELECTRON initialize; ~ **à la ferraille** *vt* MECANIQUE scrap; ~ **à feu** *vt* ESPACE *propulsion* ignite, PRODUCTION *haut fourneau* blow in; ~ **le feu à** *vt* THERMODYN kindle, set fire to, set ablaze; ~ **à flot** *vt* NAUT launch, PHYSIQUE float; ~ **hors circuit** *vt* ELECTROTEC break, isolate, power down, switch off, turn off, TV switch off; ~ **hors feu** *vt* PRODUCTION *haut* *fourneau* blow out; **~ hors service** *vt* ELECTROTEC disable; **~ hors tension** *vt* ELECTROTEC power down; **~ à jour** *vt* CONS MECA bring up to date, INFORMAT, ORDINAT update; **~ à la masse** *vt* ELECTR *raccordement*, ELECTROTEC, PHYSIQUE, TELECOM, VEHICULES *système électrique* earth (BrE), ground (AmE); **~ à la mer** *vt* NAUT *embarcations* lower, *navire* launch; **~ de niveau** *vt* CINEMAT level; **~ à niveau** *vt* CONSTR, MECANIQUE level; **~ au point** *vt* CONS MECA *projet*, CONSTR develop, INFORMAT debug, METROLOGIE *microscope* adjust, ORDINAT debug, PHOTO, PHYSIQUE focus, PRODUCTION *foret* bring into position for use; **~ au point zéro** *vt* COMMANDE zero reset, zero; **~ à poste** *vt* NAUT stow; **~ au rebut** *vt* CONSTR throw back to waste, PRODUCTION scrap; **~ sous forme irréductible** *vt* MATH *fraction* reduce to its lowest terms; **~ sous forme numérique** *vt* ELECTRON digitize; **~ sous pression** *vt* PRODUCTION get up steam, REFRIG pressurize; **~ sous tension** *vt* ELECTR *appareil* switch on, ELECTROTEC apply power to, energize, power up, turn on, PRODUCTION *matériel* turn on; **~ sur microfiche** *vt* INFORMAT, ORDINAT fiche; **~ sur orbite** *vt* ESPACE send into orbit; **~ à la terre** *vt* ELECTR *raccordement*, ELECTROTEC, TELECOM, VEHICULES *système électrique* earth (BrE), ground (AmE); **~ à terre** *vt* NAUT put ashore; **~ à un** *vt* INFORMAT *bit* set, PRODUCTION turn on; **~ à la valeur initiale** *vt* ORDINAT initialize; **~ à zéro** *vt* COMMANDE zero, zero reset, PRODUCTION turn off, *bit* set

mettre:[2] **~ le cap au nord** *vi* NAUT stand to the north; **~ en panne** *vi* NAUT heave to; **~ les gaz** *vi* AERONAUT advance the throttle; **~ au point sur l'infini** *vi* PHOTO focus for infinity; **~ au sec** *vi* NAUT ground; **~ à zéro** *vi* PRODUCTION *bit* reset

mettre:[3] **se ~ à la cape** *v réfl* NAUT heave to; **se ~ côte à côte** *v réfl* NAUT go alongside; **se ~ en grumeaux** *v réfl* AGRO ALIM cake; **se ~ en panne** *v réfl* NAUT heave to; **se ~ en tas** *v réfl* CONSTR bank, bank up

meuble[1] *adj* CHARBON *roche* fragmented, loose

meuble[2] *m* TELECOM suite of switchboards; **~ cuisine** *m* AERONAUT galley; **~ cuisine de bord** *m* AERONAUT galley; **~ manuel** *m* TELECOM manual board; **~ mécanicien** *m* AERONAUT flight engineer's panel; **~ office de bord** *m* AERONAUT galley; **~ réfrigéré** *m* REFRIG refrigeration cabinet; **~ téléphonique** *m* TELECOM telephone switchboard

meulage *m* MECANIQUE, PLAST CAOU *procédé*, PRODUCTION grinding; **~ à l'eau** *m* RESSORTS wet grinding; **~ des extrémités de ressort** *m* RESSORTS spring end grinding; **~ sec** *m* RESSORTS dry grinding

meule *f* AGRO ALIM grinder, millstone, CERAM VER grinding wheel, CONS MECA abrasive wheel, grinding wheel, wheel, MECANIQUE *outillage* abrasive wheel, grinding wheel, PAPIER grindstone, PRODUCTION grinding wheel, sharpening wheel, SECURITE abrasive wheel; **~ à affûter** *f* PRODUCTION grinding wheel, sharpening wheel; **~ affûteuse** *f* PRODUCTION grinding wheel, sharpening wheel; **~ à aiguiser** *f* PRODUCTION grinding wheel, sharpening wheel; **~ aléseuse** *f* PRODUCTION internal grinding wheel; **~ avec liant de résine synthétique** *f* CONS MECA resin-bonded wheel; **~ à base de diamant** *f* CONS MECA diamond grinding-wheel; **~ à base de nitrure de bore** *f* CONS MECA cubic boron nitride grinding-wheel; **~ boisseau** *f* PRODUCTION cup wheel; **~ courante** *f* AGRO ALIM upper millstone; **~ à cuvette** *f* PRODUCTION dished wheel; **~ à dégrossir** *f* CONS MECA rough grinding-wheel, PRO-

DUCTION roughing wheel; **~ de dégrossissage** *f* INSTRUMENT roughing wheel; **~ diamantée** *f* CONS MECA diamond grinding-wheel; **~ dure** *f* PRODUCTION hard wheel; **~ à ébarber** *f* CONS MECA trimming wheel; **~ émeri** *f* MECANIQUE *outillage*, PRODUCTION emery wheel; **~ en Carborundum** *f* (MD) PRODUCTION Carborundum wheel (TM); **~ en corindon** *f* PRODUCTION corundum wheel; **~ encrassée** *f* PRODUCTION loaded wheel; **~ en émeri** *f* PRODUCTION emery wheel; **~ en grès** *f* PRODUCTION grindstone; **~ de finition** *f* INSTRUMENT fining lap; **~ à grain fin** *f* PRODUCTION fine-grained wheel; **~ à lamelles abrasives** *f* CONS MECA abrasive flap wheel; **~ lapidaire** *f* PRODUCTION face wheel; **~ au nitrure de bore** *f* CONS MECA cubic boron nitride grinding wheel; **~ à noyau rentrant** *f* CONS MECA tub wheel, PRODUCTION cup wheel; **~ à polir** *f* PRODUCTION polishing wheel; **~ de polissage** *f* CERAM VER polishing wheel; **~ à rectifier** *f* CONS MECA truing wheel; **~ de remouleur** *f* PRODUCTION grinding wheel; **~ à satiner** *f* CONS MECA satin-finishing wheel; **~ de taille** *f* CERAM VER cutting wheel; **~ tendre** *f* PRODUCTION soft wheel; **~ tournante** *f* AGRO ALIM upper millstone; **~ travaillant sur face** *f* PRODUCTION face wheel; **~ à tronçonner** *f* CONS MECA cutoff wheel, cutting-off wheel; **~ à user** *f* PRODUCTION abrading wheel, reducing wheel; **~ verticale** *f* PRODUCTION edge runner, edge wheel, edgestone

meulé *adj* RESSORTS ground

meule-boisseau *f* CONS MECA tub wheel

meuler *vt* MECANIQUE, PRODUCTION grind

meuleton *m* PAPIER edge runner, kollergang

meuleuse: ~ à double arête *f* CERAM VER double edge grinder

meulière *f* GEOLOGIE cherty limestone, PRODUCTION millstone grit

meunerie *f* AGRO ALIM milling, milling industry

meurtrissure *f* AGRO ALIM bruise

MEV *abrév* (*mémoire vive*) ELECTRON, INFORMAT, ORDINAT RAM (*random access memory*)

MF *abrév* (*modulation de fréquence*) ELECTR, ELECTRON, ENREGISTR, ORDINAT, PHYS ONDES, PHYSIQUE, TELECOM, TV FM (*frequency modulation*)

mg *abrév* (*milligramme*) METROLOGIE mg (*milligram*)

Mg (*magnésium*) CHIMIE Mg (*magnesium*)

MHD *abrév* (*magnétohydrodynamique*) ELECTROTEC, ESPACE, GEOPHYS MHD (*magnetohydrodynamic*)

MIA *abrév* (*modulation d'impulsions en amplitude*) ELECTRON, ESPACE, INFORMAT, ORDINAT, TELECOM PAM (*pulse amplitude modulation*)

miargyrite *f* MINERAUX miargyrite

MIC *abrév* (*modulation par impulsion et codage, modulation par impulsion codée*) ELECTRON, ESPACE, INFORMAT, ORDINAT, PHYS RAYON, PHYSIQUE, TV PCM (*pulse code modulation*)

mica *m* CERAM VER, CHIMIE, ELECTR *diélectrique, isolateur*, ELECTROTEC, MATERIAUX, MINERAUX, PETR, PLAST CAOU *matière première* mica; **~ magnésien** *m* CERAM VER biotite; **~ moscovite** *m* PLAST CAOU *matière première* white mica; **~ vitrifié** *m* ELECTROTEC glass-bonded mica

micacé *adj* GEOLOGIE micaceous

micaschiste *m* GEOLOGIE micaschist

MICDA *abrév* (*modulation par impulsion et codage différentiels adaptatifs*) TELECOM ADPCM (*adaptive differential pulse code modulation*)

micelle *f* CHIMIE, PLAST CAOU micelle

mi-collé *adj* IMPRIM medium-sized

mi-course *f* CONS MECA midtravel

micrite *f* GEOLOGIE micrite

micro *m* INFORMAT, ORDINAT micro; ~ branché *m* ENREGISTR live microphone; ~ canon *m* ENREGISTR rifle microphone; ~ cravate *m* ENREGISTR lapel microphone; ~ haute fréquence *m (micro HF)* ENREGISTR RF microphone, radio frequency microphone, transmitting microphone; ~ HF *m (micro haute fréquence)* ENREGISTR RF microphone, radio frequency microphone, transmitting microphone; ~ d'intercom *m* ENREGISTR talkback microphone; ~ main *m* ENREGISTR hand mike; ~ d'ordres *m* ENREGISTR cue mike; ~ ouvert *m* ENREGISTR live microphone; ~ de reportage *m* ENREGISTR field microphone; ~ sur perche *m* CINEMAT boom mike; ~ de table *m* ENREGISTR table mike

micro- *préf* METROLOGIE micro-

micro-ampère *m* ELECTR microampere

micro-ampèremètre *m* ELECTROTEC microammeter

micro-analyse *f* CHIMIE, MATERIAUX microanalysis

micro-analytique *adj* CHIMIE microanalytic, microanalytical

microbande *f* PHYSIQUE microstrip

microbille: ~ de verre *f* CERAM VER glass microsphere

microbulle *f* OPTIQUE microbubble

microburette *f* CHIMIE microburette

microcanal *m* ELECTRON microchannel

microcasque *m* ENREGISTR headset

microchimie *f* CHIMIE microchemistry

microcinématographie *f* CINEMAT cinemicrography

microcircuit *m* ELECTRON integrated circuit, microcircuit, INFORMAT, ORDINAT microcircuit; ~ hybride *m* ELECTRON hybrid microcircuit; ~ logique *m* ELECTRON logic microcircuit

microclimat *m* METEO microclimate

microcline *m* MINERAUX microcline

microcode *m* INFORMAT, ORDINAT microcode

microconnecteur *m* MINES detonating relay

microcontrôleur *m* INFORMAT, ORDINAT microcontroller

microcosmique *adj* CHIMIE *sel* microcosmic

microcoupure *f* ELECTROTEC brownout

microcourbure *f* ELECTROTEC microbend, OPTIQUE, TELECOM microbending

microcrêpage *m* PAPIER microcrêping

microcristallin *adj* CHIMIE microcrystalline

microcuvette *f* OPTIQUE micropit

microdéformation *f* METALL microstrain

microdévitrification *f* OPTIQUE microdevitrification

microdisquette *f* INFORMAT, ORDINAT microfloppy disk

microdistillation *f* CHIMIE microdistillation

microdureté *f* METALL, PLAST CAOU microhardness

micro-électronique *f* ELECTRON, INFORMAT, ORDINAT microelectronics

micro-élément *m* CHIMIE microelement

microfalaise *f* OCEANO bluff, nip

microfarad *m* ELECTR, ELECTROTEC microfarad

microfente: à ~ *adj* TELECOM microslot

microfiche *f* IMPRIM microfiche, INFORMAT, ORDINAT fiche, microfiche

microfilm *m* IMPRIM, INFORMAT, ORDINAT, PHOTO microfilm

microfiltre *m* DISTRI EAU microfilter

microfissure *f* MECANIQUE *matériaux* hairline crack

microfluage *m* METALL microcreep

microfossile *m* GEOLOGIE microfossil

microfracture *f* OPTIQUE microcrack

microgranite *m* GEOLOGIE elvan, PETR microgranite

micrographe: ~ électronique *m* PHYS RAYON electron micrograph

micrographie *f* CRISTALL micrograph, METALL photomicrograph

microgravité *f* ASTRONOMIE, ESPACE microgravity

microgrenu *adj* GEOLOGIE microgranular

microgrès *m* GEOLOGIE siltstone

microhenry *m* ELECTR microhenry

microhm *m* ELECTROTEC microhm

micro-instruction *f* INFORMAT, ORDINAT microinstruction

micro-interrupteur *m* PRODUCTION dip switch

microlite *f* MINERAUX microlite

microlog *m* PETR microlog

micrologiciel *m* ORDINAT firmware

micromacle *f* METALL microtwin

micrométéorite *f* ASTRONOMIE micrometeorite

micromètre *m* CONS MECA micrometer, micrometer calipers (AmE), micrometer callipers (BrE), METROLOGIE *extérieur, intérieur, vertical, barre* micrometer; ~ d'épaisseur *m* PAPIER micrometer, thickness gauge; ~ à lecture digitale *m* METROLOGIE digital readout micrometer; ~ de précision *m* CONS MECA precision micrometer; ~ de profondeur *m* METROLOGIE micrometer; ~ à tambour *m* METROLOGIE dial indicating micrometer

micromètre-objectif *m* CONS MECA eyepiece micrometer

micrométrie *f* CONS MECA micrometry

micrométrique *adj* METROLOGIE micrometric

micro-micron *m* METROLOGIE micromicron

micromillimètre *m* METROLOGIE micromil, micromillimeter (AmE), micromillimetre (BrE), micron, millicron

microminiaturisation *f* ELECTRON microminiaturization

micron *m* METROLOGIE micrometer (AmE), micrometre (BrE), micromil, micromillimeter (AmE), micromillimetre (BrE), micron

micronique *adj* CONS MECA *filtre* micronic

micronisé *adj* PLAST CAOU *pigments, charges* micronized

microniser *vt* CHIMIE micronize

micro-onde *f* ELECTR, ELECTRON, PHYS ONDES, PHYSIQUE, TELECOM microwave

micro-ordinateur *m* INFORMAT, ORDINAT microcomputer

micro-organisme *m* HYDROLOGIE, POLLUTION microorganism

microperthite *f* MINERAUX microperthite

micropesanteur *f* ASTRONOMIE, ESPACE microgravity

microphone *m* ACOUSTIQUE, ELECTR *transmission*, ENREGISTR, PHYSIQUE microphone, TELECOM transmitter; ~ antidirectionnel *m* ENREGISTR astatic microphone; ~ baladeur *m* ENREGISTR roving mike; ~ bidirectionnel *m* ACOUSTIQUE, ENREGISTR bidirectional microphone; ~ à bobine mobile *m* ACOUSTIQUE moving coil microphone, ENREGISTR dynamic microphone, moving coil microphone; ~ cardioïde *m* ACOUSTIQUE, ENREGISTR cardioid microphone; ~ à cartouche de charbon *m* ACOUSTIQUE, ENREGISTR carbon microphone; ~ céramique cylindrique *m* ENREGISTR ceramic cylinder microphone; ~ combiné *m* ENREGISTR combination microphone; ~ à condensateur *m* ACOUSTIQUE condenser microphone, ENREGISTR capacitor microphone, condenser microphone; ~ à contact *m* ACOUSTIQUE contact microphone, ENREGISTR contact microphone, impact microphone; ~ **à cristal** *m* ENREGISTR crystal microphone; ~ **à décharge ionique** *m* ENREGISTR discharge microphone; ~ **à déphasage** *m* ACOUSTIQUE phase shift microphone; ~ **différentiel** *m* ACOUSTIQUE, ENREGISTR differential microphone; ~ **directionnel** *m* ACOUSTIQUE, ENREGISTR directional microphone; ~ **à électret** *m* ACOUSTIQUE electret foil microphone; ~ **électrodynamique** *m* ACOUSTIQUE electrodynamic microphone, ENREGISTR dynamic microphone, electrodynamic microphone, PHYSIQUE moving coil microphone; ~ **électromagnétique** *m* ACOUSTIQUE, ENREGISTR electromagnetic microphone; ~ **électronique** *m* ENREGISTR electronic microphone; ~ **électrostatique** *m* ACOUSTIQUE electrostatic microphone, ENREGISTR condenser microphone, electret foil microphone, electrostatic microphone; ~ **émetteur** *m* MILITAIRE wireless microphone; ~ **en cravate** *m* ENREGISTR Lavalier microphone; ~ **étalon** *m* ACOUSTIQUE standard microphone; ~ **à fil chaud** *m* ACOUSTIQUE hot wire microphone; ~ **à gradient** *m* ACOUSTIQUE gradient microphone; ~ **haute fréquence mains libres** *m* (*microphone HF mains libres*) ENREGISTR wireless headset; ~ **HF mains libres** *m* (*microphone haute fréquence mains libres*) ENREGISTR wireless headset; ~ **hypercardioïde** *m* ACOUSTIQUE hypercardioid microphone; ~ **incorporé** *m* ENREGISTR built-in microphone; ~ **à interférence** *m* ENREGISTR interference microphone; ~ **labial** *m* ACOUSTIQUE lip microphone; ~ **à magnétostriction** *m* ACOUSTIQUE magnetostriction microphone; ~ **de masque** *m* ACOUSTIQUE mask microphone; ~ **multiple** *m* ACOUSTIQUE, ENREGISTR multiple microphone; ~ **omnidirectionnel** *m* ACOUSTIQUE omnidirectional microphone, ENREGISTR astatic microphone; ~ **d'ordre** *m* CINEMAT intercom microphone; ~ **personnel** *m* ACOUSTIQUE lapel microphone; ~ **piézoélectrique** *m* ACOUSTIQUE piezoelectric microphone, piezomicrophone, ENREGISTR crystal microphone, piezoelectric microphone; ~ **à pression** *m* ACOUSTIQUE pressure microphone; ~ **de proximité** *m* ENREGISTR close talking microphone; ~ **à réflecteur parabolique** *m* ENREGISTR parabolic reflector microphone; ~ **à rotation de phase** *m* ENREGISTR phase shift microphone; ~ **à ruban** *m* ACOUSTIQUE ribbon microphone, ENREGISTR ribbon microphone, velocity microphone; ~ **à semi-conducteur** *m* ENREGISTR semiconductor microphone; ~ **semi-directionnel** *m* ACOUSTIQUE, ENREGISTR semidirectional microphone; ~ **sonde** *m* ACOUSTIQUE probe microphone; ~ **standard** *m* ENREGISTR standard microphone; ~ **téléphonique** *m* TELECOM transmitter; ~ **à vitesse** *m* ACOUSTIQUE velocity microphone

microphonique *adj* ENREGISTR microphonic
microphotogramme *m* METALL photomicrogram
microphotographie *f* CINEMAT microphotography, mike tap
microphotomètre *m* PHYS RAYON microphotometer
micropipette *f* EQUIP LAB *verrerie* micropipette
microplaquette *f* ELECTRON chip
micropli *m* GEOLOGIE crenulation, microfold
micropompe *f* CONS MECA micropump
microprocesseur *m* CONS MECA, ELECTR, ELECTRON, ESPACE *communications*, IMPRIM, INFORMAT, ORDINAT chip, microprocessor
microprogrammation *f* INFORMAT, ORDINAT microprogramming

microprogramme *m* INFORMAT, ORDINAT microprogram; ~ **de régulation** *m* TRANSPORT local program (AmE), local programme (BrE)
micropropulseur *m* ESPACE microrocket, microthruster
micropuce *f* ELECTRON microchip
microréflexion *f* ELECTROTEC microbend
microrégulation *f* TRANSPORT individual control, microcontrol
microrhéologie *f* METALL microrheology
microruban[1] *adj* TELECOM microribbon
microruban[2] *m* PHYSIQUE, TELECOM microstrip
microrupteur *m* ELECTROTEC microswitch
microscope *m* EQUIP LAB, INSTRUMENT, METROLOGIE, PHYSIQUE microscope; ~ **d'atelier** *m* METROLOGIE toolmaker's microscope; ~ **auxiliaire** *m* INSTRUMENT secondary viewing tube; ~ **à balayage** *m* TELECOM sweep microscope; ~ **binoculaire** *m* EQUIP LAB *instrument*, INSTRUMENT binocular microscope; ~ **chirurgical** *m* INSTRUMENT surgical microscope; ~ **composé** *m* INSTRUMENT, PHYSIQUE compound microscope; ~ **à contraste de phase** *m* EQUIP LAB phase contrast microscope, INSTRUMENT contrasting phase microscope, PHYSIQUE phase contrast microscope; ~ **à coupe optique** *m* INSTRUMENT light section microscope; ~ **à dissection** *m* INSTRUMENT dissecting microscope; ~ **à éclairage incident** *m* INSTRUMENT reflected light microscope; ~ **électronique** *m* ELECTRON, EQUIP LAB, INSTRUMENT, METALL, PHYSIQUE, TELECOM electron microscope; ~ **électronique à balayage** *m* ELECTR, ELECTRON, EQUIP LAB, INSTRUMENT, PHYS RAYON, PHYSIQUE scanning electron microscope; ~ **électronique à balayage avec réflecteur** *m* INSTRUMENT scanning mirror electron microscope; ~ **électronique à balayage de surface** *m* INSTRUMENT SEM, surface electron microscope; ~ **électronique à émission** *m* ELECTRON emission electron microscope; ~ **électronique à émission de champ** *m* INSTRUMENT field electron microscope, field emission microscope; ~ **électronique à filtrage en énergie** *m* INSTRUMENT energy selecting electron microscope; ~ **électronique à haute tension** *m* INSTRUMENT high-voltage electron microscope; ~ **électronique à lentilles magnétiques** *m* INSTRUMENT permanent magnet electron microscope; ~ **électronique à miroir** *m* INSTRUMENT mirror electron microscope; ~ **électronique à ombre** *m* INSTRUMENT shadow microscope; ~ **électronique à réflexion** *m* ELECTRON reflection electron microscope; ~ **électronique à transmission** *m* ELECTRON, EQUIP LAB, INSTRUMENT, NUCLEAIRE, PHYSIQUE transmission electron microscope; ~ **à émission** *m* INSTRUMENT emission microscope; ~ **à émission de champ** *m* PHYSIQUE field emission microscope; ~ **à émission ionique** *m* INSTRUMENT ion emission microscope; ~ **à émission photo-ionique** *m* INSTRUMENT photoemission electron microscope; ~ **à émission thermoélectrique** *m* INSTRUMENT thermionic emission microscope; ~ **à fil** *m* INSTRUMENT thread microscope; ~ **à fluorescence** *m* INSTRUMENT fluorescence microscope; ~ **à fort grossissement** *m* INSTRUMENT high-power microscope; ~ **à genouillère** *m* INSTRUMENT hinged body microscope; ~ **infrarouge** *m* INSTRUMENT infrared microscope; ~ **interférentiel** *m* INSTRUMENT, METALL, PHYSIQUE interference microscope; ~ **inversé** *m* INSTRUMENT inverted microscope; ~ **ionique à émission de champ** *m* INSTRUMENT, PHYSIQUE field ion microscope; ~ **de lecture** *m* IN-

STRUMENT measuring microscope, reading microscope; **~ à lumière réfléchie** *m* INSTRUMENT reflected light microscope; **~ de mesure** *m* INSTRUMENT measuring microscope, reading microscope, METROLOGIE microscope; **~ de métallographie à grand champ** *m* INSTRUMENT wide-field metallurgical microscope; **~ métallographique** *m* EQUIP LAB metallographic microscope (BrE), metalographic microscope (AmE), INSTRUMENT micrographic microscope; **~ de microphotographie** *m* INSTRUMENT photomicroscope; **~ par réflexion** *m* INSTRUMENT reflected light microscope; **~ photoélectrique** *m* INSTRUMENT photoelectric microscope; **~ à photomètre** *m* INSTRUMENT microscopic photometer; **~ à plancton** *m* INSTRUMENT plankton microscope; **~ polarisant** *m* CRISTALL polarizing microscope, EQUIP LAB polarization microscope, polarizing microscope, INSTRUMENT, PHYSIQUE polarizing microscope; **~ pour l'étude de la couche superficielle des pièces** *m* INSTRUMENT surface-finish microscope; **~ à projection** *m* INSTRUMENT projection microscope; **~ protonique** *m* INSTRUMENT proton microscope; **~ à rayons X** *m* NUCLEAIRE X-ray microscope, PHYS RAYON X-ray microscope, transmission electron microscope; **~ de recherche** *m* INSTRUMENT laboratory microscope; **~ à réflecteur** *m* INSTRUMENT reflecting microscope; **~ stéréoscopique équipé d'un zoom** *m* INSTRUMENT zoom stereomicroscope; **~ stéréoscopique à grand champ** *m* INSTRUMENT wide-field stereo microscope; **~ à surplatine hémisphérique** *m* INSTRUMENT ball stage microscope; **~ téléviseur** *m* INSTRUMENT television microscope; **~ à transmission** *m* INSTRUMENT transmitted light microscope; **~ à transmission de type Zeiss avec appareil polariseur** *m* INSTRUMENT Zeiss system transmitted light microscope with polarizer; **~ à ultraviolet** *m* PHYS RAYON ultraviolet microscope; **~ universel à grand champ** *m* INSTRUMENT universal wide-field microscope

Microscope *m* ASTRONOMIE Microscopium

microscopie *f* CHIMIE microscopy; **~ axiale interférentielle** *f* OPTIQUE axial interference microscopy, slab interferometry, TELECOM axial interference microscopy; **~ à balayage d'Auger** *f* NUCLEAIRE scanning Auger microscopy; **~ électronique** *f* ELECTRON electron microscopy; **~ à électron de transmission** *f* PHYS RAYON transmission electron microscopy; **~ à émission** *f* METALL emission microscopy; **~ optique** *f* METALL light microscopy

microseconde *f* INFORMAT, ORDINAT microsecond

microségrégation *f* METALL microsegregation

microseringue *f* EQUIP LAB *chromatographie en phase gazeuse* microsyringe

microsillon *m* ACOUSTIQUE microgroove, ENREGISTR long-playing record; **~ stéréophonique** *m* ENREGISTR stereophonic microgroove

microsonde *f* PHYS RAYON microprobe

microsphère: ~ fabriquée par le procédé sol-gel *f* NUCLEAIRE gel derived microsphere

microsphères *f pl* PLAST CAOU *pigments* microspheres

microstructure *f* CHARBON, CRISTALL, GEOLOGIE microstructure; **~ fibreuse** *f* METALL fibrous microstructure

microtamis *m* DISTRI EAU microstrainer

microtome *m* EQUIP LAB *microscopie* microtome

micro-usinage *m* PHYS RAYON micromachining

microvolt *m* ELECTR *unité de potentiel*, ELECTROTEC microvolt

MID *abrév (modulation par impulsions de durée)* ELEC-

TRON, ESPACE PDM *(pulse duration modulation)*

mi-dur *adj* MATERIAUX half-hard, medium-hard

mi-fixe *adj* CONS MECA semiportable

migmatisation *f* GEOLOGIE migmatization

migmatite *f* GEOLOGIE injection gneiss

mignonnette *f* CERAM VER miniature bottle

migration *f* CHIMIE, PETROLE *hydrocarbure*, PLAST CAOU *plastifiant* migration; **~ des joints de grains** *f* METALL grain boundary migration; **~ de plastifiant** *f* PLAST CAOU *revêtement* plasticizer migration

migrer *vi* CHIMIE, PETR migrate

mijoter *vti* AGRO ALIM simmer

milarite *f* MINERAUX milarite

mildiou *m* AGRO ALIM downy mildew, mildew; **~ de la pomme de terre** *m* AGRO ALIM potato blight

milieu:[1] **au ~ du navire** *adv* NAUT amidships, midships

milieu[2] *m* DISTRI EAU medium, ESPACE environment, PHYSIQUE medium, surroundings; **~ actif** *m* ELECTRON lasing medium, MATERIAUX active medium; **~ actif gazeux** *m* ELECTRON gaseous active medium; **~ actif laser** *m* OPTIQUE active laser medium, TELECOM laser medium; **~ actif liquide** *m* ELECTRON liquid lasing medium; **~ ambiant** *m* PRODUCTION environment; **~ aménagé** *m* POLLUTION planned environment; **~ amplifiant** *m* MATERIAUX laser material; **~ biréfringent** *m* OPTIQUE birefringent medium; **~ climatique** *m* METEO climate environment; **~ compact** *m* MATERIAUX compact medium; **~ de congélation** *m* REFRIG freezing medium; **~ du courant** *m* HYDROLOGIE midstream; **~ dense** *m* CHARBON dense medium, GENIE CHIM flotation liquid; **~ diélectrique** *m* ELECTROTEC dielectric medium; **~ dispersif** *m* GENIE CHIM, PHYSIQUE dispersive medium; **~ dissipatif** *m* PHYSIQUE dissipative medium; **~ gazeux** *m* POLLUTION gaseous medium; **~ géologique** *m* GAZ geological environment; **~ homogène** *m* PHYSIQUE homogeneous medium; **~ hostile** *m* PHYS RAYON dangerous environment, hostile environment; **~ intergalactique** *m* ASTRONOMIE intergalactic medium; **~ interplanétaire** *m* ASTRONOMIE interplanetary medium; **~ interstellaire** *m* ASTRONOMIE interstellar medium; **~ ionisé** *m* ESPACE ionized environment, plasma environment; **~ isotrope** *m* MATERIAUX isotropic medium; **~ laser** *m* OPTIQUE laser medium, TELECOM active laser medium, laser medium; **~ marécageux** *m* GEOLOGIE marshy environment, paludal environment; **~ marin** *m* POLLUTION marine environment; **~ naturel** *m* DISTRI EAU, POLLUTION natural environment; **~ non dispersif** *m* PHYSIQUE nondispersive medium; **~ opaque** *m* PHYSIQUE opaque medium; **~ palustre** *m* GEOLOGIE marshy environment, paludal environment; **~ poreux** *m* GAZ porous medium; **~ de propagation** *m* ELECTROTEC propagation medium; **~ sédimentaire** *m* GEOLOGIE sedimentary environment; **~ sédimentaire à faible énergie** *m* GEOLOGIE low-energy environment; **~ sédimentaire à forte énergie** *m* GEOLOGIE high-energy environment; **~ translucide** *m* PHYSIQUE translucent medium; **~ transparent** *m* PHYSIQUE transparent medium

mille *m* CINEMAT blip tone, sync plop; **~ anglais** *m* METROLOGIE, TRANSPORT mile; **~ carré** *m* METROLOGIE square mile; **~ marin** *m* NAUT nautical mile; **~ nautique** *m* METEO, OCEANO nautical mile

millérite *f* MINERAUX hair pyrites, millerite

milles: ~ par gallon *m pl* TRANSPORT miles per gallon, mpg

milli- *préf (m)* METROLOGIE milli-*(m)*

milliampère *m (mA)* ELECTR *unité de courant,* ELECTRO-
TEC milliampere *(mA)*

milliampèremètre *m* ELECTR, ELECTROTEC milliammeter

milliard *m* MATH billion

millibar *m* METROLOGIE millibar

millicron *m* METROLOGIE millicron

milligramme *m (mg)* METROLOGIE milligram (AmE),
milligramme (BrE) *(milligram)*

millimètre *m (mm)* METROLOGIE millimeter (AmE),
millimetre (BrE) *(mm)*

millimétrique *adj* ELECTRON *onde* millimetric

millions: **~ d'instructions par seconde** *m pl (MIPS)*
IMPRIM, INFORMAT, ORDINAT millions of instructions
per second *(MIPS)*; **~ de pieds cubes par jour** *m pl*
PETROLE *unité de volume* MCFD, millions of cubic
feet per day

milliseconde *f (ms)* INFORMAT, ORDINAT millisecond
(ms)

millivolt *m (mV)* ELECTR *unité de potentiel,* ELECTROTEC
millivolt *(mV)*

millivoltmètre *m* ELECTR millivoltmeter

milliwatt *m (mW)* ELECTR *unité de puissance* milliwatt
(mW)

milliwattmètre *m* ELECTR milliwattmeter

millstonegrit *m* PRODUCTION millstone grit

mi-marée *f* NAUT half tide

mi-mat *adj* TEXTILE semimatt

MIMD *abrév (multiflux d'instruction-multiflux de
données)* INFORMAT, ORDINAT MIMD *(multiple-
instruction multiple-data)*

mimétite *f* MINERAUX mimetene, mimetite

minage *m* CHARBON, CONSTR blasting, MINES blasting,
shot-firing

mince *adj* PRODUCTION thin

minceur *f* PRODUCTION thinness

mine *f* MILITAIRE mine, MINES blast hole, borehole, mining hole, chamber, coal mine, colliery, pit, mine, mine
chamber, quarry, shot, shot hole; **~ antichar** *f* MILI-
TAIRE antitank mine; **~ antipersonnel** *f* MILITAIRE
antipersonnel mine; **~ d'argent** *f* MINES silver mine; **~
chambrée** *f* MINES chambered hole; **~ de charbon** *f*
CHARBON coal mine, MINES coal mine, colliery, pit; **~ à
ciel ouvert** *f* MINES daylight mine, open pit mine; **~ de
couronne** *f* MINES top hole; **~ de cuivre** *f* MINES copper
mine; **~ de dégraissage** *f* MINES easer, enlarging hole,
shoulder hole; **~ de diamants** *f* MINES diamond mine;
~ d'empiétage *f* MINES breaking shot, breaking-in
hole, busting shot, breaking-in shot, bursting shot,
buster shot, center cut hole (AmE), centre cut hole
(BrE), cut hole; **~ en activité** *f* MINES active mine,
operational mine, working mine; **~ exploitée par
puits** *f* MINES shaft mine; **~ de fer** *f* CHIMIE iron ore,
MINERAUX ironstone; **~ au fond** *f* MINES drift mining; **~
à grande profondeur** *f* MINES deep mine; **~ de houille** *f*
CHARBON coal mine, MINES coal mine, colliery, pit; **~
magnétique** *f* MILITAIRE magnetic mine; **~ d'or** *f* MINES
gold mine; **~ de plomb** *f* CHIMIE graphite; **~ de relevage**
f MINES bottom hole, lifter; **~ au sol** *f* CHARBON floor
shots; **~ souterraine** *f* MINES underground mine

miné *adj* MILITAIRE *zone* mined

miner *vt* MINES undermine

minerai *m* CHARBON ore, MINES metal, mine stone,
minestuff, stone; **~ abattu** *m* MINES broken ore; **~
bocardé** *m* MINES milled ore; **~ broyé** *m* MINES broken
ore, crushed ore, milled ore; **~ brut** *m* CHARBON crude

ore; **~ complexe** *m* CHARBON complex ore; **~ contenant du métal à l'état libre** *m* MINES free milling ore; **~
dont le métal est totalement amalgamable** *m* MINES
free milling ore; **~ en place** *m* MINES unbroken ore; **~
de fer** *m* CHIMIE iron ore, MINERAUX ironstone; **~ de fer
des marais** *m* MINES meadow ore; **~ ferreux** *m* MINE-
RAUX ironstone; **~ de gangue** *m* CHARBON gangue
mineral; **~ de mercure** *m* MINES mercury ore; **~ non
abattu** *m* MINES unbroken ore; **~ d'or** *m* MINES gold
ore; **~ oxydé** *m* CHIMIE oxide ore; **~ de plomb** *m* MINES
lead ore; **~ de plomb argentifère** *m* MINES silver lead
ore; **~ rebelle** *m* MINES stubborn ore; **~ réfractaire** *m*
MINES stubborn ore; **~ riche** *m* CHARBON high-grade
ore; **~ sulfuré** *m* MINES sulfide ore (AmE), sulphide ore
(BrE); **~ à la surface** *m* MINES ore at grass; **~ de
tourbières** *m* MINES meadow ore

minerai-vrac-pétrole *m* PETROLE OBO, ore-bulk-oil

minéral[1] *adj* CHARBON mineral, CHIMIE inorganic, MINE-
RAUX mineral

minéral[2] *m* CHARBON, MINERAUX mineral; **~ des argiles**
m CHARBON clay mineral; **~ caractéristique** *m* GEO-
LOGIE *zone de métamorphisme* index mineral; **~ de
chrome** *m* CERAM VER chrome ore; **~ normatif** *m*
GEOLOGIE normative mineral; **~ uranifère** *m* NU-
CLEAIRE uranium-bearing mineral

minéralier *m* CHARBON coal ship, NAUT ore carrier

minéralier-pétrolier *m* NAUT, TRANSPORT OO, oil-ore
carrier

minéralisateur[1] *adj* CHIMIE *agent* mineralizing

minéralisateur[2] *m* CHIMIE mineralizer, EQUIP LAB *analyse*
digestion apparatus; **~ Kjeldahl** *m* EQUIP LAB *analyse
d'azote* Kjeldahl digestion apparatus

minéralisation *f* CHIMIE digestion, mineralization, GEO-
LOGIE mineralization

minéralogie *f* GEOLOGIE, PETROLE mineralogy

minéralogique *adj* GEOLOGIE mineralogic (AmE), mineralogical (BrE)

minéralogiste *m* MINERAUX mineralogist

minéralurgie *f* CHARBON mineral processing

minéraux: **~ lourds** *m pl* GEOLOGIE heavy minerals

minérogène *adj* CHARBON minerogenic, minerogenous

mines: **~ à éparpiller** *f pl* MILITAIRE scatterable mines; **~
de mazières** *f pl* MINES side holes

mineur *m* CHARBON miner; **~ au rocher** *m* CHARBON
stoneman

mini *m* INFORMAT, ORDINAT mini

miniaturisation *f* INFORMAT, ORDINAT miniaturization

minicassette *f* ENREGISTR minicassette

minière *f* MINES alluvial mining, diggings, placer; **~ à ciel
ouvert** *f* MINES daylight mine, open diggings

minime *adj* CHIMIE minute

mini-message *m* TELECOM user-to-user information

minimum: **~ d'atterrissage** *m* AERONAUT minimum
weather conditions; **~ de déviation** *m* PHYSIQUE minimum deviation; **~ de perception** *m* TELECOM minimum
payable

mini-ordinateur *m* INFORMAT, ORDINAT minicomputer

mini-pousseur *m* TRANSPORT mini pusher tug

minirail *m* TRANSPORT minirail

mini-TOP *m* ELECTRON miniature traveling-wave tube
(AmE), miniature travelling-wave tube (BrE)

minium *m* CHIMIE minium, red lead, MINERAUX minium;
~ de plomb *m* CERAM VER, PLAST CAOU *matière première* red lead

minoterie *f* AGRO ALIM milling, milling industry

minuscule *adj* CHIMIE minute

minutage m CERAM VER elutriation; ~ **des signaux** m TV station timing

minute f METROLOGIE, PHYSIQUE minute; ~ **d'angle** f CONSTR minute, PHYSIQUE arc minute; ~ **d'arc** f PHYSIQUE arc minute; ~ **dégradée** f TELECOM DM, degraded minute

minuter vt CINEMAT clock

minuterie f CINEMAT time switch, ELECTROTEC, EQUIP LAB, PHYSIQUE timer; ~ **électronique** f ELECTRON, PHOTO electronic timer

minuteur m EQUIP LAB timer

minutieusement adv CHIMIE minutely

minutieux adj CHIMIE minute

miogéosynclinal m GEOLOGIE miogeosyncline

mionite f MINERAUX meionite, mionite

MIPS abrév (millions d'instructions par seconde) IMPRIM, INFORMAT, ORDINAT MIPS (millions of instructions per second)

mirabilite f MINERAUX mirabilite

mirbane f CHIMIE mirbane

mire f CONSTR leveling pole (AmE), leveling rod (AmE), leveling staff (AmE), levelling pole (BrE), levelling rod (BrE), levellingstaff (BrE), pole, rod, staff, ELECTRON pattern, test pattern, INSTRUMENT sight; ~ **de barres** f TV bar pattern; ~ **de barres couleurs** f TV color bar test pattern (AmE), colour bar test pattern (BrE); ~ **de convergence** f ELECTRON dot generator; ~ **de définition** f CINEMAT resolution chart, TV definition test pattern; ~ **électronique** f ELECTRON electronic test pattern; ~ **étalon** f TV standard pattern; ~ **de gris** f TV gray scale (AmE), grey scale (BrE); ~ **de netteté** f CINEMAT definition chart; ~ **parlante** f CONSTR self-reading staff, speaking rod; ~ **pour usage nocturne** f MILITAIRE night sight; ~ **quadrillée** f CINEMAT cross hatch pattern; ~ **de réglage** f CINEMAT test chart, test pattern, TV grating, test pattern; ~ **à voyant** f CONSTR target levelling rod, target levelling-staff

miroir m INSTRUMENT looking glass, sighting mirror, PHYSIQUE mirror; ~ **actif** m NUCLEAIRE active mirror; ~ **adiabatique** m EN RENOUV heat mirror; ~ **ardent** m INSTRUMENT burning mirror, burning reflector; ~ **argenté** m INSTRUMENT silvered mirror; ~ **à argenture semi-transparente** m INSTRUMENT semireflecting mirror, semisilvered mirror; ~ **auxiliaire** m PHOTO auxiliary mirror; ~ **de la cavité** m INSTRUMENT cavity mirror; ~ **concave** m INSTRUMENT burning mirror, burning reflector, concave mirror, PHYSIQUE concave mirror; ~ **concentrateur** m INSTRUMENT concentrating mirror, solar concentrator; ~ **convexe** m INSTRUMENT, PHYSIQUE convex mirror; ~ **à couche secondaire** m ESPACE véhicules SSM, second surface mirror; ~ **de courtoisie** m INSTRUMENT make-up mirror, VEHICULES accessoire vanity mirror; ~ **d'un cristal** m INSTRUMENT crystallographic plane; ~ **cylindro-parabolique avec foyer tubulaire** m INSTRUMENT PTC, parabolic trough conveyor; ~ **déployable** m PHOTO swing-up mirror; ~ **de déviation** m INSTRUMENT correcting plate, secondary mirror, deviation mirror; ~ **dichroïque** m CINEMAT color splitter (AmE), colour splitter (BrE), dichroic mirror, OPTIQUE, TELECOM dichroic mirror; ~ **d'éclairage** m INSTRUMENT illuminating mirror, illumination mirror; ~ **électronique** m INSTRUMENT electron mirror; ~ **à électrons** m ELECTRON electron mirror; ~ **elliptique** m INSTRUMENT, PHYSIQUE elliptical mirror; ~ **de faille** m GEOLOGIE slickenside; ~ **fixe** m INSTRUMENT sextant horizon glass; ~ **de fracture** m CERAM VER fracture mirror; ~ **grossissant** m INSTRUMENT concave mirror; ~ **d'inversion** m INSTRUMENT inverting mirror; ~ **de Lloyd** m PHYSIQUE Lloyd's mirror; ~ **magnétique** m PHYSIQUE magnetic mirror; ~ **à main** m INSTRUMENT hand glass, hand mirror; ~ **métallique** m INSTRUMENT metallic mirror; ~ **mobile** m INSTRUMENT sextant index mirror; ~ **objectif** m ASTRONOMIE objective mirror; ~ **d'observation** m INSTRUMENT observation mirror; ~ **d'octant** m INSTRUMENT octant mirror; ~ **parabolique** m PHYSIQUE parabolic mirror; ~ **parabolique non-aluminé** m ASTRONOMIE nonmetalized parabolic mirror (AmE), nonmetallized parabolic mirror (BrE); ~ **plan** m INSTRUMENT flat mirror, plane mirror, PHYSIQUE plane mirror; ~ **plan escamotable** m ASTRONOMIE retractable plane mirror; ~ **polygonal** m INSTRUMENT, OPTIQUE polygonal mirror; ~ **primaire** m ASTRONOMIE télescope primary mirror; ~ **primaire parabolique** m INSTRUMENT main mirror; ~ **principal** m INSTRUMENT main mirror, primary mirror; ~ **réfléchissant** m INSTRUMENT reflected light mirror; ~ **réfléchissant à la surface** m INSTRUMENT surface mirror; ~ **réflecteur** m INSTRUMENT concentrating reflector; ~ **réflexe** m PHOTO reflex mirror; ~ **réticulé** m ESPACE véhicules reticulated mirror; ~ **semi-argenté** m INSTRUMENT semireflecting mirror, semisilvered mirror; ~ **semi-réfléchissant** m CERAM VER see-through mirror (AmE), two-way mirror (BrE); ~ **de sortie** m INSTRUMENT output mirror; ~ **sphérique** m EQUIP LAB, INSTRUMENT, OPTIQUE, PHYSIQUE, TELECOM spherical mirror; ~ **de surface** m INSTRUMENT surface mirror; ~ **tournant** m INSTRUMENT, PHYSIQUE rotating mirror; ~ **ultraviolet** m PHYS RAYON ultraviolet mirror

miroirs: ~ **de Fresnel** m pl PHYSIQUE Fresnel mirrors

miroiterie f CERAM VER mirror-making

mis: ~ **directement à la terre** adj ELECTROTEC directly earthed (BrE), directly grounded (AmE); ~ **en attente** adj TELECOM call-queued; ~ **en boîte** adj AGRO ALIM canned (AmE), tinned; ~ **en conserve** adj AGRO ALIM canned (AmE), tinned; ~ **en décharge** adj CHARBON dumped, stockpiled; ~ **en garde** adj TELECOM parked; ~ **à la masse** adj ELECTROTEC earthed, grounded; ~ **à niveau** adj CONSTR leveled (AmE), levelled (BrE); ~ **au point** adj PHYSIQUE focused; ~ **au repos** adj INFORMAT, ORDINAT quiescing; ~ **à la terre** adj ELECTR earthed (BrE), grounded (AmE), ELECTROTEC connected to earth (BrE), connected to ground (AmE), earthed, grounded, TELECOM earthed (BrE), grounded (AmE)

misaine f NAUT foresail

miscible adj CHIMIE, PETROLE miscible

MISD abrév (multiflux d'instruction-monoflux de donnés) INFORMAT, ORDINAT MISD (multiple-instruction single-data)

mise: ~ **à l'abri** f CONSTR housing; ~ **à l'air** f NUCLEAIRE air drain, bleeding, vent, venting; ~ **à l'arche** f CERAM VER carry-in, stacking; ~ **à l'arrêt** f NUCLEAIRE shutdown; ~ **au banc d'essai** f INFORMAT, ORDINAT benchmarking; ~ **au bassin** f NAUT docking; ~ **à bord** f NAUT shipping; ~ **à dimensions** f CONS MECA sizing; ~ **à l'eau** f NAUT navire launching; ~ **à l'échelle** f INFORMAT, ORDINAT scaling, PRODUCTION automatisme industriel input scaling; ~ **en attente** f TELECOM call queueing facility; ~ **en boîte** f AGRO ALIM canning; ~ **en caisse** f EMBALLAGE case packing; ~ **en carte de dessin jacquard** f TEXTILE card cutting; ~ **en chantier** f PRODUCTION floor bedding, planting; ~ **en charge** f

HYDROLOGIE loading; ~ **en circuit** *f* ELECTROTEC switching in, turn-on; ~ **en circulation alternée** *f* TRANSPORT tidal flow; ~ **en condition** *f* IMPRIM *papier* conditioning; ~ **en conduction** *f* ELECTROTEC turn-on; ~ **en cône** *f* AERONAUT coning; ~ **en conserve par autoclavage** *f* AGRO ALIM canning; ~ **en court-circuit** *f* ELECTROTEC shorting; ~ **en décharge** *f* POLLU MER landfilling; ~ **en drapeau** *f* AERONAUT *hélice* feathering; ~ **en drapeau automatique** *f* AERONAUT *hélice* autofeathering; ~ **en feu** *f* PRODUCTION *haut-fourneau* blowing in; ~ **en file d'attente** *f* TELECOM queue control; ~ **en forme** *f* IMPRIM, INFORMAT, ORDINAT editing, TEXTILE boarding; ~ **en forme électronique du faisceau** *f* ELECTRON electronic beam forming; ~ **en forme du faisceau** *f* ELECTRON beam shaping; ~ **en forme d'impulsion** *f* INFORMAT pulse shaping; ~ **en forme par filtre** *f* ELECTRON filter shaping; ~ **en forme de signal** *f* INFORMAT, ORDINAT signal shaping; ~ **en forme du signal** *f* PRODUCTION *automatisme industriel* signal conditioning; ~ **en forme du signal d'entrée** *f* ELECTRON input signal conditioning; ~ **en forme de signaux** *f* ELECTRON signal conditioning, signal shaping; ~ **en garde** *f* TELECOM *appel* call held, call holding, call hold; ~ **en ligne** *f* PETR line-up; ~ **en marche** *f* CONS MECA starting, ELECTROTEC turn-on, PAPIER *de la machine à papier* startup; ~ **en marche progressive** *f* PRODUCTION *automatisme industriel* soft start; ~ **en mémoire** *f* INFORMAT, ORDINAT storage; ~ **en mémoire de données** *f* NUCLEAIRE data storage; ~ **en mémoire de programme** *f* INFORMAT program storage; ~ **en mémoire tampon** *f* ORDINAT buffering; ~ **en mémoire tampon de deux mots** *f* INFORMAT double word buffering; ~ **en oeuvre** *f* BREVETS carrying out, use, GEOLOGIE implementation, INFORMAT initialization, TELECOM implementation; ~ **en oeuvre en vol** *f* ESPACE *véhicules* in-flight operation; ~ **en oeuvre au sol** *f* ESPACE *véhicules* ground operation; ~ **en page** *f* IMPRIM layout, make-up; ~ **en page en lignes** *f* IMPRIM *imposition* in-line position; ~ **en pâte** *f* PAPIER pulping; ~ **en phase** *f* ELECTRON, ENREGISTR *haut-parleur* phasing, GEOLOGIE line-up, TV phase adjustment, phase control; ~ **en phase d'impulsion** *f* TV pulse phasing; ~ **en phase des voies** *f* ENREGISTR channel phasing; ~ **en place** *f* CONSTR *canalisation* laying; ~ **en place de l'armature** *f* CONSTR steel fixing; ~ **en place de pieux** *f* CHARBON piling; ~ **en pression** *f* TRANSPORT pressurization; ~ **en rotation** *f* ESPACE *véhicules* spin-up; ~ **en route** *f* CONS MECA starting; ~ **en sac manuelle** *f* EMBALLAGE hand bagging; ~ **en séquence** *f* INFORMAT, ORDINAT sequencing; ~ **en service** *f* CONSTR, PRODUCTION commissioning; ~ **en service du système** *f* PRODUCTION system startup; ~ **en solution** *f* THERMODYN natural ageing (BrE), natural aging (AmE); ~ **en station** *f* CONSTR setup; ~ **en tampon de deux mots** *f* INFORMAT double word buffering; ~ **en tas** *f* PRODUCTION stacking; ~ **en terre** *f* CONSTR earthing (BrE), grounding (AmE); ~ **en tire-bouchon** *f* RESSORTS corkscrew set; ~ **en train** *f* CONS MECA starting, starting gear, IMPRIM pre-press; ~ **en valeur** *f* PETROLE development; ~ **en veilleuse** *f* ELECTROTEC power down feature; ~ **en voie** *f* CONS MECA *dents d'une scie* setting; ~ **d'épaisseur** *f* CONS MECA thicknessing; ~ **à la ferraille** *f* PRODUCTION scrap; ~ **à feu** *f* ESPACE *propulsion* blastoff, firing, MINES firing, PRODUCTION *haut-fourneau* blowing in; ~ **à feu électrique** *f* MINES electric blasting, electric firing, electric shotfiring; ~ **au ga-** barit par filtre passe-bande *f* ELECTRON band-pass filter shaping; ~ **hors circuit** *f* ELECTROTEC breaking of a circuit, disconnection, power down, turn-off; ~ **hors feu** *f* PRODUCTION *haut-fourneau* blowing out; ~ **hors tension** *f* ELECTROTEC, PRODUCTION power down; ~ **à jour** *f* INFORMAT update, ORDINAT update, *de fichiers* updating, TELECOM updating; ~ **à jour d'articles** *f* ORDINAT record updating; ~ **à jour d'enregistrements** *f* INFORMAT, ORDINAT record updating; ~ **à jour de fichier** *f* INFORMAT, ORDINAT file maintenance, file updating; ~ **à jour rapide** *f* TELECOM fast update; ~ **à longueur** *f* ELECTRON apodization; ~ **à la masse** *f* CH DE FER earthing (BrE), grounding (AmE), ELECTROTEC connection to earth (BrE), connection to ground (AmE), earthing (BrE), grounding (AmE), ESPACE earthing (BrE), grounding (AmE); ~ **aux molettes** *f* MINES overwind, overwinding, pulleying; ~ **au net** *f* PRODUCTION *travail* cleanup; ~ **à niveau** *f* INFORMAT retrofit, upgrade, MECANIQUE leveling (AmE), levelling (BrE), ORDINAT retrofit, PRODUCTION levelness; ~ **à niveau a posteriori** *f* PRODUCTION *fabricant* retrofit; ~ **à nu** *f* GEOLOGIE *massif intrusif* deroofing; ~ **au pilon** *f* PRODUCTION scrap; ~ **à plat** *f* ENREGISTR rough mix; ~ **au point** *f* COMMANDE adjustment, regulating, regulating, CONS MECA *foret* positioning, CONSTR development, INFORMAT, ORDINAT debugging, setup, PAPIER adjusting, adjustment, PHOTO focusing, TELECOM fine tuning; ~ **au point automatique** *f* CINEMAT autofocus, PHOTO autofocus, automatic focusing; ~ **au point de la couleur** *f* IMPRIM *photogravure* toning; ~ **au point du diaphragme** *f* COMMANDE definition adjustment, depth of focus adjustment; ~ **au point à distance** *f* TV remote control focusing; ~ **au point fixe** *f* PHOTO fixed focus; ~ **au point préalable** *f* CINEMAT prefocusing; ~ **au point du programme** *f* ORDINAT program checkout; ~ **au point sélective** *f* CINEMAT differential focusing; ~ **au point sur pellicule** *f* CINEMAT focus on film; ~ **au point à travers l'objectif** *f* CINEMAT through-the-lens focusing; ~ **de pot** *f* CERAM VER pot setting; ~ **de prix préalable** *f* EMBALLAGE prepricing; ~ **au riblon** *f* PRODUCTION scrap; ~ **sous emballage** *f* IMPRIM *expédition* housing; ~ **sous tension** *f* ELECTROTEC power up, turn-on; ~ **sur ensouple** *f* TEXTILE beaming; ~ **sur orbite** *f* ESPACE entry into orbit, orbital injection, orbiting, *véhicules* acquisition of orbit; ~ **à tension zéro** *f* TV zero volt adjustment; ~ **à la terre** *f* CH DE FER earthing (BrE), grounding (AmE), ELECTROTEC connection to earth (BrE), connection to ground (AmE), earthing (BrE), grounding (AmE), ESPACE earthing (BrE), grounding (AmE); ~ **à la terre en un seul point** *f* ELECTR *connexion d'écrans* single-point bonding; ~ **à la terre de protection multiple** *f* ELECTR *installation* protective multiple earthing (BrE), protective multiple grounding (AmE); ~ **à terris** *f* MINES dumping; ~ **des trames selon le bon angle** *f* IMPRIM *photogravure* angling

mises ~ **rapportées** *f pl* CONS MECA brazed-on tips

mispickel *m* MINERAUX mispickel

missile *m* MILITAIRE missile; ~ **aérodynamique** *m* MILITAIRE aerodynamic missile; ~ **balistique** *m* ELECTRON, ESPACE *véhicules*, MILITAIRE ballistic missile; ~ **de croisière** *m* MILITAIRE, NAUT cruise missile; ~ **navire-sous-marin** *m* MILITAIRE surface-to-underwater missile; ~ **sol-air** *m* MILITAIRE ground-to-air missile; ~ **sol-sol** *m* MILITAIRE ground-to-ground missile; ~ **stratégique** *m* MILITAIRE strategic missile; ~ **téléguidé** *m* MILITAIRE guided missile; ~ **téléguidé à grand rayon d'action** *m* MILITAIRE guided long-range missile

mission: ~ **circumterrestre** *f* ESPACE *véhicules* Earth-orbiting mission; ~ **express** *f* ESPACE *véhicules* sprint mission; ~ **interplanétaire** *f* ESPACE *véhicules* deep space mission, interplanetary mission; ~ **de longue durée** *f* ESPACE *véhicules* long mission; ~ **rapide** *f* ESPACE *véhicules* sprint mission; ~ **spatiale lointaine** *f* ESPACE *véhicules* deep space mission; ~ **vers les planètes intérieures** *f* ESPACE inner planet mission; ~ **vers les planètes supérieures** *f* ESPACE outer planet mission

mitraille *f* MILITAIRE grapeshot, PRODUCTION scrap, scrap iron

mitraillette *f* MILITAIRE submachine gun

mitrailleuse *f* MILITAIRE machine gun

mitre *f* CONSTR cowl, *couteau* bolster

mixage *m* ACOUSTIQUE mixing, ENREGISTR mixdown, PRODUCTION mixing; ~ **définitif** *m* CINEMAT, ENREGISTR final mix; ~ **en marche avant-arrière** *m* CINEMAT, ENREGISTR rock and roll mixing; ~ **magnétique original** *m* CINEMAT magnetic master; ~ **de signaux d'image à activation électronique** *m* TV *différence de couleur* color separation overlay (AmE), colour separation overlay (BrE)

mixer[1] *m* AGRO ALIM electric mixer

mixer[2] *vt* ENREGISTR mix, *multi-piste sur bi-piste stéréo* mix down, TV mix

mixeur *m* ENREGISTR, TV mixer

mixte *adj* CHIMIE mixed

mixtes *m pl* CHARBON middlings, MINES middles, middlings; ~ **définitifs** *m pl* CHARBON finished middlings; ~ **de structure** *m pl* CHARBON true middlings; ~ **de triage** *m pl* CHARBON inferior coal; ~ **vrais** *m pl* CHARBON true middlings

mixtion *f* CHIMIE mixture

mizzonite *f* MINERAUX mizzonite

MLM *abrév (modes longitudinaux multiples)* TELECOM MLM *(multilongitudinal modes)*

mm *abrév (millimètre)* METROLOGIE mm *(millimeter)*

Mn *(manganèse)* CHIMIE Mn *(manganese)*

mnémonique *adj* INFORMAT *code* mnemonic

Mo[1] *(molybdène)* CHIMIE Mo *(molybdenum)*

Mo[2] *abrév (méga-octet)* INFORMAT, ORDINAT Mb *(megabyte)*

mobile[1] *adj* CONS MECA detachable, removable, GEOLOGIE *comportement d'un élément* labile

mobile[2] *m* CONS MECA motor, mover, prime mover, MECANIQUE body in motion, TELECOM mobile radio station; ~ **du compresseur** *m* AERONAUT compressor rotor

mobilier: ~ **et agencement** *m* CONSTR furniture fixtures and fittings

mobilité *f* CHIMIE, MATERIAUX *métal*, PETR, PHYSIQUE mobility; ~ **Hall** *f* PHYSIQUE Hall mobility; ~ **d'ion** *f* PHYS RAYON ionic mobility; ~ **des porteurs** *f* PHYSIQUE carrier mobility

MOD *abrév (matière organique digestible)* RECYCLAGE DOM *(digestible organic matter)*

modacrylique *m* TEXTILE modacrylic

modalités *f pl* PRODUCTION *garantie* scope

mode:[1] ~ **menu** *adj* ORDINAT menu-driven; **en ~ non connecté** *adj* TELECOM CL, connectionless

mode[2] *m* ACOUSTIQUE, ELECTRON, GEOLOGIE *d'une*

roche, IMPRIM, INFORMAT, ORDINAT, PRODUCTION mode; ~ **d'accès** *m* ORDINAT access mode; ~ **d'alimentation** *m* CERAM VER feeding process (AmE), method of feeding (BrE); ~ **alterné** *m* ELECTRON *balayage* alternate mode; ~ **d'appauvrissement** *m* ELECTRON depletion mode; ~ **d'asservissement automatique** *m* TV autoservo mode; ~ **d'attente** *m* ESPACE *véhicules* stand-by mode; ~ **de balayage** *m* ELECTRON sweep mode; ~ **de balayage découpé** *m* ELECTRON chopped mode; ~ **commun** *m* ELECTRON common mode; ~ **de compensation du temps réel** *m* TV drop frame mode; ~ **continu** *m* ORDINAT burst mode; ~ **conversationnel** *m* INFORMAT, ORDINAT conversational mode; ~ **de correction de poste** *m* ESPACE *véhicules* station correction mode; ~ **dédié** *m* INFORMAT, ORDINAT dedicated mode; ~ **de déplétion** *m* ELECTRON depletion mode; ~ **déporté** *m* PRODUCTION *automatisme industriel* remote mode; ~ **de désintégration** *m* PHYS RAYON decay mode; ~ **de désintégration interdite** *m* PHYS RAYON *transition atomique* forbidden decay mode; ~ **différentiel** *m* ELECTRON differential mode; ~ **de diffusion** *m* INFORMAT broadcast mode; ~ **dominant** *m* PHYSIQUE dominant mode, fundamental mode; ~ **édition** *m* TV edit mode; ~ **élastique** *m* ESPACE *véhicules* elastic mode; ~ **électrique** *m* OPTIQUE TE mode, transverse electric mode; ~ **électrique transversal** *m* OPTIQUE, TELECOM TE mode, transverse electric mode; ~ **électromagnétique** *m* OPTIQUE TEM mode, transverse electromagnetic mode, electromagnetic mode; ~ **électromagnétique transversal** *m* OPTIQUE, TELECOM TEM mode, transverse electromagnetic mode; ~ **d'emploi** *m* EMBALLAGE directions for use, instructions for use, PRODUCTION instructions for use; ~ **d'enrichissement** *m* ELECTRON enhancement mode; ~ **d'exécution** *m* PRODUCTION *automatisme industriel* run mode; ~ **d'exploitation avec attente** *m* TELECOM delay-mode relay; ~ **d'exploitation avec perte** *m* TELECOM loss-mode working; ~ **de fabrication** *m* PAPIER processing; ~ **fenêtre** *m* INFORMAT pop-up window; ~ **de fonctionnement** *m* ELECTROTEC operating mode, TELECOM mode of operation; ~ **fondamental** *m* ELECTROTEC dominant mode, fundamental mode, ESPACE *véhicules* fundamental mode, OPTIQUE HE11 mode, fundamental mode, PHYSIQUE dominant mode, fundamental mode, fundamental mode; ~ **fondamental de vibration** *m* ACOUSTIQUE fundamental vibration mode; ~ **de fuite** *m* OPTIQUE, TELECOM leaky mode; ~ **de gaine** *m* OPTIQUE, TELECOM cladding mode; ~ **guidé** *m* OPTIQUE, TELECOM bound mode; ~ **du guide d'ondes** *m* TELECOM waveguide mode; ~ **hybride** *m* OPTIQUE, TELECOM hybrid mode; ~ **interactif** *m* INFORMAT, ORDINAT interactive mode; ~ **d'interrogation** *m* ELECTRON interrogation mode; ~ **lié** *m* OPTIQUE, TELECOM bound mode; ~ **longitudinal unique** *m* TELECOM SLM, single-longitudinal mode; ~ **LP** *m (mode à polarisation rectiligne)* OPTIQUE, TELECOM LP mode *(linearly polarized mode)*; ~ **de métré** *m* CONSTR method of measurement; ~ **de montage électronique** *m* TV edit mode; ~ **multiclique** *m* TELECOM multiclique mode; ~ **multidestination** *m* TELECOM multidestination mode; ~ **natif** *m* INFORMAT, ORDINAT native mode; ~ **naturel de vibration** *m* ESPACE natural mode of vibration; ~ **non interrogé** *m* PRODUCTION *automatisme industriel* unpolled mode; ~ **non lié** *m* OPTIQUE, TELECOM unbound mode; ~ **normal** *m* PHYSIQUE normal mode; ~ **normal déconnecté** *m* TELE-

COM NDM, normal disconnected mode; ~ **normal de réponse** m TELECOM NRM, normal response mode; ~ **normal de vibration** m ACOUSTIQUE, ESPACE natural mode of vibration; ~ **opératoire** m PRODUCTION procedure, TELECOM mode of operation, TEXTILE operating method; ~ **opératoire de soudage** m CONSTR welding procedure; ~ **d'opérer** m PRODUCTION modus operandi; ~ **d'oscillation** m ELECTRON oscillation mode; ~ **parallèle** m ELECTROTEC parallel form; ~ **particulier** m BREVETS embodiment; ~ **partiel** m ELECTRON harmonic mode; ~ **par transmission** m ELECTRON transmission mode; ~ **passif** m ELECTRON passive mode; ~ **point** m INFORMAT bit map; ~ **à polarisation rectiligne** m *(mode LP)* OPTIQUE, TELECOM linearly polarized mode *(LP mode)*; ~ **de programmation déportée** m PRODUCTION *automatisme industriel* remote program mode; ~ **de propagation** m OPTIQUE bound mode, propagation mode; ~ **propre** m ESPACE *véhicules* fundamental mode; ~ **propre de vibration** m ESPACE fundamental vibration mode; ~ **de rafraîchissement** m ELECTRON refresh mode; ~ **rayonnant** m OPTIQUE, TELECOM radiation mode; ~ **de réacquisition** m ESPACE *véhicules* reacquisition mode; ~ **de réalisation d'invention** m BREVETS way of carrying out the invention; ~ **de redondance** m PRODUCTION *automatisme industriel* backup mode; ~ **de réparation** m ESPACE *véhicules* restoration mode; ~ **saturé** m ELECTRON saturated mode; ~ **de secours** m ESPACE *véhicules* emergency mode; ~ **séquentiel** m ORDINAT sequence control; ~ **silencieux** m IMPRIM quiet mode; ~ **de surcharge EMCN** m TELECOM DCME overload; ~ **TE** m *(mode transversal électrique)* OPTIQUE, TELECOM TE mode, transverse electric mode; ~ **TE/TM** m PHYSIQUE TE/TM mode; ~ **TEM** m *(mode transversal électrique, mode transversal magnétique)* OPTIQUE, TELECOM TEM mode, transverse electromagnetic mode; ~ **de test déporté** m PRODUCTION *automatisme industriel* remote test mode; ~ **TM** m *(mode transversal magnétique)* OPTIQUE, TELECOM TM mode, transverse magnetic mode; ~ **de traitement** m INFORMAT, ORDINAT processing mode; ~ **de transfert synchrone** m TELECOM STM, synchronous transfer mode; ~ **de transmission** m ELECTRON transmission mode; ~ **transversal électrique** m *(mode TE, mode TEM)* OPTIQUE, TELECOM TE mode, transverse electric mode; ~ **transversal magnétique** m *(mode TM, mode TEM)* OPTIQUE, TELECOM TM mode, transverse magnetic mode

modelage m PRODUCTION modeling (AmE), modelling (BrE), pattern making

modelé m CONSTR form; ~ **dans les ombres** m PHOTO shadow detail

modèle m BREVETS design, ELECTRON pattern, ESPACE *essais*, INFORMAT model, NAUT mock-up, model, ORDINAT model, PRODUCTION pattern, TELECOM model; ~ **d'affectation du trafic** m TRANSPORT traffic assignment model; ~ **des bandes** m METALL band model; ~ **Bohr-Sommerfeld** m PHYSIQUE Bohr-Sommerfeld model; ~ **de bulles** m METALL bubble model; ~ **calcul** m GAZ mathematical model; ~ **à cases** m TELECOM compartmental model; ~ **collectif** m PHYSIQUE collective model; ~ **à compartiments** m TELECOM compartmental model; ~ **des couches** m NUCLEAIRE, PHYSIQUE shell model; ~ **de Debye** m PHYSIQUE Debye model; ~ **dynamique** m ESPACE *essais* dynamic model;

~ **d'essai** m ESSAIS test model; ~ **d'étude** m ESPACE *essais* engineering model; ~ **de faisceaux** m PHYS RAYON *noyau atomique* beam model; ~ **de fonderie** m MECANIQUE *matériaux* casting pattern; ~ **du gaz de phonons** m PHYSIQUE phonon gas model; ~ **de la goutte liquide** m PHYSIQUE liquid drop model; ~ **hiérarchique** m INFORMAT, ORDINAT hierarchical model; ~ **hydrodynamique** m EN RENOUV hydrodynamic model; ~ **d'intégration** m ESPACE *essais* integration model; ~ **de Jackson** m NUCLEAIRE Jackson model; ~ **mathématique** m ELECTRON, INFORMAT, ORDINAT mathematical model; ~ **du moment d'inertie variable** m NUCLEAIRE variable moment of inertia model; ~ **nucléaire** m PHYSIQUE nuclear model; ~ **numérique maillé** m GAZ multiphase digital model; ~ **numérique de simulation** m GAZ digital simulation model; ~ **ordre-désordre** m NUCLEAIRE order-disorder model; ~ **à particules indépendantes** m NUCLEAIRE, PHYSIQUE independent particle model; ~ **perfectionné** m PRODUCTION improved pattern, improved type; ~ **de qualification** m ESPACE *essais* qualification model; ~ **du quartet** m NUCLEAIRE quartet model; ~ **réduit** m CINEMAT miniature, scale model, GEOMETRIE, NAUT scale model, TELECOM reduced model; ~ **de référence de protocole** m TELECOM PRM, protocol reference model; ~ **de référence à sept couches** m INFORMAT, ORDINAT seven-layer reference model; ~ **du régulateur** m NUCLEAIRE governor model; ~ **relationnel** m INFORMAT, ORDINAT relational model; ~ **de réseau** m INFORMAT, ORDINAT network model; ~ **sédimentaire** m GAZ sedimentary model; ~ **de sphères dures** m CRISTALL hard sphere model; ~ **stochastique** m INFORMAT, ORDINAT stochastic model; ~ **de structure par éléments finis** m ESPACE *véhicules* finite element structural model; ~ **de transport** m POLLUTION *polluants* transport model; ~ **d'utilité** m BREVETS utility model; ~ **vectoriel** m PHYSIQUE *atome* vector model; ~ **de vol** m ESPACE *essais* flight model; ~ **de Westcott** m NUCLEAIRE Westcott model

modeler vt PRODUCTION shape, TEXTILE pattern

modeleur m PRODUCTION pattern maker

modélisation f ELECTRON, GEOLOGIE, INFORMAT, ORDINAT, QUALITE modeling (AmE), modelling (BrE); ~ **multidimensionnelle** f ORDINAT multidimensional modelling; ~ **de signaux** f ELECTRON signal modeling (AmE), signal modelling (BrE)

modéliste m CINEMAT miniature maker, model builder

modem m ELECTRON, IMPRIM *télétransmissions* modem, INFORMAT, ORDINAT dataphone (TM), modem, TELECOM modem; ~ **acoustique** m INFORMAT acoustic modem; ~ **asynchrone** m ELECTRON asynchronous modem; ~ **à couplage acoustique** m INFORMAT acoustically-coupled modem; ~ **courte distance** m ORDINAT baseband modem; ~ **en bande de base** m ORDINAT, TELECOM baseband modem; ~ **à faible vitesse de transmission** m ELECTRON low-speed modem; ~ **à grande vitesse de transmission** m ELECTRON high-speed modem; ~ **incorporé** m INFORMAT built-in modem; ~ **intégré** m ORDINAT integrated modem; ~ **à large bande** m ELECTRON wide band modem; ~ **lent** m ELECTRON low-speed modem; ~ **MDF** m ELECTRON FSK modem; ~ **à MF** m ELECTRON FM modem; ~ **à modulation de fréquence** m ELECTRON frequency modulation modem; ~ **pour fibre optique** m ELECTRON fiberoptic modem (AmE), fibreoptic modem (BrE); ~ **pour modulation par déplacement de fréquence** m ELEC-

TRON FSK modem; ~ **pour transmission asynchrone** *m* ELECTRON asynchronous modem; ~ **prêt** *m* ORDINAT, TELECOM DSR, data set ready; ~ **rapide** *m* ELECTRON high-speed modem; ~ **sur carte** *m* ELECTRON board-level modem; ~ **synchrone** *m* ELECTRON synchronous modem

modérateur[1] *adj* CONS MECA governing

modérateur[2] *m* CINEMAT restrainer, CONS MECA governor, ELECTRON moderator, INST HYDR throttle, PHYSIQUE moderator; ~ **organique** *m* NUCLEAIRE organic moderator; ~ **de vitesse** *m* CONS MECA overspeed gear, overspeeder

modérer *vt* PRODUCTION *vitesse d'une machine* check

modes: ~ **couplés** *m pl* ESPACE, OPTIQUE, TELECOM coupled modes; ~ **longitudinaux multiples** *m pl* *(MLM)* TELECOM multilongitudinal modes *(MLM)*; ~ **résonants** *m pl* PHYS RAYON *cavités optiques, lasers à gaz* resonant modes

modificateur *m* CHARBON modifier; ~ **de densité** *m* AGRO ALIM density modifier; ~ **instantané** *m* CONS MECA trip, trip gear; ~ **de réseau** *m* CERAM VER network modifier; ~ **de tension superficielle** *m* POLLU MER surface tension modifier

modificatif *m* ORDINAT amendment record

modification *f* BREVETS amendment, INFORMAT patch, MECANIQUE change order; ~ **de l'accord** *f* ELECTRON detuning; ~ **a posteriori** *f* PRODUCTION *fabricant* retrofit; ~ **de la couleur** *f* IMPRIM *photogravure, impression* color shift (AmE), colour shift (BrE); ~ **en cours d'appel** *f* TELECOM in-call modification; ~ **de l'orbite** *f* ESPACE orbit modification; ~ **technique** *f* PRODUCTION engineering change

modifier *vt* CONS MECA amend, ELECTRON modify, INFORMAT, ORDINAT modify, patch; ~ **la priorité** *vt* PRODUCTION expedite

modulaire *adj* INFORMAT, ORDINAT modular

modularité *f* INFORMAT, ORDINAT, QUALITE modularity

modulateur *m* ELECTRON, INFORMAT, ORDINAT, TELECOM, TV modulator; ~ **à absorption** *m* ELECTRON absorptive modulator; ~ **acousto-optique** *m* ELECTRON, OPTIQUE acousto-optic modulator, acousto-optical modulator; ~ **d'amplitude** *m* ELECTRON amplitude modulator; ~ **d'amplitude à quadrature** *m* ELECTRON quadrature amplitude modulator; ~ **à bande latérale unique** *m* ELECTRON single sideband modulator; ~ **couleur** *m* TV color modulator (AmE), colour modulator (BrE); ~ **à deux bandes latérales** *m* ELECTRON double sideband modulator; ~ **à diode** *m* ELECTRON diode modulator; ~ **dynamiseur** *m* ELECTRON serrodyne modulator; ~ **électro-optique** *m* ELECTRON electro-optical modulator; ~ **en anneau** *m* ENREGISTR ring modulator; ~ **équilibré** *m* ELECTRON balanced modulator; ~ **à étalement du spectre** *m* ELECTRON spread spectrum modulator; ~ **final** *m* ELECTRON final modulator; ~ **de fréquence** *m* ELECTRON, TV frequency modulator; ~ **hyperfréquence** *m* TELECOM microwave modulator; ~ **d'impulsions** *m* ELECTRON pulse modulator; ~ **à impulsions** *m* ELECTRON pulse modulator; ~ **linéaire** *m* ELECTRON linear modulator; ~ **de lumière** *m* ACOUSTIQUE light modulator, CINEMAT light valve; ~ **optique** *m* ELECTRON, TELECOM optical modulator; ~ **de phase** *m* ELECTRON, TELECOM phase modulator; ~ **à quadrature** *m* ELECTRON quadrature amplitude modulator; ~ **de sous-porteuse de chrominance** *m* ELECTRON chrominance subcarrier modulator; ~ **à**

spectre étalé *m* ELECTRON spread spectrum modulator; ~ **à transistor** *m* ELECTRON transistor modulator; ~ **à tube** *m* ELECTRON vacuum tube modulator; ~ **à tube électronique** *m* ELECTRON vacuum tube modulator

modulateur-démodulateur *m* IMPRIM *télétransmissions* modem, INFORMAT, ORDINAT modem, modulator-demodulator, TELECOM modulator-demodulator

modulation *f* ACOUSTIQUE modulation, sound modulation, ELECTR *onde*, ELECTRON, ENREGISTR, ESPACE *communications*, INFORMAT, ORDINAT, PHYS ONDES *onde*, PHYSIQUE, TELECOM modulation; ~ **acousto-optique** *f* ELECTRON acousto-optic modulation; ~ **d'amplitude** *f* ELECTR *onde*, ELECTRON *(MA)*, ENREGISTR *(MA)*, ORDINAT *(MA)*, PHYS ONDES, PHYSIQUE, TELECOM, TV *(MA)* amplitude modulation *(AM)*; ~ **d'amplitude constante** *f* ELECTRON constant amplitude modulation; ~ **d'amplitude en quadrature** *f* *(MAQ)* ELECTRON, INFORMAT, ORDINAT, TELECOM quadrature amplitude modulation *(QAM)*; ~ **d'amplitude parasite** *f* ELECTRON incidental amplitude modulation; ~ **analogique** *f* ELECTRON, PHYSIQUE analog modulation (AmE), analogue modulation (BrE); ~ **angulaire** *f* ELECTRON angle modulation; ~ **avec étalement du spectre** *f* ELECTRON spread-spectrum modulation; ~ **à balayage de tonalité sans cohérence** *f* TELECOM noncoherent swept tone modulation; ~ **à bande latérale unique** *f* ELECTRON single sideband modulation; ~ **à bandes latérales indépendantes** *f* ELECTRON independent sideband modulation; ~ **à bas niveau** *f* ELECTRON low-level modulation; ~ **basse fréquence** *f* ELECTRON audio modulation; ~ **binaire** *f* TELECOM binary modulation; ~ **BLI** *f* ELECTRON independent sideband modulation; ~ **du canal** *f* ELECTRON channel modulation; ~ **de conductivité** *f* ELECTRON conductivity modulation; ~ **continue du faisceau** *f* TV continuous beam modulation; ~ **de convergence** *f* TV focus modulation; ~ **à courant constant** *f* ELECTRON constant current modulation; ~ **dans l'étage final** *f* ELECTRON direct modulation; ~ **dans la grille** *f* TV grid modulation; ~ **dans le temps** *f* ELECTRON time modulation; ~ **delta** *f* ELECTRON, ESPACE *communications* delta modulation, ORDINAT DM, delta modulation, TELECOM delta modulation, quantization pulse modulation; ~ **delta avec compression-extension** *f* TELECOM CDM, companded delta modulation; ~ **delta à pente asservie** *f* ESPACE *communications* variable slope delta modulation; ~ **de densité** *f* ELECTRON density modulation; ~ **à déplacement minimal** *f* ELECTRON MSK, minimum-shift keying; ~ **à déplacement minimal à filtre gaussien** *f* TELECOM GMSK, Gaussian-filtered minimum shift keying; ~ **à deux bandes latérales** *f* ELECTRON double sideband modulation; ~ **différentielle** *f* ELECTRON differential modulation; ~ **différentielle par impulsions codées** *f* ELECTRON DPCM, differential pulse code modulation; ~ **de données** *f* TELECOM data modulation; ~ **Doppler** *f* ELECTRON Doppler modulation; ~ **DPSK** *f* ELECTRON DPSK, differential phase-shift keying; ~ **en bruit** *f* ENREGISTR noise modulation; ~ **en impulsion codée** *f* ENREGISTR pulse code modulation; ~ **en phase des signaux numériques** *f* TELECOM digital phase modulation; ~ **en quadrature de phase** *f* ELECTRON quadrature amplitude modulation; ~ **extérieure** *f* ELECTRON external modulation; ~ **à faible distorsion** *f* ELECTRON low-distortion modulation; ~ **d'un fais-**

ceau laser *f* ELECTRON laser-beam modulation; ~ **de fréquence** *f (MF)* ELECTR *courant alternatif,* ELECTRON, ENREGISTR, ORDINAT, PHYS ONDES, PHYSIQUE, TELECOM, TV frequency modulation *(FM)*; ~ **de fréquence asservie** *f* TELECOM tamed frequency modulation; ~ **de fréquence à bande étroite** *f* ELECTRON, TELECOM *satellite maritime* NBFM, narrow band frequency modulation; ~ **de fréquence directe** *f* ELECTRON direct frequency modulation; ~ **de fréquence d'impulsion** *f* ELECTRON, INFORMAT, ORDINAT PFM, pulse frequency modulation; ~ **de fréquence indirecte** *f* ELECTRON indirect frequency modulation; ~ **de fréquence linéaire** *f* ESPACE *communications* chirp modulation; ~ **de fréquence modifiée** *f (modulation MFM)* ELECTRON MFM modulation, modified frequency modulation *(modified frequency modulation)*; ~ **de fréquence parasite** *f* ELECTRON incidental frequency modulation; ~ **de fréquence résiduelle** *f* ELECTRON residual frequency modulation; ~ **à haut niveau** *f* ELECTRON high-level modulation; ~ **d'impulsion** *f* ELECTR *réglage,* ELECTRON pulse modulation; ~ **d'impulsion en position** *f* ESPACE PPM, pulse position modulation; ~ **d'impulsions échantillonnées** *f* ELECTRON quantized pulse modulation; ~ **d'impulsions en amplitude** *f (MIA)* ELECTRON, ESPACE, INFORMAT, ORDINAT, TELECOM pulse amplitude modulation *(PAM)*; ~ **d'impulsions en largeur** *f* ESPACE PWM, pulse width modulation; ~ **insuffisante** *f* ELECTRON undermodulation; ~ **d'intensité** *f* ELECTRON current modulation, intensity modulation; ~ **d'intervalle entre impulsions** *f* TV pulse interval modulation; ~ **inverse** *f* ELECTRON inverse modulation; ~ **à large bande** *f* ELECTRON wide band modulation; ~ **de largeur d'impulsion** *f* ELECTRON pulse width modulation; ~ **linéaire** *f* ELECTRON linear modulation; ~ **de lumière** *f* ELECTRON light modulation; ~ **de luminosité** *f* ELECTRON brightness modulation; ~ **mécanique** *f* ELECTRON mechanical modulation; ~ **MFM** *f (modulation de fréquence modifiée)* ELECTRON MFM modulation *(modified frequency modulation)*; ~ **MIC-FM** *f* ELECTRON PCM-FM modulation; ~ **multiniveau** *f* ELECTRON multilevel modulation; ~ **multiple** *f* ELECTRON multiple modulation; ~ **musicale** *f* ACOUSTIQUE sequence; ~ **négative** *f* ELECTRON negative modulation; ~ **numérique** *f* ELECTRON, PHYSIQUE, TELECOM digital modulation; ~ **d'onde porteuse** *f* PHYS ONDES carrier wave modulation; ~ **optique** *f* ELECTRON optical modulation; ~ **par l'anode** *f* ELECTRON anode modulation; ~ **parasite induite** *f* ELECTRON incidental modulation; ~ **par la base** *f* ELECTRON base modulation; ~ **par la cathode** *f* ELECTRON cathode modulation; ~ **par déplacement de fréquence** *f (MDF)* ELECTRON, INFORMAT, ORDINAT, TELECOM, TV frequency shift keying *(FSK)*; ~ **par déplacement de phase** *f (MDP)* ELECTRON, ESPACE *communications,* INFORMAT, ORDINAT, TELECOM phase shift keying *(PSK)*; ~ **par déplacement de phase bivalente** *f (MDPB)* TELECOM binary phase shift keying *(BPSK)*; ~ **par déplacement de phase cohérente** *f (MDPC)* TELECOM coherent phase-shift keying *(CPSK)*; ~ **par déplacement de phase différentielle** *f* ELECTRON DPSK, differential phase-shift keying; ~ **par déplacement de phase modifiée avec retard** *f* ELECTRON delayed MSPK, delayed modified phase-shift keying; ~ **par déplacement de phase quadrivalente** *f (MDPQ)* ELECTRON, TELECOM quad-

riphase shift keying, quaternary phase-shift keying *(QPSK)*; ~ **par diode PIN** *f* ELECTRON PIN diode modulation; ~ **par étalement du spectre** *f* TELECOM spread-spectrum modulation; ~ **par la grille** *f* ELECTRON grid modulation; ~ **par impulsion codée** *f* ELECTRON *(MIC),* INFORMAT *(MIC),* PHYS RAYON *(MIC),* PHYSIQUE, TV *(MIC)* pulse code modulation *(PCM)*; ~ **par impulsion et codage** *f (MIC)* ESPACE, ORDINAT, PHYSIQUE, TV pulse code modulation *(PCM)*; ~ **par impulsions** *f* ELECTRON pulse modulation; ~ **par impulsions de durée** *f (MID)* ELECTRON, ESPACE pulse duration modulation *(PDM)*; ~ **par impulsion et codage différentiels adaptifs** *f (MICDA)* TELECOM adaptive differential pulse code modulation *(ADPCM)*; ~ **par la plaque** *f* ELECTRON anode modulation; ~ **par réduction d'amplitude** *f* ELECTRON downward modulation; ~ **par retard de phase** *f* ELECTRON phase delay keying; ~ **par sauts d'amplitude** *f* ELECTRON amplitude shift keying; ~ **par signal de bruit** *f* TV noise modulation; ~ **par un signal sinusoïdal** *f* ELECTRON sine wave modulation; ~ **PCM différentielle** *f* ELECTRON DPCM, differential pulse code modulation; ~ **de phase** *f (MP)* ELECTRON, ENREGISTR, INFORMAT, ORDINAT, PHYSIQUE, TELECOM, TV phase modulation *(PM)*; ~ **de phase à huit états** *f* ELECTRON eight-phase shift keying; ~ **de porteuse** *f* ELECTRON carrier modulation; ~ **de position d'impulsion** *f* ELECTRON PPM, pulse position modulation, pulse phase modulation; ~ **positive** *f* ELECTRON positive modulation; ~ **de la poussée** *f* ESPACE *propulsion* thrust modulation; ~ **PSK** *f* ELECTRON phase shift keying; ~ **sans retour** *f* TELECOM nonreturn modulation; ~ **sonore** *f* ENREGISTR sound modulation; ~ **de sous-porteuse** *f* TV subcarrier modulation; ~ **de sous-porteuse de chrominance** *f* ELECTRON chrominance subcarrier modulation; ~ **spatiale** *f* ELECTRON spatial modulation; ~ **à spectre étalé** *f* ELECTRON spread-spectrum modulation; ~ **successive** *f* ELECTRON compound modulation; ~ **à taux constant** *f* ELECTRON controlled carrier modulation, floating carrier modulation, variable carrier modulation; ~ **temporelle** *f* ELECTRON time modulation; ~ **de temps d'impulsion** *f* ELECTRON pulse time modulation; ~ **de vitesse** *f* ELECTRON, PHYSIQUE, TV velocity modulation; ~ **vocale à bande étroite** *f* TELECOM NBVM, narrow band voice modulation

module *m* CONS MECA, ELECTR *appareil,* ELECTRON, INFORMAT, INST HYDR, ORDINAT module, PETR modulus, PETROLE module, PHYSIQUE modulus; ~ **d'affichage à cristaux liquides** *m* ELECTRON LCD module, liquid crystal display module; ~ **d'allongement** *m* PLAST CAOU modulus of elongation; ~ **annuel** *m* HYDROLOGIE average annual flow; ~ **d'atterrissage** *m* ESPACE *véhicules* lander, lander stage, landing stage; ~ **d'atterrissage automatique** *m* ESPACE *véhicules* unmanned lander, unmanned landing stage; ~ **à borniers** *m* PRODUCTION terminal-strip module; ~ **de cisaillement** *m* CHARBON rigidity modulus, shear modulus, CONS MECA, PETR shear modulus, PHYSIQUE modulus of rigidity, rigidity modulus, shear modulus; ~ **de Colomb** *m* AERONAUT modulus of elasticity; ~ **de commande** *m* ESPACE *véhicules* command module, TV control deck; ~ **de commande et de service** *m* ESPACE CSM, command and service module; ~ **de commande de ligne** *m* INFORMAT line driver; ~ **de compression** *m* PHYSIQUE bulk modulus,

PLAST CAOU compression modulus; **~ de déformation** *m* CHARBON deformation modulus, CONSTR strain modulus; **~ de déformation volumique** *m* CHARBON compressibility modulus; **~ de descente** *m* ESPACE *véhicules* descent stage; **~ à deux emplacements** *m* PRODUCTION *automatisme industriel* two-slot module; **~ double** *m* PRODUCTION *automatisme industriel* dual slot; **~ d'E/S** *m* PRODUCTION *automatisme industriel* I/O module; **~ d'éclairage** *m* INSTRUMENT lamphouse; **~ éjectable** *m* ESPACE *véhicules* ejectable capsule; **~ d'élasticité** *m* AERONAUT, CHARBON, CONS MECA, CONSTR modulus of elasticity, MATERIAUX elastic modulus, METALL modulus of elasticity, PETR stretch modulus, PHYSIQUE, PLAST CAOU modulus of elasticity; **~ d'élasticité cubique** *m* PHYSIQUE bulk modulus; **~ électronique** *m* AUTO electronic control unit, trigger box, ELECTRON electronic module, PRODUCTION *automatisme industriel* solid-state module; **~ enfichable** *m* ELECTROTEC plug-in module; **~ d'expérience** *m* ESPACE *véhicules* experiment module; **~ d'extension** *m* PRODUCTION expander module; **~ d'extension du système** *m* PRODUCTION *automatisme industriel* system expander module; **~ hyperfréquence** *m* ELECTRON microwave module; **~ d'instrumentation électronique** *m* NUCLEAIRE electronic instrument module; **~ d'interface déporté pour thermistances PTC** *m* PRODUCTION *automatisme industriel* remote RTD module; **~ de masse d'élasticité** *m* CONS MECA bulk modulus of elasticity; **~ de mémoire** *m* INFORMAT, ORDINAT memory module, PRODUCTION *automatisme industriel* memory cartridge; **~ mémoire RAM CMOS** *m* PRODUCTION *automatisme industriel* CMOS RAM memory module; **~ de mémoire à une rangée de broches** *m* INFORMAT, ORDINAT SIMM, single-in-line memory module; **~ multiplex numérique** *m* TELECOM DTI, digital trunk interface, digital carrier module; **~ objet** *m* INFORMAT, ORDINAT object module; **~ d'observation** *m* INSTRUMENT polarizing filter; **~ orbital** *m* ESPACE *véhicules* orbiter stage; **~ porte-objectifs** *m* INSTRUMENT lens panel; **~ porte-platine** *m* INSTRUMENT stage base; **~ de pressiomètre** *m* CHARBON pressuremeter modulus; **~ puissance** *m* PRODUCTION *automatisme industriel* power module; **~ de réaction du sol** *m* CHARBON subgrade reaction modulus; **~ de réception optique** *m* TELECOM fiberoptic receiver (AmE), fibreoptic receiver (BrE), optical receiver; **~ de réglage** *m* AERONAUT calibration module; **~ de résistance** *m* TEXTILE breaking strength; **~ de rétrofusées** *m* ESPACE *véhicules* retropack; **~ de rigidité** *m* PHYSIQUE rigidity modulus, shear modulus; **~ simple** *m* PRODUCTION single slot module, singled module; **~ de sortie** *m* PRODUCTION *automatisme industriel* output terminal; **~ sur carte** *m* ELECTRON card module; **~ à synthèse vocale** *m* PRODUCTION *automatisme industriel* speech module; **~ à touches et à voyants** *m* TELECOM key-and-lamp unit; **~ de transport synchrone** *m* TELECOM STM, synchronous transport module; **~ de transport synchrone-n** *m* TELECOM STM-n, synchronous transport module-n; **~ de volume** *m* PETR bulk modulus; **~ de Young** *m* AERONAUT modulus of elasticity, CHARBON, METALL, PETR, PETROLE *élasticité*, PHYSIQUE, PLAST CAOU Young's modulus
modulé: ~ en amplitude *adj* ELECTRON amplitude-modulated; **~ en fréquence** *adj* ELECTRON frequency-modulated; **~ par impulsion** *adj* ELECTRON pulse-modulated
moduler *vt* ELECTRON, ENREGISTR, PHYSIQUE, TELECOM, TV modulate
modulus: ~ latent *m* METALL latent modulus
moellon *m* CERAM VER grinding runner, CONSTR rubble, rubble stone, INST HYDR rock rubble
mofette *f* EN RENOUV *source chaude* mofette, MINES afterdamp, damp, foul mine gas; **~ inflammable** *f* MINES gas, pit gas
moignon *m* PRODUCTION mop-end brush
moirage *m* ACOUSTIQUE moiré pattern
moiré *m* TV moiré, moiré effect
moirure *f* PLAST CAOU *défaut de peinture* picture framing
mois: ~ anomalistique *m* ASTRONOMIE anomalistic month; **~ anomalistique lunaire** *m* ASTRONOMIE lunar anomalistic month; **~ synodique** *m* ASTRONOMIE synodic month
moisage *m* CONSTR waling
moise *f* CONSTR binding beam, brace, ledger
moiser *vt* CONSTR *étais* brace; **~ ensemble** *vt* CONSTR *des étais, pour éviter le flambage* brace together
moises *f pl* CONSTR *d'une batterie d'étais* braces, MINES dividers
mol *abrév (môle)* METROLOGIE, PHYSIQUE mol *(mole)*
molaire *adj* CHIMIE molar
molale *adj* CHIMIE molal
molalité *f* CHIMIE molality
molarite *f* PRODUCTION millstone grit
molarité *f* CHIMIE molarity
mole *f* METROLOGIE gram molecule (AmE), gramme molecule (BrE)
môle[1] *m* DISTRI EAU mole, NAUT breakwater, mole, OCEANO mole
môle[2] *f* CHIMIE, METROLOGIE *(mol)*, PHYSIQUE *(mol)* mole *(mol)*
molécule *f* PETROLE, PHYSIQUE molecule; **~ activée** *f* PHYS RAYON activated molecule; **~ diatomique** *f* PHYS RAYON diatomic molecule; **~ polaire** *f* CHIMIE, PLAST CAOU polar molecule
molécule-gramme *f* METROLOGIE gram molecule (AmE), gramme molecule (BrE)
molécules: ~ interstellaires *f pl* ASTRONOMIE interstellar molecules
moletage *m* CERAM VER grip, CONS MECA knurling, nurling, PRODUCTION milling
moleté *adj* MECANIQUE knurled, milled
moleter *vt* PRODUCTION mill
molette *f* AGRO ALIM upper millstone, AUTO starwheel, CERAM VER shaping tool, CINEMAT thumbwheel, CONS MECA cutter, cutter wheel, knurling tool, knurl, knurled nut, milled nut, nurled nut, revolving cutter, *tourneur* nurl, MINES hoisting pulley, pithead pulley, pulley, PRODUCTION crown pulley, *tourneur* milling tool, nurling tool; **~ coupante** *f* CONS MECA cutter, cutter wheel, cutting wheel, revolving cutter; **~ de coupe** *f* IMPRIM slitter; **~ de découpe** *f* CERAM VER glass-cutting wheel; **~ à dresser** *f* CONS MECA crusher, dresser cutter; **~ d'entraînement** *f* INSTRUMENT *cercle horizontal* drive knob; **~ à gorge** *f* CONS MECA grooved roller, sheave; **~ de marquage du pli** *f* IMPRIM *façonnage* creaser; **~ de mise au point** *f* INSTRUMENT central focusing wheel; **~ de perforation** *f* IMPRIM *façonnage* perforation wheel
molettes *f pl* CERAM VER edge rolls
molleton *m* TEXTILE molleton
mollir *vi* NAUT abate

molybdate *m* CHIMIE molybdate
molybdène *m* (*Mo*) CHIMIE molybdenum (*Mo*)
molybdénite *f* MINERAUX molybdenite
molybdénocre *f* MINERAUX molybdic ocher (AmE), molybdic ochre (BrE), molybdite
molybdine *f* MINERAUX molybdic ocher (AmE), molybdic ochre (BrE)
molybdite *f* MINERAUX molybdic ocher (AmE), molybdic ochre (BrE), molybdite
molysite *f* MINERAUX molysite
moment *m* CONS MECA moment, momentum, CONSTR, MECANIQUE, PHYSIQUE *force* moment; ~ **d'amortissement** *m* AERONAUT damping moment; ~ **angulaire** *m* ASTRONOMIE, PHYS PART, PHYSIQUE angular momentum; ~ **angulaire intrinsèque** *m* PHYS PART intrinsic angular momentum; ~ **angulaire orbital** *m* PHYS RAYON *fonction d'onde* orbital angular momentum; ~ **de battement** *m* AERONAUT flapping moment; ~ **de charnière** *m* AERONAUT hinge moment; ~ **cinétique** *m* AERONAUT, MECANIQUE, PHYSIQUE angular momentum; ~ **cinétique orbital** *m* PHYSIQUE orbital angular momentum; ~ **cinétique de spin** *m* PHYSIQUE spin angular momentum; ~ **cinétique total** *m* PHYSIQUE total angular momentum; ~ **d'un couple** *m* CONS MECA turning moment, twisting moment, MECANIQUE moment of couple; ~ **du couple inclinant** *m* NAUT heeling moment; ~ **du couple de redressement** *m* NAUT righting moment; ~ **dipolaire** *m* CHIMIE dipole moment; ~ **dipôle** *m* ELECTROTEC dipole moment; ~ **de dipôle électrique** *m* ELECTROTEC electric dipole moment; ~ **de dipôle électrique instantané** *m* PHYS RAYON instantaneous electric dipole moment; ~ **électrique dipolaire** *m* ELECTROTEC, PHYSIQUE electric dipole moment; ~ **électrique quadripolaire** *m* PHYS RAYON quadrupole electric moment; ~ **électromagnétique** *m* ELECTR electromagnetic moment; ~ **d'encastrement** *m* CONSTR fixed end moment; ~ **fléchissant** *m* CONSTR bending moment; ~ **de flexion** *m* CONS MECA, CONSTR, NAUT, PRODUCTION bending moment; ~ **gravitationnel** *m* ESPACE gravity gradient torque; ~ **d'inclinaison** *m* NAUT heeling moment; ~ **d'inclinaison transversale** *m* NAUT heeling moment; ~ **d'inertie** *m* CONS MECA rotational inertia, CONSTR, NAUT, PHYSIQUE moment of inertia; ~ **d'inertie de la pale** *m* AERONAUT blade moment of inertia; ~ **de lacet** *m* AERONAUT, EN RENOUV yawing moment; ~ **magnétique** *m* ELECTR, PHYS PART, PHYSIQUE magnetic moment; ~ **magnétique dipolaire** *m* PHYSIQUE magnetic dipole moment; ~ **magnétique du muon** *m* PHYS RAYON muon magnetic moment; ~ **orbital** *m* PHYS RAYON *atome* orbital moment; ~ **par rapport à un axe** *m* PHYSIQUE moment about an axis; ~ **quadripolaire** *m* PHYSIQUE quadrupole moment; ~ **quadripolaire nucléaire** *m* PHYSIQUE nuclear quadrupole moment; ~ **de redressement** *m* NAUT righting moment; ~ **redresseur** *m* AERONAUT *aérodynamique* restoring moment; ~ **de renversement** *m* CONSTR overturning moment; ~ **de roulis** *m* AERONAUT rolling moment; ~ **de rupture** *m* MECANIQUE failure moment; ~ **stabilisateur** *m* AERONAUT restoring moment; ~ **de tangage** *m* EN RENOUV pitching moment; ~ **de torsion** *m* RESSORTS torsional moment; ~ **de torsion externe** *m* CONS MECA external torque; ~ **de torsion de la pale** *m* AERONAUT blade-twisting moment; ~ **de traînée** *m* AERONAUT drag moment
monacide *m* CHIMIE monacid
monadique *adj* INFORMAT, ORDINAT monadic

monaural *adj* ACOUSTIQUE, ENREGISTR monaural
monazite *f* MATERIAUX, MINERAUX monazite
monceau *m* CONSTR heap, pile
monergol *m* CHIMIE monopropellant; ~ **liquide** *m* THERMODYN liquid monopropellant
monheimite *f* MINERAUX monheimite
moniteur *m* ELECTR, INFORMAT monitor, INSTRUMENT control screen, monitor, ORDINAT monitor, supervisor, PHYS RAYON, TELECOM monitor, TV monitor, picture monitor; ~ **d'antenne** *m* TV air monitor; ~ **bistandard** *m* TV dual-standard monitor; ~ **de caméra** *m* TV camera monitor; ~ **de contamination par poussière** *m* NUCLEAIRE dust monitor; ~ **d'émission** *m* TV master monitor; ~ **final** *m* TV air monitor; ~ **d'image et de forme d'onde** *m* TV image and waveform monitor; ~ **de retour antenne** *m* TV air monitor; ~ **RVB** *m* INFORMAT, ORDINAT RGB monitor; ~ **à six canaux** *m* INSTRUMENT six-channel monitor; ~ **de sortie** *m* TV line monitor, output monitor; ~ **vidéo** *m* ORDINAT video display
monoacétine *f* CHIMIE monoacetin
monoacide[1] *adj* CHIMIE monoacidic
monoacide[2] *m* CHIMIE monoacid
monoalcoolique *adj* CHIMIE monoalcoholic
monoamide *m* CHIMIE monoamide
monoamine *f* CHIMIE monoamine
monoaminé *adj* CHIMIE monoamino
monoatomique *adj* CHIMIE monadic, monatomic, monoatomic
monobasique *adj* CHIMIE *acide* monobasic
monobloc *m* PRODUCTION solid bloc
monochromateur *m* OPTIQUE, PHYSIQUE, TELECOM monochromator
monochromatique *adj* IMPRIM *photogravure*, OPTIQUE, PHYSIQUE monochromatic
monochrome[1] *adj* IMPRIM monochrome, *photogravure* monochromatic, INFORMAT, ORDINAT monochrome
monochrome[2] *m* CINEMAT monochrome; ~ **à quartz** *m* NUCLEAIRE quartz monochromator
monocinétique *adj* PHYSIQUE monoenergetic
monoclinal *m* GEOLOGIE monocline
monoclinique *adj* CHIMIE, CRISTALL monoclinic
monocoque *adj* ESPACE *véhicules* monocoque, NAUT single-hull
monocorde *adj* ACOUSTIQUE monochord
monocouche *f* CHIMIE monolayer
monocristal *m* CRISTALL, ELECTRON, MATERIAUX single crystal; ~ **sans dislocations** *m* MATERIAUX, METALL whisker; ~ **de semi-conducteur** *m* ELECTRON semiconductor single crystal; ~ **whisker** *m* MATERIAUX, METALL whisker
monocristalline *f* GEOLOGIE diadochy
monoénergétique *adj* PHYSIQUE monoenergetic
monoéthylénique *adj* CHIMIE *acide* monoethylenic
monofilament *m* PHYSIQUE strand, PLAST CAOU monofilament
monogénique *adj* GEOLOGIE *conglomérat* monogenetic, monomict
monohalogéné *adj* CHIMIE monohalogen
monohydrate *m* CHIMIE monohydrate
monohydraté *adj* CHIMIE monohydrated
monohydrique *adj* CHIMIE *composé* monohydric
monôme *m* MATH monomial
monomère[1] *adj* CHIMIE, PLAST CAOU monomeric
monomère[2] *m* CHIMIE, IMPRIM, MATERIAUX, PETROLE, PLAST CAOU monomer

monominéral *adj* GEOLOGIE monomineralic

monophasé *adj* ELECTR *alimentation* monophase, *réseau* single-phase, ELECTROTEC one-phase, single-phase, uniphase

monopied *m* CINEMAT unipod

monopolaire *adj* ELECTR *alimentation* monopolar

monopôle: ~ **magnétique** *m* PHYSIQUE magnetic monopole

monopoulie *f* PRODUCTION constant speed pulley

monorail *m* CH DE FER, CONSTR, MINES, TRANSPORT monorail; ~ **aérien** *m* CONS MECA runway, PRODUCTION overhead runway, overhead track; ~ **à chariots électrifiés** *m* CONS MECA overhead electrical monorail conveyor; ~ **à cheval sur poutre porteuse** *m* TRANSPORT saddlebag monorail; ~ **supporté** *m* TRANSPORT supported monorail; ~ **surélevé** *m* TRANSPORT elevated monorail; ~ **suspendu** *m* MINES monorail, TRANSPORT monorail conveyor, suspended monorail; ~ **transporteur** *m* CONS MECA runway, PRODUCTION overhead runway, overhead track

monorotor *m* AERONAUT *hélicoptère* single rotor

monosaccharide *m* CHIMIE monosaccharide

monosaccharoses *m pl* CHIMIE monosaccharoses

monospace *m* TRANSPORT minivan

monostable[1] *adj* ELECTRON, INFORMAT, ORDINAT monostable

monostable[2] *m* PHYSIQUE monostable

monostéarine *f* CHIMIE monostearin

monosubstitué *adj* CHIMIE monosubstituted

monotron *m* ELECTRON monotron

monotropique *adj* METALL *réaction* monotropic

monovalence *f* CHIMIE monovalence, monovalency, univalence

monovalent *adj* CHIMIE monovalent, univalent

monoxyde: ~ **d'azote** *m* POLLUTION nitric oxide; ~ **de carbone** *m* CHARBON, POLLUTION, VEHICULES carbon monoxide; ~ **de diazote** *m* POLLUTION nitrous oxide

mont: ~ **sous-marin** *m* OCEANO seamount

montage *m* ACOUSTIQUE dubbing, CINEMAT editing, CONS MECA fit, fitting, fixture, setting, *machine* setting up, CONSTR assembly, *pierres au moyen d'une grue* raising, CRISTALL setting, setting up, ELECTR circuit, ELECTRON mounting, ELECTROTEC arrangement, connection, ENREGISTR editing, IMPRIM make-up, stripping, METROLOGIE jig, *essai et contrôle dimensionnel* fixture, MINES raise, NAUT fitting, PAPIER erection, *machine* assembling, PHOTO *diapositive* mounting, PRODUCTION *machine* erection, TV editing, setup, VEHICULES assembly; ~ **affleurant** *m* PRODUCTION flush mount; ~ **à l'aide de goujons** *m* PRODUCTION stud mounting; ~ **alterné** *m* CINEMAT crosscutting, intercutting; ~ **amplificateur** *m* ELECTRON amplifier circuit, amplifying circuit; ~ **analogique** *m* ELECTRON analog circuit (AmE), analogue circuit (BrE); ~ **à anode commune** *m* ELECTROTEC common anode connection; ~ **astable** *m* ELECTRON astable circuit; ~ **autodyne** *m* ELECTRON autodyne; ~ **automatique** *m* TV auto-editing, automatic editing; ~ **avec code temporel** *m* CINEMAT, TV time code editing; ~ **à base commune** *m* ELECTROTEC common base connection, earthed base connection (BrE), grounded base connection (AmE); ~ **bout à bout** *m* CINEMAT first assembly; ~ **de bridage** *m* CONS MECA clamping fixture; ~ **à bride** *m* ESPACE *véhicules* flange mounting; ~ **à cathode asservie** *m* PHYSIQUE cathode follower; ~ **cathodyne** *m* ELECTROTEC ca-

thode follower; ~ **collecteur commun** *m* PHYSIQUE emitter follower; ~ **à collecteur commun** *m* ELECTROTEC common collector connection, earthed collector connection (BrE), grounded collector connection (AmE); ~ **compensateur** *m* ELECTROTEC compensator; ~ **définitif** *m* CINEMAT final cut; ~ **déphaseur** *m* ELECTRON paraphase amplifier; ~ **détecteur** *m* ELECTRON detector circuit; ~ **à drain commun** *m* ELECTROTEC common drain connection; ~ **élastique** *m* ESPACE *véhicules* shock mount; ~ **électronique** *m* TV E-E, electronic editing; ~ **à émetteur commun** *m* ELECTROTEC common emitter connection, earthed emitter connection (BrE), grounded emitter connection (AmE); ~ **émetteur-suiveur** *m* ELECTROTEC emitter follower; ~ **en A et B** *m* CINEMAT checkerboarding; ~ **en l'air** *m* CONS MECA chucking, faceplate mounting; ~ **en assemblage** *m* TV add-on edit, assemble edit; ~ **en baie** *m* EMBALLAGE rack mount; ~ **en cascade** *m* ELECTROTEC cascade arrangement, tandem arrangement; ~ **encastré** *m* ELECTR *de commutateur* flush mounting; ~ **d'un enchaînement** *m* TV insert edit; ~ **en continu** *m* CINEMAT continuity editing; ~ **en demi-pont** *m* ELECTROTEC half bridge arrangement; ~ **en étoile** *m* ELECTROTEC Y-connection, star connection; ~ **en opposition** *m* ELECTROTEC back-to-back arrangement; ~ **en page** *m* IMPRIM editing; ~ **en parallèle** *m* ELECTR parallel connection, parallel mounting, ELECTROTEC parallel arrangement, parallel connection, PHYSIQUE parallel connection; ~ **en pont** *m* ELECTR bridge circuit, bridge connection, ELECTROTEC bridge circuit; ~ **en saillie** *m* ELECTRON surface mounting; ~ **en série** *m* ELECTR series connection, series mounting, ELECTROTEC series arrangement, series connection, tandem connection, MINES, PHYSIQUE series connection; ~ **en surface** *m* ELECTR, INFORMAT, ORDINAT surface mounting; ~ **en totem pôle** *m* ELECTRON totem pole arrangement; ~ **entre pointes** *m* CONS MECA chucking between centers (AmE), chucking between centres (BrE); ~ **en triangle** *m* ELECTROTEC delta connection, mesh connection; ~ **en triangle double** *m* ELECTR double delta connection; ~ **d'essai** *m* ELECTROTEC breadboard model, ESPACE test rig; ~ **étoile-triangle** *m* ELECTROTEC star-delta connection; ~ **de fabrication** *m* MECANIQUE *outillage* jig; ~ **fin** *m* CINEMAT fine cut; ~ **flottabilité** *m* AERONAUT *hélicoptère* floating gear; ~ **à force** *m* CONS MECA force fit; ~ **à frottement doux** *m* CONS MECA push fit; ~ **à frottement dur** *m* CONS MECA drive fit, driving fit; ~ **à glissement** *m* CONS MECA running fit; ~ **à grille commune** *m* ELECTROTEC common gate connection; ~ **intégrateur** *m* ELECTROTEC integrating circuit; ~ **interne** *m* ELECTROTEC internal installation; ~ **Leblanc** *m* ELECTR *raccordement transformateur* Leblanc connection; ~ **manuel** *m* TV manual editing; ~ **manuel pour magnétoscope hélicoïdal** *m* TV physical helical editing; ~ **manuel pour magnétoscope à quatre têtes** *m* TV physical quadruplex editing; ~ **mural** *m* CONSTR wall fitting; ~ **du négatif** *m* CINEMAT negative cutting; ~ **non symétrique** *m* ELECTROTEC unsymmetrical arrangement; ~ **numérique** *m* ELECTRON digital circuit; ~ **off-line** *m* TV off-line editing; ~ **oscillateur** *m* ELECTRON oscillator circuit; ~ **papier** *m* IMPRIM paste-up, *préparation* mechanicals; ~ **par association** *m* CINEMAT relational editing; ~ **par boulons** *m* PRODUCTION bolt mounting; ~ **par insertion** *m* TV insert editing; ~ **physique** *m* TV mechanical editing; ~ **pose de ligne** *m* ELECTR *raccordement* wiring; ~ **rapide** *m* CINEMAT flash cutting; ~ **à réaction** *m* ELECTRON regenerative circuit; ~ **redresseur** *m* ELECTROTEC rectifying circuit; ~ **réglable** *m* CINEMAT adjustable lens holder; ~ **de rodage** *m* CONS MECA lapping fixture; ~ **de Rowland** *m* PHYSIQUE Rowland mounting; ~ **Scott** *m* ELECTR *connexion de transformateur* Scott connection; ~ **serré** *m* CINEMAT tight editing; ~ **au sol** *m* CONS MECA floor-mounting; ~ **sur écran** *m* IMPRIM editing; ~ **sur film** *m* IMPRIM editing; ~ **sur original** *m* TV editing on original; ~ **sur panneau** *m* ELECTR, PRODUCTION panel mounting; ~ **sur poteau** *m* PRODUCTION pole mounting; ~ **symétrique** *m* ELECTROTEC symmetrical arrangement; ~ **tête-bêche** *m* ELECTROTEC antiparallel arrangement, back-to-back arrangement; ~ **de vérification** *m* CONS MECA checking fixture

montage-papier *m* IMPRIM paper flat

montagnes: ~ **lunaires** *f pl* ASTRONOMIE lunar highlands

montant[1] *adj* CONSTR uphill

montant[2] *m* CONS MECA upright, *machine à raboter* housing, CONSTR post, stile, *échelle* side bar, upright, MECANIQUE strut, MINES post, prop, support pier, support pillar, upright, PRODUCTION *machine à raboter* standard; ~ **d'angle** *m* CONSTR corner pillar, corner post; ~ **de battement** *m* CONSTR shutting post; ~ **de busc** *m* DISTRI EAU meeting post, miter post (AmE), mitre post (BrE); ~ **de cloison** *m* NAUT bulkhead stiffener; ~ **de côtière** *m* CONSTR hinge post, hinging post, swinging post; ~ **de derrick** *m* CONSTR derrick post; ~ **d'entrée du roof** *m* NAUT companionway post; ~ **de fenêtre** *m* CONSTR jamb, jamb post; ~ **de fourche** *m* VEHICULES *motocyclette* fork leg; ~ **de guidage** *m* PETR guidepost; ~ **de guide** *m* PETR guidepost; ~ **de porte** *m* CONSTR door post, gate post, jamb, jamb post, VEHICULES door pillar

montants: ~ **à glissière incorporée** *m pl* CONS MECA *machine-outil* integral-way columns

monté: ~ **en bâti** *adj* CINEMAT, ELECTROTEC rack-mounted; ~ **en dérivation** *adj* PHYSIQUE shunt; ~ **en étoile** *adj* TELECOM star-connected; ~ **en parallèle** *adj* ELECTROTEC, PHYSIQUE connected in parallel, parallel-connected; ~ **en série** *adj* ELECTROTEC, PHYSIQUE connected in series, series-connected; ~ **en tandem** *adj* PRODUCTION *bloc de contact* tandem-mounted; ~ **sur rubis** *adj* MECANIQUE jeweled (AmE), jewelled (BrE)

monte-acides *m pl* GENIE CHIM acid egg, acid elevator

montebrasite *f* MINERAUX montebrasite

monte-charge *m* CONSTR heavy-duty lift, lifter, MECANIQUE elevator, PRODUCTION elevator, goods lift, hoist, TRANSPORT elevator; ~ **à bras pour magasin** *m* PRODUCTION handpower warehouse goods lift; ~ **en continu** *m* PRODUCTION unit load vertical conveyor; ~ **à frein de sûreté à friction** *m* PRODUCTION friction brake hoist; ~ **pour véhicule lourd** *m* TRANSPORT heavy vehicle elevator (AmE), heavy vehicle lift (BrE)

monte-coulée *m* PRODUCTION gate spool

monte-courroie *m* PRODUCTION belt mounter, belt shifter, belt shipper

montée *f* AERONAUT climb, CONSTR rise, *voûte* height above impost level, CRISTALL *dislocation* climb, GEOLOGIE *magma* uprise, HYDROLOGIE *eaux* rise, MATERIAUX climb, MINES creep, NAUT rise, TEXTILE *colle, colorant* uptake; ~ **de brûleur** *f* CERAM VER port uptake; ~ **au décollage** *f* AERONAUT climb out, initial climb out; ~ **en caisson** *f* AERONAUT chamber ascent;

~ **en pression de la vapeur** *f* INST HYDR steam raising; ~ **en régime de croisière** *f* AERONAUT cruise climb, cruise climb drift up; ~ **en température** *f* THERMODYN heat rise, temperature rise; ~ **initiale** *f* AERONAUT climb out, initial climb out; ~ **par paliers** *f* AERONAUT stepped climb

monter[1] *vt* CINEMAT cut, edit, set up, CONS MECA chuck, fit, set, wind up, CONSTR assemble, ELECTRON mount, ELECTROTEC connect, ENREGISTR *son* bring up, IMPRIM assemble, *couleur d'une photogravure* tone up, *page* build, strip, INFORMAT mount, MECANIQUE erect, fit, MINES rise, NAUT fit, install, OCEANO filet set up, ORDINAT mount, PAPIER set up, *machine* assemble, PETR rig up, PRODUCTION hoist, install, mount, rig, rig up, *bit* set, TV edit, set up; ~ **à bord de** *vt* NAUT *passagers* board; ~ **en cascade** *vt* ELECTROTEC cascade; ~ **en parallèle** *vt* ELECTROTEC connect in parallel, couple in parallel; ~ **en série** *vt* ELECTROTEC connect in series; ~ **au jour** *vt* MINES bring to the surface, hoist to the surface; ~ **progressivement** *vt* ENREGISTR *volume* fade in

monter[2] *vi* ESPACE *véhicules* climb, HYDROLOGIE, NAUT *marée* rise

monter:[3] **se** ~ *v réfl* CONS MECA fit

monteur *m* CINEMAT editor, CONS MECA fitter, MECANIQUE erector, fitter, PRODUCTION erector, TV editor; ~ **de négatif** *m* CINEMAT negative cutter; ~ **négatif** *m* CINEMAT conformer

monte-wagon *m* CH DE FER *véhicules* car elevator (AmE), wagon hoist (BrE), wagon lift (BrE)

monticellite *f* MINERAUX monticellite

monticule *m* CONSTR knoll

montmorillonite *f* CHARBON, MINERAUX, PETROLE montmorillonite

montrer *vt* ESPACE display

monture *f* ASTRONOMIE *télescope*, CINEMAT *lentille* mount, CONS MECA fitting, setting, GENIE CHIM sieve frame, INSTRUMENT spectacle frame, stand, OCEANO net frame, PHOTO mount, PRODUCTION mounting; ~ **allemande** *f* INSTRUMENT German-type mounting; ~ **altazimutale** *f* ASTRONOMIE altazimuth mounting, altazimuthal mount, altazimuthal mount, INSTRUMENT altazimuth mounting; ~ **anglaise** *f* ASTRONOMIE English mount; ~ **anglaise à axe** *f* INSTRUMENT English-type axis mounting; ~ **Angle Horaire-Déclinaison** *f* ASTRONOMIE, ESPACE Ha-Dec mount; ~ **Azimut-Elévation** *f* ASTRONOMIE, ESPACE Az-El mount; ~ **Azimut-Site** *f* ASTRONOMIE, ESPACE Az-El mount; ~ **à baïonnette** *f* INSTRUMENT, PHOTO bayonet mount; ~ **à berceau** *f* ASTRONOMIE cradle mount; ~ **C** *f* CINEMAT C-mount; ~ **coudée** *f* INSTRUMENT knee mounting; ~ **à déplacement** *f* INSTRUMENT axial radial bearing; ~ **à emboîtement** *f* CINEMAT push-fit mount, PHOTO push-on mount; ~ **en fer à cheval** *f* ASTRONOMIE horseshoe mount, INSTRUMENT horseshoe mount, horseshoe mounting; ~ **en fourche** *f* INSTRUMENT fork mounting; ~ **à fourche** *f* ASTRONOMIE fork mount; ~ **fourrée** *f* PHOTO sunk mount; ~ **à friction** *f* PHOTO slip-on sleeve; ~ **d'objectif** *f* PHOTO lens mount; ~ **réglable de scie à métaux** *f* CONS MECA adjustable hacksaw frame; ~ **rentrante** *f* PHOTO countersunk mount, countersunk setting, sunk mount, sunk setting; ~ **de roulette** *f* CERAM VER chuck block; ~ **sans verre** *f* INSTRUMENT trial frame; ~ **soudée** *f* CONS MECA welded fitting; ~ **à ventouse** *f* CINEMAT limpet mount, suction mount; ~ **à vis** *f* CINEMAT screw mount

montures *f pl* CONS MECA fittings; ~ **de télescope** *f pl* INSTRUMENT telescope mountings, telescope mounts

monzonite *f* PETR monzonite

moon-pool *m* PETR moon pool

moraillon *m* CONSTR hasp

moraine *f* CHARBON moraine, till

morasse *f* IMPRIM *typographie* brush proof

morceau *m* CHIMIE moiety, PRODUCTION scrap

morceaux: ~ **de ferraille** *m pl* PRODUCTION scrap iron

morceler[1] *vt* CONSTR break, break up

morceler:[2] **se** ~ *v réfl* CONSTR break, break up

morcellement *m* CONSTR breaking-up, MINES breakage, shatter

mordache *f* CONS MECA vice cap (BrE), vice clamp (BrE), vice jaw (BrE), vise cap (AmE), vise clamp (AmE), vise jaw (AmE), PRODUCTION gripping pad

mordant *m* CHIMIE mordant, CONS MECA biting, *cylindres d'un laminoir* biting

mordre[1] *vt* CONS MECA *objet* bite, bite into, CONSTR *vis* bite; ~ **dans** *vt* CONS MECA *objet* bite, bite into

mordre[2] *vi* CONS MECA engage, interlock, CONSTR *vis* bite

morénosite *f* MINERAUX morenosite

morfil *m* CONS MECA wire edge

morfiler *vt* CONS MECA *tranchant d'un couteau* remove

morflat *m* CONS MECA wire edge

morin *m* CHIMIE morin

morindine *f* CHIMIE morindin

morion *m* MINERAUX morion

morphine *f* CHIMIE morphine

morpholine *f* CHIMIE, LESSIVES morpholine

morphologie *f* MATERIAUX morphology

morphoscopique *adj* GEOLOGIE *analyse* morphometric

morphotropie *f* CHIMIE morphotropism, morphotropy

morphotropique *adj* CHIMIE morphotropic

morruol *m* CHIMIE morrhuol

mors *m* CERAM VER *canne* nose, CONS MECA jaw, *étau* cheeks, IMPRIM *reliure* joint, MECANIQUE *outillage* jaw

morsure *f* IMPRIM etching

mort: ~ **énergétique** *f* PHYSIQUE heat death; ~ **thermique** *f* PHYSIQUE heat death

mortaisage *m* CONS MECA slotting, CONSTR mortising

mortaise *f* CONS MECA slot, socket, CONSTR mortise, *d'un rabot* mouth, PRODUCTION *d'un palan* mortise; ~ **aveugle** *f* CONSTR stub mortise; ~ **passante** *f* CONSTR through-mortice

mortaiseuse *f* CONS MECA slotter, slotting machine, CONSTR, PRODUCTION mortising machine; ~ **à bielle et à manivelle** *f* CONS MECA crank-drive slotting machine; ~ **excentrique** *f* CONS MECA eccentric-drive slotting machine; ~ **à outil oscillant** *f* CONS MECA mortising machine with oscillating tool action

mortier *m* CHIMIE, CONSTR, EQUIP LAB, GENIE CHIM, MILITAIRE mortar, PRODUCTION *de bocard* mortar, mortar box; ~ **d'agate** *m* CHIMIE, MATERIAUX agate mortar; ~ **avec paroi postérieure droite** *m* MINES concentration mortar; ~ **de chaux** *m* PRODUCTION lime mortar; ~ **de gâchage** *m* GENIE CHIM mixing mortar; ~ **d'injection** *m* CONSTR grout; ~ **liquide** *m* CONSTR grout; ~ **de pose** *m* CONSTR bedding mortar; ~ **sans amalgamation intérieure** *m* MINES concentration mortar; ~ **de terre** *m* CERAM VER clay mortar

mort-mur *m* PRODUCTION *d'un four* wall

morts-terrains *m* DISTRI EAU capping, EN RENOUV cap rock, MINES dead ground, overburden, overburden; ~ **de recouvrement** *m pl* MINES strippings

morue *f* AERONAUT horizontal stabilizer centre fishplate

morvénite *f* MINERAUX morvenite

MOS:[1] *abrév (semi-conducteur à oxyde métallique)* ORDINAT MOS *(metal-oxide semiconductor)*

MOS[2] ~ **complémentaire** *m* ORDINAT CMOS, compatible MOS

mosaïque *f* AGRO ALIM, ELECTRON mosaic; ~ **de verre** *f* CERAM VER glass mosaic

mosandrite *f* MINERAUX mosandrite

mot *m* INFORMAT, ORDINAT word; ~ **d'adresse de canal** *m* ORDINAT CAW, channel address word; ~ **de commande** *m* INFORMAT, ORDINAT control word; ~ **de commande du canal** *m* INFORMAT, ORDINAT channel command word; ~ **de données** *m* INFORMAT, ORDINAT data word; ~ **d'état** *m* INFORMAT, ORDINAT status word; ~ **d'état de canal** *m* INFORMAT, ORDINAT channel status word; ~ **d'état du processeur** *m* INFORMAT, ORDINAT processor status word; ~ **d'état du programme** *m* INFORMAT, ORDINAT PSW, program status word; ~ **facultatif** *m* INFORMAT, ORDINAT optional word; ~ **particulier** *m* ESPACE *communications* UW, burst word, unique word; ~ **de passe** *m* INFORMAT, ORDINAT, TELECOM password; ~ **de recherche** *m* INFORMAT, ORDINAT search word; ~ **réservé** *m* INFORMAT, ORDINAT reserved word; ~ **de synchronisation** *m* TELECOM *satellite maritime* syncword

mot-clé *m* INFORMAT keyword; ~ **en contexte** *m* INFORMAT, ORDINAT KWIC, keyword in context; ~ **hors contexte** *m* INFORMAT, ORDINAT KWOC, keyword out of context

moteur:[1] **à** ~ *adj* ELECTROTEC motor-driven

moteur[2] *m* ACOUSTIQUE driver, AUTO motor, CONS MECA engine, motor, mover, prime mover, ELECTR, ELECTROTEC, ESPACE motor, NAUT, VEHICULES engine; **■ a** ~ **aérobie** *m* AERONAUT air breathing engine; ~ **à air chaud** *m* TRANSPORT hot air engine; ~ **à air comprimé** *m* CONS MECA compressed air engine, MINES compressed air motor; ~ **alimenté en gaz** *m* GAZ gas engine; ~ **à allumage par compression** *m* CONS MECA compression ignition engine; ~ **alternatif** *m* AERONAUT piston engine, reciprocating engine, CONS MECA reciprocating engine; ~ **alternatif à combustion interne** *m* TRANSPORT reciprocating internal combustion engine; ~ **antidéflagrant** *m* THERMODYN fireproof motor, flameproof motor; ~ **antigrisouteux** *m* ELECTROTEC fireproof motor, flameproof motor; ~ **antitangage** *m* ESPACE *propulsion* pitch-thruster; ~ **d'apogée** *m* ESPACE *propulsion* apogee motor; ~ **arrière** *m* VEHICULES rear engine; ~ **à l'arrière** *m* AUTO rear engine, rear-mounted engine, VEHICULES rear-mounted engine; ~ **asservi** *m* CONS MECA relay; ~ **asynchrone** *m* CH DE FER asynchronous motor, CINEMAT wild motor, ELECTR, ELECTROTEC asynchronous motor, induction motor, PRODUCTION induction motor, TRANSPORT asynchronous motor; ~ **asynchrone à bagues** *m* ELECTROTEC slip-ring induction motor; ~ **asynchrone compensé** *m* ELECTR compensated induction motor; ~ **asynchrone diphasé** *m* ELECTROTEC two-phase motor; ~ **asynchrone linéaire** *m* ELECTROTEC linear electric motor; ~ **asynchrone monophasé** *m* ELECTROTEC single-phase induction motor; ~ **asynchrone polyphasé** *m* ELECTROTEC polyphase induction motor; ~ **asynchrone à rotor bobiné** *m* ELECTROTEC wound rotor induction motor; ~ **asynchrone synchronisé** *m* ELECTR, ELECTROTEC synchronous induction motor; ~ **asynchrone triphasé** *m* ELECTROTEC three-phase induction motor; ~ **at-**

mosphérique *m* AUTO unsupercharged engine; ~ **auto-synchrone** *m* ELECTROTEC self-starting synchronous motor; ~ **auxiliaire** *m* CONS MECA auxiliary engine, ELECTR auxiliary motor; ~ **avant** *m* AUTO front engine; ~ **à l'avant** *m* VEHICULES front-mounted engine; **~ b** ~ **à bague de déphasage** *m* ELECTR shaded-pole motor, split pole motor; ~ **à bagues** *m* ELECTR slip-ring motor, ELECTROTEC wound rotor induction motor; ~ **à bagues collectrices** *m* ELECTR slip-ring motor; ~ **à balancier** *m* ELECTR swivel bearing motor; ~ **bicylindrique** *m* CONS MECA double cylinder engine, double engine, duplex engine, duplex cylinder engine; ~ **bipolaire** *m* ELECTR two-pole motor; ~ **blindé** *m* ELECTR, ELECTROTEC enclosed motor; ~ **à bougie d'allumage** *m* CONS MECA spark ignition engine; ~ **à boule chaude** *m* AUTO hot bulb engine; ~ **à bride** *m* ELECTR flange motor; ~ **bypass** *m* AERONAUT bypass engine; **~ c** ~ **à caractéristique shunt** *m* ELECTR flat response motor; ~ **à carburateur** *m* AUTO carburetor engine (AmE), carburettor engine (BrE); ~ **au centre** *m* AUTO center engine (AmE), centre engine (BrE), mid-engine; ~ **à champ glissant** *m* TRANSPORT traveling-field motor (AmE), travelling-field motor (BrE); ~ **à champ d'ondes progressives** *m* ELECTR traveling-wave motor (AmE), travelling-wave motor (BrE); ~ **à charge stratifiée** *m* TRANSPORT stratified charge engine; ~ **à circuit Rankine** *m* TRANSPORT Rankine-cycle engine; ~ **à collecteur** *m* ELECTR commutator motor, ELECTROTEC collector motor, commutator motor, TRANSPORT commutator motor; ~ **à combustible liquide** *m* THERMODYN liquid fuel engine; ~ **à combustion** *m* TRANSPORT combustion engine; ~ **à combustion externe** *m* TRANSPORT external combustion engine; ~ **à combustion interne** *m* AUTO, ELECTROTEC, MECANIQUE, PETROLE, PRODUCTION, TRANSPORT, VEHICULES internal combustion engine; ~ **à combustion pauvre** *m* THERMODYN lean-burn engine; ~ **de commande** *m* CINEMAT drive motor, COMMANDE servomotor; ~ **à commande de tension d'induit** *m* ELECTR armature-controlled motor; ~ **compensé** *m* ELECTR compensated motor; ~ **compound** *m* CONS MECA compound expansion engine, ELECTR compound motor, compound-wound motor, ELECTROTEC compound winding motor; ~ **à compression** *m* ENREGISTR compression driver; ~ **à condensateur** *m* ELECTR capacitor start motor, ELECTROTEC capacitor motor, capacitor start motor; ~ **à condensateur à deux capacités** *m* ELECTR capacitor start-and-run motor, dual-capacitor motor; ~ **à condensateur permanent** *m* ELECTROTEC capacitor start-run motor, permanent magnet split capacitor motor; ~ **à couple élevé** *m* MECANIQUE high-torque motor; ~ **à couple torque** *m* PRODUCTION constant motor torque; ~ **à courant alternatif** *m* ELECTR, ELECTROTEC AC motor, alternating current motor, PHYSIQUE AC motor, alternate current motor; ~ **à courant continu** *m* ELECTR, ELECTROTEC, PHYSIQUE DC motor, direct current motor; ~ **à courant continu à collecteur** *m* ELECTROTEC brush-type DC motor, brush-type direct current motor, commutator DC motor, commutator direct current motor; ~ **à courant continu à excitation série** *m* ELECTROTEC series DC motor, series direct current motor; ~ **à courant continu sans collecteur** *m* ELECTROTEC brushless DC motor, brushless direct current motor; ~ **critique** *m* AERONAUT critical engine; ~ **critique hors de fonctionnement** *m* AERONAUT critical

engine inoperative; ~ **à crosses** *m* NAUT crosshead engine; ~ **cuirassé** *m* ELECTR enclosed motor, shell-type motor; ~ **à cylindrée fixe** *m* PRODUCTION *système hydraulique* fixed displacement motor; ~ **à cylindrée variable** *m* PRODUCTION *système hydraulique* variable displacement motor; ~ **à cylindres en ligne** *m* AUTO in-line engine, CONS MECA in-line cylinder engine, straight engine; ~ **à cylindres en V** *m* CONS MECA V-cylinder engine, VEHICULES V-type engine; ~ **à cylindres opposés à plat** *m* VEHICULES flat engine; ~ **à cylindres parallèles** *m* AUTO U-type engine; **~ d** ~ **de démarrage** *m* CONS MECA starter motor, starting motor, ELECTR starting motor; ~ **à démarrage direct** *m* ELECTR across-the-line motor; ~ **à démarrage par condensateur** *m* ELECTROTEC capacitor start motor; ~ **demi-enfermé** *m* ELECTR semienclosed motor; ~ **à dérivation** *m* AERONAUT bypass engine; ~ **à détente** *m* CONS MECA expansion engine; ~ **à deux combustibles** *m* TRANSPORT dual fuel engine; ~ **à deux cylindres** *m* TRANSPORT twin engine; ~ **à deux cylindres opposés à plat** *m* AUTO flat twin engine; ~ **à deux temps** *m* AUTO, CONS MECA, MECANIQUE, NAUT, TRANSPORT, VEHICULES two-stroke engine; ~ **deux temps à trois lumières** *m* AUTO three-part two-stroke engine; ~ **diesel** *m* AUTO, NAUT, PRODUCTION, TRANSPORT, VEHICULES diesel engine; ~ **diesel amélioré** *m* TRANSPORT improved diesel engine; ~ **diesel à chambre d'accumulation** *m* AUTO air cell diesel engine; ~ **diesel-électrique** *m* TRANSPORT diesel-electric engine; ~ **diesel-hydraulique** *m* CONS MECA diesel-hydraulic engine; ~ **diesel lent** *m* NAUT low-speed diesel engine, TRANSPORT slow-running diesel engine; ~ **diesel à préchambre** *m* TRANSPORT indirect injection diesel engine; ~ **diphasé** *m* ELECTR, ELECTROTEC two-phase motor; ~ **à double cage** *m* ELECTR double squirrel cage motor; ~ **à double flux** *m* AERONAUT bypass engine; ~ **à double piston** *m* AUTO twin-piston engine; ~ **à double vitesse** *m* ELECTR double speed motor; **~ e** ~ **d'écureuil** *m* PRODUCTION squirrel cage motor; ~ **d'éjection de secours** *m* ESPACE launch escape motor; ~ **électrique** *m* ELECTROTEC electric motor, electromotor, TRANSPORT electric motor; ~ **électrique à bride** *m* MECANIQUE flange motor; ~ **électrique à courant alternatif** *m* ELECTROTEC AC motor, alternating current motor; ~ **électrique à faible vitesse** *m* ELECTROTEC low-speed electric motor; ~ **électrique de fusée** *m* CONS MECA electric rocket engine; ~ **électrique linéaire** *m* ELECTR linear induction motor, ELECTROTEC linear electric motor; ~ **électrique shunt** *m* ELECTR shunt motor; ~ **en cage d'écureuil** *m* ELECTR, ELECTROTEC squirrel cage motor; ~ **en dérivation** *m* ELECTROTEC shunt motor, shunt-wound motor; ~ **à engrenages** *m* MECANIQUE geared motor; ~ **en ligne** *m* CONS MECA, NAUT in-line engine; ~ **à enroulement auxiliaire** *m* ELECTROTEC split phase motor; ~ **à enroulement auxiliaire de démarrage** *m* ELECTR split phase motor; ~ **à enroulement en court-circuit** *m* ELECTR shaded-pole motor; ~ **d'entraînement** *m* CINEMAT, ELECTR drive motor, ENREGISTR motor drive, PHOTO drive motor; ~ **en V** *m* AUTO V-engine, NAUT V-engine, Vee engine; ~ **en W** *m* AUTO W-type engine; ~ **en X** *m* AUTO X-type engine; ~ **d'épuisement** *m* DISTRI EAU draining engine, pumping engine; ~ **équilibré** *m* ELECTR balanced armature unit; ~ **d'érection** *m* CONSTR leveling motor (AmE), levelling motor (BrE); ~ **à essence** *m* NAUT, THERMODYN gasoline engine (AmE), petrol engine (BrE), VEHICULES gas engine (AmE), gasoline engine (AmE), petrol engine (BrE); ~ **étanche aux poussières** *m* ELECTR dustproof motor; ~ **excitateur** *m* ELECTR self-excited motor; ~ **à excitation compound** *m* ELECTR, ELECTROTEC compound motor; ~ **à excitation indépendante** *m* ELECTR separately excited motor; ~ **à excitation mixte** *m* ELECTR compound motor; ~ **à excitation série** *m* ELECTROTEC series motor; ~ **à expansion compound** *m* CONS MECA compound expansion engine; ~ **à explosion** *m* CONS MECA internal combustion engine; ~ **à explosion externe** *m* CONS MECA external combustion engine; ~ **d'extraction** *m* MINES draft engine (AmE), draught engine (BrE), mine hoist, drawing engine, winding engine, hoist, hoisting engine;

~ f ~ **à faible course** *m* VEHICULES short-stroke engine; ~ **à faible poussée** *m* ESPACE *propulsion* low-thrust motor; ~ **fermé** *m* ELECTR totally enclosed motor, ELECTROTEC enclosed motor; ~ **flottant** *m* AUTO floating engine; ~ **à fluide organique** *m* TRANSPORT organic fluid engine; ~ **fractionnaire** *m* ELECTR stepper motor, stepping motor, ELECTROTEC FHP motor, fractional horsepower motor; ~ **de frein** *m* ELECTR brake motor; ~ **de freinage** *m* ESPACE descent engine;

~ g ~ **à gaz** *m* CONS MECA gas engine, PRODUCTION gas engine, gas motor, *haut-fourneau* gas engine, THERMODYN gas engine; ~ **à gaz liquéfié** *m* TRANSPORT liquid gas engine; ~ **à gaz naturel** *m* TRANSPORT natural gas engine; ~ **à gaz de pétrole liquéfié** *m* AUTO LPG engine, liquid petroleum gas engine; ~ **générateur** *m* ELECTROTEC motor generator; ~ **à grande vitesse** *m* ELECTR high-speed motor;

~ h ~ **à haute tension** *m* ELECTR high-voltage motor; ~ **hermétique** *m* ELECTR sealed motor; ~ **horaire** *m* ASTRONOMIE declination drive; ~ **horizontal** *m* AUTO, VEHICULES horizontal engine, transverse engine; ~ **hors-bord** *m* NAUT outboard engine; ~ **à huile lourde** *m* AUTO heavy-oil engine; ~ **hybride** *m* TRANSPORT dual fuel system, hybrid engine; ~ **hydraulique** *m* CONS MECA hydraulic motor; ~ **à hystérésis** *m* ELECTROTEC hysteresis motor;

~ i ~ **incliné** *m* AUTO slanter engine; ~ **incompensé** *m* ELECTROTEC noncompensated motor; ~ **incorporé** *m* ELECTROTEC built-in motor; ~ **à induction** *m* ELECTROTEC, PHYSIQUE, TRANSPORT induction motor; ~ **d'inférence** *m* ELECTROTEC, INFORMAT, ORDINAT inference engine; ~ **à injection directe** *m* TRANSPORT direct injection engine; ~ **interlock** *m* CINEMAT selsyn motor; ~ **inversible** *m* ELECTR reversing motor; ~ **ionique** *m* ESPACE ion engine, ion thruster; ~ **ionique à effet Hall** *m* ESPACE Hall ion-thruster;

~ l ~ **latéral** *m* ESPACE strap-on booster; ~ **linéaire** *m* ELECTROTEC linear electric motor, TRANSPORT linear motor; ~ **linéaire asynchrone** *m* TRANSPORT asynchronous linear induction motor; ~ **linéaire à flux transversal** *m* TRANSPORT transverse-flux linear motor, transverse-flux machine; ~ **linéaire de grande puissance** *m* TRANSPORT high-power linear motor; ~ **linéaire à inducteur** *m* TRANSPORT linear induction motor, vehicle-mounted short primary linear motor; ~ **linéaire à simple inducteur** *m* TRANSPORT SLIM, single linear inductor motor, single primary-type linear motor;

~ m ~ **de mise en rotation** *m* ESPACE spin thruster; ~ **monocylindrique** *m* AUTO one-cylinder engine, CONS MECA one-cylinder engine, single cylinder engine; ~ **monophasé** *m* ELECTR, ELECTROTEC single-phase motor; ~ **à mouvement alternatif** *m* AERONAUT piston engine, reciprocating engine, CONS MECA reciprocating engine;

~ n ~ **non réversible** *m* ELECTR nonreversible motor; ~ **non synchrone** *m* CINEMAT wild motor;

~ p ~ **pas-à-pas** *m* CINEMAT, ELECTROTEC, INFORMAT, ORDINAT stepper motor; ~ **pas-à-pas à aimant permanent** *m* ELECTROTEC permanent magnet stepper motor; ~ **pas-à-pas à cliquet** *m* ELECTROTEC solenoid stepper motor; ~ **pas-à-pas à réluctance** *m* ELECTROTEC variable reluctance stepper motor; ~ **pas-à-pas à trois phases** *m* ELECTROTEC three-phase stepper motor; ~ **de périgée** *m* ESPACE perigee kick motor; ~ **à phases compensées** *m* ELECTR all-watt motor; ~ **à piston** *m* AUTO, CONS MECA piston engine; ~ **à piston à mouvement alternatif** *m* TRANSPORT reciprocating internal combustion engine; ~ **à pistons** *m* AERONAUT reciprocating piston engine; ~ **à pistons fourreaux** *m* NAUT trunk piston engine; ~ **à pistons à mouvement alternatif** *m* VEHICULES reciprocating engine; ~ **à pistons opposés** *m* CONS MECA opposed piston engine; ~ **à pistons rotatifs** *m* VEHICULES *moteur Wankel* rotary engine; ~ **plat** *m* AUTO flat engine, underfloor engine, ELECTROTEC pancake motor, VEHICULES flat engine; ~ **pneumatique** *m* AERONAUT air motor, CONS MECA air engine, pneumatic motor, *rotation* air motor; ~ **polycarburant** *m* AUTO, THERMODYN, TRANSPORT multifuel engine; ~ **polycylindrique** *m* AUTO multicylinder engine; ~ **polyphasé** *m* ELECTR, ELECTROTEC polyphase motor; ~ **à pompes** *m* DISTRI EAU pumping engine; ~ **de positionnement** *m* COMMANDE servomotor; ~ **à poudre** *m* ESPACE *propulsion* solid fuel booster; ~ **pour brûleur à mazout** *m* CONS MECA oil burner motor; ~ **à poussée vectorielle** *m* ESPACE vectored thrust engine; ~ **de propulsion** *m* NAUT propulsion engine; ~ **à propulsion MHD** *m* ESPACE plasma engine, plasma thruster; ~ **à propulsion plasmique** *m* ESPACE plasma engine, plasma thruster; ~ **de puissance fractionnaire** *m* ELECTR fractional horsepower motor;

~ q ~ **à quartz** *m* CINEMAT crystal motor; ~ **quatre cylindres à plat** *m* TRANSPORT flat-four engine; ~ **à quatre temps** *m* AUTO, CONS MECA, MECANIQUE, NAUT, VEHICULES four-stroke engine;

~ r ~ **rapide** *m* MECANIQUE high-speed engine; ~ **à réaction** *m* AERONAUT jet engine, ELECTR reaction motor, ESPACE, MECANIQUE jet engine; ~ **à réaction d'induit** *m* ELECTR armature reaction-excited machine; ~ **refroidi à l'air** *m* CONS MECA air-cooled motor; ~ **refroidi à l'air forcé** *m* ELECTR forced ventilation motor; ~ **à refroidissement par air** *m* VEHICULES air-cooled engine; ~ **à refroidissement par eau** *m* AUTO liquid-cooled engine; ~ **à refroidissement par l'eau** *m* AUTO, VEHICULES water-cooled engine; ~ **à réluctance** *m* ELECTR, ELECTROTEC, TRANSPORT reluctance motor; ~ **à réluctance variable** *m* TRANSPORT variable reluctance motor; ~ **à répulsion** *m* ELECTR, ELECTROTEC repulsion motor; ~ **à répulsion-induction** *m* ELECTROTEC repulsion-induction motor; ~ **réversible** *m* ELECTROTEC, TRANSPORT reversible motor; ~ **rotatif** *m* AUTO rotary engine, rotary piston engine, TRANSPORT revolving cylinder engine, rotating piston engine; ~ **rotatif Wankel** *m* AUTO, THERMODYN, VEHICULES Wankel rotary engine; ~ **à rotor bobiné** *m*

ELECTR phase-wound rotor motor, ELECTROTEC wound rotor motor; ~ **à rotor noyé** m MECANIQUE *hydraulique* canned motor; ~ **de roulage et d'extraction** m MINES hauling and winding engine;

~ s ~ **sans balai** m ELECTR brushless motor; ~ **sans détente** m CONS MECA nonexpansion engine; ~ **sans soupape** m AUTO sleeve valve engine; ~ **sans soupapes** m AUTO valveless engine; ~ **selsyn** m CINEMAT selsyn motor; ~ **semi-diesel** m AUTO, CONS MECA semi-diesel engine; ~ **de séparation** m ESPACE *propulsion* separation motor; ~ **série** m ELECTR, ELECTROTEC series motor, series-wound motor; ~ **série à courant continu** m ELECTROTEC series DC motor, series direct current motor; ~ **à un seul cylindre** m CONS MECA one-cylinder engine, single cylinder engine; ~ **shunt** m ELECTROTEC shunt motor, shunt-wound motor; ~ **à soufflante canalisée** m AERONAUT ducted fan engine; ~ **à soupapes bilatérales** m AUTO T-head engine; ~ **à soupapes en tête** m AUTO I-head engine, OHV engine, overhead valve engine; ~ **à soupapes en tête et latérales** m AUTO F-head engine; ~ **à soupapes latérales** m AUTO L-head engine, side-valve engine; ~ **à soupapes symétriques** m AUTO DOHC engine; ~ **à spires Frager** m ELECTROTEC shaded-pole motor; ~ **à stator bobiné** m ELECTROTEC wound stator motor; ~ **super carré** m AUTO oversquare engine; ~ **suralimenté** m NAUT turbocharged engine; ~ **synchrone** m CINEMAT, ELECTR, ELECTROTEC, PHYSIQUE, TRANSPORT synchronous motor; ~ **synchrone à aimants permanents** m ELECTROTEC permanent magnet synchronous motor; ~ **synchrone polyphasé** m ELECTROTEC polyphase synchronous motor; ~ **synchrone triphasé** m ELECTROTEC three-phase synchronous motor; ~ **à synchronisation automatique** m CINEMAT selsyn motor;

~ t ~ **thermique** m MECANIQUE, PHYSIQUE heat engine, THERMODYN thermal engine; ~ **de traction à courant continu** m TRANSPORT direct current traction motor; ~ **triphasé** m ELECTR, ELECTROTEC, PRODUCTION three-phase motor, TRANSPORT three-phase alternomotor, three-phase induction motor; ~ **tubulaire** m TRANSPORT tubular motor; ~ **à turbo-statoréacteur** m TRANSPORT turbo-ramjet;

~ u ~ **universel** m ELECTR all-current motor (AmE), all-mains motor (BrE), universal motor, ELECTROTEC universal motor;

~ v ~ **V4** m AUTO V-four engine, V4 engine; ~ **V6** m AUTO V-six engine, V6 engine; ~ **V8** m AUTO V-eight engine, V8 engine; ~ **à vapeur** m AUTO, INST HYDR, TRANSPORT steam-engine; ~ **de ventilateur** m REFRIG fan motor; ~ **à ventilateur enveloppé** m CONS MECA ducted fan engine; ~ **ventilé** m ELECTR ventilated motor; ~ **vernier** m ESPACE *propulsion* vernier motor; ~ **vertical** m AUTO, VEHICULES vertical engine; ~ **vireur** m ELECTR torque motor; ~ **à vitesse réglable** m ELECTR adjustable speed motor; ~ **à vitesse réglable et variable** m ELECTR adjustable varying speed motor; ~ **à vitesse variable** m CONSTR variable speed motor, MECANIQUE adjustable speed motor;

~ w ~ **Wankel** m CONS MECA, THERMODYN, TRANSPORT, VEHICULES Wankel engine; ~ **Warren** m TRANSPORT Warren engine

moteur:[3] **un ~ hors de fonctionnement** *loc* AERONAUT one engine inoperative

moteur-fusée m CONS MECA, ESPACE *propulsion* rocket engine, MILITAIRE rocket motor; ~ **chimique** m CONS MECA chemical rocket engine; ~ **électronique** m ESPACE electron bombardment thruster, electronic rocket engine; ~ **à propergol solide** m CONS MECA solid propellant rocket engine

moteurs:[1] **à ~ en tandem** *adj* TRANSPORT push-pull

moteurs:[2] **tous ~ en fonctionnement** *loc* AERONAUT all engines operating

motif m CHIMIE *chaîne* unit, ELECTRON pattern; ~ **binaire de contrôle** m ELECTRON test pattern; ~ **de contrôle** m ELECTRON test pattern; ~ **optique** m ELECTRON optical pattern; ~ **primaire** m ELECTRON master pattern; ~ **programmé** m INFORMAT, ORDINAT sprite; ~ **reproduit** m ELECTRON replicated pattern

motifs m pl BREVETS *opposition ou nullité* grounds; ~ **caractéristiques** m pl CONS MECA *profil de rugosité* characteristic shape

motionnel *adj* ACOUSTIQUE *impédance* motional

moto: ~ **grande routière** f TRANSPORT heavyweight motorcycle; ~ **grosse cylindrée** f TRANSPORT large capacity motorcycle; ~ **à quatre cylindres** f TRANSPORT four-cylinder motorcycle

motobasculeur m CONSTR dumper

motocompresseur: ~ **hermétique** m REFRIG hermetically-sealed compressor unit; ~ **ouvert** m REFRIG open-type compressor unit

motopompe f POLLU MER motor pump

motorboating m ELECTRON motorboating

motoréducteur m MECANIQUE geared motor

motorgrader m CONSTR grader

motorisé *adj* MECANIQUE motor-driven

motoriste m ESPACE engine manufacturer

motor-sailer m NAUT motor sailer

motrice f CH DE FER *véhicules* power car, IMPRIM carriage A, TRANSPORT carriage A, driving unit, rail motor car; ~ **de tramway** f CH DE FER tramway motor unit

mots: ~ **à la seconde** m pl IMPRIM *télétransmissions* words per second

motte f (Fra) CERAM VER batch pile, CONSTR clod, lump; ~ **de recouvrement** f PRODUCTION cake, loam cake

mottramite f MINERAUX mottramite

mou m NAUT, TELECOM slack

mouche f CONS MECA planet gear, planet gearing; ~ **à scie** f AGRO ALIM saw fly

Mouche f ASTRONOMIE Musca

moucheté *adj* EMBALLAGE, GEOLOGIE mottled

moucheter vt TEXTILE speckle

mouchette f CONSTR bench plane, jack plane

moudre vt PRODUCTION grind, mill

mouflage m PETROLE blocks

moufle m AERONAUT hoisting block, CERAM VER muffle, CONS MECA block and tackle, chain block, pulley block, sheave, sheave block, MAT CHAUFF muffle, NAUT pulley block, PRODUCTION muffle, tackle block; ~ **à chaîne** m CONS MECA chain block; ~ **à estrope double** m CONS MECA purchase block; ~ **fixe** m CONS MECA standing block, PETR, PETROLE crown block; ~ **mobile** m CONS MECA runner, running block, PETR, PETROLE traveling block (AmE), travelling block (BrE), PRODUCTION hoisting block; ~ **plongeur** m CERAM VER immersion muffle; ~ **à poulies** m CONS MECA sheave pulley block; ~ **de sécurité** m SECURITE safety pulley block; ~ **à trois poulies** m CONS MECA three-sheave block

moufler vt PRODUCTION rig

mouillabilité f PETR, PLAST CAOU *adhésifs* wettability

mouillage m CHIMIE moistening, wetting, CONS MECA wetting, NAUT anchorage, anchoring ground, *action ou location* mooring; ~ **de mines** m NAUT minelaying; ~ **à sec** m TEXTILE wetting of dry material

mouillant[1] *adj* CHIMIE wetting

mouillant[2] m PHOTO, PLAST CAOU *additif* wetting agent

mouille f HYDROLOGIE *cours d'eau* bed, OCEANO bottom

mouillé *adj* THERMODYN humid, wet; ~ **sur mouillé** *adj* PLAST CAOU *application de peinture* wet on wet

mouillement m CHIMIE, CONS MECA wetting

mouiller[1] *vt* CHIMIE wet, NAUT *bateau, bouée* moor, PHYSIQUE wet, THERMODYN moisten

mouiller[2] *vi* NAUT anchor, bring up, drop anchor

mouilleur: ~ **de mines** m MILITAIRE minelayer, NAUT minelayer, minelaying ship

moulage m ACOUSTIQUE, ELECTROTEC molding (AmE), moulding (BrE), ESPACE potting, GAZ, MATERIAUX, NAUT, PLAST CAOU *procédé* molding (AmE), moulding (BrE), PRODUCTION founding, molding (AmE), moulding (BrE), *métal* casting; ~ **d'acier** m NAUT steel casting; ~ **capillaire** m PRODUCTION capillary molding (AmE), capillary moulding (BrE); ~ **centrifuge** m PRODUCTION centrifugal casting; ~ **au contact** m CERAM VER contact molding (AmE), contact moulding (BrE), hand lay-up, PLAST CAOU hand lay-up; ~ **à la croûte** m CERAM VER forming with sheets, molding with clay batts (AmE), moulding with clay batts (BrE), molding with clay sheets (AmE), moulding with clay sheets (BrE); ~ **à découvert** m PRODUCTION open-sand molding (AmE), open-sand moulding (BrE); ~ **en châssis** m CONS MECA box casting, PRODUCTION box molding (AmE), box moulding (BrE), flask molding (AmE), flask moulding (BrE); ~ **en coquille** m CONS MECA gravity casting, PRODUCTION chill casting; ~ **en fonte trempée** m PRODUCTION chill casting, chilled iron casting; ~ **en fosse** m PRODUCTION bedding in; ~ **en pièces battues** m PRODUCTION false core molding (AmE), false core moulding (BrE); ~ **et revêtement rotatifs de fibre avec du vernis** m EMBALLAGE rotary molding of fiber and rollercoat varnishing (AmE), rotary moulding of fibre and rollercoat varnishing (BrE); ~ **à froid** m PLAST CAOU cold molding (AmE), cold moulding (BrE), THERMODYN cold casting; ~ **au gabarit** m PRODUCTION strickle molding (AmE), strickle moulding (BrE), sweep molding (AmE), sweep moulding (BrE); ~ **à la main** m PLAST CAOU hand lay-up; ~ **des métaux** m PRODUCTION metal founding; ~ **par centrifugation** m CERAM VER centrifugal casting; ~ **par compression** m EMBALLAGE, PLAST CAOU compression molding (AmE), compression moulding (BrE); ~ **par embouage** m PLAST CAOU slush molding (AmE), slush moulding (BrE); ~ **par injection** m EMBALLAGE, MATERIAUX, PLAST CAOU *plastiques*, PRODUCTION injection molding (AmE), injection moulding (BrE); ~ **par injection-gonflage** m PLAST CAOU injection blow molding (AmE), injection blow moulding (BrE); ~ **par injection-soufflage** m PLAST CAOU injection blow molding (AmE), injection blow moulding (BrE); ~ **par réaction** m MATERIAUX reaction molding (AmE), reaction moulding (BrE); ~ **par soufflage** m CERAM VER mold blowing (AmE), mould blowing (BrE); ~ **par transfert** m PLAST CAOU transfer molding (AmE), transfer moulding (BrE); ~ **des pâtes** m PLAST CAOU *procédé* slush molding (AmE), slush moulding (BrE); ~ **des pièces en fonte** m PRODUCTION iron founding;

~ **de prémix** m CERAM VER dough molding (AmE), dough moulding (BrE); ~ **à la presse** m CERAM VER compression molding (AmE), compression moulding (BrE); ~ **sur plaque-modèle** m PRODUCTION card molding (AmE), card moulding (BrE), plate molding (AmE), plate moulding (BrE); ~ **au trousseau** m PRODUCTION strickle molding (AmE), strickle moulding (BrE), sweep molding (AmE), sweep moulding (BrE)

moulages m pl CERAM VER structural glass

moule m AGRO ALIM mold (AmE), mould (BrE), CONS MECA die, MATERIAUX mold (AmE), mould (BrE), NAUT mold (AmE), mould (BrE), OCEANO *filet* kibble, mesh pin, PAPIER casting box, PLAST CAOU *presse* mold (AmE), mould (BrE), PRODUCTION matrix, mold (AmE), mould (BrE); ~ **aspirant** m CERAM VER suction mold (AmE), suction mould (BrE); ~ **de bague** m CERAM VER neck ring; ~ **basculant** m CERAM VER tilting mold (AmE), tilting mould (BrE); ~ **de bouchonnage** m CONS MECA encapsulation mold (AmE), encapsulation mould (BrE); ~ **brûlé** m CERAM VER burnt mold (AmE), burnt mould (BrE); ~ **à coins** m PLAST CAOU split mold (AmE), split mould (BrE); ~ **conformateur** m CERAM VER bending mold (AmE), bending mould (BrE); ~ **cylindrique** m GENIE CHIM grinding cylinder; ~ **à double cavité** m CERAM VER double cavity mold (AmE), double cavity mould (BrE); ~ **ébaucheur** m CERAM VER blank mold (AmE), blank mould (BrE), parison mold (AmE), parison mould (BrE); ~ **à échappement** m PLAST CAOU flash mold (AmE), flash mould (BrE); ~ **à une empreinte** m CONS MECA single impression mold (AmE), single impression mould (BrE); ~ **à empreintes multiples** m CONS MECA, PLAST CAOU multi-impression mold (AmE), multi-impression mould (BrE); ~ **enduit** m (Bel) *(cf moule à moulé-tourné)* CERAM VER paste mold (AmE), paste mould (BrE); ~ **en grand plateau** m CONS MECA *production de joint d'étanchéité et garniture en caoutchouc* large plate mold (AmE), large plate mould (BrE); ~ **en mousse** m CONS MECA structural foam mold (AmE), structural foam mould (BrE); ~ **en plein** m CERAM VER hot mold (AmE), hot mould (BrE); ~ **de fonderie** m CONS MECA mold for casting (AmE), mould for casting (BrE); ~ **de fonderie à basse pression** m CONS MECA low-pressure for casting; ~ **de gueuses** m PRODUCTION pig mold (AmE), pig mould (BrE); ~ **à injection** m CERAM VER injection mold (AmE), injection mould (BrE); ~ **à lingots** m PRODUCTION ingot mold (AmE), ingot mould (BrE); ~ **mâle** m PLAST CAOU *presse* positive mold (AmE), positive mould (BrE); ~ **moulé-tourné** m (Fra) *(cf moule enduit)* CERAM VER paste mold (AmE), paste mould (BrE); ~ **à noyau** m CONSTR *barrage* core; ~ **ouvrant** m CERAM VER split mold (AmE), split mould (BrE); ~ **à pièces dévissables** m CONS MECA unscrewing parts mold (AmE), unscrewing parts mould (BrE); ~ **portatif** m PLAST CAOU *matériel* portable mold (AmE), portable mould (BrE); ~ **positif** m PLAST CAOU *presse* positive mold (AmE), positive mould (BrE); ~ **pour caoutchouc** m CONS MECA mold for rubber (AmE), mould for rubber (BrE), rubber mold (AmE), rubber mould (BrE); ~ **pour compression** m CONS MECA compression mold (AmE), compression mould (BrE); ~ **pour compression thermodurcissable** m CONS MECA thermosetting mold (AmE), thermosetting mould

(BrE); ~ **pour la confiserie** *m* CONS MECA confectionery mold (AmE), confectionery mould (BrE); ~ **pour
coulée à chaud à empreintes multiples** *m* CONS MECA
multi-impression hot runner mold (AmE), multi-impression hot runner mould (BrE); ~ **pour fonderie à la
cire perdue** *m* CONS MECA investment mold for casting
(AmE), lost wax mold for casting (AmE), investment
mould for casting (BrE), lost wax mould for casting
(BrE); ~ **pour fonderie par gravité** *m* CONS MECA gravity mold for casting (AmE), gravity mould for
casting (BrE); ~ **pour fonderie sous pression** *m* CONS
MECA die casting die, pressure mold for casting
(AmE), pressure mould for casting (BrE); ~ **pour
formage sous vide** *m* CONS MECA vacuum-forming
mold (AmE), vacuum-forming mould (BrE); ~ **pour
injection de caoutchouc** *m* CONS MECA injection mold
for rubber (AmE), injection mould for rubber (BrE);
~ **pour injection thermodurcissable** *m* CONS MECA
injection mold for thermosetting resins (AmE), injection mould for thermosetting resins (BrE); ~ **pour
injection de thermoplastique** *m* CONS MECA injection
mold for thermoplastics (AmE), injection mould for
thermoplastics(BrE); ~ **pour matières minérales** *m*
CONS MECA *verre, céramique, béton* mold for mineral
materials (AmE), mould for mineral materials
(BrE); ~ **pour moulage par coulée** *m* CONS MECA,
PLAST CAOU casting mold (AmE), casting mould
(BrE); ~ **pour moulage rotatif** *m* CONS MECA rotational
mold (AmE), rotational mould (BrE); ~ **pour mousse
à peau intégrée** *m* CONS MECA mold for structural
foam (AmE), mould for structural foam (BrE); ~ **pour
plastiques** *m* CONS MECA mold for plastics (AmE),
mould for plastics (BrE); ~ **pour plastiques thermo-
durcis** *m* CONS MECA mold for thermoset plastics
(AmE), mould for thermoset plastics (BrE); ~ **pour
polyester chargé de verre** *m* CONS MECA mold for
GRP (AmE), mold for glass-reinforced polyester
(AmE), mould for GRP (BrE), mould for glass-reinforced polyester (BrE); ~ **pour produits alimentaires**
m CONS MECA mold for food products (AmE), mould
for food products (BrE); ~ **pour la savonnerie** *m* CONS
MECA soap mold (AmE), soap mould (BrE); ~ **pour
thermoplastiques** *m* CONS MECA mold for thermoplastics (AmE), mould for thermoplastics (BrE),
thermoplastic mold (AmE), thermoplastic mould
(BrE), thermosetting mold (AmE), thermosetting
mould (BrE); ~ **pour la verrerie** *m* CONS MECA mold for
glassware (AmE), mould for glassware (BrE); ~ **rayé**
m CERAM VER scratched mold (AmE), scratched
mould (BrE); ~ **à réservoir** *m* CERAM VER font mold
(AmE), font mould (BrE); ~ **de sable** *m* PRODUCTION
sand mold (AmE), sand mould (BrE); ~ **à saumons** *m*
PRODUCTION pig mold (AmE), pig mould (BrE); ~
semi-positif *m* PLAST CAOU *presse* semipositive mold
(AmE), semipositive mould (BrE); ~ **de soufflage
pour plastiques** *m* CONS MECA blow mold (AmE),
blow mould (BrE); ~ **sous vide** *m* CONS MECA vacuum
mold (AmE), vacuum mould (BrE); ~ **stratifié** *m*
CONS MECA, PLAST CAOU lamination mold (AmE),
lamination mould (BrE); ~ **de terre** *m* PRODUCTION
loam mold (AmE), loam mould (BrE); ~ **de transfert**
m CONS MECA *caoutchouc, thermodurcissable* transfer
mold (AmE), transfer mould (BrE); ~ **à triple cavité** *m*
CERAM VER triple-cavity mold (AmE), triple-cavity
mould (BrE)
moulé[1] *adj* PAPIER molded (AmE), moulded (BrE),

PRODUCTION cast
moulé:[2] **être** ~ *vi* PRODUCTION be cast
mouleau: ~ **à glace** *m* REFRIG ice can
mouler[1] *vt* CERAM VER mold (AmE), mould (BrE), CONS
MECA, PRODUCTION *fonte* cast; ~ **d'avance** *vt* CONSTR
precast; ~ **sous pression** *vt* CONS MECA die-cast
mouler:[2] **se** ~ *v réfl* PRODUCTION be cast, cast
moulerie *f* PRODUCTION molding floor (AmE), moulding floor (BrE)
mouleur *m* CERAM VER former, PRODUCTION molder
(AmE), moulder (BrE), pattern molder (AmE), pattern moulder (BrE); ~ **en faïence** *m* CERAM VER
hollow ware presser; ~ **en porcelaine** *m* CERAM VER
china caster, porcelain caster
moulière *f* OCEANO mussel bed
moulin *m* PAPIER, PLAST CAOU, PRODUCTION mill; ~
d'amalgamation *m* PRODUCTION grinding pan, pan
mill, pan; ~ **à billes** *m* PLAST CAOU ball mill; ~ **à
bocards** *m* PRODUCTION stamp mill, stamping mill; ~ **à
boulets** *m* MINES ball mill; ~ **à cylindres** *m* AGRO ALIM,
GENIE CHIM roller mill, PRODUCTION crushing roll,
rolls; ~ **à galets** *m* AGRO ALIM ball mill; ~ **à granules** *m*
GENIE CHIM granulating crusher; ~ **à marée** *m* EN
RENOUV tide mill; ~ **marémoteur** *m* EN RENOUV tide
mill; ~ **mélangeur** *m* GENIE CHIM mixing mill; ~ **à
meules** *m* CONSTR stone mill; ~ **à poudre** *m* PRODUC-
TION powder mill; ~ **à préparer l'argile** *m* CERAM VER
clay mill; ~ **à scie** *m* CONSTR sawmill
moulinet *m* CONS MECA fly, DISTRI EAU, HYDROLOGIE
current meter, OCEANO reel; ~ **à bitords** *m* TEXTILE
spun yarn winch
moulure *f* CONSTR molding (AmE), moulding (BrE)
moulurière *f* CONSTR molding machine (AmE), moulding machine (BrE)
mousqueton *m* CONS MECA clevis, clip hook, safety
hook, spring hook, NAUT snap shackle
moussage *m* CERAM VER, GENIE CHIM, PETROLE *comportement de liquides*, PRODUCTION *système hydraulique*
foaming
moussant *m* GENIE CHIM foamer, foaming agent,
LESSIVES foamer
mousse *f* AGRO ALIM, CERAM VER, CHARBON foam,
CHIMIE foam, scum, IMPRIM *équilibre encre-eau* scum,
LESSIVES, MATERIAUX, PAPIER foam, PLAST CAOU
frothing, *plastique, élastomère* foam, TEXTILE foam; ~
avec cellules fermées *f* EMBALLAGE close cell foam; ~
de calage en feuille *f* EMBALLAGE flow foam wrap; ~
carbonique *f* THERMODYN extinguishing foam; ~ **au
chocolat** *f* POLLU MER, POLLUTION chocolate mousse;
~ **d'Irlande** *f* AGRO ALIM Irish moss, carrageen; ~ **de
latex** *f* PLAST CAOU latex foam; ~ **perlée** *f* AGRO ALIM
carrageen; ~ **de plastique à alvéoles fermées** *f* PLAST
CAOU closed-cell cellular plastic; ~ **de plastique à
alvéoles ouvertes** *f* REFRIG open cell foamed plastic; ~
de plastique expansé *f* REFRIG expanded cellular plastic; ~ **de plastique extrudé** *f* REFRIG extruded cellular
plastic; ~ **de platine** *f* CHIMIE platinum sponge; ~ **de
polyester** *f* PLAST CAOU polyester foam; ~ **de polyéther**
f PLAST CAOU polyether foam; ~ **de polyuréthane** *f*
MATERIAUX *matière plastique*, NAUT, PLAST CAOU
polyurethane foam
mousseline *f* IMPRIM super
mousser *vti* GENIE CHIM, TEXTILE foam
mousseux *adj* GENIE CHIM, TEXTILE foamy
mousson *f* HYDROLOGIE inspection gallery, METEO
maritime equatorial air, monsoon

moût *m* AGRO ALIM *breuvage* wort

mouton *m* CHARBON pile hammer, pile ram, CONSTR drop hammer (AmE), monkey, pile hammer (AmE), piling hammer, pile driver, *marteau-pilon* ram, *sonnette* ram, PHYSIQUE ram, PRODUCTION head, *marteau-pilon* hammer head, tup, *sonnette* tup; ~ **de battage** *m* CONSTR drop hammer (AmE), monkey, pile hammer (AmE), piling hammer; ~ **comprimé** *m* CONSTR *air ou diesel* pile driver; ~ **à déclic** *m* CHARBON drop hammer, CONSTR trip pile driver; ~ **pneumatique** *m* CHARBON pneumatic ram; ~ **scié côté fleur** *m* IMPRIM skiver

moutonnage *m* CERAM VER cockled surface, CONSTR pile driving

moutonneux *adj* IMPRIM *impression* mottled

mouture *f* AGRO ALIM milling process, PRODUCTION grinding

mouvement:[1] **à ~ alternatif** *adj* CONS MECA reciprocating

mouvement[2] *m* CONS MECA movement, EMBALLAGE *marchandise* flow, IMPRIM *table d'encrage* oscillation, INFORMAT transaction, MECANIQUE motion, ORDINAT transaction, PHYSIQUE *particule* motion; ~ **absolu** *m* CHIMIE absolute movement, PHYSIQUE absolute motion; ~ **accéléré** *m* MECANIQUE accelerated motion; ~ **d'aéronef** *m* AERONAUT aircraft movement; ~ **alternatif** *m* CONS MECA alternating motion, reciprocating motion, PETROLE reciprocal movement; ~ **alterné** *m* CONS MECA alternating motion, balancing motion; ~ **arrière** *m* IMPRIM backward motion; ~ **ascendant et descendant** *m* CONS MECA up-and-down motion; ~ **d'avance et de recul** *m* CONS MECA back-and-forth motion, backward-and-forward motion; ~ **d'avancement** *m* PRODUCTION feed motion; ~ **d'avance principal** *m* CONS MECA main feed motion; ~ **basculaire** *m* CONS MECA seesaw motion, swinging movement; ~ **basculant** *m* CONS MECA balancing motion; ~ **de bascule** *m* CONS MECA swinging movement; ~ **brownien** *m* PHYS RAYON, PHYSIQUE Brownian motion, Brownian movement; ~ **circulaire** *m* PHYSIQUE circular motion; ~ **composé** *m* MECANIQUE compound motion; ~ **de déplacement** *m* PRODUCTION feed motion; ~ **descendant** *m* PRODUCTION downward motion; ~ **diurne** *m* ASTRONOMIE diurnal motion; ~ **électrophorétique** *m* NUCLEAIRE electrophoretic migration; ~ **d'enroulement** *m* CONS MECA winding motion; ~ **enrouleur** *m* CONS MECA winding motion; ~ **épirogénique** *m* GEOLOGIE epeirogenic movement; ~ **à griffe** *m* CINEMAT claw movement; ~ **harmonique simple** *m* PHYS ONDES, PHYSIQUE simple harmonic motion; ~ **hélicoïdal** *m* NUCLEAIRE helicoidal motion; ~ **d'horlogerie** *m* MECANIQUE clockwork; ~ **inversé** *m* CINEMAT reverse action; ~ **inviscide** *m* PHYS FLUID inviscid motion; ~ **de lacet** *m* ESPACE *pilotage* wobble; ~ **de machine** *m* PRODUCTION machine motion; ~ **de la marée** *m* EN RENOUV tidal movement; ~ **non-uniforme** *m* PHYSIQUE nonuniform motion; ~ **ondulatoire** *m* PHYS ONDES wave motion; ~ **oscillatoire** *m* PHYSIQUE vibration; ~ **des particules en spirale** *m* NUCLEAIRE particle spiraling (AmE), particle spiralling (BrE); ~ **planétaire** *m* CONS MECA planet gear, planet gearing; ~ **de pression** *m* PRODUCTION feed motion; ~ **propre** *m* ASTRONOMIE proper motion; ~ **rapide** *m* TV fast motion; ~ **rectiligne** *m* MECANIQUE, PHYSIQUE motion in a straight line, rectilinear motion, rectilinear motion; ~ **de recul** *m* CONS MECA backward motion, backward movement, IMPRIM backward motion, INST HYDR *piston* instroke; ~ **relatif** *m* PHYSIQUE relative motion; ~ **retardé** *m* CONS MECA retarded motion; ~ **rétrograde** *m* ASTRONOMIE retrograde motion; ~ **rotatif** *m* CINEMAT rotary movement; ~ **à secousses** *m* CONS MECA shaking motion; ~ **sinusoïdal** *m* PHYSIQUE sinusoidal motion; ~ **de surfaçage** *m* CONS MECA surfacing motion; ~ **de terrain** *m* GAZ ground movement; ~ **thermique au hasard** *m* PHYS RAYON *atomes émettants* random thermal motion; ~ **de traînée** *m* AERONAUT *pale d'hélicoptère* hunting, lagging; ~ **de translation** *m* CONS MECA translation, translatory motion; ~ **turbulent** *m* PHYS FLUID turbulent motion; ~ **uniforme** *m* PHYSIQUE uniform motion; ~ **universel** *m* PHYS FLUID universal motion; ~ **de va-et-vient** *m* CONS MECA reciprocating motion; ~ **vrai** *m* NAUT true motion

mouvements: ~ **de coulissage** *m pl* GEOLOGIE strike-slip movements; ~ **des navires** *m pl* NAUT shipping intelligence; ~ **de stock** *m pl* PRODUCTION stock movements; ~ **de stock prévus** *m pl* PRODUCTION planned stock movements

moyen[1] *adj* GEOLOGIE middle, PHYSIQUE average

moyen:[2] ~ **d'évacuation** *m* SECURITE means of escape; ~ **de fortune** *m* PRODUCTION makeshift; ~ **de production** *m* PRODUCTION resource

moyen-courrier *m* AERONAUT medium-range aircraft, medium-range airliner

moyennage: ~ **de signaux** *m* ELECTRON signal averaging

moyenne *f* INFORMAT mean, MATH average, mean, ORDINAT mean, PHYSIQUE average; ~ **arithmétique** *f* MATH, ORDINAT arithmetic mean; ~ **fréquence** *f* ELECTROTEC MF, medium frequency; ~ **géométrique** *f* ORDINAT geometric mean; ~ **harmonique** *f* (*cf moyenne arithmétique*) MATH harmonic mean; ~ **mobile autorégressive** *f* ORDINAT ARMA, autoregressive moving average; ~ **pondérée** *f* PRODUCTION weighted average; ~ **de temps de bon fonctionnement** *f* (*MTBF*) ESPACE, INFORMAT, MECANIQUE, ORDINAT, QUALITE mean time between failures (*MTBF*); ~ **de temps entre pannes** *f* ELECTROTEC mean time between failures; ~ **des vitesses instantanées** *f* TRANSPORT average spot speed; ~ **des vitesses de parcours** *f* TRANSPORT average overall travel speed

moyens: ~ **de communication interactifs** *m pl* ORDINAT interactive media; ~ **d'essais servo-hydrauliques** *m pl* CONS MECA servohydraulic test equipment; ~ **de fuite** *m pl* SECURITE *incendie, bâtiment* means of escape; ~ **industriels** *m pl* MECANIQUE engineering facilities; ~ **de production** *m pl* PRODUCTION production facilities; ~ **techniques** *m pl* TV facilities, production facilities; ~ **techniques studio** *m pl* TV studio facilities; ~ **techniques vidéo** *m pl* TV videotape facilities

moyeu *m* CONS MECA *manivelle* boss, INFORMAT, MECANIQUE, ORDINAT, VEHICULES *roue* hub; ~ **à charnière** *m* CONSTR door hinge hub; ~ **conique** *m* VEHICULES tapered hub; ~ **d'hélice** *m* AERONAUT propeller hub, NAUT propeller boss, propeller hub; ~ **de rotor** *m* AERONAUT *hélicoptère* rotor hub

MP *abrév* (*modulation de phase*) ELECTRON, ENREGISTR, INFORMAT, ORDINAT, PHYSIQUE, TELECOM, TV PM (*phase modulation*)

MPF *abrév* (*multiplexage par partage des fréquences*) ORDINAT, PHYSIQUE FDM (*frequency-division multiplexing*)

MRC *abrév* (*multiplexage par répartition de code*) TELECOM CDM (*code-division multiplexing*)

MRF *abrév* (*multiplexage par répartition en fréquence*)

ELECTRON, ORDINAT, PHYSIQUE, TELECOM FDM *(frequency-division multiplexing)*

MRL *abrév (multiplexage par répartition en longueur d'onde)* TELECOM WDM *(wavelength division multiplexing)*

MRT *abrév (multiplexage par répartition dans le temps)* ELECTRON, ESPACE, INFORMAT, ORDINAT, TELECOM TDM *(time-division multiplexing)*

ms *abrév (milliseconde)* INFORMAT, ORDINAT ms *(millisecond)*

mSv-year *m* PHYS RAYON mSv-year

MTBF *abrév (moyenne de temps de bon fonctionnement)* ESPACE, INFORMAT, MECANIQUE, ORDINAT, QUALITE MTBF *(mean time between failures)*

muciforme *adj* CHIMIE muciform

mucilagineux *adj* CHIMIE mucilaginous

mucine *f* CHIMIE mucin

mucipare *adj* CHIMIE muciferous, mucipheric

mucique *adj* CHIMIE mucic

mucoïtine-sulfurique *adj* CHIMIE *acide* mucoitin-sulfuric (AmE), mucoitin-sulphuric (BrE)

muconique *adj* CHIMIE muconic

mucoprotéine *f* CHIMIE mucoprotein

muet *adj* IMPRIM mute

mullite *f* MINERAUX mullite

multi-adressage *m* TELECOM multi-addressing

multibroche *adj* ELECTROTEC multipin

multicellulaire *adj* ACOUSTIQUE *haut-parleur* multicellular

multichaînage *m* INFORMAT, ORDINAT multithreading

multiconnexion *f* ELECTROTEC mass termination

multicoque *f* NAUT multihull

multicouche[1] *adj* ESPACE *véhicules* multilayer

multicouche[2] *f* CHIMIE multilayer

multidenté *adj* CHIMIE multidentate

multifaisceau[1] *adj* ESPACE *communications* multibeam

multifaisceau[2] *m* OCEANO multibeam echo sounder, multibeam sounder

multifilaire *adj* CONS MECA multiwire

multifilament: ~ **traité en long** *m* TEXTILE multifilament machine

multiflux: ~ **d'instruction-monoflux de donnés** *m (MISD)* INFORMAT, ORDINAT multiple-instruction single-data *(MISD)*; ~ **d'instruction-multiflux de données** *m (MIMD)* INFORMAT, ORDINAT multiple-instruction multiple-data *(MIMD)*

multi-images *f* CINEMAT split screen

multilisse *m* CONS MECA multistringer

multimédia *adj* ORDINAT multimedia

multimètre *m* ELECTROTEC, TV multimeter; ~ **numérique** *m* ELECTROTEC digital multimeter

multiphasé *adj* ELECTR *moteur* multiphase, *réseau à courant alternatif, moteur* polyphase

multiple[1] *adj* CHIMIE multiple

multiple[2] *m* METROLOGIE *unité de mesure*, PETR multiple

multiplet *m* PHYS RAYON, PHYSIQUE multiplet; ~ **de charge** *m* PHYS RAYON charge multiplet

multiplex: ~ **numérique** *m* ELECTRON digital multiplex; ~ **optique** *m* ELECTRON optical multiplex; ~ **temporel** *m* TELECOM time-division multiplex, TV time multiplex

multiplexage *m* ESPACE *communications*, INFORMAT, ORDINAT multiplexing, TELECOM channeling (AmE), channelling (BrE), multiplexing; ~ **analogique** *m (MA)* PHYSIQUE frequency-division multiplexing *(FDM)*; ~ **dans le temps** *m* TELECOM time-division multiplexing; ~ **en fréquence** *m* TELECOM frequency

multiplexing; ~ **en longueur d'onde** *m* OPTIQUE wavelength multiplexing, TELECOM wavelength division multiplexing; ~ **d'informations** *m* ELECTRON data multiplexing; ~ **MIC** *m* ELECTRON PCM multiplexing; ~ **numérique** *m* ELECTRON, PHYSIQUE digital multiplexing; ~ **optique** *m* ELECTRON optical multiplexing; ~ **par partage des fréquences** *m (MPF)* ORDINAT, PHYSIQUE frequency-division multiplexing *(FDM)*; ~ **par partage du temps** *m* PHYSIQUE time-division multiplexing; ~ **par répartition de code** *m (MRC)* TELECOM code-division multiplexing *(CDM)*; ~ **par répartition dans le temps** *m (MRT)* ELECTRON, INFORMAT, ORDINAT, PHYSIQUE, TELECOM time-division multiplexing *(TDM)*; ~ **par répartition en fréquence** *m (MRF)* ELECTRON, ORDINAT, PHYSIQUE, TELECOM frequency-division multiplexing *(FDM)*; ~ **par répartition en longueur d'onde** *m (MRL)* TELECOM wavelength-division multiplexing *(WDM)*; ~ **par répartition en temps** *m (MRT)* ESPACE *communications* time-division multiplexing *(TDM)*; ~ **de signaux** *m* ELECTRON signal multiplexing; ~ **spectral** *m* TELECOM wavelength-division multiplexing; ~ **temporel** *m* ELECTRON, INFORMAT, ORDINAT time-division multiplexing, PHYSIQUE, TELECOM time multiplexing; ~ **temporel asynchrone** *m* TELECOM ATDM, asynchronous time-division multiplexing

multiplexer *vt* ELECTRON, INFORMAT, ORDINAT, TELECOM multiplex

multiplexeur *m* ELECTRON, INFORMAT, ORDINAT multiplex, multiplexer, mux, TELECOM multiplexer, mux, TV multiplex, multiplexer, mux; ~ **aiguilleur** *m* TELECOM switching multiplexer, switching mux, switching statistical multiplexer; ~ **de données** *m* INFORMAT, ORDINAT data channel multiplexer, TELECOM, TRANSPORT data multiplexer; ~ **insertion-extraction** *m* TELECOM add-drop multiplexer; ~ **MIC** *m* ELECTRON PCM multiplexer; ~ **numérique** *m* ELECTRON digital multiplex, TELECOM DM, digital multiplexer; ~ **optique** *m* ELECTRON, TV optical multiplexer; ~ **à répartition dans le temps** *m* ELECTRON time-division multiplexer; ~ **à répartition de fréquence** *m* ELECTRON frequency-division multiplexer; ~ **statistique** *m* INFORMAT, ORDINAT statistical multiplexer, statmux; ~ **synchrone** *m* TELECOM SM, synchronous multiplexer; ~ **temporel** *m* ELECTRON time-division multiplexer

multiplicande *m* INFORMAT, MATH, ORDINAT multiplicand

multiplicateur *m* ELECTRON, INFORMAT, ORDINAT multiplier, TELECOM multiplicator, multiplier; ~ **binaire** *m* ELECTRON, TELECOM binary multiplier; ~ **de couple** *m* CONS MECA torque multiplier; ~ **d'électrons** *m* ELECTRON, PHYS RAYON electron multiplier; ~ **d'électrons secondaires** *m* TV secondary emission multiplier; ~ **de focale** *m* CINEMAT teleconverter lens; ~ **de fréquence** *m* ELECTRON, TELECOM frequency multiplier; ~ **de fréquence à diode** *m* ELECTRON diode frequency multiplier; ~ **de fréquence à réactance** *m* ELECTRON reactance-frequency multiplier; ~ **de pression** *m* INST HYDR intensifier; ~ **à quatre quadrants** *m* ELECTRON four-quadrant multiplier; ~ **de tension** *m* ELECTR *circuit redresseur*, ELECTROTEC voltage multiplier

multiplicatif *adj* MATH multiplicative

multiplication *f* CONS MECA gear ratio, INFORMAT, MATH, ORDINAT multiplication; ~ **binaire** *f* ELECTRON binary multiplication; ~ **de fréquence** *f* ELECTRON frequency multiplication; ~ **numérique** *f* ELECTRON digital

multiplication; ~ **des pistes** *f* ENREGISTR track spreading; ~ **de la pression** *f* PRODUCTION *système hydraulique* pressure intensification
multiplicité *f* PHYSIQUE multiplicity
multiplier *vt* INFORMAT, ORDINAT multiply; ~ **par** *vt* MATH multiply by
multiplieur *m* ELECTRON multiplier; ~ **numérique** *m* ELECTRON digital multiplier; ~ **parallèle** *m* ELECTRON parallel multiplier
multipolaire *adj* ELECTR *machine* multipolar
multipôle *m* PHYSIQUE multipole
multiport *adj* INFORMAT, ORDINAT multiport
multiprocesseur *m* INFORMAT, ORDINAT multiprocessor; ~ **distribué** *m* INFORMAT, ORDINAT distributed array processor
multiprogrammation *f* INFORMAT, ORDINAT multiprogramming, multithreading
multirelève *f* TELECOM multipolling
multistandard *adj* TV multistandard
multitoron *m* NAUT multistrand
multitraitement *m* INFORMAT, ORDINAT multiprocessing
multivibrateur *m* ELECTRON, PHYSIQUE, TELECOM multivibrator; ~ **astable** *m* ELECTRON astable multivibrator; ~ **bistable** *m* ELECTRON bistable multivibrator; ~ **monostable** *m* ELECTRON monostable multivibrator, one-shot multivibrator; ~ **monté en diviseur** *m* ELECTRON dividing multivibrator; ~ **à retard** *m* ELECTRON delay multivibrator
multivoies *adj* NAUT multichannel
mumétal *m* PHYSIQUE mu-metal
munir: ~ **de** *vt* CONS MECA fit with; ~ **d'une étiquette** *vt* TELECOM time-tag
munitions *f pl* MILITAIRE ammunition; ~ **à agents multiples** *f pl* MILITAIRE *guerre chimique* multiagent munitions
munjeestine *f* CHIMIE munjistin
munjistine *f* CHIMIE munjistin
muon *m* PHYS PART, PHYSIQUE muon
mur *m* CHARBON bottom, *couche de houille* floor, CONSTR wall, GEOLOGIE *filon ou couche* footwall, MINES foot, footwall, *couche* floor, *d'une galerie de mine* wall, *filon* ledger, ledger wall; ~ **antibruit** *m* SECURITE noise-abating wall; ~ **d'appui** *m* CONSTR breast wall, supporting wall; ~ **aveugle** *m* CONSTR blank wall; ~ **bombé** *m* CONSTR bulged wall; ~ **borgne** *m* CONSTR blind wall; ~ **bouclé** *m* CONSTR bulged wall; ~ **de la chaleur** *m* TRANSPORT thermal barrier; ~ **de chute** *m* DISTRI EAU lift wall; ~ **de cloison** *m* CONSTR partition wall; ~ **de clôture** *m* CONSTR boundary wall, enclosing wall; ~ **coupe-feu** *m* PETROLE *sécurité* firewall, THERMODYN fire stop; ~ **déflecteur** *m* PAPIER baffle wall, deflector; ~ **de démarcation** *m* CONSTR party wall; ~ **déversé** *m* CONSTR overhanging wall; ~ **d'écran** *m* CERAM VER shadow wall; ~ **en aile** *m* CONSTR return wall, wingwall; ~ **en briques** *m* CONSTR brick wall; ~ **d'enceinte** *m* CONSTR enclosing wall; ~ **en encorbellement** *m* CONSTR overhanging wall; ~ **en pierre** *m* CONSTR stonewall; ~ **en pierres sèches** *m* CONSTR dry stone wall; ~ **en retour** *m* CONSTR flank wall, return wall; ~ **en surplomb** *m* CONSTR overhanging wall; ~ **forjeté** *m* CONSTR overhanging wall; ~ **masqué** *m* CONSTR blind wall; ~ **du micron** *m* ELECTRON micron barrier; ~ **mitoyen** *m* CONSTR party wall; ~ **orbe** *m* CONSTR blind wall, dead wall; ~ **de parapet** *m* CONSTR breast wall; ~ **portant** *m* CONSTR load-bearing wall; ~ **porté** *m* CONSTR load-bearing wall; ~ **porteur** *m*

CONSTR load-bearing wall; ~ **de refend** *m* CONSTR cross wall; ~ **de remblai** *m* MINES building, pack wall; ~ **de remplissage** *m* CONSTR infill wall; ~ **de retenue** *m* CONSTR retaining wall; ~ **de revêtement** *m* CONSTR breast wall, face wall, retaining wall; ~ **de séparation** *m* CONSTR partition; ~ **de soubassement** *m* CONSTR base wall, basement wall; ~ **de soutènement** *m* CONSTR retaining wall; ~ **de soutènement cantilever** *m* CONSTR cantilever retaining wall; ~ **de soutènement-encorbellement** *m* CONSTR cantilever retaining wall; ~ **de soutien** *m* CONSTR supporting wall; ~ **suspendu** *m* CONSTR overhanging wall; ~ **de terrasse** *m* CONSTR breast wall, retaining wall; ~ **de tête** *m* CONSTR head wall
murage *m* CONSTR walling
muraille *f* CONSTR wall; ~ **qui pousse** *f* CONSTR bulging wall
muraillement *m* CONSTR walling
murailler *vt* MINES wall, wall in, wall up
murchisonite *f* MINERAUX murchisonite
murer *vt* MINES wall, wall in, wall up
muret *m* CONSTR small wall
muretin: ~ **en pierres sèches** *m* MINES building, pack, pack wall; ~ **de remblai** *m* MINES building
murette: ~ **garde-ballast** *f* CH DE FER ballast retainer
murexide *f* CHIMIE murexide
mûrir *vt* THERMODYN age
mur-rideau *m* CERAM VER adjustable curtain wall, CONSTR curtain wall
muscarine *f* CHIMIE muscarine
muscovite *f* MINERAUX muscovite
musoir *m* NAUT pier head, OCEANO mole head, pier head, spit
mutarotation *f* CHIMIE *sucre* mutarotation
mutateur *m* ELECTROTEC grid-controlled mercury arc rectifier; ~ **polyanodique** *m* ELECTROTEC multianode rectifier
mutation: ~ **radioinduite** *f* PHYS RAYON radiation-induced mutation
muting *m* PETR muting
mutité *f* ACOUSTIQUE muteness
Mutuelle: ~ **de protection et d'indemnisation** *f* POLLU MER Protection and Indemnity Association
mV *abrév* (*millivolt*) ELECTR, ELECTROTEC mV (*millivolt*)
mW *abrév* (*milliwatt*) ELECTR mW (*milliwatt*)
MW *abrév* (*mégawatt*) ELECTR MW (*megawatt*)
Mx *abrév* (*maxwell*) ELECTROTEC Mx (*maxwell*)
mycoprotéine *f* AGRO ALIM mycoprotein
mycotoxine *f* AGRO ALIM mycotoxin
mylonite *f* GEOLOGIE crush breccia, crush rock, mylonite; ~ **pulvérente** *f* GEOLOGIE fault gouge; ~ **recristallisée** *f* GEOLOGIE phyllonite
myocine *f* CHIMIE myocin
myrcène *m* CHIMIE myrcene
myria- *préf* METROLOGIE myria-
myriagramme *m* METROLOGIE myriagram (AmE), myriagramme (BrE)
myristine *f* CHIMIE myristin
myristique *adj* CHIMIE myristic, *acide* tetradecanoic
myristyle *adj* CHIMIE myristyl
myronique *adj* CHIMIE *acide* myronic
myrosine *f* CHIMIE myrosin
mysorine *f* MINERAUX mysorin
mytiliculture *f* OCEANO mussel breeding, mussel culture
mytilotoxine *f* CHIMIE mytilotoxine

N

n *abrév (nano-)* METROLOGIE n *(nano-)*

N[1] CHIMIE N

N[2] *abrév (newton)* ELECTR, METROLOGIE, PHYSIQUE N *(newton)*

Na *(sodium)* CHIMIE Na *(sodium)*

nable *m* NAUT drain; **~ de remplissage** *m* NAUT filling plate

nacelle *f* AERONAUT nacelle, ESPACE *véhicules* basket, gondola, pod; **~ amovible** *f* AERONAUT detachable pod; **~ à combustion** *f* EQUIP LAB *analyse* combustion boat; **~ moteur** *f* AERONAUT engine pod; **~ de pastille** *f* NUCLEAIRE dishing shallow depression; **~ de pesée** *f* EQUIP LAB weighing boat; **~ de signal** *f* CH DE FER signal structure; **~ de visite** *f* CONSTR *pont* inspection platform

nacrite *f* MINERAUX nacrite

nadir *m* ASTRONOMIE nadir

nagatélite *f* NUCLEAIRE nagatelite

nagyagite *f* MINERAUX nagyagite

naine *f* ASTRONOMIE, ESPACE dwarf, dwarf star; **~ blanche** *f* ASTRONOMIE white dwarf; **~ brune** *f* ASTRONOMIE brown dwarf; **~ noire** *f* ASTRONOMIE black dwarf; **~ rouge** *f* ASTRONOMIE red dwarf

naissance *f* ASTRONOMIE *étoile* birth, CONSTR *voûte* spring

nannofossile *m* GEOLOGIE nannofossil

nano- *préf (n)* METROLOGIE nano-*(n)*

nanoseconde *f* INFORMAT, METROLOGIE, ORDINAT, PHYSIQUE, TV nanosecond

nantokite *f* MINERAUX nantokite

napalm *m* CHIMIE, MILITAIRE, THERMODYN napalm

naphta *m (cf naphte)* CHIMIE, PETROLE, THERMODYN naphtha; **~ de charbon** *m (cf naphte de charbon)* CHARBON coal naphtha; **~ minéral** *m (cf naphte minéral)* CHARBON coal oil, mineral naphtha; **~ natif** *m (cf naphte natif)* CHARBON coal oil

naphtacène *m* CHIMIE naphthacene

naphtalène *m* CHIMIE naphthalene

naphtalénique *adj* CHIMIE naphthalenic

naphtaléno-disulfonique *adj* CHIMIE naphthalenedisulfonic (AmE), naphthalenedisulphonic (BrE)

naphtaline *f* CHIMIE, LESSIVES naphthalene

naphtalino-disulfoné *adj* CHIMIE naphthalenedisulfonic (AmE), naphthalenedisulphonic (BrE)

naphte *m (cf naphta)* CHIMIE, PETROLE, THERMODYN naphtha; **~ minéral** *m* CHARBON coal oil, mineral naphtha PETR earth oil; **~ natif** *m* CHARBON coal oil, PETR earth oil; **~ de pétrole** *m* PETR petroleum naphtha

naphténate *m* CHIMIE naphthenate; **~ de calcium** *m* PLAST CAOU *peinture, polyesters* calcium naphthenate; **~ de cobalt** *m* PLAST CAOU *peintures, polyesters* cobalt naphthenate; **~ de plomb** *m* PLAST CAOU *peintures, polyesters* lead naphthenate

naphtène *m* CHIMIE naphthene

naphténique *adj* CHIMIE naphthenic

naphtionique *adj* CHIMIE naphthionic

naphtoïque *adj* CHIMIE naphthoic

naphtol *m* CHIMIE naphthol

naphtolate *m* CHIMIE naphtholate

naphtol-sulfonique *adj* CHIMIE naphtholsulfonic (AmE), naphtholsulphonic (BrE)

naphtoquinone *f* CHIMIE naphthoquinone

naphtoyle *m* CHIMIE naphthoyl

naphtylamine *f* CHIMIE naphthylamine

naphtyle *m* CHIMIE naphthyl

naphtylène *m* CHIMIE naphthylene

naphtylique *adj* CHIMIE naphthylic

nappage: **~ fin** *m* TEXTILE fine batt; **~ grossier** *m* TEXTILE coarse batt

nappe *f* CERAM VER blanket, bundle, ESPACE *véhicules* ply, GAZ pool, GEOMETRIE *cône*, HYDROLOGIE, INST HYDR nappe, OCEANO netting, POLLU MER *mazout ou huile sur l'eau* slick, PRODUCTION *eau, pétrole* body, TEXTILE batt, lap; **~ adhérente** *f* HYDROLOGIE adhering nappe; **~ aérée** *f* DISTRI EAU ventilated nappe; **~ alluviale** *f* HYDROLOGIE alluvial nappe; **~ aquifère** *f* GAZ aquifer; **~ de capteurs solaires** *f* EN RENOUV array blanket; **~ captive** *f* CHARBON, DISTRI EAU confined ground water; **~ de carcasse en diagonale** *f* TEXTILE bias ply; **~ de charriage** *f* GEOLOGIE fold nappe, overthrust block, overthrust sheet; **~ chauffante** *f* REFRIG heater mat; **~ d'eau souterraine** *f* CHARBON ground water, DISTRI EAU ground water level; **~ envers** *f* TEXTILE backside batt; **~ d'hydrocarbures** *f* PETROLE, POLLUTION hydrocarbon slick; **~ de lave** *f* GEOLOGIE lava plateau; **~ libre** *f* CHARBON unconfined ground water, DISTRI EAU free ground water, HYDROLOGIE free nappe; **~ noyée** *f* HYDROLOGIE drowned nappe; **~ de pétrole** *f* PETROLE, POLLUTION oil slick; **~ de photopiles** *f* EN RENOUV array blanket; **~ phréatique** *f* CONSTR ground water level, DISTRI EAU ground water, ground water level, ground water supply, GEOLOGIE water table, HYDROLOGIE ground water level, water table, ground water, ground water level, PETROLE water table; **~ pour ouatinage** *f* TEXTILE wadding; **~ souterraine** *f* DISTRI EAU subsoil water, HYDROLOGIE underground nappe, water table; **~ à surface libre** *f* HYDROLOGIE free nappe; **~ tissée** *f* TEXTILE woven fabric

napper *vt* AGRO ALIM coat

narangine *f* AGRO ALIM narangin

narcéine *f* CHIMIE narceine

narcose: **~ à l'azote** *f* OCEANO nitrogen narcosis

narcotine *f* CHIMIE narcotine

narcotique[1] *adj* CHIMIE, OCEANO narcotic

narcotique[2] *m* CHIMIE opiate

narguilé *m* OCEANO hookah, narghile, surface air supply, surface demand lifeline

naringénine *f* CHIMIE naringenin

naringine *f* CHIMIE naringin

NASA *abrév (Agence nationale de l'aéronautique et de l'espace)* ESPACE NASA *(National Aeronautics and Space Administration)*

natif *adj* MINERAUX native

natrium *m* CHIMIE natrium

natrolite *f* MINERAUX natrolite

natron *m* MINERAUX natron

natronitre *m* MINERAUX soda niter (AmE), soda nitre (BrE)

nature *adj* AGRO ALIM unflavored (AmE), unflavoured (BrE)

nature-identique *adj* AGRO ALIM nature-identical

naturel *m* MATH natural number

naumannite *f* MINERAUX naumannite

nautique *adj* NAUT nautical

nautophone *m* NAUT horn

naval *adj* NAUT naval

navette *f* AERONAUT shuttle train, CONSTR shuttle train, ESPACE *véhicules*, INST HYDR shuttle, MINES bulldog casing spear, NAUT shuttle ferry, OCEANO fisherman's needle, netting needle, TEXTILE, TRANSPORT, TV shuttle; ~ spatiale *f* ESPACE *véhicules*, TELECOM Earth-to-orbit shuttle, space shuttle

navigabilité *f* AERONAUT airworthiness, NAUT navigability, POLLU MER seaworthiness

navigable *adj* NAUT navigable

navigation:[1] de ~ *adj* NAUT navigational

navigation[2] *f* NAUT navigation, sailing, shipping, TRANSPORT navigation; ~ aérienne *f* AERONAUT, TRANSPORT aeronautics; ~ astrale *f* AERONAUT celestial navigation; ~ astronomique *f* AERONAUT celestial navigation, NAUT astronavigation, celestial navigation, astronomical navigation; ~ côtière *f* HYDROLOGIE coastal navigation, coastal shipping, NAUT, OCEANO coastal navigation, pilotage, TRANSPORT cabotage; ~ dépendante *f* ESPACE dependent navigation; ~ Doppler *f* ESPACE, PETR Doppler navigation; ~ à l'estime *f* AERONAUT, NAUT dead reckoning, OCEANO navigation by dead reckoning; ~ fluviale *f* NAUT inland navigation, TRANSPORT river navigation; ~ géodésique *f* NAUT geodesic navigation; ~ hauturière *f* NAUT deep-sea navigation, ocean navigation; ~ hyperbolique *f* NAUT hyperbolic navigation; ~ indépendante *f* ESPACE independent navigation; ~ intérieure *f* NAUT inland navigation; ~ au long cours *f* NAUT deep-sea navigation, ocean navigation; ~ loxodromique *f* NAUT rhumb line navigation; ~ par inertie *f* ESPACE, OCEANO inertial navigation; ~ par radar *f* AERONAUT, TRANSPORT radar navigation; ~ radioélectrique *f* NAUT radio navigation; ~ sans visibilité *f* ESPACE blind navigation; ~ à la sonde *f* NAUT navigation by sounding; ~ stellaire *f* ESPACE stellar navigation; ~ sur coque *f* TRANSPORT navigation afloat; ~ à la voile *f* NAUT sailing

naviguer *vi* NAUT navigate, sail; ~ à feux masqués *vi* NAUT *navire* darken

naviplane *m* TRANSPORT naviplane

navire *m* NAUT, OCEANO, POLLU MER, TRANSPORT boat, ship, vessel; ~ à ailes portantes *m* NAUT hydrofoil; ~ allégeur *m* POLLU MER lighterer, lightering vessel; ~ amiral *m* NAUT command ship, flagship; ~ annexe *m* NAUT tender; ~ articulé *m* TRANSPORT articulated ship; ~ d'assistance *m* PETR, PETROLE support vessel; ~ auxiliaire *m* NAUT auxiliary vessel; ~ baleinier *m* OCEANO factory ship, whale factory ship, whaler, whaling ship; ~ câblier *m* NAUT, TELECOM cable ship; ~ charbonnier *m* NAUT coal ship, collier; ~ de charge *m* NAUT cargo ship, freighter; ~ à chargement horizontal et vertical *m* TRANSPORT rolo ship; ~ à chargement vertical *m* TRANSPORT lift on-off ship; ~ collecteur *m* NAUT, TRANSPORT feeder ship; ~ combiné *m* TRANSPORT combination bulk carrier, combined vessel; ~ de commerce *m* NAUT merchant ship; ~ conteneur du type catamaran *m* TRANSPORT barge-aboard-catamaran ship; ~ de croisière *m* NAUT cruise ship; ~ dépollueur *m* POLLU MER, POLLUTION depolluting ship, oil recovery vessel, oil clearance vessel; ~ à deux hélices *m* NAUT twin-screw steamer; ~ à effet de surface *m* NAUT surface effect ship; ~ en acier *m* NAUT steel vessel; ~ en charge *m* NAUT ship loading; ~ en perdition *m* NAUT ship in distress; ~ d'excursion *m* TRANSPORT excursion steamer; ~ de forage *m* NAUT, PETR, PETROLE drill ship, ship-type rig; ~ frigorifique *m* NAUT cold storage ship, REFRIG refrigerated cargo vessel, TRANSPORT refrigeration ship; ~ de guerre *m* MILITAIRE, NAUT man-of-war, warship; ~ de haute mer *m* POLLU MER seagoing vessel, TRANSPORT sea vessel; ~ à une hélice *m* NAUT single screw ship; ~ hydrographique *m* NAUT hydrographic survey vessel, ocean survey vessel; ~ inférieur aux normes *m* TRANSPORT substandard ship; ~ jumeau *m* NAUT sister ship; ~ à manutention verticale *m* NAUT lift-on-lift-off vessel; ~ marchand *m* NAUT merchant ship, merchantman; ~ marchand à vide *m* NAUT light vessel, lightship; ~ de mer *m* NAUT ocean going ship, seagoing vessel; ~ météorologique *m (cf navire-météo)* METEO, NAUT weather ship; ~ mixte *m* NAUT auxiliary engine sailing ship, cargo and passenger ship, mixed cargo ship; ~ monocoque *m* TRANSPORT single-hull ship; ~ à moteur *m* NAUT motor ship, motor vessel; ~ multicoque *m* TRANSPORT multihulled ship; ~ non prioritaire *m* NAUT give-way vessel; ~ océanique *m* POLLU MER seagoing vessel; ~ océanographique *m* OCEANO oceanographic research ship; ~ OCO *m* TRANSPORT OCO carrier, oil-coal-ore carrier; ~ à passagers *m* TRANSPORT passenger ship; ~ de pêche *m* NAUT, OCEANO fishing vessel; ~ pétrolier *m* NAUT oil tanker, POLLU MER, POLLUTION crude carrier; ~ polytherme *m* NAUT reefer ship; ~ à un pont *m* NAUT single-decked ship; ~ porte-barges *m* NAUT float-on-float-off vessel, TRANSPORT barge-carrying ship; ~ porte-barges Seabee *m* TRANSPORT Seabee carrier; ~ porte-barges de type LASH *m* TRANSPORT lighter aboard ship carrier; ~ porte-barges du type LASH *m* TRANSPORT LASH carrier; ~ porte-chalands *m* TRANSPORT barge carrier; ~ porte-chalands HDW *m* TRANSPORT HDW barge carrier; ~ porte-conteneurs *m* TRANSPORT CTS, container transport ship, container ship; ~ porte-conteneurs cellulaire *m* TRANSPORT cellular container ship; ~ porte-palettes *m* TRANSPORT pallet ship; ~ porteur de type catamaran *m* TRANSPORT bacat ship, barge-aboard-catamaran ship; ~ pour charges palettisées *m* TRANSPORT palletized cargo carrier; ~ pour le transport en vrac *m* NAUT bulk carrier; ~ de ravitaillement *m* PETROLE supply boat; ~ ravitailleur *m* NAUT supply vessel; ~ de recherche océanographique *m* NAUT oceanographic research ship; ~ de relevage *m* NAUT salvage vessel; ~ sauveteur *m* NAUT salvage vessel; ~ de secours *m* NAUT rescue ship; ~ semi-porte conteneur *m* TRANSPORT semicontainer ship; ~ de servitude *m* NAUT support vessel; ~ de soutien *m* PETROLE support vessel; ~ support multitâche *m* PETROLE multipurpose vessel; ~ sur lest *m* NAUT ship in ballast; ~ transbordeur *m* CH DE FER train ferry; ~ transporteur de vrac sec *m* NAUT, TRANSPORT dry bulk carrier, dry cargo ship; ~ à turbine *m* NAUT turbine vessel; ~ **à turbines à gaz** *m* NAUT gas turbine ship; ~ **du type roll-on/roll-off** *m* NAUT roll-on/roll-off vessel; ~ **du type TRISEC** *m* TRANSPORT TRISEC ship, planing hull-type ship; ~ **usine** *m* NAUT, REFRIG factory ship; ~ **à vapeur** *m* NAUT steamer, steamship; ~ **à voiles** *m* NAUT sailing ship

navire-annexe *m* NAUT auxiliary vessel

navire-citerne *m* NAUT, POLLU MER, TRANSPORT tanker

navire-école *m* NAUT training ship

navire-hôpital *m* NAUT hospital ship

navire-mère *m* NAUT, TRANSPORT mother ship

navire-météo *m (cf navire météorologique)* METEO, NAUT weather ship

navires: *m pl* NAUT shipping; ~ **désarmés** *m pl* NAUT idle shipping; ~ **inemployés** *m pl* NAUT idle shipping

navisphère *f* OCEANO nautical celestial globe

Nb *(niobium)* CHIMIE Nb *(niobium)*

Nd *(néodyme)* CHIMIE Nd *(neodymium)*

Ne *(néon)* CHIMIE Ne *(neon)*

nébuleuse *f* ASTRONOMIE, ESPACE nebula; ~ **anneau** *f* ASTRONOMIE, ESPACE Ring Nebula; ~ **cométaire** *f* ASTRONOMIE, ESPACE cometary nebula; ~ **du Crabe** *f* ASTRONOMIE, ESPACE Crab nebula; ~ **de la Dentelle du Cygne** *f* ASTRONOMIE, ESPACE Veil Nebula; ~ **diffuse** *f* ASTRONOMIE, ESPACE diffuse nebula; ~ **à émission** *f* ASTRONOMIE, ESPACE emission nebula; ~ **froide de faible densité** *f* ASTRONOMIE, ESPACE cold low-density nebula; ~ **noire** *f (cf nébuleuse obscure)* ASTRONOMIE, ESPACE dark nebula; ~ **obscure** *f (cf nébuleuse noire)* ASTRONOMIE, ESPACE dark nebula; ~ **Orion** *f* ASTRONOMIE, ESPACE Orion Nebula; ~ **planétaire** *f* ASTRONOMIE, ESPACE planetary nebula; ~ **à raies d'émission** *f* ASTRONOMIE, ESPACE emission nebula; ~ **à raies d'émission lumineuses et chaudes** *f* ASTRONOMIE, ESPACE hot bright and radiating nebula; ~ **Tête de Cheval** *f* ASTRONOMIE, ESPACE Horsehead nebula; ~ **du Trapèze** *f* ASTRONOMIE, ESPACE Trapezium Nebula; ~ **de type HI** *f* ASTRONOMIE, ESPACE HI-type nebula, HII-type nebula; ~ **de Veil** *f* ASTRONOMIE, ESPACE Veil Nebula

nébulisation *f* IMPRIM *lubrification* oil mist

nébuliseur *m* CHIMIE nebulizer

nébulium *m* CHIMIE nebulium

nébulosité *f* ASTRONOMIE nebulosity, METEO cloud amount, NAUT cloud cover

nécessaire *m* CONS MECA outfit; ~ **à réparations** *m* PRODUCTION repair outfit

nef: ~ **de montage** *f* NAUT assembly hall

négatif[1] *adj* ELECTR *électrode* negative

négatif[2] *m* CINEMAT, IMPRIM, PHOTO negative; ~ **avec trucages** *m* CINEMAT optical negative; ~ **monté** *m* CINEMAT cut negative; ~ **original** *m* CINEMAT master negative, original; ~ **original non monté** *m* CINEMAT original uncut negative; ~ **d'origine** *m* PHOTO straight negative; ~ **par contact** *m* PHOTO contact negative; ~ **pour transparence** *m* CINEMAT background negative; ~ **réalisé par contact** *m* IMPRIM *reproduction* internegative; ~ **de sélection** *m* CINEMAT separation negative; ~ **de sélection trichrome** *m* PHOTO color separation negative (AmE), colour separation negative (BrE); ~ **son** *m* CINEMAT negative track, sound negative; ~ **son optique** *m* CINEMAT optical sound negative; ~ **sous-exposé** *m* CINEMAT thin negative; ~ **sur papier** *m* PHOTO paper negative; ~ **à trois bandes** *m* CINEMAT three-strip negative

négation *f* INFORMAT, ORDINAT negation

négaton *m* ELECTRON, PHYS PART negatron

négatoscope *m* CINEMAT light box, light table, PHOTO negative viewer

négliger *vt* PRODUCTION, SECURITE overlook

négociant: ~ **en lainages** *m* TEXTILE wool merchant

nègre *m* CINEMAT flag, nigger

neige *f* ELECTRON, METEO, REFRIG snow, TV noise, snow; ~ **acide** *f* POLLUTION acid snow; ~ **carbonique** *f* CHIMIE dry ice, REFRIG carbon dioxide snow; ~ **douce** *f* METEO soft snow; ~ **fondante** *f* REFRIG slush; ~ **normale** *f* POLLUTION clean snow; ~ **propre** *f* POLLUTION clean snow; ~ **roulée** *f* METEO soft hail

neiger *vi* METEO snow

neigeux *adj* METEO snowy

néoabiétique *adj* CHIMIE neoabietic

néodyme *m (Nd)* CHIMIE neodymium *(Nd)*

néoergostérol *m* CHIMIE neoergosterol

néon *m (Ne)* CHIMIE neon *(Ne)*

néoprène *m* CHIMIE, CONSTR, EMBALLAGE, PLAST CAOU neoprene

néotectonique *adj* GEOLOGIE neotectonic

néovolcanique *adj* GEOLOGIE neovolcanic

néozoïque *m* GEOLOGIE Neozoic, Neozoic era

néper *m* ACOUSTIQUE, ELECTRON, PHYSIQUE neper

néphélémétrie *f* CHIMIE nephelometry

néphéline *f* MINERAUX nepheline, nephelite; ~ **syénite** *f* CERAM VER nepheline syenite

néphélinite *f* PETR nephelinite, nephelinyte

néphélomètre *m* EQUIP LAB *analyse, turbidité* nephelometer

néphrite *f* MINERAUX nephrite

neptunium *m (Np)* CHIMIE neptunium *(Np)*

nerf *m* IMPRIM *reliure* band, MINES horse, PLAST CAOU *caoutchouc* nerve

nérol *m* CHIMIE nerol

nervure *f* AERONAUT *aéronef*, ESPACE *véhicules*, IMPRIM rib, MECANIQUE fin, rib, NUCLEAIRE *plaque support des guides de grappes* fin, rib, PAPIER, PRODUCTION rib; ~ **d'enroulement** *f* CERAM VER lapping rib; ~ **en treillis** *f* AERONAUT lattice rib; ~ **d'entretoisage** *f* CONS MECA *du banc d'un tour* cross-girth, PRODUCTION *du banc d'un tour* crossbar; ~ **d'extrémité** *f* AERONAUT end rib; ~ **de fermeture de chapelle** *f* AERONAUT fin stub top rib; ~ **forte** *f* AERONAUT main rib; ~ **de glissière** *f* AERONAUT flap track rib; ~ **glissière** *f* AERONAUT flap track rib; ~ **de positionnement** *f* PRODUCTION locating rib; ~ **de rive** *f* AERONAUT end rib

nervuré *adj* MECANIQUE ribbed

net *adj* CINEMAT sharp, IMPRIM *photogravure, impression* keen

netteté *f* CINEMAT definition, sharpness, IMPRIM *photogravure, impression*, PHOTO sharpness; ~ **des coins** *f* TV corner detail; ~ **des contours** *f* PHOTO acutance

nettoyage[1]: **pour ~ des surfaces difficiles** *adj* LESSIVES heavy-duty

nettoyage[2] *m* DISTRI EAU *des écluses* cleanup, PETROLE *fond marin* debris removal, POLLU MER cleanup, PRODUCTION cleaning, cleanup, dressing; ~ **chimique du charbon** *m* POLLUTION chemical coal cleaning; ~ **en place** *m* AGRO ALIM CIP, cleaning in place; ~ **du littoral** *m* POLLU MER shoreline cleanup; ~ **par ultrasons** *m* AERONAUT, CINEMAT, ENREGISTR, TV ultrasonic cleaning; ~ **à sec** *m* LESSIVES dry-cleaning; ~ **à la vapeur** *m* POLLU MER steam cleaning

nettoyages: **pour ~ faciles** *adj* LESSIVES light-duty

nettoyant *m* GENIE CHIM detergent

nettoyer *vt* PAPIER clean, PRODUCTION clean out, *la grille* clean, *une pièce coulée* dress; ~ **par le feu** *vt* THERMODYN burn off; ~ **à sec** *vt* TEXTILE dry-clean

nettoyeur *m* GENIE CHIM purifier, SECURITE cleaner; ~ **de bande** *m* MINES belt cleaner; ~ **de surface modulaire** *m* EMBALLAGE modular surface cleaner

nettoyeuse *f* PRODUCTION cleaning machine

neuraminique *adj* CHIMIE *acide* neuraminic

neurodine *f* CHIMIE neurodine

neurone *m* INFORMAT, ORDINAT neuron

neutralisant[1] *adj* CHIMIE neutralizing

neutralisant[2] *m* CHIMIE neutralizer

neutralisation *f* CHARBON neutralization, CHIMIE neutralization, neutralizing, ELECTR *de charge*, ELECTROTEC, HYDROLOGIE, LESSIVES neutralization, PETROLE sweetening, PLAST CAOU *chimie* neutralization; ~ **de charge** *f* ELECTR *électrostatique* charge neutralization; ~ **d'odeur** *f* GENIE CHIM odor control (AmE), odour control (BrE)

neutraliser *vt* CONS MECA deactivate, ESPACE *véhicules* passivate, PRODUCTION override

neutraliseur *m* ESPACE *communications* tone disabler, *propulsion* neutralizer

neutralité *f* CHIMIE neutrality, PHYS PART neutral state

neutre *adj* CHIMIE *sel*, ELECTR neutral, PHYS RAYON uncharged, PHYSIQUE neutral

neutrino *m* PHYS PART, PHYSIQUE neutrino; ~ **électronique** *m* PHYSIQUE electron neutrino; ~ **muon** *m* PHYSIQUE muon neutrino; ~ **muonique** *m* PHYS PART, PHYSIQUE muon neutrino; ~ **tau** *m* PHYS PART tau neutrino; ~ **tauique** *m* PHYSIQUE tauon neutrino; ~ **tauonique** *m* PHYS PART tau neutrino; ~ *m* PHYS PART muon neutrino

neutron *m* ELECTR *particule neutre*, PETR, PHYS PART, PHYS RAYON, PHYSIQUE neutron; ~ **apparaissant au moment de l'émission** *m* NUCLEAIRE nascent neutron; ~ **différé** *m* PHYSIQUE delayed neutron; ~ **diffusé** *m* NUCLEAIRE scattered neutron; ~ **de fission** *m* PHYS RAYON fission neutron; ~ **de fission non modéré** *m* NUCLEAIRE unmoderated fission neutron; ~ **immédiat** *m* PHYS RAYON *neutron de fission* prompt neutron; ~ **instantané** *m* PHYSIQUE prompt neutron; ~ **lent** *m* PHYSIQUE slow neutron; ~ **prompt** *m* PHYSIQUE prompt neutron; ~ **rapide** *m* NUCLEAIRE fast neutron; ~ **retardé** *m* PHYS RAYON delayed neutron; ~ **thermique** *m* NUCLEAIRE, PHYS RAYON *à mouvement lent*, PHYSIQUE thermal neutron; ~ **ultrafroid** *m* NUCLEAIRE ultracold neutron; ~ **vierge** *m* NUCLEAIRE first flight neutron, uncollided neutron, virgin neutron

névé *m* HYDROLOGIE glacier snow

névianskite *f* MINERAUX nevyanskite

newton *m (N)* ELECTR, METROLOGIE, PHYSIQUE newton *(N)*

newtonien *adj* ASTRONOMIE, PHYSIQUE Newtonian

nez:[1] **sur ~** *adj* NAUT trimmed by the head

nez:[2] **sur ~** *adv* NAUT down by the head

nez[3] *m* CONS MECA *d'un mandrin, d'un arbre porte-foret, d'un outil* nose, CONSTR *de marche* nosing; ~ **d'arbre** *m* CONS MECA extension shaft; ~ **basculant** *m* AERONAUT droop nose; ~ **de broche** *m* CONS MECA spindle nose; ~ **cylindrique fileté** *m* CONS MECA punch shank; ~ **cylindrique pour pigeonneau** *m* CONS MECA spigot holder; ~ **du mandrin** *m* CONS MECA mandrel nose, mandril nose, spindle nose; ~ **de marche** *m* CONSTR nosing plane; ~ **de raccord** *m* CONSTR nosepiece, stud coup-

ling, stud union; ~ **renifleur** *m* GAZ sniffer device; ~ **de vilebrequin** *m* AUTO crankshaft front end

Ni *(nickel)* CHIMIE Ni *(nickel)*

nialamide *m* CHIMIE nialamide

niccolite *f* MINERAUX niccolite, nickeline

niche *f* CONS MECA housing, CONSTR manhole, refuge hole, shelter; ~ **d'arrachement** *f* GEOLOGIE scar, slip scar, GEOPHYS scaur, scaw; ~ **d'écrémage** *f* CERAM VER skim pocket (AmE), skimming pocket (BrE); ~ **d'enfournement** *f* CERAM VER doghouse (BrE), filling end (AmE); ~ **murale** *f* CONSTR wall box; ~ **de refuge** *f* CONSTR manhole, refuge hole, shelter

nickel *m* CHIMIE niccolum, CHIMIE *(Ni)* nickel *(Ni)*

nickelage *m* ELECTR *procédé*, MATERIAUX nickel plating, PRODUCTION nickel plating, nickelage, nickeling (AmE), nickelling (BrE)

nickel-cadmium *m* MATERIAUX nickel cadmium

nickéleux *adj* CHIMIE nickelous

nickéline *f* MINERAUX kupfernickel

nickélique *adj* CHIMIE nickelic

nickelocène *m* CHIMIE nickelocene

nickelure *f* PRODUCTION nickelure

nicol *m* PHYSIQUE Nicol prism

nicols: ~ **croisés** *m pl* PHYSIQUE crossed Nicols

nicotinamide *f* CHIMIE niacinamide

nicotine *f* CHIMIE nicotine

nicotinique *adj* CHIMIE *acide* nicotinic

nicotyrine *f* CHIMIE nicotyrine

nid *m* CERAM VER bird's nest, MINES *de minerai* nest; ~ **d'abeilles** *m* AERONAUT honeycomb, CONSTR honeycombing, ESPACE honeycomb; ~ **de poule** *m* CONSTR, VEHICULES *route* pothole

nida *m* AERONAUT, ESPACE honeycomb

nifé *m* GEOPHYS barysphere, centrosphere, core, earth core

nimbo-stratus *m (Ns)* METEO nimbostratus *(Ns)*

niobite *f* CHIMIE columbite, niobite, MINERAUX niobite

niobium *m (Nb)* CHIMIE niobium *(Nb)*

nit *m* METROLOGIE nit (AmE)

nitramine *f* CHIMIE nitramine, nitroamine

nitraniline *f* CHIMIE nitroaniline

nitrant *m* CHIMIE nitriding

nitratage *m* CHIMIE nitration

nitrate *m* CHIMIE, POLLUTION nitrate; ~ **d'ammonium et fuel-oil** *m* MINES ANFO, ammonium nitrate fuel oil, prills-and-oil; ~ **d'argent** *m* CHIMIE silver nitrate; ~ **de cellulose** *m* CINEMAT celluloid, PLAST CAOU *plastiques, peintures* cellulose nitrate; ~ **de péroxoacétyle** *m* POLLUTION peroxoacetylnitrate; ~ **de potassium** *m* AGRO ALIM, CHIMIE potassium nitrate; ~ **de sodium** *m* CERAM VER natronitre, soda niter (AmE), soda nitre (BrE), sodium nitrate (BrE), CHIMIE sodium nitrate; ~ **de soude** *m* CHIMIE sodium nitrate

nitrate-fioul *m* MINES ANFO, ammonium nitrate fuel oil, prills-and-oil

nitrate-fuel *m* MINES ANFO, ammonium nitrate fuel oil, prills-and-oil

nitrate-huile *m* MINES ANFO, ammonium nitrate fuel oil, prills-and-oil

nitratine *f* CHIMIE nitratine

nitration *f* CHIMIE nitration; ~ **en phase vapeur** *f* GENIE CHIM vapor phase nitration (AmE), vapour phase nitration (BrE)

nitratite *f* MINERAUX nitratine, nitratite

nitrazine *f* CHIMIE nitrazine

nitre *m* CHIMIE niter (AmE), nitre (BrE), potassium

nitrate, saltpeter (AmE), saltpetre (BrE)
nitré *adj* CHIMIE nitrated
nitrer *vt* CHIMIE nitrate
nitréthane *m* CHIMIE nitroethane
nitreux *adj* CHIMIE nitrous
nitrifiant *adj* CHIMIE nitrifying, nitrosifying
nitrification *f* CHIMIE, HYDROLOGIE nitrification
nitrifier[1] *vt* CHIMIE nitrify
nitrifier:[2] **se ~** *v réfl* CHIMIE nitrify
nitrile *m* CHIMIE nitrile
nitrine *f* CHIMIE nitrin
nitrique *adj* CHIMIE nitric
nitrite *m* CHIMIE nitrite
nitritoïde *adj* CHIMIE nitritoid
nitrobenzène *m* CHIMIE nitrobenzene
nitrocellulose *f* CHIMIE nitrocellulose
nitrocellulosique *adj* CHIMIE nitrocellulosic
nitrochloroforme *m* CHIMIE nitrochloroform
nitro-éthane *m* CHIMIE nitroethane
nitroforme *m* CHIMIE nitroform
nitroglucose *f* CHIMIE nitroglucose
nitroglycérine *f* CHIMIE, MILITAIRE, MINES nitroglycerine
nitroindole *m* CHIMIE nitroindole
nitromannitol *m* CHIMIE nitromannite
nitrométhane *m* CHIMIE nitromethane
nitromètre *m* CHIMIE nitrometer
nitron *m* CHIMIE nitron
nitronaphtaline *f* CHIMIE nitronaphthalene
nitronium *m* CHIMIE nitronium
nitroparaffine *f* CHIMIE nitroparaffin
nitrophénol *m* CHIMIE nitrophenol
nitrosate *m* CHIMIE nitrosate
nitrosation *f* CHIMIE nitrosation
nitrosite *f* CHIMIE nitrosite
nitrosochlorure *m* CHIMIE nitrosochloride
nitrosubstitué *adj* CHIMIE nitrosubstituted
nitrosulfurique *adj* CHIMIE *acide* nitrosulfuric (AmE), nitrosulphuric (BrE)
nitrosyle *m* CHIMIE nitrosyl
nitrotartarique *adj* CHIMIE nitrotartaric
nitrotoluène *m* CHIMIE nitrotoluene
nitrox *m* OCEANO nitrox
nitruration *f* CHIMIE nitridation, nitriding, CONS MECA nitriding, MATERIAUX nitridation, nitriding, PRODUCTION nitride hardening; **~ en phase gazeuse** *f* THERMODYN gas nitriding; **~ à gaz** *f* THERMODYN gas nitriding
nitrure *m* CHIMIE nitride; **~ de bore** *m* CONS MECA cubic boron nitride; **~ de silicium** *m* ELECTRON silicon nitride; **~ de tellure** *m* ELECTROTEC tellurium nitride
nitrurer *vt* CHIMIE nitride
nitryle *m* CHIMIE nitroxyl, nitryl
nival *adj* METEO snowy
nivation *f* CHIMIE nivation
niveau:[1] **au ~ de la mer** *adj* METEO at sea level
niveau:[2] **de ~** *adv* CONSTR at grade
niveau[3] *m* CINEMAT, CONSTR, ELECTRON, EMBALLAGE *de remplissage*, ENREGISTR level, GEOLOGIE bed, layer, horizon, INFORMAT level, MECANIQUE elevation, *outillage* level, MINES level, lift, ORDINAT, PHYS RAYON *d'irradiation externe* level, POLLUTION *d'émission* level, *de pollution* level, PRODUCTION gage glass (AmE), gauge glass (BrE), TRANSPORT *de service* level;
~ à l'abri du gel *m* CHARBON frost-free level; **~ d'accélération acoustique** *m* ACOUSTIQUE sound acceleration level; **~ accepteur** *m* ELECTRON acceptor level; **~ d'acidité** *m* CONSTR *système hydraulique* acid level, POLLUTION acidity level; **~ à alcool** *m* CONSTR spirit level; **~ d'alidade** *m* INSTRUMENT plate level; **~ ancien des sols** *m* CONSTR old ground level; **~ aquifère** *m* EN RENOUV aquifer; **~ d'arasement de pieu** *m* CHARBON pile cutoff level; **~ audio instable** *m* ENREGISTR variable audio level; **~ d'audition** *m* ACOUSTIQUE level above threshold;
~ des bacs *m* PETROLE pit lever; **~ de base des vagues** *m* OCEANO wave base, wave trough level; **~ de blanc** *m* TV bright level, white level; **~ de bruit** *m* ENREGISTR, PHYS ONDES, TELECOM noise level; **~ à bulle** *m* MECANIQUE *outillage* bubble level, METROLOGIE level, spirit level; **~ à bulle d'air** *m* CONSTR air level, level, spirit level; **~ à bulle indépendant sur la lunette** *m* CONS MECA striding level;
~ de la charge *m* PRODUCTION stock line; **~ à cheval** *m* CONS MECA striding level; **~ cible d'irradiation** *m* NUCLEAIRE target burn-up, target irradiation; **~ de la composante continue** *m* TV DC level; **~ des composants** *m* ELECTRON component level; **~ de contrainte élevé** *m* PRODUCTION elevated stress level; **~ de contrôle** *m* QUALITE inspection level; **~ de crête de signal** *m* TV peak signal; **~ critique d'eau** *m* DISTRI EAU critical water level;
~ de densité d'énergie *m* ACOUSTIQUE sound energy density level; **~ donneur** *m* ELECTRON donor level; **~ de dopage** *m* ELECTRON doping level;
~ d'eau *m* CHIMIE, DISTRI EAU water level; **~ de l'eau d'aval** *m* EN RENOUV tailwater level; **~ d'eau en aval** *m* HYDROLOGIE downstream level; **~ d'eau intermédiaire** *m* DISTRI EAU intermediate water level; **~ de l'eau phréatique** *m* CONSTR ground water level; **~ d'écoute** *m* CINEMAT reproduction level; **~ d'écrêtage** *m* ELECTRON, TV clipping level; **~ d'électrolyte** *m* AUTO acid level; **~ électronique** *m* METROLOGIE level; **~ d'émergence de la nappe d'eau** *m* CHARBON ground water table; **~ des émissions parasites** *m* ESPACE *communications* spurious emission level; **~ d'empreinte magnétique** *m* TV print-through level; **~ énergétique** *m* GEOPHYS, PHYS PART, PHYS RAYON, PHYSIQUE energy level; **~ énergétique d'un atome** *m* NUCLEAIRE atomic energy level; **~ énergétique de vibration de la molécule** *m* PHYS RAYON molecular vibrational energy level; **~ d'énergie** *m* GEOPHYS, PHYS PART *d'un atome*, PHYS RAYON *d'un atome*, PHYSIQUE energy level; **~ d'énergie accepteur** *m* ELECTRON acceptor level; **~ d'énergie donneur** *m* ELECTRON donor level; **~ d'énergie zéro** *m* NUCLEAIRE zero energy level; **~ d'enregistrement** *m* ENREGISTR recording level; **~ d'entrée** *m* TELECOM, TV input level; **~ d'entrée du signal audiofréquence** *m* ENREGISTR audio signal input level; **~ d'équilibre** *m* OCEANO hydrostatic level, still water, mean sea level; **~ d'étiage** *m* DISTRI EAU low-water level;
~ de Fermi *m* PHYSIQUE Fermi level; **~ de fond** *m* MINES bottom level, POLLUTION background level;
~ de givrage *m* REFRIG frost level indicator;
~ d'habilitation *m* INFORMAT, ORDINAT clearance level; **~ hydraulique** *m* PETROLE *géologie, écoulement des fluides* hydraulic head; **~ hydrostatique** *m* HYDROLOGIE water table, OCEANO mean sea level;
~ d'impuretés *m* ELECTRON impurity level; **~ d'incrustation** *m* TV key level; **~ initial** *m* POLLUTION *eau* initial level; **~ d'injection** *m* ELECTRON injection

level; ~ **d'insonie** *m* ACOUSTIQUE loudness level; ~ **instantané de nuisance** *m* POLLUTION instantaneous concentration; ~ **d'intensité** *m* ELECTROTEC *sonore* intensity level, PHYS RAYON level of intensity; ~ **d'intensité acoustique** *m* ACOUSTIQUE, PHYSIQUE sound intensity level; ~ **d'intensité sonore** *m* ENREGISTR sound intensity level; ~ **interfacial** *m* CONS MECA interface level; ~ **d'intervention** *m* CH DE FER maintenance level; ~ **d'isolement assigné** *m* ELECTR *tension d'essai* rated insulation level; ~ **d'isolement nominal** *m* ELECTR *tension d'essai* rated insulation level; ~ **d'isosonie** *m* PHYSIQUE loudness level;

~ l ~ **de lecture** *m* ENREGISTR playback level; ~ **ligne** *m* ENREGISTR, TV line level; ~ **du liquide** *m* EMBALLAGE liquid level; ~ **liquide** *m* PETROLE *raffinerie* liquid level; ~ **logique** *m* ELECTRON, INFORMAT, ORDINAT logic level; ~ **logique bas** *m* ELECTRON low logic level; ~ **logique haut** *m* ELECTRON high logic level; ~ **de luminosité** *m* IMPRIM *photogravure* luminance; ~ **à lunette** *m* CONSTR leveling instrument (AmE), levelling instrument (BrE), surveyor's level, *lunette fixe* dumpy level, *reposant* dans des étriers en forme de fourche Y-level;

~ m ~ **maximal du signal bleu** *m* TV blue peak level; ~ **maximal du signal rouge** *m* TV red peak level; ~ **maximal du signal vert** *m* TV green peak level; ~ **maximum de crue** *m* HYDROLOGIE maximum flood level; ~ **de la mer** *m* CONSTR, DISTRI EAU, EN RENOUV, NAUT sea level; ~ **de mi-marée** *m* OCEANO half tide level; ~ **minimal du bleu** *m* TV blue black level; ~ **minimal du signal rouge** *m* TV red black level; ~ **minimal du signal vert** *m* TV green black level; ~ **de mise à jour** *m* ORDINAT release level; ~ **de modulation** *m* PHYS ONDES modulation level; ~ **à moteur** *m* INSTRUMENT motor-driven level; ~ **moyen annuel** *m* DISTRI EAU annual mean water level; ~ **moyen de la mer** *m* NAUT, OCEANO mean sea level;

~ n ~ **de la nappe aquifère** *m* DISTRI EAU ground water level; ~ **de la nappe phréatique** *m* DISTRI EAU phreatic level; ~ **de noir** *m* TV black level, pedestal; ~ **normal** *m* NUCLEAIRE ground level, normal level, normal energy level; ~ **normalisé du bruit de choc** *m* ACOUSTIQUE normalized impact sound level; ~ **normal de stockage** *m* PRODUCTION carry level;

~ o ~ **original des sols** *m* CONSTR old ground level;
~ p ~ **de parole** *m* ENREGISTR speech level; ~ **de pente** *m* CONSTR slope level; ~ **piézométrique** *m* PETROLE piezometric head; ~ **à pinnules** *m* CONSTR sighted level; ~ **de pointe** *m* ENREGISTR peak level; ~ **de pointe d'enregistrement** *m* ENREGISTR peak recording level; ~ **de pollution naturelle** *m* POLLUTION background level; ~ **de la porteuse** *m* ELECTRON carrier level; ~ **potentiométrique** *m* PETROLE potentiometric head, potentiometric level; ~ **de pression acoustique** *m* ACOUSTIQUE, PHYSIQUE sound pressure level; ~ **de pression sélectif** *m* ENREGISTR band pressure level; ~ **pseudopotentiométrique** *m* PETROLE pseudopotentiometric head; ~ **de puissance acoustique** *m* ACOUSTIQUE, PHYSIQUE sound power level;

~ q ~ **de qualité** *m* METROLOGIE standard of quality; ~ **de qualité acceptable** *m* (*NQA*) QUALITE acceptable quality level (*AQL*); ~ **de quantification** *m* ELECTRON, INFORMAT, ORDINAT quantization level;
~ r ~ **de recépage de pieux** *m* CONSTR pile cutoff level; ~ **de réception** *m* ELECTRON reception level; ~ **de réduction des sondes** *m* NAUT chart datum, OCEANO

sounding datum, sounding datum level; ~ **de référence** *m* CINEMAT zero level, ELECTRON reference level, ENREGISTR reference volume, zero level; ~ **de référence audio** *m* ENREGISTR, TV reference audio level; ~ **de remplissage** *m* EMBALLAGE fill level; ~ **repère** *m* GEOLOGIE datum horizon, key horizon; ~ **de risque** *m* QUALITE criticality; ~ **de ronronnement** *m* ENREGISTR rumble level;

~ s ~ **de saturation** *m* ENREGISTR saturation level; ~ **de sensation d'intensité** *m* ENREGISTR loudness level; ~ **de service** *m* PRODUCTION service level; ~ **de signal** *m* TELECOM signal level; ~ **du signal** *m* ELECTRON signal level; ~ **de son direct** *m* ENREGISTR direct sound level; ~ **sonore** *m* ACOUSTIQUE sound level, IMPRIM noise level, POLLUTION sound pressure level, SECURITE noise level; ~ **sonore de référence** *m* ENREGISTR reference audio level; ~ **de sortie** *m* ENREGISTR, TELECOM, TV output level; ~ **de sortie de chrominance** *m* TV chrominance carrier output; ~ **de sortie de luminance** *m* TV luminance carrier output; ~ **de spectre d'intensité** *m* ENREGISTR intensity spectrum level; ~ **sphérique** *m* INSTRUMENT circular level; ~ **statique d'un fluide** *m* PETR static fluid level; ~ **de suppression** *m* TV blanking level; ~ **de suppression de ligne** *m* TV line blanking level; ~ **de surcharge** *m* ELECTROTEC, ENREGISTR overload level;

~ t ~ **de tarification** *m* TELECOM charge rate; ~ **technique** *m* PRODUCTION engineering issue level; ~ **de tension** *m* PRODUCTION voltage level; ~ **de transmission du bruit de choc** *m* ACOUSTIQUE impact sound transmission level;

~ v ~ **de vent géostrophique** *m* GEOPHYS geostrophic wind level; ~ **de version** *m* INFORMAT release level; ~ **vidéo** *m* TV video level; ~ **vidéo comprimé** *m* TV compressed video level; ~ **vidéo faible** *m* TV low-level video; ~ **vidéo oscillant** *m* TV fluttering video level; ~ **visible** *m* REFRIG gage glass (AmE), gauge glass (BrE); ~ **de vitesse acoustique** *m* ACOUSTIQUE acoustic velocity level; ~ **de vol** *m* AERONAUT flight level

niveau:[4] **être au ~ de** *vi* PRODUCTION be flush with; **être de ~ avec** *vi* PRODUCTION be flush with
nivelée *f* CONSTR observation
niveler *vt* CONSTR bone, level, PRODUCTION level
nivelette *f* CH DE FER grade stake (AmE), level indicator (BrE), CONSTR boning rod, boning stick
niveleuse *f* CONSTR grader, leveling machine (AmE), levelling machine (BrE), grader, motor grader, POLLU MER grader, TRANSPORT grader, road grader; ~ **à lame** *f* TRANSPORT motor grader
nivellement *m* CONSTR leveling (AmE), levelling (BrE), *d'une voie entre deux points* boning, PRODUCTION leveling (AmE), levelling (BrE), smoothing; ~ **de charges** *m* PRODUCTION production smoothing; ~ **de la voie** *m* CH DE FER surfacing of the road (AmE), surfacing of the track (BrE)
nivénite *f* NUCLEAIRE nivenite
nivosité *f* METEO snowfall
No (*nobélium*) CHIMIE No (*nobelium*)
nobélium *m* (*No*) CHIMIE nobelium (*No*)
noble *adj* CHIMIE *métal, gaz* noble
nocif *adj* CHIMIE noxious, PETROLE, SECURITE harmful
nocivité *f* POLLUTION harmfulness
nocturne *adj* ASTRONOMIE nocturnal; ~ **lumineux** *adj* ASTRONOMIE noctilucent
nodulation *f* CONS MECA coring
nodule *m* CERAM VER, CHARBON, CHIMIE, GEOLOGIE no-

dule; ~ **de corrosion** m NUCLEAIRE corrosion nodule; ~ **en forme de rognon** m GEOLOGIE *de silex, marne* kidney stone; ~ **de manganèse** m GEOLOGIE manganese nodule; ~ **polymétallique** m GEOLOGIE manganese nodule

noeud m ACOUSTIQUE, ASTRONOMIE node, CONS MECA cluster, CONSTR *d'une penture* knuckle, CRISTALL, ELECTR *circuit*, ELECTROTEC node, EN RENOUV *vitesse nautique* knot, GEOMETRIE, INFORMAT, METALL node, NAUT hitch, knot, ORDINAT node, PAPIER knot, PHYS ONDES, PHYSIQUE, TELECOM *de réseau* node, TEXTILE knot; ~ **d'accès** m TELECOM access node; ~ **d'anguille** m NAUT timber hitch; ~ **ascendant** m ESPACE ascending node; ~ **de bois** m NAUT timber hitch; ~ **de bosse** m NAUT stopper knot; ~ **de cabestan** m NAUT clove hitch; ~ **de carrick** m NAUT carrick bend; ~ **de chaise** m NAUT bowline; ~ **de communication** m TRANSPORT traffic center (AmE), traffic centre (BrE); ~ **à commutation de paquets** m TELECOM PSN, packet switching node; ~ **coulant** m NAUT *cordage* loop; ~ **descendant** m ESPACE descending node; ~ **d'écoute** m NAUT becket bend, sheet bend; ~ **d'empattement** m CONSTR T-joint; ~ **en forme de huit** m NAUT figure-of-eight knot; ~ **étendu** m METALL extended node; ~ **ferroviaire** m CH DE FER major railroad junction (AmE), major railway junction (BrE), railroad center (AmE), railway centre (BrE), TRANSPORT railroad junction (AmE), railway junction (BrE); ~ **imparfait** m ACOUSTIQUE partial node; ~ **de jambe de chien** m NAUT sheepshank; ~ **de jonction** m CONSTR butt joint; ~ **de jonction renforcé** m CONS MECA double strap butt joint; ~ **d'orin** m NAUT fisherman's bend; ~ **partiel** m ELECTROTEC partial node; ~ **de pêcheur** m NAUT fisherman's bend; ~ **pincé** m METALL constricted node; ~ **plat** m NAUT reef knot; ~ **de réseau** m CRISTALL lattice point; ~ **de ride simple** m NAUT single Matthew Walker; ~ **de soudure** m CONSTR wipe joint, wiped joint; ~ **de transit international** m *(NTI)* TELECOM international gateway node, international packet-switching gateway exchange; ~ **de transmission** m TELECOM transmission node; ~ **de vache** m NAUT granny knot

noir m IMPRIM *papier, encres* black; ~ **animal** m AGRO ALIM blood black; ~ **de carbone** m PETROLE, PLAST CAOU *pigment, charge* carbon black; ~ **de carbone activé** m PLAST CAOU *pigment, charge* activated carbon black; ~ **de couche** m PRODUCTION blackwash; ~ **et blanc** m CINEMAT monochrome, IMPRIM B&W, black and white; ~ **d'étuve** m PRODUCTION blackwash; ~ **FF** m PLAST CAOU *charge pour caoutchouc* FF carbon black, fine furnace carbon black; ~ **HEF** m PLAST CAOU *pigment, charge pour caoutchouc* high elongation furnace carbon black; ~ **HMF** m PLAST CAOU *pigment, charge pour caoutchouc* HMF carbon black, high modulus furnace carbon black; ~ **HPC** m PLAST CAOU *pigment, charge pour caoutchouc* HPC carbon black, hard processing channel carbon black; ~ **MPC** m PLAST CAOU *pigment, charge pour caoutchouc* MPC carbon black, medium-processing channel carbon black; ~ **MT** m PLAST CAOU *pigment, charge pour caoutchouc* MT carbon black, medium thermal carbon black; ~ **perturbé** m TV noisy blacks; ~ **pour grisaille** m CERAM VER black stain; ~ **de référence** m TV reference black; ~ **SRF** m PLAST CAOU SRF carbon black, semireinforcing carbon black; ~ **de la trichromie** m IMPRIM *photogravure* three-color black (AmE), three-colour black (BrE); ~ **d'uranium** m NU-

CLEAIRE uranium black, varied pitchblende

noirci adj THERMODYN burnt, *par la chaleur* blackened

noircir vt CINEMAT black out, THERMODYN *par chaleur* blacken

noircissage m PRODUCTION blackening

noircissement m CERAM VER blackening, darkening, PRODUCTION blackening, blacking; ~ **des gris** m TV black crush

noix f CONS MECA *pour chaîne calibrée* sheave, CONSTR groove, *d'un robinet* plug, EQUIP LAB *pince* bosshead; ~ **d'articulation** f CONS MECA hinge yoke; ~ **de réglage arrière** f PHOTO *d'un soufflet* back adjustment; ~ **de réglage frontale** f PHOTO *d'un soufflet* front standard adjustment; ~ **vomique** f CHIMIE nux vomica

nolisage m NAUT charter

nom m INFORMAT, ORDINAT name; ~ **alternatif** m ORDINAT alias; ~ **commercial** m BREVETS trading name; ~ **de donnée** m INFORMAT, ORDINAT data name; ~ **de fichier** m INFORMAT, ORDINAT filename; ~ **générique** m INFORMAT, ORDINAT generic name; ~ **d'un point d'entrée** m TELECOM log-in; ~ **de procédure** m INFORMAT, ORDINAT procedure name; ~ **qualifié** m INFORMAT, ORDINAT qualified name; ~ **symbolique** m INFORMAT, ORDINAT symbolic name; ~ **trivial** m CHIMIE trivial name; ~ **de l'utilisateur** m INFORMAT, ORDINAT user name; ~ **de variable** m INFORMAT, ORDINAT variable name

nombre m CHIMIE number, ELECTRON quantity, INFORMAT number; ~ **d'Abbé** m CERAM VER Abbé value, PHYSIQUE Abbé number; ~ **d'ailes** m EN RENOUV blade quantity; ~ **aléatoire** m INFORMAT, MATH, ORDINAT random number; ~ **atomique** m CHIMIE, PHYS PART, PHYSIQUE atomic number; ~ **baryonique** m PHYS PART, PHYSIQUE baryon number; ~ **binaire** m TELECOM bit; ~ **de bobines** m CINEMAT reelage; ~ **cardinal** m MATH cardinal number; ~ **de colis** m PRODUCTION quantity packing; ~ **complexe** m INFORMAT, MATH complex number; ~ **composé** m MATH composite number; ~ **de coordination** m CHIMIE, CRISTALL, METALL coordination number; ~ **entier naturel** m GEOMETRIE natural whole number; ~ **en virgule flottante** m INFORMAT floating point number; ~ **de fractionnements** m PRODUCTION number; ~ **de Froude** m PHYSIQUE Froude number; ~ **générateur** m INFORMAT, ORDINAT generation number; ~ **guide** m PHOTO guide number; ~ **d'heures de vol** m AERONAUT flying time; ~ **imaginaire** m MATH imaginary number; ~ **irrationnel** m INFORMAT irrational number, MATH surd; ~ **isotopique** m PHYS PART isotopic number; ~ **leptonique** m PHYSIQUE lepton number; ~ **de Mach** m AERONAUT, PHYSIQUE Mach number; ~ **de Mach maximal admissible** m AERONAUT maximum permissible Mach number; ~ **magique** m PHYSIQUE magic number; ~ **de masse** m PHYS PART mass number, PHYSIQUE mass number, nucleon number; ~ **de mots utilisés** m PRODUCTION word usage; ~ **moyen des bits par échantillon** m TELECOM average bits per sample; ~ **naturel** m MATH natural number; ~ **de neutrons** m PHYSIQUE neutron number; ~ **de neutrons produits par fission** m PHYSIQUE neutron yield; ~ **de neutrons produits par neutron absorbé** m PHYSIQUE neutron yield, eta factor; ~ **de nucléons** m PHYSIQUE nucleon number; ~ **d'onde** m ACOUSTIQUE, CHIMIE, PHYS ONDES wave number; ~ **ordinal** m GEOMETRIE ordinal, INFORMAT serial number; ~ **de pales** m EN RENOUV blade quantity; ~ **par échantillon** m ESSAIS *d'éprouvettes* number per sample; ~ **des particules** m

METALL particle number; ~ **de passes** *m* CONSTR number of passes; ~ **de Poisson** *m* CHARBON Poisson's ratio; ~ **premier** *m* MATH prime number; ~ **de protons** *m (Z)* PHYS PART proton number *(Z)*; ~ **pseudo-aléatoire** *m* INFORMAT, ORDINAT pseudo random number; ~ **quantique** *m* CHIMIE, NUCLEAIRE, PHYS PART, PHYSIQUE quantum number; ~ **quantique azimutal** *m* PHYS RAYON azimuthal quantum number, orbital quantum number; ~ **quantique magnétique** *m* PHYSIQUE magnetic quantum number; ~ **quantique du moment cinétique orbital** *m* PHYSIQUE azimuthal quantum number, orbital angular momentum quantum number, orbital quantum number; ~ **quantique du moment cinétique total** *m* PHYSIQUE total angular momentum quantum number; ~ **quantique orbital** *m* PHYSIQUE azimuthal quantum number, orbital angular momentum quantum number, orbital quantum number; ~ **quantique d'oscillations** *m* PHYSIQUE vibrational quantum number; ~ **quantique principal** *m* AERONAUT main quantum number, PHYSIQUE principal quantum number; ~ **quantique rotatoire** *m* PHYSIQUE rotational quantum number; ~ **quantique de spin** *m* PHYSIQUE spin quantum number; ~ **quantique de vibrations** *m* PHYSIQUE vibrational quantum number; ~ **de rapports** *m* TEXTILE *d'un dessin, d'une armure* number of repeats; ~ **rationnel** *m* INFORMAT, MATH rational number; ~ **réel** *m* INFORMAT, MATH real number; ~ **de Reynolds** *m* AERONAUT *aérodynamique*, EN RENOUV, PHYS FLUID, PHYSIQUE *(Re)* Reynolds number; ~ **de Reynolds élevé** *m* PHYS FLUID high Reynolds number; ~ **de Reynolds faible** *m* PHYS FLUID low Reynolds number; ~ **de Schmidt** *m* PHYSIQUE Schmidt number; ~ **de Sommerfield** *m* EN RENOUV *énergie marémotrice* Sommerfield number; ~ **volumique électronique** *m* PHYSIQUE electron density; ~ **de Wolf** *m (R)* ASTRONOMIE Wolf number *(R)*

nombres: ~ **inversement proportionnels** *m pl* MATH inversely proportional numbers; ~ **ordinaux finis et transfinis** *m pl* GEOMETRIE finite and infinite ordinals

nomenclature *f* ASTRONOMIE, CHIMIE, GEOLOGIE, ORDINAT, PHYSIQUE nomenclature, PRODUCTION bill of material, nomenclature; ~ **arborescente** *f* PRODUCTION multilevel bill of material, indented bill of material; ~ **des astéroïdes** *f* ASTRONOMIE asteroid nomenclature; ~ **de fabrication** *f* PRODUCTION *production* manufacturing bill of material; ~ **de montage** *f* PRODUCTION assembly list, assembly sheet; ~ **multiniveaux** *f* PRODUCTION multilevel bill of material; ~ **multivineuse** *f* PRODUCTION indented bill of material; ~ **des pièces** *f* PRODUCTION names of parts; ~ **des variantes produit** *f* PRODUCTION product variant

nominal *adj* CONS MECA indicated

non: ~ **adhérisé** *adj* TEXTILE *tissu* undipped; ~ **affecté** *adj* MATERIAUX free; ~ **agréé** *adj* TELECOM nonapproved; ~ **altéré** *adj* GEOLOGIE fresh, unaltered; ~ **amplifié** *adj* TELECOM *circuit* unamplified; ~ **apprêté** *adj* PAPIER without finish; ~ **aqueux** *adj* CHIMIE nonaqueous; ~ **biodégradable** *adj* RECYCLAGE nondegradable; ~ **capacitif** *adj* ELECTROTEC *charge* noncapacitive; ~ **chargé** *adj* CINEMAT unloaded, ELECTR uncharged; ~ **circulaire** *adj* TEXTILE open-ended; ~ **cokéfiant** *adj* CHARBON noncoking; ~ **collant** *adj* CHARBON noncaking; ~ **collé** *adj* PAPIER unsized; ~ **coloré** *adj* AGRO ALIM, COULEURS colorless (AmE), colourless (BrE); ~ **combiné** *adj* CHIMIE free, uncombined; ~ **comestible** *adj* AGRO ALIM unfit for human consumption; ~ **con-**

densé *adj* INFORMAT, ORDINAT unpacked; ~ **conforme à l'original** *adj* IMPRIM *photogravure, impression* out-of-true; ~ **conforme aux normes établies** *adj* CHIMIE substandard; ~ **congelable** *adj* AERONAUT antifreezing; ~ **conjugué** *adj* CHIMIE nonconjugated; ~ **corrosif** *adj* MATERIAUX noncorrosive; ~ **cristallin** *adj* GEOLOGIE amorphous, noncrystalline; ~ **cuit** *adj* THERMODYN unbaked, unfired; ~ **déformé** *adj* ELECTRON undistorted; ~ **dilué** *adj* CHIMIE *acide concentré* undiluted; ~ **dissocié** *adj* METALL *dislocation* undissociated; ~ **dopé** *adj* MATERIAUX *semi-conducteur* undoped; ~ **durci** *adj* PLAST CAOU *plastiques, caoutchouc* uncured; ~ **enrichi** *adj* NUCLEAIRE *uranium* unenriched; ~ **épuisé** *adj* NUCLEAIRE *uranium* unburned; ~ **éteint** *adj* CHIMIE unslaked; ~ **ferreux** *adj* CHIMIE nonferrous; ~ **fissionné** *adj* NUCLEAIRE *charge nucléaire* unfissioned; ~ **gradué** *adj* CHIMIE ungraduated; ~ **gras** *adj* AGRO ALIM nonfat; ~ **grisouteux** *adj* CHIMIE sweet, MINES nonfiery; ~ **habité** *adj* ESPACE *véhicules* unmanned; ~ **incorporé à la carte** *adj* ELECTRON off board; ~ **incorporé à la puce** *adj* ELECTRON off chip; ~ **inflammable** *adj* EMBALLAGE noninflammable; ~ **ionique** *adj* LESSIVES nonionic; ~ **lacté** *adj* AGRO ALIM nondairy; ~ **linéaire** *adj* ELECTR nonlinear; ~ **magnétique** *adj* MATERIAUX nonmagnetic, earth-free (BrE) PHYSIQUE nonmagnetic; ~ **maîtrisable** *adj* COMMANDE out-of-control; ~ **manoeuvrable** *adj* NAUT not under command; ~ **mis à la terre** *adj* ELECTR *circuit, appareil* ground-free (AmE); ~ **miscible** *adj* AGRO ALIM immiscible; ~ **modulé** *adj* ESPACE *communications* unmodulated; ~ **moulé** *adj* (Bel) *(cf mal rendu)* CERAM VER not blown up; ~ **orienté** *adj* GEOLOGIE *texture* unoriented; ~ **perforé** *adj* TELECOM *bande* unperforated; ~ **planifié** *adj* PRODUCTION unplanned; ~ **plastifié** *adj* PLAST CAOU unplasticized; ~ **plastique** *adj* CONSTR nonplastic; ~ **polaire** *adj* CHIMIE nonpolar; ~ **polarisé** *adj* INFORMAT, ORDINAT unbiased; ~ **polluant** *adj* AUTO, MECANIQUE antipollution; ~ **polymérisé** *adj* PLAST CAOU *plastiques, caoutchouc* uncured; ~ **pondéré** *adj* ENREGISTR *niveau de bruit* unweighted; ~ **ponté** *adj* NAUT open; ~ **poreux** *adj* GAZ nonporous; ~ **prévu** *adj* PRODUCTION *travail* unplanned; ~ **raffiné** *adj* AGRO ALIM unrefined; ~ **réactif** *adj* CHIMIE nonreactive; ~ **recuit** *adj* MATERIAUX *verre* unannealed; ~ **relativiste** *adj* ASTRONOMIE nonrelativist; ~ **rémanent** *adj* INFORMAT nonvolatile; ~ **répertorié** *adj* PRODUCTION not listed; ~ **reproductible** *adj* EMBALLAGE nonreproductible; ~ **retour à zéro** *adj* TELECOM NRZ, nonreturn to zero; ~ **retour à zéro inversé** *adj* TELECOM NRZI, nonreturn to zero inverted; ~ **réutilisable** *adj* INFORMAT, ORDINAT nonreusable; ~ **saturé** *adj* AGRO ALIM *graisse*, CHIMIE unsaturated, GEOLOGIE undersaturated, PETROLE *hydrocarbure*, PLAST CAOU *polyester* unsaturated; ~ **stoechiométrique** *adj* CHIMIE, MATERIAUX nonstoichiometric; ~ **synchrone** *adj* TV asynchronous, nonsync, out-of-sync; ~ **tachant** *adj* PLAST CAOU nonstaining; ~ **tissé** *adj* IMPRIM, TEXTILE nonwoven; ~ **valide** *adj* TELECOM *message* invalid; ~ **volatil** *adj* INFORMAT, ORDINAT nonvolatile; ~ **vulcanisé** *adj* PLAST CAOU *plastiques, caoutchouc* uncured, THERMODYN unvulcanized

nonacosane *m* CHIMIE nonacosane

nonane *m* CHIMIE nonane

non-circularité *f* TELECOM *de la gaine* noncircularity

non-conducteur *m* ELECTR *isolateur*, MATERIAUX *chaleur* nonconductor

non-conformité *f* PRODUCTION nonconformance, QUALITE nonconformity

non-conformités: **~ par individu** *f pl* QUALITE nonconformities per item; **~ par unité** *f pl* QUALITE nonconformities per item; **~ pour cent individus** *f pl* QUALITE nonconformities per hundred items; **~ pour cent unités** *f pl* QUALITE nonconformities per hundred items

non-conservation: **~ de la parité** *f* PHYSIQUE nonconservation of parity

non-fonctionnement *m* CONS MECA failure

non-métal *m* CHIMIE *métalloïde* nonmetal

nononique *adj* CHIMIE nononic

nonose *f* CHIMIE nonose

non-réperfusion *f* CHIMIE no-reflow

nontronite *f* MINERAUX nontronite

nonyle *m* CHIMIE nonyl

nonylène *m* CHIMIE nonylene

nonylique *adj* CHIMIE nonylic

noradrénaline *f* CHIMIE noradrenalin

norateur *m* PHYSIQUE norator

norbergite *f* MINERAUX norbergite

norbornadiène *f* CHIMIE norbornadiene

norbornane *f* CHIMIE norbornane

norbornylène *f* CHIMIE norbornylene

nord:[1] **du ~** *adj* NAUT northerly, north; **~ en haut** *adj* NAUT north-up

nord:[2] **~ magnétique** *m* GEOPHYS magnetic north; **~ vrai** *m* NAUT true north

nordé *m* NAUT northeast

nord-est:[1] **du ~** *adj* NAUT *vent* northeasterly NAUT northeast

nord-est[2] *m* NAUT nor'easter, northeast, northeaster

nord-est-quart-est *adv* NAUT northeast by east

nord-est-quart-nord *adv* NAUT northeast by north

nord-nord-est *m* NAUT north-northeast

nord-nord-ouest *m* NAUT north-northwest

nord-ouest:[1] **du ~** *adj* NAUT *vent* northwesterly NAUT northwest

nord-ouest[2] *m* NAUT nor'wester, northwest, northwester

nord-ouest-quart-nord *adv* NAUT northwest by north

nord-quart-nord-ouest *m* NAUT northwest by west

nord-quart-nord-est *adv* NAUT north by east

nord-quart-nord-ouest *adv* NAUT north by west

noréphédrine *f* CHIMIE norephedrine

noria *f* INST HYDR bucket pump

norite *m* PETR norite

normal *adj* PHYSIQUE normal

normale *f* GEOMETRIE normal, perpendicular, PETR normal; **~ commune** *f* CONS MECA common normal; **~ commune des profils** *f* CONS MECA common normal, line of action, train of action; **~ de contact** *f* CONS MECA common normal, line of action, train of action

normalisation *f* GAZ standardization, INFORMAT normalization, standardization, METALL normalization, ORDINAT normalization, standardization, PHYSIQUE, QUALITE, TELECOM, TV standardization

normaliser *vt* CHIMIE standardize, MECANIQUE *matériaux* normalize, QUALITE standardize

normalité *f* CHIMIE, QUALITE normality

normanite *f* MINES normanite

norme *f* CONS MECA standard specification, GEOLOGIE norm, IMPRIM, INFORMAT, ORDINAT standard, PHYSIQUE modulus, standard, QUALITE, TELECOM, TV standard; **~ de balayage** *f* TV scanning standard; **~**

britannique *f* CONS MECA BSS, British Standards Specification; **~ de codage** *f* TELECOM coding standard; **~ de diffusion** *f* TV broadcast standard; **~ d'émission** *f* POLLUTION emission standard; **~ EMS** *f (spécification de mémoire étendue)* ORDINAT EMS *(expanded memory specification)*; **~ d'enregistrement magnétique** *f* ENREGISTR magnetic recording standard; **~ française** *f* CONS MECA French standard; **~ à fréquences basses** *f* TV low-band standard; **~ d'homologation** *f* QUALITE approval standard; **~ industrielle** *f* INFORMAT, ORDINAT industrial standard; **~ de l'installation** *f* NUCLEAIRE in-house standard; **~ internationale** *f* CONSTR international standard; **~ ISO** *f* QUALITE ISO standard; **~ obligatoire** *f* CONSTR mandatory standard; **~ de rejet d'effluent** *f* RECYCLAGE effluent standard; **~ relative aux émissions atmosphériques** *f* POLLUTION ambient emission standard; **~ relative à la qualité de l'air ambiant** *f* POLLUTION ambient quality standard; **~ de sécurité** *f* SECURITE safety requirement; **~ de télévision** *f* TV television standard; **~ de l'usine** *f* NUCLEAIRE in-house standard

Norme: **~ de télécommunication européenne** *f* TELECOM ETS, European Telecommunication Standard

normes: **~ et codes locaux appropriés** *f pl* PRODUCTION local standards and code of practice; **~ d'environnement** *f pl* POLLU MER, POLLUTION environmental quality standards

normorphine *f* CHIMIE normorphine

nornarcéine *f* CHIMIE nornarceine

nornicotine *f* CHIMIE nornicotine

noropianique *adj* CHIMIE *acide* noropianic

norvaline *f* CHIMIE norvaline

noscapine *f* CHIMIE opianine

noséane *f* MINERAUX nosean, noselite

noséite *f* MINERAUX nosean, noselite

noséite *f* MINERAUX nosean, noselite

notarisation *f* TELECOM notarisation

notation *f* INFORMAT, TELECOM notation; **~ à base fixe** *f* INFORMAT fixed base notation, fixed radix notation; **~ à base multiple** *f* INFORMAT mixed-base notation, mixed-radix notation; **~ binaire** *f* INFORMAT, ORDINAT binary notation; **~ décimale** *f* MATH, TELECOM decimal notation; **~ en puissance dix** *f* MATH scientific notation; **~ en virgule fixe** *f* INFORMAT fixed point notation; **~ en virgule flottante** *f* INFORMAT floating point notation; **~ infixée** *f* INFORMAT, ORDINAT infix notation; **~ octale** *f* INFORMAT octal notation; **~ polonaise** *f* INFORMAT Polish notation; **~ polonaise inversée** *f* INFORMAT reverse Polish notation, suffix notation, ORDINAT suffix notation; **~ préfixée** *f* INFORMAT Polish notation, prefix notation; **~ sans parenthèses** *f* INFORMAT parenthesis-free notation; **~ suffixée** *f* INFORMAT postfix notation, suffix notation, reverse Polish notation, ORDINAT suffix notation; **~ de syntaxe abstraite numéro un** *f* TELECOM ASN1, abstract syntax notation one

note *f* ACOUSTIQUE note; **~ de chargement** *f* NAUT shipping note; **~ différentielle** *f* ENREGISTR difference note; **~ enharmonique** *f* ACOUSTIQUE enharmonic note; **~ marginale** *f* IMPRIM side note; **~ modale** *f* ACOUSTIQUE modal note; **~ moyenne d'opinion** *f* TELECOM MOS, mean opinion score; **~ de respect des délais** *f* PRODUCTION timeliness rating; **~ sensible** *f* ACOUSTIQUE leading note; **~ tonale** *f* ACOUSTIQUE tonal note

notebook *m* INFORMAT, ORDINAT notebook

notice: **~ technique** *f* CH DE FER technical instructions

notification *f* BREVETS communication, POLLU MER notification; **~ EDI** *f* TELECOM EDI notification, EDIN; **~ d'encombrement explicite** *f* TELECOM ECN, explicit congestion notification; **~ d'encombrement explicite émise vers l'arrière** *f* TELECOM BECN, backward explicit congestion notification; **~ d'encombrement explicite émise vers l'avant** *f* TELECOM FECN, forward explicit congestion notification; **~ négative** *f* TELECOM NN, negative notification; **~ de non-remise** *f* TELECOM NDN, nondelivery notification; **~ positive** *f* TELECOM PN, positive notification; **~ retransmise** *f* TELECOM forwarded notification

nouage *m* TEXTILE knotting

noue *f* CONSTR valley

nouer *vt* TEXTILE knot

noueux *adj* TEXTILE knotty

nouméite *f* MINERAUX noumeaite, noumeite

nourrice *f* AERONAUT feeder tank, TRANSPORT jerry can; **~ de gueuse** *f* PRODUCTION sow; **~ de secours** *f* AERONAUT emergency supply tank

nourrissant *adj* AGRO ALIM nutritious, nutritive

nourriture: **~ de base** *f* AGRO ALIM staple

nouveau *adj* CHIMIE argent new, MATERIAUX fresh

nouveauté *f* BREVETS novelty

nouvelle: **~ lune** *f* ASTRONOMIE new moon; **~ méthode autrichienne de percement des tunnels** *f* CONSTR NATM, New Austrian Tunnelling Method; **~ prise** *f* CINEMAT retake

nouvelles: **~ maritimes** *f pl* NAUT shipping intelligence

nova *f* ASTRONOMIE nova; **~ naine** *f* ASTRONOMIE dwarf nova

novocaïne *f* CHIMIE novocaine

novolaque *f* PLAST CAOU novolac

noyage *m* HYDROLOGIE flooding; **~ du coeur** *m* NUCLEAIRE *ligne* core flooding train

noyau *m* ASTRONOMIE *d'une galaxie* nucleus, CINEMAT bobbin, core, CONS MECA *d'une vis d'Archimède* newel, CONSTR core, *barrage* core, *d'une vis* core, *d'un escalier tournant* newel, ELECTR *machine électrique, transformateur* core, ELECTROTEC core, magnetic core, ESPACE *astronomie*, HYDROLOGIE core, INFORMAT kernel, nucleus, MATERIAUX nucleus, NUCLEAIRE *de l'écoulement* core, ORDINAT kernel, nucleus, PHYS PART nucleus, PHYSIQUE core, nucleus, PRODUCTION core pin, newel, nucleus, *d'un cylindre broyeur* core, TV *d'une bobine* hub; **~ à air** *m* ELECTROTEC air core; **~ aplati** *m* NUCLEAIRE oblate nucleus; **~ atomique** *m* NUCLEAIRE, PHYS PART atomic nucleus; **~ benzénique** *m* CHIMIE benzene ring; **~ de bobine** *m* ELECTR coil core; **~ brut en métal dur** *m* CONS MECA as sintered hard metal pellet; **~ chambré** *m* PRODUCTION chambered core; **~ chélaté** *m* HYDROLOGIE chelate; **~ de comète** *m* ASTRONOMIE, ESPACE comet core; **~ compact** *m* ASTRONOMIE dense core; **~ composé** *m* NUCLEAIRE, PHYS RAYON, PHYSIQUE compound nucleus; **~ de condensation** *m* METEO, POLLUTION condensation nucleus; **~ condensé** *m* CHIMIE condensed ring; **~ de courant** *m* OCEANO current core; **~ du descendant radioactif** *m* PHYS RAYON daughter nuclide; **~ droit** *m* ELECTROTEC I-core; **~ d'électro-aimant** *m* ELECTROTEC magnet core; **~ en acier au silicium** *m* ELECTROTEC silicon steel core; **~ en ferrite** *m* ELECTR *transformateur, ordinateur*, ELECTROTEC, INFORMAT ferrite core; **~ en fil** *m* ELECTR *transformateur* wire-wound core; **~ en fils** *m* ELECTROTEC wire core; **~ en fusion** *m* ESPACE *astronomie* molten core; **~ en plas-**

tique de 50 mm *m* CINEMAT T-core; **~ en terre** *m* PRODUCTION loam core; **~ à entrefer** *m* ELECTROTEC gapped core; **~ escamotable** *m* CONS MECA *moule d'injection* collapsible core; **~ d'étoile** *m* ASTRONOMIE stellar core; **~ de fer** *m* ELECTROTEC iron core; **~ de fer divisé** *m* ELECTROTEC powdered iron core; **~ de fer doux** *m* ELECTROTEC soft-iron core; **~ feuilleté** *m* ELECTR *générateur, moteur, transformateur*, ELECTROTEC laminated core; **~ à fibres** *m* TV fiber core (AmE), fibre core (BrE); **~ hexagonal** *m* CHIMIE six-membered ring; **~ image** *m* PHYSIQUE mirror nucleus; **~ impair-impair** *m* PHYSIQUE odd-odd nucleus; **~ impair-pair** *m* PHYS RAYON, PHYSIQUE odd-even nucleus; **~ d'induit** *m* ELECTR *moteur, générateur*, ELECTROTEC armature core; **~ instable** *m* PHYS PART unstable nucleus; **~ intégral** *m* NUCLEAIRE kernel; **~ de l'intégrale de diffusion** *m* NUCLEAIRE *neutron* diffusion kernel; **~ interne** *m* GEOLOGIE *de la Terre* inner core; **~ lunaire** *m* ASTRONOMIE lunar core; **~ maçonné** *m* CONSTR bricked up core; **~ magnétique** *m* ELECTROTEC, INFORMAT magnetic core; **~ magnétique droit** *m* ELECTROTEC I-core; **~ magnétique feuilleté** *m* ELECTROTEC laminated core; **~ magnétique réglable** *m* ELECTROTEC adjustable core; **~ métallique** *m* ASTRONOMIE *d'une planète* metallic core; **~ miroir** *m* PHYSIQUE mirror nucleus; **~ mobile** *m* ELECTR *transformateur* movable core; **~ ouvert** *m* ELECTR *transformateur* open core; **~ pair-impair** *m* PHYSIQUE even-odd nucleus; **~ pair-pair** *m* PHYSIQUE even-even nucleus; **~ plongeur** *m* ELECTROTEC plunger; **~ rapporté** *m* CONS MECA, PRODUCTION removable insert; **~ rapporté mobile** *m* CONS MECA *moule d'injection* spring-loaded core; **~ récepteur rétractable** *m* CINEMAT collapsible take-up core; **~ de recul** *m* PHYSIQUE recoil nucleus; **~ réglable** *m* ELECTROTEC adjustable core, slug; **~ de relais** *m* ELECTROTEC relay core; **~ de salinité** *m* OCEANO sea salt nucleus; **~ saturé** *m* ELECTROTEC saturated core; **~ de sécurité** *m* INFORMAT, ORDINAT security kernel; **~ à six éléments** *m* CHIMIE six-membered ring **~ superlourd** *m* PHYSIQUE superheavy nucleus; **~ synchroniseur** *m* AUTO trigger wheel; **~ du système d'exploitation** *m* ORDINAT operating system kernel; **~ terrestre** *m* EN RENOUV Earth's core, GEOPHYS barysphere, centrosphere, core, earth core; **~ de tête magnétique** *m* TV magnetic head core; **~ torique** *m* ELECTROTEC toroidal core; **~ toroïdal** *m* ELECTROTEC toroidal core, NUCLEAIRE ring core, toroidal core; **~ de transformateur** *m* ELECTR, ELECTROTEC transformer core; **~ troussé** *m* PRODUCTION struck-up core, swept-up core; **~ d'uranium** *m* NUCLEAIRE uranium nucleus; **~ de vis à crémaillère** *m* CONS MECA unscrewing core

noyautage *m* PRODUCTION coring, coring out

noyauter *vt* PRODUCTION core, core out

noyauterie *f* PRODUCTION core making, making of cores

noyé *adj* HYDROLOGIE flooded

noyer *vt* AUTO flood, DISTRI EAU submerge, MECANIQUE flood, MINES *grisou* baffle, NAUT *soute* flood

Np *(neptunium)* CHIMIE Np *(neptunium)*

NQA *abrév (niveau de qualité acceptable)* QUALITE AQL *(acceptable quality level)*

Ns *abrév (nimbo-stratus)* METEO Ns *(nimbostratus)*

NTI *abrév (noeud de transit international)* TELECOM IGN *(international gateway node)*

nu *adj* ELECTROTEC bare

nuage: **~ de charge** *m* PHYS RAYON charge cloud; **~ chaud** *m* METEO warm cloud; **~ électronique** *m* PHYS

RAYON, TV electron cloud; ~ **en queue-de-chat** *m* METEO spindrift cloud; ~ **galactique** *m* ESPACE galactic cloud; ~ **de gaz** *m* GAZ gas cloud; ~ **d'hydrogène moléculaire** *m* ASTRONOMIE molecular hydrogen cloud; ~ **interstellaire** *m* ASTRONOMIE interstellar cloud; ~ **lumineux** *m* METEO luminous cloud; ~ **moléculaire** *m* ASTRONOMIE molecular cloud; ~ **noctilumineux** *m* METEO luminous cloud; ~ **nocturne lumineux** *m* METEO luminous cloud, noctilucent cloud; ~ **d'Oort** *m* ASTRONOMIE Oort cloud; ~ **phosphorescent** *m* METEO noctilucent cloud; ~ **de plasma** *m* GEOPHYS plasma cloud; ~ **sombre d'hydrogène moléculaire** *m* ASTRONOMIE dark cloud of molecular hydrogen; ~ **surfondu** *m* METEO supercooled cloud; ~ **zodiacal** *m* ASTRONOMIE zodiacal cloud

nuageage *m* PLAST CAOU *peinture* blushing

nuages: ~ **de Magellan** *m pl* ASTRONOMIE Magellanic Clouds

nuançage *m* PLAST CAOU tinting, *peinture* shading

nuance *f* COULEURS color hue (AmE), colour hue (BrE), PLAST CAOU *peinture* color tone (AmE), colour tone (BrE)

nuancier: ~ **de couleurs** *m* IMPRIM *photogravure* color chart (AmE), colour chart (BrE)

nucléaire *adj* ELECTR *puissance*, MILITAIRE, NUCLEAIRE, PHYSIQUE nuclear

nucléation *f* MATERIAUX *cristallographie*, METALL, METEO nucleation; ~ **de fissure** *f* METALL crack nucleation; ~ **orientée** *f* METALL oriented nucleation

nucléide *m* PHYSIQUE nuclide; ~ **père** *m* PHYS RAYON parent nuclide

nucléides: ~ **images** *m pl* PHYSIQUE mirror nuclides; ~ **miroirs** *m pl* PHYSIQUE mirror nuclides

nucléine *f* CHIMIE nuclein

nucléique *adj* CHIMIE *acide* nucleic

nucléohistone *f* CHIMIE nucleohistone

nucléoline *f* CHIMIE nucleolin

nucléon *m* NUCLEAIRE, PHYSIQUE nucleon; ~ **périphérique** *m* NUCLEAIRE peripheral nucleon

nucléonique *f* PHYSIQUE nucleonics

nucléophile *adj* CHIMIE nucleophilic

nucléophilie *f* CHIMIE nucleophilicity

nucléus *m* PRODUCTION nucleus

nuée: ~ **ardente** *f* GEOLOGIE *éruption volcanique explosive* glowing cloud

nugget *m* MINES nugget

nuisance: ~ **d'un bruit** *f* ACOUSTIQUE noise nuisance

nuisances: ~ **acoustiques** *f pl* POLLUTION noise pollution; ~ **sonores** *f pl* SECURITE noise pollution

nuisible *adj* SECURITE harmful, injurious; ~ **aux yeux** *adj* SECURITE injurious to the eyes

nuit: ~ **américaine** *f* CINEMAT day for night, night for day

nul[1] *adj* CHIMIE *point mort* null

nul[2] *m* INFORMAT NUL, null character, MATH zero, ORDINAT NUL, null character

nullateur *m* PHYSIQUE nullator

nullité *f* BREVETS revocation

nullivalent *adj* CHIMIE zerovalent

numérateur *m* MATH numerator

numération *f* INFORMAT number representation, numeration; ~ **bactérienne** *f* DISTRI EAU bacterial count; ~ **à base** *f* INFORMAT, ORDINAT radix notation; ~ **à base fixe** *f* ORDINAT fixed base notation; ~ **à base mixte** *f* ORDINAT mixed-base notation, mixed-radix notation; ~ **décimale** *f* INFORMAT, ORDINAT decimal

notation; ~ **hexadécimale** *f* INFORMAT hexidecimal notation

numérique *adj* CINEMAT, ELECTRON, INFORMAT digital, MATH numerical, ORDINAT, PHYSIQUE, TELECOM digital

numérique-analogique *adj* CINEMAT, TV D-to-A, digital-to-analog (AmE), digital-to-analogue (BrE)

numérisation *f* ELECTRON analog-to-digital conversion (AmE), analogue-to-digital conversion (BrE), digitizing, INFORMAT digitalization, digitization, NUCLEAIRE digitization, ORDINAT digitalization, digitization, scan, scanning, PHYSIQUE digitalization, digitization, TELECOM digitalization, digitization; ~ **des images** *f* ELECTRON image digitization; ~ **parallèle** *f* ELECTRON flash analog-to-digital conversion (AmE), flash analogue-to-digital conversion (BrE); ~ **série** *f* CONSTR, ELECTRON serial analog-to-digital conversion (AmE), serial analogue-to-digital conversion (BrE); ~ **de signaux** *f* ELECTRON signal digitization; ~ **des signaux vocaux** *f* TELECOM voice digitization; ~ **sur huit bits** *f* ELECTRON eight-bit conversion; ~ **sur la puce** *f* ELECTRON on-chip analog-to-digital conversion (AmE), on-chip analogue-to-digital conversion (BrE)

numérisé *adj* ESPACE *communications* digitalized, TELECOM digitized

numériser *vt* CONS MECA *travail à trois dimensions*, ELECTRON, ENREGISTR, INFORMAT digitize, ORDINAT digitize, scan, PHYSIQUE, TV digitize

numériseur *m* ELECTRON analog-to-digital converter (AmE), analogue-to-digital converter (BrE), digitizer, INFORMAT, ORDINAT digitizer, scanner; ~ **à huit bits** *m* ELECTRON eight-bit converter; ~ **parallèle** *m* ELECTRON flash analog-to-digital converter (AmE), flash analogue-to-digital converter (BrE); ~ **série** *m* CONSTR, ELECTRON serial analog-to-digital converter (AmE), serial analogue-to-digital converter (BrE); ~ **de signaux** *m* ELECTRON signal digitizer; ~ **de signaux vidéo** *m* ELECTRON image digitizer

numéro *m* IMPRIM folio, page number, INFORMAT number; ~ **d'abonné** *m* TELECOM SN, subscriber number; ~ **d'abonné multiple** *m* TELECOM MSN, multiple-subscriber number; ~ **abrégé** *m* TELECOM abbreviated number; ~ **d'accès** *m* TELECOM access number; ~ **d'annuaire** *m* TELECOM directory number; ~ **d'appel** *m* TELECOM DN, directory number; ~ **d'appel sans frais** *m* (Can) (*cf numéro vert*) TELECOM freephone number (BrE), toll-free number (AmE); ~ **atomique** *m* CHIMIE, PHYS PART, PHYSIQUE atomic number; ~ **de bloc** *m* PETROLE block number; ~ **de bobine** *m* CINEMAT roll number; ~ **de bon** *m* PRODUCTION ticket number; ~ **de bord** *m* CINEMAT edge coding, negative number, *imprimé sur le négatif* code number, edge number; ~ **de bord imprimé** *m* CINEMAT rubber number; ~ **du cahier** *m* IMPRIM signature number; ~ **de classification d'aéronef** *m* AERONAUT aircraft classification; ~ **de code** *m* TEXTILE run number; ~ **demandé initial** *m* TELECOM original called number; ~ **désaffecté** *m* TELECOM old number; ~ **de l'émulsion** *m* PHOTO emulsion batch number; ~ **de fabrication** *m* PHOTO serial number; ~ **de jauge** *m* PRODUCTION gage number (AmE), gauge number (BrE); ~ **de ligne** *m* INFORMAT, ORDINAT line number; ~ **de lot** *m* CONSTR, EMBALLAGE batch number; ~ **de lot de fabrication** *m* PHOTO emulsion batch number; ~ **de Messier** *m* ASTRONOMIE Messier number; ~ **national** *m* TELECOM NN, national number; **~ national significatif** *m* TELECOM NSN, national significant number; **~ non attribué** *m* TELECOM spare number; **~ occupé** *m* TELECOM busy number; **~ d'opération** *m* PRODUCTION operation number; **~ d'ordre** *m* INFORMAT serial number; **~ de page** *m* IMPRIM folio, page number; **~ de phase** *m* PRODUCTION operation number; **~ de la piste** *m* AERONAUT runway number; **~ de renvoi** *m* TELECOM redirection number; **~ renvoyant l'appel** *m* TELECOM redirecting number; **~ de séquence** *m* TELECOM SN, sequence number; **~ de série** *m* BREVETS, CONS MECA, ORDINAT serial number; **~ spécial** *m* IMPRIM special edition; **~ de station de navire** *m* TELECOM ship station number; **~ universel** *m* TELECOM universal number; **~ vert** *m* (Fra) *(cf numéro d'appel sans frais)* TELECOM freephone number (BrE), TELECOM toll-free number (AmE)

numérotage *m* PHOTO numbering

numérotation *f* IMPRIM numbering, TELECOM dialing (AmE), dialling (BrE), keying, keying; **~ abrégée** *f* TELECOM abbreviated dialling (BrE), short code dialing (AmE), short code dialling (BrE); **~ abrégée à un chiffre** *f* TELECOM single digit dialing (AmE), single digit dialling (BrE); **~ en séquence** *f* IMPRIM *finition* sequential numbering; **~ incomplète** *f* TELECOM partial

dial; **~ par commande vocale** *f* TELECOM voice dialling; **~ par pression** *f* IMPRIM crash numbering; **~ sans décrocher** *f* TELECOM on-hook dialing (AmE), on-hook dialling (BrE), preseizure dialing (AmE), preseizure dialling (BrE)

numéroter[1] *vt* IMPRIM folio, PRODUCTION, TELECOM number; **~ consécutivement** *vt* BREVETS number consecutively; **~ de façon continue** *vt* BREVETS number consecutively

numéroter[2] *vi* TELECOM dial

numéroteur *m* EMBALLAGE numbering apparatus

nursery: ~ d'étoiles *f* ASTRONOMIE stellar nursery

nutation *f* ASTRONOMIE, ESPACE *astronomie*, PHYSIQUE nutation

nutriment *m* POLLU MER nutrient

nutritif[1] *adj* AGRO ALIM nutritious, nutritive

nutritif[2] *m* AGRO ALIM nutrient

nutrition *f* AGRO ALIM nutrition

nux: ~ vomica *f* CHIMIE nux vomica

nydrazide *m* CHIMIE nydrazid

nylon *m* CHIMIE, IMPRIM, PLAST CAOU *plastiques* nylon

nystatine *f* CHIMIE nystatin

O

O *(oxygène)* CHIMIE O *(oxygen)*

oasis *f* HYDROLOGIE oasis; ~ **sous-marine** *f* OCEANO deep-sea oasis, hydrothermal ecosystem

obduction *f* GEOLOGIE obduction

obélisque *f* GEOMETRIE obelisk

objectif *m* ASTRONOMIE *d'un instrument d'optique* objective, CINEMAT lens, ESPACE target, IMPRIM *optique* camera, INSTRUMENT objective, PHOTO lens, PHYSIQUE lens, objective, PRODUCTION *d'une caméra* lens; ~ **achromatique** *m* ASTRONOMIE *d'une lunette d'approche*, IMPRIM, PHOTO achromatic lens, PHYSIQUE achromat, achromatic lens; ~ **anachromatique** *m* PHOTO anachromatic lens; ~ **anamorphoseur** *m* CINEMAT anamorphic lens, anamorphoser; ~ **anastigmat** *m* PHOTO anastigmat lens, anastigmatic lens, stigmatic lens; ~ **anastigmatique** *m* CINEMAT anastigmatic lens, PHOTO anastigmatic lens, stigmatic lens; ~ **à angle moyen** *m* PHOTO medium-angle lens; ~ **aplanat** *m* PHOTO aplanatic lens; ~ **apochromatique** *m* CINEMAT apochromat, PHOTO apochromatic lens; ~ **asphérique** *m* CINEMAT aspherical lens; ~ **avec mise au point très rapprochée** *m* CINEMAT macro lens; ~ **bleui** *m* PHOTO bloomed lens; ~ **bleuté** *m* PHYSIQUE bloomed lens, coated lens, REVETEMENT coated lens; ~ **corrigé chromatiquement** *m* PHOTO color-corrected lens (AmE), colour-corrected lens (BrE); ~ **de courte focale** *m* PHOTO short-focus lens; ~ **à court foyer** *m* PHOTO short-focus lens; ~ **à décentrement** *m* CINEMAT offset lens; ~ **dédoublable** *m* PHOTO doubled lens, doublet, doublet lens; ~ **à distance focale variable** *m* CINEMAT varifocal lens, zoom lens; ~ **fish-eye** *m* CINEMAT, PHOTO fish-eye lens; ~ **à flou artistique** *m* PHOTO soft-focus lens; ~ **fluoruré** *m* PHOTO bloomed lens; ~ **à focale** *m* INSTRUMENT zoom lens; ~ **à focale fixe** *m* CINEMAT prime lens; ~ **de focale normale** *m* PHOTO standard lens; ~ **à focale variable** *m* PHOTO zoom lens; ~ **à foyer fixe** *m* PHOTO fixed focus lens; ~ **à grand angle** *m* PHOTO wide-angle lens; ~ **grand angulaire** *m* CINEMAT wide-angle lens; ~ **à grande ouverture** *m* CINEMAT wide-aperture lens, PHOTO high-speed lens, large-aperture lens; ~ **à immersion** *m* *(cf objectif sec)* EQUIP LAB *microscope* immersion lens, METALL, PHYSIQUE immersion objective; ~ **à immersion à huile** *m* EQUIP LAB oil immersion lens; ~ **à immersion à l'huile** *m* EQUIP LAB *microscope* oil immersion lens; ~ **interchangeable** *m* INSTRUMENT, PHOTO interchangeable lens; ~ **à lentilles multiples** *m* PHOTO composite lens; ~ **à lentilles non collées** *m* CINEMAT uncemented lens; ~ **de longue focale** *m* CINEMAT telephoto lens, PHOTO long-focus lens, telephoto lens; ~ **à longue focale** *m* CINEMAT long-focus lens, telephoto lens; ~ **macro** *m* CINEMAT macro lens; ~ **ménisque** *m* PHOTO meniscus lens; ~ **à miroir** *m* PHOTO mirror lens; ~ **à mise au point fixe** *m* CINEMAT fixed focus lens; ~ **multi-images** *m* CINEMAT multi-image lens; ~ **non corrigé** *m* CINEMAT uncorrected lens; ~ **normal** *m* PHOTO medium-angle lens; ~ **panoramique** *m* PHOTO panoramic lens, wide-angle lens; ~ **périscopique** *m* PHOTO periscopic lens; ~ **petit angulaire** *m* PHOTO narrow angle lens; ~ **petit champ** *m* PHOTO narrow angle lens; ~ **de Petzval** *m* CINEMAT Petzval lens; ~ **à présélecteur** *m* PHOTO lens with aperture preselector; ~ **primaire** *m* CINEMAT prime lens; ~ **de prise de vues** *m* PHOTO taking lens; ~ **de projection** *m* PHOTO projection lens; ~ **rentrant** *m* PHOTO flush mounted lens; ~ **à revêtement antiréfléchissant** *m* PHYSIQUE bloomed lens, coated lens; ~ **sec** *m (cf objectif à immersion)* EQUIP LAB *microscope* dry lens; ~ **simple** *m* PHOTO single lens; ~ **au sol** *m* MILITAIRE ground target; ~ **sphérique** *m* CINEMAT spherical lens; ~ **stigmatique** *m* PHOTO anastigmatic lens, stigmatic lens; ~ **terrestre** *m* MILITAIRE ground target; ~ **traité** *m* CINEMAT bloomed lens, coated lens, REVETEMENT coated lens; ~ **à trois lentilles** *m* PHOTO triplet lens; ~ **ultra grand angle** *m* CINEMAT fish-eye lens; ~ **de visée** *m* PHOTO viewing lens; ~ **zoom** *m* CINEMAT, INSTRUMENT zoom lens, PHOTO zoom, zoom lens

objectifs: ~ **interchangeables** *m pl* INSTRUMENT interchangeable objectives

objet *m* BREVETS subject matter, INFORMAT, ORDINAT, PHYSIQUE, PRODUCTION object; ~ **en terre réfractaire** *m* CERAM VER fireproof pottery; ~ **géré** *m* TELECOM MO, managed object; ~ **pressé** *m* CERAM VER pressing; ~ **quasi-stellaire** *m* ASTRONOMIE, ESPACE QSO, quasi-stellar object; ~ **de service d'application** *m* TELECOM ASO, application service object; ~ **spatial** *m* ESPACE object in space, orbiting object; ~ **virtuel** *m* PHYSIQUE virtual object; ~ **volant non identifié** *m (OVNI)* ASTRONOMIE, ESPACE unidentified flying object *(UFO)*

objets: ~ **en fer-blanc** *m pl* PRODUCTION tinware

oblimak *m* NUCLEAIRE oblate spheromak, oblimak

oblique[1] *adj* CONSTR slanting, GEOMETRIE oblique

oblique[2] *f* GEOMETRIE oblique stroke, PETR skew

obliquité *f* ASTRONOMIE obliquity, CONSTR, ORDINAT skew; ~ **de l'éclipse** *f* ASTRONOMIE obliquity of the eclipse

oblong *adj* GEOMETRIE oblong, MECANIQUE elongated

obscurité *f* ASTRONOMIE darkness; ~ **atmosphérique** *f* POLLUTION atmospheric obscurity

observateur *m* AERONAUT observer

observation *f* CONSTR observation, IMPRIM *épreuve, écran* viewing, NAUT observation; ~ **aérienne** *f* POLLU MER aerial reconnaissance; ~ **de radarsonde** *f* AERONAUT radarsonde observation

observatoire *m* ASTRONOMIE observatory; ~ **astronomique en orbite** *m* ASTRONOMIE orbiting astronomical observatory; ~ **astronomique orbital** *m* ESPACE orbiting astronomical observatory; ~ **astronomique sur orbite** *m* ASTRONOMIE orbiting astronomical observatory; ~ **des marées** *m* OCEANO tide station; ~ **météorologique** *m* ESPACE *communications*, METEO, NAUT weather station; ~ **solaire en orbite** *m* ASTRONOMIE orbiting solar observatory; ~ **solaire sur orbite** *m* ASTRONOMIE orbiting solar observatory; ~ **spatial** *m* ESPACE space observatory

obsidienne *f* CERAM VER obsidian
obsolescence *f* PRODUCTION obsolescence
obsolète *adj* PRODUCTION obsolete
obstacle *m* METALL obstacle, SECURITE barricade, hindrance; **~ dans un fluide stratifié** *m* PHYS FLUID obstacle in stratified fluid; **~ dans un fluide tournant** *m* PHYS FLUID obstacle in rotating fluid
obstruction *f* CONSTR obstruction, *tuyau* obstruction, MINES *de la cheminée* chute hang-up, clogging, PAPIER clogging, PRODUCTION choking, stoppage
obstruer[1] *vt* CONS MECA, PAPIER clog, PRODUCTION choke
obstruer:[2] **s'~** *v réfl* PRODUCTION choke
obtention *f* PRODUCTION procurement; **~ de cendres humides** *f* NUCLEAIRE wet ashing
obturateur *m* CINEMAT shutter, CONS MECA obturator, CONSTR cap, ESPACE *véhicules*, INSTRUMENT shutter, MAT CHAUFF obturator, MECANIQUE blind, PETROLE blowout preventer, PHOTO *d'un appareil photographique* shutter, REFRIG throttling device; **~ d'air** *m* EN RENOUV *séparation* air valve; **~ annulaire** *m* GAZ ring seal; **~ à armement préalable** *m* PHOTO preset shutter; **~ arrière** *m* CINEMAT rear shutter; **~ avec double synchronisation pour flash** *m* PHOTO XM synchronized shutter; **~ central à lamelles** *m* PHOTO leaf shutter; **~ Compur** *m* PHOTO Compur shutter; **~ au diaphragme** *m* PHOTO between-the-lens shutter; **~ à disque** *m* CINEMAT disc shutter (BrE), disk shutter (AmE); **~ d'entrée d'air dérivé** *m* AERONAUT blanking cover for fin air scoop; **~ d'évacuation d'air refroidisseur** *m* AERONAUT blanking cover for air-cooling unit outlet; **~ à fente** *m* TV slit shutter; **~ focal** *m* PHOTO focal plane shutter; **~ fonctionnant à la pose** *m* PHOTO shutter with B setting; **~ à guillotine** *m* PHOTO guillotine shutter; **~ à miroir** *m* CINEMAT reflex shutter; **~ d'objectif** *m* PHOTO lens shutter; **~ à ouverture variable** *m* CINEMAT variable aperture shutter; **~ à pales** *m* CINEMAT blade shutter; **~ à pale unique** *m* CINEMAT single blade shutter; **~ de plaque** *m* PHOTO focal plane shutter; **~ plug** *m* PRODUCTION blanking plug; **~ pour fondu** *m* CINEMAT dissolving shutter, fade shutter; **~ reflex** *m* CINEMAT mirror shutter; **~ réglable** *m* CINEMAT adjustable shutter; **~ à rideau** *m* PHOTO roller blind shutter; **~ rotatif** *m* CINEMAT revolving shutter, rotating shutter; **~ secondaire** *m* CINEMAT capping shutter; **~ à secteurs** *m* CINEMAT rotating shutter; **~ à soufflet** *m* PHOTO bellows shutter; **~ Synchro-Compur** *m* PHOTO Synchro-Compur shutter; **~ toujours armé** *m* PHOTO self-cocking shutter; **~ de tube** *m* CONS MECA pipe cap; **~ variable** *m* CINEMAT variable shutter
obturateur-raccord *m* PRODUCTION coupling blanking plug
obturation *f* CONSTR scaling, sealing up, PRODUCTION stoppage
obturer *vt* CONS MECA close up, CONSTR *un puits jaillissant* cap, DISTRI EAU clog, PRODUCTION blank off, seal, seal up, stop up, stop
obtus *adj* GEOMETRIE obtuse
obtusangle *adj* GEOMETRIE obtuse-angled, obtuse-angular
obtusité *f* GEOMETRIE obtuseness
obus *m* MILITAIRE shell; **~ chargé** *m* MILITAIRE live shell; **~ à charge nucléaire** *m* MILITAIRE nuclear shell; **~ guidé** *m* MILITAIRE smart shell; **~ perforant** *m* MILITAIRE antiarmor warhead (AmE), antiarmour warhead (BrE)

obusier *m* MILITAIRE howitzer
occlus *adj* CHIMIE *gaz* occluded
occlusion *f* CHIMIE, METEO occlusion, PRODUCTION stoppage
occultation *f* ASTRONOMIE eclipse, occultation, TELECOM shadowing; **~ lognormale** *f* TELECOM log normal shadowing
occulter *vt* CONSTR encase
occupation: **~ du spectre** *f* TELECOM spectral occupancy
océanaute *m* OCEANO aquanaut
océanique *adj* METEO oceanic
océanographe *m* METEO, OCEANO oceanographer
océanographie *f* METEO, NAUT, PETROLE oceanography
océanographique *adj* METEO oceanographical
océanologie *f* OCEANO oceanology
ocre: **~ de chrome** *f* MINERAUX chrome ocher (AmE), chrome ochre (BrE)
octacosane *m* CHIMIE octacosane
octadécane *m* CHIMIE octadecane
octadécylène *m* CHIMIE octadecyl
octaèdre[1] *adj* CHIMIE octahedral
octaèdre[2] *m* CRISTALL, GEOMETRIE octahedron
octaédrique *adj* CHIMIE, CRISTALL, GEOMETRIE octahedral
octaédrite *f* MINERAUX octahedrite
octal[1] *adj* INFORMAT octal
octal:[2] **~ codé binaire** *m* PRODUCTION *automatisme industriel* binary-coded octal
octamère *m* CHIMIE octamer
octanal *m* CHIMIE octanal
octane *m* CHIMIE octane
Octant *m* ASTRONOMIE Octans
octave *f* ACOUSTIQUE, ELECTRON, PHYSIQUE octave
octène *m* CHIMIE octene
octet *m* CHIMIE octet, ELECTRON eight-bit byte, INFORMAT byte, octet, ORDINAT octet
octode *f* ELECTRON octode
octodécylène *m* CHIMIE octadecyl
octogonal *adj* GEOMETRIE octagonal
octogone *m* GEOMETRIE octagon
octose *f* CHIMIE octose
octovalent *adj* CHIMIE octavalent, octovalent
octupôle *m* CONSTR octupole
octyle *m* CHIMIE octyl
octylène *m* CHIMIE octene
octyne *m* CHIMIE octyne
oculaire *m* ASTRONOMIE *d'un télescope*, EQUIP LAB *d'un microscope*, ESPACE eyepiece, INSTRUMENT eyepiece, eyepiece lens, PHOTO eyepiece lens, PHYSIQUE eyepiece; **~ Barlow** *m* ASTRONOMIE Barlow lens; **~ coudé** *m* INSTRUMENT star diagonal; **~ de Huygens** *m* PHYSIQUE Huygens' eyepiece; **~ du microscope de lecture** *m* INSTRUMENT microscope eyepiece; **~ orthoscopique** *m* ASTRONOMIE orthoscopic eyepiece; **~ de Ramsden** *m* PHYSIQUE Ramsden eyepiece; **~ réglable** *m* CINEMAT, PHOTO adjustable eyepiece; **~ à réticule** *m* ASTRONOMIE reticle eyepiece; **~ à réticule éclairé** *m* ASTRONOMIE illuminated reticle eyepiece; **~ de visée** *m* CINEMAT eyepiece, PHOTO viewfinder eyepiece; **~ de viseur** *m* CINEMAT viewfinder eyepiece
ocytoxique *adj* CHIMIE oxytoxic
OD *abrév* (*oxygène dissous*) POLLUTION DO (*dissolved oxygen*)
odeur *f* CHIMIE odor (AmE), odour (BrE), scent; **~ âcre** *f* POLLUTION acrid odor (AmE), acrid odour (BrE)
odomètre *m* CONSTR odometer

odontographe *m* CONS MECA odontograph
odontolite *f* MINERAUX odontolite
odorant *adj* GENIE CHIM, POLLUTION odorous
odorifique *adj* CHIMIE odoriferous
odorisant *m* PETROLE *détection des gaz* odorant
odorisation *f* GAZ odorization
oeil *m* CERAM VER, CONS MECA *d'un outil* eye, CONSTR *d'une penture* knuckle, METEO *d'un cyclone* eye, NAUT *d'un cordage, métallique* eye, *d'un cordage* loop, PRODUCTION drawhole, mouth, tap hole, *d'une aiguille* eye; ~ **de Berlin** *m* RESSORTS Berlin eye; ~ **de caractère** *m* IMPRIM, INFORMAT typeface; ~ **droit** *m* RESSORTS upturned eye; ~ **épaulé** *m* RESSORTS Berlin eye; ~ **d'une étoffe** *m* MATERIAUX sheen; ~ **fixe** *m* RESSORTS fixed loop; ~ **forgé** *m* RESSORTS forged eye; ~ **de la lettre** *m* IMPRIM z-height; ~ **de levage** *m* AERONAUT hoisting eye; ~ **magique** *m* ELECTRON magic eye; ~ **à queue filetée** *m* CONS MECA eye-bolt
oeil-de-chat *m* CONSTR, MINERAUX cat's eye (TM)
oeil-de-tigre *m* MINERAUX tiger's eye
oeillard *m* CONS MECA *d'un ventilateur, d'une pompe centrifuge* ear, *d'une meule en émeri* hole, *d'un ventilateur, d'une pompe centrifuge* intake, PRODUCTION *d'un ventilateur, d'une pompe centrifuge* intake
oeillet *m* EMBALLAGE, IMPRIM eyelet, PHOTO *de fixation de la courroie* ring, PRODUCTION eyelet; ~ **de métal** *m* PRODUCTION metal eyelet
oeilleton *m* CINEMAT eyepiece; ~ **d'oculaire** *m* CINEMAT, PHOTO eyecup; ~ **de visée** *m* PHOTO eyepiece
oellacherite *f* MINERAUX oellacherite
oenanthal *m* CHIMIE oenanthal
oenanthine *f* CHIMIE oenanthin
oenanthique *adj* CHIMIE oenanthic
oenanthol *m* CHIMIE oenanthol
oenanthylate *m* CHIMIE oenanthylate
oenanthylique *adj* CHIMIE oenanthylic
oersted *m* CONSTR oersted
oestradiol *m* CHIMIE oestradiol
oestriol *m* CHIMIE oestriol
oestrone *f* CHIMIE oestrone
oeuf: ~ **en poudre** *m* AGRO ALIM powdered egg
oeuvres: ~ **mortes** *f pl* NAUT dead works, topsides, upper works, PETROLE platform equipment; ~ **vives** *f pl* NAUT quickworks, underwater hull
office *m* AERONAUT galley; ~ **désigné** *m* BREVETS designated office; ~ **élu** *m* BREVETS elected office; ~ **récepteur** *m* BREVETS receiving office
Office: ~ **de recherches et d'essais** *m* CH DE FER Office for Research and Experiments
officier: ~ **chargé des marchandises** *m* NAUT cargo officer; ~ **en second** *m* NAUT first mate, first officer; ~ **général** *m* NAUT flag officer; ~ **marinier** *m* NAUT petty officer; ~ **mécanicien en second** *m* NAUT second engineer; ~ **navigateur** *m* NAUT navigation officer; ~ **de pont** *m* NAUT deck officer; ~ **radio** *m* NAUT radio officer
offre *m* TELECOM offer
offset *m* IMPRIM offset; ~ **en creux** *m* IMPRIM offset deep printing; ~ **sec** *m* IMPRIM dry offset
offshore *m* PETROLE offshore oil industry
ogive *f* ESPACE *véhicules* missile warhead; ~ **de guidage** *f* CONS MECA *outil* guide bush; ~ **de montant** *f* CONSTR poststaff
ohm *m* ELECTR, ELECTROTEC, METROLOGIE, PHYSIQUE ohm; ~ **étalon** *m* ELECTR standard ohm
ohmique *adj* ELECTR *résistance*, ELECTROTEC ohmic

ohmmètre *m* ELECTR, ELECTROTEC, MINES, PHYSIQUE, TELECOM ohmmeter; ~ **à magnéto** *m* ELECTR Megger (TM)
oïdium *m* AGRO ALIM powdery mildew
oignon *m* CERAM VER onion
Oiseau: ~ **Indien** *m* ASTRONOMIE Indus; ~ **de Paradis** *m* ASTRONOMIE Apus
okénite *f* MINERAUX okenite
oléandrine *f* CHIMIE oleandrin
oléate *m* CHIMIE oleate
oléfiant *adj* CHIMIE *gaz* oil-forming
oléfine *f* CHIMIE, LESSIVES, PETROLE *chimie, raffinage* olefin, olefine
oléfines *f pl* PETR olefins
oléfinique *adj* CHIMIE olefinic
oléine *f* CHIMIE olein
oléique *adj* CHIMIE *acide, ether* oleic
oléobromie *f* PHOTO bromoil print
oléoduc *m* NAUT pipeline, PETR, PETROLE, TRANSPORT oil pipeline
oléomètre *m* CHIMIE oleometer, CONS MECA oilometer, METROLOGIE acrometer, PRODUCTION oil gage (AmE), oil gauge (BrE)
oléophile *adj* CHIMIE, POLLU MER oleophilic
oléophosphorique *adj* CHIMIE oleophosphoric
oléoréseau *m* PETROLE hydrant system
oléorésine *f* CHIMIE oleoresin
oléorésineux *adj* CHIMIE oleoresinous
oléoserveur *m* AERONAUT servicer
oléosoluble *adj* PLAST CAOU *peinture* oil-soluble
oléovitamine *f* CHIMIE oleovitamin
oléum *m* CHIMIE, LESSIVES oleum
oligoclase *f* MINERAUX oligoclase
oligo-élément *m* CHIMIE microelement, trace element, GEOLOGIE trace element, HYDROLOGIE micronutrient, POLLUTION trace element
oligomère[1] *adj* CHIMIE oligomeric
oligomère[2] *m* CHIMIE, PLAST CAOU oligomer
oligomérisation *f* MATERIAUX *chimie*, PLAST CAOU *procédé* oligomerization
oligomycine *f* CHIMIE oligomycyn
oligonite *f* MINERAUX oligon spar, oligonite
olistolithe *m* GEOLOGIE olistolith
olive *f* CERAM VER bulb, oval punt, CONSTR oval knob
olivénite *f* MINERAUX olivenite
olivine *f* MINERAUX olivine
ombellique *adj* CHIMIE *acide* umbellic
ombilical[1] *adj* GEOLOGIE *paléontologie* umbilical
ombilical[2] *m* OCEANO diver's umbilical, umbilical
ombrage: ~ **continu** *m* CINEMAT drop shadow
ombre *f* CINEMAT, IMPRIM, PHOTO shadow; ~ **aérodynamique** *f* AERONAUT blanking effect; ~ **propre** *f* ESPACE *véhicules* eigenshadow; ~ **pure** *f* PHYSIQUE umbra
ombré *adj* IMPRIM shaded
OMI *abrév (Organisation maritime internationale)* NAUT IMO *(International Maritime Organization)*
omnibus *m* CH DE FER *véhicules* local train (AmE), slow train (BrE), stopping train (AmE)
omphacite *f* MINERAUX omphacite
once *f* METROLOGIE ounce avoirdupois, ounce, ounce troy; ~ **avoirdupoids** *f* METROLOGIE ounce, ounce avoirdupois; ~ **troy** *f* METROLOGIE ounce, ounce troy
oncolithe *m* GEOLOGIE oncolith
onde *f* ACOUSTIQUE wave, CERAM VER ream, ELECTR *électromagnétique*, ELECTROTEC, NAUT, PHYS ONDES,

PHYSIQUE, TELECOM wave; ~ **A4** *f* IMPRIM *fac-similé, téléphotographie* A4 wave; ~ **acoustique** *f* ELECTROTEC acoustic wave, PHYSIQUE, TELECOM soundwave; ~ **acoustique en volume** *f* ELECTROTEC BAW, bulk acoustic wave; ~ **acoustique de surface** *f* ELECTRON, TELECOM SAW, surface acoustic wave; ~ **aérienne** *f* PETR air pulse, airwave; ~ **aérienne stationnaire** *f* PHYS ONDES stationary aerial wave; ~ **capillaire** *f* OCEANO capillary wave; ~ **carrée** *f* ELECTRON, PHYSIQUE square wave; ~ **de choc** *f* GEOPHYS, MINES, PETR, PHYS ONDES, PHYSIQUE shockwave; ~ **de choc adiabatique** *f* ESPACE *véhicules* adiabatic shockwave; ~ **de choc amont** *f* AERONAUT bow wave; ~ **de choc de la comète** *f* ASTRONOMIE comet shockwave; ~ **de choc de compression** *f* GEOPHYS shockwave; ~ **de choc géomagnétique** *f* ESPACE magnetosphere bow shock; ~ **de combustion thermonucléaire** *f* NUCLEAIRE thermonuclear combustion wave; ~ **complexe** *f* TELECOM complex wave; ~ **composée** *f* OCEANO compound tide; ~ **composite** *f* TELECOM composite wave; ~ **de compression** *f* ACOUSTIQUE, ENREGISTR compressional wave, GEOLOGIE P-wave, compressional wave; ~ **cosinusoïdale** *f* GEOMETRIE cosine wave; ~ **courte** *f* ELECTR *rayonnement*, PHYS ONDES *radio* SW, short wave; ~ **de crue** *f* HYDROLOGIE flood wave; ~ **cylindrique** *f* ACOUSTIQUE cylindrical wave; ~ **décimétrique** *f* TELECOM decametric wave; ~ **de détente** *f* AERONAUT *bang sonique* expansion wave; ~ **de détonation** *f* MINES detonation wave; ~ **diffractée** *f* PHYSIQUE diffracted wave; ~ **de dilatation** *f* GEOLOGIE dilatational wave; ~ **directe** *f* ELECTROTEC forward wave, forward-traveling wave (AmE), forward-travelling wave (BrE), GEOLOGIE direct wave, TELECOM ground wave; ~ **diurne** *f* OCEANO diurnal wave; ~ **élastique** *f* ELECTROTEC elastic wave, GEOLOGIE seismic wave, PHYSIQUE elastic wave; ~ **électrique** *f* ELECTROTEC electric wave; ~ **électromagnétique** *f* ELECTR, ELECTROTEC, PHYS ONDES, PHYSIQUE, TELECOM electromagnetic wave; ~ **électromagnétique externe** *f* PHYS RAYON external electromagnetic wave; ~ **électromagnétique hybride** *f* ELECTR *moteur* hybrid electromagnetic wave; ~ **électromagnétique transversale** *f* ELECTR transverse electromagnetic wave; ~ **entretenue** *f* ELECTROTEC CW, continuous wave, ENREGISTR continuous wave, PHYS ONDES CW, continuous wave, TV continuous wave; ~ **entretenue modulée** *f* TV modulated continuous wave; ~ **équivolumique** *f* ACOUSTIQUE shear wave; ~ **évanescente** *f* PHYSIQUE evanescent wave; ~ **explosive** *f* MINES detonation wave, explosion wave, shockwave; ~ **fondamentale** *f* OCEANO ground swell, ground wave; ~ **gravitationnelle** *f* ASTRONOMIE, PHYSIQUE gravitational wave; ~ **de gravité** *f* OCEANO gravitational wave, gravity wave, PHYS ONDES, PHYSIQUE gravity wave; ~ **guidée** *f* OPTIQUE, TELECOM guided wave; ~ **guidée optique** *f* ELECTROTEC optical guided wave; ~ **hertzienne** *f* ELECTRON, ELECTROTEC radio wave, PHYS ONDES airwave, radio wave, PHYSIQUE radio wave; ~ **hyperfréquence** *f* ELECTR, ELECTRON, PHYS ONDES, PHYSIQUE, TELECOM microwave; ~ **incidente** *f* PHYS ONDES, PHYSIQUE incident wave; ~ **d'inertie** *f* OCEANO inertial wave; ~ **interne** *f* OCEANO internal wave; ~ **inverse** *f* ELECTROTEC backward wave, *progressive* reverse traveling wave (AmE), reverse travelling wave (BrE); ~ **ionosphérique** *f* PHYSIQUE sky wave; ~ **lente** *f* ELECTROTEC slow wave; ~ **longitudinale** *f* ACOUSTIQUE longitudinal wave, GEOLOGIE P-wave, compressional wave, PHYS ONDES, PHYSIQUE longitudinal wave; ~ **longitudinale stationnaire** *f* PHYS ONDES stationary longitudinal wave; ~ **lumineuse** *f* ELECTRON, PHYS ONDES light wave; ~ **lumineuse stationnaire** *f* PHYS ONDES stationary light wave; ~ **lunaire** *f* OCEANO lunar wave; ~ **lunisolaire** *f* OCEANO lunisolar wave; ~ **magnétique** *f* ELECTROTEC magnetic wave; ~ **magnétohydrodynamique** *f* *(onde MHD)* GEOPHYS magnetohydrodynamic wave *(MHD wave)*; ~ **de marée** *f* GEOPHYS tidal wave, tsunami, NAUT tidal wave, OCEANO harmonic component, tidal component; ~ **mécanique** *f* ELECTROTEC mechanical wave; ~ **métrique** *f* TELECOM metric wave; ~ **MHD** *f* *(onde magnétohydrodynamique)* GEOPHYS MHD wave *(magnetohydrodynamic wave)*; ~ **mobile** *f* ELECTR *ligne* line transient; ~ **modulante** *f* ELECTRON, TV modulating wave; ~ **de modulation** *f* ELECTRON modulating wave; ~ **modulée** *f* ELECTRON, ENREGISTR modulated wave; ~ **moyenne** *f* ELECTR, PHYS ONDES *radio* MW, medium wave; ~ **myriamétrique** *f* TELECOM very large-scale integration circuit; ~ **nocturne** *f* AERONAUT night wave; ~ **normale** *f* ELECTROTEC fast wave; ~ **de nuit** *f* AERONAUT night wave; ~ **optique** *f* ELECTROTEC optical wave; ~ **optique guidée** *f* ELECTROTEC optical guided wave; ~ **P** *f* GEOLOGIE P-wave, dilatational wave, PHYSIQUE P-wave; ~ **périodique** *f* ELECTROTEC periodic wave; ~ **plane** *f* ACOUSTIQUE, ELECTROTEC, ESPACE, OPTIQUE, PHYSIQUE, TELECOM plane wave; ~ **plane polarisée** *f* PHYS ONDES plane-polarized wave; ~ **à polarisation rectiligne** *f* ELECTROTEC linearly-polarized wave; ~ **polarisée circulairement** *f* ACOUSTIQUE, PHYSIQUE circularly-polarized wave; ~ **polarisée elliptiquement** *f* ACOUSTIQUE, PHYSIQUE elliptically-polarized wave; ~ **polarisée linéairement** *f* ACOUSTIQUE linearly-polarized wave; ~ **polarisée rectilignement** *f* PHYSIQUE linearly-polarized wave, plane-polarized wave; ~ **porteuse** *f* ELECTRON carrier, NAUT common carrier, PHYS ONDES, PHYSIQUE, TV carrier wave; ~ **porteuse d'image** *f* IMPRIM *télétransmission, vidéo* pixel carrier, TV image carrier; ~ **de pression** *f* TELECOM pressure wave; ~ **progressive** *f* ACOUSTIQUE, ELECTRON traveling wave (AmE), travelling wave (BrE), ELECTROTEC forward wave, forward-traveling wave (AmE), forward-travelling wave (BrE), PHYS ONDES, PHYSIQUE traveling wave (AmE), travelling wave (BrE), TELECOM outward propagating wave, traveling wave (AmE), travelling wave (BrE); ~ **progressive directe** *f* ELECTROTEC forward wave, forward-traveling wave (AmE), forward-travelling wave (BrE); ~ **progressive inverse** *f* ELECTROTEC backward wave; ~ **prolongée** *f* MINES collision wave; ~ **de propagation** *f* GEOPHYS shockwave; ~ **radio** *f* ELECTRON radio wave; ~ **radioélectrique** *f* ELECTR, ELECTRON, ELECTROTEC, GEOPHYS, PHYSIQUE, TELECOM radio wave; ~ **de Rayleigh** *f* PHYSIQUE Rayleigh wave; ~ **rectangulaire** *f* ELECTROTEC rectangular wave, ENREGISTR, PHYSIQUE square wave; ~ **réfléchie** *f* ELECTROTEC backward wave, reflected wave, OCEANO, PHYS ONDES, PHYSIQUE reflected wave; ~ **de réflexion** *f* GEOPHYS reflection wave; ~ **de réfraction** *f* GEOPHYS, PETR refraction wave; ~ **régressive** *f* ELECTROTEC backward wave, reverse traveling wave (AmE), reverse travelling wave (BrE), TELECOM inward propagating wave; ~ **rétrograde** *f* MINES retonation wave; ~ **rotationnelle** *f*

ACOUSTIQUE shear wave; ~ **S** f GEOLOGIE shear wave, PHYSIQUE S-wave, secondary wave; ~ **de séisme** f GEOPHYS seismic wave, surface wave; ~ **semi-diurne** f OCEANO semidiurnal wave; ~ **sinusoïdale** f ACOUSTIQUE, ELECTR, ELECTRON sine wave, PHYS ONDES sine wave, sinusoidal wave, GEOM sine wave; ~ **sismique** f GEOLOGIE seismic wave, GEOPHYS seismic wave, surface wave, surface wave, PHYS ONDES, PHYSIQUE seismic wave; ~ **au sol** f PHYS RAYON groundwave; ~ **de sol** f TELECOM ground wave; ~ **sonore** f ACOUSTIQUE, PHYS ONDES, PHYSIQUE, TELECOM soundwave; ~ **sonore périodique** f PHYS ONDES periodic sound wave; ~ **sphérique** f ACOUSTIQUE spherical wave, ELECTROTEC sphere wave, PHYS ONDES, PHYSIQUE spherical wave; ~ **de spins** f PHYSIQUE spin wave; ~ **stationnaire** f ACOUSTIQUE, ELECTROTEC, ENREGISTR standing wave, PHYS ONDES standing wave, stationary wave, PHYSIQUE, TELECOM standing wave, stationary wave; ~ **superficielle** f GEOPHYS surface wave; ~ **supérieure** f OCEANO surface wave; ~ **de surface** f OPTIQUE surface wave; ~ **TE** f ELECTROTEC H-wave; ~ **de tempête** f OCEANO storm surge, storm tide; ~ **de tension** f ELECTROTEC voltage surge; ~ **TM** f ELECTROTEC E-wave; ~ **topographique** f OCEANO topographic wave; ~ **tourbillonnaire** f ACOUSTIQUE rotational wave; ~ **transmise** f PHYSIQUE transmitted wave; ~ **transversale** f ACOUSTIQUE, ELECTROTEC transverse wave, GEOLOGIE shear wave, PHYS ONDES, PHYSIQUE, TELECOM transverse wave; ~ **transversale électrique** f ELECTROTEC, PHYSIQUE, TELECOM transverse electric wave; ~ **transversale électromagnétique** f ELECTROTEC transverse electromagnetic wave, PHYSIQUE transverse electric and magnetic wave; ~ **transversale magnétique** f ELECTROTEC, PHYSIQUE transverse magnetic wave; ~ **ultracourte** f ELECTR, ELECTRON, PHYS ONDES, PHYSIQUE, TELECOM microwave

ondelette f PHYS ONDES wavelet

onde-marée f OCEANO tidal component

ondemètre m PHYS ONDES, PHYSIQUE wavemeter; ~ **hétérodyne** m PHYS ONDES beat frequency wavemeter, heterodyne wavemeter

ondes: ~ **brogliennes** f pl PHYSIQUE de Broglie waves; ~ **de capillarité** f pl OCEANO capillary waves; ~ **centimétriques** f pl PHYSIQUE centimeter waves (AmE), centimetre waves (BrE); ~ **de choc nucléaires** f pl PHYS RAYON nuclear shock waves; ~ **circulaires** f pl PHYS ONDES circular waves; ~ **cohérentes** f pl PHYSIQUE coherent waves; ~ **dans les fluides** f pl PHYS FLUID fluid waves; ~ **de de Broglie** f pl ELECTROTEC, PHYS RAYON, PHYSIQUE de Broglie waves; ~ **de densité** f pl ASTRONOMIE density waves; ~ **de gravité en eau profonde** f pl PHYSIQUE deep-water waves; ~ **harmoniques** f pl PHYS ONDES harmonic waves; ~ **lumineuses** f pl PHYS ONDES visible light; ~ **millimétriques** f pl PHYSIQUE millimeter waves (AmE), millimetre waves (BrE); ~ **planes parallèles** f pl PHYS ONDES d'une source éloignée plane parallel waves; ~ **polarisées** f pl PHYS ONDES polarized waves; ~ **progressives** f pl PHYS ONDES progressive waves; ~ **radar** f pl PHYS RAYON radar waves; ~ **sismiques** f pl GEOLOGIE ondes de volume body waves; ~ **sonores adiabatiques** f pl PHYS ONDES adiabatic sound waves; ~ **transversales stationnaires** f pl PHYS ONDES stationary transverse waves; ~ **ultracourtes** f pl PHYS ONDES ultrashort waves; ~ **ultrasonores** f pl PHYS ONDES ultrasonic waves

ondin m OCEANO ice ridge

ondomètre m NAUT wavemeter

ondulation f ACOUSTIQUE ripple, CONSTR ringing, ripple, ELECTROTEC current ripple, IMPRIM, PAPIER corrugation; ~ **du courant** f ELECTROTEC current ripple; ~ **efficace maximale** f PRODUCTION électricité maximum ripple current; ~ **en bande passante** f CONSTR ringing; ~ **résiduelle** f CONSTR ripple; ~ **de rouleau** f CERAM VER roller bump; ~ **de la tension** f CONSTR ripple voltage

ondulatoire adj PHYS PART wave-like

ondulé adj CERAM VER wavy, CONS MECA, PAPIER corrugated, TELECOM surface undulating

onduleur m ELECTR transducteur, ELECTRON inverter, ELECTROTEC static inverter, TELECOM inverter; ~ **synchrone** m ELECTROTEC synchronous inverter; ~ **à thyratrons** m ELECTRON thyratron inverter

onglet m CONSTR miter (AmE), mitre (BrE), IMPRIM guard, façonnage, reliure, carton index tab, miter (AmE), mitre (BrE), INFORMAT, ORDINAT tab; ~ **débordant** m IMPRIM index tab; ~ **d'encadrement** m CONSTR chamfered joint, miter joint (AmE), mitre joint (BrE); ~ **de retour** m IMPRIM finition, façonnage foldover edge

onguent m CHIMIE ointment

onyx m MINERAUX onyx; ~ **d'Algérie** m MINERAUX Algerian onyx; ~ **calcaire** m MINERAUX Algerian onyx

OOR abrév (oscillateur à ondes rétrogrades) TELECOM BWO (backward wave oscillator)

OP abrév (ordinateur personnel) INFORMAT, ORDINAT PC (personal computer)

opacifiant[1] adj CHIMIE agent opacifying

opacifiant[2] m (Fra) (cf opalisant) CERAM VER opacifier

opacimètre m CHIMIE opacimeter, PAPIER opacimeter, opacity tester

opacité f CHIMIE, IMPRIM opacity, MATERIAUX opacity, opaqueness, PAPIER, PHYS ONDES, PHYSIQUE opacity; ~ **de contraste** f PAPIER contrast ratio; ~ **d'impression** f PAPIER printing opacity; ~ **du panache** f CERAM VER plume opacity; ~ **sur fond blanc** f PAPIER opacity white backing; ~ **sur fond papier** f PAPIER opacity paper backing

opale f IMPRIM héliogravure, MINERAUX opal; ~ **au pot** f CERAM VER pot opal

opalescence f HYDROLOGIE opalescence

opaline f CERAM VER opaline

opalisant m (Bel) (cf opacifiant) CERAM VER opacifier

opaque adj IMPRIM photogravure, informatique opaque

OPEP abrév (Organisation des pays exportateurs de pétrole) PETROLE OPEC (Organization of Petroleum Exporting Countries)

opérande m INFORMAT, ORDINAT operand

opérateur[1] m CINEMAT cameraman, IMPRIM, INFORMAT, ORDINAT, PETROLE operator, TELECOM operator, switchboard operator (AmE), telephone operator (AmE), telephonist (BrE); ~ **d'actualités** m CINEMAT newsreel cameraman; ~ **arithmétique** m ORDINAT arithmetic operator; ~ **banc-titre** m CINEMAT rostrum camera operator; ~ **booléen** m INFORMAT, ORDINAT Boolean operator; ~ **de clavier-écran** m PRODUCTION VDU operator; ~ **de collisions de Krook** m NUCLEAIRE Krook's collision operator; ~ **logique** m ELECTRON logic operator, INFORMAT, ORDINAT logic operator, logical operator; ~ **de projection** m CINEMAT projectionist; ~ **de prompteur** m TV cuer; ~ **de quart** m NUCLEAIRE poste on-shift operator; ~ **de radar** m

MILITAIRE, NAUT radar operator; ~ **réalisateur** *m* CINE-MAT camera director; ~ **relationnel** *m* INFORMAT, ORDINAT relational operator

opérateur:[2] ~ **provisoirement absent** *loc* TELECOM operator temporarily unavailable

opération *f* CONS MECA, INFORMAT, MATH, ORDINAT operation, PRODUCTION stage; ~ **arithmétique** *f* ORDINAT arithmetic operation; ~ **assistée** *f* INFORMAT, ORDINAT hands-on operation; ~ **binaire** *f* ORDINAT binary operation; ~ **centralisée** *f* ORDINAT centralized operation; ~ **de changement de prises** *f* ELECTR tap change operation; ~ **à constance du nombre de ligne** *f* TV constant line number operation, drift lock; ~ **déclassée** *f* PRODUCTION out-of-sequence operation; ~ **discontinue** *f* AGRO ALIM, GENIE CHIM batchwise operation; ~ **en mode duplex** *f* ORDINAT duplex operation; ~ **en mode semi-duplex** *f* ORDINAT half-duplex operation; ~ **en mode simplex** *f* ORDINAT simplex operation; ~ **en virgule flottante** *f* INFORMAT, ORDINAT floating point operation; ~ **ET** *f* ORDINAT AND operation; ~ **de fabrication** *f* PAPIER making; ~ **de gestion interne** *f* INFORMAT housekeeping operation; ~ **hors séquence** *f* PRODUCTION out-of-sequence operation; ~ **illégale** *f* INFORMAT, ORDINAT illegal operation; ~ **logique** *f* ELECTRON logic operation, INFORMAT logic operation, logical operation, ORDINAT logical operation; ~ **machine** *f* INFORMAT, ORDINAT machine operation; ~ **manuelle** *f* INFORMAT, ORDINAT manual operation; ~ **monadique** *f* INFORMAT, ORDINAT monadic operation; ~ **NI** *f* INFORMAT, ORDINAT NOR operation; ~ **NI exclusif** *f* INFORMAT, ORDINAT equivalence operation, exclusive NOR operation; ~ **NON** *f* INFORMAT, ORDINAT NOT operation; ~ **non assistée** *f* INFORMAT, ORDINAT hands-off operation; ~ **NON-ET** *f* INFORMAT, ORDINAT NAND operation; ~ **OU** *f* INFORMAT, ORDINAT OR operation; ~ **OU exclusif** *f* INFORMAT, ORDINAT exclusive OR operation, nonequivalence operation; ~ **OU inclusif** *f* INFORMAT, ORDINAT inclusive OR operation; ~ **à plier les anneaux** *f* RESSORTS looping; ~ **privilégiée** *f* INFORMAT, ORDINAT privileged operation; ~ **de refroidissement** *f* REFRIG cooling down; ~ **de rendre rugueux** *f* CONSTR deadening; ~ **de sauvetage** *f* SECURITE rescue operation; ~ **séquentielle** *f* INFORMAT, ORDINAT serial operation; ~ **de servitude** *f* ORDINAT housekeeping operation; ~ **de seuil** *f* INFORMAT, ORDINAT threshold operation; ~ **simple** *f* CONS MECA single operation; ~ **sur chaîne** *f* INFORMAT string operation; ~ **sur fichier** *f* PRODUCTION *automatisme industriel* file operation; ~ **de téléchargement** *f* PRODUCTION *automatisme industriel* download operation; ~ **de trempe et revenu** *f* RESSORTS quenching and tempering; ~ **unaire** *f* INFORMAT, ORDINAT unary operation

opérations: ~ **distantes** *f pl* TELECOM RO, remote operations; ~ **d'entretien mineures et majeures** *f pl* AERONAUT minor and major servicing operations; ~ **de forage** *f pl* PETROLE drilling operations

opératrice *f* TELECOM operator, telephonist

operculage *m* IMPRIM *emballage* heat seal

opercule *m* INST HYDR *de valve, de clapet* cap, *de vanne d'arrêt* cutoff plate; ~ **de détente** *m* INST HYDR expansion slide; ~ **en aluminium mince** *m* EMBALLAGE foil sealing; ~ **fraîcheur** *m* EMBALLAGE freshness seal; ~ **soudé par impulsion** *m* EMBALLAGE induction inner seal; ~ **de vanne** *m* INST HYDR shuttle plate

opérer[1] *vt* PRODUCTION operate

opérer:[2] ~ **une rotation de phase** *vi* ELECTRON shift phase; ~ **un sondage** *vi* MINES put down a borehole

Ophiuchus *m* ASTRONOMIE Ophiuchus

ophtalmomètre *m* INSTRUMENT ophthalmometer

opiacé *m* CHIMIE opiate

opianique *adj* CHIMIE opianic

opianyle *m* CHIMIE opianyl

opium *m* CHIMIE opiate

opposé *adj* GEOMETRIE opposite, vertical

opposition:[1] **en** ~ **de phase** *adj* ELECTRON, PHYSIQUE in phase opposition

opposition[2] *f* ASTRONOMIE *d'une planète*, BREVETS opposition; ~ **de phase** *f* ELECTRON phase opposition, PETR phase inversion, phase reversal

optimisation *f* INFORMAT, ORDINAT optimization; ~ **de la commande adaptative** *f* COMMANDE ACO, adaptive control optimization; ~ **de la masse** *f* ESPACE *véhicules* weight optimization; ~ **à réaction** *f* COMMANDE feedback process optimization

optimiser *vt* INFORMAT, ORDINAT optimize

optimiseur: ~ **de têtes vidéo** *m* TV video head optimizer

option *f* PETROLE *contrats, permis*, PRODUCTION option; ~ **de jalonnement** *f* PRODUCTION scheduling option

options: ~ **matérielles** *f pl* PRODUCTION optional hardware

optique *f* CINEMAT lens; ~ **de condensateur** *f* PHOTO condensing lens; ~ **d'éclairage** *f* INSTRUMENT illumination optics; ~ **électronique** *f* PHYSIQUE electron optics; ~ **de fibre** *f* CERAM VER, ELECTROTEC, INFORMAT, OPTIQUE, ORDINAT, PHYSIQUE fiber optics (AmE), fibre optics (BrE); ~ **géométrique** *f* OPTIQUE geometric optics, ray optics, PHYSIQUE, TELECOM geometric optics; ~ **inverseuse de faisceau** *f* TV beam reversing lens; ~ **ondulatoire** *f* OPTIQUE physical optics, wave optics, TELECOM wave optics; ~ **physique** *f* OPTIQUE physical optics, wave optics, PHYSIQUE, TELECOM physical optics; ~ **des rayons** *f* OPTIQUE geometric optics, ray optics, TELECOM ray optics

optique-électrique *adj* TELECOM O-E, optical-electrical

optocoupleur *m* TELECOM optocoupler

optoélectronique[1] *adj* OPTIQUE, TELECOM optoelectronic

optoélectronique[2] *f* ELECTRON optronics, ELECTROTEC, INFORMAT, ORDINAT, PHYSIQUE, TELECOM optoelectronics

or *m* (*Au*) CHIMIE gold *(Au)*; ~ **alluvionnien** *m* MINES placer gold; ~ **brillant** *m* CERAM VER bright gold; ~ **flottant** *m* MINES float gold; ~ **flottant** *m* MINES floating gold; ~ **de lavage** *m* MINES placer gold; ~ **liquide** *m* CERAM VER liquid gold; ~ **transparent** *m* CERAM VER starved gold

orage: ~ **électrique** *m* METEO electrical storm; ~ **élémentaire** *m* GEOPHYS ionospheric substorm; ~ **de grêle** *m* METEO hailstorm; ~ **magnétique** *m* ESPACE *géophysique*, GEOPHYS magnetic storm; ~ **solaire** *m* GEOPHYS solar storm, substorm

orangite *f* MINERAUX orangite

orbital *adj* ESPACE, PHYS RAYON orbital

orbitale *f* PHYS RAYON orbital; ~ **antiliante atomique** *f* PHYS RAYON antibonding atomic orbital; ~ **antiliante moléculaire** *f* PHYS RAYON antibonding molecular orbital; ~ **d'un atome** *f* PHYS PART atomic orbital; ~ **atomique** *f* CHIMIE, PHYSIQUE atomic orbital; ~ **hybride** *f* CHIMIE hybrid orbital; ~ **moléculaire** *f* PHYSIQUE molecular orbital

orbite:[1] **en** ~ **autour de la Terre** *adj* ESPACE Earth-orbiting; **en** ~ **polaire** *adj* ESPACE polar-orbiting

orbite² *f* ASTRONOMIE orbit, CHIMIE orbital, ESPACE, PHYSIQUE orbit; ~ **d'attente** *f* ESPACE interim orbit, parking orbit, MILITAIRE *d'un satellite* park orbit; ~ **d'attente à proximité de la Terre** *f* ESPACE Earth parking orbit; ~ **basse** *f* ESPACE low-altitude orbit; ~ **circulaire** *f* ESPACE circular orbit; ~ **de comète** *f* ASTRONOMIE cometary orbit; ~ **de dérive** *f* ESPACE drift orbit; ~ **de descente** *f* ESPACE descent orbit; ~ **directe** *f* ESPACE direct orbit; ~ **elliptique** *f* ASTRONOMIE, PHYSIQUE elliptical orbit; ~ **en halo** *f* ESPACE halo orbit; ~ **à ensoleillement constant** *f* ESPACE sun-synchronous orbit; ~ **équatoriale** *f* ESPACE equatorial orbit; ~ **excentrique** *f* ASTRONOMIE eccentric orbit; ~ **géostationnaire** *f* PHYSIQUE geostationary orbit; ~ **géosynchrone** *f* ESPACE Earth synchronous orbit, geosynchronous orbit; ~ **hyperbolique** *f* ESPACE hyperbolic orbit; ~ **Keplérienne** *f* ESPACE Keplerian orbit; ~ **lunaire** *f* ESPACE lunar orbit; ~ **moléculaire** *f* CHIMIE molecular orbital; ~ **non perturbée** *f* ESPACE Keplerian orbit, unperturbed orbit; ~ **polaire** *f* ESPACE polar orbit; ~ **quasi-parabolique** *f* ESPACE near parabolic orbit; ~ **de rebut** *f* ESPACE graveyard orbit; ~ **rétrograde** *f* ASTRONOMIE, ESPACE retrograde orbit; ~ **des satellites géostationnaires** *f* ESPACE geostationary satellite orbit; ~ **stationnaire** *f* ESPACE stationary orbit; ~ **terrestre** *f* ESPACE Earth orbit; ~ **de transfert** *f* ESPACE transfer orbit

orbiter *vi* ESPACE orbit

orbiteur *m* ESPACE orbiter; ~ **récupérable** *m* ESPACE *véhicules* recoverable orbiter; ~ **Viking** *m* ASTRONOMIE Viking orbiter

orbitographie *f* ESPACE orbit tracking

orcéine *f* CHIMIE orcein

ordinal *m* INFORMAT serial number, MATH ordinal number

ordinateur *m* ELECTR *appareil*, INFORMAT computer, ORDINAT computer, stored program computer; ~ **de bureau** *m* INFORMAT, ORDINAT desktop computer; ~ **cible** *m* INFORMAT target computer; ~ **de cinquième génération** *m* INFORMAT, ORDINAT fifth-generation computer; ~ **de communication inter-réseau** *m* INFORMAT gateway computer; ~ **compilateur** *m* ORDINAT source machine; ~ **de compilation** *m* INFORMAT source machine; ~ **domestique** *m* ORDINAT home computer; ~ **d'exécution** *m* INFORMAT target computer; ~ **familial** *m* INFORMAT home computer; ~ **frontal** *m* TELECOM front-end processor; ~ **de haute gamme** *m* ORDINAT high end computer; ~ **hôte** *m* INFORMAT, ORDINAT host computer; ~ **hybride** *m* INFORMAT, ORDINAT hybrid computer; ~ **à jeu d'instructions complexe** *m* ORDINAT CISC, complex instruction set computer; ~ **à jeu d'instructions réduit** *m* INFORMAT, ORDINAT RISC, reduced instruction set computer; ~ **à mots de longueur fixe** *m* INFORMAT, ORDINAT fixed wordlength computer; ~ **à mots de longueur variable** *m* INFORMAT, ORDINAT variable word length computer; ~ **numérique** *m* INFORMAT, ORDINAT digital computer; ~ **parallèle** *m* INFORMAT, ORDINAT parallel computer; ~ **passerelle** *m* INFORMAT, ORDINAT gateway computer; ~ **personnel** *m* (OP) INFORMAT personal computer (PC); ~ **portable** *m* INFORMAT, ORDINAT laptop computer; ~ **portable autonome** *m* INFORMAT, ORDINAT laptop computer; ~ **de première génération** *m* INFORMAT, ORDINAT first-generation computer; ~ **à programme enregistré** *m* INFORMAT stored program computer; ~ **de quatrième génération** *m* INFORMAT,

ORDINAT fourth-generation computer; ~ **RISC** *m* INFORMAT RISC, ORDINAT RISC, reduced instruction set computer; ~ **satellite** *m* INFORMAT, ORDINAT satellite computer; ~ **secondaire intégré à un système** *m* IMPRIM satellite; ~ **de seconde génération** *m* INFORMAT, ORDINAT second-generation computer; ~ **série** *m* ORDINAT serial computer; ~ **spécialisé** *m* INFORMAT dedicated computer, special-purpose computer, ORDINAT dedicated computer; ~ **synchrone** *m* INFORMAT synchronous computer; ~ **de trafic** *m* TRANSPORT traffic computer; ~ **de troisième génération** *m* INFORMAT, ORDINAT third-generation computer

ordinatique *f* ORDINAT computer literacy

ordinogramme *m* INFORMAT flowgraph

ordonnancement *m* PRODUCTION work assembly; ~ **d'atelier** *m* PRODUCTION production scheduling; ~ **de paquets** *m* INFORMAT, ORDINAT packet sequencing

ordonnancer *vt* PRODUCTION schedule

ordonnanceur *m* ORDINAT scheduler; ~ **de programmes** *m* ORDINAT scheduler

ordonnée *f* INFORMAT, ORDINAT ordinate, PHYSIQUE y-coordinate

ordonner *vt* INFORMAT, ORDINAT order

ordre *m* ACOUSTIQUE *d'un harmonique*, CHIMIE, INFORMAT order, ORDINAT command, order; ~ **d'achat suggéré** *m* PRODUCTION recommended purchase order; ~ **d'allumage** *m* VEHICULES *moteur* firing order; ~ **architectonique** *m* CONSTR variation order; ~ **d'atterrissage** *m* AERONAUT landing sequence; ~ **de braquage de tuyère** *m* ESPACE *propulsion* engine angle command; ~ **de change** *m* CONSTR variation order; ~ **à courte distance** *m* CRISTALL, METALL short-range order; ~ **en fabrication en cours** *m* PRODUCTION open order; ~ **d'entrelacement** *m* TV interlace sequence; ~ **de fabrication** *m* PRODUCTION production order, work order; ~ **de fabrication lancé** *m* PRODUCTION open order, released order; ~ **de fabrication suggéré** *m* PRODUCTION recommended production order; ~ **de fabrication suspendu** *m* PRODUCTION held-up order; ~ **de filtre** *m* ELECTRON filter order; ~ **à grande distance** *m* CRISTALL long-range order; ~ **de grandeur** *m* INFORMAT, ORDINAT, PHYSIQUE order of magnitude; ~ **d'interclassement** *m* ORDINAT collating sequence; ~ **d'interférence** *m* PHYSIQUE order of interference; ~ **lexicographique** *m* INFORMAT lexicographic order; ~ **magnétique** *m* METALL magnetic order; ~ **de phases** *m* ELECTR *système à trois phases*, ELECTRON phase sequence; ~ **de phases positif** *m* ELECTR *générateur à courant alternatif* positive phase sequence; ~ **positif** *m* ELECTR *courant alternatif* positive sequence; ~ **prioritaire** *m* PRODUCTION priority order; ~ **de priorité** *m* INFORMAT, ORDINAT order of precedence; ~ **de réaction** *m* METALL order of reaction; ~ **suggéré** *m* PRODUCTION suggested order; ~ **de transfert en magasin** *m* PRODUCTION warehouse order

ordre-désordre *m* METALL order-disorder

ordures: ~ ménagères *f pl* AGRO ALIM kitchen waste, DISTRI EAU recirculating water economy, refuse, RECYCLAGE household waste

oreille *f* CONS MECA ear, lug, *d'une vis ailée* wing, *de levage* eyebolt, MECANIQUE, PRODUCTION *d'un châssis de fonderie* lug; ~ **d'ancre** *f* NAUT anchor fluke; ~ **artificielle** *f* ACOUSTIQUE artificial ear

organe *m* CONS MECA component, ORDINAT unit, PRODUCTION component, VEHICULES part; ~ **de commande** *m* TELECOM control unit; ~ **commun** *m*

TELECOM CE, common equipment; ~ **de commutation automatique** *m* TELECOM DSE, digital switching element; ~ **d'E/S** *m* PRODUCTION *automatisme industriel* I/O hardware; ~ **d'entrée** *m* ELECTROTEC input device; ~ **d'exécution** *m* ELECTROTEC actuator; ~ **de gestion** *m* TELECOM control unit, management unit; ~ **de mise en mouvement** *m* CONS MECA starting gear; ~ **périphérique** *m* TELECOM peripheral device; ~ **de puissance** *m* ELECTROTEC actuator; ~ **de réglage** *m* COMMANDE adjusting device, adjusting mechanism; ~ **de trafic** *m* TELECOM traffic-carrying device

organeau *m* NAUT anchor shackle; ~ **d'ancre** *m* NAUT anchor ring

organes *m pl* CONS MECA gear, mechanism; ~ **accessoires** *m pl* CONS MECA fittings; ~ **accessoires de chaudière** *m pl* INST HYDR, PRODUCTION boiler fittings; ~ **de changement de marche** *m pl* CONS MECA reversing gear; ~ **de commande** *m pl* CONS MECA driving gear; ~ **communs** *m pl* TELECOM common control equipment; ~ **de roulement** *m pl* CONS MECA running gear; ~ **de transmission** *m pl* CONS MECA transmission gear

organicien *m* CHIMIE organic chemist

organigramme *m* INFORMAT, PHYSIQUE flowchart; ~ **de données** *m* INFORMAT data flowchart

organique *adj* CHIMIE *fonction* organic

organisation: ~ **de la copie** *f* IMPRIM *composition, mise en page* copy fitting; ~ **de fichier** *f* INFORMAT, ORDINAT file organization; ~ **internationale de pêche** *f* OCEANO international fisheries organization; ~ **du passage papier** *f* IMPRIM web-up

Organisation: ~ **internationale de normalisation** *f* *(ISO)* CONS MECA, TELECOM International Standards Organization *(ISO)*; ~ **maritime internationale** *f* *(OMI)* NAUT International Maritime Organization *(IMO)*; ~ **des pays exportateurs de pétrole** *f* *(OPEP)* PETROLE Organization of Petroleum Exporting Countries *(OPEC)*

organisme *m* AERONAUT agency; ~ **agréé** *m* QUALITE approved organization; ~ **de certification** *m* QUALITE certification organisation; ~ **de contrôle** *m* NAUT regulatory agency; ~ **filtreur** *m* RECYCLAGE filter feeder; ~ **d'homologation** *m* QUALITE certification body; ~ **officiel** *m* PRODUCTION authority

organogène *adj* CHARBON organogenous

organomagnésien *m* CHIMIE organomagnesium

organométallique *adj* CHIMIE organometallic

organosol *m* CHIMIE organosol

organsin *m* TEXTILE organzine

orge: ~ **de brasserie** *f* AGRO ALIM malting barley; ~ **à malter** *f* AGRO ALIM malting barley

orgue: ~ **basaltique** *m* GEOLOGIE columnar basalt

orgues: ~ **basaltiques** *m pl* GEOLOGIE basaltic columns

orientateur-marqueur *m* MILITAIRE *parachutiste* pathfinder

orientation *f* AERONAUT heading, CONSTR bearing, bearings, orientation, ELECTRON *de faisceau* directing, ESPACE *pilotage* attitude, *véhicules* trim, IMPRIM *composition, montage, maquette* orientation, MINES bearing, PLAST CAOU *plastiques, fibres* drawing; ~ **biaxiale** *f* PLAST CAOU *feuille plastique* biaxial orientation; ~ **épitaxiale** *f* MATERIAUX *cristallographie* epitaxial orientation; ~ **des particules magnétiques** *f* TV magnetic particle orientation; ~ **de la poussée en vol** *f* ESPACE *propulsion* in-flight thrust vectoring; ~ **préférentielle** *f* CRISTALL, GEOLOGIE preferred orienta-

tion; ~ **train avant** *f* AERONAUT nose wheel steering

orientations *f pl* CONSTR *faces d'un édifice* bearings

orienté: ~ **machine** *adj* INFORMAT, ORDINAT machine-oriented; ~ **mot** *adj* INFORMAT, ORDINAT word oriented; ~ **opérateur** *adj* INFORMAT, ORDINAT user friendly

orienter[1] *vt* CONS MECA position, CONSTR orient

orienter:[2] **s'**~ *v réfl* CONSTR find one's bearings

orifice *m* CONS MECA hole, orifice, port, porthole, CONSTR opening, IMPRIM *vidange* slot, INST HYDR, MECANIQUE port, MINES mouth, PAPIER aperture, hole, PETROLE orifice, VEHICULES *moteur* port; ~ **d'accès** *m* NUCLEAIRE transfer port; ~ **d'admission** *m* AUTO inlet port (BrE), intake port (AmE), INST HYDR *d'un cylindre à vapeur* induction port, MECANIQUE intake, PAPIER, PRODUCTION inlet, VEHICULES *d'un moteur* inlet port (BrE), intake port (AmE); ~ **d'admission de vapeur** *m* INST HYDR steam port; ~ **d'arrivée** *m* DISTRI EAU *d'un réservoir* infall, PRODUCTION inlet; ~ **d'aspiration** *m* AUTO inlet, MECANIQUE intake, PRODUCTION *système hydraulique* suction port; ~ **à bord vif** *m* INST HYDR sharp-edged orifice; ~ **calibre** *m* PETROLE choke; ~ **calibré** *m* CONS MECA metering hole, PETROLE gaged restriction (AmE), gauged restriction (BrE), orifice, *canalisation* gaged orifice (AmE), gauged orifice (BrE); ~ **de charge** *m* EMBALLAGE fill hole; ~ **de chauffe** *m* PRODUCTION fire hole; ~ **de coulée du laitier** *m* PRODUCTION cinder notch; ~ **de décharge** *m* PRODUCTION outlet; ~ **de distribution** *m* INST HYDR port; ~ **d'eau** *m* PRODUCTION water port; ~ **d'échappement** *m* AUTO exhaust port, INST HYDR *d'un cylindre à vapeur* eduction port, *de décharge* exhaust port; ~ **d'écoulement de distributeur** *m* CERAM VER orifice; ~ **en parol mince** *m* INST HYDR opening in thin partition; ~ **d'entrée** *m* INST HYDR *d'un cylindre à vapeur* induction port, PRODUCTION inlet; ~ **d'évacuation** *m* PAPIER outlet; ~ **d'évacuation de vapeur** *m* INST HYDR steam port; ~ **évasé** *m* INST HYDR rounded approach orifice; ~ **de la fosse** *m* MINES pit mouth, pithead; ~ **de grandes dimensions** *m* HYDROLOGIE large orifice; ~ **immergé** *m* INST HYDR orifice, submerged orifice; ~ **d'introduction d'eau** *m* DISTRI EAU water inlet; ~ **d'introduction de l'objet** *m* INSTRUMENT specimen insertion airlock; ~ **d'introduction de vapeur** *m* INST HYDR steam inlet; ~ **noyé** *m* INST HYDR orifice, submerged orifice; ~ **ouvert à sa partie supérieure** *m* DISTRI EAU notch; ~ **percé dans une paroi épaisse** *m* INST HYDR short pipe; ~ **percé en plaque mince** *m* INST HYDR opening in thin plate; ~ **de pointe** *m* CHARBON apex; ~ **de progression** *m* AUTO bypass bore; ~ **de puits** *m* MINES shaft collar; ~ **de raccordement** *m* CONS MECA connection port; ~ **de refoulement** *m* AUTO outlet; ~ **de remplissage** *m* ESPACE *véhicules*, MECANIQUE filling hole; ~ **de remplissage d'huile** *m* AUTO oil inlet; ~ **de remplissage du moule** *m* CERAM VER baffle hole; ~ **de sortie** *m* PRODUCTION outlet; ~ **de sortie d'eau** *m* DISTRI EAU water outlet, water outlet port; ~ **standard** *m* INST HYDR percé dans une paroi mince standard orifice; ~ **de trop plein** *m* AUTO overflow hole; ~ **de vidange d'huile** *m* AUTO oil drain hole

original *m* ENREGISTR master, IMPRIM original, TV master, original; ~ **bas contraste** *m* CINEMAT low contrast original; ~ **inversible** *m* CINEMAT original; ~ **tourné** *m* CINEMAT camera original

origine: ~ **ETCD** *f* TELECOM DCE source

origines: ~ **des comètes** *f pl* ASTRONOMIE comet origins

orin *m* NAUT buoy line, buoy rope, tripping line, PETR pennant line; ~ **d'ancre** *m* NAUT anchor buoy rope

Orion *f* ASTRONOMIE Orion

orlon *m* CHIMIE orlon

ornement *m* IMPRIM *typographie, reliure* adornment, *typographie* fleuron

ornière *f* CONSTR rut

ornithurique *adj* CHIMIE ornithuric

orogène[1] *adj* GEOLOGIE orogene

orogène[2] *m* GEOLOGIE orogen

orogenèse *f* GEOLOGIE orogeny

orogénie: ~ **cimmérienne** *f* PETROLE Cimmerian orogeny, Cimmerian unconformity

orotron *m* ELECTRON orotron

orpailleur *m* MINES digger

orphelin *m* IMPRIM *composition* orphan

orpiment *m* MINERAUX orpiment

orsellinique *adj* CHIMIE orsellinic

orsellique *adj* CHIMIE orsellic

orthicon *m* ELECTRON orthicon

orthite *f* MINERAUX, NUCLEAIRE orthite

orthobasique *adj* CHIMIE orthobasic

orthocarbonique *adj* CHIMIE orthocarbonic

orthocentre *m* GEOMETRIE orthocenter (AmE), orthocentre (BrE)

orthochlorite *f* MINERAUX orthochlorite

orthochlorotoluène *m* CHIMIE orthochlorotoluene

orthochromatisation *f* CINEMAT orthochromatization

orthochromatisme *m* CINEMAT orthochromatism

orthodromie *f* AERONAUT great circle route, NAUT orthodromy

orthoformique *adj* CHIMIE orthoformic

orthogneiss *m* GEOLOGIE granite-gneiss

orthogonal *adj* GEOMETRIE orthogonal

orthogonales: ~ **de houle** *f pl* OCEANO wave propagation direction

orthohydrogène *m* CHIMIE orthohydrogen

orthophosphate *m* CHIMIE orthophosphate

orthophosphorique *adj* CHIMIE orthophosphoric

orthorhombique *adj* CRISTALL orthorhombic

orthoscopique *adj* PHYSIQUE orthoscopic

orthose *m* MINERAUX orthoclase

orthosilicate *m* CHIMIE orthosilicate

orthosilicique *adj* CHIMIE orthosilicic

orthovanadique *adj* CHIMIE orthovanadic

orthoxylène *m* CHIMIE o-xylene, PETROLE *chimie, raffinage* orthoxylene

Os *(osmium)* CHIMIE Os *(osmium)*

osazone *f* CHIMIE osazone

oscillant *adj* ELECTR, ELECTRON, PAPIER oscillating

oscillateur[1] *adj* ELECTRON oscillating

oscillateur[2] *m* CINEMAT, ELECTR, ELECTRON, ESPACE *communications*, PHYS ONDES, PHYSIQUE, TELECOM oscillator; ~ **accordable** *m* ELECTRON tunable oscillator; ~ **accordable à large bande** *m* ELECTRON wide band tunable oscillator; ~ **accordable multioctave** *m* ELECTRON multioctave tunable oscillator; ~ **accordable sur un octave** *m* ELECTRON octave band oscillator; ~ **à accord continu** *m* ELECTRON continuously-tunable oscillator; ~ **accordé électriquement** *m* ELECTRON electrically-tuned oscillator; ~ **à accord électrique** *m* ELECTRON electrically-tuned oscillator; ~ **à accord électronique** *m* ELECTRON electronically-tuned oscillator; ~ **accordé par diode varicap** *m* ELECTRON varactor-tuned oscillator; ~ **à accord**

instantané *m* ELECTRON fast-tuned oscillator; ~ **à accord mécanique** *m* ELECTRON mechanically-tuned oscillator; ~ **d'activation** *m* ELECTRON antistiction oscillator, dither oscillator, keep-alive oscillator; ~ **asservi** *m* ELECTRON locked oscillator, tracking oscillator; ~ **asservi en phase** *m* ELECTRON PLO, phase-locked oscillator; ~ **asservi à la salve de référence** *m* TV burst locked oscillator; ~ **audiofréquence** *m* ELECTRON audio frequency oscillator; ~ **à autoexcitation** *m* ELECTRON self-excited oscillator; ~ **autoexcité** *m* ELECTRON self-excited oscillator; ~ **basse fréquence** *m* ELECTRON low-frequency oscillator; ~ **de battement** *m* ELECTRON beat frequency oscillator; ~ **à battement de fréquence** *m* AERONAUT, ENREGISTR BFO, beat frequency oscillator; ~ **à battement** *m* TELECOM BFO, beat frequency oscillator; ~ **de blocage** *m* PHYSIQUE blocking oscillator; ~ **bloqué** *m* ELECTRON blocking oscillator; ~ **de brouilleur** *m* ELECTRON jammer oscillator; ~ **à cavité** *m* ELECTRON cavity oscillator; ~ **cohérent** *m* ELECTRON coherent oscillator; ~ **Colpitts** *m* ELECTRON Colpitts oscillator; ~ **commandé** *m* ELECTRON controlled oscillator; ~ **commandé en courant** *m* ELECTRON current-controlled oscillator; ~ **commandé en tension** *m* ELECTRON, ESPACE *communications*, TELECOM VCO, voltage-controlled oscillator; ~ **commandé en tension à fréquence instantanée** *m* ELECTRON set-on voltage-controlled oscillator; ~ **à couplage électronique** *m* ELECTRON electron coupling oscillator; ~ **à courant constant** *m* ELECTRON constant current oscillator; ~ **à cristal** *m* ELECTR crystal oscillator, PHYSIQUE quartz crystal oscillator; ~ **cristallin** *m* PHYS RAYON crystal oscillator; ~ **à décades** *m* ELECTRON decade oscillator; ~ **à déphasage** *m* ELECTRON phase shift oscillator; ~ **à diapason** *m* ELECTRON fork oscillator; ~ **à diode** *m* ELECTRON diode oscillator; ~ **à diode Impatt** *m* ELECTRON IMPATT oscillator; ~ **à diode varicap** *m* ELECTRON varactor-tuned oscillator; ~ **électrique** *m* ELECTRON electrical oscillator; ~ **en dent de scie** *m* ENREGISTR sawtooth oscillator; ~ **à faible dérive** *m* ELECTRON low-drift oscillator; ~ **à fréquence fixe** *m* ELECTRON fixed frequency oscillator; ~ **à fréquence porteuse** *m* ELECTRON carrier frequency oscillator; ~ **à fréquence synthétisée** *m* ELECTRON synthesized oscillator; ~ **à fréquence variable** *m* ELECTRON variable frequency oscillator; ~ **harmonique** *m* ELECTRON harmonic oscillator, sine wave oscillator, PHYSIQUE harmonic oscillator; ~ **Hartley** *m* ELECTRON Hartley oscillator; ~ **haute fréquence** *m (oscillateur HF)* ELECTRON RF oscillator, radiofrequency oscillator; ~ **hétérodyne** *m* PHYSIQUE, TV beat frequency oscillator; ~ **HF** *m (oscillateur haute fréquence)* ELECTRON RF oscillator, radiofrequency oscillator; ~ **hyperfréquence** *m* ELECTRON microwave oscillator; ~ **à impulsion** *m* ELECTRON pulsed oscillator; ~ **à interaction étendue** *m* ELECTRON extended interaction oscillator; ~ **à ligne accordée** *m* ELECTRON resonant line oscillator; ~ **local** *m* ELECTRON conversion oscillator, local oscillator, ESPACE *communications*, PHYSIQUE local oscillator, TELECOM LO, local oscillator; ~ **local asservi** *m* ELECTRON tracking local oscillator; ~ **local synthétisé** *m* ELECTRON synthesized local oscillator; ~ **maître** *m* PHYSIQUE master oscillator; ~ **à modulation de vitesse** *m* ELECTRON velocity-modulated oscillator; ~ **modulé** *m* ELECTRON modulated oscillator; ~ **non accordable** *m* ELECTRON fixed frequency oscillator; ~ **non asservi en phase** *m* ELECTRON open loop oscillator; ~ **non piloté** *m* ELECTRON free-running oscillator; ~ **à onde régressive** *m* ELECTRON backward wave oscillator; ~ **à onde régressive à faisceau droit** *m* ELECTRON linear beam backward wave oscillator; ~ **à ondes en volume** *m* ELECTRON bulk wave oscillator; ~ **à ondes rétrogrades** *m* TELECOM carcinotron, TELECOM backward wave oscillator; ~ **d'onduleur** *m* ELECTRON inverter oscillator; ~ **optique** *m* ELECTRON optical oscillator; ~ **paramétrique** *m* TELECOM parametric oscillator; ~ **paramétrique optique** *m* TELECOM optical parametric oscillator; ~ **Pierce** *m* ELECTRON Pierce oscillator; ~ **piézo-électrique** *m* ELECTR, ELECTROTEC, PHYSIQUE piezoelectric oscillator; ~ **pilote** *m* ELECTRON, PHYSIQUE master oscillator; ~ **piloté par ligne de transmission** *m* ELECTRON line-stabilized oscillator; ~ **piloté par quartz** *m* CINEMAT quartz crystal oscillator; ~ **de polarisation** *m* ELECTRON, ENREGISTR bias oscillator; ~ **à pont de Wien** *m* ELECTRON Wien bridge oscillator; ~ **programmable** *m* ELECTRON programmable oscillator; ~ **de puissance** *m* ELECTRON power oscillator; ~ **de puissance à autoexcitation** *m* ELECTRON self-excited power oscillator; ~ **de puissance autoexcité** *m* ELECTRON self-excited power oscillator; ~ **à quartz** *m* ELECTR quartz oscillator, ELECTRON crystal oscillator, quartz crystal oscillator, quartz oscillator, PHYSIQUE quartz crystal oscillator, TELECOM quartz oscillator; ~ **à quartz à compensation thermique** *m* ELECTRON temperature-compensated crystal oscillator; ~ **à quartz compensé en température** *m* ELECTRON temperature-compensated crystal oscillator; ~ **à quartz non thermostaté** *m* ELECTRON free air crystal oscillator, simple-packaged crystal oscillator; ~ **à quartz thermostaté** *m* ELECTRON temperature-controlled crystal oscillator; ~ **RC** *m* ELECTRON, ELECTROTEC RC oscillator; ~ **de réaction** *m* ELECTRON feedback oscillator; ~ **de régénération** *m* ELECTRON *sous-porteuse de chrominance* chrominance subcarrier oscillator; ~ **de régénération de la porteuse** *m* ELECTRON carrier reinsertion operator; ~ **de régénération de porteuse** *m* ELECTRON homodyne oscillator; ~ **à régulation de tension** *m* ELECTRON voltage-controlled oscillator; ~ **à régulation de tension à fréquence instantanée** *m* ELECTRON set-on voltage-controlled oscillator; ~ **à relaxation** *m* ELECTRON relaxation oscillator; ~ **à résistance négative** *m* ELECTRON, PHYSIQUE negative resistance oscillator; ~ **de rétroaction** *m* COMMANDE feedback oscillator; ~ **à sauts de fréquence** *m* ELECTRON frequency-hopping oscillator; ~ **de service** *m* ELECTRON service oscillator; ~ **synchronisé par injection** *m* ELECTRON, ESPACE *communications* injection-locked oscillator; ~ **synthétisé** *m* ELECTRON synthesized oscillator; ~ **à transistor** *m* ELECTRON transistor oscillator; ~ **à transistor à YIG** *m* ELECTRON YIG tuned transistor oscillator; ~ **à triode** *m* ELECTRON triode oscillator; ~ **à tube** *m* ELECTRON vacuum tube oscillator; ~ **à tube électronique** *m* ELECTRON electron tube oscillator, vacuum tube oscillator; ~ **ultrastable** *m* ELECTRON highly-stable oscillator; ~ **à YIG** *m* ELECTRON YIG tuned oscillator

oscillateurs: ~ **couplés** *m pl* PHYSIQUE coupled oscillators

oscillation *f* CONS MECA oscillation, pendulum motion, swaying, swaying, swinging, swinging, CONSTR ringing, ELECTR *courant alternatif*, ELECTRON oscillation, ELECTROTEC *autour de la position finale* hunting, ENREGISTR ringing, ESPACE *pilotage* wobble, PHYS ONDES oscillation, PHYSIQUE oscillation, vibration, TELECOM oscillation; ~ **acoustique** *f* ACOUSTIQUE acoustic oscillation; ~ **amortie** *f* ELECTRON, ENREGISTR damped oscillation; ~ **annulée** *f* ENREGISTR deadbeat; ~ **de Chandler** *f* ASTRONOMIE Chandler wobble; ~ **de dépassement** *f* CONSTR ringing; ~ **électrique** *f* ELECTRON electric oscillation, PHYS ONDES electrical oscillation; ~ **en dent de scie** *f* ELECTR *oscilloscope* sawtooth oscillation; ~ **entretenue** *f* ELECTRON continuous oscillation, sustained oscillation, PHYSIQUE maintained oscillation; ~ **forcée** *f* ELECTRON, PHYSIQUE forced oscillation; ~ **à la fréquence propre** *f* ELECTRON natural frequency oscillation; ~ **harmonique** *f* PHYSIQUE harmonic oscillation; ~ **d'image** *f* TV picture drift; ~ **d'incidence** *f* AERONAUT incidence oscillation; ~ **d'inertie** *f* OCEANO inertial oscillation; ~ **ionique électrostatique** *f* NUCLEAIRE *de plasma* electrostatic ion oscillation; ~ **de lacet** *f* AERONAUT *aérodynamique* snaking; ~ **libre** *f* ELECTR *galvanomètre*, ELECTRON free oscillation, PHYSIQUE free oscillation, free vibration; ~ **linéaire** *f* CONS MECA, TELECOM linear oscillation; ~ **linéaire libre** *f* CONS MECA free linear oscillation; ~ **longitudinale libre** *f* CONS MECA free longitudinal oscillation; ~ **longitudinale de longue période** *f* AERONAUT *aéronef* phugoid oscillation; ~ **mécanique** *f* ACOUSTIQUE mechanical oscillation; ~ **nonlinéaire** *f* TELECOM nonlinear oscillation; ~ **parasite** *f* PHYSIQUE parasitic oscillation, stray oscillation, TELECOM parasitic oscillation; ~ **d'un pendule** *f* CONS MECA oscillation of a pendulum; ~ **phugoïde** *f* AERONAUT phugoid oscillation; ~ **propre** *f* CONS MECA natural oscillation; ~ **de réaction** *f* ENREGISTR feedback oscillation; ~ **de relaxation** *f* ELECTRON, PHYSIQUE relaxation oscillation; ~ **d'un ressort** *f* CONS MECA oscillation of a spring; ~ **sinusoïdale** *f* ELECTRON sinusoidal oscillation; ~ **thermique** *f* THERMODYN thermal cycling; ~ **de torsion** *f* PHYSIQUE torsional oscillation; ~ **transitoire** *f* PHYSIQUE transient oscillation

oscillatoire *adj* ELECTR oscillating, TELECOM oscillatory

osciller *vi* ELECTRON oscillate, ESPACE *pilotage* wobble, PAPIER oscillate, swing, PHYS ONDES oscillate

oscillogramme *m* TV oscillogram

oscillographe *m* CHIMIE, ELECTRON, PHYS ONDES oscillograph; ~ **d'enregistrement** *m* ACOUSTIQUE recording oscillograph

oscilloscope *m* ELECTR *appareil de mesure* oscilloscope, ELECTRON, INFORMAT, ORDINAT, PHYS ONDES, PHYSIQUE, TV oscilloscope; ~ **de contrôle** *m* TV waveform monitor; ~ **à mémoire** *m* PHYSIQUE storage oscilloscope; ~ **mesureur** *m* ELECTR measuring oscilloscope; ~ **de profil** *m* TV image and waveform monitor, waveform monitor; ~ **à rayons de cathode** *m* ELECTRON, PHYSIQUE, PHYS RAYON cathode ray oscilloscope

osculateur *adj* GEOMETRIE osculatory

ose *m* CHIMIE glucose

oside *m* CHIMIE glycocide

osmiate *m* CHIMIE osmate, osmiate

osmieux *adj* CHIMIE osmious

osmique *adj* CHIMIE osmic

osmiridium *m* MINERAUX osmiridium

osmium *m (Os)* CHIMIE osmium *(Os)*

osmolarité *f* CHIMIE osmolarity

osmole *f* CHIMIE osmol, osmole

osmophore *m* CHIMIE osmophore
osmophorique *adj* CHIMIE osmophoric
osmose *f* CHIMIE, GENIE CHIM, HYDROLOGIE, PETROLE, PHYSIQUE osmosis; ~ **inverse** *f* CONSTR, GENIE CHIM, HYDROLOGIE reverse osmosis; ~ **de renversement** *f* GENIE CHIM reverse osmosis
osmotique *adj* PHYSIQUE osmotic
osmyl *f* CHIMIE osmyl
osone *f* CHIMIE osone
osotétrazine *f* CHIMIE osotetrazine
osotriazol *m* CHIMIE osotriazole
ossature *f* CONSTR framework, framing
osséine *f* CHIMIE ossein, ostein, TEXTILE bone glue
ossivibrateur *m* ACOUSTIQUE bone vibrator
ostéine *f* CHIMIE ossein, ostein
ostéolite *f* MINERAUX osteolite
ostréiculteur *m* OCEANO oyster farmer
ostréiculture *f* OCEANO oyster culture
ottrélite *f* MINERAUX ottrelite
OU: ~ **exclusif** *m* INFORMAT exjunction
ouate *f* PAPIER tissue, wadding, TEXTILE wad, wadding; ~ **de verre** *f* EMBALLAGE glass wadding
ouatinage *m* TEXTILE padding
ouatiner *vt* TEXTILE wad
oued *m* HYDROLOGIE wadi
ouest:[1] **d'~** *adj* NAUT *vent* westerly; **de l'~** *adj* NAUT west
ouest:[2] **à l'~** *adv* NAUT westwards
ouïe *f* CONS MECA *d'un ventilateur, d'une pompe centrifuge* ear, intake, PRODUCTION *d'un ventilateur, d'une pompe centrifuge* inlet; ~ **d'admission** *f* AERONAUT air scoop; ~ **d'entrée d'air** *f* AERONAUT air scoop
ouïes: ~ **de capot** *f pl* VEHICULES *carrosserie* louver (AmE), louvre (BrE)
ouillage *m* AGRO ALIM filling, ESPACE ullage
ouiller *vt* AGRO ALIM refill, ESPACE top up
ouragan *m* METEO hurricane
ouralite *f* MINERAUX uralite
ourdir *vt* TEXTILE warp
ourdissage *m* TEXTILE warping; ~ **sectionnel** *m* TEXTILE section warping, sectional warping
ourdissoir *m* TEXTILE warper; ~ **sectionnel** *m* TEXTILE sectional warping machine
ourlet *m* TEXTILE hem
outil *m* CONS MECA, INFORMAT, MECANIQUE, MINES, ORDINAT tool, PETROLE *forage* bit; ~ **d'alésage** *m* CONS MECA boring tool; ~ **à aléser** *m* CONS MECA boring cutter; ~ **biseauté** *m* CONS MECA bevel-edged flat; ~ **à calibrer** *m* CONS MECA forming tool; ~ **au carbure** *m* CONS MECA carbide tool; ~ **à chanfreiner** *m* CONS MECA bar chamfering tool, countersink; ~ **à chanfreiner à angle de 60 degrés au sommet** *m* CONS MECA countersink for 60 degrees angle; ~ **à charioter** *m* CONS MECA bar turning tool, roughing tool; ~ **à clavetage** *m* CONS MECA splining tool; ~ **de côté** *m* CONS MECA side tool; ~ **coudé** *m* CONS MECA *de tour* bent tool; ~ **coudé à charioter** *m* CONS MECA cranked turning and facing tool; ~ **coudé à charioter arrondi** *m* CONS MECA cranked round nose and turning tool; ~ **coudé à dresser les faces** *m* CONS MECA cranked facing tool; ~ **coupant** *m* CONS MECA cutting tool; ~ **de coupe** *m* MECANIQUE cutter, cutting tool; ~ **de coupe à partie active unique** *m* CONS MECA single point cutting tool; ~ **couteau** *m* CONS MECA knife tool; ~ **couteau coudé** *m* CONS MECA cranked knife tool; ~ **couteau coudé à charioter arrondi** *m* CONS MECA cranked knife tool for copy turning; ~ **à couteau à droite** *m* CONS MECA

right-hand knife tool; ~ **à crochet** *m* CONS MECA cranked tool, PRODUCTION hanging tool; ~ **à dégainer les câbles** *m* CONS MECA cable sheath stripper; ~ **à dégrafer** *m* CONS MECA staple remover; ~ **à dégrossir** *m* CONS MECA roughing tool; ~ **de diagnostique** *m* TELECOM diagnostic aid; ~ **au diamant** *m* CONS MECA diamond tool; ~ **diamanté** *m* MECANIQUE diamond tool; ~ **à dresser** *m* CONS MECA bar facing tool, facing tool, inside corner tool; ~ **à dresser les angles** *m* CONS MECA cranked finishing tool; ~ **à dresser les faces** *m* CONS MECA facing tool, facing tool for roughing; ~ **d'ébauchage** *m* CONS MECA boring tool; ~ **électrique à main** *m* SECURITE hand-held electric tool; ~ **en fibre de carbone** *m* CONS MECA carbon fiber tool (AmE), carbon fibre tool (BrE); ~ **à fileter** *m* CONS MECA threading tool; ~ **à fileter extérieurement** *m* CONS MECA outside-threading tool; ~ **à fileter intérieurement** *m* CONS MECA inside-threading tool; ~ **de finition** *m* CONS MECA boring tool; ~ **de forage** *m* CONSTR drilling tool, MINES boring tool, PETR bit, drilling bit, PETROLE drill bit; ~ **foreur** *m* CONSTR drilling tool, MINES boring tool; ~ **de forme** *m* CONS MECA forming tool; ~ **à grain-d'orge** *m* CONS MECA round-nose tool; ~ **à lamer** *m* CONS MECA counterbore; ~ **à lamer à pilote amovible** *m* CONS MECA counterbore with detachable pilot; ~ **à lamer à pilote fixe** *m* CONS MECA counterbore with solid pilot; ~ **logiciel** *m* INFORMAT, ORDINAT software tool; ~ **à main** *m* MECANIQUE, PRODUCTION hand tool; ~ **à mise rapportée en carbure** *m* CONS MECA carbide-tipped tool; ~ **à moleter** *m* MECANIQUE knurling tool; ~ **à moteur portatif** *m* CONS MECA hand-held portable power tool; ~ **motorisé** *m* MECANIQUE *outillage* power tool; ~ **de perçage pour presses** *m* CONS MECA piercing die; ~ **à planer** *m* CONS MECA planisher, planishing tool; ~ **à plaquette carbure** *m* MECANIQUE carbide-tipped tool; ~ **pneumatique** *m* CONS MECA pneumatic tool; ~ **pneumatique pour l'assemblage** *m* CONS MECA pneumatic assembly tool; ~ **à pointe** *m* CONS MECA *tour* point tool; ~ **à pointe de diamant** *m* CONS MECA diamond point, diamond point tool, diamond tool; ~ **pour emballage à vide** *m* CONS MECA vacuum packaging tool; ~ **pour rectifier les sièges de robinets** *m* CONS MECA tap reseating tool; ~ **pour tours** *m* CONS MECA turning tool; ~ **de profil conique** *m* CONS MECA dovetail form tool; ~ **à queue cylindrique** *m* CONS MECA parallel shank tool; ~ **à queue cylindrique à méplat** *m* CONS MECA flatted parallel shank tool; ~ **à rainer** *m* PRODUCTION keyway cutting tool; ~ **à rainures** *m* CONS MECA slotting tool; ~ **de repêchage** *m* PETROLE *récupération des objets perdus* fishing tool; ~ **de repêchage magnétique** *m* PETROLE magnetic fishing tool; ~ **de reproduction** *m* CONS MECA forming tool; ~ **à restaurer les filetages** *m* CONS MECA rethreading file; ~ **à restaurer les filets** *m* CONS MECA thread restorer; ~ **à saigner** *m* CONS MECA parting blade, *tour* parting tool; ~ **de sculpteur** *m* PRODUCTION carving tool; ~ **sérié** *m* CONS MECA gang tool; ~ **de sertissage** *m* CONS MECA crimping tool; ~ **de sondage** *m* CONSTR drilling tool, MINES boring tool; ~ **de supervision** *m* TELECOM supervisory aid; ~ **à surfacer** *m* CERAM VER optical tool; ~ **de tour** *m* CONS MECA turning tool; ~ **tournant** *m* GAZ rotary cutting tool; ~ **à tourner** *m* CONS MECA turning tool; ~ **à tourner intérieur** *m* MECANIQUE inside tool; ~ **de tour à plaquette en carbures métalliques** *m* CONS MECA turning tool with carbide tip; ~ **de tour à reproduire** *m* CONS MECA copying lathe tool; ~ **tricône** *m* GAZ tricone bit; ~ **à tronçonner** *m* CONS MECA cutting-off tool, parting tool, *pour porte-lame* parting-off blade

outillage *m* CONS MECA machinery, outfit, tools, *d'extrusion, de formage, presse* dies, MECANIQUE jig, PRODUCTION plant, tooling; ~ **à air comprimé** *m* CONS MECA compressed air equipment; ~ **d'ajourage pour presse** *m* CONS MECA piercing die; ~ **de cisaillage pour presse** *m* CONS MECA shearing die; ~ **de découpage fin** *m* CONS MECA *presse* fine blanking die; ~ **de découpage de flan** *m* CONS MECA *presse* blanking die; ~ **destiné aux carrosseries automobiles** *m* CONS MECA car body tooling; ~ **de drague** *m* MINES dredge plant; ~ **d'emboutissage** *m* CONS MECA dies for stamping; ~ **d'emboutissage profond** *m* CONS MECA deep drawing die; ~ **d'encochage pour presse** *m* CONS MECA notching die; ~ **en métal dur** *m* CONS MECA tungsten-carbide tooling; ~ **d'étirage** *m* CONS MECA *de formage* stretch die; ~ **d'extrusion** *m* CONS MECA extrusion die; ~ **de fixation** *m* CONS MECA holding fixture; ~ **de forgeage** *m* CONS MECA forging dies; ~ **de forgeage chaud** *m* CONS MECA hot forging die; ~ **de forgeage froid** *m* CONS MECA cold forging dies; ~ **de formage** *m* CONS MECA forming dies; ~ **de formage par explosion** *m* CONS MECA explosion dies; ~ **de frappe de formage** *m* CONS MECA coining dies; ~ **d'hydro-formage** *m* CONS MECA hydraulic bulging dies; ~ **isolé** *m pl* SECURITE insulated tooling; ~ **à main** *m* PRODUCTION hand tools; ~ **de martelage de formage** *m* CONS MECA hammer die; ~ **de matriçage de formage** *m* CONS MECA swaging die; ~ **de mines** *m* MINES mining appliances; ~ **mobile** *m* CONS MECA loose plant, portable plant; ~ **de pliage pour presse** *m* CONS MECA bending die; ~ **de poinçonnage** *m* CONS MECA dies for punching; ~ **pour cadre de plomb** *m* CONS MECA lead frame tooling; ~ **pour chantier de maintenance** *m* CONSTR onsite maintenance tools; ~ **pour couvercle fileté** *m* CONS MECA screw cap tooling; ~ **pour feuilles métalliques** *m* CONS MECA foil tooling; ~ **pour feuilles plastiques** *m* CONS MECA plastic foil tooling; ~ **pour métal pulvérisé** *m* CONS MECA powder metal die; ~ **pour mise en boîte** *m* CONS MECA canning tooling; ~ **pour poudre métallique** *m* CONS MECA dies for metallic powders; ~ **pour presses** *m* CONS MECA dies for pressing; ~ **pour prototypes** *m* CONS MECA preproduction tooling, prototype tooling; ~ **pour tôles de carrosserie automobile** *m* CONS MECA dies for motor body panels; ~ **pour tréfilage de fils à chaud** *m* CONS MECA hot wire-drawing die; ~ **de progression en étapes multiples** *m* CONS MECA multistage progression tooling; ~ **de progression pour presses** *m* CONS MECA progression dies; ~ **d'une seule commande** *m* CONS MECA one-off tooling; ~ **tranchant** *m* CONS MECA sharp-edged tool; ~ **de transfert pour presses** *m* CONS MECA transfer die

outillages: ~ **composés pour presses** *m pl* CONS MECA compound dies; ~ **multiples** *m pl* CONS MECA *outillage pour presses* combination tools

outiller *vt* CONS MECA equip, fit out, PRODUCTION equip, fit out

outilleur *m* MECANIQUE, PRODUCTION toolmaker

outils *m pl* CONS MECA tools; ~ **de chariotage** *m pl* CONS MECA slide rest tools, slide rest turning tools; ~ **à charioter** *m pl* CONS MECA slide rest tools, slide rest turning tools; ~ **coupants** *m pl* PRODUCTION edge tools; ~ **de curage** *m pl* MINES cleaning tools, flushing tools, scraping tools; ~ **de dévissage à empreintes multiples** *m pl* CONS MECA multi-impression unscrewing tools; ~ **de diagnostique** d'erreurs *m pl* ORDINAT error diagnostics; ~ **en carbure pour tours et raboteuses** *m pl* CONS MECA tungsten-carbide tipped turning and planing tools; ~ **d'entretien et de dépannage** *m pl* CONS MECA service tools; ~ **d'étaux-limeurs** *m pl* CONS MECA shaper tools; ~ **isolés** *m pl* SECURITE insulated tools; ~ **de limeuses** *m pl* CONS MECA shaper tools; ~ **de manoeuvre** *m pl* CONS MECA assembly tools; ~ **à mortaiser** *m pl* CONS MECA slotter tools, slotting tools; ~ **de mortaiseuses** *m pl* CONS MECA slotter tools, slotting tools; ~ **pour bicyclettes** *m pl* TRANSPORT bicycle tools; ~ **pour emballages sous feuilles plastiques** *m pl* CONS MECA blister pack tooling; ~ **pour freins à disque** *m pl* AUTO disc brake tools (BrE), disk brake tools (AmE); ~ **pour freins à tambour** *m pl* AUTO drum brake tools; ~ **pour tours** *m pl* CONS MECA lathe tools; ~ **à raboter** *m pl* CONSTR planing tools; ~ **de rechange** *m pl* CONS MECA spare tools; ~ **de réparation courants** *m pl* CONS MECA common repair tools; ~ **de terrassement** *m pl* CONSTR earthworking tools; ~ **de tour au cuivre** *m pl* PRODUCTION brassworking tools; ~ **à tourner en céramique d'oxyde** *m pl* CONS MECA oxide ceramic lathe tools; ~ **de tourneur sur bois** *m pl* CONSTR wood-turning tools; ~ **de tours** *m pl* CONS MECA lathe tools; ~ **tranchants** *m pl* PRODUCTION edge tools; ~ **usés** *m pl* SECURITE worn tools; ~ **de verrier** *m pl* CERAM VER glassmaker's tools

outre: ~ **flottante** *f* POLLU MER dracone

outre-mer: d'~ *adj* NAUT overseas

outremer *m* CHIMIE ultramarine

ouvarovite *f* MINERAUX uvarovite

ouvert *adj* CONS MECA open-type, INFORMAT, ORDINAT open

ouverture *f* ASTRONOMIE aperture, CHARBON mesh size, worked thickness, CONS MECA aperture, gap, hole, orifice, CONSTR opening, *d'un pont* span, ELECTROTEC opening, port, ESPACE *communications*, IMPRIM *d'un diaphragme, d'un objectif*, INFORMAT, MECANIQUE aperture, METROLOGIE *d'un palmer* capacity, MINES *d'une carrière* opening, ORDINAT aperture, PAPIER opening, PHYSIQUE aperture, PRODUCTION *contacts* break, TELECOM, TV aperture, VEHICULES *roues avant* toe-out; ~ **angulaire du faisceau** *f* ELECTRON beam angle; ~ **de bouchon** *f* MINES cut hole; ~ **de la boucle** *f* RESSORTS hook opening; ~ **de branche** *f* PRODUCTION *automatisme industriel* branch open; ~ **de chargement** *f* PLAST CAOU *moulage par injection* sprue opening; ~ **d'un circuit** *f* ELECTROTEC breaking of a circuit; ~ **du circuit au zéro du courant** *f* ELECTROTEC zero current turn off; ~ **circulaire** *f* PHYSIQUE circular aperture; ~ **du diaphragme** *f* CINEMAT F-stop, PHOTO F-number, lens stop, stop, F-stop, PHYSIQUE aperture stop; ~ **de l'ébaucheur** *f* CERAM VER blank cracking; ~ **efficace** *f* CINEMAT actual aperture; ~ **en fondu** *f* CINEMAT *apparition graduelle de l'image* fade-in; ~ **de fenêtre** *f* CONSTR window opening; ~ **de jet** *f* POLLU MER spray aperture; ~ **de lentille** *f* PHOTO lens aperture; ~ **libre** *f* PLAST CAOU *presse* daylight; ~ **de la lumière** *f* INST HYDR port opening; ~ **de maille** *f* CHARBON mesh, MECANIQUE mesh size; ~ **du moule** *f* CONS MECA daylight; ~ **numérique** *f* CONSTR, OPTIQUE, PHYSIQUE, TELECOM NA, numerical aperture; ~ **numérique d'injection** *f* OPTIQUE, TELECOM LNA, launch numerical aperture; ~ **numérique maximale** *f* OPTIQUE maximum numerical aperture; ~ **numérique théorique maximale** *f* TELECOM maximum theoretical numerical aperture; ~ **de l'objectif** f INSTRUMENT objective aperture; ~ **photométrique** f CINEMAT T-stop; ~ **relative** f PHYSIQUE F-number, relative aperture; ~ **de remplissage** f PLAST CAOU *moulage par injection* sprue opening; ~ **de session** f ORDINAT log-in, log-on; ~ **utile** f CINEMAT effective aperture; ~ **utile d'un objectif** f PHOTO effective aperture of a lens; ~ **de ventilation** f CONSTR, NUCLEAIRE vent; ~ **de visite** f MECANIQUE manhole

ouvrabilité f CERAM VER plasticity, workability

ouvrage m CH DE FER, CONSTR structure, PRODUCTION hearth, *d'un haut fourneau* crucible; ~ **d'art** m CONSTR permanent structure, permanent work; ~ **d'assainissement** m CONSTR drainage structure, storm drain; ~ **de campagne** m MILITAIRE field work; ~ **de captage d'eau** m CONSTR water extraction structure; ~ **contre les inondations** m DISTRI EAU flood control works; ~ **de crue** m EN RENOUV, HYDROLOGIE flood control works; ~ **en béton** m CONSTR concrete structure; ~ **en maçonnerie** m CONSTR masonry work; ~ **de prise d'eau** m DISTRI EAU intake structure, EN RENOUV *barrage* headwork; ~ **de soutènement** m DISTRI EAU retaining structure

ouvreau m CERAM VER glory hole; ~ **de cueillage** m CERAM VER gathering hole

ouvre-portes: ~ **d'aération** f pl SECURITE ventilation door openers; ~ **de ventilation** f pl SECURITE ventilation door openers

ouvrer vt CONS MECA work

ouvreuse f TEXTILE opener

ouvrier: ~ **d'accrochage** m MINES onsetter (BrE), platman (AmE); ~ **carrier** m MINES quarryman; ~ **dragueur** m NAUT dredger; ~ **imprimeur** m IMPRIM printing trade worker; ~ **maçon** m CONSTR bricklayer; ~ **mécanicien** m PRODUCTION mechanic; ~ **modeleur** m PRODUCTION pattern maker; ~ **mouleur** m CERAM VER mold maker (AmE), mould maker (BrE), PRODUCTION molder (AmE), moulder (BrE); ~ **de plancher** m PETROLE *forage* floorman; ~ **porcelainier** m CERAM VER porcelain maker; ~ **professionnel** m PRODUCTION highly-skilled worker; ~ **serrurier** m PRODUCTION metalworker; ~ **à la veine** m MINES getter

ouvriers: ~ **du fond** m pl MINES below-ground workers; ~ **du jour** m pl MINES above-ground workers, surface workers

ouvrir[1] vt DISTRI EAU *l'eau* turn on, ELECTROTEC break; ~ **par un volet** vt CINEMAT wipe on; ~ **au pic** vt CONSTR *la terre* break with a pick

ouvrir:[2] ~ **le diaphragme** vi CINEMAT open up, PHOTO open diaphragm; ~ **en plein** vi CONS MECA turn full on; ~ **la fibre** vi TEXTILE open fiber (AmE), open fibre (BrE); ~ **une session** vi INFORMAT log in, log on

ouvrir:[3] ~ **de ce côté** loc EMBALLAGE *instructions de manutention* open this end; ~ **ici** loc EMBALLAGE *instructions de manutention* open here

ovale:[1] **en** ~ adj GEOMETRIE oval-shaped, egg-shaped, oval

ovale[2] m GEOMETRIE oval

ovalisation f AUTO out-of-round wear, CERAM VER triangularity, CONS MECA elongation, PETR out-of-roundness, PETROLE *problème en cours de forage* ovalization, RESSORTS ovality

ovalisé adj AUTO out-of-round, CONS MECA out-of-true

overbias f ENREGISTR overbias

OVNI abrév (objet volant non identifié) ASTRONOMIE, ESPACE UFO (unidentified flying object)

ovoglobuline f CHIMIE ovoglobulin

oxacide m CHIMIE oxo acid, oxyacid

oxalacétique adj CHIMIE oxaloacetic

oxalate m CHIMIE oxalate

oxalaté adj CHIMIE oxalated

oxalique adj CHIMIE oxalic

oxalurique adj CHIMIE oxaluric

oxalyle m CHIMIE oxalyl

oxalylurée f CHIMIE oxalylurea, parabanic acid

oxalyluréide f CHIMIE oxalylurea

oxamide m CHIMIE oxamide

oxamique adj CHIMIE oxamic

oxanilide m CHIMIE oxanilide

oxanilique adj CHIMIE oxanilic

oxazine f CHIMIE oxazine

oxazole m CHIMIE oxazole

oxétone f CHIMIE oxetone

oxhydrique adj CHIMIE oxyhydric, oxyhydrogen

oximation f CHIMIE oximation

oxime f CHIMIE oxime

oxonium m CHIMIE oxonium

oxozone m CHIMIE oxozone

oxyacide m CHIMIE oxo acid, oxyacid

oxycellulose f CHIMIE oxycellulose

oxychlorure m CHIMIE oxychloride; ~ **de carbone** m CHIMIE phosgene

oxycoupage m MECANIQUE flame cutting, *procédé* oxy-cutting, PRODUCTION gas cutting, oxygen arc cutting, THERMODYN flame cutting, gas cutting; ~ **à l'arc** m CONSTR oxygen arc cutting

oxycyanure m CHIMIE oxycyanide

oxydabilité f CHIMIE oxidability, oxidizability

oxydable adj CHIMIE corrodible, oxidable, oxidizable, MATERIAUX oxidable, oxidizable

oxydant[1] adj CHIMIE, GEOLOGIE, SECURITE oxidizing

oxydant[2] m CHIMIE oxidant, oxidizer, oxidizing agent, ESPACE *propulsion* oxidizer, POLLUTION oxidizing agent, THERMODYN oxidant

oxydation f CHIMIE oxidation, oxidization, CINEMAT, ELECTR *métaux*, HYDROLOGIE, IMPRIM, POLLUTION oxidation; ~ **biologique** f HYDROLOGIE biological oxidation; ~ **interne** f METALL internal oxidation; ~ **sélective** f ELECTRON local oxidation

oxyde m CHIMIE, ENREGISTR, TV oxide; ~ **d'aluminium** m CHIMIE alumina, aluminium oxide (BrE), aluminum oxide (AmE); ~ **d'argent** m ELECTROTEC silver oxide; ~ **d'azote** m POLLUTION nitrogen oxide; ~ **azoteux** m POLLUTION nitrous oxide; ~ **azotique** m POLLUTION nitric oxide; ~ **de carbone** m CHIMIE carbon monoxide, monoxide, CONS MECA, POLLUTION carbon monoxide; ~ **de chrome** m CERAM VER chromic oxide; ~ **épais** m ELECTRON field oxide; ~ **d'éthylène** m LESSIVES ether oxide, ethylene oxide; ~ **de fer** m CHIMIE, MATERIAUX iron oxide; ~ **de fer micacé** m PLAST CAOU *pigment pour peinture* micaceous iron oxide; ~ **de fer noir** m COULEURS black iron oxide; ~ **ferreux** m CERAM VER ferrous oxide; ~ **ferrique** m ENREGISTR ferric oxide; ~ **métallique** m MATERIAUX metal oxide; ~ **nitreux** m CHIMIE, POLLUTION nitrous oxide; ~ **nitrique** m POLLUTION nitric oxide; ~ **de phényle** m CHIMIE phenoxybenzene; ~ **de propylène** m LESSIVES propylene oxide; ~ **secondaire** m ELECTRON thick oxide; ~ **de silicium** m ELECTRON silicon oxide; ~ **de soufre** m POLLUTION sulfur oxide (AmE), sulphur oxide (BrE); ~ **stannique** m CHIMIE stannic oxide; ~ **sulfureux** m CHIMIE sulfur dioxide (AmE), sulphur dioxide (BrE); ~ **de tantale** *m* ELECTROTEC tantalum oxide; ~ **d'uranium** *m* CHIMIE uranium oxide; ~ **de zinc** *m* ELECTROTEC zinc oxide; ~ **de zinc activé** *m* PLAST CAOU *charge* activated zinc oxide; ~ **de zinc plombifère** *m* MATERIAUX lead zinc oxide

oxyder[1] *vt* CHIMIE oxidize

oxyder:[2] **s'~** *v réfl* CHIMIE oxidize

oxydoréduction *f* CHIMIE oxidoreduction

oxyfluorure *m* CHIMIE oxyfluoride

oxygénable *adj* CHIMIE oxygenizable

oxygénase *f* CHIMIE oxygenase

oxygénation *f* CHIMIE, HYDROLOGIE oxygenation

oxygéné *adj* CHIMIE oxygenated, oxygenic, HYDROLOGIE oxygenated

oxygène *m (O)* CHIMIE oxygen *(O)*; ~ **dissous** *m (OD)* POLLUTION dissolved oxygen *(DO)*; ~ **liquide** *m* CHIMIE loxygen, ESPACE lox, *propulsion* liquid oxygen, THERMODYN liquid oxygen

oxygéner *vt* CHIMIE, HYDROLOGIE oxygenate

oxyhémographie *f* CHIMIE oxyhaemography (BrE), oxyhemography (AmE)

oxylignite *m* MINES liquid oxygen explosive

oxymètre *m* CHIMIE oximeter

oxymétrie *f* CHIMIE oximetry

oxymétrique *adj* CHIMIE oximetric

oxyphosphate *m* CHIMIE oxyphosphate

oxysel *m* CHIMIE oxysalt

oxysulfure *m* CHIMIE oxysulfide (AmE), oxysulphide (BrE); ~ **de carbone** *m* POLLUTION carbonyl sulfide (AmE), carbonyl sulphide (BrE)

oxytétracycline *f* CHIMIE oxytetracycline

ozalid *m* IMPRIM brown print, ozalid

ozobromie *f* PHOTO carbro printing

ozocérite *f* MINERAUX ozocerite

ozokérite *f* MINERAUX ozocerite

ozonation *f* METEO ozonization

ozone *m* CHIMIE, ESPACE, METEO ozone

ozoné *adj* HYDROLOGIE *eau* ozonized

ozoner *vti* CHIMIE, METEO ozonize

ozonide *m* CHIMIE ozonide

ozonisation *f* METEO ozonization

ozonisé *adj* CHIMIE, HYDROLOGIE *eau* ozonized

ozoniser *vti* CHIMIE, METEO ozonize

ozoniseur *m* CHIMIE ozonizer

ozonolyse *f* CHIMIE ozonolysis

ozonoscope *m* CHIMIE ozonoscope

ozonoscopique *adj* CHIMIE ozonoscopic

ozonosphère *f* ESPACE ozonosphere, *géophysique* ozone layer, METEO *géophysique* ozone layer

P

p *abrév* METROLOGIE *(peta-)* p *(peta)*, METROLOGIE *(pico-)* p *(pico-)*

P *(phosphore)* CHIMIE P *(phosphorus)*

Pa[1] *(protactinium)* CHIMIE Pa *(protactinium)*

Pa[2] *abrév (pascal)* METROLOGIE, PETROLE, PHYSIQUE Pa *(pascal)*

PABX: **~ à intégration de services** *m* TELECOM integrated services PABX

pacage: **~ en mer** *m* OCEANO marine grazing, sea ranching; **~ marin** *m* OCEANO marine grazing, sea ranching

pachnolite *f* MINERAUX pachnolite

packer *m* PETR packer

packstone *m* GEOLOGIE packstone

page *f* IMPRIM, INFORMAT, ORDINAT page; **~ d'annonces** *f* IMPRIM advertisement page; **~ de droite** *f* IMPRIM *imposition* right-hand page; **~ de gauche** *f* IMPRIM *imposition* left-hand page; **~ d'illustrations** *f* IMPRIM photo page; **~ impaire** *f* IMPRIM odd page; **~ à l'italienne** *f* IMPRIM oblong page; **~ paire** *f* IMPRIM even page; **~ sans faute** *f* IMPRIM perfectly set page; **~ de titre** *f* IMPRIM title page

pages *f pl* IMPRIM pages, pp; **~ liminaires** *f pl* IMPRIM oddments; **~ par minute** *f pl* INFORMAT, ORDINAT PPM, pages per minute

pagination *f* IMPRIM pagination, INFORMAT, ORDINAT paging; **~ automatique** *f* IMPRIM *mise en page ou imposition* automatic pagination; **~ sur demande** *f* INFORMAT, ORDINAT demand paging

paginer *vt* IMPRIM paginate, INFORMAT, ORDINAT page, paginate

pahage *m* MINES lodge

PAI *abrév (poste d'aiguillage informatisée)* CH DE FER computerized signal box (BrE), computerized switch tower (AmE)

paillasse *f* EQUIP LAB *meuble* bench

paille *f* PAPIER straw, PRODUCTION fault, scale, TV dropout; **~ de fer** *f* PRODUCTION cinder, forge scale, hammer slag, hammer scale, iron scale, nill

paillet *m* NAUT fender

pailleteur *m* MINES digger

paillette *f* MATERIAUX flake, PLAST CAOU *pigment* platelet; **~ de verre** *f* CERAM VER flake glass

paillettes: **~ métalliques** *f pl* MINES float mineral; **~ d'or** *f pl* MINES float gold, floating gold

pain: **~ azyme** *m* AGRO ALIM matzo, unleavened bread; **~ de glace** *m* REFRIG ice cake

pair *adj* INFORMAT even

paire *f* ELECTROTEC pair; **~ blindée** *f* ELECTROTEC shielded pair; **~ de câble téléphonique** *f* ELECTROTEC telephone cable pair; **~ coaxiale** *f* ELECTROTEC coaxial pair; **~ de compas** *f* CONS MECA compasses; **~ complémentaire** *f* ELECTRON complementary pair; **~ de conducteurs** *f* ELECTROTEC cable pair; **~ différentielle** *f* ELECTRON long-tail pair; **~ d'électrons** *f* PHYS PART electron pair; **~ électron-trou** *f* PHYSIQUE electron hole pair; **~ de fils** *f* ELECTROTEC *conducteurs* wire pair; **~ d'ions** *f* CHIMIE, PHYS RAYON *radiologie* ion pair; **~ de jumelles** *f* INSTRUMENT pair of binoculars; **~**

torsadée *f* ELECTROTEC, INFORMAT, ORDINAT, PRODUCTION twisted pair; **~ de transistors** *f* ELECTRON transistor pair

paires: **~ de Cooper** *f pl* PHYSIQUE Cooper pairs; **~ de jets de masse élevée** *f pl* PHYS RAYON *recherche particule* pairs of high-mass jets

palagonite *f* GEOLOGIE hyaloclastite, PETR palagonite

palan *m* CONS MECA block and tackle, purchase, CONSTR gin wheel, tackle, MECANIQUE hoist, *matériel de levage* tackle, NAUT purchase, tackle, PRODUCTION tackle, tackle and fall; **~ à chaîne** *m* CONS MECA chain pulley block, MECANIQUE *matériel de levage* chain block; **~ de chèvre** *m* PRODUCTION gin tackle; **~ à croc** *m* PRODUCTION tackle with hook block; **~ à deux brins** *m* NAUT double tackle; **~ différentiel** *m* MECANIQUE *matériel de levage* differential chain block; **~ électrique** *m* MECANIQUE *matériel de levage* electric hoist; **~ à engrenage droit** *m* CONS MECA spur-geared pulley block; **~ mousse** *m* NAUT handy billy; **~ roulant** *m* PRODUCTION traveling pulley block (AmE), travelling pulley block (BrE); **~ simple** *m* CONSTR luff tackle, PRODUCTION single tackle

palangre *f* OCEANO long line

palastre *m* CONSTR *d'une serrure* plate

palâtre *m* CONSTR *d'une serrure* box staple, plate

pale *f* AERONAUT, CONS MECA *de ventilateur, de turbine* blade, DISTRI EAU shut, shut-off, INST HYDR paddle, *de turbine* blade, vane, NAUT *d'hélice* blade, REFRIG blade; **~ d'antiscintillement** *f* CINEMAT antiflicker blade; **~ articulée** *f* AERONAUT articulated blade; **~ avançante** *f* AERONAUT advancing blade; **~ du compresseur** *f* AERONAUT compressor blade; **~ décalée** *f* AERONAUT offset blade; **~ directrice** *f* INST HYDR stationary blade; **~ fixe** *f* INST HYDR stationary blade; **~ d'hélice** *f* REFRIG fan blade; **~ incurvée** *f* INST HYDR curved vane; **~ mobile** *f* INST HYDR *de turbine* runner blade; **~ d'obturateur** *f* CINEMAT, PHOTO shutter blade; **~ principale de rotor** *f* AERONAUT main rotor blade; **~ réceptrice** *f* INST HYDR runner vane; **~ reculante** *f* AERONAUT *hélicoptère* retreating blade; **~ repliable** *f* AERONAUT folding blade; **~ de rotor** *f* AERONAUT *hélicoptère* rotor blade; **~ de scintillement** *f* CINEMAT flicker blade; **~ traînante** *f* AERONAUT hunting blade; **~ de turbine** *f* CONS MECA turbine blade; **~ de ventilateur** *f* AUTO, MECANIQUE, VEHICULES *refroidissement* fan blade

palée *f* CHARBON row of piles; **~ de port** *f* CONSTR *d'un pont* pier

paléocéanographie *f* OCEANO palaeo-oceanography (BrE), paleo-oceanography (AmE)

paléomagnétisme *m* GEOLOGIE, PHYSIQUE palaeomagnetism (BrE), paleomagnetism (AmE)

paléopente *f* GEOLOGIE palaeoslope (BrE), paleoslope (AmE)

paléopression *f* PETROLE palaeopressure (BrE), paleopressure (AmE)

paléorelief: **~ enfoui** *m* GEOLOGIE buried topography

paléozoïque *f* GEOLOGIE Palaeozoic (BrE),

Paleozoic (AmE)

palet *m* IMPRIM puck; **~ d'accouplement** *m* AERONAUT coupling buffer

palette *f* AERONAUT, CERAM VER pallet, CONS MECA *d'un ventilateur, d'une roue hydraulique* paddle, paddle board, *d'une turbine* vane, DISTRI EAU float, float-board, GAZ range, MECANIQUE vane, PRODUCTION flight, *système hydraulique* vane, TEXTILE latch, TRANSPORT pallet; **~ caisse cadrée** *f* TRANSPORT crate pallet; **~ de chargement** *f* AERONAUT pallet; **~ à côté démontable** *f* TRANSPORT pallet with loose partition; **~ de couleurs** *f* INFORMAT, ORDINAT color palette (AmE), colour palette (BrE), TEXTILE color wheel (AmE), colour wheel (BrE); **~ à deux entrées** *f* TRANSPORT two-way pallet; **~ à deux étages** *f* EMBALLAGE double platform pallet; **~ de diffuseur** *f* GENIE CHIM diffuser blade; **~ extensible** *f* EMBALLAGE expandable pallet; **~ à forer** *f* PRODUCTION conscience; **~ gerbable** *f* TRANSPORT stacking pallet; **~ graphique** *f* INFORMAT, ORDINAT paintbox, TV graphic tablet, paintbox; **~ à jeter** *f* EMBALLAGE one-way pallet; **~ de manoeuvre** *f* AERONAUT actuating plate; **~ à montants** *f* EMBALLAGE stacking pallet, TRANSPORT post pallet; **~ perdue** *f* EMBALLAGE nonreturnable pallet, nonreusable pallet, TRANSPORT expendable pallet, one-way pallet; **~ à plancher débordant** *f* TRANSPORT stevedore-type pallet, wing pallet with projecting deck; **~ plate** *f* EMBALLAGE flat pallet; **~ porte-pièce** *f* CONS MECA workholding pallet; **~ à quatre entrées** *f* EMBALLAGE four-way pallet; **~ réversible** *f* TRANSPORT reversible pallet; **~ à roulettes** *f* TRANSPORT roller pallet; **~ à un seul plancher** *f* TRANSPORT single platform pallet, single-decked pallet; **~ à simple face** *f* TRANSPORT single-faced pallet; **~ à simple planche** *f* EMBALLAGE single-faced pallet; **~ sur coussin d'air** *f* TRANSPORT hover pallet; **~ transportable classique** *f* EMBALLAGE conventional transportable pallet

palette-caisse *f* EMBALLAGE box pallet; **~ à claire-voie** *f* EMBALLAGE box pallet with mesh

palettisable *adj* EMBALLAGE, TRANSPORT palletizable

palettisation *f* EMBALLAGE palletization, TRANSPORT palletization, palletizing

palettiser *vt* EMBALLAGE, TRANSPORT palletize

palier *m* AUTO main bearing, CONS MECA bearing block, bearing surface, bush, bushing, journal bearing, journal box, pedestal, pillow, pillow block, *arbre, axe* bearing, CONSTR landing, level, ELECTR *machine*, IMPRIM *mécanique*, MECANIQUE bearing, MINES cradle, walling scaffold, walling stage, NAUT engine bearing, PETROLE plateau level, PRODUCTION plummer block, TV porch, VEHICULES bearing; **~ d'alignement** *m* AERONAUT align-reaming box; **~ à alignement** *m* AERONAUT align-reaming box; **~ antifriction** *m* CONS MECA *roulement à rouleaux*, PRODUCTION *système hydraulique* antifriction bearing; **~ arrière** *m* TV back porch; **~ à billes** *m* CONS MECA ball bearing plummet block; **~ de butée** *m* CONS MECA thrust, thrust bearing, thrust block, MECANIQUE, NAUT thrust bearing; **~ de butée à patins** *m* MECANIQUE Kingsbury bearing; **~ de comptage** *m* TELECOM metering rate; **~ de congélation** *m* REFRIG freezing plateau; **~ à coussinets lisses** *m* CONS MECA plain bearing, NUCLEAIRE journal bearing; **~ déclinaison** *m* INSTRUMENT declination bearing; **~ de décompression** *m* OCEANO decompression stop; **~ de déplacement latéral** *m* CONS MECA traverse motion bearing; **~ d'échauffement** *m* THERMODYN overheat-

ing; **~ garni d'alliage antifriction** *m* CONS MECA bearing lined with antifriction metal; **~ à gaz** *m* MECANIQUE gas bearing, NUCLEAIRE gas lubricated bearing; **~ à graissage automatique par bagues** *m* CONS MECA oiled bearings; **~ à graissage automatique par chaîne** *m* CONS MECA chain-oiled bearing; **~ graisseur à bagues** *m* CONS MECA oiled bearings; **~ de guidage** *m* CONS MECA flanged guide; **~ hydrodynamique** *m* ESPACE *véhicules* hydrodynamic bearing; **~ hydrostatique** *m* MECANIQUE hydrostatic bearing; **~ intermédiaire** *m* AUTO center bearing (AmE), centre bearing (BrE), TV breezeway; **~ lisse** *m* CONS MECA plain bearing, NUCLEAIRE journal bearing, VEHICULES plain bearing; **~ lisse avec coussinets frittés** *m* CONS MECA plain bearing made from sintered material; **~ lisse de butée** *m* CONS MECA plain thrust bearing; **~ de machine** *m* CONS MECA engine bearing; **~ magnétique** *m* ESPACE *véhicules*, MECANIQUE magnetic bearing; **~ Mitchell** *m* MECANIQUE Kingsbury bearing; **~ mural** *m* MINES wall bearing; **~ du noir** *m* TV black porch, pedestal; **~ de pied** *m* CONS MECA footstep, footstep bearing, shaft step, step, step bearing, step box; **~ à potence** *m* MINES bracket hanger, wall bracket; **~ de poussée** *m* EN RENOUV thrust bearing; **~ principal** *m* CONSTR, NAUT, VEHICULES *moteur* main bearing; **~ de production** *m* PETROLE plateau level; **~ réacteur** *m* AERONAUT engine shaft bearing; **~ renforcé** *m* PRODUCTION heavy-type plummer block; **~ de repos** *m* CONSTR half space, landing, MINES stage; **~ à rotule** *m* CONS MECA swivel bearings, swivel hanger, swivel plummer block; **~ de roulement** *m* CONS MECA rolling bearing; **~ de secours** *m* ESPACE *véhicules* backup bearing; **~ à serrage** *m* CONS MECA friction-type bearing; **~ de transmission** *m* CONS MECA shaft bearing; **~ transversal** *m* PAPIER radial bearing; **~ de trépan** *m* PETR bit bearing; **~ de vilebrequin** *m* AUTO, VEHICULES *moteur* crankshaft bearing

palier-guide *m* INSTRUMENT guide bearing

palier-manivelle *m* CONS MECA crank bearing

paliers *m pl* CONS MECA, IMPRIM *mécanique* bearings; **~ à aiguilles** *m pl* CONS MECA needle roller bearings; **~ régulés** *m pl* CONS MECA babbitted cast-iron bearings

palis *m* CONSTR pale, paling

palissade *f* CONSTR palisade

palladeux *adj* CHIMIE palladious

palladique *adj* CHIMIE palladic

palladium *m (Pd)* CHIMIE palladium *(Pd)*

pallasites *m pl* ASTRONOMIE pallasites

palle *f* DISTRI EAU shut, shut-off

palmer *m* CONS MECA micrometer, micrometer calipers (AmE), micrometer callipers (BrE), EQUIP LAB *mesure d'épaisseur*, MECANIQUE *outillage*, METROLOGIE, PHYSIQUE micrometer; **~ d'extérieur** *m* CONS MECA external micrometer; **~ d'intérieur** *m* CONS MECA internal micrometer

palmier: ~ à huile de Guinée *m* AGRO ALIM oil palm

palmique *adj* CHIMIE *acide* palmic

palmitate *m* CHIMIE palmitate

palmitine *f* CHIMIE palmin, palmitin

palmitique *adj* CHIMIE *acide* palmitic

palmitone *f* CHIMIE palmitone

palonnier *m* AERONAUT crossbar, rudder bar, rudder pedal, MECANIQUE *matériel de levage*, TRANSPORT spreader; **~ de frein** *m* VEHICULES brake compensator; **~ orientation train avant** *m* AERONAUT nose gear steering base post

palpeur *m* AERONAUT cam follower, CONS MECA follower; ~ **aiguille** *m* CONS MECA *exploration de l'état de surface* needle follower; ~ **de calibrage électronique** *m* CONS MECA electronic gaging probe (AmE), electronic gauging probe (BrE); ~ **de contrôle ultrasonore** *m* CH DE FER ultrasonic probe; ~ **à ultrasons** *m* CONSTR ultrasonic probe

palplanche *f* CHARBON sheet pile, CONSTR pile plank, sheet pile, sheeting pile, MINES lagging piece; ~ **en acier** *f* CONSTR steel pile

palplanches *f pl* CONSTR sheet piling; ~ **jointives** *f pl* CONSTR close piling, sheet piling

palustre *adj* GEOLOGIE marshy

pan *m* CONS MECA pane, CONSTR frame, framing, *d'un mur* face, *d'un comble* side; ~ **d'amalgamation** *m* PRODUCTION grinding pan, pan mill, pan; ~ **de bois** *m* CONSTR timber frame, timber framing

PAN *abrév (peroxoacétylnitrate)* POLLUTION PAN *(peroxoacetylnitrate)*

panabase *f* MINERAUX panabase

panache *m* OCEANO, PHYS FLUID *écoulement thermique* plume, POLLUTION mist, plume; ~ **à la cheminée** *m* CERAM VER stack plume; ~ **de fumée** *m* POLLUTION steam-laden emission; ~ **mantellique** *m* GEOLOGIE mantle plume

pancarte *f* CH DE FER train service indicator, washboards

panchromatique *adj* CHIMIE, CINEMAT, IMPRIM, PHOTO panchromatic

pancréatine *f* CHIMIE pancreatin

pandermite *f* MINERAUX pandermite

pané *adj* AGRO ALIM coated

panflavine *f* CHIMIE panflavine

panier: ~ **à bouteilles** *m* EMBALLAGE bottle carrier; ~ **à cartes** *m* INFORMAT card cage; ~ **à charbon** *m* CHARBON coal basket; ~ **à coke** *m* CHARBON coke basket

panne:[1] **en ~** *adj* ELECTR *défaut* out-of-order

panne[2] *f* CONS MECA breakdown, failure, CONSTR breakdown, *pièce de bois* purlin, ELECTROTEC breakdown, failure, ESPACE *qualité*, INFORMAT, MECANIQUE failure, ORDINAT crash, failure, PHYSIQUE breakdown, PRODUCTION *d'un marteau* pane, SECURITE *d'une machine*, TELECOM breakdown; ~ **d'aérage** *f* CHARBON ventilation breakdown; ~ **d'alimentation** *f* ELECTROTEC power failure, PRODUCTION power outage; ~ **d'appentis** *f* CONSTR lean-to; ~ **bombée** *f* CONS MECA ball pane, ball peen, *de marteau* ball pean; ~ **de brisis** *f* CONSTR curb, curb plate; ~ **de courant** *f* ELECTROTEC power failure; ~ **douce** *f* ORDINAT soft fail; ~ **d'électricité** *f* CINEMAT power failure; ~ **d'émetteur** *f* TV transmitter failure; ~ **faîtière** *f* CONSTR ridge beam, ridge piece, ridge plate; ~ **filière** *f* CONSTR purlin; ~ **hydraulique** *f* SECURITE hydraulic failure; ~ **induite** *f* INFORMAT, ORDINAT induced failure; ~ **de moteur** *f* NAUT engine failure, VEHICULES engine breakdown; ~ **du pilon** *f* PRODUCTION die, top die, tup die, pallet for tup, top pallet, tup pallet; ~ **de réseau** *f* ELECTROTEC power failure, TELECOM network breakdown; ~ **de secteur** *f* CINEMAT, ELECTROTEC power failure; ~ **sphérique** *f* CONS MECA ball pean, ball peen, ball pane

panneau *m* CH DE FER signal, CHARBON, CONSTR, ELECTR *commande*, GAZ panel, GEOLOGIE screen, MINES, REFRIG, TEXTILE panel, VEHICULES *route* sign; ~ **absorbant perforé** *m* ENREGISTR perforated absorbent tile; ~ **d'accès** *m* AERONAUT access panel; ~ **acoustique** *m* ENREGISTR acoustic flat, acoustic tile, fissured acoustic tile; ~ **d'affichage plat** *m* ELECTRON flat panel display; ~ **d'aggloméré avec doublure** *m* EMBALLAGE lined chipboard; ~ **antibruit en mousse** *m* SECURITE noise-abating foam panel, sound-absorbent foam panel; ~ **arrière** *m* CONS MECA back-end plate, PRODUCTION backplane; ~ **avant** *m* CONS MECA front panel; ~ **avertisseur** *m* CONSTR warning sign, PRODUCTION *automatisme industriel* annunciator panel; ~ **de bordure** *m* AERONAUT edging panel; ~ **de branchement** *m* CINEMAT jack field; ~ **de brassage** *m* TV patch board, patch panel; ~ **capteur plat** *m* EN RENOUV *énergie solaire* flat plate collector; ~ **de cellules solaires** *m* ELECTROTEC solar cell panel; ~ **central** *m* AERONAUT center panel (AmE), centre panel (BrE); ~ **de chalut** *m* OCEANO otter board, trawl board; ~ **de chargement** *m* NAUT cargo hatch, TRANSPORT cargo hatchway; ~ **de chauffage** *m* CONS MECA heating panel; ~ **chauffant** *m* THERMODYN panel heater; ~ **chauffant en verre** *m* CERAM VER glass heating panel; ~ **à claire-voie** *m* CH DE FER clear light, deadlight; ~ **de commande** *m* INFORMAT, ORDINAT control panel, TV switchboard; ~ **de contrôle** *m* TEXTILE control panel; ~ **de couverture** *m* CONSTR *à l'orifice du puits* covering; ~ **à cristaux liquides** *m* ELECTRON LCD panel, liquid crystal display panel; ~ **de déchargement** *m* NAUT cargo hatch; ~ **de descente** *m* NAUT companionway hatch, hatch cover, washboards; ~ **de disjoncteur** *m* POLLU MER breaker board; ~ **de distribution** *m* TV switchboard; ~ **dur** *m* CONSTR *marque déposée*, EMBALLAGE hardboard; ~ **d'écoutille** *m* NAUT hatch cover; ~ **d'extrémité** *m* CONS MECA end panel; ~ **de fermeture** *m* CONS MECA closing panel; ~ **final** *m* EMBALLAGE end panel; ~ **de fusible** *m* ELECTROTEC fuse board; ~ **d'identification** *m* CH DE FER rolling stock label; ~ **indicateur** *m* ESPACE *véhicules* annunciator; ~ **indicateur variable** *m* TRANSPORT variable route sign; ~ **indicateur des voies** *m* CH DE FER track diagram; ~ **isolant** *m* EMBALLAGE insulating board; ~ **isolant à double vitrage** *m* REFRIG sandwich-paned insulating panel; ~ **latéral** *m* EMBALLAGE, VEHICULES *carrosserie* side panel; ~ **lumineux** *m* CH DE FER light signal; ~ **ouvrant** *m* CONS MECA hinged panel; ~ **de particules** *m* MECANIQUE *matériaux* particle board; ~ **de plafond** *m* AERONAUT overhead panel; ~ **de plancher** *m* AERONAUT floor panel; ~ **de porte** *m* CONSTR door panel; ~ **préfabriqué** *m* REFRIG prefabricated panel; ~ **de raccordement** *m* CINEMAT patch bay, patch field, TV patch panel; ~ **radiant infrarouge** *m* GAZ infrared radiant panel; ~ **rayonnant à gaz à température élevée** *m* MAT CHAUFF high-temperature gas radiant panel; ~ **réflecteur** *m* CINEMAT bounce board, fill-in screen, reflecting screen, reflector; ~ **refroidisseur** *m* REFRIG panel cooler; ~ **routier parlant** *m* TRANSPORT talking road sign; ~ **de sécurité** *m* EQUIP LAB safety placard, safety sign; ~ **de signalisation** *m* CONSTR direction sign, road sign, TRANSPORT traffic sign; ~ **de signalisation routière** *m* VEHICULES road sign; ~ **solaire** *m* ASTRONOMIE solar panel, ELECTROTEC solar cell panel, EN RENOUV, ESPACE *véhicules*, PHYSIQUE, TELECOM solar panel; ~ **sur plafond** *m* AERONAUT overhead panel; ~ **vertical** *m* TELECOM switchboard panel; ~ **de visite** *m* AERONAUT *cellule* inspection panel; ~ **de voûte** *m* CONSTR arch panel

panneau-signal *m* CH DE FER signal; ~ **à oculaire mobile coloré** *m* CH DE FER colored light signal (AmE), coloured light signal (BrE)

panneaux: ~ **radiants à rayons infrarouges** *m pl* MAT CHAUFF infrared panel heating; ~ **de signalisation contre les accidents** *m pl* SECURITE accident prevention advertising signs

panneresse *f* CONSTR stretcher

panneton *m* CONSTR bit, *d'une clé* web; ~ **de clef** *m* CONSTR key bit

pano: ~ **filé** *m* CINEMAT flash pan, flick pan, whip pan

panonceaux: ~ **phosphorescents de sûreté** *m pl* SECURITE phosphorescent safety signs

panoramique *m* CINEMAT pan; ~ **filé** *m* CINEMAT blur pan, swish pan, zip pan; ~ **vertical** *m* CINEMAT tilt

panorimaquer:[1] ~ **vers le bas** *vt* CINEMAT tilt down

panorimaquer[2] *vi* CINEMAT pan

pansement: ~ **stérile** *m* SECURITE *pour traitement des plaies* sterile dressing

pantalon *m* CINEMAT changing bag

pantellérite *f* PETR pantellerite

pantographe *m* CH DE FER *véhicules*, CONS MECA, ELECTR *chemin de fer* pantograph

pantothénate *m* CHIMIE pantothenate; ~ **de calcium** *m* AGRO ALIM calcium pantothenate

PAO *abrév (publication assistée par ordinateur)* IMPRIM, INFORMAT, ORDINAT DTP *(desktop publishing)*

Paon *m* ASTRONOMIE Pavo

papaïne *f* AGRO ALIM, CHIMIE papain

papavéraldine *f* CHIMIE papaveraldine

papavérine *f* CHIMIE papaverine

papeterie *f* PAPIER, RECYCLAGE paper mill

papier *m* PAPIER paper, paper draw; ▪**~ a** ~ **abrasif** *m* ELECTR *nettoyage*, IMPRIM, MECANIQUE *outillage* abrasive paper; ~ **absorbant** *m* IMPRIM absorbent paper, PAPIER waterleaf paper; ~ **accordéon** *m* INFORMAT fanfold stationery, ORDINAT fanfold paper (BrE), fanfold stationery (BrE); ~ **d'agrandissement** *m* PHOTO printing paper; ~ **albuminé** *m* PAPIER albumenized paper; ~ **alfa** *m* IMPRIM esparto paper; ~ **d'aluminium** *m* AGRO ALIM, PAPIER aluminium foil (BrE), aluminum foil (AmE); ~ **antiasthmatique** *m* PAPIER asthma paper, nitrate paper; ~ **anticorrosif** *m* EMBALLAGE anticorrosion paper, corrosion preventive paper; ~ **antigel** *m* PAPIER antifreeze paper; ~ **antirouille** *m* EMBALLAGE, PAPIER antirust paper; ~ **antiternissure** *m* PAPIER antitarnish paper; ~ **apprêté** *m* IMPRIM machine-finished paper; ~ **armé** *m* MATERIAUX reinforced paper; ~ **autocollant** *m* EMBALLAGE pressure-sensitive paper, self-adhesive paper; ~ **autocopiant** *m* IMPRIM, PAPIER carbonless copy paper; ~ **avec bois** *m* IMPRIM, PAPIER wood paper; ~ **avion** *m* IMPRIM, PAPIER airmail paper; ▪**~ b** ~ **de base** *m* IMPRIM, PAPIER base paper; ~ **berzélius** *m* CERAM VER polishing paper; ~ **bible** *m* IMPRIM bible paper; ~ **bitumé** *m* PAPIER asphalt paper, tarpaper (AmE), tarred brown paper (BrE); ~ **bituminé** *m* CONSTR bituminized paper; ~ **à border** *m* PAPIER edging paper; ~ **bouffant** *m* PAPIER bulking paper, paper swelling; ~ **bromure** *m* IMPRIM bromide paper; ~ **au bromure donnant doux** *m* PHOTO soft bromide paper; ~ **au bromure donnant dur** *m* PHOTO hard bromide paper; ~ **buvard** *m* PAPIER blotting paper; ▪**~ c** ~ **calandré humide** *m* IMPRIM, PAPIER water-finished paper; ~ **à calquer** *m* CONS MECA tracing paper; ~ **à canneler** *m* PAPIER fluting corrugating paper, fluting paper; ~ **à canneler pour carton ondulé** *m* PAPIER corrugating medium, fluting medium, fluting corrugating medium; ~ **carbone** *m* IMPRIM, PAPIER carbon

paper; ~ **carton apprêté** *m* PAPIER MF paperboard, machine-finished paperboard; ~ **carton calandré** *m* PAPIER calendered paperboard; ~ **carton à plat** *m* PAPIER paper board in the flat; ~ **charbon** *m* IMPRIM carbon tissue; ~ **au charbon hélio** *m* IMPRIM gravure tissue; ~ **de chiffons** *m* IMPRIM rag paper, PAPIER all-rag paper, rag paper; ~ **chiné** *m* PAPIER veined paper; ~ **au chlorure d'argent** *m* PHOTO chloride paper; ~ **collé** *m* PAPIER sized paper, REVETEMENT coated paper; ~ **collé en surface** *m* IMPRIM surface-sized paper; ~ **collé à la pâte** *m* IMPRIM ES paper; ~ **coloré deux faces** *m* PAPIER two-side colored paper (AmE), two-side coloured paper (BrE); ~ **coloré une face** *m* PAPIER one-side colored paper (AmE), one-side coloured paper (BrE); ~ **comprimé** *m* PAPIER presspaper; ~ **conditionné** *m* IMPRIM quired paper; ~ **contrecollé** *m* PAPIER pasted paper; ~ **couché** *m* IMPRIM art paper, coated paper, PAPIER art paper, coated paper, REVETEMENT coated paper; ~ **couché anti-adhésif** *m* PAPIER release-coated paper, resilience; ~ **couché à la barre filetée** *m* PAPIER road-coated paper; ~ **couché à la brosse** *m* PAPIER brush-coated paper; ~ **couché à chaud** *m* IMPRIM hot-melt-coated paper; ~ **couché une face** *m* IMPRIM one-side art paper, one-side coated paper; ~ **couché une fois** *m* PAPIER single-coated paper; ~ **couché à lame d'air** *m* PAPIER air knife coated paper; ~ **couché à lame traînante** *m* PAPIER trailing-blade coated paper; ~ **couché machine** *m* EMBALLAGE machine-coated paper; ~ **couché mousse** *m* PAPIER bubble-coated paper; ~ **couché par émulsion** *m* PAPIER emulsion-coated paper; ~ **couché par extrusion** *m* PAPIER extrusion-coated paper; ~ **couché par fusion** *m* PAPIER hot-melt-coated paper; ~ **couché par gravure** *m* PAPIER gravure-coated paper; ~ **couché par voile** *m* PAPIER curtain-coated paper; ~ **couché à la presse encolleuse** *m* PAPIER size-press-coated paper; ~ **couché au rouleau** *m* PAPIER roll-coated paper; ~ **couché au solvant** *m* PAPIER solvent-coated paper; ~ **couché au trempé** *m* PAPIER dip-coated paper; ~ **couverture kraft** *m* EMBALLAGE kraft liner; ~ **crêpé** *m* EMBALLAGE, PAPIER crepe paper; ~ **crêpé à double face** *m* EMBALLAGE double-face crepe paper; ~ **cristal** *m* AGRO ALIM glassine; ~ **à la cuve** *m* IMPRIM hand-made paper; ▪**~ d** ~ **deux couches** *m* PAPIER two-layer paper; ~ **diélectrique** *m* PAPIER electrical insulating paper; ~ **doublé métal** *m* EMBALLAGE metallic paper; ~ **à doubler** *m* PAPIER liner paper; ~ **double toile** *m* PAPIER twin-wire paper; ~ **de doublure** *m* IMPRIM *reliure* lining paper; ~ **doublure** *m* IMPRIM coating paper; ▪**~ e** ~ **électrosensible** *m* INFORMAT, ORDINAT electrosensitive paper; ~ **d'emballage** *m* PAPIER wrapping paper; ~ **d'emballage paraffiné** *m* EMBALLAGE oil packing paper; ~ **émerisé** *m* PRODUCTION emery paper; ~ **en bobine** *m* IMPRIM roll paper; ~ **en cartouche** *m* IMPRIM cartridge paper; ~ **encollé** *m* EMBALLAGE coated paper; ~ **en continu** *m* IMPRIM continuous stationery, ORDINAT continuous forms (AmE), continuous stationery (BrE), continuous-feed paper (AmE); ~ **enduit** *m* EMBALLAGE, REVETEMENT coated paper; ~ **enduit de matière synthétique** *m* EMBALLAGE coated synthetic paper; ~ **d'enregistrement** *m* INSTRUMENT recording paper; ~ **en relief** *m* EMBALLAGE embossed paper; ~ **entoilé** *m* PAPIER cloth-lined paper, reinforced paper; ~ **entre-**

deux fils *m* PAPIER cloth-centered paper (AmE), cloth-centred paper (BrE); ~ **entre-deux toiles** *m* PAPIER cloth-centred paper (BrE); ~ **épais** *m* PHOTO double weight paper;

~ f ~ **à filer** *m* PAPIER spinning paper; ~ **fini en machine** *m* IMPRIM mill-finished paper; ~ **fini machine** *m* EMBALLAGE machine-finished paper; ~ **à la forme** *m* IMPRIM mold paper (AmE), mould paper (BrE); ~ **frictionné** *m* EMBALLAGE, IMPRIM, PAPIER MG paper, machine-glazed paper;

~ g ~ **garniture** *m* IMPRIM back lining; ~ **gaufré** *m* PAPIER embossed paper; ~ **au gélatino-bromure** *m* PHOTO bromide paper; ~ **glacé** *m* EMBALLAGE glazed paper, high gloss paper, IMPRIM, PAPIER glazed paper; ~ **glacé albumineux** *m* IMPRIM albumenized paper; ~ **gommé** *m* EMBALLAGE gummed paper; ~ **goudronné** *m* EMBALLAGE tarpaper, PAPIER *papier d'emballage* tarred brown paper; ~ **goudronné renforcé** *m* PAPIER reinforced union paper; ~ **grainé** *m* PAPIER grained paper; ~ **grand format** *m* PAPIER large paper;

~ i ~ **ignifugé** *m* PAPIER fire-resistant paper; ~ **imperméable à la graisse** *m* EMBALLAGE, PAPIER grease-resistant paper; ~ **imprégné** *m* EMBALLAGE, IMPRIM impregnated paper; ~ **imprégné d'huile** *m* EMBALLAGE oil-drenched paper; ~ **d'impression** *m* IMPRIM printing paper; ~ **indicateur** *m* EMBALLAGE, PHOTO indicator paper; ~ **infalsifiable** *m* PAPIER safety paper; ~ **ingraissable** *m* PAPIER grease-resistant paper, greaseproof paper; ~ **isolant** *m* ELECTR, PAPIER insulating paper;

~ j ~ **jacquard** *m* EMBALLAGE, PAPIER jacquard paper; ~ **joseph** *m* GENIE CHIM filter paper; ~ **journal** *m* IMPRIM, PAPIER newsprint;

~ k ~ **kraft** *m* EMBALLAGE, PAPIER kraft paper; ~ **kraft pour sacs** *m* EMBALLAGE kraft sack paper;

~ l ~ **laminé** *m* EMBALLAGE paper laminate; ~ **léger** *m* IMPRIM thin paper;

~ m ~ **machine à écrire** *m* IMPRIM bank paper; ~ **mat** *m* IMPRIM mat surface paper, matt paper, PHOTO matt paper; ~ **métallisé** *m* EMBALLAGE metalized paper (AmE), metallized paper (BrE), PAPIER foil craft; ~ **mince** *m* PAPIER lightweight paper, PHOTO single weight paper; ~ **de mise en cartes** *m* EMBALLAGE cartridge paper; ~ **de montagne** *m* MINERAUX mountain paper; ~ **mousseline** *m* PAPIER wrapping tissue; ~ **multicouches** *m* PAPIER multilayer paper;

~ n ~ **neutre** *m* IMPRIM acid-free paper; ~ **non acide** *m* EMBALLAGE, PAPIER acid-free paper; ~ **non apprêté** *m* IMPRIM, PAPIER paper without finish; ~ **non oxydant** *m* PAPIER nonrust paper; ~ **non ternissant** *m* PAPIER nontarnish paper;

~ o ~ **ondulé** *m* EMBALLAGE corrugated cardboard, corrugated paper; ~ **ozalid** *m* IMPRIM ozalid paper;

~ p ~ **de paille mixte** *m* PAPIER mixed strawpaper; ~ **paraffiné** *m* EMBALLAGE kerosene-impregnated paper (AmE), paraffin-impregnated paper (BrE), paraffin-waxed paper (BrE), wax paper, IMPRIM wax paper; ~ **paraffiné à double face** *m* EMBALLAGE double-face wax paper; ~ **parcheminé** *m* AGRO ALIM greaseproof paper, parchment paper (AmE), EMBALLAGE greaseproof paper; ~ **de pâte mécanique** *m* PAPIER mechanical woodpulp paper; ~ **peint** *m* REVETEMENT paper wallcovering; ~ **peint anaglyptique** *m* REVETEMENT Anaglypta (TM), Anaglyptic wallpaper (TM); ~ **peint ingrain** *m* REVETEMENT woodchip wall covering, woodchip wallpaper; ~ **à pliage accordéon** *m* ORDINAT fanfold paper (BrE), fanfold stationery (BrE); ~ **à pliage paravent** *m* ORDINAT fanfold paper (BrE), fanfold stationery (BrE); ~ **pour affiches** *m* PAPIER poster paper; ~ **pour billet de banque** *m* PAPIER banknote paper (BrE), onionskin paper (AmE); ~ **pour câbles électriques** *m* PAPIER paper for conductor insulation; ~ **pour calque** *m* PAPIER oil tracing paper; ~ **pour cartes géographiques** *m* PAPIER map paper; ~ **pour cartes perforées** *m* PAPIER paper for punched cards, tabulating card paper; ~ **pour cartouches** *m* PAPIER cartridge paper; ~ **pour condensateur** *m* PAPIER capacitor tissue paper; ~ **pour demi-teintes** *m* IMPRIM halftone paper; ~ **pour documents de longue conservation** *m* PAPIER archival paper, paper for long storage documents; ~ **pour doublage de caisse** *m* PAPIER crate liners; ~ **pour duplicateur à alcool** *m* PAPIER spirit duplicator copy paper; ~ **pour duplicateur à stencil** *m* PAPIER stencil duplicator copy paper; ~ **pour enveloppes postales** *m* PAPIER envelope paper; ~ **pour étiquettes** *m* IMPRIM label stock; ~ **pour impression hélio** *m* IMPRIM copperplate printing paper; ~ **pour imprimante** *m* IMPRIM print files, printout paper; ~ **pour isolants stratifiés** *m* PAPIER paper for laminated insulators; ~ **pour machine à écrire** *m* PAPIER typewriter paper; ~ **pour rouleaux de calandre** *m* PAPIER calender bowl paper; ~ **pour sacs** *m* EMBALLAGE bag paper; ~ **pour sortie d'ordinateur** *m* IMPRIM printing-out paper, printout paper; ~ **pour support carboné** *m* PAPIER carbonizing base paper; ~ **pour support carbone une fois** *m* PAPIER one-time-carbonizing base paper; ~ **pour support carbone multifois** *m* PAPIER multiple-use carbonizing base paper; ~ **pour tubes de filature** *m* PAPIER paper for textile paper tubes; ~ **procédé** *m* IMPRIM scraper board; ~ **protecteur** *m* PHOTO film backing; ~ **de protection** *m* PHOTO backing paper; ~ **pur chiffon** *m* PAPIER all-rag paper; ~ **pure paille** *m* PAPIER yellow strawpaper;

~ q ~ **quadrillé** *m* CONSTR plotting paper, PAPIER graph paper, scale paper; ~ **qui a du corps** *m* PAPIER bulky paper;

~ r ~ **RC photographique** *m* IMPRIM resin-coated paper; ~ **à réactif** *m* CHIMIE test paper; ~ **recyclé** *m* EMBALLAGE, RECYCLAGE recycled paper; ~ **réglé** *m* GEOMETRIE lined paper; ~ **renforcé** *m* EMBALLAGE reinforced paper; ~ **résistant aux acides** *m* IMPRIM acid-proof paper; ~ **résistant aux alcalis** *m* EMBALLAGE alkali-proof paper; ~ **résistant à l'état humide** *m* PAPIER wet strength paper; ~ **de revêtement pour caisses** *m* EMBALLAGE case lining paper; ~ **revêtu de bitume** *m* EMBALLAGE bitumen-coated paper;

~ s ~ **sans acide** *m* IMPRIM acid-free paper; ~ **sans bois** *m* PAPIER woodfree paper; ~ **sans cendres** *m* PAPIER ashless paper; ~ **sans pâte mécanique** *m* IMPRIM groundwood-free paper; ~ **satiné** *m* IMPRIM, PAPIER SC paper, supercalendered paper, REVETEMENT enamelled paper (AmE), enamelled paper (BrE), glazed paper; ~ **séché à l'air** *m* IMPRIM air-dry paper; ~ **de sécurité** *m* IMPRIM safety paper, PAPIER security paper; ~ **sensible** *m* PHOTO sensitive paper; ~ **de séparation** *m* EMBALLAGE anti-adhesive paper; ~ **siliconé servant de support aux adhésifs** *m* IMPRIM backing paper; ~ **simili-sulfurisé** *m* PAPIER greaseproof paper; ~ **de soie** *m* EMBALLAGE tissue paper; ~ **spécial** *m* IMPRIM safety paper; ~ **sulfurisé** *m* PAPIER, PRODUCTION *véritable* vegetable parchment; ~ **sup-**

port *m* IMPRIM, PAPIER base paper; ~ **support photographique** *m* PAPIER photographic base paper; ~ **support pour stencil** *m* PAPIER duplicating stencil base paper; ~ **support pour tenture** *m* PAPIER wallpaper base; ~ **surfacé** *m* PAPIER surface-sized paper; ~ **surglacé** *m* PAPIER imitation art paper;
~ t ~ **thermique** *m* IMPRIM thermal paper; ~ **thermocollant** *m* REVETEMENT heat-set adhesive paper; ~ **thermosoudable** *m* EMBALLAGE, REVETEMENT heat-sealable paper; ~ **de tournesol** *m* CHIMIE litmus paper; ~ **de tournesol bleu** *m* CHIMIE blue litmus paper; ~ **de tournesol rouge** *m* CHIMIE red litmus paper; ~ **trois couches** *m* PAPIER three-layer paper;
~ u ~ **ultradoux** *m* PHOTO extrasoft paper; ~ **ultradur** *m* PHOTO extrahard paper; ~ **ultraléger** *m* IMPRIM featherweight paper;
~ v ~ **vélin** *m* IMPRIM, PAPIER wove paper; ~ **vergé** *m* IMPRIM, PAPIER laid paper; ~ **vergé fini caoutchouc** *m* EMBALLAGE laid paper with rubber appearance; ~ **de verre** *m* MECANIQUE *outillage* sandpaper, PRODUCTION glasspaper, sandpaper; ~ **verré** *m* PRODUCTION glasspaper, sandpaper

papier-calque *m* CONS MECA tracing paper, PAPIER translucent drawing paper

papier-émeri *m* IMPRIM sandpaper, MECANIQUE *outillage* abrasive paper, emery paper, PRODUCTION emery paper

papier-filtre *m* CHIMIE, EQUIP LAB *filtration*, GENIE CHIM, PAPIER filter paper; ~ **sans cendres** *m* AGRO ALIM, EQUIP LAB ashless filter paper

papier-parchemin *m* AGRO ALIM greaseproof paper; ~ **végétal** *m* EMBALLAGE parchment paper

papiers: ~ **de bord** *m pl* NAUT ship's papers; ~ **pour chromatographie** *m pl* EQUIP LAB *analyse* chromatography papers; ~ **pour formulaires carbonés** *m pl* PAPIER carbonized forms

papillon *m* CONS MECA thumbnut, CONSTR butterfly nut, finger nut, INST HYDR throttle valve, PRODUCTION fly nut, hand nut, VEHICULES *carburateur* throttle; ~ **des gaz** *m* AUTO butterfly, throttle valve; ~ **de réglage** *m* AUTO throttle plate

papillonnage *m* DISTRI EAU swinging across the face

papillote *f* AGRO ALIM fruit wrapper

papillotement *m* TELECOM flickering, TV flicker; ~ **auditif** *m* ACOUSTIQUE aural flutter; ~ **chromatique** *m* TV chromatic flicker; ~ **de trame** *m* TV field rate flicker

paquebot *m* NAUT, TRANSPORT liner, passenger ship; ~ **atlantique** *m* NAUT ocean liner

paquet *m* CH DE FER *de rails* bundle, INFORMAT packet, MINES *de minerai* patch, splash, PAPIER parcel, PRODUCTION pile, TELECOM packet, TEXTILE package, packet, TRANSPORT parcel; ~ **d'appel** *m* TELECOM call setup packet; ~ **de demande de libération** *m* TELECOM clear request packet; ~ **de données** *m* ESPACE *communications* data burst, INFORMAT, ORDINAT packet, TELECOM data packet; ~ **d'eau** *m* DISTRI EAU feed; ~ **d'erreurs** *m* INFORMAT error burst; ~ **glissé** *m* GEOLOGIE landslide block; ~ **de mer** *m* OCEANO green sea, heavy sea; ~ **d'ondes** *m* PHYSIQUE wave packet; ~ **de référence** *m* ESPACE *communications* reference burst

paquetage *m* PRODUCTION piling

paqueter *vt* PRODUCTION pile

paquets *m pl* MINES *de minerai* splashes

parabanique *adj* CHIMIE parabanic

parabenzène *m* CHIMIE parabenzene

parabole *f* GEOMETRIE parabola, parabole, TV dishpan

parabolique *adj* PHYSIQUE square-law

parachor *m* CHIMIE parachor

parachute *m* ESPACE parachute, parafoil, *véhicules* chute; ~ **auxiliaire** *m* MILITAIRE auxiliary parachute; ~ **avec pilote** *m* MILITAIRE parachute with pilot; ~ **frein** *m* TRANSPORT deceleration parachute; ~ **de freinage** *m* ESPACE parabrake, *véhicules* drag chute; ~ **de queue** *m* AERONAUT drag chute, TRANSPORT brake parachute; ~ **retardateur** *m* MILITAIRE retarder parachute; ~ **stabilisateur** *m* ESPACE *véhicules* drogue chute

parachute-frein *m* ESPACE *véhicules* brake chute, drogue chute, TRANSPORT drag parachute

parachuter *vt* TRANSPORT airdrop

parachutiste *m* MILITAIRE parachutist

parachymosine *f* CHIMIE parachymosin

paracousie *f* ACOUSTIQUE paracusis

paracrésol *m* CHIMIE p-cresol, paracresol

paracyanogène *m* CHIMIE paracyanogen

paradiaphonie *f* ELECTROTEC near end crosstalk

paradichlorobenzène *m* CHIMIE paradichlorobenzene

paradière *f* OCEANO pound net

paradigme *m* INFORMAT, ORDINAT paradigm

paradoxe: ~ **des jumeaux** *m* PHYSIQUE twin paradox; ~ **de l'obscurité du ciel nocturne** *m* ASTRONOMIE paradoxical darkness of the night sky

paraffinage *m* CINEMAT waxing, IMPRIM *papier* wax impregnation

paraffine *f* CHIMIE, MATERIAUX *chimie*, PETROLE kerosene (AmE), paraffin (BrE); ~ **liquide** *f* CHIMIE liquid paraffin; ~ **solide** *f* CHIMIE paraffin wax

paraffinique *adj* CHIMIE paraffinic

parafoudre *m* ELECTR *sécurité* lightning arrester, lightning rod, ELECTROTEC arrester, lightning arrester, ESPACE *véhicules* lightning arrester, GEOPHYS lightning arrester, lightning protection fuse, SECURITE lightning protector; ~ **à éclateur** *m* ELECTR *sécurité* air gap protector; ~ **à expulsion** *m* ELECTROTEC expulsion-type lightning arrester; ~ **pour surtensions** *m* GEOPHYS lightning surge arrester

parafoudres: ~ **à haute tension** *m pl* SECURITE lightning arresters for high voltage

parafouille *m* DISTRI EAU cutoff trench, cutoff wall, OCEANO cutoff trench

paragénèse *f* GEOLOGIE mineral assemblage, paragenesis

parages *m pl* NAUT sea area, waters

paragonite *f* MINERAUX paragonite

paragraphe *m* INFORMAT, ORDINAT paragraph

parahydrogène *m* CHIMIE parahydrogen

paraisomère *m* CHIMIE paraisomer

paraison *f* CERAM VER parison

paraldéhyde *m* CHIMIE paraldehyde

paralique *adj* GEOLOGIE *milieu de transition continental ou marin* paralic

parallactique *adj* ASTRONOMIE *relatif à la parallaxe* parallactic

parallaxe *f* ASTRONOMIE, CINEMAT, CONS MECA, PHOTO, PHYSIQUE parallax; ~ **annuelle** *f* ASTRONOMIE annual parallax; ~ **diurne** *f* ASTRONOMIE diurnal parallax; ~ **héliocentrique** *f* ASTRONOMIE heliocentric parallax; ~ **trigonométrique** *f* ASTRONOMIE trigonometrical parallax

parallèle: **en** ~ *adj* ELECTROTEC shunt, PHYSIQUE in parallel ELECTR *montage*, GEOMETRIE, INFORMAT, ORDINAT, TEXTILE parallel

parallèlement: ~ **à** *adv* GEOMETRIE parallel

parallélisation *f* ELECTROTEC serial-to-parallel conversion; ~ **des fibres** *f* TEXTILE parallelization of fibers (AmE), parallelization of fibres (BrE)

paralléliseur *m* ELECTROTEC serial-to-parallel converter

parallélisme *m* CONS MECA, GEOMETRIE, IMPRIM, TEXTILE parallelism; ~ **des cambrages** *m* RESSORTS cambering parallelism

parallélogramme *m* GEOMETRIE, MECANIQUE parallelogram; ~ **des forces** *m* GEOMETRIE, PHYSIQUE parallelogram of forces; ~ **des vitesses** *m* PHYSIQUE parallelogram of velocities

paramagnétique *adj* ELECTR *matériel*, PHYSIQUE paramagnetic

paramagnétisme *m* ELECTR, PHYSIQUE paramagnetism

paramétrage *m* INFORMAT, ORDINAT parameterization

paramètre *m* ELECTRON, INFORMAT, ORDINAT, PHYSIQUE parameter; ~ **d'activation** *m* METALL activation parameter; ~ **de circulation** *m* TRANSPORT traffic parameter; ~ **dynamique** *m* INFORMAT, ORDINAT dynamic parameter; ~ **de flux axial** *m* AERONAUT inflow ratio; ~ **formel** *m* INFORMAT, ORDINAT formal parameter; ~ **H** *m* ELECTRON hybrid parameter; ~ **de Hubble** *m* ASTRONOMIE Hubble parameter; ~ **hybride** *m* ELECTRON hybrid parameter; ~ **d'impact** *m* PHYSIQUE impact parameter; ~ **de masse de l'avion** *m* AERONAUT aeroplane mass ratio (BrE), airplane mass ratio (AmE); ~ **de mot clé** *m* INFORMAT keyword parameter; ~ **pour signaux de faible amplitude** *m* ELECTRON small-signal parameter; ~ **de profil** *m* OPTIQUE profile parameter; ~ **de programme** *m* INFORMAT, ORDINAT program parameter; ~ **réel** *m* ORDINAT actual parameter; ~ **de réseau** *m* METALL lattice constant; ~ **de similitude** *m* AERONAUT *hélice* advance diameter ratio; ~ **Y** *m* ELECTRON Y-parameter; ~ **de Zener-Hollomon** *m* METALL Zener-Hollomon parameter

paramètres: ~ **de forage** *m pl* PETROLE drilling conditions; ~ **de maille** *m pl* CRISTALL cell parameters, unit cell parameters; ~ **mémorisés gérant la composition** *m pl* IMPRIM styles; ~ **de réseau** *m pl* CRISTALL lattice parameters; ~ **Z** *m pl* ELECTRON Z-parameters

paramétrique *adj* INFORMAT, ORDINAT parametric

parangonnage *m* IMPRIM alignment

parangonner *vt* IMPRIM *composition* line up, *typographie* align

paranthine *f* MINERAUX paranthine

parapet *m* CONSTR parapet

pararosaniline *f* CHIMIE pararosaniline

parasitage *m* TELECOM interference

parasite[1] *adj* ELECTRON parasitic, PHYSIQUE stray

parasite[2] *m* ELECTR *faute* interference, MINERAUX parasite

parasites *m pl* ELECTRON interference, ENREGISTR static, PHYS ONDES noise, TV interference, noise, static; ~ **atmosphériques** *m pl* ELECTRON, ELECTROTEC atmospherics, GEOPHYS atmospheric interference, atmospherics; ~ **à bande étroite** *m pl* ELECTRON narrow band interference; ~ **électromagnétiques** *m pl* ELECTROTEC, PRODUCTION *électricité* electromagnetic interference; ~ **électrostatiques** *m pl* ELECTROTEC static; ~ **à haute fréquence** *m pl* ELECTRON radio interference; ~ **industriels** *m pl* ELECTRON interference noise, ELECTROTEC industrial interference; ~ **à large bande** *m pl* ELECTRON wide band interference; ~ **magnétiques** *m pl* GEOPHYS magnetic interference; ~ **radioélectriques** *m pl* ELECTRON radio interference; ~

rayonnés *m pl* ELECTROTEC radiated interference; ~ **de télévision** *m pl* ELECTRON television interference

parasoleil *m* CINEMAT lens hood, INSTRUMENT dew cap, PHOTO hood; ~ **avec porte-filtre et porte-cache** *m* CINEMAT matt box; ~ **d'objectif** *m* PHOTO lens hood; ~ **pour objectif** *m* PHOTO lens hood

parasurtenseur *m* ELECTR surge arrester, *transmission* surge absorber

paratartarique *adj* CHIMIE paratartaric

paratonnerre *m* ELECTR *sécurité* lightning arrester, lightning rod, ELECTROTEC, GEOPHYS lightning conductor, SECURITE lightning conductor (BrE), lightning rod (AmE)

paraxylène *m* CHIMIE p-xylene, paraxylene, PETROLE paraxylene

parc *m* CONSTR yard, MINES depot, OCEANO fish pond, weir bed, TRANSPORT *voitures, camions* fleet; ~ **d'artillerie** *m* MILITAIRE artillery park; ~ **automobile** *m* CONSTR parking area; ~ **à bois** *m* MINES timberyard; ~ **à charbon** *m* CHARBON coal yard; ~ **à châssis** *m* PRODUCTION box yard; ~ **à ferraille** *m* PRODUCTION scrap yard; ~ **à fonte** *m* PRODUCTION pig iron yard, pig yard; ~ **à matières** *m* CONSTR stock yard; ~ **de stationnement** *m* CONSTR parking area; ~ **à tiges** *m* PETROLE pipe rack; ~ **voiture** *m* CH DE FER *véhicules* fleet; ~ **wagons** *m* CH DE FER fleet

parcelle *f* CONSTR block

parchemin: ~ **de veau** *m* IMPRIM calf vellum; ~ **végétal** *m* PRODUCTION *industrie du papier* vegetable parchment

parcmètre *m* TRANSPORT parking meter

parcomètre *m* TRANSPORT parking meter

parcourir[1] *vt* INFORMAT, ORDINAT browse, PHYSIQUE cover

parcourir:[2] ~ **les mers** *vi* NAUT sail over the seas

parcours *m* AERONAUT course, route, CINEMAT threading path, PHYSIQUE distance; ~ **à l'atterrissage** *m* AERONAUT landing run; ~ **d'éloignement** *m* AERONAUT reciprocal leg; ~ **libre moyen** *m* METALL mean free path; ~ **de réglage** *m* COMMANDE regulating distance

par-dessus: ~ **bord** *adv* NAUT overboard

pare-battage *m* NAUT fender

pare-boue *m* VEHICULES *carrosserie* mud flap, mudguard (BrE)

pare-brise *m* CERAM VER windscreen (BrE), windshield (AmE), CH DE FER *véhicules* driver's windscreen (BrE), driver's windshield (AmE), windscreen (BrE), windshield (AmE), ESPACE *véhicules*, VEHICULES *carrosserie* windscreen (BrE), windshield (AmE); ~ **en verre feuilleté** *m* VEHICULES *carrosserie* laminated windscreen (BrE), laminated windshield (AmE)

pare-buffle *m* AUTO bullbar

pare-chocs *m* AUTO, MECANIQUE, VEHICULES *carrosserie* bumper (BrE), fender (AmE); ~ **arrière** *m* AUTO rear bumper (BrE), rear fender (AmE); ~ **avant** *m* AUTO front bumper (BrE), front fender (AmE)

parée: ~ **d'une recherche** *f* PETR depth of an investigation

pare-écume *m* HYDROLOGIE scum baffle

pare-étincelles *m* ELECTROTEC spark suppressor, VEHICULES *moteur* flame trap

pare-feu[1] *adj* SECURITE fireproof, flameproof

pare-feu[2] *m* SECURITE fire screen, THERMODYN firebreak

pare-flamme *m* ESPACE *véhicules* flame arrester

parement *m* CONSTR facing, *d'un mur, d'un talus* face, MINES wall; ~ **aval** *m* HYDROLOGIE downstream face; ~ **extérieur** *m* CERAM VER facing block

pare-moteur *m* VEHICULES *lubrification du moteur* sump guard

parent *m* INFORMAT, ORDINAT parent

parenthèse *f* IMPRIM bracket, parenthesis

pare-poussière *m* AUTO dust seal, CHARBON dust guard, VEHICULES *levier de commande des vitesses* dust boot

parer[1] *vt* IMPRIM *reliure* pare, NAUT fend off, *cap, quai* clear, *navire* give a wide berth to, PRODUCTION trim; **~ à** *vt* SECURITE guard against

parer:[2] **~ un abordage** *vi* NAUT fend off a collision

pare-ringard *m* PRODUCTION *de porte de foyer* sill plate

pare-soleil *m* AERONAUT glare shield, AUTO, SECURITE sun visor (BrE), sun vizor (AmE)

parfaitement: ~ lié *adj* MATERIAUX perfectly bonded

parfum *m* CHIMIE scent

pargasite *f* MINERAUX pargasite

parité *f* INFORMAT, ORDINAT, PHYS RAYON, PHYSIQUE parity; **~ 8 à entrelacement de bits** *f* TELECOM BIP-8, bit interleaved parity 8, bit interleaved parity order 8; **~ entrelacée bit d'ordre 8** *f* TELECOM BIP-8, bit interleaved parity 8, bit interleaved parity order 8; **~ d'entrelacement des bits** *f* TELECOM BIP, bit interleaved parity; **~ impaire** *f* INFORMAT, ORDINAT, PHYSIQUE odd parity; **~ longitudinale** *f* INFORMAT, ORDINAT horizontal parity; **~ paire** *f* INFORMAT, ORDINAT, PHYSIQUE even parity; **~ verticale** *f* INFORMAT, ORDINAT vertical parity; **~ X à entrelacement de bits** *f* TELECOM BIP-X, bit interleaved parity-X

parking *m* CONSTR parking area

paroi *f* CONSTR, MINES, PHYS FLUID *d'un canal, d'un tuyau* wall, PRODUCTION *d'un cylindre, d'une chaudière* wall, *d'un four* wall; **~ adiabatique** *f* PHYSIQUE adiabatic wall; **~ amont** *f* CERAM VER gable wall; **~ antibruit** *f* SECURITE noise-abating wall, sound-absorbent wall; **~ d'antiphase** *f* CRISTALL antiphase boundary; **~ aval** *f* CERAM VER front wall; **~ de calorifugeage** *f* AERONAUT heat-insulating wall; **~ de cylindre** *f* AUTO, VEHICULES *moteur* cylinder wall; **~ de dislocation** *f* CRISTALL dislocation wall; **~ interne** *f* TELECOM inner wall; **~ latérale** *f* MINES *d'une galerie de mine* side, sidewall, wall; **~ latérale à claire-voie** *f* TRANSPORT sidewall with ventilation flaps; **~ mobile** *f* CINEMAT flat; **~ moulée** *f* CHARBON slurry trench wall; **~ de séparation** *f* CONSTR, NUCLEAIRE partition

parois:[1] **à ~ minces** *adj* CONS MECA thin-walled

parois[2] *f pl* MINES *d'un filon* cheeks, sidewall; **~ de séparateur** *f pl* POLLUTION scrubber walls

parole: ~ artificielle *f* TELECOM simulated speech; **~ comprimée** *f* ELECTRON compressed speech; **~ numérique** *f* ELECTRON digital speech

parpaing *m* CONSTR bond, bond stone, bonder, perpend, perpend stone, through-binder, through-stone

parquer *vt* OCEANO *huîtres* lay down

parquet *m* CONSTR floor; **~ en arête de poisson** *m* CONSTR herringbone pattern parquet flooring; **~ à point de Hongrie** *m* CONSTR herringbone pattern parquet flooring

parquetage *m* CONSTR decking

parqueter *vt* CONSTR board, floor

parre *m* CONSTR binding beam

parsec *m* PHYSIQUE parsec

partage *m* CHIMIE, ELECTROTEC partitioning, HYDROLOGIE *des eaux* braiding, INFORMAT, ORDINAT sharing, TELECOM trunking; **~ des eaux** *m* HYDROLOGIE parting of the waters; **~ de fichier** *m* INFORMAT, ORDINAT file sharing; **~ du film d'encre** *m* IMPRIM *impression* film splitting; **~ de ressources** *m* INFORMAT, ORDINAT resource sharing; **~ du temps** *m* INFORMAT, ORDINAT, TELECOM time sharing

partager *vt* INFORMAT, ORDINAT share

partance: en ~ *adj* NAUT *navire* outward bound; **en ~ pour** *adj* NAUT bound for

particulaire *adj* PHYS PART particle-like

particularisation *f* PRODUCTION customization

particule *f* ACOUSTIQUE, CHARBON, ELECTRON, PHYS PART, PHYSIQUE, SECURITE, TEXTILE particle; **~ aciculaire** *f* METALL needle-shaped particle; **~ acide** *f* POLLUTION acid particle, acidic particle; **~ alpha** *f* ASTRONOMIE, ELECTR *particule chargée*, PHYS PART, PHYS RAYON, PHYSIQUE alpha particle; **~ bêta** *f* ELECTR *particule chargée*, NUCLEAIRE, PHYS PART, PHYSIQUE beta particle; **~ bombardante** *f* NUCLEAIRE impinging particle, incident particle; **~ chargée** *f* ELECTROTEC, PHYS PART, POLLUTION charged particle; **~ cohérente** *f* METALL coherent particle; **~ à court parcours** *f* NUCLEAIRE short-range particle; **~ de désintégration** *f* PHYS PART decay particle; **~ élémentaire** *f* PHYS PART, PHYSIQUE elementary particle; **~ élémentaire de haute énergie** *f* PHYS PART high-energy elementary particle; **~ émise** *f* NUCLEAIRE outcoming particle; **~ en suspension** *f* POLLUTION suspended particle; **~ de faible parcours** *f* NUCLEAIRE short-range particle; **~ de fluide** *f* PHYS FLUID fluid particle; **~ gamma** *f* PHYS PART gamma particle; **~ germe** *f* NUCLEAIRE initiating particle; **~ à haute énergie** *f* ELECTRON high-energy particle; **~ de Higgs** *f* PHYS PART Higgs particle; **~ incidente** *f* NUCLEAIRE impinging particle, incident particle; **~ ionisante** *f* PHYS RAYON ionizing particle; **~ J** *f* PHYSIQUE J-particle; **~ lambda** *f* PHYSIQUE lambda particle; **~ lourde** *f* GAZ heavy particle; **~ magnétique** *f* TV magnetic particle; **~ mésique** *f* CHIMIE meson; **~ neutre** *f* PHYSIQUE neutral particle; **~ non enrobée** *f* NUCLEAIRE uncoated fuel particle; **~ nue** *f* NUCLEAIRE *mathématique* bare particle, mathematical particle; **~ oméga moins** *f* PHYSIQUE omega minus particle; **~ piégée** *f* NUCLEAIRE trapped particle; **~ de plasma** *f* GEOPHYS plasma particle; **~ rapide** *f* NUCLEAIRE fast particle, high-speed particle; **~ rayonnante** *f* PHYS PART radiating particle; **~ relativiste** *f* ESPACE relativistic particle; **~ secondaire** *f* NUCLEAIRE secondary particle; **~ sigma** *f* PHYSIQUE sigma particle; **~ subatomique** *f* PHYSIQUE subatomic particle; **~ tau** *f* PHYS PART *lepton lourd* tau particle; **~ à triple enrobage** *f* NUCLEAIRE triplex-coated particle; **~ virtuelle** *f* PHYS PART virtual particle; **~ virtuelle chargée** *f* PHYS PART virtual charged particle; **~ virtuelle neutre** *f* PHYS PART virtual neutral particle; **~ W** *f* PHYS PART, PHYSIQUE W-particle; **~ xi** *f* PHYSIQUE xi particle; **~ Z** *f* PHYS PART Z-particle

particules: ~ en suspension dans l'air *f pl* METEO airborne particles; **~ ferromagnétiques** *f pl* MATERIAUX ferromagnetic particles; **~ de poussière** *f pl* POLLUTION dust particles; **~ qui s'échappent sans interagir** *f pl* PHYS RAYON particles which escape without interacting; **~ solides** *f pl* POLLUTION particulate matter, solid particles; **~ suprasymétriques** *f pl* PHYS RAYON supersymmetrical particles; **~ transitoires** *f pl* PHYS PART short-lived particles

partie *f* CHIMIE moiety, INFORMAT, ORDINAT part, PRODUCTION section, VEHICULES part; **~ caractérisante** *f* BREVETS characterizing portion; **~ centrale de la coque** *f* NAUT midship body; **~ centrale du tube** *f*

INSTRUMENT tube center (AmE), tube centre (BrE); ~ **chaude** *f* AERONAUT *d'un réacteur* hot section; ~ **du domaine initial** *f* TELECOM IDP, initial domain part; ~ **à faible rendement** *f* ELECTRON low-yield region; ~ **fixe** *f* PRODUCTION stationary portion; ~ **fractionnaire** *f* INFORMAT, ORDINAT fractional part; ~ **froide** *d'un réacteur* *f* AERONAUT cold section; ~ **haute fréquence** *f* ELECTRON RF section; ~ **HF** *f* ELECTRON RF section; ~ **humide** *f* CINEMAT, PAPIER wet end; ~ **inférieure** *f* IMPRIM bottom; ~ **lisse** *f* CONS MECA *d'une vis* plain length; ~ **du matériel par laquelle pénètre la matière première** *f* IMPRIM infeed; ~ **montante** *f* IMPRIM *d'un caractère* ascender; ~ *au noir* *f* CINEMAT *d'une développeuse* wet end; ~ **non étanche** *f* AERONAUT *fuselage* nonpressurized section; ~ **ouverte d'un cahier** *f* IMPRIM *fabrication* face; ~ **ouvrière** *f* CONS MECA working part; ~ **projection d'une tireuse optique** *f* CINEMAT tailgate; ~ **propre** *f* INFORMAT, ORDINAT proper subset; ~ **radiale de la fonction d'onde** *f* PHYS RAYON radial part of the wave function; ~ **solidaire du satellite après séparation** *f* ESPACE *véhicules* afterbody; ~ **spécifique du domaine** *f* TELECOM DSP, domain-specific part; ~ **terminale déformable** *f* TRANSPORT deformable rear section; ~ **travaillante** *f* CONS MECA working part

partiel *adj* ACOUSTIQUE partial

partiellement: ~ **obligatoire** *adj (PO)* TELECOM conditionally mandatory *(CM)*

parties *f pl* CONSTR *d'une charpente* members; ~ **frottantes d'une machine** *f pl* CONS MECA wearing parts of a machine; ~ **par million** *f pl* CHIMIE PPM, parts-per-million

partir: ~ **à la dérive** *vi* CH DE FER *véhicules* run away; ~ **au lof** *vi* NAUT broach; ~ **au tapis** *vi* NAUT broach

partition *f* EMBALLAGE partition wall, ENREGISTR score, INFORMAT, ORDINAT partition

partitionné *adj* INFORMAT partitioned

partitionnement *m* INFORMAT partitioning

partitionner *vt* INFORMAT partition

parton *m* PHYSIQUE parton

parvoline *f* CHIMIE parvoline

pas:[1] ~ **en mesure de se conformer** *adj* TELECOM unable to comply; ~ **en phase** *adj* ELECTRON out-of-phase; ~ **maître de sa commande** *adj* NAUT *navire* NUC; ~ **maître de sa manoeuvre** *adj* NAUT *navire* NUC, not under command

pas[2] *m* CINEMAT pitch, CONS MECA thread, *d'un engrenage, d'une chaîne, de vis* pitch, ELECTR *bobine*, ELECTROTEC pitch, INFORMAT pitch, step, MECANIQUE *de filetage*, NAUT, OPTIQUE pitch, ORDINAT pitch, step, PHOTO *entre perforations* pitch, PHYSIQUE pitch, spacing, PRODUCTION *de séquenceur* step, TEXTILE shed; ~ **américain système Sellers** *m* CONS MECA Sellers thread, US standard thread; ~ **apparent** *m* CONS MECA apparent pitch, divided pitch; ~ **d'assemblage** *m* ELECTR *constituant d'un câble* length of lay; ~ **de l'aubage** *m* EN RENOUV *turbines* blade pitch; ~ **bâtard** *m* CONS MECA fractional pitch, odd pitch, *vis et écrous* bastard pitch; ~ **circonférentiel** *m* CONS MECA arc pitch, circular pitch; ~ **circulaire** *m* CONS MECA arc pitch, circular pitch, MECANIQUE *engrenages* circular pitch; ~ **collectif** *m* AERONAUT collective pitch; ~ **court** *m* CINEMAT short pitch; ~ **cyclique** *m* AERONAUT cyclic pitch; ~ **cyclique latéral** *m* AERONAUT lateral cyclic pitch; ~ **cyclique longitudinal** *m* AERONAUT fore-and-aft cyclic pitch; ~ **à droite** *m* CONS MECA right-hand

thread; ~ **d'écriture** *m* ORDINAT row pitch; ~ **d'écrou** *m* CONS MECA inside thread; ~ **effectif** *m* AERONAUT effective pitch; ~ **en cours d'exécution** *m* PRODUCTION *automatisme industriel* step-in effect; ~ **d'enroulement** *m* ELECTR coil pitch, *bobine* winding pitch; ~ **exact** *m* CONS MECA even pitch; ~ **de filetage** *m* CONS MECA, VEHICULES thread pitch; ~ **à fileter** *m* CONS MECA pitch to be cut; ~ **de freinage** *m* AERONAUT braking pitch, TRANSPORT brake pitch; ~ **de gaz** *m* PRODUCTION gas thread; ~ **général** *m* AERONAUT collective pitch, *hélicoptère* collective pitch angle; ~ **géométrique** *m* AERONAUT *hélice* geometric pitch; ~ **géométrique relatif** *m* AERONAUT *hélice* pitch diameter ratio; ~ **de l'hélice** *m* AERONAUT propeller pitch, RESSORTS spring pitch; ~ **d'hélice en drapeau** *m* AERONAUT feathered pitch; ~ **inter-assemblage** *m* NUCLEAIRE assembly pitch; ~ **inverse** *m* AERONAUT *hélice* reverse pitch; ~ **large** *m* CONS MECA coarse thread; ~ **long** *m* CINEMAT *des perforations* long pitch; ~ **longitudinal** *m* INFORMAT, ORDINAT row pitch; ~ **de la maille** *m* NUCLEAIRE lattice pitch, lattice pitch spacing; ~ **moyen** *m* AERONAUT mean pitch angle; ~ **multicyclique** *m* AERONAUT high-order cyclic pitch; ~ **de la nappe** *m* IMPRIM shingle distance; ~ **négatif** *m* AERONAUT reverse pitch, CINEMAT short pitch; ~ **nominal** *m* AERONAUT *hélice* standard pitch; ~ **de perforations** *m* CINEMAT perforation pitch; ~ **de pistes** *m* ENREGISTR track pitch; ~ **positif** *m* CINEMAT positive pitch, print pitch; ~ **réel** *m* CONS MECA total pitch, true pitch; ~ **du réseau** *m* NUCLEAIRE lattice pitch, lattice pitch spacing; ~ **de sillonnage** *m* ACOUSTIQUE diametral groove pitch; ~ **des sillons** *m* ENREGISTR groove spacing; ~ **système international** *m* CONS MECA international standard thread; ~ **de torsade** *m* ELECTROTEC lay; ~ **transversal** *m* INFORMAT, OPTIQUE track pitch; ~ **variable** *m* RESSORTS variable pitch; ~ **de vis** *m* CONS MECA screw pitch, screw thread; ~ **de vis de fixation** *m* PHOTO fixing thread; ~ **de la vis mère** *m* CONS MECA pitch of lead screw; ~ **Whitworth** *m* CONS MECA BSW thread, British Standard Whitworth thread, Whitworth screw thread, Whitworth thread

pas[3] **à ne ~ marcher** *loc* AERONAUT no-step; **ne ~ jeter** *loc* EMBALLAGE *inscription, étiquette de manutention* do not throw, not to be thrown; **ne ~ laisser tomber** *loc* EMBALLAGE *inscription ou étiquette de manutention* do not drop, not to be dropped; ~ **d'opérateur** *loc* TELECOM *maritime mobile* no operator available; **ne ~ renverser** *loc* EMBALLAGE *inscription ou étiquette de manutention* keep upright, to be kept upright; **ne ~ repasser** *loc* TEXTILE *instruction ou étiquette de manutention* drip-dry

pas-à-pas *m* CINEMAT inching

pascal *m (Pa)* METROLOGIE, PETROLE *unité de mesure de pression*, PHYSIQUE pascal *(Pa)*

passage *m* ASTRONOMIE transit, CERAM VER take-down, CONS MECA aperture, CONSTR thoroughfare, INFORMAT *d'un programme* running, MINES passageway, *pour les hommes* manhole, manway, NAUT fairway, ORDINAT running, PRODUCTION passage, pass; ~ **d'air** *m* CONS MECA air passage; ~ **annulaire** *m* NUCLEAIRE *interstice* annular gap; ~ **archipélagique** *m* OCEANO archipelagic passage; ~ **automatique** *m* TELECOM automatic changeover; ~ **automatique à la ligne** *m* IMPRIM, INFORMAT, ORDINAT word wrap; ~ **au bassin** *m* NAUT docking; ~ **de câbles** *m* ELECTROTEC raceway; ~ **carrossable** *m* CONSTR *d'une route* roadway; ~ **de**

chaleur *m* THERMODYN heat transition; ~ **à la claie** *m* PRODUCTION screening; ~ **clouté** *m* COMMANDE pedestrian crossing, pedestrian only crossing; ~ **commandé par piétons** *m* COMMANDE pedestrian-controlled crossing; ~ **à commande des piétons** *m* COMMANDE pedestrian-controlled crossing; ~ **au crible** *m* PRODUCTION screening; ~ **de criticité** *m* NUCLEAIRE passage of criticality; ~ **dur** *m* CONS MECA friction point; ~ **en dessus** *m* CH DE FER overpass; ~ **d'escalier** *m* CONSTR staircase, stairway; ~ **d'essai** *m* INFORMAT dry run, test run, ORDINAT dry run, test run, test run; ~ **étanche** *m* NUCLEAIRE tight penetration; ~ **à l'état conducteur** *m* ELECTROTEC turn-on; ~ **à l'état non conducteur** *m* ELECTROTEC turn-off; ~ **au gaz** *m* CHIMIE gassing; ~ **inférieur** *m* CH DE FER underpass, CONSTR underbridge, underpass, TRANSPORT railroad underbridge (AmE), railway underbridge (BrE); ~ **de la ligne** *m* NAUT crossing the line; ~ **machine** *m* CONS MECA machine run; ~ **au méridien** *m* ASTRONOMIE culmination, ESPACE *orbitographie* meridian transit; ~ **à niveau** *m* CH DE FER, CONSTR, TRANSPORT grade crossing (AmE), level crossing (BrE); ~ **normal-secours** *m* TELECOM changeover to stand-by; ~ **papier** *m* IMPRIM web lead, *impression, rotatives* web path; ~ **de paramètres** *m* INFORMAT, ORDINAT parameter passing; ~ **par zéro** *m* ELECTROTEC zero crossing; ~ **piétons** *m* CONSTR pedestrian subway; ~ **pour piétons** *m* COMMANDE pedestrian crossing, pedestrian only crossing; ~ **de programme** *m* INFORMAT, ORDINAT run; ~ **réglementé** *m* COMMANDE controlled crossing; ~ **réservé aux piétons** *m* COMMANDE pedestrian only crossing; ~ **sans issue** *m* CONSTR blind alley; ~ **souterrain** *m* CH DE FER underpass, CONSTR pedestrian subway; ~ **supérieur** *m* CH DE FER overpass, TRANSPORT flyover, railroad overbridge (AmE), railway overbridge (BrE); ~ **supérieur de chemin de fer** *m* TRANSPORT bridge under railroad (AmE), bridge under railway (BrE); ~ **supérieur de la route** *m* TRANSPORT road over railway; ~ **sur rame** *m* TEXTILE tentering; ~ **au tamis** *m* PRODUCTION sifting; ~ **traversée** *m* NUCLEAIRE penetration unit; ~ **de Vénus d'un bord à l'autre du Soleil** *m* ASTRONOMIE transit of Venus across the sun

passager[1] *adj* ESPACE passenger

passager[2] *m* AERONAUT passenger

passagers: ~ **en transit** *m pl* TRANSPORT transit passengers

passant[1] *adj* PRODUCTION *automatisme industriel* gated on

passant[2] *m* CHARBON undersize

passe *f* CONS MECA cut, operation, HYDROLOGIE navigable channel, IMPRIM overrun, overs, waste sheets, INFORMAT pass, MECANIQUE *outillage* cut, NAUT fairway, pass, ORDINAT pass, PRODUCTION going over, pass, stage; ~ **chaude** *f* PETR hot pass; ~ **de dégrossissage** *f* PRODUCTION roughing pass; ~ **étroite** *f* NAUT *entre deux caps* narrows; ~ **de fond** *f* MECANIQUE *soudage* root pass, PETR root bead, root pass; ~ **à poisson** *f* EN RENOUV fish pass; ~ **à poisson de type à débordement** *f* EN RENOUV overfall-type fish pass; ~ **de remplissage** *f* PETR filler pass; ~ **de soutien** *f* PRODUCTION backing pass; ~ **de teinture** *f* TEXTILE batch

passé *m* CHARBON undersize

passe-bande *m* ENREGISTR pass band, PETR band-pass

passe-bas *m* AERONAUT low-pass

passe-courroie *m* CONS MECA strike gear, striker, striking gear

passe-fil *m* ELECTROTEC grommet; ~ **étanche** *m* NAUT through-deck cable fitting

passe-film *m* PHOTO *d'un agrandisseur* negative carrier

passe-partout *m* CONSTR, PRODUCTION master key

passe-poil *m* CONS MECA edging

passer[1] *vt* CONSTR cross, HYDROLOGIE *l'eau, une rivière* ford, NAUT *cordage dans une poulie* reeve; ~ **à** *vt* CINEMAT cut to; ~ **à l'antenne** *vt* TV switch to air; ~ **au chinois** *vt* AGRO ALIM sift; ~ **au crible** *vt* GENIE CHIM sieve; ~ **à la filière** *vt* PRODUCTION draw; ~ **au filtre** *vt* GENIE CHIM filter; ~ **au flou** *vt* CINEMAT defocus; ~ **au large de** *vt* NAUT steer clear of; ~ **au tamis** *vt* AGRO ALIM sieve, sift, GENIE CHIM sieve; ~ **à travers** *vt* HYDROLOGIE percolate through; ~ **au travers de** *vt* HYDROLOGIE run through; ~ **à la vapeur** *vt* AGRO ALIM, TEXTILE steam

passer[2] ~ **une annonce** *vi* IMPRIM advertise; ~ **au large** *vi* NAUT *d'un navire* give a wide berth; ~ **de la marche par engrenages à la marche à la volée** *vi* CONS MECA change over from gear-drive to belt-drive; ~ **par-dessus ses berges** *vi* HYDROLOGIE *rivière* overtop its banks, burst its bank, overflow its banks; ~ **par un opérateur** *vi* TELECOM go via the circuit

passerelle *f* AERONAUT jetway, CONSTR catwalk, walkway, footbridge, walkway, ESPACE *véhicules* walkway, INFORMAT gateway, MECANIQUE catwalk, gallery, walkway, NAUT gangplank, *navire* bridge, NUCLEAIRE catwalk, ORDINAT, TELECOM gateway, TRANSPORT footbridge; ~ **de commandement** *f* NAUT bridge; ~ **de débarquement** *f* NAUT gangway; ~ **d'embarquement** *f* NAUT gangway; ~ **en dessus** *f* CH DE FER footbridge; ~ **haute** *f* NAUT flying bridge; ~ **de navigation** *f* NAUT navigating bridge; ~ **de niveau application** *f* TELECOM application level gateway; ~ **de réseau** *f* TELECOM network gateway; ~ **supérieure** *f* NAUT flying bridge; ~ **télescopique** *f* AERONAUT aerobridge, air bridge, boarding bridge, passenger bridge

passette *f* TEXTILE guide

passeur: ~ **d'échantillons** *m* NUCLEAIRE sample changer

passe-vues: ~ **automatique** *m* PHOTO automatic slide changer; ~ **va-et-vient** *m* PHOTO slide changer

passif *adj* ELECTRON, INFORMAT, ORDINAT passive

passivation *f* CHIMIE, ELECTRON, PHYSIQUE passivation; ~ **à verre** *f* ELECTRON glass passivation; ~ **au verre** *f* ELECTRON glass passivation, glassivation

passivé *adj* PHYSIQUE passivated

passiver[1] *vt* CHIMIE passivate

passiver[2] *vi* ELECTRON, PHYSIQUE passivate

passoire *f* CONSTR sieve; ~ **en grès** *f* CERAM VER earthenware sieve

passure: ~ **en colle** *f* IMPRIM gluing up

pasteurisation *f* AGRO ALIM, GENIE CHIM, THERMODYN pasteurization; ~ **HTST** *f* AGRO ALIM HTST, high-temperature short time

pasteurisé *adj* THERMODYN pasteurized

pasteuriser *vt* AGRO ALIM, GENIE CHIM, THERMODYN pasteurize

pastillage *m* CERAM VER china ornamentation, MATERIAUX pelletizing

pastille *f* ELECTRON chip, MATERIAUX, PLAST CAOU *plastiques* pellet; ~ **d'aluminium** *f* NUCLEAIRE aluminium pellet (BrE), aluminum pellet (AmE); ~ **de bioxyde d'uranium** *f* NUCLEAIRE UO_2 pellet, uranium dioxide pellet; ~ **de bioxyde d'uranium-oxyde de gadolinium** *f*

NUCLEAIRE UO2-Gd2-O3 pellet, urania-gadolinia pellet; ~ **de contact** *f* ELECTRON bonding pad; ~ **de positionnement** *f* CONS MECA locating disc (BrE), locating disk (AmE); ~ **de silicium** *f* ELECTR *électronique*, ORDINAT silicon chip; ~ **d'UO2** *f* NUCLEAIRE UO2 pellet, uranium dioxide pellet

pastilleuse: ~ **rotative à grand rendement** *f* EMBALLAGE high-speed rotary tablet compression machine

PAT *abrév (protection automatique de trains)* CH DE FER ATP (BrE) *(automatic train protection)*

pataras *m* NAUT backstay

patch: ~ **de raccordement jack** *m* ENREGISTR jack panel

pâte *f* CERAM VER body, CHIMIE mull, ESPACE *véhicules* paste, IMPRIM pulp, PAPIER pulp, stock, PLAST CAOU dough; ~ **acceptée** *f* PAPIER accepted stock; ~ **d'alfa** *f* PAPIER esparto pulp; ~ **de bambou** *f* PAPIER bamboo pulp; ~ **au bisulfite** *f* PAPIER sulfite pulp (AmE), sulphite pulp (BrE); ~ **blanchie** *f* PAPIER bleached pulp; ~ **de bois** *f* IMPRIM chemical wood pulp, paper pulp, PAPIER woodpulp; ~ **de bois chimique** *f* IMPRIM chemical pulp, chemical wood pulp; ~ **de bois de résineux** *f* PAPIER softwood pulp; ~ **de cacao** *f* AGRO ALIM cocoa mass; ~ **céramique** *f* CERAM VER clay mass; ~ **chemico-thermicomécanique de copeaux** *f* PAPIER chemicothermomechanical pulp; ~ **de chiffon** *f* PAPIER rag pulp; ~ **chimique** *f* IMPRIM chemical pulp, chemical wood pulp, PAPIER chemical pulp; ~ **au chlore** *f* PAPIER soda-chlorine pulp; ~ **combustible** *f* NUCLEAIRE paste fuel; ~ **de couchage** *f* REVETEMENT coating color (AmE), coating colour (BrE), coating slip; ~ **de cuir** *f* PAPIER leather pulp; ~ **à détacher** *f* LESSIVES detergent paste; ~ **diamantée** *f* METALL diamond paste; ~ **dissolvante** *f* PAPIER dissolving pulp; ~ **écrue** *f* PAPIER unbleached pulp; ~ **épurée** *f* PAPIER accepted stock; ~ **de feuillus** *f* PAPIER hardwood pulp; ~ **de fruits à pectine** *f* AGRO ALIM pectin jelly; ~ **grasse** *f* PAPIER wet stock; ~ **hautement blanchie** *f* PAPIER fully-bleached pulp; ~ **à haut rendement** *f* PAPIER high-yield pulp; ~ **humide** *f* PAPIER wet pulp; ~ **isolante** *f* EMBALLAGE insulating compound; ~ **kraft** *f* PAPIER kraft pulp; ~ **maigre** *f* PAPIER free stock, thin stock; ~ **mécanique** *f* EMBALLAGE mechanical woodpulp, PAPIER mechanical pulp, mechanical woodpulp; ~ **mécanique brune** *f* PAPIER brown mechanical pulp; ~ **mécanique de défibreur** *f* PAPIER groundwood pulp; ~ **mécanique de meule** *f* PAPIER groundwood; ~ **mi-blanchie** *f* PAPIER semibleached pulp; ~ **mi-chimique** *f* PAPIER semichemical pulp; ~ **de paille** *f* PAPIER straw pulp; ~ **de paille lessivée** *f* PAPIER yellow straw pulp; ~ **à papier** *f* DISTRI EAU pulp, PAPIER paper making pulp, RECYCLAGE paper pulp; ~ **pour gravure au cachet** *f* CERAM VER stamp etching paste; ~ **pour gravure mate** *f* CERAM VER matt-etching paste; ~ **pour gravure profonde** *f* CERAM VER deepetching paste; ~ **pour transformation chimique** *f* PAPIER dissolving pulp; ~ **de rodage** *f* PRODUCTION lapping compound; ~ **à roder** *f* CONS MECA, MECANIQUE grinding paste, PRODUCTION grinding paste, lapping compound; ~ **sèche** *f* PAPIER dry pulp; ~ **séchée à l'air** *f* IMPRIM, PAPIER air-dry pulp; ~ **à la soude** *f* PAPIER soda pulp; ~ **au sulfate** *f* PAPIER sulfate pulp (AmE), sulphate pulp (BrE); ~ **de sulfate** *f* PAPIER kraft pulp; ~ **au sulfite neutre** *f* PAPIER neutral sulfite pulp, neutral sulphite pulp (BrE); ~ **thermomécanique de copeaux** *f* PAPIER thermomechanical pulp; ~ **travaillée** *f* PAPIER stuff; ~ **de vieux papiers**

désencrés *f* PAPIER deinked paper stock; ~ **de viscose** *f* PRODUCTION viscose pulp

patentage *m* MAT CHAUFF *sidérurgie* patenting

patente: ~ **de santé** *f* NAUT bill of health

patère *f* CONSTR base

pathéine *f* CINEMAT cement, splicing cement

pathogène *adj* HYDROLOGIE pathogenic

patin *m* ACOUSTIQUE advance ball, CH DE FER *véhicules* shoe, CONS MECA slipper, *d'une happe* heel, *de la crosse du piston* shoe, CONSTR footing block, sole piece, *d'une enclume* foot, *d'un palier* sill plate, *d'une happe* toe, MECANIQUE pad, runner, skid, NUCLEAIRE segment, shoe, PRODUCTION muller, sole plate, *d'une cuve d'amalgamation* shoe, *d'un palier* sole, *du tiroir* face flange; ~ **à billes** *m* CONS MECA ball pad; ~ **de chenille** *m* MILITAIRE pad; ~ **de la crosse** *m* CONS MECA crosshead gib, crosshead shoe, crosshead slipper; ~ **de palier de butée** *m* MECANIQUE bearing pad; ~ **presseur** *m* CINEMAT *de la fenêtre de projection*, ENREGISTR, PHOTO pressure pad; ~ **de pression** *m* AUTO pressure pad; ~ **de queue** *m* AERONAUT tailskid; ~ **de rail** *m* CH DE FER rail base, rail flange, rail foot; ~ **à roulettes** *m* IMPRIM *manipulations* skate

patinage *m* AUTO wheel slip, PRODUCTION *des cylindres d'un laminoir* slipping; ~ **de l'embrayage** *m* AUTO, VEHICULES clutch slip; ~ **d'une roue** *m* AUTO spinning of the wheel

patine *f* CHIMIE, MATERIAUX patina

patiner *vi* CONS MECA slip

patins: ~ **d'atterrissage** *m pl* TRANSPORT landing skids; ~ **de repos** *m pl* TRANSPORT rest skids

patouille *f* CONS MECA patouillet

patouillet *m* CONS MECA patouillet

patron *m* CONS MECA template, templet, PRODUCTION former, patron, pattern, TEXTILE pattern

patrouilleur *m* MILITAIRE patrol boat, patrol craft, NAUT, POLLU MER patrol boat; ~ **motopropulsé** *m* MILITAIRE motor-propelled patrol boat

patte *f* CONS MECA holdfast, ELECTROTEC pin, EMBALLAGE tab, MECANIQUE lug, tab, NAUT becket, fluke, reef cringle, PAPIER *d'enveloppe* flap, PRODUCTION lug, tab; ~ **d'attache du moteur** *f* AUTO engine support plug, VEHICULES engine support lug; ~ **du câble** *f* MINES cable end; ~ **de chien** *f* PETR, PETROLE dogleg; ~ **à crochet** *f* CONSTR pipestrap; ~ **d'élingue** *f* CONS MECA dog, dog hook, PRODUCTION sling dog; ~ **d'extraction de module** *f* PRODUCTION *automatisme industriel* module extraction pad; ~ **de lièvre** *f* CH DE FER wing rail; ~ **de métallisation** *f* PRODUCTION bonding tab; ~ **d'oie** *f* NAUT *d'un cordage, d'une chaîne* bridle; ~ **de puce** *f* ELECTRON beam lead; ~ **de ris** *f* NAUT becket, reef cringle; ~ **de verrouillage** *f* PRODUCTION locking lab

pattes: ~ **d'araignées** *f pl* CONS MECA oil groove; ~ **d'embarcation** *f pl* NAUT boat slings; ~ **d'oies** *f pl* IMPRIM *pliage* gusset wrinkles

paumelle: ~ **double** *f* CONSTR H-hinge

pause *f* (Bel) CERAM VER *main d'oeuvre* shop, IMPRIM *photographie* exposure

pauvreté *f* MINES baseness, low grade, poor grade

pavage *m* CONSTR pavement (BrE), paving (AmE); ~ **asphaltique** *m* CONSTR asphalt surfacing; ~ **bétonné** *m* CONSTR *routes* pavement (BrE); ~ **en briques** *m* CONSTR brick pavement (BrE), brick paving (AmE); ~ **en cailloux** *m* CONSTR pebble paving (AmE), pebble pavement (BrE)

pavé *m* CERAM VER pavement light, CONSTR pavement

(BrE), paving (AmE), paving stone, set; **~ de distribution** *m* IMPRIM *composition* routing block; **~ en dalles** *m* CONSTR flagstone pavement; **~ en granit** *m* CONSTR set, sett; **~ numérique** *m* INFORMAT, ORDINAT numeric keypad; **~ tactile** *m* ORDINAT touchpad

pavement *m* CONSTR pavement (BrE), paving (AmE)

paveur *m* CONSTR pavior (AmE), paviour (BrE)

pavillon *m* CH DE FER *véhicules* roof, NAUT ensign, flag, pennant, TELECOM *de l'écouteur* earpiece, VEHICULES *carrosserie* roof; **~ acoustique** *m* ACOUSTIQUE horn; **~ alphabétique** *m* NAUT signal flag; **~ aperçu** *m* NAUT answering pennant; **~ de beaupré** *m* NAUT jack, jack flag; **~ du code** *m* NAUT code flag; **~ de compagnie** *m* NAUT house flag; **~ de complaisance** *m* NAUT flag of convenience; **~ conique** *m* ACOUSTIQUE conical horn; **~ de courtoisie** *m* NAUT courtesy ensign; **~ de départ** *m* NAUT Blue Peter; **~ exponentiel** *m* ACOUSTIQUE exponential horn; **~ à lanterneau** *m* CH DE FER *véhicules* clerestory roof; **~ de manche à air** *m* NAUT ventilator cowl; **~ marchand** *m* NAUT red ensign; **~ de partance** *m* NAUT Blue Peter; **~ de pilote** *m* NAUT pilot flag; **~ de poupe** *m* NAUT stern flag; **~ pour signaux** *m* COMMANDE signal flag; **~ Q** *m* NAUT Q-flag; **~ de quarantaine** *m* NAUT quarantine flag, yellow flag; **~ de signaux** *m* NAUT signal flag

pavois *m* NAUT bulwarks

pavoiser[1] *vt* NAUT *navire* dress

pavoiser[2] *vi* NAUT dress ship overall

pays: **~ accidenté** *m* CONSTR broken country; **~ tourmenté** *m* CONSTR broken country

paysagiste *m* PHOTO landscape photographer

Pb *(plomb)* CHIMIE Pb *(lead)*

PC *abrév* CH DE FER *(poste de commande)* control center (AmE), control centre (BrE), signal box (BrE), signal tower (AmE), switch tower (AmE)

PCS *abrév (pouvoir calorifique supérieur)* CHAUFFAGE, GAZ gross calorific value

Pd *(palladium)* CHIMIE Pd *(palladium)*

peau *f* AERONAUT, IMPRIM *encre, reliure*, PLAST CAOU *plastiques* skin; **~ de chamois** *f* CONSTR, PRODUCTION chamois; **~ de crapaud** *f* CERAM VER hogging; **~ de crocodile** *f* PLAST CAOU *défaut de caoutchouc* alligatoring; **~ crue** *f* PRODUCTION green hide; **~ décollée** *f* ESPACE *véhicules* unbonded skin; **~ d'étanchéité** *f* NUCLEAIRE liner; **~ d'orange** *f* PLAST CAOU *défaut de peinture* orange peel; **~ de porc** *f* IMPRIM pigskin; **~ rugueuse** *f* CERAM VER *de verre* pockmarks; **~ verte** *f* PRODUCTION green hide

PEB *abrév (puissance équivalente de bruit)* OPTIQUE *d'un photodétecteur*, TELECOM NEP *(noise equivalent power)*

pechblende *f* CHIMIE, MINERAUX pitchblende, NUCLEAIRE uranium black

pêche *f* NAUT haul, OCEANO fishery, fishing; **~ côtière** *f* OCEANO coastal fishery, inshore fishery; **~ au feu** *f* OCEANO light fishing; **~ hauturière** *f* NAUT deep-sea fishing, OCEANO deep-sea fishery; **~ industrielle** *f* OCEANO industrial fishery; **~ au lamparo** *f* OCEANO light fishing; **~ au large** *f* OCEANO deep-sea fishery, deep-sea fishing, offshore fishery, offshore fishing; **~ lointaine** *f* OCEANO distant water fishing; **~ minotière** *f* OCEANO fish meal fishery; **~ à pied** *f* OCEANO beach fishing, seashore fishing; **~ à la traîne** *f* OCEANO dragnet fishing, trolling fishing; **~ au vif** *f* OCEANO live bait fishing

pêcher: **~ à la drague** *vti* NAUT drag

pêcherie *f* NAUT fishery, fishing ground, OCEANO fishery; **~ sédentaire** *f* OCEANO sedentary fishery

pêcheur: **~ à la drague** *m* NAUT dredger

péchurane *m* CHIMIE pitchblende

peck *m* METROLOGIE peck

pectase *f* CHIMIE pectase

pectate *m* CHIMIE pectate

pecteux *adj* CHIMIE pectous

pectine *f* AGRO ALIM, CHIMIE pectin

pectiniculture *f* OCEANO scallop culture

pectique *adj* CHIMIE pectic

pectisable *adj* CHIMIE pectizable

pectisation *f* CHIMIE pectization

pectiser *vt* CHIMIE pectize

pectolite *f* MINERAUX pectolite

pectose *m* CHIMIE pectose

pédalage *m* GEOPHYS reverberation, PETR singing

pédale *f* CONS MECA treadle, VEHICULES *frein, embrayage* pedal; **~ d'accélérateur** *f* AUTO, VEHICULES accelerator (BrE), gas pedal (AmE); **~ de calage** *f* CH DE FER locking bar; **~ d'embrayage** *f* VEHICULES clutch pedal; **~ de frein** *f* AUTO, VEHICULES brake pedal; **~ mécanique d'aiguille** *f* CH DE FER locking bar; **~ phare code** *f* AUTO foot dimmer (AmE), foot dimmer switch (AmE), foot dip switch (BrE); **~ de verrouillage** *f* CH DE FER locking bar; **~ de verrouillage mécanique de signal** *f* CH DE FER locking bar

pédologie *f* CHARBON pedology, soil science, DISTRI EAU soil science

Pégase *m* ASTRONOMIE Flying Horse, Pegasus

pegmatite *f* MATERIAUX *géologie* pegmatite

peignage *m* CERAM VER line, CONS MECA chasing; **~ fin** *m* CERAM VER brush lines; **~ à la grande peigneuse** *m* TEXTILE hackling

peigne *m* CONS MECA chaser, cleat, screw tool, ELECTROTEC fan, laced cable fan, TEXTILE comb; **~ de câble** *m* ELECTROTEC cable harness; **~ détacheur** *m* TEXTILE doffer comb; **~ d'envergure** *m* TEXTILE leasing reed; **~ à fileter** *m* CONS MECA chaser, screw tool, thread chaser; **~ d'ourdissage** *m* TEXTILE warping reed

peigné *adj* TEXTILE combed

peigner *vt* CONS MECA chase, TEXTILE comb, hackle

peigneuse *f* TEXTILE combing machine, reed; **~ rectiligne** *f* TEXTILE rectilinear combing machine

peindre: **~ en détrempe** *vt* COULEURS distemper; **~ au pistolet** *vt* COULEURS spray

peint: **~ à l'huile** *adj* COULEURS oil-painted

peintre: **~ en majolique** *m* CERAM VER majolica painter; **~ sur faïence** *m* CERAM VER earthenware decorator; **~ sur porcelaine** *m* CERAM VER china painter; **~ sur poterie** *m* CERAM VER pottery decorator

peinturage *m* CONSTR paintwork

peinture *f* CONSTR paint, PLAST CAOU enamel, THERMODYN *laque pyrométrique* heat-sensitive paint, VEHICULES *carrosserie* paint; **~ acrylique** *f* CONSTR acrylic paint; **~ antiacide** *f* CONSTR acid-resisting paint; **~ anticorrosion** *f* COULEURS anticorrosive paint; **~ anticorrosive** *f* OPTIQUE protective coating, PLAST CAOU anticorrosive coating, *revêtement* protective coating; **~ antidérapante** *f* NAUT nonslip deck paint; **~ antifouling** *f* NAUT, PLAST CAOU antifouling paint; **~ anti-incendie** *f* COULEURS fire-resistant paint, fireproof coat, fireproof paint, PLAST CAOU fireproof coating, THERMODYN fire-resistant paint, fire-resisting paint; **~ antirouille** *f* COULEURS rust protective paint, REVETEMENT anticorrosion paint, antirust paint, rust-proofing paint; ~ **antisolaire** _f_ COULEURS, PLAST CAOU shading paint; ~ **antisonique** _f_ COULEURS sound-deadening paint; ~ **d'apprêt** _f_ COULEURS primer, priming paint, PLAST CAOU primer; ~ **à base d'eau** _f_ CONSTR water-based paint; ~ **à base de plomb** _f_ CONSTR, COULEURS lead paint; ~ **bâtiment** _f_ COULEURS, PLAST CAOU house paint; ~ **bitumineuse** _f_ CONSTR, COULEURS, PLAST CAOU bituminous paint; ~ **bouche-pores** _f_ PLAST CAOU sealer; ~ **brillante** _f_ CONSTR, COULEURS gloss paint; ~ **à la brosse** _f_ REVETEMENT brush coating; ~ **de camouflage** _f_ COULEURS camouflage paint; ~ **à la caséine** _f_ COULEURS casein paint; ~ **cellulosique** _f_ COULEURS cellulose lacquer, PLAST CAOU cellulose paint; ~ **cellulosique au pistolet** _f_ COULEURS spray cellulose paint; ~ **à la chaux** _f_ COULEURS limewash, whitewash; ~ **à la colle** _f_ COULEURS calcimine, distemper, glue color (AmE), glue colour (BrE), size colour (BrE), PLAST CAOU distemper, size color (AmE), size colour (BrE); ~ **couvrante** _f_ COULEURS masking paint, PLAST CAOU covering paint; ~ **craquelée** _f_ AERONAUT alligatoring; ~ **définitive** _f_ PLAST CAOU finishing coat, top coat of paint; ~ **dispersion** _f_ COULEURS dispersion paint; ~ **à l'eau brillante** _f_ COULEURS water enamel, water lacquer; ~ **à effet** _f_ PLAST CAOU decorative varnish; ~ **électrophorétique** _f_ COULEURS electrophoretic enamelling; ~ **électrostatique** _f_ PLAST CAOU electrostatic powder coating; ~ **électrostatique au pistolet** _f_ COULEURS electrostatic spray painting; ~ **d'émulsion** _f_ PLAST CAOU emulsion paint; ~ **émulsionnée** _f_ PLAST CAOU emulsion paint; ~ **en détrempe** _f_ PLAST CAOU distemper; ~ **en zinc** _f_ PLAST CAOU zinc coating; ~ **à faux bois** _f_ PLAST CAOU scumble; ~ **de finissage** _f_ PLAST CAOU finishing coat; ~ **de finition** _f_ COULEURS final coat, top coat; ~ **fongicide** _f_ PRODUCTION fungicide paint; ~ **au four** _f_ PLAST CAOU stoving finish; ~ **fraîche** _f_ CONSTR wet paint; ~ **gélatineuse** _f_ COULEURS size color (AmE), size colour (BrE), size paint; ~ **givrée** _f_ PLAST CAOU wrinkle paint; ~ **glycérophtalique** _f_ COULEURS glyptal resin lacquer; ~ **aux goudrons** _f_ PLAST CAOU tar coating; ~ **à graphite** _f_ COULEURS graphite paint; ~ **à l'huile** _f_ COULEURS oil paint, oil-bound paint; ~ **hydrofuge** _f_ COULEURS sealing paint, REVETEMENT waterproof paint, waterproofing; ~ **ignifuge** _f_ PLAST CAOU fireproof coating, THERMODYN fire-resistant paint, fire-resisting paint; ~ **d'imprégnation** _f_ COULEURS penetrating paint; ~ **incombustible** _f_ COULEURS fireproofing paint, PLAST CAOU fireproof coating, THERMODYN fire-resistant paint, fire-resisting paint; ~ **intumescente** _f_ COULEURS intumescent paint; ~ **isolante** _f_ COULEURS sealer; ~ **laquée** _f_ COULEURS, REVETEMENT enamel paint, varnish paint; ~ **au latex** _f_ COULEURS latex paint; ~ **luminescente** _f_ COULEURS Day-Glo paint (TM), luminescent paint, luminous paint; ~ **lumineuse** _f_ PLAST CAOU Day-Glo paint (TM); ~ **marine antisalissure** _f_ REVETEMENT antifouling composition, antifouling paint; ~ **mate** _f_ COULEURS flat paint; ~ **métallisée** _f_ COULEURS metalized paint (AmE), metallic pigment paint, metallized paint (BrE), PLAST CAOU metalized paint (AmE), metallized paint (BrE); ~ **mouillée** _f_ CONSTR wet paint; ~ **non jaunissante** _f_ PLAST CAOU nonyellowing paint; ~ **oléorésineuse** _f_ CONSTR oleoresinous paint; ~ **opaque** _f_ COULEURS masking paint; ~ **pare-feu** _f_ THERMODYN fire-resistant paint, fire-resisting paint; ~ **à pigment métallique** _f_ COULEURS metallic pigment paint; ~ **au pistolet** _f_ CONSTR spray

painting, PLAST CAOU spraying paint; ~ **de polyester** _f_ CONSTR polyester paint; ~ **pour béton** _f_ COULEURS concrete coating, concrete enamel; ~ **pour bois** _f_ COULEURS wood paint, wood stain; ~ **pour extérieur** _f_ COULEURS exterior finish, outdoor paint, outside paint; ~ **pour façades** _f_ COULEURS house paint; ~ **primaire** _f_ COULEURS first coat; ~ **primaire réactive** _f_ PLAST CAOU two-pack primer; ~ **protectrice** _f_ REVETEMENT protective coating, protective finish; ~ **résistant aux acides** _f_ COULEURS acid-proof coat; ~ **résistant aux intempéries** _f_ COULEURS weatherproof paint; ~ **au rouleau** _f_ CONSTR roller painting, COULEURS roller paint; ~ **routière** _f_ CONSTR road painting; ~ **sanitaire** _f_ COULEURS sanitary paint; ~ **sans plomb** _f_ COULEURS lead-free paint; ~ **aux silicates** _f_ COULEURS silicate paint; ~ **sous émail** _f_ COULEURS underglaze painting; ~ **sous-marine** _f_ COULEURS ship's bottom paint; ~ **structurée** _f_ COULEURS textured paint; ~ **sur porcelaine** _f_ CERAM VER china painting, painting on porcelain; ~ **sur verre** _f_ COULEURS baked glass painting; ~ **synthétique** _f_ COULEURS synthetic enamel; ~ **à la térébenthine** _f_ COULEURS sharp oil paint; ~ **thermochrome** _f_ COULEURS thermal control paint; ~ **trichromatique** _f_ PLAST CAOU tristimulus paint; ~ **vernis** _f_ CONSTR, COULEURS gloss paint; ~ **vernissante** _f_ CONSTR enamel; ~ **au verre** _f_ COULEURS silicate paint; ~ **vitrifiable sur verre** _f_ CERAM VER painting on glass; ~ **au zinc** _f_ COULEURS inorganic zinc paint

peinture-émail _f_ COULEURS enamel varnish

peinture-émulsion _f_ CONSTR emulsion paint, COULEURS emulsion paint, oil-bound water paint, PRODUCTION emulsion paint

pelage-dégainage chimique _m_ NUCLEAIRE chemical decanning, chemical decladding

pélargonate _m_ CHIMIE pelargonate

pélargonique _adj_ CHIMIE pelargonic

peler[1] _vt_ AGRO ALIM _fruit_ peel

peler:[2] ~ **une rondelle** _vi_ CONS MECA peel the lamination off a shim washer

pélite _f_ GEOLOGIE mudstone, pelite

pélitique _adj_ GEOLOGIE pelitic

pelle _f_ CONSTR shovel, DISTRI EAU shut, shut-off, EQUIP LAB scoop, INST HYDR paddle, POLLU MER shovel; ~ **automatique** _f_ NAUT shovel dredger; ~ **excavatrice mécanique** _f_ POLLU MER backhoe; ~ **à grille** _f_ CONSTR pronged shovel; ~ **mécanique** _f_ CONSTR mechanical broom, mechanical grab; ~ **de poussage** _f_ CERAM VER stowing tool; ~ **rétrocaveuse** _f_ POLLU MER backhoe; ~ **semi-automatique** _f_ CONS MECA hand-operated power shovel

pelletage _m_ CONSTR shovel work

pelletée _f_ CONSTR shovelful

pelleter _vt_ CONSTR shovel

pelleteuse _f_ CONSTR power shovel

pelleteuse-chargeuse _f_ CONSTR loading shovel

pelletiérine _f_ CHIMIE pelletierine

pelliculage _m_ IMPRIM lamination, wax laminating, varnishing; ~ **sec** _m_ IMPRIM _façonnage_ dry lamination

pellicule _f_ CHIMIE, CINEMAT, MECANIQUE, PHOTO, PRODUCTION _d'huile_ film; ~ **d'acétocellulose** _f_ EMBALLAGE cellulose acetate film; ~ **anticorrosive** _f_ EMBALLAGE anticorrosive film; ~ **autocollante** _f_ EMBALLAGE cling film; ~ **avec extrusions en couches multiples** _f_ EMBALLAGE co-extruded film; ~ **avec piste couchée** _f_ CINEMAT magnetic striped film, striped film; ~ **barrière** _f_ EMBALLAGE barrier film; ~ **à contraste élevé** _f_

CINEMAT high contrast film; ~ **couleur inversible** *f* CINEMAT color reversal film (AmE), colour reversal film (BrE); ~ **couleur multicouches** *f* CINEMAT multi-layer color film (AmE), multilayer colour film (BrE); ~ **couleur pour lumière artificielle** *f* CINEMAT A-type color film (AmE), A-type colour film (BrE); ~ **double huit** *f* CINEMAT double 8 film; ~ **à double perforation** *f* CINEMAT double perf stock; ~ **en bobine** *f* CINEMAT, PHOTO roll film; ~ **à enregistrement magnétique** *f* ENREGISTR magnetic recording film; ~ **en rouleau** *f* PHOTO roll film; ~ **exposée par la caméra** *f* CINEMAT original; ~ **inversible** *f* CINEMAT reversal film; ~ **isolante** *f* MATERIAUX insulating film; ~ **lumière artificielle** *f* CINEMAT tungsten film; ~ **lumière de jour** *f* CINEMAT daylight film; ~ **magnétique** *f* CINEMAT magnetic film, magnetic stock; ~ **monochrome** *f* CINEMAT black and white film; ~ **monocouche** *f* CINEMAT single layer film; ~ **monoperf** *f* CINEMAT single perforation film; ~ **montée par rapport au métrage tournée** *f* CINEMAT shooting ratio; ~ **nitrate** *f* CINEMAT nitrate film; ~ **noir et blanc** *f* CINEMAT black and white film; ~ **non flam** *f* CINEMAT non-flam film; ~ **panchromatique** *f* CINEMAT panchromatic film; ~ **pelable** *f* REVETEMENT protective film; ~ **périmée** *f* CINEMAT outdated film; ~ **pistée** *f* CINEMAT striped film; ~ **positive** *f* CINEMAT positive film; ~ **pour contretype** *f* PHOTO duplicating film; ~ **pour l'obtention de contretypes directs** *f* PHOTO direct duplicating film; ~ **pour protéger la surface** *f* EMBALLAGE surface protection film; ~ **pour la reproduction réduite de documents** *f* PHOTO document film; ~ **prépistée** *f* CINEMAT prestriped film; ~ **protectrice** *f* REVETEMENT coating film; ~ **rapide** *f* CINEMAT high-speed film; ~ **rétractable** *f* REVETEMENT heat shrinking foil; ~ **sensible** *f* CINEMAT fast stock, high-speed film; ~ **support acétate** *f* CINEMAT acetate film; ~ **thermorétractable** *f* THERMODYN heat-shrinkable film (BrE), heat-shrinkable wrap (AmE), shrink film (BrE), shrink-wrap; ~ **thermorétrécissable** *f* THERMODYN heat-shrinkable film (BrE), heat-shrinkable wrap (AmE), shrink film (BrE), shrink-wrap; ~ **de tirage** *f* CINEMAT print film, printing stock; ~ **tripack** *f* CINEMAT three-emulsion film; ~ **à trois couches** *f* PHOTO tripack film; ~ **de vernis** *f* REVETEMENT coating film; ~ **vierge** *f* CINEMAT raw film, raw stock, stock, unexposed film; ~ **32 mm** *f* CINEMAT double 16 film (AmE), double 16 stock (BrE)

pelliculer *vt* IMPRIM laminate

pelliculés *m pl* IMPRIM laminate

pelliplacage *m* EMBALLAGE skinpack

pellon *m* PRODUCTION pegging peen, pegging rammer

pelotage *m* CERAM VER palleting

peloton *m* TRANSPORT platoon

peluchage *m* PAPIER dusting, linting, fluffing

peluche *f* IMPRIM lint, *papier, impression* fuzz

pelure *f* ACOUSTIQUE peeling; ~ **d'oignon** *f* PAPIER cockle-finished paper

penchant[1] *adj* CONSTR leaning

penchant[2] *m* CONSTR *d'une colline* slope

penché *adj* CERAM VER bent

pencher[1] *vt* CINEMAT tilt

pencher:[2] ~ **sur le côté** *vi* NAUT *navire* list

pendage *m* GEOLOGIE, MINES, PETROLE dip; ~ **élevé** *m* GEOLOGIE high angle dip; ~ **originel** *m* GEOLOGIE initial dip

pendage-mètre *m* GEOPHYS tiltmeter

pendeloque *f* CERAM VER drop

pendre *vt* PRODUCTION hang, hang up

pendulaire *adj* MECANIQUE pendular

pendule[1] *m* GEOPHYS, MECANIQUE, PHYSIQUE pendulum; ~ **compensateur** *m* PHYSIQUE compensated pendulum; ~ **composé** *m* PHYSIQUE compound pendulum; ~ **de Foucault** *m* PHYSIQUE Foucault pendulum; ~ **pesant** *m* PHYSIQUE compound pendulum; ~ **simple** *m* PHYSIQUE simple pendulum; ~ **de torsion** *m* PHYSIQUE torsional pendulum

pendule:[2] ~ **enregistreuse** *f* SECURITE works recording clock

pêne *m* CONSTR *d'une serrure* bolt; ~ **à demi-tour** *m* CONSTR latch bolt, spring bolt; ~ **dormant** *m* CONSTR dead bolt; ~ **à ressort** *m* CONSTR latch bolt, spring bolt, PRODUCTION spring bolt; ~ **de serrure** *m* CONSTR lock bolt

pénécontemporain *adj* GEOLOGIE penecontemporaneous

pénétration *f* CONSTR bite, ELECTRON, INFORMAT, ORDINAT penetration; ~ **de l'aiguille** *f* TEXTILE needling penetration; ~ **de la chaleur** *f* THERMODYN heating depth; ~ **d'eau** *f* PRODUCTION ingress of water; ~ **d'eau dans un élément combustible** *f* NUCLEAIRE water logging; ~ **du gel** *f* CHARBON frost penetration depth; ~ **des têtes** *f* TV tip engagement, tip penetration

pénétrer *vt* HYDROLOGIE percolate through

pénétromètre *m* CONSTR, EQUIP LAB *dureté* penetrometer, PLAST CAOU *instrument* penetration tester

péniche *f* NAUT barge, canal boat; ~ **automotrice** *f* NAUT self-propelled barge; ~ **de débarquement** *f* MILITAIRE, NAUT, TRANSPORT landing craft; ~ **remorquée** *f* TRANSPORT barge, cargo barge

pénicilline *f* CERAM VER penicillin phial

péninsule *f* NAUT peninsula

pennine *f* MINERAUX pennine, penninite

penninite *f* MINERAUX pennine, penninite

pennyweight *m* METROLOGIE pennyweight

pénombre *f* ASTRONOMIE, PHYSIQUE penumbra; ~ **d'une tache solaire** *f* ASTRONOMIE sunspot penumbra

pentachlorure *m* CHIMIE pentachloride

pentaèdre[1] *adj* GEOMETRIE pentahedral

pentaèdre[2] *m* GEOMETRIE pentahedron

pentagonal *adj* GEOMETRIE pentagonal

pentagone *m* GEOMETRIE pentagon

pentaguine *f* CHIMIE pentaguine

pentalcool *m* CHIMIE pentite, pentitol

pentaméthylène *m* CHIMIE pentamethylene

pentaméthylènediamine *f* CHIMIE pentamethylenediamine

pentane *m* CHIMIE, PETROLE pentane

pentanoïque *adj* CHIMIE *acide* pentanoic

pentanol *m* CHIMIE pentanol

pentanone *f* CHIMIE pentanone

pentaprisme *m* PHOTO pentaprism

pentasulfure *m* CHIMIE pentasulfide (AmE), pentasulphide (BrE)

pentathionate *m* CHIMIE pentathionate

pentathionique *adj* CHIMIE pentathionic

pentatomique *adj* CHIMIE pentatomic

pentavalence *f* CHIMIE pentavalence, quinquevalence

pentavalent *adj* CHIMIE pentavalent, quinquevalent

pente:[1] **en** ~ *adj* CONSTR slanting

pente[2] *f* CH DE FER gradient, CHARBON slope, CINEMAT rake, CONSTR dip, downward gradient, falling gradient, grade, gradient, incline, pitch, *d'une colline* slant, slope, ELECTRON fall-off, GEOMETRIE grade, *d'une droite* gradient, *surface* slope, IMPRIM slant, PHYSIQUE gradient, slope; ~ **aérodynamique** *f* AERONAUT climb gradient; ~ **d'une ancienne surface continentale** *f* GEOLOGIE palaeoslope (BrE), paleoslope (AmE); ~ **d'attaque avant** *f* CONS MECA front rake angle; ~ **de comble** *f* CONSTR pitch of roof, roof pitch; ~ **continentale** *f* OCEANO continental slope; ~ **de conversion** *f* ELECTROTEC conversion conductance; ~ **de la courbe de portance** *f* AERONAUT lift curve slope; ~ **faible** *f* CONSTR low gradient; ~ **d'un fond de mer** *f* GEOLOGIE palaeoslope (BrE), paleoslope (AmE); ~ **d'inclinaison** *f* EN RENOUV dip; ~ **latérale** *f* AERONAUT bank; ~ **longitudinale** *f* AERONAUT pitch; ~ **montante** *f* CONSTR rising gradient; ~ **de montée** *f* AERONAUT climb gradient; ~ **normale** *f* AERONAUT normal descent angle; ~ **de la piste** *f* AERONAUT runway gradient; ~ **prodeltaïque** *f* OCEANO predelta slope; ~ **radiogoniométrique** *f* AERONAUT glide slope; ~ **raide** *f* CONSTR steep gradient, steep slope; ~ **rapide** *f* CONSTR steep gradient, steep slope; ~ **récifale** *f* OCEANO recifal slope, reef slope; ~ **transversale** *f* CONSTR crossfall

pentène *m* CHIMIE pentene
pentétrazol *m* CHIMIE pentylenetetrazol
penthiofène *m* CHIMIE penthiophene
penthiophène *m* CHIMIE penthiophene
penthotal *m* CHIMIE pentothal
pentite *f* CHIMIE pentite, pentitol
pentitol *m* CHIMIE pentite, pentitol
pentlandite *f* MINERAUX nicopyrite, pentlandite
pentode *f* ELECTRON, PHYSIQUE pentode
pentosane *m* CHIMIE pentosan
pentosazone *f* CHIMIE pentosazon
pentose *m* CHIMIE pentose
pentoside *m* CHIMIE pentosid, pentoside
pentosurique *adj* CHIMIE pentosuric
pentoxyde *m* CHIMIE pentothal, thiopental; ~ **de diazote** *m* POLLUTION nitrogen pentoxide
penture *f* CONSTR hinge, hook and hinge, ride; ~ **à T** *f* CONSTR T-hinge, butt-and-strap hinge, cross-garnet hinge, crosstail hinge, crosstailed hinge, garnet, garnet hinge
pentyle *m* CHIMIE pentyl
péonine *f* CHIMIE peonin
pépite *f* MINES nugget
PEPS *abrév (premier entré premier sorti)* ORDINAT FIFO *(first-in first-out)*
pepsinase *f* CHIMIE pepsin, pepsinum
pepsine *f* AGRO ALIM pepsin, CHIMIE pepsin, pepsinum
pepsinogène *m* CHIMIE pepsinogen
peptisable *adj* CHIMIE peptizable
peptisant *m* LESSIVES, PLAST CAOU *caoutchouc* peptizer
peptisation *f* AGRO ALIM, CHIMIE, LESSIVES peptization
peptiser *vt* CHIMIE peptizate, peptize, LESSIVES peptize
peptolyse *f* CHIMIE peptolysis
peptonisable *adj* CHIMIE peptonizable
peracétique *adj* CHIMIE peracetic
peracide *m* CHIMIE peracid
perazotate *m* CHIMIE pernitrate
perazotique *adj* CHIMIE pernitric
perborate *m* CHIMIE, LESSIVES perborate
perbromure *m* CHIMIE perbromide
perçage *m* CERAM VER preblowing, CONS MECA drilling, CONSTR boring, PAPIER drilling; ~ **à la lance** *m* PRODUCTION oxygen lancing; ~ **des matériaux à l'aide d'un laser** *m* MATERIAUX laser drilling
perçant *adj* IMPRIM *photogravure, impression* keen

percarbonate *m* CHIMIE percarbonate
perce-bouchon *m* EQUIP LAB *outil* cork borer
percée *f* AERONAUT let-down, CONS MECA break-out, CONSTR opening, MINES boring, drilling, PRODUCTION boring; ~ **directe** *f* NUCLEAIRE direct breakthrough; ~ **aux eaux** *f* DISTRI EAU boring against water, MINES tapping water; ~ **en GCA** *f* AERONAUT ground-controlled approach; ~ **technologique** *f* PRODUCTION technical breakthrough
percement *m* CONS MECA drilling, CONSTR boring, breakthrough, ELECTRON puncture, ELECTROTEC breakdown, GAZ boring, MINES bore, boring, drilling, development, drifting, driving, tunneling (AmE), tunnelling (BrE), PRODUCTION boring, perforating, perforation; ~ **aux eaux** *m* DISTRI EAU boring against water, MINES tapping water; ~ **en travers-banc** *m* MINES crosscutting; ~ **de galeries en direction** *m* MINES drifting, driving, tunneling (AmE), tunnelling (BrE); ~ **de galeries de recherche** *m* MINES drifting, driving, tunneling (AmE), tunnelling (BrE); ~ **du massif** *m* MINES holing; ~ **de recoupes** *m* MINES cross driving; ~ **de tunnels** *m* CONSTR tunneling (AmE), tunnelling (BrE)
percentile: ~ **d'ordre Q de la durée de vie** *m* NUCLEAIRE Q-percentile life
percer[1] *vt* CONS MECA drill, CONSTR bore, MECANIQUE drill, MINES bore, drill, PAPIER drill; ~ **à** *vt* MINES tap
percer[2] *vi* CONSTR hole; ~ **aux eaux accumulées** *vi* MINES bore against water; ~ **en montant** *vi* MINES rise; ~ **en travers-banc** *vi* GEOLOGIE, MINES crosscut; ~ **un sondage** *vi* CONSTR drill a borehole
perceur: ~ **de porcelaine** *m* CERAM VER china borer, china piercer, porcelain driller, porcelain piercer, porcelain borer
perceuse *f* CONS MECA, MECANIQUE drilling machine; ~ **autonome à batterie** *f* CONS MECA cordless power drill; ~ **à broches multiples** *f* PRODUCTION gang drill, multiple drilling machine, multiple-spindle drill; ~ **à colonne** *f* MECANIQUE drill press; ~ **électrique** *f* ELECTR *outil*, MECANIQUE *outillage* electric drill; ~ **d'établi** *f* CONS MECA bench drilling machine, bench drill, MECANIQUE bench drill; ~ **d'établi à colonne** *f* CONS MECA bench pillar drilling machine; ~ **et fraiseuse à coordonnées** *f* CONS MECA coordinate boring and milling machine; ~ **laser** *f* ELECTRON laser drill; ~ **à main** *f* CONS MECA breast drill, MECANIQUE *outillage* hand drill; ~ **à main à conscience** *f* CONS MECA breast drill; ~ **monobroche** *f* CONS MECA single spindle boring machine; ~ **multibroche** *f* MECANIQUE multiple drilling machine; ~ **pneumatique** *f* CONS MECA air drill; ~ **radiale** *f* MECANIQUE radial drilling machine; ~ **de rails** *f* CH DE FER rail-drilling machine; ~ **sensitive** *f* MECANIQUE drill press
perche *f* CINEMAT boom, CONSTR pole, scaffold pole, standard, ESPACE *véhicules* boom, METROLOGIE, NAUT perch, PAPIER pole, PRODUCTION belt mounter, belt shipper; ~ **de magnétomètre** *f* ESPACE *véhicules* magnetometer boom; ~ **micro** *f* ENREGISTR sound boom; ~ **de microphone** *f* ENREGISTR microphone boom; ~ **de mise à la terre** *f* GEOPHYS earth rod (BrE), ground rod (AmE), earth spike (BrE); ~ **de mise à terre** *f* CH DE FER earthing paddle (BrE), earthing pole (BrE), earthing rod (BrE), grounding paddle (AmE), grounding pole (AmE), grounding rod (AmE); ~ **de ravitaillement** *f* TRANSPORT refueling boom (AmE), refuelling boom (BrE); ~ **de ravitaillement en vol** *f*

TRANSPORT refueling in-flight system (AmE), refuelling in-flight system (BrE); ~ **son** f ENREGISTR sound boom; ~ **de sonde** f OCEANO sounding pole; ~ **à sonder** f NAUT sounding pole

perchette f CINEMAT fisher boom, fishpole boom

perchiste m CINEMAT boom operator, poleman

perchlorate m CHIMIE perchlorate; ~ **d'ammonium** m ESPACE *propulsion* ammonium perchlorate

perchloré adj CHIMIE perchlorinated

perchlorique adj CHIMIE perchloric

perchlorure m CHIMIE perchloride

perchman m ENREGISTR sound boom man

perchromate m CHIMIE perchromate

perchromique adj CHIMIE perchromic

perçoir m CONSTR auger gimlet, bore bit

percolation f AGRO ALIM, HYDROLOGIE percolation

percussion f NUCLEAIRE knock-on, PHYSIQUE impact; ~ **de bouteille** f AERONAUT extinguisher percussion

percuteur m MILITAIRE percussion needle, *d'une grenade* firing pin; ~ **d'extincteur** m AERONAUT extinguisher striker

percylite f MINERAUX percylite

perdant m OCEANO lag of the tide

perdisulfurique adj CHIMIE peroxydisulfuric (AmE), peroxydisulphuric (BrE)

perdition: en ~ adj NAUT in distress

perdre[1] vt CONSTR leak

perdre:[2] ~ **l'équilibre** vi SECURITE overbalance

perdre:[3] se ~ v réfl HYDROLOGIE go to waste, run to waste

perdu adj AGRO ALIM nonreturnable

père m ACOUSTIQUE master; ~ **nucléaire** m NUCLEAIRE, PHYS RAYON parent nuclide

péreirine f CHIMIE pereirine

péremption f PRODUCTION obsolescence

perfectionnement m CONS MECA development

perforage m MINES boring, drilling, PRODUCTION perforating, perforation

perforamètre m PAPIER burst tester, puncture tester

perforateur m INFORMAT perforator, punch, MINES borer, drill, jackhammer, rock drill, ORDINAT perforator, punch, PRODUCTION perforator; ~ **à air comprimé** m CONSTR pneumatic drill; ~ **automatique** m INFORMAT *de bande* automatic punch; ~ **à balles** m PETROLE perforating gun, *forage* gun perforator; ~ **de bande** m INFORMAT, ORDINAT tape punch; ~ **de bande de papier** m INFORMAT paper tape punch; ~ **de cartes** m INFORMAT card punch; ~ **diamanté** m PRODUCTION diamond drill; ~ **manuel** m INFORMAT, ORDINAT handpunch; ~ **mécanique** m MINES borer, drilling machine, rock drill; ~ **pneumatique** m CONS MECA compressed air drill, MECANIQUE *outillage* air drill

perforation f CINEMAT sprocket hole, INFORMAT perforation, punching, MINES boring, drilling, ORDINAT punching, PAPIER burst, puncture, PHOTO perforation, sprocket hole, PRODUCTION perforating, perforation; ~ **arrondie** f CINEMAT negative perforation; ~ **du cuvelage** f PETROLE *puits, forage* casing perforation; ~ **destinée à céder sous la traction de la main** f IMPRIM snap perforation; ~ **au diamant** f MINES diamond drilling; ~ **en grille** f CONS MECA lace punching; ~ **en liasses épaisses** f IMPRIM crash perforation; ~ **d'entraînement** f INFORMAT, ORDINAT feed hole, sprocket hole; ~ **mécanique** f MINES machine drilling; ~ **négative** f CINEMAT negative perforation; ~ **positive** f CINEMAT positive perforation; ~ **récapitulative** f IN-FORMAT, ORDINAT summary punching; ~ **rectangulaire** f CINEMAT positive perforation; ~ **transversale** f IMPRIM *impression, finition* cross perforation; ~ **à trous ronds** f IMPRIM round hole perforating; ~ **de tubage** f PETR perforated casing

perforations: ~ **au pouce** f pl IMPRIM *continu* ties per inch

perforatrice f CINEMAT perforating machine, CONSTR rock drill, INFORMAT keypunch, MINES borer, drill, drilling machine, rock drill, ORDINAT keypunch, PRODUCTION perforator; ~ **à air comprimé** f CONS MECA compressed air drill; ~ **antidéflagrante** f MINES fireproof drilling machine, flameproof drilling machine; ~ **au charbon** f CHARBON coal drill; ~ **diamantée** f PRODUCTION diamond drill; ~ **à diamants** f PRODUCTION diamond drill; ~ **mécanique** f CONSTR power drill, MINES borer, drilling machine, rock drill; ~ **à percussion** f CONSTR hammer drill; ~ **à percussion rotative hydraulique** f MINES hydraulic rotary percussion drill; ~ **percutante** f CONS MECA percussion drill, plugger, CONSTR hammer drill; ~ **percutante à main** f CONS MECA plug drill; ~ **pneumatique** f CONSTR pneumatic drill; ~ **à pointes de diamant** f PRODUCTION diamond drill; ~ **récapitulative** f INFORMAT, ORDINAT summary punch; ~ **au rocher** f CONSTR rock borer; ~ **rotative** f CONSTR rotary drill; ~ **à taquet** f CONSTR tappet valve drill

perforé adj INFORMAT perforated; ~ **sur rouleau** adj EMBALLAGE perforated on the reel

perforer vt CONS MECA drill

perforeuse f EMBALLAGE perforating machine

performance f INFORMAT, ORDINAT performance; ~ **à l'abattage** f AGRO ALIM carcass yield; ~ **ascensionnelle** f AERONAUT climb performance; ~ **du réseau** f TELECOM NP, network performance

performances: ~ **du moteur** f pl AERONAUT engine ratings

performant adj PHYSIQUE high-performance

pergélisol m CHARBON, PETROLE permafrost

perhydrol m CHIMIE perhydrol

perhydrure m CHIMIE perhydride

périapside m ASTRONOMIE *le plus proche* periapsis

périastre m ESPACE *mécanique céleste* periastron

périclase f CHIMIE periclase, MINERAUX periclase, periclasite

périclinal m GEOLOGIE pericline

péricline f MINERAUX pericline

péridot m MINERAUX peridot

péridotite f PETR peridotite

périer m PRODUCTION tapping bar

périgée m ASTRONOMIE, ESPACE *mécanique céleste*, PHYSIQUE perigee

périhélie m ASTRONOMIE, EN RENOUV, PHYSIQUE perihelion

péril m SECURITE hazard; ~ **aviaire** m AERONAUT bird strike hazard

périmé adj PRODUCTION obsolete

périmètre m CONSTR, GEOMETRIE perimeter

périodate m CHIMIE periodate

période f ACOUSTIQUE period, CONS MECA cycle, ELECTRON, GEOLOGIE period, PETR cycle, period, PHYS PART *d'un isotope radioactif* half life, PHYSIQUE period, time, PRODUCTION time interval; ~ **d'accélération** f GENIE CHIM accelerating period; ~ **d'arrêt** f ELECTROTEC off period; ~ **axiale** f ESPACE axial period; ~ **de base** f PRODUCTION time bucket, time period; ~ **de**

blocage *f* ELECTROTEC blocking period, off period; ~ **de coupure** *f* ELECTROTEC off period; ~ **de déblocage** *f* ELECTROTEC on period; ~ **de décarburation** *f* PRODUCTION boil period; ~ **de décomposition** *f* GEOLOGIE half life; ~ **de défaillance par usure** *f* QUALITE wear-out failure period; ~ **de défaillance précoce** *f* QUALITE early failure period; ~ **de défaillance rapide** *f* QUALITE early failure period; ~ **de défaillance à taux constant** *f* QUALITE constant failure rate period; ~ **de détente** *f* INST HYDR expansion duration, expansion period; ~ **d'échantillonnage** *f* PETR sample period, sample rate, PRODUCTION *automatisme industriel* sample time; ~ **d'échappement de la vapeur** *f* INST HYDR release period; ~ **d'éclipse** *f* ASTRONOMIE eclipse period; ~ **d'élaboration** *f* CINEMAT development time; ~ **élémentaire de prévision** *f* PRODUCTION forecast period; ~ **d'émission** *f* ELECTROTEC on-air period; ~ **erronée** *f* TELECOM EP, erroneous period; ~ **des étincelles** *f* PRODUCTION slag formation period; ~ **de faible charge** *f* ELECTR *alimentation* off-peak period; ~ **des flammes** *f* PRODUCTION boil period; ~ **de fonctionnement** *f* ELECTROTEC on period; ~ **des fumées** *f* PRODUCTION fining period; ~ **de groupage** *f* PRODUCTION time bucket, time period; ~ **d'homologation** *f* QUALITE approval period; ~ **d'horloge** *f* ELECTRON clock period; ~ **humide** *f* POLLUTION wet period; ~ **d'intégration** *f* ELECTROTEC integration period; ~ **de livraison** *f* EMBALLAGE delivery delay; ~ **minimale sans erreur** *f* TELECOM MEFP, minimum error-free pad; ~ **d'un nucléide radioactif** *f* NUCLEAIRE radioactive half life; ~ **d'occupation totale** *f* TELECOM busy period; ~ **d'oscillation** *f* ELECTR *courant alternatif* period of oscillation, ELECTRON oscillation period; ~ **de polarité géomagnétique** *f* GEOLOGIE magnetic interval, polarity epoch; ~ **de précipitation** *f* POLLUTION wet period; ~ **propre** *f* ELECTRON natural period, GEOPHYS free oscillation period; ~ **radioactive** *f* GEOLOGIE, PHYSIQUE half life; ~ **de réapprovisionnement** *f* PRODUCTION reorder period; ~ **de récurrence** *f* ELECTRON pulse repetition interval, pulse repetition period; ~ **de régulation** *f* AERONAUT cycling; ~ **de repos** *f* AERONAUT rest period, ELECTRON idle period; ~ **de révolution** *f* ESPACE *orbitographie* orbital period; ~ **sans émission** *f* CONSTR off-air period; ~ **de scorification** *f* PRODUCTION slag formation period; ~ **sèche** *f* POLLUTION rain-free period; ~ **sidérale** *f* ASTRONOMIE sidereal period; ~ **de solstice** *f* ESPACE solstitial period; ~ **spatiale** *f* ELECTRON spatial period; ~ **temporelle** *f* ELECTRON time period; ~ **de vague** *f* NAUT wave period

périodicité *f* CRISTALL, ELECTRON periodicity

périodique *adj* ELECTR *courant alternatif* periodic, ELECTRON oscillating, periodic, MATH recurring, PHYSIQUE periodic

periodure *m* CHIMIE periodide

périphérie *f* CONSTR periphery

périphérique *m* ELECTROTEC peripheral device, INFORMAT device, peripheral, peripheral device, ORDINAT peripheral, peripheral device, TELECOM peripheral; ~ **téléphonique** *m* TELECOM telephony-rated device

périphériques *m pl* IMPRIM ancillaries

périscope *m* CINEMAT periscope, snorkel, ESPACE *véhicules*, NAUT, PHYSIQUE periscope; ~ **panoramique** *m* NUCLEAIRE panorama periscope

péritectoïde *m* METALL peritectoid

perlage *m* IMPRIM sweating

perle *f* CERAM VER bead; ~ **de borax** *f* CONSTR borax bead; ~ **descendue** *f* (Bel) *(cf rupture totale due à la goutte)* CERAM VER bead down; ~ **nacrée** *f* CERAM VER mother-of-pearl bead; ~ **de verre** *f* CERAM VER slug

perlé *adj* PRODUCTION beaded

perles: ~ **de coke** *f pl* CHARBON globular coke

perlite *f* MATERIAUX *métallurgie* pearlite, PETR pearlstone, perlite; ~ **divisée** *f* METALL divorced pearlite; ~ **expansée** *f* CHAUFFAGE expanded perlite; ~ **lamellaire** *f* METALL lamellar pearlite; ~ **non lamellaire** *f* METALL nonlamellar pearlite

perlon *m* CHIMIE perlon

permafrost *m* INST HYDR permafrost

permagel *m* PETROLE permafrost

permalloy *m* ELECTR *magnétisme*, PHYSIQUE permalloy

permanence: **en** ~ *adv* PRODUCTION unconditionally

permanganate *m* CHIMIE, HYDROLOGIE permanganate; ~ **de potasse** *m* CHIMIE potassium permanganate; ~ **de potassium** *m* CHIMIE potassium permanganate

permanganique *adj* CHIMIE permanganic

perméabilité *f* CHARBON, CHIMIE, CONSTR, ELECTR *magnétisme*, EN RENOUV, ESSAIS, GAZ, HYDROLOGIE, MATERIAUX, PETR, PETROLE, PHYSIQUE, PLAST CAOU, TEXTILE permeability; ~ **absolue** *f* ELECTR *magnétisme* absolute permeability, ELECTROTEC permeability of free space, ESSAIS, PETR absolute permeability; ~ **de l'air** *f* ELECTROTEC permeability of air; ~ **à l'air** *f* CHAUFFAGE, IMPRIM air permeability; ~ **complexe** *f* ELECTR *circuit à courant alternatif* complex permeability; ~ **à l'eau** *f* PLAST CAOU water permeability; ~ **au fluide** *f* CHAUFFAGE fluid permeability; ~ **au gaz** *f* PLAST CAOU, THERMODYN gas permeability; ~ **à la graisse** *f* EMBALLAGE permeability to grease; ~ **incrémentielle** *f* ESSAIS incremental permeability; ~ **intrinsèque** *f* ELECTR *électromagnétisme* intrinsic permeability; ~ **magnétique** *f* ELECTR, ELECTROTEC, PETR magnetic permeability; ~ **magnétique absolue** *f* ELECTROTEC absolute permeability; ~ **réelle** *f* PETR effective permeability; ~ **relative** *f* ELECTR *électromagnétisme*, ELECTROTEC, ESSAIS relative permeability, PETR effective permeability, PHYSIQUE relative permeability; ~ **à la vapeur** *f* CHAUFFAGE, THERMODYN vapor permeability (AmE), vapour permeability (BrE); ~ **du vide** *f* ELECTROTEC, PHYSIQUE permeability of free space

perméable *adj* CHIMIE, CONSTR, HYDROLOGIE, PETR permeable

perméamètre *m* CHARBON permeameter

perméance *f* *(cf réluctance)* ELECTR *magnétisme*, ELECTROTEC permeance, EN RENOUV perviousness, PAPIER, PHYSIQUE permeance; ~ **à la vapeur** *f* CHAUFFAGE vapor permeance (AmE), vapour permeance (BrE)

Permien *m* PETROLE Permian period

permis *m* PETROLE *prospection, exploitation* licence (BrE), license (AmE); ~ **de construire** *m* CONSTR planning permission; ~ **d'embarquement** *m* NAUT shipping note; ~ **d'exploitation** *m* PETROLE production licence (BrE), production license (AmE); ~ **d'exploration** *m* PETROLE exploration licence (BrE), exploration license (AmE); ~ **de navigation** *m* NAUT ship's passport; ~ **d'urbanisation** *m* CONSTR planning permission

permission: ~ **à terre** *f* NAUT shore leave

permittivité *f* ELECTR *condensateur* permittivity, ELECTROTEC electric constant, permittivity, ESPACE, PHYSIQUE, TELECOM permittivity; ~ **absolue** *f* ELECTR *champ électrique* absolute permittivity, ELECTROTEC absolute permittivity, permittivity of free space; ~ **de l'air** *f* ELECTROTEC permittivity of air; ~ **relative** *f* ELECTR *électromagnétisme*, ELECTROTEC relative permittivity, PHYSIQUE dielectric constant, relative permittivity; ~ **du vide** *f* ELECTROTEC electric constant, permittivity of free space, permittivity of free space

permonosulfurique *adj* CHIMIE permonosulfuric (AmE), permonosulphuric (BrE)

permutation *f* ELECTR *connexions d'écrans* crossbonding, INFORMAT permutation, swapping, MATH permutation, ORDINAT permutation, swapping; ~ **circulaire** *f* INFORMAT, ORDINAT end-around shift; ~ **continue** *f* ELECTR *connexions d'écrans* continuous cross bonding; ~ **ternaire** *f* ELECTR *connexions d'écrans* sectionalized cross-bonding

permuter *vti* INFORMAT, ORDINAT swap

peroxoacétylnitrate *m (PAN)* POLLUTION peroxoacetylnitrate *(PAN)*

peroxophosphate *m* CHIMIE peroxophosphate

peroxyacide *m* CHIMIE peroxy acid

peroxydation *f* CHIMIE peroxidation

peroxyde *m* CHIMIE peroxide; ~ **d'acétylbenzoyle** *m* AGRO ALIM benzoyl peroxide; ~ **d'azote** *m* POLLUTION nitrogen peroxide; ~ **de benzoyle** *m* AGRO ALIM, PLAST CAOU *polyesters* benzoyl peroxide; ~ **d'hydrogène** *m* CHIMIE, ESPACE *propulsion* hydrogen peroxide

peroxyder *vt* CHIMIE peroxidize

perpendiculaire[1] *adj* GEOMETRIE perpendicular, right-angled

perpendiculaire:[2] ~ **arrière** *f* NAUT aft perpendicular; ~ **avant** *f* NAUT forward perpendicular; ~ **milieu** *f* NAUT perpendicular amidships

perpendiculaire:[3] **à** *prép* GEOMETRIE at right angles to, perpendicular to

perpendiculaires: ~ **entre eux** *adj* METROLOGIE *mesure en coordonnées d'axes* perpendicular to each other

perré: ~ **en moellons** *m* CONSTR riprap

perrhénate *m* CHIMIE perrhenate

perrhénique *adj* CHIMIE perrhenic

Persée *m* ASTRONOMIE Perseus

Perséides *m pl* ASTRONOMIE Perseids

persel *m* CHIMIE persalt

perseulose *m* CHIMIE perseulose

persienne *f* AUTO, CONSTR, ENREGISTR louver (AmE), louvre (BrE)

persistance *f* CINEMAT afterimage, ELECTR *de tube cathodique* persistence, ELECTRON persistence, *d'écran* afterglow, TV afterglow, retentivity; ~ **lumineuse** *f* ORDINAT afterglow; ~ **rétinienne** *f* CINEMAT persistence of vision; ~ **variable** *f* ELECTRON variable persistence

personnalisation *f* ELECTRON customization

personnalisé *adj* ELECTRON custom-designed, customized

personnel *m* PRODUCTION manpower; ~ **d'accompagnement** *m* CH DE FER *véhicules* train crew; ~ **anti-incendie** *m* SECURITE firefighting personnel; ~ **commercial de bord** *m* AERONAUT cabin attendants; ~ **de conduite** *m* CH DE FER driving crew; ~ **navigant** *m* AERONAUT flight crew; ~ **navigant commercial** *m (PNC)* AERONAUT cabin crew; ~ **au sol** *m* AERONAUT ground staff

perspective: ~ **auditive** *f* ENREGISTR auditory perspective; ~ **sonore** *f* ENREGISTR acoustic perspective

persulfate *m* CHIMIE persulfate (AmE), persulphate (BrE)

perte *f* BREVETS *de la priorité* loss, CONSTR leak, *de la lame d'une machine* inclination, DISTRI EAU *d'eau* leakage, ELECTROTEC leakage, loss, EN RENOUV *de chaleur*, INST HYDR *de chaleur* loss, NUCLEAIRE degradation, energy degradation, thindown, OPTIQUE loss, PETROLE mud losses, *boue de forage* losses, POLLU MER leakage, PRODUCTION wastage, waste, SECURITE leak, TELECOM loss; ~ **acoustique par absorption** *f* ENREGISTR acoustic absorption loss; ~ **de brillant** *f* IMPRIM *impression* dry back; ~ **calorifique** *f* THERMODYN heat loss; ~ **de chaleur** *f* CHAUFFAGE, PHYSIQUE, REFRIG heat loss; ~ **de chaleur brute** *f* CHAUFFAGE gross heat loss; ~ **de chaleur nette** *f* CHAUFFAGE net heat loss; ~ **de charge** *f* INST HYDR pressure loss, *déperdition de pression* loss of pressure, MAT CHAUFF, PETROLE pressure drop, RESSORTS loss of load; ~ **de chauffage** *f* ELECTR *résistance* heat loss; ~ **de circulation** *f* PETROLE loss of returns, lost circulation; ~ **de couplage** *f* OPTIQUE, TELECOM coupling loss; ~ **de courbure** *f* ELECTROTEC bending loss; ~ **à la cuisson** *f* AGRO ALIM baking loss; ~ **cumulative** *f* INFORMAT, ORDINAT walk down; ~ **dans le cuivre** *f* ELECTR *transformateur*, ELECTROTEC, PHYSIQUE copper loss; ~ **dans le fer** *f* ELECTR *transformateur* iron loss, PHYSIQUE core loss, iron loss; ~ **dans le noyau** *f* ELECTR *transformateur* core loss; ~ **à la découpe** *f* CERAM VER cutting loss; ~ **diélectrique** *f* ELECTR, ELECTROTEC, PHYSIQUE dielectric loss; ~ **due à la diffusion inverse** *f* NUCLEAIRE back diffusion loss; ~ **due au pointage** *f* TELECOM pointing loss; ~ **électrique** *f* ELECTR *appareil* electric loss; ~ **en courbe** *f* TELECOM corner loss, loss around a corner; ~ **en eau libre** *f* PETR filtrate loss; ~ **d'énergie** *f* CONS MECA loss of power, ELECTR, GAZ energy loss; ~ **d'énergie électronique** *f* PHYS RAYON electron energy loss; ~ **d'énergie au moteur** *f* PRODUCTION *automatisme industriel* motor power loss; ~ **d'énergie par ion** *f* PHYS RAYON ionization loss; ~ **d'énergie par ionisation** *f* PHYS PART ionization loss; ~ **d'énergie par rayonnement** *f* PHYS PART radiation loss; ~ **en matières nutritives** *f* AGRO ALIM nutrient loss; ~ **d'entrefer** *f* ACOUSTIQUE, ENREGISTR, TV gap loss; ~ **d'épissure** *f* TELECOM splice loss; ~ **extrinsèque de raccordement** *f* OPTIQUE extrinsic joint loss, extrinsic junction loss, misalignment loss, TELECOM extrinsic joint loss, misalignment loss; ~ **au feu** *f* CHARBON, POLLUTION ignition loss; ~ **de feuille** *f* CERAM VER loss of sheet; ~ **de filtrat** *f* PETR filtrate loss; ~ **de force** *f* RESSORTS loss of load; ~ **d'humidité** *f* THERMODYN humidity loss; ~ **hydraulique** *f* NUCLEAIRE *fuite* hydraulic loss, velocity loss; ~ **d'image** *f* CINEMAT cutoff, TV picture failure; ~ **d'infiltration de l'air** *f* MAT CHAUFF air infiltration loss; ~ **d'information** *f* INFORMAT drop-out; ~ **d'information par affaiblissement** *f* ORDINAT drop-out; ~ **d'insertion** *f* OPTIQUE, PHYSIQUE insertion loss, TELECOM insertion loss, low-insertion loss; ~ **intrinsèque de raccordement** *f* OPTIQUE, TELECOM intrinsic joint loss; ~ **d'isolement** *f* TELECOM low insulation loss; ~ **de lecture** *f* ACOUSTIQUE reproducing loss, TV reproduction loss; ~ **maritime** *f* NAUT marine loss; ~ **de multitrame** *f* TELECOM LOM, loss of multiframe; ~ **de niveau** *f* ELECTROTEC, TV drop-out; ~ **ohmique** *f* PHYSIQUE ohmic loss; ~ **d'oxyde** *f* CINEMAT oxide build-up, TV oxide shedding; ~ **par absorption** *f* ELECTROTEC, TV absorption loss; ~ **par calcination** *f* POLLUTION ignition loss; ~ **par courant de Foucault** *f* PHYSIQUE, TV eddy current loss; ~ **par débordement** *f* ESPACE *com-*

munications spillover loss; ~ **par décalage latéral** *f* TELECOM lateral offset loss; ~ **par décentrement transversal** *f* OPTIQUE, TELECOM lateral offset loss, transverse offset loss; ~ **par démagnétisation** *f* ENREGISTR demagnetization loss; ~ **par dépointage** *f* ESPACE *communications* pointing loss; ~ **par déréglage d'azimut** *f* TV azimuth loss; ~ **par désalignement angulaire** *f* OPTIQUE, TELECOM angular misalignment loss; ~ **par désalignement de la tête** *f* ENREGISTR head misalignment loss; ~ **par effet d'espacement tête-bande** *f* TV spacing loss; ~ **par effet Joule** *f* ELECTR *résistance* Joule's heat loss; ~ **par effet de masque** *f* ESPACE *communications* blocking loss; ~ **par épaisseur de couche magnétique** *f* TV thickness loss; ~ **par espacement longitudinal** *f* OPTIQUE longitudinal gap loss, longitudinal offset loss, TELECOM longitudinal offset loss; ~ **par évaporation** *f* DISTRI EAU, GENIE CHIM evaporation loss; ~ **par frottement** *f* EN RENOUV friction loss; ~ **par hystérésis** *f* ELECTROTEC, PHYSIQUE, PLAST CAOU hysteresis loss; ~ **par inclinaison axiale** *f* OPTIQUE, TELECOM angular misalignment loss; ~ **par inondation** *f* EN RENOUV flood loss; ~ **par réflexion** *f* ELECTRON, ENREGISTR reflection loss; ~ **par réfraction** *f* ENREGISTR refraction loss; ~ **par séparation longitudinale** *f* OPTIQUE longitudinal offset loss; ~ **par séparation terminale** *f* OPTIQUE, TELECOM gap loss; ~ **par la ventilation** *f* MAT CHAUFF ventilation loss; ~ **de phase** *f* PRODUCTION *automatisme industriel* phase loss; ~ **de pointeur** *f* TELECOM LOP, loopback command, loss of pointer; ~ **de pression** *f* INST HYDR pressure drop; ~ **de propagation** *f* PHYSIQUE propagation loss; ~ **de puissance** *f* CONS MECA loss of power; ~ **de qualité** *f* QUALITE, TV degradation; ~ **relative de déviation angulaire** *f* ACOUSTIQUE relative angular deviation loss; ~ **de reproduction** *f* ENREGISTR playback loss; ~ **de séparation** *f* ENREGISTR spacing loss; ~ **de signal** *f* TELECOM LOS, loss of signal; ~ **de synchronisation** *f* TV synchronization loss; ~ **de tension** *f* ELECTROTEC voltage drop; ~ **à la terre** *f* ELECTR earth leakage (BrE), ground leakage (AmE); ~ **de trame** *f* TELECOM LOF, loss of frame; ~ **de transmission** *f* ACOUSTIQUE, ESPACE, TELECOM transmission loss; ~ **de travail utile** *f* CONS MECA loss of power; ~ **de verrouillage de trame** *f* *(PVT)* TELECOM loss of frame alignment *(LFA)*

pertes *f pl* PETROLE mud losses; ~ **de commutation** *f pl* ELECTROTEC switching loss; ~ **dans le compteur** *f pl* ELECTR meter losses; ~ **dans la ligne** *f pl* ELECTR *réseau d'alimentation* line losses; ~ **dans un transformateur** *f pl* ELECTROTEC transformer loss; ~ **directes** *f pl* HYDROLOGIE direct losses; ~ **dissipatives** *f pl* ELECTROTEC dissipative loss; ~ **dues au câble** *f pl* ELECTROTEC cable loss; ~ **dues à la charge** *f pl* ELECTR load loss; ~ **d'énergie** *f pl* ELECTROTEC power loss; ~ **d'enregistrement** *f pl* ENREGISTR recording loss; ~ **hydrauliques** *f pl* NUCLEAIRE *fuite* hydraulic loss; ~ **ohmiques** *f pl* ELECTR *chauffage* ohmic losses, ELECTROTEC ohmic loss; ~ **par courant** *f pl* ELECTR leakage loss; ~ **par effet Joule** *f pl* ELECTROTEC ohmic loss; ~ **par la ventilation** *f pl* ELECTR *machine* windage losses; ~ **relatives à la qualité** *f pl* QUALITE quality losses; ~ **de reproduction** *f pl* TV playback loss; ~ **au tirage** *f pl* CINEMAT *de qualité* printing loss; ~ **totales** *f pl* ELECTR total losses; ~ **à vide** *f pl* ELECTR no-load loss

perthite *f* MINERAUX perthite

pertinence *f* CONS MECA dependability

pertuis *m* DISTRI EAU sluice, NAUT narrows, sluice, straits; ~ **d'entrée** *m* DISTRI EAU inlet; ~ **de fond** *m* DISTRI EAU bottom culvert

perturbation *f* ESPACE perturbation, METEO, PETR disturbance, PHYS FLUID perturbation; ~ **atmosphérique** *f* METEO atmospheric disturbance; ~ **électromagnétique** *f* ESPACE EMI, electromagnetic interference, TELECOM electromagnetic disturbance; ~ **en boucles** *f* TV herringboning; ~ **extérieure** *f* ELECTR *faute* external disturbance; ~ **d'orbite** *f* ESPACE perturbation of orbit

perturbations: ~ **écologiques** *f pl* POLLU MER, POLLUTION ecological disruption

perturber *vt* IMPRIM offset

pervéance *f* ELECTROTEC, TELECOM perveance

pérylène *m* CHIMIE perylene

pesage *m* PAPIER weighing; ~ **et remplissage de barquettes** *m* EMBALLAGE weighing and punnet filling; ~ **à très grande exactitude** *m* EMBALLAGE ultrahigh accuracy weighing

pesanteur *f* ESPACE, MECANIQUE gravity, METROLOGIE weight, PHYSIQUE gravity

pèse-acide *m* AUTO acid hydrometer, CHIMIE acidimeter

pèse-alcool *m* AGRO ALIM spirit gage (AmE), spirit gauge (BrE)

peser *vt* PRODUCTION weigh

peson *m* METROLOGIE balance; ~ **à contrepoids** *m* CONS MECA lever balance; ~ **cylindrique** *m* METROLOGIE spiral balance; ~ **à hélice** *m* CONS MECA spring balance, METROLOGIE spiral balance; ~ **à ressort** *m* CONS MECA spring balance, METROLOGIE spiral balance

peste: ~ **rouge** *f* ELECTROTEC purple plague

pesticide *m* CHIMIE pesticide

peta- *préf (p)* METROLOGIE peta-*(p)*

pétalite *f* MINERAUX petalite

pétarade *f* VEHICULES *moteur* backfire

pétard *m* CH DE FER detonator (BrE), torpedo (AmE), MINES shot

petchblende *f* NUCLEAIRE uranium black, varied pitchblende

pète *f* CERAM VER spontaneous breaking

pétillant *adj* AGRO ALIM effervescent

pétillement: ~ **de la mer** *m* OCEANO bubbling

petit:[1] **au ~ largue** *adv* NAUT on a close reach; **à ~ point** *adv* NAUT *carte* small-scale

petit:[2] ~ **axe** *m* GEOMETRIE *d'une ellipse* minor axis; ~ **bloc** *m* GEOLOGIE cobble; ~ **bois** *m* CONSTR glass bar, glazing bar, window bar, sash bar; ~ **bois en fer** *m* CONSTR glazing bar, window bar, sash bar; ~ **caillou** *m* GEOLOGIE cobble; ~ **cheval alimentaire** *m* INST HYDR auxiliary boiler feeder; ~ **dos** *m* OCEANO baiting; ~ **échantillon** *m* TEXTILE cutting, swatch; ~ **fond** *m* GEOLOGIE shoal; ~ **galet** *m* GEOLOGIE cobble; ~ **laminoir** *m* PRODUCTION small bar mill; ~ **micro en forme de bille** *m* ENREGISTR eight-ball mike; ~ **outillage** *m* CONS MECA small tools, PRODUCTION hand tools; ~ **outillage en acier rapide** *m* CONS MECA HSS small tools, high-speed small tools, high-speed steel small tools; ~ **pas** *m* AERONAUT *hélice* fine pitch; ~ **pied de caméra** *m* CINEMAT high hat; ~ **schelem** *m* PETR small slam; ~ **signal** *m* ELECTRON small signal; ~ **temps** *m* NAUT *météorologie* light weather; ~ **train** *m* PRODUCTION small bar mill; ~ **trépied** *m* CINEMAT baby tripod

Petit: ~ **Cheval** *m* ASTRONOMIE Equuleus; ~ **Chien** *m* ASTRONOMIE Canis Minor; ~ **Lion** *m* ASTRONOMIE Leo, The Lion; ~ **Nuage de Magellan** *m* ASTRONOMIE Small

Magellanic Cloud; ~ **Renard** *m* ASTRONOMIE Vulpecula

petite:[1] **à ~ échelle** *adj* NAUT *carte* small-scale

petite:[2] **~ aiguille** *f* METROLOGIE hour hand; **~ baie** *f* OCEANO cove; **~ calorie** *f* METROLOGIE gram calory (AmE), gram centimeter (AmE), gramme calorie (BrE), gramme centimetre (BrE); **~ charpenterie en fer** *f* CONSTR ironworking; **~ chaudière** *f* CONS MECA back boiler; **~ courroie** *f* IMPRIM *mécanique* strip; **~ erse** *f* NAUT becket; **~ forge** *f* PRODUCTION portable forge; **~ mécanique** *f* CONS MECA light engineering; **~ multiplication** *f* CONS MECA low gear; **~ normale** *f* PETR short normal; **~ planète** *f* ASTRONOMIE minor planet, ESPACE *astronomie* planetoid; **~ série** *f* CONS MECA *production en petite série* short run; **~ tête** *f* CONS MECA *de bielle* small end; **~ tête de bielle** *f* CONS MECA connecting rod little end; **~ visite** *f* AERONAUT base check, minor base check, minor check; **~ vitesse** *f* CONS MECA low-speed, PRODUCTION thread speed

petite:[3] **à ~ échelle** *adj* GEOLOGIE small-scale

Petite: **~ Ourse** *f* ASTRONOMIE Little Bear, Ursa Minor

petites: **~ capitales** *f pl* IMPRIM level small caps, small caps; **~ pièces** *f pl* PRODUCTION fine castings; **~ réparations** *f pl* PRODUCTION minor repairs

petit-lait *m* AGRO ALIM whey

petits: **~ fonds** *m pl* HYDROLOGIE, NAUT shallows, shoals

pétrissage *m* AGRO ALIM, PRODUCTION kneading

pétrissement *m* PRODUCTION kneading

pétrisseur *m* GENIE CHIM dispersion kneader

pétrochimique *adj* PETROLE petrochemical

pétrographie: **~ structurale** *f* GEOLOGIE petrofabric analysis

pétrole:[1] **de ~** *adj* CHIMIE *éther* petrolic

pétrole[2] *m* CHARBON coal oil, mineral oil, CHIMIE *lampant* kerosene (AmE), kerosine, PETR earth oil, gas (AmE), petrol (BrE), oil, petroleum, rock oil, stone oil, PETROLE oil, petroleum, POLLU MER hydrocarbon; **~ altéré** *m* POLLU MER weathered oil; **~ brut** *m* PETR crude oil, rock tar, PETROLE crude, crude oil, POLLU MER, POLLUTION crude oil; **~ brut léger** *m* PETROLE light crude oil; **~ brut lourd** *m* PETROLE heavy crude oil; **~ brut qui contient ses gaz d'origine** *m* THERMODYN live oil; **~ en place** *m* PETROLE *estimation des réserves* oil in place; **~ raffiné d'éclairage** *m* THERMODYN kerosene (AmE), paraffin (BrE)

pétroléine *f* CHIMIE petrolene

pétrolier *m* NAUT oil tanker, PETROLE crude oil tanker, tanker, *transport maritime* oil tanker, TRANSPORT oil tanker, tanker; **~ brise-glace** *m* TRANSPORT icebreaking oil tanker; **~ ravitailleur** *m* TRANSPORT fuel tanker, replenishing ship; **~ sous-marin** *m* TRANSPORT submarine tanker

pétrolier-navette *m* PETROLE shuttle tanker

pétrolier-vracquier-minéralier *m* TRANSPORT OBO carrier, oil-bulk-ore carrier

pétrolifère *adj* PETR, PETROLE oil-bearing

pétrologie *f* CHARBON, PETROLE petrology

pétrosilex *m* PETR petrosilex

petzite *f* MINERAUX petzite

peuplier *m* PAPIER poplar

peut: **qui ~ être absorbé** *adj* CHIMIE adsorbable

PGCD *abrév (plus grand commun diviseur)* MATH HCF *(highest common factor)*

pH:[1] *abrév (potentiel hydrogène)* CHIMIE pH *(potential of hydrogen)*

pH[2] **~ mètre** *m* CHARBON, EQUIP LAB, METROLOGIE pH meter

phacolite *f* GEOLOGIE, MINERAUX phacolite

phage *m* AGRO ALIM bacteriophage

phanérozoïque *adj* GEOLOGIE Phanerozoic

phare *m* AUTO headlamp, headlight, NAUT lighthouse, TRANSPORT beacon, VEHICULES *éclairage* headlamp, headlight; **~ antibrouillard** *m* VEHICULES *éclairage* fog lamp; **~ d'approche** *m* AERONAUT approach light beacon; **~ d'atterrissage** *m* AERONAUT landing light; **~ de danger** *m* AERONAUT hazard beacon; **~ d'identification** *m* AERONAUT identification beacon; **~ portatif** *m* CONSTR portable light; **~ de radiocompas** *m* AERONAUT radio beacon; **~ rotatif** *m* AERONAUT rotating beacon

phares: **~ code** *m pl* VEHICULES *éclairage* dipped headlights (BrE), low beams (AmE)

pharmacolite *f* MINERAUX pharmacolite

pharmacosidérite *f* MINERAUX pharmacosiderite

phase:[1] **en ~** *adj* ELECTRON in-phase, ELECTROTEC, IMPRIM *réglages* in-step, PHYSIQUE in-phase, TV in-phase, phased

phase:[2] **en ~** *adv* PHYS ONDES in phase

phase[3] *f* CHIMIE, ELECTR *courant alternatif*, ELECTRON, ESSAIS, INFORMAT, METALL, ORDINAT, PETR, PHYSIQUE phase, PRODUCTION *électricité* live, THERMODYN, TRANSPORT phase; **~ d'apprentissage** *f* ELECTRON learning phase; **~ d'approche** *f* AERONAUT approach phase; **~ aqueuse** *f* CHARBON aqueous phase; **~ cholestérique** *f* CRISTALL cholesteric phase; **~ de chrominance** *f* TV chrominance phase; **~ de compression** *f* INST HYDR compression, compression period; **~ constante** *f* OPTIQUE constant phase; **~ couleur** *f* TV color phase (AmE), colour phase (BrE); **~ de course** *f* INST HYDR event; **~ du cycle** *f* INST HYDR event; **~ de décollage** *f* AERONAUT takeoff phase; **~ de déformation** *f* GEOLOGIE *en relation avec un épisode* deformational phase; **~ de détente de la vapeur** *f* INST HYDR cutoff point, duration of expansion of steam; **~ de développement** *f* PETROLE development phase; **~ différentielle** *f* ELECTRON DP, differential phase, TV differential phase; **~ de distributeur à tiroir** *f* INST HYDR event; **~ de distribution** *f* PRODUCTION critical event; **~ diurne** *f* ESPACE *astronomie* diurnal phase; **~ de données** *f* TELECOM data phase; **~ en quadrature** *f* ELECTRON quadrature phase; **~ d'établissement de la communication** *f* TELECOM call setup phase; **~ d'exécution** *f* INFORMAT, ORDINAT execute phase; **~ d'exploration** *f* PETROLE exploration phase; **~ gazeuse** *f* THERMODYN gaseous phase; **~ gazeuse seule** *f* THERMODYN gas-only phase, gaseous phase only; **~ d'une grandeur sinusoïdale** *f* ACOUSTIQUE phase; **~ des impulsions** *f* ELECTRON pulse phase; **~ intermétallique** *f* MATERIAUX intermetallic phase; **~ liquide seule** *f* THERMODYN liquid-only phase; **~ de marche du tiroir** *f* PRODUCTION critical event; **~ mésomorphe** *f* CRISTALL mesomorphic phase, mesophase; **~ de montée** *f* AERONAUT climb phase; **~ nématique** *f* CRISTALL nematic phase; **~ nocturne** *f* ESPACE *astronomie* nocturnal phase; **~ opposée** *f* ELECTR *courant alternatif* opposite phase; **~ parente** *f* METALL parent phase; **~ piétons** *f* TRANSPORT pedestrian phase; **~ pilote** *f* TELECOM field trial; **~ de préparation** *f* PRODUCTION setup phase; **~ de production** *f* GAZ production mode, PETROLE production phase; **~ de référence** *f* TV reference phase; **~ de régénération** *f* GAZ regeneration mode; **~ de rouge** *f* TRANSPORT red phase; **~ du signal** *f* ELECTRON signal phase; ~ **du signal de référence** *f* ELECTRON reference signal phase; ~ **smectique** *f* CRISTALL smectic phase; ~ **solide** *f* THERMODYN solid phase; ~ **du soluté** *f* MATERIAUX solute phase; ~ **de sous-porteuse** *f* TV subcarrier phase; ~ **de sous-porteuse de synchronisation couleur** *f* TV burst phase; ~ **spéciale pour tourner à gauche** *f* TRANSPORT left turn phase; ~ **stationnaire** *f* TELECOM stationary phase; ~ **à la terre** *f* PRODUCTION phase to ground; ~ **transitoire** *f* METALL transient phase; ~ **de transport** *f* TELECOM uplink transmission phase; ~ **vapeur** *f* GENIE CHIM, THERMODYN vapor phase (AmE), vapour phase (BrE); ~ **d'une vibration acoustique** *f* ACOUSTIQUE phase

phaséoline *f* CHIMIE phaseolin

phaséolunatine *f* CHIMIE phaseolunatin

phases: ~ **de la Lune** *f pl* ASTRONOMIE phases of the moon

phaseur *m* ELECTR *forme d'onde* phasor

phellandrène *m* CHIMIE phellandrene

phénacétine *f* CHIMIE phenacetin

phénacéturique *adj* CHIMIE phenaceturic

phénacite *f* MINERAUX phenacite, phenakite

phénacyle *m* CHIMIE phenacyl

phénanthraquinone *f* CHIMIE phenanthraquinone

phénanthrazine *f* CHIMIE phenanthrazine

phénanthridine *f* CHIMIE phenanthridine

phénanthridone *f* CHIMIE phenanthridone

phénanthrol *m* CHIMIE phenanthrol

phénanthroline *f* CHIMIE phenanthroline

phénate *m* CHIMIE phenate, phenolate

phénazine *f* CHIMIE phenazine

phénazocine *f* CHIMIE phenazocine

phénazone *f* CHIMIE phenazone

phénétidine *f* CHIMIE phenetidine

phénétole *m* CHIMIE phenetole

phengite *f* MINERAUX pheelgite

phéniqué *adj* CHIMIE carbolic

phéniramine *f* CHIMIE pheniramine

Phénix *m* ASTRONOMIE Phoenix

phénoblaste *f* GEOLOGIE, PETR phenocryst

phénoclaste[1] *adj* PETR phenoclast

phénoclaste[2] *m* GEOLOGIE phenoclast

phénocristal[1] *adj* GEOLOGIE, PETR phenocryst

phénocristal[2] *m* GEOLOGIE *roches éruptives*, PETR phenocryst

phénocryste *adj* GEOLOGIE, PETR phenocryst

phénol *m* HYDROLOGIE phenol

phénolate *m* CHIMIE phenolate, phenoxide

phénolique *adj* CHIMIE phenolic

phénolphtaléine *f* CHIMIE phenolphthalein

phénolsulfonique *adj* CHIMIE phenolsulfonic (AmE), phenolsulphonic (BrE)

phénomène: ~ **atmosphérique** *m* POLLUTION atmospheric phenomenon; ~ **coopératif** *m* PHYSIQUE cooperative phenomenon; ~ **dangereux** *m* QUALITE hazard; ~ **d'élargissement du papier** *m* IMPRIM *impression* fan-out; ~ **relativiste** *m* ESPACE relativity effect; ~ **tectonique** *m* PETROLE tectonic process; ~ **transitoire** *m* PHYSIQUE transient

phénomènes: ~ **d'instabilité** *m pl* PHYS FLUID instability phenomena; ~ **sismiques** *m pl* GEOPHYS seismic phenomena

phénoplaste *m* MATERIAUX, PLAST CAOU *plastiques* phenolic plastic

phénosafranine *f* CHIMIE phenosafranine

phénothiazine *f* CHIMIE phenothiazine

phénoxazine *f* CHIMIE phenoxazine

phénylacétaldéhyde *m* CHIMIE toluldehyde

phénylacétamide *m* CHIMIE phenylacetamide

phénylacétique *adj* CHIMIE phenylacetic

phénylalanine *f* CHIMIE phenylalanine

phénylamine *f* CHIMIE, IMPRIM phenylamine

phénylbenzène *m* CHIMIE diphenyl

phényle *m* CHIMIE phenyl

phénylé *adj* CHIMIE phenylated

phénylènediamine *f* CHIMIE phenylenediamine

phényléthylamine *f* CHIMIE phenylethylamine

phényléthylène *m* CHIMIE phenylethylene

phénylglycocolle *m* CHIMIE phenylglycine

phénylglycol *m* CHIMIE phenylglycol

phénylglycolique *adj* CHIMIE phenylglycolic

phénylhydrazine *f* CHIMIE phenylhydrazine

phénylhydrazone *f* CHIMIE phenylhydrazone

phénylhydroxyacétique *adj* CHIMIE phenylhydroxyacetic

phénylhydroxylamine *f* CHIMIE phenylhydroxylamine

phénylique *adj* CHIMIE phenylic

phénylmercaptan *m* CHIMIE thiophenol

phénylméthane *m* CHIMIE phenylmethane, LESSIVES toluene

phénylpropiolique *adj* CHIMIE phenylpropiolic

phénylpyrazol *m* CHIMIE phenylpyrazole

phénylurée *f* CHIMIE phenylurea

phillipsite *f* MINERAUX phillipsite

phlobaphène *m* CHIMIE phlobaphene

phlogopite *f* MINERAUX phlogopite

phlorétine *f* CHIMIE phloretin

phlorétique *adj* CHIMIE phloretic

phloridzine *f* CHIMIE phlorhizin, phloridzin, phlorrhizin

phlorol *m* CHIMIE phlorol

phoenicite *f* MINERAUX phoenicite, phoenicochroite

phoenicochroïte *f* MINERAUX phoenicite, phoenicochroite

phonation *f* ACOUSTIQUE phonation

phone *m* ACOUSTIQUE, PHYSIQUE phon

phonolite *f* PETR phonolite, phonolyte, PRODUCTION clinkstone

phonométrie *f* ENREGISTR audiometry

phonon *m* PHYSIQUE phonon

phonovision *f* OPTIQUE phonovision

phorone *f* CHIMIE phorone

phosgène *m* CHIMIE carbonyl chloride, phosgene, MILITAIRE *guerre chimique* phosgene

phosgénite *f* MINERAUX phosgenite

phospham *m* CHIMIE phospham

phosphatase *f* CHIMIE phosphatase

phosphatation *f* GENIE CHIM, LESSIVES phosphation, phosphatization

phosphate *m* CHIMIE, HYDROLOGIE, LESSIVES phosphate; ~ **de calcium** *m* AGRO ALIM calcium phosphate; ~ **de chaux** *m* CHIMIE phosphate of lime; ~ **ester** *m* LESSIVES phosphate ester; ~ **trisodique** *m* LESSIVES TSP, trisodium phosphate

phosphaté *adj* CHIMIE phosphated, phosphatic

phosphatique *adj* CHIMIE phosphatic

phosphine *f* CHIMIE phosphine

phosphite *m* CHIMIE phosphite

phosphocatalyse *f* CHIMIE phosphocatalysis

phosphoglycérique *adj* CHIMIE phosphoglyceric

phospholipide *m* AGRO ALIM phospholipid

phosphomolybdique *adj* CHIMIE phosphomolybdic

phosphonium *m* CHIMIE phosphonium

phosphore *m* CHIMIE phosphor, CHIMIE *(P)* phosphorus *(P)*

phosphoré *adj* CHIMIE phosphorated, phosphorized

phosphorescence *f* ELECTRON, NAUT, PHYS RAYON, PHYSIQUE phosphorescence, TV afterglow

phosphorique *adj* CHIMIE phosphoric

phosphoriser *vt* CHIMIE phosphorize

phosphorite *f* MINERAUX phosphorite

phosphorocalcite *f* MINERAUX phosphochalcite, phosphorochalcite

phosphorogène *adj* CHIMIE phosphorogenic

phosphorylase *f* CHIMIE phosphorylase

phosphoryle *m* CHIMIE phosphoryl

phosphorylé *adj* CHIMIE phosphorylated

phosphotungstate *m* CHIMIE phosphotungstate

phosphure *m* CHIMIE phosphide

phot *m* METROLOGIE phot

photicon *m* ELECTRON photicon

photo *f* PHOTO photograph, shot, PHYSIQUE photograph; **~ contretype** *f* PHOTO duplicate; **~ de contrôle** *f* PHOTO test shot; **~ couleur** *f* PHOTO color photography (AmE), colour photography (BrE); **~ de tournage** *f* CINEMAT production still; **~ de travail** *f* CINEMAT action still

photoamorceur *m* PLAST CAOU *durcissement de polymère* photoinitiator

photocathode *f* ELECTROTEC, PHYSIQUE, TV photocathode; **~ semi-transparente** *f* ELECTROTEC semitransparent photocathode

photocellule *f* CHIMIE photocell, PHOTO photoelectric cell

photochimie *f* CHIMIE, PHOTO photochemistry

photochimique *adj* POLLUTION photochemical

photoclinomètre *m* PETR photoclinometer

photocomposeuse *f* IMPRIM filmsetter; **~ pleine page** *f* IMPRIM image setter

photocompositeur *m* IMPRIM filmset (BrE), photocomposer (AmE)

photocompositeuse *f* IMPRIM filmset (BrE), photocomposer (AmE)

photocomposition *f* IMPRIM light setting, phototypesetting

photoconducteur *adj* ELECTRON photoconductive, PHOTO light-positive, photoconductive

photoconduction *f* ELECTRON, PHYSIQUE photoconductivity; **~ extrinsèque** *f* ELECTROTEC extrinsic photoconductivity; **~ indirecte** *f* ELECTRON indirect photoconductivity; **~ intrinsèque** *f* ELECTRON intrinsic photoconductivity

photoconductivité *f* OPTIQUE, PHYSIQUE, TELECOM photoconductivity

photocopie *f* IMPRIM *maquette, montage papier* stat; **~ blanche** *f* IMPRIM white photocopy

photocoupleur *m* ELECTROTEC optocoupler

photocourant *m* OPTIQUE light current, photocurrent, TELECOM photocurrent

photodésintégration *f* PHYSIQUE photodisintegration

photodétachement: **~ d'un électron** *m* NUCLEAIRE photodetachment

photodétecteur *m* ELECTRON photodetector, photosensor, OPTIQUE photodetector, TELECOM light detector, optical detector; **~ à semi-conducteur** *m* ELECTRON semiconductor photodetector; **~ au silicium** *m* ELECTRON silicon detector

photodétection *f* ELECTRON photodetection

photodiode *f* ELECTRON photodiode, OPTIQUE diode photodetector, photodiode, PHOTO, PHYSIQUE photodiode, TELECOM diode photodetector, photodiode; **~ à avalanche** *f* ELECTRON, OPTIQUE, TELECOM APD, avalanche photodiode; **~ à avalanche au germanium** *f* ELECTRON germanium avalanche photodiode; **~ à avalanche au silicium** *f* ELECTRON silicon avalanche photodiode; **~ à jonction par diffusion** *f* ELECTRON diffused photodiode; **~ PIN** *f* ELECTRON, OPTIQUE, TELECOM PIN photodiode; **~ au silicium** *f* ELECTRON silicon photodiode; **~ à zone de déplétion** *f* ELECTRON depletion layer photodiode

photodissociation *f* CHIMIE photodissociation

photoélectrique *adj* ELECTR *effet* photoelectric

photoélectron *m* ELECTRON photoelectron

photoémissif *adj* PHOTO photoemissive

photoémission *f* ELECTRON photoelectric emission, photoemission, OPTIQUE external photoelectric effect, photoemissive effect, TELECOM photoemissive effect

photogrammétrie *f* CONSTR, ESPACE photogrammetry; **~ aérienne** *f* GEOLOGIE aerial photographic survey

photographe *m* PHOTO photographer

photographie *f* IMPRIM photographic print, PHOTO, PHYSIQUE photograph; **~ de cristal tournant** *f* CRISTALL rotation photography; **~ en couleur** *f* PHOTO color photography (AmE), colour photography (BrE); **~ à la lumière artificielle** *f* PHOTO artificial light photography; **~ à la lumière du jour** *f* PHOTO daylight photography; **~ de nature morte** *f* PHOTO still-life photography; **~ publicitaire** *f* PHOTO advertising photography; **~ sous-marine** *f* PHOTO underwater photography; **~ sténopéique** *f* PHOTO pinhole photography; **~ trichrome** *f* PHOTO three-color photography (AmE), three-colour photography (BrE); **~ ultraviolette** *f* PHYS RAYON ultraviolet photography

photographier: **~ sur pied** *vt* PHOTO photograph with a tripod

photograver *vt* ELECTRON photoengrave

photograveur *m* IMPRIM process engraver

photogravure *f* ELECTRON photoengraving, photolithography, IMPRIM photoengraving; **~ typographique** *f* IMPRIM blockmaking

photoionisation *f* PHYSIQUE photoionization

photoluminescence *f* PHYS RAYON photoluminescence

photolyse *f* CHIMIE, EN RENOUV photolysis; **~ flash** *f* CHIMIE flash photolysis

photolytique *adj* CHIMIE photolytic

photomécanique *adj* IMPRIM photomechanical

photomètre *m* ASTRONOMIE photometer, CINEMAT light meter, MATERIAUX, PHOTO, PHYSIQUE, PLAST CAOU *instrument* photometer; **~ de flamme** *m* EQUIP LAB *analyse* flame photometer; **~ de Lummer et Brodhun** *m* PHYSIQUE Lummer-Brodhun photometer; **~ de papillotement** *m* PHYSIQUE flicker photometer

photométrie *f* MATERIAUX, PHYSIQUE photometry

photomultiplicateur *m* ELECTRON photomultiplier, INSTRUMENT multiplier phototube, photomultiplier, PHYS RAYON, PHYSIQUE photomultiplier

photon *m* OPTIQUE, PHYS PART, PHYS RAYON, PHYSIQUE photon; **~ d'annihilation** *m* PHYS RAYON annihilation photon; **~ gamma** *m* PHYS PART, PHYS RAYON gamma-ray photon; **~ à la longueur d'ondes de 21 cm** *m* ASTRONOMIE photon at 21 cm wavelength; **~ de rayonnement X** *m* NUCLEAIRE *quantum* X-ray photon, X-ray quantum; **~ ultraviolet** *m* PHYS PART ultraviolet photon; **~ UV** *m* PHYS PART ultraviolet photon

photons: ~ **de pompage** *m pl* ELECTRON pumping photons

photopile *f* ELECTR photocell, photoelectric cell, solar cell, ELECTROTEC, EN RENOUV photovoltaic cell, PHYSIQUE photocell, photoelectric cell

photopolymère *m* IMPRIM photopolymer

photopolymérisation *f* CHIMIE photopolymerization

photoréaction *f* CHIMIE photoreaction

photorécepteur *m* TELECOM light detector

photorésist *m* ELECTRON photoresist; ~ **négatif** *m* ELECTRON negative photoresist; ~ **positif** *m* ELECTRON positive photoresist

photorésistance *f* ELECTROTEC photovaristor

photorésistant *adj* PHOTO light-negative

photorésistor *m* PHYS RAYON photoresistor

photosensibilité *f* ELECTRON, PHYSIQUE photosensitivity

photosensible *adj* CINEMAT, ELECTRON, IMPRIM *photogravure* light-sensitive, PHOTO, PHYSIQUE photosensitive

photosphère *f* ASTRONOMIE, ESPACE *astronomie* photosphere; ~ **de poussière** *f* ASTRONOMIE *autour d'une protoétoile* dust photosphere

photostat *m* IMPRIM *maquette, montage papier* stat

photostyle *m* INFORMAT, ORDINAT, PHYSIQUE light pen

photosynthèse *f* CHIMIE, EN RENOUV, HYDROLOGIE photosynthesis

phototélécopie *f* TELECOM phototelegraphy

phototélégraphie *f* TELECOM facsimile telegraphy

photothyristor *m* ELECTROTEC light-activated silicon controlled rectifier

phototraceur *m* INFORMAT, ORDINAT photoplotter

phototransistor *m* ELECTRON, INFORMAT, ORDINAT, PHYS RAYON phototransistor; ~ **au silicium** *m* ELECTRON silicon phototransistor

phototube *m* ELECTRON phototube; ~ **au césium** *m* ELECTRON caesium phototube (BrE), cesium phototube (AmE); ~ **à gaz** *m* ELECTRON gas phototube; ~ **à vide** *m* ELECTRON vacuum phototube

photovoltaïque *adj* ESPACE *énergie* photovoltaic

phrase *f* INFORMAT, ORDINAT sentence

phtalamide *m* CHIMIE phthalamide

phtalate *m* CHIMIE phthalate; ~ **de dibutyle** *m* PLAST CAOU dibutyl phthalate, *plastifiant* butyl phthalate; ~ **de dioctyle** *m* PLAST CAOU *plastifiant* dioctyl phthalate

phtaléine *f* CHIMIE phthalein

phtalide *m* CHIMIE phthalide

phtaline *f* CHIMIE phthalin

phtalique *adj* CHIMIE *acide* phthalic

phtalocyanine *f* PLAST CAOU *pigment* phthalocyanine

phtanite *f* GEOLOGIE black chert, PETR phanite

phugoïde *m* AERONAUT phugoid

phycologie *f* OCEANO phycology

phyllade *m* GEOLOGIE phyllite

phyllite *f* GEOLOGIE *cristal*, PETR phyllite

phylliteux *adj* GEOLOGIE sheet silicate-bearing

phyrique *adj* GEOLOGIE *roches magmatiques* phyric

physalite *f* MINERAUX physalite

physicien: ~ **des accélérateurs** *m* PHYS PART accelerator physicist; ~ **de l'atome** *m* PHYS PART atomic physicist, nuclear physicist; ~ **expérimentateur** *m* PHYS PART experimental physicist

physique[1] *adj* INFORMAT, ORDINAT, TELECOM physical

physique:[2] **personne** ~ *f* BREVETS natural person; ~ **atomique** *f* PHYSIQUE atomic physics; ~ **de l'état solide** *f* PHYS PART, PHYSIQUE solid-state physics; ~ **des fluides** *f* PHYSIQUE fluid physics; ~ **des hautes énergies** *f* PHYS RAYON, PHYSIQUE high-energy physics; ~ **mathématique** *f* PHYSIQUE mathematical physics; ~ **nucléaire** *f* NUCLEAIRE nuclear physics, nucleonics, PHYSIQUE nuclear physics; ~ **nucléaire à basse énergie** *f* PHYS PART low-energy nuclear physics; ~ **nucléaire des énergies moyennes** *f* NUCLEAIRE medium-energy nuclear physics; ~ **des ondulatoire** *f* PHYSIQUE wave physics; ~ **des particules** *f* PHYSIQUE particle physics; ~ **quantique** *f* PHYS PART, PHYSIQUE quantum physics; ~ **des rayonnements** *f* NUCLEAIRE, PHYSIQUE radiation physics; ~ **du solide** *f* PHYS PART solid-state physics; ~ **statistique** *f* PHYSIQUE statistical physics

physostigmine *f* CHIMIE physostigmine

phytase *f* AGRO ALIM phytase

phytine *f* AGRO ALIM phytin

phytocide *adj* CHIMIE phytocidal

phytotoxique *adj* CHIMIE phytotoxic

pianine *f* CHIMIE opianine

pic *m* CHIMIE, NAUT *voile* peak, NUCLEAIRE line, maximum, peak, PRODUCTION pick; ~ **d'absorption** *m* ELECTROTEC absorption peak; ~ **avant** *m* NAUT forepeak; ~ **à charbon** *m* CHARBON coal pick; ~ **de courant** *m* ELECTR current peak; ~ **à deux pointes** *m* CHARBON, MINES mandrel, mandril; ~ **de fuite** *m* PHYS RAYON *radiation gamma* escape peak; ~ **de fuite de photons** *m* PHYS RAYON gamma ray escape peak; ~ **de fuite des rayons X** *m* PHYS RAYON X-ray escape peak; ~ **léger** *m* NUCLEAIRE light peak; ~ **de Lewis** *m* NUCLEAIRE Lewis peak; ~ **lourd** *m* NUCLEAIRE *du groupe lourd* heavy peak; ~ **père** *m* NUCLEAIRE parent mass peak, parent peak; ~ **de premier échappement** *m* PHYS RAYON *spectre de rayons gamma* single escape peak; ~ **de résonance** *m* PHYS RAYON resonance peak; ~ **de rétrodiffusion** *m* PHYS RAYON *rayonnement gamma* backscatter peak; ~ **à tête** *m* CONSTR poll pick, PRODUCTION hammer pick; ~ **à la veine** *m* CHARBON coal pick

pica *m* IMPRIM pica

piccadil *m* CERAM VER slag

pick-up *m* ENREGISTR pick-up

pico- *préf (p)* METROLOGIE pico-*(p)*

picoline *f* CHIMIE picoline

picoseconde *f* INFORMAT, ORDINAT picosecond

picot *m* ELECTROTEC pin; ~ **fond** *m* CERAM VER spike; ~ **sous la bague** *m* CERAM VER pip under finish

picotite *f* MINERAUX picotite

picrate *m* CHIMIE picrate

picrique *adj* CHIMIE picric

picrite *f* PETR picrite

picrol *m* CHIMIE picrol

picrolite *f* MINERAUX picrolite

picromérite *f* MINERAUX picromerite

picrotine *f* CHIMIE picrotin

picryle *m* CHIMIE picryl

pics: ~ **de paires** *m pl* PHYS RAYON *annihilation d'un positron* pair peaks

pictographe *m* IMPRIM pictograph

pièce:[1] **tout d'une** ~ *adj* CONS MECA, PRODUCTION all in one piece

pièce[2] *f* CONSTR *de bois* stick, PRODUCTION casting, TEXTILE, VEHICULES part; ~ **d'amarrage** *f* ESPACE *véhicules* docking piece, docking unit; ~ **d'artillerie** *f* MILITAIRE ordnance gun; ~ **battue** *f* PRODUCTION drawback, false core; ~ **brute de fonderie** *f* PRODUCTION rough casting; ~ **brute d'usinage** *f* PRODUCTION blank; ~ **de calage** ƒ CERAM VER tuckstone; ~ **chargée debout** ƒ CONSTR *résistance des matériaux* strut; ~ **à coller** ƒ PLAST CAOU *adhésifs* adherend; ~ **coudée** ƒ CONSTR bend; ~ **coulée** ƒ PLAST CAOU *article*, PRODUCTION casting; ~ **coulée en coquille** ƒ PRODUCTION chill casting, chilled iron casting; ~ **découpée** ƒ RESSORTS outpiece; ~ **à demeure** ƒ CONS MECA fixture; ~ **détachée** ƒ NAUT, VEHICULES spare part; ~ **d'écartement** ƒ CONS MECA distance bar, distance piece spacer, distance piece, CONSTR *entre les barreaux d'une grille* distance piece; ~ **d'écartement de la tête de bobine** ƒ NUCLEAIRE end winding spacer, overhang spacer; ~ **entière** ƒ TEXTILE full-length cloth, whole piece; ~ **d'espacement d'entrefer** ƒ ENREGISTR gap spacer; ~ **estampée** ƒ MECANIQUE *matériaux* drop forging; ~ **faciale filtrante contre les particules** ƒ SECURITE filtering facepiece for protection against particles; ~ **factice** ƒ CONS MECA dummy part; ~ **de fixation des tubes de discussion** ƒ INSTRUMENT discussion tube arrangement; ~ **fixe** ƒ CONS MECA fixture; ~ **de fonderie** ƒ CONS MECA, IMPRIM *typographie*, PRODUCTION casting; ~ **fondue** ƒ PRODUCTION casting; ~ **fondue en coquille** ƒ PRODUCTION chill casting, chilled iron casting; ~ **fondue au sable** ƒ PRODUCTION sand casting; ~ **de fonte** ƒ PRODUCTION casting; ~ **de forge** ƒ PRODUCTION forging; ~ **de forge dégrossie** ƒ PRODUCTION roughed forging; ~ **forgée** ƒ MECANIQUE *matériaux*, PRODUCTION forging; ~ **forgée en titane** ƒ ESPACE *véhicules* titanium forging; ~ **forgée pour matrice à ouverture** ƒ CONS MECA open die forging; ~ **manquée** ƒ PRODUCTION spoiled casting; ~ **moulée** ƒ MATERIAUX, MECANIQUE *matériaux*, PAPIER casting, PRODUCTION casting, molded casting (AmE), moulded casting (BrE); ~ **à nez** ƒ CERAM VER plate block; ~ **à noyaux** ƒ PRODUCTION cored casting; ~ **permutable** ƒ CONS MECA interchangeable part; ~ **polaire** ƒ ELECTROTEC pole piece, pole shoe, ENREGISTR, PHYSIQUE pole piece, TV pole tip; ~ **pour partitionner** ƒ EMBALLAGE partitioning insert; ~ **de rapport** ƒ PRODUCTION drawback, false core, loose piece; ~ **rapportée** ƒ CONS MECA, EMBALLAGE insert, PRODUCTION drawback, false core, insert, loose piece; ~ **rapportée en PVC** ƒ EMBALLAGE PVC insert fitment; ~ **rapportée d'évacuation d'air** ƒ CONS MECA air vent pin; ~ **rapportée mobile** ƒ PLAST CAOU spring-loaded core; ~ **rapportée de refroidissement** ƒ CONS MECA cooling spirals; ~ **de rechange** ƒ CONS MECA spare part, spare, VEHICULES spare part; ~ **de recouvrement** ƒ INSTRUMENT cover; ~ **de renfort** ƒ CONS MECA stiffener; ~ **de serrage** ƒ MECANIQUE clamp; ~ **de tête** ƒ NUCLEAIRE headpiece; ~ **troussée** ƒ PRODUCTION strickled casting, struck-up casting, swept-up casting; ~ **à usiner** ƒ MECANIQUE workpiece; ~ **d'usure** ƒ CHARBON wearing part, CONS MECA wear part, GAZ wearing part; ~ **venue de forge** ƒ PRODUCTION forging; ~ **à vis** ƒ CONS MECA screw piece

pièces ƒ pl CONS MECA machinery, CONSTR *d'une charpente* members; ~ **d'automobile** ƒ pl VEHICULES motorcar parts; ~ **composantes thermoplastiques** ƒ pl CONS MECA thermoplastic components; ~ **coupées** ƒ pl SECURITE cut pieces; ~ **d'embarquement** ƒ pl NAUT shipping documents; ~ **moyennes** ƒ pl PRODUCTION average castings

pied:[1] **à ~ d'oeuvre** adj CONSTR on site, site-delivered
pied:[2] **à ~ d'oeuvre** adv CONSTR on site
pied[3] *m* CINEMAT stand, CONS MECA standard, *de bielle* small end, CONSTR support, *d'une colline* bottom,

INSTRUMENT base, *de trépied* leg, METROLOGIE, NAUT *mesure* foot, PRODUCTION tripod; ~ **"boule"** *m* CINEMAT geared center column (AmE), geared centre column (BrE); ~ **ajustable** *m* CINEMAT telescopic tripod; ~ **d'aube** *m* AERONAUT blade root; ~ **de bielle** *m* AUTO connecting rod small end, small end, CONS MECA connecting rod little end, VEHICULES small end, *moteur* connecting rod small end; ~ **de bord** *m* CERAM VER root; ~ **carré** *m* METROLOGIE square foot; ~ **à coulisse** *m* CONS MECA caliper gage (AmE), calliper gauge (BrE), sliding caliper gage (AmE), sliding calipers (AmE), sliding calliper gauge (BrE), sliding callipers (BrE), EQUIP LAB *mesure de longueur ou d'écartement* calipers (AmE), callipers (BrE), MECANIQUE *outillage* caliper (AmE), calliper (BrE), METROLOGIE beam caliper (AmE), beam caliper gage (AmE), beam calliper (BrE), beam calliper gauge (BrE), RESSORTS slide caliper (AmE), slide calliper (BrE); ~ **à coulisse à vernier** *m* MECANIQUE *outillage* vernier calipers (AmE), vernier callipers (BrE), METEO vernier caliper (AmE), vernier calliper (BrE), PHYSIQUE vernier calipers (AmE), vernier callipers (BrE); ~ **courant** *m* METROLOGIE running foot; ~ **de la courbe** *m* PHOTO toe region of curve; ~ **cube** *m* METROLOGIE, PETROLE *unité de mesure de volume anglo-saxonne* cubic foot; ~ **d'éclairage** *m* PHOTO lighting stand, reflector stand; ~ **en forme de fer à cheval** *m* EQUIP LAB *microscope* horseshoe foot; ~ **à fourche** *m* CONS MECA *pour machine à percer* U-shaped base plate; ~ **linéaire** *m* METROLOGIE running foot; ~ **de mât** *m* NAUT mast foot; ~ **de mouton vibrant** *m* CONSTR vibrating sheepsfoot roller; ~ **photographique** *m* PHOTO camera stand, tripod; ~ **pliant** *m* CINEMAT collapsible stand; ~ **de poitrine** *m* CINEMAT body brace, chestpod; ~ **de positionnement** *m* CONS MECA locator; ~ **de positionnement cylindrique** *m* CONS MECA dowel pin parallel; ~ **de positionnement cylindrique à trou taraudé** *m* CONS MECA dowel pin with extracting thread; ~ **à quatre brisures** *m* PHOTO fourfold tripod stand; ~ **de table** *m* CINEMAT table top tripod, PHOTO table tripod; ~ **de talus** *m* CHARBON slope toe; ~ **à tête panoramique graduée** *m* PHOTO pan head tripod; ~ **à trois branches** *m* PRODUCTION tripod stand, tripod; ~ **à trois branches coulissantes** *m* METROLOGIE adjustable tripod; ~ **à trois branches extensibles** *m* PHOTO extension tripod

pied-de-biche *m* CONS MECA eccentric hook, CONSTR claw, claw bar, nail claw, INST HYDR gab, gab hook, hook gear, MECANIQUE *outillage* crowbar

pied-de-boeuf *m* MINES lifting dog
pied-de-chèvre *m* CONSTR claw, nail claw
pied-droit *m* CONS MECA upright, CONSTR pier, pillar, MINES post, prop, support pier, support pillar, wall
piédestal *m* CHARBON footing
pieds: ~ **à coulisse** *m* pl METROLOGIE calipers (AmE), callipers (BrE); ~ **à coulisse à vernier** *m* pl METROLOGIE vernier calipers (AmE), vernier callipers (BrE); ~ **par seconde** *m* pl CINEMAT feet per second

piège *m* ELECTROTEC choke, line choking coil, GAZ trap, GENIE CHIM separator, trap, PETR, PETROLE trap, POLLUTION sink, REFRIG trap, TELECOM choke; ~ **à absorption** *m* GENIE CHIM absorber trap, NUCLEAIRE adsorption trap; ~ **anticlinal** *m* PETROLE anticlinal trap; ~ **à l'aspiration** *m* REFRIG dead end trap; ~ **de condensation** *m* GENIE CHIM condensation trap; ~ **à crasse** *m* GAZ dross filter; ~ **froid** *m* REFRIG cold trap;

~ **d'hydrocarbures** m PETROLE *géologie du pétrole* hydrocarbon trap, oil trap; ~ **à ions** m ELECTRON, TV ion trap; ~ **par discordance** m PETROLE *formation des hydrocarbures* unconformity trap; ~ **par faille** m PETROLE *formation des hydrocarbures* fault trap; ~ **pétrolifère** m PETROLE hydrocarbon trap, oil trap; ~ **de polarisation** m ENREGISTR bias trap; ~ **à porteurs de charge** m ELECTROTEC trapping site; ~ **réversible** m MATERIAUX *cristallographie* reversible trap; ~ **à sable** m PETROLE sand trap; ~ **stratigraphique** m PETROLE stratigraphic trap; ~ **structural** m PETROLE structural tap; ~ **thermique** m NUCLEAIRE heat trap; ~ **à vapeur** m GENIE CHIM vapor trap (AmE), vapour trap (BrE)

piégeage m POLLUTION rainout
piège-condenseur m EQUIP LAB *verrerie* condensing trap; ~ **pour pompe à vide** m EQUIP LAB trap for vacuum pump
piéger vt POLLU MER entrap
piémontite f MINERAUX piedmontite
pierraille f DISTRI EAU break stone
pierre: ~ **à aiguiser** f CONS MECA honing stone, PRODUCTION hone, honestone, oilstone, whetstone; ~ **d'aimant** f MINERAUX lodestone; ~ **d'arrachement** f CONSTR toothing stone; ~ **d'attente** f CONSTR toothing stone; ~ **à bâtir** f CONSTR building stone; ~ **de bornage** f CONSTR boundary stone; ~ **bornale** f CONSTR boundary stone; ~ **calcaire** f CHIMIE limestone; ~ **cassée** f CONSTR broken stone; ~ **à chaux** f CHIMIE limestone; ~ **de clavage** f CONSTR *maçonnerie* binding stone; ~ **de construction** f CONSTR building stone; ~ **de croix** GEOLOGIE, MINES cross stone; ~ **de dévitrification** f CERAM VER devitrification stone; ~ **équarrie** f CONSTR building stone; ~ **à feu** f CERAM VER firestone; ~ **à huile** f CONS MECA *abrasifs*, PRODUCTION oilstone; ~ **à liards** f GEOLOGIE nummulitic limestone; ~ **lithographique** f CHIMIE lithographic slate, lithographic stone; ~ **de lune** f MINERAUX moonstone; ~ **de meule** f PRODUCTION millstone grit; ~ **meulière** f PRODUCTION millstone grit; ~ **de miel** f MINERAUX honey stone; ~ **de mine** f MINES metal, mine stone, minestuff, stone; ~ **à morfiler** f PRODUCTION oilstone; ~ **noire** f CERAM VER black speck; ~ **parée** f CONSTR dressed stone; ~ **de pavage** f CONSTR paving stone; ~ **à plâtre** f CHIMIE gypsum, CONSTR plaster rock, plaster stone; ~ **ponce** f CERAM VER, GEOLOGIE pumice, MINERAUX pumice stone; ~ **à roder** f MECANIQUE *outillage* honing stone; ~ **de savon** f MINERAUX soapstone; ~ **de soleil** f MINERAUX sunstone; ~ **de superfinissage** f CONS MECA superfinishing honing stone, superfinishing stone; ~ **de taille** f CONSTR building stone, cut stone; ~ **taillée** f CONSTR building stone, dressed stone; ~ **verte** f CONSTR greenstone
pierres: ~ **concassées** f pl CONSTR crushed stone
pierreux adj CONSTR stony
piétage m AERONAUT cover strip of root rib, CINEMAT edge numbering; ~ **femelle** m CONS MECA locating hole; ~ **mâle** m CONS MECA locating stud
pieu m CHARBON pile, CONSTR pile, post, spile, stake; ~ **d'amarrage** m NAUT mooring pile, mooring post; ~ **à cohésion** m CHARBON cohesion pile; ~ **combiné** m CHARBON composite pile; ~ **composé** m CHARBON segmented pile; ~ **en acier** m CHARBON steel pile; ~ **en béton** m CHARBON concrete pile; ~ **en bois** m CHARBON wooden pile; ~ **en milieu pulvérulent** m CHARBON friction pile; ~ **flottant** m CHARBON floating pile; ~ **de fondation** m CONSTR datum; ~ **à friction** m CONSTR

friction pile; ~ **intermédiaire** m CHARBON middle pile segment; ~ **moulé dans un avant-puits** m CHARBON prebored pile; ~ **moulé dans le sol** m CHARBON cast-in-place pile, in situ pile; ~ **pour remblai** m CHARBON embankment pile; ~ **poussé** m CHARBON jacked pile; ~ **de sécurité** m CONSTR life preserver
pieux m pl CONSTR piling, spiling; ~ **en acier** m pl PETROLE piling
piézodiffusion f NUCLEAIRE barodiffusion
piézo-électricité f CRISTALL, ELECTROTEC piezoelectricity
piézo-électrique adj CRISTALL, ELECTROTEC piezoelectric
piézomètre m CHARBON, CONSTR piezometer
pige: ~ **rigide** f METROLOGIE measuring rod
pigeonite f MINERAUX pigeonite
pigeonneau: ~ **fileté** m CONS MECA *bloc à colonnes* coupling spigot with thread
pigment m CERAM VER, CHIMIE, COULEURS pigment, IMPRIM coloring matter (AmE), colouring matter (BrE), PLAST CAOU *peinture*, TEXTILE pigment; ~ **d'aluminium** m COULEURS silver bronze powder; ~ **à base de chromate de plomb et bleu de phthalocyanine** m COULEURS lead chrome-phthalocyanine blue pigment; ~ **à base d'oxyde de fer** m COULEURS iron oxide pigment; ~ **à base d'oxyde de titane** m COULEURS titanium oxide pigment; ~ **blanc** m COULEURS white pigment; ~ **blanc en poudre** m COULEURS white pigmented powder; ~ **bleu de fer** m COULEURS iron blue pigment; ~ **bleuté** m COULEURS blue glaze pigment; ~ **de bronze** m COULEURS bronze, bronze pigment; ~ **bronze** m COULEURS bronze; ~ **de charge** m PLAST CAOU *mélange* extender; ~ **à la chaux** m COULEURS lime pigment; ~ **au chromate de baryum** m COULEURS barium chromate pigment; ~ **au chromate de plomb** m COULEURS lead chrome green pigment; ~ **au chromate de strontium** m COULEURS strontium chromate pigment; ~ **au chromate de zinc** m COULEURS zinc chromate pigment; ~ **de chrome** m COULEURS chromic oxide pigment; ~ **coloré** m COULEURS colored pigment (AmE), coloring pigment (AmE), coloured pigment (BrE), colouring pigment (BrE); ~ **de fer** m COULEURS iron pigment; ~ **à grand teint** m PLAST CAOU *peinture, matière première* high purity pigment; ~ **laque** m COULEURS lake pigment; ~ **de lissage** m PLAST CAOU *peinture* flatting pigment; ~ **luminescent** m COULEURS luminescent pigment; ~ **minéral** m COULEURS mineral color (AmE), mineral colour (BrE), mineral pigment; ~ **nacré** m PLAST CAOU nacreous pigment; ~ **à nuancer** m COULEURS shading-off pigment, stainer pigment; ~ **opacifiant** m COULEURS opaque pigment; ~ **organique** m COULEURS organic pigment; ~ **organométallique** m COULEURS metallo-organic pigment (BrE), metalo-organic pigment (AmE); ~ **d'outremer** m COULEURS ultramarine pigment; ~ **d'oxyde de fer** m COULEURS iron oxide pigment; ~ **de poudre de zinc** m COULEURS zinc dust pigment; ~ **végétal** m COULEURS plant pigment
pigmentation f TEXTILE pigmentation
pigmenté adj COULEURS pigmented
pigmenter vt TEXTILE pigment
pignon m AUTO pinion, CONS MECA gear, pinion, CONSTR gable, PRODUCTION sprocket, VEHICULES *boîte de vitesses* pinion; ~ **d'arbre intermédiaire** m AUTO countershaft gear; ~ **d'attaque** m AUTO drive pinion shaft, pinion gear, CONS MECA driving gear, driving

pinion, VEHICULES *arbre de transmission* drive pinion; ~ d'attaque du différentiel *m* AUTO drive line; ~ de brûleur *m* CERAM VER port back wall (BrE), port endwall (AmE); ~ de chaîne *m* CONS MECA rag wheel; ~ à chaîne *m* MECANIQUE sprocket wheel, VEHICULES *transmission de motocyclette* sprocket; ~ à chevrons *m* CONS MECA herringbone gear; ~ cloche *m* CONS MECA bell gear; ~ de commande *m* CONS MECA driving pinion; ~ conique *m* CONS MECA bevel gear; ~ conique de différentiel *m* VEHICULES *transmission* differential bevel gear; ~ de démarreur *m* AUTO drive pinion, VEHICULES *moteur* starter motor pinion; ~ denté *m* MECANIQUE *engrenages* gear wheel; ~ à denture droite *m* AUTO straight-tooth meshing gear; ~ de deuxième vitesse *m* AUTO second gear; ~ de distribution *m* AUTO crankshaft gear, timing gear, VEHICULES *commande de l'arbre à cames* timing gear; ~ d'entraînement *m* CONS MECA driving pinion; ~ d'entraînement à chaîne *m* VEHICULES drive sprocket; ~ d'entraînement de pellicule *m* PHOTO film transport sprocket; ~ entraîneur *m* AUTO clutch gear, main drive gear, transmission pinion, VEHICULES *boîte de vitesses* drive pinion; ~ à ergot *m* CONS MECA pick-up gear; ~ et crémaillère *m* CONS MECA rack-and-pinion; ~ excentrique *m* CONS MECA eccentric gear; ~ fou *m* VEHICULES *boîte de vitesses* idle gear; ~ de Galle *m* CONS MECA rag wheel, sprocket wheel; ~ hélicoïdal *m* CONS MECA helical gear; ~ inverseur *m* AUTO, VEHICULES *boîte de vitesses* reverse idler gear; ~ de marche arrière *m* AUTO, VEHICULES *boîte de vitesses* reverse gear; ~ planétaire *m* AUTO differential side gear; ~ récepteur *m* VEHICULES *boîte de vitesses* countershaft gear; ~ satellite *m* CONS MECA planet gear; ~ de troisième vitesse *m* AUTO third gear

pignons: ~ d'arbres à cames *m pl* CONS MECA camshaft gears

PILA *abrév (présentation de l'identification de la ligne appelante)* TELECOM CLID *(calling line identification display)*

pilastre *m* CONSTR *de rampe d'escalier* newel, newel post

PILC *abrév (présentation de l'identification de la ligne connectée)* TELECOM COLP *(connected line identification presentation)*

pile *f* CERAM VER stack, CONSTR pile, ELECTR battery, *source* cell, *à plusieurs éléments* primary battery, ELECTROTEC pile, INFORMAT, ORDINAT, PAPIER *de papier* stack, PHYSIQUE battery, TELECOM battery, cell; ~ alcaline *f* ELECTROTEC alkaline battery, alkaline cell, alkaline storage cell; ~ amorçable *f* ELECTROTEC reserve battery; ~ amorçable à l'eau *f* ELECTROTEC water-activated battery; ~ à l'argent *f* ELECTROTEC silver oxide cell; ~ atomique *f* NUCLEAIRE atomic pile, nuclear reactor, PHYSIQUE atomic pile; ~ atomique transportable *f* NUCLEAIRE aspatron; ~ d'attente *f* AERONAUT holding stack, stack; ~ au bioxyde de manganèse *f* ELECTROTEC zinc-manganese dioxide cell; ~ blanchisseuse *f* PAPIER bleacher, bleaching washer; ~ de Bunsen *f* ELECTR Bunsen cell; ~ câblée *f* INFORMAT, ORDINAT hardware stack; ~ cadmium *f* ELECTR cadmium cell; ~ calomel *f* ELECTR *électrode* calomel electrode; ~ de cassettes *f* CERAM VER bung of saggars; ~ charbon-zinc *f* ELECTROTEC zinc-carbon cell; ~ au chlorure d'argent *f* ELECTROTEC zinc-silver cell; ~ au chlorure d'argent-magnésium *f* ELECTROTEC magnesium silver chloride cell; ~ au chlorure de zinc *f* ELECTROTEC zinc chloride cell; ~ à combustible *f* ES-

PACE *énergie*, THERMODYN fuel cell; ~ de concentration *f* ELECTR concentration cell; ~ à dépolarisation par l'air *f* ELECTROTEC air cell, air-depolarized battery; ~ désagrégeante *f* PAPIER beater-breaker; ~ directe *f* INFORMAT, ORDINAT push-up stack, TRANSPORT direct cell, primary fuel cell; ~ directe à hydrogène-oxygène *f* TRANSPORT direct hydrogen-oxygen cell; ~ directe méthanol-air *f* TRANSPORT direct methanol-air cell; ~ électrique *f* ELECTROTEC electric cell, galvanic cell, primary cell; ~ à électrolyte liquide *f* ELECTROTEC wet cell; ~ à un élément *f* ELECTROTEC one-element cell; ~ épuisée *f* TELECOM flat battery; ~ étalon *f* ELECTR, ELECTROTEC, PHYSIQUE standard cell; ~ étalon au cadmium *f* ELECTROTEC Weston standard cell; ~ étalon Weston *f* ELECTR, ELECTROTEC Weston standard cell; ~ froide directe à hydrogène *f* TRANSPORT direct cold hydrogen cell; ~ galvanique *f* ELECTR galvanic cell, voltaic cell, ELECTROTEC galvanic cell; ~ à haute température *f* TRANSPORT high-temperature fuel cell; ~ à haute température à électrolyte solide *f* TRANSPORT high-temperature solid electrolyte cell; ~ image *f* NUCLEAIRE image reactor; ~ incorporée *f* ELECTROTEC internal battery; ~ indirecte *f* TRANSPORT secondary fuel cell; ~ inversée *f* INFORMAT, ORDINAT push-down stack; ~ Leclanché *f* ELECTROTEC, EQUIP LAB *électricité* Leclanché cell; ~ au lithium *f* ELECTROTEC lithium battery; ~ de maintien de la mémoire *f* PRODUCTION backup battery; ~ au mercure *f* ELECTROTEC mercury cell, *à plusieurs éléments* mercury battery; ~ au méthanol *f* TRANSPORT methanol cell; ~ nucléaire *f* CONSTR nuclear cell, NUCLEAIRE nuclear reactor, pile, reactor; ~ à l'oxyde d'argent *f* ELECTROTEC silver oxide cell, zinc-silver oxide cell, *à plusieurs éléments* silver oxide battery; ~ à oxydoréduction *f* EQUIP LAB *analyse, électrochimie* oxidation reduction cell, redose cell; ~ de papier *f* IMPRIM pile; ~ de polarisation *f* ELECTROTEC bias battery; ~ de port *f* CONSTR *pont* pier; ~ raffineuse *f* PAPIER beater, refiner; ~ rechargeable *f* ELECTROTEC rechargeable battery, PHYSIQUE rechargeable cell; ~ redox *f* TRANSPORT redox cell; ~ régénérable *f* TRANSPORT regenerative cell; ~ de requêtes *f* INFORMAT, ORDINAT request stack; ~ de sauvegarde *f* PRODUCTION *électricité* battery backup; ~ sèche *f* ELECTR, ELECTROTEC, PHYSIQUE dry cell; ~ secondaire *f* ELECTR, ELECTROTEC secondary cell; ~ de secours *f* PRODUCTION backup battery; ~ sigma *f* NUCLEAIRE sigma pile; ~ solaire *f* ASTRONOMIE, ELECTR, PHYS RAYON, PHYSIQUE solar cell, TV solar battery; ~ de soutènement *f* MINES self-advancing chock; ~ à sulfure de cadmium *f* ELECTR cadmium sulfide cell (AmE), cadmium sulphide cell (BrE); ~ thermoélectrique *f* ELECTROTEC thermopile; ~ de Volta *f* ELECTROTEC galvanic cell; ~ voltaïque *f* ELECTROTEC voltaic pile; ~ Weston *f* ELECTROTEC Weston standard cell; ~ au zinc *f* ELECTROTEC zinc battery

piler *vt* PRODUCTION pound

pilier *m* CERAM VER, CONSTR, GEOPHYS, MINES *de charbon, de minerai, de stérile* pillar; ~ d'arc-boutant *m* CONSTR flying buttress; ~ de charbon *m* CHARBON coal pillar; ~ de protection de puits *m* MINES bottom pillar, shaft safety pillar; ~ de soutènement *m* MINES supporting pillar; ~ de voûte *m* MINES arch pillar

pilocarpidine *f* CHIMIE pilocarpidine

pilocarpine *f* CHIMIE pilocarpine

pilon *m* CHARBON ram, CHIMIE pestle, CONSTR earth rammer, rammer, *d'un marteau-pilon* ram, EQUIP LAB,

GENIE CHIM pestle, PRODUCTION forge hammer, hammer, head, pounder, power hammer, tup, *d'un marteau-pilon* hammer head, *de bocard, ou analogue* stamp; ~ **à chute**libre *m* CONSTR free falling stamp, PRODUCTION gravity stamp; ~ **diesel** *m* CHARBON diesel hammer; ~ **hydraulique** *m* EN RENOUV hydraulic ram

pilonnage *m* PRODUCTION drop forging

pilonnement *m* OCEANO, PETROLE *d'une plate-forme flottante, d'un navire de forage* heave

pilonner *vt* AGRO ALIM crush, pound, CONSTR ram, PRODUCTION tamp

pilot *m* CONSTR pile, spile

pilotage *m* COMMANDE control, CONSTR pile driving, pile work, piling, spiling, NAUT pilotage, NUCLEAIRE fine control, regulating, TELECOM steering; ~ **automatique transparent** *m* AERONAUT limited authority autopilot; ~ **manuel** *m* COMMANDE hand signalling (BrE); ~ **par quartz** *m* CINEMAT crystal control, crystal sync, ENREGISTR crystal control; ~ **piézo-électrique** *m* AERONAUT crystal control; ~ **des requêtes** *m* INFORMAT inquiry control

pilote *m* AERONAUT pilot, INFORMAT driver, NAUT pilot, ORDINAT driver, TELECOM pilot; ~ **d'allumage** *m* CONS MECA pilot flame; ~ **automatique** *m* AERONAUT, ESPACE, NAUT, TRANSPORT automatic pilot, autopilot; ~ **de commande** *m* COMMANDE pilot, regulating pilot; ~ **d'écran** *m* INFORMAT, ORDINAT display driver; ~ **d'essai** *m* AERONAUT test pilot; ~ **hauturier** *m* NAUT deep-sea pilot; ~ **de périphérique** *m* INFORMAT device driver, peripheral driver, ORDINAT device driver; ~ **de régulation** *m* COMMANDE pilot, regulating pilot; ~ **thermostaté** *m* ELECTRON temperature-controlled crystal oscillator

piloté: ~ **par informatique** *adj* TELECOM computer-controlled; ~ **par menu** *adj* INFORMAT, ORDINAT menu-driven; ~ **par touche** *adj* INFORMAT, ORDINAT key-driven

piloter *vt* AERONAUT pilot, CONSTR pile, ENREGISTR monitor, NAUT sail, *un bateau* pilot

pilots *m pl* CONSTR piling, spiling

pilulier *m* CERAM VER tablet bottle

pimarique *adj* CHIMIE *acide* pimaric

pimélique *adj* CHIMIE *acide* pimelic

pimélite *f* MINERAUX pimelite

pinacol *m* CHIMIE pinacol, pinacone

pinacoline *f* CHIMIE pinacoline, pinacolone

pinacolique *adj* CHIMIE pinacolic

pinardier *m* NAUT wine tanker

pince *f* CONS MECA clamp, clip, *outils* pliers, CONSTR claw, crow, crowbar, nail claw, pinch cock, ELECTR *outil* clip, EQUIP LAB *pour tube* clip, *support* clamp, MECANIQUE clip, MINES gad, *pour câble guide* gland, TEXTILE clip, VEHICULES *outil* pliers; ~ **américaine** *f* CONS MECA collet; ~ **à anneaux** *f* CONS MECA ring pliers; ~ **d'arrêt** *f* CHIMIE pinch cock, CONS MECA clamp; ~ **à batterie** *f* ELECTROTEC battery clip; ~ **à bécher** *f* EQUIP LAB beaker holder; ~ **à becs coudés** *f* CONS MECA bent-nose pliers; ~ **à becs longs** *f* MECANIQUE *outillage* long-nose pliers; ~ **à becs parallèles** *f* NUCLEAIRE parallel-jaw tong; ~ **de bord** *f* CERAM VER edge holder; ~ **brucelles** *f* EQUIP LAB tweezers; ~ **à circlip** *f* CONS MECA circlip pliers; ~ **cisailleuse** *f* CONSTR cutting pliers; ~ **à cosse de batterie** *f* CONS MECA battery terminal pliers; ~ **coupante diagonale** *f* CONS MECA diagonal cutter, MECANIQUE *outillage* angle cutter; ~

coupante en bout *f* PRODUCTION end cutting nippers; ~ **à creuset** *f* EQUIP LAB crucible tongs; ~ **crocodile** *f* CINEMAT alligator clamp, gaffer grip, CONS MECA, ELECTR *raccordement* alligator clip, crocodile clip, ELECTROTEC alligator clip; ~ **de croqueur** *f* CERAM VER cutter's pliers; ~ **de débouchage de trou de coulée** *f* PRODUCTION tapping bar; ~ **à dénuder** *f* CONS MECA wire stripping pliers, IMPRIM *électricité* cable sprinter; ~ **de développement** *f* PHOTO developing clip, developing tongs; ~ **à donner la voie aux scies** *f* CONSTR plier saw set; ~ **emporte-pièce à tourniquet** *f* CONS MECA revolving punch pliers; ~ **à équarrir** *f* CERAM VER glazier's pliers; ~ **exécutant les actions des doigts** *f* NUCLEAIRE finger action tool; ~ **de film** *f* PHOTO film clip; ~ **à fionner** *f* CERAM VER chipping tool; ~ **à freiner** *f* CONS MECA lockwire pliers; ~ **de fusible** *f* PRODUCTION *électricité* fuse clip; ~ **à genouillère** *f* PRODUCTION lever grip tongs; ~ **à levier** *f* CONSTR crow, crowbar; ~ **à mâchoires** *f* EQUIP LAB *support* clamp with jaws, retort clamp; ~ **de Mohr** *f* EQUIP LAB *tuyau en caoutchouc* Mohr's clip; ~ **de montage** *f* PRODUCTION exchange clip; ~ **motoriste** *f* CONS MECA slip joint pliers; ~ **multiprise** *f* CONS MECA multigrip pliers; ~ **à ouvrir** *f* CERAM VER pucella, reaming tool; ~ **à papier** *f* PHOTO print tongs; ~ **à pied-de-biche** *f* CONSTR claw bar, jim crow; ~ **plate** *f* CONS MECA flat-nose pliers, MECANIQUE *outillage* flat-nosed pliers, PRODUCTION flat-nose pliers, flat-nosed pliers; ~ **plate à bec-de-canard** *f* CONS MECA duckbill pliers (BrE), needle nose pliers (AmE); ~ **de plombage** *f* EMBALLAGE lead sealing pliers; ~ **à poitrine** *f* TEXTILE bustline ruffle; ~ **pour tubes** *f* CONSTR tube clip; ~ **pour tubes à essais** *f* EQUIP LAB test tube holder; ~ **à rails** *f* CH DE FER rail tongs; ~ **réglable** *f* CONS MECA multigrip pliers; ~ **réglable à crémaillère** *f* CONS MECA slip joint multigrip pliers; ~ **à ressort** *f* CONS MECA spring clip; ~ **à rodage** *f* EQUIP LAB *support* ground glass joint clamp; ~ **ronde** *f* CONS MECA round-nose pliers; ~ **à segments** *f* CONS MECA piston ring pliers; ~ **de serrage** *f* CONS MECA holding collet; ~ **à sertir** *f* CONS MECA crimping pliers, ELECTR *outil*, MECANIQUE *outillage* crimping tool; ~ **à sertir les cosses** *f* CONS MECA terminal crimper; ~ **de taille** *f* TEXTILE waist dart; ~ **à talon** *f* CONSTR pinching bar; ~ **thermocouple** *f* ELECTROTEC thermocouple; ~ **de tirage** *f* PHOTO print tongs; ~ **à torsade** *f* PRODUCTION joint-twisting pliers; ~ **universelle** *f* CINEMAT set clamp, CONSTR pinch cock; ~ **universelle gainée** *f* CONS MECA sheathed-combination pliers

pinceau *m* MECANIQUE *outillage* brush, PLAST CAOU *peinture* paintbrush; ~ **à badigeon** *m* COULEURS flat brush, whitewash brush; ~ **fin** *m* ESPACE *communications* spot beam; ~ **de lecture** *m* OPTIQUE read beam; ~ **lumineux** *m* OPTIQUE light beam; ~ **pour balance** *m* EQUIP LAB *analyse* balance brush; ~ **soufflant** *m* CINEMAT blower brush

pince-cisaille *f* CONSTR cutting pliers

pincée: ~ **tectonique** *f* GEOLOGIE upthrusted wedge

pince-étau *f* CONS MECA lock grip pliers (BrE), locking pliers (AmE), vise grips (AmE), vice grips (BrE)

pince-levier *f* MECANIQUE handspike

pincement *m* VEHICULES *roues avant* toe-in; ~ **négatif** *m* VEHICULES *roues avant* toe-out; ~ **positif** *m* VEHICULES *roues avant* toe-in

pince-monseigneur *f* MECANIQUE *outillage* jemmy (BrE), jimmy (AmE)

pincer *vt* PRODUCTION grip

pinces *f pl* CERAM VER, CONS MECA pliers, CONSTR tongs, ELECTR pliers, PRODUCTION nippers; **~ articulées pour monter les pierres de taille** *f pl* PRODUCTION lever grip tongs; **~ à bec** *f pl* CERAM VER pinchers; **~ à becs courts** *f pl* CONS MECA short-nose pliers, short-nosed pliers; **~ à becs plats** *f pl* PRODUCTION flat-nose pliers, flat-nosed pliers; **~ à becs ronds** *f pl* CONS MECA round-nose pliers; **~ à combinaisons** *f pl* CONS MECA combination pliers; **~ à cônes** *f pl* CONS MECA cone pliers; **~ coupantes** *f pl* CONSTR cutting nippers; **~ coupantes diagonales** *f pl* CONS MECA diagonal cutting nippers; **~ coupantes sur côté** *f pl* CONS MECA side cutting nippers; **~ à emporte-pièce à revolver** *f pl* CONS MECA revolving head punch; **~ et transporteurs de fil** *f pl* TEXTILE grippers and yarn carriers; **~ à gaz** *f pl* CONSTR gas pliers; **~ longues** *f pl* PRODUCTION long-nosed pliers; **~ à mâchoires pointues** *f pl* CONS MECA needle-nose pliers; **~ à plomber** *f pl* CONS MECA sealing pliers; **~ pour agrafer** *f pl* EMBALLAGE stapling pliers; **~ réglables à deux positions** *f pl* CONS MECA lip joint pliers; **~ de serrage** *f pl* PRODUCTION nippers; **~ serre-tubes à chaîne** *f pl* CONS MECA chain pipe wrench; **~ de sûreté** *f pl* SECURITE *barils, bidons, seaux* safety clamps; **~ à tuyaux** *f pl* CONSTR pipe tongs

pincette *f* CONS MECA elliptic spring

pincettes *f pl* CONSTR tongs

pinceurs *m pl* IMPRIM *plieuses, rotatives* pinch roller

pinène *m* CHIMIE pinene

pinique *adj* CHIMIE pinic

pinite *f* MINERAUX pinite

pinnule *f* CONSTR sight, vane; **~ à charnière** *f* CONSTR folding sight

pinonique *adj* CHIMIE pinonic

pinte *f* METROLOGIE pint

piochage *m* CONSTR picking

pioche *f* CONSTR pickax (AmE), pickaxe (BrE), PRODUCTION pick, pickax (AmE); **~ à bec plat et pointu** *f* CONSTR chisel-and-point pick, PRODUCTION pickax(AmE), pickaxe (BrE); **~ à bec pointu et marteau** *f* PRODUCTION hammer pick; **~ à bec pointu et tête** *f* CONSTR poll pick; **~ à bourrer** *f* CONSTR beater, beating pick; **~ à défricher** *f* CONSTR mattock; **~ à défricher à hache** *f* CONSTR mattock; **~ ordinaire** *f* PRODUCTION pickax (AmE), pickaxe (BrE); **~ à tasser et pointer** *f* CONSTR beater; **~ de terrassier** *f* PRODUCTION pickax (AmE), pickaxe (BrE)

pioche-hache *f* CONSTR mattock

piochement *m* CONSTR picking

piocher *vt* CONSTR pick, *terre* break with a pick

pion *m* PHYS PART *(méson pi)*, PHYSIQUE pion; **~ de centrage** *m* CONS MECA guide pin; **~ d'entraînement** *m* CONS MECA drive pin; **~ de verrouillage** *m* CONS MECA locking pin

pipe: **~ de cueillage** *f* CERAM VER boot; **~ en terre glaise** *f* CERAM VER clay pipe

pipécoline *f* CHIMIE pipecoline

pipe-line *m* CONS MECA, CONSTR, INFORMAT, ORDINAT, PETROLE, POLLUTION, TRANSPORT pipeline

pipe-linier *m* TRANSPORT pipeliner

pipérazine *f* CHIMIE piperazine

pipéridéine *f* CHIMIE piperideine

pipéridine *f* CHIMIE hexahydropyridine, piperidine

pipérique *adj* CHIMIE piperic

pipéronal *m* CHIMIE heliotropin, piperonal

pipérylène *m* CHIMIE piperylene

pipette *f* EQUIP LAB *verrerie, analyse* pipette; **~ à bord**

large *f* CHIMIE wide band pipette; **~ graduée** *f* EQUIP LAB *verrerie, analyse* graduated pipette; **~ jaugée** *f* EQUIP LAB *verrerie, analyse* graduated pipette; **~ Pasteur** *f* EQUIP LAB, *verrerie, analyse* Pasteur pipette

piquage *m* CERAM VER impression, MECANIQUE *hydraulique* branch pipe, PETROLE drain tap, PRODUCTION scaling

piqué[1] *adj* CINEMAT sharp

piqué[2] *m* AERONAUT, ESPACE *véhicules* dive; **~ en spirale** *m* AERONAUT spiral dive; **~ en vol** *m* AERONAUT dive; **~ simple** *m* TEXTILE single jersey

pique-feu *m* PRODUCTION poker, prick bar, pricker

piquer[1] *vt* CHARBON hew, CONSTR *un tuyau sur un autre* branch, PRODUCTION *une chaudière* descale

piquer[2] *vi* AERONAUT, ESPACE *véhicules* dive; **~ de l'avant** *vi* NAUT go down by the bows

piquet *m* CONSTR peg, picket, stake; **~ de terre** *m* ELECTR *raccordement* earth bar (BrE), ground bar (AmE), earth rod (BrE), ground rod (AmE), earthing rod (BrE), grounding rod (AmE), GEOPHYS earth rod (BrE), ground rod (AmE), earth spike (BrE), ground spike (AmE)

piquetage *m* CONSTR staking

piqueur *m* CHARBON digger; **~ à la veine** *m* MINES getter

piqûre *f* CERAM VER (Bel) burn mark, pit, rod proof; **~ à cheval** *f* IMPRIM saddle stitching; **~ d'épingle** *f* PLAST CAOU *défaut de peinture* pinhole; **~ à plat** *f* IMPRIM stab stitching, stabbing

piratage *m* TV bootleg

PIRE *abrév* *(puissance isotrope rayonnée équivalente)* ESPACE *communications* EIRP *(equivalent isotropically-radiated power)*

pis-aller *m* PRODUCTION makeshift

pisciculture *f* AGRO ALIM, OCEANO fish breeding (AmE), fish farming (BrE), pisciculture

piscine: **~ supérieure** *f* NUCLEAIRE upper containment pool

pisé *m* CERAM VER tamping clay, CONSTR loam

pissée *f* PRODUCTION break-out

pissette *f* CHIMIE, EQUIP LAB wash bottle

pistage *m* CINEMAT magnetic striping, ENREGISTR *de la tête sur la bande* striping, tracking, MILITAIRE tracking; **~ magnétique** *m* ENREGISTR magnetic striping

piste *f* AERONAUT landing strip, runway, ENREGISTR track, INFORMAT strip, *de ruban perforé, magnétique* track, OPTIQUE, ORDINAT *magnétique*, TV track; **~ d'alignement sonore** *f* ENREGISTR buzz track; **~ d'asservissement** *f* ENREGISTR, TV control track; **~ d'asservissement temporel** *f* ENREGISTR, TV control track time code; **~ d'atterrissage** *f* AERONAUT landing strip, TRANSPORT landing path; **~ audio** *f* TV audio track, soundtrack; **~ avec approche aux instruments** *f* AERONAUT instrument approach runway; **~ centrale** *f* ENREGISTR center track (AmE), centre track (BrE); **~ de commande** *f* TV control track; **~ commentaire** *f* ENREGISTR commentary track; **~ de compensation** *f* CINEMAT balance stripe; **~ compressée** *f* ENREGISTR squeeze track; **~ concentrique** *f* OPTIQUE concentric track; **~ de contrôle** *f* ENREGISTR control track, INFORMAT, ORDINAT audit trail, TV control track; **~ cyclable** *f* CONSTR cycle track, TRANSPORT cycle path; **~ à densité variable** *f* TV variable density track; **~ de dérapage** *f* VEHICULES skid pad; **~ du dialogue** *f* TV dialogue track; **~ DIN** *f* ENREGISTR center track (AmE), centre track (BrE); **~ d'enregistrement** *f* ACOUSTIQUE, INFORMAT, ORDINAT recording track; **~**

en service *f* AERONAUT active runway (AmE), runway in use (BrE); **~ de garde** *f* ENREGISTR guard track; **~ de glissance** *f* CONSTR skid track; **~ horaire** *f* ENREGISTR clock track; **~ image** *f* TV video track; **~ latérale** *f* CINEMAT edge stripe, edge track; **~ magnétique** *f* CINEMAT stripe; **~ magnétique centrale** *f* CINEMAT magnetic center track (AmE), magnetic centre track (BrE); **~ magnétique de compensation** *f* CINEMAT magnetic balance track, TV balancing magnetic stripe; **~ magnétique couchée** *f* CINEMAT magnetic sound stripe, ENREGISTR magnetic stripe; **~ métronome** *f* ENREGISTR click track; **~ d'ordres** *f* TV cue track, cue track address codes; **~ parole** *f* ENREGISTR speech track, voice track; **~ de patinage** *f* CONSTR skid track; **~ de perforation** *f* INFORMAT punching track; **~ périphérique** *f* AERONAUT perimeter track; **~ pilote hors norme** *f* TV nonstandard control track; **~ principale** *f* AERONAUT primary runway; **~ RCA** (MD) *f* ENREGISTR variable area soundtrack; **~ de référence** *f* ENREGISTR guide track; **~ de repérage** *f* TV cue track; **~ de réserve** *f* INFORMAT, ORDINAT spare track; **~ de roulement** *f* CONS MECA runway, TRANSPORT apron taxiway; **~ de sécurité** *f* TV guard band; **~ son** *f* CINEMAT track; **~ son à densité constante** *f* ENREGISTR variable width soundtrack; **~ son à densité fixe** *f* ENREGISTR variable area soundtrack; **~ son à densité variable** *f* ENREGISTR variable density soundtrack; **~ son internationale** *f* CINEMAT M and E track, Music and Effects track; **~ de son magnétique** *f* ENREGISTR magnetic soundtrack; **~ son optique** *f* CINEMAT optical track; **~ sonore** *f* CINEMAT audio track, soundtrack, ENREGISTR soundtrack, TV audio track 1, audio track, soundtrack; **~ sonore 2** *f* TV *piste d'ordre* audio track 2; **~ sonore de bourdonnement** *f* ENREGISTR buzz track; **~ sonore magnétique** *f* CINEMAT magnetic soundtrack; **~ sonore multiple** *f* ENREGISTR multiple soundtrack; **~ sonore optique** *f* ENREGISTR optical soundtrack; **~ sonore de programme 1** *f* TV audio track 1, program audio track (AmE), programme audio track (BrE); **~ de synchronisation** *f* INFORMAT, ORDINAT clock track; **~ témoin** *f* ENREGISTR guide track; **~ vidéo** *f* TV video track; **~ à vue** *f* AERONAUT noninstrument runway; **~ Western Electric** (MD) *f* ENREGISTR variable density soundtrack

pistes: **~ par pouce** *f pl* IMPRIM, INFORMAT, ORDINAT TPI, tracks per inch

pistolage: **~ à la flamme** *m* REVETEMENT plast spraying

pistolet *m* CONS MECA latch, MINES borer, drill, jackhammer, rock drill, chisel; **~ à colle** *m* CONS MECA bonding gun; **~ d'étiquetage** *m* EMBALLAGE labeler (AmE), labeller (BrE); **~ à extrusion** *m* CONS MECA extrusion gun; **~ de fixation** *m* EMBALLAGE attaching gun; **~ à fusée éclairante** *m* MILITAIRE flare pistol; **~ graisseur** *m* CONSTR grease gun; **~ lance-fusée** *m* MILITAIRE rocket pistol, NAUT Very pistol; **~ oléopneumatique** *m* AUTO airdraulic gun; **~ à peinture** *m* CONS MECA paint spray, POLLU MER spray gun; **~ pour soudage des goujons** *m* CONSTR stud welding gun; **~ pulvérisateur** *m* CONS MECA sprayer nozzle, POLLU MER spray gun; **~ sableur** *m* IMPRIM air eraser

pistolet-mitrailleur *m* MILITAIRE submachine gun

piston *m* AUTO piston, CONS MECA plunger, plunger piston, ram, ELECTROTEC plunger, INST HYDR, MECANIQUE, MINES, NAUT, PHYSIQUE, VEHICULES *moteur* piston; **~ à air** *m* CONS MECA air piston; **~ autothermique** *m* AUTO autothermic piston; **~ bimétal** *m* AUTO bimetal piston; **~ à clapet** *m* CONS MECA piston with clack-valve; **~ de commande** *m* CONS MECA control piston; **~ compensateur** *m* INST HYDR balancing piston; **~ à contre-tige** *m* CONS MECA piston with extended rod, piston with tailrod; **~ de court-circuit** *m* PHYSIQUE adjustable short circuit; **~ équilibreur** *m* INST HYDR balancing piston; **~ à fenêtres** *m* AUTO full slipper piston; **~ de guide d'ondes** *m* ELECTROTEC waveguide plunger; **~ à jupe découpée** *m* AUTO semi-slipper piston; **~ de levage** *m* PRODUCTION *système hydraulique* lift piston, lifting piston; **~ massif** *m* INST HYDR solid piston; **~ nervuré** *m* AUTO ribbed piston; **~ à piège** *m* ELECTROTEC choke plunger; **~ à plateau** *m* INST HYDR disc piston (BrE), disk piston (AmE); **~ plein** *m* CONS MECA plunger, plunger piston, ram, INST HYDR solid piston; **~ plongeur** *m* CONS MECA plunger, plunger piston, ram, INST HYDR solid piston, MECANIQUE plunger, PLAST CAOU *presse* ram; **~ pneumatique** *m* CONS MECA air piston; **~ primaire** *m* AUTO front piston, primary piston; **~ racleur** *m* PETR pig, scraper, PETROLE go devil, pig; **~ robinet** *m* CERAM VER hand bellows; **~ secondaire** *m* AUTO secondary piston; **~ à segments** *m* INST HYDR piston; **~ à vapeur** *m* INST HYDR steam piston; **~ de vérin** *m* CONS MECA cylinder piston rod

pistonnage *m* CHARBON jigging, PETR swabbing, PETROLE surge, swab

pistonphone *m* ACOUSTIQUE piston phone

pitchpin *m* NAUT pitch pine

piton *m* CONSTR screw eye, MECANIQUE eyebolt, NAUT ring bolt; **~ de filière** *m* NAUT eyebolt; **~ à oeil** *m* NAUT eyebolt; **~ à vis** *m* CONSTR screw eye

pitticite *f* MINERAUX pitticite, pittizite

pittizite *f* MINERAUX pitticite, pittizite

pivalique *adj* CHIMIE pivalic

pivot *m* CONS MECA pin, pivot, *d'une mèche à trois pointes, d'un foret à téton* center point (AmE), centre point (BrE), INSTRUMENT, MECANIQUE pivot, NUCLEAIRE king journal, pivot, trunnion, PHYSIQUE fulcrum; **~ d'attelage** *m* VEHICULES *semi-remorque* fifth wheel kingpin; **~ de bogie** *m* VEHICULES *remorque* bogie pin (BrE), bogie pivot (BrE), truck pin (AmE), truck pivot (AmE); **~ central** *m* CONS MECA kingbolt, kingpin, main pin, pintle, *d'une plaque tournante* center pin (AmE), centre pin (BrE); **~ d'entraînement** *m* CH DE FER, CONS MECA catch pin; **~ d'essieu avant** *m* MECANIQUE *véhicules* kingpin; **~ de fusée** *m* AUTO steering knuckle, VEHICULES *remorque* pivot pin

pivotant *adj* MECANIQUE hinged, pivoted

pivoter[1] *vt* INFORMAT, ORDINAT rotate

pivoter[2] *vi* MECANIQUE slew

pixel *m* IMPRIM *infographie*, INFORMAT, ORDINAT pixel

pixels: **~ par pouce** *m pl* INFORMAT, ORDINAT pixels per inch

placage *m* CERAM VER patching, CONSTR veneering, ELECTROTEC plating, ESPACE *véhicules* cladding, PRODUCTION plating; **~ par soudage** *m* MECANIQUE cladding

placard *m* CERAM VER (Bel) patch block, NAUT locker; **~ suspendu** *m* EQUIP LAB *meuble* wall cupboard

place:[1] **sur ~** *adj* CONSTR on the spot

place:[2] **sur ~** *adv* CONSTR, MECANIQUE in situ

place[3] *f* CERAM VER shop, VEHICULES *habitacle* seat

placer[1] *m* MINES alluvial mining, diggings, placer

placer:[2] **~ ensemble** *vt* PRODUCTION bundle

placette *f* CONSTR piazzetta

plafond *m* AERONAUT ceiling, CONSTR *d'un bassin, d'un réservoir* floor, ESPACE *véhicules* ceiling altitude, float altitude, METEO ceiling, MINES *d'une mine* roof, NAUT deckhead; ~ **de ballast** *m* NAUT tank top; ~ **de double fond** *m* NAUT inner bottom plating; ~ **insonorisant** *m* SECURITE sound-absorbent ceiling; ~ **nuageux** *m* AERONAUT cloudbase; ~ **opérationnel** *m* AERONAUT operational ceiling; ~ **pratique** *m* AERONAUT *aéronef* service ceiling; ~ **de service** *m* AERONAUT service ceiling; ~ **utile** *m* AERONAUT dry weight, service ceiling; ~ **d'utilisation** *m* AERONAUT service ceiling

plafonnier *m* AERONAUT overhead light, ELECTR *éclairage* ceiling fitting, NAUT deckhead light

plage *f* ASTRONOMIE plage, GEOLOGIE beach, foreshore, NAUT beach, PHYS RAYON *du bruit de fond* spectrum; ~ **d'accord automatique** *f* ELECTRON follow range; ~ **d'accord électronique** *f* ELECTRON electronic tuning range; ~ **arrière** *f* NAUT afterdeck, bridge deck; ~ **d'avance transversale automatique** *f* PRODUCTION automatic crossfeed range; ~ **balayée** *f* TV raster; ~ **d'une barre de contrôle** *f* IMPRIM *contrôle de qualité* step; ~ **de capacité** *f* PRODUCTION *électricité* nominal capacitance; ~ **de connexion** *f* ELECTROTEC pad; ~ **de contraste** *f* TV dynamic range; ~ **de couleur** *f* IMPRIM *photogravure* key; ~ **de couleurs** *f* IMPRIM *contrôle de qualité* step; ~ **d'ébullition** *f* PETROLE *distillation fractionnée* boiling range; ~ **en terrasse** *f* GEOPHYS raised beach; ~ **floculaire** *f* ASTRONOMIE flocculus; ~ **de fusion** *f* THERMODYN melting range; ~ **d'incréments d'avance** *f* CONS MECA wheelfeed increment range; ~ **d'insensibilité** *f* ELECTROTEC dead band; ~ **de mesure** *f* PRODUCTION *système hydraulique* gage (AmE), gauge (BrE); ~ **de modulation** *f* ACOUSTIQUE modulated space; ~ **neutre** *f* ELECTROTEC dead band, neutral zone; ~ **de pivotements sens anti-horaire** *f* CONS MECA swivel range counter clockwise; ~ **de pivotements sens horaire** *f* CONS MECA swivel range clockwise; ~ **de régulation** *f* ELECTROTEC regulation range; ~ **de synchronisation** *f* ELECTRON capture range; ~ **de températures** *f* MATERIAUX, THERMODYN temperature range; ~ **de températures intrinsèques** *f* ELECTRON intrinsic temperature range; ~ **de tension** *f* PRODUCTION *électricité* rated voltage; ~ **d'utilisation** *f* PRODUCTION operational range; ~ **de vol** *f* AERONAUT flight level

plagioclase *m* MINERAUX plagioclase

plain:[1] **au** ~ *adj* NAUT aground
plain:[2] **au** ~ *adv* NAUT aground

plaine: ~ **abyssale** *f* GEOLOGIE, OCEANO, PETR abyssal plain; ~ **alluviale** *f* DISTRI EAU alluvial plain, HYDROLOGIE flood plain; ~ **alluviale d'inondation** *f* HYDROLOGIE flood plain; ~ **côtière** *f* GEOLOGIE coastal plain; ~ **deltaïque** *f* GEOLOGIE delta plain; ~ **d'inondation** *f* DISTRI EAU, GEOLOGIE, HYDROLOGIE flood plain; ~ **de lave** *f* GEOLOGIE lava plateau; ~ **littorale** *f* GEOLOGIE coastal plain

plan[1] *adj* CONSTR flat, GEOLOGIE even, planar, PAPIER even; **d'un** ~ *adj* GEOMETRIE planar
plan:[2] **dans le** ~ *adv* CINEMAT in shot
plan[3] *m* CERAM VER flat optical tool, CINEMAT shot, CONS MECA layout, CONSTR incline, GEOMETRIE plane, NAUT *architecture navale* drawing, plan, PRODUCTION schedule, *surface* even;
~ **a** ~ **d'accolement** *m* CRISTALL habit plane; ~ **d'acheminement** *m* TELECOM traffic routing strategy; ~ **d'aménagement** *m* NAUT accommodation plan; ~

des **aménagements** *m* NAUT general arrangement plan; ~ **américain** *m* CINEMAT close medium shot; ~ **d'assemblage** *m* MECANIQUE assembly drawing; ~ **automoteur** *m* CONS MECA incline, CONSTR gravity incline, gravity plane, gravity road; ~ **avec cache** *m* CINEMAT mask shot; ~ **avec mouvement vertical** *m* CINEMAT tilt shot; ~ **avec transparence** *m* CINEMAT process shot; ~ **axial** *m* GEOLOGIE *d'un pli* axial plane;
~ **b** ~ **de Babcock** *m* TELECOM Babcock plan; ~ **basal** *m* MATERIAUX basal plane; ~ **de base** *m* METALL basal plane; ~ **de Benioff** *m* GEOLOGIE Benioff plane;
~ **c** ~ **de câblage** *m* ELECTR wiring diagram, NUCLEAIRE schematic wiring diagram; ~ **cache-contrecache** *m* CINEMAT composite shot, matte shot; ~ **cadastral** *m* CONSTR cadastral survey; ~ **de cargo** *m* NAUT cargo plan; ~ **central** *m* AERONAUT center wing section (AmE), centre wing section (BrE); ~ **de circulation** *m* TRANSPORT traffic management; ~ **de cisaillement** *m* METALL plane of shear; ~ **de clivage** *m* CHIMIE cleavage plane; ~ **des cloisons** *m* NAUT bulkhead plan; ~ **de comparaison** *m* CONSTR datum, datum level, datum plane; ~ **conjugué** *m* METALL, PHYSIQUE conjugate plane; ~ **continu** *m* CH DE FER continuous surface; ~ **de coupe** *m* CINEMAT cutaway shot; ~ **des couples** *m* CONS MECA frame plan, NAUT hull drawings;
~ **d** ~ **de déformation** *m* GEOLOGIE *schistosité, gneissosité* kink plane; ~ **de détail** *m* CINEMAT insert shot; ~ **directeur du plan** *m* PRODUCTION master production schedule; ~ **directeur de production** *m* PRODUCTION production plan; ~ **de disposition des pieux** *m* CHARBON pile situation plan; ~ **de disposition des voies à deux fréquences** *m* TELECOM two-frequency channeling plan (AmE), two-frequency channelling plan (BrE); ~ **à double effet avec chaîne à deux bouts** *m* MINES cut chain incline; ~ **du double fond** *m* NAUT double bottom plan; ~ **à double niveau** *m* TELECOM dual-level plan;
~ **e** ~ **E** *m* ELECTROTEC E-plane; ~ **d'eau** *m* HYDROLOGIE sheet of water, *au-dessus d'un déversoir* flow, OCEANO sheet of water; ~ **d'échantillonnage** *m* METROLOGIE sampling plan; ~ **d'élingage** *m* NAUT lashing plan; ~ **d'empilement compact** *m* MATERIAUX *métallurgie* close-packed plane; ~ **en contre plongée** *m* CINEMAT ground angle shot, low shot; ~ **en double Babcock** *m* TELECOM double Babcock plan; ~ **en plongée** *m* CINEMAT high angle shot; ~ **d'ensemble** *m* CINEMAT establishing shot, long shot, wide shot, CONS MECA assembly drawing, CONSTR construction plan, general arrangement, MECANIQUE general arrangement drawing, NUCLEAIRE general drawing;
~ **f** ~ **de faille** *m* GEOLOGIE fault plane; ~ **fixe** *m* CINEMAT still shot; ~ **fixe horizontal** *m* AERONAUT tailplane; ~ **fixe vertical** *m* AERONAUT tail fin; ~ **focal** *m* CINEMAT, ELECTRON, PHYSIQUE focal plane; ~ **focal antérieur** *m* PHOTO front focal plane; ~ **focal postérieur** *m* PHOTO rear focal plane; ~ **de forme** *m* CONS MECA outline drawing; ~ **des formes** *m* CONS MECA body plan, frame plan, lines drawing, lines plan, NAUT sheer draft, sheer drawing; ~ **de fracture** *m* GEOPHYS fracture plane;
~ **g** ~ **général** *m* CINEMAT establishing shot, long shot; ~ **géométrique** *m* GEOMETRIE ground plane; ~ **de glissement** *m* CRISTALL slip plane, NUCLEAIRE glide plane; ~ **graphique** *m* PRODUCTION diagram;
~ **h** ~ **H** *m* ELECTROTEC H-plane; ~ **d'habitus** *m* ME-

TALL habit plane; **~ horizontal** *m* GEOMETRIE horizontal plane;

~ i ~ **d'image** *m* PHOTO focal plane; **~ image** *m* CINEMAT image plane; **~ d'implantation** *m* MECANIQUE layout drawing; **~ d'incidence** *m* PHYSIQUE plane of incidence; **~ incliné** *m* CINEMAT angle shot, CONSTR incline, inclined plane, GEOMETRIE, PHYSIQUE inclined plane; **~ incliné automoteur** *m* CONS MECA incline, self-acting incline, self-acting plane, CONSTR gravity incline, gravity plane, gravity road, MINES brow; **~ incliné automoteur à simple effet** *m* MINES jig, jig brow, jig plane;

~ j ~ **de jauge** *m* CONS MECA *d'un assemblage* gauge plane (AmE), gauge plane (BrE); **~ de joint** *m* CONS MECA mating surfaces, PRODUCTION parting line;

~ l ~ **large** *m* CINEMAT wide shot; **~ de livraison** *m* PRODUCTION delivery schedule; **~ de luminance zéro** *m* TV alychne, zero luminance plane; **~ de lutte contre l'incendie** *m* NAUT fire control plan;

~ m ~ **de maclage** *m* METALL twinning plane; **~ maillé** *m* TELECOM lattice plan; **~ de maquette** *m* CINEMAT model shot; **~ de masse** *m* PHYSIQUE earth plane (BrE), ground plane (AmE); **~ de mâture** *m* NAUT rigging drawing; **~ mi-moyen** *m* CINEMAT medium close-up; **~ miroir** *m* CINEMAT mirror shot, CRISTALL mirror plane; **~ de montage** *m* CONSTR construction plan, PRODUCTION erection plan; **~ moyen** *m* CINEMAT medium shot, mid-shot; **~ moyen approché** *m* CINEMAT close medium shot; **~ muet** *m* CINEMAT mute shot; **~ multi-images** *m* CINEMAT composite shot;

~ n ~ **neutre de la bande** *m* TV tape neutral plane; **~ nodal** *m* PHOTO nodal plane; **~ de numérotage privé** *m (PNP)* TELECOM private numbering plan *(PNP)*;

~ o ~ **oblique** *m* CINEMAT angle shot, tilted shot; **~ d'occupation du sol** *m* DISTRI EAU zoning plan; **~ de l'ouvrage** *m* CONSTR construction plan;

~ p ~ **à partir d'une grue** *m* CINEMAT boom shot; **~ de pellicule** *m* CINEMAT film plane; **~ de pilotage** *m* AERONAUT control plane; **~ de polarisation** *m* OPTIQUE plane of polarization, PHYSIQUE plane; **~ des ponts** *m* NAUT deck plan; **~ principal** *m* AERONAUT *aéronef* mainplane; **~ à profilé d'aile** *m* NAUT aerofoil (BrE), airfoil (AmE); **~ de protection contre l'incendie** *m* SECURITE fire protection plan; **~ de protection contre la pollution thermique** *m* POLLUTION heat load plan; **~ pyramidal** *m* METALL pyramidal plane;

~ q ~ **qualité** *m* QUALITE quality plan;

~ r ~ **raccord** *m* CINEMAT bridging shot; **~ refait** *m* CINEMAT retake; **~ de référence structure** *m* AERONAUT airframe reference plane; **~ de réflexion** *m* CRISTALL mirror plane; **~ de réflexion avec glissement** *m* CRISTALL glide plane; **~ de réfraction des vagues** *m* NAUT wave refraction diagram; **~ du réseau ferroviaire** *m* CH DE FER, TRANSPORT railroad map (AmE), railway map (BrE); **~ réticulaire** *m* CRISTALL lattice plane; **~ de roulement** *m* CH DE FER running surface;

~ s ~ **de séparation** *m* GEOLOGIE joint plane; **~ de séparation eau-huile** *m* POLLU MER oil-water interface; **~ séquence** *m* CINEMAT long take; **~ à simple effet** *m* MINES jig, jig brow, jig plane; **~ de la surface** *m* MINES plat; **~ de sustentation** *m* EN RENOUV aerofoil (BrE), airfoil (AmE); **~ de symétrie** *m* CONS MECA plane of symmetry, CRISTALL mirror plane, METALL plane of symmetry; **~ de symétrie avec glissement** *m* CRISTALL glide plane;

~ t ~ **de tir** *m* MINES blasting pattern; **~ de tore** *m*

ELECTROTEC core plane; **~ de tournage** *m* CINEMAT schedule; **~ tourné en muet** *m* CINEMAT wild shot; **~ tourné en vol** *m* CINEMAT aerial shot; **~ tourné sous l'eau** *m* CINEMAT underwater shot; **~ de transition** *m* CINEMAT bridging shot; **~ de translation** *m* CRISTALL, METALL translation plane; **~ de transport** *m* CH DE FER traffic schedule; **~ transversal** *m* NAUT cross-sectional drawing; **~ de travail** *m* PRODUCTION work surface; **~ de travail de la table** *m* CONS MECA table work surface; **~ des travaux souterrains** *m* MINES plat; **~ travelling** *m* CINEMAT dolly shot, tracking shot; **~ très rapproché** *m* CINEMAT very close-up; **~ de tuyautage** *m* NAUT piping plan;

~ u ~ **d'urbanisme** *m* CONSTR town planning map; **~ d'urgence** *m* POLLU MER contingency plan;

~ v ~ **de vagues** *m* OCEANO wave refraction diagram; **~ vertical** *m* GEOMETRIE vertical plan; **~ des voies** *m* CH DE FER track diagram; **~ de voilure** *m* NAUT sail plan; **~ de vol** *m* AERONAUT flight plan; **~ de vol déposé en vol** *m* AERONAUT air-filed flight plan; **~ de vol répétitif** *m* AERONAUT repetitive flight plan; **~ des volumes** *m* NAUT capacity plan

planage *m* CONS MECA planishing, surfacing, CONSTR grading, planing

planche *f* CERAM VER battledore, CHARBON rib, CONSTR board, deal, strickle board, NAUT plank; **~ d'ambiance** *f* CONS MECA general assembly, general layout drawing; **~ de bord** *f* AERONAUT instrument panel, AUTO dashboard, instrument panel; **~ de bord mécanicien** *f* AERONAUT flight engineer's panel; **bouvetée** *f* CONSTR matchboard; **~ à dessin** *f* CONSTR, MECANIQUE, NAUT drawing board; **~ d'échafaud** *f* CONSTR scaffold board; **~ d'égout** *f* CONSTR eaves board; **~ d'essai** *f* CONSTR test section, trial strip; **~ expérimentale** *f* CONSTR experimental section; **~ à noyaux** *f* PRODUCTION core board; **~ photographique** *f* IMPRIM photographic plate; **~ à pied** *f* CONSTR toe board; **~ de roulis** *f* NAUT leeboard; **~ de tête** *f* NAUT headboard; **~ à trousser** *f* PRODUCTION loam board, sweep board; **~ à voile** *f* NAUT sailboard

planchéiage *m* CONSTR boarding, decking, SECURITE flooring

planchéier *vt* CONSTR board, floor

plancher *m* *d'un bâtiment, d'une maison* floor, MINES *d'une cage d'extraction* deck, NAUT cabin sole, floor, VEHICULES *carrosserie* floor pan; **~ cabine** *m* AERONAUT cabin floor; **~ chauffant** *m* ELECTR underfloor heating; **~ continu** *m* CONSTR continuous slab; **~ double** *m* CONSTR double floor; **~ en bois** *m* PRODUCTION wooden dunnage; **~ de forage** *m* PETR drill floor; **~ incombustible** *m* SECURITE fireproof floor; **~ de manoeuvre** *m* MINES battery, brace, bracket, PETROLE derrick floor, drilling floor, rig floor; **~ pressurisé** *m* AERONAUT pressurized floor; **~ de repos** *m* MINES stage; **~ de sole** *m* (Fra) *(cf poutrellage de fond)* CERAM VER grillage; **~ sur poutre** *m* CONSTR double floor; **~ sur poutre pan de bois** *m* CONSTR framed floor; **~ de travail** *m* CERAM VER working platform; **~ volant** *m* MINES cradle, walling scaffold, walling stage

planches *f pl* CONSTR boarding; **~ en chicane** *f pl* CONSTR baffle boards; **~ en cuivre rouge** *f pl* CONSTR copper sheets

planchette *f* CONSTR plane table, spokeshave, PRODUCTION conscience; **~ d'objectif** *f* PHOTO lens panel; **~ de pression à ressort** *f* CINEMAT spring pressure plate; **~ de tir** *f* MILITAIRE *artillerie* range card

planchettes *f pl* CERAM VER footboards
planchon: ~ **de coupée** *m* NAUT gangplank
plane *f* CONS MECA planisher, planishing tool, CONSTR drawknife
planéité *f* PRODUCTION flatness
planer *vt* CONSTR shoot, MECANIQUE plane
planétaire[1] *adj* ASTRONOMIE, MECANIQUE *engrenages* planetary
planétaire[2] *m* AUTO sun gear; ~ **primaire** *m* AERONAUT first-stage planet gear
planétarium *m* ASTRONOMIE orrery, planetarium
planète *f* ASTRONOMIE planet; ~ **acide** *f* POLLUTION acid earth; ~ **extérieure** *f* ASTRONOMIE outer planet; ~ **géante gazeuse** *f* ASTRONOMIE gas giant; ~ **inférieure** *f* ASTRONOMIE inferior planet; ~ **intérieure** *f* ASTRONOMIE inner planet; ~ **supérieure** *f* ASTRONOMIE outer planet, superior planet; ~ **tellurique** *f* ASTRONOMIE, ESPACE telluric planet; ~ **terrestre** *f* ASTRONOMIE terrestrial planet
planètes: ~ **géantes** *f pl* ASTRONOMIE giant planets; ~ **troyennes** *f pl* ASTRONOMIE Trojan group
planétoïde *m* ASTRONOMIE planetoid, ESPACE *astronomie* minor planet, planetoid
planeur *m* AERONAUT glider, CONS MECA planisher, MILITAIRE glider; ~ **orbital** *m* ESPACE *véhicules*, TRANSPORT orbital glider; ~ **de transport** *m* MILITAIRE transport glider
planificateur: ~ **des programmes** *m* INFORMAT scheduler
planification *f* TELECOM planning; ~ **des besoins en matières** *f* PRODUCTION material requirement planning; ~ **cadencée** *f* PRODUCTION timed-phased planning; ~ **des capacités** *f* PRODUCTION capacity requirement planning; ~ **échelonnée** *f* PRODUCTION timed-phased planning; ~ **globale** *f* PRODUCTION rough-cut planning; ~ **par période** *f* PRODUCTION timed-phased planning; ~ **de la production** *f* QUALITE production planning; ~ **de programmes** *f* INFORMAT, ORDINAT program scheduling; ~ **de la qualité** *f* QUALITE quality planning; ~ **des ressources de l'entreprise** *f* PRODUCTION manufacturing resource planning
planifié: ~ **ferme** *adj* PRODUCTION firm-planned
planifier *vt* PRODUCTION schedule, TELECOM plan
planimètre *m* CONSTR, GEOMETRIE planimeter
planimétrie *f* GEOMETRIE planimetry
planisphère *m* ASTRONOMIE planisphere
planning: ~ **d'atelier** *m* PRODUCTION Gantt chart; ~ **avant le vol** *m* AERONAUT preflight planning; ~ **en vol** *m* AERONAUT *météorologie* in-flight operational planning; ~ **de production** *m* PRODUCTION production planning; ~ **tableau** *m* PRODUCTION Gantt chart
plans: ~ **intersectés** *m pl* GEOMETRIE intersecting planes; ~ **nodaux** *m pl* PHYSIQUE nodal planes; ~ **principaux** *m pl* PHYSIQUE principal planes
plante: ~ **indicatrice** *f* CONS MECA indicator plant
planter *vt* CONSTR set, *un jalon dans le sol* set
plaque *f* CONS MECA, ELECTR *pile*, ELECTROTEC plate, IMPRIM plate, zinc plate, MECANIQUE, METALL plate, NAUT *métallique* sheet, PRODUCTION *de fonte* plate; ~ **absorbante** *f* NUCLEAIRE absorber plate; ~ **absorbeur** *f* EN RENOUV absorber plate; ~ **d'accrochage** *f* CONS MECA catch plate; ~ **d'accumulateur** *f* ELECTR accumulator plate, ELECTROTEC battery plate; ~ **à accumulation** *f* TV target electrode; ~ **d'aluminium anodisée** *f* IMPRIM anodized aluminium plate (BrE), anodized aluminum plate (AmE); ~ **d'amalgamation**

f CHARBON amalgamation plate; ~ **d'amalgamation intérieure** *f* CONS MECA inside amalgamation plate; ~ **d'amiante** *f* TEXTILE asbestos mat; ~ **d'ancrage** *f* CHARBON anchor plate, CONSTR anchoring plate; ~ **d'appui** *f* CONSTR bedplate; ~ **d'appui du ressort de traction** *f* CH DE FER *véhicules* draw gear spring plate; ~ **d'arrêt** *f* CONS MECA *moules d'injection* bridge plate; ~ **arrière** *f* CONS MECA *de foyer* back sheet; ~ **d'assise** *f* CONSTR baseplate, bedplate, foundation plate, sole plate; ~ **d'autel** *f* CONSTR bridge plate; ~ **d'avant-foyer** *f* PRODUCTION coking plate, deadplate, dumb plate; ~ **de base** *f* CONS MECA baseplate, *d'une machine* bedplate, CONSTR baseplate, foundation plate, sole plate, PETROLE template, *forage*en mer bedplate; ~ **de base provisoire** *f* PETR temporary guide base; ~ **de base temporaire** *f* PETR template drilling, temporary guide base; ~ **de batterie** *f* AUTO, ELECTROTEC battery plate; ~ **de béton** *f* GEOPHYS concrete base; ~ **bimétallique** *f* IMPRIM bimetal plate; ~ **du bleu** *f* IMPRIM *préimpression* blue printer; ~ **de blindage** *f* CONSTR, MECANIQUE armor plate (AmE), armour plate (BrE); ~ **de butée** *f* CONS MECA thrust plate, PHOTO stop plate; ~ **de centrage** *f* CINEMAT aperture plate; ~ **chauffante** *f* EQUIP LAB hotplate, GENIE CHIM boiling plate; ~ **de choc** *f* CHARBON impact plate, CONS MECA *bloc à colonnes* percussion plate; ~ **collectrice** *f* ELECTRON backplate; ~ **au collodiobromure d'argent** *f* PHOTO silver bromide collodion plate; ~ **au collodion** *f* PHOTO collodion plate; ~ **de condensateur** *f* ELECTR capacitor plate; ~ **conscience** *f* PRODUCTION conscience; ~ **de constructeur** *f* ELECTR *appareil*, MECANIQUE name plate; ~ **continentale** *f* GEOLOGIE continental plate; ~ **de contre-feu** *f* PRODUCTION forge back; ~ **de couloir** *f* CINEMAT aperture plate; ~ **de cuivre** *f* IMPRIM copperplate; ~ **de déflection** *f* ESPACE *véhicules* deflection plate; ~ **de dessous** *f* CONSTR bottom plate; ~ **de détente** *f* INST HYDR expansion plate; ~ **dévêtisseuse** *f* CONS MECA stripper plate, *moule d'injection* retaining plate; ~ **de déviation** *f* AERONAUT *tube rayon cathodique* deflector plate, ELECTRON, TV deflection plate; ~ **de déviation horizontale** *f* ELECTRON horizontal deflection plate; ~ **de déviation verticale** *f* ELECTRON vertical deflection plate; ~ **de durcissement des fonds** *f* REFRIG bottomer slab; ~ **d'éjection** *f* CONS MECA, PLAST CAOU ejector plate; ~ **d'embase** *f* MECANIQUE baseplate; ~ **en porcelaine** *f* CERAM VER porcelain plate; ~ **enveloppante** *f* IMPRIM wraparound plate; ~ **en verre** *f* EQUIP LAB glass plate; ~ **d'extracteur** *f* CONS MECA drift plate; ~ **extrême d'induit** *f* ELECTR *machine* armature end plate; ~ **d'extrémité** *f* IMPRIM *livres et piles sur stackers* endboard, PRODUCTION end plate; ~ **de fabricant** *f* ELECTR *appareil* name plate; ~ **de fer** *f* PRODUCTION iron plate; ~ **de fermeture** *f* CONS MECA cover plate; ~ **à filtrer en porcelaine** *f* CERAM VER porcelain filter plate; ~ **de fixation** *f* INSTRUMENT baseplate; ~ **flexo pour l'impression du carton** *f* IMPRIM box die; ~ **de fond** *f* CONSTR bottom plate, foundation plate, PRODUCTION loam plate, *d'un moule en terre* bottom plate; ~ **de fondation** *f* CONSTR baseplate, bedplate, foundation plate, sole plate, NAUT bedplate, PAPIER baseplate; ~ **de fonte** *f* PRODUCTION iron plate; ~ **à four** *f* AGRO ALIM baking sheet; ~ **de friction** *f* CONS MECA chafing plate, wear plate, wearing plate, PRODUCTION friction plate; ~ **de frottement** *f* CONS MECA chafing plate, wear plate, wearing plate, PRODUCTION friction plate; ~ **à godet** *f* EQUIP LAB *analyse* spotting plate, spotting tile; ~ **de guidage** *f* CONS MECA finger guide plate, *bloc à colonnes* guide plate; ~ **d'identification** *f* CONS MECA name plate, SECURITE identification tag; ~ **d'identification de l'élingue** *f* SECURITE sling identification tag; ~ **d'immatriculation** *f* AUTO, VEHICULES license plate (AmE), numberplate (BrE); ~ **imprimante moulée** *f* IMPRIM *flexographie* molded printing plate (AmE), moulded printing plate (BrE); ~ **d'induit** *f* TRANSPORT rotor plate; ~ **inférieure** *f* CONSTR bottom plate; ~ **instrumentale** *f* INSTRUMENT instrument mounting plate; ~ **isolante** *f* ELECTROTEC insulating plate; ~ **de jonction** *f* ELECTROTEC junction plate; ~ **lithographique** *f* IMPRIM lithoplate; ~ **de mesure** *f* PRODUCTION *automatisme industriel* gaging plate (AmE), gauging plate (BrE); ~ **de montage** *f* CONS MECA baseplate, PRODUCTION flange plate; ~ **de moule sans coulée** *f* CONS MECA runnerless mold plate (AmE), runnerless mould plate (BrE); ~ **multimétallique** *f* IMPRIM multimetal plate; ~ **négative** *f* AUTO negative plate, IMPRIM *copie* negative plate, negative working plate; ~ **du noir** *f* IMPRIM *préimpression* black printer; ~ **à noyaux** *f* PRODUCTION core plate; ~ **de numéro** *f* CONS MECA number plate; ~ **obturatrice** *f* AERONAUT blanking plate; ~ **offset en papier** *f* IMPRIM paper plate; ~ **de parquet** *f* MECANIQUE floor plate; ~ **perforée** *f* NUCLEAIRE perforated plate; ~ **perforée pour dessiccateurs** *f* GENIE CHIM desiccator screen; ~ **photographique** *f* INSTRUMENT, PHOTO photographic plate; ~ **plane** *f* PHYS FLUID flat plate; ~ **polie** *f* PHOTO glazing sheet; ~ **porte-empreinte** *f* CONS MECA *moules d'injection* bolster plate, cavity plate; ~ **porte-matrice pour découpage fin** *f* CONS MECA *bloc à colonnes* baseplate for fine blanking; ~ **porte-modèle** *f* PRODUCTION carded pattern, match plate; ~ **porte-modèles** *f* PRODUCTION pattern plate; ~ **porte-poinçon** *f* CONS MECA *bloc à colonnes* punch plate; ~ **porte-poinçon ronde** *f* PRODUCTION round pinch plate; ~ **positive** *f* AUTO positive plate; ~ **pour culture** *f* EQUIP LAB *bactériologie* culture plate, petridish; ~ **de pré-éjection** *f* PLAST CAOU feel plate; ~ **de pression à rappel** *f* PRODUCTION *serre-fils* self-lifting pressure plate; ~ **de propreté** *f* CONSTR finger plate; ~ **de protection** *f* PRODUCTION guard plate; ~ **de rappel fermeture** *f* CONS MECA core slide retaining plate; ~ **à rebord** *f* CONSTR flange plate; ~ **de recouvrement** *f* PRODUCTION covering plate, top plate; ~ **de recouvrement des interrupteurs** *f* PRODUCTION switch cover plate; ~ **de redresseur** *f* ELECTROTEC rectifier anode; ~ **de refroidissement** *f* CERAM VER deadplate; ~ **de réglage** *f* COMMANDE adjusting plate; ~ **de renfort** *f* CONS MECA stiffening plate; ~ **de répartition des canaux d'injection** *f* CONS MECA *moule d'injection* feed plate; ~ **de repérage de signal** *f* CH DE FER signal identification plate; ~ **de réverbération** *f* ENREGISTR reverberation plate; ~ **de revêtement** *f* PRODUCTION lining plate; ~ **de sécurité** *f* PRODUCTION safety guard plate; ~ **sensible à la lumière** *f* IMPRIM light-sensitive plate; ~ **signalétique** *f* CONS MECA, ELECTR name plate; ~ **signalétique du moteur** *f* PRODUCTION motor nameplate; ~ **de signalisation** *f* SECURITE indicator plate; ~ **stratifiée** *f* CONSTR, PLAST CAOU *plastiques* laminated sheet; ~ **striée** *f* PRODUCTION checker plate (AmE), checkered plate (AmE), chequer plate (BrE), chequered plate (BrE); ~ **supérieure** *f* CONS MECA top plate, NUCLEAIRE cover plate, cover slab, roof shielding plate; ~ **support** *f* ESPACE *véhicules* support plate,

NUCLEAIRE tie plate; ~ **support du sommier** *f* NUCLEAIRE grid support plate; ~ **support supérieure** *f* NUCLEAIRE upper tie plate; ~ **terminale** *f* PRODUCTION end plate; ~ **de terre** *f* GEOPHYS earth plate; ~ **tournante** *f* TRANSPORT hub, turntable; ~ **trichrome** *f* PHOTO three-color plate (AmE), three-colour plate (BrE); ~ **de trou d'homme** *f* CONSTR manhole door, manhole plate; ~ **tubulaire** *f* NUCLEAIRE tube plate, PRODUCTION flue plate, flue sheet; ~ **tubulaire de foyer** *f* CH DE FER *véhicules* firebox tube plate, CONS MECA back tube sheet; ~ **usinée** *f* CONS MECA machined rectangular plate; ~ **de Widmannstätten** *f* METALL Widmannstätten plate

plaqué:[1] or *adj* CHIMIE gold-plated
plaqué:[2] ~ **en métal** *m* REVETEMENT metal coat, metal coating, metal plating
plaque-frein *f* CONS MECA locking plate
plaque-modèle *f* PRODUCTION carded pattern, match plate, pattern plate; ~ **en bois** *f* PRODUCTION matchboard
plaquer *vt* ELECTROTEC electroplate, plate, MECANIQUE *procédé* plate, REVETEMENT line, metal-coat
plaques: ~ **alésées et simples** *f pl* CONS MECA bored and plain plates; ~ **à déviation** *f pl* PHYS RAYON deflection plates; ~ **de déviation verticale** *f pl* PHYSIQUE vertical deflecting plates; ~ **estampées à vide** *f pl* SECURITE negative pressure signs; ~ **imprimantes produites par laser** *f pl* IMPRIM laser-produced printing plates; ~ **d'insonorisation** *f pl* SECURITE acoustic boards; ~ **d'isolation sans amiante** *f pl* SECURITE asbestos-free insulating plates; ~ **de moules** *f pl* CONS MECA mold plates (AmE), mould plates (BrE); ~ **pour la déviation horizontale** *f pl* PHYSIQUE horizontal deflecting plates; ~ **de serrage** *f pl* PRODUCTION side plates
plaque-signal *f* ELECTRON signal plate
plaquette *f* ELECTRON chip, wafer, INSTRUMENT padded bridge; ~ **amovible en métal dur** *f* CONS MECA *outils de coupe* indexable hard metal insert; ~ **antiusure** *f* ESPACE *véhicules* antifret plate; ~ **d'arrêt** *f* CONS MECA lockplate; ~ **d'avertissement** *f* SECURITE warning label; ~ **céramique** *f* GAZ ceramic tile; ~ **de circuits intégrés** *f* ELECTRON integrated circuit wafer; ~ **enduite de résist** *f* ELECTRON resist-coated wafer; ~ **en semi-conducteur** *f* ELECTRON semiconductor wafer; ~ **en silicium** *f* ELECTRON silicon wafer; ~ **épitaxiée** *f* ELECTRON epitaxial wafer; ~ **de fourchette de débrayage** *f* AUTO throw-out fork strut; ~ **de frein** *f* AUTO, MECANIQUE brake pad, VEHICULES brake pad, *frein à disque* pad; ~ **de frein à disque** *f* AUTO disc brake pad (BrE), disk brake pad (AmE); ~ **d'identification** *f* CONS MECA name plate; ~ **d'instructions** *f* PRODUCTION instruction plate; ~ **non épitaxiée** *f* ELECTRON bulk wafer; ~ **d'obturation** *f* AERONAUT blanking plate; ~ **porte-écrou** *f* CONS MECA gang channel; ~ **de progressivité** *f* VEHICULES *embrayage* cushion spring; ~ **sur panneau** *f* CONS MECA placard; ~ **d'usure** *f* CONS MECA wear pad
plaquette-frein *f* CONS MECA lockplate
plaquettes: ~ **en carbures métalliques** *f pl* CONS MECA carbide tips; ~ **à jeter en métal dur** *f pl* CONS MECA throwaway tips
plaqueur *m* PRODUCTION plater
plasma *m* ELECTRON, ESPACE, GAZ, MINERAUX, PHYS PART, PHYSIQUE plasma; ~ **d'hydrogène** *m* GAZ hydrogen plasma; ~ **inductif** *m* GAZ inductive plasma; ~ **quark-gluon** *m* PHYS PART quark-gluon plasma; ~

thermique *m* GAZ thermic plasma

plasmatron *m* GAZ plasmatron

plaste *m* CHIMIE plastid

plastic *m* MINES plastic explosive

plasticité *f* CHARBON, MATERIAUX, METALL plasticity, PLAST CAOU plasticity, *plastiques, peintures* flow; ~ **cristalline** *f* METALL crystal plasticity; ~ **Mooney** *f* PLAST CAOU Mooney viscosity

plastide *m* CHIMIE plastid

plastifiant *m* CHIMIE plasticizer, CONSTR plasticizer, plasticizer admixture, plastifying admixture, PLAST CAOU *additif pour le caoutchouc* softener, *plastiques, caoutchouc, revêtements, adhésifs* plasticizer; ~ **extérieur** *m* PLAST CAOU *ingrédient de mélange* external plasticizer; ~ **intérieur** *m* PLAST CAOU *ingrédient de mélange* internal plasticizer; ~ **non migratoire** *m* PLAST CAOU *plastiques, revêtements* nonmigratory plasticizer

plastification *f* REVETEMENT plastic covering; ~ **à chaud** *f* REVETEMENT plast spraying

plastifié *adj* REVETEMENT plastic-coated

plastifier *vt* PLAST CAOU *plastiques, caoutchouc, revêtements, adhésifs* plasticize

plastimètre *m* PLAST CAOU *instrument* plastimeter

plastine *f* CHIMIE plastin

plastique *m* MINES plastic explosive, PETROLE, PLAST CAOU, REFRIG plastic; ~ **acrylique** *m* EMBALLAGE acrylic plastic, PLAST CAOU Lucite; ~ **alvéolaire** *m* PLAST CAOU, REFRIG cellular plastic; ~ **alvéolaire à cellules ouvertes** *m* PLAST CAOU open-cell cellular plastic; ~ **armé de verre** *m* PRODUCTION glass-reinforced plastic; ~ **biodégradable** *m* RECYCLAGE biodegradable plastic; ~ **cellulaire à cellules fermées** *m* REFRIG closed-cell foamed plastic; ~ **chargé verre** *m* EMBALLAGE glass fiber reinforced plastic (AmE), glass fibre reinforced plastic (BrE); ~ **expansé** *m* PLAST CAOU cellular plastic, expanded plastic; ~ **isocyanate** *m* MATERIAUX *polyuréthanes* isocyanate plastic; ~ **mousse** *m* PLAST CAOU expanded plastic, foamed plastic; ~ **phénolique** *m* PLAST CAOU phenolic plastic; ~ **pour la construction** *m* MATERIAUX structural plastic; ~ **renforcé** *m* CERAM VER, EMBALLAGE, MATERIAUX, PLAST CAOU reinforced plastic; ~ **renforcé à la fibre de verre** *m* PLAST CAOU glass fiber reinforced plastic (AmE), glass fibre reinforced plastic (BrE); ~ **rigide** *m* PLAST CAOU rigid plastic; ~ **stratifié** *m* ELECTR *isolateur*, NAUT laminated plastic; ~ **stratifié au verre textile** *m* EMBALLAGE glass fiber laminate (AmE), glass fibre laminate (BrE)

plastisol *m* PLAST CAOU *plastiques* plastisol

plastomère *m* CHIMIE, PETROLE plastomer

plastron *m* PRODUCTION conscience

plat[1] *adj* CONSTR flat, GEOLOGIE even, planar

plat[2] *m* CONS MECA scale, scale pan, MECANIQUE flat, METROLOGIE *d'une balance* bowl; à ~ *m* PAPIER *du papier* flatness; ~ **cuisiné** *m* AGRO ALIM ready meal; ~ **cuisiné réfrigéré** *m* AGRO ALIM cook-chill meal; ~ **d'évaporation** *m* GENIE CHIM evaporating basin, evaporating dish, evaporating pan; ~ **laminé calibré** *m* METALL sized rolled flat iron; ~ **d'un livre** *m* IMPRIM *reliure* flat; ~ **sur la bobine qui la fait tourner faux-rond** *m* IMPRIM *papier* flat spot

platain *m* OCEANO flat, shallow, shoal

plat-bord *m* CONSTR scaffold board, NAUT covering board

plat-coin *m* CONSTR plug

plateau *m* ACOUSTIQUE turntable, CERAM VER slab, CHIMIE plate, *de colonne de fractionnement* tray, CINEMAT acting area, set, floor, stage, CONS MECA chuck plate, disc (BrE), disk (AmE), face chuck, faceplate, faceplate chuck, plate, table, *d'un tour* chuck, *d'un cylindre* cylinder head, head, *d'une presse* plate, *d'une machine-outil, d'une machine à mouler* platen, *d'une machine-outil* plate, CONSTR scaffold board, EQUIP LAB *d'une balance* pan, *matériel général* tray, IMPRIM pile board, INFORMAT platter, METROLOGIE *d'une balance* bowl, ORDINAT platter, PETROLE plateau, PRODUCTION *d'un soufflet* board; ~ **de l'agrandisseur** *m* PHOTO baseboard; ~ **alvéolé** *m* EMBALLAGE compartmented tray; ~ **antivibratoire** *m* EQUIP LAB *balance* antivibration table; ~ **d'appui d'embrayage** *m* VEHICULES clutch drive plate; ~ **d'assemblage** *m* EMBALLAGE collating transit tray; ~ **avant de cylindre** *m* INST HYDR *locomotive ou machine à vapeur fixe* front cylinder cover, front cylinder head; ~ **de balance** *m* CONS MECA scale, scale pan; ~ **de barbotage** *m* CHIMIE uniflex tray, GENIE CHIM bubble tray; ~ **de blocage** *m* AUTO sun gear control plate; ~ **chauffant** *m* PLAST CAOU *presse* heated platten; ~ **de commande du rotor arrière** *m* AERONAUT pitch change spider; ~ **continental** *m* GEOPHYS continental plate, NAUT, OCEANO, PETROLE continental shelf; ~ **cyclique fixe** *m* AERONAUT nonrotating star; ~ **de cylindre** *m* PRODUCTION cylinder cover, cylinder head; ~ **de dessus** *m* CONS MECA top plate; ~ **diviseur** *m* CONS MECA division plate, index dial, index plate, MECANIQUE index table; ~ **diviseur rotatif** *m* CONS MECA rotary dividing table; ~ **de division** *m* CONS MECA division plate, index dial, index plate; ~ **à double coulisse** *m* CONS MECA compound table, table with compound slides; ~ **des ébaucheurs** *m* CERAM VER blank table; ~ **d'enregistrement** *m* ENREGISTR recording stage; ~ **enrouleur de fibre** *m* TELECOM fiber coiling plate (AmE), fibre coiling plate (BrE); ~ **des finisseurs** *m* CERAM VER blow table; ~ **fixe** *m* CONS MECA stationary plate; ~ **de flette** *m* CERAM VER horizontal grinding disc, horizontal grinding disk (AmE); ~ **flottant** *m* CONS MECA floating platen; ~ **de frein** *m* AUTO brake anchor plate, brake shield, VEHICULES backing plate, brake plate; ~ **de friction** *m* AUTO driven plate assembly, CONS MECA friction disc (BrE), friction disk (AmE); ~ **de glace** *m* REFRIG ice slab; ~ **à griffes** *m* CONS MECA jaw chuck; ~ **à hauteur variable** *m* CONS MECA table which can be raised or lowered; ~ **insonorisé** *m* CINEMAT, ENREGISTR sound stage; ~ **d'instruments** *m* INSTRUMENT instrument basin; ~ **marginal** *m* OCEANO marginal plateau; ~ **mobile** *m* PHOTO tilting baseboard; ~ **porte-charge** *m* AERONAUT cargo carrier support; ~ **porte-chariot à avance continue** *m* CONS MECA continuous-feed head; ~ **porte-chariot à fraiser** *m* CONS MECA milling head; ~ **porte-chariot à surfacer** *m* CONS MECA facing head; ~ **porte-coussinets** *m* CONS MECA *d'une machine à tarauder les tiges ou les tubes* screwing chuck, screwing head, PRODUCTION *d'une machine à tarauder les tiges ou les tubes* die-head; ~ **porte-ferrasse** *m* CERAM VER runner back; ~ **porte-feutres** *m* CERAM VER polishing runner; ~ **porte-pièce** *m* CONS MECA work plate; ~ **pousse-toc** *m* CONS MECA catch plate, dog chuck, driver chuck, driver plate, point chuck, take-about chuck; ~ **presseur** *m* CINEMAT platen; ~ **de pression** *m* AUTO driven plate, driven plate assembly, pressure plate, VEHICULES *embrayage* pressure plate; ~ **de**

pression d'embrayage *m* CONS MECA clutch pressure plate; ~ **à quatre griffes indépendantes** *m* CONS MECA four-jaw independent chuck; ~ **à rainures** *m* CONS MECA slotted table; ~ **à rainures hélicoïdales** *m* CONS MECA scroll chuck; ~ **rectangulaire magnétique type lourd** *m* CONS MECA heavy-duty rectangular magnetic chuck; ~ **à secousses** *m* PRODUCTION bumping tray, shaking tray; ~ **à serrage concentrique à trois mors** *m* CONS MECA three-jaw concentric gripping chuck; ~ **sinus** *m* MECANIQUE *outillage* sine table; ~ **sous-marin** *m* OCEANO submarine plateau; ~ **support de segments** *m* AUTO brake carrier plate; ~ **à toc** *m* CONS MECA dog chuck, driver chuck, driver plate, point chuck, take-about chuck; ~ **tournant** *m* MECANIQUE turntable; ~ **tournant porte-pièces** *m* CONS MECA *éléments standard pour machine-outils* rotary table; ~ **à trois griffes concentriques** *m* CONS MECA three-jaw concentric gripping chuck; ~ **à trous muni de poupées à pompe** *m* CONS MECA chuck faceplate with dogs

plateau-étau *m* CONS MECA vice plate (BrE), vise plate (AmE)

plateau-manivelle *m* CONS MECA wheel crank, PRODUCTION disc crank (BrE), disk crank (AmE)

plateau-toc *m* CONS MECA catch plate, dog chuck, driver chuck, driver plate, point chuck, take-about chuck

plateaux: ~ **de serrage** *m pl* PRODUCTION side plates

plate-bande *f* CONSTR flange, flange plate, flat arch, platband, *d'une poutre composée* boom, boom plate

plate-curve *f* MINES *dans un puits abandonné* dam

plate-forme *f* CH DE FER road bed, subgrade, track bed, CONS MECA platform, CONSTR footing block, plate, pole plate, roof plate, wall plate, ESPACE bus, INFORMAT platform, NAUT shelf, ORDINAT platform, PETROLE platform, rig, PRODUCTION landing, platform; ~ **d'accrochage** *f* PETR, PETROLE footboard (AmE), monkey board (BrE); ~ **d'appontage d'hélicoptère** *f* NAUT helicopter pad; ~ **d'attente de circulation** *f* AERONAUT *aéroport* holding apron, holding bay; ~ **d'atterrissage pour hélicoptère** *f* TRANSPORT helicopter landing deck; ~ **auto-élévatrice** *f* PETR jackup platform, PETROLE jackup rig; ~ **carbonatée** *f* GEOLOGIE carbonate platform; ~ **de chargement** *f* CONSTR loading platform, PRODUCTION charging platform, charging scaffold, TRANSPORT loading platform; ~ **de collecte de données** *f* ESPACE DCP, data collection platform, METEO data collection platform; ~ **continentale** *f* GEOLOGIE *sous-marine* continental shelf, *émergée* continental platform, GEOPHYS continental platform, NAUT, OCEANO continental shelf; ~ **deltaïque** *f* OCEANO deltaic platform; ~ **élévatrice** *f* PRODUCTION platform lift; ~ **en acier** *f* PETROLE jacket platform, steel platform; ~ **en béton** *f* PETROLE *exploitation en mer* concrete platform; ~ **en mer** *f* PETROLE offshore platform; ~ **d'exploration** *f* ESPACE *véhicules* exploration platform, scan platform, PETROLE exploration rig; ~ **flottante** *f* OCEANO floating platform, ice shelf, PETROLE *exploitation en mer* floating rig; ~ **de forage** *f* NAUT, PETR, PETROLE drilling platform; ~ **de forage en mer** *f* CONSTR marine drilling rig; ~ **gyroscopique** *f* CINEMAT gyroscopic tripod head, ESPACE *véhicules* gyro-stabilized platform; ~ **d'hébergement** *f* PETROLE accommodation rig, flotel, hotel rig, *en mer* accommodation platform, *exploitation en mer* hotel platform; ~ **hybride** *f* PETROLE *exploitation en mer* hybrid platform; ~ **immergée** *f* PETR submersible platform; ~ **à inertie** *f*

CONS MECA inertial platform; ~ **inertielle** *f* ESPACE inertial navigation platform; ~ **inertielle liée** *f* ESPACE *véhicules* strapdown inertial platform; ~ **insulaire** *f* OCEANO insular shelf; ~ **de lancement** *f* ESPACE *véhicules* launch platform; ~ **de levage** *f* AERONAUT lifting platform; ~ **littorale** *f* OCEANO bench, coastal platform; ~ **marine à câbles tendus** *f* PETROLE TBP, tethered buoyant platform; ~ **d'observation interplanétaire** *f* ASTRONOMIE IMP, interplanetary monitoring platform; ~ **de production** *f* PETR, PETROLE production platform; ~ **de quartier** *f* PETR quarter platform; ~ **roulante élévatrice** *f* CONSTR portable hoisting platform; ~ **semi-submersible** *f* PETR semisubmersible platform, PETROLE semisubmersible rig; ~ **stabilisée** *f* ESPACE *véhicules* stabilized platform; ~ **submersible** *f* PETR submersible platform; ~ **de surpression** *f* PETROLE *canalisations* booster platform; ~ **terminale** *f* PETROLE terminal platform; ~ **des terrassements** *f* CH DE FER track bed; ~ **de travail** *f* CONSTR working platform; ~ **de vissage** *f* PETROLE stabbing board; ~ **de la voie** *f* (*cf plate-forme*) CH DE FER road bed, subgrade, track bed

plate-forme-poids *f* PETROLE gravity platform

plate-formeur *m* PETROLE platforming

platelage *m* CONSTR *d'un pont* flooring

platier *m* OCEANO reef flat

platin *m* OCEANO flat, shallow, shoal

platine[1] *m* (*Pt*) CHIMIE platinum (*Pt*)

platine[2] *f* CONS MECA lockplate, CONSTR *d'une serrure* plate, EQUIP LAB *microscope* stage, ESPACE *véhicules* support plate, INSTRUMENT microscope stage, microscopic stage, object stage, specimen stage, stage, PLAST CAOU *presse* platten, TEXTILE sinker; ~ **à chariot** *f* INSTRUMENT mechanical stage; ~ **à coordonnées** *f* PHOTO mechanical stage; ~ **d'enregistrement** *f* ENREGISTR tape deck; ~ **d'enregistreur sur bande** *f* ENREGISTR recording tape deck; ~ **de fenêtre** *f* CINEMAT aperture plate, film aperture assembly; ~ **de magnétophone** *f* ACOUSTIQUE tape deck; ~ **d'objectif** *f* PHOTO lens mounting plate; ~ **de pile** *f* PAPIER beater plate, bedplate; ~ **rotative** *f* METROLOGIE *indexage, appareil de mesure et de réglage* rotary table; ~ **rotative universelle** *f* INSTRUMENT universal stage; ~ **tournante** *f* EQUIP LAB *microscope* revolving stage; ~ **universelle** *f* CRISTALL universal stage

platinique *adj* CHIMIE platinic

platiniridium *m* CHIMIE platiniridium, platinum-iridium

platinochlorure *m* CHIMIE platinochloride

platinoïde *adj* MATERIAUX platinoid

platinotron *m* PHYSIQUE platinotron

plat-pont *m* NAUT flush deck

plâtrage *m* CERAM VER (Bel) laying on plaster, CONSTR plastering, plasterwork, REVETEMENT plaster coating

plâtre *m* CONSTR plaster; ~ **de moulage** *m* CONSTR plaster of Paris; ~ **de perlite** *m* CHAUFFAGE perlite plaster; ~ **du puits** *m* MINES pithead works

plâtrer *vt* CONSTR plaster

plâtrerie *f* CONSTR plastering, plasterwork

plâtrière *f* MINES gypsum quarry

plâtroir *m* CONS MECA plastering trowel

plats: **sur** ~ *adj* CONS MECA across flats

plattnérite *f* MINERAUX plattnerite

plaxage *m* REVETEMENT acrylic resin coating

Playertypie *f* PHOTO reflex printing method

Pléiades *f pl* ASTRONOMIE Pleiades

plein[1] *adj* MATERIAUX solid; **au** ~ *adj* NAUT aground; ~

d'eau *adj* NAUT waterlogged; **de ~ fouet** *adj* SECURITE head-on

plein:[2] **au ~** *adv* NAUT aground

plein[3] *m* AERONAUT fueling (AmE), fuelling (BrE), CONS MECA tooth; **~ bateau** *m* NAUT *de passagers* boatload; **~ cadre** *m* CINEMAT full frame; **~ de l'eau** *m* HYDRO-LOGIE high water; **~ soleil** *m* ESPACE *véhicules* full sunlight; **~ tuyau** *m* INST HYDR full pipe, opening in thick wall

pleine:[1] **~ couleur** *adj* IMPRIM full-color (AmE), full-colour (BrE); **~ reliure** *adj* IMPRIM full-bound

pleine:[2] **à ~ ouverture** *adv* CINEMAT wide open; **en ~ activité** *adv* CONS MECA in full swing, in full working order; **en ~ exploitation** *adv* CONS MECA in full swing, in full working order; **en ~ marche** *adv* CONS MECA in full swing, in full working order

pleine:[3] **~ charge** *f* AERONAUT, ELECTR *générateur* full-load; **~ charge d'eau** *f* INST HYDR full head of water; **eau** *f* OCEANO open sea, open seas; **~ lune** *f* (*cf phases de la Lune*) ASTRONOMIE full moon; **~ lune d'automne** *f* ASTRONOMIE harvest moon; **~ marche avant** *f* CONS MECA full gear forward, full-forward gear; **~ mer** *f* NAUT high tide, high water, OCEANO high tide, open sea; **~ mer inférieure** *f* OCEANO lower high water; **~ mer supérieure** *f* OCEANO higher high water; **~ ouverture** *f* PHOTO full aperture; **~ piste** *f* ACOUSTIQUE, ENREGISTR full track; **~ poussée** *f* ESPACE *propulsion* full thrust

pleins *m pl* CONS MECA *d'une roue d'engrenage* teeth; **~ phares** *m pl* VEHICULES *éclairage* full beam headlights (BrE), high beams (AmE)

plenum: **~ supérieur** *m* NUCLEAIRE top plenum, upper plenum

pleurage *m* ACOUSTIQUE wow, ENREGISTR, TV flutter, wow; **~ et scintillement** *m* ENREGISTR, TV wow and flutter; **~ de tourne-disque** *m* ENREGISTR turntable wow

plexiglas *m* NAUT Perspex (TM), PLAST CAOU Lucite (TM), Perspex (TM); **~ de saumon d'aile** *m* AERO-NAUT Plexiglass fairing

pli *m* AUTO ply, CERAM VER bend, buckle, CONS MECA, ESPACE ply, GEOLOGIE, PAPIER, PETR fold, TEXTILE crease, pleat, VEHICULES *d'un pneu* ply; **~ accordéon** *m* IMPRIM *façonnage* fanfold, *imposition et produits sur rotatives* concertina fold; **~ cassant** *m* TEXTILE knife pleat; **~ coffré** *m* GEOLOGIE box fold; **~ concentrique** *m* GEOLOGIE parallel fold; **~ couché** *m* GEOLOGIE recumbent fold, TEXTILE flat pleat; **~ de coulée** *m* CERAM VER lap mark; **~ creux** *m* TEXTILE inverted pleat; **~ crevé** *m* CERAM VER parison check, parison crack; **~ delta** *m* IMPRIM *impression, façonnage* delta fold; **~ déversé** *m* GEOLOGIE overfold, PETR aliasing error, foldover; **~ droit** *m* GEOLOGIE upright fold; **~ d'ébauche** *m* CERAM VER blank tear; **~ en accordéon** *m* GEOLOGIE chevron fold, zigzag fold; **~ en chevron** *m* GEOLOGIE chevron fold; **~ en fourreau** *m* GEOLOGIE sheath fold; **~ en genou** *m* GEOLOGIE knee fold; **~ d'équerre** *m* IMPRIM *plieuse sur rotative* chopper fold, *rotatives* quarter fold; **~extérieur** *m* TEXTILE top ply; **~ de fluage** *m* GEOLOGIE flow fold; **~ de fond** *m* EMBAL-LAGE bottom fold; **~ formé de couches ayant gardé la même épaisseur** *m* GEOLOGIE parallel fold; **~ français** *m* IMPRIM French folder, French fold; **~ à la française** *m* IMPRIM French fold, French folder; **~ isoclinal** *m* PETR isoclinal fold; **~ isopaque** *m* GEOLOGIE parallel fold; **~ marqué mais non replié** *m* IMPRIM *façonnage* crease; **~ médian** *m* IMPRIM centerfold (AmE), centre-

fold (BrE); **~ monoclinal** *m* GEOLOGIE homocline, PETR monocline fold; **~ oblique** *m* GEOLOGIE inclined fold; **~ ouvert** *m* PETR open fold; **~ parallèle** *m* GEO-LOGIE parallel fold, IMPRIM *plieuses rotatives* jaw fold; **~ paravent** *m* IMPRIM *façonnage* fanfold, zigzag fold; **~ ptygmatique** *m* GEOLOGIE ptygmatic fold; **~ renversé** *m* GEOLOGIE inverted fold, overturned fold; **~ semblable** *m* GEOLOGIE similar fold, PETR similar folding; **~ synclinal** *m* CONS MECA synclinal flexure, synclinal fold; **~ synclinal en forme d'auge** *m* GEOLOGIE canoe fold; **~ transverse** *m* GEOLOGIE cross-fold; **~ zigzag** *m* IMPRIM accordion fold, *façonnage* fanfold, z-fold, *imposition et produits sur rotative* concertina fold

pliage *m* CERAM VER bending, PAPIER folding, PRODUC-TION bending, folding, RESSORTS *de la boucle* bending; **~ accordéon** *m* PRODUCTION fanfold; **~ à froid** *m* MECANIQUE cold bending

plié: **~ et assemblé** *adj* IMPRIM *façonnage, brochure* folded and collated

plier[1] *vt* CONSTR bend, *osier* bend, EMBALLAGE crease, IMPRIM, PAPIER fold

plier:[2] **se ~** *v réfl* CONSTR bend

plieuse *f* IMPRIM folder unit, folder, PAPIER folding machine, roll crimper, PRODUCTION folding machine; **~ à carton** *f* CONS MECA folding machine for card-board; **~ à lame** *f* IMPRIM blade folder; **~ à lames prenantes et engageantes** *f* IMPRIM *rotatives* nip and tuck folder; **~ à poches** *f* IMPRIM buckle folder machine, pocket folding machine; **~ à triangle** *f* IMPRIM *machine* former folder

pli-faille *m* GEOLOGIE *flanc inverse étiré* stretch thrust; **~ couché** *m* GEOLOGIE overthrust fold

plinthe *f* CONSTR baseboard (AmE), mopboard (AmE), skirt board, skirting, skirting board (BrE), wash-board

pliofilm *m* CHIMIE pliofilm

pliolite *f* CHIMIE pliolit

plis: **~ avec bouillons** *m pl* CERAM VER lap blisters; **~ de couverture** *m pl* GEOLOGIE drape folds; **~ en écailles** *m pl* GEOLOGIE shear folding; **~ en échelon** *m pl* GEO-LOGIE en echelon folds; **~ en relais** *m pl* GEOLOGIE en echelon folds; **~ de fond** *m pl* GEOLOGIE drape folds; **~ de froid** *m pl* CERAM VER cold mold (AmE), cold mould (BrE), cold surface; **~ parallèles** *m pl* GEOLOGIE concentric folds; **~ de revêtement** *m pl* GEOLOGIE drape folds

plissage *m* TEXTILE pleating

plissé *adj* TEXTILE pleated

plissement *m* ESSAIS fold, GEOLOGIE folding, IMPRIM *papier* flute, PRODUCTION folding; **~ concentrique par flexion** *m* GEOLOGIE flexural slip folding; **~ en retour** *m* GEOLOGIE back folding; **~ secondaire** *m* GEOLOGIE refolding

plisser *vt* IMPRIM *liasses en continu* crimp, TEXTILE crease

plisseur *m* TEXTILE pleater

plissotement *m* GEOLOGIE buckling

pliure *f* PRODUCTION folding, TEXTILE raised edge; **~ accordéon** *f* IMPRIM, PAPIER accordion fold

plomb:[1] **à ~** *adv* CONSTR plumb

plomb[2] *m* CHIMIE *(Pb)* lead *(Pb)*, CONSTR plumb line, *d'un fil à plomb* bob, plumb bob, ELECTR *d'un circuit* fuse; **~ contrôle au travail** *m* SECURITE lead control at work; **~ corné** *m* MINERAUX horn lead; **~ déposé électrolytiquement** *m* REVETEMENT electroplated terne; **~ d'encrier** *m* IMPRIM clump; **~ en feuilles** *m*

CONSTR sheet lead; ~ **en saumon** *m* PRODUCTION pig lead; ~ **fusible pour chaudière à vapeur** *m* INST HYDR fusible plug for steam boiler; ~ **optique** *m* INSTRUMENT optical plummet; ~ **rouge** *m* MINERAUX red lead ore; ~ **de sécurité** *m* INST HYDR safety plug; ~ **de sonde** *m* NAUT sounding lead; ~ **spongieux** *m* AUTO sponge lead; ~ **sulfuré** *m* CHIMIE galena, MINERAUX galena, galenite, lead glance; ~ **tétraéthyle** *m* AUTO tetraethyl lead, CHIMIE lead tetraethyl, tetraethyl lead

plombage *m* CONSTR plumbing, EMBALLAGE lead seal, PAPIER blackening, PRODUCTION leading

plombagine *f* CHIMIE graphite, plumbago

plombate *m* CHIMIE plumbate

plomber *vt* CONSTR lead, plumb, plumb, REVETEMENT coat, enamel

plomberie *f* CONSTR plumbing

plombeux *adj* CHIMIE plumbous

plombier *m* CONSTR plumber

plombifère *adj* MINES lead-bearing

plombinage *m* COULEURS black lead

plombique *adj* CHIMIE plumbic

plommure *f* CERAM VER glazed pottery

plongé *adj* PHYSIQUE immersed

plongée *f* CONSTR *de la lunette d'un théodolite* plunging, OCEANO, PETR diving; ~ **autonome** *f* PETR scuba diving; ~ **en apnée** *f* OCEANO skin dive, skin diving; ~ **profonde** *f* PETR deep-water diving; ~ **à saturation** *f* OCEANO saturation dive, saturation diving, PETR saturated diving, PETROLE saturation diving; ~ **sous-marine autonome** *f* NAUT scuba diving

plongement *m* GEOLOGIE pitch, *de l'axe d'un pli* plunge, GEOMETRIE *topologie* immersion

plonger *vt* EMBALLAGE, PRODUCTION dip

plongeur *m* CH DE FER point lock plunger, CONS MECA plunger, plunger piston, ram, OCEANO, PETR diver, PHYSIQUE adjustable short circuit, VEHICULES *cylindre de frein, d'embrayage* plunger; ~ **chauffant** *m* EQUIP LAB immersion heater; ~ **à saturation** *m* PETROLE saturation diver; ~ **sous-marin** *m* NAUT deep-sea diver

plot *m* ELECTROTEC contact block, jack; ~ **de contact** *m* VEHICULES *allumage* point; ~ **d'entrée** *m* PRODUCTION inbound stock point; ~ **magnétique avec extracteur** *m* CONS MECA magnetic holdfast; ~ **radar** *m* AERONAUT radar blip

plots: ~ **à soufflage magnétique** *m pl* CONS MECA magnetic blowout contacts

ployé: ~ **à la vapeur** *adj* NAUT steamed

ployer[1] *vti* CONSTR bend

ployer:[2] **se ~** *v réfl* CONSTR bend

pluie: ~ **acide** *f* GAZ acid rain; ~ **diluvienne** *f* METEO deluge; ~ **effective** *f* METEO effective precipitation; ~ **efficace** *f* METEO effective precipitation; ~ **de météore** *f* ASTRONOMIE meteor storm; ~ **de mousson** *f* METEO monsoon rain; ~ **normale** *f* POLLUTION clean rain; ~ **ordinaire** *f* POLLUTION clean rain; ~ **propre** *f* POLLUTION clean rain; ~ **pure** *f* POLLUTION clean rain; ~ **utile** *f* METEO useful rain

pluies: ~ **acides** *f pl* POLLUTION acid rain, acidic rain

plumbate *m* CHIMIE plumbite

plumbicon *m* ELECTRON plumbicon

plumer *vt* AGRO ALIM pluck

plurivalent *adj* CHIMIE plurivalent, polyvalent

plus:[1] **au ~ près** *adj* NAUT close-hauled

plus:[2] **au ~ près bon plein** *adv* NAUT full and by; **au ~ tard** *adv* PRODUCTION latest

plus:[3] ~ **grand commun diviseur** *m (PGCD)* MATH greatest common divisor, highest common factor *(HCF)*; ~ **grand diamètre admis au-dessus du banc** *m* CONS MECA swing of the bed, swing over bed; ~ **grand diamètre admis au-dessus des chariots** *m* CONS MECA swing of the rest, swing over saddle; ~ **grand diamètre admissible** *m* CONS MECA swing; ~ **petit commun multiple** *m (PPCM)* MATH, ORDINAT least common multiple, lowest common multiple *(LCM)*; ~ **petit commun multiple des dénominateurs** *m (PPCMD)* MATH least common denominator, lowest common denominator *(LCD)*

plus:[4] ~ **basses eaux** *f pl* CONSTR low-water mark; ~ **hautes eaux** *f pl* CONSTR high water level; ~ **hautes eaux des grandes marées ordinaires** *f pl* EN RENOUV HWOST, high water ordinary spring tide

plusieurs: **à ~ constituants** *adj* CHIMIE multicomponent; **à ~ épaisseurs** *adj* EMBALLAGE multiply; **à ~ gammes** *adj* ELECTR multirange

pluton *m* GEOLOGIE pluton

plutonium *m (Pu)* CHIMIE plutonium *(Pu)*

pluviomètre *m* CONSTR rain gage (AmE), rain gauge (BrE), DISTRI EAU precipitation gage (AmE), precipitation gauge (BrE), rain gage (AmE), rain gauge (BrE), EN RENOUV, EQUIP LAB *instrument*, METEO rain gage (AmE), rain gauge (BrE)

Pm *(prométhéum)* CHIMIE Pm *(promethium)*

PMA *abrév (prise maximale autorisée)* OCEANO TAC *(total allowable catch)*

PMB *abrév (point mort bas)* MECANIQUE BDC *(bottom dead centre)*, MINES *(puissance au mortier balistique)* WS *(weight strength)*

PMH *abrév (point mort haut)* AUTO, VEHICULES TDC *(top dead centre)*

PNA *abrév (potentiel de neutralisation de l'acide)* POLLUTION ANC *(acid neutralizing capacity)*

PNC *abrév (personnel navigant commercial)* AERONAUT cabin crew

pneu *m* TRANSPORT, VEHICULES tire (AmE), tyre (BrE); ~ **à bavette** *m* AERONAUT chine tire (AmE), chine tyre (BrE); ~ **à carcasse radiale** *m* PLAST CAOU radial ply tire (AmE), radial ply tyre (BrE), VEHICULES radial tire (AmE), radial tyre (BrE); ~ **classique** *m* PLAST CAOU, VEHICULES crossply tire (AmE), crossply tyre (BrE); ~ **clouté** *m* VEHICULES studded tire (AmE), studded tyre (BrE); ~ **crevé** *m* VEHICULES flat tire (AmE), flat tyre (BrE); ~ **diagonal** *m* PLAST CAOU diagonal ply tire (AmE), diagonal ply tyre (BrE), crossply tire (AmE), crossply tyre (BrE), VEHICULES bias ply tire (AmE), crossply tyre (BrE); ~ **haute pression** *m* TRANSPORT, VEHICULES high-pressure tire (AmE), high-pressure tyre (BrE); ~ **lisse** *m* VEHICULES bald tire (AmE), bald tyre (BrE), plain tread tire (AmE), plain tread tyre (BrE); ~ **neige** *m* VEHICULES snow tire (AmE), snow tyre (BrE); ~ **à plat** *m* VEHICULES flat tire (AmE), flat tyre (BrE); ~ **radial** *m* PLAST CAOU radial ply tire (AmE), radial ply tyre (BrE), VEHICULES radial tire (AmE), radial tyre (BrE); ~ **rechapé** *m* VEHICULES retreaded tire (AmE), retreaded tyre (BrE); ~ **sans chambre d'air** *m* VEHICULES tubeless tire (AmE), tubeless tyre (BrE); ~ **sans sculpture** *m* VEHICULES plain tread tire (AmE), plain tread tyre (BrE); ~ **usé** *m* VEHICULES bald tire (AmE), bald tyre (BrE)

pneumaticité *f* MATERIAUX pneumaticity

pneumatique[1] *adj* CONS MECA, PHYSIQUE, VEHICULES pneumatic

pneumatique[2] *m* TRANSPORT, VEHICULES pneumatic tire (AmE), pneumatic tyre (BrE); ~ **ballon** *m* AUTO balloon tire (AmE), balloon tyre (BrE); ~ **à carcasse diagonale** *m* VEHICULES bias ply tire (AmE), crossply tyre (BrE); ~ **à carcasse radiale** *m* PLAST CAOU radial ply tire (AmE), radial ply tyre (BrE) VEHICULES radial tire (AmE), radial tyre (BrE); ~ **classique** *m* PLAST CAOU crossply tire (AmE), crossply tyre (BrE); ~ **clouté** *m* VEHICULES studded tire (AmE), studded tyre (BrE); ~ **crevé** *m* VEHICULES flat tire (AmE), flat tyre (BrE); ~ **diagonal** *m* PLAST CAOU crossply tire (AmE), crossply tyre (BrE), diagonal ply tire (AmE), diagonal ply tyre (BrE), VEHICULES bias ply tire (AmE), crossply tyre (BrE); ~ **haute pression** *m* TRANSPORT, VEHICULES high-pressure tire (AmE), high-pressure tyre (BrE); ~ **lisse** *m* VEHICULES bald tire (AmE), bald tyre (BrE), plain tread tire (AmE), plain tread tyre (BrE); ~ **neige** *m* VEHICULES snow tire (AmE), snow tyre (BrE); ~ **à plat** *m* VEHICULES flat tire (AmE), flat tyre (BrE); ~ **radial** *m* PLAST CAOU radial ply tire (AmE), radial ply tyre (BrE), VEHICULES radial tire (AmE), radial tyre (BrE); ~ **rechapé** *m* VEHICULES retreaded tire (AmE), retreaded tyre (BrE); ~ **sans chambre d'air** *m* VEHICULES tubeless tire (AmE), tubeless tyre (BrE); ~ **sans sculpture** *m* VEHICULES plain tread tire (AmE), plain tread tyre (BrE); ~ **usé** *m* VEHICULES bald tire (AmE), bald tyre (BrE)

pneumatique[3] *f* PHYSIQUE pneumatics

pneumatolyse *f* GEOLOGIE pneumatolysis

PNP *abrév (plan de numérotage privé)* TELECOM PNP *(private numbering plan)*

PNR *abrév (point de non-retour)* AERONAUT point of no return

Po *(polonium)* CHIMIE Po *(polonium)*

PO *abrév (partiellement obligatoire)* TELECOM CM *(conditionally mandatory)*

pochage *m* CERAM VER ladling

poche *f* CERAM VER ladle, CHARBON pocket, MINES bag, cavity, PRODUCTION casting ladle, foundry ladle, ladle; ~ **d'air** *f* AERONAUT air pocket, airlock; ~ **à armature fixe et à anse démontable** *f* PRODUCTION bull ladle; ~ **avec armature à fourche** *f* PRODUCTION shank, shank ladle; ~ **à chariot** *f* PRODUCTION car ladle; ~ **de coulée** *f* CONS MECA bull ladle, PRODUCTION casting ladle, foundry ladle; ~ **de coulée suspendue** *f* PRODUCTION crane ladle; ~ **doseuse** *f* MINES loading pocket; ~ **de fonderie** *f* PRODUCTION casting ladle, foundry ladle; ~ **de fondeur** *f* PRODUCTION foundry ladle; ~ **à fonte** *f* PRODUCTION casting ladle, foundry ladle; ~ **à fourche** *f* PRODUCTION shank, shank ladle; ~ **à laitier** *f* PRODUCTION slag pot; ~ **de liquide** *f* REFRIG liquid slug; ~ **de minerai** *f* MINES pocket; ~ **montée sur wagonnet** *f* PRODUCTION car ladle; ~ **pour grues** *f* PRODUCTION crane ladle; ~ **simple** *f* PRODUCTION single bag; ~ **de vidange** *f* PRODUCTION drain cup; ~ **volcanique souterraine** *f* GEOPHYS subterranean volcano

poché *adj* MINES bunchy

pocher *vt* CERAM VER ladle

pochette *f* PHOTO *de papier photographique* pack; ~ **autocollante** *f* EMBALLAGE self-seal pocket envelope; ~ **postale** *f* PAPIER correspondence envelope, correspondence pocket; ~ **pour négatif** *f* PHOTO negative sleeve

pocheur *m* CERAM VER ladler

pochoir *m* CERAM VER, IMPRIM stencil, PRODUCTION stencil, stencil plate

podocarpique *adj* CHIMIE podocarpic

podomètre *m* PHYSIQUE pedometer

podophylline *f* CHIMIE podophyllin

poêle: ~ **à flamber** *m* PRODUCTION chauffer, devil, fire lamp, kettle, lamp, lantern

poids:[1] **de** ~ **faible** *adj* INFORMAT low-order; **de** ~ **fort** *adj* INFORMAT high-order, most significant, ORDINAT high-order, most significant; **de** ~ **le plus faible** *adj* INFORMAT, ORDINAT least significant; **de** ~ **le plus fort** *adj* INFORMAT, ORDINAT most significant

poids[2] *m* IMPRIM *papiers* weight, METROLOGIE weight, weights, *d'une balance romaine* bob, PAPIER, PHYSIQUE weight; ~ **approximatif** *m* EMBALLAGE approximate weight; ~ **atomique** *m* CHIMIE atomic weight; ~ **avoirdupois** *m* METROLOGIE avoirdupois weight; ~ **de base** *m* IMPRIM *papier* basic weight; ~ **des boues** *m* PETROLE mud weight; ~ **brut** *m* EMBALLAGE, METROLOGIE, TEXTILE gross weight; ~ **de calcul au décollage** *m* AERONAUT design takeoff mass; ~ **de calcul pour les évolutions au sol** *m* AERONAUT design taxi weight; ~ **de la couche** *m* IMPRIM *papier* coating weight; ~ **curseur** *m* METROLOGIE *d'une balance romaine* bob; ~ **au décollage** *m* ESPACE *véhicules* liftoff weight; ~ **embarqué** *m* NAUT shipping weight; ~ **d'encre par unité de surface** *m* PAPIER ink coverage ratio; ~ **en ordre de marche** *m* ESPACE *véhicules* operating weight; ~ **d'essieu** *m* CONSTR axle load; ~ **étalon** *m* EQUIP LAB calibration weight; ~ **étalons** *m pl* METROLOGIE standard weights; ~ **et mesures** *m pl* METROLOGIE weights and measures; ~ **d'expédition** *m* PRODUCTION shipping weight; ~ **facturé** *m* TEXTILE invoice weight; ~ **faible** *m* METROLOGIE short weight; ~ **du foret** *m* PETR bit weight; ~ **fort** *m* METROLOGIE overweight; ~ **lourd** *m* TRANSPORT HGV, heavy goods vehicle, heavy lorry (BrE), heavy truck (AmE), VEHICULES heavy lorry (BrE), heavy truck (AmE); ~ **maximum** *m* EMBALLAGE maximum weight; ~ **maximum en charge** *m* VEHICULES gross vehicle weight, maximum total weight; ~ **de la mèche** *m* PETR bit weight; ~ **minimum** *m* EMBALLAGE minimum weight; ~ **moléculaire** *m* PETROLE molecular weight; ~ **mort** *m* CONSTR dead load, MECANIQUE dead-weight; ~ **net** *m* TEXTILE net weight; ~ **de l'outil** *m* PETR bit weight; ~ **de poil** *m* TEXTILE pile weight; ~ **propre** *m* CONSTR dead load; ~ **du rotor** *m* EN RENOUV rotor weight; ~ **roulant** *m* CONSTR live load, moving load, rolling load; ~ **sec** *m* AERONAUT *moteur*, EMBALLAGE dry weight; ~ **spécifique** *m* CHARBON unit weight, IMPRIM *papier* basic weight, PETROLE density, specific gravity, PLAST CAOU, TEXTILE specific gravity; ~ **sur l'outil** *m* PETROLE *forage* WOB, weight on bit; ~ **du tissu** *m* TEXTILE fabric weight; ~ **total autorisé en charge** *m (PTAC)* VEHICULES *réglementation* total permissible laden weight (BrE), total permissible loaded weight (AmE) *(total permissible laden weight)*; ~ **total en charge** *m* TRANSPORT AUW, all-up weight, VEHICULES *(PTC)* gross vehicle weight *(GVW)*; ~ **total maximal autorisé** *m (PTMA)* VEHICULES *réglementation* total permissible weight; ~ **total maximum** *m (PTM)* VEHICULES gross vehicle weight, maximum total weight *(GVW)*; ~ **du trépan** *m* PETR bit weight; ~ **troy** *m* METROLOGIE troy weight; ~ **à vide** *m* AERONAUT dry weight, EMBALLAGE tare weight, ESPACE *véhicules* dry weight poignée *f* CINEMAT handgrip, CONSTR door handle, EMBALLAGE, ESPACE *véhicules* handle, INSTRUMENT carrying handle, MECANIQUE, MINES handle, PHOTO handgrip, PRODUCTION handle; ~ à action verticale *f* PRODUCTION vertical lever; ~ amovible *f* CONS MECA detachable handle; ~ anatomique *f* CINEMAT contour grip; ~ du coffre *f* VEHICULES boot handle (BrE), trunk handle (AmE); ~ de commande du sectionneur *f* PRODUCTION *automatisme industriel* switch-operating handle; ~ crosse *f* PHOTO rifle grip; ~ à déclencheur *f* CINEMAT handgrip with shutter release, trigger grip; ~ d'interrupteur *f* ELECTROTEC switch handle; ~ de largage de parachute *f* AERONAUT parachute release handle; ~ de manutention *f* EMBALLAGE carrying handle; ~ à piles *f* PHOTO battery grip; ~ de porte *f* CONSTR, VEHICULES door handle; ~ renforcée intégrée *f* EMBALLAGE integral reinforced handle; ~ sphérique *f* CONS MECA ball knob; ~ tournante *f* VEHICULES *guidon de motocyclette* twist grip; ~ de transport *f* EMBALLAGE, MECANIQUE carrying handle; ~ à ventouses *f* CERAM VER hand sucker; ~ de verrouillage *f* CONSTR locking handle

poignée-déclencheur *f* PHOTO pistol grip with shutter release

poil *m* TEXTILE nap, pile; ~ non coupé *m* TEXTILE uncut pile; ~ de scorie *m* PRODUCTION cinder wool

poinçon *m* CERAM VER feeder plunger, plunger, CONS MECA joggle piece, joggle post, solid punch, CONSTR awl, *d'une ferme de comble* crown post, king rod, MECANIQUE punch, PRODUCTION driver, hallmark, maker's mark, mark; ~ de centrage *m* MECANIQUE center punch (AmE), centre punch (BrE); ~ à cloche de centrage *m* CONS MECA bell centering punch (AmE), bell centring punch (BrE); ~ à collerette avec éjecteur *m* CONS MECA perforating ejector punch; ~ cylindrique à démontage rapide *m* CONS MECA ball lock round punch; ~ cylindrique à tête conique *m* CONS MECA round punch with conical head; ~ ébauche cylindrique à tête cylindrique *m* CONS MECA head-type punch blank; ~ d'emboutissage *m* CONS MECA drawing punch; ~ de garantie *m* PRODUCTION hallmark, maker's mark, mark; ~ à la machine *m* CONS MECA machine punch; ~ à main *m* PRODUCTION hand-punch; ~ à oeil *m* PRODUCTION eyed punch

poinçonnage *m* PRODUCTION punching, stamping

poinçonnement *m* GEOLOGIE impingement, indenter tectonics, PRODUCTION punching

poinçonner *vt* MECANIQUE punch, PRODUCTION punch, stamp

poinçonneuse *f* CINEMAT punch, CONS MECA punching machine; ~ de contrôle *f* TRANSPORT ticket punch; ~ à copier *f* CONS MECA copy punch press; ~ duplex *f* CONS MECA duplex lever punch, duplex punching bear; ~ à levier *f* PRODUCTION lever punching machine; ~ à main *f* CONS MECA screw bear; ~ multiple *f* PRODUCTION gang punch, multiple-punching machine; ~ à vis *f* CONS MECA screw punching bear; ~ à vis simple *f* CONS MECA screw bear, screw punching bear

poinçonneuse-cisaille *f* CONS MECA punching and shearing machine, shearing and punching machine; ~ à levier *f* PRODUCTION lever punching-and-shearing machine

point:[1] au ~ *adj* PHOTO in focus; de ~ fort *adj* ORDINAT high-order; ~ à point *adj* INFORMAT, ORDINAT, TELECOM point-to-point

point[2] *m* ESPACE *véhicules* fix, GEOMETRIE point, IMPRIM full point, full stop (BrE), period (AmE), point, INFORMAT point, NAUT position, *sur la carte* plot, ORDINAT point, PAPIER dot, TEXTILE dot, stitch; **~ a** ~ d'accès *m* TELECOM access port, port; ~ d'accès asynchrone *m* TELECOM asynchronous port; ~ d'accès électronique *m* PHYSIQUE port; ~ d'accès public *m* TELECOM public dial-up port; ~ d'accès au service *m* TELECOM SAP, service access point; ~ d'accès au service de réseau *m* TELECOM NSAP, network service access point; ~ d'accès au service de transport *m* TELECOM TSAP, transport service access point; ~ d'accès synchrone *m* TELECOM synchronous port; ~ d'accès vidéotex *m* TELECOM videotex gateway; ~ d'action du réglage *m* COMMANDE regulating point; ~ d'alignement *m* NAUT leading mark; ~ d'allumage *m* AUTO ignition point, spark timing; ~ d'amure *m* NAUT tack; ~ d'aniline *m* PLAST CAOU aniline value; ~ d'anticheminement *m* CH DE FER mid-point anchor; ~ d'approche finale *m* AERONAUT final approach fix, final approach point; ~ d'appui *m* CONS MECA bearing point, point of support, PETROLE supply base, PHYSIQUE fulcrum; ~ d'arrêt *m* AERONAUT *aérodynamique*, PHYS FLUID, PHYSIQUE stagnation point; ~ astronomique *m* ESPACE astro fix, NAUT astronomical position; ~ d'attaque *m* CRISTALL etch pit; ~ d'attente *m* AERONAUT holding point; ~ d'attente de circulation *m* AERONAUT taxi holding position; ~ d'atterrissage *m* AERONAUT touchdown; ~ azéotrope *m* REFRIG azeotropic point; ~ d'azéotropie *m* REFRIG azeotropic point; **~ b** ~ de bâti *m* TEXTILE hacking stitch; ~ de branchement *m* ELECTRON, ORDINAT *programme* branch point; ~ brillant *m* CERAM VER seed; **~ c** ~ de captation éloigné *m* TV remote pickup point; ~ de charge *m* INFORMAT, ORDINAT load point; ~ chaud *m* CERAM VER hot spot, spring zone; ~ de coincement *m* CONS MECA pinch point; ~ de commande *m* PRODUCTION order point; ~ commun de profondeur *m* PETR common depth point; ~ de commutation *m* TELECOM switching point; ~ de commutation auxiliaire *m* TELECOM auxiliary switching point; ~ de commutation large bande *m* TELECOM broadband crosspoint; ~ de compression *m* INST HYDR compression point; ~ concourant *m* GEOMETRIE point of concurrence; ~ de conflit *m* TRANSPORT conflict point, point of conflict; ~ de congélation *m* NAUT freezing point, PHYS FLUID congealing point, pour point, PHYSIQUE, REFRIG freezing point, VEHICULES *huile* pour point; ~ de connexion *m* TELECOM crosspoint; ~ de connexion CMOS *m* TELECOM CMOS crosspoint; ~ de connexion à contacts scellés *m* TELECOM reed relay crosspoint; ~ de connexion à deux fils *m* TELECOM two-wire crosspoint; ~ de connexion à diode *m* TELECOM diode crosspoint; ~ de connexion électronique *m* TELECOM electronic crosspoint; ~ de connexion à maintien électrique *m* TELECOM electrically-held crosspoint; ~ de connexion à maintien magnétique *m* TELECOM magnetically-latched crosspoint; ~ de connexion métallique *m* TELECOM metallic crosspoint; ~ de connexion optique *m* TELECOM optical center (AmE), optical centre (BrE), optical switching crosspoint; ~ de connexion optoélectronique *m* TELECOM optoelectronic crosspoint; ~ de connexion à quatre fils *m* TELECOM four-wire crosspoint; ~ de connexion remreed *m* TELECOM remreed crosspoint; ~ de connexion à

semi-conducteur *m* TELECOM semiconductor crosspoint; ~ **de connexion à thyristor** *m* TELECOM SCR crosspoint, silicon-controlled rectifier crosspoint; ~ **de contact** *m* CONS MECA *des cercles primitifs* pitch point, PHYSIQUE point of contact; ~ **de contrôle** *m* ORDINAT checkpoint; ~ **de contrôle de présence du signal de queue** *m* CH DE FER tail-end marker trackside detector; ~ **de convergence** *m* TV crossover; ~ **de côte** *m* TEXTILE ribbed stitch; ~ **de couleur** *m* TEXTILE scintillation; ~ **de coupe** *m* CINEMAT cutting point; ~ **de coupure du câble électrique** *m* CH DE FER electric cable joint; ~ **de coupure en fréquence** *m* ELECTRON frequency cutoff; ~ **de cristallisation** *m* GENIE CHIM crystallization point; ~ **critique** *m* PHYSIQUE critical point; ~ **de Curie** *m* ELECTR *paramagnétisme*, PETR, REFRIG Curie point; ~ **de Curie paramagnétique** *m* PHYS RAYON paramagnetic Curie point;

~ d ~ **de dégel** *m* CHIMIE thawing point; ~ **de départ** *m* CONS MECA starting point, TRANSPORT assembly point; ~ **de dérivation** *m* ELECTRON branch point; ~ **de détente** *m* INST HYDR expansion point; ~ **de distribution primaire** *m* TELECOM cabinet; ~ **de distribution secondaire** *m* TELECOM pillar; ~ **de drisse** *m* NAUT head; ~ **dur** *m* CONS MECA friction point;

~ e ~ **d'ébullition** *m* AGRO ALIM, PHYSIQUE, PLAST CAOU, THERMODYN boiling point; ~ **d'échantillonnage** *m* QUALITE sampling point; ~ **d'éclair** *m* CHIMIE, PETROLE flash point, PHYSIQUE flash point, ignition point, PLAST CAOU, REFRIG, THERMODYN flash point; ~ **d'éclair à vase clos** *m* PLAST CAOU *essai* closed-cup flash point; ~ **d'écoulement** *m* IMPRIM *fluidique* flow point, PETROLE pour point, *viscosité* flow point, PHYS FLUID flow point, REFRIG pour point; ~ **d'écoute** *m* NAUT clew; ~ **d'électrode** *m* ELECTR electrode tip; ~ **d'embouteillage** *m* PRODUCTION bottleneck; ~ **d'émergence tronqué** *m* METALL flat-bottomed etch pit; ~ **d'enfoncement** *m* CERAM VER sinking point; ~ **d'entrée** *m* INFORMAT, ORDINAT entry point, TELECOM inlet, TV edit-in, *début d'un nouvel enregistrement* in point, in-edit; ~ **d'équilibre** *m* AERONAUT balance point; ~ **équitemps** *m* AERONAUT *navigation* equaltime point; ~ **d'essai** *m* INFORMAT benchmark; ~ **estimé** *m* NAUT dead reckoning position, estimated position, OCEANO dead reckoning position, dead reckoning; ~ **eutectique** *m* MATERIAUX, METALL eutectic point; ~ **d'évitement** *m* CH DE FER passing point, turnout; ~ **d'évitement sans personnel** *m* CH DE FER unmanned passing point, unmanned turnout;

~ f ~ **de feu** *m* REFRIG fire point; ~ **fin** *m* CERAM VER seed; ~ **fixe** *m* AERONAUT *moteur* run-up, CONSTR fixed point; ~ **fixé** *m* CONSTR *arpentage* base, benchmark; ~ **fixe d'amarrage** *m* PETR deadman; ~ **fixe de clé** *m* PETROLE backup post; ~ **fixe réacteur** *m* AERONAUT engine run-up; ~ **de floculation** *m* GENIE CHIM flocculation point; ~ **de fluage** *m* THERMODYN melting point; ~ **de fonctionnement** *m* ELECTROTEC operating point; ~ **de formation de gouttes** *m* PHYS FLUID drop point; ~ **de fuite** *m* CHARBON breakthrough point, GEOMETRIE vanishing point; ~ **de fusion** *m* CHIMIE, MATERIAUX, METEO, PAPIER, PHYSIQUE, PLAST CAOU, REFRIG, TEXTILE melting point, THERMODYN fusing point, melting point;

~ g ~ **gamma** *m* ASTRONOMIE, ESPACE vernal point; ~ **de gel** *m* EMBALLAGE, THERMODYN *de l'eau* freezing point; ~ **de gelée blanche** *m* REFRIG frost point; ~ **géodésique** *m* NAUT geodesic station; ~ **de givre** *m*

REFRIG frost point; ~ **de la glace fondante** *m* PHYSIQUE ice point; ~ **de goutte** *m* REFRIG drop point; ~ **de grainage** *m* GENIE CHIM granulation pitch;

~ h ~ **harmonique** *m* GEOMETRIE harmonic point;

~ i ~ **identifié** *m* AERONAUT pinpoint; ~ **d'ignition** *m* NAUT flash point; ~ **d'impact** *m* AERONAUT stagnation point, touchdown, ESPACE *véhicules* touchdown point; ~ **d'impact de l'air** *m* IMPRIM *séchage* air impingement; ~ **d'impact du faisceau** *m* TV beam impact point; ~ **imprécis** *m* IMPRIM *photogravure* soft dot; ~ **d'inflammabilité** *m* AGRO ALIM, NAUT flash point; ~ **d'inflammation** *m* CHAUFFAGE *température*, CHIMIE flash point, PETROLE ignition point, PHYSIQUE flash point, REFRIG fire point, flash point, THERMODYN flash point, kindling point; ~ **d'interception** *m* ESPACE *orbitographie* intercept point; ~ **intermédiaire** *m* NAUT way point; ~ **d'intersection** *m* CONSTR intersection point, GEOMETRIE point of intersection;

~ j ~ **de jonction** *m* ELECTROTEC junction point;

~ l ~ **lambda** *m* PHYSIQUE lambda point; ~ **de liquéfaction** *m* PHYS FLUID pour point; ~ **logique** *m* ELECTRON node; ~ **de lumière** *m* CINEMAT printer point; ~ **lumineux** *m* ELECTRON light spot;

~ m ~ **de mesure du bruit à l'approche** *m* AERONAUT approach noise measurement point; ~ **de mesure du bruit latéral** *m* AERONAUT lateral noise measurement point; ~ **de mesure survolé au décollage** *m* AERONAUT flyover noise measurement point; ~ **milieu** *m* AERONAUT point of no return; ~ **milieu du secondaire** *m* ELECTROTEC secondary center tap (AmE), secondary centre tap (BrE); ~ **de mire** *m* CONSTR leveling point (AmE), levelling point (BrE); ~ **miroir commun** *m* GEOLOGIE, PETR common depth point; ~ **de montage** *m* CONS MECA division point; ~ **de montée de câble** *m* ELECTROTEC cable distribution point; ~ **mort** *m* CINEMAT dead spot, MECANIQUE dead center (AmE), dead centre (BrE), neutral, VEHICULES *boîte de vitesses* neutral, *moteur, piston* dead center (AmE), dead centre (BrE); ~ **mort AV** *m* CONS MECA crank-end dead center (AmE), crank-end dead centre (BrE); ~ **mort bas** *m* (*PMB*) MECANIQUE bottom dead center (AmE), bottom dead centre (BrE) (*BDC*); ~ **mort haut** *m* (*PMH*) AUTO, VEHICULES *piston* top dead center (AmE), top dead centre (BrE) (*TDC*); ~ **mou** *m* IMPRIM *photogravure* soft dot;

~ n ~ **de Néel** *m* REFRIG Néel point; ~ **neutre** *m* PHYSIQUE neutral point; ~ **de non-retour** *m* (*PNR*) AERONAUT point of no return;

~ o ~ **observé** *m* ASTRONOMIE position by astrocalculation, NAUT fix, observed position, OCEANO estimated reckoning, observed position; ~ **observé par radio** *m* AERONAUT radio fix; ~ **d'osculation** *m* GEOMETRIE point of osculation;

~ p ~ **par relèvements successifs** *m* NAUT running fix; ~ **perdu** *m* CONSTR turning point; ~ **de poser** *m* TRANSPORT spot; ~ **de prélèvement** *m* CHARBON sampling point, ELECTROTEC tapping point, QUALITE sampling point;

~ r ~ **radiant** *m* ASTRONOMIE radiant; ~ **radio** *m* AERONAUT radio fix; ~ **de ramollissement** *m* PLAST CAOU, REFRIG, TEXTILE softening point; ~ **de rapprochement maximum** *m* NAUT closest point of approach; ~ **de réapprovisionnement** *m* PRODUCTION reorder point; ~ **de réarmement bas** *m* PRODUCTION *automatisme industriel* low reset; ~ **de référence** *m* ACOUSTIQUE, GEOMETRIE reference point; ~ **de référence de déter-**

mination du bruit en approche *m* AERONAUT approach reference noise measurement point; ~ de référence interne *m* TELECOM IRP, internal reference point; ~ de repère *m* AERONAUT landmark, CHIMIE set point, CONSTR benchmark, datum, datum point, fixed point, landmark, mark point, MECANIQUE benchmark, MILITAIRE, NAUT landmark, ORDINAT benchmark; ~ de reprise *m* INFORMAT, ORDINAT restart point, TEXTILE darning stitch; ~ du réseau *m* CRISTALL lattice point; ~ de rosée *m* AERONAUT, AGRO ALIM, CHAUFFAGE, METEO dew point, NUCLEAIRE dew point temperature, PAPIER, PETR, PHYSIQUE, REFRIG dew point; ~ de rosée équivalent *m* REFRIG apparatus dew point; ~ de rupture *m* ORDINAT breakpoint, TEXTILE breaking length;

~ s ~ de saturation *m* ESPACE *communications* saturation point; ~ de sédimentation maximum *m* GEOLOGIE depocenter (AmE), depocentre (BrE); ~ de selle *m* METALL saddle point; ~ sémaphore *m* TELECOM SP, signaling point (AmE), signalling point (BrE); ~ de sinus *m* METROLOGIE sine center (AmE), sine centre (BrE); ~ de solidification *m* MATERIAUX congealing point, REFRIG solidification point; ~ du solstice *m* ASTRONOMIE, ESPACE solstitial point; ~ de sortie *m* INFORMAT, ORDINAT exit point, TELECOM outlet, TV edit-out, *d'un montage* out-edit, out-point; ~ sous-satellite *m* ESPACE *mécanique* subsatellite point; ~ subsurface *m* PETR depth point; ~ de surjet *m* TEXTILE oversewing, stitch; ~ de survol *m* ESPACE *orbitographie* fly-by point;

~ t ~ de tangence *m* GEOMETRIE point of tangency; ~ de test *m* NUCLEAIRE test jack, TELECOM test point; ~ de touché *m* AERONAUT touchdown; ~ de trame *m* IMPRIM picture dot, *photogravure* halftone dot; ~ de transfert sémaphore *m* TELECOM STP, signaling transfer point (AmE), signalling transfer point (BrE); ~ de transition *m* NUCLEAIRE transition point, transition temperature; ~ de triangulation *m* CONSTR triangulation point; ~ triple *m* METALL, PHYSIQUE, THERMODYN triple point; ~ de trouble *m* LESSIVES, REFRIG cloud point; ~ typographique *m* IMPRIM typographic point;

~ v ~ de vaporisation *m* GENIE CHIM evaporating point; ~ de vente *m* INFORMAT, ORDINAT POS, point of sale; ~ de vente électronique *m* ORDINAT EPOS, electronic point of sale; ~ de vérification *m* ESPACE checkpoint; ~ vernal *m* ASTRONOMIE, ESPACE vernal point;

~ z ~ zénithal *m* ASTRONOMIE, ESPACE zenith point

pointage *m* ESPACE *communications* pointing, MECANIQUE *soudage* tack welding, MILITAIRE *artillerie* sighting, *radar* plotting, NAUT plotting, PRODUCTION timekeeping; ~ des marchandises *m* PRODUCTION tally; ~ radar *m* NAUT radar plotting; ~ des temps *m* PRODUCTION time recording

point-à-point *adv* IMPRIM dot-to-dot

pointe *f* CINEMAT spike, CONS MECA center (AmE), centre (BrE), point, scriber, *de poupée mobile* dead center (AmE), dead centre (BrE), CONSTR brad, point, nail, scriber, NAUT point, TELECOM transient; ~ d'aiguille *f* CH DE FER tip of switch tongue; ~ avant amovible *f* AERONAUT detachable nose cone; ~ avant du fuselage *f* AERONAUT nose cone; ~ de charge *f* ELECTR peak load, *réseau* load peak; ~ de coeur *f* CH DE FER switch diamond; ~ à cône Morse *f* CONS MECA Morse taper center (AmE), Morse taper centre

(BrE); ~ conique *f* ENREGISTR nose cone; ~ de contact *f* CONS MECA prod, ELECTR *raccordement* plug pin, ELECTRON whisker; ~ de contrainte en battement *f* AERONAUT flapping stress peak; ~ de courant *f* ELECTROTEC current surge; ~ de crue *f* HYDROLOGIE flood peak; ~ de demande *f* GAZ peak demand; ~ de diamant *f* CONS MECA diamond point, diamond point tool, diamond tool, CONSTR diamond pencil, diamond point, diamond tool, glass cutter, glass cutter's diamond, glazier's diamond; ~ en diamant *f* ENREGISTR diamond stylus; ~ de fission *f* NUCLEAIRE fission spike; ~ de fusée-sonde *f* ESPACE nose cone; ~ de mouleur *f* PRODUCTION sprig; ~ de pieu *f* CHARBON pile point, pile tip; ~ de la poupée fixe *f* CONS MECA live center (AmE), live centre (BrE); ~ de la poupée mobile *f* CONS MECA back center (AmE), back centre (BrE); ~ pour engager la feuille *f* PAPIER leader, tail end; ~ de pression *f* INST HYDR pressure surge; ~ de puissance *f* ELECTROTEC power surge; ~ de résonance *f* ENREGISTR resonance peak; ~ réticulaire *f* METALL lattice point; ~ sèche *f* CINEMAT scribe; ~ sharp end *f* PHYSIQUE point; ~ de tension *f* ELECTROTEC spike, voltage spike; ~ de tension admissible *f* PRODUCTION withstand impulse, withstand impulse voltage; ~ de touche *f* ELECTROTEC test prod; ~ de tour *f* CONS MECA lathe center (AmE), lathe centre (BrE); ~ de traçage *f* CONSTR scriber; ~ à tracer *f* CONS MECA, ELECTRON scriber; ~ transitoire *f* PRODUCTION transient; ~ à trois dents *f* CONS MECA fork center (AmE), fork centre (BrE), *tour* prong center (AmE), prong centre (BrE)

pointé: ~ des arrivées *m* GEOLOGIE *des temps des premières arrivées* picking of arrivals, selection of arrivals

pointeau *m* AUTO float needle, fuel inlet valve, needle valve, CONS MECA center pop (AmE), center punch (AmE), centre pop (BrE), centre punch (BrE), needle valve, prick punch, punch, tapered needle, CONSTR pin valve, EQUIP LAB needle, *instrument* pointer, PRODUCTION finder point punch; ~ de carburateur *m* VEHICULES carburetor needle (AmE), carburettor needle (BrE); ~ de débit visible *m* CONS MECA sightfeed needle valve; ~ de mécanicien *m* CONS MECA center pop (AmE), center punch (AmE), centre pop (BrE), centre punch (BrE), prick punch, punch, PRODUCTION finder point punch

Pointel *m* TELECOM Telepoint

pointer *vt* MILITAIRE *canon* range

pointerolle *f* CHARBON dresser

pointes: ~ de bruit *f pl* ELECTRON grass; ~ polaires *f pl* TV pole tip

pointeur *m* INFORMAT pointer, INSTRUMENT edge, ORDINAT pointer, PRODUCTION checker, timekeeper, TELECOM pointer; ~ de fin *m* PRODUCTION *automatisme industriel* end pointer; ~ solaire *m* GEOPHYS sun tracker; ~ du système *m* PRODUCTION *automatisme industriel* system pointer

pointillage *m* CERAM VER stippling

pointillés *m pl* IMPRIM leaders

points: ~ cardinaux *m pl* ASTRONOMIE, NAUT, PHYSIQUE cardinal points; ~ circulaires dans l'infinité *m pl* GEOMETRIE circular points at infinity; ~ de conduite *m pl* IMPRIM leader dots, leaders; ~ de conflit *m pl* TRANSPORT traffic cuts; ~ conjugués *m pl* PHYSIQUE conjugate points; ~ entremêlés *m pl* TEXTILE meshed stitches; ~ nodaux *m pl* PHYSIQUE nodal points; ~ principaux *m pl* PHYSIQUE principal points

pointu *adj* IMPRIM *photogravure, impression* keen

pointures *f pl* IMPRIM pins, *rotatives* withdrawing pins; ~ **droites** *f pl* IMPRIM *plieuses rotatives* straight-shank pins

poire *f* CONS MECA cone, cone pulley, speed cone, step cone, EQUIP LAB blow ball, bulb, METROLOGIE *d'une balance romaine* bob; ~ **en caoutchouc** *f* EQUIP LAB *pipette* rubber bulb; ~ **à pipetter** *f* EQUIP LAB *analyse* pipetting bulb

poise *m* METROLOGIE poise

poison *m* SECURITE poison; ~ **de catalyseur** *m* POLLUTION catalyst poison

poisseux[1] *adj* AGRO ALIM sticky, PLAST CAOU sticky, *adhésifs* tacky

poisseux[2] *m* IMPRIM *encres, colles* tack

poisson *m* PETROLE fish

Poisson: ~ **Austral** *m* ASTRONOMIE Piscis Austrinus; ~ **Volant** *m* ASTRONOMIE Volans

Poissons *m pl* ASTRONOMIE Pisces, The Fishes

poitrail *m* CONSTR breast summer, bressummer

poivres: ~ **dans le papier** *m pl* PAPIER specks

poix *f* CERAM VER, CONSTR, PAPIER *dû à la résine* pitch; ~ **de houille** *f* CHARBON coal tar pitch; ~ **liquide** *f* CONSTR tar

polaire[1] *adj* CHIMIE polar

polaire[2] *f* ASTRONOMIE, GEOMETRIE polar

Polaire *f* ASTRONOMIE Polaris

polarimètre *m* CHIMIE, EQUIP LAB *analyse*, PHYS RAYON, PHYSIQUE polarimeter

polarimétrie *f* CHIMIE polarimetry

polarimétrique *adj* CHIMIE polarimetric

polarisabilité *f* CHIMIE, PHYSIQUE polarizability

polarisable *adj* CHIMIE polarizable

polarisant *adj* OPTIQUE polarizer

polarisation *f* ELECTR polarization, ELECTROTEC bias, polarization, ENREGISTR bias, biasing, magnetic bias, ESPACE *communications* polarization, INFORMAT, ORDINAT bias, PHOTO, PHYS RAYON, PHYSIQUE, TELECOM polarization, TV biasing, magnetic bias; ~ **atomique** *f* PHYS RAYON atomic polarization; ~ **automatique** *f* ELECTROTEC self-bias; ~ **à champ transversal** *f* ENREGISTR cross field bias; ~ **circulaire** *f* PHYSIQUE, TELECOM circular polarization; ~ **circulaire droite** *f* ESPACE *communications* right-hand circular polarization; ~ **circulaire gauche** *f* ESPACE *communications* LHCP, left-hand circular polarization; ~ **circulaire de la lumière** *f* PHYS RAYON circular polarization of light; ~ **diélectrique** *f* ELECTROTEC dielectric polarization; ~ **dipolaire** *f* PHYSIQUE orientational polarization; ~ **directe** *f* ELECTROTEC, PHYSIQUE forward bias; ~ **du drain** *f* ELECTROTEC drain bias; ~ **électrique** *f* ELECTR *diélectrique*, PHYSIQUE electric polarization; ~ **d'électrode** *f* ELECTROTEC electrode bias; ~ **électronique** *f* PHYS RAYON, PHYSIQUE electronic polarization; ~ **elliptique** *f* ESPACE *communications* elliptical polarization, PHYS RAYON elliptic polarization, PHYSIQUE elliptical polarization; ~ **en courant alternatif** *f* ENREGISTR AC bias; ~ **en courant continu** *f* ENREGISTR DC bias, TV DC biasing; ~ **de la gâchette** *f* ELECTROTEC gate bias; ~ **de la grille** *f* ELECTROTEC gate bias, grid bias; ~ **horizontale** *f* ELECTROTEC, PHYSIQUE, TELECOM horizontal polarization; ~ **inverse** *f* ELECTROTEC, PHYSIQUE reverse bias; ~ **ionique** *f* PHYSIQUE ionic polarization; ~ **linéaire** *f* TELECOM linear polarization; ~ **magnétique** *f* ACOUSTIQUE magnetic polarization, ELECTROTEC magnetic bias, magnetic polarization, TV bias; ~ **magnétique par courant alternatif** *f* TV AC magnetic biasing; ~ **mécanique** *f* ELECTROTEC mounting polarization; ~ **négative** *f* ELECTROTEC negative bias; ~ **oblique** *f* ELECTROTEC slant polarization; ~ **d'onde électromagnétique** *f* ELECTROTEC electromagnetic wave polarization; ~ **des ondes** *f* TELECOM wave polarization; ~ **optimum** *f* ENREGISTR optimal bias; ~ **optique** *f* TELECOM optical polarization; ~ **d'orientation** *f* PHYSIQUE orientational polarization; ~ **orthogonale** *f* TELECOM orthogonal polarization; ~ **d'une pile** *f* ELECTROTEC cell polarization; ~ **positive** *f* ELECTROTEC positive bias; ~ **rectiligne** *f* ELECTROTEC, TELECOM linear polarization; ~ **spontanée** *f* GEOPHYS self-potential; ~ **d'un transistor** *f* ELECTRON transistor bias; ~ **verticale** *f* ELECTROTEC, PHYSIQUE, TELECOM vertical polarization; ~ **du vide** *f* NUCLEAIRE vacuum polarization

polariscope *m* CERAM VER polarizing microscope, strain viewer, PHYSIQUE polariscope

polarisé *adj* PHYSIQUE biased

polariser *vt* ELECTROTEC bias, OPTIQUE polarize

polariseur *m* EQUIP LAB *microscope*, ESPACE *communications*, METALL, OPTIQUE polarizer, PHOTO polarizing filter, PHYSIQUE, TELECOM polarizer

polarité *f* CHIMIE *optique, magnétique*, ELECTR *d'une pile, d'une machine*, ELECTROTEC, PHYSIQUE, TV polarity; ~ **d'impulsion** *f* ELECTRON pulse polarity; ~ **négative du signal image** *f* TV negative picture phase, negative video signal; ~ **positive du signal image** *f* TV positive picture phase; ~ **de la tension** *f* ELECTROTEC voltage polarity

polarogramme *m* CHIMIE polarogram

polarographie *f* CHIMIE polarography

polarographique *adj* CHIMIE polarographic

polaroïd *m* (MD) PHYS RAYON, PHYSIQUE Polaroid (TM)

polaron *m* PHYSIQUE polaron

pôle *m* ELECTR *d'un commutateur, d'un aimant, d'une machine* pole, ELECTROTEC pole, *de l'alimentation* rail, GEOLOGIE end member, GEOMETRIE, METROLOGIE, PHYSIQUE pole; ~ **analogue** *m* CRISTALL analogous pole; ~ **antilogue** *m* CRISTALL antilogous pole; ~ **auxiliaire** *m* ELECTR *moteur à courant continu* interpole; ~ **de champ** *m* ELECTROTEC field pole; ~ **de commutation** *m* ELECTR *machine* commutating pole; ~ **électrique** *m* ELECTROTEC electric pole; ~ **de filtre** *m* ELECTRON filter pole; ~ **fixe** *m* ELECTR *moteur* fixed pole; ~ **géomagnétique** *m* GEOPHYS geomagnetic pole; ~ **géomagnétique Nord** *m* GEOPHYS North magnetic pole; ~ **géomagnétique sud** *m* GEOPHYS south geomagnetic pole; ~ **de la lentille** *m* PHOTO lens vertex; ~ **lisse** *m* ELECTR *machine* nonsalient pole; ~ **magnétique** *m* ELECTR, GEOPHYS magnetic pole, PETR unit magnetic pole, PHYSIQUE magnetic pole; ~ **de mélange** *m* GEOLOGIE end member; ~ **négatif** *m* ELECTR *borne*, ELECTROTEC negative pole; ~ **Nord** *m* PHYSIQUE north pole; ~ **Nord galactique** *m* ASTRONOMIE north galactic pole; ~ **nord magnétique** *m* PHYSIQUE magnetic north pole; ~ **positif** *m* ELECTR *raccordement* positive pole, ELECTROTEC anode; ~ **principal** *m* ELECTR *borne* main pole; ~ **saillant** *m* ELECTR *machine*, ELECTROTEC salient pole; ~ **sud** *m* PHYSIQUE south pole; ~ **sud galactique** *m* ASTRONOMIE south galactic pole; ~ **sud magnétique** *m* PHYSIQUE magnetic south pole

polecat *m* CINEMAT polecat

pôles: ~ **célestes** *m pl* ASTRONOMIE celestial poles; ~ **de même nom** *m pl* ELECTR *magnétisme*, PHYSIQUE like poles; **~ de nom contraire** *m pl* ELECTR *magnétisme*, PHYSIQUE unlike poles

poli:[1] **~ au feu** *adj* CERAM VER fire-polished; **~ partout** *adj* CONS MECA *outil* bright all over

poli[2] *m* PHYSIQUE optically-smooth surface, PRODUCTION polishing; **~ éclatant** *m* PRODUCTION brilliant polish; **~ au feu** *m* CERAM VER fire finish; **~ miroir** *m* MECANIQUE mirror finish

polianite *f* MINERAUX polianite

police *f* IMPRIM *fonderie* font (BrE), fount (AmE); **~ de caractères** *f* IMPRIM font (BrE), fount (AmE)

polices: **~ de caractères d'édition** *f pl* IMPRIM book fonts

polir *vt* MECANIQUE polish, PRODUCTION buff

poli-rond *m* CERAM VER disc polishing (BrE), disk polishing (AmE)

polissable *adj* MATERIAUX polishable

polissage *m* CONS MECA honing, MATERIAUX buffing, flattening, lapping, MECANIQUE burnishing, METALL, PLAST CAOU *opération*, PRODUCTION polishing; **~ à l'acide** *m* CERAM VER acid polishing; **~ chimique** *m* METALL chemical polishing; **~ électrolytique** *m* METALL, RESSORTS electropolishing; **~ humide** *m* PRODUCTION wet polishing; **~ au liège** *m* CERAM VER cork polishing; **~ mécanique** *m* CONS MECA, METALL mechanical polishing; **~ à reflets** *m* CONS MECA mirror finish; **~ au tonneau** *m* MATERIAUX tumbling, PRODUCTION barrel finishing

polisseur *m* CERAM VER, PRODUCTION polisher

polisseuse *f* MATERIAUX polishing apparatus

polissoir *m* CERAM VER flattening tool, lap, polisher, CONS MECA polishing head, polishing lathe; **~ en drap** *m* CERAM VER cloth polisher; **~ en feutre** *m* CERAM VER felt polisher; **~ en papier** *m* CERAM VER paper polisher; **~ à la poix** *m* CERAM VER pitch polisher

politique: **~ de qualité** *f* QUALITE quality policy; **~ de sécurité** *f* TELECOM security policy; **~ de sécurité fondée sur l'identité** *f* TELECOM identity-based security policy

polluant *m* POLLU MER, POLLUTION pollutant; **~ acidifiant** *m* POLLUTION acidic precursor; **~ de l'air** *m* POLLUTION air pollutant; **~ aquatique** *m* DISTRI EAU aquatic pollutant; **~ atmosphérique** *m* POLLUTION air pollutant, air polluting substance; **~ des eaux** *m* POLLUTION water pollutant; **~ précurseur** *m* POLLUTION precursor pollutant

polluants: **~ des sols** *m pl* POLLUTION soil pollutants

pollucite *f* MINERAUX pollucite

pollué *adj* POLLUTION polluted

polluer *vt* POLLUTION, QUALITE, SECURITE pollute

pollueur *m* SECURITE pollutant

pollution *f* CHIMIE pollution, MATERIAUX contamination, QUALITE, SECURITE pollution; **~ de l'air** *f* POLLUTION, SECURITE air pollution; **~ atmosphérique** *f* POLLUTION air pollution, atmospheric pollution; **~ atmosphérique par des particules en suspension** *f* POLLUTION particulate air pollution; **~ de base** *f* POLLUTION background pollution; **~ des eaux** *f* DISTRI EAU, HYDROLOGIE, POLLUTION *du niveau initial* water pollution; **~ radioactive** *f* POLLUTION radioactive pollution; **~ solide** *f* POLLUTION material pollution; **~ des sols** *f* POLLUTION land pollution, soil pollution; **~ thermique** *f* POLLUTION, THERMODYN thermal pollution

polonium *m (Po)* CHIMIE polonium *(Po)*

polyacrylamide *m* PETROLE polyacrylamide

polyacrylate *m* CHIMIE, PLAST CAOU polyacrylate

polyacrylonitrile *m* CHIMIE polyacrylonitrile

polyamide *m* CHIMIE, MATERIAUX *matières plastiques*, PLAST CAOU, TEXTILE polyamide

polyamine *f* PLAST CAOU polyamine; **~ aliphatique** *f* PLAST CAOU *adhésifs, revêtements* aliphatic polyamine

polyatomique *adj* CHIMIE, GAZ polyatomic

polybasite *f* MINERAUX polybasite

polybutadiène *m* ESPACE *propulsion* polybutadiene

polybutylène *m* PLAST CAOU polybutylene

polycarbonate *m* ELECTR *diélectrique*, MATERIAUX *matières plastiques*, PLAST CAOU polycarbonate

polychloroprène *m* PLAST CAOU neoprene

polychlorure: **~ de vinyle** *m* CONSTR, ELECTROTEC, MATERIAUX, PLAST CAOU polyvinyl chloride

polychromatique *adj* CERAM VER *verre* polychromatic

polychrome *adj* IMPRIM polychrome

polycondensation *f* CHIMIE polycondensation

polycrase *f* MINERAUX polycrase

polycristal *m* MATERIAUX polycrystal

polycristallin *adj* MATERIAUX polycrystalline

polycyclique *adj* CHIMIE polycyclic

polydenté *adj* CHIMIE polydentate

polydiméthylsiloxane *m* CHIMIE polydimethylsiloxane

polyécran *m* TV multiscreen

polyèdre[1] *adj* GEOMETRIE polyhedral

polyèdre[2] *m* CRISTALL, GEOMETRIE, METALL polyhedron; **~ irrégulier** *m* GEOMETRIE irregular polyhedron

polyène *m* CHIMIE polyene

polyénique *adj* CHIMIE polyenic

polyester *m* MATERIAUX *matières plastiques*, NAUT, PLAST CAOU, TEXTILE polyester; **~ armé** *m* MECANIQUE *matériaux* GRP, glass reinforced polyester; **~ saturé** *m* PLAST CAOU saturated polyester

polyestérification *f* CHIMIE polyesterification

polyéthylène *m* CHIMIE polyethylene, polythene, ELECTR *isolateur*, EMBALLAGE, MATERIAUX *matières plastiques* polyethylene, NAUT polyethylene, polythene, PETROLE polyethylene, polythene, PLAST CAOU, TEXTILE polyethylene; **~ chloré** *m* PLAST CAOU chlorinated polyethylene; **~ à haute densité** *m* EMBALLAGE HDPE, high-density polyethylene, MATERIAUX *matières plastiques* high-density polyethylene

polyéthylène-glycol *m* LESSIVES polyethylene glycol

polyéthylène-téréphtalate *m* ELECTR *diélectrique*, PLAST CAOU polyethylene terephthalate

polyfonctionnel *adj* CHIMIE polyfunctional

polygonal *adj* GEOMETRIE polygonal

polygone *m* GEOMETRIE polygon; **~ des forces** *m* PHYSIQUE polygon; **~ plan** *m* GEOMETRIE plane polygon; **~ régulier** *m* GEOMETRIE regular polygon

polygonisation *f* METALL polygonization

polyhalite *f* MINERAUX polyhalite

polyimide *m* ELECTRON, PLAST CAOU polyimide

polyinsaturé *adj* AGRO ALIM, CHIMIE polyunsaturated

polyisoprène *m* CHIMIE, PLAST CAOU *caoutchouc* polyisoprene

polymère[1] *adj* CHIMIE polymeric

polymère[2] *m* CHIMIE, PETROLE, PLAST CAOU, PRODUCTION, TEXTILE polymer; **~ d'addition** *m* PLAST CAOU addition polymer; **~ atactique** *m* PLAST CAOU atactic polymer; **~ de condensation** *m* PLAST CAOU condensation polymer; **~ en échelle** *m* PLAST CAOU ladder polymer; **~ greffé** *m* PLAST CAOU graft polymer; **~ implanté** *m* PLAST CAOU graft polymer; **~ linéaire** *m* PLAST CAOU linear polymer; **~ ramifié** *m* PLAST CAOU branched polymer

polymérie *f* CHIMIE polymeria, polymerism

polymérisation *f* CHIMIE, MATERIAUX polymerization, MECANIQUE *matériaux* curing, NAUT curing, polymerization, PETROLE, PLAST CAOU polymerization, TEXTILE curing; **~ d'addition** *f* PLAST CAOU *procédé* addition polymerization; **~ en émulsion** *f* PLAST CAOU *procédé* emulsion polymerization; **~ en masse** *f* LESSIVES block polymerization; **~ en perles** *f* NUCLEAIRE bead polymerization; **~ en solution** *f* PLAST CAOU solution polymerization; **~ en suspension** *f* PLAST CAOU *procédé* suspension polymerization; **~ implantée** *f* PLAST CAOU *procédé* graft polymerization; **~ par condensation** *f* PLAST CAOU *procédé* condensation polymerization; **~ par greffage** *f* PLAST CAOU *procédé* graft polymerization

polymériser *vt* CHIMIE, PAPIER polymerize, PLAST CAOU, TEXTILE cure, polymerize

polymériseuse *f* TEXTILE polymerizer

polyméthacrylate *m* PLAST CAOU polymeth acrylate; **~ d'hexyle** *m* PLAST CAOU polyhexyl methacrylate; **~ de méthyle** *m* PLAST CAOU polymethyl methacrylate

polyméthylène *m* CHIMIE polymethylene

polymignite *f* MINERAUX polymignite

polymorphisme *m* METALL polymorphism

polynôme *m* INFORMAT polynomial, MATH multinomial, polynomial, ORDINAT, PHYSIQUE polynomial; **~ réductible** *m* INFORMAT, ORDINAT reducible polynomial

polynômes: ~ de Legendre *m pl* PHYSIQUE Legendre polynomials

polynucléotide *m* CHIMIE polynucleotide

polyol *m* CHIMIE, PLAST CAOU polyol

polyoléfine *f* MATERIAUX, PLAST CAOU, TEXTILE polyolefin

polyoxyéthylène *m* CHIMIE polyoxyethylene

polyoxyméthylène *m* CHIMIE, PLAST CAOU POM, polyoxymethylene

polypeptide *m* CHIMIE polypeptide

polyphasé *adj* ELECTRON multiphase, ELECTROTEC polyphase, GEOLOGIE *métamorphisme, déformation* multiphase, polyphase

polyphénol *m* CHIMIE polyphenol

polyphosphate: ~ de sodium *m* AGRO ALIM sodium polyphosphate

polypier *m* GEOLOGIE coral

polypnée *f* OCEANO fast breathing, polypnea

polypropylène *m* CHIMIE, ELECTR *isolateur*, MATERIAUX, NAUT, PETROLE, PLAST CAOU, TEXTILE polypropylene

polyptyque *m* CINEMAT split screen

polysaccharide: ~ du genre laminaria *m* CHIMIE laminarin

polysilicium *m* ELECTRON polysilicon

polysiloxane *m* PLAST CAOU polysiloxane

polystyrène *m* CHIMIE polystyrene, polyvinylbenzene, MATERIAUX *matières plastiques*, PLAST CAOU polystyrene; **~ expansé** *m* PLAST CAOU Styrofoam (AmE, TM), expanded polystyrene; **~ mousse** *m* EMBALLAGE Styrofoam (AmE, TM), expanded polystyrene

polystyrène-choc *m* PLAST CAOU impact polystyrene

polysulfone *f* CHIMIE, MATERIAUX polysulfone (AmE), polysulphone (BrE)

polysulfure *m* CHIMIE, PLAST CAOU polysulfide (AmE), polysulphide (BrE)

polytène *m* CHIMIE polytene

polyterpène *m* CHIMIE polyterpene

polytétrafluoréthylène *m* PLAST CAOU Fluon (TM), polytetrafluoroethylene

polythène *m* CHIMIE polyethylene, polythene

polyuréthane *m* MATERIAUX *matières plastiques*, PLAST CAOU, TEXTILE polyurethane; **~ cellulaire** *m* PLAST CAOU *caoutchouc synthétique* polyurethane foam

polyuréthanique *adj* PLAST CAOU polyurethane

polyvalence *f* CHIMIE multivalence, polyvalence, polyvalency

polyvalent *adj* CHIMIE polyvalent

polyvinylacétal *m* PLAST CAOU polyvinyl acetal

polyvinylacétate *m* PLAST CAOU polyvinyl acetate

polyvinylchlorure *m (PVC)* CONSTR, ELECTROTEC, MATERIAUX, PLAST CAOU polyvinyl chloride *(PVC)*; **~ non plastifié** *m* PLAST CAOU unplasticized polyvinyl chloride; **~ rigide** *m* EMBALLAGE rigid PVC

polyvinyle *m* CHIMIE, TEXTILE polyvinyl

polyvinyléther *m* PLAST CAOU polyvinyl ether

polyvinylpyrrolidone *m* LESSIVES PVP, polyvinylpyrrolidone

pomme *f* CONSTR knob, NAUT *de mât* truck

pommette *f* CONSTR knob

pompage *m* AERONAUT *turbomachine* surge, CONS MECA hub extractor, DISTRI EAU pumping, pumping out, ELECTR *machine*, ELECTROTEC hunting, MINES pumping, REFRIG hunting, TV fluttering of brightness level, picture flutter; **~ du compresseur** *m* AERONAUT compressor stall, compressor surge; **~ d'essai** *m* INST HYDR pumping test; **~ de gain** *m* ENREGISTR gain pumping; **~ optique** *m* ELECTRON, NUCLEAIRE, PHYS RAYON *procédé laser*, PHYSIQUE optical pumping; **~ par faisceau d'électrons** *m* ELECTRON electron beam pumping

pompe *f* DISTRI EAU pump, INSTRUMENT diffusion pump, MINES, NAUT pump, NUCLEAIRE discharge nozzle, PHYSIQUE, POLLU MER, REFRIG pump;

~ a **~ d'accélération** *f* MECANIQUE booster pump, VEHICULES *carburateur* accelerator pump; **~ à action directe** *f* DISTRI EAU direct acting pump, direct action pump; **~ à air** *f* CONS MECA, PHYSIQUE air pump; **~ alimentaire de chaudière** *f* MAT CHAUFF boiler feed pump; **~ d'alimentation** *f* CONS MECA fuel pump, MAT CHAUFF feed pump, POLLU MER supply pump, PRODUCTION feed pump; **~ d'amorçage** *f* AERONAUT primer pump; **~ d'appoint** *f* CONS MECA booster pump; **~ aspirante** *f* AGRO ALIM suction pump, CONS MECA aspiring pump, DISTRI EAU suction pump, INST HYDR aspiration pump, aspiring pump, suction pump, TEXTILE suction pump; **~ aspirante et foulante** *f* DISTRI EAU lift-and-force pump; **~ aspirante et refoulante** *f* DISTRI EAU lift-and-force pump; **~ d'assèchement** *f* POLLU MER stripping pump; **~ asynchrone** *f* ELECTROTEC induction pump; **~ auto-amorçante** *f* INST HYDR self-priming pump; **~ auto-amorçante à eau usée** *f* NUCLEAIRE self-priming dirty-water pump; **~ auto-aspirante** *f* VEHICULES *carburant* self-priming pump; **~ auto-étanchéifiante** *f* EMBALLAGE self-sealing pump; **~ autonome portative** *f* EQUIP LAB *échantillonnage* portable pump; **~ auxiliaire** *f* ESPACE *propulsion* fuel backup pump;

~ b **~ de balayage** *f* PRODUCTION *système hydraulique* scavenge pump; **~ à boue** *f* MINES mud pump, sludge pump, sludger, PETR mud pump, PETROLE mud pump, slush pump; **~ à bras** *f* PRODUCTION hand pump;

~ c **~ de cale** *f* NAUT bilge pump; **~ à carburant** *f* AERONAUT, VEHICULES fuel pump; **~ à carburant haute pression** *f* VEHICULES fuel high-pressure pump; **~ de cargaison** *f* NAUT, POLLU MER cargo pump; **~ cen-**

trifuge _f_ GENIE CHIM centrifugal pump, INST HYDR turbine pump, POLLU MER, REFRIG centrifugal pump; ~ **centrifuge à aspiration en bout** _f_ CONS MECA end suction centrifugal pump; ~ **à chaîne** _f_ DISTRI EAU chain pump; ~ **à chaleur** _f_ CHAUFFAGE, CONS MECA, MECANIQUE, PHYSIQUE, THERMODYN heat pump; ~ **à chapelet** _f_ DISTRI EAU chain pump, chapelet, paternoster pump; ~ **à charge** _f_ ELECTROTEC charge pump; ~ **à chute libre** _f_ PRODUCTION free delivery pump, free fall pump; ~ **cinétique** _f_ CONS MECA kinetic pump; ~ **de circulation** _f_ AGRO ALIM circulation pump, INST HYDR circulating pump, PETROLE mud pump, slush pump, REFRIG circulation pump; ~ **clapet** _f_ PRODUCTION flap valve pump; ~ **à combustible** _f_ MECANIQUE _véhicules_, NAUT fuel pump; ~ **à commande par courroie** _f_ PRODUCTION belt pump, belt-driven pump; ~ **de compression** _f_ INST HYDR compression pump; ~ **à conduction** _f_ ELECTROTEC conduction pump; ~ **à courroie** _f_ PRODUCTION belt pump, belt-driven pump; ~ **à crépine** _f_ POLLU MER strainer pump; ~ **cryotechnique** _f_ ESPACE _véhicules_ cryopump;

~ **d** ~ **à débit constant** _f_ CONS MECA constant flow pump; ~ **à débit fixe** _f_ PRODUCTION _système hydraulique_ fixed delivery pump; ~ **à débit réglable** _f_ CONS MECA adjustable discharge pump, variable discharge pump; ~ **à débit variable** _f_ CONS MECA adjustable discharge pump, variable discharge pump, PRODUCTION _système hydraulique_ variable delivery pump; ~ **demi-rotative** _f_ DISTRI EAU semirotary pump; ~ **à diaphragme** _f_ DISTRI EAU, POLLU MER diaphragm pump; ~ **à diffusion** _f_ CONS MECA, PHYSIQUE diffusion pump; ~ **à doser** _f_ EMBALLAGE dosing pump; ~ **doseuse** _f_ EQUIP LAB _manutention de fluides_ metering pump; ~ **à double effet** _f_ INST HYDR duplex pump; ~ **de drague** _f_ NAUT dredge pump; ~ **dragueuse** _f_ CONSTR pump dredge, pump dredger; ~ **duplex** _f_ INST HYDR duplex pump;

~ **e** ~ **à eau** _f_ AUTO, VEHICULES _refroidissement_ water pump; ~ **à eau usée** _f_ NUCLEAIRE dirty-water pump; ~ **d'échantillonnage** _f_ EQUIP LAB sampling pump; ~ **à écoulement axial** _f_ CONS MECA axial flow pump; ~ **à éjecteur** _f_ CONS MECA ejector pump; ~ **électromagnétique** _f_ NUCLEAIRE electromagnetic pump; ~ **élévatoire** _f_ DISTRI EAU lift pump, GENIE CHIM airlift pump; ~ **à engrenages** _f_ AUTO, PLAST CAOU _pompage de liquides_, PRODUCTION _système hydraulique_, REFRIG gear pump; ~ **en ligne** _f_ AUTO multicylinder injection pump; ~ **entraînée par réacteur** _f_ AERONAUT engine-driven pump; ~ **éolienne** _f_ EN RENOUV windmill pump; ~ **d'épreuve** _f_ DISTRI EAU test pump; ~ **d'épuisement** _f_ DISTRI EAU drainage pump, MINES dewatering pump; ~ **à ergol** _f_ ESPACE _propulsion_ fuel pump; ~ **à essence** _f_ AUTO fuel pump, VEHICULES _carburant_ fuel pump, gas pump (AmE), gasoline pump (AmE), petrol pump (BrE); ~ **à essence à commande électromagnétique** _f_ VEHICULES _alimentation en carburant_ electric fuel pump; ~ **à essence à commande mécanique** _f_ VEHICULES _alimentation en carburant_ mechanical fuel pump; ~ **à essence à dépression** _f_ AUTO vacuum fuel pump; ~ **à essence mécanique** _f_ AUTO mechanical fuel pump; ~ **à essence à membrane** _f_ VEHICULES _alimentation en carburant_ diaphragm fuel pump; ~ **à essence à piston** _f_ AUTO plunger fuel pump; ~ **éthylglycol** _f_ AERONAUT de-icing pump; ~ **d'évacuation d'air** _f_ CONS MECA aspiring pump; ~ **à évaporation** _f_ GENIE CHIM evaporating pump; ~ **d'extraction des conden-**

sats _f_ GENIE CHIM condensate pump;

~ **f** ~ **à feu** _f_ CONSTR fire pump, THERMODYN fire engine; ~ **à flux axial** _f_ MINES axial flow pump; ~ **à flux mélangé** _f_ MINES mixed flow pump; ~ **de forage** _f_ DISTRI EAU borehole pump; ~ **foulante** _f_ DISTRI EAU plunger pump, ram pump, PRODUCTION force pump;

~ **g** ~ **de gavage** _f_ CONS MECA booster pump, ESPACE _propulsion_ boost pump, MECANIQUE, TRANSPORT booster pump; ~ **à godets** _f_ DISTRI EAU chapelet, paternoster pump; ~ **de graissage** _f_ CONS MECA grease gun; ~ **à graisse** _f_ VEHICULES _outil_ grease gun;

~ **h** ~ **haute pression pour abatteuse à tambour** _f_ MINES shearer-high pressure pump; ~ **hélice** _f_ TRANSPORT screw pump; ~ **hélico-centrifuge** _f_ CONS MECA mixed flow pump; ~ **hélicoïde** _f_ CONS MECA axial pump; ~ **à huile** _f_ AUTO, CONSTR oil pump, MECANIQUE lubricating pump, REFRIG, VEHICULES _lubrification_ oil pump; ~ **à huile à engrenages** _f_ AUTO gear-type oil pump;

~ **i** ~ **d'incendie** _f_ CONSTR, SECURITE, THERMODYN fire pump; ~ **à incendie** _f_ SECURITE, THERMODYN fire engine; ~ **à induction** _f_ ELECTROTEC induction pump; ~ **d'injection** _f_ AUTO fuel injection pump, CONS MECA, CONSTR, NAUT injection pump; ~ **d'injection de carburant** _f_ VEHICULES fuel injection pump; ~ **ionique** _f_ PHYSIQUE ion pump; ~ **ionique par vaporisation** _f_ GENIE CHIM evaporation pump; ~ **d'ions** _f_ CONS MECA ion pump;

~ **j** ~ **à jet** _f_ NUCLEAIRE jet pump;

~ **l** ~ **de lubrification et sa tuyauterie** _f_ CONS MECA oil pump and pipe connections, pump and connections, PRODUCTION lubricating pump and pipe connections;

~ **m** ~ **magnétohydrodynamique** _f (pompe MHD)_ ELECTROTEC magnetohydrodynamic pump; ~ **à main** _f_ PRODUCTION, SECURITE _matériel pour combattre l'incendie_ hand pump; ~ **à main portative** _f_ SECURITE _à incendie_ stirrup pump; ~ **à maîtresse-tige** _f_ MINES bull pump; ~ **de mélange** _f_ PAPIER fan pump, mixing pump; ~ **MHD** _f (pompe magnétohydrodynamique)_ ELECTROTEC MHD pump; ~ **moléculaire** _f_ PHYSIQUE molecular pump; ~ **à mouvement alternatif** _f_ DISTRI EAU reciprocating pump;

~ **p** ~ **péristaltique** _f_ EQUIP LAB _manutention des liquides_ peristaltic pump; ~ **à pied** _f_ AUTO, CONS MECA foot pump; ~ **à piston** _f_ DISTRI EAU, PRODUCTION _système hydraulique_ piston pump; ~ **à piston plein** _f_ INST HYDR solid piston pump; ~ **à piston plongeur** _f_ DISTRI EAU plunger pump, ram pump, PRODUCTION force pump; ~ **à pistons axiaux** _f_ MECANIQUE axial piston pump; ~ **à plongeur** _f_ DISTRI EAU plunger pump, ram pump, INST HYDR solid piston pump, PRODUCTION force pump; ~ **pouvant fonctionner noyée** _f_ DISTRI EAU subaqueous pump, submerged pump; ~ **à presse-étoupe** _f_ NUCLEAIRE glanded pump; ~ **de pression** _f_ DISTRI EAU pressure pump; ~ **primaire volumétrique** _f_ CONS MECA positive displacement pump; ~ **primaire volumétrique à vide** _f_ CONS MECA positive displacement vacuum pump; ~ **de puisard des eaux de fuite** _f_ NUCLEAIRE leakage water pump; ~ **de purge** _f_ DISTRI EAU drip pump;

~ **q** ~ **à quatre corps et à engrenages** _f_ PRODUCTION four-throw geared pump;

~ **r** ~ **refoulante** _f_ CHARBON pressure pump, DISTRI EAU plunger pump, ram pump, PRODUCTION force pump; ~ **de refoulement** _f_ INST HYDR pressure pump; ~ **relais** _f_ MECANIQUE booster pump; ~ **de reprise** _f_

VEHICULES *carburateur* accelerator pump; ~ **de réservoir d'eau traitée** *f* NUCLEAIRE waste condensate pump; ~ **rotative** *f* DISTRI EAU, PHYSIQUE rotary pump; ~ **rotative à ailettes** *f* DISTRI EAU vane pump; ~ **rotative à distributeur** *f* AUTO distributor injection pump; ~ **rotative à palettes** *f* DISTRI EAU, PRODUCTION *système hydraulique* vane pump;

~ s ~ **à sable** *f* MINES sludge pump, sludger; ~ **à saumure** *f* REFRIG brine pump; ~ **à schlamm** *f* MINES slurry pump; ~ **de secours** *f* PRODUCTION *système hydraulique* stand-by pump; ~ **semi-rotative** *f* DISTRI EAU semirotary pump; ~ **de service** *f* PRODUCTION *système hydraulique* duty pump; ~ **de servodirection** *f* AUTO power steering pump; ~ **de sondage** *f* CONSTR borehole pump; ~ **à sorption** *f* PHYSIQUE sorption pump; ~ **à soufflet** *f* EQUIP LAB bellows pump; ~ **soulevante** *f* DISTRI EAU lift pump; ~ **à sublimation** *f* GENIE CHIM evaporation pump; ~ **submersible** *f* MINES submersible pump; ~ **suceuse** *f* DISTRI EAU suction pump, INST HYDR aspiration pump, aspiring pump, suction pump; ~ **de suralimentation** *f* CONS MECA booster pump, ESPACE *propulsion* boost pump, TRANSPORT booster pump; ~ **suspendue** *f* MINES slung pump, suspended pump;

~ t ~ **à tarer les injecteurs** *f* AUTO, CONS MECA injector test pump; ~ **de transfert** *f* POLLU MER transfer pump; ~ **de treuil** *f* AERONAUT hoist pump; ~ **à trois corps** *f* DISTRI EAU three-throw pump; ~ **turbine** *f* DISTRI EAU turbopump, EN RENOUV pump turbine;

~ v ~ **à vélo** *f* TRANSPORT bicycle pump; ~ **à vide** *f* AGRO ALIM vacuum air pump, vacuum pump, CONS MECA, EQUIP LAB, PHYSIQUE vacuum pump, POLLU MER vacuum pump, vacuum unit; ~ **à vide cinétique** *f* MECANIQUE kinetic vacuum pump; ~ **à vide élevé** *f* CONS MECA low-pressure vacuum pump; ~ **à vide préliminaire** *f* CONS MECA high-pressure vacuum pump; ~ **à vis** *f* POLLU MER, PRODUCTION *système hydraulique*, TRANSPORT screw pump; ~ **à volant** *f* PRODUCTION hand flywheel pump; ~ **volante** *f* MINES slung pump, suspended pump; ~ **volumétrique** *f* INST HYDR, PRODUCTION *système hydraulique* positive displacement pump

pomper[1] *vt* DISTRI EAU pump, pump out, ELECTRON evacuate, PRODUCTION churn, feed

pomper[2] *vti* NAUT pump

pompes: ~ **d'épuisement** *f pl* DISTRI EAU pumping equipment, pumping plant

ponçage *m* CERAM VER, PLAST CAOU *procédé de finissage* sanding, PRODUCTION pumicing, sandpapering

ponce *f* GEOLOGIE pumice, MINERAUX pumice stone

ponceau *m* CONSTR, HYDROLOGIE culvert; ~ **avec dalles** *m* CONSTR box culvert

poncer *vt* PRODUCTION sandpaper

ponceuse: ~ **à bande étroite** *f* CONS MECA narrow belt sanding machine; ~ **à disque** *f* CONS MECA disc sanding machine (BrE), disk sanding machine (AmE); ~ **orbitale** *f* CONS MECA orbital sander; ~ **orbitale rotative** *f* CONS MECA rotary orbital sander; ~ **vibrante** *f* CONS MECA finishing sander

poncif *m* PRODUCTION face dust

ponctuel *adj* PHYSIQUE point

pondération *f* INFORMAT, ORDINAT weighting; ~ **de Galerkin** *f* NUCLEAIRE Galerkin weighting

pont *m* CERAM VER shut-off, CONS MECA bridge, gang piece, gap bridge, CONSTR bridge, *de grue roulante* bridge, ELECTR bridge, ELECTROTEC bridge circuit, INFORMAT, INSTRUMENT bridge, NAUT deck, ORDINAT bridge, PRODUCTION bridge, fire bridge, flame bridge, furnace bridge; ~ **d'alimentation** *m* TELECOM transmission bridge; ~ **alternatif** *m* PHYSIQUE alternating current bridge; ~ **d'Anderson** *m* ELECTR *circuit* Anderson bridge; ~ **à arches surbaissées** *m* CONSTR bridge with diminished arches; ~ **arrière** *m* AUTO rear axle assembly, rear axle housing assembly, NAUT afterdeck, VEHICULES *transmission* rear axle assembly; ~ **arrière à double démultiplication** *m* AUTO double reduction rear axle; ~ **auto-équilibré** *m* ELECTROTEC self-balancing switch; ~ **avant** *m* NAUT foredeck; ~ **Bailey** *m* CONSTR, MILITAIRE Bailey bridge; ~ **banjo** *m* VEHICULES *essieu arrière* banjo-type housing; ~ **basculant** *m* NAUT lifting bridge; ~ **à bascule** *m* CONSTR balance bridge, bascule bridge, counterpoise bridge, drawbridge, weigh bridge; ~ **de bateaux** *m* MILITAIRE pontoon bridge, NAUT floating bridge, TRANSPORT pontoon bridge; ~ **biais** *m* CONSTR oblique bridge, skew bridge; ~ **bow-string** *m* CONSTR bowstring bridge; ~ **à bras égaux** *m* ELECTR *circuit* equal arm bridge; ~ **à câbles** *m* CONSTR cable-stayed bridge; ~ **cambré** *m* NAUT cambered deck; ~ **cantilever** *m* CONSTR cantilever bridge; ~ **de capacité** *m* ELECTR *circuit* capacity bridge; ~ **de chargement** *m* PRODUCTION charging platform, charging scaffold, landing, platform; ~ **de chevalets** *m* CONSTR trestle bridge; ~ **de conférence** *m* TELECOM conference bridge; ~ **console** *m* CONSTR cantilever bridge; ~ **à contrepoint** *m* CONSTR counterpoise bridge; ~ **à corde** *m* ELECTROTEC slide bridge; ~ **de coulée** *m* PRODUCTION ladle crane; ~ **de courant alternatif** *m* ESSAIS alternating current bridge; ~ **à courant continu** *m* ELECTROTEC DC bridge; ~ **de déversement** *m* TRANSPORT tipping platform; ~ **de Dion** *m* AUTO Dion axle; ~ **dormant** *m* CONSTR footbridge; ~ **double** *m* ELECTR double bridge; ~ **doublé** *m* NAUT sheathed deck; ~ **double de Kelvin** *m* ELECTR double Kelvin bridge; ~ **double de Thompson** *m* ELECTR double Thompson bridge; ~ **de la dunette** *m* NAUT afterdeck; ~ **dunette** *m* NAUT poop deck; ~ **des embarcations** *m* NAUT, TRANSPORT boat deck; ~ **des emménagements** *m* NAUT saloon deck; ~ **en arc** *m* CONSTR arched beam bridge; ~ **en bois** *m* CONSTR timber bridge; ~ **en charpente** *m* CONSTR frame bridge; ~ **en courant alternatif** *m* ELECTR *mesure* alternating current bridge; ~ **en dos d'âne** *m* CONSTR hog-backed bridge; ~ **en encorbellement** *m* CONSTR cantilever bridge; ~ **en pierre** *m* CONSTR stone bridge; ~ **en poutres** *m* CONSTR girder bridge; ~ **en treillis** *m* CONSTR lattice bridge, truss bridge; ~ **d'envol** *m* NAUT flight deck, TRANSPORT landing deck; ~ **ferroviaire** *m* CONSTR railroad bridge (AmE), railway bridge (BrE); ~ **fixe** *m* CERAM VER curtain; ~ **flottant** *m* MILITAIRE floating bridge, VEHICULES *transmission* floating axle; ~ **de gaillard arrière** *m* NAUT afterdeck; ~ **à hauban** *m* CONSTR cable-stayed bridge; ~ **d'impédance** *m* ELECTROTEC impedance bridge; ~ **d'inductance** *m* ELECTROTEC inductance bridge; ~ **inférieur** *m* NAUT lower deck, PETR cellar deck; ~ **intégral** *m* ELECTR full bridge; ~ **de jauges** *m* ELECTROTEC strain gage bridge (AmE), strain gauge bridge (BrE); ~ **de Kelvin** *m* ELECTR, ELECTROTEC, PHYSIQUE Kelvin bridge; ~ **léger** *m* NAUT spar deck; ~ **levant** *m* CONSTR drawbridge, lifting bridge, lifting bridge, TRANSPORT lift bridge; ~ **de manoeuvre** *m* NAUT hurricane deck; ~ **de mesure** *m* CONS MECA measuring bridge; ~ **de**

mesure de capacité *m* ELECTR capacitance bridge; ~
de mesure de conductance *m* ELECTR conductance
bridge; ~ de mesure à corde *m* ELECTROTEC slide wire
bridge; ~ de mesure de distorsion *m* ENREGISTR distor-
tion-measuring bridge; ~ métallique *m* CONSTR iron
bridge, steel bridge; ~ de Miller *m* ELECTR *circuit*
Miller bridge; ~ mobile *m* NAUT movable bridge; ~
moteur *m* AUTO, VEHICULES *transmission* driving axle;
~ de Nernst *m* ELECTROTEC Nernst bridge; ~ d'Owen *m*
ELECTR *circuit* Owen bridge; ~ par-dessus *m* CH DE
FER overpass; ~ à péage *m* CONSTR toll bridge; ~ pour
routes *m* CONSTR highway bridge, road bridge; ~ à
poutres *m* CONSTR girder bridge; ~ à poutres armées
m CONSTR truss bridge; ~ à poutres à consoles *m*
CONSTR cantilever bridge; ~ à poutres en caisson *m*
CONSTR box-girder bridge; ~ des premières *m* NAUT
saloon deck; ~ principal *m* NAUT main deck; ~ promenade *m* NAUT promenade deck; ~ provisoire *m*
CONSTR temporary bridge; ~ de radeaux *m* NAUT
floating bridge; ~ ras *m* NAUT flush deck; ~ de redresseurs *m* ELECTROTEC rectifier bridge; ~ des répéteurs
m TELECOM repeater deck; ~ à résonance *m* ELECTR
mesure resonance bridge; ~ roulant *m* CINEMAT overhead crane, CONS MECA cranage, CONSTR drawbridge,
overhead crane, roller bridge, rolling bridge, running
bridge, MECANIQUE overhead crane, traveling crane
(AmE), travelling crane (BrE), PRODUCTION overhead crane, traveler (AmE), traveller (BrE), traveling
crane (AmE), travelling crane (BrE); ~ roulant de 20
tonnes *m* CONS MECA cranage up to 20 tonnes capacity; ~ roulant d'atelier *m* PRODUCTION shop traveler
(AmE), shop traveller (BrE); ~ roulant de chargement *m* TRANSPORT transtainer, transtainer crane; ~
roulant à électro-aimant de levage *m* PRODUCTION
magnet crane; ~ roulant à électro-aimant porteur *m*
PRODUCTION magnet crane; ~ Schering *m* ELECTRO-
TEC, PHYSIQUE Schering bridge; ~ supérieur *m* NAUT
upper deck; ~ sur chevalets *m* CONSTR trestle bridge; ~
surélevé *m* NAUT raised deck; ~ sur tréteaux *m* CONSTR
trestle bridge; ~ suspendu *m* CONSTR suspension
bridge; ~ suspendu à chaînes *m* CONSTR chain bridge;
~ à tablier inférieur *m* CONSTR bottom road bridge,
overbridge, through bridge; ~ à tablier supérieur *m*
CONSTR deck bridge, top-road bridge, undergrade
bridge; ~ de teugue *m* NAUT anchor deck; ~ thermique
m CHAUFFAGE, THERMODYN heat bridge; ~ de thermistances *m* ELECTROTEC thermistor bridge; ~ de
Thomson *m* ELECTR Thomson bridge; ~ tournant *m*
CONSTR drawbridge, pivot bridge, swing bridge, swivel bridge, turn bridge, turning bridge, NAUT swing
bridge; ~ de transbordement *m* TRANSPORT loading
bridge; ~ à travées égales *m* CONSTR bridge with
equal bays; ~ à trompette *m* VEHICULES *pont arrière*
split housing; ~ à trompettes *m* AUTO split housing; ~
universel *m* ELECTR *mesure* universal bridge; ~ verseur
m CERAM VER casting crane; ~ viaduc *m* CONSTR viaduct; ~ des voitures *m* TRANSPORT car deck; ~ volant *m*
CONSTR flying bridge; ~ de Wheatstone *m* ELECTR,
ELECTROTEC, PHYSIQUE Wheatstone bridge; ~ de Wien
m ELECTRON, PHYSIQUE Wien bridge
pontage *m* NAUT decking
pont-bascule: ~ pour véhicules routiers *m* TRANSPORT
road vehicle weighing machine
pont-char *m* MILITAIRE *pour surmonter les tranchées
antichar* bridging tank
ponté *adj* NAUT decked, PRODUCTION bridged

pontée *f* NAUT deck cargo, deck load
ponter *vt* ELECTROTEC shunt
pontet *m* MILITAIRE trigger guard
pont-grue *m* CONSTR bridge crane
pontier *m* NAUT bridge keeper
pontil *m* CERAM VER ground base, punty (BrE), sticking-
up iron (AmE); ~ à boîte *m* CERAM VER cashey box; ~
à griffes *m* CERAM VER gadget
ponton *m* CONSTR, NAUT pontoon, PETR barge, pontoon, TRANSPORT ferry landing stage, pontoon; ~
d'accostage *m* TRANSPORT landing pontoon, landing
stage; ~ de forage *m* PETR drilling barge; ~ à pipe-line
m PETR lay barge
ponton-grue *m* NAUT floating crane
pont-rail *m* TRANSPORT railroad bridge (AmE), railway
bridge (BrE)
pont-redresseur *m* ELECTROTEC bridge rectifier
pont-route *m* CONSTR highway bridge, road bridge,
TRANSPORT road bridge
pooling *m* PETROLE *commerce, blocs* unitization
popeline *f* TEXTILE poplin
population: ~ d'électrons *f* ESPACE electron population;
~ inversée *f* ELECTRON inverted population
populine *f* CHIMIE populin
porcelaine *f* CERAM VER china, porcelain, TEXTILE porcelain; ~ artistique *f* CERAM VER artistic porcelain, craft
porcelain, studio porcelain; ~ dure *f* CERAM VER hard
porcelain; ~ électrotechnique *f* ELECTROTEC
electrotechnical porcelain; ~ à haute tension *f* ELECTR
high-voltage porcelain; ~ pour ménage *f* CERAM VER
household porcelain; ~ de rebut *f* CERAM VER porcelain reject; ~ tendre *f* CERAM VER soft porcelain; ~
tendre anglaise *f* CERAM VER English china, bone
china
pore *m* CHARBON pore, void, GAZ pore
poreux *adj* CHIMIE unglazed, EN RENOUV, MATERIAUX
porous
porosimètre *m* PAPIER porosimeter, porosity tester; ~ à
aspiration *m* PAPIER suction porosimeter, suction porosity tester; ~ à cylindre *m* PAPIER densometer
porosité *f* ACOUSTIQUE, CHARBON, CHIMIE, CONSTR, DIS-
TRI EAU, EN RENOUV, GAZ porosity, GEOLOGIE pore
space, MATERIAUX, METALL porosity, PAPIER porosity,
des papiers et des cartons absorption capacity,
absorptive capacity, PETR, PETROLE, PLAST CAOU porosity; ~ effective *f* PETR effective porosity; ~ efficace *f*
HYDROLOGIE *du sol* absorptive capacity, porosity; ~
ouverte *f* CERAM VER apparent porosity; ~ du pain *f*
AGRO ALIM bread texture; ~ secondaire *f* PETR secondary porosity
porpézite *f* MINERAUX porpezite
porphine *f* CHIMIE porphin
porphyrique *adj* GEOLOGIE *structure de roche ignée* porphyritic
porphyroblastique *adj* GEOLOGIE *roche* porphyroblastic
porphyroïde *adj* GEOLOGIE *roche* porphyritic
porphyropsine *f* CHIMIE porphyropsin
porque *f* NAUT, OCEANO web frame
port *m* EMBALLAGE carriage, IMPRIM, INFORMAT port,
NAUT harbor (AmE), harbour (BrE), port, ORDINAT
port, PRODUCTION carriage, TRANSPORT carriage,
port; ~ d'accostage *m* ESPACE *véhicules* docking port;
~ d'aéroglisseurs *m* NAUT, TRANSPORT hoverport; ~
d'armement *m* NAUT port of commissioning, port of
documentation (AmE), port of registry (BrE); ~
artificiel *m* NAUT artificial port; ~ d'attache *m* NAUT

home port, port of registration, port of registry; ~ **de chargement** *m* NAUT shipping port; ~ **de chevalement** *m* CONSTR trestle shore; ~ **de commerce** *m* NAUT commercial port, trading port; ~ **d'éclatement** *m* TRANSPORT offshore terminal; ~ **en eau profonde** *m* NAUT deep-water harbor (AmE), deep-water harbour (BrE); ~ **en lourd** *m* NAUT cargo capacity, dead weight, PETROLE dead-weight, deadweight tonnage; ~ **en lourd utile** *m* PETROLE dead weight tons; ~ **d'entrée/sortie** *m* INFORMAT, ORDINAT input/output port; ~ **d'escale** *m* NAUT port of call; ~ **fluvial** *m* NAUT river port; ~ **franc** *m* NAUT, TRANSPORT free port; ~ **d'immatriculation** *m* NAUT port of registry; ~ **imprimante** *m* IMPRIM printer port; ~ **à marée** *m* NAUT tidal harbor (AmE), tidal harbour (BrE), tidal port; ~ **maritime** *m* NAUT seaport; ~ **de mer** *m* NAUT seaport; ~ **naturel** *m* NAUT natural harbor (AmE), natural harbour (BrE); ~ **parallèle** *m* INFORMAT, ORDINAT parallel port; ~ **de pêche** *m* NAUT fishing port; ~ **de périphérique** *m* INFORMAT, ORDINAT terminal port; ~ **pétrolier** *m* TRANSPORT tanker terminal; ~ **pétrolier en mer** *m* TRANSPORT offshore port; ~ **de plaisance** *m* NAUT marina; ~ **à roulage direct** *m* NAUT roll-on/roll-off port; ~ **de toute marée** *m* NAUT deep-water harbor (AmE), deep-water harbour (BrE); ~ **de transit** *m* NAUT port of transit

portabilité *f* TELECOM call portability

portable *adj* INFORMAT, ORDINAT portable

portail *m* CONSTR launching gantry; ~ **ignifugé** *m* SECURITE fire protection gate

portance *f* AERONAUT lift, CHARBON bearing capacity, EN RENOUV, PHYSIQUE lift; ~ **aérodynamique** *f* TRANSPORT aerodynamic lift; ~ **hydrodynamique** *f* TRANSPORT hydrodynamic lift; ~ **maximum** *f* AERONAUT maximum lift; ~ **de la pale** *f* AERONAUT hélicoptère blade lift; ~ **totale** *f* TRANSPORT total lift

portant: au ~ *adv* NAUT downwind

porte *f* CONSTR, ELECTRON, INFORMAT gate, ORDINAT gate, port, PHYSIQUE gate, PRODUCTION *servant à constater le jeu d'un mécanisme* door, REFRIG refrigerant distributor, VEHICULES *carrosserie* door; ~ **d'accès** *f* AERONAUT access door; ~ **d'accostage** *f* REFRIG port door; ~ **d'aérage** *f* CONSTR ventilating door, MINES air door, ventilation door; ~ **d'amont** *f* DISTRI EAU *d'une écluse de canal* crown gate, *d'une écluse* head gate, EN RENOUV *barrages* head gate; ~ **analogique** *f* ELECTRON analog gate (AmE), analogue gate (BrE); ~ **anti-incendie** *f* SECURITE fire door; ~ **arrière** *f* AUTO rear door; ~ **automatique** *f* CONSTR self-closing door; ~ **d'aval** *f* DISTRI EAU *d'une écluse de canal* aft gate, *d'une écluse* tailgate; ~ **aveugle** *f* CONSTR blank door; ~ **de bassin de marée** *f* NAUT floodgate; ~ **blindée** *f* SECURITE security door; ~ **de caisson** *f* CERAM VER tower door; ~ **cargo** *f* AERONAUT loading door; ~ **de chargement** *f* PRODUCTION charging door, TRANSPORT tail loading gate; ~ **du coffre** *f* VEHICULES boot lid (BrE), trunk lid (AmE); ~ **à coulisse** *f* CONSTR sliding door; ~ **coupe-feu** *f* PRODUCTION fire door, SECURITE fire-resistant door, THERMODYN fire door; ~ **déclenchant la synchronisation de la sous-porteuse** *f* TV burst gate; ~ **à diode** *f* ELECTRON diode gate; ~ **d'écluse** *f* DISTRI EAU canal lock-gate, lock gate, HYDROLOGIE lock gate, NAUT floodgate, lock gate; ~ **d'écluse de canal** *f* DISTRI EAU canal lock-gate; ~ **à enfournage** *f* PRODUCTION charging door; ~ **d'entrée** *f* NAUT washboards; ~ **de l'équipage** *f* AERONAUT crew door; ~ **ET** *f* ELEC-TRON, ORDINAT, PHYSIQUE AND gate; ~ **ET inclusif** *f* ELECTRON inclusive AND gate; ~ **fausse** *f* CONSTR blank door; ~ **à flot** *f* NAUT tide gate; ~ **de foyer** *f* PRODUCTION fire door; ~ **à glissant** *f* CONSTR sliding door; ~ **glissante** *f* CONSTR sliding shutter; ~ **à guichet** *f* MINES gage door (AmE), gauge door (BrE), ventilation door, regulating door; ~ **ignifugée** *f* SECURITE fire protection door; ~ **inverseuse** *f* ELECTRON inverter gate; ~ **d'isolation contre les fumées** *f* SECURITE smoke protection door; ~ **isolée contre le bruit** *f* SECURITE sound-insulated door, soundproof door; ~ **à lever** *f* CONSTR lift; ~ **logique** *f* ELECTRON, INFORMAT, ORDINAT, PHYSIQUE logic gate; ~ **logique d'entrée** *f* ELECTRON input gate; ~ **logique intégrée** *f* ELECTRON integrated logic gate; ~ **logique majoritaire** *f* ELECTRON majority gate; ~ **logique optique** *f* ELECTRON optical logic gate; ~ **majoritaire** *f* ELECTRON majority gate; ~ **MOS** *f* ELECTRON MOS gate, metal-oxide semiconductor gate; ~ **NI** *f* ELECTRON, INFORMAT, ORDINAT, PHYSIQUE NOR gate; ~ **NI exclusif** *f* ELECTRON exclusive NOR gate, INFORMAT, ORDINAT equivalence gate, exclusive NOR gate; ~ **NON** *f* ELECTRON, INFORMAT, ORDINAT, PHYSIQUE NOT gate; ~ **NON-ET** *f* ELECTRON, INFORMAT, ORDINAT, PHYSIQUE NAND gate; ~ **NON-ET à trois entrées** *f* ELECTRON three-input NAND gate; ~ **NON-OU** *f* PHYSIQUE NOR gate; ~ **optique** *f* ELECTRON optical logic gate; ~ **OU** *f* ELECTRON, INFORMAT, ORDINAT, PHYSIQUE OR gate; ~ **OU exclusif** *f* ELECTRON, INFORMAT, ORDINAT exclusive OR gate; ~ **OU inclusif** *f* ELECTRON, INFORMAT, ORDINAT inclusive OR gate; ~ **d'ouvreau** *f* CERAM VER tweel block; ~ **poinçon carré à bille** *f* CONS MECA *bloc à colonnes* square ball lock retainer; ~ **de protection contre les bruits** *f* SECURITE *tôle d'acier* noise abatement door, sound-absorbent door; ~ **quantifiée** *f* TV quantized gate; ~ **à rabat** *f* CONSTR flap door; ~ **régulatrice d'air** *f* CHARBON regulator door; ~ **roulante** *f* CONSTR rolling door; ~ **de secours** *f* CONSTR emergency door; ~ **de sécurité** *f* CONSTR safety door; ~ **de sélection d'amplitude** *f* ELECTRON amplitude gate; ~ **à seuil** *f* ELECTRON threshold gate; ~ **de signal couleur** *f* TV color gate (AmE), colour gate (BrE); ~ **de soute** *f* AERONAUT cargo compartment door; ~ **à tambour** *f* CINEMAT light trap; ~ **tournante** *f* CONSTR swing door; ~ **du train avant** *f* AERONAUT nose gear door; ~ **du train principal** *f* AERONAUT main landing gear door; ~ **de transfert** *f* ELECTROTEC transfer gate; ~ **à trois entrées** *f* ELECTRON three-input gate; ~ **à trois états** *f* ELECTRON three-state gate; ~ **va-et-vient** *f* CONSTR swing door, swinging door; ~ **validée** *f* ELECTRON enabled gate; ~ **de vidange** *f* PRODUCTION mud plug; ~ **de visite** *f* AERONAUT inspection panel, ESPACE *véhicules* inspection hatch, PRODUCTION inspection cover, inspection door; ~ **vissée** *f* PRODUCTION plug door; ~ **vitrée** *f* CONSTR glass door, glazed door

porté: à blanc *adj* THERMODYN white-hot; ~ **au rouge** *adj* THERMODYN red-hot

porte-accessoire *m* CINEMAT accessory shoe

porte-à-faux:[1] **en ~** *adj* MECANIQUE cantilevered

porte-à-faux[2] *m* CONSTR overhang, NUCLEAIRE boom, jib, PAPIER cantilever, VEHICULES *carrosserie* overhang

porte-aiguille *m* ENREGISTR needle holder

porte-ampoule *m* INSTRUMENT X-ray tube stand

porteau: ~ en treillis *m* CONSTR lattice tower

porte-avions *m* NAUT aircraft carrier, flat top, TRANS-

PORT aircraft carrier

porte-balais m ELECTR *machine* brush holder, ELECTROTEC brush holder, brush rod; ~ **en levier** m ELECTR *machine* arm-type brush holder

porte-barges m NAUT barge carrier, TRANSPORT barge carrier, lighter carrier; ~ **LASH** m TRANSPORT lighter aboard ship carrier

porte-broche m CONS MECA grinding spindle carrier

porte-câble m ELECTROTEC cable clamp

porte-cache m CINEMAT mask attachment, matte box, PHOTO matte box

porte-caches m CINEMAT effects box

porte-chaîne m CONSTR chainman

porte-charbon m CINEMAT carbon holder, ELECTROTEC carbon holder lamp

porte-cliché: ~ **inclinable** m PHOTO *d'un agrandisseur* tilting head

porte-conteneurs m NAUT container ship

porte-copie m IMPRIM *ateliers de composition* page bearer

porte-coussinets m CONS MECA *d'une machine à tarauder les tiges ou les tubes* screwing chuck, screwing head, PRODUCTION *d'une machine à tarauder les tiges ou les tubes* die-head

porte-couteaux m PAPIER knife holder

porte-culbuteurs m VEHICULES *moteur, soupape* rocker box

porte-cylindres m PAPIER holder, roller

porte-documents m IMPRIM copy frame

portée f BREVETS scope, CONS MECA bearing surface, boss, *d'un arbre, d'un axe* bearing, *de la main* reach, CONSTR projection, set-off, *d'une pierre, d'une gouttière au delà d'un mur* projection, *d'une grue* radius, *d'un pont, d'une grue roulante, d'une poutre, d'un comble* span, DISTRI EAU *d'un cours d'eau, d'un déversoir* discharge, ELECTRON, ESPACE *communications* range, INFORMAT scope, METROLOGIE chain, MILITAIRE *d'un projectile* range, *d'une arme* range, NAUT *d'un radar* range, ORDINAT scope, PHYSIQUE range, PRODUCTION bearing, print, seating, steady pin, RESSORTS seat, seating, TELECOM, TV range; ~ **d'arbre** f CONS MECA bearing end; ~ **d'axe** f CONS MECA bearing end; ~ **de calage de l'essieu** f CONS MECA axle seat; ~ **conique** f AUTO tapered axle end; ~ **distale** f ESPACE far range; ~ **diurne** f AERONAUT day range; ~ **géographique** f NAUT geographical range; ~ **nocturne** f AERONAUT night range; ~ **de noyau** f PRODUCTION bearing, core print, print, seating, steady pin; ~ **proximale** f ESPACE near range; ~ **radar** f MILITAIRE radar range; ~ **de remmoulage** f PRODUCTION bearing, core print, print, seating, steady pin; ~ **de soupape** f AUTO valve mating surface, VEHICULES *moteur* valve face; ~ **sur la tranche** f ELECTROTEC side wiping; ~ **utile** f MILITAIRE effective range; ~ **de visée** f MILITAIRE sighting range; ~ **visuelle** f MILITAIRE range of vision; ~ **visuelle de piste** f AERONAUT runway visual range; ~ **de voix** f NAUT hailing distance

porte-échantillons m INSTRUMENT specimen stage, NUCLEAIRE sample holder, specimen holder

porte-électrode m CONSTR, ELECTROTEC electrode holder

porte-éprouvette m NUCLEAIRE sample holder, specimen holder

porte-équerre m CONS MECA angle plate

porte-fenêtre f CERAM VER French window, patio door, CONSTR French casement, French doors (AmE), French windows (BrE)

portefeuille: ~ **de produits** m PRODUCTION product range

porte-filière m CONS MECA circular die-stock, screw plate, screw stock, stock, PRODUCTION die-stock; ~ **oblique** m CONS MECA screw plate stock

porte-film m CINEMAT rack, PHOTO film holder

porte-filtre m CINEMAT, TV filter holder

porte-fleuret m MINES drill holder

porte-foret m CONS MECA bit holder, drill, drill holder; ~ **à foret** m CONS MECA piercer

porte-fusée m AUTO steering knuckle pin

porte-fusible m ELECTROTEC fuse carrier, fuse holder, TV fuse holder

porte-garniture m CONS MECA packing retainer

porte-goutte m PRODUCTION *d'un fer à souder* copper bit

porte-injecteur m AUTO injection nozzle holder, nozzle holder

porte-lame m CONS MECA blade holder; ~ **pour tour** m CONS MECA cutter bar

porte-lampe m ELECTROTEC lamp holder

porte-lunette m CONS MECA *d'une machine à tarauder* screwing chuck, screwing head, PRODUCTION *d'une machine à tarauder* die-head; ~ **revolver** m CONS MECA revolving die-head

porte-mâchoire m CONS MECA jaw holder

portemanteau m NAUT davit

porte-masque m ELECTRON mask carrier

porte-matrice m CONS MECA bolster, *dans une presse* die holder, *de marteau-pilon* anvil die, PRODUCTION die holder

porte-mèche m CONS MECA bit holder, drill, drill holder; ~ **à changement rapide** m CONS MECA quick change drill chuck

porte-meule m PRODUCTION emery wheel attachment, wheel head

porte-mire m CONSTR staff holder

porte-moule: ~ **de bague** m CERAM VER neck ring holder

porte-négatif m PHOTO negative carrier, printing stage

porte-noyau m PRODUCTION bearing, print, seating, steady pin

porte-objectif: ~ **à soufflet** m PHOTO bellows attachment

porte-objectifs m INSTRUMENT objective nosepiece, objective turret

porte-objet m INSTRUMENT microscope stage, microscopic stage, object stage

porte-outil m CONS MECA tool holder, *d'une machine à raboter* head, *pour centre d'usinage* tool-holding fixture, MINES chuck; ~ **articulé** m CONS MECA jointed tool holder; ~ **à double coulisse** m CONS MECA compound tool holder; ~ **entraîné** m CONS MECA driven tool holder; ~ **de reproduction** m CONS MECA forming tool holder; ~ **revolver** m CONS MECA revolving tool holder, turret head, turret, PRODUCTION monitor; ~ **revolver à quatre faces** m CONS MECA four-tool tool post, four-tool turret; ~ **à serrage rapide** m CONS MECA rapid change tool holder; ~ **à tourelle carrée** m CONS MECA four-tool tool post, four-tool turret

porte-page m IMPRIM page shoe, *ateliers de composition* page bearer

porte-piles m ELECTR battery housing, IMPRIM *machines* pile board, PRODUCTION battery housing

porte-poinçon m CONS MECA *de presse* punch holder; ~ **à bille** m CONS MECA ball lock retainer

porte-protecteur: ~ **de train** m AERONAUT landing gear boot retainer

porte-puce *m* ELECTRON chip carrier; ~ **non enfichable** *m* ELECTROTEC leadless chip carrier; ~ **à souder** *m* ELECTROTEC leadless chip carrier

porter[1] *vt* CONSTR carry, NAUT chart, PAPIER carry; ~ **à l'écran** *vt* CINEMAT film; ~ **à fusion** *vt* THERMODYN fuse, melt; ~ **au journal de bord** *vt* NAUT log; ~ **sur une carte** *vt* NAUT chart; ~ **à température** *vt* THERMODYN heat up

porter:[2] ~ **un relèvement** *vi* NAUT plot a bearing

porter:[3] **se ~ comme** *v réfl* CONSTR act as

porte-rideau *m* VEHICULES *carrosserie* roll-up door

portes: ~ **battantes** *f pl* CONSTR folding doors; ~ **repliantes** *f pl* CONSTR folding doors

porte-sac *m* EMBALLAGE bag holder

porte-satellite *m* AERONAUT planet pinion cage, AUTO planet carrier

porte-scie *m* CONS MECA saw frame; ~ **à découper** *m* PRODUCTION fret saw, fret saw frame; ~ **à métaux** *m* CONS MECA hacksaw, hacksaw frame; ~ **à repercer** *m* PRODUCTION fret saw, fret saw frame

porte-tampon *m* PRODUCTION bott stick

porte-taraud *m* CONS MECA tap holder

porte-têtes *m* TV head assembly

porte-tube *m* EQUIP LAB *support* tube holder, INSTRUMENT limb top

porteur[1] *adj* NAUT buoyant

porteur[2] *m* ELECTROTEC charge carrier, IMPRIM *mécanique, machines* bearer, *personnel* carrier, PHYSIQUE carrier; ~ **à l'arche** *m* CERAM VER taker-in; ~ **central** *m* OPTIQUE central load-bearing element, central strength member; ~ **de charge** *m* ELECTROTEC, ESPACE *véhicules* charge carrier; ~ **d'électricité** *m* PHYS RAYON electric current carrier; ~ **majoritaire** *m* ELECTRON, PHYSIQUE majority carrier; ~ **minoritaire** *m* ELECTRON, PHYSIQUE minority carrier

porteuse *f* ELECTRON, ENREGISTR, ESPACE *communications*, IMPRIM *télétransmission*, INFORMAT carrier, MINES bearer, crown bearer, ORDINAT, PHYSIQUE, TELECOM carrier, TV carrier, carrier wave; ~ **acoustique** *f* ELECTRON acoustic carrier; ~ **AM** *f* ELECTRON AM carrier; ~ **audio** *f* ELECTRON sound carrier; ~ **commune** *f* TV common carrier; ~ **de données** *f* TELECOM data carrier; ~ **FM** *f* ELECTRON FM carrier; ~ **à haute fréquence** *f* *(porteuse HF)* ELECTRON high-frequency carrier *(HF carrier)*; ~ **HF** *(porteuse à haute fréquence)* *f* ELECTRON HF carrier *(high-frequency carrier)*; ~ **image** *f* ELECTRON picture carrier, TV vision carrier; ~ **d'impulsion** *f* ELECTRON pulse carrier; ~ **modulée** *f* ELECTRON, TV modulated carrier; ~ **modulée en amplitude** *f* ELECTRON amplitude-modulated carrier; ~ **modulée en fréquence** *f* ELECTRON FM carrier; ~ **monovoie** *f* ESPACE *communications*, TELECOM SCPC, single-channel per carrier; ~ **multidestination** *f* ESPACE *communications* multidestination carrier; ~ **multivoie** *f* ESPACE *communications* multichannel carrier; ~ **optique** *f* ELECTRON optical carrier; ~ **pilote** *f* TELECOM pilot carrier; ~ **son** *f* ELECTRON, ENREGISTR sound carrier; ~ **vidéo** *f* ELECTRON picture carrier, TV image carrier, video carrier; ~ **zéro** *f* TV zero carrier

porte-vent *m* PRODUCTION belly pipe, blast pipe, blowpipe

portillon *m* CONS MECA flap

portine *f* (Fra) *(cf couvercle)* CERAM VER stopper

portique *m* CH DE FER gantry crane, CONSTR gantry, NUCLEAIRE gantry crane; ~ **de chargement** *m* TRANSPORT loading bridge; ~ **roulant** *m* NAUT traveling gantry (AmE), travelling gantry (BrE)

ports: ~ **de la métropole** *m pl* NAUT home ports

posage *m* CONSTR laying; ~ **de tuyaux** *m* CONSTR pipe laying

pose *f* CINEMAT time exposure, CONS MECA fixing, CONSTR laying, *de bornes* setting, PHOTO time exposure, PHYSIQUE exposure, TELECOM *d'un câble* laying; ~ **de bornes-signaux** *f* CONSTR monumenting; ~ **de câbles** *f* ELECTR *alimentation*, ELECTROTEC cable laying; ~ **de la canalisation** *f* CONSTR laying of piping; ~ **de coronographe** *f* ASTRONOMIE coronograph exposure; ~ **exagérée** *f* PHOTO overexposure; ~ **instantanée** *f* PHOTO instantaneous exposure; ~ **d'origine** *f* IMPRIM *emballage* one-up; ~ **de la quille** *f* NAUT keel laying; ~ **de rails** *f* CH DE FER rail laying, track laying; ~ **sur la forme imprimante** *f* IMPRIM repeat; ~ **de tuyaux** *f* CONSTR pipe laying; ~ **de verres** *f* CONSTR glazing; ~ **de vitres** *f* CERAM VER glazing; ~ **de la voie** *f* CH DE FER plate laying; ~ **des voies** *f* CONSTR track-laying

posé: ~ **sur appui simple** *adj* CONSTR simply-supported

posé-décollé *m* AERONAUT touch-and-go landing

posemètre *m* CINEMAT exposure meter, PHOTO, PHYSIQUE exposure meter, light meter; ~ **d'agrandissement** *m* PHOTO enlarging meter; ~ **d'agrandissement à minuterie** *m* PHOTO exposure timer; ~ **couplé** *m* PHOTO exposure meter using needle-matching system

poser[1] *vt* CONSTR fix, *tuyau* lay, *béton* pour, *rivet* set, *serrure* fix, NAUT *câble*, TELECOM lay; ~ **une pierre dans le sens de son lit de carrière** *vt* CONSTR set a stone in the sense of its natural bed; ~ **une pierre en délit** *vt* CONSTR set a stone bed out

poser:[2] ~ **le dernier raccord** *vi* PETROLE *canalisation* flange up; ~ **les fondements** *vi* CONSTR *d'une maison* lay the foundations; ~ **des planches de côté** *vi* CONSTR set edgeways; ~ **des tuiles sur le comble d'un bâtiment** *vi* CONSTR tile the roof of a building

poser:[3] **se ~** *v réfl* ESPACE *véhicules* touch down

pose-tubes *m* CONS MECA, CONSTR pipe layer

poseuse: ~ **de panneaux de voie** *f* CH DE FER track panel laying machine; ~ **de travées de voie** *f* CH DE FER track panel laying machine

positif[1] *adj* ELECTR positive

positif[2] *m* IMPRIM positive; ~ **double bande avec son magnétique** *m* CINEMAT sepmag; ~ **double bande avec son optique** *m* CINEMAT sepopt; ~ **grain fin pour contretype** *m* CINEMAT fine-grain master; ~ **image seule** *m* CINEMAT silent print; ~ **intermédiaire** *m* CINEMAT intermediate positive; ~ **muet** *m* CINEMAT silent print; ~ **pour contretype** *m* CINEMAT master positive; ~ **pour contretyper** *m* CINEMAT dupe positive; ~ **pour transparence** *m* CINEMAT background film; ~ **de sélection** *m* CINEMAT separation positive; ~ **son** *m* CINEMAT sound positive; ~ **son optique** *m* CINEMAT optical sound positive; ~ **transparent** *m* IMPRIM transparent positive

position *f* CONS MECA location, IMPRIM lay, NAUT position, TELECOM operating position; ~ **adressable** *f* ORDINAT addressable location; ~ **arrêt** *f* ELECTROTEC off-period; ~ **des balais** *f* ELECTROTEC brush position; ~ **du bit** *f* INFORMAT, ORDINAT bit position; ~ **de droite** *f* INFORMAT low-order position; ~ **en hauteur** *f* NUCLEAIRE height position; ~ **fermée** *f* ELECTR *relais* closed position; ~ **de fermeture** *f* ELECTR *relais* closed position, ELECTROTEC on-position; ~ **identifiée** *f* AERONAUT, TRANSPORT pinpoint; ~ **d'impression** *f* IN-

FORMAT, ORDINAT print position; ~ **d'impulsion** *f* ELECTRON pulse position; ~ **marche** *f* ELECTROTEC on-position; ~ **de mémoire** *f* INFORMAT memory location, storage location; ~ **de mise à la terre** *f* ELECTR *commutateur* earthing position (BrE), grounding position (AmE); ~ **du navire** *f* NAUT ship's position; ~ **d'opératrice** *f* TELECOM operator position; ~ **optimale stéréo** *f* ENREGISTR stereo seat; ~ **ouverte** *f* ELECTR *relais* open position; ~ **d'ouverture** *f* ELECTROTEC off-period; ~ **de réglage** *f* AERONAUT *aéronef* rigging position; ~ **de repos** *f* CONS MECA off-position, PRODUCTION home position; ~ **solide** *f* RESSORTS solid position; ~ **sur l'orbite** *f* ESPACE station, stationary point; ~ **de synchronisation finale** *f* ORDINAT postamble; ~ **de synchronisation initiale** *f* ORDINAT preamble; ~ **télex** *f* TELECOM telex position; ~ **terminale** *f* TELECOM auxiliary service position; ~ **de transit** *f* TELECOM traffic operator position; ~ **de travail** *f* PRODUCTION operative contacts; ~ **de verrouillage** *f* PRODUCTION *automatisme industriel* latching position

positionnement *m* CINEMAT registration, CONS MECA location; ~ **arrière** *m* AERONAUT, TRANSPORT *aéroport* nose-out positioning; ~ **avant** *m* AERONAUT, TRANSPORT nose-in positioning; ~ **du commutateur rotatif** *m* PRODUCTION *automatisme industriel* thumb wheel setting; ~ **dynamique** *m* PETR, PETROLE dynamic positioning; ~ **des formes** *m* IMPRIM *finition, emballage* nest; ~ **parallèle** *m* AERONAUT, TRANSPORT parallel positioning

positionner *vt* CONS MECA position, INFORMAT set
positionneur *m* CONS MECA positioner
positon *m* PHYSIQUE positon, positron
positron *m* PHYSIQUE positon, positron
possédant: le pouvoir rotatoire *adj* CHIMIE chiral
posséder: ~ sa courbe de lit *vi* CONSTR be at grade; ~ **sa pente-limite** *vi* CONSTR be at grade; ~ **son profil d'équilibre** *vi* CONSTR be at grade
possibilité: ~ de capture *f* OCEANO catchability coefficient; ~ **de commande manuelle** *f* PRODUCTION manual override; ~ **de commercialisation** *f* TEXTILE marketability; ~ **de se déplacer** *f* TELECOM roaming capability; ~ **d'émission en différé** *f* TELECOM store-and-forward facility; ~ **de surimpression** *f* ELECTRON write-through capability; ~ **de vol stationnaire** *f* AERONAUT hovering capability
possibilités: ~ d'armurage *f pl* TEXTILE patterning capacities, scope
postaccentuation *f* ENREGISTR, TV postemphasis
postbrûleur *m* TRANSPORT afterburner, exhaust gas combustion
postchauffage *adj* PRODUCTION postheating
postcombustion *f* AERONAUT, CONS MECA afterburner, THERMODYN afterburning, TRANSPORT reheat; ~ **thermique** *f* TRANSPORT thermal postcombustion
postcompensation *f* ENREGISTR postequalization
poste[1] *m* CERAM VER *main d'oeuvre* shop, CONSTR, ELECTR *réseau* substation, ESPACE *communications* shift, INFORMAT station, NAUT post, ORDINAT station, PRODUCTION crew, TELECOM extension, instrument; ~ **abaisseur** *m* ELECTR *transformateur* step down station; ~ **d'aiguillage informatisé** *m* (Fra) *(PAI)* CH DE FER computerized signal box (BrE), computerized switch tower (AmE); ~ **d'amarrage** *m* NAUT mooring berth, POLLU MER mooring; ~ **aval** *m* PRODUCTION forward station; ~ **avant** *m* NAUT forecastle; ~ **de butte**

m TRANSPORT classification yard tower; ~ **central** *m* CH DE FER *(PC)* signal box (BrE), switch tower (AmE), TRANSPORT master controller; ~ **de charge** *m* ELECTROTEC charging station, TRANSPORT charging point; ~ **de chargement** *m* TRANSPORT truck-to-truck operation, truck-to-truck system; ~ **à clavier** *m* TELECOM push-button telephone; ~ **à clavier mixte** *m* TELECOM *de numérotation* dual-signaling telephone (AmE), dual-signalling telephone (BrE); ~ **de commande** *m* CH DE FER control center (AmE), control centre (BrE), signal box (BrE), signal tower (AmE), switch tower (AmE), ELECTR *contrôle* control room; ~ **de commandement** *m* CH DE FER *(PC)* control center (AmE), control centre (BrE), signal box (BrE), signal tower (AmE), switch tower (AmE) NAUT control room; ~ **de commande du réseau** *m* ELECTR *contrôle* net control station; ~ **de commutation extérieure** *m* ELECTR *commutateur* outdoor switchgear; ~ **de comptage** *m* TRANSPORT counting station; ~ **de comptage permanent** *m* TRANSPORT continuous counting station; ~ **de conversion** *m* ELECTR *réseau* substation for frequency conversion, *transformateur* converter station, converting station; ~ **de courant** *m* CONSTR substation; ~ **de distribution** *m* ELECTR *alimentation, distribution* switching station, *réseau* distribution substation, ELECTROTEC distribution station; ~ **de données prêt** *m* ORDINAT, TELECOM DSR, data set ready; ~ **électrique** *m* ELECTR *réseau de distribution* electric power substation; ~ **électrique extérieur** *m* ELECTR *matériel* outdoor electrical installation; ~ **élévateur** *m* ELECTR *transformateur* step-up station; ~ **d'emballage** *m* EMBALLAGE packing station; ~ **émetteur** *m* TV transmitter; ~ **en dérivation** *m* ELECTR *réseau* tapped substation, tee-off substation; ~ **en piquage** *m* ELECTR *réseau* tapped substation, tee-off substation; ~ **d'enroulage** *m* PAPIER reeling end; ~ **d'entrée** *m* PRODUCTION gateway; ~ **d'équipage** *m* AERONAUT cockpit, crew compartment, crew station, flight compartment, flight deck, NAUT crew's quarters, mess deck; ~ **d'essai** *m* TELECOM test position; ~ **d'exploitation déporté** *m* TELECOM remote operating terminal; ~ **à fréquences vocales** *m* TELECOM MF telephone; ~ **graphique** *m* INFORMAT, ORDINAT graphics work station; ~ **d'incendie** *m* SECURITE fire post; ~ **d'incendie fixe** *m* SECURITE stationary firefighting installation; ~ **d'intercommunication** *m* TELECOM key telephone set; ~ **intérieur** *m* TELECOM internal extension; ~ **d'interrogation** *m* INFORMAT, ORDINAT inquiry station; ~ **des matelots** *m* NAUT mess deck; ~ **de mesure** *m* NUCLEAIRE measuring desk, test assembly, test rig; ~ **météorologique** *m* METEO meteorological station; ~ **d'opérateur** *m* TELECOM operator position, operator's telephone; ~ **d'opérateur de classe A** *m* TELECOM key-per-line console (BrE), key-per-trunk console (AmE); ~ **d'opérateur de classe B** *m* TELECOM switched-loop console; ~ **de pilotage** *m* AERONAUT cockpit, crew compartment, flight compartment, flight deck, ESPACE *véhicules*, NAUT cockpit; ~ **pilote** *m* AERONAUT cockpit; ~ **de pliage** *m* IMPRIM folding station; ~ **de poursuite par radar** *m* TRANSPORT radar tracking station; ~ **de premier secours** *m* NAUT first-aid post, SECURITE first-aid treatment room; ~ **principal** *m* *(PP)* ELECTRON main station *(MS)*; ~ **radio de bord** *m* NAUT radio room; ~ **de radio portatif** *m* MILITAIRE backpack radio; ~ **à rayon X** *m* PETR X-ray station; ~ **à relais à**

commande informatique m *(PRCI)* CH DE FER computer-controlled all-relay interlocking unit; ~ **de sauvetage** m NAUT lifeboat station, SECURITE rescue station; ~ **de secours** m SECURITE ambulance station, emergency center (AmE), emergency centre (BrE), TELECOM emergency telephone; ~ **de sectionnement** m CH DE FER switching station (BrE), tie station (AmE); ~ **de soudage** m PETR welding station; ~ **de soudage oxyacétylénique** m PRODUCTION oxyacetylene welding equipment; ~ **supplémentaire** m TELECOM extension; ~ **de surveillance** m TELECOM observation telephone; ~ **téléphonique sans cordon** m TELECOM cordless telephone; ~ **téléphonique sur autoroute** m TRANSPORT emergency telephone; ~ **de télévision** m TV television set; ~ **à touches musicales** m TELECOM MF telephone; ~ **de transformation** m ELECTR *réseau d'alimentation* transformer substation; ~ **de travail** m CONS MECA, EMBALLAGE, INFORMAT, ORDINAT, PRODUCTION work station, TELECOM terminal; ~ **de travail graphique** m INFORMAT, ORDINAT graphics work station; ~ **de travail d'ingénieur** m INFORMAT engineering work station; ~ **de travail initial** m PRODUCTION gateway; ~ **de travail propre** m REFRIG cleanwork station; ~ **de travail technique** m ORDINAT engineering work station; ~ **de ventilation** m CONSTR fan station

poste:[2] ~ **aérienne** f AERONAUT, TRANSPORT airmail

postégalisation f ENREGISTR postequalization

postes: ~ **d'embarcation** m pl NAUT boat stations

postformable adj PLAST CAOU *plastiques* postforming

postillon m CONS MECA bumping hammer

postlumination f CINEMAT, PHOTO flashing

postprocesseur m INFORMAT, ORDINAT postprocessor

postsécheur m PAPIER afterdryer

postsonorisation f ACOUSTIQUE postscoring

postsuppression f TV final blanking

postsynchronisation f CINEMAT lip sync, ENREGISTR postsynchronization

postsynchroniser vt CINEMAT dub, postsynchronize

post-tectonique adj GEOLOGIE *métamorphisme après déformation* postkinematic

post-traitement m ELECTRON postprocessing

postulat m MATH postulate; ~ **du parallélisme d'Euclide** m GEOMETRIE Euclid's parallel postulate

pot m CHIMIE crucible, IMPRIM *colle* pot, PRODUCTION crucible, melter, melting pot; ~ **catalytique** m AUTO, POLLUTION catalytic converter (BrE), catalytic muffler (AmE); ~ **coulé** m CERAM VER slip cast pot; ~ **couvert** m CERAM VER closed pot, covered pot; ~ **cru** m CERAM VER green pot, unfired pot; ~ **de détente** m AUTO exhaust muffler (AmE), exhaust silencer (BrE); ~ **d'échappement** m MECANIQUE, VEHICULES muffler (AmE), silencer (BrE); ~ **d'équilibrage** m AERONAUT plenum chamber; ~ **à pression** m CONSTR pressure vessel; ~ **primaire** m AUTO premuffler; ~ **de purge** m PETROLE steam trap, *tuyauterie, raffinerie* catchpot; ~ **vibrant** m ESPACE *essais* vibration generator

potable adj AGRO ALIM, DISTRI EAU potable

potasse f CERAM VER, CHIMIE potash; ~ **caustique** f CHIMIE potassium hydroxide, LESSIVES caustic potash

potassique adj GEOLOGIE potassic

potassium m *(K)* CHIMIE potassium *(K)*

pot-au-noir m METEO *zone équatoriale de calmes* doldrums, equatorial calms

poteau m CONSTR pole, post, ELECTROTEC *ligne* pylon, NAUT *amarrage, marque de hauts-fonds* post; ~ **d'ancrage** m CERAM VER buckstay, CONSTR anchor post; ~ **d'angle** m CONSTR corner pillar, corner post; ~ **battant** m CONSTR shutting post, striking post, DISTRI EAU meeting post, miter post (AmE), mitre post (BrE); ~ **de bornage** m CONSTR boundary post; ~ **busqué** m DISTRI EAU meeting post, miter post (AmE), mitre post (BrE); ~ **caténaire** m CH DE FER catenary support; ~ **cornier** m CONSTR corner pillar, corner post; ~ **de guidage** m PETR guidepost; ~ **d'huisserie** m CONSTR door post, jamb, jamb post, post; ~ **indicateur** m CONSTR finger post, guidepost; ~ **indicateur de déclivité** m CH DE FER gradient post; ~ **indicateur de pente** m CH DE FER gradient post; ~ **indicateur de pentes et rampes** m CH DE FER gradient post; ~ **jumelé** m CH DE FER twin pole, twin post; ~ **kilométrique** m CH DE FER milepost; ~ **tourillon** m CONSTR hanging post, DISTRI EAU *porte d'écluse* heel post, quoin post; ~ **de vanne** m DISTRI EAU staple post

poteaux m pl NAUT piles; ~ **dans les angles** m pl MINES *pour relier les cadres* studdles

potée f CERAM VER rouge, PRODUCTION loam; ~ **d'émeri** f CONS MECA emery powder ~ **d'étain** f CERAM VER putty, CONSTR putty, putty powder

potelet m CERAM VER monkey pot

potelle f MINES hitch

potence f AERONAUT hoist arm, CH DE FER post bracket, CONSTR bracket, INSTRUMENT arm, stand; ~ **angulaire** f CONSTR angle bracket; ~ **d'assemblage** f CONSTR angle bracket; ~ **à colonne** f INSTRUMENT pillar stand; ~ **cornière** f CONSTR angle bracket; ~ **de hissage** f CONSTR portable crane; ~ **de manutention** f AERONAUT derrick; ~ **à signaux** f pl CH DE FER signal structure; ~ **de treuil** f AERONAUT hoist arm

potentiel m ELECTR, ELECTROTEC, ESPACE, PHYSIQUE potential; ~ **absolu** m ELECTR absolute potential; ~ **accélérateur** m ELECTROTEC driving potential; ~ **d'arrêt** m PHYSIQUE stopping potential; ~ **chimique** m PHYSIQUE chemical potential; ~ **de contact** m ELECTR contact potential; ~ **de croissance des algues** m HYDROLOGIE algal growth potential; ~ **de deuxième ionisation** m PHYSIQUE second ionization potential; ~ **disruptif** m ELECTROTEC breakdown voltage; ~ **électrique** m ELECTR *champ* electric potential, ELECTROTEC electric potential, electrical potential, PHYSIQUE electric potential; ~ **d'électrode** m ELECTR, PHYSIQUE electrode potential; ~ **d'équilibre** m GEOPHYS EP, equilibrium potential; ~ **évoqué auditif** m ACOUSTIQUE hearing-evoked potential; ~ **d'extinction** m ELECTROTEC extinction potential; ~ **flottant** m ELECTROTEC floating potential; ~ **gravitationnel** m PHYSIQUE gravitational potential; ~ **hydrogène** m *(pH)* CHIMIE potential of hydrogen *(pH)*; ~ **d'ionisation** m PHYS RAYON, PHYSIQUE ionization potential; ~ **lunisolaire** m ESPACE lunisolar potential; ~ **magnétique** m ELECTROTEC magnetic potential; ~ **de neutralisation de l'acide** m *(PNA)* POLLUTION acid neutralizing capacity *(ANC)*; ~ **nucléaire** m PHYS RAYON nuclear potential; ~ **de première ionisation** m PHYSIQUE first ionization potential; ~ **quadripolaire** m NUCLEAIRE quadrupole potential; ~ **redox** m POLLUTION oxidation reduction potential; ~ **retardé** m PHYSIQUE retarded potential; ~ **scalaire** m ELECTROTEC, PHYSIQUE scalar potential; ~ **scalaire magnétique** m PHYSIQUE magnetic scalar potential; ~ **de sédimentation** m GENIE CHIM sedimentation potential; ~ **Tabakin** m NUCLEAIRE Tabakin potential; ~ **de la terre** m ELECTR earth potential

(BrE), ground potential (AmE); ~ **terrestre** *m* ESPACE Earth potential (BrE), ground potential (AmE), GEOPHYS geopotential; ~ **thermodynamique** *m* PHYSIQUE, THERMODYN thermodynamic potential; ~ **vecteur** *m* ELECTROTEC, PHYSIQUE vector potential; ~ **vecteur magnétique** *m* PHYSIQUE magnetic vector potential; ~ **de vitesse** *m* EN RENOUV velocity potential; ~ **de Yukawa** *m* PHYSIQUE Yukawa potential; ~ **zéro** *m* ELECTROTEC null voltage

potentiomètre *m* CINEMAT potentiometer, CONSTR potentiometer, *résistance* potentiometer, ELECTRO-TEC potentiometer, ENREGISTR pot, potentiometer, EQUIP LAB *électrochimie*, MATERIAUX, PAPIER, PHYSIQUE potentiometer, TV voltage divider; ~ **d'affichage** *m* ELECTR read-out potentiometer; ~ **ajustable** *m* ELECTROTEC trimming potentiometer; ~ **bobiné** *m* ELECTR wire-wound potentiometer; ~ **de codage** *m* ESPACE *communications* encoding potentiometer; ~ **à couche** *m* ELECTR nonwirewound potentiometer; ~ **à courant alternatif** *m* ELECTR AC potentiometer; ~ **à courant continu** *m* ELECTR direct current potentiometer, *relais* DC potentiometer; ~ **général** *m* TV master control fader; ~ **à glissière** *m* ELECTROTEC slide potentiometer; ~ **hélicoïdal** *m* ELECTR helipot, multiturn potentiometer, *résistance* helical potentiometer; ~ **inductif** *m* ELECTR *autotransformateur* inductive potential divider; ~ **linéaire** *m* ELECTROTEC linear potentiometer, ENREGISTR fader; ~ **logarithmique** *m* ELECTROTEC logarithmic potentiometer; ~ **de magnétorésistance** *m* ELECTR magnetoresistor potentiometer; ~ **multitour** *m* ELECTROTEC multiturn potentiometer; ~ **non linéaire** *m* CONSTR nonlinear potentiometer; ~ **de panoramique** *m* ENREGISTR pan pot; ~ **principal de gain** *m* ENREGISTR master gain control; ~ **à prises** *m* ELECTROTEC tapped control; ~ **de réglage** *m* AERONAUT adjusting potentiometer, ELECTR *résistance* preset pot, ELECTROTEC control potentiometer; ~ **du réglage de champ** *m* ELECTR *résistance* pot-type field rheostat; ~ **rotatif** *m* ELECTR, ELECTROTEC rotary potentiometer; ~ **trimmer** *m* ELECTR *résistance* trimming potentiometer; ~ **vernier** *m* ELECTR vernier potentiometer; ~ **de vitesse** *m* PRODUCTION speed pot

poterie *f* CERAM VER crockery ware, pottery, pot room, PRODUCTION pottery; ~ **artistique** *f* CERAM VER artistic pottery, craft pottery, studio pottery; ~ **commune** *f* CERAM VER coarse pottery, earthenware; ~ **de Delft** *f* CERAM VER Delft, delftware; ~ **de grès** *f* CERAM VER stoneware; ~ **de santé** *f* CERAM VER sanitary ware

poubelle *f* NUCLEAIRE storage canister, waste canister

pouce *m* METROLOGIE inch; ~ **anglais** *m* METROLOGIE inch; ~ **carré** *m* METROLOGIE square inch; ~ **cube** *m* METROLOGIE cubic inch

pouces: ~ **par seconde** *m pl (PPS)* ENREGISTR, INFORMAT inches per second *(IPS)*

poudingue *m* GEOLOGIE conglomerate

poudrage *m* CINEMAT oxide build-up, PAPIER *de papier couché* dusting, powdering, TV oxide shedding; ~ **exécuté sur les quatre côtés** *m* IMPRIM four-way dusting, four-way powdering; ~ **des récoltes** *m* AERONAUT crop-dusting

poudre:[1] **en ~** *adj* CERAM VER powdered, GENIE CHIM pulverized; **à ~** *adj* ELECTROTEC powder-filled

poudre[2] *f* CHIMIE powder, ESPACE solid propellant, PAPIER, PLAST CAOU *charges, pigments* powder; ~ **d'amiante** *f* IMPRIM agalite, PAPIER asbestos powder;

~ **à blanchir** *f* AGRO ALIM bleaching powder; ~ **de bronze** *f* COULEURS, IMPRIM *finition* bronze powder; ~ **à canon** *f* MILITAIRE gunpowder; ~ **frittée** *f* GENIE CHIM sintering powder; ~ **de lait** *f* AGRO ALIM milk powder; ~ **de lait écrémé** *f* AGRO ALIM skimmed milk powder; ~ **à lever** *f* AGRO ALIM chemical leavening, raising agent; ~ **de métal** *f* METALL metal powder; ~ **à mouler** *f* PLAST CAOU *plastiques* molding powder (AmE), moulding powder (BrE); ~ **de petit-lait** *f* AGRO ALIM whey powder; ~ **pour revêtement électrostatique** *f* REVETEMENT coating powder; ~ **à récurer** *f* LESSIVES scouring powder

poudrerie *f* PRODUCTION powder mill, powder works

poudreuse *f* IMPRIM *impression* dusting unit

poudrière *f* MINES explosives magazine, powder store, magazine

poudrin *m* HYDROLOGIE spindrift

poulie *f* CONS MECA pulley block, pulley, pulley sheave, pulley wheel, sheave, wheel, CONSTR gin wheel, tackle, MINES pulley, NAUT block, pulley, PHYSIQUE pulley; ~ **d'assemblage** *f* CONS MECA, PRODUCTION made block; ~ **d'attaque** *f* PRODUCTION driving pulley; ~ **bombée** *f* CONS MECA round-faced pulley, rounding pulley, PRODUCTION crown-face pulley, crowned pulley, crowning pulley; ~ **à chape croisée** *f* CONS MECA gin block, whip gin; ~ **de chevalement** *f* MINES hoisting pulley, pithead pulley, pulley; ~ **de chèvre** *f* PRODUCTION gin pulley; ~ **à chicane** *f* CONS MECA rag wheel, spider wheel; ~ **de commande** *f* PRODUCTION driving pulley; ~ **conductrice** *f* PRODUCTION driving pulley; ~ **conduite** *f* CONS MECA follower; ~ **à corde** *f* CONS MECA V-pulley, grooved wheel, pulley for gut band, sheave; ~ **coupée** *f* CONS MECA return block; ~ **à courroie** *f* CONS MECA band pulley, PRODUCTION belt pulley; ~ **à croc** *f* CONS MECA hook block; ~ **démontable** *f* CONS MECA parting pulley; ~ **différentielle** *f* NUCLEAIRE *moufle* differential chain block, PHYSIQUE differential pulley; ~ **à émerillon** *f* CONS MECA swivel block; ~ **à empreintes** *f* CONS MECA chain sheave, indented wheel, PRODUCTION cupped chain sheave; ~ **en deux pièces** *f* CONS MECA parting pulley, split pulley; ~ **en dos d'âne** *f* CONS MECA round-faced pulley, PRODUCTION crown-face pulley, crowned pulley, crowning pulley; ~ **en une pièce** *f* CONS MECA solid pulley; ~ **d'entraînement** *f* CONS MECA driving pulley, VEHICULES *alternateur* drive pulley; ~ **étagée** *f* CONS MECA cone, cone pulley, speed cone, step cone; ~ **excentrique** *f* CONS MECA eccentric disc (BrE), eccentric disk (AmE), eccentric sheave; ~ **fixe** *f* CONS MECA runner, standing block, NAUT standing block, PRODUCTION fast pulley, tight pulley; ~ **folle** *f* CONS MECA dead pulley, idle pulley, idler pulley; ~ **à fouet** *f* PRODUCTION tail block; ~ **à gorge** *f* CONS MECA grooved pulley, grooved roller, scored pulley, sheave; ~ **à gradins** *f* CONS MECA cone, cone pulley, speed cone, step cone; ~ **isolante** *f* ELECTROTEC reel insulator; ~ **à joue** *f* CONS MECA flange pulley; ~ **menante** *f* PRODUCTION driving pulley; ~ **menée** *f* CONS MECA follower; ~ **mobile** *f* CONS MECA runner, running block, PRODUCTION hoisting block; ~ **à mortaise** *f* CONS MECA, PRODUCTION mortise block; ~ **motrice** *f* CONS MECA *palan à chaîne sans fin* nearing-up pulley, PRODUCTION driving pulley; ~ **de moufle** *f* CONS MECA pulley, pulley sheave, pulley wheel, sheave; ~ **mouflée** *f* CONS MECA sheave; ~ **à noix** *f* CONS MECA *chaîne calibrée* sheave; ~ **ovale** *f* CONS MECA oval pulley; ~

plate *f* CONS MECA straight-faced pulley; **~ porte-lame** *f* CONS MECA saw pulley; **~ à rebord** *f* CONS MECA flange pulley; **~ de renvoi** *f* CONS MECA return pulley, return wheel, tail pulley, PRODUCTION tail sheave, turn pulley; **~ de renvoi avec tige filetée** *f* CONSTR screw pulley; **~ de renvoi à plat** *f* CONSTR side pulley; **~ de renvoi à pont** *f* CONSTR axle pulley; **~ de retour** *f* CONS MECA return pulley, return wheel, NAUT lead block, leading block, PRODUCTION tail sheave, turn pulley; **~ à sangle** *f* CONS MECA band pulley; **~ tendeuse** *f* CONS MECA binding pulley; **~ de tension** *f* CONS MECA idler, jockey, jockey roller, jockey wheel, tension pulley, tension roller, tightening pulley, PAPIER jockey pulley, jockey roller, PRODUCTION belt idler; **~ tournée et alésée** *f* PRODUCTION turned-and-bored pulley; **~ de transmission** *f* PRODUCTION driving pulley; **~ triple** *f* CONS MECA three-sheave block; **~ de ventilateur** *f* AUTO, VEHICULES *refroidissement* fan pulley; **~ à violon** *f* NAUT fiddle block

poulie-guide *f* CONS MECA guide, guide pulley, idler, leading-on pulley, runner, PRODUCTION belt idler

poulier *m* OCEANO bar, shingle bank

poulies : **~ folles et fixes** *f pl* PRODUCTION fast and loose pulleys

poulie-support *f* MINES hat roller

poulie-volant *f* CONS MECA fly pulley

poundal *m* METROLOGIE poundal

poupe *f* NAUT stern

Poupe *f* ASTRONOMIE Puppis

poupée *f* CONS MECA dog, head, *tour, fraiseuse horizontale* headstock, *tour* poppet head, NAUT gypsy, warping drum, warping head; **~ blindée** *f* CONS MECA ironclad headstock, totally-enclosed headstock; **~ de cabestan** *f* NAUT capstan drum, PETR cathead; **~ courante** *f* CONS MECA deadhead, footstock, headstock, loose head, loose headstock, sliding headstock, sliding poppet, tailstock; **~ diviseuse à commande mécanique** *f* CONS MECA mechanical dividing head; **~ diviseuse et sa contre-pointe** *f* CONS MECA dividing heads; **~ fixe** *f* CONS MECA head, headstock, *tour* live head, MECANIQUE headstock, PRODUCTION *tour* fast head, fast headstock; **~ à friction** *f* CONS MECA friction headstock; **~ à griffes** *f* CONS MECA faceplate dog, faceplate jaw; **~ mobile** *f* CONS MECA back puppet, backhead, deadhead, footstock, headstock, loose head, loose headstock, sliding headstock, sliding poppet, tailstock; **~ à monopoulie** *f* PRODUCTION constant-speed belt head; **~ à pompe** *f* CONS MECA dog, screw dog; **~ de tour** *f* CONS MECA lathe headstock, lathe head; **~ de tour à boîte de vitesse intégrée** *f* CONS MECA all-gear head, all-geared headstock

pourcentage *m* TEXTILE content, percentage; **~ de déclivité** *m* TV percentage tilt; **~ de fibres** *m* TEXTILE fiber content (AmE), fibre content (BrE); **~ d'immobilisation** *m* CH DE FER *véhicules* percentage awaiting repair; **~ d'individus non conformes** *m* QUALITE percentage of non-conforming items; **~ de mélange** *m* TEXTILE blend ratio; **~ de poids-frein** *m* CH DE FER braked weight percentage; **~ de rebut** *m* PRODUCTION scrap factor; **~ de synchronisation** *m* TV percentage synchronization; **~ d'unités non conformes** *m* QUALITE percentage of non-conforming items

pourpre : **~ rétinien** *m* CHIMIE erythropsin

pourri *adj* AGRO ALIM putrid

pourrir *vi* AGRO ALIM putrefy, CONSTR rot

pourrissage *m* CERAM VER ageing (BrE), aging (AmE); **~**

des fibres *m* PAPIER rotting

pourriture *f* CONSTR *du bois* rotting, NAUT rot; **~ sèche** *f* NAUT dry rot

poursuite *f* ESPACE *communications*, MILITAIRE *radar*, OCEANO, TELECOM tracking; **~ automatique** *f* ASTRONOMIE *d'un télescope* automatic tracking, ESPACE *communications* autotracking, NAUT automatic tracking; **~ dans l'espace lointain** *f* ASTRONOMIE deep space tracing; **~ en fréquence** *f* ESPACE *communications* frequency tracking; **~ laser** *f* ELECTRON laser tracking; **~ par radar** *f* AERONAUT, MILITAIRE radar tracking; **~ spatiale** *f* ESPACE *communications*, MILITAIRE space tracking; **~ télémesure et télécommande** *f (PTT)* ESPACE *communications* tracking telemetry and command *(TTC)*

poursuiteur *m* CINEMAT follow spot

poursuivre *vt* BREVETS prosecute

pourtour *m* CONSTR periphery

pourvoir : **~ de** *vt* CONS MECA fit with, PRODUCTION provide with, supply with

poussage *m* MINES forepoling, lagging, poling, TRANSPORT push towing

pousse *f* AGRO ALIM raising power, MINES stythe; **~ des pâtons** *f* AGRO ALIM raising power

poussé : **~ à la côte** *adj* NAUT blown ashore; **~ au large** *adj* NAUT blown out to sea

poussée *f* AERONAUT, CONS MECA thrust, CONSTR *d'une voûte* thrust, *terres* thrust, ESPACE *propulsion* thrust, *véhicules* thrust, INST HYDR pressure, NAUT buoyancy, PHYS FLUID buoyancy, surge, PHYSIQUE thrust, *exercée par un fluide* buoyancy, upthrust, POLLU MER, PRODUCTION *système hydraulique* thrust; **~ active des terres** *f* CHARBON active earth pressure; **~ aérodynamique** *f* AERONAUT aerodynamic pressure; **~ d'Archimède** *f* PHYS FLUID buoyancy, surge, PHYSIQUE buoyancy, upthrust; **~ axiale** *f* ESPACE *propulsion* azimuth thrust; **~ axiale maximale** *f* EN RENOUV maximum axial thrust; **~ au banc d'essai** *f* AERONAUT static thrust; **~ brute** *f* AERONAUT gross thrust; **~ dans le vide** *f* ESPACE *propulsion* vacuum thrust; **~ d'eau** *f* PETR water drive; **~ de fréquence** *f* ELECTRON frequency pushing; **~ garantie** *f* AERONAUT guaranteed thrust; **~ de gaz** *f* GAZ gas drive; **~ de gel** *f* METEO frost heave; **~ horizontale** *f* EN RENOUV side thrust; **~ hydraulique** *f* EN RENOUV hydraulic thrust; **~ hydrodynamique** *f* HYDROLOGIE hydrodynamic thrust; **~ hydrostatique** *f* AERONAUT, NAUT buoyancy; **~ inverse** *f* AERONAUT reverse thrust; **~ latérale** *f* ACOUSTIQUE side thrust; **~ nominale** *f* ESPACE *dans le vide, propulsion* nominal thrust; **~ phytoplanctonique** *f* OCEANO algal bloom, phytoplankton bloom, red tide; **~ au point fixe** *f* AERONAUT static thrust; **~ de régime** *f* ESPACE *propulsion* full thrust; **~ du rotor** *f* AERONAUT *hélicoptère* rotor thrust; **~ statique** *f* AERONAUT, MILITAIRE static thrust; **~ de terre passive** *f* CONSTR passive earth pressure; **~ unitaire** *f* ESPACE *propulsion* unit thrust; **~ vectorielle** *f* ESPACE *propulsion* vectored thrust; **~ du vent** *f* METEO wind pressure; **~ au vide** *f* CONSTR bulging, thrust passing outside material

pousse-pointe *m* CONSTR nail set, set

pousser[1] *vt* CINEMAT *au développement* push, CONS MECA drive, drive in, CONSTR *menuiserie* stick, *moulure, baguette sur un joint* run, *un chemin* carry, PHOTO push; **~ à l'alignement** *vt* CONSTR *mur* throw back into alignment

pousser:[2] **~ en dehors** *vi* CONSTR bulge; **~ au vide** *vi*

CONSTR bulge

pousser[3] *vti* INFORMAT, ORDINAT push

pousse-toc *m* CONS MECA driving dog

pousseur *m* ESPACE booster, NAUT pusher tug, PRODUCTION pushing jack, TRANSPORT push tow, push tug, pusher tug, towboat; ~ **hydraulique** *m* MINES hydraulic ram; ~ **hydraulique pour convoyeurs** *m* MINES hydraulic conveyor ram; ~ **pneumatique** *m* MINES air leg, jack leg

poussier *m* CHARBON coal dust; ~ **de houille** *m* CHARBON coal dust; ~ **isolant** *m* PRODUCTION parting dust, parting sand; ~ **de sable brûlé** *m* PRODUCTION parting dust, parting sand

poussière *f* CHARBON, CONSTR, POLLUTION, SECURITE dust; ~ **d'acier allié** *f* CHARBON steel alloy dust; ~ **d'acier au carbone** *f* CHARBON carbon steel dust; ~ **d'acier inoxydable** *f* CHARBON stainless steel dust; ~ **de charbon** *f* CHARBON, POLLUTION coal dust; ~ **de ciment** *f* CONSTR cement dust; ~ **de coke** *f* CHARBON coke dust; ~ **cosmique** *f* ASTRONOMIE, ESPACE meteor dust; ~ **de diamant** *f* MINES diamond dust, diamond powder; ~ **d'eau** *f* HYDROLOGIE spindrift, spray; ~ **de fumée** *f* CHARBON flue dust; ~ **incombustible** *f* MINES stone dust; ~ **inerte** *f* CHARBON stone dust; ~ **de papier** *f* IMPRIM fuzz, *papier, impression* lint; ~ **provenant de four à arc électrique** *f* CHARBON EAF dust; ~ **radioactive** *f* MILITAIRE *guerre nucléaire* radioactive dust; ~ **de silice cristalline** *f* SECURITE silica dust; ~ **stérile** *f* CHARBON stone dust; ~ **de tirage** *f* CINEMAT printed dirt; ~ **de verre** *f* CERAM VER glass dust; ~ **zodiacale** *f* ASTRONOMIE zodiacal dust

poussières *f pl* POLLUTION particulate materials; ~ **abrasives** *f pl* SECURITE abrasive dust; ~ **aériennes** *f pl* SECURITE airborne dust; ~ **en suspension dans l'air** *f pl* SECURITE airborne dust; ~ **interplanétaires** *f pl* ASTRONOMIE interplanetary dust; ~ **interstellaires** *f pl* ASTRONOMIE interstellar dust; ~ **microscopiques** *f pl* SECURITE microscopic dust; ~ **de verre** *f pl* CERAM VER loose glass

poussiéreux *adj* CHARBON, SECURITE dust-laden

poussoir *m* MECANIQUE push rod, PRODUCTION plunger, VEHICULES *moteur* cam following, *soupape de moteur* tappet; ~ **à commande hydraulique** *m* AUTO hydraulic valve lifter; ~ **de débrayage rapide** *m* AERONAUT autopilot disengage push button; ~ **de démoulage** *m* CERAM VER push-up; ~ **à galet** *m* AUTO roller tappet; ~ **latéral à galet** *m* PRODUCTION side-push roller; ~ **à plateau** *m* AUTO flat-bottomed tappet; ~ **pneumatique** *m* MINES air leg, jack leg; ~ **à réarmement** *m* PRODUCTION *automatisme industriel* reset push; ~ **à ressort** *m* CONS MECA spring ejector; ~ **de soupape** *m* AUTO push rod, valve tappet, tappet, INST HYDR valve tappet, VEHICULES *moteur* valve lifter

poutrage *m* CONSTR beams

poutraison *f* CONSTR beams

poutre *f* CONS MECA beam, CONSTR balk (AmE), baulk (BrE), beam, binding beam, GAZ, MECANIQUE, NAUT girder, PHYSIQUE beam; ~ **à âme pleine** *f* CONSTR built-up girder, plate web girder; ~ **appuyée** *f* CONSTR *résistance des matériaux* supported beam; ~ **armée** *f* CONSTR trussed beam, trussed girder; ~ **bow-string** *f* CONSTR bowstring girder; ~ **cantilever** *f* CONSTR cantilever beam; ~ **centrale du fuselage** *f* AERONAUT fuselage center box (AmE), fuselage centre box (BrE); ~ **composée** *f* CONSTR built-up girder, composite girder, compound girder; ~ **conductrice** *f*

TRANSPORT guide beam; ~ **conjuguée** *f* CONSTR compound girder; ~ **continue** *f* CONSTR continuous beam; ~ **de contreventement** *f* CONSTR wind bracing; ~ **en acier** *f* CONSTR steel beam; ~ **en bois sous-bandée** *f* CONSTR trussed wooden beam; ~ **en caisson** *f* CONSTR box girder; ~ **encastrée** *f* CONS MECA built-in beam, CONSTR cased beam, encased beam, fixed beam; ~ **encastrée à une extrémité** *f* CONS MECA beam fixed at one end; ~ **encastrée à une extrémité et chargée à l'autre** *f* CONSTR *résistance des matériaux* cantilever loaded at free end; ~ **en double T** *f* CONSTR H-beam, H-girder, I-beam, I-girder; ~ **en fer** *f* CONSTR steel beam; ~ **en forme de T inversé** *f* TRANSPORT U-shaped track girder; ~ **en porte-à-faux** *f* CONSTR cantilever beam, unsupported beam, *résistance des matériaux* free beam; ~ **en simple T** *f* CONSTR T-beam; ~ **en T** *f* CONSTR T-beam; ~ **en T inversé** *f* TRANSPORT inverted T-shaped track girder; ~ **en tôle** *f* CONSTR plate girder, plate iron girder; ~ **en tôles** *f* CONSTR built-up girder; ~ **en tôle section rectangulaire** *f* CONSTR box girder; ~ **en treillis** *f* CONSTR lattice, lattice beam, lattice girder, lattice truss, open-web girder, skeleton girder, MECANIQUE lattice girder; ~ **évidée** *f* CONSTR lattice, lattice beam, lattice girder, lattice truss, open-web girder, skeleton girder; ~ **de fer** *f* CONSTR iron girder; ~ **guide creuse** *f* TRANSPORT hollow-type track girder; ~ **à jour** *f* CONSTR lattice, lattice beam, lattice girder, lattice truss, open-web girder, skeleton girder; ~ **laminée à froid** *f* THERMODYN CRJ, cold-rolled joist; ~ **à larges ailes** *f* CONSTR broad flange girder; ~ **métallique** *f* NAUT girder; ~ **mixte** *f* CONSTR composite girder; ~ **optique** *f* OPTIQUE optical head; ~ **de plancher** *f* CONSTR summer, summer beam, summer tree; ~ **porteuse** *f* TRANSPORT guideway, track girder; ~ **porteuse fermée** *f* TRANSPORT closed box girder; ~ **porteuse à section rectangulaire** *f* TRANSPORT box section track girder; ~ **principale** *f* AERONAUT keel; ~ **de rive** *f* CONSTR stringer; ~ **sablière** *f* CONSTR plate, roof plate, wall plate; ~ **secondaire** *f* CONSTR trimmed joist; ~ **simple** *f* CONSTR simple beam; ~ **sous-bandée** *f* CONSTR trussed beam; ~ **de treuil** *f* AERONAUT hoist boom; ~ **tubulaire** *f* CONSTR box girder

poutre-caisson *f* CONSTR box girder

poutre-console *f* PHYSIQUE cantilever beam

poutrellage: ~ **de fond** *m* (Bel) *(cf plancher de sole)* CERAM VER grillage

poutrelle *f* CONSTR H-beam, H-iron, I-beam, I-girder, joist, girder, MECANIQUE girder; ~ **à croisillons** *f* CONSTR lattice, lattice beam, lattice girder, lattice truss, open-web girder, skeleton girder; ~ **métallique en arceau** *f* CONSTR lattice girder arch; ~ **métallique de treillis et arceau** *f* CONSTR lattice girder arch

poutre-navire *f* NAUT hull girder, ship girder

pouvoir *m* BREVETS authorization, CONS MECA power, PHYSIQUE power, rating; ~ **abrasif** *m* PAPIER abrasiveness; ~ **absorbant** *m* EMBALLAGE absorbency, MECANIQUE *matériaux* absorbing capacity, PAPIER absorbency, absorbtiveness; ~ **absorbant de chaleur** *m* THERMODYN *d'un four* heat-absorbing power; ~ **d'arrêt** *m* PHYSIQUE stopping power; ~ **d'arrêt atomique total** *m* PHYSIQUE total atomic stopping power; ~ **d'arrêt linéique relatif** *m* PHYSIQUE relative linear stopping power; ~ **d'arrêt linéique total** *m* PHYSIQUE total linear stopping power; ~ **d'arrêt massique relatif** *m* PHYSIQUE relative mass stopping power; ~ **d'arrêt massique total** *m* PHYSIQUE total mass stopping power; ~ **calorifique** *m* CHAUFFAGE, PETROLE calorific value, THERMODYN caloric power, calorific power, heating power, thermal power; ~ **calorifique inférieur** *m* CHAUFFAGE net calorific value; ~ **calorifique supérieur** *m* (*PCS*) CHAUFFAGE, GAZ gross calorific value; ~ **calorifuge** *m* THERMODYN heat insulation effectiveness, heat insulation power; ~ **chromatique de résolution** *m* PHYSIQUE chromatic resolving power; ~ **collant** *m* MATERIAUX tackiness; ~ **colorant** *m* COULEURS coloring power (AmE), coloring value (AmE), colouring power (BrE), colouring value (BrE), PLAST CAOU *peinture* color strength (AmE), colour strength (BrE); ~ **convergent** *m* PHOTO *d'un objectif* refractive power; ~ **de coupure** *m* ELECTR *d'un interrupteur, d'un fusible*, ELECTROTEC breaking capacity; ~ **de coupure en court-circuit** *m* PRODUCTION short circuit interrupting current; ~ **couvrant** *m* PLAST CAOU hiding power, *peinture* covering power, REVETEMENT coating property; ~ **débitant** *m* PRODUCTION *d'un ventilateur* capacity of output; ~ **de définition** *m* PHOTO resolving power; ~ **détergent** *m* LESSIVES detergency, detergent power; ~ **discriminateur de filtre** *m* ELECTRON filter discrimination; ~ **dispersif** *m* PHYSIQUE dispersive power; ~ **d'échange cationique** *m* POLLUTION cation exchange capacity; ~ **émanateur** *m* PHYS RAYON emanating power; ~ **de fermeture** *m* ELECTR *relais*, ELECTROTEC making capacity; ~ **feutrant** *m* PAPIER felting power; ~ **de formation de gaz** *m* AGRO ALIM gassing power; ~ **inducteur spécifique** *m* ELECTROTEC specific inductive capacity; ~ **neutralisant des acides** *m* POLLUTION acid neutralizing capacity; ~ **de prédiction** *m* POLLUTION predictive capability; ~ **de ralentissement** *m* NUCLEAIRE, PHYSIQUE slowing-down power; ~ **réactif** *m* CHIMIE reagency; ~ **réfléchissant du papier** *m* IMPRIM *optique, impression* reflectance; ~ **réflecteur** *m* ELECTROTEC reflectance; ~ **réfringent** *m* PHOTO refractive power; ~ **de résolution** *m* METALL, PHYSIQUE resolving power; ~ **rotatoire** *m* PHYSIQUE rotatory power, specific rotation; ~ **de rupture** *m* ELECTR *d'un interrupteur, d'un fusible* breaking capacity; ~ **séparateur** *m* CINEMAT, ELECTRON resolving power, GENIE CHIM separation effect, NUCLEAIRE separating power, separative effort, PHOTO, PHYSIQUE resolving power; ~ **séparateur unitaire** *m* NUCLEAIRE elementary separative power; ~ **thermoélectrique** *m* ELECTROTEC, PHYSIQUE thermoelectric power

PP *abrév (poste principal)* ELECTRON MS *(main station)*

PPCM *abrév (plus petit commun multiple)* MATH, ORDINAT LCM *(least common multiple, lowest common multiple)*

PPCMD *abrév (plus petit commun multiple des dénominateurs)* MATH LCD *(least common denominator)*

PPS *abrév (pouces par seconde)* ENREGISTR, ORDINAT IPS *(inches per second)*

Pr *(praséodyme)* CHIMIE Pr *(praseodymium)*

pragma *m* INFORMAT, ORDINAT pragma

pragmatique *f* INFORMAT, ORDINAT pragmatics

prase *m* MINERAUX prase

praséodyme *m (Pr)* CHIMIE praseodymium *(Pr)*

praséolite *f* MINERAUX praseolite

praticien *m* PRODUCTION practician

pratique *adj* MECANIQUE *outillage* handy

pratiquer: ~ **le découvert** *vi* MINES remove an overburden; ~ **la découverte** *vi* MINES remove an overburden; ~ **un trou** *vi* CONSTR hole; ~ **un trou de**

sonde *vi* CONSTR bore, drill a borehole, MINES bore, drill, put down a borehole

PRCI *abrév (poste à relais à commande informatique)* CH DE FER computer-controlled all-relay interlocking unit

préaccentuation *f* ACOUSTIQUE, ENREGISTR, ESPACE *communications*, PHYSIQUE, TV pre-emphasis; ~ **vidéo** *f* TV video pre-emphasis

préaération *f* HYDROLOGIE preaeration

préaffecter *vt* ORDINAT prestore

préaffichage *m* ELECTRON presetting

préambule *m* BREVETS preamble, precharacterizing portion, ESPACE *communications* preamble

préamplificateur *m* ELECTRON preamp, preamplifier, ENREGISTR preamplifier, ESPACE *communications* head amplifier, preamplifier, PETR, PHYSIQUE, TELECOM preamplifier; ~ **à faible bruit** *m* ELECTRON low-noise preamplifier

préamplification *f* ELECTRON, ENREGISTR, ESPACE, PETR, PHYSIQUE, TELECOM preamplification

préassigner *vt* TELECOM designate

préattaque *f* CHARBON preleaching

préavertissement *m* CH DE FER outer distant signal

précalage *m* IMPRIM *machines* make-ready

précambrien[1] *adj* GEOLOGIE Precambrian

précambrien[2] *m* GEOLOGIE Precambrian

précautions: ~ **contre l'incendie** *f pl* SECURITE fire precautions; ~ **contre les poussières** *f pl* SECURITE precautions against dust; ~ **à prendre** *f pl* SECURITE precautions to be taken; ~ **de sécurité** *f* SECURITE safety precaution; ~ **spéciales** *f pl* SECURITE special precautions

précession *f* ASTRONOMIE, ESPACE, PHYSIQUE precession; ~ **des équinoxes** *f* ASTRONOMIE precession of the equinoxes; ~ **de Larmor** *f* PHYSIQUE Larmor precession

préchambre *f* VEHICULES *moteur diesel* prechamber; ~ **de combustion** *f* TRANSPORT combustion prechamber

précharge *f* RESSORTS initial tension

préchauffage *m* CH DE FER, CONSTR, MAT CHAUFF, MATERIAUX, METALL, PLAST CAOU *plastiques, caoutchouc* preheating

préchauffer *vt* CONSTR, MAT CHAUFF, REFRIG, THERMODYN preheat

préchauffeur *m* MAT CHAUFF, PETROLE, VEHICULES *moteur diesel* preheater

précipitabilité *f* CHIMIE precipitability

précipitant *m* CHIMIE precipitant, precipitator, GENIE CHIM precipitating agent

précipitateur *m* CHIMIE precipitator; ~ **électrostatique** *m* POLLUTION ESP, electrostatic precipitator

précipitation *f* CHIMIE, CONSTR, MATERIAUX, METALL, METEO precipitation, POLLUTION deposition, THERMODYN natural ageing (BrE), natural aging (AmE); ~ **chimique** *f* HYDROLOGIE chemical precipitation; ~ **continue** *f* METALL continuous precipitation; ~ **efficace** *f* METEO effective precipitation; ~ **primaire** *f* HYDROLOGIE primary precipitation

précipitations *f pl* METEO rainfall; ~ **acides** *f pl* POLLUTION acid pollution, acid precipitation, acid rain; ~ **humides** *f pl* POLLUTION wet precipitation; ~ **naturelles** *f pl* POLLUTION clean rain; ~ **normales** *f pl* POLLUTION clean rain; ~ **sèches** *f pl* POLLUTION dry precipitation

précipité[1] *adj* CHIMIE precipitated

précipité[2] *m* CHIMIE, GENIE CHIM, METALL, PETROLE precipitate; ~ **de gaz** *m* METALL gas precipitate; ~

intermétallique *m* MATERIAUX intermetallic precipitate; ~ **de transition** *m* METALL transitional precipitate

précipiter[1] *vti* GENIE CHIM separate

précipiter:[2] **se ~** *v réfl* GENIE CHIM precipitate

précis *adj* MECANIQUE, PHYSIQUE accurate

préciser *vt* SECURITE *détails* specify

précision *f* CONS MECA accuracy, INFORMAT precision, MECANIQUE, METROLOGIE accuracy, ORDINAT, PHYSIQUE accuracy, precision, PRODUCTION exactitude, exactness; ~ **d'alignement** *f* TV registration accuracy; ~ **des engrenages parallèles** *f* CONS MECA accuracy of parallel gears; ~ **d'étalonnage** *f* MATERIAUX calibration accuracy; ~ **de huit bits** *f* ELECTRON eight-bit accuracy; ~ **de point** *f* NAUT accuracy of ship's position; ~ **de pointage** *f* ESPACE *communications* pointing accuracy; ~ **des points de consigne** *f* NUCLEAIRE set point accuracy; ~ **de poursuite** *f* ESPACE *communications* tracking accuracy; ~ **simple** *f* ORDINAT single precision

préclimatisation *f* CH DE FER precooling

précoce *adj* GEOLOGIE early, PLAST CAOU *caoutchouc* scorchy

précombustion *f* THERMODYN precombustion

précompensation *f* ENREGISTR pre-equalization

précompresseur *m* REFRIG booster compressor

préconcentré *m* CHARBON preconcentrate; ~ **d'uranium** *m* NUCLEAIRE uranium preconcentrate

préconformation *f* RESSORTS presetting; ~ **à chaud** *f* RESSORTS hot presetting; ~ **à froid** *f* RESSORTS cold presetting

préconformer *vt* RESSORTS preset

précontrainte *f* RESSORTS prestressing; ~ **à chaud** *f* RESSORTS hot prestressing; ~ **extérieure** *f* CONSTR external prestressing; ~ **à froid** *f* RESSORTS cold prestressing

précontrôle *m* TV preview

précontrôler *vt* TV preview

précorrection *f* ACOUSTIQUE predistortion

précouche *f* CHARBON precoating

précriblage *m* CHARBON prescreening, scalping

précuisiné *adj* AGRO ALIM precooked

précuit *adj* AGRO ALIM precooked

précurseur *m* NUCLEAIRE parent nuclide, POLLUTION precursor pollutant; ~ **acide** *m* POLLUTION acidic precursor; ~ **d'acides** *m* POLLUTION acidic precursor

prédécapage: ~ **à l'acide** *m* NUCLEAIRE acid prepickling

prédécesseur: ~ **en droit** *m* BREVETS legal predecessor, predecessor in title

prédécoupage *m* MINES presplit basting, presplitting

prédéfinir *vt* INFORMAT, ORDINAT preset

prédéformation *f* METALL prestrain

prédélivreur: ~ **à tambour** *m* TEXTILE drum feeder

prédicat *m* INFORMAT predicate, MATH quantifier, ORDINAT predicate

prédisposé: ~ **aux accidents** *adj* SECURITE accident-prone

préenregistré *adj* INFORMAT, ORDINAT, TELECOM prerecorded

préenregistrer *vt* ENREGISTR prerecord, INFORMAT, ORDINAT prestore, TV prerecord

préfabrication *f* NAUT prefabrication

préfabriqué *adj* CONSTR precast

préfabriquer *vt* CONSTR precast

préfiltrage *m* ELECTRON prefiltering

préfiltre *m* DISTRI EAU primary filter, ELECTRON prefilter; ~ **d'ordre deux** *m* ELECTRON second order prefilter; ~ **à plusieurs cellules** *m* ELECTRON multisection prefilter;

~ **du second ordre** *m* ELECTRON second order prefilter

préfixe *m* INFORMAT, ORDINAT, TELECOM prefix; ~ **de conduit** *m* TELECOM POH, path overhead; ~ **interurbain** *m* TELECOM direct distance dialing access code (AmE), subscriber trunk dialling access code (BrE)

préformage *m* PLAST CAOU *procédé, plastiques* preforming

préforme *f* CERAM VER, OPTIQUE, TELECOM preform

préformeuse: ~ **à piston** *f* CONS MECA piston-type preforming unit

prégnane *m* CHIMIE pregnane

préhnite *f* MINERAUX prehnite

préhnitène *m* CHIMIE, MINERAUX prehnitene

préhnitique *adj* CHIMIE, MINERAUX prehnitic

préimprégnation *f* CERAM VER preimpregnation, prepegging

préimprégné *m* PLAST CAOU *stratifié* prepreg

préimprimé *adj* EMBALLAGE preprinted

préionisation *f* PHYS RAYON preionization

préjudiciable *adj* SECURITE injurious

prélart *m* CONSTR tarpaulin

prélèvement *m* DISTRI EAU sampling, ELECTROTEC tapping, PHYSIQUE sample, tapping; ~ **d'air d'un compresseur** *m* CONS MECA compressor air bleed; ~ **d'échantillons** *m* ESSAIS, PRODUCTION sampling; ~ **d'échantillons lié aux problèmes de santé** *m* SECURITE health-related sampling; ~ **par lots** *m* PRODUCTION batch sampling

prélever *vt* INFORMAT, ORDINAT fetch, PHYSIQUE sample, tap, *un échantillon* take

préleveur *m* EQUIP LAB *échantillonnage* sampling device

prélumination *f* PHOTO flashing

prémagnétisation *f* ENREGISTR magnetic bias, premagnetization, TV bias, biasing, magnetic bias

prémaquette *f* IMPRIM dummy

premier:[1] **au ~ plan** *adv* PHOTO in the foreground

premier:[2] ~ **amplificateur à fréquence intermédiaire** *m* ELECTRON first IF amplifier; ~ **changeur de fréquence** *m* ELECTRON first mixer; ~ **entré premier sorti** *m* *(PEPS)* ORDINAT first-in first-out *(FIFO)*; ~ **étage** *m* ESPACE booster, just stage; ~ **faux pont** *m* NAUT second deck; ~ **harmonique** *m* ELECTRON first harmonic; ~ **maître** *m* NAUT chief petty officer; ~ **membre d'une équation** *m* PHYSIQUE left-hand side; ~ **montage** *m* CINEMAT first assembly, rough cut; ~ **oscillateur local** *m* ELECTRON first local oscillator; ~ **petit quart** *m* MILITAIRE first dogwatch; ~ **plan** *m* CINEMAT foreground; ~ **plan du film** *m* CINEMAT opening shot; ~ **poste de travail** *m* PRODUCTION gateway; ~ **principe de la thermodynamique** *m* PHYSIQUE first law; ~ **quart** *m* MILITAIRE first watch; ~ **quartier** *m* *(cf phases de la Lune)* ASTRONOMIE first quarter; ~ **raccordement au réseau** *m* NUCLEAIRE first connection to grid; ~ **stade** *m* METALL initial stage; ~ **taraud** *m* PRODUCTION entering tap; ~ **voisin** *m* CRISTALL nearest neighbor (AmE), nearest neighbour (BrE); ~ **vol** *m* AERONAUT maiden flight

première: ~ **anode** *f* ELECTROTEC first anode; ~ **charge fissile** *f* NUCLEAIRE initial fissile charge; ~ **copie** *f* CINEMAT answer print; ~ **copie standard** *f* CINEMAT first trial composite; ~ **couche** *f* PLAST CAOU *revêtement* base coat; ~ **couche d'un couchage** *f* PAPIER precoating; ~ **cuisson** *f* CERAM VER first firing, first oxidizing firing; ~ **divergence** *f* NUCLEAIRE first critical experiment, first divergence; ~ **fréquence**

intermédiaire ƒ ELECTRON first intermediate frequency; ~ **génération** ƒ INFORMAT, ORDINAT first generation; ~ **image du plan** ƒ CINEMAT *sur caméra avec lampe de marquage* flash frame; ~ **injection** ƒ ELECTRON first injection; ~ **passe** ƒ PETR stringer head

premières: ~ **arrivées** ƒ pl GEOLOGIE *onde sismique* first arrivals

premiers: ~ **secours** m pl SECURITE first aid, first-aid work; ~ **voisins** m pl METALL first nearest neighbours

prémixer vt CINEMAT predub

prémontage m CINEMAT assembly

prémonter[1] vt CINEMAT pre-edit

prémonter[2] vi CINEMAT assemble edit

prenant: ~ **à la chaleur** adj THERMODYN heat-setting

prendre[1] vt ~ **en remorque** vt NAUT tow; PRODUCTION grip

prendre[2] vi MATERIAUX congeal; ~ **de l'arc** vi NAUT hog; ~ **contre le fil** vi CONSTR *du bois* work against the grain; ~ **effet** vi CONS MECA become effective, take effect; ~ **de l'erre** vi NAUT gather way; ~ **fond** vi NAUT bite, grip; ~ **du gîte** vi NAUT cant over; ~ **du jeu** vi CONS MECA *clavetage* work loose; ~ **le large** vi NAUT sail away; ~ **la mer** vi NAUT put to sea, set sail; ~ **un ris** vi NAUT reef; ~ **sa source** vi HYDROLOGIE rise

preneur m CHARBON grip; ~ **d'encre** m IMPRIM *machines* ink ductor

préparation ƒ AGRO ALIM mix, mixture, IMPRIM *machines* make-ready, PHOTO *des bains* making-up, PRODUCTION setup; ~ **avec immobilisation** ƒ PRODUCTION internal setup; ~ **de bandes son pour mixage** ƒ CINEMAT track-laying; ~ **d'un bord droit** ƒ CONSTR square-edge preparation; ~ **de chanfreins** ƒ MECANIQUE *soudage* edge preparation; ~ **de données** ƒ INFORMAT, ORDINAT data preparation; ~ **en temps masqué** ƒ PRODUCTION external setup; ~ **de fichier** ƒ INFORMAT, ORDINAT file preparation; ~ **interne** ƒ PRODUCTION internal setup; ~ **de joints** ƒ CONSTR joint preparation; ~ **mécanique** ƒ CHARBON dressing; ~ **mécanique du charbon** ƒ CHARBON coal dressing, coal preparation; ~ **mécanique du minerai** ƒ MINES ore dressing; ~ **par jet d'abrasif** ƒ CONSTR shot-blasting; ~ **de la pâte** ƒ PAPIER stock preparation; ~ **de surface** ƒ CONSTR surface preparation

préparé adj AGRO ALIM cooked, dressed, prepared

préparer: ~ **la gomme** vi IMPRIM base

prépistage m CINEMAT prestriping

préplastification ƒ PLAST CAOU preplasticizing

préplieuse ƒ IMPRIM *plieuses, rotatives* plough folder (BrE), plow folder (AmE)

préposé: ~ **au tir** m CHARBON blaster, shot firer

préprint m IMPRIM preprint, *emballage* lining paper

préprocesseur m INFORMAT, ORDINAT preprocessor

préprogrammé adj INFORMAT, ORDINAT preprogrammed

préréfrigéré adj AGRO ALIM precooled

prérefroidisseur m REFRIG precooler

prérégler vt ENREGISTR preset

prérégulateur: ~ **à thyristors** m ELECTROTEC SCR preregulator

prérégulation: ~ **par thyristors** ƒ ELECTROTEC SCR preregulation

prérodage m CONS MECA honing, preliminary seating

près: ~ **de l'avant** adv NAUT fine on the bow; ~ **de terre** adv NAUT inshore

presbyacousie ƒ ACOUSTIQUE presbyacusis (BrE), presbycusis (AmE)

prescription ƒ SECURITE requirement, safety requirement; ~ **technique** ƒ METROLOGIE technical requirement

prescriptions: ~ **pour la santé et la sécurité** ƒ pl SECURITE health and safety requirements; ~ **de sécurité** ƒ pl TRANSPORT safety specifications; ~ **de sécurité et de surveillance** ƒ pl SECURITE safety requirements and supervision; ~ **de sécurité pour l'électricité** ƒ pl SECURITE electrical safety requirements; ~ **techniques de sécurité** ƒ pl SECURITE technical safety requirements; ~ **d'utilisation** ƒ pl EMBALLAGE handling and installing instructions

présécheur m PAPIER predryer

présélecteur m ELECTRON, MAT CHAUFF preselector, TV subswitcher, VEHICULES *boîte de vitesses* preselector; ~ **de diaphragme** m PHOTO aperture preselector; ~ **de vitesse** m VEHICULES *boîte de vitesses* preselector

présélection: ~ **des canaux** ƒ TV presetting of channels; ~ **de diaphragme** ƒ CINEMAT diaphragm presetting

présentation ƒ AERONAUT *d'un vol* approach, CONS MECA layout, ESPACE display; ~ **de l'identification de la ligne appelante** ƒ *(PILA)* TELECOM calling line identification display, calling line identification presentation *(CLIP)*; ~ **de l'identification de la ligne connectée** ƒ *(PILC)* TELECOM connected line identification presentation *(COLP)*; ~ **sous carte** ƒ EMBALLAGE visual carded packaging; ~ **visuelle** ƒ INFORMAT soft copy

présenter[1] vt CONS MECA position, CONSTR *un tenon à une mortaise* try, ELECTRON, ESPACE display

présenter:[2] ~ **un balourd** vi METROLOGIE be out of balance; ~ **un dépassement négatif** vi ELECTRON undershoot; ~ **un phénomène d'eutrophisation** vi RECYCLAGE eutrophy; ~ **des risques pour la sécurité** vi SECURITE be a safety risk; ~ **une sous-modulation** vi ELECTRON undershoot

présentoir: ~ **frigorifique** m REFRIG refrigerated display case

présérie ƒ PRODUCTION preproduction

préservatif: ~ **pour produits alimentaires** m AGRO ALIM food preservative

préservation: ~ **de l'ouïe** ƒ SECURITE hearing conservation, protecting the hearing

présomption ƒ BREVETS presumption

présonorisation ƒ ENREGISTR playback

presqu'île ƒ HYDROLOGIE peninsula, spit, NAUT peninsula

presque: ~ **calme** m NAUT light airs

pressage m ACOUSTIQUE molding (AmE), moulding (BrE), CERAM VER, ENREGISTR pressing; ~ **automatique** m CERAM VER automatic pressing; ~ **à chaud** m MATERIAUX, METALL hot pressing; ~ **hydraulique** m CONS MECA hydraulic pressing; ~ **industriel** m OPTIQUE disc mastering (BrE), disk mastering (AmE), mastering; ~ **semi-automatique** m CERAM VER semi-automatic pressing; ~ **simple** m CERAM VER straight pressing

pressboard m PAPIER pressboard

presse ƒ CONS MECA clamp, cramp, PAPIER press, TEXTILE press, press-finishing machine, presser bar; ~ **d'agglomération** ƒ GENIE CHIM sintering pallet, sintering pan; ~ **à l'argile** ƒ CERAM VER clay press; ~ **ascendante** ƒ PLAST CAOU *moulage* upstroke press; ~ **à balancier** ƒ CONS MECA friction screw, PRODUCTION fly press; ~ **à balles** ƒ PAPIER baling press; ~ **à bandes de type Cameron** ƒ IMPRIM *rotatives* belt press; ~ **à border** ƒ PRODUCTION flanger, flanging machine, flanging press; ~ **à boues** ƒ HYDROLOGIE sludge press; ~ **à bras** ƒ IMPRIM hand press; ~ **à cage à ressorts** ƒ CERAM VER spring cage press; ~ **à carrelages** ƒ CERAM VER tile press; ~ **à cintrer** ƒ CONS MECA bending press; ~ **à coller** ƒ CINEMAT joiner, splicer, CONS MECA G-clamp, G-cramp, cramp; ~ **à coller à sec** ƒ PHOTO dry-mounting press; ~ **coucheuse** ƒ PAPIER couch press; ~ **coucheuse aspirante** ƒ PAPIER suction couch press; ~ **à cylindre** ƒ PRODUCTION rolling press; ~ **de découpage** ƒ CONS MECA blanking press; ~ **découpage fin** ƒ CONS MECA fine blanking press; ~ **de découpage volante** ƒ PRODUCTION fly press; ~ **à découper** ƒ CONS MECA blanking press, PAPIER die-stamping press, punching press; ~ **demi-laize** ƒ IMPRIM *rotatives* half-width printing press; ~ **descendante** ƒ PLAST CAOU downstroke press; ~ **à deux couleurs** ƒ IMPRIM two-color press (AmE), two-colour press (BrE); ~ **à double révolution** ƒ IMPRIM two-revolution press; ~ **d'ébauchage** ƒ CONS MECA blanking press; ~ **à écorces** ƒ PAPIER bark press; ~ **à emballer** ƒ PAPIER bundling press; ~ **à emboutir** ƒ CONS MECA drawing press, PRODUCTION flanger, flanging machine, flanging press; ~ **en blanc** ƒ IMPRIM stop cylinder press; ~ **encolleuse** ƒ PAPIER size press; ~ **à épreuve à plat** ƒ IMPRIM *machines* flat-bed proofing press; ~ **d'essai** ƒ CONS MECA tryout press; ~ **essoreuse** ƒ PAPIER dewatering press; ~ **à étirer les tubes** ƒ PRODUCTION tube-drawing press; ~ **à façonner les briques** ƒ CERAM VER brick molding machine (AmE), brick moulding machine (BrE); ~ **à faire les balles** ƒ EMBALLAGE baling press; ~ **à filage** ƒ MATERIAUX extruder; ~ **à filtrer** ƒ AGRO ALIM filter press; ~ **à forger** ƒ PRODUCTION forging press; ~ **à forger à quatre colonnes** ƒ PRODUCTION four-column forging press; ~ **à froid pour rivets** ƒ CONS MECA rivet cold press; ~ **à gaufrer** ƒ IMPRIM stamping press; ~ **à genouillère** ƒ CERAM VER toggle press; ~ **hélio** ƒ IMPRIM copperplate printing press; ~ **humide** ƒ PAPIER wet press; ~ **hydraulique** ƒ EQUIP LAB, PLAST CAOU hydraulic press, SECURITE power press; ~ **à imprimer** ƒ IMPRIM printing press; ~ **d'imprimerie rapide** ƒ IMPRIM printing fly press; ~ **à imprimer rotative** ƒ IMPRIM rotary printing press; ~ **inférieure** ƒ PAPIER bottom press; ~ **à injection** ƒ PLAST CAOU *plastiques* injection molding press (AmE), injection moulding press (BrE), SECURITE injection machine, injection molding machine (AmE), injection moulding machine (BrE); ~ **à levier** ƒ CERAM VER side lever press, CONS MECA lever press; ~ **lisse** ƒ PAPIER pinhole; ~ **lisseuse** ƒ PAPIER smoothing press; ~ **à macquer** ƒ PRODUCTION crocodile squeezer; ~ **à mandriner** ƒ CONS MECA arbor press; ~ **mécanique à bâti en col de cygne** ƒ CONS MECA open front mechanical power press; ~ **à molette** ƒ PAPIER marking press; ~ **montante** ƒ PAPIER reversed press; ~ **à mouvement descendant** ƒ PLAST CAOU downstroke press; ~ **offset** ƒ EMBALLAGE offset press, IMPRIM offset printing press, PAPIER smoothing press; ~ **à passage direct** ƒ PAPIER straight-through press; ~ **à pastilles** ƒ PLAST CAOU preforming press; ~ **à plaquer** ƒ CONS MECA veneering press; ~ **à plat** ƒ IMPRIM flat-bed cylinder press; ~ **à plusieurs étages** ƒ PLAST CAOU multiple daylight press, platten press; ~ **à poinçons sériés** ƒ CONS MECA gang press; ~ **pour plaques en argile** ƒ CERAM VER clay plate press; ~ **principale** ƒ PAPIER main press; ~ **rainurée** ƒ PAPIER grooved press; ~ **recto-verso** ƒ IMPRIM two-cylinder press; ~ **à refouler** ƒ CONS MECA upsetting-press; ~ **rotative** ƒ IMPRIM rotary

printing machine; ~ **rotative offset** ƒ EMBALLAGE offset rotary press; ~ **à sertir** ƒ PRODUCTION flanging press; ~ **à toile synthétique** ƒ PAPIER press fabric, press felt; ~ **de transfert à chaud** ƒ EMBALLAGE thermal transfer printer; ~ **typo** ƒ IMPRIM letterpress printing machine; ~ **à vis** ƒ CONS MECA G-clamp, G-cramp, screw clamp, screw press, vice press (BrE), vise press (AmE), PAPIER screw press

presse-étoupe *m* CONS MECA packing gland, stuffing box, ESPACE *pyrotechnie* gland, packing gland, MECANIQUE, PETROLE *canalisations, raffinerie* gland, PRODUCTION stuffing box; ~ **avec joints** *m* PRODUCTION packing gland; ~ **étanche à la vapeur** *m* INST HYDR steam packing gland

presse-film *m* PHOTO pressure plate

presse-filtre *m* EQUIP LAB *filtration* filter press

presse-garniture *m* CONS MECA gland, PRODUCTION stuffing box

presse-pâte *m* PAPIER pulp machine, pulp saver, wet machine

presser:[1] ~ **pour parler** *adj* TELECOM push-to-talk

presser[2] *vt* PAPIER press, PRODUCTION squeeze

presses: ~ **étagées** ƒ *pl* PAPIER press stack, stacked presses

presseur *m* CERAM VER presser, CINEMAT, PHOTO pressure plate; ~ **démontable** *m* PHOTO detachable pressure plate; ~ **latéral** *m* CINEMAT edge guide; ~ **à ressort** *m* PHOTO spring-mounted pressure plate

presseur-guide *m* CINEMAT pressure guide

pressiomètre *m* CHARBON pressiometer

pression:[1] **en** ~ *adj* CONS MECA in steam, under steam, INST HYDR under steam; **sous** ~ *adj* CONS MECA in steam, under steam, INST HYDR under steam

pression[2] ƒ AERONAUT, CONSTR, ELECTROTEC, ESPACE, GAZ, INST HYDR, MATERIAUX, MECANIQUE, PAPIER, PHYSIQUE pressure, PRODUCTION feed, feeding, REFRIG pressure; ~ **absolue** ƒ REFRIG absolute pressure; ~ **acoustique** ƒ ENREGISTR acoustic pressure, PHYSIQUE, POLLUTION sound pressure; ~ **acoustique de crête** ƒ ACOUSTIQUE peak sound pressure; ~ **acoustique effective** ƒ POLLUTION effective sound pressure; ~ **acoustique efficace** ƒ ACOUSTIQUE effective sound pressure; ~ **acoustique instantanée** ƒ ACOUSTIQUE instantaneous sound pressure; ~ **acoustique maximale** ƒ ACOUSTIQUE maximum sound pressure, pressure amplitude; ~ **acoustique de référence** ƒ ACOUSTIQUE, POLLUTION reference sound pressure; ~ **d'admission** ƒ AERONAUT manifold pressure, TRANSPORT boost pressure; ~ **d'admission d'air** ƒ AERONAUT air intake pressure; ~ **d'air** ƒ CONS MECA air pressure; ~ **d'alimentation** ƒ CHARBON inlet pressure; ~ **anormale** ƒ GEOLOGIE, PETROLE abnormal pressure; ~ **d'arrêt** ƒ AERONAUT impact pressure, PHYS FLUID stagnation pressure; ~ **atmosphérique** ƒ GAZ, METEO, PHYSIQUE atmospheric pressure; ~ **automatique** ƒ CONS MECA self-acting feed; ~ **barométrique** ƒ METEO barometric pressure; ~ **basse** ƒ GAZ low-pressure; ~ **de bruit** ƒ ACOUSTIQUE *d'un microphone* inherent noise pressure; ~ **de bulle** ƒ PETR bubble point pressure; ~ **de cabine** ƒ AERONAUT, ESPACE *véhicules* cabin pressure; ~ **de condensation** ƒ REFRIG condensing pressure; ~ **de couverture** ƒ CHARBON overburden pressure; ~ **critique** ƒ CHAUFFAGE, PHYSIQUE critical pressure; ~ **critique de refoulement** ƒ CONS MECA *d'une pompe à vide* critical backing pressure; ~ **dans le roc** ƒ CHARBON rock pressure; ~ **de décharge** ƒ CONS MECA discharge pressure; ~

de déclenchement *f* AERONAUT calibration pressure; ~ de détonation *f* MINES detonation pressure; ~ différentielle *f* PETROLE differential pressure; ~ différentielle de cabine *f* AERONAUT cabin differential pressure; ~ différentielle au tapis *f* CERAM VER back pressure; ~ dynamique *f* AERONAUT dynamic pressure, impact pressure, METEO dynamic pressure; ~ de l'eau *f* CONSTR, DISTRI EAU water pressure, INST HYDR water pressure, *hauteur piézométrique* head of water pressure, MAT CHAUFF, TEXTILE water pressure; ~ de l'eau interstitielle *f* CHARBON pore water pressure; ~ d'éclatement *f* CERAM VER, EMBALLAGE, PAPIER bursting pressure; ~ d'écoulement *f* PETR flowing pressure; ~ effective *f* CONS MECA, MECANIQUE active pressure, REFRIG gage pressure (AmE), gauge pressure (BrE); ~ effective de la vapeur *f* INST HYDR, NUCLEAIRE effective steam pressure; ~ élevée *f* PHYSIQUE high-pressure; ~ en puits fermé *f* PETROLE shut-in pressure; ~ en régime permanent *f* CONS MECA steady-state pressure; ~ en tête de puits *f* EN RENOUV, PETR wellhead pressure; ~ d'épreuve *f* CONS MECA proof pressure; ~ d'équilibre *f* REFRIG balance pressure; ~ d'essai *f* REFRIG test pressure; ~ d'essai hydraulique *f* REFRIG hydraulic proof pressure; ~ d'étalonnage *f* INST HYDR rating pressure; ~ exercée sur le sol *f* CHARBON soil pressure; ~ extérieure *f* MATERIAUX atmospheric pressure; ~ du fluide *f* PHYS FLUID fluid pressure; ~ de fonctionnement *f* ESPACE *propulsion* operating pressure; ~ de fond *f* PETR bottom hole pressure; ~ de formation *f* GEOLOGIE, PETROLE formation pressure; ~ de formation anormale négative *f* PETROLE subnormal pressure; ~ de formation anormale positive *f* PETR overpressure, PETROLE abnormal pressure, geopressure, positive abnormal pressure; ~ de formation normale *f* GEOLOGIE, PETROLE hydrostatic pressure, normal pressure; ~ de fracturation *f* GEOLOGIE, PETROLE fracture pressure; ~ de freinage *f* AUTO brake pressure; ~ de gaz *f* GAZ, PHYSIQUE gas pressure; ~ gazeuse *f* PHYSIQUE gas pressure; ~ du gaz interstitiel *f* CHARBON pore gas pressure; ~ géostatique *f* GEOLOGIE lithostatic pressure, PETROLE geostatic pressure, overburden pressure; ~ de gisement *f* PETR reservoir energy; ~ de gonflage *f* PRODUCTION inflation pressure; ~ hydrostatique *f* CHARBON, GAZ, GEOLOGIE, HYDROLOGIE, OCEANO, PETROLE, PHYS FLUID, REFRIG hydrostatic pressure; ~ d'impression *f* IMPRIM printing pressure; ~ initiale de réservoir *f* PETR initial reservoir pressure; ~ d'injection *f* PETROLE pump pressure; ~ d'injectivité *f* PETROLE *forage* leak-off pressure; ~ intérieure *f* DISTRI EAU internal pressure; ~ interstitielle *f* CHARBON, PETROLE pore pressure; ~ à levier *f* CONS MECA lever feed; ~ de la ligne de tangence entre les rouleaux *f* IMPRIM nip pressure; ~ linéaire *f* PAPIER linear pressure, nip pressure; ~ lithostatique *f* GEOLOGIE lithostatic pressure; ~ à la main par levier *f* CONS MECA hand lever feed; ~ maximale admissible *f* PRODUCTION total line value, *automatisme industriel* maximum allowable pressure; ~ motrice *f* CONS MECA driving pressure; ~ de moulage par injection *f* EMBALLAGE injection molding pressure (AmE), injection moulding pressure (BrE); ~ moyenne efficace au frein *f* AERONAUT brake mean-effective pressure; ~ moyenne en régime permanent *f* CONS MECA *dans un conduit fermé* average steady state pressure; ~ normale *f* PETR standard pressure; ~ normale de formation *f* PETR normal formation pressure;

~ normale de gisement *f* PETR normal formation pressure; ~ osmotique *f* GEOPHYS, PETROLE, PHYSIQUE, REFRIG osmotic pressure; ~ partielle *f* CHIMIE, PHYSIQUE partial pressure; ~ de pêche *f* OCEANO fishing pressure; ~ pneumatique *f* CONS MECA air pressure; ~ de pore *f* PETROLE pore pressure; ~ pulsée *f* PRODUCTION *système hydraulique* pulsating pressure; ~ de radiation *f* ACOUSTIQUE, ASTRONOMIE, PART PHYS, PHYS RAYON, PHYSIQUE radiation pressure; ~ de rayonnement *f* ASTRONOMIE, PHYS PART radiation pressure; ~ du rayonnement solaire *f* ESPACE *véhicules* solar radiation pressure; ~ de refoulement *f* DISTRI EAU delivery pressure, REFRIG discharge pressure; ~ réglée *f* CONS MECA controlled pressure; ~ de réservoir *f* PETR, PETROLE reservoir pressure; ~ de la roche *f* CHARBON mountain mass, rock pressure; ~ de la roche-magasin *f* PETROLE formation pressure; ~ de service *f* REFRIG operating pressure; ~ de service maximale *f* REFRIG design pressure; ~ de silo *f* CHARBON silo pressure; ~ sonore *f* ESPACE *véhicules* acoustic pressure, PHYSIQUE sound pressure; ~ statique *f* ACOUSTIQUE static pressure, INST HYDR static head, PETR, PETROLE shut-in pressure, REFRIG static pressure; ~ de suralimentation *f* AERONAUT *excès de pression*, ESPACE *propulsion* boost pressure; ~ de sustentation *f* TRANSPORT lifting pressure; ~ de tarage *f* PRODUCTION *système hydraulique* set pressure; ~ des terres *f* CHARBON earth pressure; ~ des terres au repos *f* CHARBON earth pressure at rest; ~ de la vapeur *f* INST HYDR, MAT CHAUFF steam pressure, vapor pressure (AmE), vapour pressure (BrE), PHYSIQUE, REFRIG vapor pressure (AmE), vapour pressure (BrE), TEXTILE steam pressure; ~ de la vapeur saturante *f* PHYSIQUE saturated vapor pressure (AmE), saturated vapour pressure (BrE); ~ du vent *f* METEO wind pressure, PRODUCTION blast pressure; ~ à vis *f* CONS MECA screw feed

pressostat *m* CHIMIE pressurestat, PAPIER pressure controller, PRODUCTION *contacteur de pression* pressure switch, REFRIG pressostat; ~ différentiel *m* REFRIG pressure differential cutout; ~ d'huile *m* REFRIG oil pressostat; ~ de sécurité *m* REFRIG safety cutout; ~ de sécurité de basse pression *m* REFRIG low-pressure safety cutout; ~ de sécurité de haute pression *m* REFRIG high-pressure safety cutout; ~ de sécurité d'huile *m* REFRIG oil pressure safety cutout; ~ à soufflets *m* PRODUCTION *système hydraulique* bellows-type pressure switch

presspahn *m* ELECTR pressboard, *isolation* insulating board, PAPIER presspahn-transformer board

pressurisation *f* AERONAUT pressurization; ~ cabine *f* AERONAUT cabin pressurization; ~ non régulée *f* ESPACE *véhicules* blowdown pressurization

pressurisé *adj* MECANIQUE pressurized

prestataire: ~ de service *m* TELECOM SP, service provider; ~ de service de maintenance *m* TELECOM MSP, maintenance service provider

prestation *f* PRODUCTION commissioned work

préstocker *vt* INFORMAT, ORDINAT prestore

présure *f* AGRO ALIM rennet, rennin

prêt *adj* INFORMAT, ORDINAT ready; ~ au débit *adj* AGRO ALIM *bière* finished; ~ à émettre *adj* ORDINAT ready-to-send, TELECOM ready-for-sending; ~ à l'emploi *adj* PHOTO ready-made; ~ à être activé *adj* TELECOM ready-to-activate; ~ pour la photogravure *adj* IMPRIM camera-ready; ~ à transmettre *adj* INFORMAT ready-

to-send
prêt-à-monter *m* CONS MECA kit
prétannage *m* CINEMAT prehardener
prétorsion *f* RESSORTS pretwist
prétraité *adj* CHIMIE pretreated, ELECTRON preprocessed, MATERIAUX pretreated
prétraitement *m* CHARBON pretreatment, CHIMIE pretreating, ELECTRON preprocessing, HYDROLOGIE primary treatment, MATERIAUX pretreating, pretreatment, PETROLE separation
prétrempé *adj* RESSORTS prehardened
preuve: ~ **entière** *f* BREVETS conclusive evidence; ~ **de réception** *f* MATERIAUX acceptance test; ~ **de l'utilisation** *f* BREVETS evidence of use
prévaporisation *f* CHIMIE preflashing
prévenir *vt* SECURITE *accidents* prevent
prévention: ~ **des accidents** *f* SECURITE accident prevention; ~ **de crue** *f* DISTRI EAU flood prevention; ~ **incendie** *f* THERMODYN fire prevention; ~ **des pertes** *f* QUALITE loss prevention; ~ **des risques** *f* SECURITE *en construction* hazard prevention
prévide *m* PHYSIQUE fore vacuum
prévisible *adj* TELECOM *interruption* foreseen
prévision *f* DISTRI EAU, INFORMAT, ORDINAT forecasting; ~ **intrinsèque** *f* PRODUCTION intrinsic forecast; ~ **météo** *f* ESPACE, METEO, METROLOGIE weather forecast; ~ **météorologique** *f* METEO weather forecast, weather report, METROLOGIE weather forecast, NAUT weather report; ~ **de serrage** *f* CONS MECA allowance for shrinkage; ~ **statistique** *f* PRODUCTION statistical forecasting; ~ **du temps** *f* METEO weather forecast; ~ **de trafic** *f* CH DE FER traffic forecast
prévoiler *vt* CINEMAT preflash, prefog
pricéite *f* MINERAUX priceite
primage *m* INST HYDR priming
primaire *m* ELECTROTEC primary, PLAST CAOU, PRODUCTION, REVETEMENT primer; ~ **anticorrosion** *m* COULEURS anticorrosive primer; ~ **antirouille** *m* COULEURS antirusting primer; ~ **d'atelier** *m* REVETEMENT shop priming; ~ **respirant** *m* PLAST CAOU *peinture* permeable primer
prime: ~ **de sauvetage** *f* NAUT salvage award
primer *vt* INST HYDR *chaudière à vapeur* prime
primitif *m* CONS MECA dividing circle, pitch circle, pitch line
primitive *f* INFORMAT, ORDINAT primitive
primuline *f* CHIMIE primuline
principaux: ~ **intervalles de la gamme diatonique** *m pl* ACOUSTIQUE main intervals on the diatonic scale
principe *m* CHIMIE *d'une substance* ingredient; ~ **de l'action minimale** *m* PHYSIQUE principle of least action; ~ **d'addition et de division** *m* ELECTRON *de fréquence* add-and-divide principle; ~ **anthropique** *m* ASTRONOMIE anthropic principle; ~ **d'Archimède** *m* PHYSIQUE Archimedes' principle; ~ **de combinaison de Ritz** *m* PHYSIQUE Ritz combination principle; ~ **de complémentarité** *m* PHYSIQUE principle of complementarity; ~ **de correspondance** *m* PHYSIQUE correspondence principle, principle of correspondence; ~ **d'entropie maximale** *m* PHYS RAYON maximum entropy principle, principle of maximum entropy; ~ **d'équivalence** *m* PHYSIQUE principle of equivalence; ~ **d'exclusion** *m* CHIMIE exclusion principle; ~ **d'exclusion de Pauli** *m* PHYS PART, PHYSIQUE Pauli exclusion principle; ~ **de Fermat** *m* PHYSIQUE Fermat's principle; ~ **de Frank-Condon** *m* PHYSIQUE Frank-Condon

principle; ~ **de Huygens** *m* PHYS RAYON, PHYSIQUE Huygens' principle; ~ **d'incertitude** *m* PHYSIQUE uncertainty principle; ~ **d'incertitude de Heisenberg** *m* PHYS PART Heisenberg uncertainty principle; ~ **de Mach** *m* PHYSIQUE Mach's principle; ~ **de moindre action** *m* PHYSIQUE principle; ~ **de Pascal** *m* PHYSIQUE Pascal's principle; ~ **de Pauli** *m* CHIMIE Pauli principle; ~ **pollueur-payeur** *m* POLLUTION polluter pays principle; ~ **de superposition** *m* PHYS ONDES *effet combiné des deux ondes* principle of superposition, PHYSIQUE principle of superposition; ~ **topologique abstrait** *m* GEOMETRIE abstract topological principle; ~ **des travaux virtuels** *m* PHYSIQUE principle of virtual work; ~ **zéro** *m* PHYSIQUE, THERMODYN zeroth law
principes: ~ **directeurs** *m pl* CONS MECA guidelines; ~ **d'étude ergonomique** *m pl* SECURITE *sécurité des machines* ergonomic design principles
prioritaire *adj* MECANIQUE overriding
priorité *f* BREVETS priority, INFORMAT, ORDINAT precedence, priority; ~ **antérieure** *f* BREVETS earlier priority; ~ **interne** *f* PRODUCTION internal priority; ~ **d'interruption** *f* INFORMAT, ORDINAT interrupt priority; ~ **des opérateurs** *f* INFORMAT, ORDINAT operator precedence; ~ **de passage** *f* AERONAUT *circulation* right-of-way; ~ **de perte de cellule** *f* TELECOM CLP, cell loss priority
prise:[1] **en** ~ *adj* PRODUCTION *boîte de vitesse* engaged; **avec** ~ **arrière** *adj* ELECTR *commutateur, interrupteur* back-connected
prise[2] *f* CHIMIE sample, CINEMAT connector, jack, jack plug, plug, socket, *d'un plan* take, CONS MECA engagement, engaging, intake, mesh, meshing, pitching, CONSTR set, *des chaux, des ciments* setting, ELECTR *enroulement* tap, *raccordement* tapping, ELECTROTEC tap, GENIE CHIM *durcissement* setting, NAUT *pêche* haul, OCEANO catch, haul, PRODUCTION grip, hold, socket, TELECOM outlet (AmE), seizure, socket outlet (BrE), TV plug; ~ **additive** *f* ELECTR plus tapping; ~ **d'air** *f* AERONAUT air scoop, CONS MECA air inlet, air intake, EQUIP LAB vent, NAUT air intake; ~ **d'air variable** *f* TRANSPORT variable geometry inlet, variable geometry intake; ~ **automatique** *f* PAPIER lick-up, pick-up; ~ **cannon** *f* CINEMAT cannon plug; ~ **coaxiale** *f* ELECTROTEC coaxial connector; ~ **à collet** *f* ELECTROTEC *raccordement* socket with shrouded contacts; ~ **de conscience du consommateur** *f* TEXTILE consumer awareness; ~ **constante** *f* AUTO *boîte de vitesses*, VEHICULES *boîte de vitesses* constant mesh; ~ **de contact** *f* AERONAUT touchdown; ~ **de coque** *f* AERONAUT fuselage ground connection; ~ **de courant** *f* ELECTR power outlet, socket, ELECTRON socket, ELECTROTEC current collector, outlet, plug box, IMPRIM plug, PHYSIQUE socket, VEHICULES *électrique* plug socket; ~ **de courant femelle** *f* ELECTR, EQUIP LAB *alimentation en électricité* electric socket; ~ **de courant irréversible** *f* ELECTR *raccordement* nonpolarized plug, nonreversible plug; ~ **de courant mâle** *f* ELECTR, EQUIP LAB *alimentation en électricité* electric plug; ~ **de déclencheur souple** *f* PHOTO cable release socket; ~ **à deux fiches** *f* ELECTR *raccordement* two-contacts connector; ~ **DIN** *f* ELECTR *raccordement* multiconductor locking plug; ~ **directe** *f* CONS MECA direct drive; ~ **directe du réseau** *f* TELECOM DOD, direct outward dialing (AmE), direct outward dialling (BrE); ~ **double** *f* TELECOM double seizure; ~ **d'eau** *f* CONSTR water intake, DISTRI EAU offtake, EN RENOUV water

intake, HYDROLOGIE intake, water intake; ~ **d'eau à incendie** f THERMODYN fire hydrant; ~ **d'eau à la mer** f NAUT seacock; ~ **d'éclairage** f ELECTR light wall socket; ~ **embrochable** f ELECTR *accessoire de câble* plug-in termination, *raccordement* plug-type connection, plug-type outlet; ~ **en charge** f INFORMAT support; ~ **enfichable** f ELECTR *accessoire de câble* plug-in termination, TELECOM socket outlet; ~ **en glace** f THERMODYN freeze-up; ~ **en saillie** f ELECTR *raccordement* surface socket; ~ **d'entraînement des accessoires** f AERONAUT accessory drive; ~ **d'essai** f CHIMIE sample, QUALITE test portion; ~ **d'un faisceau** f AERONAUT beam capture; ~ **femelle** f CINEMAT jack socket, ELECTR outlet box, *raccordement* plug receptacle; ~ **femelle étanche à l'eau** f ELECTR *raccordement* watertight socket outlet; ~ **femelle du prolongateur** f ELECTR *raccordement* socket coupler; ~ **femelle de prolongation** f ELECTR *raccordement* portable socket outlet; ~ **de flash** f PHOTO flash contact; ~ **de flash F et X** f PHOTO flash socket for F and X contact; ~ **de gaz latérale** f PRODUCTION downcomer, downtake; ~ **haute tension** f NUCLEAIRE high-potential socket; ~ **d'huile** f PLAST CAOU *pigment pour peinture* oil absorption; ~ **de jack** f ELECTROTEC jack; ~ **de main** f SECURITE hand hold; ~ **mâle** f ELECTR *raccordement* plug; ~ **mâle de courant** f ELECTR *raccordement* plug; ~ **mâle et femelle** f ELECTR coupler plug and socket connection, hickey (AmE); ~ **mâle du prolongateur** f ELECTR *raccordement* socket plug; ~ **de masse** f NAUT electrical earth connector (BrE), electrical ground connector (AmE); ~ **maximale autorisée** f *(PMA)* OCEANO total allowable catch, total authorized catch; ~ **médiane** f ELECTR *transformateur* CT, center tap (AmE), centre tap (BrE); ~ **médiane au secondaire** f ELECTROTEC secondary center tap (AmE), secondary centre tap (BrE); ~ **mobile de connecteur** f ELECTR coupler connector, coupler socket connector; ~ **de montage en surface** f ELECTR *raccordement* surface-mounted socket; ~ **de mouvement** f AERONAUT power takeoff; ~ **multiple** f ELECTR *raccordement* multiple socket, TELECOM multiple seizure, TV multiple-outlet plug; ~ **murale** f ELECTR *raccordement* wall outlet, wall socket; ~ **par unité d'effort** f OCEANO catch per unit effort; ~ **pour casque** f ENREGISTR headphone jack; ~ **pour jeux de barres** f ELECTR *raccordements* bus duct plug-in unit; ~ **pour remorque** f AUTO, ELECTR *automobile* connector socket for trailer; ~ **de pression** f AERONAUT pressure inlet; ~ **au primaire** f ELECTROTEC primary tap; ~ **principale** f ELECTR *raccordement* principal tapping; ~ **programmable** f ELECTROTEC plug timer, time switch; ~ **à puissance réduite** f ELECTR reduced power tapping; ~ **de ravitaillement en vol** f TRANSPORT flight refueling probe (AmE), flight refuelling probe (BrE), in-flight refueling probe (AmE), in-flight refuelling probe (BrE); ~ **de rinçage** f CONS MECA flushing connector; ~ **S** f TELECOM S-universal access; ~ **au secondaire** f ELECTROTEC secondary tap; ~ **au secteur** f ELECTR *raccordement* electrical plug (AmE), mains plug (BrE); ~ **secteur** f ELECTROTEC electrical outlet (AmE), mains socket (BrE); ~ **de sécurité** f ELECTR *raccordement* Home Office socket (BrE), shockproof socket; ~ **de son** f ACOUSTIQUE sound take; ~ **soustractive** f ELECTR minus tapping; ~ **sur l'enroulement** f ELECTROTEC secondary tap; ~ **sur socle** f ELECTR *raccordement* surface socket; ~ **téléphonique** f TELECOM

plug and socket; ~ **de terre** f CONSTR earthing (BrE), grounding (AmE), ELECTR *raccordement* earth connection (BrE), earth wire (BrE), ground connection (AmE), ground wire (AmE), ELECTROTEC earth plate (BrE), ground plate (AmE), earth terminal (BrE), ground terminal (AmE); ~ **de terre de sécurité** f ELECTR *raccordement* safety earth (BrE), safety ground (AmE); ~ **de terre simple** f ELECTR *raccordement* single earth (BrE), single ground (AmE); ~ **de terre superficielle** f ELECTR *raccordement* surface earthing connection (BrE), surface grounding connection (AmE); ~ **de terre symétrique** f ELECTR *raccordement* midpoint earthing (BrE), midpoint grounding (AmE); ~ **de terre du système** f ELECTR *raccordement* system earth (BrE), system ground (AmE); ~ **de transformateur** f ELECTROTEC transformer tap; ~ **tripolaire** f ELECTR *raccordement* three-pin socket; ~ **universelle** f TELECOM S-universal access; ~ **de vapeur** f INST HYDR intake, steam cock, steam valve; ~ **de vapeur de l'injecteur** f INST HYDR injection cock, injector throttle; ~ **de vidange** f CONS MECA drain connector; ~ **de vue** f CINEMAT, PHOTO shot; ~ **de vue d'archive** f CINEMAT stock shot; ~ **de vue au crépuscule** f PHOTO twilight shot; ~ **de vue éloignée** f CINEMAT long shot; ~ **de vue en contre-plongée** f PHOTO low-angle shot; ~ **de vue en infrarouge** f PHOTO infrared photography; ~ **de vue à la lumière du jour** f PHOTO daylight exposure; ~ **de vue au ralenti** f CINEMAT low-speed photography; ~ **de vues aériennes** f PHOTO aerial photography; ~ **de vues avec son direct** f CINEMAT sound take; ~ **de vues en infrarouge** f CINEMAT infrared cinematography; ~ **de vues et enregistrement sonore sur la même bande** f CINEMAT single system; ~ **de vues image par image** f CINEMAT time lapse photography; ~ **de vue à très grande vitesse** f CINEMAT ultrahigh-speed photography

prise:[3] **être en ~** *vi* CONS MECA engage, mesh

prises: ~ **d'eau sur cours d'eau** f pl DISTRI EAU tapping streams; ~ **de vues** f pl CINEMAT shooting

prismation f GEOLOGIE columnar jointing, prismatic jointing; ~ **basaltique** f GEOLOGIE columnar jointing, prismatic jointing

prisme m CERAM VER, EQUIP LAB, GEOMETRIE, OPTIQUE, PHYSIQUE, TELECOM prism; ~ **d'accrétion** m GEOLOGIE accretionary prism; ~ **d'Amici** m PHYSIQUE Amici prism, direct vision prism, roof prism; ~ **basculant** m OPTIQUE dove prism; ~ **de déviation** m INSTRUMENT, TELECOM deviation prism; ~ **diviseur** m CINEMAT beam-splitting prism; ~ **diviseur de rayons** m CINEMAT prism beam splitter; ~ **en toit** m PHOTO pentaprism, PHYSIQUE direct vision prism, roof prism; ~ **de marée** m EN RENOUV tidal prism; ~ **de Nicol** m PHYSIQUE Nicol prism; ~ **objectif** m ASTRONOMIE objective prism; ~ **de petit angle** m PHYSIQUE small angle prism; ~ **polariseur** m INSTRUMENT polarizing prism; ~ **de Porro** m INSTRUMENT Porro prism; ~ **à redressement** m INSTRUMENT image erecting prism, inverting prism; ~ **réfléchissant** m OPTIQUE reflecting prism; ~ **réflecteur** m INSTRUMENT reflecting prism; ~ **à réflexion totale** m INSTRUMENT reflecting prism; ~ **réfringent** m OPTIQUE refracting prism; ~ **rotatif** m CINEMAT intermittent prism; ~ **solaire polariseur** m INSTRUMENT polarizing sun prism; ~ **tournant** m OPTIQUE rotating prism; ~ **à vision directe** m PHYSIQUE Amici prism, direct vision prism, roof prism

prismes: ~ **de déviation** m pl INSTRUMENT

beam-splitting prisms

prisonnier *m* CONS MECA blind stud bolt, standing bolt, stud, stud bolt; **~ à clavette** *m* CONS MECA cotter stud bolt

prix: **~ des communications** *m* TELECOM call charges; **~ courant** *m* TEXTILE market price; **~ coûtant** *m* PRODUCTION cost, cost price; **~ de fabrication** *m* PRODUCTION cost, cost price; **~ de fabrique** *m* PRODUCTION cost, cost price; **~ forfaitaire** *m* PRODUCTION contract price; **~ à la ligne** *m* IMPRIM *composition* line rate; **~ magasin** *m* PRODUCTION warehouse price; **~ de rachat** *m* PETROLE *commerce* buy-back price; **~ rendu** *m* PETROLE *commerce* landed price; **~ de renouvellement** *m* PRODUCTION replacement price; **~ de revient** *m* PRODUCTION cost, cost price; **~ de revient de la surface** *m* EMBALLAGE cost of space; **~ de revient total** *m* TV program cost (AmE), programme cost (BrE); **~ de revient unitaire** *m* PRODUCTION product cost; **~ de transport par eau** *m* NAUT waterage

probabilité *f* INFORMAT, MATH, ORDINAT probability; **~ de dépassement d'un temps d'attente** *f* TELECOM probability of excess delay; **~ d'erreur humaine** *f* QUALITE human error probability; **~ d'erreurs** *f* TELECOM error probability; **~ de fausse alarme** *f* TELECOM false alarm probability; **~ de fission spontanée** *f* PHYS RAYON spontaneous fission probability; **~ de lancement réussi** *f* ESPACE *véhicules* launch success probability; **~ mathématique** *f* MATH mathematical chance, mathematical probability; **~ de non-fuite d'un neutron thermique** *f* NUCLEAIRE thermal neutron nonleakage probability; **~ thermodynamique** *f* PHYSIQUE, THERMODYN thermodynamic probability; **~ de transition** *f* PHYSIQUE transition probability

problème *m* BREVETS problem; **~ des cartes trichromatiques** *m* GEOMETRIE three-color map problem (AmE), three-colour map problem (BrE); **~ du cube** *m* GEOMETRIE cube problem; **~ des deux électrons** *m* NUCLEAIRE two-electron problem; **~ à n corps** *m* ESPACE many-body problem; **~ des trois corps** *m* ASTRONOMIE three-body problem

procaïne *f* CHIMIE procaine

procédé *m* CHARBON process, CONSTR way, PAPIER process, PHYSIQUE method, PRODUCTION process, way, QUALITE, TEXTILE process; **~ acide** *m* PAPIER acid process; **~ additif** *m* ELECTRON additive process; **~ d'ajourage** *m* PRODUCTION notching process; **~ à l'albumine** *m* PHOTO albumen process; **~ d'alimentation par débordement** *m* CERAM VER overflow process; **~ d'analyse** *m* TV scanning process; **~ aspiré-soufflé** *m* CERAM VER suck-and-blow process; **~ d'assemblage** *m* PRODUCTION joining process; **~ aval de fabrication** *m* TEXTILE downstream process; **~ Bessemer** *m* PRODUCTION Bessemer process; **~ de bouclier** *m* CH DE FER shield tunneling (AmE), shield tunnelling (BrE); **~ des boues activées** *m* DISTRI EAU activated sludge process; **~ au catalyseur fluide** *m* GENIE CHIM fluid-catalyst process; **~ catalytique** *m* POLLUTION catalytic process; **~ des chambres** *m* GENIE CHIM chamber process; **~ de chargement sur résidus** *m* POLLUTION load on top process; **~ de cimentage** *m* CONSTR cementation process; **~ de codage** *m* ELECTRON coding scheme; **~ à la colle synthétique** *m* IMPRIM polyvinyl process; **~ au collodion** *m* IMPRIM collodion process; **~ au collodion humide** *m* IMPRIM collodion process, wet-collodion process, wet-plate process, PHOTO wet-collodion process; **~ de copie négative** *m*

IMPRIM negative copying process; **~ couleur par synthèse additive** *m* CINEMAT additive color process (AmE), additive colour process (BrE); **~ de craquage catalytique fluide** *m* CHIMIE orthoforming; **~ de CVD activé au plasma** *m* ELECTRON plasma-activated chemical vapor deposition (AmE), plasma-activated chemical vapour deposition (BrE); **~ de cyanuration** *m* CHIMIE cyanide process; **~ de dépôt chimique en phase vapeur activé au plasma** *m* ELECTRON PCVD, plasma-activated chemical vapor deposition (AmE), plasma-activated chemical vapourdeposition (BrE); **~ destructif** *m* EMBALLAGE destruction process; **~ de désulfuration** *m* CHIMIE mercaptol process; **~ de désulfuration catalytique** *m* CHIMIE unifining; **~ de diffusion thermique** *m* NUCLEAIRE thermal diffusion process; **~ discontinu** *m* PAPIER batch processing; **~ du double creuset** *m* OPTIQUE, TELECOM double crucible technique; **~ "dye transfer"** *m* CINEMAT dye transfer process; **~ en couleur par synthèse additive** *m* CINEMAT additive color system (AmE), additive colour system (BrE); **~ d'enregistrement** *m* ENREGISTR recording process; **~ d'enregistrement "noiseless"** *m* ENREGISTR noiseless recording system; **~ d'épuration d'effluent** *m* RECYCLAGE effluent purification process; **~ d'épuration par boues activées** *m* DISTRI EAU activated sludge process; **~ d'étirage** *m* CERAM VER horizontal drawing process; **~ d'étirage vertical par le haut** *m* CERAM VER updraw process; **~ d'extraction** *m* PETROLE *forage, raffinage, etc* extraction process; **~ FINGAL** *m* NUCLEAIRE FINGAL process; **~ de flottation** *m* CHARBON flotation process; **~ fond bleu** *m* CINEMAT blue screen process; **~ à la fonte et au minerai** *m* PRODUCTION pig-and-ore process; **~ de frittage** *m* GENIE CHIM sintering technique; **~ de frittage par réaction** *m* NUCLEAIRE reaction sintering process; **~ au gélatino-bromure d'argent** *m* PHOTO gelatino-bromide process; **~ de Haber** *m* CHIMIE Haber process; **~ héliothermique** *m* EN RENOUV heliothermal process; **~ Imax** *m* CINEMAT Imax process; **~ d'immersion** *m* EMBALLAGE dipping process; **~ d'impression** *m* IMPRIM printing process; **~ industriel** *m* POLLUTION industrial process; **~ d'injection** *m* NAUT injection procedure; **~ d'injection de ciment** *m* CONSTR cement injection process; **~ inversible** *m* CINEMAT direct positive process, reversal process; **~ d'inversion des couleurs** *m* PHOTO color reversal process (AmE), colour reversal process (BrE); **~ KALC** *m* NUCLEAIRE KALC process, krypton absorption in liquid carbon dioxide; **~ LD** *m* MATERIAUX LD process; **~ de Leblanc** *m* LESSIVES Leblanc process; **~ lithographique** *m* ELECTRON lithographic process, IMPRIM lithography; **~ mesa** *m* ELECTRON mesa process; **~ mixte** *m* ELECTRON mixed process; **~ MOS canal n à grille silicium** *m* ELECTRON n-channel silicon gate MOS process; **~ moulé-tourné** *m* CERAM VER paste mold blowing (AmE), paste mould blowing (BrE), turn mold blowing (AmE), turn mould blowing (BrE); **~ de mouture** *m* AGRO ALIM milling process; **~ Ozalid** *m* (MD) IMPRIM Ozalid process (TM); **~ panavision** *m* CINEMAT panavision system; **~ Pantone** *m* IMPRIM Pantone process; **~ par échange d'ions** *m* OPTIQUE, TELECOM ion exchange technique; **~ par flottage** *m* MINES flotation process; **~ par osmose** *m* GENIE CHIM osmosis process; **~ par synthèse additive des couleurs** *m* PHOTO additive color process (AmE), additive colour process (BrE); **~ par transfert hydrotypique** *m* PHOTO dye transfer process; ~ **planar** m ELECTRON planar process; ~ **poly I** m ELECTRON single-level polysilicon process; ~ **au poly-silicium à simple couche** m ELECTRON single-level polysilicon process; ~ **pour changer d'un système à un autre** m EMBALLAGE changeover procedure; ~ **pressé-soufflé-tourné** m CERAM VER paste-mold press-and-blow process (AmE), paste-mould press-and-blow process (BrE); ~ **radicalaire** m PLAST CAOU polymérisation radical process; ~ **de récupération** m PETROLE recovery process; ~ **de reformage catalytique** m CHIMIE isoforming; ~ **Schüfftan** m CINEMAT Schüfftan process; ~ **de séparation** m GENIE CHIM separation process; ~ **à simple diffusion** m ELECTRON single diffusion process; ~ **de Solvay** m LESSIVES Solvay's ammonia soda process, Solvay's process; ~ **de soudage** m CONSTR welding process; ~ **de soufflage d'oxygène par le fond** m MATERIAUX, METALL oxygen bottom blowing; ~ **soufflé-soufflé** m CERAM VER blow-and-blow process; ~ **soufflé-tourné** m CERAM VER paste-mold blowing (AmE), paste-mould blowing (BrE); ~ **soustractif** m CINEMAT subtractive process; ~ **de soyage à chaud** m CONS MECA hot-dimpling process; ~ **stéréovision** m TV stereovision; ~ **stochastique** m PHYSIQUE stochastic process; ~ **TBP** m NUCLEAIRE TBP process; ~ **de la tige dans le tube** m OPTIQUE, TELECOM rod-in-tube technique; ~ **trichrome** m CINEMAT three-color process (AmE), three-colour process (BrE); ~ **verneuil au plasma** m OPTIQUE plasma-activated chemical vapor deposition (AmE), plasma-activated chemical vapour deposition (BrE), vapor phase verneuil method (AmE), vapour phase verneuil method (BrE)

procéder: ~ **à une étude** vi POLLU MER survey

procédés: ~ **d'assurance de la qualité selon la norme BS 5750** m pl CONS MECA quality assurance procedure to BS 5750

procédure f BREVETS processing, proceedings, INFORMAT, ORDINAT, QUALITE procedure; ~ **d'approche** f ESPACE véhicules approach procedure; ~ **d'approche finale** f AERONAUT landing procedure; ~ **d'approche aux instruments** f AERONAUT instrument approach procedure; ~ **d'approche interrompue** f AERONAUT missed-approach procedure; ~ **d'approche de précision** f AERONAUT precision approach procedure; ~ **d'arrêt du moteur** f ESPACE propulsion shutdown procedure; ~ **d'arrivée** f TELECOM incoming procedure; ~ **d'attente** f AERONAUT holding procedure; ~ **de commande de liaison** f ORDINAT link protocol; ~ **de commande de transmission synchrone** f ORDINAT SDLC, synchronous data link control; ~ **de contrôle** f METROLOGIE inspection procedure; ~ **de contrôle de l'environnement** f SECURITE environmental testing procedure; ~ **de départ** f TELECOM outgoing procedure; ~ **détaillée** f TELECOM DP, detailed procedure; ~ **d'essai des systèmes de freinage** f CONS MECA test procedures for braking systems; ~ **HDLC** f (procédure de liaison de données à haut niveau) ORDINAT HDLC (high-level data link control); ~ **d'initialisation du système** f ORDINAT initial setup procedure; ~ **de liaison** f ORDINAT data link control protocol; ~ **de liaison de données à haut niveau** f (procédure HDLC) ORDINAT high-level data link control (HDLC); ~ **de libération** f TELECOM clearing procedure; ~ **d'opposition** f BREVETS opposition proceedings; ~ **orale** f BREVETS oral proceedings; ~ **de premier secours** f SECURITE first-aid procedure; ~ **de recherche par divi**sion binaire f TELECOM binary search procedure; ~ **de rendez-vous** f ESPACE véhicules rendezvous procedure; ~ **de secours** f AERONAUT emergency procedure; ~ **de stationnement** f AERONAUT docking procedure

processeur m INFORMAT, ORDINAT, TELECOM processor; ~ **acousto-optique** m ELECTRON acousto-optic processor; ~ **actif** m TELECOM active processor; ~ **asservi** m ORDINAT slave processor; ~ **associatif** m TELECOM associative processor; ~ **central** m ORDINAT central processor; ~ **de communications** m TELECOM communications processor; ~ **de commutation** m TELECOM switching processor; ~ **de commutation de messages** m TELECOM message switching processor; ~ **de commutation de paquets** m TELECOM packet switching processor; ~ **d'écran** m INFORMAT, ORDINAT display processor; ~ **en tranches** m ORDINAT bit slice processor; ~ **d'entrée** m ORDINAT IP, input processor; ~ **d'entrée/sortie** m INFORMAT input/output processor, ORDINAT IOP, input/output processor; ~ **en virgule flottante** m INFORMAT, ORDINAT FPP, floating point processor; ~ **esclave** m INFORMAT, ORDINAT slave processor; ~ **frontal** m ORDINAT FEP, front-end processor; ~ **maître** m TELECOM master processor; ~ **matriciel** m ORDINAT array processor; ~ **nodal** m ORDINAT node processor; ~ **de noeud** m INFORMAT node processor; ~ **périphérique** m INFORMAT, ORDINAT peripheral processor; ~ **pipeline** m INFORMAT, ORDINAT pipeline processor; ~ **régional** m TELECOM RP, regional processor; ~ **relationnel** m INFORMAT, ORDINAT relational processor; ~ **de réserve** m TELECOM stand-by processor; ~ **secondaire** m PRODUCTION backup processor; ~ **de secours** m PRODUCTION automatisme industriel hot backup; ~ **de signal** m TV SP, signal processor; ~ **de signaux** m ELECTRON SP, signal processor; ~ **de traitement des appels** m TELECOM CP, call processor

processus m CHARBON, INFORMAT, ORDINAT, QUALITE process; ~ **d'ablation et compression** m NUCLEAIRE ablation; ~ **adaptatif** m ORDINAT adaptive process; ~ **cascade** m PHYS RAYON cascade process; ~ **chimique atmosphérique** m POLLUTION atmospheric chemical process; ~ **de contrôle** m PRODUCTION supervisory process; ~ **de coupe des lisières** m TEXTILE selvage cutting process; ~ **de cuisson** m IMPRIM de la plaque baking process; ~ **de désulfuration humide** m POLLUTION wet desulfurization process (AmE), wet desulphurization process (BrE); ~ **de désulfuration sec** m POLLUTION dry desulfurization process (AmE), dry desulphurization process (BrE); ~ **d'écoulement** m TEXTILE flow-in process; ~ **endothermique** m MATERIAUX, PETROLE raffinage endothermic process; ~ **exothermique** m PETROLE raffinage exothermic process; ~ **hydrothermal** m EN RENOUV hydrothermal process; ~ **industriel** m POLLUTION industrial process; ~ **itératif** m INFORMAT, ORDINAT iterative process, POLLUTION iteration; ~ **limité par la sortie** m INFORMAT output-limited process; ~ **limité par la vitesse des périphériques en sortie** m ORDINAT output-limited process; ~ **de mesure** m METROLOGIE measurement process; ~ **de recombinaison** m ELECTRON recombination process; ~ **de signal optique** m PHYS RAYON optical signal processing; ~ **thermodynamique** m THERMODYN thermodynamic process; ~ **de transformation** m GAZ transformation process; ~ **Umklapp** m NUCLEAIRE de réorientation Umklapp process, flopover process procès-verbal: ~ de recette *m* MECANIQUE *contrats* acceptance report

prodigiosus *m* CHIMIE prodigiosin

producteur *m* GAZ producer

production *f* CHARBON get, output, production, MINES output, production, yield, PRODUCTION generating, yield, generation, output, TEXTILE production, turnout, yield; ~ à la chaîne *f* PRODUCTION mass production; ~ de chaleur *f* THERMODYN heat generation; ~ à la commande *f* PRODUCTION custom manufacture, custom production, job shop, order shop; ~ discontinue *f* PRODUCTION discrete manufacturing, intermittent production; ~ d'électricité *f* NUCLEAIRE electricity generated; ~ en continu *f* PRODUCTION continuous production; ~ d'énergie *f* ELECTROTEC power generation; ~ d'énergie par réaction thermonucléaire *f* NUCLEAIRE thermonuclear power generation; ~ d'essai *f* PETR test production; ~ excédentaire *f* PETR excessive production; ~ du four *f* CERAM VER pull; ~ frigorifique *f* REFRIG refrigeration output; ~ de gaz naturel *f* POLLUTION gas recovery; ~ d'hélium *f* ASTRONOMIE helium production; ~ journalière *f* CINEMAT dailies, rushes; ~ de lithium *f* ASTRONOMIE lithium production; ~ de masse *f* PRODUCTION mass production; ~ maximale équilibrée *f* OCEANO maximal sustainable yield; ~ nette *f* GEOPHYS net output; ~ de paires *f* PHYS PART, PHYSIQUE pair production; ~ par expansion de gaz dissous *f* PETR solution gas drive; ~ par lots *f* PRODUCTION batch process; ~ de la parole *f* TELECOM speech production; ~ par projets *f* PRODUCTION project production; ~ par sections homogènes *f* PRODUCTION intermittent production; ~ spécifique *f* CERAM VER production per unit area; ~ de tissu *f* TEXTILE cloth turnout; ~ de vapeur *f* INST HYDR steam raising, NAUT steam generation; ~ vidéo en reportage *f* TV ENG, electronic news gathering

productique: ~ intégrée *f* ORDINAT CIM, computer-integrated manufacturing

productivité *f* PRODUCTION productiveness, productivity; ~ de la main-d'oeuvre *f* PRODUCTION labor productivity (AmE), labour productivity (BrE)

produire[1] *vt* TEXTILE yield

produire:[2] ~ de la vapeur *vi* PRODUCTION raise steam

produire:[3] se ~ *v réfl* PRODUCTION be generated

produit *m* INFORMAT, ORDINAT product, PRODUCTION yield, QUALITE product; ~ d'addition *m* MATERIAUX additive, PETR dope; ~ adoucissant *m* TEXTILE softening agent; ~ alimentaire *m* AGRO ALIM foodstuff; ~ alimentaire préparé à l'avance *m* EMBALLAGE heat-and-eat food; ~ anti-agglomérant *m* AGRO ALIM anticaking agent; ~ antigélif *m* CONSTR antifreeze; ~ antiretrait *m* CONSTR antishrinkage admixture; ~ antistatique *m* TEXTILE antistatic agent; ~ antitirant *m* IMPRIM *encre, vernis et colle* detack; ~ d'apprêt *m* TEXTILE finishing agent; ~ aromatique *m* AGRO ALIM flavor (AmE), flavoring (AmE), flavour (BrE), flavouring (BrE); ~ assouplissant *m* LESSIVES fabric softener, TEXTILE softening agent; ~ avec emballage thermorétractable *m* EMBALLAGE shrink-wrapped product; ~ de base *m* PETROLE feedstock; ~ blanc *m* POLLU MER white product; ~ blanchissant *m* AGRO ALIM bleaching agent; ~ cartésien *m* INFORMAT Cartesian product; ~ de convolution *m* ELECTRON convolution product; ~ de cure *m* CONSTR curing compound; ~ démulsifiant *m* POLLUTION demulsi-

fying product; ~ dérivé *m* CHIMIE derived product; ~ désinfectant *m* SECURITE disinfectant; ~ desséchant *m* EMBALLAGE drying agent; ~ de la distillation *m* CHIMIE distillate, distillation, MATERIAUX, PETROLE, THERMODYN distillation; ~ à écoulement libre *m* EMBALLAGE free flow product; ~ en bande continue *m* IMPRIM *impression* continuous web product; ~ à épurer *m* GENIE CHIM purifying agent; ~ d'étanchéité *m* VEHICULES sealant; ~ d'étanchéité de dessous de carrosserie *m* VEHICULES underbody protection, undercoat (AmE), underseal (BrE); ~ d'évaporation *m* GENIE CHIM evaporation product; ~ de filtrage *m* GENIE CHIM filtrate; ~ filtré *m* GENIE CHIM filtrate; ~ fini *m* MATERIAUX finished product; ~ imprégnant *m* CHIMIE saturant; ~ intermédiaire *m* MATERIAUX *chimie* intermediate, PETROLE *raffinage* intermediate chemical; ~ d'intermodulation *m* ELECTRON, ESPACE *communications* intermodulation product, TELECOM IM, intermodulation product; ~ ionique *m* CHIMIE ionic product; ~ laitier *m* AGRO ALIM dairy produce, dairy product; ~ de lavage *m* LESSIVES detergent, washing agent; ~ lessiviel *m* LESSIVES detergent, washing adjuvant, washing auxiliary; ~ lyophilisé *m* EMBALLAGE freeze-dried product; ~ naturel *m* AGRO ALIM whole food; ~ de nettoyage *m* INSTRUMENT cleaning fluid, LESSIVES cleaning agent, cleaning material; ~ de nettoyage pour l'industrie *m* LESSIVES industrial cleaning material; ~ non alimentaire *m* EMBALLAGE nonfood product; ~ passé *m* GENIE CHIM filtrate; ~ pétrolier *m* MATERIAUX, POLLUTION petroleum product; ~ polluant *m* SECURITE polluting agent; ~ polymérisé *m* MATERIAUX polymer; ~ de première distillation *m* PETROLE straight-run product; ~ raffiné *m* POLLU MER refined product; ~ de réduction *m* POLLUTION reducing product; ~ sans fuite *m* PRODUCTION leak-free product; ~ scalaire *m* PHYSIQUE scalar product; ~ scellant *m* IMPRIM sealant; ~ de scellement *m* CONSTR sealing compound; ~ secondaire *m* CHIMIE, PRODUCTION by-product; ~ de solubilité *m* CHIMIE solubility product; ~ surgelé *m* EMBALLAGE frozen product; ~ de surmoulage *m* ESPACE *véhicules* potting compound; ~ à teneur réduit en sodium *m* AGRO ALIM reduced salt food, reduced sodium; ~ tensio-actif *m* POLLUTION surfactant; ~ de tête *m* AGRO ALIM first runnings, fore-runnings; ~ d'unisson *m* TEXTILE leveling agent (AmE), levelling agent (BrE); ~ vectoriel *m* PHYSIQUE vector product

produits *m pl* BREVETS goods, PHYSIQUE *d'inertie* products; ~ abrasifs agglomérés *m pl* CONS MECA bonded abrasive products; ~ chimiques *m pl* PAPIER chemicals; ~ chimiques pour développement couleur *m pl* PHOTO color processing chemicals (AmE), colour processing chemicals (BrE); ~ de consommation *m pl* EMBALLAGE consumer goods; ~ en carton ondulé *m pl* EMBALLAGE corrugated products; ~ en cellulose moulée *m pl* PAPIER molded pulp products (AmE), moulded pulp products (BrE); ~ finis *m pl* TEXTILE finished goods; ~ d'intermodulation *m pl* ELECTRON cross products; ~ de lavage *m pl* PRODUCTION washings; ~ lavés *m pl* PRODUCTION washings; ~ logiciels *m pl* TELECOM software products; ~ nouveaux *m pl* CONS MECA new products; ~ pétrochimiques *m pl* PETROLE petrochemicals; ~ pétrochimiques de base *m pl* PETROLE basic petrochemicals; ~ de préparation de montage *m pl* IMPRIM *films de support, de masquage* planning products; ~ réfrigérés *m* EMBALLAGE chilled

goods; ~ **du tamisage** *m pl* PRODUCTION siftings
profil *m* CONS MECA cross section, outline, section, section, INFORMAT, NAUT, ORDINAT, PHYSIQUE profile, PRODUCTION *d'une poutre, d'un rail* cross section, TRANSPORT *d'un pneu* tread; ~ **aérodynamique** *m* AERONAUT aerofoil (BrE), airfoil (AmE), VEHICULES *carrosserie* aerodynamic shape; ~ **de bandage** *m* CH DE FER tire profile (AmE), tyre profile (BrE); ~ **bathymétrique** *m* OCEANO bottom profile; ~ **de came** *m* AERONAUT cam contour, MECANIQUE cam shape, VEHICULES *moteur* cam profile; ~ **de concentration d'impuretés** *m* ELECTRON impurity concentration profile; ~ **de dent** *m* CONS MECA tooth profile; ~ **de dopage** *m* ELECTRON doping profile; ~ **de dopage en cloche** *m* ELECTRON low-high-low doping profile; ~ **en long** *m* CH DE FER, CONSTR longitudinal section; ~ **en travers** *m* CONS MECA, CONSTR *d'une route* cross section; ~ **à gradient d'indice** *m* OPTIQUE graded index profile, TELECOM ; ~ **d'impulsion** *m* TELECOM pulse profile; ~ **d'indice** *m* OPTIQUE index profile, refractive index profile, TELECOM *de réfraction* index profile; ~ **d'indice à gradient** *m* OPTIQUE graded index profile, TELECOM ; ~ **d'indice à loi en puissance** *m* OPTIQUE alpha profile, power law and index profile, TELECOM power law and index profile; ~ **d'indice parabolique** *m* OPTIQUE parabolic profile index, quadratic profile, TELECOM parabolic profile; ~ **d'indice de réfraction** *m* OPTIQUE refractive index profile; ~ **d'indice à saut** *m* OPTIQUE, TELECOM step index profile; ~ **d'indice à saut équivalent** *m* OPTIQUE, TELECOM ESI profile, equivalent step index profile; ~ **inversé** *m* GEOPHYS reversed profile; ~ **à loi en puissance** *m* OPTIQUE alpha profile, power law and index profile, TELECOM power law and index profile; ~ **à mécanique quantique** *m* PHYS RAYON *raies spectrales* quantum mechanical line shape; ~ **de pale** *m* AERONAUT *hélicoptère* blade profile; ~ **parabolique** *m* OPTIQUE parabolic profile, quadratic profile, TELECOM parabolic profile; ~ **de paramètre** *m* TELECOM parameter profile; ~ **prévisionnel de stock** *m* PRODUCTION inventory profile; ~ **pseudosonique** *m* PETROLE pseudosonic profile; ~ **de la raie spectrale** *m* PHYS RAYON spectral line profile; ~ **du rail** *m* CH DE FER *véhicules* rail profile, rail section; ~ **de règle** *m* CONSTR screed profile; ~ **de rugosité** *m* CONS MECA roughness profile; ~ **à saut d'indice** *m* OPTIQUE, TELECOM step index profile; ~ **du sillon** *m* ACOUSTIQUE groove shape; ~ **sismique vertical** *m (PSV)* PETROLE *levé sismique* vertical seismic profile *(VSP)*; ~ **de sonde** *m* OCEANO sounding line, sounding profile; ~ **spatial** *m* POLLUTION spatial pattern; ~ **des températures** *m* THERMODYN temperature profile; ~ **transversal** *m* CONS MECA, CONSTR *d'une route* cross section; ~ **de vitesse** *m* PHYSIQUE velocity profile
profilage *m* AERONAUT fairing, CONS MECA profiling
profilé[1] *adj* AERONAUT streamlined, CONS MECA sectional, ESPACE, PHYSIQUE, VEHICULES *carrosserie* streamlined
profilé[2] *m* CONS MECA section, MATERIAUX steel section, NAUT section, steel section; ~ **de bordure** *m* CONS MECA edging; ~ **à boudin** *m* CONS MECA beaded extrusion; ~ **en métal** *m* NAUT steel section; ~ **en U** *m* MECANIQUE channel; ~ **d'étanchéité** *m* CONS MECA extruded seal; ~ **laminé** *m* NAUT rolled section; ~ **plié** *m* PRODUCTION bending; ~ **standard** *m* ESPACE standard shape; ~ **stratifié** *m* PLAST CAOU *plastiques* laminated section

profil-limite *m* CH DE FER gage clearance (AmE), gauge clearance (BrE)
profilomètre *m* CONS MECA contour follower; ~ **d'état de surface à contact** *m* CONS MECA contact profile meter
profils: ~ **d'emballage** *m pl* EMBALLAGE packaging profiles; ~ **et tolérances de filetage** *m pl* CONS MECA screw thread profiles and tolerances
profond: peu ~ *adj* NAUT shallow
profondeur *f* NAUT *d'eau* depth; ~ **d'aile** *f* AERONAUT chord; ~ **de carène** *f* NAUT extreme depth, molded draft (AmE), moulded draught (BrE), rabbet draft (AmE), rabbet draught (BrE); ~ **de cémentation** *f* CONS MECA case depth; ~ **de champ** *f* CINEMAT, METALL, PHOTO, PHYSIQUE, TV depth of field; ~ **du champ** *f* TELECOM field depth; ~ **de compensation** *f* OCEANO compensation depth; ~ **de coupe** *f* CONS MECA depth of cut; ~ **du creux** *f* CONS MECA dedendum, depth below pitch line; ~ **de destruction** *f* OCEANO collapse depth, maximum depth; ~ **d'eau** *f* EN RENOUV, HYDROLOGIE depth of water; ~ **d'entrefer** *f* ACOUSTIQUE, TV gap depth; ~ **équivalente** *f* PETROLE *forage* equivalent depth; ~ **de foyer** *f* CINEMAT, GEOPHYS, PHOTO, PHYSIQUE depth of focus; ~ **du foyer** *f* GEOLOGIE focal depth; ~ **de frottement** *f* OCEANO depth of frictional influence; ~ **de gravure** *f* IMPRIM *hélio* engraving depth; ~ **de l'hypocentre** *f* GEOLOGIE focal depth; ~ **d'immersion** *f* TRANSPORT depth of immersion; ~ **indiquée sur la carte** *f* NAUT charted depth; ~ **d'investigation** *f* GEOPHYS depth of investigation; ~ **de modulation** *f* ELECTRON modulation depth, PHYSIQUE modulation depth, modulation factor; ~ **de la nappe phréatique** *f* DISTRI EAU ground water depth; ~ **optique** *f* OCEANO optical depth; ~ **de pale** *f* AERONAUT blade depth; ~ **de passe** *f* CONS MECA, MECANIQUE *outillage* depth of cut; ~ **de pénétration** *f* CONSTR, ELECTRON penetration depth, ESSAIS, NUCLEAIRE depth of penetration; ~ **de réglage** *f* CONSTR screed height; ~ **de service** *f* OCEANO operating depth, operational depth; ~ **thermométrique** *f* OCEANO thermometric depth
profondimètre *m* OCEANO depth gage (AmE), depth gauge (BrE), depth meter
progestérone *f* CHIMIE progesterone
progiciel *m* INFORMAT, ORDINAT package, software package, PHYSIQUE software package; ~ **d'application** *m* INFORMAT, ORDINAT application package; ~ **graphique** *m* INFORMAT, ORDINAT graphic software package
progradation *f* OCEANO progradation
prograde *adj* GEOLOGIE creeping
programmable: ~ **par masque** *adj* INFORMAT, ORDINAT mask-programmable
programmateur *m* ELECTROTEC time switch, INFORMAT, ORDINAT programmer unit, scheduler; ~ **horaire** *m* EQUIP LAB *durée* program timer (AmE), programme timer (BrE); ~ **à horloge** *m* REFRIG timer; ~ **de mémoire morte** *m* INFORMAT, ORDINAT programming unit; ~ **de PROM** *m* INFORMAT, ORDINAT PROM programmer; ~ **de travaux** *m* INFORMAT, ORDINAT job scheduler; ~ **des travaux** *m* INFORMAT scheduler
programmathèque *f* ORDINAT program library
programmation *f* INFORMAT programming, ORDINAT coding, programming, TV scheduling; ~ **de base** *f* PRODUCTION fundamental programing (AmE), fundamental programming (BrE); ~**convexe** *f* ORDINAT convex programming; ~ **dynamique** *f* ORDINAT

dynamic programming; ~ **en cours d'exécution** *f* PRO-DUCTION *automatisme industriel* on-line programing (AmE), on-line programming (BrE); ~ **en cours de fonctionnement** *f* PRODUCTION *automatisme industriel* on-line programing (AmE), on-line programming (BrE); ~ **d'impulsion** *f* PRODUCTION one-shot programing (AmE), one-shot programming (BrE); ~ **d'impulsion sur front de descente** *f* PRODUCTION *automatisme industriel* trail-edge one-shot programing (AmE), trail-edge one-shot programming (BrE), trailing-edge one-shot; ~ **d'impulsion sur front de montée** *f* PRODUCTION leading-edge one-shot programing (AmE), leading-edge one-shot programming (BrE), *automatisme industriel* leading-edge one shot; ~ **linéaire** *f* ELECTRON linear programing (AmE), linear programming (BrE), - ORDINAT linear programming; ~ **mathématique** *f* ORDINAT mathematical programming; ~ **modulaire** *f* ORDINAT modular programming; ~ **non linéaire** *f* INFORMAT, ORDINAT nonlinear programming; ~ **paramétrée** *f* INFORMAT skeletal coding; ~ **séquentielle** *f* INFORMAT serial programming; ~ **série** *f* ORDINAT serial programming; ~ **structurée** *f (PS)* INFORMAT, ORDINAT structured programming *(SP)*; ~ **système** *f* INFORMAT, ORDINAT systems programming; ~ **à temps d'accès minimal** *f* INFORMAT miniaturization, minimum-access programming, ORDINAT minimum-access programming

programme *m* INFORMAT, ORDINAT program, TELECOM program (AmE), programme (BrE); ~ **d'affectation du trafic** *m* TRANSPORT traffic assignment program (AmE), traffic assignment programme (BrE); ~ **d'aide** *m* INFORMAT, ORDINAT help program; ~ **d'analyse** *m* ORDINAT trace program; ~ **Apollo d'exploration de la lune** *m* ASTRONOMIE Apollo program of moon exploration (AmE), Apollo programme of moon exploration (BrE); ~ **d'application** *m* ORDINAT application program; ~ **d'arrière-plan** *m* ORDINAT background program; ~ **d'autopsie** *m* INFORMAT, ORDINAT postmortem program; ~ **auxiliaire** *m* INFORMAT support program; ~ **d'avant-plan** *m* ORDINAT foreground program; ~ **de bibliothèque** *m* ORDINAT library program; ~ **de césure et justification** *m* IMPRIM hyphenation and justification programme; ~ **de chargement** *m* ORDINAT loader; ~ **de chargement initial** *m* ORDINAT IPL, initial program load; ~ **de coloriage de l'écran** *m* ORDINAT screen painter; ~ **de commande automatique** *m* ORDINAT APT, automatic programming tool; ~ **de déverminage** *m* INFORMAT, ORDINAT debugger; ~ **de diagnostic** *m* INFORMAT, ORDINAT diagnostic program; ~ **d'erreurs** *m* ORDINAT error program; ~ **espion** *m* INFORMAT spoofing program; ~ **d'essai** *m* CHARBON trial; ~ **d'essais** *m* METROLOGIE test program (AmE), test programme (BrE); ~ **de fabrication** *m* PRODUCTION production schedule; ~ **de forage** *m* PETROLE drilling program (AmE), drilling programme (BrE); ~ **de formatage** *m* ORDINAT formatter; ~ **de formation** *m* CONS MECA training scheme; ~ **générateur** *m* ORDINAT generating program; ~ **de gestion de bibliothèque** *m* ORDINAT librarian program; ~ **horodateur** *m* ORDINAT dating program; ~ **hydrologique international** *m* DISTRI EAU international hydrological program (AmE), international hydrological programme (BrE); ~ **de livraison** *m* PRODUCTION delivery schedule; ~ **mémorisé** *m* INFORMAT, ORDINAT stored program; ~ **de mise au point**

m INFORMAT, ORDINAT debugger; ~ **objet** *m* INFORMAT, ORDINAT object program; ~ **pilote** *m* TV pilot; ~ **piloté par menu** *m* ORDINAT menu-driven application; ~ **de plus courte distance** *m* TRANSPORT shortest-path program (AmE), shortest-path programme (BrE); ~ **de pompage** *m* PETR pumping schedule; ~ **de poussée** *m* ESPACE *propulsion* thrust program (AmE), thrust programme (BrE); ~ **de prévision du trafic** *m* TRANSPORT traffic forecasting program (AmE), traffic forecasting programme (BrE); ~ **de production** *m* PETR flow schedule; ~ **de recherche d'itinéraire** *m* TRANSPORT shortest-route program (AmE), shortest-route programme (BrE), traffic routing program (AmE), traffic routing programme (BrE); ~ **de régulation** *m* TRANSPORT control program (AmE), control programme (BrE); ~ **de régulation de la circulation** *m* TRANSPORT traffic control program (AmE), traffic control programme (BrE); ~ **résident** *m* ORDINAT resident program; ~ **de sécurité routière** *m* TRANSPORT road safety program (AmE), road safety programme (BrE); ~ **de service** *m* INFORMAT, ORDINAT service program; ~ **de signalisation** *m* TRANSPORT semaphoric program (AmE), semaphoric programme (BrE), traffic signals program (AmE), traffic signals programme (BrE); ~ **de simulation** *m* INFORMAT, ORDINAT simulation program; ~ **de soudage** *m* CONSTR welding program (AmE), welding programme (BrE); ~ **source** *m* INFORMAT, ORDINAT source program; ~ **spatial** *m* ESPACE space program (AmE), space programme (BrE); ~ **superviseur** *m* INFORMAT, ORDINAT run-time system; ~ **thermique** *m* CERAM VER annealing schedule; ~ **de traçage** *m* INFORMAT trace program; ~ **de traitement automatique de diagraphies** *m* PETROLE program for computer processing wire line logs; ~ **translatable** *m* INFORMAT, ORDINAT relocatable program; ~ **de tri** *m* INFORMAT, ORDINAT sort program; ~ **utilitaire** *m* INFORMAT, ORDINAT utility program; ~ **de vérification orthographique** *m* INFORMAT spell-checker; ~ **vidéo** *m* TV videoware

programmé *adj* INFORMAT, ORDINAT programmed
programmer *vt* INFORMAT, ORDINAT program, TELECOM schedule, TV program (AmE), programme (BrE)
programmes: ~ **utilitaires** *m pl* ORDINAT utilities
programmeur *m* INFORMAT, ORDINAT programmer
progression *f* MATH progression, sequence
projecteur *m* CINEMAT *d'éclairage* projector, ELECTR floodlight, ELECTROTEC floodlight, searchlight, IN-STRUMENT acuity projector, MILITAIRE searchlight, PHOTO projector, VEHICULES *éclairage* headlamp; ~ **de 10 kw** *m* CINEMAT skylite; ~ **de 500 watts focalisable** *m* CINEMAT pup; ~ **de 5 kw** *m* CINEMAT skylite; ~ **800 watts à quartz** *m* CINEMAT redhead; ~ **d'ambiance** *m* CINEMAT flood, scoop, soft source; ~ **antibrouillard** *m* VEHICULES *éclairage* fog lamp; ~ **à arc** *m* CINEMAT arc projector; ~ **à arc 10.000 watts** *m* CINEMAT brute; ~ **avec son magnétique** *m* CINEMAT magnetic film projector; ~ **ciné** *m* ELECTR *éclairage* cinema projector (BrE), movie projector (AmE); ~ **convergent** *m* ELECTR *éclairage* focusing lamp, intensive projector; ~ **de décrochement** *m* CINEMAT kicker light; ~ **en nappe** *m* ELECTR *éclairage* apron floodlight; ~ **à faisceau concentré** *m* ELECTR *éclairage* spotlight; ~ **à faisceau dirigé** *m* CINEMAT spot, spotlight; ~ **flood 500 watts** *m* CINEMAT basher; ~ **focalisable** *m* CINEMAT multibroad; ~ **intensif** *m* ELECTR *éclairage* cone light; ~ **à lentilles** *m* PHOTO spotlight; ~ **à longue portée** *m*

VEHICULES *éclairage* spotlight; ~ **à lumière unie** *m* CINEMAT *sans faisceau* flood; ~ **à main** *m* ELECTR *éclairage* pistol light; ~ **de mesure optique** *m* CONS MECA optical measuring projector; ~ **de motifs** *m* CINEMAT pattern projector; ~ **ponctuel** *m* ELECTR *raccordement* Houdini eye-light; ~ **de pont** *m* NAUT deck light; ~ **pour les décors** *m* ELECTR *éclairage* scenery lamp; ~ **pour diapositives** *m* PHOTO slide projector; ~ **de poursuite** *m* CINEMAT follow spot; ~ **de profil** *m* METROLOGIE profile projector; ~ **sans lentille** *m* CINEMAT open-face spotlight; ~ **de silhouettes** *m* CINEMAT pattern projector; ~ **de spectres** *m* PHYS RAYON spectrum projector; ~ **spot** *m* PHOTO spotlight; ~ **spot de 500 watts** *m* CINEMAT baby; ~ **spot de 750 watts** *m* CINEMAT baby; ~ **stroboscopique** *m* ESPACE strobe light projector; ~ **de studio avec Fresnel de 10 kw** *m* CINEMAT tenner; ~ **de télécinéma** *m* TV telecine machine; ~ **de texte** *m* TV prompter; ~ **vidéo** *m* TV video projector

projecteurs: ~ **jumelés** *m pl* CINEMAT twin projectors

projectile *m* MILITAIRE missile, projectile; ~ **à décollage assisté** *m* MILITAIRE rocket assisted projectile

projection *f* CONSTR projection, spatter, CRISTALL, GEOMETRIE, IMPRIM, PHOTO *d'une image*, PHYSIQUE projection; ~ **d'abrasif** *f* CONSTR grit blasting; ~ **arrière** *f* CINEMAT back projection; ~ **conique** *f* GEOMETRIE conical projection; ~ **équivalente** *f* GEOLOGIE equa-area projection; ~ **de face** *f* CINEMAT front projection; ~ **à flamme** *f* NUCLEAIRE flame spraying; ~ **de forme conique** *f* GEOMETRIE conical projection; ~ **frontale** *f* CINEMAT front projection, reflex projection; ~ **gnomonique** *f* NAUT gnomonic projection; ~ **horizontale** *f* NAUT half-breadth plan; ~ **image par image d'un décor réel** *f* CINEMAT *pour création de cache* rotoscope; ~ **d'image par spectroscopie électronique** *f* PHYS RAYON electron spectroscopic imaging; ~ **le long de l'axe c** *f* CRISTALL projection along the c-axis; ~ **longitudinale** *f* NAUT sheer plan; ~ **de Mercator** *f* ESPACE, NAUT Mercator projection; ~ **de métal fondu** *f* SECURITE *vêtement de protection* molten metal splash; ~ **orthodromique** *f* ESPACE orthodromic projection; ~ **orthogonale** *f* GEOMETRIE orthogonal projection; ~ **par transparence** *f* CINEMAT back projection, rear projection; ~ **de sable** *f* PRODUCTION sandblasting; ~ **stéréographique** *f* CRISTALL, METALL stereographic projection; ~ **de tungstène** *f* CONSTR tungsten spatter; ~ **de vapeur** *f* INST HYDR steam jet; ~ **verticale du rejet** *f* GEOLOGIE normal throw

projectionniste *m* CINEMAT projectionist

projections: ~ **volcaniques** *f pl* GEOLOGIE ejecta, ejectamenta, volcanic ejecta, volcanic ejectamenta

projet *m* CONSTR design, INFORMAT project, NAUT plan, ORDINAT project, PRODUCTION draft (AmE), draught (BrE); ~ **d'aménagement hydraulique** *m* HYDROLOGIE water resource development project; ~ **d'aménagement par irrigation** *m* HYDROLOGIE irrigation project; ~ **économique** *m* PETROLE *commerce, prospection* economic project; ~ **hydro-électrique** *m* CONSTR hydroelectric project; ~ **de norme internationale** *m* TELECOM DIS, draft international standard; ~ **pilote** *m* PETROLE development project, pilot project; ~ **à réservoir** *m* EN RENOUV *hydro-électricité* storage scheme

projeter[1] *vt* CINEMAT project, screen, CONSTR design, GEOMETRIE project, MINES *la bourre* force, ORDINAT image, TELECOM plan

projeter:[2] ~ **des étincelles** *vi* ELECTROTEC arc

prolongateur *m* EQUIP LAB *alimentation en électricité* extension lead, *verrerie* extension tube; ~ **de pieu** *m* CHARBON follower; ~ **téléphonique** *m* TELECOM telephone extension cable

prolongation *f* CONS MECA extension

prolongement *m* CONS MECA extension; ~ **d'arrêt** *m* AERONAUT *piste* stopway; ~ **de l'axe de piste** *m* AERONAUT extended runway centerline (AmE), extended runway centreline (BrE); ~ **occasionnellement roulable** *m* AERONAUT stopway

prolonger *vt* CONS MECA *durée de service des outils* extend

PROM[1] *abrév* *(ROM programmable)* INFORMAT, ORDINAT PROM *(programmable read-only memory)*

PROM[2] ~ **effaçable** *f* INFORMAT, ORDINAT EPROM, erasable PROM

prométhéum *m* *(Pm)* CHIMIE promethium *(Pm)*

promontoire *m* NAUT headland, promontory

promoteur *m* CHIMIE promoter; ~ **d'adhésion** *m* PLAST CAOU adhesion promoter

prompteur *m* TV autocue, prompter

prontosil *m* CHIMIE prontosil

propadiène *m* CHIMIE propadiene

propagation *f* INFORMAT, ORDINAT, TELECOM propagation; ~ **acoustique** *f* ELECTROTEC acoustic wave propagation; ~ **du déchirement** *f* PLAST CAOU *essai, défaut* tear propagation; ~ **des ondes** *f* PHYS ONDES propagation of waves, PHYSIQUE wave propagation; ~ **des ondes acoustiques** *f* ELECTROTEC acoustic wave propagation; ~ **des ondes hertziennes** *f* PHYS RAYON radio wave propagation; ~ **par trajets multiples** *f* TELECOM multipath propagation; ~ **rectiligne** *f* PHYS ONDES *des ondes lumineuses*, PHYSIQUE, TV rectilinear propagation; ~ **du son** *f* ENREGISTR sound propagation; ~ **sous-marine** *f* TELECOM underwater propagation; ~ **souterraine** *f* TELECOM subterranean propagation; ~ **des vagues** *f* EN RENOUV wave propagation

propager[1] *vt* PHYS ONDES propagate

propager:[2] **se** ~ *v réfl* OPTIQUE propagate

propane *m* CHIMIE, PETROLE propane

propanier *m* PETROLE propane tanker

propanoïque *adj* CHIMIE propanoic

propanol *m* CHIMIE propanol

propanone *f* CHIMIE propanone

propargyle *m* CHIMIE propargyl

propédeutique *f* CHIMIE propaedeutics

propène *m* CHIMIE propene, propylene, PETROLE propene

propénoïque *adj* CHIMIE propenoic

propényle *m* CHIMIE isoallyl, propenyl

propénylique *adj* CHIMIE propenylic

propergol *m* CHIMIE propellant, ESPACE *propulsion* propellant fuel, MILITAIRE propelled charge; ~ **hybride** *m* ESPACE *propulsion* hybrid propellent, lithergol; ~ **liquide** *m* ESPACE *propulsion* liquid propellant, THERMODYN liquid fuel, liquid propellant, lithergol; ~ **solide** *m* ESPACE *propulsion* solid propellant

proportion *f* CHIMIE proportion, MATH ratio; ~ **gaz-huile** *f* PETROLE *production* GOR, gas-to-oil ratio; ~ **d'individus non conformes** *f* QUALITE proportion of nonconforming items; ~ **d'unités non conformes** *f* QUALITE proportion of nonconforming items

proportions: ~ **de l'écran** *f pl* CINEMAT screen ratio; ~ **multiples** *f pl* CHIMIE multiple proportions; ~ **réci-**

proques *f pl* CHIMIE equivalent proportions; ~ **trigon-ométriques** *f pl* GEOMETRIE *d'un angle* trigonometrical ratio

proposition: ~ **d'ordre** *f* PRODUCTION suggested order

propreté: ~ **de l'environnement** *f* SECURITE environmental cleanliness; ~ **de l'environnement dans les espaces clos** *f* SECURITE environmental cleanliness in enclosed spaces

propriétaire *m* INFORMAT, ORDINAT owner; ~ **de navire** *m* NAUT shipowner

propriété *f* CHIMIE property, CONS MECA characteristic, GAZ, GEOMETRIE, MATERIAUX property; ~ **diélectrique** *f* ELECTR dielectric property; ~ **dynamique** *f* PLAST CAOU dynamic property; ~ **en volume** *f* METALL bulk property; ~ **industrielle** *f* BREVETS industrial property; ~ **intellectuelle** *f* BREVETS intellectual property; ~ **liante** *f* MATERIAUX bonding property; ~ **thermique** *f* THERMODYN thermal property; ~ **topologique** *f* GEOMETRIE topological property

propriétés *f pl* GEOMETRIE *des angles*, TEXTILE properties; ~ **communes des ondes électromagnétiques** *f pl* PHYS RAYON common properties of electromagnetic waves; ~ **de drapage** *f pl* TEXTILE draping properties; ~ **élastiques** *f pl* PHYS FLUID elastic properties; ~ **électriques** *f pl* CONSTR electrical properties; ~ **en profondeur** *f pl* ELECTRON bulk properties; ~ **géométriques** *f pl* GEOMETRIE geometric properties; ~ **géotechniques** *f pl* GEOLOGIE geotechnical properties; ~ **isolantes** *f pl* EMBALLAGE insulating properties; ~ **mécaniques** *f pl* CONS MECA, CONSTR, PHYS FLUID, PLAST CAOU mechanical properties; ~ **pétrophysiques** *f pl* GEOLOGIE geotechnical properties; ~ **physiques** *f pl* PHYSIQUE physical properties; ~ **piézo-électriques** *f pl* ELECTROTEC piezoelectric properties; ~ **plastiques** *f pl* PHYS FLUID plastic properties; ~ **de resserrage de la maille** *f pl* TEXTILE self-healing properties; ~ **rhéologiques** *f pl* PHYS FLUID rheological properties

propulsant *m* CHIMIE propellant, MILITAIRE rocket propellant

propulseur *m* CONS MECA propeller, ESPACE thruster, *véhicules* engine, power plant, PAPIER impeller, propeller, POLLUTION propellant; ~ **d'accélération** *m* ESPACE booster; ~ **d'appoint** *m* ESPACE *véhicules* booster; ~ **arrière** *m* NAUT stern thruster; ~ **auxiliaire** *m* ESPACE strap-on booster; ~ **avant** *m* NAUT bow thruster; ~ **diesel-électrique** *m* TRANSPORT diesel-electric drive; ~ **électrothermique** *m* ESPACE electrothermal booster, resistojet; ~ **d'étrave** *m* NAUT bow thruster; ~ **à fusée à ions** *m* ESPACE *véhicules* ion rocket engine; ~ **ionique** *m* ESPACE *véhicules* ion rocket; ~ **ionique à choc électronique** *m* ESPACE electron impact ion engine; ~ **à jet d'eau rotatif** *m* TRANSPORT rotatable water-jet; ~ **latéral** *m* ESPACE strap-on booster, NAUT side thruster; ~ **latéral arrière** *m* NAUT stern thruster; ~ **monergol** *m* ESPACE monopropellant thruster; ~ **de poupe** *m* NAUT stern thruster; ~ **à propergol solide** *m* ESPACE *véhicules* solid propellant rocket, solid-fuelled rocket; ~ **récupérable** *m* ESPACE recoverable thruster

propulsif *adj* CONS MECA impulsive

propulsion:[1] **à ~ nucléaire** *adj* NAUT, TRANSPORT nuclear-powered

propulsion[2] *f* CHIMIE, CONS MECA, ESPACE, NAUT propulsion, VEHICULES *transmission* drive; ~ **arrière** *f* TRANSPORT, VEHICULES *transmission* rear-wheel drive; ~ **biliquide** *f* ESPACE liquid bipropellant propulsion; ~

colloïdale *f* ESPACE colloid propulsion; ~ **hybride** *f* TRANSPORT hybrid propulsion; ~ **à hydrazine** *f* ESPACE hydrazine propulsion; ~ **ionique** *f* ESPACE ion propulsion, ionic propulsion; ~ **nucléaire** *f* ESPACE nuclear propulsion; ~ **par fusée** *f* ESPACE rocket propulsion; ~ **par galets installés sur la voie** *f* TRANSPORT propulsion by stationary drive wheels; ~ **par hélice** *f* TRANSPORT propeller drive; ~ **par jet d'eau** *f* TRANSPORT hydrojet propulsion, water jet propulsion; ~ **par jet hydraulique** *f* TRANSPORT hydraulic jet propulsion; ~ **par laser** *f* ESPACE laser propulsion; ~ **par pression d'air** *f* TRANSPORT propulsion by air pressure; ~ **par turbines** *f* NAUT turbine propulsion; ~ **par vis d'Archimède à pas variable** *f* TRANSPORT propulsion by spiral drive with varying pitch; ~ **à réaction** *f* AERONAUT reaction jet propulsion, ESPACE jet propulsion, propulsion by reaction, rocket propulsion, MILITAIRE jet propulsion; ~ **à voile solaire** *f* ESPACE solar sail propulsion

propylamine *f* CHIMIE propylamine

propyle *m* CHIMIE propyl

propylène *m* CHIMIE, MATERIAUX, PETROLE propylene

propylique *adj* CHIMIE propylic

propyne *m* CHIMIE propyne

propynoïque *adj* CHIMIE propynoic

prorogation: ~ **des délais** *f* BREVETS extension of time limits

prosopite *f* MINERAUX prosopite

prospecteur *m* PETROLE doodlebugger

prospection *f* MINES prospecting, prospection, PETROLE prospecting; ~ **aéroportée** *f* GEOLOGIE airborne survey; ~ **géophysique** *f* GEOPHYS geophysical prospecting; ~ **magnétique** *f* GEOPHYS magnetic survey; ~ **magnéto-tellurique** *f* GEOPHYS magneto-telluric prospecting; ~ **sismique** *f* CONSTR seismic survey, GEOPHYS seismic prospection

prospectus *m pl* IMPRIM dodgers

protactinium *m (Pa)* CHIMIE protactinium *(Pa)*

protagon *m* CHIMIE protagon

protéase *f* CHIMIE protease

protecteur[1] *adj* SECURITE protective

protecteur[2] *m* EQUIP LAB *sécurité* shield, PRODUCTION, SECURITE guard; ~ **en fil de fer** *m* PRODUCTION wire guard; ~ **de ligne** *m* GEOPHYS line protector; ~ **de machine** *m* SECURITE machine cage; ~ **de mandrin** *m* CONS MECA chuck guard; ~ **d'oreilles** *m* ACOUSTIQUE ear protection; ~ **de poignets** *m* SECURITE wrist protector; ~ **à thyristor** *m* ELECTROTEC crowbar

protecteurs: ~ **individuels pour les yeux** *m pl* SECURITE personal eye protectors; ~ **industriels pour oreilles** *m pl* SECURITE industrial hearing protectors; ~ **industriels pour les yeux** *m pl* SECURITE industrial eye protectors; ~ **pour cheveux** *m pl* SECURITE hair protectors; ~ **pour oreilles** *m pl* SECURITE hearing protectors

protection:[1] **de ~** *adj* SECURITE protective

protection[2] *f* ELECTROTEC protection, ESPACE protection, shielding, INFORMAT protection, ORDINAT protection, PHYSIQUE coating, protective coating, PRODUCTION finishing, protection coating, SECURITE guard, guarding, protection, *des bâtiments* safeguarding; ~ **antibruit** *f* CONSTR acoustic fencing, noise barrier; ~ **antigaz** *f* MILITAIRE *guerre chimique* protection against gas; ~ **automatique de trains** *f (PAT)* CH DE FER automatic train protection *(ATP)*; ~ **biologique** *f* NUCLEAIRE biological shield; ~ **des bords** *f* EMBALLAGE edge protection; ~ **cathodique** *f* CHAR-

BON, HYDROLOGIE cathodic protection; ~ de chaîne *f* SECURITE chaincase; ~ climatique *f* SECURITE climatic protection; ~ conditionnelle *f* BREVETS conditional protection; ~ contre l'appel de courant *f* ELECTROTEC inrush current protection; ~ contre le bruit *f* ENREGISTR noise shield; ~ contre le bruit et les secousses *f* SECURITE *construction mécanique* noise and vibration protection; ~ contre les charges électrostatiques *f* CONS MECA antistatic protection; ~ contre les courts-circuits *f* ELECTROTEC, PRODUCTION short circuit protection; ~ contre les défauts à la terre *f* ELECTR earth fault protection (BrE), ground fault protection (AmE); ~ contre l'écriture *f* ORDINAT write protect; ~ contre l'égouttement d'eau *f* PRODUCTION protection against dripping water; ~ contre les erreurs *f* ELECTRON, TELECOM error protection; ~ contre l'exposition au travail *f* SECURITE protection against exposure at work; ~ contre la foudre *f* ELECTROTEC, GEOPHYS lightning protection; ~ contre l'incendie *f* SECURITE fire protection; ~ contre les inversions de polarité *f* ELECTROTEC reverse voltage protection; ~ contre la mer *f* METEO sea defence (BrE), sea defense (AmE); ~ contre les microcoupures *f* ELECTR, PRODUCTION power loss ride-through; ~ contre les pannes de phase *f* PRODUCTION *automatisme industriel* phase failure protection; ~ contre les paquets de mer *f* NAUT protection against heavy seas; ~ contre les radiations *f* ELECTROTEC, PHYS RAYON radiation protection; ~ contre les rayonnements *f* MILITAIRE *guerre nucléaire* protection against radiation, POLLUTION, SECURITE radiation protection; ~ contre la rouille *f* EMBALLAGE rust protection; ~ contre les surcharges *f* ELECTR *circuit, appareil*, ELECTROTEC overload protection; ~ contre les surcharges de courte durée *f* ELECTROTEC short-term protection; ~ contre les surcharges momentanées *f* ELECTR, PRODUCTION momentary overload protection; ~ contre la surintensité de courant *f* ELECTR *sécurité* overcurrent protection; ~ contre les surintensités *f* ELECTROTEC overcurrent protection, PRODUCTION transient protection; ~ contre les surtensions *f* ELECTR *sécurité* excess voltage protection, overvoltage protection, ELECTROTEC overvoltage protection, surge protection; ~ contre la survitesse *f* CONS MECA overspeed protection; ~ contre les transitoires en entrée *f* PRODUCTION *électricité* input transient protection; ~ côtière *f* HYDROLOGIE coastal defence (BrE), coastal defense (AmE); ~ différentielle de courant *f* ELECTR current differential protection; ~ des données *f* INFORMAT, ORDINAT data protection; ~ en écriture *f* INFORMAT write protect, write protection, ORDINAT write protection; ~ de l'environnement *f* POLLUTION, PRODUCTION, RECYCLAGE environmental protection; ~ de fichier *f* INFORMAT, ORDINAT file protection; ~ fixe *f* SECURITE fixed guard; ~ individuelle *f* SECURITE personal protection; ~ de ligne *f* ELECTR *réseau d'alimentation* line protection; ~ de machine *f* SECURITE machine guard; ~ à maximum de courant *f* ELECTR *sécurité* overcurrent protection; ~ mémoire *f* INFORMAT, ORDINAT memory protection, storage protection; ~ de numéro de séquence *f* TELECOM SNP, sequence number protection; ~ par chaussures contre les brûlures *f* SECURITE footwear for protection against burns; ~ par mot de passe *f* INFORMAT, ORDINAT password protection; ~ par thyristor *f* ELECTROTEC crowbar; ~ pendant le soudage *f* SECURITE

welding protection; ~ pleine et entière *f* BREVETS full protection; ~ des points de coincements sur les rouleaux *f* CONS MECA protection of pinch points on idlers; ~ provisoire *f* BREVETS provisional protection; ~ de réseau *f* ELECTR *alimentation* network protection; ~ des rivages *f* DISTRI EAU shore protection; ~ de section de multiplexage *f* TELECOM MSP, multiplex section protection; ~ sélective des champs *f* TELECOM selective field protection; ~ structurelle contre l'incendie *f* SECURITE structural fire protection; ~ de talus *f* CONSTR slope protection; ~ thermique *f* AERONAUT heat shield, ESPACE thermal protection, OPTIQUE thermal wrap; ~ des yeux du visage et du cou *f* SECURITE eye face and neck protection

protégé *adj* PRODUCTION *borne* shrouded, SECURITE guarded; ~ contre l'humidité *adj* MATERIAUX moisture-proof; ~ contre les intempéries *adj* SECURITE weatherproof; ~ contre les moisissures *adj* PRODUCTION fungus-proof; ~ contre la poussière *adj* PRODUCTION dust-tight; ~ contre les poussières *adj* CONS MECA, SECURITE dustproof; ~ par fusible *adj* ELECTROTEC fuse-protected

protège-chaîne *m* CONS MECA chain guard

protège-conducteur *m* SECURITE *pour chariot de manutention à grande levée* overhead guard

protège-fusible *m* ELECTR, PRODUCTION fuse cover

protège-matelas *m* TEXTILE mattress cover

protéger *vt* ESPACE shield, INFORMAT, ORDINAT protect; ~ contre *vt* SECURITE guard against, protect against

protéine *f* CHIMIE protein; ~ animale spécifique *f* AGRO ALIM animal protein factor; ~ brute *f* AGRO ALIM crude protein; ~ du lait *f* AGRO ALIM milk protein; ~ végétale *f* AGRO ALIM vegetable protein; ~ végétale texturée *f* AGRO ALIM TVP, textured vegetable protein

protéique *adj* CHIMIE *substance* proteinic

protérozoïque *m* GEOLOGIE proterozoic

protide *m* CHIMIE protid, protide

protobastite *f* MINERAUX protobastite

protocole *m* CHIMIE, ESPACE, IMPRIM, INFORMAT, ORDINAT, TELECOM protocol; ~ d'accès de ligne *m* TELECOM LAP, line access protocol; ~ de bout en bout *m* INFORMAT, ORDINAT end-to-end protocol; ~ commun d'information de gestion *m* TELECOM CMIP, common management information protocol; ~ de convergence du mode non connecté *m* TELECOM CLCP, connectionless convergence protocol; ~ de la couche physique *m* INFORMAT, ORDINAT physical layer protocol; ~ de couche réseau en mode connexion *m* TELECOM CONP, connection-oriented network layer protocol; ~ de couche réseau sans connexion *m* TELECOM CLNP, connectionless network layer protocol; ~ d'échange de signaux *m* INFORMAT, ORDINAT signaling protocol (AmE), signalling protocol (BrE); ~ d'exploitation *m* CONS MECA performance specification; ~ d'interfonctionnement *m* TELECOM IWP, interworking protocol; ~ de liaison *m* INFORMAT link protocol; ~ monovoie *m* ORDINAT single-channel protocol; ~ multivoie *m* INFORMAT, ORDINAT multi-channel protocol; ~ N *m* TELECOM N-protocol; ~ de réservation rapide *m* TELECOM FRP, fast-reservation protocol; ~ de session *m* TELECOM SP, session protocol; ~ de transfert *m* INFORMAT, ORDINAT transfer protocol; ~ de transmission *m* INFORMAT data link control protocol; ~ univoie *m* INFORMAT single-channel protocol

protoétoile *f* ASTRONOMIE protostar

protolithe *m* GEOLOGIE protolith
protolyse *f* CHIMIE protolysis
proton *m* CHIMIE, ELECTROTEC, PHYS PART, PHYS RAYON, PHYSIQUE proton; ~ **à haute énergie** *m* ESPACE high-energy proton; ~ **solaire** *m* GEOPHYS solar proton
protoplanète *f* ASTRONOMIE protoplanet
prototype *m* INFORMAT, NAUT, ORDINAT prototype
protoxyde *m* CHIMIE monoxide, protoxide
protubérance *f* ASTRONOMIE prominence, CONS MECA boss, ESPACE prominence
proue:[1] **à ~ renflée** *adj* NAUT *navire* bluff-bowed
proue[2] *f* NAUT bow, prow, stem
proustite *f* MATERIAUX *minéralogie*, MINERAUX proustite
provenance *f* HYDROLOGIE *de l'eau* source, TELECOM call origin
province: ~ **faunistique** *f* GEOLOGIE faunal province, faunistic province; ~ **métallogénique** *f* GEOLOGIE metallogenetic province (BrE), metalogenetic province (AmE); ~ **pétrolière** *f* PETROLE petroleum province
provision *f* PRODUCTION allowance; ~ **d'eau assurée** *f* DISTRI EAU assured water supply; ~ **d'eau douce** *f* DISTRI EAU freshwater stock; ~ **de réseau ouvert** *f* TELECOM ONP, open network provision
provoquer: ~ **un appel d'air** *vi* CONS MECA create a draft (AmE), create a draught (BrE); ~ **une émulsion** *vi* IMPRIM *impression* emulsify
proximité: ~ **des marchés** *f* TEXTILE market closeness
prulaurasine *f* CHIMIE prulaurasin
prussiate *m* CHIMIE prussiate
PS *abrév* (*programmation structurée*) INFORMAT, ORDINAT SP (*structured programming*)
pseudacide *m* CHIMIE pseudoacid
pseudoaléatoire *adj* TELECOM pseudorandom
pseudoclivage *m* GEOLOGIE false cleavage
pseudocode *m* INFORMAT, ORDINAT pseudocode
pseudoenclenchement *m* TV pseudolock
pseudoimage *f* PHOTO circle of least confusion
pseudoinstruction *f* INFORMAT, ORDINAT pseudoinstruction
pseudoionone *f* CHIMIE pseudo ionone
pseudolangage *m* INFORMAT, ORDINAT pseudolanguage
pseudomalachite *f* MINERAUX pseudomalachite
pseudomère *m* CHIMIE pseudomer
pseudomérie *f* CHIMIE pseudomerism
pseudomérique *adj* CHIMIE pseudomeric
pseudomorphe *m* GEOLOGIE *métamorphisme* pseudomorph
pseudonitrol *m* CHIMIE pseudonitrole
pseudoplastique *m* CHIMIE pseudoplastic
pseudosaphir *m* MINERAUX sapphire quartz
pseudosphère *f* GEOMETRIE pseudosphere
pseudostéréophonie *f* ENREGISTR pseudostereophony
pseudotachylite *f* GEOLOGIE flinty crush rock
psilomélane *f* MINERAUX psilomelane
PSV *abrév* (*profil sismique vertical*) PETROLE VSP (*vertical seismic profile*)
psychotrine *f* CHIMIE psychotrine
psychromètre *m* EQUIP LAB *humidité*, PAPIER, PHYSIQUE, REFRIG psychrometer; ~ **à aspiration** *m* REFRIG aspiration psychrometer; ~ **ventilé** *m* REFRIG aspirated psychrometer
psychrométrie *f* PHYSIQUE psychrometry
Pt (*platine*) CHIMIE Pt (*platinum*)
PTAC *abrév* (*poids total autorisé en charge*) VEHICULES total permissible laden weight (BrE), total permissible loaded weight (AmE)

PTC[1] *abrév* (*poids total en charge*) VEHICULES GVW (*gross vehicle weight*)
PTC:[2] ~ **pour enroulement** *m* PRODUCTION *automatisme industriel* winding RTD; ~ **pour paliers** *m* PRODUCTION *automatisme industriel* bearing RTD
ptéridine *f* CHIMIE pterin
ptérine *f* CHIMIE pterin
PTM *abrév* (*poids total maximum*) VEHICULES GVW (*gross vehicle weight*)
PTMA *abrév* (*poids total maximal autorisé*) VEHICULES total permissible weight
ptomaïne *f* CHIMIE ptomaine
PTT *abrév* (*poursuite télémesure et télécommande*) ESPACE *communications* TTC (*tracking telemetry and command*)
Pu (*plutonium*) CHIMIE Pu (*plutonium*)
publication: ~ **assistée par ordinateur** *f* (*PAO*) IMPRIM, INFORMAT desktop publishing (*DTP*), ORDINAT desktop publishing, electronic publishing; ~ **précoce** *f* BREVETS early publication
publicité: ~ **photographique** *f* PHOTO commercial photography
publier *vt* BREVETS, IMPRIM publish
publiphone *m* TELECOM payphone, public telephone, telephone kiosk; ~ **à cartes** *m* TELECOM cardphone
publipostage *m* INFORMAT, ORDINAT mailing, mailmerge
puce *f* ELECTR chip, ELECTRON chip, wafer, IMPRIM chip, *composition* footnote call-out, *typographie* bug, ORDINAT chip, TELECOM *électronique* chip; ~ **d'amplificateur opérationnel** *f* ELECTRON operational amplifier chip; ~ **amplificatrice** *f* ELECTRON amplifier chip; ~ **analogique** *f* ELECTRON analog chip (AmE), analogue chip (BrE); ~ **d'arséniure de gallium** *f* ELECTRON gallium arsenide chip; ~ **auxiliaire** *f* ELECTRON companion chip; ~ **à bosses** *f* ELECTRON inverted chip; ~ **de convertisseur** *f* ELECTRON converter chip; ~ **de cryptage** *f* ELECTRON encryption chip; ~ **à la demande** *f* ORDINAT custom chip; ~ **de diode varicap** *f* ELECTRON varactor chip; ~ **électronique** *f* ELECTR silicon chip, PHYS RAYON microchip; ~ **d'interface** *f* ELECTRON interface chip; ~ **logique programmable** *f* ELECTRON random logic chip; ~ **à matrice de portes** *f* ELECTRON gate array chip; ~ **de mémoire** *f* INFORMAT, ORDINAT memory chip; ~ **microprocesseur** *f* ELECTRON microprocessor chip; ~ **NMOS** *f* ELECTRON NMOS chip; ~ **numérique** *f* ELECTRON digital chip; ~ **optoélectronique** *f* ELECTRON optoelectronic chip; ~ **parole** *f* INFORMAT, ORDINAT speech chip; ~ **partielle** *f* ELECTRON bit slice; ~ **à pattes** *f* ELECTRON beam lead chip; ~ **personnalisée** *f* ELECTRON custom chip; ~ **à protubérances** *f* ELECTRON flip chip; ~ **de semiconducteur** *f* ELECTRON semiconductor chip; ~ **semi-personnalisée** *f* ELECTRON semicustom chip; ~ **de silicium** *f* ELECTRON, INFORMAT, ORDINAT silicon chip; ~ **spéciale** *f* ELECTRON exotic chip; ~ **spécialement conçue** *f* ELECTRON custom-designed chip; ~ **spécialisée** *f* ELECTRON dedicated chip; ~ **suppresseur d'écho** *f* ELECTRON echo-cancelling chip; ~ **de traitement de signaux** *f* ELECTRON signal-processing chip; ~ **de transistor** *f* ELECTRON transistor chip; ~ **typographique** *f* IMPRIM *composition* bullet; ~ **universelle** *f* ELECTRON general-purpose chip; ~ **vidéo** *f* ELECTRON imaging chip; ~ **VLSI** *f* INFORMAT, ORDINAT VLSI chip; ~ **vocale** *f* INFORMAT speech chip
puces *f pl* OCEANO itching, niggles

puddlage: ~ **bouillant** *m* PRODUCTION pig boiling; ~ **chaud** *m* PRODUCTION pig boiling; ~ **gras** *m* PRODUCTION pig boiling; ~ **par bouillonnement** *m* PRODUCTION pig boiling

puisage *m* DISTRI EAU *de l'eau d'un puits* drawing, ESPACE *véhicules* transfer, PETR bailing; ~ **dans un réservoir** *m* ESPACE transfer from tank

puisard *m* CONSTR catch pit, collecting pit, sinkhole, DISTRI EAU catch basin, cess pit, cesspool, sump, sump pump, EQUIP LAB sump, HYDROLOGIE sink trap, MINES sink, sinkhole, standage, sump, PETROLE, PRODUCTION *système hydraulique* sump; ~ **d'huile** *m* AERONAUT oil sump; ~ **de puits** *m* MINES sink, sump

puisatier *m* CONSTR sump man

puisement *m* DISTRI EAU *de l'eau d'un puits* drawing

puiser *vt* PHYS FLUID bail, bail out; ~ **avec des pompes** *vt* DISTRI EAU pump, pump out; ~ **à la cuiller** *vt* PRODUCTION skim, skim off

puissance *f* AUTO, CONS MECA, ELECTR, ELECTROTEC, ESPACE, MATH *d'un test de signifiance*, MECANIQUE power, MINES *d'un explosif* strength, PHYSIQUE power, PRODUCTION strength, TELECOM power; ~ **absorbée** *f* ELECTROTEC input power, power consumption, power input; ~ **absorbée maximale** *f* ELECTROTEC maximum power input; ~ **acoustique** *f* ACOUSTIQUE *d'une source* sound power, PHYSIQUE sound energy flux, sound power; ~ **acoustique instantanée** *f* ACOUSTIQUE instantaneous sound power; ~ **acoustique de référence** *f* ACOUSTIQUE reference sound power; ~ **active** *f* ELECTR *courant alternatif* active power, ELECTROTEC active power, real power, PHYSIQUE active power; ~ **aérodynamique** *f* EN RENOUV aerodynamic power; ~ **apparente** *f* ELECTR, ELECTROTEC, PHYSIQUE apparent power; ~ **apparente rayonnée** *f* TELECOM ERP, effective radiated power; ~ **assignée** *f* ELECTR rated power; ~ **de brouillage admissible** *f* ESPACE *communications* permissible level of interference; ~ **de bruit** *f* ELECTRON, NUCLEAIRE noise power; ~ **de calcul** *f* TELECOM processing power; ~ **calorifique** *f* THERMODYN caloric power, heating capacity, heating power, thermal power; ~ **de chaudière** *f* MAT CHAUFF boiler capacity; ~ **complexe** *f* ELECTR complex power; ~ **consommée** *f* ELECTROTEC power consumption; ~ **continue** *f* ELECTR *générateur* continuous output; ~ **convergente** *f* PHYS ONDES *d'une lentille* converging power; ~ **de coupure** *f* ELECTR *d'un interrupteur, d'un fusible* breaking capacity, PRODUCTION *de contacts* rating; ~ **de crête** *f* ELECTR *réseau* peaking capacity, ELECTROTEC, TV peak power; ~ **de creux** *f* NUCLEAIRE *base* base power; ~ **de décollage homologuée** *f* AERONAUT takeoff power rating; ~ **disponible** *f* CONS MECA, ELECTR *alimentation*, EN RENOUV, ENREGISTR *d'un amplificateur*, TELECOM available power; ~ **dissipée** *f* ELECTR *pertes* dissipated power; ~ **effective** *f* CONS MECA, ELECTR effective power, MECANIQUE actual power; ~ **effective en chevaux** *f* CONS MECA BHP, actual horsepower, brake horsepower, effective horsepower, MECANIQUE actual horsepower, PRODUCTION BHP, brake horsepower; ~ **électrique** *f* ELECTR, ELECTROTEC electric power, electrical power, NUCLEAIRE *d'un réacteur* electrical output, electrical power, TELECOM electrical power; ~ **électrique maximale possible** *f* NUCLEAIRE maximum capacity; ~ **électromagnétique surfacique** *f* TELECOM irradiance; ~ **d'émetteur** *f* TV transmitter power; ~ **émise** *f* TELECOM, TV radiated power; ~ **en activité** *f* ELECTROTEC active power; ~ **en**

chevaux *f* AUTO horsepower, hp, CONS MECA horsepower; ~ **en chevaux-vapeur effectifs** *f* CONS MECA BHP, brake horsepower, actual horsepower, PRODUCTION BHP, brake horsepower; ~ **en crête** *f* TELECOM *maritime mobile* peak envelope power; ~ **en heures creuses** *f* NUCLEAIRE off-peak power; ~ **d'entraînement** *f* CONS MECA drive power; ~ **d'entrée** *f* ELECTRON input signal power, PRODUCTION, TELECOM, TV input power; ~ **équivalente de bruit** *f (PEB)* OPTIQUE *d'un photodétecteur*, TELECOM noise equivalent power *(NEP)*; ~ **équivalente sur arbre** *f* CONS MECA equivalent shaft horsepower; ~ **évaporatrice** *f* GENIE CHIM evaporative capacity; ~ **d'excitation de grille** *f* ELECTROTEC grid driving power; ~ **exigée** *f* NUCLEAIRE *théorique* designed power required output; ~ **du faisceau** *f* ELECTRON beam power; ~ **fournie** *f* ELECTROTEC input power, power output; ~ **fournie par le générateur** *f* ELECTROTEC generator output power; ~ **au frein** *f* CONS MECA effective power, TRANSPORT BHP, brake horsepower, braking power; ~ **de freinage** *f* CONS MECA brake power; ~ **au frein en chevaux** *f* CONS MECA BHP, actual horsepower, brake horsepower, effective horsepower, PRODUCTION BHP, brake horsepower; ~ **frigorifique** *f* REFRIG refrigerant capacity, refrigerating capacity; ~ **frigorifique globale** *f* REFRIG overall refrigerating effect; ~ **frigorifique nette** *f* REFRIG net refrigeration effect; ~ **frigorifique utile** *f* REFRIG useful refrigerating effect; ~ **garantie** *f* NUCLEAIRE firm capacity; ~ **du générateur** *f* ELECTROTEC generator output power; ~ **hyperfréquence** *f* ELECTROTEC microwave power; ~ **indiquée en chevaux** *f* CONS MECA gross horsepower; ~ **installée** *f* ELECTR installed capacity, *alimentation* generating capacity, VEHICULES *moteur* installed power; ~ **installée brute** *f* NUCLEAIRE gross installed capacity; ~ **instantanée maximale** *f* ESPACE *propulsion* maximum instantaneous power; ~ **isotrope rayonnée équivalente** *f (PIRE)* ESPACE *communications* equivalent isotropically-radiated power *(EIRP)*; ~ **de levage** *f* CONS MECA lifting power; ~ **massique** *f* AERONAUT, CONS MECA power-weight ratio; ~ **maximale** *f* ELECTR *alimentation* maximum power, NAUT full power; ~ **maximale admissible** *f* TELECOM maximum admissible power; ~ **maximale continue** *f* AERONAUT maximum continuous power; ~ **maximale à la vitesse nominale du vent** *f* EN RENOUV maximum power at rated wind speed; ~ **maximum absorbée** *f* PRODUCTION *automatisme industriel* maximum power requirement; ~ **METO** *f* AERONAUT *maximale sauf décollage* METO power, maximum except takeoff power; ~ **au mortier balistique** *f (PMB)* MINES weight strength *(WS)*; ~ **de moteur** *f* PRODUCTION motor rating; ~ **moyenne** *f* TELECOM average power; ~ **nominale** *f* ELECTR rated power, ELECTROTEC power rating, NUCLEAIRE rated power capacity; ~ **nominale continue** *f* ELECTR *d'un générateur, d'un moteur* continuous rating; ~ **nominale en chevaux** *f* CONS MECA indicated horsepower; ~ **nucléaire** *f* PHYSIQUE nuclear power; ~ **ondulatoire** *f* PHYS ONDES wave power; ~ **optique** *f* ELECTROTEC, OPTIQUE radiant flux, radiant power, optical power, TELECOM optical power; ~ **optique d'entrée** *f* ELECTROTEC optical input power; ~ **optique de sortie** *f* TELECOM optical power output; ~ **de pêche** *f* OCEANO fishing power; ~ **de pénétration** *f* PHYS RAYON *d'un rayonnement de particule* penetrating power; ~ **phonétique** *f* ACOUSTIQUE phonetic power; ~ **de pointe**

f ELECTROTEC peak power; ~ **de pointe de sortie** *f* ENREGISTR peak power output; ~ **de prise** *f* ELECTR *d'un enroulement* tapping power; ~ **de production** *f* ELECTR generating capacity; ~ **de quadrature** *f* ELECTR *courant alternatif* quadrature power; ~ **rayonnante** *f* OPTIQUE radiant flux, radiant power, *d'un signal* optical power, PHYSIQUE radiant flux, radiant power, TELECOM radiant power; ~ **rayonnée** *f* TELECOM radiated power; ~ **de rayonnement** *f* TV radiated power; ~ **réactive** *f* ELECTR *courant alternatif*, ELECTROTEC, PHYSIQUE reactive power; ~ **reçue** *f* COMMANDE incoming power, received power, signal strength; ~ **de régulation** *f* COMMANDE regulating power; ~ **relative** *f* ELECTROTEC relative power; ~ **de résolution** *f* ASTRONOMIE *d'un télescope* resolving power; ~ **de rupture** *f* ELECTR *d'un interrupteur, d'un fusible* breaking capacity; ~ **sans injection d'eau** *f* AERONAUT *moteur* dry power; ~ **de serrage** *f* PRODUCTION holding power; ~ **du signal** *f* ELECTRON signal power; ~ **du signal d'entrée** *f* ELECTRON input signal power; ~ **de sortie** *f* ELECTR output, output power, ELECTROTEC output power, power output, TELECOM output power; ~ **de sortie en mode continu** *f* ENREGISTR continuous power output; ~ **de sortie du générateur** *f* ELECTROTEC generator output power; ~ **de sortie optique** *f* ELECTROTEC optical output power; ~ **de sortie à la saturation** *f* ELECTRON saturation output power; ~ **surfacique** *f* ESPACE power flux density, power per unit area, specific power, GAZ surface power; ~ **surfacique acoustique instantanée** *f* ACOUSTIQUE instantaneous sound power per unit area; ~ **surfacique acoustique moyenne** *f* ACOUSTIQUE average sound power per unit area; ~ **de sustentation** *f* TRANSPORT lifting power; ~ **thermique** *f* CONS MECA, THERMODYN thermal output; ~ **thermique du générateur de vapeur** *f* NUCLEAIRE thermal steam generator output; ~ **thermique volumique** *f* NUCLEAIRE heat output density; ~ **unitaire** *f* NUCLEAIRE unit capacity, unit output; ~ **utile** *f* CONS MECA effective power, EN RENOUV, GAZ power output; ~ **utile maximale** *f* ELECTR *d'un générateur* maximum output; ~ **de ventilateur** *f* CHAUFFAGE fan performance; ~ **vocale de crête** *f* ACOUSTIQUE peak speech power; ~ **vocale instantanée** *f* ACOUSTIQUE instantaneous speech power; ~ **vocale moyenne** *f* ACOUSTIQUE average speech power; ~ **volumique** *f* EN RENOUV power density, GAZ volumic power

puits:[1] **dans le ~** *adj* PETROLE downhole
puits[2] *m* CERAM VER riser, CHARBON pit, shaft, CONSTR hole, DISTRI EAU pit, HYDROLOGIE well, METALL sink, MINES shaft, PETR well, PETROLE hole, well bore, well, POLLUTION sink; ~ **absorbant** *m* DISTRI EAU absorbing well, MINES drain well; ~ **d'aérage** *m* MINES air shaft, ventilation shaft; ~ **à ancre** *m* NAUT anchor well; ~ **d'appel** *m* MINES downcast, downcast shaft, intake shaft; ~ **d'appel d'air** *m* MINES downcast, downcast shaft, intake shaft; ~ **artésien** *m* DISTRI EAU artesian well; ~ **à balancier** *m* PETROLE beam well; ~ **blindé** *m* MINES ironclad shaft, metal-lined shaft; ~ **boisé** *m* CONSTR timbered shaft; ~ **borgne** *m* CONSTR blind pit, blind shaft; ~ **à cabestan** *m* CONSTR capstan pit; ~ **à câbles** *m* ELECTR manhole, *alimentation* cable manhole, ELECTROTEC cable shaft; ~ **de captage d'eau brute** *m* HYDROLOGIE collector well; ~ **central** *m* MINES main shaft, PETROLE moon pool; ~ **à chaînes** *m* NAUT cable locker, chain locker; ~ **de chaleur** *m* ELECTRO-

TEC heat sink; ~ **collecteur** *m* CONSTR collecting pit, MINES sump shaft; ~ **à condensat** *m* PETR condensate well; ~ **de contrôle** *m* GAZ observation well; ~ **creux** *m* DISTRI EAU deep well; ~ **de décharge** *m* DISTRI EAU relief well; ~ **de décompression** *m* DISTRI EAU relief well; ~ **de découverte** *m* PETR discovery well; ~ **de délinéation** *m* PETROLE appraisal well; ~ **de désactivation** *m* NUCLEAIRE *refroidissement, décroissance* cooling cavity, decay cavity; ~ **de développement** *m* PETROLE development well; ~ **dévié** *m* PETR deviation well, PETROLE deviated well, directional well; ~ **de drainage** *m* DISTRI EAU injection well, MINES drain shaft, drainage well; ~ **des échelles** *m* MINES ladder road, ladder shaft, ladder way; ~ **d'électrons** *m* NUCLEAIRE electron sink; ~ **en mer** *m* POLLUTION offshore well; ~ **en opération** *m pl* GAZ operating wells; ~ **en tôle d'acier au bore** *m* NUCLEAIRE boronated steel absorber; ~ **d'entrée** *m* MINES downcast, downcast shaft, intake shaft; ~ **d'entrée d'air** *m* MINES downcast, downcast shaft, intake shaft; ~ **d'épuisement** *m* DISTRI EAU pumping shaft, MINES sump shaft; ~ **éruptif** *m* PETR flowing well; ~ **d'essai** *m* CHARBON test pit; ~ **d'estimation** *m* PETR appraisal well; ~ **d'évaluation** *m* PETR appraisal well; ~ **d'exhaure** *m* DISTRI EAU pumping shaft, MINES sump shaft; ~ **d'exploitation** *m* GAZ operating well; ~ **d'exploration** *m* PETR exploration well, exploratory well, wildcat well, PETROLE exploration well; ~ **d'extension** *m* PETROLE step-out well, outstep well, *forage* extension well; ~ **d'extraction** *m* MINES hoisting shaft, winding shaft; ~ **filtrant** *m* DISTRI EAU filter well, GENIE CHIM filtering well; ~ **foré** *m* DISTRI EAU artesian well, bored well; ~ **de gaz** *m* PETR gas well; ~ **à gaz** *m* PETR gas well; ~ **de gravitation** *m* ASTRONOMIE *d'un trou noir* gravitational well; ~ **improductif** *m* PETR duster; ~ **incliné** *m* MINES incline shaft, inclined shaft; ~ **d'infiltration** *m* DISTRI EAU dry well, soaking pit; ~ **d'injection** *m* DISTRI EAU pressure well, PETR, PETROLE injection well; ~ **d'injection d'air** *m* PETROLE air input well; ~ **intérieur** *m* MINES internal shaft, staple, staple pit, staple shaft; ~ **d'intervention** *m* PETR relief well; ~ **jaillissant** *m* HYDROLOGIE artesian well, geyser; ~ **de mine** *m* MINES mine shaft; ~ **d'obligation** *m* PETROLE *contrats, permis d'exploitation* obligatory well; ~ **d'observation** *m* DISTRI EAU observation well; ~ **de pétrole** *m* PETR oil well; ~ **de pompage** *m* CHARBON pumping pit, pumping well; ~ **de pompe** *m* DISTRI EAU pump shaft; ~ **de potentiel** *m* PHYSIQUE potential well; ~ **principal** *m* MINES main shaft; ~ **productif** *m* PETR production well; ~ **de production** *m* GAZ, PETR, PETROLE production well; ~ **profond** *m* DISTRI EAU, HYDROLOGIE deep well; ~ **quantique** *m* PHYS RAYON quantum well; ~ **de recharge** *m* DISTRI EAU recharge well; ~ **de recherche** *m* MINES discovery shaft, exploration shaft, PETR exploratory well, wildcat well; ~ **de refoulement d'air** *m* MINES downcast, downcast shaft, intake shaft; ~ **revêtu** *m* HYDROLOGIE cased well; ~ **de roue** *m* AERONAUT *atterrisseur* wheel well; ~ **satellite** *m* PETR satellite well; ~ **sec** *m* PETR dry hole, duster, PETROLE dry hole, dry well; ~ **de secours** *m* PETR relief well; ~ **au secret** *m* PETROLE tight hole; ~ **de sonar** *m* OCEANO sonar hole; ~ **de sondage** *m* PETR wildcat well; ~ **sous-marin** *m* POLLUTION subsea well; ~ **thermique** *m* ESPACE heat sink; ~ **thermométrique** *m* PETROLE thermowell; ~ **de travail** *m* MINES winding shaft; ~ **tubé** *m* HYDROLOGIE bored well, cased well, drilled well; ~ **de ventilation** *m*

MINES air shaft, ventilation shaft; ~ **vertical** *m* MINES vertical shaft; ~ **de Yukawa** *m* NUCLEAIRE Yukawa well

pulégone *f* CHIMIE pulegone

pulpe *f* CHARBON pulp, slurry, PRODUCTION pulp

pulsar *m* ASTRONOMIE pulsar; ~ **binaire** *m* ASTRONOMIE binary pulsar; ~ **du Crabe** *m* ASTRONOMIE Crab pulsar; ~ **optique** *m* ASTRONOMIE optical pulsar; ~ **à rayons X** *m* ASTRONOMIE X-ray pulsar

pulsation *f* ELECTROTEC pulsation, PHYS ONDES pulse, PHYSIQUE pulsatance; ~ **angulaire** *f* ACOUSTIQUE angular pulsing

pulsoréacteur *m* AERONAUT pulsating jet engine, pulse jet, TRANSPORT aeropulse, pulsojet

pulvérin *m* CHARBON coal dust, HYDROLOGIE spray; ~ **incombustible** *m* MINES stone dust; ~ **rocheux** *m* MINES stone dust; ~ **schisteux** *m* MINES stone dust

pulvérisateur *m* AGRO ALIM dust mill, CHIMIE sprayer, CONSTR, DISTRI EAU pulverizer, EMBALLAGE, EQUIP LAB *analyse* atomizer, GENIE CHIM atomizer, pulverizer, *broyeur* grinding device, PAPIER atomizer, sprayer, pulverizer, PETROLE sprayer, POLLU MER spray gun, PRODUCTION spray, spray producer; ~ **de liquide** *m* GENIE CHIM spray diffuser, vaporizer

pulvérisateur-mélangeur *m* PRODUCTION, TRANSPORT pulvimixer

pulvérisation *f* CERAM VER shear spray, CHARBON, CHIMIE pulverization, HYDROLOGIE spraying, NUCLEAIRE *pour un solide* comminution, PHYS FLUID spray; ~ **agricole** *f* AERONAUT crop-dusting; ~ **cathodique** *f* ELECTROTEC cathode sputtering, sputtering, METALL cathode sputtering; ~ **de dispersants** *f* POLLU MER dispersant spraying; ~ **d'eau** *f* DISTRI EAU water pulverizing; ~ **électrique** *f* NUCLEAIRE electrospraying; ~ **ionique** *f* CHIMIE ion sputtering; ~ **par décharge luminescente** *f* NUCLEAIRE glow discharge sputtering; ~ **de saumure** *f* REFRIG brine spray

pulvérisé *adj* GENIE CHIM pulverized, PLAST CAOU *pigments, charges, plastiques* powdered

pulvériser *vt* CHARBON, CHIMIE, CONSTR, GENIE CHIM pulverize, PAPIER atomize, powder, spray, POLLU MER spray

pulvérulence *f* GENIE CHIM pulverizing equipment, MATERIAUX powderiness

pulvérulent *adj* CHARBON powder form, GENIE CHIM pulverulent, GEOLOGIE, MATERIAUX powdery

punaise *f* IMPRIM *typographie* bug

pupille: ~ **d'entrée** *f* PHYSIQUE entrance pupil; ~ **de sortie** *f* PHYSIQUE exit pupil

pupinisation *f* ELECTROTEC coil loading

pupitre *m* ELECTR *contrôle*, NAUT console, TELECOM *dirigeur* switchboard; ~ **automatique** *m* TELECOM automanual switchboard, automatic switchboard; ~ **de commande automatique** *m* TELECOM automanual switchboard, automatic switchboard; ~ **de commande** *m* CH DE FER driving desk, ELECTR control console, INSTRUMENT control desk, NAUT console, TV control console, switchboard; ~ **de commande debout** *m* NUCLEAIRE bench board; ~ **de commande du réacteur** *m* NUCLEAIRE reactor control board; ~ **de contrôle** *m* ELECTR control console; ~ **d'éclairage** *m* CINEMAT lighting console; ~ **de mixage** *m* CINEMAT sound control desk, ENREGISTR mixing desk, sound console; ~ **principal de commande** *m* IMPRIM master control desk; ~ **de prise de son** *m* ACOUSTIQUE sound take desk; ~ **de régie** *m* TV control console, production console; ~ **de régie finale** *m* TV master control panel; ~ **de régie image** *m* TV vision mixer; ~ **de trucages** *m* TV special effects generator

pur[1] *adj* POLLU MER neat

pur:[2] ~ **chiffon** *m* PAPIER all-rag paper

pureau *m* CONSTR bare, margin

pureté *f* GAZ purity; ~ **de l'air** *f* POLLUTION air purity; ~ **de polarisation** *f* ESPACE *communications* polarization purity; ~ **radioactive** *f* PHYS RAYON radioactive purity

purge *f* CONS MECA *des freins* bleeding, DISTRI EAU draining, INFORMAT, ORDINAT purging, PETROLE bleeding, purging, REFRIG bleed-off; ~ **de l'air** *f* NUCLEAIRE air drain, bleeding, vent, venting; ~ **des freins** *f* AUTO brake bleeder unit; ~ **sous pression** *f* DISTRI EAU blowdown

purgé: ~ **par gaz** *adj* EMBALLAGE gas-flushed

purger *vt* CHARBON bleed off, CONS MECA bleed, DISTRI EAU blow down, blow off, drain, MECANIQUE drain, PETR bleed down, PRODUCTION *cylindre* drain

purgeur *m* AUTO bleed valve, CH DE FER *véhicules* drain valve, CONSTR cylinder cock, drain cock, drain-off cock, drip cock, PETROLE steam trap; ~ **d'air** *m* EMBALLAGE air purger, NUCLEAIRE air drain valve, air vent; ~ **automatique** *m* INST HYDR steam trap; ~ **à flotteur** *m* INST HYDR float trap; ~ **d'huile** *m* REFRIG oil drain; ~ **de vapeur** *m* PAPIER steam trap; ~ **de vapeur d'eau** *m* CONS MECA steam trap

purificateur *m* CHIMIE, GENIE CHIM purifier

purification: ~ **de l'eau** *f* GENIE CHIM water purification; ~ **du gaz** *f* GAZ gas cleaning; ~ **par fusion en zones** *f* METALL zone refining

purifier *vt* CHARBON clean, CHIMIE purify, DISTRI EAU purify, GENIE CHIM clarify

purin *m* RECYCLAGE slurry

purine *f* CHIMIE purine

purpurine *f* CHIMIE purpurin

purpuroxanthine *f* CHIMIE purpuroxanthin

putréfaction: **en** ~ *adj* AGRO ALIM putrescent, putrid

putréfier: **se** ~ *v réfl* AGRO ALIM putrefy

putrescent *adj* AGRO ALIM putrescent

PVC *abrév (polyvinylchlorure)* CONSTR, ELECTROTEC, MATERIAUX, PLAST CAOU PVC *(polyvinyl chloride)*

PVT *abrév (perte de verrouillage de trame)* TELECOM LFA *(loss of frame alignment)*

pyargyrite *f* MINERAUX pyrargyrite

pycnite *f* MINERAUX pycnite

pycnomètre *m* EQUIP LAB *densité* density bottle, pycnometer, pyknometer, PETROLE, PHYSIQUE pycnometer, pyknometer

pylône *m* AERONAUT pylon, CONSTR lattice tower, pylon, trellis post, tower, ELECTR *réseau* pylon, tower, ELECTROTEC pylon, PRODUCTION standard; ~ **d'antenne** *m* NAUT aerial mast, antenna mast; ~ **d'arrêt** *m* ELECTR terminal tower, *réseau* dead end tower; ~ **central** *m* AERONAUT control pedestal; ~ **en treillis** *m* ELECTR *ligne aérienne* lattice tower; ~ **d'étai** *m* ELECTR dead end tower; ~ **étayé** *m* ELECTR dead end tower; ~ **de haubanage** *m* ELECTR span pole, *ligne aérienne* stay pole, anchoring tower; ~ **à haubans** *m* ELECTR span pole, *ligne aérienne* stay pole, anchoring tower; ~ **hertzien** *m* TELECOM microwave tower; ~ **de lignes électriques aériennes** *m* ELECTR *réseau* transmission tower; ~ **porteur** *m* ELECTR *réseau* supporting pylon; ~ **repliable** *m* AERONAUT folding pylon; ~ **de téléphérique** *m* TRANSPORT cable support; ~ **de**

transposition *m* ELECTR *réseau* transposition tower

pyr *m* METROLOGIE decimal candle

pyramide *f* ELECTR *réseau de distribution* tower, GEOMETRIE pyramid; ~ **alimentaire** *f* POLLUTION ecological pyramid

pyran *m* CHIMIE pyran

pyranne *m* CHIMIE pyran

pyrannose *m* CHIMIE pyranose

pyranomètre *m* EN RENOUV pyranometer; ~ **spectral** *m* EN RENOUV spectral pyranometer

pyrargyrite *f* MINERAUX argyrythrose

pyrazine *f* CHIMIE pyrazine

pyrazol *m* CHIMIE pyrazole

pyrazoline *f* CHIMIE pyrazoline

pyrazolone *f* CHIMIE pyrazolone

pyrène *m* CHIMIE pyrene

pyrhéliomètre *m* EN RENOUV pyrheliometer

pyridazine *f* CHIMIE pyridazin

pyridine *f* CHIMIE pyridine

pyridone *f* CHIMIE pyridone

pyrimidine *f* CHIMIE pyrimidine

pyrite *f* MINERAUX iron pyrite, pyrite, MINES iron pyrite, pyrite, , sulphur ore (BrE); ~ **aurifère** *f* MINERAUX auriferous pyrites; ~ **blanche** *f* MINERAUX white iron pyrites; ~ **de cuivre** *f* MINERAUX copper pyrites; ~ **de fer** *f* MINERAUX iron pyrite, pyrite, MINES iron pyrite, pyrite, sulfur ore (AmE), sulphur ore (BrE); ~ **jaune** *f* MINERAUX iron pyrite, pyrite, MINES iron pyrite, pyrite, sulfur ore (AmE), sulphur ore (BrE); ~ **martiale** *f* MINERAUX iron pyrite, pyrite

pyrites *f pl* MINERAUX pyrites

pyritique *adj* MATERIAUX, MINERAUX pyritic

pyroacétique *adj* CHIMIE pyroacetic

pyroarséniate *m* CHIMIE pyroarsenate

pyroborique *adj* CHIMIE pyroboric

pyrocatéchine *f* CHIMIE pyrocatechin

pyrochlore *m* MINERAUX pyrochlore

pyrochroïte *f* MINERAUX pyrochroite

pyroélectricité *f* CRISTALL pyroelectricity

pyroélectrique *adj* CRISTALL pyroelectric

pyrogallique *adj* CHIMIE *acide* pyrogallic

pyrogallol[1] *adj* CHIMIE *acide* pyrogallic

pyrogallol[2] *m* CHIMIE pyrogallol

pyrogénation *f* THERMODYN pyrogenic reaction

pyrogène *adj* THERMODYN pyrogenic

pyrolusite *f* MINERAUX pyrolusite

pyrolyse *f* AGRO ALIM, CHIMIE, GAZ, MATERIAUX pyrolysis

pyrolytique *adj* CHIMIE pyrolytic

pyroméconique *adj* CHIMIE pyromeconic

pyromellique *adj* CHIMIE pyromellitic

pyromètre *m* CHARBON, ELECTR, EQUIP LAB *mesure de température*, PHYS RAYON, PHYSIQUE, THERMODYN pyrometer; ~ **chromatique** *m* THERMODYN colorimetric pyrometer; ~ **à couleurs** *m* PHYS RAYON color pyrometer (AmE), colour pyrometer (BrE); ~ **à disparition de filament** *m* PHYSIQUE disappearing filament pyrometer; ~ **optique** *m* PHYS RAYON, PHYSIQUE optical pyrometer; ~ **à rayonnement** *m* EQUIP LAB *mesure de température*, GEOPHYS, PHYSIQUE radiation pyrometer; ~ **à rayonnement total** *m* PHYSIQUE total radiation pyrometer

pyrométrie *f* PHYSIQUE, THERMODYN pyrometry

pyrométrique *adj* THERMODYN pyrometric

pyromorphite *f* MINERAUX pyromorphite

pyromucique *adj* CHIMIE *acide* pyromucic

pyrone *f* CHIMIE pyrone

pyrope *m* MINERAUX pyrope

pyrophorique *adj* CHIMIE pyrophoric

pyrophosphate *m* CHIMIE pyrophosphate

pyrophosphoreux *adj* CHIMIE pyrophosphorous

pyrophosphorique *adj* CHIMIE pyrophosphoric

pyrophyllite *f* MINERAUX, PETROLE pyrophyllite

pyrorthite *f* MINERAUX pyrorthite

pyrosclérite *f* MINERAUX pyrosclerite

pyroscope *m* PHYSIQUE pyroscope

pyrostat *m* PHYSIQUE pyrostat

pyrostibite *f* MINERAUX pyrostibite

pyrosulfate *m* CHIMIE pyrosulfate (AmE), pyrosulphate (BrE)

pyrosulfite *m* CHIMIE pyrosulfite (AmE), pyrosulphite (BrE)

pyrosulfurique *adj* CHIMIE pyrosulfuric (AmE), pyrosulphuric (BrE)

pyrosulfuryle *adj* CHIMIE pyrosulfuryl (AmE), pyrosulphuryl (BrE)

pyrotechnie *f* ESPACE pyrotechnics

pyroxène *m* MINERAUX pyroxene

pyrrhotine *f* MINERAUX pyrrhotine, pyrrhotite

pyrrhotite *f* MINERAUX magnetic pyrites

pyrrol *m* CHIMIE pyrrole

pyrrole *m* CHIMIE pyrrole

pyrrolidine *f* CHIMIE pyrrolidine

pyrrolidone *f* CHIMIE pyrrolidone

pyrroline *f* CHIMIE pyrroline

pyruvate *m* CHIMIE pyruvate

pyruvique *adj* CHIMIE pyruvic

Q

Q: ~ **mètre** *m* PHYSIQUE Q-meter

QMAC *abrév (qualité moyenne après contrôle)* QUALITE AOQ *(average outgoing quality)*

quadrac *m* ELECTROTEC quadrac

quadrangulaire *adj* GEOMETRIE quadrangular

quadrant *m* ASTRONOMIE, GEOMETRIE quadrant

quadratin *m (em)* IMPRIM emquad *(em)*

quadratique *adj* CRISTALL tetragonal, MATH quadratic, PHYSIQUE square-law

quadrature:[1] **en ~** *adj* ELECTRON, PHYSIQUE in quadrature

quadrature[2] *f* ASTRONOMIE, ELECTRON, EN RENOUV, INFORMAT, ORDINAT, PHYSIQUE, TV quadrature; ~ **du cercle** *f* GEOMETRIE quadrature, squaring the circle; ~ **gaussienne** *f* INFORMAT, ORDINAT Gaussian quadrature; ~ **de phase** *f* ELECTR quadrature, ELECTRON phase quadrature

quadrature:[3] **être en ~ avance** *vi* PHYSIQUE lead in phase by half pi; **être en ~ retard** *vi* PHYSIQUE lag

quadribasique *adj* CHIMIE quadribasic

quadrichromie *f* IMPRIM four-color printing (AmE), four-colour process (BrE), *impression* four-color process (AmE), four-colour printing (BrE)

quadricycle *m* CHIMIE quadricycle

quadrilatère[1] *adj* GEOMETRIE four-sided, quadrilateral

quadrilatère[2] *m* GEOMETRIE quadrangle

quadrillage *m* CINEMAT graticule, TV grating, raster; ~ **de l'écran cathodique** *m* IMPRIM raster

quadriphase *adj* ELECTRON four-phase

quadriplace *m* AERONAUT four-seat aircraft

quadripolaire *adj* ELECTR four-polar, four-pole

quadripôle *m* ELECTR *réseau* network, quadripole, ELECTROTEC *réseau* four-terminal network, quadripole, PHYSIQUE *réseau* quadripole; ~ **actif** *m* ELECTROTEC active quadripole; ~ **linéaire** *m* ELECTR *réseau* linear four-terminal network; ~ **passif** *m* ELECTROTEC passive quadripole

quadriréacteur *m* AERONAUT four-engine jet aircraft

quadrivecteur *m* PHYSIQUE four vector

quadroxyde *m* CHIMIE quadroxide

quadruplet *m* PHYSIQUE quartet

quadrupôle *m* ELECTROTEC, PHYSIQUE quadrupole; ~ **électrique** *m* ELECTROTEC electric quadrupole

quai *m* CH DE FER, CONSTR platform, NAUT dock, pier, quay, wharf, TRANSPORT quay; ~ **d'armement** *m* NAUT fitting-out berth; ~ **de charbonnage** *m* TRANSPORT coal wharf; ~ **de chargement** *m* TRANSPORT freight depot (AmE), goods depot (BrE), loading dock; ~ **à conteneurs** *m* TRANSPORT container wharf; ~ **d'embarquement** *m* TRANSPORT boarding platform; ~ **en îlot** *m* CH DE FER island platform; ~ **pétrolier** *m* TRANSPORT oil pier; ~ **surélevé** *m* CH DE FER elevated platform

qualificatif: ~ **du code d'identification** *m* TELECOM identification code qualifier; ~ **des informations d'autorisation** *m* TELECOM authorization information qualifier; ~ **de référence du destinataire** *m* TELECOM recipient reference qualifier

qualification: ~ **de contrôle d'approche** *f* AERONAUT approach control rating; ~ **entretien d'aéronef** *f* AERONAUT aircraft maintenance rating; ~ **pour usage spatial** *f* ESPACE space qualification; ~ **radar** *f* AERONAUT radar rating; ~ **radar d'approche de précision** *f* AERONAUT precision approach radar rating; ~ **radar d'approche de surveillance** *f* AERONAUT surveillance approach radar rating; ~ **révisions d'aéronef** *f* AERONAUT aircraft overhaul rating; ~ **de vol aux instruments** *f* AERONAUT instrument rating; ~ **de vol aux instruments monopilote** *f* AERONAUT single pilot instrument rating; ~ **de vol aux instruments pilote unique** *f* AERONAUT single pilot instrument rating

qualitatif *adj* CHIMIE qualitative

qualité *f* ACOUSTIQUE quality, MATERIAUX *de l'acier* grade; ~ **des agrégats** *f* CONSTR quality of aggregate; ~ **antenne** *f* TV *d'une émission* air quality, broadcast quality; ~ **boulangère** *f* AGRO ALIM baking quality; ~ **brouillon** *f* IMPRIM draft quality; ~ **de carburant** *f* AERONAUT fuel grade; ~ **courrier** *f* IMPRIM, ORDINAT LQ, letter quality; ~ **dégradée** *f* TELECOM lower quality of service; ~ **de l'eau** *f* DISTRI EAU quality of water, water quality, EN RENOUV, HYDROLOGIE water quality; ~ **d'eau potable** *f* DISTRI EAU drinking water quality; ~ **économique** *f* QUALITE economic quality; ~ **d'écoulement du trafic** *f* TELECOM grade of service; ~ **d'écoute** *f* CINEMAT quality of reproduction; ~ **estimée** *f* QUALITE assessed quality; ~ **de fonctionnement** *f* ORDINAT performance; ~ **intolérable** *f* TELECOM unacceptable quality; ~ **listage** *f* PRODUCTION draft quality; ~ **moyenne après contrôle** *f (QMAC)* QUALITE average outgoing quality *(AOQ)*; ~ **ordinaire** *f* PRODUCTION common quality; ~ **de papier** *f* EMBALLAGE paper grade; ~ **de papier utilisée pour imprimer** *f* EMBALLAGE printings; ~ **par dessin** *f* CONS MECA quality through design; ~ **de pénétration** *f* CONSTR penetration grade; ~ **de planéité** *f* CONS MECA *des faces de mesure* flatness quality; ~ **pseudo-courrier** *f* INFORMAT, ORDINAT NLQ, near letter quality; ~ **de service** *f* TELECOM QOS, quality of service, grade of service; ~ **sonore** *f* TELECOM sound quality; ~ **téléphonique** *f* TELECOM *circuit* voice grade; ~ **de transmission** *f* TELECOM transmission quality; ~ **de vitrage** *f* CERAM VER glazing quality

qualités: ~ **nautiques** *f pl* NAUT seakeeping qualities

quantificateur *m* ELECTRON, INFORMAT quantizer, MATH quantifier, ORDINAT, TELECOM quantizer

quantification *f* ELECTRON, INFORMAT, ORDINAT, PHYSIQUE quantization; ~ **des blocs** *f* TELECOM block quantization; ~ **des lots** *f* PRODUCTION lot sizing; ~ **des ordres** *f* PRODUCTION lot sizing; ~ **du risque** *f* QUALITE risk quantification; ~ **de signal** *f* TELECOM signal quantization; ~ **du signal d'entrée** *f* ELECTRON input signal quantization; ~ **spatiale** *f* PHYSIQUE spatial quantization

quantifier *vt* CONSTR quantify, ELECTRON, INFORMAT, ORDINAT quantize

quantique *adj* PHYSIQUE quantum

quantitatif *adj* CHIMIE quantitative

quantité *f* ELECTRON quantity; ~ **analogique** *f* INFORMAT, ORDINAT analog quantity; ~ **de chaleur** *f* PHYSIQUE quantity of heat; ~ **critique** *f* NUCLEAIRE chain reacting amount, critical amount; ~ **de décision** *f* INFORMAT decision content; ~ **économique** *f* PRODUCTION economic order quantity; ~ **en stock** *f* PRODUCTION stock on hand; ~ **expédiée** *f* PRODUCTION shipped quantity; ~ **fixe de réapprovisionnement** *f* PRODUCTION fixed order quantity; ~ **de froid** *f* CHARBON cold content; ~ **d'information** *f* INFORMAT information content; ~ **de lumière** *f* PHYSIQUE quantity of light; ~ **de matière** *f* PHYSIQUE amount of substance; ~ **minimale détectable** *f* POLLUTION lower limit of detectability; ~ **de mouvement** *f* CONS MECA, MECANIQUE, PHYSIQUE momentum; ~ **de mouvement électromagnétique** *f* PHYSIQUE electromagnetic momentum; ~ **négative** *f* GEOMETRIE minus amount; ~ **photométrique énergétique** *f* NUCLEAIRE radiant quantity; ~ **du premier ordre** *f* GEOMETRIE first-order quantity; ~ **réalisée** *f* PRODUCTION quantity completed; ~ **de réapprovisionnement** *f* PRODUCTION reorder quantity; ~ **rebutée** *f* PRODUCTION rejected quantity, scrap quantity; ~ **rejetée** *f* PRODUCTION quantity declared unfit; ~ **restante** *f* PRODUCTION *du stock* balance; ~ **du second ordre** *f* GEOMETRIE second-order quantity; ~ **à soustraire** *f* INFORMAT subtrahend

quantum *m* INFORMAT, ORDINAT *théorie*, PHYS PART, PHYSIQUE quantum; ~ **d'action** *m* PHYSIQUE quantum of action; ~ **de flux** *m* PHYSIQUE flux quantum; ~ **de rayonnement gamma** *m* PHYS PART gamma ray quantum

quarantaine *f* TRANSPORT quarantine

quarantièmes: ~ **rugissants** *m pl* NAUT roaring forties, OCEANO roaring forties, westerlies

quark *m* PHYS PART, PHYSIQUE quark; ~ **bas** *m* PHYS PART, PHYSIQUE down quark; ~ **de beauté** *m* PHYS PART beauty quark, bottom quark, PHYSIQUE beauty quark; ~ **aventurine** *m* MINERAUX aventurine quartz; ~ **bleu** *m* PHYSIQUE blue quark; ~ **bottom** *m* PHYSIQUE bottom quark; ~ **charmé** *m* PHYS PART charm quark, PHYSIQUE charmed quark; ~ **étrange** *m* PHYS PART, PHYSIQUE strange quark; ~ **haut** *m* PHYS PART up quark; ~ **rouge** *m* PHYSIQUE red quark; ~ **de sommet** *m* PHYS PART top quark; ~ **top** *m* PHYS PART, PHYSIQUE top quark; ~ **up** *m* PHYSIQUE up quark; ~ **vert** *m* PHYSIQUE green quark

quart:[1] **de** ~ *adj* NAUT on watch

quart[2] *m* METROLOGIE quart, PETROLE shift (BrE), tour (AmE); ~ **de cercle** *m* CONS MECA *d'un compas*, GEOMETRIE quadrant; ~ **de longueur d'onde** *m* ELECTRON quarter wavelength; ~ **de masque** *m* SECURITE quarter mask; ~ **au mouillage** *m* MILITAIRE anchor watch; ~ **de nuit** *m* MILITAIRE *service de veille de quatre heures sur un bateau* night watch; ~ **de ton** *m* IMPRIM *photogravure* quarter tone

quart-de-rond *m* CONSTR ovolo, quarter round

quarte *f* ACOUSTIQUE fourth, ELECTROTEC, PHYSIQUE quad; ~ **en étoile** *f* ELECTROTEC, PHYSIQUE star quad; ~ **juste** *f* ACOUSTIQUE perfect fourth; ~ **à paires combinables** *f* ELECTROTEC multiple twin quad

quarter *m* METROLOGIE quarter

quartet *m* INFORMAT, ORDINAT nibble; ~ **inférieur** *m* PRODUCTION *automatisme industriel* lower nibble

quartier: ~ **tournant** *m* CONSTR quarter space

quartier-maître *m* NAUT quartermaster

quarto *m* PRODUCTION four-high

quartz *m* CINEMAT quartz crystal, ELECTRON, MATERIAUX, MINERAUX, PHYSIQUE quartz; ~ **aventurine** *m* MINERAUX aventurine quartz; ~ **bleu** *m* MINERAUX blue quartz, sapphire quartz; ~ **citrine** *m* MINERAUX citrine, citrine quartz; ~ **enfumé** *m* MINERAUX smoky quartz; ~ **de filtrage** *m* ELECTRON filter crystal; ~ **fondu** *m* OPTIQUE, TELECOM fused quartz; ~ **fumé** *m* MINERAUX smoky quartz; ~ **naturel** *m* ELECTRON mother crystal; ~ **oeil-de-chat** *m* MINERAUX cat's eye quartz; ~ **à or libre** *m* MATERIAUX free milling quartz; ~ **d'oscillateur** *m* ELECTRON oscillator crystal; ~ **d'oscillateur local** *m* ELECTRON receive crystal; ~ **pilote** *m* ELECTRON oscillator crystal; ~ **thermostaté** *m* ELECTRON temperature-controlled crystal

quartzeux *adj* GEOLOGIE quartzose

quartz-iode *m* CINEMAT quartz iodine

quartzite *f* CONSTR, GEOLOGIE, MATERIAUX quartzite; ~ **sédimentaire** *f* GEOLOGIE orthoquartzite, quartzarenite

quasar *m* ASTRONOMIE quasar, ESPACE QSS, quasistellar radio source

quasi-abordage *m* AERONAUT near collision, near miss, ESPACE near miss

quasi-collision *f* AERONAUT near collision, near miss, ESPACE near miss

quasi-particule *f* PHYSIQUE quasi-particle

quasi-statique *adj* ESPACE *véhicules* quasi-statical

quassine *f* CHIMIE quassin

quaternaire *adj* CHIMIE quaternary

quaternion *m* MATH quaternion

quatre:[1] **en** ~ **épaisseurs** *adj* PRODUCTION *courroie* four-ply; **à** ~ **plis** *adj* PRODUCTION *courroie* four-ply; **à** ~ **têtes** *adj* TV quadruplex

quatre:[2] ~ **roues motrices** *f pl* AUTO, VEHICULES *transmission* four-wheel drive

quatre-mâts *m* NAUT four master

quatrième: ~ **génération** *f* INFORMAT, ORDINAT fourth generation

quercétine *f* CHIMIE quercetin, quercitin

quercitannique *adj* CHIMIE quercitannic

quercite *f* CHIMIE quercite

quercitol *m* CHIMIE quercite

question: ~ **à l'étude** *f* CONS MECA subject under investigation

quête *f* NAUT *du mât* rake

queue *f* CONS MECA tailrod, *d'un outil* shank, *d'une lime* tang, DISTRI EAU *d'une vanne* stem, ELECTRON, IMPRIM *plaques et blanchets*, INFORMAT, ORDINAT tail, TRANSPORT *d'un avion* tail, *d'un train* rear; ~ **d'aronde** *f* CONSTR, MECANIQUE dovetail, fantail; ~ **de l'avion** *f* AERONAUT aircraft tail unit; ~ **de calibrage** *f* PETR calibration tail; ~ **de cochon** *f* CONSTR auger gimlet, ELECTROTEC pigtail; ~ **cométaire** *f* ASTRONOMIE cometary tail; ~ **de la comète** *f* ASTRONOMIE cometary tail; ~ **cône Morse** *f* CONS MECA Morse taper shank; ~ **de distillation** *f* GENIE CHIM, THERMODYN distillation tail; ~ **d'étalonnage** *f* PETR calibration tail; ~ **de foret avec cônes** *f* CONS MECA Morse taper shank drill; ~ **de la magnétosphère** *f* ESPACE *géophysique* geomagnetic tail, magnetotail; ~ **de morue** *f* COULEURS flat brush, whitewash brush; ~ **d'onde** *f* ELECTRON trailing edge; ~ **de paraison** *f* CERAM VER gob tail; ~ **de pierre larmée** *f* CERAM VER tail; ~ **de pignon conique d'attaque** *f* AERONAUT *hélicoptère* input bevel pinion shaft; ~ **de piston** *f* CONS MECA tail piston rod; ~ **de poussée** *f*

ESPACE *propulsion* thrust decay; **~ de rat** *f* CONS MECA rat-tail file; **~ de soupape** *f* INST HYDR rod, stem, valve rod, valve spindle, valve stem; **~ de vanne** *f* INST HYDR gate stem

quiescent *adj* CHIMIE quiescent

qui: **~ est là** *loc* TELECOM who are you, WRU

quille *f* AERONAUT hull, CONSTR plug, stone wedge, NAUT keel; **~ d'angle** *f* AERONAUT chine; **~ de dérive** *f* NAUT drop keel; **~ lestée** *f* NAUT ballast keel; **~ de roulis** *f* NAUT bilge keel

quinaldine *f* CHIMIE quinaldine

quinaldinique *adj* CHIMIE quinaldinic, *acide* quinaldic

quinalizarine *f* CHIMIE quinalizarin

quinamine *f* CHIMIE quinamine

quincaillerie *f* MECANIQUE hardware

quincite *f* MINERAUX quincite

quinhydrone *f* CHIMIE quinhydrone

quinicine *f* CHIMIE quinicine

quinidine *f* CHIMIE quinidine

quinine *f* CHIMIE quinine

quinique *adj* CHIMIE quininic, *acide* quinic

quinite *f* CHIMIE quinite, quinitol

quinoa *m* CHIMIE quinoa

quinoïde *adj* CHIMIE quinoid, quinonoid

quinoléine *f* CHIMIE quinoline

quinoléique *adj* CHIMIE quinolinic

quinone *f* CHIMIE quinone

quinophtalone *f* CHIMIE quinaldine

quinovine *f* CHIMIE quinovin

quinoxaline *f* CHIMIE quinoxaline

quinoyle *m* CHIMIE quinoyle

quinquefide *adj* CHIMIE quinquefid

quintal *m* METROLOGIE centner; **~ métrique** *m* METROLOGIE metric centner, metric quintal, quintal

quinte *f* ACOUSTIQUE fifth; **~ juste** *f* ACOUSTIQUE perfect fifth

quintet *m* PHYSIQUE quintet

quitter: **~ le navire** *vi* NAUT abandon ship; **~ un port** *vi* NAUT sail away

quota *m* OCEANO catch quota

quotient *m* INFORMAT, ORDINAT quotient

R

Ra *(radium)* CHIMIE Ra *(radium)*

RA *abrév (réparations accidentelles)* CH DE FER minor repairs

rabasneuse *f* MINES dintheader

rabat *m* IMPRIM *emballage* overlap, TEXTILE *d'une poche* flap

rabat-eau *m* PRODUCTION splash guard, splash wing, splashboard, splasher

rabattable *adj* CONS MECA folding, hinged

rabattement *m* DISTRI EAU *de nappe*, PETROLE drawdown

rabattoir *m* CONSTR beater, bossing mallet, PRODUCTION lead dresser; **~ d'ardoisier** *m* CONSTR slate knife

rabattre *vt* PRODUCTION fold back, fold down, fold over, TEXTILE stitch down; **~ le bord de** *vt* PRODUCTION flange; **~ la collerette de** *vt* CONSTR bead over, PRODUCTION flange

rabbittite *f* NUCLEAIRE rabbittite

râble *m* CERAM VER skimming rod, PRODUCTION rake

rabot *m* CONSTR plane; **~ cintré** *m* CONSTR compass plane; **~ denté** *m* CONSTR tooth plane, toothing plane; **~ à dents** *m* CONSTR tooth plane; **~ à deux rainures** *m* CONSTR double-ended match plane; **~ d'établi** *m* CONSTR bench plane, jointer; **~ à languette** *m* CONSTR tonguing plane; **~ à lumière de côté** *m* CONSTR side plane; **~ à rainurer** *m* CONSTR rebate plane

rabotage *m* CONSTR planing

raboter *vt* CONSTR *le champ d'une planche* shoot, MECANIQUE plane

raboteuse *f* CONSTR planer (AmE), planing machine (BrE), MECANIQUE planer (AmE); **~ à deux montants** *f* CONS MECA double housing planing machine; **~ à un montant** *f* CONS MECA open-side planing machine; **~ de rails** *f* CH DE FER rail-planing machine; **~ à table mobile** *f* CONS MECA carriage planing machine

rabot-racloir *m* CONSTR scraping plane

raccagnac *m* CONS MECA ratchet, ratchet brace

raccommodage *m* PRODUCTION mending, repairing, repair, TEXTILE darning, mending

raccommoder *vt* PRODUCTION repair, TEXTILE darn, mend

raccord *m* CINEMAT connector, CONS MECA coupling, CONSTR connection, union, union cock, EQUIP LAB *verrerie* connector, MECANIQUE fitting, OPTIQUE *fibres optiques* joint, TELECOM joint, splice, VEHICULES *système électrique* coupling; **~ d'air** *m* CONS MECA air connection; **~ banjo** *m* CONS MECA banjo union; **~ à boulon à charnière** *m* CONS MECA *tubes* hinged bolt fitting; **~ à braser pour capillarité** *m* CONS MECA *pour tubes en cuivre* capillary solder fitting; **~ à bride** *m* CONS MECA flanged union; **~ de buse plongeante** *m* CONS MECA *moule d'injection* sprue bush; **~ des câbles** *m* ELECTR cable connector; **~ capillaire** *m* CONS MECA capillary filling; **~ de chargement** *m* REFRIG charging connection; **~ de circuit de pression** *m* PRODUCTION *système hydraulique* in-line pressure connection; **~ à circulation d'eau** *m* DISTRI EAU water fitting; **~ de compression** *m* CONS MECA *tuyauterie* compressed

fitting; **~ de conduit** *m* PRODUCTION conduit hub; **~ coudé** *m* CONS MECA bend coupling, CONSTR elbow union, union elbow; **~ à coude d'équerre** *m* CONS MECA right-angled bend coupling; **~ à culotte** *m* PRODUCTION breeching piece; **~ à emboîtement** *m* MECANIQUE socket joint; **~ en croix** *m* CONS MECA cross union; **~ en équerre** *m* CONSTR elbow union; **~ d'entrée** *m* PRODUCTION *système hydraulique* inlet connection; **~ de fibres optiques** *m* TELECOM fiberoptic splice (AmE), fibreoptic splice (BrE); **~ fileté** *m* CONS MECA screwed fitting, threaded fitting; **~ fileté pour tubes** *m* CONS MECA screwed pipe coupling; **~ flexible** *m* CONS MECA flexible coupling; **~ de graissage** *m* CONS MECA lubrication fitting; **~ inférieur** *m* NUCLEAIRE *d'un assemblage combustible* bottom fitting; **~ de jonction en T** *m* EQUIP LAB T-piece; **~ de jonction en Y** *m* EQUIP LAB Y-piece; **~ multifibre** *m* TELECOM multifiber joint (AmE), multifibre joint (BrE); **~ pendant la suppression de trame** *m* TV interfield cut; **~ de pompe** *m* DISTRI EAU pump connection; **~ pour tubes** *m* CONS MECA pipe coupling, pipe fitting; **~ pour tuyaux** *m* PRODUCTION hose coupling; **~ pour tuyaux flexibles** *m* CONS MECA hose connection; **~ presse-étoupe** *m* CONS MECA gland; **~ rapide** *m* CONS MECA quick-release pipe coupling, CONSTR hose coupler, PRODUCTION *système hydraulique* quick-release coupling; **~ à rodage conique** *m* EQUIP LAB *verrerie* conical ground glass point; **~ à rodage mâle et femelle** *m* EQUIP LAB *verrerie* cone and socket joint; **~ de serrage conique** *m* CONS MECA conical clamping connection; **~ de sortie** *m* PRODUCTION *système hydraulique* outlet connection; **~ symétrique** *m* CONS MECA symmetric pipe coupling; **~ à T** *m* CONSTR T-piece union, tee-piece union, union T; **~ taraudé** *m* CONS MECA tapped fitting; **~ de tuyau** *m* CONSTR connections, NUCLEAIRE discharge nozzle; **~ de tuyau amovible** *m* CONS MECA detachable union; **~ de tuyaux** *m* CONSTR pipe connection, pipe coupling, pipe union, PRODUCTION hose coupling; **~ à verrou bascule** *m* CONS MECA swing bolt coupling; **~ à vis** *m* NUCLEAIRE screwed joint, threaded joint

raccordé *adj* ELECTR *circuit* connected, ESPACE strapdown-mounted, PHYSIQUE connected

raccordement *m* CONS MECA connection, CONSTR union, *routes* interchange, ELECTR joint, *circuit* connection, ELECTROTEC connection, INFORMAT attachment, MECANIQUE mating, ORDINAT attachment, PAPIER splicing, PHYSIQUE connection; **~ d'aile** *m* TRANSPORT wing fillet; **~ avec étanchéité** *m* CONS MECA *filetage de tuyauterie* pressure-tight joint; **~ collectif** *m* OPTIQUE multifiber joint (AmE), multifibre joint (BrE); **~ d'entrée d'air réacteur** *m* AERONAUT engine air intake extension; **~ à fiches** *m* ELECTROTEC plug connection; **~ du flexible** *m* MINES flexible hose connection, flexible hose coupling, flexible hose union; **~ frigorifique** *m* REFRIG refrigerant connection; **~ global** *m* OPTIQUE multifiber joint (AmE), multifibre joint (BrE); **~ de guide d'ondes** *m* ELECTROTEC waveguide coupling; **~**

d'une ligne de transmission *m* ELECTROTEC line interfacing; **~ par modem** *m* ELECTRON modem interfacing; **~ pour tubes** *m* CONS MECA pipe connection; **~ de servomoteur à fraction de tour** *m* CONS MECA part-turn actuator attachment; **~ de servomoteurs** *m* CONS MECA actuator attachment

raccorder *vt* CINEMAT connect, patch, CONSTR join, ELECTROTEC connect, connect up, plug in, IMPRIM patch, PHYSIQUE, PRODUCTION connect, TV patch, plug in

raccorderie *f* PRODUCTION fittings

raccourcir *vt* CINEMAT *au montage* trim, MILITAIRE *la portée*, PAPIER shorten

raccourcissement *m* GEOLOGIE, PAPIER *des fibres* shortening; **~ dû au froid** *m* REFRIG cold shortening

raccrocher *vi* TELECOM hang up

racémate *m* CHIMIE racemate

racémique *adj* CHIMIE *acide* racemic

racémisant *adj* CHIMIE racemizing

racémisation *f* CHIMIE racemization

racémiser *vt* CHIMIE racemize

racine *f* INFORMAT, ORDINAT root; **~ carrée** *f* MATH square root; **~ de la soudure** *f* CONSTR root of weld

rack: **~ d'E/S** *m* PRODUCTION *automatisme industriel* I/O rack; **~ d'entrée complémentaire** *m* PRODUCTION *automatisme industriel* complementary input rack

raclage *m* PRODUCTION scraping

racle *f* IMPRIM squeegee, *héliogravure* doctor blade, *héliogravure, flexographie* knife, PAPIER doctor, TEXTILE squeegee; **~ à air comprimé** *f* PLAST CAOU air knife, *matériel pour revêtement* airbrush; **~ alternative** *f* IMPRIM reciprocating blade; **~ à arêtes réglables** *f* IMPRIM *héliogravure, flexographie* adjustable edge doctor blade; **~ d'égouttage** *f* PAPIER foil; **~ d'essuyage** *f* IMPRIM doctor blade; **~ latérale** *f* IMPRIM *héliogravure, flexographie* edge doctor

racler *vt* POLLU MER scrape

raclette *f* CERAM VER, CINEMAT squeegee, CONS MECA scraper, PHOTO squeegee, POLLU MER scraper; **~ pour tubes de chaudière** *f* PRODUCTION tube-scraper

racleur *m* CHARBON scraper, MINES slusher, PETR pig, PETROLE go devil, pig, POLLU MER scraper; **~ de boues** *m* HYDROLOGIE sludge scraper; **~ à chaînes sans fin** *m* HYDROLOGIE chain scraper

racloir *m* AGRO ALIM scraper, CONSTR scraper, spokeshave, PAPIER doctor blade, scraper

racon *m* NAUT racon

rad *m* PHYS RAYON rad

radar *m* AERONAUT, ASTRONOMIE, MILITAIRE, NAUT, PHYS RAYON, PHYSIQUE, TELECOM radar; **~ acoustique** *m* PHYS ONDES sound ranging; **~ aéroporté** *m* TELECOM airborne radar; **~ aéroporté à balayage latéral** *m* POLLU MER SLAR, sideways-looking airborne radar; **~ d'autoguidage** *m* NAUT homing radar; **~ à courte portée** *m* MILITAIRE short-range radar; **~ à impulsions synchronisées** *m* PHYS RAYON coherent pulse radar, radar with coherent pulse; **~ à longue portée** *m* MILITAIRE long-range radar; **~ de navigation** *m* NAUT navigation radar; **~ à ondes entretenues** *m* NAUT continuous wave radar; **~ à ondes ultracourtes** *m* MILITAIRE ultrashort wave radar; **~ de poursuite** *m* ESPACE *communications* tracking radar, MILITAIRE pursuit radar; **~ de rendez-vous** *m* ESPACE *véhicules* rendezvous radar; **~ routier à ondes continues** *m* TRANSPORT continuous wave radar detector; **~ routier à pulsation** *m* TRANSPORT pulsed radar detector; **~**

ultrasonique *m* PHYS RAYON ultrasonic radar; **~ de veille** *m* MILITAIRE surveillance radar; **~ de veille air** *m* NAUT air search radar; **~ de veille lointaine** *m* NAUT early warning radar; **~ de veille surface** *m* NAUT surface search radar

radargraphie *f* ESPACE radar image

radariste *m* NAUT radar operator

rade *f* NAUT, OCEANO roads, roadstead; **~ foraine** *f* NAUT, OCEANO open roadstead

radeau *m* NAUT raft; **~ de bois** *m* CONSTR timber raft; **~ de sauvetage** *m* NAUT, SECURITE life raft

radial *adj* MECANIQUE radial

radian *m* ELECTR, ELECTRON, GEOMETRIE, PHYSIQUE radian

radiance *f* PHYSIQUE radiance

radiant *adj* PHYSIQUE, THERMODYN radiant

radiateur *m* AUTO radiator, ELECTR *diode Zener* heat sink, MECANIQUE radiator, PRODUCTION *système hydraulique* heat sink, THERMODYN, VEHICULES *refroidissement* radiator; **~ à accumulation** *m* CHAUFFAGE storage heater; **~ à ailettes** *m* AUTO finned radiator; **~ chauffant** *m* CHAUFFAGE, THERMODYN radiant heater; **~ à convection** *m* THERMODYN convector heater; **~ à débit horizontal** *m* AUTO crossflow radiator; **~ à débit vertical** *m* AUTO upright radiator; **~ à eau chaude** *m* CONS MECA hot water heater; **~ électrique** *m* ELECTR electric fire, electric heater; **~ électrique à accumulation** *m* THERMODYN electric storage heater; **~ à foyer rayonnant** *m* PHYS RAYON radiant heater; **~ à gaz** *m* CONS MECA gas-fired heater, THERMODYN gas fire; **~ à l'huile** *m* VEHICULES oil cooler; **~ intégral** *m* PHYS RAYON black body radiator, total radiator; **~ à nids d'abeille** *m* AUTO honeycomb radiator, ribbon cellular radiator; **~ panneau** *m* MAT CHAUFF flat radiator; **~ à rayonnement** *m* THERMODYN radiant heater; **~ secondaire** *m* CHAUFFAGE aftercooler; **~ soufflant** *m* MAT CHAUFF, THERMODYN fan heater; **~ à tubes d'air** *m* AUTO tube and fin radiator; **~ tubulaire** *m* AUTO flanged tube radiator, tubular radiator

radiatif *adj* PHYS RAYON, THERMODYN radiative

radiation *f* BREVETS cancelation (AmE), cancellation (BrE), ELECTRON, METEO, OPTIQUE, PHYS RAYON, PHYSIQUE, POLLUTION, THERMODYN, TV radiation; **~ actinique** *f* PHYS RAYON actinic light, actinic radiation; **~ annuelle de fond** *f* PHYS RAYON annual natural background radiation; **~ bêta** *f* PHYS RAYON beta radiation; **~ blanche** *f* PHYS RAYON white radiation; **~ de corps noir** *f* PHYS RAYON black body radiation; **~ de cyclotron** *f* PHYS RAYON cyclotron radiation; **~ de fond** *f* PHYS RAYON background radiation; **~ infrarouge** *f* PHYS RAYON infrared radiation; **~ monochromatique** *f* PHYS RAYON homogeneous stimulus, monochromatic radiation; **~ non-ionisante** *f* PHYS RAYON nonionizing radiation; **~ parasite** *f* PHYS RAYON stray radiation; **~ de résonance** *f* PHYS RAYON resonance radiation; **~ secondaire** *f* PHYS RAYON secondary radiation; **~ ultraviolette** *f* EN RENOUV, PHYS RAYON ultraviolet radiation

radical *m* CHIMIE group, hexad, radical, GAZ, MATH, PLAST CAOU *groupe d'atomes* radical; **~ acide** *m* CHIMIE acid radical; **~ libre** *m* AGRO ALIM, CHIMIE free radical; **~ octavalent** *m* CHIMIE octad

radier *m* CHARBON invert, mat, raft, CONSTR apron, invert, inverted arch, DISTRI EAU *du sas d'une écluse* floor, HYDROLOGIE apron, INST HYDR reversed arch; **~**

en béton *m* HYDROLOGIE concrete apron

radio:[1] ~ navigant *m* NAUT radio operator; ~ ralliement *m* ESPACE *véhicules*, MILITAIRE homing, TELECOM radio homing; ~ repérage *m* TRANSPORT radio direction finding; ~ taxi *m* TRANSPORT radio taxicab

radio:[2] ~ de bord *f* TRANSPORT radio equipment; ~ portable *f* CONSTR hand-held mobile radio; ~ portative *f* MILITAIRE manpack radio; ~ de ralliement *f* AERONAUT radio beacon; ~ télécommande *f* TRANSPORT radio telecontrol

radioactif *adj* PHYS PART, PHYS RAYON, PHYSIQUE, SECURITE radioactive

radioactinium *m* CHIMIE, PHYS RAYON radioactinium

radioactivimètre *m* PHYS RAYON radioactivity meter

radioactivité *f* CHIMIE, MILITAIRE *guerre nucléaire*, NUCLEAIRE, PHYS PART, PHYS RAYON, PHYSIQUE radioactivity; ~ ambiante *f* PHYS RAYON ambient radioactivity, environmental radioactivity; ~ artificielle *f* PHYS PART induced radioactivity, PHYS RAYON, PHYSIQUE artificial radioactivity; ~ induite *f* PHYS PART induced radioactivity; ~ naturelle *f* PHYS RAYON, PHYSIQUE natural radioactivity; ~ résiduelle *f* PHYS RAYON residual radioactivity

radioaltimètre *m* AERONAUT radio altimeter

radioamateur *m* TELECOM radio amateur

radioanalyse *f* PHYS RAYON radioanalysis, radiolysis

radioastrométrie *f* ASTRONOMIE, ESPACE, PHYSIQUE radio astrometry

radioastronomie *f* ASTRONOMIE, ESPACE, PHYSIQUE radio astronomy

radiobalise *f* AERONAUT compass locator, radio beacon; ~ de détresse *f* TELECOM ELT, emergency locator transmitter; ~ en éventail *f* AERONAUT fan marker beacon; ~ individuelle de repérage *f* NAUT personal location beacon; ~ de localisation de sinistre *f* NAUT, TELECOM EPIRB, emergency position-indicating radio beacon; ~ maritime *f* NAUT maritime radio beacon; ~ médiane *f* AERONAUT middle marker; ~ moyenne *f* AERONAUT middle marker

radioborne *f* AERONAUT marker beacon, radio beacon; ~ en éventail *f* AERONAUT, NAUT fan marker beacon; ~ extérieure *f* AERONAUT outer marker; ~ intérieure *f* AERONAUT inner marker; ~ intermédiaire *f* AERONAUT middle marker

radiocarbone *m* PHYS RAYON, PHYSIQUE radiocarbon

radiocarottage *m* EN RENOUV well logging

radiocassette *f* ENREGISTR radiocassette, radiorecorder

radiocésium *m* PHYS RAYON radiocaesium (BrE), radiocesium (AmE)

radiochimie *f* CHIMIE radiochemistry

radiochimique *adj* CHIMIE radiochemical

radiochromatographie *f* PHYS RAYON radiochromatography

radiocobalt *m* CHIMIE, PHYS RAYON radiocobalt

radiocommunication *f* NAUT, TELECOM, TRANSPORT radiocommunication; ~ par paquets *f* TELECOM packet radio

radiocompas *m* AERONAUT automatic direction finder, radio beacon, radio compass, TRANSPORT radio compass; ~ automatique *m* TRANSPORT automatic direction finder

radiocristallographie *f* PHYS RAYON X-ray crystallography

radiodiagnostic *m* PHYS RAYON radiodiagnosis

radiodiffractomètre *m* PHYS RAYON crystal spectrometer

radiodiffusion *f* ESPACE broadcasting, TELECOM broadcasting, radio broadcasting; ~ directe par satellite *f* TELECOM, TV direct satellite broadcasting, direct broadcasting by satellite; ~ régionale *f* TRANSPORT area broadcasting; ~ sonore *f* TELECOM sound broadcasting

radioélectrique *adj* PHYSIQUE radio

radioélément *m* PHYS RAYON radioactive element

radioémetteur *m* PHYSIQUE radio transmitter

radioendommagement *m* PHYS RAYON radiation damage

radiofréquence *f (RF)* ELECTRON, ELECTROTEC, ENREGISTR, TELECOM, TRANSPORT, TV radio frequency *(RF)*

radiogène *adj* PHYSIQUE radiogenic

radiogénique *adj* PHYSIQUE radiogenic

radiogonio *m* NAUT RDF, radio direction finder

radiogoniomètre *m* AERONAUT, NAUT RDF, radio direction finder, PHYS RAYON, PHYSIQUE radiogoniometer; ~ automatique *m* AERONAUT automatic direction finder, NAUT radio compass; ~ à tube cathodique *m* TELECOM cathode ray direction finder

radiogoniométrie *f* AERONAUT homing, PHYS RAYON radiogoniometry, radiolocation, PHYSIQUE radio direction finding, radiogoniometry, TELECOM DF, direction finding, radio direction finding, TRANSPORT radio position fixing; ~ automatique *f* AERONAUT, TELECOM ADF, automatic direction finding; ~ visuelle à deux canaux de réception *f* TELECOM dual-carrier visual direction finding

radiogramme: ~ chiffré *m* MILITAIRE radio code message

radiographe *m* INSTRUMENT X-ray photograph, radiograph, PHYS RAYON X-ray photograph

radiographie *f* INSTRUMENT X-ray image, X-ray photography, radiography, PHOTO X-radiograph, PHYS RAYON, PHYSIQUE radiography; ~ aux particules chargées *f* NUCLEAIRE charged particle radiography; ~ à résolution en temps *f* NUCLEAIRE time resolved radiography

radiographier *vt* INSTRUMENT X-ray, radiograph

radioguidage *m* TELECOM radioguidance; ~ routier *m* TRANSPORT route guidance by radio

radioguidé *m* MILITAIRE radio-guided flight

radioguider *vt* TRANSPORT radioguide

radio-interféromètre *m* GEOPHYS radio interferometer

radio-iode *m* CHIMIE radioiodine

radio-iodine *m* PHYS RAYON radioiodine

radio-isomère *m* CHIMIE radioisomer

radio-isotope *m* CHIMIE, PHYS PART, PHYS RAYON, PHYSIQUE radioisotope; ~ de période longue *m* PHYS RAYON long-lived radioisotope

radiolarite *f* GEOLOGIE radiolarian chert

radiolecteur: ~ de cassettes *m* VEHICULES *accessoire* radiocassette deck

radiolite *f* MINERAUX radiolite

radiolocalisation *f* MILITAIRE *radar* radiolocation

radiologie *f* PHYS RAYON radiology

radioluminescence *f* PHYS RAYON radioluminescence

radiolyse *f* CHIMIE, PHYS RAYON radiolysis; ~ d'eau *f* NUCLEAIRE water decomposition under irradiation, water radiolysis

radiomessagerie *f* TELECOM radio paging

radiométallographie *f* PHYS RAYON X-ray metallography

radiomètre *m* EN RENOUV, GEOPHYS, PHYSIQUE radiometer; ~ acoustique *m* ACOUSTIQUE acoustic radiometer

radiométrie *f* CHIMIE, GEOPHYS radiometry

radiométrique *adj* GEOPHYS radiometric
radiomicromètre *m* CONS MECA radiomicrometer
radiomimétique *adj* CHIMIE radiomimetic
radionavigant *m* NAUT radio officer
radionavigation *f* AERONAUT, NAUT, TRANSPORT radio navigation
radionucléide *m* PHYS RAYON, PHYSIQUE radionuclide; **~ naturel** *m* PHYS RAYON, PHYSIQUE natural radionuclide
radio-opaque *adj* PHYS RAYON radio-opaque
radiophare *m* AERONAUT radio beacon, NAUT maritime radio beacon, PHYS RAYON, TRANSPORT radio beacon; **~ d'alignement** *m* AERONAUT, TRANSPORT radio range; **~ d'alignement de descente** *m* TRANSPORT glide path beacon, glide path localizer; **~ d'alignement de piste** *m* TRANSPORT localizer; **~ d'approche** *m* TRANSPORT radio marker; **~ à axes** *m* AERONAUT radio range; **~ circulaire** *m* AERONAUT radio beacon; **~ omnidirectionnel VHF** *m* AERONAUT VHF omnidirectional radio range, VOR, omnidirectional radiorange, TRANSPORT VHFO, very high-frequency omnirange; **~ pour radar** *m* TRANSPORT radar beacon; **~ de rappel** *m* AERONAUT homing beacon; **~ à rayonnement circulaire** *m* AERONAUT radio beacon; **~ de repérage d'urgence** *m* AERONAUT emergency location beacon; **~ répondeur** *m* AERONAUT responder beacon
radiophonie *f* TELECOM wireless telephony
radiophotographie *f* ESPACE, MATERIAUX, PHYS RAYON fluorography, photofluorography
radiorécepteur *m* PHYSIQUE radio receiver
radiorésistance *f* ELECTROTEC radiation hardness, NUCLEAIRE radiation resistance
radiosensibilité *f* PHYS RAYON radio sensitivity
radiosonde *f* GEOPHYS, TELECOM radiosonde
radiosource *f* ASTRONOMIE, ESPACE radio source, radio star, PHYS RAYON radio source
radiospectrographe *m* PHYS RAYON X-ray spectrograph
radiospectromètre *m* PHYS RAYON X-ray spectrometer
radiostrontium *m* PHYS RAYON radiostrontium
radiotachymètre *m* TRANSPORT radar speed meter
radiotechnicien *m* MILITAIRE radiomechanic
radiotéléphone *m* CONSTR radiotelephone, TRANSPORT radiophone; **~ VHF** *m* NAUT VHF radio telephone
radiotéléphoner *vt* TRANSPORT radiophone
radiotéléphonie: ~ cellulaire *f* INFORMAT, ORDINAT cellular radio
radiotélescope *m* ASTRONOMIE, INSTRUMENT, PHYSIQUE radio telescope; **~ à antenne fixe** *m* ASTRONOMIE fixed reflector radio telescope; **~ complètement orientable** *m* ASTRONOMIE fully-steerable radio telescope, steerable radio telescope
radiotélévision: ~ communautaire *f* TV community broadcasting
radiothérapie *f* PHYS RAYON radiation treatment, radiotherapy
radiotoxicité *f* PHYS RAYON radiotoxicity
radium *m* (*Ra*) CHIMIE radium (*Ra*)
radome *m* AERONAUT, ESPACE *communications*, NAUT, TELECOM, TRANSPORT radome; **~ humide** *m* TELECOM wet radome
radon *m* (*Rn*) CHIMIE radon (*Rn*)
radoub:[1] **en ~** *adv* NAUT *navire* under repair
radoub[2] *m* NAUT refitting
radouber *vt* NAUT grave, *la coque* refit, repair
rafale *f* AERONAUT gust, INFORMAT *erreurs* burst, METEO gust, squall, MILITAIRE *de mitrailleuse* burst, NAUT

gust, ORDINAT *erreurs* burst; **~ descendante** *f* AERONAUT down gust; **~ d'erreurs** *f* INFORMAT, ORDINAT error burst; **~ de neige** *f* METEO snow flurry; **~ de pluie** *f* METEO cloudburst
raffinage *m* CHIMIE refinement, PAPIER beating, freeness, refining, PETROLE refining; **~ de copeaux** *m* PAPIER chip refining; **~ par solvants** *m* PETROLE solvent refining; **~ du plomb** *m* PRODUCTION lead refining; **~ des résidus** *m* PETROLE residue refining process; **~ zonal** *m* CRISTALL zone refining
raffiné *adj* PAPIER beaten, refined, POLLU MER refined
raffinement *m* CRISTALL, INFORMAT, ORDINAT refinement
raffiner *vt* PAPIER beat, refine
raffinerie *f* PETROLE, PRODUCTION refinery; **~ de sel** *f* PRODUCTION salt refinery, salt works
raffineur *m* PAPIER refiner; **~ atmosphérique** *m* PAPIER atmospheric refiner, nonpressurized refiner; **~ à boulets** *m* PAPIER ball mill
raffinose *m* CHIMIE mellitose, raffinose
raffûtage *m* CONS MECA resharpening
rafraîchir *vt* ELECTRON, INFORMAT, ORDINAT refresh
rafraîchissement *m* ELECTRON, INFORMAT, ORDINAT refresh; **~ d'image** *m* INFORMAT, ORDINAT image refreshing; **~ périodique** *m* ELECTRON periodic refresh; **~ pour le confort** *m* REFRIG comfort cooling; **~ prioritaire** *m* PRODUCTION immediate update; **~ prioritaire d'entrée** *m* PRODUCTION *automatisme industriel* immediate input date; **~ prioritaire de sortie** *m* PRODUCTION *automatisme industriel* immediate output date
ragage *m* NAUT chafing
raide *adj* TEXTILE crisp, stiff
raideur *f* ACOUSTIQUE, CONS MECA stiffness, CONSTR steepness, PHYSIQUE rigidity, stiffness, RESSORTS rate, TEXTILE stiffness; **~ acoustique** *f* ACOUSTIQUE, PHYSIQUE acoustic stiffness; **~ du front** *f* ELECTRON edge steepness; **~ du ressort** *f* RESSORTS spring rate
raidir *vt* CONS MECA tighten, NAUT *un câble* haul taut
raidissage: ~ transversal *m* NAUT transverse framing
raidissement *m* CONS MECA stiffening, tightening, ESPACE *véhicules* stiffening
raidisseur *m* CONS MECA strainer, CONSTR wire strainer, wire stretcher, ESPACE *véhicules*, NAUT stiffener; **~ de cloison** *m* NAUT bulkhead stiffener
raie *f* CRISTALL, ELECTRON line, OPTIQUE spectral line, PHYS RAYON line, TELECOM spectral line; **~ d'absorption** *f* ASTRONOMIE *spectrale*, PHYSIQUE absorption line; **~ d'absorption interstellaire** *f* ASTRONOMIE *spectres des étoiles* interstellar absorption line; **~ D du sodium** *f* PHYSIQUE sodium D-line; **~ d'émission** *f* PHYSIQUE emission line; **~ de Fraunhofer** *f* ASTRONOMIE, PHYSIQUE Fraunhofer line; **~ de Kikuchi** *f* NUCLEAIRE Kikuchi line; **~ de Kossel** *f* NUCLEAIRE *courbe, ligne* Kossel line; **~ de résonance** *f* PHYS RAYON resonance line; **~ de la série de Balmer** *f* PHYS PART *spectre de l'hydrogène* Balmer series line; **~ spectrale** *f* ASTRONOMIE *spectres des étoiles*, OPTIQUE, PHYS RAYON, TELECOM spectral line; **~ spectrale de la couronne solaire** *f* PHYS RAYON coronal emission line; **~ spectrale d'hydrogène** *f* PHYS RAYON hydrogen spectral line; **~ spectrale laser** *f* PHYS RAYON laser spectral line; **~ du spectre** *f* PHYSIQUE spectral line
rail *m* CH DE FER rail, CINEMAT track, *travelling* track, NAUT track, TRANSPORT rail; **~ central** *m* CH DE FER monorail, TRANSPORT center rail (AmE), centre rail

(BrE); ~ **collecteur** *m* CONS MECA busbar; ~ **conducteur** *m* ELECTR *chemin de fer* conductor rail, TRANSPORT conductor rail, live rail, third rail; ~ **de contact** *m* ELECTR *chemin de fer*, ELECTROTEC conductor rail, TRANSPORT contact rail; ~ **crémaillère** *m* CH DE FER rack rail; ~ **denté** *m* CH DE FER rack rail; ~ **DIN** *m* PRODUCTION *automatisme industriel* DIN rail; ~ **à double champignon** *m* CH DE FER double-headed rail, *voie* bullheaded rail; ~ **échancré** *m* CH DE FER scalloped rail; ~ **encastré** *m* CH DE FER *voie* grooved rail; ~ **en U** *m* CONSTR bridge rail; ~ **exfolié** *m* CH DE FER *voie* flaked rail; ~ **à gorges** *m* CH DE FER *voie* grooved rail; ~ **de guidage** *m* CH DE FER *voie* checkrail, TRANSPORT center rail (AmE), centre rail (BrE), guiderail; ~ **isolé** *m* CH DE FER *voie* insulated rail; ~ **méplat** *m* CH DE FER strap rail; ~ **de montage** *m* PRODUCTION mounting rail; ~ **noyé** *m* CH DE FER sunken rail; ~ **paramagnétique** *m* TRANSPORT paramagnetic rail; ~ **à pont** *m* CONSTR bridge rail; ~ **porteur** *m* TRANSPORT bearing rail; ~ **de raccord** *m* CH DE FER *voie* closure rail; ~ **de réaction** *m* CH DE FER reaction rail, TRANSPORT inductive reaction rail; ~ **de roulement** *m* CH DE FER *voie* running rail; ~ **de stabilisation** *m* TRANSPORT stabilization rail; ~ **de sûreté** *m* TRANSPORT safety rail; ~ **de sustentation** *m* TRANSPORT supporting rail; ~ **de tramway** *m* TRANSPORT streetcar track (AmE) tramline (BrE), tramway (BrE); ~ **de transaction** *m* CONS MECA running rail; ~ **de translation** *m* CONSTR crane rail; ~ **de travelling** *m* CINEMAT dolly track

rail-guide *m* CONS MECA guiderail

rail-route *m* TRANSPORT railroad (AmE), railway (BrE), road rail

rails: sur ~ *adj* TRANSPORT rail mounted

rainage *m* IMPRIM scoring

rainé *adj* PAPIER grooved, scored

rainer[1] *m* IMPRIM score

rainer[2] *vt* CERAM VER edge with a groove

rainurage *m* CONS MECA slotting, CONSTR fluting, PRODUCTION groove, grooving

rainure:[1] **à ~** *adj* PRODUCTION grooved

rainure[2] *f* CONS MECA slot, CONSTR flute, groove, MECANIQUE groove, NUCLEAIRE groove, slot, OPTIQUE, PAPIER, PRODUCTION groove; ~ **de bridage** *f* CONS MECA clamp slot; ~ **de cale** *f* CONS MECA keyway; ~ **de clavetage** *f* CONS MECA keyway; ~ **de clavette** *f* CONS MECA keyway, MECANIQUE keyslot, keyway; ~ **en T** *f* CONS MECA T-slot; ~ **en V** *f* CONS MECA, ELECTRON V-groove; ~ **de fixation** *f* REFRIG fin slot; ~ **de graissage** *f* CONS MECA oil groove

rainuré *adj* PRODUCTION slotted

rainures: à ~ *adj* PRODUCTION grooved

rainureuse *f* CONS MECA slot-drilling machine

raison:[1] **en ~ inverse de** *adv* CONS MECA in inverse proportion, in inverse ratio, inversely as

raison[2] *f* MATH common ratio, ratio; ~ **de l'équipe** *f* CONS MECA gear ratio; ~ **inverse** *f* CONS MECA inverse ratio, reciprocal ratio, MATH inverse ratio; ~ **du renvoi** *f* TELECOM redirecting reason

raison:[3] **à ~ de** *prép* METROLOGIE at the rate of

raisonnement: ~ par récurrence *m* INFORMAT, ORDINAT mathematical induction

rajeunissement *m* GEOLOGIE reactivation, rejuvenation, PETROLE rejuvenation; ~ **des âges** *m* GEOLOGIE overprinting, resetting

rajustement *m* CONS MECA refitting, PRODUCTION repairing

rajuster *vt* PRODUCTION repair

ralenti[1] *adj* PHYSIQUE decelerated

ralenti[2] *m* CINEMAT slow motion, VEHICULES *moteur* idling; ~ **de prise de terrain** *m* AERONAUT approach idling conditions

ralentir[1] *vt* CHIMIE retard, ESPACE *la rotation* despin

ralentir:[2] **~ l'allure** *vi* CONS MECA reduce speed

ralentir[3] *vti* MECANIQUE, PHYSIQUE decelerate

ralentissement *m* CONS MECA slackening, IMPRIM *rotatives* drag, MECANIQUE, PHYSIQUE deceleration; ~ **des neutrons** *m* NUCLEAIRE slowing down; ~ **de la rotation** *m* ESPACE *véhicules* spin down

ralentisseur *m* PHYS RAYON *énergie atomique*, PHYSIQUE moderator, TRANSPORT retarder; ~ **sur échappement** *m* VEHICULES *freinage* exhaust brake

ralingue *f* NAUT bolt rope

ralliement *m* AERONAUT homing; ~ **par radar** *m* TRANSPORT radar homing

rallier: ~ la terre *vi* NAUT stand inshore

rallonge *f* CINEMAT extension cable, extension lead, CONS MECA extension piece, lengthening piece, lengthening rod, CONSTR bore rod, boring rod, MINES drill pipe, drill rod, rod; ~ **de pieu** *f* CHARBON pile block; ~ **de raccord** *f* CONS MECA *refroidissement de moule d'injection* extension connector plug; ~ **à soufflet** *f* CINEMAT extension bellows unit; ~ **de trépied** *f* PHOTO tripod extension

rallumeur *m* CONS MECA igniter

ralstonite *f* MINERAUX ralstonite

RAM: ~ dynamique *f* INFORMAT, ORDINAT dynamic RAM; ~ **statique** *f* ORDINAT SRAM, static RAM

ramassage *m* POLLU MER collection, RECYCLAGE refuse collection, waste collection

ramasse-pâte *m* PAPIER pulp saver, save-all

ramasser: ~ à la pelle *vt* CONSTR shovel

rambarde *f* INST HYDR breasting parapet, MECANIQUE handrail, NAUT, SECURITE guardrail

rame *f* CH DE FER train set, *véhicules* train rake, IMPRIM ream, NAUT oar, PETROLE string; ~ **automotrice** *f* TRANSPORT multiple-unit train, rail motor coach, railcar; ~ **de cyclorama** *f* CINEMAT strip light; ~ **élargisseuse** *f* TEXTILE stenter frame; ~ **de papier** *f* EMBALLAGE, PAPIER ream; ~ **à picots** *f* TEXTILE pin frame, pin stenter; ~ **à pinces** *f* TEXTILE clip frame, clip stenter; ~ **réversible** *f* TRANSPORT push-pull train; ~ **de tramway** *f* TRANSPORT streetcar (AmE), tram (BrE); ~ **à turbine à gaz** *f* TRANSPORT RTG train, gas turbine train; ~ **de wagons** *f* MINES rake of hutches

rameau: ~ de pistonnement *m* CH DE FER air pressure relief duct, pressure relief duct, CONSTR piston relief duct

ramendage *m* OCEANO net mending

ramendeur *m* OCEANO net mender, net repairer

ramener: ~ à zéro *vt* CONS MECA reset to zero, set to zero

ramer *vi* NAUT row, scull

ramification *f* DISTRI EAU branching; ~ **de fissures** *f* METALL crack branching

ramifié *adj* CHIMIE branched

ramifier: se ~ *v réfl* CONSTR branch, branch off

ramollissage *m* CERAM VER sagging

ramollissement *m* GAZ softening

ramonage *m* PRODUCTION *des tubes de chaudière* cleaning

ramoner *vt* CONSTR *une cheminée* sweep, PRODUCTION *des tubes à fumée* clean

ramoneur *m* PETROLE go devil, pig

rampage *m* PLAST CAOU cissing
rampant[1] *adj* CONSTR rampant
rampant[2] *m* CONSTR *d'un comble* slope, PRODUCTION neck
rampe *f* AERONAUT ramp, CH DE FER bank, CINEMAT footlights, CONSTR grade, gradient, incline, railing, upgrade, *balustrade* balustrade, handrail, *d'une colline* slope, ELECTROTEC, GEOPHYS, MINES, PAPIER ramp, PETR pontoon, ramp, stinger; ~ **d'accès** *f* CONSTR access ramp, TRANSPORT acceleration lane, access ramp, vehicle ramp; ~ **d'allumage** *f* AERONAUT ignition harness; ~ **articulée** *f* PETR articulated stinger; ~ **de charge** *f* NUCLEAIRE ramp change of load; ~ **de chargement** *f* AERONAUT loading ramp; ~ **de chevrons** *f* CONSTR pitch of roof, roof pitch; ~ **de courant** *f* PRODUCTION *électricité* current ramp; ~ **de culbuteurs** *f* AUTO rocker arm assembly; ~ **de distribution** *f* AERONAUT manifold, CONS MECA oil distributor, PRODUCTION feed rack, lubricating rack; ~ **de distribution de la couche** *f* IMPRIM *moteurs, machines, liasses de papier* manifold; ~ **d'escalier** *f* CONSTR elbow height handrail; ~ **d'évacuation** *f* AERONAUT escape chute, ESPACE *véhicules* chute, escape chute; ~ **fixée** *f* PETR fixed stinger; ~ **à gaz annulaire** *f* THERMODYN gas ring; ~ **de graissage** *f* CONS MECA oil distributor, PRODUCTION feed rack, lubricating rack; ~ **de graissage à départs multiples** *f* PRODUCTION multiple feed rack; ~ **de guidage** *f* CONS MECA guide ramp; ~ **hélicoïdale** *f* CINEMAT focusing mount, CONS MECA helical groove; ~ **inclinée** *f* PETR inclined ramp; ~ **de lancement** *f* ESPACE launch ramp, launching ramp; ~ **de lancement pour engins téléguidés** *f* MILITAIRE launching ramp for guided missiles; ~ **lumineuse** *f* PHOTO bank; ~ **de poste** *f* PETROLE stinger; ~ **de pulvérisation** *f* POLLU MER spray boom; ~ **rigide** *f* PETR rigid stinger; ~ **de soufflage** *f* AERONAUT hot air gallery; ~ **de soufflage d'air** *f* PAPIER air shower; ~ **de 0,0X** *f* CONSTR gradient of x in 1000, gradient of x%.; ~ **de 0m** *f* CONSTR gradient of x in 1000, gradient of x%.
rancher *m* CH DE FER stanchion, upright
rang *m* INFORMAT row, MATH rank, ORDINAT row; ~ **d'un harmonique** *m* ELECTRON harmonic order
rangée *f* CRISTALL line, ELECTROTEC bank, INFORMAT *de bandes*, ORDINAT *de bandes* row; ~ **de géophones** *f* GEOLOGIE seismic array; ~ **de mailles** *f* TEXTILE course; ~ **de mailles endroit** *f* TEXTILE course of face stitches; ~ **de mailles envers** *f* TEXTILE course of reverse stitches; ~ **de pieux** *f* CHARBON row of piles; ~ **réticulaire** *f* CRISTALL lattice row
rangées: ~ **de mailles paires et impaires** *f pl* TEXTILE even and odd courses; ~ **à la minute** *f pl* TEXTILE courses per minute
rangement *m* INFORMAT, ORDINAT order; ~ **en mémoire tampon** *m* INFORMAT, ORDINAT buffering; ~ **pour les cartes électroniques** *m* IMPRIM rack
ranger[1] *vt* INFORMAT, ORDINAT order; ~ **en mémoire tampon** *vt* ORDINAT buffer
ranger:[2] **se ~ à quai** *v réfl* NAUT berth
rankiniser *vt* CONS MECA *les diagrammes de rendement d'une machine polycylindrique* combine
RAP *abrév* (*récupération assistée du pétrole*) PETROLE EOR (*enhanced oil recovery*)
râpage *m* CONSTR rasping
râpe *f* CONSTR rasp
rapide[1] *adj* ELECTROTEC *relais* fast-acting, MECANIQUE high-speed

rapide[2] *m* HYDROLOGIE rapid
rapidité: ~ **de transfert de données** *f* TELECOM data transfer rate
rapiéçage *m* PRODUCTION patching, patching up, patchwork
rapiècement *m* PRODUCTION patching, patching up, patchwork
rapiécer *vt* INFORMAT patch
rappel:[1] **à ~** *adj* PRODUCTION *automatisme industriel* self-lifting
rappel[2] *m* INFORMAT, ORDINAT roll in, TELECOM recall; ~ **automatique** *m* TELECOM automatic recall; ~ **du dernier numéro** *m* TELECOM last number recall, last number redial; ~ **de manche** *m* AERONAUT beeper trim; ~ **sur le matériel** *m* PRODUCTION hardware review
rappelé: ~ **par ressort** *adj* PRODUCTION *système hydraulique* spring-loaded
rappeler *vt* INFORMAT, ORDINAT roll in
rappel-transfert *m* ORDINAT roll in-roll out
rapport *m* ESPACE payoff, MATH, PHYSIQUE ratio; ~ **d'agrandissement** *m* CINEMAT magnification factor; ~ **air-combustible** *m* TRANSPORT air-fuel ratio; ~ **d'amplification** *m* ENREGISTR amplification ratio; ~ **d'anamorphose** *m* CINEMAT lens squeeze ratio; ~ **des axes** *m* CRISTALL axial ratio; ~ **de battage de pieux** *m* CHARBON pile-driving record; ~ **de branchement** *m* PHYSIQUE branching ratio; ~ **de cadrage** *m* ORDINAT aspect ratio; ~ **de chaleur sensible** *m* REFRIG sensible heat ratio; ~ **des chaleurs massiques** *m* PHYSIQUE ratio; ~ **des chaleurs spécifiques** *m* THERMODYN adiabatic coefficient; ~ **coeur-gaine** *m* TELECOM core-cladding ratio; ~ **de compression** *m* CONS MECA, ELECTRON compression ratio; ~ **de contraste** *m* TV contrast ratio; ~ **creux-tirant d'eau** *m* NAUT depth to draught ratio; ~ **cyclique** *m* PHYSIQUE mark-space ratio; ~ **débit-capacité** *m* TRANSPORT V-C ratio, volume capacity ratio; ~ **du défaut de masse** *m* PHYSIQUE packing fraction; ~ **de démultiplication** *m* VEHICULES *boîte de vitesses* gear ratio; ~ **de démultiplication de commande** *m* AERONAUT control gearing ratio; ~ **de détente** *m* ESPACE pressure ratio; ~ **de diffusion thermique** *m* PHYSIQUE thermal diffusion ratio; ~ **des dimensions de l'image** *m* CINEMAT picture ratio; ~ **de données dans la bande des fréquences vocales** *m* TELECOM voice-band data ratio; ~ **de données numériques sans restriction** *m* TELECOM unrestricted digital data ratio; ~ **dose-effet** *m* POLLUTION dose response relationship; ~ **eau-ciment** *m* CONSTR water-cement ratio; ~ **eau-pétrole** *m* PETR WOR, water-oil ratio; ~ **d'élancement** *m* MECANIQUE aspect ratio; ~ **d'embranchement** *m* PHYSIQUE branching ratio; ~ **d'endurance** *m* NUCLEAIRE endurance ratio; ~ **d'engrenage** *m* CONS MECA gear ratio; ~ **d'enroulement** *m* RESSORTS spring index; ~ **entre les doses et les effets** *m* POLLUTION dose response relationship; ~ **entre les doses et les réactions** *m* POLLUTION dose response relationship; ~ **d'erreurs** *m* INFORMAT, ORDINAT error report; ~ **d'essai** *m* INFORMAT, ORDINAT test report; ~ **de finesse** *m* AERONAUT, CONS MECA fineness ratio; ~ **de flèche** *m* RESSORTS deflection ratio; ~ **de format** *m* CINEMAT aperture ratio, aspect ratio; ~ **gain-température de bruit** *m* (*G-T*) ESPACE *communications* gain-to-noise temperature ratio (*G-T*); ~ **gaz-pétrole** *m* PETR GOR, gas-to-oil ratio; ~ **gyromagnétique** *m* PHYSIQUE gyromagnetic ratio;

~ **image** *m* CINEMAT camera log, camera report; ~ **d'impédance** *m* ENREGISTR impedance ratio; ~ **d'impédance à basse température** *m* PRODUCTION *électricité* impedance ratio at low temperature; ~ **impulsionnel** *m* TELECOM impulsiveness ratio; ~ **initial** *m* GEOLOGIE initial ratio; ~ **d'inventaire fissile** *m* NUCLEAIRE fissile inventory ratio; ~ **isotopique** *m* PHYS PART abundance ratio of isotopes; ~ **labo** *m* CINEMAT lab report; ~ **lambda** *m* AUTO air ratio; ~ **largeur-hauteur** *m* ELECTROTEC aspect ratio; ~ **largeur-hauteur de l'image** *m* CINEMAT aspect ratio; ~ **liqueur-poids de tissu** *m* TEXTILE liquor-to-goods ratio; ~ **longueur-largeur** *m* TRANSPORT aspect ratio; ~ **des luminances** *m* CINEMAT brightness ratio, PHYS RAYON luminance ratio; ~ **de luminosité** *m* TV brightness ratio; ~ **manométrique du réacteur** *m* AERONAUT engine pressure ratio; ~ **masse-luminosité** *m* ASTRONOMIE *des étoiles de la séquence principale* mass-luminosity relationship; ~ **de mélange carburant-combinant** *m* ESPACE *propulsion* fuel oxidizer mixture ratio; ~ **neutronique** *m* EN RENOUV neutron log; ~ **d'ondes stationnaires** *m* *(ROS)* PHYSIQUE standing-wave ratio *(SWR)*, voltage standing-wave ratio *(VSWR)*, TELECOM standing-wave ratio *(SWR)*; ~ **de pas** *m* ELECTR *constituant d'un câble* lay ratio; ~ **poids en charge-poids à vide** *m* TRANSPORT load-no charge ratio; ~ **de pont** *m* AUTO differential ratio, VEHICULES *pont arrière* axle ratio; ~ **de la portance à la traînée** *m* AERONAUT L-D ratio, lift-drag ratio; ~ **porteuse/brouillage** *m* TELECOM CIR, carrier-to-interface ratio; ~ **porteuse-bruit thermique du récepteur** *m* TELECOM carrier-to-receiver thermal-no-noise ratio; ~ **porteuse-densité de bruit** *m* TELECOM carrier-to-noise density ratio; ~ **porteuse-densité de bruit d'intermodulation** *m* TELECOM carrier-to-intermodulation noise density ratio; ~ **de la porteuse sur le bruit** *m* ENREGISTR carrier-to-noise ratio; ~ **pour montage** *m* CINEMAT continuity sheet; ~ **poussée-masse** *m* ESPACE *propulsion* thrust-to-mass ratio, thrust-to-weight ratio; ~ **poussée-poids** *m* ESPACE *propulsion* thrust-to-mass ratio, thrust-to-weight ratio; ~ **de pressions moteur** *m* AERONAUT engine pressure ratio; ~ **de puissance crête à la puissance moyenne** *m* NUCLEAIRE peak-to-average power ratio; ~ **de puissance porteuse utile-porteuse brouilleuse** *m* TELECOM wanted-to-unwanted carrier power ratio; ~ **de rayons gamma** *m* EN RENOUV gamma ray log; ~ **de recherche** *m* BREVETS search report; ~ **réciproque** *m* CONS MECA inverse ratio, reciprocal ratio; ~ **de réduction** *m* CHARBON reduction ratio; ~ **de réjection en mode commun** *m* ELECTRON common mode rejection ratio; ~ **de résistivité** *m* EN RENOUV resistivity log; ~ **sable-argile** *m* PETROLE sand-shale ratio; ~ **scripte** *m* CINEMAT continuity sheet; ~ **des sections** *m* ESPACE nozzle expansion area ratio; ~ **signal-bruit** *m* ACOUSTIQUE, ELECTRON SNR, signal-to-noise ratio, ENREGISTR SNR, dynamic range, signal-to-noise ratio, INFORMAT, ORDINAT, PETR, PHYSIQUE, TELECOM, TV SNR, signal-to-noise ratio; ~ **signal-bruit à l'entrée** *m* ELECTRON input signal-to-noise ratio; ~ **signal-bruit pondéré** *m* ENREGISTR weighted signal-to-noise ratio; ~ **SINAD** *m* TELECOM SINAD ratio; ~ **de sondage** *m* CHARBON sounding record; ~ **spontané** *m* EN RENOUV spontaneous log; ~ **du surface** *m* CHARBON relative grain area; ~ **de surrégénération** *m* NUCLEAIRE net breeding rate; ~ **sustentation-résistance à l'avance-**

ment *m* TRANSPORT lift-to-drag ratio; ~ **de sveltesse** *m* RESSORTS slenderness ratio; ~ **de température** *m* EN RENOUV temperature log; ~ **des températures** *m* THERMODYN temperature ratio; ~ **des teneurs isotopiques** *m* NUCLEAIRE abundance ratio of isotopes; ~ **de test** *m* INFORMAT, ORDINAT test report; ~ **thermique** *m* THERMODYN temperature ratio; ~ **du trafic journalier au trafic à l'heure chargée** *m* TELECOM day to busy hour ratio; ~ **de la traînée à la poussée** *m* NAUT lift-drag ratio; ~ **de transfert** *m* TV transfer ratio; ~ **de transformation** *m* AUTO turns ratio, ELECTR turn ratio, winding ratio, ELECTROTEC turns ratio, MECANIQUE gear ratio, PHYSIQUE turns ratio; ~ **de transformation assigné** *m* ELECTR rated voltage ratio; ~ **de transformation de courant** *m* ELECTR current transformation ratio; ~ **de transformation nominal** *m* ELECTR rated voltage ratio; ~ **de transmission** *m* AUTO transmission ratio; ~ **de vide** *m* PRODUCTION void ratio; ~ **de vitesse périphérique** *m* EN RENOUV tip speed ratio; ~ **vitesse tête-vitesse bande** *m* TV head-to-tape velocity; ~ **volumétrique** *m* THERMODYN compression ratio; ~ **de Wylie** *m* PETR Wylie relationship

rapporte: qui se ~ à la masse *adj* CHIMIE molar
rapporté *adj* CONS MECA detachable, IMPRIM *illustration* tipped in
rapporter *vt* CONSTR join on, plot, IMPRIM tip on
rapporteur *m* GEOMETRIE, METROLOGIE *mécanique, optique*, NAUT protractor; ~ **circulaire** *m* GEOMETRIE circular protractor; ~ **universel** *m* METROLOGIE universal level protractor
rapprochement *m* ESPACE *véhicules* approach
rapprocher *vt* IMPRIM close up
raquette *f* CH DE FER avoiding line
rare *adj* CHIMIE rare, *gaz* noble
raréfaction *f* PHYS ONDES, PHYSIQUE rarefaction
ras: au ~ de terre *adj* CONSTR even with the ground, level with the ground
rase: au ~ terre *adj* CONSTR even with the ground, level with the ground
rassemblement *m* PRODUCTION collection; ~ **de données** *m* TELECOM data collection
rassissement *f* AGRO ALIM retrogradation, staling
raté *m* MINES misfire; ~ **d'allumage** *m* MINES misfire; ~ **d'amorçage** *m* ELECTROTEC misfire; ~ **de shunt** *m* CH DE FER de-shunting
râteau *m* CONSTR rake
râtelier *m* CINEMAT film horse, pin rack; ~ **d'armes** *m* MILITAIRE arms rack, rack; ~ **magnétique** *m* CONSTR magnetic tool rack
ratière *f* TEXTILE dobby
ratile *f* CHIMIE ratile
ratio: de décroissance *m* TV decay rate; ~ **harmonique** *m* GEOMETRIE harmonic ratio; ~ **homme-machine** *m* PRODUCTION man-machine ratio
rattaches *f pl* TEXTILE transfer tails
rattrapage: ~ de jeu *m* MECANIQUE compensation for wear; ~ **du jeu** *m* CONS MECA taking up play; ~ **sur orbite** *m* ESPACE orbital catch-up; ~ **de l'usure** *m* MECANIQUE compensation for wear
rattraper[1] *vt* NAUT *un autre navire* overhaul
rattraper:[2] ~ **le jeu** *vi* MECANIQUE compensate for wear; ~ **l'usure** *vi* MECANIQUE compensate for wear
RAV *abrév (revue d'aptitude au vol)* ESPACE *gestion* FRR *(flight readiness review)*
ravine *f* HYDROLOGIE torrent
ravinement *m* AERONAUT guttering, CH DE FER erosion; ~

et remblayage *m* GEOLOGIE scour-and-fill; ~ de remblai *m* CH DE FER washout

raviner *vt* CONSTR, GEOLOGIE channel

ravitaillement *m* CONS MECA refueling (AmE), refuelling (BrE); ~ air-air *m* MILITAIRE air-to-air refueling (AmE), air-to-air refuelling (BrE); ~ en carburant *m* AERONAUT, POLLU MER refueling (AmE), refuelling (BrE); ~ en essence *m* TRANSPORT refueling (AmE), refuelling (BrE); ~ en vol *m* TRANSPORT refueling in flight (AmE), refuelling in flight (BrE)

ravitailler *vt* NAUT provision; ~ en combustible *vt* TRANSPORT refuel

ravitailleur *m* NAUT tender, PETROLE supply boat; ~ de forage en mer *m* TRANSPORT offshore drilling rig supply vessel

raviver[1] *vt* SECURITE break out again

raviver:[2] se ~ *v réfl* SECURITE break out again

rayage *m* CERAM VER scoring

rayé *adj* PAPIER striped

rayer: ~ l'âme *vi* MILITAIRE rifle

rayeuse: ~ laser *f* ELECTRON laser scriber

rayon *m* CINEMAT beam, CONSTR shelf, ELECTRON ray, GEOMETRIE radius, OPTIQUE radius, ray, PHYSIQUE radius, TELECOM ray; ~ d'action *m* AERONAUT operating range, range, ESPACE *véhicules* range, MILITAIRE *d'un missile* operating range; ~ d'action absolu *m* MILITAIRE absolute range; ~ d'actionnement *m* PRODUCTION operating radius; ~ d'action par charge *m* TRANSPORT *véhicules électriques* useful working range; ~ d'action tactique *m* MILITAIRE tactical radius of action; ~ alpha *m* PHYSIQUE alpha ray; ~ d'anode *m* PHYS RAYON anode ray; ~ d'arrondi sous la tête *m* CONS MECA *sous la tête de boulon, vis* radius; ~ atomique *m* CHIMIE, NUCLEAIRE atomic radius; ~ d'autonomie par charge *m* TRANSPORT range of action per charge; ~ axial *m* OPTIQUE axial radius, axial ray, TELECOM axial ray; ~ bêta *m* ELECTR, NUCLEAIRE, PHYSIQUE beta ray; ~ de Bohr *m* PHYSIQUE Bohr radius; ~ de la boucle *m* RESSORTS hook radius; ~ de braquage *m* CONSTR *auto* lock; ~ canal *m* PHYSIQUE canal ray; ~ de cathode *m* PHYS RAYON cathode ray; ~ cathodique *m* ELECTRON cathode ray, electron ray, PHYSIQUE, TV cathode ray; ~ du cercle primitif *m* AERONAUT pitch radius; ~ de cintrage *m* MECANIQUE bending radius, PRODUCTION bend radius; ~ classique *m* PHYSIQUE classical radius; ~ cosmique *m* ASTRONOMIE cosmic ray; ~ de courbure *m* GEOMETRIE radius of curvature, RESSORTS bending radius; ~ de dégagement *m* PRODUCTION swing radius; ~ delta *m* NUCLEAIRE, PHYS RAYON delta ray; ~ extraordinaire *m* PHYSIQUE extraordinary ray; ~ focalisé *m* PHYS ONDES focused beam; ~ de fuite *m* OPTIQUE, TELECOM leaky ray; ~ gamma *m* ELECTRON, PETR, PHYS ONDES, PHYS RAYON gamma ray, PHYSIQUE gamma rays; ~ de giration *m* CONS MECA, CONSTR radius of gyration; ~ horizontal *m* CONSTR horizontal radius; ~ d'incidence *m* PHYS ONDES incident ray; ~ incident *m* PHYSIQUE incident ray; ~ ionique *m* CRISTALL, PHYS RAYON ionic radius; ~ laser *m* PHYS ONDES laser beam; ~ de lumière *m* CINEMAT light ray; ~ lumineux *m* OPTIQUE light beam, light ray, PHYSIQUE light ray; ~ de magasin *m* EMBALLAGE storing shelf; ~ méridien *m* OPTIQUE meridian ray; ~ non méridien *m* OPTIQUE nonmeridian ray, skew ray, TELECOM skew ray; ~ oblique *m* CERAM VER skew ray; ~ optique *m* OPTIQUE light ray, optical ray; ~ ordinaire *m* PHYSIQUE ordinary ray; ~ de pale *m* AERO-

NAUT *hélicoptère* blade radius; ~ paraxial *m* OPTIQUE, PHYSIQUE, TELECOM paraxial ray; ~ de pliage *m* PRODUCTION bending radius; ~ positif *m* ELECTRON positive ray; ~ primitif *m* CONS MECA pitch radius; ~ principal *m* PHYSIQUE principal ray; ~ de raccordement *m* CONS MECA fillet; ~ de raccordement vertical *m* CONSTR vertical curve radius; ~ réfléchi *m* PHYS ONDES, PHYSIQUE reflected ray; ~ réfracté *m* OPTIQUE *dans une fibre optique*, PHYSIQUE, TELECOM refracted ray; ~ du rotor *m* AERONAUT *hélicoptère* rotor radius; ~ de Schwarzschild *m* PHYSIQUE Schwarzschild radius; ~ tunnel *m* OPTIQUE leaky ray, TELECOM tunneling ray (AmE), tunnelling ray (BrE); ~ ultraviolet *m* PHYS ONDES ultraviolet ray; ~ de Van der Waals *m* PHYSIQUE Van der Waals radius; ~ X *m* ELECTR, ELECTRON, ESPACE, METALL, PHYS ONDES, PHYSIQUE X-ray; ~ X dur *m* PHYS RAYON, PHYSIQUE hard X-ray; ~ X mou *m* PHYS RAYON, PHYSIQUE soft X-ray

rayonnant *adj* PHYS RAYON radiating, radiative, PHYSIQUE, THERMODYN radiant

rayonne *f* PLAST CAOU *type de polymère*, TEXTILE rayon

rayonnement *m* ELECTRON radiation, ESPACE radiation, *communications* irradiation, METEO, NUCLEAIRE, OPTIQUE radiation, PHYS RAYON emission, radiation, PHYSIQUE, POLLUTION, TELECOM, THERMODYN, TV radiation; ~ ambiant *m* PHYSIQUE background radiation; ~ d'annihilation *m* PHYS RAYON annihilation radiation; ~ atmosphérique *m* METEO atmospheric radiation; ~ atomique *m* NUCLEAIRE atomic radiation; ~ bêta *m* PHYS RAYON beta emission; ~ calorifique *m* EMBALLAGE, THERMODYN heat radiation; ~ Cerenkov *m* PHYS RAYON, PHYSIQUE Cerenkov radiation; ~ de chaleur *m* THERMODYN heat dissipation; ~ cohérent *m* OPTIQUE, TELECOM coherent radiation; ~ du corps noir *m* ASTRONOMIE, PHYSIQUE black body radiation; ~ cosmique *m* ESPACE cosmic radiation, PHYSIQUE cosmic rays; ~ cosmologique *m* PHYSIQUE cosmic background radiation, microwave background radiation; ~ diffus *m* EN RENOUV, ESPACE diffuse radiation; ~ diffusé *m* PHYS RAYON scattered radiation; ~ direct *m* EN RENOUV direct radiation; ~ dur *m* PHYS RAYON hard radiation; ~ électromagnétique *m* ELECTR *phénomène fondamental*, ELECTROTEC, METEO, OPTIQUE, PHYS ONDES, PHYS RAYON, PHYSIQUE, PRODUCTION, TELECOM eletromagnetic radiation; ~ émis *m* PHYS RAYON emitted radiation; ~ de faible énergie *m* PHYS RAYON low-energy radiation; ~ de fond *m* ASTRONOMIE, PHYSIQUE background radiation; ~ fossile *m* ASTRONOMIE relict radiation, ESPACE big bang radiation, fossil radiation, relict radiation; ~ de freinage *m* PHYS RAYON, PHYSIQUE bremsstrahlung; ~ de fuites *m* ELECTROTEC leakage radiation; ~ gamma *m* ELECTR gamma radiation, PHYS RAYON gamma emission, gamma radiation, PHYSIQUE gamma radiation; ~ gamma instantané *m* PHYS RAYON *en analyse d'activation* instant gamma radiation; ~ de grande énergie *m* PHYS RAYON high-energy radiation; ~ à haute énergie *m* PHYS RAYON high-energy radiation; ~ incohérent *m* PHYSIQUE, TELECOM incoherent radiation; ~ infrarouge *m* EN RENOUV, ESPACE, PHYS ONDES infrared radiation, PHYS RAYON infrared light, PHYSIQUE, POLLUTION infrared radiation; ~ infrarouge lointain *m* PHYSIQUE far infrared; ~ infrarouge proche *m* PHYSIQUE near infra red; ~ ionisant *m* ELECTR, PHYS ONDES, PHYS RAYON, PHYSIQUE, POLLUTION ionizing radiation; ~ laser *m* ELECTRON, PHYS

RAYON laser radiation; ~ **à longueur d'ondes** *m* PHYS RAYON millimeter wavelength emission (AmE), millimetre wavelength emission (BrE); ~ **de lumière** *m* NUCLEAIRE light radiation; ~ **micro-onde de corps noir** *m* ASTRONOMIE microwave background radiation; ~ **mixte** *m* PHYS RAYON mixed radiation; ~ **moléculaire** *m* ASTRONOMIE molecular radiation; ~ **monochromatique** *m* OPTIQUE, TELECOM monochromatic radiation; ~ **monoénergétique** *m* PHYSIQUE homogeneous radiation; ~ **mou** *m* PHYS RAYON soft radiation; ~ **nocturne** *m* GEOPHYS net output; ~ **nucléaire** *m* PHYS RAYON nuclear radiation; ~ **optique** *m* ELECTROTEC optical power source, OPTIQUE, TELECOM optical radiation; ~ **parasite** *m* TV parasitic radiation; ~ **parasite par conduction** *m* TELECOM conducted spurious emission; ~ **par les coffrets** *m* TELECOM cabinet radiation; ~ **de plasma** *m* GAZ plasma radiation; ~ **solaire** *m* EN RENOUV, GEOPHYS, PHYS RAYON, POLLUTION solar radiation; ~ **à spectre uniforme** *m* ESPACE white radiation; ~ **spontané** *m* PHYS RAYON spontaneous emission; ~ **synchrotron** *m* ASTRONOMIE synchrotron radiation, PHYS RAYON, PHYSIQUE synchrotron emission; ~ **terrestre** *m* GEOPHYS earth radiation; ~ **thermique** *m* NUCLEAIRE thermal flash, thermal radiation, PHYS RAYON *des solides incandescents* thermal emission, PHYSIQUE thermal radiation, THERMODYN heat radiation, thermal radiation; ~ **ultraviolet** *m* ESPACE ultraviolet radiation, OPTIQUE ultraviolet, PHYSIQUE, POLLUTION ultraviolet radiation; ~ **ultraviolet lointain** *m* ELECTROTEC deep ultraviolet radiation, PHYSIQUE far ultraviolet; ~ **ultraviolet proche** *m* PHYSIQUE near ultraviolet; ~ **universel** *m* PHYSIQUE cosmic background radiation, microwave background radiation; ~ **visible** *m* ESPACE visible radiation, OPTIQUE light, visible radiation, TELECOM visible radiation; ~ **X** *m* PHYS RAYON X-ray radiation; ~ **X secondaire** *m* PHYS RAYON secondary X-ray radiation; ~ **yrast** *m* NUCLEAIRE yrast radiation

rayonner[1] *vt* ELECTRON beam, PHYS RAYON, THERMODYN, TV radiate; ~ **en faisceau** *vt* ELECTRON beam

rayonner[2] *vi* PHYS RAYON radiate

rayure *f* CINEMAT, IMPRIM *surfaces* scratch, MILITAIRE rifling, PLAST CAOU scratch, TV glitch; ~ **en chaîne** *f* TEXTILE stripiness in the warp; ~ **horizontale** *f* CINEMAT transversal scratch; ~ **longitudinale** *f* CINEMAT longitudinal scratch; ~ **sur le support** *f* PHOTO base scratch

rayures: ~ **parallèles** *f pl* PHOTO tramlines

raz *m* NAUT, OCEANO *marée* race; ~ **de marée** *m* GEOPHYS tidal wave, tsunami, NAUT tidal wave, tide race

Rb *(rubidium)* CHIMIE Rb *(rubidium)*

RC *abrév (résistance-capacité)* ELECTRON, ELECTROTEC RC *(resistance-capacitance)*

RCC *abrév (réseau commuté canadien)* TELECOM CSN *(Canadian Switched Network)*

RCD *abrév (réseau de communication de données)* TELECOM data communication network

RCL *abrév (réseau de communication local)* TELECOM local communications network

RDF *abrév (revue de définition finale)* ESPACE *gestion* FDR *(final design review)*

Re[1] *abrév* PHYS FLUID *(nombre de Reynolds)* R *(Reynolds number)*

Re[2] *(rhénium)* CHIMIE Re *(rhenium)*

réa *f* CONS MECA pulley, pulley sheave, pulley wheel, sheave, NAUT sheave

réaccoster *vt* ESPACE *véhicules* redock

réacheminement *m* TELECOM rerouting

réacheminer *vt* TELECOM redirect

réactance *f* ELECTR, ELECTROTEC, ENREGISTR, ESSAIS, PHYSIQUE reactance; ~ **acoustique** *f* ACOUSTIQUE, ELECTROTEC, PHYSIQUE acoustic reactance; ~ **à air** *f* ELECTR air reactor; ~ **de capacité** *f* ELECTROTEC capacitive reactance; ~ **capacitive** *f* ELECTR *circuit à courant alternatif*, PHYSIQUE capacitive reactance; ~ **d'un condensateur** *f* ELECTROTEC capacitor reactance; ~ **directe** *f* ELECTR positive phase sequence reactance; ~ **en série** *f* ELECTROTEC series reactance; ~ **inductive** *f* ELECTR, ELECTROTEC, PHYSIQUE inductive reactance; ~ **d'induit** *f* ELECTR *machine* armature reactance; ~ **de limitation de courant** *f* ELECTR current-limiting reactor; ~ **mécanique** *f* ACOUSTIQUE mechanical reactance; ~ **négative** *f* ELECTROTEC negative reactance; ~ **à ordre de phases positif** *f* ELECTR positive phase sequence reactance; ~ **de la prise de terre** *f* ELECTROTEC earthing reactor (BrE), grounding reactor (AmE); ~ **statique** *f* ELECTROTEC blocked reactance

réactant *m* CHIMIE reactant

réacteur *m* AERONAUT jet engine, AUTO, CHIMIE, ELECTROTEC reactor, NUCLEAIRE nuclear reactor, pile, reactor, TRANSPORT jet engine; ~ **d'accélérateur linéaire** *m* NUCLEAIRE LADR, linear-accelerator-driven reactor; ~ **à arc** *m* CONS MECA arc jet engine; ~ **bouillant à cycle direct** *m* NUCLEAIRE direct cycle boiling reactor; ~ **catalytique** *m* GENIE CHIM, MATERIAUX catalytic reactor; ~ **à chargement en discontinu** *m* NUCLEAIRE batch reactor; ~ **à coeur gazeux** *m* NUCLEAIRE gaseous core reactor; ~ **à coeur à germes** *m* NUCLEAIRE seed core reactor; ~ **à combustible nitrure** *m* NUCLEAIRE nitride-fueled reactor (AmE), nitride-fuelled reactor (BrE); ~ **convertisseur thermique** *m* NUCLEAIRE thermal converter reactor; ~ **critique différé** *m* NUCLEAIRE delayed critical reactor; ~ **de dessalement** *m* NUCLEAIRE desalination reactor; ~ **à deux phases** *m* NUCLEAIRE two-phase reactor; ~ **diphasique** *m* NUCLEAIRE two-phase reactor; ~ **à double flux** *m* AERONAUT dual-flow jet engine, TRANSPORT bypass engine, fan engine, fan jet, turbofan; ~ **à eau bouillante** *m* PHYSIQUE BWR, boiling water reactor; ~ **à eau bouillante à circulation naturelle** *m* NUCLEAIRE natural circulation boiling water reactor; ~ **à eau légère excité par accélérateur** *m* NUCLEAIRE accelerator-driven light water reactor; ~ **à eau lourde** *m* NUCLEAIRE heavy water reactor; ~ **à eau sous pression** *m* NUCLEAIRE PWR, pressurized-water reactor; ~ **à l'ébullition** *m* NUCLEAIRE boiling reactor; ~ **d'ébullition modéré à l'eau lourde** *m* NUCLEAIRE boiling heavy water-moderated reactor; ~ **en autorotation** *m* AERONAUT engine windmilling; ~ **en forme d'une plaque infinie** *m* NUCLEAIRE slab pile, slab reactor; ~ **enrichi** *m* NUCLEAIRE *combustible* enriched reactor; ~ **en rotation libre** *m* AERONAUT engine windmilling; ~ **d'entraînement** *m* NUCLEAIRE training reactor; ~ **d'épitaxie** *m* ELECTRON epitaxy reactor; ~ **d'essais de matériaux** *m* NUCLEAIRE MTR, materials testing reactor; ~ **à faisceau sorti** *m* NUCLEAIRE beam reactor; ~ **à fluide bouillant** *m* NUCLEAIRE boiling reactor; ~ **gros porteur** *m* TRANSPORT jumbo jet; ~ **à haute température à éléments** *m* NUCLEAIRE block-type element-fueled high temperature reactor (AmE), block-type element-fuelled high temperature reactor

(BrE); ~ **à haut flux** *m* NUCLEAIRE *de neutrons* high flux reactor; ~ **hétérogène** *m* NUCLEAIRE heterogeneous reactor; ~ **homogène** *m* TRANSPORT homogeneous reactor; ~ **hybride à eau légère** *m* NUCLEAIRE LWHR, light water hybrid reactor; ~ **à injection d'air** *m* TRANSPORT AIR, air injection reactor; ~ **de laboratoire** *m* NUCLEAIRE laboratory reactor; ~ **Magnox** *m* NUCLEAIRE magnox reactor; ~ **de mesure** *m* NUCLEAIRE measurements reactor; ~ **à miroirs à champ renversé** *m* NUCLEAIRE field reversed mirror reactor; ~ **à miroir tandem** *m* NUCLEAIRE TMR, tandem mirror fusion reactor; ~ **mobile** *m* NUCLEAIRE transportable reactor; ~ **modéré au béryllium** *m* NUCLEAIRE beryllium moderated reactor; ~ **négatif** *m* NUCLEAIRE negative flux image reactor, negative reactor; ~ **à neutrons rapides** *m* NUCLEAIRE fast reactor; ~ **nu** *m* NUCLEAIRE *sans réflecteur* bare reactor; ~ **nucléaire** *m* ELECTR *générateur* nuclear reactor, NUCLEAIRE nuclear reactor, pile, reactor, PHYSIQUE nuclear reactor; ~ **nucléaire naturel** *m* NUCLEAIRE fossil nuclear reactor, natural nuclear reactor; ~ **nucléaire de puissance** *m* CONSTR nuclear reactor; ~ **pile de puissance nulle** *m* NUCLEAIRE zero energy reactor, zero power reactor; ~ **pile à uranium** *m* NUCLEAIRE uranium reactor; ~ **pilote** *m* AERONAUT master engine; ~ **pour l'étude des effets de rayonnement** *m* NUCLEAIRE radiation effects reactor; ~ **préfabriqué** *m* NUCLEAIRE package reactor; ~ **presque critique** *m* NUCLEAIRE near critical reactor; ~ **presque régénérateur** *m* NUCLEAIRE quasi-breeder reactor; ~ **de puissance en série** *m* NUCLEAIRE series produced power reactor; ~ **de radiochimie** *m* NUCLEAIRE chemonuclear fuel reactor; ~ **rapide à lit de boulets quasistatique** *m* NUCLEAIRE settled bed fast reactor; ~ **à réflecteur de béryllium** *m* NUCLEAIRE beryllium reflected reactor; ~ **refroidi à l'eau** *m* NUCLEAIRE light-water-cooled reactor, water-cooled reactor; ~ **refroidi au gaz** *m* NUCLEAIRE gas-cooled nuclear power plant; ~ **refroidi par azote** *m* NUCLEAIRE nitrogen-cooled reactor; ~ **refroidi par un écoulement en phase dispersée** *m* NUCLEAIRE dispersion-cooled reactor; ~ **refroidi au sodium** *m* NUCLEAIRE sodium-cooled reactor; ~ **refroidi à vapeur saturée** *m* NUCLEAIRE saturated steam-cooled heater; ~ **sec** *m* AERONAUT dry engine; ~ **secondaire** *m* NUCLEAIRE secondary reactor; ~ **sigma** *m* NUCLEAIRE sigma pile; ~ **source** *m* NUCLEAIRE neutron source reactor, source reactor; ~ **sous eau** *m* NUCLEAIRE underwater reactor; ~ **à stabilité inhérente** *m* NUCLEAIRE inherently stable reactor; ~ **surrégénérateur** *m* NUCLEAIRE, PHYSIQUE breeder reactor; ~ **surrégénérateur refroidi au gaz** *m* NUCLEAIRE GCBR, gas-cooled breeder reactor; ~ **à suspension solide** *m* NUCLEAIRE FSR, flowable solids reactor; ~ **thermique** *m* PHYS RAYON thermal reactor, TRANSPORT thermal exhaust manifold reactor; ~ **à thorium** *m* NUCLEAIRE thorium fueled reactor (AmE), thorium fuelled reactor (BrE); ~ **transportable** *m* NUCLEAIRE package reactor, transportable reactor; ~ **travaillant à une seule pression** *m* NUCLEAIRE one-cycle reactor; ~ **à ultra haute température** *m* NUCLEAIRE ultrahigh temperature reactor; ~ **à uranium-eau lourde** *m* NUCLEAIRE uranium heavy water reactor

réactif[1] *adj* ELECTR *courant alternatif* wattless

réactif[2] *m* CHARBON, CHIMIE, PHOTO reagent; ~ **antivoile** *m* CINEMAT, PHOTO antifogging agent; ~ **collecteur** *m* CHARBON collecting reagent; ~ **cupro-alcalin** *m* CHIMIE Fehling's solution

réaction *f* AERONAUT jet propulsion, CHIMIE reaction, reagency, COMMANDE reaction, response, CONS MECA interaction, ELECTRON, ENREGISTR, INFORMAT, ORDINAT feedback, PHYSIQUE reaction, TV feedback circuit; ~ **absorbante de neutrons** *f* NUCLEAIRE neutron-absorbing reaction; ~ **acoustique** *f* ENREGISTR acoustic feedback; ~ **de Cannizzaro** *f* CHIMIE Cannizzaro reaction; ~ **capacitive** *f* ELECTROTEC capacitive feedback; ~ **catalytique** *f* GAZ catalytic reaction; ~ **chimique des radiations** *f* PHYS RAYON radiation induced reaction; ~ **critique** *f* PHYS RAYON critical reaction; ~ **de deutérium catalysée** *f* NUCLEAIRE catalyzed deuterium reaction; ~ **de Diels-Alder** *f* CHIMIE Diels-Alder reaction; ~ **d'échange d'énergie** *f* NUCLEAIRE energy exchange reaction; ~ **en chaîne** *f* CONS MECA chain reaction, METALL autocatalytic effect, chain reaction, PHYS RAYON *des neutrons en fission nucléaire*, PHYSIQUE chain reaction; ~ **endothermique** *f* EN RENOUV *énergie solaire*, GAZ endothermic reaction; ~ **en phase vapeur** *f* ELECTRON vapor phase reaction (AmE), vapour phase reaction (BrE); ~ **eutétique** *f* METALL eutetic reaction; ~ **au freinage** *f* TRANSPORT brake reaction; ~ **de Friedel-Craft** *f* CHIMIE Friedel-Crafts reaction; ~ **inductive** *f* ELECTROTEC inductive feedback; ~ **d'induit** *f* ELECTR *machine*, ELECTROTEC armature reaction; ~ **interférence du premier ordre** *f* PHYS RAYON primary interference; ~ **inverse** *f* NUCLEAIRE *en retour, de recombinaison* back reaction, reverse reaction; ~ **isotherme** *f* METALL isothermal reaction; ~ **monomoléculaire** *f* CHIMIE monomolecular reaction; ~ **monophasée** *f* METALL monophase reaction; ~ **négative** *f* ELECTRON, ENREGISTR negative feedback; ~ **normale** *f* PHYSIQUE normal reaction; ~ **nucléaire** *f* ASTRONOMIE *étoiles en activité*, CHIMIE, PHYS RAYON, PHYSIQUE nuclear reaction; ~ **nucléaire induite** *f* NUCLEAIRE artificial nuclear reaction, induced nuclear reaction; ~ **nucléaire secondaire** *f* NUCLEAIRE secondary nuclear reaction; ~ **par voie humide** *f* CHIMIE wet reaction; ~ **péritectique** *f* METALL peritectic reaction; ~ **photonucléaire directe** *f* NUCLEAIRE direct photonuclear effect; ~ **positive** *f* COMMANDE positive feedback, ELECTRON regenerative feedback, ENREGISTR, PHYS RAYON positive feedback; ~ **du premier ordre** *f* CHIMIE, METALL first-order reaction; ~ **des radicaux libres** *f* PLAST CAOU free radical reaction; ~ **de Salpeter** *f* NUCLEAIRE Salpeter process, triple alpha process; ~ **sans diffusion** *f* METALL diffusionless reaction; ~ **sous-critique** *f* PHYS RAYON subcritical reaction; ~ **supracritique** *f* PHYS RAYON supercritical reaction; ~ **tactile** *f* PRODUCTION tactile feedback; ~ **thermonucléaire** *f* ASTRONOMIE, NUCLEAIRE, PHYSIQUE thermonuclear reaction; ~ **de transfert** *f* NUCLEAIRE transfer reaction; ~ **de transfert de nombreux nucléons** *f* NUCLEAIRE many-nuclear transfer reaction; ~ **ultrarapide** *f* CHIMIE ultrarapid reaction

réactivation *f* CHARBON, CHIMIE reactivation; ~ **du hot-melt par la chaleur** *f* IMPRIM *brochure* heat reactivation

réactiver *vt* CHIMIE *un catalyseur* reactivate

réactivité *f* NUCLEAIRE, PHYSIQUE reactivity; ~ **de l'empoisonnement xénon** *f* NUCLEAIRE xenon poisoning reactivity

réajustement: ~ **atomique** *m* METALL atomic shuffling

réalésage *m* AUTO reboring

réaléser *vt* AUTO rebore, CONS MECA counterbore, rebore, VEHICULES *moteur, cylindre* rebore

réalgar *m* MINERAUX realgar, red arsenic

réalimentation: ~ **du frein** *f* CH DE FER *véhicules* refilling the brake; ~ **naturelle d'eau souterraine** *f* DISTRI EAU natural groundwater recharge

réalisateur *m* CINEMAT film director; ~ **de dessin animé** *m* CINEMAT animation director

réalisation *f* INFORMAT, ORDINAT implementation, instance; ~ **anticipée** *f* PRODUCTION advance termination

réaliser *vt* BREVETS *invention* make, CINEMAT direct, TV produce; ~ **en tôlerie** *vt* MECANIQUE fabricate

réalité: ~ **virtuelle** *f* ORDINAT virtual reality

réallumage *m* ESPACE *véhicules* reignition

réamorcer *vt* CONS MECA *injecteur* restart

réanimateur *m* SECURITE resuscitator

réappliquer *vt* COMMANDE feed back

réapprovisionnement *m* PRODUCTION restocking

réarmement: ~ **à distance** *m* PRODUCTION *automatisme industriel* remote reset

réarmer *vt* NAUT refit

réarpentage *m* CONSTR resurvey

réarrangement *m* CHIMIE *moléculaire* rearrangement; ~ **Beckmann** *m* CHIMIE Beckmann rearrangement; ~ **radial** *m* NUCLEAIRE *combustible* radial shift, radial shuffling

réavalement: ~ **d'un puits** *m* MINES shaft deepening

rebanchage *m* MINES *du mur* lifting

rebâtir *vt* CONSTR rebuild

rebobinage *m* ELECTR *générateur, moteur*, TEXTILE rewinding

rebobiner[1] *vt* ENREGISTR, INFORMAT, ORDINAT, PAPIER, TEXTILE rewind

rebobiner[2] *vi* CINEMAT backwind

rebobineuse *f* PAPIER rewinder

rebondir *vi* MILITAIRE rebound

rebondissement *m* PLAST CAOU rebound; ~ **à l'atterrissage** *m* AERONAUT bounced landing; ~ **de contacts** *m* AUTO contact chatter, ELECTR contact bounce, contact chatter, PRODUCTION *électricité* contact bounce

rebord *m* CONS MECA flange, ledge, *d'un tiroir, d'une lumière de cylindre* edge, CONSTR ledge, selvage, selvedge, *d'une serrure* edge plate, EQUIP LAB *ouverture*, PRODUCTION flange; ~ **de roue** *m* VEHICULES wheel flange

rebouchage *m* PETROLE plugging

rebouché *adj* PETROLE *puits* junked

rebouilleur *m* PETROLE reboiler

rebranchement *m* ELECTROTEC reconnection

rebrancher *vt* ELECTROTEC reconnect

rebroussement: ~ **des lèvres d'une faille** *m* GEOLOGIE fault drag

rebroyage *m* PRODUCTION regrinding

rebroyer *vt* CHARBON regrind

rebrûlage *m* CERAM VER edge fusion, edge melting, fire polishing

rebrûleuse *f* CERAM VER fire finisher

rebullage *m* CERAM VER reboil

rebut *m* INFORMAT, ORDINAT rejection, PRODUCTION refuse, scrap, spoiled casting, QUALITE nonacceptance, rejection; ~ **à l'entrée et à la sortie** *m* ORDINAT GIGO, garbage-in/garbage-out; ~ **d'uranium** *m* NUCLEAIRE uranium scrap

rebuter *vt* CONS MECA discard, QUALITE reject, TEXTILE discard, reject

rebuts *m pl* MECANIQUE junk, MINES barren ground, deads, waste ground, waste, PRODUCTION garbage (AmE), rubbish (BrE), rejects, waste, TEXTILE reject, seconds

recadrage *m* TV *de films* pan and scan

recadrer *vt* CINEMAT crop, reframe

recalage: ~ **de gyro** *m* AERONAUT gyro resetting; ~ **rapide** *m* AERONAUT fast slaving

recaler *vt* MECANIQUE reset

récalescence *f* PHYSIQUE recalescence

récent *adj* GEOLOGIE late, late-stage

recépage *m* CONSTR *de pieux, des pilotis* cutting-off

récépissé: ~ **de documents** *m* BREVETS receipt for documents

réceptacle: ~ **de vapeur** *m* INST HYDR steam dome

récepteur *m* CERAM VER trough, CONS MECA indicator, ELECTRON receiver, ELECTROTEC *d'énergie électrique* sink, ESPACE receiver, INFORMAT, INST HYDR, ORDINAT sink, PETROLE receiver, PHYSIQUE load, receiver, POLLUTION receptor, TELECOM pager, receiver, signal receiver, TRANSPORT, TV receiver; ~ **alphanumérique** *m* TELECOM alphanumeric pager; ~ **d'antenne** *m* TV off-air monitor; ~ **d'appel** *m* TELECOM call indicating device, pager; ~ **à bande étroite** *m* TELECOM narrow band receiver; ~ **de contrôle final** *m* TV master monitor; ~ **de courant** *m* ELECTROTEC current sink, sink; ~ **double** *m* CONS MECA dual indicator; ~ **à fibre optique** *m* ELECTROTEC fiberoptic receiver (AmE), fibreoptic receiver (BrE); ~ **gonio** *m* NAUT DF receiver, direction finding receiver; ~ **de guidage** *m* ESPACE *véhicules* guidance receiver; ~ **d'information** *m* ELECTROTEC data sink; ~ **intégré PIN-TEC** *m* OPTIQUE, TELECOM PIN-FET integrated receiver; ~ **à large bande** *m* TELECOM wide band receiver; ~ **de modem** *m* ELECTRON modem receiver; ~ **monochrome** *m* TV monochrome receiver; ~ **noir et blanc** *m* TV monochrome receiver; ~ **optique** *m* OPTIQUE optical receiver, TELECOM fiberoptic receiver (AmE), fibroptic receiver (BrE), optical receiver, optical receiver, receive fiber optic terminal device (AmE), receive fibre optic terminal device (BrE); ~ **optoélectronique** *m* TELECOM fiberoptic receiver (AmE), optoelectronic receiver; ~ **d'ordres** *m* ESPACE *véhicules* command receiver; ~ **photoélectrique** *m* OPTIQUE photoelectric receiver, TELECOM optical detector; ~ **portable** *m* TELECOM portable receiver; ~ **portatif** *m* TELECOM hand-held receiver; ~ **de prothèse auditive sans fil** *m* TELECOM wireless hearing aid receiver; ~ **de radiomessagerie** *m* TELECOM Message-master (TM), message pager; ~ **retour antenne** *m* TV off-air monitor; ~ **de signalisation MF** *m (récepteur de signalisation multifréquence)* TELECOM multifrequency receiver; ~ **de signalisation multifréquence** *m (récepteur de signalisation MF)* TELECOM multifrequency receiver; ~ **de signaux** *m* TELECOM signal receiver; ~ **téléphonique** *m* ACOUSTIQUE telephone earphone; ~ **de télévision** *m* ELECTRON, PHYSIQUE television receiver; ~ **témoin** *m* TV monitor; ~ **terrestre** *m* ESPACE *communications* Earth receiver; ~ **TV numérique** *m* TV digital TV receiver

réception:[1] **à** ~ **seule** *adj* INFORMAT, ORDINAT receive only

réception[2] *f* DISTRI EAU uptake, ESPACE acceptance, INFORMAT receipt, reception, MINES landing, ORDINAT receipt, reception, QUALITE acceptance; ~ **directe** *f* TV off-air pick-up; ~ **des données** *f* TELECOM received data; ~ **en diversité dans le temps** *f* TELECOM time diversity reception; ~ **de fabrication** *f* PRODUCTION shop receipt; ~ **du faisceau** *f* NUCLEAIRE acceptance of a beam; ~ **fournisseur** *f* PRODUCTION delivery; ~ **de la fréquence-image** *f* ELECTRON image frequency interference; ~ **par battements** *f* TV carrier difference system; ~ **des produits** *f* QUALITE receipt of goods; ~ **provisoire** *f* CONSTR completion; **à ~ seule** *f* INFORMAT receive only; ~ **seule** *f* INFORMAT, ORDINAT receive only

recette *f* CERAM VER top floor, IMPRIM *imprimerie* delivery, MECANIQUE *contrats* acceptance, MINES landing stage, landing station, lodge, onsetting, plane table, platt, plat; ~ **d'à haut** *f* MINES bank; ~ **à eau** *f* MINES lodge room; ~ **en usine** *f* MECANIQUE *contrats* factory acceptance; ~ **de fin de fabrication** *f* PRODUCTION shop receipt; ~ **du jour** *f* MINES bank; ~ **de puits** *f* MINES pit landing

recevoir *vt* INFORMAT, ORDINAT receive

rechange: ~ **de lampe** *f* PHOTO lamp replacement

recharge *f* ELECTROTEC recharging, HYDROLOGIE recharge, PRODUCTION filler; ~ **artificielle** *f* HYDROLOGIE artificial recharge; ~ **des batteries** *f* CONSTR recharging batteries

rechargé: en dur *adj* CONS MECA hard faced

rechargeable *adj* PHOTO rechargeable

rechargement *m* CONSTR, repaving, resurfacing, PRODUCTION reloading; ~ **des batteries** *m* CONSTR recharging batteries; ~ **bidirectionnel** *m* NUCLEAIRE bidirectional refueling (AmE), bidirectional refuelling (BrE); ~ **dur** *m* NUCLEAIRE hardfacing; ~ **sans arrêt** *m* NUCLEAIRE *combustible* hot refueling (AmE), hot refuelling (BrE), on-load refueling (AmE), on-load refuelling (BrE)

recharger *vt* CINEMAT reload, ELECTROTEC recharge, INFORMAT, ORDINAT, PHOTO reload

réchaud *m* THERMODYN *à bois, au charbon, à gaz, électrique, au mazout* cooker; ~ **électrique** *m* THERMODYN electric hot plate

réchauffage *m* AERONAUT heating, CERAM VER comeback, reheat (AmE), reheating (BrE), warming-in, MATERIAUX reheating, THERMODYN *au four* comeback; ~ **d'aiguilles** *m* CH DE FER points heating; ~ **de la soudure** *m* MATERIAUX postheating

réchauffe *f* CERAM VER comeback, THERMODYN afterburning, *au four* comeback, TRANSPORT reheat

réchauffer *vt* REFRIG reheat

réchauffeur *m* PRODUCTION heater; ~ **d'air** *m* CONS MECA air reheater, MAT CHAUFF, PAPIER air heater, THERMODYN blast preheater; ~ **d'air à régénération** *m* SECURITE regenerative airheater; ~ **d'air rotatif** *m* MAT CHAUFF rotary air heater; ~ **d'air tubulaire** *m* MAT CHAUFF tubular air heater; ~ **d'air électrique** *m* arc heater, electric arc heater, electric heater; ~ **de combustible** *m* AUTO carburetor jacket (AmE), carburettor jacket (BrE), heat riser tube; ~ **à combustibles solides** *m* CONS MECA solid fuel heater; ~ **diélectrique** *m* CONS MECA dielectric heater; ~ **d'eau d'alimentation** *m* CHAUFFAGE, PRODUCTION feedwater heater; ~ **électrique pour cuvette** *m* PHOTO dish heater; ~ **à immersion** *m* MAT CHAUFF immersion heater; ~ **à multicombustibles** *m* CONS MECA multifuel heater; ~ **pour cuve profonde** *m* PHOTO tank heater; ~ **radiant** *m* CONS MECA radiant heater

recherche *f* BREVETS search, INFORMAT retrieval, searching, search, MINES prospecting, prospection, ORDINAT retrieval, search, searching; ~ **appliquée** *f* POLLUTION applied research; ~ **arborescente** *f* INFORMAT, ORDINAT tree search; ~ **atomique** *f* NUCLEAIRE atomic research; ~ **auprès de collisionneurs** *f* PHYS PART research with colliders; ~ **avant arrière** *f* TV shuttle search; ~ **binaire** *f* INFORMAT, ORDINAT binary chop, binary search; ~ **dans une table** *f* INFORMAT, ORDINAT table lookup; ~ **dichotomique** *f* INFORMAT, ORDINAT Fibonacci search, dichotomizing search; ~ **documentaire** *f* INFORMAT IR, document retrieval, information retrieval, ORDINAT IR, information retrieval, document retrieval; ~ **des données** *f* ORDINAT data retrieval; ~ **en arrière** *f* INFORMAT, ORDINAT backtracking; ~ **d'erreurs** *f* QUALITE error retrieval; ~ **d'erreurs dans la mémoire** *f* PRODUCTION *automatisme industriel* memory tracking; ~ **et extraction de texte** *f* INFORMAT text search; ~ **et sauvetage** *f* NAUT search and rescue; ~ **de Fibonacci** *f* INFORMAT, ORDINAT Fibonacci search, dichotomizing search; ~ **forestière** *f* POLLUTION forestry research; ~ **hiérarchique** *f* INFORMAT, ORDINAT tree search; ~ **indexée** *f* INFORMAT, ORDINAT indexing; ~ **d'information** *f* INFORMAT data retrieval; ~ **minière magnétique** *f* GEOPHYS magnetic prospecting; ~ **minière par secousses provoquées** *f* GEOPHYS seismic prospecting; ~ **nucléaire** *f* PHYS RAYON nuclear research; ~ **opérationnelle** *f* *(RO)* INFORMAT, ORDINAT operational research, operations research; ~ **par chaînage** *f* INFORMAT, ORDINAT chaining search; ~ **par méthode sismique** *f* GEOPHYS seismic exploration method; ~ **par mot clé** *f* INFORMAT, ORDINAT keyword retrieval; ~ **de personnes** *f* TELECOM paging service; ~ **séquentielle** *f* INFORMAT, ORDINAT sequential search; ~ **du son en marche avant-arrière** *f* ENREGISTR rocking; ~ **spatiale** *f* ESPACE space research; ~ **spatiale au moyen de vols habités** *f* ESPACE manned space research; ~ **sur place** *f* CHARBON field investigation

rechercher *vt* ELECTROTEC locate, INFORMAT, ORDINAT seek

récif *m* NAUT, OCEANO reef; ~ **artificiel** *m* OCEANO artificial reef; ~ **corallien** *m* GEOLOGIE coral reef, OCEANO coral, coral reef; ~ **frangeant** *m* OCEANO fringing reef

récif-barrière *m* OCEANO barrier reef

récipient *m* CHIMIE receiver, receptacle, recipient, EQUIP LAB vessel, *verrerie* receiver, PHYSIQUE, TEXTILE vessel; ~ **de la centrifugeuse** *m* GENIE CHIM extractor basket; ~ **composite** *m* EMBALLAGE composite container; ~ **consigné** *m* EMBALLAGE returnable container; ~ **d'égouttement** *m* PRODUCTION *système hydraulique* drip tray; ~ **en forme de poire** *m* EQUIP LAB *verrerie* pear-shaped vessel; ~ **en grès** *m* CERAM VER earthenware jar; ~ **en polyoléfine** *m* EMBALLAGE polyolefin container; ~ **en polyéthythène** *m* EMBALLAGE polyethylene container; ~ **en verre** *m* EMBALLAGE glass container; ~ **de sécurité** *m* EQUIP LAB safety container, SECURITE *stockage de liquides inflammables* safety vessel; ~ **séparateur** *m* GENIE CHIM decantation tank; ~ **de séparation** *m* GENIE CHIM decantation glass, decantation vessel, refining glass; ~ **sous pression** *m* PETROLE pressure equipment, REFRIG pressure vessel; ~ **style bécher** *m* PRODUCTION beaker-type container; ~ **à unités multiples** *m* EMBALLAGE multiunit container

récipient-dose *m* EMBALLAGE unit-dose container

réciproque[1] *adj* CONS MECA converse, inverse, MATH inverse

réciproque[2] *f* CONS MECA inverse, GEOMETRIE, INFORMAT

reciprocal, MATH inverse, reciprocal, ORDINAT reciprocal

recirculation: ~ **des gaz brûlés** *f* THERMODYN waste gas heat recovery; ~ **des gaz de carter** *f* TRANSPORT exhaust recirculation; ~ **des gaz de carter accompagnée d'injection d'air** *f* TRANSPORT exhaust gas recirculation with air injection; ~ **des produits de fission** *f* NUCLEAIRE recirculation of fission products

réciter: ~ **la rose des vents** *vi* NAUT box the compass

recoin *m* CONSTR recess

recollage: ~ **sur bande pour impression en continu** *f* IMPRIM conti-snap

recollement *m* PHYS FLUID *de tourbillons* reattachment; ~ **turbulent** *m* PHYS FLUID turbulent reattachment

récolte *f* PRODUCTION yield; ~ **d'or** *f* MINES gold cleanup

récolter *vt* MINES *l'or des plaques* clean up, wash

recombinaison *f* ELECTRON, PHYSIQUE recombination; ~ **électron trou** *f* NUCLEAIRE electron hole recombination; ~ **radiative** *f* ELECTRON radiative recombination

recommandation *f* ESPACE *du CCITT ou du CCIR* recommendation; ~ **de sécurité** *f* AERONAUT safety recommendation

recompression *f* OCEANO recompression

reconditionnement *m* CONS MECA reconditioning, PETROLE *forage* workover, PRODUCTION reconditioning

reconditionner *vt* PRODUCTION recondition

reconduction: ~ **de droits** *f* PETROLE retention of rights

reconfigurable *adj* INFORMAT, ORDINAT reconfigurable

reconfiguration *f* INFORMAT, ORDINAT reconfiguration

reconfigurer *vt* INFORMAT, ORDINAT reconfigure

recongeler *vt* REFRIG refreeze

reconnaissance *f* ACOUSTIQUE, INFORMAT, ORDINAT recognition, PRODUCTION inspection; ~ **de caractères** *f* INFORMAT, ORDINAT character recognition; ~ **des formes** *f* ELECTRON, INFORMAT, TELECOM pattern recognition; ~ **géologique** *f* PETROLE geological survey; ~ **géophysique** *f* GEOPHYS geophysical exploration, PETROLE geophysical survey; ~ **magnétique de caractères** *f* (RMC) INFORMAT, ORDINAT magnetic ink character recognition (MICR); ~ **optique des caractères** *f* (ROC) IMPRIM, INFORMAT, ORDINAT optical character recognition (OCR); ~ **de la parole** *f* INFORMAT, ORDINAT speech recognition, TELECOM voice recognition; ~ **du sol** *f* CHARBON soil exploration

reconnaître *vt* INFORMAT acknowledge, MINES prove, ORDINAT acknowledge

reconnecter *vt* ELECTROTEC reconnect

reconnexion *f* ELECTROTEC reconnection

reconstruction *f* CONSTR rebuilding, reconstruction

reconstruire *vt* CONSTR rebuild, INFORMAT, ORDINAT reconstruct

recoupe *f* MINES cross drift, cross drive, cross entry, crossheading, offset drive, drift, offset; ~ **d'aérage** *f* MINES crossheading; ~ **de blé** *f* AGRO ALIM middlings

recoupement: ~ **par bombardement** *m* PHYS RAYON cross bombardment

recouper[1] *vt* GEOLOGIE cross, intersect, MINES cross drive, tap

recouper:[2] ~ **un filon** *vi* MINES cut a lode

recoupettes *f pl* AGRO ALIM middlings bran

recours *m* BREVETS appeal

recouvert *adj* REVETEMENT coated

recouvrement *m* CONSTR lap, overlapping, overlap, EMBALLAGE coating, GEOLOGIE, IMPRIM overlap, INFORMAT overlay, MATERIAUX overlapping, MINES overburden, ORDINAT overlay, TV *des têtes* crossover, overlap; ~ **à l'admission** *m* INST HYDR outside lap, *d'un distributeur de vapeur* steam lap; ~ **de chrome dur** *m* CONS MECA *pour outillages, jauges, etc* hard chrome plating; ~ **à l'échappement** *m* INST HYDR inside cover, *d'un tiroir de distribution* inside lap slide valve; ~ **en discordance angulaire** *m* GEOLOGIE toplap; ~ **extérieur** *m* INST HYDR outside lap; ~ **de fréquence** *m* TV frequency overlap; ~ **intérieur** *m* INST HYDR inside cover, inside lap slide valve; ~ **négatif** *m* PRODUCTION clearance; ~ **perforé** *m* EMBALLAGE perforated overlap; ~ **de protection** *m* REVETEMENT protective bonnet, protective cover, protective covering, protective sheathing; ~ **de tiroir** *m* INST HYDR lap; ~ **d'un tiroir distributeur** *m* INST HYDR lap

recouvrir *vt* PRODUCTION *un palier* line; ~ **d'une couche de béton appliquée par projection** *vt* CONSTR spray with shotcrete; ~ **de glace** *vt* GEOLOGIE glaciate

recristallisation *f* CHIMIE, CRISTALL, METALL recrystallization; ~ **secondaire** *f* METALL secondary recrystallization; ~ **tertiaire** *f* METALL tertiary recrystallization

rectangle *m* GEOMETRIE oblong, rectangle; ~ **de Berne** *m* CH DE FER Berne rectangle

rectangulaire *adj* GEOMETRIE rectangular

rectangularité *f* GEOMETRIE rectangularity

rectifiage: ~ **frontal** *m* PRODUCTION face grinding

rectificateur *m* CHIMIE rectifier; ~ **d'huile** *m* REFRIG oil still

rectificatif *m* CONS MECA amendment, correction

rectification *f* CHIMIE rectification, redistillation, CONS MECA rectification, MECANIQUE grinding, PRODUCTION extra labor (AmE), extra labour (BrE), straightening; ~ **des clapets à boisseau** *f* PRODUCTION valve spool grinding; ~ **cylindrique** *f* CONS MECA, MECANIQUE cylindrical grinding; ~ **en coordonnées** *f* CONS MECA jig grinding; ~ **en plan** *f* CONS MECA surface grinding; ~ **extérieure** *f* RESSORTS surface rectification; ~ **des filetages** *f* CONS MECA thread grinding; ~ **intérieure** *f* CONS MECA internal grinding; ~ **de précision** *f* PRODUCTION precision grinding; ~ **de profilage** *f* CONS MECA form grinding; ~ **des profils** *f* CONS MECA profile grinding; ~ **sans centre** *f* CONS MECA centerless grinding (AmE), centerless precision grinding (AmE), centreless grinding (BrE), centreless precision grinding (BrE); ~ **sec** *f* CONS MECA dry precision grinding; ~ **du tir** *f* MILITAIRE fire correction; ~ **universelle** *f* PRODUCTION universal grinding

rectifié *adj* CHIMIE rectified, RESSORTS ground; ~ **visuellement** *adj* IMPRIM *composition informatique* optically letter-spaced

rectifier *vt* CHIMIE redistil, CONS MECA amend, true, true up, CONSTR *le tracé d'une route* straighten, MECANIQUE grind, PRODUCTION grind, straighten, VEHICULES *soupapes de moteur* reseat

rectifieuse *f* CONS MECA grinding machine, MECANIQUE grinder; ~ **cylindrique** *f* MECANIQUE cylindrical grinder; ~ **cylindrique universelle compacte à CNC** *f* CONS MECA compact CNC universal cylindrical grinding machine; ~ **à haute vitesse** *f* CONS MECA high-speed grinding machine; ~ **de profil optique** *f* CONS MECA optical profile grinder; ~ **sans centre** *f* MECANIQUE centerless grinder (AmE), centreless grinder (BrE)

rectiligne *adj* CONS MECA rectilinear, MECANIQUE rectilineal

recto *m* PAPIER recto

reçu: ~ **de bord** *m* NAUT mate's receipt

recueil: ~ **de données** *m* TELECOM data collection; ~ **des eaux de pluie** *m* DISTRI EAU rainwater catchment

recuire *vt* CERAM VER, MECANIQUE *procédé* anneal; ~ **en pot** *vt* THERMODYN pot anneal

recuisson *f* CERAM VER annealing

recuit[1] *adj* CRISTALL, THERMODYN annealed; ~ **doux** *adj* RESSORTS soft-annealed; ~ **en atmosphère contrôlée** *adj* THERMODYN annealed under gas

recuit[2] *m* CRISTALL, ELECTRON, MAT CHAUFF, METALL annealing, THERMODYN anneal, annealing; ~ **d'a-doucissement** *m* METALL soft annealing, THERMODYN soft anneal; ~ **d'adoucissement complet** *m* THERMO-DYN dead soft anneal; ~ **d'affinage** *m* THERMODYN grain-refining anneal; ~ **blanc** *m* MAT CHAUFF bright annealing; ~ **de coalescence** *m* THERMODYN dead anneal, soft anneal; ~ **complet** *m* THERMODYN dead soft anneal, soft anneal; ~ **de détente** *m* THERMODYN stress-relieving anneal; ~ **d'élimination des tensions** *m* THERMODYN stress-relieving anneal; ~ **en caisse** *m* MAT CHAUFF close annealing; ~ **isochrone** *m* METALL isochronal annealing; ~ **isothermique** *m* METALL isothermal annealing; ~ **au laser** *m* ELECTRON laser annealing; ~ **de mise en solution** *m* METALL solution annealing; ~ **par faisceau d'électrons** *m* ELECTRON electron beam annealing; ~ **de précipitation** *m* GENIE CHIM precipitation annealing, THERMODYN precipita-tion anneal; ~ **rapide** *m* CERAM VER rapid annealing

recul *m* CONS MECA backward motion, backward move-ment, recoil, MECANIQUE, MILITAIRE *d'une arme à feu, d'un canon* recoil, NAUT *du vent* backing; ~ **d'entrée** *m* ESPACE *communications d'un TOP* input back-off; ~ **à la fission** *m* NUCLEAIRE fission recoil; ~ **du piston** *m* INST HYDR piston back stroke; ~ **de sortie** *m* ESPACE *communications* output back-off

reculer: ~ **d'un espace** *vi* INFORMAT, ORDINAT back-space

reculoire *f* MINES drag, safety drag bar

récupérage: ~ **de matériaux mélangés** *m* EMBALLAGE multimaterial recycling

récupérateur *m* CERAM VER, MAT CHAUFF recuperator, POLLU MER recovery device, POLLUTION recovery de-vice, skimmer, PRODUCTION recuperator; ~ **autopropulsé** *m* POLLU MER self-propelled skimmer; ~ **à bande** *m* POLLU MER, POLLUTION belt skimmer; ~ **à bande absorbante** *m* POLLUTION absorbent belt skim-mer; ~ **à bande transporteuse** *m* POLLUTION conveyor belt skimmer; ~ **centrifuge** *m* POLLU MER centrifugal skimmer; ~ **de chaleur** *m* THERMODYN heat econ-omizer; ~ **du coeur** *m* NUCLEAIRE core catcher, melting core catcher; ~ **à corde flottante** *m* POLLU MER rope skimmer; ~ **à courroie** *m* POLLU MER, POLLUTION belt skimmer; ~ **à courroie oléophile** *m* POLLU MER oleophilic belt skimmer; ~ **à déversoir** *m* POLLU MER, POLLUTION weir skimmer; ~ **à disque** *m* POLLU MER, POLLUTION disc skimmer (BrE), disk skimmer (AmE); ~ **dynamique** *m* POLLU MER hydrodynamic skimmer; ~ **mécanique** *m* POLLUTION oil recovery skimmer; ~ **à seuil** *m* POLLU MER weir skimmer; ~ **à succion directe** *m* POLLU MER direct suction skimmer; ~ **à tambour** *m* POLLU MER drum skimmer; ~ **à vortex** *m* POLLU MER vortex skimmer, POLLUTION cyclone recovery skimmer

récupération *f* AERONAUT salvage, CHARBON recovery, CHIMIE recuperation, ESPACE *véhicules*, INFORMAT re-covery, NAUT recovery, salvage, OCEANO, ORDINAT, PETR recovery, PETROLE reclaiming, PLAST CAOU re-covery, POLLU MER collection, recovery, POLLUTION recovery, RECYCLAGE reclamation, recovery, salvag-ing, TEXTILE recovery, retrieval; ~ **d'air dynamique** *f* AERONAUT ram recovery; ~ **après surcharge** *f* ELEC-TROTEC recovery from dynamic loads; ~ **de l'argent** *f* CINEMAT silver recovery; ~ **assistée du pétrole** *f* *(RAP)* PETROLE enhanced oil recovery *(EOR)*; ~ **de barrage** *f* POLLU MER boom retrieval; ~ **de chaleur** *f* CHAUFFAGE, RECYCLAGE, THERMODYN heat recovery; ~ **de la chaleur perdue** *f* THERMODYN waste heat recovery; ~ **d'énergie** *f* THERMODYN energy recovery, energy recuperation, energy regeneration; ~ **de l'énergie** *f* RECYCLAGE energy recovery; ~ **de fichier** *f* INFORMAT, ORDINAT file recovery; ~ **finale** *f* PETR ulti-mate recovery; ~ **des matériaux** *f* RECYCLAGE materials reclamation; ~ **de métal** *f* CHARBON metal recovery; ~ **de place en mémoire** *f* INFORMAT, ORDI-NAT garbage collection; ~ **des positions inutilisées** *f* INFORMAT, ORDINAT garbage collection; ~ **primaire** *f* PETR, PETROLE primary recovery; ~ **secondaire** *f* PETR, PETROLE secondary recovery; ~ **du solvant** *f* AGRO ALIM, IMPRIM solvent recovery; ~ **tertiaire** *f* PETROLE tertiary recovery; ~ **thermique** *f* THERMODYN waste heat recovery

récupérer *vt* CHARBON, IMPRIM *papiers, huiles* recover, INFORMAT, ORDINAT restore, PAPIER save, POLLUTION recover, RECYCLAGE recover, salvage, TELECOM re-cover

récurer *vt* LESSIVES scour

récurrence *f* INFORMAT, ORDINAT recursion

récurrent *adj* INFORMAT, ORDINAT recursive

récursif *adj* INFORMAT, ORDINAT recursive

recuvelage *m* CONSTR recasing

recyclable *adj* RECYCLAGE recyclable

recyclage *m* CERAM VER, CHARBON recycling, CHIMIE rerun, *des acides* recycling, CONSTR recycling, GEO-LOGIE cycling, MATERIAUX, POLLUTION, PRODUCTION recycling, TELECOM recycle; ~ **des cartonnages** *m* EMBALLAGE recycling of paper cartons; ~ **des déchets** *m* RECYCLAGE waste recycling; ~ **des eaux résiduaires** *m* NUCLEAIRE wastewater recycling operation; ~ **des gaz de carter** *m* AUTO PCV, positive crankcase venti-lation, VEHICULES *moteur* positive crankcase ventilation

recycler *vt* CHARBON recirculate, CONSTR recycle, IMPRIM *papiers, huiles* recover, METALL reblow, POLLUTION recover, recycle, PRODUCTION recycle, RECYCLAGE recover, recycle

redan *m* AERONAUT hull step

redémarrage *m* INFORMAT, ORDINAT restart; ~ **automatique** *m* INFORMAT, ORDINAT PFR, power fail restart

redémarrer *vt* ORDINAT, TELECOM restart

redevance *f* BREVETS royalties, PETROLE royalty; ~ **d'aéroport** *f* AERONAUT airport charge; ~ **d'atterris-sages** *f* AERONAUT landing charge (BrE), landing fee (AmE)

redéveloppement *m* CINEMAT redevelopment

rediffuser *vt* TV rebroadcast

rediffusion *f* TV repeat

redistillation *f* CHIMIE rerun

redistribution *f* ELECTROTEC redistribution; ~ **des charges** *f* ELECTROTEC spill

redondance:[1] **en** ~ *adj* TELECOM stand-by, stand-by working

redondance[2] *f* INFORMAT, ORDINAT, TELECOM redundancy

redondant *adj* INFORMAT, ORDINAT redundant

redoublement *m* PRODUCTION relining

redox *m* CHIMIE redox

redressage *m* PRODUCTION straightening

redressé *adj* CHIMIE rectified

redressement:[1] **à ~ automatique** *adj* NAUT self-righting

redressement[2] *m* CONS MECA, ELECTR, ELECTROTEC rectification, PRODUCTION *de tubes faussés ou gauchis* straightening, TV *d'une image* inversion; **~ d'une alternance** *m* ELECTROTEC half-wave rectification; **~ demi-onde** *m* ELECTR half-wave rectification, single wave rectification, ELECTROTEC half-wave rectification; **~ à deux alternances** *m* ELECTR full-wave rectification; **~ par effet thermoélectronique** *m* ELECTROTEC thermionic rectification; **~ pleine onde** *m* ELECTR, ELECTROTEC full-wave rectification; **~ d'une seule alternance** *m* ELECTROTEC half-wave rectification; **~ du signal de chrominance** *m* TV subcarrier rectification

redresser *vt* CONS MECA true, true up, ELECTR *courant alternatif*, ELECTROTEC rectify, PRODUCTION rectify, *une tige faussée* straighten

redresse-tubes *m* PRODUCTION drift, swage

redresseur *m* AUTO, CINEMAT, ELECTR *courant alternatif et courant continu*, ELECTROTEC, ENREGISTR, PHYSIQUE rectifier, PRODUCTION drift, swage, TELECOM rectifier unit, rectifier, VEHICULES *système électrique* rectifier; **~ à une alternance** *m* ELECTROTEC, PHYSIQUE half-wave rectifier; **~ à arc** *m* ELECTROTEC arc rectifier; **~ biphasé** *m* ELECTR single way modulator, single way rectifier; **~ de charge d'accumulateurs** *m* ELECTR charging rectifier; **~ à court temps de transition inverse** *m* ELECTROTEC fast reverse-recovery rectifier; **~ à cuve scellée** *m* ELECTROTEC sealed rectifier; **~ à décharge luminescente** *m* ELECTROTEC glow discharge rectifier; **~ demi-onde** *m* ELECTR, ELECTROTEC, PHYSIQUE half-wave rectifier; **~ à deux alternances** *m* ELECTROTEC, PHYSIQUE full-wave rectifier; **~ à double alternance** *m* PHYSIQUE full-wave rectifier; **~ électrolytique** *m* ELECTR, ELECTROTEC electrolytic rectifier; **~ en pont** *m* ELECTR, ELECTROTEC bridge rectifier; **~ au germanium** *m* ELECTR, ELECTROTEC germanium rectifier; **~ de grande puissance** *m* ELECTROTEC high-power rectifier; **~ à haute tension** *m* ELECTR high-voltage rectifier; **~ hexaphasé** *m* ELECTROTEC six-phase rectifier; **~ à ignitrons** *m* ELECTROTEC ignitron rectifier; **~ indirect** *m* ELECTR indirect rectifier; **~ à jonction PN** *m* ELECTROTEC p-n rectifier; **~ métal** *m* ELECTR metal rectifier; **~ métal-semiconducteur** *m* ELECTROTEC metallic rectifier; **~ monoanodique** *m* ELECTROTEC single anode rectifier; **~ monophasé en pont** *m* ELECTR single-phase bridge rectifier; **~ à ordre de phases** *m* ELECTR *système à trois phases* phase sequence rectifier; **~ à l'oxyde de cuivre** *m* ELECTROTEC copper-oxide rectifier; **~ parfait** *m* ELECTROTEC ideal rectifier; **~ pleine onde** *m* ELECTROTEC, PHYSIQUE full-wave rectifier; **~ point-plaque** *m* ELECTR point plate rectifier; **~ polyanodique** *m* ELECTROTEC multianode rectifier; **~ pour commutation rapide** *m* ELECTROTEC fast-switching power rectifier; **~ pour lampe à arc** *m* CINEMAT arc rectifier; **~ de puissance** *m* ELECTR power rectifier; **~ sec** *m* ELECTROTEC metallic rectifier; **~ de secteur** *m* ELECTR current rectifier (AmE), mains

rectifier (BrE); **~ au sélénium** *m* ELECTR, ELECTROTEC, PHYSIQUE selenium rectifier; **~ à semi-conducteur** *m* ELECTR, ELECTROTEC semiconductor rectifier; **~ au silicium** *m* ELECTR, ELECTROTEC, PHYSIQUE silicon rectifier; **~ au silicium commandé** *m* ELECTROTEC, PHYSIQUE SCR, silicon-controlled rectifier; **~ à simple alternance** *m* PHYSIQUE half-wave rectifier; **~ thermoionique** *m* ELECTROTEC thermionic rectifier; **~ THT** *m* TV EHT rectifier; **~ à vapeur de mercure** *m* ELECTROTEC mercury arc rectifier, mercury rectifier, mercury vapor rectifier (AmE), mercury vapour rectifier (BrE); **~ à vide définitif** *m* ELECTROTEC sealed rectifier

réducteur *m* CHIMIE reducer, reducing agent, *corps* reductant, CINEMAT reducer, CONS MECA gear head, CONSTR reducer, reducing pipe fitting, PRODUCTION *système hydraulique* gearbox; **~ de bruit** *m* ENREGISTR, TELECOM noise reducer; **~ de charge** *m* COMMANDE regulating switch; **~ de débit** *m* PRODUCTION *système hydraulique* throttle valve; **~ de décharge** *m* COMMANDE regulating switch; **~ épicyclique** *m* NAUT epicyclic gear; **~ épicycloïdal** *m* NAUT epicyclic gear; **~ d'essieu monté** *m* TRANSPORT wheel and axle drive; **~ de mesure** *m* ELECTR instrument transformer; **~ de pression** *m* AERONAUT pressure reducer, CONS MECA, PRODUCTION *système hydraulique* pressure-reducing valve; **~ de pression pour air comprimé** *m* CONS MECA airline pressure regulator; **~ de pression proportionnel** *m* PRODUCTION *système hydraulique* proportional pressure reducing valve; **~ de puissance** *m* REFRIG capacity reducer; **~ de tuyau** *m* CONSTR pipe reducer; **~ de vitesse** *m* CONS MECA speed reducer, PAPIER speed governor, speed reducer

réductif *adj* CHIMIE reductive

réduction *f* CHARBON, CHIMIE reduction, IMPRIM *photographique, électronique* crimp, POLLU MER mitigation; **~ d'altitude** *f* GEOPHYS free air reduction; **~ de Bouguer** *f* GEOPHYS Bouguer correction; **~ de bruit** *f* ENREGISTR noise reduction; **~ catalytique** *f* MATERIAUX catalytic reduction process; **~ catalytique sélective** *f* POLLUTION selective catalytic reduction; **~ des coûts du montage mécanique** *f* CONS MECA cost reduction in mechanical assembly; **~ de données** *f* INFORMAT, ORDINAT data reduction; **~ des émissions de SO2** *f* POLLUTION sulfur dioxide reduction (AmE), sulphur dioxide reduction (BrE); **~ en lit fluidisé** *f* GENIE CHIM fluidized bed reduction; **~ en trame** *f* TEXTILE weft density; **~ d'erreurs** *f* TELECOM error correction; **~ des étincelles** *f* ELECTROTEC spark suppression; **~ finale** *f* AUTO final drive; **~ finale à double rapport** *f* AUTO two-speed final drive; **~ finale à vis sans fin** *f* AUTO worm gear final drive; **~ granulométrique** *f* CHARBON particle size reduction; **~ du niveau sonore** *f* IMPRIM noise reduction; **~ du pH** *f* POLLUTION pH depression; **~ du plan d'image** *f* TV cropping; **~ de production** *f* TEXTILE cutback; **~ sur facture** *f* IMPRIM abatement; **~ au zénith** *f* ESPACE zenith reduction

réduire[1] *vt* CHIMIE *oxyde* reduce, IMPRIM *photographiquement, électroniquement* crimp, PHOTO *l'éclairage* dim, PRODUCTION thin, thin out; **~ en cendres** *vt* CHIMIE reduce to ashes, THERMODYN destroy by fire; **~ en poudre** *vt* CHIMIE reduce to powder; **~ par ébullition** *vt* AGRO ALIM boil down, GENIE CHIM thicken by boiling; **~ la taille des points de** *vt* IMPRIM sharpen

réduire[2] *vi* CHARBON reduce, THERMODYN *par ébullition* boil away; **~ l'effet de la commande** *vi* PRODUCTION back off; ~ **les gaz** *vi* AERONAUT throttle back; ~ **la largeur de bande** *vi* ELECTRON band-limit; ~ **progressivement le volume** *vi* ENREGISTR fade down; ~ **la vitesse** *vi* CONS MECA reduce speed

réduit: ~ **en cendres** *adj* THERMODYN incinerated

réécrire *vt* INFORMAT, ORDINAT rewrite

réécriture *f* INFORMAT, ORDINAT rewrite

reef *m* MINES reef

réel *adj* INFORMAT, ORDINAT real

réembarquement *m* NAUT reshipment, reshipping

réembobinage *m* CINEMAT take-up, TV rewinding

réembobiner *vt* CINEMAT rewind

réembobineuse *f* CINEMAT, PHOTO rewinder

réémettre *vt* TELECOM retransmit, TV rebroadcast

réempilage *m* EMBALLAGE restackability

réenclencher *vt* CINEMAT reset

réenclencheur: ~ **automatique** *m* ELECTR *interrupteur* automatic circuit recloser

réenregistrement *m* ACOUSTIQUE rerecording, ENREG-ISTR dubbing, rerecording; ~ **interpiste** *m* ENREGISTR cross-track recording

réenroulement: ~ **au moteur** *m* CINEMAT motor rewind

réenrouler *vt* CINEMAT rewind

réenrouleuse *f* CINEMAT rewinder

réétalonnage *m* NUCLEAIRE recalibration

réétalonné *adj* PHYS RAYON recalibrated

réétalonnement *m* PHYS RAYON recalibration

réétiquetage: ~ **de boîtes** *m* EMBALLAGE can relabeling (AmE), can relabelling (BrE)

réexécuter *vt* INFORMAT rerun

réexpédition *f* NAUT reshipment

réextraction *f* CHARBON re-extraction

refaire *vt* PRODUCTION repair

réfection *f* PRODUCTION repairing, repair, restoration, *de joints* remaking

réfectoire *m* NAUT mess

refend *m* CONSTR cross wall

refendeuse *f* IMPRIM slitter

refendeuse-enrouleuse *f* EMBALLAGE slitting and re-winding machine, *pour feuilles* slit rewind machine

refendeuse-imprimeuse *f* EMBALLAGE slitting and print-ing machine

refendre *vt* CONSTR rip, *l'ardoise* split, EMBALLAGE, PA-PIER slit; ~ **en deux** *vt* CONSTR *un arbre* split in two

refente *f* CONSTR cleaving, ripping, splitting, EMBAL-LAGE, PAPIER slitting; ~ **d'ardoises** *f* CONSTR slate splitting; ~ **d'une bobine** *f* PAPIER slitting

référence *f* INFORMAT, ORDINAT reference, PRODUCTION catalog number (AmE), catalogue number (BrE); ~ **d'appel** *f* TELECOM call reference; ~ **d'application** *f* TELECOM application reference; ~ **de contrôle de l'échange** *f* TELECOM interchange control reference; ~ **du destinataire** *f* TELECOM recipient reference; ~ **ex-terne** *f* INFORMAT, ORDINAT external reference; ~ **du fuselage** *f* AERONAUT fuselage datum line; ~ **locale** *f* TELECOM local reference; ~ **de phase** *f* TV phase refer-ence; ~ **de pièce** *f* EMBALLAGE part number; ~ **de tension** *f* ELECTROTEC voltage reference

référentiel *m* INFORMAT, ORDINAT repository, universal set, PHYSIQUE frame; ~ **galiléen** *m* PHYSIQUE Galilean frame; ~ **d'inertie** *m* ESPACE inertial reference frame, inertial reference system; ~ **du laboratoire** *m* PHYSIQUE laboratory frame

refilmer *vt* CINEMAT reshoot

réfléchir *vt* PHYSIQUE reflect

réfléchissement *m* GEOPHYS reverberation

réflectance *f* ASTRONOMIE, ELECTROTEC, EN RENOUV, ES-PACE, OPTIQUE reflectance, PHYSIQUE reflectance, reflection factor; ~ **spectrale** *f* PHYSIQUE spectral re-flectance

réflecteur *m* CONS MECA, ELECTRON reflector, ELECTRO-TEC reflector electrode, repeller, ESPACE *communications*, INSTRUMENT, PHOTO, PHYSIQUE, TRANSPORT reflector; ~ **argenté** *m* INSTRUMENT sil-vered reflector; ~ **à armilles** *m* INSTRUMENT circular reflector; ~ **de concentration** *m* INSTRUMENT concen-trating reflector; ~ **conformé** *m* ESPACE *communications* shaped reflector; ~ **décalé** *m* ESPACE *communications* offset reflector; ~ **à éclairage** *m* IN-STRUMENT indirect light reflector; ~ **à foyer réglable** *m* PHOTO variable focus reflector; ~ **lambertien** *m* OP-TIQUE lambertian reflector; ~ **métallique** *m* INSTRUMENT metal reflector; ~ **miroir à lumière froide** *m* CINEMAT cold mirror reflector; ~ **orientable** *m* PHOTO swivel-mounted reflector; ~ **parabolique** *m* CINEMAT, MILITAIRE, PHOTO parabolic reflector; ~ **parabolique de 5 kw** *m* CINEMAT skypan; ~ **parabo-lique radar** *m* AERONAUT radar dish; ~ **parapluie** *m* CINEMAT umbrella; ~ **à pince** *m* PHOTO clamping re-flector; ~ **plan** *m* INSTRUMENT planar reflector; ~ **principal** *m* ESPACE *communications* main reflector; ~ **radar** *m* NAUT radar reflector; ~ **rigide** *m* ESPACE *communications* rigid reflector; ~ **secondaire** *m* ES-PACE *communications* secondary reflector, subreflector; ~ **solaire optique** *m* ESPACE *véhicules* OSR, optical solar reflector; ~ **souple** *m* ESPACE *com-munications* flexible reflector

réflection: ~ **interne** *f* PHOTO lens flare

réflectivité *f* CHAUFFAGE, EN RENOUV, ESPACE reflectiv-ity; ~ **spéculaire** *f* ESPACE reflectivity

réflectographie *f* PHOTO reflex printing method

réflectomètre *m* PAPIER reflectance meter, reflec-tometer, PLAST CAOU reflectometer, *peintures, instrument* gloss meter

réflectométrie: ~ **optique dans le domaine temporel** *f* OPTIQUE OTDR, optical time domain reflectometry, backscattering technique, TELECOM OTDR, optical time domain reflectometry

reflet *m* CINEMAT flare, glare, PHYS ONDES *dans un miroir* reflection, POLLU MER sheen; ~ **gênant** *m* CINEMAT burn; ~ **interne** *m* CINEMAT lens flare; ~ **irisé** *m* CERAM VER iridescence; ~ **métallique** *m* CERAM VER luster (AmE), lustre (BrE); ~ **sur cellule** *m* CINEMAT cell flare

refléter *vt* PHYSIQUE reflect

reflex: ~ **monoculaire** *m* PHOTO single-lens reflex ca-mera

réflexion *f* ACOUSTIQUE, CRISTALL, ELECTRON, ESPACE *communications*, GEOMETRIE reflection, GEOPHYS re-flection wave, MATH dissymmetry, OPTIQUE, PHYS ONDES, PHYSIQUE, TELECOM reflection; ~ **de Bragg** *f* CRISTALL Bragg reflection; ~ **diffuse** *f* ELECTROTEC, PHYS RAYON diffuse reflection; ~ **en direct** *f* ENREGISTR forward scattering; ~ **de Fresnel** *f* OPTIQUE, TELECOM Fresnel reflection; ~ **interne** *f* PHYS RAYON internal reflection; ~ **interne totale** *f* CERAM VER, PHYS ONDES total internal reflection; ~ **par l'ionosphère** *f* PHYS ONDES reflection from ionosphere; ~ **partielle** *f* PHYS ONDES *des ondes lumineuses* partial reflection; ~ **de pointe** *f* PETR reflection peak; ~ **des rayons X** *f* PHYS RAYON X-ray reflection; ~ **sélective** *f* PHYSIQUE selec-tive reflection; ~ **sismique** *f* GEOPHYS reflection shooting; ~ **spéculaire** *f* CINEMAT, PHYSIQUE, TELECOM specular reflection; ~ **totale** *f* OPTIQUE, PHYSIQUE, TELECOM total reflection

réflexions: ~ **absentes** *f pl* CRISTALL absent reflection; ~ **par trajets multiples** *f pl* TELECOM multipath reflections

reflux *m* CHIMIE reflux, DISTRI EAU backflow, GENIE CHIM reflux, INST HYDR *de l'eau d'aval* backing up, NAUT ebb tide, ebb, OCEANO ebb, falling tide, PETROLE reflux

refondre *vt* PRODUCTION recast

reformage *m* PETROLE reforming; ~ **catalytique** *m* MATERIAUX, PETROLE catalytic reforming; ~ **thermique** *m* PETROLE thermal reforming

reformatage *m* INFORMAT, ORDINAT reformatting

réforming: ~ **à la vapeur** *m* MATERIAUX steam reforming

refouillement *m* CONSTR recess

refouiller *vt* CONSTR recess

refoulement *m* AERONAUT push back, CERAM VER blow-back, CH DE FER *véhicules* backing, CONS MECA discharge, CONSTR battering, DISTRI EAU delivery, INST HYDR backflow, backset, MINES forcing, forcing down, REFRIG discharge, TRANSPORT push back; ~ **des dents d'une scie** *m* CONS MECA setting; ~ **en bourrelet** *m* CERAM VER thickening; ~ **des têtes de boulons** *m* PRODUCTION jumping bolt heads

refouler[1] *vt* CONS MECA drive, drive in, PRODUCTION *un cercle de roue, la tête d'un boulon* jump, *un rivet* close, TRANSPORT push back

refouler[2] *vi* CH DE FER *véhicules* back up, CONS MECA set

refouloir *m* MILITAIRE *artillerie* rammer; ~ **automatique** *m* MILITAIRE *artillerie* automatic rammer

réfractaire[1] *adj* CHIMIE refractory, EMBALLAGE heat-resistant, ESPACE heat-resistant, heat-resisting, MAT CHAUFF fire-resistant, heat-resistant, refractory, MATERIAUX refractory, PHYSIQUE, SECURITE heat-resistant, THERMODYN fireproof, flameproof, refractory

réfractaire[2] *m* CERAM VER, PRODUCTION refractory; ~ **fritté** *m* CERAM VER sintered refractory; ~ **de magnésie-chrome** *m* CERAM VER magnesite chrome refractory; ~ **de spinelle** *m* CERAM VER spinel refractory; ~ **de zircon** *m* CERAM VER zircon refractory; ~ **de zircone** *m* CERAM VER zirconia refractory

réfractarité *f* MATERIAUX refractory quality

réfracter *vt* PHYSIQUE refract

réfracteur *m* GEOPHYS refractor

réfraction *f* GEOPHYS refraction wave, NAUT, OPTIQUE, PHYS ONDES *d'une onde lumineuse*, PHYSIQUE refraction; ~ **atmosphérique** *f* ASTRONOMIE atmospheric refraction; ~ **double** *f* PHYS RAYON double refraction; ~ **optique** *f* TELECOM optical refraction; ~ **sismique** *f* GEOPHYS refraction shooting

réfractivité: ~ **moléculaire** *f* PHYSIQUE molecular refractivity

réfractomètre *m* EQUIP LAB refractometer, INSTRUMENT optometer, refractometer, PHYS RAYON, PHYSIQUE refractometer; ~ **d'Abbé** *m* PHYSIQUE Abbé refractometer; ~ **binaire** *m* INSTRUMENT binocular refractometer; ~ **à immersion** *m* INSTRUMENT dipping refractometer; ~ **de Pulfrich** *m* PHYSIQUE Pulfrich refractometer; ~ **de Rayleigh** *m* PHYSIQUE Rayleigh refractometer

réfrigérant[1] *adj* CHIMIE refrigerant, REFRIG chilling, frigorific, refrigerating, THERMODYN refrigerant

réfrigérant[2] *m* CHIMIE condenser, EMBALLAGE cooling, cooling agent, EQUIP LAB *verrerie* condenser, MATERI-AUX coolant, NUCLEAIRE cooler, heat exchanger, PETROLE cooler, POLLUTION refrigerant, THERMODYN heat exchanger, refrigerator, VEHICULES *moteur* coolant; ~ **à ailettes** *m* THERMODYN finned cooler; ~ **atmosphérique** *m* NUCLEAIRE air cooler, THERMODYN cooling tower; ~ **à cheminée** *m* CONSTR chimney cooler, PRODUCTION, THERMODYN cooling tower; ~ **à reflux** *m* EQUIP LAB *verrerie* reflux condenser; ~ **tubulaire** *m* AGRO ALIM tubular cooler

réfrigérateur *m* EMBALLAGE refrigeration machine, PHYSIQUE refrigerator, REFRIG ice refrigerator, refrigerator, THERMODYN compression plant, fridge, freezer, refrigerator; ~ **à absorption** *m* REFRIG absorption refrigerator, THERMODYN absorption-type refrigerator; ~ **à biberons** *m* REFRIG nursery refrigerator; ~ **à compartiment congélateur** *m* REFRIG fridge freezer; ~ **à compresseur** *m* CONS MECA compression refrigerator; ~ **à compression** *m* THERMODYN compression refrigerator; ~ **à dilution** *m* PHYSIQUE, REFRIG dilution refrigerator; ~ **à dilution d'hélium** *m* PHYSIQUE helium dilution refrigerator; ~ **à gaz** *m* CONS MECA, REFRIG, THERMODYN gas refrigerator; ~ **à liquides** *m* CONS MECA liquid cooler; ~ **ménager** *m* CONS MECA domestic refrigerator, refrigerator, REFRIG domestic refrigerator, household refrigerator

réfrigérateur-congélateur *m* REFRIG dual-temperature refrigerator

réfrigération *f* AGRO ALIM refrigeration, REFRIG refrigerating, THERMODYN cooling to low temperature, refrigeration; ~ **mécanique** *f* CONS MECA mechanical refrigeration; ~ **par déshydratation** *f* AGRO ALIM dehydrofreezing; ~ **par immersion dans l'eau glacée** *f* REFRIG flood-type cooling; ~ **par jet d'air froid** *f* REFRIG jet cooling; ~ **par saumure** *f* AGRO ALIM brine cooling; ~ **primaire** *f* REFRIG chilling process; ~ **primaire des carcasses** *f* REFRIG carcass chilling; ~ **rapide** *f* REFRIG quick chill, rapid chill, THERMODYN rapid cooling; ~ **à récupération partielle de frigorigène** *f* REFRIG partial recovery refrigeration system

réfrigération-choc *f* REFRIG shock chilling

réfrigéré *adj* AGRO ALIM chilled, REFRIG refrigerated

réfrigérer[1] *vt* REFRIG, chill, refrigerate THERMODYN refrigerate; ~ **par compression** *vt* CONS MECA refrigerate by compression; ~ **sous vide** *vt* THERMODYN freeze-dry

réfrigérer[2] *vi* REFRIG chill, refrigerate

réfringence: ~ **spécifique** *f* ESPACE *communications*, PHYSIQUE refractivity

refroidi *adj* THERMODYN chilled, cooled; ~ **à l'air** *adj* CONS MECA, IMPRIM *mécanique*, PAPIER air-cooled; ~ **par l'air** *adj* ELECTR *matériel*, THERMODYN air-cooled; ~ **par l'eau** *adj* GAZ, PRODUCTION water-cooled; ~ **par l'eau de mer** *adj* THERMODYN sea water-cooled; ~ **par gaz** *adj* THERMODYN gas-cooled; ~ **par de l'huile** *adj* THERMODYN oil-cooled; ~ **par liquide** *adj* THERMODYN liquid-cooled; ~ **par du métal liquide** *adj* THERMODYN liquid-metal-cooled

refroidir:[1] ~ **brusquement** *vt* MECANIQUE *procédé* chill; ~ **par l'air** *vt* THERMODYN air-cool; ~ **par l'eau** *vt* CHIMIE *l'air* water-cool; ~ **par ventilateur** *vt* THERMODYN fan cool; ~ **rapidement** *vt* CHIMIE quench

refroidir[2] *vti* CERAM VER cool down, PAPIER cool, REFRIG chill, cool, TEXTILE cool, THERMODYN chill, cool

refroidissement:[1] **à ~** *adj* THERMODYN *par eau* water-cooled; **à ~ à l'air** *adj* CONS MECA air-cooled; **à ~ d'eau** *adj* PRODUCTION water-cooled; **à ~ au gaz** *adj* THER-

MODYN *par gaz* gas-cooled; à ~ **par l'air** *adj* THERMODYN air-cooled; à ~ **par eau** *adj* TEXTILE water-cooled
refroidissement² *m* CERAM VER, CONS MECA, GAZ cooling, PLAST CAOU *procédé* chilling, PRODUCTION *d'un haut-fourneau* slacking, REFRIG chilling, cooling, refrigerating, TEXTILE cooling, THERMODYN chilling; ~ **absorbant** *m* EN RENOUV absorption cooling; ~ **des agrégats** *m* REFRIG aggregate cooling; ~ **à air aspiré** *m* REFRIG forced draft cooling (AmE), forced draught cooling (BrE); ~ **à air forcé** *m* REFRIG forced draft cooling (AmE), forced draught cooling (BrE); ~ **de l'ambiance** *m* REFRIG environment cooling; ~ **brusque** *m* REFRIG chilling; ~ **à convection naturelle** *m* NUCLEAIRE natural convection cooling; ~ **dans le pot** *m* CERAM VER pot cooling; ~ **diphasique** *m* NUCLEAIRE two-phase cooling; ~ **électronique** *m* PHYS PART electron cooling; ~ **de l'environnement** *m* REFRIG environment cooling; ~ **forcé** *m* CONS MECA forced cooling; ~ **forcé à l'air** *m* CONS MECA forced air cooling; ~ **forcé à l'eau** *m* CONS MECA forced water cooling; ~ **forcé à l'huile** *m* CONS MECA forced oil cooling; ~ **à frigorigène perdu** *m* REFRIG total loss refrigeration system; ~ **à huile** *m* ELECTR *transformateur* oil cooling; ~ **hydraulique** *m* REFRIG hydro cooling; ~ **localisé** *m* REFRIG spot cooling; ~ **magnétique** *m* REFRIG magnetic cooling; ~ **naturel** *m* THERMODYN natural cooling; ~ **par ablation** *m* ESPACE ablative cooling; ~ **par ailettes** *m* NUCLEAIRE fin cooling, rib cooling; ~ **par air** *m* AUTO air cooling; ~ **par l'air** *m* ELECTROTEC air cooling; ~ **par air forcé** *m* THERMODYN fan cooling, rapid air cooling; ~ **par aspersion** *m* REFRIG spray cooling; ~ **par chemise** *m* NUCLEAIRE jacket cooling; ~ **par circulation d'huile** *m* THERMODYN air-or-oil cooling; ~ **par combustible** *m* THERMODYN fuel cooling; ~ **par convection** *m* THERMODYN convection cooling; ~ **par convection naturelle** *m* REFRIG natural convection cooling; ~ **par détente directe** *m* REFRIG direct expansion refrigeration system; ~ **par eau** *m* AUTO, MATERIAUX, TEXTILE water-cooling; ~ **par évaporation** *m* GENIE CHIM evaporation cooling, REFRIG, THERMODYN evaporative cooling; ~ **par film** *m* ESPACE film cooling; ~ **par film fluide** *m* TRANSPORT film cooling; ~ **par fluide perdu** *m* ESPACE dump cooling; ~ **par l'huile** *m* CONS MECA oil cooling; ~ **par immersion** *m* REFRIG flood-type cooling, immersion cooling; ~ **par jet d'air** *m* REFRIG air blast cooling; ~ **par jet d'air froid** *m* REFRIG jet cooling; ~ **par liquide** *m* THERMODYN liquid cooling; ~ **par pression d'air** *m* REFRIG pressure cooling; ~ **par pression gazeuse** *m* REFRIG pressure cooling; ~ **par radiation** *m* THERMODYN radiant cooling; ~ **par récupération** *m* REFRIG, THERMODYN regenerative cooling; ~ **par soufflerie** *m* REFRIG air blast cooling; ~ **par surface d'écoulement** *m* REFRIG surface cooling; ~ **par transpiration** *m* ESPACE sweat cooling, GAZ, REFRIG transpiration cooling; ~ **par vaporisation** *m* GENIE CHIM evaporation cooling; ~ **par ventilateur** *m* THERMODYN fan cooling; ~ **par le vide** *m* REFRIG vacuum cooling; ~ **pelliculaire** *m* ESPACE, TRANSPORT film cooling; ~ **rapide** *m* CERAM VER chilling, quenching, THERMODYN rapid cooling; ~ **stochastique** *m* PHYS PART stochastic cooling; ~ **thermoélectrique** *m* REFRIG thermoelectric cooling; ~ **à tirage naturel** *m* THERMODYN natural draft cooling (AmE), natural draught cooling (BrE); ~ **type fontaine** *m* CONS MECA *moule pour fonderie sous pression* water-cooling cascade

refroidisseur *m* CHAUFFAGE, CONS MECA cooler, NUCLEAIRE cooler, heat exchanger, PAPIER, PRODUCTION, REFRIG cooler, TEXTILE cooling system, THERMODYN cooler; ~ **à accumulation de glace** *m* REFRIG ice bank cooler; ~ **à air** *m* REFRIG air cooler; ~ **d' air à chaleur sensible** *m* REFRIG sensitive heat air cooler; ~ **à air à double écartement d'ailettes** *m* REFRIG two-way finned cooler; ~ **à bière** *m* REFRIG beer cooler; ~ **à bouteille** *m* REFRIG bottle-type liquid cooler; ~ **de bouteilles** *m* REFRIG bottle cooler; ~ **à convection** *m* THERMODYN convection cooler; ~ **à eau** *m* REFRIG water chiller; ~ **à gaz** *m* REFRIG gas cooler; ~ **d'huile** *m* ELECTR REFRIG, THERMODYN oil cooler; ~ **intermédiaire** *m* REFRIG interstage cooler; ~ **intermédiaire à détente** *m* REFRIG flashstage cooler; ~ **à lait** *m* REFRIG milk cooler; ~ **à lait en bidons** *m* REFRIG churn milk cooler; ~ **à lait par collier d'aspersion** *m* REFRIG sparge ring cooler; ~ **à lait par immersion** *m* REFRIG immersion milk cooler; ~ **à lait par ruissellement** *m* REFRIG cascade milk cooler; ~ **à moût** *m* REFRIG wort cooler; ~ **à pulvérisation** *m* REFRIG spray-type cooler; ~ **à rayonnement** *m* THERMODYN radiant cooler; ~ **à ruissellement** *m* REFRIG irrigation cooler; ~ **à saumure** *m* REFRIG brine cooler; ~ **à tambour** *m* REFRIG drum cooler; ~ **à tambour agitateur** *m* REFRIG spin chiller; ~ **à tambour rotatif** *m* REFRIG spin chiller; ~ **à tampon humide** *m* REFRIG wetted pad evaporative cooler; ~ **à tourniquet** *m* REFRIG turbine cooler; ~ **de type humide** *m* REFRIG wet-type cooler; ~ **de type sec** *m* REFRIG dry-type cooler; ~ **vibrant à tourbillon** *m* GENIE CHIM fluidized bed vibro-cooler

refuge *m* CONSTR manhole, refuge hole, shelter; ~ **pour piétons** *m* TRANSPORT safety island

refus *m* BREVETS refusal, MINES *du crible* oversize, QUALITE nonacceptance; ~ **de broyage** *m* AGRO ALIM break tailings; ~ **de criblage** *m* GENIE CHIM sieving residue; ~ **du crible** *m* PRODUCTION riddlings

refuser *vi* NAUT veer forward

régalage *m* CONSTR grading, leveling (AmE), levelling (BrE)

regard *m* CERAM VER observation hole, CONS MECA inspection hole, sight hole, spy hole, CONSTR *d'un aqueduc, d'un égout* inspection chamber, manhole, DISTRI EAU pit, ESPACE *véhicules* inspection hatch, inspection hole, MECANIQUE inspection door, PETROLE sight glass, *raffinerie* gage glass (AmE), gauge glass (BrE), PRODUCTION peep hole, *d'un fourneau, d'un cubilot* eye, *servant à constater le jeu d'un mécanisme* door; ~ **d'accès** *m* NUCLEAIRE access port; ~ **de lavage** *m* PRODUCTION hand hole, mud door, washout hole; ~ **de nettoyage** *m* PRODUCTION cleaning door, cleaning hole; ~ **de service** *m* HYDROLOGIE manhole; ~ **de visite** *m* HYDROLOGIE manhole, PRODUCTION inspection cover, inspection door; ~ **de visite latéral** *m* CERAM VER pigeon hole

regarnir *vt* CONS MECA repack, PAPIER *un rouleau* refill, VEHICULES *freins* reline

regarnissage *m* CONS MECA refitting, reflector

regazéification *f* GAZ regasification

regel *m* PHYSIQUE regelation

régélation *f* PHYSIQUE regelation

regeler *vi* REFRIG regel

régénérateur¹ *adj* ESPACE *communications* regenerative

régénérateur² *m* CINEMAT replenisher, ELECTRON, ESPACE *communications* regenerator, PRODUCTION recuperator, TELECOM regenerator; ~ **d'impulsion** *m*

ELECTRON pulse regenerator; ~ **de signaux** *m* ELECTRON signal regenerator

régénération *f* CHIMIE *d'une substance*, CINEMAT, DISTRI EAU, ELECTRON, ESPACE *communications*, INFORMAT, ORDINAT regeneration, PETROLE reclaiming, TELECOM regeneration; ~ **d'huile** *f* CONS MECA oil reclaiming; ~ **d'image** *f* ORDINAT image refreshing; ~ **d'impulsion** *f* ELECTRON, PHYSIQUE pulse regeneration, TV pulse restoration; ~ **numérique** *f* ELECTRON digital regeneration; ~ **des signaux** *f* ELECTRON signal regeneration

régénérer *vt* INFORMAT, ORDINAT regenerate

régie *f* ENREGISTR control room, TV central control room, control center (AmE), control centre (BrE), control room, studio control room; ~ **centrale** *f* TV MCR, master control room; ~ **de continuité** *f* TV NCR, network control room; ~ **finale** *f* TV NCR, network control room, continuity control, master control; ~ **image** *f* TV video control room, vision control room; ~ **image-lumière** *f* TV lighting and vision control room; ~ **mobile** *f* TV mobile control unit; ~ **de production** *f* TV production control room; ~ **de son** *f* CINEMAT, ENREGISTR sound control room, audio control room; ~ **de studio** *f* TV control room

régime:[1] **en ~ permanent** *adj* PHYSIQUE steady-state; **en ~ stationnaire** *adj* PHYSIQUE steady-state

régime[2] *m* CONS MECA normal conditions, normal working conditions, ELECTROTEC operating conditions, HYDROLOGIE *d'un cours d'eau* regime, VEHICULES *moteur* engine speed, revs; ~ **banane** *m* NUCLEAIRE banana regime; ~ **caractéristique** *m* PHYSIQUE rating; ~ **à charge maximale** *m* ELECTR *alimentation* on-peak conditions; ~ **continu** *m* ELECTR *matériel* continuous duty; ~ **de croisière** *m* AERONAUT cruising power; ~ **dangereux** *m* SECURITE unsafe conditions; ~ **dynamique** *m* ELECTROTEC dynamic conditions; ~ **établi** *m* ELECTROTEC steady-state; ~ **de frein moteur** *m* VEHICULES overrun; ~ **de fusion** *m* THERMODYN melting range; ~ **de grands signaux** *m* ELECTRON large-signal conditions; ~ **hydraulique** *m* GAZ hydraulic status; ~ **d'impulsion** *m* ELECTRON ELECTROTEC pulsed mode; ~ **linéaire** *m* ELECTROTEC linear conditions; ~ **maximum rotor** *m* AERONAUT *hélicoptère* maximum rotor speed; ~ **de montée** *m* AERONAUT climb setting; ~ **moteur** *m* AERONAUT, AUTO engine speed; ~ **non linéaire** *m* CONSTR nonlinear condition; ~ **permanent** *m* ELECTR steady-state, *matériel* constant duty, ELECTROTEC, PHYSIQUE steady-state; ~ **plein** *m* AERONAUT full throttle; ~ **de pointe** *m* VEHICULES *moteur* peak engine speed, peak revs; ~ **de prise** *m* ELECTR tapping duty; ~ **quasi-permanent** *m* PHYSIQUE quasi-steady state; ~ **quasi-stationnaire** *m* PHYSIQUE quasi-steady state; ~ **rotor** *m* AERONAUT *hélicoptère* rotor speed; ~ **de saturation** *m* ELECTROTEC saturation conditions; ~ **sinusoïdal** *m* ELECTROTEC sinusoidal conditions; ~ **stationnaire** *m* PHYSIQUE steady-state; ~ **statique** *m* ELECTROTEC static conditions; ~ **transitoire** *m* ELECTR transient condition, transient state, ELECTROTEC transient condition; ~ **des vents** *m* METEO wind conditions

région *f* ASTRONOMIE region, CONSTR area, GEOMETRIE, GEOPHYS region; ~ **des calmes** *f* METEO doldrums; ~ **des calmes équatoriaux** *f* METEO equatorial calms; ~ **carbonifère** *f* CHARBON coal field; ~ **de champ lointain** *f* OPTIQUE, TELECOM far-field region; ~ **de champ proche** *f* OPTIQUE, TELECOM near field region; ~ **collectrice** *f* POLLUTION receptor region; ~ **couverte** *f* TV

footprint; ~ **dopée négativement** *f* PHYSIQUE negatively doped region; ~ **dopée positivement** *f* PHYSIQUE positively skewed doped region; ~ **effondrée** *f* MINES caved area; ~ **émettrice** *f* POLLUTION source area; ~ **de Fraunhofer** *f* ESPACE *communications* Fraunhofer region; ~ **de Fresnel** *f* INFORMAT, TELECOM Fresnel region; ~ **de glissement facile** *f* METALL easy glide region; ~ **de haute pression** *f* METEO barometric maximum; ~ **HI** *f* ASTRONOMIE HI region; ~ **HII** *f* ASTRONOMIE HII region; ~ **imprimante** *f* IMPRIM printing area; ~ **morte** *f* NUCLEAIRE *de fluide* stagnant area, wake area, wake space; ~ **neigeuse** *f* METEO snow belt; ~ **nourricière** *f* GEOLOGIE *à l'origine des éléments détritiques ou magmas* source area, source region; ~ **réceptrice** *f* POLLUTION receptor region; ~ **routière** *f* TRANSPORT traffic region; ~ **de soudure** *f* NUCLEAIRE weld region; ~ **source** *f* GEOLOGIE *à l'origine des éléments détritiques ou magmas* source area, source region, POLLUTION source area; ~ **de striction** *f* MATERIAUX necking region; ~ **terminale** *f* AERONAUT *aéroport* terminal area

régisseur *m* ELECTROTEC controller; ~ **de ligne** *m* ELECTROTEC line controller; ~ **de mémoire** *m* ELECTROTEC memory controller; ~ **de plateau** *m* TV studio manager; ~ **de processus** *m* ELECTROTEC process controller; ~ **de tube cathodique** *m* ELECTRON CRT controller

registre *m* BREVETS register, CERAM VER feeder gate, CHAUFFAGE, CONSTR damper, ELECTROTEC register, IMPRIM *impression* fit, INFORMAT, ORDINAT register, PRODUCTION draft regulator (AmE), draught regulator (BrE), *d'un fourneau* register, REFRIG damper, TELECOM register; ~ **d'adresse** *m* ORDINAT address register; ~ **d'adresse de base** *m* ORDINAT base address register; ~ **aéronautique** *m* AERONAUT aeronautical register; ~ **d'appels** *m* TELECOM CR, call register; ~ **de contrôle** *m* INFORMAT, ORDINAT control register; ~ **de contrôle de séquence** *m* INFORMAT, ORDINAT sequence control register; ~ **à coulisses** *m* CHAUFFAGE slide damper; ~ **de cumul** *m* INFORMAT, ORDINAT accumulator register; ~ **à décalage** *m* ELECTRON, INFORMAT, ORDINAT, PRODUCTION *automatisme industriel*, TELECOM shift register; ~ **à décalage analogique** *m* INFORMAT, ORDINAT analog shift register; ~ **de décalage binaire** *m* ORDINAT shift register; ~ **à décalage bouclé** *m* PRODUCTION *automatisme industriel* circulating shift register; ~ **à décalage à droite** *m* PRODUCTION *automatisme industriel* shift right register; ~ **à décalage à gauche** *m* PRODUCTION *automatisme industriel* shift left register; ~ **à deux états** *m* TELECOM two-state register; ~ **d'égalisation** *m* REFRIG equalizing damper; ~ **d'entrée/sortie** *m* INFORMAT, ORDINAT input/output register; ~ **d'état** *m* INFORMAT, ORDINAT status register; ~ **à glissières** *m* CHAUFFAGE hit and miss damper, REFRIG slide damper; ~ **d'horloge** *m* INFORMAT clock register, timer, ORDINAT clock register, timer; ~ **d'index** *m* INFORMAT, ORDINAT index register; ~ **d'instruction** *m* INFORMAT, ORDINAT instruction register; ~ **intermédiaire** *m* INFORMAT, ORDINAT temporary register; ~ **manuel** *m* CHAUFFAGE manual damper; ~ **mémoire de données** *m* INFORMAT, ORDINAT MDR, memory data register; ~ **obturateur** *m* CERAM VER back tweel; ~ **d'opération** *m* INFORMAT, ORDINAT operation register; ~ **à organe mobile unique** *m* CONS MECA single-leaf damper; ~ **à organes mobiles multiples** *m* CONS MECA multiple leaf damper; ~ **à papillon** *m* REFRIG butterfly damper; ~ **à persiennes** *m* REFRIG multileaf damper; ~ **pivotant** *m* CHAUFFAGE butterfly damper; ~ **d'une procédure de contrôle** *m* METROLOGIE inspection record; ~ **de réglage du vent** *m* PRODUCTION blast gate; ~ **régulateur** *m* CERAM VER front tweel, PRODUCTION draft regulator (AmE), draught regulator (BrE); ~ **de sécurité** *m* CONSTR safety record; ~ **tampon** *m* ORDINAT buffer register; ~ **tampon des commandes** *m* PRODUCTION *automatisme industriel* command buffer; ~ **de vapeur** *m* INST HYDR throttle; ~ **à volet** *m* REFRIG single leaf damper

Registre: ~ **international des substances potentiellement toxiques** *m* (*RISCPT*) POLLUTION International Register of Potentially Toxic Chemicals (*IRPTC*)

registreux *m* EQUIP LAB chart recorder

réglable *adj* COMMANDE adjustable, adjusting, CONS MECA, MECANIQUE adjustable; ~ **à volonté** *adj* CONS MECA adjustable at will

réglage:[1] **de** ~ *adj* COMMANDE, CONS MECA adjusting; **à** ~ **automatique** *adj* COMMANDE self-adjusting; **à** ~ **continu** *adj* ELECTRON continuously adjustable

réglage[2] *m* AERONAUT, CHARBON setting, CHIMIE regulation, COMMANDE adjustment, regulating, regulation, CONS MECA adjustment, regulating, regulation, ruling, CRISTALL adjustment, ELECTR control, ELECTRON, IMPRIM adjustment, NUCLEAIRE fine control, regulating, PRODUCTION, TV setup; ~ **de l'alignement de piste** *m* AERONAUT *système d'atterrissage aux instruments* course alignment; ~ **altimétrique** *m* AERONAUT altimeter setting; ~ **d'amplitude** *m* PHYS ONDES amplitude control; ~ **de l'amplitude** *m* ELECTRON amplitude adjustment; ~ **de l'amplitude verticale** *m* TV vertical amplitude control; ~ **approximatif** *m* ELECTR coarse adjustment; ~ **automatique** *m* COMMANDE self-adjustment, ELECTR *commande* automatic control; ~ **automatique des antiretours** *m* NAUT clearscan; ~ **automatique de la durée de pose** *m* PHOTO automatic exposure; ~ **automatique en fonction de l'intensité de la lumière** *m* SECURITE automatic adjustment to light intensity; ~ **automatique de la fréquence** *m* ELECTR *alimentation* automatic frequency control; ~ **automatique du gain** *m* ENREGISTR AGC, automatic gain control; ~ **automatique de la tension** *m* ELECTR automatic voltage control; ~ **avec immobilisation** *m* PRODUCTION internal setup; ~ **d'azimut** *m* TV azimuth adjustment; ~ **brosse plis** *m* PRODUCTION fold brush setting; ~ **de cadrage** *m* TV centering control (AmE), centring control (BrE); ~ **du cadrage** *m* TV framing control; ~ **de la caméra** *m* TV camera line-up; ~ **des caméras** *m* TV camera matching; ~ **de centrage de trame** *m* TV field centering control (AmE), field centring control (BrE); ~ **des charbons** *m* CINEMAT arc feed control; ~ **de chrominance** *m* TV chroma control; ~ **continu** *m* ELECTRON continuous adjustment, ORDINAT continuous control; ~ **du contraste** *m* CINEMAT, TV contrast control; ~ **de courant** *m* ELECTR current regulation; ~ **de la course pendant la marche de la machine** *m* CONS MECA adjustment of the stroke without stopping the machine; ~ **de cylindre** *m* TEXTILE roller setting; ~ **de décentrement vertical** *m* TV vertical centering control (AmE), vertical centring control (BrE); ~ **électronique** *m* ELECTRON electronic tuning; ~ **électronique de vitesse** *m* TRANSPORT electronic speed control; ~ **en longueur** *m* COMMANDE length adjustment; ~ **en phase** *m* ELECTR *courant alternatif* quadrature control; ~ **externe** *m* PRODUCTION external setup; ~ **fin** *m* ELECTRON, NUCLEAIRE, TV fine adjustment; ~ **de fréquence** *m* ELECTRON frequency adjustment; ~ **de la fréquence d'accord** *m* ELECTRON frequency tuning; ~ **de la fréquence de lignes** *m* TV horizontal hold control; ~ **fréquence-puissance** *m* ELECTR *machine* load frequency control; ~ **de gain** *m* ELECTRON gain adjustment, gain setting; ~ **gorge-à-gorge** *m* IMPRIM *machines* gap-to-gap adjustment; ~ **de la hauteur de l'image** *m* CINEMAT vertical control; ~ **d'inclinaison** *m* CINEMAT tilt control; ~ **interne** *m* PRODUCTION internal setup; ~ **de lacet** *m* EN RENOUV yaw adjustment; ~ **de la largeur** *m* COMMANDE width adjustment; ~ **de la largeur de l'image** *m* TV horizontal deflection control; ~ **linéaire** *m* ENREGISTR slide control; ~ **de la linéarité** *m* TV linearity control; ~ **de la linéarité horizontale** *m* TV line linearity control; ~ **de la linéarité de trame** *m* TV vertical linearity control; ~ **de luminosité** *m* TV brightness control; ~ **à la main** *m* COMMANDE manual adjustment; ~ **manuel du gain** *m* ELECTRON manual gain control; ~ **de mise au point** *m* CINEMAT focus pulling, NUCLEAIRE final position setting, limit setting, PHOTO focus setting; ~ **de modulation** *m* TV output control; ~ **moteur** *m* AUTO tuning; ~ **de netteté** *m* TV sharpness control; ~ **de niveau** *m* ELECTRON level adjustment; ~ **du niveau** *m* EMBALLAGE level control; ~ **du niveau du noir** *m* TV pedestal level control; ~ **de l'obturateur** *m* PHOTO shutter speed setting; ~ **de pale** *m* AERONAUT blade setting; ~ **de pas** *m* AERONAUT pitch setting; ~ **du pas des pales** *m* AERONAUT blade pitch setting; ~ **de la pénétration par réaction** *m* COMMANDE feedback penetration control; ~ **du pH** *m* CHARBON pH control; ~ **de phase** *m* TV phase adjustment; ~ **de piste** *m* TV track adjustment; ~ **des plages** *m* PRODUCTION *automatisme industriel* range adjustment; ~ **de la polarité** *m* TV polarity control; ~ **de position** *m* PRODUCTION dwell setting; ~ **de précision** *m* CONS MECA precision setting, PRODUCTION fine adjustment; ~ **de la profondeur de champ** *m* COMMANDE depth of focus adjustment; ~ **de la puissance** *m* REFRIG capacity control; ~ **à réaction** *m* COMMANDE feedback control; ~ **de saturation de la couleur** *m* TV chroma control; ~ **des soupapes** *m* AUTO valve setting; ~ **du spot lumineux** *m* TV scanning spot control; ~ **de la stabilité horizontale** *m* TV horizontal hold control; ~ **de la stabilité verticale** *m* TV frame synchronization control; ~ **de la synchronisation de trame** *m* TV vertical hold control; ~ **du télescope** *m* ASTRONOMIE setting up a telescope; ~ **de température** *m* THERMODYN temperature control; ~ **de tension** *m* ELECTR voltage control; ~ **de la tension de la bande** *m* ENREGISTR, TV tape tension control; ~ **des têtes** *m* TV head adjustment; ~ **de la tête vidéo** *m* TV video head alignment; ~ **du tir** *m* MILITAIRE *artillerie* registration fire; ~ **de tonalité** *m* ENREGISTR tone control; ~ **de valeur fixe** *m* COMMANDE fixed command control; ~ **vertical** *m* COMMANDE, INSTRUMENT height adjustment; ~ **de vitesse** *m* AERONAUT pitch control, ELECTR *machine* speed control; ~ **de volume** *m* ENREGISTR gain control; ~ **de zéro** *m* TV zero volt adjustment; ~ **du zéro** *m* NUCLEAIRE zero adjustment, zero setting

réglant *adj* COMMANDE regulating

Règle *f* ASTRONOMIE Norma

réglé *adj* PHYS RAYON tuned; ~ **en usine** *adj* MECANIQUE factory adjusted

règle f BREVETS rule, CONS MECA rule, straightedge, CONSTR, GEOMETRIE ruler, INFORMAT, ORDINAT rule; ~ **des altitudes quadrantales** f AERONAUT *altitudes de vol précisées* quadrantal height rule; ~ **d'Ampère** f ELECTR *électromagnétisme* Ampère's rule; ~ **articulée** f CONSTR folding rule (AmE), jointed rule (BrE), zigzag rule (AmE); ~ **à calculer** f INFORMAT, ORDINAT slide rule; ~ **de coupeur** f CERAM VER cutter's lath, cutter's straight edge; ~ **à couteau** f METROLOGIE knife-edge rule; ~ **de découpe automatique** f CERAM VER vitrea cutter; ~ **droite** f METROLOGIE straightedge; ~ **à ergots** f CINEMAT peg bar; ~ **d'estimateur** f CERAM VER straightedge; ~ **étalon** f METROLOGIE length bar; ~ **graduée** f CERAM VER cutter's table ruler; ~ **de la main droite** f ELECTR *électromagnétisme*, PHYSIQUE right-hand rule; ~ **de la main gauche** f ELECTR *électromagnétisme*, PHYSIQUE left-hand rule; ~ **des phases** f CHIMIE phase rule; ~ **des phases de Gibbs** f NUCLEAIRE Gibbs phase rule, phase rule; ~ **plate de contrôle en acier** f METROLOGIE steel straight edge; ~ **de production** f INFORMAT, ORDINAT production rule; ~ **de sélection** f NUCLEAIRE, PHYSIQUE selection rule; ~ **des sommes de Kuhn-Thomas-Reich** f NUCLEAIRE Kuhn-Thomas-Reich sum rule; ~ **de tire-bouchon** f ELECTR *électromagnétisme*, ELECTROTEC, PHYSIQUE corkscrew rule; ~ **à tracer des parallèles** f CONS MECA parallel rule, parallel ruler; ~ **des trois doigts de la main droite** f ELECTROTEC right-hand rule

règlement m SECURITE regulation; ~ **applicable de navigabilité** m AERONAUT appropriate airworthiness requirement; ~ **simplifié** m TELECOM easy payment; ~ **technique** m CONSTR technical regulation

réglementation: ~ **de l'espace aérien** f AERONAUT airspace restriction

règlements: ~ **de chemin de fer** m pl CH DE FER railroad regulations (AmE), railway regulations (BrE); ~ **définis par un article de loi** m pl SECURITE statutory regulations; ~ **relatifs aux lieux de travail** m pl SECURITE workplace regulations; ~ **relatifs au meulage des métaux** m pl SECURITE *meulage à sec et à l'eau* metal-grinding regulations; ~ **de sécurité** m pl SECURITE safety regulations; ~ **de sécurité des meules abrasives** m pl SECURITE *aspects de condition, vitesse, marquage, usage, et entreposage* abrasive wheels regulations; ~ **spéciaux** m pl SECURITE special regulations

régler[1] vt CONSTR *un instrument de nivellement* adjust, IMPRIM rule, set, MECANIQUE *mettre au point* adjust, PHYS ONDES *sur une fréquence* tune, PRODUCTION *un litige* settle, TV *une machine* set up

régler:[2] ~ **le tir** vi MILITAIRE range; ~ **la venue du vent** vi PRODUCTION *d'une machine soufflante* regulate the draft (AmE), regulate the draught (BrE)

règles: ~ **de l'air** f pl AERONAUT rules of the air; ~ **d'approvisionnement** f pl PRODUCTION ordering policy, ordering rules; ~ **de coulée** f pl CERAM VER iron slips; ~ **étalons graduées** f pl METROLOGIE line-graduated master scales; ~ **de Fleming** f pl ELECTR *électromagnétisme* Fleming's rules; ~ **de Hund** f pl PHYSIQUE Hund rules; ~ **parallèles** f pl NAUT parallel ruler; ~ **de sécurité** f pl SECURITE safety rules; ~ **de vol aux instruments** f pl AERONAUT instrument flight rules

règle-support: ~ **magnétique** f CONS MECA magnetic rack

réglette f CONS MECA square ruler, CONSTR batten, ME-

TROLOGIE divided beam; ~ **de bordure** f PAPIER deckle board; ~ **de jacks** f ELECTROTEC jack strip; ~ **de montage** f ENREGISTR editing block, tape splicer

régleur m PAPIER adjuster, regulator; ~ **d'ajustage** m COMMANDE adjusting device; ~ **de centrage** m TV tracking control; ~ **de pédale** m VEHICULES *frein, embrayage* pedal adjuster; ~ **de synchronisation** m TV hold control; ~ **de temps de pose** m PHOTO shutter speed control; ~ **de vitesse** m PHOTO shutter speed control

régolithe m ASTRONOMIE, GEOLOGIE *roches ou sédiments altérés sur place* regolith

regravage: ~ **du point** m IMPRIM re-etching

régression f GEOLOGIE *retrait de la mer*, INFORMAT, MATH *statistiques*, ORDINAT regression

regroupement m PRODUCTION collection; ~ **de données** m INFORMAT, ORDINAT data collection; ~ **des informations en mémoire** m INFORMAT, ORDINAT garbage collection

régularisation f CONSTR grading, DISTRI EAU regularization, river training; ~ **d'un cours d'eau** f HYDROLOGIE river training; ~ **du niveau** f DISTRI EAU storage level regulation; ~ **de pente** f CONSTR grading

régulariser vt CONSTR grade; ~ **la pente de** vt CONSTR grade

régulateur[1] adj COMMANDE regulating

régulateur[2] m AUTO equalizer bar, governor, speed limiter, CINEMAT governor, COMMANDE control unit, generator regulator, controller, regulator, CONS MECA, ELECTROTEC governor, regulator, EN RENOUV governor, EQUIP LAB regulator, INST HYDR throttle, NAUT governor, TELECOM regulator, VEHICULES *limitation du régime* governor; ~ **abaisseur** m ESPACE *véhicules* bucking regulator; ~ **abaisseur-élévateur** m ESPACE *véhicules* buck-boost regulator; ~ **à action différentielle** m COMMANDE differential regulator, lead controller; ~ **à action intégrale** m COMMANDE floating action controller, integral action regulator; ~ **à ailettes** m COMMANDE fly governor, fly regulator; ~ **d'alimentation** m COMMANDE feed regulator, feeding regulator, PRODUCTION feed box; ~ **altimétrique** m AERONAUT barometric controller; ~ **d'amenée** m COMMANDE feed regulator; ~ **d'arc** m ELECTR arc regulator; ~ **automatique** m COMMANDE automatic regulator, CONS MECA automatic regulator, self-acting regulator, EN RENOUV automatic governor; ~ **automatique de débit des eaux usées** m HYDROLOGIE automatic sewage flow regulator; ~ **automatique de niveau** m COMMANDE automatic level regulator, IAGC, instantaneous automatic gain control, IAVC, instantaneous automatic volume control; ~ **automatique de vitesse** m AUTO automatic speed control device; ~ **à bascule autonome** m COMMANDE relay control system; ~ **basse pression** m REFRIG low-pressure controller; ~ **biphase** m TRANSPORT two-phase controller; ~ **à boules** m COMMANDE pendulum governor, pendulum regulator, CONS MECA ball governor, PRODUCTION fly ball governor; ~ **de carburant** m AERONAUT fuel control unit; ~ **de carrefour** m TRANSPORT local controller, local intersection controller; ~ **centrifuge** m COMMANDE centrifugal regulator, *vitesse* governor, CONS MECA ball governor, MECANIQUE governor; ~ **centrifuge à contact** m COMMANDE centrifugal contact governor, centrifugal contact regulator; ~ **de champ** m ELECTROTEC field regulator; ~ **de charge** m ESPACE discharge regulator, *véhicules* charging regulator; ~ **combiné haute-basse pression** *m* REFRIG dual pressure controller; ~ **à commande thermostatique** *m* PRODUCTION *système hydraulique* thermostatically-controlled valve; ~ **à commande par détection de trafic** *m* TRANSPORT traffic-adjusted controller; ~ **conjoncteur-disjoncteur** *m* COMMANDE contact-discontact regulator, generator regulator, regulator, voltage regulator; ~ **à contacts vibrants** *m* COMMANDE vibrating contact regulator; ~ **à corrélation intégrale** *m* COMMANDE floating action controller; ~ **de couleur** *m* COMMANDE *télévision* color control (AmE), colour control (BrE); ~ **coulissant** *m* COMMANDE roller-type governor, roller-type regulator; ~ **à coulisse** *m* COMMANDE slider control regulator, slider control; ~ **à curseur** *m* COMMANDE cursor control regulator, cursor control; ~ **de débit** *m* COMMANDE flow rate controller, PRODUCTION flow controller, *système hydraulique* flow control valve; ~ **de débit d'une pompe à air** *m* CONS MECA air pump throttle; ~ **de débit de vapeur** *m* INST HYDR steam governor; ~ **à découpage** *m* ELECTROTEC switching regulator; ~ **de densité** *m* PAPIER consistency regulator; ~ **à dépression** *m* AUTO suction-type governor; ~ **à dérivation** *m* COMMANDE derivative control regulator, derivative control unit; ~ **à 2 étages** *m* AUTO two-contact regulator; ~ **à deux niveaux** *m* COMMANDE two-stage controller, two-stage regulator; ~ **dévolteur** *m* ESPACE *véhicules* bucking regulator; ~ **différentiel** *m* COMMANDE differential governor; ~ **différentiel de pression** *m* COMMANDE differential pressure controller; ~ **à distance** *m* COMMANDE remote control unit; ~ **d'éclairage** *m* COMMANDE dimming resistance; ~ **d'écoulement** *m* COMMANDE flow governor, flow regulator, EN RENOUV discharge regulator; ~ **électronique** *m* AUTO transistorized regulator; ~ **élévateur** *m* ESPACE boosting regulator; ~ **élévateur de tension** *m* ESPACE *véhicules* boosting regulator; ~ **en cascade** *m* COMMANDE cascade controller, follow-up controller, follower controller, servofollower; ~ **enregistreur** *m* COMMANDE level recorder controller; ~ **à flotteur** *m* COMMANDE float regulator; ~ **à force centrifuge** *m* PRODUCTION fly ball governor; ~ **à force centrifuge et dépression** *m* AERONAUT centrifugal and vacuum governor; ~ **de freinage** *m* TRANSPORT braking governor; ~ **de gaz** *m* COMMANDE gas regulator; ~ **des graves** *m* COMMANDE bass control; ~ **grossier** *m* COMMANDE coarse regulator; ~ **haute-basse pression** *m* REFRIG dual pressure controller; ~ **de haute pression** *m* REFRIG high-pressure controller; ~ **d'hélice** *m* AERONAUT propeller governor; ~ **hydromécanique** *m* EN RENOUV hydromechanical governor; ~ **à induction** *m* COMMANDE, ELECTR *transformateur* induction regulator; ~ **intégral** *m* COMMANDE floating action controller; ~ **d'intensité** *m* ELECTROTEC current regulator; ~ **de luminance** *m* TV brightness control; ~ **à main** *m* COMMANDE manual regulator; ~ **manométrique de pression** *m* COMMANDE manometric pressure governor, manometric pressure regulator, pressure governor, pressure regulator; ~ **à masse centrale** *m* CONS MECA loaded governor; ~ **de mode** *m* COMMANDE mode control; ~ **monophase** *m* TRANSPORT one-phase controller; ~ **multiphase** *m* TRANSPORT multiphase controller; ~ **de niveau** *m* ELECTRON volume-limiting amplifier; ~ **de niveau enregistrant** *m* COMMANDE level recorder controller; ~ **de niveau de verre** *m* CERAM VER glass level controller; ~ **optimal** *m* NUCLEAIRE optimal

controller; ~ **d'oxygène** *m* ESPACE *véhicules* oxygen regulator; ~ **par poursuite** *m* COMMANDE servocontroller, servogovernor, servoloop regulator; ~ **par tout ou rien** *m* AERONAUT hit or miss governor; ~ **du pH** *m* CHARBON pH controller; ~ **pneumatique** *m* COMMANDE pneumatic governor; ~ **à poids** *m* COMMANDE gravity governor, gravity regulator, weight governor; ~ **potentiométrique** *m* COMMANDE potentiometer controller; ~ **précis** *m* COMMANDE precision regulator; ~ **de présélecteur de vitesse constante** *m* VEHICULES *conduite* cruise control; ~ **de pression** *m* COMMANDE pressure regulating valve, pressure regulator, ELECTROTEC, INST HYDR pressure regulator, REFRIG pressure controller; ~ **de pression d'eau** *m* COMMANDE water pressure regulator; ~ **de pression du gaz** *m* COMMANDE gas pressure governor, gas pressure regulator; ~ **de pression hydraulique** *m* PAPIER load governor; ~ **de pression de la vapeur** *m* COMMANDE steam pressure regulator; ~ **de profondeur** *m* PETR depth controller; ~ **proportionnel** *m* COMMANDE P-controller, proportional action controller, proportional control unit, proportional controller; ~ **proportionnel de débit** *m* PRODUCTION *système hydraulique* proportional control valve; ~ **proportionnel de pression** *m* COMMANDE proportional pressure controller; ~ **de puissance** *m* REFRIG capacity controller; ~ **de quantité** *m* COMMANDE quantity governor; ~ **rapide** *m* COMMANDE quick-acting regulator; ~ **de rendement** *m* COMMANDE output regulator; ~ **de réseau** *m* COMMANDE network regulator; ~ **à ressort** *m* CONS MECA spring governor; ~ **de roulis** *m* AERONAUT lateral trim; ~ **série** *m* ELECTROTEC series regulator; ~ **shunt** *m* ELECTROTEC shunt regulator; ~ **de signalisation** *m* COMMANDE, TRANSPORT traffic signal controller; ~ **survolteur** *m* ESPACE *véhicules* boosting regulator; ~ **survolteur-dévolteur** *m* ESPACE *véhicules* buck-boost regulator; ~ **de température** *m* COMMANDE temperature regulator, thermoregulator, MAT CHAUFF, PRODUCTION temperature regulator, REFRIG temperature controller; ~ **de tension** *m* AUTO, COMMANDE, ELECTR, ELECTROTEC, INFORMAT, ORDINAT, PRODUCTION, TV, VEHICULES *système électrique* voltage regulator; ~ **thermique** *m* PRODUCTION *système hydraulique* temperature regulator; ~ **à thyristors** *m* ELECTROTEC SCR regulator; ~ **de tirage** *m* MAT CHAUFF draft regulator (AmE), draught regulator (BrE); ~ **à tiroir** *m* INST HYDR slide throttle valve; ~ **variable d'affaiblissement** *m* COMMANDE fading regulator, variable attenuator; ~ **de vitesse** *m* COMMANDE speed regulator, CONS MECA governor, speed governor, EN RENOUV speed control device; ~ **de vitesse asservie** *m* TV velocity control servo; ~ **de vitesse constante** *m* VEHICULES *conduite* cruise control; ~ **à volant d'inertie** *m* CONS MECA inertia governor; ~ **de Watt** *m* CONS MECA ball governor, PRODUCTION fly ball governor

régulation *f* COMMANDE control, regulation, ELECTROTEC regulation, ESPACE control, TELECOM regulation; ~ **des accès** *f* TRANSPORT access road control (AmE), slip road control (BrE); ~ **à action directe** *f* COMMANDE direct acting control; ~ **automatique** *f* COMMANDE automatic control, CONS MECA automatic regulation; ~ **automatique de la vitesse** *f* TRANSPORT automatic speed control; ~ **autonome** *f* NUCLEAIRE independent control; ~ **de la capacité** *f* PRODUCTION production smoothing; ~ **à cascade simple** *f*

COMMANDE single cascade control, single cascade regulation; ~ **de chaleur** *f* COMMANDE heat control; ~ **de la convergence** *f* TRANSPORT merging control; ~ **des couloirs de circulation** *f* TRANSPORT corridor control; ~ **du courant** *f* COMMANDE current regulation; ~ **du débit** *f* DISTRI EAU outlet flow control, TRANSPORT *sur autoroute* control of flow; ~ **à dérivation** *f* ELECTR derivative control; ~ **à deux positions** *f* COMMANDE flicker control; ~ **d'une déviation** *f* COMMANDE deviation control; ~ **directe** *f* COMMANDE direct acting control; ~ **à échelons multiples** *f* COMMANDE multiple-step regulation; ~ **d'écoulement** *f* PRODUCTION flow control; ~ **électronique** *f* COMMANDE electronic control; ~ **en boucle fermée de position** *f* COMMANDE closed-loop position control; ~ **en cascade** *f* COMMANDE cascade control, sequential control; ~ **d'énergie** *f* COMMANDE energy control; ~ **des espacements entre véhicules** *f* TRANSPORT headway control; ~ **des espacements minimaux entre véhicules** *f* TRANSPORT control of minimum headway; ~ **flottante** *f* COMMANDE floating control; ~ **de fréquence** *f* TELECOM frequency regulation; ~ **hydraulique** *f* COMMANDE hydraulic control; ~ **indépendante du débit dans le canal individuel** *f* NUCLEAIRE individual channel flow control; ~ **d'intensité** *f* ELECTROTEC current regulation; ~ **linéaire** *f* COMMANDE, ELECTR linear control; ~ **de maintien** *f* COMMANDE fixed command control, regulation; ~ **de mise à la terre** *f* PRODUCTION *électricité* earthing regulation (BrE), grounding regulation (AmE); ~ **naturelle** *f* ELECTRON inherent feedback, inherent regulation; ~ **du niveau** *f* ELECTRON leveling (AmE), levelling (BrE); ~ **par anticipation** *f* INFORMAT, ORDINAT feed-forward control; ~ **par découpage** *f* ELECTROTEC switching regulation; ~ **par paliers** *f* COMMANDE step control, step regulation; ~ **par plus ou moins** *f* COMMANDE flicker control; ~ **par rapport à la charge** *f* ELECTROTEC load regulation; ~ **par thyristors** *f* ELECTROTEC SCR regulation; ~ **par tout ou rien** *f* COMMANDE flicker control; ~ **de phase** *f* TELECOM phase regulation; ~ **de position** *f* COMMANDE positioning control; ~ **à positions multiples** *f* COMMANDE multiple-step control, multiple-step regulation; ~ **de pression en marche normale** *f* PRODUCTION *système hydraulique* pressure control normal; ~ **de pression en marche de secours** *f* PRODUCTION *système hydraulique* pressure control emergency; ~ **à programme** *f* COMMANDE programmable regulation, time pattern control; ~ **des rampes d'accès** *f* TRANSPORT access road metering (AmE), slip road metering (BrE); ~ **rhéostatique** *f* COMMANDE rheostat control; ~ **secteur** *f* ELECTROTEC line regulation; ~ **série** *f* ELECTROTEC linear regulation, series regulation; ~ **statistique des cotes** *f* COMMANDE statistical quality control; ~ **de synchro** *f* COMMANDE synchronization control; ~ **de tension** *f* ELECTROTEC voltage regulation; ~ **de tension continue** *f* ELECTR direct voltage regulation; ~ **thermique** *f* ESPACE temperature control regulation, thermal control; ~ **thermique passive** *f* ESPACE PTC, passive thermal control; ~ **variométrique** *f* AERONAUT pressure rate-of-change regulating; ~ **de vitesse** *f* COMMANDE speed control, speed regulation, ELECTR *machine* speed control, TRANSPORT cruise control device

régule *m* METALL regulus

réguler[1] *vt* ESPACE control

réguler:[2] ~ **un palier** *vi* PRODUCTION line

régulier *adj* CHIMIE uniform, IMPRIM regular

rehausse: ~ **pour palette** *f* TRANSPORT pallet collar

rehaussement *m* CONSTR heightening, *d'un mur* raising

rehausser *vt* IMPRIM *une teinte* bring up, TEXTILE enhance; ~ **l'arôme de** *vt* AGRO ALIM enhance; ~ **la couleur de** *vt* IMPRIM touch up; ~ **le goût de** *vt* AGRO ALIM enhance

rehausseur: ~ **de saveur** *m* AGRO ALIM flavor enhancer (AmE), flavour enhancer (BrE)

réhumectable *adj* IMPRIM *façonnage, finition* remoistenable

reillère *f* PRODUCTION flume, leat

rein *m* CONSTR *d'une voûte* flank, haunch, *d'une voûte* spandrel

réinjecter *vt* COMMANDE feed back

réinjection *f* ELECTRON feedback, reflection, PETROLE reinjection; ~ **positive** *f* COMMANDE positive feedback

réintégration *f* CHIMIE reintegration

rejalonnement *m* PRODUCTION rescheduling

réjecteur *m* ELECTRON rejector

réjection: ~ **à la fréquence intermédiaire** *f* ELECTRON, TELECOM IF rejection, intermediate frequency rejection; ~ **des harmoniques** *f* ELECTRON harmonic rejection; ~ **d'intermodulation** *f* ENREGISTR crosstalk rejection; ~ **du mode commun** *f* ELECTRON common mode rejection; ~ **des parasites** *f* ELECTRON interference rejection

rejet *m* BREVETS refusal, rejection, CHARBON refuse, CONSTR tailings, GEOLOGIE displacement, MINES leap, NUCLEAIRE effluent, *d'une barre de commande* fast insertion, POLLU MER, POLLUTION discharge, QUALITE nonacceptance, rejection, RECYCLAGE discharge; ~ **accidentel** *m* POLLU MER, POLLUTION accidental discharge; ~ **de chaleur** *m* CHAUFFAGE heat rejection, RECYCLAGE heat discharge; ~ **en bas** *m* MINES downcast; ~ **en mer** *m* POLLU MER, POLLUTION discharge at sea; ~ **horizontal** *m* GEOLOGIE horizontal displacement, horizontal separation; ~ **intentionnel** *m* POLLU MER, POLLUTION intentional discharge; ~ **net** *m* GEOLOGIE dip slip; ~ **souterrain** *m* DISTRI EAU underground waste disposal; ~ **de transaction d'entrée** *m* TELECOM ITR, input transaction rejected; ~ **transversal** *m* GEOLOGIE dip slip; ~ **vertical** *m* GEOLOGIE vertical throw

rejeter *vt* POLLU MER discharge, dump, POLLUTION discharge, QUALITE reject, RECYCLAGE discharge, dump

rejets: ~ **thermiques** *m pl* RECYCLAGE thermal discharge

rejeu *m* GEOLOGIE reactivation, rejuvenation

rejointoyer *vt* CONSTR repoint

relâchement *m* CONS MECA slackening, ELECTROTEC drop-out, release, RESSORTS relaxation; ~ **de ruban** *m* ENREGISTR tape spill

relâcher[1] *vt* GAZ, PRODUCTION release

relâcher[2] *vi* MECANIQUE, RESSORTS relax

relais *m* CINEMAT, ELECTR *interrupteur*, ELECTROTEC, EQUIP LAB relay, HYDROLOGIE silt, INFORMAT relay, repeater, ORDINAT, PHYSIQUE, TELECOM, VEHICULES *système électrique* relay; ~ **a** ~ **d'absence de courant** *m* ELECTR no-voltage release relay; ~ **d'accélération** *m* ELECTR acceleration relay; ~ **accordé** *m* ELECTR tuned relay; ~ **à action différée** *m* ELECTR definitive time relay, differential relay, marginal relay, time lag relay, time-delay relay, time-locking relay; ~ **à action instantanée** *m* ELECTR instantaneous relay, trip relay; ~ **à action lente** *m* ELECTR slow-acting relay; ~ **actionné par le courant**

de travail *m* ELECTR working current relay; ~ **à action rapide** *m* ELECTR high-speed relay, trip relay; ~ **d'amorçage** *m* MINES booster; ~ **ampèremétrique** *m* COMMANDE automatic control switch, ELECTR automatic control switch, automatic current controller, overcurrent relay, overload relay; ~ **d'annonciateur** *m* ELECTR line relay; ~ **à armature** *m* ELECTROTEC armature relay; ~ **à armature à courant alternatif** *m* ELECTROTEC AC armature relay; ~ **avertisseur** *m* ELECTR alarm relay; ~ **avertisseur de givrage** *m* AERONAUT ice detector relay;

~ b ~ **balancé** *m* ELECTR balance relay; ~ **de balance électrodynamique** *m* ELECTR current balance relay; ~ **bistable** *m* ELECTROTEC bistable relay;

~ c ~ **à cage** *m* ELECTROTEC cage relay; ~ **capacitif** *m* ELECTR capacitance relay; ~ **à cascade** *m* ELECTR stepping switch; ~ **centrifuge** *m* ELECTR centrifugal relay; ~ **clignoteur** *m* ELECTROTEC sequence relay; ~ **de commande** *m* ELECTR control relay; ~ **à commande photoélectrique** *m* ELECTROTEC photoelectrically-operated relay; ~ **commun** *m* TELECOM trunk system; ~ **de commutation** *m* ELECTR changeover relay; ~ **à un contact interrupteur** *m* ELECTROTEC SPST relay; ~ **à un contact inverseur** *m* ELECTROTEC SPDT relay; ~ **à contacts inverseurs** *m* ELECTROTEC changeover relay; ~ **de couche réseau** *m* TELECOM NLR, network layer relay; ~ **à couplage optique** *m* ELECTROTEC photo-coupled solid-state relay; ~ **de coupure** *m* ELECTR cutoff relay, switch relay, ELECTROTEC disconnect relay; ~ **de courant** *m* ELECTR current relay, undercurrent relay; ~ **à courant alternatif** *m* ELECTR alternating current relay, ELECTROTEC AC relay; ~ **à courant continu** *m* ELECTR direct current relay, ELECTROTEC DC relay;

~ d ~ **de déclenchement** *m* PHOTO trigger relay; ~ **déclencheur** *m* ELECTR release relay; ~ **de défaut à la terre** *m* PRODUCTION earth fault tray (BrE), ground fault tray (AmE); ~ **dépendant du temps** *m* ELECTR time dependent relay; ~ **de détente** *m* ELECTR tripping relay; ~ **de détonation** *m* MINES detonating relay; ~ **à deux circuits** *m* ELECTR two-element relay; ~ **à deux contacts interrupteurs** *m* ELECTROTEC DPST relay; ~ **à deux contacts inverseurs** *m* ELECTROTEC DPDT relay; ~ **à deux paliers** *m* ELECTR two-stage relay; ~ **à deux seuils** *m* ELECTR two-stage relay; ~ **différentiel** *m* ELECTR balancing relay, differential protection relay, differential relay, ELECTROTEC differential relay; ~ **de diffusion** *m* TV booster station; ~ **à direction** *m* ELECTR unbiased polarized relay; ~ **directionnel** *m* ELECTR directional relay, discriminating relay, reverse current relay, ELECTROTEC directional relay; ~ **directionnel de puissance** *m* ELECTR PDR, power directional relay; ~ **à double armature** *m* ELECTR double-armature relay; ~ **à double contact interrupteur** *m* ELECTROTEC DPST relay; ~ **à double contact inverseur** *m* ELECTROTEC DPDT relay; ~ **double repos** *m* ELECTR break-break contact; ~ **double travail** *m* ELECTR make-make contact; ~ **DPDT** *m* ELECTROTEC DPDT relay; ~ **DPST** *m* ELECTROTEC DPST relay;

~ e ~ **électrique** *m* ELECTR electric relay, electric relay, electrical relay; ~ **électrodynamique** *m* ELECTR electrodynamic relay; ~ **électromagnétique** *m* ELECTROTEC electromagnetic relay; ~ **électromécanique** *m* ELECTROTEC electromechanical relay; ~ **électronique** *m* ELECTR electronic relay; ~ **électrostatique** *m* ELECTR electrostatic relay;

~ **en boîtier DIP** *m* ELECTROTEC DIP relay; ~ **d'encaissement** *m* ELECTR coin box relay; ~ **d'enclenchement** *m* ELECTROTEC interlock relay; ~ **encliqueté** *m* ELECTR latching relay; ~ **enfichable** *m* ELECTROTEC plug-in relay; ~ **en position enclenchée** *m* PRODUCTION energized relay; ~ **à enroulement de maintien** *m* ELECTROTEC dual-coil latching relay; ~ **et détecteurs photoélectriques** *m pl* EMBALLAGE photoelectric light barriers and scanners; ~ **excité** *m* ELECTROTEC operate relay; ~ **extra-plat** *m* ELECTROTEC flat relay;

~ f ~ **à fermeture** *m* ELECTR make relay; ~ **de fréquence** *m* ELECTROTEC frequency relay;

~ g ~ **galvanométrique** *m* ELECTROTEC instrument-type relay, meter-type relay; ~ **à gaz** *m* ELECTRON gas-filled relay;

~ h ~ **hertzien** *m* ELECTROTEC link relay, radio relay, TELECOM, TV microwave link; ~ **hydraulique** *m* AERONAUT antisurge valve;

~ i ~ **d'impédance** *m* ELECTR impedance relay; ~ **à impédance** *m* ELECTROTEC reactance relay; ~ **d'impulsion** *m* ELECTR pulse relay; ~ **à impulsions** *m* ELECTROTEC impulse relay; ~ **indifférent** *m* ELECTR neutral armature, nonpolarized relay; ~ **indirect** *m* ELECTR secondary relay; ~ **à induction** *m* ELECTR, ELECTROTEC induction relay; ~ **instantané** *m* ELECTROTEC instantaneous relay; ~ **d'intensité** *m* ELECTROTEC current relay, PRODUCTION overload relay; ~ **interrupteur bipolaire** *m* ELECTROTEC DPST relay; ~ **interrupteur unipolaire** *m* ELECTROTEC single-pole single-throw relay; ~ **inverseur** *m* ELECTR changeover relay; ~ **inverseur bipolaire** *m* ELECTROTEC DPDT relay; ~ **inverseur unipolaire** *m* ELECTROTEC SPDT relay; ~ **à inversion de phase** *m* ELECTR reverse phase relay;

~ l ~ **à lames souples** *m* ELECTR reed contact relay, ELECTROTEC reed relay; ~ **à lames vibrantes** *m* ELECTR reed contact relay; ~ **latching** *m* ELECTR latching relay;

~ m ~ **magnétique de surcharge** *m* ELECTR magnetic overload relay; ~ **magnéto-électrique** *m* ELECTR moving coil relay, permanent magnet relay; ~ **de maintien** *m* ELECTROTEC guarding relay; ~ **à maximum** *m* ELECTR overcurrent relay, overload relay, surge relay; ~ **à maximum et minimum** *m* ELECTR over-and-under current relay; ~ **à maximum d'intensité** *m* ELECTR overload relay; ~ **à maximum de tension** *m* ELECTR maximum voltage relay, overvoltage relay, ELECTROTEC overvoltage relay; ~ **mécanique** *m* CONS MECA bell crank block; ~ **à mercure** *m* ELECTR mercury relay; ~ **de mesure** *m* ELECTROTEC measuring relay; ~ **miniature** *m* ELECTROTEC miniature relay; ~ **à minimum** *m* ELECTR undercurrent relay, underload relay; ~ **à minimum de courant** *m* ELECTR minimum current relay; ~ **à minimum de puissance** *m* ELECTR minimum power relay; ~ **de mise hors circuit** *m* ELECTROTEC disconnect relay; ~ **mobile** *m* TV portable relay; ~ **modulateur** *m* AERONAUT chopper;

~ n ~ **N** *m* TELECOM N-relay; ~ **nominal** *m* TELECOM mobile-to-base relay; ~ **non inverseur** *m* ELECTROTEC single throw relay; ~ **non polarisé** *m* CONSTR nonpolarized relay, ELECTR neutral relay, nonpolarized relay, ELECTROTEC neutral polar relay; ~ **non temporisé** *m* ELECTROTEC instantaneous relay; ~ **à noyau plongeur** *m* ELECTR solenoid relay, ELECTROTEC plunger relay, solenoid relay;

~ o ~ **optique** *m* CINEMAT light valve, ELECTROTEC

optical relay;

~ p ~ **à palette** *m* ELECTR vane-type relay, ELECTROTEC armature relay; ~ **de passage** *m* TELECOM base-to-mobile relay; ~ **photoélectrique** *m* ELECTR, ELECTROTEC photoelectric relay; ~ **photoélectrique à tube** *m* ELECTROTEC phototube relay; ~ **à plusieurs positions** *m* ELECTR multiposition relay; ~ **à point nul** *m* ELECTR residual relay; ~ **polarisé** *m* ELECTR, ELECTROTEC biased relay, polarized relay; ~ **polyphasé** *m* ELECTR phase-balance relay; ~ **à position neutre** *m* ELECTROTEC neutral relay; ~ **principal de commande** *m* PRODUCTION master control relay; ~ **de programme** *m* TV program repeater (AmE), programme repeater (BrE); ~ **de protection** *m* ELECTROTEC protective relay; ~ **de protection à alliage eutectique** *m* PRODUCTION eutectic alloy overload relay; ~ **de protection thermique à bilames** *m* PRODUCTION *automatisme industriel* thermal bimetallic overlay relay; ~ **de puissance** *m* ELECTROTEC, PRODUCTION power relay; ~ **de puissance active** *m* ELECTR active power relay;

~ r ~ **radar** *m* TRANSPORT radar relay station; ~ **de recalage rapide** *m* AERONAUT fast slaving relay; ~ **à réenclenchement** *m* ELECTR self-resetting relay; ~ **à repos central** *m* ELECTR center stable relay (AmE), centre stable relay (BrE); ~ **retardé** *m* ELECTR delay relay, time lag relay, time-delay relay, ELECTROTEC time-delay relay;

~ s ~ **sélecteur** *m* ELECTROTEC selector relay; ~ **à semi-conducteur** *m* ELECTROTEC semiconductor relay, solid-state relay; ~ **à semi-conducteur à commande optique** *m* ELECTROTEC optically-coupled solid-state relay; ~ **sensible** *m* ELECTROTEC sensing relay; ~ **à séquence** *m* ELECTROTEC sequence relay; ~ **séquentiel** *m* ELECTR slave relay; ~ **à simple contact interrupteur** *m* ELECTROTEC SPST relay; ~ **à simple contact inverseur** *m* ELECTROTEC SPDT relay; ~ **SPDT** *m* ELECTROTEC SPDT relay; ~ **SPST** *m* ELECTROTEC SPST relay; ~ **statique** *m* ELECTR static relay, ELECTROTEC solid-state relay, TELECOM static relay; ~ **subminiature** *m* ELECTROTEC subminiature relay; ~ **synchronisé** *m* ELECTR synchronizing relay;

~ t ~ **tabatière** *m* ELECTR box relay; ~ **télécommandé** *m* ELECTR distance relay; ~ **téléphonique** *m* ELECTROTEC telephone relay; ~ **de télévision** *m* ELECTROTEC television relay; ~ **temporisé** *m* ELECTR, ELECTROTEC delay relay; ~ **temporisé à la fermeture** *m* ELECTROTEC on-delay relay; ~ **temporisé à l'ouverture** *m* ELECTROTEC off-delay relay; ~ **temporisé au relâchement** *m* ELECTROTEC slow-operate relay; ~ **à temps dépendant** *m* ELECTR inverse time relay; ~ **de tension** *m* ELECTROTEC voltage relay; ~ **thermique** *m* ELECTR hot wire relay, thermal relay, ELECTROTEC thermal relay, PRODUCTION overload relay; ~ **à tige** *m* ELECTROTEC, TELECOM reed relay; ~ **à tiges accordées** *m* ELECTROTEC resonant reed relay; ~ **à tiges à contacts mouillés au mercure** *m* ELECTROTEC mercury-wetted reed relay; ~ **tout-ou-rien** *m* ELECTR, ELECTROTEC all-or-nothing relay; ~ **au travail** *m* ELECTROTEC operate relay; ~ **à trois positions** *m* ELECTR three-step relay;

~ u ~ **universel** *m* ELECTROTEC general-purpose relay;

~ v ~ **de verrouillage** *m* ELECTR latching relay; ~ **à verrouillage** *m* ELECTR interlock relay, interlocking relay, ELECTROTEC latching relay; ~ **de verrouillage de l'alimentation** *m* PRODUCTION *automatisme industriel* power interlock relay; ~ **à verrouillage électrique** *m*

ELECTROTEC lock-up relay, magnetic latching relay; ~ **à verrouillage sans enroulement de maintien** *m* ELECTROTEC single coil latching relay

relais-maître *m* PRODUCTION *automatisme industriel* master control relay

relais-moteur *m* CONS MECA relay

relance *f* ESPACE *mécanique* swing-by, INFORMAT, ORDINAT retry, TELECOM reconnection; ~ **préventive** *f* PRODUCTION pre-expediting, predelivery reminder; ~ **sur point de contrôle** *f* ORDINAT checkpoint recovery

relancer *vt* INFORMAT, ORDINAT reboot, restart

relarger *vt* CHIMIE salt out

relation *f* INFORMAT, ORDINAT relation; ~ **débit-densité** *f* TRANSPORT volume density relationship; ~ **de dispersion** *f* PHYSIQUE dispersion relation; ~ **homme-machine** *f (RHM)* TELECOM man-machine relationship; ~ **de maclage** *f* MATERIAUX twinning relationship; ~ **origine-destination** *f* TRANSPORT O-D equation, origin and destination equation; ~ **période-luminosité** *f* ASTRONOMIE period-luminosity relation; ~ **de Planck** *f* PHYSIQUE Planck's law; ~ **de Planck-Einstein** *f* PHYSIQUE Planck's law; ~ **vitesse-débit** *f* TRANSPORT speed flow relationship; ~ **vitesse-densité** *f* TRANSPORT speed-density relationship; ~ **de Wylie** *f* PETR Wylie relationship

relationnel *adj* INFORMAT, ORDINAT relational

relations: ~ **d'Ehrenfest** *f pl* PHYSIQUE Ehrenfest's equations

relativiste *adj* PHYSIQUE relativistic

relativité *f* PHYSIQUE relativity

relaxation *f* ELECTR *oscillation*, METALL, PLAST CAOU, RESSORTS relaxation; ~ **des contraintes** *f* CERAM VER stress relaxation, ESSAIS stress relief

relevage *m* CONS MECA lifting; ~ **hydraulique du sol** *m* CHARBON hydraulic bottom heave

relevé *m* AERONAUT plot, CHIMIE reading; ~ **des communications** *m* TELECOM call logging; ~ **de formes** *m* NAUT rise of floor; ~ **géophysique** *m* GEOLOGIE geophysical survey; ~ **du terrain** *m* CONSTR plotting ground; ~ **de varangue** *m* NAUT rise of floor; ~ **des varangues** *m* NAUT deadrise

relève: ~ **de dérangement** *m* TELECOM fault clearance

relèvement *m* CONSTR *d'un mur* raising, MINES *des galeries éboulés* clearing, fall cleanup, NAUT bearing; ~ **au compas** *m* AERONAUT, GEOLOGIE, NAUT compass bearing; ~ **constant** *m* NAUT steady bearing; ~ **et enregistrement automatiques de la position des navires** *m* TELECOM automatic location registration of ships; ~ **des fréquences élevées** *m* ELECTRON peaking; ~ **inverse** *m* AERONAUT *navigation* reciprocal bearing; ~ **magnétique** *m* AERONAUT, GEOPHYS magnetic bearing; ~ **du mouillage** *m* NAUT anchor bearing; ~ **au radar** *m* NAUT radar bearing; ~ **radio** *m* AERONAUT radio fix; ~ **radiogoniométrique** *m* AERONAUT, NAUT radio bearing; ~ **d'urgence** *m* TELECOM emergency attention; ~ **de la voie** *m* CH DE FER track raising

relever[1] *vt* AGRO ALIM enhance, CONSTR plot, PHYSIQUE record

relever:[2] ~ **une galerie éboulée** *vi* MINES clear a fall; ~ **un plan** *vi* POLLU MER survey; ~ **un pointé** *vi* NAUT *radar* plot the position; ~ **un volume** *vi* PRODUCTION read a volume

releveur *m* CERAM VER estimator, uprighter; ~ **de goût** *m* AGRO ALIM flavor enhancer (AmE), flavour enhancer (BrE)

reliage *m* CONSTR connection

relié *adj* ESPACE *véhicules* strapdown-mounted, PHYSIQUE connected; ~ **demi-teinte** *adj* IMPRIM half-bound; ~ **en demi-cuir** *adj* IMPRIM quarter-bound; ~ **en dur** *adj* IMPRIM hard-bound; ~ **sans couture** *adj* IMPRIM perfect-bound

relief *m* CONSTR form; ~ **sonore** *m* ENREGISTR sound perspective

relier *vt* ELECTROTEC connect, link, patch, INFORMAT attach, connect, ORDINAT, PHYSIQUE, PRODUCTION connect, TELECOM link up

relieur *m* IMPRIM bookbinder

reliquat *m* CHIMIE residue

relique *adj* GEOLOGIE *minéral, structure* relic, relictual

reliure *f* IMPRIM bindery, bookbinding, casing-in; ~ **avec mors et ficelles** *f* IMPRIM inboard binding; ~ **demi-peau** *f* IMPRIM half-binding; ~ **en veau pleine** *f* IMPRIM calf binding; ~ **flexible** *f* IMPRIM limp binding; ~ **à la Hollandaise** *f* IMPRIM yapp binding; ~ **à la main** *f* IMPRIM hand binding; ~ **sans couture** *f* IMPRIM perfect binding; ~ **souple** *f* IMPRIM limp binding, soft-cover binding, yapp edges

reloger *vt* INFORMAT, ORDINAT roll in

réluctance *f (cf perméance)* ELECTR *magnétisme*, ELECTROTEC reluctance, EN RENOUV imperviousness, PHYSIQUE reluctance

réluctivité *f* ELECTR *magnétisme*, PHYSIQUE reluctivity

rem *m* PHYS RAYON rem

rémanence *f* ELECTR, ELECTROTEC, ENREGISTR remanence, NAUT afterglow, PETR remanence, PHYS RAYON aftereffect, PHYSIQUE remanence, retentivity, TV image retention, lag; ~ **d'image** *f* TV burn, image lag; ~ **magnétique** *f* ELECTR, PRODUCTION *automatisme industriel* residual magnetism; ~ **par compression** *f* PLAST CAOU compression set; ~ **variable** *f* ELECTRON variable persistence

rémanent: ~ **de supernova** *m* ASTRONOMIE supernova remnant

rembarquer[1] *vti* NAUT *passagers* re-embark

rembarquer:[2] **se** ~ *v réfl* NAUT *passagers* re-embark

remblai *m* CH DE FER embankment, railroad embankment (AmE), railway embankment (BrE), CHARBON bank, fill, stowing dirt, CONSTR backfill, MINES embankment, gob, pack, packing, POLLUTION backfill, PRODUCTION slag dump, slag heap, slag tip; ~ **d'embouage** *m* MINES slush; ~ **rocheux** *m* CONSTR rock fill; ~ **de tuf** *m* GEOLOGIE tuff deposit

remblayage *m* MINES filling, packing, stowing, POLLUTION backfill

remblayer *vt* CONSTR backfill, *un fossé* fill up, MINES bank up, pack, stow, fill

remblayeuse *f* CONSTR back filler, MINES stowing equipment, TRANSPORT back filler

rembobineuse: ~ **automatique** *f* PHOTO automatic rewinder

rembourrage *m* CONS MECA padding, EMBALLAGE padding, wadding, PRODUCTION stuffing, TEXTILE wadding

rembourré *adj* MECANIQUE padded

rembourrement *m* CONS MECA padding

rembourrer *vt* TEXTILE pad

remboursement *m* BREVETS refund, reimbursement

remède *m* TELECOM corrective measure

remédier: ~ **à** *vt* PRODUCTION *l'usure* make good

remettre *vt* CONS MECA *machines en marche* restart; ~ **en état** *vt* NAUT *un navire* refit, PRODUCTION repair; ~ **en marche** *vt* AERONAUT *moteur* restart; ~ **à l'état initial** *vt*

INFORMAT, ORDINAT reset; ~ **à flot** *vt* NAUT refloat; ~ **à neuf** *vt* PRODUCTION recondition; ~ **au point de départ** *vt* CINEMAT reset; ~ **à zéro** *vt* CHIMIE zero, CINEMAT reset, zero, CONS MECA reset to zero, set to zero, ENREGISTR, ESSAIS *instrument* zero, INFORMAT, MECANIQUE, ORDINAT reset, TV zero

remisage *m* CH DE FER *véhicules* stabling

remise *f* NUCLEAIRE *d'une centrale* checkout, handover; ~ **en culture** *f* POLLUTION *d'un terrain, d'eau* recultivation; ~ **en état** *f* NAUT refit, refitting, PETROLE *fond marin* restoration, PRODUCTION repairing; ~ **en forme d'impulsion** *f* TV pulse regeneration; ~ **en marche** *f* AERONAUT *moteur* restart; ~ **en marche en moulinet** *f* AERONAUT windmilling restart; ~ **en pression par air comprimé** *f* PETROLE *d'un gisement* air repressuring; ~ **en valeur** *f* POLLUTION *d'un terrain* rehabilitation, *des terres, des eaux* reclamation; ~ **à l'état initial** *f* INFORMAT, ORDINAT reset; ~ **à l'heure** *f* ESPACE *communications* clock recovery; ~ **à locomotives** *f* CH DE FER locomotive depot, roundhouse, *véhicules* engine shed; ~ **à machines** *f* CH DE FER *véhicules* engine shed; ~ **de pas** *f* AERONAUT pitch increase; ~ **physique** *f* TELECOM PD, physical delivery; ~ **à zéro** *f* CONS MECA, GEOLOGIE overprinting, resetting, INFORMAT, ORDINAT clear to zero, PRODUCTION overprinting, resetting; ~ **à zéro du temporisateur** *f* PRODUCTION *automatisme industriel* timer reset

remodelage *m* PETROLE revamping, TRANSPORT lifting, restyling

remodeler *vt* TRANSPORT restyle

remontage *m* MINES raising, rising

remonte *f* CONS MECA lifting, MINES drawing, hoisting, raising, PRODUCTION hoisting

remontée *f* CONS MECA lifting, MINES drawing, hoisting, raising, OCEANO ascent, PHYS FLUID uplift, PRODUCTION hoisting; ~ **capillaire** *f* CHARBON capillary rise; ~ **d'eau** *f* OCEANO upwelling; ~ **en ballon** *f* OCEANO balloon surfacing, ballooning; ~ **de fluide** *f* PHYS FLUID surge; ~ **du train de tiges** *f* PETROLE coming out of hole

remonte-glace *m* AUTO window winder

remonter[1] *vt* CINEMAT *un film* re-edit, CONS MECA reset, wind up, CONSTR reassemble, IMPRIM *une couleur* bring up, MINES hoist, raise, rise, PRODUCTION hoist, TV re-edit; ~ **au jour** *vt* MINES bring to the surface, hoist to the surface; ~ **à la surface** *vt* MINES bring to the surface, hoist to the surface

remonter:[2] ~ **le courant** *vi* HYDROLOGIE *d'une rivière* go upstream; ~ **le cours** *vi* HYDROLOGIE *d'un fleuve* go upstream; ~ **le minerai au jour** *vi* MINES hoist ore, raise ore; ~ **le minerai à la surface** *vi* MINES hoist ore, raise ore; ~ **la piste** *vi* AERONAUT backtrack; ~ **au vent** *vi* NAUT claw off

remorquage *m* NAUT towage, towing, TRANSPORT aeroplane tow launch (BrE), airplane tow launch (AmE); ~ **de barrage flottant** *m* POLLU MER boom towing

remorque *f* CH DE FER *véhicules*, CONSTR, MECANIQUE *véhicules* trailer, NAUT tow rope, towline, TRANSPORT, VEHICULES trailer; ~ **basculant en arrière** *f* TRANSPORT rear tipping trailer; ~ **à bateaux** *f* TRANSPORT boat carriage, boat trailer; ~ **de camping** *f* VEHICULES caravan (BrE), house trailer (AmE), trailer (AmE); ~ **à fond plat** *f* CONSTR low bed trailer (BrE), low boy trailer (AmE); ~ **à fourgon frigorifique** *f* REFRIG refrigerated trailer; ~ **polyvalente** *f* TRANSPORT all-purpose trailer remorquer *vt* NAUT, POLLU MER, TRANSPORT tow; ~ en arbalète *vt* NAUT tow astern; ~ en flèche *vt* NAUT tow astern

remorqueur *m* NAUT, PETR tug, POLLU MER tugboat, VEHICULES towing vehicle; ~ d'assistance *m* NAUT salvage tug; ~ d'avion *m* TRANSPORT aircraft tractor, aircraft tug; ~ de cible *m* MILITAIRE target tug; ~ de haute mer *m* NAUT salvage tug, sea tug, TRANSPORT salvage tug, sea tug; ~ de planeur *m* MILITAIRE glider tug; ~ de rivière *m* TRANSPORT river tug; ~ de sauvetage *m* NAUT, TRANSPORT salvage tug; ~ de sauvetage en mer *m* TRANSPORT sea salvage tug; ~ spatial *m* ESPACE *véhicules* space tug

remoulage *m* PRODUCTION remolding (AmE), remoulding (BrE)

remouler *vt* PRODUCTION recast

rémouleur *m* PRODUCTION grinder

remous *m* AERONAUT slipstream, DISTRI EAU backwater, headwater, HYDROLOGIE backwash, eddy, NAUT eddy, OCEANO dead water, eddy, swirl; ~ d'hélice *m* AERONAUT propeller wash

remplacement *m* CONS MECA exchange; ~ de câblage *m* ELECTR *alimentation* rewiring

rempli: ~ de gaz *adj* THERMODYN gas-filled

remplir *vt* CONSTR *un fossé* fill up, INFORMAT, ORDINAT pad, PRODUCTION *une citerne, une lampe, un tonneau vide* fill; ~ de zéros *vt* INFORMAT zero fill, zeroize, ORDINAT zero fill, zeroize

remplissage:[1] à ~ pulvérulent *adj* ELECTROTEC powder filled

remplissage[2] *m* AGRO ALIM filling, CERAM VER filling point, *du four* filling, CONSTR filling, ESPACE transfer, transfer from tank, GAZ filling, GEOLOGIE *d'un bassin ou filon* infilling, INFORMAT filling, padding, NUCLEAIRE filling, ORDINAT filling, padding; ~ aseptique *m* AGRO ALIM aseptic filling; ~ à l'azote *m* ESPACE *des réservoirs des véhicules* nitrogen purging; ~ de carburant *m* AERONAUT fueling (AmE), fuelling (BrE); ~ à chaud *m* EMBALLAGE hot filling; ~ à deux vitesses *m* EMBALLAGE two-speed filling; ~ filonien *m* MINES lode filling; ~ géotropique *m* GEOLOGIE geotropic filling; ~ à niveau constant *m* ESPACE *véhicules* ullage; ~ numérique *m* TELECOM digital filling; ~ par le fond *m* EMBALLAGE bottom filling; ~ par gravité *m* AERONAUT gravity refueling (AmE), gravity refuelling (BrE), ESPACE *véhicules* gravity filling, gravity refueling (AmE), gravity refuelling (BrE); ~ par injection *m* EMBALLAGE injection filling; ~ par poids continu *m* EMBALLAGE continuous motion weight filling; ~ rotatif *m* EMBALLAGE rotary filling; ~ de sacs *m* EMBALLAGE bag filling; ~ sous pression *m* EMBALLAGE pressure filling; ~ sous vide *m* AGRO ALIM vacuum filling; ~ stérilisé *m* EMBALLAGE aseptic filling; ~ volumétrique *m* EMBALLAGE volume filling

remplisseuse: ~ de bouteilles *f* AGRO ALIM bottle filler, bottling machine; ~ de cartons *f* EMBALLAGE carton filler; ~ de poudre en godets *f* EMBALLAGE in cup powder filling machine; ~ de sacs *f* EMBALLAGE sack filling machine; ~ volumétrique *f* EMBALLAGE volumetric filling unit

remploi *m* RECYCLAGE reuse

remployer *vt* RECYCLAGE reuse

remuer *vt* CONSTR *le sol* disturb, GENIE CHIM, IMPRIM, PHOTO *les épreuves* agitate; ~ à la pelle *vt* CONSTR shovel

renard *m* CHARBON piping, HYDROLOGIE mechanical piping, piping

rencontre *f* CONSTR meeting, MINES strike; ~ électron-positron *f* PHYS PART electron-positron encounter

rencontrer[1] *vt* MINES strike

rencontrer[2] *vi* MINES *le fond solide* bottom

rencontrer:[3] se ~ *v réfl* DISTRI EAU meet

rendement *m* CHARBON, CHIMIE yield, CONS MECA efficiency, output, performance, ELECTR *appareil* efficiency, ELECTRON yield, ENREGISTR efficiency, ESPACE payoff, *communications* efficiency, GAZ output, yield, INFORMAT yield, MECANIQUE efficiency, MINES output, production, yield, NUCLEAIRE efficiency, yield, ORDINAT, PAPIER, PETROLE yield, PHYSIQUE efficiency, PRODUCTION capacity, efficiency, output, yield, *d'une machine* duty, TEXTILE yield; ~ à l'abattage *m* AGRO ALIM carcass dressing percentage, carcass yield; ~ acoustique *m* ENREGISTR acoustic efficiency; ~ adiabatique *m* PHYSIQUE, THERMODYN adiabatic efficiency; ~ d'ailette *m* REFRIG fin efficiency; ~ Auger *m* PHYSIQUE Auger yield; ~ du bocard *m* PRODUCTION mill result; ~ calorifique *m* THERMODYN calorific output, heat efficiency, heat output; ~ calorique *m* THERMODYN caloric power; ~ de canon *m* TV gun efficiency; ~ de capteur *m* EN RENOUV collector efficiency; ~ à charge partielle *m* CONS MECA part-load efficiency; ~ de chaudière *m* MAT CHAUFF boiler efficiency; ~ de combustion *m* ESPACE *propulsion*, THERMODYN combustion efficiency; ~ de couplage *m* OPTIQUE, TELECOM coupling efficiency; ~ électrique *m* ELECTROTEC electric efficiency, electrical efficiency; ~ d'émission secondaire *m* ELECTRON secondary emission ratio; ~ en carcasse *m* AGRO ALIM carcass yield; ~ énergétique *m* OPTIQUE *d'une source optique*, TELECOM source power efficiency, THERMODYN energy efficiency; ~ en puissance *m* ENREGISTR power efficiency; ~ d'ensemble *m* PRODUCTION aggregate output; ~ en verre *m* CERAM VER glass yield; ~ de l'étage *m* ELECTRON stage efficiency; ~ de fabrication *m* ELECTRON fabrication yield; ~ d'un four *m* CERAM VER furnace performance; ~ global *m* EN RENOUV overall efficiency; ~ à l'habillage *m* AGRO ALIM carcass yield; ~ horaire *m* EMBALLAGE hourly output; ~ hydraulique *m* EN RENOUV hydraulic efficiency; ~ d'illumination *m* ESPACE *communications* illumination efficiency; ~ industriel *m* PRODUCTION commercial coefficient; ~ ionique *m* PHYS RAYON ionic yield; ~ journalier moyen *m* EN RENOUV, PRODUCTION average daily output; ~ lumineux *m* PHOTO light output; ~ mécanique *m* CONS MECA, EN RENOUV mechanical efficiency; ~ moyen *m* THERMODYN average output; ~ des neutrons *m* PHYS PART neutron yield; ~ des neutrons thermiques *m* NUCLEAIRE thermal neutron yield; ~ des plaquettes *m* ELECTRON wafer yield; ~ quantique *m* OPTIQUE, PHYS RAYON *d'un laser* quantum efficiency, PHYSIQUE quantum efficiency, quantum yield, TELECOM quantum efficiency; ~ quantique différentiel *m* OPTIQUE, TELECOM differential quantum efficiency; ~ quantique de la luminescence *m* PHYS RAYON luminescence quantum yield; ~ des rayons X *m* NUCLEAIRE X-ray yield; ~ de redressement *m* ELECTROTEC rectification efficiency; ~ du rotor *m* AERONAUT *hélicoptère* rotor efficiency; ~ de surrégénération *m* NUCLEAIRE breeding process efficiency; ~ de sustentation *m* AERONAUT lighting efficiency; ~ thermique *m* AUTO, CHAUFFAGE, PHYSIQUE thermal efficiency, THERMODYN heat efficiency, heat rate, heatthroughput, thermal dissociation, thermal efficiency, thermal output; ~ **total** *m* PRODUCTION aggregate output; ~ **de trame** *m* ESPACE *communications* frame efficiency; ~ **d'un transformateur** *m* ELECTR transformer efficiency; ~ **de turbine** *m* EN RENOUV turbine efficiency, turbine output; ~ **de tuyère** *m* ESPACE *véhicules* nozzle efficiency; ~ **volumétrique** *m* AUTO, EN RENOUV volumetric efficiency

rendez-vous: ~ **spatial** *m* ESPACE space rendezvous, spatial rendezvous, *orbitographie* space rendezvous; ~ **sur orbite terrestre** *m* ESPACE *orbitographie* Earth orbit rendezvous; ~ **syncopal** *m* OCEANO shallow water blackout

rendre[1] *vt* PRODUCTION return; ~ **automatique** *vt* COMMANDE automate; ~ **basique** *vt* CHIMIE basify; ~ **à l'épreuve de feu** *vt* THERMODYN fireproof; ~ **étanche** *vt* NAUT seal; ~ **inerte** *vt* ESPACE *véhicules* passivate; ~ **inviolable** *vt* EMBALLAGE tamperproof; ~ **rugueux artificiellement** *vt* NUCLEAIRE artificially roughen

rendre:[2] ~ **la main** *vi* AERONAUT ease forward

rendu: ~ **correct** *m* PHOTO accurate reproduction; ~ **des couleurs** *m* CINEMAT color rendition (AmE), colour rendition (BrE); ~ **des détails** *m* TV detail rendition; ~ **des valeurs** *m* ENREGISTR tone reproduction, PHOTO reproduction of tonal values

rendus: ~ **et rabais** *m pl* PRODUCTION returns and allowances

renflement *m* CONS MECA boss, bulge, PRODUCTION *sur une pièce venue de fonte* boss; ~ **équatorial** *m* ASTRONOMIE equatorial bulge

renflouage *m* AERONAUT, NAUT salvage, TRANSPORT salvaging

renflouer *vt* NAUT float off, *un navire échoué* refloat

renfoncement: ~ **dans le texte** *m* IMPRIM *composition* indent

renfoncer *vt* IMPRIM indent

renforçage *m* CONSTR bracing, PHOTO intensification, PRODUCTION strengthening

renforçateur: ~ **de moussage** *m* LESSIVES foam boosting; ~ **de mousse** *m* LESSIVES foam boosting; ~ **de nettoyage** *m* LESSIVES dry-cleaning agent; ~ **à sel de chrome** *m* PHOTO chrome intensifier

renforcé: ~ **nylon** *adj* EMBALLAGE nylon-reinforced

renforcement *m* CONS MECA backing, CONSTR bracing, reinforcement, reinforcing, EMBALLAGE backing, MATERIAUX reinforcement, PHOTO intensification, PRODUCTION strengthening, TEXTILE backing; ~ **des aigus** *m* ENREGISTR treble boost; ~ **chimique** *m* PHOTO chemical intensification; ~ **des coins** *m* EMBALLAGE corner reinforcement; ~ **discontinu** *m* MATERIAUX discontinuous reinforcement; ~ **fragile** *m* MATERIAUX *céramique* brittle reinforcement; ~ **des graves** *m* ELECTRON bass boost; ~ **latent** *m* PHOTO latensification; ~ **au mercure** *m* PHOTO mercury intensification; ~ **par armature métallique** *m* CERAM VER wire mesh reinforcement; ~ **pour réclame suspendue par un ruban** *m* EMBALLAGE tape-hanging display reinforcement; ~ **à radiation** *m* ELECTROTEC radiation hardening

renforcer *vt* MECANIQUE boost

renfort *m* CONS MECA backing, brace, doubler, CONSTR haunch, NAUT stiffener; ~ **carré** *m* CONSTR haunch; ~ **en chaperon** *m* CONSTR haunch; ~ **pneumatique** *m* TEXTILE tire reinforcement (AmE), tyre reinforcement (BrE)

reniflard *m* AUTO breather pipe, breather, CONS MECA breather, DISTRI EAU rose, strainer, tailpiece, wind bore, PRODUCTION breather, *système hydraulique* air breather; ~ **de carter** *m* VEHICULES *de vilebrequin* breather; ~ **de carterin** *m* VEHICULES *moteur* crankcase breather

rénine *f* AGRO ALIM rennin

reniveIlement *m* CONSTR releveling (AmE), relevelling (BrE)

renmoulage *m* PRODUCTION coring, coring up, *de moules* setting up; ~ **de noyaux** *m* PRODUCTION coring, coring up

renmouler *vt* PRODUCTION core, core up

renonciation *f* BREVETS waiving

renouvellement *m* BREVETS renewal, CINEMAT replenishment, DISTRI EAU turnover, PRODUCTION renovation; ~ **de l'air** *m* AERONAUT air renewal; ~ **des fonds océaniques** *m* OCEANO seafloor renewal, seafloor spreading

renseignement *m* IMPRIM information; ~ **électronique** *m* ELECTRON electronic intelligence

renseignements: ~ **pour la sélection** *m pl* PRODUCTION selection information

rentable *adj* PRODUCTION cost-effective

rentrant *adj* GEOMETRIE re-entrant, reflex, INFORMAT, ORDINAT re-entrant

rentrée *f* PETROLE *pour reconditionnement* going in hole; ~ **des cannelures** *f* PRODUCTION draft (AmE), draught (BrE); ~ **dans l'atmosphère** *f* ESPACE *orbitographie* atmospheric re-entry

rentrer *vt* IMPRIM *un alinéa* indent, *une composition, une ligne* indent, NAUT *amarres* heave in, *avirons* ship, *une embarcation* haul up; ~ **son pavillon** *vt* NAUT strike colors (AmE), strike colours (BrE)

renverse *f* OCEANO turn; ~ **de la marée** *f* NAUT turn

renversement *m* CONS MECA *de marche*, MINES *aérage* reversing, PRODUCTION rolling over; ~ **de l'ébaucheur** *m* CERAM VER blank mold turnover (AmE), blank mould turnover (BrE); ~ **de la vapeur** *m* INST HYDR reversing steam

renverser[1] *vt* CONS MECA reverse

renverser:[2] ~ **la marche** *vi* CONS MECA reverse the motion; ~ **la vapeur** *vi* HYDROLOGIE reverse the steam

renvoi *m* CONS MECA counter driving motion, countermotion, counter gear, countershaft, countershaft and accessories, lever, reversing lever, GEOPHYS reverberation, INFORMAT, ORDINAT reference; ~ **adhérent** *m* CONS MECA self-contained countershaft, self-contained driving motion; ~ **d'angle** *m* AUTO, VEHICULES *différentiel* ring and pinion gearing; ~ **d'appel** *m* TELECOM call diversion; ~ **automatique** *m* (Can) TELECOM automatic call transfer; ~ **avec tige filetée** *m* CONSTR screw pulley; ~ **de chaîne** *m* CONS MECA chain sprocket; ~ **de combinateur** *m* AERONAUT mixer bellcrank; ~ **intermédiaire** *m* AERONAUT intermediate gearbox; ~ **de mouvement** *m* CONS MECA counter driving motion, countermotion, counter gear, countershaft, countershaft and accessories; ~ **de mouvement adhérent au bâti** *m* CONS MECA self-contained countershaft, self-contained driving motion; ~ **de mouvement à double vitesse** *m* CONS MECA two-speed counter motion; ~ **de mouvement se fixant au plafond** *m* CONS MECA overhead motion; ~ **de mouvement se fixant au sol** *m* CONS MECA countershaft for floor; ~ **de mouvement à simple vitesse** *m* CONS MECA single speed counter motion; ~ **d'organigramme** *m* INFORMAT, ORDINAT flowchart connector; ~ **à plat** *m*

CONSTR side pulley; ~ **à pont** *m* CONSTR axle pulley; ~ **de sonnette** *m* CONS MECA bell crank; ~ **temporaire de l'installation** *m* TELECOM installation call forwarding; ~ **temporaire de l'ITA** *m* TELECOM installation call forwarding; ~ **temporaire du terminal** *m* TELECOM terminal call forwarding; ~ **tendeur** *m* CONS MECA tension block; ~ **du terminal** *m* TELECOM terminal call forwarding

renvois: ~ **de mouvement** *m pl* CONS MECA countershafting

renvoyer *vt* INFORMAT, ORDINAT return

réoxygénation *f* DISTRI EAU reaeration, POLLUTION reoxidation

répandeuse *f* TRANSPORT spreader; ~ **de goudron** *f* TRANSPORT road tarring machine

répandre[1] *vt* PHYSIQUE give off, PRODUCTION *du sable* spread

répandre:[2] **se** ~ *v réfl* POLLU MER spread

réparation:[1] **en** ~ *adv* CONS MECA under repair, CONSTR undergoing repairs

réparation[2] *f* MINES *d'un guidage* rodding, NAUT refit, refitting, repair, PRODUCTION mending, repair, repairing; ~ **automatique** *f* TEXTILE automatic repair

réparations: ~ **accidentelles** *f pl (RA)* CH DE FER minor repairs; ~ **peu importantes** *f pl* PRODUCTION minor repairs

réparer *vt* ELECTRON, NAUT repair, PRODUCTION repair, *l'usure* make good

réparti *adj* INFORMAT, ORDINAT distributed

répartir *vt* PRODUCTION apportion, *des travaux* dispatch

répartiteur *m* CINEMAT break-out box, CONS MECA adaptor, ELECTR *raccordement* terminal block, INFORMAT dispatcher, MINES stage loader, ORDINAT dispatcher, PAPIER distributor, flow distributor, spreader, TELECOM distribution frame, TRANSPORT dispatcher; ~ **d'avarie** *m* NAUT average adjuster; ~ **de charge** *m* ELECTR *réseau* load dispatcher; ~ **à double face** *m* TELECOM double-sided distribution frame; ~ **d'entrée** *m* TELECOM MDF, main distribution frame; ~ **de freinage** *m* AUTO brake power distributor; ~ **de groupe primaire** *m* TELECOM group distribution frame; ~ **de hautes fréquences** *m* TELECOM high-frequency distribution frame; ~ **intermédiaire** *m (RI)* TELECOM intermediate distribution frame *(IDF)*; ~ **de jonction** *m* TELECOM JDF, junction distribution frame, TDF, trunk distribution frame; ~ **mixte** *m* TELECOM CDF, combined distribution frame; ~ **monoface** *m* TELECOM single-sided distribution frame; ~ **numérique** *m* TELECOM digital distribution frame; ~ **optique** *m* TELECOM OFF, optical flexibility frame; ~ **principal de station de répéteurs** *m* TELECOM main repeater distribution frame; ~ **de signaux** *m* TV signal splitter

répartition *f* BREVETS apportionment, CERAM VER, CONS MECA *de l'effort transversal* distribution, POLLUTION *géographique* spatial distribution, PRODUCTION *des travaux* dispatching; ~ **de charges** *f* AERONAUT, CONSTR load distribution; ~ **dans le temps** *f* ELECTRON time division; ~ **d'écoulement non-visqueux** *f* PHYS FLUID inviscid flow distribution; ~ **d'erreurs** *f* MATH error distribution; ~ **exponentielle** *f* INFORMAT, ORDINAT exponential distribution; ~ **de gaines d'air** *f* REFRIG duct distribution; ~ **gaussienne** *f* INFORMAT, ORDINAT Gaussian distribution; ~ **granulométrique** *f* CHIMIE particle size distribution; ~ **d'intensité** *f* PHYS RAYON *spectrographie* intensity distribution; ~ **intrin-**

sèque *f* PHYS RAYON *de fréquences* intrinsic distribution; ~ **isotropique** *f* ASTRONOMIE *des galaxies* isotropic distribution; ~ **de lumière** *f* OPTIQUE far-field diffraction pattern, far-field radiation pattern; ~ **des modes à l'équilibre** *f* OPTIQUE, TELECOM equilibrium mode distribution, steady state condition; ~ **des modes hors équilibre** *f* OPTIQUE, TELECOM nonequilibrium mode distribution; ~ **au moyen d'une formule** *f* MATERIAUX breakdown; ~ **normale** *f* INFORMAT normal distribution; ~ **des pistes** *f* ENREGISTR tracking configuration, TV track configuration; ~ **de probabilité des amplitudes** *f* TELECOM APD, amplitude probability distribution; ~ **sonore** *f* ENREGISTR sound distribution; ~ **statistique** *f* INFORMAT, ORDINAT probability distribution

repassage:[1] ~ **superflu** *adj* TEXTILE noniron, wash-and-wear

repassage[2] *m* CONS MECA sharpening, PRODUCTION whetting, TEXTILE ironing, pressing

repasser *vt* CINEMAT roll back, CONS MECA sharpen, INFORMAT rerun, NAUT *le gréement* overhaul, ORDINAT rerun, PRODUCTION *les filets* chase, TEXTILE iron

repêchage *m* ESPACE *véhicules en mer* recovery, PETR, PETROLE *d'un objet perdu* fishing

repêcher *vt* NAUT *un homme à la mer* rescue

repérage *m* ACOUSTIQUE cueing, CONS MECA identification, CONSTR marking, IMPRIM register, MILITAIRE position finding, PRODUCTION labeling (AmE), labelling (BrE), TELECOM locating, TV reconnaissance; ~ **automatique des déplacements** *m* TELECOM automatic roaming; ~ **du bruit des machines** *m* CONS MECA *acoustique* noise labeling (AmE), noise labelling (BrE); ~ **circonférentiel** *m* IMPRIM *contrôle qualité* circumferential register; ~ **défectueux** *m* IMPRIM *contrôle qualité* misregister; ~ **diagonal** *m* IMPRIM diagonal register; ~ **exact de l'impression** *m* EMBALLAGE accurate print registration; ~ **latéral** *m* IMPRIM side register; ~ **linéaire** *m* IMPRIM *contrôle qualité* linear register; ~ **par le son** *m* PHYS ONDES sound ranging; ~ **photoélectrique** *m* EMBALLAGE photoelectric register control; ~ **point sur point** *m* IMPRIM register; ~ **radio** *m* NAUT radio fix; ~ **à tétons** *m* IMPRIM *précalage* pin register; ~ **très précis** *m* IMPRIM hairline register; ~ **des voies au repos** *m* TELECOM MIC, marked idle channel

reperçage *m* PRODUCTION fret cutting, fret sawing

répercussion *f* MINES *d'une explosion* backlash

répercussions: ~ **élastiques** *f pl* PHYS FLUID turbulence elastic aftereffects

repère *m* CINEMAT cue, CONS MECA index, item number, CONSTR benchmark, datum, datum point, reference mark, ENREGISTR cue dot, cue, IMPRIM *fabrication* lay, METROLOGIE scale mark, NAUT guiding mark, PHYSIQUE coordinate system, PRODUCTION guiding mark, mark; ~ **d'alignement** *m* IMPRIM *machines* alignment mark; ~ **d'angle** *m* IMPRIM angle mark; ~ **d'approche** *m* AERONAUT approach fix, approach point; ~ **d'approche finale** *m* AERONAUT final approach fix, final approach point; ~ **d'approche initiale** *m* AERONAUT initial approach fix, initial approach point; ~ **d'approche intermédiaire** *m* AERONAUT intermediate approach fix, intermediate approach point; ~ **de bande** *m* ORDINAT tape mark; ~ **barycentrique** *m* PHYSIQUE center of mass coordinates (AmE), centre of mass coordinates (BrE); ~ **de centrage** *m* CERAM VER lug, pip; ~ **de départ** *m* CINEMAT printer start mark, start mark, TV start mark; ~ **de distribution** *m* AUTO timing mark; ~ **de fin de bande** *m* INFORMAT end of tape marker, ORDINAT EOT marker, end of tape marker; ~ **de fonction des composants** *m* PRODUCTION *automatisme industriel* component identification marker; ~ **inertiel** *m* PHYSIQUE inertial frame; ~ **de ligne de marche** *m* INSTRUMENT baseline; ~ **de niveau horizontal** *m* AERONAUT leveling mark (AmE), levelling mark (BrE); ~ **du niveau d'huile** *m* VEHICULES *lubrification* oil level mark; ~ **de position** *m* CONSTR benchmark; ~ **radio** *m* AERONAUT radio fix; ~ **de rogne** *m* IMPRIM trim mark; ~ **son** *m* ENREGISTR audio cue; ~ **sur diaphragme** *m* CINEMAT click stop; ~ **de visée** *m* INSTRUMENT graticule

repérer *vt* CINEMAT line up, NAUT locate

répertoire *m* CONS MECA index, INFORMAT, ORDINAT catalog (AmE), catalogue (BrE), repertoire, directory, TELECOM telephone directory, telephone number list; ~ **d'aide principale** *m* PRODUCTION *automatisme industriel* master help directory; ~ **d'aides** *m* PRODUCTION help directory; ~ **encoché** *m* IMPRIM side index; ~ **de fichier** *m* INFORMAT, ORDINAT file directory; ~ **imprimante** *m* IMPRIM printer directory; ~ **d'instructions** *m* INFORMAT, ORDINAT instruction repertoire; ~ **de programmes** *m* INFORMAT, ORDINAT contents directory

répertorier *vt* PRODUCTION *des données* document

répétabilité *f* METROLOGIE *des mesurages* repeatability

répéter *vt* IMPRIM *mots* double

répéteur *m* ELECTRON carrier repeater, repeater, ESPACE *communications* repeater, transponder, INFORMAT, ORDINAT repeater, PHYSIQUE, TELECOM repeater, transponder; ~ **analogique** *m* ELECTRON nonregenerative repeater; ~ **immergé** *m* TELECOM submerged repeater; ~ **de ligne** *m* TELECOM line repeater; ~ **non régénérateur** *m* ELECTRON nonregenerative repeater; ~ **numérique** *m* ELECTRON digital regenerator; ~ **optique** *m* OPTIQUE, TELECOM optical repeater; ~ **optique immergé** *m* TELECOM submerged optical repeater; ~ **de programme** *m* TV program repeater (AmE), programme repeater (BrE); ~ **à quatre fils** *m* ELECTRON four-wire repeater; ~ **régénérateur** *m* ELECTRON regenerative repeater; ~ **régénérateur optique** *m* OPTIQUE optical regenerative receiver, TELECOM optical regenerative repeater; ~ **sur câble** *m* ELECTROTEC cable repeater; ~ **unidirectionnel** *m* ELECTRON one-way repeater

répétiteur *m* ESPACE *véhicules* repeater; ~ **de cap** *m* AERONAUT heading repeater; ~ **de compas** *m* NAUT compass repeater; ~ **optique** *m* ELECTRON optical stepper

répétition *f* INFORMAT, ORDINAT retry; ~ **du dernier numéro** *f* TELECOM last number redial

répétitivité: ~ **du positionnement** *f* CONS MECA *machine-outil* positioning repeatability

repiquage *m* CINEMAT sound transfer, ENREGISTR rerecording, IMPRIM imprinting, imprint, overprinting, surprint, PHOTO spotting; ~ **avec formes en relief et forte pression** *m* IMPRIM *typographie* crash printing; ~ **en son optique** *m* CINEMAT optical transfer; ~ **magnétique** *m* CINEMAT magnetic transfer; ~ **par estampage à chaud** *m* IMPRIM *façonnage* hot-stamp imprint; ~ **vidéo** *m* TV videotape dubbing

repiquer *vt* ENREGISTR transfer, IMPRIM imprint, overprint, tip on, PHOTO retouch, TV dub, duplicate

replanir *vt* CONSTR clean off

replanissage *m* CONSTR cleaning off

repli: ~ **de laminage** *m* RESSORTS lap, seam

repliage: ~ **de la pale** *m* AERONAUT blade folding

repliement: ~ **du spectre** *m* ELECTRON aliasing

réplique: ~ **au carbone** *f* NUCLEAIRE carbon replica

répondeur *m* AERONAUT *communications* responder, TELECOM telephone answering machine, transponder; ~ **téléphonique** *m* TELECOM telephone answering machine; ~ **vocal** *m* INFORMAT, ORDINAT audio response unit

réponse *f* ACOUSTIQUE response, COMMANDE reaction, response, ELECTRON reply, response, ENREGISTR, INFORMAT, ORDINAT response, TELECOM blip, response; ~ **A-associate** *f* TELECOM AARE; ~ **acoustique** *f* COMMANDE audio response; ~ **amplitude-amplitude** *f* ELECTRON amplitude-amplitude response; ~ **amplitude-fréquence** *f* ELECTRON amplitude-frequency response, frequency response; ~ **des basses** *f* ENREGISTR bass response; ~ **aux basses fréquences** *f* ELECTRON low-frequency response; ~ **au courant** *f* ACOUSTIQUE response to current; ~ **dans la bande passante** *f* ELECTRON pass band response; ~ **directionnelle** *f* ELECTRON directional response; ~ **dynamique** *f* TELECOM dynamic response; ~ **à un échelon** *f* ELECTRON step function response; ~ **en amplitude** *f* ELECTRON amplitude response; ~ **en amplitude de filtre** *f* ELECTRON filter amplitude response; ~ **en champ libre** *f* ENREGISTR free field response; ~ **en fréquence** *f* ELECTRON, ENREGISTR, OPTIQUE, TELECOM frequency response; ~ **en fréquence de filtre** *f* ELECTRON filter frequency response; ~ **en fréquence de la tête** *f* TV head response; ~ **en passe-bas** *f* ELECTRON low-pass response; ~ **en phase** *f* COMMANDE, ELECTRON phase response; ~ **en phase de filtre** *f* ELECTRON filter phase response; ~ **en régime transitoire** *f* ELECTROTEC transient response; ~ **en température** *f* ELECTROTEC temperature response; ~ **de filtre** *f* ELECTRON filter response; ~ **de fréquence** *f* TELECOM frequency response; ~ **fréquentielle** *f* PHYS ONDES frequency response; ~ **impulsionnelle** *f* OPTIQUE, PETR, TELECOM impulse response; ~ **impulsionnelle finie** *f* ELECTRON FIR, finite impulse response; ~ **impulsionnelle infinie** *f* ELECTRON IIR, infinite impulse response; ~ **d'impulsions** *f* PETR impulse response; ~ **indicielle** *f* COMMANDE indicial response, transient response, ELECTRON indicial response; ~ **infinie à une impulsion** *f* TELECOM IIR, infinite impulse response; ~ **linéaire** *f* ENREGISTR flat response; ~ **à la puissance** *f* ACOUSTIQUE response to power; ~ **radar** *f* AERONAUT radar response; ~ **rapide** *f* COMMANDE rapid response; ~ **au signal d'entrée** *f* ELECTRON input response; ~ **au signal unité** *f* TV surge characteristic, transient response; ~ **spatiale** *f* ELECTRON spatial response; ~ **à la tension** *f* ACOUSTIQUE response to voltage; ~ **transitoire** *f* ELECTROTEC transient response; ~ **uniforme** *f* ELECTRON, ENREGISTR flat response; ~ **uniforme en fréquence** *f* ENREGISTR flat frequency response; ~ **vocale** *f* ELECTRON, TELECOM audio response, voice response

report *m* ELECTRON carry, IMPRIM transfer, *copie* repeat, *fabrication des plaques* step-and-repeat, INFORMAT *arithmétique*, ORDINAT *arithmétique* carry; ~ **de charge** *m* ELECTR *alimentation* load transfer; ~ **circulaire** *m* INFORMAT, ORDINAT end-around carry; ~ **en cascade** *m* ELECTRON cascaded carry; ~ **parallèle** *m* INFORMAT, ORDINAT carry look-ahead, look-ahead; ~ **partiel** *m* INFORMAT, ORDINAT partial carry

reportage: ~ **en direct** m TV live coverage; ~ **en extérieur** m TV field pick-up

repos:[1] **au** ~ adj ELECTROTEC quiescent, PRODUCTION nonoperating

repos:[2] **au** ~ adv PRODUCTION off delay

repos[3] m CONSTR landing, PRODUCTION contacts break

repose-pied m VEHICULES motocyclette footrest

repousser vt NAUT fend off

repousseur:[1] ~ **d'eau** adj REVETEMENT water-repellent

repousseur[2] m POLLU MER herding agent

repoussoir m CONSTR pin punch

reprendre vt INFORMAT, ORDINAT restart

représentant: ~ **de la sécurité** m SECURITE safety representative

représentation f INFORMAT, ORDINAT representation; ~ **binaire** f ELECTRON bit mapping, INFORMAT binary representation, ORDINAT bit map; ~ **de connaissances** f INFORMAT, ORDINAT knowledge representation; ~ **de données** f INFORMAT, ORDINAT data representation; ~ **en valeur signée** f INFORMAT, ORDINAT signed magnitude representation; ~ **en virgule variable** f INFORMAT, ORDINAT variable point representation; ~ **fil de fer** f INFORMAT, ORDINAT wireframe representation; ~ **géométrique** f GEOMETRIE des nombres entiers geometric representation; ~ **graphique** f INFORMAT graphical representation, MATH diagram, graph, ORDINAT graphical representation; ~ **numérique** f ELECTRON digital representation, INFORMAT, ORDINAT digital representation, numeric representation; ~ **simplifiée** f CONS MECA des trous de centre simplified representation

représenter vt ORDINAT image; ~ **graphiquement** vt MATH graph; ~ **par une image** vt INFORMAT image

reprise f AUTO, CONS MECA pick-up, INFORMAT fallback, restart, ORDINAT fallback, rerun, restart, PRODUCTION moulage cold shot, cold shut, TELECOM call retrieval, TEXTILES darning, VEHICULES moteur engine pick-up; ~ **après erreur** f INFORMAT, ORDINAT error recovery; ~ **après incident** f INFORMAT failure recovery, fallback, ORDINAT failure recovery; ~ **de carburant** f AERONAUT fueling (AmE), fuelling (BrE); ~ **commerciale d'humidité** f ESSAIS textiles, TEXTILE commercial moisture regain; ~ **conventionnelle d'humidité** f ESSAIS, TEXTILE conventional moisture regain; ~ **élastique** f PLAST CAOU essai de plasticité recovery; ~ **en secours** f INFORMAT, ORDINAT backup; ~ **en sous-oeuvre** f CONSTR underpinning; ~ **d'humidité** f ESSAIS, PAPIER, TEXTILE moisture regain; ~ **d'humidité dans l'atmosphère normale** f ESSAIS textiles moisture regain in the standard atmosphere; ~ **vidéo** f CINEMAT video assist

repriser vt TEXTILE darn

reproducteur: ~ **de bande** m INFORMAT, ORDINAT tape reproducer; ~ **de bandes perforées** m INFORMAT punch tape reproducer (AmE), punched tape producer (BrE), ORDINAT punch tape reproducer (AmE), punched tape reproducer (BrE); ~ **de cartes perforées** m INFORMAT punch card reproducer (AmE), punched card reproducer (BrE), ORDINAT punch card reproducer (AmE), punched card reproducer (BrE); ~ **sonore optique** m ENREGISTR optical sound reproducer

reproductibilité f METROLOGIE des mesurages reproducibility; ~ **de fréquence** f ELECTRON frequency retrace

reproduction f ACOUSTIQUE reproducing, reproduction, ENREGISTR playback, replay, reproduction, TV playback, replay; ~ **des demi-teintes** f IMPRIM photogravure halftone reproduction; ~ **de diapositives** f PHOTO slide duplication; ~ **différée** f ENREGISTR playback; ~ **fidèle de la tonalité** f IMPRIM tone reproduction; ~ **instantanée** f TV instant replay; ~ **photomécanique** f IMPRIM photomechanical transfer; ~ **de son** f TV audio playback

reproduire vt ENREGISTR replay, reproduce, INFORMAT, ORDINAT duplicate

reprofilage m CONSTR reprofiling

reprographie f INFORMAT, ORDINAT reprographics

reprojeter vt CINEMAT roll back

répudiation f TELECOM repudiation

répulsion f ELECTROTEC, PHYSIQUE repulsion; ~ **coulombienne** f PHYSIQUE Coulomb repulsion; ~ **magnétique** f ELECTROTEC magnetic repulsion

requête f BREVETS, INFORMAT, ORDINAT request

RER abrév (réseau express régional) CH DE FER regional express railroad (AmE), regional express railway (BrE)

résazurine f CHIMIE resazurin

réseau:[1] **en** ~ adj TELECOM networked

réseau[2] m CHIMIE lattice, CONSTR network, system, ELECTR electrical supply (BrE), mains (BrE), mains supply (BrE), supply network (AmE), grid, alimentation network, power grid, ELECTRON pattern, ELECTROTEC linear network, mains (BrE), network, power grid, supply network (AmE), ESPACE communications network, véhicules lattice, INFORMAT network, NUCLEAIRE lattice, ORDINAT network, PETR array, PHYSIQUE, PLAST CAOU, PRODUCTION, de fils, TRANSPORT network, TV network, raster;

~ a ~ **d'accès** m TELECOM access network; ~ **actif** m ELECTROTEC active network; ~ **d'adaptation d'impédance** m ELECTROTEC, PHYSIQUE impedance matching network; ~ **aérien** m ELECTR transmission line network, ELECTROTEC overhead system, TELECOM overhead network; ~ **d'alimentation** m ELECTR supply network, ELECTROTEC electricity supply system, power system; ~ **d'alimentation en énergie** m ESPACE véhicules power distribution network; ~ **d'antennes** m ASTRONOMIE, ESPACE antenna array; ~ **d'antennes à très longue ligne de base** m (VLBA) ASTRONOMIE Very Long Baseline Array (VLBA); ~ **arborescent** m ELECTR treed system, INFORMAT, ORDINAT tree network, TELECOM tree and branch network, tree network; ~ **d'assainissement** m CONSTR storm sewer system, RECYCLAGE drainage system, sewer system, sewerage system; ~ **d'assainissement mixte** m DISTRI EAU combined sewer system; ~ **atténuateur** m ELECTRON pad; ~ **atténuateur en T** m ELECTROTEC T-network; ~ **avec blocage** m ELECTROTEC blocking network;

~ b ~ **basse tension** m ELECTR alimentation low-voltage network; ~ **bilatéral** m ELECTROTEC bidirectional network; ~ **à blocage** m TELECOM blocking network; ~ **de bobine** m ESSAIS coil arrangement; ~ **bouclé** m ELECTR ring main system; ~ **de Bravais** m CRISTALL Bravais lattice;

~ c ~ **câblé** m TV cabled network; ~ **de câbles** m ELECTROTEC cable network; ~ **de câbles souterrains** m CONSTR underground cabling; ~ **de canalisations** m CONSTR piping network; ~ **ccc** m CRISTALL bcc lattice; ~ **cellulaire** m TELECOM cellular network; ~ **centré** m METALL body-centered lattice (AmE), body-centred lattice (BrE); ~ **centré sur base** m METALL base-centered lattice (AmE), base-centred lattice (BrE);

~ **CFC** *m* CHIMIE, CRISTALL FCC lattice; ~ **de circulation aérienne** *m* AERONAUT air traffic pattern; ~ **classique** *m* TELECOM ordinary network; ~ **client** *m* TELECOM CN, customer network; ~ **de Clos** *m* TELECOM Clos network; ~ **de Clos imparfait** *m* TELECOM sub-Clos network; ~ **de communication** *m* INFORMAT, ORDINAT communication network, telecommunication network; ~ **de communication de données** *m* *(RCD)* TELECOM data communication network; ~ **de communication local** *m* *(RCL)* TELECOM local communications network; ~ **de commutation** *m* TELECOM switching network; ~ **à commutation de circuits** *m* INFORMAT, ORDINAT circuit-switched network, TELECOM circuit switching network, circuit-switched network; ~ **à commutation de messages** *m* INFORMAT, ORDINAT message-switched network, TELECOM message switching network, store-and-forward switching network; ~ **à commutation de paquets** *m* TELECOM packet switching network; ~ **de commutation par paquets** *m* INFORMAT, ORDINAT PSN, packet-switched network; ~ **commuté** *m* ELECTROTEC, INFORMAT, ORDINAT, TELECOM switched network; ~ **commuté canadien** *m* *(RCC)* TELECOM Canadian Switched Network *(CSN)*; ~ **compact** *m* METALL close-packed lattice; ~ **de compensation thermique** *m* ELECTROTEC temperature-compensating network; ~ **compensé par bobine d'extinction** *m* ELECTR resonant earthed neutral system (BrE), resonant grounded neutral system (AmE); ~ **concave** *m* PHYSIQUE *de Rowland* concave grating; ~ **de concentration** *m* TELECOM concentration network; ~ **de conduites** *m* CONSTR system of pipes; ~ **de conduits** *m* CONSTR piping network; ~ **conformateur** *m* TV shaping network; ~ **connecté** *m* ELECTR connected network; ~ **de connexion** *m* ELECTROTEC switching network, TELECOM distribution network, switching network; ~ **de connexion à bande étroite** *m* TELECOM narrow band switching network; ~ **de connexion à large bande** *m* TELECOM broadband switching network, wide band switching network; ~ **de connexion numérique** *m* TELECOM digital switching network; ~ **de connexion optique** *m* TELECOM OSN, optical switching network; ~ **de connexion à relais à tiges** *m* ELECTROTEC reed relay switching network; ~ **de connexion sans blocage** *m* ELECTROTEC nonblocking network; ~ **de connexion temporel** *m* TELECOM time-division network; ~ **correcteur** *m* TELECOM equalizer circuit; ~ **de correction** *m* TELECOM equalizer circuit; ~ **à courant alternatif** *m* ELECTR, ELECTROTEC alternating current network; ~ **à courant continu** *m* ELECTR direct current network, ELECTROTEC DC network; ~ **de courant linéaire** *m* ELECTR *alimentation* linear current network; ~ **cristallin** *m* CRISTALL crystal lattice, ELECTRON lattice, MATERIAUX crystal network; ~ **cubique centré** *m* CRISTALL body-centered cubic lattice (AmE), body-centred cubic lattice (BrE); ~ **cubique simple** *m* CRISTALL simple cubic lattice;

~ **d** ~ **décentralisé** *m* INFORMAT, ORDINAT distributed network; ~ **déphaseur** *m* ELECTR *courant alternatif*, PHYSIQUE phase-shifting network; ~ **de destination** *m* TELECOM DN, destination network; ~ **à deux accès** *m* ELECTROTEC two-port network; ~ **à deux conducteurs** *m* ELECTR double wire system; ~ **à deux fils** *m* ELECTR two-wire network, two-wire system; ~ **du diamant** *m* METALL diamond lattice; ~ **de diffraction** *m* MATERIAUX *chromatographie*, OPTIQUE, PHYS ONDES, PHYSIQUE, TELECOM diffraction grating; ~ **de diffusion** *m* TV broadcasting network; ~ **de diodes** *m* TELECOM diode array; ~ **diphasé** *m* ELECTR two-phase network, ELECTROTEC two-phase system; ~ **de dispersion** *m* GENIE CHIM dispersion grating; ~ **distribué** *m* INFORMAT, ORDINAT distributed network; ~ **de distribution** *m* CONSTR distribution network, DISTRI EAU mains (BrE), supply network (AmE), ELECTR distribution network, distribution system, ELECTROTEC distribution network, distribution system, supply main, REFRIG *d'air, de fluides* duct work, TELECOM distribution network; ~ **de distribution d'énergie** *m* ELECTROTEC electric power system, power grid; ~ **de données** *m* INFORMAT, ORDINAT, TELECOM data network; ~ **double** *m* ELECTR duplicate supply; ~ **dual** *m* PHYSIQUE dual network;

~ **e** ~ **d'échantillonnage** *m* QUALITE sampling network; ~ **d'éclairage** *m* ELECTROTEC lighting system; ~ **d'égouts** *m* HYDROLOGIE sewer network; ~ **électrique** *m* PHYSIQUE electrical network; ~ **électrique actif** *m* ELECTROTEC active network; ~ **électrique bilatéral** *m* ELECTROTEC bidirectional network; ~ **électrique de bord** *m* AERONAUT aircraft electrical system (AmE), aircraft mains; ~ **électrique à courant alternatif** *m* ELECTROTEC alternating current network; ~ **électrique en treillis** *m* ELECTROTEC lattice network; ~ **en anneau** *m* INFORMAT, ORDINAT, TELECOM ring network; ~ **en anneau à jeton** *m* INFORMAT, ORDINAT token passing network; ~ **en arbre** *m* TELECOM tree and branch network; ~ **en boucle** *m* ELECTR ring main system, INFORMAT loop network, ring network, ORDINAT loop network; ~ **en delta** *m* ELECTR two-wire delta network, ELECTROTEC delta network; ~ **en double T** *m* ELECTROTEC twin-T network; ~ **en échelette** *m* PHYSIQUE blazed grating, echelette grating; ~ **en échelle** *m* ELECTROTEC, PHYSIQUE ladder network; ~ **en échelon** *m* PHYSIQUE echelon grating; ~ **d'énergie** *m* ESPACE *véhicules* power distribution network; ~ **en étoile** *m* ESPACE star network, *communications* mesh network, INFORMAT, ORDINAT, TELECOM star network; ~ **en étoile commuté** *m* TELECOM switched-star network; ~ **en fil métallique** *m* CONSTR wire netting; ~ **en H ponté** *m* ELECTROTEC bridged-H network; ~ **en L** *m* ELECTROTEC L-network; ~ **en pont** *m* ELECTROTEC bridge circuit; ~ **en T** *m* PHYSIQUE T-network; ~ **en T ponté** *m* ELECTROTEC bridged-T network; ~ **en treillis** *m* ELECTROTEC lattice network; ~ **en Y** *m* PHYSIQUE Y-network; ~ **d'équilibrage** *m* ELECTROTEC balancing network; ~ **équilibré** *m* ELECTR, ELECTROTEC balanced network; ~ **d'espace** *m* CRISTALL space lattice; ~ **à étages** *m* TELECOM multistage network; ~ **à étages multiples** *m* TELECOM multistage network; ~ **étoilé** *m* INFORMAT, ORDINAT, TELECOM star network; ~ **d'expansion** *m* TELECOM expansion network; ~ **express régional** *m* *(RER)* CH DE FER regional express railroad (AmE), regional express railway (BrE);

~ **f** ~ **à faces centrées** *m* METALL face-centered lattice (AmE), face-centred lattice (BrE); ~ **ferroviaire** *m* TRANSPORT railroad network (AmE), railway network (BrE); ~ **à fibre optique** *m* ELECTROTEC fiberoptic network (AmE), fibreoptic network (BrE); ~ **de files d'attente** *m* TELECOM queueing network; ~ **de fil de fer barbelé** *m* MILITAIRE barbed wire entanglement;

~ **g** ~ **de gaz** *m* PETROLE *système de distribution* gas grid; ~ **de gazoducs** *m* THERMODYN gas grid; ~ **de**

gestion SDH *m* TELECOM SDH management network, SMN; **~ de gestion des télécommunications** *m (RGT)* TELECOM telecommunications management network *(TMN)*;

~ h ~ hexagonal compact *m* NUCLEAIRE HCP lattice, hexagonal close-packed lattice; **~ hydrographique** *m* GEOLOGIE drainage pattern, HYDROLOGIE water system;

~ i ~ d'installation d'abonnés *m* TELECOM SPN, subscriber premises network; **~ d'intégration** *m* AERONAUT integrating network; **~ interactif** *m* TELECOM interactive network; **~ interconnecté** *m* ELECTR interconnected network, interconnected systems, meshnetwork, meshed network; **~ d'interconnexion** *m (RI)* TELECOM interconnection network; **~ international de transmission par paquets** *m* TELECOM international packet-switched data network; **~ intra-ZAA** *m* TELECOM local area network; **~ isolateur** *m* ELECTROTEC line pad;

~ l ~ de lignes spécialisées *m* INFORMAT, ORDINAT leased line network; **~ linéaire** *m* ELECTROTEC, PHYSIQUE linear network; **~ local** *m* TELECOM local network; **~ local d'entreprise** *m (RLE)* INFORMAT, ORDINAT, TELECOM local area network *(LAN)*; **~ local de raccordement** *m* TELECOM local distribution network; **~ logique programmable** *m* INFORMAT, ORDINAT PLA, programmable logic array; **~ à logique programmable par l'utilisateur** *m* INFORMAT, ORDINAT FPLA, field programmable logic array; **~ à logique programmée** *m* INFORMAT, ORDINAT PLA, programmed logic array;

~ m ~ maillé *m* ELECTR INFORMAT, ORDINAT mesh network, meshed network; **~ métropolitain** *m* TELECOM metropolitan network; **~ MIA** *m* TELECOM PAM network; **~ mobile terrestre public** *m* TELECOM public mobile network; **~ de modulation par impulsions d'amplitude** *m* TELECOM pulse amplitude modulation network; **~ mondial** *m* TELECOM *communications* worldwide network; **~ de moyenne tension** *m* ELECTROTEC medium-voltage system;

~ n ~ national d'interconnexion *m* NUCLEAIRE *production et transport d'électricité* national grid; **~ navigable** *m* NAUT inland waterway; **~ neuronal** *m* INFORMAT, ORDINAT neural network; **~ à neutre directement à la terre** *m* ELECTR solidly-earthed neutral system (BrE), solidly-grounded neutral system (AmE); **~ à neutre isolé** *m* ELECTR isolated neutral system; **~ à neutre non-directement à la terre** *m* ELECTR impedance earthed neutral system (BrE), impedance grounded neutral system (AmE); **~ non blocable** *m* TELECOM strictly nonblocking network; **~ non bloquant** *m* TELECOM nonblocking network; **~ non linéaire** *m* CONSTR nonlinear network; **~ numérique** *m* TELECOM DN, digital network; **~ numérique à intégration des services** *m (RNIS)* TELECOM integrated services digital network *(ISDN)*; **~ numérique avec intégration des services à large bande** *m (RNIS-LB)* TELECOM wide band integrated services digital network, broadband integrated services digital network *(B-ISDN)*; **~ numérique intégré** *m (RNI)* TELECOM integrated digital network *(IDN)*;

~ o ~ officiel de télétransmission *m* IMPRIM common carrier; **~ optique passif** *m* TELECOM PON, passive optical network; **~ d'ordinateurs** *m* INFORMAT, ORDINAT, TELECOM computer network; **~ d'ordres** *m*

ENREGISTR studio address system; **~ d'ordre supérieur** *m* TELECOM high-order network;

~ p ~ de parole-données *m* TELECOM speech-data network; **~ par réflexion** *m* PHYSIQUE reflection grating; **~ à partage de ressources** *m* INFORMAT, ORDINAT resource-sharing network; **~ par transmission** *m* PHYSIQUE transmission grating; **~ passif** *m* ELECTR, ELECTROTEC passive network; **~ de Pétri** *m* INFORMAT, ORDINAT Petri net; **~ de phase** *m* ELECTR *courant alternatif* phase grid; **~ pi** *m* ELECTROTEC, PHYSIQUE pi network; **~ pilote** *m* ELECTR pilot network; **~ polyphasé** *m* ELECTR polyphase network; **~ de poursuite et de saisie de données dans l'espace** *m* MILITAIRE STADAN, space tracking and data acquisition network; **~ primaire** *m* ELECTR high-voltage grid, high-voltage system; **~ privé** *m* TELECOM private network; **~ public** *m* TELECOM public network; **~ public commuté** *m* TELECOM *télétransmissions* PSN, public switched network; **~ public de données** *m* INFORMAT, ORDINAT PDN, public data network; **~ public de transmission de données** *m* INFORMAT, ORDINAT PDN, public data network;

~ q ~ quadrillé *m* CINEMAT graticule;

~ r ~ radial *m* ELECTR radial system; **~ ramifié** *m* DISTRI EAU arterial system; **~ réarrangeable** *m* TELECOM rearrangeable non-blocking network; **~ réciproque** *m* CRISTALL reciprocal lattice; **~ à réflexion** *m* PHYS ONDES reflection grating; **~ régional de radioguidage** *m* TRANSPORT regional radio warning system; **~ à relais à tiges** *m* ELECTROTEC reed relay switching network; **~ replié** *m* TELECOM folded network; **~ de réserve** *m* ELECTR stand-by supply; **~ de résistances** *m* ELECTROTEC resistor network; **~ résistif** *m* PRODUCTION impedance network; **~ routier** *m* TRANSPORT road system; **~ rural** *m* ELECTROTEC rural district, TELECOM rural network;

~ s ~ séparatif *m* DISTRI EAU separate sewerage system; **~ du service fixe des télécommunications aéronautiques** *m* AERONAUT aeronautical fixed telecommunication network; **~ simple** *m* ELECTR single supply; **~ au sol** *m* TELECOM ground network; **~ spatial** *m* CRISTALL space lattice; **~ spatial-temporel-spatial** *m* TELECOM space-time-space network; **~ STS** *m* TELECOM space-time-space network; **~ synchrone** *m* INFORMAT synchronous network; **~ de synchronisation** *m* TELECOM synchronization network;

~ t ~ de télécommunication *m* INFORMAT, ORDINAT telecommunication network, TELECOM telecommunications network, TV news network; **~ de télédistribution** *m* TV broadcasting network; **~ télématique** *m* INFORMAT, ORDINAT data communication network; **~ téléphonique** *m* TELECOM telephone network, voice network; **~ téléphonique classique** *m* TELECOM traditional telephone network; **~ téléphonique commuté** *m* TELECOM public switched telephone network, TELECOM switched telephone network; **~ téléphonique ignifuge** *m* CONSTR fireproof telephone system; **~ téléphonique privé** *m* TELECOM private telephone network; **~ téléphonique public** *m* TELECOM public telephone network; **~ téléphonique public commuté** *m* TELECOM PSTN, public switched telephone network; **~ de télévision par câbles** *m* TELECOM cable television network; **~ temporel-spatial-temporel** *m* TELECOM time-space-time network; **~ thermique équivalent** *m* THERMODYN equivalent thermal network; **~ de traction** *m* ELECTR traction network; ~ **transfrontalier** *m* TELECOM cross-border system; ~ **de transmission** *m* INFORMAT, ORDINAT communication network, TELECOM transmission network; ~ **de transmission de données à longues distances** *m* IMPRIM wide area network; ~ **de transmission de données par paquets** *m (TRANSPAC)* TELECOM packet data transmission network; ~ **de transport** *m* GAZ transmission network, TELECOM data transport network, trunk network; ~ **de transport d'énergie** *m* ELECTROTEC power transmission network; ~ **triphasé** *m* ELECTR three-phase supply network, ELECTROTEC three-phase system; ~ **à trois fils** *m* ELECTROTEC three-wire current (AmE), three-wire mains (BrE); ~ **de tubes réfrigérants** *m* REFRIG pipe-cooling grids; ~ **de tubes servant à transporter un liquide** *m* CONSTR system of tubing for conveying a liquid; ~ **de type bus** *m* INFORMAT, ORDINAT bus network;

~ **u** ~ **unitaire** *m* HYDROLOGIE combined sewer; ~ **urbain** *m* TELECOM urban network;

~ **v** ~ **à valeur ajoutée** *m (RVA)* INFORMAT, ORDINAT, TELECOM value-added network *(VAN)*; ~ **à voie étroite** *m* CH DE FER light railway (BrE);

~ **z** ~ **de zone locale** *m* TELECOM local area network; ~ **de zone urbaine** *m* TELECOM MAN, metropolitan area network

réserpine *f* CHIMIE reserpine

réservation *f* PRODUCTION allocation, allotment; ~ **physique** *f* PRODUCTION staging

réserve:[1] **de** ~ *adj* ORDINAT backup, QUALITE stand-by, TELECOM stand-by, stand-by working; **en** ~ *adj* INFORMAT, ORDINAT stand-by, TELECOM stand-by, stand-by working

réserve[2] *f* IMPRIM *dans un texte* window, *héliogravure* resist; ~ **à l'acide** *f* IMPRIM acid resist, top; ~ **de combustible** *f* AERONAUT fuel reserve; ~ **de composition** *f* CERAM VER mixed batch store; ~ **de flottabilité** *f* NAUT reserve buoyancy; ~ **de flottaison** *f* TRANSPORT reserve buoyancy; ~ **à glace** *f* REFRIG ice storage room; ~ **d'oxygène** *f* SECURITE *incendie, explosion* oxygen supply; ~ **de périphérique** *f* INFORMAT, ORDINAT device reserve

réservé: ~ **à un emploi spécifique** *adj* PRODUCTION reserved for special use; ~ **aux instruments** *adj* AERONAUT instrument restricted

réserver: ~ **une communication** *vi* TELECOM book a call

réserves *f pl* AERONAUT reserves; ~ **possibles** *f pl* PETROLE possible reserves; ~ **probables** *f pl* PETR, PETROLE probable reserves; ~ **prouvées** *f pl* PETROLE proven reserves; ~ **récupérables** *f pl* PETROLE recoverable reserves; ~ **sûres** *f pl* PETR proven reserves

réservoir *m* CONS MECA *d'un compresseur d'air* receiver, *ménagé sous le banc* drop-pan, tray, DISTRI EAU cistern, flume, reservoir, ESPACE *de récupération* disposal tank, *véhicules* tank, HYDROLOGIE reservoir, MECANIQUE tank, MINES bunker, ore bin, NAUT tank, PETR reservoir, supply vessel, PETROLE reservoir, storage tank, tank, PHYS FLUID reservoir, POLLUTION tank, PRODUCTION tank, trough, REFRIG, TRANSPORT tank, VEHICULES *carburant, huile* reservoir, tank; ~ **additionnel** *m* ESPACE *véhicules* additional tank; ~ **d'aile** *m* AERONAUT wing tank; ~ **d'air** *m* CONS MECA air box, air receiver; ~ **d'air comprimé** *m* CONS MECA air receiver; ~ **d'alimentation** *m* PETROLE *raffinerie* feed tank; ~ **d'aspiration** *m* INST HYDR suction tank; ~ **de carburant** *m* AERONAUT, VEHICULES fuel tank; ~ **de**

chaleur *m* REFRIG heat reservoir; ~ **de chasse** *m* DISTRI EAU flush box, flush tank; ~ **à combustible** *m* MECANIQUE *véhicules* fuel tank; ~ **de compensation** *m* HYDROLOGIE compensation reservoir; ~ **cryogénique** *m* ESPACE *véhicules* cryogenic tank; ~ **cryogénique à pression** *m* CONS MECA cryogenic pressure vessel; ~ **à débit non réglable** *m* HYDROLOGIE detention reservoir; ~ **déshydrateur** *m* AUTO receiver dehydrator, receiver dryer; ~ **de détente** *m* CONS MECA expansion vessel; ~ **des drains du circuit primaire** *m* NUCLEAIRE reactor coolant drain tank; ~ **d'eau** *m* MINES water reservoir, NUCLEAIRE water accumulator; ~ **à eau** *m* DISTRI EAU cistern, water tank, NAUT water tank; ~ **d'eau chaude** *m* MAT CHAUFF hot water tank; ~ **à eau chaude sous pression** *m* MAT CHAUFF pressurized hot water tank; ~ **d'eau filtrée** *m* HYDROLOGIE purified water reservoir, purified water tank; ~ **d'eau portatif** *m* MILITAIRE portable water storage tank; ~ **des eaux pluviales** *m* HYDROLOGIE rainwater reservoir; ~ **d'eaux usées** *m* ESPACE *véhicules* disposal tank, wastewater tank; ~ **d'échantillonnage** *m* NUCLEAIRE *du bâti* sample admission vessel; ~ **d'écrêtement des crues** *m* DISTRI EAU detention reservoir; ~ **égalisateur** *m* REFRIG equalizer tank; ~ **d'emmagasinage** *m* PETROLE accumulator tank, PRODUCTION storage reservoir, storage tank; ~ **d'encre** *m* IMPRIM *machines* ink tank; ~ **enterré** *m* DISTRI EAU earth reservoir; ~ **d'équilibre** *m* REFRIG balance tank; ~ **d'ergol** *m* ESPACE *véhicules* fuel tank; ~ **d'essence** *m* AUTO fuel tank, VEHICULES fuel tank, *carburant* gas tank (AmE), gasoline tank (AmE), petrol tank (BrE); ~ **d'expansion** *m* AUTO supply tank; ~ **flexible pour carburant** *m* MILITAIRE flexible oil storage tank; ~ **de flottabilité** *m* NAUT air tank, buoyancy tank, flotation tank; ~ **de fluide** *m* CONS MECA fluid receiver; ~ **de fluide hydraulique** *m* CONS MECA hydraulic fluid reservoir, INST HYDR hydraulic reservoir; ~ **à gaz** *m* PETR gas reservoir, PRODUCTION gas tank, gasholder; ~ **à gaz de condensation** *m* PETR condensate gas reservoir; ~ **de gaz de pressurisation** *m* ESPACE *véhicules* pressurizing gas tank; ~ **haute pression** *m* ESPACE *véhicules* high-pressure tank; ~ **d'huile** *m* CONSTR, ELECTROTEC oil tank, MINES, PETR oil reservoir; ~ **d'hydrogène** *m* ESPACE *véhicules* hydrogen tank; ~ **inférieur** *m* AUTO lower tank; ~ **intégré** *m* CONS MECA built-in tank, integral tank; ~ **intermédiaire** *m* CONS MECA *d'une machine à détente* receiver; ~ **journalier** *m* NUCLEAIRE *groupes de secours* day tank, day-fuel tank; ~ **de liquide** *m* REFRIG liquid receiver; ~ **de liquide de freins** *m* CONS MECA brake fluid tank; ~ **de mélange** *m* GENIE CHIM mixing vessel; ~ **de mélange d'acide borique** *m* NUCLEAIRE boric acid blender; ~ **à membrane élastomère** *m* ESPACE *véhicules* elastomer membrane tank; ~ **de minerai** *m* MINES ore bin; ~ **de pétrole** *m* PETR oil reservoir; ~ **de pétrole brut** *m* PETR oil reservoir; ~ **pour liquide de freins** *m* AUTO brake fluid reservoir; ~ **de préparation** *m* NUCLEAIRE *de produits chimiques* batching tank; ~ **à pression** *m* CONS MECA pressure vessel; ~ **à pression cuit** *m* CONS MECA fired pressure vessel; ~ **à pression à membrane** *m* CONS MECA diaphragm pressure vessel; ~ **à pression sans soudure** *m* CONS MECA seamless pressure vessel; ~ **à pression vêtu** *m* CONS MECA clad pressure vessel; ~ **réfrigérant intermédiaire** *m* PRODUCTION *d'un compresseur d'air* intercooler; ~ **de régulation** *m* HYDROLOGIE detention reservoir; ~ **relais** *m* NUCLEAIRE day tank, day-fuel tank; ~ **de retenue d'eau** *m* HYDROLOGIE catchment basin, reservoir, storage basin; ~ **à retour de saumure** *m* REFRIG brine return tank; ~ **de rétrolavage** *m* NUCLEAIRE backwash tank; ~ **de sécurité** *m* TRANSPORT safety gas tank (AmE), safety gasoline tank (AmE), safety petrol tank (BrE); ~ **souple** *m* AERONAUT *ne faisant pas partie de la cellule* bladder tank; ~ **souple flottant** *m* POLLU MER dracone; ~ **souterrain** *m* GAZ underground storage system; ~ **sphérique** *m* ESPACE *véhicules* spherical tank; ~ **de stockage** *m* EN RENOUV storage basin, ESPACE *véhicules* storage tank, PETR flow tank, storage tank; ~ **de stockage des effluents** *m* NUCLEAIRE active effluent holdup tank; ~ **de stockage inférieur** *m* EN RENOUV lower storage basin; ~ **de stockage de sécurité** *m* SECURITE safety storage tank; ~ **de stockage supérieur** *m* EN RENOUV upper storage basin; ~ **supérieur** *m* AUTO radiator header; ~ **tampon** *m* PETR flow tank, REFRIG accumulator, battery; ~ **à tension de surface** *m* ESPACE *véhicules* surface tension tank; ~ **thermique** *m* PHYSIQUE heat reservoir; ~ **de turbine** *m* DISTRI EAU open turbine chamber, INST HYDR open turbine chamber, openturbine pit; ~ **de vapeur** *m* CONS MECA steam receiver

résidant *adj* INFORMAT, ORDINAT resident; ~ **en mémoire** *adj* INFORMAT, ORDINAT memory-resident; ~ **sur disque** *adj* INFORMAT, ORDINAT disk resident

résider *vi* INFORMAT, ORDINAT reside

résidu *m* AGRO ALIM bottoms, residue, waste, CHARBON tailings, tails, CHIMIE residue, CONSTR tailings, DISTRI EAU residue, GENIE CHIM sediment, LESSIVES slurry, PETROLE bottoms, residue, POLLU MER, POLLUTION residue; ~ **d'argent** *m* PHOTO residual silver; ~ **de combustion** *m* THERMODYN combustion deposit; ~ **de connexion** *m* TELECOM connection overhead; ~ **de détergents** *m* LESSIVES washing powder slurry; ~ **de distillation** *m* GENIE CHIM, THERMODYN distillation tail; ~ **sec** *m* HYDROLOGIE dry matter, solid matter; ~ **de section** *m* TELECOM section overhead; ~ **stérile** *m* CONSTR tailings; ~ **de trajet** *m* TELECOM POH, path overhead

résiduaire *adj* CHIMIE residuary

résiduel *adj* CHIMIE residuary, GEOLOGIE *d'un minéral, d'une structure* relic, relictual, INFORMAT, ORDINAT residual

résiliation *f* TELECOM cease

résilience *f* CONS MECA, INFORMAT resilience, MECANIQUE *matériaux* impact strength, NUCLEAIRE impact strength, notch toughness, toughness, ORDINAT, PAPIER resilience, PHYSIQUE impact strength, PLAST CAOU, TEXTILE resilience; ~ **au choc** *f* MATERIAUX impact toughness; ~ **de la mie** *f* AGRO ALIM crumb elasticity

résilient *adj* MATERIAUX resilient

résine *f* CHIMIE, MATERIAUX, NAUT, PLAST CAOU *plastiques, polymères*, TEXTILE resin; ~ **acétonique** *f* EMBALLAGE, PLAST CAOU acetone resin; ~ **acrylique** *f* EMBALLAGE, MECANIQUE *matériaux*, PLAST CAOU *plastiques, peintures, adhésifs* acrylic resin; ~ **alkyde** *f* PLAST CAOU *liant de peinture* alkyd resin; ~ **amino** *f* PLAST CAOU *plastiques, peintures, adhésifs* amino resin; ~ **d'aniline-formaldéhyde** *f* EMBALLAGE aniline formaldehyde resin; ~ **artificielle** *f* MATERIAUX synthetic resin; ~ **de coumarone** *f* PLAST CAOU coumarone resin; ~ **crésolique** *f* PLAST CAOU cresol resin; ~ **échangeuse d'ions** *f* MATERIAUX ion exchange resin; ~ **époxidique** *f* CONSTR epoxy resin; ~ **époxy** *f*

ELECTR *isolation* epoxy resin; ~ **époxyde** *f* CHIMIE, ELECTR *isolation*, EMBALLAGE, MATERIAUX, PLAST CAOU epoxy resin; ~ **époxyde acrylée** *f* PLAST CAOU *peintures, adhésifs* acrylated epoxy resin; ~ **d'esters** *f* LESSIVES ester resin; ~ **à l'état A** *f* PLAST CAOU A-stage resin; ~ **à l'état B** *f* PLAST CAOU B-stage resin; ~ **à l'état C** *f* PLAST CAOU C-stage resin; ~ **fluorocarbonée** *f* PLAST CAOU fluorocarbon resin; ~ **de gaïacol** *f* AGRO ALIM guaiac gum, gum guaiacum; ~ **à hydrocarbures** *f* MATERIAUX hydrocarbon resin; ~ **de mélamine** *f* ELECTR *isolation* melamine resin, PLAST CAOU melamine formaldehyde resin; ~ **phénolique** *f* ELECTR *isolation*, PLAST CAOU phenolic resin; ~ **de polyester** *f* CHIMIE polyester, polyester resin; ~ **polyuréthane** *f* CONSTR polyurethane resin; ~ **pour moulage en coquilles** *f* PLAST CAOU shell molding resin (AmE), shell moulding resin (BrE); ~ **de résorcine** *f* PLAST CAOU resorcinol resin; ~ **synthétique** *f* MATERIAUX artificial resin, PETROLE, PLAST CAOU synthetic resin; ~ **d'urée** *f* MATERIAUX urea resin; ~ **urée-formaldéhyde** *f* ELECTR *isolation* urea-formaldehyde resin; ~ **urée-formol** *f* PLAST CAOU urea-formaldehyde resin

résist *m* ELECTRON resist; ~ **développé au plasma** *m* ELECTRON plasma-developed resist; ~ **multicouche** *m* ELECTRON multilayer resist; ~ **négatif** *m* ELECTRON negative resist; ~ **optique** *m* ELECTRON optical resist; ~ **optique négatif** *m* ELECTRON negative photoresist; ~ **photosensible** *m* ELECTRON photoresist; ~ **positif** *m* ELECTRON positive resist; ~ **pour faisceau d'électrons** *m* ELECTRON electron beam resist; ~ **pour rayons X** *m* ELECTRON X-ray resist; ~ **à rayons X** *m* ELECTRON X-ray resist

résistance *f* AUTO resistor, CHARBON strength, CONS MECA resistance, tenacity, toughness, ELECTR resistance, *conducteur* resistor, ELECTROTEC resistance, resistor, GAZ strength, MATERIAUX resistance, tensile strength, strength, METALL strength, MINES *de la mine* drag, resistance, NAUT drag, PAPIER strength, PETR resistance, PHYSIQUE resistance, resistor, *de charge* load resistance, PLAST CAOU, TELECOM resistance, TEXTILE resistance, strength;

~ a ~ **à l'abrasion** *f* MATERIAUX, PAPIER, PLAST CAOU abrasion resistance, TEXTILE fastness to rubbing; ~ **aux acides** *f* PLAST CAOU acid resistance; ~ **à l'acidité** *f* POLLUTION acid tolerance; ~ **acoustique** *f* ACOUSTIQUE acoustic resistance; ~ **d'adhésion** *f* MATERIAUX bonding resistance, PLAST CAOU bond strength; ~ **aérodynamique** *f* TRANSPORT aerodynamic drag, aerodynamical levitation; ~ **agglomérée** *f* ELECTROTEC carbon composition resistor; ~ **d'aiguille** *f* ENREGISTR needle drag; ~ **ajustable** *f* ELECTROTEC adjustable resistor; ~ **aux alcalis** *f* PLAST CAOU alkali resistance; ~ **à l'allongement** *f* PLAST CAOU yield strength; ~ **d'amortissement** *f* ELECTR damping resistor, ELECTROTEC snubber resistor, PHYSIQUE damping resistance; ~ **anhydre à la traction** *f* TEXTILE oven-dry tensile strength; ~ **d'antenne** *f* PHYSIQUE aerial resistance; ~ **à l'arrachage** *f* PAPIER pick resistance, surface bonding strength; ~ **à l'arrachement** *f* CONS MECA resistance to tearing, MATERIAUX pullout resistance;

~ b ~ **à bagues** *f* ELECTROTEC ferrule resistor; ~ **ballast** *f* ELECTR ballast resistor, load resistor, ELECTROTEC ballast resistor, barretter; ~ **de la base** *f* ELECTROTEC base resistance; ~ **à base pincée** *f* ELECTROTEC pinched resistor; ~ **bobinée** *f* ELECTROTEC, PHYSIQUE wire-wound resistor; ~ **bobinée inductive** *f*

ELECTROTEC inductive wirewound resistor; ~ **bobinée non inductive** *f* CONSTR noninductive resistor; ~ **bobinée de précision** *f* ELECTROTEC precision wirewound resistor; ~ **bobinée de puissance** *f* ELECTROTEC power wire-wound resistor; ~ **de bouclage** *f* ELECTROTEC terminating resistor; ~ **au brouillard salin** *f* CERAM ver salt spray test;

~ c ~ **capacitive** *f* ELECTROTEC capacitive resistance; ~ **au carbone** *f* ELECTROTEC carbon resistor, organic resistor; ~ **carbone** *f* ELECTROTEC carbon resistor, organic resistor; ~ **de carbone aggloméré** *f* PHYSIQUE carbon resistor; ~ **de la carène** *f* NAUT hull resistance; ~ **à la chaleur** *f* PLAST CAOU heat resistance, THERMODYN heat resistance, resistance to heat; ~ **au charbon** *f* PHYSIQUE carbon resistor; ~ **de charge** *f* ELECTROTEC load resistor; ~ **de la charge** *f* ELECTROTEC load resistance; ~ **à chaud** *f* THERMODYN hot strength; ~ **de chauffage** *f* ELECTR heating resistor; ~ **de chauffage de carter** *f* REFRIG crankcase heater; ~ **chauffante** *f* AERONAUT heating resistor; ~ **chimique** *f* PLAST CAOU chemical resistance; ~ **aux chocs** *f* CONS MECA resistance to impact, resistance to shock, EMBALLAGE impact resistance, PLAST CAOU impact strength, shock resistance; ~ **aux chocs et à l'usure** *f* CONS MECA shock and wear resistance; ~ **aux chocs thermiques** *f* THERMODYN resistance to thermal shock; ~ **chutrice** *f* ELECTROTEC dropping resistor, voltage dropping resistor; ~ **au cisaillement** *f* CHARBON shear strength, CONS MECA resistance to shearing, shearing strength, shearing tenacity, MECANIQUE *matériaux* shear strength, PLAST CAOU adhesive shear strength, shear strength, RESSORTS shear resistance, shear strength; ~ **à collier** *f* ELECTROTEC adjustable resistor; ~ **à la compression** *f* CONS MECA retroactive tenacity, EMBALLAGE, MECANIQUE *matériaux* compression strength, PLAST CAOU compressive strength; ~ **à la congélation-décongélation** *f* REFRIG freeze-thaw resistance; ~ **de contact** *f* ELECTR *entre deux métaux*, ELECTROTEC contact resistance; ~ **de contact des balais** *f* ELECTR *machine* brush contact resistance; ~ **de contre-réaction** *f* ELECTROTEC feedback resistor; ~ **à la corrosion** *f* CONSTR, MATERIAUX, PLAST CAOU corrosion resistance; ~ **à couche** *f* ELECTROTEC film resistor; ~ **à couche de carbone** *f* ELECTROTEC carbon film resistor; ~ **à couche épaisse** *f* ELECTRON thick-film resistor, ELECTROTEC metal glaze resistor; ~ **à couche métallique** *f* ELECTROTEC metal film resistor; ~ **à couches minces** *f* ELECTRON thin-film resistor; ~ **de couplage** *f* ELECTR coupling resistance; ~ **au craquelage** *f* PLAST CAOU crack resistance; ~ **au creep** *f* PLAST CAOU creep resistance; ~ **critique** *f* ELECTR critical resistance;

~ d ~ **au débit en amont** *f* PRODUCTION *système hydraulique* upstream resistance; ~ **de décharge** *f* ELECTR discharge resistor; ~ **au déchirement** *f* CONS MECA resistance to tearing, PLAST CAOU tear resistance, tear strength, POLLU MER resistance to tearing; ~ **à la déchirure** *f* IMPRIM *papiers*, TEXTILE tear strength; ~ **de défaut** *f* ELECTROTEC fault resistance; ~ **de détection** *f* ELECTROTEC sensing resistor; ~ **de détection de courant** *f* ELECTROTEC current-sensing resistor; ~ **diagonale** *f* NAUT diagonal strength; ~ **diélectrique** *f* ELECTR *condensateur* dielectric resistance, dielectric strength; ~ **directe** *f* ELECTR positive phase sequence resistance, *semi-conducteur* forward resistance; ~ **discrète** *f* ELECTROTEC discrete resistor; ~ **due au vent**

f PHYS FLUID wind resistance; ~ **dynamique** *f* ELECTR dynamic resistance;

~ e ~ **à l'éclatement** *f* EMBALLAGE bursting strength, resistance to shattering, PAPIER, PLAST CAOU, TEXTILE bursting strength; ~ **à l'écoulement** *f* ACOUSTIQUE flow resistance, PHYS FLUID resistance to flow; ~ **à l'écrasement** *f* CONS MECA resistance to crushing, retroactive tenacity, IMPRIM *carton* flat crush resistance, PAPIER crushing resistance, TEXTILE crush resistance; ~ **effective** *f* ELECTROTEC, PHYSIQUE effective resistance; ~ **à l'effet corona** *f* PLAST CAOU corona resistance; ~ **électrique** *f* ELECTR, ELECTROTEC, PHYSIQUE electric resistance; ~ **élevée** *f* PHYSIQUE high resistance; ~ **en bande** *f* ELECTROTEC reeled resistor; ~ **en courant alternatif** *f* ELECTROTEC AC resistance; ~ **en courant continu** *f* ELECTROTEC DC resistance, ohmic resistance; ~ **en dérivation** *f* ELECTR shunt, ELECTROTEC shunt resistor; ~ **d'enduit** *f* ELECTR *machine* armature resistance; ~ **en fil bobiné** *f* ELECTR wire-wound resistor; ~ **en parallèle** *f* ELECTR parallel-connected resistance, ELECTROTEC parallel resistance, shunt resistance, shunt resistor; ~ **en série** *f* ELECTR series-connected resistance; ~ **d'entrée** *f* ELECTROTEC input resistance; ~ **d'équilibrage** *f* ELECTR balancing resistor; ~ **équivalente** *f* ELECTR equivalent resistance; ~ **à l'essence** *f* PLAST CAOU gasoline resistance (AmE), petrol resistance (BrE); ~ **à l'état humide** *f* PAPIER, PLAST CAOU wet strength; ~ **extérieure** *f* ELECTROTEC external resistor; ~ **externe** *f* ELECTR external resistance; ~ **extrême** *f* CONS MECA ultimate strength;

~ f ~ **faible** *f* PHYSIQUE low resistance; ~ **à la fatigue** *f* AERONAUT, ESPACE *véhicules*, MECANIQUE *matériaux* fatigue strength; ~ **au feu** *f* PLAST CAOU fire resistance, SECURITE fire-resistance; ~ **de filament** *f* ELECTR *tube* filament resistance; ~ **fixe** *f* ELECTR, ELECTROTEC, PHYSIQUE fixed resistor; ~ **au flambage** *f* CONS MECA resistance to buckling; ~ **flexible** *f* ELECTROTEC flexible resistor; ~ **à la flexion** *f* CONS MECA resistance to bending, stiffness, IMPRIM, MECANIQUE *matériaux* flexural strength, NUCLEAIRE bending strength, flexural strength, PAPIER bending strength, PLAST CAOU flexing resistance, flexural strength; ~ **aux flexions répétées** *f* PLAST CAOU flexing endurance; ~ **au fluage** *f* CHARBON creep strength, MATERIAUX creep resistance, METALL creep strength, PLAST CAOU creep resistance; ~ **à force de rupture** *f* METALL rupture strength; ~ **de forte valeur** *f* ELECTROTEC large-value resistor; ~ **de freinage** *f* TRANSPORT braking resistance; ~ **à froid** *f* ELECTROTEC cold resistance, THERMODYN cold strength; ~ **de frottement** *f* MECANIQUE frictional drag, NAUT frictional resistance; ~ **de fuite** *f* PHYSIQUE leakage resistance; ~ **de fuite de grille** *f* PHYSIQUE grid leak resistor;

~ g ~ **gâchette-cathode** *f* ELECTROTEC gate-to-cathode resistor; ~ **au glissement** *f* CONS MECA resistance to sliding;

~ h ~ **de Hall** *f* PHYSIQUE Hall resistance; ~ **à l'humidité** *f* PLAST CAOU wet strength; ~ **hybride intégrée** *f* ELECTROTEC integrated hybrid resistor;

~ i ~ **inductive** *f* ELECTROTEC inductive resistor; ~ **d'induit** *f* ELECTROTEC armature resistance; ~ **aux intempéries** *f* CONSTR weathering resistance; ~ **interne** *f* ELECTR *pile* internal resistance; ~ **d'isolement** *f* ELECTROTEC, PHYSIQUE insulation resistance;

~ k ~ **kilométrique** *f* TEXTILE breaking length;

~ l ~ **au laminage** *f* TEXTILE laminating resistance; ~

de lamination *f* EMBALLAGE laminating strength; ~ au lavage *f* TEXTILE fastness to washing; ~ de limitation du courant *f* ELECTR limiting resistor; ~ limite *f* CONS MECA ultimate strength; ~ limite au cisaillement *f* CONS MECA ultimate shear strength; ~ linéaire *f* ELECTR, ELECTROTEC, PHYSIQUE linear resistor; ~ linéique *f* PHYSIQUE resistance per unit length; ~ de lissage *f* ELECTR smoothing resistor; ~ à la lumière *f* PLAST CAOU light fastness; ~ à la lumière solaire *f* PLAST CAOU sunlight resistance;

~ m ~ magnétique *f* ELECTROTEC magnetic resistance; ~ aux matières grasses *f* PLAST CAOU grease resistance; ~ mécanique *f* ACOUSTIQUE mechanical resistance, MATERIAUX mechanical strength; ~ mécanique des trichites *f* MATERIAUX whisker strength; ~ métallique *f* ELECTR metallic resistor; ~ de la mine *f* MINES mine resistance; ~ de mise à l'échelle *f* ELECTROTEC scalar resistor; ~ au mouvement *f* MECANIQUE drag;

~ n ~ négative *f* ELECTR, ELECTROTEC negative resistance; ~ au nitrure de tellure *f* ELECTROTEC tellurium nitride resistor; ~ non bobinée *f* CONSTR nonwire-wound resistor; ~ non inductive *f* ELECTR noninductive resistor; ~ non linéaire *f* ELECTR nonlinear resistor, ELECTROTEC varistance, TELECOM nonlinear resistance;

~ o ~ d'obscurité *f* ELECTROTEC, NUCLEAIRE dark resistance; ~ ohmique *f* ELECTR ohmic resistance, ELECTROTEC ohmic resistance, pure resistance; ~ ordinaire *f* ELECTROTEC general-purpose resistor; ~ à ordre des phases positives *f* ELECTR positive phase sequence resistance; ~ à l'ozone *f* PLAST CAOU ozone resistance;

~ p ~ par carré *f* ELECTROTEC sheet resistance; ~ passive *f* CONS MECA resistance to motion; ~ permanente à la traction *f* CONS MECA endurance tensile strength; ~ au pliage *f* EMBALLAGE folding strength; ~ à la pointe *f* CHARBON point resistance; ~ de polarisation *f* ELECTROTEC, PHYSIQUE bias resistor; ~ de pont *f* ELECTR bridge resistance; ~ de précision *f* ELECTROTEC power resistor; ~ à prises *f* ELECTROTEC tapped resistor; ~ proportionnée *f* ELECTR *pont* proportionate arm, ratio arm; ~ de protection *f* ELECTROTEC protection resistor; ~ de puissance *f* ELECTROTEC power resistor; ~ pure *f* ELECTROTEC pure resistance;

~ r ~ à radiation *f* ELECTROTEC radiation hardness; ~ ramenée au primaire *f* ELECTROTEC reflected resistance; ~ de rayonnement *f* PHYSIQUE radiation resistance; ~ aux rayures *f* PLAST CAOU scratch resistance; ~ de réglage *f* ELECTROTEC regulating resistance; ~ de rencontre *f* TRANSPORT impact resistance; ~ résiduelle *f* CHARBON residual strength, ELECTROTEC residual resistance; ~ au retrait *f* TEXTILE shrink resistance; ~ à roulement *f* VEHICULES *pneus* road resistance, rolling resistance; ~ à la rupture *f* CONS MECA tensile strength, ultimate strength, CONSTR ultimate strength, MECANIQUE ultimate tensile strength, *matériaux* breaking strength, PLAST CAOU breaking strength, fracture toughness, ultimate tensile strength; ~ à la rupture fragile *f* METALL brittle fracture resistance; ~ à la rupture par compression *f* CONS MECA ultimate crushing strength; ~ à la rupture par flexion *f* CONS MECA ultimate bending strength; ~ à la rupture par traction *f* CONS MECA ultimate tensile strength, NUCLEAIRE ultimate tensile stress, PAPIER, PHYSIQUE tensile strength; ~ à la rupture par traction

"zero span" *f* PRODUCTION *industrie du papier* zero span tensile strength; ~ à la rupture par traction dans la direction z *f* PRODUCTION *industrie du papier* z-direction tensile strength;

~ s ~ à la salissure *f* TEXTILE resistance to soiling; ~ secondaire *f* ELECTROTEC secondary resistance; ~ à semi-conducteur *f* ELECTROTEC semiconductor resistor; ~ sensible à la température *f* ELECTROTEC temperature-dependent resistor; ~ sensible à la tension *f* ELECTROTEC voltage-dependent resistor; ~ série *f* ELECTR series resistor, ELECTROTEC series resistance; ~ série du collecteur *f* ELECTROTEC series collector resistance; ~ à sorties radiales *f* ELECTROTEC radial lead resistor; ~ spécifique *f* ELECTR, ELECTROTEC specific resistance; ~ spécifique à l'écoulement *f* ACOUSTIQUE flow resistivity; ~ stabilisatrice *f* ELECTROTEC bleeder resistor; ~ superficielle *f* CHARBON skin resistance, surface resistance, ESSAIS surface resistance; ~ de surface *f* CHAUFFAGE surface resistance;

~ t ~ à température basse *f* PLAST CAOU low-temperature resistance; ~ de la terre *f* ELECTR earth resistance (BrE), ground resistance (AmE); ~ thermique *f* CHAUFFAGE, PHYSIQUE, THERMODYN thermal resistance; ~ thermosensible *f* ELECTROTEC thermistor; ~ à la torsion *f* CONS MECA resistance to twisting, torsional strength, torsional tenacity; ~ à la traction *f* CONS MECA resistance to tension, tensile strength, MECANIQUE *matériaux*, PHYSIQUE, PLAST CAOU, TEXTILE tensile strength; ~ à la transpiration *f* TEXTILE fastness to perspiration;

~ u ~ ultime à la traction *f* METALL ultimate tensile strength; ~ à l'usure *f* MATERIAUX wear resistance, METROLOGIE durability, TEXTILE wear resistance; ~ utile *f* ESSAIS effective resistance;

~ v ~ de vague *f* NAUT wave resistance; ~ à la vapeur *f* CHAUFFAGE vapor resistance (AmE), vapour resistance (BrE); ~ variable *f* ELECTR adjustable resistor, variable resistor, ELECTROTEC variable resistance, variable resistor, PHYSIQUE variable resistor; ~ vive *f* CONS MECA resilience

résistance-capacité *f (RC)* ELECTRON, ELECTROTEC resistance-capacitance *(RC)*

résistances: ~ appariées *f pl* ELECTROTEC matched resistors

résistant *adj* CHIMIE fast, PLAST CAOU resistant; ~ à l'abrasion *adj* IMPRIM abrasion-resistant, MECANIQUE *matériaux*, REVETEMENT abrasion-proof; ~ aux acides *adj* EMBALLAGE acid-resistant, IMPRIM acid-proof, acid-resistant, PAPIER acid-proof; ~ aux alcalis *adj* LESSIVES alkali-fast, alkali-proof, PAPIER alkali-proof; ~ aux attaques chimiques *adj* EMBALLAGE chemically resistant; ~ à la chaleur *adj* EMBALLAGE heat-proof, ESPACE, MATERIAUX heat-resistant, THERMODYN heat-proof, heat-resistant, heat-resisting; ~ au chaud *adj* THERMODYN heat-proof, heat-resistant, heat-resisting; ~ aux chocs *adj* EMBALLAGE shock-proof, METROLOGIE resistant to impact; ~ à la décoloration *adj* COULEURS bleaching-resistant; ~ à l'eau *adj* EMBALLAGE, TEXTILE water-resistant; ~ au feu *adj* ELECTR *matériel* fireproof, SECURITE fire-resistant, fireproof, THERMODYN fire-resistant, fire-resisting, refractory; ~ aux flammes *adj* SECURITE, THERMODYN fireproof, flameproof; ~ au gel *adj* CHARBON *sol* frost-resistant; ~ à l'huile *adj* PLAST CAOU oil-resistant; ~ à l'humidité *adj* EMBALLAGE moisture-resistant, THERMODYN humidity-resistant; ~ aux

insectes *adj* EMBALLAGE insect-proof; ~ **aux intempéries** *adj* PAPIER, SECURITE weatherproof; ~ **aux liquides** *adj* EMBALLAGE liquid-proof; ~ **à la lumière** *adj* COULEURS light-fast, sunfast, EMBALLAGE stable-to-light, IMPRIM fade-proof, *papiers, encres* fade-resistant; ~ **au moisi** *adj* EMBALLAGE mold-resistant (AmE), mould-resistant (BrE); ~ **aux odeurs** *adj* EMBALLAGE odor-proof (AmE), odour-proof (BrE); ~ **à la pourriture** *adj* EMBALLAGE antirot; ~ **à l'usure** *adj* EMBALLAGE wear resistant; ~ **au vieillissement** *adj* EMBALLAGE ageing-resistant (BrE), aging-resistant (AmE)

résister *vt* PRODUCTION *des manipulations brutales* stand

résisteur *m* ELECTR resistor

résistif *adj* ELECTROTEC resistive

résistivimètre *m* GEOPHYS resistivity meter

résistivité *f* CHARBON, CHAUFFAGE, ELECTR resistivity, ELECTROTEC specific resistance, MATERIAUX, PETR, PETROLE, PHYSIQUE, PLAST CAOU resistivity; ~ **apparente** *f* PETR apparent resistivity; ~ **électrique** *f* PLAST CAOU electrical resistivity; ~ **en couche** *f* ELECTROTEC sheet resistance; ~ **en profondeur** *f* ELECTROTEC bulk resistivity; ~ **de formation** *f* PETR formation resistivity; ~ **de masse** *f* ELECTR mass resistivity; ~ **spécifique** *f* ELECTROTEC resistivity; ~ **superficielle** *f* ELECTROTEC surface resistivity; ~ **thermique** *f* CHAUFFAGE thermal resistivity; ~ **à la vapeur** *f* CHAUFFAGE vapor resistivity (AmE), vapour resistivity (BrE); ~ **volumique** *f* ELECTROTEC, ESSAIS volume resistivity; ~ **volumique électrique** *f* ESSAIS volume resistivity

résite *f* PLAST CAOU resite

résitole: ~ **à l'état B** *m* PLAST CAOU B-stage resin

résol *m* PLAST CAOU resol; ~ **à l'état A** *m* PLAST CAOU A-stage resin

résolution *f* ACOUSTIQUE, CINEMAT, ESSAIS resolution, INFORMAT resolution, *graphique* definition, ORDINAT definition, resolution, TV resolution; ~ **angulaire** *f* ASTRONOMIE angular resolution; ~ **de l'écran** *f* IMPRIM screen resolution; ~ **géographique** *f* POLLUTION spatial resolution; ~ **géométrique du faisceau** *f* NUCLEAIRE geometric beam resolution; ~ **spatiale** *f* POLLUTION spatial resolution; ~ **temporelle** *f* PHYS RAYON, POLLUTION temporal resolution

résonance *f* CHIMIE, ELECTR *circuit à courant alternatif*, ELECTRON, ENREGISTR, PHYS ONDES, PHYSIQUE, TELECOM resonance; ~ **d'amplitude** *f* PHYSIQUE amplitude resonance; ~ **de bielle de commande** *f* AERONAUT control rod resonance; ~ **de Briet et Wigner** *f* NUCLEAIRE Briet-Wigner resonance, single level resonance; ~ **cyclotronique** *f* TELECOM cyclotronic resonance; ~ **dans une cavité** *f* ELECTRON cavity resonance; ~ **magnétique** *f* ELECTROTEC, PHYSIQUE magnetic resonance; ~ **magnétique électronique** *f* PHYSIQUE ESR, electron spin resonance; ~ **magnétique nucléaire** *f* *(RMN)* CHIMIE, PETROLE, PHYS RAYON, PHYSIQUE nuclear magnetic resonance *(NMR)*; ~ **mécanique** *f* PHYSIQUE mechanical resonance; ~ **de la membrane** *f* ENREGISTR cone resonance; ~ **de la membrane à l'air libre** *f* ENREGISTR free air cone resonance; ~ **à un niveau** *f* NUCLEAIRE Briet-Wigner resonance, single level resonance; ~ **optique** *f* ELECTRON optical resonance; ~ **parallèle** *f* ELECTRON, PHYSIQUE parallel resonance; ~ **paramagnétique** *f* ELECTR, ELECTRON paramagnetic resonance; ~ **paramagnétique électronique** *f* PHYSIQUE EPR, electron

paramagnetic resonance, paramagnetic resonance; ~ **quadripolaire** *f* NUCLEAIRE quadrupole resonance; ~ **série** *f* ELECTROTEC, PHYSIQUE series resonance; ~ **au sol** *f* AERONAUT ground resonance; ~ **de spin électronique** *f* PHYS PART, PHYSIQUE ESR, electron spin resonance; ~ **des tensions** *f* ELECTR *circuit à courant alternatif* acceptor resonance; ~ **de vitesse** *f* PHYSIQUE velocity resonance

résonant *adj* PHYSIQUE resonant

résonateur *m* ELECTRON, TELECOM resonator; ~ **acoustique** *m* ELECTRON acoustic resonator; ~ **acoustique de Helmholtz** *m* ACOUSTIQUE Helmholtz resonator; ~ **de cavité** *m* TELECOM cavity resonator; ~ **coaxial** *m* ELECTRON coaxial resonator; ~ **diélectrique** *m* TELECOM dielectric resonator; ~ **électrique** *m* ELECTRON electrical resonator; ~ **électromagnétique** *m* ELECTRON electromagnetic resonator; ~ **d'entrée** *m* ELECTRON input resonator; ~ **à flexion** *m* ELECTRON flexure-mode resonator; ~ **de Helmholtz** *m* ACOUSTIQUE, PHYSIQUE Helmholtz resonator; ~ **à hyperfréquences** *m* ELECTRON, TELECOM microwave resonator; ~ **à jet de césium** *m* ELECTRON caesium beam resonator (BrE), cesium beam resonator (AmE); ~ **à ondes en volume** *m* ELECTRON bulk wave resonator; ~ **optique** *m* PHYS RAYON *création laser*, TELECOM optical resonator; ~ **piézoélectrique** *m* ELECTROTEC piezoelectric resonator; ~ **à quartz** *m* ELECTRON crystal resonator, quartz resonator

résonnant *adj* PHYSIQUE resonant

résorcine *f* CHIMIE resorcinol

résorcinol *m* CHIMIE resorcinol

résorcylique *adj* CHIMIE resorcylic

résorufine *f* CHIMIE resorufine

respect: ~ **des délais** *m* PRODUCTION deadline conformity; ~ **de la vie privée** *m* TELECOM privacy

respirateur *m* SECURITE breathing apparatus, respirator, *à filtre antioxyde de carbone* carbon monoxide filter self-rescue, respirator self-rescue apparatus

respiration: ~ **liquidienne** *f* OCEANO fluid breathing, liquid breathing

respiratoire *adj* SECURITE respiratory

resplendissant *adj* THERMODYN *de lumière* ablaze

responsabilité *f* POLLU MER liability; ~ **EDIM** *f* TELECOM EDIM responsibility; ~ **du fait du produit** *f* QUALITE product liability

responsable *m* POLLU MER supervisor; ~ **d'atelier** *m* PRODUCTION unit supervisor; ~ **de la conception des systèmes** *m* TELECOM system designer; ~ **des méthodes** *m* CONS MECA methods manager; ~ **du plan** *m* PRODUCTION master scheduler; ~ **de la sécurité** *m* SECURITE safety officer

ressac *m* NAUT undercurrent, OCEANO backwash, surf, underset, undertow

ressaut *m* CONSTR offset, projection, set-off, *d'une pierre, d'une gouttière au delà d'un mur* projection, HYDROLOGIE hydraulic jump; ~ **hydraulique** *m* HYDROLOGIE upsurge

resserrement *m* MINES contraction, nip, pinch; ~ **de l'image** *m* TV image contraction

resserrer: se ~ *v réfl* PHYSIQUE contract

ressort:[1] **à** ~ *adj* PRODUCTION *système hydraulique* spring-loaded

ressort[2] *m* CONS MECA, MATERIAUX, MECANIQUE, PHYSIQUE, VEHICULES spring; ~ **d'acier** *m* RESSORTS steel spring; ~ **aminci** *m* RESSORTS tapered spring; ~ **à bague** *m* RESSORTS ring spring; ~ **de balai** *m* ELECTRO-

TEC brush spring; ~ **à barillet** *m* RESSORTS barrel spring; ~ **à barre** *m* RESSORTS round bar spring; ~ **bilame** *m* RESSORTS double leaf spring; ~ **à boudin** *m* CONS MECA spiral spring, MECANIQUE coil spring, helical spring, PHYSIQUE helical spring; ~ **caoutchouc** *m* CONS MECA *bloc à colonnes* rubber buffer; ~ **chargé** *m* RESSORTS loaded spring; ~ **de clavette** *m* AUTO insert spring; ~ **compensateur** *m* CONS MECA equalizer spring, RESSORTS auxiliary spring, helper spring; ~ **de compression** *m* CONS MECA open coil spring, open spiral spring, INST HYDR, RESSORTS compression spring; ~ **de compression formé à froid** *m* RESSORTS cold-formed compression spring; ~ **conique** *m* RESSORTS conical spring, tapered spring; ~ **de contact** *m* ELECTR *relais* contact spring; ~ **cylindrique** *m* PRODUCTION cylindrical spring; ~ **à demi-pincette** *m* CONS MECA half elliptic spring; ~ **elliptique** *m* RESSORTS elliptic spring; ~ **d'embrayage** *m* CONS MECA, RESSORTS, VEHICULES clutch spring; ~ **en crosse** *m* RESSORTS cross spring; ~ **en épingle** *m* CONS MECA hairpin spring; ~ **en hélice** *m* RESSORTS coil spring; ~ **enroulé à froid** *m* RESSORTS cold-wound spring; ~ **en spirale** *m* CONS MECA coil spring, coiled spring, spiral-coiled spring; ~ **en volute** *m* CONS MECA volute spring; ~ **à fil profilé** *m* RESSORTS section wire spring; ~ **de flexion** *m* CONS MECA flexion spring, spring subjected to bending; ~ **forgé** *m* RESSORTS tapered spring; ~ **de friction** *m* CONS MECA friction spring; ~ **de gâchette** *m* MILITAIRE *d'une arme à feu* rear spring; ~ **à gaz** *m* CONS MECA gas spring; ~ **hélicoïdal** *m* AUTO coil spring, PHYSIQUE helical spring, RESSORTS, VEHICULES *suspension* coil spring; ~ **hélicoïdal cylindrique** *m* RESSORTS cylindrical helical spring; ~ **hélicoïdal cylindrique de compression** *m* RESSORTS cylindrical helical compression spring; ~ **hélicoïdal cylindrique enroulé à chaud** *m* RESSORTS hot-coiled cylindrical helical spring; ~ **hélicoïdal cylindrique enroulé à froid** *m* RESSORTS cold-coiled cylindrical spring; ~ **hélicoïdal cylindrique de traction** *m* RESSORTS cylindrical helical extension spring; ~ **hélicoïdal à fil rond** *m* CONS MECA *bloc à colonnes* round section coil spring; ~ **à lames** *m* CONS MECA, VEHICULES *suspension* leaf spring; ~ **à lames étagées** *m* CONS MECA leaf spring, plate spring; ~ **à lames multiples** *m* CONS MECA multiple blade spring; ~ **à lames superposées** *m* CONS MECA leaf spring; ~ **du levier de débrayage** *m* AUTO release lever spring; ~ **monolame** *m* RESSORTS monoleaf spring; ~ **parabolique** *m* RESSORTS parabolic spring; ~ **de percussion** *m* MILITAIRE *d'une arme à feu* striker spring; ~ **à pincette** *m* CONS MECA, RESSORTS elliptic spring; ~ **plat** *m* CONS MECA blade spring, RESSORTS flat spring; ~ **de pression** *m* VEHICULES *embrayage* pressure plate spring; ~ **principal** *m* MILITAIRE *du mécanisme de percussion* main spring; ~ **progressif** *m* RESSORTS progressive rate spring; ~ **de rappel** *m* AUTO retracting spring, return spring, CONS MECA close coil spring, close spiralspring, drawback spring, PRODUCTION return spring; ~ **de rappel de fourchette** *m* VEHICULES *embrayage* fork return spring; ~ **de rappel des segments de frein** *m* AUTO brake release spring; ~ **de réglage** *m* COMMANDE adjustment spring; ~ **de retenue** *m* MINES retaining spring; ~ **de retour** *m* MILITAIRE recoil spring; ~ **de rupteur** *m* AUTO breaker spring; ~ **semi-elliptique** *m* RESSORTS semielliptic spring; ~ **de sommier** *m* PRODUCTION hourglass spring; ~ **de soupape** *m* AUTO, VEHICULES *moteur*

valve spring; ~ **spirale** *m* CONS MECA hairspring, RESSORTS spiral spring; ~ **de sûreté** *m* MILITAIRE safety spring; ~ **de suspension** *m* RESSORTS suspension spring; ~ **de tension** *m* CONS MECA tension spring; ~ **de torsion** *m* CONS MECA spring subjected to torsion, torsion spring; ~ **de traction** *m* CONS MECA, RESSORTS extension spring; ~ **transversal** *m* CH DE FER transverse spring; ~ **trilame** *m* RESSORTS three-leaf spring; ~ **uréthane** *m* CONS MECA *bloc à colonnes* urethane buffer; ~ **de voiture** *m* CONS MECA carriage spring, leaf spring

ressorts: ~ **de séparation** *m pl* ESPACE *véhicules* spring release device

ressoudage *m* PRODUCTION resoldering

ressoudure *f* PRODUCTION resoldering

ressource *f* INFORMAT, ORDINAT, POLLU MER, PRODUCTION resource; ~ **critique** *f* INFORMAT critical resource, ORDINAT critical resource; ~ **OSI** *f* TELECOM OSI resource, open systems interconnection resource

ressources: ~ **en eaux souterraines** *f pl* DISTRI EAU ground water resources; ~ **géothermiques** *f pl* EN RENOUV geothermal resources; ~ **identifiées** *f pl* EN RENOUV identified resources; ~ **logicielles** *f pl* INFORMAT, ORDINAT software resources; ~ **matérielles** *f pl* INFORMAT, ORDINAT hardware resources

ressuage *m* MATERIAUX sweat; ~ **fluorescent** *m* MECANIQUE fluorescent penetration test; ~ **réfrigéré** *m* REFRIG carcass chilling

restauration *f* CINEMAT *d'un film* regeneration, INFORMAT reset, restore, METALL recovery, ORDINAT reset, restore; ~ **de fichier** *f* INFORMAT, ORDINAT file restore; ~ **d'images** *f* INFORMAT, ORDINAT image restoration

restaurer *vt* INFORMAT, ORDINAT restore

reste *m* INFORMAT, MATH, ORDINAT remainder, PRODUCTION *du stock* balance; ~ **à livrer** *m* PRODUCTION quantity backorder, subsequent delivery

rester: ~ **à la hauteur de** *vt* TEXTILE keep up with

restes: ~ **de supernova** *m pl* ASTRONOMIE supernova residues

restitution *f* INFORMAT, ORDINAT restitution

restricteur *m* PRODUCTION *système hydraulique* restrictor; ~ **à deux voies** *m* PRODUCTION *système hydraulique* two-way restrictor

restriction: ~ **de l'identification de la ligne appelante** *f* *(RILA)* TELECOM calling line identification restriction *(CLIR)*; ~ **de l'identification de la ligne connectée** *f (RILC)* TELECOM connected line identification restriction *(COLR)*

restylage *m* TRANSPORT lifting, restyling

restyler *vt* TRANSPORT restyle

résultante *f* CONS MECA, MATH, PHYSIQUE resultant

résultat *m* MECANIQUE effect, METROLOGIE *de l'examen* result, TELECOM response; ~ **brut** *m* METROLOGIE uncorrected result; ~ **corrigé** *m* METROLOGIE *compte tenu des erreurs présumées* corrected result

résumé *m* INFORMAT, ORDINAT abstract, summary, TELECOM summary

résumer *vt* INFORMAT, ORDINAT abstract, summarize

resurchauffe *f* CHAUFFAGE reheat

resurchauffer *vt* CHAUFFAGE reheat

resurchauffeur *m* CHAUFFAGE reheater

résurgence *f* HYDROLOGIE resurgence

résurgent *adj* DISTRI EAU resurgent

résynchroniser *vt* TELECOM resynchronize

rétablir: ~ **l'alimentation** *vi* PRODUCTION provide power

rétablissement *m* AERONAUT *manoeuvre de vol* recovery;

~ **du signal** *m* TELECOM signal restoration

rétamage *m* PRODUCTION retinning

retard:[1] **en ~** *adj* ELECTROTEC lagging

retard[2] *m* ELECTR delay, lag, time delay, time lag, ELECTRON, ESPACE *communications*, INFORMAT delay, NUCLEAIRE delay, hangover, ORDINAT delay, PRODUCTION lag, TELECOM, TRANSPORT delay, TV delay time, lag; ~ **à l'admission** *m* INST HYDR *d'un distributeur de vapeur* steam lap; ~ **aérodynamique** *m* AERONAUT aerodynamic lag; ~ **à l'appel** *m* ELECTROTEC operate lag; ~ **de chrominance** *m* TV chroma delay; ~ **conjoncturel** *m* TRANSPORT operational delay; ~ **différentiel** *m* ELECTRON differential delay; ~ **échelonné** *m* ELECTRON tapped delay; ~ **de fabrication** *m* MECANIQUE backlog; ~ **de groupe** *m* ELECTROTEC group delay; ~ **de luminance** *m* TV luminance delay; ~ **de la lune** *m* ASTRONOMIE retardation of moon; ~ **de la marée** *m* EN RENOUV, OCEANO lagging of the tide; ~ **moyen par véhicule** *m* TRANSPORT average delay per vehicle; ~ **d'ordre élevé** *m* ELECTRON high-order delay; ~ **de phase** *m* ELECTR phase lag, *courant alternatif* lag, ELECTRON lag, phase lag, PHYSIQUE phase lag; ~ **au relâchement** *m* ELECTROTEC release lag; ~ **à la retombée** *m* ELECTROTEC release lag; ~ **du signal** *m* ELECTRON, TELECOM signal delay; ~ **variable** *m* TELECOM variable delay

retardateur *m* AERONAUT lagging system, CINEMAT restrainer, CONSTR retarding agent, PLAST CAOU *matière première* retarder, TEXTILE retarding agent

retardation *f* MECANIQUE, PHYSIQUE deceleration

retardé *adj* PHYSIQUE decelerated

retarder[1] *vt* CHIMIE inhibit, ELECTR *relais, commutateur*, ELECTRON delay, ESPACE *véhicules* retard

retarder[2] *vti* MECANIQUE, PHYSIQUE decelerate

retardeur *m* PAPIER retarder; ~ **de grillage** *m* PLAST CAOU antiscorching agent

retassement *m* MATERIAUX shrinking

retassure *f* CERAM VER void

rétène *m* CHIMIE retene

retenir *vt* CHIMIE *un gaz* occlude, INFORMAT, ORDINAT carry

rétention *f* CHIMIE, DISTRI EAU, HYDROLOGIE retention; ~ **de l'eau** *f* DISTRI EAU, HYDROLOGIE water retention

retenu: ~ **en position verrouillée** *adj* PRODUCTION locked down; ~ **par les glaces** *adj* NAUT icebound; ~ **par le mauvais temps** *adj* NAUT weather-bound

retenue *f* DISTRI EAU impounding reservoir, INFORMAT carry digit, NAUT guy, ORDINAT carry digit, PRODUCTION borrow; ~ **à bille** *f* CONS MECA *outils* ball lock; ~ **de bôme** *f* NAUT boom guy; ~ **d'eau** *f* EN RENOUV pondage; ~ **d'envasement** *f* DISTRI EAU silt storage space

réticulage *m* IMPRIM EBC, electron beam curing

réticulaire *adj* AERONAUT network-like

réticulation *f* CHIMIE *polymère* cross-linkage, cross-linking, CINEMAT frilling, reticulation, wrinkling, IMPRIM *encres, polymères*, PHOTO reticulation; ~ **sous rayonnement** *f* PLAST CAOU *polymérisation* radiation cross linking

Réticule *m* ASTRONOMIE Reticulum

réticule *m* ASTRONOMIE *d'un oculaire de télescope* reticle, CHIMIE cross-link, CINEMAT graticule, reticle, ELECTRON reticle, IMPRIM, INFORMAT cross hair, INSTRUMENT reticle, ORDINAT cross hair, TV graticule; ~ **d'optique** *m* METROLOGIE optical graticule

réticuler *vt* PLAST CAOU *polymérisation* cross-link

retient *m* CONS MECA lockplate

retient-graisse *m* CONS MECA grease retainer, oil seal

rétigraphe *f* CRISTALL precession camera

rétinalite *f* MINERAUX retinalite

rétinasphalte *m* MINERAUX retinasphalt

rétinellite *f* MINERAUX retinellite

rétinite *f* MINERAUX pitchstone, retinite

retiration *f* IMPRIM backing up, perfect printing, perfecting

retire-goupille *m* CONS MECA pin extractor

retirer[1] *vt* AGRO ALIM tap, CINEMAT reprint, INFORMAT, ORDINAT roll out

retirer:[2] **se ~** *v réfl* HYDROLOGIE recede, subside

retirure *f* PRODUCTION draw

retombée *f* CONSTR *d'une voûte* spring, PETROLE *forage* caving, PHYS RAYON, PHYSIQUE, POLLUTION fallout, REFRIG drop; ~ **radioactive** *f* NUCLEAIRE, POLLUTION radioactive fallout; ~ **de voûte** *f* CERAM VER skew block (AmE), skewback block (BrE)

retombées *f pl* POLLUTION fallout; ~ **acides** *f pl* POLLUTION acid fallout; ~ **acides humides** *f pl* POLLUTION wet acidic fallout; ~ **acides sèches** *f pl* POLLUTION dry acidic fallout; ~ **atmosphériques** *f pl* POLLUTION atmospheric fallout; ~ **globales** *f pl* POLLUTION bulk deposition; ~ **humides** *f pl* POLLUTION wet deposition; ~ **nucléaires** *f pl* NUCLEAIRE radioactive fallout; ~ **de polluants** *f pl* POLLUTION contamination fallout; ~ **des polluants** *f pl* POLLUTION pollutant deposition; ~ **sèches** *f pl* POLLUTION dry deposition; ~ **totales** *f pl* POLLUTION total deposition

retomber *vt* PRODUCTION *un bit* reset

retordage *m* CERAM VER twisting

retordeuse *f* TEXTILE twister

retorte *m* CHIMIE, EQUIP LAB retort

retouche *f* CERAM VER retouching, touching up, IMPRIM touching up, *photographie, photogravure* retouching, PHOTO retouching, PLAST CAOU *peinture* refinishing, PRODUCTION extra labor (AmE), extra labour (BrE)

retoucher *vt* IMPRIM *les plaques* add and delete, *photogravure* touch up, PHOTO retouch, spot

retour:[1] **de ~** *adj* NAUT *cargaison* homeward-bound; **en ~** *adj* NAUT inward bound; ~ **antenne** *adj* TV off-air

retour:[2] **de ~** *adv* NAUT homeward

retour[3] *m* ESPACE payoff, INFORMAT return, INST HYDR *du piston* instroke, ORDINAT return; ~ **antenne** *m* TV line monitor; ~ **d'arc** *m* ELECTROTEC arc back; ~ **automatique** *m* ELECTR *réglage* automatic reset; ~ **de balayage** *m* ELECTRON retrace; ~ **à blanc** *m* CONS MECA noncutting return, *d'un outil* idle return; ~ **au carburateur** *m* AUTO blowback; ~ **de chariot** *m* ORDINAT CR, carriage return; ~ **commun** *m* TELECOM common return; ~ **de courant** *m* ELECTROTEC reverse current; ~ **des déchets** *m* CERAM VER admix, scrap return; ~ **d'eau** *m* DISTRI EAU check valve, INST HYDR backflow; ~ **d'écoute** *m* ENREGISTR feedback circuit, foldback, TV audio feedback circuit; ~ **en arrière** *m* CINEMAT flashback; ~ **en boucle fermée** *m* PRODUCTION closed-loop feedback; ~ **en surface** *m* OCEANO ascent; ~ **à l'exploitation** *m* TELECOM return to service; ~ **du faisceau** *m* ELECTRON flyback, retrace, TV beam return; ~ **de flamme** *m* CONSTR backfire, flashback, THERMODYN *soudure* flashback, VEHICULES *moteur* backfire; ~ **au fonctionnement normal** *m* TELECOM error recovery; ~ **de liquide à haute pression** *m* REFRIG dump trap liquid return; ~ **manuel** *m* ELECTR *commande* manual reset; ~ **de mer** *m* NAUT sea clutter; ~ **de palan** *m*

PRODUCTION monkey block; **~ par la masse** *m* ELECTROTEC earth return (BrE), ground return (AmE); **~ par terre** *m* ELECTROTEC earth return (BrE), ground return (AmE), GEOPHYS earth return, TELECOM earth return (BrE), ground return (AmE); **~ de pluie** *m* NAUT rain clutter; **~ au point de départ** *m* INST HYDR backset; **~ rapide** *m* ENREGISTR fast rewind; **~ de signal** *m* TV feedback circuit; **~ du spot de ligne** *m* TV line flyback; **~ à la terre** *m* PRODUCTION *électricité* earth return (BrE), ground return (AmE); **~ de trame** *m* TV field flyback; **~ à vide** *m* CONS MECA *d'un outil* idle return, noncutting return

retour-arrière *m* IMPRIM *clavier* backspace

retour-chariot *m* IMPRIM soft return

retournement *m* CERAM VER turnover; **~ de la sphère** *m* GEOMETRIE *topologie* reversal of the sphere

retourner *vt* CONSTR *le sol* disturb, INFORMAT, ORDINAT return

rétraction: **~ au figeage** *f* EMBALLAGE shrinkage on solidification

retrait *m* CERAM VER, CINEMAT shrinkage, CONS MECA contraction, CONSTR recess, retreat, *du ciment* shrinkage, shrinking, HYDROLOGIE *des eaux* recession, INFORMAT roll out, METALL shrinkage, ORDINAT roll out, PAPIER, PLAST CAOU, PRODUCTION shrinkage; **~ différentiel** *m* TEXTILE differential shrinkage; **~ de graphite** *m* NUCLEAIRE graphite shrinkage; **~ au moulage** *m* PLAST CAOU mold shrinkage (AmE), mould shrinkage (BrE); **~ de pellicule** *m* PHOTO film shrinkage; **~ résiduel** *m* TEXTILE residual shrinkage; **~ de séchage** *m* CONSTR *du ciment* drying shrinkage; **~ des sous-couleurs** *m* IMPRIM under-color removal (AmE), under-colour removal (BrE); **~ de stock** *m* PRODUCTION material issue

retraite *f* CONSTR manhole, recess, refuge hole, setback, shelter, HYDROLOGIE *des eaux* recession

retraitement *m* PRODUCTION, RECYCLAGE reprocessing

retraiter *vt* CHARBON reclean, retreat, PRODUCTION retreat, RECYCLAGE reprocess

retranché *adj* MILITAIRE dug-in

retransmission: **~ EDI** *f* TELECOM EDI forwarding

rétrécir[1] *vt* PAPIER, TEXTILE shrink

rétrécir:[2] **se ~** *v réfl* PHYSIQUE contract

rétrécissement *m* CERAM VER tank neck, CINEMAT shrinkage, CONSTR shrinking, PHYSIQUE contraction, shrinkage, PRODUCTION shrinkage, TELECOM shrinkage, shrinking, TEXTILE shrinkage; **~ brusque de section** *m* INST HYDR sudden contraction of cross section; **~ de la ligne** *m* TV underlap

retréfilé *adj* REVETEMENT *zingué* drawn

rétreindre *vt* MECANIQUE swage

rétreint *m* CONS MECA necking

rétroaction *f* COMMANDE, ELECTRON, ENREGISTR, INFORMAT, NUCLEAIRE, ORDINAT, PHYS ONDES, TV feedback; **~ capacitive** *f* ELECTROTEC capacitive feedback; **~ inhérente** *f* NUCLEAIRE inherent feedback; **~ positive** *f* COMMANDE positive feedback

rétroappel *m* TELECOM recall

rétrochargeuse *f* CONSTR back loader

rétrocharriage *m* GEOLOGIE *transport vers la zone interne d'une chaîne* back thrusting

rétrocompatibilité *f* TV reverse compatibility

rétrocouplage *m* ELECTROTEC cross coupling

rétrodiffuser *vti* OPTIQUE backscatter

rétrodiffuseur *m* NUCLEAIRE backscatterer

rétrodiffusion *f* ELECTRON backscattering, ESPACE backscatter, backscattering, NUCLEAIRE back diffusion, OPTIQUE, PHYS RAYON, TELECOM backscattering

rétrofit *m* PRODUCTION retrofit

rétroflexion *f* PHYS RAYON retroreflection

rétrofusée *f* ESPACE *propulsion* retrorocket, TRANSPORT retardation rocket, retrorocket

rétrogradation: **~ automatique** *f* VEHICULES *boîte de vitesses* automatic gear lever (BrE), automatic gearshift (AmE); **~ forcée** *f* AUTO, VEHICULES *boîte de vitesses automatique* kick down

rétrograde *adj* ESPACE retrograde

rétrogradeur *m* AUTO kick down switch

rétrolavage *m* NUCLEAIRE backflushing

rétromorphose *f* GEOLOGIE retrograde metamorphism, retrogressive metamorphism

rétroprojection *f* CINEMAT rear projection

rétrorsine *f* CHIMIE retrorsine

rétroviseur *m* AUTO, rear-view mirror, INSTRUMENT driving mirror, rear-view mirror, VEHICULES *accessoire* mirror, rear-view mirror; **~ extérieur** *m* VEHICULES *accessoire* side mirror; **~ orientable** *m* VEHICULES *accessoire* adjustable rear-view mirror

réunion *f* CONSTR connection, joining; **~ de chantier** *f* CONSTR site meeting

réunir *vt* CERAM VER adjust, fit, true up, CONSTR join, DISTRI EAU collect, PRODUCTION connect

réutilisable *adj* INFORMAT, ORDINAT reusable

réutilisation: **~ de fréquence** *f* ESPACE *communications*, TELECOM frequency reuse

réveil: **~ automatique** *m* TELECOM alarm call; **~ avertisseur** *m* EQUIP LAB *durée* sub timer alarm; **~ téléphonique** *m* TELECOM alarm call

révélateur *m* CINEMAT, PHOTO developer; **~ chromogène** *m* PHOTO color developer (AmE), colour developer (BrE); **~ compensateur** *m* PHOTO compensating developer; **~ donnant doux** *m* PHOTO developer for soft contrast; **~ doux** *m* PHOTO soft developer; **~ épuisé** *m* PHOTO exhausted developer; **~ à grain fin** *m* CINEMAT, PHOTO fine grain developer; **~ pour développement en bain unique** *m* PHOTO single bath developer; **~ rapide** *m* PHOTO fast developer

revendeur: **~ en gros** *m* PRODUCTION wholesale supplier

revendication: **~ autorisée** *f* BREVETS admissible claim; **~ dépendante** *f* BREVETS dependent claim; **~ indépendante** *f* BREVETS independent claim

revendiquer *vt* BREVETS claim

revenir: **~ en surface** *vi* NAUT return to surface; **~ entre ses repères** *vi* CONSTR come back to the center of its run (AmE), come back to the centre of its run (BrE)

revenu[1] *adj* CRISTALL, MECANIQUE *matériaux*, RESSORTS tempered

revenu[2] *m* METALL, NUCLEAIRE, RESSORTS tempering, THERMODYN anneal, annealing; **~ net** *m* PETROLE *finance* net income

réverbération *f* ACOUSTIQUE, ENREGISTR reverberation

réverbère *m* CONS MECA reflector

revers:[1] **à ~ de soie** *adj* TEXTILE faced with silk

revers[2] *m* TEXTILE facing; **~ de cuesta** *m* GEOLOGIE dip slope

réversibilité *f* CHIMIE, MATERIAUX, PHYSIQUE, TRANSPORT reversibility

réversible *adj* CHIMIE, PHYSIQUE reversible

revêtement *m* AERONAUT *aéronef* skin, CONSTR coating, facing, lining, overlay, revetment, splashback, ESPACE *véhicules* cladding, skin, MATERIAUX coating, MECANIQUE, MINES *d'un puits de mine* lining, NUCLEAIRE

weld overlay cladding, weld-deposited cladding, OP-
TIQUE fiber coating (AmE), fibre coating (BrE), PETR
coating, PHYSIQUE coating, protective coating, PLAST
CAOU *peintures, adhésifs* coating, PRODUCTION coating, revetment, coating, lining; ~ **anodique** *m*
REVETEMENT anodic coating; ~ **antibruit** *m* ESPACE
véhicules acoustic blanket, SECURITE noise reduction;
~ **anticorrosion** *m* NUCLEAIRE anticorrosion coating;
~ **antiréfléchissant** *m* TELECOM antireflective coating;
~ **antireflet** *m* TELECOM antiglare coating; ~ **asphaltique** *m* CONSTR asphalt tanking; ~ **d'assemblage** *m*
ELECTR *isolation d'un câble* inner covering; ~ **béton** *m*
PETR concrete coating; ~ **bicouche** *m* CONSTR DBST,
double bituminous surface treatment, TELECOM
double-layer coating; ~ **de bitume** *m* REVETEMENT
bitumen coating; ~ **de bitume pour tubes** *m* CONS
MECA bitumen pipe coating; ~ **de câble** *m* PLAST CAOU
cable sheathing; ~ **de cailloutage** *m* CONSTR roughcast; ~ **calorifique du corps du cylindre** *m* PRODUCTION
cylinder lagging; ~ **céramique de surface** *m* REVETE-
MENT ceramic coating; ~ **à chaud** *m* REVETEMENT hot
dip metal coating; ~ **de chaudière** *m* INST HYDR boiler
jacketing; ~ **de contact** *m* REVETEMENT dip coat, dip
coating; ~ **coupe-feu** *m* NUCLEAIRE *de surface* fire-retardant coat; ~ **de surface** *m* PLAST CAOU knife
spreading; ~ **décoratif** *m* REVETEMENT appearance
cover; ~ **électrolytique à cuve rotative** *m* PRODUCTION
barrel plating; ~ **en bain fluidisé** *m* GENIE CHIM
fluidized bed coating; ~ **en béton** *m* CONSTR concrete
lining; ~ **en caoutchouc** *m* REVETEMENT rubber coating; ~ **en caoutchouc mou antibruit** *m* SECURITE
antinoise soft rubber lining; ~ **en chrome dur** *m* RE-
VETEMENT hard chrome plating, hard plating; ~ **en
graphite** *m* NUCLEAIRE graphite coating; ~ **en lit fluidisé** *m* REVETEMENT fluidized bed coating; ~ **en nitrure
de titane** *m* CONS MECA titanium nitride coating; ~ **en
plâtre** *m* CONSTR rendering; ~ **en poudre** *m* COULEURS,
PLAST CAOU powder coating; ~ **étain-zinc** *m* REVETE-
MENT tin-zinc finish; ~ **ETFE** *m* TELECOM epoxy buffer;
~ **extérieur en papier** *m* REVETEMENT paper covering; ~
de film *m* EMBALLAGE film coating; ~ **galvanique** *m*
REVETEMENT electrodeposit, electroplating; ~
galvanoplastique partiel *m* REVETEMENT partial plating; ~ **ignifuge** *m* THERMODYN fire-resistant coating,
fire-resisting coating; ~ **intérieur** *m* EMBALLAGE interior lining, REVETEMENT lining; ~ **intérieur en papier** *m*
EMBALLAGE paper liner, REVETEMENT paper lining; ~
interne de studio *m* ENREGISTR studio lining; ~ **isolant
de chaudière** *m* INST HYDR boiler jacket; ~ **de joint** *m*
PETR joint coating; ~ **magnétique** *m* ENREGISTR magnetic coating; ~ **métallique** *m* CONS MECA metallic
coating, EMBALLAGE metal coating, metallic coating,
REVETEMENT metal coat, metal coating, metal plating,
TELECOM metallic coating, TV metal coating; ~ **monocouche** *m* CONSTR SBST, single bituminous surface
treatment; ~ **mural** *m* COULEURS wall paint; ~ **non-mé-
tallique** *m* REVETEMENT nonmetallic coating; ~ **non
retréfilé** *m* REVETEMENT finally galvanized coating; ~
organique *m* REVETEMENT organic coating; ~ **de paraffine** *m* EMBALLAGE kerosene coating (AmE), paraffin
coating (BrE); ~ **par couches antiréfléchissantes** *m*
PRODUCTION antireflective coating, blooming, coating, lumenizing; ~ **pare-feu** *m* THERMODYN
fire-resistant coating, fire-resisting coating; ~ **par immersion** *m* EMBALLAGE, PRODUCTION dip coating,
REVETEMENT immersion plating; ~ **par poudre** *m* -

REVETEMENT powder coating; ~ **par projection** *m* RE-
VETEMENT spray coating; ~ **par rouleau inverse** *m*
PLAST CAOU, REVETEMENT reverse roll coating; ~ **par
rouleau de transfert** *m* REVETEMENT kiss roll coating; ~
partiel *m* REVETEMENT partial coating, partial plating;
~ **par trempage** *m* PLAST CAOU dip coating; ~ **par voie
chimique** *m* NUCLEAIRE chemical coating; ~ **au pistolet à chaud** *m* REVETEMENT thermal spraying; ~ **au
pistolet à flamme** *m* REVETEMENT flame spray coating;
~ **plastique** *m* REVETEMENT, TELECOM plastic coating; ~
primaire *m* OPTIQUE primary coating, TELECOM epoxy
buffer, primary coating; ~ **protecteur** *m* REVETEMENT
protective bonnet, protective cover, protective
covering, protective sheathing, surface protection; ~
de protection cathodique *m* REVETEMENT cathodic
oxide coating; ~ **de protection pelable** *m* EMBALLAGE
peelable protective coating; ~ **réfractaire** *m* MAT
CHAUFF, REVETEMENT refractory lining; ~ **réfractaire
de surface** *m* REVETEMENT refractory coating, refractory wash; ~ **de résine silicone** *m* TELECOM silica
coating; ~ **aux résines synthétiques** *m* REVETEMENT
plastic laminate covering; ~ **résistant aux acides** *m*
REVETEMENT acid-proof lining, SECURITE acid-resisting covering; ~ **résistant aux alcalins** *m* SECURITE
installations industrielles alkaline-resistant lining; ~
de retenue *m* DISTRI EAU reservoir lining; ~ **au rouleau**
m PLAST CAOU, REVETEMENT roll coating; ~ **secondaire** *m* OPTIQUE buffering, fiber buffer (AmE), fiber
jacket (AmE), fibre buffer (BrE), fibrejacket (BrE),
secondary coating, TELECOM secondary coating; ~
sélectif *m* EN RENOUV selective coating, REVETEMENT
pattern plating; ~ **silice** *m* TELECOM silica coating; ~
transparent *m* REVETEMENT transparent coating; ~ **au
trempé** *m* REVETEMENT dip coat, dip coating; ~ **zingué
à chaud** *m* REVETEMENT hot dip galvanised coating; ~
zingué non retréfilé *m* REVETEMENT finally galvanized
coating

revêtir *vt* MINES *un puits de mine* line, PLAST CAOU
procédé coat, PRODUCTION *un fourneau* line, REVETE-
MENT coat, line, TEXTILE face; ~ **d'une couche
antireflet** *vt* REVETEMENT coat lenses; ~ **d'émail** *vt*
REVETEMENT enamel; ~ **d'étain-nickel** *vt* REVETEMENT
nickel-plate

revêtu *adj* REVETEMENT coated; ~ **de matière plastique**
adj REVETEMENT plastic-coated

revif *m* OCEANO priming

réviser *vt* IMPRIM revise, NAUT *une machine*, PAPIER
maintenance overhaul

révision *f* AERONAUT *matériel* overhaul, IMPRIM second
proof; ~ **générale** *f* NUCLEAIRE general maintenance,
major overhaul; ~ **du moteur** *f* NAUT engine overhaul

revolin *m* METEO, NAUT eddy wind, OCEANO cross ripple,
eddy wind

révolution *f* CONS MECA revolution, turn, ESPACE *orbitographie*, GEOMETRIE *d'un solide* revolution

revolver *m* CONS MECA turret, turret head, EQUIP LAB
microscope revolving nosepiece, PRODUCTION monitor; ~ **à objectifs** *m* INSTRUMENT objective nosepiece,
objective turret; ~ **d'ordonnance** *m* MILITAIRE service
pistol; ~ **porte-objectifs** *m* INSTRUMENT revolving
nosepiece

revue *f* IMPRIM review; ~ **d'aptitude au lancement** *f*
ESPACE *gestion* launch readiness review; ~ **d'aptitude
au vol** *f* (*RAV*) ESPACE *gestion* flight readiness review
(*FRR*); ~ **de conception intermédiaire** *f* ESPACE *gestion* intermediate design review; ~ **de conception**

système *f* ESPACE *gestion* SDR, system design review; **~ de conformité du premier article** *f* ESPACE *gestion* FACR, first article configuration review; **~ critique de définition** *f* ESPACE *gestion* CDR, critical design review; **~ de définition finale** *f (RDF)* ESPACE final design review *(FDR)*; **~ de définition préliminaire** *f* ESPACE *gestion* PDR, preliminary design review; **~ de prononcé de qualification** *f* ESPACE *gestion* qualification test review; **~ de qualification** *f* ESPACE qualification test review

RF *abrév (radiofréquence)* ELECTRON, ELECTROTEC, ENREGISTR, TELECOM, TRANSPORT, TV RF *(radio frequency)*

RGT *abrév (réseau de gestion des télécommunications)* TELECOM TMN *(telecommunications management network)*

Rh *(rhodium)* CHIMIE Rh *(rhodium)*

rhabillage *m* CERAM VER, PRODUCTION *de meules en émeri* dressing

rhabilleur *m* PRODUCTION dresser; **~ pantographe** *m* CONS MECA *meules* pantograph dresser; **~ pour meules** *m* CONS MECA wheel dresser; **~ pour meules d'émeri** *m* PRODUCTION emery wheel dresser; **~ de rayon tangentiel** *m* CONS MECA tangent radius dresser

rhaetizite *f* MINERAUX rhaetizite

rhamnétine *f* CHIMIE rhamnetin

rhamnite *m* CHIMIE rhamnitol

rhamnitol *m* CHIMIE rhamnitol

rhamnose *f* CHIMIE rhamnose

rhénique *adj* CHIMIE rhenic

rhénium *m (Re)* CHIMIE rhenium *(Re)*

rhéologie *f* CHARBON, GAZ, PHYS FLUID, PHYSIQUE, PLAST CAOU rheology

rhéomètre *m* CHARBON flowmeter

rhéostat *m* AUTO rheostat, CINEMAT dimmer, ELECTR, ELECTROTEC, EQUIP LAB, PHYSIQUE rheostat; **~ d'ajustage** *m* COMMANDE adjusting rheostat; **~ d'arc** *m* ELECTR arc rheostat; **~ de champ** *m* ELECTR field regulator, field rheostat; **~ à commande manuelle** *m* CINEMAT manual dimmer; **~ à curseur** *m* ELECTR slide rheostat; **~ cylindrique** *m* ELECTR cylinder rheostat; **~ de démarrage** *m* ELECTR, ELECTROTEC starting rheostat; **~ de démarrage à liquide** *m* ELECTR liquid starter resistance, liquid starting resistance; **~ en pont** *m* ELECTR potentiometer rheostat; **~ d'excitation** *m* ELECTROTEC field rheostat; **~ liquide** *m* ELECTR liquid rheostat; **~ à liquide** *m* ELECTROTEC liquid controller, liquid starter; **~ régulateur d'intensité** *m* ELECTR current regulator

rhéostat-démarreur: **~ en série** *m* ELECTR series starter

RHM *abrév (relation homme-machine)* TELECOM man-machine relationship

rhodite *f* MINERAUX rhodite, rhodium gold

rhodium *m (Rh)* CHIMIE rhodium *(Rh)*

rhodizite *f* MINERAUX rhodizite

rhodochrosite *f* MINERAUX rhodochrosite

rhodonite *f* MINERAUX rhodonite

rhombe *m* GEOMETRIE rhomb, rhombus

rhomboédrique *adj* CRISTALL rhombohedral, trigonal

rhomboïdal *adj* GEOMETRIE rhomboid

rhomboïde *m* GEOMETRIE rhomboid

rhumbatron *m* ELECTRON rhumbatron

rhyolite *f* PETR rhyolite, rhyolyte

RI *abrév* TELECOM *(répartiteur intermédiaire)* IDF *(intermediate distribution frame)*, TELECOM *(réseau d'interconnexion)* interconnection network

riblon *m* PRODUCTION scrap, swarf

riboflavine *f* CHIMIE riboflavin

ribonucléique *adj* CHIMIE ribonucleic

riche: **~ en gaz** *adj* THERMODYN gassy; **~ en protéines** *adj* AGRO ALIM high-protein

richesse *f* MINES strength; **~ de mélange** *f* ESPACE mixture composition

ricinoléique *adj* CHIMIE ricinoleic

ricochet *m* MILITAIRE ricochet

ridage *m* PLAST CAOU *défaut de peinture* crawling

ride *f* HYDROLOGIE ripple, NAUT *de hauban* lanyard; **~ de courant** *f* GEOLOGIE *sédimentologie* current ripple, ripple mark; **~ de glace** *f* OCEANO ice ridge, ice ripple; **~ de plage** *f* OCEANO ripple mark, sand ripple, PETR ripple mark

rideau *m* TEXTILE curtain; **~ d'air** *m* MAT CHAUFF, REFRIG, TRANSPORT air curtain; **~ coupe-feu** *m* THERMODYN fire curtain; **~ de fer** *m* SECURITE *protection antifeu* safety curtain; **~ flexible** *m* PHOTO roller blind shutter; **~ de fumée** *m* MILITAIRE smoke screen; **~ fumigène** *m* MILITAIRE smoke screen; **~ d'injection** *m* CONSTR *barrage* grout curtain; **~ d'obscurcissement** *m* TEXTILE blackout curtain; **~ d'obstruction** *m* VEHICULES *radiateur* blind; **~ de protection pour soudeurs** *m* SECURITE welder's protective curtain; **~ de radiateur** *m* VEHICULES *refroidissement* radiator blind; **~ de stabilité** *m* TRANSPORT stability curtain

ridelle *f* CONS MECA *d'un camion* ledge; **~ arrière** *f* TRANSPORT tailgate

rides: **~ de fond** *f pl* HYDROLOGIE bottom ripples; **~ d'interférence** *f pl* GEOLOGIE interference ripples

ridoir *m* MECANIQUE turnbuckle, NAUT bottle screw, rigging screw, turnbuckle, OCEANO turnbuckle

riébeckite *f* MINERAUX riebeckite

riffle: **~ à losanges** *m* DISTRI EAU diamond riffle

riflard *m* CONSTR jack plane

rifloir *m* CONS MECA riffler

rigide *adj* PRODUCTION *fil* solid

rigidité *f* CONS MECA stiffness, PAPIER rigidity, stiffness, PHYSIQUE rigidity, RESSORTS rate, stiffness; **~ diélectrique** *f* ELECTR *condensateur* dielectric resistance, dielectric strength, disruptive strength, ELECTROTEC dielectric strength, disruptive strength, MATERIAUX, PHYSIQUE dielectric strength; **~ flexionnelle** *f* PHYSIQUE flexural rigidity; **~ latérale** *f* RESSORTS lateral stiffness; **~ du moyeu de battement** *f* AERONAUT hub flapping stiffness; **~ spécifique** *f* ESPACE *véhicules* specific stiffness

rigole *f* CONS MECA gutter, CONSTR channel, chute, ditch, gutter, DISTRI EAU ditch, flume, INST HYDR race, raceway; **~ d'assèchement** *f* CONSTR gutter, DISTRI EAU drainage ditch; **~ de drainage** *f* DISTRI EAU drainage ditch; **~ d'évacuation** *f* DISTRI EAU discharge flume; **~ pour recevoir l'eau de savon** *f* CONS MECA sud-channel; **~ pour recevoir l'huile** *f* CONS MECA oil channel; **~ de vidange** *f* DISTRI EAU outlet channel

rigueur: **~ à la décongélation** *m* REFRIG thaw rigor

RILA *abrév (restriction de l'identification de la ligne appelante)* TELECOM CLIR *(calling line identification restriction)*

RILC *abrév (restriction de l'identification de la ligne connectée)* TELECOM COLR *(connected line identification restriction)*

rinçage *m* CINEMAT wash, IMPRIM washing, MECANIQUE, PRODUCTION flushing

rincer *vt* DISTRI EAU scour

rinceur *m* PAPIER shower; ~ **de bordure** *m* PAPIER trim shower; ~ **oscillant** *m* PAPIER oscillating shower; ~ **rotatif** *m* PAPIER rotating shower

ringard *m* PRODUCTION prick bar, pricker, staff; ~ **à crochet** *m* PRODUCTION rake; ~ **à lance** *m* PRODUCTION prick bar, pricker

riper *vi* NAUT *cargaison* shift, PETROLE *la tour de forage* skid

ripidolite *f* MINERAUX ripidolite

ripper *m* CONSTR ripper

rippeur *m* CONSTR ripper

ripple-mark *f* GEOLOGIE, HYDROLOGIE ripple mark

ris *m* NAUT *voile*, OCEANO *voile* reef

RISCPT *abrév* (*Registre international des substances potentiellement toxiques*) POLLUTION IRPTC (*International Register of Potentially Toxic Chemicals*)

risée *f* NAUT *vent* cat's paw

risette *f* NAUT *vent* cat's paw

risque *m* AERONAUT hazard, QUALITE hazard, major hazard, risk, SECURITE hazard, risk; ~ **d'asphyxie** *m* SECURITE risk of suffocation; ~ **aviaire** *m* AERONAUT bird strike hazard; ~ **biologique** *m* SECURITE biological hazard; ~ **du brasage** *m* SECURITE brazing hazard; ~ **chimique** *m* SECURITE chemical hazard; ~ **dû aux machines à bois** *m* SECURITE woodworking machinery hazard; ~ **dû à la scie à ruban étroit** *m* SECURITE narrow bandsaw hazard; ~ **dû aux vibrations transmises à la main** *m* SECURITE hand-transmitted vibration hazard; ~ **dû aux vibrations transmises par des objets** *m* SECURITE body-transmitted vibration hazard; ~ **économique** *m* QUALITE economic risk; ~ **d'exposition** *m* PHYS RAYON risk of exposure, SECURITE *radiation* exposure risk, risk of exposure; ~ **d'incendie** *m* SECURITE, THERMODYN fire hazard; ~ **d'incendie dû à l'électricité** *m* SECURITE electrical fire risk; ~ **individuel** *m* QUALITE individual risk; ~ **inhérent à l'emploi de scies passe-partout** *m* SECURITE crosscut saw hazard; ~ **lié à l'électricité** *m* SECURITE electrical hazard; ~ **du métier** *m* SECURITE occupational hazard; ~ **de la microbiologie** *m* SECURITE microbiological hazard; ~ **pathogène** *m* SECURITE pathogenic hazard; ~ **potentiel** *m* SECURITE potential hazard; ~ **pour l'environnement** *m* QUALITE environmental risk; ~ **pour la santé** *m* SECURITE health hazard; ~ **pour la sécurité** *m* SECURITE safety hazard, safety risk; ~ **relatif** *m* MATH relative risk; ~ **social** *m* QUALITE societal risk

rivage *m* GEOLOGIE, NAUT coast, shore, coastline, shoreline

rive *f* HYDROLOGIE margin, shoreline, *d'une rivière, d'un étang, d'un lac* bank, NAUT bank, PRODUCTION *d'un four* lip

rivé *adj* PRODUCTION clinched

river[1] *vt* PRODUCTION clinch

river:[2] **se ~** *v réfl* PRODUCTION be clinched

riverain *adj* DISTRI EAU riparian, HYDROLOGIE riparian, riverside

rivet *m* CONS MECA, CONSTR, MECANIQUE, PRODUCTION rivet; ~ **aveugle** *m* CONS MECA blind rivet; ~ **bifurqué** *m* CONSTR slotted clinch rivet, slotted rivet, PRODUCTION bifurcated rivet; ~ **de chaudière** *m* INST HYDR boiler rivet; ~ **de chaudronnerie** *m* INST HYDR boiler rivet; ~ **à clin** *m* CONS MECA clinch rivet; ~ **à corps fendu** *m* CONS MECA bifurcated rivet; ~ **creux** *m* CONS MECA hollow rivet; ~ **à deux pointes** *m* CONS MECA bifurcated rivet; ~ **en cuivre rouge** *m* CONSTR copper

rivet; ~ **explosif** *m* MECANIQUE explosive-type rivet, PRODUCTION pop rivet; ~ **pour courroie** *m* PRODUCTION belt rivet; ~ **à tête affleurée** *m* CONS MECA flush head rivet; ~ **à tête bombée** *m* PRODUCTION button head rivet; ~ **à tête chaudronnée** *m* PRODUCTION brazier head rivet; ~ **à tête conique** *m* CONSTR cone head rivet, steeple head rivet; ~ **à tête cylindrique** *m* CONSTR cheese head rivet, pan head rivet; ~ **à tête en arc de cercle** *m* PRODUCTION button head rivet; ~ **à tête en goutte-de-suif** *m* PRODUCTION button head rivet; ~ **à tête en pointe de diamant** *m* CONSTR cone head rivet, steeple head rivet; ~ **à tête fraisée** *m* CONSTR countersunk head rivet; ~ **à tête fraisée et goutte de suif** *m* CONS MECA oval countersunk rivet, raised countersunk rivet, CONSTR bullhead rivet, bullheaded rivet, countersunk buttonhead rivet; ~ **à tête goutte de suif** *m* PRODUCTION brazier head rivet; ~ **à tête hémisphérique** *m* CONSTR cup head rivet; ~ **à tête noyée** *m* PRODUCTION flat countersunk rivet; ~ **à tête perdue** *m* PRODUCTION flat countersunk rivet; ~ **à tête ronde** *m* CONSTR cup head rivet; ~ **à tête tronconique** *m* CONS MECA pan head rivet, CONSTR cone head rivet; ~ **tubulaire** *m* CONS MECA hollow rivet

rivetage *m* CONS MECA, CONSTR, MECANIQUE, PRODUCTION riveting; ~ **à bande de recouvrement** *m* PRODUCTION butt riveting; ~ **à clin** *m* PRODUCTION lap riveting; ~ **à froid** *m* CONSTR cold riveting; ~ **au marteau** *m* PRODUCTION hammer riveting

riveter: ~ **à chaud** *vt* CONS MECA hot rivet

riveteuse *f* INST HYDR *fixation des dômes des chaudières* dome riveter

riveuse *f* CONSTR riveter, riveting machine; ~ **à martelage** *f* CONS MECA percussion rivet

rivière *f* DISTRI EAU, HYDROLOGIE, NAUT river; ~ **absorbante** *f* DISTRI EAU gaining stream; ~ **capturée** *f* DISTRI EAU beheaded river; ~ **côtière** *f* DISTRI EAU coastal river; ~ **en tresse** *f* GEOLOGIE braided river; ~ **franchissable** *f* HYDROLOGIE navigable river; ~ **souterraine** *f* HYDROLOGIE subterranean river, underground river; ~ **au stade de jeunesse** *f* HYDROLOGIE young river

rivoir *m* CONSTR riveter, riveting hammer, riveting machine; ~ **pneumatique** *m* PRODUCTION pneumatic riveter

rivolin *m* OCEANO eddy wind

rivure *f* CONS MECA riveting, CONSTR riveting, *d'une charnière* hinge pin, pin, MECANIQUE riveting, PRODUCTION *d'un rivet* head; ~ **d'assemblage** *f* PRODUCTION joint riveting; ~ **à bande de recouvrement** *f* PRODUCTION flush riveting; ~ **à couvre-joint** *f* PRODUCTION butt riveting, flush riveting; ~ **à éclisser** *f* PRODUCTION butt riveting; ~ **en quinconce** *f* PRODUCTION cross-riveting; ~ **étanche** *f* CONSTR tight riveting; ~ **à franc-bord** *f* PRODUCTION butt riveting, flush riveting; ~ **prisonnière** *f* CONSTR countersunk riveting; ~ **prisonnière fraisée** *f* CONSTR countersunk riveting; ~ **à un rang de rivets** *f* CONSTR single-riveted butt joint; ~ **à un rang de rivets à clin** *f* CONSTR single-riveted lap joint; ~ **à recouvrement** *f* EMBALLAGE, PRODUCTION lap riveting; ~ **saillante** *f* CONS MECA raised head; ~ **simple à recouvrement** *f* CONSTR single-riveted lap joint

rizerie *f* AGRO ALIM rice mill

RLE *abrév* (*réseau local d'entreprise*) INFORMAT, ORDINAT, TELECOM LAN (*local area network*)

RLS: ~ **par satellite** *m* TELECOM satellite EPIRB, satellite emergency position indicating radio beacon

RMC *abrév (reconnaissance magnétique de caractères)* INFORMAT, ORDINAT MICR *(magnetic ink character recognition)*

RMN *abrév (résonance magnétique nucléaire)* CHIMIE, PETROLE, PHYS RAYON, PHYSIQUE NMR *(nuclear magnetic resonance)*

Rn *(radon)* CHIMIE Rn *(radon)*

RNI *abrév (réseau numérique intégré)* TELECOM IDN *(integrated digital network)*

RNIS:[1] *abrév (réseau numérique à intégration des services)* TELECOM ISDN *(integrated services digital network)*

RNIS[2] ~ **à large bande** *m (RNIS-LB)* TELECOM broadband ISDN, wide band ISDN *(B-ISDN)*

RNIS-LB *abrév (réseau numérique avec intégration des services à large bande, RNIS à large bande)* TELECOM B-ISDN *(broadband integrated services digital network)*

RO *abrév (recherche opérationnelle)* INFORMAT, ORDINAT OR *(operational research)*

roable *m* PRODUCTION rake

roadster *m* TRANSPORT roadster

roatle *m* PRODUCTION rake

robe *f* TV cone

robinet *m* CONSTR bib, bibcock, cock, faucet (AmE), tap (BrE), spigot, stopcock, valve, EQUIP LAB cock, INST HYDR stop valve, *allant au cylindre* cutoff device, MECANIQUE faucet (AmE), valve, *hydraulique* cock, PETROLE *raffinerie* valve; ~ **d'admission d'air** *m* CONS MECA air inlet cock; ~ **d'air** *m* CONS MECA air tap; ~ **à air** *m* PETROLE air vent; ~ **d'alimentation** *m* PRODUCTION feed cock; ~ **d'amorçage** *m* DISTRI EAU priming cock; ~ **d'arrêt** *m* CONSTR stop valve, stopcock, EQUIP LAB stopcock, INST HYDR cutoff device, shutter, NAUT shut-off valve; ~ **d'arrêt à soupape** *m* CONSTR screw-down stopvalve; ~ **d'arrêt de vapeur** *m* INST HYDR steam stop valve; ~ **d'arrosage** *m* DISTRI EAU flood cock, jet cock, PRODUCTION cooler cock; ~ **de batterie** *m* AUTO battery master switch; ~ **à bec courbe** *m* CONS MECA bib tap, bibcock; ~ **à bec droit** *m* CONSTR straight-nose cock; ~ **à boisseau conique et à clef** *m* CONSTR plug cock; ~ **à boisseau sphérique** *m* INST HYDR globe valve; ~ **à boulet** *m* CONS MECA globe cock; ~ **de carburant** *m* AERONAUT fuel cock; ~ **à carré** *m* CONS MECA tap with square head; ~ **de charge** *m* PRODUCTION feed cock; ~ **de chute de pression** *m* CONS MECA depressurization valve; ~ **à clef** *m* CONSTR plug cock; ~ **à cloche** *m* INST HYDR bell valve; ~ **à col de cygne** *m* CONSTR swan neck cock; ~ **de commande à pédale** *m* AUTO, CONS MECA treadle brake valve; ~ **de compression** *m* INST HYDR compression cock; ~ **de conduite de gaz** *m* PRODUCTION gas cock, gas tap; ~ **coupe-feu** *m* AERONAUT fuel shut-off cock; ~ **à deux eaux** *m* DISTRI EAU two-way cock; ~ **à deux faces** *m* DISTRI EAU twin cock; ~ **à deux voies** *m* DISTRI EAU two-way cock, EQUIP LAB two-way tap; ~ **de drainage** *m* CONS MECA drain valve; ~ **d'eau** *m* EQUIP LAB faucet (AmE), tap (BrE), stopcock (BrE), water tap; ~ **de fermeture** *m* CONSTR stopcock; ~ **à flotteur** *m* CONS MECA, CONSTR ball cock, INST HYDR ball valve, float valve; ~ **de freinage** *m* CH DE FER *véhicules* brake valve, INST HYDR butterfly throttle valve, throttle, throttle valve; ~ **de freinage d'une pompe à air** *m* CONS MECA air pump throttle; ~ **de gaz** *m* PRODUCTION gas tap, gas valve; ~ **à gaz** *m* PRODUCTION gas cock, gas tap; ~

graisseur *m* CONS MECA oil cock, PRODUCTION grease cock; ~ **à guillotine** *m* CONS MECA gate valve; ~ **de hauteur d'eau** *m* DISTRI EAU gage cock (AmE), gauge cock (BrE), test cock, trial cock, try cock; ~ **hydraulique** *m* CONSTR water cock; ~ **d'incendie** *m* SECURITE fire point; ~ **d'isolation de soupape** *m* INST HYDR valve cock; ~ **d'isolement** *m* CONSTR cutoff cock, PRODUCTION isolating valve; ~ **de jauge** *m* DISTRI EAU gage cock (AmE), gauge cock (BrE), test cock, trial cock, try cock; ~ **mélangeur de sécurité** *m* CONS MECA safety mixing tap; ~ **à passage intégral** *m* CONSTR nonrestricted valve; ~ **à pointeau** *m* CHIMIE, CONS MECA, EQUIP LAB needle valve; ~ **pour conduite d'eau** *m* CONSTR water cock; ~ **pour eau** *m* CONSTR water cock; ~ **pour fûts** *m* CONSTR butt cock; ~ **de prise d'eau** *m* CONSTR water valve; ~ **de prise de vapeur** *m* INST HYDR steam cock, steam valve; ~ **de puisage** *m* CONS MECA draw-off tap; ~ **de pulvérisation** *m* CONS MECA spray tap; ~ **de purge** *m* CONS MECA bleed valve, CONSTR cylinder cock, drain-off cock, drain cock, waste cock, DISTRI EAU bleeding cock, bleeding valve, PRODUCTION *système hydraulique* drain cock; ~ **purgeur** *m* CONSTR cylinder cock, drain-off cock, drain cock, drip cock, waste cock; ~ **à quatre eaux** *m* DISTRI EAU four-way cock; ~ **à quatre voies** *m* DISTRI EAU four-way cock; ~ **se refermant automatiquement** *m* CONSTR self-closing cock (BrE), self-closing faucet (AmE); ~ **régulateur** *m* INST HYDR governor valve; ~ **à repoussoir** *m* CONSTR push-button faucet (AmE), push-button tap (BrE); ~ **à ressort** *m* CONSTR self-closing cock (BrE), self-closing faucet (AmE); ~ **de souffleur** *m* PRODUCTION blower cock; ~ **à soupape** *m* CONSTR screw-down valve; ~ **sphérique** *m* CONS MECA ball valve; ~ **de sûreté** *m* CONS MECA safety cock; ~ **à tête** *m* CONSTR tap with crutch key; ~ **à tournant sphérique** *m* MECANIQUE ball valve; ~ **à tournant sphérique à bride** *m* CONS MECA flanged ball valve; ~ **à trois eaux** *m* CONSTR switch cock, three-way cock; ~ **à trois voies** *m* CONSTR switch cock, three-way cock, INST HYDR switch valve, three-wayvalve; ~ **de vapeur** *m* INST HYDR steam cock; ~ **de vidange** *m* CONS MECA drain cock, DISTRI EAU purge cock, purging cock, PRODUCTION mud cock, VEHICULES *radiateur* drain cock; ~ **de vidange d'eau** *m* DISTRI EAU water drain cock; ~ **de vidange du radiateur** *m* AUTO radiator drain cock, VEHICULES *refroidissement* radiator drain tap; ~ **à vis** *m* EQUIP LAB screw valve; ~ **à vis de pression** *m* CONSTR screw-down cock

robinet-coffret *m* CONS MECA main tap

robinetier *m* CONSTR brass smith

robinetterie *f* CONSTR brass foundry, cocks and fittings; ~ **industrielle** *f* CONS MECA industrial valves; ~ **mélangeur** *f* CONS MECA combination tap assembly; ~ **de sûreté** *f* SECURITE safety valves and fittings, *pour distributeurs d'eau chaude* safety fittings

robinet-vanne *m* CONS MECA gate valve, DISTRI EAU sluicevalve, water gate

robot *m* INFORMAT, ORDINAT robot; ~ **d'appels** *m* TELECOM call sender; ~ **d'assemblage** *m* MECANIQUE assembly robot; ~ **dans le coeur** *m* NUCLEAIRE in-core power manipulator; ~ **industriel** *m* SECURITE industrial robot; ~ **manipulateur industriel** *m* CONS MECA, PRODUCTION manipulating industrial robot; ~ **sous-marin** *m* OCEANO autonomous submersible, unmanned submersible

robotique *f* INFORMAT, ORDINAT robotics

robuste *adj* EMBALLAGE tough

robustesse *f* ESSAIS, INFORMAT robustness, MATERIAUX strength, ORDINAT robustness

roc *m* CHARBON rock

ROC *abrév (reconnaissance optique des caractères)* IMPRIM, INFORMAT, ORDINAT OCR *(optical character recognition)*

rocade: ~ **littorale** *f* CONSTR coastal ring road

rocailleux *adj* CONSTR stony

roche *f* CHARBON, GEOLOGIE, NAUT rock; ~ **acide** *f* CHIMIE acidic rock, GEOLOGIE acid rock, acidic rock; ~ **biogénétique** *f* PETR biogenic rock; ~ **clastique** *f* GEOLOGIE clastic rocks; ~ **clastique terrigène** *f* GEOLOGIE clastic terrigenous rock, siliciclastic rock; ~ **concassée** *f* CHARBON crushed aggregate; ~ **couverture** *f* GEOLOGIE *d'un gisement, d'un réservoir,* PETR *d'un gisement, d'un réservoir* cap rock; ~ **cristallophyllienne** *f* GEOLOGIE foliated crystalline rock; ~ **détritique** *f* GEOLOGIE clastic rocks, fragmental rock; ~ **effusive** *f* GEOLOGIE extrusive rock; ~ **d'épanchement** *f* EN RENOUV extrusive rock, igneous rock; ~ **ferrugineuse** *f* GEOLOGIE ironstone; ~ **foliée** *f* GEOLOGIE foliated crystalline rock; ~ **ignée** *f* EN RENOUV, GEOLOGIE, PETR igneous rock; ~ **imperméable** *f* GAZ watertight caprock; ~ **intrusive de semi-profondeur** *f* GEOLOGIE hypabyssal rock; ~ **intrusive stratifiée** *f* GEOLOGIE layered igneous rock; ~ **magasin** *f* GEOLOGIE host rock, PETROLE reservoir; ~ **magmatique** *f* GEOLOGIE igneous rock; ~ **mère** *f* GEOLOGIE, PETR, PETROLE source rock; ~ **mère du diamant** *f* MINES diamond matrix; ~ **métamorphique** *f* EN RENOUV metamorphic rock; ~ **métavolcanique** *f* GEOLOGIE metavolcanic; ~ **phosphatée** *f* PETR phosphate rock; ~ **plutonienne** *f* GEOPHYS plutonic rock; ~ **pyroclastique** *f* GEOLOGIE pyroclastic rock; ~ **pyroclastique à cristaux** *f* GEOLOGIE crystal tuff; ~ **pyroclastique vitreuse** *f* GEOLOGIE hyaloclastite; ~ **réservoir** *f* GAZ reservoir rock, GEOLOGIE host rock, reservoir rock, PETR carrier bed, PETROLE reservoir rock; ~ **saline** *f* GEOLOGIE evaporite; ~ **sédimentaire** *f* CHARBON, PETR, PETROLE sedimentary rock; ~ **sédimentaire métamorphisée** *f* GEOLOGIE metasediment; ~ **siliceuse non-détritique** *f* GEOLOGIE siliceous nondetrital rock; ~ **silicoclastique** *f (cf silicoclastites)* GEOLOGIE siliciclastic rock; ~ **subautochtone** *f* GEOLOGIE *déplacée sur une courte distance* para-autochthonous unit; ~ **de type acide** *f* GEOLOGIE acid rock, acidic rock; ~ **de type intermédiaire** *f* GEOLOGIE intermediate rock; ~ **ultrabasique** *f* GEOLOGIE ultrabasic rock, ultramafic rock, ultramafite; ~ **ultramafique** *f* GEOLOGIE ultramafic rock; ~ **verte** *f* GEOLOGIE greenstone; ~ **volcanique** *f* GEOLOGIE extrusive rock; ~ **volcanique métamorphisée** *f* GEOLOGIE metavolcanic; ~ **zoogène** *f* PETR zoogenic rock

rocher[1] *m* MINES stone, NAUT rock

rocher[2] *vt* PRODUCTION flux

roches: ~ **encaissantes** *f pl* MINES country rocks; ~ **intercalaires** *f pl* GEOLOGIE country rocks

rochet *m* CONSTR brace

rochetage *m* NUCLEAIRE ratchetting

rodage *m* CONS MECA *d'une voiture* breaking in (AmE), running in (BrE), *d'une surface* honing, ESPACE burn-in, MECANIQUE breaking-in, PRODUCTION grinding, lapping; ~ **aux boues de carbure de silicium et de diamant** *m* CONS MECA lapping with silicon carbide and diamond slurries; ~ **en verre** *m* EQUIP LAB ground glass joint

roder *vt* MECANIQUE hone, lap, PRODUCTION lap, *cylindre, bouchon de verre* grind, VEHICULES *moteur, voiture* run in; ~ **à la pierre** *vt* MECANIQUE *outillage* hone

rodoir *m* PRODUCTION lap, lapping tool; ~ **en cuivre rouge** *m* PRODUCTION copper lap; ~ **en plomb** *m* PRODUCTION lead lap; ~ **pneumatique de soupapes** *m* AUTO air-operated valve grinder; ~ **pour transmissions** *m* CONS MECA shaft lap

roentgen *m* PHYS RAYON, PHYSIQUE R, roentgen, röntgen

roentgen-film *m* INSTRUMENT X-ray film

rognage *m* CERAM VER chipping, shearing-off; ~ **de bords** *m* CHIMIE trimerization

rogne *f* IMPRIM, PAPIER trim

rogner *vt* IMPRIM, PAPIER trim

rognoir *m* CONS MECA scraper

rognure *f* CONSTR shaving, PRODUCTION cutting

rognures *f pl* EMBALLAGE offcut, PAPIER shavings, trimmings; ~ **de papier** *f pl* EMBALLAGE paper chips

roidir *vt* CONS MECA tighten

rôle: ~ **d'équipage** *m* NAUT crew list, PETROLE ship's articles

ROM:[1] *abrév* ELECTRON, ELECTROTEC, INFORMAT, ORDINAT ROM, read-only memory

ROM[2] ~ **effaçable électriquement** *f* INFORMAT, ORDINAT EEROM, electrically-erasable ROM; ~ **optique** *f* INFORMAT, ORDINAT optical ROM; ~ **programmable** *f (PROM)* INFORMAT, ORDINAT programmable read-only memory *(PROM)*

romain *m* IMPRIM Roman type

romaine *f* CONS MECA lever scales

roméite *f* MINERAUX romeite

rompre[1] *vt* CHIMIE rupture, ELECTROTEC *un circuit* break

rompre:[2] **se** ~ *v réfl* CHIMIE rupture, CONSTR break

rompu *adj* NAUT broken

ronce *f* CONSTR barbed wire; ~ **artificielle** *f* CONSTR barbed wire

rond: ~ **de gant** *m* NUCLEAIRE glove port

rondelle *f* CONS MECA tap washer, washer, CONSTR washer, PRODUCTION trim washer, RESSORTS, VEHICULES *vis, boulon* washer; ~ **d'ajustage** *f* COMMANDE adjustment washer; ~ **d'amiante** *f* CERAM VER asbestos roll disc (BrE), asbestos roll disk (AmE); ~ **d'appui** *f* AUTO thrust washer; ~ **d'arrêt** *f* MECANIQUE lock washer; ~ **autolubrifiante** *f* CONS MECA oil ring; ~ **biseautée** *f* CONS MECA beveled washer (AmE), bevelled washer (BrE); ~ **de blocage** *f* CONS MECA bend-up lock washer, locking washer; ~ **de blocage pour colonne conique** *f* CONS MECA washer for tapered guide pillar; ~ **bombée** *f* CONS MECA dished washer; ~ **de butée** *f* CONS MECA ring-type thrust washer, thrust washer, PRODUCTION thrust washer; ~ **carrée** *f* CONS MECA square washer; ~ **de centrage** *f* CONS MECA location spigot; ~ **de compensation** *f* CONS MECA round distance piece; ~ **cuvette** *f* CONS MECA cup washer; ~ **à denture extérieure** *f* CONS MECA serrated lockwasher; ~ **élastique** *f* CONS MECA spring washer; ~ **en amiante** *f* CONS MECA asbestos washer; ~ **en étoile** *f* PRODUCTION star washer; ~ **d'équilibrage** *f* AERONAUT balance washer; ~ **extra-serrante** *f* CONS MECA heavy-duty lock washer; ~ **de feutre** *f* CONS MECA felt washer; ~ **de freinage à lamelle** *f* CONS MECA bend-up lock washer; ~ **de frottement** *f* CONS MECA friction ring; ~ **fuselée** *f* CONS MECA taper washer; ~ **fusible** *f* INST HYDR safety plug; ~ **fusible pour chaudière** *f* INST

HYDR fusible plug for steam boiler; ~ **Grower** *f* CONS MECA bend-up lock washer, lock washer; ~ **joint** *f* CONS MECA gasket; ~ **à languette** *f* MECANIQUE tab washer; ~ **de liège** *f* CONS MECA cork washer; ~ **de montage** *f* CONS MECA base washer; ~ **d'objectif** *f* PHOTO lens flange; ~ **d'obturation** *f* CONS MECA blank washer, blind washer; ~ **ondulée** *f* RESSORTS waved washer; ~ **plane** *f* VEHICULES plain washer; ~ **plate** *f* CONS MECA flat washer, plain washer; ~ **plate à crans** *f* CONS MECA tooth lock washer; ~ **plate pour boulonnerie métrique** *f* CONS MECA plain washer for metric bolts screws and nuts; ~ **pleine** *f* CONS MECA blind washer; ~ **rectangulaire** *f* CONS MECA lockplate; ~ **ressort** *f* CONS MECA disc spring (BrE), disk spring (AmE); ~ **à ressort** *f* CONS MECA crinkle washer, spring washer; ~ **de serrage** *f* PRODUCTION clamp washer; ~ **de sertissage** *f* CONS MECA crimping washer; ~ **à siège sphérique** *f* CONS MECA spherical seat washer; ~ **tournée** *f* CONS MECA turned washer
rondelle-éventail *f* CONS MECA lock washer
rondelle-frein *f* CONS MECA lock washer
rondin *m* PAPIER log
rond-point *m* CONSTR rotary (AmE), roundabout (BrE), traffic circle (AmE)
ronds: ~ **à béton** *m pl* CONSTR reinforced concrete rounds; ~ **lisses** *m pl* CONSTR reinforced concrete rounds
ronflement *m* AERONAUT, ELECTROTEC hum, ESPACE, NUCLEAIRE chugging; ~ **au démarrage** *m* TV starting hum; ~ **de relais** *m* ELECTROTEC relay hum; ~ **du secteur** *m* ELECTROTEC electrical hum (AmE), mains hum (BrE); ~ **de transformateur** *m* ENREGISTR transformer hum
ronfleur *m* ELECTROTEC, IMPRIM, TELECOM buzzer
ronronnement *m* ACOUSTIQUE rumble, AUTO rumble (BrE), rumble seat (AmE)
rood *m* METROLOGIE rood
roquet *m* CERAM VER bobbin
roquette *f* MILITAIRE rocket; ~ **à charge atomique** *f* MILITAIRE atomic rocket
ROS *abrév (rapport d'ondes stationnaires)* ESPACE SWR *(standing-wave ratio)*, VSWR *(voltage standing-wave ratio)*, TELECOM SWR *(standing-wave ratio)*
rosace *f* CERAM VER rosette, ELECTROTEC rose; ~ **de plafond** *f* ELECTR, ELECTROTEC ceiling rose; ~ **de raccordement** *f* TELECOM block terminal
rosaline *f* CERAM VER pink glass
rose: ~ **du compas** *f* NAUT compass card; ~ **des courants** *f* OCEANO current rose; ~ **des vents** *f* EN RENOUV, METEO wind rose, NAUT compass card
rotamètre *m* PAPIER, PHYSIQUE rotameter
rotary *m* TELECOM rotary system
rotateur: ~ **mécanique** *m* AUTO positive-type valve rotator; ~ **de soupape** *m* AUTO, VEHICULES *moteur* valve rotator
rotatif *adj* GEOMETRIE rotational
rotation[1] *f* AERONAUT *d'aéronef* turnaround, CHIMIE rotation, ESPACE rotation, spin, GEOMETRIE, INFORMAT, ORDINAT rotation, PAPIER revolution, PHYSIQUE rotation; ~ **anticyclonique** *f* METEO anticyclonic rotation; ~ **de l'arc** *f* RESSORTS angular rotation; ~ **des axes de coordonnées** *f* GEOMETRIE rotation of coordinate axes; ~ **cyclonique** *f* METEO cyclonic rotation; ~ **dans le sens antihoraire** *f* MECANIQUE anticlockwise rotation, counterclockwise rotation, PRODUCTION counter-

clockwise rotation; ~ **dans le sens horaire** *f* MECANIQUE clockwise rotation; ~ **différentielle** *f* ASTRONOMIE *d'une galaxie* differential rotation; ~ **de Faraday** *f* ESPACE Faraday rotation; ~ **galactique** *f* ASTRONOMIE galactic rotation; ~ **journalière** *f* PRODUCTION daily use; ~ **de la lune** *f* ASTRONOMIE moon's rotation; ~ **de phase** *f* ELECTRON phase shift; ~ **pince** *f* NUCLEAIRE tongue rotation; ~ **des stocks** *f* PRODUCTION inventory turnover, stock turnover
rotation:[2] **être en ~** *vi* ESPACE spin
rotationnel *m* ELECTRON curl, PHYS FLUID vorticity, *d'un vecteur* curl, PHYSIQUE curl, vorticity; ~ **correspondant au tourbillon** *m* PHYS FLUID *équations des mouvements des fluides* curl corresponding to vorticity
rotative *f* IMPRIM reel-fed press, web press; ~ **avec façonnage** *f* IMPRIM in-line web press; ~ **en continu** *f* IMPRIM in-line web press; ~ **à journal** *f* IMPRIM newspaper rotary press; ~ **offset** *f* IMPRIM web-fed offset rotary press, *machines* web offset press; ~ **pour la couleur** *f* IMPRIM multicolor rotary printing machine (AmE), multicolour rotary printing machine (BrE); ~ **de presse** *f* IMPRIM newspaper rotary press
rotatoire *adj* GEOMETRIE rotational
roténone *f* CHIMIE rotenone
rothoffite *f* MINERAUX rothoffite
rotor *m* AERONAUT *hélicoptère*, AUTO, CHARBON, ELECTR *générateur*, ELECTROTEC, PHYSIQUE, TRANSPORT, VEHICULES rotor; ~ **d'allumeur** *m* VEHICULES distributor rotor; ~ **anticouple** *m* AERONAUT *hélicoptère* tail rotor; ~ **articulé** *m* AERONAUT articulated rotor; ~ **auxiliaire** *m* AERONAUT auxiliary rotor; ~ **balancé** *m* EN RENOUV teetered rotor; ~ **bobiné** *m* ELECTROTEC wound rotor; ~ **à cage** *m* ELECTROTEC cage rotor; ~ **de compresseur** *m* AERONAUT *turbomachine* impeller; ~ **diphasé** *m* ELECTROTEC two-phase rotor; ~ **de distribution** *m* AUTO rotor arm; ~ **en cage d'écureuil** *m* ELECTROTEC squirrel cage rotor; ~ **à godets de centrifugeur** *m* EQUIP LAB centrifuge rotor; ~ **libre** *m* AERONAUT free rotor; ~ **massif** *m* ELECTR *machine* solid rotor; ~ **non bobiné** *m* CONSTR nonwound rotor; ~ **à pôles saillants** *m* ELECTROTEC salient pole rotor; ~ **principal** *m* AERONAUT main rotor; ~ **de queue** *m* TRANSPORT antitorque rotor, tail rotor; ~ **rigide** *m* AERONAUT *hélicoptère*, CONS MECA rigid rotor; ~ **soufflé** *m* AERONAUT jet flapped rotor; ~ **sustentateur** *m* AERONAUT lifting rotor; ~ **à tambour biologique** *m* HYDROLOGIE biorotor; ~ **triphasé** *m* ELECTROTEC three-phase rotor; ~ **de turbine** *m* INST HYDR turbine wheel with vanes, turbine wheel; ~ **de ventilateur** *m* CONS MECA blower wheel
rotule *f* CONS MECA ball, swivel, IMPRIM *mécanique*, PHOTO ball and socket, VEHICULES *direction* ball joint; ~ **d'articulation** *f* CONS MECA hinge and ball joint; ~ **de direction supérieure** *f* CONS MECA upper ball joint; ~ **de fourchette de débrayage** *f* AUTO throw-out fork pivot; ~ **de friction** *f* CONS MECA friction ball; ~ **de joint de cardan** *f* AUTO torque ball; ~ **lisse** *f* CONS MECA spherical plain bearing; ~ **lisse à contact radial** *f* CONS MECA spherical plain radial bearing
rouage *m* CONS MECA cogwheel, gear work, gear, gear wheel, gearing, mill gearing, toothed wheel
roue *f* CONS MECA wheel, MINES crib, curb, TRANSPORT, VEHICULES wheel; ~ **d'angle** *f* CONS MECA bevel wheel; ~ **d'arbre à cames** *f* CONS MECA camshaft gear; ~ **arrière** *f* TRANSPORT rear wheel; ~ **à aubes** *f* AERONAUT

impeller, DISTRI EAU paddle wheel, INST HYDR breast wheel, NAUT paddle wheel; ~ **à auges** *f* EN RENOUV *turbines* runner; ~ **à auges intégrales** *f* EN RENOUV *turbines* integral runner; ~ **à augets** *f* CONSTR bucket wheel; ~ **à augets en dessus** *f* DISTRI EAU overshot water wheel, overshot wheel; ~ **avant** *f* AERONAUT nose gear wheel, TRANSPORT front wheel; ~ **de Barlow** *f* ELECTROTEC Faraday disc (BrE), Faraday disk (AmE), PHYSIQUE Barlow's wheel; ~ **à boudin** *f* CONS MECA flange wheel; ~ **à bourrelet** *f* CONS MECA flange wheel; ~ **calée** *f* CONS MECA fixed wheel, PRODUCTION fast wheel; ~ **à chaîne** *f* CONS MECA chain pulley, chain sheave, chain wheel; ~ **de champ** *f* CONS MECA crown wheel; ~ **à chien** *f* CONS MECA click wheel, dog wheel, ratch, ratchet, ratchet wheel; ~ **cinétique** *f* ESPACE *véhicules* momentum wheel; ~ **à cliquet** *f* CONS MECA click wheel, dog wheel, ratch, ratchet, ratchet wheel; ~ **conduite** *f* CONS MECA follower; ~ **conique** *f* CONS MECA bevel ring, cone wheel; ~ **conique hypoïde** *f* MECANIQUE *engrenages* hypoid bevel gear; ~ **de correction** *f* CONS MECA translating wheel; ~ **crantée** *f* PRODUCTION toothed wheel; ~ **dentée** *f* AUTO sprocket, CONS MECA cogwheel, gear, gear wheel, rack wheel, toothed wheel, MECANIQUE *engrenages* gear wheel; ~ **dentée en partie** *f* CONS MECA mutilated wheel; ~ **à dents** *f* CONS MECA cogwheel, rack wheel, toothed wheel; ~ **à dents creuses** *f* CONS MECA enveloping tooth wheel; ~ **à dents droites** *f* CONS MECA straight-tooth wheel; ~ **à denture creuse** *f* CONS MECA enveloping tooth wheel; ~ **à denture droite** *f* CONS MECA straight-tooth wheel; ~ **directrice** *f* TRANSPORT guide wheel, VEHICULES steered wheel; ~ **diviseuse** *f* CONS MECA dividing wheel, division wheel; ~ **de division** *f* CONS MECA dividing wheel, division wheel; ~ **droite** *f* CONS MECA spur gear, spur wheel; ~ **élastique** *f* TRANSPORT elastic wheel; ~ **élévatoire** *f* CONS MECA elevating wheel, lifting wheel; ~ **élévatrice à godets** *f* TRANSPORT scoop wheel elevator, scoop wheel feeder; ~ **à empreintes** *f* CONS MECA chain sheave, indented wheel, PRODUCTION cupped chain sheave; ~ **en dessus** *f* DISTRI EAU overshot water wheel, overshot wheel; ~ **d'engrenage** *f* CONS MECA cogwheel, gear, gear wheel, pitch wheel, toothed wheel; ~ **d'entraînement** *f* CINEMAT driving wheel; ~ **épaulée** *f* CONS MECA flanged gear, shrouded gear, shrouding gear; ~ **de filetage** *f* CONS MECA change wheel; ~ **à fileter** *f* CONS MECA change wheel; ~ **fixe** *f* CONS MECA fixed wheel, PRODUCTION fast wheel; ~ **folle** *f* CONS MECA loose wheel; ~ **de friction** *f* CONS MECA friction wheel; ~ **de frottement** *f* CONS MECA friction wheel; ~ **à godets** *f* CONSTR bucket wheel; ~ **à gorge** *f* CONS MECA grooved roller, sheave; ~ **à grande vitesse spécifique** *f* EN RENOUV high specific speed wheel; ~ **hélicoïdale** *f* CONS MECA screw wheel, spiral wheel; ~ **hydraulique** *f* TEXTILE water wheel; ~ **d'impression** *f* INFORMAT, ORDINAT print wheel; ~ **intermédiaire** *f* CONS MECA idler, intermediate wheel, runner, stud wheel; ~ **à lamelles sur tige** *f* CONS MECA *abrasifs sur support* flap wheel with shaft; ~ **libre** *f* AUTO starter gear, CONS MECA freewheel; ~ **maîtresse** *f* CONS MECA leader, master wheel; ~ **manante** *f* VEHICULES *transmission* drive wheel; ~ **menante** *f* CONS MECA driver, driving wheel; ~ **menée** *f* CONS MECA driven wheel, follower; ~ **à mentonnet** *f* CONS MECA flange wheel; ~ **mobile** *f* CONS MECA *d'une turbine, d'un pompe centrifuge* runner, NUCLEAIRE *motrice* impeller, PRODUCTION *d'une pompe cen-*

trifuge impeller, *d'une turbine* wheel; ~ **motrice** *f* AUTO drive wheel, CONS MECA driver, driving wheel, TRANSPORT driving wheel; ~ **à palettes** *f* DISTRI EAU, NAUT paddle wheel; ~ **parasite** *f* CONS MECA idler, intermediate wheel, runner, stud wheel; ~ **Pelton** *f* EN RENOUV Pelton wheel; ~ **Pelton à arbre horizontal** *f* EN RENOUV horizontal shaft Pelton Wheel; ~ **Pelton à arbre vertical** *f* EN RENOUV vertical shaft Pelton Wheel; ~ **pignon** *f* AUTO sprocket; ~ **à pignon** *f* CONS MECA pinion wheel; ~ **pivotante** *f* CONS MECA castor; ~ **planétaire** *f* CONS MECA planet gear, planet wheel, planetary pinion, VEHICULES *différentiel* planet wheel, side gear; ~ **pleine** *f* VEHICULES disc centre wheel (BrE), disk center wheel (AmE); ~ **porteuse** *f* TRANSPORT carrying wheel; ~ **de potier** *f* CERAM VER potter's wheel; ~ **qui engrène une vis sans fin** *f* CONS MECA wheel which engages a worm; ~ **à rais** *f* CONS MECA spoke wheel; ~ **à rayons** *f* CONS MECA spoke wheel, VEHICULES spoke wheel, wire wheel; ~ **de réaction** *f* ESPACE *véhicules* reaction wheel; ~ **à réaction** *f* DISTRI EAU reaction water wheel, reaction wheel; ~ **de rechange** *f* CONS MECA change wheel; ~ **relevable** *f* VEHICULES retractable wheel; ~ **à rochet** *f* CONS MECA click wheel, dog wheel, ratch, ratchet, ratchet wheel; ~ **de secours** *f* AUTO spare tire (AmE), spare tyre (BrE), spare wheel; ~ **de stabilisation** *f* TRANSPORT stabilizing wheel; ~ **de translation** *f* CONS MECA runner, running wheel, *pour chariot de pont roulant* rail wheel, PRODUCTION traveling wheel (AmE), travelling wheel (BrE); ~ **de transmission** *f* CONS MECA driving wheel; ~ **de turbine** *f* NAUT turbine wheel; ~ **à tuyaux** *f* DISTRI EAU reaction water wheel, reaction wheel; ~ **de verrouillage** *f* AUTO parking gear, parking lock gear; ~ **à vis sans fin** *f* CONS MECA worm wheel; ~ **à voile plein** *f* VEHICULES disc centre wheel (BrE), disk center wheel (AmE)

roues: ~ **en diabolo** *f pl* AERONAUT dual wheels, twin wheels; ~ **et poulies à chaînes** *f pl* CONS MECA chain and sprocket wheels; ~ **jumelées** *f pl* AERONAUT *train d'atterrissage* dual wheels, twin wheels

rouet *m* CONS MECA cogwheel, pulley, pulley sheave, pulley wheel, sheave, MINES crib, curb, PRODUCTION mortise wheel, TEXTILE spinning wheel

roue-turbine: ~ **à impulsion** *f* PRODUCTION impulse wheel

rouf *m* NAUT coachroof

rouf-passerelle *m* NAUT bridge house

rouge:[1] ~ **d'Angleterre** *m* PRODUCTION rouge; ~ **antenne** *m* TV cue light; ~ **blanc** *m* THERMODYN white heat; ~ **de cochenille** *m* AGRO ALIM cochineal; ~ **à polir** *m* PRODUCTION rouge; ~ **vert bleu** *m* *(RVB)* INFORMAT, ORDINAT, TV red green blue *(RGB)*

rouge:[2] **être** ~ *vi* THERMODYN glow

rougeoyer *vi* MATERIAUX glow red

rouillage *m* MATERIAUX rust

rouille *f* AGRO ALIM, CHIMIE, MATERIAUX, MECANIQUE, PAPIER, VEHICULES *carrosserie* rust; ~ **superficielle** *f* CONSTR surface rust

rouilleuse *f* CHARBON holing machine, nicking machine, shearing machine

rouillure *f* CHIMIE rustiness

rouissage *m* TEXTILE retting; ~ **à terre** *m* TEXTILE dew retting

roulage *m* MINES drawing, TRANSPORT roll-on/roll-off; ~ **du papier** *m* PAPIER curl, curling

roulante *f* GEOMETRIE rolling circle

rouleau *m* CINEMAT roll, spool, EMBALLAGE coil, IMPRIM

printing roller, roller, *plieuses, rotatives* pinch roller, MECANIQUE coil, roller, NAUT roller, PAPIER roll, PHYS ONDES wave, PLAST CAOU *calandre, enduiseuse* cylinder, *matériel* roller, PRODUCTION *de fil*, RESSORTS coil, TEXTILE roll; ~ **d'alimentation** *m* AGRO ALIM feed roller, IMPRIM pick-up roll, PAPIER feed roll, feeding roll; ~ **anilox** *m* IMPRIM *flexographie* anilox roll; ~ **antiflexion** *m* PAPIER antideflection roll; ~ **d'appel** *m* IMPRIM *rotatives* pull roller; ~ **d'appel avant le triangle** *m* IMPRIM *plieuses, rotatives* roller top of former; ~ **d'application** *m* EMBALLAGE application roller; ~ **aspirant** *m* PAPIER suction roll; ~ **avec racle** *m* IMPRIM doctor roll; ~ **barboteur** *m* IMPRIM pan roller, *machines* dip roller; ~ **de bassine** *m* IMPRIM dipping roller, pan roller, *machines* dip roller; ~ **brisé** *m* PAPIER bowed roll, spreader roll; ~ **broyeur** *m* CONS MECA *pour filetages* crushing roll; ~ **de calandre** *m* PAPIER calender bowl, calender roll; ~ **compresseur** *m* CONSTR roller, TRANSPORT road roller; ~ **concasseur** *m* GENIE CHIM crusher roll; ~ **de contrepression** *m* IMPRIM *machines* backing roller; ~ **de couchage** *m* IMPRIM *papier* press roll; ~ **débiteur** *m* IMPRIM *rotatives* infeed roller; ~ **débiteur** *m* IMPRIM *machines, papier* metering roller, TV supply roll; ~ **déplisseur** *m* EMBALLAGE mount hope roller, spread roll, IMPRIM *rotatives* mount hope roller, PAPIER spread roll; ~ **distributeur** *m* IMPRIM doctor roll, *machines, encre et mouillage* metering roller; ~ **de distribution** *m* IMPRIM *machines* lay-on roller; ~ **égalisateur** *m* PAPIER doctor roll, evener roll; ~ **égoutteur** *m* PAPIER dandy roll; ~ **embarqueur** *m* PAPIER leading-in roll; ~ **encreur tramé** *m* IMPRIM *flexographie* anilox roll; ~ **d'encrier** *m* IMPRIM *machines* ink fountain roller; ~ **en cuir grainé** *m* IMPRIM roller; ~ **enducteur** *m* PAPIER applicator roll; ~ **d'enduction** *m* IMPRIM *machines* lay-on roller, *papiers, films* superspreader roller; ~ **d'engagement de la bande** *m* IMPRIM *rotatives* leading-in roller; ~ **entraîné** *m* PAPIER follower roll; ~ **d'entraînement** *m* IMPRIM *machine* forwarding roller; ~ **d'entraînement de toile** *m* PAPIER wire-drive roll; ~ **entraîneur** *m* CONS MECA feed roll, feed roller, PAPIER draw roll; ~ **d'entrée** *m* IMPRIM *machines* breast roller; ~ **d'essorage** *m* IMPRIM *héliogravure, flexographie* squeeze roller, PHOTO squeegee; ~ **essoreur** *m* PAPIER dewatering roll, squeeze roll, wringer roll; ~ **essoreur en caoutchouc** *m* CINEMAT rubber squeegee; ~ **et presse rotative coupante** *m* EMBALLAGE roller and rotary cutting press; ~ **exprimeur** *m* TEXTILE squeezing roller; ~ **de feuille** *m* PAPIER paper roll; ~ **de feutre** *m* PAPIER felt carrying roll, felt roll; ~ **filigraneur** *m* PAPIER dandy roll, watermark roll; ~ **fixe** *m* CERAM VER backup roll; ~ **de formation** *m* PAPIER forming roll; ~ **de foulon** *m* PAPIER wringer roll; ~ **de friction** *m* PRODUCTION friction roller; ~ **de front** *m* IMPRIM *machines* breast roller; ~ **garni** *m* IMPRIM *machines* resilient covered roller; ~ **gaufreur** *m* PAPIER embossing roll; ~ **gravé** *m* IMPRIM gravure roller; ~ **de guidage** *m* PRODUCTION guide roller; ~ **guide** *m* PAPIER guide roll, leading roll, PRODUCTION, TEXTILE guide roller; ~ **de guide** *m* CERAM VER roller; ~ **guide-toile** *m* PAPIER wire-guide roll; ~ **d'impression** *m* PLAST CAOU *matériel* impression roller; ~ **d'imprimerie** *m* PLAST CAOU *matériel* printing roll; ~ **inférieur de calandre** *m* PAPIER king roll; ~ **lamineur** *m* CERAM VER casting roller; ~ **leveur aspirant** *m* PAPIER pick-up roll; ~ **leveur sur forme ronde** *m* PAPIER baby press; ~ **lisse** *m* CONSTR smooth roller; ~ **marieur** *m* PLAST CAOU *revêtement de tapis* marriage roll; ~ **mouilleur** *m* EMBALLAGE damping roll; ~ **à papier de tenture** *m* CONS MECA seam roller; ~ **du passage-papier** *m* IMPRIM *rotatives* lead roll; ~ **perforé** *m* PAPIER holy roll, rectifier roll; ~ **à pieds de mouton** *m* CONSTR sheepsfoot roller; ~ **pinceur** *m* IMPRIM *machines* nipping roller; ~ **placé au dessus de la plieuse** *m* IMPRIM *rotatives* roller top of former; ~ **plieur** *m* CERAM VER bending roller, IMPRIM folding roller; ~ **plongé** *m* IMPRIM *machines* dip roller; ~ **pneumatique** *m* IMPRIM air cylinder; ~ **à pneus** *m* CONSTR pneumatic tired roller (AmE), pneumatic tyred roller (BrE); ~ **porteur** *m* CERAM VER carrying roller, CONS MECA carrying idler, PAPIER king roll, winding drum; ~ **premier pli** *m* IMPRIM *plieuses, rotatives* pinch roller; ~ **preneur** *m* IMPRIM *impression* pick-up roll; ~ **de presse coucheuse** *m* PAPIER press roll; ~ **de presse humide** *m* PAPIER wet press roll; ~ **de presse lisse** *m* PAPIER plain press roll; ~ **presseur** *m* CERAM VER pressure roller, CINEMAT pinch roller, PAPIER lump breaker, rider roll, roll; ~ **rainuré** *m* PAPIER grooved roll; ~ **ramasse-pétouilles** *m* IMPRIM *impression* pick-up roll; ~ **refroidisseur** *m* IMPRIM *périphériques de rotatives*, PLAST CAOU chill roll; ~ **de renvoi** *m* CONS MECA return roller; ~ **de renvoi de feuille** *m* PAPIER fly roll; ~ **de retour de toile** *m* PAPIER wire-return roll; ~ **de sacs** *m* EMBALLAGE bag reel; ~ **de sacs détachables en polythène** *m* EMBALLAGE polyethylene bags on the roll; ~ **souffleur** *m* PAPIER air roll, blow roll; ~ **de soutien** *m* PAPIER backing roll; ~ **spiralé** *m* PAPIER worm roll; ~ **supérieur** *m* PAPIER top roll; ~ **support** *m* IMPRIM *machines* backing roller, PAPIER bed roll; ~ **tendeur** *m* CONS MECA binding pulley, tension roller, PAPIER stretch roll, tension roller; ~ **de tension** *m* CONS MECA idler, jockey, jockey roller, jockey wheel, tension pulley, tightening pulley, PRODUCTION belt idler; ~ **de tête** *m* PAPIER breast roll; ~ **de toile** *m* PAPIER wire roll; ~ **de tôle piquée** *m* IMPRIM *rotatives* gravure roller; ~ **toucheur** *m* IMPRIM *machine* form roller; ~ **tramé** *m* IMPRIM screen roller; ~ **tramé spécial** *m* IMPRIM chanelled screen roller; ~ **à trous borgnes** *m* PAPIER blind drill roll; ~ **de ventilation de poche d'air** *m* PAPIER pocket ventilation roll; ~ **à vernis** *m* REVETEMENT coating roller system; ~ **vibrant** *m* CONSTR vibrating roller

roulement *m* CONS MECA working, *fonctionnement* running, *mécanisme* bearing, *organes* running gear, IMPRIM *mécanique*, PAPIER bearing, PRODUCTION campaign, *d'un haut-fourneau* run; ~ **à aiguilles** *m* CONS MECA, IMPRIM *mécanique* needle bearing; ~ **à anneau mince** *m* CONS MECA thin-ring bearing; ~ **de l'arbre primaire** *m* VEHICULES *embrayage* input shaft bearing; ~ **d'articulation** *m* CONS MECA knuckle bearing; ~ **à l'atterrissage** *m* AERONAUT landing run; ~ **à billes** *m* CONS MECA, MECANIQUE, VEHICULES ball bearing; ~ **à billes avec gorge** *m* CONS MECA grooved ball bearing; ~ **à billes à contact oblique** *m* MECANIQUE angular ball bearing; ~ **à billes en fil d'acier** *m* CONS MECA wire steel race ball bearing; ~ **à billes à gorge profonde** *m* CONS MECA deep groove ball bearing; ~ **à billes miniatures** *m* CONS MECA miniature ball bearing; ~ **à billes pour charge moyenne** *m* PRODUCTION medium-type ball bearings; ~ **à billes pour forte charge** *m* CONS MECA heavy-duty ball bearing; ~ **au décollage** *m* AERONAUT takeoff run; ~ **linéaire** *m* CHAUFFAGE linear bearings; ~ **de magnéto** *m* CONS MECA magneto bearing;

~ **de palier** *m* CONS MECA plummer block, plummer block bearing; ~ **pilote** *m* AUTO pilot bearing; ~ **de poussée** *m* VEHICULES *moteur* overrun; ~ **principal** *m* CONSTR main bearing; ~ **radial à rouleaux cylindriques** *m* CONS MECA radial cylindrical roller bearing; ~ **à rotule** *m* VEHICULES self-aligning bearing; ~ **de roue** *m* VEHICULES wheel bearing; ~ **à rouleaux** *m* CONS MECA, VEHICULES roller bearing; ~ **à rouleaux barriques** *m* CONS MECA barrel roller bearing; ~ **à rouleaux bombés** *m* CONS MECA barrel-shaped roller bearing; ~ **à rouleaux coniques** *m* CONS MECA taper rolling bearings, VEHICULES tapered roller bearing; ~ **à rouleaux cylindriques** *m* CONS MECA cylindrical roller bearing; ~ **à rouleaux cylindriques axiaux** *m* CONS MECA axial cylindrical roller bearing; ~ **à rouleaux obliques** *m* MECANIQUE angular roller bearing; ~ **sur coussin d'air** *m* CINEMAT air bearing

roulement-guide *m* AUTO pilot bearing

rouler[1] *vt* NAUT coil, PAPIER, TEXTILE curl

rouler[2] *vi* CONS MECA run; ~ **en roue libre** *vi* VEHICULES coast; ~ **au sol** *vi* AERONAUT taxi

roulette *f* CONS MECA follower, wheel, GEOMETRIE roulette, MECANIQUE roller, METROLOGIE measure, measuring tape, ribbon, tape measure, PRODUCTION caster; ~ **d'acier** *f* METROLOGIE steel measuring tape; ~ **d'arpenteur** *f* CONSTR surveyor's tape; ~ **d'assemblage** *f* CERAM VER gathering shoe; ~ **à gabarit** *f* CERAM VER former roller; ~ **de nez** *f* AERONAUT nose gear wheel; ~ **pivotante** *f* CONS MECA castor; ~ **de queue** *f* AERONAUT tail wheel

roulettes: ~ **de séparation** *f pl* CERAM VER split rollers

roulier *m* NAUT roll-on/roll-off vessel, TRANSPORT ro-ro, roll-on/roll-off, roll-on/roll-off vessel

roulis *m* ESPACE *pilotage* ripple, roll, NAUT rolling, PHYSIQUE roll; ~ **hollandais** *m* AERONAUT *aéronef à l'aile en flèche* Dutch roll

roulisse *f* MINES crib, curb

rouloir *m* TEXTILE wind-up apparatus

roulottage *m* TEXTILE *du jersey* curling

rousture *f* OCEANO lashing, packing

routage *m* INFORMAT, ORDINAT, TELECOM routing; ~ **centralisé** *m* INFORMAT, ORDINAT centralized routing; ~ **météorologique** *m* NAUT weather routing

route:[1] **en** ~ **pour** *adj* NAUT bound for; **en** ~ **vers l'espace** *adj* ESPACE space-bound

route:[2] **en** ~ *adv* NAUT under way

route[3] *f* AERONAUT course, route, CONSTR highway, road, way, ESPACE course, INFORMAT, NAUT, ORDINAT route, TRANSPORT road, route, VEHICULES road; ~ **d'accès** *f* TRANSPORT access road (AmE), slip road (BrE); ~ **aérienne** *f* AERONAUT airway; ~ **aérienne internationale** *f* AERONAUT international air route; ~ **commerciale** *f* NAUT main trading route; ~ **au compas** *f* NAUT course to steer; ~ **de dégagement** *f* TRANSPORT bypass road; ~ **départementale** *f* TRANSPORT secondary road; ~ **à deux voies** *f* CONSTR two-way road; ~ **à double chaussée** *f* CONSTR divided highway (AmE), dual carriageway (BrE); ~ **empierrée** *f* CONSTR metalled road (BrE), paved road (AmE); ~ **en eau profonde** *f* OCEANO deep-water route; ~ **en surface** *f* NAUT course through the water; ~ **escarpée** *f* CONSTR steep road; ~ **ferrée** *f* CONSTR metalled road (BrE), paved road (AmE); ~ **fond** *f* NAUT course made good; ~ **du grand cercle** *f* AERONAUT great circle route, NAUT great circle course; ~ **guidée** *f* TRANSPORT guided road; ~ **inverse** *f* NAUT reciprocal course;

~ **magnétique** *f* AERONAUT magnetic heading; ~ **maritime** *f* NAUT sea link, sea route, OCEANO sea lane, seaway; ~ **de mer** *f* NAUT sea route; ~ **de montagne** *f* CONSTR mountain road; ~ **de navigation** *f* NAUT shipping lane, shipping route; ~ **orthodromique** *f* AERONAUT great circle route, NAUT great circle course; ~ **à péage** *f* CONSTR toll road; ~ **principale** *f* CONSTR main road, major road, TRANSPORT main road; ~ **provisoire** *f* CONSTR temporary road; ~ **rugueuse** *f* CONSTR rough road; ~ **secondaire** *f* CONSTR minor road; ~ **à sens unique** *f* CONSTR one-way road; ~ **de sortie** *f* TRANSPORT arterial road; ~ **surface** *f* NAUT leeway track; ~ **à terre-plein central** *f* CONSTR divided highway (AmE), dual carriageway (BrE); ~ **transversale** *f* CONSTR bypath, byroad, byway

routeur *m* INFORMAT, ORDINAT router

routier[1] *adj* TRANSPORT road-bound

routier[2] *m* TRANSPORT long-haul truck driver; ~ **aéronautique** *m* AERONAUT aeronautical route chart

roving: ~ **direct** *m* CERAM VER direct roving

RTC *abrév (réseau téléphonique commuté)* TELECOM STN *(switched telephone network)*

ru *m* HYDROLOGIE brook, rivulet

Ru *(ruthénium)* CHIMIE Ru *(ruthenium)*

ruban *m* CERAM VER, ELECTR *isolation* tape, ELECTROTEC line, trace, IMPRIM ribbon, *rotatives* narrow web, INFORMAT ribbon, MECANIQUE tape, METROLOGIE measure, measuring tape, ribbon, tape measure, ORDINAT ribbon, PLAST CAOU *article* tape, TEXTILE narrow fabric, sliver, tape, top; ~ **d'acier** *m* METROLOGIE steel measuring tape; ~ **adhésif** *m* CINEMAT splicing tape, EMBALLAGE, MECANIQUE *matériaux* adhesive tape, PLAST CAOU adhesive tape, self-adhesive tape; ~ **adhésif repositionnable** *m* IMPRIM pressure-sensitive adhesive; ~ **d'aluminium** *m* EMBALLAGE aluminium tape (BrE), aluminum tape (AmE); ~ **d'arrachage** *m* EMBALLAGE tear tape; ~ **autocollant** *m* EMBALLAGE pressure-sensitive tape, self-adhesive tape; ~ **autocollant destiné à fermer les cartons** *m* EMBALLAGE, PAPIER sealing tape; ~ **autocollant en polyéthylène** *m* EMBALLAGE polyethylene self-adhesive tape; ~ **autocollant en polyvinyle chloride** *m* EMBALLAGE PVC pressure-sensitive tape; ~ **autocollant laminé** *m* EMBALLAGE self-adhesive laminated tape; ~ **cache** *m* CINEMAT masking tape; ~ **chauffant** *m* EQUIP LAB heating tape; ~ **collant après chauffage** *m* EMBALLAGE heat-fix tape; ~ **converti** *m* TEXTILE converted top; ~ **double face adhésive** *m* EMBALLAGE double-sided tape; ~ **d'effaçage du raccord de la piste sonore** *m* ENREGISTR blooping tape; ~ **encreur** *m* ORDINAT inked ribbon; ~ **étroit** *m* ELECTRON fine line; ~ **de fixage** *m* EMBALLAGE gummed paper tape; ~ **de frein** *m* VEHICULES *embrayage* brake band; ~ **isolant** *m* ELECTR insulating tape, ELECTROTEC adhesive insulating tape, adhesive tape, insulating tape, PRODUCTION *électricité* electrical tape; ~ **luminescent** *m* TV phosphor strip; ~ **magnétique** *m* TV magnetic tape; ~ **de Möbius** *m* GEOMETRIE *topologie* Möbius strip; ~ **peigné** *m* TEXTILE combed top; ~ **perforé** *m* TELECOM perforated tape, punched tape; ~ **pour balles** *m* EMBALLAGE bale hoop; ~ **pour protéger la surface** *m* EMBALLAGE surface protection tape; ~ **de sable** *m* OCEANO sand ribbon; ~ **thermocollant** *m* EMBALLAGE heat seal tape; ~ **turbo** *m* TEXTILE turbo-top

rubanage *m* OPTIQUE tape wrap

rubané *adj* GEOLOGIE banded, laminated

rubellite *f* MINERAUX rubellite

rubérythrique *adj* CHIMIE *acide* ruberythric

rubicelle *f* MINERAUX rubicelle

rubicon *m* CERAM VER first pair of rollers

rubidium *m (Rb)* CHIMIE rubidium *(Rb)*

rubijervine *f* CHIMIE rubijervine

rubine *f* CHIMIE fuchsin, rubin

rubis *m* CONSTR, GEOLOGIE, MINERAUX ruby; ~ **du Brésil** *m* MINERAUX Brazilian ruby; ~ **direct** *m* CERAM VER pot ruby; ~ **par réchauffement** *m* CERAM VER flash ruby

rubis-balais *m* MINERAUX balas ruby

rubrique *f* IMPRIM column, ORDINAT data field

rude *adj* MATERIAUX *au toucher* rough

rudites *f pl* GEOLOGIE rudaceous rocks, rudites

rue: ~ **de tourbillons** *f* PHYS FLUID *forme des écoulements* vortex street

rugosimètre *m* METROLOGIE surface roughness standard

rugosité *f* MECANIQUE, PAPIER roughness, PETR rugosity; ~ **de surface** *f* CONS MECA, CONSTR surface roughness

rugueux *adj* PAPIER rough

ruine *f* METALL failure

ruisseau *m* HYDROLOGIE rivulet, stream, NAUT creek; ~ **affluent** *m* HYDROLOGIE affluent stream

ruisseler *vi* HYDROLOGIE run down, run off, stream

ruisselet *m* HYDROLOGIE rill, rivulet, run, small stream, streamlet, stream

ruissellement *m* CONSTR, DISTRI EAU, EN RENOUV runoff, HYDROLOGIE flow, running off over the surface, runoff, trickling, POLLUTION runoff; ~ **acide** *m* POLLUTION acid runoff; ~ **sur les troncs** *m* POLLUTION stem flow

rupteur *m* AUTO breaker, CINEMAT switch, ELECTROTEC interrupter, ORDINAT burster; ~ **à deux lignes** *m* AUTO dual point breaker; ~ **double** *m* AUTO two-system contact breaker

rupture:[1] **à ~ brusque** *adj* PRODUCTION *contact* snap-action

rupture[2] *f* CHARBON break, CHIMIE rupture, CONS MECA failure, CRISTALL failure, fracture, CRYSTALL rupture, MATERIAUX failure, fracture, METALL rupture, NUCLEAIRE fracture, impact fracture, PAPIER break, QUALITE fracture; ~ **de base** *f* CONSTR base failure; ~ **brutale de gaine** *f* NUCLEAIRE fast burst; ~ **aux chocs** *f* NUCLEAIRE impact fracture; ~ **de cisaillement** *f* METALL shear fracture; ~ **de contact** *f* VEHICULES contact breaker; ~ **cristalline** *f* METALL crystalline fracture; ~ **diélectrique** *f* ELECTR dielectric breakdown; ~ **ductile** *f* CRISTALL, METALL ductile fracture; ~ **en coin** *f* METALL wedge-type fracture; ~ **en cône et coupe** *f* METALL cup-and-cone fracture; ~ **fibreuse** *f* METALL, NUCLEAIRE fibrous fracture; ~ **du fil de chaîne** *f* PRODUCTION warp breakage; ~ **fragile** *f* CRISTALL, METALL brittle fracture; ~ **de fragilité** *f* MECANIQUE brittle fracture; ~ **à fragilité** *f* RESSORTS brittle fracture; ~ **de gaine en fin de vie** *f* NUCLEAIRE end of life cladding rupture; ~ **à grains** *f* METALL crystalline fracture; ~ **granulaire** *f* NUCLEAIRE granular fracture; ~ **inclinée** *f* METALL slant fracture; ~ **instable** *f* METALL unstable fracture; ~ **intergranulaire** *f* RESSORTS intergranular fracture; ~ **d'isolation** *f* ELECTR insulation breakdown; ~ **de matrice** *f* MATERIAUX matrix failure; ~ **à nerfs** *f* METALL fibrous fracture, NUCLEAIRE gliding fracture, sliding fracture; ~ **par cavitation** *f* METALL cavitation failure; ~ **par fatigue** *f* CRISTALL fatigue fracture; ~ **par fluage** *f* RESSORTS creep rupture; ~ **par glissement** *f* NUCLEAIRE gliding fracture, sliding fracture; ~ **par surcharge** *f* RESSORTS overload fracture; ~ **de pente** *f* GEOLOGIE break-of-slope; ~ **plate** *f* METALL normal rupture; ~ **de profil** *f* GEOLOGIE knickpoint (BrE), nickpoint (AmE); ~ **progressive** *f* CHARBON progressive failure; ~ **des rails** *f* TRANSPORT rail break; ~ **retardée** *f* METALL delayed fracture; ~ **semifragile** *f* METALL semibrittle fracture; ~ **du sol** *f* CHARBON base failure; ~ **de stock** *f* PRODUCTION out-of-stock situation, runout, shortage, stock shortage; ~ **de talus** *f* CHARBON slope failure; ~ **totale due à la goutte** *f* (Fra) *(cf perle descendue)* CERAM VER bead down

rushes *m pl* CINEMAT dailies, rushes

ruthénique *adj* CHIMIE ruthenic

ruthénium *m (Ru)* CHIMIE ruthenium *(Ru)*

rutherfordium *m* CHIMIE rutherfordium

rutile *m* CHIMIE, MINERAUX rutile

RVA *abrév (réseau à valeur ajoutée)* INFORMAT, ORDINAT, TELECOM VAN *(value-added network)*

RVB *abrév (rouge vert bleu)* INFORMAT, ORDINAT, TV RGB *(red green blue)*

rythmage *m* ELECTRON clocking

rythme *m* ACOUSTIQUE rhythm, CINEMAT pace

rythmer *vt* ELECTRON clock

rythmeur *m* ELECTRON clock

S

s *abrév (seconde)* METROLOGIE s *(second)*

S :[1] **~ de suspension** *m* CONS MECA S-hook, S-shaped hook

S [2] *(soufre)* CHIMIE S *(sulfur, sulphur)*

S [3] *abrév (siemens)* METROLOGIE S *(siemens)*

sablage *m* CONSTR, MATERIAUX sandblasting, MECANIQUE grit blasting, sandblasting, NAUT sandblasting, PRODUCTION sanding

sable *m* CONSTR grit, PETR sand, PRODUCTION molding sand (AmE), moulding sand (BrE), sand; **~ armé de fibres** *m* CONSTR fiber-reinforced sand (AmE), fibre-reinforced sand (BrE); **~ asphaltique** *m* PETROLE tar sand; **~ bouillant** *m* HYDROLOGIE quicksand; **~ boulant** *m* CHARBON, HYDROLOGIE quicksand; **~ brûlé** *m* PRODUCTION burned sand, dead sand; **~ de carrière** *m* MINES pit sand; **~ de chantier** *m* PRODUCTION floor sand, heap sand; **~ de dragage** *m* CONSTR dredging sand; **~ d'étuve** *m* PRODUCTION baked sand; **~ étuvé** *m* PRODUCTION baked sand; **~ fin** *m* CHARBON, CONSTR fine sand; **~ fin pour béton** *m* CONSTR fines; **~ flottant** *m* CHARBON quicksand; **~ de fonderie** *m* CONSTR foundry sand, PRODUCTION foundry sand, molding sand (AmE), moulding sand (BrE); **~ glauconieux vert** *m* GEOLOGIE greensand; **~ gris** *m* PRODUCTION burned sand, dead sand; **~ gros avec cailloux** *m* CONSTR coarse gravelly sand; **~ grossier** *m* GEOLOGIE, MINES coarse sand; **~ de moulage** *m* PRODUCTION foundry sand, molding sand (AmE), moulding sand (BrE); **~ mouvant** *m* HYDROLOGIE, OCEANO quicksand; **~ noir ferrugineux** *m* PRODUCTION black iron sand; **~ à noyaux** *m* PRODUCTION core sand; **~ pour noyautage** *m* PRODUCTION core sand; **~ de râperie** *m* PRODUCTION burned sand, dead sand; **~ recuit** *m* PRODUCTION baked sand; **~ de remplissage** *m* PRODUCTION *fonderie* floor sand; **~ terrain** *m* MINES pit sand; **~ usé** *m* CERAM VER burgee, spent grinding sand; **~ de verrerie** *m* CERAM VER glassmaking sand; **~ vert** *m* PRODUCTION greensand; **~ vieux** *m* PRODUCTION floor sand

sablé : **~ moucheté** *m* CERAM VER peppered sandblast; **~ uni** *m* CERAM VER plain sandblast

sabler *vt* MECANIQUE sandblast, PRODUCTION sand

sablerie *f* PRODUCTION sand shop

sables : **~ calcaréo-siliceux** *m pl* GEOLOGIE calcareous grits; **~ pétrolifères** *m pl* PETR oil sands

sableuse *f* CERAM VER sandblast apparatus, PRODUCTION sandblast machine

sableux *adj* GEOLOGIE sandy

sablier *m* CERAM VER hourglass, PAPIER riffler, sand-table

sablière *f* CONSTR plate, pole plate, roof plate, wall plate; **~ basse** *f* CONSTR sill, *d'un pan de bois* ground-sill; **~ de comble** *f* CONSTR plate, pole plate, roof plate, wall plate; **~ haute** *f* CONSTR head plate, plate

sablon *m* CONSTR, PETR fine sand

sabord : **~ de chargement** *m* NAUT cargo port

saborder *vt* NAUT scuttle

sabot *m* CH DE FER *véhicules* shoe, CHARBON pile shoe, CONS MECA shoe, *d'un étau-lime, d'une machine à raboter* tool box, CONSTR hanger, ELECTR *commutateur* collector shoe, MINES *d'un pilon*, VEHICULES *frein* shoe; **~ arrière** *m* AERONAUT tailskid; **~ coupant** *m* MINES drive shoe; **~ de cuvelage** *m* GAZ casing shoe, PETROLE *d'un puits, forage* casing set; **~ de Denver** *m* TRANSPORT clamp; **~ de fixation** *m* PHOTO mounting foot; **~ de formation** *m* PAPIER forming shoe; **~ de frein** *m* CH DE FER *véhicules* brake block, CONS MECA brake block, brake shoe, VEHICULES *d'un vélo* brake block, *d'un frein à disque* pad; **~ HP** *m* PRODUCTION *système hydraulique* HP shoe; **~ de pieu** *m* CONSTR pile shoe; **~ de pilon** *m* PRODUCTION stamp shoe; **~ de queue** *m* AERONAUT tailskid; **~ à roc** *m* CHARBON rock shoe; **~ de rouleau** *m* PRODUCTION *système hydraulique* roller shoe; **~ tranchant** *m* MINES drive shoe; **~ à vis** *m* CONSTR screw shoe

saboteuse : **~ de traverses** *f* CH DE FER railroad tie-adzing machine (AmE), railway tie-adzing machine (BrE), sleeper-adzing machine (BrE), tie-adzing machine (AmE)

sabotier *m* (Sui) *(cf enrayeur)* CH DE FER *personnel* shunter

sabre *m* INST HYDR *d'une distribution Corliss* lifting rod

sac *m* CHARBON bag, EMBALLAGE bag, sack, IMPRIM bag, MINES bag, cavity; **~ accessoire** *m* PHOTO gadget bag; **~ avec bulles d'air** *m* EMBALLAGE air bubble bag; **~ avec extrémité plate** *m* EMBALLAGE flat-end sack; **~ carré** *m* EMBALLAGE *avec goussets* square bag; **~ de chargement** *m* CINEMAT changing bag; **~ de cuisson** *m* EMBALLAGE boil in bag; **~ doublé** *m* EMBALLAGE lined bag; **~ en matériel mince aplati** *m* EMBALLAGE lay-flat film bag; **~ en papier** *m* EMBALLAGE paper bag, paper sack; **~ en plastique pour casier** *m* EMBALLAGE bin liner; **~ gonflable** *m* AUTO air bag; **~ à noir** *m* PRODUCTION blacking bag; **~ de parachute** *m* MILITAIRE parachute pack; **~ à plusieurs épaisseurs** *m* EMBALLAGE multiply sack, multiwall sack; **~ poubelle** *m* EMBALLAGE liner bag; **~ pour les détritus** *m* EMBALLAGE garbage bag (AmE), refuse sack (BrE); **~ à poussière** *m* CHARBON dust catcher, PRODUCTION dusting bag, SECURITE *aspirateur, ventilateur* dust bag; **~ pouvant être inséré** *m* EMBALLAGE insertable sack; **~ de sable** *m* SECURITE sandbag

saccharate *m* CHIMIE saccharate

saccharide *m* CHIMIE saccharide

saccharimètre *m* PHYSIQUE saccharimeter

saccharine *f* CHIMIE saccharin

saccharique *adj* CHIMIE saccharic

saccoblaste *m* CHIMIE saccoblast

sachet *m* EMBALLAGE bag, pack (AmE), sachet (BrE), paper bag, pouch, IMPRIM bag; **~ de cuisson** *m* EMBALLAGE boilable pouch; **~ dans une boîte métallique** *m* EMBALLAGE bag in a can; **~ desséchant** *m* EMBALLAGE desiccant bag; **~ dessiccant** *m* EMBALLAGE moisture-absorbent bag; **~ à dosage simple** *m* EMBALLAGE unit-dose packet (AmE), unit-dose sachet (BrE); **~ à extrémités arrondies** *m* EMBALLAGE *pour l'emballage sous vide* round ended pouch; **~ à fermeture par**

pression et glissière *m* EMBALLAGE zip lock bag; ~ **soluble** *m* EMBALLAGE soluble sachet

sacs: ~ **perforés en rouleau** *m pl* EMBALLAGE perforated bags on a roll

SADO *abrév (Système d'acquisition de données océaniques)* OCEANO ODAS *(Ocean Data Acquisition System)*

safflorite *f* MINERAUX safflorite

safran *m* AGRO ALIM saffron, NAUT rudder blade; ~ **de gouvernail** *m* NAUT rudder blade

safranine *f* CHIMIE safranin, safranine

safrol *m* CHIMIE safrol, safrole

safrole *m* CHIMIE safrol, safrole

sagénite *f* MINERAUX sagenite

Sagittaire *m* ASTRONOMIE Sagittarius

saignée *f* CONS MECA groove, CONSTR cut, trench, PRODUCTION nick

saigner *vt* CONSTR *un fossé*, DISTRI EAU drain

saillie *f* CONS MECA addendum, boss, height above pinch line, *d'une mèche* land, *d'une dent d'engrenage* point, CONSTR depth of thread, ledge, offset, projection, set-off, *d'une pierre, d'une gouttière au delà d'un mur* projection, IMPRIM *reliure* joint, *typographie* kern; ~ **de la pointe polaire** *f* TV tip protrusion

saisie *f* NAUT arrest, seizure, SECURITE entanglement; ~ **de données** *f* ELECTRON data entry, INFORMAT data capture, data entry, ORDINAT data capture

saisir[1] *vt* ELECTRON enter, IMPRIM keyboard, NAUT lash, seize, PRODUCTION grip; ~ **au clavier** *vt* INFORMAT keyboard

saisir:[2] ~ **la bouée** *vi* NAUT pick up a mooring

saisissage *m* NAUT lashing

saison: ~ **des pluies** *f* METEO rainy season; ~ **sèche** *f* METEO dry season

saisonnalité *f* PRODUCTION seasonal behavior (AmE), seasonal behaviour (BrE), seasonality

SAL *abrév (signalisation automatique lumineuse)* CH DE FER automatic light signals

salacétol *m* CHIMIE salacetol

salage *m* AGRO ALIM salting, OCEANO salt curing

salaison *f* AGRO ALIM salting

salbande *f* MINES gouge, pug, selvage, selvedge; ~ **argileuse** *f* MINES gouge, pug, selvage, selvedge

salée *adj* CONSTR *eau* brackish

saleté *f* IMPRIM smudge, QUALITE dirt; ~ **de tirage** *f* CINEMAT printed dirt

salicine *f* CHIMIE salicin

salicylate *m* CHIMIE salicylate; ~ **de phényle** *m* CHIMIE salol

salicyle *m* CHIMIE salicyl

salicylé *adj* CHIMIE salicylated

salicylique *adj* CHIMIE *acide* salicylic

salifère *adj* GEOLOGIE salt-bearing

salifiable *adj* CHIMIE salifiable

saligénine *f* CHIMIE saligenin

salin *adj* DISTRI EAU, HYDROLOGIE saline

salinisation *f* HYDROLOGIE salinization

salinité *f* CHIMIE, DISTRI EAU, EN RENOUV salinity, GAZ salt content, HYDROLOGIE salinity, saltiness, NAUT, PETR, PETROLE salinity

salinomètre *m* CHARBON, OCEANO salinometer

salite *f* MINERAUX sahlite, salite

salle *f* CONSTR room; ~ **anéchoïque** *f* ACOUSTIQUE anechoic room; ~ **avec conditionnement d'air** *f* EMBALLAGE climatic chamber; ~ **blanche** *f* ELECTRON, EQUIP LAB clean room, ESPACE white room, REFRIG clean room; ~ **des chaudières** *f* MAT CHAUFF boiler room; ~ **de chauffe** *f* INST HYDR boiler room; ~ **climatisée** *f* EMBALLAGE climatic chamber; ~ **de commandes** *f* ELECTR *contrôle* control room; ~ **de commande électrique** *f* NUCLEAIRE electrical control board, electrical control room; ~ **de commande de radiographie** *f* INSTRUMENT X-ray control room; ~ **des défileurs** *f* ENREGISTR machine room; ~ **d'enregistrement** *f* ENREGISTR recording room; ~ **d'essais et mesures** *f* TELECOM test room; ~ **d'exploitation** *f* TELECOM operations room; ~ **de finissage** *f* EMBALLAGE salle; ~ **des gabarits** *f* NAUT mold loft (AmE), mould loft (BrE); ~ **d'inspection avec température contrôlée** *f* CONS MECA temperature-controlled inspection room; ~ **de la machine** *f* MINES hoist room, winder house; ~ **des machines** *f* ENREGISTR machine room, NUCLEAIRE turbine building, turbine house, PRODUCTION engine room; ~ **de montage** *f* CINEMAT editing room, NAUT assembly hall; ~ **de projection** *f* CINEMAT screening room, viewing theatre; ~ **de réchauffage** *f* REFRIG warming room; ~ **de rédaction** *f* TV newsroom; ~ **de rédaction du journal** *f* TV editorial newsroom; ~ **de régie** *f* TV control room; ~ **réverbérante** *f* ACOUSTIQUE reverberation room; ~ **sourde** *f* ACOUSTIQUE dead room, PHYSIQUE anechoic room, dead room; ~ **à tracer** *f* NAUT mold loft (AmE), mould loft (BrE); ~ **de vision** *f* CINEMAT screening room, viewing theatre

salmanazar *m* CERAM VER salmanazar

salmonelle *f* AGRO ALIM salmonella

salmonellose *f* AGRO ALIM salmonella

salmoniculteur *m* OCEANO salmon breeder, salmon farmer

salmoniculture *f* OCEANO salmon culture

salol *m* CHIMIE salol

salopette *f* SECURITE overalls; ~ **pour l'industrie** *f* SECURITE industrial overalls

salpêtre *m* AGRO ALIM, CERAM VER saltpeter (AmE), saltpetre (BrE), CHIMIE niter (AmE), nitre (BrE), potassium nitrate, saltpeter (AmE), saltpetre (BrE), PRODUCTION saltpeter (AmE), saltpetre (BrE)

salse *f* EN RENOUV mud volcano

saltation *f* HYDROLOGIE saltation

salvarsan: ~ **606** *m* CHIMIE salvarsan

salve *f* ESPACE *communications* burst, MILITAIRE *d'un canon* round, salvo, *d'une arme à feu* volley, TELECOM, TV burst; ~ **alternante** *f* TV alternating burst; ~ **de commande** *f* ESPACE *communications* control burst; ~ **couleur** *f* TV color burst (AmE), colour burst (BrE); ~ **laser** *f* ELECTRON laser burst; ~ **multiple** *f* TV multiburst; ~ **de neutrons** *f* NUCLEAIRE neutron burst; ~ **de référence** *f* TV color burst (AmE), colour burst (BrE); ~ **de signaux d'accès** *f* TELECOM access burst signal; ~ **de trafic** *f* ESPACE *communications* traffic burst

samarium *m (Sm)* CHIMIE samarium *(Sm)*

samarskite *f* MINERAUX samarskite

sandbergérite *f* MINERAUX sandbergerite

sandwich: ~ **treillis** *m* ESPACE mesh sandwich

sangle *f* POLLU MER webbing, PRODUCTION strap; ~ **de frein** *f* AUTO brake band, CONS MECA brake strap; ~ **de remorquage** *f* TRANSPORT tow strap; ~ **de sauvetage** *f* AERONAUT rescue strap

sanidine *f* MINERAUX sanidine

sans:[1] ~ **acide** *adj* EMBALLAGE *papier* acidless, IMPRIM, PAPIER acid-free; ~ **action** *adj* CHIMIE inactive; ~ **additif** *adj* AGRO ALIM additive-free; ~ **apprêt** *adj* PAPIER, REVETEMENT unfinished; ~ **carbone** *adj* IMPRIM *papier* carbonless; ~ **cargaison** *adj* POLLU MER unladen; ~ **cellulose** *adj* EMBALLAGE woodfree; ~ **cendres** *adj* PAPIER ashless; ~ **charge** *adj* RESSORTS unloaded; ~ **chauffeur** *adj* TRANSPORT *véhicules* driverless; ~ **colle** *adj* PAPIER unsized; ~ **conducteur** *adj* TRANSPORT driverless; ~ **connexion** *adj* TELECOM CL, connectionless; ~ **contamination de l'environnement** *adj* EMBALLAGE environment friendly, environmentally friendly; ~ **coupure** *adj* TELECOM break-free; ~ **couture** *adj* IMPRIM *reliure* unsewn, TEXTILE seamless; ~ **défaillance** *adj* TELECOM fault-free; ~ **défaut** *adj* PAPIER flawless; ~ **différence** *adj* NAUT *de tirant d'eau* on even keel; ~ **eau** *adj* LESSIVES waterless; ~ **élution** *adj* CHIMIE *chromatographie* nonelution; ~ **encre** *adj* EMBALLAGE *système à jet d'encre* inkless; ~ **engrenage** *adj* CONS MECA gearless; ~ **fin** *adj* PAPIER endless; ~ **friction** *adj* CONS MECA frictionless; ~ **frottement** *adj* MECANIQUE frictionless; ~ **fumée** *adj* SECURITE smokeless; ~ **garnissage** *adj* CHIMIE unlined; ~ **gigue** *adj* ELECTRON jitter-free; ~ **gluten** *adj* AGRO ALIM gluten-free; ~ **graduations** *adj* CHIMIE ungraduated; ~ **grains** *adj* PHOTO grainless; ~ **gras** *adj* AGRO ALIM nonfat; ~ **maintien** *adj* ORDINAT *caractère* nonlocking; ~ **matière grasse** *adj* AGRO ALIM nonfat; ~ **noeud** *adj* TEXTILE knotless; ~ **odeur** *adj* GENIE CHIM, MATERIAUX odorless (AmE), odourless (BrE); ~ **ordre** *adj* CHIMIE random; ~ **pertes** *adj* ELECTR *diélectrique* lossfree, ELECTROTEC lossless; ~ **pilote** *adj* ESPACE *véhicules* unmanned; ~ **prises** *adj* ELECTR *bobine* untapped; ~ **rainure** *adj* CONS MECA *petit outillage* fluteless; ~ **réaction** *adj* CHIMIE nonreactive; ~ **recul** *adj* MILITAIRE recoilless; ~ **scintillement** *adj* INFORMAT, ORDINAT flicker free; ~ **scorie** *adj* THERMODYN *charbon* free from slag; ~ **solvant** *adj* IMPRIM solventless; ~ **soudure** *adj* PRODUCTION weldless; ~ **structure définie** *adj* GEOLOGIE massive; ~ **verrouillage** *adj* INFORMAT nonlocking

sans:[2] ~ **interagir** *adv* PHYS RAYON without interacting

sans:[3] ~ **empattement** *m* IMPRIM sanserif

sans:[4] ~ **addition de sucre** *loc* AGRO ALIM no added sugar; ~ **garantie du gouvernement** *loc* (*SGDG*) BREVETS no government guarantee; ~ **rapport avec** *loc* MATH incommensurable with

sans-différence *m* NAUT, TRANSPORT even keel

santé:[1] ~ **de l'environnement** *f* SECURITE environmental health

santé:[2] **la ~ la sécurité et le bien-être** *loc* SECURITE *de personnes au travail* health safety and welfare

santonine *f* CHIMIE santonin

santonique *adj* CHIMIE *acide* santonic

sapelli *m* NAUT sapele

sapement *m* CONSTR undermining, MINES sapping

saper *vt* MINES undermine

saphir *m* ELECTRON, MINERAUX sapphire; ~ **bleu** *m* MINERAUX blue sapphire

saphirine *f* MINERAUX sapphirine

sapogénine *f* CHIMIE sapogenin

saponase *f* CHIMIE lipase

saponifiant[1] *adj* CHIMIE saponifying

saponifiant[2] *m* CHIMIE saponifier

saponification *f* CHIMIE saponification

saponifier[1] *vt* CHIMIE *de la graisse* saponify

saponifier:[2] **se ~** *v réfl* CHIMIE saponify

saponine *f* CHIMIE saponin

saponite *f* MINERAUX saponite

sapropèle *m* GEOLOGIE sapropel deposit, sapropelic deposit, OCEANO sapropel

SAR *abrév* (*signalisation automatique routière*) CH DE FER automatic traffic light signals

sarcine *f* CHIMIE sarcine

sarcolactique *adj* CHIMIE sarcolactic

sarcolite *f* MINERAUX sarcolite

sarcosine *f* CHIMIE sarcosin, sarcosine

sarde *m* MINERAUX sard

sardinal *m* OCEANO sardine net

sardineau *m* OCEANO sardine net

sardinier *m* OCEANO sardine boat

sardoine *f* MINERAUX sardonyx

sarkinite *f* MINERAUX sarkinite

saros *f* ASTRONOMIE saros

sarrau: ~ **de protection** *m* SECURITE protective gown

sartorite *f* MINERAUX sartorite

sas *m* CHARBON sieve, CINEMAT light trap, CONSTR sieve, DISTRI EAU chamber, coffer, INSTRUMENT specimen chamber, NAUT lock chamber, lock, TRANSPORT boat tank; ~ **d'aérage** *m* MINES airlock; ~ **à air** *m* DISTRI EAU *d'un caisson*, IMPRIM, MINES, REFRIG, SECURITE *entrée-sortie* airlock; ~ **de communication** *m* ESPACE *véhicules* airlock, connecting tunnel; ~ **coupe-feu** *m* THERMODYN fire lobby, firelock; ~ **d'écluse** *m* DISTRI EAU lock chamber; ~ **à gaz** *m* NUCLEAIRE gas lock; ~ **d'incendie** *m* THERMODYN fire lobby, firelock; ~ **de secours** *m* NUCLEAIRE emergency air lock

sassage *m* MINES jigging

sassement *m* MINES jigging, POLLU MER screening

sasser *vt* POLLU MER screen

sasseur *m* MINES jig

sassolite *f* MINERAUX sassoline, sassolite

satcom *m* (*communications par satellite*) NAUT satcom (*satellite communications*)

satellite *m* AERONAUT, ASTRONOMIE satellite, AUTO differential pinion, planet gear, planetary pinion, side gear, CONS MECA planet gear, ESPACE *véhicules*, IMPRIM, PHYSIQUE satellite, TELECOM dependent exchange, remote switching system, TRANSPORT satellite, VEHICULES *différentiel* pinion gear; ~ **actif** *m* ESPACE *véhicules* active satellite; ~ **additionnel** *m* ESPACE *véhicules* piggyback satellite; ~ **artificiel** *m* ASTRONOMIE, TELECOM artificial satellite; ~ **astronomique infrarouge** *m* (*IRAS*) ASTRONOMIE infrared astronomical satellite (*IRAS*); ~ **à autonomie d'acheminement restreinte** *m* TELECOM discriminating satellite exchange; ~ **berger** *m* ASTRONOMIE shepherd satellite; ~ **central** *m* TELECOM satellite exchange; ~ **de collecte de données** *m* ESPACE *véhicules* data collection satellite; ~ **de communications** *m* NAUT comsat, communications satellite; ~ **à défilement** *m* ESPACE nonsynchronous satellite; ~ **de détection d'explosions nucléaires** *m* ESPACE *véhicules* nuclear detection satellite; ~ **de détection des ressources terrestres** *m* ESPACE *véhicules* Earth resources research satellite; ~ **de différentiel** *m* VEHICULES *transmission* differential spider pinion; ~ **de diffusion** *m* TV broadcasting satellite; ~ **discriminateur** *m* TELECOM discriminating satellite exchange; ~ **à double rotation** *m* ESPACE *véhicules* dual-spin satellite; ~ **en laisse** *m* ESPACE *véhicules* tethered satellite; ~ **en orbite** *m* ESPACE orbiting satellite; ~ **d'étude de l'environnement** *m* ESPACE *véhicules* environment survey satellite; ~ **géostationnaire** *m* ESPACE *véhicules*, NAUT, PHYSIQUE, TELECOM, TV geostationary satellite; ~ **géosynchrone** *m* ESPACE *véhicules* Earth synchronous satellite; ~ **héliosynchrone** *m* ESPACE *véhicules* sun-synchronous satellite;

~ **infrarouge** m ASTRONOMIE infrared satellite; ~ **maintenu à poste** m ESPACE *véhicules* station keeping satellite; ~ **météorologique** m ESPACE *véhicules* meteorological satellite; ~ **naturel** m ASTRONOMIE natural satellite; ~ **d'observation** m ESPACE *véhicules* observation satellite; ~ **d'observation militaire** m ESPACE *véhicules* military observation satellite; ~ **d'observation de la Terre** m ESPACE *véhicules* Earth observation satellite; ~ **passif** m TV passive satellite; ~ **à plateforme contrarotative** m ESPACE *véhicules* dual-spin satellite; ~ **polyvalent** m ESPACE *véhicules* utility satellite; ~ **de radiodiffusion** m ESPACE *véhicules* broadcasting satellite, radio broadcast satellite; ~ **de radiodiffusion directe** m ESPACE, TV direct broadcast satellite; ~ **réflecteur** m ESPACE *véhicules* passive satellite, reflecting satellite; ~ **relais** m ESPACE, TV relay satellite; ~ **relais de données** m ESPACE *véhicules* DRS, data relay satellite; ~ **répéteur** m ESPACE *véhicules* repeater satellite; ~ **sous-synchrone** m ESPACE *véhicules* subsynchronous satellite; ~ **sur orbite équatoriale** m ESPACE *véhicules* equatorial orbiting satellite; ~ **de surveillance** m ESPACE *véhicules* monitoring satellite, surveillance satellite; ~ **synchrone** m ESPACE *véhicules* synchronous satellite; ~ **de télécommunications** m ESPACE *véhicules* communication satellite; ~ **de télécommunications maritimes** m ESPACE *véhicules* maritime satellite; ~ **de télédétection** m ESPACE *véhicules* remote sensing satellite; ~ **de télédétection terrestre** m ESPACE *véhicules* Earth remote sensing satellite; ~ **de télédiffusion** m ESPACE *véhicules* television broadcast satellite; ~ **terrestre** m ESPACE *véhicules* Earth satellite; ~ **de transmission directe** m TV real-time repeater satellite; ~ **de transmission en direct** m TELECOM DBS, direct broadcasting satellite; ~ **Uhuru** m ASTRONOMIE Uhuru satellite

Satellite: ~ **Explorer** m ASTRONOMIE Explorer satellite; ~ **Explorer pour l'étude dans l'ultraviolet** m ASTRONOMIE International Ultraviolet Explorer Satellite, IUE; ~ **international ultraviolet Explorer** m ASTRONOMIE International Ultraviolet Explorer Satellite

satellites: ~ **bergers de Saturne** m pl ASTRONOMIE Saturn's shepherd satellites; ~ **Cosmos** m pl ASTRONOMIE Cosmos satellites; ~ **galiléens** m pl ASTRONOMIE Galilean satellites; ~ **planétaires** m pl ASTRONOMIE planetary satellites

satin m TEXTILE satin

satinage m PAPIER smooth finish, supercalenderizing

satiné[1] adj EMBALLAGE glossy

satiné[2] m CERAM VER satin etch, EMBALLAGE gloss

satiner vt TEXTILE glaze

satineuse f EMBALLAGE calender

satisfaire: ~ **à** vt SECURITE meet

satnav m *(appareil de navigation par satellites)* NAUT satnav *(satellite navigator)*

saturation f CHIMIE, ELECTR *magnétisme*, ELECTRON, ELECTROTEC saturation, INFORMAT overflow, saturation, METEO, NUCLEAIRE saturation, ORDINAT overflow, saturation, PHYSIQUE, REFRIG, TV saturation; ~ **du blanc** f TV white saturation; ~ **des couleurs** f ELECTRON color saturation (AmE), colour saturation (BrE); ~ **de courant anodique** f ELECTROTEC anode saturation; ~ **d'eau** f PETR water saturation; ~ **en eau** f PETR water saturation; ~ **en eau irréductible** f PETR irreducible water saturation; ~ **en gaz** f PETR gas saturation; ~ **en huile** f PETR oil saturation; ~ **en huile résiduelle** f PETR ROS, residual oil saturation; ~ **en**

pétrole f PETR oil saturation; ~ **d'équilibre** f PETR equilibrium saturation; ~ **d'hydrocarbures** f PETR hydrocarbon saturation; ~ **magnétique** f ELECTR, ELECTROTEC magnetic saturation; ~ **magnétique ca** f ESSAIS magnetic saturation AC; ~ **magnétique cc** f ESSAIS magnetic saturation DC; ~ **numérique** f PETR flat topping; ~ **résiduelle en eau** f PETR residual water saturation; ~ **striée** f TV saturation banding; ~ **de température** f ELECTRON temperature saturation; ~ **d'un transistor** f ELECTRON transistor saturation

saturé adj CHIMIE saturated, saturate, CINEMAT, REFRIG saturated; ~ **d'eau** adj PAPIER saturated, soggy

sauce f IMPRIM *papier* coating mix; ~ **de couchage** f PAPIER coating color (AmE), coating colour (BrE), slip, slurry

saucier m CONS MECA *de cabestan* pawl bitt

saucisson m MINES dummy cartridge

sauf[1] adj SECURITE safe

sauf:[2] ~ **erreurs ou omissions** loc IMPRIM *devis, contrats* error and omissions excepted

saumâtre adj AGRO ALIM, CONSTR, DISTRI EAU *eau*, GEOLOGIE *milieu sédimentaire, faune* brackish, HYDROLOGIE brackish, briny, salty, *eau* brackish, saline, OCEANO *eau* brackish

saumon m AERONAUT *d'aéronef* wing tip, PRODUCTION ingot, pig; ~ **de fonte** m PRODUCTION pig of iron; ~ **de pale** m AERONAUT blade tip cap; ~ **de plomb** m PRODUCTION pig of lead; ~ **de voilure** m AERONAUT wing tip

saumurage m AGRO ALIM brine cooling, OCEANO brine pickling

saumure f CHIMIE, GAZ, HYDROLOGIE brine, NUCLEAIRE brine, saline solution, salt liquor, OCEANO brine, hot brines, REFRIG brine

saunerie f AGRO ALIM saltern, PRODUCTION salt refinery, salt works

saupoudrage m CHIMIE sprinkling; ~ **de cultures** m AERONAUT crop-dusting

saupoudrer vt AGRO ALIM dust, CHIMIE sprinkle

saurissage m OCEANO bloating, curing

saussurite f PETR saussurite

saut m HYDROLOGIE waterfall, INFORMAT jump, skip, METALL jump, ORDINAT branch, jump, skip; ~ **avec permutation** m ORDINAT exchange jump; ~ **de bande** m INFORMAT, ORDINAT tape skip; ~ **conditionnel** m ORDINAT conditional jump; ~ **en chute libre** m MILITAIRE *parachutage* free fall jump; ~ **inconditionnel** m INFORMAT, ORDINAT unconditional jump; ~ **d'indice équivalent** m OPTIQUE, TELECOM ESI refractive index difference; ~ **de ligne** m IMPRIM *imprimantes, photocomposeuses*, INFORMAT, ORDINAT, TELECOM LF, line feed; ~ **de mode** m OPTIQUE mode hopping, mode jumping, TELECOM mode hopping, mode jumping; ~ **de montage** m CINEMAT jump cut; ~ **de mouton** m CONSTR cattle grid, sheep's leap; ~ **de papier** m INFORMAT paper skip, paper slew (AmE), paper throw (BrE), ORDINAT paper skip; ~ **de pile** m PAPIER backfall; ~ **de potentiel** m PHYSIQUE voltage step; ~ **quantique** m PHYS PART quantum leap; ~ **de tension** m ELECTR voltage jump, PHYSIQUE voltage step

sautage m MINES blasting, shot-firing; ~ **en pochées** m MINES chambering, springing; ~ **par mines pochées** m MINES chambering, springing; ~ **par pans** m MINES bench blasting

saute f PETROLE surge

sauter[1] vt IMPRIM skip

sauter[2] *vi* NAUT *vent* shift, PRODUCTION fly, fly off; **~ en parachute** *vi* AERONAUT bail out, bale out

sauterelle *f* CONSTR apron conveyor, METROLOGIE bevel square, MINES loading belt, TRANSPORT apron conveyor; **~ graduée** *f* METROLOGIE bevel protractor

sauteuse *f* CONS MECA scroll saw, CONSTR jigsaw, PRODUCTION fret saw

sautillement *m* TV *de l'image* flutter, jitter

sauts: ~ de fréquence *m pl* TELECOM frequency hopping; **~ de fréquence rapides** *m pl* ELECTRON fast frequency hopping; **~ de fréquence du signal** *m pl* ELECTRON signal agility

sauvegarde:[1] **de ~** *adj* INFORMAT, ORDINAT backup

sauvegarde[2] *f* INFORMAT, ORDINAT save, POLLUTION safe keeping, PRODUCTION *mémoire* backup

sauvegarder *vt* IMPRIM record, INFORMAT, ORDINAT back up, save

sauver *vt* NAUT salvage, ORDINAT save, SECURITE rescue

sauvetage *m* NAUT rescue, *d'un navire* salvage, SECURITE rescue; **~ aérien en mer** *m* NAUT air-sea rescue; **~ aéromaritime** *m* NAUT air-sea rescue; **~ air-mer** *m* NAUT air-sea rescue; **~ des naufragés d'un désastre aérien** *m* MILITAIRE air-sea rescue

sauveteur *m* NAUT lifeboatman

saveur *f* AGRO ALIM flavor (AmE), flavour (BrE); **~ de quark** *f* PHYS PART flavor of quark (AmE), flavour of quark (BrE)

savoir-faire *m* BREVETS, CONSTR know-how

savon *m* CHIMIE, TEXTILE soap; **~ dégraisseur** *m* LESSIVES scouring soap; **~ de montagne** *m* MINERAUX mountain soap; **~ ponce** *m* LESSIVES pumice soap; **~ de récurage** *m* LESSIVES scrubbing soap

savonnage *m* CERAM VER smoothing

savoyarde *f* TRANSPORT tilt-type semitrailer

Sb *(antimoine)* CHIMIE Sb *(stibium)*

Sc *(scandium)* CHIMIE Sc *(scandium)*

scalaire[1] *adj* INFORMAT, MATH, ORDINAT scalar

scalaire[2] *m* MATH, PHYSIQUE scalar

SCAM *abrév (sens contraire des aiguilles d'une montre)* CONS MECA CCW *(counterclockwise)*

scandium *m (Sc)* CHIMIE scandium *(Sc)*

scannage *m* ESPACE scanning

scanner *m* IMPRIM, INFORMAT, ORDINAT, PHYS RAYON scanner; **~ à balayage** *m* PHYS RAYON radar scanner; **~ de code à barres** *m* ORDINAT bar code scanner; **~ holographique** *m* ORDINAT holographic scanner; **~ optique** *m* ORDINAT optical scanner; **~ à plat** *m* INFORMAT, ORDINAT flat-bed scanner; **~ à tambour** *m* IMPRIM *photogravure* drum scanner

scannériser *vt* INFORMAT scan

scanneur *m* INFORMAT, TV scanner

scanning *m* IMPRIM electronic scanning

scanographie *f* PHYS RAYON scanning; **~ à haute résolution** *f* PHYS RAYON high-resolution scan; **~ microscopique aux ions** *f* PHYS RAYON scanning ion microscopy

scaphandre *m* ESPACE *véhicules* full-pressure suit, OCEANO diving suit, PETR wetsuit; **~ articulé** *m* OCEANO articulated diving suit; **~ autonome** *m* NAUT scuba, OCEANO aqualung; **~ spatial** *m* ESPACE spacesuit

scaphandrier *m* OCEANO, PETR diver

scapolite *f* MINERAUX scapolite

scarificateur *m* CONSTR lawn rake kit, scarifier, TRANSPORT road plough (BrE), road plow (AmE), road ripper, scarifier

scarification *f* CONSTR scarification

scarifier *vt* CONSTR scarify

scatol *m* CHIMIE skatol, skatole

scatolcarbonique *adj* CHIMIE skatolecarboxylic

scatoxylsulfate *m* CHIMIE skatoxylsulfate (AmE), skatoxylsulphate (BrE)

scatoxylsulfurique *adj* CHIMIE skatoxylsulfuric (AmE), skatoxylsulphuric (BrE)

scellage *m* CERAM VER laying up, laying yard, CONSTR scaling, sealing up, IMPRIM *emballage* heat seal; **~ à chaud** *m* PLAST CAOU heat sealing; **~ sur plâtre** *m* (Fra) *(cf plâtrage)* CERAM VER laying on plaster; **~ sur toile** *m* CERAM VER laying on cloth; **~ à vide** *m* CONS MECA vacuum seal

scellé[1] *adj* POLLU MER sealed

scellé:[2] **~ à froid** *m* IMPRIM *emballage* coldseal; **~ de sécurité** *m* SECURITE tamperproof seal

scellement *m* CONSTR sealing, NUCLEAIRE encapsulation, SECURITE bolting; **~ à coulis** *m* CONSTR slurry seal; **~ hermétique** *m* TELECOM hermetic sealing; **~ par boulons** *m* SECURITE bolting; **~ à sable** *m* CONSTR sand seal

sceller *vt* NAUT seal, PRODUCTION seal, seal up

scénario *m* CINEMAT scenario, screenplay, script, treatment, INFORMAT, ORDINAT script, PRODUCTION scenario

scénariste *m* TV script writer

scène: ~ en direct *f* CINEMAT live action; **~ glace** *f* CINEMAT glass shot; **~ de liaison** *f* CINEMAT connecting scene; **~ sonore** *f* ENREGISTR sound stage

scheelite *f* MINERAUX scheelite

scheelitine *f* MINERAUX scheelitine

scheerérite *f* MINERAUX scheererite

schefférite *f* MINERAUX schefferite

scheidage *m* CHARBON sorting; **~ d'épuration** *m* MINES ragging; **~ préalable** *m* MINES ragging; **~ préliminaire** *m* MINES ragging

scheider *vt* CHARBON cull by hand, sort by hand, cull, hand-pick, MINES cull, sort

schéma *m* CONS MECA scheme, ELECTRON, ESPACE pattern, ORDINAT schema, PRODUCTION diagram; **~ de balayage de radar** *m* TRANSPORT radar scan pattern; **~ de branchement** *m* ELECTROTEC connection diagram; **~ de branchement d'entrée** *m* PRODUCTION input connection diagram; **~ de câblage** *m* AUTO, ELECTR, TELECOM wiring diagram, TV circuit diagram; **~ de chargement de la bande** *m* ENREGISTR tape transport geometry; **~ cinématique** *m* CONS MECA kinematic diagram; **~ de circuit** *m* ELECTROTEC circuit diagram; **~ du circuit de combustible** *m* NAUT fuel system diagram; **~ du circuit électrique** *m* NAUT electrical wiring diagram; **~ des circuits** *m* NUCLEAIRE schematic wiring diagram; **~ des connexions** *m* ELECTR *d'un circuit* circuit diagram; **~ des connexions de base** *m* NUCLEAIRE *d'un circuit* basic circuit diagram; **~ de distribution** *m* AUTO timing diagram; **~ équivalent** *m* ELECTRON, ELECTROTEC equivalent circuit; **~ d'exploitation d'un réseau** *m* ELECTR system operational diagram; **~ fonctionnel** *m* INFORMAT functional diagram, ORDINAT block diagram; **~ fonctionnel synoptique** *m* ELECTROTEC block diagram; **~ d'impédance** *m* ESSAIS impedance diagram; **~ de lavage** *m* MINES flow sheet; **~ logique** *m* ELECTRON, INFORMAT, PRODUCTION *automatisme industriel* logic diagram; **~ de montage** *m* CONS MECA assembly plan, PRODUCTION mounting layout; **~ de principe** *m* CONS MECA block diagram, functional diagram, PETROLE *ingé-*

niérie, organigramme flow sheet; ~ **des quarks et des leptons** m PHYS PART quark-lepton scheme; ~ **à relais** m PRODUCTION automatisme industriel ladder diagram; ~ **d'un réseau** m ELECTR system diagram; ~ **synoptique** m TELECOM block diagram; ~ **de temporisation** m PRODUCTION automatisme industriel timing diagram; ~ **de traitement** m CHARBON flow sheet; ~ **unifilaire** m ELECTR réseau single line diagram

schème m PRODUCTION diagram

schiste m PETROLE shale; ~ **argileux à graptolites** m GEOLOGIE graptolitic shale; ~ **bitumineux** m GEOLOGIE bituminous shale, kerogenite, PETR oil shale; ~ **bleu** m GEOLOGIE blue schist; ~ **charbonneux** m GEOLOGIE carbonaceous shale; ~ **à glaucophane** m GEOLOGIE blue schist; ~ **lustré** m GEOLOGIE lustrous schist; ~ **tacheté** m GEOLOGIE métamorphisme de contact spotted slate; ~ **vert** m GEOLOGIE roche métamorphique ou faciès greenschist

schisteux adj GEOLOGIE foliated, schistose, shaly

schistosité f GEOLOGIE cleavage, foliation, des schistes cristallins schistosity; ~ **de fracturation** f GEOLOGIE axial plane foliation

schlague f CERAM VER stringy knot

schlamms m CHARBON slime, slurry, PRODUCTION sludge; ~ **épais** m CHARBON thickened slime, thickened slurry

schoopage m REVETEMENT metal coating

schorl m MINERAUX schorl; ~ **rouge** m MINERAUX red schorl

schreibersite f MINERAUX schreibersite

schuilingite f NUCLEAIRE schuilingite

schwarzembergite f MINERAUX schwarzembergite

schwatzite f MINERAUX schwatzite

sciage m CERAM VER sawing out, CONSTR sawing, bois saw timber; ~ **du diamant** m PRODUCTION diamond cleaving; ~ **électrique** m NUCLEAIRE electrical sawing

scie f CONS MECA, MECANIQUE outillage saw; ~ **alternative** f PRODUCTION reciprocating saw; ~ **alternative à main** f PRODUCTION handpower hacksaw; ~ **alternative à tronçonner** f PRODUCTION crosscut saw, log crosscutting machine; ~ **à arc** f NUCLEAIRE arc saw; ~ **à base de diamant** f CONS MECA diamond saw; ~ **à base de nitrure de bore** f CONS MECA cubic boron nitride saw; ~ **à béton** f CONSTR concrete saw; ~ **à bûches** f CONSTR wood saw; ~ **à chaîne** f CONS MECA chain saw; ~ **à chantourner** f CONS MECA scroll saw, turning saw, CONSTR jigsaw, PRODUCTION fret saw; ~ **à châssis** f PRODUCTION frame saw; ~ **circulaire** f CONS MECA annular saw, circular saw; ~ **circulaire à axe fixe** f PRODUCTION fixed spindle circular saw bench; ~ **circulaire à segments rapportés** f CONS MECA segmental circular saw; ~ **continue** f CONS MECA continuous saw; ~ **à couper en travers** f PRODUCTION crosscut saw; ~ **à découper** f CONSTR jigsaw, PRODUCTION fret saw, fret saw blade; ~ **à découper électrique** f PRODUCTION fret saw; ~ **à dents** f CONS MECA saw with teeth; ~ **à diamants** f CERAM VER diamond slitting wheel; ~ **à dos** f CONSTR back saw, tenon saw; ~ **égoïne** f CONSTR handsaw; ~ **à élaguer** f CONS MECA pruning saw; ~ **électrique** f ELECTR outil electric saw; ~ **d'entre-lames** f CONS MECA undercutting saw; ~ **à froid** f CONS MECA cold saw; ~ **à guichet** f CONSTR compass saw, keyhole saw, lock saw; ~ **de long** f PRODUCTION long saw; ~ **à main** f CONSTR handsaw; ~ **mécanique** f CONS MECA power saw, sawing machine; ~ **à métaux** f CONS MECA hacksaw, hacksaw frame, MECANIQUE outillage hack-

saw, PRODUCTION metal saw; ~ **mobile** f SECURITE moving saw; ~ **à mouvement alternatif** f CONS MECA alternating saw, hacksaw; ~ **ordinaire** f PRODUCTION frame saw; ~ **passe-partout** f PRODUCTION crosscut saw; ~ **à plusieurs lames** f PRODUCTION gang saw; ~ **de poche** f CONS MECA flexible wire saw; ~ **à raccourcir** f CONSTR tenon saw; ~ **à refendre** f CONSTR cleaving saw; ~ **à ruban** f CONS MECA band-saw, band-sawing machine; ~ **à ruban pour le débit des bois en grume** f PRODUCTION log band mill; ~ **à ruban verticale** f CONS MECA vertical handsaw; ~ **segmentée** f CONS MECA pour l'usinage de la pierre segmented saw; ~ **à tenon** f CONSTR back saw, tenon saw; ~ **à tôles** f CONS MECA plate saw; ~ **à tourner** f CONSTR compass saw; ~ **de travers** f PRODUCTION crosscut saw; ~ **trépan** f CONS MECA hole saw; ~ **verticale alternative à plusieurs lames** f PRODUCTION log frame

science: ~ **de l'alimentation** f AGRO ALIM food science; ~ **des aliments** f AGRO ALIM food science; ~ **de l'eau** f DISTRI EAU hydroscience; ~ **de l'ingénieur** f CONS MECA engineering; ~ **sonique** f ENREGISTR sonics; ~ **des ultrasons** f PHYS ONDES ultrasonics

scientifique adj CHIMIE scientific

scier vt MECANIQUE saw; ~ **en travers** vt PRODUCTION crosscut

scierie f CONSTR, MINES sawmill

scintillateur m ASTRONOMIE, PHYS RAYON scintillator

scintillation f ASTRONOMIE, ESPACE, PHYSIQUE scintillation, TELECOM flutter, scintillation; ~ **ionosphérique** f ASTRONOMIE ionospheric scintillation

scintillement m ACOUSTIQUE flutter, CINEMAT flicker, ENREGISTR flutter, INFORMAT, ORDINAT flicker, PRODUCTION sparkling, TV image flicker; ~ **de chrominance** m TV chroma flutter

scintiller vi CINEMAT flicker

sciure f CONSTR sawdust; ~ **de bois** f CONSTR sawdust

scléroclase f MINERAUX scleroclase

scléromètre m PHYSIQUE sclerometer

scléroprotéine f AGRO ALIM scleroprotein

scolécite f MINERAUX scolecite

scooter m TRANSPORT motor scooter, scooter; ~ **sous-marin** m OCEANO minisubmersible

scopolamine f CHIMIE hyoscine

scorie f CHIMIE scum, GEOLOGIE volcaniques scoria, volcanic cinders, METALL, PAPIER slag, PRODUCTION cinder, clinker; ~ **de forge** f PRODUCTION cinder

scories f pl PRODUCTION dans poches ou moules sullage; ~ **de forge** f pl PRODUCTION forge scale, hammer slag, hammer scale, iron scale, nill, scale; ~ **de hauts fourneaux** f pl PRODUCTION blast furnace slag; ~ **de laminoir** f pl PRODUCTION mill scale, roll scale

scorodite f MINERAUX scorodite

Scorpion m ASTRONOMIE Scorpius, the Scorpion

scotch m CINEMAT splicing tape

scraper m CONS MECA, CONSTR scraper, PETR pig; ~ **à bras radial** m HYDROLOGIE radial sludge tank

scraps m pl PRODUCTION scrap; ~ **de fonderie** m pl PRODUCTION cast scrap, foundry scrap, scrap

scripte f IMPRIM script

scrutateur: ~ **des E/S** m PRODUCTION automatisme industriel I/O scanner; ~ **mécanique** m ELECTROTEC scanning switch

scrutation f ORDINAT polling; ~ **d'essai continue** f PRODUCTION automatisme industriel test continuous scan; ~ **gamma du combustible** f NUCLEAIRE gamma fuel scanning; ~ **par appel** f INFORMAT roll call polling; ~

par appel de terminaux *f* ORDINAT roll call polling; ~ **par passage de témoin** *f* ORDINAT hub polling; ~ **de programme** *f* PRODUCTION *automatisme industriel* program scanning (AmE), programme scanning (BrE); ~ **unique d'essai** *f* PRODUCTION *automatisme industriel* test single scan

scruter *vt* PRODUCTION *automatisme industriel* scan

scruteur *m* ELECTROTEC commutator

Sculpteur *m* ASTRONOMIE Sculptor

sculpture *f* VEHICULES *pneu* tread design

SDS *abrév (surdébit de section)* TELECOM SOH *(section overhead)*

SDSM *abrév (surdébit de section de multiplexage)* TELECOM multiplex section overhead

SDSR *abrév (surdébit de section de régénération)* TELECOM regenerator section overhead

Se *(sélénium)* CHIMIE Se *(selenium)*

séance: ~ **d'enregistrement** *f* ENREGISTR recording session; ~ **d'enregistrement de musique** *f* ENREGISTR scoring session; ~ **de mixage** *f* ENREGISTR rerecording session

seau *m* CONSTR, EQUIP LAB *récipient*, INST HYDR bucket; ~ **au benne à câble** *m* CONSTR bucket; ~ **plein** *m* CONSTR bucketful

sébacique *adj* CHIMIE sebacic

sébile *f* MINES pan

sec[1] *adj* TEXTILE dry, THERMODYN dried, dry; **au ~** *adj* NAUT aground; ~ **absolu** *adj* PAPIER bone dry, oven-dry; ~ **à l'absolu** *adj* TEXTILE bone dry

sec:[2] **au ~** *adv* NAUT aground

SECAM *abrév (séquentiel couleur à mémoire)* TV SECAM

sécant *adj* GEOLOGIE crosscutting, cutting, GEOMETRIE secant

sécante *f* GEOMETRIE secant, *d'un angle* secant

séchage:[1] **à ~ rapide** *adj* EMBALLAGE, TEXTILE quick-drying

séchage[2] *m* AGRO ALIM desiccation, CHARBON, CHIMIE drying, MAT CHAUFF dehumidification, PAPIER, PETROLE, PLAST CAOU *procédé*, TEXTILE, THERMODYN drying; ~ **à l'air** *m* IMPRIM air drying; ~ **entraînant une perte de brillant** *m* IMPRIM *d'une encre* dry down; ~ **à l'étuve** *m* CONSTR kiln drying; ~ **au four** *m* REVETEMENT stoving; ~ **de mousse** *m* AGRO ALIM foam mat drying; ~ **de mousse sous vide** *m* AGRO ALIM foam vacuum drying; ~ **par convection** *m* THERMODYN convection drying; ~ **par convection forcée** *m* IMPRIM forced convection edge; ~ **par distillation** *m* MATERIAUX distillation drying; ~ **par pulvérisation** *m* LESSIVES spray drying; ~ **par soufflage** *m* CINEMAT impingement drying; ~ **à plaques sous vide** *m* AGRO ALIM vacuum contact plate process; ~ **sous vide** *m* AGRO ALIM vacuum drying; ~ **de surface par bombardement d'électrons** *m* IMPRIM EBC, electron beam curing; ~ **de surface par faisceau d'électrons** *m* IMPRIM EBC, electron beam curing

séché *adj* AGRO ALIM desiccated, THERMODYN dried; ~ **à l'air** *adj* AGRO ALIM, EMBALLAGE, IMPRIM *papier*, PAPIER air-dried; ~ **au four** *adj* PRODUCTION kiln dried, THERMODYN kiln dried, oven-dried; ~ **par congélation** *adj* GENIE CHIM freeze-dried; ~ **par pulvérisation** *adj* LESSIVES spray-dried

sécher[1] *vt* CHARBON dry, SECURITE air, THERMODYN dry out, dry; ~ **à l'air** *vt* PAPIER air-dry; ~ **à la chaleur** *vt* THERMODYN dry by heat; ~ **au four** *vt* THERMODYN kiln dry; ~ **par de l'air froid** *vt* THERMODYN dry by cold air; ~

par chauffage *vt* THERMODYN dry by heat

sécher[2] *vi* CHARBON dry

sécheresse *f* TEXTILE dryness

sécherie *f* PAPIER dryer section; ~ **à cylindres sécheurs superposés** *f* PAPIER bank of dryers, stacked dryer section; ~ **à feuille aéroportée** *f* PAPIER air float dryer; ~ **monocylindrique** *f* PAPIER yankee dryer; ~ **multicylindrique** *f* PAPIER multicylinder dryer section

sécheur *m* CHARBON, CONS MECA dryer, EMBALLAGE drying oven, IMPRIM *rotative*, THERMODYN dryer; ~ **à air** *m* IMPRIM air dryer; ~ **à coussins d'air** *m* IMPRIM air flotation dryer; ~ **embarqueur** *m* PAPIER baby dryer; ~ **de feutre** *m* PAPIER felt dryer; ~ **frictionneur** *m* PAPIER yankee dryer; ~ **à infrarouge** *m* IMPRIM infrared dryer; ~ **à lattes** *m* PAPIER slat dryer; ~ **pour bandes transporteuses** *m* GENIE CHIM belt dryer; ~ **pour moule abrasif** *m* CONS MECA dryer for grinding wheel; ~ **rotatif** *m* THERMODYN *à tambour* drum dryer; ~ **rotatif à mazout** *m* MAT CHAUFF *station d'enrobage* oil-fired rotary dryer; ~ **à rouleaux** *m* IMPRIM roller dryer; ~ **à tambour** *m* CHARBON drum dryer, GENIE CHIM granulator; ~ **de vapeur** *m* INST HYDR steam dryer; ~ **à vide** *m* CHARBON vacuum dryer

sécheuse *f* EMBALLAGE drying machine, IMPRIM dryer, PHOTO print dryer; ~ **de film** *f* CINEMAT film drying machine

sécheuse-glaceuse *f* PHOTO dryer glazer

séchoir *m* AGRO ALIM desiccator, drying cupboard, drying kiln, drying oven, CHIMIE, CONS MECA, IMPRIM *papier* dryer, MAT CHAUFF dehumidifier, PRODUCTION drying chamber, drying house, drying room, drying stove, TEXTILE dryer, tumbledryer, THERMODYN dryer; ~ **à convection** *m* THERMODYN convection dryer; ~ **à cylindre** *m* AGRO ALIM drum dryer; ~ **à deux cylindres** *m* AGRO ALIM double drum dryer; ~ **électrique** *m* ELECTR *appareil*, MAT CHAUFF electric dryer; ~ **en lit fluidisé** *m* GENIE CHIM, MAT CHAUFF *combustion* fluidized bed dryer; ~ **de film** *m* PHOTO film dryer; ~ **filtre** *m* GENIE CHIM filter dryer; ~ **à lit fluidisé** *m* AGRO ALIM fluidized bed dryer; ~ **par rayonnement** *m* PAPIER radiant dryer; ~ **par tambours perforés** *m* GENIE CHIM sieve dryer; ~ **rotatif** *m* AGRO ALIM drum dryer, PRODUCTION rotary dryer; ~ **à soufflage d'air chaud** *m* TEXTILE hot air impingement dryer; ~ **sous vide** *m* AGRO ALIM vacuum dryer; ~ **à tambour** *m* AGRO ALIM, TEXTILE drum dryer; ~ **tubulaire** *m* TEXTILE tubular dryer

séchoir-tunnel *m* AGRO ALIM drying tunnel

second *m* NAUT first mate, first officer; ~ **amplificateur à fréquence intermédiaire** *m* ELECTRON second IF amplifier; ~ **capitaine** *m* NAUT mate; ~ **choix** *m* IMPRIM *papier* diamond, TEXTILE trash; ~ **développement** *m* CINEMAT redevelopment; ~ **maître** *m* NAUT petty officer; ~ **membre** *m* MATH, PHYSIQUE *d'une équation* right-hand side; ~ **oscillateur local** *m* ELECTRON second local oscillator; ~ **taraud** *m* CONS MECA plug tap, second tap; ~ **voisin** *m* CRISTALL second nearest neighbor (AmE), second nearest neighbour (BrE)

secondaire[1] *adj* PHYS RAYON secondary

secondaire:[2] ~ **du transformateur** *m* PRODUCTION *automatisme industriel* transformer secondary

seconde:[1] ~ **anode** *adj* ELECTROTEC second anode; ~ **fréquence intermédiaire** *adj* ELECTRON second intermediate frequency; **de ~ génération** *adj* INFORMAT, ORDINAT second generation

seconde[2] *f* ACOUSTIQUE, METROLOGIE, PHYSIQUE second;

~ d'angle *f* CONSTR second, PHYSIQUE arc second, second; **~ d'arc** *f* ASTRONOMIE arc second; **~ avec erreur** *f* TELECOM ES, errored second; **~ avec perte de trame** *f* TELECOM FLS, frame loss second; **~ gravement erronée** *f* NAUT, TELECOM SES, severely errored second; **~ d'indisponibilité** *f* TELECOM UAS, unavailable second; **~ majeure** *f* ACOUSTIQUE major second; **~ mineure** *f* ACOUSTIQUE minor second; **~ de perte du verrouillage de trame** *f* TELECOM OFS, out-of-frame second

seconde-lumière *f* ASTRONOMIE light second

seconds: ~ voisins *m pl* METALL next nearest neighbors (AmE), next nearest neighbours (BrE)

secourir *vt* SECURITE rescue

secouriste *m* SECURITE *personne* first aider

secours:[1] **de ~** *adj* ESPACE *véhicules* emergency, INFORMAT backup, stand-by, MECANIQUE emergency, ORDINAT backup, PRODUCTION standing by, SECURITE emergency INFORMAT backup

secours[2] *m* SECURITE assistance, rescue; **~ d'urgence** *m pl* SECURITE first aid

secousse *f* CONS MECA jerk, shake, shaking, shock, ESPACE buffet, jerk, shock, *véhicules* judder, PRODUCTION jar, jarring; **~ électrique** *f* SECURITE electric shock

secousses *f pl* AERONAUT buffeting

secret: ~ des conversations *m* TELECOM voice privacy; **~ de l'identité du demandeur** *m* TELECOM calling line identification restriction

secrétaire: ~ de plateau *m* CINEMAT script person

secteur *m* CONSTR sector, ELECTROTEC grid, power grid, GEOMETRIE, INFORMAT, NAUT *d'un feu*, ORDINAT, PETROLE sector, VEHICULES *boîte automatique* gate; **~ brassicole** *m* AGRO ALIM brewing industry; **~ de changement de marche** *m* CONS MECA quadrant; **~ de contrôle** *m* AERONAUT *circulation* control sector; **~ crénelé** *m* CONS MECA quadrant, toothed sector, toothed segment, sectorgear, sector wheel, segment gear; **~ denté** *m* AUTO sector gear, CONS MECA quadrant, toothed segment, sector gear, sector wheel, segment gear, toothed sector, VEHICULES *direction* sector gear; **~ denté de l'appareil de mise en marche** *m* CONS MECA quadrant; **~ de disque** *m* INFORMAT, ORDINAT disk sector; **~ du gouvernail** *m* NAUT rudder quadrant; **~ de manette** *m* AERONAUT control lever quadrant; **~ maritime** *m* NAUT maritime industry; **~ des produits de consommation** *m* EMBALLAGE consumer goods sector; **~ spatial** *m* ESPACE *communications, gestion* space segment; **~ sphérique** *m* GEOMETRIE spherical sector; **~ terrien** *m* ESPACE *communications, gestion* ground segment; **~ des transports maritimes** *m* NAUT maritime industry

secteurs: à ~ fixes *adj* ORDINAT *disque* hard-sectored

section *f* CONS MECA cross section, section, CONSTR *d'un bâtiment* vertical section, DISTRI EAU *d'un cours d'eau, d'un canal découvert* cross section, *d'une rivière* reach, GEOMETRIE, INFORMAT section, MATERIAUX cross section, NAUT, ORDINAT, PETR section, PRODUCTION section, *d'une poutre, d'un rail* cross section, TEXTILE section; **~ d'absorption zéro de neutrons** *f* NUCLEAIRE zero neutron-absorption cross section; **~ administrative** *f* CONSTR administrative area; **~ arrière** *f* NAUT aft section; **~ atomique efficace** *f* NUCLEAIRE atomic cross section; **~ de bobine** *f* ELECTR coil section; **~ de câble** *f* ELECTROTEC cable section; **~ de capture** *f* PETR capture cross section; **~ centrale de voilure** *f* AERONAUT center wing section (AmE), centre wing section (BrE); **~ de**

chemin de fer *f* TRANSPORT railroad line (AmE), railway line (BrE); **~ de contraction** *f* INST HYDR contracted section; **~ critique** *f* INFORMAT, ORDINAT critical section; **~ dangereuse** *f* CONS MECA *résistance des matériaux* section of maximum intensity of stress; **~ droite** *f* NAUT cross section; **~ effective** *f* MECANIQUE effective cross-sectional area; **~ efficace** *f* PHYSIQUE cross section; **~ efficace de diffusion** *f* PHYSIQUE scattering cross section; **~ efficace de fission** *f* PHYSIQUE fission cross section; **~ efficace de Thomson** *f* PHYSIQUE Thomson cross section; **~ d'égale résistance** *f* CONS MECA section of uniform strength; **~ d'encastrement** *f* CONSTR *d'une poutre, d'une colonne* embedment; **~ de l'equipement** *f* CH DE FER Way and Works Department (BrE); **~ horizontale** *f* NAUT *du plan des formes* waterplane; **~ libre de passage d'air** *f* REFRIG free area; **~ macroscopique efficace** *f* NUCLEAIRE cross section density, macroscopic cross section; **~ maximale des câbles** *f* PRODUCTION terminal capacity; **~ de multiplexage** *f* TELECOM MS, multiplex section; **~ neutre** *f* CH DE FER *voie* dead sector, neutral section; **~ nominale de passage** *f* NUCLEAIRE NB, nominal bore; **~ numérique** *f* TELECOM DS, digital section; **~ d'or** *f* GEOMETRIE golden section; **~ de la pale** *f* AERONAUT blade cross section; **~ radar** *f* AERONAUT radar unit; **~ rectangulaire** *f* CONSTR rectangular cross section; **~ de régénération** *f* TELECOM RS, regenerator section; **~ retouches** *f* PRODUCTION rework center (AmE), rework centre (BrE); **~ de segment** *f* AUTO ring joint; **~ de surrégénération** *f* NUCLEAIRE breeding section; **~ tampon** *f* CH DE FER overlap section; **~ totale** *f* REFRIG core area; **~ transversale** *f* CONS MECA, METALL cross section, NAUT midship section, transverse section, PRODUCTION *d'une poutre, d'un rail* cross section, TELECOM transverse section, TEXTILE cross section; **~ de tube** *f* PETR joint; **~ de tuyère** *f* ESPACE *propulsion* nozzle area; **~ utile** *f* MECANIQUE effective cross-sectional area

sectionné *adj* CONS MECA sectional

sectionnel *adj* CONS MECA, GEOMETRIE sectional

sectionnement *m* ELECTR *réseau d'alimentation* sectionalization

sectionneur *m* CH DE FER cutout, disconnector, ELECTR *interrupteur* disconnecting switch, *réseau d'alimentation* sectionalizing switch, ELECTROTEC disconnecting switch, isolating switch, PRODUCTION *électricité* disconnect switch; **~ à actionneur rotatif** *m* PRODUCTION rod operated disconnect switch; **~ d'alimentation secteur** *m* PRODUCTION *automatisme industriel* main power disconnect; **~ de barres** *m* ELECTR *commutateur* busbar sectionalizing switch; **~ de câble** *m* ELECTROTEC cable isolator; **~ à coupure en charge** *m* ELECTR *commutateur* load switch; **~ de ligne** *m* ELECTR *réseau d'alimentation* line isolating switch; **~ de protection** *m* ELECTROTEC isolating switch; **~ de terre** *m* ELECTR *commutateur* earthing switch (BrE), grounding switch (AmE)

sections: ~ horizontales *f pl* NAUT water lines; **~ longitudinales** *f pl* NAUT buttock lines, buttocks; **~ obliques** *f pl* NAUT diagonal lines; **~ transversales** *f pl* NAUT ordinates, stations

sectorisation:[1] **à ~ logicielle** *adj* INFORMAT soft-sectored; **à ~ matérielle** *adj* INFORMAT *disque* hard-sectored

sectorisation:[2] **~ logicielle** *f* INFORMAT, ORDINAT soft sectoring; **~ matérielle** *f* INFORMAT, ORDINAT hard sectoring

sectorisé: ~ matériellement adj ORDINAT hard-sectored; **~ par programme** adj ORDINAT soft-sectored

séculaire adj GEOPHYS secular

sécurisé adj INFORMAT trusted

sécurité:[1] **en ~** adj SECURITE safe; **à ~ intégrée** adj ESPACE integrated safety, MECANIQUE fail-safe; **à ~ intrinsèque** adj ELECTROTEC fail-safe, intrinsically safe, ESPACE fail-safe

sécurité[2] f INFORMAT security, MECANIQUE safety, ORDINAT, PRODUCTION security, QUALITE safety, SECURITE safety, *condition, sentiment* security; **~ active des véhicules automobiles** f TRANSPORT active motor vehicle safety; **~ anti-incendie** f SECURITE fire safety; **~ du cyclotron** f PHYS RAYON cyclotron safety; **~ en usinage** f SECURITE safety in working; **~ de fichier** f INFORMAT, ORDINAT file security; **~ de fonctionnement** f CONS MECA reliability; **~ informatique** f INFORMAT, ORDINAT computer security; **~ intrinsèque** f COMMANDE fail-safe system; **~ maritime** f NAUT maritime safety; **~ de la navigation aérienne par radar** f TRANSPORT radar air traffic control; **~ de la navigation fluviale** f NAUT river safety; **~ nucléaire** f SECURITE nuclear safety; **~ passive des véhicules automobiles** f TRANSPORT passive motor vehicle safety; **~ physique** f TELECOM physical security; **~ du public** f SECURITE crowd safety; **~ des routes** f SECURITE road safety; **~ routière** f CONSTR, TRANSPORT road safety; **~ du système** f INFORMAT, ORDINAT system security; **~ de transmission** f INFORMAT, ORDINAT transmission security; **~ au travail** f SECURITE industrial safety, occupational safety, safety at work, work safety

sédentaire adj CHARBON sedentary

sédiment m CHARBON sediment, CHIMIE deposit, sediment, settlings, DISTRI EAU sediment, GENIE CHIM precipitate, sediment, PETROLE, RECYCLAGE sediment; **~ détritique** m GEOLOGIE clastic rocks, OCEANO detrital sediment; **~ marin** m OCEANO marine sediment

sédimentation f CHARBON settling, CHIMIE, DISTRI EAU, PETROLE, PHYSIQUE, PLAST CAOU *pigments, charges,* POLLUTION, RECYCLAGE sedimentation; **~ biogénique** f GEOLOGIE biogenic sedimentation; **~ chimique** f GEOLOGIE chemical sedimentation; **~ rythmique avec séquences** f GEOLOGIE cyclic sedimentation

sédimenter vi CHARBON, GENIE CHIM settle

sédiments: ~ argileux déposés en avant d'un delta m pl GEOLOGIE prodelta clays; **~ de forage** m pl CHARBON chippings, drilling debris, cuttings; **~ de prodelta** m pl GEOLOGIE prodelta clays; **~ à stratification inclinée dans la direction du cou** m pl GEOLOGIE coset deposits

segment m AUTO ring, CONS MECA, GEOMETRIE, INFORMAT, ORDINAT segment, VEHICULES *d'un piston* ring, *d'un frein* shoe; **~ du collecteur** m ELECTROTEC commutator segment; **~ de compression** m VEHICULES *du moteur, du piston* compression ring; **~ conique** m AUTO tapered compression ring; **~ de droite** m GEOMETRIE line segment; **~ de feu** m AUTO, VEHICULES *d'un piston* top compression ring; **~ de frein** m AUTO, MECANIQUE, VEHICULES brake shoe; **~ ISA** m TELECOM ISA segment; **~ de piston** m AUTO, CONS MECA piston ring, INST HYDR ring, MECANIQUE, VEHICULES *moteur* piston ring; **~ de près** m CERAM VER short vision segment; **~ primaire** m AUTO primary shoe; **~ de programme** m INFORMAT, ORDINAT program part; **~ racleur** m AUTO, VEHICULES *d'un piston* oil control ring; **~ racleur à expansion** m AUTO oil expander ring; **~ racleur à fentes** m AUTO slotted oil control ring; **~ racleur à trois pièces** m AUTO three-piece oil control ring; **~ secondaire** m AUTO secondary sleeve; **~ tendu** m VEHICULES *d'un frein* trailing shoe; **~ de transition** m AERONAUT *atterrissage* transition segment; **~ UNA** m TELECOM UNA segment; **~ UNB** m TELECOM UNB segment; **~ UNH** m TELECOM UNH segment

segmentaire adj GEOMETRIE segmental

segmentation f CHIMIE segmentation, GAZ merogenesis, INFORMAT, ORDINAT segmentation; **~ et réassemblage** f TELECOM SAR, segmentation and reassembly; **~ et réassemblage sous-couche** f TELECOM segmentation and reassembly sublayer

segmenté adj ORDINAT partitioned

segmenter vt INFORMAT segment, ORDINAT partition, segment

segments m pl CONS MECA *de piston* packing rings

ségrégation f CERAM VER, CHIMIE, CONSTR, MATERIAUX, NUCLEAIRE segregation

seiche f EN RENOUV *du niveau de l'eau* seiche, OCEANO bore, seiche

seille f CONSTR bucket

séisme m GEOPHYS earthquake; **~ anthropogénique** m POLLUTION man-made earthquake; **~ sous-marin** m OCEANO seaquake

séismicité f ESPACE seismicity, GEOLOGIE seismic activity, GEOPHYS seismicity

séismique adj CONSTR, GEOPHYS, PETROLE seismic

séismogénique adj GEOPHYS seismogenic

séismogramme m PETR seismogram

séismographe m CONSTR, GAZ seismograph, GEOPHYS horizontal seismograph, seismometer, PHYSIQUE seismograph; **~ horizontal** m GEOPHYS horizontal seismograph, seismometer; **~ vertical** m GEOPHYS vertical seismograph

séismologie f GEOPHYS, PHYSIQUE seismology

séismologiste f GEOPHYS seismologist

séismologue f GEOPHYS seismologist

séismomètre m GEOPHYS horizontal seismograph, seismometer

séismosondage m PETROLE checkshot

séismotectonique f GEOPHYS seismotectonics

sel m CHIMIE halide, salt, PETROLE salt; **~ acide** m AGRO ALIM acid salt; **~ ammoniac** m CHIMIE sal ammoniac; **~ ferrique** m LESSIVES iron salt; **~ gemme** m AGRO ALIM, CHIMIE, GAZ rock salt, GEOLOGIE salt rock, MINERAUX rock salt; **~ gemme sédimentaire** m GAZ sedimentary rock salt; **~ marin** m AGRO ALIM sea salt; **~ à mater** m CERAM VER matt-etching salt; **~ neutre** m CHIMIE normal salt; **~ d'onium** m CHIMIE onium salt; **~ de pétrole** m CHIMIE petroleum jelly; **~ rose** m CHIMIE pink salt; **~ de Seignette** m AGRO ALIM, CHIMIE, ELECTROTEC Rochelle salt; **~ sodique** m CHIMIE sodium salt

sélecteur m CINEMAT switch, ELECTROTEC *téléphonique,* INFORMAT, ORDINAT, TELECOM selector, TV switch, VEHICULES *transmission automatique* selector; **~ de balai** m ELECTR *machine* brush selector; **~ à barres croisées** m ELECTROTEC crossbar selector; **~ à bouton standard** m PRODUCTION standard knob selector; **~ de canal** m ENREGISTR channel selector switch, TELECOM channel selector, TV channel selector switch, multichannel selector; **~ de cap** m AERONAUT heading selector; **~ de circuit** m PRODUCTION *système hydraulique* shuttle valve; **~ à clé** m PRODUCTION cylinder lock operator, *automatisme industriel* key-operated selector switch; **~ de combustible** m MAT CHAUFF fuel selector; **~ de contrôle** m ELECTROTEC control switch; **~ en charge** m

ELECTR *commutateur* selector switch; **~ de fréquence** *m* TELECOM frequency selector; **~ marche/arrêt** *m* CONS MECA on/off switch; **~ de mode** *m* ELECTROTEC grating; **~ de mode de fonctionnement** *m* AERONAUT course selector; **~ de niveau de carburant** *m* AERONAUT fuel level selector; **~ de normes** *m* TV standards selector; **~ omnidirectionnel** *m* AERONAUT omnibearing selector; **~ d'ondes métriques et décimétriques** *m* TV VHF and UHF tuner; **~ au pied** *m* VEHICULES *boîte de vitesses de motocyclette* foot change lever (BrE), foot gearshift (AmE); **~ de piste** *m* TV track selector; **~ des plages d'étude** *m* INSTRUMENT measurement range selector; **~ de prises** *m* ELECTR *commutateur* tap selector; **~ de programmes** *m* TELECOM program selector (AmE), programme selector (BrE); **~ rotatif** *m* CINEMAT rotary switch, ELECTROTEC uniselector; **~ de route** *m* AERONAUT course selector; **~ de tension** *m* ELECTROTEC line voltage selector, voltage selector; **~ à tête à encoche** *m* PRODUCTION coin slot selector switch; **~ tout ou rien** *m* CONS MECA hit or miss selector valve; **~ de vitesse** *m* CINEMAT, ENREGISTR speed selector, TV tape speed control; **~ de vitesses à temps de vol** *m* NUCLEAIRE time of flight velocity selector; **~ de vol** *m* AERONAUT mode selector switch; **~ des zones de mesure** *m* INSTRUMENT measurement range selector

sélectif *adj* MATERIAUX selective

sélection *f* IMPRIM *photogravure* separation, INFORMAT, ORDINAT selection, TELECOM dialing (AmE), dialling (BrE); **~ automatique** *f* TELECOM automatic dialing (AmE), automatic dialling (BrE); **~ de bande** *f* ELECTRON band separation; **~ à bascule** *f* PRODUCTION *automatisme industriel* toggle selection; **~ des couleurs** *f* CINEMAT color separation (AmE), colour separation (BrE), IMPRIM color separation (AmE), colour separation (BrE), *photogravure* halftone selection, TV color separation (AmE), colour separation (BrE); **~ de dimensions** *f* CONS MECA *pour la boulonnerie* selected sizes; **~ directe à un poste** *f* TELECOM DDI (BrE), direct dialling in (BrE), DID (AmE), direct inward dialing (AmE); **~ à distance de l'abonné demandé** *f* TELECOM DDD (AmE), direct distance dialing (AmE), STD (BrE), subscriber trunk dialling (BrE); **~ de forçage** *f* PRODUCTION *automatisme industriel* force selection; **~ indirecte** *f* IMPRIM indirect process, three-way process; **~ indirecte en deux temps** *f* IMPRIM *photomécanique* indirect color separation (AmE), indirect colour separation (BrE); **~ de mode déporté** *f* PRODUCTION *automatisme industriel* remote mode selection; **~ par porte** *f* ELECTRON gating; **~ de la tension** *f* ELECTROTEC input tapping

sélectionner[1] *vt* INFORMAT *une fonction* set

sélectionner:[2] **~ les couleurs** *vi* IMPRIM *photogravure* break for colors (AmE), break for colours (BrE)

sélectivité *f* ELECTRON, PHYSIQUE selectivity; **~ pour la voie adjacente** *f* TELECOM adjacent channel rejection ratio; **~ vis à vis de la voie adjacente** *f* TELECOM adjacent channel selectivity

séléniate *m* CHIMIE selenate

sélénié *adj* CHIMIE selenious, selenous

sélénieux *adj* CHIMIE selenious, selenous

sélénique *adj* CHIMIE *acide* selenic

sélénite *m* CHIMIE, MINERAUX selenite

séléniteux *adj* CHIMIE selenitic

sélénium *m (Se)* CHIMIE selenium *(Se)*

séléniure *m* CHIMIE selenide; **~ d'argent** *m* CHIMIE silver selenide

sélénocyanate *m* CHIMIE selenocyanate

sélénocyanique *adj* CHIMIE selenocyanic

sélénographie *f* ASTRONOMIE selenography

sélénologie *f* ASTRONOMIE selenology

self: **~ antiparasite** *f* ELECTR suppressor choke; **~ de filtrage** *f* ELECTR *inducteur* smoothing choke, *réseau* filter choke

self-induction *f* ELECTR *bobine*, PHYSIQUE self-induction

selfmètre *m* ELECTR inductance meter

self-service *m* EMBALLAGE self-service

sellaïte *f* MINERAUX sellaite

selle *f* RESSORTS saddle; **~ d'arrêt** *f* CONS MECA packing piece; **~ symétrique** *f* GEOMETRIE *topologie* symmetric saddle shape

seller: se ~ *v réfl* MINES sink

sellette *f* VEHICULES *d'une semi-remorque* fifth wheel

sels: **~ hydrofuges** *m pl* REVETEMENT waterproofing salts; **~ nutritifs** *m pl* HYDROLOGIE nutrient salts

sémantique *f* INFORMAT, ORDINAT semantics

sémaphore *m* COMMANDE arm signal, semaphore signal, INFORMAT semaphore, NAUT signal station, ORDINAT semaphore

séméline *f* MINERAUX semelin, semeline

semelle *f* CH DE FER *véhicules* shoe, CONS MECA crossslide, packing piece, slipper, *d'une presse* plate, *de la crosse du piston* gib shoe, shoe, CONSTR footing block, foundation, head beam, plate, wall plate, roof plate, sole piece, sole plate, tread, *d'une poutre* flange, *d'un palier* sill plate, *d'un rabot* sole, ESPACE *véhicules* sole plate, GEOLOGIE sole, IMPRIM base, MINES die, sill, sill piece, sole, sole piece, *d'un cadre de boisage* groundsill, *d'une mine* seat, PRODUCTION sole plate, *d'une cuve d'amalgamation* die, *d'un palier* sole; **~ antidérapante** *f* SECURITE *chaussure* nonslip sole, slip-resistant sole; **~ de la crosse** *f* CONS MECA crosshead gib, crosshead shoe, crosshead slipper; **~ de cylindre** *f* VEHICULES *moteur* cylinder flange; **~ dans le chausson en caoutchouc** *f* CONSTR pad inside rubber boot; **~ élargie** *f* CHARBON pad foundation, slab; **~ inférieure** *f* CONSTR bottom flange; **~ de palier** *f* CONS MECA base of plummer block; **~ de pieu** *f* CHARBON pile footing; **~ de sabot de frein sans flasque** *f* CH DE FER flangeless brake block; **~ de support à main** *f* CONS MECA handrest socket

semelles *f pl* PLAST CAOU *caoutchouc* soling

semence *f* CONS MECA tin tack, NUCLEAIRE seed assembly, seed element, spike

semi-automatique *adj* CONS MECA semiautomatic

semi-carbazide *f* CHIMIE semicarbazide

semi-carbazone *f* CHIMIE semicarbazone

semi-conducteur *m* ELECTRON, ORDINAT, PHYSIQUE semiconductor; **~ amorphe** *m* ELECTRON amorphous semiconductor; **~ condensé** *m* ELECTROTEC compensated semiconductor; **~ dégénéré** *m* ELECTRON degenerate semiconductor; **~ dopé** *m* ELECTRON doped semiconductor; **~ électronique** *m* NUCLEAIRE electronic semiconductor; **~ extrinsèque** *m* ELECTRON, ORDINAT, PHYSIQUE extrinsic semiconductor; **~ faiblement dopé** *m* ELECTRON lightly doped semiconductor; **~ intrinsèque** *m* ELECTRON I-type semiconductor, intrinsic semiconductor, INFORMAT, ORDINAT, PHYSIQUE intrinsic semiconductor; **~ massif** *m* ELECTRON bulk semiconductor; **~ monocristallin** *m* ELECTRON single crystal semiconductor; **~ non épitaxié** *m* ELECTRON bulk semiconductor; **~ à oxyde métallique** *m (MOS)* ORDINAT metal-oxide semiconductor *(MOS)*; **~ à**

oxyde métallique complémentaire *m* ORDINAT CMOS, compatible metal-oxide semiconductor; ~ **polycristallin** *m* ELECTRON polycrystalline semiconductor; ~ **à transitions indirectes** *m* ELECTRON indirect gap semiconductor; ~ **de type N** *m* ELECTRON, PHYSIQUE n-type semiconductor; ~ **de type N+** *m* ELECTRON n$^+$-type semiconductor; ~ **de type N faiblement dopé** *m* ELECTRON n$^-$-type semiconductor; ~ **de type N fortement dopé** *m* ELECTRON n$^+$-type semiconductor; ~ **de type P** *m* ELECTRON, PHYSIQUE p-type semiconductor; ~ **de type P$^+$** *m* ELECTRON p$^+$-semiconductor; ~ **de type P faiblement dopé** *m* ELECTRON p$^-$-semiconductor; ~ **de type P fortement dopé** *m* ELECTRON p$^+$-semiconductor

semi-conducteurs: à ~ *adj* ORDINAT, TV solid-state
semi-coquille: ~ **lunetterie** *f* CERAM VER micoquille
semidine *f* CHIMIE semidine
semi-duplex[1] *adj* ORDINAT HDX, half-duplex
semi-duplex[2] *m* INFORMAT half-duplex, half-duplex operation
semi-fini *adj* PRODUCTION semifinished
semi-fixe *adj* CONS MECA semiportable
semi-gélatine: ~ **dynamite** *f* MINES semigelatin, semigelatin dynamite, semigelatin explosive
semi-métro *m* TRANSPORT tramway metro, underground tramway
semi-ouvré *adj* PRODUCTION semifinished
semi-personnalisé *adj* INFORMAT, ORDINAT semicustom
semi-polaire *adj* CHIMIE semipolar
semi-portique *m* NUCLEAIRE gantry with hoist
semi-remorque *f* TRANSPORT, VEHICULES semitrailer; ~ **citerne** *f* TRANSPORT tank semitrailer; ~ **rail-route** *f* TRANSPORT railroad semitrailer (AmE), railway semitrailer (BrE)
sénarmontite *f* MINERAUX senarmontite
sénestre *adj* GEOLOGIE sinistral
sénévol *m* AGRO ALIM mustard oil
senne *f* NAUT seine net, OCEANO dragnet, seine, tow net; ~ **coulissante** *f* OCEANO purse seine; ~ **danoise** *f* OCEANO Danish seine; ~ **de plage** *f* OCEANO beach seine, lampara
senneur *m* OCEANO seiner
sens:[1] **dans le ~ horaire** *adj* ELECTROTEC CW, clockwise; **de ~ direct** *adj* PHYSIQUE right-handed
sens:[2] **dans le ~ de défilement du papier** *adv* IMPRIM *traitements complémentaires* in-line; **dans le ~ travers** *adv* IMPRIM *papier* crosswise; **dans le ~ du vent** *adv* METEO downwind, leeward; **en ~ travers** *adv* IMPRIM against the grain
sens[3] *m* GEOLOGIE *d'un vecteur* sense, HYDROLOGIE *d'un fleuve* direction of flow, *d'un courant* drift; ~ **de câblage** *m* ELECTR direction of lay; ~ **de circulation** *m* INFORMAT, ORDINAT flow direction; ~ **contraire des aiguilles d'une montre** *m (SCAM)* CONS MECA counterclockwise *(CCW)*; ~ **du courant** *m* ELECTROTEC current direction; ~ **de l'émulsion** *m* CINEMAT emulsion position; ~ **d'enroulement** *m* RESSORTS direction of coiling, hand, winding direction; ~ **d'enroulement droit** *m* RESSORTS right-hand coiling; ~ **d'enroulement gauche** *m* RESSORTS left-hand coiling; ~ **d'étirage** *m* RESSORTS direction of wiredrawing; ~ **des fibres** *m* IMPRIM grain; ~ **inverse** *m* ELECTROTEC reverse direction; ~ **inverse horaire** *m (SIH)* CONS MECA counterclockwise *(CCW)*; ~ **de laminage** *m* RESSORTS direction of rolling; ~ **de la liaison** *m* INFORMAT *dans un organigramme*, ORDINAT *transmission* flow direction; ~ **machine** *m* IMPRIM grain direction, *papiers* machine

direction, PAPIER machine direction; ~ **de la marche** *m* CH DE FER direction of traffic; ~ **marin** *m* NAUT seamanship; ~ **de non-conduction** *m* ELECTROTEC inverse direction; ~ **papier** *m* IMPRIM grain direction; ~ **de torsion** *m* TEXTILE direction of twist; ~ **transversal de la bande** *m* IMPRIM *impression* cross web; ~ **travers** *m* IMPRIM cross direction, *dans la rotative* short grain, *rotatives* cross grain, PAPIER cross direction
sensibilisateur *m* CINEMAT, IMPRIM sensitizer
sensibilisation *f* PHOTO sensitization
sensibiliser *vt* CINEMAT, PHOTO sensitize
sensibilité *f* CHARBON, ELECTR *d'un instrument*, ELECTROTEC, ENREGISTR, ESPACE *communications*, INFORMAT sensitivity, MINES explosive sensitivity, sensitivity, OPTIQUE, ORDINAT, PHYSIQUE sensitivity, TELECOM responsivity, sensitivity; ~ **de l'accord électronique** *f* ELECTRON electronic tuning sensitivity; ~ **à l'amorce** *f* MINES sensitivity to initiation; ~ **à la chaleur** *f* PLAST CAOU heat sensitivity; ~ **chromatique** *f* CINEMAT color response (AmE), colour response (BrE); ~ **à la corrosion** *f* NUCLEAIRE corrodibility; ~ **aux criques de trempe** *f* THERMODYN heat treatment crack sensitivity; ~ **de la déviation** *f* ELECTRON deflection sensitivity; ~ **directionnelle** *f* TV directional selectivity; ~ **d'écart angulaire** *f* AERONAUT *entre deux sens ou deux axes* angular displacement sensitivity; ~ **de l'émulsion** *f* CINEMAT emulsion speed; ~ **énergétique** *f* OPTIQUE sensitivity; ~ **énergique** *f* TELECOM responsivity; ~ **aux erreurs** *f* TELECOM error susceptibility; ~ **aux fissures de trempe** *f* THERMODYN heat treatment crack sensitivity; ~ **à la lumière** *f* PHYS RAYON sensitivity to light; ~ **à l'onde explosive** *f* MINES propagation sensitivity; ~ **de référence** *f* TELECOM reference sensibility; ~ **spectrale** *f* CINEMAT spectral sensitivity, OPTIQUE spectral sensibility, TELECOM spectral responsivity; ~ **tangentielle** *f* PHYSIQUE tangential signal sensitivity; ~ **aux variations hygrométriques** *f* PAPIER hygrosensibility
sensibilité-limite: ~ **de détection** *f* POLLUTION lower limit of detectability
sensible: ~ **à l'infrarouge** *adj* PHOTO, PHYS RAYON infrared-sensitive; ~ **à la lumière** *adj* CINEMAT light-sensitive, photosensitive, ELECTRON, IMPRIM *photogravure*, PHOTO light-sensitive; ~ **à la pression** *adj* IMPRIM pressure-sensitive
sensitogramme *m* CINEMAT wedge print
sensitométrie *f* ACOUSTIQUE, CINEMAT sensitometry
sentier *m* CONSTR path
sentinelle *f* IMPRIM *codes et marques*, INFORMAT, ORDINAT sentinel
séparabilité *f* NUCLEAIRE separability
séparable *adj* CHIMIE separable
séparateur *m* CHARBON separator, stripper, CONS MECA separator, CRISTALL separator, trap, DISTRI EAU, ELECTR *câble*, GENIE CHIM, INFORMAT separator, MATERIAUX separator, trap, MINES ore separator, separator, ORDINAT IS, information separator, separator, PETR, POLLU MER, TELECOM separator; ~ **d'air** *m* CONS MECA air separator; ~ **d'articles** *m* ORDINAT RS, record separator; ~ **centrifuge** *m* GENIE CHIM centrifugal, centrifugal separator, NUCLEAIRE inertial separator; ~ **à chicanes** *m* GENIE CHIM baffle-type separator; ~ **des courants de circulation** *m* COMMANDE traffic bollard; ~ **d'eau** *m* PETROLE water knock out; ~ **d'eau de condensation** *m* CHAUFFAGE steam trap; ~ **électrique** *m* POLLUTION ESP, electrostatic precipita-

tor; ~ **d'éléments de données** *m* TELECOM data element separator; ~ **d'éléments de données constitutifs** *m* TELECOM component data element separator; ~ **d'enregistrements** *m* INFORMAT RS, record separator; ~ **de fichier** *m* INFORMAT, ORDINAT file separator; ~ **à force centrifuge** *m* GENIE CHIM centrifugal force sizer; ~ **à gaz** *m* NUCLEAIRE gas stripper; ~ **de groupes** *m* ORDINAT GS, group separator; ~ **à hélice** *m* CHARBON spiral classifier; ~ **d'huile** *m* HYDROLOGIE oil separator, oil trap, REFRIG oil separator; ~ **humide** *m* POLLUTION wet scrubber; ~ **d'impulsions** *m* TV pulse separator; ~ **d'impuretés** *m* REFRIG scale trap; ~ **laveur** *m* POLLUTION venturi scrubber; ~ **laveur à garnissage** *m* POLLUTION packed bed scrubber; ~ **laveur à plateaux** *m* POLLUTION plate column scrubber; ~ **magnétique** *m* CHARBON, MINES, PRODUCTION magnetic separator; ~ **magnétique à rubans** *m* CHARBON magnetic separator; ~ **à minerai** *m* MINES ore separator; ~ **de mots** *m* ORDINAT word delimiter; ~ **à pulvérisation** *m* POLLUTION preformed spray scrubber; ~ **rotatif** *m* CHARBON trommel washer; ~ **de signaux** *m* TV signal splitter; ~ **des signaux de synchronisation** *m* TV sync separator; ~ **de synchronisation couleur** *m* TV burst separator; ~ **à tambour** *m* CHARBON drum cobber, drum separator; ~ **à tissu filtrant** *m* POLLUTION fabric filter; ~ **de vapeur** *m* INST HYDR steam separator

séparateurs: ~ **aérauliques** *m pl* SECURITE cleaning equipment

séparation *f* CHARBON, CHIMIE separation, CONSTR division, partition, ESPACE separation, *véhicules* kick-off, IMPRIM *photogravure* separation, PETROLE separation, treatment, TEXTILE separation; ~ **de l'air** *f* GENIE CHIM air separation; ~ **angulaire** *f* TELECOM angular separation; ~ **chromatique** *f* TV color separation (AmE), colour separation (BrE); ~ **cinétique** *f* NUCLEAIRE kinetic separation; ~ **entre canaux** *f* ENREGISTR channel separation; ~ **entre plis** *f* PLAST CAOU *d'un pneu en caoutchouc* ply separation; ~ **en vol** *f* NUCLEAIRE kinetic separation; ~ **des fibres** *f* MATERIAUX fiber debonding (AmE), fibre debonding (BrE); ~ **du film d'encre** *f* IMPRIM film splitting; ~ **des fréquences** *f* ELECTRON frequency separation; ~ **géométrique** *f* NUCLEAIRE separation by geometry; ~ **des isotopes** *f* PHYS PART isotope separation; ~ **des isotopes magnétiques** *f* NUCLEAIRE magnetic isotope separation; ~ **isotopique** *f* PHYS PART isotope separation; ~ **magnétique** *f* CERAM VER drawing; ~ **des modes** *f* ELECTRON mode separation; ~ **par air** *f* AGRO ALIM air classification, air separation; ~ **par écumage** *f* GENIE CHIM foam separation; ~ **des particules** *f* PHYS PART particle separation; ~ **par turbine** *f* AGRO ALIM turboseparation; ~ **secondaire** *f* NUCLEAIRE secondary separation; ~ **stéréo** *f* ENREGISTR stereo separation

séparer[1] *vt* CHIMIE separate, separate out, GAZ separate; ~ **par congélation** *vt* REFRIG freeze out; ~ **par filtration** *vt* GENIE CHIM filter out

séparer[2] *vti* GENIE CHIM precitate, separate

séparer:[3] **se ~ en dissociation** *v réfl* GENIE CHIM separate out; **se ~ en flocons** *v réfl* GENIE CHIM flocculate, separate as flocculent preparation; **se ~ par précipitation** *v réfl* CHIMIE separate, separate out, GENIE CHIM precipitate, separate out

sépiolite *f* MINERAUX sepiolite

septième *f* ACOUSTIQUE seventh; ~ **majeure** *f* ACOUSTIQUE major seventh; ~ **mineure** *f* ACOUSTIQUE minor seventh

septivalent *adj* CHIMIE septivalent

séquence *f* GEOLOGIE sequence; ~ **d'appel** *f* ORDINAT calling sequence, TELECOM call sequence; ~ **d'approche** *f* AERONAUT approach sequence; ~ **d'atterrissage** *f* AERONAUT landing sequence; ~ **binaire** *f* INFORMAT, ORDINAT, TELECOM binary sequence; ~ **binaire pseudoaléatoire** *f* TELECOM PRBS, pseudorandom binary sequence; ~ **brève** *f* CINEMAT flash; ~ **de bruit pseudoaléatoire** *f* NAUT pseudonoise sequence; ~ **de cadencement** *f* ELECTRON clocking sequence; ~ **de classement** *f* INFORMAT collating sequence; ~ **de comblement** *f* GEOLOGIE *par régression* shallowing-up sequence; ~ **de commutation de couleurs** *f* TV color sampling sequence (AmE), colour sampling sequence (BrE); ~ **de contrôle** *f* TELECOM check sequence; ~ **directe** *f* TELECOM DS, direct sequence; ~ **d'échappement** *f* INFORMAT, ORDINAT escape sequence; ~ **d'empilement** *f* CRISTALL stacking sequence; ~ **ESC** *f* INFORMAT, ORDINAT escape sequence; ~ **d'exécution** *f* INFORMAT, ORDINAT control sequence; ~ **de fonctionnement de l'automate programmable** *f* PRODUCTION *automatisme industriel* PC control sequence; ~ **de freinage** *f* ESPACE *véhicules* retrosequence; ~ **de freinage par rétrofusées** *f* ESPACE retrorocket sequence; ~ **d'images** *f* TELECOM image sequence; ~ **de manoeuvres** *f* ELECTR *commutateur* switching sequence; ~ **de marquage** *f* TELECOM marking sequence; ~ **négative** *f* GEOLOGIE coarsening-up sequence; ~ **numérique de pseudo-bruit** *f* TELECOM digital pseudo-noise sequence; ~ **des opérations** *f* PRODUCTION operations sequence, process chart; ~ **paramétrable** *f* INFORMAT, ORDINAT skeletal coding; ~ **à pas de pèlerin** *f* PRODUCTION backstep sequence; ~ **positive** *f* ELECTR *courant alternatif* positive sequence, GEOLOGIE fining-up sequence; ~ **de saut** *f* PRODUCTION *automatisme industriel* jump routine; ~ **de scrutation** *f* PRODUCTION *automatisme industriel* scanning sequence; ~ **sédimentaire** *f* GEOLOGIE depositional sequence, sedimentary sequence; ~ **sédimentaire rythmique** *f* GEOLOGIE cyclothem; ~ **de soudage** *f* CONSTR welding sequence; ~ **de l'utilisateur** *f* ORDINAT own coding; ~ **utilisateur** *f* INFORMAT own coding; ~ **de vol** *f* ESPACE *véhicules* flight sequence, in-flight sequence

séquenceur *m* ELECTROTEC sequencing

séquenceur *m* ELECTROTEC, INFORMAT, ORDINAT, PRODUCTION *automatisme industriel*, TELECOM sequencer; ~ **fixe** *m* TELECOM fixed sequencer; ~ **programmable** *m* TELECOM programmable sequencer

séquentiel[1] *adj* INFORMAT sequential, serial, ORDINAT sequential

séquentiel:[2] ~ **couleur à mémoire** *m* *(SECAM)* TV SECAM

sergé *m* TEXTILE twill

sergent *m* CONSTR joiner's cramp, sash clamp, sash cramp

sérialisation *f* ELECTROTEC serialization

sérialiser *vt* ELECTROTEC, INFORMAT, ORDINAT serialize

sérialiseur *m* ELECTROTEC serializer

séricite *f* MINERAUX sericite

séricito-schiste *m* GEOLOGIE *roche métamorphique* sericite schist

série:[1] **en ~** *adj* IMPRIM serial, PHYSIQUE in series, TELECOM, INFORMAT, ORDINAT serial

série[2] *f* CONS MECA *de postes de travail*, ELECTR *circuit* series, GEOLOGIE sequence, series, set, INFORMAT, MATH, ORDINAT series, PRODUCTION batch; ~ **d'ac-**

tinides *f* PHYS RAYON actinide series; ~ **aromatique** *f* CHIMIE aromatic series; ~ **Balmer** *f* PHYSIQUE Balmer series; ~ **de Brackett** *f* PHYSIQUE Brackett series; ~ **chronologique** *f* ORDINAT time series; ~ **condensée** *f* GEOLOGIE *complète mais peu épaisse* condensed sequence; ~ **de désintégration radioactive** *f* PHYS RAYON radioactive decay series; ~ **électrochimique des tensions** *f* CHIMIE *éléments* electrochemical series; ~ **de Fourier** *f* CRISTALL, PHYSIQUE Fourier series; ~ **harmonique** *f* ACOUSTIQUE harmonic series; ~ **homologue** *f* MATERIAUX, PETROLE *raffinage* homologous series; ~ **ignée** *f* GEOLOGIE igneous suite; ~ **isomorphe** *f* CRISTALL isomorphous series; ~ **de Lyman** *f* PHYS RAYON, PHYSIQUE Lyman series; ~ **magmatique** *f* GEOLOGIE igneous suite; ~ **d'objectifs** *f* CINEMAT set of lenses; ~ **paraffinique** *f* PETROLE paraffin series; ~ **de Paschen** *f* PHYSIQUE Paschen series; ~ **de Pfund** *f* PHYSIQUE Pfund series; ~ **de plaques négatives** *f* AUTO negative bank; ~ **de plaques positives** *f* AUTO positive bank; ~ **de poids** *f* METROLOGIE weights; ~ **radioactive** *f* PHYS RAYON radioactive series; ~ **de roues de filetage** *f* CONS MECA set of change wheels; ~ **de roues pour les variations de vitesse des avances** *f* CONS MECA set of change wheels; ~ **rythmique** *f* GEOLOGIE rhythmic beds; ~ **de tamis** *f* GENIE CHIM sieve set; ~ **temporelle** *f* INFORMAT time series

série-parallèle *adj* INFORMAT, ORDINAT serial-parallel

sérigraphie *f* IMPRIM serigraphy, TEXTILE silk-screen printing

seringue *f* EQUIP LAB syringe; ~ **à usage unique** *f* EQUIP LAB *analyse* disposable syringe

sérotonine *f* CHIMIE enteramine, serotonin

Serpent *m* ASTRONOMIE Serpens

serpentage *m* (Bel) CERAM VER snaking, CERAM VER curled edge

serpenter *vi* HYDROLOGIE meander

serpentin *m* CHAUFFAGE *d'un échangeur* coil, EQUIP LAB *d'un alambic* worm, *distillation* serpent coil, NUCLEAIRE cooling coil, OPTIQUE fiber helix (AmE), fibre helix (BrE); ~ **accumulateur** *m* REFRIG hold-over coil; ~ **de chauffage** *m* REFRIG heating coil; ~ **à grille** *m* PRODUCTION grid coil; ~ **réchauffeur** *m* CHAUFFAGE heating coil, *transmission thermique* calorifier; ~ **réfrigérant** *m* CONS MECA cooling oil; ~ **de refroidissement** *m* GAZ cooling coil; ~ **refroidisseur** *m* REFRIG cooling coil; ~ **à vapeur** *m* CHAUFFAGE steam coil

serpentine *f* MINERAUX serpentine

serpentinisation *f* EN RENOUV serpentinization

serrage *m* CONS MECA depth of cut, screwing up, throttling, *d'une vis* screwing, *d'un joint* tightening, *rétrécissement* shrinkage, shrinkage allowance, CONSTR compaction, driving in, *d'une vis* driving, MECANIQUE *dans un étau* clamping, *outillage* chucking, MINES *dans une galerie de mine* dam, PRODUCTION grip, *du sable d'un moule* packing, *à pied* tramping; ~ **du frein** *m* CH DE FER *véhicules* brake application; ~ **de puissance** *m* PRODUCTION power torquing; ~ **du sable** *m* PRODUCTION tramping

serre *f* CONS MECA clip, NAUT stringer, PRODUCTION *pour oreilles de châssis* dog; ~ **de bouchain** *f* NAUT bilge stringer

serre-câble *m* ELECTROTEC cable tensioner, PRODUCTION wire-rope clamp, VEHICULES *système électrique, commande* cable clip

serrée *f* MINES contraction, nip, pinch

serre-fil: ~ **terminal à rappel** *f* PRODUCTION *automatisme industriel* self-lifting terminal clamp

serre-fils *m* CONS MECA clamp; ~ **de mise à la terre** *m* PRODUCTION *électricité* earth connector (BrE), ground connector (AmE)

serre-flan *m* CONS MECA draw ring

serre-frein *m* CH DE FER *véhicules* brakeman

serre-joints *m* AUTO car clamp, CONS MECA G-cramp, CONSTR joiner's cramp; sash clamp, sash cramp; ~ **à coins** *m* EMBALLAGE glue press

serrement *m* CONS MECA tightening, MINES contraction, nip, pinch

serrer[1] *vt* CINEMAT crop, CONS MECA screw, take in, tighten, *vis* tighten, CONSTR bind, drive, drive in, DISTRI EAU *nappes aquifères* shut off, MECANIQUE clamp, PRODUCTION grip, hold, *tôle* close; ~ **avec une bride** *vt* PRODUCTION clamp; ~ **à bloc** *vt* CONS MECA *vis* tighten up hard

serrer[2] *vi* VEHICULES brake; ~ **le frein** *vi* VEHICULES apply the brake

serre-tête *m* SECURITE *protecteurs d'oreilles, industriels* earmuffs

serre-tubes *m* CONS MECA tube wrench, CONSTR pipe wrench, PRODUCTION cylinder wrench; ~ **à chaînes** *m* CONS MECA, VEHICULES central locking

serrure *f* CONSTR, SECURITE, VEHICULES *carrosserie* lock; ~ **antivol sur la direction** *f* VEHICULES steering column lock; ~ **bénarde** *f* CONSTR pinned key lock; ~ **à bosse** *f* CONSTR spring lock; ~ **à broche** *f* CONSTR piped key lock; ~ **de coffre** *f* CONSTR box lock; ~ **à combinaisons** *f* CONSTR combination lock, puzzle lock; ~ **à demi-tour** *f* CONSTR latch lock; ~ **à droite** *f* CONSTR right-hand lock; ~ **encastrée** *f* CONSTR flush lock; ~ **encloisonnée** *f* CONSTR lock; ~ **entaillée** *f* CONSTR flush lock; ~ **à garnitures** *f* CONSTR warded lock; ~ **à gorge** *f* CONSTR tumbler lock; ~ **à larder** *f* CONSTR mortise lock; ~ **à mortaiser** *f* CONSTR mortise lock; ~ **à pêne à demi-tour** *f* CONSTR spring lock; ~ **à pêne dormant** *f* CONSTR deadlock, dormant lock; ~ **de porte** *f* VEHICULES door lock; ~ **à ressort** *f* CONSTR latch lock, spring lock; ~ **de sécurité** *f* CONSTR safety lock; ~ **de sûreté à gorges mobiles** *f* CONSTR tumbler lock

serrurerie *f* CONSTR ironworking, locksmithery, locksmithing, lockwork, PRODUCTION ironwork, metalwork, metalworking; ~ **d'art** *f* CONSTR art metalwork; ~ **de bâtiment** *f* CONSTR builders' hardware

serrurier *m* CONSTR locksmith, PRODUCTION metalworker; ~ **en bâtiment** *m* CONSTR builders' hardware merchant; ~ **mécanicien** *m* PRODUCTION mechanic

sertir *vt* EMBALLAGE, MECANIQUE, MINES crimp; ~ **par replis** *vt* PRODUCTION crimp

sertissage *m* MINES, PRODUCTION crimping

sérum-albumine *m* AGRO ALIM blood albumin

servant: ~ **de hausse** *m* MILITAIRE *artillerie* setter sight

servante: ~ **d'outillage** *f* CONS MECA roller tool chest

serveur *m* INFORMAT, ORDINAT server, TELECOM applications processor; ~ **à accès multiples** *m* TELECOM S-universal interface; ~ **de communication** *m* INFORMAT, ORDINAT communication server; ~ **en mode non connecté** *m* TELECOM CLS, connectionless server; ~ **de fichier** *m* INFORMAT, ORDINAT file server; ~ **d'impression** *m* INFORMAT, ORDINAT print server; ~ **de message** *m* TELECOM IMP, interface message processor; ~ **de messagerie** *m* TELECOM mail server; ~ **de messagerie vocale** *m* TELECOM voice message processor; ~ **de noms** *m* TELECOM name server; ~ **de**

terminaux *m* INFORMAT, ORDINAT terminal server; ~ de transfert fiable *m* TELECOM RTS, reliable transfer server; ~ vidéotex *m* TELECOM videotex server

service:[1] en ~ *adj* ELECTROTEC on

service[2] *m* INFORMAT, ORDINAT service, PRODUCTION utility, QUALITE service; ~ aux abonnés *m* TELECOM subscriber service; ~ des abonnés absents *m* TELECOM absent subscriber service, answering service; ~ aérien interurbain *m* AERONAUT intercity air service; ~ d'amateur *m* TELECOM amateur radio service; ~ amélioré *m* TELECOM enhanced service; ~ des annonces *m* IMPRIM advertising department; ~ d'appoint *m* TRANSPORT backup service; ~ après vente *m* CONSTR, QUALITE after sales service; ~ d'assistance annuaire *m* TELECOM directory assistance, directory enquiries (BrE), directory information (AmE); ~ automatique de cartes de crédit *m* TELECOM automatic credit card service; ~ avec confirmation *m* TELECOM confirmed service; ~ de bas niveau *m* TELECOM lower-level service; ~ à bord *m* ESPACE *véhicules* housekeeping; ~ CA *m* PRODUCTION *électricité* AC-operated service; ~ de circuit commuté audio *m* TELECOM audio bearer service; ~ de circuit commuté en canal B non transparent *m* TELECOM sixty-four kbps restricted service; ~ de circuit commuté en canal B transparent *m* TELECOM clear sixty-four service; ~ de circuit commuté de parole *m* TELECOM speech service; ~ de circuit virtuel sur canal B *m (service CVB)* TELECOM B-channel virtual circuit service; ~ des colis *m* TRANSPORT parcels office; ~ de communication virtuelle *m* INFORMAT, ORDINAT virtual call service; ~ commun d'information de gestion *m* TELECOM CMIS, common management information service; ~ commun de transfert d'informations de gestion *m* TELECOM CMIS, common management information service; ~ commuté *m* TELECOM switched service; ~ commuté de données multimégabit *m* TELECOM SMDS, switched multimegabit data service; ~ complémentaire *m* TELECOM facility; ~ confirmé *m* TELECOM confirmed service; ~ confort *m* TELECOM custom calling service; ~ continu *m* ELECTR *matériel* continuous duty; ~ contractuel d'emballage thermoformé *m* EMBALLAGE contract blister packaging service; ~ de contrôle d'approche *m* AERONAUT approach control service; ~ du contrôle de la circulation aérienne *m* AERONAUT air traffic control service; ~ de la couche physique *m* TELECOM PLS, physical layer service; ~ de couche réseau sans connexion *m* TELECOM CLNS, connectionless network layer service, connectionless mode network service; ~ courrier électronique *m* ORDINAT electronic mail service; ~ CVB *m (service de circuit virtuel sur canal B)* TELECOM B-channel virtual circuit service; ~ au débit de base *m* TELECOM basic rate service; ~ de dépannage *m* TELECOM FRC, fault reception center (AmE), fault reception centre (BrE); ~ de données à haut débit en mode non connecté *m* TELECOM CBDS, connectionless broadband data service; ~ des eaux *m* DISTRI EAU water supply; ~ d'entretien efficace *m* SECURITE *méthodes de travail sûres* good housekeeping; ~ étalonnage *m* METROLOGIE calibration service; ~ d'études *m* NAUT design department; ~ d'études techniques *m* CONS MECA technical service; ~ exclusif de fret *m* AERONAUT all-freight service; ~ d'exploitation internationale *m* TELECOM international operations service; ~ d'exploration de la Terre par satellite *m* ESPACE *communications* Earth exploration satellite service; ~

fixe aéronautique *m* AERONAUT *réseau de stations au sol* aeronautical fixed network (AmE), aeronautical fixed service (BrE), aeronautical fixed system (AmE); ~ fixe par satellite *m* ESPACE *communications* FSS, fixed satellite service; ~ de gestion d'aire de trafic *m* AERONAUT apron management service; ~ hors vacation *m* TELECOM night service; ~ d'information aéronautique *m* AERONAUT aeronautical information service; ~ d'information de vol *m* AERONAUT flight information service; ~ ininterrompu *m* ELECTR *appareil* uninterrupted duty; ~ intensif *m* PRODUCTION heavy duty; ~ intérieur *m* AERONAUT domestic service; ~ intermittent *m* ELECTR *matériel* intermittent duty; ~ intersatellite *m* ESPACE *communications* intersatellite service; ~ de liaison de données *m* TELECOM DLS, data link service; ~ long-courrier *m* AERONAUT long-haul service; ~ de météorologie par satellite *m* ESPACE *communications* meteorological satellite service; ~ météorologique *m* METEO weather bureau; ~ mixte parole *m* TELECOM alternate speech service; ~ mobile aéronautique par satellite *m* ESPACE *communications* aeronautical mobile satellite service; ~ mobile maritime par satellite *m* NAUT maritime mobile satellite service; ~ mobile par satellite *m* ESPACE *communications* mobile satellite service; ~ N *m* TELECOM N-service; ~ de navette *m* AERONAUT, TRANSPORT shuttle service; ~ de niveau élevé *m* TELECOM higher-level service; ~ nominal temporaire *m* ELECTR *matériel* short-time rating; ~ non confirmé *m* TELECOM nonconfirmed service; ~ de nuit *m* TELECOM night service; ~ de parole *m* TELECOM speech service; ~ physique *m* TELECOM PhS, physical service; ~ public d'informations enregistrées *m* TELECOM recorded public information service; ~ de radiodiffusion par satellite *m* ESPACE *communications* broadcasting satellite service; ~ de radiologie *m* INSTRUMENT X-ray unit; ~ de radionavigation aéronautique *m* AERONAUT aeronautical radio navigation service; ~ radiotéléphonique mobile *m (SRM)* TELECOM mobile telephone service *(MTS)*; ~ réception *m* PRODUCTION receiving department, reception department; ~ de recherche spatiale *m* ESPACE *communications* space research service; ~ régulier *m* TRANSPORT scheduled service; ~ des renseignements *m* TELECOM directory assistance, directory enquiries (BrE), directory information (AmE); ~ de réseau *m* TELECOM NS, network service; ~ de réseau avec connexion *m* TELECOM CONS, connection-oriented mode network service; ~ restreint *m* TELECOM restricted service; ~ RNIS à large bande *m* TELECOM B-ISDN service, broadband ISDN service; ~ sans confirmation *m* TELECOM nonconfirmed service; ~ sans restriction *m* TELECOM unrestricted service; ~ de sauvetage et de lutte contre l'incendie *m* AERONAUT rescue and firefighting service; ~ de sécurité *m* TELECOM security service; ~ simplifié *m* TELECOM night service; ~ supplémentaire *m* TELECOM supplementary service; ~ support *m* TELECOM bearer service; ~ support à 64 kbit/s avec restriction *m* TELECOM sixty-four kbps restricted bearer service; ~ support à 64 kbit/s sans restriction *m* TELECOM sixty-four kbps unrestricted service; ~ support audiofréquence *m* TELECOM audio bearer service; ~ support CCBNT type audio *m* TELECOM audio bearer service; ~ support CCBNT type parole *m* TELECOM speech service; ~ support de circuit virtuel *m* TELECOM virtual-circuit bearer service; ~ support à commutation de circuits *m* TELECOM circuit

mode bearer service; ~ **support en mode circuit** *m*
TELECOM circuit mode bearer service; ~ **support en
mode paquet** *m* TELECOM packet mode bearer service,
packet-switched bearer service; ~ **support en mode
trame** *m* TELECOM FMBS, frame-mode bearer service;
~ **support non transparent** *m* TELECOM nontransparent
bearer service; ~ **support sans connexion** *m* TELECOM
connectionless bearer service; ~ **support sans restriction** *m* TELECOM unrestricted bearer service; ~ **support
de signalisation d'usager** *m* TELECOM user-signaling
bearer service (AmE), user-signalling bearer service
(BrE); ~ **à supports multiples** *m* TELECOM multibearer
service; ~ **support terminal** *m* TELECOM transparent
bearer service; ~ **support transparent** *m* TELECOM clear
channel capability; ~ **de surveillance** *m* TELECOM observation service; ~ **à tarif fixe** *m* TELECOM flat-rate
service; ~ **technique** *m* CONS MECA, MECANIQUE engineering department; ~ **de téléappel** *m* TELECOM paging
service; ~ **tout-cargo** *m* AERONAUT all-cargo service; ~
de transfert avec restriction *m* TELECOM restricted
information transfer service; ~ **de transfert d'informations avec accusé de réception** *m* TELECOM AITS,
acknowledged information transfer service; ~ **de
transfert d'informations sans accusé de réception** *m*
TELECOM UITS, unacknowledged information transfer service; ~ **de transfert sans restriction** *m* TELECOM
clear channel capability, unrestricted information
transfer service; ~ **trucages** *m* CINEMAT special effects
department; ~ **à vide** *m* ELECTR *moteur* idling
services *m pl* BREVETS services; ~ **de communication** *m pl*
TELECOM CS, communication services; ~ **généraux** *m
pl* PETROLE utilities; ~ **publics** *m pl* DISTRI EAU public
utilities; ~ **de sauvetage** *m pl* SECURITE rescue services;
~ **de trafic des navires** *m pl* NAUT vessel traffic services;
~ **d'urgence** *m pl* TELECOM emergency services; ~ **à
valeur ajoutée** *m pl* TELECOM value-added services
servir: ~ **d'équipier** *vi* NAUT crew
servitude:[1] **de** ~ *adj* ESPACE *véhicules* ancillary, TRANS-
PORT utility
servitude[2] *f* ESPACE *véhicules* utility; ~ **de passage** *f*
AERONAUT *aéroport* right-of-way
servitudes: ~ **avion** *f pl* AERONAUT equipment services; ~
passagers *f pl* AERONAUT cabin services; ~ **rampe** *f pl*
AERONAUT ramp services; ~ **au sol** *f pl* AERONAUT
ground service equipment
servo *m* VEHICULES *frein, direction* servo; ~ **de frein** *m*
VEHICULES brake servo; ~ **régulateur de pas cyclique** *m*
AERONAUT cyclic pitch servo trim
servocommande *f* AERONAUT, CINEMAT servocontrol,
COMMANDE servocontrol, servocontrol mechanism,
servomechanism, ELECTROTEC servocontrol, TRANS-
PORT booster control, servocontrol; ~ **auxiliaire** *f* CONS
MECA auxiliary servocontrol; ~ **direction** *f* AERONAUT
rudder power unit
servodébrayage *m* AUTO clutch slave cylinder
servodirection *f* AUTO power steering, VEHICULES
power-assisted steering; ~ **intégrée au boîtier** *f* AUTO
self-contained power steering system; ~ **timonerie** *f*
AUTO linkage power steering system
servodistributeur *m* CONS MECA servovalve
servofrein *m* AUTO power booster, servobrake, TRANS-
PORT power brake, servobrake, VEHICULES
power-assisted brake; ~ **hydraulique** *m* AUTO hydraulic brake servo
servomécanisme *m* COMMANDE servo, ELECTROTEC, IN-
FORMAT, ORDINAT, PHYSIQUE, TV servomechanism; ~

optique *m* ELECTROTEC optical servo
servomoteur:[1] **à** ~ *adj* COMMANDE servo-driven
servomoteur[2] *m* COMMANDE adjusting motor, regulating motor, servodrive, servomotor, CONS MECA relay,
ELECTROTEC, EN RENOUV, NUCLEAIRE servomotor,
TRANSPORT servo unit; ~ **de l'aube directrice** *m* EN
RENOUV guide vane servomotor; ~ **du cabestan** *m*
CINEMAT, ENREGISTR capstan servo; ~ **à courant alternatif** *m* ELECTROTEC AC servomotor, alternating
current servomotor; ~ **à courant continu** *m* ELECTRO-
TEC DC servomotor; ~ **multitour pour robinetterie** *m*
CONS MECA multiturn valve actuator; ~ **à simple effet**
m EN RENOUV single-acting servomotor
servopositionneur *m* COMMANDE servopositioner
servorotor *m* AERONAUT control rotor
servosoupape *f* COMMANDE servovalve
servovanne *f* PRODUCTION *système hydraulique* servovalve
sesquestrène *m* CHIMIE sequestrene
sesquiterpénique *adj* CHIMIE sesquiterpenoid
session *f* INFORMAT, ORDINAT session
set *m* IMPRIM set
seuil *m* ACOUSTIQUE threshold, CONSTR mudsill, sill,
d'un dormant de porte groundsill, *d'une porte*
threshold, DISTRI EAU *d'un barrage, d'un déversoir*
crest, *d'une écluse de canal* sill, ELECTRON, ESPACE
threshold, HYDROLOGIE sill, submerged bar, INFOR-
MAT threshold, NAUT, OCEANO sill, ORDINAT, PHYSIQUE
d'audition threshold, PRODUCTION breakpoint, *d'un
bocard* sill; ~ **absolu** *m* TV *de luminance* absolute
threshold; ~ **d'absorption** *m* CRISTALL absorption
edge; ~ **d'amplitude** *m* ELECTRON amplitude threshold;
~ **d'audition** *m* ACOUSTIQUE hearing threshold level,
POLLUTION threshold of audibility; ~ **de bruit** *m* EN-
REGISTR noise floor; ~ **de brûleur** *m* CERAM VER port
apron; ~ **critique** *m* TRANSPORT *de visibilité* limit; ~
décalé *m* AERONAUT *d'une piste* displaced threshold; ~
de déclenchement des alarmes *m* TELECOM alarm
setting; ~ **de détection** *m* OPTIQUE detection threshold,
sensitivity, TELECOM detection threshold; ~ **de différence couleur** *m* TV color threshold (AmE), colour
threshold (BrE); ~ **différentiel** *m* ACOUSTIQUE differential threshold, ENREGISTR difference limen; ~
différentiel de fréquence *m* ACOUSTIQUE differential
threshold of frequency; ~ **différentiel de niveau de
pression acoustique** *m* ACOUSTIQUE differential threshold of sound pressure level; ~ **différentiel relatif** *m*
ACOUSTIQUE relative differential threshold; ~ **de dou-
leur** *m* PHYSIQUE threshold; ~ **d'écluse** *m* DISTRI EAU
clap sill, lock sill, miter sill (AmE), mitre sill (BrE); ~
d'effet laser *m* OPTIQUE laser effect threshold, TELE-
COM lasing threshold; ~ **flottant autoréglable** *m* POLLU
MER self-adjusting floating weir; ~ **d'ionisation** *m* GAZ
ionization threshold; ~ **de luminescence** *m* TV luminescence threshold; ~ **normal d'audition** *m*
ACOUSTIQUE normal hearing threshold; ~ **normal
d'audition douloureuse** *m* ACOUSTIQUE normal threshold of painful hearing; ~ **normalisé d'audition** *m*
ACOUSTIQUE standardized threshold hearing; ~ **observé** *m* NUCLEAIRE *d'une réaction* observed
threshold; ~ **d'olfaction** *m* HYDROLOGIE odor threshold (AmE), odour threshold (BrE); ~
photoélectrique *m* PHYSIQUE photoelectric threshold;
~ **de piste** *m* AERONAUT runway threshold; ~ **de porte**
m CONSTR door sill; ~ **prédéterminé** *m* PRODUCTION *de
la tension* threshold level; ~ **de réapprovisionnement**

m PRODUCTION order point; ~ **de rentabilité** *m* TEXTILE breakeven point; ~ **de sensibilité** *m* CINEMAT gradient speed; ~ **de signal** *m* TELECOM signal threshold; ~ **des taux de rotation faibles** *m* PRODUCTION slow-moving percentage; ~ **visuel de l'éclairement lumineux** *m* AERONAUT visual threshold of illumination

seuillage *m* ESPACE thresholding

seuiller *vt* ESPACE threshold

seul: ~ **inventeur** *m* BREVETS sole inventor

seule: ~ **couche** *adj* REVETEMENT single-layer; **à une ~ voie par porteuse** *adj* ESPACE single-channel per carrier

sévérité *f* MINERAUX severite

sevranite *f* MINES perchlorate explosive

sexadécimal *adj* INFORMAT sexadecimal

sextant *m* NAUT sextant; ~ **périscopique** *m* ESPACE *véhicules* periscopic sextant

Sextant *m* ASTRONOMIE Sextans

sextet *m* PHYSIQUE sextant, sextet

sexvalent *adj* CHIMIE hexavalent

seybertite *f* MINERAUX seybertite

SGBD *abrév (système de gestion de bases de données)* INFORMAT, ORDINAT, TELECOM DBMS *(database management system)*

SGDG *abrév (sans garantie du gouvernement)* BREVETS no government guarantee

SGML *abrév (Langage standard généralisé de balisage)* IMPRIM, INFORMAT SGML *(Standard Generalized Mark-up Language)*

SHC *abrév (conteneur spécial hors-cotes)* TRANSPORT SHC *(superhigh cube)*

shed *m* CONSTR sawtooth roof, shed roof, square to roof

shunt *m* ELECTR *résistance*, ELECTROTEC, PHYSIQUE shunt; ~ **d'ampèremètre** *m* ELECTROTEC galvanometer shunt, instrument shunt; ~ **de galvanomètre** *m* ELECTR *résistance* galvanometer shunt; ~ **thermique** *m* THERMODYN heat shunt; ~ **universel** *m* ELECTR *résistance* universal shunt

shunter *vt* ELECTROTEC shunt

Si *(silicium)* CHIMIE Si *(silicium)*

SI *abrév (système international d'unités)* METROLOGIE SI *(international system of units)*

SIA *abrév (signal d'indication d'alarme)* TELECOM AIS *(alarm indication signal)*

sibérite *f* MINERAUX siberite

sibilance *f* ENREGISTR sibilance

siccamètre *m* PAPIER drying meter

siccatif[1] *adj* GENIE CHIM desiccative, THERMODYN siccative

siccatif[2] *m* AGRO ALIM desiccant, siccative, IMPRIM *encres*, PLAST CAOU *peinture* dryer, THERMODYN desiccant, drying agent, siccative

siccité *f* CHARBON dryness, PAPIER dry content, dryness, TEXTILE dryness; ~ **commerciale théorique** *f* PAPIER *de la pâte* theoretical commercial dryness

side-car *m* TRANSPORT side car

sidéral *adj* ASTRONOMIE sidereal

sidérite *f* ASTRONOMIE, MINERAUX siderite

sidérochrome *m* MINERAUX chromite

sidéromélane *f* PETR sideromelane

sidérose *f* MINERAUX siderite

siège *m* CONS MECA seat, seating, EQUIP LAB *de laboratoire* laboratory stool, INST HYDR *de soupape, de clapet*, MECANIQUE seat, NUCLEAIRE *d'une soupape* seat, seating, PRODUCTION *système hydraulique*, RES-SORTS, TRANSPORT, VEHICULES *habitacle* seat; ~ **arrière** *m* VEHICULES *motocyclette* pillion; ~ **avant** *m* AUTO front seat; ~ **de bonde** *m* CONS MECA plug seat; ~ **branlant** *m* INST HYDR *de soupape, de clapet* danaide, dancing seat; ~ **de charbonnage** *m* CHARBON coalworks, colliery, MINES coalworks; ~ **de clapet** *m* CONS MECA clapper seat, INST HYDR valve seat; ~ **conique** *m* INST HYDR valve; ~ **couchette** *m* VEHICULES reclining seat; ~ **éjectable** *m* AERONAUT ejection seat, ejector seat; ~ **mécanicien** *m* AERONAUT flight engineer's seat; ~ **oscillant** *m* INST HYDR *de clapet* fluttering seat, *de clapet, de soupape* loose seat; ~ **passager** *m* AERONAUT, TRANSPORT passenger seat; ~ **du ressort** *m* AUTO spring seat; ~ **de rotule** *m* CONS MECA ball socket seat; ~ **de soupape** *m* AUTO, VEHICULES *moteur* valve seat

siemens *m* METROLOGIE, PHYSIQUE siemens

sievert *m (Sv)* PHYS RAYON, PHYSIQUE sievert *(Sv)*

sifflement *m* ENREGISTR whistling

sifflet *m* ELECTRON whistle; ~ **d'alarme à flotteur** *m* INST HYDR float-controlled alarm whistle; ~ **avertisseur** *m* CONS MECA alarm whistle; ~ **de déviation** *m* PETROLE *forage* whipstock

SIG *abrév (système intégré de gestion)* INFORMAT, ORDINAT MIS *(management information system)*

sigle: ~ **de qualité** *m* EMBALLAGE quality mark

signal *m* ACOUSTIQUE, ELECTRON, ENREGISTR, INFORMAT, NAUT, ORDINAT, PHYSIQUE, TV signal;

▪ a ~ **d'acceptation d'appel** *m* TELECOM call acceptance signal; ~ **d'accusé de réception** *m* TELECOM acknowledgement signal; ~ **acoustique** *m* COMMANDE audible signal, CONS MECA, ELECTRON acoustic signal, TELECOM audible signal, sound signal; ~ **d'action** *m* COMMANDE action signal; ~ **actionné par télécommande** *m* TRANSPORT remote control sign; ~ **d'alarme** *m* COMMANDE alarm signal, danger signal, distress signal, emergency signal, NAUT alarm signal, SECURITE alarm; ~ **aléatoire** *m* ELECTRON, TELECOM random signal; ~ **d'amplitude excessive** *m* ELECTRON hard-over signal; ~ **analogique** *m* ELECTRON analog signal (AmE), analogue signal (BrE), ORDINAT analog signal, PHYSIQUE, TELECOM analog signal (AmE), analogue signal (BrE); ~ **d'appel en instance** *m* TELECOM call waiting indication; ~ **appliqué à la base** *m* ELECTRON base drive signal; ~ **appliqué à l'entrée** *m* ELECTRON input signal; ~ **d'arrêt d'émission** *m* COMMANDE cease sending signal, stop-send signal; ~ **d'asservissement** *m* ENREGISTR, TV control track signal; ~ **d'attaque de la grille** *m* ELECTRON gate drive signal; ~ **audio** *m* COMMANDE, ELECTRON audio signal; ~ **audiofréquence** *m* ELECTRON audio signal; ~ **d'autorisation** *m* COMMANDE, INFORMAT enabling signal; ~ **avancé** *m* COMMANDE advance warning sign; ~ **avancé d'avertissement** *m* CH DE FER distant caution signal; ~ **d'avertissement** *m* COMMANDE warning signal, SECURITE warning sign, TV cue; ~ **d'avertissement à distance** *m* CH DE FER distant caution signal; ~ **avertisseur** *m* COMMANDE, NAUT, PRODUCTION warning signal; ~ **avertisseur d'accident** *m* TRANSPORT accident advisory sign; ~ **avertisseur acoustique** *m* COMMANDE audible alarm, audible warning; ~ **avertisseur de bouchon** *m* TRANSPORT queue warning sign; ~ **avertisseur d'incident** *m* TRANSPORT incident warning sign; ~ **avertisseur lumineux** *m* COMMANDE warning light; ~ **avertisseur de verglas** *m* TRANSPORT ice warning sign; ~ **d'avis aux navigateurs** *m* TELECOM navigation warning signal;

~ b ~ **à bande étroite** *m* ELECTRON, TELECOM narrow band signal; ~ **à bande latérale atténuée** *m* ELECTRON vestigial sideband signal; ~ **à bande latérale unique** *m* ELECTRON single sideband signal; ~ **à bande réduite** *m* ELECTRON band-limited signal; ~ **des barres verticales et horizontales** *m* COMMANDE checkerboard signal; ~ **de bas niveau** *m* PRODUCTION low-level signal; ~ **à bas niveau** *m* ELECTRON low-level signal; ~ **à basse fréquence** *m* ELECTRON low-frequency signal; ~ **de battement** *m* ELECTRON beat signal; ~ **BF** *m* ELECTRON low-frequency signal; ~ **binaire** *m* ELECTRON, INFORMAT, ORDINAT, TELECOM binary signal; ~ **bipolaire** *m* TELECOM bipolar signal; ~ **bipolaire alternant** *m* TELECOM AMI, alternate mark inversion; ~ **bleu** *m* ELECTRON blue signal; ~ **de blocage** *m* ELECTRON turn-off pulse; ~ **de bourrage DX** *m* TELECOM DX-stuffing signal; ~ **de branchement** *m* ELECTRON turn-on pulse; ~ **à bras** *m* COMMANDE arm signal, semaphore signal; ~ **de brouillage** *m* ELECTRON jamming signal; ~ **brouilleur** *m* ESPACE *communications* interfering signal, spurious signal; ~ **de bruit** *m* TV noise signal; ~ **de bruit aléatoire** *m* ELECTRON random noise signal; ~ **de bruit blanc** *m* ELECTRON white noise signal; ~ **de brume** *m* NAUT fog signal; ~ **B-Y** *m* TV B-Y signal;

~ c ~ **de cadrage** *m* COMMANDE framing signal, TV phasing signal; ~ **de calibrage** *m* ELECTRON calibration signal; ~ **de caméra** *m* TV camera signal; ~ **de capteur** *m* COMMANDE, ELECTRON sensor signal; ~ **carré** *m* ELECTRON, PHYSIQUE square wave, TELECOM square waveform; ~ **chromatique** *m* TV color signal (AmE), colour signal (BrE); ~ **de chrominance** *m* COMMANDE chrominance signal, color signal (AmE), colour signal (BrE), ELECTRON, ESPACE *communications* chrominance signal, TV chrominance signal, color signal (AmE), colour signal (BrE); ~ **de clé** *m* TV keying signal; ~ **clignotant** *m* COMMANDE intermittent signal; ~ **à cocarde** *m* CH DE FER disc signal (BrE), disk signal (AmE); ~ **codé** *m* ELECTRON encoded signal; ~ **codé en binaire** *m* ELECTRON binary-coded signal; ~ **de commande** *m* COMMANDE, ELECTRON control signal, TV control signal, pilot signal; ~ **de commande de mise en porteuse** *m* TELECOM transmitter turn-on signal; ~ **de commande numérique** *m* TELECOM DCS, digital command signal; ~ **commutateur** *m* TV keying signal; ~ **de commutation** *m* COMMANDE switch signal; ~ **de commutation de pailles** *m* TV drop-out switch signal; ~ **à compansion** *m* ELECTRON companded signal; ~ **de comparaison** *m* COMMANDE compare signal; ~ **compensateur d'ombrage** *m* TV shading corrector; ~ **complet en couleur** *m* COMMANDE color video signal (AmE), colour video signal (BrE); ~ **complet de synchronisation** *m* COMMANDE complete synchronization signal, composite synchronization signal; ~ **complexe** *m* ELECTRON complex signal; ~ **composé** *m* COMMANDE compound signal; ~ **composite** *m* ELECTRON composite signal, TELECOM aggregate signal, TV composite signal; ~ **comprimé** *m* ELECTRON compressed signal; ~ **de compte rendu attendu** *m* TELECOM scheduled reporting signal; ~ **constant** *m* ELECTRON time invariant signal; ~ **continu** *m* ELECTRON continuous signal; ~ **de correction** *m* COMMANDE correction signal; ~ **de correction d'erreurs** *m* COMMANDE error correction signal; ~ **de couleur** *m* COMMANDE chrominance signal, color signal (AmE), colour signal (BrE), TV color signal (AmE), colour signal (BrE); ~ **couleur complet** *m* TV composite color signal (AmE), composite col-

our signal (BrE); ~ **couleur composite** *m* TV composite color signal (AmE), composite colour signal (BrE); ~ **de coupure** *m* COMMANDE cutoff signal, ELECTRON turn-off pulse; ~ **à court temps de montée** *m* ELECTRON fast rise signal;

~ d ~ **de danger** *m* SECURITE danger signal; ~ **de déblocage** *m* ELECTRON gating signal, turn-on pulse; ~ **de déclenchement de ligne** *m* TV line drive signal; ~ **déclencheur** *m* TV keying signal; ~ **découpé** *m* ELECTRON chopped signal; ~ **dégradé** *m* TV degraded signal, staircase signal; ~ **de départ** *m* ORDINAT start element; ~ **de dérangement** *m* COMMANDE malfunction signal; ~ **du détecteur** *m* ELECTRON detector signal; ~ **de détection de porteuse** *m* TELECOM carrier sense signal; ~ **de détresse** *m* AERONAUT distress signal, AUTO hazard warning system, COMMANDE danger signal, distress signal, emergency signal, NAUT distress alert, distress signal; ~ **de différence** *m* ELECTRON difference signal; ~ **de différence couleur** *m* TV color difference signal (AmE), colour difference signal (BrE); ~ **de différence de luminance** *m* TV luminance difference signal; ~ **différentiel** *m* ELECTRON differential signal; ~ **de direction** *m* COMMANDE, CONSTR direction sign; ~ **discret** *m* ELECTRON discrete signal; ~ **de disponibilité** *m* COMMANDE availability indicator; ~ **de diversion** *m* ELECTRON deception signal, false signal;

~ e ~ **d'écart** *m* AERONAUT deviation signal; ~ **échantillonné** *m* ELECTRON, TELECOM sampled signal; ~ **d'écho** *m* ELECTRON echo signal; ~ **à éclat lumineux** *m* COMMANDE flashing light signal; ~ **à éclats** *m* NAUT flashing signal; ~ **écrêté** *m* ELECTRON limited signal; ~ **écrêté à niveau constant** *m* ELECTRON hard limited signal; ~ **effacé** *m* CH DE FER off aspect; ~ **d'éjection de feuille défectueuse** *m* EMBALLAGE faulty sheet ejection signal; ~ **électrique** *m* ELECTRON electrical signal, ELECTROTEC electric signal; ~ **émis** *m* ELECTROTEC output signal; ~ **en bande de base** *m* ELECTRON baseband signal; ~ **en dents de scie** *m* ELECTROTEC ramp waveform, sawtooth waveform; ~ **en ondes entretenues** *m* ELECTROTEC CW signal; ~ **en phase** *m* ELECTRON in-phase signal; ~ **en Q** *m* *(signal en quadrature)* ELECTRON Q-signal *(quadrature signal)*; ~ **en quadrature** *m* *(signal en Q)* ELECTRON quadrature signal *(Q-signal)*; ~ **en temps réel** *m* COMMANDE real-time signal; ~ **d'entrée** *m* CH DE FER home signal (BrE), home switch (AmE), COMMANDE, ELECTRON input signal, TELECOM incoming signal, TV incoming feed, input signal; ~ **d'entrée différentiel** *m* ELECTRON differential mode signal; ~ **d'entrée interne** *m* TELECOM internal input signal; ~ **d'entrée logique** *m* ELECTRON logic input signal; ~ **d'entrée numérique** *m* ELECTRON digital input signal; ~ **d'entrée vers l'arrière** *m* TELECOM backward input signal; ~ **d'entrée vers l'avant** *m* TELECOM *maritime mobile* forward input signal; ~ **équilibré** *m* COMMANDE balance signal; ~ **d'erreur** *m* AERONAUT, COMMANDE, ELECTRON error signal; ~ **d'essai** *m* ELECTRON test signal; ~ **d'essai entre trames** *m* TV vertical interval test signal; ~ **d'état** *m* COMMANDE status signal; ~ **extérieur** *m* ELECTRON external signal;

~ f ~ **de faible amplitude** *m* ELECTRON small signal; ~ **à faible amplitude** *m* ELECTRON low-amplitude signal; ~ **du faisceau** *m* ELECTRON beam signal; ~ **fermé** *m* CH DE FER signal at danger; ~ **de fermeture de rampe** *m* TRANSPORT ramp closure sign; ~ **FI** *m* ELECTRON, TELE-

COM IF signal; ~ **de fin de bobine** *m* CINEMAT run out signal; ~ **de fin de communication** *m* TELECOM end of communication signal; ~ **de fin de parcours** *m* CH DE FER lower pantograph final warning sign; ~ **FM** *m* ELECTRON FM signal; ~ **fourni en l'absence du pilotage** *m* ELECTRON free-running signal; ~ **à fréquence élevée** *m* ELECTRON high-frequency signal; ~ **à fréquence HF** *m* ELECTRON HF signal; ~ **à fréquence intermédiaire** *m* ELECTRON, TELECOM, TV intermediate frequency signal; ~ **de fréquences audibles** *m* ENREGISTR audio frequency signal; ~ **à fréquence vocale** *m* ELECTRON tone signal;

~ g ~ **de grande amplitude** *m* ELECTRON high-amplitude signal, large signal;

~ h ~ **harmonique** *m* ELECTRON harmonic; ~ **à haute fréquence** *m* ELECTRON HF signal, RF section; ~ **à haut niveau** *m* ELECTRON high-level signal; ~ **HF** *m* ELECTRON HF signal; ~ **horaire** *m* ELECTRON, NAUT time signal; ~ **d'horloge** *m* COMMANDE clock signal, ELECTRON clock signal, timing signal; ~ **hydrographique** *m* OCEANO hydrographic signal; ~ **hyperfréquence** *m* ELECTRON microwave signal;

~ i ~ **d'identification** *m* TV identification signal; ~ **d'identification d'émetteur** *m* TRANSPORT transmitter identification signal; ~ **d'identification d'émission** *m* TV program identification signal (AmE), programme identification signal (BrE); ~ **d'identification de trafic** *m* TRANSPORT traffic information identification signal; ~ **image** *m* ELECTRON image signal, picture signal; ~ **d'image complet** *m* TV video signal; ~ **d'image effectif** *m* TV effective picture signal; ~ **impulsionnel** *m* ELECTRON pulse signal; ~ **impulsionnel élémentaire** *m* ELECTRON single pulse signal; ~ **d'incident** *m* COMMANDE malfunction signal; ~ **incident** *m* ELECTRON incident signal; ~ **d'indication d'alarme** *m (SIA)* TELECOM alarm indication signal *(AIS)*; ~ **d'indication d'alarme de section de multiplexage** *m (SM-SIA)* TELECOM multiplex section alarm indication signal; ~ **indirect** *m* ELECTRON long-way signal; ~ **d'inoccupation** *m* TELECOM FLS, free line signal; ~ **d'interdiction** *m* COMMANDE disabling signal, inhibiting signal, ELECTRON inhibiting signal; ~ **d'interruption** *m* INFORMAT, ORDINAT interrupt signal; ~ **d'intervention** *m* COMMANDE intervention signal;

~ l ~ **à large bande** *m* ELECTRON, TELECOM wide band signal; ~ **à limitation de vitesse variable** *m* TRANSPORT variable speed message sign; ~ **logique** *m* ELECTRON logic signal; ~ **de la logique interne** *m* PRODUCTION *automatisme industriel* internal logic signal; ~ **de luminance** *m* ESPACE *communications* luminance signal, TV Y-signal, luminance signal; ~ **lumineux** *m* COMMANDE, ELECTRON feedback light signal; ~ **lumineux actionné par le trafic** *m* TRANSPORT traffic-actuated signal;

~ m ~ **de main** *m* COMMANDE hand signal; ~ **de manoeuvre** *m* CH DE FER shunting signal; ~ **masqué** *m* CH DE FER concealed signal; ~ **maximal** *m* ELECTRON maximum signal; ~ **minimal** *m* ELECTRON minimum signal; ~ **minimal détectable** *m* ELECTRON minimum detectable signal; ~ **minimal utilisable** *m* ELECTRON threshold signal; ~ **de mise en action** *m* NUCLEAIRE actuating signal; ~ **de mise en phase** *m* ELECTRON phasing signal; ~ **de mode commun** *m* ELECTRON common mode signal; ~ **modulant** *m* ELECTRON, ENREGISTR modulating signal; ~ **de modulation** *m* ELECTRON modulating signal; ~ **modulé** *m* TELECOM modulated signal; ~ **modulé en amplitude** *m* ELECTRON AM signal; ~ **mo**dulé en fréquence *m* ELECTRON FM signal; ~ **monochrome** *m* ESPACE *communications* monochrome signal; ~ **multiplex** *m* ELECTRON, INFORMAT, ORDINAT multiplex signal;

~ n ~ **de neutralisation d'alarme** *m (SNA)* TELECOM alarm indication signal *(AIS)*; ~ **à niveau logique** *m* PRODUCTION logic level signal; ~ **non récurrent** *m* ELECTRON one-shot signal; ~ **noyé dans le bruit** *m* ELECTRON signal buried in noise; ~ **numérique** *m* ELECTRON, INFORMAT, ORDINAT, PHYSIQUE, TELECOM digital signal; ~ **numérique parallèle** *m* ELECTRON parallel digital signal; ~ **numérique série** *m* ELECTRON serial digital signal; ~ **numérisé** *m* ELECTRON digitized signal;

~ o ~ **d'occupation** *m* ORDINAT busy signal; ~ **OK** *m* TELECOM *maritime mobile* OK-signal; ~ **d'ombrage** *m* TV shading signal; ~ **optique** *m* COMMANDE visual signal, ELECTRON, TELECOM optical signal; ~ **optoacoustique** *m* INFORMAT, ORDINAT visual-audible signal; ~ **orthogonal** *m* TELECOM orthogonal signal; ~ **de l'oscillateur local** *m* ELECTRON local oscillator signal; ~ **d'ouverture de porte** *m* ELECTRON gating signal;

~ p ~ **parasite** *m* ELECTRON interference signal; ~ **de parole** *m* TELECOM speech signal; ~ **à pavillon** *m* NAUT flag signal; ~ **périodique** *m* ELECTRON, TELECOM periodic signal; ~ **perturbateur** *m* ELECTRON interfering signal; ~ **phonique** *m* COMMANDE, NAUT sound signal; ~ **de pilotage** *m* COMMANDE command signal; ~ **à portée optique** *m* ELECTRON line-of-sight signal; ~ **de préannonce** *m* CH DE FER outer distant signal; ~ **de protection de train** *m* CH DE FER train-protecting signal; ~ **pseudoaléatoire** *m* TELECOM pseudorandom signal;

~ q ~ **Q** *m* TV Q-signal; ~ **quantifié** *m* ELECTRON quantized signal;

~ r ~ **radio** *m* ELECTRON, ELECTROTEC radio signal; ~ **radioélectrique** *m* ELECTRON, ELECTROTEC radio signal; ~ **de rafraîchissement** *m* ELECTRON refresh signal; ~ **rectangulaire** *m* PHYSIQUE square wave; ~ **reçu** *m* ELECTRON incoming signal, received signal; ~ **récurrent** *m* ELECTRON repetitive signal; ~ **de référence** *m* COMMANDE, ELECTRON reference signal; ~ **de référence couleur** *m* TV color reference signal (AmE), colour reference signal (BrE); ~ **réfléchi** *m* ELECTRON echo, reflected signal; ~ **réflectorisé** *m* CH DE FER reflectorized board, scotchlight signal; ~ **de refoulement** *m* CH DE FER backing signal, backup signal; ~ **répétiteur** *m* CH DE FER repeating signal, NAUT repeater signal; ~ **de réponse** *m* TELECOM answer signal; ~ **de retour** *m* ELECTRON back signal, feedback signal; ~ **de rétroaction** *m* COMMANDE feedback signal, ELECTRON feedback signal, loop feedback signal; ~ **rouge** *m* ELECTRON red signal; ~ **routier variable** *m* TRANSPORT variable message sign; ~ **R-Y** *m* TV R-Y signal;

~ s ~ **saturant** *m* ELECTRON saturating signal; ~ **de sécurité** *m* SECURITE safety sign; ~ **sinusoïdal** *m* ELECTRON, TELECOM sinusoidal signal; ~ **sonar** *m* ELECTRON sonar signal; ~ **sonore** *m* CH DE FER *véhicules*, COMMANDE, ELECTRON sound signal, ENREGISTR audible signal, ORDINAT chirp, TELECOM audible signal, sound signal; ~ **sonore d'évacuation d'urgence** *m* SECURITE audible emergency evacuation signal; ~ **de sortie** *m* COMMANDE, ELECTROTEC, TELECOM output signal, TV outgoing feed, output signal; ~ **de sortie échantillonné** *m* COMMANDE sampled output signal, sampled output; ~ **de sortie logique** *m* ELECTRON logic output signal; ~ **de sortie numérique** *m* ELECTRON digital output signal; ~ **de la sous-porteuse couleur** *m* TV chrominance subcarrier signal; ~ **de sous-porteuse en phase orthogonale** *m* TV quadrature phase subcarrier signal; ~ **à spectre étalé** *m* ELECTRON, NAUT spread spectrum signal; ~ **à spectre replié** *m* ELECTRON aliased signal; ~ **de suppression** *m* ELECTRON, TV blanking signal; ~ **de suppression différé** *m* TV delayed blanking signal; ~ **de suppression et de synchronisation** *m* TV blanking and sync signal; ~ **de synchro** *m* CINEMAT sync pulse; ~ **de synchronisation** *m* ELECTRON timing signal, TV driving signal; ~ **de synchronisation complet** *m* TV composite synchronization signal; ~ **de synchronisation composite** *m* TV composite synchronization signal; ~ **de synchronisation couleur** *m* TV color sync signal (AmE), colour sync signal (BrE); ~ **de synchronisation de trame** *m* TV vertical sync pulse;

~ t ~ **de télécommunications** *m* ELECTRON communications signal; ~ **télégraphique** *m* ELECTRON telegraph signal; ~ **de télévision** *m* ELECTRON television signal; ~ **de top de synchronisation** *m* TV supersync signal; ~ **tout-ou-rien** *m* COMMANDE on/off signal; ~ **de trafic** *m* ELECTRON traffic signal; ~ **transmis en retour** *m* TELECOM looped signal; ~ **transmis par la ligne** *m* ELECTRON line signal; ~ **transmis par porte** *m* ELECTRON gated signal; ~ **transmis par un répéteur** *m* ELECTRON repeated signal; ~ **de transmission cocanalisée** *m* TV interleaved transmission signal; ~ **de transmission FM** *m* PHYS RAYON FM transmitting signal; ~ **à trois niveaux** *m* ELECTRON three-level signal; ~ **truqué** *m* ELECTRON exotic signal; ~ **type** *m* TV standard measuring signal;

~ u ~ **UHF** *m* ELECTRON UHF signal; ~ **utile** *m* ELECTRON wanted signal;

~ v ~ **valable** *m* COMMANDE valid signal; ~ **de validation** *m* COMMANDE enabling signal, ELECTRON enable signal, ORDINAT enabling signal; ~ **variant dans le temps** *m* ELECTRON time-varying signal; ~ **à variation temporelle** *m* ELECTRON time-varying signal; ~ **de verrouillage de trame** *m* COMMANDE framing signal, TELECOM FAS, frame alignment signal; ~ **vers l'arrière** *m* COMMANDE backward signal; ~ **VHF** *m* ELECTRON VHF signal; ~ **vidéo** *m* ELECTRON image signal, picture signal, video signal, ESPACE *communications*, PHYSIQUE video signal, TELECOM picture signal, video signal, TV camera signal, video signal; ~ **vidéo complet** *m* TV composite video signal; ~ **vidéo composite** *m* TV composite video signal; ~ **visible** *m* COMMANDE visible signal; ~ **vision à suppression** *m* TV video signal with blanking; ~ **visualisé** *m* ELECTRON displayed waveform; ~ **vocal** *m* COMMANDE voice signal; ~ **vocal codé** *m* TELECOM encrypted speech; ~ **vocal numérisé** *m* TELECOM digitized speech; ~ **à voie libre** *m* CH DE FER line clear signal; ~ **V-Y** *m* TV G-Y signal;

~ w ~ **wig-wag** *m* CH DE FER wig-wag signal

signaler[1] *vt (cf composer)* ELECTRON (Can) signal, INFORMAT, ORDINAT flag, SECURITE *accident* report, TELECOM *numéro* dial

signaler[2] *vti* NAUT signal

signalétique *f* CH DE FER information signs

signaleur: ~ **multifréquence** *m* TELECOM MF sender-receiver, multifrequency sender-receiver

signalisateur *m* COMMANDE signaling device (AmE), signalling device (BrE); ~ **à commande automatique de traversée** *m* COMMANDE *dans la rue* automatically-controlled crossing signal; ~ **à commande automatique** *m* COMMANDE automatically-controlled signaling device (AmE), automatically-controlled signalling device (BrE)

signalisation *f* CONS MECA indicating, CONSTR road signs, ESPACE *communications*, INFORMAT, NAUT, ORDINAT signaling (AmE), signalling (BrE), TELECOM signaling (AmE), signalling (BrE), signaling network (AmE), signalling network (BrE), VEHICULES *accessoires* indicators; ~ **automatique lumineuse** *f (SAL)* CH DE FER *de passage à niveau* automatic light signals; ~ **automatique routière** *f (SAR)* CH DE FER automatic traffic light signals; ~ **canal par canal** *f* TELECOM CAS, channel-associated signaling (AmE), channel-associated signalling (BrE); ~ **de connexion et déconnexion** *f* TELECOM connect and disconnect signaling (AmE), connect and disconnect signalling (BrE); ~ **coordonnée** *f* TRANSPORT linked traffic signal control; ~ **des défauts** *f* COMMANDE error indication, malfunction indication; ~ **en cabine** *f* CH DE FER *véhicules* cab signal; ~ **d'erreur** *f* PRODUCTION fault reporting; ~ **hors-bande** *f* ESPACE *communications* out-of-band signaling (AmE), out-of-band signalling (BrE); ~ **intrabande** *f* ESPACE *communications* in-band signaling (AmE), in-band signalling (BrE); ~ **latérale** *f* CH DE FER trackside signaling (AmE), trackside signalling (BrE); ~ **logique de défauts** *f* PRODUCTION *automatisme industriel* logical fault indication; ~ **manuelle** *f* COMMANDE hand signaling (AmE), hand signalling (BrE); ~ **à matrice lumineuse** *f* TRANSPORT matrix signalization; ~ **multifréquence** *f* ELECTRON tone signaling (AmE), tone signalling (BrE); ~ **par canal sémaphore** *f* TELECOM common channel signaling (AmE), common channel signalling (BrE); ~ **par cloches** *f* CH DE FER bell code signaling (AmE), bell code signalling (BrE); ~ **par fréquences vocales** *f* ELECTRON tone signaling (AmE), tone signalling (BrE); ~ **routière** *f* COMMANDE traffic control signals; ~ **des rues** *f* COMMANDE street signals; ~ **sémaphore** *f* TELECOM common channel signaling (AmE), common channel signalling (BrE); ~ **TRON et RON** *f* TELECOM E and M signaling (AmE), E and M signalling; ~ **d'usager à usager** *f* TELECOM UUS, user-to-user signaling (AmE), user-to-user signalling (BrE)

signature *f* INFORMAT, ORDINAT signature; ~ **électronique** *f* ORDINAT electronic signature; ~ **numérique** *f* TELECOM digital signature

signaux: ~ **auditifs** *m pl* SECURITE auditory signals; ~ **à fréquences proches** *m pl* ELECTRON close frequency signals; ~ **manuels** *m pl* SECURITE *levage mécanique* hand signals; ~ **à multiplexage temporel** *m pl* ELECTRON time-division multiplexed signals; ~ **multiplexés par répartition dans le temps** *m pl* ELECTRON time-division multiplexed signals; ~ **à plusieurs voies** *m pl* TV multipath signals; ~ **RVB** *m pl* TV tristimulus signals; ~ **de synchronisation mixtes** *m pl* TV mixed syncs; ~ **vocaux numériques non-linéaires** *m pl* TELECOM nonlinear digital speech

signe *m* INFORMAT, ORDINAT sign; ~ **d'alerte** *m* SECURITE warning sign; ~ **d'approbation** *m* METROLOGIE approval sign; ~ **d'effacement** *m* IMPRIM *préparation de copie* deleatur; ~ **d'interdiction** *m* SECURITE prohibition sign; ~ **obligatoire** *m* SECURITE mandatory sign; ~ **d'omission** *m* IMPRIM caret; ~ **de parallélisme** *m* IMPRIM parallel mark; ~ **de polarité** *m* ELECTR *d'une pile* polarity sign; ~ **de ponctuation** *m* IMPRIM punctuation mark; **~ de référence** *m* BREVETS reference sign; **~ de secours** *m* SECURITE emergency sign; **~ typographique** *m* IMPRIM *composition* bullet

signes: ~ de correction *m pl* IMPRIM proof correction marks; **~ de sécurité contre l'incendie** *m pl* SECURITE fire safety signs

signification *f* BREVETS notification

SIH *abrév (sens inverse horaire)* CONS MECA CCW *(counterclockwise)*

silane *m* CHIMIE, PLAST CAOU *type de polymère* silane

silence *m* ACOUSTIQUE rest; **~ modulé** *m* CINEMAT ambience track, silent track, ENREGISTR unmodulated track; **~ radio** *m* TELECOM blackout

silencieux[1] *adj* IMPRIM *niveau sonore* mute, MATERIAUX, SECURITE noiseless

silencieux[2] *m* ACOUSTIQUE damper, AUTO, MECANIQUE muffler (AmE), silencer (BrE), TELECOM squelch, VEHICULES *échappement* muffler (AmE), silencer (BrE); **~ d'aspiration** *m* MECANIQUE inlet muffler (AmE), inlet silencer (BrE); **~ à chicanes** *m* AUTO baffle muffler (AmE), baffle silencer (BrE); **~ à commande par tonalités** *m* TELECOM tone squelch system; **~ moteur** *m* CONS MECA engine muffler (AmE), engine silencer (BrE); **~ de piste** *m* AERONAUT jet noise suppressor; **~ de soufflage** *m* AERONAUT aerator muffler (AmE), aerator silencer (BrE); **~ de sous-porteuse** *m* TELECOM CTCSS, continuous tone-controlled squelch system

silentbloc *m* CONS MECA flexible mounting, ESPACE *véhicules* shock mount

silex *m* GEOLOGIE flint; **~ meulier** *m* PRODUCTION millstone grit; **~ noir** *m* PETR phanite

silexites *f pl* GEOLOGIE cherty beds

silhouette *f* IMPRIM *mode, détourage* figure

silicagel *m* CHAUFFAGE silica aerogel, EMBALLAGE silica gel

silicate *m* CHIMIE silicate; **~ d'aluminium** *m* LESSIVES aluminium silicate (BrE), aluminum silicate (AmE); **~ de calcium** *m* LESSIVES calcium silicate; **~ double** *m* CHIMIE metasilicate; **~ de potasse** *m* CHIMIE *de soude* waterglass; **~ de sodium** *m* LESSIVES sodium silicate; **~ synthétique** *m* MATERIAUX synthetic silicate

silicates *m pl* MATERIAUX silicates

silice *f* CERAM VER, CHIMIE, ELECTRON, MATERIAUX, MINERAUX, PHYSIQUE silica; **~ colloïdale** *f* LESSIVES colloidal silica; **~ fondue** *f* CERAM VER fused silica, OPTIQUE fused silica, vitreous silica, TELECOM fused silica; **~ gratinée de plastique** *f* OPTIQUE, TELECOM PCS, plastic-clad silica; **~ précipitée** *f* PLAST CAOU *charge, pigment* precipitated silica; **~ vitreuse** *f* CERAM VER, OPTIQUE, TELECOM vitreous silica

siliceux *adj* CHIMIE siliceous

silicium *m (Si)* CHIMIE silicium, silicon *(Si)*; **~ amorphe** *m* ELECTRON amorphous silicon; **~ dopé N** *m* ELECTRON n-type silicon; **~ monocristallin** *m* ESPACE mono-crystalline silicon; **~ polycristallin** *m* ELECTRON polycrystalline silicon; **~ sur saphir** *m* ELECTRON SOS, silicon on sapphire; **~ de type N** *m* ELECTRON n-type silicon; **~ de type P** *m* ELECTRON p-type silicon

siliciure *m* CHIMIE silicide, siliciuret

silico-aluminate *m* LESSIVES aluminium silicate (BrE), aluminum silicate (AmE)

siliconage *m* CERAM VER siliconing (BrE), siliconizing (AmE)

silicone *f* CHIMIE, ELECTR *polymère*, ELECTROTEC, MATERIAUX, PLAST CAOU silicone

silicophényle *m* CHIMIE silicophenyl

silicotitanate *m* CHIMIE silicotitanate

silicotungstate *m* CHIMIE silicotungstate

silicotungstique *adj* CHIMIE silicotungstic

sillage *m* NAUT wake, *du navire* track, OCEANO track, wake, PHYS FLUID, PHYSIQUE, POLLU MER wake; **~ amont** *m* PHYS FLUID *écoulement autour d'un obstacle* upstream wake; **~ dormant** *m* NUCLEAIRE stagnant area, wake area, wake space; **~ de torpille** *m* MILITAIRE torpedo furrow, torpedo track

sillimanite *f* MINERAUX sillimanite

sillon *m* ACOUSTIQUE groove, GEOLOGIE furrow, OPTIQUE, PRODUCTION groove; **~ d'amorçage** *m* ENREGISTR lead-in groove; **~ blanc** *m* ACOUSTIQUE blank groove; **~ concentrique** *m* ENREGISTR concentric groove; **~ final** *m* ACOUSTIQUE finishing groove; **~ de fin d'enregistrement** *m* ENREGISTR lead-out groove; **~ houiller** *m* CHARBON coal belt; **~ interplage** *m* ACOUSTIQUE lead-over groove; **~ large** *m* ACOUSTIQUE coarse groove; **~ modulé** *m* ACOUSTIQUE modulated groove; **~ prélittoral** *m* OCEANO offshore trough; **~ récifal** *m* OCEANO reef furrow; **~ sous-marin** *m* OCEANO deep-sea trough; **~ de train** *m* CH DE FER *horaire* available train path

sillonnement: ~ d'usure *m* CONS MECA grooving

silo *m* ESPACE silo; **~ de charbon** *m* MINES coal bunker

siloxane *m* CHIMIE siloxane

silt *m* GEOLOGIE silt

simbleau *m* PRODUCTION centering bridge (AmE), centring bridge (BrE)

simili[1] *adj* IMPRIM *reliure* half-bound

simili[2] *f* IMPRIM *photogravure* halftone; **~ détourée** *f* IMPRIM *typographie* blocked-out halftone

similicuir *m* PAPIER artificial leather, PLAST CAOU leatherette

similigravure *f* IMPRIM halftone process, *photogravure* halftone reproduction, PHOTO halftone block

similitude *f* BREVETS similarity; **~ dynamique** *f* PHYS FLUID dynamic similarity

simple:[1] **~ tarif** *m* ELECTR *consommation* flat-rate tariff; **~ tirage de la chambre** *m* PHOTO single camera extension

simple:[2] **~ précision** *f* INFORMAT single precision

simplement: ~ appuyé *adj* CONSTR simply-supported

simplex[1] *adj* INFORMAT, ORDINAT, TELECOM simplex

simplex:[2] **~ à deux fréquences** *m* TELECOM two-frequency simplex

simplifier *vt* MATH simplify

simulateur *m* AERONAUT simulator, ELECTRON simulator, trainer, INFORMAT, ORDINAT, TELECOM simulator; **~ de circulation** *m* TRANSPORT traffic simulator; **~ de combat aérien** *m* MILITAIRE air combat simulator; **~ en temps réel** *m* ELECTRON real-time simulator; **~ d'entrées** *m* PRODUCTION *automatisme industriel* input simulator; **~ d'environnement spatial** *m* ESPACE environmental test chamber; **~ logique** *m* ELECTRON logic simulator; **~ de pilotage** *m* AERONAUT flight simulator, link trainer; **~ de réseau** *m* INFORMAT, ORDINAT network simulator; **~ de sensation** *m* ESPACE feel simulator; **~ de vol** *m* AERONAUT, INFORMAT, ORDINAT flight simulator

simulation *f* ELECTRON, ESSAIS, GAZ, INFORMAT, ORDINAT simulation, PRODUCTION scenario; **~ de la circulation** *f* TRANSPORT simulation of traffic, traffic simulation; **~ en temps réel** *f* ELECTRON real-time simulation; **~ logique** *f* ELECTRON logic simulation; **~ de nuances** *f* INFORMAT dithering; **~ de signaux** *f* ELECTRON signal simulation simuler *vt* INFORMAT, ORDINAT simulate

simultané[1] *adj* INFORMAT concurrent, simultaneous, OR-DINAT simultaneous

simultané:[2] ~ antenne *m* TV off-air recording

simultanéité *f* PHYSIQUE simultaneity

sin *m* (*sinus*) GEOMETRIE, INFORMAT, MATH, ORDINAT sin (*sine*)

sinapine *f* CHIMIE sinapine

sinapique *adj* CHIMIE *acide* sinapic

singe *m* CONS MECA jig, milling jig, PRODUCTION former

singularité *f* ASTRONOMIE, PHYSIQUE singularity

singulet *m* PHYSIQUE singlet

sinus *m* (*sin*) GEOMETRIE *d'un angle*, INFORMAT, MATH, ORDINAT sine (*sin*); ~ naturel *m* GEOMETRIE *d'un angle* natural sine

sinusoïdal *adj* ELECTR *onde* sinusoidal

sinusoïde *f* GEOMETRIE, INFORMAT sinusoid, MATH sine curve, sinusoid, ORDINAT sinusoid, PHYSIQUE sine wave

siphon *m* CONSTR drain trap, stench trap, stink trap, trap, EQUIP LAB siphon, HYDROLOGIE siphon, siphon conduit, PHYSIQUE siphon; ~ à débordement *m* EN RENOUV *barrages* siphon spillway; ~ en S *m* CONSTR S-trap; ~ à filtre *m* GENIE CHIM filter siphon; ~ horizontal *m* CONSTR running trap

sirène *f* NAUT siren, PRODUCTION hooter, SECURITE alarm; ~ d'alarme *f* PRODUCTION hooter; ~ d'alerte *f* SECURITE siren; ~ d'incendie *f* SECURITE fire siren

Sirius *m* ASTRONOMIE Sirius

sirop *m* CERAM VER wavy cord

sisal *m* NAUT sisal

site *m* ESPACE altitude, elevation angle; ~ banal *m* TRANSPORT nonreserved space; ~ de décharge *m* RE-CYCLAGE dump site, dumping ground, landfill, tip; ~ d'évacuation *m* CONSTR disposal site; ~ propre *m* TRANSPORT exclusive site; ~ réactif *m* CHIMIE reactive site

sitostérol *m* CHIMIE sitosterol

situation *f* CONSTR location; ~ de la marée *f* OCEANO phase lag, tidal epoch, tide phase; ~ météorologique *f* ESPACE weather pattern; ~ à la rampe *f* AERONAUT ramp status; ~ réglementaire du vol *f* AERONAUT flight status; ~ du stock *f* PRODUCTION inventory reporting; ~ de trafic *f* TRANSPORT traffic situation; ~ d'urgence *f* NUCLEAIRE emergency condition

sixte *f* ACOUSTIQUE sixth; ~ majeure stricte *f* ACOUSTIQUE major sixth; ~ mineure *f* ACOUSTIQUE minor sixth

skiatron *m* ELECTRON skiatron

skidder *m* TRANSPORT skidder

skip: ~ à bascule *m* CONSTR dump skip

skuttérudite *f* MINERAUX skutterudite

skybus *m* TRANSPORT skybus

slamming *m* NAUT slamming

slimes *f pl* PRODUCTION sludge

slip *m* NAUT *de halage, de carénage* slipway

slogan: ~ accroche *m* IMPRIM catchline

sloop *m* NAUT sloop

slot: ~ d'extension *m* INFORMAT, ORDINAT expansion slot

slug *m* METROLOGIE slug

sluice *m* MINES sluice; ~ de décharge *m* DISTRI EAU tailsluice; ~ à pente ménagée *m* DISTRI EAU graded sluice; ~ de tête *m* DISTRI EAU head sluice

Sm (*samarium*) CHIMIE Sm (*samarium*)

smaltite *f* MINERAUX smaltite

smaragdite *f* MINERAUX smaragdite

SMCN *abrév* (*système de multiplication de circuit numérique*) TELECOM DCMS (*digital circuit multiplication system*)

SMDSM *abrév* (*système mondial de détresse et de sécurité en mer*) NAUT GMDSS (*Global Marine Distress and Safety System*)

smectite *f* CHARBON, CHIMIE smectite, LESSIVES bentonite, PETROLE smectite

smithsonite *f* MINERAUX smithsonite

smog *m* POLLUTION smog; ~ oxydant *m* POLLUTION photochemical smog; ~ photochimique *m* POLLUTION photochemical smog; ~ photochimique oxydant *m* POLLUTION photochemical smog

SM-SIA *abrév* (*signal d'indication d'alarme de section de multiplexage*) TELECOM multiplex section alarm indication signal

Sn (*étain*) CHIMIE Sn (*tin*)

SNA *abrév* (*signal de neutralisation d'alarme*) TELECOM AIS (*alarm indication signal*)

SNCB *abrév* (*Société nationale des chemins de fer belges*) CH DE FER Belgian National Railways

SNCF *abrév* (*Société nationale des chemins de fer français*) CH DE FER French National Railways

SNHP *abrév* (*syndrome nerveux des hautes pressions*) OCEANO high-pressure nervous syndrome

snorkel *m* CINEMAT periscope, snorkel

soc *m* IMPRIM *rotatives* plough (BrE), plow (AmE)

société: ~ certifiée *f* QUALITE certified company; ~ de classification *f* NAUT classification society; ~ pétrolière *f* PRODUCTION petroleum company; ~ de surveillance *f* SECURITE security firm

Société: ~ nationale des chemins de fer belges (*SNCB*) CH DE FER Belgian National Railways; ~ nationale des chemins de fer français (*SNCF*) CH DE FER French National Railways

socle *m* CONS MECA pedestal, GEOLOGIE basement, IN-STRUMENT baseplate, MECANIQUE pedestal, PETR basement; ~ de connecteur *m* ELECTROTEC connector socket; ~ continental *m* GEOPHYS continental mass; ~ cristallin *m* GEOLOGIE crystalline basement; ~ de fixation *m* CONS MECA mounting base; ~ insulaire *m* OCEANO insular shelf; ~ de machine *m* MECANIQUE engine pedestal; ~ métamorphique *m* GEOLOGIE basement complex; ~ de prise de courant *m* ELECTROTEC outlet; ~ à roulettes *m* PRODUCTION stand on wheels

socle-support *m* INSTRUMENT base, pedestal base; ~ de la platine *m* INSTRUMENT stage base

sodalite *f* MATERIAUX, MINERAUX sodalite

sodique *adj* CHIMIE, GEOLOGIE sodic

sodium *m* CHIMIE (*Na*) sodium (*Na*)

soffite *m* CONSTR soffit

software *m* PETR software; ~ spécifique existant sous une forme hardware *m* IMPRIM firmware

soie *f* CONS MECA fang, tongue, *d'une lime* tang, *d'un couteau, d'un ciseau* tang, TEXTILE silk; ~ de manivelle *f* CONS MECA crankpin

soin: ~ d'hygiène *m* SECURITE health care

sol *m* CHARBON ground, soil, GEOPHYS soil, MINES foot, footwall, *d'un filon* ledger, ledger wall, PRODUCTION *d'une fonderie* floor; ~ d'argile *m* CHARBON clay, clay soil; ~ à blocs *m* CHARBON boulder soil; ~ à coefficient d'uniformité élevé *m* CHARBON multigraded soil; ~ cohésif *m* CHARBON cohesive soil; ~ contractable *m* CHARBON contractant soil, contractible soil; ~ à couches alternées *m* CHARBON zonal soil; ~ difficile *m* CONSTR difficult ground; ~ expansible *m* CHARBON

swelling soil; ~ **gelé** *m* CHARBON frozen ground; ~ **à grains fins** *m* CHARBON fine soil; ~ **à grains grossiers** *m* CHARBON coarse soil; ~ **de granulométrie complexe** *m* CHARBON graded soil; ~ **à granulométrie uniforme** *m* CHARBON even-grained soil; ~ **marécageux** *m* CONSTR swampy soil; ~ **marin** *m* PETROLE mud line; ~ **moyen** *m* CHARBON intermediate type of soil; ~ **naturel** *m* POLLUTION unspoilt land; ~ **passif au gel** *m* CHARBON nonfrost-susceptible soil; ~ **pulvérulent** *m* CHARBON noncohesive soil; ~ **résistant** *m* CHARBON cohesive soil; ~ **sans perturbation artificielle** *m* POLLUTION unspoilt land; ~ **saturé d'eau** *m* CHARBON saturated soil; ~ **sédimentaire** *m* CHARBON sedimentary soil; ~ **de sulfure** *m* CHARBON sulfide soil (AmE), sulphide soil (BrE); ~ **tendre** *m* CONSTR soft ground
solaire *adj* ASTRONOMIE, CONSTR solar
solanidine *f* CHIMIE solanidine
solarimètre *m* EN RENOUV solarimeter
solarisation *f* CINEMAT, PHOTO solarization
solde *m* PRODUCTION *du stock* balance
sole *f* CONSTR baseplate, footing block, sole piece, sole plate, INST HYDR reversed arch, MINES groundsill, pavement (BrE), sill, sill piece, sole piece, sole, *d'une galerie de mine* floor, PRODUCTION coking plate, deadplate, dumb plate, sole, *d'un four électrique* hearth; ~ **du chantier** *f* MINES stope floor; ~ **gravière** *f* CONSTR mudsill
soleil *m* ASTRONOMIE sun; ~ **calme** *m* ASTRONOMIE quiet sun; ~ **moyen** *m* ASTRONOMIE mean sun
solénoïde *m* AUTO sodium-cooled valve, ELECTR *bobine*, ELECTROTEC, PHYSIQUE, PRODUCTION, REFRIG solenoid, TV electromagnet, solenoid, VEHICULES *démarreur* solenoid; ~ **d'arrêt** *m* PRODUCTION lockout solenoid; ~ **de vidange** *m* CONS MECA drain solenoid
solidaire *adj* CONS MECA embodied, integral
solide[1] *adj* CHIMIE solid, TEXTILE fast; ~ **au chlore** *adj* LESSIVES chlorine-fast; ~ **à la lumière** *adj* COULEURS colorfast (AmE), colourfast (BrE), light-fast, IMPRIM fast-to-light
solide[2] *m* GEOMETRIE *cube, cône, sphère*, PHYSIQUE solid; ~ **d'égale résistance** *m* CONS MECA solid of uniform strength; ~ **invariable** *m* PHYSIQUE rigid body; ~ **polycristallin** *m* CRISTALL polycrystalline solid; ~ **de révolution** *m* GEOMETRIE solid of revolution
solidification *f* AGRO ALIM caking, MATERIAUX *d'un bain fondu* solidification, METALL, PHYSIQUE solidification
solidité *f* EN RENOUV solidity, METALL strength, TEXTILE fastness, toughness; ~ **de coquille** *f* AGRO ALIM shell strength; ~ **de couleur** *f* PLAST CAOU colorfastness (AmE), colourfastness (BrE); ~ **de la couleur** *f* COULEURS color fastness (AmE), colour fastness (BrE); ~ **d'un joint** *f* EMBALLAGE joint strength; ~ **à la lumière** *f* TEXTILE fastness to light; ~ **de teinture** *f* COULEURS color fastness (AmE), colour fastness (BrE)
solidus *m* CHIMIE solidus
solin *m* CONSTR fillet gutter
solivage *m* CONSTR beams, joisting
solive *f* CONSTR beam, binder, joist, EMBALLAGE joist; ~ **bâtarde** *f* CONSTR trimmed joist; ~ **boiteuse** *f* CONSTR trimmed joist; ~ **d'enchevêtrure** *f* CONSTR landing trimmer, trimmed joist; ~ **en fer à double T** *f* CONSTR H-beam, H-girder, I-beam, I-girder; ~ **de plafond** *f* CONSTR ceiling joist; ~ **de plancher** *f* CONSTR floor joist; ~ **de tête** *f* CONSTR head beam
soliveau *m* CONSTR girder, joist
sollicitation *f* ESPACE *véhicules* actuation, loading,

stress, METALL load, PHYSIQUE strength, stress; ~ **dynamique** *f* METALL dynamic loading; ~ **au hasard** *f* METALL random loading; ~ **répétée** *f* METALL repeated loading; ~ **stochastique** *f* METALL stochastic loading; ~ **variable** *f* METALL varying loading
sollicité: ~ **par une force** *adj* PHYSIQUE acted upon by a force
solliciter *vt* PHYSIQUE act upon, stress
solstice *m* ASTRONOMIE, ESPACE solstice; ~ **d'été** *m* ASTRONOMIE summer solstice; ~ **d'hiver** *m* ASTRONOMIE winter solstice
solubilisant *m* CHIMIE solutizer
solubilité *f* CHARBON, CHIMIE, PLAST CAOU solubility; ~ **limitée** *f* METALL restricted solubility
soluble *adj* CHIMIE, PETROLE soluble; ~ **dans l'eau** *adj* TEXTILE water-soluble; ~ **dans l'huile** *adj* CHIMIE oil-soluble; ~ **en milieu alcalin** *adj* LESSIVES alkali-soluble
soluté *m* AGRO ALIM, MATERIAUX solute
solution *f* CHIMIE liquor, solution, GEOMETRIE *d'un problème* solution; ~ **acide** *f* AGRO ALIM acid solution; ~ **aqueuse d'ammoniaque** *f* PAPIER ammonia hydrate, ammonical hydroxide; ~ **aqueuse de formol** *f* CHIMIE formalin; ~ **d'attaque** *f* METALL etching solution; ~ **de blanchiment** *f* PAPIER bleaching liquor; ~ **de chlorure de calcium** *f* PRODUCTION bleach liquor; ~ **de couchage** *f* REVETEMENT coating color (AmE), coating colour (BrE), coating slip; ~ **désordonnée** *f* METALL random solution; ~ **d'entretien** *f* CINEMAT replenishing solution; ~ **forte** *f* CHIMIE strong solution; ~ **de gomme adragante** *f* IMPRIM bed; ~ **de lixiviation** *f* GENIE CHIM leach liquor; ~ **de mouillage** *f* IMPRIM dampening etch; ~ **normale** *f* CHIMIE normal solution; ~ **régénératrice** *f* PHOTO replenisher; ~ **saline** *f* NUCLEAIRE brine, saline solution, salt liquor; ~ **saturée** *f* PETR saturated solution; ~ **solide** *f* CHIMIE, CRISTALL solid solution, GEOLOGIE diadochy, solid solution; ~ **solide désordonnée** *f* MATERIAUX disordered solid solution; ~ **solide interstitielle** *f* CRISTALL interstitial solid solution; ~ **solide ordonnée** *f* METALL ordered solid solution; ~ **solide de substitution** *f* CRISTALL substitutional solid solution; ~ **standard** *f* CHIMIE standard solution; ~ **sursaturée** *f* CHIMIE supersaturated solution; ~ **tampon** *f* AGRO ALIM, PRODUCTION buffer solution
solvabilité *f* CHIMIE solvency
solvant *m* AGRO ALIM, CHARBON solvent, CHIMIE dissolver, solvent, CINEMAT solvent, GENIE CHIM dissolvent, dissolver, LESSIVES, METALL, PLAST CAOU *matière première*, POLLUTION, TEXTILE solvent; ~ **actif** *m* EMBALLAGE active solvent; ~ **aliphatique** *m* PETROLE aliphatic solvent; ~ **aprotique** *m* CHIMIE aprotic solvent; ~ **d'extraction** *m* AGRO ALIM extractant; ~ **aux halogénures d'hydrocarbones** *m* POLLUTION halogenated hydrocarbon solvent; ~ **non-polaire** *m* PLAST CAOU nonpolar solvent; ~ **sélectif** *m* CHIMIE, PETROLE selective solvent
solvatation *f* CHIMIE solvation
solvate *m* CHIMIE solvate
solvaté *adj* CHIMIE solvated
solvatisation *f* CHIMIE solvation
solvatisé *adj* CHIMIE *colloïde* solvated
sombre *adj* GEOLOGIE dark-colored (AmE), dark-coloured (BrE)
sombrer *vi* NAUT founder, go down, sink
sommaire *m* CINEMAT outline
sommation *f* PETR stack; ~ **horizontale** *f* PETR horizontal

stack; ~ **hydrographique** *f* EN RENOUV summation hydrograph

somme *f* INFORMAT, MATH, ORDINAT sum, PETR stack; ~ **de contrôle** *f* ELECTRON checksum; ~ **des états électroniques** *f* NUCLEAIRE electronic partition function

sommet *m* CONSTR *d'une voûte* crown, CRISTALL vertex, ESPACE apex, GEOMETRIE vertex, *d'un cône* apex, MINES *d'un filon* apex, PAPIER apex, peak, top, PETROLE *d'un derrick* crown, PHYSIQUE, TELECOM vertex; ~ **du derrick** *m* PETROLE derrick crown; ~ **de talus** *m* CHARBON slope top

sommier *m* CONSTR impost, springer, springer stone, springing, stringer, transom, PRODUCTION bearer; ~ **du coeur** *m* NUCLEAIRE core grid structure; ~ **de porte** *m* CONSTR lintel; ~ **transversal** *m* PRODUCTION *d'une grille de foyer* cross bearer; ~ **de voûte en briques** *m* CONSTR brick arch bearer

son *m* ACOUSTIQUE sound, tone, ENREGISTR, PHYSIQUE sound; ~ **ambiant** *m* ENREGISTR ambient noise; ~ **d'archives** *m* ENREGISTR stock sound; ~ **associé à l'image** *m* CINEMAT married sound; ~ **de battement** *m* PHYS ONDES beat note; ~ **de combinaison** *m* ACOUSTIQUE combination sound; ~ **complexe** *m* ACOUSTIQUE complex tone; ~ **dans l'image** *m* TV sound on vision; ~ **désynchronisé** *m* CINEMAT asynchronous sound; ~ **direct** *m* ENREGISTR live sound; ~ **fondamental** *m* ACOUSTIQUE fundamental tone; ~ **hululé** *m* ACOUSTIQUE howling; ~ **inversible** *m* CINEMAT sound direct positive; ~ **musical** *m* ACOUSTIQUE tone; ~ **non synchrone** *m* CINEMAT asynchronous sound, wild track; ~ **optique** *m* CINEMAT optical sound; ~ **partiel** *m* ACOUSTIQUE partial; ~ **périodique** *m* ACOUSTIQUE periodic tone; ~ **photographique** *m* CINEMAT optical sound; ~ **piloté** *m* CINEMAT pilot tone sound; ~ **plein** *m* ENREGISTR round tone; ~ **résultant** *m* ACOUSTIQUE combination tone; ~ **séparé** *m* CINEMAT unmarried sound; ~ **seul** *m* CINEMAT unmarried sound; ~ **stéréophonique** *m* ENREGISTR stereophonic sound; ~ **stéréophonique à trois pistes** *m* ENREGISTR three-track stereo; ~ **synchrone** *m* ENREGISTR synchronous sound; ~ **tétraphonique** *m* CINEMAT surround sound

sonar *m* MILITAIRE sonic depth finder, NAUT, OCEANO, PHYS RAYON sonar; ~ **à balayage** *m* OCEANO scanning sonar; ~ **panoramique** *m* OCEANO scanning sonar

sondage *m* CONSTR borehole, boreholing, hole, MINES blast hole, borehole, drill hole, bore, boring, drilling, NAUT sounding, OCEANO echo sounding, sounding, PETR borehole, PETROLE hole, well bore, well, PRODUCTION sounding; ~ **de battage** *m* MINES churn drilling; ~ **à chute libre** *m* CONSTR free fall boring, free fall drilling; ~ **dévié** *m* PETR crooked hole; ~ **au diamant** *m* MINES diamond drilling; ~ **dynamique** *m* CHARBON dynamic sounding; ~ **exécuté au hasard** *m* MINES gopher hole; ~ **à grande profondeur** *m* MINES deep boring, deep drilling; ~ **à la grenaille d'acier** *m* CONSTR boring by shot drills, MINES shot boring, shot drilling; ~ **au hasard** *m* MINES gopher hole; ~ **non-tubé** *m* PETR uncased hole; ~ **par battage** *m* CONSTR boring by percussion; ~ **par battage à la tige** *m* CONSTR boring by percussion with rods; ~ **par rodage** *m* CONSTR boring by rotation, MINES rotary drilling; ~ **par segments capables** *m* OCEANO fixed angle sounding; ~ **par ultrasons** *m* NAUT echo sounding, PHYS ONDES ultrasonic sounding; ~ **percutant** *m* MINES churn drilling; ~ **au pilon** *m* CHARBON ram penetration test; ~ **profond** *m* MINES deep borehole, deep drillhole; ~ **de recherche** *m*

PETROLE exploratory drilling; ~ **de roc** *m* CHARBON rock sounding; ~ **au trépan** *m* CONSTR boring with the bit

sonde *f* CHARBON, ELECTR *mesure*, ESPACE *véhicules*, GAZ probe, MINES borer, drilling machine, rock drill, boring machine, NAUT sounding line, OCEANO detector, probe, sounding, sounding lead, PHYSIQUE probe, sensor, POLLU MER sensing element; ~ **d'accostage** *f* ESPACE *véhicules* docking probe; ~ **d'adaptation** *f* ELECTROTEC slug; ~ **altimétrique** *f* TRANSPORT radar altimeter; ~ **à carottes** *f* MINES core borer, core drill; ~ **de cyclage** *f* AERONAUT cycling thermoresistor; ~ **à déclenchement par touches** *f* CONS MECA touch trigger probe; ~ **d'échantillonnage** *f* QUALITE *d'eau* sampling probe; ~ **électromagnétique** *f* AERONAUT flux gate (AmE), flux valve (BrE); ~ **électronique** *f* NUCLEAIRE electron probe; ~ **d'espace Hélios** *f* ASTRONOMIE Helios space probe; ~ **d'espace lointain** *f* ESPACE *véhicules* deep space probe; ~ **d'espace Voyager** *f* ASTRONOMIE Voyager space probe; ~ **de givrage** *f* AERONAUT icing probe; ~ **à grille** *f* NUCLEAIRE grid probe; ~ **de Hall** *f* PHYS RAYON, PHYSIQUE Hall probe; ~ **interplanétaire** *f* ESPACE *véhicules* interplanetary probe; ~ **lambda** *f* AUTO lambda probe; ~ **de ligne de mesure** *f* ELECTROTEC slotted line probe; ~ **lointaine** *f* ESPACE *véhicules* deep space probe; ~ **lunaire** *f* ESPACE *véhicules* lunar probe; ~ **de Magellan** *f* ASTRONOMIE Magellan spacecraft; ~ **magnétique** *f* NUCLEAIRE magnetic probe; ~ **de mesure de la température** *f* PRODUCTION temperature sending device; ~ **microphonique** *f* ACOUSTIQUE, ENREGISTR probe microphone; ~ **orbitale** *f* ESPACE *véhicules* orbiter; ~ **pendulaire** *f* CERAM VER pendulum floater; ~ **percutante** *f* MINES churn drill, percussion drill; ~ **planétaire** *f* ESPACE *véhicules* planetary probe; ~ **à pointes de diamant** *f* PRODUCTION diamond drill; ~ **à pointes de diamant et à tube carottier** *f* PRODUCTION diamond core drill; ~ **de posemètre** *f* PHOTO light meter probe; ~ **de prospection** *f* MINES temper screw, testing drill; ~ **réciprocale** *f* PETR reciprocal probe; ~ **de régulation** *f* REFRIG probe; ~ **spatiale** *f* ASTRONOMIE, ESPACE *véhicules* space probe; ~ **spatiale en orbite** *f* ASTRONOMIE orbiting space probe; ~ **spatiale Galilée** *f* ASTRONOMIE Galilean space probe; ~ **spatiale Giotto** *f* ASTRONOMIE Giotto spacecraft; ~ **spatiale Hélios** *f* ASTRONOMIE Helios space probe; ~ **spatiale Mariner** *f* ASTRONOMIE Mariner space probe; ~ **spatiale Pioneer** *f* ASTRONOMIE Pioneer spacecraft; ~ **spatiale Venera** *f* ASTRONOMIE Venera space probe; ~ **de surchauffe** *f* AERONAUT overheat thermoresistor; ~ **de température** *f* AUTO temperature sensor, MATERIAUX heat sensor, PRODUCTION temperature detector, THERMODYN heat sensor, temperature probe; ~ **de température carburant** *f* AERONAUT fuel temperature probe; ~ **de température extérieure** *f* AERONAUT outside air temperature probe; ~ **de température d'huile** *f* AERONAUT oil temperature probe; ~ **thermique** *f* THERMODYN temperature probe

sonder *vt* ESSAIS bore, NAUT, OCEANO sound

sondeur *m* NAUT depth finder, depth sounder, sounder, OCEANO depth recorder, depth sounder; ~ **au diamant** *m* MINES diamond driller; ~ **à écho** *m* NAUT echo sounder; ~ **de filet** *m* OCEANO netsonde; ~ **ionosphérique** *m* GEOPHYS ionospheric recorder; ~ **multifaisceau** *m* OCEANO echo sounder, multibeam echo sounder, multibeam sounder; ~ **par ultrasons** *m* NAUT echo sounder; ~ **de radar** *m* MILITAIRE radar scanner; ~ de **sédiment** *m* OCEANO sediment probe, sediment sounder, sub-bottom profiler; ~ **de vase** *m* OCEANO sediment probe, sediment sounder, sub-bottom profiler

sondeuse *f* MINES borer, drill, drilling machine, jackhammer, rock drill, boring machine; ~ **à carottes** *f* MINES core borer, core drill; ~ **à couronne** *f* MINES angled drill, annular borer; ~ **à couronne à dents d'acier** *f* MINES calyx drill; ~ **à diamant** *f* PRODUCTION diamond drill; ~ **à grenaille d'acier** *f* MINES shot drill; ~ **rotative à carottage continu** *f* MINES rotary continuous-core drill

sone *m* ACOUSTIQUE, PHYSIQUE sone

sonie *f* ACOUSTIQUE, PHYSIQUE loudness

sonificateur *m* EQUIP LAB ultrasound generator

sonique *adj* PHYSIQUE sonic

sonner *vi* TELECOM ring

sonnerie *f* ELECTROTEC call bell, TELECOM ringing; ~ **d'alarme** *f* SECURITE alarm bell, warning bell; ~ **d'appel** *f* ELECTROTEC call bell; ~ **d'avertissement** *f* COMMANDE signal bell; ~ **continue** *f* ELECTROTEC continuous ringing bell; ~ **de poste** *f* TELECOM extension bell; ~ **téléphonique** *f* TELECOM telephone bell

sonnette *f* CHARBON pile driver, CONSTR gin, pile driver, postdriver, ram, piling frame, MECANIQUE *chantier* drop pile hammer; ~ **d'alarme** *f* ELECTR alarm bell; ~ **électrique** *f* ELECTR electric bell; ~ **à trembleur** *f* ELECTR trembler bell

sonneur *m* CONSTR pile driver

sonographe *m* OCEANO sound channel

sonomètre *m* ACOUSTIQUE sound level meter, PHYS ONDES, PHYSIQUE sonometer, SECURITE sound exposure meter, sound level meter; ~ **de poche** *m* SECURITE personal sound exposure meter

sonore *adj* ENREGISTR audio

sonoriser *vt* CINEMAT dub

sonothèque *f* ENREGISTR sound archive

sorbant *m* POLLU MER sorbent

sorbite *f* CHIMIE sorbite

sorbitol *m* CHIMIE sorbitol

sorbonne *f* EQUIP LAB fume hood

sorbose *m* CHIMIE sorbose

sorcière *f* CERAM VER witch mirror

sorption *f* DISTRI EAU, MATERIAUX sorption

sortance *f* ELECTROTEC, INFORMAT, ORDINAT fan-out

sortant *adj* NAUT *d'un port* outward bound, TELECOM outgoing

sortie *f* CONS MECA outlet, CONSTR way out, DISTRI EAU outfall, outflow, ELECTROTEC lead, output, IMPRIM output, *imprimerie* delivery, INFORMAT exit, output, ORDINAT output, *instruction* exit, PRODUCTION delivery, outlet, TELECOM outlet, output port, read-out, TV output; ~ **d'air de dégivrage** *f* AERONAUT de-icing air outlet; ~ **alternative** *f* ELECTROTEC AC output, alternating current output; ~ **amplificateur de ligne** *f* PRODUCTION *automatisme industriel* line driver output; ~ **de l'amplificateur vertical** *f* ELECTRON vertical amplifier output; ~ **analogique** *f* INSTRUMENT analog output (AmE), analogue output (BrE); ~ **d'arche** *f* CERAM VER end of lehr; ~ **asservie** *f* CONS MECA controlled outlet; ~ **asymétrique** *f* ELECTROTEC single-ended output, unbalanced output; ~ **continue** *f* ELECTROTEC DC output, direct current output; ~ **de coque** *f* NAUT seacock; ~ **dans l'espace** *f* ESPACE space step-out; ~ **directe** *f* ELECTRON direct output; ~ **dissymétrique** *f* ESPACE *communications* unbalanced

output; ~ **de données** *f* INSTRUMENT data output; ~ **de l'eau** *f* DISTRI EAU, REFRIG water outlet, water outlet port; ~ **électrique** *f* ELECTRON, ELECTROTEC electrical output; ~ **en accumulation** *f* IMPRIM *rotatives* collect run; ~ **en courant** *f* ELECTROTEC current output; ~ **en courant alternatif** *f* ELECTROTEC AC output, alternating current output; ~ **en courant continu** *f* ELECTROTEC DC output, direct current output; ~ **en temps réel** *f* INFORMAT, ORDINAT real-time output; ~ **flottante** *f* ELECTROTEC floating output; ~ **gardée** *f* ELECTROTEC guarded output; ~ **du générateur** *f* ELECTROTEC generator output; ~ **de la génératrice** *f* ELECTROTEC generator output; ~ **imprimante** *f* IMPRIM printer output; ~ **imprimée** *f* INFORMAT printout; ~ **latérale de piste** *f* AERONAUT runoff; ~ **ligne** *f* ENREGISTR line out, TV line out, line output; ~ **de livres un par un** *f* IMPRIM *brochure* one-up; ~ **de machine** *f* IMPRIM front delivery; ~ **de la magnéto** *f* ELECTROTEC generator output; ~ **à la masse** *f* PRODUCTION *électricité* output earth short (BrE), output ground short (AmE); ~ **de matière** *f* PRODUCTION material issue; ~ **nominale** *f* INFORMAT, ORDINAT rated output; ~ **non équilibrée** *f* ELECTROTEC single-ended output; ~ **non mémorisée** *f* PRODUCTION *automatisme industriel* nonretentive output; ~ **numérique** *f* ELECTRON digital output; ~ **numérique série** *f* INFORMAT, ORDINAT serial digital output; ~ **optique** *f* ELECTROTEC optical output; ~ **ordinateur sur microfilm** *f* ORDINAT COM, computer output on microfilm; ~ **pendant le déroulement du programme** *f* ORDINAT runtime output; ~ **pendant l'exécution du programme** *f* ORDINAT runtime output; ~ **de piste** *f* AERONAUT exit taxiway; ~ **à plat** *f* IMPRIM flat-sheet delivery, sheeter; ~ **pour périphérique** *f* PRODUCTION *automatisme industriel* peripheral port; ~ **prioritaire** *f* PRODUCTION *automatisme industriel* immediate output; ~ **radiale** *f* ELECTROTEC radial lead; ~ **redressée** *f* ELECTROTEC rectified output; ~ **de robinet** *f* CONS MECA valve outlet; ~ **de secours** *f* CONSTR, SECURITE emergency exit, THERMODYN fire exit; ~ **séquenceur** *f* PRODUCTION *automatisme industriel* sequencer output; ~ **de stock** *f* PRODUCTION material issue; ~ **sur huit bits** *f* ELECTRON eight-bit output; ~ **sur imprimante** *f* IMPRIM *photogravure* hard copy, TELECOM printout; ~ **du train d'atterrissage** *f* AERONAUT landing gear extension; ~ **à trois états** *f* ELECTRON three-state output; ~ **de tuyère** *f* PHYSIQUE nozzle exit; ~ **d'usine** *f* PRODUCTION ex works; ~ **de vapeur** *f* INST HYDR steam outlet; ~ **du vent** *f* CONS MECA air outlet; ~ **vidéo** *f* TV video output; ~ **vocale** *f* INFORMAT, ORDINAT voice output

sorties: ~ **complémentaires** *f pl* ELECTRON complementary outputs

sortir[1] *vt* CINEMAT *film* release

sortir[2]: ~ **du système** *vi* INFORMAT, ORDINAT log off, log out, sign off

SOS *m* TRANSPORT SOS

soubassement *m* CONSTR base, GEOLOGIE substratum, underlying rock, PETR basement, PETROLE bedrock; ~ **de patinoire** *m* REFRIG rink floor

soubresaut *m* CHIMIE bumping

souche: ~ **de cheminée** *f* CONSTR chimney stack

souchevage *m* MINES holing, jad, kerving, kirving

souchevé *adj* MINES holed

souchever *vt* MINES hole

soucheveur *m* MINES cutter

soucoupe: ~ **plongeante** *f* (*SP*) OCEANO diving saucer

soudabilité *f* CONS MECA, MATERIAUX, METALL weldability

soudable *adj* PRODUCTION solderable

soudage *m* CONS MECA welding, CONSTR, MATERIAUX soldering, PLAST CAOU *enveloppe plastique* heat sealing, *procédé* welding, PRODUCTION soldering, welding, SECURITE, THERMODYN welding; ~ **aluminothermique** *m* CH DE FER, CONSTR thermit welding; ~ **à l'arc** *m* CONSTR, ELECTR *application*, MECANIQUE arc welding, THERMODYN arc welding, *avec fil électrode* metal arc welding; ~ **à arc automatique** *m* CONS MECA automatic arc welding; ~ **à l'arc avec électrode enrobée** *m* NUCLEAIRE SMAW, shielded metal arc welding; ~ **à l'arc avec fil fourré** *m* CONSTR flux-cored arc welding; ~ **à l'arc électrique** *m* PRODUCTION, THERMODYN electric arc welding; ~ **à l'arc à électrodes de carbone** *m* PRODUCTION carbon arc welding; ~ **à l'arc en atmosphère inerte** *m* PRODUCTION inert gas welding; ~ **à l'arc manuel** *m* CONSTR manual arc welding; ~ **à l'arc sous flux en poudre** *m* CONSTR submerged arc welding; ~ **à l'arc sous gaz actif avec fil fourré** *m* CONSTR flux-cored arc welding with active-gas shielding; ~ **à l'arc sous protection gazeuse avec fil électrode** *m* CONSTR gas-shielded metal arc welding; ~ **à l'argon** *m* PRODUCTION argon arc welding; ~ **autogène** *m* MECANIQUE gas welding; ~ **bout à bout** *m* MECANIQUE butt welding, PRODUCTION butt seam welding; ~ **au chalumeau** *m* MECANIQUE, THERMODYN oxyacetylene welding; ~ **des connexions** *m* ELECTROTEC wire bonding; ~ **à décharge** *m* PRODUCTION discharge welding; ~ **à droite** *m* PRODUCTION backward welding; ~ **dur** *m* NUCLEAIRE hardfacing; ~ **électrique** *m* ELECTR electric welding; ~ **électrique sous laitier** *m* MECANIQUE electroslag welding; ~ **en arrière** *m* MECANIQUE, PRODUCTION backhand welding; ~ **en atmosphère inerte** *m* CONS MECA inert gas welding; ~ **en bout** *m* CONSTR, MECANIQUE butt welding; ~ **en bout par résistance** *m* THERMODYN upset welding; ~ **en bout par résistance pure** *m* CONSTR resistance butt welding; ~ **en continu** *m* EMBALLAGE band sealing; ~ **en montant** *m* MECANIQUE uphand welding; ~ **de flamme** *m* THERMODYN flashback; ~ **à flamme** *m* PLAST CAOU flame welding; ~ **à la forge** *m* CONSTR, PRODUCTION forge welding; ~ **à franc-bord** *m* MECANIQUE butt welding; ~ **à froid** *m* CONS MECA, MECANIQUE cold pressure welding; ~ **à gaz** *m* THERMODYN gas welding; ~ **des goujons** *m* CONSTR stud welding; ~ **à l'hydrogène atomique** *m* NUCLEAIRE atomic hydrogen welding; ~ **intérieur** *m* MECANIQUE inside welding; ~ **au laser** *m* CONSTR, ELECTRON, MATERIAUX, PRODUCTION laser welding; ~ **MAG** *m* CONSTR, THERMODYN MAG welding, metal active gas welding; ~ **manuel à l'arc** *m* CONS MECA, MECANIQUE manual metal arc welding; ~ **de métaux** *m* MATERIAUX metal bonding; ~ **MIG** *m* CONSTR, THERMODYN MIG welding, metal inert gas welding; ~ **à la molette** *m* CONSTR resistance seam welding; ~ **oxyacétylénique** *m* CONSTR, PRODUCTION oxyacetylene welding, THERMODYN gas welding, oxyacetylene welding; ~ **par aluminothermie** *m* CONSTR thermit welding; ~ **par bossages** *m* CONSTR projection welding; ~ **par étincelage** *m* CONSTR, PRODUCTION flash welding; ~ **par faisceau d'électrons** *m* CONSTR, NUCLEAIRE electron beam welding; ~ **par faisceau laser** *m* CONSTR laser beam welding; ~ **par force magnétique** *m* NUCLEAIRE magnetic force welding; ~ **par friction** *m* CONSTR friction welding; ~ **par fusion** *m* CONSTR, PRODUCTION, THERMODYN fusion welding; ~ **par impulsion** *m* EMBALLAGE impulse heat sealer; ~ **par induction** *m* PRODUCTION induction welding; ~ **par points** *m* CONS MECA resistance spot welding, ELECTR resistance spot welding, spot welding; ~ **par pression** *m* CONSTR, PRODUCTION, THERMODYN pressure welding; ~ **par pression à froid** *m* CONSTR cold pressure welding; ~ **par projection** *m* PRODUCTION projection welding; ~ **par rapprochement** *m* PRODUCTION butt welding; ~ **par refusion** *m* ELECTROTEC reflow soldering; ~ **par résistance** *m* CONSTR, ELECTR *procédé*, THERMODYN resistance welding; ~ **par résistance par étincelage** *m* CONSTR flash welding; ~ **par résistance par points** *m* CONSTR spot welding; ~ **par ultrasons** *m* PLAST CAOU *procédé* ultrasonic welding, THERMODYN ultrasonic sealing, ultrasonic welding; ~ **des plastiques** *m* CONS MECA plastic welding; ~ **de saillies** *m* CONSTR projection welding; ~ **au solvant** *m* PLAST CAOU *procédé* solvent welding; ~ **sous l'eau** *m* PETR, THERMODYN underwater welding; ~ **sous flux électroconducteur** *m* MATERIAUX submerged arc welding; ~ **sous laitier** *m* CONSTR electroslag welding; ~ **sous laitier électroconducteur** *m* NUCLEAIRE electroslag welding; ~ **sur bande** *m* ELECTROTEC tap automated bonding; ~ **TIG** *m* CONSTR TIG welding, tungsten inert gas welding; ~ **ultrasonique** *m* THERMODYN ultrasonic sealing; ~ **vertical sous laitier** *m* CONSTR electroslag welding

soudaineté: ~ de l'incendie *f* SECURITE suddenness of conflagration

soudant *m* PRODUCTION sparkling heat

soude *f* CERAM VER soda, CHIMIE caustic soda, sodium hydroxide, soda, PAPIER soda; ~ **calcinée** *f* LESSIVES soda ash; ~ **carbonatée** *f* CHIMIE natron; ~ **caustique** *f* CHIMIE caustic soda, sodium hydroxide, LESSIVES caustic soda; ~ **en cristaux** *f* CHIMIE washing soda; ~ **granulaire** *f* METALL granular ash

soudé *adj* PRODUCTION, THERMODYN welded; ~ **au laiton** *adj* THERMODYN brazed

souder *vt* CONSTR solder, MECANIQUE, PAPIER, THERMODYN weld

soudeur *m* MECANIQUE *personne* welder, PRODUCTION *personne* solderer, SECURITE *personne* welder, TELECOM jointer, splicer cable, *outil* cable jointer; ~ **à l'arc** *m* MECANIQUE arc welder

soudeuse: ~ de barquettes *f* EMBALLAGE tray sealer; ~ **en continu** *f* EMBALLAGE band sealer

soudo-brasage *m* CONSTR braze welding, bronze welding

soudo-brasure *f* PRODUCTION brazing

soudoir *m* PRODUCTION copper bit

soudure:[1] ~ **non traitée thermiquement** *adj* PRODUCTION as welded

soudure[2] *f* AGRO ALIM *de boîte métallique* soldered seam, CERAM VER fusing, sealing, welding, seal, MECANIQUE seam, METALL weld, NUCLEAIRE weld, welding seam, PRODUCTION butt seal, soldering, welding, weld, SECURITE welding, THERMODYN weld; ~ **d'angle** *f* MECANIQUE fillet weld; ~ **d'argent** *f* PRODUCTION silver solder; ~ **avec verres intermédiaires** *f* CERAM VER graded seal; ~ **bout à bout** *f* CONS MECA butt weld; ~ **chaude** *f* ELECTR *thermocouple* hot junction; ~ **à chaude portée** *f* PRODUCTION lap welding, scarf weld, scarf welding, lap weld; ~ **circulaire** *f* NUCLEAIRE girth weld, ring weld; ~ **concave** *f* NUCLEAIRE concave weld, light weld; ~ **continue** *f* NUCLEAIRE seam weld; ~ **au**

cuivre *f* CONSTR brass solder, PRODUCTION brazing solder; ~ **défectueuse** *f* ELECTR *raccordement* dry joint; ~ **à électrolaitier** *f* MATERIAUX electroslag welding; ~ **en bout** *f* PRODUCTION butt weld; ~ **enrobée** *f* ELECTR *raccordements* cored solder; **à l'étain** *f* ELECTROTEC solder, IMPRIM *mécanique* soldering; ~ **d'étanchéité** *f* NUCLEAIRE sealing weld; ~ **forte** *f* SECURITE brazing; ~ **froide** *f* ELECTR *thermocouple*, ELECTROTEC cold junction; ~ **grasse** *f* PRODUCTION fine solder; ~ **à gueule-de-loup** *f* PRODUCTION cleft weld, cleft welding, split weld, split welding, tongue weld, tongue welding; ~ **à haute fréquence** *f* EMBALLAGE high-frequency welding; ~ **maigre** *f* PRODUCTION coarse solder; ~ **à noeud** *f* CONSTR wipe joint, wiped joint; ~ **oxyacétylénique** *f* PRODUCTION oxyacetylene welding; ~ **par aluminothermie** *f* MECANIQUE aluminothermic welding; ~ **par amorces** *f* PRODUCTION lap welding, scarf weld, scarf welding, lap weld; ~ **par encollage** *f* PRODUCTION butt weld, butt welding, jump weld, jump welding; ~ **par la fonte liquide** *f* PRODUCTION burning, casting on; ~ **par induction** *f* ELECTR *procédé* induction welding; ~ **par rapprochement** *f* PRODUCTION butt weld, jump welding, jump weld; ~ **par recouvrement** *f* EMBALLAGE, NUCLEAIRE lap weld; ~ **des plombiers** *f* CONSTR plumber's solder; ~ **provisionnelle** *f* MATERIAUX tack weld; ~ **à recouvrement** *f* PRODUCTION lap welding, scarf weld, scarf welding, lap weld; ~ **de soutien** *f* PRODUCTION back weld; ~ **sur chantier** *f* NUCLEAIRE field weld, site weld; ~ **de thermocouple** *f* PRODUCTION hot junction

soufflage *m* CERAM VER (Bel) blowing, CHARBON blow-off, blowout, METALL blow, PLAST CAOU *procédé de moulage* blow molding (AmE), blow moulding (BrE), PRODUCTION blow, blowing; ~ **d'arc** *m* ELECTROTEC arc suppression; ~ **bouche** *m* CERAM VER offhand working; ~ **à la bouche** *m* CERAM VER mouth blowing; ~ **en cylindres** *m* CERAM VER cylinder process; ~ **en plateaux** *m* CERAM VER crown process; ~ **de feuille** *m* PLAST CAOU film blowing; ~ **final** *m* CERAM VER final blow; ~ **de fonté** *m* CONSTR *béton* honeycombing; ~ **magnétique** *m* ELECTROTEC magnetic blowout; ~ **au moule** *m* (Bel) CERAM VER mold blowing (AmE), mould blowing (BrE); ~ **par le vide** *m* CERAM VER vacuum blowing; ~ **de verre** *m* CERAM VER glass-blowing

soufflante *f* AGRO ALIM, AUTO blower, CONS MECA piston blower, MECANIQUE blower, PRODUCTION blower, blowing engine, REFRIG blower, TRANSPORT fan, VEHICULES fan, *système de refroidissement* blower; ~ **axiale** *f* SECURITE axial blower; ~ **axiale contrarotative** *f* TRANSPORT counter-revolving axial fan; ~ **canalisée** *f* TRANSPORT ducted fan; ~ **non-carénée** *f* AERONAUT *moteur* unducted fan; ~ **de sustentation** *f* TRANSPORT lift fan

soufflard *m* CERAM VER sting-out; ~ **de grisou** *m* MINES gas feeder, gas fissure, gas vent

souffle *m* AERONAUT blast, *de l'hélice* slipstream, ESPACE *communications* thermal noise, *véhicules* blast; ~ **des réacteurs** *m* AERONAUT engine jet wash; ~ **du rotor** *m* AERONAUT *hélicoptère* rotor stream

soufflé: ~ **bouche** *adj* CERAM VER free-blown

souffler[1] *vt* PAPIER, PRODUCTION *cubilot, le feu* blow

souffler:[2] ~ **en rafales** *vi* METEO gust; ~ **fort** *vi* METEO gust

soufflerie *f* AERONAUT wind tunnel, CERAM VER (Bel) bushing blower, CONS MECA air blowing, ESPACE, PHYSIQUE wind tunnel, PRODUCTION, VEHICULES *système de refroidissement* blower; ~ **à air chaud** *f* EQUIP LAB hot air blower; ~ **à arc bref** *f* AERONAUT hot shot wind tunnel; ~ **de forge** *f* PRODUCTION forge bellows; ~ **à hélice** *f* REFRIG propeller fan; ~ **libre** *f* PHYSIQUE open-jet wind tunnel; ~ **à veine guidée** *f* PHYSIQUE closed throat wind tunnel

soufflet *m* CINEMAT bellows, CONS MECA bellows, piston blower, MECANIQUE, PHOTO bellows, PRODUCTION bellows, blowing engine; ~ **cylindrique à simple vent** *m* CONS MECA single blast circular bellows; ~ **de dilatation** *m* MECANIQUE expansion bellows; ~ **de forge** *m* CONS MECA blacksmith's bellows, PRODUCTION forge bellows; ~ **de parasoleil** *m* CINEMAT lens hood bellows; ~ **de peau** *m* PHOTO leather bellows; ~ **de protection** *m* AERONAUT boot; ~ **réglable de contre-jour** *m* CINEMAT adjustable lens hood barrel; ~ **à tirage variable** *m* PHOTO extension bellows

soufflette *f* PAPIER air bell, blistering; ~ **à écran d'air** *f* PRODUCTION air screen blow gun

souffleur *m* CERAM VER blower, bushing blower, MINES gas feeder, gas fissure, gas vent, PRODUCTION blower; ~ **au chalumeau** *m* CERAM VER glass-blower

soufflure *f* GAZ gas pocket, PAPIER blow, PRODUCTION air hole, blister, blow, blowhole

soufrage *m* CERAM VER sulfuring (AmE), sulphuring (BrE)

soufre *m (S)* CHIMIE sulfur (AmE), sulphur (BrE) *(S)*; ~ **atmosphérique** *m* POLLUTION atmospheric sulfur (AmE), atmospheric sulphur (BrE); ~ **combiné** *m* PLAST CAOU *caoutchouc* combined sulfur (AmE), combined sulphur (BrE); ~ **en bâton** *m* CHIMIE stick of sulfur (AmE), stick of sulphur (BrE); ~ **en canon** *m* CHIMIE roll sulfur (AmE), roll sulphur (BrE); ~ **extractif** *m* PLAST CAOU *caoutchouc* extractable sulfur (AmE), extractable sulphur (BrE); ~ **libre** *m* PLAST CAOU *caoutchouc* free sulfur (AmE), free sulphur (BrE); ~ **total** *m* PLAST CAOU *caoutchouc* total sulfur (AmE), total sulphur (BrE)

soufré *adj* CHIMIE thionic

souille *f* OCEANO bed, trench

soulèvement *m* CONS MECA lifting, GEOLOGIE uplift, SECURITE *manuel* lifting; ~ **par congélation** *m* REFRIG *du sol* frost heave

soulever[1] *vt* IMPRIM *sujet, question* bring up, MECANIQUE lift; ~ **avec la pince** *vt* CONS MECA lever, lever up; ~ **au cric** *vt* VEHICULES *carrosserie* jack; ~ **incorrectement** *vt* SECURITE lift incorrectly; ~ **au moyen d'un levier** *vt* CONS MECA lever, lever up

soulever:[2] ~ **ici** *loc* EMBALLAGE *inscription, étiquette de manutention* lift here

soulève-rails *m* CH DE FER rail lifter

souligner *vt* IMPRIM highlight, outline, underline, *maquette, photogravure* accentuate, enhance

soumettre *vt* BREVETS submit; ~ **à l'action d'un glacier** *vt* GEOLOGIE glaciate

soumission *f* MECANIQUE *contrats* bid; ~ **des travaux à distance** *f* INFORMAT, ORDINAT RJE, remote job entry

soupape *f* AUTO valve, CONS MECA pressure relief valve, CONSTR valve, INST HYDR eduction valve, valve, *dont le clapet retombe par gravité* drop valve, MECANIQUE valve, MINES throttle valve, NUCLEAIRE, PETROLE *raffinerie*, PHYSIQUE, POLLU MER, REFRIG, VEHICULES *moteur* valve; ~ **d'admission** *f* AUTO induction valve, inlet valve, CONS MECA admission valve, IMPRIM intake valve, INST HYDR induction valve, inlet valve, intake valve, VEHICULES inlet valve; ~ **d'admission de vapeur**

f INST HYDR steam valve; ~ **à aiguille** *f* NUCLEAIRE needle valve; ~ **d'air** *f* CONS MECA air valve; ~ **d'alimentation automatique** *f* COMMANDE regulating feed valve; ~ **d'amortissement à deux voies** *f* AUTO, CONS MECA two-way damper valve; ~ **d'amortisseur de choc** *f* CONS MECA dashpot valve; ~ **d'amplification de pression de l'accélérateur** *f* AUTO throttle pressure boost valve; ~ **d'arrêt** *f* AUTO check valve, CONSTR cutoff valve, stop valve; ~ **d'arrêt à boulet** *f* NUCLEAIRE ball check valve; ~ **d'arrêt de retenue** *f* CONS MECA check valve; ~ **d'arrêt d'urgence à action rapide** *f* NUCLEAIRE fast-acting trip valve; ~ **d'arrivée d'air** *f* CONS MECA air vent valve; ~ **d'aspiration** *f* AUTO suction throttling valve; ~ **basse pression à flotteur** *f* REFRIG low-pressure float valve; ~ **à boulet** *f* PAPIER ball valve; ~ **à charnière** *f* INST HYDR leaf valve; ~ **à clapet** *f* AUTO poppet valve, CONS MECA clack valve, INST HYDR clapper, clapper valve, flap valve; ~ **à coulisse** *f* VEHICULES *moteur* slide valve; ~ **de décharge** *f* AUTO oil relief valve plunger, CONS MECA unloading valve, INST HYDR exhaust valve, pressure relief valve, MECANIQUE, VEHICULES *lubrification* relief valve; ~ **de décompression** *f* COMMANDE relief valve, CONS MECA depressurization valve; ~ **de dépression** *f* AUTO, VEHICULES *refroidissement* vacuum valve; ~ **de dérivation** *f* INST HYDR deflecting valve; ~ **de détente** *f* INST HYDR expansion valve, *de vapeur* relief valve, PETROLE relief valve, REFRIG expansion valve; ~ **de détente manuelle** *f* REFRIG hand expansion valve; ~ **de dilatation** *f* CONS MECA expansion valve, safety valve; ~ **à disque** *f* INST HYDR disc valve (BrE), disk valve (AmE), REFRIG globe valve; ~ **de dosage** *f* CONS MECA metering valve; ~ **d'échappement** *f* AUTO, EQUIP LAB exhaust valve, INST HYDR exhaust valve, outlet valve, VEHICULES *moteur* exhaust valve; ~ **d'éjection** *f* CONS MECA ejector valve; ~ **en tête** *f* VEHICULES *moteur* overhead valve; ~ **d'équilibrage** *f* INST HYDR equilibrium valve; ~ **d'équilibrage à manchon** *f* INST HYDR equilibrium valve, sleeve pattern; ~ **d'étranglement** *f* CONS MECA throttle valve; ~ **d'évacuation d'air** *f* AGRO ALIM air bleed valve; ~ **d'expansion** *f* INST HYDR expansion valve; ~ **à flotteur** *f* CHAUFFAGE float valve, CONS MECA ball valve, INST HYDR, REFRIG float valve; ~ **de freinage** *f* CH DE FER *véhicules* brake valve; ~ **à gaz** *f* ELECTROTEC gas-filled rectifier; ~ **de Gockel** *f* EQUIP LAB *distillation* antisplash head; ~ **grillée** *f* VEHICULES *moteur* burnt valve; ~ **haute pression à flotteur** *f* REFRIG high-pressure float valve; ~ **d'inversion** *f* INST HYDR reversing valve; ~ **mélangeuse** *f* CONS MECA mixing valve; ~ **modulatrice de servo-piston** *f* AUTO servomodulator valve; ~ **moteur** *f* CONS MECA engine valve; ~ **à niveau** *f* CONS MECA retention valve; ~ **de non-retour** *f* AUTO check valve; ~ **à opercule conique** *f* INST HYDR cone valve; ~ **de pied** *f* CONS MECA foot valve; ~ **pneumatique avec commande à distance** *f* CONS MECA remote-controlled pneumatic valve; ~ **à pointeau** *f* EN RENOUV needle valve; ~ **de prélèvement d'air** *f* AERONAUT air bleed valve; ~ **de purge** *f* INST HYDR pet-valve, NAUT drain valve, REFRIG blow-off valve; ~ **de purge d'air** *f* CONS MECA air inlet valve, air vent valve; ~ **purgeur** *f* REFRIG blow-off valve; ~ **rectifier** *f* ELECTROTEC multianode rectifier; ~ **de reflux** *f* INST HYDR reflux valve; ~ **de refoulement** *f* INST HYDR delivery valve; ~ **régulatrice** *f* AUTO main regulator valve; ~ **régulatrice de pression** *f* COMMANDE pressure regulating valve; ~ **de renversement** *f* INST HYDR reversing valve; ~ **de réservoir** *f* INST HYDR tank valve; ~ **à ressort** *f* INST HYDR spring valve, spring-loaded valve; ~ **de retenue** *f* CONS MECA nonreturn valve, INST HYDR back pressure valve; ~ **de retenue à clapet** *f* DISTRI EAU check valve; ~ **de séquence** *f* CONS MECA sequence valve; ~ **à siège plan** *f* REFRIG globe valve; ~ **à siège simple** *f* INST HYDR single-seated valve; ~ **à soufflet** *f* CONS MECA bellows valve; ~ **stellitée** *f* AUTO stellite valve; ~ **de sûreté** *f* EN RENOUV relief valve, INST HYDR release valve, relief valve, safety valve, MECANIQUE, PRODUCTION *système hydraulique* safety valve, REFRIG relief valve, SECURITE safety valve; ~ **de sûreté à contrepoids** *f* ASTRONOMIE, INST HYDR steam balance; ~ **de sûreté à ressort** *f* REFRIG spring-loaded pressure relief valve; ~ **de surpression du convertisseur** *f* AUTO pressure boost valve; ~ **de trop-plein** *f* INST HYDR escape valve, overflow valve; ~ **à tulipe** *f* PRODUCTION poppet valve; ~ **de vidange** *f* CONS MECA drain valve

soupape-champignon *f* AUTO mushroom valve, poppet valve

soupape-clapet *f* AUTO mushroom valve, poppet valve

soupirail *m* CONSTR vent, vent hole, PRODUCTION air hole

souplesse *f* ACOUSTIQUE compliance, MATERIAUX suppleness

source *f* ELECTRON, ELECTROTEC source, GEOLOGIE *à l'origine des éléments détritiques ou magmas* source area, source region, HYDROLOGIE spring head, *d'eau vive* spring, *d'une rivière* source, INFORMAT, ORDINAT, PHYSIQUE source, POLLUTION emission source; ~ **acoustique ponctuelle** *f* ACOUSTIQUE pinpoint acoustic source; ~ **acoustique simple** *f* ACOUSTIQUE single acoustic source; ~ **d'alimentation extérieure** *f* AERONAUT ground power supply; ~ **alternative** *f* ELECTROTEC AC source, alternating current source; ~ **de bruit** *f* ELECTRON noise source, POLLUTION noise source, sound source; ~ **de bruit aléatoire** *f* ELECTRON random noise source; ~ **de bruit blanc** *f* ELECTRON white noise source; ~ **de bruit de référence** *f* ENREGISTR reference noise source; ~ **de chaleur** *f* REFRIG heat source; ~ **chaude** *f* ASTRONOMIE radio source; ~ **de contact** *f* DISTRI EAU contact spring; ~ **de courant** *f* ELECTROTEC, PHYSIQUE current source; ~ **de courant alternatif** *f* ELECTROTEC AC source, alternating current source; ~ **de courant à haute fréquence** *f* ELECTROTEC RF current source; ~ **de dépression** *f* DISTRI EAU depression spring; ~ **de déversement** *f* DISTRI EAU depression spring; ~ **diffuse** *f* POLLUTION area emission source; ~ **d'eau souterraine** *f* CHARBON ground water supply; ~ **d'électrons** *f* ELECTRON electron source, INSTRUMENT electron gun; ~ **éloignée** *f* POLLUTION distant source; ~ **émettrice** *f* POLLUTION emission source; ~ **d'émission** *f* POLLUTION emission source; ~ **d'énergie** *f* CONS MECA power producer, ELECTROTEC power source, ESPACE *véhicules* energy source, GAZ energy form; ~ **d'énergie hydraulique** *f* INST HYDR hydraulic pressure supply; ~ **d'énergie nucléaire** *f* ESPACE nuclear power supply; ~ **d'énergie renouvelable** *f* EN RENOUV, PHYSIQUE renewable source of energy; ~ **étalon de laboratoire** *f* NUCLEAIRE laboratory standard; ~ **étendue** *f* POLLUTION area emission source; ~ **d'excitation** *f* PHYS RAYON excitation source; ~ **extérieure** *f* ELECTRON external source, POLLUTION foreign source; ~ **extérieure de signaux** *f* ELECTRON external signal source; ~ **externe** *f* POLLU-

TION foreign source; ~ de faille *f* DISTRI EAU fault spring; ~ fixe *f* POLLUTION stationary emission source; ~ de Frank-Read *f* CRISTALL Frank-Read source; ~ de fréquence *f* ELECTRON frequency source; ~ de fréquence à quartz *f* ELECTRON quartz frequency source; ~ froide d'ultime secours *f* NUCLEAIRE ultimate heat sink; ~ hydrothermale *f* OCEANO hot springs, hydrothermal vent; ~ d'hyperfréquences *f* ELECTRON microwave signal source; ~ illuminée *f* PHYS RAYON illuminated source; ~ à impédance nulle *f* ELECTROTEC zero impedance source; ~ d'informations *f* INFORMAT, ORDINAT information source; ~ infrarouge *f* ASTRONOMIE infrared source; ~ intarissable *f* HYDROLOGIE perennial spring; ~ intérieure *f* POLLUTION internal source; ~ intermittente *f* DISTRI EAU intermittent spring; ~ d'ions *f* PHYSIQUE ion source; ~ d'ions à arc à flamme découverte *f* NUCLEAIRE open arc ion source; ~ d'ions à cathode creuse *f* NUCLEAIRE hollow cathode ion source; ~ d'ions à métal liquide *f* PHYS RAYON liquid metal ion source; ~ karstique *f* DISTRI EAU karstic spring; ~ lambertienne *f* OPTIQUE TELECOM lambertian radiator, lambertian source; ~ linéaire *f* POLLUTION line source; ~ locale *f* POLLUTION local emission source; ~ de lumière *f* ELECTRON light source; ~ lumineuse *f* OPTIQUE, PHOTO light source, PHYS RAYON luminous source, PHYSIQUE light source; ~ lumineuse du photomètre *f* INSTRUMENT photometric light source; ~ majeure *f* POLLUTION major source; ~ de messages *f* INFORMAT, ORDINAT message source; ~ millimétrique *f* ELECTRON millimeter wave source (AmE), millimetre wave source (BrE); ~ mince *f* NUCLEAIRE thin source; ~ minérale *f* DISTRI EAU mineral spring; ~ mobile *f* POLLUTION transportation source; ~ non blindée *f* NUCLEAIRE free source, unshielded source; ~ d'ondes millimétriques *f* ELECTRON millimeter wave source (AmE), millimetre wave source (BrE); ~ pérenne *f* HYDROLOGIE perennial spring; ~ permanente *f* HYDROLOGIE perennial spring; ~ de polarisation *f* ELECTROTEC bias source; ~ de pollution *f* POLLUTION pollution emitter, pollution source; ~ ponctuelle *f* CINEMAT, PHOTO, PHYSIQUE, POLLUTION point source; ~ ponctuelle centrée *f* NUCLEAIRE collimated point source; ~ à quartz *f* ELECTRON quartz frequency source; ~ quasi-stellaire *f* ASTRONOMIE *avec émissions radio* quasi-stellar source; ~ de la radiation *f* PHYS RAYON radiation source; ~ de radiation non-constante *f* PHYS RAYON nonuniform source of radiation; ~ radioactive *f* ASTRONOMIE radio source; ~ de rayonnement *f* ELECTRON, NUCLEAIRE radiation source; ~ de rayonnement de freinage *f* NUCLEAIRE bremsstrahlung source; ~ de rayons X *f* NUCLEAIRE X-ray source; ~ à rayons X *f* ASTRONOMIE X-ray source; ~ de rythme de multiplexeur *f* TELECOM MTS, multiplexer timing source; ~ salée *f* DISTRI EAU saline spring, HYDROLOGIE saline spring, saltbed; ~ saline *f* HYDROLOGIE saline spring, saltbed; ~ saumâtre *f* HYDROLOGIE saline spring, saltbed; ~ scellée *f* NUCLEAIRE encapsulated source, sealed source; ~ secondaire *f* OPTIQUE secondary source; ~ de signaux différentiels *f* ELECTRON differential signal source; ~ de signaux hyperfréquence *f* ELECTRON microwave signal source; ~ de signaux programmable *f* ELECTRON programmable signal generator; ~ sonore *f* ACOUSTIQUE sound source; ~ sonore réelle *f* ACOUSTIQUE real sound source; ~ sonore virtuelle *f* ACOUSTIQUE virtual sound source; ~ submergée *f* DISTRI EAU submerged spring; ~

de tension *f* ELECTROTEC, PHYSIQUE voltage source; ~ à tension constante *f* ELECTR, ELECTROTEC constant voltage source; ~ de tension continue *f* ELECTROTEC DC voltage source, direct current voltage source; ~ de tension extérieure *f* ELECTROTEC external voltage source; ~ thermale *f* HYDROLOGIE, THERMODYN thermal spring; ~ vive *f* HYDROLOGIE spring

sources: ~ alignées *f pl* POLLUTION line source; ~ à sursauts *f pl* ASTRONOMIE bursters

sourcier *m* HYDROLOGIE dowser

sourdine *f* CONS MECA baffle

sourdre *vi* HYDROLOGIE spring

souricière *f* PETROLE fishing socket, overshot; ~ en cas d'incendie *f* SECURITE firetrap

souris *f* IMPRIM puck, INFORMAT, ORDINAT mouse; ~ à connexion parallèle *f* INFORMAT, ORDINAT parallel mouse; ~ à deux boutons *f* INFORMAT, ORDINAT two-button mouse; ~ à trois boutons *f* INFORMAT, ORDINAT three-button mouse

sous-acétate *m* CHIMIE subacetate

sous-adressage *m* TELECOM subaddressing; ~ des terminaux *m* TELECOM terminal subaddressing

sous-adresse *f* TELECOM subaddress

sous-alimentation *f* REFRIG starving

sous-azotate *m* CHIMIE subnitrate

sous-barbe *f* NAUT bobstay

sous-biez *m* DISTRI EAU backwater

sous-carbonate *m* CHIMIE subcarbonate

sous-cave *f* MINES holing, jad, kerving, kirving

sous-cavé *adj* MINES holed

sous-caver *vt* MINES hole

sous-centrale *f* ELECTROTEC substation

sous-chaîne *f* INFORMAT, ORDINAT substring

sous-champ: ~ inférieur *m* TELECOM lower subfield; ~ supérieur *m* TELECOM upper subfield

sous-charge *f* NUCLEAIRE underload

sous-charriage *m* GEOLOGIE underthrust

souschevage *m* MINES jad, kerving

souschevé *adj* MINES holed

souschever *vt* MINES hole

souscheveur *m* MINES cutter

sous-chlorure *m* CHIMIE subchloride

sous-compacté *adj* PETR undercompacted

sous-compaction *f* PETR undercompaction, PETROLE *argiles* compaction disequilibrium

sous-couche *f* CHIMIE undercoat, CONSTR sub-base, undercoat, COULEURS undercoat, PHYS FLUID sublayer, PHYSIQUE subshell, REVETEMENT backing, TEXTILE sublayer; ~ de convergence *f* TELECOM CS, convergence sublayer; ~ de convergence de transmission *f* TELECOM transmission convergence sublayer, transmission convergence; ~ électronique *f* PHYS RAYON *structure atomique* electronic subshell; ~ de support physique *f* TELECOM physical medium sublayer

sous-courant *m* OCEANO subsurface current, undercurrent

sous-détail *m* CONSTR *finance* breakdown

sous-développé *adj* CINEMAT, IMPRIM *photographie* underdeveloped

sous-développer *vt* PHOTO underdevelop

sous-dominant *adj* ACOUSTIQUE subdominant

sous-dominante *f* ACOUSTIQUE subdominant

sous-écartement *m* CH DE FER tight to gage (AmE), tight to gauge (BrE)

sous-ensemble *m* INFORMAT, MATH, ORDINAT subset

sous-étage *m* MINES sublevel, substage
sous-étampe: ~ **pour fers ronds** *f* PRODUCTION bottom swage
sous-exploitation *f* OCEANO underfishing
sous-exposé *adj* IMPRIM *photographie* underexposed
sous-exposer *vt* CINEMAT, PHOTO underexpose
sous-exposition *f* PHOTO underexposure
sous-garde *f* MILITAIRE trigger guard
sous-habillage *m* IMPRIM *d'une plaque, d'un planchet* backing
sous-harmonique[1] *adj* ACOUSTIQUE subharmonic
sous-harmonique:[2] ~ **inférieur** *m* ELECTRON lower harmonic
sous-intensité *f* PRODUCTION undercurrent
sous-jacent *adj* GEOLOGIE underlying
sous-licence *f* BREVETS sublicence (BrE), sublicense (AmE)
sous-lot *m* PRODUCTION *de fractionnement* sublot
sous-marin[1] *adj* NAUT undersea
sous-marin:[2] ~ **crache-plongeur** *m* OCEANO diver lockout submersible
sous-modulation *f* ELECTRON, ENREGISTR undermodulation
sous-multiple *m* METROLOGIE *d'une unité de mesure* submultiple
sous-multiplexer *vt* TELECOM submultiplex
sous-multitrame *m* TELECOM SMF, submultiframe
sous-munition *f* MILITAIRE submunition
sous-naine *f* ASTRONOMIE *type d'étoile* subdwarf
sous-nitrate *m* CHIMIE subnitrate
sous-niveau *m* MINES, PHYSIQUE sublevel
sous-normal *m* GEOMETRIE subnormal
sous-orage: ~ **ionosphérique** *m* GEOPHYS ionospheric substorm
sous-oscillation *f* TV underswing
sous-passage *m* CONSTR underbridge
sous-porteuse *f* ESPACE *communications*, TV subcarrier; ~ **de chrominance** *f* ELECTRON chrominance subcarrier, TV chrominance subcarrier, color subcarrier (AmE), colour subcarrier (BrE); ~ **couleur** *f* TV chrominance subcarrier; ~ **couleur de référence** *f* TV chrominance subcarrier reference; ~ **stéréo** *f* ENREGISTR stereo subcarrier
sous-poutre *f* CONSTR bridging piece
sous-pression *f* CONS MECA underpressure
sous-produit *m* CHARBON, CHIMIE, CONS MECA, PETROLE by-product, PRODUCTION by-product, *à rebuter* scrap
sous-programme *m* INFORMAT, ORDINAT subprogram, subroutine; ~ **de gestion** *m* INFORMAT control routine
sous-réaction *f* CHIMIE side reaction
sous-refroidisseur *m* REFRIG subcooler
sous-répertoire *m* ORDINAT subdirectory
sous-réseau *f* TELECOM subnetwork; ~ **de gestion SDH** *m* TELECOM SDH management subnetwork, SMS
sous-saturation *f* METALL undersaturation
sous-saturé *adj* GEOLOGIE undersaturated
sous-sel *m* CHIMIE subsalt
sous-sol[1] *adj* GAZ underground
sous-sol[2] *m* MINES undersoil, PAPIER basement
sous-station *f* ELECTROTEC, PRODUCTION substation; ~ **électrique** *f* ELECTR *réseau de distribution* electric power substation; ~ **à redresseurs** *f* ELECTROTEC rectifier substation; ~ **de sectionnement** *f* ELECTROTEC switching substation; ~ **de transformation** *f* ELECTR *réseau d'alimentation*, ELECTROTEC transformer substation

sous-système *m* ESPACE *véhicules*, INFORMAT, ORDINAT, TELECOM subsystem; ~ **d'accès** *m* TELECOM access subsystem; ~ **d'alimentation en énergie** *m* ESPACE *véhicules* power subsystem; ~ **de commande de connexion sémaphore** *m* (SSCS) TELECOM signaling connection control part (AmE), signalling connection control part (BrE); ~ **de contrôle de signalisation** *m* TELECOM ISCP, international signaling control part (AmE), international signalling control part (BrE); ~ **de gestion des transactions** *m* (SSGT) TELECOM transaction capabilities application part; ~ **de localisation des véhicules** *m* TELECOM vehicle location subsystem; ~ **pour l'exploitation la maintenance et la gestion** *m* (SSEM) TELECOM operating and maintenance application part; ~ **pour la gestion des transactions** *m* TELECOM transaction management subsystem; ~ **radio** *m* TELECOM radio subsystem; ~ **de télémesure télécommande et localisation** *m* (TTL) ESPACE *communications* telemetry command and ranging subsystem (TCR); ~ **de transport de messages** *m* (SSTM) TELECOM message transfer part; ~ **usager réseau** *m* (SSUR) TELECOM ISDN user part; ~ **utilisateur pour le RNIS** *m* TELECOM ISDN user part; ~ **utilisateur téléphonie** *m* (SSUT) TELECOM telephone user part
sous-tâche *f* INFORMAT, ORDINAT subtask
sous-tangente *f* GEOMETRIE subtangent
sous-tendre *vt* GEOMETRIE subtend
sous-tension *f* PRODUCTION undervoltage
sous-titrage *m* CHIMIE undertitration, TV subtitling
sous-titre *m* CINEMAT subtitle
sous-titrer *vt* CINEMAT subtitle
sous-titreur *m* TV subtitler
soustracteur *m* INFORMAT, ORDINAT subtractor; ~ **binaire** *m* ELECTRON binary subtractor; ~ **complet** *m* INFORMAT, ORDINAT full subtractor; ~ **numérique** *m* ELECTRON digital subtractor; ~ **série** *m* ELECTRON serial subtractor
soustraction *f* INFORMAT, MATH, ORDINAT subtraction; ~ **binaire** *f* ELECTRON binary subtraction
soustraire *vt* INFORMAT, MATH, ORDINAT subtract
sous-traitance *f* PRODUCTION subcontracting
sous-traitant *m* PRODUCTION subcontractor
sous-type *m* INFORMAT, ORDINAT subtype
sous-variétés: ~ **à surface minimale** *f pl* GEOMETRIE minimal submanifolds
sous-verse *f* CHARBON underflow
sous-virage *m* VEHICULES *direction* understeer
soutage *m* NAUT bunkering
soute *f* AERONAUT cargo compartment, hold, CHARBON bunker, pit, shaft, ESPACE *véhicules* bay, cargo hold, hold, cargo bay, payload bay, NAUT bunker, locker, POLLU MER bunker, pit, shaft, POLLUTION bunker tank, TRANSPORT cargo hold, hold; ~ **à bagages** *f* TRANSPORT baggage compartment (AmE), luggage compartment (BrE); ~ **à bombes** *f* MILITAIRE bomb bay; ~ **à charbon** *f* CH DE FER *véhicules*, CHARBON coal bunker; ~ **à combustible** *f* PRODUCTION fuel bunker; ~ **à eau** *f* CH DE FER *véhicules* water tank; ~ **à voiles** *f* NAUT sail locker
soutènement *m* CONSTR propping, support, supporting; ~ **avec bouclier** *m* MINES shield support; ~ **des extrémités de taille** *m* MINES face and support system
soutenir *vt* CONS MECA carry, hold up, support, PAPIER back, support
souterrain *m* CONSTR substructure, tunnel

soutien *m* CONSTR, INFORMAT support, PAPIER backing, support; ~ **après vente** *m* QUALITE after sales servicing; ~ **logistique** *m* AERONAUT logistic support

soutirage *m* AGRO ALIM racking, MECANIQUE bleeding, NUCLEAIRE air drain, bleeding, vent, venting

soutirer *vt* AGRO ALIM, CHARBON tap, MECANIQUE bleed

soutireuse: ~ **à bouteilles** *f* AGRO ALIM bottle filler, bottling machine

soya *m* PLAST CAOU soya

soyage *m* PLAST CAOU *peinture* silking

SP *abrév (soucoupe plongeante)* OCEANO diving saucer

spaniolite *f* MINERAUX spaniolite

spartalite *f* MINERAUX spartalite

spartéine *f* CHIMIE spartein

spath: ~ **brunissant** *m* MINERAUX brown spar; ~ **calcaire** *m* GEOLOGIE calcite, lime spar; ~ **fluor** *m* CERAM VER fluorite (BrE), fluorspar (AmE), CHIMIE fluorite (BrE), fluorspar; ~ **lourd** *m* PETROLE *forage*, PLAST CAOU *pigment* barytes; ~ **pesant** *m* PETR, PETROLE barytes; ~ **satiné** *m* MINERAUX satin spar

spatiabiliser *vt* ESPACE *véhicules* adapt to space conditions

spatial: ~ **ergol** *m* THERMODYN fuel

spatialisé *adj* ESPACE space-bound

spatialiser *vt* ESPACE *véhicules* send into space

spatial-temporel-spatial *m (STS)* ESPACE space-time-space *(STS)*

spationaute *m* ESPACE astronaut, cosmonaut

spationef *m* ESPACE spacecraft

spatioporté *adj* ESPACE *véhicules* spaceborne

spatule *f* CERAM VER paddle, pallet, EQUIP LAB spatula

spécialisé *adj* INFORMAT, ORDINAT dedicated

spécialiste: ~ **très hautement qualifié** *m* CONS MECA artificer

spécificateur: ~ **de la section de la table de données** *m* PRODUCTION *automatisme industriel* data table section specifier

spécification *f* CONSTR, INFORMAT, ORDINAT, TEXTILE specification; ~ **de changement notifié** *f* TRANSPORT MC, master change, SCN, specification change notice; ~ **de contrôle** *f* QUALITE inspection specification; ~ **d'essai** *f* ESPACE *véhicules* test specification; ~ **des matériaux** *f* QUALITE materials specification; ~ **du matériel** *f* QUALITE equipment specification; ~ **de mémoire étendue** *f (norme EMS)* ORDINAT expanded memory specification *(EMS)*; ~ **du procédé** *f* QUALITE process specification; ~ **du produit** *f* PRODUCTION, QUALITE product specification; ~ **de programme** *f* INFORMAT, ORDINAT program specification; ~ **de réception** *f* QUALITE acceptance specification; ~ **technique** *f* CONSTR technical specification; ~ **unifiée** *f* PRODUCTION standard specification

spécifications: ~ **de transmission pour filtres ultraviolets** *f pl* SECURITE transmission requirements for ultraviolet filters

spécifier *vt* TEXTILE itemize

spécifique *adj* PHYSIQUE per unit mass, specific

spécimen *m* CHARBON, CHIMIE, PLAST CAOU *essai* specimen

spècle *m* ESPACE *véhicules* speckle

spectranalyse: ~ **moléculaire** *f* PHYS RAYON molecular spectroanalysis

spectre *m* ASTRONOMIE, CINEMAT, ELECTRON, ENREGISTR, ESPACE spectrum, PHOTO chromatic spectrum, PHYS RAYON, PHYSIQUE spectrum; ~ **d'abondance** *m* GEOLOGIE *diagramme des abondances relatives* abundance pattern; ~ **d'absorption** *m* ESPACE absorption spectrum, dark-line spectrum, PAPIER absorption range, PHYS RAYON, PHYSIQUE absorption spectrum; ~ **d'absorption X** *m* NUCLEAIRE, PHYSIQUE X-ray absorption spectrum; ~ **acoustique** *m* ACOUSTIQUE acoustical spectrum, ENREGISTR acoustic spectrum, POLLUTION sound pressure spectrum; ~ **d'activation de fluorescence** *m* PHYS RAYON fluorescence excitation spectrum; ~ **d'amplitudes** *m* PETR, PHYS ONDES amplitude spectrum; ~ **d'arc** *m* PHYSIQUE arc spectrum; ~ **atomique** *m* NUCLEAIRE, PHYSIQUE atomic spectrum; ~ **audible** *m* ENREGISTR audible spectrum; ~ **de bandes** *m* PHYS RAYON, PHYSIQUE band spectrum; ~ **bêta** *m* PHYS RAYON beta ray spectrum; ~ **calorifique** *m* THERMODYN heat spectrum; ~ **caractéristique rayons X** *m* PHYS RAYON characteristic X-ray spectrum; ~ **continu** *m* ACOUSTIQUE, ELECTRON, ESPACE, PHYS RAYON, PHYSIQUE continuous spectrum; ~ **continu d'électrons** *m* NUCLEAIRE electron continuum; ~ **diagramme** *m* MATERIAUX spectrum; ~ **de diffraction** *m* PHYS RAYON diffraction spectrum; ~ **discontinu** *m* PHYS RAYON discontinuous spectrum; ~ **dispersé** *m* MATERIAUX dispersion spectrum; ~ **électromagnétique** *m* ELECTRON, ELECTROTEC, PHYS RAYON electromagnetic spectrum; ~ **d'émission** *m* ESPACE, PHYSIQUE emission spectrum; ~ **énergétique** *m* ESPACE energy spectrum; ~ **d'énergie** *m* EN RENOUV spectral energy distribution; ~ **d'étincelles** *m* PHYS RAYON spark spectrum; ~ **de fission de Watt** *m* NUCLEAIRE Watt's fission spectrum; ~ **de flamme** *m* PHYSIQUE, THERMODYN flame spectrum; ~ **de fréquences** *m* ELECTRON, ENREGISTR, INFORMAT frequency spectrum, METALL frequency distribution, ORDINAT, PHYS ONDES frequency spectrum; ~ **des fréquences radioélectriques** *m* ELECTRON radio spectrum; ~ **des hautes fréquences** *m* ELECTRON high-frequency spectrum; ~ **HF** *m* ELECTRON HF spectrum; ~ **de la houle** *m* OCEANO sea state spectrum, wave spectrum; ~ **infrarouge** *m* PHYS RAYON, PHYSIQUE infrared spectrum; ~ **d'ions** *m* PHYS RAYON ion spectrum; ~ **de la lumière** *m* PHYS ONDES light spectrum; ~ **de masse** *m* PHYS RAYON, PHYSIQUE mass spectrum; ~ **des mésons légers** *m* PHYS RAYON light meson spectrum; ~ **de micro-ondes** *m* PHYS RAYON microwave spectrum; ~ **moléculaire** *m* PHYSIQUE molecular spectrum; ~ **d'ondes** *m* PHYS ONDES wave spectrum; ~ **optique** *m* ELECTRON, OPTIQUE, PHYS RAYON, TELECOM optical spectrum; ~ **permis** *m* NUCLEAIRE allowed spectrum; ~ **photoélectronique** *m* NUCLEAIRE X-ray photoelectron spectrum; ~ **prismatique** *m* PHYS RAYON prismatic spectrum; ~ **de puissances** *m* ELECTROTEC power spectrum; ~ **pur** *m* PHYS RAYON pure spectrum; ~ **radio** *m* PHYS RAYON radio spectrum; ~ **radioélectrique** *m* ELECTRON radio spectrum; ~ **de raies** *m* ACOUSTIQUE, OPTIQUE, PHYS RAYON, PHYSIQUE, TELECOM line spectrum; ~ **de rayonnement** *m* GEOPHYS radiation spectrum, PHYS RAYON emission spectrum; ~ **du rayonnement nucléaire** *m* PHYS RAYON nuclear radiation spectrum; ~ **des rayons bêta** *m* PHYSIQUE beta ray spectrum; ~ **de rayons gamma** *m* PHYS RAYON gamma-ray spectrum; ~ **des rayons X** *m* PHYS RAYON X-ray spectrum; ~ **de repliement** *m* ELECTRON aliased spectrum; ~ **de réponse à bande étroite** *m* NUCLEAIRE narrow band response spectrum; ~ **résolu dans le temps** *m* PHYS RAYON time-resolved spectrum; ~ **de résonance** *m* PHYS ONDES resonance spectrum; ~ **de rotation** *m* PHYS RAYON rotation spectrum, PHYSIQUE rotational spectrum; ~ **secondaire** *m* PHOTO ghost; ~ **thermique** *m* THERMODYN thermal spectrum; ~ **de transmission** *m* NUCLEAIRE transmission spectrum; ~ **de la turbulence** *m* PHYS FLUID spectrum of turbulence; ~ **de vibration-rotation** *m* PHYSIQUE vibration-rotation spectrum; ~ **des vibrations** *m* PHYSIQUE vibrational spectrum; ~ **visible** *m* PHYSIQUE visible spectrum; ~ **de vol** *m* AERONAUT flight spectrum

spectres: ~ **d'énergie et de dissipation de la turbulence** *m pl* PHYS FLUID energy and dissipation spectra in turbulence

spectrochimique *adj* CHIMIE, MATERIAUX spectrochemical

spectrographe *m* PHYS RAYON, PHYSIQUE spectrograph; ~ **acoustique** *m* ACOUSTIQUE sound spectrograph; ~ **magnétique** *m* GEOPHYS magnetic spectrograph; ~ **de masse** *m* PHYS RAYON, PHYSIQUE mass spectrograph; ~ **prismatique** *m* PHYS RAYON prismatic spectrograph; ~ **à rayons X** *m* INSTRUMENT X-ray diffractometer, X-ray spectrograph; ~ **à réseau** *m* NUCLEAIRE diffraction spectrograph, grating spectrograph; ~ **à réseau sous vide** *m* PHYS ONDES vacuum grating spectrograph; ~ **semi-circulaire bêta** *m* NUCLEAIRE semicircular beta spectrograph

spectrographie: ~ **de masse à sonde laser** *f* NUCLEAIRE laser probe mass spectrography; ~ **à rayons X** *f* NUCLEAIRE X-ray spectrography

spectrohéliographe *m* ASTRONOMIE spectroheliograph

spectrohélioscope *m* ASTRONOMIE spectrohelioscope

spectromètre *m* EN RENOUV, GAZ, MATERIAUX, PHYS ONDES, PHYSIQUE, TELECOM spectrometer; ~ **d'absorption** *m* EQUIP LAB *analyse* absorption spectrometer; ~ **d'absorption atomique** *m* EQUIP LAB *analyse* atomic absorption spectrometer; ~ **à coïncidence à scintillation** *m* NUCLEAIRE scintillation coincidence spectrometer; ~ **à coïncidence à trois faisceaux** *m* NUCLEAIRE triple-beam coincidence spectrometer; ~ **à fluorescence de rayons X** *m* PHYS RAYON fluorescent X-ray spectrometer; ~ **infrarouge** *m* PHYS RAYON infrared spectrometer; ~ **de masse** *m* EQUIP LAB *analyse*, MATERIAUX, PHYSIQUE mass spectrometer; ~ **de masse cycloïdale** *m* NUCLEAIRE trochoidal mass analyzer, trochoidal mass spectrometer; ~ **de masse à désorption par champ électrique** *m* NUCLEAIRE field desorption mass spectrometer; ~ **à rayons gamma** *m* PHYS ONDES, PHYS RAYON gamma ray spectrometer; ~ **scanographique** *m* PHYS RAYON scanning spectrometer; ~ **à scintillation** *m* PHYS RAYON scintillation spectrometer; ~ **Slätis-Siegbahn** *m* NUCLEAIRE Slätis-Siegbahn spectrometer

spectrométrie *f* GAZ spectometry, PETROLE, TELECOM spectrometry; ~ **d'absorption** *f* TELECOM absorption spectrometry; ~ **de masse** *f* CHIMIE, MATERIAUX, PHYSIQUE mass spectrometry; ~ **à rayons alpha** *f* PHYS RAYON alpha ray spectrometry; ~ **à rayons X** *f* NUCLEAIRE X-ray spectrometry, X-ray spectroscopy

spectrophotomètre *m* PHYSIQUE spectrophotometer; ~ **d'absorption** *m* PHYS RAYON absorption spectrophotometer; ~ **d'absorption atomique** *m* PHYS RAYON *analyse chimique* atomic absorption spectrophotometer; ~ **à infrarouge** *m* CHIMIE, EQUIP LAB *analyse* infrared spectrophotometer; ~ **monofaisceau** *m* PHYS RAYON single beam spectrophotometer; ~ **à UV-visible** *m* EQUIP LAB *analyse* ultraviolet-visible spectrophotometer

spectrophotométrie *f* PHYSIQUE spectrophotometry; ~ **cinétique** *f* PHYS RAYON kinetic spectrophotometry; ~ **dans l'infrarouge** *f* CHIMIE infrared spectrophotometry; ~ **dans l'ultraviolet** *f* CHIMIE ultraviolet spectrophotometry

spectroradiomètre *m* EN RENOUV spectroradiometer

spectroscope *m* PHYS ONDES, PHYSIQUE spectroscope

spectroscopie *f* CHIMIE, PHYS RAYON, PHYSIQUE spectroscopy; ~ **d'absorption** *f* PHYS RAYON absorption spectroscopy; ~ **atomique** *f* PHYS RAYON atomic spectroscopy; ~ **électronique** *f* PHYSIQUE electron spectroscopy; ~ **électronique Auger** *f* CHIMIE, PHYSIQUE AES, Auger electron spectroscopy; ~ **de flamme** *f* THERMODYN flame spectroscopy; ~ **de flamme en émission** *f* PHYSIQUE flame emission spectroscopy; ~ **de Fourier** *f* PHYSIQUE Fourier transform spectroscopy; ~ **à hyperfréquences** *f* PHYSIQUE microwave spectroscopy; ~ **à infrarouge** *f* CHIMIE, PHYSIQUE infrared spectroscopy; ~ **laser** *f* PHYS RAYON laser spectroscopy; ~ **laser colinéaire** *f* PHYS RAYON collinear laser spectroscopy; ~ **de masse aux ions secondaires** *f* PHYSIQUE SIMS, secondary ion mass spectrometry; ~ **de micro-ondes** *f* PHYS RAYON microwave spectroscopy; ~ **par absorption** *f* PHYSIQUE absorption spectroscopy; ~ **par absorption atomique** *f* CHIMIE, PHYSIQUE atomic absorption spectroscopy; ~ **de la perte d'énergie électronique** *f* PHYS RAYON electron energy loss spectroscopy; ~ **de photo-électrique** *f* CHIMIE ESCA, electron spectroscopy for chemical analysis; ~ **de photo-électrique X** *f* PHYSIQUE X-ray photoelectron spectroscopy; ~ **photo-électrique X** *f* CHIMIE X-ray photoelectron spectroscopy XPS; ~ **photoélectronique** *f* MATERIAUX photoelectron spectroscopy; ~ **Raman** *f* PHYS RAYON, PHYSIQUE Raman spectroscopy; ~ **des réactions nucléaires** *f* NUCLEAIRE reaction spectroscopy; ~ **à résonance magnétique** *f* PHYS RAYON magnetic resonance spectroscopy

spermidine *f* CHIMIE spermidine

spermine *f* CHIMIE spermin, spermine

sperrylite *f* MINERAUX sperrylite

spessartite *f* MINERAUX spessartine, spessartite

sphalérite *f* CHIMIE zinc blende, MINERAUX sphalerite

sphène *m* MINERAUX sphene

sphère *f* GEOMETRIE, MATERIAUX, PHYSIQUE sphere; ~ **céleste** *f* ASTRONOMIE celestial sphere; ~ **de Fermi** *f* PHYSIQUE Fermi sphere; ~ **de réflexion** *f* CRISTALL sphere of reflection

sphéricité *f* GEOMETRIE sphericity

sphérique *adj* GEOMETRIE spherical

sphéroïdal *adj* GEOMETRIE spheroidal

sphéroïde *m* GEOMETRIE, PHYSIQUE spheroid; ~ **allongé** *m* GEOMETRIE prolate spheroid; ~ **aplati** *m* GEOMETRIE oblate spheroid

sphérolite *m* GEOLOGIE spherulite

sphérolithe *m* PETR spherulite

sphéromak: ~ **aplati** *m* NUCLEAIRE oblate spheromak, oblimak

sphéromètre *m* PHYSIQUE spherometer

sphérosidérite *f* MINERAUX spherosiderite

sphingosine *f* CHIMIE sphingosine

sphragidite *f* MINERAUX sphragidite

spicule *f* ASTRONOMIE spicule

spilite *f* PETR spilite

spilosite *f* PETR spilosite

spin *m* PHYS PART *de proton, de neutron*, PHYS RAYON, PHYSIQUE spin; ~ **demi-entier** *m* PHYSIQUE half integral spin; ~ **de l'électron** *m* CHIMIE electron spin; ~ **électronique** *m* CHIMIE electron spin; ~ **entier** *m* PHYSIQUE integral spin; ~ **impair-impair** *m* NUCLEAIRE *d'un noyau* odd-odd spin; ~ **isobarique** *m* PHYSIQUE isobaric spin, isotopic spin, isospin; ~ **isotopique** *m* PHYSIQUE isobaric spin, isotopic spin, isospin; ~ **nucléaire** *m* PHYS RAYON, PHYSIQUE nuclear spin; ~ **3/2** *m* PHYS PART spin 3/2

spinastérol *m* CHIMIE spinasterol
spinelle *m* CHIMIE, MINERAUX spinel
spinnaker *m* NAUT spinnaker
spiral *adj* CONS MECA spiral
spiralage *m* ELECTROTEC helixing
spirale:¹**à** ~ *adj* CONS MECA spiral; **en** ~ *adj* CONS MECA, GEOMETRIE spiral
spirale² *f* CONS MECA, GEOMETRIE spiral; ~ **de croissance** *f* METALL growth spiral; ~ **d'Ekman** *f* OCEANO Ekman spiral; ~ **engagée** *f* AERONAUT spiral dive; ~ **hyperbolique** *f* CONS MECA reciprocal spiral; ~ **de la qualité** *f* QUALITE quality spiral
spiraloïde *adj* CONS MECA spiral
spiranne *m* CHIMIE spiran, spirane
spire *f* CONS MECA coil, spire, turn, ELECTR enroulement, ELECTROTEC turn, OPTIQUE spiral track, RESSORTS coil; ~ **d'amortissement** *f* RESSORTS damper coil, damping coil; ~ **de départ du sillon** *f* ACOUSTIQUE lead-in groove; ~ **en court-circuit** *f* ELECTROTEC shorted turn; ~ **d'extrémité** *f* RESSORTS end coil, extreme coil; ~ **jointive** *f* RESSORTS close wound coil; ~ **morte** *f* RESSORTS dead coil, inactive coil; ~ **multiple** *f* PHOTO multiunit tank spiral; ~ **non jointive** *f* ELECTROTEC loosely-wound turn; ~ **porte-film** *f* PHOTO developing reel (AmE), developing spiral (BrE), developing spool (AmE); ~ **rapprochée** *f* RESSORTS closed coil; ~ **de silence** *f* ELECTROTEC slug; ~ **de sortie du sillon** *f* ACOUSTIQUE lead-out groove; ~ **terminale** *f* RESSORTS end coil; ~ **terminale amincie rapprochée et meulée** *f* RESSORTS closed and ground tapered end; ~ **terminale fermée et meulée** *f* RESSORTS ground closed end; ~ **terminale ouverte** *f* RESSORTS open end; ~ **terminale ouverte et meulée** *f* RESSORTS open-and-ground end; ~ **terminale rapprochée** *f* RESSORTS closed end; ~ **terminale rapprochée et meulée** *f* RESSORTS closed and ground end; ~ **terminale saillante** *f* RESSORTS projecting end
spires: ~ **actives** *f pl* RESSORTS active coils; ~ **serrées** *f pl* RESSORTS close coils, tight coils; ~ **totales** *f pl* RESSORTS total coils, total turns
spiroïdal *adj* CONS MECA, GEOMETRIE spiral
spliures *f pl* CERAM VER cullet crush, splinters
spodumène *m* MINERAUX spodumene
spoiler *m* AERONAUT *d'aéronef* spoiler
spondée *m* ACOUSTIQUE spondee
spongiculture *f* OCEANO sponge culture
spongine *f* CHIMIE spongine
spongolithe *m* GEOLOGIE sponge bed
spoolage *m* ORDINAT spooling
spooleur *m* INFORMAT, ORDINAT spooler
spot *m* CINEMAT spot, spotlight; ~ **250 watt** *m* CINEMAT inky, inky-dink; ~ **lumineux** *m* ELECTRON focal spot; ~ **lumineux décalant** *m* TV hopping patch; ~ **mobile** *m* TV flying spot; ~ **radar** *m* NAUT radar blip
spotmètre *m* CINEMAT spotmeter
spots: ~ **successifs** *m pl* TV back-to-back commercials
sprinkler *m* SECURITE fire sprinkler, sprinkler
squalane *m* CHIMIE squalane

squalène *m* CHIMIE squalene
squelette: ~ **noir** *m* IMPRIM *photogravure* skeleton black, *préimpression* black printer; ~ **du sol** *m* CHARBON soil skeleton
squid *abrév* (*interféromètre quantique*) PHYSIQUE squid (*superconducting quantum interference device*)
Sr (*strontium*) CHIMIE Sr (*strontium*)
SRI *abrév* (*système de référence intermédiaire*) TELECOM IRS (*information reference system*)
SRM *abrév* (*service radiotéléphonique mobile*) TELECOM MTS (*mobile telephone service*)
SSCS *abrév* (*sous-système de commande de connexion sémaphore*) TELECOM signaling connection control part (AmE), signalling connection control part (BrE)
SSEM *abrév* (*sous-système pour l'exploitation la maintenance et la gestion*) TELECOM operating and maintenance application part
SSGT *abrév* (*sous-système de gestion des transactions*) TELECOM transaction capabilities application part
SSTM *abrév* (*sous-système de transport de messages*) TELECOM message transfer part
SSUR *abrév* (*sous-système usager réseau*) TELECOM ISDN user part
SSUT *abrév* (*sous-système utilisateur téléphonie*) TELECOM telephone user part
stabilisant *m* CERAM VER stabilizer, CHIMIE stabilizer, stabilizing agent
stabilisateur *m* AERONAUT *d'aéronef* stabilizer, AUTO stabilizer bar, CHARBON, CHIMIE, CINEMAT, ELECTR, NAUT, PETROLE, PHOTO, PLAST CAOU *ingrédient de mélange* stabilizer, VEHICULES *suspension* antiroll bar, stabilizer; ~ **automatique** *m* MILITAIRE *d'engin téléguidé* stabilizer, TRANSPORT ASE, automatic stabilization equipment, stabilizer; ~ **de flamme** *m* AERONAUT flame holder; ~ **de fréquence** *m* ELECTR frequency stabilizer; ~ **gyroscopique** *m* AERONAUT, CINEMAT gyrostabilizer; ~ **de tension** *m* ELECTROTEC voltage stabilizer
stabilisation *f* CHARBON, CHIMIE *d'une préparation*, ELECTR, ESPACE *pilotage*, GAZ, NAUT stabilization, PAPIER maturing, PLAST CAOU *procédé*, QUALITE, REFRIG stabilization, RESSORTS prestressing; ~ **des boues** *f* HYDROLOGIE sludge stabilization; ~ **à chaud** *f* RESSORTS stress relieving; ~ **à la chaux** *f* CONSTR lime stabilization; ~ **chimique** *f* HYDROLOGIE chemical stabilization; ~ **au ciment** *f* CONSTR cement stabilization; ~ **contrarotative** *f* ESPACE *pilotage* dual-spin stabilization; ~ **double par rotation** *f* ESPACE *pilotage* dual-spin stabilization; ~ **de l'échantillon** *f* QUALITE sample stabilization; ~ **en azimut** *f* NAUT azimuth stabilization; ~ **du froid** *f* REFRIG cold stabilization; ~ **à froid** *f* RESSORTS cold prestressing; ~ **latérale** *f* TRANSPORT sway stabilization; ~ **d'orientation** *f* AERONAUT attitude control; ~ **par asservissement** *f* COMMANDE servostabilization; ~ **par gradient de gravité** *f* ESPACE *pilotage* gravity gradient stabilization; ~ **par gyroscope** *f* TRANSPORT gyro stabilization; ~ **par position basse du centre de gravité** *f* TRANSPORT stabilization by low center of gravity (AmE), stabilization by low centre of gravity (BrE); ~ **par rotation** *f* ESPACE *pilotage* spin stabilization; ~ **profonde** *f* CHARBON deep stabilization; ~ **de la rotation** *f* ESPACE *pilotage* stabilization of rotation; ~ **des sols** *f* CONSTR soil stabilization; ~ **superficielle** *f* CHARBON shallow stabilization; ~ **sur trois axes** *f* ESPACE *pilotage* three-axis stabilization; ~ **de la taille et de l'organisation des grains** *f* IMPRIM *surfaces sensibles*

ripening

stabilisé *adj* CHIMIE stabilized; **~ par la chaleur** *adj* THERMODYN heat-stabilized

stabilité *f* CHARBON, CHIMIE, INFORMAT, MINES, NAUT, ORDINAT, TELECOM stability; **~ absolue** *f* TELECOM absolute stability; **~ d'assiette** *f* AERONAUT trim stability; **~ à la chaleur** *f* PLAST CAOU heat stability; **~ chimique** *f* CHARBON chemical stability; **~ de la couche limite** *f* PHYS FLUID boundary layer stability; **~ dimensionnelle** *f* CINEMAT, EMBALLAGE, ESSAIS, IMPRIM *film et impression*, NUCLEAIRE, PAPIER dimensional stability; **~ directionnelle** *f* ESPACE *pilotage* directional stability; **~ dynamique** *f* AERONAUT, TELECOM dynamic stability; **~ d'émulsion** *f* GENIE CHIM emulsion persistence; **~ en cap** *f* ESPACE *pilotage* directional stability; **~ en fréquence à court terme** *f* ELECTRON short-term frequency stability; **~ en lacet** *f* ESPACE *pilotage* directional stability; **~ en phase** *f* ELECTR *courant alternatif* phase stability; **~ en roulis** *f* AERONAUT rolling stability; **~ à l'état intact** *f* NAUT intact stability; **~ au froid** *f* REFRIG chill proofing; **~ horizontale** *f* TV horizontal hold; **~ d'image** *f* CINEMAT image steadiness; **~ initiale** *f* NAUT initial stability; **~ intrinsèque** *f* PHYS FLUID intrinsic stability; **~ latérale** *f* RESSORTS, TRANSPORT lateral stability; **~ longitudinale** *f* TRANSPORT longitudinal stability; **~ à long terme** *f* ELECTRON long-term stability; **~ manche bloqué** *f* AERONAUT fixed stick stability; **~ mécanique** *f* PLAST CAOU mechanical stability; **~ de mousse** *f* GENIE CHIM foam persistence; **~ de phase** *f* TELECOM phase stability; **~ de route** *f* TRANSPORT directional stability; **~ statique** *f* AERONAUT *navigabilité* static stability; **~ de stockage** *f* EMBALLAGE shelf stability; **~ d'un système asservi** *f* COMMANDE servostability; **~ de talus** *f* CHARBON slope stability; **~ thermique** *f* EMBALLAGE heat stability, PLAST CAOU thermal stability, THERMODYN heat stability; **~ transversale** *f* AERONAUT *d'aéronef* rolling stability, NAUT transverse stability; **~ verticale** *f* TRANSPORT vertical stability

stabilotron *m* PHYSIQUE stabilotron

stable *adj* CHIMIE stable, ELECTRON jitter-free; **~ à la chaleur** *adj* THERMODYN heat-stable, temperature-stable

stachydrine *f* CHIMIE stachydrine

stachyose *m* CHIMIE stachyose

stade *m* PRODUCTION stage; **~ de fabrication** *m* PAPIER stage; **~ de finition** *m* TEXTILE finishing stage; **~ du prototype** *m* PHYS RAYON prototype stage

stadiomètre *m* CONSTR stadimeter, stadiometer

stalagmomètre *m* PHYSIQUE stalagmometer

stalle *f* TRANSPORT box

stand *m* IMPRIM *exposition* booth

standard[1] *adj* INFORMAT, ORDINAT standard

standard[2] *m* PHYSIQUE standard, TELECOM PBX switchboard, switchboard, telephone switchboard; **~ à clefs** *m* TELECOM cordless switchboard; **~ à magnéto** *m* TELECOM magneto switchboard

standardisation *f* CHIMIE, PHYSIQUE standardization

standardisé *adj* IMPRIM customized

standardiser *vt* CHIMIE standardize

standardiste *m* TELECOM operator, switchboard operator

stannate *m* CHIMIE stannate

stanneux *adj* CHIMIE stannous

stannique *adj* CHIMIE stannic

stannite *f* MINERAUX stannite, tin pyrites

starter *m* ELECTR *interrupteur* line starter (AmE), starter (BrE), ELECTROTEC glow switch, MECANIQUE *véhicules*, VEHICULES *carburateur* choke; **~ automatique** *m* AUTO automatic choke; **~ au néon** *m* ELECTROTEC glow switch

stassfurtite *f* MINERAUX stassfurtite

statif *m* EQUIP LAB *support* retort stand, INSTRUMENT stand; **~ à colonne** *m* INSTRUMENT pillar stand

station *f* ELECTROTEC, INFORMAT, ORDINAT station, TRANSPORT railroad depot (AmE), station (BrE); **~ asservie** *f* INFORMAT, ORDINAT slave station; **~ aval** *f* ESPACE downrange station; **~ balnéaire** *f* POLLU MER seaside resort; **~ de base** *f* MILITAIRE, TELECOM base station; **~ centrale** *f* GAZ central station; **~ de communication** *f* TELECOM on-board communication station; **~ de commutation** *f* ELECTR *alimentation, distribution* switching station; **~ de conversion** *f* ELECTR *transformer* converter station, converting station; **~ de convertisseurs** *f* ELECTR *réseau* substation for frequency conversion; **~ de coordination du réseau** *f* ESPACE *communications* NCS, network coordination station; **~ côtière** *f* TELECOM coastal station; **~ de culbutage** *f* CONSTR dumping station; **~ de décompression** *f* COMMANDE pressure relief station; **~ de données** *f* INFORMAT, ORDINAT data station; **~ d'échange de batteries** *f* TRANSPORT battery exchange point; **~ électrique** *f* ELECTROTEC electric power station, generating plant, power plant; **~ émettrice** *f* TV broadcasting station, key station; **~ émettrice d'informations** *f* TELECOM information sending station; **~ d'émission** *f* TV broadcasting station; **~ en dérivation** *f* TRANSPORT off-line docking station; **~ d'énergie** *f* TELECOM power plant; **~ d'énergie nucléaire** *f* CONSTR nuclear power plant, nuclear power station; **~ d'enregistrement de la marée** *f* OCEANO tide station; **~ d'enrobage** *f* PETR field joint station; **~ d'épuisement** *f* DISTRI EAU pump station; **~ d'épuration** *f* DISTRI EAU, HYDROLOGIE purification plant, MINES water-cleansing plant, RECYCLAGE purification plant; **~ d'épuration à boues actives** *f* HYDROLOGIE activated sludge treatment plant; **~ d'épuration collective** *f* DISTRI EAU community sewage works; **~ d'épuration des eaux usées** *f* HYDROLOGIE sewage treatment plant, sewage works, RECYCLAGE sewage treatment plant, wastewater treatment plant; **~ d'essence** *f* TRANSPORT petrol station (BrE), road gasoline station (AmE); **~ d'exhaure** *f* CONSTR pumping station; **~ de filtration rapide** *f* HYDROLOGIE rapid filter plant; **~ fixe aéronautique** *f* AERONAUT aeronautical fixed station; **~ de force motrice** *f* CONS MECA power station; **~ génératrice d'énergie** *f* CONS MECA power station; **~ à haute tension** *f* ELECTROTEC high-tension power supply; **~ hydraulique** *f* HYDROLOGIE waterworks; **~ hydroélectrique** *f* ELECTROTEC hydroelectric power plant, hydroelectric power station; **~ inférieure** *f* TRANSPORT valley station; **~ interdite** *f* TELECOM station barred; **~ de jaugeage** *f* DISTRI EAU gaging station (AmE), gauging station (BrE); **~ de lâchage de ballons** *f* ESPACE balloon release station; **~ lâcheuse de ballons** *f* ESPACE balloon release station; **~ libre-service** *f* TRANSPORT self-service station; **~ de limitation de pression** *f* COMMANDE pressure limiting station; **~ météorologique** *f* ESPACE, METEO, NAUT weather station; **~ météorologique aéronautique** *f* AERONAUT aeronautical meteorological station; **~ météorologique automatique** *f* METEO automatic weather station; **~**

météorologique d'observation *f* METEO meteorological station; ~ **mobile** *f* ESPACE, IMPRIM, TELECOM MS, mobile station; ~ **mobile aéronautique** *f* ESPACE mobile aeronautical station; ~ **mobile maritime** *f* ESPACE mobile maritime station; ~ **mobile terrestre** *f* ESPACE mobile land station, TELECOM LMS, land mobile station; ~ **orbitale** *f* ESPACE *véhicules* orbital station; ~ **d'oxydation totale** *f* DISTRI EAU comprehensive treatment plant; ~ **piquet radar** *f* TRANSPORT radar picket station; ~ **de pompage** *f* CONSTR, DISTRI EAU, NAUT pumping station, PETR booster station, pumping station; ~ **de pompage des eaux usées** *f* HYDROLOGIE sewage pumping station; ~ **de pompe** *f* DISTRI EAU pump station; ~ **de poursuite** *f* ESPACE *communications* tracking station; ~ **de poursuite radar** *f* MILITAIRE radar tracking station; ~ **principale** *f* INFORMAT, ORDINAT master station; ~ **radar** *f* NAUT radar station; ~ **radio** *f* AERONAUT ground radio station; ~ **radiogoniométrique** *f* AERONAUT radio direction finding station; ~ **à rayons X** *f* PETR X-ray station; ~ **de réception d'informations** *f* TELECOM IRS, information receiver station; ~ **de réception terrestre** *f* TV receiving Earth station; ~ **de référence** *f* ESPACE *communications* reference station; ~ **relais** *f* TV relay station; ~ **de relèvement** *f* HYDROLOGIE boosting station; ~ **de réseau** *f* INFORMAT, ORDINAT network station; ~ **de revêtement** *f* PETR dope station; ~ **satellite** *f* TV affiliate; ~ **de sauvetage** *f* NAUT lifeboat station; ~ **de signal** *f* COMMANDE signal station; ~ **sismique** *f* GEOPHYS seismic station; ~ **au sol** *f* ESPACE ground station; ~ **spatiale** *f* ESPACE *véhicules* space station; ~ **supérieure** *f* TRANSPORT top station; ~ **de taxi** *f* TRANSPORT taxi rank; ~ **terminale d'usager local** *f* TELECOM LUT, local user terminal; ~ **de Terre** *f* ESPACE *communications* terrestrial station; ~ **terrestre** *f* ESPACE *communications* terrestrial station, TV Earth station; ~ **terrestre transportable** *f* ESPACE *communications* transportable Earth station; ~ **terrienne** *f* ESPACE *communications* Earth station, TELECOM, TV Earth station; ~ **terrienne côtière** *f* NAUT coast Earth station; ~ **terrienne embarquée** *f* ESPACE *communications* airborne Earth station, ship-borne Earth station; ~ **terrienne de navire** *f* NAUT ship Earth station; ~ **terrienne de télécommande** *f* ESPACE *communications* command Earth station; ~ **de traitement des déchets** *f* RECYCLAGE waste treatment plant; ~ **de traitement de l'eau** *f* DISTRI EAU water treatment plant MINES water-cleansing plant; ~ **de transfert** *f* MINES transfer station; ~ **de travail graphique** *f* INFORMAT, ORDINAT graphics work station; ~ **utilisatrice locale** *f* NAUT local user terminal

stationnaire *adj* MECANIQUE fixed

station-relais *f* PETROLE *canalisations* booster platform

station-service *f* PRODUCTION service station, TRANSPORT gasoline station (AmE), petrol station (BrE), service station; ~ **batterie** *f* TRANSPORT battery loading point; ~ **moteur** *m* AUTO engine shop; ~ **vidange** *f* AUTO oil change shop

statique[1] *adj* ELECTROTEC, INFORMAT, ORDINAT static

statique[2] *f* ELECTROTEC, PHYSIQUE statics; ~ **des fluides** *f* PHYSIQUE hydrostatics

statistique *f* INFORMAT, MATH, ORDINAT statistics

statistiques: ~ **de Bose-Einstein** *f pl* PHYSIQUE Bose-Einstein statistics; ~ **de Fermi-Dirac** *f pl* PHYSIQUE Fermi-Dirac statistics; ~ **quantiques** *f pl* PHYSIQUE quantum statistics

stator *m* AUTO, ELECTR *d'une machine*, ELECTROTEC, PHYSIQUE stator; ~ **bobiné** *m* ELECTROTEC wound stator; ~ **compresseur** *m* AERONAUT compressor stator; ~ **diphasé** *m* ELECTROTEC two-phase stator; ~ **à pôles saillants** *m* ELECTROTEC salient pole stator; ~ **triphasé** *m* ELECTROTEC three-phase stator

statoréacteur *m* AERONAUT athodyd, ramjet engine, ramjet, THERMODYN ramjet engine, TRANSPORT aerothermodynamic duct, athodyd, ramjet engine

staurotide *f* MINERAUX staurolite, staurotide

Steadicam *m* CINEMAT Steadicam

stéarate *m* CHIMIE stearate

stéarine *f* CHIMIE stearin

stéarique *adj* CHIMIE stearic

stéaryle *m* CHIMIE stearyl

stéatite *f* MINERAUX steatite

Steenbeck *m* CINEMAT *table de montage* Steenbeck

steinmannite *f* MINERAUX steinmannite

stellaire *adj* ASTRONOMIE, ESPACE stellar

stencil: ~ **pour l'adresse** *m* EMBALLAGE address stencil

sténopé *m* PHOTO, PHYSIQUE pinhole

stéphanite *f* MINERAUX psaturose, stephanite

stéradian *m* ELECTRON, GEOMETRIE, PHYSIQUE steradian

stercorite *f* MINERAUX stercorite

stère *m* METROLOGIE stere

stéréo *adj* ENREGISTR stereo

stéréochimie *f* CHIMIE stereochemistry

stéréo-isomère *m* CHIMIE stereoisomer

stéréomicroscope *m* EQUIP LAB stereomicroscope

stéréophonie *f* ACOUSTIQUE, ENREGISTR stereophony; ~ **codée** *f* ENREGISTR encoded stereo

stéréophotogrammétrie *f* MATERIAUX stereophotogrammetry

stéréoscope *m* PHOTO stereoscope

stéréoscopie *f* PHOTO stereoscopy

stérile *adj* CHARBON barren, dead, sterile, GEOLOGIE barren, MINES barren, hungry

stériles *m pl* MINES barren ground, leavings, deads, waste ground, mullock (BrE), waste rock, waste, PRODUCTION waste

stérilisation: ~ **force 10** *f* AGRO ALIM botulinum cook

stérilisé *adj* AGRO ALIM sterilized

stérique *adj* CHIMIE steric

sternbergite *f* MINERAUX sternbergite

stéroïde *m* CHIMIE steroid

stérol *m* CHIMIE sterol

stibiconite *f* MINERAUX stibiconite, stibilite

stibieux *adj* CHIMIE stibious

stibine *f* IMPRIM *non chimique* antimony, MINERAUX stibnite

stibique *adj* CHIMIE antimonic

stibnite *f* CHIMIE stibnite

stigmastérol *m* CHIMIE stigmasterol

stigmomètre *m* PHOTO split image rangefinder

stilb *m* METROLOGIE stilb

stilbène *m* CHIMIE stilbene

stilbite *f* MINERAUX stilbite

stilpnomélane *f* MINERAUX stilpnomelane

stimulation *f* PETR stimulation; ~ **de gisements d'hydrocarbures liquides** *f* PETR oil stimulation

stimuler *vt* PHYS RAYON *absorption de radiation* stimulate

stochastique *adj* INFORMAT, MATH, ORDINAT stochastic

stock *m* MINES arch, support pillar, OCEANO fish stock, PRODUCTION inventory; ~ **atelier** *m* PRODUCTION floor stock, in-process inventory; ~ **comptable** *m* PRODUC-

TION system stock; ~ **au contrôle** m PRODUCTION stock at inspection; ~ **contrôlé** m EMBALLAGE accepted stock; ~ **disponible** m PRODUCTION available inventory, available stock, picking stock;~ **disponible prévisionnel** m PRODUCTION planned projected available stock; ~ **dormant** m PRODUCTION inactive inventory; ~ **en cours** m PRODUCTION in-process inventory; ~ **en cours d'approvisionnement** m PRODUCTION stock on order; ~ **en début de période** m PRODUCTION opening stock; ~ **en rupture** m PRODUCTION out-of-stock situation, runout, stock-out; ~ **existant** m PRODUCTION stock on hand; ~ **inactif** m PRODUCTION inactive inventory; ~ **physique** m PRODUCTION stock on hand; ~ **prévisionnel** m PRODUCTION projected available stock; ~ **projeté** m PRODUCTION projected available stock; ~ **réservé** m PRODUCTION allocated stock; ~ **de sécurité** m PRODUCTION safety stock; ~ **stratégique** m PRODUCTION hedge, hedging

stockage m IMPRIM *manutention*, INFORMAT, ORDINAT, PHOTO *de pellicule*, POLLU MER, SECURITE *des matières dangereuses* storage; ~ **définitif** m NUCLEAIRE ultimate waste disposal; ~ **de données** m INFORMAT, ORDINAT data storage; ~ **d'eau** m EN RENOUV pondage; ~ **en cavité souterraine** m THERMODYN underground storage; ~ **d'énergie** m THERMODYN energy storage; ~ **de l'énergie pendant les heures creuses** m NUCLEAIRE off-peak energy storage; ~ **et transfert des données sur disquettes** m IMPRIM store and forward; ~ **flottant** m PETROLE spar; ~ **d'information** m TV information storage; ~ **optique** m OPTIQUE optical storage; ~ **des particules** m PHYS PART particle storage; ~ **souterrain** m DISTRI EAU, GAZ, THERMODYN underground storage; ~ **superficiel** m HYDROLOGIE surface storage; ~ **tampon** m PETR flow tank

stockage-restitution: ~ **des données** m INFORMAT, ORDINAT ISR, information storage and retrieval

stocker vt CHARBON, INFORMAT, ORDINAT store

stoechiométrie f CHIMIE stoichiometry

stoechiométrique adj CHIMIE, MATERIAUX stoichiometric

stolzite f MINERAUX stolzite

stone m METROLOGIE stone

stop m COMMANDE stop light, CONSTR halt sign, INFORMAT, ORDINAT stop

stopper[1] vt INFORMAT, ORDINAT halt, stop

stopper:[2] ~ **les machines** vi NAUT stop engines

stoppeur m NAUT bow stopper

stot m MINES arch, support pillar

stracou m CERAM VER annealing lehr

strapage m PHYSIQUE strapping

strapontin m VEHICULES *siège* folding seat (AmE), tip-up seat (BrE)

strate f CHARBON stratum, CRISTALL layer line, GEOLOGIE bed, layer; ~ **de craie** f CONSTR chalk strata; ~ **perméable** f HYDROLOGIE aquafer, aquifer, water-bearing stratum

stratégie: ~ **de régulation** f TRANSPORT regulation strategy

stratification f CHARBON stratification, EMBALLAGE laminating, EN RENOUV *des eaux* stratification, GEOLOGIE layering, PAPIER laminating, PETR bedding, stratification, PLAST CAOU lamination; ~ **de la charge** f TRANSPORT charge stratification; ~ **de courant** f GEOLOGIE current bedding; ~ **en feston** f GEOLOGIE *à dépressions marquées* festoon cross-bedding, trough cross-bedding; ~ **en film** f EMBALLAGE film lamination;

~ **entrecroisée** f GEOLOGIE cross-bedding, *à dépressions marquées* festoon cross-bedding, trough cross-bedding; ~ **lenticulaire** f GEOLOGIE lensing; ~ **transverse en chevrons** f GEOLOGIE herringbone cross lamination

stratifié[1] adj CHARBON stratified, NAUT *plastiques*, PLAST CAOU laminated

stratifié[2] m ELECTRON, IMPRIM, MATERIAUX, MECANIQUE *matériaux* laminate, PLAST CAOU laminated plastic, *plastiques* laminate; ~ **ordinaire** m ELECTRON general-purpose laminate; ~ **pour circuits imprimés** m ELECTRON printed circuit laminate; ~ **verre-époxy** m ELECTRON glass epoxy laminate

stratifier vt CHARBON stratify

stratifiés m pl IMPRIM laminate

stratifil m PLAST CAOU *fibre de verre* roving; ~ **bouclé** m CERAM VER spun roving; ~ **poilu** m CERAM VER hairy roving; ~ **de verre textile** m CERAM VER roving; ~ **de verre textile torsion zéro** m CERAM VER no-twist roving

stratigraphie f CHARBON stratigraphy

strato-cumulus m AERONAUT *météorologie*, METEO stratocumulus

stratosphère f METEO stratosphere

stratotype m GEOLOGIE type section

stratovision f TV airborne television

stratovolcan m GEOPHYS stratovolcano

stratus m METEO stratus; ~ **fractus** m METEO stratus fractus

streamer m IMPRIM streamer, ORDINAT tape streamer

stress: ~ **acide** m POLLUTION acid stress; ~ **d'acidité** m POLLUTION acid stress

strict adj ACOUSTIQUE just

striction f MATERIAUX necking, METALL neck, PHYSIQUE necking; ~ **de diamètre** f METALL necking; ~ **en bande** f NUCLEAIRE belt pinch; ~ **hélicoïdale** f NUCLEAIRE screw pinch; ~ **toroïdale** f NUCLEAIRE toroidal pinch effect

strie f METALL striation, PAPIER scratch, streak, PRODUCTION checkering (AmE), chequering (BrE), groove

strié adj PRODUCTION grooved

strier vt PRODUCTION checker (AmE), chequer (BrE)

stries f pl PHYS FLUID streaklines; ~ **d'acier à arêtes vives** f pl PRODUCTION sharp ridges of steel

strioscopie f PHYSIQUE Schlieren photography

strip: ~ **bande** f PRODUCTION strip

striure f PRODUCTION checkering (AmE), chequering (BrE)

stroboscope m PHYS ONDES, PHYSIQUE stroboscope

stromeyérite f MINERAUX stromeyerite

strontianite f MINERAUX strontianite

strontique adj CHIMIE strontic

strontium m *(Sr)* CHIMIE strontium *(Sr)*; ~ **radioactif** m CHIMIE radiostrontium

strophantine f CHIMIE strophanthin

stross: ~ **central** m MINES center core (AmE), centre core (BrE)

structural adj CONSTR structural

structure f CONSTR, INFORMAT, ORDINAT structure, PAPIER *de la feuille* formation, PETR fabric, PHYSIQUE *de l'atome* structure; ~ **d'affaissement tectonique** f GEOLOGIE gravity collapse structure; ~ **alvéolaire** f AERONAUT, CONSTR honeycomb structure, GEOLOGIE *altération* honeycomb structure, honeycomb texture; ~ **amorphe** f PLAST CAOU amorphous structure; ~ **anormale** f METALL abnormal structure; ~ **arborescente** f INFORMAT tree structure; ~ **atomique** f PHYS

PART atomic structure; ~ **atomistique** *f* NUCLEAIRE atomistic structure; ~ **aust**é**nitique** *f* RESSORTS austenitic structure; ~ **band**é**e** *f* METALL banded structure; ~ **de bandes** *f* MATERIAUX *semi-conducteurs* band structure; ~ **de bloc** *f* ORDINAT block structure; ~ **à carrousel** *f* ESPACE *communications* carousel structure; ~ **cellulaire** *f* TELECOM cellular structure; ~ **cellulaire-dendritique** *f* MATERIAUX cellular-dendritic structure; ~ **compacte** *f* CRISTALL close-packed structure; ~ **de coulée** *f* MATERIAUX, METALL as cast structure; ~ **cristalline** *f* CHARBON, CRISTALL, MATERIAUX, METALL crystal structure; ~ **de défaut** *f* METALL defect structure; ~ **dendritique** *f* MATERIAUX dendritic structure; ~ **2B+D** *f* TELECOM 2B+D arrangement; ~ **de domaines** *f* PHYSIQUE domain structure; ~ **de données** *f* INFORMAT, ORDINAT data model, data structure; ~ **d'E/S** *f* PRODUCTION *automatisme industriel* I/O designation; ~ **des écoulements turbulents** *f* PHYS FLUID structure of turbulent flows; ~ **d'effondrement gravitaire** *f* GEOLOGIE gravity collapse structure; ~ **électronique** *f* NUCLEAIRE electronic structure; ~ **élémentaire d'un réseau** *f* ELECTR system pattern; ~ **en arbre** *f* TELECOM tree structure; ~ **en bandes** *f* MATERIAUX banded structure; ~ **en béton** *f* CONSTR concrete structure; ~ **en couches** *f* CRISTALL layer structure; ~ **en couches d'application** *f* TELECOM ALS, application layer structure; ~ **en couches d'application étendue** *f* TELECOM XALS, extended application layer structure; ~ **en domaines** *f* METALL domain structure; ~ **en écailles** *f* GEOLOGIE *de nappes de charriage de même direction* imbricated structure; ~ **en étoile** *f* TELECOM star structure; ~ **en nid d'abeille** *f* GEOLOGIE *altération* honeycomb structure, honeycomb texture; ~ **de l'espace-temps** *f* PHYS RAYON structure of space time; ~ **d'essai** *f* CRISTALL trial structure; ~ **feuilletée** *f* MATERIAUX laminated structure; ~ **de fichier** *f* INFORMAT, ORDINAT file structure; ~ **filamenteuse** *f* ASTRONOMIE filigree formation; ~ **fine** *f* PHYS RAYON *spectroscopie d'atome*, PHYSIQUE fine structure; ~ **fluidale** *f* GEOLOGIE fluidal structure, *roches magmatiques* fluidal texture, *texture magmatique* laminar structure; ~ **gonflable** *f* CONSTR inflated structure; ~ **des grains** *f* CHARBON grain structure; ~ **granulaire** *f* MATERIAUX grain structure, granular structure; ~ **grumeleuse** *f* CONS MECA crumb structure; ~ **hexagonale compacte** *f* CRISTALL hcp, hexagonal close-packed structure; ~ **horizontale** *f* ELECTRON lateral structure; ~ **à horsts et dépressions tectoniques** *f* GEOLOGIE basin-and-range structure; ~ **hyperfine** *f* PHYS RAYON *de la matière*, PHYSIQUE hyperfine structure; ~ **interne** *f* PHYS PART *du proton* internal structure; ~ **interne d'une planète** *f* ASTRONOMIE planetary interior; ~ **lamellaire** *f* METALL lamellar structure; ~ **lamifiée** *f* EMBALLAGE lamination; ~ **de langage** *f* ORDINAT language construct; ~ **légère alvéolée** *f* EMBALLAGE lightweight honeycomb structure; ~ **lenticulaire oeillée** *f* GEOLOGIE augen structure; ~ **de liste** *f* INFORMAT, ORDINAT list structure; ~ **litée** *f* GEOPHYS layered structure; ~ **à longue période** *f* CRISTALL long period structure; ~ **manufacturée** *f* ESPACE *véhicules* fabricated structure; ~ **métallique** *f* CONSTR metallic structure; ~ **modulée** *f* METALL modulated structure; ~ **monocoque** *f* ESPACE *véhicules spatiaux* monocoque structure; ~ **nida** *f* AERONAUT honeycomb structure; ~ **orientée** *f* GEOLOGIE directional fabric, directional structure; ~ **de plaquettes** *f* METALL platelet structure; ~ **de pont** *f* NAUT deck structure; ~ **de**

programme *f* INFORMAT, ORDINAT program structure; ~ **résistante** *f* AERONAUT primary structure; ~ **à retard** *f* PHYSIQUE slow-wave structure; ~ **du schéma à relais** *f* PRODUCTION *automatisme industriel* ladder diagram format; ~ **secondaire** *f* ESPACE *véhicules* secondary structure; ~ **sédimentaire** *f* PETR depositional fabric; ~ **à simple niveau de masquage** *f* ELECTRON single layer masking structure; ~ **sorbitique** *f* RESSORTS sorbitic structure; ~ **spatiale** *f* POLLUTION spatial pattern; ~ **de support** *f* INSTRUMENT pedestal base; ~ **tarifaire** *f* TELECOM tariff structure; ~ **de la trame numérique** *f* TELECOM digital frame structure; ~ **TS** *f* TELECOM TS network; ~ **de type CFC** *f* CRISTALL FCC-based structure; ~ **de Widmannstätten** *f* METALL Widmannstätten structure

structure-guide *f* PETR permanent guide base, permanent guide structure
structure-poids *f* PETROLE gravity platform
structures: ~ **orientées parallèles aux linéations tectoniques** *f pl* GEOLOGIE *en forme de crêtes et sillons* mullion structure
struvite *f* MINERAUX struvite
STS *abrév (spatial-temporel-spatial)* ESPACE STS *(space-time-space)*
stub *m* PHYSIQUE stub
studio *m* CINEMAT studio, ENREGISTR continuity studio; ~ **actif** *m* ENREGISTR live studio; ~ **de doublage** *m* CINEMAT dubbing theater (AmE), dubbing theatre (BrE); ~ **d'enregistrement** *m* ENREGISTR recording studio; ~ **de mixage** *m* ENREGISTR dubbing studio; ~ **réverbérant** *m* ENREGISTR live studio; ~ **son** *m* ENREGISTR sound studio; ~ **à zone active et à zone morte** *m* ENREGISTR live-end dead-end studio
stupéfiant[1] *adj* CHIMIE stupefacient
stupéfiant[2] *m* CHIMIE stupefacient
style: ~ **maison** *m* IMPRIM house style
stylet: ~ **d'enregistreur** *m* GEOPHYS pen
stylo *m* IMPRIM wand; ~ **à cartouche** *m* IMPRIM cartridge pen; ~ **à pointe de diamant** *m* EQUIP LAB *marquage* diamond-tipped pen
styphnate *m* CHIMIE styphnate
styracine *f* CHIMIE styracitol
styramate *m* CHIMIE styramate
styrène *m* CHIMIE, MATERIAUX *matières plastiques*, PETROLE styrene
styrène-acrylonitrile-butadiène *m* PLAST CAOU ABS, acrylonitrile-butadiene-styrene
styrol *m* CHIMIE styrene
styrolène *m* CHIMIE styrene, styrolene
SUAC *abrév (message d'acceptation de service supplémentaire)* TELECOM FAA *(facility accepted message)*
suage *m* PRODUCTION swage
subdiviser[1] *vt* MINES *courant d'air* split
subdiviser:[2] **se ~** *v réfl* CONSTR split
subdivision *f* CONSTR splitting
subduction *f* PETROLE subduction
subérate *m* CHIMIE suberate
subérification *f* CHIMIE suberification
subérine *f* CHIMIE suberin
subérique *adj* CHIMIE suberic
subérone *f* CHIMIE suberone
subéryle *m* CHIMIE suberyl
subérylique *adj* CHIMIE suberylic
subir: ~ **un dommage** *vi* BREVETS suffer damage
subjectile *m* PLAST CAOU substrate

sublimable *adj* CHIMIE sublimable

sublimat *m* CHIMIE sublimate

sublimation *f* CHIMIE, PHYSIQUE sublimation

sublimatoire *m* CHIMIE sublimatory

sublime *m* CHIMIE sublimate

sublimé[1] *adj* CHIMIE sublimed

sublimé[2] *m* CHIMIE, PETROLE sublimate

sublimer *vt* CHIMIE sublime; ~ **sous vide** *vt* PHOTO evaporate

submergé *adj* HYDROLOGIE flooded

submerger *vt* DISTRI EAU submerge

submersible *m* OCEANO submersible

submersion *f* CHIMIE submergence, submersion, DISTRI EAU inundation

subrécargue *m* NAUT supercargo

subsidence *f* GEOLOGIE, METEO, PETROLE, POLLUTION subsidence; ~ **du fond** *f* MATERIAUX subsidence

substance *f* CHIMIE substance; ~ **adaptatrice d'indice** *f* OPTIQUE, TELECOM index-matching material; ~ **biodégradable** *f* POLLUTION biodegradable substance; ~ **cancérigène** *f* SECURITE carcinogenic substance; ~ **cancérogène** *f* SECURITE carcinogenic substance; ~ **carcinogène** *f* CHIMIE carcinogen; ~ **combustible** *f* THERMODYN combustible; ~ **corrosive** *f* SECURITE corrosive substance; ~ **dangereuse** *f* SECURITE dangerous substance, hazardous substance; ~ **diamagnétique** *f* ELECTR diamagnetic material; ~ **diffusante** *f* NUCLEAIRE scattering medium; ~ **dissoute** *f* AGRO ALIM solute; ~ **ferromagnétique** *f* ELECTR ferromagnetic material; ~ **fluorescente** *f* PHYS RAYON fluorescent substance; ~ **irritante** *f* SECURITE irritant substance; ~ **luminescente** *f* ELECTRON phosphorescent material, PHYSIQUE phosphor; ~ **magnétique** *f* MATERIAUX magnetic substance; ~ **miscible** *f* POLLUTION miscible substance; ~ **nocive** *f* SECURITE harmful substance; ~ **nutritive** *f* AGRO ALIM nutrient; ~ **odorante** *f* GENIE CHIM odorizer; ~ **opaque** *f* PHYS RAYON opaque substance; ~ **optiquement active** *f* OPTIQUE, TELECOM optically active material; ~ **oxydante** *f* SECURITE oxidizing substance; ~ **phosphorescente** *f* ELECTRON phosphorescent material; ~ **radioactive** *f* POLLUTION, SECURITE radioactive substance; ~ **retenue après immersion** *f* TEXTILE dip pickup; ~ **révélatrice** *f* CHIMIE tracer substance; ~ **toxique** *f* SECURITE toxic substance; ~ **traceur** *f* CHIMIE tracer substance; ~ **translucide** *f* PHYS RAYON translucent substance; ~ **transparente** *f* PHYS RAYON transparent substance; ~ **volatile** *f* GEOLOGIE volatile

substituant *m* CHIMIE substituent

substituer *vt* IMPRIM overwrite

substitut: ~ **de sel** *m* AGRO ALIM salt substitute; ~ **de térébenthine** *m* COULEURS turpentine substitute

substitution *f* CHIMIE metathesis, substitution, IMPRIM *composition* overstrike; ~ **isomorphe** *f* CRISTALL isomorphous replacement; ~ **de paramètres** *f* INFORMAT, ORDINAT parameter substitution

substrat *m* ELECTRON base, ORDINAT, PHYSIQUE, PLAST CAOU, TELECOM substrate; ~ **amorphe** *m* ELECTRON amorphous substrate; ~ **de circuit hybride à couches épaisses** *m* ELECTRON thick-film hybrid circuit substrate; ~ **de circuit hybride à couches minces** *m* ELECTRON thin-film hybrid circuit substrate; ~ **de circuit imprimé** *m* ELECTRON printed circuit substrate; ~ **de circuit intégré** *m* ELECTRON integrated circuit substrate; ~ **dopé N** *m* ELECTRON n-type substrate; ~ **double face** *m* ELECTRON double-sided substrate; ~ **en**

arséniure de gallium *m* ELECTRON gallium arsenide substrate; ~ **en saphir** *m* ELECTRON sapphire substrate; ~ **en semi-conducteur** *m* ELECTRON semiconductor substrate; ~ **en verre** *m* ELECTRON glass substrate; ~ **isolant** *m* ELECTROTEC, ESPACE *thermique* insulating substrate; ~ **N** *m* ELECTRON n-type substrate; ~ **passif** *m* ELECTRON passive substrate; ~ **piézo-électrique** *m* ELECTROTEC piezoelectric substrate; ~ **plaqué** *m* ELECTRON metal-clad substrate; ~ **pour hyperfréquences** *m* ELECTRON microwave substrate; ~ **semi-isolant** *m* ELECTRON semi-insulating substrate; ~ **de silicium** *m* ELECTRON silicon substrate; ~ **de silicium de type P** *m* ELECTRON p-type silicon substrate; ~ **de type N** *m* ELECTRON n-type substrate

substratum *m* GEOLOGIE substratum, underlying rock, PETROLE substratum

substructure *f* CONSTR, PETROLE substructure

subsurface *f* OCEANO subsurface zone

subtilisation *f* CHIMIE volatilization

succédané: ~ **de lait** *m* AGRO ALIM nondairy creamer

succession: ~ **des couches** *f* CHARBON bed sequence, seam sequence, layer sequence; ~ **de renflements** *f* CERAM VER gobbing

succinate *m* CHIMIE succinate

succinimide *f* CHIMIE succinimide

succinique *adj* CHIMIE succinic

succinite *f* MINERAUX succinite

succinyle *m* CHIMIE succinyl

succion *f* CONS MECA suction; ~ **d'Ekman** *f* OCEANO Ekman forcing; ~ **thermohaline** *f* OCEANO thermohaline pumping

sucette *f* IMPRIM *de machine* forwarding sucker

suceuse *f* OCEANO suction dredge

sucrage *m* AGRO ALIM sugaring

sucrase *f* AGRO ALIM saccharase, sucrase

sucrate *m* CHIMIE sucrate

sucre *m* CHIMIE sugar; ~ **de canne** *m* AGRO ALIM, CHIMIE cane sugar; ~ **caramélisé** *m* AGRO ALIM caramel sugar (AmE), caramelized sugar (BrE); ~ **en morceaux** *m* AGRO ALIM lump sugar; ~ **de fermentation** *m* AGRO ALIM dietary sugar; ~ **filé** *m* AGRO ALIM pulled sugar; ~ **de fruit** *m* AGRO ALIM fructose, fruit sugar; ~ **inverti** *m* AGRO ALIM, CHIMIE invert sugar; ~ **de lait** *m* CHIMIE lactose; ~ **de raisin** *m* AGRO ALIM grape sugar, CHIMIE glucose; ~ **tiré** *m* AGRO ALIM pulled sugar

sucré *adj* AGRO ALIM sweetened

sud:[1] **du** ~ *adj* NAUT southerly, south

sud:[2] ~ **magnétique** *m* GEOPHYS magnetic south

sud-est:[1] **du** ~ *adj* NAUT southeasterly, southeast

sud-est[2] *m* NAUT southeaster, southeasterly wind

sud-est-quart-est[1] *adj* NAUT southeast by east

sud-est-quart-est[2] *m* NAUT southeast by east

sud-est-quart-sud[1] *adj* NAUT southeast by south

sud-est-quart-sud[2] *m* NAUT southeast by south

SUDM *abrév* (*message de demande de service supplémentaire*) TELECOM FAR (*facility request message*)

sud-ouest:[1] **du** ~ *adj* NAUT southwesterly NAUT southwest

sud-ouest[2] *m* NAUT southwest

sud-ouest-quart-ouest[1] *adj* NAUT southwest by west

sud-ouest-quart-ouest[2] *m* NAUT southwest by west

sud-ouest-quart-sud[1] *adj* NAUT southwest by south

sud-ouest-quart-sud[2] *m* NAUT southwest by south

sud-quart-sud-est *m* NAUT south by southeast

sud-quart-sud-ouest[1] *adj* NAUT south by southwest

sud-quart-sud-ouest[2] *m* NAUT south by southwest

sud-sud-est[1] *adj* NAUT south-southeast
sud-sud-est[2] *m* NAUT south-southeast
sud-sud-ouest[1] *adj* NAUT south-southwest
sud-sud-ouest[2] *m* NAUT south-southwest
suffixe *m* INFORMAT, ORDINAT suffix
suie *f* CERAM VER soot
suif *m* TEXTILE tallow; **~ minéral** *m* MINERAUX mineral tallow, mountain tallow
suintement *m* AGRO ALIM percolation, CHIMIE, DISTRI EAU seepage, GAZ creep, seepage, HYDROLOGIE ooze, oozing, POLLU MER seepage
suinter *vi* CHIMIE seep
suite *f* INFORMAT stream, suite, MATH progression, sequence, ORDINAT stream, suite; **~ binaire** *f* ELECTRON bit string; **~ convergente** *f* MATH convergent sequence; **~ de Fibonacci** *f* MATH Fibonacci sequence; **~ de Fourier** *f* MATH Fourier series; **~ géométrique** *f* MATH geometric sequence; **~ d'impulsions** *f* ELECTRON pulse sequence; **~ de message** *f* TELECOM COM, continuation of message; **~ de passages** *f* TELECOM series of links; **~ de segments emboîtés** *f* MATH nested intervals
suivant: ~ l'ordre indiqué *loc* BREVETS in the order specified
suiveur *m* ESPACE tracker; **~ des pièces** *m* PRODUCTION expeditor; **~ stellaire** *m* ESPACE star tracker
suivi: ~ d'atelier *m* PRODUCTION manufacturing follow-up; **~ de fabrication** *m* PRODUCTION manufacturing follow-up; **~ de piste** *m* TV tracking; **~ de production** *m* PRODUCTION manufacturing follow-up; **~ de projet** *m* CONSTR project monitoring; **~ du réseau** *m* NUCLEAIRE grid following behavior (AmE), grid following behaviour (BrE); **~ de stock** *m* PRODUCTION inventory reporting; **~ de train** *m* CH DE FER train describer, train supervision number
suivre[1] *vt* NAUT *la route de l'aller* sail; **~ la direction de** *vt* HYDROLOGIE flow along; **~ à la trace** *vt* INFORMAT, ORDINAT trace
suivre:[2] **~ le cap fixé** *vi* NAUT be on course; **~ le point** *vi* CINEMAT follow focus, pull focus, rack focus; **~ sans alinéa** *vi* IMPRIM run on
sujet:[1] **~ à l'influence de la température** *adj* THERMODYN temperature-dependent
sujet[2] *m* TV scope
sulfacide *m* CHIMIE thioacid
sulfafurazol *m* CHIMIE sulfafurazole (AmE), sulphafurazole (BrE)
sulfaguanidine *f* CHIMIE sulfaguanidine (AmE), sulphaguanidine (BrE)
sulfamate *m* CHIMIE sulfamate (AmE), sulphamate (BrE)
sulfamide *m* CHIMIE sulfa drug (AmE), sulpha drug (BrE), sulfamide (AmE), sulphamide (BrE), sulfonamide (AmE), sulphonamide (BrE)
sulfamique *adj* CHIMIE *acide* sulfamic (AmE), sulphamic (BrE)
sulfanates: ~ de calcium *m pl* PETROLE calcium petroleum sulfanates (AmE), calcium petroleum sulphanates (BrE)
sulfanilamide *f* CHIMIE sulfanilamide (AmE), sulphanilamide (BrE)
sulfanilate *m* CHIMIE sulfanilate (AmE), sulphanilate (BrE)
sulfanilique *adj* CHIMIE *acide* sulfanilic (AmE), sulphanilic (BrE)
sulfapyridine *f* CHIMIE sulfapyridine (AmE), sulphapyridine (BrE)

sulfarsénique *adj* CHIMIE thioarsenic, *acide* sulfarsenic (AmE), sulpharsenic (BrE)
sulfarséniure *m* CHIMIE sulfarsenide (AmE), sulpharsenide (BrE)
sulfatation *f* LESSIVES sulfation (AmE), sulphation (BrE)
sulfate *m* CHIMIE, POLLUTION sulfate (AmE), sulphate (BrE); **~ d'aluminium** *m* HYDROLOGIE aluminium sulphate (BrE), aluminum sulfate (AmE); **~ basique** *m* CHIMIE subsulfate (AmE), subsulphate (BrE); **~ de calcium** *m* AGRO ALIM calcium sulfate (AmE), calcium sulphate (BrE); **~ de chaux** *m* CHIMIE sulfate of lime (AmE), sulphate of lime (BrE); **~ de cuivre** *m* CHIMIE blue vitriol, bluestone, copper sulfate (AmE), copper sulphate (BrE), IMPRIM cupric sulfate (AmE), cupric sulphate (BrE), PHOTO copper sulfate (AmE), copper sulphate (BrE); **~ de diméthyle** *m* CHIMIE dimethyl sulfate (AmE), dimethyl sulphate (BrE); **~ de magnésium** *m* LESSIVES magnesium sulfate (AmE), magnesium sulphate (BrE); **~ neutre de sodium** *m* LESSIVES sodium sulfate (AmE), sodium sulphate (BrE); **~ de plomb** *m* CHIMIE lead sulfate (AmE), lead sulphate (BrE); **~ de potassium** *m* LESSIVES potassium sulfate (AmE), potassium sulphate (BrE); **~ de sodium** *m* CHIMIE sodium sulfate (AmE), sodium sulphate (BrE); **~ de sodium commercial** *m* AGRO ALIM block salt cake (BrE), salt cake (AmE); **~ de soude** *m* CERAM VER salt cake
sulfathiazole *m* CHIMIE sulfathiazole (AmE), sulphathiazole (BrE)
sulfatide *m* CHIMIE sulfatide (AmE), sulphatide (BrE)
sulfhydrate *m* CHIMIE hydrosulfide (AmE), hydrosulphide (BrE), sulfhydrate (AmE), sulphydrate (BrE)
sulfhydrique *adj* CHIMIE sulfhydric (AmE), sulphydric (BrE)
sulfine *f* CHIMIE sulfonium (AmE), sulphonium (BrE)
sulfinique *adj* CHIMIE sulfinic (AmE), sulphinic (BrE)
sulfinyle *m* CHIMIE sulfinyl (AmE), sulphinyl (BrE)
sulfite *m* CHIMIE sulfite (AmE), sulphite (BrE); **~ neutre** *m* PAPIER neutral sulfite (AmE), neutral sulphite (BrE)
sulfocarbonate *m* CHIMIE thiocarbonate
sulfochloration *f* LESSIVES sulfochlorination (AmE), sulphochlorination (BrE)
sulfochlorure *m* CHIMIE sulfur chloride (AmE), sulphur chloride (BrE)
sulfocyanate *m* CHIMIE thiocyanate
sulfocyanique *adj* CHIMIE thiocyanic
sulfolane *m* CHIMIE sulfolane (AmE), sulpholane (BrE), PETROLE sulfolane (AmE), sulpholane (BrE)
sulfolène *m* PETROLE sulfolene (AmE), sulpholene (BrE)
sulfonate *m* CHIMIE sulfonate (AmE), sulphonate (BrE)
sulfonation *f* CHIMIE, LESSIVES sulfonation (AmE), sulphonation (BrE)
sulfone *m* CHIMIE, LESSIVES sulfone (AmE), sulphone (BrE); **~ de diméthyle** *m* CHIMIE dimethyl sulfone (AmE), dimethyl sulphone (BrE)
sulfoné *adj* CHIMIE sulfonated (AmE), sulphonated (BrE), sulfonic (AmE), sulphonic (BrE)
sulfonique *adj* CHIMIE sulfonic (AmE), sulphonic (BrE)
sulfonyle *m* CHIMIE sulfonyl (AmE), sulphonyl (BrE)
sulforation *f* LESSIVES sulfation (AmE), sulphation (BrE)
sulfosalicylique *adj* CHIMIE *acide* sulfosalicylic (AmE), sulphosalicylic (BrE)
sulfuration *f* CHIMIE sulfuration (AmE), sulphuration

(BrE), sulfurization (AmE), sulphurization (BrE), thiation

sulfure *m* CHIMIE sulfide (AmE), sulphide (BrE); **~ de carbone** *m* AGRO ALIM carbon disulfide (AmE), carbon disulphide (BrE); **~ de carbonyle** *m* POLLUTION carbonyl sulfide (AmE), carbonyl sulphide (BrE); **~ d'hydrogène** *m* POLLUTION hydrogen sulfide (AmE), hydrogen sulphide (BrE); **~ mercurique noir** *m* MINERAUX metacinnabarite; **~ de plomb** *m* CHIMIE lead sulfide (AmE), lead sulphide (BrE)

sulfureux *adj* CHIMIE *acide* sulfurous (AmE), sulphurous (BrE)

sulfurique *adj* CHIMIE sulfuric (AmE), sulphuric (BrE)

sulfurisation *f* CHIMIE sulfuration (AmE), sulphuration (BrE), sulfurization (AmE), sulphurization (BrE)

sulfuriser *vt* CHIMIE sulfurize (AmE), sulphurize (BrE)

sulfuryle *m* CHIMIE sulfuryl (AmE), sulphfuryl (BrE)

sulphonium *m* CHIMIE sulfonium (AmE), sulphonium (BrE)

sultame *f* CHIMIE sultam

sultone *f* CHIMIE sultone

sumatrole *f* CHIMIE sumatrol

superamas *m* ASTRONOMIE *de galaxies* supercluster; **~ de galaxies de la Vierge** *m* ASTRONOMIE Virgo supercluster

supercalandre *f* PAPIER supercalender

supercalculateur *m* ORDINAT supercomputer

supercarburant *m* AUTO premium fuel (BrE), premium gasoline (AmE), PETROLE premium fuel (BrE), premium gasoline (AmE), premium gas (AmE), premium grade petrol (BrE), VEHICULES premium grade gas (AmE), premium grade gasoline (AmE), premium grade petrol (BrE)

superficie *f* CONSTR, PAPIER area; **~ totale** *f* CONSTR *d'un champ* total area

superficiel *adj* MINES above ground, surface

superfluide *m* PHYSIQUE superfluid

superfluidité *f* CHIMIE, PHYSIQUE superfluidity

supericonoscope *m* ELECTRON image iconoscope

supérieur *adj* GEOLOGIE upper

super-informatique *f* INFORMAT, ORDINAT supercomputing

superluminescence *f* OPTIQUE, TELECOM superluminescence, superradiance

supermini *m* INFORMAT, ORDINAT supermini

supernova *f* ASTRONOMIE, ESPACE supernova

super-ordinateur *m* INFORMAT supercomputer

superpétrolier *m* TRANSPORT mammoth tanker, supertanker

superphosphate *m* CHIMIE superphosphate; **~ de chaux** *m* CHIMIE superphosphate of lime

superplasticité *f* MATERIAUX superplasticity

superplastifiant *m* CONSTR superplasticizer

super-polissage *m* PRODUCTION mirror finish

superposé *adj* CHIMIE supernatant

superposer *vt* INFORMAT *données* overwrite, TV superimpose

superposition *f* INFORMAT *données* overwriting, METALL overlapping, ORDINAT *données* overwriting; **~ des dépôts par progradation** *f* GEOLOGIE regressive overlap; **~ d'instructions** *f* INFORMAT, ORDINAT overwriting; **~ de strates en progradation** *f* GEOLOGIE offlap; **~ de strates en transgression** *f* GEOLOGIE onlap

superréseau *m* CRISTALL superlattice

superstring *m* PHYS RAYON superstring

superstructure *f* CONSTR, NAUT superstructure

supersynchrotron: **~ à protons** *m* PHYS PART proton supersynchrotron

superviseur *m* INFORMAT supervisor, *programme* executive, ORDINAT control routine, supervisor, *programme* executive, POLLU MER supervisor, TELECOM network supervisor; **~ actif** *m* TELECOM active supervisor; **~ de secours** *m* TELECOM backup supervisor

supplément: **~ d'affaiblissement** *m* TELECOM excess attenuation

supplémentaire *adj* CONS MECA, IMPRIM additional, TEXTILE incremental

support *m* CHIMIE stand, CINEMAT *d'une pellicule* base, CONS MECA holder, pedestal, pillow, pillow block, rest, standard, CONSTR supporting, *d'une voûte* support, EMBALLAGE backing, ENREGISTR base, tape base, EQUIP LAB stand, *de tube à essai* rack, IMPRIM base paper, INFORMAT carrier, medium, support, INST HYDR bracket, MATERIAUX carrier, substrate, MECANIQUE bracket, NAUT foot, strut, NUCLEAIRE base frame, underframe, ORDINAT carrier, medium, support, PRODUCTION chaplet; **~ d'acétate** *m* IMPRIM acetate base; **~ antistatique** *m* PHOTO antistatic backing; **~ d'appui** *m* INSTRUMENT handrest; **~ d'arbre porte-fraise** *m* CONS MECA *d'une fraiseuse* arbor support; **~ de bande** *m* TV base film, tape base; **~ de base** *m* NUCLEAIRE base frame; **~ de batterie** *m* AUTO battery cradle; **~ de burettes** *m* EQUIP LAB burette stand; **~ de butée de débrayage** *m* AUTO release bearing hub; **~ de caméra** *m* CINEMAT camera bracket, camera mount; **~ de carton** *m* EMBALLAGE cardboard backing; **~ de centrage** *m* INSTRUMENT centering suction holder (AmE), centring suction holder (BrE); **~ central** *m* NAUT center girder (AmE), centre girder (BrE); **~ de chambre** *m* PHOTO camera mount; **~ à chariot** *m* CONS MECA turning rest, *tour* slide head, slide rest; **~ à chariot à double coulisse** *m* CONS MECA compound slide rest; **~ à chariot à mouvement longitudinal et transversal** *m* CONS MECA compound slide rest; **~ à chariot pivotant** *m* CONS MECA swivel slide rest; **~ à colonne** *m* INSTRUMENT pillar stand; **~ de communication** *m* INFORMAT, ORDINAT communication medium; **~ des contacts mobiles** *m* PRODUCTION *électricité* movable contact crossbar; **~ de couche** *m* PAPIER coating base paper; **~ de coussinet** *m* PRODUCTION bearing bracket; **~ de culbuteur** *m* AUTO rocker arm support; **~ disque** *m* OPTIQUE disc platter (BrE), disk platter (AmE); **~ de données** *m* INFORMAT, ORDINAT data carrier, data medium, DM; **~ double** *m* PRODUCTION stud, stud chaplet; **~ élévateur** *m* EQUIP LAB jack; **~ en acétate de cellulose** *m* CINEMAT cellulose acetate base; **~ en caoutchouc** *m* VEHICULES *du moteur* rubber mounting; **~ en nitrate de cellulose** *m* CINEMAT cellulose nitrate base; **~ en plateau à hauteur variable** *m* PRODUCTION stand with rising table; **~ d'enregistrement** *m* ENREGISTR, INFORMAT, ORDINAT recording medium; **~ d'enregistrement magnétique** *m* ORDINAT magnetic media; **~ en triacétate de cellulose** *m* CINEMAT cellulose triacetate base; **~ en V pour le traçage** *m* CONS MECA V-block; **~ estar** *m* CINEMAT estar base; **~ à éventail** *m* CONS MECA hand rest, *d'un tour* T-rest; **~ à faible retrait** *m* CINEMAT low-shrink base; **~ de fil** *m* TEXTILE package sleeve, tube; **~ de filtre** *m* EQUIP LAB filter support; **~ de fixation** *m* INSTRUMENT support arm; **~ flam** *m* CINEMAT nitrate base; **~ flexible** *m* CINEMAT gooseneck; **~ flottant** *m* PETR support vessel; **~ de gauchissement** *m* AERONAUT lateral cyclic control support; ~ **des glissières** *m* CONS MECA guide bearer, guide cross tie, guide yoke, motion plate, spectacle plate; ~ **d'impression** *m* IMPRIM substrate; ~ **d'impression dont les surfaces ont été traitées** *m* IMPRIM *flexographie* face stock; ~ **d'informations** *m* INFORMAT, ORDINAT data carrier, data medium, DM; ~ **isolant** *m* ELECTROTEC post insulator; ~ **de jambe du train** *m* AERONAUT landing gear leg support; ~ **de jauge** *m* METROLOGIE gage stand (AmE), gauge stand (BrE); ~ **latéral** *m* NAUT side girder; ~ **magnétique** *m* ACOUSTIQUE, ELECTROTEC magnetic medium, INFORMAT magnetic media; ~ **magnétique à défilement** *m* ELECTROTEC moving magnet medium; ~ **magnétique d'information** *m* ELECTROTEC magnetic storage medium; ~ **à main** *m* CONS MECA hand rest, turning rest, CONSTR *pour tourner en l'air* pillar hand rest; ~ **du masque compensé thermiquement** *m* TV temperature-compensated shadow mask mount; ~ **de mémoire** *m* INFORMAT, ORDINAT storage medium; ~ **de microphone** *m* ENREGISTR microphone stand; ~ **mobile** *m* INSTRUMENT mobile mounting; ~ **de montage** *m* NUCLEAIRE *chevalet* fitting stand, PRODUCTION mounting bracket; ~ **de moteur** *m* AUTO engine support; ~ **de moufle** *m* CERAM VER muffle support; ~ **mural** *m* TELECOM wall bracket; ~ **mylar** *m* TV mylar base; ~ **de nitrate** *m* CINEMAT, PHOTO nitrate base; ~ **non effaçable** *m* OPTIQUE write-once medium; ~ **non flam** *m* CINEMAT safety base; ~ **non inscriptible** *m* OPTIQUE read-only medium; ~ **à noyaux** *m* PRODUCTION core rack; ~ **d'objectif** *m* CINEMAT cradle; ~ **optique** *m* INFORMAT, OPTIQUE, ORDINAT optical medium; ~ **optique inscriptible une seule fois** *m* OPTIQUE write-once optical medium; ~ **d'outil** *m* CONS MECA tool rest; ~ **d'outils pour tours** *m* CONS MECA lathe tool post; ~ **physique** *m* TELECOM physical medium sublayer; ~ **à pinces** *m* PHOTO clamp; ~ **polyester** *m* CINEMAT polyester base; ~ **de porte-forêt** *m* CONS MECA drilling pillar; ~ **porte-fraise** *m* PRODUCTION *d'une machine* overhanging arm; ~ **pour enregistrement magnétique** *m* TV magnetic recording medium; ~ **pour entonnoir** *m* EQUIP LAB *filtration* funnel stand; ~ **pour pipettes** *m* EQUIP LAB *analyse* pipette stand; ~ **profondeur** *m* AERONAUT fore-and-aft cyclic control support; ~ **de quartz** *m* ELECTRON crystal holder; ~ **de quartz en verre** *m* ELECTROTEC glass holder; ~ **de radiateur** *m* AUTO radiator support; ~ **de remorquage** *m* VEHICULES towing bracket; ~ **de reproduction** *m* PHOTO copy stand; ~ **de résistance** *m* ELECTROTEC resistor core; ~ **simple** *m* PRODUCTION staple; ~ **de tablier** *m* PAPIER apron board; ~ **teinté** *m* CINEMAT tinted base; ~ **télescopique** *m* INSTRUMENT telescopic support; ~ **de thermistance** *m* ELECTROTEC thermistor mount; ~ **du train avant** *m* AERONAUT nose gear saddle; ~ **de transmission** *m* INFORMAT, OPTIQUE, ORDINAT transmission medium, TELECOM transmission bearer; ~ **transparent** *m* CINEMAT clear base; ~ **triacétate** *m* CINEMAT triacetate base; ~ **à trois pieds** *m* PRODUCTION tripod stand; ~ **de tube** *m* ELECTROTEC tube socket; ~ **du tube à rayons X** *m* INSTRUMENT X-ray tube stand; ~ **de tubes à essai** *m* EQUIP LAB test tube rack; ~ **de turbine** *m* AERONAUT engine cradle; ~ **de tuyauterie** *m* MECANIQUE hanger pipe; ~ **de tuyaux** *m* CONS MECA pipe support; ~ **universel** *m* PHOTO optical bench; ~ **vide** *m* INFORMAT, ORDINAT empty medium; ~ **vierge** *m* INFORMAT, ORDINAT blank medium, virgin medium; ~ **de la voie** *m* CH DE FER supporting column, TRANSPORT pedestal, pillar

supporter[1] *vt* CONS MECA carry, hold up, support, *charge, contrainte* bear

supporter:[2] ~ **les coûts des stocks** *vi* TEXTILE bear stock-holding costs

supports: ~ **pour filet de camouflage** *m pl* MILITAIRE camouflage supports

suppresseur *m* ELECTR *antiparasitage*, TELECOM suppressor; ~ **antiparasite** *m* ELECTR suppressor capacitor; ~ **de bruit** *m* ENREGISTR noise suppressor; ~ **de chrominance** *m* TV color kill (AmE), colour kill (BrE); ~ **d'écho** *m* ELECTRON ES, echo suppressor, echo canceller, ESPACE *communications*, INFORMAT, ORDINAT, TELECOM ES, echo suppressor; ~ **de rétroaction** *m* COMMANDE feedback suppressor; ~ **des transitoires** *m* ELECTROTEC transient suppressor, despiking circuit

suppression *f* ELECTROTEC *des parasites*, ESSAIS suppression, INFORMAT delete character, deletion, suppression, ORDINAT, TELECOM deletion, TV blanking; ~ **des bruits** *f* ELECTROTEC noise suppression; ~ **d'écho** *f* ELECTRON echo cancellation, echo suppression; ~ **des explosions** *f* SECURITE explosion suppression; ~ **du faisceau** *f* ELECTRON beam blanking, blanking, trace blanking, TV beam blanking; ~ **de ligne** *f* TV horizontal blanking, line blanking; ~ **des lobes secondaires** *f* ELECTRON side lobe cancellation; ~ **de la porteuse** *f* ELECTRON, TELECOM carrier suppression; ~ **progressive** *f* PHYS ONDES phase-out; ~ **du retour** *f* TV flyback blanking; ~ **des signaux reçus sur les lobes secondaires** *f* ELECTRON side lobe cancellation; ~ **de synchronisation** *f* TV sync blanking; ~ **de trame** *f* ELECTRON, INFORMAT, ORDINAT, TV vertical blanking; ~ **verticale** *f* TV vertical blanking; ~ **des zéros** *f* INFORMAT, ORDINAT zero suppression

supprimer[1] *vt* IMPRIM kill, INFORMAT, ORDINAT delete, suppress

supprimer:[2] ~ **la pression** *vi* NUCLEAIRE depressurize

supraconducteur[1] *adj* MATERIAUX superconductive

supraconducteur[2] *m* ELECTR, ELECTRON, MATERIAUX, PHYSIQUE, TELECOM superconductor; ~ **de première espèce** *m* ELECTRON soft superconductor

supraconductibilité *f* PHYSIQUE superconductivity

supraconduction *f* ELECTR, ELECTRON superconductivity

supraconductivité *f* ELECTR, INFORMAT, MATERIAUX, ORDINAT, PHYS RAYON, PHYSIQUE superconductivity; ~ **à haute température** *f* PHYSIQUE high-temperature superconductivity

supracorde *f* PHYS RAYON superstring

supragranulation *f* ASTRONOMIE *de la surface solaire* supergranulation

supra-haute: ~ **fréquence** *f* ELECTRON SHF, superhigh frequency

supraréfraction *f* ESPACE *communications* super-refraction

sûr *adj* SECURITE safe

suractivation *f* ESPACE *véhicules* activity overvoltage

suraffinage *m* PRODUCTION overrefining

suralésage *m* CONS MECA counterbore

suraléser *vt* PRODUCTION counterbore

suralimentation *f* AERONAUT supercharge, AUTO, CH DE FER *véhicules* supercharging, CONS MECA overfeed, overfeeding, NAUT turbocharging, REFRIG overfeeding, TEXTILE overfeed

suralimenter *vt* ESPACE *véhicules* boost

suralimenteur *m* VEHICULES *moteur* compressor
suramortissement *m* PHYSIQUE overdamping
suramplificateur *m* VEHICULES booster
suranné *adj* MATERIAUX out of date
surarrimage *m* NAUT overstowage
surbalayage *m* TV overscan
surbau *m* AERONAUT, NAUT coaming
surbroyage *m* CHARBON overgrinding
surbroyé *adj* CHARBON overground
surcapacité *f* AERONAUT *transport aérien* overcapacity
surcharge *f* CONSTR overload, ELECTR *d'un accumulateur* overcharge, *du courant* overload, ELECTROTEC, EMBALLAGE, ENREGISTR, ESPACE *communications*, GAZ overload, HYDROLOGIE surcharge, INFORMAT, ORDINAT, PHYSIQUE overload, PRODUCTION overloading, overload, overstress, overstressing, overworking, *d'un pilon* head, TELECOM overload; ~ **EMCN** *f* TELECOM DCME overload; ~ **d'épreuve** *f* INST HYDR test pressure; ~ **neige** *f* CONSTR snow loading; ~ **normale de fonctionnement** *f* PRODUCTION operating overload; ~ **de pilon** *f* PRODUCTION stamp boss, stamp head; ~ **de transmission** *f* TELECOM transmission overload
surchargé *adj* EMBALLAGE overweight, HYDROLOGIE surcharged, PHYSIQUE, TELECOM overloaded
surchargement *m* METALL overstressing
surcharger *vt* CONSTR overload, weigh down, ELECTR *circuit, composant*, ELECTROTEC overload, IMPRIM overprint, TELECOM, TV overload
surchauffage *m* CHIMIE superheating, ELECTROTEC, MATERIAUX overheating, METALL superheating, PRODUCTION, THERMODYN overheating, superheating
surchauffe *f* PHYSIQUE superheating, PRODUCTION excessive heat, overheating, superheating, REFRIG superheat, SECURITE overheating, THERMODYN over temperature, overheating, VEHICULES *moteur* overheating
surchauffer *vt* CHAUFFAGE, MAT CHAUFF superheat, THERMODYN overheat
surchauffeur *m* CHAUFFAGE, MAT CHAUFF, PRODUCTION superheater; ~ **à convection** *m* MAT CHAUFF convection superheater; ~ **à rayonnement** *m* MAT CHAUFF radiant superheater; ~ **de vapeur** *m* CHAUFFAGE steam superheater, PRODUCTION superheater
surcompoundage *m* ELECTROTEC overcompounding
surcompression *f* AERONAUT supercharge
surconcentration *f* ESPACE *véhicules* concentration overvoltage
surcourse *f* PRODUCTION *automatisme industriel* overtravel
surcuisson *f* PLAST CAOU *défaut de plastique, de caoutchouc* overcure
surcuit *adj* THERMODYN dead-burned
surdébit *m* TELECOM overhead; ~ **de section** *m* (*SDS*) TELECOM section overhead (*SOH*); ~ **de section de multiplexage** *m* (*SDSM*) TELECOM multiplex section overhead; ~ **de section de régénération** *m* (*SDSR*) TELECOM regenerator section overhead
surdéveloppement *m* CERAM VER overstriking, CINEMAT overdevelopment
surdévelopper *vt* PHOTO overdevelop
surdiamétrage *m* CONS MECA oversizing
surdimensionné *adj* CONS MECA oversize
surdi-mutité *f* ACOUSTIQUE deaf-muteness
surdité *f* ACOUSTIQUE deafness; ~ **professionnelle** *f* ACOUSTIQUE professional deafness
surdosage *m* CHIMIE overdosage

sureau *m* AGRO ALIM elderflower
surécartement *m* CH DE FER gage widening (AmE), gauge widening (BrE), wide to gage (AmE), wide to gauge (BrE)
surélévation *f* CONSTR heightening, superelevation
surélèvement *m* CONSTR heightening
suremballeuse *f* EMBALLAGE exterior packaging machine
surépaisseur *f* MECANIQUE allowance, oversize; ~ **pour usinage** *f* PRODUCTION allowance for machining, machining allowance, tooling allowance
surestarie *f* PETROLE demurrage
sûreté:[1] **à ~ intégrée** *adj* ELECTR, TRANSPORT fail-safe
sûreté[2] *f* MECANIQUE, QUALITE, SECURITE safety; ~ **de fonctionnement** *f* CONS MECA, ELECTROTEC, PRODUCTION reliability, QUALITE dependability; ~ **intégrée** *f* COMMANDE fail-safe system; ~ **du tir** *f* MILITAIRE fire safety; ~ **du transport maritime** *f* SECURITE marine safety; ~ **des transports** *f* SECURITE transportation safety; ~ **des transports par voie ferrée** *f* SECURITE rail safety
surexcursion *f* ESPACE *communications* overdeviation
surexploitation *f* HYDROLOGIE *d'eau souterraine* overextraction, OCEANO overfishing
surexposer *vt* CINEMAT, PHOTO overexpose
surexposition *f* PHOTO, PHYS RAYON *à une radiation ionisante* overexposure
surf *m* PHYS ONDES surfing
SURF *abrév* (*message de refus de service supplémentaire*) TELECOM FRJ (*facility rejected message*)
surfaçage *m* CERAM VER surface working, CONS MECA facing, surfacing; ~ **rigide** *m* CONSTR rigid construction; ~ **souple** *m* CONSTR flexible construction
surface:[1] **à la ~** *adv* MINES above ground; **en ~** *adv* CHARBON above ground
surface[2] *f* ASTRONOMIE *d'un trou noir* boundary, BREVETS surface, CONSTR area, GEOMETRIE surface, MINES grass, NAUT surface, PAPIER area, surface, PHYSIQUE surface; ~ **active** *f* MATERIAUX *chimie* active surface; ~ **d'adhérence** *f* PAPIER adhesive surface; ~ **alaire** *f* AERONAUT design wing area; ~ **aléatoire** *f* TELECOM mixed terrain; ~ **d'appui** *f* MECANIQUE seat, PLAST CAOU *presse* land, RESSORTS bearing surface; ~ **d'assise** *f* CONSTR bedding surface; ~ **du bain** *f* THERMODYN *fonderie* meniscus; ~ **caustique** *f* PHYSIQUE caustic surface; ~ **chauffante** *f* THERMODYN effective heating surface, heating surface; ~ **de chauffe** *f* MAT CHAUFF, THERMODYN heating surface; ~ **à coller** *f* PLAST CAOU *adhésifs* adherend; ~ **concave** *f* GEOMETRIE concave surface; ~ **de condensation refroidie à l'air** *f* CONS MECA air-cooled surface condenser; ~ **conique** *f* GEOMETRIE *composée de deux nappes* conical surface; ~ **de contact** *f* CONS MECA surface of contact, GEOLOGIE contact, MATERIAUX contact surface; ~ **de contact eau-gaz** *f* PETR gas-water contact; ~ **de contact huile-eau** *f* PETR oil-water contact; ~ **de contact huile-gaz** *f* PETR gas-oil contact; ~ **conventionnelle de la voilure** *f* AERONAUT *navigabilité* design wing area; ~ **convexe** *f* GEOMETRIE convex surface; ~ **couverte** *f* REFRIG diffusion area; ~ **criblante** *f* CHARBON screening surface; ~ **dégagée** *f* MINES free end, free face; ~ **du disque balayé** *f* AERONAUT disc area (BrE), disk area (AmE); ~ **de drainage** *f* PETR drainage area; ~ **d'eau perchée** *f* DISTRI EAU apparent water table; ~ **d'échange** *f* REFRIG heat transfer surface; ~ **d'écriture** *f* ORDINAT recording surface; ~ **d'enregistrement** *f* IN-

FORMAT recording surface; ~ **équiphase** f ELECTROTEC equiphase surface; ~ **équipotentielle** f ELECTR *électrostatique*, ELECTROTEC, ESPACE, PHYSIQUE equipotential surface; ~ **équipotentielle terrestre** f GEOPHYS equipotential surface; ~ **équivalente** f ESPACE *communications* effective area, equivalent area; ~ **des étages** f CONSTR *d'un bâtiment* floorspace; ~ **extérieure** f EMBALLAGE exterior surface; ~ **de Fermi** f PHYSIQUE Fermi surface; ~ **de la flottaison** f NAUT waterplane; ~ **frontale** f CONS MECA frontal area; ~ **frottante** f CONS MECA bearing surface, wearing surface, PRODUCTION rubbing surface; ~ **de frottement** f CONS MECA bearing surface, wearing surface, PRODUCTION rubbing surface; ~ **gauche** f RESSORTS warped surface; ~ **géométrique** f GEOMETRIE geometric surface; ~ **de glissement** f CHARBON slip surface; ~ **grenaillée** f RESSORTS shot-peened surface; ~ **de grille** f CONSTR grate area; ~ **d'image** f CINEMAT image area; ~ **immergée** f NAUT wetted surface; ~ **d'imposition** f IMPRIM *copie* imposing surface; ~ **imprimante repoussant l'encre** f IMPRIM *plaques* blind image; ~ **de joint** f CERAM VER sealing surface; ~ **à lames** f CHAUFFAGE *échangeurs* finned surface; ~ **libre** f MINES free end, free face, PHYSIQUE *d'un liquide* free surface; ~ **lisse** f CONS MECA plain surface; ~ **magnétique** f NUCLEAIRE magnetic flux surface; ~ **minimale** f GEOMETRIE minimal surface; ~ **de la nappe phréatique** f DISTRI EAU ground water table; ~ **de nappe suspendue** f HYDROLOGIE perched water table; ~ **nette de l'aile** f AERONAUT net wing area; ~ **nodale** f ACOUSTIQUE node; ~ **d'onde** f ACOUSTIQUE wavefront, ELECTROTEC wave surface, OPTIQUE wavefront, PHYSIQUE wave surface, TELECOM wavefront; ~ **opaque** f MATERIAUX dull surface; ~ **de la page** f IMPRIM image area; ~ **de piston** f CONS MECA piston area, piston surface; ~ **plane** f CONS MECA plain surface, MATERIAUX plane surface; ~ **portante** f CONS MECA bearing surface, NAUT aerofoil (BrE), airfoil (AmE); ~ **primitive** f CONS MECA pitch surface; ~ **projetée** f CONSTR projected area; ~ **de la puce** f ELECTRON chip area; ~ **de référence** f GEOLOGIE DP, datum plane, TELECOM reference surface; ~ **de révolution** f GEOMETRIE surface of revolution; ~ **rugueuse** f CONS MECA, RESSORTS rough surface; ~ **sélective** f EN RENOUV selective surface; ~ **sensible** f PHOTO emulsion; ~ **de séparation** f PETR interface; ~ **spécifique** f PLAST CAOU specific surface area; ~ **de surchauffe** f PRODUCTION superheater heating surface; ~ **terrestre** f ESPACE terrestrial surface; ~ **thermoconductrice** f THERMODYN heat transfer surface; ~ **touche du clavier** f IMPRIM keycap; ~ **de translation** f MATERIAUX *cristallographie* gliding plane; ~ **très absorbante** f IMPRIM *papiers, supports* hungry surface; ~ **unie** f CONS MECA plain surface; ~ **usinée** f MECANIQUE machined surface; ~ **d'usure** f TEXTILE wearing surface; ~ **utile** f CONS MECA useful surface; ~ **de voilure** f NAUT sail area

surfacé adj PHOTO optically flat; ~ **au kaolin** adj IMPRIM clay-coated

surfacer: ~ **dur** vt CONS MECA hard-face

surfaces: ~ **sensibles sur films** f pl IMPRIM *chimie du film, photogravure* key coatings on film

surfaceuse-disqueuse f CONS MECA surface sander

surfacique adj PHYSIQUE per unit area

surfactant m CHIMIE surfactant

surfondu adj PHYSIQUE supercooled

surforage m PETR washover

surfusion f GENIE CHIM, METALL, PHYSIQUE supercooling

surgelage: ~ **par immersion** m EMBALLAGE dip freezing

surgélation f EMBALLAGE, REFRIG, THERMODYN deep-freezing, quick freezing

surgelé adj AGRO ALIM deep-frozen, frozen, EMBALLAGE deep-frozen, REFRIG, THERMODYN deep-frozen, quick-frozen

surgeler vt AGRO ALIM deep-freeze, PHYSIQUE freeze, REFRIG, THERMODYN deep-freeze, quick-freeze

surhaussement m CH DE FER cant, superelevation of track, CONSTR heightening, raising

surimposition: ~ **de fond faux** f TV patterning

surimpression f ACOUSTIQUE rerecording, CINEMAT multiple exposure, overprint, EMBALLAGE overprinting, ENREGISTR sound on sound, IMPRIM overlay, overprinting, surprint, TV overlay; ~ **par enroulement électronique** f IMPRIM wrapped overlay; ~ **de suppression** f TV super blanking pulse

surimpressionner vt CINEMAT super, TV superimpose

surimpressions: ~ **multiples** f pl PHOTO multiple exposure

surimprimer vt IMPRIM overprint

surintensité f ELECTROTEC overcurrent; ~ **de courant** f ELECTR excess current, overcurrent

surisolation f REFRIG superinsulation

surjaler vti NAUT *ancre* foul

surjeu m ACOUSTIQUE playback

surlargeur f CONSTR curve widening; ~ **de courbe** f CONSTR curve widening

surligner vt IMPRIM *stabilo-composition* overscore

surliure f NAUT whipping

surlongueur f OPTIQUE fiber excess length (AmE), fibre excess length (BrE)

surmenage m PRODUCTION overworking

surmodulation f ENREGISTR overmodulation

surmoduler vt PRODUCTION overdrive

surmultiplicateur m AUTO, VEHICULES *boîte de vitesses* overdrive

surmultiplication f MECANIQUE overdrive

surmultipliée f AUTO overdrive

surnageant adj CHIMIE supernatant

suroît m NAUT *vent* sou'wester, southwester

suroscillation f TV intermediate multiple ringing; ~ **en début de ligne** f TV scan rings

suroxydation f CHIMIE peroxidation

suroxyde m CHIMIE peroxide

suroxyder vt CHIMIE overoxidize

suroxygénation f CERAM VER oxygen boosting, oxygen enrichment

suroxygéner vt CHIMIE superoxygenate

surpêche f OCEANO overfishing

surplomb m CONSTR overhang

surplombement m CONSTR overhanging

surplus: ~ **d'énergie** m THERMODYN excess energy

surpoids m EMBALLAGE excess weight

surpresseur m PETROLE booster pump

surpression f AERONAUT, PETR overpressure, PRODUCTION surge pressure, surge, REFRIG excess pressure; ~ **d'admission** f AERONAUT *excès de pression* boost pressure; ~ **de crête en air libre** f AERONAUT *de bang sonique* free air peak overpressure; ~ **interstitielle** f CHARBON pore overpressure; ~ **de vapeur** f NUCLEAIRE effective steam pressure

surproduction f PRODUCTION overproduction

surrection f GEOLOGIE uplift

surréfrigération f REFRIG superchilling

surrefroidissement: ~ **flash** m NUCLEAIRE *par détente* flash subcooling, flash undercooling

surrégénérateur *m* ESPACE breeder; ~ **rapide** *m* PHYSIQUE fast-breeder reactor

surrégénération *f* NUCLEAIRE breeding process

surrégime: en ~ *adv* PRODUCTION *système hydraulique* over speed

sursalure *f* OCEANO hypersalinity

sursaturation *f* CHIMIE supersaturation, TV oversaturation

sursaturé *adj* HYDROLOGIE waterlogged, POLLUTION supersaturated

sursaturer *vt* CHIMIE supersaturate

sursécher *vt* PAPIER overdry

sursel *m* CHIMIE supersalt

sursoufflage *m* PRODUCTION afterblow

surstructure *f* CRISTALL superlattice

surteindre *vt* TEXTILE cross-dye, overdye

surtension *f* ELECTR excess voltage, overvoltage, ELECTROTEC overvoltage, surge, GEOPHYS lightning surge, PHYSIQUE overvoltage, PRODUCTION overpressure, TELECOM voltage surge; ~ **atmosphérique** *f* GEOPHYS lightning surge; ~ **de foudre** *f* ELECTR lightning surge; ~ **transitoire** *f* ELECTROTEC dynamic overvoltage

surveillance *f* ESPACE, PRODUCTION monitoring, QUALITE, SECURITE *des travailleurs* surveillance, TELECOM monitoring, supervision, TEXTILE monitoring; ~ **aérienne** *f* POLLU MER aerial surveillance; ~ **des échantillons** *f* QUALITE sample surveillance; ~ **électronique** *f* TELECOM electronic surveillance; ~ **et gestion des réseaux** *f* TELECOM network supervision and management; ~ **et maintenance** *f* TELECOM monitoring and maintenance; ~ **minutieuse** *f* SECURITE close supervision; ~ **par radar** *f* MILITAIRE radar surveillance, TRANSPORT radar monitoring, radar surveillance; ~ **de la qualité** *f* QUALITE quality surveillance; ~ **de la qualité en production** *f* TEXTILE on-line quality monitoring; ~ **radar** *f* AERONAUT radar monitoring; ~ **de la radiation** *f* PHYS RAYON radiation monitoring; ~ **de rayonnement** *f* ESPACE *véhicules* radiation monitoring; ~ **sur site** *f* NUCLEAIRE in situ monitoring; ~ **de la température** *f* MINES temperature-monitoring unit; ~ **de temporisation** *f* TELECOM time-out supervision; ~ **du trafic** *f* COMMANDE traffic surveillance

surveillant *m* CONSTR *des travaux publics* surveyor, SECURITE supervisor; ~ **de la voie** *m* CH DE FER lineman

surveiller *vt* ENREGISTR, INFORMAT, ORDINAT monitor, POLLU MER survey, PRODUCTION monitor

surverse *f* CHARBON overflow

survêtement *m* TEXTILE outerwear

survirage *m* AUTO, VEHICULES *direction* oversteer

survirer *vi* AUTO oversteer

survireur *adj* AUTO oversteer

survitesse *f* CONS MECA, MECANIQUE overspeed; ~ **maximale du moteur** *f* AERONAUT maximum engine overspeed

survitrage *m* CERAM VER overglazing

survol *m* AERONAUT, ESPACE fly-by

survoler *vt* INFORMAT, ORDINAT browse

survoltage *m* ELECTROTEC overvoltage

survolter *vt* ELECTROTEC boost

survolteur *m* ELECTROTEC booster; ~ **d'induction** *m* ELECTROTEC induction voltage regulator

survolteur-dévolteur *m* ELECTROTEC reversible booster

survulcanisation *f* PLAST CAOU *défaut de plastique, de caoutchouc* overcure

susceptance *f* ELECTR *réactance*, ELECTROTEC, PHYSIQUE susceptance

susceptibilité *f* ELECTR *réactance*, PHYSIQUE susceptibility; ~ **diamagnétique** *f* PHYS RAYON diamagnetic susceptibility; ~ **diélectrique** *f* ELECTR dielectric susceptibility; ~ **électrique** *f* ELECTROTEC, PHYSIQUE electric susceptibility; ~ **magnétique** *f* ELECTR, PETR, PHYSIQUE magnetic susceptibility

susceptible: ~ d'application industrielle *adj* BREVETS susceptible of industrial application

sus-dominante *f* ACOUSTIQUE submediant

suspendre[1] *vt* PRODUCTION hang, hang up

suspendre:[2] **~ l'exploitation** *vi* MINES cease work

suspendu *adj* INFORMAT, ORDINAT suspended, PRODUCTION *ordre de fabrication* held up; ~ **sur coque** *adj* TRANSPORT hull-borne

suspens: en ~ *adj* PRODUCTION outstanding

suspension *f* AUTO, CHIMIE suspension, CONS MECA holding up, suspension, ELECTROTEC, MINES, PHYSIQUE, PLAST CAOU suspension, PRODUCTION hanging, hanging up; ~ **active** *f* TRANSPORT active suspension; ~ **anti-plongée** *f* VEHICULES antidive suspension; ~ **aqueuse** *f* NUCLEAIRE water slurry, water suspension; ~ **argileuse** *f* DISTRI EAU clay suspension; ~ **arrière** *f* AUTO rear suspension; ~ **arrière à roues indépendantes** *f* AUTO, VEHICULES independent rear suspension; ~ **articulée** *f* CONS MECA hinged suspension, suspension with linkages; ~ **asymétrique** *f* TRANSPORT *de monorail* asymmetric suspension; ~ **avant** *f* AUTO front suspension; ~ **avant à roues indépendantes** *f* AUTO, VEHICULES independent front suspension; ~ **avant du type MacPherson** *f* AUTO MacPherson strut front suspension; ~ **à barre** *f* CONS MECA bar hanger; ~ **bifilaire** *f* ELECTR, PHYSIQUE bifilar suspension; ~ **à la cardan** *f* CONS MECA Cardan's suspension, gimbal suspension, MECANIQUE gimbal, NAUT gimbal mounting; ~ **à deux bras transversaux** *f* AUTO parallel arm-type suspension; ~ **élastique du pendule** *f* GEOPHYS pendulum suspension spring; ~ **hydrolastique** *f* AUTO hydroelastic suspension; ~ **hydropneumatique** *f* VEHICULES hydropneumatic suspension; ~ **MacPherson** *f* AUTO MacPherson strut; ~ **du moteur sur tampons de caoutchouc** *f* AUTO rubber engine mounting; ~ **oléo-pneumatique** *f* AUTO hydropneumatic suspension; ~ **par quadrilatères** *f* AUTO double wishbone suspension, trapezoid arm-type suspension; ~ **pendulaire** *f* TRANSPORT pendulum suspension, *de monorail* pendulum vehicle suspension; ~ **pendulaire de la caisse** *f* TRANSPORT pendulum suspension; ~ **pneumatique** *f* TRANSPORT *de monorail* pneumatic suspension; ~ **sans contact** *f* TRANSPORT noncontact suspension; ~ **secondaire** *f* TRANSPORT secondary suspension; ~ **de la sonde** *f* MINES suspension of the rods; ~ **sur coussin** *f* TRANSPORT cushion borne; ~ **de tubing** *f* PETR tubing hanger; ~ **unifilaire** *f* ELECTR *d'un instrument* unifilar suspension

sustentation *f* AERONAUT lift; ~ **à dépression dynamique** *f* TRANSPORT vacuum suspension; ~ **électrodynamique** *f* TRANSPORT electrodynamic levitation; ~ **électrodynamique à flux nul** *f* TRANSPORT null flux suspension; ~ **électromagnétique** *f* TRANSPORT electromagnetic levitation; ~ **magnétique** *f* TRANSPORT magnetic levitation, magnetic suspension; ~ **magnétique par aimants permanents** *f* TRANSPORT levitation by permanent magnets; ~ **mixte** *f* TRANSPORT mixed levitation; ~ **par aimant à supraconductivité** *f* TRANS-

PORT superconducting magnet levitation; ~ **par cous-sin d'air** *f* TRANSPORT air cushion levitation

sus-tonique *f* ACOUSTIQUE supertonic

susuroît *m* NAUT south-southwest

Sv *abrév (sievert)* PHYS RAYON, PHYSIQUE Sv *(sievert)*

syénite *f* CHIMIE syenite

sylvanite *f* MINERAUX sylvanite

sylvestrène *m* CHIMIE sylvestrene

sylvinite *f* MINERAUX sylvinite

sylvite *f* MINERAUX sylvine, sylvite

symbole *m* CHIMIE, INFORMAT symbol; ~ **abstrait** *m* INFORMAT abstract symbol; ~ **graphique** *m* SECURITE *pour plans de protection contre l'incendie* graphical symbol; ~ **logique** *m* INFORMAT, ORDINAT logic symbol; ~ **d'organigramme** *m* INFORMAT flowchart symbol; ~ **séparateur** *m* ORDINAT separator symbol; ~ **de séparation** *m* INFORMAT separator symbol; ~ **de terminaison** *m* INFORMAT, ORDINAT terminal symbol; ~ **de terre de sécurité** *m* PRODUCTION *électricité* safety earth symbol (BrE), safety ground symbol (AmE)

symboles: ~ **en images** *m pl* SECURITE *substances dangereuses* pictorial symbols; ~ **identiques consécutifs** *m pl* TELECOM CID, consecutive identical digits; ~ **typographiques inhabituels** *m pl* IMPRIM *composition* arbitrary signs

symétrie *f* CHIMIE, GEOMETRIE symmetry; ~ **amont-aval** *f* PHYS FLUID upstream-downstream symmetry; ~ **axiale** *f* GEOMETRIE axial symmetry; ~ **charge-parité** *f* PHYS RAYON charge parity symmetry; ~ **cristalline** *f* CRISTALL crystal symmetry; ~ **de groupe ponctuel** *f* CRISTALL point group symmetry; ~ **rotatoire** *f* GEOMETRIE rotational symmetry

symétrique *adj* CHIMIE symmetrical, GEOMETRIE symmetric, symmetrical, INFORMAT, ORDINAT symmetric

SYN *abrév (caractère de synchronisation)* INFORMAT, ORDINAT SYN *(synchronous idle character)*

synchro *m* AUTO synchromesh, synchronizer; ~ **détecteur de tangage** *m* AERONAUT pitch detector synchro

synchrocyclotron *m* PHYSIQUE synchrocyclotron

synchrone *adj* CINEMAT in sync, ELECTRON synchronous, IMPRIM *réglages* in-step, INFORMAT, ORDINAT synchronous, TV in sync

synchronisateur *m* ELECTRON pulser, ELECTROTEC synchronizer

synchronisation:[1] **de ~** *adj* ELECTR *alimentation en courant alternatif* synchronizing

synchronisation[2] *f* AUTO, CONS MECA synchronization, ELECTRON clocking, lock, timing, ENREGISTR, ESPACE *communications* synchronization, INFORMAT clocking, synchronization, timing, ORDINAT clocking, synchronization, timing, TELECOM synchronization, TV *magnétoscope* pixlock; ~ **défectueuse** *f* TV degraded sync; ~ **d'émetteurs secondaires** *f* TV slavelock; ~ **extérieure** *f* ELECTRON external synchronization; ~ **externe** *f* TV slaving; ~ **des feux** *f* TRANSPORT synchronization; ~ **horizontale** *f* TV horizontal sync; ~ **labiale** *f* CINEMAT lip sync; ~ **des modes** *f* ELECTRON mode locking; ~ **mutuelle** *f* TELECOM mutual synchronization; ~ **par impulsion** *f* TV pulse sync; ~ **par injection** *f* ELECTRON injection locking; ~ **du réseau** *f* TV locking; ~ **sans fil** *f* CINEMAT cordless sync; ~ **de trame** *f* ESPACE *communications* frame synchronization; ~ **des trames couleurs** *f* TV color framing (AmE), colour framing (BrE)

synchronisé *adj* CINEMAT in sync, sunk up

synchroniser[1] *vt* CINEMAT, TV sync, synchronize

synchroniser:[2] ~ **les rushes** *vi* CINEMAT sync dailies

synchroniseur *m* ELECTR *machine*, INFORMAT, ORDINAT synchronizer; ~ **de cap** *m* AERONAUT heading synchronizer; ~ **final** *m* INFORMAT postamble; ~ **initial** *m* INFORMAT preamble; ~ **numérique** *m* TV digital framer; ~ **de tangage** *m* AERONAUT pitch synchro

synchroniseuse *f* CINEMAT synchronizer; ~ **d'images** *f* CINEMAT picture synchronizer; ~ **à quatre tambours** *f* CINEMAT four-way synchronizer

synchronisme:[1] **en ~** *adj* ELECTROTEC in-step

synchronisme[2] *m* CONS MECA, ELECTRON, ENREGISTR synchronism; ~ **des lèvres** *m* ENREGISTR lip sync; ~ **de montage** *m* TV edit sync; ~ **de tirage** *m* CINEMAT printer sync

synchrotrame *f* TV field sync

synchrotransformateur *m* ELECTROTEC control transformer, solid synchrotransformer

synchrotron *m* PHYS PART, PHYSIQUE synchrotron; ~ **à électrons** *m* PHYS PART electron synchrotron; ~ **à protons** *m* PHYS PART proton synchrotron

synclinal *m* PETROLE syncline; ~ **bordier** *m* GEOLOGIE rim syncline; ~ **coffré** *m* GEOLOGIE canoe fold

synclinorium *m* GEOLOGIE synclinorium

synderme *m* PAPIER leatherfiber board (AmE), leatherfibre board (BrE)

syndicat *m* IMPRIM union

syndrome: ~ **articulaire des hautes pressions** *m* OCEANO hyperbaric arthralgia; ~ **nerveux des hautes pressions** *m (SNHP)* OCEANO high-pressure nerve syndrome, high-pressure nervous syndrome

synéclise *f* GEOLOGIE furrow

synérèse *f* AGRO ALIM, CHIMIE, PLAST CAOU syneresis

synergie *f* LESSIVES synergism, synergy, PLAST CAOU *effet* synergism effect, synergistic effect

synergique[1] *adj* CHIMIE synergetic, synergistic

synergique[2] *m* AGRO ALIM synergist

synergiste *m* LESSIVES synergist

synforme *f* GEOLOGIE synform

syngénite *f* MINERAUX syngenite

synopsis *m* CINEMAT outline, treatment

synorogénique *adj* GEOLOGIE synorogenic

synschisteux *adj* GEOLOGIE synschistous

syntactique *adj* CHIMIE syntactic

syntaxe *f* INFORMAT, ORDINAT syntax; ~ **des instructions** *f* PRODUCTION *automatisme industriel* instruction syntax; ~ **de transfert** *f* TELECOM transfer syntax

syntectonique *adj* GEOLOGIE syntectonic

synthèse *f* CHIMIE, GAZ synthesis; ~ **additive** *f* IMPRIM *couleur* additive synthesis; ~ **électronique de la parole** *f* ELECTRON electronic speech synthesis; ~ **de filtre** *f* ELECTRON filter synthesis; ~ **de fréquence** *f* ELECTRON frequency synthesis; ~ **de fréquence directe** *f* ELECTRON direct frequency synthesis; ~ **de fréquence indirecte** *f* ELECTRON indirect frequency synthesis; ~ **Friedel-Crafts** *f* LESSIVES Friedel-Crafts synthesis; ~ **numérique de la parole** *f* ELECTRON digital speech synthesis; ~ **d'ouverture** *f* ASTRONOMIE aperture synthesis; ~ **oxo** *f* LESSIVES oxo process, oxo synthesis; ~ **de la parole** *f* ELECTRON, INFORMAT, ORDINAT, TELECOM speech synthesis; ~ **des réseaux** *f* ELECTR *alimentation*, ELECTROTEC network synthesis; ~ **de signaux** *f* ELECTRON signal synthesis, waveform synthesis

synthétique *adj* CHIMIE synthetic

synthétiseur *m* ENREGISTR, TELECOM synthesizer; ~ **d'écriture** *m* TV character generator; ~ **de fréquence** *m*

ELECTRON frequency synthesizer; ~ **à fréquence fixe** m ELECTRON fixed frequency synthesizer; ~ **de fréquence à synthèse directe** m ELECTRON direct frequency synthesizer; ~ **de fréquence à synthèse indirecte** m ELECTRON indirect frequency synthesizer; ~ **hyperfréquence** m ELECTRON microwave synthesizer; ~ **d'impulsion** m ELECTRON pulse synthesizer; ~ **de parole** m ENREGISTR vocoder, INFORMAT, ORDINAT speech synthesizer; ~ **vidéo** m TV video synthesizer; ~ **vocal** m INFORMAT vocoder

synthol m CHIMIE synthol

syntonine f CHIMIE syntonin

syntonisation f TELECOM tuning; ~ **par bouton-poussoir** f COMMANDE push-button tuning

syntoniseur m ENREGISTR, TV tuner; ~ **stéréo** m ENREGISTR stereo tuner; ~ **UHF** m TV UHF tuner

syringique adj CHIMIE syringic

systématique f ORDINAT systems engineering

Système: ~ **d'acquisition de données océaniques** m *(SADO)* OCEANO Ocean Data Acquisition System, Oceanic Data Acquisition System *(ODAS)*; ~ **mondial de détresse et de sécurité en mer** m *(SMDSM)* NAUT Global Marine Distress and Safety System *(GMDSS)*; ~ **mondial de surveillance**continue de l'environnement m POLLUTION Global Environment Monitoring System; ~ **mondial de télécommunications** m TELECOM Global Telecommunications System

système m GEOLOGIE, INFORMAT, ORDINAT, PRODUCTION, TELECOM system;

- a ~ **d'abonné à courant porteur** m TELECOM one-plus-one carrier system; ~ **absolu** m ESSAIS *de bobine* absolute system; ~ **d'accrochage de la plaque** m IMPRIM *machines* plate lockup system; ~ **acoustique** m ACOUSTIQUE acoustic system; ~ **d'acquisition de données** m PHYS RAYON data recovery system; ~ **actif** m ACOUSTIQUE active system; ~ **adaptatif** m COMMANDE, ORDINAT adaptive system; ~ **adiabatique** m THERMODYN adiabatic system; ~ **d'adressage** m ORDINAT addressing system; ~ **aérien d'appui feu avancé** m AERONAUT advanced airborne fire support system; ~ **d'affichage** m CONS MECA read-out system; ~ **d'affichage embarqué** m TRANSPORT in-vehicle visual display; ~ **d'alarme et d'enregistrement** m SECURITE *pour application industrielle* alarm and logging system; ~ **d'alimentation** m PAPIER feeding system; ~ **d'alimentation automatique** m EMBALLAGE automatic feeding system; ~ **d'allumage** m ESPACE *propulsion* ignition system, lighting system; ~ **ALOHA** m TELECOM ALOHA system; ~ **ALOHA crénelé** m TELECOM slotted ALOHA system; ~ **alterné** m TRANSPORT limited progressive system; ~ **alvéolé de protection** m EMBALLAGE honeycomb protection system; ~ **d'amplification d'impulsions** m PRODUCTION *automatisme industriel* hard fired gate drive; ~ **anaglyphe** m CINEMAT anaglyph process; ~ **analogique** m TELECOM analog system (AmE), analogue system (BrE); ~ **analogique relatif** m ORDINAT analog incremental system; ~ **anamorphoseur** m CINEMAT anamorphic system; ~ **d'ancrage** m NUCLEAIRE anchorage system; ~ **ANPN** m TRANSPORT ANPN, army navy performance number; ~ **à antennes-relais sans amplification** m TELECOM non-boosted antenna repeater system; ~ **antiblocage** m VEHICULES antilocking system; ~ **antibloquant** m VEHICULES antilock brake system, antilock system; ~ **antibloquant de roue** m VEHICULES antilock brake system; ~ **anticollision embarqué** m AERONAUT air-

borne collision avoidance system; ~ **antivibratoire Tyler** m CINEMAT Tyler mount; ~ **d'appel sélectif** m TELECOM SELCAL, selective calling system; ~ **d'appel d'urgence** m TRANSPORT emergency call system; ~ **d'approche contrôlée au sol** m AERONAUT ground-controlled approach system; ~ **d'approche contrôlée du sol** m AERONAUT ground-controlled approach system; ~ **aquatique** m DISTRI EAU aquatic system; ~ **d'archivage avec juke-box** m OPTIQUE jukebox filing system; ~ **d'archivage à don** m OPTIQUE optical data disc document filing system (BrE), optical data disk document filing system (AmE), optical disc filing system (BrE), optical disk filing system (AmE); ~ **d'archivage sur disque optique numérique** m OPTIQUE optical data disc document filing system (BrE), optical data diskdocument filing system (AmE), optical disc filing system (BrE), optical disk filing system (AmE); ~ **d'armes** m MILITAIRE weapons system; ~ **d'armes intégré** m AERONAUT integrated weapon system; ~ **d'arrêt complémentaire** m NUCLEAIRE backup reactor, secondary shutdown system; ~ **d'arrêt progressif automatique** m PRODUCTION automatic ramp down; ~ **d'aspersion** m NUCLEAIRE water spray system; ~ **d'assemblage** m EMBALLAGE collating system; ~ **asservi** m COMMANDE servosystem, ELECTRON closed-loop control system, ELECTROTEC feedback control system, TV servosystem; ~ **asservi adaptatif** m ELECTROTEC adaptive control system; ~ **asservi linéaire** m ELECTROTEC linear feedback control system; ~ **asservi du second ordre** m ELECTROTEC second order servo; ~ **d'asservissement** m COMMANDE automatic control system, ESPACE *communications* servosystem; ~ **à atmosphère raréfiée** m TRANSPORT evacuated system; ~ **d'atténuation** m AERONAUT *balisage lumineux* dimmer system; ~ **d'atterrissage** m TRANSPORT landing system; ~ **d'atterrissage automatique** m TRANSPORT autoland; ~ **d'atterrissage hyperfréquences** m AERONAUT MLS, microwave landing system; ~ **d'atterrissage aux instruments** m AERONAUT, ESPACE *véhicules*, TRANSPORT ILS, instrument landing system; ~ **d'atterrissage radiogoniométrique** m AERONAUT ILS, instrument landing system; ~ **d'autobus express sur voie réservée** m TRANSPORT busway for rapid transit; ~ **autocommandé** m INFORMAT adaptive control system; ~ **autogérant** m TV self-controlling system; ~ **automatique de détection d'incendie** m SECURITE automatic fire detection system; ~ **automatique d'extinction des incendies** m COMMANDE automatic fire-extinguishing system; ~ **d'automatisme** m PRODUCTION programmable controller system, *automatisme industriel* automatic control system; ~ **d'automatisme réparti** m PRODUCTION distributed control system; ~ **auto-organisateur** m INFORMAT, ORDINAT self-organizing system; ~ **d'autopositionnement** m AERONAUT autopositioning unit; ~ **avec arrêts intermédiaires** m TRANSPORT system with intermediate stops; ~ **avec neutre à la terre** m ELECTR earthed neutral system (BrE), grounded neutral system (AmE); ~ **avec unités de transport de longueur finie** m TRANSPORT system with transportation units of intermediate length; ~ **avec ventilation pour couper et éjecter les déchets** m EMBALLAGE ejector-type trim exhaust system; ~ **d'avertissement de nuages et de collision** m TRANSPORT cloud collision warning system; ~ **d'avertissement sonore** m EMBALLAGE *fermeture de sécurité pour enfants* audible warning system; ~ **avertisseur** m SECURITE alarm system; ~ **avertisseur anti-effraction** m SECURITE burglar alarm;

-b ~ **de balayage** m PRODUCTION *hydraulique* scavenge system; ~ **de ballon porteur de charge** m MILITAIRE load-carrying balloon system; ~ **à banc de filtres** m TELECOM filter bank system; ~ **à bande élargie** m TELECOM extended bandwidth system; ~ **à barre non régulée** m ESPACE *thermique* unregulated bus system; ~ **à barre régulée** m ESPACE *thermique* regulated bus system; ~ **barrique** m AERONAUT pressure system; ~ **BI** m ORDINAT IOS, integrated office system; ~ **bielle-manivelle** m CONS MECA crank and connecting rod system; ~ **bifilaire** m ELECTROTEC two-wire system; ~ **binaire** m INFORMAT binary system; ~ **bipolaire** m ELECTR *machine* two-pole system; ~ **de bloc** m CH DE FER block system; ~ **bouclé** m REFRIG bootstrap system; ~ **bureautique intégré** m TELECOM integrated office system;

-c ~ **à cabine sur rail** m TRANSPORT cabin system on rail; ~ **de calage des aubes** m AERONAUT blade spacing system; ~ **caloporteur à cycle fermé** m NUCLEAIRE closed cycle cooling system; ~ **de camouflage** m MILITAIRE camouflage system; ~ **de carburant moteur** m CONS MECA engine fuel system; ~ **cardinal** m NAUT cardinal system; ~ **à cartes** m INFORMAT card system; ~ **CATV** m TELECOM cable television system; ~ **cellulaire** m TELECOM cellular system; ~ **à cellules** m TELECOM cellular system, cellular technique; ~ **centimètre-gramme-seconde** m *(système CGS)* METROLOGIE centimeter-gram-second system (AmE), centimetre-gramme-second system (BrE); ~ **centralisé** d'aspiration m SECURITE central vacuum cleaning system; ~ **centré** m PHYSIQUE centered system (AmE), centred system (BrE); ~ **du centre de masse** m MECANIQUE center of mass system (AmE), centre of mass system (BrE); ~ **Centrex** m (MD) TELECOM Centrex system (TM); ~ **de certification** m QUALITE certification system; ~ **CGS** m *(système centimètre-gramme-seconde)* METROLOGIE CGS system; ~ **de chargement automatique** m PHOTO automatic loading system; ~ **de chargement rapide** m PHOTO rapid loading system; ~ **de chauffage** m THERMODYN heating plant, heating system; ~ **de chauffage de la chemise** m NUCLEAIRE jacket heating system; ~ **à chutes** m PRODUCTION scrap process; ~ **de circulation** m CONS MECA *installation de graissage centralisé* circulating system; ~ **CLASS** m TRANSPORT containerized lighter aboard ship system; ~ **de classification** m QUALITE classification system; ~ **clé en main** m INFORMAT, ORDINAT turnkey system; ~ **de climatisation** m ESPACE *véhicules* environmental control system; ~ **de codage-décodage** m TRANSPORT code-decode system; ~ **de codage à quatre signatures** m TELECOM *air mobile* four-signature coding system; ~ **de codage simple** m EMBALLAGE single head system; ~ **à coeur réparti spécialisé** m TELECOM function division system; ~ **à coeur réparti universel** m TELECOM centralized traffic division system; ~ **collecteur** m POLLU MER manifold system; ~ **de combustion contrôlée** m TRANSPORT controlled combustion system; ~ **de commande adaptative** m MECANIQUE *régulation* adaptive control system; ~ **de commande d'attitude et d'orbite** m ESPACE *véhicules* AOCS, attitude and orbit control system; ~ **de commande** m AERONAUT, COMMANDE control system, ORDINAT command system, TELECOM

control system, TEXTILEdrive system; ~ **à commande centrale** m TELECOM common control switching system; ~ **à commande centralisée** m TELECOM centralized control system, centralized system, common control system; ~ **à commande directe** m TELECOM directory control system; ~ **à commande indirecte** m TELECOM indirect control system; ~ **à commande par impulsions inverses** m TELECOM revertive control system; ~ **à commande répartie** m TELECOM distributed control system; ~ **de commande à distance** m COMMANDE remote control system; ~ **de commande électronique** m ELECTRON electronic control system; ~ **de commande en chaîne fermée** m COMMANDE servosystem; ~ **de commande et contrôle** m ORDINAT CSM, command and control system; ~ **de commande et de visualisation** m ESPACE *pilotage* control and display unit; ~ **de commande manuelle** m CONSTR manual control; ~ **de commande numérique** m COMMANDE digital control system, numerical control system; ~ **de commande piéton** m COMMANDE pedestrian control system; ~ **de commande de processus** m INFORMAT process control system; ~ **de communication** m INFORMAT, ORDINAT communication system; ~ **de communication auditive embarqué** m TRANSPORT in-vehicle aural communication system; ~ **de communication par câble rayonnant** m TELECOM radiating cable communication system; ~ **de commutation** m TELECOM, TV switching system; ~ **de commutation analogique** m TELECOM analog switching system (AmE), analogue switching system (BrE); ~ **à commutation de circuits** m TELECOM circuit switching system; ~ **de commutation électromécanique** m TELECOM electromechanical switching system; ~ **de commutation électronique** m TELECOM ESS, electronic switching system; ~ **de commutation électronique de messages** m TELECOM EMS, electronic message system; ~ **de commutation en modulation de fréquence** m TELECOM FDS system, frequency-division switching system; ~ **de commutation intégrée** m TELECOM integrated digital exchange; ~ **de commutation de messages** m TELECOM message switching system; ~ **de commutation MIC** m TELECOM PCM switching system, PCM system; ~ **de commutation MIC intégrée** m TELECOM integrated digital exchange; ~ **de commutation multidébit** m TELECOM multirate switching system; ~ **de commutation numérique** m TELECOM digital switching system; ~ **de commutation optique** m TELECOM optical switching system; ~ **de commutation à relais** m ELECTROTEC relay switching system; ~ **de commutation semi-automatique** m TELECOM semiautomatic system; ~ **de commutation spatiale** m TELECOM spaced division switching system; ~ **de commutation temporelle** m TELECOM time-division switching system, time-division system; ~ **de commutation tout optique** m TELECOM all-optical switching system; ~ **comparatif** m ESSAIS *réseaux de bobines* comparative system; ~ **à compression** m REFRIG compression system; ~ **à compression-expansion** m ENREGISTR compander; ~ **de comptage à haute vitesse sur baies multiples** m EMBALLAGE high-speed multirack counting system; ~ **de comptes rendus des navires** m TELECOM ship reporting system; ~ **de condensateur** m PHOTO condenser system; ~ **de conduite de processus industriel** m ORDINAT process control system; ~ **de connexion électromécanique** m TELECOM crossbar system; ~ **de conteneurs industriels pour le transport en vrac** m

EMBALLAGE industrial bulk container system; ~ **de contrôle** m COMMANDE, ELECTR, TEXTILE control system; ~ **de contrôle de processus** m INFORMAT process control system; ~ **de contrôle de la radioactivité d'effluent** m RECYCLAGE effluent monitor; ~ **de contrôle de vol automatique** m AERONAUT automatic flight control system; ~ **de coordonnées** m PHYSIQUE coordinate system; ~ **de coordonnées cartésiennes** m ELECTRON Cartesian coordinate system; ~ **de coordonnées géocentriques** m ASTRONOMIE geocentric coordinate system; ~ **de coordonnées horizontales** m ASTRONOMIE horizontal coordinate system; ~ **de coton modifié** m TEXTILE modified cotton system, modified system; ~ **à coulée à chaud** m CONS MECA hot runner system; ~ **couleur PAL** m TV PAL color system (AmE), PAL colour system (BrE); ~ **de coupe irrégulière** m IMPRIM *presse* shear cutter; ~ **crénelé** m TELECOM slotted system; ~ **crénelé à trame** m TELECOM frame-slotted system; ~ **cristallin** m CRISTALL crystal system; ~ **crossbar** m TELECOM crossbar system; ~ **cubique** m METALL cubic system;

~ d ~ **décentralisé** m TELECOM decentralized system; ~ **de décontamination** m NUCLEAIRE decontamination system; ~ **déflecteur du faisceau** m TV beam-positioning system; ~ **de démarrage verrouillable** m CONS MECA key-locked starting system; ~ **dépoussiéreur** m CONSTR dust suppression system, EMBALLAGE dust removal system; ~ **de dérivation** m NUCLEAIRE *d'une turbine* steam dumping system, turbine bypass system; ~ **de désembuage** m VEHICULES *accessoire* demister system; ~ **de déshuilage** m GAZ oil removing system; ~ **desservant des zones étendues** m TELECOM wide area system; ~ **détachable** m EMBALLAGE peelable system; ~ **de détection d'incendie et d'alarme** m SECURITE fire detection and alarm system; ~ **de détection de porteuse** m TELECOM carrier sense system; ~ **de détection de rupture de gaine** m NUCLEAIRE burst can, burst slug, failed element detection system; ~ **de détection au sol** m TRANSPORT detection system outside the vehicle; ~ **de détresse radioélectrique** m TELECOM distress radio call system; ~ **à deux calculateurs** m TELECOM dual-processor system; ~ **à deux calculateurs en partage de trafic** m TELECOM dual-processor load-sharing system; ~ **de deux ensembles de diaclases symétriques** m GEOLOGIE conjugate jointing; ~ **à deux fils** m ELECTROTEC two-wire system; ~ **à deux nucléons** m NUCLEAIRE two-nucleon system; ~ **différentiel** m ESSAIS *réseaux de bobines* differential system; ~ **dioptrique** m ASTRONOMIE dioptric system; ~ **diphasé** m ELECTR *réseau* two-phase system; ~ **de distribution** m DISTRI EAU, ELECTR *réseau*, ELECTROTEC distribution system; ~ **de distribution avec pompe** m EMBALLAGE pump dispenser system; ~ **de division de faisceau** m CINEMAT beam-splitting system; ~ **de données de vol** m ESPACE *communications* flight data system; ~ **double** m TELECOM dual-processor system; ~ **à doubles rouleaux** m IMPRIM two-roll system;

~ e ~ **EBCS** m TRANSPORT EBCS, European barge carrier system; ~ **d'échange de textes en mode message** m TELECOM MOTIS, message-oriented text interchange system; ~ **d'échappement** m VEHICULES exhaust system; ~ **d'échouage** m TRANSPORT landing system; ~ **des effluents radioactifs** m NUCLEAIRE active effluent system; ~ **d'éjection** m PLAST CAOU *presse* ejector; ~ **d'éjection de secours** m ESPACE *véhicules* launch escape system; ~ **électronique antiblocage** m

TRANSPORT electronic anti-locking device; ~ **électronique antiblocage des roues** m TRANSPORT electronic anti-skid system; ~ **électronique à relais à tige** m TELECOM reed relay system; ~ **d'emballage en boîtes de métal** m IMPRIM in-can system; ~ **d'emballage pliable pouvant être réutilisé** m EMBALLAGE collapsible and reusable packaging system; ~ **d'emballage thermoformé** m EMBALLAGE thermoforming packaging system; ~ **embarqué de détection** m TRANSPORT detection system inside the vehicle; ~ **émetteur-récepteur** m TELECOM transponder system; ~ **d'emmagasinage sous conditions climatiques contrôlées** m EMBALLAGE controlled environment storage system; ~ **d'enclenchement** m SECURITE *mécanique, hydraulique, électrique ou pneumatique* interlocking system; ~ **d'enclenchement informatisé** m CH DE FER SSI, solid-state interlocking (BrE), computerized interlocking system; ~ **d'encollage à froid** m EMBALLAGE cold glueing system; ~ **en microsynchronisme** m TELECOM hot stand-by system; ~ **en mode de secours** m TELECOM stand-by system; ~ **en partage de charge** m TELECOM load sharing system; ~ **en partage de fonctions** m TELECOM functionally-divided system; ~ **en partage de trafic** m TELECOM traffic division system; ~ **en pipeline** m TELECOM pipeline system; ~ **d'enregistrement binaural** m ENREGISTR binaural sound system; ~ **d'enregistrement multipiste** m ENREGISTR multi-track recording system; ~ **d'enregistrement sonore** m ENREGISTR sound recording system; ~ **à enregistreurs** m TELECOM register-controlled system; ~ **en répartition géographique** m TELECOM segmented multiprocessor system; ~ **en réplique synchrone** m TELECOM parallel synchronous system; ~ **d'enroulage du tissu** m TEXTILE take-up system; ~ **en temps réel** m INFORMAT, ORDINAT real-time system; ~ **d'entraînement de caméra** m CINEMAT camera drive; ~ **d'entraînement à griffe** m CINEMAT claw feed system; ~ **à entraînement mécanique** m TELECOM motor-driven system; ~ **d'entrée** m CONS MECA intake system; ~ **d'entretien autocontrôlé** m TRANSPORT self-regulating maintenance system; ~ **d'épreuves** m IMPRIM *électronique, informatique* proofing system; ~ **d'équilibre** m GEOPHYS equilibrium system; ~ **d'essai non destructif** m CONS MECA nondestructive testing system; ~ **d'étalonnage modulaire** m METROLOGIE modular gaging system (AmE), modular gauging system (BrE); ~ **d'étanchéité** m CONSTR system of seals; ~ **d'étiquetage avec code à barres** m EMBALLAGE bar code labeling system (AmE), bar code labelling system (BrE); ~ **d'étiquetage modulaire** m EMBALLAGE modular labeling system (AmE), modular labelling system (BrE); ~ **d'étiquetage à voies multiples** m EMBALLAGE multilane labeling system (AmE), multilane labelling system (BrE); ~ **d'étirage** m TEXTILE drafting system; ~ **d'évacuation des fumées de soudage** m SECURITE welding smoke extraction system; ~ **d'évacuation à piston hydraulique** m CONSTR hydraulic piston discharger; ~ **expert** m INFORMAT, ORDINAT expert system; ~ **d'exploitation** m ORDINAT, TELECOM OS, operating system; ~ **d'exploitation à disque** m *(DOS)* INFORMAT, ORDINAT disk operating system *(DOS)*; ~ **d'exploitation distribué** m ORDINAT distributed operating system; ~ **d'exploitation de réseau** m ORDINAT NOS, network operating system; ~ **d'extraction des déchets** m EMBALLAGE waste extraction system; ~ **d'extrémité** m TELECOM end system;

~ f ~ **de fabrication directe des formes imprimantes** *m* IMPRIM direct-to-plate imaging system; ~ **à fentes** *m* ESPACE *communications* slit system; ~ **fermé** *m* THERMODYN closed system; ~ **de fichiers de base** *m* PRODUCTION *automatisme industriel* root file system; ~ **de filature** *m* TEXTILE spinning system; ~ **à film d'air** *m* TRANSPORT air film system; ~ **de fixation** *m* MINES retainer; ~ **flexible de rechange d'outils** *m* CONS MECA *pour moulage par injection* flexible tool changing system; ~ **de flottabilité de secours** *m* AERONAUT emergency flotation gear; ~ **flottant** *m* PRODUCTION undergrounded system; ~ **de freinage** *m* CONS MECA braking system, VEHICULES brake system; ~ **de freinage automatique** *m* COMMANDE automatic braking system; ~ **de freinage à quatre roues** *m* VEHICULES four-wheel brake system; ~ **de freinage de secours** *m* VEHICULES secondary brake system; ~ **de frein à disque** *m* AUTO, CONSTR disc braking system (BrE), disk braking system (AmE); ~ **frigorifique** *m* REFRIG refrigeration system; ~ **frigorifique à absorption** *m* REFRIG absorption refrigeration system; ~ **frigorifique à éjection** *m* REFRIG ejector cycle refrigeration system; ~ **frigorifique préassemblé** *m* REFRIG factory assembled system;

~ g ~ **à générateur synchroniseur** *m* ENREGISTR, TV genlocking; ~ **à générateur verrouillé** *m* ENREGISTR, TV genlocking; ~ **à genouillère** *m* MECANIQUE bell crank system; ~ **de gestion de bases de données** *m (SGBD)* INFORMAT, ORDINAT database management system *(DBMS)*, TELECOM database management software, database management system (DBMS); ~ **Giorgi** *m* METROLOGIE Giorgi system; ~ **de gradation** *m* AERONAUT *balisage lumineux* dimmer system; ~ **de graissage** *m* AUTO lubricating system, PRODUCTION *hydraulique* lubrication system; ~ **de graissage des paliers** *m* PRODUCTION *hydraulique* bearing lubrication system; ~ **à griffe** *m* CINEMAT pin movement; ~ **de guidage** *m* OPTIQUE tracking mechanism; ~ **de guidage et de navigation** *m* ESPACE *pilotage* guidance navigation system; ~ **de guidage par adhérence** *m* TRANSPORT adhesion system, system with guidance by adhesion; ~ **à guidage par forme** *m* TRANSPORT system with compulsory guidance by physical means; ~ **de guidage pour l'accostage** *m* AERONAUT docking guidance system; ~ **guidé de transport public collectif** *m* TRANSPORT guided public mass transportation system;

~ h ~ **de haut-parleur** *m* ACOUSTIQUE, ENREGISTR loudspeaker system; ~ **héliocentrique** *m* ASTRONOMIE heliocentric system; ~ **hertzien** *m* TELECOM microwave system; ~ **hiérarchisé** *m* TELECOM hierarchical system; ~ **d'homologation** *m* QUALITE approval system; ~ **hybride** *m* TELECOM, TRANSPORT hybrid system; ~ **hydraulique** *m* INST HYDR hydraulic system; ~ **hydraulique de freinage** *m* CONS MECA hydraulic brake system; ~ **hyperbolique de localisation** *m* NAUT hyperbolic position-fixing system;

~ i ~ **d'identification** *m* TRANSPORT vehicle tagging; ~ **à impulsions inverses** *m* TELECOM revertive control system; ~ **indépendant** *m* ESPACE *communications* stand-alone system; ~ **indicateur de fuite** *m* SECURITE leakage indicator system; ~ **indirect de refroidissement** *m* REFRIG indirect expansion refrigeration system; ~ **inducteur** *m* PHYSIQUE inducing system; ~ **d'information** *m* TELECOM information system; ~ **informatique** *m* ELECTR computer system, INFORMAT data

processing system, ORDINAT IS, information system, TELECOM computer system; ~ **informatique hors ligne** *m* NUCLEAIRE off-line computer; ~ **d'injection** *m* MATERIAUX injection system; ~ **d'injection K-Jetronic** *m* AUTO K-Jetronic fuel injection system; ~ **d'injection de résine pour boulons de toit** *m* MINES resin roof-bolting system; ~ **insensible aux défaillances** *m* ORDINAT fault-tolerant system; ~ **intégré** *m* TELECOM integrated system; ~ **intégré de gestion** *m (SIG)* INFORMAT, ORDINAT management information system *(MIS)*; ~ **interactif** *m* TELECOM interactive system; ~ **d'interception automatique** *m* TELECOM automatic intercept system; ~ **d'intercommunication** *m* TELECOM house exchange system, key telephone system; ~ **d'intercommunications électronique** *m* TELECOM electronic key system; ~ **intermédiaire** *m* TELECOM IS, intermediate system; ~ **international de référence** *m* POLLUTION IRS, international referral system; ~ **international d'unités** *m* METROLOGIE international system of units, PHYSIQUE SI units; ~ **d'interrogation séquentiel** *m* TELECOM polling system; ~ **isolé** *m* PHYSIQUE isolated system;

~ j ~ **à jet d'encre** *m* EMBALLAGE, ORDINAT ink jet system;

~ l ~ **latéral** *m* NAUT lateral system; ~ **de lecture** *m* CONS MECA read-out system; ~ **de lecture optique de caractères** *m* EMBALLAGE optical character reading system; ~ **de levée des supports de filature** *m* TEXTILE doffing devices; ~ **lié** *m* ESPACE *véhicules* strapdown system; ~ **de ligne coaxiale** *m* TELECOM coaxial line system; ~ **de localisation** *m* PETR position reference system; ~ **à logique câblée** *m* TELECOM wired-logic system; ~ **de lubrification centralisé** *m* CONS MECA centralized lubricating system;

~ m ~ **de maclage** *m* METALL twinning system; ~ **de magasinage mélangeur distributeur** *m* EMBALLAGE mix and dispense storage system; ~ **à mailles** *m* TELECOM link system; ~ **maître-esclave** *m* INFORMAT, ORDINAT master-slave system; ~ **de manoeuvre en orbite** *m* ESPACE *pilotage* OMS, orbital maneuvering system (AmE), orbital manoeuvring system (BrE); ~ **manuel** *m* TELECOM manual system; ~ **à marquage centralisé** *m* TELECOM marker control system, marker system; ~ **mécanique** *m* ACOUSTIQUE, CONS MECA *de réfrigération, de graissage, de transmissions hydrauliques* mechanical system; ~ **à mémoire** *m* TV memory system; ~ **à mémoire commune** *m* ORDINAT shared memory system; ~ **à mémoire partagée** *m* INFORMAT shared memory system; ~ **à mémoire virtuelle** *m* INFORMAT, ORDINAT VMS, virtual memory system; ~ **Mercator** *m* NAUT Mercator projection; ~ **de messagerie** *m* TELECOM MHS, message handling system; ~ **de messagerie EDI** *m* TELECOM EDI messaging system, EDIMS; ~ **de messagerie électronique** *m* TELECOM EMS, electronic message system; ~ **de messagerie interpersonnelle** *m* TELECOM interpersonal messaging system; ~ **de mesure** *m* ELECTR measuring system; ~ **de mesure absolue** *m* ELECTRON absolute measuring system; ~ **de mesures** *m* ELECTR system of units; ~ **de mesures analogique** *m* ORDINAT analog measuring system; ~ **météorologique** *m* METEO weather system; ~ **mètre-kilogramme-seconde-ampère** *m (système MKSA)* METROLOGIE Giorgi system, meter kilogram-second-ampere-system (AmE), metre kilogramme-second-ampere-system (BrE); ~ **métrique** *m* METROLOGIE metric system; ~ **de micro-**

analyse par dispersion en énergie *m* CHIMIE EDAX, energy dispersive analysis by X-rays; ~ **de mise au point du télescope** *m* ASTRONOMIE telescope focusing mechanism; ~ **de mise à la terre** *m* PRODUCTION *électricité* earthing electrode system (BrE), grounding electrode system (AmE); ~ **mixte local et transit** *m* TELECOM combined local-toll system; ~ **MKSA** *m* *(système mètre-kilogramme-seconde-ampère)* MÉTROLOGIE Giorgi system, MKSA system *(meter kilogram-second-ampere-system, metre kilogramme-second-ampere-system)*; ~ **à modulation numérique** *m* TELECOM digital modulation system; ~ **mondial de localisation** *m* NAUT global positioning system; ~ **de monitorage** *m* PHYS RAYON *radiation ionisante* monitoring system; ~ **monoclinique** *m* METALL monoclinic system; ~ **monoconducteur** *m* ELECTR *câble* single wire system; ~ **monopoutre** *m* TRANSPORT monobeam system; ~ **monoprocesseur** *m* TELECOM single processor common-control system; ~ **de mouillage à lame d'air** *m* IMPRIM air doctor dampening system; ~ **de moulage de pâte** *m* EMBALLAGE pulp molding system (AmE), pulp moulding system (BrE); ~ **multiaccès** *m* INFORMAT, ORDINAT multiaccess system; ~ **multicellulaire** *m* TELECOM cellular system; ~ **multimodal** *m* TRANSPORT multiple mode transportation system; ~ **de multiplication de circuit numérique** *m* *(SMCN)* TELECOM digital circuit multiplication system *(DCMS)*; ~ **multiprocesseur** *m* TELECOM multiprocessor system; ~ **de multiprogrammation** *m* INFORMAT, ORDINAT multiprogramming system; ~ **de multitraitement** *m* INFORMAT, ORDINAT multiprocessing system; ~ **multiutilisateur** *m* INFORMAT, ORDINAT multiuser system;

~ **n** ~ **de navigation inertielle** *m* AERONAUT, NAUT INS, inertial navigation system; ~ **de navigation par inertie** *m* AERONAUT, NAUT INS, inertial navigation system; ~ **de navigation par satellites** *m* NAUT system of satellite navigation; ~ **à niveaux multiples** *m* TELECOM multilevel system; ~ **non compartimenté** *m* PRODUCTION bucketless system; ~ **non équilibré** *m* TELECOM unbalanced system; ~ **de noyaux condensés** *m* GENIE CHIM condensed system; ~ **NTSC** *m* TV NTSC system (AmE), National Television Standards Committee system (AmE); ~ **nuageux** *m* METEO cloud system; ~ **de numération** *m* INFORMAT number system;

~ **o** ~ **d'ondes stationnaires** *m* ELECTROTEC standing wave; ~ **optique** *m* ELECTRON optical system, OPTIQUE imaging mechanism, imaging system; ~ **optique à faisceau d'ions** *m* PHYS RAYON ion beam optical system; ~ **optique d'identification de caractères** *m* EMBALLAGE OCR system, optical character reading system; ~ **optique Leitz** *m* INSTRUMENT Leitz system; ~ **d'organisation du trafic** *m* NAUT routing system; ~ **oscillant** *m* ELECTRON oscillatory system; ~ **ouvert** *m* INFORMAT, ORDINAT, TELECOM, THERMODYN open system;

~ **p** ~ **PAL** *m* TV PAL; ~ **panel** *m* TELECOM panel system; ~ **partagé du type "dispatching"** *m* TELECOM trunked dispatch system; ~ **pas à pas** *m* TELECOM progressive switching magazine, step-by-step system; ~ **passif** *m* ACOUSTIQUE, EN RENOUV passive system; ~ **passif des ceintures de sécurité** *m* TRANSPORT passive seat belt system; ~ **à perte sèche** *m* PRODUCTION *système hydraulique* dead loss system; ~ **pilote** *m* ENREGISTR pilot system; ~ **à piste de contrôle sur les trous d'entraînement** *m* ENREGISTR sprocket hole control track system; ~ **à plusieurs antennes réparties** *m*

TELECOM distributed multi-antenna system; ~ **à plusieurs conducteurs** *m* ELECTR multiple-wire system; ~ **pneumatique de freinage** *m* CONS MECA pneumatic brake system; ~ **des points de répartition primaire et secondaire** *m* TELECOM cab and pillar distribution service; ~ **des points typographiques** *m* IMPRIM point system; ~ **à ponts multiples** *m* TRANSPORT multidecking system; ~ **à porteuse analogique** *m* INFORMAT, ORDINAT analog carrier system; ~ **à porteuse monovoie** *m* ESPACE *communications* SCPC, single-channel per carrier; ~ **à porteuses décalées** *m* TV offset carrier system; ~ **de positionnement de sachets** *m* EMBALLAGE bag placing system; ~ **de positions automatisées de téléphonistes** *m* (Can) TELECOM operator system; ~ **de positions d'opératrices** *m* TELECOM operator system; ~ **de positions de téléphonistes** *m* (Can) TELECOM operator system; ~ **de poursuite** *m* TELECOM tracking system; ~ **de poursuite pas à pas** *m* ESPACE *communications* step track system; ~ **pour tester les matériaux** *m* TEXTILE materials testing system; ~ **préventif** *m* SECURITE protective restraint system; ~ **de prisme diviseur** *m* CINEMAT beam-splitting system; ~ **programmable pour la protection de moteurs** *m* PRODUCTION *automatisme industriel* programable motor protector (AmE), programmable motor protector (BrE); ~ **de programmation orienté objet** *m* INFORMAT, ORDINAT object-oriented programming system; ~ **à programme câblé** *m* TELECOM WPC system, wired-program control system (AmE), wired-programme control system, hard-wired programable switching system (AmE), hard-wired programmable switching system (BrE); ~ **à programme enregistré** *m* TELECOM stored program switching system (AmE), stored programme switching system (BrE); ~ **propulsif** *m* ESPACE propulsion system; ~ **de propulsion** *m* ESPACE propulsion system; ~ **de propulsion à hydrazine** *m* ESPACE *véhicules* hydrazine propulsion system; ~ **de pulsation de faisceau** *m* NUCLEAIRE *couperet* beam pulser, mechanical chopper;

~ **q** ~ **quadratique** *m* METALL tetragonal system; ~ **qualité** *m* QUALITE quality system; ~ **à quatre fils** *m* ELECTROTEC four-wire system;

~ **r** ~ **radar anticollision actif** *m* AERONAUT active beacon collision avoidance system; ~ **radioélectrique d'appel** *m* TELECOM radiopaging system; ~ **de radiorepérage par satellite** *m* NAUT radio determination satellite system; ~ **radio sol-air à voie simple** *m* MILITAIRE SINCGARS, single channel ground and airborne radio system; ~ **rail-roue** *m* TRANSPORT steel wheel on steel rail system; ~ **de ramassage** *m* POLLU MER collection device; ~ **à rayonnement guidé** *m* TELECOM guided radiation system; ~ **de rechange d'outils** *m* CONS MECA tool changing system; ~ **de recherche documentaire** *m* INFORMAT, ORDINAT information retrieval system; ~ **de recherche et de sauvetage maritimes par satellite** *m* TELECOM SAMSARS, satellite-aided maritime search and rescue system; ~ **de récupération** *m* POLLU MER recovery system; ~ **à réenclenchement automatique** *m* IMPRIM *électronique* autoreclosing system; ~ **de référence intermédiaire** *m* *(SRI)* TELECOM information reference system *(IRS)*; ~ **refroidi à gaz** *m* CONS MECA gas welded system; ~ **de refroidissement** *m* CONSTR, ELECTR *machine*, TEXTILE cooling system; ~ **à refroidissement d'air** *m* CONS MECA air-cooled system; ~ **de refroidissement du bouclier** *m*

NUCLEAIRE shield cooling system; ~ de refroidisse-ment à cycle fermé m NUCLEAIRE closed cycle cooling system; ~ de refroidissement en route m REFRIG over-the-road system; ~ à refroidissement par l'eau m CONS MECA water-cooled system; ~ de refroidissement de la protection biologique m NUCLEAIRE biological protec-tion cooling system; ~ de refroidissement scellé m AUTO sealed cooling system; ~ de réglage m ELECTR control system; ~ de réglage à auto-adaptation m COMMANDE adaptive regulating system; ~ de réglage et de commande m COMMANDE automatic control system; ~ de réglage des surfaces par rayon laser m CONSTR laser grading system; ~ de régulation m COM-MANDE controller, regulation system, ELECTROTEC regulator; ~ de régulation de la circulation m TRANS-PORT traffic regulation system; ~ de régulation progressive m TRANSPORT progressive system; ~ de réinjection m COMMANDE feedback system; ~ à relais m ELECTROTEC relay switching system; ~ de relais à deux fréquences m TELECOM two-frequency relay system; ~ relié à la terre m PRODUCTION earthed system (BrE), grounded system (AmE); ~ de remise physique m TELECOM PDS, physical delivery system; ~ de remplis-sage en soufflant combiné avec fermeture m EMBAL-LAGE blow fill seal system; ~ de remplissage jumelé pour sacs m EMBALLAGE twin bagging system; ~ de reproduction sonore m ENREGISTR sound reproduc-tion system; ~ de réservation de places m TRANSPORT passenger reservation system; ~ à retard artificiel m ENREGISTR artificial delay system; ~ retardataire m AERONAUT lagging system; ~ de rétroaction m COM-MANDE feedback system; ~ de rétrovision m TRANSPORT rear-view system; ~ robotique pour palet-tiser et mettre sous film étirable m EMBALLAGE robotic palletizing and stretch system; ~ rotatif m TELECOM rotary system; ~ rotatif à commande indirecte m TELE-COM rotary system;

~ s ~ sans fin m TRANSPORT system with endless transportation units; ~ de sas m NUCLEAIRE airlock system; ~ SECAM m TV SECAM system; ~ de séchage m GAZ drying system, gas drying plant; ~ de sécurité automatique m TRANSPORT passive occupant restraint system; ~ de sécurité électrosensible m SECURITE fixé aux presses à commande mécanique electrosensitive safety system; ~ semi-automatique m TELECOM semi-automatic system; ~ séparatif d'assainissement m DISTRI EAU separate sewerage system; ~ séquentiel à mémoire m TV sequential color with memory system (AmE), sequential colour with memory system (BrE); ~ de serrage à ouverture rapide m CONS MECA quick-release clamping system; ~ à signal décalé m TV offset signal method; ~ de signalisation m TELECOM signaling system (AmE), signalling system (BrE); ~ solaire m ASTRONOMIE solar system; ~ solaire actif m EN RENOUV active solar system; ~ solaire passif m CONSTR passive solar system; ~ à son hi-fi m TV hi-fi sound; ~ de sonorisation cabine m AERONAUT public address sys-tem; ~ souple de protection collective m MILITAIRE guerre chimique collective protective system; ~ spatial m TELECOM spaced division system; ~ stabilisateur portable m CINEMAT panaglide; ~ de stabilisation arti-ficielle m TRANSPORT ASE, automatic stabilization equipment; ~ de stabilisation par gaz froid m ESPACE pilotage cold gas system; ~ strapdown m ESPACE vé-hicules strapdown system; ~ Strowger m TELECOM Strowger system, step-by-step system; ~ à structure

déconcentrée m TELECOM fully distributed control system; ~ à structure démocratique m TELECOM non-hierarchical system; ~ à structure éclatée m TELECOM fully distributed control system; ~ à structure hiérar-chique m TELECOM hierarchical system; ~ à structure multimicro m TELECOM multimicroprocessor system; ~ à suppression de porteuse m TV suppressed carrier system; ~ de surveillance d'espace et de poursuite m MILITAIRE SPADATS, space detection and tracking system; ~ de surveillance radar m MILITAIRE radar surveillance system; ~ suspendu m TRANSPORT sus-pended system; ~ de sustentation multijupe m TRANSPORT multiple-skirt system, multiskirt system; ~ synchronisé m TRANSPORT simultaneous system;

~ t ~ de télécommande m SECURITE remote control system; ~ de télépaiement m ORDINAT EFTS, elec-tronic funds transfer system; ~ téléphonique à touches m TELECOM key telephone system; ~ de télévi-sion à balayage lent m TV slow-scan television system; ~ de télévision par câbles m TELECOM cable television system; ~ temporel m TELECOM time-division switch-ing system, time-division system; ~ tétragonal m METALL tetragonal system; ~ thermodynamique m THERMODYN thermodynamic system; ~ à tolérance de pannes m INFORMAT fault-tolerant system; ~ tout à relais m TELECOM relay system; ~ de traitement m INFORMAT computer system; ~ de traitement de don-nées m INFORMAT, NUCLEAIRE data processing system; ~ de traitement de l'information m TELECOM informa-tion processing system; ~ de traitement d'information m INFORMAT data processing system; ~ de traitement numérique m NUCLEAIRE digital process computer system; ~ de traitement de travaux m INFORMAT, ORDI-NAT job processing system; ~ de transfert de messages m TELECOM MTS, message transfer system; ~ de transmission m ELECTROTEC transmission sys-tem; ~ de transmission de données m TELECOM data transfer system; ~ de transmission d'énergie m CONS MECA power transmission system; ~ de transmission à fibre optique m ELECTROTEC fiberoptic transmission system (AmE), fibreoptic transmission system (BrE); ~ de transmission mécanique m CONS MECA mechan-ical transmission system; ~ de transmission optique m OPTIQUE optical transmission system; ~ de trans-mission pneumatique m CONS MECA pneumatic transmission system; ~ de transmission sur fibre op-tique m OPTIQUE optical fiber transmission system (AmE), optical fibre transmission system (BrE); ~ de transport m CONSTR transportation system; ~ de transport automatique m TRANSPORT automatic transportation system; ~ de transport continu m TRANSPORT continuous transportation system; ~ de transport en commun à accès continu m TRANSPORT continuous access public transport system; ~ de transporteur à bandes m CONSTR conveyor system; ~ transporteur de manutention m EMBALLAGE conveyor handling system; ~ de transport de fil m TEXTILE yarn carrier assembly; ~ de transport guidé m TRANSPORT track-guided transport system; ~ de transport léger et guidé m CH DE FER guided light transport system; ~ de transport pour film sous vide m EMBALLAGE vacuum film transport system; ~ de transport rapide m CH DE FER RTS, rapid transit system; ~ de transport spatial m ESPACE STS, véhicules space transportation system; ~ triclinique m METALL triclinic system; ~ triphasé déséquilibré m ELECTR à courant alternatif unbalanced three-phase system; **~ triphasé à quatre fils** *m* ELECTR three-phase four-wire system; **~ à trois fils** *m* ELECTR third wire system, ELECTROTEC three-wire system; **~ à trois voies** *m* ENREGISTR three-way system; **~ de tuyauterie** *m* CONS MECA *robinetterie, installations* pipework system;

~ u **~ unitaire** *m* HYDROLOGIE combined sewer; **~ unitaire d'assainissement** *m* DISTRI EAU combined sewer system;

~ v **~ de vapeur d'étanchéité** *m* NUCLEAIRE gland steam system; **~ de ventilation des appareils de peinture au pistolet** *m* SECURITE paint-spraying apparatus ventilation system; **~ de ventilation par extraction** *m* SECURITE extractor fan system; **~ de verrouillage** *m* CINEMAT interlock device; **~ de verrouillage électrique** *m* ENREGISTR interlocking system; **~ VHS** *m* TV VHS, video home system; **~ VHS-C** *m* TV VHS-C system, video home system-compact; **~ vibrant** *m* PHYS ONDES *qui engendre des ondes* vibrating system; **~ de vidange** *m* NAUT drainage system; **~ de vidéodisque** *m* OPTIQUE videodisc system (BrE), videodisk system (AmE); **~ de visée reflex** *m* PHOTO reflex housing; **~ visuel de lecture de caractères** *m* EMBALLAGE character reading vision system; **~ de vitesse affichée** *m* TRANSPORT displayed speed system; **~ de voie intégrale** *m* TRANSPORT multipurpose material pipeline; **~ à volets mobiles** *m* ESPACE *communications* shutter system; **~ de volets soufflés** *m* AERONAUT blown-flap system

systèmes: **~ antierreurs** *m pl* PRODUCTION fail-safe work methods; **~ couplés** *m pl* PHYSIQUE coupled systems; **~ de déclenchement** *m pl* PHYS RAYON triggering systems; **~ électroniques de préparation des formes imprimantes** *m pl* IMPRIM imaging systems; **~ de filtres pour poussières et fibres** *m pl* SECURITE *industrie textile* filtering plants for dust and fibres; **~ infographiques** *m pl* IMPRIM imaging systems; **~ laser de surveillance** *m pl* PHYS RAYON laser monitoring systems

syzygie *f* ASTRONOMIE, GEOMETRIE syzygy

T

T *abrév* CONS MECA *(té)* T *(tee)*, METROLOGIE *(téra-)* T *(tera-)*, PHYSIQUE *(tesla)* T *(tesla)*

Ta *(tantale)* CHIMIE Ta *(tantalum)*

tab: ~ **automatique de compensation** *m* AERONAUT balance tab; ~ **de réglage d'incidence de pale** *m* AERONAUT blade trim tab

tabergite *f* MINERAUX tabergite

table *f* CHARBON table, CONS MECA *d'un cylindre de laminoir* barrel, *d'une enclume* block, *d'une machine-outil* plate, *d'une machine à mouler* table, CONSTR *d'une poutre* tread, GEOMETRIE, INFORMAT, ORDINAT table, PRODUCTION face, *d'un cylindre de laminoir* body, *d'une enclume* crown; ~ **d'agrandisseur** *f* PHOTO enlarger baseboard; ~ **d'aiguilletage accrue** *f* TEXTILE needling penetration; ~ **d'alimentation** *f* EMBALLAGE feeding table; ~ **d'amalgamation** *f* CHARBON amalgamating table; ~ **d'angiographie** *f* INSTRUMENT angiographic examination table; ~ **d'animation** *f* CINEMAT animation bench, peg board; ~ **ascendante** *f* CONS MECA raising table; ~ **Atwater** *f* AGRO ALIM Atwater table; ~ **basculante** *f* CERAM VER rocking table; ~ **à bascule** *f* CONS MECA lift-up table; ~ **de calcul d'adresses** *f* INFORMAT hash table; ~ **à cartes** *f* NAUT chart table; ~ **circulaire automatique** *f* CONS MECA self-acting circular table; ~ **de collage** *f* IMPRIM *prépresse* splicing table; ~ **de concentration** *f* CHARBON concentrating table; ~ **à consulter** *f* INFORMAT, ORDINAT look-up table; ~ **de conversion** *f* METROLOGIE conversion table; ~ **du cosinus** *f* GEOMETRIE cosine table; ~ **de coulée** *f* CERAM VER casting table; ~ **de décision** *f* INFORMAT decision table; ~ **de décompression** *f* PETR decompression table; ~ **de découpe** *f* CERAM VER cutter's table; ~ **de découpe basculante** *f* CERAM VER tilt table; ~ **de démoulage** *f* REFRIG ice dump table; ~ **de déplacement rectiligne** *f* CONS MECA slide unit; ~ **à dessin** *f* CONSTR drawing board; ~ **de distributeur** *f* INST HYDR seat of a slide-valve; ~ **de données** *f* PRODUCTION *automatisme industriel* data table; ~ **des données** *f* PRODUCTION image table; ~ **des données d'entrée** *f* PRODUCTION input image table; ~ **de données étendue** *f* PRODUCTION *automatisme industriel* expanded data table; ~ **à double coulisse** *f* CONS MECA compound table, table with compound slides; ~ **à double équerre** *f* CONS MECA table with top and side faces; ~ **élévatrice** *f* MECANIQUE elevating table; ~ **d'encrage** *f* IMPRIM vibrator, *machines* oscillator; ~ **d'entrée** *f* IMPRIM *machines* feed table; ~ **d'épandage** *f* PRODUCTION spreading table; ~ **d'équerre à rainures** *f* CONS MECA slotted box table; ~ **d'étalonnage** *f* ORDINAT calibration chart; ~ **d'état des canaux** *f* INFORMAT, ORDINAT channel status table; ~ **d'examen radiologique** *f* INSTRUMENT X-ray examination table; ~ **de fabrication** *f* PAPIER wire end; ~ **fixe** *f* CERAM VER fixed table; ~ **des forçages** *f* PRODUCTION force table; ~ **des fumées** *f* SECURITE *classification* smoke chart; ~ **d'harmonie** *f* PHYS ONDES sounding board; ~ **de hash-code** *f* ORDINAT hash table; ~ **à hauteur variable** *f* CONS MECA table which can be raised or lowered; ~ **horizontale** *f* TELE-COM keyshelf; ~ **d'imposition** *f* IMPRIM *copie* imposing surface; ~ **inclinable** *f* CONS MECA tilting table; ~ **s'inclinant sous tout angle** *f* CONS MECA table canting to any angle; ~ **inclinée à aire plane** *f* MINES plane table; ~ **de lancement** *f* ESPACE launcher, MILITAIRE *d'une fusée* launch station; ~ **des lumières** *f* INST HYDR portface; ~ **de marge** *f* IMPRIM *machines* feedboard; ~ **de mesure** *f* METEO bed gage (AmE), bed gauge (BrE); ~ **de mixage** *f (cf pupitre de mixage)* ENREGISTR mixing desk, sound console; ~ **mobile** *f* CERAM VER moving table; ~ **de montage** *f* CINEMAT editing machine, IMPRIM *prépresse* splicing machine; ~ **de montage horizontale** *f* CINEMAT flat-bed editing table, table editing machine; ~ **de montage à quatre plateaux** *f* CINEMAT four-plate; ~ **de mouillage** *f* IMPRIM *machines* oscillator, vibrator; ~ **à numériser** *f* INFORMAT, ORDINAT digitizing tablet; ~ **d'opérations** *f* INFORMAT, ORDINAT operation table; ~ **de pages** *f* INFORMAT, ORDINAT page table; ~ **à papier** *f* IMPRIM bank; ~ **plate en porte-à-faux** *f* PAPIER cantilevered Fourdrinier; ~ **plate de fabrication** *f* PAPIER Fourdrinier; ~ **plate sortante** *f* PAPIER roll-out Fourdrinier; ~ **de plongée** *f* OCEANO decompression chart; ~ **pneumatique** *f* CHARBON pneumatic table; ~ **porte-pièces** *f* CONS MECA work plate; ~ **porte-pièces à rainures à double coulisse** *f* CONS MECA compound-slotted worktable; ~ **à rainures** *f* CONS MECA slotted table; ~ **à rainures de montage** *f* CONS MECA slotted table; ~ **de recette** *f* IMPRIM fly board; ~ **de renversement** *f* PRODUCTION roll-over table; ~ **de repassage** *f* CHARBON cleaner jig; ~ **de rotation** *f* PETR, PETROLE rotary table; ~ **rotative** *f* CONS MECA revolving table; ~ **de roulement** *f* CH DE FER running surface, tread; ~ **secoueuse** *f* CHARBON griddle, riddle, shaking table, sieve table, vibrating table, PRODUCTION shaking table; ~ **à secousses** *f* CHARBON oscillating table, vibrating table, shaking table, CONS MECA concussion table, EMBALLAGE jarring table, MINES joggling table, PRODUCTION bumping table, shaking table; ~ **de sinus** *f* GEOMETRIE, METROLOGIE sine table; ~ **à soudure avec aspirateur** *f* SECURITE welding table with vacuum apparatus; ~ **statistique** *f* QUALITE statistical table; ~ **de symboles** *f* INFORMAT symbol table; ~ **de tir** *f* MILITAIRE range table; ~ **tournante** *f* CONS MECA revolving table; ~ **traçante** *f* INFORMAT plotter, plotting board, NAUT plotting table, ORDINAT plotter, plotting board; ~ **de travail** *f* INSTRUMENT workbench; ~ **de triage** *f* MINES picking table; ~ **de vérité** *f* INFORMAT, ORDINAT truth table; ~ **vibrante** *f* CERAM VER vibrating table; ~ **de vie** *f* MATH life table

Table *f* ASTRONOMIE Mensa

tableau *m* DISTRI EAU *d'une vanne* frame, IMPRIM *tableautage* chart, INFORMAT, MATH *de nombres* array, TELECOM board, TRANSPORT display; ~ **d'affichage** *m* ORDINAT, TELECOM bulletin board; ~ **arrière** *m* NAUT transom, transom plate; ~ **de bord** *m* AERONAUT control panel, instrument panel, AUTO instrument panel, NAUT control panel, instrument panel, PRODUCTION instruction panel, instrument panel, management chart, management report, VEHICULES *accessoires* instrument panel; ~ **de brassage** *m* TV patch board; ~ **calculateur** *m* PHOTO exposure calculating chart; ~ **de caractères** *m* INFORMAT string array; ~ **de codes de défauts** *m* PRODUCTION *automatisme industriel* fault code chart; ~ **de codes d'identification de défaut** *m* PRODUCTION fault identification code chart; ~ **de commande** *m* CONSTR control panel, ELECTR control board, ESPACE *pilotage*, MECANIQUE control panel; ~ **de commande à bouton-poussoir** *m* ELECTR *contrôle, réglage* push-button control panel; ~ **commutateur à cordons** *m* TELECOM cord switchboard; ~ **commutateur sans cordons** *m* TELECOM cordless switchboard; ~ **de commutation** *m* ELECTROTEC, TV switchboard; ~ **comptable** *m* IMPRIM spreadsheet; ~ **de connexions** *m* ELECTROTEC plugboard, INFORMAT patch board, plugboard, ORDINAT jack panel (BrE), patch board, patch panel (AmE), plugboard; ~ **de contrôle** *m* ELECTR test board; ~ **de dépannage** *m* CONS MECA fault-finding table; ~ **distributeur** *m* ELECTR, VEHICULES distributing board; ~ **de distribution** *m* ELECTROTEC distribution board, switchboard, TELECOM distribution board; ~ **de distribution électrique** *m* NUCLEAIRE electrical control board, electrical control room; ~ **de distribution à fusibles** *m* ELECTR distribution fuse board; ~ **électrique** *m* NAUT electrical panel, switch panel; ~ **du flux thermique** *m* THERMODYN heat flow diagram; ~ **de graissage** *m* MECANIQUE lubrication chart; ~ **indicateur des avances** *m* CONS MECA feed chart; ~ **d'instruments** *m* INSTRUMENT instrument board, VEHICULES *habitacle* dashboard; ~ **lumineux des alarmes** *m* AERONAUT, SECURITE general warning panel; ~ **à monocordes** *m* TELECOM single cord switchboard; ~ **périodique** *m* CHIMIE periodic table; ~ **de planning** *m* PRODUCTION planning board; ~ **de progression de vol** *m* AERONAUT flight progress board; ~ **de raccordement** *m* CINEMAT patch bay, patch field, TV patch board; ~ **de répartition brute des ressources** *m* PRODUCTION rough capacity load table; ~ **de répartition du travail de la production** *m* CINEMAT production strip board; ~ **de suivi d'atelier** *m* PRODUCTION Gantt chart; ~ **synoptique** *m* ELECTR *commutateur* mimic board, synoptical switchboard; ~ **systolique** *m* INFORMAT, ORDINAT systolic array

tableautage *m* IMPRIM tabular work

table-image *f* PRODUCTION image table; ~ **d'entrée** *f* PRODUCTION input image table; ~ **des sorties** *f* PRODUCTION *automatisme industriel* output image table

tabler *vt* CHARBON table

tablette *f* CERAM VER tray (BrE), tray bar (AmE), CONSTR shelf, INFORMAT, ORDINAT tablet; ~ **graphique** *f* IMPRIM board, INFORMAT, ORDINAT graphics tablet; ~ **horizontale** *f* TELECOM keyshelf; ~ **à numériser** *f* INFORMAT data tablet, digitizing tablet, ORDINAT digitizing tablet; ~ **Rand** *f* INFORMAT Rand tablet, ORDINAT Rand tablet, data tablet

tableur *m* INFORMAT spreadsheet; ~ **électronique** *m* ORDINAT spreadsheet

tablier *m* CONSTR *d'un pont* apron, deck, IMPRIM *impression*, PAPIER, PRODUCTION, SECURITE apron, VEHICULES *habitacle* dashboard; ~ **en cuir** *m* SECURITE leather apron; ~ **de protection** *m* SECURITE protective apron; ~ **releveur** *m* PRODUCTION *de laminoir* lifting table; ~ **d'un tour** *m* CONS MECA apron of a lathe; ~ **de vanne** *m* INST HYDR shuttle plate

tabouret ~ **de laboratoire** *m* EQUIP LAB *meuble* laboratory stool

tabulaire *adj* INFORMAT, ORDINAT tabular

tabulation *f* INFORMAT tabulation, ORDINAT tab, tabulation, PRODUCTION tab; ~ **horizontale** *f* ORDINAT HT, horizontal tabulation; ~ **verticale** *f* INFORMAT, ORDINAT VT, vertical tabulation

tabuler *vt* INFORMAT, ORDINAT tab, tabulate

TAC *abrév* CH DE FER *(train autos-couchettes)* véhicules motorail, POLLUTION *(taux d'appauvrissement en cations)* cation denudation rate

tache *f* CERAM VER sugar, IMPRIM *impression* smudge, PAPIER *salissure*, QUALITE stain, TEXTILE blotch; ~ **d'acide** *f* CERAM VER acid mark; ~ **Airy** *f* ASTRONOMIE Airy disc (BrE), Airy disk (AmE); ~ **d'Airy** *f* PHYSIQUE Airy disc (BrE), Airy disk (AmE); ~ **blanche** *f* ASTRONOMIE *de Saturne* great white spot; ~ **cathodique** *f* ELECTROTEC cathode spot; ~ **centrale** *f* PHOTO ghost; ~ **claire** *f* CERAM VER clear spot; ~ **de diffraction** *f* CRISTALL diffraction spot; ~ **de diffusion** *f* PHOTO circle of confusion; ~ **de goutte d'eau dans la feuille** *f* PAPIER drop watermark; ~ **de graisse** *f* CERAM VER dope mark, grease mark; ~ **ionique** *f* ELECTRON ion burn, TV ion spot; ~ **de jour** *f* CERAM VER bloach; ~ **lumineuse** *f* CINEMAT flare spot; ~ **rouge** *f* ASTRONOMIE *de Jupiter* great red spot; ~ **rouge de Jupiter** *f* ASTRONOMIE Jupiter's red spot; ~ **solaire** *f* ASTRONOMIE, GEOPHYS sunspot; ~ **sur la peau** *f* AGRO ALIM skin blemish

tâche *f* INFORMAT, ORDINAT, QUALITE task; ~ **de premier plan** *f* INFORMAT foreground job

tachéomètre *m* CONSTR, PHYSIQUE tacheometer, tachymeter; ~ **électro-optique** *m* INSTRUMENT electro-optical distance measuring instrument

tachéométrie *f* CONSTR tacheometry

tacher *vt* PLAST CAOU *défaut*, QUALITE stain

taches *f pl* MINES *de minerai* splashes; ~ **d'albédo** *f pl* ASTRONOMIE albedo features

tacheture *f* TEXTILE speckle

tachydrite *f* MINERAUX tachhydrite, tachydrite

tachygraphe *m* AUTO trip mileage indicator, trip odometer (AmE), trip recorder (BrE), TRANSPORT tachograph

tachylite *f* PETR basalt glass

tachymètre *m* AUTO speedometer, CINEMAT camera speed checker, tachometer, CONS MECA motion indicator, revolution indication, speed indicator, IMPRIM tacho, tachometer, PHYSIQUE, TV tachometer; ~ **de haute précision** *m* CONS MECA high-sensitivity tachometer, precision tachometer

tachyon *m* PHYSIQUE tachyon

tactique *adj* MILITAIRE *vol* tactical

taffetas *m* TEXTILE taffeta

TAI *abrév (Temps atomique international)* ASTRONOMIE IAT *(International Atomic Time)*

tailings *m pl* CONSTR tailings

taillage ~ **par fraise-mère** *m* CONS MECA hob cutting

taillanderie *f* PRODUCTION edge tool making, edge tools

taillandier *m* PRODUCTION toolmaker

taillant *m* CONS MECA cutting edge, MINES drill bit

taille:[1] ~ **côtes plates** *adj* CERAM VER faceted (AmE), facetted (BrE); **à ~ croisée** *adj* PRODUCTION *lime* double-cut

taille[2] *f* CERAM VER cut, decorative cutting, smoothing, CHARBON breast, face, stall, CONSTR dressing, MINES chamber, room, PRODUCTION *d'une lime, d'une râpe* cut, *des dents des roues d'engrenage* cutting, TEXTILE *d'un vêtement* size, waist, waistline; ~ **de l'alvéole** *f*

IMPRIM *héliogravure* cell definition; ~ **bâtarde** *f* CONS MECA *d'une lime, d'une râpe* bastard cut; ~ **blanche** *f* CERAM VER gray cutting (AmE), grey cutting (BrE); ~ **brute** *f* CONSTR rough dressing, spalling; ~ **d'un champ** *f* INFORMAT, ORDINAT field length; ~ **chassante** *f* MINES drift stope; ~ **demi-douce** *f* CONS MECA second cut; ~ **de l'échantillon** *f* ELECTRON sample size; ~ **effective de grain** *f* CHARBON effective grain size; ~ **en dentelle** *f* CERAM VER lacing; ~ **en diamants** *f* CERAM VER diamond cut pattern; ~ **en dressant au bélier** *f* MINES diagonal ram longwall face; ~ **en dressant à marteaux-piqueurs** *f* MINES vertical pneumatic pick longwall face; ~ **d'engrenage en chevrons** *f* CONS MECA chevron-cut gears; ~ **des engrenages** *f* CONS MECA gear cutting; ~ **en râpe** *f* CONSTR rasp cut; ~ **de fichier** *f* INFORMAT, ORDINAT file size; ~ **de grain** *f* CHARBON, CRISTALL, METALL grain size; ~ **grosse** *f* CONS MECA rough cut; ~ **horizontale à havage** *f* MINES horizontal cut longwall face; ~ **horizontale à rabot** *f* MINES horizontal ploughed longwall face (BrE), horizontal plowed longwall face (AmE); ~ **de lot** *f* PRODUCTION lot size; ~ **mi-douce** *f* CONS MECA second cut; ~ **montante** *f* CHARBON rise face, rise workings, MINES raise stope; ~ **moyenne** *f* PRODUCTION middle cut; ~ **non polie** *f* CERAM VER matt cutting; ~ **des particules** *f* METALL, NUCLEAIRE particle size; ~ **des pierres** *f* CONSTR stone dressing; ~ **profonde** *f* CERAM VER deep cut; ~ **à la roue** *f* CERAM VER brilliant cutting; ~ **rude** *f* CONS MECA rough cut; ~ **des signaux échantillonnés** *f* ELECTRON sampled data size filter

taillé: ~ **dans la masse** *adj* PRODUCTION cut from the solid, cut from the solid banks

taille-douce *f* IMPRIM *impression* intaglio

taille-gravure *f* CERAM VER intaglio

tailler *vt* MECANIQUE *outillage*, PRODUCTION *crémaillère, dents d'une lime* cut; ~ **en pointe** *vt* CONSTR point; ~ **par éclats** *vt* PRODUCTION chip

tailleur *m* CONSTR cutter, hewer; ~ **de pierre** *m* CONSTR stone dresser, stonemason

tailleuse: ~ **d'engrenages** *f* CONS MECA gear cutter, gear-cutting machine

tain *m* PRODUCTION quicksilvering, silvering

talc *m* CERAM VER, MATERIAUX, MINERAUX talc

taler: **se** ~ *v réfl* CONSTR bind

tallol *f* CHIMIE tall oil

taloche *f* CONSTR float, hawk

talon *m* CERAM VER heel, CONS MECA heel, *d'un essieu* collar, CONSTR ogee, MECANIQUE *soudage* root, VEHICULES *d'un pneu* bead; ~ **d'angle** *m* IMPRIM corner stub; ~ **d'aube** *m* AERONAUT blade root; ~ **de barrage** *m* CERAM VER floater lug (BrE), floater notcher (AmE)

talonique *adj* CHIMIE talonic

talonnage: ~ **d'aiguille** *m* CH DE FER forcing open the points

talonner *vi* NAUT touch bottom

talose *m* CHIMIE talose

talqueur *m* PRODUCTION talcking unit

talure *f* AGRO ALIM bruise

talus *m* CHARBON slope, CONSTR slope, *d'un fossé* bank, *d'un mur, d'un remblai* batter, *de terre* bank, GEOPHYS scree, OCEANO *sous-marin* continental slope, escarpment, scarp, submarine slope; ~ **continental** *m* GEOLOGIE *sous-marin*, GEOPHYS, PETROLE continental slope; ~ **naturel** *m* CONSTR *des terres* angle of repose

talutage *m* CONSTR *d'un fossé* battering

taluter *vt* CONSTR weather, *fossé* batter

talweg *m* CONSTR, GEOLOGIE talweg, thalweg

tambour *m* CINEMAT drum, roller, CONS MECA *de treuil* barrel, INFORMAT, INST HYDR *de turbine à vapeur* drum, MECANIQUE barrel, drum, NAUT warping drum, OCEANO net drum, net roller, reel, ORDINAT, PAPIER drum, PRODUCTION drum, *pour malaxage, lavage, etc* drum, *transmission de force* drum, TEXTILE tumble dryer; ~ **d'analyse** *m* TV drum scanner; ~ **de bobinage** *m* CERAM VER spindle; ~ **bouleteur** *m* CHARBON balling drum; ~ **de broyage** *m* GENIE CHIM grinding drum; ~ **de câble** *m* ELECTR, EMBALLAGE cable drum; ~ **de commande** *m* CERAM VER timing drum; ~ **conique** *m* CONS MECA cone drum, PRODUCTION fusee wheel; ~ **de couverture** *m* PAPIER deckle pulley; ~ **cribleur** *m* GENIE CHIM classifying drum; ~ **débiteur** *m* CINEMAT feed sprocket; ~ **débourbeur** *m* CONSTR drum washer; ~ **denté** *m* CINEMAT sprocket; ~ **denté d'entraînement** *m* CINEMAT drive sprocket; ~ **denté inférieur** *m* CINEMAT bottom sprocket; ~ **dessableur** *m* PRODUCTION cleaning barrel, rattler, rattling barrel, rumbler, shaking machine, shaking mill, tumbler, tumbling barrel, tumbling box, tumbling drum, tumbling mill; ~ **de développement** *m* CINEMAT developing drum, PHOTO developing drum, processing drum; ~ **écorceur** *m* PAPIER barking drum, drum debarker; ~ **à écrans** *m* AUTO trigger wheel; ~ **d'embrayage** *m* AUTO, CONS MECA clutch drum; ~ **d'enregistrement** *m* ENREGISTR recording drum; ~ **d'enroulement** *m* CINEMAT take-up sprocket; ~ **enrouleur** *m* PAPIER reel drum; ~ **d'entraînement** *m* CINEMAT film drum, TRANSPORT driving drum, TV drive sprocket; ~ **épaississeur** *m* GENIE CHIM thickener drum; ~ **filtrant** *m* GENIE CHIM filter drum; ~ **de frein** *m* CONS MECA, MECANIQUE, VEHICULES brake drum; ~ **d'impression** *m* INFORMAT, ORDINAT print drum; ~ **imprimeur** *m* EMBALLAGE impression pad; ~ **à inertie** *m* CONS MECA inertia reel; ~ **à laquer** *m* REVETEMENT coating drum; ~ **laveur** *m* CONSTR drum washer, PAPIER washing drum; ~ **de lecture** *m* ENREGISTR sound drum, TV scanning drum; ~ **de machine d'extraction** *m* MINES hoisting drum; ~ **magnétique** *m* ELECTROTEC, INFORMAT magnetic drum; ~ **moteur** *m* CONS MECA motorized driving pulley; ~ **photoconducteur** *m* OPTIQUE photoconducting drum; ~ **de pliage** *m* IMPRIM *machine* folding drum; ~ **presseur** *m* CINEMAT pressure roller; ~ **de séchage** *m* CINEMAT film drying drum, LESSIVES drying cylinder, drying drum; ~ **à sécher** *m* CONSTR drying drum; ~ **sécheur** *m* TEXTILE drying cylinder, THERMODYN drum dryer; ~ **tamiseur** *m* GENIE CHIM sieve drum; ~ **de têtes** *m* TV head drum; ~ **à têtes magnétiques** *m* TV head drum; ~ **de treuil** *m* NAUT winch drum

tamis *m* CHARBON screen, sieve, CONSTR, EQUIP LAB sieve, HYDROLOGIE screen, sieve, MECANIQUE, MINES *d'un bocard à minerai*, PAPIER screen, PRODUCTION gauze, *d'un bocard à minerai* grate, RECYCLAGE screen, sieve; ~ **à châssis vibrant** *m* EMBALLAGE vibratory sifter; ~ **de contrôle** *m* CONS MECA test sieve; ~ **déschlammeur** *m* CHARBON depulping screen; ~ **déslimeur** *m* CHARBON desliming screen; ~ **métallique** *m* PRODUCTION *pour entonnoir* gauze strainer; ~ **moléculaire** *m* CHIMIE molecular sieve; ~ **de mouleur** *m* PRODUCTION foundry riddle; ~ **plat** *m* IMPRIM *sérigraphie* flat screen; ~ **rotatif** *m* CONSTR rotary screen, HYDROLOGIE drum screen; ~ **roulant** *m* PRODUCTION traveling belt screen (AmE), travelling belt screen (BrE); ~ **à secousses** *m* CHIMIE vibrating screen; ~ **à**

tambour *m* GENIE CHIM mixing sieve, HYDROLOGIE drum screen; ~ **vibrant** *m* PETR shale shaker; ~ **vibratoire** *m* PETR shale shaker

tamisage *m* CONSTR filtering, screening, sifting, sieving, GENIE CHIM sieving, NUCLEAIRE screening, POLLU MER screening, sieving, POLLUTION sieving, PRODUCTION sifting; ~ **de contrôle** *m* CONS MECA test sieving, GENIE CHIM sieve test; ~ **à main** *m* CHARBON hand screening

tamiser *vt* AGRO ALIM sieve, sift, CHIMIE screen, CONSTR screen, sift, GENIE CHIM classify, sieve, HYDROLOGIE sieve, POLLU MER screen

tamiseur *m* EQUIP LAB sample divider, sieve shaker

tampan *m* CONSTR dowel

tampon *m* AGRO ALIM buffer salt, AUTO engine mounting, CH DE FER buffer, *sur wagon ou voiture* bumper (AmE), damper (BrE), CHIMIE buffer, CONS MECA internal cylindrical gage (AmE), internal cylindrical gauge (BrE), CONSTR plug, plug gage (AmE), plug gauge (BrE), ELECTROTEC buffer, IMPRIM buffer, print buffer, INST HYDR *de vapeur dans le cylindre* cushion, ORDINAT, PLAST CAOU *contrôle de pH* buffer, PRODUCTION boat, bott, plug, TV buffer; ~ **d'aspiration d'échangeur thermique** *m* REFRIG heat exchanger suction accumulator; ~ **de caoutchouc** *m* AUTO rubber pad; ~ **de contrôle** *m* PRODUCTION inspection stamp; ~ **entre** *m* MECANIQUE go plug; ~ **d'entrée** *m* INFORMAT, ORDINAT input buffer; ~ **d'entrée/sortie** *m* INFORMAT, ORDINAT input/output buffer; ~ **latéral** *m* PETR sidewall pad; ~ **de lavage** *m* PRODUCTION washout plug; ~ **obturateur** *m* CONS MECA obturating plug, sealing plug; ~ **d'ouate** *m* CHIMIE wadding, TEXTILE wad of cotton wool; ~ **passe** *m* CONS MECA go gage (AmE), go gauge (BrE); ~ **passe pas** *m* CONS MECA *trous* no-go gage (AmE), no-go gauge (BrE); ~ **de pression** *m* ENREGISTR pressure pad; ~ **à ressort** *m* CH DE FER spring bumper (AmE), spring damper (BrE); ~ **sec** *m* CH DE FER spring bumper (AmE), spring damper (BrE); ~ **de sortie** *m* INFORMAT, ORDINAT output buffer; ~ **à tolérance** *m* CONS MECA limit internal gauge (BrE), plug gage (AmE), plug gauge (BrE); ~ **de vidange** *m* PRODUCTION emptying plug; ~ **à vis** *m* CONSTR screw plug

tampon-jauge *m* CONS MECA plug gage (AmE), plug gauge (BrE)

tamponnage *m* CHIMIE buffer action, neutralization, CONSTR plugging, LESSIVES buffer action, ORDINAT buffering

tamponnement *m* CHIMIE buffer action, *d'une solution* neutralization, CONS MECA plugging, SECURITE collision

tamponner *vt* CHIMIE buffer, DISTRI EAU *voie d'eau* stop, ORDINAT buffer, PRODUCTION stop, stop up, SECURITE crash into

tangage *m* AERONAUT, ESPACE *pilotage* pitch, NAUT, PHYSIQUE pitch, pitching

tangence *f* GEOMETRIE tangency

tangent *adj* GEOMETRIE tangent

tangente *f* GEOMETRIE *d'un angle*, INFORMAT, ORDINAT tangent; ~ **au cercle** *f* GEOMETRIE tangent to the circle

tangentiel *adj* GEOMETRIE, MECANIQUE, PHYSIQUE tangential

tangon *m* NAUT spinnaker boom; ~ **écarteur** *m* POLLU MER jib boom

tangonner *vi* NAUT boom out

tanguer *vi* NAUT pitch

tanin *m* CHIMIE tannin

tank: ~ **à sédimentation** *m* DISTRI EAU sedimentation tank; ~ **de soutirage** *m* AGRO ALIM bottling tank

tanker *m* TRANSPORT refueler (AmE), refueller (BrE)

tannage *m* CHIMIE tannage, CINEMAT tanning

tannant *m* PHOTO hardener

tannate *m* CHIMIE tannate

tannin *m* CHIMIE tannin

tannique *adj* CHIMIE *acide* tannic

tantalate *m* CHIMIE tantalate

tantale *m (Ta)* CHIMIE tantalum *(Ta)*

tantalique *adj* CHIMIE tantalic

tantalite *f* MINERAUX tantalite

tapage *m* CONS MECA knocking

tape: ~ **de trou d'homme** *f* MECANIQUE manhole cover

taper[1] *vt* INFORMAT, ORDINAT type

taper[2] *vi* CONS MECA knock

taphrogenèse *f* GEOLOGIE rift tectonics, taphrogenesis

tapiolite *f* MINERAUX tapiolite

tapis *m* CERAM VER lehr belt, MECANIQUE belt; ~ **accélérateur pour piétons** *m* TRANSPORT acceleration device; ~ **aiguilleté** *m* TEXTILE needloom carpet; ~ **antistatique** *m* ORDINAT antistatic mat; ~ **asphaltique** *m* CONSTR asphalt surfacing; ~ **bouclé** *m* TEXTILE loop-pile carpet; ~ **de corde** *m* TEXTILE cord carpet; ~ **en grande largeur** *m* TEXTILE broadloom carpet; ~ **haircord** *m* TEXTILE haircord carpet; ~ **isolant** *m* ELECTR insulating mat; ~ **de mousse** *m* AERONAUT foam blanket; ~ **non tissé** *m* TEXTILE nonwoven carpet; ~ **roulant** *m* CONSTR conveyor, REVETEMENT enamelling line (AmE), enamelling line (BrE), TRANSPORT moving carpet, moving floor; ~ **roulant rapide** *m* TRANSPORT high-speed passenger conveyor; ~ **texturé** *m* TEXTILE textured carpet; ~ **tissé** *m* TEXTILE woven carpet; ~ **touffe** *m* TEXTILE tufted carpet

tapure *f* NUCLEAIRE capillary crack, hairline crack, PRODUCTION contraction crack, shrinkage crack

taque *f* PRODUCTION *de fonte* plate; ~ **d'assise** *f* CONSTR baseplate, foundation plate, sole plate; ~ **porte-pièce** *f* CONS MECA *machine-outils* workholding fixed table; ~ **de soubassement** *f* CONSTR baseplate

taquer *vt* IMPRIM jog

taquet *m* CONS MECA cleat, stop, tappet, CONSTR button, MINES catch, dog, prop, rest, NAUT cleat, lug, VEHICULES *moteur* cam following, *soupape de moteur* tappet; ~ **d'amarre** *m* NAUT mooring cleat; ~ **coinceur** *m* NAUT cam cleat, jam cleat; ~ **définissant un point d'un tableau** *m* IMPRIM *tableautage, composition* tab stop; ~ **de détente** *m* INST HYDR expansion cam; ~ **de front** *m* IMPRIM *machines* front guide; ~ **de tournage** *m* NAUT belaying cleat

taquets *m pl* MINES cage sheets, cage shuts, fangs, kep

taqueur *m* IMPRIM *rotatives, façonnage* kicker

tarage *m* MECANIQUE rating, PRODUCTION calibration, *système hydraulique* pressure setting; ~ **d'un ressort** *m* METROLOGIE scaling a spring

taraud *m* CONS MECA, MECANIQUE *outillage* tap; ~ **accrocheur** *m* MINES grabbing tap; ~ **aléseur** *m* CONS MECA reamer tap; ~ **conique** *m* PRODUCTION entering tap; ~ **cylindrique** *m* CONS MECA plug tap, straight tap, third tap; ~ **demi-conique** *m* CONS MECA plug tap, second tap; ~ **à denture interrompue** *m* CONS MECA interrupted tooth tap; ~ **à droite** *m* CONS MECA right-hand tap; ~ **ébaucheur** *m* PRODUCTION entering tap; ~ **à filet carré** *m* CONS MECA square thread tap; ~ **fileté Acme** *m* CONS MECA Acme thread tap; ~ **à filets rectifiés** *m* CONS MECA ground thread tap; ~ **finisseur** *m* CONS MECA bottoming tap, plug tap, straight tap, third tap; ~ **à gaz** *m* PRODUCTION gas tap; ~ **intermédiaire** *m* CONS MECA plug tap, second tap; ~ **à main** *m* PRODUCTION hand tap; ~ **matrice** *m* CONS MECA hob, hob tap, master tap; ~ **mère** *m* CONS MECA hob, hob tap, master tap; ~ **au pas métrique** *m* CONS MECA tap with metric thread; ~ **au pas Whitworth** *m* CONS MECA tap with Whitworth thread; ~ **pour fileter l'entretoise de chaudière** *m* CONS MECA boiler stay screwing tap; ~ **pour machine à queue longue** *m* CONS MECA long-shank top; ~ **pour machines** *m* CONS MECA machine tap; ~ **pour tuyauteries** *m* CONSTR pipe tap; ~ **à rainures hélicoïdales** *m* CONS MECA twist tap; ~ **sans rainures** *m* CONS MECA fluteless screwing tap

taraudage *m* CONS MECA screwing, tapping; ~ **des tuyaux** *m* CONSTR pipe screwing, pipe threading

tarauder *vt* CONS MECA screw, PRODUCTION tap

taraudeuse *f* CONS MECA screw machine, screwing and tapping machine, screwing machine, tapping machine, threader

tardif *adj* GEOLOGIE late, late-stage

tardimagmatique *adj* GEOLOGIE late-stage magmatic

tare *f* EMBALLAGE, TEXTILE tare

tarer *vt* CONS MECA measure, *ressort* scale

tarière *f* CHARBON auger, CONS MECA *perceuse* auger bit, CONSTR, MINES auger; ~ **à cuiller** *f* CONSTR spoon auger; ~ **à double spire** *f* CONS MECA screw auger; ~ **à glaise** *f* MINES earth auger, earth borer, mud bit, surface auger; ~ **rubanée** *f* CONS MECA screw auger; ~ **à tire-bouchon** *f* CONS MECA screw auger; ~ **torse** *f* CONS MECA screw auger; ~ **à vrille** *f* CONSTR gimlet

tarif *m* TELECOM tariff; ~ **d'accès** *m* TELECOM access charge rate; ~ **blanc** *m* TELECOM medium rate; ~ **bleu** *m* (Fra) TELECOM cheap call rate; ~ **bleu nuit** *m* (Fra) TELECOM cheap call; ~ **excursion avec achat anticipé** *m* AERONAUT APEX fare, advance purchase excursion fare; ~ **minimum** *m* TELECOM minimum charge; ~ **de nuit** *m* ELECTR *alimentation* night tariff; ~ **pour usages multiples** *m* ELECTR *alimentation* all-in tariff; ~ **de raccordement** *m* TELECOM initial connection charge; ~ **réduit** *m* TELECOM reduced rate; ~ **rouge** *m* (Fra) TELECOM peak rate; ~ **des terminaux** *m* TELECOM apparatus charge rate; ~ **du trafic** *m* TELECOM call charge rate; ~ **de transport pour marchandises** *m* EMBALLAGE freight rate

tarifer: ~ à *vt* TELECOM charge at

tarification *f* TELECOM call charge rate

tarir *vti* DISTRI EAU run dry, HYDROLOGIE dry up, run dry

tarissement *m* HYDROLOGIE drying up

tarmac *m* CONSTR tarmac, tarmacadam

tarmacadam *m* CONSTR tarmac, tarmacadam

tarnissure *f* MATERIAUX tarnishing

tartrate *m* CHIMIE tartrate

tartre *m* AGRO ALIM boiler scale, lime scale, CHIMIE tartar, INST HYDR boiler scale, LESSIVES boiler scale, scale, PRODUCTION fur, scale; ~ **brut** *m* CHIMIE argol

tartré *adj* CHIMIE tartrated

tartrifuge *m* PRODUCTION disincrustant

tartrique *adj* CHIMIE *acide* tartaric

tartronique *adj* CHIMIE tartronic

tartronylurée *f* CHIMIE tartronylurea

tas *m* CERAM VER (Bel) course, CONSTR heap, pile, INFORMAT, ORDINAT heap, PRODUCTION bottom die, bottom pallet, die, dolly, pallet for anvil; ~ **à bouteroller** *m* CONSTR rivet dolly, PRODUCTION dolly; ~ **de déblais** *m* CONSTR, RECYCLAGE waste heap; ~ **de déchets** *m*

CONSTR, RECYCLAGE waste heap; ~ **de grillage** *m* PRODUCTION open heap; ~ **inférieur** *m* PRODUCTION bottom die, bottom pallet, die, pallet for anvil; ~ **inférieur de l'empilage** *m* CERAM VER secondary checkers; ~ **à planer** *m* CONS MECA planishing stake; ~ **de rejets** *m* MINES dump heap, waste dump

tas-étampe *m* PRODUCTION swage block

tasmanite *f* MINERAUX tasmanite

tasseau *m* CONS MECA cleat, CONSTR strip, *de bois* cleat, MINES holing prop, *placé dans la sous-cave* punch prop; ~ **d'éjection** *m* CONS MECA spacer block; ~ **d'établi** *m* CONSTR bench stake; ~ **de fixation des glissières** *m* CONS MECA guide block, slide bar carrier, slide block

tassement *m* CHARBON settlement, CONSTR base failure, settlement, settling, GEOLOGIE compaction, MINES sinking, squeeze, squeezing, PRODUCTION draw, draw-down, sinking; ~ **différentiel** *m* CONSTR differential settlement; ~ **initial** *m* CHARBON initial settlement; ~ **des noirs** *m* TV black compression; ~ **primaire** *m* CHARBON primary settlement; ~ **secondaire** *m* CHARBON secondary settlement

tasser[1] *vt* MINES squeeze

tasser:[2] **se ~** *v réfl* MINES sink

tassomètre *m* GENIE CHIM settlement meter

tâtonner *vi* GEOMETRIE proceed by trial and error

tatronylurée *f* CHIMIE dialuric acid

taud *m* NAUT canopy, *de soleil* awning

tauon *m* PHYSIQUE tauon

Taureau *m* ASTRONOMIE Taurus, The Bull

Taurides *f pl* ASTRONOMIE Taurids

taurine *f* CHIMIE taurine

tauriscite *f* MINERAUX tauriscite

taurocholate *m* CHIMIE taurocholate

taurocholique *adj* CHIMIE taurocholic

tautomérie *f* CHIMIE tautomerism; ~ **céto-énolique** *f* CHIMIE keto-enol tautomerism

tautomérisation *f* CHIMIE tautomerization

taux *m* METROLOGIE rate, REFRIG ratio; ~ **d'aboutissement des appels** *m* TELECOM call success rate; ~ **d'abrasion** *m* MECANIQUE *matériaux* abrasion factor; ~ **d'accrétion** *m* ASTRONOMIE *de la masse* accretion rate; ~ **d'accrétion de la masse** *m* ASTRONOMIE mass accretion rate; ~ **d'activité** *m* ESPACE *communications* activity factor; ~ **d'appauvrissement en cations** *m* (*TAC*) POLLUTION cation denudation rate; ~ **d'appel des abonnés** *m* TELECOM subscriber calling rate; ~ **d'appels intempestifs** *m* TELECOM false calling rate; ~ **d'application** *m* CONSTR application rate, rate of spread; ~ **d'appoint** *m* CONS MECA make-up rate; ~ **d'attrition** *m* PRODUCTION shrinkage factor; ~ **d'audience** *m* TV rating; ~ **d'avancement** *m* CONSTR rate of progress; ~ **de bourrage** *m* TELECOM stuffing rate; ~ **de casse** *m* PAPIER, TEXTILE breakage rate; ~ **de cendres** *m* AGRO ALIM ash content; ~ **de changement d'air** *m* MAT CHAUFF rate of air change; ~ **de charge** *m* PETROLE capacity factor (AmE), load factor (BrE); ~ **de combustion** *m* NUCLEAIRE burnup fraction; ~ **de compression** *m* CONS MECA, REFRIG, VEHICULES *moteur* compression ratio; ~ **de comptage** *m* ELECTRON counting rate; ~ **de concentration** *m* CHARBON, EN RENOUV concentration ratio; ~ **constant** *m* TELECOM constant rate; ~ **de contre-réaction** *m* ELECTRON feedback ratio; ~ **de conversion** *m* POLLUTION transformation rate, TRANSPORT conversion degree; ~ **de cure** *m* CONSTR rate of curing; ~ **de décroissance** *m*

ACOUSTIQUE, TV decay rate; ~ **de défaillance** *m* ELEC-TROTEC, INFORMAT, ORDINAT, QUALITE, TELECOM failure rate; ~ **de défaillances instantanées** *m* QUALITE instantaneous failure rate; ~ **de défaut** *m* ELECTRON defect density; ~ **de dénudation des cations** *m (TDC)* POLLUTION cation denudation rate; ~ **de dépôt** *m* POLLUTION deposition rate; ~ **de désintégration** *m* PHYS RAYON decay rate; ~ **de désintégration radiative** *m* PHYS RAYON radiative decay rate; ~ **de désintégration radioactive** *m* PHYS RAYON radioactive decay rate; ~ **de dessiccation** *m* REFRIG desiccation ratio; ~ **de dilution** *m* AERONAUT *turboréacteur, turbosoufflante* bypass ratio; ~ **de disponibilité en énergie** *m* ELECTRO-TEC energy availability factor; ~ **d'écoute** *m* TV rating; ~ **d'efficacité** *m* PRODUCTION performance efficiency; ~ **d'efficacité de combustion** *m* THERMODYN combustion efficiency; ~ **d'élimination** *m* POLLUTION washout rate; ~ **d'élimination des cations** *m* POLLUTION cation denudation rate; ~ **d'élimination de la chaleur** *m* NUCLEAIRE *vitesse* heat rejection rate; ~ **d'ellipticité** *m* ESPACE axial ratio; ~ **d'émission le plus bas possible** *m* POLLUTION lowest achievable emission rate; ~ **d'épandage** *m* POLLU MER application rate; ~ **d'épuisement** *m* PETROLE depletion rate; ~ **d'érosion** *m* ESPACE *véhicules* erosion rate; ~ **d'erreurs** *m* ELECTRON, INFORMAT, ORDINAT, TELECOM error rate; ~ **d'erreurs binaires** *m (TEB)* ELECTRON, ORDINAT, TELECOM binary error rate, bit error rate *(BER)*; ~ **d'erreurs sur les bits** *m (TEB)* ELECTRON, ORDINAT, TELECOM binary error rate, bit error rate *(BER)*; ~ **d'erreurs sur les blocs** *m* ORDINAT block error rate; ~ **d'expansion** *m* GEOLOGIE *du plancher océanique* spreading rate; ~ **d'extinction** *m* TELECOM EX, extinction ratio; ~ **d'extraction** *m* AGRO ALIM extraction rate; ~ **de fautes de frappe** *m* INFORMAT keying error rate; ~ **de fluctuation** *m* ACOUSTIQUE flutter factor; ~ **de fuite** *m* NUCLEAIRE leak rate; ~ **d'harmoniques** *m* ELECTRON relative harmonic content; ~ **horaire au zénith** *m* ASTRONOMIE zenithal hourly rate; ~ **d'huile** *m* PLAST CAOU *résine alkyde, vernis* oil length; ~ **d'humidité** *m* DISTRI EAU moisture content; ~ **d'impulsion** *m* TV pulse rate factor; ~ **de l'insertion de la trame** *m* TEXTILE pick rate; ~ **d'Ionisation** *m* PHYS PART ionization rate; ~ **de lacet** *m* ESPACE *véhicules* yaw rate; ~ **de lavage** *m* POLLUTION washout rate; ~ **de mélange** *m* CONSTR mixing rate; ~ **de modulation** *m* ELECTRON percentage modulation, PHYSIQUE modulation depth, modulation factor; ~ **de montée** *m* AERONAUT rate of climb; ~ **de mouvements de fichier** *m* INFORMAT file activity ratio; ~ **de mouvements de fichiers** *m* ORDINAT file activity ratio; ~ **de mutilation** *m* ESPACE *communications* freeze-out fraction; ~ **de neutrons** *m* PHYS PART neutron yield; ~ **d'obéissance** *m* TRANSPORT degree of compliance, obedience level; ~ **d'occupation** *m* CONSTR occupancy rate; ~ **d'ondulation** *m* CONSTR ripple factor; ~ **de panne** *m* CONS MECA, TELECOM failure rate; ~ **de pénétration** *m* PETROLE ROP, rate of penetration; ~ **de perte métastable** *m* PHYS RAYON metastable loss rate; ~ **de plané** *m* AERONAUT glide ratio; ~ **de pleurage** *m* TV *son* flutter rate; ~ **de réaction** *m* COMMANDE feedback factor, feedback ratio; ~ **de réaction** *m* ELECTRON feedback ratio; ~ **de rebut** *m* PRODUCTION scrap factor, scrapping factor, shrinkage factor; ~ **de recombinaison** *m* PHYSIQUE recombination rate; ~ **de régulation** *m* COMMANDE regulation ratio; ~ **de remplissage** *m* REFRIG storage factor; ~ **de rencontre** *m* POLLU MER encounter rate; ~

de répétition des impulsions *m* PHYSIQUE PRR, pulse repetition rate; ~ **de restitution d'énergie** *m* METALL crack extension force; ~ **de rétroaction** *m* ELECTRON feedback ratio; ~ **de rotation** *m* PHYS FLUID swirl, PRODUCTION *stock* turnover; ~ **de rotation des stocks** *m* PRODUCTION inventory turnover, stock turnover; ~ **de saturation** *m* TRANSPORT load value; ~ **de sécurité** *m* CONSTR safety record; ~ **de siccité** *m* REFRIG dryness ratio; ~ **de soutirage** *m* HYDROLOGIE extraction rate; ~ **de transfert de chaleur** *m* MAT CHAUFF rate of heat transfer; ~ **de transfert thermique** *m* IMPRIM *refroidisseurs, rotatives* H-rate; ~ **de transformation** *m* POLLUTION transformation rate; ~ **de travail** *m* RESSORTS working stress; ~ **d'usure** *m* CONSTR wear rate, MECANIQUE *matériaux* abrasion factor; ~ **d'utilisation machine** *m* PRODUCTION machine utilization degree; ~ **de vapeur sèche** *m* CHAUFFAGE dryness fraction of steam, steam quality; ~ **de virage** *m* AERONAUT rate of turn

tavelure *f* AGRO ALIM scab, CERAM VER pocking

taxation *f* TELECOM charge rate

taxe *f* BREVETS fee, TELECOM charge; ~ **aéroportuaire** *f* AERONAUT airport charge; ~ **annuelle** *f* BREVETS renewal fee; ~ **forfaitaire** *f* BREVETS flat-rate fee

taxeur *m* TELECOM call accounting device

taxi: ~ **aérien** *m* AERONAUT air taxi; ~ **sans chauffeur** *m* TRANSPORT self-drive taxi

taximètre *m* NAUT pelorus

taylorite *f* MINERAUX taylorite

Tb *(terbium)* CHIMIE Tb *(terbium)*

Tc *(technétium)* CHIMIE Tc *(technetium)*

TD *abrév (traitement de données)* ELECTRON, INFORMAT, ORDINAT, TELECOM DP *(data processing)*

TDC *abrév (taux de dénudation des cations)* POLLUTION cation denudation rate

TdT *abrév (traitement de texte)* INFORMAT, ORDINAT WP *(word processing)*

Te *(tellure)* CHIMIE Te *(tellurium)*

té *m (T)* CONS MECA tee *(T)*; ~ **de commande de pas** *m* AERONAUT pitch change beam; ~ **de dessin** *m* CONS MECA T-square; ~ **double** *m* CONSTR cross; ~ **de raccordement** *m* CONS MECA T-connection

TEB *abrév (taux d'erreurs binaires, taux d'erreurs sur les bits)* ELECTRON, ORDINAT, TELECOM BER *(binary error rate, bit error rate)*

TEC:[1] *abrév (transistor à effet de champ)* ELECTRON, OPTIQUE, ORDINAT, PHYSIQUE FET *(field-effect transistor)*

TEC[2] ~ **à canal P** *m* ELECTRON p-channel FET; ~ **discret à canal N** *m* ELECTRON n-channel discrete FET; ~ **à enrichissement** *m* ELECTRON enhancement mode FET; ~ **à grille isolée** *m* ELECTRON IGFET, insulated gate FET; ~ **à hétérojonction** *m* ELECTRON heterojunction FET; ~ **intégré à canal P** *m* ELECTRON p-channel integrated FET; ~ **à jonction** *m* ELECTRON junction FET; ~ **à jonction intégré à canal P** *m* ELECTRON p-channel integrated junction FET

technétium *m (Tc)* CHIMIE technetium *(Tc)*

technicien *m* CONS MECA, PRODUCTION technician; ~ **en matériel thermique** *m* CONS MECA heating technician; ~ **méthodes** *m* CONS MECA methods engineer

technique *f* MECANIQUE engineering; ~ **d'affichage par électroluminescence à couches minces** *f* ELECTRON TFEL display technology; ~ **des afficheurs électroluminescents à couches minces** *f* ELECTRON TFEL display technology; ~ **aseptique** *f* SECURITE aseptic engineering; ~ **d'automatisme à coût réduit** *f* CONS MECA low cost automation technique; ~ **bipolaire** *f* ELECTRON bipolar technology; ~ **bipolaire fusionnée** *f* ELECTRON merged bipolar technology; ~ **du canal N** *f* ELECTRON n-channel technology; ~ **de codage à fréquence synchrone** *f* TELECOM SFET, synchronous frequency encoding technique; ~ **de combustion** *f* THERMODYN combustion engineering; ~ **de commande** *f* COMMANDE control technique; ~ **de commandes à distance** *f* COMMANDE remote control technique; ~ **de comparaison des épreuves progressives** *f* IMPRIM swatching-out; ~ **des composants à semi-conducteur** *f* ELECTRON semiconductor technology; ~ **de comptage par impulsions** *f* TELECOM *maritime mobile* pulse-counting technique; ~ **des couches épaisses** *f* ELECTRON thick-film technology; ~ **des couches minces** *f* ELECTRON thin-film technology; ~ **de datation 39-Ar/40-Ar par paliers de température** *f* GEOLOGIE Ar-Ar step heating method; ~ **de déblayage** *f* CONSTR digging technique; ~ **des dernières lueurs pulsées** *f* PHYS RAYON pulsed afterglow technique; ~ **de détachement de la feuille de son talon** *f* IMPRIM *continu* snap-out; ~ **de différence de teneur en métaux lourds** *f* NUCLEAIRE heavy metal difference technique; ~ **digitale** *f* MATERIAUX digital technique; ~ **de discrimination de phase** *f* ESSAIS phase discrimination technique; ~ **de dissymétrie de pont** *f* ESSAIS bridge unbalance technique; ~ **de distorsion préalable** *f* TELECOM predistortion technique; ~ **de distribution** *f* EMBALLAGE distribution technique; ~ **DMOS** *f* ELECTRON DMOS technology; ~ **d'élimination** *f* POLLU MER cleanup technique; ~ **à fibre optique** *f* ELECTROTEC fiberoptic technology (AmE), fibreoptic technology (BrE); ~ **de forage** *f* CONSTR digging technique; ~ **de frittage et d'infiltration** *f* GENIE CHIM sintering and infiltration technique; ~ **du froid** *f* AGRO ALIM refrigeration engineering; ~ **des fusées** *f* MILITAIRE rocketry; ~ **de gestion de la qualité** *f* QUALITE quality engineering; ~ **de la grille au silicium** *f* ELECTRON silicon gate technology; ~ **d'impulsion** *f* ESSAIS pulse technique; ~ **des jauges de déformation** *f* CONS MECA strain gage technique (AmE), strain gauge technique (BrE); ~ **de marquage** *f* NUCLEAIRE labeling technique (AmE), labelling technique (BrE); ~ **de mélange** *f* GENIE CHIM mixing technique; ~ **de métallisation sous vide** *f* GENIE CHIM vapor deposition technique (AmE), vapour deposition technique (BrE); ~ **minière** *f* MINES mining engineering; ~ **mixte** *f* ELECTRON mixed technology; ~ **MOS** *f* ELECTRON MOS technology, metal-oxide semiconductor technology; ~ **de nettoyage** *f* POLLU MER cleanup technique; ~ **de percement** *f* CONSTR tunnelling technique (AmE), tunnelling technique (BrE); ~ **de pointe** *f* CONSTR state-of-the-art technique; ~ **des réacteurs** *f* NUCLEAIRE reactor engineering; ~ **de rendez-vous** *f* TRANSPORT rendezvous maneuver (AmE), rendezvous manoeuvre (BrE); ~ **de rétrodiffusion** *f* OPTIQUE OTDR, backscattering technique, optical time domain reflectometry; ~ **sanitaire** *f* DISTRI EAU sanitary engineering; ~ **de séparation** *f* GENIE CHIM separation process; ~ **de la somme et de la différence** *f* ENREGISTR sum-and-difference technique; ~ **de stabilisation de la couleur** *f* IMPRIM *photogravure* achromatic color removal (AmE), achromatic colour removal (BrE); ~ **de télécommande** *f* COMMANDE remote control technique; ~ **de télétransmission** *f* COMMANDE remote transmission technique; ~ **de tir-**

age *f* PHOTO printing technique; ~ **de tressage** *f* TEXTILE braiding technique; ~ **du vide** *f* CONS MECA vacuum technology; ~ **de zone flottante** *f* NUCLEAIRE floating zone melting method

techniques: ~ **de couchage préréglé** *f pl* IMPRIM *papiers, films* premetered techniques (AmE), premetred techniques (BrE); ~ **de couchage à la racle** *f pl* IMPRIM flood and doctor techniques; ~ **cryogéniques** *f pl* THERMODYN low-temperature techniques; ~ **d'échantillonnage de l'air** *f pl* SECURITE air sampling techniques; ~ **d'ennoblissement** *f pl* TEXTILE finishing techniques; ~ **d'invasion** *f pl* PHYS RAYON invasive techniques; ~ **de soulèvement manuel** *f pl* SECURITE manual lifting techniques; ~ **de soulèvement manuel correct** *f pl* SECURITE correct manual lifting techniques

technologie *f* CONS MECA technology; ~ **biergol** *f* TRANSPORT *propulsion* bi-ergol technology; ~ **des couches épaisses** *f* ESPACE *véhicules* thick-film technology; ~ **du décapage chimique** *f* NUCLEAIRE acid pickling technology; ~ **diergol** *f* ESPACE *propulsion* di-ergol technology; ~ **énergétique** *f* POLLUTION energy technology; ~ **des faisceaux de particules** *f* PHYS PART particle beam technology; ~ **des hyperfréquences** *f* ESPACE *véhicules* microwave technology; ~ **informatique** *f* ORDINAT computer technology; ~ **de manutention des matériaux en vrac** *f* CONS MECA bulk solids handling technology; ~ **de pointe** *f* INFORMAT, ORDINAT advanced technology; ~ **propre** *f* POLLUTION clean technology; ~ **des salles de transaction** *f* TELECOM dealer room technology; ~ **spatiale** *f* TRANSPORT space technology; ~ **des surgénérateurs** *f* NUCLEAIRE fast-breeder reactor technology

teck *m* NAUT teak

tectite *m* ASTRONOMIE tektite

tectogenèse *f* PETROLE tectogenesis

tectonique[1] *adj* GEOLOGIE, PETROLE tectonic

tectonique[2] *f* PETROLE tectonics; ~ **d'écoulement** *f* GEOLOGIE gravity gliding; ~ **d'entraînement** *f* GEOLOGIE gravity gliding; ~ **des plaques** *f* GEOLOGIE plate tectonics; ~ **de rifts** *f* GEOLOGIE rift tectonics; ~ **du sel** *f* GEOLOGIE salt tectonics; ~ **tangentielle** *f* GEOLOGIE tangential tectonics

Téflon *m* (MD) CHIMIE Teflon (TM); ~ **aluminisé** *m* (MD) ESPACE aluminized Teflon (TM)

teindre *vt* COULEURS dye, stain, PHOTO dye; ~ **avant tissage** *vt* TEXTILE yarn-dye; ~ **en colorants solides** *vt* COULEURS dye fast; ~ **en cramoisi** *vt* COULEURS crimson; ~ **en effet changeant** *vt* COULEURS shot-dye; ~ **en nuances foncées** *vt* COULEURS sadden; ~ **en pièce** *vt* TEXTILE dye in the piece; ~ **en pourpre** *vt* COULEURS purple; ~ **en vert** *vt* COULEURS green; ~ **légèrement** *vt* COULEURS tincture; ~ **au rouge turc** *vt* COULEURS dye turkey red; ~ **sous pression** *vt* TEXTILE dye under pressure

teint[1] *adj* COULEURS dyed; ~ **dans la masse** *adj* TEXTILE spun-dyed; ~ **en bourre** *adj* TEXTILE stock-dyed; ~ **en câble** *adj* TEXTILE tow-dyed; ~ **en gâteau** *adj* TEXTILE cake-dyed; ~ **en mèche** *adj* TEXTILE slubbing-dyed; ~ **en pièce** *adj* TEXTILE piece-dyed; ~ **en ruban** *adj* TEXTILE top-dyed; ~ **légèrement** *adj* COULEURS tinted; ~ **sur bobines** *adj* COULEURS cop-dyed; ~ **sur encolleuse** *adj* TEXTILE slasher-dyed

teint[2] *m* CHIMIE dye

teinte *f* COULEURS tinge, tint, tonality, IMPRIM shade, tint, tone, *parasite ou voile* tint, *photogravure* chroma,

PHOTO tint; ~ **claire** *f* COULEURS light tone; ~ **défec-tueuse** *f* COULEURS off-color shade (AmE), off-colour shade (BrE); ~ **dominante** *f* IMPRIM *photogravure, impression* hue; ~ **dominante restant égale tout au long du tirage** *f* IMPRIM *impression* hue consistency; ~ **légère** *f* CERAM VER tint; ~ **mélangée** *f* COULEURS secondary color (AmE), secondary colour (BrE); ~ **neutre** *f* COULEURS neutral tint; ~ **nuageuse** *f* COULEURS hum; ~ **propre** *f* COULEURS self-color (AmE), self-colour (BrE); ~ **sombre** *f* COULEURS dark tone; ~ **unie** *f* COULEURS plain color (AmE), plain colour (BrE), solid color (AmE), solid colour (BrE)

teinter *vt* COULEURS stain, tinge, tint

teinture:[1] ~ **solide** *adj* EMBALLAGE colorfast (AmE), colourfast (BrE)

teinture[2] *f* CHIMIE dye, COULEURS dyeing, tincture, TEXTILE dyeing, mock; ~ **avec addition de solvant** *f* COULEURS solvent dyeing; ~ **à bronzer** *f* COULEURS bronzing tincture; ~ **à la brosse** *f* COULEURS brush dyeing; ~ **aux colorants de cuve** *f* COULEURS vat dyeing; ~ **de comparaison** *f* COULEURS comparative dyeing; ~ **à l'eau** *f* COULEURS water stain; ~ **en autoclave** *f* COULEURS kettle dyeing; ~ **en bourre** *f* COULEURS loose dyeing; ~ **en boyau** *f* COULEURS rope dyeing; ~ **en continu** *f* COULEURS continuous dyeing; ~ **en cuve autoclave** *f* COULEURS pressure dyeing; ~ **en deux tons** *f* COULEURS two-tone dyeing; ~ **en écheveaux sous pression** *f* COULEURS pressure hank dyeing; ~ **en fil** *f* TEXTILE yarn dyeing; ~ **en rubans de peigné** *f* COULEURS top dyeing; ~ **de fond** *f* COULEURS bottom dyeing; ~ **au foulard** *f* TEXTILE pad dyeing; ~ **à froid** *f* COULEURS cold dyeing; ~ **hors-ton** *f* COULEURS off-shade dyeing; ~ **d'iode** *f* COULEURS tincture of iodine; ~ **au jigger** *f* COULEURS jig dyeing; ~ **mate** *f* COULEURS dead dyeing; ~ **au métachrome** *f* COULEURS metachrome dyeing, monochrome dyeing; ~ **au naphtol** *f* COULEURS naphthol dyeing; ~ **par foulardage** *f* COULEURS pad dyeing; ~ **par immersion** *f* COULEURS dip dyeing; ~ **partielle** *f* COULEURS localized dyeing; ~ **pigmentaire** *f* COULEURS pigment dyeing; ~ **pour bois** *f* COULEURS wood stain; ~ **pour caramel** *f* COULEURS browning, burnt sugar coloring (AmE), burnt sugar colouring (BrE), caramel, sugar dye; ~ **pour emballages** *f* COULEURS package dyeing; ~ **propre** *f* COULEURS self-shade; ~ **rose** *f* COULEURS pink coloration; ~ **sur barre à tourniquet** *f* COULEURS star dyeing; ~ **sur bobines** *f* COULEURS package dyeing; ~ **sur chaîne** *f* COULEURS warp dyeing; ~ **sur ensouple** *f* TEXTILE beam dyeing; ~ **sur fil** *f* COULEURS raw-stock dyeing; ~ **sur mèche de banc** *f* TEXTILE roving dyeing; ~ **sur mordançage** *f* PHOTO mordant dyeing; ~ **terne** *f* COULEURS dead dyeing; ~ **au tonneau** *f* COULEURS drum dyeing; ~ **uniforme** *f* COULEURS level dyeing, plain dyeing; ~ **à l'unisson** *f* TEXTILE level dyeing; ~ **vitale** *f* COULEURS vital stain

teinturerie *f* COULEURS dye room, dye shop, dyehouse

teinturier *m* COULEURS dyer, stainer; ~ **d'échantillons** *m* COULEURS swatch dyer; ~ **en laine** *m* COULEURS woollen dyer

tel: ~ **vu tel imprimé** *adj* (*WYSIWYG*) INFORMAT, ORDINAT what you see is what you get (*WYSIWYG*)

téléalarme *f* COMMANDE remote alarm

téléalerte *f* TELECOM reminder alarm service

téléalimentation *f* ELECTROTEC remote power supply

téléappel *m* TELECOM paging

télécabine *f* TRANSPORT passenger ropeway; ~ **à câble**

sans fin *f* TRANSPORT gondola cableway

télécarte *f* TELECOM phonecard, telephone card

téléchargeable *adj* INFORMAT, ORDINAT, TELECOM downloadable

téléchargement *m* INFORMAT, ORDINAT, TELECOM downloading, remote loading

télécharger *vt* INFORMAT, ORDINAT, TELECOM download

télécinéma *m* TV film pick-up, film scanner, telecine, telecine machine

télécollecte *f* TELECOM electronic funds transfer

télécommande *f* CINEMAT remote control, COMMANDE remote control, telecontrol, CONSTR, ELECTR, MECANIQUE, PHOTO, TELECOM remote control; ~ **à infrarouge** *f* CONS MECA infrared remote control; ~ **à passerelle** *f* COMMANDE remote bridge control

télécommandé *adj* COMMANDE remote-controlled, TRANSPORT radio-controlled, TV remote-controlled

télécommunications *f pl* INFORMAT, ORDINAT, PHYSIQUE, TRANSPORT telecommunications; ~ **à l'échelle du globe** *f pl* TELECOM worldwide communications; ~ **optique** *f pl* TELECOM optical communications; ~ **par câble** *f pl* TELECOM cable communications; ~ **par faisceau laser** *f pl* ELECTRON laser communications; ~ **par satellite** *f pl* TELECOM satellite communications; ~ **spatiales** *f pl* TELECOM space communications

télécommutation *f* TV remote switching

téléconférence *f* ORDINAT, TELECOM teleconference, TV conference network

télécopie *f* TELECOM facsimile, fax; ~ **rapide** *f* TELECOM high-speed facsimile

télécopieur *m* INFORMAT, ORDINAT, TELECOM facsimile machine, fax, fax machine

télécouplage *m* COMMANDE remote control, remote-controlled switching

télédétection *f* COMMANDE remote detection, ESPACE, GEOLOGIE, ORDINAT, POLLU MER remote sensing, TELECOM remote detection; ~ **aéroportée** *f* POLLU MER airborne remote sensing

télédiffusion *f* ESPACE broadcasting, TELECOM broadcasting, television broadcasting, TV broadcasting; ~ **de paquets** *f* TELECOM packet broadcasting

télédistribution *f* TV cablecast, piped television, teledistribution, wired broadcasting

télédynamique *adj* CONS MECA teledynamic

télé-écriture *f* ORDINAT data communication, TELECOM telewriting

téléfilm *m* TV television film

téléflex *m* CONS MECA flexible control

télégestion *f* TELECOM remote management

télégramme: ~ **par câble** *m* ELECTROTEC cablegram

télégraphe: ~ **de menuisier** *m* CONSTR joiner's bevel

télégraphie: ~ **fac-similée** *f* TELECOM facsimile telegraphy

téléguidage: ~ **électrique** *m* TRANSPORT radio remote control

téléguider *vt* COMMANDE remote control

téléimprimeur *m* TELECOM TTY, teleprinter (BrE), teletype, teletypewriter (AmE); ~ **émetteur-récepteur** *m* ORDINAT ASR, automatic send-receive

téléinformatique *f* COMMANDE remote data processing, TELECOM remote data processing, teleinformatics

télélogiciel *m* INFORMAT, ORDINAT telesoftware

télémaintenance *f* ESPACE housekeeping, *communications* housekeeping telemetry, QUALITE housekeeping, housekeeping telemetry, TELECOM remote maintenance

télémanipulateur *m* OCEANO remote manipulator, remote operator; **~ universel** *m* NUCLEAIRE universal manipulator

télémarketing *m* TELECOM telemarketing

télématique *f* INFORMAT, ORDINAT data communication, TELECOM IT, information technology, telematic, telematics

télémécanique *f* CONS MECA telemechanics

télémécanisme *m* CONS MECA telemechanism

télémesure *f* ELECTR, ESPACE *communications*, MILITAIRE telemetry, NUCLEAIRE remote metering, telemetry, PHYSIQUE telemetry

télémesures: ~ de maintenance *f pl* ESPACE *véhicules* housekeeping telemetry

télémètre *m* CINEMAT distance meter, rangefinder, CONS MECA telemeter, ELECTRON rangefinder, MILITAIRE telemeter, *artillerie* rangefinder, NAUT distance finder, rangefinder, PHOTO rangefinder; **~ couplé avec l'objectif** *m* PHOTO coupled rangefinder; **~ laser** *m* ELECTRON laser rangefinder; **~ de nuages** *m* AERONAUT ceilometer, cloudbase measuring instrument; **~ optique** *m* PHOTO optical rangefinder; **~ de plafond** *m* AERONAUT ceilometer, cloudbase measuring instrument; **~ de plafond de nuages** *m* AERONAUT ceilometer; **~ radar** *m* MILITAIRE radar telemeter

télémétrie *f* CONS MECA telemetry, ELECTRON, ESPACE range finding, INFORMAT, ORDINAT, TELECOM telemetry; **~ inertielle** *f* ESPACE *communications* inertial sensing system; **~ laser** *f* TELECOM laser telemetry

télémétrographe *m* CONS MECA telemetrograph

téléobjectif *m* ASTRONOMIE lens, CINEMAT long-focus lens, telephoto lens, PHOTO telelens, telephoto lens, PHYSIQUE telephoto lens; **~ inversé** *m* CINEMAT retrofocus lens

télépaiement *m* TELECOM electronic funds transfer

télépéage *m* TRANSPORT toll payment

téléphérique *m* TRANSPORT cableway; **~ pour passagers** *m* TRANSPORT passenger ropeway

téléphone: ~ appelant *m* TELECOM calling telephone; **~ appelé** *m* TELECOM called telephone; **~ de cabine** *m* AERONAUT cabin telephone; **~ à cadran** *m* TELECOM dial telephone; **~ à clavier** *m* (Can) *(cf téléphone à touches)* TELECOM push-button telephone; **~ à poussoirs** *m* (Can) TELECOM key telephone set; **~ répondeur enregistreur** *m* TELECOM telephone answering machine; **~ sans fil** *m* TELECOM cordless telephone; **~ à touches** *m* *(cf téléphone à clavier)* TELECOM push-button telephone; **~ de voiture** *m* TRANSPORT car telephone

téléphoner: ~ à *vt* TELECOM call

téléphonie *f* INFORMAT, ORDINAT, PHYSIQUE telephony

téléphoniste *m* TELECOM operator, telephonist

téléprompteur *m* TV camera prompting system

téléréglage: ~ de caméra *m* TV CCU, camera control unit

télérégulé *adj* COMMANDE remote-controlled

téléréunion *f* TELECOM meet-me conference call

télérupteur *m* COMMANDE remote-controlled switch

télescopable *adj* CONS MECA collapsible

télescopage *m* CONS MECA telescoping

Télescope *m* ASTRONOMIE Telescopium

télescope *m* ASTRONOMIE, ESPACE telescope, INSTRUMENT reflector telescope, spyglass, telescope, PHYSIQUE telescope; **~ achromatique** *m* ASTRONOMIE achromatic telescope; **~ astronomique** *m* INSTRUMENT astronomical telescope; **~ Cassegrain** *m* ASTRONOMIE,

PHYSIQUE Cassegrain telescope; **~ détecteur à microrubans de silicium** *m* PHYS RAYON silicon microstrip detector telescope; **~ de Gregory** *m* PHYSIQUE Gregorian telescope; **~ infrarouge** *m* ASTRONOMIE infrared telescope; **~ infrarouge du Royaume-Uni** *m* *(UKIRT)* ASTRONOMIE UK Infrared Telescope *(UKIRT)*; **~ à lentilles** *m* INSTRUMENT refracting telescope, refractor, refractor telescope; **~ à miroir** *m* INSTRUMENT reflecting telescope, reflector telescope; **~ à miroir parabolique** *m* ASTRONOMIE parabolic mirror telescope; **~ monoculaire** *m* INSTRUMENT monocular telescope; **~ multimiroirs** *m* ASTRONOMIE multimirror telescope; **~ de Newton** *m* ASTRONOMIE, PHYSIQUE Newtonian telescope; **~ optique** *m* ASTRONOMIE, ESPACE optical telescope; **~ panoramique** *m* INSTRUMENT panoramic telescope; **~ protonique** *m* INSTRUMENT proton telescope; **~ à rayons X** *m* ASTRONOMIE X-ray telescope; **~ à réflecteur** *m* ASTRONOMIE reflecting telescope, INSTRUMENT reflecting telescope, reflector telescope, PHYSIQUE reflecting telescope; **~ à réflexion** *m* INSTRUMENT reflecting telescope, reflector telescope; **~ réversible** *m* INSTRUMENT transit telescope; **~ de Schmidt** *m* ASTRONOMIE Schmidt telescope; **~ solaire** *m* INSTRUMENT solar telescope; **~ spatial** *m* ASTRONOMIE space telescope; **~ spatial Hubble** *m* ASTRONOMIE Hubble space telescope; **~ à tour** *m* INSTRUMENT domeless telescope, tower telescope; **~ zénithal** *m* ESPACE zenith telescope

télescopique *adj* MECANIQUE telescopic

téléscripteur *m* INFORMAT, ORDINAT TTY, teletype, teletypewriter, TELECOM teleprinter (BrE), teletypewriter (AmE), telewriter; **~ émetteur-récepteur à clavier** *m* ORDINAT keyboard send-receive, teletype

téléservice *m* TELECOM teleservice

télésiège *m* TRANSPORT chair lift

téléski *m* TRANSPORT drag lift

télésouffleur *m* TV autocue, camera prompting system, prompter

téléspectateur *m* TELECOM television viewer, TV viewer

télésurveillance *f* COMMANDE remote control, TELECOM, TV remote monitoring

télésurveillé *adj* ESPACE unattended

télétest *m* INFORMAT, ORDINAT remote test

télétex *m* INFORMAT, ORDINAT teletex

Télétexte *m* (MD) INFORMAT, ORDINAT, TELECOM teletext (TM), TV broadcast videographics, teletext (TM)

téléthermomètre *m* THERMODYN remote temperature gage (AmE), remote temperature gauge (BrE)

téléthermométrie *f* THERMODYN remote temperature monitoring

télétraitement *m* INFORMAT teleprocessing; **~ de données** *m* COMMANDE remote data processing; **~ par lots** *m* COMMANDE remote batch control, INFORMAT, ORDINAT remote batch processing

télétransmission: ~ de données *f* COMMANDE remote data processing, remote data transmission

télétravail *m* ORDINAT telecommuting, TELECOM teleworking

télétype *m* INFORMAT, ORDINAT, TELECOM TTY, teletype

télévente *f* TELECOM telesales

téléviser *vt* TV telecast, televise

téléviseur *m* PHYSIQUE television receiver

télévision: ~ à balayage lent *f* TELECOM slow-scan television; **~ couleur** *f* TV color television (AmE), colour television (BrE); **~ à définition améliorée** *f* TV EDTV, extended definition television; **~ en circuit fermé** *f* TV

CCTV, closed-circuit television; **~ en noir et blanc** *f* TV black and white television; **~ expérimentale** *f* TV experimental television; **~ à haute définition** *f* *(TVHD)* TELECOM, TV high-definition television *(HDTV)*; **~ interactive** *f* TV interactive television; **~ numérique** *f* TV digital television; **~ à péage** *f* TELECOM pay television, TV pay TV; **~ à péage par câble** *f* TV pay cable; **~ projetée** *f* TV projection television; **~ sur grand écran** *f* TV projection television

télex *m* INFORMAT, ORDINAT, TELECOM telex

télex-plus *m* TELECOM telex-plus

tellurate *m* CHIMIE tellurate

tellure *m* *(Te)* CHIMIE tellurium *(Te)*; **~ auroplombifère** *m* MINERAUX black tellurium, foliated tellurium

tellureux *adj* CHIMIE tellurous

tellurhydrique *m* MINERAUX telluric ocher (AmE), telluric ochre (BrE)

tellurique *adj* ASTRONOMIE, CHIMIE, EN RENOUV telluric

tellurite *f* CHIMIE tellurite, MINERAUX telluric ocher (AmE), telluric ochre (BrE), tellurite

telluromètre *m* CONSTR tellurometer, ELECTR earth resistance meter (BrE), ground resistance meter (AmE)

tellurure *m* CHIMIE telluride

TEM *abrév (électromagnétique transverse)* ELECTROTEC TEM *(transverse electromagnetic)*

témoin *m* CERAM VER marker, MINES core, core sample, drill core, PLAST CAOU *essai* test specimen, VEHICULES *accessoire* pilot lamp (AmE), pilot light (BrE); **~ d'antenne** *m* TV line monitor; **~ de défaut** *m* PRODUCTION fault indicator; **~ de forçage** *m* PRODUCTION *automatisme industriel* forcing indicator; **~ de frein** *m* VEHICULES brake warning light; **~ de mise sous tension** *m* PRODUCTION *automatisme industriel* power indicator; **~ au néon** *m* ELECTR *lampe* neon glow lamp; **~ de pression d'huile** *m* AUTO oil pressure warning light; **~ de profondeur** *m* PRODUCTION *moulage en terre* depth gage (AmE), depth gauge (BrE); **~ de signalisation de détresse** *m* VEHICULES *accessoire de sécurité* hazard warning lights; **~ d'usure de plaquettes de frein** *m* AUTO brake lining wear indicator

tempérament *m* ACOUSTIQUE temperament; **~ égal** *m* ACOUSTIQUE equal temperament

température:[1] **à ~ contrôlée** *adj* THERMODYN temperature-controlled; **à ~ élevée** *adj* CHAUFFAGE, PHYSIQUE high-temperature

température[2] *f* PETROLE, PHYSIQUE, REFRIG, TEXTILE, THERMODYN temperature; **~ absolue** *f* AGRO ALIM absolute zero, CHIMIE absolute temperature, ESPACE *thermique* Kelvin temperature, PHYSIQUE, REFRIG absolute temperature, THERMODYN Kelvin temperature, absolute temperature; **~ ambiante** *f* EMBALLAGE, GAZ, MAT CHAUFF, METALL, METROLOGIE ambient temperature, PHYSIQUE, THERMODYN ambient temperature, room temperature; **~ ambiante normale** *f* REFRIG standard ambient temperature; **~ d'arrêt de fissuration** *f* METALL crack arrest temperature; **~ d'aspiration** *f* REFRIG suction temperature; **~ de blocage** *f* GEOLOGIE blocking temperature; **~ de Boyle-Mariotte** *f* PHYSIQUE Boyle temperature; **~ de bruit** *f* ELECTROTEC, ESPACE *communications* noise temperature; **~ de bruit du ciel** *f* ESPACE *communications* sky noise temperature; **~ de cabine** *f* AERONAUT cabin temperature; **~ Celsius** *f* PHYSIQUE Celsius temperature; **~ centrale maximale combustible** *f* NUCLEAIRE maximum fuel central temperature; **~ compensée** *f* THERMODYN offset temperature; **~ de congélation** *f* PHYSIQUE freezing

point; **~ contrôlée** *f* CHAUFFAGE controlled temperature; **~ de coulée** *f* MATERIAUX casting temperature; **~ de couleur** *f* CINEMAT Kelvin temperature, color temperature (AmE), colour temperature (BrE); **~ critique** *f* CHAUFFAGE, PETROLE, PHYSIQUE, REFRIG, THERMODYN critical temperature; **~ de cueillage** *f* CERAM VER gathering temperature; **~ de cuisson** *f* CERAM VER firing temperature; **~ de Curie** *f* PHYS RAYON, PHYSIQUE Curie temperature; **~ de Debye** *f* PHYSIQUE Debye temperature; **~ de décharge** *f* THERMODYN discharge temperature; **~ de détonation** *f* MINES detonating point, detonation temperature; **~ différentielle** *f* PETROLE differential temperature; **~ d'ébullition** *f* PLAST CAOU *d'un solvant* boiling point; **~ effective** *f* THERMODYN effective temperature; **~ d'Einstein** *f* PHYSIQUE Einstein temperature; **~ élevée** *f* PHYSIQUE high-temperature; **~ empirique** *f* THERMODYN empirical temperature; **~ en tête de puits** *f* EN RENOUV wellhead temperature; **~ d'entrée** *f* POLLUTION inlet temperature; **~ d'entrée d'air** *f* REFRIG entering air temperature; **~ en valeur Celsius** *f* PRODUCTION Celsius temperature; **~ équivalente de bruit** *f* ESPACE *communications* equivalent noise temperature; **~ d'évaporation** *f* REFRIG evaporating temperature; **~ excédentaire** *f* THERMODYN excess temperature; **~ externe de calcul** *f* MAT CHAUFF design outside temperature; **~ de façonnage** *f* EMBALLAGE forming temperature; **~ de fermeture** *f* GEOLOGIE blocking temperature; **~ de filament** *f* ELECTR *d'un tube* filament temperature; **~ de fléchissement** *f* CERAM VER sag point, self-sagging temperature; **~ de fluage** *f* CERAM VER flow point; **~ de fonctionnement** *f* AERONAUT, ESPACE *thermique*, REFRIG operating temperature; **~ de frittage** *f* GENIE CHIM sintering heat; **~ de fusion** *f* PHYSIQUE melting point, THERMODYN heat of fusion; **~ de fusion commençante** *f* REFRIG initial fusion temperature; **~ des gaz d'échappement** *f* AERONAUT exhaust gas temperature; **~ de la glace fondante** *f* PHYSIQUE ice point; **~ à la goulotte** *f* PETROLE *en tête de puits* flow line temperature; **~ de goutte** *f* CERAM VER gob temperature; **~ d'ignition** *f* THERMODYN *plasma* critical temperature; **~ inférieure de recuit** *f* CERAM VER lower annealing temperature; **~ d'inflammation** *f* AUTO flash point; **~ intérieure** *f* EMBALLAGE internal temperature; **~ intrinsèque** *f* ELECTRON intrinsic temperature; **~ d'inversion** *f* ELECTR *thermocouple*, PHYSIQUE inversion temperature; **~ Kelvin** *f* ESPACE, THERMODYN Kelvin temperature; **~ limite de la gaine** *f* NUCLEAIRE cladding temperature limit; **~ de Littleton** *f* CERAM VER Littleton softening point; **~ maximale de la gaine** *f* NUCLEAIRE PCT, peak cladding temperature; **~ de la mer** *f* NAUT sea temperature; **~ moyenne** *f* REFRIG average mean temperature; **~ de Néel** *f* ELECTR *antiferromagnétisme* Néel temperature, PHYSIQUE Néel point; **~ normale** *f* *(TPN)* PHYSIQUE standard temperature *(STP)*; **~ de la pièce** *f* PHYSIQUE room temperature; **~ au point de rosée** *f* CHAUFFAGE dew point, THERMODYN dew point temperature; **~ de pourriture** *f* EMBALLAGE decomposition temperature; **~ de ramollissement dilatométrique** *f* CERAM VER deformation point; **~ de rayonnement du corps noir** *f* PHYSIQUE black body temperature; **~ de référence** *f* METROLOGIE reference temperature, PETR standard temperature; **~ de refoulement** *f* REFRIG discharge temperature; **~ de repassage** *f* TEXTILE safe ironing temperature; **~ de saturation** *f* REFRIG saturation temperature; **~ de ser-**

vice *f* PRODUCTION operation temperature; ~ **solaire par couleur** *f* ASTRONOMIE sun's color temperature (AmE), sun's colour temperature (BrE); ~ **de sortie** *f* POLLUTION outlet temperature; ~ **de spin** *f* PHYSIQUE spin temperature; ~ **de stockage** *f* PRODUCTION storage temperature; ~ **supérieure à la normale** *f* THERMODYN excess temperature; ~ **supérieure de recuit** *f* CERAM VER upper annealing temperature; ~ **de la surface de la mer** *f* NAUT sea surface temperature; ~ **des surfaces accessibles au toucher** *f* SECURITE *machines* temperature of touchable surfaces; ~ **thermodynamique** *f* PHYSIQUE thermodynamic temperature, REFRIG absolute temperature, THERMODYN Kelvin temperature; ~ **au thermomètre mouillé** *f* CHAUFFAGE wet bulb temperature; ~ **au thermomètre sec** *f* CHAUFFAGE dry bulb temperature; ~ **de thermosoudage** *f* EMBALLAGE heat seal temperature; ~ **de transformation** *f* CERAM VER transformation point, transformation temperature; ~ **de transition** *f* METALL transition temperature, NUCLEAIRE transition point, transition temperature, PHYSIQUE, REFRIG transition temperature; ~ **de transition de rupture** *f* MECANIQUE *matériaux* brittle fracture transition temperature; ~ **de transition vitreuse** *f* MATERIAUX, PLAST CAOU glass transition temperature; ~ **de travail** *f* CERAM VER working temperature; ~ **de trouble** *f* LESSIVES cloud point; ~ **de tuyère** *f* AERONAUT jet pipe temperature; ~ **de vaporisation** *f* PHYSIQUE boiling point, REFRIG evaporating temperature; ~ **de vitrification** *f* CERAM VER maturing temperature; ~ **de zéro** *f* THERMODYN zero degrees

températures: ~ **maximales de la surface** *f pl* SECURITE surface temperature limits

tempête *f* METEO storm; ~ **centenaire** *f* PETROLE *exploitation en mer* hundred year storm; ~ **magnétique** *f* ASTRONOMIE geomagnetic storm, magnetic storm; ~ **de neige** *f* METEO snowstorm

tempo *m* ACOUSTIQUE tempo

temporisateur *m* INFORMAT, ORDINAT interval timer, PRODUCTION *automatisme industriel*, TELECOM timer; ~ **en cascade** *m* PRODUCTION *automatisme industriel* cascading timer; ~ **à mémoire au repos** *m* PRODUCTION *automatisme industriel* retentive timer-off day; ~ **à mémoire au travail** *m* PRODUCTION *automatisme industriel* retentive timer-on, retentive timer-on delay; ~ **non asservi** *m* PRODUCTION free-running timer; ~ **programmable** *m* ELECTRON PIT, programable interval timer (AmE), programmable interval timer (BrE); ~ **au repos** *m* PRODUCTION *automatisme industriel* timer-off delay; ~ **sans mémoire** *m* PRODUCTION *automatisme industriel* nonretentive timer; ~ **de supervision** *m* TELECOM *maritime mobile* supervisory timer; ~ **au travail** *m* PRODUCTION *automatisme industriel* timer-on delay

temporisation *f* ELECTRON time delay, ELECTROTEC delay, PRODUCTION *automatisme industriel* clock rate, TELECOM delay time, time delay, *maritime mobile* time-out; ~ **de décalage** *f* PRODUCTION *automatisme industriel* shift clock rate, shift clock register

temporisé: ~ **à 1** *adj* PRODUCTION pulse on; ~ **à 0** *adj* PRODUCTION pulse off

temporiser *vt* ELECTRON, ELECTROTEC delay

temps:[1] **en ~ réel** *adj* ELECTRON real-time; ~ **réel en ligne** *adj* INFORMAT, ORDINAT OLRT, on-line real-time

temps:[2] **en ~ réel** *adv* ELECTRON real-time

temps[3] *m* ACOUSTIQUE time, AUTO stroke, ELECTRON, ESPACE, INFORMAT, ORDINAT, PHYSIQUE time;

~ a ~ **d'aberration** *m* ASTRONOMIE light time; ~ **d'accélération** *m* ORDINAT acceleration time; ~ **d'accès** *m* ELECTROTEC access time, IMPRIM access time, read time, OPTIQUE, ORDINAT access time; ~ **d'acheminement** *m* PRODUCTION move time; ~ **d'acquisition de régime stable de synthétiseur** *m* TELECOM synthesizer settling time; ~ **d'addition ou de soustraction** *m* ORDINAT add-subtract time; ~ **d'aller** *m* TV forward stroke interval; ~ **alloué** *m* PRODUCTION standard time; ~ **anormal** *m* NAUT freak weather; ~ **d'antenne** *m* TV airtime, on-air time; ~ **apparent** *m* ASTRONOMIE *solaire* apparent time; ~ **d'approche** *m* AERONAUT approach time; ~ **d'arrêt** *m* INFORMAT fault time, MECANIQUE downtime, dwell time, ORDINAT downtime, fault time, PRODUCTION downtime; ~ **atomique** *m* ASTRONOMIE atomic time; ~ **d'attaque** *m* ENREGISTR attack time; ~ **d'attente** *m* INFORMAT, ORDINAT, latency, stand-by time, TELECOM, TV queueing time; ~ **d'avance** *m* ELECTRON lead time;

~ b ~ **beau-fixe** *m* NAUT settled weather; ~ **bloc** *m* AERONAUT block time, block-to-block time, ramp-to-ramp time; ~ **de blocage** *m* ELECTROTEC turn-off time; ~ **de bobinage** *m* CERAM VER running time; ~ **de bon fonctionnement** *m* ORDINAT uptime;

~ c ~ **civil du fuseau** *m* NAUT zone time; ~ **clair** *m* NAUT clear weather; ~ **codé** *m* ENREGISTR time code; ~ **de commutation** *m* ELECTROTEC switching time; ~ **de conditionnement** *m* MATERIAUX stabilization time; ~ **de connexion** *m* INFORMAT, ORDINAT connect time; ~ **de conservation** *m* ELECTROTEC *de l'information* retention time, storage time, *de la charge* storage time; ~ **de contact** *m* HYDROLOGIE *avec d'air* aeration time; ~ **de cuisson** *m* PLAST CAOU curing time; ~ **de cycle** *m* INFORMAT, ORDINAT cycle time, PRODUCTION lead time, service cycle;

~ d ~ **de déblocage** *m* ELECTRON, ELECTROTEC turn-on time; ~ **de décélération** *m* INFORMAT, ORDINAT deceleration time; ~ **de déclenchement** *m* PRODUCTION trip time; ~ **de décompression** *m* PETR decompression time; ~ **de décroissance** *m* ELECTRON decay rate, PHYSIQUE decay time, fall time, TV decay rate; ~ **de défaillance** *m* INFORMAT fault time; ~ **de défaillance non détectée** *m* NUCLEAIRE undetected failure time; ~ **de dégradation** *m* PETR decay time; ~ **de démarrage** *m* INFORMAT start time, TV preroll, preroll time; ~ **de déplacement** *m* PRODUCTION move time; ~ **de dépôt** *m* GENIE CHIM settling time, TELECOM submission time; ~ **de désaturation** *m* ELECTROTEC storage time; ~ **de descente** *m* ELECTRON decay time, fall time, INFORMAT, ORDINAT decay time, PHYSIQUE decay time, fall time; ~ **de descente d'impulsion** *m* ENREGISTR, TELECOM pulse decay time; ~ **de détente** *m* INST HYDR *de la vapeur* expansion duration, expansion period; ~ **différentiel** *m* ELECTRON differential time; ~ **de digestion** *m* HYDROLOGIE digestion time; ~ **disponible** *m* ORDINAT available time; ~ **de durcissement** *m* PLAST CAOU curing time;

~ e ~ **d'échappement** *m* AUTO exhaust stroke; ~ **d'échauffement** *m* MATERIAUX heating-up time; ~ **écoulé** *m* INFORMAT, ORDINAT elapsed time; ~ **d'écriture** *m* ELECTROTEC, INFORMAT, ORDINAT write time; ~ **effectif de congélation** *m* REFRIG effective freezing time; ~ **d'élévation** *m* PETR rise time; ~ **d'émission** *m* TELECOM airtime, on-air time; ~ **des éphémérides** *m* ASTRONOMIE ephemeris time; ~ **d'exécution** *m* INFORMAT execution time, PRODUCTION run-time; ~ d'exploitation *m* ORDINAT productive time; ~ **d'exposition avant assemblage** *m* PLAST CAOU *adhésifs* open assembly time; ~ **d'extinction** *m* ELECTRON decay time;

~ f ~ **fait** *m* NAUT settled weather; ~ **fixe** *m* NAUT settled weather; ~ **de fonctionnement** *m* AERONAUT flying time, PRODUCTION operating time;

~ g ~ **de garde** *m* ESPACE *communications* guard time; ~ **de garnissage des machines** *m* TEXTILE setup time; ~ **de gélatinisation** *m* EMBALLAGE gel time; ~ **de gélification** *m* PLAST CAOU gel time; ~ **de gravure** *m* ELECTRON writing time;

~ i ~ **d'immobilisation** *m* AERONAUT, INFORMAT downtime; ~ **imparti** *m* ORDINAT time-out; ~ **impropre** *m* PHYSIQUE *relativité* improper time; ~ **d'inactivité** *m* INFORMAT idle time; ~ **d'indisponibilité** *m* NUCLEAIRE downtime, outage time, unavailability time, TELECOM UAT, unavailable time; ~ **d'induction** *m* METALL induction period; ~ **d'instruction en double commande** *m* AERONAUT dual instruction time; ~ **d'intégration** *m* ELECTRON, ELECTROTEC integration time; ~ **interopération** *m* PRODUCTION interoperation time; ~ **interopératoire** *m* PRODUCTION interoperative time; ~ **d'intervention** *m* TELECOM out-of-service time; ~ **d'inversion** *m* TELECOM turnaround time; ~ **d'inversion de ligne** *m* INFORMAT, ORDINAT turnaround time;

~ l ~ **laiteux** *m* METEO white-out; ~ **de lancement** *m* ENREGISTR run-up time; ~ **de latence** *m* INFORMAT latency; ~ **de lecture** *m* INFORMAT, ORDINAT read time;

~ m ~ **machine** *m* INFORMAT, ORDINAT machine time, PRODUCTION run-time; ~ **de maintenance** *m* NUCLEAIRE turnaround time; ~ **de maintien** *m* ESPACE *communications* hangover time, hold time, INFORMAT, ORDINAT hold time, TELECOM hangover time; ~ **maniable** *m* NAUT moderate weather; ~ **de manipulation** *m* TEXTILE handling time; ~ **de manoeuvre** *m* COMMANDE response time; ~ **de manutention** *m* PRODUCTION move time; ~ **de marche** *m* TRANSPORT running time; ~ **de mémorisation** *m* ELECTRON decay time, ELECTROTEC storage time; ~ **de mise en attente** *m* TELECOM, TV queueing time; ~ **de mise en fonctionnement** *m* THERMODYN warm-up time; ~ **de mise en route** *m* PRODUCTION set up time; ~ **de mise à température** *m* THERMODYN heating time, heating-up curve, heating-up time; ~ **de mixage** *m* PETR mixing time; ~ **de montée** *m* AERONAUT *bang sonique*, CONSTR, ENREGISTR, INFORMAT, ORDINAT, PHYSIQUE rise time; ~ **de montée en vitesse** *m* PAPIER acceleration time; ~ **de montée du front d'impulsion** *m* TV leading-edge pulse time; ~ **de montée de la porteuse** *m* TELECOM transmitter turn-on time; ~ **mort** *m* INFORMAT, ORDINAT dead time, idle time, PETROLE downtime, PRODUCTION slack time, TV dead air, downtime; ~ **morts** *m pl* PETROLE *forage* lost time; ~ **moyen d'attente** *m* TRANSPORT average stopped time; ~ **moyen de bon fonctionnement** *m* ESPACE *qualité*, MECANIQUE, QUALITE mean time between failures; ~ **moyen entre pannes** *m* ELECTROTEC, INFORMAT, ORDINAT mean time between failures; ~ **moyen entre réparations** *m* ESPACE *qualité* MTBR, mean time between removals; ~ **moyen local** *m* NAUT local mean time; ~ **moyen de réparation** *m* ELECTROTEC, INFORMAT, ORDINAT MTTR, mean time to repair;

~ n ~ **nécessaire à une fonction pour opérer** *m* IMPRIM clearing time; ~ **nominal de congélation** *m* REFRIG nominal freezing time;

~ o ~ **d'obtention** *m* PRODUCTION lead time; ~ **d'obtention total** *m* PRODUCTION procurement lead time, replenishment lead time; ~ **d'obturation** *m* PHOTO shutter speed; ~ **d'occupation** *m* TELECOM holding time; ~ **opératoire** *m* PRODUCTION run-time; ~ **d'ouverture** *m* ELECTROTEC opening time;

~ p ~ **de panne** *m* AERONAUT downtime; ~ **de parcours** *m* CH DE FER journey time, TRANSPORT overall travel time; ~ **de parcours moyen** *m* TRANSPORT average journey time; ~ **par pièce** *m* PRODUCTION time per piece, time per unit; ~ **partagé** *m* INFORMAT, ORDINAT time sharing; ~ **partiel réalisé à ce jour** *m* PRODUCTION partial time to date; ~ **de passage** *m* TRANSPORT green period; ~ **passé** *m* PRODUCTION spent capacity; ~ **de pénétration de la chaleur** *m* THERMODYN heat penetration time; ~ **de perception-réaction** *m* TRANSPORT perception-reaction time, reaction time; ~ **de Planck** *m* ASTRONOMIE Planck time; ~ **de pose** *m* CINEMAT exposure duration, PHOTO exposure, exposure time; ~ **de positionnement** *m* INFORMAT setup time, OPTIQUE radial positioning time, seek time, ORDINAT setup time; ~ **de précalage** *m* IMPRIM make-ready time, *machines* lead time; ~ **de préparation** *m* AGRO ALIM bench time, PRODUCTION setup time; ~ **de prise** *m* PLAST CAOU *polymérisation* setting time; ~ **de prise d'antenne** *m* TV on-air time; ~ **productif** *m* INFORMAT productive time; ~ **de propagation** *m* ELECTRON circuit delay, gate delay, ESPACE *communications* propagation delay, travel time; ~ **de propagation entre boîtiers** *m* ELECTRON interchip signal delay; ~ **de propagation entre circuits** *m* ELECTRON intercircuit signal delay; ~ **de propagation de groupe** *m* ESPACE *communications* envelope delay, TELECOM group transmission delay; ~ **de propagation de groupe modal différentiel** *m* OPTIQUE, TELECOM differential mode delay, multimode group delay; ~ **de propagation par porte** *m* ELECTRON gate delay; ~ **de propagation de phase** *m* TV phase delay; ~ **de propagation des signaux entre boîtiers** *m* ELECTRON interchip signal delay; ~ **de propagation des signaux entre circuits** *m* ELECTRON intercircuit signal delay; ~ **propre** *m* PHYSIQUE proper time;

~ r ~ **de réaction** *m* TEXTILE lead time; ~ **de recherche** *m* INFORMAT, ORDINAT seek time; ~ **de recouvrement inverse** *m* ELECTRON reverse recovery time; ~ **de récupération** *m* ELECTRON dead time; ~ **de recyclage** *m* PHOTO recycling time; ~ **réel** *m* CINEMAT, INFORMAT, ORDINAT real-time; ~ **de réglage** *m* PRODUCTION setup time; ~ **de relâchement** *m* ELECTR *diélectrique* relaxation time, ELECTROTEC release time; ~ **de relaxation** *m* ELECTR *diélectrique*, METALL relaxation time; ~ **de remontée de la boue** *m* PETROLE *du fond jusqu'à la surface* lag time; ~ **de réparation** *m* INFORMAT, ORDINAT repair time; ~ **de réponse** *m* ELECTRON, INFORMAT, METROLOGIE, ORDINAT, TELECOM response time; ~ **de réponse à l'appel** *m* ELECTROTEC operate time; ~ **de réponse en température** *m* NUCLEAIRE temperature lag; ~ **de retard** *m* TELECOM delay time; ~ **de retardement** *m* DISTRI EAU lag; ~ **de retour** *m* ELECTR *relais* drop-out time, ENREGISTR release time; ~ **de retournement** *m* INFORMAT, ORDINAT turnaround time; ~ **de retour à zéro** *m* ELECTROTEC decay time; ~ **de réverbération** *m* ENREGISTR reverberation time; ~ **rude** *m* NAUT rough weather;

~ s ~ **de scrutation** *m* PRODUCTION *automatisme industriel* scan time; ~ **de scrutation des E/S** *m* PRODUCTION *automatisme industriel* I/O scan time; ~

de scrutation de programme *m* PRODUCTION *automatisme industriel* program scan time (AmE), programme scan time (BrE); **~ section** *m* PETR record time; **~ de sécurité** *m* PRODUCTION protection time; **~ de séjour** *m* CERAM VER, TEXTILE *dans un séchoir à rame* dwell time; **~ de serrage des freins** *m* TRANSPORT braking time; **~ de service** *m* TELECOM service time; **~ sidéral** *m* ASTRONOMIE, ESPACE *mesures* sidereal time; **~ sidéral local** *m* ASTRONOMIE Local Sidereal Time; **~ sidéral moyen de Greenwich** *m* ASTRONOMIE GMAT, Greenwich Mean Astronomical Time; **~ solaire moyen** *m* ESPACE *mesures* mean solar time; **~ solaire moyen de Greenwich** *m* PHYSIQUE Greenwich Mean Time; **~ de sonnerie** *m* TELECOM ringing period; **~ de stabilisation** *m* OPTIQUE stabilization time; **~ standard** *m* PRODUCTION standard time; **~ de stockage** *m* ELECTROTEC storage time; **~ de suppression** *m* PHYSIQUE decay time, fall time; **~ sûr** *m* NAUT settled weather; **~ t** **~ de traitement** *m* INFORMAT, ORDINAT processing time; **~ de trajet** *m* GEOPHYS travel time, PETR transit time; **~ de transfert** *m* PRODUCTION move time, transit time, transportation time; **~ de transfert d'un mot** *m* INFORMAT, ORDINAT word time; **~ de transit** *m* ELECTROTEC, NUCLEAIRE, PETR, PHYSIQUE transit time, PRODUCTION transit time, transportation time; **~ de transport** *m* PRODUCTION move time, transit time; **~ de travail cumulé** *m* PRODUCTION cumulative working time; **~ de travail quotidien** *m* PRODUCTION working time percentage; **~ u** **~ unitaire** *m* PRODUCTION time per piece, time per unit, unit time; **~ universel** *m* *(TU)* ASTRONOMIE, ESPACE *mesures* Universal Time *(UT)*; **~ universel coordonné** *m* TELECOM UTC, universal time coordinated; **~ utile de trame** *m* TV active field period; **~ utilisable** *m* INFORMAT uptime; **~ v** **~ variable** *m* PETR time variant; **~ de vert** *m* TRANSPORT green phase; **~ de vol** *m* AERONAUT flying time; **~ de vol en solo** *m* AERONAUT solo flight time; **~ de vol estimé** *m* AERONAUT estimated flight time

Temps: ~ atomique international *m* *(TAI)* ASTRONOMIE International Atomic Time *(IAT)*; **~ moyen de Greenwich** *m* *(TMG)* ESPACE, PHYSIQUE Greenwich Mean Time *(GMT)*

ténacité *f* CONS MECA stiffness, tenacity, toughness, MATERIAUX, METALL, PHYSIQUE, PLAST CAOU toughness, TEXTILE tenacity; **~ extrême** *f* CONS MECA ultimate strength; **~ au noeud** *f* TEXTILE knot strength; **~ de rupture** *f* PLAST CAOU fracture toughness

tenaille *f* CONSTR pincers, tongs, PRODUCTION nippers; **~ à bec recourbé** *f* PRODUCTION elbow tongs; **~ à cornières** *f* PRODUCTION elbow tongs; **~ à forger** *f* CONSTR smith's pliers; **~ de forgeron** *f* CONS MECA blacksmith's tongs; **~ pour boulons** *f* PRODUCTION bolt tongs; **~ à rails** *f* CH DE FER rail tongs; **~ à vis** *f* CONS MECA hand vice (BrE), hand vise (AmE)

tenailles *f pl* CONSTR pincers, tongs, PRODUCTION nippers; **~ coupantes** *f pl* CONSTR cutting nippers; **~ de mécanicien** *f pl* CONS MECA end nippers; **~ à mors coupants** *f pl* CONSTR cutting nippers

tendance *f* TEXTILE trend; **~ barométrique** *f* METEO barometrical variation; **~ à cabrer** *f* AERONAUT tail heaviness; **~ au flambage** *f* AERONAUT elastic instability; **~ géographique** *f* POLLUTION spatial trend; **~ au grillage** *f* PLAST CAOU *de caoutchouc* scorching tendency; **~ momostable** *f* ELECTROTEC sticking; **~ normale** *f* GEOLOGIE, PETROLE normal trend; **~ à piquer** *f* AERO-

NAUT nose heaviness; **~ de pression** *f* METEO pressure tendency; **~ spatiale** *f* POLLUTION spatial trend; **~ temporelle** *f* POLLUTION time trend

tendances *f pl* TEXTILE directions

tendard *m* MINES stretcher piece

tender:[1] **~ en arrière** *adv* CH DE FER *véhicules* smokestack first

tender[2] *m* CH DE FER *véhicules* tender

tendeur *m* CH DE FER wire strainer, CINEMAT tension roller, CONS MECA strainer, stretcher, take-up, tightener, PAPIER stretcher, tightener, VEHICULES *chaîne* tensioner; **~ articulé** *m* CONSTR *pour fils* devil's claw, lion's claw; **~ de chaîne** *m* PAPIER chain tightener, VEHICULES *transmission, motocyclette* chain tensioner; **~ de courroie** *m* AUTO belt idler; **~ de feutre** *m* PAPIER felt stretcher; **~ à pouce articulé** *m* CONSTR devil's claw, lion's claw; **~ de segments de piston** *m* VEHICULES *outil* piston ring clamp; **~ de toile** *m* PAPIER wire stretcher; **~ à vis** *m* CONS MECA screw tightener, straining screw, stretching screw, union screw

tendeurs: ~ de nipples *m pl* TRANSPORT bicycle nipple adjusters

tendon *m* NUCLEAIRE steel tendon, tendon

tendre[1] *adj* GEOLOGIE *couches* incompetent

tendre[2] *vt* CONS MECA *courroie* tighten, PAPIER, TEXTILE stretch

tendromètre *m* AGRO ALIM tenderometer

teneur *f* CHARBON assay grade, assay value, content, CONS MECA tenor, METALL content, MINES content, grade, tenor, PAPIER content, PLAST CAOU concentration, content, PRODUCTION grade; **~ calorifique** *f* THERMODYN thermal content; **~ en acide** *f* EMBALLAGE acid content; **~ en alcalis** *f* LESSIVES alkali content; **~ en alumine** *f* CHARBON alumina content; **~ en argent** *f* PHOTO silver content; **~ en argile** *f* CHARBON clay content; **~ en boue** *f* DISTRI EAU mud content; **~ en carbone** *f* MATERIAUX carbon content; **~ en cendres** *f* AGRO ALIM, PAPIER, PRODUCTION ash content; **~ en eau** *f* CHARBON water content, water ratio, CHIMIE moisture content, CONSTR moisture content, water content, DISTRI EAU, EMBALLAGE, ESSAIS moisture content, OPTIQUE water content, PAPIER *du papier* moisture content, PHYSIQUE water content, REFRIG moisture content; **~ en eau résiduelle** *f* OPTIQUE residual water content; **~ en gaz** *f* GAZ gas factor, THERMODYN gas content; **~ en gris** *f* IMPRIM *photogravure, impression* gray contents (AmE), grey contents (BrE); **~ en humidité** *f* AGRO ALIM, CHARBON, PHYSIQUE, TEXTILE moisture content; **~ en jus** *f* AGRO ALIM juice content; **~ en masse** *f* NUCLEAIRE mass fraction, weight fraction; **~ en matière organique** *f* HYDROLOGIE organic matter content; **~ en matière sèche** *f* PAPIER dry solids content; **~ en minerai** *f* MINES ore contents; **~ en paraffine** *f* REFRIG wax content; **~ en poussière** *f* POLLUTION dust content; **~ en produits solides** *f* IMPRIM *encres* solid content; **~ en sel** *f* OCEANO salt content; **~ en silice** *f* MINES *du minerai* silica content; **~ en soufre** *f* PETROLE sulfur content (AmE), sulphur content (BrE); **~ en substances nutritives** *f* AGRO ALIM nutrient content; **~ isotopique** *f* NUCLEAIRE isotopic abundance; **~ limite** *f* CHARBON cutoff grade; **~ maximale des émissions** *f* POLLUTION maximum emission concentration; **~ moyenne** *f* MINES medium grade; **~ nominale** *f* IMPRIM nominal content; **~ oléfinique** *f* CHIMIE olefinic content; **~ optimale de l'eau** *f* CONSTR optimum moisture content; **~ optimum**

en eau *f* CONSTR optimum moisture content; ~ **de rejet** *f* NUCLEAIRE *d'une cascade* enrichment tails, tail assay

teneurmètre: ~ **d'eau schlammeuse de minerais à rayons gamma** *m* NUCLEAIRE gamma ore pulp content meter; ~ **en béryllium** *m* NUCLEAIRE beryllium content meter

tenir[1] *vt* CONS MECA carry, hold up, support; ~ **compte de** *vt* METROLOGIE make allowance for

tenir:[2] ~ **la barre** *vi* NAUT steer; ~ **bon** *vi* PRODUCTION hold, hold fast; ~ **le coup** *vi* PRODUCTION hold up; ~ **ferme** *vi* PRODUCTION hold, hold fast

tennantite *f* MINERAUX tennantite

tenon *m* CONSTR tenon; ~ **bâtard** *m* CONSTR barefaced tenon; ~ **éhonté** *m* CONSTR barefaced tenon; ~ **épaulé** *m* CONSTR shouldered tenon; ~ **invisible** *m* CONSTR stub, stub tenon; ~ **passant** *m* CONSTR through-tenon; ~ **à rainure et languette** *m* CONSTR tongue-and-groove joint; ~ **simple d'extrémité de tige de piston** *m* CONS MECA rod-end plain eye

tenoneuse *f* CONS MECA tenoning machine; ~ **simple** *f* CONS MECA single end tenoning machine

tenons: ~ **d'entraînement** *m pl* CONS MECA *pour outils à queue cylindrique* driving tenons; ~ **à rotule d'extrémité de tige de piston** *m pl* CONS MECA rod-end spherical eyes

ténorite *f* MINERAUX tenorite

tenseur *m* CONS MECA strainer, stretcher, tightener, MATH tensor; ~ **de contraintes** *m* PHYSIQUE stress tensor; ~ **de déformation** *m* PHYSIQUE strain tensor

tensio-actif[1] *adj* CHIMIE surface-active

tensio-actif[2] *m* CHIMIE surfactant, wetting agent, LESSIVES surfactant, PHYSIQUE surface tension, surfactant

tensiomètre *m* EQUIP LAB *instrument* hydrostatic balance, surface tension meter, METROLOGIE strain gauge, OCEANO dynamometer, strain gage (AmE), strain gauge (BrE), tensiometer

tension:[1] **sous** ~ *adj* ELECTR live, *circuit* alive, energized, ELECTROTEC alive, energized, live, PHYSIQUE live; **à ~ directe ca/cc** *adj* PRODUCTION full voltage AC/DC

tension[2] *f* CHARBON stress, CONS MECA strain, tightening, *d'un ressort* tension, CONSTR stretching, ELECTR voltage, ELECTROTEC power, tension, voltage, INST HYDR pressure, PHYSIQUE tension, voltage, POLLU MER stress, TELECOM voltage, TEXTILE tension, VEHICULES *système électrique, allumage* voltage;

~ a ~ **d'accélération** *f* ELECTR *particules chargées*, ELECTROTEC accelerating voltage; ~ **accélératrice** *f* ELECTR *particules chargées*, ELECTROTEC accelerating voltage; ~ **active** *f* ELECTR *courant alternatif* active voltage, *potentiel* active potential, ELECTROTEC, PHYSIQUE active voltage; ~ **admissible** *f* ELECTROTEC permissible voltage; ~ **d'alimentation** *f* PHYSIQUE, PRODUCTION supply voltage; ~ **d'alimentation unique** *f* ELECTROTEC single supply voltage; ~ **alternative** *f* ELECTR, ELECTROTEC alternating voltage; ~ **d'amorçage** *f* ELECTROTEC breakdown voltage, firing voltage, PHYSIQUE, TELECOM breakdown voltage; ~ **de l'anode** *f* ELECTROTEC anode voltage; ~ **anodique** *f* ELECTROTEC anode voltage; ~ **d'appel** *f* ELECTROTEC operate voltage, pick-up voltage; ~ **appliquée** *f* ELECTR impressed voltage; ~ **appliquée à l'anode** *f* ELECTROTEC anode voltage; ~ **appliquée à l'entrée** *f* ELECTROTEC input voltage; ~ **d'arc** *f* ELECTR peak arc voltage; ~ **assignée** *f* ELECTR rated voltage; ~ **assignée d'un enroulement** *f* ELECTR rated voltage of a winding; ~ **d'avalanche** *f* ELECTR avalanche voltage;

~ b ~ **de la bande** *f* ENREGISTR, TV tape tension; ~ **de bruit** *f* ELECTROTEC noise voltage, random voltage;

~ c ~ **ca redressé double alternance** *f* PRODUCTION full-wave rectified AC voltage; ~ **de charge** *f* ELECTR *accumulateur* charging voltage; ~ **de chauffage** *f* ELECTROTEC heater voltage; ~ **de choc** *f* ELECTR, ELECTROTEC impulse voltage; ~ **de cisaillement** *f* PHYSIQUE shear stress; ~ **de claquage** *f* CONS MECA, ELECTR *diélectrique*, ELECTROTEC, PHYSIQUE breakdown voltage; ~ **de commande** *f* PRODUCTION control voltage; ~ **compensatrice** *f* ELECTR compensating voltage; ~ **composée** *f* ELECTR phase-to-phase voltage (BrE), *réseau triphasé* line-to-line voltage (AmE); ~ **constante** *f* ELECTR constant voltage; ~ **continue** *f* ELECTROTEC DC voltage; ~ **continue bas niveau** *f* ELECTR, PRODUCTION low-level DC voltage; ~ **continue à vide** *f* ELECTR no-load direct voltage; ~ **de contournement** *f* ELECTROTEC flashover voltage; ~ **de contournement sec** *f* ELECTR *arc* dry flashover voltage; ~ **de courroie de transmission** *f* CONS MECA belt tension; ~ **de courroie trapézoïdale** *f* CONS MECA V-belt tension; ~ **crénelée** *f* TV square wave voltage; ~ **de crête** *f* ELECTR *réseau* peak value, ELECTROTEC, PHYSIQUE, TV peak voltage; ~ **critique** *f* ELECTR, ELECTROTEC critical voltage;

~ d ~ **de déclenchement** *f* TV triggering voltage; ~ **de déplacement du point neutre** *f* ELECTR *réseau* neutral point displacement voltage; ~ **différentielle** *f* ELECTROTEC differential voltage; ~ **de diode** *f* ELECTRON diode voltage; ~ **directe** *f* ELECTR, PRODUCTION full voltage; ~ **disruptive** *f* ELECTR disruptive voltage, *diélectrique* breakdown voltage, ELECTROTEC breakdown voltage, disruptive voltage;

~ e ~ **d'échelon assignée** *f* ELECTR *transformateur* rated step voltage; ~ **d'échelon assignée maximale** *f* ELECTR *changeur de prise* maximum rated step voltage; ~ **d'échelon nominale** *f* ELECTR *transformateur* rated step voltage; ~ **d'éclatement** *f* ELECTR *arc* spark-over voltage; ~ **effective** *f* CONS MECA effective tension; ~ **efficace** *f* CHARBON effective stress, ELECTROTEC effective voltage; ~ **élévatrice** *f* TV booster voltage; ~ **en charge** *f* ELECTROTEC on-load voltage; ~ **en circuit fermé** *f* ELECTR on-load voltage, ELECTROTEC closed-circuit voltage; ~ **en circuit ouvert** *f* ELECTR, ELECTROTEC open circuit voltage; ~ **en dents de scie** *f* ELECTROTEC ramp voltage, sawtooth voltage, PHYSIQUE sawtooth voltage; ~ **en étoile** *f* ELECTR star voltage; ~ **en hexagone** *f* ELECTR hexagon voltage; ~ **en régime** *f* CONSTR *en volts* normal voltage; ~ **d'enroulement** *f* CINEMAT winding tension; ~ **d'entrée** *f* ELECTR, ELECTROTEC, PRODUCTION input voltage; ~ **à l'entrée** *f* ELECTR, ELECTROTEC, PRODUCTION input voltage; ~ **entre phases** *f* ELECTR *réseau* phase-to-phase voltage; ~ **d'entretien** *f* ELECTROTEC keep-alive voltage; ~ **d'essai** *f* ELECTR test voltage; ~ **étoilée** *f* ELECTR star voltage; ~ **d'excitation** *f* ELECTR *machine* field voltage; ~ **d'excitation d'alternateur** *f* ELECTR alternator field voltage; ~ **extérieure** *f* ELECTROTEC external voltage; ~ **d'extinction** *f* ELECTROTEC extinction potential;

~ f ~ **du faisceau électronique** *f* TV electron beam voltage; ~ **de fonctionnement** *f* ELECTR working voltage, *d'un réseau* operating voltage, ELECTROTEC operating voltage;

~ g ~ **de la gâchette** *f* ELECTROTEC gate voltage; ~ **de**

la grille *f* ELECTROTEC gate voltage; ~ **grille-source** *f* ELECTROTEC gate-to-source voltage;

~ h ~ **de Hall** *f* PHYSIQUE Hall voltage;

~ i ~ **d'impulsion** *f* ELECTR impulse voltage; ~ **d'induction** *f* ELECTROTEC induction voltage; ~ **induite** *f* ELECTR *transformateur* secondary voltage, *électromagnétisme* induced voltage, ELECTROTEC induction voltage, TELECOM induced voltage; ~ **initiale inverse** *f* ELECTR initial inverse voltage; ~ **instantanée** *f* ELECTR instantaneous voltage; ~ **interfaciale** *f* POLLU MER interfacial tension; ~ **inverse** *f* ELECTR, ELECTROTEC reverse voltage, PRODUCTION inverse voltage; ~ **d'isolement** *f* ELECTR, PRODUCTION insulation withstand voltage; ~ **d'isolement nominale** *f* ELECTR, PRODUCTION rated insulation voltage;

~ l ~ **de ligne** *f* ELECTR *réseau* line voltage, METALL line tension; ~ **linéaire** *f* ELECTROTEC linear voltage;

~ m ~ **maximale** *f* ELECTR maximum voltage; ~ **à mesurer** *f* ELECTR measured voltage; ~ **minimale** *f* ELECTR minimum voltage; ~ **de mode commun** *f* ELECTROTEC common mode voltage; ~ **moyenne** *f* ELECTROTEC medium voltage;

~ n ~ **négative** *f* ELECTROTEC negative voltage; ~ **négative en valeur relative** *f* ELECTROTEC relatively negative voltage; ~ **à niveau logique** *f* PRODUCTION *automatisme industriel* logic level voltage; ~ **de noeud** *f* ELECTR *circuit* nodal voltage; ~ **nominale** *f* ELECTR rated voltage, ELECTROTEC full voltage, rated voltage; ~ **nominale de court-circuit** *f* ELECTR *transformateur* impedance voltage at rated current; ~ **nominale d'un système** *f* ELECTR *d'un réseau* nominal voltage; ~ **non régulée** *f* ELECTROTEC unregulated voltage; ~ **normale** *f* CHARBON normal stress; ~ **nulle** *f* ELECTR, ELECTROTEC null voltage, zero voltage;

~ o ~ **d'ondulation** *f* ELECTRON ripple voltage; ~ **ondulée** *f* CONSTR ripple voltage;

~ p ~ **par rapport à la masse** *f* ELECTROTEC voltage to earth (BrE), voltage to ground (AmE); ~ **par rapport à la terre** *f* ELECTROTEC voltage to earth (BrE), voltage to ground (AmE); ~ **de phase** *f* ELECTR *réseau* phase voltage; ~ **phase-neutre** *f* ELECTR phase-to-neutral voltage (BrE), *réseau* line-to-neutral voltage (AmE); ~ **phase-terre** *f* ELECTR *réseau d'alimentation* line-to-earth voltage (BrE), line-to-ground voltage (AmE); ~ **de pliage** *f* PLAST CAOU bending stress; ~ **de pointe inverse** *f* ELECTR peak inverse voltage; ~ **de polarisation** *f* PHYSIQUE bias voltage; ~ **de polarisation d'électrode** *f* ELECTROTEC electrode bias voltage; ~ **positive en valeur relative** *f* ELECTROTEC relatively positive voltage; ~ **de préconsolidation** *f* CHARBON preconsolidation pressure; ~ **primaire** *f* ELECTR *d'un transformateur*, ELECTROTEC primary voltage;

~ q ~ **de quadrature** *f* ELECTR *circuit à courant alternatif* quadrature voltage; ~ **de quasi-crête** *f* TELECOM quasi-peak voltage;

~ r ~ **réactive** *f* ELECTR *circuit à courant alternatif*, PHYSIQUE reactive voltage; ~ **de réamorçage** *f* ELECTROTEC reignition voltage; ~ **de rebobinage** *f* CINEMAT, ENREGISTR rewind tension; ~ **de récupération** *f* TV booster voltage; ~ **redressée** *f* ELECTROTEC rectified voltage; ~ **de référence** *f* ELECTROTEC reference voltage; ~ **réfléchie** *f* ELECTROTEC reflected voltage; ~ **de réglage** *f* ELECTR adjusting voltage; ~ **régulée** *f* ELECTROTEC regulated voltage; ~ **de relâchement** *f* ELECTROTEC drop-out voltage; ~ **de repos** *f* EN RENOUV open circuit voltage; ~ **du réseau** *f* ELECTR

alimentation mains voltage (BrE), supply voltage (AmE), ELECTROTEC line voltage; ~ **résiduelle** *f* CONSTR residual stress; ~ **de rétablissement** *f* ELECTR *commutateur* recovery voltage; ~ **de retenue** *f* ENREGISTR back tension; ~ **de retombée** *f* ELECTROTEC drop-out voltage; ~ **de rétroaction** *f* ELECTROTEC feedback voltage; ~ **de ronflement** *f* ELECTROTEC hum voltage; ~ **de rupture** *f* ELECTROTEC disruptive voltage, interrupting voltage, kickback, PHYSIQUE breakdown voltage;

~ s ~ **de saturation** *f* ELECTROTEC saturation voltage; ~ **secondaire** *f* ELECTR *d'un transformateur*, ELECTROTEC secondary voltage; ~ **du secteur** *f* ELECTROTEC line voltage, mains voltage (BrE), supply voltage (AmE), TV mains voltage (BrE), supply voltage (AmE); ~ **de service** *f* ELECTR *d'un réseau*, ELECTROTEC operating voltage; ~ **de seuil** *f* ELECTROTEC threshold voltage, TV threshold voltage, tilt mixer; ~ **sinusoïdale** *f* ELECTROTEC, PHYSIQUE sinusoidal voltage; ~ **de sortie** *f* ELECTR, ELECTROTEC, TELECOM, TV output voltage; ~ **de sortie continue bas niveau** *f* PRODUCTION *automatisme industriel* low-level DC out; ~ **de sortie régulée** *f* ELECTROTEC regulated output voltage; ~ **de la source** *f* ELECTR open circuit voltage; ~ **superficielle** *f* CHARBON, CONSTR, PHYSIQUE, PLAST CAOU surface tension; ~ **de suppression** *f* TV blanking voltage; ~ **de surcharge** *f* ELECTR *circuit, appareil* overload voltage;

~ t ~ **de tenue** *f* ELECTR *installation* withstand voltage; ~ **transitoire** *f* ELECTR transient voltage;

~ u ~ **d'utilisation** *f* PRODUCTION operating voltage;

~ v ~ **de vapeur** *f* INST HYDR pressure, PETROLE vapor pressure (AmE), vapour pressure (BrE); ~ **à variation lente** *f* ELECTROTEC slowly varying voltage; ~ **du vent** *f* OCEANO wind stress; ~ **à vide** *f* ELECTROTEC open circuit voltage;

~ z ~ **de Zener** *f* PHYSIQUE Zener voltage

tensionneur *m* CONS MECA, PETR tensioner

tentative: ~ **d'appel** *f* TELECOM call attempt; ~ **d'appel répétée** *f* TELECOM repeated call attempt; ~ **automatique** *f* TELECOM automatic attempt; ~ **manuelle** *f* TELECOM manual attempt; ~ **de perturbation** *f* INFORMAT spoofing; ~ **de perturbation d'un système** *f* INFORMAT spoofing; ~ **de prise** *f* ORDINAT, TELECOM bid

tenthrède *f* AGRO ALIM saw fly

ténu *adj* PRODUCTION thin

tenue:[1] ~ **à la foudre** *adj* ELECTROTEC lightning-resistant

tenue[2] *f* CONS MECA hold-up; ~ **de cap** *f* AERONAUT heading hold; ~ **à la fatigue** *f* RESSORTS fatigue resistance; ~ **au feu** *f* PLAST CAOU fire resistance; ~ **de fichier** *f* INFORMAT, ORDINAT file maintenance; ~ **à la flexion** *f* TELECOM flexibility strength; ~ **au froid** *f* REFRIG chill proofing; ~ **à la mer** *f* NAUT seakeeping qualities; ~ **à la mer et au vent** *f* TRANSPORT wind and sea state capability handling; ~ **du papier** *f* IMPRIM paper substance; ~ **du plein** *f* OCEANO full-tide duration; ~ **de plongée** *f* NAUT wetsuit; ~ **à radiation** *f* TELECOM radiation hardness; ~ **de stationnaire** *f* AERONAUT hover control; ~ **à la traction** *f* TELECOM tensile strength; ~ **à la viscosité-température** *f* THERMODYN viscosity-temperature characteristics; ~ **au vol** *f* AERONAUT airworthiness

ténuité *f* PRODUCTION thinness

téphroïte *f* MINERAUX tephroite

téra- *préf* (T) METROLOGIE tera-(T)

téraoctet *m* OPTIQUE terabyte

terbium *m* (Tb) CHIMIE terbium (Tb)

térébenthène *m* CHIMIE terebenthene

térébenthine *f* CHIMIE, COULEURS, PLAST CAOU *pour peinture* turpentine

térébique *adj* CHIMIE *acide* terebic

téréphtalate *m* CHIMIE terephthalate

Tergal *m* (MD) NAUT Dacron (TM), Terylene (TM), PLAST CAOU Tergal (TM)

terme *m* INFORMAT, MATH, ORDINAT term; ~ **soustractif** *m* INFORMAT subtrahend

termes: ~ **du même ordre** *m pl* MATH terms of the same degree; ~ **spectraux** *m pl* PHYSIQUE spectral terms

terminaison *f* IMPRIM hairstroke, INFORMAT, ORDINAT termination; ~ **à broches** *f* PRODUCTION pin termination; ~ **de bus** *f* INFORMAT, ORDINAT bus terminator; ~ **de commutateur** *f* TELECOM ET, exchange termination; ~ **de conduit d'ordre inférieur** *f* TELECOM LPT, lower-order path termination; ~ **de conduit d'ordre supérieur** *f* TELECOM HPT, higher-order path termination; ~ **de ligne** *f* IMPRIM, TELECOM LT, line termination; ~ **numérique réseau** *f* TELECOM digital subscriber access unit; ~ **de réseau** *f* TELECOM NT, network termination; ~ **de réseau 1 pour le RNIS-LB** *f* TELECOM B-ISDN network termination 1, NT1-LB; ~ **de réseau 2 pour le RNIS-LB** *f* TELECOM B-ISDN network termination 2, NT2-LB; ~ **de réseau pour le RNIS-LB** *f* TELECOM B-ISDN network termination, NT-LB; ~ **de section de multiplexage** *f* TELECOM MST, multiplex section termination; ~ **de section de régénération** *f* TELECOM RST, regenerator section termination; ~ **de segment** *f* TELECOM segment terminator

terminal[1] *adj* GEOLOGIE late, late-stage

terminal[2] *m* AERONAUT, INFORMAT, ORDINAT, PETROLE, TELECOM, TRANSPORT terminal; ~ **AMRT** *m* ESPACE *communications* TDMA terminal; ~ **des bagages** *m* TRANSPORT baggage terminal; ~ **à bananes** *m* TRANSPORT banana handling terminal; ~ **de bord** *m* NAUT, TELECOM shipboard terminal; ~ **de commande** *m* TELECOM CT, control terminal; ~ **de concentration numérique des conversations** *m* TELECOM digital circuit multiplication equipment; ~ **à conteneurs** *m* TRANSPORT container terminal; ~ **de données** *m* INFORMAT, ORDINAT data terminal; ~ **de données prêt** *m* TELECOM data terminal ready; ~ **à écran** *m* TELECOM screen terminal; ~ **éloigné** *m* INFORMAT, ORDINAT remote terminal; ~ **en mode paquet** *m* INFORMAT, ORDINAT packet mode terminal; ~ **d'exploitation éloigné** *m* TELECOM remote operating terminal; ~ **de fibre optique** *m* TELECOM fiberoptic terminal device (AmE), fibreoptic terminal device (BrE); ~ **inactif** *m* INFORMAT, ORDINAT dormant terminal; ~ **intelligent** *m* INFORMAT, ORDINAT intelligent terminal, smart terminal; ~ **de liaison optique** *m* OPTIQUE fiberoptic terminal device (AmE), fibreoptic terminal device (BrE); ~ **de ligne** *m* TELECOM line terminal; ~ **de ligne plésiochrone** *m* TELECOM plesiosynchronous line terminal; ~ **muet** *m* INFORMAT, ORDINAT dumb terminal; ~ **de poche** *m* TELECOM hand-held terminal, pocket terminal; ~ **portatif** *m* NAUT portable terminal; ~ **pour conteneurs** *m* TRANSPORT container berth; ~ **de programmation portatif** *m* PRODUCTION *automatisme industriel* hand-held programmer; ~ **spécialisé travaux** *m* ORDINAT job oriented terminal; ~ **téléphonique** *m* TELECOM telephone terminal; ~ **de télétraitement** *m* INFORMAT, ORDINAT RBT, remote batch terminal; ~ **de traitement de données** *m* TELE-COM data terminal; ~ **de transmission de données** *m* INFORMAT, ORDINAT data communication terminal; ~ **vidéo** *m* INFORMAT, ORDINAT video terminal; ~ **de vidéotex** *m* TV viewdata terminal; ~ **virtuel** *m* INFORMAT, ORDINAT VT, virtual terminal; ~ **virtuel de réseau** *m* INFORMAT, ORDINAT NVT, network virtual terminal; ~ **voyageurs** *m* TRANSPORT passenger terminal

terminateur *m* ASTRONOMIE terminator

terminer: **se ~ en biseau** *v réfl* GEOLOGIE die out, wedge out

ternaire *adj* CHIMIE ternary

terne *adj* DISTRI EAU cloudy, MATERIAUX, TEXTILE dull, lusterless (AmE), lustreless (BrE)

ternissement *m* CERAM VER staining

ternitrate *m* CHIMIE ternitrate

terpadiène *m* CHIMIE terpadiene

terpène *m* CHIMIE terpene

terpénique *adj* CHIMIE terpenic

terpine *f* CHIMIE terpinol

terpinène *m* CHIMIE terpinene

terpinéol *m* CHIMIE terpineol

terpinol *m* CHIMIE terpin, terpinol

terpinolène *m* CHIMIE terpinolene

terpolymère *m* CHIMIE, PLAST CAOU *type de polymère* terpolymer

terrain *m* GEOLOGIE terrain, POLLUTION surface area; ~ **d'alluvions** *m* MINES placer ground; ~ **d'atterrissage de dégagement** *m* ESPACE *véhicules* alternate landing site; ~ **carbonifère** *m* MINES coal measures, coal-bearing rock; ~ **couvert de cratères** *m* ASTRONOMIE cratered terrain; ~ **encaissant** *m* MINES country rocks; ~ **d'essai** *m* VEHICULES test ground; ~ **ferme** *m* CONSTR firm ground, solid; ~ **graveleux** *m* CHARBON gravel; ~ **houiller** *m* MINES coal measures, coal-bearing rock; ~ **limoneux** *m* CHARBON silt; ~ **meuble** *m* CONSTR soft ground; ~ **pierreux** *m* CONSTR stony ground; ~ **plat** *m* CONSTR even ground; ~ **réhabilité** *m* POLLUTION reclaimed area; ~ **remis en valeur** *m* POLLUTION reclaimed area; ~ **de sable fin** *m* CHARBON fine sand; ~ **sablonneux** *m* CHARBON sand, sandy ground; ~ **de studio** *m* CINEMAT lot; ~ **uni** *m* CONSTR even ground

terrains: ~ **de couverture** *m pl* MINES overplacement, strippings; ~ **de dragage** *m pl* MINES dredging ground; ~ **de recouvrement** *m pl* MINES overplacement, strippings

terramycine *f* CHIMIE terramycin

terrane *m* GEOLOGIE terrane

terraplane *m* TRANSPORT terraplane

terrasse: ~ **de colature** *f* AERONAUT drainage terrace; ~ **continentale** *f* OCEANO continental terrace; ~ **de plage** *f* GEOLOGIE beach berm; ~ **de travertin** *f* GEOPHYS fiorite terrace, siliceous sinter terrace, sinter terrace

terrassement *m* CONSTR earthmoving, earthwork; ~ **en remblai** *m* CONSTR earthwork embankment, MINES embankment

terrasser *vt* CONSTR bank, *mur* bank up with earth, MINES bank up, dam, fill, pack, stow

terrasseur *m* CONSTR digging machine

terre:[1] **à ~** *adj* NAUT, PETROLE ashore, onshore

terre:[2] **à ~** *adv* NAUT ashore, onshore

terre[3] *f* CHARBON earth (BrE), ground (AmE), CONSTR brickearth, ELECTR *raccordement* earth (BrE), ground (AmE), ELECTROTEC earth (BrE), ground (AmE), protective conductor, NAUT land, PRODUCTION ground, loam, TELECOM earth (BrE), ground (AmE), VE-HICULES *système électrique* earth (BrE), ground

(AmE); ~ **d'alluvions aurifères** *f* MINES pay dirt; ~ **arable** *f* CHARBON topsoil; ~ **aurifère** *f* MINES pay dirt; ~ **à blanchir** *f* CERAM VER bleaching clay; ~ **à briques** *f* CONSTR brickearth; ~ **à cassettes** *f* CERAM VER saggar clay; ~ **cuite** *f* CERAM VER burnt earthenware, fired earthenware, terracotta; ~ **décolorante** *f* LESSIVES bleaching earth; ~ **à diatomées** *f* AGRO ALIM diatomaceous earth, GEOLOGIE diatomaceous earth, kieselguhr, HYDROLOGIE, REFRIG diatomaceous earth; ~ **forte** *f* CONSTR loam; ~ **à foulon** *f* CHIMIE smectite, GEOLOGIE *argile smectique* fuller's earth; ~ **grasse** *f* CONSTR loam; ~ **humus** *f* CONSTR topsoil; ~ **minérale** *f* CHARBON mineral soil; ~ **mobile** *f* CHARBON running ground, running soil; ~ **organique** *f* CHARBON organic soil; ~ **de pipe** *f* CONSTR pipe clay; ~ **à porcelaine** *f* CERAM VER china clay, porcelain clay; ~ **de signalisation** *f* TELECOM signal ground; ~ **sous le vent** *f* NAUT lee shore; ~ **végétale** *f* CONSTR humus, topsoil, GEOLOGIE loam; ~ **verte** *f* MINERAUX green earth

Terre: **de** ~ *adj* ESPACE terrestrial

terreau *m* CHIMIE humus; ~ **argileux** *m* CONSTR clay loam; ~ **sableux** *m* CONSTR sandy loam

terres: ~ **de couverture** *f pl* MINES strippings

terrestre *adj* ESPACE land, terrestrial

terrien *adj* ESPACE earth

terrigène *adj* GEOLOGIE terrigenous

terril *m* CONSTR dump site, MINES dump, slack heap, slag heap, spoil heap, tip heap (BrE)

terris *m* MINES dump site (AmE), dumping ground, tailings area, tip area (BrE)

terrou *m* MINES gas, pit gas

tertiaire *adj* GEOLOGIE tertiary

tertiobutylbenzène *m* CHIMIE tert-butylbenzene

tertre *m* CONSTR knoll

térylène *m* (MD) CHIMIE Terylene (TM)

tesla *m* (*T*) PHYSIQUE tesla (*T*)

tessélite *f* MINERAUX tesselite

tessou: ~ **de briques** *m* CONSTR hardcore

test *m* INFORMAT, ORDINAT test; ~ **de bits** *m* PRODUCTION *automatisme industriel* bit examining; ~ **déporté** *m* PRODUCTION *automatisme industriel* remote test; ~ **de diagnostic** *m* INFORMAT, ORDINAT diagnostic test; ~ **de diagnostic interne** *m* PRODUCTION *automatisme industriel* internal diagnostic test; ~ **d'étalonnage** *m* CINEMAT *bande d'essai pour cameraman* cinex strip; ~ **de floculation** *m* GENIE CHIM flocculation test; ~ **fonctionnel** *m* INFORMAT, ORDINAT functional test; ~ **d'humidité** *m* EMBALLAGE moisture test; ~ **d'injectivité** *m* PETROLE LOT, leak-off test; ~ **paramétrique** *m* TELECOM parametric test; ~ **de performance** *m* INFORMAT, ORDINAT benchmark; ~ **de recette** *m* TELECOM acceptance test; ~ **saute-mouton** *m* INFORMAT, ORDINAT leapfrog test; ~ **de signifiance** *m* MATH significance test; ~ **de signification** *m* INFORMAT, ORDINAT significance test; ~ **sur limites** *m* PRODUCTION *automatisme industriel* limit test; ~ **triangulaire** *m* AGRO ALIM triangle test; ~ **à "1"** *m* PRODUCTION *automatisme industriel* examine-on; ~ **à "O"** *m* PRODUCTION *automatisme industriel* examine-off;

testeur: ~ **de formation** *m* PETR formation tester

testudoculture *f* OCEANO turtle culture

têt *m* THERMODYN melting crucible; ~ **de coupellation** *m* CHIMIE cupel

tête *f* CINEMAT *d'un trépied* head, CONS MECA stub end, *d'un coin* head, *d'un rivet* head, *d'une dent d'engrenage* point, *de bielle* butt, CONSTR crutch key, *d'un pieu* head, *d'un gond* pintle, INFORMAT head, MECANIQUE *de piston* crown, MINES apex, *de pilon de bocard* boss, NUCLEAIRE *d'un assemblage combustible* top fitting, upper end fitting, ORDINAT head, PRODUCTION *d'un cabestan* drumhead, *d'un marteau* face, *d'un pilon* head, *d'une vis, d'un boulon, d'un clou* head, *d'un rivet* head, *d'un marteau* head; ~ **d'abattage** *f* MINES cutting head; ~ **d'accouplement de frein** *f* CH DE FER *véhicules* brake hose coupling head; ~ **d'actionnement** *f* PRODUCTION operating head; ~ **affleurante** *f* PRODUCTION flush head, flush operated; ~ **alignée** *f* ENREGISTR in-line head; ~ **d'allumeur** *f* AUTO distributor cap; ~ **d'application** *f* EMBALLAGE *pour étiquettes* applicator head; ~ **autodirectrice** *f* ESPACE *véhicules* homing head; ~ **d'avertisseur de givrage** *f* AERONAUT ice probe; ~ **d'axe** *f* CONS MECA driving head; ~ **basculante** *f* PHOTO pan and tilt head; ~ **à bascule** *f* CINEMAT cradle head; ~ **de bélier** *f* CONS MECA change hook; ~ **de bielle** *f* AUTO big end, connecting rod big end, CONS MECA connecting rod big end, connecting rod end, end of connecting rod, large end of connecting rod, pitman head, VEHICULES big end; ~ **de bielle à cage fermée** *f* CONS MECA box connecting rod end; ~ **de bielle à chape** *f* CONS MECA strap connecting rod end; ~ **de bielle à fourche** *f* CONS MECA fork head; ~ **de boulon** *f* CONS MECA, MECANIQUE bolthead; ~ **de câble** *f* CINEMAT cable terminal box, ELECTROTEC cable head; ~ **de cavottier** *f* CONSTR cutter head; ~ **chercheuse** *f* MILITAIRE homing device, TV scanning head; ~ **de cheval** *f* CONS MECA quadrant, quadrant plate, *d'un tour à fileter* swing frame, tangent plate; ~ **de la comète** *f* ASTRONOMIE *chevelure, noyau* comet's head; ~ **de contrôle** *f* ENREGISTR monitor head; ~ **couleur** *f* CINEMAT *tireuse*, PHOTO color head (AmE), colour head (BrE); ~ **coup-de-poing** *f* PRODUCTION mushroom head; ~ **de coupe** *f* CONSTR cutter head; ~ **à crosse** *f* PRODUCTION knob lever operator; ~ **de détection de givrage** *f* AERONAUT ice probe; ~ **du diamant** *f* CERAM VER block; ~ **de direction** *f* VEHICULES steering head; ~ **double de percussion** *f* CONS MECA dual discharge head; ~ **d'éclairement** *f* PHOTO lamphousing; ~ **d'écrémage** *f* POLLU MER skimming head; ~ **d'écriture** *f* INFORMAT, ORDINAT write head; ~ **d'effacement** *f* ENREGISTR, INFORMAT, ORDINAT erase head, TV erase head, erasing head; ~ **d'effacement à double entrefer** *f* ENREGISTR double gap erase head; ~ **d'effacement en courant continu** *f* ENREGISTR DC erase head; ~ **d'effacement à haute fréquence** *f* ENREGISTR HF erase head; ~ **d'émulsionnage** *f* CINEMAT coating head; ~ **en anneau** *f* ENREGISTR ring head; ~ **à encoche** *f* PRODUCTION coin slot operator; ~ **en ferrite** *f* ENREGISTR, TV ferrite head; ~ **d'enregistrement** *f* ENREGISTR recording head, INFORMAT, ORDINAT record head, recording head, TV recording head; ~ **d'enregistrement et de lecture** *f* ENREGISTR record-playback head; ~ **d'enregistrement et de reproduction différée** *f* ENREGISTR record-playback head; ~ **d'éruption** *f* PETR Christmas tree, PETROLE wellhead; ~ **d'éruption en pleine eau** *f* PETROLE wet tree; ~ **d'extrusion** *f* CONS MECA extrusion head; ~ **de fissure** *f* METALL crack tip; ~ **fixe** *f* INFORMAT, ORDINAT fixed head; ~ **de flèche** *f* CONSTR arrowhead; ~ **fluide** *f* CINEMAT fluid head; ~ **à friction** *f* CONS MECA ratchet stop; ~ **du gisement** *f* MINES rock capping; ~ **à graver** *f* IMPRIM engraving head; ~ **gyroscopique** *f* CINEMAT gyroscopic head; ~ **de hache** *f* CONSTR ax head (AmE), axe head (BrE); ~ **hexagonale**

f MECANIQUE hexagon head; ~ **d'impression** *f* IMPRIM printing head, INFORMAT, ORDINAT print head, PAPIER printing head; ~ **d'injection** *f* PETROLE swivel; ~ **de lecture** *f* ACOUSTIQUE pick-up head, CINEMAT playback head, ENREGISTR replay head, IMPRIM scanning head, INFORMAT, OPTIQUE, ORDINAT read head, TV reproducing head; ~ **de lecture de disque** *f* OPTIQUE disc head (BrE), disk head (AmE); ~ **de lecture-écriture** *f* INFORMAT, OPTIQUE, ORDINAT read-write head; ~ **de lecture monophonique** *f* ACOUSTIQUE monophonic pick-up; ~ **de lecture optique** *f* CINEMAT optical sound head; ~ **de lecture stéréophonique** *f* ACOUSTIQUE stereophonic pick-up; ~ **de lettre** *f* IMPRIM letterhead; ~ **de ligne ferroviaire** *f* CONSTR railhead; ~ **magnétique** *f* ACOUSTIQUE, ENREGISTR, INFORMAT, ORDINAT, TV magnetic head; ~ **magnétique annulaire** *f* TV ring head; ~ **magnétique d'effacement** *f* ACOUSTIQUE erasing magnetic head, TV magnetic erasing head; ~ **magnétique encrassée** *f* TV clogged head; ~ **magnétique d'enregistrement** *f* ACOUSTIQUE recording magnetic head; ~ **magnétique de lecture** *f* ACOUSTIQUE reproducing magnetic head; ~ **magnétique mixte** *f* ACOUSTIQUE recording-reproducing magnetic head; ~ **magnétisée** *f* ENREGISTR magnetized head; ~ **de manche pilote** *f* AERONAUT control column boss; ~ **à manivelle** *f* CINEMAT cradle gear head, geared head; ~ **de marteau** *f* CONSTR beetle head; ~ **de mât** *f* NAUT masthead; ~ **de mesure** *f* MATERIAUX probe; ~ **mobile de convoyeur** *f* MINES conveyor drive; ~ **motrice** *f* MINES drive; ~ **nodale** *f* CINEMAT nodal head; ~ **optique** *f* OPTIQUE optical head; ~ **optique à laser** *f* OPTIQUE laser head, laser pick-up head; ~ **de palastre** *f* CONSTR *d'une serrure* selvage, selvedge; ~ **panoramique** *f* CINEMAT pan and tilt head; ~ **panoramique Moy** *f* CINEMAT Moy head; ~ **de perçage multiple** *f* CONS MECA multidrill head, multiple-spindle drilling head; ~ **perforante** *f* PAPIER puncture head; ~ **de pièce** *f* TEXTILE head-end; ~ **de pied** *f* PHOTO tripod head; ~ **de pieu** *f* CHARBON pile head; ~ **de pilon** *f* PRODUCTION stamp boss, stamp head; ~ **de piston** *f* AUTO piston head, CONS MECA slipper block, PRODUCTION crosshead of piston, VEHICULES *moteur* piston crown; ~ **de piston guidée par quatre glissières** *f* CONS MECA crosshead with 4-bar guide; ~ **plate trapézoïdale** *f* CONS MECA *rivet* pan head; ~ **porte-foret** *f* CONS MECA drill head; ~ **porte-fraise** *f* CONS MECA cutter head, milling head; ~ **porte-outil** *f* CONS MECA tool head; ~ **de production** *f* PETROLE wellhead; ~ **de production au sec** *f* PETROLE dry tree; ~ **de puits** *f* EN RENOUV, GAZ, PETR wellhead, PETROLE casing head, wellhead; ~ **de puits sous-marine** *f* PETROLE subsea wellhead; ~ **de raccordement au point de vente** *f* EMBALLAGE point of sale terminal; ~ **de radiographie** *f* INSTRUMENT X-ray head; ~ **de reproduction** *f* CINEMAT, TV playback head; ~ **de reproduction sonore optique** *f* ENREGISTR optical sound head; ~ **de rotor** *f* AERONAUT *hélicoptère* rotor head; ~ **du rotor** *f* AERONAUT *hélicoptère* spider unit; ~ **de rotor principal** *f* AERONAUT main rotor head; ~ **à rotule** *f* CINEMAT, PHOTO ball and socket head; ~ **de rubrique** *f* IMPRIM straddle; ~ **saillante** *f* CONS MECA raised head; ~ **de sécurité** *f* ESPACE *véhicules* safety unit; ~ **à six pans** *f* CONS MECA, MECANIQUE hexagon head; ~ **de sonde** *f* MINES swivel, swivel rod; ~ **sonore** *f* ENREGISTR audio head, TV sound head; ~ **de soufflage** *f* CERAM VER blow head; ~ **de soupape** *f* AUTO valve disc (BrE), valve disk (AmE), valve head; ~ **à tige à**

ressort *f* PRODUCTION wobble stick operating head; ~ **à tige à ressort en fil métallique** *f* PRODUCTION wire wobble stick head; ~ **à tige à ressort en nylon** *f* PRODUCTION wobble stick head; ~ **à tige souple à ressort** *f* PRODUCTION cat whisker head; ~ **de trépied** *f* CINEMAT tripod head; ~ **de tubage** *f* CONSTR casing head; ~ **de tube** *f* CONSTR casing head; ~ **de tube à vis** *f* CONS MECA screw casing head; ~ **de vérification d'enregistrement** *f* TV video confidence head; ~ **vidéo** *f* TV video head; ~ **vidéo rotative** *f* TV rotary video head; ~ **de vis** *f* CONS MECA screw head

têtes:[1] **à ~ multiples** *adj* TEXTILE multihead

têtes[2] *f pl* AGRO ALIM first runnings, fore-runnings; ~ **décalées** *f pl* ENREGISTR staggered heads; ~ **magnétiques décalées** *f pl* TV staggered heads; ~ **magnétiques empilées** *f pl* TV stacked heads

Téthys *m* GEOLOGIE Tethyan realm, Tethys Ocean

têtière *f* CONSTR selvage, selvedge, *d'une serrure* edge plate, IMPRIM *mise en page* head, NAUT head, headboard; ~ **d'un tableau sur plusieurs colonnes** *f* IMPRIM *composition* straddle

téton *m* CONS MECA tit, *d'une mèche à trois pointes d'un foret à téton* center point (AmE), centre point (BrE); ~ **d'assemblage** *m* MECANIQUE locating pin; ~ **de blocage** *m* CONS MECA locking stud; ~ **de centrage** *m* CONS MECA centering pin (AmE), centring pin (BrE), locating spigot, ELECTROTEC aligning plug; ~ **d'entraînement** *m* CINEMAT drive pin; ~ **de la filière** *m* CERAM VER nozzle

tétrabasique *adj* CHIMIE tetrabasic

tétraborate: ~ **de sodium** *m* LESSIVES borax

tétrabrométhane *m* CHIMIE tetrabromoethane

tétrabrométhylène *m* CHIMIE tetrabromoethylene

tétrabromure *m* CHIMIE tetrabromide

tétracarbonyle *m* CHIMIE tetracarbonyl

tétrachloréthane *m* CHIMIE tetrachlorethane, tetrachloroethane

tétrachloréthylène *m* CHIMIE tetrachloroethylene

tétrachlorométhane *m* CHIMIE tetrachloromethane

tétrachlorure *m* CHIMIE tetrachloride; ~ **de carbone** *m* CHIMIE carbon tetrachloride

tétracorde *f* ACOUSTIQUE tetrachord; ~ **diatonique** *f* ACOUSTIQUE diatonic tetrachord

tétradymite *f* MINERAUX tetradymite

tétraèdre[1] *adj* CHIMIE, GEOMETRIE tetrahedral

tétraèdre[2] *m* CRISTALL, GEOMETRIE tetrahedron; ~ **régulier** *m* GEOMETRIE regular tetrahedron

tétraédrique *adj* CHIMIE, CRISTALL tetrahedral

tétraédrite *f* MINERAUX tetrahedrite

tétraéthyle *m* CHIMIE tetraethyl

tétragone *m* GEOMETRIE tetragon

tétrahydrobenzène *m* CHIMIE tetrahydrobenzene

tétrahydroglyoxaline *f* CHIMIE tetrahydroglyoxaline

tétrahydronaphtalène *m* CHIMIE tetrahydronaphthalene, tetralin

tétrahydroquinone *f* CHIMIE tetrahydroquinone

tétrahydroxyquinone *f* CHIMIE tetrahydroxyquinone

tétraiodofluorescéine *f* CHIMIE tetraiodofluorescein

tétraline *f* CHIMIE tetrahydronaphthalene, tetralin

tétramère *adj* CHIMIE tetrameric

tétraméthyle *adj* CHIMIE tetramethyl

tétraméthylène *m* CHIMIE tetramethylene

tétramine *f* CHIMIE tetramine

tétranitrol *m* CHIMIE tetranitrol

tétrapack *m* (MD) AGRO ALIM tetrapak (TM)

tétraphonie *f* ACOUSTIQUE quadraphony

tétrapolaire *adj* ELECTR *générateur* four-polar, four-pole

tétrasulfide *m* CHIMIE tetrasulfide (AmE), tetrasulphide (BrE)

tétrathionique *adj* CHIMIE *acide* tetrathionic

tétratomicité *f* CHIMIE tetratomicity

tétravalence *f* CHIMIE quadrivalence, tetravalence, tetravalency

tétravalent *adj* CHIMIE quadrivalent, tetravalent

tétrazène *m* CHIMIE tetrazene

tétrazine *f* CHIMIE tetrazine

tétrazole *m* CHIMIE tetrazole

tétrode *f* ELECTRON, PHYSIQUE tetrode; **~ à gaz** *f* ELECTRON gas tetrode

tétrolique *adj* CHIMIE tetrolic

tétrose *m* CHIMIE tetrose

tétroxyde *m* CHIMIE tetroxide

tétryl *m* CHIMIE tetryl

têtu *m* CONSTR sledge, sledgehammer, PRODUCTION hammer

teugue *f* NAUT anchor deck

texasite *f* MINERAUX texasite

texte *m* INFORMAT, ORDINAT text; **~ en clair** *m* TELECOM clear text; **~ intégral** *m* INFORMAT, ORDINAT full text; **~ au kilomètre** *m* IMPRIM *non-formaté* text stream; **~ de message** *m* INFORMAT, ORDINAT message text

textiles: **~ de maison** *m pl* TEXTILE home textiles; **~ de production nationale** *m pl* TEXTILE home-produced textiles

texturage: **~ des moules** *m* CONS MECA mold texturing (AmE), mould texturing (BrE)

texture *f* GEOLOGIE fabric, PAPIER formation; **~ aérée du pain** *f* AGRO ALIM bread texture; **~ fibreuse** *f* CRISTALL fibrous texture, METALL fiber texture (AmE), fibre texture (BrE); **~ fluidale** *f* GEOLOGIE *roches magmatiques* fluidal structure, fluidal texture; **~ de la mie** *f* AGRO ALIM crumb texture; **~ sphérolitique** *f* GEOLOGIE, MATERIAUX spherulitic texture

TGD *abrév (transport à grande distance)* POLLUTION long-range transport

TGDPA *abrév (transport à grande distance des polluants aéroportés)* POLLUTION long-range transport of air pollutants, long-range transport of airborne pollutants

TGTB *abrév (très gros transporteur de brut)* PETROLE VLCC *(very large crude carrier)*

TGV *abrév (train expérimental à grande vitesse, train à grande vitesse)* CH DE FER APT *(advanced passenger train)*, HST *(high-speed train)*

Th *(thorium)* CHIMIE Th *(thorium)*

thalassogène *adj* GEOLOGIE *marine* hydrogenous

thalleux *adj* CHIMIE thallous

thallique *adj* CHIMIE thallic

thallium *m (Tl)* CHIMIE thallium *(Tl)*

thalweg *m* CONSTR, GEOLOGIE talweg, thalweg

thébaïne *f* CHIMIE thebaine

théine *f* CHIMIE theine

thénardite *f* MINERAUX thenardite

théobromine *f* CHIMIE theobromine

théodolite *m* CONSTR, INSTRUMENT theodolite; **~ à boussole** *m* CONSTR surveyor's transit; **~ électronique et digital** *m* CONSTR electronic digital theodolite; **~ à lunette centrale** *m* CONSTR transit, transit theodolite; **~ à lunette centrée** *m* CONSTR transit, transit theodolite; **~ universel** *m* INSTRUMENT one second theodolite

théophylline *f* CHIMIE theophylline

théorème *m* PHYSIQUE theorem; **~ d'Ampère** *m* ELECTR Ampère's theorem, PHYSIQUE Ampère's law; **~ d'Ampère-Laplace** *m* ELECTR Ampère-Laplace theorem; **~ d'Archimède** *m* PHYSIQUE Archimedes' principle; **~ de Babinet** *m* PHYSIQUE Babinet's principle; **~ de Bernoulli** *m* PHYSIQUE Bernoulli's theorem; **~ de Carnot** *m* PHYSIQUE Carnot's theorem; **~ de compensation** *m* ELECTR, PHYSIQUE compensation theorem; **~ de Coulomb** *m* ELECTR *champ électrique*, PHYSIQUE Coulomb's theorem; **~ d'Earnshaw** *m* PHYSIQUE Earnshaw's theorem; **~ d'échantillonnage** *m* PETR sampling theorem; **~ de Gauss** *m* ELECTR *champ électrique* Gauss' theorem, PHYSIQUE Gauss' law, Gauss' theorem; **~ de la limite centrée** *m* MATH central limit theorem; **~ de Norton** *m* PHYSIQUE Norton's theorem; **~ de Pascal** *m* PHYSIQUE Pascal's principle; **~ PCT** *m* PHYSIQUE CPT theorem; **~ de Poynting** *m* PHYSIQUE Poynting's theorem; **~ de Pythagore** *m* GEOMETRIE Pythagoras' theorem; **~ de réciprocité** *m* ELECTROTEC, PHYSIQUE reciprocity theorem; **~ de Thévenin** *m* PHYSIQUE Thévenin's theorem; **~ du viriel** *m* PHYSIQUE virial theorem

théorie *f* PHYSIQUE theory; **~ d'Abbé** *f* PHYSIQUE *de la formation des images* Abbé theory; **~ additive de couleur** *f* IMPRIM additive color theory (AmE), additive colour theory (BrE); **~ des bandes** *f* PHYSIQUE band theory; **~ des bandes d'état solide** *f* PHYS RAYON band theory of solids; **~ BCS** *f* ELECTRON, PHYSIQUE BCS theory, Bardeen-Cooper-Schrieffer theory; **~ de Bjernim de l'association des ions** *f* PHYS RAYON Bjernim association theory of ions; **~ du champ ligand** *f* CHIMIE ligand field theory; **~ du chaos** *f* MATH chaos theory; **~ de choc d'élargissement des raies** *f* PHYS RAYON *raies spectrales* impact theory of line broadening; **~ cinétique du gaz** *f* PHYSIQUE kinetic theory; **~ des circuits** *f* ELECTROTEC circuit theory; **~ de codage** *f* INFORMAT, ORDINAT coding theory; **~ de la communication** *f* INFORMAT, ORDINAT communication theory; **~ de la commutation** *f* INFORMAT, ORDINAT switching theory; **~ de la décision** *f* MATH decision theory; **~ de Deybe-Hückel** *f* CHIMIE Deybe-Hückel theory; **~ des écoulements laminaires** *f* PHYS FLUID laminar flow theory; **~ électrofaible** *f* PHYS PART electroweak theory, particle beam technology, PHYSIQUE electroweak theory; **~ électronique des métaux** *f* PHYS RAYON electron theory of metals; **~ des ensembles** *f* MATH set theory; **~ d'explosion cosmogonique initiale** *f* PHYSIQUE Big Bang Theory; **~ d'explosion cosmogonique primitive** *f* PHYSIQUE Big Bang Theory; **~ des files d'attente** *f* INFORMAT, ORDINAT queueing theory; **~ floue** *f* ORDINAT fuzzy theory; **~ de grande unification** *f* PHYS PART, PHYSIQUE GUT, grand unified theory; **~ graphique** *f* MATH graph theory; **~ des groupes** *f* MATH group theory; **~ de l'information** *f* ELECTRON, INFORMAT, ORDINAT information theory; **~ des jeux** *f* MATH game theory; **~ des noeuds** *f* GEOMETRIE knot theory; **~ des nombres** *f* MATH number theory, theory of numbers; **~ des nombres transcendants** *f* MATH theory of transcendental numbers; **~ ondulatoire de la lumière** *f* PHYS ONDES wave theory of light; **~ des ordinaux** *f* GEOMETRIE theory of ordinals; **~ des probabilités** *f* MATH probability theory; **~ des quanta** *f* CHIMIE, ESPACE, NUCLEAIRE, PHYS PART quantum theory; **~ quantique** *f* CHIMIE, PHYS PART quantum theory; **~ quantique de champ** *f* PHYSIQUE quantum field theory; **~ quantique de rayonnement** *f* PHYS RAYON quantum theory of radiation; ~ **du rayon effectif** *f* NUCLEAIRE theory of effective radius; ~ **de réinjection** *f* COMMANDE feedback theory; ~ **de la relativité générale** *f* ASTRONOMIE, PHYSIQUE general theory of relativity; ~ **de la relativité restreinte** *f* PHYSIQUE special theory; ~ **des réseaux** *f* ELECTROTEC network theory; ~ **de rétroaction** *f* COMMANDE feedback theory; ~ **de la séparation de Kynch** *f* NUCLEAIRE Kynch's separation theory; ~ **de Stokes** *f* PHYS FLUID Stokes' theory

théorique *adj* CHIMIE, PHYSIQUE theoretical

thérapie: ~ **infrarouge** *f* PHYS RAYON infrared therapy

théréphtalique *adj* CHIMIE terephthalic

thermal *adj* THERMODYN thermal

thermalisation: ~ **des neutrons** *f* PHYS RAYON neutron thermalization

thermaliser *vt* CHIMIE *eau* thermalize

thermicien *m* ESPACE *véhicules* heat transfer engineer, THERMODYN heat physicist

thermion *m* THERMODYN thermion

thermionique *adj* THERMODYN thermionic

thermique[1] *adj* PHYSIQUE, REFRIG thermal, THERMODYN thermal, thermic

thermique[2] *f* THERMODYN science of heat

thermiquement: ~ **conducteur** *adj* THERMODYN heat-conducting

thermistance *f* ELECTROTEC, PHYSIQUE, REFRIG, TELECOM thermistor

thermite *f* CHIMIE thermite

thermoanalyse *f* THERMODYN thermal analysis, thermoanalysis

thermobalance *f* CHIMIE thermobalance

thermochimie *f* CHIMIE thermochemistry

thermochimique *adj* MATERIAUX thermochemical

thermocline *f* OCEANO thermocline

thermocollable *adj* PAPIER heat-sealing, thermoforming

thermocollage *m* REVETEMENT heat sealing, THERMODYN thermal bonding

thermocolorimètre *m* CINEMAT *analyseur de couleur* color analyzer (AmE), color temperature meter (AmE), colour analyzer (BrE), colour temperature meter (BrE), kelvinometer, PHOTO color temperature meter (AmE), colour temperature meter (BrE)

thermoconducteur *adj* THERMODYN heat-conducting

thermoconductibilité *f* THERMODYN heat conductivity

thermoconductible *adj* THERMODYN heat-conducting

thermoconductivité: ~ **unitaire** *f* THERMODYN unit conductance

thermocontact *m* ELECTROTEC temperature-controlled switch, thermal switch

thermocouple *m* ELECTR *mesure*, EQUIP LAB *mesure de température*, NUCLEAIRE, PETROLE, PHYSIQUE, THERMODYN thermocouple; ~ **gainé** *m* NUCLEAIRE sheathed thermocouple

thermodiffusion *f* THERMODYN thermal diffusion, thermodiffusion

thermodurci *adj* PLAST CAOU thermoset, THERMODYN heat-hardened

thermodurcir *vt* THERMODYN heat harden

thermodurcissable *adj* CHIMIE, MECANIQUE *matériaux*, PLAST CAOU, THERMODYN thermosetting

thermodurcissant *adj* THERMODYN heat-setting

thermodurcissement *m* THERMODYN heat hardening, hot curing

thermodynamique[1] *adj* MATERIAUX, THERMODYN thermodynamic

thermodynamique[2] *f* CHIMIE, CONSTR, PHYSIQUE thermodynamics; ~ **appliquée** *f* CONS MECA applied thermodynamics; ~ **classique** *f* THERMODYN classic thermodynamics; ~ **linéaire** *f* THERMODYN linear thermodynamics

thermoélectricité *f* ELECTROTEC, PHYSIQUE thermoelectricity

thermoélectrique *adj* ELECTROTEC thermoelectrical, thermoelectric, PHYSIQUE, THERMODYN thermoelectric

thermofixage *m* TEXTILE heat setting, thermofixing

thermofixation *f* TEXTILE heat setting

thermofixer: ~ **à sec** *vt* TEXTILE dry-heat-set

thermoformage *m* GAZ thermoforming, THERMODYN heat forming; ~ **directement d'un rouleau** *m* EMBALLAGE thermoforming automatically from the reel

thermoformé *adj* THERMODYN heat-formed

thermoformer *vt* THERMODYN heat-form

thermoformeuse: ~ **sous vide** *f* EMBALLAGE vacuum thermoforming machine

thermofusible *adj* THERMODYN *matières plastiques* heat-fusible

thermogène *adj* THERMODYN calorific, heat-generating

thermographe *m* EQUIP LAB *enregistrement de températures* thermograph, thermohygrograph, NUCLEAIRE, PHYSIQUE, THERMODYN thermograph

thermographie *f* MILITAIRE, PHYS RAYON, THERMODYN thermal imaging

thermogravimétrie *f* PLAST CAOU *analyse* thermogravimetry, THERMODYN thermal gravimetric analysis

thermoguidé *adj* THERMODYN *missile* heat-seeking

thermoluminescence *f* PHYS RAYON, PHYSIQUE thermoluminescence, THERMODYN thermoluminescence, thermophosphorescence

thermoluminescent *adj* THERMODYN thermoluminescent

thermolyse *f* THERMODYN thermal decomposition, thermolysis

thermomagnétique *adj* THERMODYN thermomagnetic

thermomagnétisme *m* THERMODYN thermomagnetism

thermomètre *m* EQUIP LAB *instrument*, PHYSIQUE, REFRIG, THERMODYN thermometer; ~ **à alcool** *m* REFRIG alcohol thermometer; ~ **avertisseur** *m* CONS MECA alarm thermometer; ~ **de Beckmann** *m* PHYSIQUE Beckmann thermometer; ~ **à boule mouillée** *m* REFRIG, THERMODYN wet bulb thermometer; ~ **à boule sèche** *m* THERMODYN dry bulb thermometer; ~ **à cadran** *m* REFRIG dial thermometer; ~ **calorimétrique** *m* THERMODYN calorimetric thermometer; ~ **à cuvette** *m* PHOTO dish thermometer; ~ **de développement** *m* PHOTO developing tank thermometer; ~ **différentiel** *m* THERMODYN differential thermometer; ~ **à dilatation de gaz** *m* PHYSIQUE gas thermometer; ~ **à dilatation solide** *m* REFRIG solid expansion thermometer; ~ **à distance** *m* THERMODYN remote temperature gage (AmE), remote temperature gauge (BrE); ~ **enregistreur** *m* THERMODYN recording thermometer, thermograph; ~ **de fond** *m* PETR DWT, deep well thermometer; ~ **à gaz** *m* REFRIG gas thermometer; ~ **à lecture directe** *m* REFRIG indicating thermometer; ~ **à lecture à distance** *m* REFRIG remote reading thermometer; ~ **à liquide** *m* THERMODYN liquid thermometer; ~ **magnétique** *m* REFRIG magnetic thermometer; ~ **à maxima et minima** *m* EQUIP LAB *température*, THERMODYN maximum-minimum thermometer; ~ **à maximums et minimums** *m* CHAUFFAGE,

PHYSIQUE maximum-minimum thermometer; ~ à **mercure** m PHYSIQUE, REFRIG mercury thermometer; ~ **mouillé** m REFRIG, THERMODYN wet bulb thermometer; ~ **à réservoir mouillé** m THERMODYN wet bulb thermometer; ~ **à réservoir sec** m THERMODYN dry bulb thermometer; ~ **à résistance électrique** m PHYSIQUE, REFRIG resistance thermometer; ~ **à résistance de platine** m PHYSIQUE platinum resistance thermometer; ~ **sec** m CHAUFFAGE, REFRIG, THERMODYN dry bulb thermometer; ~ **à stockage thermique** m REFRIG thermal storage thermometer; ~ **à tension de vapeur** m REFRIG vapor pressure thermometer (AmE), vapour pressure thermometer (BrE); ~ **à thermocouples** m ELECTROTEC thermocouple thermometer

thermométrie f PHYSIQUE, THERMODYN thermometry
thermométrique adj THERMODYN thermometric
thermonatrite f MINERAUX thermonatrite
thermoneutralité f CHIMIE thermoneutrality
thermophone f ACOUSTIQUE thermophone
thermopile f ELECTROTEC, ESPACE énergie, PHYSIQUE thermopile
thermoplasticité f PLAST CAOU thermoplasticity
thermoplastique[1] adj MATERIAUX, MECANIQUE matériaux, NAUT, PLAST CAOU, TEXTILE thermoplastic
thermoplastique[2] m NAUT thermoplastic
thermoplongeur m CONS MECA, ELECTR chauffage, ELECTROTEC immersion heater, MECANIQUE heater, immersion heater
thermopompe f THERMODYN heat pump
thermopropulseur m AERONAUT thermal jet engine
thermorégulateur m COMMANDE temperature regulator
thermorégulation f ESPACE thermal control, MAT CHAUFF thermostat control
thermorésistant adj ESPACE heat-resistant, PETROLE thermostable
thermorétractable adj THERMODYN heat-shrinkable, shrinkable
thermorétracté adj THERMODYN heat-shrunk
thermorétréci adj THERMODYN heat-shrunk
thermorétrécir vt THERMODYN heat shrink
thermorétrécissable adj THERMODYN heat-shrinkable, shrinkable
thermorétrécissement m REVETEMENT, THERMODYN heat shrinking
thermoscellable adj THERMODYN heat-sealable
thermoscellage m REVETEMENT, THERMODYN heat sealing; ~ **par induction** m EMBALLAGE heat induction sealing
thermoscellé adj THERMODYN heat-sealed
thermosceller vt THERMODYN heat seal
thermoscelleuse: ~ **par induction** f EMBALLAGE induction sealer
thermosensible adj PLAST CAOU, THERMODYN heat-sensitive
thermosiphon m EN RENOUV thermosiphon
thermosoudable adj REVETEMENT heat-sealing, THERMODYN heat-sealable
thermosoudage m EMBALLAGE heat lamination, IMPRIM emballage thermosealing, REVETEMENT, THERMODYN heat sealing
thermosoudant adj THERMODYN matières plastiques heat-fusible
thermosoudé adj THERMODYN heat-sealed
thermosouder vt THERMODYN heat seal
thermosoudeur m EQUIP LAB sac en polyethylène heat seal apparatus

thermosoudeuse: ~ **sous vide** f EMBALLAGE vacuum heatsealer
thermosoudure f EMBALLAGE heat sealing, heat welding
thermosphère f GEOPHYS thermosphere
thermostabilisé adj THERMODYN heat-stabilized
thermostabilité f MATERIAUX thermostability
thermostable adj CHIMIE thermostable, THERMODYN heat-stable, temperature-stable, thermostable
thermostat m AUTO thermostat, COMMANDE heat valve, thermoregulator, thermostat, CONSTR, ELECTR, EQUIP LAB, MAT CHAUFF, PHYSIQUE thermostat, PRODUCTION système hydraulique temperature switch, REFRIG, THERMODYN, VEHICULES refroidissement thermostat; ~ **d'ambiance** m COMMANDE, REFRIG room thermostat; ~ **à bulbe** m REFRIG remote bulb thermostat; ~ **local** m COMMANDE, THERMODYN room thermostat; ~ **mouillé** m THERMODYN water thermostat; ~ **de radiateur** m COMMANDE radiator thermostat; ~ **de sécurité d'huile** m REFRIG oil temperature cutout; ~ **de sécurité de refoulement** m REFRIG high discharge temperature cutout; ~ **de type à sonde** m PRODUCTION bulb-type temperature switch; ~ **de type à tube capillaire** m PRODUCTION capillary-type temperature switch; ~ **de zéro** m COMMANDE zero thermostat
thermostatique[1] adj COMMANDE, REFRIG, THERMODYN thermostatic
thermostatique[2] f THERMODYN thermostatics
thesaurus m INFORMAT, ORDINAT thesaurus
thévétine f CHIMIE thevetin
thial m CHIMIE thial, thioaldehyde
thialdine f CHIMIE thialdine
thiamine f CHIMIE aneurin, torulin
thiazine f CHIMIE thiazine, thioindamine
thiazole m CHIMIE thiazole
thiazoline f CHIMIE thiazoline
thibaude f TEXTILE carpet underlay
thio- préf CHIMIE thio-
thioacétique adj CHIMIE thioacetic
thioacide m CHIMIE thioacid
thioalcool m AGRO ALIM thiol, CHIMIE thioalcohol, thiol, PETROLE mercaptan
thioaldéhyde m CHIMIE thial, thioaldehyde
thioamide m CHIMIE thioamide
thiocarbamide f CHIMIE thiocarbamide
thiocarbanilide m CHIMIE thiocarbanilide
thiocarbonate m CHIMIE thiocarbonate
thiocarbonique adj CHIMIE thiocarbonic
thiocétone f CHIMIE thioketone, thione
thiocyanate m CHIMIE thiocyanate
thiocyanique adj CHIMIE thiocyanic
thiodiphénylamine f CHIMIE phenothiazine, thiodiphenylamine
thioéther m CHIMIE thioether
thiofène m CHIMIE thiophene
thioflavine f CHIMIE thioflavin
thioglycolique adj CHIMIE thioglycolic
thiogomme f CHIMIE thioplast
thio-indamine f CHIMIE thioindamine
thio-indigo m CHIMIE thioindigo
thiol m CHIMIE thioalcohol, thiol, PETROLE mercaptan
thiolate m CHIMIE thiolate
thionaphtène m CHIMIE thionaphthene
thionate m CHIMIE thionate
thionation f CHIMIE thionation
thione m CHIMIE thione
thionéine f CHIMIE thioneine

thionine *f* CHIMIE thionine
thionique *adj* CHIMIE thionic
thionyle *m* CHIMIE thionyl
thiopental *m* CHIMIE thiopental
thiophène *m* CHIMIE thiophene
thiophénol *m* CHIMIE thiophenol
thiophosgène *m* CHIMIE thiophosgene
thiosulfate *m* CHIMIE thiosulfate (AmE), thiosulphate (BrE); ~ **de sodium** *m* CHIMIE sodium thiosulfate (AmE), sodium thiosulphate (BrE)
thiosulfurique *adj* CHIMIE thiosulfuric (AmE), thiosulphuric (BrE)
thio-urée *f* CHIMIE thiocarbamide, thiourea
thioxanthone *m* CHIMIE thioxanthone
thioxène *m* CHIMIE thioxene
thixotrope *adj* CHIMIE, PHYSIQUE, PLAST CAOU thixotropic
thixotropie *f* CHARBON, CHIMIE thixotropy, IMPRIM *encres* false body, PETR, PHYSIQUE thixotropy
thixotropique *adj* CHIMIE thixotropic
tholoïde *m* GEOLOGIE cumulo-dome, tholoid dome
thomsénolite *f* MINERAUX thomsenolite
thomsonite *f* MINERAUX thomsonite
thonaire *m* OCEANO tunny net
thonier *m* OCEANO tuna boat, tunny boat
thorianite *f* MINERAUX thorianite
thorine *f* CHIMIE thoria
thorique *adj* CHIMIE thoric
thorite *f* MINERAUX thorite
thorium *m* *(Th)* CHIMIE thorium *(Th)*
thréose *m* CHIMIE threose
THT *abrév (très haute tension)* ELECTROTEC, TV EHT *(extra high tension)*
thulite *f* MINERAUX thulite
thulium *m* *(Tm)* CHIMIE thulium *(Tm)*
thumper *m* PETR thumper
thuringite *f* MINERAUX thuringite
thuyane *m* CHIMIE thujane
thuyène *m* CHIMIE thujene
thuyone *m* CHIMIE absinthole
thymol *m* CHIMIE thymol
thymolphtaléine *f* CHIMIE thymolphthalein
thyratron *m* CHIMIE, ELECTRON, PHYSIQUE thyratron; ~ **à l'hydrogène** *m* ELECTRON hydrogen thyratron
thyristor *m* ELECTR, ELECTROTEC, PHYSIQUE, TELECOM thyristor; ~ **à l'état bloqué** *m* ELECTRON off thyristor; ~ **de grande puissance** *m* ELECTROTEC high-power SCR; ~ **de protection** *m* ELECTROTEC crowbar; ~ **de puissance** *m* TELECOM power thyristor; ~ **au silicium** *m* ELECTROTEC, TELECOM SCR, silicon-controlled rectifier
thyronine *f* CHIMIE thyronine
thyroxine *f* CHIMIE thyroxin, thyroxine
Ti *(titane)* CHIMIE Ti *(titanium)*
ticket *m* PRODUCTION docket; ~ **de mélange** *m* PRODUCTION batch card; ~ **de réception** *m* PRODUCTION delivery ticket
tiède *adj* THERMODYN tepid
tiemannite *f* MINERAUX tiemannite
tierce *f* ACOUSTIQUE third; ~ **majeure** *f* ACOUSTIQUE major third; ~ **mineure** *f* ACOUSTIQUE minor third
tiergol *m* ESPACE tripropellant
tiers *m* BREVETS third party
tiers-point *m* CONS MECA three-square file; ~ **double** *m* PRODUCTION double-ended handsaw file
tiffanyite *f* MINERAUX tiffanyite

tige *f* CONS MECA rod, *d'un boulon, d'un clou* shank, *d'une vis* stem, CONSTR *d'une vis* barrel, *d'un rivet* pale, *d'une clef* shank, stem, DISTRI EAU rod, spear, EQUIP LAB, MECANIQUE, MINES rod, PHYSIQUE stem; ~ **d'actionnement** *f* PRODUCTION *automatisme industriel* operating shaft; ~ **d'agitateur** *f* EQUIP LAB stirrer blade; ~ **d'ancrage** *f* CHARBON anchor rod; ~ **bouclée** *f* PRODUCTION *automatisme industriel* looped rod; ~ **de captage** *f* ELECTROTEC lightning rod; ~ **carrée d'entraînement** *f* PETR, PETROLE kelly; ~ **de centrage** *f* CONS MECA centering rod (AmE), centring rod (BrE); ~ **de chauffe-bain électrique** *f* PHOTO heater element; ~ **collectrice** *f* ELECTROTEC lightning rod; ~ **de commande des gaz** *f* AUTO throttle control rod; ~ **de commande du piston** *f* CONS MECA sucker rod; ~ **crantée** *f* CONS MECA notched stem; ~ **de crémaillère** *f* AUTO control rod; ~ **de crochet de traction** *f* CH DE FER *véhicules* draw hook bar; ~ **de démontage** *f* NUCLEAIRE disconnect rod, unloading rod; ~ **d'éjection** *f* CONS MECA knock-out rod, MECANIQUE ejector pin; ~ **d'embrayage** *f* VEHICULES clutch rod; ~ **d'entraînement** *f* PETROLE kelly; ~ **d'excentrique** *f* CONS MECA eccentric rod; ~ **de fer** *f* PRODUCTION iron rod; ~ **de fleuret** *f* MINES drill rod; ~ **de forage** *f* MINES drill rod, PETR drill pipe, drill rod, PETROLE drill pipe; ~ **de frein** *f* VEHICULES brake connecting rod, *système de freinage* brake rod; ~ **d'injecteur** *f* AUTO nozzle holder spindle; ~ **de jaugeage** *f* PRODUCTION gage (AmE), gauge (BrE), stock indicator, test rod; ~ **de laiton** *f* EN RENOUV *pompe d'éolienne* brass rod; ~ **de manoeuvre** *f* INST HYDR *d'une distribution Corliss* lifting rod; ~ **de manoeuvre d'aiguille** *f* CH DE FER points rod; ~ **à oeil** *f* PRODUCTION eyed rod; ~ **de paratonnerre** *f* ELECTROTEC, GEOPHYS lightning rod; ~ **du pilon** *f* PRODUCTION stamp stem; ~ **de piston** *f* AUTO, CH DE FER *véhicules*, CONS MECA, PRODUCTION *système hydraulique* piston rod; ~ **polie** *f* EN RENOUV *pompe d'éolienne* polished rod; ~ **de pompage** *f* EN RENOUV *pompe d'éolienne* sucker rod; ~ **de pompe** *f* DISTRI EAU pump rod, spear; ~ **de poussée** *f* CONS MECA push rod; ~ **de poussoir** *f* AUTO tappet stem, valve push rod, SECURITE push stick; ~ **à poussoir latéral** *f* PRODUCTION side push rod; ~ **de rallonge** *f* CONS MECA extension piece, lengthening piece, lengthening rod; ~ **de rappel** *f* CONS MECA drawbar; ~ **de réglage** *f* COMMANDE adjusting spindle; ~ **de repérage** *f* CONS MECA centering pin (AmE), centring pin (BrE); ~ **rouge** *f* EN RENOUV *pompe d'éolienne* red rod; ~ **de sonde** *f* CONSTR bore rod, boring rod, MINES drill pipe, drill rod, rods; ~ **de soupape** *f* AUTO valve shaft, CH DE FER *véhicules* valve rod, INST HYDR rod, stem, valve rod, valve spindle, valve stem, VEHICULES *moteur* valve stem; ~ **souple à ressort** *f* PRODUCTION cat whisker; ~ **de surcharge** *f* MINES sinker bar; ~ **de suspension** *f* CH DE FER *véhicules* suspension rod; ~ **de tiroir** *f* INST HYDR slide rod, stem; ~ **de traction** *f* CH DE FER *véhicules* drawbar; ~ **de transmission** *f* CONS MECA flat rod, string rod, transmission rod; ~ **de vanne** *f* INST HYDR gate stem; ~ **de vérin** *f* CONS MECA cylinder rod, PRODUCTION jack rod
tige-poussoir *f* AUTO nozzle holder spindle
tiges *f pl* NUCLEAIRE linkage
tiglique *adj* CHIMIE tiglic
tille: ~ **de couvreur** *f* CONSTR roofer's hammer
timbrage *m* IMPRIM stamping
timbre *m* ACOUSTIQUE timbre, INST HYDR *d'une chaudière à vapeur* test plate, PHYS ONDES timbre,

PRODUCTION *d'une chaudière à vapeur* badge plate; ~ **de chaudière** *m* INST HYDR boiler test plate

timbrer *vt* PRODUCTION *chaudière* badge

timon *m* VEHICULES *remorque* drawbar

timonerie *f* MECANIQUE gear, NAUT signaling (AmE), signalling (BrE), wheel house, VEHICULES *direction, embrayage, freins* linkage; ~ **d'accélérateur** *f* VEHICULES *carburateur* accelerator linkage; ~ **de carburateur** *f* VEHICULES carburetor linkage (AmE), carburettor linkage (BrE); ~ **de direction** *f* AUTO steering linkage; ~ **de frein** *f* CH DE FER *véhicules* brake rigging, VEHICULES brake linkage; ~ **de frein compensé** *f* CH DE FER *véhicules* compensated brake rigging; ~ **du papillon** *f* VEHICULES *carburateur* throttle linkage

timonérie: ~ **d'accélérateur** *f* TRANSPORT accelerator linkage

tincalconite *f* MINERAUX tincalconite

tinctorial *adj* COULEURS tinctorial

tinkal *m* MINERAUX tincal

tintement *m* ACOUSTIQUE tinnitus

tir *m* PETROLE shot; ~ **d'artillerie** *m* MILITAIRE artillery fire; ~ **avec bouchon** *m* MINES breaking shot, breaking-in shot, buster shot, opening shot; ~ **de barrage** *m* MILITAIRE curtain of fire, *artillerie* barrage; ~ **de bruit** *m* PETR noise analysis; ~ **coup par coup** *m* MILITAIRE repetition fire, MINES shot-by-shot firing; ~ **de couverture** *m* MILITAIRE covering fire; ~ **de cratère** *m* MINES crater cut; ~ **décalé** *m* MILITAIRE indirect fire; ~ **à départs successifs** *m* MINES rotation firing; ~ **dispersé** *m* MILITAIRE *artillerie* ragged fire; ~ **électrique** *m* MINES electric blasting, electric shotfiring, electric firing; ~ **électrique des coups de mine** *m* MINES electric firing; ~ **d'emblée** *m* MILITAIRE rapid fire; ~ **en enfilade** *m* MILITAIRE raking fire; ~ **en plusieurs rangées** *m* MINES multiple row blasting; ~ **instantané** *m* MINES instantaneous firing, simultaneous firing, simultaneous shot firing; ~ **de mines** *m* MINES blasting, shot-firing; ~ **périmétrique** *m* MINES perimeter blasting, smooth blasting, smooth wall blasting; ~ **primaire** *m* MINES primary blasting; ~ **de réglage** *m* MILITAIRE *artillerie* ranging fire; ~ **secondaire** *m* MINES secondary blasting

tirage *m* CONS MECA traction, *de plan* blueprint, CONSTR draft (AmE), draught (BrE), IMPRIM combination run, print run, INFORMAT hard copy, MAT CHAUFF draft (AmE), draught (BrE), MINES blasting, quarrying, PAPIER draw, PHOTO positive, print, printing, *d'un soufflet* extension, PLAST CAOU *plastiques, fibres* drawing, PRODUCTION drawing, wire drawing; ~ **aller-et-retour** *m* CINEMAT back-and-forth printing; ~ **arrière** *m* CINEMAT back focus; ~ **avec moins de lumière** *m* CINEMAT printing down; ~ **avec sortie en nappe** *m* IMPRIM *rotatives* straight run; ~ **de la chambre** *m* PHOTO camera extension; ~ **de copies en série** *m* CINEMAT release printing; ~ **de coups de mine** *m* MINES shot-firing; ~ **court** *m* IMPRIM *impression* short run; ~ **en accéléré** *m* CINEMAT skip frame printing; ~ **en boucle** *m* CINEMAT loop printing; ~ **en conduite** *m* TELECOM pulling in; ~ **en lumière diffuse** *m* CINEMAT opal printing; ~ **en plein** *m* PHOTO full frame print; ~ **en surimpression** *m* CINEMAT bipack; ~ **d'épaisseur** *m* CONS MECA thicknessing; ~ **de fil-à-fil** *m* CINEMAT section printing; ~ **forcé** *m* CONSTR, MAT CHAUFF forced draft (AmE), forced draught (BrE); ~ **humide** *m* CINEMAT fluid-gate printing, liquid gate printing, wet gate; ~ **image par image** *m* CINEMAT step printing; ~ **induit** *m*

CONS MECA, MAT CHAUFF induced draft (AmE), induced draught (BrE); ~ **inversé** *m* CINEMAT reverse printing; ~ **de monocristaux** *m* ELECTRON single crystal growth; ~ **naturel** *m* MAT CHAUFF natural draft (AmE), natural draught (BrE); ~ **optique anamorphosé** *m* CINEMAT anamorphosing printing; ~ **optique désanamorphosé recadré** *m* CINEMAT scanning printing; ~ **optique normal** *m* CINEMAT one-to-one printing; ~ **optique par agrandissement** *m* CINEMAT blowup printing; ~ **du papier** *m* PAPIER paper draw, paper machine; ~ **par contact** *m* PHOTO contact printing; ~ **par immersion** *m* CINEMAT liquid gate printing, wet gate; ~ **par réduction** *m* PHOTO reduction print; ~ **photographique** *m* IMPRIM, PHOTO shot; ~ **photo opaque à analyser par réflexion** *m* IMPRIM *photogravure* reflection print; ~ **plus sombre** *m* CINEMAT printing down; ~ **répété de la même image** *m* CINEMAT multiple frame printing; ~ **du soufflet** *m* PHOTO bellows extension; ~ **à travers le dos du papier** *m* PHOTO printing in; ~ **à travers le support** *m* CINEMAT printing through the base, PHOTO reverse printing

tirant *m* CERAM VER tie rod, CONS MECA tension piece, tie, tie bar, tie bolt, tie rod, CONSTR stay, stay bolt, stay rod, stretcher, IMPRIM *encres* tack, MECANIQUE, NAUT tie rod; ~ **d'air** *m* NAUT air draft (AmE), air draught (BrE); ~ **d'amarrage** *m* AERONAUT mooring ring; ~ **articulé permettant la dilatation de la plaque** *m* CONS MECA flexible stay bolt; ~ **de la colle** *m* IMPRIM wet track; ~ **d'eau** *m* NAUT, TRANSPORT draft (AmE), draught (BrE); ~ **d'eau maximal** *m* NAUT extreme draft (AmE), extreme draught (BrE); ~ **d'eau maximal d'exploitation** *m* NAUT deepest seagoing draft (AmE), deepest seagoing draught (BrE); ~ **d'eau moyen** *m* NAUT mean draft (AmE), mean draught (BrE); ~ **d'eau sur quille** *m* NAUT molded draft (AmE), moulded draught (BrE); ~ **de ferme** *m* CONSTR truss rod; ~ **d'une ferme de comble** *m* CONSTR stringer, *en bois* tie beam, *métallique* tie bar, tie rod

tirants: ~ **de bâti** *m pl* CONS MECA *de tour* bed bars

tiré *adj* CERAM VER *jambe* drawn

tire-aiguille *m* CONS MECA extractor

tire-bouchon *m* NUCLEAIRE helical instability

tire-bourre *m* CONS MECA worm screw

tire-braise *m* PRODUCTION rake

tire-clou *m* CONSTR nail extractor, EMBALLAGE nail puller

tire-fil *m* CERAM VER pull roll

tire-fond *m* CH DE FER railroad tie screw (AmE), railway sleeper screw (BrE), sleeper screw (BrE), tie screw (AmE), screw spike, CONSTR lag screw

tirefonner *vt* CH DE FER fasten with sleeper screws (BrE), fasten with tie screws (AmE)

tirefonneuse *f* CH DE FER railroad tie screwdriver (AmE), railway sleeper screwdriver (BrE), sleeper screwdriver (BrE), tie screwdriver (AmE), spike driver (AmE)

tire-goupille *m* CONS MECA pin extractor

tirer[1] *vt* CINEMAT print, strike, *un contre-type* dupe, IMPRIM print, pull, NAUT draw, PHOTO print, PRODUCTION draw, *des trous d'air* pierce; ~ **à l'argue** *vt* PRODUCTION draw; ~ **deux fois** *vt* CINEMAT doubleprint; ~ **d'un four** *vt* PRODUCTION *briques* draw out of a kiln; ~ **de largeur** *vt* CONSTR *planche* reduce to width; ~ **standard** *vt* CINEMAT marry up

tirer[2] *vi* CONSTR draw; ~ **à blanc** *vi* MILITAIRE fire a blank; ~ **un bord** *vi* NAUT make a tack; ~ **des bords** *vi* NAUT tack; ~ **les images plusieurs fois** *vi* CINEMAT stretch frame print; ~ **une image sur deux** *vi* CINEMAT skip frame; ~ **au vide** *vi* CONSTR bulge

tirés-à-part *m pl* IMPRIM off-prints

tire-sonde *m* MINES drill rod grab

tiret *m* IMPRIM hyphen, *composition* dash

tirette *f* CERAM VER cutout; ~ **à main** *f* NUCLEAIRE hand wire pull, hand-operated pull; ~ **de volet de départ** *f* AUTO manual choke control

tireur: ~ **embusqué** *m* MILITAIRE sniper; ~ **isolé** *m* MILITAIRE sniper

tireuse *f* CINEMAT, PHOTO printer; ~ **additive** *f* CINEMAT additive printer; ~ **automatique** *f* PHOTO automatic printer; ~ **en continu** *f* EMBALLAGE continuous printer; ~ **multiple** *f* CINEMAT cascade printer; ~ **optique** *f* CINEMAT optical printer, projection printer; ~ **optique Oxberry** *f* CINEMAT Oxberry optical printer; ~ **par contact** *f* CINEMAT contact printer; ~ **par contact image par image** *f* CINEMAT intermittent contact printer, step contact printer; ~ **par immersion** *f* CINEMAT wet gate printer; ~ **par synthèse additive** *f* CINEMAT additive color printer (AmE), additive colour printer (BrE); ~ **pour la copie par contact** *f* PHOTO contact printer; ~ **pour copies standard** *f* CINEMAT positive release printer; ~ **soustractive** *f* CINEMAT subtractive color printer (AmE), subtractive colour printer (BrE)

tiroir *m* CONS MECA slide, slider, ELECTR *unité* plug-in unit, INST HYDR shuttle, slide box, slide, slide valve, PAPIER end deckle, PRODUCTION drawback, false core, *système hydraulique* spool; ~ **à admission retardée** *m* INST HYDR late admission slide valve; ~ **d'Allen** *m* CONS MECA Allen valve; ~ **à canal** *m* CONS MECA Allen valve; ~ **de compensation** *m* PRODUCTION *système hydraulique* compensating spool; ~ **compensé** *m* CONS MECA balanced slide valve; ~ **cylindrique** *m* CONS MECA piston valve; ~ **débrochable** *m* ELECTR *unité* draw-out unit; ~ **de détente** *m* CONS MECA auxiliary valve, INST HYDR expansion valve, riding cutoff valve, PRODUCTION independent cutoff valve; ~ **de distribution** *m* INST HYDR slide box; ~ **à échappement retardé** *m* INST HYDR late release slide valve; ~ **en D** *m* INST HYDR D-valve; ~ **équilibré** *m* CONS MECA balanced slide valve; ~ **d'étranglement** *m* VEHICULES *carburateur* throttle slide; ~ **d'expansion** *m* CONS MECA auxiliary valve, INST HYDR expansion valve, riding cutoff valve, PRODUCTION independent cutoff valve; ~ **de freinage** *m* INST HYDR slide throttle valve; ~ **à glace** *m* REFRIG ice cube tray; ~ **à grille** *m* PRODUCTION gridiron valve; ~ **à orifices multiples** *m* PRODUCTION multiported valve; ~ **oscillant** *m* PRODUCTION swinging valve; ~ **à piston** *m* CONS MECA piston valve; ~ **porte-filtre** *m* PHOTO sliding filter drawer; ~ **à recouvrement** *m* INST HYDR lap valve; ~ **rond** *m* CONS MECA piston valve; ~ **rotatif** *m* PRODUCTION swinging valve, VEHICULES *moteur à deux-temps* rotary disc valve (BrE), rotary disk valve (AmE); ~ **sans recouvrement** *m* INST HYDR lapless valve; ~ **simple** *m* INST HYDR plain slide valve; ~ **à tuile de détente** *m* PRODUCTION independent cutoff valve; ~ **à vapeur** *m* INST HYDR steam valve

tisard *m* PRODUCTION stoke hole, stoking door

tisonnier *m* PRODUCTION poker; ~ **d'allumage** *m* CONS MECA ignition poker; ~ **à gaz** *m* CONS MECA gas poker

tissage *m* TEXTILE weaving

tissé: ~ **à la demande** *adj* TEXTILE custom-ordered

tisser *vt* TEXTILE weave

tissu *m* ESPACE fabric, TEXTILE cloth, fabric; ~ **d'ameublement** *m* TEXTILE furnishing fabric, home furnishing, upholstery; ~ **apparent** *m* TEXTILE facing fabric; ~ **apprêté** *m* TEXTILE crisp linen, finished fabric; ~ **armuré** *m* TEXTILE dobby-weave fabric; ~ **bouillonné** *m* TEXTILE bubble type; ~ **chaîne et trame** *m* TEXTILE woven fabric; ~ **de chemiserie** *m* TEXTILE shirting; ~ **chenillé** *m* TEXTILE chenille fabric; ~ **croisé** *m* TEXTILE chafer; ~ **dentelé** *m* TEXTILE lacy fabric; ~ **de doublure** *m* TEXTILE backing fabric, lining fabric; ~ **de drap de lit** *m* TEXTILE sheeting; ~ **en boyau** *m* TEXTILE fabric in rope form; ~ **enduit** *m* MATERIAUX, PLAST CAOU *article*, REVETEMENT coated fabric; ~ **enduit imperméable** *m* REVETEMENT waterproof tissue; ~ **en pièce** *m* TEXTILE piece goods; ~ **entraîneur** *m* TEXTILE leader cloth; ~ **fantaisie** *m* TEXTILE fancy woven fabric; ~ **filtrant** *m* DISTRI EAU filter cloth, GENIE CHIM filter cloth, filter press cloth, sieve cloth; ~ **haut-module** *m* MATERIAUX *fibre de verre* high modulus fabric; ~ **huilé** *m* EMBALLAGE oilcloth; ~ **imprégné** *m* EMBALLAGE impregnated fabric; ~ **imprimé** *m* TEXTILE printed fabric; ~ **jacquard** *m* TEXTILE jacquard fabric; ~ **léger pour ameublement** *m* TEXTILE lightweight furnishing fabric; ~ **léger pour habillement** *m* TEXTILE lightweight apparel fabric; ~ **à mailles** *m* TEXTILE knitted fabric; ~ **métis** *m* TEXTILE union cloth; ~ **mille-raies** *m* TEXTILE millerayes, stripe fabric; ~ **non tissé** *m* TEXTILE nonwoven fabric; ~ **ouaté** *m* PAPIER soft tissue; ~ **peigné** *m* TEXTILE combed wool fabric; ~ **pour complet** *m* TEXTILE suiting; ~ **pour filtre** *m* GENIE CHIM filter press cloth, sieve cloth; ~ **pour panneau amovible** *m* TEXTILE panel fabric; ~ **pour rideaux de fenêtre** *m* TEXTILE casement cloth; ~ **pour robe** *m* TEXTILE dress material; ~ **pour tamisage** *m* TEXTILE bolting fabric; ~ **pour veste** *m* TEXTILE jacketing; ~ **pour vêtements imperméables à l'air** *m* SECURITE *résistant aux liquides dangereux* air-impermeable clothing material; ~ **de protection thermique** *m* SECURITE heat-protective material; ~ **qui ressemble à la dentelle** *m* TEXTILE lacy fabric; ~ **rachel** *m* TEXTILE directionally-structured raschel goods; ~ **à revêtement poromère** *m* PLAST CAOU *article* poromeric-coated fabric; ~ **serré** *m* TEXTILE firmly set fabric; ~ **silionne** *m* EMBALLAGE glass fabric; ~ **de taille** *m* TEXTILE waistsize; ~ **uni** *m* TEXTILE plain fabric; ~ **de verre** *m* NAUT glass cloth, PLAST CAOU *plastiques* fiberglass (AmE), fibreglass (BrE)

titanate *m* CHIMIE titanate

titane *m* *(Ti)* CHIMIE titanium *(Ti)*; ~ **oxydé** *m* CHIMIE ratile

titaneux *adj* CHIMIE titanous

titanique *adj* CHIMIE titanic

titanite *f* MINERAUX titanite

titanyle *m* CHIMIE titanyl

titiller *vt* VEHICULES *carburateur* flood

titrage *m* CHARBON titration, CHIMIE standardization, titration, LESSIVES titration; ~ **du brut** *m* PETROLE crude assay; ~ **en retour** *m* CHIMIE back titration; ~ **par défaut** *m* CHIMIE undertitration; ~ **potentiométrique** *m* CHIMIE electrometric titration

titration *f* ESSAIS volumetric analysis; ~ **automatique** *f* EQUIP LAB *analyse* automatic titration; ~ **complexométrique** *f* CHIMIE complexometric titration; ~ **conductimétrique** *f* CHIMIE conductimetric titration

titre:[1] **au** ~ *adj* CONS MECA standard

titre:[2] **à** ~ **gratuit** *adv* TELECOM free of charge

titre[3] *m* BREVETS *de l'invention* title, CHIMIE titre, *d'une* *solution* strength, CINEMAT caption, title, CONS MECA tenor, IMPRIM headline, head, title, INFORMAT heading, MINES content, grade, tenor, ORDINAT heading, PRODUCTION grade; ~ **de colonne incliné** *m* IMPRIM *composition* angled column head; ~ **courant** *m* IMPRIM running head, running title, text label, *mise en page, maquette* telltale; ~ **au dos** *m* IMPRIM *du livre* back title; ~ **encadré** *m* IMPRIM boxed head; ~ **en or fin** *m* MINES gold grade, gold tenor; ~ **en vapeur** *m* INST HYDR steam quality; ~ **du fil** *m* TEXTILE count; ~ **fin** *m* TEXTILE fine count; ~ **de jauge** *m* PRODUCTION gage number (AmE), gauge number (BrE); ~ **molaire** *m* REFRIG mole titer (AmE), mole titre (BrE); ~ **provisoire** *m* CINEMAT working title; ~ **de rubrique** *m* IMPRIM header; ~ **de la vapeur** *m* INST HYDR relative dryness

titrer *vt* CHARBON titrate, CHIMIE standardize, titrate; ~ **en retour** *vt* CHIMIE back titrate

titres: ~ **déroulants** *m pl* CINEMAT roller titles

titreur *m* TV title keyer

titreuse: ~ **à tambour** *f* CINEMAT drum titler

titrimètre *m* CHIMIE titrator

titrimétrie *f* CHIMIE titrimetry

titulaire *m* BREVETS owner, proprietor; ~ **du brevet** *m* BREVETS patent proprietor; ~ **du contrat** *m* QUALITE contractor

TJD *abrév (traversée-jonction double)* CH DE FER double diamond crossing with slips

Tl *(thallium)* CHIMIE Tl *(thallium)*

Tm *(thulium)* CHIMIE Tm *(thulium)*

TMG *abrév (Temps moyen de Greenwich)* ESPACE, PHYSIQUE GMT *(Greenwich Mean Time)*

TO *abrév (traversée oblique)* CH DE FER diamond crossing

toboggan *m* SECURITE toboggan, TRANSPORT freight chute (AmE), goods chute (BrE), parcels chute; ~ **d'évacuation** *m* AERONAUT emergency slide, escape chute; ~ **gonflable** *m* AERONAUT inflatable slide; ~ **de secours** *m* AERONAUT emergency slide, escape chute

toc *m* CONS MECA dog, driver, turning carrier, MECANIQUE dog; ~ **à coussinets** *m* CONS MECA jaw dog; ~ **en acier estampé** *m* PRODUCTION drop-forged steel dog; ~ **d'entraînement** *m* CONS MECA catch pin; ~ **pour tourneur** *m* CONS MECA turning carrier; ~ **de tour** *m* CONS MECA lathe carrier, lathe dog; ~ **à vis** *m* CONS MECA screw dog

tocophérol *m* AGRO ALIM tocopherol

toile *f* IMPRIM linen, NAUT *à voile* canvas, PAPIER wire, PRODUCTION flash, TEXTILE canvas, VEHICULES *vilebrequin* web; ~ **abrasive** *f* CONS MECA abrasive cloth, emery cloth; ~ **antiroulis** *f* NAUT lee canvas; ~ **d'araignée** *f* CONS MECA pinion web; ~ **à bâches** *f* CONSTR tarpaulin; ~ **à bluter** *f* CERAM VER bolting cloth; ~ **caoutchoutée** *f* REVETEMENT rubberized cloth; ~ **cirée** *f* PLAST CAOU, TEXTILE oilcloth; ~ **émeri** *f* MECANIQUE *outillage*, PRODUCTION emery cloth; ~ **émeri fine** *f* CONS MECA crocus cloth, fine emery cloth; ~ **émerisée** *f* PRODUCTION emery cloth; ~ **en fil de fer** *f* PRODUCTION iron wire gauze; ~ **en fil de laiton** *f* CONSTR brass wire gauze; ~ **filtrante** *f* DISTRI EAU filter cloth; ~ **de filtre** *f* DISTRI EAU filter cloth; ~ **de formation** *f* PAPIER forming fabric; ~ **frictionnée** *f* REVETEMENT rubberized cloth; ~ **de jute** *f* EMBALLAGE jute sacking, TEXTILE hessian; ~ **de lin** *f* TEXTILE linen; ~ **à matelas** *f* TEXTILE mattress ticking; ~ **métallique** *f* PAPIER wire cloth, PRODUCTION gauze, wire cloth, wire gauze; ~ **pour filtre-presses** *f* GENIE CHIM filter cloth; ~ **de relieur** *f*

IMPRIM art canvas; ~ **de sauvetage** *f* SECURITE jumping sheet; ~ **de scellage** *f* CERAM VER bench cloth; ~ **sécheuse** *f* TEXTILE dryer fabric; ~ **de soutien** *f* PAPIER backing wire; ~ **synthétique** *f* PAPIER fabric; ~ **tailleur** *f* TEXTILE interlining material; ~ **de tamisage** *f* GENIE CHIM sieve netting; ~ **de tension** *f* PHOTO pressure cloth; ~ **de traction** *f* PAPIER power fabric; ~ **transporteuse** *f* PRODUCTION apron, conveyor belt, traveling apron (AmE), travelling apron (BrE); ~ **de triage** *f* MINES canvas table, picking belt, PRODUCTION sorting belt; ~ **unie** *f* PAPIER plain weave; ~ **vernie** *f* PLAST CAOU, TEXTILE oilskin; ~ **verrée** *f* PRODUCTION glass cloth; ~ **à voiles** *f* NAUT sailcloth

toiles: ~ **d'aérage** *f pl* MINES brattice cloth

toilette *f* NAUT head; ~ **étanche** *f* CH DE FER *véhicules* controlled emission toilet

toit *m* CONSTR roof, GEOLOGIE cap rock, MINES *d'une mine, d'un filon*, VEHICULES *carrosserie* roof; ~ **avec entrait** *m* CONSTR collar roof; ~ **batière** *m* CONSTR couple roof; ~ **de la couche** *m* MINES roof; ~ **d'une couche** *m* GEOLOGIE hanging wall; ~ **décapotable** *m* VEHICULES convertible hood, convertible top; ~ **en coupole** *m* CONSTR dome roof; ~ **en croupe et faîte** *m* CONSTR hip-and-ridge roof; ~ **en dos d'âne** *m* CONSTR couple roof; ~ **ouvrant** *m* VEHICULES *carrosserie* sunroof; ~ **pivotant** *m* TRANSPORT swiveling roof (AmE), swivelling roof (BrE)

toit-dalle *m* NUCLEAIRE cover plate, cover slab, roof shielding plate

toiture *f* CONSTR roof, roofing; ~ **en tuiles** *f* CERAM VER tiling; ~ **à scimple** *f* CONSTR lean-to roof

tokamak *m* PHYSIQUE tokamak

tôle *f* CERAM VER bow and warp (AmE), warped sheet (BrE), pad, ELECTROTEC lamination, MATERIAUX plate, sheet metal, MECANIQUE plate, *matériaux* sheet, NAUT plate, NUCLEAIRE sheet, PRODUCTION plate, plate iron; ~ **d'acier** *f* MATERIAUX steel sheet, VEHICULES *carrosserie* sheet steel; ~ **d'arcasse** *f* NAUT transom plate; ~ **bandeau** *f* NAUT faceplate; ~ **de blindage** *f* CONSTR armor plate (AmE), armour plate (BrE); ~ **de bouchain** *f* NAUT bilge plate, bulkhead plate; ~ **de chaudronnerie** *f* INST HYDR boiler plate; ~ **de coffrage** *f* REVETEMENT coating sheet; ~ **collée** *f* CONSTR bonded steel plate; ~ **composée** *f* MATERIAUX bonded metal; ~ **de coup de feu** *f* PRODUCTION flame plate; ~ **de criblage** *f* CHARBON screen plate; ~ **de cuivre** *f* CONSTR copper sheets; ~ **émaillée** *f* PRODUCTION enameled iron (AmE), enamelled iron (BrE); ~ **à émailler** *f* REVETEMENT enameling sheet (AmE), enamelling sheet (BrE); ~ **en acier au silicium** *f* ELECTROTEC silicon steel lamination; ~ **entretoise** *f* NAUT cross tie; ~ **d'enveloppe** *f* PRODUCTION jacket; ~ **d'enveloppe du corps du cylindre** *f* PRODUCTION cylinder casing; ~ **d'enveloppe extérieure** *f* INST HYDR clothing plate; ~ **de fer** *f* PRODUCTION iron sheeting, plate iron; ~ **de fermeture** *f* CONS MECA cover plate; ~ **laminée** *f* REVETEMENT lamination sheet; ~ **larmée** *f* MECANIQUE *matériaux* bulb plate; ~ **magnétique** *f* ELECTROTEC lamination, stamping; ~ **magnétique découpée** *f* ELECTROTEC stamping; ~ **du noyau** *f* ELECTROTEC core lamination; ~ **ondulée** *f* CONSTR corrugated iron; ~ **ondulée en fer** *f* CONSTR corrugated iron, corrugated sheet iron; ~ **pare-feu** *f* AERONAUT fire wall; ~ **perforée** *f* CHARBON, CONSTR punched plate, NUCLEAIRE *à tamisage* perforated plate, screen plate; ~ **de pied** *f* NAUT heel plate; ~ **de pont** *f* NAUT deck plate; **~ pour bordages** *f* CONSTR flange plate; **~ pour foyers** *f* PRODUCTION furnace plate **~ de quille** *f* NAUT keel plate; **~ rivée** *f* CONSTR riveted plate; **~ du rotor** *f* ELECTROTEC rotor lamination; **~ de séparation** *f* CONS MECA, MINES baffle; **~ au silicium** *f* MATERIAUX silicon sheet; **~ du stator** *f* ELECTROTEC stator lamination; **~ striée** *f* PRODUCTION checker plate (AmE), checkered plate (AmE), chequer plate (BrE), chequered plate (BrE); **~ supérieure** *f* NAUT rider plate; **~ de tête** *f* NAUT head plate; **~ de transfert** *f* GENIE CHIM deflector plate; **~ de varangue** *f* NAUT floor plate

tôle-chicane *f* GENIE CHIM baffle plate

tolérance:[1] **à ~ de fautes** *adj* INFORMAT fault-tolerant; **à ~ de pannes** *adj* ORDINAT fault-tolerant

tolérance[2] *f* CONS MECA clearance, limit, margin, tolerance, MATERIAUX, MECANIQUE tolerance, PRODUCTION allowance, QUALITE, TEXTILE tolerance; **~ à l'acidité** *f* POLLUTION acid tolerance; **~ de cylindricité** *f* RESSORTS out-of-roundness tolerance; **~ à défaut** *f* ELECTROTEC fault tolerance; **~ en moins** *f* CONS MECA margin under; **~ en plus** *f* CONS MECA margin over; **~ d'enroulement** *f* RESSORTS coiling tolerance; **~ d'excentration** *f* MECANIQUE concentricity tolerance; **~ de parallélisme** *f* RESSORTS parallelism tolerance, tolerance of parallelism; **~ de perpendicularité** *f* RESSORTS squareness tolerance; **~ de planéité** *f* CONS MECA flatness tolerance; **~ sur le bord** *f* PRODUCTION edge range limit; **~ sur brut** *f* CONS MECA general tolerance; **~ sur la capacité** *f* PRODUCTION capacitance tolerance; **~ sur le diamètre du coeur** *f* OPTIQUE, TELECOM core diameter tolerance; **~ sur le diamètre de la gaine** *f* OPTIQUE cladding diameter tolerance; **~ sur les dimensions** *f* CONS MECA size margin; **~ sur l'épaisseur** *f* CONS MECA thickness margin; **~ sur la longueur** *f* CONS MECA length margin; **~ temps-température** *f* REFRIG t-t-t, time-temperature-tolerance; **~ d'usinage** *f* CONS MECA allowance; **~ d'usure** *f* CH DE FER rail wear tolerance; **~ de verticalité** *f* CERAM VER verticality tolerance

tolérancement *m* CONS MECA, PRODUCTION tolerancing; **~ géométrique** *m* CONS MECA geometric tolerancing

tolérances: ~ de fabrication *f pl* RESSORTS manufacturing tolerances

tolérant: ~ à l'acide *adj* POLLUTION acid-resistant; **~ aux défauts** *adj* ELECTROTEC fault-tolerant; **~ aux fautes** *adj* INFORMAT fault-tolerant

tôlerie *f* PRODUCTION plateworks, plating, sheet iron works

tolite *f* CHIMIE trotyl

toluate *m* CHIMIE toluate

toluène *m* CHIMIE, LESSIVES, PETROLE, PLAST CAOU *solvant* toluene; **~ diisocyanate** *m* PLAST CAOU *agent de durcissement* TDI, toluene diisocyanate

toluidine *f* CHIMIE toluidine

toluique *adj* CHIMIE toluic

tolunitrile *m* CHIMIE tolunitrile

toluol *m* CHIMIE toluene, toluol

toluquinoléine *f* CHIMIE toluquinoline

toluyle *m* CHIMIE toluyl

toluylène *m* CHIMIE toluylene

tolyle *m* CHIMIE tolyl

tolylénique *adj* CHIMIE tolylene

tombé: ~ de métier *m* TEXTILE loom state

tombée *f* CONSTR collapse, MINES caving, caving in, collapse, *du toit* subsidence

tomber[1] *vt* CONS MECA *bord* flange; **~ dans le domaine de** *vt* BREVETS fall within the scope of

tomber:[2] **~ dans la mer** *vi* HYDROLOGIE discharge into the sea, outfall to sea; **~ en déliquescence** *vi* CHIMIE deliquesce; **~ en efflorescence** *vi* CHIMIE effloresce; **~ en panne** *vi* CONSTR break down, MECANIQUE fail, TEXTILE break down; **~ en travers** *vi* NAUT broach; **~ à la mer** *vi* NAUT fall overboard

tombereau *m* CONSTR dumper, TRANSPORT dump truck

tomodensitomètre *m* PHYS ONDES scanner

tomographie *f* CONS MECA tomography

ton *m* ACOUSTIQUE key, whole tone, IMPRIM tone, PHOTO hue, shade, tone; **~ continu** *m* IMPRIM continuous tone; **~ hululé** *m* ACOUSTIQUE warble; **~ majeur** *m* ACOUSTIQUE major whole tone; **~ mineur** *m* ACOUSTIQUE minor whole tone; **~ plein** *m* PLAST CAOU *peinture* deep color tone (AmE), deep colour tone (BrE); **~ relatif** *m* ACOUSTIQUE relative tone; **~ subjectif** *m* ACOUSTIQUE subjective tone

tonalite *f* PETR tonalite

tonalité *f* ACOUSTIQUE key, ENREGISTR tonality, IMPRIM tone value, tone, *photogravure, impression* hue, TELECOM tone; **~ chromatique** *f* IMPRIM hue; **~ d'entrée d'un tiers** *f* TELECOM third-party warning tone; **~ d'étalonnage** *f* ENREGISTR line-up tone; **~ pilote** *f* ENREGISTR neo-pilot tone, pilot tone

tondeuse *f* CONSTR lawn mower, TEXTILE *pour moutons* shearing machine

tondre *vt* TEXTILE crop, shear

toner *m* IMPRIM toner

tonie *f* ACOUSTIQUE pitch

tonique *f* ACOUSTIQUE keynote

tonnage *m* METROLOGIE tonnage, NAUT tonnage, *d'un navire de guerre* displacement; **~ brut** *m* NAUT gross tonnage; **~ inemployé** *m* NAUT idle shipping; **~ net** *m* NAUT net tonnage, register tonnage

tonne *f* METROLOGIE metric ton, metric tonne, ton, tonne, MINES bucket, kibble, tub, PETROLE metric ton, PHYSIQUE tonne, PRODUCTION hoisting bucket; **~ courte** *f* METROLOGIE net ton, short ton, ton; **~ de déplacement** *f* NAUT ton of displacement; **~ forte** *f* METROLOGIE gross ton, long ton, ton; **~ à lisier** *f* POLLU MER vacuum tanker; **~ métrique** *f* METROLOGIE metric ton, ton, tonne

tonneau *m* AERONAUT *acrobaties* roll, AGRO ALIM barrel, PRODUCTION tub; **~ d'affrètement** *m* NAUT shipping ton; **~ à dessabler** *m* PRODUCTION cleaning barrel, rattler, rattling barrel, shaking barrel, tumbler, tumbling box, tumbling drum, tumbling mill, tumbling barrel; **~ dessableur** *m* PRODUCTION rattler, rattling barrel, shaking barrel, shaking mill, tumbler, tumbling box, tumbling drum, tumbling mill, rumbler, shaking machine, tumbling barrel; **~ à eau** *m* CONSTR water butt; **~ d'encombrement** *m* NAUT measured ton; **~ de jauge** *m* NAUT gross ton, register ton; **~ à malaxer le mortier** *m* CONSTR mortar mixer; **~ à mortier** *m* CONSTR mortar mixer

tonnelet *m* CHIMIE keg

tonner *vi* METEO thunder

tonnerre *m* METEO thunder

tonnes: ~ de port en lourd *f* PETROLE tonnes dead weight

tonture *f* NAUT *du pont* camber, *du pont* sheer; **~ arrière** *f* NAUT sheer aft; **~ avant** *f* NAUT sheer forward

top: ~ d'enchaînement *m* TV changeover cue; **~ de réseau** *m* TV network cue; **~ de synchronisation** *m* CINEMAT sync beep, ENREGISTR sound pulse

TOP:[1] *abrév* (*tube à onde progressive*) ELECTRON, ESPACE, PHYSIQUE, TELECOM TWT (*traveling-wave tube,*

travelling-wave tube)

TOP[2] ~ **en bande X** *m* ELECTRON X-band traveling-wave tube (AmE), X-band travelling-wave tube (BrE); ~ **en ondes millimétriques** *m* ELECTRON millimeter wave-traveling wave tube (AmE), millimetre wave travelling-wave tube (BrE); ~ **millimétrique** *m* ELECTRON millimeter wave traveling wave tube (AmE), millimetre wave travelling-wave tube (BrE)

topaze *f* MINERAUX topaz; ~ **rose** *f* MINERAUX pink topaz

topazolite *f* MINERAUX topazolite

topogramme: ~ **mémoire** *m* INFORMAT, ORDINAT memory map; ~ **à rayons X** *m* CRISTALL X-ray topogram

topographe *m* CONSTR topographer

topographie *f* CONSTR topography; ~ **mémoire** *f* INFORMAT, ORDINAT memory map; ~ **aux rayons X** *f* METALL X-ray topography; ~ **sous-marine** *f* OCEANO bottom topography, submarine relief, submarine topography

topologie *f* GEOMETRIE, INFORMAT, ORDINAT topology; ~ **différentielle** *f* GEOMETRIE differential topology; ~ **en anneau** *f* INFORMAT, ORDINAT ring topology; ~ **en arbre** *f* INFORMAT, ORDINAT tree topology; ~ **en bus** *f* INFORMAT, ORDINAT bus topology; ~ **en étoile** *f* INFORMAT, ORDINAT star topology; ~ **en flocon de neige** *f* INFORMAT, ORDINAT snowflake topology; ~ **d'interconnexion** *f* INFORMAT, ORDINAT interconnection topology; ~ **de réseau** *f* INFORMAT, ORDINAT network topology

topologue *m* GEOMETRIE topologist

torbérite *f* MINERAUX torbernite

torbernite *f* MINERAUX torbernite, NUCLEAIRE copper uranite, torbernite

torche *f* CONSTR, GAZ torch, PETROLE *d'une plateforme, d'une raffinerie* flare, THERMODYN gas flare; ~ **ciné** *f* CINEMAT sun gun; ~ **de foin** *f* PRODUCTION hay band, hay rope; ~ **pour soudage MIG-MAG** *f* CONSTR torch for MIG-MAG welding; ~ **pour soudage plasma** *f* CONSTR torch for plasma welding; ~ **pour soudage TIG** *f* CONSTR torch for TIG welding

torcher *vt* THERMODYN burn off

torchère *f* PETROLE flare stack

torchis *m* CONSTR cob

tordre *vt* POLLU MER wring

tore *m* ELECTROTEC core, magnetic core, GEOMETRIE torus, ORDINAT core, PHYS RAYON *recherche de fusion nucléaire* torus, TELECOM threading ring; ~ **à deux trous** *m* GEOMETRIE two-hole torus; ~ **en feuillard enroulé** *m* ELECTROTEC tape-wound core; ~ **européen conjoint** *m (JET)* NUCLEAIRE, PHYS RAYON Joint European Torus *(JET)*; ~ **de ferrite** *m* ELECTROTEC, ORDINAT ferrite core; ~ **magnétique** *m* ELECTROTEC magnetic core, ORDINAT bead, core, magnetic core; ~ **à trois trous** *m* GEOMETRIE three-hole torus

tornade *f* METEO tornado; ~ **éphémère** *f* METEO short-lived tornado

toron *m* ESPACE *véhicules* harness, strand, OPTIQUE, PHYSIQUE, PRODUCTION strand; ~ **de câble** *m* ELECTR *conducteur* stranded conductor; ~ **de cuivre** *m* PRODUCTION copper braid

torose *f* OCEANO hummocks, hummocky ice

torpille *f* MILITAIRE, MINES, NAUT torpedo, PLAST CAOU *boudineuse* mandrel, mandril, *presse à extrusion* torpedo

torpilleur *m* NAUT torpedo boat

torque: ~ **à rotor bloqué** *f* ELECTR *machine* locked rotor torque

torr *m* PHYSIQUE torr

torréfacteur *m* PRODUCTION torrefier

torréfaction *f* AGRO ALIM roasting, PRODUCTION roasting, torrefaction

torrent *m* HYDROLOGIE torrent; ~ **de lumière** *m* THERMODYN blaze; ~ **permanent** *m* HYDROLOGIE continuous flood; ~ **persistant** *m* HYDROLOGIE continuous flood, continuous high flow

torrentiel *adj* METEO torrential

torsadé *adj* TELECOM twisted together

torse *f* CONS MECA screw auger

torsiomètre *m* EQUIP LAB, INSTRUMENT torsion meter, PAPIER torsional tear tester

torsion:[1] **de** ~ *adj* MECANIQUE torsional

torsion[2] *f* CONS MECA torsion, twisting, MATERIAUX, METALL torsion, NUCLEAIRE *des lignes de champ*, PAPIER twist, PHYS FLUID *tourbillon de fond* twisting, PHYSIQUE torsion, TEXTILE twist; ~ **aérodynamique** *f* AERONAUT aerodynamic twist; ~ **avec cisaillement** *f* NUCLEAIRE twist with shear; ~ **nulle** *f* TEXTILE zero twist; ~ **S** *f* TEXTILE S-twist; ~ **Z** *f* TEXTILE Z-twist

torticolis: ~ **de dislocation** *m* METALL dislocation kink

tortillement *m* PRODUCTION kink

tortilleur *m* TRANSPORT twister

tosyle *m* CHIMIE tosyl

total *m* INFORMAT sum, ORDINAT sum, tally; ~ **autorisé de captures** *m* OCEANO total allowable catch; ~ **de contrôle** *m* INFORMAT batch total, control total, ORDINAT batch total, checksum, control total

totalement: ~ **compatible** *adj* ELECTROTEC plug compatible

totalisateur: ~ **d'heures de marche** *m* MECANIQUE elapsed time counter; ~ **partiel** *m* VEHICULES *instrument* odometer (AmE), trip counter (BrE)

touage *m* NAUT towage, towing

Toucan *m* ASTRONOMIE Tucana

touchau *m* CONS MECA test needle, touch needle

touche *f* CINEMAT key, CONS MECA milling jig, *d'une machine à fraiser* profiling roller, ELECTROTEC, IMPRIM, INFORMAT, ORDINAT key, TELECOM button, TV *d'un clavier* key; ~ **d'activation** *f* ORDINAT hot key; ~ **d'appel** *f* ELECTROTEC call button; ~ **arrêt** *f* TV stop key; ~ **de commande** *f* INFORMAT, ORDINAT control key; ~ **de commande du curseur** *f* ORDINAT cursor key; ~ **du curseur** *f* INFORMAT cursor key; ~ **de cycle unique** *f* PRODUCTION *automatisme industriel* single scan key; ~ **directe** *f* INFORMAT, ORDINAT hot key; ~ **échappement** *f* ORDINAT escape key; ~ **d'échappement** *f* INFORMAT escape key; ~ **à effleurement** *f* ELECTROTEC touch switch; ~ **d'enregistrement** *f* TV record button; ~ **de fonction** *f* INFORMAT, ORDINAT function key; ~ **de forçage** *f* PRODUCTION forcing key; ~ **à impulsion** *f* PRODUCTION *automatisme industriel* momentary push key; ~ **de justification** *f* IMPRIM justification key; ~ **non attribuée** *f* INFORMAT, ORDINAT undefined key; ~ **non définie** *f* INFORMAT undefined key; ~ **prise de ligne** *f* TELECOM line seizure button; ~ **programmable** *f* INFORMAT, ORDINAT soft key; ~ **de rappel** *f* COMMANDE reset button; ~ **répétition** *f* TV repeat key; ~ **de tabulation** *f* INFORMAT, ORDINAT TAB, tabulator key; ~ **de test à "1"** *f* PRODUCTION *automatisme industriel* examine-on key; ~ **de test à "O"** *f* PRODUCTION *automatisme industriel* examine-off key; ~ **de verrouillage** *f* PRODUCTION *automatisme industriel* latch key

toucher[1] *m* TEXTILE handle; ~ **doux** *m* TEXTILE soft handle; ~ **dur** *m* TEXTILE hard handle; ~ **ferme** *m*

TEXTILE firm handle; ~ **nerveux** *m* TEXTILE crisp handle, lively handle; ~ **plein** *m* TEXTILE full handle; ~ **rêche** *m* TEXTILE harsh handle; ~ **soyeux** *m* TEXTILE silk-like handle

toucher:[2] ~ **le but** *vi* MILITAIRE *sur une cible* score a hit; ~ **le fond** *vi* NAUT ground

toucheur: ~ **d'encre** *m* IMPRIM *machines* ink form roller

touer *vt* NAUT kedge, warp, *chaland* tow; ~ **avec ancre** *vt* NAUT kedge; ~ **avec point fixe** *vt* NAUT warp

touffe *f* MINES stythe, TEXTILE tuft

touline: ~ **de passage** *f* NAUT messenger, messenger line

toupilleuse *f* CONSTR spindle molding machine (AmE), spindle moulding machine (BrE)

tour[1] *m* CONS MECA revolution, turning lathe, turn, turn, ELECTROTEC turn, MECANIQUE lathe, PHYSIQUE turn, PRODUCTION lathe, RESSORTS turn; ~ **à archet** *m* CONS MECA bow lathe; ~ **automatique** *m* MECANIQUE automatic lathe, screw machine; ~ **automatique à copier** *m* CONS MECA automatic copying lathe; ~ **automatique pour le travail en mandrin** *m* CONS MECA automatic chucking lathe; ~ **avec porte-outil revolver** *m* CONS MECA turret lathe, PRODUCTION monitor lathe; ~ **avec tourelle revolver** *m* CONS MECA turret lathe, PRODUCTION monitor lathe; ~ **ayant deux vis mères indépendantes et de pas différent** *m* CONS MECA twin-screw lathe; ~ **à banc droit** *m* CONS MECA plain bed lathe; ~ **à banc rompu** *m* CONS MECA gap lathe; ~ **à barre prismatique** *m* CONS MECA gantry lathe; ~ **à bâti** *m* CONS MECA bed lathe; ~ **bibroche** *m* CONS MECA twin-spindle lathe; ~ **à bois** *m* CONSTR wood-turning lathe; ~ **à chariot** *m* CONS MECA slide lathe; ~ **à charioter** *m* CONS MECA slide lathe, sliding lathe; ~ **à combinaisons** *m* CONS MECA combination lathe; ~ **à copier** *m* CONS MECA copying lathe, forming lathe; ~ **à cuivre** *m* CONSTR brass-finisher's lathe; ~ **à cylindrer** *m* CONS MECA plain turning lathe; ~ **à décolleter** *m* MECANIQUE screw machine; ~ **à décolleter automatique** *m* MECANIQUE automatic screw machine; ~ **à dégager** *m* CONS MECA relieving lathe; ~ **à dépouiller** *m* CONS MECA relieving lathe; ~ **à détalonner** *m* CONS MECA backing-off lathe; ~ **double à roues montées** *m* CONS MECA double wheel lathe; ~ **en l'air** *m* CONS MECA face lathe, surfacing and boring lathe; ~ **en l'air à plateau horizontal** *m* CONS MECA turning mill; ~ **en l'air à plateau vertical** *m* CONS MECA face lathe, surfacing and boring lathe; ~ **en l'air sur banc** *m* CONS MECA bed-type surfacing and boring lathe; ~ **en l'air sur taque** *m* CONS MECA floor-type surfacing and boring lathe; ~ **entre-pointes** *m* CONS MECA center lathe (AmE), centre lathe (BrE), centering lathe (AmE), centring lathe (BrE); ~ **à essieux** *m* CONS MECA axle lathe; ~ **d'établi** *m* CONS MECA, MECANIQUE bench lathe; ~ **à facer** *m* CONS MECA face lathe; ~ **à fileter** *m* CONS MECA screw cutting lathe; ~ **de gravure** *m* CERAM VER engraving lathe; ~ **à marche rapide** *m* CONS MECA speed lathe; ~ **mort et deux demi-clefs** *m* NAUT round turn and two half hitches; ~ **à noyaux** *m* PRODUCTION core lathe; ~ **d'outillage** *m* CONS MECA toolmaker's lathe; ~ **à outils multiples** *m* CONS MECA multiple-tool lathe, multitool lathe; ~ **parallèle à fileter charioter et surfacer** *m* CONS MECA self-acting sliding lathe, sliding surfacing and screw-cutting lathe; ~ **parallèle très renforcé** *m* CONS MECA heavy-duty lathe; ~ **de pâtisserie** *m* REFRIG refrigerated bakery slab; ~ **de piste en approche** *m* AERONAUT circling approach; ~ **à plateau horizontal** *m* CONS MECA turning mill; ~ **à pointes** *m* CONS MECA

center lathe (AmE), centre lathe (BrE), centering lathe (AmE), centring lathe (BrE), pole lathe; ~ **de potier** *m* CERAM VER pallet, potter's wheel, throwing wheel; ~ **à poulies** *m* CONS MECA pulley lathe, pulley-turning lathe; ~ **pour arbres de transmission** *m* CONS MECA shafting lathe; ~ **pour bâtons ronds** *m* PRODUCTION rounding machine; ~ **rapide** *m* CONS MECA speed lathe; ~ **à repousser** *m* CONS MECA chasing lathe; ~ **à reproduire** *m* CONS MECA copy milling lathe; ~ **revolver** *m* CONS MECA, MECANIQUE capstan lathe, turret lathe, PRODUCTION monitor lathe; ~ **à revolver pour le décolletage et la façonnage** *m* CONS MECA cutting-off and forming lathe; ~ **de robinetterie** *m* CONSTR brass-finisher's lathe; ~ **simple** *m* CONS MECA plain lathe, plain ungeared lathe; ~ **à simple harnais d'engrenage** *m* CONS MECA single-geared lathe; ~ **à singer** *m* CONS MECA copying lathe, forming lathe; ~ **de spire** *m* CONS MECA turn; ~ **de tailleur** *m* CERAM VER cutting frame; ~ **à touche** *m* CONS MECA copying lathe, forming lathe; ~ **à tourelle hexagonale** *m* CONS MECA hexagon turret lathe; ~ **à trains montés** *m* CONS MECA double wheel lathe; ~ **à tronçonner** *m* CONS MECA cutting-off lathe; ~ **vertical** *m* CONS MECA boring and turning mill

tour:[2] ~ **d'absorption** *f* AGRO ALIM, CHARBON absorption tower, GENIE CHIM, PAPIER absorption column, absorption tower; ~ **basculante** *f* EN RENOUV *énergie éolienne* tiltable tower; ~ **de blanchiment** *f* PAPIER bleaching tower; ~ **de charbon à coke** *f* MINES coke-cooling tower; ~ **de composition** *f* CERAM VER batch tower; ~ **de concentration** *f* GENIE CHIM concentration column; ~ **de contrôle** *f* AERONAUT, TRANSPORT control tower; ~ **de décantation pour fines** *f* GENIE CHIM settling pit; ~ **de diffusion** *f* GENIE CHIM diffusion tower; ~ **d'éjection de secours** *f* ESPACE launch escape system; ~ **d'extinction du coke** *f* MINES coke-quenching tower; ~ **d'extraction** *f* MINES head frame, pithead frame, winding tower; ~ **à fines** *f* MINES coke-cooling tower; ~ **de forage** *f* EN RENOUV, PETROLE derrick; ~ **de fractionnement** *f* GENIE CHIM fractionating column; ~ **de guet** *f* MILITAIRE watchtower; ~ **hertzienne** *f* TELECOM microwave tower; ~ **de lancement** *f* ESPACE launch tower, *véhicules* launching tower; ~ **de lavage** *f* GENIE CHIM scrubber, washing column, washing tower; ~ **d'observation** *f* MILITAIRE observation tower; ~ **de prise d'eau** *f* HYDROLOGIE intake tower; ~ **de puissance** *f* EN RENOUV *énergie solaire* power tower; ~ **de réfrigération** *f* CONS MECA, GENIE CHIM cooling tower; ~ **de refroidissement** *f* CHAUFFAGE, CONSTR cooling tower, IMPRIM *périphériques de rotatives* chilling tower, PRODUCTION, REFRIG cooling tower; ~ **de refroidissement sec** *f* REFRIG dry cooling tower; ~ **de sauvetage** *f* ESPACE *véhicules* emergency escape tower; ~ **de séchage** *f* AGRO ALIM drying tower; ~ **solaire** *f* EN RENOUV solar tower; ~ **de télescope solaire** *f* INSTRUMENT solar telescope tower

touraille *f* AGRO ALIM drying kiln, drying oven, kiln

tourbe *f* CHARBON, CHIMIE peat; ~ **fibreuse** *f* CHARBON fibrous peat; ~ **de marais** *f* CHARBON bog peat

tourbillon *m* CHARBON, ESPACE *véhicules* vortex, HYDROLOGIE eddy, vortex, whirlpool, MECANIQUE *hydraulique* vortex, NAUT eddy, swirl, vortex, PHYSIQUE eddy, vortex; ~ **élevé localement** *m* PHYS FLUID locally high vorticity; ~ **d'extrémité d'aile** *m* AERONAUT wing tip vortex; ~ **d'extrémité de pale** *m* AERONAUT blade tip vortex; ~ **de vent** *m* METEO, NAUT whirlwind

tourbillonnement: ~ **des arbres** m CONS MECA whirling of shafts; ~ **de fond** m PHYS FLUID background vorticity

tourbillonner vi NAUT eddy

tourbillons: ~ **d'apex** m pl EN RENOUV tip loss; ~ **derrière des obstacles** m pl PHYS FLUID trailing vortices; ~ **liés** m pl PHYS FLUID attached eddies

tourelle f CINEMAT, CONS MECA, MECANIQUE, MILITAIRE d'un char d'assaut turret, PRODUCTION monitor; ~ **à action automatique** f MILITAIRE d'un char d'assaut self-propelled turret; ~ **des filtres** f IMPRIM photogravure filter turret; ~ **d'objectifs** f CINEMAT, IMPRIM, OPTIQUE lens turret; ~ **d'observation** f OCEANO survey diving bell; ~ **de plongée** f OCEANO diving bell; ~ **porte-objectifs** f INSTRUMENT objective nosepiece, objective turret; ~ **revolver** f CONS MECA turret, turret head, PRODUCTION monitor; ~ **revolver pour six outils** f CONS MECA six-tool capstan; ~ **à trois objectifs** f CINEMAT three-lens turret

touret m CONS MECA bow lathe, piercer, pulley for gut band, ELECTROTEC cable drum, MINES swivel, OCEANO cable drum, drum, winch drum, reel; ~ **électrique** m CONS MECA bench grinder; ~ **hydraulique** m MINES water swivel; ~ **à meuler** m MECANIQUE grinder; ~ **pour câbles** m ELECTROTEC cable drum; ~ **pour flexibles** m PETR cable reel, reel; ~ **pour polisseurs** m CONS MECA polishing head; ~ **de pousseur** m CONS MECA pour polisseurs polishing lathe

tourette f CONS MECA circular diamond cutting apparatus

tourillon m AUTO journal, CHARBON trunnion, CONS MECA stub, trunnion, d'un arbre gudgeon, d'un cylindre de laminoir journal, CONSTR pin, MECANIQUE journal, trunnion, NUCLEAIRE king journal, pivot, trunnion, d'un palier journal, PRODUCTION d'un tambour de treuil gudgeon, d'une lanterne gudgeon, d'un cylindre de laminoir neck, d'un châssis de fonderie swivel, VEHICULES bearing, journal, trunnion; ~ **de crosse** m CONS MECA crosshead pin, gudgeon, gudgeon pin, INST HYDR de machine à vapeur pin of cross-head; ~ **de manivelle** m CONS MECA crankpin; ~ **de suspension de la coulisse** m CONS MECA link bearing, suspension stud; ~ **de la tête de piston** m CONS MECA crosshead pin, gudgeon, gudgeon pin

tourmaline f MINERAUX, PHYSIQUE tourmaline; ~ **bleue** f MINERAUX blue tourmaline; ~ **brune** f MINERAUX brown tourmaline

tournage m CINEMAT shooting, CONS MECA d'un arbre coudé turning; ~ **d'un accéléré** m CINEMAT time lapse photography; ~ **à deux caméras** m CINEMAT double take; ~ **en l'air** m CONS MECA turning on the face plate; ~ **en extérieurs** m CINEMAT exterior, location shooting; ~ **en playback** m CINEMAT shooting to playback; ~ **en synchrone** m CINEMAT synchronized shooting; ~ **entre pointes** m CONS MECA turning between centers (AmE), turning between centres (BrE); ~ **image par image** m CINEMAT single frame filming; ~ **par animation** m CINEMAT bench work

tournant: ~ **faux-rond** adj IMPRIM rouleaux, cylindres, bobines out-of-round

tourné adj CONS MECA turned-in-the-lathe

tourne-à-gauche m CONS MECA tap wrench, MINES brace head, brace key, rod-turning tool, tiller, PRODUCTION pour donner la voie aux scies swage; ~ **de manoeuvre** m MINES rod-turning tool, tiller; ~ **pour donner la voie aux scies** m CONS MECA saw set, set, PRODUCTION jumper; ~ **de support** m MINES rod support, suppor-

ting fork

tourne-disque m ACOUSTIQUE, ENREGISTR record player, turntable

tourner[1] vt CERAM VER throw, CINEMAT film, film shoot, shoot, tourelle rack, CONS MECA turn; ~ **pour relâcher** vt PRODUCTION twist to release, automatisme industriel twist-release; ~ **à une vitesse inférieure à la normale** vt CINEMAT under-crank; ~ **à une vitesse supérieure à la normale** vt CINEMAT overcrank

tourner[2] vi CONS MECA run, NAUT veer; ~ **au ralenti** vi MECANIQUE, VEHICULES moteur idle; ~ **sur soi-même** vi ESPACE spin; ~ **à vide** vi MECANIQUE idle

tournesol m CHIMIE litmus

tournette f CERAM VER trammel

tourneur m CERAM VER thrower, turner, MECANIQUE lathe operator; ~ **de porcelaine** m CERAM VER china thrower, porcelain thrower

tournevis m CONS MECA screwdriver, turnscrew, VEHICULES outil screwdriver; ~ **détecteur de tension** m CONS MECA voltage tester screwdriver; ~ **dynamométrique** m CONS MECA torque screwdriver; ~ **à frapper** m CONS MECA impact screwdriver; ~ **au fût** m CONS MECA screwdriver bit; ~ **pour vilebrequin** m CONS MECA screwdriver bit; ~ **de syntonisation** m CONS MECA tuning screwdriver; ~ **à tête plate** m PRODUCTION flat-head screwdriver

tourniquet m CONS MECA latch, PRODUCTION d'un ventilateur wheel; ~ **de cabestan** m CONSTR roller; ~ **de ventilateur** m CONS MECA, SECURITE fan wheel

tournure f PRODUCTION turnings

tours: ~ **au mètre** m pl TEXTILE turns per meter (AmE), turns per metre (BrE); ~ **par minute** m pl AUTO, CINEMAT, PHYSIQUE revolutions per minute; ~ **par pouce** m pl TEXTILE turns per inch

tourtia f CONSTR glauconite marl

tout-venant m CHARBON raw material, CONSTR all-in ballast, MINES mine run, run-of-mine, run-of-mine coal

toxicité f CHIMIE, PETROLE, PLAST CAOU, POLLU MER, SECURITE toxicity

toxicologie f SECURITE toxicology

toxine f QUALITE toxin

toxique[1] adj CHARBON, PETROLE, SECURITE toxic

toxique[2] m CHIMIE toxicant, SECURITE poison

toxistérol m CHIMIE toxisterol

TPN abrév (température normale) PHYSIQUE STP (standard temperature)

traçabilité f METROLOGIE traceability

traçage m CERAM VER marking out, CINEMAT, CONS MECA tracing, INFORMAT plotting, MINES mine development, d'un gîte opening up, NAUT lofting, ORDINAT plotting; ~ **par radar de la trajectoire de vol** m MILITAIRE, TRANSPORT radar plotting; ~ **au rocher** m MINES development by rock chutes

trace f ELECTRON, GAZ, INFORMAT, MATERIAUX, ORDINAT, PETR trace, POLLU MER swath, PRODUCTION mark; ~ **acoustique** f ACOUSTIQUE soundtrack; ~ **acoustique symétrique** f ACOUSTIQUE symmetrical sound track; ~ **de l'axe** f GEOLOGIE du pli en surface axial trace; ~ **bilatérale** f ACOUSTIQUE dual track; ~ **croisée** f PETR crossplot; ~ **de gain** f PETR gain trace; ~ **de glissement** f METALL slip marking; ~ **nucléaire** f NUCLEAIRE nuclear track, track; ~ **d'oscilloscope** f ELECTRON oscilloscope trace; ~ **pilote** f ACOUSTIQUE control track; ~ **de pression tectonique** f GEOLOGIE pressure shadow; ~ **de la pulvérisation** f POLLU MER spraypath; ~ **saillante** f PRODUCTION *laissée sur une petite moulée* ridge; ~ **de satellite** f ESPACE satellite track; ~ **de séchage** f CINEMAT watermark; ~ **unilatérale** f ACOUSTIQUE unilateral track

tracé m CH DE FER *de ligne* route, CONSTR *d'une ligne, d'un alignement* running, *projection horizontale* alignment, ELECTRON pattern, EMBALLAGE layout, HYDROLOGIE *d'une rivière* course, IMPRIM blind embossing, layout, INFORMAT plot, *d'une carte* layout, MILITAIRE *topographie* plotting, NAUT plotting, *sur la carte* plot, ORDINAT plot, PRODUCTION layout; ~ **de câble** m ELECTR *alimentation* cable run; ~ **de chargement** m CINEMAT lacing path; ~ **dendritique du réseau hydrographique** m HYDROLOGIE dendritic drainage pattern; ~ **du flux thermique** m THERMODYN heat flow line; ~ **généré par des points correctement imprimés** m IMPRIM *photogravure, impression* rosette; ~ **de l'heure** m GEOPHYS time trace; ~ **inférieur** m HYDROLOGIE lower track; ~ **des motifs** m ELECTRON pattern generation; ~ **parasite sur un écran cathodique** m IMPRIM, INFORMAT hash; ~ **polygonal** m CONSTR traverse; ~ **de la puce** m ELECTRON chip layout; ~ **de la quille hors membres** m NAUT *étude du navire* baseline; ~ **de la route** m NAUT plotting; ~ **des secousses** m GEOPHYS seismic wave trace

tracelet m CONSTR scratch awl, PRODUCTION marking awl

tracement m CONS MECA tracing

tracer[1] vt CONSTR plot, *itinéraire* mark out, GEOMETRIE plot, trace, GEOPHYS record, trace, IMPRIM score, MATH *courbe* trace, *graphique* plot, MINES develop, *un filon jusqu'à l'origine* chase, NAUT *bureau d'études* draw, *route* plot; ~ **la coupe de** vt CONSTR *pierre* line out; ~ **au couteau** vt IMPRIM score

tracer:[2] ~ **les formes** vi NAUT lay down the lines

traceret m CONSTR scratch awl, scribe awl, scriber, scribing awl, PRODUCTION marking awl

traces: ~ **de développement** f pl CINEMAT processing marks; ~ **de pinceau** f pl CERAM VER brush marks; ~ **de serrage** f pl CINEMAT stress marks

tracés: ~ **parasites** m pl IMPRIM *en surface d'un adhésif* feathers

traceur m CERAM VER tracer, IMPRIM pen ruling machine, INFORMAT plotter, MILITAIRE tracer, NAUT draftsman (AmE), draughtsman (BrE), loftsman, NUCLEAIRE isotopic tracer, tracer, labeled atom (AmE), labelled atom (BrE), tagged atom, tracer atom, ORDINAT plotter, PETR tracer, PRODUCTION draftsman (AmE), draughtsman (BrE); ~ **biochimique** m POLLUTION biochemical tracer; ~ **de courbes** m ESPACE X-Y plotter, INFORMAT graph plotter, graphics plotter, ORDINAT graph plotter, graphics plotter; ~ **électrostatique** m INFORMAT, ORDINAT electrostatic plotter; ~ **incrémentiel** m INFORMAT, ORDINAT incremental plotter; ~ **mécanicien** m PRODUCTION mechanical draftsman (AmE), mechanical draughtsman (BrE); ~ **numérique** m INFORMAT, ORDINAT digital plotter; ~ **à plat** m INFORMAT, ORDINAT flat-bed plotter; ~ **à plume** m INFORMAT pen plotter, ORDINAT pen plotter (AmE), pen recorder (BrE); ~ **radioactif** m PHYS RAYON, PHYSIQUE radioactive tracer; ~ **de route** m AERONAUT course tracer; ~ **à tambour** m INFORMAT drum plotter, ORDINAT barrel plotter (BrE), drum plotter (AmE)

trackball m INFORMAT, ORDINAT trackball

traçoir m CONS MECA scriber, *d'une mèche à trois pointes*

nicker, CONSTR scratch awl, scribe awl, scriber, scribing awl, PRODUCTION marking awl

tractage m AERONAUT, TRANSPORT towing

tracteur m CONSTR, INFORMAT, ORDINAT, TRANSPORT tractor, VEHICULES towing vehicle, tractor; ~ **à bagages** m TRANSPORT luggage trolley; ~ **à chenilles** m MILITAIRE caterpillar tractor; ~ **forestier** m TRANSPORT short-haul skidder; ~ **à picots** m IMPRIM tractor feed; ~ **routier** m TRANSPORT road tractor, trailer-towing machine; ~ **de semi-remorque** m TRANSPORT semitrailer motor vehicle, semitrailer towing vehicle, semitrailer truck; ~ **sur chenilles** m CONSTR tracked tractor

tracteur-char m MILITAIRE tank bulldozer, tank dozer

traction:[1] **à ~ avant** adj TRANSPORT front-wheel drive

traction[2] f CH DE FER *véhicules* traction, CONS MECA pulling, tension, traction, CONSTR traction, METALL tension, VEHICULES *transmission* drive; ~ **arrière** f AUTO, TRANSPORT rear-wheel drive; ~ **avant** f AUTO, TRANSPORT front-wheel drive; ~ **d'hélice** f TRANSPORT propeller thrust

tractopelle f CONSTR tracked tractor, POLLU MER backhoe

traducteur m INFORMAT, ORDINAT language translator, translator, TELECOM translator; ~ **toroïdal** m TELECOM ring translator

traduction f INFORMAT, ORDINAT translation; ~ **assistée par ordinateur** f ORDINAT computer-assisted translation; ~ **dynamique d'adresse** f ORDINAT DAT, dynamic address translation

trafic m INFORMAT, ORDINAT traffic, TELECOM calls, TRANSPORT traffic; ~ **aérien** m TRANSPORT air traffic; ~ **d'aéroport** m AERONAUT airport traffic; ~ **d'arrivée** m TELECOM incoming call, terminating traffic; ~ **de banlieue** m TRANSPORT suburban traffic; ~ **commercial** m TRANSPORT business traffic, commercial traffic; ~ **de débordement** m TELECOM overflow traffic; ~ **de départ** m TELECOM originating traffic; ~ **de destination** m TRANSPORT terminating traffic; ~ **discontinu** m TRANSPORT stop-and-go traffic; ~ **écoulé** m TELECOM traffic carried; ~ **efficace** m TELECOM effective traffic; ~ **en transit** m TRANSPORT external traffic; ~ **entrant** m TELECOM incoming traffic, TRANSPORT entering traffic, inbound traffic, inward traffic; ~ **fluvial** m NAUT, TRANSPORT river traffic; ~ **de groupage** m CH DE FER *véhicules* groupage traffic; ~ **habitation travail** m TRANSPORT commuter traffic, home to work traffic; ~ **d'heure de pointe** m TRANSPORT peak hour traffic, peak load traffic, peak period traffic, rush hour traffic; ~ **intermodal** m CH DE FER *véhicules* intermodal traffic; ~ **interne** m TELECOM internal traffic; ~ **interne-externe** m TRANSPORT originating traffic; ~ **journalier** m TELECOM day traffic; ~ **local** m TELECOM local traffic; ~ **lourd** m TRANSPORT HGV traffic; ~ **de marchandises à longue distance** m TRANSPORT long-distance freight traffic (AmE), long-distance goods traffic (BrE); ~ **multimodal** m CH DE FER *véhicules* multimodal traffic; ~ **normal** m TRANSPORT normal traffic; ~ **offert** m TELECOM traffic offered; ~ **perdu** m TELECOM lost traffic; ~ **de pointe** m CH DE FER peak hour traffic, TRANSPORT peak load traffic, peak period traffic; ~ **poissonnien** m TELECOM Poisson traffic; ~ **professionnel** m TRANSPORT work traffic; ~ **de projet** m TRANSPORT design volume; ~ **de pur hasard** m TELECOM pure chance traffic; ~ **régularisé** m TELECOM smooth traffic; ~ **sortant** m TELECOM outgoing traffic, TRANSPORT outbound traffic, outward traffic; ~ **de**

transit *m* TELECOM transit traffic, TRANSPORT bypassable traffic, through traffic; **~ urbain** *m* TRANSPORT urban traffic; **~ voyageurs** *m* TRANSPORT passenger transport

traille *f* TRANSPORT ferry cable

train *m* CONS MECA *d'engrenages* cluster, *de cylindres* battery, GAZ *de tiges* string, PRODUCTION mill, rolls, VEHICULES *roues* set of wheels; **~ à adhérence totale** *m* TRANSPORT total adherence train; **~ aéromagnétique** *m* TRANSPORT aeromagnetic train; **~ arrière** *m* VEHICULES *transmission* rear axle; **~ articulé** *m* TRANSPORT articulated train; **~ d'atterrissage** *m* AERONAUT landing gear, undercarriage, ESPACE *véhicules* landing gear, undercarriage, TRANSPORT landing gear; **~ d'atterrissage en tandem de diabolos** *m* AERONAUT dual tandem wheel undercarriage; **~ d'atterrissage semi-actif** *m* AERONAUT semiactive landing gear; **~ d'atterrissage tricycle** *m* AERONAUT tricycle landing gear; **~ autos-couchettes** *m (TAC)* CH DE FER *véhicules* car sleeper train, motorail; **~ avant** *m* AERONAUT nose gear, nose wheel, VEHICULES *roues, transmission* front axle; **~ baladeur** *m* CONS MECA sliding gear train; **~ de bétonnage** *m* CH DE FER *véhicules* concreting train; **~ à billettes** *m* CONS MECA billetting rolls; **~ de bits** *m* ORDINAT bit stream; **~ de bits en continu** *m* TELECOM CBO, continuous bit stream oriented; **~ blindé** *m* MILITAIRE armored train (AmE), armoured train (BrE); **~ blooming** *m* PRODUCTION cogging mill; **~ à blooms** *m* PRODUCTION cogging mill; **~ de bois** *m* CONSTR timber raft, NAUT raft; **~ collecteur** *m* CH DE FER *véhicules* pick-up freight train (AmE), pick-up goods train (BrE), way freight train (AmE); **~ commercial** *m* CH DE FER *véhicules* revenue-earning train; **~ complémentaire** *m* CH DE FER *véhicules* relief train; **~ à coussin magnétique** *m* TRANSPORT magnetic cushion train; **~ de cylindres** *m* CONS MECA train of rolls, PRODUCTION set of rolls; **~ de cylindres de laminage** *m* CONS MECA battery of rolls; **~ de désherbage chimique** *m* CH DE FER *véhicules* weed-killing train; **~ désherbeur** *m* CH DE FER *véhicules* weed-killing train; **~ à desserte limitée** *m* CH DE FER *véhicules* limited train (AmE), semifast train (BrE); **~ duo** *m* PRODUCTION two-high mill, two-high rolls, two-high train; **~ ébaucheur** *m* CONS MECA blooming mill, PRODUCTION puddle bar train, puddle train, roughing rolls, puddle rolls; **~ en correspondance** *m* CH DE FER connecting train; **~ d'engrenages** *m* CONS MECA gear train, train of gearing, gear work, multiple of gearing, VEHICULES *boîte de vitesses* gear train, set of gears; **~ d'engrenages commandé par manivelle** *m* PHOTO geared center column (AmE), geared centre column (BrE); **~ d'engrenages épicycloïdal** *m* MECANIQUE epicyclic gear train; **~ d'engrenages planétaire** *m* MECANIQUE epicyclic gear train; **~ en partance** *m* CH DE FER train about to depart; **~ épicycloïdal** *m* AUTO planetary gear set, CONS MECA epicyclic gear train, epicyclic train; **~ expérimental à grande vitesse** *m (TGV)* CH DE FER advanced passenger train *(APT)*, high speed train *(HST)*; **~ express** *m* CH DE FER *véhicules* express train, fast train, TRANSPORT express train (BrE), fast train (AmE); **~ de forage** *m* PETR drill column, drill stem, drill string, PETROLE drill pipe; **~ de galets de la cabine** *m* TRANSPORT cabin pulley cradle; **~ à grande vitesse** *m (TGV)* CH DE FER advanced passenger train *(APT)*, high-speed train *(HST)*; **~ de grande ligne** *m* TRANSPORT

express train (BrE), fast train (AmE); **~ à gros profilés** *m* CONS MECA heavy-section rolls; **~ GVT** *m* TRANSPORT GVT train, gravity vacuum transit train; **~ d'impulsion** *m* ELECTRON, INFORMAT, ORDINAT pulse train; **~ d'impulsions numériques** *m* TELECOM digital pulse stream; **~ indéformable** *m* CH DE FER *véhicules* train that cannot be split up; **~ interurbain** *m* TRANSPORT intercity train; **~ interville** *m* TRANSPORT intercity train; **~ de laminage** *m* CONS MECA battery of rolls; **~ de laminage d'aciers marchands** *m* CONS MECA bar mill; **~ de laminoir** *m* PRODUCTION roll train, rolling mill roll, rolling mill train; **~ limité** *m* CH DE FER *véhicules* limited train (AmE), semifast train (BrE); **~ de machine** *m* CONS MECA wire mill, PRODUCTION looping mill, rod mill; **~ de marchandises** *m* CH DE FER *véhicules* freight train; **~ de messageries direct** *m* CH DE FER *véhicules* through parcel service; **~ de meulage des rails** *m* CH DE FER *véhicules* rail-grinding train; **~ océanique** *m* TRANSPORT bulk ship train; **~ omnibus** *m* CH DE FER *véhicules* local train (AmE), slow train (BrE), stopping train (AmE); **~ d'ondes** *m* ACOUSTIQUE, PHYS ONDES, PHYSIQUE wave train; **~ de pêche** *m* OCEANO fishing gear; **~ de petits fers** *m* PRODUCTION small bar mill; **~ planétaire** *m* AUTO planetary gear system, planetary gears, CONS MECA planetary gear train; **~ porteur** *m* TV pulse carrier; **~ postal** *m* CH DE FER mail train; **~ de présérie** *m* CH DE FER *véhicules* preproduction train; **~ principal** *m* AERONAUT main landing gear; **~ de puddlage** *m* PRODUCTION puddle bar train, puddle rolls, puddle train; **~ de ramassage** *m* CH DE FER *véhicules* feeder train; **~ réversible** *m* PRODUCTION reversing mill; **~ robot** *m* TRANSPORT brain train; **~ de roues** *m* CONS MECA wheel train; **~ des rouleaux d'encrage** *m* IMPRIM *machines* inking train; **~ de rouleaux transporteur** *m* CONS MECA roller conveyor; **~ de roulement** *m* VEHICULES *transmission* drive train; **~ routier** *m* TRANSPORT heavy motor lorry (BrE), heavy motor truck (AmE), road train; **~ routier à longue distance** *m* TRANSPORT long-distance road train; **~ routier à passagers** *m* TRANSPORT passenger road train; **~ sauvage** *m* TRANSPORT spot train; **~ de serpentage** *m* CONS MECA wire mill, PRODUCTION looping mill, rod mill; **~ à serpenter** *m* CONS MECA wire mill, PRODUCTION looping mill, rod mill; **~ spontané** *m* TRANSPORT spot train; **~ thermostat** *m* REFRIG power system; **~ de tiges** *m* PETROLE drill string; **~ de tôlerie** *m* CONS MECA plate mill; **~ trio** *m* CONS MECA three-high mill, three-high rolls, three-high train; **~ voyageurs** *m* TRANSPORT passenger train; **~ de wagons** *m* MINES rake of hutches

traînage *m* CINEMAT streaking, METALL drag, TV afterglow, afterimage, lag

traînard *m* CONS MECA saddle

train-bloc *m* CH DE FER *véhicules* block train; **~ de conteneurs** *m* CH DE FER *véhicules* freightliner train

traîneau: **~ d'ensouillage par injection** *m* PETR jet sled

traînée *f* AERONAUT, EN RENOUV *énergie éolienne* drag, ESPACE trail, *véhicules* drag, MECANIQUE, NAUT drag, PAPIER streak, PHYS FLUID, PHYSIQUE drag, TRANSPORT drag, resistance to forward motion; **~ de captation** *f* TRANSPORT captation drag, ram drag; **~ de compressibilité** *f* AERONAUT compressibility drag; **~ de condensation** *f* AERONAUT condensation trail; **~ due aux projections** *f* AERONAUT *décollage* spray drag; **~ d'échappement** *f* AERONAUT exhaust trail; **~ d'étain** *f* CERAM VER tin streak; **~ de forme** *f* AERONAUT form drag; ~ **de friction** *f* AERONAUT friction drag; ~ **de frottement** *f* AERONAUT friction drag; ~ **houillère** *f* CHARBON coal belt; ~ **humide** *f* PAPIER damp streak, moisture expansion; ~ **hydrodynamique** *f* TRANSPORT hydrodynamic drag; ~ **induite** *f* AERONAUT induced drag; ~ **lumineuse** *f* ESPACE afterglow, phosphorescence; ~ **lumineuse de comète** *f* ASTRONOMIE comet tar; ~ **magnétique** *f* TRANSPORT magnetic drag; ~ **d'onde** *f* TRANSPORT wave drag; ~ **parasite** *f* AERONAUT parasitic drag; ~ **de pression** *f* AERONAUT pressure drag; ~ **de prise d'air** *f* TRANSPORT ram drag; ~ **de profil** *f* AERONAUT profile drag; ~ **d'une sphère** *f* PHYS FLUID drag on a sphere; ~ **totale** *f* TRANSPORT total drag

traînées: ~ **colorées** *f pl* CERAM VER color streaks (AmE), colour streaks (BrE), smoke (AmE)

train-ferry *m* TRANSPORT rail ferry

train-poste *m* CH DE FER mail train

train-tube *m* TRANSPORT tube train

train-type *m* CH DE FER *véhicules* test train

trait *m* ELECTRON line, IMPRIM *composition* line, *photogravure* line work, MINES hoist, lift; ~ **du cadran** *m* ELECTR scale division; ~ **de centre** *m* PRODUCTION *axe médian* center line (AmE), centre line (BrE); ~ **de centre pour affûtage régulier** *m* PRODUCTION grinding line; ~ **de côte** *m* OCEANO coastline, shoreline; ~ **de coupe** *m* GEOLOGIE *d'une carte* line of section; ~ **de division** *m* CONS MECA dividing circle, pitch circle, pitch line, pitch line; ~ **fin** *m* ELECTRON fine line, IMPRIM fine line, hairline; ~ **de jauge** *m* EQUIP LAB *d'une pipette, d'une burette, d'une fiole* graduation mark; ~ **de repère** *m* PRODUCTION guiding line; ~ **de scie** *m* CONS MECA saw kerf, CONSTR saw cut

traité *adj* REVETEMENT coated; ~ **cryogéniquement** *adj* CONS MECA cryogenically treated

traitement *m* CHARBON, INFORMAT, ORDINAT processing, PETROLE processing, treatment, PRODUCTION process, TELECOM handling, processing, TEXTILE treatment; ~ **acide** *m* PETR acidizing; ~ **adaptatif des signaux** *m* ELECTRON adaptive signal processing; ~ **de l'air** *m* REFRIG air treatment; ~ **anaérobie** *m* RECYCLAGE anaerobic treatment; ~ **analogique des signaux** *m* ELECTRON analog signal processing (AmE), analogue signal processing (BrE); ~ **antireflet** *m* CINEMAT blooming, ESPACE *véhicules* antireflection coating; ~ **antiretrait** *m* CINEMAT deshrinking process; ~ **antirétrécissement** *m* TEXTILE antishrink treatment; ~ **antirouille** *m* CONS MECA rust proofing; ~ **d'appel** *m* TELECOM CC, call control; ~ **d'appels** *m* TELECOM call handling; ~ **d'arrière-plan** *m* INFORMAT, ORDINAT background processing; ~ **automatique** *m* PRODUCTION batch mode; ~ **automatique de données** *m* ORDINAT ADP, automatic data processing; ~ **autonome** *m* ORDINAT off-line processing; ~ **biologique** *m* POLLUTION biological treatment; ~ **biologique de l'eau** *m* DISTRI EAU biological water treatment; ~ **à bord** *m* ESPACE *communications* on-board processing; ~ **des boues** *m* RECYCLAGE sludge processing; ~ **de chaîne** *m* INFORMAT string manipulation; ~ **chelatant** *m* HYDROLOGIE chelating, chelation; ~ **chimique** *m* CHARBON chemical treatment; ~ **chimique de l'eau** *m* DISTRI EAU chemical water treatment; ~ **aux chloramines** *m* HYDROLOGIE chlorine-ammonia process; ~ **cohérent des signaux** *m* ELECTRON coherent signal processing; ~ **concurrent** *m* ORDINAT concurrent processing; ~ **contre les rayures** *m* CINEMAT antiscratch solution; ~ **couleur** *m* CINEMAT color processing (AmE), colour

processing (BrE); ~ **des déchets** *m* RECYCLE waste processing, waste treatment; ~ **des demandes** *m* INFORMAT, ORDINAT inquiry processing, query processing; ~ **différé** *m* PRODUCTION batch mode; ~ **différé d'entrées-sorties** *m* INFORMAT spooling; ~ **direct** *m* INFORMAT, ORDINAT in-line processing; ~ **distribué** *m* INFORMAT, ORDINAT distributed processing; ~ **à distribution ouverte** *m* TELECOM ODP, open distribution processing; ~ **de données** *m (TD)* ELECTRON, INFORMAT, ORDINAT, TELECOM data processing *(DP)*; ~ **à l'eau** *m* CHARBON, CONS MECA wet treatment; ~ **des eaux** *m* CHARBON, GENIE CHIM, HYDROLOGIE water treatment, NUCLEAIRE *chimique* water conditioning process, water treatment; ~ **des eaux de chaudière** *m* HYDROLOGIE feedwater treatment, MAT CHAUFF boiler water treatment; ~ **des eaux d'égout** *m* POLLUTION sewage sludge; ~ **des eaux usées** *m* HYDROLOGIE, POLLUTION, RECYCLAGE wastewater treatment; ~ **de l'écran** *m* IMPRIM *sérigraphie* screen processing; ~ **élaboré des signaux** *m* ELECTRON advanced signal processing; ~ **électronique de données** *m* ORDINAT EDP, electronic data processing; ~ **électronique des signaux** *m* ELECTRON electronic signal processing; ~ **en différé** *m* INFORMAT off-line processing; ~ **en direct** *m* INFORMAT, ORDINAT on-line processing; ~ **en parallèle** *m* ELECTRON, INFORMAT, TELECOM parallel processing; ~ **en séquence** *m* ORDINAT sequential processing; ~ **en temps réel** *m* INFORMAT, ORDINAT real-time processing; ~ **d'erreurs** *m* INFORMAT, ORDINAT error control; ~ **d'événements** *m* INFORMAT, ORDINAT event handling; ~ **de fichier** *m* INFORMAT, ORDINAT file processing; ~ **final** *m* EMBALLAGE final treatment, NUCLEAIRE tail-end process; ~ **fréquenciel** *m* ELECTRON frequency domain signal processing; ~ **à froid** *m* CERAM VER cold end coating; ~ **d'images** *m* ELECTRON image processing, INFORMAT picture processing, ORDINAT image processing, picture processing, TELECOM image processing; ~ **immédiat** *m* INFORMAT in-line processing; ~ **de l'information** *m* ELECTRON, INFORMAT, ORDINAT IP, information processing; ~ **initial** *m* NUCLEAIRE head end process; ~ **intégré des données** *m* INFORMAT IDP, integrated data processing; ~ **intégré de l'information** *m* INFORMAT IDP, integrated data processing; ~ **intermittent** *m* GENIE CHIM batch processing; ~ **irrétrécissable** *m* TEXTILE nonshrink treatment; ~ **de liste** *m* INFORMAT, ORDINAT list processing; ~ **du minerai** *m* MINES ore treatment; ~ **mouillé ou à sec** *m* TEXTILE wet-dry processing treatment; ~ **multitâche** *m* INFORMAT, ORDINAT multitasking; ~ **de normalisation** *m* MAT CHAUFF *procédé de four* normalizing; ~ **numérique** *m* ELECTRON, TELECOM digital processing; ~ **numérique des images** *m* ELECTRON digital image processing; ~ **numérique réparti** *m* NUCLEAIRE distributed digital processing; ~ **numérique de signaux** *m* ELECTRON DSP, digital signal processing, INFORMAT, ORDINAT digital signal processing; ~ **optique** *m* TELECOM optical processing; ~ **optique des signaux** *m* ELECTRON electro-optical signal processing, optical signal processing; ~ **par faisceau d'électrons** *m* ELECTRON electron beam processing; ~ **par lots** *m* IMPRIM, INFORMAT, ORDINAT batch processing; ~ **de la parole** *m* INFORMAT, ORDINAT, TELECOM speech processing; ~ **par priorités** *m* ORDINAT priority processing; ~ **par rayonnement** *m* NUCLEAIRE radiation processing; ~ **par trempe et revenu** *m* THERMODYN heat treatment; ~

par voie humide *m* CONS MECA wet treatment; ~ **perma-film** *m* CINEMAT antiscratch solution; ~ **physique de l'eau** *m* DISTRI EAU physical water treatment; ~ **pipeline** *m* ELECTRON, INFORMAT pipelining; ~ **de la plaque** *m* IMPRIM *copie* plate processing; ~ **des plaquettes** *m* ELECTRON wafer processing; ~ **pneumatique** *m* CHARBON pneumatic handling, pneumatic treatment; ~ **préalable** *m* ELECTRON preprocessing, MATERIAUX pretreatment; ~ **préliminaire du pétrole** *m* PETR field processing; ~ **de premier plan** *m* INFORMAT, ORDINAT foreground processing; ~ **préventif pour bois** *m* CONSTR wood preservative; ~ **prioritaire** *m* INFORMAT priority processing; ~ **réduit** *m* ORDINAT graceful degradation; ~ **réduit en cas d'incident grave** *m* ORDINAT graceful degradation; ~ **de relaxation** *m* MAT CHAUFF stress relieving; ~ **réparti** *m* PRODUCTION *automatisme industriel* distributed processing; ~ **de secours** *m* SECURITE emergency treatment; ~ **de secours d'urgence** *m* SECURITE first-aid procedure; ~ **séquentiel** *m* IMPRIM batch processing, INFORMAT sequential processing; ~ **série** *m* INFORMAT, ORDINAT serial processing; ~ **de signaux** *m* ELECTRON, INFORMAT, ORDINAT, TELECOM signal processing; ~ **de signaux dans le domaine temporel** *m* ELECTRON time-domain signal processing; ~ **de signaux en temps réel** *m* ELECTRON real-time signal processing; ~ **de signaux par circuit à CCD** *m* ELECTRON CCD signal processing; ~ **simultané** *m* ELECTRON, INFORMAT concurrent processing; ~ **de surface** *m* CERAM VER, MATERIAUX surface treatment; ~ **de surface à chaud** *m* CERAM VER hot end coating; ~ **de surface optique** *m* CINEMAT coating; ~ **sur la puce** *m* ELECTRON on-chip processing; ~ **symbolique** *m* INFORMAT, ORDINAT symbolic processing; ~ **temporel des signaux** *m* ELECTRON time-domain signal processing; ~ **de texte** *m (TdT)* INFORMAT, ORDINAT text processing, word processing *(WP)*; ~ **thermique** *m* CHARBON heat treatment, MATERIAUX heat treatment, thermal treatment, METALL, THERMODYN heat treatment; ~ **thermique de précipitation** *m* PRODUCTION precipitation heat treatment; ~ **thermique sous vide** *m* METALL vacuum heat treatment; ~ **de transactions** *m* INFORMAT, ORDINAT TP, transaction processing; ~ **ultérieur** *m* ELECTRON postprocessing; ~ **vectoriel** *m* INFORMAT, ORDINAT vector processing

traiter *vt* AGRO ALIM process, CHARBON mill, treat, CINEMAT, INFORMAT, ORDINAT process; ~ **à l'acide nitrique** *vt* CHIMIE nitrate; ~ **à chaud** *vt* THERMODYN heat treat; ~ **par maturation artificielle** *vt* THERMODYN artificially age

trajectographie *f* ESPACE, PHYS RAYON *observation de particules* trajectography

trajectoire *f* AERONAUT path, trajectory, ASTRONOMIE track, ESPACE path, trajectory, NAUT path, *navire, radar* track, PHYSIQUE path, trajectory; ~ **d'approche courbe en azimut** *f* AERONAUT *système d'atterrissage hyperfréquences* curved azimuth approach path; ~ **d'approche finale** *f* AERONAUT final approach path; ~ **d'approche initiale** *f* AERONAUT initial approach path; ~ **d'approche segmentée** *f* AERONAUT segmented approach path; ~ **d'attente** *f* AERONAUT holding path; ~ **d'atterrissage** *f* AERONAUT glide path; ~ **balistique** *f* ESPACE ballistic path, ballistic trajectory; ~ **banane** *f* NUCLEAIRE banana orbit, banana trajectory; ~ **de collision** *f* ESPACE collision course; ~ **de décollage** *f* AERONAUT takeoff flight path; ~ **de descente** *f* ESPACE

descent path; ~ **de l'éclair** *f* ELECTR *conducteur* lightning path; ~ **électronique** *f* TV electron path; ~ **d'électrons** *f* NUCLEAIRE electron path, electron trajectory; ~ **en approche** *f* AERONAUT approach path; ~ **en ligne brisée** *f* AERONAUT segmented approach path; ~ **garantie** *f* AERONAUT guaranteed flight path; ~ **horizontale** *f* MILITAIRE *artillerie* flat trajectory; ~ **d'injection** *f* ESPACE injection orbit; ~ **moyenne** *f* MILITAIRE *artillerie* mean trajectory; ~ **de pulvérisation** *f* POLLU MER spraypath; ~ **d'un rayon** *f* GEOLOGIE, PETR ray path; ~ **de rendez-vous** *f* ESPACE rendezvous trajectory; ~ **segmentée** *f* AERONAUT segmented approach path; ~ **de totalité** *f* ASTRONOMIE *d'une éclipse solaire totale* track of totality; ~ **de vol** *f* AERONAUT flight path; ~ **de vol assignée** *f* AERONAUT assigned flight path; ~ **de vol exigée** *f* AERONAUT required flight path; ~ **de vol indiquée** *f* AERONAUT indicated flight path; ~ **de vol prévue** *f* AERONAUT intended flight path; ~ **de vol réelle** *f* AERONAUT actual flight path

trajectoires: ~ **planétaires autour du soleil** *f pl* ASTRONOMIE planetary paths

trajet *m* ELECTROTEC, ESPACE, PHYSIQUE path; ~ **de conversation** *m* TELECOM speech path; ~ **du courant** *m* ELECTROTEC current path; ~ **descendant de la liaison de connexion** *m* TELECOM down link feeder link; ~ **de faisceau lumineux** *m* INSTRUMENT illumination beam path, illumination path; ~ **mixte** *m* ESPACE mixed path; ~ **multiple** *m* ESPACE multiple path; ~ **optique** *m* PHYSIQUE optical path; ~ **de propagation** *m* ELECTROTEC propagation path; ~ **sismique** *m* PETROLE seismic path; ~ **suivant un grand cercle** *m* ESPACE great circle path; ~ **de transmission** *m* TELECOM transmission path; ~ **virtuel** *m* TELECOM VP, virtual path

trajets: ~ **des particules ballottées par des molécules turbulentes** *m pl* PHYS RAYON *mouvement brownien* particle trajectories buffeted by turbulent molecules

tramail *m* OCEANO trammel net

trame *f* CINEMAT screen, ELECTRON frame, ESPACE *communications* frame, screening, weft, IMPRIM frame, screen, INFORMAT, ORDINAT frame, raster, PAPIER *d'un tissu* weft, PRODUCTION *automatisme industriel* raster, TELECOM frame, TEXTILE *d'un tissu* weft, TV field, raster; ~ **de balayage** *f* ELECTRON raster; ~ **à couleurs** *f* TV color field (AmE), colour field (BrE); ~ **écrue** *f* TEXTILE loom state weft; ~ **EMCN** *f* TELECOM DCME frame; ~ **fine** *f* IMPRIM *photogravure* fine screen; ~ **grossière** *f* IMPRIM coarse screen; ~ **d'identification numérique** *f* TELECOM digital identification frame; ~ **d'image** *f* TV picture frame; ~ **sémaphore de message** *f* TELECOM MSU, message signal unit; ~ **serrée** *f* IMPRIM fine screen; ~ **simili** *f* IMPRIM screen; ~ **à 25%** *f* IMPRIM *photogravure* quarter tone; ~ **à 75%** *f* IMPRIM three-quarter tone

tramé *m* IMPRIM *photogravure* base tint; ~ **direct** *m* IMPRIM *photogravure* direct screen

trames: ~ **mécaniques** *f pl* IMPRIM *utilisées par les illustrateurs* zip-a-tone

tramway *m* TRANSPORT tramway; ~ **articulé** *m* TRANSPORT articulated tramway; ~ **express** *m* TRANSPORT express tramway

tranchage *m* PRODUCTION cutting-off, slabbing, *d'un seul coup d'une pièce de fer* cutting-off; ~ **des feuilles de placage** *m* CONSTR cutting veneers

tranchant[1] *adj* CONS MECA sharp

tranchant[2] *m* CONS MECA cutting edge, edge, *d'un coin* point, CONSTR *d'un outil* cutting edge, MECANIQUE edge; ~ **diamanté** *m* PRODUCTION diamond cutting; ~ **de lame** *m* CONSTR bit

tranche *f* CONSTR *de pierre* slab, INFORMAT slice, NUCLEAIRE unit, ORDINAT slice; ~ **de couleur** *f* IMPRIM colored edge (AmE), coloured edge (BrE); ~ **dorée** *f* IMPRIM gilt edge; ~ **extérieure** *f* IMPRIM fore edge; ~ **horaire** *f* TV slot; ~ **mouchetée** *f* IMPRIM sprinkled edge; ~ **nucléaire** *f* ELECTR nuclear tranche; ~ **de silicium** *f* ORDINAT wafer; ~ **de temps** *f* ELECTRON time slot, INFORMAT, ORDINAT time slice

tranchée *f* CH DE FER cutting, railroad cutting (AmE), railway cutting (BrE), CHARBON trench, CONSTR cut, cutting, ditch, trench, MINES surface cut, trench, PETR ditch, trench, POLLU MER trench; ~ **de câble** *f* ELECTR *alimentation* cable trench; ~ **parafouille** *f* CONSTR cutoff ditch; ~ **de prospection** *f* MINES exploration trench; ~ **de recherches** *f* MINES exploration trench

tranchée-abri *f* MILITAIRE dug-out

tranchefile *f* IMPRIM *reliure* headband; ~ **inférieure** *f* IMPRIM tailband; ~ **supérieure** *f* IMPRIM headband

trancher *vt* CONSTR *feuilles de placage* cut, PRODUCTION cutoff

trancheuse *f* CONSTR ditcher, rock channeler (AmE), rock channeller (BrE), trench cutter, MINES bar channeler (AmE), bar channeller (BrE), quarrying machine, *machine* channeler (AmE), channeller (BrE), rock channeler (AmE), rock channeller (BrE); ~ **montée sur rails** *f* MINES track channeler (AmE), track channeller (BrE); ~ **pour le bois de bout** *f* CONS MECA trimmer, CONSTR paring machine

transaction *f* INFORMAT, ORDINAT transaction

transatlantique *m* TRANSPORT ocean liner

transbordement *m* NAUT, PETROLE transshipment

transborder *vt* NAUT *passagers, cargaison* transship

transbordeur *m* NAUT ferryboat, ferry, TRANSPORT ferryboat; ~ **fluvial** *m* NAUT river ferry; ~ **pour voitures** *m* NAUT, TRANSPORT car ferry

transcendent *adj* MATH transcendental

transcodage *m* TELECOM transcoding, TV standards conversion

transcodeur *m* ELECTROTEC code converter, TELECOM transcoder, TV standards converter, transcoder; ~ **vidéo** *m* TV video frequency converter

transconductance *f* ELECTROTEC, PHYSIQUE transconductance

transconteneur *m* TRANSPORT transcontainer

transcrire *vt* INFORMAT, ORDINAT transcribe

transducteur *m* ACOUSTIQUE, ELECTR, ELECTROTEC, INFORMAT, ORDINAT transducer, PHYSIQUE magnetic amplifier, saturable reactor, transducer, transductor, TELECOM transducer; ~ **actif** *m* ELECTR, ELECTROTEC active transducer; ~ **autogénérateur** *m* ELECTROTEC self-generating transducer; ~ **à balance de forces** *m* ELECTROTEC force balance transducer; ~ **bilatéral** *m* ELECTROTEC bidirectional transducer, bilateral transducer; ~ **électrique** *m* ELECTROTEC electric transducer; ~ **électroacoustique** *m* ACOUSTIQUE, ELECTROTEC electroacoustic transducer; ~ **électromécanique** *m* ACOUSTIQUE, ELECTROTEC electromechanical transducer; ~ **d'entrée** *m* ELECTROTEC input transducer; ~ **interdigital** *m* TELECOM IDT, interdigital transducer; ~ **linéaire** *m* ACOUSTIQUE, ELECTROTEC linear transducer; ~ **magnétique** *m* ELECTROTEC transductor; ~ **magnétostrictif** *m* ELECTROTEC magnetostrictive transductor; ~ **à magnétostriction** *m* ELECTROTEC magnetostrictive transductor; ~ **de mesure** *m* METROLOGIE measuring transducer; ~ **non réversible** *m* ELECTROTEC unidirectional transducer; ~ **optoélectronique** *m* ELECTROTEC optoelectronic transducer; ~ **passif** *m* ELECTROTEC passive transducer; ~ **photoactif** *m* ELECTROTEC photoactive transducer; ~ **photoélectrique** *m* ELECTROTEC photoelectric transducer; ~ **piézoélectrique** *m* ELECTROTEC piezoelectric transducer; ~ **de pression** *m* PRODUCTION *système hydraulique* pressure transducer; ~ **réciproque** *m* ACOUSTIQUE reciprocal transducer; ~ **réversible** *m* ACOUSTIQUE, ELECTROTEC reversible transducer; ~ **de sortie** *m* ELECTROTEC output transducer; ~ **symétrique** *m* ELECTROTEC symmetrical transducer

transestérification *f* CHIMIE cross-esterification, LESSIVES ester interchange

transférer *vt* ENREGISTR. INFORMAT, ORDINAT transfer; ~ **en mémoire auxiliaire** *vt* INFORMAT, ORDINAT roll out; ~ **de petit format en format professionnel** *vt* TV dub up

transfert *m* BREVETS, ESPACE *véhicules*, IMPRIM transfer, INFORMAT, ORDINAT staging, transfer, TELECOM hand off, through-connection, transfer; ~ **d'appel** *m* TELECOM call transfer; ~ **automatique** *m* TELECOM automatic call transfer; ~ **bidirectionnel** *m* INFORMAT bidirectional flow; ~ **bilatéral** *m* ORDINAT bidirectional flow; ~ **de blocs** *m* INFORMAT, ORDINAT block transfer; ~ **de carburant** *m* AERONAUT fuel transfer; ~ **de chaleur** *m* MAT CHAUFF heat transfer, PHYSIQUE heat sink, heat transfer, PLAST CAOU, REFRIG heat transfer, THERMODYN thermal conduction; ~ **de charge** *m* NUCLEAIRE charge transfer, TELECOM load transfer; ~ **de données** *m* INFORMAT, ORDINAT data transfer; ~ **de données demandé** *m* TELECOM data transfer requested; ~ **de l'ébauche** *m* CERAM VER blank transfer; ~ **électronique de fonds** *m* TELECOM EFT, electronic funds transfer; ~ **électronique de fonds au point de vente** *m* TELECOM EFTPOS, electronic funds transfer at point of sale; ~ **en bloc bidirectionel** *m* PRODUCTION bidirectional block transfer; ~ **en bloc écriture** *m* PRODUCTION *automatisme industriel* block transfer write; ~ **en bloc lecture** *m* PRODUCTION block transfer read; ~ **d'encre** *m* IMPRIM ink transfer; ~ **en entrée** *m* INFORMAT copy-in; ~ **d'énergie** *m* GEOPHYS, THERMODYN energy transfer; ~ **d'énergie par vibration** *m* PHYS ONDES *onde progressive* energy transference by vibration; ~ **d'énergie résonante** *m* PHYS RAYON *entre atomes* resonant energy transfer; ~ **en magasin** *m* PRODUCTION warehouse delivery; ~ **en mémoire centrale** *m* INFORMAT, ORDINAT roll in; ~ **en mémoire centrale/sur mémoire auxiliaire** *m* INFORMAT roll-in/roll-out; ~ **en parallèle** *m* INFORMAT, ORDINAT parallel transfer; ~ **en parallèle par bits** *m* INFORMAT, ORDINAT bit parallel transfer; ~ **en série par bits** *m* INFORMAT, ORDINAT bit serial transfer; ~ **en sortie** *m* INFORMAT copy-out; ~ **entre les cellules** *m* TELECOM intercell hand-off, switching call-in-progress; ~ **de fichier** *m* INFORMAT, ORDINAT file transfer; ~ **de film sur vidéo** *m* CINEMAT, TV film-to-tape transfer; ~ **du glissement** *m* MATERIAUX slip transfer; ~ **d'humidité** *m* REFRIG, TEXTILE moisture transfer; ~ **d'image** *m* TELECOM image transfer; ~ **interdit** *m* TELECOM TFP, transfer prohibited; ~ **interorbital** *m* ESPACE *trajectographie* transfer orbit; ~ **linéique d'énergie** *m* PHYS RAYON, PHYSIQUE linear energy transfer; ~ **de masse** *m* ASTRONOMIE *entre des étoiles binaires proches* mass transfer, GAZ transfer of mass; ~ **de masse du carbone**

m NUCLEAIRE carbon mass transfer; ~ **de messages** *m* INFORMAT, ORDINAT message transfer, TELECOM MT, message transfer; ~ **de modulation** *m* ELECTRON re-modulation; ~ **par blocs** *m* INFORMAT, ORDINAT block transfer; ~ **par octet** *m* PRODUCTION *automatisme industriel* put byte; ~ **périphérique** *m* INFORMAT, ORDINAT peripheral transfer; ~ **radiatif** *m* ASTRONOMIE, PHYS RAYON radiative transfer; ~ **restreint** *m* TELECOM TFR, transfer restricted; ~ **sans heurts** *m* PRODUCTION bumpless transfer; ~ **série** *m* INFORMAT, ORDINAT serial transfer, serial transmission; ~ **sous contrôle** *m* TELECOM TFC, controlled transfer; ~ **de stock** *m* PRODUCTION stock transfer; ~ **sur film** *m* TV film transfer; ~ **thermique** *m* GAZ thermal transfer, thermic transfer; ~ **de vidéo sur pellicule** *m* CINEMAT tape-to-film transfer

Transfert: ~ **temporel asynchrone** *m (TTA)* TELECOM Asynchronous Transfer Mode *(ATM)*

transfilage *m* OCEANO lacing

transfini *adj* MATH transfinite

transformateur *m* ELECTR *courant alternatif-continu*, ELECTROTEC, PHYSIQUE, TELECOM transformer; ~ **abaisseur** *m* ELECTR step-down transformer; ~ **abaisseur de tension** *m* ELECTROTEC step-down transformer; ~ **accordé** *m* ELECTROTEC tuned transformer; ~ **d'adaptation** *m* ELECTR, ELECTROTEC matching transformer; ~ **d'adaptation d'impédance** *m* ELECTROTEC impedance matching transformer; ~ **à air** *m* ELECTR air transformer, air-cooled transformer, ELECTROTEC air core transformer; ~ **d'alimentation** *m* ELECTR current transformer (AmE), mains transformer (BrE), feeding transformer, ELECTRON current transformer (AmE), mains transformer (BrE), ELECTROTEC line coupling transformer, power transformer; ~ **d'allumage** *m* ELECTROTEC ignition transformer; ~ **d'amortissement** *m* ELECTROTEC neutral compensator; ~ **auxiliaire** *m* ELECTR auxiliary transformer; ~ **auxiliaire du bloc** *m* NUCLEAIRE *pile* unit auxilliary transformer; ~ **blindé** *m* ELECTROTEC shielded transformer; ~ **de chauffage** *m* ELECTROTEC filament transformer; ~ **à cinq colonnes** *m* ELECTR five-legged transformer; ~ **à colonnes** *m* ELECTR core-type transformer; ~ **de couplage** *m* ELECTR coupling transformer; ~ **de courant** *m* ELECTR current transformer (AmE), mains transformer (BrE), ELECTROTEC current transformer; ~ **à courant constant** *m* ELECTROTEC constant current transformer; ~ **à courant continu** *m* ELECTROTEC DC transformer; ~ **de courant séquentiel** *m* PRODUCTION *automatisme industriel* sequence current transformer; ~ **de crête** *m* ELECTR peaking transformer; ~ **cuirassé** *m* ELECTR, ELECTROTEC shell-type transformer; ~ **dans l'huile** *m* ELECTROTEC oil transformer; ~ **de déclenchement de thyristor** *m* ELECTROTEC SCR trimmer transformer; ~ **de démarrage** *m* ELECTROTEC starting transformer; ~ **déphaseur** *m* ELECTR phase-shifting transformer; ~ **dévolteur** *m* ELECTROTEC booster transformer; ~ **différentiel** *m* ELECTR, ELECTROTEC differential transformer; ~ **différentiel à translation** *m* ELECTROTEC linear variable differential transformer; ~ **à double enroulement** *m* ELECTR double-wound transformer; ~ **élévateur** *m* ELECTR, PHYSIQUE step-up transformer; ~ **élévateur de tension** *m* ELECTROTEC step-up transformer; ~ **en barres** *m* ELECTR bar-type transformer; ~ **à enroulement mobile** *m* ELECTROTEC variable ratio transformer; ~ **à enroulements séparés** *m* ELECTR separate winding transformer; ~ **d'entrée** *m* ELECTRO-TEC, PHYSIQUE input transformer; ~ **d'étalonnage** *m* NUCLEAIRE calibrating transformer; ~ **à fer** *m* ELECTROTEC core-type transformer; ~ **à fer saturé** *m* ELECTROTEC saturable transformer; ~ **de fréquence** *m* ELECTR frequency transformer; ~ **de grande puissance** *m* ELECTR high-power transformer; ~ **à haute fréquence** *m* ELECTROTEC HF transformer, high-frequency transformer; ~ **à haute tension** *m* ELECTR high-voltage transformer; ~ **hermétique** *m* ELECTR sealed transformer; ~ **HF** *m* ELECTROTEC HF transformer; ~ **HT** *m* ELECTR high-voltage transformer; ~ **à huile** *m* ELECTROTEC oil-cooled transformer; ~ **immergé dans l'huile** *m* ELECTR oil-immersed transformer; ~ **d'impulsion** *m* ELECTROTEC, PHYSIQUE pulse transformer; ~ **d'intensité** *m* ELECTROTEC current transformer; ~ **intermédiaire** *m* ELECTROTEC interstage transformer; ~ **isolant** *m* PRODUCTION *automatisme industriel* isolation transformer; ~ **d'isolement** *m* ELECTROTEC isolation transformer; ~ **de liaison** *m* ELECTROTEC coupling transformer; ~ **de mesure** *m* ELECTR, ELECTROTEC instrument transformer, TELECOM test transformer; ~ **de microphone** *m* ENREGISTR microphone transformer; ~ **monophasé** *m* ELECTROTEC single-phase transformer; ~ **à noyau** *m* ELECTR core-type transformer, ELECTROTEC core transformer; ~ **à noyau de fer** *m* ELECTR, ELECTROTEC iron core transformer; ~ **à noyau magnétique** *m* ELECTROTEC core-type transformer; ~ **à noyau ouvert** *m* ELECTR open core transformer; ~ **à noyau toroïdal** *m* ELECTROTEC toroidal transformer; ~ **de papier** *m* PAPIER converter; ~ **parfait** *m* ELECTROTEC ideal transformer; ~ **pas à pas** *m* PRODUCTION *automatisme industriel* step transformer; ~ **à plusieurs enroulements** *m* ELECTR multiwinding transformer; ~ **à point milieu** *m* ELECTROTEC double-wound transformer; ~ **polyphasé** *m* ELECTR, ELECTROTEC polyphase transformer; ~ **à poteaux** *m* ELECTR pole-type transformer, *ligne aérienne* pole-mounted transformer; ~ **pour radiographie** *m* INSTRUMENT X-ray transformer; ~ **à prises** *m* ELECTR, ELECTROTEC tapped transformer; ~ **de puissance** *m* PRODUCTION power transformer; ~ **de puissance type sec** *m* ELECTROTEC dry-type power transformer; ~ **de redresseur** *m* ELECTROTEC rectifier transformer; ~ **réducteur** *m* PHYSIQUE, PRODUCTION *automatisme industriel* step-down transformer; ~ **refroidi par l'air** *m* ELECTR air-cooled transformer; ~ **refroidi par huile** *m* ELECTR oil-cooled transformer; ~ **à refroidissement par l'air soufflé** *m* ELECTR air blast transformer; ~ **à refroidissement par l'eau** *m* ELECTR water-cooled transformer; ~ **à refroidissement par huile** *m* ELECTR, ELECTROTEC oil-cooled transformer; ~ **réglable** *m* COMMANDE regulating transformer; ~ **de réglage** *m* COMMANDE regulating transformer; ~ **régulateur** *m* ELECTROTEC regulation transformer, PRODUCTION constant voltage transformer; ~ **régulateur de tension** *m* ELECTROTEC voltage-regulating transformer; ~ **résistant à la foudre** *m* ELECTR lightning proof transformer; ~ **de retour de spot** *m* TV flyback transformer; ~ **rotatif** *m* ELECTROTEC rotary transformer; ~ **sans fer** *m* ELECTROTEC air core transformer; ~ **sans noyau** *m* ELECTROTEC air core transformer; ~ **sans noyau de fer** *m* ELECTR air core transformer; ~ **sans noyau magnétique** *m* ELECTROTEC air core transformer; ~ **saturable** *m* ELECTROTEC saturable transformer; ~ **saturé** *m* ELECTROTEC saturated transformer; ~ **sec** *m* ELECTR dry-type transformer; ~

secteur *m* ELECTROTEC current transformer (AmE), mains transformer (BrE); **~ de sonnerie** *m* ELECTR, ELECTROTEC bell transformer; **~ de sortie** *m* ELECTR, ELECTROTEC, ENREGISTR, PHYSIQUE output transformer; **~ de soudage** *m* ELECTROTEC welding transformer; **~ statique** *m* ELECTROTEC static transformer; **~ sur poteau** *m* ELECTR pole-type transformer, *ligne aérienne* pole-mounted transformer; **~ survolteur** *m* ELECTR booster, booster transformer, ELECTROTEC booster transformer, PHYSIQUE, TV step-up transformer; **~ survolteur-dévolteur** *m* ELECTR series transformer; **~ de synchronisation** *m* PRODUCTION synchronization transformer; **~ de tension** *m* ELECTR, ELECTROTEC potential transformer, voltage transformer; **~ de tension continue** *m* ELECTR direct current transformer; **~ toroïdal** *m* ELECTROTEC toroidal transformer; **~ toroïdal à fer saturé** *m* ELECTROTEC saturated toroidal transformer; **~ triphasé** *m* ELECTROTEC three-phase transformer; **~ triphasé de mise à la terre** *m* ELECTR three-phase earthing transformer (BrE), three-phase grounding transformer (AmE); **~ à trois enroulements** *m* ELECTR triple-wound transformer, ELECTROTEC three-winding transformer; **~ de type sec à enroulements non encapsulés** *m* ELECTR nonencapsulated winding dry-type transformer; **~ variable** *m* COMMANDE regulating transformer, ELECTR adjustable transformer, ELECTROTEC variable transformer, EQUIP LAB regulating transformer

transformation *f* ELECTROTEC transformation, INFORMAT transform, MATERIAUX transformation, MATH function, ORDINAT transform, PAPIER converting; **~ adiabatique** *f* METALL adiabatic transformation, THERMODYN adiabatic process; **~ affine** *f* METALL affine transformation; **~ de coordonnées** *f* ELECTRON coordinate transformation; **~ des déchets** *f* RECYCLAGE waste processing; **~ delta-étoile** *f* ELECTR *raccordement* delta-to-star conversion; **~ en coke** *f* CHARBON coking; **~ d'énergie** *f* ELECTR energy transformation; **~ d'énergie électrique** *f* ELECTR *réseau* transformation of electricity; **~ étoile-triangle** *f* ELECTR, PHYSIQUE *raccordement* star-to-delta conversion, star-to-delta transformation, star-delta transformation; **~ eutectique** *f* METALL eutectic transformation; **~ fenêtre clôture** *f* INFORMAT, ORDINAT viewing transformation, window transformation; **~ de Fourier** *f* ELECTRON, PHYSIQUE Fourier transformation; **~ de Fourier rapide** *f* ELECTRON FFT, fast Fourier transform, ORDINAT FFT, fast Fourier transform; **~ de Galilée** *f* PHYSIQUE Galilean transformation; **~ gel-sol** *f* LESSIVES peptization; **~ de Laplace** *f* ELECTRON Laplace transformation, PHYSIQUE Laplace transform, Laplace transformation; **~ de Lorentz** *f* PHYSIQUE Lorentz transformation; **~ martensitique** *f* CRISTALL, MATERIAUX martensitic transformation; **~ massive** *f* METALL massive reaction; **~ ordre-désordre** *f* CRISTALL order-disorder transformation; **~ ortho-para** *f* NUCLEAIRE ortho-para conversion; **~ péritectique** *f* MATERIAUX peritectic transformation; **~ polymorphe** *f* CRISTALL polymorphic transformation; **~ spinodale** *f* MATERIAUX spinodal instability; **~ thermodynamique** *f* THERMODYN thermodynamic transformation

transformations: **~ de phase** *f pl* THERMODYN phase transformations

transformée *f* MATH transform; **~ de Fourier** *f* CRISTALL, ELECTRON, PHYSIQUE Fourier transform; **~ de Fourier**

discrète *f* ELECTRON discrete Fourier transform; **~ de Fourier rapide** *f* ELECTRON fast Fourier transform; **~ de Laplace** *f* MATH Laplace transform

transformer *vt* AGRO ALIM process, INFORMAT, ORDINAT transform, PAPIER convert; **~ en coke** *vt* CHARBON coke; **~ en mousse** *vt* GENIE CHIM foam

transgression *f* GEOLOGIE transgression

transistor *m* ELECTRON, INFORMAT, ORDINAT, PHYSIQUE transistor; **~ amplificateur** *m* ELECTRON amplifying transistor; **~ amplificateur de puissance** *m* ELECTRON power amplifier transistor; **~ ballast** *m* ELECTRON pass transistor, series-pass transistor; **~ bipolaire** *m* ELECTRON, ORDINAT, PHYSIQUE, TELECOM bipolar transistor; **~ bipolaire CMOS** *m* ORDINAT BiCMOS transistor; **~ bipolaire discret** *m* ELECTRON discrete bipolar transistor; **~ bipolaire de grande puissance** *m* ELECTRON high-power bipolar transistor; **~ bipolaire intégré** *m* ELECTRON integrated bipolar transistor; **~ bipolaire de puissance** *m* ELECTRON bipolar power transistor; **~ bipolaire au silicium** *m* ELECTRON silicon bipolar transistor; **~ bipolaire vertical** *m* ELECTRON vertical bipolar transistor; **~ CMOS** *m* ELECTRON CMOS transistor; **~ de commutation de puissance** *m* ELECTRON power switching transistor; **~ de commutation rapide** *m* ELECTRON high-speed switching transistor; **~ à couches minces** *m* ELECTRON thin-film transistor; **~ de déblocage** *m* ELECTRON gating transistor; **~ DMOS** *m* ELECTRON DMOS transistor; **~ à double diffusion** *m* ELECTRON double diffused transistor; **~ à effet de champ** *m* ELECTRON, field-effect transistor, INFORMAT TEC, field-effect transistor, OPTIQUE, ORDINAT, PHYSIQUE field-effect transistor; **~ à effet de champ à accès Schottky** *m* ELECTRON Schottky barrier FET; **~ à effet de champ à déplétion** *m* ELECTRON depletion-mode FET; **~ à effet de champ au silicium** *m* ELECTRON silicon FET; **~ à effet de champ vertical** *m* ELECTRON vertical field effect transistor; **~ à émetteur et collecteur diffusés** *m* ELECTRON diffused emitter-collector transistor; **~ épitaxial** *m* ELECTRON epitaxial transistor; **~ à l'état bloqué** *m* ELECTRON off transistor; **~ d'excursion basse à canal N** *m* ELECTRON n-channel pulldown transistor; **~ au germanium** *m* ELECTRON germanium transistor; **~ à grille auto-alignée** *m* ELECTRON self-aligned transistor; **~ à grille au silicium** *m* ELECTRON silicon gate transistor; **~ haute fréquence** *m* ELECTRON HF transistor, high-frequency transistor; **~ haut et bas** *m* PRODUCTION up and lower transistor switch; **~ HF** *m* ELECTRON HF transistor; **~ horizontal** *m* ELECTRON lateral transistor; **~ hyperfréquence** *m* ELECTRON microwave transistor; **~ intégré** *m* ELECTRON on-chip transistor; **~ inverseur** *m* ELECTRON inverting transistor; **~ à jonction** *m* ELECTRON, PHYSIQUE junction transistor; **~ à jonction par alliage** *m* ELECTRON alloy junction transistor; **~ à jonction par diffusion et alliage** *m* ELECTRON diffused alloy transistor; **~ laminé** *m* ELECTRON laminar transistor; **~ latéral** *m* ELECTRON lateral transistor; **~ de lecture** *m* ELECTRON read transistor; **~ mélangeur** *m* ELECTRON mixing transistor; **~ de mémorisation** *m* ELECTRON memory transistor; **~ mésa** *m* ELECTRON mesa transistor; **~ MESFET** *m* ELECTRON MESFET, metal semiconductor field effect transistor; **~ MIS** *m* (*transistor multipoint d'état secondaire*) ELECTRON MIS transistor; **~ monté en base commune** *m* ELECTRON common base transistor; **~ monté en diode** *m* ELECTRON diode-connected transistor; ~ **monté en drain commun** *m* ELECTRON common drain transistor; ~ **monté en émetteur commun** *m* ELECTRON common emitter transistor; ~ **monté en grille commune** *m* ELECTRON common gate transistor; ~ **monté en source commune** *m* ELECTRON common source transistor; ~ **MOS** *m* ELECTRON MOS transistor, metal-oxide semiconductor transistor; ~ **MOS à l'arséniure de gallium** *m* ELECTRON gallium arsenide MOS transistor; ~ **MOS à canal court** *m* ELECTRON short channel MOS transistor; ~ **MOS canal N intégré** *m* ELECTRON n-channel integrated MOS transistor; ~ **MOS canal P à déplétion** *m* ELECTRON p-channel depletion mode MOS transistor; ~ **MOS canal P à enrichissement** *m* ELECTRON p-channel enhancement mode MOS transistor; ~ **MOS intégré** *m* ELECTRON integrated MOS transistor; ~ **MOS intégré à canal N** *m* ELECTRON n-channel integrated MOS transistor; ~ **MOS de puissance verticale** *m* ELECTRON vertical power MOS transistor; ~ **MOS vertical** *m* ELECTRON vertical MOS transistor; ~ **multicollecteur** *m* ELECTRON multicollector transistor; ~ **multiémetteur** *m* ELECTRON multiemitter transistor; ~ **multipoint d'état secondaire** *m (transistor MIS)* ELECTRON multipoint indication secondary status transistor; ~ **NMOS** *m* ELECTRON NMOS transistor; ~ **non connecté** *m* ELECTRON uncommitted transistor; ~ **NPN** *m* ELECTRON NPN transistor; ~ **parasite** *m* ELECTRON parasitic transistor; ~ **passivé** *m* ELECTRON passivated transistor; ~ **planar bipolaire** *m* ELECTRON planar bipolar transistor; ~ **planar épitaxial au silicium** *m* ELECTRON silicon epitaxial planar transistor; ~ **PNP** *m* ELECTRON, PHYSIQUE PNP transistor; ~ **à pointes** *m* ELECTRON cat's whisker transistor, point contact transistor; ~ **pour forts courants** *m* ELECTRON high-current transistor; ~ **pour petits signaux** *m* ELECTRON small-signal transistor; ~ **pour signaux à bas niveau** *m* ELECTRON low-level transistor; ~ **de puissance** *m* ELECTRON power amplifier transistor, power transistor; ~ **de puissance à commutation rapide** *m* ELECTRON fast-switching power transistor; ~ **de puissance employé comme transistor ballast** *m* ELECTRON series pass power transistor; ~ **de puissance hyperfréquence** *m* ELECTRON microwave power transistor; ~ **de puissance MOS** *m* ELECTRON MOS power transistor, metal-oxide semiconductor power transistor; ~ **quantique** *m* ELECTRON quantum transistor; ~ **réalisé sur la puce** *m* ELECTRON on-chip transistor; ~ **de régulation** *m* ELECTRON series-pass transistor; ~ **saturé** *m* ELECTRON saturated transistor; ~ **Schottky** *m* ELECTRON Schottky clamped transistor; ~ **série** *m* ELECTRON series-pass transistor; ~ **tétrode** *m* ELECTRON tetrode transistor; ~ **du type bipolaire** *m* ELECTRON bipolar transistor; ~ **unijonction** *m* ELECTRON unijunction transistor; ~ **unijonction programmable** *m* ELECTRON programmable unijunction transistor; ~ **unipolaire** *m* ELECTRON majority carrier transistor; ~ **de verrouillage** *m* ELECTRON latching transistor; ~ **VMOS** *m* ELECTRON VMOS transistor

transistorisé *adj* TV solid-state

transistors: ~ **appariés** *m pl* ELECTRON matched transistors; ~ **complémentaires** *m pl* ELECTRON complementary transistors

transit *m* NUCLEAIRE transit

transitaire *m* NAUT forwarding agent (BrE), freight agent (AmE), TRANSPORT forwarding agent (BrE), freight agent (AmE)

transiter *vi* TELECOM pass through; ~ **par les opératrices** *vi* TELECOM go via the circuit

transition *f* ELECTROTEC tapered section; ~ **avec inversion de spin** *f* PHYS PART spin reversal transition; ~ **du deuxième ordre** *f* PHYSIQUE second order transition; ~ **ductile-fragile** *f* METALL ductile brittle transition, tough-brittle transition; ~ **en vol** *f* AERONAUT flight transition; ~ **de l'état fondamental** *f* PHYS PART ground state transition; ~ **fragile-ductile** *f* NUCLEAIRE brittle ductile transition; ~ **de guides d'ondes** *f* ELECTROTEC waveguide transition; ~ **interdite** *f* PHYS RAYON *en noyaux atomiques*, PHYSIQUE forbidden transition; ~ **isomérique** *f* PHYS RAYON isomeric transition; ~ **laser** *f* PHYS RAYON laser transition; ~ **magnétique** *f* METALL magnetic transition; ~ **montante** *f* ELECTRON low-to-high transition; ~ **musicale** *f* ENREGISTR segue; ~ **non favorisée** *f* NUCLEAIRE forbidden transition, unfavored transition (AmE), unfavoured transition (BrE); ~ **non-radiative** *f* PHYS RAYON radiationless transition; ~ **optique** *f* PHYS RAYON optical transition; ~ **permise** *f* PHYSIQUE allowed transition; ~ **positronique faible** *f* NUCLEAIRE weak positron transition; ~ **du premier ordre** *f* PHYSIQUE first-order transition; ~ **progressive** *f* OPTIQUE tapered transition, TELECOM progressive transition; ~ **progressive de fibre optique** *f* OPTIQUE, TELECOM tapered fiber (AmE), tapered fibre (BrE); ~ **quantique** *f* PHYS PART quantum leap; ~ **radiative** *f* PHYS RAYON radiative transition; ~ **rectangulaire-circulaire** *f* ELECTROTEC rectangular-to-circular transition; ~ **de turbulence** *f* PHYS FLUID transition to turbulence; ~ **du vrai au faux** *f* PRODUCTION *automatisme industriel* true-to-false transition

transitions: ~ **dipôles magnétiques** *f pl* PHYS RAYON magnetic dipole transitions; ~ **permises du dipôle électrique** *f pl* PHYS RAYON allowed electron dipole transitions; ~ **quadripôles électriques** *f pl* PHYS RAYON electric quadrupole transitions; ~ **spontanées** *f pl* PHYS RAYON spontaneous transitions

transitoire[1] *adj* ELECTROTEC, PHYSIQUE transient

transitoire[2] *f* ELECTROTEC, TELECOM transient

translatable *adj* INFORMAT, ORDINAT relocatable

translater *vt* INFORMAT, ORDINAT relocate, translate

translateur *m* CONSTR repeating coil

translation *f* CONS MECA translation, translatory motion, GEOMETRIE translation, INFORMAT relocation, MINES *du personnel* transportation, ORDINAT relocation, PHYSIQUE translation, PRODUCTION *d'un pont roulant* traveling (AmE), travelling (BrE), *du chariot d'un pont roulant* traversing; ~ **du chariot d'un pont roulant** *f* CONS MECA racking the carriage of a traveling crane (AmE), racking the carriage of a travelling crane (BrE); ~ **panoramique** *f* INFORMAT, ORDINAT panning

translitération *f* INFORMAT, ORDINAT transliteration

translitérer *vt* INFORMAT, ORDINAT transliterate

translittération *f* INFORMAT, ORDINAT transliteration

translittérer *vt* INFORMAT, ORDINAT transliterate

translucide *adj* CHIMIE translucent

translucidité *f* MATERIAUX translucence, translucency, PHYS RAYON translucence

transmanche *adj* NAUT cross-channel

transmetteur: ~ **de gauchissement** *m* AERONAUT aileron follow-up; ~ **de jaugeur** *m* AERONAUT fuel level transmitter; ~ **de modem** *m* ELECTRON modem transmitter; ~ **de pas** *m* AERONAUT blade pitch transmitter; ~ **de pression** *m* INST HYDR pressure transmitter

transmettre *vt* INFORMAT, NAUT, ORDINAT transmit, TV *signal* air, broadcast, feed; **~ par ligne** *vt* TV pipe

transmission *f* AUTO power train, transmission, CONS MECA drive, driving, driving gear, shaft, shafting, transmission gear, transmission, ELECTR *réseau*, INFORMAT transmission, MECANIQUE drive, transmission, ORDINAT, PHYSIQUE, TELECOM transmission, TV TX, transmission, VEHICULES drive train, transmission; **~ à air comprimé** *f* CONS MECA compressed air system; **~ analogique** *f* TELECOM analog transmission (AmE), analogue transmission (BrE); **~ anisochrone** *f* INFORMAT anisochronous transmission; **~ asynchrone** *f* INFORMAT, ORDINAT asynchronous transmission; **~ automatique** *f* AUTO, MECANIQUE, TELECOM, VEHICULES automatic transmission; **~ binaire synchrone** *f* ORDINAT BISYNC, BSC, binary synchronous communication; **~ de chaleur** *f* CHAUFFAGE heat transmission, REFRIG heat transfer, THERMODYN heat transmission; **~ codée** *f* TELECOM coded transmission; **~ cohérente** *f* TELECOM coherent transmission; **~ à courroie plate** *f* CONS MECA flat belt drive; **~ à courroie trapézoïdale** *f* CONS MECA V-belt drive; **~ à courroie trapézoïdale multiple** *f* CONS MECA multi-V-belt, multiple V-belt drive; **~ à deux bandes latérales** *f* TV double sideband transmission; **~ différée** *f* TELECOM store-and-forward transmission, TV delayed broadcast; **~ de données** *f* INFORMAT, ORDINAT data communication, data transmission; **~ électrique** *f* ELECTR *réseau* electric linkage (AmE), electric transmission (BrE); **~ en bloc** *f* TELECOM block transmission; **~ en clair** *f* TELECOM clear transmission; **~ d'énergie** *f* ELECTROTEC power transmission, transmission of energy; **~ d'énergie à commande par courroie** *f* CONS MECA power transmission by belt drive; **~ en mode sans connexion** *f* TELECOM connectionless mode transmission; **~ en multiplex** *f* TV multiplex transmission; **~ en parallèle** *f* INFORMAT, ORDINAT, TELECOM parallel transmission; **~ flexible** *f* CONS MECA flexible shaft; **~ à grande puissance** *f* TELECOM high-power transmission; **~ Hotchkiss** *f* VEHICULES Hotchkiss drive; **~ hydraulique** *f* CONS MECA hydraulic drive, hydraulic fluid power, hydraulic transmission system, MECANIQUE fluid drive; **~ hydraulique et pneumatique** *f* CONS MECA fluid power systems; **~ hydrostatique** *f* MECANIQUE hydrostatic transmission; **~ d'image** *f* TELECOM image transmission; **~ intermédiaire** *f* CONS MECA counter driving motion, countermotion, counter gear, countershaft, countershaft and accessories, countershafting; **~ intermédiaire se fixant au sol** *f* CONS MECA countershaft for floor; **~ isochrone** *f* INFORMAT, ORDINAT isochronous transmission; **~ à large bande** *f* TELECOM wide band transmission; **~ linéaire des commandes** *f* TRANSPORT continuous automatic train control; **~ du maximum d'énergie** *f* ELECTROTEC maximum power transmission; **~ mécanique** *f* EN RENOUV mechanical transmission; **~ mécanique à courroie trapézoïdale** *f* CONS MECA V-belt speed transmission; **~ non synchrone** *f* TELECOM asynchronous transmission; **~ numérique** *f* TELECOM digital transmission; **~ numérique avec compression** *f* TELECOM compressed digital transmission; **~ oblique** *f* AERONAUT inclined drive shaft; **~ d'ondes** *f* TELECOM wave transmission; **~ de paquets** *f* INFORMAT packet transmission; **~ par arbre apparent** *f* VEHICULES Hotchkiss drive; **~ par câble** *f* TV cable transmission; **~ par chaîne** *f* CONS MECA, MECANIQUE chain drive; **~ par courant continu** *f* ELECTRON DC signaling (AmE), DC signalling (BrE); **~ par courroie** *f* PRODUCTION belt drive; **~ par double porteuse** *f* TELECOM dual-carrier transmission; **~ par engrenages** *f* CONS MECA, MECANIQUE gear drive; **~ par engrenages coniques** *f* CONS MECA bevel gear drive; **~ par fibres optiques** *f* OPTIQUE, TELECOM fiberoptic transmission (AmE), fibreoptic transmission (BrE), optical fiber transmission (AmE), optical fibre transmission (BrE); **~ par friction** *f* CONS MECA friction drive; **~ par frottement** *f* CONS MECA friction gear, friction gearing; **~ par onde porteuse supprimée** *f* ELECTRON suppressed carrier transmission; **~ par paquets** *f* TELECOM packet transmission; **~ par pignons coniques** *f* CONS MECA bevel gear drive; **~ par poulie unique et boîte de vitesse intégrée** *f* CONS MECA all-gear single-pulley drive; **~ par satellite** *f* TELECOM satellite transmission; **~ par système optoélectronique** *f* ORDINAT optical transmission; **~ par tube de poussée** *f* VEHICULES torque tube drive; **~ par vis sans fin précise** *f* CONS MECA fine worm drive; **~ pneumatique** *f* CONS MECA pneumatic fluid power; **~ poste à poste** *f* PRODUCTION *automatisme industriel* point-to-point communication; **~ pour centrifuge** *f* CONS MECA centrifuge drive; **~ principale** *f* CONS MECA main drive, main shaft; **~ au rotor principal** *f* AERONAUT main drive shaft; **~ secondaire** *f* CONS MECA counter driving motion, countermotion, counter gear, countershaft, countershaft and accessories, countershafting; **~ secondaire se fixant au sol** *f* CONS MECA countershaft for floor; **~ secondaire à placer en l'air** *f* CONS MECA overhead motion; **~ à signal unipolaire** *f* INFORMAT neutral transmission; **~ du son** *f* TELECOM sound transmission; **~ supérieure** *f* CONS MECA top driving apparatus; **~ à suppression d'onde porteuse** *f* ELECTRON suppressed carrier transmission; **~ synchrone** *f* INFORMAT, ORDINAT, TELECOM synchronous transmission; **~ synchrone par courroies** *f* CONS MECA synchronous belt drive; **~ thermique** *f* CHAUFFAGE thermal transmission, THERMODYN heat transmission; **~ au travers de filtre** *f* GENIE CHIM filter transmittance; **~ à vitesse variable** *f* CONS MECA variable speed drive

transmittance *f* PHYS ONDES *coefficient*, PHYSIQUE transmittance; **~ spectrale** *f* PHYSIQUE spectral transmittance

transmitteur: **~ de profondeur** *m* AERONAUT elevator follow-up

transmodulation *f* ELECTRON cross modulation, TV cross modulation, intermodulation, superimposed interference

transmultiplexeur *m* TELECOM TMUX, transmultiplexer

transmutation *f* NUCLEAIRE *d'un élément*, PHYS RAYON, PHYSIQUE transmutation; **~ radioactive** *f* PHYS RAYON radioactive transmutation

transonore *adj* CINEMAT *d'un écran* transoral

transordinateur *m* ORDINAT transputer

TRANSPAC *abrév (réseau de transmission de données par paquets)* TELECOM packet data transmission network

transparence *f* IMPRIM, PLAST CAOU transparency; **~ électronique** *f* TV overlay

transparent[1] *adj* GEOLOGIE hyaline, INFORMAT, ORDINAT, TELECOM transparent, TEXTILE sheer; **~ aux UV** *adj* CERAM VER (Bel) UV-transmitting

transparent:[2] **~ superposable** *m* CINEMAT transparent overlay

transpercement *m* IMPRIM *encre et papier* breakthrough

transpiration: ~ **thermique des gaz** *f* GAZ transpiration of gases

transpolarisation *f* ESPACE *communications* depolarization

transpondeur *m* ESPACE *communications*, PHYSIQUE transponder; ~ **pour sonde en espace lointain** *m* ESPACE deep space transponder; ~ **pour sonde lointaine** *m* ESPACE deep space transponder

transport *m* GAZ transmission, INFORMAT, ORDINAT transport, TEXTILE carrying; ~ **aérien** *m* AERONAUT air transport, TRANSPORT air transport, airlift; ~ **automatique rapide** *m* TRANSPORT rapid automatic transport; ~ **de chaleur** *m* REFRIG heat transfer, THERMODYN heat convection; ~ **de charge par élingue** *m* AERONAUT external load carrying; ~ **à ciel ouvert** *m* MINES surface conveyance; ~ **combiné** *m* REFRIG intermodal transport; ~ **combiné minerai-vrac-pétrole** *m* TRANSPORT combination bulk carrier; ~ **continu** *m* TRANSPORT continuous transport; ~ **de l'électricité** *m* THERMODYN electricity transmission; ~ **à l'élingue** *m* AERONAUT, MILITAIRE *hélicoptères* sling transport; ~ **en commun individualisé** *m* TRANSPORT automated personal rapid transit; ~ **en commun personnalisé** *m* TRANSPORT PRT, personal rapid transport; ~ **d'énergie** *m* THERMODYN energy transmission; ~ **d'énergie électrique** *m* ELECTR *réseau* transmission, ELECTROTEC electric power transmission; ~ **d'énergie haute tension en courant continu** *m* ELECTROTEC DC high-tension power transmission; ~ **en tube** *m* TRANSPORT TVS, tube vehicle, tube vehicle system, tubular transportation; ~ **en tube à dépression** *m* TRANSPORT transport in low-pressure tube; ~ **fluvial** *m* NAUT inland water transport; ~ **de fond** *m* HYDROLOGIE bed load transport; ~ **frigorifique** *m* AGRO ALIM, TRANSPORT refrigerated transport; ~ **de gaz par canalisation** *m* TRANSPORT long-distance gas transport; ~ **à grande distance** *m* *(TGD)* POLLUTION long-range transport; ~ **à grande distance des polluants aéroportés** *m* *(TGDPA)* POLLUTION long-range transport of air pollutants, long-range transport of airborne pollutants; ~ **hectométrique** *m* TRANSPORT short distance transport; ~ **interurbain** *m* TRANSPORT intercity transport; ~ **à longue distance** *m* TRANSPORT long-haul carriage; ~ **de marchandises par conduites** *m* TRANSPORT tube transportation; ~ **maritime** *m* EMBALLAGE carriage by sea, NAUT sea transport, seaborne trade; ~ **de matières en vrac** *m* EMBALLAGE bulk transport; ~ **par bac** *m* NAUT ferrying; ~ **par canalisation** *m* CONSTR pipage; ~ **par chemin de fer à courte distance** *m* TRANSPORT regional railroad traffic (AmE), regional railway traffic (BrE); ~ **par conduite** *m* TRANSPORT pipeline transportation; ~ **par eau** *m* NAUT water carriage, waterage; ~ **par ferry** *m* NAUT ferrying; ~ **par mer** *m* NAUT sea carriage; ~ **par voie d'eau** *m* NAUT water transport; ~ **par voie ferrée** *m* TRANSPORT rail transport, railroad transport (AmE), railway transport (BrE); ~ **pneumatique de matériaux en vrac** *m* CONS MECA pneumatic conveying of bulk materials; ~ **de point à point** *m* TRANSPORT point-to-point transport; ~ **routier** *m* CONSTR, TRANSPORT road transport; ~ **sous contrôle de température** *m* REFRIG transport under controlled temperature; ~ **sous froid** *m* REFRIG refrigerated transport; ~ **supersonique** *m* AERONAUT SST, supersonic transport; ~ **sur achats** *m* PRODUC-

TION incoming freight; ~ **à la surface** *m* MINES surface conveyance; ~ **terrestre à grande vitesse** *m* TRANSPORT high-speed ground transportation; ~ **de troupes** *m* NAUT troopship; ~ **ultrarapide** *m* TRANSPORT super-high-speed traffic, ultrahigh-speed traffic; ~ **urbain continu** *m* TRANSPORT nonstop rapid transit system, nonstop urban transportation; ~ **de voyageurs** *m* TRANSPORT passenger service

transportable *adj* INFORMAT, ORDINAT portable, transportable

transportation: ~ **d'énergie électrique** *f* ELECTR *réseau* conversion of electricity

transporté: ~ **par l'eau** *adj* HYDROLOGIE waterborne; ~ **par mer** *adj* NAUT *marchandises* seaborne

transporter[1] *vt* TEXTILE carry; ~ **au moyen d'une canalisation** *vt* CONSTR pipe

transporter:[2] ~ **la force motrice** *vi* CONS MECA convey power

transporteur *m* CONS MECA transporter, EMBALLAGE conveyor, IMPRIM *ateliers* carriage, PAPIER conveyor, PRODUCTION, TEXTILE carrier, TRANSPORT common carrier; ~ **aérien** *m* AERONAUT airline, EMBALLAGE aerial conveyor; ~ **aérien d'apport** *m* AERONAUT feeder airline; ~ **d'automobiles** *m* TRANSPORT pure car carrier; ~ **d'automobiles et de camions** *m* TRANSPORT pure car and truck carrier; ~ **à bande** *m* EMBALLAGE band conveyor, belt conveyor, MINES belt conveyor, conveyor belt, TRANSPORT conveyor belt; ~ **de brut** *m* NAUT crude carrier; ~ **à chaîne** *m* CONS MECA chain conveyor; ~ **de chargement** *m* MINES load conveyor; ~ **à chenilles** *m* MECANIQUE *véhicules* crawler; ~ **combiné minerai-vrac-pétrole** *m* TRANSPORT OBO carrier, oil-bulk-ore carrier; ~ **à courroie** *m* MINES belt conveyor, conveyor belt, PRODUCTION band conveyor, belt conveyor; ~ **à courroie muni de rouleaux porteurs** *m* CONS MECA belt conveyor with carrying idlers; ~ **exclusif de fret** *m* AERONAUT all-cargo carrier; ~ **de fil** *m* TEXTILE yarn carrier; ~ **de gaz naturel liquéfié** *m* NAUT LNG tanker; ~ **de gaz de pétrole liquéfié** *m* NAUT LPG tanker; ~ **à godets** *m* CONSTR bucket conveyor; ~ **à godets basculants** *m* TRANSPORT tipping bucket conveyor; ~ **maritime** *m* NAUT sea carrier; ~ **de minerai sous forme liquide** *m* TRANSPORT OSO tanker, ore-slurry-oil tanker, slurry tanker; ~ **à palettes** *m* PRODUCTION flight conveyor, push-plate conveyor, scraper conveyor, trough conveyor; ~ **à palettes métalliques** *m* CONS MECA *engins de manutention continue* apron conveyor; ~ **par inertie** *m* CONS MECA oscillating conveyor; ~ **par secousses** *m* CONS MECA oscillating conveyor; ~ **à plateaux** *m* EMBALLAGE apron conveyor; ~ **pour compte propre** *m* TRANSPORT industrial carrier; ~ **régional** *m* AERONAUT regional carrier; ~ **routier** *m* TRANSPORT road hauler (AmE), road haulier (BrE); ~ **suspendu** *m* EMBALLAGE overhead conveyor; ~ **à toile sans fin** *m* PRODUCTION band conveyor, belt conveyor; ~ **à vibrations** *m* AGRO ALIM vibration conveyor; ~ **à vis** *m* CONS MECA screw conveyor, CONSTR conveyor, PAPIER screw conveyor; ~ **à vis sans fin** *m* PRODUCTION screw conveyor, spiral conveyor

transporteur-gerbeur *m* EMBALLAGE stacking conveyor

transporteur-trembleur *m* PRODUCTION shaker conveyor

transporteuse *f* CONS MECA transporter; ~ **à palettes** *f* PRODUCTION flight conveyor, push-plate conveyor, scraper conveyor, trough conveyor; ~ **à vis sans fin** *f* EMBALLAGE screw conveyor

transports: ~ **et communications** *m pl* TRANSPORT transport and communications; ~ **maritimes** *m pl* NAUT shipping; ~ **routiers** *m pl* TRANSPORT road haulage

transposition *f* ACOUSTIQUE, ELECTR *de câbles isolés* transposition; ~ **de fréquence** *f* ENREGISTR frequency transposition, TV frequency translation

transputer *m* INFORMAT transputer

transrouleur *m* EMBALLAGE gravity roller, gravity roller conveyor

transsonique *adj* AERONAUT, PHYSIQUE, TRANSPORT transonic

transsuder *vt* AGRO ALIM sweat

transuranique *adj* PHYS RAYON transuranic

transvasement *m* GENIE CHIM decantation

transvaser *vt* CHIMIE, GENIE CHIM decant

transversal[1] *adj* NAUT transverse; ~ **électrique** *adj* OPTIQUE, TELECOM TE, transverse electric

transversal:[2] ~ **du pont** *m* NAUT deck transverse

transversale *f* GEOMETRIE transversal

transversalement *adv* NAUT athwartships; ~ **dans la plieuse** *adv* IMPRIM *impression* crosswise

trapèze *m* GEOMETRIE kite, trapezium

trapézoïde[1] *adj* GEOMETRIE trapezoidal

trapézoïde[2] *m* GEOMETRIE trapezoid

trappe *f* AERONAUT hatch, ASTRONOMIE dome shutter, CONSTR flap, trap, trap door, ESPACE *véhicules* hatch, INFORMAT trap, VEHICULES *carburant* filler compartment flap; ~ **de cheminée** *f* CONSTR chute gate, MINES chute door, chute gate; ~ **de dilatation** *f* INST HYDR expansion trap; ~ **à essence** *f* VEHICULES *carburant* filler compartment flap; ~ **de fond** *f* EMBALLAGE bottom flap; ~ **de plancher** *f* AERONAUT floor hatch; ~ **sous train** *f* AERONAUT main gear sliding door

trauma: ~ **sonore** *m* ACOUSTIQUE acoustic trauma

travail:[1] **au** ~ *adv* PRODUCTION *automatisme industriel* on delay

travail[2] *m* INFORMAT, ORDINAT job, PHYSIQUE work, PRODUCTION workmanship, *contacts* make, work; ~ **à l'aérographe** *m* IMPRIM airbrushing; ~ **d'art** *m* CONSTR permanent structure, permanent work; ~ **d'assemblage manuel** *m* EMBALLAGE hand assembled work; ~ **du chalumeau** *m* CONSTR blowpiping; ~ **à chaud** *m* CERAM VER, METALL hot working; ~ **au cisaillement** *m* CONS MECA shearing stress; ~ **à l'eau** *m* MINES spatter work; ~ **à l'écrasement** *m* CONS MECA positive stress; ~ **emmagasiné** *m* PRODUCTION stored up energy; ~ **en couleurs** *m* IMPRIM colorwork (AmE), colourwork (BrE); ~ **en équipage double** *m* AERONAUT double crew operation; ~ **en main** *m* PRODUCTION work-in-hand, work-in-progress; ~ **en progrès** *m* PRODUCTION work-in-hand, work-in-progress; ~ **en régie** *m* PRODUCTION commissioned work; ~ **en studio** *m* PHOTO studio work; ~ **à l'entreprise** *m* PRODUCTION contract work; ~ **à l'extension** *m* CONS MECA tensile stress; ~ **d'extraction** *m* ELECTROTEC, PHYSIQUE work function; ~ **au forfait** *m* PRODUCTION contract work; ~ **humide** *m* CERAM VER wet polishing; ~ **à la main** *m* IMPRIM handwork, PRODUCTION hand working, handwork, manual labor (AmE), manual labour (BrE); ~ **manuel** *m* PRODUCTION hand working, handwork, manual labor (AmE), manual labour (BrE); ~ **mécanique** *m* CONS MECA machine work, mechanical energy; ~ **des métaux** *m* PRODUCTION metalworking; ~ **moteur** *m* CONS MECA mechanical energy; ~ **nuisible** *m* CONS MECA loss; ~ **de nuit** *m* SECURITE night work; ~ **à la pelle** *m* CONSTR shovel work; ~ **posté** *m* PRODUCTION shift

work; ~ **de premier plan** *m* ORDINAT foreground job; ~ **des résistances passives** *m* CONS MECA loss due to friction; ~ **à la séchée** *m* CERAM VER wet and dry polishing; ~ **de séparation unitaire** *m* NUCLEAIRE unit separative power; ~ **de sortie** *m* ELECTROTEC work function; ~ **sur mors battu** *m* CERAM VER making on blowpipe; ~ **sur poste soufflé** *m* CERAM VER making on a post, working on blown post; ~ **au tour** *m* PRODUCTION lathe work; ~ **de tour** *m* PRODUCTION lathe work; ~ **à la traction** *m* CONS MECA tensile stress; ~ **de trait** *m* IMPRIM line work; ~ **utile** *m* CONS MECA power

travaillant: ~ **avec formes tridimensionnelles** *adj* CONS MECA three-dimensional form working; ~ **dans les deux sens de marche** *adj* CONS MECA *machine à raboter* double-cutting

travailler[1] *vt* CONS MECA work, CONSTR *bois* trim, PRODUCTION machine, tool; ~ **à pleine charge** *vt* CONS MECA work to full capacity; ~ **à plein rendement** *vt* CONS MECA work to full capacity; ~ **sur pied** *vt* PHOTO work with tripod

travailler[2] *vi* CONS MECA run; ~ **à contre-fil** *vi* CONSTR *du bois* work against the grain; ~ **en l'entreprise** *vi* PRODUCTION do work on contract; ~ **en sous-sol** *vi* CONSTR work underground; ~ **au forfait** *vi* PRODUCTION do work on contract

travaux: ~ **de construction** *m pl* CONSTR construction site, construction work; ~ **de déblaiement** *m pl* CONSTR clearing operations; ~ **de dragage** *m pl* NAUT dredging operations; ~ **électriques** *m pl* PETR electrical survey; ~ **en couche** *m pl* CHARBON seam work, MINES seam working, seam work; ~ **en régie** *m pl* CONSTR dayworks; ~ **en roche** *m pl* MINES rock work; ~ **en tranchées** *m pl* CONSTR trench work; ~ **d'exploitation** *m pl* CHARBON mining; ~ **d'exploration** *m pl* MINES exploration work; ~ **de fondation** *m pl* CHARBON foundation; ~ **d'injection** *m pl* CONSTR grouting; ~ **d'installation** *m pl* ELECTR *alimentation* electrical installation work; ~ **de mines** *m pl* CHARBON mining; ~ **miniers** *m pl* CHARBON mining; ~ **paysagers** *m pl* CONSTR landscaping; ~ **de percement** *m pl* CONSTR tunneling work (AmE), tunnelling work (BrE); ~ **de premier établissement** *m pl* MINES dead-work, development work; ~ **préparatoires** *m pl* MINES dead-work, development work; ~ **provisoires** *m pl* CONSTR temporary works; ~ **publics** *m pl* CONSTR, DISTRI EAU public works; ~ **de relèvement** *m pl* CONSTR clearing operations; ~ **au rocher** *m pl* MINES mullocking; ~ **routiers** *m pl* TRANSPORT road works; ~ **de sauvetage** *m pl* SECURITE rescue work; ~ **de terrassement** *m pl* CONSTR earthwork; ~ **théoriques** *m pl* PHYSIQUE theoretical work; ~ **de ville** *m pl* IMPRIM *impression* jobbing

trave *f* CONSTR single notch joint

travée *f* CONSTR bay, span, *d'un pont, d'une poutre, d'un comble* span, MECANIQUE *atelier* bay, MINES lift, stage, TELECOM suite

travelling: ~ **de poursuite** *m* CINEMAT traveling dolly (AmE), travelling dolly (BrE); ~ **réalisé à la truca** *m* CINEMAT optical zoom

travers:[1] **de** ~ **à droite** *adj* GEOMETRIE positively skewed; **de** ~ **à gauche** *adj* GEOMETRIE negatively skewed; **à** ~ **l'objectif** *adj* CINEMAT through-the-lens

travers:[2] **à** ~ **de l'avant** *adv* NAUT across the bow; **en** ~ *adv* NAUT *du navire* athwartships; **par le** ~ *adv* ESPACE abeam, NAUT abeam, abreast, athwartships; **au** ~ **de la page** *adv* IMPRIM across the page

travers-banc *m* MINES cross cut, crosscutting; ~ **au rocher** *m* MINES stone drift

traverse *f* CH DE FER cross tie (AmE), sleeper (BrE), grade crossing (AmE), level crossing (BrE), tie (AmE), CONS MECA *d'un châssis de fonderie* bar, CONSTR crossbar, crossbeam, crossover, crosspiece, head beam, lintel, rail, sill, transom, traverse, MINES crossheading, NAUT transverse beam, PHYSIQUE crosshead, PRODUCTION stay, *d'un châssis de fonderie* crossbar, TRANSPORT grade crossing (AmE), level crossing (BrE), VEHICULES *carrosserie* cross-member; ~ **d'aiguille** *f* CH DE FER crossing timber; ~ **du bas** *f* CONSTR *d'un bâti de porte, d'un châssis de fenêtre* bottom rail; ~ **basse** *f* CONSTR *d'un bâti de porte, d'un châssis de fenêtre* bottom rail; ~ **béton** *f* CONSTR concrete sleeper (BrE), concrete tie (AmE); ~ **bois** *f* CONSTR wooden sleeper (BrE), wooden tie (AmE); ~ **de couple** *f* CONS MECA frame crossbeam; ~ **crevassée** *f* CH DE FER split railroad tie (AmE), split sleeper (BrE); ~ **danseuse** *f* CH DE FER dancing sleeper (BrE), dancing tie (AmE), pumping sleeper (BrE), *véhicules* bogie bolster, truck bolster (AmE); ~ **d'envergure** *f* TEXTILE lease rod; ~ **d'essieu** *f* AUTO front suspension cross-member; ~ **de fondation** *f* CONSTR mudsill, PRODUCTION *d'un bocard* sill; ~ **du haut** *f* CONSTR *d'un bâti de porte, d'un châssis de fenêtre* top rail, PRODUCTION *du derrick* crown block; ~ **du milieu** *f* CONSTR *d'une porte* lock rail, middle rail; ~ **monobloc en béton** *f* CH DE FER monobloc concrete sleeper (BrE), monobloc concrete tie (AmE); ~ **de nez** *f* PRODUCTION nose sill; ~ **porte-tampons** *f* CH DE FER *véhicules* buffer beam; ~ **pour tubes** *f* CONS MECA pipe cross; ~ **support de plancher** *f* AERONAUT floor beam

traversée *f* CH DE FER crossover, diamond crossing, power supply duct, ELECTROTEC, ESPACE *véhicules* feedthrough, MECANIQUE penetration, NAUT crossing, passage; ~ **d'aller** *f* NAUT outward passage; ~ **combinée** *f* CH DE FER nonstandard diamond crossing; ~ **diagonale** *f* CH DE FER scissor crossing; ~ **électrique** *f* NUCLEAIRE *passage* electric penetration; ~ **isolante** *f* ELECTROTEC feedthrough insulator; ~ **jonction double** *f (TJD)* CH DE FER double diamond crossing with slips; ~ **jonction simple** *f* CH DE FER single diamond crossing with slips; ~ **oblique** *f (TO)* CH DE FER diamond crossing; ~ **de paroi** *f* MECANIQUE feedthrough; ~ **de retour** *f* NAUT homeward passage

traversée-bretelle *f* CONSTR double crossover, double crossover road

traverser *vt* CONSTR bridge, cross, GEOLOGIE cross, HYDROLOGIE run through, *un fleuve* ford

traversier *m* (Can) NAUT, TRANSPORT ferry, ferryboat

traversière *f* NAUT breast line

traversin *m* NAUT crosspiece

traversine *f* NAUT *entre deux navires* gangplank

travertin *m* EN RENOUV travertine; ~ **calcaire** *m* GEOLOGIE calcareous tufa, sinter

TRC *abrév (tube à rayons cathodiques)* ELECTR, ELECTRON, IMPRIM, ORDINAT, SECURITE, TV CRT *(cathode ray tube)*

trébuchet *m* EQUIP LAB balance, physical balance, METROLOGIE beam support; ~ **ordinaire** *m* EQUIP LAB scales; ~ **à plateaux** *m* EQUIP LAB pan scales

tréfilage *m* PRODUCTION wire drawing; ~ **à froid** *m* RESSORTS cold drawing

tréfilé *adj* CONS MECA *fil* drawn; ~ **dur** *adj* RESSORTS hard drawn

tréfiler *vt* PRODUCTION draw

tréfilerie *f* PRODUCTION wire drawing, wire works

tréfileur *m* PRODUCTION wiredrawer

trèfle: ~ **occultable** *m* AERONAUT dimmer cap

tréhalose *f* CHIMIE trehalose

treillage *m* CONSTR lattice, lattice work, netting, network, trellis, trellis work; ~ **métallique en losange** *m* CONSTR diamond wire lattice

treillis *m* CHIMIE lattice, CONSTR lattice, lattice work, netting, network, trellis work, trellis, ESPACE, MATH *dans les graphiques* lattice; ~ **d'armature** *m* CONSTR mat reinforcement; ~ **métallique** *m* CERAM VER wire mesh, CONSTR wire netting, EQUIP LAB *chauffage, support* wire gauze; ~ **à pointe** *m* TV dot grating

tréma *m* IMPRIM *composition* diaeresis

trémail *m* OCEANO trammel net

tremblement *m* AERONAUT buffeting, CONS MECA shaking; ~ **de mer** *m* GEOPHYS submarine earthquake; ~ **tectonique** *m* GEOPHYS tectonic quake; ~ **de terre** *m* GEOPHYS earth tremor, earthquake; ~ **de terre sous-marin** *m* GEOPHYS seaquake; ~ **volcanique** *m* GEOPHYS volcanic quake

trembleur *m* ELECTROTEC trembler

trémie *f* CONSTR bunker, feed hopper, opening, MECANIQUE bin, hopper, MINES bunker system, PAPIER, PRODUCTION hopper; ~ **d'alimentation** *f* CONSTR, MECANIQUE *procédé*, PRODUCTION feed hopper, TEXTILE hopper; ~ **charbon** *f* MAT CHAUFF fuel hopper; ~ **de chargement** *f* PRODUCTION feed hopper; ~ **d'entrée** *f* EMBALLAGE feed hopper; ~ **à minerai** *f* MINES ore bin, ore hopper; ~ **à tout-venant** *f* MINES raw coal bunker; ~ **vibratoire** *f* EMBALLAGE vibratory hopper

trémolite *f* MINERAUX tremolite

trémolo *m* ACOUSTIQUE tremolo

trémorine *f* CHIMIE tremorine

trempabilité *f* CRISTALL, RESSORTS hardenability

trempage *m* EMBALLAGE immersion coating, PAPIER dipping, dumping, soaking, TEXTILE soaking; ~ **à coeur** *m* RESSORTS full hardening, through hardening; ~ **dans la poudre fluidisée** *m* GENIE CHIM fluidized bed sintering

trempe *f* AGRO ALIM mash, CERAM VER dip, machine start-up, MATERIAUX hardening, quenching, METALL quench, quenching, NUCLEAIRE quench hardening; ~ **à coeur** *f* RESSORTS full hardening, through hardening; ~ **différée** *f* THERMODYN delayed hardening; ~ **différenciée** *f* CERAM VER zone toughening; ~ **à l'eau** *f* METALL water quenching; ~ **en coquille** *f* PRODUCTION chill hardening, chilling; ~ **étagée** *f* RESSORTS marquenching, step quenching, THERMODYN delayed hardening; ~ **gamma** *f* NUCLEAIRE gamma quench; ~ **à l'huile** *f* THERMODYN oil quenching; ~ **interrompue** *f* THERMODYN delayed hardening; ~ **irrégulière** *f* CERAM VER uneven temper; ~ **isothermique** *f* METALL isothermal quenching; ~ **lente** *f* METALL slow quenching; ~ **de nitruration au titane** *f* CONS MECA titanium nitride hardening; ~ **par induction** *f* ELECTROTEC, MATERIAUX, METALL induction hardening; ~ **structurale** *f* PRODUCTION precipitation hardening; ~ **à la vapeur** *f* METALL vapor quenching (AmE), vapour quenching (BrE)

trempé *adj* CRISTALL quenched; ~ **à coeur** *adj* RESSORTS full-hardened, through hardened; ~ **à l'eau** *adj* THERMODYN water-hardened; ~ **et revenu** *adj* THERMODYN heat-treated; ~ **à l'huile** *adj* THERMODYN oil-hardened, oil-quenched; ~ **mûri** *adj* THERMODYN artificially-aged, heat-treated

tremper[1] *vt* AGRO ALIM soak, MECANIQUE chill, quench, METALL quench, PAPIER dip, dump, soak, PRODUCTION chill, chill harden, dip, TEXTILE steep, THERMODYN age, artificially age, heat treat, quench; ~ **en coquille** *vt* PRODUCTION chill, chill harden; ~ **et faire revenir** *vt* THERMODYN heat treat; ~ **à flamme** *vt* THERMODYN flame harden; ~ **à l'huile** *vt* THERMODYN oil quench; ~ **sélectivement** *vt* THERMODYN flash harden

tremper[2] *vi* TEXTILE soak

trempeur: ~ **de biscuit** *m* CERAM VER biscuit dipper

trenail *m* CONSTR treenail, trenail, trunnel

trépan *m* CONSTR bore bit, MINES boring chisel, chisel, chisel bit, drill bit, drilling bit, PETROLE drill bit, *forage* bit; ~ **aléseur** *m* PETROLE reamer, reaming bit; ~ **annulaire** *m* PETROLE annular bit; ~ **d'attaque** *m* PETROLE spudding bit; ~ **de battage** *m* PETROLE spudding bit; ~ **batteur** *m* MINES churn drill bit; ~ **bêche** *m* PETROLE spudding bit; ~ **à biseau** *m* MINES chisel bit, chopping bit, cutting bit, PETROLE chisel bit; ~ **à boue** *m* PETROLE mud bit; ~ **carbure** *m* CONS MECA carbide-tipped hole saw; ~ **carbure pour béton** *m* CONS MECA core drill carbide tipped for concrete; ~ **carottier** *m* MINES core bit, core cutter, core lifter, PETROLE core bit; ~ **composé** *m* MINES boring head, cutter head; ~ **à concrétion carbure** *m* CONS MECA tungsten-carbide-grit hole saw; ~ **à cônes** *m* PETROLE cone bit; ~ **à couronne** *m* PETROLE crown bit; ~ **découpeur** *m* MINES core bit, core cutter, core lifter; ~ **à deux taillants** *m* PETROLE four-wing bit; ~ **à diamant** *m* PETROLE diamond bit; ~ **à disque** *m* PETROLE disc bit (BrE), disk bit (AmE); ~ **à effacement** *m* PETROLE collapsible bit; ~ **en croix** *m* PETROLE crossbit, star bit; ~ **en queue de poisson** *m* PETROLE fishtail bit; ~ **excentrique** *m* MINES eccentric bit, eccentric chisel, PETROLE *forage* eccentric bit; ~ **de forage au câble** *m* PETROLE cable drilling bit; ~ **hélicoïdal** *m* PETROLE spiral bit; ~ **à jets** *m* PETROLE jet bit; ~ **à lames** *m* PETROLE blade bit, drag bit; ~ **Mère Hubbard** *m* PETROLE Mother Hubbard bit; ~ **à molettes** *m* PETROLE rock bit, roller bit; ~ **à pastilles** *m* PETROLE insert bit; ~ **pilote** *m* PETROLE pilot bit; ~ **plat** *m* MINES flat chisel, plain bit; ~ **pour forage rotary** *m* PETROLE rotary bit; ~ **pour formations dures** *m* PETROLE hard formation bit; ~ **pour roches** *m* PETROLE rock bit; ~ **pour sondage au câble** *m* PETROLE churn drill; ~ **pour sondage percutant** *m* PETROLE borer bit; ~ **quadricône** *m* PETROLE quadricone bit; ~ **à quatre lames** *m* PETROLE four-way bit; ~ **à redans** *m* PETROLE step bit; ~ **réglable** *m* PETROLE expansion bit; ~ **sec** *m* PETROLE claying bar; ~ **simple** *m* MINES flat chisel, plain bit; ~ **tranchant** *m* MINES chisel bit, chopping bit, cutting bit; ~ **à tranchant en croix** *m* MINES star bit; ~ **trancheur** *m* PETROLE chisel bit; ~ **tricône** *m* PETROLE three-cone bit, tricone bit; ~ **à turbine** *m* PETROLE turbodrill; ~ **usé** *m* PETROLE dull bit, *forage* worn bit

trépan-benne *m* CONSTR hammer grab

trépaneur *m* CONS MECA trepanner

trépidation *f* ESPACE *véhicules* judder

trépied *m* CINEMAT, EQUIP LAB *support*, INSTRUMENT, MINES, PHOTO, PRODUCTION tripod; ~ **à branches courtes** *m* CINEMAT top hat; ~ **à coulisse** *m* METROLOGIE adjustable tripod; ~ **extensible** *m* PHOTO extension tripod; ~ **de table** *m* CINEMAT table top tripod

tresse *f* CERAM VER, ELECTR *câble*, ELECTROTEC braid, NAUT sennet, PRODUCTION gasket, TEXTILE braiding, braid; ~ **de blindage** *f* ELECTROTEC braid; ~ **de coton** *f* ELECTROTEC, TEXTILE cotton braid; ~ **de cuivre** *f* PRODUCTION copper braid; ~ **en chanvre** *f* PRODUCTION hemp gasket; ~ **de métallisation** *f* PRODUCTION bonding jumper; ~ **de mise à la masse** *f* ESPACE bonding strap, PRODUCTION bonding jumper; ~ **ronde** *f* ELECTROTEC braided wire

tresser *vt* ELECTROTEC braid

tréteau *m* CONSTR trestle, NUCLEAIRE holding pedestal, pedestal, PRODUCTION horse; ~ **de noyauteur** *m* PRODUCTION core trestle

treuil *m* CONSTR winch, windlass, MECANIQUE *matériel de levage* hoist, NAUT, POLLU MER winch, PRODUCTION crab, hoisting crab, hoist, TRANSPORT hoist; ~ **à air comprimé** *m* PETROLE, PRODUCTION air hoist; ~ **d'applique** *m* MINES bracket crab, PRODUCTION gypsy winch; ~ **à bras** *m* PRODUCTION crab winch, hand winch; ~ **de câble** *m* ELECTROTEC, TRANSPORT cable winch; ~ **à câble** *m* ELECTROTEC, TRANSPORT cable winch; ~ **à chaîne** *m* CONS MECA chain hoist; ~ **de chargement** *m* NAUT, TRANSPORT cargo winch; ~ **d'extraction** *m* CONSTR gin wheel, tackle, PRODUCTION hoisting crab; ~ **de forage** *m* MINES drilling winch, hoist, PETR, PETROLE draw works; ~ **hydraulique** *m* MINES hydraulic winch; ~ **de levage** *m* CONSTR gin wheel, tackle, NAUT cargo winch; ~ **à manivelle** *m* PRODUCTION crab winch, hand winch; ~ **de manoeuvre** *m* CONSTR shunting winch, MINES drilling winch, hoist; ~ **à noix** *m* CONSTR lifting gear; ~ **pneumatique** *m* CONS MECA air hoist; ~ **réacteur** *m* AERONAUT engine hoist; ~ **roulant** *m* NUCLEAIRE crab, trolley; ~ **à tension constante** *m* NAUT self-tensioning winch

treuilliste *m* AERONAUT hoist operator

tri *m* CHARBON grading, INFORMAT, ORDINAT sort, sorting, QUALITE grading; ~ **alphanumérique** *m* INFORMAT, ORDINAT alphanumeric sort; ~ **ascendant** *m* INFORMAT, ORDINAT ascending sort; ~ **binaire** *m* INFORMAT, ORDINAT binary sort; ~ **des déchets** *m* RECYCLAGE waste sorting; ~ **descendant** *m* INFORMAT, ORDINAT backward sort; ~ **en ordre décroissant** *m* INFORMAT, ORDINAT backward sort; ~ **externe** *m* INFORMAT, ORDINAT external sort; ~ **de fusionnement** *m* INFORMAT, ORDINAT external sort; ~ **interne** *m* INFORMAT, ORDINAT internal sort; ~ **par bloc** *m* INFORMAT, ORDINAT block sort; ~ **par permutation** *m* INFORMAT, ORDINAT bubble sort

triac *m* ELECTR *thyristor*, ELECTROTEC triac

triacétate *m* TEXTILE triacetate; ~ **de cellulose** *m* PLAST CAOU cellulose triacetate

triacétine *f* CHIMIE triacetin

triacétonamine *f* CHIMIE triacetonamin, triacetonamine

triacide *m* CHIMIE triacid

triade *f* CHIMIE triad

triage *m* CH DE FER sorting, *véhicules* classification, CHARBON sorting, EMBALLAGE grading, PAPIER sorting, PETROLE processing, separation, treatment, QUALITE grading; ~ **à tamis** *m* GENIE CHIM sieve classification

trialcool *m* CHIMIE triol

triamyle *m* CHIMIE triamyl

triangle *m* CINEMAT spider, spreader, GEOMETRIE triangle, IMPRIM *plieuse* former; ~ **aigu** *m* GEOMETRIE acute triangle; ~ **d'avertissement** *m* SECURITE warning triangle; ~ **de base** *m* METALL basic triangle; ~ **à chape** *m* CONS MECA clevis link; ~ **congruent** *m* GEOMETRIE congruent triangle; ~ **des couleurs** *m* PHYSIQUE color triangle (AmE), colour triangle (BrE), TV chromaticity diagram; ~ **équilatéral** *m* GEOMETRIE equiangular triangle; ~ **des forces** *m* CONSTR, PHYSIQUE triangle of forces; ~ **isocèle** *m* GEOMETRIE isosceles triangle; ~ **oblique** *m* GEOMETRIE oblique triangle, VEHICULES *essieu arrière* semitrailing arm; ~ **obtus** *m* GEOMETRIE obtuse triangle; ~ **polaire** *m* GEOMETRIE polar triangle; ~ **pour creusets** *m* EQUIP LAB *support* pipe clay triangle; ~ **rectangle** *m* GEOMETRIE right angle triangle; ~ **rectiligne** *m* GEOMETRIE plane triangle; ~ **scalène** *m* GEOMETRIE scalene triangle; ~ **sphérique** *m* GEOMETRIE spherical triangle; ~ **sur roulettes** *m* CINEMAT spider dolly

Triangle *m* ASTRONOMIE Triangulum; ~ **austral** *m* ASTRONOMIE Triangulum Australe

triangulaire *adj* GEOMETRIE triangular

triangulation *f* CONSTR, ESPACE, GEOMETRIE, METROLOGIE triangulation; ~ **du train** *f* AERONAUT landing gear bracing installation

trianguler *vt* GEOMETRIE triangulate

trias *m* PETROLE Triassic period

triazole *m* CHIMIE triazole

tribasique *adj* CHIMIE tribasic

triboélectricité *f* ELECTR *phénomène* frictional electricity, PHYSIQUE triboelectricity

triboélectrique *adj* TRANSPORT *détecteur* triboelectric

triboluminescence *f* PHYSIQUE triboluminescence

tribord *m* ESPACE *véhicules*, NAUT starboard

tributaire *adj* HYDROLOGIE tributary, PRODUCTION dependent; ~ **de la vitesse de sortie** *adj* INFORMAT output-limited

tributyrine *f* CHIMIE tributyrin

tricarballylique *adj* CHIMIE tricarballylic

trichite *f* CRISTALL whisker, PETR trichite

trichloracétique *adj* CHIMIE trichloroacetic

trichloréthylène *m* CHIMIE trichlorethylene, trichloroethylene, LESSIVES trichlorethylene

trichlorure *m* CHIMIE terchloride, trichloride

trichroïque *adj* PHYSIQUE trichroic

trichroïsme *m* PHYSIQUE trichroism, trigger

trichrome *adj* INSTRUMENT *filtre* trichromatic

trichronomie *f* IMPRIM *impression* three-color printing (AmE), three-colour printing (BrE)

tricinate *m* CHIMIE styphnate

triclinique *adj* CHIMIE, CRISTALL triclinic

tricoises *f pl* CONSTR pincers

tricosane *f* CHIMIE tricosane

tricot: ~ **circulaire** *m* TEXTILE circular-knitted fabric; ~ **sans trame** *m* TEXTILE weft-knitted fabric; ~ **de verre textile** *m* CERAM VER knitted glass fabric

tricotage *m* TEXTILE hose knitting, knitting; ~ **chaîne** *m* TEXTILE warp knitting; ~ **rectiligne** *m* TEXTILE flat knitting

tricoter *vt* TEXTILE knit

tricoteurs: ~ **au mètre** *m pl* TEXTILE yard good knitters

tricrésol *m* CHIMIE tricresol

tricrésyle *m* CHIMIE tricresyl

tricyclique *adj* CHIMIE tricyclic

tridimensionnel *adj* PHYSIQUE three-dimensional

tridymite *f* MINERAUX tridymite

trièdre[1] *adj* GEOMETRIE trihedral

trièdre[2] *m* GEOMETRIE trihedron; ~ **de référence** *m* AERONAUT pitch roll and yaw axes; ~ **de référence d'inertie** *m* ESPACE inertial frame, pitch roll and yaw axes

trier *vt* AGRO ALIM grade, GENIE CHIM classify, separate, GEOLOGIE grade, IMPRIM, INFORMAT, ORDINAT sort

triester *m* CHIMIE triester

triéthanolamine *m* LESSIVES triethanolamine

trieur *m* CERAM VER sorter, MINES ore separator, separator; ~ **électromagnétique** *m* MINES magnetic separator; ~ **magnétique** *m* MINES, NUCLEAIRE *parateur* magnetic separator; ~ **de noeuds** *m* PAPIER knotter screen

trieuse *f* EMBALLAGE sorting machine; ~ **de chiffons** *f* PAPIER rag sorter; ~ **de documents** *f* INFORMAT, ORDINAT document sorter

trifurcation *f* ELECTR trifurcator, *accessoire de câble* trifurcating box

trigatron *m* ELECTRON trigatron

trigger: ~ **de Schmitt** *m* PHYSIQUE Schmitt trigger

triglycéride *m* CHIMIE, LESSIVES triglyceride

trigma *m* NUCLEAIRE plugged mirror, trigma

trigonal *adj* CRISTALL trigonal

trigonométrie *f* GEOMETRIE trigonometry; ~ **parallactique** *f* ASTRONOMIE parallactic trigonometry; ~ **plane** *f* GEOMETRIE plane trigonometry

trigonométrique *adj* GEOMETRIE trigonometric, trigonometrical

trihydrate *m* CHIMIE trihydrate

trihydrique *adj* CHIMIE trihydric

trihydrol *m* CHIMIE trihydrol

triiodure *m* CHIMIE triiodide

trilatéral *m* GEOMETRIE trilateral

trille *f* ACOUSTIQUE trill

trim: ~ **de profondeur** *m* AERONAUT elevator trim

trimellique *adj* CHIMIE trimellitic

trimellitique *adj* CHIMIE trimellitic

trimère *m* CHIMIE, PLAST CAOU trimer

trimériser *vt* CHIMIE trimerize

trimésique *adj* CHIMIE trimesic

trimétallique *adj* IMPRIM *plaque* trimetallic

triméthylbenzène *m* CHIMIE trimethylbenzene

triméthylbutane *m* CHIMIE triptane

triméthylcarbinol *m* CHIMIE trimethylcarbinol

triméthylène *m* CHIMIE trimethylene

triméthylpyridine *f* CHIMIE trimethylpyridine

trimoléculaire *adj* CHIMIE thermolecular, trimolecular

trimorphe *adj* CHIMIE trimorphic, trimorphous

trimorphisme *m* CHIMIE trimorphism

trimyristine *f* CHIMIE trimyristin

tringle *f* CONS MECA rod; ~ **de fer** *f* PRODUCTION iron rod; ~ **de fourchette** *f* AUTO release rod, VEHICULES *embrayage* fork push rod; ~ **de manoeuvre d'aiguille** *f* CH DE FER point-operating stretcher, throw rod; ~ **de manoeuvre de régulateur** *f* INST HYDR throttle reach rod, throttle rod, throttle stem; ~ **de manoeuvre de signal** *f* CH DE FER signal-operating rod; ~ **de pédale de débrayage** *f* VEHICULES clutch pedal push rod; ~ **du régulateur** *f* CONS MECA governor rod; ~ **de suspension** *f* MINES hand dog, hanging rod; ~ **de talon** *f* AUTO bead core; ~ **de tirage** *f* CONS MECA pull rod; ~ **de tirage de frein** *f* VEHICULES brake connecting rod, brake rod

tringlerie *f* CONS MECA, MECANIQUE, VEHICULES *direction, embrayage, freins* linkage; ~ **de frein** *f* CONS MECA brake linkage; ~ **de gaz** *f* AUTO carburetor linkage (AmE), carburettor linkage (BrE)

trinitré[1] *adj* CHIMIE trinitrated

trinitré[2] *m* CHIMIE trinitrate, *composé* trinitro-compound

trinitrine *f* CHIMIE trinitrin

trinitrobenzène *m* CHIMIE trinitrobenzene

trinitrocrésol *m* CHIMIE trinitrocresol
trinitrophénol *m* CHIMIE trinitrophenol
trinitrorésorcinate *m* CHIMIE styphnate
trinitrorésorcine *f* CHIMIE styphnic acid
trinitrotoluène *m* CHIMIE trinitrotoluene, trotyl
trinôme *m* MATH trinomial
trinquette *f* NAUT forestaysail, storm sail
trio *m* CONS MECA three-high mill, three-high rolls, three-high train
triode *f* ELECTRON, PHYSIQUE triode; ~ à cathode chaude *f* ELECTRON thermionic triode, thermionic tube; ~ à cible *f* ELECTRON EBS, electron-bombarded semiconductor; ~ EBS *f* ELECTRON EBS, electron-bombarded semiconductor; ~ à électrodes planes *f* ELECTRON planar triode; ~ à gaz *f* ELECTRON gas triode; ~ à vide *f* ELECTRON vacuum triode
triode-hexode *f* ELECTRON triode-hexode
triol *m* CHIMIE triol
trioléine *f* CHIMIE triolein
triose *f* CHIMIE triose
trioxyde *m* CHIMIE teroxide, trioxide
trioxyméthylène *m* CHIMIE trioxane, trioxymethylene
tripalmitine *f* CHIMIE tripalmitin
triparanol *m* CHIMIE triparanol
triphane *m* MINERAUX triphane
triphasé *adj* ELECTR *réseau* three-phase, ELECTROTEC three-phase, triphase, PHYSIQUE three-phase
triphasique *adj* CHIMIE triphasic
triphénol *m* CHIMIE triphenol
triphile *adj* CHIMIE triphilic
triphosphate: ~ d'adénosine *m* AGRO ALIM adenosine triphosphate
triphylite *f* MINERAUX triphyline, triphylite
triple: ~ écran *m* CINEMAT triptych screen
triplet *m* NUCLEAIRE triplet, PHOTO triplet lens, PHYSIQUE triplet
triplite *f* MINERAUX triplite
tripol *m* PETR tripolite
tripolite *f* MINERAUX tripolite
triptane *m* CHIMIE triptane
trisection *f* GEOMETRIE *d'un angle* trisection
trisnitrate *m* CHIMIE trisnitrate
trisodique *adj* CHIMIE trisodium
tristandard *adj* TV triple-standard
tristéarate: ~ de glycéryle *m* CHIMIE glyceryl tristearate
tristéarine *f* CHIMIE tristearin
trisubstitué *adj* CHIMIE trisubstituted
tritane *m* CHIMIE tritan
trithionique *adj* CHIMIE trithionic
triticine *f* CHIMIE triticin
trité *adj* NUCLEAIRE tritiated
tritium *m* CHIMIE, PHYSIQUE tritium
tritoxyde *m* CHIMIE tritoxide
triturateur *m* CONS MECA triturator, PAPIER pulper; ~ en discontinu *m* PAPIER batch pulper
trituration *f* CHIMIE grinding, triturating, PAPIER slushing, PRODUCTION grinding
trituré *adj* GENIE CHIM pulverized
triturer *vt* CHIMIE grind, triturate, GENIE CHIM grind, pulverize, PRODUCTION grind
trityle *m* CHIMIE trityl
trivalence *f* CHIMIE tervalence, trivalence, trivalency
trivalent *adj* CHIMIE tervalent, trivalent
troctolite *f* PETR troctolite, troctolyte
troegérite *f* MINERAUX troegerite, trögerite
troïlite *f* MINERAUX troilite

trois: à ~ dimensions *adj* MATERIAUX three-dimensional, tridimensional; à ~ phases *adj* ELECTROTEC three-phase; à ~ voies *adj* MECANIQUE three-way
trois-carrés *m* CONS MECA three-square file, tri-square file
troisième[1] *m* MATH third; ~ cuisson *m* CERAM VER third firing; ~ principe de la thermodynamique *m* PHYSIQUE third law of thermodynamics; ~ rail *m* CH DE FER third rail, ELECTR conductor rail; ~ taraud *m* CONS MECA plug tap, straight tap, third tap
troisième[2] ~ de couverture *f* IMPRIM *maquette* inside back cover; ~ génération *f* INFORMAT, ORDINAT third generation; ~ harmonique *f* ELECTRON third harmonic
trois-mâts: ~ goélette à huniers *m* TRANSPORT bark schooner (AmE), barque schooner (BrE)
trois-quarts *m* CONS MECA three-square file
trolley *m* CONS MECA runner, PRODUCTION traveling runner (AmE), traveling trolley (AmE), travelling runner (BrE), travelling trolley (BrE), trolley, TRANSPORT trolley
trolleybus *m* TRANSPORT trolleybus; ~ articulé *m* TRANSPORT articulated trolleybus; ~ souterrain *m* TRANSPORT underground trolleybus
trombe *f* METEO spout, OCEANO waterspout; ~ d'eau *f* METEO cloudburst, NAUT waterspout; ~ marine *f* METEO waterspout
trommel *m* CHARBON revolving screen, trommel, CONSTR *préparation mécanique des minerais* rotary screen, MINES revolving screen; ~ classeur *m* GENIE CHIM classifying drum; ~ des fins *m* PRODUCTION fine trommel; ~ des gros *m* MINES coarse trommel; ~ rotatif Bradford *m* CHARBON Bradford breaker
trompe *f* CONS MECA nozzle; ~ d'alarme *f* PRODUCTION hooter; ~ à eau à vide *f* EQUIP LAB *filtration* filter pump; ~ évasée *f* MINES chimney
tromperie *f* INFORMAT, ORDINAT spoofing
trompette *f* CONS MECA *d'un étau-limeur* ram, NAUT reed; ~ de pont *f* AUTO split housing; ~ de pont arrière *f* AUTO rear axle flared tube; ~ de roue conique *f* AERONAUT bevel gear housing, bevel ring flared stub shaft
trompeur *adj* BREVETS misleading
trona *m* LESSIVES sodium sesquicarbonate, MINERAUX trona
tronc: ~ d'arbre équarri *m* CONSTR balk (AmE), baulk (BrE); ~ de l'atome *m* NUCLEAIRE atomic trunk; ~ commun *m* TELECOM common highway; ~ de cône *m* GEOMETRIE frustum-truncated cone; ~ de pyramide *m* GEOMETRIE truncated pyramid
troncature *f* GEOMETRIE truncating, truncation, INFORMAT, ORDINAT truncation
tronçon *m* CONS MECA, CONSTR, DISTRI EAU, PETROLE section, TELECOM length, section; ~ de guide d'ondes *m* ELECTROTEC waveguide section; ~ de mesure en guide d'ondes *m* ELECTROTEC waveguide slotted section; ~ de route sans droits de trafic *m* AERONAUT, TRANSPORT blind sector without traffic rights; ~ de voie *m* CH DE FER track section
tronçonnage *m* PRODUCTION cutting-off, *d'un tube* cutting-off pieces; ~ d'une bobine *m* PAPIER slitting
tronçonnement *m* PRODUCTION cutting-off
tronçonner *vt* PRODUCTION cutoff
tronçonneuse *f* CONS MECA chain saw; ~ à meule *f* CONS MECA abrasive cutoff machine; ~ à meule et rectifieuse de fonderie *f* CONS MECA foundry abrasive cutoff and grinding machine; ~ pour feuillard de cerclage *f* EMBALLAGE iron band cutter

tronquer *vt* GEOMETRIE, INFORMAT, ORDINAT truncate

troostite *f* METALL, MINERAUX troostite

tropine *f* CHIMIE tropine

tropique *adj* CHIMIE *acide* tropic

tropopause *f* METEO tropopause

troposphère *f* ESPACE *géophysique*, METEO troposphere

trop-plein *m* CH DE FER overflow valve, CONS MECA *d'un injecteur* overflow, CONSTR waste pipe, wastewater, DISTRI EAU overflow, overflow pipe, surplus water, weir, HYDROLOGIE, MECANIQUE overflow

trottoir *m* CONSTR footway, pavement (BrE), path, walkway, pavement (BrE), sidewalk (AmE), OCEANO lithothamnion ridge, wave-cut bench; **~ de chargement** *m* CH DE FER *véhicules* loading platform; **~ roulant** *m* AERONAUT moving sidewalk (AmE), passenger conveyor, CONSTR moving platform (BrE), moving sidewalk (AmE), traveling sidewalk (AmE), travelling platform (BrE), TRANSPORT moving pavement (BrE), moving sidewalk (AmE); **~ roulant articulé** *m* TRANSPORT articulated-type moving pavement (BrE), articulated-type moving sidewalk (AmE); **~ roulant à bande continue** *m* TRANSPORT belt-type moving pavement (BrE), belt-type moving sidewalk (AmE); **~ roulant à cabines** *m* TRANSPORT cabin conveyor, cabin-type moving pavement (BrE), cabin-type moving sidewalk (AmE)

trou *m* CONS MECA, ELECTROTEC hole, MINES blast hole, drill hole, NUCLEAIRE electron positive hole, hole, OCEANO hole, PETROLE hole, well, well bore, PHYSIQUE hole; **~ d'abattage** *m* MINES bench hole; **~ d'accès** *m* CONSTR *abri* manhole; **~ d'aération** *m* CONS MECA air vent; **~ d'air** *m* PRODUCTION sand vent, *d'un moule* vent, vent hole; **~ d'allégement** *m* AERONAUT, MECANIQUE lightening hole; **~ de bonde** *m* PRODUCTION *système hydraulique* bunghole; **~ borgne** *m* CONSTR blind hole; **~ de bouchon** *m* MINES cut hole; **~ de bougie** *m* AUTO spark plug hole; **~ de boulon** *m* CONS MECA bolt hole; **~ de bras** *m* PRODUCTION hand hole, mud door, washout hole; **~ de centrage** *m* CONS MECA center hole (AmE), centre hole (BrE); **~ de cheville** *m* CONSTR dowel hole, draw bore; **~ de clef** *m* CONSTR *d'un robinet* plug hole; **~ de côté** *m* MINES rib hole, trimmer; **~ de coulée** *m* CERAM VER tapping hole, PRODUCTION cast gate, down runner, pouring hole, sprue hole, drawhole, funnel, gate, jet, mouth, pouring gate, runner, running gate, tap hole; **~ de couronne** *m* MINES backhole, top hole; **~ à crasse** *m* PRODUCTION cinder notch; **~ de dégagement** *m* MINES easer, easer hole, relief hole, reliever, reliever hole; **~ de dégraissage** *m* MINES easer, easer hole, relief hole, reliever, reliever hole; **~ échancré** *m* CONS MECA *d'une filière* notched hole; **~ d'écoulement** *m* CONSTR weephole; **~ d'écrémage** *m* CERAM VER skimming hole; **~ d'effaçage du raccord de la piste sonore** *m* ENREGISTR bloop punch; **~ électronique** *m* NUCLEAIRE electron positive hole, hole; **~ embrevé** *m* CONS MECA dimpled hole; **~ d'épingle** *m* CINEMAT, PAPIER pinhole; **~ d'évent** *m* CONSTR vent, vent hole, PRODUCTION air hole, riser; **~ de forage** *m* CHARBON, GEOLOGIE borehole; **~ fraisé** *m* PRODUCTION countersunk hole; **~ de front** *m* MINES breast hole, face hole; **~ de graissage** *m* CONS MECA oil hole; **~ graisseur** *m* CONS MECA oil hole; **~ de gueuse** *m* PRODUCTION drawhole, mouth, tap hole; **~ d'homme** *m* CONS MECA manhole, CONSTR *abri* inspection chamber, manhole, ELECTR *alimentation*, ESPACE, MECANIQUE, NUCLEAIRE manhole, PETROLE manway; **~**

hors calibre *m* PETR overgage hole (AmE), overgauge hole (BrE); **~ humide** *m* MINES wet hole; **~ incliné** *m* MINES incline hole, inclined hole; **~ d'index** *m* ORDINAT *d'une disquette* index hole; **~ de jaumière** *m* NAUT rudder port; **~ à laitier** *m* PRODUCTION breast hole, cinder notch; **~ libre** *m* PETR empty hole; **~ lisse** *m* CONS MECA *destiné à recevoir un boulon* bolt hole; **~ à main** *m* PRODUCTION hand hole, mud door, washout hole; **~ métallisé** *m* ELECTR *carte de circuits imprimés* metalized hole (AmE), metallized hole (BrE), ELECTRON plated-through hole; **~ de mine** *m* MINES blast hole, borehole, mining hole, chamber, mine chamber, shot hole; **~ de mine vertical** *m* MINES vertical hole; **~ noir** *m* ASTRONOMIE, ESPACE, PHYSIQUE black hole; **~ noir d'une masse solaire** *m* ASTRONOMIE solar mass black hole; **~ noir primordial** *m* ASTRONOMIE primordial black hole; **~ noir sans rotation** *m* ASTRONOMIE nonrotating black hole; **~ non tubé** *m* PETR open hole; **~ oblong** *m* MECANIQUE elongated hole; **~ ovalisé** *m* CONS MECA elongated hole; **~ de passage** *m* CONS MECA clearance hole; **~ percé de part en part** *m* CONSTR thoroughfare hole; **~ perdu** *m* PETROLE *forage* lost hole; **~ de piétage** *m* CONS MECA locating hole; **~ pilote** *m* CONS MECA pilot hole; **~ de prospection** *m* MINES exploration pit, prospect hole; **~ de rat** *m* PETR rat hole, PETROLE mouse hole, rat hole; **~ de regard** *m* ESPACE *véhicules* peep hole; **~ de relevage** *m* MINES lifter, lifter hole; **~ de repérage** *m* INFORMAT *d'une disquette* index hole; **~ de sable** *m* PRODUCTION *dans une pièce venue de fonte* sand hole; **~ de la scorie** *m* PRODUCTION cinder notch; **~ sec** *m* MINES dry hole; **~ de sel** *m* PRODUCTION hand hole, mud door, washout hole; **~ de serrure** *m* PETROLE *forage* key seating; **~ de sondage** *m* GEOLOGIE, GEOPHYS borehole; **~ de sondage sismique** *m* GEOPHYS seismic borehole; **~ de sonde** *m* CONSTR borehole, hole, GAZ borehole, MINES blast hole, borehole, drill hole, PETR borehole; **~ de sonde pratiqué sec** *m* MINES dry hole; **~ souffleur** *m* OCEANO blowhole; **~ de souris** *m* EN RENOUV *appareil de forage géothermique*, PETR, PETROLE mouse hole; **~ sous-calibré** *m* PETR undergage hole (AmE), undergauge hole (BrE); **~ taraudé** *m* CONS MECA *destiné à recevoir un boulon* bolt hole, NUCLEAIRE threaded hole, PRODUCTION tapped hole; **~ de toit** *m* MINES backhole, top hole; **~ traversant la pièce de part en part** *m* CONSTR thoroughfare hole; **~ de traversée** *m* PHYSIQUE feedthrough; **~ de visée** *m* MILITAIRE *d'une arme à feu* sight hole; **~ de visite** *m* CONSTR *abri* inspection chamber, manhole, ESPACE manhole

trouble[1] *adj* DISTRI EAU cloudy

trouble[2] *m* OCEANO push net; **~ au froid** *m* REFRIG chilling injury

trouée: **~ d'approche** *f* AERONAUT approach funnel; **~ de décollage** *f* AERONAUT takeoff funnel; **~ dégagée** *f* CONS MECA clearway; **~ d'évacuation** *f* AERONAUT *lutte contre l'incendie* fire rescue path

trouer *vt* CONSTR hole

troupes: **~ portées** *f pl* MILITAIRE lorried troops

trous: **~ de positionnement** *m pl* CINEMAT registration holes

trousquin *m* CONSTR joiner's gage (AmE), joiner's gauge (BrE)

troussage *m* PRODUCTION strickling, sweeping, sweeping up

trousse *f* CONS MECA outfit, set, MINES crib, curb, NUCLEAIRE kit, PRODUCTION former, templet, kit, strickle, sweep, template, VEHICULES *outils* case; ~ **d'analyse d'eau** *f* EQUIP LAB water analysis kit; ~ **d'objectifs** *f* PHOTO set of supplementary lenses; ~ **de premiers secours** *f* SECURITE first-aid box, first-aid kit; ~ **à réparations** *f* PRODUCTION repair outfit

trousseau *m* CONS MECA outfit, PRODUCTION kit, rig, spindle and sweep; ~ **à potence murale** *m* PRODUCTION horse; ~ **transportable** *m* PRODUCTION gig

troussequin *m* CONS MECA scribing block, CONSTR carpenter's gage (AmE), carpenter's gauge (BrE), joiner's gage (AmE), joiner's gauge (BrE), scribing gage (AmE), scribing gauge (BrE)

troussequiner *vti* CONSTR scribe

trousser *vt* PRODUCTION sweep, sweep up

truc *m* TRANSPORT large capacity truck

truca *f* CINEMAT trick printer

trucage *m* CINEMAT optical; ~ **par cache contre-cache** *m* CINEMAT traveling matte (AmE), travelling matte (BrE); ~ **à la prise de vue** *m* CINEMAT in-camera effect

trucages *m pl* CINEMAT effects, special effects, TV FX, effects; ~ **réalisés à la prise de vues** *m pl* CINEMAT camera opticals

truelle *f* CONSTR brick trowel, bricklayer's trowel, trowel; ~ **à coeur** *f* CONSTR heart trowel; ~ **à feuille de laurier** *f* PRODUCTION leaf, leaf-shaped trowel; ~ **à mortier** *f* CONSTR brick trowel, bricklayer's trowel; ~ **à plâtre** *f* CONSTR plastering trowel

truqueur: ~ **électronique** *m* TV matting amplifier

trusquin *m* CONS MECA scribing block, CONSTR carpenter's gage (AmE), carpenter's gauge (BrE), joiner's gage (AmE), joiner's gauge (BrE), mortise gage (AmE), mortise gauge (BrE), scribing gage (AmE), scribing gauge (BrE), MECANIQUE *outillage* surface gage (AmE), surface gauge (BrE), PRODUCTION marking gage (AmE), marking gauge (BrE); ~ **à combinaisons** *m* CONS MECA combination surface gage (AmE), combination surface gauge (BrE); ~ **de côté** *m* CONSTR scratch gage (AmE), scratch gauge (BrE); ~ **à couper** *m* CONSTR *de menuisier* cutting gage (AmE), cutting gauge (BrE); ~ **à double traçoir** *m* CONSTR mortise gage (AmE), mortise gauge (BrE); ~ **de hauteur à vernier** *m* METROLOGIE vernier height gage (AmE), vernier height gauge (BrE); ~ **à main** *m* CONSTR scratch gage (AmE), scratch gauge (BrE); ~ **à marbre** *m* CONS MECA scribing block; ~ **à pointe** *m* CONSTR scribing gage (AmE), scribing gauge (BrE), PRODUCTION marking gage (AmE), marking gauge (BrE); ~ **porte-planche** *m* PRODUCTION spindle arm; ~ **de profondeur à vernier** *m* METROLOGIE vernier depth gage (AmE), vernier depth gauge (BrE); ~ **à tracer** *m* CONS MECA marking gage (AmE), marking gauge (BrE)

trusquiner *vti* CONSTR scribe, PRODUCTION mark

truxilline *f* CHIMIE truxilline

truxillique *adj* CHIMIE truxillic

tryptique *adj* CHIMIE tryptic

tryptomine *f* CHIMIE tryptomin, tryptomine

tscheffkinite *f* MINERAUX tscheffkinite, tschewkinite

tschermigite *f* MINERAUX tschermakite, tschermigite

tsunami *m* GEOPHYS, OCEANO tidal wave, tsunami

TTA *abrév (Transfert temporel asynchrone)* TELECOM ATM *(Asynchronous Transfer Mode)*

TTL *abrév (sous-système de télémesure télécommande et localisation)* ESPACE *communications* TCR *(telemetry command and ranging subsystem)*

TU *abrév (temps universel)* ASTRONOMIE, ESPACE UT *(Universal Time)*

tuba *m* OCEANO snorkel

tubage *m* CHARBON pipe casing, CONSTR tubing, MECANIQUE, PETR casing; ~ **à joint à insertion** *m* PRODUCTION inserted joint casing; ~ **perforé** *m* PETR perforated casing; ~ **d'un puits** *m* DISTRI EAU casing pipe

tube *m* CONSTR, ELECTRON, EQUIP LAB, ESPACE *communications* tube, INSTRUMENT body, main scope tube, OPTIQUE tube, PETROLE pipe, *puits, forage* casing, PHYSIQUE tube, valve;

~ a ~ **absorbant** *m* GENIE CHIM absorber tube; ~ **absorbeur** *m* EQUIP LAB *verrerie* absorption tube; ~ **d'accélération** *m* GENIE CHIM accelerating tube; ~ **accumulateur de saumure** *m* REFRIG brine drum; ~ **d'acier au carbone à basse tension** *m* MAT CHAUFF low-tensile carbon steel tube; ~ **adaptateur** *m* TEXTILE cheese adaptor; ~ **à ailettes** *m* MECANIQUE finned tube; ~ **à ailettes extérieures** *m* PRODUCTION gilled tube; ~ **d'aluminium** *m* EMBALLAGE aluminium tube (BrE), aluminum tube (AmE); ~ **d'amenée d'air chaud** *m* AERONAUT hot air duct; ~ **amorcé** *m* ELECTRON fired tube; ~ **amplificateur** *m* ELECTRON amplifier tube; ~ **amplificateur hyperfréquence** *m* ELECTRON microwave amplifier tube; ~ **amplificateur de lumière** *m* TV image intensifier tube; ~ **amplificateur de puissance** *m* ELECTRON power amplifier tube; ~ **analyseur** *m* ELECTRON pick-up tube, television camera tube, *de caméra de télévision* camera tube, TV pick-up tube; ~ **analyseur à cible multiplicatrice au silicium** *m* ELECTRON silicon-intensifier target camera tube; ~ **analyseur à grand gamma** *m* ELECTRON high-gamma camera tube; ~ **analyseur infrarouge** *m* ELECTRON thermal-imaging tube; ~ **analyseur à spot mobile** *m* TV flying-spot tube scanner; ~ **à anode tournante** *m* CONSTR rotating anode tube; ~ **aplati** *m* EMBALLAGE lay flat tubing; ~ **avec pli central** *m* EMBALLAGE center folding tubing (AmE), centre folding tubing (BrE);

~ b ~ **à bande étroite** *m* ELECTRON narrow band tube; ~ **binoculaire** *m* INSTRUMENT binocular head; ~ **de Bourdon** *m* PETROLE Bourdon gage (AmE), Bourdon gauge (BrE); ~ **broyeur à galets en silex** *m* PRODUCTION pebble mill; ~ **brûleur** *m* PRODUCTION *d'une lampe à souder* flame tube;

~ c ~ **de caméra** *m* TV camera tube, pick-up tube; ~ **capillaire** *m* EQUIP LAB *verrerie*, PETROLE, PHYSIQUE capillary tube; ~ **capillaire blindé** *m* PRODUCTION armored capillary (AmE), armoured capillary (BrE); ~ **carottier** *m* MINES core barrel, core tube; ~ **à cathode chaude** *m* ELECTRON hot cathode gas tube, hot cathode tube, thermionic valve; ~ **à cathode froide** *m* ELECTRON cold cathode tube; ~ **à cathode liquide** *m* ELECTROTEC mercury pool tube; ~ **cathodique** *m* ORDINAT cathode ray tube; ~ **cathodique à balayage cavalier** *m* ELECTRON vector scan cathode ray tube; ~ **cathodique à balayage récurrent** *m* ELECTRON raster scan cathode ray tube; ~ **cathodique bifaisceau** *m* ELECTRON dual-beam cathode-ray tube; ~ **cathodique à deux faisceaux** *m* ELECTRON dual-beam cathode-ray tube, TV double-gun tube; ~ **cathodique à déviation électrostatique** *m* ELECTRON electrostatic CRT; ~ **cathodique à faisceau divisé** *m* TV split beam cathode ray tube; ~ **cathodique à mémoire** *m* ELECTRON storage tube; ~ **cathodique monofaisceau** *m* ELECTRON single beam cathode ray tube; ~ **cathodique multifaisceau** *m* ELECTRON multibeam CRT, multibeam cathode ray tube; **~ cathodique à pénétration** m ELEC-TRON penetration CRT; **~ cathodique à postaccélération** m ELECTRON postaccelerator CRT; **~ cathodique sans postaccélération** m ELECTRON mono-accelerator CRT; **~ cathodique à vide élevé** m TV high-vacuum cathode ray tube; **~ à cathode de mercure** m ELECTRON mercury pool tube; **~ à centrifugeur** m EQUIP LAB *séparation* centrifuge tube; **~ à champs croisés** m ELECTRON, PHYSIQUE crossed field tube; **~ changeur de fréquence** m ELECTRON mixer tube; **~ de chaudière** m CONS MECA boiler tube; **~ de chauffage** m NUCLEAIRE heater rod; **~ chauffant** m REFRIG heating coil; **~ à claire-voie** m INSTRUMENT body tube; **~ collecteur** m CHIMIE yoke; **~ de commutation** m ELECTRON switching tube; **~ de commutation à gaz** m ELECTRON gas-filled switching tube; **~ compteur** m ELECTRON counter tube; **~ compteur à cathode froide** m ELECTRON cold cathode counter tube; **~ compteur de neutrons** m NUCLEAIRE neutron counter tube; **~ compteur de radiation** m ELECTRON radiation counter tube; **~ compteur sonde** m NUCLEAIRE counter tube probe; **~ concentrique** m GAZ concentric pipe; **~ de condensation** m NUCLEAIRE downcomer, vent pipe; **~ conducteur** m MINES conductor pipe, drill casing, guide tube; **~ à cône métallique** m ELECTRON metal cone tube; **~ congélateur** m PRODUCTION freezing tube; **~ convertisseur** m INSTRUMENT converter tube; **~ convertisseur d'image à infrarouge** m TV infrared image converter; **~ convertisseur d'images** m ELECTRON image converter tube; **~ coudé** m MECANIQUE knee bend; **~ à coude brusque** m ELECTRON sharp cutoff tube; **~ à coupes optiques** m INSTRUMENT light section tube; **~ de Crookes** m ELECTRON Crookes tube; **~ à culot local** m ELECTRON loctal tube;

~ d ~ **à décharge** m ELECTR *ampoule* glow discharge lamp, ELECTRON, PHYSIQUE discharge tube; **~ à décharge d'arc** m ELECTROTEC arc discharge tube; **~ à décharge luminescente** m ELECTRON glow discharge tube; **~ à décharge lumineuse** m ELECTR *éclairage* discharge lamp; **~ de dégagement de vapeur** m INST HYDR steam pipe; **~ détecteur pour échantillonnage rapide** m SECURITE *air des lieux de travail* detector tubes for short-term sampling; **~ à déviation** m PHYS RAYON deflection tube; **~ de dilatation** m INST HYDR boiler tube expander; **~ diode** m ELECTRON diode tube, NUCLEAIRE diode, diode tube; **~ dissecteur** m ELECTRON image dissector, TV dissector tube; **~ distillateur** m GENIE CHIM distilling tube; **~ de distillation** m GENIE CHIM distilling tube; **~ donneur** m PRODUCTION delivery tube;

~ e ~ **d'eau** m AUTO, CHAUFFAGE water tube; **~ à éclair** m ELECTRON flash tube; **~ d'écran** m NUCLEAIRE heating surface tube; **~ d'élargissement** m EQUIP LAB *verrerie* expansion tube; **~ électromètre** m ELECTRON, ELECTROTEC electrometer tube; **~ électronique** m ELECTRON electron tube, electronic tube, electronic valve, valve, INSTRUMENT body tube, microscope body, microscope tube; **~ électronique à gaz** m ELECTRON gas tube; **~ électronique industriel** m ELECTRON industrial electronic tube; **~ à émission secondaire** m ELECTRON secondary emission tube; **~ d'emmanchement** m CONS MECA drift tube; **~ en acier au carbone** m CONS MECA carbon steel tool; **~ en acier étiré sans soudure** m CONS MECA solid-drawn steel tube; **~ en acier inoxydable** m CONS MECA stainless steel tube; **~ en carton** m EMBALLAGE cardboard tube; **~ en épingle à**

cheveux m CONS MECA hairpin tube; **~ en ondes millimétriques** m ELECTRON millimeter wave tube (AmE), millimetre wave tube (BrE); **~ en porcelaine** m CERAM VER porcelain tube; **~ enroulé** m EMBALLAGE laminated tube; **~ en U** m EQUIP LAB *verrerie* U-tube; **~ à enveloppe en verre** m ELECTRON glass tube; **~ en verre** m ELECTRON glass tube, EQUIP LAB *verrerie* glass tubing; **~ en verre de débit visible** m CONS MECA sight-feed glass; **~ en verre soufflé** m EQUIP LAB *verrerie* blown glass tube; **~ épanoui** m PRODUCTION flared tube; **~ à essai** m EQUIP LAB *verrerie* test tube; **~ d'étambot** m NAUT stern tube; **~ externe** m GAZ outside pipe;

~ f ~ **de faible section** m EQUIP LAB *verrerie* narrow bore tube; **~ à faisceau droit** m ELECTRON linear beam tube, linear tube; **~ à faisceau d'électrons** m ELECTRON electron beam tube; **~ à faisceau en forme** m ELECTRON shaped beam tube; **~ à faisceau rentrant** m ELECTRON re-entrant beam tube; **~ de Field** m NUCLEAIRE Field tube; **~ de filature** m TEXTILE ring tube; **~ finisseur à galets** m PRODUCTION pebble mill; **~ à flamme** m AERONAUT liner; **~ flash** m ELECTRON flash tube; **~ fluorescent** m ELECTR *éclairage* fluorescent tube, PHYS RAYON fluorescent discharge tube, PHYSIQUE fluorescent lamp; **~ fluorescent au néon** m PHYS RAYON neon fluorescent tube; **~ de forte section** m EQUIP LAB *verrerie* wide-bore tube; **~ frigorifique** m PRODUCTION freezing tube; **~ de fumée** m CHAUFFAGE smoke tube, NUCLEAIRE fire tube, flame tube, flue tube;

~ g ~ **à gaz** m ELECTRON gas tube, gas-filled tube; **~ à gaz à cathode chaude** m ELECTRON hot cathode tube; **~ à gaz inerte** m ELECTRON rare gas tube; **~ Geiger** m PHYS RAYON Geiger counter, Geiger tube; **~ de Geiger-Müller** m PHYSIQUE Geiger-Müller tube; **~ de Geissler** m ELECTRON Geissler tube; **~ de glissement** m ELECTRON drift tube; **~ de grande puissance** m ELECTRON high-power tube; **~ à grille de commande** m ELECTRON grid-controlled tube; **~ à grille au culot** m ELECTRON single-ended tube; **~ à grille-écran** m ELECTRON screen grid tube; **~ de guidage** m CONS MECA guide tube; **~ guide** m MINES drill casing; **~ guide en graphite** m NUCLEAIRE graphite guide tube; **~ guide de sondage** m MINES drill casing;

~ h ~ **hyperfréquence** m CONS MECA microwave tube, ELECTRON microwave tube, slow-wave tube, velocity-modulated tube, wide band tube; **~ hyperfréquence de type M** m ELECTRON M-type microwave tube;

~ i ~ **image** m ELECTRON television picture tube, TV camera tube; **~ image couleur à trois canons** m ELECTRON three-gun color picture tube (AmE), three-gun colour picture tube (BrE); **~ image couleur à trois faisceaux** m ELECTRON three-beam color picture tube (AmE), three-beam colour picture tube (BrE); **~ image à mémoire** m ELECTRON image storage tube; **~ image orthicon** m ELECTRON image orthicon; **~ immergé compact** m GAZ compact immersion tube; **~ indicateur** m ELECTRON indicator tube; **~ indicateur de niveau** m PRODUCTION gage glass (AmE), gauge glass (BrE); **~ d'installation** m ELECTR *alimentation* conduit; **~ intensificateur** m ELECTRON intensifier tube; **~ intensificateur d'image** m ELECTRON image intensifier, image intensifier tube; **~ intensificateur d'images à microcanaux** m ELECTRON microchannel image intensifier; **~ intensificateur d'images de rayons X** m INSTRUMENT X-ray amplifier tube; **~ à interaction courte** m ELECTRON short-interaction tube; **~ à inter-**

action répartie *m* ELECTRON extended interaction tube; ~ **isolant** *m* ELECTR *installation* insulated conduit;

~ k ~ **de Kundt** *m* PHYSIQUE Kundt's tube;

~ l ~ **lance-torpilles** *m* MILITAIRE torpedo launching tube; ~ **à large bande** *m* ELECTRON wide band tube; ~ **laveur** *m* EQUIP LAB *verrerie* washing tube; ~ **lisse** *m* CONSTR plain tube;

~ m ~ **à masque** *m* ELECTRON, TV shadow mask tube; ~ **à masque perforé** *m* ELECTRON shadow mask tube; ~ **à mémoire** *m* ELECTRON charge storage tube, memory tube, storage tube, INFORMAT, ORDINAT storage tube; ~ **à mémoire enregistreur** *m* ELECTRON recording storage tube; ~ **à mémoire à grille** *m* ELECTRON barrier grid storage tube, mesh storage tube; ~ **à mémoire à grille d'arrêt** *m* ELECTRON barrier grid storage tube; ~ **à mémoire monocanon** *m* ELECTRON single gun storage tube; ~ **à mémoire à persistance variable** *m* ELECTRON variable persistence storage tube; ~ **à mémoire à projection** *m* ELECTRON expansion storage tube; ~ **à mémoire à vision directe** *m* ELECTRON direct view storage tube, display storage tube; ~ **métallique** *m* ELECTRON metal tube; ~ **micro-ondes** *m* CONS MECA microwave tube; ~ **millimétrique** *m* ELECTRON millimeter wave tube (AmE), millimetre wave tube (BrE); ~ **à modulation de vitesse** *m* ELECTRON velocity-modulated tube, ESPACE transit time tube; ~ **monoanodique** *m* ELECTRON single anode tube; ~ **monofaisceau** *m* ELECTRON single beam tube; ~ **montant** *m* CONSTR riser; ~ **monté en diode** *m* ELECTRON diode-connected tube; ~ **multicanon** *m* ELECTRON multigun tube; ~ **multi-électrode** *m* ELECTRON multielectrode tube; ~ **multigrille** *m* ELECTRON multigrid tube; ~ **multiple** *m* ELECTRON multiple-unit tube; ~ **à multiplicateur d'électrons** *m* ELECTRON electron multiplier tube;

~ n ~ **au néon** *m* ELECTR *éclairage*, ELECTROTEC, PHYSIQUE neon tube; ~ **de niveau d'eau** *m* PRODUCTION gage glass (AmE), gauge glass (BrE); ~ **Nixie** *m* ELECTRON Nixie tube; ~ **non amorcé** *m* ELECTRON unfired tube; ~ **à noyaux** *m* PRODUCTION core tube;

~ o ~ **octal** *m* ELECTRON octal tube; ~ **à onde électronique** *m* ELECTRON electron wave tube; ~ **à onde lente** *m* ELECTRON microwave tube, slow-wave tube; ~ **à onde normale** *m* ELECTRON fast wave tube; ~ **à onde progressive** *m* (TOP) ELECTRON, ESPACE *communications*, PHYSIQUE traveling-wave tube (AmE), travelling-wave tube (BrE) (TWT), TELECOM traveling waveguide (AmE), traveling-wave tube (AmE), travelling waveguide (BrE), travelling-wave tube (BrE) (TWT); ~ **à onde progressive en bande X** *m* ELECTRON X-band TWT, X-band traveling-wave tube (AmE), X-band travelling-wave tube (BrE); ~ **à onde progressive à hélice** *m* ELECTRON helix traveling-wave tube (AmE), helix travelling-wave tube (BrE); ~ **à onde progressive millimétrique** *m* ELECTRON millimeter wave traveling-wave tube (AmE), millimetre wave travelling-wave tube (BrE); ~ **à onde régressive** *m* ELECTRON, PHYSIQUE backward wave tube, TELECOM backward wave guide; ~ **oscillateur hyperfréquence** *m* ELECTRON microwave oscillator tube; ~ **de l'oscillateur local** *m* ELECTRON local oscillator tube; ~ **oscillateur à onde régressive** *m* ELECTRON backward wave oscillator; ~ **d'oscilloscope** *m* ELECTRON oscilloscope tube;

~ p ~ **à pente variable** *m* ELECTRON exponential tube,

variable mu tube; ~ **perdu non crépiné** *m* PETROLE *forage* blank liner; ~ **perforateur** *m* MINES casing pipe, drive pipe, drive sampler, drive tube; ~ **perforé** *m* PETR perforated pipe; ~ **à persistance variable** *m* ELECTRON variable persistence storage tube; ~ **phare** *m* ELECTRON disc seal tube (BrE), disk seal tube (AmE); ~ **de phase** *m* TV gated beam tube; ~ **photoélectrique** *m* ELECTRON photoelectric tube, phototube; ~ **photoélectrique à gaz** *m* ELECTRON gas phototube; ~ **photomultiplicateur** *m* ELECTRON electron multiplier phototube, photomultiplier; ~ **photosensible** *m* ELECTRON photosensitive tube; ~ **de Pitot** *m* PHYSIQUE Pitot tube; ~ **à plusieurs grilles** *m* ELECTRON multigrid tube; ~ **pneumatique vertical** *m* NUCLEAIRE vertical rabbit; ~ **à polarisation automatique** *m* ELECTRON self-biased tube; ~ **porte-oculaire** *m* ASTRONOMIE *d'une lunette* eye tube, INSTRUMENT drawtube, eyepiece holder; ~ **porte-vent** *m* PRODUCTION blast pipe; ~ **à potasse** *m* EQUIP LAB *verrerie* potash bulb; ~ **pour dosage** *m* CHIMIE measuring tube; ~ **pour échangeur thermique** *m* CONS MECA heat exchanger tube; ~ **pour expédition postale** *m* EMBALLAGE mailing tube (AmE), postal tube (BrE); ~ **pour transmission postale** *m* EMBALLAGE mailing tube (AmE), postal tube (BrE); ~ **pour vérin** *m* CONS MECA cylinder barrel; ~ **de poussée** *m* AUTO torque tube; ~ **de présentation** *m* ELECTRON display tube; ~ **de projection à col court** *m* ELECTRON short-neck projection tube; ~ **de projection court** *m* ELECTRON short-neck projection tube; ~ **prolongateur** *m* PETROLE marine riser, riser, riser pipeline; ~ **protecteur électrique** *m* ELECTROTEC electric conduit; ~ **protecteur pour pyromètre** *m* SECURITE pyrometer protection tube; ~ **de puissance** *m* ELECTRON power amplifier tube, power tube;

~ r ~ **de raccordement** *m* CONS MECA coupling tube; ~ **de raccordement d'eau** *m* DISTRI EAU waterway; ~ **radar** *m* ELECTRON radar tube; ~ **radiogène** *m* INSTRUMENT X-ray tube; ~ **rallonge** *m* CINEMAT, PHOTO extension tube; ~ **à rayons cathodiques** *m* (TRC) ELECTR *visualisation*, ELECTRON, IMPRIM, ORDINAT, SECURITE, TV cathode ray tube (CRT); ~ **à rayons X** *m* CRISTALL, ELECTRON, INSTRUMENT, PHYS RAYON X-ray tube; ~ **de réception** *m* ELECTRON receiving tube; ~ **redresseur** *m* ELECTRON rectifier tube; ~ **redresseur à gaz** *m* ELECTROTEC gas-filled rectifier; ~ **de réduction** *m* EQUIP LAB *verrerie* reduction tube; ~ **de référence de tension** *m* ELECTROTEC voltage reference tube; ~ **réfractaire** *m* MAT CHAUFF refractory tube; ~ **refroidi par air** *m* ELECTRON air-cooled tube; ~ **de refroidissement** *m* CONS MECA cooling tube; ~ **à refroidissement par l'eau** *m* ELECTRON water-cooled tube; ~ **de regroupement** *m* ELECTRON drift tube; ~ **rentrant** *m* PHOTO telescopic tube; ~ **de retour de fumée** *m* PRODUCTION return flue, return tube; ~ **de revêtement** *m* CHARBON pipe casing, MINES lining tube; ~ **rigide** *m* CONS MECA rigid pipe; ~ **rouge** *m* ELECTRON red tube; ~ **rubanné** *m* EMBALLAGE spirally wound tube; ~ **à rubans fluorescents** *m* TV index tube;

~ s ~ **à sable** *m* MINES sludge pump, sludger; ~ **sans soudure en cuivre corroyé** *m* CONS MECA seamless wrought copper tube; ~ **à une seule grille** *m* ELECTRON single grid tube; ~ **à sorties au culot** *m* ELECTRON single-ended tube; ~ **souple** *m* EMBALLAGE collapsible tube; ~ **sous pression** *m* CONS MECA pressure pipe; ~ **stabilisateur de tension** *m* ELECTROTEC voltage regulator tube, voltage stabilizer tube; ~ **de stellarator en**

forme de huit *m* NUCLEAIRE *8* figure-of-eight stellarator tube; ~ **support** *m* TEXTILE cheese tube; ~ **surchauffeur** *m* PRODUCTION superheater pipe; ~ **de sûreté** *m* EQUIP LAB *verrerie* safety funnel, safety tube; **~ t** ~ **tétrode** *m* ELECTRON tetrode tube; ~ **thermoionique** *m* ELECTR *radio* thermionic tube (AmE), thermionic valve (BrE); ~ **de Thièle** *m* EQUIP LAB *point de fusion* Thiele tube; ~ **TR** *m* ELECTRON TR tube; ~ **triode** *m* ELECTRON triode tube; ~ **à trois électrodes** *m* ELECTRON three-electrode tube; ~ **à trois grilles** *m* ELECTRON three-grid tube; ~ **de type M** *m* ELECTRON M-type microwave tube, M-type tube; ~ **de type O** *m* ELECTRON O-type microwave tube, O-type tube; **~ v** ~ **de ventilation** *m* CONSTR vent pipe; ~ **de venturi** *m* PHYSIQUE venturi meter, venturi tube; ~ **à vide** *m* ELECTRON, INFORMAT, ORDINAT, PHYSIQUE, TV vacuum tube; ~ **à vide partiel** *m* ELECTRON soft tube; ~ **à vide poussé** *m* ELECTRON hard tube, high-vacuum tube; ~ **vidicon** *m* ELECTRON vidicon tube

tube-cuiller *m* MINES sludge pump, sludger

tube-foyer *m* NUCLEAIRE fire tube, flame tube, flue tube, PRODUCTION *d'une chaudière* flue

tube-gaine: ~ **pour câbles** *m* ELECTR *alimentation* conduit

tube-gland *m* ELECTRON acorn tube

tube-guide *m* MINES conductor pipe, guide tube

tuber *vt* CONSTR line, *puits* case

tubérine *f* CHIMIE tuberin

tubes *m pl* CONSTR tubing, EN RENOUV *récepteur à plaques plates* tubes; ~ **aplatis avec gousset** *m pl* EMBALLAGE gusseted layflat tubing; ~ **appariés** *m pl* ELECTRON matched tubes

tube-tirant *m* PRODUCTION stay tube

tubing *m* PETR tubing; ~ **de production** *m* PETROLE production string, production tubing

tubiste *m* OCEANO caisson worker

tubulure *f* AERONAUT radiator hose, CONSTR *d'un robinet* tailpipe, EN RENOUV nozzle, PRODUCTION passage; ~ **d'admission** *f* AUTO inlet manifold (BrE), intake manifold (AmE); ~ **d'aspiration** *f* DISTRI EAU suction pipe, tailpipe; ~ **d'échappement** *f* NUCLEAIRE vent nozzle; ~ **d'échappement d'air** *f* MECANIQUE *air comprimé* air discharge nozzle; ~ **d'entrée du caloporteur primaire** *f* NUCLEAIRE *fluide* reactor coolant inlet nozzle; ~ **d'entrée de l'eau d'alimentation** *f* NUCLEAIRE feedwater inlet nozzle; ~ **de prise de vapeur** *f* INST HYDR steamway; ~ **de refoulement** *f* DISTRI EAU delivery pipe, head pipe; ~ **de remplissage** *f* AUTO radiator filler neck; ~ **transfert** *f* PRODUCTION transfer tube

tuer *vt* PETROLE *un puits* kill

tuf *m* CONSTR tufa, GEOLOGIE calcareous tufa, sinter, PETR tuff; ~ **volcanique** *m* GEOLOGIE lithic tuff

tuffeau *m* GEOLOGIE sandy chalk

tuilage *m* CINEMAT film wrinkling, wrinkling, PAPIER curl, curling

tuile *f* CERAM VER, CONSTR tile, ESPACE *véhicules* thermal protection tile, tile; ~ **arêtière** *f* CONSTR hip tile; ~ **de béton** *f* CONSTR concrete roofing tile; ~ **canal** *f* CONSTR arched tile, crown tile; ~ **cornière** *f* CONSTR corner tile; ~ **creuse** *f* CERAM VER gutter tile, CONSTR arched tile, crown tile; ~ **en dos d'âne** *f* CONSTR saddle tile; ~ **en S** *f* CONSTR pantile; ~ **faîtière** *f* CERAM VER ridge tile, CONSTR crest tile; ~ **glacée** *f* CONSTR glazed tile; ~ **plate** *f* CERAM VER flat tile, CONSTR crown tile, plain tile; ~ **à rebord** *f* CONSTR flange tile; ~ **vernie** *f* CERAM VER encaustic tile; ~ **vernissée** *f* CONSTR glazed tile; ~ **de**

verre *f* CERAM VER glass roof tile

tuilerie *f* CERAM VER tile factory, tilery

tuiles: ~ **insonorisantes** *f pl* SECURITE soundproof tiles

tuilier *m* CERAM VER tile burner, tile kiln, tile maker, tiler, CONSTR tiler

tulipage *m* AERONAUT gyro caging

tuner *m* TELECOM tuner

tungstate *m* CHIMIE, MATERIAUX tungstate

tungstène *m* CHIMIE wolfram, CHIMIE tungsten

tungstique *adj* CHIMIE tungstic, wolframic

tungstosilicate *m* CHIMIE tungstosilicate

tunnel *m* CONSTR tunnel, ELECTRON drift tunnel, EN RENOUV *hydroélectricité*, IMPRIM *de mise sous film rétractable*, REFRIG tunnel; ~ **d'accostage** *m* ESPACE *véhicules* docking tunnel; ~ **de l'arbre de transmission** *m* VEHICULES *transmission* drive shaft tunnel (AmE), propeller shaft tunnel (BrE); ~ **de chauffe** *m* EMBALLAGE heating tunnel; ~ **de congélation** *m* REFRIG freezing tunnel; ~ **d'étuvage** *m* CONSTR curing tunnel; ~ **ferroviaire** *m* CONSTR railroad tunnel (AmE), railway tunnel (BrE); ~ **pour emballage thermorétractable de manchons** *m* EMBALLAGE shrink tunnel for sleeve sealing; ~ **de prospection** *m* MINES prospect tunnel; ~ **de recherches** *m* MINES prospect tunnel; ~ **de réfrigération** *m* AGRO ALIM cooling tunnel; ~ **de refroidissement** *m* REFRIG cooling tunnel; ~ **de séchage** *m* EMBALLAGE drying tunnel, IMPRIM tunnel; ~ **de service** *m* CONSTR service tunnel; ~ **thermorétractable pour manchons** *m* EMBALLAGE shrink tunnel for sleeving; ~ **à vent** *m* CONSTR wind tunnel

tunnelier *m* CONSTR mole, tunnel-boring machine

turbidimètre *m* CHIMIE turbidimeter, EQUIP LAB *instrument, analyse* turbidity meter, OCEANO turbidimeter, turbidity meter

turbidimétrie *f* CHIMIE turbidimetry

turbidite *m* GEOLOGIE turbidite

turbidité *f* CHIMIE, EN RENOUV turbidity, GAZ cloudiness, HYDROLOGIE turbidity

turbine *f* AUTO impeller, turbine, ELECTR *générateur*, EN RENOUV, INST HYDR, MECANIQUE, NAUT turbine, VEHICULES turbine, *pompe* impeller; ~ **d'action** *f* PRODUCTION impulse turbine; ~ **à action** *f* CONS MECA, MECANIQUE, PRODUCTION impulse turbine; ~ **à action directe** *f* INST HYDR action turbine; ~ **à action-réaction** *f* INST HYDR reaction and impulse turbine; ~ **aérogénérateur** *f* EN RENOUV wind turbine generator; ~ **à air** *f* CONS MECA air turbine; ~ **à air chaud** *f* NUCLEAIRE heat turbine; ~ **à air chaud et à circuit fermé** *f* TRANSPORT closed cycle hot air turbine; ~ **américaine** *f* INST HYDR combined flow turbine; ~ **atmosphérique** *f* CONS MECA air turbine; ~ **à aubes garnies** *f* INST HYDR limit turbine; ~ **axiale** *f* INST HYDR journal turbine; ~ **centrifuge** *f* INST HYDR outward flow turbine; ~ **centripète** *f* PRODUCTION inward flow turbine; ~ **à condensation** *f* MAT CHAUFF condensing turbine; ~ **à débit axial** *f* INST HYDR parallel flow turbine; ~ **à débit parallèle** *f* INST HYDR parallel flow turbine; ~ **de détente** *f* AERONAUT expansion turbine, REFRIG expansion turbine, turboexpander; ~ **à eau** *f* THERMODYN water turbine; ~ **à écoulement inversé** *f* EN RENOUV reverse flow turbine; ~ **à engrenages** *f* MECANIQUE geared turbine; ~ **éolienne** *f* EN RENOUV wind turbine; ~ **éolienne à axe vertical** *f* EN RENOUV vertical axis wind turbine; ~ **à étages de vitesse** *f* INST HYDR velocity stage turbine; ~ **Francis** *f* EN RENOUV Francis turbine; ~ **à gaz** *f* AERONAUT gas turbine engine, MECANIQUE, NAUT,

PRODUCTION, THERMODYN, TRANSPORT gas turbine; ~ **à gaz à circuit fermé** *f* TRANSPORT closed cycle gas turbine; ~ **à gaz à circuit ouvert** *f* TRANSPORT open cycle gas turbine; ~ **à gaz d'échappement** *f* AUTO exhaust gas turbine; ~ **à gaz à piston libre** *f* CONS MECA free piston gas turbine; ~ **haute pression** *f* TRANSPORT fan jet turbine; ~ **à hélice** *f* EN RENOUV propeller turbine; ~ **hélico-centripète** *f* INST HYDR combined flow turbine; ~ **hélicoïdale** *f* INST HYDR axial flow turbine; ~ **hélicoïde** *f* INST HYDR parallel flow turbine; ~ **hydraulique** *f* EN RENOUV, THERMODYN water turbine; ~ **immergée** *f* INST HYDR drowned turbine, submerged turbine; ~ **à impulsion** *f* CONS MECA impulse turbine, INST HYDR action turbine, MECANIQUE, PRODUCTION impulse turbine; ~ **à injection intégrale** *f* INST HYDR full-injection turbine; ~ **à injection totale** *f* INST HYDR full-injection turbine; ~ **libre** *f* AERONAUT free turbine; ~ **à libre déviation** *f* INST HYDR action turbine, PRODUCTION impulse turbine; ~ **limite** *f* INST HYDR limit turbine; ~ **linéaire** *f* TRANSPORT linear turbine; ~ **mixte** *f* INST HYDR combined flow turbine; ~ **noyée** *f* INST HYDR drowned turbine, submerged turbine; ~ **à paliers lisses** *f* INST HYDR journal turbine; ~ **parallèle** *f* INST HYDR axial flow turbine, journal turbine; ~ **Pelton** *f* EN RENOUV Pelton turbine; ~ **à pression** *f* INST HYDR pressure turbine, reaction turbine; ~ **à réaction** *f* EN RENOUV reaction turbine, INST HYDR pressure turbine, reaction turbine, MECANIQUE reaction turbine; ~ **à réaction nulle** *f* INST HYDR limit turbine; ~ **de réfrigération** *f* CONS MECA cooling turbine; ~ **simple** *f* INST HYDR single stage turbine; ~ **à vapeur** *f* INST HYDR, MAT CHAUFF, NAUT steam turbine; ~ **à vapeur d'échappement** *f* CHAUFFAGE exhaust steam turbine, exhaust turbine; ~ **à vapeur de mercure** *f* CONS MECA mercury vapor turbine (AmE), mercury vapour turbine (BrE); ~ **à veine moulée** *f* INST HYDR limit turbine; ~ **à vent** *f* CONS MECA wind turbine

turbo *m* TEXTILE turbo-stapler
turbo-alimentation *f* IMPRIM slot feeding
turbo-alternateur *m* ELECTR *générateur* turbo-alternator, ELECTROTEC turbo-alternator, turbogenerator, PHYSIQUE turbogenerator
turbocombustible *m* ESPACE turbine fuel
turbocompresseur *m* AUTO turbosupercharger, NAUT turbocompressor, VEHICULES *moteur* turbocharger; ~ **de construction radiale et axiale** *m* CONS MECA radial and axial turbocompressor; ~ **à gaz** *m* AUTO exhaust turbocharger; ~ **à suralimentation** *m* CONS MECA turbocharger
turbodétendeur *m* REFRIG turboexpander
turboforage *m* PETR turbodrilling, PETROLE turbine drilling
turboforeuse *f* PETROLE turbodrill
turbogénérateur *m* ELECTROTEC turbogenerator
turbogénératrice *f* ELECTROTEC turbogenerator
turbomachine *f* AERONAUT gas turbine engine, THERMODYN gas turbine, turboshaft engine
turbomélangeur *m* PRODUCTION turbomixer
turbomoléculaire *adj* CONS MECA turbomolecular
turbomoteur *m* AERONAUT gas turbine, gas turbine engine, turbine engine, AUTO turbine engine, THERMODYN gas turbine
turbopompe *f* DISTRI EAU, ESPACE *propulsion* turbopump, INST HYDR turbine pump, NAUT turbopump
turbopropulseur *m* AERONAUT turboprop, *moteur* turbopropeller, TRANSPORT propjet engine

turboréacteur *m* AERONAUT *moteur* turbojet, THERMODYN gas turbine, jet engine, turbojet engine, TRANSPORT jet turbine engine, jet turbine, turbojet; ~ **à double flux** *m* TRANSPORT bypass engine, ducted fan turbo engine; ~ **double flux** *m* AERONAUT bypass engine; ~ **à double flux** *m* THERMODYN bypass engine, fan jet engine, turbofan engine, TRANSPORT turbofan; ~ **à ventilateur** *m* CONS MECA turbofan engine
turboséparation *f* AGRO ALIM air separation, turboseparation
turbosoufflante *f* AERONAUT *moteur* turbofan, NAUT turbocharger
turbotrain *m* TRANSPORT turbotrain; ~ **à grande vitesse** *m* TRANSPORT high-speed gas turbine motor coach (BrE), high-speed gas turbine railcar (AmE)
turbulence *f* AUTO, EN RENOUV turbulence, ESPACE buffet, turbulence, METEO, PHYS FLUID turbulence; ~ **de convection** *f* AERONAUT convective turbulence; ~ **en air clair** *f* AERONAUT clear air turbulence; ~ **en ciel clair** *f* AERONAUT clear air turbulence; ~ **en spirale** *f* PHYS FLUID spiral turbulence; ~ **de grille** *f* PHYS FLUID grid turbulence; ~ **homogène isotrope** *f* PHYS FLUID homogeneous isotropic turbulence; ~ **isotrope** *f* PHYS FLUID isotropic turbulence; ~ **au moyen d'une grille** *f* PHYS FLUID grid turbulence; ~ **de sillage** *f* AERONAUT wake turbulence
turbulences: ~ **d'extrémité** *f pl* EN RENOUV tip loss; ~ **d'extrémité de pale** *f pl* EN RENOUV tip loss
turbulent *adj* METEO, PHYS FLUID turbulent
turc: ~ **à tête inclinable** *m* CONS MECA jackscrew with self-adjusting head
turgescence *f* AGRO ALIM turgor
turgite *f* MINERAUX turgite
turjite *f* MINERAUX turgite
turnapull *m* CONSTR turnapull scraper
turquoise *f* MINERAUX turquoise; ~ **orientale** *f* MINERAUX oriental turquoise
tuyau *m* CONSTR chimney, funnel, hose, pipe, MECANIQUE pipe, MINES stock, tree, PETROLE, PHYS FLUID pipe, PRODUCTION hose, *d'une cheminée* flue; ~ **adducteur** *m* INST HYDR flow pipe; ~ **d'admission** *m* INST HYDR induction pipe; ~ **d'aération** *m* MINES ventilation pipe; ~ **d'air** *m* CONS MECA air pipe; ~ **d'air comprimé** *m* CONSTR air hose; ~ **d'alimentation** *m* PRODUCTION feed pipe; ~ **d'amenée** *m* CONS MECA feedwater pump, CONSTR supply pipe, INST HYDR head pipe, NUCLEAIRE feeder pipe, inlet jumper, pigtail; ~ **d'amenée d'eau** *m* DISTRI EAU water supply pipe; ~ **d'argile à joint ouvert** *m* CONSTR open-jointed clayware pipe; ~ **armé** *m* CONSTR armored hose (AmE), armoured hose (BrE); ~ **arrière** *m* VEHICULES *échappement* tailpipe; ~ **d'arrivée** *m* PRODUCTION feed pipe, inlet pipe; ~ **d'arrivée d'air** *m* CONS MECA air inlet pipe; ~ **d'arrivée du gaz** *m* THERMODYN gas pipe; ~ **d'arrosage** *m* DISTRI EAU squirt hose; ~ **d'aspiration** *m* DISTRI EAU suction hose, suction pipe, SECURITE *matériel de lutte contre l'incendie* suction hose; ~ **d'aspiration en caoutchouc** *m* DISTRI EAU rubber suction hose; ~ **d'assainissement** *m* DISTRI EAU soil pipe; ~ **bifurqué** *m* CONSTR forked pipe; ~ **à bride** *m* CONS MECA flanged fitting, CONSTR flange pipe; ~ **de câble** *m* ELECTROTEC cable duct; ~ **de cheminée** *m* CHAUFFAGE flue lining, CONSTR chimney flue, chimney, funnel; ~ **collecteur** *m* MECANIQUE header pipe; ~ **de conduite** *m* CONSTR conduit, conduit pipe; ~ **conique** *m* CONS MECA taper pipe; ~ **coudé** *m* CONSTR bend; ~ **court** *m* INST HYDR short pipe; ~ **à**

couture *m* CONS MECA seamed pipe; ~ de descente *m* CONSTR leader, rainwater downpipe (BrE), rainwater downspout (AmE), stack pipe; ~ de descente des eaux pluviales *m* CONSTR leader, rainwater downpipe (BrE), rainwater downspout (AmE); ~ de discharge *m* DISTRI EAU discharge pipe; ~ distributeur *m* DISTRI EAU distributing pipe; ~ de drainage *m* CONSTR drainpipe; ~ d'eau *m* DISTRI EAU water pipe; ~ d'eau écrasable *m* CONS MECA collapsible water hose; ~ d'échappement *m* AERONAUT exhaust pipe, AUTO tailpipe, NAUT, THERMODYN exhaust pipe; ~ d'écoulement *m* DISTRI EAU discharge pipe; ~ d'écoulement du trop-plein *m* CONSTR waste pipe, DISTRI EAU overflow, overflow pipe; ~ élévatoire *m* CONSTR lift pipe; ~ à emboîtement *m* CONSTR socket pipe; ~ en béton *m* CONSTR concrete pipe; ~ en caoutchouc *m* EQUIP LAB *raccord* rubber tubing, PLAST CAOU rubber hose; ~ en caoutchouc pour la vapeur *m* CONS MECA rubber hose for steam; ~ en col de cygne *m* CONS MECA gooseneck pipe; ~ en fonte ductile *m* CONS MECA ductile iron pipe; ~ en fonte grise *m* CONS MECA gray iron pipe (AmE), grey iron pipe (BrE); ~ en plomb *m* CONSTR lead piping; ~ en poterie *m* CERAM VER earthenware pipe; ~ en tôle *m* CONSTR sheet iron pipe; ~ à essence *m* PLAST CAOU fuel hose, gasoline hose (AmE), petrol hose (BrE); ~ évacuateur *m* INST HYDR flow pipe; ~ d'évacuation d'une pompe à air *m* CONS MECA air pump exhaust pipe; ~ d'évacuation de vapeur *m* INST HYDR steam pipe; ~ de fer *m* CONSTR iron pipe; ~ flexible *m* CONS MECA hosepipe, ESPACE *véhicules*, MECANIQUE, MINES, PAPIER, PRODUCTION hose; ~ flexible à armature textile *m* CONS MECA *transmission hydraulique* textile reinforced hose; ~ flexible à essence *m* VEHICULES *carburant* gas hose (AmE), gasoline hose (AmE), petrol hose (BrE); ~ flexible renforcé par des fils métalliques *m* CONS MECA wire reinforced hose; ~ flexible de ventilation *m* VEHICULES *refroidissement* radiator vent hose; ~ de fonçage *m* CHARBON well casing; ~ de fonte *m* CONSTR cast-iron pipe, iron pipe; ~ de fonte à bride *m* CONSTR flanged cast-iron pipe; ~ à fourche *m* MECANIQUE breeches pipe; ~ de frein *m* VEHICULES brake hose; ~ de frein à air *m* PLAST CAOU air brake hose; ~ de gaz *m* CONSTR, THERMODYN gas pipe; ~ à gaz *m* CONSTR, THERMODYN gas pipe; ~ de graissage *m* PRODUCTION oil pipe; ~ hydraulique *m* PLAST CAOU hydraulic hose; ~ d'incendie *m* CONSTR, SECURITE fire hose; ~ d'incendie à toile plate *m* SECURITE flat canvas hose; ~ d'injection *m* AUTO delivery pipe, INST HYDR injection pipe; ~ isolant *m* CONS MECA insulation pipe; ~ métallique *m* CONS MECA flexible metallic hose, flexible steel piping; ~ métallique flexible à agrafage simple *m* CONS MECA single overlap flexible metal hose; ~ métallique flexible agrafé *m* CONS MECA strip-wound flexible metal hose; ~ montant *m* CONSTR riser; ~ moulé *m* PLAST CAOU molded hose (AmE), moulded hose (BrE); ~ perforé *m* AGRO ALIM sparge pipe; ~ poreux à joint ouvert *m* CONSTR open-jointed porous pipe; ~ portevent *m* PRODUCTION belly pipe; ~ de pression à bride *m* CONS MECA flanged pressure pipe; ~ principal de vapeur *m* INST HYDR main steam pipe; ~ de prise d'eau *m* PRODUCTION feed pipe, water pipe; ~ protégé *m* CONSTR armored hose (AmE), armoured hose (BrE); ~ de refoulement *m* DISTRI EAU delivery hose, delivery pipe; ~ de refoulement semi-rigide *m* SECURITE semi-rigid delivery hose; ~ de refroidissement des gaz *m* GENIE CHIM baffle tube; ~ de remplissage *m* NAUT filling pipe; ~ de remplissage d'huile *m* AUTO oil filler pipe; ~ renforcé de fils métallique *m* PLAST CAOU wire reinforced hose; ~ résistant à l'essence et à l'huile *m* PLAST CAOU gasoline and oil resistant hose (AmE), petrol and oil resisting hose (BrE); ~ résistant à l'huile *m* PLAST CAOU oil-resisting hose; ~ sans soudure *m* CONS MECA seamless pipe; ~ serpentin *m* CONSTR coil; ~ soudé *m* CONS MECA seamed pipe; ~ souple *m* CONSTR flexible hose, EQUIP LAB *connexion* hose; ~ souple d'incendie *m* THERMODYN fire hose; ~ de terre *m* CONSTR earthenware pipe; ~ tressé *m* PLAST CAOU braided hose; ~ de trop-plein *m* DISTRI EAU overflow, overflow pipe, VEHICULES *refroidissement* overflow pipe; ~ de vapeur *m* INST HYDR steam pipe; ~ de ventilation *m* MINES ventilation pipe; ~ de vidange *m* DISTRI EAU outlet pipe; ~ de vidange des escarbilles *m* PRODUCTION cinder chute, cinder pocket

tuyautage *m* CONSTR piping, tubing; ~ de fer *m* CONSTR iron piping

tuyauterie *f* CONS MECA pipeline, CONSTR connections, pipe connections, pipes and fittings, pipeworks, piping, tubing, MECANIQUE duct, pipework, PETROLE piping, PRODUCTION tube works; ~ d'adduction de vapeur *f* INST HYDR steam supply pipe; ~ d'alimentation *f* AUTO fuel line; ~ à bride *f* CONS MECA *en fonte* flanged pipeline; ~ bridée *f* CONS MECA clamped pipe connection; ~ en fonte *f* CONS MECA cast-iron pipeline; ~ flexible *f* CONS MECA flexible tubing; ~ flexible d'alimentation en air *f* CONS MECA air hose; ~ de frein *f* VEHICULES brake line; ~ d'intercommunication *f* AERONAUT crossfeed line; ~ plastique *f* CONS MECA plastic pipeline; ~ pour fluides *f* CONS MECA fluid pipeline; ~ de raccordement *f* PRODUCTION *système hydraulique* interconnecting pipework; ~ souple *f* CONS MECA flexible pipe; ~ souple d'alimentation de frein pneumatique *f* CONS MECA air brake hose; ~ souple de vapeur *f* INST HYDR steam hose

tuyauteur *m* CONSTR pipe fitter

tuyaux *m pl* CONSTR piping; ~ de fer *m pl* CONSTR iron piping

tuyère *f* AERONAUT expansion nozzle, CHARBON, EN RENOUV nozzle, ESPACE *propulsion* jet nozzle, jet pipe, *véhicules* nozzle, GAZ nozzle, PHYSIQUE jet, nozzle, PRODUCTION blast nozzle, nose, tue iron, nosepiece, nozzle, tuyère, *d'un injecteur, d'une soufflerie* nozzle; ~ de carburant *f* VEHICULES fuel line; ~ convergente *f* CONS MECA *d'un injecteur* combining cone, combining nozzle, combining tube; ~ débit *f* CONS MECA flow nozzle; ~ de déflexion *f* AERONAUT *d'un aéronef* thrust-vectoring nozzle; ~ divergente *f* PRODUCTION *d'un injecteur* delivery cone, delivery nozzle, delivery tube; ~ d'éjection *f* AERONAUT jet nozzle; ~ d'éjection des gaz *f* AERONAUT exhaust nozzle; ~ en régime sonique *f* AERONAUT choked nozzle; ~ d'essence *f* VEHICULES *carburant* fuel line; ~ d'extrémité de pale *f* AERONAUT blade tip nozzle; ~ d'injection de l'eau lourde *f* NUCLEAIRE heavy water spray nozzle; ~ à lobes *f* AERONAUT notched nozzle; ~ multilobe *f* AERONAUT multitube nozzle; ~ multitube *f* AERONAUT multitube nozzle; ~ orientable *f* ESPACE *propulsion* rotatable nozzle, thrust-vectoring nozzle; ~ d'orientation *f* AERONAUT thrust-vectoring nozzle; ~ de postcombustion *f* VEHICULES *moteur* afterburner; ~ pour réchauffeur à vapeur *f* CONS MECA steam heating jet; ~ propulsive *f* AERONAUT propelling nozzle; ~ second-

aire *f* AERONAUT *moteur* secondary nozzle; ~ **à vapeur** *f* INST HYDR steam nozzle; ~ **de ventilateur** *f* AUTO fan shroud

TVHD *abrév (télévision à haute définition)* TELECOM, TV HDTV *(high-definition television)*

tweeter *m* ENREGISTR tweeter

twin-douci *m* CERAM VER twin grinder

twin-poli *m* CERAM VER twin polisher, twin polishing

tympan *m* CONSTR spandrel, DISTRI EAU scoop waterwheel, scoop wheel, IMPRIM tympan, INST HYDR tympanus

tympe *f* PRODUCTION tymp

type[1] *adj* CONS MECA standard; ~ **non pivotant** *adj* CONS MECA nonswiveling (AmE), nonswivelling (BrE)

type:[2] **de ~ soulevant** *adv* PRODUCTION *système hydraulique* pop-up type

type[3] *m* CHARBON *de pieu, terre*, INFORMAT, ORDINAT type; ~ **abstrait** *m* INFORMAT abstract data type; ~ **abstrait de données** *m* INFORMAT abstract data type; ~ **booléen** *m* INFORMAT, ORDINAT Boolean type; ~ **de caractère** *m* INFORMAT, ORDINAT character type; ~ **de codage** *m* TELECOM EIT, encoded information type, coding type; ~ **complexe** *m* INFORMAT, ORDINAT complex type; ~ **de conditionnement** *m* PRODUCTION packing type; ~ **de données** *m* INFORMAT, ORDINAT data type; ~ **encapsulé** *m* INFORMAT, ORDINAT encapsulated type; ~ **d'enregistrement** *m* INFORMAT, ORDINAT record class; ~ **entier** *m* INFORMAT, ORDINAT integer type; ~ **énumératif** *m* INFORMAT, ORDINAT enumeration type; ~ **d'information** *m* TELECOM IT, information type; ~ **d'informations codées** *m* TELECOM EIT, encoded information type; ~ **de ligne** *m* INFORMAT, ORDINAT line style; ~ **logique** *m* INFORMAT, ORDINAT Boolean type, logical type; ~ **N** *m* ELECTRON n-type; ~ **de numéro** *m* TELECOM TON, type of number; ~ **privé** *m* INFORMAT, ORDINAT private type; ~ **de produit** *m* QUALITE product type; ~ **réel** *m* INFORMAT, ORDINAT real type; ~ **de retrait de stock** *m* PRODUCTION stock issue status; ~ **de roche** *m* CHARBON, PETR rock type; ~ **scalaire** *m* INFORMAT, ORDINAT scalar type; ~ **de segment** *m* TELECOM ST, segment type; ~ **structuré** *m* INFORMAT, ORDINAT structured type; ~ **tropical** *m* NUCLEAIRE tropical type

typhon *m* METEO typhoon

typographie *f* EMBALLAGE letterpress printing, IMPRIM block printing, typography, *impression* letterpress

typographique *adj* IMPRIM letterpress

typon *m* CERAM VER stencil silk

tyrosamine *f* CHIMIE tyrosamine

tyrosine *f* CHIMIE tyrosine

U

U *(uranium)* CHIMIE U *(uranium)*

UA *abrév (unité astronomique)* ASTRONOMIE AU *(astronomical unit)*

UAD *abrév (unité administrative)* TELECOM AU *(administrative unit)*

UAO *abrév (utilisation apparente d'oxygène)* OCEANO apparent utilization of oxygen

ubitron *m* ELECTRON ubitron

UC *abrév (unité centrale)* INFORMAT, ORDINAT, TELECOM CPU *(central processing unit)*

U-galène *f* NUCLEAIRE uranium galena

UGPB *abrév (ultragros porteur de brut)* PETROLE ULCC *(ultralarge crude carrier)*

UHF *abrév (ultrahaute fréquence)* ELECTRON, PHYS ONDES, TELECOM, TV UHF *(ultrahigh frequency)*

UHT *abrév* AGRO ALIM *(longue-conservation)* UHT *(ultra heat treated)* AGRO ALIM *(ultrahaute température)* UHT *(ultrahigh temperature)*

UKIRT *abrév (télescope infrarouge du Royaume-Uni)* ASTRONOMIE UKIRT *(UK Infrared Telescope)*

ULA *abrév (unité arithmétique et logique)* ORDINAT ALU *(arithmetic and logic unit)*

uléxine *f* CHIMIE cytisine, ulexine

ulexite *f* MINERAUX ulexite

ullmannite *f* MINERAUX ullmannite

ulmine *f* CHIMIE ulmin

ulmique *adj* CHIMIE *acide* ulmic, ulmous

ultracentrifugation *f* CHIMIE, NUCLEAIRE ultracentrifugation

ultracentrifugeur *m* CHIMIE ultracentrifuge

ultracentrifugeuse *f* NUCLEAIRE, PHYSIQUE ultracentrifuge

ultrachimique *adj* CHIMIE ultrachemical

ultrachromatographie *f* CHIMIE ultrachromatography

ultracompact *adj* PRODUCTION ultrasmall

ultrafiltration *f* CHIMIE, GENIE CHIM ultrafiltration

ultrafiltratum *m* CHIMIE ultrafiltrate

ultrafiltre *m* CHIMIE ultrafilter

ultragros: ~ **porteur de brut** *m (UGPB)* PETROLE ultralarge crude carrier *(ULCC)*

ultrahaute: ~ **fréquence** *f (UHF)* ELECTRON, PHYS ONDES, TELECOM, TV ultrahigh frequency *(UHF)*; ~ **température** *f* AGRO ALIM ultrahigh temperature *(UHT)*

ultramicroanalyse *f* CHIMIE ultratrace, NUCLEAIRE ultramicroanalysis

ultramicroscope *m* CHIMIE ultramicroscope

ultramicroscopie *f* CHIMIE ultramicroscopy

ultramicroscopique *adj* CHIMIE ultramicroscopic

ultramylonite *f* GEOLOGIE ultramylonite

ultrason *m* ACOUSTIQUE, PHYS RAYON, PHYSIQUE ultrasound

ultrasonore *adj* PHYS ONDES supersonic

ultrasons *f pl* PHYS ONDES ultrasonics

ultravide *f* THERMODYN ultravacuum

ultraviolet[1] *adj (UV)* OPTIQUE ultraviolet *(UV)*

ultraviolet[2] *m (UV)* ESPACE ultraviolet *(UV)*; ~ **lointain** *m* ESPACE vacuum ultraviolet, PHYS RAYON far

ultraviolet; ~ **proche** *m* PHYS RAYON near ultraviolet

unaire *adj* INFORMAT, ORDINAT unary

undécane *m* CHIMIE undecane

undécanoïque *adj* CHIMIE *acide* undecanoic

undécylénique *adj* CHIMIE *acide* undecyllnic

uni[1] *adj* PRODUCTION *surface* even, TEXTILE plain

uni:[2] ~ **de pavement** *m* CONSTR pavement surface evenness

uniaxe *adj* CRISTALL uniaxial

unicité *f* BREVETS *du brevet européen* unity

unidimensionnel *adj* PHYSIQUE one-dimensional

unidirectionnel *adj* ACOUSTIQUE *microphone*, ELECTR *courant*, ELECTROTEC, ENREGISTR *microphone*, TELECOM unidirectional

unification: ~ **des méthodes d'essai** *f* CONS MECA standardization of test methods

unifié *adj* ESPACE *propulsion*, INFORMAT *architecture*, ORDINAT *architecture* unified

unifier *vt* CONS MECA, PRODUCTION standardize

uniforme *adj* GEOLOGIE even

unilatéral *adj* TELECOM unidirectional

union *f* CONSTR joining, union, INFORMAT union

Union: ~ **européenne des alcools d'eaux-de-vie et spiritueux** *f* AGRO ALIM European Alcohol Brandy and Spirit Union; ~ **internationale des télécommunications** *f* TELECOM International Telecommunication Union

uniphasé *adj* ELECTR *conducteur* uniphase

unipolaire *adj* ELECTR *alimentation* monopolar, *borne* single-pole, *dynamo, générateur* unipolar, ELECTRON one-pole, *transistor* unipolar, ELECTROTEC, INFORMAT, NUCLEAIRE *arc*, ORDINAT unipolar, TV single-pole

unique: ~ **inventeur** *m* BREVETS sole inventor

unir[1] *vt* CONSTR join, PRODUCTION level; ~ **ensemble** *vt* CONSTR join

unir:[2] **s'** ~ *v réfl* CHIMIE, MATERIAUX unite

unisson *m* ACOUSTIQUE unison

unité:[1] ~ **de stockage** *f* INFORMAT storage device

unité[2] *f* CHIMIE, ELECTR unit, ESSAIS item, GEOLOGIE *terme lithostratigraphique* unit, INFORMAT drive, unit, NUCLEAIRE *d'une centrale nucléaire* unit, ORDINAT drive, unit, PHYSIQUE, TELECOM unit; ~ **absolue** *f* CONS MECA, ELECTR fundamental unit; ~ **d'accélération** *f* PETR gravity unit; ~ **d'accès** *f* TELECOM AU, access unit; ~ **d'accès EDI** *f* TELECOM EDI access unit, EDI-AU; ~ **d'accès de remise physique** *f* TELECOM physical delivery access unit; ~ **à accès série** *f* INFORMAT serial access device; ~ **d'accès au service de remise physique** *f* TELECOM PDAU, physical delivery access unit; ~ **d'accès aux services télex** *f* TELECOM telex access unit; ~ **d'acquisition décentralisée** *f* COMMANDE RAU, remote acquisition unit; ~ **administrative** *f (UAD)* TELECOM administrative unit *(AU)*; ~ **d'affichage** *f* ORDINAT VDU; ~ **d'affluents** *f* TELECOM TU, tributary unit; ~ **d'aire** *f* METROLOGIE unit of area; ~ **Angström** *f* AGRO ALIM Angström unit; ~ **d'appel automatique** *f* INFORMAT, ORDINAT ACU, automatic calling unit; ~

arithmétique *f* ORDINAT AU, arithmetic unit; ~ arithmétique et logique *f (ULA)* ORDINAT arithmetic and logic unit *(ALU)*; ~ astronomique *f (UA)* ASTRONOMIE astronomic unit, astronomical unit *(AU)*; ~ avionique d'hélicoptère *f* AERONAUT helicopter avionics package; ~ à bande magnétique *f* INFORMAT, ORDINAT magnetic tape unit, tape transport, tape unit; ~ de broche d'usinage *f* CONS MECA spindle unit; ~ de capacité *f* PRODUCTION resource unit; ~ à cartouche *f* INFORMAT cartridge drive; ~ centrale INFORMAT *(UC)*, ORDINAT *(UC) de traitement* central processing unit *(CPU)*, TELECOM *de commande* central control, TELECOM *(UC) de traitement* central processing unit *(CPU)*; ~ centrale de traitement *f* ORDINAT central processing unit; ~ chronostratigraphique *f* GEOLOGIE *stratigraphie* chronostratigraphic unit; ~ de coloriage de l'écran *f* INFORMAT screen painter; ~ de commande *f* ELECTR, ELECTROTEC control unit, PRODUCTION ordering unit, TELECOM control system, control unit; ~ de commutation pour effets spéciaux *f* TV effects bank; ~ de comptage *f* ORDINAT tally; ~ de connexion *f* TELECOM switching network complex; ~ de contrôle *f* COMMANDE, ELECTR, IMPRIM, INFORMAT, ORDINAT control unit; ~ de conversion en différé *f* TELECOM store-and-forward conversion facility; ~ de conversion en temps réel *f* TELECOM real-time conversion facility; ~ de craquage catalytique *f* PETROLE cat cracker, catalytic cracking plant; ~ déportée *f* TELECOM remote unit; ~ de dépoussiérage *f* CONSTR dedusting unit; ~ dérivée *f* CONS MECA, PHYSIQUE derived unit; ~ de dessalage *f* CONSTR desalination plant; ~ de dessalement *f* CONSTR desalination plant; ~ de disque *f* INFORMAT, ORDINAT disk drive, disk unit; ~ de disque CD-ROM *f* OPTIQUE CD-ROM disc drive (BrE), CD-ROM disk drive (AmE), CD-ROM drive; ~ de disque effaçable *f* OPTIQUE erasable disc drive (BrE), erasable disk drive (AmE), erasable optical drive; ~ de disque magnétique *f* INFORMAT, ORDINAT disk unit; ~ de disque optique *f* OPTIQUE optical disc drive (BrE), optical disk drive (AmE), optical drive; ~ de disque souple *f* INFORMAT, ORDINAT floppy disk drive; ~ de disquette *f* INFORMAT, ORDINAT diskette drive; ~ distante *f* TELECOM RU, remote unit; ~ de distillation au brut *f* PETROLE CDU, crude distillation unit; ~ de données du protocole *f* TELECOM PDU, protocol data unit; ~ de données du protocole d'application *f* TELECOM APDU, application protocol data unit; ~ de données du protocole N *f* TELECOM N-protocol data unit; ~ de données du protocole de présentation *f* TELECOM PPDU, presentation protocol data unit; ~ de données du protocole de réseau *f* TELECOM NPDU, network protocol data unit; ~ de données du protocole de session *f* TELECOM SPDU, session protocol data unit; ~ de données du protocole de la sous-couche convergence *f* TELECOM CSPDU, convergence sublayer protocol data unit; ~ de données du protocole de transport *f* TELECOM TPDU, transport protocol data unit; ~ de données de service *f* TELECOM SDU, service data unit; ~ de données de service AAL *f* TELECOM AAL service data unit, AAL-SDU; ~ de données de service ATM *f* TELECOM ATM service data unit, ATM-SDU; ~ de données de service N *f* TELECOM N-service data unit; ~ de dose absorbée *f* PHYS RAYON unit of absorbed dose; ~ d'effort de pêche *f* OCEANO unit of fishing effort; ~

électromagnétique *f* ELECTR electromagnetic unit; ~ d'énergie *f* THERMODYN unit of energy; ~ enfichable *f* ELECTR plug-in unit; ~ d'enregistrement et de retransmission *f* TELECOM SFU, store-and-forward unit; ~ d'entraînement de disque *f* INFORMAT, ORDINAT disk drive; ~ d'entraînement de disque optique *f* OPTIQUE optical disc drive (BrE), optical disk drive (AmE), optical drive; ~ d'entrée *f* INFORMAT, ORDINAT input device; ~ d'entrée/sortie *f* INFORMAT, ORDINAT input/output device; ~ d'entropie *f* THERMODYN unit of entropy; ~ de l'exposition *f* PHYS RAYON unit of exposure; ~ d'extension à couple thermoélectrique *f* PRODUCTION *automatisme industriel* thermocouple expander; ~ fonctionnelle *f* INFORMAT, ORDINAT, TELECOM FU, functional unit; ~ fonctionnelle d'interfonctionnement *f* TELECOM IFU, interworking functional unit; ~ fondamentale *f* CONS MECA fundamental unit; ~ de force *f* CONS MECA force unit, unit of force; ~ de gravité *f* PETR gravity unit; ~ d'hydroforming *f* MATERIAUX hydroforming plant; ~ indépendante *f* PRODUCTION stand-alone unit; ~ internationale *f* ELECTR international unit; ~ d'invention *f* BREVETS unity of invention; ~ légale de longueur *f* METROLOGIE legal unit of length; ~ lithostratigraphique *f* GEOLOGIE lithostratigraphic unit; ~ de longueur *f* METROLOGIE unit of length; ~ de lubrification *f* CONSTR lubricating unit; ~ de masse atomique *f* PHYS PART, PHYSIQUE atomic mass unit; ~ de masse atomique chimique *f* NUCLEAIRE atomic weight unit, chemical atomic mass unit; ~ de mesure *f* METROLOGIE, PETROLE unit of measurement; ~ de mesure d'intermodulation *f* ENREGISTR crosstalk unit; ~ mobile de mesure *f* GAZ mobile logging unit; ~ d'oeuvre *f* PRODUCTION production unit of measure; ~ optique *f* OPTIQUE optical disc drive (BrE), optical disk drive (AmE), optical drive; ~ optique de lecture-écriture *f* OPTIQUE read-write optical drive; ~ para-autochtone *f* GEOLOGIE para-autochthonous unit; ~ périphérique *f* ELECTROTEC peripheral device, INFORMAT, ORDINAT peripheral unit, TELECOM peripheral module; ~ de poids *f* METROLOGIE weight unit; ~ de poids atomique *f* (UPA) NUCLEAIRE atomic weight unit, chemical atomic mass unit *(AWU)*; ~ pratique *f* CONS MECA practical unit; ~ de production *f* PRODUCTION facility; ~ de programme *f* INFORMAT, ORDINAT program unit; ~ de protocole *f* TELECOM PU, protocol unit; ~ de puissance *f* CONS MECA power unit; ~ de raccordement *f* TELECOM IM, line connection unit, interface module; ~ de raccordement d'abonnés *f* TELECOM line interface module, line module; ~ de raccordement d'abonnés distants *f* TELECOM long-line relay set; ~ de rayonnement *f* PHYS RAYON radiation unit; ~ de reconnaissance de la parole *f* TELECOM voice recognizer; ~ récurrente *f* CHIMIE recurring unit; ~ de refroidissement et de convoiement *f* CONS MECA, MINES cooling and conveying unit; ~ remplaçable en ligne *f* ELECTROTEC LRU, line replaceable unit; ~ à réponse vocale *f* INFORMAT audio response unit, TELECOM voice response unit; ~ de sauvegarde sur cartouche magnétique *f* INFORMAT streamer, streaming tape drive; ~ SI *f* ELECTR, PHYSIQUE SI unit; ~ au sol *f* CINEMAT strip light; ~ de stockage *f* IMPRIM storage cell, POLLUTION storage facility, PRODUCTION stock unit, storage unit; ~ de surface *f* METROLOGIE unit of area; ~ de surveillance *f* TELECOM monitor unit; ~ de tir automatique *f* MILITAIRE automatic firing unit; ~ de traitement de signaux *f* TELECOM SP, signal processor; ~ transistorisée *f* ELECTRON solid-state device; ~ de transport passive *f* TRANSPORT passive transport unit; ~ d'utilisation *f* PRODUCTION production unit of measure; ~ vidéo mobile *f* TV OB unit, outside broadcast unit; ~ de visualisation *f* PHYSIQUE visual display unit; ~ de voiture particulière *f* (UVP) TRANSPORT passenger car unit (PCU); ~ de volume *f* ACOUSTIQUE volume unit

univalence *f* CHIMIE monovalence, monovalency

univalent *adj* CHIMIE monadic, monovalent, univalent

univers *m* ASTRONOMIE universe, MATH *théorie des ensembles* universal set; ~ cyclique *m* ASTRONOMIE cyclic universe; ~ elliptique *m* ASTRONOMIE elliptical universe; ~ fermé *m* ASTRONOMIE closed universe; ~ hyperbolique *m* ASTRONOMIE hyperbolic universe; ~ oscillant *m* ASTRONOMIE oscillating universe; ~ ouvert *m* ASTRONOMIE open universe; ~ visible *m* ASTRONOMIE observable universe

universel *adj* ELECTROTEC, MECANIQUE *outillage* general-purpose

UPA *abrév (unité de poids atomique)* NUCLEAIRE AWU *(atomic weight unit)*

upérisation *f* AGRO ALIM uperization, THERMODYN ultra-pasteurization

uraminé *adj* CHIMIE uramido

uranate *m* CHIMIE uranate

urane *m* CHIMIE uranium oxide

uraneux *adj* CHIMIE uranous

uranide *m* CHIMIE uranide

uranifère *adj* CHIMIE, PHYS RAYON uranium-bearing

uraninite *f* MINERAUX uraninite

uranique *adj* CHIMIE uranic

uranium *m* (U) CHIMIE uranium (U); ~ appauvri *m* MILITAIRE depleted uranium; ~ dégradé *m* MILITAIRE depleted uranium; ~ enrichi *m* PHYSIQUE enriched uranium; ~ frais *m* NUCLEAIRE fresh uranium, uranium free from its daughters; ~ très enrichi *m* NUCLEAIRE highly-enriched uranium

uranophyllite *f* NUCLEAIRE copper uranite, torbernite

uranyle *m* CHIMIE uranyl

urao *m* LESSIVES sodium sesquicarbonate

urazol *m* CHIMIE urazole

urée *f* CHIMIE, LESSIVES urea

uréide *m* CHIMIE ureide

uréido- *préf* CHIMIE ureido-

uréique *adj* CHIMIE ureal, ureic

uréotélique *adj* CHIMIE *acide* ureotelic

uréthane *m* CHIMIE urethane

urgence:[1] **d'~** *adj* ESPACE *véhicules*, MECANIQUE, SECURITE emergency

urgence[2] *f* PRODUCTION expedition, SECURITE emergency case

uridine *f* CHIMIE uridine

urique *adj* CHIMIE *acide* uric

urobilinogène *m* CHIMIE urobilinogen

urographie *f* INSTRUMENT pyelography

uronique *adj* CHIMIE *acide* uronic

uroptérine *f* CHIMIE uropterin

urotropine *f* CHIMIE hexamethyltetramine, urotropin, urotropine

uroxanique *adj* CHIMIE uroxanic

usage:[1] **à ~ intensif** *adj* MECANIQUE heavy-duty; **d'~ général** *adj* MECANIQUE *outillage* general-purpose

usage[2] *m* BREVETS use, working; ~ antérieur *m* BREVETS prior use; ~ frauduleux *m* TELECOM fraudulent use; ~

général *m* LESSIVES general-purpose; ~ national *m* TELECOM NU, national use; ~ public *m* BREVETS public use; ~ sans risques *m* SECURITE *de meule, échelle, outil électrique à main* safe use, *de machine manuelle* safety

usagé *adj* POLLUTION *huile* used

usager *m* TELECOM user; ~ inscrit sur le registre *m* BREVETS registered user; ~ de la route *m* TRANSPORT road user

usages: ~ maritimes *m pl* NAUT seamanship

usé *adj* MECANIQUE worn, TEXTILE worn-out

user *vt* CONS MECA wear, wear down, wear off, wear out, MATERIAUX abrade, wear, PAPIER abrade, TEXTILE wear out; ~ par abrasion *vt* MECANIQUE, PAPIER abrade

useur: ~ sur porcelaine *m* CERAM VER porcelain polisher

usinabilité *f* CONS MECA, MATERIAUX machinability, MECANIQUE ease of machining; ~ à chaud *f* CONS MECA hot strength

usinage *m* CONS MECA, MECANIQUE machining, PRODUCTION machining, tooling; ~ chimique *m* PRODUCTION chemical milling; ~ en série *m* PRODUCTION gang machining, multiple machining; ~ hélicoïdal *m* CONS MECA helicoidal machining; ~ au laser *m* MECANIQUE laser machining; ~ par électro-érosion *m* CONS MECA EDM, electrodischarge machining; ~ par étincelage *m* CONS MECA electrospark machining, spark machining; ~ par faisceau d'électrons *m* ELECTRON electron beam machining; ~ par ultrasons *m* NUCLEAIRE, PHYS RAYON ultrasonic machining; ~ par voie chimique *m* MECANIQUE chemical machining; ~ de précision *m* CONS MECA precision machining; ~ tridimensionnel *m* CONS MECA three-dimensional machining

usine *f* ELECTROTEC station, MECANIQUE factory, PRODUCTION factory, plant, works, SECURITE factory; ~ d'affinage de métaux *f* PRODUCTION metal refinery; ~ à l'argile *f* CERAM VER clayworks; ~ d'assainissement *f* HYDROLOGIE sewage treatment plant, sewage works; ~ chimique *f* GENIE CHIM chemical plant; ~ de dessalement *f* GENIE CHIM desalination plant, desalinization plant; ~ d'électricité thermique *f* THERMODYN thermal power station; ~ électrique *f* ELECTROTEC electric power station, electric utility, generating plant, power plant; ~ électrique marémotrice *f* ELECTROTEC tidal power plant, EN RENOUV tidal power station; ~ électrique à mazout *f* CHAUFFAGE oil-fired power station; ~ électrosolaire *f* ELECTROTEC solar electric power station; ~ d'énergie à vapeur *f* ELECTROTEC steam-electric power station; ~ d'enrichissement du minerai *f* NUCLEAIRE ore enrichment plant; ~ d'enrichissement à ultracentrifugation *f* NUCLEAIRE ultracentrifuge enrichment plant; ~ en service avant 1975 *f* POLLUTION existing plant; ~ d'épuration de l'eau *f* HYDROLOGIE water treatment plant; ~ existante *f* POLLUTION existing plant; ~ de fabrication de sacs *f* EMBALLAGE bag factory; ~ au fil de l'eau *f* EN RENOUV *hydroélectricité* run-of-river station; ~ à force motrice *f* ELECTROTEC generating plant, power station; ~ de force motrice *f* ELECTROTEC generating plant, power station; ~ à gaz *f* PRODUCTION gas works; ~ génératrice *f* CONS MECA power station, ELECTROTEC generating plant, power plant; ~ hydraulique *f* HYDROLOGIE waterworks; ~ hydroélectrique *f* ELECTROTEC, EN RENOUV hydroelectric power plant, hydroelectric power station; ~ laitière *f* AGRO ALIM dairy plant; ~ marémotrice *f* OCEANO tidal power station; ~ métallurgique d'affinage *f* PRODUCTION metal refinery; ~ de papeterie *f* RECYCLAGE paper mill; ~ pétrochimique *f*

PETROLE petrochemical plant; **~ pilote** f CHARBON pilot plant; **~ de potabilisation** f CONSTR water treatment plant; **~ de préfabrication** f CONSTR precasting works; **~ de raffinage** f PRODUCTION refinery; **~ à rails** f CH DE FER rail mill; **~ de régénération des huiles usées** f RECYCLAGE oil regeneration plant; **~ de retraitement** f RECYCLAGE reprocessing plant; **~ de séparation isotopique d'uranium** f NUCLEAIRE uranium isotope separation plant; **~ sidérurgique** f PRODUCTION ironworks; **~ thermique** f ELECTROTEC thermal electric power plant, thermal electric power station; **~ de traitement des déchets** f RECYCLAGE waste treatment plant

usiné *adj* MECANIQUE machined; **~ partout** *adj* MECANIQUE machined-all-over

usiner *vt* MECANIQUE machine, PRODUCTION machine, tool, *pièce venue de fonte* machine; **~ une dépouille** *vt* CONS MECA back off

ustensile *m* CONSTR, PRODUCTION utensil; **~ en porcelaine** *m* CERAM VER porcelain utensil; **~ d'imprimerie** *m* IMPRIM printer's supply

ustensiles: ~ d'imprimerie *m pl* IMPRIM printing implements

usure f CONS MECA attrition, wear, wear and tear, wearing, MATERIAUX, MECANIQUE wear, NUCLEAIRE wastage, PAPIER, POLLU MER, TEXTILE wear; **~ abrasive** f CONSTR abrasive wear; **~ détérioration** f TEXTILE wear and tear; **~ mécanique** f CONSTR, PRODUCTION mechanical wear; **~ normale** f CONS MECA wear and tear; **~ d'outil** f PETROLE bit wear; **~ par abrasion** f PLAST CAOU abrasive wear; **~ par frottement** f CONSTR, IMPRIM, PAPIER attrition, PRODUCTION fretting; **~ provenant de la tôle mécanique** f IMPRIM wire wear; **~ de tête** f TV head wear

usurpation: ~ d'identité f TELECOM masquerade

utile[1] *adj* MECANIQUE effective

utile:[2] **~ de la machine** *m* CERAM VER machine tray; **~ à rouleaux** *m* CERAM VER roller tray

utilisable *adj* POLLUTION *déchets*, PRODUCTION *déchets* usable

utilisateur *m* INFORMAT, ORDINAT, SECURITE *personne* user; **~ EDI** *m* TELECOM EDI user; **~ final** *m* INFORMAT, ORDINAT, TELECOM end user; **~ inscrit au registre** *m* BREVETS registered user; **~ de la messagerie EDI** *m* TELECOM EDI messaging user, EDIMG user; **~ des rivières** *m* NAUT river user; **~ du service CMISE** *m* TELECOM CMISE service user; **~ du service CMISE exécuteur** *m* TELECOM performing CMISE service user; **~ du service CMISE lanceur** *m* TELECOM invoking CMISE service user

utilisation: ~ apparente d'oxygène f *(UAO)* OCEANO apparent utilization of oxygen; **~ des eaux usées comme engrais** f RECYCLAGE sewage farming; **~ de l'emplacement** f EMBALLAGE economy of space; **~ future** f TELECOM future use; **~ hebdomadaire** f PRODUCTION week utilization; **~ des microprocesseurs dans les systèmes de calibrage** f CONS MECA application of microprocessors to gaging systems (AmE), application of microprocessors to gauging systems (BrE); **~ du poste de charge** f PRODUCTION work center utilization (AmE), work centre utilization (BrE); **~ sans risques** f SECURITE *des explosifs* safe use

utiliser: ~ avant la date *loc* EMBALLAGE *indication sur l'emballage* use by date

utilitaire[1] *adj* PRODUCTION, TRANSPORT utility

utilitaire[2] *m* PRODUCTION, TRANSPORT utility

UV *abrév (ultraviolet)* ESPACE, OPTIQUE UV *(ultraviolet)*

uvarovite f MINERAUX uvarovite

uvitique *adj* CHIMIE uvitic

UVP *abrév (unité de voiture particulière)* TRANSPORT PCU *(passenger car unit)*

V

V ;[1] *(vanadium)* CHIMIE V *(vanadium)*

V[2] *abrév* CONS MECA *(V de mécanicien)* V-block, METROLOGIE *(volt)* V *(volt)*

V[3] ~ **de mécanicien** *m* *(V)* CONS MECA V-block

V1 *abrév (vitesse de décision)* AERONAUT V1 *(decision speed)*

vacciniine *f* CHIMIE vacciniin

vaciller *vi* AERONAUT, ESPACE wobble

vacuolaire *adj* GEOLOGIE, PETROLE *géologie* vuggy, vughy, vugular

vacuole *f* GEOLOGIE druse, vug

vacuomètre *m* PETROLE vacuum gage (AmE), vacuum gauge (BrE)

va-et-vient[1] *adj* CONS MECA reciprocating

va-et-vient[2] *m* CONS MECA alternating motion, oscillation, reciprocating motion, swinging, to-and-fro, TEXTILE coming and going; ~ **d'un pendule** *m* CONS MECA oscillation of a pendulum

vague *f* NAUT, PHYS ONDES *marine* wave; ~ **d'air** *f* PETR air pulse; ~ **anormale** *f* OCEANO freak wave, phenomenal wave; ~ **capillaire** *f* OCEANO, PHYSIQUE capillary wave; ~ **centenaire** *f* PETROLE *exploitation en mer* hundred year wave; ~ **de chaleur** *f* METEO, THERMODYN heatwave; ~ **déferlante** *f* OCEANO breaker, breaking wave; ~ **d'étrave** *f* NAUT bow wave; ~ **de fond** *f* NAUT ground wave, tidal wave; ~ **porteuse** *f* NAUT carrier wave; ~ **significative** *f* OCEANO significant wave; ~ **de tempête** *f* OCEANO storm surge, storm tide

vaguelette *f* OCEANO capillary wave, PHYS ONDES wavelet

vaisseau *m* NAUT, PAPIER vessel; ~ **de guerre** *m* NAUT man-of-war, warship; ~ **Soyuz** *m* ESPACE Soyuz craft; ~ **spatial** *m* ESPACE *véhicules* space vehicle, spacecraft, spaceship; ~ **spatial Hélios** *m* ASTRONOMIE Helios spacecraft

vaisseau-mère *m* ESPACE mother ship

valence *f* CHIMIE valency, METALL, PHYSIQUE valence; ~ **homopolaire** *f* NUCLEAIRE covalence, covalency

valentinite *f* MINERAUX valentinite

valéramide *m* CHIMIE valeramide

valérate *m* CHIMIE valerate

valérique *adj* CHIMIE *acide* valeric

valéryle *m* CHIMIE valeryl

valérylène *m* CHIMIE valerylene

valet *m* EQUIP LAB *de la platine d'un microscope* clip; ~ **d'arrêt** *m* CONS MECA latch; ~ **d'établi** *m* CONS MECA holdfast; ~ **de menuisier** *m* CONS MECA holdfast; ~ **de la platine** *m* EQUIP LAB *d'un microscope*, INSTRUMENT stage clip

valeur *f* CHIMIE reading, TELECOM value; ~ **absolue** *f* CHIMIE, MATH, ORDINAT absolute value, PHYSIQUE modulus; ~ **d'acidité** *f* AGRO ALIM acid value; ~ **aéronautique** *f* AERONAUT airworthiness; ~ **ajoutée directe** *f* CONS MECA value added; ~ **assignée** *f* ELECTR nominal value, rated value, rating, NUCLEAIRE desired value, index value; ~ **booléenne** *f* INFORMAT, ORDINAT Boolean value; ~ **boulangère** *f* AGRO ALIM baking quality; ~ **calorifique** *f* PHYSIQUE, THERMODYN ca-

lorific value; ~ **de la cause** *f* TELECOM cause value; ~ **chromatique d'une couleur** *f* IMPRIM *photogravure* color lightness (AmE), colour lightness (BrE); ~ **de contrôle cryptographique** *f* TELECOM cryptographic check value; ~ **crête** *f* ELECTRON peak value; ~ **de crête** *f* ELECTRON, PHYSIQUE, TELECOM peak value; ~ **crête-à-crête** *f* PHYSIQUE peak-to-peak value; ~ **d'une division échelon** *f* METROLOGIE scale interval; ~ **échantillonnée** *f* ELECTRON sampled value; ~ **effective** *f* COMMANDE feedback value, ELECTROTEC effective value; ~ **efficace** *f* ELECTROTEC, ENREGISTR, OPTIQUE, PHYSIQUE, TELECOM RMS value, root mean square value; ~ **en douane** *f* NAUT bonded value; ~ **en eau** *f* PHYSIQUE water equivalent; ~ **établie sur l'horloge chien de garde** *f* PRODUCTION *automatisme industriel* watchdog timer set valve; ~ **d'étalon** *f* MATERIAUX calibration value; ~ **d'étalonnage** *f* PRODUCTION scaling value; ~ **de gris** *f* PHOTO tonal value; ~ **indiquée** *f* NUCLEAIRE indicated value; ~ **instantanée** *f* COMMANDE, ELECTR *tension*, PHYSIQUE instantaneous value; ~ **d'interruption** *f* PRODUCTION interrupt value; ~ **d'iode** *f* AGRO ALIM iodine number, iodine value; ~ **limite** *f* TELECOM limiting value; ~ **logique** *f* INFORMAT, ORDINAT logical value; ~ **de lux** *f* PHOTO lux value; ~ **maximale** *f* ELECTRON peak value; ~ **moyenne** *f* ELECTR, PHYSIQUE average value, mean value; ~ **moyenne quadratique** *f* ELECTR mean square value; ~ **négative du laplacien** *f* NUCLEAIRE laplacian; ~ **nominale** *f* ELECTR *appareil* rated value, rating, MECANIQUE rating; ~ **nominale de commutation des moteurs** *f* PRODUCTION *automatisme industriel* motor switching; ~ **nominale de tension inverse** *f* PRODUCTION inverse voltage rating; ~ **numérique** *f* METROLOGIE numerical value; ~ **ohmique** *f* ELECTROTEC ohmic value; ~ **de panification** *f* AGRO ALIM baking quality; ~ **de paramètre** *f* TELECOM PV, parameter value; ~ **de paramètre erronée** *f* TELECOM parameter out-of-range class; ~ **par défaut** *f* TELECOM default value; ~ **de pas indiquée** *f* AERONAUT indicated pitch angle; ~ **du pH** *f* HYDROLOGIE pH number, pH value; ~ **de présélection** *f* PRODUCTION *automatisme industriel* preset value; ~ **propre** *f* ELECTRON, ORDINAT, PHYSIQUE eigenvalue; ~ **Q** *f* PHYSIQUE Q-value; ~ **quadratique moyenne** *f* CONSTR, ELECTRON, MATH, TELECOM RMS, root mean square value; ~ **réelle** *f* IMPRIM actual value; ~ **de remplacement** *f* PRODUCTION *production* replacement cost valuation; ~ **des retombées** *f* POLLUTION deposition value; ~ **de saponification** *f* AGRO ALIM saponification number; ~ **de seuil** *f* ELECTRON threshold value, TV limen; ~ **théorique de charge** *f* RESSORTS theoretical load value; ~ **à titre impératif** *f* RESSORTS critical value; ~ **à titre indicatif** *f* RESSORTS guiding dimension, reference value

valeurs: ~ **d'émission acoustique** *f pl* CONS MECA *des machines* noise emission value; ~ **d'exploitation** *f pl* PETROLE inventory, stock

validation *f* ELECTRON enabling, INFORMAT, ORDINAT validation, QUALITE approval, validation; ~ **de don-**

nées *f* INFORMAT, ORDINAT data validation, data vet

valider *vt* ELECTRON enable, INFORMAT, ORDINAT enable, validate

validité *f* BREVETS validity, MATERIAUX soundness, TELECOM validity; ~ **avion** *f* AERONAUT aircraft effectivity

vallée *f* MINES diphead; ~ **axiale** *f* GEOLOGIE median valley, rift valley; ~ **centrale de la dorsale médio-océanique** *f* GEOLOGIE median valley; ~ **d'énergie** *f* NUCLEAIRE energy valley; ~ **noyée** *f* HYDROLOGIE drowned valley; ~ **sèche** *f* HYDROLOGIE dry valley; ~ **sous-marine** *f* OCEANO submarine valley

valorisation *f* CHARBON enrichment, upgrading; ~ **de stock** *f* PRODUCTION inventory valuation

valve *f* CONS MECA, INST HYDR, VEHICULES *pneu* valve; ~ **à flotteur** *f* CONS MECA float valve; ~ **à gaz** *f* PRODUCTION *haut fourneau* gas valve; ~ **de gonflage** *f* CONS MECA *pneu* air valve; ~ **de mise en pression** *f* AERONAUT pressurizing valve; ~ **oscillante** *f* PRODUCTION swinging valve; ~ **pneumatique** *f* CONS MECA pneumatic valve; ~ **à pointeau** *f* CONS MECA needle valve; ~ **de réduction** *f* CONS MECA reducing valve

vanadate *m* CHIMIE vanadate

vanadeux *adj* CHIMIE vanadous

vanadifère *adj* CHIMIE vanadiferous

vanadinite *f* MINERAUX vanadinite

vanadiolite *f* MINERAUX vanadiolite

vanadique *adj* CHIMIE *acide* vanadic

vanadite *m* CHIMIE vanadite

vanadium *m* (*V*) CHIMIE vanadium (*V*)

vanadyle *m* CHIMIE vanadyl

vannage *m* GEOLOGIE winnowing, INST HYDR gating

vanne *f* DISTRI EAU gate, penstock, shut, shut-off, sluice, sluicegate, water gate, EN RENOUV sluicegate, *barrages* sluice, EQUIP LAB *matériel général*, ESPACE *véhicules* valve, HYDROLOGIE gate, valve, INST HYDR cutoff device, shutter, *de turbine* gate, MECANIQUE valve, NAUT cock, floodgate, sluice, NUCLEAIRE, PETROLE *raffinerie*, PHYSIQUE, POLLU MER valve, PRODUCTION *d'un ventilateur* shutter, RECYCLAGE sluice, REFRIG valve; ~ **d'admission** *f* IMPRIM intake valve; ~ **d'admission d'air** *f* AERONAUT air intake valve; ~ **d'admission de vapeur** *f* INST HYDR steam valve; ~ **d'aiguillage** *f* PRODUCTION *système hydraulique* director valve; ~ **à aiguille** *f* CHIMIE needle valve; ~ **à air** *f* IMPRIM *séchage* airlock; ~ **d'air chaud** *f* AERONAUT hot air valve; ~ **d'alimentation** *f* PETROLE *raffinerie* feed valve; ~ **antiretour** *f* CONSTR nonreturn valve; ~ **d'arrêt** *f* INST HYDR stop valve, PAPIER check valve; ~ **d'arrêt d'une turbine** *f* NUCLEAIRE turbine stop valve; ~ **d'aspiration** *f* REFRIG suction valve; ~ **automatique** *f* PETROLE, REFRIG automatic valve; ~ **basculante** *f* EN RENOUV flap gate, *barrages* tilting gate, HYDROLOGIE flap gate, tilting gate; ~ **de chasse** *f* DISTRI EAU flush gate; ~ **de cheminée** *f* PRODUCTION *appareil à air chaud, haut fourneau* chimney valve; ~ **à chenille** *f* HYDROLOGIE roller gate; ~ **de climatisation** *f* CONS MECA air conditioning master valve; ~ **à commande thermostatique** *f* REFRIG thermostatically-controlled valve; ~ **de commande de sens** *f* CONS MECA direction control valve; ~ **à coulisse** *f* DISTRI EAU sash gate, EN RENOUV *barrages* sliding sluice gate; ~ **de coupure** *f* PRODUCTION shut-off valve; ~ **cylindrique** *f* EN RENOUV *barrages* drum gate; ~ **de dégivrage planeur** *f* AERONAUT aerofoil de-icing valve (BrE), airfoil de-icing valve (AmE); ~ **de dégivrage réacteur** *f* AERONAUT engine anti-icing gate valve; ~ **de dépressurisation** *f* CONS MECA depressurization valve;

~ **de dérivation** *f* EQUIP LAB bypass valve; ~ **de dérivation des gaz chauds** *f* REFRIG hot gas bypass valve; ~ **d'échappement** *f* PAPIER exhaust valve; ~ **d'écluse** *f* DISTRI EAU draw gate; ~ **à écoulement direct** *f* EN RENOUV straight-flow valve; ~ **équilibrée** *f* EN RENOUV balanced valve; ~ **d'éruption** *f* COMMANDE blowout preventer; ~ **d'étranglement** *f* CHARBON choker valve, throttle valve; ~ **à fermeture instantanée** *f* DISTRI EAU quick closing valve; ~ **de flux** *f* AERONAUT flux gate (AmE), flux valve (BrE); ~ **hydraulique** *f* CONS MECA, REFRIG hydraulically-operated valve; ~ **d'injection** *f* EQUIP LAB *chromatographie en phase gazeuse* injection valve; ~ **d'injection de liquide** *f* REFRIG liquid injection valve; ~ **instantanée** *f* REFRIG snap-action valve; ~ **d'inversion** *f* PRODUCTION *système hydraulique* changeover valve; ~ **d'isolement** *f* ESPACE *véhicules*, PRODUCTION *système hydraulique* isolation valve; ~ **d'isolement de manomètre** *f* PRODUCTION *système hydraulique* gage isolating valve (AmE), gauge isolating valve (BrE); ~ **d'isolement principal** *f* NUCLEAIRE main isolating valve; ~ **lançoire** *f* DISTRI EAU head gate; ~ **à membrane** *f* CONS MECA diaphragm valve; ~ **de modération de débit d'eau** *f* REFRIG water-regulating valve; ~ **motrice** *f* DISTRI EAU head gate; ~ **à opercule coulissant** *f* INST HYDR gate valve; ~ **papillon** *f* CONS MECA butterfly valve, EN RENOUV *barrages* balanced disc valve (BrE), balanced disk valve (AmE), butterfly valve, INST HYDR butterfly valve, throttle valve; ~ **papillon à fermeture rapide** *f* CONS MECA butterfly valve; ~ **à passage direct** *f* NAUT seacock; ~ **plongeante** *f* DISTRI EAU floodgate, HYDROLOGIE falling sluice; ~ **à pointeau** *f* REFRIG needle valve; ~ **pressostatique** *f* REFRIG pressure-controlled valve; ~ **principale** *f* MAT CHAUFF main valve; ~ **de prise de vapeur** *f* INST HYDR steam valve; ~ **proportionnelle** *f* PRODUCTION *système hydraulique* proportional valve; ~ **de purge** *f* CHAUFFAGE *chaudières* blowdown valve, EN RENOUV *appareil de forage géothermique* purge valve, PETROLE bleed valve; ~ **pyrotechnique** *f* ESPACE pyrotechnic valve; ~ **réductrice de pression** *f* REFRIG pressure-reducing valve; ~ **de refoulement** *f* REFRIG discharge valve; ~ **de réglage** *f* EQUIP LAB *de fluides* regulating valve; ~ **de réglage de vent** *f* PRODUCTION blast gate; ~ **de régulation** *f* GAZ adjusting valve, control valve, MECANIQUE control valve; ~ **de régulation pneumatique** *f* CONS MECA pneumatically-operated valve; ~ **régulatrice** *f* INST HYDR regulator gate; ~ **régulatrice de débit** *f* DISTRI EAU flow-regulating valve; ~ **de remplissage** *f* ESPACE *véhicules* filling valve; ~ **de répartition** *f* CONS MECA distribution valve; ~ **restricto-changeuse** *f* REFRIG restrictor valve; ~ **rotative** *f* EN RENOUV rotary valve; ~ **à roues fixes** *f* EN RENOUV *barrages* fixed roller sluice gate; ~ **à roues libres** *f* EN RENOUV *barrages* free roller sluice gate; ~ **à secteur** *f* EN RENOUV *barrages* radial gate, sector gate; ~ **de sectionnement** *f* EQUIP LAB isolating valve; ~ **de sectionnement automatique** *f* PETROLE automatic isolating valve; ~ **de sécurité** *f* GAZ, MAT CHAUFF safety valve; ~ **de sécurité de fond** *f* PETROLE downhole safety valve, storm choke; ~ **de sécurité de subsurface** *f* PETR downhole safety valve; ~ **à solénoïde** *f* REFRIG solenoid valve; ~ **à soufflet** *f* REFRIG bellows valve; ~ **télécommandée automatique** *f* REFRIG servo-operated valve; ~ **de tête de puits** *f* EN RENOUV wellhead valve; ~ **thermostatique** *f* CONS MECA thermostatic valve; ~ **de travail** *f* DISTRI EAU head gate; **~ de trop plein** f INST HYDR overflow valve; **~ à vent froid** f PRODUCTION *appareil à air chaud, haut fourneau* cold blast valve; **~ de vidange** f ESPACE *véhicules* jettison valve

vanne-limiteur: **~ de débit** f CONS MECA flow control valve

vannelle f DISTRI EAU gate, sluicevalve, water gate, INST HYDR paddle

vanne-pilote f MECANIQUE control valve

vanner vt INST HYDR gate

vantail m CONSTR *d'une porte* leaf; **~ de fenêtre** m CONSTR casement window

vantelle f DISTRI EAU gate, sluicevalve, water gate, INST HYDR paddle

vapeur[1] m NAUT steamboat, steamer

vapeur[2] f CHIMIE fume, vapor (AmE), vapour (BrE), EN RENOUV, INST HYDR, MAT CHAUFF steam, METALL vapor (AmE), vapour (BrE), PAPIER, PHYSIQUE steam, POLLUTION vapor (AmE), vapour (BrE), TEXTILE steam, THERMODYN vapor (AmE), vapour (BrE); **~ achetée au dedans** f NUCLEAIRE service steam; **~ d'eau** f INST HYDR steam; **~ d'eau lourde** f NUCLEAIRE heavy water vapor (AmE), heavy water vapour (BrE); **~ d'échappement** f AGRO ALIM exhaust steam, INST HYDR dead steam, exhaust steam, THERMODYN dead steam; **~ épuisée** f INST HYDR, THERMODYN dead steam; **~ fraîche** f INST HYDR live steam, NUCLEAIRE live steam, main steam, THERMODYN live steam; **~ humide** f EN RENOUV wet steam, MAT CHAUFF saturated steam; **~ inflammable** f SECURITE flammable vapor (AmE), flammable vapour (BrE); **~ instantanée** f REFRIG flash gas; **~ de mercure** f CHIMIE, CONSTR mercury vapor (AmE), mercury vapour (BrE); **~ principale** f NUCLEAIRE live steam, main steam; **~ saturée** f CHAUFFAGE saturated steam, PHYSIQUE saturated vapor (AmE), saturated vapour (BrE), THERMODYN saturated steam; **~ sèche** f EN RENOUV, MAT CHAUFF dry steam; **~ de service** f NUCLEAIRE service steam; **~ de soufre** f GAZ sulfur steam (AmE), sulphur steam (BrE); **~ surchauffée** f CHAUFFAGE, MAT CHAUFF, PHYSIQUE superheated steam; **~ d'uranium atomique** f NUCLEAIRE atomic uranium vapor (AmE), atomic uranium vapour (BrE); **~ vive** f INST HYDR live steam, NUCLEAIRE live steam, main steam; **~ de zinc** f CHARBON zinc vapor (AmE), zinc vapour (BrE)

vapeurs f pl POLLUTION steam emission, SECURITE fumes; **~ de colle** f pl SECURITE adhesive fumes; **~ de laque** f pl SECURITE lacquer fumes; **~ de peinture** f pl SECURITE paint fumes

vapocraquage m PETROLE steam cracking

vaporeformage m PETROLE steam reforming

vaporeux adj CHIMIE vaporous

vaporisateur m CHIMIE sprayer, vaporizer, DISTRI EAU pulverizer, GENIE CHIM atomizer, evaporating apparatus, evaporator, PRODUCTION spray, spray producer; **~ d'eau** m DISTRI EAU pulverizer

vaporisation f AUTO, GAZ, GENIE CHIM vaporization, MATERIAUX evaporation, PHYSIQUE vaporization; **~ par laser** f PHYS RAYON laser vaporization

vaporisé adj THERMODYN vaporized

vaporiser[1] vt CHIMIE vaporize, GENIE CHIM evaporate, vaporize, POLLU MER spray, THERMODYN vaporize

vaporiser:[2] **se ~** v réfl CHIMIE vaporize

vaporiseur m GENIE CHIM evaporating apparatus, evaporator, THERMODYN vaporizer

Vapotron m (MD) ELECTRON Vapotron (TM)

varangue f NAUT cabin sole reinforcement, floor

varech m AGRO ALIM kelp

variabilité: **~ spatiale** f POLLUTION spatial variability

variable[1] adj MATH variable, METEO changeable, unsettled

variable[2] f CHIMIE variate, INFORMAT, MATH, ORDINAT variable; **~ aléatoire** f ELECTRON, INFORMAT, MATH, ORDINAT random variable; **~ booléenne** f INFORMAT, ORDINAT Boolean variable; **~ commandée** f COMMANDE regulated variable, regulating variable; **~ dépendante** f MATH *dans une fonction* dependent variable; **~ globale** f INFORMAT, ORDINAT global variable; **~ locale** f INFORMAT, ORDINAT local variable; **~ logique** f INFORMAT, ORDINAT logical variable; **~ rhéologique** f METALL rheological variable

variables: **~ irrégulières** f pl ASTRONOMIE irregular variables; **~ macroscopiques** f pl PHYSIQUE macroscopic variables

variamine f CHIMIE variamine

variance f INFORMAT, MATH *statistiques*, ORDINAT, PHYSIQUE variance

variante f PRODUCTION option

variateur: **~ d'avance** m VEHICULES *allumage* advance mechanism; **~ électronique de vitesse** m TRANSPORT electronic speed controller; **~ de lumière** m ELECTR dimmer switch

variation:[1] **à ~ rapide** adj ELECTRON *signal* fast-changing

variation[2] f CONS MECA variation, ELECTR fluctuation, NAUT compass error; **~ absolue de la vitesse de rotation** f ELECTR *machine* absolute speed variation; **~ de courant** f ELECTR current fluctuation; **~ cyclique principale** f AERONAUT primary cyclic variation; **~ dans le temps** f POLLUTION temporal fluctuation; **~ diurne** f NAUT diurnal variation; **~ d'échelle** f INFORMAT, ORDINAT zooming; **~ d'éclat** f ASTRONOMIE brightness variation; **~ de flux macroscopique** f NUCLEAIRE macroscopic flux variation; **~ de fréquence** f ELECTRON frequency change; **~ de gain** f ELECTRON gain change; **~ d'induction** f ELECTR *bobine* self-inductance variation; **~ latérale** f GEOLOGIE *de faciès* lateral variation; **~ linéaire de la capacité** f ELECTROTEC straight-line capacitance; **~ linéaire de la fréquence** f ELECTROTEC straight-line frequency; **~ magnétique** f GEOPHYS magnetic declination, magnetic variation; **~ magnétique diurne** f GEOPHYS magnetic daily variation; **~ magnétique diurne des jours calmes** f GEOPHYS magnetic solar quiet day variation; **~ magnétique diurne lunaire** f GEOPHYS magnetic lunar daily variation; **~ du pas de la pale** f AERONAUT blade pitch variation; **~ périodique** f GEOPHYS periodic variation; **~ de phase** f ELECTR *courant alternatif* phase variation, TV shift; **~ de pression** f GAZ, PHYS ONDES *d'une onde stationnaire* pressure variation; **~ de pression d'eau** f TEXTILE water gradient pressure; **~ séculaire** f ASTRONOMIE secular variation, GEOPHYS secular change, secular variation; **~ séculaire géomagnétique** f GEOPHYS geomagnetic secular variation; **~ spatiale** f POLLUTION geographic variation; **~ de stock** f PRODUCTION inventory change; **~ de température** f REFRIG temperature variation; **~ temporelle** f POLLUTION temporal variation; **~ de temps** f PETR time variant; **~ de vitesse** f PHYS FLUID velocity fluctuation

variations: **~ systématiques** f pl QUALITE systematic variations

varicap f TV varactor diode

varier:[1] vt ENREGISTR *un niveau* fade

varier² *vi* ELECTR fluctuate

variété *f* GEOMETRIE *topologie* manifold; ~ **à trois dimensions** *f* GEOMETRIE three-dimensional manifold

variocoupleur *m* ELECTROTEC variocoupler

variomètre *m* AERONAUT rate-of-climb indicator, vertical speed indicator, ELECTROTEC variometer, ESPACE *véhicules, mesures* VSI, vertical speed indicator; ~ **étalonné** *m* ELECTROTEC inductometer; ~ **magnétique** *m* GEOPHYS magnetic variometer

variscite *f* MINERAUX variscite

varistance *f* ELECTROTEC varistance, PHYSIQUE, PRODUCTION varistor; ~ **au carbure de silicium** *f* ELECTROTEC silicon carbide varistor

varistor *f* ELECTR *résistance* varistor; ~ **à l'oxyde de zinc** *f* ELECTROTEC zinc oxide varistor

varlet *m* CONS MECA V-bob, MINES *d'une pompe de mine* quadrant

varlope *f* CONSTR bench plane, jointer, jointing plane, try plane; ~ **des bennes** *f* CONSTR bench plane

varloper *vt* CONSTR try, try up

varlopeuse *f* CONS MECA trying-up machine

varve *f* GEOLOGIE varve

vase¹ *m* AGRO ALIM beaker, CHIMIE beaker, retort, PHYSIQUE retort, vessel; ~ **d'absorption** *m* GENIE CHIM absorber, absorption cell, absorption vessel; ~ **clarificateur** *m* GENIE CHIM precipitating tank, precipitation tank; ~ **à clarifier** *m* GENIE CHIM precipitating tank, precipitation tank, settling tank, settling tub, settling vat; ~ **clos** *m* EQUIP LAB closed vessel, GENIE CHIM retort; ~ **clos pour la multiplication des bactéries** *m* AGRO ALIM bacteria propagation tank; ~ **conique** *m* EQUIP LAB *verrerie* conical beaker; ~ **de Dewar** *m* EQUIP LAB *isolation*, GENIE CHIM, PHYSIQUE Dewar flask; ~ **en verre** *m* EMBALLAGE glass jar; ~ **évaporateur** *m* GENIE CHIM evaporating basin, evaporating dish, evaporating pan; ~ **d'expansion** *m* AUTO, CHAUFFAGE, MECANIQUE expansion tank; ~ **de filtration** *m* EQUIP LAB filtration flask; ~ **à filtration** *m* GENIE CHIM filtering cup; ~ **à fond rond** *m* EQUIP LAB *verrerie* round-bottomed flask

vase² *f* AGRO ALIM, CHIMIE sludge, DISTRI EAU slime, sludge, HYDROLOGIE ooze, silt, slime, sludge, MINES mud, REFRIG liquid receiver; ~ **calcaire** *f* GEOLOGIE calcareous ooze; ~ **de fond** *f* DISTRI EAU bottom deposit; ~ **pélagique** *f* GEOLOGIE pelagic ooze; ~ **tampon** *f* REFRIG accumulator, battery; ~ **tampon d'aspiration** *f* REFRIG suction accumulator

vaseline: ~ **industrielle** *f* CHIMIE petrolatum

vases: ~ **communicants** *m pl* EQUIP LAB communicating vessels

vasière *f* HYDROLOGIE mudflat

vasopressine *f* CHIMIE vasopressin

vasque *f* DISTRI EAU basin

vastringue *f* CONSTR spokeshave

vauquelinite *f* MINERAUX vauquelinite

VCO: ~ **à fréquence instantanée** *m* ELECTRON set-on voltage-controlled oscillator

VD *abrév (Vigneron-Dahl)* OCEANO Vigneron-Dahl trawl

veau *m* IMPRIM calf leather

vecteur *m* ELECTR *électromagnétisme*, ELECTROTEC, ESPACE, GEOMETRIE, INFORMAT, MATH, ORDINAT, PHYSIQUE vector; ~ **de base** *m* PHYSIQUE basis vector; ~ **boson intermédiaire** *m* PHYSIQUE intermediate vector boson; ~ **de Burgers** *m* CRISTALL Burgers vector; ~ **champ** *m* ELECTROTEC field vector; ~ **de fuite** *m* AERO-

NAUT *bang sonique* trailing vector; ~ **d'interruptions** *m* INFORMAT, ORDINAT interrupt vector; ~ **d'onde** *m* PHYSIQUE wave vector; ~ **d'onde de Fermi** *m* PHYSIQUE Fermi wave vector; ~ **de position** *m* GEOMETRIE, PHYSIQUE position vector; ~ **de Poynting** *m* PHYSIQUE Poynting's vector; ~ **de propagation** *m* ELECTROTEC wave vector; ~ **propre** *m* ELECTRON, ORDINAT, PHYSIQUE eigenvector; ~ **tournant** *m* ESSAIS phasor; ~ **unitaire** *m* PHYSIQUE unit vector

vecteur-poussée *m* ESPACE *propulsion* thrust vector

vecteurscope *m* TV vectorscope

vectoriel *adj* GEOMETRIE, PHYSIQUE vectorial

vectorisé *adj* ESPACE *véhicules* vectored

vedette *f* NAUT launch, motorboat; ~ **automobile** *f* NAUT motorboat; ~ **de défense côtière** *f* NAUT seaward defence boat; ~ **de défense vers le large** *f* NAUT seaward defence boat; ~ **de la douane** *f* NAUT customs patrol boat, revenue cutter; ~ **garde-pêche** *f* OCEANO fishery protection vessel, fishing patrol boat; ~ **lance-torpilles** *f* MILITAIRE torpedo boat; ~ **rapide** *f* TRANSPORT motor cruiser; ~ **de sauvetage** *f* AERONAUT rescue boat; ~ **de surveillance** *f* MILITAIRE, NAUT patrol boat; ~ **de surveillance côtière** *f* MILITAIRE, NAUT patrol boat

véhicule *m* CHIMIE *pour un mélange* vehicle, ESPACE craft, vehicle, IMPRIM carriage, *encres* binder, MECANIQUE, TRANSPORT vehicle; ~ **aéré** *m* REFRIG ventilated vehicle; ~ **aérosuspendu** *m* TRANSPORT suction-suspended vehicle; ~ **amphibie** *m* MILITAIRE amphibious vehicle; ~ **d'atterrissage** *m* ESPACE landing vehicle; ~ **autochenilles** *m* MILITAIRE half track vehicle; ~ **autoportant rigide** *m* TRANSPORT self-supporting rigid vehicle; ~ **à batterie** *m* ELECTROTEC battery vehicle; ~ **blindé de combat** *m* MILITAIRE AFV, armored fighting vehicle (AmE), armoured fighting vehicle (BrE); ~ **à chenilles** *m* VEHICULES tracked vehicle; ~ **commandé à distance** *m* MILITAIRE remote piloted vehicle; ~ **à coussin d'air** *m* TRANSPORT ACV, air cushion vehicle; ~ **à effet de sol** *m* TRANSPORT GEM, ground effect machine, SEV, surface effect vehicle; ~ **électrique** *m* TRANSPORT electric vehicle; ~ **électrique à accumulateur** *m* TRANSPORT battery-powered electric vehicle; ~ **électrique routier** *m* TRANSPORT electric road vehicle; ~ **électrique urbain** *m* TRANSPORT urban electric vehicle; ~ **d'entretien** *m* TRANSPORT service vehicle; ~ **frigorifique** *m* CONS MECA, REFRIG refrigerated vehicle; ~ **à grande vitesse hypothétique** *m* TRANSPORT HHSV, high hypothetical speed vehicle; ~ **hybride** *m* TRANSPORT hybrid vehicle; ~ **logistique lunaire** *m* ESPACE LLV, lunar logistics vehicle; ~ **lourd de dépannage** *m* MILITAIRE, TRANSPORT wrecker; ~ **de manipulation des bagages** *m* TRANSPORT baggage loader; ~ **à moteur à essence** *m* POLLUTION gasoline engine vehicle (AmE), petrol engine vehicle (BrE); ~ **à moteur et à propulsion arrière** *m* AUTO rear engine rear wheel drive; ~ **orbital** *m* ESPACE orbital vehicle; ~ **pour combattre l'incendie** *m* SECURITE firefighting vehicle; ~ **pour voies ferrées super rapides** *m* TRANSPORT superhigh-speed rail vehicle; ~ **à quatre roues motrices** *m* TRANSPORT four-wheel drive vehicle; ~ **de rentrée** *m* ESPACE re-entry vehicle; ~ **de rentrée en orbite terrestre** *m* ESPACE Earth capture vehicle; ~ **de sauvetage** *m* AERONAUT rescue vehicle, ESPACE escape module, rescue vehicle; ~ **sous-marin** *m* OCEANO submersible, underwater vehicle, PETR submersible, underwater vehicle; ~ **spatial** *m*

ASTRONOMIE, ESPACE spacecraft; ~ **sur coussin d'air** *m* NAUT air cushion vehicle, TRANSPORT hovering craft; ~ **sur rails** *m* TRANSPORT rail vehicle; ~ **à suspension supérieure** *m (VSS)* TRANSPORT suspended vehicle system *(SVS)*; ~ **à sustentation sans contact** *m* TRANSPORT contactless support vehicle, support vehicle with non contact suspension; ~ **terrestre** *m* ESPACE land vehicle; ~ **terrestre guidé** *m* TRANSPORT track-guided vehicle; ~ **tout-terrain** *m* TRANSPORT AT vehicle, all-terrain vehicle; ~ **tracteur** *m* TRANSPORT tow vehicle, traction engine, tractive unit; ~ **de transfert interorbital** *m* ESPACE OTV, orbital transfer vehicle; ~ **de transfert orbital** *m* ESPACE OTV, orbital transfer vehicle; ~ **transporteur de troupes** *m* MILITAIRE troop-carrying vehicle; ~ **utilitaire** *m* VEHICULES commercial vehicle; ~ **utilitaire électrique** *m* TRANSPORT commercial electric vehicle, general-purpose electric vehicle

véhiculer *vt* TELECOM carry

veille *f* NAUT lookout; ~ **météorologique** *f* ESPACE, METEO weather watch

veiller *vi* NAUT keep a lookout

veilleuse *f* AUTO sidelight, ELECTROTEC power down, GAZ pilot lamp (AmE), pilot light (BrE)

veine *f* CONSTR vein, MINES lode, seam, vein, PHYSIQUE jet, working section; ~ **centrale** *f* MINES main lode; ~ **de courant** *f* OCEANO current stream; ~ **d'eau** *f* NUCLEAIRE gap, water gap; ~ **d'essai** *f* PHYSIQUE test section; ~ **gazeuse** *f* GAZ gaseous vein; ~ **transversale** *f* MINES cross vein, crosslode

veinule *f* MINES stringer, *de minerai* thread

vélin *m* PAPIER wove

vélocimètre *m* PHYSIQUE velocimeter

vélocimétrie *f* PHYSIQUE velocimetry

vélocité *f* PHYSIQUE velocity

vélomoteur *m* TRANSPORT light motorcycle with kickstarter; ~ **tout-terrain** *m* TRANSPORT scrambler, scrambling motor cycle

velours *m* TEXTILE velvet; ~ **côtelé** *m* TEXTILE corduroy; ~ **panne** *m* TEXTILE panne

venasquite *f* MINERAUX venasquite

vendre: à ~ avant le *loc* EMBALLAGE *indication de la date* sell by

venir: ~ à la coulée *vi* PRODUCTION be cast; ~ **de fonte** *vi* PRODUCTION be cast

vent:[1] **sous le ~** *adj* METEO downwind, NAUT alee, leeward; **au ~** *adj* METEO, NAUT windward; ~ **en poupe** *adj* EN RENOUV downwind

vent:[2] **au ~** *adv* NAUT windward; ~ **arrière** *adv* EN RENOUV, NAUT downwind; ~ **debout** *adv* NAUT in stays; ~ **en poupe** *adv* EN RENOUV downwind; **sous le ~** *adv* METEO leeward, NAUT alee, leeward

vent[3] *m* CONS MECA draft (AmE), draught (BrE), METEO wind; ~ **alizé** *m* METEO trade wind; ~ **apparent** *m* NAUT apparent wind; ~ **arrière** *m* AERONAUT downwind, tailwind, EN RENOUV downwind, METEO tailwind, NAUT following wind; ~ **contraire** *m* NAUT foul wind, *météorologie* headwind; ~ **debout** *m* AERONAUT, METEO, NAUT *météorologie* headwind; ~ **dominant** *m* METEO prevailing wind; ~ **frais** *m* METEO strong breeze; ~ **géostrophique** *m* GEOPHYS geostrophic wind; ~ **grand large** *m* NAUT quarter wind; ~ **de haute altitude** *m* METEO upper wind; ~ **de haute atmosphère** *m* METEO upper wind; ~ **au large** *m* NAUT offshore wind; ~ **du large** *m* NAUT onshore wind; ~ **latéral** *m* AERONAUT cross wind; ~ **du nord** *m* NAUT north wind; ~ **du**

nord-est *m* NAUT northeast wind; ~ **du nord-ouest** *m* NAUT northwest wind; ~ **régnant** *m* METEO prevailing wind; ~ **solaire** *m* ASTRONOMIE, ESPACE, GEOPHYS, PHYSIQUE solar wind; ~ **soufflé** *m* CONS MECA forced draft (AmE), forced draught (BrE); ~ **stellaire** *m* ASTRONOMIE stellar wind; ~ **du sud** *m* NAUT south wind; ~ **du sud-est** *m* NAUT southeast wind; ~ **du sud-ouest** *m* NAUT southwest wind; ~ **de surface** *m* METEO surface wind; ~ **de terre** *m* NAUT offshore wind; ~ **vrai** *m* NAUT true wind

venteuse *f* NUCLEAIRE air drain valve, air vent

ventilateur *m* AUTO cooling fan, engine fan, fan, CONS MECA fan, fan blower, CONSTR fan, vent pipe, ventilating fan, ventilator, ELECTR *appareil* fan, EQUIP LAB *meuble, sécurité* extraction fan, MECANIQUE blower, fan, MINES fan, mine fan, *à la surface* surface ventilating fan, ventilating fan, NAUT ventilator, PAPIER, PHYSIQUE fan, PRODUCTION blower, fan, REFRIG fan, SECURITE ventilator, TRANSPORT, VEHICULES fan; ~ **amplificateur** *m* MINES booster ventilation fan; ~ **aspirant** *m* CHAUFFAGE *chaudières* exhaust fan, CONS MECA exhaust fan, induced draft fan (AmE), induced draught fan (BrE), suction fan, MECANIQUE, PAPIER exhaust fan; ~ **aspirateur mural** *m* CONS MECA porthole fan; ~ **à aubes profilées** *m* REFRIG aerofoil fan (BrE), airfoil fan (AmE); ~ **axial** *m* CHAUFFAGE axial flow fan, SECURITE axial ventilator, TRANSPORT axial flow lift fan; ~ **axial à aubage directeur** *m* REFRIG vane axial fan; ~ **axial à gaz de combustion** *m* CONS MECA combustion axial gas fan; ~ **brasseur d'air** *m* REFRIG circulating fan; ~ **centrifuge** *m* CHAUFFAGE centrifugal fan, radial flow fan, REFRIG centrifugal fan, TRANSPORT centrifugal flow fan; ~ **de chauffage** *m* CONS MECA fan heater; ~ **à courant transversal** *m* CHAUFFAGE crossflow fan, radial flow fan; ~ **débrayable** *m* AUTO power fan; ~ **déplaceur** *m* PRODUCTION displacement fan; ~ **de désembuage** *m* AERONAUT defogging fan; ~ **à deux ouïes** *m* CONS MECA, REFRIG double inlet fan; ~ **électrique** *m* SECURITE electric fan; ~ **enveloppé** *m* CONS MECA *tournant dans une enveloppe* ducted fan; ~ **extracteur** *m* CONS MECA, GENIE CHIM extractor fan; ~ **de fonderie** *m* PRODUCTION foundry blower; ~ **foulant** *m* CONS MECA compressing fan, plenum fan, plenum ventilator, PRODUCTION compressing fan, force fan; ~ **à haute technologie** *m* REFRIG high-performance fan; ~ **à hélice** *m* CHAUFFAGE, CONS MECA, REFRIG propeller fan; ~ **hélico-centrifuge** *m* REFRIG mixed flow fan; ~ **hélicoïde** *m* REFRIG propeller fan; ~ **négatif** *m* CONS MECA exhaust fan, induced draft fan (AmE), induced draught fan (BrE), suction fan; ~ **portatif** *m* CONS MECA portable fan; ~ **positif** *m* CONS MECA compressing fan, plenum fan, plenum ventilator, PRODUCTION compressing fan, force fan; ~ **de puits** *m* MINES mine fan; ~ **réchauffeur** *m* AERONAUT heater blower; ~ **de refoulement de poussière** *m* SECURITE dust exhaust fan; ~ **de refroidissement** *m* CINEMAT, VEHICULES cooling fan; ~ **à une seule ouïe** *m* CONS MECA single inlet fan; ~ **soufflant** *m* CONS MECA compressing fan, plenum fan, plenum ventilator, PAPIER blower, PRODUCTION blower, force fan; ~ **statique** *m* PRODUCTION displacement fan; ~ **à turbine éolienne** *m* REFRIG wind turbine fan; ~ **ventilé** *m* REFRIG ventilated fan; ~ **volumogène** *m* PRODUCTION displacement fan

ventilation *f* CONSTR ventilating, ventilation, MAT CHAUFF, MINES, NAUT, REFRIG, SECURITE, THERMODYN, VEHICULES *moteur, habitacle* ventilation; ~ **d'air** *f* EM-

BALLAGE aeration; ~ **d'air frais** f CONS MECA air cooling; ~ **autonome** f EMBALLAGE self-venting system; ~ **de carter** f VEHICULES *moteur* crankcase ventilation; ~ **forcée** f CONS MECA air blowing, forced ventilation; ~ **de marche** f TEXTILE breakdown; ~ **mécanique par insufflation** f CONS MECA forced draft (AmE), forced draught (BrE), pressure draught (BrE); ~ **naturelle** f NUCLEAIRE natural ventilation; ~ **du réacteur** f AERONAUT cranking; ~ **sous plancher** f REFRIG underfloor ventilation

ventilé adj SECURITE, THERMODYN ventilated

ventiler vt AGRO ALIM, CHARBON aerate, SECURITE, THERMODYN ventilate

ventimètre m NAUT ventimeter

ventouse f CERAM VER cupping glass, CONS MECA sucker, CONSTR ventiduct, IMPRIM sucker, PRODUCTION draft hole (AmE), draught hole (BrE); ~ **d'aération** f EN RENOUV air valve; ~ **de centrage** f INSTRUMENT sucker; ~ **d'entraînement** f IMPRIM *machine* forwarding sucker

ventre m ACOUSTIQUE antinode, loop, CERAM VER belly, CONSTR *d'un mur* bulge, ELECTR *d'onde* antinode, NAUT *navire*, PRODUCTION belly; ~ **de courant** m ELECTROTEC current antinode; ~ **d'onde antinoeud** m ELECTR, PHYS ONDES, PHYSIQUE antinode; ~ **de tension** m ELECTROTEC voltage antinode

ventrier f CONSTR binding beam

vents: ~ **de l'est** m pl METEO easterlies; ~ **de l'ouest** m pl METEO westerlies; ~ **périodiques** m pl METEO periodical winds

venturi m CONS MECA, VEHICULES venturi tube

venu: ~ **à la coulée** adj PRODUCTION cast; ~ **de fonderie** adj MECANIQUE *matériaux* integrally cast; ~ **de fonte** adj PRODUCTION cast; ~ **de forge** adj PRODUCTION forged in one piece

venue f DISTRI EAU irruption, GEOLOGIE *de magma* uprise, HYDROLOGIE *d'eau*, MINES *d'eau* inrush, PETROLE *problème de forage* kick; ~ **d'eau** f DISTRI EAU influx of water, water inflow, water irruption; ~ **d'eau importante** f HYDROLOGIE large inflow of water; ~ **d'eau souterraine** f HYDROLOGIE ground water inrush; ~ **du vent** f CONS MECA draft (AmE), draught (BrE), indraught (BrE), indraught of air (BrE), inlet

vératramine f CHIMIE veratramine

vératrine f CHIMIE cevadine, veratrine

vératrique adj CHIMIE veratric

vératrol m CHIMIE veratrol

vératrole m CHIMIE veratrol

verdi adj GEOLOGIE *altération des silex* green-stained

verdière f OCEANO sea grass bed

verge: ~ **de balance** f CONS MECA scale beam, METROLOGIE balance beam; ~ **de fer** f PRODUCTION iron rod; ~ **de piston** f CONS MECA piston rod

vergence f GEOLOGIE facing direction, PHYSIQUE power

vergeures f pl PAPIER laid lines

verglas m METEO glazed frost, REFRIG glaze

vérificateur: ~ **d'angle de pale** m AERONAUT blade angle check gage (AmE), blade angle check gauge (BrE); ~ **de copie** m CINEMAT print viewer; ~ **de film** m CINEMAT film checker; ~ **lisse** m CONS MECA plain gage (AmE), plain gauge (BrE); ~ **lisse de filetage pour tuyauterie** m CONS MECA plain gage for pipe threads (AmE), plain gauge for pipe threads (BrE); ~ **pour quartz** m CINEMAT crystal checker; ~ **de pression des pneus** m COMMANDE tire pressure gage (AmE), tyre pressure gauge (BrE)

vérification f CONS MECA check, *par calibres à limites*

verification, EMBALLAGE check, checking, INFORMAT check, verification, ORDINAT check, verification; ~ **assistée par ordinateur** f ORDINAT CAT, computer-aided testing; ~ **automatique** f COMMANDE ASC, automatic sequence control, INFORMAT, ORDINAT automatic check; ~ **avant la mise sous tension** f PRODUCTION prepower check; ~ **d'étalonnage** f AERONAUT calibration test; ~ **de matériel** f INFORMAT hardware check; ~ **matérielle** f ORDINAT hardware check; ~ **périodique** f AERONAUT routine inspection; ~ **du poids** f EMBALLAGE check weighing; ~ **primitive** f METROLOGIE initial verification; ~ **d'une procédure de contrôle** f METROLOGIE audit of inspection procedure; ~ **de programme** f INFORMAT, ORDINAT program verification; ~ **au sol** f AERONAUT ground test; ~ **systématique** f AERONAUT routine inspection; ~ **visuelle** f EMBALLAGE machine vision verification; ~ **vrai-faux** f PRODUCTION *automatisme industriel* true-false check

vérificatrice f INFORMAT, ORDINAT verifier

vérifier vt CHIMIE test, CINEMAT *la fenêtre d'exposition* check, *le synchronisme* check, COMMANDE verify, INFORMAT check, verify, METROLOGIE check, ORDINAT check, verify, SECURITE check

vérin m AERONAUT actuator, AUTO power cylinder, COMMANDE jack, regulator, CONS MECA jack, jackscrew, lifting jack, lifting screw, screw jack, screw lifting jack, *à vis* handscrew, CONSTR ram, MECANIQUE jack, ram, PRODUCTION jack, *système hydraulique* cylinder, TRANSPORT actuator; ~ **des aubes de guidage** m AERONAUT intake guide vane ram; ~ **à bille des volets** m AERONAUT flap jack; ~ **à bouteille** m CONS MECA bottle jack; ~ **de calage** m CONS MECA jackscrew; ~ **de calage avec tête à rotule** m CONS MECA jackscrew with self-adjusting head; ~ **à chariot** m CONS MECA traversing jack; ~ **correcteur d'effort** m AERONAUT pitch-correcting unit; ~ **creux** m CONS MECA hollow ram; ~ **de décrochage** m AERONAUT pitch-correcting unit; ~ **hydraulique** m CONSTR hydraulic jack, INST HYDR hydraulic actuating cylinder, hydraulic jack, MECANIQUE hydraulic jack; ~ **d'immobilisation** m CINEMAT safety jack; ~ **multiple** m CONS MECA lift pull and push jack and cramp; ~ **pneumatique** m CONS MECA air cylinder, air jack, air pin block, air piston; ~ **à simple tige** m CONS MECA single piston rod cylinder, PRODUCTION *système hydraulique* simple rod cylinder; ~ **télescopique** m CONS MECA telescopic jack; ~ **universel** m AUTO universal jack; ~ **à vis** m CONS MECA handscrew, lifting jack, lifting screw, screw jack, screw lifting jack

vérine f OCEANO hookrope, tripping line

vermiculite f CHAUFFAGE, MINERAUX, REFRIG vermiculite

verni adj REVETEMENT enamel-covered, enameled (AmE), enamelled (BrE), varnished; ~ **par salage** adj COULEURS, REVETEMENT salt-glazed

vernier m CONS MECA, MECANIQUE, METROLOGIE *échelle* vernier

vernir vt COULEURS, REVETEMENT varnish; ~ **par immersion** vt COULEURS, REVETEMENT dip-varnish; ~ **au tampon** vt COULEURS French polish; ~ **au vernis à cuire** vt COULEURS, REVETEMENT enamel, stove enamel

vernis m CHIMIE, CONSTR varnish, COULEURS enamel, varnish, ELECTR *isolation*, IMPRIM varnish, PLAST CAOU *peinture* enamel, *revêtement* varnish, PRODUCTION lacquer, REVETEMENT lacquer, varnish; ~ **acétocellulosique** m COULEURS acetyl cellulose lacquer; ~ **à l'acétone** m COULEURS acetone lacquer; ~ **à l'acétylcellulose** m COULEURS acetyl cellulose lacquer;

~ **adhésif** m COULEURS adhesive varnish; ~ **à l'alcool** m COULEURS spirit lacquer, spirit varnish; ~ **antiacide** m COULEURS acid-proof enamel; ~ **anticryptogamique** m COULEURS fungicidal varnish; ~ **antiflash** m COULEURS antiflash varnish; ~ **à l'asphalte** m COULEURS asphalt varnish, black japan; ~ **d'automobile** m REVETEMENT car polish; ~ **de barrière de finition** m REVETEMENT coating varnish; ~ **à base de résines alkydes** m REVETEMENT alkyd resin varnish; ~ **brillant** m COULEURS brilliant varnish, REVETEMENT glazing varnish; ~ **à bronzer** m COULEURS bronze lacquer, bronze varnish; ~ **cellulosique** m COULEURS cellulose lacquer; ~ **collant** m COULEURS adhesive varnish; ~ **conducteur** m REVETEMENT conductive lacquer, conductive varnish; ~ **copal** m COULEURS copal varnish; ~ **corsé** m COULEURS long oil varnish; ~ **court en huile** m COULEURS short-oil varnish; ~ **à couvrir** m PLAST CAOU *peinture* resist coating; ~ **craquelant** m REVETEMENT strain-indicating lacquer; ~ **craqueleur** m COULEURS wrinkle paint; ~ **cristallisant** m REVETEMENT frosted lacquer; ~ **à cuire** m PLAST CAOU *peinture* stoving enamel varnish; ~ **d'ébéniste** m REVETEMENT polish; ~ **d'ébéniste au shellac** m REVETEMENT French polish; ~ **à effet** m PLAST CAOU *peinture* decorative varnish; ~ **à effet de structure** m REVETEMENT structural varnish; ~ **d'émaillage** m REVETEMENT insulating lacquer; ~ **d'emballage déchirable** m REVETEMENT package lacquer; ~ **enduit** m REVETEMENT finishing varnish; ~ **épargne** m REVETEMENT long oil varnish; ~ **à l'essence** m REVETEMENT turpentine varnish; ~ **faible** m REVETEMENT short-oil varnish; ~ **fait à froid** m REVETEMENT cold cut varnish; ~ **de finition** m COULEURS finishing varnish, REVETEMENT coating varnish; ~ **flatting** m REVETEMENT flatting varnish; ~ **fongicide** m COULEURS, REVETEMENT fungicidal varnish; ~ **fort** m REVETEMENT long oil varnish; ~ **givré** m REVETEMENT frosted lacquer; ~ **à la gomme-laque** m COULEURS, REVETEMENT lac varnish, shellac varnish; ~ **gras** m REVETEMENT long oil varnish; ~ **à l'huile** m REVETEMENT oleoresinous varnish; ~ **à l'huile de lin** m REVETEMENT linseed oil lacquer; ~ **à immersion** m REVETEMENT dipping varnish; ~ **à imprégnation** m ELECTR *isolation*, REVETEMENT impregnating varnish; ~ **d'impression** m IMPRIM printing varnish; ~ **incolore** m COULEURS clear varnish; ~ **isolant** m ELECTR *isolation* insulating varnish, REVETEMENT insulating varnish, isolac; ~ **isolant pour noeuds** m COULEURS knot varnish; ~ **knotting** m COULEURS knot varnish; ~ **de laque** m COULEURS brilliant varnish; ~ **lithographique** m REVETEMENT lithographic oil, lithographic varnish; ~ **long en huile** m COULEURS, REVETEMENT long oil varnish; ~ **maigre** m REVETEMENT short-oil varnish; ~ **à masquer** m REVETEMENT opaque, resist; ~ **mat** m REVETEMENT mat lacquer; ~ **de miroiterie** m CERAM VER protective paint; ~ **oléorésineux** m REVETEMENT oleoresinous varnish; ~ **pelable** m REVETEMENT protective film; ~ **pelable de protection** m REVETEMENT protective film; ~ **au pinceau** m REVETEMENT painting varnish; ~ **au plomb** m REVETEMENT lead glazing; ~ **à poncer** m COULEURS, REVETEMENT flatting varnish; ~ **à porcelaine** m CERAM VER porcelain varnish; ~ **pour le béton** m REVETEMENT concrete coating; ~ **pour découpage** m REVETEMENT stamping varnish; ~ **pour fer-blanc** m REVETEMENT tin plate varnish; ~ **pour les ferrures** m REVETEMENT iron black; ~ **pour fils** m REVETEMENT wire enamel; ~ **pour plancher** m REVETEMENT floor varnish; ~ **pour sérigraphie**

m REVETEMENT screen varnish; ~ **protecteur** m REVETEMENT protecting lacquer; ~ **pyrométrique** m REVETEMENT temperature-indicating lacquer; ~ **de renforcement** m COULEURS stiffening dope, stiffening varnish; ~ **à résine** m REVETEMENT gum lac, gum lake; ~ **de résinyle** m REVETEMENT resin oil varnish; ~ **résistant aux acides** m EMBALLAGE acid-proof varnish, REVETEMENT acid-proof enamel; ~ **ridé** m REVETEMENT wrinkle paint; ~ **séchant au four** m MATERIAUX baking varnish; ~ **au sel** m REVETEMENT salt glaze; ~ **au shellac** m REVETEMENT shellac varnish; ~ **siccatif** m REVETEMENT drying varnish; ~ **soudable** m REVETEMENT solderable lacquer; ~ **au succin** m REVETEMENT amber varnish; ~ **de surimpression** m IMPRIM overprint varnish, *finition* overprint lacquer; ~ **synthétique** m COULEURS synthetic varnish; ~ **synthétique long en huile** m COULEURS synthetic long-oil varnish; ~ **à la térébenthine** m COULEURS turpentine varnish; ~ **à tracer** m PRODUCTION layout dye; ~ **transparent** m COULEURS transparent lacquer; ~ **au trempé** m REVETEMENT dipping varnish; ~ **de vérification des contraintes** m REVETEMENT stress coating; ~ **zapon** m NUCLEAIRE, REVETEMENT zapon lacquer

vernis-émail m REVETEMENT baked enamel, stove enamel

vernissage m CINEMAT *d'une copie* lacquering, CONSTR varnishing, EMBALLAGE enameling (AmE), enamelling (BrE), IMPRIM *façonnage* varnishing, *finition* glazing, PRODUCTION varnishing, REVETEMENT glass glazing, varnishing; ~ **de fond** m REVETEMENT undercoat; ~ **intérieur** m EMBALLAGE internal lacquering; ~ **mat** m REVETEMENT mat enameling (AmE), mat enamelling (BrE); ~ **par immersion** m EMBALLAGE immersion painting; ~ **au vernis à cuivre** m REVETEMENT enameling (AmE), enamelling (BrE)

vernissé adj CERAM VER glazed

vernisser vt REVETEMENT enamel, varnish

vernisseur m REVETEMENT varnish maker, varnisher; ~ **à la laque** m REVETEMENT enameller

vernisseuse f REVETEMENT varnishing machine

véronal m CHIMIE veronal

verranne f CERAM VER staple fiber (AmE), staple fibre (BrE)

verre m CERAM VER, CHIMIE glass, INSTRUMENT glass, lens;

~ a ~ **absorbant** m CERAM VER radiation-shielding glass; ~ **d'albâtre** m CERAM VER alabaster glass; ~ **antiéblouissement** m CERAM VER antidazzle glass; ~ **antique** m CERAM VER *en cylindres* antique glass; ~ **antique étiré** m CERAM VER antique drawn glass; ~ **antiréfléchissant** m CERAM VER nonreflecting glass; ~ **armé** m CONSTR armored glass (AmE), armoured glass (BrE); ~ **armé à mailles carrées soudées** m CERAM VER Georgian wired glass; ~ **armé à mailles hexagonales** m CERAM VER hexagonal mesh-wired glass; ~ **athermane** m CERAM VER heat-absorbing glass; ~ **aventurine** m CERAM VER aventurine;

~ b ~ **de base** m CERAM VER base glass, parent glass; ~ **blindé** m CERAM VER armored glass (AmE), armoured glass (BrE); ~ **bombé** m CERAM VER bent glass; ~ **borosilicaté** m CERAM VER, CHAUFFAGE, EQUIP LAB *verrerie* borosilicate glass; ~ **à bouteilles** m CERAM VER bottle glass; ~ **brut coulé** m CERAM VER rough cast glass; ~ **brut refroidi dans le pot** m CERAM VER transfer glass;

~ c ~ **cabal** m CERAM VER cabal glass; ~ **de calcin** m

(Fra) *(cf verre de groisil)* CERAM VER glass melted from cullet; ~ **calorifuge** *m* THERMODYN heat-resisting glass; ~ **cannelé** *m* (Fra) *(cf verre flûté)* CERAM VER reeded glass; ~ **à cannelures croisées** *m* CERAM VER cross-reeded glass; ~ **cathédrale** *m* CERAM VER cathedral glass; ~ **cellulaire** *m* CERAM VER foam glass, CHAUFFAGE cellular glass; ~ **de centrage muni d'un réticule** *m* CERAM VER centering lens with ruled cross (AmE), centring lens with ruled cross (BrE); ~ **de chalcogénure** *m* CERAM VER chalcogenide glass; ~ **de chlorure** *m* CERAM VER chloride glass; ~ **clivé** *m* CERAM VER cleaved glass; ~ **collé** *m* CERAM VER cemented glass; ~ **de composition** *m* (Fra) *(cf verre frais)* CERAM VER glass melted from batch only; ~ **concave-convexe** *m* INSTRUMENT concave-convex lens; ~ **de contact** *m* CERAM VER contact lens; ~ **à couche** *m* CERAM VER coated glass; ~ **coulé** *m* CERAM VER cast glass; ~ **de couleur** *m* CERAM VER colored glass (AmE), coloured glass (BrE); ~ **coupe-feu** *m* SECURITE firebreak glass; ~ **court** *m* CERAM VER short glass; ~ **couvre-objet** *m* CERAM VER microscope slide; ~ **craquelé** *m* CERAM VER crackled glass; ~ **creux** *m* CERAM VER hollow ware; ~ **creux doublé** *m* CERAM VER cased hollow ware; ~ **creux doublé à l'opale** *m* CERAM VER ply glass; ~ **creux taillé** *m* CERAM VER cut glass; ~ **de Crookes** *m* CERAM VER Crookes glass; ~ **culinaire** *m* THERMODYN ovenproof glass;

~ d ~ **demi-blanc** *m* CERAM VER half white glass; ~ **demi-brut** *m* CERAM VER selected chunks; ~ **dépoli** *m* CINEMAT *pour faire la mise au point* focusing screen, ground glass; ~ **dépoli à échelons de Fresnel** *m* PHOTO ground glass with Fresnel lens; ~ **dépoli à microprismes** *m* PHOTO ground glass screen with microprism spot; ~ **dépoli de la mise au point** *m* PHOTO focusing screen; ~ **dépoli de projection** *m* INSTRUMENT ground glass screen, matt screen, projection screen; ~ **dépoli à quadrillage** *m* PHOTO ground glass screen with reticule; ~ **diathermane** *m* CERAM VER heat-transmitting glass; ~ **dichroïque** *m* CERAM VER dichroic glass; ~ **dopé au césium** *m* ESPACE caesium-doped glass (BrE), cesium-doped glass (AmE); ~ **doublé** *m* CERAM VER flashed glass (BrE), overlay (AmE); ~ **à double foyer** *m* CERAM VER, INSTRUMENT bifocal lens; ~ **doublé à l'opale** *m* CERAM VER flashed opal; ~ **dur** *m* CERAM VER hard glass; ~ **durci** *m* CONSTR toughened glass;

~ e ~ **d'éclairage** *m* CERAM VER lighting glass; ~ **d'emballage** *m* CERAM VER container glass; ~ **en cylindres** *m* CERAM VER blown sheet (AmE), cylinder glass (BrE); ~ **en plateaux** *m* CERAM VER crown glass; ~ **en poudre** *m* CERAM VER powdered glass; ~ **épais** *m* CERAM VER crystal sheet glass (AmE), thick sheet glass (BrE); ~ **expansé** *m* CERAM VER foamed glass; ~ **extra-blanc** *m* CERAM VER flint; ~ **extra-mince** *m* CERAM VER extra thin sheet glass;

~ f ~ **à faibles pertes diélectriques** *m* CERAM VER low-loss glass; ~ **à feu** *m* THERMODYN ovenproof glass; ~ **feuilleté** *m* CERAM VER, TRANSPORT laminated glass; ~ **feuilleté avec couche intermédiaire en fibres de verre** *m* CERAM VER ply glass; ~ **feuilleté coloré** *m* CERAM VER tinted laminated glass; ~ **filé** *m* CERAM VER spun glass, CHAUFFAGE glass fiber (AmE), glass fibre (BrE); ~ **filé imprégné** *m* NUCLEAIRE *à la bakélite* glass reinforced laminate; ~ **filtre** *m* PHOTO filter screen; ~ **flotté** *m* CERAM VER float glass; ~ **flûté** *m* (Bel) *(cf verre cannelé)* CERAM VER reeded glass; ~ **fondu** *m* CERAM VER metal, molten glass; ~ **frais** *m* (Bel) *(cf verre de*

composition) CERAM VER glass melted from batch only; ~ **fritté** *m* CERAM VER fritted glass, sintered glass; ~ **fumé** *m* CERAM VER smoked glass;

~ g ~ **de germaniure** *m* CERAM VER germanide glass; ~ **givré à l'acide** *m* CERAM VER acid-etched frosted glass; ~ **givré à la colle** *m* CERAM VER ice-patterned glass; ~ **à glace** *m* CERAM VER plate glass; ~ **goutte d'eau** *m* CERAM VER dewdrop glass; ~ **à graduations Schellbach** *m* CERAM VER Schellbach tubing; ~ **granulé** *m* CERAM VER granulated glass; ~ **gris** *m* CERAM VER neutral tinted glass; ~ **de groisil** *m* (Bel) *(cf verre de calcin)* CERAM VER glass melted from cullet;

~ h ~ **horticole** *m* CERAM VER horticultural glass;

~ i ~ **imprimé** *m* CERAM VER figured rolled glass (BrE), patterned glass (AmE); ~ **inactinique** *m* CERAM VER document glass; ~ **incolore** *m* CERAM VER colorless glass (AmE), colourless glass (BrE); ~ **intermédiaire** *m* CERAM VER intermediate sealing glass (BrE), solder glass (AmE); ~ **inverse** *m* CERAM VER invert glass; ~ **isolant insonorisant** *m* SECURITE noise protective insulating glass, soundproof insulating glass; ~ **isolant de protection contre le feu** *m* SECURITE insulating glass for fire protection;

~ j ~ **jardinier translucide imprimé** *m* CERAM VER horticultural cast glass;

~ l ~ **laiteux** *m* CERAM VER milk glass; ~ **laiteux au phosphate** *m* CERAM VER white phosphate opal; ~ **de laitier** *m* CERAM VER slag glass; ~ **laminé** *m* CERAM VER rolled glass; ~ **long** *m* CERAM VER slow-setting glass; ~ **luminescent** *m* CERAM VER luminescent glass; ~ **de lunette** *m* INSTRUMENT spectacle lens; ~ **à lunettes** *m* CERAM VER spectacle glass;

~ m ~ **martelé** *m* CERAM VER hammered glass; ~ **maté à cannelures** *m* CERAM VER reedlyte glass; ~ **maté au sable** *m* CERAM VER frosted glass; ~ **à médicaments** *m* CERAM VER dispensing glass; ~ **métallique** *m* MATERIAUX metallic glass; ~ **mince** *m* CERAM VER thin sheet glass; ~ **monté cuivre** *m* CERAM VER copper light; ~ **de montre** *m* EQUIP LAB *verrerie* watch glass;

~ n ~ **négatif** *m* INSTRUMENT negative lens surface; ~ **neutre** *m* CERAM VER neutral glass; ~ **neutre blanc type I** *m* CERAM VER neutral white glass; ~ **neutre brun type I** *m* CERAM VER neutral amber glass; ~ **non décoré** *m* CERAM VER blank glass;

~ o ~ **ondulé** *m* CERAM VER corrugated glass; ~ **ondulé armé** *m* CERAM VER corrugated wired glass; ~ **opale** *m* CERAM VER opal glass; ~ **opale au fluorure** *m* CERAM VER fluoride opal glass; ~ **opale au phosphate** *m* CERAM VER phosphate opal glass; ~ **opalescent** *m* CERAM VER opalescent glass; ~ **opaque** *m* CERAM VER opaque glass; ~ **optique** *m* INSTRUMENT lens, optical glass, PHOTO optical glass; ~ **d'optique flint** *m* CERAM VER optical flint;

~ p ~ **panchro** *m* CINEMAT pan glass; ~ **pare-flamme** *m* CERAM VER fireproof glass, flameproof glass; ~ **de passivation** *m* CERAM VER passivation glass; ~ **perdu** *m* EMBALLAGE no-return bottle, nonreturnable bottle; ~ **photosensible** *m* CERAM VER photosensitive glass; ~ **à pied** *m* CERAM VER stemware; ~ **piqué** *m* (Bel) *(cf verre puceux)* CERAM VER seedy glass; ~ **plan** *m* METROLOGIE optical flat; ~ **plan-concave** *m* INSTRUMENT planoconcave lens; ~ **plat** *m* CERAM VER flat glass; ~ **plat à facettes** *m* INSTRUMENT flat lens; ~ **positif** *m* INSTRUMENT positive lens surface; ~ **potassique** *m* CERAM VER potash glass; ~ **pour boussoles** *m* CERAM VER compass lens; ~ **pour dosimètre** *m* CERAM VER dosimeter glass; ~

pour échange ionique *m* CERAM VER ion exchange glass; ~ **pour encadrement** *m* CERAM VER picture glass; ~ **pour lampe de Wood** *m* CERAM VER Wood's glass; ~ **pour laser** *m* CERAM VER laser glass; ~ **pour niveau** *m* CERAM VER gage glass (AmE), gauge glass (BrE); ~ **pour revêtement de cuve** *m* CERAM VER tank lining glass; ~ **pour thermomètres** *m* CERAM VER thermometer glass; ~ **pour tubes** *m* CERAM VER tubing glass; ~ **pressé** *m* CERAM VER pressed glass (BrE), pressware (AmE); ~ **presseur** *m* CINEMAT platen; ~ **prismatique** *m* CERAM VER prismatic glass; ~ **de protection** *m* SECURITE protective glass; ~ **de protection contre les rayons X** *m* CERAM VER, INSTRUMENT, SECURITE X-ray protective glass; ~ **de protection pour lunettes de soudeur** *m* SECURITE protective glass for welder's goggles; ~ **puceux** *m* (Fra) *(cf verre piqué)* CERAM VER seedy glass;

~ r ~ **résiduel dans le pot** *m* CERAM VER bottom glass; ~ **résistant aux attaques chimiques** *m* CERAM VER *pour laboratoire* chemically-resistant glass; ~ **résistant au choc thermique** *m* CERAM VER heat-resisting glass; ~ **rubis au sélénium** *m* CERAM VER selenium ruby glass;

~ s ~ **sans hydroxyles** *m* CERAM VER hydroxyl-free glass; ~ **satiné** *m* CERAM VER satin finish glass; ~ **de sécurité** *m* CERAM VER, CONSTR safety glass, TRANSPORT safety glass, shatterproof glass; ~ **de sécurité armé** *m* CERAM VER wired cast glass, wired safety glass; ~ **de sécurité feuilleté armé** *m* CERAM VER laminated safety glass; ~ **de signalisation** *m* CERAM VER signal glass; ~ **de silice** *m* METALL silica glass; ~ **simple** *m* CERAM VER single thickness sheet glass (BrE), single thickness window glass (AmE); ~ **soluble** *m* CERAM VER, LESSIVES soluble glass, water glass; ~ **sombre** *m* CERAM VER dark glass; ~ **sonore** *m* CERAM VER crystal glass; ~ **soufflé** *m* PRODUCTION blown glass; ~ **soufflé bouche** *m* CERAM VER hand-blown glass, mouth-blown glass; ~ **de sulfure** *m* CERAM VER sulfide glass (AmE), sulphide glass (BrE);

~ t ~ **teinté** *m* CERAM VER tinted glass; ~ **tendre** *m* CERAM VER soft glass; ~ **aux terres rares** *m* CERAM VER rare earth glass; ~ **de toiture** *m* CERAM VER plain rolled glass; ~ **translucide** *m* CERAM VER translucent glass; ~ **trempé** *m* CERAM VER tempered glass, toughened glass, CONSTR toughened glass, TRANSPORT tempered glass, toughened glass; ~ **à trempe différenciée** *m* CERAM VER zone-toughened glass; ~ **à triple foyer** *m* CERAM VER trifocal glass;

~ v ~ **vierge** *m* CERAM VER pristine glass; ~ **de visée interchangeable** *m* PHOTO interchangeable focusing screen; ~ **à vitres** *m* CERAM VER sheet glass, CONSTR window glass

verrerie *f* EQUIP LAB glassware; ~ **d'emballage à col étroit** *f* CERAM VER narrow-neck container; ~ **d'emballage à col large** *f* CERAM VER wide-mouth containers; ~ **pour limonadiers** *f* CERAM VER hotel glassware

verres: ~ **bifocaux fusionnés** *m pl* CERAM VER fused bifocals; ~ **bifocaux d'une seule pièce** *m pl* CERAM VER solid bifocals; ~ **protecteurs** *m pl* CERAM VER eye protection glasses

verrière *f* AERONAUT canopy, CERAM VER glass roof

verrou *m* CONSTR bolt, latch, lock, EMBALLAGE latch, INFORMAT lock, MECANIQUE catch, ORDINAT lock; ~ **à la capucine** *m* CONSTR *serrurerie* tower bolt; ~ **à coquille** *m* CONSTR barrel bolt; ~ **à coulisse** *m* CONSTR bolt; ~ **à crochet** *m* EMBALLAGE hooked lock; ~ **de fermeture** *m* CONSTR locking bolt; ~ **glissant** *m* CONS

MECA sliding bolt; ~ **d'interdiction de levage** *m* AERONAUT landing gear safety lock; ~ **à platine** *m* CONSTR *serrurerie* tower bolt; ~ **de porte** *m* CONSTR door bolt; ~ **à ressort** *m* CONS MECA latch, CONSTR spring bolt; ~ **de sécurité** *m* SECURITE security bolt; ~ **de sûreté** *m* CONSTR safety lock; ~ **de train rentré** *m* AERONAUT landing gear retraction lock, landing gear uplock

verrouillage *m* AERONAUT, CINEMAT interlock, CONS MECA bolting, CONSTR locking, ELECTROTEC interlock, latching, IMPRIM lock, INFORMAT, ORDINAT, PRODUCTION interlock, SECURITE bolting, latching, TELECOM alignment, VEHICULES *carrosserie* lock; ~ **anormal** *m* ESPACE latch-up; ~ **à baïonnette** *m* EMBALLAGE, MECANIQUE bayonet catch; ~ **de carter** *m* CINEMAT housing lock; ~ **centralisé** *m* VEHICULES *portes* central locking; ~ **de clavier** *m* INFORMAT, ORDINAT keyboard lockout; ~ **de différentiel** *m* VEHICULES *transmission* differential lock; ~ **double bande** *m* CINEMAT sepmag lock; ~ **de fréquence** *m* TELECOM frequency alignment; ~ **hydraulique** *m* INST HYDR hydraulic locking; ~ **mécanique** *m* CONS MECA mechanical locking; ~ **de multitrame** *m* TELECOM MFA, multiframe alignment; ~ **du niveau** *m* TV clamping; ~ **par baïonnette** *m* ELECTROTEC bayonet coupling; ~ **de phase** *m* TELECOM, TV phase alignment, phase locking; ~ **de porte** *m* VEHICULES door locking mechanism; ~ **des portes** *m* CH DE FER *véhicules* door locking; ~ **position train sorti** *m* AERONAUT down lock; ~ **réciproque** *m* MECANIQUE interlocking; ~ **retardé** *m* TV controlled delay lock; ~ **sans mémoire** *m* PRODUCTION *automatisme industriel* nonretentive latch; ~ **du signal couleur** *m* TV color lock (AmE), colour lock (BrE); ~ **sur fréquence latérale** *m* TV side lock; ~ **sur front** *m* ELECTRON edge latching; ~ **de trame** *m* ESPACE *communications* frame alignment, TELECOM frame alignment, frame synchronization, TV frame alignment, framing; ~ **de trame de base** *m* TELECOM BFA, basic frame alignment

verrouiller *vt* CH DE FER *une aiguille*, CINEMAT lock, CONSTR bolt, ELECTROTEC interlock, IMPRIM lock, INFORMAT, MECANIQUE, ORDINAT latch, lock

verrouilleur: ~ **de synchronisation** *m* ENREGISTR, TV genlock

vers:[1] ~ **le large** *adj* NAUT seaward; ~ **la terre** *adj* NAUT shoreward

vers:[2] ~ **l'arrière** *adv* NAUT astern; ~ **le continent** *adv* GEOLOGIE landward; ~ **le large** *adv* GEOLOGIE offshore, NAUT seaward; ~ **la métropole** *adv* NAUT homeward; ~ **le nord** *adv* NAUT northwards; ~ **le nord-est** *adv* NAUT northeastwards; ~ **le nord-ouest** *adv* NAUT northwestwards; ~ **l'ouest** *adv* NAUT westwards; ~ **le sud** *adv* NAUT southwards; ~ **le sud-est** *adv* NAUT southeastwards; ~ **le sud-ouest** *adv* NAUT southwestwards; ~ **la terre** *adv* GEOLOGIE landward, NAUT shoreward

versage *m* CONSTR dumping (AmE), tipping (BrE)

versant *m* CONSTR *d'une colline* slope, *d'un comble* slope, DISTRI EAU drainage basin

Verseau *m* ASTRONOMIE Aquarius, Water Carrier

versène *m* CHIMIE versene

verser:[1] ~ **des indemnités** *vi* SECURITE compensate

verser:[2] **se** ~ **dans** *v réfl* HYDROLOGIE *rivière* flow into

verseur *m* CHARBON dump truck (AmE), tipper (BrE), CONSTR dump (AmE), tip (BrE), dump truck (AmE), tipper (BrE)

version *f* INFORMAT, ORDINAT release, version, PRODUCTION version; ~ **bêta** *f* ORDINAT beta version; ~ **doublée** *f* CINEMAT dubbed version; ~ **électrolytique** *f* ELECTRO-

TEC electrolytic unit; **~ hermétique** *f* ELECTROTEC hermetically-sealed unit; **~ de syntaxe** *f* TELECOM syntax version

verso *m* EMBALLAGE *d'une étiquette* back, IMPRIM verso, *impression, reliure* backside, *impression* lower side, PAPIER back

vert[1] *adj* THERMODYN unfired; **~ de chrome** *adj* CERAM VER chrome green

vert:[2] **~ de cuivre** *m* CHIMIE green mineral; **~ primaire** *m* TV green primary

vert-de-gris *m* CHIMIE verdigris

vertical[1] *adj* AUTO *carburateur* updraft (AmE), updraught (BrE), GEOMETRIE vertical

vertical:[2] **~ du plan des formes** *m* CONS MECA body plan, frame plan, lines drawing, lines plan

verts: ~ simultanés *m pl* TRANSPORT opposing green

vésiculeux *adj* GEOLOGIE vesicular

vesou *m* AGRO ALIM cane juice

vestibule: ~ d'accès *m* CH DE FER *véhicules* vestibule (BrE)

vésuvianite *f* MINERAUX vesuvianite

vésuvine *f* CHIMIE vesuvin

vêtement *m* TEXTILE apparel, garment; **~ de plongée** *m* OCEANO diving suit, wetsuit

vêtements *m pl* SECURITE clothing; **~ antiflamme** *m pl* SECURITE fireproof clothing, flameproof clothing; **~ à cotte de mailles** *m pl* SECURITE chain mail garments; **~ à l'épreuve des intempéries** *m pl* SECURITE weatherproof clothing; **~ de laboratoire** *m pl* SECURITE laboratory clothing; **~ lumineux** *m pl* SECURITE luminous clothing; **~ matelassés** *m pl* SECURITE padded clothing; **~ pour l'industrie** *m pl* SECURITE industrial clothing; **~ pour salles aseptisées** *m pl* SECURITE aseptic room clothing; **~ de protection** *m pl* MILITAIRE, SECURITE protective clothing; **~ de protection antistatiques** *m pl* SECURITE antistatic protective clothing; **~ de protection contre la chaleur** *m pl* SECURITE heat-protective clothing; **~ de protection contre la chaleur et le feu** *m pl* SECURITE protective clothing against heat and fire; **~ de protection contre la chaleur sans amiante** *m pl* SECURITE asbestos-free protective clothing; **~ à protection intégrale** *m pl* SECURITE overall protective suits; **~ de protection à jeter** *m pl* SECURITE disposable protective clothing; **~ de protection pour services de sauvetage** *m pl* SECURITE protective clothing for rescue services; **~ de protection thermique** *m pl* SECURITE heat-proof protective clothing; **~ de signalisation** *m pl* SECURITE luminous and colored protective clothing (AmE), luminous and coloured protective clothing (BrE); **~ de travail** *m pl* CONSTR, TEXTILE working clothes

vêture: ~ isolante *f* CONSTR insulating wall panel

veuve *f* IMPRIM *composition, mise en page* widow

VHF *abrév (très haute fréquence)* ELECTRON, ESPACE, PHYS ONDES, TELECOM, TV VHF *(very high-frequency)*

viaduc *m* CONSTR viaduct

viaille *f* MINES cross drift, cross drive, crossheading, offset drive, drift, offset

vibrateur *m* PETROLE shale shaker; **~ à béton** *m* CONSTR poker vibrator

vibration *f* IMPRIM *mécanique*, MECANIQUE, METALL vibration, PHYSIQUE oscillation, vibration, SECURITE vibration; **~ acoustique** *f* ACOUSTIQUE acoustic vibration; **~ aéroélastique** *f* AERONAUT flutter; **~ de l'aube directrice** *f* EN RENOUV guide vane vibration; **~ forcée** *f* ACOUSTIQUE, PHYSIQUE forced vibration; **~ libre** *f* ACOUSTIQUE free vibration; **~ mécanique** *f* ACOUSTIQUE mechanical vibration; **~ moteur** *f* AERONAUT engine vibration; **~ transmise par les mains** *f* SECURITE hand-transmitted vibration

vibrational *adj* PHYSIQUE vibration

vibrations: ~ amorties *f pl* PHYS ONDES damped vibrations; **~ de déformation** *f pl* PHYS RAYON bending vibrations

vibrato *m* ACOUSTIQUE vibrato

vibrer *vt* CONSTR vibrate

vibreur *m* AERONAUT chopper, CONSTR, ELECTROTEC vibrator; **~ de remplissage** *m* EMBALLAGE filling vibrator; **~ de silo** *m* MINES bunker vibrator; **~ sonore** *m* ELECTROTEC, IMPRIM, TELECOM, TRANSPORT buzzer

vibro-compacteur *m* CONSTR vibrating roller

vibrocompaction *f* NUCLEAIRE vibrocompaction

vibrocrible *m* CHARBON vibrating screen

vibroseis *m* PETR vibroseis

vibrotassement *m* NUCLEAIRE vibrocompaction

vice: ~ de construction *m* CONSTR constructional defect

vicinal *adj* CHIMIE vicinal

vidage *m* CONSTR dewatering, INFORMAT, ORDINAT change dump, dump; **~ binaire** *m* ORDINAT binary dump; **~ à la demande** *m* INFORMAT, ORDINAT snapshot dump; **~ dynamique** *m* INFORMAT, ORDINAT dynamic dump; **~ d'écran** *m* INFORMAT, ORDINAT screen dump; **~ mémoire** *m* INFORMAT, ORDINAT core dump, memory dump; **~ de secours** *m* INFORMAT, ORDINAT rescue dump; **~ sélectif** *m* INFORMAT, ORDINAT selective dump; **~ statique** *m* INFORMAT, ORDINAT static dump; **~ sur bande** *m* INFORMAT, ORDINAT tape dump

vidange *f* AGRO ALIM ullage, CONS MECA drainage, DISTRI EAU drawoff, PRODUCTION *système hydraulique* drainage; **~ du cockpit** *f* NAUT cockpit drainage; **~ de combustible** *f* ESPACE *véhicules* fuel dumping; **~ des eaux usées** *f* RECYCLAGE wastewater disposal; **~ en vol** *f* AERONAUT in-flight dumping; **~ de fond** *f* DISTRI EAU, HYDROLOGIE bottom outlet; **~ d'huile** *f* VEHICULES *lubrification* oil change; **~ du radiateur** *f* AUTO radiator draining

vidanger[1] *vt* AERONAUT jettison, MECANIQUE, RECYCLAGE drain

vidanger:[2] **~ carburant en vol** *vi* ESPACE *véhicules* dump fuel in flight

vidanges *f pl* EMBALLAGE empties

vide:[1] **sous ~** *adj* PHYSIQUE, PRODUCTION under vacuum INFORMAT, ORDINAT empty; **à ~** *adj* AERONAUT no-load, CONS MECA light-running, light, PHYSIQUE vacuum, PRODUCTION empty; **à ~ poussé** *adj* MECANIQUE high-vacuum

vide[2] *m* AGRO ALIM ullage, CHARBON interstice, void, CHIMIE vacuum, void, CONS MECA gap, space, ESPACE, MATERIAUX, MECANIQUE, PAPIER, PETROLE, PHYSIQUE vacuum, PRODUCTION fire room, *d'une vis* groove, *d'un haut fourneau* tunnel, REFRIG, TEXTILE, TV vacuum; **~ absolu** *m* REFRIG absolute vacuum; **~ bas** *m* PHYSIQUE low vacuum; **~ grossier** *m* PHYSIQUE rough vacuum; **~ limite** *m* THERMODYN ultimate vacuum; **~ naturel** *m* GAZ natural void; **~ normal** *m* CH DE FER *véhicules* normal vacuum; **~ peu poussé** *m* PHYSIQUE low vacuum, rough vacuum; **~ poussé** *m* ELECTRON hard vacuum, PHYSIQUE high vacuum; **~ primaire** *m* PHYSIQUE low vacuum, rough vacuum; **~ secondaire** *m* PHYSIQUE ultrahigh vacuum; **~ très poussé** *m* PHYSIQUE, REFRIG ultrahigh vacuum

vidéo *f* INFORMAT, ORDINAT, TELECOM, TV video; ~ **inverse** *f* INFORMAT, ORDINAT reverse video; ~ **PAD** *f* TELECOM videotex PAD; ~ **portative** *f* TV portable pack

vidéocassette *f* TV videocassette

vidéoclip *m* TV videoclip

vidéoconférence: ~ **à images animées** *f* TELECOM full-motion videoconferencing; ~ **à images fixes** *f* TELECOM slow-scan videoconferencing

vidéodisque *m* OPTIQUE videodisc, videodisk (AmE), TV videodisc (BrE), videodisk (AmE); ~ **analogique** *m* OPTIQUE analog videodisk (AmE), analogue videodisc (BrE), capacitance disc (BrE), capacitance disk (AmE); ~ **capacitif** *m* OPTIQUE capacitance disc (BrE), capacitance disk (AmE); ~ **à gravure superficielle** *m* OPTIQUE surface-written videodisc (BrE), surface-written videodisk (AmE); ~ **interactif** *m* OPTIQUE interactive videodisc (BrE), interactive videodisk (AmE); ~ **laser** *m* OPTIQUE laser videodisc (BrE), laser videodisk (AmE); ~ **numérique** *m* OPTIQUE digital videodisc (BrE), digital videodisk (AmE), digitally-encoded videodisc (BrE), digitally-encoded videodisk (AmE); ~ **optique** *m* OPTIQUE optical videodisc (BrE), optical videodisk (AmE); ~ **synchrone** *m* OPTIQUE synchronous videodisc (BrE), synchronous videodisk (AmE)

vidéofréquence[1] *adj* PHYSIQUE video frequency

vidéofréquence[2] *f* TELECOM, TV video frequency

vidéographie *f* INFORMAT, ORDINAT, TELECOM videography; ~ **interactive** *f* INFORMAT, ORDINAT videotex, TELECOM interactive videography, videotex

vide-ordures *m* RECYCLAGE garbage chute (AmE), rubbish chute (BrE)

vidéo-sur-vidéo *adj* TV E-E, E-to-E, electronic-to-electronic

vidéotex *m* INFORMAT, ORDINAT, TELECOM videotex; ~ **interactif** *m* TELECOM interactive videotex

vidéothèque *f* TV videotape library

vidéotransmission *f* TELECOM video transmission

vider *vt* DISTRI EAU *l'eau d'une cuve* run off, ELECTRON evacuate, MECANIQUE drain, NAUT bail out, PHYS FLUID bail, bail out

videur: ~ **d'arche** *m* CERAM VER lehr assistant; ~ **de moule** *m* CERAM VER mold emptier (AmE), mould emptier (BrE)

vide-vite *m* AERONAUT fuel dump valve, jettison valve, ESPACE *véhicules* fuel dump valve, jettison valve

vidicon *m* ELECTRON vidicon; ~ **intensificateur** *m* ELECTRON intensifier vidicon

vie *f* MINES *d'une mine* life, lifetime, QUALITE life; ~ **aquatique** *f* DISTRI EAU aquatic life; ~ **atmosphérique** *f* POLLUTION atmospheric lifetime; ~ **du combustible dans le coeur** *f* NUCLEAIRE in-core fuel life; ~ **en pot** *f* PLAST CAOU *adhésifs* pot life; ~ **extra-terrestre** *f* ASTRONOMIE, ESPACE extraterrestrial life; ~ **moyenne** *f* PHYSIQUE average life, lifetime, mean life; ~ **opérationnelle** *f* ESPACE *véhicules* service life

vieilles: ~ **fontes** *f pl* PRODUCTION cast scrap, foundry scrap, scrap; ~ **fontes de poterie** *f pl* PRODUCTION pot scrap

vieilli *adj* MATERIAUX, THERMODYN aged

vieillir *vt* METALL, PAPIER, THERMODYN age

vieillissement *m* CINEMAT *d'une pellicule*, CONSTR, CRISTALL *d'un alliage*, ELECTR *matériel*, EMBALLAGE, IMPRIM *papier, film, chimie*, PAPIER, PLAST CAOU *peintures, plastiques*, TELECOM ageing (BrE), aging

(AmE); ~ **accéléré** *m* PRODUCTION, THERMODYN *métal* artificial ageing (BrE), artificial aging (AmE); ~ **après trempe** *m* METALL, NUCLEAIRE quench ageing (BrE), quench aging (AmE); ~ **en étuve** *m* PLAST CAOU *procédé* oven ageing (BrE), oven aging (AmE); ~ **étagé** *m* PLAST CAOU interrupted ageing (BrE), interrupted aging (AmE); ~ **naturel** *m* METALL, PLAST CAOU *plastiques, peintures* natural ageing (BrE), natural aging (AmE); ~ **par écrouissage** *m* RESSORTS age hardening; ~ **préalable** *m* TELECOM preageing; ~ **progressif** *m* PLAST CAOU *plastiques, caoutchouc, revêtements* progressive ageing (BrE), progressive aging (AmE); ~ **thermique** *m* PLAST CAOU heat ageing

vierge *adj* INFORMAT, ORDINAT blank, virgin

Vierge *f* ASTRONOMIE *constellation zodiacale* The Virgin, Virgo

vieux: ~ **papiers** *m pl* PAPIER, RECYCLAGE waste paper; ~ **sable** *m* PRODUCTION floor sand, heap sand

vif *adj* CONS MECA sharp, sharp-edged

vif-argent *m* CHIMIE quicksilver

vigie[1] *f* NAUT lookout; ~ **de frein** *f* CH DE FER *véhicules* brake cabin

vigie:[2] **être de** ~ *vi* NAUT keep a lookout

Vigneron-Dahl *m* (*VD*) OCEANO Vigneron-Dahl trawl

vignettage *m* CINEMAT vignetting

vignette *f* CINEMAT mask, IMPRIM *pour livres* vignette, *typographie* fleuron; ~ **typographique représentant une main** *f* IMPRIM composition fist

vilebrequin *m* AUTO crankshaft, CONS MECA bit brace, bit stock, crankshaft, stock, CONSTR *pour forerie* brace, MECANIQUE, NAUT, VEHICULES *moteur* crankshaft; ~ **à cliquet** *m* CONSTR ratchet, ratchet brace; ~ **à conscience** *m* CONS MECA breast drill

vinasse: ~ **de distillerie** *f* AGRO ALIM distillery residue

vinique *adj* CHIMIE *alcool, éther* vinic

vinylacétylène *m* CHIMIE vinylacetylene

vinylation *f* CHIMIE vinylation

vinylbenzène *m* CHIMIE vinylbenzene

vinyle *m* CHIMIE vinyl

vinylidène *m* CHIMIE vinylidene

vinylite *f* CHIMIE vinylite

vinylogue[1] *adj* CHIMIE vinylogous

vinylogue[2] *m* CHIMIE vinylog

vinylpyridine *f* CHIMIE vinylpyridine

violation: ~ **de code** *f* TELECOM CV, code violation; ~ **de la parité** *f* PHYSIQUE nonconservation of parity

viole *f* CONSTR timber jack

violurique *adj* CHIMIE violuric

virage *m* CINEMAT dye toning, toning, CONSTR *d'une grue* slewing round, slewing, swinging round, turning, PHOTO dye toning, toning; ~ **dérapé** *m* AERONAUT flat turn; ~ **en deux bains** *m* PHOTO two-bath toning; ~ **en montée** *m* AERONAUT climb turn; ~ **en sépia** *m* PHOTO sepia toning; ~ **à l'or** *m* PHOTO gold toning; ~ **par sulfuration** *m* PHOTO sulfide toning (AmE), sulphide toning (BrE); ~ **à plat** *m* AERONAUT flat turn; ~ **de procédure** *m* AERONAUT landing pattern turn; ~ **serré** *m* AERONAUT steep turn

virement: ~ **électronique** *m* INFORMAT, ORDINAT electronic funds transfer

virer[1] *vt* IMPRIM tone

virer[2] *vi* AERONAUT bank, ESPACE *véhicules* bank, turn, NAUT cast, turn, veer, *navire* heave; ~ **de bord** *vi* NAUT go about, tack; ~ **vent arrière** *vi* NAUT wear

vireur *m* NAUT turning gear, NUCLEAIRE slewing gear, turning gear

virgule *f* CONS MECA lifter, wipe, wiper, IMPRIM comma; ~ **décimale** *f* INFORMAT, MATH, ORDINAT decimal point, PHYSIQUE point; ~ **fixe** *f* INFORMAT, TELECOM fixed point; ~ **flottante** *f* INFORMAT, TELECOM floating point

viridine *f* CHIMIE viridine

virole *f* CHARBON shell, CONS MECA clip, MECANIQUE collar, ferrule, NUCLEAIRE *d'un échangeur de chaleur*, PAPIER shell, PRODUCTION strake, thimble, *de corps cylindrique, d'une chaudière* shell plate, TELECOM ferrule; ~ **d'air de combustion** *f* CONS MECA *d'un brûleur à gaz* air regulator; ~ **conique** *f* ESPACE *véhicules* conical shell, shroud; ~ **de corps** *f* NUCLEAIRE shell course, shell section; ~ **cylindrique** *f* ESPACE *véhicules* cylindrical shell; ~ **intérieure de réacteur** *f* AERONAUT inner engine shroud; ~ **de raccordement** *f* CONS MECA coupling ring; ~ **supérieure** *f* NUCLEAIRE upper shell assembly

virtuel *adj* INFORMAT, ORDINAT virtual

virure *f* NAUT strake; ~ **d'aération** *f* NAUT air course; ~ **d'axe** *f* NAUT king plank; ~ **de bouchain** *f* NAUT bilge strake; ~ **de carreau** *f* NAUT sheerstrake; ~ **de galbord** *f* NAUT garboard strake; ~ **de gouttière** *f* NAUT deck stringer; ~ **d'hiloire** *f* NAUT tie plate; ~ **de quille** *f* NAUT keel strake

virus *m* INFORMAT, ORDINAT virus

vis *f* CONS MECA, MECANIQUE, NAUT, PAPIER, PLAST CAOU *extrudeuse*, VEHICULES screw; ~ **d'accord** *f* PHYSIQUE tuning screw; ~ **d'adaptation** *f* ELECTROTEC *d'impédance* tuning screw; ~ **ailée** *f* CONS MECA butterfly screw, thumbscrew, wing screw, winged screw, CONSTR butterfly screw; ~ **à ailettes** *f* CONSTR butterfly screw; ~ **d'ajustage** *f* COMMANDE adjusting screw, adjustment screw; ~ **Allen à tête hexagonale** *f* IMPRIM *mécanique* Allen screw; ~ **d'Archimède** *f* INST HYDR *convoyage de liquides ou de solides granuleux* Archimedeans c r e w, Archimedes' screw; ~ **d'arrêt** *f* PRODUCTION clamp screw, clamping screw; ~ **arrêtoir** *f* CONS MECA footscrew, leveling screw (AmE), levelling screw (BrE); ~ **d'assemblage** *f* CONS MECA connecting screw; ~ **à billes** *f* CONS MECA ball screw; ~ **de blocage** *f* CONS MECA lock screw, PRODUCTION clamp screw, clamping screw, setscrew; ~ **de blocage du mouvement approximatif de latitude** *f* INSTRUMENT latitude coarse motion clamp; ~ **de blocage du mouvement en site** *f* INSTRUMENT vertical clamp; ~ **de blocage du réglage approximatif d'azimut** *f* INSTRUMENT azimuth coarse motion clamp; ~ **à bois** *f* CONSTR wood screw; ~ **à bois en laiton à tête ronde** *f* CONSTR brass round head woodscrew; ~ **à bois pointé à tête carrée** *f* CONSTR pointed square head coach screw; ~ **à bois à tête carrée** *f* CONSTR lag screw; ~ **à bois à tête plate fraisée** *f* CONSTR countersunk woodscrew; ~ **à bois à tête plate rayée** *f* CONSTR countersunk woodscrew; ~ **de borne cruciforme** *f* PRODUCTION terminal screw; ~ **de bride** *f* CONS MECA footscrew, leveling screw (AmE), levelling screw (BrE); ~ **de butée** *f* PHOTO, PRODUCTION stop screw; ~ **du butée du papillon** *f* VEHICULES *carburateur* throttle stop screw; ~ **cachée** *f* CONS MECA *d'un étau, ou analogue* protected screw; ~ **de calage** *f* CONS MECA footscrew, leveling screw (AmE), levelling screw (BrE); ~ **calante** *f* COMMANDE adjusting screw, adjustment screw, CONS MECA footscrew, leveling screw(AmE), levelling screw (BrE), INSTRUMENT levelling screw; ~ **de carrosserie** *f* CONS MECA coach screw; ~ **de centrage** *f* CONS MECA centering screw (AmE), centring screw (BrE); ~ **de changement de marche** *f* CONS MECA reversing screw; ~ **à collerette** *f* CONS MECA flanged bolt; ~ **de commande de compteur de vitesse** *f* AUTO speedometer drive gear; ~ **de couvercle protégé** *f* PRODUCTION shrouded cover screw; ~ **creuse** *f* CONS MECA hollow bolt, inside screw, PRODUCTION inside screw; ~ **de culasse** *f* CONS MECA cylinder head stud, MILITAIRE breech screw; ~ **décolletée** *f* CONS MECA bright bolt; ~ **différentielle** *f* CONS MECA compound screw; ~ **à droite** *f* CONS MECA right-hand screw, right-handed screw; ~ **élévatoire** *f* INST HYDR Archimedean screw, Archimedes' screw; ~ **à empreinte cruciforme** *f* CONS MECA cruciform head fastener; ~ **à empreinte Phillips** *f* (MD) CONS MECA Phillips screw (TM); ~ **à empreinte Posidriv** *f* (MD) CONS MECA Posidriv screw (TM); ~ **en blanc** *f* CONS MECA screw blank; ~ **d'encrier** *f* IMPRIM *machine* fountain screw; ~ **en laiton** *f* CONS MECA brass screw; ~ **d'épinglage** *f* CONS MECA locating screw; ~ **d'établi** *f* CONSTR bench screw; ~ **femelle** *f* CONS MECA inside screw, PRODUCTION internal screw; ~ **à fente** *f* CONS MECA slotted screw; ~ **à un filet** *f* CONS MECA single-threaded screw; ~ **à filet carré** *f* CONS MECA square thread screw, square-threaded screw; ~ **à filet droite et gauche** *f* CONS MECA right-and-left screw; ~ **à filet rectangulaire** *f* CONS MECA square thread screw, square-threaded screw; ~ **à filets convergents** *f* PRODUCTION hourglass screw; ~ **à filet triangulaire** *f* CONS MECA, MECANIQUE V-threaded screw; ~ **de fixation** *f* CONS MECA, CONSTR fixing screw; ~ **de fixation du distributeur** *f* AUTO distributor clamp bolt; ~ **de fixation pour tête de trépied** *f* CINEMAT tripod screw; ~ **fraise** *f* CONS MECA hob; ~ **globique** *f* PRODUCTION hourglass screw; ~ **globoïde** *f* PRODUCTION hourglass screw; ~ **imperdable** *f* CONS MECA captive screw; ~ **macrométrique** *f* INSTRUMENT coarse adjustment screw; ~ **mâle** *f* CONS MECA male screw, outside screw, PRODUCTION external screw; ~ **mécanique** *f* CONS MECA, PRODUCTION machine screw; ~ **mère** *f* CONS MECA *d'un tour*, PRODUCTION lead screw; ~ **à métaux** *f* CONS MECA, PRODUCTION machine screw; ~ **à métaux à collet carré** *f* CONS MECA square neck bolt; ~ **à métaux fendue à tête cylindrique** *f* CONS MECA slotted cheese-head screw; ~ **à métaux à tête bombée** *f* CONS MECA cup head bolt; ~ **micrométrique** *f* CONS MECA micrometer screw, INSTRUMENT fine adjustment; ~ **moletée** *f* CONS MECA knurled screw, thumbscrew; ~ **monte-et-baisse** *f* CONS MECA elevating screw; ~ **à mouvement lent de rotation** *f* CONS MECA slow-motion screw; ~ **à noyau plein** *f* CONSTR solid-newel stair; ~ **à oeil** *f* CONSTR capstan screw, capstan-headed screw; ~ **à oreilles** *f* CONS MECA butterfly screw, thumbscrew, wing screw, winged screw; ~ **de pas allongé** *f* CONS MECA, CONSTR long pitch screw; ~ **à pas carré** *f* CONS MECA square thread screw, square-threaded screw; ~ **à pas contraires** *f* CONS MECA compound screw, right-and-left screw; ~ **à pas couché de haute précision** *f* CONS MECA finely-threaded micrometer screw; ~ **à pas fin** *f* CONSTR fine pitch screw; ~ **à pas rapide** *f* CONS MECA long pitch screw, CONSTR coarse pitch screw; ~ **platinée** *f* AUTO contact breaker point (BrE), points (AmE), MECANIQUE *véhicules* ignition point; ~ **pleine** *f* CONS MECA male screw, outside screw, PRODUCTION external screw; ~ **à plusieurs filets** *f* PRODUCTION multiple-threaded screw; ~ **pneumatique** *f* MINES screw fan; ~ **à pompe** *f* CONS MECA shrouding screw; ~

préfiletée *f* EMBALLAGE continuous thread, ct; ~ de pression *f* CONS MECA pressure screw, setscrew; ~ de purge *f* AUTO bleeder screw; ~ de rallonge *f* MINES *du câble de forage* temper screw; ~ de rappel *f* CONS MECA drag screw, draw screw, temper screw, MECANIQUE drag screw; ~ de rappel du mouvement en azimut *f* INSTRUMENT horizontal tangent screw; ~ de rappel du mouvement en site *f* INSTRUMENT vertical tangent screw; ~ de rappel pour le mouvement lent *f* CONS MECA slow-motion adjusting screw; ~ de réglage *f* COMMANDE adjusting screw, adjustment screw, regulating screw, CONS MECA adjusting screw, regulating screw, IMPRIM *mécanique*, MECANIQUE, PRODUCTION adjusting screw; ~ de réglage de la bulle *f* CONSTR *d'un instrument de nivellement* bubble nut; ~ de réglage du condensateur *f* INSTRUMENT condenser adjustment knob; ~ de réglage de hausse *f* INSTRUMENT elevation adjusting screw; ~ de réglage latéral *f* INSTRUMENT windage adjustment screw; ~ de réglage de ralenti *f* AUTO, VEHICULES *carburateur* idle adjustment screw; ~ régulatrice *f* COMMANDE adjusting screw, adjustment screw, regulating screw; ~ sans fin *f* CONS MECA endless screw, perpetual screw, MECANIQUE worm; ~ sans tête *f* CONS MECA grub screw, set screw, MECANIQUE headless screw; ~ sans tête fendue *f* CONS MECA slotted headless screw; ~ sans tête à six pans *f* CONS MECA hexagon socket screw with flat point; ~ sans tête à tige lisse *f* CONS MECA grub screw; ~ de serrage *f* CONS MECA tightening screw; ~ à six pans creux *f* CONS MECA, MECANIQUE hexagon socket screw; ~ tangente *f* CONS MECA tangent screw; ~ taraudeuse à bout plat *f* CONS MECA flat and self-tapping screw; ~ de tension *f* CONS MECA straining screw, stretching screw, tension screw, union screw; ~ de tension en bout *f* PRODUCTION terminal tensioning screw; ~ à tête bombée *f* CONS MECA saucer head screw; ~ à tête cylindrique *f* CONS MECA head cap screw, CONSTR cheese head screw, pan head screw, MECANIQUE, PRODUCTION cheese head screw; ~ à tête cylindrique bombée *f* CONS MECA, PRODUCTION fillister head machine screw; ~ à tête cylindrique bombée large *f* CONS MECA pan head screw; ~ à tête cylindrique bombée large à empreinte cruciforme *f* CONS MECA cross-recessed pan head screw; ~ à tête cylindrique forcée *f* CONS MECA drilled fillister head screw; ~ à tête en goutte-de-suif *f* CONS MECA raised head screw; ~ à tête fendue *f* CONS MECA slotted head screw; ~ à tête fraisée *f* CONSTR, MECANIQUE countersunk head screw; ~ à tête fraisée bombée *f* CONS MECA oval head screw; ~ à tête hexagonale *f* MECANIQUE hexagon head screw; ~ à tête noyée *f* CONS MECA countersunk screw; ~ à tête plate *f* PRODUCTION binding head screw, pan head screw; ~ à tête rectangulaire *f* CONS MECA hammer head screw, square head screw; ~ à tête romaine *f* CONSTR capstan screw, capstan-headed screw; ~ à tête ronde *f* CONS MECA round-headed screw; ~ à tête saillante *f* CONS MECA raised head screw; ~ à tête à six pans *f* PRODUCTION hexagon head screw; ~ à téton *f* CONS MECA teat screw, tit screw; ~ à tôle *f* CONS MECA sheet metal screw; ~ à tôle à tête cylindrique large fendue *f* CONS MECA slotted pan head tapping screw; ~ à tôle à tête fraisée fendue *f* CONS MECA slotted countersunk head tapping screw; ~ transporteuse *f* PRODUCTION screw conveyor, spiral conveyor; ~ à trois filets *f* CONS MECA three-threaded screw

vis-bouchon: ~ d'un orifice de purge *f* CONS MECA bleed screw

viscine *f* CHIMIE viscin

viscocoupleur *m* VEHICULES *transmission* viscous clutch

visco-élasticité *f* PLAST CAOU viscoelasticity

viscomètre *m* EQUIP LAB *instrument*, GENIE CHIM, PETROLE, PHYS FLUID, PHYSIQUE, PLAST CAOU *instrument* viscometer, viscosimeter; ~ capillaire *m* CHIMIE, EQUIP LAB capillary viscometer, capillary viscosimeter; ~ à chute de bille *m* EQUIP LAB *viscosité des liquides* falling sphere viscometer

viscoplastique *adj* GAZ, MATERIAUX viscoplastic

viscoréducteur *m* PETROLE visbreaker

viscose *f* CHIMIE viscose

viscosimètre *m* EQUIP LAB *instrument*, GENIE CHIM, PETROLE, PHYS FLUID, PHYSIQUE, PLAST CAOU *instrument* viscometer, viscosimeter; ~ capillaire *m* CHIMIE, EQUIP LAB *débit d'un liquide* capillary viscometer, capillary viscosimeter; ~ type Ostwald *m* EQUIP LAB *viscosité de liquides* Ostwald viscometer

viscosité *f* AGRO ALIM ropiness, CHARBON viscosity, CHIMIE thickness, viscidity, viscosity, GAZ, MATERIAUX, PETR, PETROLE viscosity, PHYS FLUID viscidity, viscosity, PHYSIQUE, PLAST CAOU, THERMODYN viscosity; ~ absolue *f* MATERIAUX absolute viscosity; ~ Brookfield *f* PLAST CAOU Brookfield viscosity; ~ cinématique *f* EN RENOUV, MECANIQUE *matériaux*, PHYS FLUID, PHYSIQUE, REFRIG kinematic viscosity; ~ dynamique *f* EN RENOUV, PHYS FLUID, PHYSIQUE, PLAST CAOU dynamic viscosity; ~ intrinsèque *f* PHYS FLUID intrinsic viscosity; ~ Mooney *f* PLAST CAOU Mooney viscosity; ~ relative *f* PHYS FLUID relative viscosity

viscostatique *adj* CHIMIE viscostatic

visée *f* CONSTR observation, sight, sighting, NAUT sight; ~ optique *f* ESPACE *mesures* optical sight; ~ réflexe *f* CINEMAT through-the-lens reflex

viser *vt* PHOTO *un appareil photographique* sight

viseur *m* CINEMAT finder, viewfinder, ESPACE viewfinder, INSTRUMENT sight, PHOTO finder, viewfinder; ~ de bombardement *m* MILITAIRE bombsight; ~ à cadre lumineux *m* PHOTO bright line viewfinder; ~ à capuchon *m* PHOTO viewfinder with hood; ~ à chambre noire *m* PHOTO reflecting viewfinder; ~ à champ variable *m* CINEMAT director's finder, multifocal finder; ~ coudé *m* CINEMAT angular viewfinder; ~ donnant une image redressée *m* PHOTO erect image viewfinder; ~ de l'écran fluorescent *m* INSTRUMENT final image tube; ~ électronique *m* TV camera monitor; ~ gyroscopique de tir *m* MILITAIRE gyroscopic sight; ~ à image redressée *m* PHOTO reversal finder; ~ à imagerie thermique *m* THERMODYN thermal-imaging sight; ~ inversé *m* CINEMAT reversal finder; ~ latéral *m* CINEMAT offset viewfinder, side finder; ~ de mine *m* MINES lining sight; ~ multifocal *m* CINEMAT director's finder, multifocal finder, zoom viewfinder; ~ multiformat *m* PHOTO universal viewfinder; ~ obscur *m* PHOTO reflecting viewfinder; ~ optique *m* IMPRIM optical viewfinder; ~ orientable *m* CINEMAT orientable viewfinder; ~ pliant *m* PHOTO collapsible finder; ~ de la première image *m* INSTRUMENT intermediate-image screen; ~ redresseur *m* CINEMAT reversal finder; ~ reflex *m* PHOTO reflex viewfinder; ~ à renvoi d'angle *m* PHOTO right angle finder; ~ sans parallaxe *m* CINEMAT direct viewfinder, parallax-free viewfinder; ~ sportif *m* PHOTO sports finder; ~ thermoscopique *m* THERMODYN thermal-imaging sight

visibilité:[1] en ~ *adv* TELECOM line of sight

visibilité[2] *f* METEO, NAUT, PHYSIQUE visibility; ~ **de dépassement** *f* TRANSPORT passing sight distance; ~ **en vol** *f* AERONAUT flight visibility; ~ **au sol** *f* AERONAUT ground visibility

visible *m* OPTIQUE, TELECOM visible light

visière *f* SECURITE face visor, visor, *en celluloïd* eyeshade; ~ **de protection** *f* SECURITE safety visor

visioconférence *f* ESPACE, TELECOM videoconference

visionnage *m* TV monitoring

visionner *vt* CINEMAT *un film* project, screen, view, TV preview

visionneuse *f* CINEMAT print viewer; ~ **à pile sèche** *f* PHOTO battery-powered viewer; ~ **pour diapositives** *f* PHOTO slide viewer

visiophone *m* TELECOM videophone

visite *f* CONS MECA check, NAUT *navire* surveying, PRODUCTION, SECURITE inspection; ~ **après-vol** *f* AERONAUT postflying check; ~ **de la chaudière** *f* SECURITE boiler inspection

vis-mère *f* CONS MECA feed screw, lead screw, guide screw, leading screw, MECANIQUE feed screw, lead screw; ~ **à billes** *f* CONS MECA ball circulating lead screw, circulating ball lead screw

visqueux *adj* AGRO ALIM viscous, CHIMIE thick, viscid, viscous, PHYS FLUID viscid, viscous, PHYSIQUE viscous

vissage *m* CONS MECA screwing, screwing up, PETROLE screwing in, screwing up, screwing

vissé *adj* CONS MECA, MATERIAUX screwed

visser[1] *vt* CONS MECA screw, CONSTR drive, drive in, MECANIQUE screw

visser:[2] **se ~** *v réfl* CONS MECA, PRODUCTION thread

visserie *f* CONSTR nut and bolt works, nuts and bolts, PRODUCTION screw works

visseuse: ~ **autonome à batterie** *f* CONS MECA cordless power screwdriver

visu *m* ORDINAT display device, PHYSIQUE visual display unit, TV video display unit

visualisation *f* ELECTRON imaging, ESPACE display, IMPRIM *épreuves, observations* viewing, INFORMAT display, visualization, ORDINAT display, visualization; ~ **à balayage cavalier** *f* ELECTRON directed beam display; ~ **des cartes électriques** *f* NAUT electronic chart display; ~ **de défaut** *f* TELECOM fault display; ~ **par flux d'électrons** *f* ELECTRON electron imaging; ~ **radar** *f* AERONAUT radar display; ~ **tête basse** *f* AERONAUT, ESPACE *véhicules* head-down display; ~ **tête haute** *f* AERONAUT, ESPACE *véhicules* head-up display

visualiser *vt* ELECTRON, ESPACE, TELECOM display

visuel *m* ORDINAT display device, PHYSIQUE visual display unit

vit: ~ **de mulet** *m* NAUT gooseneck

vitelline *f* CHIMIE vitellin

vitesse *f* ACOUSTIQUE, CONS MECA, ELECTRON, HYDROLOGIE *d'un courant*, MECANIQUE velocity, PAPIER speed, PHYS ONDES velocity, PHYSIQUE speed, velocity, TEXTILE, TRANSPORT speed;
~ **a** ~ **absolue** *f* MECANIQUE absolute velocity; ~ **absolue de l'eau** *f* EN RENOUV absolute water velocity; ~ **d'absorption** *f* DISTRI EAU rate of absorption; ~ **d'accès** *f* ELECTROTEC access speed; ~ **d'accroissement du courant** *f* ELECTROTEC rate of current rise; ~ **d'accroissement de la tension** *f* ELECTROTEC rate of voltage rise; ~ **acoustique de référence** *f* ACOUSTIQUE reference sound velocity; ~ **acquise** *f* INST HYDR velocity head; ~ **adiabatique** *f* THERMODYN *refroidissement, échauffement* adiabatic lapse rate; ~ **de l'air** *f* MAT CHAUFF air velocity; ~ **anémométrique** *f* AERONAUT airspeed; ~ **angulaire** *f* CONS MECA, ELECTROTEC, EN RENOUV, ESPACE, PHYSIQUE angular velocity; ~ **angulaire constante** *f* OPTIQUE, ORDINAT CAV, constant angular velocity; ~ **angulaire de lacet** *f* AERONAUT angular yaw rate; ~ **angulaire de précession** *f* EN RENOUV angular velocity of precession; ~ **angulaire de rotation de rotor** *f* AERONAUT angular rotor speed; ~ **angulaire de roulis** *f* AERONAUT angular roll rate; ~ **angulaire de tangage** *f* AERONAUT angular pitch rate; ~ **angulaire de virage** *f* AERONAUT rate of turn; ~ **apparente** *f* GEOPHYS apparent velocity; ~ **d'approche** *f* AERONAUT, ESPACE, TRANSPORT approach speed; ~ **d'approche à l'atterrissage** *f* AERONAUT, ESPACE landing approach speed; ~ **d'approche de référence** *f* AERONAUT reference landing approach speed; ~ **ascensionnelle** *f* AERONAUT climbing speed, rate of climb, ESPACE *véhicules* RC, rate of climb, climbing speed; ~ **d'attente** *f* AERONAUT holding speed; ~ **d'atterrissage** *f* AERONAUT, TRANSPORT landing speed; ~ **d'aube** *f* EN RENOUV vane velocity; ~ **des aubes** *f* EN RENOUV blade speed; ~ **d'auge** *f* EN RENOUV bucket velocity; ~ **d'avance du chariot porte-outil** *f* CONS MECA saddle feed rate; ~ **d'avancement** *f* PETROLE drilling rate, rate of penetration; ~ **d'avancement normalisée** *f* PETROLE NDR, *forage* normalized drilling rate; ~ **axiale** *f* EN RENOUV axial velocity;
~ **b** ~ **badin** *f* AERONAUT indicated air speed; ~ **de balayage** *f* AERONAUT scanning rate, scanning speed, INFORMAT, ORDINAT scanning rate, scanning speed, TV scanning speed; ~ **de bande** *f* TV tape speed;
~ **c** ~ **de cabrage** *f* AERONAUT rotation speed; ~ **de calcul** *f* AERONAUT *navigabilité* design airspeed; ~ **de calcul d'atterrissage** *f* AERONAUT design landing speed; ~ **de calcul en air turbulent** *f* AERONAUT *navigabilité* design rough air speed; ~ **de calcul en atmosphère agitée** *f* AERONAUT design rough air speed; ~ **de calcul en croisière** *f* AERONAUT *navigabilité* design cruising speed; ~ **de calcul en piqué** *f* AERONAUT *navigabilité* design diving speed; ~ **de calcul pour l'intensité de rafale maximale** *f* AERONAUT *navigabilité* design speed for maximum gust intensity; ~ **de calcul volets sortis** *f* AERONAUT *navigabilité* design flaps extended speed; ~ **de cale à cale** *f* TRANSPORT block speed; ~ **de la chaîne de fabrication** *f* EMBALLAGE line speed; ~ **de choc** *f* METALL impact velocity; ~ **circonférentielle du rotor** *f* AERONAUT *hélicoptère* rotor tip velocity; ~ **de cisaillement** *f* PLAST CAOU rate of shear, shear rate; ~ **de combustion** *f* THERMODYN rate of combustion; ~ **commerciale** *f* AERONAUT block speed, PRODUCTION average speed including stoppages, TRANSPORT block speed, schedule speed; ~ **de commutation** *f* ELECTROTEC switching speed; ~ **de conception** *f* TRANSPORT design speed; ~ **de congélation** *f* REFRIG freezing rate; ~ **constante** *f* TRANSPORT constant speed; ~ **de conversion** *f* ELECTRON conversion rate; ~ **de coordination** *f* TRANSPORT progression speed; ~ **corrigée** *f* AERONAUT calibrated airspeed; ~ **corrigée en vol** *f* AERONAUT *au cours d'une manoeuvre de décrochage normale* minimum calibrated speed; ~ **cosmique** *f* ESPACE cosmic velocity; ~ **de coupe** *f* CONS MECA cutting speed; ~ **du courant** *f* NAUT current rate; ~ **de crête** *f* DISTRI EAU peak velocity; ~ **critique** *f* AERONAUT, ESPACE, MECANIQUE critical speed, PHYSIQUE critical velocity, TRANSPORT critical speed; ~ **critique de croissance** *f* MATERIAUX critical growth

rate; ~ **de croisière** f AERONAUT, NAUT cruising speed;
~ d ~ **de décantation** f GENIE CHIM decantation rate, decantation speed, settling speed; ~ **de décision** f *(V1)* AERONAUT decision speed *(V1)*; ~ **de décollage** f AERONAUT takeoff speed, unstick speed; ~ **de décroissance** f ELECTRON decay rate; ~ **de défilement** f ACOUSTIQUE groove speed, tape speed, ENREGISTR running speed, tape speed, TV tape speed; ~ **de déplacement** f NUCLEAIRE rate of travel; ~ **de déplacement de la table** f CONS MECA table traverse speed; ~ **de déplacement traverse** f PHYSIQUE crosshead displacement rate; ~ **de dépôt** f GENIE CHIM decantation rate, decantation speed, POLLUTION deposition velocity; ~ **de dérive** f METALL drift velocity; ~ **descensionnelle** f AERONAUT rate of descent; ~ **de détonation** f MINES VOD, detonation velocity, velocity of detonation; ~ **de dislocation** f METALL dislocation velocity; ~ **de durcissement** f PLAST CAOU *plastiques* rate of cure;
~ e ~ **d'eau relative** f EN RENOUV relative water velocity; ~ **économique** f NAUT economical speed; ~ **d'écoulement** f CHARBON, HYDROLOGIE velocity of flow, PHYS FLUID flow speed, REFRIG velocity of flow; ~ **d'écriture** f ELECTRON writing speed; ~ **effective de marche** f MECANIQUE actual running speed; ~ **d'éjection** f ESPACE *propulsion* jet velocity; ~ **d'emballement** f EN RENOUV *turbines* runaway speed; ~ **en amont** f PHYSIQUE free stream velocity; ~ **en DIN** f PHOTO *rapidité d'émulsion, standard industriel Allemand* DIN speed; ~ **en fin de combustion** f ESPACE *propulsion* burnout velocity; ~ **en surface** f NAUT surface speed; ~ **d'entraînement** f METALL drift velocity; ~ **d'entrée** f INST HYDR inlet velocity; ~ **d'envol** f AERONAUT liftoff speed; ~ **équivalente au sol** f AERONAUT equivalent airspeed; ~ **d'essai** f ESSAIS test speed, NAUT trial speed; ~ **d'expansion** f GEOLOGIE spreading rate; ~ **d'exploration** f AERONAUT *radar* scanning speed; ~ **d'expulsion** f PETROLE expulsion rate;
~ f ~ **faible** f TELECOM low-speed; ~ **de figeage** f CERAM VER setting rate; ~ **de fissuration** f METALL crack velocity; ~ **de fluage** f MATERIAUX creep rate, PLAST CAOU rate of flow; ~ **de fuite** f ASTRONOMIE recession velocity; ~ **Furling** f EN RENOUV *énergie éolienne* Furling speed;
~ g ~ **génératrice** f EN RENOUV generator speed; ~ **de glissement** f MATERIAUX *cristallographie* slip rate; ~ **de groupe** f ACOUSTIQUE, GEOPHYS, OPTIQUE, PHYSIQUE group velocity, TELECOM envelope velocity, group velocity, TRANSPORT group velocity;
~ h ~ **hypersonique** f PHYSIQUE hypersonic speed;
~ i ~ **idéale** f EN RENOUV ideal velocity; ~ **d'impression** f INFORMAT, ORDINAT print speed; ~ **indiquée** f AERONAUT indicated airspeed; ~ **infrasonique** f PHYSIQUE infrasonic speed; ~ **initiale** f ESPACE *propulsion* initial velocity; ~ **d'inscription** f ELECTRON writing speed; ~ **instantanée** f TRANSPORT spot speed;
~ l ~ **de lacet** f ESPACE *véhicules* yaw rate; ~ **de lecture** f ENREGISTR playback speed, INFORMAT, ORDINAT reading rate; ~ **au lever des roues** f AERONAUT unstick speed; ~ **de libération** f ASTRONOMIE, ESPACE, PHYSIQUE escape velocity; ~ **limite** f AERONAUT, ESPACE, PHYSIQUE terminal velocity; ~ **limite d'impact** f AERONAUT limit rate of descent at touchdown; ~ **limite de piqué** f AERONAUT design diving speed; ~ **linéaire constante** f OPTIQUE, ORDINAT CLV, constant linear velocity; ~ **linéaire du sillon** f ENREGISTR groove speed;

~ **de la lumière** f PHYS ONDES speed of light;
~ m ~ **de marche** f NAUT cruising speed, TRANSPORT running speed; ~ **de maturation** f CONSTR rate of curing; ~ **maximale** f AERONAUT, NAUT maximum speed; ~ **maximale de l'arbre** f EN RENOUV *énergie éolienne* maximum shaft speed; ~ **maximale en exploitation** f AERONAUT maximum permissible operating speed; ~ **maximale en palier au régime moteur nominal** f AERONAUT maximum speed in level flight with rated power; ~ **maximale permise** f TRANSPORT speed limit; ~ **maximale réalisable** f TRANSPORT operating speed; ~ **maximale au seuil** f AERONAUT maximum threshold speed; ~ **maximale de sortie du train d'atterrissage** f AERONAUT maximum landing gear operating speed; ~ **maximale de tenue mécanique** f PRODUCTION slew speed; ~ **maximale du train d'atterrissage sorti** f AERONAUT maximum landing gear extended speed; ~ **maximale volets sortis** f AERONAUT maximum flap extended speed; ~ **maximum de conception** f VEHICULES maximum design speed; ~ **du métier** f TEXTILE loom speed; ~ **de meule** f CONS MECA wheel spindle speed; ~ **de meule périphérique** f CONS MECA peripheral wheel speed; ~ **minimale de contrôle à l'approche** f AERONAUT minimum control speed during landing approach; ~ **minimale de contrôle en air libre** f AERONAUT minimum control speed in the air; ~ **minimale de contrôle au sol** f AERONAUT minimum control speed on the ground; ~ **minimale de déjaugeage** f AERONAUT minimum unstick speed; ~ **minimale de démonstration au seuil** f AERONAUT minimum demonstrated threshold speed; ~ **minimale de sécurité au décollage** f AERONAUT minimum takeoff safety speed; ~ **de montée** f AERONAUT climbing speed, rate of climb, ELECTRON edge rate, ELECTROTEC rate of rise; ~ **de montée de la charge** f METALL rate of loading; ~ **moyenne** f TRANSPORT mean speed; ~ **moyenne de marche** f TRANSPORT average running speed; ~ **moyenne de production** f IMPRIM average running speed; ~ **moyenne du vent** f EN RENOUV average wind speed, mean wind speed;
~ n ~ **nominale de rafale** f AERONAUT nominal gust velocity; ~ **nominale du vent** f EN RENOUV rated wind speed; ~ **de nucléation** f METALL nucleation rate; ~ **de numérisation** f ORDINAT scan rate;
~ o ~ **des ondes** f PHYS ONDES wave velocity; ~ **orbitale** f ASTRONOMIE orbital velocity;
~ p ~ **des pales** f EN RENOUV blade speed; ~ **parabolique** f ASTRONOMIE, ESPACE parabolic velocity; ~ **de parcours** f TRANSPORT overall travel speed; ~ **d'une particule** f ACOUSTIQUE particle velocity; ~ **périphérique** f AERONAUT circumferential speed, EN RENOUV peripheral velocity; ~ **de phase** f PETR, PHYSIQUE phase velocity; ~ **de pointe de volume** f ENREGISTR peak volume velocity; ~ **de précession** f ESPACE precession rate; ~ **de prise de vues** f CINEMAT camera speed; ~ **de projection** f CINEMAT projection speed; ~ **de propagation** f PHYS ONDES, TELECOM propagation velocity, THERMODYN *de la flamme* rate of spread; ~ **de propagation des fissures** f NUCLEAIRE crack propagation rate; ~ **de propagation de l'onde** f PHYS ONDES wave propagation speed; ~ **propre** f AERONAUT TAS, airspeed, true air speed;
~ q ~ **quadratique moyenne** f PHYSIQUE mean square velocity;
~ r ~ **radiale** f ASTRONOMIE, EN RENOUV radial velocity; ~ **de rafraîchissement** f INFORMAT, ORDINAT

refresh rate; ~ **de rapprochement** *f* NAUT closing speed; ~ **de réaction** *f* CHIMIE, METALL reaction rate; ~ **de rebobinage** *f* ORDINAT rewind speed; ~ **de récession** *f* ASTRONOMIE recession velocity; ~ **de réchauffement** *f* THERMODYN rate of heating; ~ **de recombinaison** *f* ELECTRON recombination rate; ~ **recommandée** *f* TRANSPORT recommended speed; ~ **réelle de transfert de données** *f* INFORMAT effective data transfer rate; ~ **de réembobinage** *f* INFORMAT rewind speed; ~ **de refroidissement** *f* REFRIG, THERMODYN rate of cooling; ~ **de régime** *f* CONS MECA working speed, TRANSPORT operating speed; ~ **de réglage** *f* COMMANDE regulating speed; ~ **relative** *f* CONS MECA, PHYSIQUE relative velocity; ~ **relative d'eau** *f* EN RENOUV relative water velocity; ~ **relative tête-bande** *f* TV head-to-tape speed; ~ **de réponse** *f* ELECTR *relais* closing speed; ~ **de restauration** *f* METALL recovery rate; ~ **retardée** *f* CONS MECA retarded velocity; ~ **de révolution orbitale** *f* PHYSIQUE orbital velocity; ~ **de rotation** *f* AERONAUT, CONS MECA rotation speed, EN RENOUV rotating speed, rotation speed, rotational speed, PETROLE rotating speed, rotation speed, VEHICULES revs;

~ s ~ **des sauts** *f* METALL jump rate; ~ **de séchage** *f* THERMODYN rate of drying; ~ **de sécurité** *f* AERONAUT, TRANSPORT safety speed; ~ **de sédimentation** *f* CERAM VER Stokes' velocity, CHARBON settling speed, GENIE CHIM decantation rate, decantation speed, settling speed, MATERIAUX, PETROLE sedimentation rate, POLLUTION deposition velocity, RECYCLAGE sedimentation rate; ~ **de signal enregistré** *f* ACOUSTIQUE recorded velocity; ~ **sismique** *f* GEOLOGIE, PETR seismic velocity; ~ **au sol** *f* AERONAUT ground speed; ~ **du son** *f* ACOUSTIQUE, PHYS ONDES velocity of sound; ~ **sonique** *f* PHYSIQUE speed of sound; ~ **de sortie** *f* INST HYDR exit velocity; ~ **spécifique** *f* EN RENOUV specific speed; ~ **supérieure à celle de la lumière** *f* ASTRONOMIE, PHYSIQUE superluminal velocity; ~ **supersonique** *f* PHYSIQUE supersonic speed; ~ **surface** *f* NAUT speed through the water; ~ **sur le fond** *f* NAUT speed over the ground; ~ **synchrone** *f* ELECTR *moteur*, EN RENOUV synchronous speed;

~ t ~ **tangentielle** *f* EN RENOUV tangential velocity; ~ **de toucher des roues** *f* AERONAUT touchdown speed; ~ **de tranche** *f* PETROLE *levé sismique* interval velocity; ~ **de transfert** *f* INFORMAT, ORDINAT transfer rate; ~ **de transfert de données** *f* INFORMAT, ORDINAT data transfer rate; ~ **de translation** *f* TRANSPORT translation speed; ~ **de transmission** *f* ELECTROTEC transmission rate, INFORMAT, ORDINAT transmission speed, PRODUCTION transmission rate, TELECOM transmission speed; ~ **de transmission de données** *f* ORDINAT data rate; ~ **de transmission en bauds** *f* INFORMAT, ORDINAT baud rate; ~ **transsonique** *f* AERONAUT, PHYSIQUE, TRANSPORT transonic speed; ~ **de travail** *f* CONS MECA working speed;

~ v ~ **des vagues** *f* OCEANO wave velocity; ~ **de variation de phase** *f* TELECOM phase change velocity; ~ **variée** *f* CONS MECA variable velocity; ~ **du vent** *f* EN RENOUV wind speed, wind velocity, METEO wind speed, wind velocity; ~ **du vent au cube** *f* EN RENOUV wind velocity cubed; ~ **du vent en entrée** *f* EN RENOUV cut-in wind speed; ~ **du vent en sortie** *f* EN RENOUV cutout wind speed; ~ **du vent résiduel** *f* EN RENOUV survival wind speed; ~ **verticale de descente** *f* AERONAUT rate of descent; ~ **de virage** *f* AERONAUT rate of turn; ~ **de**

vulcanisation *f* PLAST CAOU *caoutchouc* rate of cure

vitrage *m* CERAM VER, CONSTR, EN RENOUV *capteur plat* glazing; ~ **antiexplosion** *m* CERAM VER explosion-proof glazing; ~ **antiouragan** *m* CERAM VER antistorm glazing; ~ **athermique** *m* CERAM VER heat-absorbing glazing; ~ **double** *m* CERAM VER double glazing unit; ~ **multiple** *m* CERAM VER multiple glazing unit; ~ **solaire** *m* CERAM VER solar control glass

vitrail *m* CERAM VER stained glass window; ~ **au plomb** *m* CERAM VER leaded light

vitre *f* VEHICULES *carrosserie* window; ~ **arrière** *f* VEHICULES *carrosserie* rear window; ~ **de porte** *f* VEHICULES door glass; ~ **de visualisation** *f* REFRIG sight glass

vitrer *vt* CERAM VER glaze

vitrerie *f* CERAM VER glazing industry

vitreux *adj* CHIMIE vitreous, GEOLOGIE hyaline

vitrier *m* CONSTR glass cutter, glazier

vitrifiant *m* CERAM VER glass former

vitrification *f* CHIMIE vitrification

vitrifié *adj* CERAM VER fired-on, COULEURS glazed

vitrifier *vt* CERAM VER glaze, REVETEMENT glaze, vitrify

vitrine *f* CERAM VER display window, REFRIG display case; ~ **à basse température** *f* REFRIG low-temperature display case; ~ **frigorifique** *f* REFRIG refrigerated display cabinet, refrigerated showcase

vitriol *m* CHIMIE oil of vitriol, sulfuric acid (AmE), sulphuric acid (BrE), vitriol, vitriolic acid; ~ **bleu** *m* CHIMIE blue vitriol, bluestone; ~ **vert** *m* CHIMIE ferrous sulfate (AmE), ferrous sulphate (BrE), green vitriol

vitriolisation *f* CHIMIE vitriolization

vitrocéramique *f* CERAM VER, NUCLEAIRE glass ceramic

vitrofibre *f* EMBALLAGE glass wool

vitrorésine *f* CERAM VER organic glass

vive:[1] **à ~ arête** *adj* CONS MECA sharp, sharp-edged

vive[2] *f* OCEANO weever; ~ **arête** *f* CERAM VER sharp finish

vivianite *f* MINERAUX vivianite

vivier *m* OCEANO fish tank

VLA *abrév (très grand réseau d'antennes)* ASTRONOMIE VLA *(Very Large Array)*

VLBA *abrév (réseau d'antennes à très longue ligne de base)* ASTRONOMIE VLBA *(Very Long Baseline Array)*

vobulateur *m* ELECTRON wobbulator

vobulation *f* ELECTRON wobbulation

vocodeur *m* ORDINAT vocoder, TELECOM voice coder

vogésite *f* PETR vogesite (AmE), vogesyte (BrE)

voie:[1] **par ~ maritime** *adj* TRANSPORT seaborne

voie:[2] **par ~ de mer** *adv* NAUT by sea

voie[3] *f* AERONAUT *atterrisseur* tread, AUTO, CH DE FER track, CHIMIE method, process, way, CONS MECA set, CONSTR road, thoroughfare, way, ELECTRON subchannel, ELECTROTEC, ENREGISTR, INFORMAT channel, MECANIQUE *véhicules* track, MINES level, roadway, ORDINAT channel, TELECOM channel, path, TRANSPORT track, TV channel; ~ **d'accélération** *f* CONSTR acceleration lane; ~ **d'accès** *f* TELECOM access channel, TRANSPORT access road (AmE), slip road (BrE); ~ **d'acheminement** *f* TELECOM route; ~ **d'acheminement détourné** *f* TELECOM alternative route; ~ **d'air** *f* MINES airhead, airheading, ventilation drive, airway; ~ **analogique** *f* INFORMAT, ORDINAT analog channel; ~ **d'appel** *f* TELECOM calling channel; ~ **d'appel unilatéral** *f* TELECOM paging channel; ~ **d'approche** *f* AERONAUT landing lane; ~ **d'ascente** *f* CONSTR climbing lane; ~ **audio** *f* ENREGISTR audio channel; ~ **d'autobus équipée**

d'un **système de guidage** ƒ TRANSPORT bus lane equipped with guiding device; ~ **de caméra** ƒ TV CCU, camera control unit, camera channel; ~ **de chaînage** ƒ ORDINAT linkage path; ~ **de chargement** ƒ TRANSPORT loading siding; ~ **de circulation** ƒ AERONAUT *aéroport* taxiway, NAUT traffic lane; ~ **de circulation d'aire de trafic** ƒ AERONAUT apron taxiway; ~ **de classement** ƒ CH DE FER *véhicules* marshalling track (BrE), switching track (AmE), sorting siding; ~ **classique** ƒ CH DE FER standard track; ~ **de communication** ƒ INFORMAT, ORDINAT communication channel; ~ **de commutation** ƒ TV bus; ~ **de concentration des vides** ƒ CH DE FER empties siding; ~ **de contournement** ƒ CH DE FER loop line; ~ **de contrôle de réseau** ƒ INFORMAT, ORDINAT network control channel; ~ **de débranchement** ƒ CH DE FER siding; ~ **de décélération** ƒ TRANSPORT deceleration lane; ~ **de décharge principale** ƒ ELECTROTEC main gap; ~ **de dédoublement** ƒ CH DE FER relief track; ~ **de dépassement** ƒ CONSTR overtaking lane, passing lane; ~ **descendante** ƒ CH DE FER down line; ~ **de désintégration muonique** ƒ PHYS RAYON muon decay track; ~ **de desserte** ƒ CH DE FER line serving a siding, CONSTR service road; ~ **de données** ƒ INFORMAT, ORDINAT data channel, TELECOM DCC, data communication channel; ~ **à double écartement** ƒ CH DE FER mixed gage track (AmE), mixed gauge track (BrE); ~ **d'eau** ƒ CONSTR leak; ~ **d'écart** ƒ CH DE FER recessing siding; ~ **d'échange** ƒ CH DE FER interchange track; ~ **d'écoulement** ƒ DISTRI EAU water adit, MINES offset, offtake; ~ **d'effets** ƒ TV special effects bus; ~ **élastique** ƒ TRANSPORT resilient rail; ~ **d'embranchement** ƒ CH DE FER branch line, siding; ~ **en alignement** ƒ CH DE FER *véhicules* straight track; ~ **d'enchaînement** ƒ INFORMAT linkage path; ~ **en estacade** ƒ CH DE FER elevated track; ~ **en forme de double L** ƒ TRANSPORT channel track; ~ **en ligne droite** ƒ CH DE FER straight track; ~ **en raquette** ƒ CH DE FER loop line; ~ **d'enregistrement** ƒ ENREGISTR recording channel; ~ **en remblai** ƒ CH DE FER railroad embankment (AmE), railway embankment (BrE); ~ **en surélévation** ƒ TRANSPORT aerial guideway; ~ **en tranchée** ƒ CH DE FER cutting; ~ **d'entrée d'air** ƒ CHARBON intake airway; ~ **d'établissement** ƒ TELECOM setup channel; ~ **d'évitement** ƒ CH DE FER passing track; ~ **exclusive** ƒ TELECOM dedicated channel; ~ **exploitée** ƒ CH DE FER track in service; ~ **à faible circulation** ƒ CONSTR low traffic road, minor road; ~ **ferrée** ƒ MINES rail track, TRANSPORT railroad line (AmE), railway line (BrE), railroad track (AmE), railway track (BrE); ~ **ferrée aérienne** ƒ CONS MECA runway, PRODUCTION overhead runway, overhead track; ~ **de fond** ƒ MINES bottom level, bottom road; ~ **de garage** ƒ CH DE FER holding siding, TRANSPORT siding; ~ **impaire** ƒ CH DE FER downline; ~ **impraticable** ƒ CH DE FER out-of-service track; ~ **libre** ƒ CH DE FER line clear; ~ **maîtresse** ƒ MINES level road, mainway; ~ **mal modulée** ƒ ENREGISTR unbalanced channel; ~ **maritime** ƒ NAUT sea link; ~ **d'un mètre** ƒ CH DE FER meter gage (AmE), metre gauge (BrE); ~ **de mobile** ƒ TELECOM reversal control channel; ~ **d'un multiplex** ƒ ELECTRON multiplex channel; ~ **navigable** ƒ HYDROLOGIE, NAUT waterway; ~ **neutralisée** ƒ TELECOM blanked-off channel; ~ **de niveau** ƒ MINES level; ~ **à niveau** ƒ TRANSPORT guideway at grade; ~ **normale** ƒ CH DE FER standard gauge; ~ **noyée** ƒ CH DE FER sunken track; ~ **occupée** ƒ CH DE FER line occupied, occupied track; ~ **de passage** ƒ PRODUCTION *système hydraulique* flow path; ~ **porteuse** ƒ TELECOM

BC, bearer channel; ~ **poutre** ƒ TRANSPORT supporting track; ~ **principale** ƒ CH DE FER main line, main track, CHARBON entry, main gate, CONSTR main line, main track, MINES mainway; ~ **principale d'entrée d'air** ƒ MINES main intake airway; ~ **principale de retour d'air** ƒ MINES main return airway; ~ **publique** ƒ CONSTR highway, public road; ~ **Q** ƒ ELECTRON Q-channel; ~ **de raccordement** ƒ CH DE FER, CONSTR siding; ~ **de ralentissement** ƒ TRANSPORT access road (AmE), deceleration lane, slip road (BrE); ~ **de remisage** ƒ CH DE FER holding siding, TRANSPORT storage siding; ~ **de réparations** ƒ CH DE FER repair track (BrE), rip track (AmE); ~ **de report** ƒ CH DE FER relief track; ~ **de retour** ƒ ENREGISTR return channel, INFORMAT, ORDINAT return channel, reverse channel, TELECOM return path; ~ **de retour d'air** ƒ MINES return airway; ~ **de rocade** ƒ TRANSPORT bypass; ~ **de roulage** ƒ MINES haulage way; ~ **de roulement** ƒ CONS MECA runway, *pour billes* race; ~ **sans ballast** ƒ TRANSPORT ballastless track; ~ **de secours** ƒ CH DE FER auxiliary track; ~ **de signalisation non-spécialisée** ƒ TELECOM nondedicated signalling channel; ~ **son** ƒ ENREGISTR audio channel; ~ **de sortie** ƒ TV outgoing channel; ~ **de sortie rapide** ƒ AERONAUT *aéroport* high-speed exit taxiway, rapid exit taxiway; ~ **de sous-triage** ƒ CH DE FER advance classification track; ~ **support** ƒ TELECOM BC, bearer channel; ~ **surélevée** ƒ CONSTR elevated runway, TRANSPORT aerial guideway, elevated track; ~ **de taille** ƒ CHARBON conveyor road, gate road; ~ **de télécommande** ƒ ESPACE command channel; ~ **téléphonique** ƒ CH DE FER main line, INFORMAT voice channel, voice-band, ORDINAT, TELECOM voice channel; ~ **d'une tête** ƒ TV head channel; ~ **de tête** ƒ MINES top road; ~ **de traçage** ƒ MINES development heading; ~ **de trafic** ƒ TELECOM working channel; ~ **de trafic au repos** ƒ TELECOM idle working channel; ~ **du train d'atterrissage** ƒ AERONAUT landing gear track; ~ **de tram** ƒ CONSTR tram track; ~ **de transbordement** ƒ CH DE FER transfer track (AmE), transshipment track (BrE); ~ **de translation** ƒ CONS MECA runway; ~ **de transmission** ƒ INFORMAT, ORDINAT transmission channel, TELECOM transmission channel, transmission path; ~ **de transmission de données** ƒ INFORMAT, ORDINAT data transmission channel; ~ **de transmission par satellite** ƒ TV satellite channel; ~ **de transport** ƒ CHARBON, MINES haulage road; ~ **de triage** ƒ CH DE FER shunting track, *véhicules* classification siding, sorting line, TRANSPORT classification siding, classification track, shunting siding, shunting track; ~ **de trucages** ƒ TV effects bus; ~ **d'usine** ƒ CH DE FER *voie* factory siding; ~ **vidéo** ƒ TV video channel; ~ **virtuelle** ƒ TELECOM VC, virtual channel; ~ **virtuelle diffusée de signalisation** ƒ TELECOM BSVC, broadcast signaling virtual channel (AmE), broadcast signalling virtual channel (BrE); ~ **virtuelle de signalisation** ƒ TELECOM SVC, signaling virtual channel (AmE), signalling virtual channel (BrE)

Voie: ~ **Lactée** ƒ ASTRONOMIE *galaxie* Milky Way

voies: ~ **conjuguées doubles** ƒ pl MINES double entries

voile:[1] **sous** ~ *adj* NAUT under canvas

voile[2] *m* ACOUSTIQUE fog, warp, CERAM VER bloom, milkiness, staple tissue, CINEMAT fog, *sur une pellicule* veil, CONS MECA buckle, buckling, PHOTO fog, PLAST CAOU *peintures, plastiques, caractéristique* haze, PRODUCTION coat, TEXTILE voile, TV black shading; ~ **argentique** *m* CINEMAT silver fog; ~ **atmosphérique** *m*

CINEMAT aerial fog, PHOTO atmospheric haze; ~ **chimique** *m* CINEMAT chemical fogging; ~ **de développement** *m* CINEMAT development fog; ~ **dichroïque** *m* CINEMAT, PHOTO dichroic fog; ~ **électronique** *m* TV clouding; ~ **de fond** *m* PHOTO base fog; ~ **latéral** *m* CINEMAT edge flare, edge fogging; ~ **au magenta** *m* IMPRIM *impression* blushing; ~ **marginal** *m* CINEMAT edge flare, edge fogging; ~ **d'oxydation** *m* CINEMAT air fog; ~ **voilage** *m* NUCLEAIRE *déformation* buckling

voile[3] *f* NAUT canvas, sail, sheet; ~ **d'artimon** *f* NAUT mizzen; ~ **de cape** *f* NAUT trysail; ~ **de carde** *f* TEXTILE web; ~ **d'étanchéité** *f* CONSTR grout curtain; ~ **de netteté** *f* IMPRIM *impression* fog; ~ **au rouge** *f* IMPRIM *impression* flushing; ~ **solaire** *f* ESPACE *véhicules* solar sail

voilé *adj* CINEMAT light-struck, CONS MECA out-of-true

voiler *vt* ACOUSTIQUE, CINEMAT fog, CONS MECA buckle, PHOTO fog

voilerie *f* NAUT sail loft

Voiles *f pl* ASTRONOMIE Vela

voilier *m* NAUT sailboat (AmE), sailing boat (BrE), sailmaker, TRANSPORT sailboat (AmE), sailing boat (BrE); ~ **de croisière** *m* TRANSPORT coastal cruiser

voilure *f* CONSTR *du bois* warping, PRODUCTION *d'une tôle de chaudière* buckling; ~ **en double delta** *f* AERONAUT double delta wing; ~ **en flèche** *f* TRANSPORT arrowhead wing, swept-back wing; ~ **en porte-à-faux** *f* AERONAUT cantilever wing; ~ **fixe** *f* AERONAUT fixed wing; ~ **à flèche inverse** *f* AERONAUT forward-swept wing; ~ **à flèche négative** *f* AERONAUT forward-swept wing; ~ **médiane** *f* AERONAUT center wing section (AmE), centre wing section (BrE); ~ **de parachutage** *f* AERONAUT parachute canopy; ~ **de parachute** *f* AERONAUT parachute canopy; ~ **tronquée** *f* TRANSPORT clipped wing

voiture *f* AUTO automobile, car, CH DE FER carriage, coach (BrE), TRANSPORT automobile, VEHICULES automobile, car; ~ **amphibie** *f* NAUT amphibian; ~ **articulée** *f* TRANSPORT articulated car; ~ **à caisse inclinable** *f* TRANSPORT tilting body coach; ~ **de chemin de fer à crémaillère** *f* TRANSPORT rack railroad trailer (AmE), rack railway trailer (BrE); ~ **à cinq portes** *f* TRANSPORT hatchback car; ~ **à deux volumes** *f* VEHICULES hatchback automobile, hatchback car; ~ **des dunes** *f* TRANSPORT dune buggy; ~ **électronique** *f* TRANSPORT electronic car; ~ **expérimentale de sécurité** *f* TRANSPORT ESV, experimental safety vehicle; ~ **à gaz** *f* TRANSPORT gas-fueled car (AmE), gas-fuelled car (BrE); ~ **à hayon arrière** *f* VEHICULES hatchback automobile, hatchback car; ~ **à jetons** *f* TRANSPORT public automobile; ~ **mixte** *f* VEHICULES dual-purpose vehicle; ~ **non compartimentée** *f* TRANSPORT saloon coach; ~ **non polluante** *f* TRANSPORT clean air car; ~ **particulière** *f* TRANSPORT passenger car, VEHICULES passenger automobile, passenger car, private vehicle; ~ **à passagers** *f* TRANSPORT passenger car, passenger coach; ~ **plate-forme passive** *f* TRANSPORT passive flat car; ~ **postale** *f* TRANSPORT mail van; ~ **propre** *f* TRANSPORT clean air car; ~ **radio** *f* TRANSPORT radio patrol car; ~ **de reconnaissance** *f* MILITAIRE reconnaissance vehicle; ~ **de tête** *f* TRANSPORT carriage A; ~ **tout usage** *f* MILITAIRE, VEHICULES utility vehicle; ~ **de tramway** *f* TRANSPORT streetcar (AmE), tram (BrE); ~ **travelling** *f* CINEMAT camera car; ~ **à trois portes** *f* TRANSPORT hatchback car; ~ **à vapeur** *f* TRANSPORT steam car; ~ **à voyageurs** *f* TRANSPORT railroad carriage (AmE), railway carriage (BrE)

voitureabilité *f* CONSTR rideability

voiture-bar *f* CH DE FER buffet car (AmE), buffet coach (BrE)

voiture-buffet *f* CH DE FER *véhicules* buffet car (AmE), buffet coach (BrE)

voiture-salon *f* CH DE FER *véhicules* club car

voix *f* INFORMAT, ORDINAT voice; ~ **artificielle** *f* ACOUSTIQUE artificial voice; ~ **de l'hélium** *f* OCEANO helium voice

vol *m* AERONAUT, ESPACE flight; ~ **accompagné** *m* TRANSPORT passenger flight; ~ **affrété avec réservation à l'avance** *m* AERONAUT advance booking charter; ~ **affrété tout-cargo** *m* AERONAUT all-cargo charter flight; ~ **captif** *m* ESPACE captive flight; ~ **contrôlé** *m* AERONAUT controlled flight; ~ **contrôlé à distance** *m* MILITAIRE remote-controlled flight; ~ **de convoyage** *m* AERONAUT ferry flight; ~ **de cycle** *m* INFORMAT, ORDINAT cycle stealing; ~ **direct** *m* AERONAUT direct flight; ~ **en ascendance thermique** *m* THERMODYN thermal soaring; ~ **en autorotation** *m* AERONAUT autorotation flight; ~ **en dérapage** *m* AERONAUT drifting flight; ~ **en double commande** *m* AERONAUT dual instruction; ~ **en formation** *m* AERONAUT formation flight; ~ **en palier** *m* AERONAUT level flight; ~ **en régime stabilisé** *m* AERONAUT steady flight; ~ **d'entraînement** *m* AERONAUT training flight; ~ **d'épreuve** *m* AERONAUT proving flight; ~ **d'essai** *m* AERONAUT, ESPACE test flight; ~ **d'étalonnage** *m* AERONAUT calibration flight; ~ **habité** *m* ESPACE manned flight; ~ **horizontal** *m* AERONAUT level flight; ~ **aux instruments** *m* AERONAUT instrument flying, TRANSPORT instrument flight; ~ **intérieur** *m* AERONAUT domestic flight; ~ **interplanétaire** *m* ESPACE interplanetary flight; ~ **libre** *m* ESPACE free flight; ~ **de longue distance** *m* TRANSPORT long-distance flight; ~ **de nuit** *m* AERONAUT night flight; ~ **orbital** *m* ESPACE orbital flight; ~ **plané** *m* AERONAUT gliding flight; ~ **porté** *m* ESPACE *véhicules* captive flight; ~ **radio guidé** *m* MILITAIRE radio-guided flight; ~ **de réception** *m* AERONAUT acceptance flight, acceptance trial, TRANSPORT acceptance flight; ~ **de reconnaissance de route** *m* AERONAUT route familiarization flight; ~ **régulier** *m* AERONAUT scheduled flight; ~ **à la remorque** *m* AERONAUT, TRANSPORT aerotow flight; ~ **sans escale** *m* AERONAUT nonstop flight; ~ **sans visibilité** *m* AERONAUT blind flight; ~ **spatial** *m* ESPACE space flight; ~ **stationnaire** *m* AERONAUT hovering; ~ **statique** *m* TRANSPORT static hovering; ~ **téléguidé** *m* MILITAIRE remote-controlled flight; ~ **de transport exclusif de fret** *m* AERONAUT all-freight service; ~ **de transport exclusif de poste** *m* AERONAUT all-mail service; ~ **vers l'arrière** *m* AERONAUT backward flight; ~ **à vue du sol** *m* AERONAUT contact flight

volage *m* CERAM VER batch dust

volant *m* AUTO steering wheel, CONS MECA driving wheel, fly, flywheel, hand wheel, wheel, CONSTR *d'une poutre, d'un comble* span, PRODUCTION fly, flywheel, REFRIG flywheel, VEHICULES *direction* steering wheel; ~ **d'aileron** *m* AERONAUT aileron control wheel; ~ **à ailettes** *m* COMMANDE fly governor, fly regulator; ~ **de chasse** *m* CONS MECA driving wheel, fly, flywheel; ~ **de commande** *m* CONS MECA driving wheel, fly, flywheel; ~ **de compensation** *m* CINEMAT balance wheel; ~ **de direction** *m* AERONAUT steering control wheel, VEHICULES steering wheel; ~ **à disque plein expérimental** *m* CONS MECA experimental solid disc flywheel (BrE), experimental solid disk flywheel (AmE); ~ **d'entraîne-ment** *m* CONS MECA driving wheel, fly, flywheel; ~ **d'inertie** *m* ESPACE *véhicules* momentum wheel, MECANIQUE flywheel; ~ **d'inertie sur paliers magnétiques** *m* ESPACE *véhicules* magnetic bearing momentum wheel; ~ **de machine** *m* CONS MECA engine flywheel; ~ **magnétique** *m* ELECTROTEC magnetic flywheel; ~ **à main** *m* CONS MECA hand wheel; ~ **à manivelle** *m* CONS MECA hand wheel; ~ **de manoeuvre** *m* CONS MECA operating hand wheel, MECANIQUE hand wheel; ~ **moteur** *m* AUTO, VEHICULES flywheel; ~ **à poignée** *m* CONS MECA hand wheel; ~ **à poignées radiales** *m* CONS MECA pilot wheel; ~ **de pointage en direction** *m* MILITAIRE *artillerie* training wheel; ~ **de pointage en élévation** *m* MILITAIRE *artillerie* elevating wheel; ~ **porte-lame** *m* CONS MECA saw pulley; ~ **pour commande à bras** *m* CONS MECA hand wheel; ~ **de scie à ruban** *m* CONS MECA band wheel, band-saw pulley; ~ **de serrage** *m* CONS MECA friction wheel

volatil *adj* CHIMIE ethereal, volatile, INFORMAT, PLAST CAOU, TEXTILE volatile

volatilisation *f* CHIMIE volatilization

volatiliser[1] *vt* CHIMIE volatilize

volatiliser:[2] **se ~** *v réfl* CHIMIE volatilize GENIE CHIM evaporate

volatilité *f* CHIMIE, MATERIAUX, METALL, PLAST CAOU, TEXTILE volatility; ~ **relative** *f* MATERIAUX relative volatility

volborthite *f* MINERAUX volborthite

volcan: ~ **bouclier** *m* GEOLOGIE shield volcano; ~ **de boue** *m* PETROLE mud volcano; ~ **composé** *m* GEOLOGIE composite volcano; ~ **en activité** *m* GEOLOGIE active volcano; ~ **éteint** *m* GEOLOGIE extinct volcano; ~ **sous-marin** *m* GEOLOGIE guyot, seamount; ~ **de type hawaïen** *m* GEOLOGIE Hawaiian-type volcano

volcanique *adj* GEOLOGIE, PETR *géologie* volcanic

volcanisme *m* ASTRONOMIE, GEOLOGIE volcanism, GEOPHYS vulcanicity; ~ **intraplaque** *m* GEOLOGIE intraplate volcanism; ~ **planétaire** *m* ASTRONOMIE planetary volcanism

volée *f* CONSTR flight, *d'une grue* boom, jib, MINES cross drift, cross drive, crossheading, offset drive, drift, offset, round; ~ **droite** *f* CONSTR straight flight; ~ **d'escalier** *f* CONSTR flight of stairs

voler: ~ **à un cap** *vt* TRANSPORT steer

volet *m* AERONAUT *aéronef* flap, CHARBON toggle, CINEMAT flag, nigger, wipe, CONS MECA *d'un ventilateur, d'une roue hydraulique* paddle, paddle board, CONSTR shield, shutter, DISTRI EAU float, EMBALLAGE flap, ESPACE *véhicules* flap, shutter, MECANIQUE flap, PRODUCTION *pour protéger l'ouvrier contre les accidents* guard, screen, shutter, SECURITE screen, TRANSPORT spoiler; ~ **d'aération** *m* MECANIQUE louver (AmE), louvre (BrE); ~ **d'air** *m* MECANIQUE *véhicules* choke; ~ **d'atterrissage** *m* TRANSPORT landing flap; ~ **batteur** *m* NAUT wave maker; ~ **de bord d'attaque** *m* TRANSPORT droop flap, leading edge flap; ~ **de bord de fuite** *m* AERONAUT trailing-edge flap; ~ **de capot** *m* AERONAUT *moteur* cowl flap; ~ **carré** *m* CINEMAT box wipe; ~ **de compensation** *m* AERONAUT balance tab, trim tab (AmE), trimming tab (BrE); ~ **de courbure** *m* AERONAUT *aéronef* flap; ~ **de départ** *m* AUTO choker plate, VEHICULES *carburateur* choke; ~ **extérieur** *m* EMBALLAGE outer flap; ~ **à fente** *m* AERONAUT *aéronef* slot flap; ~ **hypersustentateur** *m* AERONAUT *aéronef* flap, TRANSPORT wing flap; ~ **d'intrados** *m* AERONAUT *aéro-*

nef split flap; ~ **latéral** *m* CINEMAT push-off wipe; ~ **mécanique** *m* CONSTR rolling shutter; ~ **pare-feu** *m* CINEMAT dowser; ~ **de protection de l'objectif** *m* PHOTO lens cover slide; ~ **de refroidissement** *m* AERONAUT cooling flap; ~ **réglable** *m* CINEMAT barndoor; ~ **rentrant** *m* EMBALLAGE tuck-in flap; ~ **à rideau** *m* CONSTR rolling shutter; ~ **rotatif** *m* CINEMAT spin wipe; ~ **roulant** *m* CONSTR rolling shutter, sliding shutter; ~ **soufflé** *m* AERONAUT *contrôle de la couche limite* blown-flap; ~ **vertical** *m* CINEMAT vertical wipe

volets: ~ **à recouvrement** *m pl* EMBALLAGE overlapping flaps

volice *f* CONSTR lath

volige *f* CONSTR batten, lath, slate lath; ~ **chanlattée** *f* CONSTR eaves board, fascia, fascia board

voligeage *m* CONSTR battening, lathing

voliger *vt* CONSTR batten

volt *m* ELECTR, ELECTROTEC, METROLOGIE, PHYSIQUE volt

voltage *m* ELECTROTEC voltage

voltamètre *m* CHIMIE, ELECTROTEC, PHYSIQUE voltameter (BrE), voltammeter (AmE)

voltige *f* IMPRIM *encres* misting

voltmètre *m* ELECTR, ELECTROTEC, PHYSIQUE voltmeter; ~ **alternatif** *m* ELECTROTEC AC voltmeter; ~ **analogique** *m* ELECTROTEC analog voltmeter (AmE), analogue voltmeter (BrE); ~ **astatique** *m* ELECTR astatic voltmeter; ~ **Cardew** *m* ELECTR Cardew voltmeter; ~ **continu** *m* ELECTROTEC DC voltmeter; ~ **à courant continu** *m* ELECTROTEC DC voltmeter; ~ **de crête** *m* ELECTR peak voltmeter, TV peak program meter (AmE), peak programme metre (BrE); ~ **différentiel** *m* ELECTR differential voltmeter; ~ **électrostatique** *m* ELECTR static voltmeter; ~ **ferrodynamique** *m* ELECTR iron core voltmeter; ~ **à fil chaud** *m* ELECTR hot wire voltmeter; ~ **magnéto-électrique** *m* ELECTR moving coil voltmeter; ~ **numérique** *m* ELECTROTEC digital voltmeter; ~ **pour courant alternatif** *m* ELECTR alternating current voltmeter, ELECTROTEC AC voltmeter; ~ **sélectif** *m* ELECTR selective voltmeter; ~ **à tension continue** *m* ELECTROTEC DC voltmeter

volume:[1] **à ~ réduit** *adj* EMBALLAGE space-saving

volume[2] *m* ACOUSTIQUE volume, CERAM VER bulk, CHIMIE volume, CONSTR *d'une pierre* bulk, ENREGISTR, GEOMETRIE volume, IMPRIM *papier* bulk, INFORMAT, MATH, ORDINAT, PHYSIQUE, TEXTILE volume; ~ **apparent** *m* MATERIAUX, PETR bulk volume; ~ **après tassement** *m* GENIE CHIM settled volume; ~ **atomique** *m* NUCLEAIRE atomic volume; ~ **brut** *m* EMBALLAGE gross volume; ~ **critique** *m* CHAUFFAGE critical volume; ~ **équivalent de sensation d'intensité** *m* ENREGISTR loudness volume equivalent; ~ **libre** *m* ESPACE *véhicules*, MECANIQUE ullage; ~ **massique** *m* PHYSIQUE specific volume, REFRIG humid volume; ~ **des modes** *m* OPTIQUE, TELECOM mode volume; ~ **molaire** *m* PHYSIQUE molar volume; ~ **mort** *m* ESPACE *véhicules* ullage; ~ **optique des modes** *m* OPTIQUE, TELECOM effective mode volume; ~ **des pores** *m* CHARBON pore volume, GEOLOGIE pore space, PETR pore volume; ~ **de référence** *m* ACOUSTIQUE reference volume; ~ **résiduel** *m* ESPACE *véhicules* ullage; ~ **de révolution** *m* GEOMETRIE volume of rotation; ~ **sonore** *m* ACOUSTIQUE volume; ~ **total stockable** *m* GAZ total storage volume; ~ **de vapeur d'une chaudière** *m* INST HYDR steam space; ~ **de vide** *m* TEXTILE void volume

volumètre *f* ACOUSTIQUE volumeter

volumétrique *adj* MATERIAUX, METALL volumetric

volumique *adj* PHYSIQUE per unit volume

volutine *f* CHIMIE volutin

vomicine *f* CHIMIE vomicine

vorscheidage *m* MINES ragging

vortex *m* CHARBON, ESPACE vortex, HYDROLOGIE vortex, whirlpool, METEO, PHYS FLUID vortex; ~ **de diffusion** *m* PHYS FLUID vorticity diffusion

vorticité *m* PHYS FLUID vorticity

votator *m* AGRO ALIM votator

vousseau *m* CONSTR arch stone, voussoir, PRODUCTION quoin

voussette *f* (Bel) *(cf voûtain de chambre)* CERAM VER rider arch

voussoir *m* CONSTR arch stone, voussoir, binding stone, lining segment, PRODUCTION quoin; ~ **de clé** *m* CONSTR key, keystone

voûtain: ~ **de chambre** *m* (Fra) *(cf voussette)* CERAM VER rider arch

voûte *f* CERAM VER crown, CONSTR arch, vault, *d'un tunnel, d'une caverne* roof, NAUT counter, fantail, PAPIER arch, PRODUCTION *d'un fourneau* dome; ~ **d'allumage** *f* CHAUFFAGE ignition arch; ~ **aplatie** *f* CONSTR four-centered arch (AmE), four-centred arch (BrE); ~ **d'arête** *f* CONSTR groined vault; ~ **biaise** *f* CONSTR oblique arch; ~ **bombée** *f* CONSTR segmental arch; ~ **de brûleur** *f* CERAM VER port crown (BrE), uptake crown (AmE); ~ **du couvercle** *f* NUCLEAIRE *calotte* cover cap; ~ **elliptique** *f* CONSTR elliptical arch; ~ **en anse de panier** *f* CONSTR basket handle arch; ~ **en arc de cercle** *f* CONSTR segmental arch; ~ **en arc de cloître** *f* CONSTR groined vault; ~ **en berceau** *f* CONSTR tunnel vault, wagon vault; ~ **en briques** *f* CONSTR brick arch; ~ **en fer à cheval** *f* CONSTR horseshoe arch; ~ **en plein cintre** *f* CONSTR round arch, semicircular arch; ~ **exhaussée** *f* CONSTR stilted arch; ~ **outrepassée** *f* CONSTR horseshoe arch; ~ **plate** *f* CERAM VER front arch, jack arch, CONSTR flat arch, platband; ~ **de plein cintre** *f* CONSTR round arch, semicircular arch; ~ **à quatre centres** *f* CONSTR four-centered arch (AmE), four-centred arch (BrE); ~ **rampante** *f* CONSTR rising arch; ~ **renversée** *f* CONSTR reversed arch; ~ **surbaissée** *f* CERAM VER flying arch, CONSTR diminished arch, scheme arch, segmental arch, skene arch; ~ **surélevée** *f* CONSTR stilted arch; ~ **surhaussée** *f* CONSTR stilted arch; ~ **surmontée** *f* CONSTR stilted arch; ~ **triangulaire** *f* CONSTR triangular arch; ~ **à trois centres** *f* CONSTR three-centered arch (AmE), three-centred arch (BrE)

voûté *adj* CONSTR arched

voûter[1] *vt* CONSTR, MINES arch

voûter:[2] **se** ~ *v réfl* MINES arch

voyage: ~ **aller-retour** *m* ESPACE *véhicules* round trip; ~ **dans l'espace** *m* ESPACE space travel; ~ **inaugural** *m* ESPACE, NAUT maiden voyage; ~ **interplanétaire** *m* ESPACE interplanetary travel

voyageur *m* TRANSPORT passenger

voyageur-kilomètre *m* TRANSPORT passenger kilometer (AmE), passenger kilometre (BrE)

voyant *m* CINEMAT pilot lamp (AmE), CONSTR sighting board, target, vane, EMBALLAGE inspection window, NAUT top mark, REFRIG sight glass; ~ **d'antenne** *m* TV cue light; ~ **de baisse de niveau** *m* CONS MECA low-level warning light; ~ **de défaut** *m* PRODUCTION fault light; ~ **de défaut de masse** *m* PRODUCTION *électricité* ground

detector light; ~ **électrique** *m* AERONAUT indicator light; ~ **des entrées** *m* PRODUCTION *automatisme industriel* input section indicator; ~ **d'état** *m* PRODUCTION switch indicator, *automatisme industriel* status indicator; ~ **d'état de fusible coupé** *m* PRODUCTION fuse blown status indicator; ~ **d'états des E/S** *m* PRODUCTION *automatisme industriel* I/O status indicator; ~ **de fusible claqué** *m* PRODUCTION fuse blown status indicator; ~ **de fusible fusé** *m* PRODUCTION blown fuse indicator; ~ **d'huile** *m* REFRIG oil sight glass; ~ **indicateur** *m* CINEMAT, TV tally light; ~ **d'indication d'alarme** *m* TELECOM alarm indication lamp; ~ **lumineux** *m* AERONAUT indicator light, warning light, CH DE FER indicator lamp, PRODUCTION indicator light; ~ **lumineux pousser-test** *m* PRODUCTION push-to-test pilot light, *automatisme industriel* push-to-test indicating light; ~ **magnétique** *m* CONS MECA magnetic indicator; ~ **marche** *m* PRODUCTION run indicator; ~ **de mise en service** *m* CINEMAT on/off pilot light; ~ **multilampes** *m* PRODUCTION *électricité* cluster indicator light; ~ **d'occupation** *m* TELECOM status lamp; ~ **zéro direction** *m* AERONAUT rudder trim light

vrac: **en** ~ *adv* CHARBON, TRANSPORT in bulk

vracquier *m* NAUT, TRANSPORT bulk carrier

vraie: ~ **grandeur** *f* CONS MECA, PRODUCTION actual size

vraisemblance *f* MATH, ORDINAT likelihood

vraquier: ~ **sec** *m* NAUT, TRANSPORT dry bulk carrier

vrillage *m* CERAM VER twisting, EMBALLAGE *déformation d'une feuille de papier ou de carton* curl, RESSORTS corkscrew set

vrille *f* AERONAUT *manoeuvre de vol* spin, CONSTR auger gimlet, gimlet; ~ **déclenchée** *f* AERONAUT controlled spin; ~ **façon suisse** *f* CONSTR shell gimlet; ~ **à plat** *f* AERONAUT flat spin; ~ **à torsade** *f* CONSTR twist gimlet

VSS *abrév* *(véhicule à suspension supérieure)* TRANSPORT SVS *(suspended vehicle system)*

vue:[1] **à** ~ **exempté** *adj* AERONAUT visual exempted

vue[2] *f* ASTRONOMIE seeing, PHOTO shot; ~ **coupée** *f* CONS MECA cutaway view; ~ **éclatée** *f* CONS MECA, MECANIQUE exploded view; ~ **en coupe** *f* CONS MECA sectional drawing, sectional view; ~ **en plan** *f* CONS MECA plan drawing, plan view; ~ **d'ensemble** *f* CONS MECA *dessin technique* general plan; ~ **de face** *f* CONS MECA front elevation; ~ **panoramique** *f* PHOTO panoramic photograph

vu-imprimé *adj* *(WYSIWYG)* INFORMAT, ORDINAT what you see is what you get *(WYSIWYG)*

vulcanisation *f* CHIMIE vulcanization, PLAST CAOU curing, *caoutchouc* vulcanization, *peintures, plastiques, caoutchouc* hardening, *prématurée* scorch, THERMODYN vulcanization; ~ **en continu** *f* PLAST CAOU *procédé* continuous vulcanization; ~ **en étuve** *f* PLAST CAOU *caoutchouc* air cure

vulcanisé *adj* THERMODYN vulcanized

vulcaniser *vt* PLAST CAOU cure, THERMODYN heat cure, vulcanize

vulcanite *f* CHIMIE vulcanite, PLAST CAOU *caoutchouc* ebonite, vulcanite

vulnérabilité: ~ **électromagnétique** *f* ELECTROTEC electromagnetic vulnerability

VU-mètre *f* ACOUSTIQUE VI-meter ENREGISTR, TV VI meter, volume indicator meter

W

W[1] *(tungstène)* CHIMIE W *(tungsten)*

W[2] *abrév (watt)* ELECTR, ELECTROTEC, METROLOGIE, PHYSIQUE W *(watt)*

wackestone *m* GEOLOGIE wacke, wackestone

wad *m* MINERAUX wad, OCEANO tide flat

wagnérite *f* MINERAUX wagnerite

wagon *m* CH DE FER *véhicules* car (AmE), carriage, wagon (BrE), TRANSPORT *chemins de fer* car (AmE), wagon (BrE); **~ à attelage souple** *m* CH DE FER *véhicules* cushion car (AmE), cushion wagon (BrE); **~ autodéchargeable** *m* CH DE FER *véhicules* self-discharging car (AmE), self-discharging wagon (BrE); **~ avarié** *m* CH DE FER *véhicules* damaged car (AmE), damaged wagon (BrE); **~ à bâche** *m* CH DE FER *véhicules* sheeted car (AmE), sheeted wagon (BrE); **~ basculant avec bec** *m* CH DE FER scoop tipper, TRANSPORT scoop dump car (AmE), scoop dump wagon (BrE), scoop tipper; **~ à basculement automatique** *m* CH DE FER *véhicules* self-tipping car (AmE), self-tipping wagon (BrE); **~ à basculement à becs** *m* CH DE FER *véhicules* suspended-load trolley set; **~ basculeur** *m* CH DE FER *véhicules* tip-up car (AmE), tip-up wagon (BrE); **~ à benne basculante** *m* TRANSPORT dump car (AmE), dump wagon (BrE); **~ à bestiaux** *m* CH DE FER *véhicules* cattle car (AmE), cattle wagon (BrE); **~ à bogies à toit pivotant** *m* TRANSPORT bogie wagon with swivelling roof (BrE), truck car with swiveling roof (AmE); **~ de brouettage** *m* CH DE FER *véhicules* car for internal yard use (AmE), wagon for internal yard use (BrE); **~ de chargement** *m* MINES larry, larry car; **~ citerne** *m* CH DE FER *véhicules* tank car (AmE), tank wagon (BrE), CONSTR tanker truck, MINES tank car (AmE), tank wagon (BrE), TRANSPORT rail tank car (AmE), rail tank wagon (BrE), tank barge, tank car (AmE), tank wagon (BrE); **~ complet** *m* CH DE FER box wagon (BrE), carload (AmE); **~ de course** *m* CH DE FER *véhicules* regular part load car (AmE), regular part load wagon (BrE); **~ couvert** *m* CH DE FER *véhicules* boxcar (AmE), covered car (AmE), covered wagon (BrE), TRANSPORT freight van (AmE), goods van (BrE); **~ à culbutage latéral** *m* CH DE FER *fret* side dump car (AmE), side dump wagon (BrE); **~ à déchargement** *m* TRANSPORT truck car (AmE), truck wagon (BrE); **~ à déchargement automatique** *m* TRANSPORT self-discharge car (AmE), self-discharge wagon (BrE), self-discharge freight car (AmE), self-discharge goods wagon (BrE); **~ à déchargement par le fond** *m* CH DE FER *véhicules* hopper car (AmE), hopper wagon (BrE); **~ découvert** *m* CH DE FER gondola car (AmE), open wagon (BrE); **~ à la dérive** *m* CH DE FER *véhicules* runaway car (AmE), runaway wagon (BrE); **~ dérouleur** *m* CH DE FER overhead drum car (AmE), overhead drum wagon (BrE); **~ à déversement arrière** *m* CH DE FER *véhicules* back-discharge car (AmE), back-discharge wagon (BrE), rear dump car (AmE); **~ étanche** *m* CH DE FER *véhicules* pressure-sealed car (AmE), pressure-sealed wagon (BrE); **~ à évidement**

central *m* CH DE FER *véhicules* depressed deck car (AmE), well wagon (BrE); **~ freiné** *m* CH DE FER *véhicules* braked car (AmE), braked wagon (BrE); **~ frigorifique** *m* CH DE FER *véhicules* refrigerated car (AmE), refrigerated wagon (BrE), REFRIG refrigerated truck, TRANSPORT refrigerated car (AmE), refrigerated wagon (BrE); **~ frigorifique à bac d'extrémité** *m* REFRIG end bunker refrigerated truck; **~ de groupage** *m* CH DE FER *véhicules* groupage car (AmE), groupage wagon (BrE), TRANSPORT pooling car (AmE); **~ grumier** *m* CH DE FER *véhicules* timber car (AmE), timber wagon (BrE); **~ isolé** *m* REFRIG insulated truck; **~ isotherme** *m* REFRIG insulated truck; **~ kangourou** *m* CH DE FER *véhicules* depressed deck car (AmE), kangaroo type wagon, well wagon (BrE); **~ lits** *m* CH DE FER *véhicules* sleeping car; **~ à marchandises** *m* TRANSPORT railroad freight car (AmE), railway freight coach (BrE); **~ à minerai** *m* MINES hutch; **~ ouvert autodéchargeur à bogies** *m* TRANSPORT bogie open self-discharge wagon (BrE), truck open self-discharge car (AmE); **~ de particulier** *m* CH DE FER *véhicules* private car (AmE), *véhicules* private wagon (BrE); **~ plat** *m* CH DE FER *véhicules* flat car (AmE), flat wagon (BrE), flat-bed car (AmE), flat-bed wagon (BrE), TRANSPORT flat car (AmE), flat wagon (BrE); **~ porte-conteneur** *m* TRANSPORT container car (AmE), container wagon (BrE); **~ porte-rails** *m* CH DE FER rail-carrying car (AmE), rail-carrying wagon (BrE); **~ porteur** *m* CH DE FER carrier car (AmE), carrier wagon (BrE); **~ pour les expéditions en détail** *m* TRANSPORT freight car (AmE), freight van (AmE), freight wagon (BrE), goods van (BrE); **~ pour le personnel** *m* MINES manriding car; **~ pupitre** *m* CH DE FER *véhicules* trestle car (AmE), trestle wagon (BrE); **~ raccord** *m* CH DE FER *véhicules* match truck; **~ à ranchers** *m* TRANSPORT flat car (AmE), flat wagon (BrE), flat car with side stakes (AmE), flat wagon with side stakes (BrE); **~ réfrigéré à bac plafonnier** *m* REFRIG overhead bunker refrigerated truck; **~ réservoir** *m* MINES tank car; **~ Schnabel** *m* CH DE FER *véhicules* Schnabel car (AmE), Schnabel wagon (BrE); **~ de secours** *m* CH DE FER *véhicules* breakdown car (AmE), breakdown wagon (BrE); **~ de service à groupe diesel-électrique** *m* CH DE FER diesel generator unit service car (AmE), diesel generator unit service wagon (BrE)

wagonnet *m* CH DE FER skip car (AmE), skip wagon (BrE), small tip wagon (BrE), spoil car (AmE), tip car (AmE), tip wagon (BrE), CHARBON buggy, car (AmE), wagon (BrE), MINES car (AmE), truck, wagon (BrE), hurley, tram, tub, TRANSPORT trailer wagon (AmE), wagon car (BrE); **~ à caisse basculante** *m* CHARBON tip box car, tipping mine car; **~ verseur** *m* TRANSPORT tilting car (AmE), tilting wagon (BrE), tilting skip

walchowite *f* MINERAUX walchowite

warfarine *f* CHIMIE warfarin

washout: **~ atmosphérique** *m* POLLUTION washout

watt *m (W)* ELECTR, ELECTROTEC, METROLOGIE, PHYSIQUE watt *(W)*

wattage *m* PHYSIQUE wattage; ~ **physique** *m* PHYSIQUE wattage

wattheure *f* ELECTR, ELECTROTEC, PHYSIQUE watt-hour

wattheuremètre *m* PHYSIQUE watt-hour meter

wattmètre *m* ELECTR, PHYSIQUE wattmeter; ~ **électrodynamique** *m* ELECTR dynamometer wattmeter; ~ **ferrodynamique** *m* ELECTR ferrodynamic wattmeter; ~ **à fil chaud** *m* ELECTR hot wire wattmeter; ~ **à palette** *m* ELECTR vane wattmeter

wavellite *f* MINERAUX wavellite

Wb *abrév (weber)* METROLOGIE, PHYSIQUE Wb *(weber)*

weber *m (Wb)* ELECTR, ELECTROTEC, METROLOGIE, PHYSIQUE weber *(Wb)*

webstérite *f* MINERAUX websterite

wehnelt *m* ELECTROTEC control grid

wernérite *f* MINERAUX wernerite

whewellite *f* MINERAUX whewellite

whisker *m* METALL whisker

whitneyite *f* MINERAUX rhombique, whitneyite

willémite *f* MINERAUX willemite

williamsite *f* MINERAUX williamsite

wiluite *f* MINERAUX wiluite

winch *m* NAUT winch

withamite *f* MINERAUX withamite

withérite *f* MINERAUX witherite

wittichénite *f* MINERAUX wittichenite

wittichite *f* MINERAUX wittichenite

wobulateur *m* ELECTRON tracking generator

wöhlérite *f* MINERAUX woehlerite, wöhlerite

wolfram *m* CHIMIE tungsten, wolfram

wolframite *f* CHIMIE, MINERAUX wolframite

wolfsbergite *f* MINERAUX wolfsbergite

wollastonite *f* MINERAUX wollastonite

woofer *m* ENREGISTR woofer

wulfénite *f* MINERAUX wulfenite

wurtzite *f* MINERAUX wurtzite

WYSIWYG *abrév (tel vu tel imprimé, vu-imprimé)* INFORMAT, ORDINAT WYSIWYG *(what you see is what you get)*

X

xanthate *m* CHIMIE xanthate
xanthéine *f* CHIMIE xanthein
xanthène *m* CHIMIE xanthene
xanthine *f* CHIMIE xanthine
xanthique *adj* CHIMIE xanthic
xanthocréatine *f* CHIMIE xanthocreatinine
xanthogène *m* CHIMIE xanthein
xanthogénique *adj* CHIMIE xanthogenic
xanthone *f* CHIMIE xanthone
xanthophyllite *f* MINERAUX xanthophyllite
xanthoprotéique *adj* CHIMIE xanthoproteic
xanthosine *f* CHIMIE xanthosine
xanthotoxine *f* CHIMIE xanthotoxin
xanthoxyline *f* CHIMIE xanthoxylin
xanthydrol *m* CHIMIE xanthydrol
xanthyle *m* CHIMIE xanthyl
Xe *(xénon)* CHIMIE Xe *(xenon)*
xénocristal *m* GEOLOGIE xenocryst
xénolite *f* GEOLOGIE xenolith

xénomorphe *adj* GEOLOGIE xenomorphic
xénon *m (Xe)* CHIMIE xenon *(Xe)*
xénotime *f* MINERAUX xenotime
xérographie *f* ELECTR *reproduction*, ELECTRON, GAZ, IN-FORMAT, ORDINAT xerography
xylanthite *f* CHIMIE xylanthite
xylène *m* CHIMIE, LESSIVES, PETROLE, PLAST CAOU *solvant* xylene
xylènethiol *m* CHIMIE xylenethiol
xylénol *m* CHIMIE xylenol
xylidine *m* CHIMIE xylidine
xylite *f* CHIMIE xylite
xylitol *m* AGRO ALIM, CHIMIE xylitol
xylol *m* CHIMIE xylol
xylonite *f* PLAST CAOU xylonite
xylose *m* CHIMIE xylose
xylotile *m* MINERAUX xylotile
xylyle *m* CHIMIE xylyl
xylylène *m* CHIMIE xylylene

Y

Y *(yttrium)* CHIMIE Y *(yttrium)*

yacht: ~ **de croisière** *m* NAUT, TRANSPORT cruiser

YAG *abrév (grenat d'yttrium et d'aluminium)* ELECTRON YAG *(yttrium aluminium garnet)*

yard *m* METROLOGIE yard; ~ **carré** *m* METROLOGIE square yard; ~ **cube** *m* METROLOGIE cubic yard

yawl *m* NAUT yawl

Yb *(ytterbium)* CHIMIE Yb *(ytterbium)*

YIG *abrév (grenat d'yttrium ferreux)* ELECTRON YIG *(yttrium iron garnet)*

youyou *m* NAUT dinghy

ytterbine *f* CHIMIE ytterbia

ytterbium *m (Yb)* CHIMIE ytterbium *(Yb)*

yttria *m* CHIMIE yttria

yttrite *f* MINERAUX yttrite

yttrium *m (Y)* CHIMIE yttrium *(Y)*

yttrocérite *f* CHIMIE, MINERAUX yttrocerite

yttrocolumbite *f* NUCLEAIRE yttrocolumbite

yttrogummite *f* NUCLEAIRE yttrogummite

yttrotantalite *f* MINERAUX yttrotantalite

yttrotitanite *f* MINERAUX yttrotitanite

Z

Z ^{1} *m* PHYSIQUE Z-coordinate

Z ^{2} *abrév (nombre de protons)* PHYS PART Z *(proton number)*

ZAA *abrév (zone à autonomie d'acheminement)* TELECOM group switching center catchment area (AmE), group switching center exchange area (AmE), group switching centre catchment area (BrE), group switching centre exchange area (BrE)

zapon: ~ **liquide** *m* CINEMAT blooping ink

zaponner *vt* CINEMAT bloop

zaratite *f* MINERAUX zaratite

zéaxanthine *f* CHIMIE zeaxanthin

zéine *f* CHIMIE, PLAST CAOU zein

zénith *m* ASTRONOMIE, ESPACE, NAUT zenith

zéolite *f* CHIMIE, LESSIVES, MATERIAUX, MINERAUX zeolite

zéphyr *m* METEO zephyr

zéro *m* CHIMIE, MATH, METROLOGIE *d'un appareil de mesure* zero; ~ **absolu** *m* CHIMIE, PHYSIQUE, REFRIG, THERMODYN absolute zero; ~ **des cartes** *m* NAUT chart datum; ~ **électrique** *m* ELECTR, INSTRUMENT electrical zero; ~ **en tête** *m* PRODUCTION *automatisme industriel* leading zero

zéromètre *m* ELECTR, INSTRUMENT null galvanometer

zéros: ~ **de filtre** *m* ELECTRON filter zeros

zeunérite *f* MINERAUX zeunerite

zietrisikite *f* CHIMIE zietrisikite

zinc *m (Zn)* CHIMIE zinc *(Zn)*; ~ **électrolytique** *m* MATERIAUX electrolytic zinc; ~ **plombifère** *m* MATERIAUX lead zinc

zincate *m* CHIMIE zincate

zincide *adj* CHIMIE zincoid

zincifère *adj* CHIMIE zincky

zincique *adj* CHIMIE zincic

zincite *f* MINERAUX zincite

zinckénite *f* MINERAUX zinckenite

zincon *m* CHIMIE zincon

zinconite *f* MINERAUX zinconize

zincosite *f* MINERAUX zincosite, zinkøsite

zingage *m* CHIMIE zincking, MATERIAUX galvanizing, PRODUCTION galvanization, REVETEMENT zinc coating; ~ **à froid** *m* MATERIAUX electrolytic galvanizing

zingibérène *m* CHIMIE zingiberene

zingué *adj* MECANIQUE *matériaux* galvanized

zinguer *vt* CONSTR zinc, PRODUCTION galvanize

zingueux *adj* CHIMIE zincky, zincous

zinnwaldite *f* MINERAUX zinnwaldite

zircaloy *m* NUCLEAIRE zircaloy, zirconium base alloy

zircon *m* CERAM VER, MATERIAUX, MINERAUX zircon

zirconate *m* CHIMIE zirconate

zircone *f* CERAM VER, CHIMIE zirconia

zirconifluorure *m* CHIMIE zirconifluoride

zirconique *adj* CHIMIE zirconic

zirconium *m (Zr)* CHIMIE zirconium *(Zr)*

zirconyle *m* CHIMIE zirconyl

Zn *(zinc)* CHIMIE Zn *(zinc)*

zodiaque *m* ASTRONOMIE zodiac

zoïsite *f* MINERAUX zoisite

zonation *f* GEOLOGIE *des minéraux* zoning

zone *f* CONSTR area, CRISTALL, GEOLOGIE *subdivision d'un étage* zone, ORDINAT area, zone;

~ a ~ **d'accumulation pétrolière** *f* PETROLE zone of petroleum accumulation; ~ **active** *f* ELECTRON active region, ENREGISTR live end; ~ **affectée thermiquement** *f* MECANIQUE, THERMODYN *soudage* heat-affected zone; ~ **affichée à l'écran** *f* IMPRIM image; ~ **d'affinage** *f* CERAM VER refining zone; ~ **altérée** *f* PETR low-velocity layer, weathering; ~ **anacoustique** *f* ENREGISTR zone of silence; ~ **d'analyse** *f* TV scanning area; ~ **appauvrie** *f* METALL denuded zone; ~ **d'appauvrissement** *f* ELECTRON depletion layer; ~ **d'arrêt d'autobus** *f* TRANSPORT bus bay; ~ **aurorale** *f* ESPACE auroral zone; ~ **des aurores polaires** *f* GEOPHYS auroral belt; ~ **à autonomie d'acheminement** *f (Z.A.A.)* TELECOM local exchange area, trunk switching exchange area, TELECOM group switching center catchment area (AmE), group switching center exchange area (AmE), group switching centre catchment area (BrE), group switching centre exchange area (BrE); ~ **aveugle** *f* PETR blind zone; ~ **axiale** *f* GEOLOGIE *d'une dorsale* axial rift zone;

~ b ~ **balayée** *f* TV scanning area; ~ **de la base** *f* ELECTRON base region; ~ **de basse pression** *f* METEO low, low-pressure area, low-pressure zone; ~ **Benioff** *f* EN RENOUV *ressources géothermiques* Benioff zone; ~ **de bombardement** *f* MILITAIRE bombing area; ~ **bordière** *f* GEOLOGIE margin; ~ **de braise** *f* CERAM VER conditioning zone; ~ **de Brillouin** *f* METALL, PHYSIQUE Brillouin zone; ~ **de brouillage** *f* TV interference area; ~ **de broyage tectonique** *f* GEOLOGIE crush belt; ~ **broyée** *f* GEOLOGIE shear zone;

~ c ~ **calme** *f* NAUT doldrums; ~ **chargée de combustible extérieur** *f* NUCLEAIRE outer fueled zone (AmE), outer fuelled zone (BrE); ~ **de chauffage** *f* THERMODYN heating zone; ~ **cisaillée** *f* GEOLOGIE shear zone; ~ **de coeur** *f* OPTIQUE, TELECOM core area; ~ **du collecteur** *f* ELECTROTEC collector region; ~ **commune** *f* INFORMAT, ORDINAT common area; ~ **de conditionnement** *f* PRODUCTION packaging area; ~ **de conduction** *f* ELECTROTEC conducting zone; ~ **conductrice** *f* ELECTROTEC conducting zone; ~ **de contact entre deux rouleaux** *f* PAPIER nip; ~ **contiguë** *f* OCEANO contiguous zone; ~ **de contrôle** *f* INFORMAT, ORDINAT control field; ~ **de coordination** *f* ESPACE coordination area; ~ **de couverture** *f* ESPACE coverage area; ~ **de couverture d'un satellite** *f* TV satellite coverage area;

~ d ~ **dangereuse** *f* SECURITE danger area, danger zone, hazardous zone; ~ **de décrochement entre deux plaques lithosphériques** *f* GEOLOGIE conservative plate-margin; ~ **déformable** *f* AUTO crumple zone, TRANSPORT collapsible section; ~ **dénucléarisée** *f* MILITAIRE nuclear-free zone; ~ **de dépassement de capacité** *f* INFORMAT, ORDINAT overflow area; ~ **de déplacement** *f* NUCLEAIRE displacement spike; ~ **de déplétion** *f* ELECTRON, PHYSIQUE depletion layer;

~ e ~ **de l'émetteur** *f* ELECTROTEC emitter region; ~ **émettrice** *f* ELECTROTEC emitter region; ~ **d'emprunt** *f*

CONSTR borrow pit; ~ **en arrière du récif** *f* GEOLOGIE back reef; ~ **d'encollage lié à un schéma** *f* IMPRIM *façonnage, continu* pad; ~ **d'enracinement** *f* GEOLOGIE root zone; ~ **d'entrée** *f* INFORMAT, ORDINAT input area; ~ **envahie** *f* PETR invaded zone; ~ **de l'épicentre** *f* GEOPHYS epicentral area; ~ **d'extinction** *f* GAZ extinction zone;

~ f ~ **formante** *f* ACOUSTIQUE formant; ~ **formantique** *f* ACOUSTIQUE formant; ~ **de fracture** *f* GEOPHYS fracture zone; ~ **de Fresnel** *f* TELECOM Fresnel zone; ~ **de frittage** *f* CERAM VER fritting zone;

~ g ~ **de gaz** *f* GAZ gas band; ~ **Guinier-Preston** *f* CRISTALL GP, Guinier-Preston zone;

~ h ~ **de haute pression** *f* METEO high, high-pressure area, high-pressure zone;

~ i ~ **imprimante** *f* IMPRIM *impression* image area; ~ **imprimante texte et illustrations** *f* IMPRIM *plaques et films* image; ~ **imprimée avec texte et image** *f* IMPRIM *impression* image; ~ **inactive** *f* INFORMAT, ORDINAT dead zone; ~ **d'influence** *f* DISTRI EAU area of influence; ~ **d'initialisation** *f* PRODUCTION *automatisme industriel* boot area; ~ **intacte** *f* POLLUTION unspoilt land; ~ **interdite** *f* NAUT prohibited area; ~ **intertidale** *f* POLLU MER intertidal zone; ~ **intertropicale** *f* METEO equatorial zone; ~ **d'invasion** *f* PETR invaded zone;

~ l ~ **de largage** *f* ESPACE *véhicules* drop zone; ~ **lavée** *f* PETR flushed zone; ~ **libre** *f* ORDINAT free field; ~ **littorale** *f* GEOLOGIE littoral zone; ~ **locale** *f* TELECOM LCA, local calling area;

~ m ~ **de mauvais temps** *f* METEO bad weather zone; ~ **de mémorisation des messages** *f* PRODUCTION *automatisme industriel* message store area; ~ **métamorphique** *f* GEOLOGIE metamorphic zone; ~ **de métamorphisme** *f* GEOLOGIE metamorphic zone; ~ **de migration** *f* ELECTRON drift region; ~ **mobile** *f* GEOLOGIE mobile belt; ~ **morte** *f* ENREGISTR dead end, dead zone, PETR blind zone;

~ n ~ **navale d'exercices** *f* OCEANO naval exercise area, naval maneuvers zone (AmE), naval manoeuvres zone (BrE); ~ **de navigation** *f* OCEANO navigation zone; ~ **neigeuse** *f* METEO snow belt; ~ **néritique** *f* GEOLOGIE neritic zone; ~ **non imprimée** *f* IMPRIM *impression* blank; ~ **non-reconnue** *f* CONSTR unproved area;

~ o ~ **obscure cathodique** *f* ELECTROTEC cathode dark space; ~ **obscure de Crookes** *f* ELECTRON Crookes dark space; ~ **obscure de Faraday** *f* ELECTRON Faraday dark space; ~ **d'ombre** *f* TV poor reception area, shadow area; ~ **d'onde** *f* PHYS RAYON wave zone; ~ **orogénique** *f* GEOLOGIE mobile belt, orogenic zone; ~ **où les foyers ouverts sont interdits** *f* POLLUTION smokeless zone;

~ p ~ **de pêche** *f* OCEANO exclusive fishing zone, fishing zone; ~ **de perforation lié à un schéma** *f* IMPRIM *façonnage, continu* pad; ~ **P faiblement dopée** *f* ELECTRON p⁻-region; ~ **P fortement dopée** *f* ELECTRON p⁺-region; ~ **photosynthétique** *f* OCEANO photosynthetic layer; ~ **piétonne** *f* TRANSPORT pedestrian area, pedestrian zone, pedestrian-only crossing zone; ~ **piétons** *f* TRANSPORT pedestrian area, pedestrian zone, pedestrian-only crossing zone; ~ **de pilotage** *f* NAUT pilot waters, OCEANO pilotage waters, pilotage zone; ~ **de point fixe** *f* AERONAUT run-up area; ~ **de précipitations** *f* GENIE CHIM, METEO precipitation area; ~ **de précipitations acides** *f* POLLUTION acid rain zone, acidic area; ~ **de production** *f* PETR pool; ~ **productive**

f PETR pay zone; ~ **productive effective** *f* PETR net pay zone; ~ **productrice** *f* PETROLE pay zone; ~ **prouvée** *f* PETROLE proven area;

~ r ~ **de rassemblement** *f* NAUT assembly area; ~ **de réaction** *f* CHARBON reaction zone; ~ **de recherche** *f* INFORMAT, ORDINAT seek area; ~ **de refroidissement** *f* AGRO ALIM cooling section, CERAM VER cooling zone; ~ **de réglage** *f* COMMANDE regulating limits, regulating range; ~ **réservée aux piétons** *f* TRANSPORT pedestrian area, pedestrian zone, pedestrian-only crossing zone; ~ **réservée au texte** *f* IMPRIM text area; ~ **de retombées acides** *f* POLLUTION acid rain zone, acidic area; ~ **à risque** *f* SECURITE *pour appareillage électrique* hazardous zone;

~ s ~ **de saturation** *f* HYDROLOGIE zone of saturation; ~ **de saut** *f* MILITAIRE drop zone, dropping zone; ~ **de séchage** *f* AGRO ALIM drying area, drying section; ~ **de sécurité agréée** *f* SECURITE approved safety area; ~ **de sécurité de cadrage** *f* CINEMAT safe action area; ~ **de service** *f* ESPACE service area; ~ **de silence** *f* ENREGISTR zone of silence; ~ **de sortie** *f* INFORMAT, ORDINAT output area; ~ **source** *f* OCEANO cold water downwelling zone; ~ **sous-compactée** *f* GEOLOGIE, PETR undercompacted zone; ~ **sous douane** *f* NAUT bonded area; ~ **de stationnement** *f* CONSTR lay-by, turnout; ~ **de stockage temporaire** *f* IMPRIM *bande de papier en rotative* buffer; ~ **de subduction** *f* PETROLE subduction zone;

~ t ~ **tempérée** *f* METEO temperate zone; ~ **de tension** *f* TEXTILE stretching zone; ~ **de terrain profondément altérée** *f* CONSTR area of deep weathering; ~ **torride** *f* METEO torrid zone; ~ **de totalité** *f* ASTRONOMIE *d'une éclipse solaire* path of totality; ~ **de touché des roues** *f* AERONAUT touchdown zone; ~ **de transition** *f* ELECTRON crossover area, PETR, PETROLE transition zone; ~ **de transit principale** *f* TELECOM main trunk exchange area; ~ **de transit secondaire** *f* TELECOM second-tier trunk exchange area; ~ **de travail** *f* INFORMAT work area, working area, NUCLEAIRE operation area, ORDINAT work area, working area; ~ **de tremblements de terre** *f* GEOPHYS seismic zone; ~ **de type P⁻** *f* ELECTRON p⁻-region; ~ **de type P⁺** *f* ELECTRON p⁺-region;

~ u ~ **de l'utilisateur** *f* INFORMAT, ORDINAT UA, user area; ~ **d'utilisation** *f* PRODUCTION operational range;

~ v ~ **de vidage mémoire** *f* PRODUCTION *automatisme industriel* dump area; ~ **vide** *f* INFORMAT, ORDINAT clear zone

Zone: ~ **internationale des fonds marins** *f* OCEANO International Sea Bed Area

zoné *adj* GEOLOGIE, PETR banded

zonéographie *f* GEOLOGIE *d'un terrain métamorphique* zonation

zones: ~ **d'étirage** *f pl* TEXTILE draft zones (AmE), draught zones (BrE); ~ **externes** *f pl* GEOLOGIE *d'une chaîne ou orogène* externides; ~ **de flexure** *f pl* GEOLOGIE *crénulations en bandes* kink bands; ~ **imprimantes ne prenant pas l'encre sur la plaque** *f pl* IMPRIM *impression* drop-out; ~ **internes** *f pl* GEOLOGIE *d'une chaîne orogène* internides; ~ **de travail à haute risque** *f pl* SECURITE high-risk areas of work

zoom *m* CINEMAT zoom, zoom lens, IMPRIM *photogravure, composition, optique,* INFORMAT, ORDINAT ZOOM, PHOTO zoom, zoom lens; ~ **arrière** *m* INFORMAT, ORDINAT zoom out; ~ **avant** *m* INFORMAT, ORDINAT zoom in; ~ **à commande électrique** *m* CINEMAT mo-

torized zoom lens
zoomer *vt* CINEMAT, PHOTO zoom
zoostérol *m* CHIMIE zoosterol
zootaxie *f* CHIMIE zootaxy
zootaxique *adj* CHIMIE zootaxic
zooxanthine *f* CHIMIE zooxanthine
zorgite *f* MINERAUX zorgite

Zr *(zirconium)* CHIMIE Zr *(zirconium)*
zunyite *f* MINERAUX zunyite
zymase *f* CHIMIE zymase
zymine *f* CHIMIE zymin
zymique *adj* CHIMIE zymic
zymohydrolyse *f* CHIMIE zymohydrolysis

Abbreviations/Abréviations

A *abrév (ampère)* ELECTR, ELECTROTEC, METROLOGIE, PHYSIQUE A *(ampere)*

ADAC *abrév (avion à décollage et atterrissage courts)* AERONAUT, TRANSPORT STOL aircraft *(short takeoff and landing aircraft)*

ADAO *abrév (avion à décollage et atterrissage ordinaires)* AERONAUT CTOL aircraft *(conventional takeoff and landing aircraft)*

ADAR *abrév (avion à décollage et atterrissage réduits)* AERONAUT RTOL aircraft *(reduced takeoff and landing aircraft)*

ADAS *abrév (avion à décollage et atterrissage silencieux)* AERONAUT QTOL aircraft *(quiet takeoff and landing aircraft)*

ADAV *abrév (avion à décollage et atterrissage verticaux)* AERONAUT VTOL aircraft *(vertical takeoff and landing aircraft)*

ADN *abrév (acide désoxyribonucléique)* CHIMIE DNA *(deoxyribonucleic acid)*

AMES *abrév (accès multiple par étalement du spectre)* ESPACE SSMA *(spread spectrum multiple access)*

AMRC *abrév (accès multiple par répartition en code)* ESPACE communications CDMA *(code-division multiple access)*

AMRF *abrév (accès multiple à répartition en fréquence)* ESPACE, TELECOM FDMA *(frequency-division multiple access)*

AMRT *abrév (accès multiple par répartition dans le temps)* ELECTRON, ESPACE, INFORMAT, TELECOM TDMA *(time-division multiple access)*

ANSI *abrév (Institut américain de normalisation)* TELECOM ANSI *(American National Standards Institute)*

AR *abrév* CONS MECA *(arrière)* head-end, INFORMAT *(accusé de réception)*, ORDINAT *(accusé de réception)*, TELECOM *(accusé de réception)* ACK *(acknowledgement)*

ASCII *abrév* IMPRIM, INFORMAT, ORDINAT ASCII, American Standard Code for Information Interchange

ASE *abrév (Agence spatiale européenne)* ASTRONOMIE, ESPACE ESA *(European Space Agency)*

ATD *abrév (analyse thermique différentielle)* CONSTR, PLAST CAOU, POLLUTION, THERMODYN DTA *(differential thermal analysis)*

ATOP *abrév (amplificateur à tube à ondes progressives)* ELECTRON, ESPACE communications TWTA *(traveling-wave tube amplifier, travelling-wave tube amplifier)*

ATS *abrév (agent technique de saturation)* OCEANO caisson master, life support technician

b *abrév (barn)* PHYS PART b *(barn)*

BASIC *abrév* INFORMAT, ORDINAT BASIC, beginner's all-purpose symbolic instruction code

BDR *abrév (base de données relationnelles)* INFORMAT, ORDINAT, TELECOM RDB *(relational database)*

BF *abrév (basse fréquence)* ELECTR, ELECTRON, ELECTROTEC, PHYS RAYON, TELECOM LF *(low-frequency)*

BHT *abrév (hydroxytoluène butylé)* AGRO ALIM BHT *(butylated hydroxytoluene)*

BLU *abrév (bande latérale unique)* TELECOM SSB *(single sideband)*

BOP *abrév* COMMANDE *(bloc obturateur de puits)* BOP *(blowout preventer)*, GAZ *(bloc d'obturation de puits)* BOP *(blowout preventer)*, OCEANO *(bloc obturateur de puits)*, PETR *(bloc d'obturation de puits)*, PETROLE *(bloc obturateur de puits)* BOP *(blowout preventer)*

BPS *abrév (bits par seconde)* ORDINAT BPS *(bits per second)*

Bq *abrév (becquerel)* METROLOGIE, PHYS RAYON, PHYSIQUE Bq *(becquerel)*

c *abrév (centi-)* METROLOGIE c *(centi-)*

C *abrév* ELECTR *(coulomb)*, ELECTROTEC *(coulomb)* C *(coulomb)*, METROLOGIE *(centigrade)* C *(centigrade)*, METROLOGIE *(Celsius)* C *(Celsius)*, METROLOGIE *(coulomb)*, PHYSIQUE *(coulomb)* C *(coulomb)*

CA *abrév (courant alternatif)* ELECTR, ELECTRON, ELECTROTEC, ENREGISTR, PHYSIQUE, TELECOM, TV AC *(alternating current)*

CAC *abrév (contrôle automatique de chrominance)* TV ACC *(automatic chrominance control)*

CAF *abrév* COMMANDE *(contrôle automatique de fréquence)*, ELECTR *(commande automatique de fréquence)*, ELECTRON *(commande automatique de fréquence)*, ENREGISTR *(contrôle automatique de fréquence)*, PHYSIQUE *(commande automatique de fréquence)*, PRODUCTION *(commande automatique de fréquence)*, TELECOM *(commande automatique de fréquence)*, TV *(contrôle automatique de fréquence)* AFC *(automatic frequency control)*

CAG *abrév* COMMANDE *(contrôle automatique de gain)*, ELECTRON *(commande automatique de gain)*, GEOPHYS *(contrôle automatique de gain)*, TELECOM *(commande automatique de gain)* AGC *(automatic gain control)*

CAM *abrév (corde aérodynamique moyenne)* AERONAUT MAC *(mean aerodynamic chord)*

CAN *abrév (convertisseur analogique-numérique)* ELECTRON ADC *(analog-to-digital converter, analogue-to-digital converter)*, ORDINAT ADC *(analog-to-digital converter)*, PHYSIQUE, TELECOM ADC *(analog-to-digital converter, analogue-to-digital converter)*

CAO *abrév (conception assistée par ordinateur)* ELECTR, IMPRIM, MECANIQUE, ORDINAT, PRODUCTION, TELECOM CAD *(computer-aided design)*

CAP *abrév (capacité d'absorption des protons)* PHYS RAYON proton absorptive capacity

CAV *abrév (commande automatique de volume)* COMMANDE, ELECTROTEC, OPTIQUE, PHYSIQUE AVC *(automatic volume control)*

Cc *abrév (cirro-cumulus)* METEO Cc *(cirrocumulus)*

CC *abrév (courant continu)* CH DE FER, ELECTRON, ELECTROTEC, ENREGISTR, PRODUCTION, TELECOM, TV DC *(direct current)*

CCD *abrév (dispositif à couplage de charge, circuit CCD)* ASTRONOMIE, ELECTRON, ELECTROTEC, ORDINAT, PHYSIQUE, TELECOM, TV CCD *(charge-coupled device)*

CCIR *abrév (Comité consultatif international des radio-communications)* TELECOM CCIR *(International Radio Consultative Committee)*

CCITT *abrév (Comité consultatif international télégraphique et téléphonique)* TELECOM CCITT *(International Telegraph and Telephone Consultative Committee)*

CCL *abrév (contrôle de charge de ligne)* TELECOM LLC *(line load control)*

CCV *abrév (commutateur de circuits virtuels)* TELECOM VCS *(virtual-circuit switch)*

cd *abrév (candela)* ELECTROTEC, METROLOGIE, OPTIQUE, PHYSIQUE cd *(candela)*

CDA *abrév (couche de demi-atténuation)* NUCLEAIRE, PHYSIQUE HVL *(half value layer)*

CD-ROM *abrév (disque compact ROM)* INFORMAT, OPTIQUE, ORDINAT CD-ROM *(compact disk-read only memory)*

CEC *abrév (capacité d'échange cationique)* GEOLOGIE, PETROLE, POLLUTION CEC *(cation exchange capacity)*

CERN *abrév (Conseil européen pour la recherche nucléaire)* PHYS PART CERN *(European Organization for Nuclear Research)*

CFAO *abrév (conception et fabrication assistées par ordinateur)* ORDINAT, PRODUCTION CADCAM *(computer-aided design and manufacture)*

CFC *abrév* CHIMIE *(cubique à faces centrées)*, CRISTALL *(cubique à faces centrées)* FCC *(face-centered cubic, face-centred cubic)*, EMBALLAGE *(chlorofluorocarbone)*, POLLUTION *(chlorofluorocarbone)* CFC *(chlorofluorocarbon)*

CG *abrév (convertisseur de gestion)* TELECOM charge-metering converter

CGL *abrév (chromatographie gaz-liquide)* POLLUTION, THERMODYN gas liquid chromatography

CGS *abrév* METROLOGIE *(centimètre-gramme-seconde)* CGS *(centimetre-gramme-second)*, POLLUTION *(chromatographie gaz-solide)* gas solid chromatography

Ci *abrév (cirrus)* METEO Ci *(cirrus)*

CI *abrév* ELECTR *(circuit intégré)*, ELECTRON *(circuit intégré)* IC *(integrated circuit)*, ELECTRON *(circuit imprimé)*, INFORMAT *(circuit imprimé)* PC *(printed circuit)*, ORDINAT *(circuit intégré)* IC *(integrated circuit)*, ORDINAT *(circuit imprimé)* PC *(printed circuit)*, PHYSIQUE *(circuit intégré)* IC *(integrated circuit)*, PHYSIQUE *(circuit imprimé)* PC *(printed circuit)*, TELECOM *(circuit intégré)* IC *(integrated circuit)*, TELECOM *(circuit imprimé)* PC *(printed circuit)*, TV *(circuit intégré)* IC *(integrated circuit)*, TV *(circuit imprimé)* PC *(printed circuit)*

CIRD *abrév (code d'identification de réseau de données)* TELECOM DNIC *(data network identification code)*

CIRT *abrév (code d'identification de réseau télex)* TELECOM telex network identification code

CL50 *abrév (concentration létale à 50%)* POLLUTION median lethal concentration

CLF *abrév (combustion sur lit fluidisé)* POLLUTION fluidized bed combustion

CLHP *abrév (chromatographie liquide à haute pression)* AGRO ALIM, CHIMIE, EQUIP LAB, POLLUTION HPLC *(high-pressure liquid chromatography)*

CMI *abrév (concentration maximale d'immixtion)* POLLUTION maximum emission concentration

CMS *abrév (composant monté en surface)* ELECTRON, TELECOM SMC *(surface-mounted component)*

CN *abrév (commande numérique)* COMMANDE, CONS MECA, PRODUCTION NC *(numerical control)*

CNA *abrév* ELECTRON *(convertisseur numérique-analogique)* DAC *(digital-to-analog converter, digital-to-analogue converter)*, ORDINAT *(convertisseur numérique-analogique)* DAC *(digital-to-analog converter)*, POLLUTION *(capacité de neutralisation des acides)* ANC *(acid neutralizing capacity)*, TV *(convertisseur numérique-analogique)* DAC *(digital-to-analog converter, digital-to-analogue converter)*

CNC *abrév (concentration numérique des conversations)* TELECOM DSI *(digital speech interpolation)*

CNP *abrév (concentration numérique de la parole)* TELECOM digital speech compression

CNS *abrév (concentrateur numérique satellite)* TELECOM digital satellite concentrator

COD *abrév (carbone organique dissous)* POLLUTION dissolved organic carbon

COO *abrév (conception orientée objet)* INFORMAT, ORDINAT OOD *(object-oriented design)*

CPG *abrév (chromatographie en phase gazeuse)* AGRO ALIM, CHIMIE, MATERIAUX gas chromatography

CPP *abrév (concentré de protéines de poisson)* OCEANO FPC *(fish protein concentrate)*

CPS *abrév (caractères par seconde)* IMPRIM, ORDINAT CPS *(characters per second)*

CPUE *abrév (prise par unité d'effort)* OCEANO CUE *(catch per unit effort)*

CRC *abrév (contrôle de redondance cyclique)* COMMANDE, ELECTRON, ORDINAT CRC *(cyclical redundancy check)*

Cs *abrév (cirro-stratus)* METEO Cs *(cirrostratus)*

CSMA *abrév (accès multiple par détection de porteuse)* TELECOM CSMA *(carrier sense multiple access)*

CSMA-CD *abrév (accès multiple par détection de porteuse avec détection de collision)* ELECTRON, INFORMAT, ORDINAT CSMA-CD *(carrier sense multiple access with collision detection)*

CT *abrév (centre de transit)* TELECOM trunk transit exchange

CTV *abrév (conteneur virtuel)* TELECOM virtual container

Cu *abrév (cumulus)* METEO Cu *(cumulus)*

CUP *abrév (coefficient d'utilisation pratique)* MINES WS *(weight strength)*

CVCP *abrév (concentration volumique critique de pigment)* REVETEMENT peinture CPVC *(critical pigment volume concentration)*

D *abrév (dé)* PHYSIQUE dee

da *abrév (déca)* METROLOGIE da *(deca-)*

DAV *abrév (dépôt axial en phase vapeur)* OPTIQUE, TELECOM VAD *(vapor phase axial deposition, vapour phase axial deposition)*

dB *abrév (décibel)* ACOUSTIQUE, ENREGISTR, PHYS RAYON, PHYSIQUE, POLLUTION dB *(decibel)*

DBE *abrév (densité de boue équivalente)* PETROLE forage EMW *(Equivalent Mud Weight)*

DBO *abrév (demande biochimique d'oxygène)* AGRO ALIM, HYDROLOGIE, PETROLE, POLLUTION BOD *(biochemical oxygen demand)*

DBV *abrév (débit binaire variable)* TELECOM VBR *(variable bit rate)*

DCA *abrév (défense contre avions)* MILITAIRE air defence

DCB *abrév (décimal codé binaire)* ORDINAT BCD *(binary-coded decimal)*

DCO *abrév (demande chimique d'oxygène)* CHIMIE, HYDROLOGIE, POLLUTION COD *(chemical oxygen demand)*

DCV *abrév (dépôt chimique en phase vapeur)* ELECTRON, OPTIQUE, TELECOM CVD *(chemical vapor deposition, chemical vapour deposition)*

ddp *abrév (différence de potentiel)* PHYSIQUE pd *(potential difference)*

DEL *abrév (diode électroluminescente)* ELECTR affichage, ELECTRON, INFORMAT, OPTIQUE, ORDINAT, PHYS RAYON, PHYSIQUE, TELECOM, TV LED *(light-emitting diode)*

DIN *abrév (Deutsche Industrienorm)* CONS MECA DIN *(Deutsche Industrienorm)*

DL *abrév (dose létale)* PHYSIQUE, POLLUTION LD *(lethal dose)*

DL50 *abrév (dose létale médiane, dose létale 50%)* NUCLEAIRE, PHYS RAYON, POLLUTION, SECURITE LD50 *(median lethal dose)*

DLM *abrév (dose létale moyenne)* NUCLEAIRE, PHYS RAYON, POLLUTION, SECURITE MLD *(mean lethal dose)*

DON *abrév* INFORMAT *(disque optique non effaçable)* WOOD *(write-once optical disk)*, OPTIQUE *(disque optique numérique)* digital optical disk

DOS *abrév (système d'exploitation à disque)* INFORMAT, ORDINAT DOS *(disk operating system)*

DP *abrév (discriminateur de protocole)* TELECOM PD *(protocol discriminator)*

DRASC *abrév (diffusion Raman anti-Stokes cohérente)* PHYSIQUE CARS *(coherent anti-Stokes Raman scattering)*

DSL *abrév (diode superluminescente)* OPTIQUE, TELECOM SLD *(superluminescent diode)*

DTC *abrév (dispositif à transfert de charges)* ELECTROTEC, ESPACE *véhicules,* PHYSIQUE, TELECOM CTD *(charge transfer device)*

DVT *abrév (défaut de verrouillage trame)* TELECOM out-of-frame

E *abrév (exa-)* METROLOGIE E *(exa-)*

EAA *abrév (équipement d'appel automatique)* INFORMAT, ORDINAT ACU *(automatic calling unit)*

EAO *abrév (enseignement assisté par ordinateur)* ORDINAT CAL *(computer-assisted learning)*

EDI *abrév* TELECOM *(échange de données informatisées, échange de documents informatisés)* EDI *(electronic document interchange)*

EGA *abrév (adaptateur graphique couleur)* ORDINAT carte EGA *(enhanced graphics adaptor)*

EMCN *abrév (équipement de multiplication de circuit numérique)* TELECOM DCME *(digital circuit multiplication equipment)*

EPR *abrév (exploitation privée reconnue)* TELECOM recognized private operating agency

E/S *abrév (entrée/sortie)* ORDINAT, PRODUCTION I/O *(input/output)*

ESC *abrév (échappement)* INFORMAT, ORDINAT ESC *(escape)*

ETCD *abrév (équipement terminal de circuit de données)* TELECOM DCE *(data circuit terminal equipment)*

ETD *abrév (équipement terminal de données)* AERONAUT, ORDINAT, TELECOM DTE *(data terminal equipment)*

ETTD *abrév (équipement terminal de traitement de données)* AERONAUT, ORDINAT, TELECOM DTE *(data terminal equipment)*

ETTD-F *abrév (équipement terminal de traitement de données fixe)* TELECOM fixed data processing terminal equipment

ETTD-MT *abrév (équipement terminal mobile terrestre de traitement de données)* TELECOM mobile data processing terminal equipment

eV *abrév (électron-volt)* ELECTROTEC, METROLOGIE, PHYS PART, PHYSIQUE eV *(electronvolt)*

f *abrév (femto-)* METROLOGIE f *(femto-)*

F *abrév (farad)* METROLOGIE F *(farad)*

FAO *abrév (fabrication assistée par ordinateur)* ELECTR, ORDINAT, TELECOM CAM *(computer-aided manufacture)*

fcém *abrév (force contre-électromotrice)* ELECTR, ELECTROTEC, PHYSIQUE bemf *(back electromotive force, back emf)*, cemf *(counter-electromotive force, counter emf)*

fém *abrév (force électromotrice)* ELECTR, ELECTROTEC, PHYSIQUE emf *(electromotive force)*

FI *abrév (fréquence intermédiaire)* ELECTRON, TELECOM IF *(intermediate frequency)*

fmm *abrév (force magnétomotrice)* ELECTR, PHYSIQUE mmf *(magnetomotive force)*

FNE *abrév (fumée normalisée équivalente)* POLLUTION equivalent standard smoke

FOB *abrév (franco à bord)* NAUT *commerce, transport maritime* FOB *(free on board)*

FPB *abrév (filtre passe-bande)* ELECTR, ELECTRON, ENREGISTR, INFORMAT, ORDINAT, PHYSIQUE, TELECOM, TV BPF *(band-pass filter)*

G *abrév (giga-)* METROLOGIE G *(giga-)*

GBD *abrév (gestion de base de données)* INFORMAT, ORDINAT DBM *(database management)*

GFU *abrév (groupe fermé d'usagers)* INFORMAT, ORDINAT, TELECOM CUG *(closed user group)*

GMCN *abrév (gain de l'équipement de multiplication de circuit numérique)* TELECOM DCMG *(digital circuit multiplication gain)*

GNL *abrév (gaz naturel liquéfié)* GAZ, PETROLE, THERMODYN LNG *(liquefied natural gas)*

GNS *abrév (gaz naturel de synthèse)* GAZ, PETROLE SNG *(synthetic natural gas)*

GPL *abrév (gaz de pétrole liquéfié)* CHAUFFAGE, GAZ, PETROLE, THERMODYN, TRANSPORT LPG *(liquefied petroleum gas)*

G-T *abrév (rapport gain-température de bruit)* ESPACE *facteur de qualité* G-T *(gain-to-noise temperature ratio)*

GUA *abrév (groupe d'unités administratives)* TELECOM administrative unit group

Gy *abrév (gray)* METROLOGIE, PHYS RAYON, PHYSIQUE Gy *(gray)*

h *abrév (hecto-)* METROLOGIE h *(hecto-)*

H *abrév (henry)* ELECTR *unité d'inductance,* ELECTROTEC, METROLOGIE, PHYSIQUE H *(henry)*

Ha *abrév (humidité relative de l'air)* METEO relative humidity of the air

HC *abrév (conteneur hors-cotes)* TRANSPORT HC *(high*

cube container)

HDP *abrév (hauteur des pointes)* CONS MECA height of centers (AmE), height of centres (BrE)

HF *abrév (haute fréquence)* AERONAUT, ELECTR, ELECTRON, ELECTROTEC HF *(high-frequency)*

hlp *abrév (haut le pied)* CH DE FER *véhicules* running light

HNS *abrév (hiérarchie numérique synchrone)* TELECOM SDH *(synchronous digital hierarchy)*

HPA *abrév (heure prévue d'arrivée)* AERONAUT, NAUT ETA *(estimated time of arrival)*

HT *abrév (haute tension)* ELECTR *alimentation,* ELECTROTEC, PHYSIQUE HT *(high-tension),* HV *(high-voltage)*

Hz *abrév (hertz)* ELECTR, ELECTROTEC, METROLOGIE, PETR, PHYSIQUE, TV Hz *(hertz)*

IA *abrév (intelligence artificielle)* ORDINAT, TELECOM AI *(artificial intelligence)*

IAO *abrév (instruction assistée par ordinateur)* ORDINAT CAI *(computer-assisted instruction)*

ID *abrév (identification)* INFORMAT, ORDINAT ID *(identification)*

IDI *abrév (identificateur du domaine initial)* TELECOM IDI *(initial domain identifier)*

IGD *abrév (message d'interrogation de groupe de circuits demande)* TELECOM CQM *(circuit group query request message)*

IGR *abrév (message d'interrogation de groupe de circuits réponse)* TELECOM CQR *(circuit group query response message)*

I²L *abrév (logique intégrée à injection)* ELECTRON I²L *(integrated injection logic)*

ILA *abrév (identification de la ligne appelante)* TELECOM CLI *(calling line identification)*

IN *abrév (indice de netteté)* TELECOM AI *(articulation index)*

IND *abrév (message de demande d'information)* TELECOM INR *(information request message)*

IR *abrév (infrarouge)* OPTIQUE, PHYS RAYON, PHYSIQUE IR *(infrared)*

IRAS *abrév (satellite astronomique infrarouge)* ASTRONOMIE IRAS *(infrared astronomical satellite)*

ISO *abrév* CONS MECA *(Organisation internationale de normalisation)* ISO *(International Standards Organization),* INFORMAT *(interconnexion de systèmes ouverts),* ORDINAT *(interconnexion de systèmes ouverts)* OSI *(open systems interconnection),* TELECOM *(Organisation internationale de normalisation)* ISO *(International Standards Organization),* TELECOM *(interconnexion de systèmes ouverts)* OSI *(open systems interconnection)*

J *abrév (joule)* AGRO ALIM, ELECTR, MECANIQUE, METROLOGIE, PHYSIQUE, THERMODYN J *(joule)*

JET *abrév (tore européen conjoint)* NUCLEAIRE, PHYS RAYON *recherche de fusion* JET *(Joint European Torus)*

k *abrév (kilo-)* METROLOGIE k *(kilo-)*

K *abrév (kelvin)* METROLOGIE, PHYSIQUE, THERMODYN K *(kelvin)*

Kcal *abrév (kilocalorie)* AGRO ALIM Kcal *(kilocalorie)*

kCi *abrév (kilocurie)* CHIMIE kCi *(kilocurie)*

keV *abrév (kilo-électronvolt)* CHIMIE keV *(kilo-electronvolt)*

kg *abrév (kilogramme)* METROLOGIE kg *(kilogram, kilogramme)*

km *abrév (kilomètre)* METROLOGIE km *(kilometer, kilometre)*

kn *abrév (kilonème)* CHIMIE kn *(kilonem)*

ko *abrév (kilo-octet)* INFORMAT, ORDINAT kb *(kilobyte)*

kV *abrév (kilovolt)* ELECTROTEC kV *(kilovolt)*

kW *abrév (kilowatt)* ELECTR, ELECTROTEC kW *(kilowatt)*

l *abrév (litre)* METROLOGIE l *(litre)*

LEAR *abrév (anneau d'antiprotons de basse énergie)* PHYS PART LEAR *(low-energy antiproton ring)*

LEP *abrév (grand collisionneur électron-positron)* PHYS PART LEP *(large electron-positron collider)*

LGN *abrév (liquide de gaz naturel)* GAZ, PETROLE NGL *(natural gas liquid)*

LIB *abrév (message de libération)* TELECOM REL *(release message)*

lm *abrév (lumen)* METROLOGIE lm *(lumen)*

LPM *abrév (lignes par minute)* INFORMAT, ORDINAT LPM *(lines per minute)*

LQMAC *abrév (limite de qualité moyenne après contrôle)* QUALITE AOQL *(average outgoing quality limit)*

LRS *abrév (long rail soudé)* CH DE FER CWR *(continuous welded rail)*

LSI *abrév (intégration à grande échelle)* ELECTRON, INFORMAT, NAUT, ORDINAT, PHYSIQUE, TELECOM LSI *(large-scale integration)*

lx *abrév (lux)* METROLOGIE lx *(lux)*

m *abrév (milli-)* METROLOGIE m *(milli-)*

M *abrév (méga-)* METROLOGIE M *(mega-)*

mA *abrév (milliampère)* ELECTR, ELECTROTEC mA *(milliampere)*

MA *abrév* ELECTRON *(modulation d'amplitude),* ENREGISTR *(modulation d'amplitude),* ORDINAT *(modulation d'amplitude)* AM *(amplitude modulation),* PHYSIQUE *(multiplexage analogique)* FDM *(frequency-division multiplexing),* TV *(modulation d'amplitude)* AM *(amplitude modulation)*

MAD *abrév (demande de modification d'appel)* TELECOM CMR *(call modification request message)*

MAE *abrév (message de modification d'appel effectuée)* TELECOM CMC *(call modification completed message)*

MAQ *abrév (modulation d'amplitude en quadrature)* ELECTRON, INFORMAT, ORDINAT, TELECOM QAM *(quadrature amplitude modulation)*

MAR *abrév (message de refus de modification d'appel)* TELECOM CMRJ *(call modification reject message)*

MDF *abrév (modulation par déplacement de fréquence)* ELECTRON, INFORMAT, ORDINAT, TELECOM, TV FSK *(frequency shift keying)*

MDP *abrév (modulation par déplacement de phase)* ELECTRON, ESPACE *communications,* INFORMAT, ORDINAT PSK *(phase shift keying)*

MDPB *abrév (modulation par déplacement de phase bivalente)* TELECOM BPSK *(binary phase shift keying)*

MDPC *abrév (modulation par déplacement de phase cohérente)* TELECOM CPSK *(coherent phase shift keying)*

MDPQ *abrév (modulation par déplacement de phase quadrivalente)* ELECTRON, TELECOM QPSK *(quadriphase shift keying, quatenary phase-shift keying)*

MEV *abrév (mémoire vive)* ELECTRON, INFORMAT,

ORDINAT RAM *(random access memory)*

MF *abrév (modulation de fréquence)* ELECTR, ELECTRON, ENREGISTR, ORDINAT, PHYS ONDES, PHYSIQUE, TELECOM, TV FM *(frequency modulation)*

mg *abrév (milligramme)* METROLOGIE mg *(milligram)*

MHD *abrév (magnétohydrodynamique)* ELECTROTEC, ESPACE, GEOPHYS MHD *(magnetohydrodynamic)*

MIA *abrév (modulation d'impulsions en amplitude)* ELECTRON, ESPACE, INFORMAT, ORDINAT, TELECOM PAM *(pulse amplitude modulation)*

MIC *abrév* ELECTRON *(modulation par impulsion et codage, modulation par impulsion codée)*, ESPACE, INFORMAT, ORDINAT, PHYS RAYON, PHYSIQUE, TV PCM *(pulse code modulation)*

MICDA *abrév (modulation par impulsions et codage différentiels adaptatifs)* TELECOM ADPCM *(adaptive differential pulse code modulation)*

MID *abrév (modulation par impulsions de durée)* ELECTRON, ESPACE PDM *(pulse duration modulation)*

MIMD *abrév (multiflux d'instruction-multiflux de données)* INFORMAT, ORDINAT MIMD *(multiple-instruction multiple-data)*

MIPS *abrév (millions d'instructions par seconde)* IMPRIM, INFORMAT, ORDINAT MIPS *(millions of instructions per second)*

MISD *abrév (multiflux d'instruction-monoflux de donnés)* INFORMAT, ORDINAT MISD *(multiple-instruction single-data)*

MLM *abrév (modes longitudinaux multiples)* TELECOM MLM *(multilongitudinal modes)*

mm *abrév (millimètre)* METROLOGIE mm *(millimeter)*

Mo *abrév (méga-octet)* INFORMAT, ORDINAT Mb *(megabyte)*

MOD *abrév (matière organique digestible)* RECYCLAGE DOM *(digestible organic matter)*

mol *abrév (môle)* METROLOGIE, PHYSIQUE mol *(mole)*

MOS *abrév (semi-conducteur à oxyde métallique)* ORDINAT MOS *(metal-oxide semiconductor)*

MP *abrév (modulation de phase)* ELECTRON, ENREGISTR, INFORMAT, ORDINAT, PHYSIQUE, TELECOM, TV PM *(phase modulation)*

MPF *abrév (multiplexage par partage des fréquences)* ORDINAT, PHYSIQUE FDM *(frequency-division multiplexing)*

MRC *abrév (multiplexage par répartition de code)* TELECOM CDM *(code-division multiplexing)*

MRF *abrév (multiplexage par répartition en fréquence)* ELECTRON, ORDINAT, PHYSIQUE, TELECOM FDM *(frequency-division multiplexing)*

MRL *abrév (multiplexage par répartition en longueur d'onde)* TELECOM WDM *(wavelength division multiplexing)*

MRT *abrév (multiplexage par répartition dans le temps)* ELECTRON, ESPACE, INFORMAT, ORDINAT, TELECOM TDM *(time-division multiplexing)*

ms *abrév (milliseconde)* INFORMAT, ORDINAT ms *(millisecond)*

MTBF *abrév (moyenne de temps de bon fonctionnement)* ESPACE, INFORMAT, MECANIQUE, ORDINAT, QUALITE MTBF *(mean time between failures)*

mV *abrév (millivolt)* ELECTR, ELECTROTEC mV *(millivolt)*

mW *abrév (milliwatt)* ELECTR mW *(milliwatt)*

MW *abrév (mégawatt)* ELECTR MW *(megawatt)*

Mx *abrév (maxwell)* ELECTROTEC Mx *(maxwell)*

n *abrév (nano-)* METROLOGIE n *(nano-)*

N *abrév (newton)* ELECTR, METROLOGIE, PHYSIQUE N *(newton)*

NASA *abrév (Agence nationale de l'aéronautique et de l'espace)* ESPACE NASA *(National Aeronautics and Space Administration)*

NQA *abrév (niveau de qualité acceptable)* QUALITE AQL *(acceptable quality level)*

Ns *abrév (nimbo-stratus)* METEO Ns *(nimbostratus)*

NTI *abrév (noeud de transit international)* TELECOM IGN *(international gateway node)*

OD *abrév (oxygène dissous)* POLLUTION DO *(dissolved oxygen)*

OMI *abrév (Organisation maritime internationale)* NAUT IMO *(International Maritime Organization)*

OOR *abrév (oscillateur à ondes rétrogrades)* TELECOM BWO *(backward wave oscillator)*

OP *abrév (ordinateur personnel)* INFORMAT, ORDINAT PC *(personal computer)*

OPEP *abrév (Organisation des pays exportateurs de pétrole)* PETROLE OPEC *(Organization of Petroleum Exporting Countries)*

OVNI *abrév (objet volant non identifié)* ASTRONOMIE, ESPACE UFO *(unidentified flying object)*

p *abrév* METROLOGIE *(peta-)* p *peta-)*, METROLOGIE *(pico-)* p *(pico-)*

Pa *abrév (pascal)* METROLOGIE, PETROLE, PHYSIQUE Pa *(pascal)*

PAI *abrév (poste d'aiguillage informatisé)* CH DE FER computerized signal box (BrE), computerized switch tower (AmE)

PAN *abrév (peroxoacétylnitrate)* POLLUTION PAN *(peroxoacetylnitrate)*

PAO *abrév (publication assistée par ordinateur)* IMPRIM, INFORMAT, ORDINAT DTP *(desktop publishing)*

PAT *abrév (protection automatique de trains)* CH DE FER ATP (BrE) *(automatic train protection)*

PC *abrév (poste de commande)* CH DE FER control center (AmE), control centre (BrE), signal box (BrE), signal tower (AmE), switch tower (AmE)

PCS *abrév (pouvoir calorifique supérieur)* CHAUFFAGE, GAZ gross calorific value

PEB *abrév (puissance équivalente de bruit)* OPTIQUE *d'un photodétecteur*, TELECOM NEP *(noise equivalent power)*

PEPS *abrév (premier entré premier sorti)* ORDINAT FIFO *(first-in first-out)*

PGCD *abrév (plus grand commun diviseur)* MATH HCF *(highest common factor)*

pH *abrév (potentiel hydrogène)* CHIMIE pH *(potential of hydrogen)*

PILA *abrév (présentation de l'identification de la ligne appelante)* TELECOM CLID *(calling line identification display)*

PILC *abrév (présentation de l'identification de la ligne connectée)* TELECOM COLP *(connected line identification presentation)*

PIRE *abrév (puissance isotrope rayonnée équivalente)* ESPACE *communications* EIRP *(equivalent isotropically-radiated power)*

PMA *abrév (prise maximale autorisée)* OCEANO TAC *(total allowable catch)*

PMB *abrév* MECANIQUE *(point mort bas)* BDC *(bottom dead center)*, MINES *(puissance au mortier balistique)*

WS *(weight strength)*

PMH *abrév (point mort haut)* AUTO, VEHICULES TDC *(top dead centre)*

PNA *abrév (potentiel de neutralisation de l'acide, pouvoir neutralisant des acides)* POLLUTION ANC *(acid neutralizing capacity)*

PNC *abrév (personnel navigant commercial)* AERONAUT cabin crew

PNP *abrév (plan de numérotage privé)* TELECOM PNP *(private numbering plan)*

PNR *abrév (point de non-retour)* AERONAUT point of no return

PO *abrév (partiellement obligatoire)* TELECOM CM *(conditionally mandatory)*

PP *abrév (poste principal)* ELECTRON MS *(main station)*

PPCM *abrév (plus petit commun multiple)* MATH, ORDINAT LCM *(least common multiple, lowest common multiple)*

PPCMD *abrév (plus petit commun multiple des dénominateurs)* MATH LCD *(least common denominator)*

PPS *abrév (pouces par seconde)* ENREGISTR, ORDINAT IPS *(inches per second)*

PRCI *abrév (poste à relais à commande informatique)* CH DE FER computer-controlled all-relay interlocking unit

PROM *abrév (ROM programmable)* INFORMAT, ORDINAT PROM *(programmable read-only memory)*

PS *abrév (programmation structurée)* INFORMAT, ORDINAT SP *(structured programming)*

PSV *abrév (profil sismique vertical)* PETROLE VSP *(vertical seismic profile)*

PTAC *abrév (poids total autorisé en charge)* VEHICULES total permissible laden weight (BrE), total permissible loaded weight (AmE)

PTC *abrév (poids total en charge)* VEHICULES GVW *(gross vehicle weight)*

PTM *abrév (poids total maximum)* VEHICULES GVW *(gross vehicle weight)*

PTMA *abrév (poids total maximal autorisé)* VEHICULES total permissible weight

PTT *abrév (poursuite télémesure et télécommande)* ESPACE communications TTC *(tracking telemetry and command)*

PVC *abrév (polyvinylchlorure)* CONSTR, ELECTROTEC, MATERIAUX, PLAST CAOU PVC *(polyvinyl chloride)*

PVT *abrév (perte de verrouillage de trame)* TELECOM LFA *(loss of frame alignment)*

QMAC *abrév (qualité moyenne après contrôle)* QUALITE AOQ *(average outgoing quality)*

RA *abrév (réparations accidentelles)* CH DE FER minor repairs

RAP *abrév (récupération assistée du pétrole)* PETROLE EOR *(enhanced oil recovery)*

RAV *abrév (revue d'aptitude au vol)* ESPACE gestion FRR *(flight readiness review)*

RC *abrév (résistance-capacité)* ELECTRON, ELECTROTEC RC *(resistance-capacitance)*

RCC *abrév (réseau commuté canadien)* TELECOM CSN *(Canadian Switched Network)*

RCD *abrév (réseau de communication de données)* TELECOM data communication network

RCL *abrév (réseau de communication local)* TELECOM local communications network

RDF *abrév (revue de définition finale)* ESPACE gestion

FDR *(final design review)*

Re *abrév (nombre de Reynolds)* PHYS FLUID *Re (Reynolds number)*

RER *abrév (réseau express régional)* CH DE FER regional express railroad (AmE), regional express railway (BrE)

RF *abrév (radiofréquence)* ELECTRON, ELECTROTEC, ENREGISTR, TELECOM, TRANSPORT, TV RF *(radio frequency)*

RGT *abrév (réseau de gestion des télécommunications)* TELECOM TMN *(telecommunications management network)*

RHM *abrév (relation homme-machine)* TELECOM man-machine relationship

RI *abrév* TELECOM *(répartiteur intermédiaire)* IDF *(intermediate distribution frame)*, TELECOM *(réseau d'interconnexion)* interconnection network

RILA *abrév (restriction de l'identification de la ligne appelante)* TELECOM CLIR *(calling line identification restriction)*

RILC *abrév (restriction de l'identification de la ligne connectée)* TELECOM COLR *(connected line identification restriction)*

RISCPT *abrév (Registre international des substances potentiellement toxiques)* POLLUTION IRPTC *(International Register of Potentially Toxic Chemicals)*

RLE *abrév (réseau local d'entreprise)* INFORMAT, ORDINAT, TELECOM LAN *(local area network)*

RMC *abrév (reconnaissance magnétique de caractères)* INFORMAT, ORDINAT MICR *(magnetic ink character recognition)*

RMN *abrév (résonance magnétique nucléaire)* CHIMIE, PETROLE, PHYS RAYON, PHYSIQUE NMR *(nuclear magnetic resonance)*

RNI *abrév (réseau numérique intégré)* TELECOM IDN *(integrated digital network)*

RNIS *abrév (réseau numérique à intégration des services)* TELECOM ISDN *(integrated services digital network)*

RNIS-LB *abrév (réseau numérique avec intégration des services à large bande, RNIS à large bande)* TELECOM B-ISDN *(broadband integrated services digital network)*

RO *abrév (recherche opérationnelle)* INFORMAT, ORDINAT OR *(operational research)*

ROC *abrév (reconnaissance optique des caractères)* IMPRIM, INFORMAT, ORDINAT OCR *(optical character recognition)*

ROM *abrév* ELECTRON, ELECTROTEC, INFORMAT, ORDINAT ROM, read-only memory

ROS *abrév (rapport d'ondes stationnaires)* ESPACE SWR *(standing-wave ratio)*, VSWR *(voltage standing-wave ratio)*, TELECOM SWR *(standing-wave ratio)*

RTC *abrév (réseau téléphonique commuté)* TELECOM STN *(switched telephone network)*

RVA *abrév (réseau à valeur ajoutée)* INFORMAT, ORDINAT, TELECOM VAN *(value-added network)*

RVB *abrév (rouge vert bleu)* INFORMAT, ORDINAT, TV RGB *(red green blue)*

s *abrév (second)* METROLOGIE s *(second)*

S *abrév (siemens)* METROLOGIE S *(siemens)*

SADO *abrév (Système d'acquisition de données océaniques)* OCEANO ODAS *(Ocean Data Acquisition System)*

SAL *abrév (signalisation automatique lumineuse)* CH DE

FER automatic light signals

SAR *abrév (signalisation automatique routière)* CH DE FER automatic traffic light signals

SCAM *abrév (sens contraire des aiguilles d'une montre)* CONS MECA CCW *(counterclockwise)*

SDS *abrév (surdébit de section)* TELECOM SOH *(section overhead)*

SDSM *abrév (surdébit de section de multiplexage)* TELECOM multiplex section overhead

SDSR *abrév (surdébit de section de régénération)* TELECOM regenerator section overhead

SECAM *abrév (séquentiel couleur à mémoire)* TV SECAM

SGBD *abrév (système de gestion de bases de données)* INFORMAT, ORDINAT, TELECOM DBMS *(database management system)*

SGDG *abrév (sans garantie du gouvernement)* BREVETS no government guarantee

SGML *abrév (langage standard généralisé de balisage)* IMPRIM, INFORMAT SGML *(Standard Generalized Mark-up Language)*

SHC *abrév (conteneur spécial hors-cotes)* TRANSPORT SHC *(superhigh cube)*

SI *abrév (système international d'unités)* METROLOGIE SI *(international system of units)*

SIA *abrév (signal d'indication d'alarme)* TELECOM AIS *(alarm indication signal)*

SIG *abrév (système intégré de gestion)* INFORMAT, ORDINAT MIS *(management information system)*

SIH *abrév (sens inverse horaire)* CONS MECA CCW *(counterclockwise)*

SMCN *abrév (système de multiplication de circuit numérique)* TELECOM DCMS *(digital circuit multiplication system)*

SMDSM *abrév (système mondial de détresse et de sécurité en mer)* NAUT GMDSS *(Global Marine Distress and Safety System)*

SM-SIA *abrév (signal d'indication d'alarme de section de multiplexage)* TELECOM multiplex section alarm indication signal

SNA *abrév (signal de neutralisation d'alarme)* TELECOM AIS *(alarm indication signal)*

SNCB *abrév (Société nationale des chemins de fer belges)* CH DE FER Belgian National Railways

SNCF *abrév (Société nationale des chemins de fer français)* CH DE FER French National Railways

SNHP *abrév (syndrome nerveux des hautes pressions)* OCEANO high-pressure nervous syndrome

SP *abrév (soucoupe plongeante)* OCEANO diving saucer

squid *abrév (interféromètre quantique)* PHYSIQUE squid *(superconducting quantum interference device)*

SRI *abrév (système de référence intermédiare)* TELECOM IRS *(information reference system)*

SRM *abrév (service radiotéléphonique mobile)* TELECOM MTS *(mobile telephone service)*

SSCS *abrév (sous-système de commande de connexion sémaphore)* TELECOM signaling connection control part (AmE), signalling connection control part (BrE)

SSEM *abrév (sous-système pour l'exploitation, la maintenance et la gestion)* TELECOM operating and maintenance application part

SSGT *abrév (sous-système de gestion des transactions)* TELECOM transaction capabilities application part

SSTM *abrév (sous-système de transport de messages)* TELECOM message transfer part

SSUR *abrév (sous-système usager réseau)* TELECOM

ISDN user part

SSUT *abrév (sous-système utilisateur téléphonie)* TELECOM telephone user part

STS *abrév (spatial-temporel-spatial)* ESPACE STS *(space-time-space)*

SUAC *abrév (message d'acceptation de service supplémentaire)* TELECOM FAA *(facility accepted message)*

SUDM *abrév (message de demande de service supplémentaire)* TELECOM FAR *(facility request message)*

SURF *abrév (message de refus de service supplémentaire)* TELECOM FRJ *(facility rejected message)*

Sv *abrév (sievert)* PHYS RAYON, PHYSIQUE Sv *(sievert)*

SYN *abrév (caractère de synchronisation)* INFORMAT, ORDINAT SYN *(synchronous idle character)*

T *abrév* CONS MECA *(té)* T *(tee)*, METROLOGIE *(téra-)* T *(tera-)*, PHYSIQUE *(tesla)* T *(tesla)*

TAC *abrév* CH DE FER *(train autos-couchettes)* véhicules motorail, POLLUTION *(taux d'appauvrissement en cations)* cation denudation rate

TAI *abrév (Temps atomique international)* ASTRONOMIE IAT *(International Atomic Time)*

TD *abrév (traitement de données)* ELECTRON, INFORMAT, ORDINAT, TELECOM DP *(data processing)*

TDC *abrév (taux de dénudation des cations)* POLLUTION cation denudation rate

TdT *abrév (traitement de texte)* INFORMAT, ORDINAT WP *(word processing)*

TEB *abrév (taux d'erreurs binaires, taux d'erreurs sur les bits)* ELECTRON, ORDINAT, TELECOM BER *(binary error rate, bit error rate)*

TEC *abrév (transistor à effet de champ)* ELECTRON, OPTIQUE, ORDINAT, PHYSIQUE FET *(field-effect transistor)*

TEM *abrév (électromagnétique transverse)* ELECTROTEC TEM *(transverse electromagnetic)*

TGD *abrév (transport à grande distance)* POLLUTION long-range transport

TGDPA *abrév (transport à grande distance des polluants aéroportés)* POLLUTION long-range transport of air pollutants, long-range transport of airborne pollutants

TGTB *abrév (très gros transporteur de brut)* PETROLE VLCC *(very large crude carrier)*

TGV *abrév (train expérimental à grande vitesse, train à grande vitesse)* CH DE FER APT *(advanced passenger train)*, HST *(high-speed train)*

THT *abrév (très haute tension)* ELECTROTEC, TV EHT *(extra high tension)*

TJD *abrév (traversée-jonction double)* CH DE FER double diamond crossing with slips

TMG *abrév (Temps moyen de Greenwich)* ESPACE, PHYSIQUE GMT *(Greenwich Mean Time)*

TO *abrév (traversée oblique)* CH DE FER diamond crossing

TOP *abrév (tube à onde progressive)* ELECTRON, ESPACE, PHYSIQUE, TELECOM TWT *(traveling-wave tube, travelling-wave tube)*

TPN *abrév (température normale)* PHYSIQUE STP *(standard temperature)*

TRANSPAC *abrév (réseau de transmission de données par paquets)* TELECOM packet data transmission network

TRC *abrév (tube à rayons cathodiques)* ELECTR, ELECTRON, IMPRIM, ORDINAT, SECURITE, TV CRT *(cathode ray tube)*

TTA *abrév (Transfert temporel asynchrone)* TELECOM ATM *(Asynchronous Transfer Mode)*

TTL *abrév (sous-système de télémesure, télécommande et localisation)* ESPACE *communications* TCR *(telemetry command and ranging subsystem)*

TU *abrév (temps universel)* ASTRONOMIE, ESPACE UT *(Universal Time)*

TVHD *abrév (télévision à haute définition)* TELECOM, TV HDTV *(high-definition television)*

UA *abrév (unité astronomique)* ASTRONOMIE AU *(astronomical unit)*

UAD *abrév (unité administrative)* TELECOM AU *(administrative unit)*

UAO *abrév (utilisation apparente d'oxygène)* OCEANO apparent utilization of oxygen

UC *abrév (unité centrale)* INFORMAT, ORDINAT, TELECOM CPU *(central processing unit)*

UGPB *abrév (ultragros porteur de brut)* PETROLE ULCC *(ultralarge crude carrier)*

UHF *abrév (ultrahaute fréquence)* ELECTRON, PHYS ONDES, TELECOM, TV UHF *(ultrahigh frequency)*

UHT *abrév (longue-conservation)* AGRO ALIM UHT *(ultra heat treated)*

UKIRT *abrév (télescope infrarouge du Royaume-Uni)* ASTRONOMIE UKIRT *(UK Infrared Telescope)*

ULA *abrév (unité arithmétique et logique)* ORDINAT ALU *(arithmetic and logic unit)*

UPA *abrév (unité de poids atomique)* NUCLEAIRE AWU *(atomic weight unit)*

UV *abrév (ultraviolet)* ESPACE, OPTIQUE UV *(ultraviolet)*

UVP *abrév (unité de voiture particulière)* TRANSPORT PCU *(passenger car unit)*

V *abrév* CONS MECA *(V de mécanicien)* V-block, METRO-LOGIE *(volt)* V *(volt)*

V1 *abrév (vitesse de décision)* AERONAUT V1 *(decision speed)*

VD *abrév (Vigneron-Dahl)* OCEANO Vigneron-Dahl trawl

VHF *abrév (très haute fréquence)* ELECTRON, ESPACE, PHYS ONDES, TELECOM, TV VHF *(very high-frequency)*

VLA *abrév (très grand réseau d'antennes)* ASTRONOMIE VLA *(Very Large Array)*

VLBA *abrév (réseau d'antennes à très longue ligne de base)* ASTRONOMIE VLBA *(Very Long Baseline Array)*

VSS *abrév (véhicule à suspension supérieure)* TRANSPORT SVS *(suspended vehicle system)*

W *abrév (watt)* ELECTR, ELECTROTEC, METROLOGIE, PHYSIQUE W *(watt)*

Wb *abrév (weber)* METROLOGIE, PHYSIQUE Wb *(weber)*

WYSIWYG *abrév (tel vu tel imprimé, vu-imprimé)* INFORMAT, ORDINAT WYSIWYG *(what you see is what you get)*

YAG *abrév (grenat d'yttrium et d'aluminium)* ELECTRON YAG *(yttrium aluminium garnet)*

YIG *abrév (grenat d'yttrium ferreux)* ELECTRON YIG *(yttrium iron garnet)*

Z *abrév (nombre de protons)* PHYS PART Z *(proton number)*

ZAA *abrév (zone à autonomie d'acheminement)* TELECOM group switching center catchment area (AmE), group switching center exchange area (AmE), group switching centre catchment area (BrE), group switching centre exchange area (BrE)

Conversion tables/
Tables de conversion

1 Length / Longueur

		metre *mètre*	inch *pouce*	foot *pied*	yard *yard*	rod *rod*	mile *mile*
1 metre *mètre*	=	1	39.37	3.281	1.093	0.1988	6.214×10^{-4}
1 inch *pouce*	=	2.54×10^{-2}	1	0.083	0.02778	5.050×10^{-3}	1.578×10^{-5}
1 foot *pied*	=	0.3048	12	1	0.3333	0.0606	1.894×10^{-4}
1 yard *yard*	=	0.9144	36	3	1	0.1818	5.682×10^{-4}
1 rod *rod*	=	5.029	198	16.5	5.5	1	3.125×10^{-3}
1 mile *mile*	=	1609	63360	5280	1760	320	1

1 imperial standard yard = 0.914 398 41 metre / 1 yard standard légal = 0,914 398 41 mètre
1 yard (scientific) = 0.9144 metre (exact) / 1 yard (scientifique) = 0,9144 mètre (exactement)
1 US yard = 0.914 401 83 metre / 1 yard US = 0,914 401 83 mètre
1 English nautical mile = 6080 ft = 1853.18 metres / 1 mile marin anglais = 6080 pieds = 1853,18 mètres
1 international nautical mile = 1852 metres = 6076.12 ft / 1 mile marin international = 1852 mètres = 6076,12 pieds

2 Area / Superficie

		sq. metre $mètre^2$	sq. inch $pouce^2$	sq. foot $pied^2$	sq.yard $yard^2$	acre acre	sq. mile $mile^2$
1 sq. metre $mètre^2$	=	1	1550	10.76	1.196	2.471×10^{-4}	3.861×10^{-7}
1 sq. inch $pouce^2$	=	6.452×10^{-4}	1	6.944×10^{-3}	7.716×10^{-4}	1.594×10^{-7}	2.491×10^{-10}
1 sq. foot $pied^2$	=	0.0929	144	1	0.1111	2.296×10^{-5}	3.587×10^{-8}
1 sq. yard $yard^2$	=	0.8361	1296	9	1	2.066×10^{-4}	3.228×10^{-7}
1 acre acre	=	4.047×10^3	6.273×10^6	4.355×10^4	4840	1	1.563×10^{-3}
1 sq. mile $mile^2$	=	259.0×10^4	4.015×10^9	2.788×10^7	3.098×10^6	640	1

1 are = 100 sq. metres = 0.01 hectare / 1 are = 100 mètres carrés = 0,01 hectare
1 circular mil= 5.067×10^{-10} sq. metre / 1 millimètre circulaire = $5,067 \times 10^{-10}$ mètres carrés
　　　　　　 = 7.854×10^{-7} sq. in / = $7,854 \times 10^{-7}$ pouces carrés
1 acre (statute) = 0.4047 hectare / 1 acre (légal) = 0,4047 hectare

3 Volume / Volume

		cubic metre mètre cube	cubic inch pouce cube	cubic foot pied cube	UK gallon gallon UK	US gallon gallon US
1 cubic metre mètre cube	=	1	6.102×10^4	35.31	220.0	264.2
1 cubic in pouce cube	=	1.639×10^{-5}	1	5.787×10^{-4}	3.605×10^{-3}	4.329×10^{-3}
1 cubic ft pied cube	=	2.832×10^{-2}	1728	1	6.229	7.480
1 UK gallon* gallon UK	=	4.546×10^{-3}	277.4	0.1605	1	1.201
1 US gallon† gallon US	=	3.785×10^{-3}	231.0	0.1337	0.8327	1

* volume of 10 lb of water at 62 ° F / volume de 10 lb d'eau à 62 ° F
† volume of 8.328 28 lb of water at 60 ° F / volume de 8,328 28 lb d'eau à 60 ° F
1 cubic metre = 999.972 litres / 1 mètre cube = 999,972 litres
1 acre foot = 271 328 UK gallons = 1233 cubic metres / 1 acre pied = 271 328 gallons UK = 1233 mètres cube

until 1976 the litre was equal to 1000.028 cm^3 (the volume of 1 kg of water at maximum density) but then it was revalued to be 1000 cm^3 exactly

jusqu'en 1976 le litre était égal à 1000,028 cm^3 (volume de 1 kg d'eau à la masse volumique maximale) mais il a été depuis redéfini à 1000 cm^3 exactement

4 Angle / Angle

		degree *degré*	minute *minute*	second *seconde*	radian *radian*	revolution *tour*
1 degree *degré*	=	1	60	3600	1.745×10^{-2}	2.778×10^{-3}
1 minute *minute*	=	1.677×10^{-2}	1	60	2.909×10^{-4}	4.630×10^{-5}
1 second *seconde*	=	2.778×10^{-4}	$1.667 \times 10{-2}$	1	4.848×10^{-6}	7.716×10^{-7}
1 radian *radian*	=	57.30	3438	2.063×10^{5}	1	0.1592
1 revolution *tour*	=	360	2.16×10^{4}	1.296×10^{6}	6.283	1

1 mil = 10^{-3} radian / 1 millième (d'artillerie) = 10^{-3} radian

5 Time / Temps

		year *année*	solar day *jour (solaire moyen)*	hour *heure*	minute *minute*	second *seconde*
1 year *année*	=	1	365.24*	8.766×10^{3}	5.259×10^{5}	3.156×10^{7}
1 solar day *jour (solaire moyen)*	=	2.738×10^{-3}	1	24	1440	8.640×10^{4}
1 hour *heure*	=	1.141×10^{-4}	4.167×10^{-2}	1	60	3600
1 minute *minute*	=	1.901×10^{-6}	6.944×10^{-4}	1.667×10^{-2}	1	60
1 second *seconde*	=	3.169×10^{-8}	1.157×10^{-5}	2.778×10^{-4}	1.667×10^{-2}	1

1 year = 366.24 sidereal days / 1 année = 366,24 jours sidéraux
1 sidereal day = 86 164.090 6 seconds / 1 jour sidéral = 86 164,090 6 secondes
*exact figure = 365.242 192 64 in A.D. 2000 / *chiffre exact = 365,242 192 64 en l'an 2000 A.D.

6 Mass / Masse

		kilogram *kilogramme*	pound *livre*	slug *slug*	metric slug *slug métrique*	UK ton *tonne UK*	US ton *tonne US*	u
1 kilogram *kilogramme*	=	1	2.205	6.852×10^{-2}	0.1020	9.842×10^{-4}	11.02×10^{-4}	6.024×10^{26}
1 pound *livre*	=	0.4536	1	3.108×10^{-2}	4.625×10^{-2}	4.464×10^{-4}	5.000×10^{-4}	2.732×10^{26}
1 slug *slug*	=	14.59	32.17	1	1.488	1.436×10^{-2}	1.609×10^{-2}	8.789×10^{27}
1 metric slug *slug métrique*	=	9.806	21.62	0.6720	1	9.652×10^{-3}	1.081×10^{-2}	5.907×10^{27}
1 UK ton *tonne UK*	=	1016	2240	69.62	103.6	1	1.12	6.121×10^{29}
1 US ton *tonne US*	=	907.2	2000	62.16	92.51	0.8929	1	5.465×10^{29}
1 u	=	1.660×10^{-27}	3.660×10^{-27}	1.137×10^{-28}	1.693×10^{-28}	1.634×10^{-30}	1.829×10^{-30}	1

1 imperial standard pound = 0.453 592 338 kilogram / 1 livre standard légale = 0,453 592 338 kilogramme
1 US pound = 0.453 592 427 7 kilogram / 1 livre US = 0,453 592 427 7 kilogramme
1 international pound = 0.453 592 37 kilogram / 1 livre internationale = 0,453 592 37 kilogramme
1 tonne = 10^3 kilograms / 1 tonne = 10^3 kilogramme
1 troy pound = 0.373 242 kilogram / 1 livre troy = 0,373 242 kilogramme

7 Force / Force

		dyne *dyne*	newton *newton*	pound force *livre poids*	poundal *poundal*	*gram force *gramme poids*
1 dyne *dyne*	=	1	10^{-5}	2.248×10^{-6}	7.233×10^{-5}	1.020×10^{-3}
1 newton *newton*	=	10^5	1	0.2248	7.233	102.0
1 pound force *livre poids*	=	4.448×10^5	4.448	1	32.17	453.6
1 poundal *poundal*	=	1.383×10^4	0.1383	3.108×10^{-2}	1	14.10
1 gram force *gramme poids*	=	980.7	980.7×10^{-5}	2.205×10^{-3}	7.093×10^{-2}	1

* not recognized officially in France / unité non légal en France

8 Power / Puissance

		Btu per hr Btu/h	ft lb s^{-1} $livre$ $pied/s$	kg metre s^{-1} $kilogramme$ $mètre/s$	cal s^{-1} $calorie/s$	*HP $cheval$-$vapeur$	watt $watt$
1 Btu per hour $Btu\ par\ heure$	=	1	0.2161	2.987×10^{-2}	6.999×10^{-2}	3.929×10^{-4}	0.2931
1 ft lb per second $livre\ pied\ par\ seconde$	=	4.628	1	0.1383	0.3239	1.818×10^{-3}	1.356
1 kg metre per second $kilogramme\ mètre\ par$ $seconde$	=	33.47	7.233	1	2.343	1.315×10^{-2}	9.807
1 cal per second $calorie\ par\ seconde$	=	14.29	3.087	4.268×10^{-1}	1	5.613×10^{-3}	4.187
1 HP $cheval$-$vapeur$	=	2545	550	76.04	178.2	1	745.7
1 watt $watt$	=	3.413	0.7376	0.1020	0.2388	1.341×10^{-3}	1

1 international watt = 1.000 19 absolute watt / 1 watt international = 1,000 19 watt absolu
* not recognized officially in France / unité non légal en France

9 Energy, work, heat / Energie, travail, chaleur

	Btu *Btu*	joule *joule*	ft lb *livre pied*	cm^{-1} *cm^{-1}*	**cal *calorie*	kW h *kilowattheure*	electron volt *électron volt*	kg* *kilogramme*	u*
1 Btu *Btu*	=	1	1.055×10^3	778.2	5.312×10^{25}	252	2.930×10^{-4}	6.585×10^{21}	1.174×10^{-14}	7.074×10^{12}
1 joule *joule*	=	9.481×10^{-4}	1	7.376×10^{-1}	5.035×10^{22}	2.389×10^{-1}	2.778×10^{-7}	6.242×10^{18}	1.113×10^{-17}	6.705×10^9
1 ft lb *livre pied*	=	1.285×10^{-3}	1.356	1	6.828×10^{22}	3.239×10^{-1}	3.766×10^{-7}	8.464×10^{18}	1.507×10^{-17}	9.092×10^9
1 cm^{-1} *cm^{-1}*	=	1.883×10^{-26}	1.986×10^{-23}	1.465×10^{-23}	1	4.745×10^{-24}	5.517×10^{-30}	1.240×10^{-4}	2.210×10^{-40}	1.332×10^{-13}
1 cal 15°C *calorie 15°C*	=	3.968×10^{-3}	4.187	3.088	2.108×10^{23}	1	1.163×10^{-6}	2.613×10^{19}	4.659×10^{-17}	2.807×10^{10}
1 kW h *kilowattheure*	=	3412	3.600×10^6	2.655×10^6	1.813×10^{29}	8.598×10^5	1	2.247×10^{25}	4.007×10^{-11}	2.414×10^{16}
1 electron volt *électron volt*	=	1.519×10^{-22}	1.602×10^{-19}	1.182×10^{-19}	8.066×10^3	3.827×10^{-20}	4.450×10^{-26}	1	1.783×10^{-36}	1.074×10^{-9}
1 kg* *kilogramme*	=	8.521×10^{13}	8.987×10^{16}	6.629×10^{16}	4.525×10^{39}	2.147×10^{16}	2.497×10^{10}	5.610×10^{35}	1	6.025×10^2
1 u*	=	1.415×10^{-13}	1.492×10^{-10}	1.100×10^{-10}	7.513×10^{12}	3.564×10^{-11}	4.145×10^{-17}	9.31×10^8	1.660×10^{-27}	1

* from the mass–energy relationship $E = mc^2$ / à partir du rapport énergie–masse $E = mc^2$
**not recognized officially in France / unité non légal en France

10 Pressure / Pression

	=	standard atmosphere *atmosphère normale*	kg force cm^{-2} *kg poids cm^{-2}*	dyne cm^{-2} *dyne cm^{-2}*	pascal *pascal*	pound force in^{-2} *livre poids pouce^{-2}*	pound force ft^{-2} *livre poids pied^{-2}*	millibar *millibar*	*torr *torr*	barometric in. Hg *pouce Hg barométrique*
1 standard atmosphere *atmosphère normale*	=	1	1.033	1.013×10^6	1.013×10^5	14.70	2116	1013	760	29.92
1 kg force cm^{-2} *kg poids cm^{-2}*	=	0.9678	1	9.804×10^5	9.804×10^4	14.22	2048	980.7	735.6	28.96
1 dyne cm^{-2} *dyne cm^{-2}*	=	9.869×10^{-7}	10.20×10^{-7}	1	0.1	14.50×10^{-6}	2.089×10^{-3}	10^{-3}	750.1×10^{-6}	29.53×10^{-6}
1 pascal *pascal*	=	9.869×10^{-6}	10.20×10^{-6}	10	1	14.50×10^{-5}	2.089×10^{-2}	10^{-2}	750.1×10^{-5}	29.53×10^{-5}
1 pound force in^{-2} *livre poids pouce^{-2}*	=	6.805×10^{-2}	7.031×10^{-2}	6.895×10^4	6.895×10^3	1	144	68.95	51.71	2.036
1 pound force ft^{-2} *livre poids pied^{-2}*	=	4.725×10^{-4}	4.882×10^{-4}	478.8	47.88	6.944×10^{-3}	1	47.88×10^{-2}	0.3591	14.14×10^{-3}
1 millibar *millibar*	=	0.9869×10^{-3}	1.020×10^{-3}	10^3	10^2	14.50×10^{-3}	2.089	1	0.7500	29.53×10^{-3}
1 torr *torr*	=	1.316×10^{-3}	1.360×10^{-3}	1.333×10^2	1.333×10^3	1.934×10^{-2}	2.784	1.333	1	3.937×10^{-2}
1 barometric in. Hg *pouce Hg barométrique*	=	3.342×10^{-2}	3.453×10^{-2}	3.386×10^4	3.386×10^3	4.912×10^{-1}	70.73	33.87	25.40	1

1 torr = 1 barometric mmHg density 13.5951 g cm^{-3} at 0° C and acceleration due to gravity 980.665 cm/s^{-2}.

1 torr = 1 millimètre de mercure conventionnel à une masse volumique de 13,5951 g cm^{-3} à 0° C et pour une accélération due à la pesanteur de 980,665 cm/s^{-2}

* The torr is not recognized officially in France / Le torr est une unité non légal en France

1 dyne cm^{-2} = 1 barad / 1 dyne cm^{-2} = 1 barad

11 Magnetic flux / Flux magnétique

		*maxwell *maxwell*	kiloline *kiloline*	weber *weber*
1 maxwell (1 line) *maxwell (1 ligne)*	=	1	10^{-3}	10^{-8}
1 kiloline *kiloline*	=	10^3	1	10^{-5}
1 weber *weber*	=	10^8	10^5	1

*not recognized officially in France / unité non légal en France

12 Magnetic flux density / Densité de flux magnétique

		*gauss *gauss*	weber m^{-2} (tesla) *weber m^{-2} (tesla)*	gamma *gamma*	maxwell cm^{-2} *maxwell cm^{-2}*
1 gauss (line cm^{-2}) *gauss (ligne cm^{-2})*	=	1	10^{-4}	10^5	1
1 weber m^{-2} (tesla) *weber m^{-2} (tesla)*	=	10^4	1	10^9	10^4
1 gamma *gamma*	=	10^{-5}	10^{-9}	1	10^{-5}
1 maxwell cm^{-2} *maxwell cm^{-2}*	=	1	$10-4$	10^5	1

*not recognized officially in France / unité non légal en France

13 Magnetomotive force / Force magnétomotrice

		abamp turn *abampère tour*	amp turn *ampère tour*	*gilbert *gilbert*
1 abampere turn *abampère tour*	=	1	10	12.57
1 ampere turn *ampère tour*	=	10^{-1}	1	1.257
1 gilbert *gilbert*	=	7.958×10^{-2}	0.7958	1

*not recognized officially in France / unité non légal en France

14   Magnetic field strength / Intensité de champ magnétique

		amp turn cm^{-1} *ampère tour cm^{-1}*	amp turn m^{-1} *ampère tour m^{-1}*	*oersted *oersted*
1 amp turn cm^{-1} *ampère tour cm^{-1}*	=	1	10^2	1.257
1 amp turn m^{-1} *ampère tour m^{-1}*	=	10^{-2}	1	1.257×10^{-2}
1 oersted *oersted*	=	0.7958	79.58	1

*not recognized officially in France / unité non légal en France

15   Illumination / Eclairement lumineux

		lux *lux*	*phot *phot*	foot-candle *bougie pied*
1 lux $(1 \mathrm{m}\, \mathrm{m}^{-2})$ *lux ($1 \mathrm{m}\, \mathrm{m}^{-2}$)*	=	1	10^{-4}	9.29×10^{-2}
1 phot $(1 \mathrm{m}\, \mathrm{cm}^{-2})$ *phot ($1 \mathrm{m}\, \mathrm{cm}^{-2}$)*	=	10^4	1	929
1 foot-candle $(1 \mathrm{m}\, \mathrm{ft}^{-2})$ *bougie pied ($1 \mathrm{m}\, \mathrm{pied}^{-2}$)*	=	10.76	10.76×10^{-4}	1

*not recognized officially in France / unité non légal en France

16 Luminance / Luminance lumineuse

		*nit *nit*	*stilb *stilb*	cd ft^{-2} *candela pied^{-2}*	apostilb *apostilb*	*lambert *lambert*	foot-lambert *lambert pied*
1 nit (cd m^{-2}) *nit (candela m^{-2})*	=	1	10^{-4}	9.29×10^{-2}	π	$\pi \times 10^{-4}$	0.292
1 stilb (cd cm^{-2}) *stilb (candela cm^{-2})*	=	10^{4}	1	929	$\pi \times 10^{4}$	π	2920
1 cd ft^{-2} *candela (pied^{-2})*	=	10.76	1.076×10^{-3}	1	33.8	3.38×10^{-3}	π
1 apostilb (1m m^{-2}) *apostilb (1m m^{-2})*	=	$1/\pi$	$1/(\pi \times 10^{4})$	2.96×10^{-2}	1	10^{-4}	9.29×10^{-2}
1 lambert (1m cm^{-2}) *lambert (1m cm^{-2})*	=	$1/(\pi \times 10^{-4})$	$1/\pi$	296	10^{4}	1	929
1 foot lambert *or* equivalent foot candle *lambert pied* ou *bougie pied équivalent*	=	3.43	3.43×10^{-4}	$1/\pi$	10.76	1.076×10^{-3}	1

luminous intensity of candela = 98.1% that of international candle
intensité lumineuse de la candela = 98,1% de celle de la bougie internationale
1 lumen = flux emitted by 1 candela into unit solid angle
1 lumen = flux lumineux émis par dans l'angle solide de
1 stéradian par une source ayant une intensité lumineuse de
1 candela
*not recognized officially in France / unité non légal en France

Chemical elements/Eléments chimiques

Symbol/Symbole	Elément	Element	Numéro atomique/ Atomic number
Ac	Actinium	Actinium	89
Ag	Argent	Silver	47
Al	Aluminium	Aluminium	13
Am	Américium	Americium	95
Ar	Argon	Argon	18
As	Arsenic	Arsenic	33
At	Astate	Astatine	85
Au	Or	Gold	79
B	Bore	Boron	5
Ba	Baryum	Barium	56
Be	Béryllium	Beryllium	4
Bi	Bismuth	Bismuth	83
Bk	Berkélium	Berkelium	97
Br	Brome	Bromine	35
C	Carbone	Carbon	6
Ca	Calcium	Calcium	20
Cd	Cadmium	Cadmium	48
Ce	Cérium	Cerium	58
Cf	Californium	Californium	98
Cl	Chlore	Chlorine	17
Cm	Curium	Curium	96
Co	Cobalt	Cobalt	27
Cr	Chrome	Chromium	24
Cs	Césium	Caesium	55
Cu	Cuivre	Copper	29
Dy	Dysprosium	Dysprosium	66
Er	Erbium	Erbium	68
Es	Einsteinium	Einsteinium	99
Eu	Europium	Europium	63
F	Fluor	Fluorine	9
Fe	Fer	Iron	26
Fm	Fermium	Fermium	100
Fr	Francium	Francium	87
Ga	Gallium	Gallium	31
Gd	Gadolinium	Gadolinium	64
H	Hydrogène	Hydrogen	1
He	Hélium	Helium	2
Hf	Hafnium	Hafnium	72
Hg	Mercure	Mercury	80
Ho	Holmium	Holmium	67
I	Iodine	Iodine	53
In	Indium	Indium	49
Ir	Iridium	Iridium	77
K	Potassium	Potassium	19

Kr	Krypton	Krypton	36
La	Lanthane	Lanthanum	57
Li	Lithium	Lithium	3
Lr	Lawrençium	Lawrencium	103
Lu	Lutétium	Lutetium	71
Md	Mendelévium	Mendelevium	101
Mg	Magnésium	Magnesium	12
Mn	Manganèse	Manganese	25
Mo	Molybdène	Molybdenum	42
N	Azote	Nitrogen	7
Na	Sodium	Sodium	11
Nb	Niobium	Niobium	41
Nd	Néodyme	Neodymium	60
Ne	Néon	Neon	10
Ni	Nickel	Nickel	28
No	Nobélium	Nobelium	102
Np	Neptunium	Neptunium	93
O	Oxygène	Oxygen	8
Os	Osmium	Osmium	76
P	Phosphore	Phosphorus	15
Pa	Proctactinium	Proctactinium	91
Pb	Plomb	Lead	82
Pd	Palladium	Palladium	46
Pm	Prométhium	Promethium	61
Po	Polonium	Polonium	84
Pr	Praséodyme	Praseodymium	59
Pt	Platine	Platinum	78
Ra	Radium	Radium	88
Rb	Rubudium	Rubudium	37
Re	Rhénium	Rhenium	75
Rh	Rhodium	Rhodium	45
Rn	Radon	Radon	86
Ru	Ruthénium	Ruthenium	44
S	Soufre	Sulphur	16
Sb	Antimoine	Antimony	51
Sc	Scandium	Scandium	21
Se	Sélénium	Selenium	34
Si	Silicium	Silicon	14
Sm	Samarium	Samarium	62
Sn	Etain	Tin	50
Sr	Strontium	Strontium	38
Ta	Tantale	Tantalum	73
Tb	Terbium	Terbium	65
Tc	Technétium	Technetium	43
Te	Tellure	Tellurium	52
Th	Thorium	Thorium	90
Ti	Titane	Titanium	22
Tl	Thallium	Thallium	81
Tm	Thulium	Thulium	69
U	Uranium	Uranium	92
V	Vanadium	Vanadium	23
W	Tungstène	Tungsten	74
Xe	Xénon	Xenon	54
Y	Yttrium	Yttrium	39

Yb	Ytterbium	Ytterbium	70
Zn	Zinc	Zinc	30
Zr	Zirconium	Zirconium	40